2005–2006

Accredited Institutions *of* Postsecondary Education

Includes Candidates for Accreditation and Accredited Programs at Other Facilities

Edited by Kenneth A. Von Alt

Published by the American Council on Education
Washington, DC

In consultation with the Council for Higher Education Accreditation

Additional copies of this directory are available from:
Praeger Publishers
An imprint of Greenwood Publishing Group, Inc.
88 Post Road West
Westport, CT 06881-5007
(203) 226-3571
(800) 225-5800
http://www.greenwood.com

American Council on Education
One Dupont Circle NW
Washington, DC 20036

Printed in the United States of America

printing number
1 2 3 4 5 6 7 8 9 10

Library of Congress Cataloging in Publication Data

The Library of Congress has cataloged this serial as follows:

Accredited institutions of postsecondary education
published by the American Council on Education, Washington, DC

v.; 24 cm.

Annual
Began with issue for 1976–77.
A directory of accredited institutions, professionally accredited programs, and candidates for accreditation.
Description based on: 1980–81.
Spine title: Accredited Institutions of Postsecondary Education.

ISBN 1-57356-627-6
ISSN 0270-1715 = Accredited institutions of postsecondary education, programs, candidates.

I. Education, Higher—United States—Directories   I. American Council on Education.
II. Title: Accredited Institutions of Postsecondary Education.
   [DNLM: L901 A172]

L901.A48   378.73   81-641495
                                                       AACR2   MARC-S

Table of Contents

Abbreviations and Terms Used in this Directory v
About this Directory vii
How to Use this Directory ix

Accredited Degree-Granting Institutions 1
    Degree-Granting Institutions (United States) 3
    Degree-Granting Institutions (Outside the United States)..431

Accredited Non–Degree-Granting Institutions 439
    Non–Degree-Granting Institutions (United States) 441
    Non–Degree-Granting Institutions (Outside the United States)...................................646

Accredited Programs at Other Facilities...649
    Accredited Programs (United States)...651
    Accredited Programs (Outside the United States) 711

Major Institutional Changes 719

Candidates for Accreditation 741
    Degree-Granting Candidate Institutions (United States)...743
    Degree-Granting Candidate Institutions (Outside the United States) 752
    Non–Degree-Granting Candidate Institutions (United States)....................................753
    Non–Degree-Granting Candidate Institutions (Outside the United States)..................762

Appendices 763
    A. An Overview of U.S. Accreditation...765
    B. Recognized Accrediting Organizations 769
    C. Joint Statement on Transfer and Award of Academic Credit...................................789

Institutional Index...793

Abbreviations and Terms Used in this Directory

Accred. ....institutional accreditor; national or regional
CHEA............................Council for Higher Education Accreditation
Enroll ....student enrollment or headcount
FTE Enroll.....................full-time equivalent (enrollment calculation)
Prelim. ....preliminary
Prof. Accred. ....specialized or professional accreditor of programs within an institution
URL..............................unique Internet address (Uniform Resource Locator)
USDE............................United States Department of Education

Degree Abbreviations

C...................................certificate/diploma
A...................................associate degree or equivalent
B...................................baccalaureate (bachelor's) degree or equivalent
M..................................master's degree or equivalent
P...................................first professional degree; a degree program requiring a minimum of two years of postsecondary education for entrance and a total of six years of postsecondary education for completion
D...................................doctoral degree or equivalent

Calendar Terms

3-3................................academic year of three equal terms
4-1-4 ....academic year of two 4-month terms with a 1-month intersession
4-4-x ....academic year of two 4-month terms with one term of flexible length
Quarter.........................quarter (academic year of four equal terms)
Semester ....semester (academic year of two equal terms)
Trimester......................trimester (academic year of three 15-week terms, with students typically attending two of the three terms)

About this Directory

Accredited Institutions of Postsecondary Education (AIPE) is published annually by the American Council on Education (ACE). The list of accredited institutions and programs in this directory is compiled from the regional, faith-based, private career, professional, and specialized accrediting organizations recognized by the nongovernmental, nonprofit Council for Higher Education Accreditation (CHEA) and/or the U.S. Department of Education (USDE). Appendix A contains a thorough explanation of the accreditation process. The data provided by the accreditors for this directory have been reformatted, but have not otherwise been edited or changed.

Accreditation decisions are made throughout the year; therefore, this annual directory may not contain the most up-to-date information. Users should check with the accreditor for the most current accreditation status. (Addresses, names, and telephone numbers of persons to contact begin on page 777.)

Institutional accreditation granted by a regional, faith-based, or private career accreditor applies to the institution as a whole. Degree-granting and non–degree-granting institutions, within and in some cases outside the United States, are listed in this directory (see Table of Contents).

An individual program or department within a larger institution may be separately accredited by a professional or specialized organization and is included in the display for the larger institution. A separate section lists individually accredited programs at non-accredited, non-educational facilities such as hospitals and clinics (see page 649).

Many disciplines have no established, recognized professional accreditation organization. Therefore, no listings for such departments appear in the directory. The user should note that the institutional accreditation listings include only separately accredited programs, and not a complete list of programs available at the institution.

The dynamic arena of higher education is marked by major changes in organizational structure. To help users locate information for institutions that have modified their identifying information, this directory includes a section listing closures, mergers, and name changes, by state (see page 719). Each instance appears in three consecutive editions before it is removed. Name changes are cross-referenced in the index.

A final section of this directory lists institutions designated as "candidates for accreditation." These institutions are described as progressing toward accreditation with a recognized accrediting organization, but are not ensured of achieving accredited status.

Please take time to review the section How to Use this Directory for guidelines on interpreting the listings (see page ix). For further clarification regarding entries in the directory, contact Kenneth A. Von Alt, database editor, American Council on Education, One Dupont Circle NW, Washington, DC 20036; (202) 939-9382; e-mail: ken_von_alt@ace.nche.edu. For clarification about accreditation or the recognition process, contact the Council for Higher Education Accreditation, One Dupont Circle NW, Suite 510, Washington, DC 20036-1110; (202) 955-6126; e-mail: chea@chea.org.

How to Use this Directory

Because this directory is divided into several sections, the user is advised to begin his or her search using the index located in the back of this directory. Arranged alphabetically by institution name, the index contains numerous cross-references that make it easier to locate institutions that may use shorter or alternate names, have undergone a name change, merged with another institution, or closed altogether.

The data in every institutional entry are consistently arranged, although not every type of information is available for every institution. The following example demonstrates how a typical entry is arranged.

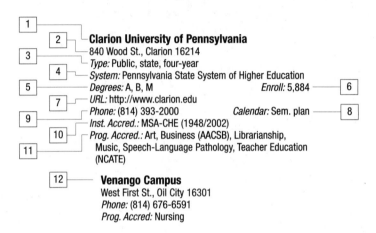

1. Institution name.

2. Address.

3. Type of institution (e.g., public), type of controlling entity (e.g., state), and specific organizational characteristics (e.g., four year).

4. Name of controlling system or entity, public or private (e.g., Ohio Board of Regents).

5. Degrees offered.

6. Enrollment figure, based on most recent enrollment data from the U.S. Department of Education.

7. Web address of institution (Uniform Resource Locator).

8. Type of academic calendar.

9. Main institutional telephone number.

10. Institutional accreditator acronym, date of first accreditation or candidacy/date of most recent renewal or reaffirmation, and, when applicable, accreditation status (e.g., probation, warning). (Consult the specific accrediting body for dates of interruption in or limitations on accreditation status.)

11. Specialized accreditation by any of 65 professional accrediting agencies, including one umbrella organization representing 17 joint review committees.

12. Branch campus(es).

Accredited Degree-Granting Institutions

ALABAMA

Air University
55 LeMay Plaza South, Maxwell AFB 36112-6335
Type: Public, federal, four-year
Degrees: A, M
URL: http://www.au.af.mil
Phone: (334) 953-2014
Inst. Accred.: SACS (2004)

Community College of the Air Force
130 West Maxwell Blvd., Simler Hall, Ste. 104,
Maxwell AFB 36112-6613
Phone: (334) 953-7848
Prog. Accred: Radiography, Surgical Technology

School of Advanced Air and Space Studies
600 Chennault Circle, Maxwell AFB 36112
Phone: (304) 953-5886

School of Health Sciences Campus
3790th MSTG, Sheppard AFB, TX 76311
Phone: (817) 676-2700
Prog. Accred: Physical Therapy Assisting

Alabama Agricultural and Mechanical University
PO Box 1357, Normal 35762
Type: Public, state, four-year
System: Alabama Commission on Higher Education
Degrees: A, B, M, P, D   *Enroll:* 5,881
URL: http://www.aamu.edu
Phone: (256) 372-5000   *Calendar:* Sem. plan
Inst. Accred.: SACS (1963/2004)
Prog. Accred.: Business (AACSB), Engineering (civil,
electrical, mechanical), Engineering Technology
(electrical, mechanical), Family and Consumer Science,
Forestry, Planning, Rehabilitation Counseling, Social
Work, Speech-Language Pathology, Teacher Education
(NCATE)

Alabama Southern Community College
PO Box 2000, Monroeville 36461
Type: Public, state, two-year
System: State of Alabama Department of Postsecondary
Education
Degrees: A   *Enroll:* 1,029
URL: http://www.ascc.edu
Phone: (251) 575-3156   *Calendar:* Sem. plan
Inst. Accred.: SACS (1992/1995)

Thomasville Campus
Highway 43, South, Thomasville 36784
Phone: (205) 636-9642

Alabama State University
915 South Jackson St., Montgomery 36101-0271
Type: Public, state, four-year
System: Alabama Commission on Higher Education
Degrees: A, B, M, P, D   *Enroll:* 5,065
URL: http://www.alasu.edu
Phone: (334) 229-4100   *Calendar:* Sem. plan
Inst. Accred.: SACS (1966/2001)
Prog. Accred.: Business (ACBSP), Music, Occupational
Therapy, Physical Therapy, Social Work, Teacher
Education (NCATE)

American College of Computer and Information Sciences
2101 Magnolia Ave., Ste. 200, Birmingham 35205-2827
Type: Private, proprietary, four-year
Degrees: B, M   *FTE Enroll:* 100
URL: http://www.accis.edu
Phone: (205) 323-6191   *Calendar:* Sem. plan
Inst. Accred.: DETC (2000/2005)

Andrew Jackson University
10 Old Montgomery Hwy., Birmingham 35209-6726
Type: Private, independent, four-year
Degrees: A, B, M   *FTE Enroll:* 144
URL: http://www.aju.edu
Phone: (205) 871-9288
Inst. Accred.: DETC (1998/2003)

Athens State University
300 North Beaty St., Athens 35611
Type: Public, state, four-year
System: State of Alabama Department of Postsecondary
Education
Degrees: B   *Enroll:* 1,633
URL: http://www.athens.edu
Phone: (256) 233-8100   *Calendar:* Sem. plan
Inst. Accred.: SACS (1955/2000)
Prog. Accred.: Business (ACBSP), Teacher Education
(NCATE)

Auburn University
Auburn University 36849-5206
Type: Public, state, four-year
System: Auburn University System
Degrees: B, M, P, D   *Enroll:* 21,271
URL: http://www.auburn.edu
Phone: (334) 844-4000   *Calendar:* Sem. plan
Inst. Accred.: SACS (1922/2004)
Prog. Accred.: Accounting, Art, Audiology, Business
(AACSB), Clinical Psychology, Computer Science,
Construction Education, Counseling, Counseling
Psychology, Engineering (aerospace, agricultural,
chemical, civil, computer, electrical, industrial, materials,
mechanical, textile), Family and Consumer Science,
Forestry, Interior Design, Journalism, Landscape
Architecture, Marriage and Family Therapy, Music,
Nursing, Pharmacy, Public Administration, Rehabilitation
Counseling, Social Work, Speech-Language Pathology,
Teacher Education (NCATE), Theatre, Veterinary Medicine

Auburn University at Montgomery
PO Box 244023, Montgomery 36124-4023
Type: Public, state, four-year
System: Auburn University System
Degrees: B, M, P   *Enroll:* 3,928
URL: http://www.aum.edu
Phone: (334) 244-3000   *Calendar:* Sem. plan
Inst. Accred.: SACS (1968/1998)
Prog. Accred.: Business (AACSB), Clinical Lab Scientist, Nursing, Nursing Education, Public Administration, Teacher Education (NCATE)

Bevill State Community College
PO Box 800, Sumiton 35148
Type: Public, state, two-year
System: State of Alabama Department of Postsecondary Education
Degrees: A   *Enroll:* 3,090
URL: http://www.bscc.edu
Phone: (205) 648-3271   *Calendar:* Sem. plan
Inst. Accred.: SACS (1994/1999)
Prog. Accred.: Clinical Lab Technology, EMT (Paramedic), Nursing, Practical Nursing

Brewer Campus
2631 Temple Ave. North, Fayette 35555
Phone: (205) 932-3221

Walker College
1411 Indiana Ave., Jasper 35501
Phone: (205) 387-0511

Birmingham-Southern College
900 Arkadelphia Rd., Birmingham 35254
Type: Private, United Methodist Church, four-year
System: Alabama Association of Independent Colleges and Universities
Degrees: B, M   *Enroll:* 1,348
URL: http://www.bsc.edu
Phone: (205) 226-4600   *Calendar:* 4-1-4 plan
Inst. Accred.: SACS (1922/2004)
Prog. Accred.: Business (AACSB), Music, Teacher Education (NCATE)

Bishop State Community College
351 North Broad St., Mobile 36603-5898
Type: Public, state, two-year
System: State of Alabama Department of Postsecondary Education
Degrees: A   *Enroll:* 3,621
URL: http://www.bishop.edu
Phone: (251) 690-6801   *Calendar:* Sem. plan
Inst. Accred.: SACS (1992/2005)
Prog. Accred.: Business (ACBSP), Culinary Education, Funeral Service Education (Mortuary Science), Health Information Technician, Nursing, Physical Therapy Assisting

Baker Gains Central Campus
1365 Martin Luther King Ave., Mobile 36603-5362
Phone: (334) 405-4400

Carver Campus
414 Stanton St., Mobile 36617
Phone: (334) 473-8692

Southwest Campus
925 Dauphin Island Pkwy., Mobile 36605-3299
Phone: (334) 479-7476

Calhoun Community College
PO Box 2216, Decatur 35609-2216
Type: Public, state, two-year
System: State of Alabama Department of Postsecondary Education
Degrees: A   *Enroll:* 5,367
URL: http://www.calhoun.edu
Phone: (256) 306-2500   *Calendar:* Sem. plan
Inst. Accred.: SACS (1968/2002)
Prog. Accred.: Dental Assisting, Nursing, Practical Nursing

Central Alabama Community College
1675 Cherokee Rd., PO Box 699, Alexander City 35011
Type: Public, state, two-year
System: State of Alabama Department of Postsecondary Education
Degrees: A   *Enroll:* 1,346
URL: http://www.cacc.edu
Phone: (256) 234-6346   *Calendar:* Sem. plan
Inst. Accred.: SACS (1969/2005)
Prog. Accred.: Nursing

Chattahoochee Valley Community College
PO Box 1000, 2602 College Dr., Phenix City 36869
Type: Public, state, two-year
System: State of Alabama Department of Postsecondary Education
Degrees: A   *Enroll:* 1,300
URL: http://www.cvcc.cc.al.us
Phone: (334) 291-4900   *Calendar:* Sem. plan
Inst. Accred.: SACS (1976/2002)
Prog. Accred.: Nursing

Columbia Southern University
25326 Canal Rd., Orange Beach 36561
Type: Private, proprietary, four-year
Degrees: A, B, M   *FTE Enroll:* 313
URL: http://www.columbiasouthern.edu
Phone: (251) 981-3771
Inst. Accred.: DETC (2001)

Concordia College Selma
1804 Green St., PO Box 1329, Selma 36701
Type: Private, Lutheran Church-Missouri Synod, four-year
System: Concordia University System
Degrees: A, B   *Enroll:* 764
URL: http://www.concordiaselma.edu
Phone: (334) 874-5700   *Calendar:* Sem. plan
Inst. Accred.: SACS (1983/1999)

Enterprise-Ozark Community College
600 Plaza Dr., PO Box 1300, Enterprise 36331
Type: Public, state, two-year
System: State of Alabama Department of Postsecondary
  Education
Degrees: A   *Enroll:* 1,459
URL: http://www.eocc.edu
Phone: (334) 347-2623   *Calendar:* Sem. plan
Inst. Accred.: SACS (1969/2005)

Aviation Campus
3405 South US 231, Ozark 36360
Phone: (334) 774-5113

Faulkner University
5345 Atlanta Hwy., Montgomery 36109-3378
Type: Private, Church of Christ, four-year
System: Alabama Association of Independent Colleges
  and Universities
Degrees: A, B, D   *Enroll:* 2,058
URL: http://www.faulkner.edu
Phone: (334) 272-5820   *Calendar:* Sem. plan
Inst. Accred.: SACS (1971/1999)

Gadsden State Community College
PO Box 227, 1001 George Wallace Dr., Gadsden 35902-
0227
Type: Public, state, two-year
System: State of Alabama Department of Postsecondary
  Education
Degrees: A   *Enroll:* 4,133
URL: http://www.gadsdenstate.edu
Phone: (256) 549-8200   *Calendar:* Sem. plan
Inst. Accred.: SACS (1968/2002)
Prog. Accred.: Business (ACBSP), Clinical Lab Technology,
  EMT (Paramedic), Nursing, Radiography

Ayers Campus
1801 Coleman Rd., PO Box 1647, Anniston 36202-
1647
Phone: (256) 835-5400

George C. Wallace State Community College—Dothan
1141 Wallace Dr., Dothan 36303-9234
Type: Public, state, two-year
System: State of Alabama Department of Postsecondary
  Education
Degrees: A   *Enroll:* 2,659
URL: http://www.wallace.edu
Phone: (334) 983-3521   *Calendar:* Sem. plan
Inst. Accred.: SACS (1969/2002)
Prog. Accred.: Diagnostic Medical Sonography, EMT
  (Paramedic), Health Information Technician, Medical
  Assisting (AMA), Nursing, Physical Therapy Assisting,
  Practical Nursing, Radiography, Respiratory Therapy

Sparks Campus
3235 South Eufaula Ave., PO Drawer 580, Eufaula
36072-0580
Phone: (334) 687-3543

George Corley Wallace State Community College—Selma
PO Box 2530, 3000 Earl Goodwin Pkwy., Selma 36702-
2530
Type: Public, state, two-year
System: State of Alabama Department of Postsecondary
  Education
Degrees: A   *Enroll:* 1,362
URL: http://www.wccs.edu
Phone: (334) 876-9227   *Calendar:* Sem. plan
Inst. Accred.: SACS (1974/1999)
Prog. Accred.: Nursing, Practical Nursing

H. Councill Trenholm State Technical College
1225 Air Base Blvd., PO Box 9039, Montgomery 36108
Type: Public, state, two-year
System: State of Alabama Department of Postsecondary
  Education
Degrees: A   *Enroll:* 503
URL: http://www.trenholmtech.cc.al.us
Phone: (334) 420-4200   *Calendar:* Sem. plan
Inst. Accred.: COE (1972/2005)
Prog. Accred.: Culinary Education, Dental Assisting,
  Dental Laboratory Technology, EMT (Paramedic),
  Medical Assisting (AMA), Practical Nursing

Patterson Campus
3920 Troy Hwy., Montgomery 36116
Phone: (334) 288-1080
Prog. Accred: Dental Assisting, Dental Laboratory
  Technology

Heritage Christian University
3625 Helton Dr., PO Box HCU, Florence 35630-9977
Type: Private, Churches of Christ, four-year
Degrees: A, B, M   *Enroll:* 85
URL: http://www.hcu.edu
Phone: (256) 766-6610   *Calendar:* Sem. plan
Inst. Accred.: ABHE (1988/1999)

Herzing College—Birmingham Campus
280 West Valley Ave., Birmingham 35209
Type: Private, proprietary, four-year
System: Herzing College Corporate Offices
Degrees: A, B   *Enroll:* 336
URL: http://www.herzing.edu
Phone: (205) 916-2800   *Calendar:* Sem. plan
Inst. Accred.: ACCSCT (1971/2004), NCA-HLC (2004,
  Indirect accreditation through Herzing College
  Corporate Offices, Milwaukee, WI)

Huntingdon College
1500 East Fairview Ave., Montgomery 36106-2148
Type: Private, United Methodist Church, four-year
System: Alabama Association of Independent Colleges
  and Universities
Degrees: A, B   *Enroll:* 642
URL: http://www.huntingdon.edu
Phone: (334) 833-4222   *Calendar:* Sem. plan
Inst. Accred.: SACS (1928/2000, Probation)
Prog. Accred.: Music

J.F. Drake State Technical College
3421 Meridian St., North, Huntsville 35811
Type: Public, state, two-year
System: State of Alabama Department of Postsecondary
Education
Degrees: A   *Enroll:* 573
URL: http://www.dstc.cc.al.us
Phone: (256) 539-8161   *Calendar:* Qtr. plan
Inst. Accred.: COE (1971/2001)

J.F. Ingram State Technical College
PO Box 220350, 5375 Ingram Rd., Deatsville 36022
Type: Public, state, two-year
System: State of Alabama Department of Postsecondary
Education
Degrees: A   *Enroll:* 500
Phone: (334) 285-7870   *Calendar:* Qtr. plan
Inst. Accred.: COE (1977/2004)

Jacksonville State University
700 Pelham Rd., Jacksonville 36265
Type: Public, state, four-year
System: Alabama Commission on Higher Education
Degrees: B, M, P   *Enroll:* 7,323
URL: http://www.jsu.edu
Phone: (256) 782-5781   *Calendar:* Sem. plan
Inst. Accred.: SACS (1935/2003)
Prog. Accred.: Art, Business (AACSB), Electronic
Technology, Industrial Technology, Music, Nursing,
Nursing Education, Social Work, Teacher Education
(NCATE), Theatre

James H. Faulkner State Community College
1900 Hwy. 31 South, Bay Minette 36507
Type: Public, state, two-year
System: State of Alabama Department of Postsecondary
Education
Degrees: A   *Enroll:* 2,308
URL: http://www.faulkner.cc.al.us
Phone: (251) 580-2100   *Calendar:* Sem. plan
Inst. Accred.: SACS (1970/1995)
Prog. Accred.: Culinary Education, Dental Assisting

Jefferson Davis Community College
PO Box 958, 220 Alco Dr., Brewton 36427
Type: Public, state, two-year
System: State of Alabama Department of Postsecondary
Education
Degrees: A   *Enroll:* 1,087
URL: http://www.jdcc.edu
Phone: (251) 867-4832   *Calendar:* Sem. plan
Inst. Accred.: SACS (1994/1999)
Prog. Accred.: Nursing

Jefferson State Community College
2601 Carson Rd., Birmingham 35215-3098
Type: Public, state, two-year
System: State of Alabama Department of Postsecondary
Education
Degrees: A   *Enroll:* 4,280
URL: http://www.jeffersonstate.edu
Phone: (205) 853-1200   *Calendar:* Sem. plan
Inst. Accred.: SACS (1968/2003)
Prog. Accred.: Business (ACBSP), Clinical Lab Technology,
Construction Education, Culinary Education, Funeral
Service Education (Mortuary Science), Nursing, Physical
Therapy Assisting, Radiography

Judson College
PO Box 120, 302 Bibb St., Marion 36756
Type: Private, Alabama Baptist Convention, four-year
System: Alabama Association of Independent Colleges
and Universities
Degrees: B   *Enroll:* 334
URL: http://www.judson.edu
Phone: (334) 683-5100   *Calendar:* Sem. plan
Inst. Accred.: SACS (1925/2005)
Prog. Accred.: Music

Lurleen B. Wallace Community College
PO Box 1418, Andalusia 36420
Type: Public, state, two-year
System: State of Alabama Department of Postsecondary
Education
Degrees: A   *Enroll:* 742
URL: http://www.lbw.edu
Phone: (334) 222-6591   *Calendar:* Sem. plan
Inst. Accred.: SACS (1972/1997)
Prog. Accred.: EMT (Paramedic)

MacArthur Campus
1708 North Main St., PO Drawer 910, Opp 36467
Phone: (334) 493-3573

Marion Military Institute
1101 Washington St., Marion 36756
Type: Private, independent, two-year
Degrees: A   *Enroll:* 173
URL: http://www.marionmilitary.edu
Phone: (334) 683-2306   *Calendar:* Sem. plan
Inst. Accred.: SACS (1926/1994, Warning)

Miles College
PO Box 3800, Birmingham 35208
Type: Private, Christian Methodist Episcopal Church,
four-year
System: Alabama Association of Independent Colleges
and Universities
Degrees: A, B   *Enroll:* 1,593
URL: http://www.miles.edu
Phone: (205) 929-1000   *Calendar:* Sem. plan
Inst. Accred.: SACS (1969/2003)
Prog. Accred.: Social Work

Northeast Alabama Community College
PO Box 159, 138 Lowell Barron Hwy., Rainsville 35986
Type: Public, state, two-year
System: State of Alabama Department of Postsecondary
  Education
Degrees: A   *Enroll:* 1,383
URL: http://www.nacc.edu
Phone: (256) 228-6001   *Calendar:* Sem. plan
Inst. Accred.: SACS (1969/2005)
Prog. Accred.: Nursing

Northwest-Shoals Community College
PO Box 2545, 800 George Wallace Blvd., Muscle Shoals
35662
Type: Public, state, two-year
System: State of Alabama Department of Postsecondary
  Education
Degrees: A   *Enroll:* 3,203
URL: http://nwscc.edu
Phone: (256) 331-5200   *Calendar:* Sem. plan
Inst. Accred.: SACS (1994/1999)
Prog. Accred.: Nursing

Oakwood College
7000 Adventist Blvd., NW, Huntsville 35896
Type: Private, Seventh-Day Adventist Church, four-year
System: Alabama Association of Independent Colleges
  and Universities
Degrees: A, B   *Enroll:* 1,672
URL: http://www.oakwood.edu
Phone: (256) 726-7000   *Calendar:* Sem. plan
Inst. Accred.: SACS (1958/2001)
Prog. Accred.: Business (ACBSP), Social Work, Teacher
  Education (NCATE)

Prince Institute of Professional Studies
7735 Atlanta Hwy., Montgomery 36117-4231
Type: Private, proprietary, two-year
Degrees: A   *Enroll:* 71
URL: http://www.princeinstitute.edu
Phone: (334) 271-1670   *Calendar:* Qtr. plan
Inst. Accred.: ACICS (1984/2002)

Reid State Technical College
I-65 at Hwy. 83, PO Box 588, Evergreen 36401
Type: Public, state, two-year
System: State of Alabama Department of Postsecondary
  Education
Degrees: A   *Enroll:* 606
URL: http://www.rstc.cc.al.us
Phone: (251) 578-1313   *Calendar:* Sem. plan
Inst. Accred.: COE (1972/2005)
Prog. Accred.: Business (ACBSP)

Remington College—Mobile
828 Downtowner Loop West, Mobile 36609-5404
Type: Private, proprietary, four-year
System: Education America, Inc.
Degrees: A, B   *Enroll:* 475
URL: http://www.remingtoncollege.edu
Phone: (251) 343-8200   *Calendar:* Qtr. plan
Inst. Accred.: ACCSCT (1986/2003)

Little Rock Campus
19 Remington Rd., Little Rock, AR 72204
Phone: (501) 312-0007

Memphis Campus
2731 Nonconnah Blvd., Memphis, TN 38132-2110
Phone: (901) 345-1000

Nashville Campus
441 Donelson Pike, Ste. 150, Nashville, TN 37214
Phone: (615) 889-5520

Samford University
800 Lakeshore Dr., Birmingham 35229
Type: Private, Southern Baptist Church, four-year
System: Alabama Association of Independent Colleges
  and Universities
Degrees: A, B, M, P, D   *Enroll:* 4,109
URL: http://www.samford.edu
Phone: (205) 726-2011   *Calendar:* Sem. plan
Inst. Accred.: ATS (1996), SACS (1920/1996)
Prog. Accred.: Athletic Training, Business (AACSB), Law,
  Liberal Education, Music, Nursing, Nursing Education,
  Pharmacy, Teacher Education (NCATE)

Shelton State Community College
9500 Old Greensboro Rd., Tuscaloosa 35405-8522
Type: Public, state, two-year
System: State of Alabama Department of Postsecondary
  Education
Degrees: A   *Enroll:* 4,089
URL: http://www.sheltonstate.edu
Phone: (205) 391-2211   *Calendar:* Sem. plan
Inst. Accred.: SACS (1994/1999)
Prog. Accred.: EMT (Paramedic), Nursing, Respiratory
  Therapy, Respiratory Therapy Technology

Snead State Community College
PO Box 734, Boaz 35957-0734
Type: Public, state, two-year
System: State of Alabama Department of Postsecondary
  Education
Degrees: A   *Enroll:* 1,353
URL: http://www.snead.edu
Phone: (256) 593-5120   *Calendar:* Sem. plan
Inst. Accred.: SACS (1941/2003)
Prog. Accred.: Veterinary Technology

Southeastern Bible College
2545 Valleydale Rd., Birmingham 35244-2083
Type: Private, nondenominational, four-year
System: Alabama Association of Independent Colleges
and Universities
Degrees: A, B   *Enroll:* 205
URL: http://www.sebc.edu
Phone: (205) 970-9200   *Calendar:* Sem. plan
Inst. Accred.: ABHE (1962/2004)

Southern Christian University
1200 Taylor Rd., Montgomery 36117-3553
Type: Private, Church of Christ, four-year
Degrees: B, M, D   *Enroll:* 558
URL: http://www.southernchristian.edu
Phone: (334) 387-3877   *Calendar:* Sem. plan
Inst. Accred.: SACS (1989/2005)

Southern Union State Community College
PO Box 1000, Wadley 36276
Type: Public, state, two-year
System: State of Alabama Department of Postsecondary
Education
Degrees: A   *Enroll:* 3,610
URL: http://www.suscc.edu
Phone: (256) 395-2211   *Calendar:* Sem. plan
Inst. Accred.: SACS (1994/1996)
Prog. Accred.: EMT (Paramedic), Nursing, Practical
Nursing, Radiography

Spring Hill College
4000 Dauphin St., Mobile 36608-1791
Type: Private, Roman Catholic Church, four-year
System: Alabama Association of Independent Colleges
and Universities
Degrees: B, M   *Enroll:* 1,225
URL: http://www.shc.edu
Phone: (251) 380-3030   *Calendar:* Sem. plan
Inst. Accred.: SACS (1922/1995)
Prog. Accred.: Business (ACBSP), Nursing Education

Stillman College
PO Box 1430, 3600 Stillman Blvd., Tuscaloosa 35403
Type: Private, Presbyterian Church (USA), four-year
System: Alabama Association of Independent Colleges
and Universities
Degrees: B   *Enroll:* 1,148
URL: http://www.stillman.edu
Phone: (205) 349-4240   *Calendar:* Sem. plan
Inst. Accred.: SACS (1953/2000)

T.A. Lawson State Community College
3060 Wilson Rd., SW, Birmingham 35221
Type: Public, state, two-year
System: State of Alabama Department of Postsecondary
Education
Degrees: A   *Enroll:* 1,884
URL: http://www.lawsonstate.edu
Phone: (205) 925-2515   *Calendar:* Sem. plan
Inst. Accred.: SACS (1968/2002)
Prog. Accred.: Business (ACBSP), Nursing

Bessemer Campus
PO Box 308, 1100 Ninth Ave., SW, Bessemer 35022
Phone: (205) 426-7374
Prog. Accred: Dental Assisting, Practical Nursing

Talladega College
627 West Battle St., Talladega 35160
Type: Private, Church of Christ, four-year
System: Alabama Association of Independent Colleges
and Universities
Degrees: B   *Enroll:* 434
URL: http://www.talladega.edu
Phone: (256) 362-0206   *Calendar:* Sem. plan
Inst. Accred.: SACS (1931/1999, Probation)

Troy University
University Ave., Troy 36082
Type: Public, state, four-year
System: Troy State University System
Degrees: A, B, M, P   *Enroll:* 12,716
URL: http://www.troy.edu
Phone: (334) 670-3000   *Calendar:* Sem. plan
Inst. Accred.: SACS (1934/2003)
Prog. Accred.: Accounting, Athletic Training, Business
(AACSB), Business (ACBSP), Counseling, Music,
Nursing, Social Work, Teacher Education (NCATE)

Atlantic Region Campus
5425 Robin Hood Rd., Ste. B-1, Norfolk, VA 23513
Phone: (757) 451-8202

Florida Region Campus
81 Beal Pkwy. SE, Fort Walton Beach, FL 32548-5327
Phone: (850) 244-7414

Pacific Region Campus
Okinawa, 47, Japan
Phone: 011 81 611-734-3930

Phenix City Campus
One University Place, Phenix City 36869
Phone: (334) 448-5106

Southeast Region Campus
PO Box 4790, Columbus, GA 31914
Phone: (866) 288-2105

Western Region Campus
5825 Delmonico Dr., Ste. 120, Colorado Springs, CO
80919

Phone: (719) 265-8769

Troy University Dothan
PO Box 8368, 3601 U.S. Hwy. 231 North, Dothan 36304-0368
Type: Public, state, four-year
System: Troy State University System
Degrees: A, B, M, P   *Enroll:* 1,271
URL: http://www.tsud.edu
Phone: (334) 983-6556   *Calendar:* Sem. plan
Inst. Accred.: SACS (1985/2000)
Prog. Accred.: Business (ACBSP), Teacher Education (NCATE)

Troy University Montgomery
231 Montgomery St., PO Drawer 4419, Montgomery 36103-4419
Type: Public, state, four-year
System: Troy State University System
Degrees: A, B, M, P   *Enroll:* 2,323
URL: http://www.tsum.edu
Phone: (334) 834-1400   *Calendar:* Sem. plan
Inst. Accred.: SACS (1983/1999)
Prog. Accred.: Business (ACBSP)

Tuskegee University
308 Kresge Center, Tuskegee 36088
Type: Private, independent, four-year
System: Alabama Association of Independent Colleges and Universities
Degrees: B, M, D   *Enroll:* 2,682
URL: http://www.tuskegee.edu
Phone: (334) 727-8011   *Calendar:* Sem. plan
Inst. Accred.: SACS (1933/1998)
Prog. Accred.: Business (AACSB), Clinical Lab Scientist, Engineering (aerospace, chemical, electrical, mechanical), Nursing, Occupational Therapy, Social Work, Teacher Education (NCATE), Veterinary Medicine

United States Sports Academy
One Academy Dr., Daphne 36526
Type: Private, independent, four-year
System: Alabama Association of Independent Colleges and Universities
Degrees: B, M, D   *Enroll:* 228
URL: http://www.ussa.edu
Phone: (251) 626-3303   *Calendar:* Sem. plan
Inst. Accred.: SACS (1983/1998)

The University of Alabama
PO Box 870100, Tuscaloosa 35487-0100
Type: Public, state, four-year
System: University of Alabama System
Degrees: B, M, P, D   *Enroll:* 18,302
URL: http://www.ua.edu
Phone: (205) 348-6010   *Calendar:* Sem. plan
Inst. Accred.: SACS (1897/2005)
Prog. Accred.: Accounting, Art, Athletic Training, Audiology, Business (AACSB), Clinical Psychology, Computer Science, Counseling, Dance, Dietetics (coordinated), Engineering (aerospace, chemical, civil, computer, electrical, industrial, mechanical,

metallurgical, mineral), English Language Education, Family and Consumer Science, Interior Design, Journalism, Law, Librarianship, Music, Nursing, Nursing Education, Rehabilitation Counseling, Social Work, Speech-Language Pathology, Teacher Education (NCATE), Theatre

The University of Alabama at Birmingham
1530 3rd Ave. South, Birmingham 35294-0150
Type: Public, state, four-year
System: University of Alabama System
Degrees: B, M, D   *Enroll:* 13,022
URL: http://www.uab.edu
Phone: (205) 934-4011   *Calendar:* Sem. plan
Inst. Accred.: SACS (1970/2005)
Prog. Accred.: Accounting, Advanced Education in General Dentistry, Applied Science (industrial hygiene), Art, Blood Bank Technology, Business (AACSB), Clinical Lab Scientist, Clinical Psychology, Combined Prosthodontics, Cytotechnology, Dental Assisting, Dental Hygiene, Dental Laboratory Technology, Dental Public Health, Dentistry, Dietetics (internship), EMT (Paramedic), Endodontics, Engineering (civil, electrical, materials, mechanical), General Dentistry, General Practice Residency, Health Information Administration, Health Services Administration, Maxillofacial Prosthetics, Medicine, Music, Nuclear Medicine Technology, Nurse Anesthesia Education, Nursing, Nursing Education, Occupational Therapy, Optometric Residency, Optometry, Oral and Maxillofacial Pathology, Oral and Maxillofacial Surgery, Orthodontic and Dentofacial Orthopedics, Pediatric Dentistry, Periodontics, Physical Therapy, Physician Assistant, Prosthodontics, Psychology Internship, Public Administration, Public Health, Radiography, Radiation Therapy, Rehabilitation Counseling, Respiratory Therapy, Social Work, Teacher Education (NCATE)

The University Hospital in Birmingham
618 18th St. South, 125 West Pavilion, Birmingham 35249
Phone: (205) 934-5748
Prog. Accred: Clinical Pastoral Education

The University of Alabama in Huntsville
301 Sparkman Dr., Huntsville 35899
Type: Public, state, four-year
System: University of Alabama System
Degrees: B, M, D   *Enroll:* 5,495
URL: http://www.uah.edu
Phone: (256) 824-6767   *Calendar:* Sem. plan
Inst. Accred.: SACS (1970/1995)
Prog. Accred.: Business (AACSB), Computer Science, EMT (Paramedic), Engineering (aerospace, chemical, civil, computer, electrical, industrial, mechanical, optical/optics), Music, Nursing, Nursing Education

University of Mobile
5735 College Pkwy., Mobile 36613
Type: Private, Southern Baptist Church, four-year
System: Alabama Association of Independent Colleges and Universities
Degrees: A, B, M   *Enroll:* 1,502
URL: http://www.umobile.edu
Phone: (251) 675-5990   *Calendar:* Sem. plan
Inst. Accred.: SACS (1968/2003)
Prog. Accred.: Business (ACBSP), Music, Nursing, Nursing Education

University of Montevallo
Station 6001, Montevallo 35115-6001
Type: Public, state, four-year
System: Alabama Commission on Higher Education
Degrees: B, M, P   *Enroll:* 2,766
URL: http://www.montevallo.edu
Phone: (205) 665-6000   *Calendar:* Sem. plan
Inst. Accred.: SACS (1925/2000)
Prog. Accred.: Art, Audiology, Business (AACSB), Counseling, Family and Consumer Science, Music, Social Work, Speech-Language Pathology, Teacher Education (NCATE)

The University of North Alabama
UNA - Box 5004, Florence 35632-0001
Type: Public, state, four-year
System: Alabama Commission on Higher Education
Degrees: B, M, P   *Enroll:* 4,769
URL: http://www.una.edu
Phone: (256) 765-4100   *Calendar:* Sem. plan
Inst. Accred.: SACS (1934/2002)
Prog. Accred.: Applied Science (industrial hygiene), Art, Business (ACBSP), Music, Nursing, Social Work, Teacher Education (NCATE)

University of South Alabama
307 University Blvd., Mobile 36688-0002
Type: Public, state, four-year
System: Alabama Commission on Higher Education
Degrees: B, M, P, D   *Enroll:* 10,948
URL: http://www.usouthal.edu
Phone: (334) 460-6101   *Calendar:* Sem. plan
Inst. Accred.: SACS (1968/2003)
Prog. Accred.: Audiology, Business (AACSB), Clinical Lab Scientist, Computer Science, EMT (Paramedic), Engineering (chemical, civil, computer, electrical, mechanical), Medicine, Music, Nursing, Nursing Education, Occupational Therapy, Physical Therapy, Physician Assistant, Radiography, Respiratory Therapy, Speech-Language Pathology, Teacher Education (NCATE)

The University of West Alabama
205 North Washington St., Station 1, Livingston 35470
Type: Public, state, four-year
System: Alabama Commission on Higher Education
Degrees: A, B, M, P   *Enroll:* 2,045
URL: http://www.uwa.edu
Phone: (205) 652-3400   *Calendar:* Sem. plan
Inst. Accred.: SACS (1938/2002)
Prog. Accred.: Athletic Training, Business (ACBSP), Nursing, Teacher Education (NCATE)

Virginia College
65 Bagby Dr., Birmingham 35219
Type: Private, proprietary, four-year
Degrees: A, B, M   *Enroll:* 2,241
URL: http://www.vc.edu
Phone: (205) 802-1200   *Calendar:* Qtr. plan
Inst. Accred.: ACICS (1990/2001)

Austin Campus
6301 East Hwy. 290, Austin, TX 78723
Phone: (512) 371-3500

Culinard at Virginia College
195 Vulcan Rd., Birmingham 35209
Phone: (205) 802-1200
Prog. Accred: Culinary Education

Gulf Coast Biloxi Campus
920 Cedar Lake Rd., Biloxi, MS 39532
Phone: (228) 392-2994

Huntsville Campus
2800-A Bob Wallace Ave., Huntsville 35805
Phone: (256) 533-7387

Jackson Campus
5360 I-55 North, Jackson, MS 39211
Phone: (601) 977-0960

VC Tech Campus
2790 Pelham Pkwy., Pelham 35124
Phone: (205) 943-2100

Virginia College Online
500 Century Park South, Ste. 200, Birmingham 35226
Phone: (205) 397-6600

Wallace State Community College
PO Box 2000, 801 Main St., Hanceville 35077-2000
Type: Public, state, two-year
System: State of Alabama Department of Postsecondary Education
Degrees: A   *Enroll:* 3,823
URL: http://www.wallacestate.edu
Phone: (256) 352-8000   *Calendar:* Sem. plan
Inst. Accred.: SACS (1978/2005)
Prog. Accred.: Clinical Lab Technology, Dental Assisting, Dental Hygiene, Diagnostic Medical Sonography, EMT (Paramedic), Health Information Technician, Medical Assisting (AMA), Nursing, Occupational Therapy Assisting, Physical Therapy Assisting, Radiography, Respiratory Therapy

ALASKA

Alaska Bible College
200 College Rd., PO Box 289, Glennallen 99588-0289
Type: Private, nondenominational, four-year
Degrees: A, B   *FTE Enroll:* 35
URL: http://www.akbible.edu
Phone: (907) 822-3201   *Calendar:* Sem. plan
Inst. Accred.: ABHE (1982/2003)

Alaska Pacific University
4101 University Dr., Anchorage 99508-4672
Type: Private, independent, four-year
Degrees: A, B, M   *Enroll:* 490
URL: http://www.alaskapacific.edu
Phone: (907) 561-1266   *Calendar:* Sem. plan
Inst. Accred.: NWCCU (1981/2003)

Charter College
2221 East Northern Lights Blvd., Ste. 120, Anchorage
99508
Type: Private, proprietary, four-year
Degrees: A, B   *Enroll:* 240
URL: http://www.chartercollege.edu
Phone: (907) 227-1000   *Calendar:* Qtr. plan
Inst. Accred.: ACICS (1988/2003)

Ilisagvik College
PO Box 749, NARL Facilities, Barrow 99723
Type: Private, independent, two-year
Degrees: A   *Enroll:* 180
URL: http://www.ilisagvik.cc
Phone: (907) 852-3333   *Calendar:* Sem. plan
Inst. Accred.: NWCCU (2002)

Prince William Sound Community College
PO Box 97, Valdez 99686
Type: Public, state, two-year
System: University of Alaska Anchorage
Degrees: A   *Enroll:* 327
URL: http://www.uaa.alaska.edu/pwscc
Phone: (907) 834-1660   *Calendar:* Sem. plan
Inst. Accred.: NWCCU (1989/1999)

Sheldon Jackson College
801 Lincoln St., Sitka 99835
Type: Private, independent, four-year
Degrees: A, B   *Enroll:* 134
URL: http://www.sj-alaska.edu
Phone: (907) 747-5222   *Calendar:* 4-1-4 plan
Inst. Accred.: NWCCU (1966/1998, Probation)

University of Alaska Anchorage
3211 Providence Dr., Anchorage 99508
Type: Public, state, four-year
System: University of Alaska System
Degrees: A, B, M   *Enroll:* 10,760
URL: http://www.uaa.alaska.edu
Phone: (907) 786-1800   *Calendar:* Sem. plan
Inst. Accred.: NWCCU (1974/2003)
Prog. Accred.: Applied Science (surveying/geomatics),
   Art, Business (AACSB), Clinical Lab Technology, Dental
   Assisting, Dental Hygiene, Engineering (civil),
   Journalism, Massage Therapy, Medical Assisting (AMA),
   Music, Nursing, Social Work

Kenai Peninsula College
34820 College Dr., Soldotna 99669
Phone: (907) 262-0330

Kodiak College
117 Benny Benson Dr., Kodiak 99615
Phone: (907) 486-4161

Matanuska-Susitna College
Box 2889, Palmer 99645
Phone: (907) 745-9774

University of Alaska Fairbanks
PO Box 757500, 320 Signers' Hall, Fairbanks 99775-
6725
Type: Public, state, four-year
System: University of Alaska System
Degrees: A, B, M, D   *Enroll:* 6,009
URL: http://www.uaf.edu
Phone: (907) 474-7581   *Calendar:* Sem. plan
Inst. Accred.: NWCCU (1934/2001)
Prog. Accred.: Accounting, Business (AACSB), Computer
   Science, Engineering (civil, electrical,
   geological/geophysical, mechanical, mining, petroleum),
   Forestry, Journalism, Music, Social Work

Bristol Bay Campus
PO Box 1070, Dillingham 99576
Phone: (800) 478-5109

Chukchi Campus
PO Box 297, Kotzebue 99752
Phone: (907) 442-3400

Kuskokwim Campus
UAF-College of Rural Alaska, PO Box 368, Bethel
99559
Phone: (907) 543-4502

Northwest Campus
Pouch 400, Nome 99762
Phone: (907) 443-2201

University of Alaska Southeast
11120 Glacier Hwy., Juneau 99801
Type: Public, state, four-year
System: University of Alaska System
Degrees: A, B, M   *Enroll:* 1,818
URL: http://www.uas.alaska.edu
Phone: (907) 465-6457   *Calendar:* Sem. plan
Inst. Accred.: NWCCU (1983/1998)

Ketchikan Campus
2600 Seventh Ave., Ketchikan 99901
Phone: (907) 225-6177

Sitka Campus
1332 Seward Ave., Sitka 99835
Phone: (907) 747-7701
Prog. Accred: Health Information Technician

AMERICAN SAMOA

American Samoa Community College

PO Box 2609, Pago Pago 96799
Type: Public, state, two-year
Degrees: A   *Enroll:* 1,052
URL: http://www.amsamoacc.as
Phone: (684) 699-9155   *Calendar:* Sem. plan
Inst. Accred.: WASC-JR. (1976/2003, Warning)

ARIZONA

American Indian College
of the Assemblies of God
10020 North 15th Ave., Phoenix 85021
Type: Private, General Council of the Assemblies of God,
four-year
Degrees: A, B   *Enroll:* 74
URL: http://www.aicag.edu
Phone: (602) 944-3335   *Calendar:* Sem. plan
Inst. Accred.: NCA-HLC (1988/2003)

Apollo College—Phoenix Campus
8503 North 27th Ave., Phoenix 85051
Type: Private, proprietary, two-year
System: U.S. Education Corporation
Degrees: A   *Enroll:* 2,262
URL: http://www.apollocollege.com
Phone: (602) 864-1571
Inst. Accred.: ABHES (1991/2002)
Prog. Accred.: Respiratory Therapy

Albuquerque Campus
5301 Central Ave., NE, Ste. 101, Albuquerque, NM
87108
Phone: (505) 254-7777
Prog. Accred: Medical Assisting (ABHES), Medical
Laboratory Technology

Mesa Campus
630 West Southern Ave., Mesa 85210-5004
Phone: (480) 831-6585
Prog. Accred: Medical Assisting (ABHES), Respiratory
Therapy

Tucson Campus
3550 North Oracle Rd., Tucson 85705
Phone: (520) 888-5885
Prog. Accred: Medical Assisting (ABHES)

Westside Campus
2701 West Bethany Home Rd., Phoenix 85017
Phone: (602) 433-1333
Prog. Accred: Radiography

Argosy University Phoenix
2301 West Dunlap, Ste. 211, Phoenix 85021
Type: Private, proprietary, four-year
System: Argosy University
Degrees: M, D
URL: http://www.argosyu.edu
Phone: (602) 216-2600   *Calendar:* Tri. plan
Inst. Accred.: NCA-HLC (1981/2001, *Indirect accreditation
through Argosy University, Chicago, IL*)
Prog. Accred.: Clinical Psychology

Arizona Automotive Institute
6829 North 46th Ave., Glendale 85301-3597
Type: Private, proprietary, two-year
Degrees: A   *Enroll:* 677
URL: http://www.azautoinst.com
Phone: (623) 934-7273   *Calendar:* Qtr. plan
Inst. Accred.: ACCSCT (1972/2000)

Arizona School of Acupunture and
Oriental Medicine
4646 East Fort Lowell Rd., Ste. 105, Tuscon 85712
Type: Private, proprietary, four-year
Degrees: M
URL: http://azschacu.edu
Phone: (520) 795-0787   *Calendar:* Qtr. plan
Inst. Accred.: ACAOM (2003)
Prog. Accred.: Acupuncture

Arizona State University
PO Box 872803, Tempe 85287-2803
Type: Public, state, four-year
System: Arizona Board of Regents
Degrees: B, M, D   *Enroll:* 41,617
URL: http://www.asu.edu
Phone: (480) 965-9011   *Calendar:* Sem. plan
Inst. Accred.: NCA-HLC (1931/2003)
Prog. Accred.: Accounting, Art, Audiology, Business
(AACSB), Clinical Lab Scientist, Clinical Psychology,
Computer Science, Construction Education, Counseling,
Counseling Psychology, Engineering (aerospace,
bioengineering, chemical, civil, computer, electrical,
industrial, materials, mechanical), Health Services
Administration, Interior Design, Journalism, Landscape
Architecture, Law, Music, Nursing, Planning, Psychology
Internship, Public Administration, Public Health,
Recreation and Leisure Services, School Psychology,
Social Work, Speech-Language Pathology

East Campus
7001 East Williams Field Rd., Mesa 85212
Phone: (480) 727-3278
Prog. Accred: Dietetics (internship), Engineering
Technology (aerospace, electrical, manufacturing),
Industrial Technology

Arizona State University West
PO Box 37100, Phoenix 85069-7100
Type: Public, state, four-year
System: Arizona Board of Regents
Degrees: B, M   *Enroll:* 5,033
URL: http://www.west.asu.edu
Phone: (602) 543-5500   *Calendar:* Sem. plan
Inst. Accred.: NCA-HLC (1992/1997)
Prog. Accred.: Accounting, Business (AACSB), Recreation
and Leisure Services, Social Work

Arizona Western College
PO Box 929, Yuma 85366
Type: Public, state/local, two-year
System: State Board of Directors for Community Colleges
of Arizona
Degrees: A   *Enroll:* 3,272
URL: http://www.azwestern.edu
Phone: (520) 317-6000   *Calendar:* Sem. plan
Inst. Accred.: NCA-HLC (1968/1999)
Prog. Accred.: Nursing

The Art Center Design College
2525 North Country Club Rd., Tucson 85716-2505
Type: Private, proprietary, four-year
Degrees: A, B   *Enroll:* 284
URL: http://www.theartcenter.edu
Phone: (520) 325-0123   *Calendar:* Qtr. plan
Inst. Accred.: ACCSCT (1992/2002)
Prog. Accred.: Interior Design

Albuquerque Campus
5041 Indian School Rd. NE, Ste. 100, Albuquerque,
NM 87110
Phone: (505) 254-7575

The Bryman School
2250 West Peoria Ave., Bldg. A, Ste. 100, Phoenix 85029
Type: Private, proprietary, two-year
System: High-Tech Institute
Degrees: A   *Enroll:* 1,319
URL: http://www.brymanschool.edu
Phone: (602) 274-4300
Inst. Accred.: ACCSCT (1989/2005)
Prog. Accred.: Medical Assisting (ABHES), Medical
Assisting (CAAHEP)

The Bryman School—Tempe
8945 South Harl Dr., Ste. 102, Tempe 85284
Type: Private, proprietary, two-year
System: High-Tech Institute
Degrees: A
URL: http://www.brymanschool.edu
Phone: (480) 776-1100
Inst. Accred.: ACCSCT (2004)

Central Arizona College
8470 North Overfield Rd., Coolidge 85228
Type: Public, local, two-year
System: State Board of Directors for Community Colleges
of Arizona
Degrees: A   *Enroll:* 3,022
URL: http://www.centralaz.edu
Phone: (520) 426-4444   *Calendar:* Sem. plan
Inst. Accred.: NCA-HLC (1973/2003)
Prog. Accred.: Nursing

Aravaina Campus
Star Route 887, Winkleman 85292
Phone: (529) 357-2000

Superstition Mountain Campus
273 Old West Hwy., Apache Juction 85219
Phone: (480) 288-4005

Chandler-Gilbert Community College
2626 East Pecos Rd., Chandler 85225-2499
Type: Public, state/local, two-year
System: Maricopa County Community College District
Degrees: A   *Enroll:* 4,156
URL: http://www.cgc.maricopa.edu
Phone: (480) 732-7000   *Calendar:* Sem. plan
Inst. Accred.: NCA-HLC (1992/1997)

Williams Center
7360 East Tahoe Ave., Mesa 85212
Phone: (480) 988-8000

Chaparral College
4585 East Speedway Blvd., Ste. 204, Tucson 85712
Type: Private, proprietary, four-year
Degrees: A, B   *Enroll:* 383
URL: http://www.chap-col.edu
Phone: (520) 327-6866   *Calendar:* Qtr. plan
Inst. Accred.: ACICS (1969/2000)

Cochise College
4190 West Hwy. 80, Douglas 85607
Type: Public, state/local, two-year
System: State Board of Directors for Community Colleges
of Arizona
Degrees: A   *Enroll:* 2,692
URL: http://www.cochise.edu
Phone: (520) 364-7943   *Calendar:* Sem. plan
Inst. Accred.: NCA-HLC (1969/1996)
Prog. Accred.: Nursing

Coconino County Community College
2800 South Lonetree Rd., Flagstaff 86001-2701
Type: Public, state/local, two-year
System: State Board of Directors for Community Colleges
of Arizona
Degrees: A   *Enroll:* 1,454
URL: http://www.coconino.edu
Phone: (928) 527-1222   *Calendar:* Sem. plan
Inst. Accred.: NCA-HLC (1996/2002)

College of the Humanities and Sciences
Harrison Middleton University
1105 East Broadway, Tempe 85282
Type: Private, independent, four-year
Degrees: A, B, M
URL: http://www.chumsci.edu
Phone: (480) 317-5955
Inst. Accred.: DETC (2003)

CollegeAmerica
1800 South Military Rd., Flagstaff 86001
Type: Private, proprietary, two-year
Degrees: A
URL: http://www.collegeamerica.edu
Phone: (928) 526-0763
Inst. Accred.: ABHES (1982/2005)

Phoenix Campus
6533 North Black Canyon Hwy., Phoenix 85015
Phone: (800) 622-2894

Collins College
1140 South Priest Dr., Tempe 85281-5206
Type: Private, proprietary, four-year
System: Career Education Corporation
Degrees: A, B   *Enroll:* 1,945
URL: http://www.collinscollege.edu
Phone: (480) 966-3000
Inst. Accred.: ACCSCT (1981/2000)

DeVry University Phoenix
2149 West Dunlap Ave., Phoenix 85021-2995
Type: Private, proprietary, four-year
System: DeVry University
Degrees: A, B, M   *Enroll:* 1,936
URL: http://www.devry.edu/phoenix
Phone: (602) 870-9222   *Calendar:* Sem. plan
Inst. Accred.: NCA-HLC (2002, *Indirect accreditation through DeVry University, Oakbrook Terrace, IL*)
Prog. Accred.: Engineering Technology (computer)

Diné College
1 Circle Dr., PO Box 126, Tsaile 86556
Type: Public, tribal, four-year
System: American Indian Higher Education Consortium
Degrees: A, B   *Enroll:* 1,234
URL: http://www.dinecollege.edu
Phone: (928) 724-6800   *Calendar:* Sem. plan
Inst. Accred.: NCA-HLC (1976/2002)

Shiprock Campus
PO Box 580, Shiprock, NM 87420-0580
Phone: (505) 368-3501

Eastern Arizona College
615 North Stadium Ave., Thatcher 85552
Type: Public, state/local, two-year
System: State Board of Directors for Community Colleges of Arizona
Degrees: A   *Enroll:* 2,393
URL: http://www.eac.edu
Phone: (520) 428-8233   *Calendar:* Sem. plan
Inst. Accred.: NCA-HLC (1966/1996)

Estrella Mountain Community College
3000 North Dysart Rd., Avondale 85323-1000
Type: Public, state/local, two-year
System: Maricopa County Community College District
Degrees: A   *Enroll:* 2,574
URL: http://www.emc.maricopa.edu
Phone: (623) 935-8000   *Calendar:* Sem. plan
Inst. Accred.: NCA-HLC (1997/2002)

Everest College
10400 North 25th Ave., Ste. 190, Phoenix 85021
Type: Private, proprietary, four-year
System: Corinthian Colleges, Inc
Degrees: A, B   *Enroll:* 416
URL: http://www.everest-college.com
Phone: (602) 942-4141
Inst. Accred.: NCA-HLC (1997/2001)

Frank Lloyd Wright School of Architecture
12621 North Frank Lloyd Wright Blvd., Scottsdale 85261-4430
Type: Private, independent, four-year
Degrees: B, M   *FTE Enroll:* 21
URL: http://www.taliesin.edu
Phone: (480) 860-2700   *Calendar:* 12-mos. pr
Inst. Accred.: NCA-HLC (1987/2005, Warning)

Gateway Community College
108 North 40th St., Phoenix 85034
Type: Public, state/local, two-year
System: Maricopa County Community College District
Degrees: A   *Enroll:* 3,377
URL: http://www.gatewaycc.edu
Phone: (602) 392-5000   *Calendar:* Sem. plan
Inst. Accred.: NCA-HLC (1971/2000)
Prog. Accred.: Nursing, Physical Therapy Assisting, Radiography, Respiratory Therapy, Respiratory Therapy Technology

Glendale Community College
6000 West Olive Ave., Glendale 85302
Type: Public, state/local, two-year
System: Maricopa County Community College District
Degrees: A   *Enroll:* 10,980
URL: http://www.gc.maricopa.edu
Phone: (623) 845-3000   *Calendar:* Sem. plan
Inst. Accred.: NCA-HLC (1967/2002)
Prog. Accred.: Nursing

Grand Canyon University
3300 West Camelback Rd., PO Box 11097, Phoenix 85061-1097
Type: Private, proprietary, four-year
Degrees: B, M   *Enroll:* 2,009
URL: http://www.grand-canyon.edu
Phone: (602) 589-2500   *Calendar:* Sem. plan
Inst. Accred.: NCA-HLC (1968/1997)
Prog. Accred.: Business (ACBSP), Nursing, Nursing Education

High-Tech Institute—Phoenix
1515 East Indian School Rd., Phoenix 85014-4901
Type: Private, proprietary, four-year
System: High-Tech Institute
Degrees: A, B   *Enroll:* 1,352
URL: http://www.hightechschools.com
Phone: (602) 279-9700
Inst. Accred.: ACCSCT (1984/2004)

Atlanta Campus
1090 Northchase Pkwy., Marietta, GA 30067
Phone: (770) 988-9877

International Baptist College
2150 East Southern Ave., Tempe 85282-7504
Type: Private, independent Baptist, four-year
Degrees: A, B, M, D   *FTE Enroll:* 81
URL: http://www.tri-citybaptist.org
Phone: (480) 838-7070   *Calendar:* Sem. plan
Inst. Accred.: TRACS (2000)

International Import-Export Institute
2432 W. Peoria, Ste. 1026, Phoenix 85029
Type: Private, independent, four-year
Degrees: B   *FTE Enroll:* 297
URL: http://www.iiei.edu
Phone: (602) 648-5750   *Calendar:* Sem. plan
Inst. Accred.: DETC (2003)

International Institute of the Americas
6049 North 43rd Ave., Phoenix 85019-1600
Type: Private, proprietary, four-year
Degrees: A, B   *Enroll:* 563
URL: http://www.iia.edu
Phone: (602) 242-6265
Inst. Accred.: ACICS (1982/2001)

Albuquerque Campus
4201 Central Ave., NW, Ste. J, Albuquerque, NM
87105-1649
Phone: (505) 880-2877

Mesa Campus
925 South Gilbert Rd., Ste. 201, Mesa 85204-4448
Phone: (480) 545-8755

Tucson Campus
5441 East 22nd St., Ste. 125, Tucson 85711-5450
Phone: (520) 748-9799

West Valley Campus
4136 North 75th Ave., Ste. 211, Phoenix 85033-3169
Phone: (623) 849-8208

ITT Technical Institute
1455 West River Rd., Tucson 85704
Type: Private, proprietary, four-year
System: ITT Educational Services, Inc.
Degrees: A, B   *Enroll:* 349
URL: http://www.itt-tech.edu
Phone: (520) 408-7488   *Calendar:* Qtr. plan
Inst. Accred.: ACICS (1999/2003)

ITT Technical Institute
5005 South Wendler Dr., Tempe 85282
Type: Private, proprietary, four-year
System: ITT Educational Services, Inc.
Degrees: A, B   *Enroll:* 467
URL: http://www.itt-tech.edu
Phone: (602) 437-7500   *Calendar:* Qtr. plan
Inst. Accred.: ACICS (1999/2004)

Albuquerque Campus
5100 Masthead St., NE, Albuquerque, NM 87109-
4366
Phone: (505) 828-1114

Saint Rose Campus
140 James Dr. East, Saint Rose, LA 70087
Phone: (504) 463-0338

Lamson College
1126 North Scottsdale Rd., Ste. 17, Tempe 85281-1700
Type: Private, proprietary, two-year
Degrees: A   *Enroll:* 265
URL: http://www.lamsoncollege.com
Phone: (480) 898-7000   *Calendar:* Qtr. plan
Inst. Accred.: ACICS (1981/2002)

Long Technical College
13450 North Black Canyon Hwy., Ste. 104, Phoenix
85029-6323
Type: Private, proprietary, two-year
System: Kaplan Higher Education Corporation
Degrees: A   *Enroll:* 107
URL: http://www.longtechnicalcollege.com
Phone: (602) 548-1955
Inst. Accred.: ACCSCT (1981/2000)
Prog. Accred.: Medical Assisting (AMA), Respiratory
Therapy Technology

Long Technical College—East Valley
4646 East Van Buren St., Ste. 350, Phoenix 85008-6952
Type: Private, proprietary, two-year
System: Kaplan Higher Education Corporation
Degrees: A
URL: http://www.longtechnicalcollege.com
Phone: (602) 252-2171
Inst. Accred.: ACICS (1981/2000)

Mesa Community College
1833 West Southern Ave., Mesa 85202
Type: Public, state/local, two-year
System: Maricopa County Community College District
Degrees: A   *Enroll:* 14,280
URL: http://www.mc.maricopa.edu
Phone: (480) 461-7000   *Calendar:* Sem. plan
Inst. Accred.: NCA-HLC (1967/2005)
Prog. Accred.: Funeral Service Education (Mortuary
Science), Nursing

Red Mountain Campus
2305 North Power Rd., Mesa 85215
Phone: (480) 654-7200

Metropolitan College—Phoenix Campus
4129 East Van Buren St., Ste. 100, Phoenix 85008-6940
Type: Private, proprietary, four-year
System: Wyandotte Collegiate Systems
Degrees: A, B   *Enroll:* 168
URL: http://www.metropolitancollege.edu
Phone: (602) 955-5900   *Calendar:* Tri. plan
Inst. Accred.: ACCSCT (1992/2000, Probation)

Mohave Community College
1971 Jagerson Ave., Kingman 86401
Type: Public, state/local, two-year
System: State Board of Directors for Community Colleges
of Arizona
Degrees: A   *Enroll:* 2,510
URL: http://www.mohave.edu
Phone: (928) 757-4331   *Calendar:* Sem. plan
Inst. Accred.: NCA-HLC (1981/2003)

Lake Havasu Campus
1977 West Acoma Blvd., Lake Havasu City 86403
Phone: (520) 855-7812

Mohave Valley Campus
3400 Hwy. 95, Bullhead City 86442
Phone: (520) 758-3926

North Mohave Campus
480 South Central, PO Box 980, Colorado City 86021
Phone: (520) 875-2799

Northcentral University
505 West Whipple St., Prescott 86301-1747
Type: Private, proprietary, four-year
Degrees: B, M, D   *FTE Enroll:* 939
URL: http://www.ncu.edu
Phone: (928) 541-7777   *Calendar:* Sem. plan
Inst. Accred.: NCA-HLC (2003)

Northern Arizona University
Box 4092, Flagstaff 86011-4092
Type: Public, state, four-year
System: Arizona Board of Regents
Degrees: B, M, D   *Enroll:* 15,032
URL: http://www.nau.edu
Phone: (928) 523-9011   *Calendar:* Sem. plan
Inst. Accred.: NCA-HLC (1930/1998)
Prog. Accred.: Business (AACSB), Computer Science,
Construction Education, Counseling, Dental Hygiene,
Engineering (civil, computer, electrical,
environmental/sanitary, mechanical), Forestry, Music,
Nursing, Nursing Education, Physical Therapy, Public
Health, Recreation and Leisure Services, Social Work,
Speech-Language Pathology

Northland Pioneer College
PO Box 610, Holbrook 86025-0610
Type: Public, state/local, two-year
System: State Board of Directors for Community Colleges
of Arizona
Degrees: A   *Enroll:* 2,188
URL: http://www.npc.edu
Phone: (928) 524-7600   *Calendar:* Sem. plan
Inst. Accred.: NCA-HLC (1980/2000)

Little Colorado Campus
1400 East 3rd St., Winslow 86047-4404
Phone: (520) 289-6511

Painted Desert Campus
993 East Hermosa Dr., Holbrook 86025
Phone: (520) 524-7311

Silver Creek Campus
1610 South Main St., Snowflake 85937-5614
Phone: (520) 536-6211

White Mountain Campus
1001 West Deuce of Clubs, Show Low 85901-6211
Phone: (520) 532-6111

Paradise Valley Community College
18401 North 32nd St., Phoenix 85032
Type: Public, state/local, two-year
System: Maricopa County Community College District
Degrees: A   *Enroll:* 4,009
URL: http://www.pvc.maricopa.edu
Phone: (602) 787-6500   *Calendar:* Sem. plan
Inst. Accred.: NCA-HLC (1990/2005)

The Paralegal Institute, Inc.
2933 West Indian School Rd., PO Box 11408, Phoenix
85061-1408
Type: Private, proprietary, two-year
Degrees: A   *FTE Enroll:* 203
URL: http://www.theparalegalinstitute.com
Phone: (602) 212-0501
Inst. Accred.: DETC (1979/2003)

Phoenix College
1202 West Thomas Rd., Phoenix 85013
Type: Public, state/local, two-year
System: Maricopa County Community College District
Degrees: A   *Enroll:* 6,586
URL: http://www.pc.maricopa.edu
Phone: (602) 285-7500   *Calendar:* Sem. plan
Inst. Accred.: NCA-HLC (1928/1996)
Prog. Accred.: Dental Assisting, Dental Hygiene, Health
Information Technician, Nursing

Phoenix Seminary
13402 N. Scottsdale Rd., Ste. B-185, Scottsdale 85254
Type: Private, four-year
Degrees: M, D
URL: http://www.phoenixseminary.edu/pages/home.htm
Phone: (480) 443-1020   *Calendar:* Sem. plan
Inst. Accred.: ATS (2000)

Pima County Community College District
401 North Bonita Ave., Tucson 85709-5001
Type: Public, state/local, two-year
System: State Board of Directors for Community Colleges of Arizona
Degrees: A   *Enroll:* 16,728
URL: http://www.pima.edu
Phone: (520) 206-4500   *Calendar:* Sem. plan
Inst. Accred.: NCA-HLC (1975/2001)
Prog. Accred.: Dental Assisting, Dental Hygiene, Dental Laboratory Technology, Nursing, Radiography, Respiratory Therapy, Respiratory Therapy Technology

Community Campus
401 N. Bonita Ave., Tucson 85709-5000
Phone: (520) 206-3933

Desert Vista Campus
5901 South Calle Santa Cruz, Tucson 85709-6001
Phone: (520) 206-5025

Downtown Campus
1255 North Stone Ave., Tucson 85709-3002
Phone: (520) 206-6135

East Campus
8181 East Irvington Rd., Tucson 85709-4000
Phone: (520) 206-7000

Northwest Campus
7600 North Shannon Rd., Tucson 85709-7500
Phone: (520) 206-2090

West Campus
2202 West Anklam Rd., Tucson 85709-0001
Phone: (520) 206-6600
Prog. Accred.: Dental Assisting, Dental Hygiene, Dental Laboratory Technology

Pima Medical Institute
3350 East Grant Rd., Ste. 200, Tucson 85716
Type: Private, proprietary, two-year
Degrees: A   *Enroll:* 581
URL: http://www.pmi.edu
Phone: (520) 326-1600
Inst. Accred.: ABHES (1982/2003)
Prog. Accred.: Diagnostic Medical Sonography, Medical Assisting (ABHES), Radiography, Respiratory Therapy, Respiratory Therapy Technology

Albuquerque Campus
2201 San Pedro Dr., NE, Building 3, Ste. 100, Albuquerque, NM 87110
Phone: (505) 881-1234
Prog. Accred.: Medical Assisting (ABHES), Radiography

Chula Vista Campus
780 Bay Blvd., Ste. 101, Chula Vista, CA 91910
Phone: (619) 425-3200
Prog. Accred.: Medical Assisting (ABHES), Radiography

Colorado Springs Campus
370 Printers Pkwy., Colorado Springs, CO 80910
Phone: (719) 482-7462
Prog. Accred.: Medical Assisting (ABHES)

Denver Campus
1701 West 72nd Ave., Ste. 130, Denver, CO 80221
Phone: (303) 426-1800
Prog. Accred.: Medical Assisting (ABHES), Ophthalmic Medical Technology, Radiography, Respiratory Therapy, Respiratory Therapy Technology

Las Vegas Campus
3333 East Flamingo Rd., Las Vegas, NV 89121-4329
Phone: (702) 458-9650
Prog. Accred.: Medical Assisting (ABHES)

Mesa Campus
957 South Dobson Rd., Mesa 85202
Phone: (480) 644-0267
Prog. Accred.: Medical Assisting (ABHES)

Renton Campus
555 South Renton Village Place, Renton, WA 98055
Phone: (425) 228-9600
Prog. Accred.: Medical Assisting (ABHES)

Seattle Campus
1627 Eastlake Ave. East, Seattle, WA 98102
Phone: (206) 322-6100
Prog. Accred.: Medical Assisting (ABHES), Ophthalmic Medical Technology, Radiography

Prescott College
220 Grove Ave., Prescott 86301
Type: Private, independent, four-year
Degrees: B, M, D   *Enroll:* 919
URL: http://www.prescott.edu
Phone: (520) 778-2090   *Calendar:* Qtr. plan
Inst. Accred.: NCA-HLC (1984/2000)

RainStar University
4130 North Goldwater Blvd., Rm. 110, Scottsdale 85251
Type: Private, proprietary, four-year
Degrees: A, M
URL: http://www.rainstaruniversity.com
Phone: (480) 423-0375   *Calendar:* Qtr. plan
Inst. Accred.: ACCSCT (2001)
Prog. Accred.: Acupuncture

The Refrigeration School
4210 East Washington St., Phoenix 85034-1816
Type: Private, proprietary, two-year
Degrees: A   *Enroll:* 247
URL: http://www.refrigerationschool.com
Phone: (602) 275-7133
Inst. Accred.: ACCSCT (1973/2000)

Rio Salado Community College
2323 W. 14th St., Tempe 85281-6950
Type: Public, state/local, two-year
System: Maricopa County Community College District
Degrees: A   *Enroll:* 5,594
URL: http://www.riosalado.edu
Phone: (480) 517-8000   *Calendar:* Sem. plan
Inst. Accred.: NCA-HLC (1981/2002)
Prog. Accred.: Dental Hygiene

Scottsdale Community College
9000 East Chaparral Rd., Scottsdale 85250-2699
Type: Public, state/local, two-year
System: Maricopa County Community College District
Degrees: A   *Enroll:* 6,297
URL: http://www.sc.maricopa.edu
Phone: (480) 423-6000   *Calendar:* Sem. plan
Inst. Accred.: NCA-HLC (1975/1997)
Prog. Accred.: Interior Design, Nursing

Scottsdale Culinary Institute
8100 East Camelback Rd., Ste. 1001, Scottsdale 85251-3940
Type: Private, proprietary, two-year
System: Career Education Corporation
Degrees: A   *Enroll:* 1,241
URL: http://www.scichefs.com
Phone: (480) 990-3773
Inst. Accred.: ACCSCT (1989/2000)
Prog. Accred.: Culinary Education

South Mountain Community College
7050 South 24th St., Phoenix 85040
Type: Public, state/local, two-year
System: Maricopa County Community College District
Degrees: A   *Enroll:* 2,084
URL: http://www.southmountaincc.edu
Phone: (602) 243-8000   *Calendar:* Sem. plan
Inst. Accred.: NCA-HLC (1984/1999)

Southwest College of Naturopathic Medicine and Health Sciences
2140 East Broadway Rd., Tempe 85282
Type: Private, proprietary, four-year
Degrees: D   *Enroll:* 306
URL: http://www.scnm.edu
Phone: (480) 858-9100
Inst. Accred.: NCA-HLC (2004)
Prog. Accred.: Naturopathic Medicine

Southwestern College
2625 East Cactus Rd., Phoenix 85032-7042
Type: Private, independent, four-year
Degrees: A, B   *Enroll:* 249
URL: http://www.southwesterncollege.edu
Phone: (602) 992-6101   *Calendar:* Sem. plan
Inst. Accred.: ABHE (1977/1998), NCA-HLC (1992/2002)

Thunderbird, The Garvin Graduate School of International Management
15249 North 59th Ave., Glendale 85306
Type: Private, independent, four-year
Degrees: M   *Enroll:* 1,095
URL: http://www.t-bird.edu
Phone: (602) 978-7250   *Calendar:* Tri. plan
Inst. Accred.: NCA-HLC (1969/1996)
Prog. Accred.: Business (AACSB)

Tucson Design College
1030 North Alvernon Way, Tucson 85711
Type: Private, independent, four-year
Degrees: A, B
URL: http://www.designcollege.org
Phone: (520) 881-2900
Inst. Accred.: ACICS (2003)

Universal Technical Institute
10695 West Pierce St., Avondale 85323
Type: Private, proprietary, two-year
Degrees: A   *Enroll:* 1,867
URL: http://www.uticorp.com
Phone: (623) 245-4600
Inst. Accred.: ACCSCT (1968/2004)

Glendale Heights Campus
601 Regency Dr., Glendale Heights, IL 60139-2208
Phone: (630) 529-2662

NASCAR Technical Institute
220 Byers Creek Rd., Mooresville, NC 28117
Phone: (704) 658-1950

Rancho Cucamonga Campus
9494 Haven Ave., Rancho Cucamonga, CA 91730
Phone: (909) 484-1929

University of Advancing Technology
2625 West Baseline Rd., Tempe 85283-1042
Type: Private, independent, four-year
Degrees: A, B, M   *Enroll:* 800
URL: http://www.uat.edu
Phone: (602) 383-8228
Inst. Accred.: ACICS (1992/2001)

University of Arizona
712 Administration Bldg., PO Box 210066, Tucson 85721-0066
Type: Public, state, four-year
System: Arizona Board of Regents
Degrees: B, M, P, D   *Enroll:* 32,835
URL: http://www.arizona.edu
Phone: (520) 621-2211   *Calendar:* Sem. plan
Inst. Accred.: NCA-HLC (1917/2000)
Prog. Accred.: Accounting, Art, Audiology, Business (AACSB), Clinical Lab Scientist, Clinical Psychology, Dance, Dietetics (internship), Engineering (aerospace, agricultural, bioengineering, chemical, civil, computer, electrical, geological/geophysical, industrial, materials, mechanical, mining, systems), Journalism, Landscape Architecture, Law, Librarianship, Medicine, Music, Nursing, Nursing Education, Perfusion, Pharmacy, Planning, Psychology Internship, Public Administration, Public Health, Rehabilitation Counseling, School Psychology, Speech-Language Pathology, Theatre

The Arizona International College
1615 East Helen St., Bldg. 410E, Tucson 85719-4511
Phone: (520) 626-0600

Sierra Vista Campus
1140 N. Colombo, Sierra Vista 85635
Phone: (602) 629-0335

University of Phoenix
4615 East Elwood St., Phoenix 85040
Type: Private, proprietary, four-year
System: Apollo Group, Inc.
Degrees: A, B, M, D   *Enroll:* 7,892
URL: http://www.phoenix.edu
Phone: (480) 966-9577
Inst. Accred.: NCA-HLC (1978/2003)
Prog. Accred.: Nursing, Nursing Education

Albuquerque Campus
7471 Pan American Freeway, NE, Albuquerque, NM 87109
Phone: (505) 821-4800

Atlanta Campus
8200 Roberts Dr., Ste. 300, Dunwoody, GA 30350
Phone: (678) 731-0555

Boise Campus
3080 Gentry Way, Ste. 150, Meridian, ID 83642
Phone: (208) 888-1505

Boston Campus
100 Grossman Dr., Ste. 201, Braintree, MA 02184
Phone: (781) 843-0844

Central Massachusetts Campus
One Research Dr., Westborough, MA 01581
Phone: (508) 614-4100

Charlotte Campus
3800 Arco Corporate Dr., Charlotte, NC 28273
Phone: (704) 504-5409

Chicago Campus
1500 McConner Pkwy., Ste. 700, Schaumburg, IL 60173
Phone: (847) 413-1922

Cincinnati Campus
110 Boggs Ln., Ste. 149, Cincinnati, OH 45246
Phone: (513) 772-9600

Cleveland Campus
5005 Rockside Rd., Ste. 325, Independence, OH 44131
Phone: (216) 447-8807

Colorado Campus
10004 Park Meadows Dr., Lone Tree, CO 80124
Phone: (303) 694-9093

Columbus, Georgia Campus
18 9th St., Columbus, GA 31901
Phone: (800) 697-8223

Columbus, Ohio Campus
8405 Pulsar Place, Ste. 120, Columbus, OH 43240
Phone: (800) 697-8223

Dallas Campus
12400 Colt Rd., Churchill Towers, Ste. 200, Dallas, TX 75251
Phone: (972) 385-1055

Ft. Lauderdale Campus
600 North Pine Island Rd., Ste. 500, Plantation, FL 33324
Phone: (954) 382-5303

Hawaii Campus
827 Fort St., Honolulu, HI 96813
Phone: (808) 536-2686

Houston Campus
11451 Katy Freeway, Ste. 100, Houston, TX 77079
Phone: (713) 465-9966

Indianapolis Campus
7999 Knue Rd., Ste. 150, Indianapolis, IN 46250
Phone: (317) 585-8610

Jacksonville Campus
4500 Salisbury Rd., Ste. 150, Jacksonville, FL 32216
Phone: (904) 636-6645

Kansas City Campus
901 East 104th St., Ste. 301, Kansas City, MO 64131
Phone: (816) 943-9600

Las Vegas Campus
333 North Rancho Dr., #300, Las Vegas, NV 89106
Phone: (702) 638-7279

Louisiana Campus
One Galleria Blvd., Ste. 725, Metairie, LA 70001
Phone: (504) 461-8852

University of Phoenix *(continued)*

Maryland Campus
8830 Stanford Blvd., Ste. 100, Columbia, MD 21045
Phone: (410) 872-9001

Metro Detroit Campus
5480 Corporate Dr., Ste. 240, Troy, MI 48098
Phone: (248) 925-4100

Milwaukee Campus
13890 Bishops Dr., Ste. 110, Brookfield, WI 53005
Phone: (262) 785-0608

Nashville Campus
616 Marriott Dr., Ste. 150, Nashville, TN 37214
Phone: (615) 872-0188

Netherlands Campus
Rivium le Straat 1, 2909 LE Capelle a/d Ijssel, Rotterdam
Phone: 011 31 10 288-6344

Northern Virginia Campus
11710 Plaza America Dr., Ste. 2000, Reston, VA 20190
Phone: (703) 435-4402

Oklahoma City Campus
6501 North Broadway Extension, Ste. 100, Oklahoma City, OK 73116
Phone: (405) 842-8007

Online Campus
3201 East Elwood St., Phoenix 85034
Phone: (602) 387-7000

Oregon Campus
13221 Southwest 68th Pkwy., #500, Tigard, OR 97223
Phone: (503) 403-2900

Orlando Campus
2290 Lucien Way, Ste. 400, Maitland, FL 32751
Phone: (407) 667-0555

Philadelphia Campus
170 South Warner Rd., Wayne, PA 19087-9971
Phone: (610) 989-0880

Phoenix Hohokam Campus
4605 East Elmwood St., Phoenix 85072-2076
Phone: (480) 804-7400
Prog. Accred: Counseling

Pittsburgh Campus
Penn Center West Six, Ste. 100, Pittsburgh, PA 15276
Phone: (412) 747-9000

Puerto Rico Campus
PO Box 3870, RD 177 KM 2.0 (Los Filtros), Guaynabo, PR 00970-3870
Phone: (787) 731-5400

Reno Campus
5370 Kietzke Ln., Ste. 102, Reno, NV 89511
Phone: (775) 828-7999

Sacramento Campus
1760 Creekside Oaks Dr., #100, Sacramento, CA 95833
Phone: (916) 923-2107

St. Louis Campus
13801 Riverport Dr., Ste. 100, Riverport Executive Center II, St. Louis, MO 63043
Phone: (314) 298-9755

Salt Lake Campus
5251 Green St., Salt Lake City, UT 84123
Phone: (801) 263-1444
Prog. Accred: Counseling

San Diego Campus
11682 El Camino Real, 2nd Flr., San Diego, CA 92130
Phone: (858) 509-4300

Southern Arizona Campus
5099 East Grant Rd., #120, Tucson 85712
Phone: (520) 881-6512
Prog. Accred: Counseling

Southern Colorado Campus
5475 Tech Center Dr., #130, Colorado Springs, CO 80919
Phone: (719) 599-5282

Spokane Campus
1330 North Washington St., Spokane, WA 99201-2446
Phone: (800) 697-8223

Tampa Campus
100 Tampa Oaks Blvd., Ste. 200, Temple Terrace, FL 33637
Phone: (813) 626-7911

Tulsa Campus
10810 East 45th St., Ste. 103, Tulsa, OK 74146
Phone: (918) 622-4877

Vancouver Campus
885 West Georgia St., Vancouver, BC, Canada V6C 3E8
Phone: (604) 408-6606

Washington Campus
7100 Fort Dent Way, #100, Seattle, WA 98188
Phone: (206) 268-5800

West Michigan Campus
318 River Ridge Dr., NW, Grand Rapids, MI 49544
Phone: (616) 956-5100

Wichita Campus
3020 North Cypress Dr., Wichita, KS 67226
Phone: (316) 630-8121

Western International University
9215 North Black Canyon Hwy., Phoenix 85021
Type: Private, proprietary, four-year
System: Apollo Group, Inc.
Degrees: A, B, M   *Enroll:* 2,138
URL: http://www.wintu.edu
Phone: (602) 943-2311   *Calendar:* Sem. plan
Inst. Accred.: NCA-HLC (1984/2005)

London Campus
3 Muirfield Crescent, Glengall Bridge West,
Millharbour, United Kingdom E14 9SZ
Phone: 0171 345 8277

Yavapai College
1100 East Sheldon St., Prescott 86301
Type: Public, state/local, two-year
System: State Board of Directors for Community Colleges
  of Arizona
Degrees: A   *Enroll:* 3,636
URL: http://www.yc.edu
Phone: (520) 445-7300   *Calendar:* Sem. plan
Inst. Accred.: NCA-HLC (1975/2003)
Prog. Accred.: Nursing

ARKANSAS

Arkansas Baptist College
1600 Bishop St., Little Rock 72202
Type: Private, Southern Baptist Church, four-year
Degrees: A, B   *Enroll:* 304
URL: http://www.arbaptcol.edu
Phone: (501) 374-7856   *Calendar:* Sem. plan
Inst. Accred.: NCA-HLC (1987/1995)
Prog. Accred.: Teacher Education (NCATE)

Arkansas Northeastern College
PO Drawer 1109, Blytheville 72316
Type: Public, state/local, two-year
System: Arkansas Department of Higher Education
Degrees: A   *Enroll:* 1,546
URL: http://www.anc.edu
Phone: (870) 762-1020   *Calendar:* Sem. plan
Inst. Accred.: NCA-HLC (1980/2002)
Prog. Accred.: Nursing

Burdette Center
Box 36, I-55 and Hwy. 148, Burdette 72321
Phone: (870) 763-1486
Prog. Accred: Dental Assisting

Paragould Campus
4601 Linwood Dr., Paragould 72450
Phone: (870) 239-3200

Arkansas State University
PO Box 10, State University 72467
Type: Public, state, four-year
System: Arkansas State University System Office
Degrees: A, B, M, P, D   *Enroll:* 8,873
URL: http://www.astate.edu
Phone: (870) 972-2100   *Calendar:* Sem. plan
Inst. Accred.: NCA-HLC (1928/2003)
Prog. Accred.: Art, Athletic Training, Business (AACSB),
   Clinical Lab Scientist, Clinical Lab Technology,
   Counseling, Engineering (general), Journalism, Music,
   Nursing, Physical Therapy, Physical Therapy Assisting,
   Public Administration, Radiation Therapy, Radiography,
   Rehabilitation Counseling, Social Work, Speech-
   Language Pathology, Teacher Education (NCATE)

Arkansas State University Mountain Home
1600 South College St., Mountain Home 72653
Type: Public, state, two-year
System: Arkansas State University System Office
Degrees: A
URL: http://www.asumh.edu
Phone: (870) 508-6100   *Calendar:* Sem. plan
Inst. Accred.: NCA-HLC (2003)
Prog. Accred.: Funeral Service Education (Mortuary
   Science)

Arkansas State University—Beebe
PO Box 1000, Beebe 72012
Type: Public, state, two-year
System: Arkansas State University System Office
Degrees: A   *Enroll:* 2,539
URL: http://www.asub.edu
Phone: (501) 882-8356   *Calendar:* Sem. plan
Inst. Accred.: NCA-HLC (1971/2002)
Prog. Accred.: Clinical Lab Technology

Arkansas State University—Newport
7648 Victory Blvd., Newport 72112
Type: Public, state, two-year
System: Arkansas State University System Office
Degrees: A
URL: http://www.asun.edu
Phone: (870) 512-7800   *Calendar:* Sem. plan
Inst. Accred.: NCA-HLC (2002)

Arkansas Tech University
Russellville 72801-2222
Type: Public, state, four-year
System: Arkansas Department of Higher Education
Degrees: A, B, M, P   *Enroll:* 5,626
URL: http://www.atu.edu
Phone: (479) 968-0389   *Calendar:* Sem. plan
Inst. Accred.: NCA-HLC (1930/2004)
Prog. Accred.: Business (AACSB), Engineering (electrical,
   mechanical), Health Information Administration, Medical
   Assisting (AMA), Music, Nursing, Recreation and Leisure
   Services, Teacher Education (NCATE)

Ozark Campus
1700 Helberg Ln., Ozark 72949-2013
Phone: (479) 667-2117

Black River Technical College
Highway 304 East, PO Box 468, Pocahontas 72455
Type: Public, state, two-year
System: Arkansas Department of Higher Education
Degrees: A   *Enroll:* 1,335
URL: http://www.blackrivertech.org
Phone: (870) 248-4000   *Calendar:* Sem. plan
Inst. Accred.: NCA-HLC (1997/2002)
Prog. Accred.: Respiratory Therapy Technology

Central Baptist College
1501 College Ave., Conway 72032
Type: Private, Missionary Baptist Association, four-year
Degrees: A, B   *Enroll:* 377
URL: http://www.cbc.edu
Phone: (501) 329-6872   *Calendar:* Sem. plan
Inst. Accred.: NCA-HLC (1993/1998)

Cossatot Community College of the University of Arkansas
PO Box 960, 183 Hwy. 399, DeQueen 71832
Type: Public, state, two-year
System: University of Arkansas System Administration
Degrees: A   *Enroll:* 608
URL: http://www.cccua.edu
Phone: (870) 584-4471   *Calendar:* Sem. plan
Inst. Accred.: NCA-HLC (1998/2003)
Prog. Accred.: Business (ACBSP)

Crowley's Ridge College
100 College Dr., Paragould 72450-9731
Type: Private, Churches of Christ, two-year
Degrees: A   *Enroll:* 145
URL: http://www.crowleysridgecollege.edu
Phone: (870) 236-6901   *Calendar:* Sem. plan
Inst. Accred.: NCA-HLC (2000/2005)

East Arkansas Community College
1700 Newcastle Rd., Forrest City 72335-9598
Type: Public, state/local, two-year
System: Arkansas Department of Higher Education
Degrees: A   *Enroll:* 1,053
URL: http://www.eacc.edu
Phone: (870) 633-4480   *Calendar:* Sem. plan
Inst. Accred.: NCA-HLC (1979/1999)
Prog. Accred.: Nursing

Ecclesia College
9163 Nations Dr., Springdale 72762
Type: Private, independent, four-year
Degrees: B
URL: http://www.ecclesiacollege.org
Phone: (479) 248-7236   *Calendar:* Sem. plan
Inst. Accred.: ABHE (2005)

Harding University
Box 10773, 900 East Center Ave., Searcy 72149-0001
Type: Private, Churches of Christ, four-year
Degrees: B, M, D   *Enroll:* 4,461
URL: http://www.harding.edu
Phone: (501) 279-4274   *Calendar:* Sem. plan
Inst. Accred.: NCA-HLC (1954/1995)
Prog. Accred.: Business (ACBSP), Marriage and Family Therapy, Music, Nursing, Social Work, Teacher Education (NCATE)

Henderson State University
1100 Henderson St., Arkadelphia 71999-0001
Type: Public, state, four-year
System: Arkansas Department of Higher Education
Degrees: A, B, M   *Enroll:* 3,132
URL: http://www.hsu.edu
Phone: (870) 230-5091   *Calendar:* Sem. plan
Inst. Accred.: NCA-HLC (1934/2002)
Prog. Accred.: Business (AACSB), Music, Nursing, Teacher Education (NCATE)

Hendrix College
1600 Washington Ave., Conway 72032-3080
Type: Private, United Methodist Church, four-year
Degrees: B, M   *Enroll:* 1,047
URL: http://www.hendrix.edu
Phone: (501) 450-1273   *Calendar:* Tri. plan
Inst. Accred.: NCA-HLC (1924/1999)
Prog. Accred.: Music, Teacher Education (NCATE)

John Brown University
2000 West University Sreet, Siloam Springs 72761
Type: Private, independent, four-year
Degrees: A, B, M   *Enroll:* 1,683
URL: http://www.jbu.edu
Phone: (479) 524-9500   *Calendar:* Sem. plan
Inst. Accred.: NCA-HLC (1962/2002)
Prog. Accred.: Construction Education, Engineering (general), Teacher Education (NCATE)

Lyon College
PO Box 2317, Batesville 72503
Type: Private, Presbyterian Church, four-year
Degrees: B   *Enroll:* 466
URL: http://www.lyon.edu
Phone: (870) 793-4201   *Calendar:* Sem. plan
Inst. Accred.: NCA-HLC (1959/2002)
Prog. Accred.: Teacher Education (NCATE)

Mid-South Community College
2000 West Broadway St., West Memphis 72301-3829
Type: Public, state, two-year
System: Arkansas Department of Higher Education
Degrees: A   *Enroll:* 610
URL: http://www.midsouthcc.edu
Phone: (870) 733-6722   *Calendar:* Sem. plan
Inst. Accred.: NCA-HLC (1999/2004)

National Park Community College at Hot Springs
101 College Dr., Hot Springs National Park 71913
Type: Public, state/local, two-year
System: Arkansas Department of Higher Education
Degrees: A   *Enroll:* 1,951
URL: http://www.npcc.edu
Phone: (501) 760-4222   *Calendar:* Sem. plan
Inst. Accred.: NCA-HLC (1981/2002)
Prog. Accred.: Business (ACBSP), Clinical Lab Technology, Health Information Technician, Nursing, Radiography

North Arkansas College
1515 Pioneer Ridge, Harrison 72601
Type: Public, state/local, two-year
System: Arkansas Department of Higher Education
Degrees: A   *Enroll:* 1,521
URL: http://www.northark.edu
Phone: (870) 391-3000   *Calendar:* Sem. plan
Inst. Accred.: NCA-HLC (1979/2001)
Prog. Accred.: Clinical Lab Technology, Nursing, Radiography, Surgical Technology

NorthWest Arkansas Community College
One College Dr., Bentonville 72712-5091
Type: Public, state/local, two-year
System: Arkansas Department of Higher Education
Degrees: A *Enroll:* 2,697
URL: http://www.nwacc.edu
Phone: (501) 636-9222 *Calendar:* Sem. plan
Inst. Accred.: NCA-HLC (1995)
Prog. Accred.: Physical Therapy Assisting, Respiratory Therapy Technology

Ouachita Baptist University
410 Ouachita St., Arkadelphia 71998
Type: Private, Southern Baptist Church, four-year
Degrees: A, B *Enroll:* 1,504
URL: http://www.obu.edu
Phone: (870) 245-5000 *Calendar:* Sem. plan
Inst. Accred.: NCA-HLC (1927/2001)
Prog. Accred.: Business (AACSB), Music, Teacher Education (NCATE)

Ouachita Technical College
One College Circle, PO Box 816, Malvern 72104
Type: Public, state, two-year
System: Arkansas Department of Higher Education
Degrees: A *Enroll:* 809
URL: http://www.otcweb.edu
Phone: (501) 332-3658 *Calendar:* Sem. plan
Inst. Accred.: NCA-HLC (1996/2001)

Ozarka College
PO Box 10, Melbourne 72556
Type: Public, state, two-year
System: Arkansas Department of Higher Education
Degrees: A *Enroll:* 697
URL: http://www.ozarka.edu
Phone: (870) 368-7371 *Calendar:* Sem. plan
Inst. Accred.: NCA-HLC (1996/2001)

Philander Smith College
One Trudie Kibbe Reed Dive, Little Rock 72202
Type: Private, United Methodist Church, four-year
Degrees: B *Enroll:* 799
URL: http://www.philander.edu
Phone: (501) 370-5275 *Calendar:* Sem. plan
Inst. Accred.: NCA-HLC (1949/1997)
Prog. Accred.: Business (ACBSP), Social Work, Teacher Education (NCATE)

Phillips Community College of the University of Arkansas
1000 Campus Dr., Box 785, Helena 72342-0785
Type: Public, state/local, two-year
System: University of Arkansas System Administration
Degrees: A *Enroll:* 1,406
URL: http://www.pccua.edu
Phone: (870) 338-6474 *Calendar:* Sem. plan
Inst. Accred.: NCA-HLC (1972/1995)
Prog. Accred.: Business (ACBSP), Clinical Lab Technology, Nursing, Phlebotomy

DeWitt Campus
1210 Ricebelt Ave. Hwy. 165, DeWitt 72042
Phone: (870) 946-3506

Stuttgart Campus
2807 Hwy. 165 South, Stuttgart 72160
Phone: (870) 673-4201

Pulaski Technical College
3000 West Scenic Rd., North Little Rock 72118-3399
Type: Public, state/local, two-year
System: Arkansas Department of Higher Education
Degrees: A *Enroll:* 4,001
URL: http://www.pulaskitech.edu
Phone: (501) 821-2216 *Calendar:* Sem. plan
Inst. Accred.: NCA-HLC (1997/2002)
Prog. Accred.: Dental Assisting, Occupational Therapy, Respiratory Therapy Technology

Rich Mountain Community College
1100 College Dr., Mena 71953
Type: Public, state/local, two-year
System: Arkansas Department of Higher Education
Degrees: A *Enroll:* 659
URL: http://www.rmcc.edu
Phone: (479) 394-7622 *Calendar:* Sem. plan
Inst. Accred.: NCA-HLC (1990/2005)

South Arkansas Community College
PO Box 7010, El Dorado 71731-7010
Type: Public, state/local, two-year
System: Arkansas Department of Higher Education
Degrees: A *Enroll:* 628
URL: http://www.southark.edu
Phone: (870) 864-7107 *Calendar:* Sem. plan
Inst. Accred.: NCA-HLC (1983/1996)
Prog. Accred.: Clinical Lab Technology, Occupational Therapy Assisting, Physical Therapy Assisting, Radiography

Southeast Arkansas College
1900 Hazel St., Pine Bluff 71603
Type: Public, state/local, two-year
System: Arkansas Department of Higher Education
Degrees: A *Enroll:* 1,557
URL: http://www.seark.edu
Phone: (870) 543-5900 *Calendar:* Sem. plan
Inst. Accred.: NCA-HLC (1996/2001)
Prog. Accred.: Radiography

Southern Arkansas University
PO Box 9392, Magnolia 71754-9392
Type: Public, state, four-year
System: Arkansas Department of Higher Education
Degrees: A, B, M   *Enroll:* 2,679
URL: http://www.saumag.edu
Phone: (870) 235-4001   *Calendar:* Sem. plan
Inst. Accred.: NCA-HLC (1929/2003)
Prog. Accred.: Business (AACSB), Music, Nursing, Social
    Work, Teacher Education (NCATE)

Southern Arkansas University—Tech
SAU Tech Station, PO Box 3499, East Camden 71711-
1599
Type: Public, state, two-year
System: Arkansas Department of Higher Education
Degrees: A   *Enroll:* 719
URL: http://www.sautech.edu
Phone: (870) 574-4500   *Calendar:* Sem. plan
Inst. Accred.: NCA-HLC (1980/2000)

University of Arkansas at Fayetteville
Administration Bldg. 425, Fayetteville 72701
Type: Public, state, four-year
System: University of Arkansas System Administration
Degrees: B, M, P, D   *Enroll:* 14,076
URL: http://www.uark.edu
Phone: (479) 575-2000   *Calendar:* Sem. plan
Inst. Accred.: NCA-HLC (1924/1997)
Prog. Accred.: Accounting, Clinical Psychology,
    Counseling, Engineering (agricultural, chemical, civil,
    computer, electrical, environmental/sanitary, industrial,
    mechanical), Family and Consumer Science, Interior
    Design, Journalism, Landscape Architecture, Law,
    Music, Nursing, Nursing Education, Radiography,
    Recreation and Leisure Services, Rehabilitation
    Counseling, Social Work, Speech-Language Pathology,
    Teacher Education (NCATE)

University of Arkansas at Fort Smith
5210 Grand Ave., PO Box 3649, Fort Smith 72913-3649
Type: Public, state, four-year
System: Arkansas Department of Higher Education
Degrees: A, B   *Enroll:* 4,602
URL: http://www.uafortsmith.edu
Phone: (501) 788-7000   *Calendar:* Sem. plan
Inst. Accred.: NCA-HLC (1973/2005)
Prog. Accred.: Dental Hygiene, Nursing, Radiography,
    Surgical Technology

University of Arkansas at Little Rock
2801 South University Ave., Little Rock 72204
Type: Public, state, four-year
System: University of Arkansas System Administration
Degrees: A, B, M, P, D   *Enroll:* 8,719
URL: http://www.ualr.edu
Phone: (501) 569-3000   *Calendar:* Sem. plan
Inst. Accred.: NCA-HLC (1929/2000)
Prog. Accred.: Art, Audiology, Business (AACSB),
    Computer Science, Construction Education, Engineering
    (systems), Engineering Technology (computer, electrical,
    mechanical), Health Services Administration, Law,
    Music, Nursing, Public Administration, Social Work,
    Speech-Language Pathology, Teacher Education
    (NCATE), Theatre

University of Arkansas at Monticello
PO Box 3596, Monticello 71655-3596
Type: Public, state, four-year
System: University of Arkansas System Administration
Degrees: A, B, M   *Enroll:* 2,540
URL: http://www.uamont.edu
Phone: (870) 367-6811   *Calendar:* Sem. plan
Inst. Accred.: NCA-HLC (1928/1995)
Prog. Accred.: Business (AACSB), Forestry, Music,
    Nursing, Social Work, Teacher Education (NCATE)

University of Arkansas at Pine Bluff
1200 North University Dr., Pine Bluff 71611
Type: Public, state, four-year
System: University of Arkansas System Administration
Degrees: A, B, M   *Enroll:* 3,012
URL: http://www.uapb.edu
Phone: (870) 543-8000   *Calendar:* Sem. plan
Inst. Accred.: NCA-HLC (1950/1997)
Prog. Accred.: Art, Family and Consumer Science,
    Industrial Technology, Music, Nursing, Social Work,
    Teacher Education (NCATE)

University of Arkansas Community College at Batesville
2005 White Dr., PO Box 3350, Batesville 72503
Type: Public, state, two-year
System: University of Arkansas System Administration
Degrees: A   *Enroll:* 963
URL: http://www.uaccb.edu
Phone: (870) 793-7581   *Calendar:* Sem. plan
Inst. Accred.: NCA-HLC (1998/2003)
Prog. Accred.: Nursing, Surgical Technology

University of Arkansas Community College at Hope
2500 South Main, PO Box 140, Hope 71802-0140
Type: Public, state, two-year
System: University of Arkansas System Administration
Degrees: A   *Enroll:* 846
URL: http://www.uacch.edu
Phone: (870) 777-5722   *Calendar:* Sem. plan
Inst. Accred.: NCA-HLC (1997/2001)
Prog. Accred.: Funeral Service Education (Mortuary
    Science), Respiratory Therapy Technology

University of Arkansas Community College at Morrilton
One Bruce St., Morrilton 72110
Type: Public, state, two-year
System: Arkansas Department of Higher Education
Degrees: A   *Enroll:* 1,231
URL: http://www.uaccm.edu
Phone: (501) 354-2465   *Calendar:* Sem. plan
Inst. Accred.: NCA-HLC (1997/2002)

University of Arkansas for Medical Sciences
4301 West Markham St., Little Rock 72205
Type: Public, state, four-year
System: University of Arkansas System Administration
Degrees: A, B, M, P, D   *Enroll:* 1,858
URL: http://www.uams.edu
Phone: (501) 686-5000   *Calendar:* Sem. plan
Inst. Accred.: NCA-HLC (1987/1997)
Prog. Accred.: Clinical Lab Scientist, Clinical Pastoral Education, Cytotechnology, Dental Hygiene, Diagnostic Medical Sonography, Dietetics (internship), Health Information Technician, Medicine, Nuclear Medicine Technology, Nursing, Nursing Education, Pharmacy, Psychology Internship, Radiography, Respiratory Therapy, Respiratory Therapy Technology, Surgical Technology

Area Health Education Center Northwest
2907 East Joyce St., Fayetteville 72703-5011
Phone: (479) 521-8269
Prog. Accred: Radiography

Area Health Education Center Southwest
300 East 6th St., Texarkana 71854
Phone: (870) 779-6000
Prog. Accred: Radiography

University of Central Arkansas
201 Donaghey Ave., Conway 72035
Type: Public, state, four-year
System: Arkansas Department of Higher Education
Degrees: A, B, M, P, D   *Enroll:* 8,876
URL: http://www.uca.edu
Phone: (501) 450-5000   *Calendar:* Sem. plan
Inst. Accred.: NCA-HLC (1931/2000)
Prog. Accred.: Art, Business (AACSB), Dietetics (internship), Music, Nursing, Occupational Therapy, Physical Therapy, Speech-Language Pathology, Teacher Education (NCATE), Theatre

University of the Ozarks
415 North College Ave., Clarksville 72830
Type: Private, Presbyterian Church (USA), four-year
Degrees: A, B   *Enroll:* 708
URL: http://www.ozarks.edu
Phone: (501) 979-1000   *Calendar:* Sem. plan
Inst. Accred.: NCA-HLC (1931/2003)
Prog. Accred.: Teacher Education (NCATE)

Williams Baptist College
201 Fulbright Ave., Walnut Ridge 72476
Type: Private, Southern Baptist, four-year
Degrees: A, B   *Enroll:* 567
URL: http://www.wbcoll.edu
Phone: (870) 886-6741   *Calendar:* Sem. plan
Inst. Accred.: NCA-HLC (1963/2002)
Prog. Accred.: Teacher Education (NCATE)

CALIFORNIA

Academy of Art University
79 New Montgomery St., San Francisco 94105
Type: Private, independent, four-year
Degrees: B, M   *Enroll:* 5,322
URL: http://www.academyart.edu
Phone: (415) 274-2200   *Calendar:* Qtr. plan
Inst. Accred.: ACICS (1998/2001)
Prog. Accred.: Art, Interior Design

Academy of Chinese Culture and Health Sciences
1601 Clay St., Oakland 94612
Type: Private, proprietary, four-year
Degrees: M   *Enroll:* 151
URL: http://www.acchs.edu
Phone: (510) 763-7787   *Calendar:* Tri. plan
Inst. Accred.: ACAOM (1992/2004)

Acupuncture and Integrative Medicine College, Berkeley
2550 Shattuck Ave., Berkeley 94704
Type: Private, proprietary, four-year
Degrees: M
URL: http://www.aic-berkeley.edu
Phone: (510) 666-8248   *Calendar:* Qtr. plan
Inst. Accred.: ACAOM (2000/2003, Probation)

Allan Hancock College
800 South College Dr., Santa Maria 93454-6368
Type: Public, state/local, two-year
System: Allan Hancock Joint Community College District
Degrees: A   *Enroll:* 5,959
URL: http://www.hancockcollege.edu
Phone: (805) 922-6966   *Calendar:* Sem. plan
Inst. Accred.: WASC-JR. (1952/2004)

Alliant International University—Fresno
5130 East Clinton Way, Fresno 93727-2014
Type: Private, independent, four-year
System: Alliant International University
Degrees: A, B, M, D   *Enroll:* 288
URL: http://www.alliant.edu/fresno
Phone: (559) 456-2777   *Calendar:* Sem. plan
Inst. Accred.: WASC-SR. (1977/1998, *Indirect accreditation through Alliant International University, San Francisco, CA*)
Prog. Accred.: Clinical Psychology, Psychology Internship

Alliant International University—Irvine
2500 Michelson Dr., Bldg. 400, Irvine 92612-1548
Type: Private, independent, four-year
System: Alliant International University
Degrees: A, B, M, D
URL: http://www.alliant.edu/irvine.htm
Phone: (949) 833-2651   *Calendar:* Sem. plan
Inst. Accred.: WASC-SR. (1977/1998, *Indirect accreditation through Alliant International University, San Francisco, CA*)
Prog. Accred.: Marriage and Family Therapy

Alliant International University—Los Angeles
1000 South Fremont Ave., Unit 5, Alhambra 91803-1360
Type: Private, independent, four-year
System: Alliant International University
Degrees: A, B, M, D   *Enroll:* 544
URL: http://www.alliant.edu/la
Phone: (626) 284-2777   *Calendar:* Sem. plan
Inst. Accred.: WASC-SR. (1977/1998, *Indirect accreditation through Alliant International University, San Francisco, CA*)
Prog. Accred.: Clinical Psychology

Alliant International University—San Diego Cornerstone Court
6161 Cornerstone Ct. East, San Diego 92121-3710
Type: Private, independent, four-year
System: Alliant International University
Degrees: A, B, M, D   *Enroll:* 1,482
URL: http://www.alliant.edu/sandiego
Phone: (858) 623-2777   *Calendar:* Sem. plan
Inst. Accred.: WASC-SR. (1977/1998, *Indirect accreditation through Alliant International University, San Francisco, CA*)
Prog. Accred.: Clinical Psychology

Alliant International University—San Diego Scripps Ranch
10455 Pomerado Rd., San Diego 92131-1799
Type: Private, independent, four-year
System: Alliant International University
Degrees: A, B, M, D   *Enroll:* 1,085
URL: http://www.alliant.edu/sandiego.htm
Phone: (858) 271-4300   *Calendar:* Sem. plan
Inst. Accred.: WASC-SR. (1977/1998, *Indirect accreditation through Alliant International University, San Francisco, CA*)
Prog. Accred.: Marriage and Family Therapy

Alliant International University— San Francisco Bay
1005 Atlantic Ave., Alameda 94501
Type: Private, independent, four-year
System: Alliant International University
Degrees: A, B, M, D   *Enroll:* 590
URL: http://www.alliant.edu/sfbay
Phone: (510) 523-2300   *Calendar:* Sem. plan
Inst. Accred.: WASC-SR. (1977/1989, *Indirect accreditation through Alliant International University, San Francisco, CA*)
Prog. Accred.: Clinical Psychology

American Academy of Dramatic Arts West
1336 North LaBrea Ave., Hollywood 90028
Type: Private, independent, two-year
Degrees: A   *Enroll:* 255
URL: http://www.aada.org
Phone: (323) 464-2777   *Calendar:* Sem. plan
Inst. Accred.: WASC-JR. (1981/2003)
Prog. Accred.: Theatre

American Baptist Seminary of the West
2606 Dwight Way, Berkeley 94704-3029
Type: Private, American Baptist Churches, USA, four-year
System: Graduate Theological Union
Degrees: M   *Enroll:* 55
URL: http://www.absw.edu
Phone: (510) 841-1905   *Calendar:* Sem. plan
Inst. Accred.: ATS (1938/2004)

American College of Traditional Chinese Medicine
455 Arkansas St., San Francisco 94107-2813
Type: Private, proprietary, four-year
Degrees: M   *Enroll:* 249
URL: http://www.actcm.org
Phone: (415) 282-7600   *Calendar:* Qtr. plan
Inst. Accred.: ACAOM (1991/2001)

American Conservatory Theater
30 Grant Ave., 6th Flr., San Francisco 94108-5800
Type: Private, independent, four-year
Degrees: M   *Enroll:* 49
URL: http://www.act-sfbay.org
Phone: (415) 439-2350   *Calendar:* Sem. plan
Inst. Accred.: WASC-SR. (1984/1998)

The American Film Institute
2021 North Western Ave., Los Angeles 90027
Type: Private, independent, four-year
Degrees: M   *Enroll:* 298
URL: http://www.afionline.org
Phone: (323) 856-7600   *Calendar:* 24-mos. pr
Inst. Accred.: WASC-SR. (2002)
Prog. Accred.: Art

American Graduate University
733 North Dodsworth Ave., Covina 91724
Type: Private, proprietary, four-year
Degrees: M
URL: http://www.agu.edu
Phone: (626) 966-4576
Inst. Accred.: DETC (1998/2003)

American River College
4700 College Oak Dr., Sacramento 95841-4286
Type: Public, state/local, two-year
System: Los Rios Community College District
Degrees: A   *Enroll:* 13,917
URL: http://www.arc.losrios.edu
Phone: (916) 484-8011   *Calendar:* Sem. plan
Inst. Accred.: WASC-JR. (1959/2004)
Prog. Accred.: Funeral Service Education (Mortuary Science), Respiratory Therapy

Antelope Valley College
3041 West Ave. K, Lancaster 93536-5426
Type: Public, state/local, two-year
System: Antelope Valley Community College District
Degrees: A   *Enroll:* 6,093
URL: http://www.avc.edu
Phone: (661) 722-6300   *Calendar:* Sem. plan
Inst. Accred.: WASC-JR. (1952/2005)

Argosy University Orange County
3501 West Sunflower Ave., Ste. 110, Santa Ana 92704-9888
Type: Private, proprietary, four-year
System: Argosy University
Degrees: M, D
URL: http://www.argosyu.edu
Phone: (714) 940-0025   *Calendar:* Tri. plan
Inst. Accred.: NCA-HLC (1981/2001, *Indirect accreditation through Argosy University, Chicago, IL*)

Argosy University San Francisco Bay Area
999 Canal Blvd., Point Richmond 94804
Type: Private, proprietary, four-year
System: Argosy University
Degrees: M, D
URL: http://www.argosyu.edu
Phone: (510) 215-0277   *Calendar:* Tri. plan
Inst. Accred.: NCA-HLC (1981/2001, *Indirect accreditation through Argosy University, Chicago, IL*)
Prog. Accred.: Clinical Psychology

Art Center College of Design
1700 Lida St., Pasadena 91103
Type: Private, independent, four-year
Degrees: B, M   *Enroll:* 1,501
URL: http://www.artcenter.edu
Phone: (626) 396-2200   *Calendar:* Tri. plan
Inst. Accred.: WASC-SR. (1955/1997)
Prog. Accred.: Art

The Art Institute of California—San Diego
7650 Mission Valley Rd., San Diego 92108-3277
Type: Private, proprietary, four-year
System: Education Management Corporation
Degrees: A, B   *Enroll:* 1,263
URL: http://www.taac.edu
Phone: (858) 598-1200   *Calendar:* Qtr. plan
Inst. Accred.: ACCSCT (1986/2001)

The Art Institute of California—San Francisco
1170 Market St., San Francisco 94102-4908
Type: Private, proprietary, four-year
System: Education Management Corporation
Degrees: A, B   *Enroll:* 800
URL: http://www.aisf.artinstitutes.edu
Phone: (415) 865-0198   *Calendar:* Qtr. plan
Inst. Accred.: ACICS (2000/2005, Probation)

Aviation and Electronic School of America
201 South Railroad St., Colfax 95713
Type: Private, proprietary, two-year
Degrees: A
URL: http://www.aesa.com
Phone: (530) 346-6792
Inst. Accred.: COE (1999/2005)

San Diego Campus
7905 Silverton Aveenue, Ste. 101, San Diego 92126
Phone: (858) 566-2184

Azusa Pacific University
901 East Alosta Ave., PO Box 7000, Azusa 91702-7000
Type: Private, independent, four-year
Degrees: A, B, M, P, D   *Enroll:* 6,241
URL: http://www.apu.edu
Phone: (626) 812-3434   *Calendar:* 4-1-4 plan
Inst. Accred.: ATS (1990/2001), WASC-SR. (1964/2001)
Prog. Accred.: Clinical Psychology, Nursing, Nursing
  Education, Physical Therapy, Social Work, Teacher
  Education (NCATE)

Bakersfield College
1801 Panorama Dr., Bakersfield 93305-1299
Type: Public, state/local, two-year
System: Kern Community College District
Degrees: A   *Enroll:* 8,138
URL: http://www.bakersfieldcollege.edu
Phone: (661) 395-4011   *Calendar:* Sem. plan
Inst. Accred.: WASC-JR. (1952/2001)
Prog. Accred.: Radiography

Barstow College
2700 Barstow Rd., Barstow 92311-6699
Type: Public, state/local, two-year
System: Barstow Community College District
Degrees: A   *Enroll:* 1,691
URL: http://www.barstow.edu
Phone: (760) 252-2411   *Calendar:* Sem. plan
Inst. Accred.: WASC-JR. (1962/2000)

Bethany University
800 Bethany Dr., Scotts Valley 95066
Type: Private, Assemblies of God, four-year
Degrees: A, B, M   *Enroll:* 486
URL: http://www.bethany.edu
Phone: (831) 438-3800   *Calendar:* 4-1-4 plan
Inst. Accred.: WASC-SR. (1966/2001)

Bethesda Christian University
730 North Euclid St., Anaheim 92801
Type: Private, Full Gospel World Mission, four-year
Degrees: B, M
URL: http://www.bcu.edu
Phone: (714) 517-1945   *Calendar:* Sem. plan
Inst. Accred.: ABHE (1997/2001)

Biola University
13800 Biola Ave., La Mirada 90639-0001
Type: Private, independent, four-year
Degrees: B, M, P, D   *Enroll:* 4,292
URL: http://www.biola.edu
Phone: (562) 903-6000   *Calendar:* 4-1-4 plan
Inst. Accred.: ATS (1978/1995), WASC-SR. (1961/2005)
Prog. Accred.: Art, Business (ACBSP), Clinical Psychology,
  Music, Nursing

Brooks College
4825 East Pacific Coast Hwy., Long Beach 90804
Type: Private, proprietary, two-year
System: Career Education Corporation
Degrees: A   *Enroll:* 1,339
URL: http://www.brookscollege.edu
Phone: (562) 597-6611   *Calendar:* Qtr. plan
Inst. Accred.: WASC-JR. (1977/2004)
Prog. Accred.: Interior Design

Sunnyvale Campus
1120 Kifer Rd., Sunnyvale 94086
Phone: (408) 328-5700

Brooks Institute of Photography
801 Alston Rd., Santa Barbara 93108
Type: Private, proprietary, four-year
System: Career Education Corporation
Degrees: A, B, M   *Enroll:* 2,154
URL: http://www.brooks.edu
Phone: (805) 690-7667   *Calendar:* Tri. plan
Inst. Accred.: ACICS (1984/2001)

Ventura Campus
5301 North Ventura Ave., Ventura 93001
Phone: (805) 585-8000

Bryman College—Ontario
520 North Euclid Ave., Ontario 91762-3591
Type: Private, proprietary, two-year
System: Corinthian Colleges, Inc
Degrees: A
URL: http://www.bryman-college.com
Phone: (909) 984-5027
Inst. Accred.: ACCSCT (1986/2003)

Bryman College—West Los Angeles
3000 South Robertson Blvd., Ste. 300, Los Angeles
90034-9158
Type: Private, proprietary, two-year
System: Corinthian Colleges, Inc
Degrees: A   *Enroll:* 1,333
URL: http://www.bryman-college.com
Phone: (310) 840-5777
Inst. Accred.: ACCSCT (1987/2004)

Bryman College—Whittier
12449 Putnam St., Whittier 90602-3198
Type: Private, proprietary, two-year
System: Corinthian Colleges, Inc
Degrees: A
URL: http://www.bryman-college.com
Phone: (562) 945-9191
Inst. Accred.: ACCSCT (1988/2000)

Butte College
3536 Butte Campus Dr., Oroville 95965-8399
Type: Public, state/local, two-year
System: Butte-Glenn Community College District
Degrees: A   *Enroll:* 7,667
URL: http://www.butte.edu
Phone: (530) 895-2511   *Calendar:* Sem. plan
Inst. Accred.: WASC-JR. (1972/2003)
Prog. Accred.: Respiratory Therapy

Cabrillo College
6500 Soquel Dr., Aptos 95003-3119
Type: Public, state/local, two-year
System: Cabrillo Community College District
Degrees: A   *Enroll:* 7,738
URL: http://www.cabrillo.edu
Phone: (831) 479-6100   *Calendar:* Sem. plan
Inst. Accred.: WASC-JR. (1961/2001)
Prog. Accred.: Dental Hygiene, Medical Assisting (AMA),
   Radiography

California Baptist University
8432 Magnolia Ave., Riverside 92504
Type: Private, Southern Baptist Church, four-year
Degrees: B, M   *Enroll:* 1,914
URL: http://www.calbaptist.edu
Phone: (909) 689-5771   *Calendar:* Sem. plan
Inst. Accred.: WASC-SR. (1961/2000)
Prog. Accred.: Business (ACBSP), Music

California Christian College
4881 East University Ave., Fresno 93703-3599
Type: Private, Free Will Baptist Church, four-year
Degrees: A, B
URL: http://www.calchristiancollege.org
Phone: (559) 251-4215   *Calendar:* Sem. plan
Inst. Accred.: TRACS (1993/2003)

California Coast University
700 North Main St., Santa Ana 92701
Type: Private, proprietary, four-year
Degrees: B, M   *FTE Enroll:* 312
URL: http://www.calcoast.edu
Phone: (714) 547-9625   *Calendar:* Sem. plan
Inst. Accred.: DETC (2005)

California College of the Arts
1111 Eigth St., San Francisco 94107-2247
Type: Private, independent, four-year
Degrees: B, M   *Enroll:* 1,389
URL: http://www.ccac-art.edu
Phone: (415) 703-9500   *Calendar:* Tri. plan
Inst. Accred.: WASC-SR. (1954/1998)
Prog. Accred.: Art, Interior Design

Oakland Campus
5212 Broadway, Oakland 94618
Phone: (510) 594-3600

California College San Diego
2820 Camino Del Rio South, Ste. 300, San Diego 92108-3821
Type: Private, proprietary, four-year
Degrees: A, B
URL: http://www.cc-sd.edu
Phone: (619) 295-5785
Inst. Accred.: ACCSCT (1992/2004)

California Culinary Academy
625 Polk St., San Francisco 94102-3368
Type: Private, proprietary, two-year
System: Career Education Corporation
Degrees: A   *Enroll:* 2,523
URL: http://www.baychef.com
Phone: (415) 771-3536
Inst. Accred.: ACCSCT (1982/2000)
Prog. Accred.: Culinary Education

California Design College
3440 Wilshire Blvd., Los Angeles 90010
Type: Private, proprietary, four-year
System: Education Management Corporation
Degrees: A, B
URL: http://www.cdc.edu
Phone: (213) 251-3636   *Calendar:* Qtr. plan
Inst. Accred.: ACICS (1995/2004)

California Institute of Integral Studies
1453 Mission St., 4th Flr., San Francisco 94103
Type: Private, independent, four-year
Degrees: B, M, D   *Enroll:* 647
URL: http://www.ciis.edu
Phone: (415) 575-6100   *Calendar:* Qtr. plan
Inst. Accred.: WASC-SR. (1981/2001)
Prog. Accred.: Clinical Psychology

California Institute of Technology
1200 East California Blvd., Pasadena 91125-0001
Type: Private, independent, four-year
Degrees: B, M, D   *Enroll:* 2,172
URL: http://www.caltech.edu
Phone: (626) 395-6811   *Calendar:* Qtr. plan
Inst. Accred.: WASC-SR. (1949/1998)
Prog. Accred.: Engineering (chemical, electrical,
   engineering physics/science)

California Institute of the Arts
24700 McBean Pkwy., Valencia 91355
Type: Private, independent, four-year
Degrees: B, M   *Enroll:* 1,259
URL: http://www.calarts.edu
Phone: (661) 255-1050   *Calendar:* Sem. plan
Inst. Accred.: WASC-SR. (1955/2000)
Prog. Accred.: Art, Dance, Music, Theatre

California Lutheran University
60 West Olsen Rd., Thousand Oaks 91360
Type: Private, Evangelical Lutheran Church in America, four-year
Degrees: B, M   *Enroll:* 2,503
URL: http://www.clunet.edu
Phone: (805) 492-2411   *Calendar:* 4-1-4 plan
Inst. Accred.: WASC-SR. (1962/2005)

California Maritime Academy
200 Maritime Academy Dr., PO Box 1392, Vallejo 94590
Type: Public, state, four-year
System: California State University System
Degrees: B   *Enroll:* 654
URL: http://www.csum.edu
Phone: (707) 654-1000   *Calendar:* Tri. plan
Inst. Accred.: WASC-SR. (1977/2002)
Prog. Accred.: Engineering (mechanical), Engineering Technology (facilities, naval architecture/marine)

California National University for Advanced Studies
8550 Balboa Blvd., Ste. 210, Northridge 91325
Type: Private, proprietary, four-year
Degrees: B, M
URL: http://www.cnuas.edu
Phone: (818) 830-2411   *Calendar:* Tri. plan
Inst. Accred.: DETC (1998/2003)

California Polytechnic State University— San Luis Obispo
San Luis Obispo 93407
Type: Public, state, four-year
System: California State University System
Degrees: B, M   *Enroll:* 17,574
URL: http://www.calpoly.edu
Phone: (805) 756-1111   *Calendar:* Qtr. plan
Inst. Accred.: WASC-SR. (1951/2000)
Prog. Accred.: Art, Business (AACSB), Computer Science, Construction Education, Counseling, Engineering (aerospace, agricultural, architectural, civil, computer, electrical, environmental/sanitary, industrial, manufacturing, materials, mechanical), Forestry, Industrial Technology, Landscape Architecture, Music, Planning, Recreation and Leisure Services

California State Polytechnic University— Pomona
3801 West Temple Ave., Pomona 91768
Type: Public, state, four-year
System: California State University System
Degrees: B, M   *Enroll:* 17,084
URL: http://www.csupomona.edu
Phone: (909) 869-7659   *Calendar:* Qtr. plan
Inst. Accred.: WASC-SR. (1970/2001)
Prog. Accred.: Art, Business (AACSB), Computer Science, Dietetics (internship), Engineering (aerospace, chemical, civil, computer, electrical, industrial, manufacturing, mechanical), Engineering Technology (civil/construction, electrical, general, surveying), Landscape Architecture, Planning, Veterinary Technology

California State University—Bakersfield
9001 Stockdale Hwy., Bakersfield 93311-1099
Type: Public, state, four-year
System: California State University System
Degrees: B, M, D   *Enroll:* 6,617
URL: http://www.csubak.edu
Phone: (661) 664-2011   *Calendar:* Qtr. plan
Inst. Accred.: WASC-SR. (1970/2000)
Prog. Accred.: Business (AACSB), Nursing, Nursing Education, Public Administration, Social Work, Teacher Education (NCATE)

California State University—Chico
400 West First St., Chico 95929
Type: Public, state, four-year
System: California State University System
Degrees: B, M   *Enroll:* 14,376
URL: http://www.csuchico.edu
Phone: (530) 898-4636   *Calendar:* Sem. plan
Inst. Accred.: WASC-SR. (1949/1996)
Prog. Accred.: Art, Business (AACSB), Computer Science, Construction Education, Dietetics (internship), Engineering (civil, computer, electrical, mechanical), Industrial Technology, Journalism, Music, Nursing, Nursing Education, Public Administration, Recreation and Leisure Services, Social Work, Speech-Language Pathology

California State University—Dominguez Hills
1000 East Victoria St., Carson 90747
Type: Public, state, four-year
System: California State University System
Degrees: B, M   *Enroll:* 9,469
URL: http://www.csudh.edu
Phone: (310) 243-3300   *Calendar:* Sem. plan
Inst. Accred.: WASC-SR. (1965/2001)
Prog. Accred.: Business (AACSB), Business (ACBSP), Clinical Lab Scientist, Computer Science, Music, Nursing, Occupational Therapy, Orthotist/Prothetist, Public Administration, Teacher Education (NCATE), Theatre

California State University—East Bay
25800 Carlos Bee Blvd., Hayward 94542-3011
Type: Public, state, four-year
System: California State University System
Degrees: B, M   *Enroll:* 10,854
URL: http://www.csuhayward.edu
Phone: (510) 885-3000   *Calendar:* Qtr. plan
Inst. Accred.: WASC-SR. (1961/2001)
Prog. Accred.: Art, Business (AACSB), Music, Nursing, Public Administration, Speech-Language Pathology, Teacher Education (NCATE)

California State University—Fresno
5241 North Maple Ave., Mailstop 48, Fresno 93740-8027
Type: Public, state, four-year
System: California State University System
Degrees: B, M, D   *Enroll:* 18,723
URL: http://www.csufresno.edu
Phone: (559) 278-4240   *Calendar:* Sem. plan
Inst. Accred.: WASC-SR. (1949/2005)
Prog. Accred.: Athletic Training, Business (AACSB),
  Construction Education, Counseling, Dietetics
  (internship), Engineering (civil, computer, electrical,
  industrial, mechanical, surveying), Industrial
  Technology, Interior Design, Music, Nursing, Physical
  Therapy, Public Administration, Public Health,
  Recreation and Leisure Services, Rehabilitation
  Counseling, Social Work, Speech-Language Pathology,
  Teacher Education (NCATE), Theatre

California State University—Fullerton
PO Box 34080, Fullerton 92834
Type: Public, state, four-year
System: California State University System
Degrees: B, M   *Enroll:* 25,572
URL: http://www.fullerton.edu
Phone: (714) 278-2011   *Calendar:* Sem. plan
Inst. Accred.: WASC-SR. (1961/2000)
Prog. Accred.: Accounting, Art, Business (AACSB),
  Computer Science, Dance, Engineering (civil, electrical,
  mechanical), Journalism, Music, Nurse Anesthesia
  Education, Nursing, Nursing Education, Public
  Administration, Speech-Language Pathology, Teacher
  Education (NCATE), Theatre

California State University—Long Beach
1250 Bellflower Blvd., Long Beach 90840
Type: Public, state, four-year
System: California State University System
Degrees: B, M, D   *Enroll:* 28,401
URL: http://www.csulb.edu
Phone: (562) 985-4111   *Calendar:* Sem. plan
Inst. Accred.: WASC-SR. (1957/2002)
Prog. Accred.: Art, Audiology, Business (AACSB),
  Computer Science, Dance, Dietetics (internship),
  Engineering (aerospace, chemical, civil, computer,
  electrical, mechanical), Engineering Technology
  (computer, electrical, manufacturing), English Language
  Education, Family and Consumer Science, Health
  Services Administration, Music, Nursing, Nursing
  Education, Phlebotomy, Physical Therapy, Psychology
  Internship, Public Administration, Public Health,
  Radiation Therapy, Recreation and Leisure Services,
  Social Work, Speech-Language Pathology, Teacher
  Education (NCATE), Theatre

California State University—Los Angeles
5151 State University Dr., Los Angeles 90032-4226
Type: Public, state, four-year
System: California State University System
Degrees: B, M, D   *Enroll:* 15,862
URL: http://www.calstatela.edu
Phone: (323) 343-3000   *Calendar:* Qtr. plan
Inst. Accred.: WASC-SR. (1954/1999)
Prog. Accred.: Art, Audiology, Business (AACSB),
  Counseling, Dietetics (coordinated), Engineering (civil,
  electrical, mechanical), Music, Nursing, Public
  Administration, Rehabilitation Counseling, Social Work,
  Speech-Language Pathology, Teacher Education
  (NCATE)

California State University—Monterey Bay
100 Campus Center, Building 1, Seaside 93955-8001
Type: Public, state, four-year
System: California State University System
Degrees: B, M, D   *Enroll:* 3,397
URL: http://csumb.edu
Phone: (831) 582-3538   *Calendar:* Sem. plan
Inst. Accred.: WASC-SR. (2003)

California State University—Northridge
18111 Nordhoff St., Northridge 91330
Type: Public, state, four-year
System: California State University System
Degrees: B, M   *Enroll:* 26,827
URL: http://www.csun.edu
Phone: (818) 677-2121   *Calendar:* Sem. plan
Inst. Accred.: WASC-SR. (1958/2000)
Prog. Accred.: Applied Science (occupational health and
  safety), Art, Athletic Training, Audiology, Business
  (AACSB), Computer Science, Counseling, Dietetics
  (internship), Engineering (civil, electrical,
  environmental/sanitary, mechanical), Family and
  Consumer Science, Interior Design, Journalism, Music,
  Nursing Education, Physical Therapy, Public Health,
  Radiography, Recreation and Leisure Services, Speech-
  Language Pathology, Teacher Education (NCATE),
  Theatre

California State University—Sacramento
6000 J St., Sacramento 95819-6016
Type: Public, state, four-year
System: California State University System
Degrees: B, M, D   *Enroll:* 23,391
URL: http://www.csus.edu
Phone: (916) 278-6011   *Calendar:* Sem. plan
Inst. Accred.: WASC-SR. (1951/1997)
Prog. Accred.: Art, Athletic Training, Audiology, Business
  (AACSB), Computer Science, Construction Education,
  Engineering (civil, computer, electrical, mechanical),
  Engineering Technology (mechanical), Interior Design,
  Music, Nursing, Nursing Education, Physical Therapy,
  Recreation and Leisure Services, Rehabilitation
  Counseling, Social Work, Speech-Language Pathology,
  Theatre

California State University—San Bernardino
5500 University Pkwy., San Bernardino 92407-2397
Type: Public, state, four-year
System: California State University System
Degrees: B, M   *Enroll:* 13,787
URL: http://www.csusb.edu
Phone: (909) 880-5000   *Calendar:* Qtr. plan
Inst. Accred.: WASC-SR. (1965/2004)
Prog. Accred.: Art, Business (AACSB), Computer Science, Music, Nursing, Nursing Education, Public Administration, Rehabilitation Counseling, Social Work, Theatre

California State University—San Marcos
333 South Twin Oaks Valley Rd., San Marcos 92096-0001
Type: Public, state, four-year
System: California State University System
Degrees: B, M, D   *Enroll:* 6,166
URL: http://www.csusm.edu
Phone: (760) 750-4000   *Calendar:* Sem. plan
Inst. Accred.: WASC-SR. (1993/2000)
Prog. Accred.: Business (AACSB), Teacher Education (NCATE)

California State University—Stanislaus
801 West Monte Vista Ave., Turlock 95382
Type: Public, state, four-year
System: California State University System
Degrees: B, M   *Enroll:* 6,225
URL: http://lead.csustan.edu
Phone: (209) 667-3082   *Calendar:* 4-1-4 plan
Inst. Accred.: WASC-SR. (1963/1998)
Prog. Accred.: Art, Business (AACSB), Music, Nursing, Nursing Education, Public Administration, Social Work, Teacher Education (NCATE), Theatre

Stockton Campus
612 East Magnolia St., Stockton 95202-1846
Phone: (209) 467-5300

California Western School of Law
350 Cedar St., San Diego 92101
Type: Private, independent, four-year
Degrees: P   *Enroll:* 915
URL: http://www.cwsl.edu
Phone: (619) 239-0391   *Calendar:* Tri. plan
Inst. Accred.: ABA (1962/2000)

Cañada College
4200 Farm Hill Blvd., Redwood City 94061-1099
Type: Public, state/local, two-year
System: San Mateo County Community College District
Degrees: A   *Enroll:* 2,637
URL: http://www.canadacollege.edu
Phone: (650) 306-3100   *Calendar:* Sem. plan
Inst. Accred.: WASC-JR. (1970/2001)
Prog. Accred.: Radiography

Cerritos College
11110 Alondra Blvd., Norwalk 90650-6296
Type: Public, state/local, two-year
System: Cerritos Community College District
Degrees: A   *Enroll:* 11,901
URL: http://www.cerritos.edu
Phone: (562) 860-2451   *Calendar:* Sem. plan
Inst. Accred.: WASC-JR. (1959/2002)
Prog. Accred.: Dental Assisting, Dental Hygiene, General Practice Residency, Nursing, Physical Therapy Assisting

Cerro Coso Community College
3000 College Heights Blvd., Ridgecrest 93555-9571
Type: Public, state/local, two-year
System: Kern Community College District
Degrees: A   *Enroll:* 1,931
URL: http://www.cerrocoso.edu
Phone: (760) 384-6100   *Calendar:* Sem. plan
Inst. Accred.: WASC-JR. (1975/1995)

Chabot College
25555 Hesperian Blvd., Hayward 94545-2447
Type: Public, state/local, two-year
System: Chabot-Las Positas Community College District
Degrees: A   *Enroll:* 6,564
URL: http://www.chabotcollege.edu
Phone: (510) 723-6600   *Calendar:* Sem. plan
Inst. Accred.: WASC-JR. (1963/2003)
Prog. Accred.: Dental Hygiene, Health Information Technician, Medical Assisting (CAAHEP)

Chaffey College
5885 Haven Ave., Rancho Cucamonga 91737-3002
Type: Public, state/local, two-year
System: Chaffey Community College District
Degrees: A   *Enroll:* 9,401
URL: http://www.chaffey.edu
Phone: (909) 987-1737   *Calendar:* Sem. plan
Inst. Accred.: WASC-JR. (1952/2004)
Prog. Accred.: Dental Assisting, Nursing, Radiography

Chapman University
One University Dr., Orange 92866
Type: Private, Disciples of Christ, four-year
Degrees: A, B, M, P, D   *Enroll:* 4,600
URL: http://www.chapman.edu
Phone: (714) 997-6815   *Calendar:* 4-1-4 plan
Inst. Accred.: WASC-SR. (1956/2005)
Prog. Accred.: Business (AACSB), Law (ABA only), Music, Physical Therapy

Charles R. Drew University of Medicine and Science
1731 East 120th St., Los Angeles 90059
Type: Private, independent, four-year
Degrees: A, B, M, D   *Enroll:* 445
URL: http://www.cdrewu.edu
Phone: (323) 563-4800   *Calendar:* Sem. plan
Inst. Accred.: WASC-SR. (1995/2003)
Prog. Accred.: Dietetics (coordinated), General Practice Residency, Health Information Technician, Nuclear Medicine Technology, Nurse (Midwifery), Oral and Maxillofacial Surgery, Physician Assistant, Radiography

Church Divinity School of the Pacific
2451 Ridge Rd., Berkeley 94709-1217
Type: Private, Province of the Pacific of the Episcopal
Church, four-year
System: Graduate Theological Union
Degrees: B, M, P, D   *Enroll:* 91
URL: http://www.cdsp.edu
Phone: (510) 204-0700   *Calendar:* Qtr. plan
Inst. Accred.: ATS (1945/2004), WASC-SR. (1978/2004)

Citrus College
1000 West Foothill Blvd., Glendora 91741-1899
Type: Public, state/local, two-year
System: Citrus Community College District
Degrees: A   *Enroll:* 6,870
URL: http://www.citruscollege.edu
Phone: (626) 963-0323   *Calendar:* Sem. plan
Inst. Accred.: WASC-JR. (1952/2004)
Prog. Accred.: Dental Assisting

City College of San Francisco
50 Phelan Ave., San Francisco 94112-1898
Type: Public, state/local, two-year
System: San Francisco Community College District
Degrees: A   *Enroll:* 19,710
URL: http://www.ccsf.edu
Phone: (415) 239-3000   *Calendar:* Sem. plan
Inst. Accred.: WASC-JR. (1952/2000)
Prog. Accred.: Culinary Education, Dental Assisting,
Health Information Technician, Medical Assisting (AMA),
Radiation Therapy, Radiography

City of Hope National Medical Center
1500 East Duarte Rd., Duarte 91010-3000
Type: Private, independent, four-year
Degrees: D
URL: http://www.cityofhope.org
Phone: (626) 256-8775   *Calendar:* Sem. plan
Inst. Accred.: WASC-SR. (2001)
Prog. Accred.: Radiation Therapy

The Claremont Graduate University
150 East 10th St., Claremont 91711
Type: Private, independent, four-year
System: Claremont University Consortium
Degrees: M, D   *Enroll:* 1,752
URL: http://www.cgu.edu
Phone: (909) 621-8000   *Calendar:* Sem. plan
Inst. Accred.: WASC-SR. (1949/2002)
Prog. Accred.: Business (AACSB)

Claremont McKenna College
500 East 9th St., Bauer Center, Claremont 91711-6400
Type: Private, independent, four-year
System: Claremont University Consortium
Degrees: B, M   *Enroll:* 1,137
URL: http://www.mckenna.edu
Phone: (909) 621-8111   *Calendar:* Sem. plan
Inst. Accred.: WASC-SR. (1949/2000)

Claremont School of Theology
1325 North College Ave., Claremont 91711
Type: Private, independent, four-year
System: Claremont University Consortium
Degrees: M, P, D   *Enroll:* 358
URL: http://www.cst.edu
Phone: (909) 447-2500   *Calendar:* Sem. plan
Inst. Accred.: ATS (1944/2003), WASC-SR. (1949/1994,
Warning)

Coastline Community College
11460 Warner Ave., Fountain Valley 92708-2597
Type: Public, state/local, two-year
System: Coast Community College District
Degrees: A   *Enroll:* 2,630
URL: http://coastline.cccd.edu
Phone: (714) 546-7600   *Calendar:* Sem. plan
Inst. Accred.: WASC-JR. (1978/2001)

Cogswell Polytechnical College
1175 Bordeaux Dr., Sunnyvale 94089-1299
Type: Private, independent, four-year
Degrees: A, B   *Enroll:* 280
URL: http://www.cogswell.edu
Phone: (408) 541-0100   *Calendar:* Sem. plan
Inst. Accred.: WASC-SR. (1977/2001)

The Colburn School of Performing Arts
200 South Grand Ave., Los Angeles 90012
Type: Private, independent, four-year
Degrees: B
URL: http://www.colburnschool.edu
Phone: (213) 621-2200   *Calendar:* Sem. plan
Inst. Accred.: NASM (1980/1995)

Coleman College
7380 Pkwy. Dr., La Mesa 91942-1532
Type: Private, independent, four-year
Degrees: A, B, M   *Enroll:* 652
URL: http://www.coleman.edu
Phone: (619) 465-3990   *Calendar:* Qtr. plan
Inst. Accred.: ACICS (1967/2001)

San Marcos Campus
1284 West San Marcos Blvd., San Marcos 92069
Phone: (760) 747-3990

College of Alameda
555 Atlantic Ave., Alameda 94501-2109
Type: Public, state/local, two-year
System: Peralta Community College District
Degrees: A   *Enroll:* 2,624
URL: http://www.peralta.cc.ca.us/coa/coa.htm
Phone: (510) 522-7221   *Calendar:* Sem. plan
Inst. Accred.: WASC-JR. (1973/1999, Warning)
Prog. Accred.: Dental Assisting

College of Marin
835 College Ave., Kentfield 94904-2509
Type: Public, state/local, two-year
System: Marin Community College District
Degrees: A   *Enroll:* 3,603
URL: http://www.marin.cc.ca.us
Phone: (415) 457-8811   *Calendar:* Sem. plan
Inst. Accred.: WASC-JR. (1952/1999, Warning)
Prog. Accred.: Dental Assisting, Nursing

Indian Valley Campus
1800 Ignacio Blvd., Novato 94949
Phone: (415) 457-8811

College of San Mateo
1700 West Hillsdale Blvd., San Mateo 94402-3784
Type: Public, state/local, two-year
System: San Mateo County Community College District
Degrees: A   *Enroll:* 6,203
URL: http://collegeofsanmateo.edu
Phone: (650) 574-6161   *Calendar:* Sem. plan
Inst. Accred.: WASC-JR. (1952/2001)
Prog. Accred.: Dental Assisting

College of the Canyons
26455 North Rockwell Canyon Rd., Santa Clarita 91355-1899
Type: Public, state/local, two-year
System: Santa Clarita Community College District
Degrees: A   *Enroll:* 7,979
URL: http://www.coc.cc.ca.us
Phone: (661) 259-7800   *Calendar:* Sem. plan
Inst. Accred.: WASC-JR. (1972/2003)
Prog. Accred.: Nursing

College of the Desert
43-500 Monterey Ave., Palm Desert 92260-2499
Type: Public, state/local, two-year
System: Desert Community College District
Degrees: A   *Enroll:* 4,369
URL: http://www.dccd.cc.ca.us
Phone: (760) 346-8041   *Calendar:* Sem. plan
Inst. Accred.: WASC-JR. (1963/2005)
Prog. Accred.: Nursing, Respiratory Therapy

College of the Redwoods
7351 Tompkins Hill Rd., Eureka 95501-9301
Type: Public, state/local, two-year
System: Redwoods Community College District
Degrees: A   *Enroll:* 3,963
URL: http://www.redwoods.edu
Phone: (707) 476-4100   *Calendar:* Sem. plan
Inst. Accred.: WASC-JR. (1967/2000)
Prog. Accred.: Dental Assisting

College of the Sequoias
915 South Mooney Blvd., Visalia 93277-2234
Type: Public, state/local, two-year
System: College of the Sequoias Community College District
Degrees: A   *Enroll:* 6,691
URL: http://www.sequoias.cc.ca.us
Phone: (559) 730-3700   *Calendar:* Sem. plan
Inst. Accred.: WASC-JR. (1952/2001)

College of the Siskiyous
800 College Ave., Weed 96094-2899
Type: Public, state/local, two-year
System: Siskiyou Joint Community College District
Degrees: A   *Enroll:* 1,471
URL: http://www.siskiyous.edu
Phone: (530) 938-4461   *Calendar:* Sem. plan
Inst. Accred.: WASC-JR. (1961/2004)

Columbia College
11600 Columbia College Dr., Sonora 95370-8518
Type: Public, state/local, two-year
System: Yosemite Community College District
Degrees: A   *Enroll:* 1,806
URL: http://www.yosemite.cc.ca.us/columbia
Phone: (209) 588-5100   *Calendar:* Sem. plan
Inst. Accred.: WASC-JR. (1972/2000)
Prog. Accred.: Culinary Education

Columbia College Hollywood
18618 Oxnard St., Tarzana 91356-1411
Type: Private, independent, four-year
Degrees: A, B   *Enroll:* 148
URL: http://www.columbiacollege.edu
Phone: (818) 345-8414   *Calendar:* Qtr. plan
Inst. Accred.: ACCSCT (1979/2004)

Compton Community College
1111 East Artesia Blvd., Compton 90221
Type: Public, state/local, two-year
System: Compton Community College District
Degrees: A   *Enroll:* 3,888
URL: http://www.compton.edu
Phone: (310) 900-1600   *Calendar:* Sem. plan
Inst. Accred.: WASC-JR. (1952/1999, Probation)

Concord Law School
10866 Wilshire Blvd., Ste. 1200, Los Angeles 90024
Type: Private, proprietary, four-year
Degrees: B, P
URL: http://www.concord.kaplan.edu
Phone: (310) 824-6980   *Calendar:* Sem. plan
Inst. Accred.: DETC (2000/2004)

Concorde Career College
12951 Euclid St., Ste. 101, Garden Grove 92840
Type: Private, proprietary, two-year
Degrees: A   *Enroll:* 569
URL: http://www.concordecareercolleges.com
Phone: (714) 703-1900
Inst. Accred.: ACCSCT (1968/2001)
Prog. Accred.: Medical Assisting (CAAHEP)

Concorde Career College
12412 Victory Blvd., North Hollywood 91606
Type: Private, proprietary, two-year
Degrees: A   *Enroll:* 726
URL: http://www.concordecareercolleges.com
Phone: (818) 766-8151
Inst. Accred.: ACCSCT (1973/2003)
Prog. Accred.: Respiratory Therapy Technology, Surgical
   Technology

Concorde Career College
201 East Airport Dr., Ste. A, San Bernardino 92408
Type: Private, proprietary, two-year
Degrees: A   *Enroll:* 644
URL: http://www.concordecareercolleges.com
Phone: (909) 884-8891
Inst. Accred.: ACCSCT (1968/2005)
Prog. Accred.: Medical Assisting (AMA), Practical Nursing

Concorde Career College
4393 Imperial Ave., Ste. 100, San Diego 92113
Type: Private, proprietary, two-year
Degrees: A
URL: http://www.concordecareercolleges.com
Phone: (619) 688-0800
Inst. Accred.: ACCSCT (1969/2002)

Concordia University Irvine
1530 Concordia West, Irvine 92612
Type: Private, Lutheran Church-Missouri Synod, four-year
System: Concordia University System
Degrees: A, B, M   *Enroll:* 1,576
URL: http://www.cui.edu
Phone: (949) 854-8002   *Calendar:* Sem. plan
Inst. Accred.: WASC-SR. (1981/2005)

Contra Costa College
2600 Mission Bell Dr., San Pablo 94806-3195
Type: Public, state/local, two-year
System: Contra Costa Community College District
Degrees: A   *Enroll:* 3,659
URL: http://www.contracosta.edu
Phone: (510) 235-7800   *Calendar:* Sem. plan
Inst. Accred.: WASC-JR. (1952/2002)
Prog. Accred.: Dental Assisting, Montessori Teacher
   Education

Copper Mountain College
6162 Rotary Way, PO Box 1398, Joshua Tree 92252
Type: Public, state/local, two-year
System: Copper Mountain Community College District
Degrees: A   *Enroll:* 1,009
URL: http://www.cmccd.cc.ca.us
Phone: (760) 366-3791   *Calendar:* Sem. plan
Inst. Accred.: WASC-JR. (2001)

Cosumnes River College
8401 Center Pkwy., Sacramento 95823-5799
Type: Public, state/local, two-year
System: Los Rios Community College District
Degrees: A   *Enroll:* 8,157
URL: http://www.crc.losrios.edu
Phone: (916) 691-7344   *Calendar:* Sem. plan
Inst. Accred.: WASC-JR. (1972/2004)
Prog. Accred.: Health Information Technician, Medical
   Assisting (AMA), Veterinary Technology

Crafton Hills College
11711 Sand Canyon Rd., Yucaipa 92399-1799
Type: Public, state/local, two-year
System: San Bernardino Community College District
Degrees: A   *Enroll:* 2,957
URL: http://www.craftonhills.edu
Phone: (909) 794-2161   *Calendar:* Sem. plan
Inst. Accred.: WASC-JR. (1975/2002)
Prog. Accred.: EMT (Paramedic), Respiratory Therapy,
   Respiratory Therapy Technology

Cuesta College
PO Box 8106, San Luis Obispo 93403-8106
Type: Public, state/local, two-year
System: San Luis Obispo Community College District
Degrees: A   *Enroll:* 6,511
URL: http://www.cuesta.edu
Phone: (805) 546-3100   *Calendar:* Sem. plan
Inst. Accred.: WASC-JR. (1968/2003)

Cuyamaca College
900 Rancho San Diego Pkwy., El Cajon 92019-4304
Type: Public, state/local, two-year
System: Grossmont-Cuyamaca Community College
   District
Degrees: A   *Enroll:* 3,770
URL: http://www.cuyamaca.edu
Phone: (619) 660-4000   *Calendar:* Sem. plan
Inst. Accred.: WASC-JR. (1980/2002)

Cypress College
9200 Valley View St., Cypress 90630-5897
Type: Public, state/local, two-year
System: North Orange County Community College District
Degrees: A   *Enroll:* 7,500
URL: http://www.cypresscollege.edu
Phone: (714) 484-7000   *Calendar:* Sem. plan
Inst. Accred.: WASC-JR. (1968/2005)
Prog. Accred.: Dental Assisting, Dental Hygiene, Funeral
   Service Education (Mortuary Science), Health
   Information Technician, Nursing, Radiography

De Anza College
21250 Stevens Creek Blvd., Cupertino 95014-5797
Type: Public, state/local, two-year
System: Foothill-DeAnza Community College District
Degrees: A   *Enroll:* 14,770
URL: http://www.deanza.fhda.edu
Phone: (408) 864-5678   *Calendar:* Qtr. plan
Inst. Accred.: WASC-JR. (1969/2000)
Prog. Accred.: Medical Assisting (CAAHEP)

Deep Springs College
Dyer, NV 89010-9803
Type: Private, independent, two-year
Degrees: A *FTE Enroll:* 26
URL: http://www.deepsprings.edu
Phone: (760) 872-2000 *Calendar:* Sem. plan
Inst. Accred.: WASC-JR. (1952/2005)

Defense Language Institute Foreign Language Center
Presidio of Monterey 93944
Type: Public, federal, two-year
Degrees: A *Enroll:* 3,102
URL: http://pom-www.army.mil
Phone: (831) 242-5000
Inst. Accred.: WASC-JR. (1979/2000)

Dell'Arte Internatinal School of Physical Theater
PO Box 816, Blue Lake 95525
Type: Private, independent, four-year
Degrees: M
URL: http://www.dellarte.com
Phone: (707) 668-5663
Inst. Accred.: NAST (1990/2002)

Design Institute of San Diego
8555 Commerce Ave., San Diego 92121
Type: Private, independent, four-year
Degrees: B, P *Enroll:* 377
URL: http://www.disd.edu
Phone: (858) 566-1200 *Calendar:* Sem. plan
Inst. Accred.: ACICS (1995/2005)
Prog. Accred.: Interior Design

DeVry University Irvine
3333 Michelson Dr., Ste. 420, Irvine 92612-1682
Type: Private, proprietary, four-year
Degrees: M
URL: http://www.devry.edu
Phone: (949) 752-5631 *Calendar:* Sem. plan
Inst. Accred.: NCA-HLC (2002, *Indirect accreditation through DeVry University, Oakbrook Terrace, IL*)

DeVry University Pomona
901 Corporate Center Dr., Pomona 91768-2642
Type: Private, proprietary, four-year
System: DeVry University
Degrees: A, B, M *Enroll:* 6,102
URL: http://www.devry.edu/pomona
Phone: (800) 533-3879 *Calendar:* Sem. plan
Inst. Accred.: NCA-HLC (2002, *Indirect accreditation through DeVry University, Oakbrook Terrace, IL*)
Prog. Accred.: Engineering Technology (electrical)

Fremont Campus
6600 Dumbarton Circle, Fremont 94555
Phone: (510) 574-1100

Long Beach Campus
3880 Kilroy Airport Way, Long Beach 90806-2449
Phone: (800) 597-1333
Prog. Accred.: Engineering Technology (electrical)

West Hills Campus
22801 Roscoe Blvd., West Hills 91304
Phone: (818) 713-8111

Diablo Valley College
321 Golf Club Rd., Pleasant Hill 94523-1544
Type: Public, state/local, two-year
System: Contra Costa Community College District
Degrees: A *Enroll:* 12,077
URL: http://www.dvc.edu
Phone: (925) 685-1230 *Calendar:* Sem. plan
Inst. Accred.: WASC-JR. (1952/2002)
Prog. Accred.: Culinary Education, Dental Assisting, Dental Hygiene

Dominican School of Philosophy and Theology
2401 Ridge Rd., Berkeley 94709
Type: Private, independent, four-year
System: Graduate Theological Union
Degrees: B, M, P *Enroll:* 80
URL: http://www.dspt.edu
Phone: (510) 849-2030 *Calendar:* Sem. plan
Inst. Accred.: ATS (1978/2002), WASC-SR. (1964/2002)

Dominican University of California
50 Acacia Ave., San Rafael 94901
Type: Private, Roman Catholic Church, four-year
Degrees: B, M *Enroll:* 1,405
URL: http://www.dominican.edu
Phone: (415) 457-4440 *Calendar:* Sem. plan
Inst. Accred.: WASC-SR. (1949/1999)
Prog. Accred.: Nursing, Nursing Education, Occupational Therapy

Don Bosco Technical Institute
1151 San Gabriel Blvd., Rosemead 91770
Type: Private, Roman Catholic Church, two-year
Degrees: A *Enroll:* 251
URL: http://www.boscotech.edu
Phone: (626) 940-2000 *Calendar:* Sem. plan
Inst. Accred.: WASC-JR. (1972/2002)

Dongguk Royal University
440 South Shatto Place, Los Angeles 90020
Type: Private, independent, four-year
Degrees: M *Enroll:* 400
URL: http://www.dru.edu
Phone: (213) 487-0110 *Calendar:* Qtr. plan
Inst. Accred.: ACAOM (1994/2004)

East Los Angeles College
1301 Cesar Chavez Ave., Monterey Park 91754-6099
Type: Public, state/local, two-year
System: Los Angeles Community College District
Degrees: A   *Enroll:* 11,395
URL: http://www.elac.edu
Phone: (323) 265-8662   *Calendar:* Sem. plan
Inst. Accred.: WASC-JR. (1952/2003)
Prog. Accred.: Health Information Technician, Respiratory
Therapy

El Camino College
16007 Crenshaw Blvd., Torrance 90506-0002
Type: Public, state/local, two-year
System: El Camino Community College District
Degrees: A   *Enroll:* 13,663
URL: http://www.elcamino.edu
Phone: (310) 532-3670   *Calendar:* Sem. plan
Inst. Accred.: WASC-JR. (1952/2002)
Prog. Accred.: Nursing, Radiography, Respiratory Therapy

Emperor's College of Traditional Oriental Medicine
1807-B Wilshire Blvd., Santa Monica 90403
Type: Private, proprietary, four-year
Degrees: M   *Enroll:* 280
URL: http://www.emperors.edu
Phone: (310) 453-8300   *Calendar:* Qtr. plan
Inst. Accred.: ACAOM (1989/2001)

Los Angeles Campus
3625 West 6th St., Ste. 220, Los Angeles 90020
Phone: (213) 738-8833

Empire College
3035 Cleveland Ave., Santa Rosa 95403
Type: Private, proprietary, two-year
Degrees: A
URL: http://www.empcol.edu
Phone: (707) 546-4000   *Calendar:* Sem. plan
Inst. Accred.: ACICS (1969/2000)

Evergreen Valley College
3095 Yerba Buena Rd., San Jose 95135-1598
Type: Public, state/local, two-year
System: San Jose-Evergreen Community College District
Degrees: A   *Enroll:* 5,387
URL: http://www.evc.edu
Phone: (408) 274-7900   *Calendar:* Sem. plan
Inst. Accred.: WASC-JR. (1977/1998, Warning)
Prog. Accred.: Nursing

Expression College for Digital Arts
6601 Shellmound St., Emeryville 94608-1021
Type: Private, proprietary, four-year
Degrees: B
URL: http://www.expression.edu
Phone: (510) 654-2934   *Calendar:* Qtr. plan
Inst. Accred.: ACCSCT (2005)

Fashion Careers College
1923 Morena Blvd., San Diego 92110
Type: Private, proprietary, two-year
Degrees: A   *Enroll:* 106
URL: http://www.fashioncollege.com
Phone: (619) 275-4700
Inst. Accred.: ACICS (1983/2001)

The Fashion Institute of Design and Merchandising
919 South Grand Ave., Los Angeles 90015
Type: Private, independent, two-year
Degrees: A   *Enroll:* 2,816
URL: http://www.fidm.com
Phone: (213) 624-1200   *Calendar:* Qtr. plan
Inst. Accred.: WASC-JR. (1978/2005)
Prog. Accred.: Art, Interior Design

Costa Mesa Campus
17590 Gillette Ave., Irvine 92614
Phone: (949) 851-6500

San Diego Campus
1010 Second Ave., Ste. 200, San Diego 92101
Phone: (619) 235-2049

San Francisco Campus
55 Stockton St., San Francisco 94108
Phone: (415) 675-5200

Feather River College
570 Golden Eagle Ave., Quincy 95971-6023
Type: Public, state/local, two-year
System: Feather River Community College District
Degrees: A   *Enroll:* 838
URL: http://www.frcc.cc.ca.us
Phone: (530) 283-0202   *Calendar:* Sem. plan
Inst. Accred.: WASC-JR. (1973/2000)

Fielding Graduate University
2112 Santa Barbara St., Santa Barbara 93105
Type: Private, independent, four-year
Degrees: M, D   *Enroll:* 1,546
URL: http://www.fielding.edu
Phone: (805) 687-1099   *Calendar:* Tri. plan
Inst. Accred.: WASC-SR. (1982/1999)
Prog. Accred.: Clinical Psychology

Five Branches Institute College of Traditional Chinese Medicine
200 7th Ave., Ste. 115, Santa Cruz 95062
Type: Private, proprietary, four-year
Degrees: M   *Enroll:* 168
URL: http://www.fivebranches.edu
Phone: (831) 476-9424   *Calendar:* Sem. plan
Inst. Accred.: ACAOM (1996/2003)

Folsom Lake College
100 Scholar Way, Folsom 95630
Type: Public, state/local, two-year
System: Los Rios Community College District
Degrees: A
URL: http://www.flc.losrios.edu
Phone: (916) 608-6500   *Calendar:* Sem. plan
Inst. Accred.: WASC-JR. (2004)

Foothill College
12345 El Monte Rd., Los Altos Hills 94022-4599
Type: Public, state/local, two-year
System: Foothill-DeAnza Community College District
Degrees: A   *Enroll:* 9,067
URL: http://www.foothill.fhda.edu
Phone: (650) 949-7777   *Calendar:* Qtr. plan
Inst. Accred.: WASC-JR. (1959/2000)
Prog. Accred.: Dental Assisting, Dental Hygiene,
   Radiography, Respiratory Therapy, Veterinary
   Technology

Foundation College San Diego
5353 Mission Center Rd., Ste. 100, San Diego 92108-
1306
Type: Private, independent, two-year
Degrees: A
URL: http://www.foundationcollege.org
Phone: (619) 683-3273
Inst. Accred.: ACCSCT (2001)

Franciscan School of Theology
1712 Euclid Ave., Berkeley 94709
Type: Private, Roman Catholic Church, four-year
System: Graduate Theological Union
Degrees: M   *Enroll:* 68
URL: http://www.fst.edu
Phone: (510) 848-5232   *Calendar:* Qtr. plan
Inst. Accred.: ATS (1975/1998), WASC-SR. (1975/1998)

Fresno City College
1101 East University Ave., Fresno 93741-0001
Type: Public, state/local, two-year
System: State Center Community College District
Degrees: A   *Enroll:* 12,111
URL: http://www.fresnocitycollege.com
Phone: (559) 442-4600   *Calendar:* Sem. plan
Inst. Accred.: WASC-JR. (1952/2000)
Prog. Accred.: Dental Hygiene, Health Information
   Technician, Radiography, Respiratory Therapy

Fresno Pacific University
1717 South Chestnut Ave., Fresno 93702
Type: Private, Mennonite Brethren, four-year
Degrees: A, B, M   *Enroll:* 1,586
URL: http://www.fresno.edu
Phone: (559) 453-2000   *Calendar:* Sem. plan
Inst. Accred.: WASC-SR. (1961/2003)

Fuller Theological Seminary
135 North Oakland Ave., Pasadena 91182
Type: Private, independent, four-year
Degrees: M, D   *Enroll:* 1,790
URL: http://www.fuller.edu
Phone: (626) 584-5200   *Calendar:* Qtr. plan
Inst. Accred.: ATS (1957/2000), WASC-SR. (1969/2003)
Prog. Accred.: Clinical Psychology

Fullerton College
321 East Chapman Ave., Fullerton 92534
Type: Public, state/local, two-year
System: North Orange County Community College District
Degrees: A   *Enroll:* 11,337
URL: http://www.fullcoll.edu
Phone: (714) 992-7000   *Calendar:* Sem. plan
Inst. Accred.: WASC-JR. (1952/2005)

Gavilan College
5055 Santa Teresa Blvd., Gilroy 95020-9599
Type: Public, state/local, two-year
System: Gavilan Joint Community College District
Degrees: A   *Enroll:* 2,499
URL: http://www.gavilan.edu
Phone: (408) 847-1400   *Calendar:* Sem. plan
Inst. Accred.: WASC-JR. (1952/2001)

Glendale Community College
1500 North Verdugo Rd., Glendale 91208-2894
Type: Public, state/local, two-year
System: Glendale Community College District
Degrees: A   *Enroll:* 8,029
URL: http://www.glendale.edu
Phone: (818) 240-1000   *Calendar:* Sem. plan
Inst. Accred.: WASC-JR. (1952/2004)

Golden Gate Baptist Theological Seminary
201 Seminary Dr., Mill Valley 94941-3197
Type: Private, Southern Baptist Convention, four-year
Degrees: M, P, D   *Enroll:* 281
URL: http://www.ggbts.edu
Phone: (415) 380-1300   *Calendar:* Sem. plan
Inst. Accred.: ATS (1962/2001), WASC-SR. (1971/2003)
Prog. Accred.: Music

Golden Gate University
536 Mission St., San Francisco 94105-2968
Type: Private, independent, four-year
Degrees: A, B, M, P, D   *Enroll:* 2,594
URL: http://www.ggu.edu
Phone: (415) 442-7000   *Calendar:* Tri. plan
Inst. Accred.: WASC-SR. (1959/2002)
Prog. Accred.: Law

Sacramento Campus
3620 Northgate Blvd., Sacramento 95834
Phone: (916) 648-1446

Seattle Campus
1326 5th Ave., Ste. 310, Seattle, WA 98101
Phone: (206) 622-9996

Golden West College
15744 Golden West St., Huntington Beach 92647-0592
Type: Public, state/local, two-year
System: Coast Community College District
Degrees: A   *Enroll:* 7,536
URL: http://www.gwc.info
Phone: (714) 892-7711   *Calendar:* Sem. plan
Inst. Accred.: WASC-JR. (1969/2001)
Prog. Accred.: Nursing

The Golf Academy of San Diego
1910 Shadowridge Dr., Ste. 111, Vista 92083
Type: Private, proprietary, two-year
System: San Diego Golf Academy
Degrees: A
URL: http://www.sdgagolf.com
Phone: (760) 734-1208   *Calendar:* Sem. plan
Inst. Accred.: ACICS (1982/2000)

The Golf Academy of Arizona
One San Marcos Place, Chandler, AZ 85224
Phone: (480) 875-1574

The Golf Academy of Hawaii
45-550 Kionaole Rd., Kaneohe, Oahu, HI 96744
Phone: (808) 247-7088

The Golf Academy of the Carolinas
1303 Azalea Ct., Myrtle Beach, SC 29577
Phone: (843) 236-0481

The Golf Academy of the South
1200 East Altamonte Dr., Unit 1010, Altamonte
Springs, FL 32701
Phone: (407) 699-1990

Graduate Theological Union
2400 Ridge Rd., Berkeley 94709
Type: Private, independent, four-year
System: Graduate Theological Union
Degrees: M, D   *Enroll:* 246
URL: http://www.gtu.edu
Phone: (510) 649-2400   *Calendar:* Sem. plan
Inst. Accred.: ATS (1969/2001), WASC-SR. (1966/2005)

Grossmont College
8800 Grossmont College Dr., El Cajon 92020-1799
Type: Public, state/local, two-year
System: Grossmont-Cuyamaca Community College
   District
Degrees: A   *Enroll:* 10,745
URL: http://www.grossmont.gcccd.cc.ca.us
Phone: (619) 644-7000   *Calendar:* Sem. plan
Inst. Accred.: WASC-JR. (1963/2002)
Prog. Accred.: Cardiovascular Technology, Nursing,
   Occupational Therapy Assisting, Respiratory Therapy

Hartnell College
156 Homestead Ave., Salinas 93901-1697
Type: Public, state/local, two-year
System: Hartnell Community College District
Degrees: A   *Enroll:* 4,999
URL: http://www.hartnell.cc.ca.us
Phone: (831) 755-6700   *Calendar:* Sem. plan
Inst. Accred.: WASC-JR. (1952/2001)
Prog. Accred.: Veterinary Technology

Harvey Mudd College
301 East 12th St., Claremont 91711
Type: Private, independent, four-year
System: Claremont University Consortium
Degrees: B, M   *Enroll:* 702
URL: http://www.hmc.edu
Phone: (909) 621-8120   *Calendar:* Sem. plan
Inst. Accred.: WASC-SR. (1959/2000)
Prog. Accred.: Engineering (general)

Heald College—Concord
5130 Commercial Circle, Concord 94520
Type: Private, independent, two-year
System: Heald Colleges
Degrees: A   *Enroll:* 694
URL: http://www.heald.edu
Phone: (925) 288-5800   *Calendar:* Qtr. plan
Inst. Accred.: WASC-JR. (1983/2000)

Heald College—Fresno
255 West Bullard Ave., Fresno 93704
Type: Private, independent, two-year
System: Heald Colleges
Degrees: A   *Enroll:* 709
URL: http://www.heald.edu
Phone: (559) 438-4222   *Calendar:* Qtr. plan
Inst. Accred.: WASC-JR. (1983/2000)

Heald College—Hayward
25500 Industrial Blvd., Hayward 94545
Type: Private, independent, two-year
System: Heald Colleges
Degrees: A   *FTE Enroll:* 359
URL: http://www.heald.edu
Phone: (510) 783-2100   *Calendar:* Qtr. plan
Inst. Accred.: WASC-JR. (1983/2000)

Heald College—Roseville
Seven Sierra Gate Plaza, Roseville 95678
Type: Private, independent, two-year
System: Heald Colleges
Degrees: A   *Enroll:* 549
URL: http://www.heald.edu
Phone: (916) 789-8600   *Calendar:* Qtr. plan
Inst. Accred.: WASC-JR. (1983/2000)

Heald College—Sacramento
2910 Prospect Park Dr., Rancho Cordova 95670
Type: Private, independent, two-year
System: Heald Colleges
Degrees: A *Enroll:* 514
URL: http://www.heald.edu
Phone: (916) 638-1616 *Calendar:* Qtr. plan
Inst. Accred.: WASC-JR. (1983/2000)

Heald College—Salinas
1450 North Main St., Salinas 93906
Type: Private, independent, two-year
System: Heald Colleges
Degrees: A *Enroll:* 538
URL: http://www.heald.edu
Phone: (831) 443-1700 *Calendar:* Qtr. plan
Inst. Accred.: WASC-JR. (1983/2000)

Heald College—San Francisco
350 Mission St., San Francisco 94105
Type: Private, independent, two-year
System: Heald Colleges
Degrees: A *Enroll:* 507
URL: http://www.heald.edu
Phone: (415) 808-3000 *Calendar:* Qtr. plan
Inst. Accred.: WASC-JR. (1983/2000)

Heald College—San Jose
341 Great Mall Pkwy., Milpitas 95035
Type: Private, independent, two-year
System: Heald Colleges
Degrees: A *FTE Enroll:* 294
URL: http://www.heald.edu
Phone: (408) 934-4900 *Calendar:* Qtr. plan
Inst. Accred.: WASC-JR. (1983/2000)

Heald College—Stockton
1605 East March Ln., 2nd Flr., Stockton 95210
Type: Private, independent, two-year
System: Heald Colleges
Degrees: A *Enroll:* 591
URL: http://www.heald.edu
Phone: (209) 477-1114 *Calendar:* Qtr. plan
Inst. Accred.: WASC-JR. (1983/2000)

Hebrew Union College—Jewish Institute of Religion
3077 University Ave., Los Angeles 90007-3796
Type: Private, Union for Reform Judaism, four-year
System: Hebrew Union College—Jewish Institute of
  Religion Central Office
Degrees: B, M, D *Enroll:* 95
URL: http://www.huc.edu
Phone: (213) 749-3424 *Calendar:* Sem. plan
Inst. Accred.: WASC-SR. (1960/2003)

High-Tech Institute—Sacramento
1111 Howe Ave., Ste. 250, Sacramento 95825
Type: Private, proprietary, two-year
System: High-Tech Institute
Degrees: A
URL: http://www.hightechinstitute.edu
Phone: (916) 929-9700
Inst. Accred.: ACCSCT (1994/2005)
Prog. Accred.: Medical Assisting (ABHES)

Holmes Institute
2600 West Magnolia Blvd., Burbank 91505
Type: Private, proprietary, four-year
Degrees: M
URL: http://www.holmesinstitute.com
Phone: (818) 556-2238
Inst. Accred.: DETC (2003)

Holy Names University
3500 Mountain Blvd., Oakland 94619-1699
Type: Private, Roman Catholic Church, four-year
Degrees: B, M *Enroll:* 673
URL: http://www.hnu.edu
Phone: (510) 436-1000 *Calendar:* Sem. plan
Inst. Accred.: WASC-SR. (1949/2003)
Prog. Accred.: Nursing, Nursing Education

Hope International University
2500 East Nutwood Ave., Fullerton 92831
Type: Private, Christian Churches/Churches of Christ,
  four-year
Degrees: A, B, M *Enroll:* 796
URL: http://www.hiu.edu
Phone: (714) 879-3901 *Calendar:* 4-1-4 plan
Inst. Accred.: WASC-SR. (1969/2005)

Humboldt State University
1 Harpst St., Arcata 95521-8999
Type: Public, state, four-year
System: California State University System
Degrees: B, M *Enroll:* 7,035
URL: http://www.humboldt.edu
Phone: (707) 826-3311 *Calendar:* Sem. plan
Inst. Accred.: WASC-SR. (1949/1998)
Prog. Accred.: Art, Engineering (environmental/sanitary),
  Forestry, Music, Nursing, Nursing Education, Social Work

Humphreys College
6650 Inglewood St., Stockton 95207
Type: Private, independent, four-year
Degrees: A, B, P *Enroll:* 659
URL: http://www.humphreys.edu
Phone: (209) 478-0800 *Calendar:* Qtr. plan
Inst. Accred.: WASC-SR. (1992/2004)

ICR Graduate School
10946 Woodside Ave. North, Santee 92071
Type: Private, nondenominational, four-year
Degrees: M
URL: http://www.icr.edu
Phone: (619) 448-0900 *Calendar:* Sem. plan
Inst. Accred.: TRACS (1990/1999)

Imperial Valley College
380 East Aten Rd., PO Box 158, Imperial 92251
Type: Public, state/local, two-year
System: Imperial Community College District
Degrees: A   *Enroll:* 4,286
URL: http://www.imperial.edu
Phone: (760) 352-8320   *Calendar:* Sem. plan
Inst. Accred.: WASC-JR. (1952/2001)

Institute of Computer Technology
3200 Wilshire Blvd., Ste. 400, Los Angeles 90010-1308
Type: Private, proprietary, four-year
Degrees: A, B   *Enroll:* 184
URL: http://www.ictcollege.edu
Phone: (213) 381-3333
Inst. Accred.: ACICS (2003)

Institute of Transpersonal Psychology
744 San Antonio Rd., Palo Alto 94303-4613
Type: Private, independent, four-year
Degrees: M, D   *Enroll:* 350
URL: http://www.itp.edu
Phone: (650) 493-4430   *Calendar:* Sem. plan
Inst. Accred.: WASC-SR. (1998)

Interior Designers Institute
1061 Camelback Rd., Newport Beach 92660-3228
Type: Private, proprietary, four-year
Degrees: A, B   *Enroll:* 260
URL: http://www.idi.edu
Phone: (949) 675-4451   *Calendar:* Qtr. plan
Inst. Accred.: ACCSCT (1987/2003)
Prog. Accred.: Interior Design

International Technological University
756 San Aleso Ave., Sunnyvale 94085
Type: Private, proprietary, four-year
Degrees: B, M   *Enroll:* 74
URL: http://www.itu.edu
Phone: (408) 752-0991   *Calendar:* Sem. plan
Inst. Accred.: ACICS (2001, Probation)

Irvine Valley College
5500 Irvine Center Dr., Irvine 92720-4399
Type: Public, state/local, two-year
System: South Orange County Community College
  District
Degrees: A   *Enroll:* 4,297
URL: http://www.ivc.edu
Phone: (949) 451-5100   *Calendar:* Sem. plan
Inst. Accred.: WASC-JR. (1988/2005)

ITT Technical Institute
525 North Muller Ave., Anaheim 92801
Type: Private, proprietary, four-year
System: ITT Educational Services, Inc.
Degrees: A, B   *Enroll:* 630
URL: http://www.itt-tech.edu
Phone: (714) 535-3700   *Calendar:* Qtr. plan
Inst. Accred.: ACICS (1999/2003)

ITT Technical Institute
10863 Gold Center Dr., Rancho Cordova 95670-6034
Type: Private, proprietary, four-year
System: ITT Educational Services, Inc.
Degrees: A, B   *Enroll:* 521
URL: http://www.itt-tech.edu
Phone: (916) 851-3900   *Calendar:* Qtr. plan
Inst. Accred.: ACICS (1999/2004)

Kansas City Campus
1740 West 92nd St., Ste. 100, Kansas City, MO 64114
Phone: (816) 276-1400

Modesto-Stockton Campus
16916 South Harlan Rd., Lathrop 95330
Phone: (209) 858-0077

Oxnard Area Campus
2051 Solar Dr., Ste. 150, Oxnard 93030
Phone: (805) 988-0143

ITT Technical Institute
630 East Brier Dr., Ste. 150, San Bernardino 92408-2800
Type: Private, proprietary, four-year
System: ITT Educational Services, Inc.
Degrees: A, B   *Enroll:* 914
URL: http://www.itt-tech.edu
Phone: (909) 889-3800   *Calendar:* Qtr. plan
Inst. Accred.: ACICS (1999/2003)

ITT Technical Institute
9680 Granite Ridge Dr., San Diego 92123-2662
Type: Private, proprietary, four-year
System: ITT Educational Services, Inc.
Degrees: A, B   *Enroll:* 963
URL: http://www.itt-tech.edu
Phone: (858) 571-8500   *Calendar:* Qtr. plan
Inst. Accred.: ACICS (1999/2004)

ITT Technical Institute
12669 Encinitas Ave., Sylmar 91342-3664
Type: Private, proprietary, four-year
System: ITT Educational Services, Inc.
Degrees: A, B   *Enroll:* 743
URL: http://www.itt-tech.edu
Phone: (818) 364-5151   *Calendar:* Qtr. plan
Inst. Accred.: ACICS (1999/2003)

ITT Technical Institute
20050 South Vermont Ave., Torrance 90502
Type: Private, proprietary, four-year
System: ITT Educational Services, Inc.
Degrees: A, B   *Enroll:* 640
URL: http://www.itt-tech.edu
Phone: (310) 380-1555   *Calendar:* Qtr. plan
Inst. Accred.: ACICS (1999/2003)

ITT Technical Institute
1530 West Cameron Ave., West Covina 91790-2767
Type: Private, proprietary, four-year
System: ITT Educational Services, Inc.
Degrees: A, B   *Enroll:* 810
URL: http://www.itt-tech.edu
Phone: (626) 960-8681   *Calendar:* Qtr. plan
Inst. Accred.: ACICS (1999/2004)

Jesuit School of Theology at Berkeley
1735 LeRoy Ave., Berkeley 94709-1193
Type: Private, Roman Catholic Church, four-year
System: Graduate Theological Union
Degrees: M, P, D   *Enroll:* 142
URL: http://www.jstb.edu
Phone: (510) 841-8804   *Calendar:* Sem. plan
Inst. Accred.: ATS (1971/1999), WASC-SR. (1971/2000)

John F. Kennedy University
100 Ellinwood Way, Pleasant Hill 94523
Type: Private, independent, four-year
Degrees: B, M, P, D   *Enroll:* 963
URL: http://www.jfku.edu
Phone: (925) 969-3300   *Calendar:* Qtr. plan
Inst. Accred.: WASC-SR. (1977/2000)
Prog. Accred.: Clinical Psychology

Keck Graduate Institute of Applied Life Science
535 Watson Dr., Claremont 91711
Type: Private, independent, four-year
System: Claremont University Consortium
Degrees: M, D
URL: http://www.kgi.edu
Phone: (909) 607-7855   *Calendar:* Sem. plan
Inst. Accred.: WASC-SR. (2004)

The King's College and Seminary
14800 Sherman Way, Los Angeles 91405-2233
Type: Private, interdenominational, four-year
Degrees: A, B, M, D
URL: http://www.kingscollege.edu
Phone: (818) 779-8040   *Calendar:* Qtr. plan
Inst. Accred.: ABHE (2002), TRACS (2001)

La Sierra University
4700 Pierce St., Riverside 92515-8247
Type: Private, Seventh-Day Adventist, four-year
Degrees: A, B, M, P, D   *Enroll:* 1,669
URL: http://www.lasierra.edu
Phone: (909) 785-2000   *Calendar:* Qtr. plan
Inst. Accred.: WASC-SR. (1960/2002)
Prog. Accred.: Music, Social Work

Laguna College of Art and Design
2222 Laguna Canyon Rd., Laguna Beach 92651-1136
Type: Private, independent, four-year
Degrees: B   *Enroll:* 306
URL: http://www.lagunacollege.edu
Phone: (949) 376-6000   *Calendar:* Sem. plan
Inst. Accred.: WASC-SR. (1997/2005)
Prog. Accred.: Art

Lake Tahoe Community College
One College Dr., South Lake Tahoe 96150-4524
Type: Public, state/local, two-year
System: Lake Tahoe Community College District
Degrees: A   *Enroll:* 1,632
URL: http://www.ltcc.cc.ca.us
Phone: (530) 541-4660   *Calendar:* Qtr. plan
Inst. Accred.: WASC-JR. (1979/2000)

Laney College
900 Fallon St., Oakland 94607-4893
Type: Public, state/local, two-year
System: Peralta Community College District
Degrees: A   *Enroll:* 5,941
URL: http://www.peralta.cc.ca.us/laney
Phone: (510) 834-5740   *Calendar:* Sem. plan
Inst. Accred.: WASC-JR. (1956/2003, Warning)

Las Positas College
3033 Collier Canyon Rd., Livermore 94550-7650
Type: Public, state/local, two-year
System: Chabot-Las Positas Community College District
Degrees: A   *Enroll:* 3,202
URL: http://www.laspositascollege.edu
Phone: (925) 373-5800   *Calendar:* Sem. plan
Inst. Accred.: WASC-JR. (1991/2003)

Lassen College
PO Box 3000, Susanville 96130-3000
Type: Public, state/local, two-year
System: Lassen Community College District
Degrees: A   *Enroll:* 1,347
URL: http://www.lassencollege.edu
Phone: (530) 257-6181   *Calendar:* Sem. plan
Inst. Accred.: WASC-JR. (1952/2002)

Life Chiropractic College West
25001 Industrial Blvd., Hayward 94545
Type: Private, independent, four-year
Degrees: P   *Enroll:* 488
URL: http://www.lifewest.edu
Phone: (510) 780-4500   *Calendar:* Sem. plan
Inst. Accred.: CCE (1987/2003)

LIFE Pacific College
1100 West Covina Blvd., San Dimas 91773-3298
Type: Private, International Church of Foursquare Gospel,
  four-year
Degrees: A, B   *Enroll:* 393
URL: http://www.lifepacific.edu
Phone: (909) 599-5433   *Calendar:* Sem. plan
Inst. Accred.: ABHE (1980/2001), WASC-SR. (2004)

Lincoln University
401 Fifteenth St., Oakland 94612
Type: Private, state, four-year
Degrees: B, M   *Enroll:* 110
URL: http://www.lincolnuca.edu
Phone: (510) 628-8016   *Calendar:* Sem. plan
Inst. Accred.: ACICS (1990/2001)

Logos Evangelical Seminary
9358 Telstar Ave., El Monte 91731
Type: Private, Evangelical Formosan Church, four-year
Degrees: M, D
URL: http://www.les.edu
Phone: (626) 571-5110
Inst. Accred.: ATS (1999)

Loma Linda University
Loma Linda 92350-0001
Type: Private, Seventh-Day Adventist Church, four-year
Degrees: A, B, M, P, D   *Enroll:* 2,936
URL: http://www.llu.edu
Phone: (909) 558-1000   *Calendar:* Qtr. plan
Inst. Accred.: WASC-SR. (1960/1999)
Prog. Accred.: Clinical Lab Scientist, Clinical Pastoral
    Education, Clinical Psychology, Combined
    Prosthodontics, Cytotechnology, Dental Hygiene,
    Dentistry, Diagnostic Medical Sonography, Dietetics
    (coordinated), Endodontics, General Practice Residency,
    Health Information Administration, Marriage and Family
    Therapy, Medicine, Nuclear Medicine Technology,
    Nursing, Nursing Education, Occupational Therapy,
    Occupational Therapy Assisting, Oral and Maxillofacial
    Surgery, Orthodontic and Dentofacial Orthopedics,
    Pediatric Dentistry, Periodontics, Pharmacy, Phlebotomy,
    Physical Therapy, Physical Therapy Assisting, Physician
    Assistant, Public Health, Radiation Therapy,
    Radiography, Respiratory Therapy, Social Work, Speech-
    Language Pathology, Surgical Technology

Long Beach City College
4901 East Carson St., Long Beach 90808-1706
Type: Public, state/local, two-year
System: Long Beach Community College District
Degrees: A   *Enroll:* 12,328
URL: http://www.lbcc.edu
Phone: (562) 938-4353   *Calendar:* Sem. plan
Inst. Accred.: WASC-JR. (1952/2003)
Prog. Accred.: Nursing, Radiography

Los Angeles City College
855 North Vermont Ave., Los Angeles 90029-3590
Type: Public, state/local, two-year
System: Los Angeles Community College District
Degrees: A   *Enroll:* 8,852
URL: http://www.lacitycollege.edu
Phone: (323) 953-4000   *Calendar:* Sem. plan
Inst. Accred.: WASC-JR. (1952/2003)
Prog. Accred.: Dental Laboratory Technology,
    Radiography

Los Angeles County College of Nursing and Allied Health
1200 North State St., Muir Hall, Rm. 114, Los Angeles 90033
Type: Public, local, two-year
Degrees: A   *Enroll:* 86
URL: http://www.dhs.co.la.ca.us/lacusc/lacnah
Phone: (323) 226-4911   *Calendar:* Sem. plan
Inst. Accred.: WASC-JR. (1995/2001)

Los Angeles Harbor College
1111 Figueroa Place, Wilmington 90744-2397
Type: Public, state/local, two-year
System: Los Angeles Community College District
Degrees: A   *Enroll:* 5,018
URL: http://www.lahc.cc.ca.us
Phone: (310) 522-8200   *Calendar:* Sem. plan
Inst. Accred.: WASC-JR. (1952/2000)
Prog. Accred.: Nursing

Los Angeles Mission College
13356 Eldridge Ave., Sylmar 91342-3200
Type: Public, state/local, two-year
System: Los Angeles Community College District
Degrees: A   *Enroll:* 3,794
URL: http://www.lamission.cc.ca.us
Phone: (818) 364-7600   *Calendar:* Sem. plan
Inst. Accred.: WASC-JR. (1978/2001)

Los Angeles Pierce College
6201 Winnetka Ave., Woodland Hills 91371-0001
Type: Public, state/local, two-year
System: Los Angeles Community College District
Degrees: A   *Enroll:* 9,420
URL: http://www.piercecollege.com
Phone: (818) 347-0551   *Calendar:* Sem. plan
Inst. Accred.: WASC-JR. (1952/2001)
Prog. Accred.: Nursing, Veterinary Technology

Los Angeles Southwest College
1600 West Imperial Hwy., Los Angeles 90047-4899
Type: Public, state/local, two-year
System: Los Angeles Community College District
Degrees: A   *Enroll:* 2,939
URL: http://www.lasc.edu
Phone: (323) 241-5225   *Calendar:* Sem. plan
Inst. Accred.: WASC-JR. (1970/2000)

Los Angeles Trade-Technical College
400 West Washington Blvd., Los Angeles 90015-4108
Type: Public, state/local, two-year
System: Los Angeles Community College District
Degrees: A   *Enroll:* 7,193
URL: http://www.lattc.edu
Phone: (213) 744-9500   *Calendar:* Sem. plan
Inst. Accred.: WASC-JR. (1952/2003)
Prog. Accred.: Culinary Education, Nursing

Los Angeles Valley College
5800 Fulton Ave., Van Nuys 91401-4096
Type: Public, state/local, two-year
System: Los Angeles Community College District
Degrees: A   *Enroll:* 8,925
URL: http://www.lavc.cc.ca.us
Phone: (818) 781-1200   *Calendar:* Sem. plan
Inst. Accred.: WASC-JR. (1952/2001)
Prog. Accred.: Nursing, Respiratory Therapy

Los Medanos College
2700 East Leland Rd., Pittsburg 94565-5197
Type: Public, state/local, two-year
System: Contra Costa Community College District
Degrees: A *Enroll:* 4,417
URL: http://www.losmedanos.edu
Phone: (925) 439-2181 *Calendar:* Sem. plan
Inst. Accred.: WASC-JR. (1977/2002)

Loyola Marymount University
One LMU Dr., Los Angeles 90045-2659
Type: Private, Roman Catholic Church, four-year
Degrees: B, M, P, D *Enroll:* 8,013
URL: http://www.lmu.edu
Phone: (310) 338-2700 *Calendar:* Sem. plan
Inst. Accred.: WASC-SR. (1949/2003)
Prog. Accred.: Art, Business (AACSB), Dance, Engineering
  (civil, electrical, mechanical), Law, Music, Teacher
  Education (NCATE), Theatre

Maric College
9055 Balboa Ave., San Diego 92123
Type: Private, proprietary, two-year
System: Kaplan Higher Education Corporation
Degrees: A *Enroll:* 1,211
URL: http://www.mariccollege.edu
Phone: (858) 279-4500 *Calendar:* Qtr. plan
Inst. Accred.: ACCSCT (1982/2003)
Prog. Accred.: Medical Assisting (ABHES)

North County Campus
2022 University Dr., Vista 92083
Phone: (760) 630-1555
Prog. Accred: Medical Assisting (ABHES)

Maric College—Modesto
5172 Kiernan Ct., Salida 95368
Type: Private, proprietary, two-year
System: Kaplan Higher Education Corporation
Degrees: A
URL: http://www.andoncollege.com
Phone: (209) 571-8777
Inst. Accred.: ACCSCT (2002)
Prog. Accred.: Medical Assisting (ABHES)

Maric College—North Hollywood
6180 Laurel Canyon Blvd., Ste. 101, North Hollywood
91606-3231
Type: Private, proprietary, two-year
System: Kaplan Higher Education Corporation
Degrees: A
URL: http://www.moderntec.com
Phone: (818) 763-2563
Inst. Accred.: ACCSCT (1987/2003)

Marymount College
30800 Palos Verdes Dr. East, Rancho Palos Verdes
90275-6299
Type: Private, Roman Catholic Church, two-year
Degrees: A *Enroll:* 652
URL: http://www.marymountpv.edu
Phone: (310) 377-5501 *Calendar:* Sem. plan
Inst. Accred.: WASC-JR. (1971/2001)

The Master's College and Seminary
21726 West Placerita Canyon Rd., New Hall 91321-1200
Type: Private, independent, four-year
Degrees: B, M, P, D *Enroll:* 1,248
URL: http://www.masters.edu
Phone: (661) 259-3540 *Calendar:* Sem. plan
Inst. Accred.: WASC-SR. (1975/2003)

Mendocino College
PO Box 3000, Ukiah 95482-0300
Type: Public, state/local, two-year
System: Mendocino-Lake Community College District
Degrees: A *Enroll:* 2,284
URL: http://www.mendocinocollege.edu
Phone: (707) 468-3071 *Calendar:* Sem. plan
Inst. Accred.: WASC-JR. (1980/2002)

Menlo College
1000 El Camino Real, Atherton 94027-4301
Type: Private, independent, four-year
Degrees: A, B, M *Enroll:* 628
URL: http://www.menlo.edu
Phone: (650) 688-3800 *Calendar:* 4-1-4 plan
Inst. Accred.: WASC-SR. (1952/2000)

Mennonite Brethren Biblical Seminary
4824 East Butler Ave., Fresno 93727-5097
Type: Private, Mennonite Brethren Churches, four-year
Degrees: M *Enroll:* 126
URL: http://www.mbseminary.edu
Phone: (559) 251-8628 *Calendar:* 4-1-4 plan
Inst. Accred.: ATS (1977/2001), WASC-SR. (1972/2002)

Merced College
3600 M St., Merced 95348-2898
Type: Public, state/local, two-year
System: Merced Community College District
Degrees: A *Enroll:* 5,736
URL: http://www.mccd.edu
Phone: (209) 384-6000 *Calendar:* Sem. plan
Inst. Accred.: WASC-JR. (1965/2005)
Prog. Accred.: Radiography

Merritt College
12500 Campus Dr., Oakland 94619-3196
Type: Public, state/local, two-year
System: Peralta Community College District
Degrees: A *Enroll:* 3,231
URL: http://www.merritt.edu
Phone: (510) 531-4911 *Calendar:* Sem. plan
Inst. Accred.: WASC-JR. (1956/2003, Warning)
Prog. Accred.: Radiography

Mills College
5000 MacArthur Blvd., Oakland 94613
Type: Private, independent, four-year
Degrees: B, M, D *Enroll:* 1,138
URL: http://www.mills.edu
Phone: (510) 430-2096 *Calendar:* Sem. plan
Inst. Accred.: WASC-SR. (1949/1999)

Mira Costa College
One Barnard Dr., Oceanside 92056-3899
Type: Public, state/local, two-year
System: MiraCosta Community College District
Degrees: A   *Enroll:* 6,061
URL: http://www.miracosta.edu
Phone: (760) 757-2121   *Calendar:* Sem. plan
Inst. Accred.: WASC-JR. (1952/2004)

Mission College
3000 Mission College Blvd., Santa Clara 95054-1897
Type: Public, state/local, two-year
System: West Valley-Mission College District
Degrees: A   *Enroll:* 4,538
URL: http://www.missioncollege.org
Phone: (408) 988-2200   *Calendar:* Sem. plan
Inst. Accred.: WASC-JR. (1979/2002)

Modesto Junior College
435 College Ave., Modesto 95350-5800
Type: Public, state/local, two-year
System: Yosemite Community College District
Degrees: A   *Enroll:* 9,789
URL: http://mjc.yosemite.cc.ca.us
Phone: (209) 575-6498   *Calendar:* Sem. plan
Inst. Accred.: WASC-JR. (1952/2000)
Prog. Accred.: Dental Assisting, Medical Assisting (AMA), Respiratory Therapy

Monterey Institute of International Studies
460 Pierce St., Monterey 93940
Type: Private, independent, four-year
Degrees: B, M   *Enroll:* 707
URL: http://www.miis.edu
Phone: (831) 647-4100   *Calendar:* Sem. plan
Inst. Accred.: WASC-SR. (1961/1998)
Prog. Accred.: Business (AACSB)

Monterey Peninsula College
980 Fremont St., Monterey 93940-4799
Type: Public, state/local, two-year
System: Monterey Peninsula Community College District
Degrees: A   *Enroll:* 5,611
URL: http://www.mpc.edu
Phone: (831) 646-4000   *Calendar:* Sem. plan
Inst. Accred.: WASC-JR. (1952/2004)
Prog. Accred.: Dental Assisting, Nursing

Moorpark College
7075 Campus Rd., Moorpark 93021-1695
Type: Public, state/local, two-year
System: Ventura County Community College District
Degrees: A   *Enroll:* 8,783
URL: http://www.moorparkcollege.edu
Phone: (805) 378-1400   *Calendar:* Sem. plan
Inst. Accred.: WASC-JR. (1969/2005)
Prog. Accred.: Nursing, Radiography

Mount Saint Mary's College
12001 Chalon Rd., Los Angeles 90049-1599
Type: Private, Roman Catholic Church, four-year
Degrees: A, B, M, D   *Enroll:* 1,770
URL: http://www.msmc.la.edu
Phone: (310) 954-4000   *Calendar:* 4-1-4 plan
Inst. Accred.: WASC-SR. (1949/2003)
Prog. Accred.: Music, Nursing, Nursing Education, Physical Therapy Assisting

Doheny Campus
10 Chester Place, Los Angeles 90007
Phone: (310) 746-0450

Mount San Antonio College
1100 North Grand Ave., Walnut 91789-1399
Type: Public, state/local, two-year
System: Mount San Antonio Community College District
Degrees: A   *Enroll:* 14,172
URL: http://www.mtsac.edu
Phone: (909) 594-5611   *Calendar:* Sem. plan
Inst. Accred.: WASC-JR. (1952/2005)
Prog. Accred.: Radiography, Respiratory Therapy, Veterinary Technology

Mount San Jacinto College
1499 North State St., San Jacinto 92583-2399
Type: Public, state/local, two-year
System: Mount San Jacinto Community College District
Degrees: A   *Enroll:* 5,875
URL: http://www.msjc.cc.ca.us
Phone: (909) 487-6752   *Calendar:* Sem. plan
Inst. Accred.: WASC-JR. (1965/2000)
Prog. Accred.: Nursing

Mount Sierra College
101 East Huntington Dr., Monrovia 91016-3414
Type: Private, proprietary, four-year
Degrees: B
URL: http://www.mtsierra.edu
Phone: (626) 873-2138   *Calendar:* Sem. plan
Inst. Accred.: ACCSCT (1996/2002)

MTI College of Business and Technology
5221 Madison Ave., Sacramento 95841
Type: Private, proprietary, two-year
Degrees: A   *Enroll:* 783
URL: http://www.mticollege.com
Phone: (916) 339-1500   *Calendar:* Qtr. plan
Inst. Accred.: WASC-JR. (1999/2002)

Musicians Institute
1655 North McCadden Place, Los Angeles 90028-6115
Type: Private, proprietary, four-year
Degrees: A, B
URL: http://www.mi.edu
Phone: (323) 462-1384   *Calendar:* Qtr. plan
Inst. Accred.: NASM (1980/1995)

Napa Valley College
2277 Napa-Vallejo Hwy., Napa 94558-6236
Type: Public, state/local, two-year
System: Napa Valley Community College District
Degrees: A   *Enroll:* 3,882
URL: http://www.napavalley.edu
Phone: (707) 253-3000   *Calendar:* Sem. plan
Inst. Accred.: WASC-JR. (1952/2004)
Prog. Accred.: Respiratory Therapy

Upper Valley Campus
1088 College Ave., St. Helena 94574
Phone: (707) 967-2900

The National Hispanic University
14271 Story Rd., San Jose 95127-3823
Type: Private, independent, four-year
Degrees: B   *Enroll:* 352
URL: http://www.nhu.edu
Phone: (408) 254-6900   *Calendar:* Sem. plan
Inst. Accred.: ACICS (1993/2004), WASC-SR. (2002)

National Institute of Technology—Long Beach
2161 Technology Place, Long Beach 90810
Type: Private, proprietary, two-year
System: Corinthian Colleges, Inc
Degrees: A
URL: http://www.nitschools.com
Phone: (562) 437-0501
Inst. Accred.: ACCSCT (1975/2004)

National Polytechnic College of Engineering and Oceaneering
Los Angeles Harbor, 272 South Fries Ave., Wilmington 90744-6399
Type: Private, independent, two-year
System: National University System
Degrees: A   *Enroll:* 288
URL: http://www.natpoly.edu
Phone: (310) 834-2501   *Calendar:* Qtr. plan
Inst. Accred.: WASC-JR. (1982/2004)

Advanced College of Technology
10085 Scripps Ranch Ct., Ste. D, San Diego 92131
Phone: (858) 547-4160

Honolulu Campus
10 Sand Island Pkwy., Honolulu, HI 96819
Phone: (808) 599-3597

National University
11255 North Torrey Pines Rd., La Jolla 92037-1011
Type: Private, independent, four-year
System: National University System
Degrees: A, B, M, P   *Enroll:* 13,148
URL: http://www.nu.edu
Phone: (858) 642-8000   *Calendar:* 12-mos. pr
Inst. Accred.: WASC-SR. (1977/2001)
Prog. Accred.: Nursing, Nursing Education

New College of California
777 Valencia St., San Francisco 94110
Type: Private, independent, four-year
Degrees: B, M, P, D   *Enroll:* 950
URL: http://www.newcollege.edu
Phone: (415) 437-3460   *Calendar:* Sem. plan
Inst. Accred.: WASC-SR. (1976/2002, Warning)

NewSchool of Architecture and Design
1249 F St., San Diego 92101
Type: Private, indepepndent, four-year
Degrees: B, M
URL: http://www.newschoolarch.edu
Phone: (619) 235-4100   *Calendar:* Qtr. plan
Inst. Accred.: ACICS (1994/2003)

Northwestern College
2317 Gold Meadow Way, Gold River 95670
Type: Private, proprietary, two-year
Degrees: A   *Enroll:* 1,155
URL: http://www.ntcollege.com
Phone: (916) 649-2400
Inst. Accred.: ACCSCT (1999/2004)

Northwestern Polytechnic University
117 Fourier Ave., Freemont 94539
Type: Private, independent, four-year
Degrees: B, M   *Enroll:* 281
URL: http://www.npu.edu
Phone: (510) 657-5911   *Calendar:* Sem. plan
Inst. Accred.: ACICS (1998/2001)

Notre Dame de Namur University
1500 Ralston Ave., Belmont 94002-1997
Type: Private, Roman Catholic Church, four-year
Degrees: B, M   *Enroll:* 1,254
URL: http://www.ndnu.edu
Phone: (650) 593-1601   *Calendar:* Sem. plan
Inst. Accred.: WASC-SR. (1955/1999)
Prog. Accred.: Music

Occidental College
1600 Campus Rd., Los Angeles 90041-3314
Type: Private, independent, four-year
Degrees: B, M   *Enroll:* 1,843
URL: http://www.oxy.edu
Phone: (323) 259-2691   *Calendar:* Sem. plan
Inst. Accred.: WASC-SR. (1949/2001)

Ohlone College
PO Box 3909, 43600 Mission Blvd., Fremont 94539-3909
Type: Public, state/local, two-year
System: Ohlone Community College District
Degrees: A   *Enroll:* 5,219
URL: http://www.ohlone.edu
Phone: (510) 659-6000   *Calendar:* Sem. plan
Inst. Accred.: WASC-JR. (1970/2002)
Prog. Accred.: Nursing, Physical Therapy Assisting, Respiratory Therapy

Orange Coast College
2701 Fairview Rd., PO Box 5005, Costa Mesa 92628
Type: Public, state/local, two-year
System: Coast Community College District
Degrees: A *Enroll:* 13,570
URL: http://www.orangecoastcollege.edu
Phone: (714) 432-0202 *Calendar:* Sem. plan
Inst. Accred.: WASC-JR. (1952/2001)
Prog. Accred.: Business (ACBSP), Culinary Education,
  Dental Assisting, Diagnostic Medical Sonography,
  Electroneurodiagnostic Technology, Medical Assisting
  (AMA), Radiography, Respiratory Therapy

Otis College of Art and Design
9045 Lincoln Blvd., Westchester 90045
Type: Private, independent, four-year
Degrees: B, M *Enroll:* 1,048
URL: http://www.otis.edu
Phone: (310) 665-6800 *Calendar:* Sem. plan
Inst. Accred.: WASC-SR. (1956/2000)
Prog. Accred.: Art

Oxnard College
4000 South Rose Ave., Oxnard 93033-6699
Type: Public, state/local, two-year
System: Ventura County Community College District
Degrees: A *Enroll:* 3,907
URL: http://www.oxnardcollege.edu
Phone: (805) 986-5800 *Calendar:* Sem. plan
Inst. Accred.: WASC-JR. (1978/2005)
Prog. Accred.: Dental Hygiene

Pacific College of Oriental Medicine
7445 Mission Valley Rd., Ste. 105, San Diego 92108
Type: Private, proprietary, four-year
Degrees: M *Enroll:* 361
URL: http://www.pacificcollege.edu
Phone: (619) 574-6909 *Calendar:* Tri. plan
Inst. Accred.: ACAOM (1995/2004)

Chicago Campus
3646 North Broadway, 2nd Flr., Chicago, IL 60613
Phone: (773) 477-4822

Pacific Graduate School of Psychology
940 East Meadow Dr., Palo Alto 94303
Type: Private, independent, four-year
Degrees: D *Enroll:* 303
URL: http://www.pgsp.edu
Phone: (650) 843-3413 *Calendar:* Qtr. plan
Inst. Accred.: WASC-SR. (1986/2001)
Prog. Accred.: Clinical Psychology

Pacific Lutheran Theological Seminary
2770 Marin Ave., Berkeley 94708-1597
Type: Private, Evangelical Lutheran Church in America,
  four-year
System: Graduate Theological Union
Degrees: M *Enroll:* 80
URL: http://www.plts.edu
Phone: (510) 524-5264 *Calendar:* Sem. plan
Inst. Accred.: ATS (1964/1998)

Pacific Oaks College
5 Westmoreland Place, Pasadena 91103-3592
Type: Private, independent, four-year
Degrees: B, M *Enroll:* 457
URL: http://www.pacificoaks.edu
Phone: (626) 397-1300 *Calendar:* Sem. plan
Inst. Accred.: WASC-SR. (1959/2002)

Pacific School of Religion
1798 Scenic Ave., Berkeley 94709
Type: Private, independent, four-year
System: Graduate Theological Union
Degrees: M, P, D *Enroll:* 162
URL: http://www.psr.edu
Phone: (510) 848-0528 *Calendar:* Sem. plan
Inst. Accred.: ATS (1938/1997), WASC-SR. (1971/2002)

Pacific States University
1516 South Western Ave., Los Angeles 90006
Type: Private, independent, four-year
Degrees: A, B, M *Enroll:* 128
URL: http://www.psuca.edu
Phone: (323) 731-2383 *Calendar:* Qtr. plan
Inst. Accred.: ACICS (1996/2004)

Pacific Union College
One Angwin Ave., Angwin 94508-9707
Type: Private, Seventh-Day Adventist Church, four-year
Degrees: A, B, M *Enroll:* 1,446
URL: http://www.puc.edu
Phone: (707) 965-6234 *Calendar:* Qtr. plan
Inst. Accred.: WASC-SR. (1951/2000)
Prog. Accred.: Music, Nursing, Social Work

Pacifica Graduate Institute
249 Lambert Rd., Carpinteria 93013
Type: Private, proprietary, four-year
Degrees: M, D *Enroll:* 551
URL: http://www.pacifica.edu
Phone: (805) 969-3626 *Calendar:* Qtr. plan
Inst. Accred.: WASC-SR. (1997/2001)

Palmer College of Chiropractic-West
90 East Tasman Dr., San Jose 95134
Type: Private, independent, four-year
System: Palmer Chiropractic University System
Degrees: D *Enroll:* 424
URL: http://www.palmer.edu
Phone: (408) 944-6000 *Calendar:* Qtr. plan
Inst. Accred.: CCE (1985/2001)
Prog. Accred.: Chiropractic Education

Palo Verde College
One College Dr., Blythe 92225
Type: Public, state/local, two-year
System: Palo Verde Community College District
Degrees: A *Enroll:* 2,148
URL: http://www.paloverde.cc.ca.us
Phone: (760) 921-5500 *Calendar:* Sem. plan
Inst. Accred.: WASC-JR. (1951/2002)

Palomar College
1140 West Mission Rd., San Marcos 92069-1487
Type: Public, state/local, two-year
System: Palomar Community College District
Degrees: A *Enroll:* 13,024
URL: http://www.palomar.edu
Phone: (760) 744-1150 *Calendar:* Sem. plan
Inst. Accred.: WASC-JR. (1951/2002)
Prog. Accred.: Dental Assisting, Nursing

Pardee Rand Graduate School
1776 Main St., Santa Monica 90401-3208
Type: Private, independent, four-year
Degrees: D *Enroll:* 83
URL: http://www.prgs.edu
Phone: (310) 393-0411 *Calendar:* Qtr. plan
Inst. Accred.: WASC-SR. (1975/2000)

Pasadena City College
1570 East Colorado Blvd., Pasadena 91106-2003
Type: Public, state/local, two-year
System: Pasadena Area Community College District
Degrees: A *Enroll:* 14,841
URL: http://www.pasadena.edu
Phone: (626) 585-7123 *Calendar:* Sem. plan
Inst. Accred.: WASC-JR. (1952/2003)
Prog. Accred.: Dental Assisting, Dental Hygiene, Dental Laboratory Technology, Medical Assisting (AMA), Nursing, Radiography

Patten University
2433 Coolidge Ave., Oakland 94601
Type: Private, Christian Evangelical Church of America, four-year
Degrees: A, B, M *Enroll:* 428
URL: http://www.patten.edu
Phone: (510) 261-8500 *Calendar:* Sem. plan
Inst. Accred.: WASC-SR. (1980/1999)

Pepperdine University
24255 Pacific Coast Hwy., Malibu 90263
Type: Private, Churches of Christ, four-year
Degrees: B, M, P, D *Enroll:* 6,089
URL: http://www.pepperdine.edu
Phone: (310) 506-4000 *Calendar:* Tri. plan
Inst. Accred.: WASC-SR. (1949/2001)
Prog. Accred.: Business (AACSB), Clinical Psychology, Law, Music

Phillips Graduate Institute
5445 Balboa Blvd., Encino 91316-1509
Type: Private, independent, four-year
Degrees: M, D *Enroll:* 250
URL: http://www.pgi.edu
Phone: (818) 386-5600 *Calendar:* Sem. plan
Inst. Accred.: WASC-SR. (1983/2005)

Pitzer College
1050 North Mills Ave., Claremont 91711-6101
Type: Private, independent, four-year
System: Claremont University Consortium
Degrees: B *Enroll:* 912
URL: http://www.pitzer.edu
Phone: (909) 621-8000 *Calendar:* Sem. plan
Inst. Accred.: WASC-SR. (1965/1999)

Platt College
7470 North Figueroa St., Los Angeles 90041-1717
Type: Private, proprietary, two-year
Degrees: A *Enroll:* 142
URL: http://www.plattcollege.edu
Phone: (323) 258-8050
Inst. Accred.: ACCSCT (1987/2004)

Platt College
3901 MacArthur Blvd., Newport Beach 92660
Type: Private, proprietary, two-year
Degrees: A *Enroll:* 142
URL: http://www.plattcollege.edu
Phone: (949) 833-2300
Inst. Accred.: ACCSCT (1985/2001)

Ontario Campus
3700 Inland Empire Blvd., Ste. 400, Ontario 91764-4609
Phone: (909) 941-9410

Platt College San Diego
6250 El Cajon Blvd., San Diego 92115-3919
Type: Private, proprietary, two-year
Degrees: A *Enroll:* 293
URL: http://www.platt.edu
Phone: (619) 265-0107
Inst. Accred.: ACCSCT (1985/2003)

Point Loma Nazarene University
3900 Lomaland Dr., San Diego 92106
Type: Private, Church of the Nazarene, four-year
Degrees: A, B, M *Enroll:* 2,831
URL: http://www.ptloma.edu
Phone: (619) 849-2200 *Calendar:* Sem. plan
Inst. Accred.: WASC-SR. (1949/1997)
Prog. Accred.: Business (ACBSP), Music, Nursing, Nursing Education

Pomona College
550 North College Ave., Claremont 91711
Type: Private, independent, four-year
System: Claremont University Consortium
Degrees: B *Enroll:* 1,529
URL: http://www.pomona.edu
Phone: (909) 621-8131 *Calendar:* Sem. plan
Inst. Accred.: WASC-SR. (1949/2002)

Porterville College
100 East College Ave., Porterville 93257-5901
Type: Public, state/local, two-year
System: Kern Community College District
Degrees: A   *Enroll:* 2,107
URL: http://www.portervillecollege.edu
Phone: (559) 791-2200   *Calendar:* Sem. plan
Inst. Accred.: WASC-JR. (1952/2001)

Professional Golfers Career College
26109 Ynez Rd., PO Box 892319, Temecul 92589-2319
Type: Private, proprietary, two-year
Degrees: A   *Enroll:* 185
URL: http://www.progolfed.com
Phone: (909) 693-2963   *Calendar:* Sem. plan
Inst. Accred.: ACICS (1996/2000)

Orlando Campus
16349 Phil Ritson Way, PO Box 2818, Windermere, FL
34786-2818
Phone: (407) 905-2200

Queen of the Holy Rosary College
43326 Mission Blvd., Mission San Jose 94539
Type: Private, Roman Catholic Church, two-year
Degrees: A   *FTE Enroll:* 79
URL: http://www.msjdominicans.org
Phone: (510) 657-2468   *Calendar:* Sem. plan
Inst. Accred.: WASC-JR. (1979/2000)

Reedley College
995 North Reed Ave., Reedley 93654-2099
Type: Public, state/local, two-year
System: State Center Community College District
Degrees: A   *Enroll:* 7,534
URL: http://www.reedleycollege.com
Phone: (559) 638-3641   *Calendar:* Sem. plan
Inst. Accred.: WASC-JR. (1952/2000)
Prog. Accred.: Dental Assisting

Remington College—San Diego
123 Camino de la Reina, North Bldg., Ste. 100, San
Diego 92108
Type: Private, proprietary, four-year
System: Education America, Inc.
Degrees: A, B, M   *Enroll:* 391
URL: http://www.remingtoncollege.edu
Phone: (619) 686-8600   *Calendar:* Qtr. plan
Inst. Accred.: ACICS (1998/2002)

Colorado Springs Campus
6050 Erin Park Dr., Colorado Springs, CO 80918-3401
Phone: (719) 532-1234

Denver Campus
11011 West 6th Ave., Lakewood, CO 80215-5501
Phone: (303) 445-0500

Honolulu Campus
1111 Bishop St., Ste. 400, Honolulu, HI 96813-2811
Phone: (808) 942-1000

Tempe Campus
875 West Elliot Rd., Ste. 126, Tempe, AZ 85284-1133
Phone: (480) 834-1000

Rio Hondo College
3600 Workman Mill Rd., Whittier 90601-1699
Type: Public, state/local, two-year
System: Rio Hondo Community College District
Degrees: A   *Enroll:* 8,641
URL: http://www.riohondo.edu
Phone: (562) 692-0921   *Calendar:* Sem. plan
Inst. Accred.: WASC-JR. (1967/2002)

Riverside City College
4800 Magnolia Ave., Riverside 92506-1293
Type: Public, state/local, two-year
System: Riverside Community College District
Degrees: A   *Enroll:* 15,332
URL: http://www.rcc.edu
Phone: (951) 222-8000   *Calendar:* Sem. plan
Inst. Accred.: WASC-JR. (1952/2001)
Prog. Accred.: Nursing

Moreno Valley Campus
16130 Lasselle St., Moreno Valley 92551-2045
Phone: (909) 485-6100
Prog. Accred: Physician Assistant

Sacramento City College
3835 Freeport Blvd., Sacramento 95822-1386
Type: Public, state/local, two-year
System: Los Rios Community College District
Degrees: A   *Enroll:* 10,616
URL: http://www.scc.losrios.edu
Phone: (916) 558-2111   *Calendar:* Sem. plan
Inst. Accred.: WASC-JR. (1952/2004)
Prog. Accred.: Dental Assisting, Dental Hygiene,
   Occupational Therapy Assisting, Physical Therapy
   Assisting

Saddleback College
28000 Marguerite Pkwy., Mission Viejo 92692-3699
Type: Public, state/local, two-year
System: South Orange County Community College
District
Degrees: A   *Enroll:* 8,473
URL: http://www.saddleback.edu
Phone: (949) 582-4500   *Calendar:* Sem. plan
Inst. Accred.: WASC-JR. (1971/2005)
Prog. Accred.: Nursing

Sage College
12125 Day St., Bldg. L, Moreno Valley 92557-6720
Type: Private, proprietary, two-year
Degrees: A
URL: http://www.cscrriverside.com
Phone: (909) 781-2727   *Calendar:* Qtr. plan
Inst. Accred.: ACICS (1986/2003)

Saint John's Seminary
5012 Seminary Rd., Camarillo 93012-2598
Type: Private, Roman Catholic Church, four-year
Degrees: B, M, P   *Enroll:* 92
URL: http://www.stjohnsem.edu
Phone: (805) 482-2755   *Calendar:* Sem. plan
Inst. Accred.: ATS (1976/2002), WASC-SR. (1951/2002)

Saint Mary's College of California
1928 St. Mary's Rd., Moraga 94556
Type: Private, Roman Catholic Church, four-year
Degrees: A, B, M, D   *Enroll:* 3,497
URL: http://www.stmarys-ca.edu
Phone: (925) 631-4000   *Calendar:* 4-1-4 plan
Inst. Accred.: WASC-SR. (1949/2003)
Prog. Accred.: Montessori Teacher Education, Nursing
Education

Saint Patrick's Seminary and University
320 Middlefield Rd., Menlo Park 94025-3596
Type: Private, Roman Catholic Church, four-year
Degrees: M, P   *Enroll:* 85
URL: http://www.stpatricksseminary.org
Phone: (650) 325-5621   *Calendar:* Sem. plan
Inst. Accred.: ATS (1971/2004), WASC-SR. (1971/2005)

Salvation Army College for Officer Training at Crestmont
30840 Hawthorne Blvd., Rancho Palos Verdes 90274
Type: Private, independent, two-year
Degrees: A
URL: http://www.crestmont.edu
Phone: (310) 377-0481   *Calendar:* Qtr. plan
Inst. Accred.: WASC-JR. (1990/2002, Probation)

Samra University of Oriental Medicine
3000 South Robertson Blvd., 4th Flr., Los Angeles 90034
Type: Private, proprietary, four-year
Degrees: M   *Enroll:* 199
URL: http://www.samra.edu
Phone: (310) 202-6444   *Calendar:* Qtr. plan
Inst. Accred.: ACAOM (1989/2003)

Samuel Merritt College
370 Hawthorne Ave., Oakland 94609
Type: Private, independent, four-year
Degrees: B, M   *Enroll:* 779
URL: http://www.samuelmerritt.edu
Phone: (510) 869-6511   *Calendar:* 4-1-4 plan
Inst. Accred.: WASC-SR. (1984/2001)
Prog. Accred.: Nurse Anesthesia Education, Nursing,
Nursing Education, Occupational Therapy, Physical
Therapy, Physician Assistant

California College of Podiatric Medicine at Sameul Merritt College
1210 Scott St., San Francisco 94115
Phone: (415) 563-3444
Prog. Accred: Podiatry

San Bernardino Valley College
701 South Mt. Vernon Ave., San Bernardino 92410-2798
Type: Public, state/local, two-year
System: San Bernardino Community College District
Degrees: A   *Enroll:* 5,974
URL: http://www.valleycollege.edu
Phone: (909) 888-6511   *Calendar:* Sem. plan
Inst. Accred.: WASC-JR. (1952/2003)
Prog. Accred.: Nursing

San Diego Christian College
2100 Greenfield Dr., El Cajon 92019
Type: Private, Shadow Mountain Community Church,
four-year
Degrees: B   *Enroll:* 516
URL: http://www.sdcc.edu
Phone: (619) 441-2200   *Calendar:* Sem. plan
Inst. Accred.: WASC-SR. (1984/2001)

San Diego City College
1313 12th Ave., San Diego 92101-4787
Type: Public, state/local, two-year
System: San Diego Community College District
Degrees: A   *Enroll:* 7,190
URL: http://www.sdcity.edu
Phone: (619) 388-3400   *Calendar:* Sem. plan
Inst. Accred.: WASC-JR. (1952/2005)

San Diego Mesa College
7250 Mesa College Dr., San Diego 92111-4996
Type: Public, state/local, two-year
System: San Diego Community College District
Degrees: A   *Enroll:* 11,724
URL: http://www.sdmesa.edu
Phone: (619) 388-2600   *Calendar:* Sem. plan
Inst. Accred.: WASC-JR. (1966/1998)
Prog. Accred.: Dental Assisting, Health Information
Technician, Interior Design, Medical Assisting (AMA),
Physical Therapy Assisting, Radiography

San Diego Miramar College
10440 Black Mountain Rd., San Diego 92126-2999
Type: Public, state/local, two-year
System: San Diego Community College District
Degrees: A   *Enroll:* 4,234
URL: http://www.sdmiramar.edu
Phone: (858) 536-7800   *Calendar:* Sem. plan
Inst. Accred.: WASC-JR. (1982/2005)

San Diego State University
5500 Campanile Dr., San Diego 92182-8143
Type: Public, state, four-year
System: California State University System
Degrees: B, M, D   *Enroll:* 27,661
URL: http://www.sdsu.edu
Phone: (619) 594-5200   *Calendar:* Sem. plan
Inst. Accred.: WASC-SR. (1949/2005)
Prog. Accred.: Accounting, Applied Science (industrial hygiene), Art, Athletic Training, Audiology, Business (AACSB), Clinical Psychology, Dietetics (internship), Engineering (aerospace, civil, computer, electrical, environmental/sanitary, mechanical), Health Services Administration, Interior Design, Marriage and Family Therapy, Nursing, Nursing Education, Public Administration, Public Health, Recreation and Leisure Services, Rehabilitation Counseling, Social Work, Speech-Language Pathology, Teacher Education (NCATE), Theatre

San Francisco Art Institute
800 Chestnut St., San Francisco 94133
Type: Private, independent, four-year
Degrees: B, M   *Enroll:* 592
URL: http://www.sfai.edu
Phone: (415) 771-7020   *Calendar:* Sem. plan
Inst. Accred.: WASC-SR. (1954/2005)
Prog. Accred.: Art

San Francisco Conservatory of Music
1201 Ortega St., San Francisco 94122
Type: Private, independent, four-year
Degrees: B, M   *Enroll:* 307
URL: http://www.sfcm.edu
Phone: (415) 564-8086   *Calendar:* Sem. plan
Inst. Accred.: WASC-SR. (1960/2003)
Prog. Accred.: Music

San Francisco State University
1600 Holloway Ave., San Francisco 94132
Type: Public, state, four-year
System: California State University System
Degrees: B, M, D   *Enroll:* 24,179
URL: http://www.sfsu.edu
Phone: (415) 338-1111   *Calendar:* Sem. plan
Inst. Accred.: WASC-SR. (1949/2001)
Prog. Accred.: Art, Audiology, Business (AACSB), Clinical Lab Scientist, Computer Science, Counseling, Dietetics (internship), Engineering (civil, electrical, mechanical), Family and Consumer Science, Journalism, Music, Nursing, Nursing Education, Physical Therapy, Public Health, Recreation and Leisure Services, Rehabilitation Counseling, Social Work, Speech-Language Pathology, Teacher Education (NCATE), Theatre

San Francisco Theological Seminary
105 Seminary Rd., San Anselmo 94960
Type: Private, Presbyterian Church (USA), four-year
System: Graduate Theological Union
Degrees: M, P, D   *Enroll:* 323
URL: http://www.sfts.edu
Phone: (415) 451-2800   *Calendar:* Sem. plan
Inst. Accred.: ATS (1938/1997), WASC-SR. (1973/2001)

San Joaquin College of Law
901 Fifth St., Clovis 93612-1312
Type: Private, independent, four-year
Degrees: M, P, D   *Enroll:* 142
URL: http://www.sjcl.edu
Phone: (559) 323-2100   *Calendar:* Sem. plan
Inst. Accred.: WASC-SR. (1993/1999)

San Joaquin Delta College
5151 Pacific Ave., Stockton 95207-6370
Type: Public, state/local, two-year
System: San Joaquin Delta Community College District
Degrees: A   *Enroll:* 10,181
URL: http://www.deltacollege.org
Phone: (209) 954-5151   *Calendar:* Sem. plan
Inst. Accred.: WASC-JR. (1952/2002)
Prog. Accred.: Culinary Education, Nursing

San Joaquin Valley College—Visalia
8400 West Mineral King Ave., Visalia 93291-9283
Type: Private, proprietary, two-year
System: San Joaquin Valley College System
Degrees: A   *Enroll:* 622
URL: http://www.sjvc.com
Phone: (559) 651-2500   *Calendar:* Sem. plan
Inst. Accred.: WASC-JR. (1994/2001)
Prog. Accred.: Dental Hygiene, Physician Assistant, Respiratory Therapy

Bakersfield Campus
201 New Stine Rd., Bakersfield 93309-2606
Phone: (661) 834-0126
Prog. Accred: Respiratory Therapy

Fresno Aviation Campus
4985 E. Andersen Ave., Fresno 93727-1501
Phone: (559) 453-0380

Fresno Campus
295 East Sierra Ave., Fresno 93710
Phone: (209) 448-8282

Modesto Campus
1700 McHenry Village Way, Ste. 6, Modesto 95350
Phone: (209) 527-7582

Rancho Cucamonga Campus
10641 Church St., Rancho Cucamonga 91703-6862
Phone: (909) 948-7582

San Jose City College
2100 Moorpark Ave., San Jose 95128-2799
Type: Public, state/local, two-year
System: San Jose-Evergreen Community College District
Degrees: A   *Enroll:* 4,962
URL: http://www.sjcc.edu
Phone: (408) 298-2181   *Calendar:* Sem. plan
Inst. Accred.: WASC-JR. (1953/1998, Warning)
Prog. Accred.: Dental Assisting

San Jose State University
One Washington Square, San Jose 95192-0031
Type: Public, state, four-year
System: California State University System
Degrees: B, M   *Enroll:* 22,644
URL: http://www.sjsu.edu
Phone: (408) 924-1000   *Calendar:* Sem. plan
Inst. Accred.: WASC-SR. (1949/1995)
Prog. Accred.: Art, Business (AACSB), Computer Science, Dance, Dietetics (internship), Engineering (aerospace, chemical, civil, computer, electrical, industrial, materials, mechanical), Industrial Technology, Journalism, Librarianship, Music, Nursing, Nursing Education, Occupational Therapy, Planning, Public Administration, Public Health, Recreation and Leisure Services, Social Work, Speech-Language Pathology, Teacher Education (NCATE), Theatre

Santa Ana College
1530 West 17th St., Santa Ana 92706-3398
Type: Public, state/local, two-year
System: Rancho Santiago Community College District
Degrees: A   *Enroll:* 10,917
URL: http://www.sac.edu
Phone: (714) 564-6000   *Calendar:* Sem. plan
Inst. Accred.: WASC-JR. (1952/2002)
Prog. Accred.: Nursing, Occupational Therapy Assisting

Santa Barbara Business College
211 South Real Rd., Bakersfield 93309
Type: Private, proprietary, two-year
Degrees: A
URL: http://www.sbbcollege.edu
Phone: (661) 835-1100   *Calendar:* Qtr. plan
Inst. Accred.: ACICS (1985/2002)

Santa Barbara Business College
5266 Hollister Ave., Santa Barbara 93111
Type: Private, proprietary, two-year
Degrees: A
URL: http://www.sbbcollege.com
Phone: (805) 967-9677   *Calendar:* Qtr. plan
Inst. Accred.: ACICS (1976/2002)

Santa Barbara Business College
303 East Plaza Dr., Santa Maria 93454
Type: Private, proprietary, two-year
Degrees: A
URL: http://www.sbbcollege.com
Phone: (805) 922-8256   *Calendar:* Qtr. plan
Inst. Accred.: ACICS (1976/2002)

Ventura Campus
4839 Market St., Ventura 93003
Phone: (805) 339-2999

Santa Barbara City College
721 Cliff Dr., Santa Barbara 93109-2394
Type: Public, state/local, two-year
System: Santa Barbara Community College District
Degrees: A   *Enroll:* 9,139
URL: http://www.sbcc.edu
Phone: (805) 965-0581   *Calendar:* Sem. plan
Inst. Accred.: WASC-JR. (1952/2003)
Prog. Accred.: Culinary Education, Dental Assisting, Health Information Administration, Nursing, Radiography

Santa Barbara College of Oriental Medicine
1919 State St., Ste. 207, Santa Barbara 93101
Type: Private, proprietary, four-year
Degrees: M   *Enroll:* 5,206
URL: http://www.sbcom.edu
Phone: (805) 898-1180   *Calendar:* Tri. plan
Inst. Accred.: ACAOM (1995/2002)

Santa Clara University
500 El Camino Real, Santa Clara 95053-0015
Type: Private, Roman Catholic Church, four-year
Degrees: B, M, P, D   *Enroll:* 6,492
URL: http://www.scu.edu
Phone: (408) 554-4000   *Calendar:* Qtr. plan
Inst. Accred.: WASC-SR. (1949/2000)
Prog. Accred.: Accounting, Business (AACSB),
  Engineering (civil, computer, electrical, mechanical),
  Law

Santa Monica College
1900 Pico Blvd., Santa Monica 90405-1628
Type: Public, state/local, two-year
System: Santa Monica Community College District
Degrees: A   *Enroll:* 13,046
URL: http://www.smc.edu
Phone: (310) 434-4000   *Calendar:* Sem. plan
Inst. Accred.: WASC-JR. (1952/2004)
Prog. Accred.: Nursing, Respiratory Therapy

Santa Rosa Junior College
1501 Mendocino Ave., Santa Rosa 95401-4395
Type: Public, state/local, two-year
System: Sonoma County Junior College District
Degrees: A   *Enroll:* 13,615
URL: http://www.santarosa.edu
Phone: (707) 527-4011   *Calendar:* Sem. plan
Inst. Accred.: WASC-JR. (1952/2003)
Prog. Accred.: Dental Assisting, Dental Hygiene,
  Radiography

Petaluma Campus
680 Sonoma Mountain Pkwy., Petaluma 94952
Phone: (707) 778-3801

Santiago Canyon College
8045 East Chapman Ave., Orange 92869-4512
Type: Public, state/local, two-year
System: Rancho Santiago Community College District
Degrees: A
URL: http://www.sccollege.edu
Phone: (714) 628-4900   *Calendar:* Sem. plan
Inst. Accred.: WASC-JR. (2000)

Saybrook Graduate School and Research Center
747 Front St., 3rd Flr., San Francisco 94111-1920
Type: Private, independent, four-year
Degrees: M, D   *Enroll:* 548
URL: http://www.saybrook.edu
Phone: (415) 433-9200
Inst. Accred.: WASC-SR. (1984/2001)

Scripps College
1030 North Columbia Ave., Claremont 91711
Type: Private, independent, four-year
System: Claremont University Consortium
Degrees: B   *Enroll:* 827
URL: http://www.scrippscollege.edu
Phone: (909) 621-8224   *Calendar:* Sem. plan
Inst. Accred.: WASC-SR. (1949/2002)

The Scripps Research Institute
10550 North Torrey Pines Rd., TCP 19, La Jolla 92037
Type: Private, independent, four-year
Degrees: D
URL: http://www.scripps.edu
Phone: (858) 784-8469   *Calendar:* 9-mos. pro
Inst. Accred.: WASC-SR. (1993/1999)

Shasta Bible College and Graduate School
2951 Goodwater Ave., Redding 96002
Type: Private, Baptist Church, four-year
Degrees: A, B, M   *Enroll:* 94
URL: http://www.shasta.edu
Phone: (530) 221-4275   *Calendar:* Sem. plan
Inst. Accred.: TRACS (1997/2002)

Shasta College
1115 Old Oregon Trail, PO Box 496006, Redding 96049-6006
Type: Public, state/local, two-year
System: Shasta-Tehama-Trinity Joint Community College
  District
Degrees: A   *Enroll:* 4,919
URL: http://www.shastacollege.edu
Phone: (530) 225-4600   *Calendar:* Sem. plan
Inst. Accred.: WASC-JR. (1952/2000)
Prog. Accred.: Dental Hygiene

Sierra College
5000 Rocklin Rd., Rocklin 95677-3397
Type: Public, state/local, two-year
System: Sierra Joint Community College District
Degrees: A   *Enroll:* 10,138
URL: http://www.sierracollege.edu
Phone: (530) 624-3333   *Calendar:* Sem. plan
Inst. Accred.: WASC-JR. (1952/2001)

Silicon Valley College
41350 Christy St., Fremont 94538
Type: Private, proprietary, four-year
Degrees: A, B   *Enroll:* 463
URL: http://www.siliconvalley.edu
Phone: (510) 623-9966
Inst. Accred.: ACCSCT (1991/2001)
Prog. Accred.: Medical Assisting (CAAHEP)

Emeryville Campus
1400 65th St., Ste. 200, Emeryville 94608
Phone: (510) 601-0133

San Jose Campus
6201 San Ignacio Ave., San Jose 95119
Phone: (408) 360-0840

Walnut Creek Campus
2800 Mitchell Dr., Walnut Creek 94598
Phone: (925) 280-0235

Silicon Valley University
2160 Lundy Ave., Ste. 110, San Jose 95131
Type: Private, independent, four-year
Degrees: B, M   *FTE Enroll:* 100
URL: http://www.svuca.edu
Phone: (408) 435-8989   *Calendar:* Tri. plan
Inst. Accred.: ACICS (2003)

Simpson University
2211 College View Dr., Redding 96003-8606
Type: Private, Christian and Missionary Alliance, four-year
Degrees: A, B, M   *Enroll:* 1,088
URL: http://www.simpsonca.edu
Phone: (530) 224-5600   *Calendar:* 4-1-4 plan
Inst. Accred.: WASC-SR. (1969/2005)

Skyline College
3300 College Dr., San Bruno 94066-1698
Type: Public, state/local, two-year
System: San Mateo County Community College District
Degrees: A   *Enroll:* 4,324
URL: http://skylinecollege.edu
Phone: (650) 738-4100   *Calendar:* Sem. plan
Inst. Accred.: WASC-JR. (1971/2001)
Prog. Accred.: Respiratory Therapy

Soka University of America
1 University Dr., Aliso Viejo 92656
Type: Private, independent, four-year
Degrees: B
URL: http://www.soka.edu
Phone: (949) 480-4000
Inst. Accred.: AALE (2005), WASC-SR. (2005)

Solano Community College
4000 Suisun Valley Rd., Fairfield 94534-3197
Type: Public, state/local, two-year
System: Solano County Community College District
Degrees: A   *FTE Enroll:* 5,555
URL: http://www.solano.edu
Phone: (707) 864-7000   *Calendar:* Sem. plan
Inst. Accred.: WASC-JR. (1952/2000)

Sonoma College—Petaluma
1304 South Point Blvd., Ste. 280, Petaluma 94954
Type: Private, proprietary, two-year
Degrees: A   *Enroll:* 108
URL: http://www.sonomacollege.com
Phone: (707) 283-0800   *Calendar:* Sem. plan
Inst. Accred.: ABHES (1995/2003)
Prog. Accred.: Physical Therapy Assisting

San Francisco Campus
301 Howard St., Ste. 510, San Francisco 94105
Phone: (415) 543-1833

Sonoma State University
1801 East Cotati Ave., Rohnert Park 94928
Type: Public, state, four-year
System: California State University System
Degrees: B, M, D   *Enroll:* 7,377
URL: http://www.sonoma.edu
Phone: (707) 664-2880   *Calendar:* Sem. plan
Inst. Accred.: WASC-SR. (1963/1999)
Prog. Accred.: Art, Business (AACSB), Counseling, Music,
Nursing

South Coast College
2011 West Chapman Ave., Orange 92868-2616
Type: Private, proprietary, two-year
Degrees: A
URL: http://www.southcoastcollege.com
Phone: (714) 635-6464
Inst. Accred.: ACICS (1984/2002)

Southern California College of Optometry
2575 Yorba Linda Blvd., Fullerton 92631-1699
Type: Private, independent, four-year
Degrees: A, B, P, D   *Enroll:* 381
URL: http://www.scco.edu
Phone: (714) 870-7226   *Calendar:* Qtr. plan
Inst. Accred.: WASC-SR. (1961/2001)
Prog. Accred.: Optometric Residency, Optometry

Southern California Institute of Architecture
960 East Third St., Los Angeles 90013
Type: Private, independent, four-year
Degrees: B, M, P   *Enroll:* 301
URL: http://www.sciarc.edu
Phone: (213) 613-2200   *Calendar:* Sem. plan
Inst. Accred.: WASC-SR. (1995/2002)

Southern California Institute of Technology
1900 West Crescent Ave., Building B, Anaheim 92801
Type: Private, proprietary, four-year
Degrees: A, B   *Enroll:* 400
URL: http://202.54.10.85
Phone: (714) 520-5552
Inst. Accred.: ACCSCT (1994/2004)

Southern California Seminary
2075 East Madison Ave., El Cajon 92019-1108
Type: Private, independent, four-year
Degrees: A, B, M, D   *Enroll:* 162
URL: http://www.socalsem.edu
Phone: (619) 442-9841   *Calendar:* Tri. plan
Inst. Accred.: TRACS (2001)

Fundación ABRE
Santo Domingo St., 34, Santiponce (Seville), Spain
41970
Phone: 011 34 955 997 555

Southern California University of Health Sciences

16200 East Amber Valley Dr., PO Box 1166, Whittier 90609-1166
Type: Private, independent, four-year
Degrees: B, M, P, D   *Enroll:* 638
URL: http://www.scuhs.edu
Phone: (562) 947-8755   *Calendar:* Sem. plan
Inst. Accred.: WASC-SR. (1993/1998)
Prog. Accred.: Acupuncture, Chiropractic Education

Southwestern College

900 Otay Lakes Rd., Chula Vista 91910-7299
Type: Public, state/local, two-year
System: Southwestern Community College District
Degrees: A   *Enroll:* 10,513
URL: http://www.swc.cc.ca.us
Phone: (619) 421-6700   *Calendar:* Sem. plan
Inst. Accred.: WASC-JR. (1964/2003)
Prog. Accred.: Dental Hygiene, Nursing, Surgical Technology

Stanford University

Stanford 94305
Type: Private, independent, four-year
Degrees: B, M, P, D   *Enroll:* 14,599
URL: http://www.stanford.edu
Phone: (650) 723-2300   *Calendar:* Qtr. plan
Inst. Accred.: WASC-SR. (1949/2000)
Prog. Accred.: Business (AACSB), Clinical Pastoral Education, Counseling Psychology, Engineering (chemical, civil, electrical, environmental/sanitary, industrial, mechanical), Law, Medicine, Physician Assistant

Starr King School for the Ministry

2441 LeConte Ave., Berkeley 94709
Type: Private, Unitarian Universalist, four-year
System: Graduate Theological Union
Degrees: M   *Enroll:* 73
Phone: (510) 845-6232   *Calendar:* Sem. plan
Inst. Accred.: ATS (1978/1998)

Taft College

29 Emmons Park Dr., Taft 93268-2317
Type: Public, state/local, two-year
System: West Kern Community College District
Degrees: A   *Enroll:* 2,301
URL: http://www.taftcollege.edu
Phone: (661) 763-7700   *Calendar:* Sem. plan
Inst. Accred.: WASC-JR. (1952/2003)
Prog. Accred.: Dental Hygiene

Thomas Aquinas College

10000 North Ojai Rd., Santa Paula 93060
Type: Private, Roman Catholic Church, four-year
Degrees: B   *Enroll:* 332
URL: http://www.thomasaquinas.edu
Phone: (805) 525-4417   *Calendar:* Sem. plan
Inst. Accred.: WASC-SR. (1980/2002), AALE (1997/2002)

Thomas Jefferson School of Law

2121 San Diego Ave., San Diego 92110-2905
Type: Private, independent, four-year
Degrees: P, D   *Enroll:* 731
URL: http://www.tjsl.edu
Phone: (619) 297-9700   *Calendar:* Sem. plan
Inst. Accred.: WASC-SR. (1976/2002)
Prog. Accred.: Law (ABA only)

Touro University International

5665 Plaza Dr., Cypress 90630
Type: Private, independent, four-year
Degrees: B, M, D
URL: http://www.tourou.edu
Phone: (714) 816-0366   *Calendar:* Sem. plan
Inst. Accred.: WASC-SR. (2005)

Touro University—California

1310 Johnson Ln., Mare Island, Vallejo 94592
Type: Private, independent, four-year
Degrees: D
URL: http://www.tumi.edu
Phone: (707) 638-5200   *Calendar:* Sem. plan
Inst. Accred.: WASC-SR. (2005)
Prog. Accred.: Osteopathy, Physician Assistant

Trinity Life Bible College

5225 Hillsdale Blvd., Sacramento 95842
Type: Private, Assemblies of God Church, four-year
Degrees: A, B   *Enroll:* 139
URL: http://www.tlbc.edu
Phone: (916) 348-4689   *Calendar:* Qtr. plan
Inst. Accred.: TRACS (2004)

The United States Naval Postgraduate School

One University Circle, Room M12, Monterey 93943-5002
Type: Public, federal, four-year
Degrees: B, M, D   *Enroll:* 1,690
URL: http://www.nps.edu
Phone: (831) 656-2441   *Calendar:* Qtr. plan
Inst. Accred.: WASC-SR. (1955/1999)
Prog. Accred.: Business (AACSB), Engineering (aerospace, electrical, mechanical), Public Administration

University of California, Berkeley
Berkeley 94720
Type: Public, state, four-year
System: University of California Office of the President
Degrees: B, M, P, D *Enroll:* 31,498
URL: http://www.berkeley.edu
Phone: (510) 642-6000 *Calendar:* Sem. plan
Inst. Accred.: WASC-SR. (1949/2003)
Prog. Accred.: Business (AACSB), Clinical Psychology, Computer Science, Dietetics (internship), Engineering (chemical, civil, computer, electrical, industrial, mechanical, nuclear), Forestry, Health Services Administration, Interior Design, Journalism, Landscape Architecture, Law, Optometric Residency, Optometry, Planning, Psychology Internship, Public Health, School Psychology, Social Work

UC Berkeley Extension
1995 University Ave., Berkeley 94720-7007
Phone: (510) 642-4111
Prog. Accred: Interior Design

University of California, Davis
One Shields Ave., Davis 95616
Type: Public, state, four-year
System: University of California Office of the President
Degrees: B, M, P, D *Enroll:* 27,641
URL: http://www.ucdavis.edu
Phone: (530) 752-1011 *Calendar:* Qtr. plan
Inst. Accred.: WASC-SR. (1954/2003)
Prog. Accred.: Business (AACSB), Clinical Lab Scientist, Clinical Pastoral Education, Computer Science, Engineering (aerospace, agricultural, chemical, civil, computer, electrical, materials, mechanical), Landscape Architecture, Law, Medicine, Physician Assistant, Psychology Internship, Veterinary Medicine

University of California, Hastings College of the Law
200 McAllister St., San Francisco 94102
Type: Public, state, four-year
System: University of California Office of the President
Degrees: P *Enroll:* 1,257
URL: http://www.uchastings.edu
Phone: (415) 565-4600 *Calendar:* Sem. plan
Inst. Accred.: ABA (1939/2002)

University of California, Irvine
501 Administration, Irvine 92697-1000
Type: Public, state, four-year
System: University of California Office of the President
Degrees: B, M, P, D *Enroll:* 23,513
URL: http://www.uci.edu
Phone: (949) 824-5011 *Calendar:* Qtr. plan
Inst. Accred.: WASC-SR. (1965/2001)
Prog. Accred.: Business (AACSB), Clinical Lab Scientist, Engineering (aerospace, chemical, civil, computer, electrical, environmental/sanitary, materials, mechanical), Medicine, Planning, Psychology Internship

University of California, Los Angeles
405 Hilgard Ave., Los Angeles 90095-1405
Type: Public, state, four-year
System: University of California Office of the President
Degrees: B, M, P, D *Enroll:* 36,146
URL: http://www.ucla.edu
Phone: (310) 825-4321 *Calendar:* Qtr. plan
Inst. Accred.: WASC-SR. (1949/1998)
Prog. Accred.: Advanced Education in General Dentistry, Applied Science (industrial hygiene), Business (AACSB), Clinical Pastoral Education, Clinical Psychology, Combined Prosthodontics, Computer Science, Cytotechnology, Dental Public Health, Dentistry, Endodontics, Engineering (aerospace, chemical, civil, computer, electrical, materials, mechanical), General Dentistry, General Practice Residency, Health Services Administration, Law, Librarianship, Maxillofacial Prosthetics, Medicine, Microbiology, Nurse (Midwifery), Nursing, Nursing Education, Oral and Maxillofacial Surgery, Orthodontic and Dentofacial Orthopedics, Pediatric Dentistry, Periodontics, Planning, Psychology Internship, Public Health, Social Work, Theatre

UCLA Extension
10995 Le Conte Ave., Los Angeles 90024-2883
Phone: (310) 825-9971
Prog. Accred: Interior Design

University of California, Riverside
900 University Ave., Riverside 92521-4009
Type: Public, state, four-year
System: University of California Office of the President
Degrees: B, M, D *Enroll:* 16,429
URL: http://www.ucr.edu
Phone: (951) 827-1012 *Calendar:* Qtr. plan
Inst. Accred.: WASC-SR. (1956/1998)
Prog. Accred.: Business (AACSB), Engineering (chemical, computer, electrical, environmental/sanitary, mechanical), School Psychology

University of California, San Diego
9500 Gilman Dr., La Jolla 92093-0321
Type: Public, state, four-year
System: University of California Office of the President
Degrees: B, M, P, D *Enroll:* 23,476
URL: http://www.ucsd.edu
Phone: (858) 534-2230 *Calendar:* Qtr. plan
Inst. Accred.: WASC-SR. (1964/1998)
Prog. Accred.: Engineering (aerospace, bioengineering, chemical, civil, electrical, mechanical), Medicine, Nurse (Midwifery), Pharmacy, Psychology Internship

University of California, San Francisco
513 Parnassus Ave., San Francisco 94143
Type: Public, state, four-year
System: University of California Office of the President
Degrees: B, M, P, D   *Enroll:* 2,763
URL: http://www.ucsf.edu
Phone: (415) 476-9000   *Calendar:* Qtr. plan
Inst. Accred.: WASC-SR. (1976/1999)
Prog. Accred.: Advanced Education in General Dentistry,
   Clinical Pastoral Education, Combined Prosthodontics,
   Dental Hygiene, Dental Public Health, Dentistry,
   Dietetics (internship), Endodontics, General Dentistry,
   General Practice Residency, Medicine, Nurse
   (Midwifery), Nursing, Nursing Education, Oral and
   Maxillofacial Surgery, Orthodontic and Dentofacial
   Orthopedics, Pediatric Dentistry, Periodontics,
   Pharmacy, Physical Therapy, Psychology Internship

University of California, Santa Barbara
Santa Barbara 93106-2030
Type: Public, state, four-year
System: University of California Office of the President
Degrees: B, M, D   *Enroll:* 20,358
URL: http://www.ucsb.edu
Phone: (805) 893-8000   *Calendar:* Qtr. plan
Inst. Accred.: WASC-SR. (1949/2001)
Prog. Accred.: Combined Professional-Scientific
   Psychology, Computer Science, Dance, Engineering
   (chemical, electrical, mechanical), Psychology
   Internship

University of California, Santa Cruz
1156 High St., Santa Cruz 95064
Type: Public, state, four-year
System: University of California Office of the President
Degrees: B, M, D   *Enroll:* 14,560
URL: http://www.ucsc.edu
Phone: (831) 459-2058   *Calendar:* Qtr. plan
Inst. Accred.: WASC-SR. (1965/2005)
Prog. Accred.: Engineering (computer, electrical),
   Psychology Internship

University of Judaism
15600 Mulholland Dr., Bel Air 90077
Type: Private, independent, four-year
Degrees: B, M   *Enroll:* 280
URL: http://www.uj.edu
Phone: (310) 476-9777   *Calendar:* Sem. plan
Inst. Accred.: WASC-SR. (1961/1996)

University of La Verne
1950 Third St., La Verne 91750
Type: Private, independent, four-year
Degrees: A, B, M, P, D   *Enroll:* 5,357
URL: http://www.ulv.edu
Phone: (909) 593-3511   *Calendar:* 4-1-4 plan
Inst. Accred.: WASC-SR. (1955/2000)
Prog. Accred.: Clinical Psychology

High Desert Campus
15447 Anacapa Rd., Ste. 100, Victorville 92392

Inland Empire Campus
10535 Foothill Blvd., Ste. 400, Ranch Cucamonga
91730
Phone: (909) 484-3858

Kern County Campus
1600 Truxton Ave., Ste. 100, Bakersfield 93301
Phone: (661) 328-1430

Orange County Campus
12951 Euclid St., Ste. 100, Garden Grove 92840-5214
Phone: (714) 534-4860

San Fernando Valley Campus
4001 West Alameda Ave., Ste. 300, Burbank 91505
Phone: (818) 846-4008

Ventura County Campus
2001 Solar Dr., Ste. 250, Oxnard 93030
Phone: (805) 981-8030

University of Redlands
PO Box 3080, 1200 East Colton Ave., Redlands 92373
Type: Private, independent, four-year
Degrees: B, M, P, D   *Enroll:* 4,309
URL: http://www.redlands.edu
Phone: (909) 793-2121   *Calendar:* Sem. plan
Inst. Accred.: WASC-SR. (1949/2003)
Prog. Accred.: Music, Speech-Language Pathology

University of San Diego
5998 Alcala Park, San Diego 92110-2492
Type: Private, Roman Catholic Church, four-year
Degrees: B, M, P, D   *Enroll:* 6,629
URL: http://www.sandiego.edu
Phone: (619) 260-4600   *Calendar:* 4-1-4 plan
Inst. Accred.: WASC-SR. (1956/2001)
Prog. Accred.: Accounting, Business (AACSB),
   Engineering (electrical, industrial), Law, Marriage and
   Family Therapy, Nursing, Nursing Education, Psychology
   Internship

University of San Francisco
2130 Fulton St., San Francisco 94117-1080
Type: Private, Roman Catholic Church, four-year
Degrees: B, M, P, D   *Enroll:* 7,623
URL: http://www.usfca.edu
Phone: (415) 422-6136   *Calendar:* Sem. plan
Inst. Accred.: WASC-SR. (1949/1998)
Prog. Accred.: Business (AACSB), Law, Nursing, Nursing
   Education

University of Southern California
University Park, Los Angeles 90089-0012
Type: Private, independent, four-year
Degrees: B, M, P, D   *Enroll:* 28,753
URL: http://www.usc.edu
Phone: (213) 740-2311   *Calendar:* Sem. plan
Inst. Accred.: WASC-SR. (1949/1998)
Prog. Accred.: Accounting, Advanced Education in
General Dentistry, Business (AACSB), Clinical
Psychology, Combined Prosthodontics, Computer
Science, Counseling Psychology, Dental Hygiene,
Dentistry, Dietetics (internship), Endodontics,
Engineering (aerospace, chemical, civil, computer,
electrical, environmental/sanitary, industrial,
mechanical), General Dentistry, General Practice
Residency, Health Services Administration, Journalism,
Law, Medicine, Music, Nurse (Midwifery), Nurse
Anesthesia Education, Nursing, Nursing Education,
Occupational Therapy, Oral and Maxillofacial Surgery,
Orthodontic and Dentofacial Orthopedics, Pediatric
Dentistry, Periodontics, Pharmacy, Physical Therapy,
Physician Assistant, Planning, Psychology Internship,
Public Administration, Public Health, Radiography,
Social Work

University of the Pacific
3601 Pacific Ave., Stockton 95211
Type: Private, independent, four-year
Degrees: B, M, P, D   *Enroll:* 5,712
URL: http://www.uop.edu
Phone: (209) 946-2344   *Calendar:* Sem. plan
Inst. Accred.: WASC-SR. (1949/2000)
Prog. Accred.: Art, Business (AACSB), Computer Science,
Dentistry, Engineering (civil, computer, electrical,
engineering management, engineering physics/science,
mechanical), General Dentistry, Law, Music, Orthodontic
and Dentofacial Orthopedics, Pharmacy, Physical
Therapy, Speech-Language Pathology, Teacher
Education (NCATE)

The University of West Los Angeles
1155 West Arbor Vitae St., Inglewood 90301-2902
Type: Private, independent, four-year
Degrees: B, M, P   *Enroll:* 227
URL: http://www.uwla.edu
Phone: (310) 342-5200   *Calendar:* Tri. plan
Inst. Accred.: WASC-SR. (1983/2003)

San Fernando Valley Campus
21300 Oxnard St., Woodland Hills 91367
Phone: (818) 883-0529

Vanguard University of Southern California
55 Fair Dr., Costa Mesa 92626
Type: Private, Southern California District of the
Assemblies of God, four-year
Degrees: B, M   *Enroll:* 1,723
URL: http://www.vanguard.edu
Phone: (714) 556-3610   *Calendar:* 4-1-4 plan
Inst. Accred.: WASC-SR. (1964/1997)

Ventura College
4667 Telegraph Rd., Ventura 93003-3899
Type: Public, state/local, two-year
System: Ventura County Community College District
Degrees: A   *Enroll:* 6,793
URL: http://www.vcccd.net
Phone: (805) 654-6400   *Calendar:* Sem. plan
Inst. Accred.: WASC-JR. (1952/2005)

Victor Valley College
18422 Bear Valley Rd., Victorville 92392-5849
Type: Public, state/local, two-year
System: Victor Valley Community College District
Degrees: A   *Enroll:* 5,776
URL: http://www.vvc.edu
Phone: (760) 245-4271   *Calendar:* Sem. plan
Inst. Accred.: WASC-JR. (1963/2005)
Prog. Accred.: Nursing, Respiratory Therapy

Victory Montessori Training Institute
444 South Sierra Madre Blvd., Pasadena 91107
Type: Private, independent, four-year
Degrees: B
Phone: (626) 577-8007
Inst. Accred.: MACTE (1997)

Vista Community College
2020 Milvia St., Berkeley 94704-1183
Type: Public, state/local, two-year
System: Peralta Community College District
Degrees: A   *Enroll:* 1,678
URL: http://vista.peralta.edu
Phone: (510) 981-2800   *Calendar:* Sem. plan
Inst. Accred.: WASC-JR. (1981/2003, Warning)

West Coast University
4021 Rosewood Ave., Los Angeles 90004-6818
Type: Private, proprietary, four-year
Degrees: A, B
URL: http://www.westcoastuniversity.com
Phone: (877) 505-4928
Inst. Accred.: ACICS (2002)

West Hills Community College
300 Cherry Ln., Coalinga 93210
Type: Public, state/local, two-year
System: West Hills Community College District
Degrees: A   *Enroll:* 2,673
URL: http://www.westhillscollege.com
Phone: (559) 935-0801   *Calendar:* Sem. plan
Inst. Accred.: WASC-JR. (1952/1999, Warning)

West Los Angeles College
9000 Overland Ave., Culver City 90230
Type: Public, state/local, two-year
System: Los Angeles Community College District
Degrees: A   *Enroll:* 4,786
URL: http://www.wlac.edu
Phone: (310) 287-4200   *Calendar:* Sem. plan
Inst. Accred.: WASC-JR. (1971/2000)
Prog. Accred.: Dental Hygiene

West Valley College
14000 Fruitvale Ave., Saratoga 95070-5698
Type: Public, state/local, two-year
System: West Valley-Mission College District
Degrees: A   *Enroll:* 5,599
URL: http://www.westvalley.edu
Phone: (408) 867-2200   *Calendar:* Sem. plan
Inst. Accred.: WASC-JR. (1966/2002)
Prog. Accred.: Interior Design, Medical Assisting
  (CAAHEP)

Western Career College
8909 Folsom Blvd., Sacramento 95826-9823
Type: Private, proprietary, two-year
System: U.S. Education Corporation
Degrees: A
URL: http://www.westerncollege.edu
Phone: (916) 361-1660   *Calendar:* Sem. plan
Inst. Accred.: WASC-JR. (2001)
Prog. Accred.: Medical Assisting (CAAHEP)

Pleasant Hill Campus
380 Civic Dr., Ste. 300, Pleasant Hill 94523
Phone: (925) 609-6650
Prog. Accred: Medical Assisting (CAAHEP)

San Leandro Campus
15555 East 14th St., Ste. 500, San Leandro 94578
Phone: (510) 276-3888

Western College of Southern California
10900 East 183rd St., Ste. 290, Cerritos 90703-5342
Type: Private, proprietary, two-year
System: U.S. Education Corporation
Degrees: A   *Enroll:* 149
URL: http://www.westerncollegesocal.com
Phone: (562) 809-5100
Inst. Accred.: ACCSCT (1986/2004)

Western State University College of Law
1111 North State College Blvd., Fullerton 92831
Type: Private, proprietary, four-year
System: Education Management Corporation—Argosy
  Education Group
Degrees: D   *Enroll:* 415
URL: http://www.wsulaw.edu
Phone: (714) 738-1000   *Calendar:* Sem. plan
Inst. Accred.: WASC-SR. (1976/2004)
Prog. Accred.: Law (ABA only)

Western University of Health Sciences
309 East Second St., College Plaza, Pomona 91766-1889
Type: Private, independent, four-year
Degrees: B, M, P, D   *Enroll:* 1,537
URL: http://www.westernu.edu
Phone: (909) 623-6116   *Calendar:* Sem. plan
Inst. Accred.: WASC-SR. (1996/2001)
Prog. Accred.: Nursing Education, Osteopathy, Pharmacy,
  Physical Therapy, Physician Assistant, Veterinary
  Medicine

Westminster Theological Seminary in California
1725 Bear Valley Pkwy., Escondido 92027-4128
Type: Private, nondenominational, four-year
Degrees: M, P, D   *Enroll:* 98
URL: http://www.wscal.edu
Phone: (760) 480-8474   *Calendar:* 4-1-4 plan
Inst. Accred.: ATS (1997/2002), WASC-SR. (1984/2002)

Westmont College
955 La Paz Rd., Santa Barbara 93108-1089
Type: Private, independent, four-year
Degrees: B   *Enroll:* 1,337
URL: http://www.westmont.edu
Phone: (805) 565-6000   *Calendar:* Sem. plan
Inst. Accred.: WASC-SR. (1957/2005)

Westwood College of Aviation Technology—Los Angeles
8911 Aviation Blvd., inglewood 90301-2904
Type: Private, proprietary, two-year
Degrees: A
URL: http://www.westwoodcollege.com
Phone: (310) 337-4442
Inst. Accred.: COE (1988/2000)

Westwood College—Long Beach
3901 Via Oro Ave., Ste. 103, Long Beach 90810
Type: Private, proprietary, four-year
Degrees: A, B
URL: http://www.westwood.edu
Phone: (310) 522-2088
Inst. Accred.: ACCSCT (1973/2003)

Westwood College—Los Angeles
3460 Wilshire Blvd., Ste. 700, Los Angeles 90010-2210
Type: Private, proprietary, four-year
Degrees: A, B   *Enroll:* 617
URL: http://www.westwood.edu
Phone: (213) 739-9999
Inst. Accred.: ACICS (1991/2001)

Chicago Loop Campus
17 North State St., 3rd Flr., Chicago, IL 60602
Phone: (312) 739-0850

River Oaks Campus
80 River Oaks Center, Ste. D-49, Calumet City, IL
60409
Phone: (708) 832-1988

Westwood Aviation Institute—Houston
8880 Telephone Rd., Houston, TX 77061-5114
Phone: (713) 645-4444

Whittier College
13406 East Philadelphia St., PO Box 634, Whittier 90608
Type: Private, independent, four-year
Degrees: B, M, P, D   *Enroll:* 2,184
URL: http://www.whittier.edu
Phone: (562) 907-4200   *Calendar:* 4-1-4 plan
Inst. Accred.: WASC-SR. (1949/2002, Probation)
Prog. Accred.: Law, Social Work

William Howard Taft University
3700 South Susan St., Office 200, Santa Ana 92704
Type: Private, independent, four-year
Degrees: M, P　　　　　　　　　　　　　　*FTE Enroll:* 289
URL: http://www.taftu.edu
Phone: (714) 850-4800
Inst. Accred.: DETC (2003)

William Jessup University
333 Sunset Blvd., Rocklin 95765
Type: Private, independent, four-year
Degrees: A, B　　　　　　　　　　　　　　*Enroll:* 318
URL: http://www.jessup.edu
Phone: (916) 577-2200　　　　　　*Calendar:* Sem. plan
Inst. Accred.: ABHE (1969/2000), WASC-SR. (2002)

Woodbury University
7500 Glenoaks Blvd., Burbank 91510-7846
Type: Private, independent, four-year
Degrees: B, M　　　　　　　　　　　　*Enroll:* 1,122
URL: http://www.woodbury.edu
Phone: (818) 767-0888　　　　　　*Calendar:* Sem. plan
Inst. Accred.: WASC-SR. (1961/1998)
Prog. Accred.: Business (ACBSP), Interior Design

The Wright Institute
2728 Durant Ave., Berkeley 94702
Type: Private, independent, four-year
Degrees: D　　　　　　　　　　　　　　*Enroll:* 286
URL: http://www.wrightinst.edu
Phone: (510) 841-9230　　　　　　*Calendar:* Tri. plan
Inst. Accred.: WASC-SR. (1977/1995)
Prog. Accred.: Clinical Psychology

WyoTech—Fremont
200 Whitney Place, Fremont 94539
Type: Private, proprietary, two-year
System: Corinthian Colleges, Inc
Degrees: A　　　　　　　　　　　　　*Enroll:* 1,397
URL: http://www.wyotech.com
Phone: (510) 490-6900
Inst. Accred.: ACCSCT (1977/2004)

Oakland Campus
9636 Earhart Rd., Oakland International Airport,
Oakland 94621
Phone: (510) 569-8436

WyoTech—Sacramento
980 Riverside Pkwy., West Sacramento 95605
Type: Private, proprietary, two-year
System: Corinthian Colleges, Inc
Degrees: A
URL: http://www.wyotech.com
Phone: (916) 376-8888
Inst. Accred.: ACCSCT (2004)

Yeshiva Ohr Elchonon-Chabad/West Coast Talmudic Seminary
7215 Waring Ave., Los Angeles 90046
Type: Private, independent, four-year
Degrees: B　　　　　　　　　　　　　　*Enroll:* 75
Phone: (323) 937-3763　　　　　　*Calendar:* Sem. plan
Inst. Accred.: AARTS (1983/2000)

Yo San University of Traditional Chinese Medicine
13315 West Washington Blvd., Los Angeles 90066-5162
Type: Private, independent, four-year
Degrees: M　　　　　　　　　　　　　　*Enroll:* 115
URL: http://www.yosan.edu
Phone: (310) 577-3000　　　　　　*Calendar:* Tri. plan
Inst. Accred.: ACAOM (1993/2003)

Yuba College
2088 North Beale Rd., Marysville 95901-7699
Type: Public, state/local, two-year
System: Yuba Community College District
Degrees: A　　　　　　　　　　　　*Enroll:* 5,022
URL: http://www.yccd.edu/yuba
Phone: (530) 741-6700　　　　　　*Calendar:* Sem. plan
Inst. Accred.: WASC-JR. (1952/2000)
Prog. Accred.: Radiography, Veterinary Technology

COLORADO

Adams State College
208 Edgemont Blvd., Alamosa 81102-0001
Type: Public, state, four-year
System: Colorado Commission on Higher Education
Degrees: A, B, M   *Enroll:* 4,319
URL: http://www.adams.edu
Phone: (719) 589-7011   *Calendar:* Sem. plan
Inst. Accred.: NCA-HLC (1950/1997)
Prog. Accred.: Counseling, Music, Teacher Education (NCATE)

Aims Community College
5401 West 20th St., PO Box 69, Greeley 80632
Type: Public, state/local, two-year
Degrees: A   *Enroll:* 3,250
URL: http://www.aims.edu
Phone: (970) 330-8000   *Calendar:* Qtr. plan
Inst. Accred.: NCA-HLC (1977/1999)
Prog. Accred.: Radiography

Fort Lupton Campus
260 College Ave., Fort Lupton 80621
Phone: (303) 857-4022

Loveland Campus
104 East Fourth St., Loveland 80637
Phone: (970) 667-4611

American Graduate School of Management
385 Inverness Pkwy., Ste. 310, Englewood 80112
Type: Private, independent, four-year
Degrees: M
URL: http://www.agsm.edu
Phone: (303) 991-1575
Inst. Accred.: DETC (2005)

American Health Science University
1010 South Joliet, Ste. 107, Aurora 80012-3150
Type: Private, proprietary, four-year
Degrees: M
URL: http://www.ahsu.edu
Phone: (303) 340-2054
Inst. Accred.: DETC (1996/2002)

Arapahoe Community College
5900 South Santa Fe Dr., PO Box 9002, Littleton 80160-9002
Type: Public, state, two-year
System: Colorado Community College System
Degrees: A   *Enroll:* 4,171
URL: http://www.arapahoe.edu
Phone: (303) 794-1550   *Calendar:* Sem. plan
Inst. Accred.: NCA-HLC (1970/1997)
Prog. Accred.: Clinical Lab Technology, Funeral Service Education (Mortuary Science), Health Information Technician, Medical Assisting (AMA), Physical Therapy Assisting

The Art Institute of Colorado
1200 Lincoln St., Denver 80203-2983
Type: Private, proprietary, four-year
System: Education Management Corporation
Degrees: A, B   *Enroll:* 1,898
URL: http://www.aic.aii.edu
Phone: (303) 837-0825   *Calendar:* Qtr. plan
Inst. Accred.: ACICS (2000/2003)
Prog. Accred.: Culinary Education

The Art Institute of California—Orange County
3601 Sunflower Ave., Santa Ana, CA 92704
Phone: (714) 830-0200

The Art Institute of Phoenix
2233 West Dunlap, Phoenix, AZ 85021
Phone: (602) 678-4300
Prog. Accred: Culinary Education

Aspen University
501 South Cherry St., Ste. 350, Denver 80246-1326
Type: Private, proprietary, four-year
Degrees: B, M
URL: http://www.aspen.edu
Phone: (303) 333-4334
Inst. Accred.: DETC (1993/2003)

Bel-Rea Institute of Animal Technology
1681 South Dayton St., Denver 80231-3048
Type: Private, independent, two-year
Degrees: A   *Enroll:* 737
URL: http://www.bel-rea.com
Phone: (303) 751-8700   *Calendar:* Qtr. plan
Inst. Accred.: ACCSCT (1975/2003)
Prog. Accred.: Veterinary Technology

Blair College
1815 Jet Wing Dr., Colorado Springs 80916
Type: Private, proprietary, two-year
System: Corinthian Colleges, Inc
Degrees: A   *Enroll:* 393
URL: http://blair-college.com
Phone: (719) 574-1082   *Calendar:* Qtr. plan
Inst. Accred.: ACICS (1953/2002)
Prog. Accred.: Medical Assisting (CAAHEP)

Boulder College of Massage Therapy
6255 Longbow Dr., Boulder 80301
Type: Private, proprietary, two-year
Degrees: A
URL: http://www.bcmt.org
Phone: (303) 530-2100
Inst. Accred.: ACCSCT (1990/2001)

Cambridge College
350 Blackhawk St., Aurora 80011
Type: Private, proprietary, two-year
System: High-Tech Institute
Degrees: A
URL: http://www.cambridgecollege.com
Phone: (303) 338-9700
Inst. Accred.: ACCSCT (1997/2004)
Prog. Accred.: Medical Assisting (ABHES), Surgical
Technology

Seattle Campus
14432 SE Eastgate Way, Ste. 100, Bellevue, WA
98007
Phone: (425) 747-3433

College for Financial Planning
6161 South Syracuse Way, Greenwood Village 80111-
4707
Type: Private, proprietary, four-year
System: Apollo Group, Inc.
Degrees: M   *FTE Enroll:* 5,975
URL: http://www.fp.edu
Phone: (303) 220-1200
Inst. Accred.: NCA-HLC (1994/2004)

CollegeAmerica—Colorado Springs
3645 Citadel Dr. South, Colorado Springs 80909
Type: Private, proprietary, four-year
Degrees: A, B
URL: http://www.collegeamerica.edu
Phone: (719) 637-0600
Inst. Accred.: ACCSCT (2002/2004)

CollegeAmerica—Denver
1385 South Colorado Blvd., Ste. A-512, Denver 80222-
1912
Type: Private, proprietary, four-year
Degrees: A, B
URL: http://www.collegeamerica.com
Phone: (303) 691-9756
Inst. Accred.: ACCSCT (1984/2004)

CollegeAmerica—Fort Collins
4601 South Mason St., Fort Collins 80525
Type: Private, proprietary, four-year
Degrees: A, B
URL: http://www.collegeamerica.com
Phone: (970) 223-6060
Inst. Accred.: ACCSCT (2001/2003)

Colorado Christian University
8787 West Alameda Ave., Lakewood 80226
Type: Private, independent, four-year
Degrees: A, B, M   *Enroll:* 1,366
URL: http://www.ccu.edu
Phone: (303) 963-3000   *Calendar:* Sem. plan
Inst. Accred.: NCA-HLC (1981/2001)

Colorado College
14 East Cache la Pourde St., Colorado Springs 80903
Type: Private, independent, four-year
Degrees: B, M   *Enroll:* 1,960
URL: http://www.coloradocollege.edu
Phone: (719) 389-7000   *Calendar:* Sem. plan
Inst. Accred.: NCA-HLC (1915/1998)

Colorado Mountain College
831 Grand Ave., Glenwood Springs 81602
Type: Public, state/local, two-year
Degrees: A   *Enroll:* 2,868
URL: http://www.coloradomtn.edu
Phone: (970) 945-7486   *Calendar:* Sem. plan
Inst. Accred.: NCA-HLC (1974/2002)
Prog. Accred.: Veterinary Technology

Alpine Campus
1370 Bob Adams Dr., Steamboat Springs 80477
Phone: (970) 870-4444

Aspen Campus
255 Sage Way, Aspen 81611
Phone: (970) 925-77400

Rifle Campus
703 Railroad Ave., Rifle 81650
Phone: (970) 625-1871

Roaring Fork Campus
3000 County Rd. 114, Glenwood Springs 81601
Phone: (303) 945-7841

Timberline Campus
901 South Hwy. 24, Leadville 80461
Phone: (719) 486-2015

Colorado Northwestern Community College
500 Kennedy Dr., Rangely 81648
Type: Public, state/local, two-year
System: Colorado Community College System
Degrees: A   *Enroll:* 1,105
URL: http://www.cncc.edu
Phone: (970) 562-1105   *Calendar:* Sem. plan
Inst. Accred.: NCA-HLC (1976/2003)
Prog. Accred.: Dental Hygiene

Craig Campus
50 College Dr., Craig 81625
Phone: (970) 824-7071

Colorado School of Healing Arts
7655 West Mississippi, Ste. 100, Lakewood 80226
Type: Private, proprietary, two-year
Degrees: A
URL: http://www.csha.net
Phone: (303) 986-2320
Inst. Accred.: ACCSCT (1998/2003)

Colorado School of Mines
1500 Illinois St., Golden 80401
Type: Public, state, four-year
System: Colorado Commission on Higher Education
Degrees: B, M, P, D   *Enroll:* 3,426
URL: http://www.mines.edu
Phone: (303) 273-3280   *Calendar:* Sem. plan
Inst. Accred.: NCA-HLC (1929/2003)
Prog. Accred.: Engineering (chemical, engineering physics/science, general, geological/geophysical, metallurgical, mining, petroleum), English Language Education

The Colorado School of Professional Psychology
555 East Pikes Peak Ave., Ste. 108, Colorado Springs 80903
Type: Private, independent, four-year
Degrees: M, D
URL: http://www.cospp.edu
Phone: (877) 442-0505
Inst. Accred.: NCA-HLC (2003)

Colorado School of Trades
1575 Hoyt St., Lakewood 80215-2996
Type: Private, proprietary, two-year
Degrees: A   *Enroll:* 122
URL: http://www.gunsmithing.com
Phone: (303) 233-4697
Inst. Accred.: ACCSCT (1973/2001)

Colorado School of Traditional Chinese Medicine
1441 York St., Ste. 202, Denver 80206-2127
Type: Private, independent, four-year
Degrees: M
URL: http://www.traditionalhealing.net
Phone: (303) 329-6355   *Calendar:* Sem. plan
Inst. Accred.: ACAOM (2002)

Colorado State University
Fort Collins 80523
Type: Public, state, four-year
System: Colorado Commission on Higher Education
Degrees: B, M, D   *Enroll:* 24,251
URL: http://www.colostate.edu
Phone: (970) 491-1101   *Calendar:* Sem. plan
Inst. Accred.: NCA-HLC (1925/2004)
Prog. Accred.: Applied Science (industrial hygiene), Business (AACSB), Construction Education, Counseling, Counseling Psychology, Dietetics (internship), Engineering (agricultural, chemical, civil, electrical, engineering physics/science, mechanical), Forestry, Industrial Technology, Interior Design, Journalism, Landscape Architecture, Marriage and Family Therapy, Music, Occupational Therapy, Psychology Internship, Recreation and Leisure Services, Social Work, Teacher Education (NCATE), Veterinary Medicine

Colorado State University—Pueblo
2200 Bonforte Blvd., Pueblo 81001-4901
Type: Public, state, four-year
System: Colorado Commission on Higher Education
Degrees: B, M   *Enroll:* 4,379
URL: http://www.colostate-pueblo.edu
Phone: (719) 549-2100   *Calendar:* Sem. plan
Inst. Accred.: NCA-HLC (1951/1997)
Prog. Accred.: Business (AACSB), Engineering (industrial), Engineering Technology (civil/construction, electrical, mechanical), Music, Nursing, Social Work

Colorado Technical University
4435 North Chestnut St., Colorado Springs 80907
Type: Private, proprietary, four-year
System: Career Education Corporation
Degrees: A, B, M, D   *Enroll:* 1,175
URL: http://www.ctucoloradosprings.com
Phone: (719) 598-0200   *Calendar:* Qtr. plan
Inst. Accred.: NCA-HLC (1980/2002)
Prog. Accred.: Engineering (computer, electrical), Engineering Technology (electrical, telecommunications)

Denver Campus
5775 Denver Tech Center Blvd., Greenwood Village 80111-3201
Phone: (303) 694-6600

North Kansas City Campus
520 East 19th Ave., North Kansas City, MO 64116
Phone: (816) 472-7400
Prog. Accred: Medical Assisting (ABHES), Radiography

Sioux Falls Campus
3901 West 59th St., Sioux Falls, SD 57108
Phone: (605) 361-0200
Prog. Accred: Medical Assisting (CAAHEP)

Community College of Aurora
16000 East Centretech Pkwy., Aurora 80011
Type: Public, state, two-year
System: Colorado Community College System
Degrees: A   *Enroll:* 2,853
URL: http://www.ccaurora.edu
Phone: (303) 360-4700   *Calendar:* Sem. plan
Inst. Accred.: NCA-HLC (1988/2003)

Community College of Denver
1111 West Colfax Ave., PO Box 173363, Denver 80217-3363
Type: Public, state, two-year
System: Colorado Community College System
Degrees: A   *Enroll:* 4,660
URL: http://ccd.rightchoice.org
Phone: (303) 556-2600   *Calendar:* Tri. plan
Inst. Accred.: NCA-HLC (1975/2004)
Prog. Accred.: Dental Hygiene, Medical Assisting (AMA), Radiation Therapy, Surgical Technology, Veterinary Technology

East Campus
3240 Humboldt St., Denver 80205
Phone: (303) 293-8737

Lowry Campus
1070 Alton Way, Building 849, Denver 80230
Phone: (303) 365-8300
Prog. Accred: Radiography

Concorde Career College
111 North Havana St., Aurora 80010
Type: Private, proprietary, two-year
Degrees: A
URL: http://www.concordecareercolleges.com
Phone: (303) 861-1151
Inst. Accred.: ACCSCT (1969/2001)
Prog. Accred.: Radiography, Surgical Technology

Denver Academy of Court Reporting
9051 Harlan St., Unit #20, Westminster 80031
Type: Private, proprietary, two-year
Degrees: A   *Enroll:* 263
URL: http://www.dacr.org
Phone: (303) 427-5292
Inst. Accred.: ACICS (1982/2003)

Denver Automotive and Diesel College
460 South Lipan St., Denver 80223-9960
Type: Private, proprietary, two-year
System: Lincoln Educational Services
Degrees: A   *Enroll:* 992
URL: http://www.dadc.com
Phone: (303) 722-5724
Inst. Accred.: ACCSCT (1968/2000)

Denver Career College
500 East 84th Ave., Ste. W-200, Thornton 80229
Type: Private, proprietary, two-year
System: Kaplan Higher Education Corporation
Degrees: A
URL: http://www.paralegal-education.com
Phone: (303) 295-0550
Inst. Accred.: ACCSCT (1979/2004)

Colorado Springs Campus
8 South Nevada, Ste. 101, Colorado Springs 80903
Phone: (719) 444-0190

Denver Seminary
PO Box 100000, Denver 80250-0100
Type: Private, Conservative Baptist Church of America (CBA), four-year
Degrees: M, D   *Enroll:* 535
URL: http://www.denverseminary.edu
Phone: (303) 761-2482   *Calendar:* Qtr. plan
Inst. Accred.: ATS (1970/2002), NCA-HLC (1972/2002)
Prog. Accred.: Counseling

DeVry University Westminster
1870 West 122nd Ave., Westmintser 80234-2010
Type: Private, proprietary, four-year
System: DeVry University
Degrees: A, B, M
URL: http://www.devry.edu/westminster
Phone: (303) 280-7400   *Calendar:* Sem. plan
Inst. Accred.: NCA-HLC (2002, *Indirect accreditation through DeVry University, Oakbrook Terrace, IL*)

Colorado Springs Campus
225 South Union Blvd., Colorado Springs 80910-3138
Phone: (719) 632-5305

Denver Campus
925 South Niagara St., Denver 80224-1658
Phone: (303) 329-3000
Prog. Accred: Physical Therapy Assisting

Fort Lewis College
1000 Rim Dr., Durango 81301-3999
Type: Public, state, four-year
System: Colorado Commission on Higher Education
Degrees: A, B   *Enroll:* 3,983
URL: http://www.fortlewis.edu
Phone: (970) 247-7010   *Calendar:* Tri. plan
Inst. Accred.: NCA-HLC (1958/1996)
Prog. Accred.: Business (AACSB), Music, Teacher Education (TEAC)

Front Range Community College
3645 West 112th Ave., Westminster 80031
Type: Public, state/local, two-year
System: Colorado Community College System
Degrees: A   *Enroll:* 8,561
URL: http://www.frcc.cc.co.us
Phone: (303) 466-8811   *Calendar:* Sem. plan
Inst. Accred.: NCA-HLC (1975/1998)
Prog. Accred.: Dental Assisting, Medical Assisting (AMA),
  Respiratory Therapy, Respiratory Therapy Technology,
  Veterinary Technology

Boulder County Campus
2190 Miller Dr., Longmont 80501
Phone: (303) 678-3722

Larimer Campus
4616 South Shields St., Fort Collins 80526
Phone: (970) 226-2500
Prog. Accred: Dental Assisting

Westminster Campus
3645 West 112th Ave., Westminster 80031
Phone: (303) 404-5550

Heritage College
12 Lakeside Ln., Denver 80212-7413
Type: Private, proprietary, two-year
Degrees: A
URL: http://www.heritage-education.com
Phone: (303) 477-7240
Inst. Accred.: ACCSCT (1989/2003)

Kansas City Campus
534 East 99th St., Kansas City, MO 64131-4203
Phone: (816) 942-5474

Iliff School of Theology
2201 South University Blvd., Denver 80210
Type: Private, United Methodist Church, four-year
Degrees: M, D   *Enroll:* 250
URL: http://www.iliff.edu
Phone: (303) 744-1287   *Calendar:* Qtr. plan
Inst. Accred.: ATS (1938/1998), NCA-HLC (1973/1998)

Institute of Business and Medical Careers
1609 Oakridge Dr., Ste. 102, Fort Collins 80525
Type: Private, proprietary, two-year
Degrees: A
URL: http://www.ibmc.edu
Phone: (970) 223-2669
Inst. Accred.: ACICS (1996/2000)

Cheyenne Campus
3425 Dell Range Blvd., Cheyenne, WY 82009
Phone: (307) 433-8363

Intellitec College—Colorado Springs
2315 East Pikes Peak Ave., Colorado Springs 80909-6030
Type: Private, proprietary, two-year
Degrees: A   *Enroll:* 427
URL: http://www.intelliteccollege.com
Phone: (719) 632-7626
Inst. Accred.: ACCSCT (1983/2000)

Emery Aviation College
1245A Aviation Way, Colorado Springs 80916-2714
Phone: (719) 591-9488

Intellitec College—Grand Junction
772 Horizon Dr., Grand Junction 81506
Type: Private, proprietary, two-year
Degrees: A   *Enroll:* 255
URL: http://www.intelliteccollege.com
Phone: (970) 245-8101
Inst. Accred.: ACCSCT (1986/2002)

Pueblo Campus
3673 Parker Blvd., Ste. 250, Pueblo 81008
Phone: (719) 542-3181

Intellitec Medical Institute
2345 North Academy Blvd., Colorado Springs 80909
Type: Private, proprietary, two-year
Degrees: A
URL: http://www.intelliteccollege.com
Phone: (719) 596-7400
Inst. Accred.: ABHES (1983/2005)
Prog. Accred.: Medical Assisting (ABHES), Medical
  Laboratory Technology, Surgical Technology

ITT Technical Institute
500 East 84th Ave., Thornton 80229
Type: Private, proprietary, four-year
System: ITT Educational Services, Inc.
Degrees: A, B   *Enroll:* 467
URL: http://www.itt-tech.edu
Phone: (303) 288-4488   *Calendar:* Qtr. plan
Inst. Accred.: ACICS (1999/2002)

Little Rock Campus
4520 South University Ave., Little Rock, AR 72204
Phone: (501) 565-5550

Liverpool Area Campus
235 Greenfield Pkwy., Liverpool, NY 13088
Phone: (315) 461-8000

Jones International University
9697 East Mineral Ave., Englewood 80112
Type: Private, independent, four-year
Degrees: B, M   *FTE Enroll:* 560
URL: http://www.jonesinternational.edu
Phone: (303) 784-8045
Inst. Accred.: NCA-HLC (1999/2001)

Lamar Community College
2401 South Main St., Lamar 81052
Type: Public, state/local, two-year
System: Colorado Community College System
Degrees: A　　　　　　　　*Enroll:* 701
URL: http://www.lcc.cccoes.edu
Phone: (719) 336-2248　　　　*Calendar:* Sem. plan
Inst. Accred.: NCA-HLC (1976/2000)

Mesa State College
1100 North Ave., Grand Junction 81501
Type: Public, state, four-year
System: Colorado Commission on Higher Education
Degrees: A, B, M　　　　　　*Enroll:* 4,879
URL: http://www.mesastate.edu
Phone: (970) 248-1020　　　　*Calendar:* Sem. plan
Inst. Accred.: NCA-HLC (1957/2004)
Prog. Accred.: Nursing, Nursing Education, Radiography

Metropolitan State College of Denver
PO Box 173362, Denver 80217-3362
Type: Public, state, four-year
System: Colorado Commission on Higher Education
Degrees: B　　　　　　　　*Enroll:* 15,198
URL: http://www.mscd.edu
Phone: (303) 556-2400　　　　*Calendar:* Sem. plan
Inst. Accred.: NCA-HLC (1971/1997)
Prog. Accred.: Art, Computer Science, Engineering
(surveying), Engineering Technology (civil/construction,
electrical, mechanical), Music, Nursing, Psychology
Internship, Recreation and Leisure Services, Social
Work, Teacher Education (NCATE)

Morgan Community College
920 Barlow Rd., Fort Morgan 80701
Type: Public, state, two-year
System: Colorado Community College System
Degrees: A　　　　　　　　*Enroll:* 758
URL: http://www.morgancc.edu
Phone: (970) 542-3100　　　　*Calendar:* Sem. plan
Inst. Accred.: NCA-HLC (1980/1996)
Prog. Accred.: Physical Therapy Assisting

The Naropa University
2130 Arapahoe Ave., Boulder 80302-6697
Type: Private, independent, four-year
Degrees: B, M　　　　　　　*Enroll:* 1,132
URL: http://www.naropa.edu
Phone: (303) 444-0202　　　　*Calendar:* Sem. plan
Inst. Accred.: NCA-HLC (1986/2001)

National Theatre Conservatory
1050 13th St., Denver 80204
Type: Private, independent, four-year
Degrees: M　　　　　　*FTE Enroll:* 23
URL: http://www.dcpa.org/page.cfm?id=23842027
Phone: (303) 446-4855　　　　*Calendar:* Sem. plan
Inst. Accred.: NCA-HLC (1992/2004)

Nazarene Bible College
1111 Academy Park Loop, Colorado Springs 80910-3704
Type: Private, Church of the Nazarene, four-year
Degrees: A, B　　　　　　　*Enroll:* 347
URL: http://www.nbc.edu
Phone: (719) 884-5000　　　　*Calendar:* Tri. plan
Inst. Accred.: ABHE (1976/1997)

Emmanuel Bible College
1605 East Elizabeth St., Pasadena, CA 91104
Phone: (626) 791-2575

Northeastern Junior College
100 College Dr., Sterling 80751
Type: Public, state/local, two-year
System: Colorado Community College System
Degrees: A　　　　　　　　*Enroll:* 1,671
Phone: (970) 522-6600　　　　*Calendar:* Sem. plan
Inst. Accred.: NCA-HLC (1964/1999)

Otero Junior College
1802 Colorado Ave., La Junta 81050
Type: Public, state, two-year
System: Colorado Community College System
Degrees: A　　　　　　　　*Enroll:* 1,155
URL: http://www.ojc.edu
Phone: (719) 384-8721　　　　*Calendar:* Sem. plan
Inst. Accred.: NCA-HLC (1967/1997)
Prog. Accred.: Nursing

Parks College
9065 Grant St., Denver 80229
Type: Private, proprietary, two-year
System: Corinthian Colleges, Inc
Degrees: A　　　　　　　　*Enroll:* 729
URL: http://www.parks-college.com
Phone: (303) 457-2757　　　　*Calendar:* Qtr. plan
Inst. Accred.: ACICS (1962/2001)
Prog. Accred.: Medical Assisting (CAAHEP)

Arlington Campus
801 North Quincy St., Ste. 500, Arlington, VA 22203
Phone: (703) 248-8887

Aurora Campus
14280 East Jewell Ave., Ste. 100, Aurora 80014
Phone: (303) 745-6244
Prog. Accred: Medical Assisting (CAAHEP)

McLean Campus
1430 Spring Hill Rd., Ste. 200, McLean, VA 22102
Phone: (703) 288-3131

Pikes Peak Community College
5675 South Academy Blvd., Colorado Springs 80906
Type: Public, state, two-year
System: Colorado Community College System
Degrees: A　　　　　　　　*Enroll:* 5,982
URL: http://www.ppcc.cccoes.edu
Phone: (800) 456-6847　　　　*Calendar:* Sem. plan
Inst. Accred.: NCA-HLC (1975/2004)
Prog. Accred.: Culinary Education, Dental Assisting

Platt College
3100 South Parker Rd., Ste. 200, Aurora 80014-3141
Type: Private, proprietary, four-year
Degrees: A, B   *Enroll:* 115
URL: http://www.plattcolorado.edu
Phone: (303) 369-5151
Inst. Accred.: ACCSCT (1986/2002)

Pueblo Community College
900 West Orman Ave., Pueblo 81004
Type: Public, state, two-year
System: Colorado Community College System
Degrees: A   *Enroll:* 3,396
URL: http://www.pcc.cccoes.edu
Phone: (719) 549-3200   *Calendar:* Sem. plan
Inst. Accred.: NCA-HLC (1979/2001)
Prog. Accred.: Culinary Education, Dental Assisting,
Dental Hygiene, Health Information Technician, Nursing,
Occupational Therapy Assisting, Ophthalmic Medical
Technology, Physical Therapy Assisting, Practical
Nursing, Respiratory Therapy, Surgical Technology

Red Rocks Community College
13300 West Sixth Ave., Lakewood 80228
Type: Public, state, two-year
System: Colorado Community College System
Degrees: A   *Enroll:* 4,087
URL: http://www.rrcc.edu
Phone: (303) 914-6600   *Calendar:* Sem. plan
Inst. Accred.: NCA-HLC (1975/1998)
Prog. Accred.: Medical Assisting (AMA), Physician
Assistant, Radiography

Regis University
3333 Regis Blvd., Denver 80221-1099
Type: Private, Roman Catholic Church, four-year
Degrees: B, M   *Enroll:* 7,839
URL: http://www.regis.edu
Phone: (303) 458-4100
Inst. Accred.: NCA-HLC (1922/2001)
Prog. Accred.: Health Information Administration, Nursing,
Nursing Education, Physical Therapy

Boulder Campus
6235 Lookout Rd., Ste. H, Boulder 80301
Phone: (303) 458-4100

Rocky Mountain College of Art and Design
1600 Pierce St., Lakewood 80214
Type: Private, proprietary, four-year
Degrees: B   *Enroll:* 380
URL: http://www.rmcad.edu
Phone: (800) 888-2787   *Calendar:* Tri. plan
Inst. Accred.: NCA-HLC (2000/2005)
Prog. Accred.: Art, Interior Design

Teikyo Loretto Heights University
3001 South Federal Blvd., Denver 80236
Type: Private, independent, four-year
Degrees: A, B   *Enroll:* 26
URL: http://www.tlhu.edu
Phone: (303) 937-4200   *Calendar:* Sem. plan
Inst. Accred.: ACICS (1995/2001)

Trinidad State Junior College
600 Prospect St., Trinidad 81082
Type: Public, state, two-year
System: Colorado Community College System
Degrees: A   *Enroll:* 1,309
URL: http://www.trinidadstate.edu
Phone: (719) 846-5011   *Calendar:* Sem. plan
Inst. Accred.: NCA-HLC (1962/2001)
Prog. Accred.: Applied Science (occupational health and
safety)

United States Air Force Academy
HQ USAFA/CC, 2304 Cadet Dr., Ste. 342, USAF Academy
80840-5001
Type: Public, federal, four-year
Degrees: B   *Enroll:* 4,149
URL: http://www.usafa.af.mil
Phone: (719) 333-3970   *Calendar:* Sem. plan
Inst. Accred.: NCA-HLC (1959/1999)
Prog. Accred.: Business (AACSB), Computer Science,
Engineering (aerospace, civil, computer, electrical,
engineering mechanics, environmental/sanitary,
mechanical)

University of Colorado at Boulder
17 UCB, Boulder 80309
Type: Public, state, four-year
System: University of Colorado Central Administration
Degrees: B, M, D   *Enroll:* 28,489
URL: http://www.colorado.edu
Phone: (303) 492-1411   *Calendar:* Sem. plan
Inst. Accred.: NCA-HLC (1913/2000)
Prog. Accred.: Audiology, Business (AACSB), Clinical
Psychology, Engineering (aerospace, architectural,
chemical, civil, electrical, environmental/sanitary,
mechanical), English Language Education, Journalism,
Law, Music, Psychology Internship, Speech-Language
Pathology, Teacher Education (NCATE)

University of Colorado at Colorado Springs
1420 Austin Bluffs Pkwy., PO Box 7150, Colorado Springs
80933-7150
Type: Public, state, four-year
System: University of Colorado Central Administration
Degrees: B, M, D   *Enroll:* 6,468
URL: http://www.uccs.edu
Phone: (719) 262-3000   *Calendar:* Sem. plan
Inst. Accred.: NCA-HLC (1970/1997)
Prog. Accred.: Business (AACSB), Computer Science,
Counseling, Engineering (computer, electrical,
mechanical), Nursing, Nursing Education, Public
Administration, Teacher Education (NCATE)

University of Colorado at Denver and Health Sciences Center
PO Box 173364, Denver 80217-3364
Type: Public, state, four-year
System: University of Colorado Central Administration
Degrees: B, M, P, D   *Enroll:* 10,194
URL: http://www.cudenver.edu
Phone: (303) 556-2400   *Calendar:* Sem. plan
Inst. Accred.: NCA-HLC (1970/2001)
Prog. Accred.: Accounting, Business (AACSB), Clinical
Pastoral Education, Computer Science, Counseling,
Dental Hygiene, Dentistry, Diagnostic Medical
Sonography, Engineering (civil, computer, electrical,
mechanical), General Practice Residency, Health
Services Administration, Landscape Architecture,
Medicine, Music, Nurse (Midwifery), Nursing, Nursing
Education, Orthodontic and Dentofacial Orthopedics,
Pharmacy, Physical Therapy, Physician Assistant,
Planning, Psychology Internship, Public Administration,
Public Health, Teacher Education (NCATE)

University of Denver
2199 South University Blvd., Denver 80208
Type: Private, United Methodist Church, four-year
Degrees: B, M, P, D   *Enroll:* 7,961
URL: http://www.du.edu
Phone: (303) 871-2000   *Calendar:* Qtr. plan
Inst. Accred.: NCA-HLC (1914/2001)
Prog. Accred.: Accounting, Art, Business (AACSB), Clinical
Psychology, Counseling Psychology, Engineering
(computer, electrical, general, mechanical), English
Language Education, Law, Librarianship, Music,
Psychology Internship, Social Work

University of Northern Colorado
Carter 4000, Campus Box 59, Greeley 80639
Type: Public, state, four-year
System: Colorado Commission on Higher Education
Degrees: B, M, P, D   *Enroll:* 11,552
URL: http://www.unco.edu
Phone: (970) 351-1890   *Calendar:* Sem. plan
Inst. Accred.: NCA-HLC (1916/2001)
Prog. Accred.: Accounting, Athletic Training, Audiology,
Business (AACSB), Counseling, Counseling Psychology,
Dietetics (internship), Music, Nursing, Nursing
Education, Public Health, Recreation and Leisure
Services, Rehabilitation Counseling, School Psychology,
Speech-Language Pathology, Teacher Education
(NCATE)

Western State College of Colorado
210 Taylor Hall, College Heights, Gunnison 81231
Type: Public, state, four-year
System: Colorado Commission on Higher Education
Degrees: B   *Enroll:* 2,282
URL: http://www.western.edu
Phone: (970) 943-2114   *Calendar:* Sem. plan
Inst. Accred.: NCA-HLC (1915/2003)
Prog. Accred.: Music, Teacher Education (TEAC)

Westwood College of Aviation Technology—Denver
10851 West 120th Ave., Broomfield 80021-3401
Type: Private, proprietary, two-year
Degrees: A   *Enroll:* 951
URL: http://www.westwood.edu
Phone: (303) 466-1714
Inst. Accred.: ACCSCT (1972/2000)

Westwood College—Denver North
7350 North Broadway, Denver 80221-3653
Type: Private, proprietary, four-year
Degrees: A, B   *Enroll:* 1,593
URL: http://www.westwood.edu
Phone: (303) 426-7000   *Calendar:* Qtr. plan
Inst. Accred.: ACCSCT (1968/2000)
Prog. Accred.: Medical Assisting (CAAHEP)

Anaheim Campus
1551 South Douglass Rd., Anaheim, CA 92806
Phone: (714) 704-2721

Houston South Campus
One Arena Place, 7322 Southwest Freeway, Houston, TX 77074
Phone: (713) 777-4433

Inland Empire Campus
20 West Seventh St., Upland, CA 91786-7148
Phone: (909) 931-7550

Westwood College—Denver South
3150 South Sheridan Blvd., Denver 80227-5548
Type: Private, proprietary, four-year
Degrees: A, B   *Enroll:* 347
URL: http://www.westwood.edu
Phone: (303) 934-2790   *Calendar:* Qtr. plan
Inst. Accred.: ACCSCT (1990/2000)

Yeshiva Toras Chaim Talmudical Seminary
1555 Stuart St., PO Box 4067, Denver 80204
Type: Private, independent, four-year
Degrees: B, M   *Enroll:* 18
Phone: (303) 629-8200   *Calendar:* Sem. plan
Inst. Accred.: AARTS (1979/2004)

CONNECTICUT

Albertus Magnus College
700 Prospect St., New Haven 06511-1189
Type: Private, Roman Catholic Church, four-year
Degrees: A, B, M   *Enroll:* 2,116
URL: http://www.albertus.edu
Phone: (203) 773-8550   *Calendar:* Sem. plan
Inst. Accred.: NEASC-CIHE (1932/2001)

Asnuntuck Community College
170 Elm St., Enfield 06082-3811
Type: Public, state, two-year
System: Board of Trustees of Connecticut Community-
Technical Colleges
Degrees: A   *Enroll:* 798
URL: http://www.acc.commnet.edu
Phone: (860) 253-3000   *Calendar:* Sem. plan
Inst. Accred.: NEASC-CIHE (1976/2005)

Bais Binyomin Academy
132 Prospect St., Stamford 06901
Type: Private, independent, four-year
Degrees: Talmudic   *FTE Enroll:* 54
Phone: (203) 325-4351   *Calendar:* Tri. plan
Inst. Accred.: AARTS (1978/2003)

Berkeley Divinity School
363 St. Ronan St., New Haven 06511
Type: Private, Episcopal Church, four-year
Degrees: M
URL: http://www.yale.edu/berkeleydivinity
Phone: (203) 764-9300   *Calendar:* Sem. plan
Inst. Accred.: ATS (1954/2001)

Briarwood College
2279 Mount Vernon Rd., Southington 06489-1057
Type: Private, proprietary, two-year
Degrees: A   *Enroll:* 468
URL: http://www.briarwood.edu
Phone: (860) 628-4751   *Calendar:* Sem. plan
Inst. Accred.: NEASC-CTCI (1982/2003)
Prog. Accred.: Dental Assisting, Funeral Service
Education (Mortuary Science), Health Information
Technician, Medical Assisting (AMA), Occupational
Therapy Assisting

Capital Community College
950 Main St., Hartford 06103
Type: Public, state, two-year
System: Board of Trustees of Connecticut Community-
Technical Colleges
Degrees: A   *Enroll:* 1,698
URL: http://www.ccc.commnet.edu
Phone: (860) 906-5000   *Calendar:* Sem. plan
Inst. Accred.: NEASC-CIHE (1975/1996)
Prog. Accred.: EMT (Paramedic), Medical Assisting (AMA),
Nursing, Radiography

Flatbush Campus
401 Flatbush Ave., Hartford 06106
Phone: (860) 527-4111

Central Connecticut State University
1615 Stanley St., New Britain 06050-4010
Type: Public, state, four-year
System: Connecticut State University System
Degrees: A, B, M, D   *Enroll:* 9,147
URL: http://www.ccsu.edu
Phone: (860) 832-3200   *Calendar:* Sem. plan
Inst. Accred.: NEASC-CIHE (1947/1998)
Prog. Accred.: Business (AACSB), Computer Science,
Construction Education, Engineering Technology
(civil/construction, manufacturing, mechanical),
Industrial Technology, Marriage and Family Therapy,
Music, Nurse Anesthesia Education, Nursing, Nursing
Education, Social Work, Teacher Education (NCATE)

Charter Oak State College
55 Paul J. Manafort Dr., New Britain 06053-2142
Type: Public, state, four-year
System: State of Connecticut Department of Higher
Education
Degrees: A, B   *Enroll:* 637
URL: http://www.cosc.edu
Phone: (860) 832-3800   *Calendar:* Sem. plan
Inst. Accred.: NEASC-CIHE (1981/1996)

Connecticut College
270 Mohegan Ave., New London 06320-4125
Type: Private, independent, four-year
Degrees: B, M   *Enroll:* 1,793
URL: http://www.connecticutcollege.edu
Phone: (860) 447-1911   *Calendar:* Sem. plan
Inst. Accred.: NEASC-CIHE (1932/1997)

Eastern Connecticut State University
83 Windham St., Willimantic 06226
Type: Public, state, four-year
System: Connecticut State University System
Degrees: A, B, M   *Enroll:* 4,245
URL: http://www.easternct.edu
Phone: (860) 465-5000   *Calendar:* Sem. plan
Inst. Accred.: NEASC-CIHE (1958/2000)
Prog. Accred.: Social Work

Fairfield University
1073 North Benson Rd., Fairfield 06824-5195
Type: Private, Society of Jesus, four-year
Degrees: B, M   *Enroll:* 4,168
URL: http://www.fairfield.edu
Phone: (203) 254-4000   *Calendar:* Sem. plan
Inst. Accred.: NEASC-CIHE (1953/1997)
Prog. Accred.: Business (AACSB), Counseling, Engineering
(electrical, mechanical), Marriage and Family Therapy,
Nursing, Nursing Education

Gateway Community College
60 Sargent Dr., New Haven 06511-5970
Type: Public, state/local, two-year
System: Board of Trustees of Connecticut Community-
Technical Colleges
Degrees: A   *Enroll:* 2,889
URL: http://www.gwctc.commnet.edu
Phone: (203) 285-2000   *Calendar:* Sem. plan
Inst. Accred.: NEASC-CIHE (1981/1996)
Prog. Accred.: Nuclear Medicine Technology, Radiation
Therapy, Radiography

North Haven Campus
88 Bassett Rd., North Haven 06473
Phone: (203) 285-2000
Prog. Accred: Engineering Technology (electrical,
mechanical), Nuclear Medicine Technology,
Radiography

Gibbs College
10 Norden Place, Norwalk 06855-1436
Type: Private, proprietary, two-year
System: Career Education Corporation
Degrees: A   *Enroll:* 1,032
URL: http://www.gibbsnorwalk.com
Phone: (203) 838-4173   *Calendar:* Sem. plan
Inst. Accred.: ACICS (1975/2001)

Farmington Campus
The Exchange, 270 Farmington Ave., Ste. 183,
Farmington 06032-1909
Phone: (860) 882-1690

Goodwin College
745 Burnside Ave., East Hartford 06108
Type: Private, independent, two-year
Degrees: A   *Enroll:* 435
URL: http://www.goodwincollege.org
Phone: (860) 528-4111
Inst. Accred.: ACICS (1983/2002), NEASC-CIHE (2004)
Prog. Accred.: Medical Assisting (ABHES), Medical
Assisting (CAAHEP)

Goodwin Institute
40 Commerce Park, Milford 06460
Phone: 203-877-9889

Stone Academy
101 Pierpont Rd., Waterbury 06705
Phone: (203) 756-5500

Hartford Seminary
77 Sherman St., Hartford 06105-2260
Type: Private, independent, four-year
Degrees: M, D   *Enroll:* 67
URL: http://www.hartsem.edu
Phone: (860) 509-9500   *Calendar:* Sem. plan
Inst. Accred.: ATS (1938/2003), NEASC-CIHE (1983/2003)

Holy Apostles College and Seminary
33 Prospect Hill Rd., Cromwell 06416
Type: Private, Roman Catholic Church, four-year
Degrees: A, B, M   *Enroll:* 136
URL: http://www.holyapostles.edu
Phone: (860) 632-3000   *Calendar:* Sem. plan
Inst. Accred.: NEASC-CIHE (1979/2005)

Housatonic Community College
900 Lafeyette Blvd., Bridgeport 06604-4704
Type: Public, state, two-year
System: Board of Trustees of Connecticut Community-
Technical Colleges
Degrees: A   *Enroll:* 2,482
URL: http://www.hctc.commnet.edu
Phone: (203) 332-5000   *Calendar:* Sem. plan
Inst. Accred.: NEASC-CIHE (1972/2002)
Prog. Accred.: Clinical Lab Technology, Occupational
Therapy Assisting

International College of Hospitality Management "Cesar Ritz"
1760 Mapleton Ave., Suffield 06078
Type: Private, proprietary, two-year
Degrees: A   *Enroll:* 45
URL: http://www.ichm.edu
Phone: (860) 668-3515
Inst. Accred.: NEASC-CTCI (1998)

Lyme Academy College of Fine Arts
84 Lyme St., Old Lyme 06371
Type: Private, independent, four-year
Degrees: B   *Enroll:* 97
URL: http://www.lymeacademy.edu
Phone: (860) 434-5232   *Calendar:* Sem. plan
Inst. Accred.: NEASC-CIHE (2001)
Prog. Accred.: Art

Manchester Community College
PO Box 1046, Manchester 06045-1046
Type: Public, state, two-year
System: Board of Trustees of Connecticut Community-
Technical Colleges
Degrees: A   *Enroll:* 3,406
URL: http://www.mcc.commnet.edu
Phone: (860) 512-3000   *Calendar:* Sem. plan
Inst. Accred.: NEASC-CIHE (1971/2002)
Prog. Accred.: Clinical Lab Technology, Culinary
Education, Occupational Therapy Assisting, Respiratory
Therapy, Surgical Technology

Middlesex Community College
100 Training Hill Rd., Middletown 06457
Type: Public, state, two-year
System: Board of Trustees of Connecticut Community-
Technical Colleges
Degrees: A   *Enroll:* 1,305
URL: http://www.mxctc.commnet.edu
Phone: (860) 343-5800   *Calendar:* Sem. plan
Inst. Accred.: NEASC-CIHE (1973/2002)
Prog. Accred.: Ophthalmic Lab Technology, Opticianry,
Radiography

Mitchell College
437 Pequot Ave., New London 06320
Type: Private, independent, four-year
Degrees: A, B *Enroll:* 675
URL: http://www.mitchell.edu
Phone: (860) 701-5000 *Calendar:* Sem. plan
Inst. Accred.: NEASC-CIHE (1956/2003)

Naugatuck Valley Community College
750 Chase Pkwy., Waterbury 06708-3089
Type: Public, state, two-year
System: Board of Trustees of Connecticut Community-
Technical Colleges
Degrees: A *Enroll:* 3,017
URL: http://www.nvcc.commnet.edu
Phone: (203) 575-8040 *Calendar:* Sem. plan
Inst. Accred.: NEASC-CIHE (1973/2002)
Prog. Accred.: Engineering Technology (automated
systems, electrical, mechanical, mechanical
drafting/design), Nursing, Physical Therapy Assisting,
Radiography

Northwestern Connecticut Community College
Park Place East, Winsted 06098-1798
Type: Public, state, two-year
System: Board of Trustees of Connecticut Community-
Technical Colleges
Degrees: A *Enroll:* 857
URL: http://www.nwctc.commnet.edu
Phone: (860) 738-6300 *Calendar:* Sem. plan
Inst. Accred.: NEASC-CIHE (1971/2003)
Prog. Accred.: Medical Assisting (AMA), Veterinary
Technology

Norwalk Community College
188 Richards Ave., Norwalk 06854-1655
Type: Public, state, two-year
System: Board of Trustees of Connecticut Community-
Technical Colleges
Degrees: A *Enroll:* 3,324
URL: http://www.ncc.commnet.edu
Phone: (203) 857-7000 *Calendar:* Sem. plan
Inst. Accred.: NEASC-CIHE (1973/2004)
Prog. Accred.: Nursing, Respiratory Therapy

Paier College of Art
20 Gorham Ave., Hamden 06517-4025
Type: Private, proprietary, four-year
Degrees: A, B *Enroll:* 221
URL: http://www.paierart.com
Phone: (203) 287-3031
Inst. Accred.: ACCSCT (1970/1999)

Post University
800 Country Club Rd., Waterbury 06723-2540
Type: Private, independent, four-year
Degrees: A, B *Enroll:* 957
URL: http://www.post.edu
Phone: (203) 596-4500 *Calendar:* Sem. plan
Inst. Accred.: NEASC-CIHE (1972/2005)

Quinebaug Valley Community College
742 Upper Maple St., Danielson 06239-1440
Type: Public, state, two-year
System: Board of Trustees of Connecticut Community-
Technical Colleges
Degrees: A *Enroll:* 866
URL: http://www.qvcc.commnet.edu
Phone: (860) 774-1160 *Calendar:* Sem. plan
Inst. Accred.: NEASC-CIHE (1978/2001)
Prog. Accred.: Medical Assisting (CAAHEP)

Quinnipiac University
Mt. Carmel Ave., Hamden 06518-1908
Type: Private, independent, four-year
Degrees: A, B, M, P, Talmudic *Enroll:* 6,529
URL: http://www.quinnipiac.edu
Phone: (203) 582-8200 *Calendar:* Sem. plan
Inst. Accred.: NEASC-CIHE (1958/1999)
Prog. Accred.: Business (AACSB), Clinical Lab Scientist,
Law, Nursing, Occupational Therapy, Pathologists'
Assistant, Perfusion, Physical Therapy, Physician
Assistant, Radiography, Respiratory Therapy, Veterinary
Technology

Rensselaer Polytechnic Institute at Hartford
275 Windsor St., Hartford 06120-2991
Type: Private, independent, four-year
Degrees: M *Enroll:* 399
URL: http://www.rh.edu
Phone: (860) 548-2400 *Calendar:* Sem. plan
Inst. Accred.: MSA-CHE (1955/2001, *Indirect*
accreditation through Rensselaer Polytechnic Institute,
Troy, NY)

Sacred Heart University
5151 Park Ave., Fairfield 06432-1000
Type: Private, Roman Catholic Church, four-year
Degrees: A, B, M, D *Enroll:* 4,403
URL: http://www.sacredheart.edu
Phone: (203) 371-7999 *Calendar:* Sem. plan
Inst. Accred.: NEASC-CIHE (1969/2003)
Prog. Accred.: Nursing, Nursing Education, Occupational
Therapy, Physical Therapy, Respiratory Therapy, Social
Work

Saint Joseph College
1678 Asylum Ave., West Hartford 06117-2791
Type: Private, independent, four-year
Degrees: B, M *Enroll:* 1,302
URL: http://www.sjc.edu
Phone: (860) 232-4571 *Calendar:* Sem. plan
Inst. Accred.: NEASC-CIHE (1938/1996)
Prog. Accred.: Dietetics (coordinated), Dietetics
(internship), Marriage and Family Therapy, Nursing,
Social Work

Saint Vincent's College
2800 Main St., Bridgeport 06606-4292
Type: Private, independent, two-year
Degrees: A   *Enroll:* 174
URL: http://www.stvincentscollege.edu
Phone: (203) 576-5513   *Calendar:* Sem. plan
Inst. Accred.: NEASC-CIHE (2004)
Prog. Accred.: Nursing, Radiography

Southern Connecticut State University
501 Crescent St., New Haven 06515-0901
Type: Public, state, four-year
System: Connecticut State University System
Degrees: A, B, M, D   *Enroll:* 9,120
URL: http://www.southernct.edu
Phone: (203) 392-5200   *Calendar:* Sem. plan
Inst. Accred.: NEASC-CIHE (1952/2001)
Prog. Accred.: Athletic Training, Audiology, Computer
   Science, Counseling, Librarianship, Marriage and Family
   Therapy, Nurse Anesthesia Education, Nursing, Nursing
   Education, Public Health, Social Work, Speech-
   Language Pathology

Three Rivers Community College
7 Mahan Dr., Norwich 06360-2479
Type: Public, state, two-year
System: Board of Trustees of Connecticut Community-
   Technical Colleges
Degrees: A   *Enroll:* 1,886
URL: http://www.trcc.commnet.edu
Phone: (860) 886-0177   *Calendar:* Sem. plan
Inst. Accred.: NEASC-CIHE (1973/2002)
Prog. Accred.: Business (ACBSP), Engineering Technology
   (civil/construction, electrical, environmental/sanitary,
   manufacturing, mechanical, nuclear), Nursing

Thames Valley Campus
574 New London Turnpike, Norwich 06360
Phone: (203) 886-0177

Trinity College
300 Summit St., Hartford 06106-3100
Type: Private, independent, four-year
Degrees: B, M   *Enroll:* 2,065
URL: http://www.trincoll.edu
Phone: (860) 297-2000   *Calendar:* Sem. plan
Inst. Accred.: NEASC-CIHE (1929/1996)
Prog. Accred.: Engineering (general)

Tunxis Community College
271 Scott Swamp Rd., Farmington 06032-3187
Type: Public, state, two-year
System: Board of Trustees of Connecticut Community-
   Technical Colleges
Degrees: A   *Enroll:* 2,244
URL: http://www.tunxis.commnet.edu
Phone: (860) 677-7701   *Calendar:* Sem. plan
Inst. Accred.: NEASC-CIHE (1975/2001)
Prog. Accred.: Dental Assisting, Dental Hygiene

United States Coast Guard Academy
15 Mohegan Ave., New London 06320-8100
Type: Public, federal, four-year
Degrees: B   *Enroll:* 983
URL: http://www.cga.edu
Phone: (860) 444-8444   *Calendar:* Sem. plan
Inst. Accred.: NEASC-CIHE (1952/2000)
Prog. Accred.: Engineering (civil, electrical, mechanical,
   naval architecture/marine)

University of Bridgeport
380 University Ave., Bridgeport 06601
Type: Private, independent, four-year
Degrees: A, B, M, D   *Enroll:* 2,483
URL: http://www.bridgeport.edu
Phone: (203) 576-4000   *Calendar:* Sem. plan
Inst. Accred.: NEASC-CIHE (1951/2004)
Prog. Accred.: Art, Business (ACBSP), Chiropractic
   Education, Dental Hygiene, Engineering (computer),
   Naturopathic Medicine

The University of Connecticut
Storrs 06269-2048
Type: Public, state, four-year
System: State of Connecticut Department of Higher Education
Degrees: B, M, P, D   *Enroll:* 19,758
URL: http://www.uconn.edu
Phone: (860) 486-2000   *Calendar:* Sem. plan
Inst. Accred.: NEASC-CIHE (1931/1996)
Prog. Accred.: Accounting, Art, Audiology, Business (AACSB), Clinical Psychology, Combined Prosthodontics, Computer Science, Cytogenetic Technology, Dietetics (coordinated), Dietetics (internship), Endodontics, Engineering (chemical, civil, computer, electrical, mechanical), English Language Education, General Dentistry, Journalism, Landscape Architecture, Law, Marriage and Family Therapy, Music, Nursing, Nursing Education, Oral and Maxillofacial Surgery, Orthodontic and Dentofacial Orthopedics, Pediatric Dentistry, Periodontics, Pharmacy, Physical Therapy, Public Administration, Public Health, Recreation and Leisure Services, School Psychology, Social Work, Speech-Language Pathology, Teacher Education (NCATE), Theatre

Avery Point Regional Campus
1084 Shennecossett Rd., Groton 06340
Phone: (860) 405-9019

Hartford Regional Campus
85 Lawler Rd., West Hartford 06117
Phone: (860) 570-9214

Stamford Regional Campus
One University Place, Stamford 06901-2315
Phone: (203) 251-8400

Torrington Regional Campus
855 University Dr., Torrington 06790
Phone: (860) 626-6800

The University of Connecticut Health Center
263 Farmington Ave., Farmington 06030
Phone: (860) 679-2000
Prog. Accred: Advanced Education in General Dentistry, Combined Prosthodontics, Cytotechnology, Dentistry, Endodontics, General Dentistry, Medicine, Oral and Maxillofacial Radiology, Oral and Maxillofacial Surgery, Orthodontic and Dentofacial Orthopedics, Pediatric Dentistry, Periodontics

Waterbury Regional Campus
32 Hillside Ave., Waterbury 06710-2288
Phone: (203) 236-9800

University of Hartford
200 Bloomfield Ave., West Hartford 06117
Type: Private, independent, four-year
Degrees: A, B, M, D   *Enroll:* 5,935
URL: http://www.hartford.edu
Phone: (860) 768-4100   *Calendar:* Sem. plan
Inst. Accred.: NEASC-CIHE (1961/2001)
Prog. Accred.: Art, Business (AACSB), Clinical Lab

Scientist, Clinical Psychology, Dance, Engineering (bioengineering, civil, computer, electrical, mechanical, metallurgical), Engineering Technology (architectural, electrical), Music, Nursing, Nursing Education, Physical Therapy, Public Administration, Radiography, Respiratory Therapy, Teacher Education (NCATE)

University of New Haven
300 Boston Post Rd., West Haven 06516
Type: Private, independent, four-year
Degrees: A, B, M, D   *Enroll:* 3,441
URL: http://www.newhaven.edu
Phone: (203) 932-7000   *Calendar:* Sem. plan
Inst. Accred.: NEASC-CIHE (1966/2000)
Prog. Accred.: Business (AACSB), Computer Science, Dental Hygiene, Engineering (chemical, civil, electrical, industrial, mechanical)

Wesleyan University
237 High St., Middletown 06457
Type: Private, independent, four-year
Degrees: B, M, D   *Enroll:* 3,024
URL: http://www.wesleyan.edu
Phone: (860) 685-2000   *Calendar:* Sem. plan
Inst. Accred.: NEASC-CIHE (1929/2002)

Western Connecticut State University
181 White St., Danbury 06810-9972
Type: Public, state, four-year
System: Connecticut State University System
Degrees: A, B, M, D   *Enroll:* 4,752
URL: http://www.wcsu.edu
Phone: (203) 837-8200   *Calendar:* Sem. plan
Inst. Accred.: NEASC-CIHE (1954/2003)
Prog. Accred.: Business (AACSB), Counseling, Music, Nursing, Social Work

Yale University
105 Wall St., New Haven 06520-8229
Type: Private, independent, four-year
Degrees: B, M, D   *Enroll:* 11,315
URL: http://www.yale.edu
Phone: (203) 432-4771   *Calendar:* Sem. plan
Inst. Accred.: NEASC-CIHE (1929/1999)
Prog. Accred.: Business (AACSB), Clinical Psychology, Engineering (chemical, electrical, mechanical), Forestry, Health Services Administration, Law, Medicine, Music, Nurse (Midwifery), Nursing, Nursing Education, Physician Assistant, Psychology Internship, Public Health

Yale University Divinity School
409 Prospect St., New Haven 06511-2167
Type: Private, interdenominational, four-year
Degrees: M
URL: http://www.yale.edu/divinity/index.html
Phone: (203) 432-5303   *Calendar:* Sem. plan
Inst. Accred.: ATS (1938/2003)

DELAWARE

Delaware State University
1200 North Dupont Hwy., Dover 19901
Type: Public, state, four-year
System: Delaware Higher Education Commission
Degrees: B, M, D　　　　　　　　　*Enroll:* 2,858
URL: http://www.desu.edu
Phone: (302) 857-6353　　　　*Calendar:* Sem. plan
Inst. Accred.: MSA-CHE (1945/2002)
Prog. Accred.: Business (AACSB), Montessori Teacher
　Education, Nursing, Nursing Education, Social Work,
　Teacher Education (NCATE)

Delaware Technical and Community College—Jack F. Owens Campus
PO Box 610, Georgetown 19947
Type: Public, state, two-year
System: Delaware Technical and Community College
　Office of the President
Degrees: A　　　　　　　　　　*Enroll:* 2,302
URL: http://www.dtcc.edu/owens
Phone: (302) 856-5400　　　　*Calendar:* Sem. plan
Inst. Accred.: MSA-CHE (1972/2003)
Prog. Accred.: Business (ACBSP), Clinical Lab Technology,
　Nursing, Occupational Therapy Assisting, Physical
　Therapy Assisting, Radiography, Respiratory Therapy

Delaware Technical and Community College—Stanton/Wilmington Campus
400 Stanton Christiana Rd., Newark 19713
Type: Public, state, two-year
System: Delaware Technical and Community College
　Office of the President
Degrees: A　　　　　　　　　　*Enroll:* 4,274
URL: http://www.dtcc.edu/stanton-wilmington
Phone: (302) 454-3900　　　　*Calendar:* Sem. plan
Inst. Accred.: MSA-CHE (1972/2003)
Prog. Accred.: Business (ACBSP), Dental Hygiene,
　Diagnostic Medical Sonography, EMT (Paramedic),
　Engineering Technology (electrical, mechanical),
　Histologic Technology, Medical Assisting (AMA), Nuclear
　Medicine Technology, Nursing, Occupational Therapy
　Assisting, Physical Therapy Assisting, Radiography,
　Respiratory Therapy

Delaware Technical and Community College—Terry Campus
100 Campus Dr., Dover 19901
Type: Public, state, two-year
System: Delaware Technical and Community College
　Office of the President
Degrees: A　　　　　　　　　　*Enroll:* 1,276
URL: http://www.dtcc.edu/terry
Phone: (302) 857-1000　　　　*Calendar:* Sem. plan
Inst. Accred.: MSA-CHE (1972/2003)
Prog. Accred.: Business (ACBSP), EMT (Paramedic),
　Nuclear Medicine Technology, Radiography

Goldey-Beacom College
4701 Limestone Rd., Wilmington 19809
Type: Private, independent, four-year
Degrees: A, B, M　　　　　　　　*Enroll:* 881
URL: http://www.gbc.edu
Phone: (302) 225-6248　　　　*Calendar:* Sem. plan
Inst. Accred.: MSA-CHE (1976/2001)
Prog. Accred.: Business (ACBSP)

University of Delaware
104 Hullihen Hall, Newark 19716
Type: Private, state, four-year
System: Delaware Higher Education Commission
Degrees: A, B, M, D　　　　　　*Enroll:* 19,086
URL: http://www.udel.edu
Phone: (302) 831-2000　　　　*Calendar:* 4-1-4 plan
Inst. Accred.: MSA-CHE (1921/2001)
Prog. Accred.: Accounting, Athletic Training, Business
　(AACSB), Clinical Lab Scientist, Clinical Psychology,
　Dietetics (internship), Engineering (chemical, civil,
　computer, electrical, environmental/sanitary,
　mechanical), Engineering Technology (agricultural,
　general), English Language Education, Music, Nursing,
　Physical Therapy, Psychology Internship, Public
　Administration, Teacher Education (NCATE)

Wesley College
120 North State St., Dover 19901-3875
Type: Private, United Methodist Church, four-year
Degrees: A, B, M　　　　　　　　*Enroll:* 1,894
URL: http://www.wesley.edu
Phone: (302) 736-2300　　　　*Calendar:* Sem. plan
Inst. Accred.: MSA-CHE (1950/1999)
Prog. Accred.: Nursing

Wilmington College
320 Dupont Hwy., New Castle 19720
Type: Private, independent, four-year
Degrees: A, B, M, D　　　　　　*Enroll:* 4,277
URL: http://www.wilmcoll.edu
Phone: (302) 328-9401　　　　*Calendar:* Tri. plan
Inst. Accred.: MSA-CHE (1975/2005)
Prog. Accred.: Counseling, Nursing, Nursing Education

DISTRICT OF COLUMBIA

American University
4400 Massachusetts Ave., NW, Washington 20016
Type: Private, United Methodist Church, four-year
Degrees: A, B, M, P, D　　　　　　　　*Enroll:* 9,330
URL: http://www.american.edu
Phone: (202) 885-1000　　　　*Calendar:* Sem. plan
Inst. Accred.: MSA-CHE (1928/2004)
Prog. Accred.: Business (AACSB), Clinical Psychology, Journalism, Law, Music, Psychology Internship, Public Administration, Teacher Education (NCATE)

The Catholic University of America
Cardinal Station, Washington 20064
Type: Private, Roman Catholic Church, four-year
Degrees: B, M, P, D　　　　　　　　*Enroll:* 4,677
URL: http://www.cua.edu
Phone: (202) 319-5000　　　　*Calendar:* Sem. plan
Inst. Accred.: ATS (1980/1995), MSA-CHE (1921/2005)
Prog. Accred.: Clinical Psychology, Engineering (bioengineering, civil, electrical, mechanical), Law, Librarianship, Music, Nursing, Social Work, Teacher Education (NCATE)

Corcoran College of Art and Design
500 17th St., NW, Washington 20006-4804
Type: Private, independent, four-year
Degrees: A, B, M　　　　　　　　*Enroll:* 453
URL: http://www.corcoran.edu
Phone: (202) 639-1800　　　　*Calendar:* Sem. plan
Inst. Accred.: MSA-CHE (1985/2003)
Prog. Accred.: Art

Georgetown Campus
1801 35th St., NW, Washington 20006
Phone: (202) 298-2540

Dominican House of Studies
487 Michigan Ave., NE, Washington 20017
Type: Private, Roman Catholic Church, four-year
Degrees: M, P　　　　　　　　*Enroll:* 55
URL: http://www.dhs.edu
Phone: (202) 529-5300　　　　*Calendar:* Sem. plan
Inst. Accred.: ATS (1976/2002), MSA-CHE (1976/2002)

Gallaudet University
800 Florida Ave., NE, Washington 20002
Type: Private, independent, four-year
Degrees: B, M, D　　　　　　　　*Enroll:* 1,496
URL: http://www.gallaudet.edu
Phone: (202) 651-5000　　　　*Calendar:* Sem. plan
Inst. Accred.: MSA-CHE (1957/2001)
Prog. Accred.: Audiology, Business (ACBSP), Clinical Psychology, Counseling, Psychology Internship, Recreation and Leisure Services, Social Work, Speech-Language Pathology, Teacher Education (NCATE)

George Washington University
2121 I St., NW, Washington 20052
Type: Private, independent, four-year
Degrees: A, B, M, P, D　　　　　　　　*Enroll:* 18,265
URL: http://www.gwu.edu
Phone: (202) 994-4949　　　　*Calendar:* Sem. plan
Inst. Accred.: MSA-CHE (1922/2003)
Prog. Accred.: Accounting, Athletic Training, Business (AACSB), Clinical Lab Scientist, Clinical Psychology, Computer Science, Counseling, Diagnostic Medical Sonography, Engineering (civil, computer, electrical, mechanical), Health Services Administration, Interior Design, Law, Medicine, Music, Physical Therapy, Physician Assistant, Psychology Internship, Public Administration, Public Health, Rehabilitation Counseling, Speech-Language Pathology, Teacher Education (NCATE)

Mount Vernon Campus
2100 Foxhall Rd., N.W., Washington 20007
Phone: (202) 625-0400
Prog. Accred: Interior Design

Georgetown University
37th and O St.s, NW, Washington 20057
Type: Private, Roman Catholic Church, four-year
Degrees: B, M, P, D　　　　　　　　*Enroll:* 12,341
URL: http://www.georgetown.edu
Phone: (202) 687-0100　　　　*Calendar:* Sem. plan
Inst. Accred.: MSA-CHE (1921/2002)
Prog. Accred.: Business (AACSB), Clinical Pastoral Education, English Language Education, Law, Medicine, Nurse (Midwifery), Nurse Anesthesia Education, Nursing, Nursing Education, Ophthalmic Medical Technology

Howard University
2400 Sixth St., NW, Washington 20059
Type: Private, independent, four-year
Degrees: B, M, P, D　　　　　　　　*Enroll:* 10,029
URL: http://www.howard.edu
Phone: (202) 806-2500　　　　*Calendar:* Sem. plan
Inst. Accred.: ATS (1940/2002), MSA-CHE (1921/1999)
Prog. Accred.: Accounting, Advanced Education in General Dentistry, Art, Audiology, Business (AACSB), Clinical Lab Scientist, Clinical Psychology, Computer Science, Counseling Psychology, Dental Hygiene, Dentistry, Dietetics (coordinated), Engineering (chemical, civil, electrical, mechanical), General Dentistry, General Practice Residency, Journalism, Law, Medicine, Music, Nursing, Nursing Education, Occupational Therapy, Oral and Maxillofacial Surgery, Orthodontic and Dentofacial Orthopedics, Pediatric Dentistry, Pharmacy, Physical Therapy, Physician Assistant, Psychology Internship, Radiation Therapy, Social Work, Speech-Language Pathology, Teacher Education (NCATE), Theatre

Joint Military Intelligence College
Defense Intell. Anlys. Ctr., 200 MacDill Blvd., Washington
20340-5100
Type: Public, federal, four-year
Degrees: B, M   *FTE Enroll:* 250
URL: http://www.dia.mil/jmic
Phone: (202) 231-3344   *Calendar:* Qtr. plan
Inst. Accred.: MSA-CHE (1983/2003)

National Defense University
Marshall Hall, Bldg. 62, Washington 20319-5066
Type: Public, federal, four-year
Degrees: M   *FTE Enroll:* 925
URL: http://www.ndu.edu
Phone: (202) 685-3912
Inst. Accred.: MSA-CHE (1997/2002)

Potomac College
4000 Chesapeake St., NW, Washington 20016
Type: Private, proprietary, four-year
Degrees: B   *Enroll:* 222
URL: http://www.potomac.edu
Phone: (202) 686-0876   *Calendar:* Sem. plan
Inst. Accred.: ACICS (1994/2003)

Northern Virginia Campus
1029 Herndon Pkwy., Herndon, VA 20170
Phone: (703) 709-5875

Southeastern University
501 I St., SW, Washington 20024-2788
Type: Private, independent, four-year
Degrees: A, B, M   *Enroll:* 588
URL: http://www.seu.edu
Phone: (202) 488-8162   *Calendar:* Qtr. plan
Inst. Accred.: MSA-CHE (1977/2001, Warning)

Strayer University
1025 15th St., NW, Washington 20005
Type: Private, proprietary, four-year
Degrees: A, B, M   *Enroll:* 10,960
URL: http://www.strayer.edu
Phone: (202) 408-2400   *Calendar:* Qtr. plan
Inst. Accred.: MSA-CHE (1981/2000)

Alexandria Campus
2730 Eisenhower Ave., Alexandria, VA 22314
Phone: (703) 329-9100

Anne Arundel Campus
1111 Berfield Blvd., Ste. 100, Millersville, MD 21108
Phone: (410) 923-4500

Arlington Campus
2121 15th St. North, Arlington, VA 22204
Phone: (703) 892-5100

Cary Campus
3200 Gateway Centre Blvd., Ste. 105, Morrsville, NC
27560
Phone: (919) 466-1150

Chamblee Campus
3355 Northeast Expressway, Ste. 100, Atlanta, GA
30341
Phone: (770) 454-9270

Chesapeake Campus
700 Independence Pkwy., Ste. 400, Chesapeake, VA
23320
Phone: (757) 382-9900

Chesterfield Campus
2820 Waterford Lake Dr., Ste. 100, Midlothian, VA
23112
Phone: (804) 763-6300

Cobb County Campus
3101 Towercreek Pkwy., Ste. 700, Atlanta, GA 30339
Phone: (770) 612-2170

Delaware County Campus
760 West Sproul Rd., Ste. 200, Springfield, PA 19064
Phone: (610) 543-2500

Fredericksburg Campus
4500 Plank Rd., Fredericksburg, VA 22407
Phone: (504) 785-8800

Greenville Campus
555 North Pleasantburg Dr., Ste. 300, Greenville, SC
29607
Phone: (864) 232-4700

Henrico Campus
11501-D Nuckols Rd., Glen Allen, VA 23059
Phone: (804) 527-1000

King of Prussia Campus
234 Mall Blvd., Ste. G50, King of Prussia, PA 19406
Phone: (610) 992-1700

Loudoun Campus
45150 Russell Branch Pkwy., Ste. 200, Ashburn, VA
20147
Phone: (703) 729-8800

Lower Bucks County Campus
3600 Horizon Blvd., Ste. 100, Trevose, PA 19053
Phone: (215) 953-5999

Manassas Campus
9990 Battleview Pkwy., Manassas, VA 20109
Phone: (703) 330-8400

Montgomery Campus
20030 Century Blvd., Ste. 300, Germantown, MD
20874
Phone: (301) 540-8066

Nashville Campus
30 Rachel Dr., Ste. 200, Nashville, TN 37214
Phone: (615) 871-2260

Strayer University *(continued)*

Newport News Campus
813 Diligence Dr., Ste. 100, Newport News, VA 23606
Phone: (757) 873-3100

North Charlotte Campus
83325 IBM Dr., Ste. 105, Charlotte, NC 28262
Phone: (704) 717-2380

North Raleigh Campus
3200 Spring Forest Rd., Ste. 3214, Raleigh, NC 27616
Phone: (919) 878-9900

Online Campus
8382-F Terminal Rd., Lorton, VA 22152
Phone: (703) 339-1850

Owings Mills Campus
500 Redland Ct., Ste. 100, Owings Mills, MD 21117
Phone: (443) 394-3339

Prince George's Campus
4710 Auth Place, 1st Flr., Suitland, MD 20746
Phone: (301) 423-3600

Shelby Oaks Campus
6211 Shelby Oaks Dr., Ste. 100, Memphis, TN 38134
Phone: (901) 383-6750

South Charlotte Campus
2430 Whitehall Park Dr., Ste. 700, Charlotte, NC 28273
Phone: (704) 587-5360

Takoma Park Campus
6830 Laurel St., NW, Washington 20012
Phone: (202) 722-8100

Thousand Oaks Campus
2620 Thousand Oaks Blvd., Ste. 1100, Memphis, TN 38118
Phone: (901) 369-0835

White Marsh Campus
9409 Philadelphia Rd., Baltimore, MD 21237
Phone: (410) 238-9000

Woodbridge Campus
13385 Minnieville Rd., Woodbridge, VA 22192
Phone: (703) 878-2800

Trinity University
125 Michigan Ave., NE, Washington 20017
Type: Private, Roman Catholic Church, four-year
Degrees: B, M   *Enroll:* 1,093
URL: http://www.trinitydc.edu
Phone: (202) 884-9000   *Calendar:* Sem. plan
Inst. Accred.: MSA-CHE (1921/2001)

University of the District of Columbia
4200 Connecticut Ave., NW, Washington 20008
Type: Public, state, four-year
Degrees: A, B, M, P   *Enroll:* 3,282
URL: http://www.udc.edu
Phone: (202) 274-5000   *Calendar:* Sem. plan
Inst. Accred.: MSA-CHE (1971/2005)
Prog. Accred.: Business (ACBSP), Engineering (civil, electrical, mechanical), Engineering Technology (architectural, civil/construction, electrical, electromechanical), Funeral Service Education (Mortuary Science), Law (ABA only), Nursing, Planning, Radiography, Respiratory Therapy, Social Work, Speech-Language Pathology

Washington Theological Union
6896 Laurel St., NW, Washington 20012-2016
Type: Private, Roman Catholic Church, four-year
Degrees: M, P   *Enroll:* 153
URL: http://www.wtu.edu
Phone: (202) 726-8800   *Calendar:* Sem. plan
Inst. Accred.: ATS (1973/1999), MSA-CHE (1973/1999)

Wesley Theological Seminary
4500 Massachusetts Ave., N.W., Washington 20016
Type: Private, United Methodist Church, four-year
Degrees: M, P, D   *Enroll:* 312
URL: http://www.wesleysem.edu
Phone: (202) 885-8600   *Calendar:* Sem. plan
Inst. Accred.: ATS (1940/2000), MSA-CHE (1975/2001)

FLORIDA

Academy for Five Element Acupuncture
1170-A East Hallendale Beach Blvd., Hallandale 33009
Type: Private, proprietary, four-year
Degrees: M
URL: http://www.acupuncturist.com
Phone: (954) 456-6336   *Calendar:* Tri. plan
Inst. Accred.: ACAOM (1998/2001)

Acupuncture and Massage College
10506 North Kendall Dr., Miami 33176
Type: Private, proprietary, four-year
Degrees: M
URL: http://www.amcollege.edu
Phone: (305) 595-9500
Inst. Accred.: ACCSCT (2003)
Prog. Accred.: Acupuncture

Angley College
230 North Woodland Blvd., Ste. 310, Deland 32720
Type: Private, proprietary, two-year
Degrees: A
URL: http://www.angley.edu
Phone: (386) 740-1215
Inst. Accred.: ACICS (2003)

Orlando Campus
3580 Aloma Ave., Ste. 5, Winter Park 32792
Phone: (407) 478-3700

Argosy University Tampa
Parkside at Tampa Bay Park, 4401 North Himes Ave., Ste. 150, Tampa 33614
Type: Private, proprietary, four-year
System: Argosy University
Degrees: M, D
URL: http://www.argosyu.edu
Phone: (813) 393-5290   *Calendar:* Tri. plan
Inst. Accred.: NCA-HLC (1981/2001, *Indirect accreditation through Argosy University, Chicago, IL*)
Prog. Accred.: Clinical Psychology

The Art Institute of Fort Lauderdale
1799 SE 17 St., Ft. Lauderdale 33316
Type: Private, proprietary, four-year
System: Education Management Corporation
Degrees: A, B   *Enroll:* 2,610
URL: http://www.aifl.edu
Phone: (954) 463-3000   *Calendar:* Qtr. plan
Inst. Accred.: ACICS (2000/2005)
Prog. Accred.: Culinary Education

ATI Career Training Center
2880 NW 62nd St., Fort Lauderdale 33309-9731
Type: Private, proprietary, two-year
Degrees: A   *Enroll:* 649
URL: http://www.aticareertraining.edu
Phone: (954) 973-4760   *Calendar:* Qtr. plan
Inst. Accred.: ACCSCT (1982/2001)

Miami Campus
One NE 19th St., Miami 33132
Phone: (305) 573-1600

ATI Career Training Center
3501 NW 9th Ave., Oakland Park 33309-5900
Type: Private, proprietary, two-year
Degrees: A   *Enroll:* 207
URL: http://www.aticareertraining.edu
Phone: (954) 563-5899   *Calendar:* Qtr. plan
Inst. Accred.: ACCSCT (1984/2002)

ATI College of Health
1395 NW 167th St., Ste. 200, Miami 33169-5745
Type: Private, proprietary, two-year
Degrees: A   *Enroll:* 313
URL: http://www.aticareertraining.edu
Phone: (305) 628-1000   *Calendar:* Qtr. plan
Inst. Accred.: ACCSCT (1979/2002)
Prog. Accred.: Respiratory Therapy, Respiratory Therapy Technology

Atlantic Institute of Oriental Medicine
100 East Broward Blvd., Ste. 100, Fort Lauderdale 33301
Type: Private, proprietary, four-year
Degrees: M
URL: http://www.atom.edu
Phone: (954) 763-9840
Inst. Accred.: ACAOM (1999/2002)

The Baptist College of Florida
5400 College Dr., Graceville 32440-1831
Type: Private, Southern Baptist Church, four-year
Degrees: A, B   *Enroll:* 517
URL: http://www.baptistcollege.edu
Phone: (850) 263-3261   *Calendar:* Sem. plan
Inst. Accred.: SACS (1981/1997)
Prog. Accred.: Music

Barry University
11300 NE Second Ave., Miami Shores 33161-6695
Type: Private, Roman Catholic Church, four-year
Degrees: B, M, P, D   *Enroll:* 7,072
URL: http://www.barry.edu
Phone: (305) 899-3000   *Calendar:* Sem. plan
Inst. Accred.: ATS (2004), SACS (1947/2003)
Prog. Accred.: Athletic Training, Business (AACSB),
  Counseling, Histologic Technology, Law (ABA only),
  Montessori Teacher Education, Nurse Anesthesia
  Education, Nursing, Nursing Education, Occupational
  Therapy, Perfusion, Physician Assistant, Podiatry, Social
  Work

South Campus
1650 Sandlake Rd., Ste. 111, Orlando 32809-9108
Phone: (407) 438-4150
Prog. Accred: Counseling

Bay Medical Center
615 North Bonita Ave., Panama City 32401
Type: Private, independent, four-year
Degrees: M   *Enroll:* 35
URL: http://www.baymedical.org/education/index.shtml
Phone: (904) 747-6051
Inst. Accred.: ABHES (2000)
Prog. Accred.: Nurse Anesthesia Education

Beacon College
105 East Main St., Leesburg 34748
Type: Private, independent, four-year
Degrees: A, B   *Enroll:* 82
URL: http://www.beaconcollege.edu
Phone: (352) 787-7660   *Calendar:* Sem. plan
Inst. Accred.: SACS (2003, Probation)

Bethune-Cookman College
640 Mary McLeod Bethune Blvd., Daytona Beach 32114-
3099
Type: Private, United Methodist Church, four-year
Degrees: B   *Enroll:* 2,687
URL: http://www.cookman.edu
Phone: (386) 481-2000   *Calendar:* Sem. plan
Inst. Accred.: SACS (1947/2000)
Prog. Accred.: Business (AACSB), Clinical Lab Scientist,
  Nursing, Teacher Education (NCATE)

Brevard Community College
1519 Clearlake Rd., Cocoa 32922-6597
Type: Public, state/local, two-year
System: Florida State Department of Education, Division
  of Community Colleges
Degrees: A   *Enroll:* 8,453
URL: http://www.brevardcc.edu
Phone: (321) 632-1111   *Calendar:* Sem. plan
Inst. Accred.: SACS (1965/2003)
Prog. Accred.: Clinical Lab Technology, Dental Assisting,
  Dental Hygiene, EMT (Paramedic), Medical Assisting
  (AMA), Radiography, Respiratory Therapy, Surgical
  Technology, Veterinary Technology

Broward Community College
111 East Las Olas Blvd., Fort Lauderdale 33301
Type: Public, local, two-year
System: Florida State Department of Education, Division
  of Community Colleges
Degrees: A   *Enroll:* 17,272
URL: http://www.broward.edu
Phone: (954) 201-6500   *Calendar:* Sem. plan
Inst. Accred.: SACS (1965/2003)
Prog. Accred.: Dental Assisting, Dental Hygiene,
  Diagnostic Medical Sonography, EMT (Paramedic),
  Health Information Technician, Medical Assisting (AMA),
  Music, Nuclear Medicine Technology, Nursing, Physical
  Therapy Assisting, Practical Nursing, Respiratory
  Therapy, Respiratory Therapy Technology

A. Hugh Adams Central Campus
3501 SW Davie Rd., Davie 33314
Phone: (954) 201-6500

Judson A. Samuels South Campus
7200 Pines Blvd., Pembroke Pines 33024
Phone: (954) 201-8835

North Campus
1000 Coconut Creek Blvd., Coconut Creek 33066
Phone: (954) 973-2240

Brown Mackie College—Miami
1501 Biscayne Blvd., Miami 33132
Type: Private, proprietary, two-year
System: Education Management Corporation
Degrees: A
URL: http://www.brownmackie.edu
Phone: (305) 341-6600   *Calendar:* Sem. plan
Inst. Accred.: ACICS (2005)

Carlos Albizu University—Miami Campus
2173 NW 99th Ave., Miami 33172
Type: Private, independent, four-year
System: Carlos Albizu—Central Administration
Degrees: B, M, D   *Enroll:* 700
URL: http://www.albizu.edu
Phone: (305) 593-1223   *Calendar:* Sem. plan
Inst. Accred.: MSA-CHE (1981/2005)
Prog. Accred.: Clinical Psychology

Central Florida Community College
PO Box 1388, 3001 SW College Rd., Ocala 34474-1388
Type: Public, state/local, two-year
System: Florida State Department of Education, Division
  of Community Colleges
Degrees: A   *Enroll:* 3,660
URL: http://www.cfcc.cc.fl.us
Phone: (352) 237-2111   *Calendar:* Sem. plan
Inst. Accred.: SACS (1964/1995)
Prog. Accred.: EMT (Paramedic), Nursing, Physical
  Therapy Assisting, Practical Nursing, Surgical
  Technology

Central Florida Institute, Inc.
30522 US Hwy. 19 North, Ste. 300, Palm Harbor 34684
Type: Private, proprietary, two-year
Degrees: A
URL: http://www.cfinstitute.com
Phone: (727) 786-4707
Inst. Accred.: ABHES (1999/2003)
Prog. Accred.: Surgical Technology

Orlando Campus
6000 Cinderlane Pkwy., Ste. 200, Orlando 32810
Phone: (407) 523-5354
Prog. Accred: Medical Assisting (ABHES)

Chipola College
3094 Indian Circle, Marianna 32446-2053
Type: Public, state/local, four-year
System: Florida State Department of Education, Division
of Community Colleges
Degrees: A, B   *Enroll:* 1,532
URL: http://www.chipola.edu
Phone: (850) 526-2761   *Calendar:* Sem. plan
Inst. Accred.: SACS (1957/1998, Probation)

City College
1401 West Cypress Creek Rd., Fort Lauderdale 33309
Type: Private, proprietary, four-year
Degrees: A, B   *Enroll:* 626
URL: http://www.citycollege.edu
Phone: (954) 492-5353   *Calendar:* Qtr. plan
Inst. Accred.: ACICS (1986/2002)

Gainesville Campus
2400 SW 13th St., Gainesville 32608
Phone: (352) 335-4000

Miami Campus
9300 South Dadeland Blvd., Ste. PH South, Miami
33156
Phone: (305) 666-9242

Clearwater Christian College
3400 Gulf-to-Bay Blvd., Clearwater 33759-4595
Type: Private, independent, four-year
Degrees: A, B   *Enroll:* 607
URL: http://www.clearwater.edu
Phone: (727) 726-1153   *Calendar:* Sem. plan
Inst. Accred.: SACS (1984/1999)

The College for Professional Studies
6409 Congress Ave., Ste. 100, Boca Raton 33487
Type: Private, proprietary (teach-out status), four-year
Degrees: A, B
URL: http://www.kaplancollege.edu
Phone: (561) 994-2522
Inst. Accred.: DETC (1993/2002)

College of Business and Technology
8991 SW 107 Ave., Ste. 200, Miami 33176
Type: Private, proprietary, two-year
Degrees: A
URL: http://www.cbt.edu
Phone: (305) 273-4499 ext 100   *Calendar:* Sem. plan
Inst. Accred.: ACICS (2003)

Flagler Campus
8230 West Flagler St., Miami 33144
Phone: (305) 273-4499 ext 200

Hialeah Campus
935 West 49 St., Hialeah 33012
Phone: (305) 273-4499 ext 300

Daytona Beach Community College
PO Box 2811, Daytona Beach 32120-2811
Type: Public, state/local, two-year
System: Florida State Department of Education, Division
of Community Colleges
Degrees: A   *Enroll:* 7,235
URL: http://www.dbcc.edu
Phone: (386) 255-8131   *Calendar:* Sem. plan
Inst. Accred.: SACS (1963/2003)
Prog. Accred.: Dental Assisting, Dental Hygiene, EMT
(Paramedic), Health Information Technician, Nursing,
Occupational Therapy Assisting, Physical Therapy
Assisting, Respiratory Therapy, Surgical Technology

DeVry University Orlando
4000 Millenia Blvd., Orlando 32839
Type: Private, proprietary, four-year
System: DeVry University
Degrees: A, B, M   *Enroll:* 1,728
URL: http://www.devry.edu/orlando
Phone: (407) 370-3131   *Calendar:* Sem. plan
Inst. Accred.: NCA-HLC (2002, *Indirect accreditation
through DeVry University, Oakbrook Terrace, IL*)

Miramar Campus
2300 Southwest 145th Ave., Miramar 33027-4150
Phone: (866) 793-3879

East West College of Natural Medicine
3808 North Tamiami Trail, Sarasota 34234
Type: Private, proprietary, four-year
Degrees: M
URL: http://www.ewcollege.org
Phone: (941) 355-9080   *Calendar:* Sem. plan
Inst. Accred.: ACAOM (1999/2004)

Eckerd College
4200 54th Ave. South, St. Petersburg 33711
Type: Private, Presbyterian Church (USA), four-year
Degrees: B   *Enroll:* 1,616
URL: http://www.eckerd.edu
Phone: (727) 867-1166   *Calendar:* 4-1-4 plan
Inst. Accred.: SACS (1966/2000)
Prog. Accred.: Liberal Education

Edison College
8099 College Pkwy., SW, PO Box 60210, Fort Myers
33906-6210
Type: Public, state/local, four-year
System: Florida State Department of Education, Division
of Community Colleges
Degrees: A, B   *Enroll:* 6,100
URL: http://www.edison.edu
Phone: (941) 489-9300   *Calendar:* Sem. plan
Inst. Accred.: SACS (1966/2001)
Prog. Accred.: Cardiovascular Technology, Dental
Assisting, Dental Hygiene, EMT (Paramedic), Nursing,
Radiography, Respiratory Therapy

Edward Waters College
1658 Kings Rd., Jacksonville 32209
Type: Private, African Methodist Episcopal Church, four-
year
Degrees: B   *Enroll:* 1,271
URL: http://www.ewc.edu
Phone: (904) 470-8000   *Calendar:* Sem. plan
Inst. Accred.: SACS (1979/2005, Warning)

Embry-Riddle Aeronautical University
600 South Clyde Morris Blvd., Daytona Beach 32114
Type: Private, independent, four-year
Degrees: A, B, M   *Enroll:* 4,532
URL: http://www.embryriddle.edu
Phone: (386) 226-6000   *Calendar:* Sem. plan
Inst. Accred.: SACS (1968/2002)
Prog. Accred.: Business (ACBSP), Engineering (aerospace,
civil, computer, engineering physics/science),
Engineering Technology (aerospace)

Arizona Campus
3200 North Willow Creek Rd., Prescott, AZ 86301
Phone: (904) 226-6000
Prog. Accred: Engineering (aerospace, computer,
electrical)

Extended Campus
600 South Clyde Morris Blvd., Daytona Beach 32114
Phone: (800) 522-6787

Everglades University
5002 T-REX Ave., Ste. 100, Boca Raton 33431
Type: Private, independent, four-year
Degrees: A, B   *Enroll:* 325
URL: http://www.evergladesuniversity.edu
Phone: (561) 912-1211   *Calendar:* Trl. plan
Inst. Accred.: ACCSCT (1993/2000)

Sarasota Campus
6151 Lake Osprey Dr., Sarasota 34240
Phone: (941) 907-2262

Flagler College
PO Box 1027, 74 King St., St. Augustine 32085-1027
Type: Private, independent, four-year
Degrees: B   *Enroll:* 2,005
URL: http://www.flagler.edu
Phone: (904) 829-6481   *Calendar:* Sem. plan
Inst. Accred.: SACS (1973/1998)

Florida Agricultural and Mechanical University
South Martin Luther King Blvd., Tallahassee 32307-3100
Type: Public, state, four-year
System: Florida Board of Education, Division of Colleges
and Universities
Degrees: B, M, P, D   *Enroll:* 12,034
URL: http://www.famu.edu
Phone: (850) 599-3000   *Calendar:* Sem. plan
Inst. Accred.: SACS (1935/1998)
Prog. Accred.: Computer Science, Engineering
(agricultural), Engineering Technology
(civil/construction, electrical), Health Information
Administration, Journalism, Law (ABA only), Nursing,
Occupational Therapy, Pharmacy, Physical Therapy,
Public Health, Respiratory Therapy, Social Work,
Teacher Education (NCATE)

Florida Atlantic University
777 Glades Rd., Boca Raton 33431-0991
Type: Public, state, four-year
System: Florida Board of Education, Division of Colleges
and Universities
Degrees: B, M, D   *Enroll:* 17,275
URL: http://www.fau.edu
Phone: (561) 297-3000   *Calendar:* Sem. plan
Inst. Accred.: SACS (1967/2002)
Prog. Accred.: Business (AACSB), Clinical Lab Scientist,
Computer Science, Engineering (civil, computer,
electrical, mechanical, ocean), Music, Nursing,
Planning, Public Administration, Social Work, Speech-
Language Pathology, Teacher Education (NCATE)

Florida Career College
1321 SW 107 Ave., Ste. 201B, Miami 33174-2521
Type: Private, proprietary, two-year
Degrees: A
URL: http://www.careercollege.edu
Phone: (305) 553-6065   *Calendar:* Qtr. plan
Inst. Accred.: ACICS (1985/2003)

Hialeah Campus
3750 West 18th Ave., Hialeah 33012
Phone: (305) 825-3231

Pembroke Pines Campus
7891 Pines Blvd., Pembroke Pines 33024-6916
Phone: (954) 965-7272

West Palm Beach Campus
6058 Okeechobee Blvd., West Palm Beach 33417-
4326
Phone: (561) 689-0550

Florida Christian College
1011 Bill Beck Blvd., Kissimmee 34744-5301
Type: Private, Christian Churches/Churches of Christ,
four-year
Degrees: A, B   *Enroll:* 230
URL: http://www.fcc.edu
Phone: (407) 847-8966   *Calendar:* Sem. plan
Inst. Accred.: ABHE (1985/1996), SACS (1995/2000)

Florida Coastal School of Law
7555 Beach Blvd., Jacksonville 32216
Type: Private, independent, four-year
Degrees: P
URL: http://www.fcsl.edu
Phone: (904) 680-7700 *Calendar:* Sem. plan
Inst. Accred.: ABA (2002)

Florida College
119 North Glen Arven Ave., Temple Terrace 33617
Type: Private, independent, four-year
Degrees: A, B *Enroll:* 472
URL: http://www.flcoll.edu
Phone: (813) 988-5131 *Calendar:* Sem. plan
Inst. Accred.: SACS (1954/1997)

Florida College of Natural Health
2001 West Sample Rd., Ste. 100, Pompano Beach 33064
Type: Private, proprietary, two-year
System: Steiner Education Group
Degrees: A *Enroll:* 265
URL: http://www.fcnh.com
Phone: (954) 975-6400
Inst. Accred.: ACCSCT (1990/2004)
Prog. Accred.: Massage Therapy

Miami Campus
7925 Northwest 12th St., Ste. 201, Miami 33126
Phone: (305) 597-9599
Prog. Accred: Massage Therapy

Orlando Campus
2600 Lake Lucien Dr., Ste. 140, Maitland 32751
Phone: (407) 261-0319
Prog. Accred: Massage Therapy

Sarasota Campus
616 67th St. Circle East, Bradenton 34208
Phone: (941) 744-1244
Prog. Accred: Massage Therapy

Florida Community College at Jacksonville
501 West State St., Jacksonville 32202-4030
Type: Public, state/local, two-year
System: Florida State Department of Education, Division of Community Colleges
Degrees: A *Enroll:* 13,717
URL: http://www.fccj.edu
Phone: (904) 633-8218 *Calendar:* Sem. plan
Inst. Accred.: SACS (1969/2004)
Prog. Accred.: Business (ACBSP), Clinical Lab Technology, Culinary Education, Dental Hygiene, EMT (Paramedic), Funeral Service Education (Mortuary Science), Health Information Technician, Histologic Technology, Nursing, Physical Therapy Assisting, Respiratory Therapy

Florida Gulf Coast University
10501 FGCU Blvd., South, Fort Myers 33965-6565
Type: Public, state, four-year
System: Florida Board of Education, Division of Colleges and Universities
Degrees: B, M *Enroll:* 4,529
URL: http://www.fgcu.edu
Phone: (239) 590-1000 *Calendar:* Sem. plan
Inst. Accred.: SACS (1999)
Prog. Accred.: Business (AACSB), Clinical Lab Scientist, Nurse Anesthesia Education, Nursing Education, Occupational Therapy, Physical Therapy, Social Work

Florida Hospital College of Health Sciences
800 Lake Estelle Dr., Orlando 32803
Type: Private, Seventh-Day Adventist Church, four-year
Degrees: A, B *Enroll:* 921
URL: http://www.fhchc.edu
Phone: (407) 303-7747 *Calendar:* Sem. plan
Inst. Accred.: SACS (1996/2001)
Prog. Accred.: Clinical Lab Scientist, Clinical Pastoral Education, Diagnostic Medical Sonography, Nursing, Occupational Therapy Assisting, Phlebotomy, Radiography

Florida Institute of Technology
150 West University Blvd., Melbourne 32901-6975
Type: Private, independent, four-year
Degrees: A, B, M, P, D *Enroll:* 3,543
URL: http://www.fit.edu
Phone: (321) 674-8000 *Calendar:* Sem. plan
Inst. Accred.: SACS (1964/2005)
Prog. Accred.: Clinical Psychology, Computer Science, Engineering (aerospace, chemical, civil, computer, electrical, mechanical, ocean)

Florida International University
11200 SW 8th St., University Park, Miami 33199-0001
Type: Public, state, four-year
System: Florida Board of Education, Division of Colleges and Universities
Degrees: A, B, M, P, D *Enroll:* 24,569
URL: http://www.fiu.edu
Phone: (305) 348-2000 *Calendar:* Sem. plan
Inst. Accred.: SACS (1974/2000)
Prog. Accred.: Accounting, Art, Business (AACSB), Computer Science, Construction Education, Counseling, Dietetics (coordinated), Dietetics (internship), Engineering (civil, computer, electrical, industrial, mechanical), Health Information Administration, Health Services Administration, Journalism, Landscape Architecture, Law (ABA only), Music, Nursing, Occupational Therapy, Physical Therapy, Public Administration, Public Health, Recreation and Leisure Services, Social Work, Speech-Language Pathology, Teacher Education (NCATE), Theatre

Florida Keys Community College
5901 West College Rd., Key West 33040-4397
Type: Public, state/local, two-year
System: Florida State Department of Education, Division of Community Colleges
Degrees: A   *Enroll:* 616
URL: http://www.firn.edu/fkcc
Phone: (305) 296-9081   *Calendar:* Sem. plan
Inst. Accred.: SACS (1968/2002, Warning)

Florida Memorial University
15800 NW 42nd Ave., Miami 33054
Type: Private, independent, four-year
Degrees: B, M   *Enroll:* 2,056
URL: http://www.fmuniv.edu
Phone: (305) 626-3600   *Calendar:* Sem. plan
Inst. Accred.: SACS (1951/2002)
Prog. Accred.: Business (ACBSP)

Florida Metropolitan University—Orange Park
805 Wells Rd., Orange Park 32073
Type: Private, independent, four-year
System: Florida Metropolitan University System
Degrees: A, B
URL: http://fmu.edu
Phone: (904) 264-9122
Inst. Accred.: ACICS (2003)

Florida Metropolitan University—Orlando North
5421 Diplomat Circle, Orlando 32810
Type: Private, indeppendent, four-year
System: Florida Metropolitan University System
Degrees: A, B, M   *Enroll:* 1,156
URL: http://fmu.edu
Phone: (407) 628-5870   *Calendar:* Qtr. plan
Inst. Accred.: ACICS (1957/2001)

Melbourne Campus
2401 North Harbor City Blvd., Melbourne 32935
Phone: (407) 253-2929
Prog. Accred: Medical Assisting (CAAHEP)

South Orlando Campus
9200 South Park Center Loop, Orlando 32819
Phone: (407) 851-2525
Prog. Accred: Medical Assisting (CAAHEP)

Florida Metropolitan University—Pinellas
2471 McMullen Booth Rd., Ste. 200, Clearwater 33759
Type: Private, independent, four-year
System: Florida Metropolitan University System
Degrees: A, B, M   *FTE Enroll:* 145
URL: http://fmu.edu
Phone: (727) 725-2688   *Calendar:* Qtr. plan
Inst. Accred.: ACICS (1971/1999)
Prog. Accred.: Medical Assisting (CAAHEP)

Jacksonville Campus
8226 Phillips Hwy., Jacksonville 32256
Phone: (904) 731-4949

Lakeland Campus
995 East Memorial Blvd., Ste. 110, Lakeland 33801-1919
Phone: (941) 686-1444

Florida Metropolitan University—Pompano Beach
225 North Federal Hwy., Pompano Beach 33062
Type: Private, independent, four-year
System: Florida Metropolitan University System
Degrees: A, B, M   *Enroll:* 1,213
URL: http://fmu.edu
Phone: (954) 783-7339   *Calendar:* Qtr. plan
Inst. Accred.: ACICS (1968/2003)

Florida Metropolitan University—Tampa
3319 West Hillsborough Ave., Tampa 33614
Type: Private, independent, four-year
System: Florida Metropolitan University System
Degrees: A, B, M   *Enroll:* 1,311
URL: http://fmu.edu
Phone: (813) 879-6000   *Calendar:* Qtr. plan
Inst. Accred.: ACICS (1966/2001)
Prog. Accred.: Medical Assisting (CAAHEP)

Brandon Campus
3924 Coconut Palm Dr., Tampa 33619
Phone: (813) 621-0041
Prog. Accred: Medical Assisting (CAAHEP)

Florida National College
4162 West 12th Ave., Hialeah 33012
Type: Private, proprietary, two-year
Degrees: A   *Enroll:* 1,298
URL: http://www.fnc.edu
Phone: (305) 821-3333   *Calendar:* 3-3 plan
Inst. Accred.: SACS (1997/2002)

Bird Road Campus
5761 SW Bird Rd., Miami 33155
Phone: (305) 663-6464

Flagler Campus
11865 SW 26th St., Unit 3, Miami 33175
Phone: (305) 226-9999 x3

Florida Southern College
111 Lake Hollingsworth Dr., Lakeland 33801-5698
Type: Private, United Methodist Church, four-year
Degrees: B, M   *Enroll:* 2,051
URL: http://www.flsouthern.edu
Phone: (863) 680-4111   *Calendar:* Sem. plan
Inst. Accred.: SACS (1935/1998)
Prog. Accred.: Nursing Education

Florida State University
Tallahassee 32306
Type: Public, state, four-year
System: Florida Board of Education, Division of Colleges
and Universities
Degrees: A, B, M, P, D   *Enroll:* 33,102
URL: http://www.fsu.edu
Phone: (850) 644-2525   *Calendar:* Sem. plan
Inst. Accred.: SACS (1915/2004)
Prog. Accred.: Accounting, Art, Business (AACSB), Clinical
Psychology, Combined Professional-Scientific
Psychology, Computer Science, Counseling, Dance,
Dietetics (internship), Engineering (chemical, civil,
computer, electrical, industrial, mechanical), Family and
Consumer Science, Interior Design, Law, Librarianship,
Marriage and Family Therapy, Medicine, Music,
Nursing, Nursing Education, Planning, Psychology
Internship, Public Administration, Recreation and
Leisure Services, Rehabilitation Counseling, Social
Work, Speech-Language Pathology, Teacher Education
(NCATE), Theatre

Florida Technical College
8711 Lone Star Rd., Jacksonville 32211
Type: Private, proprietary, two-year
Degrees: A   *Enroll:* 174
URL: http://www.flatech.edu
Phone: (904) 724-2229   *Calendar:* Qtr. plan
Inst. Accred.: ACICS (1988/2004)

Florida Technical College
1819 North Semoran Blvd., Orlando 32807
Type: Private, proprietary, two-year
Degrees: A   *Enroll:* 669
URL: http://www.flatech.edu
Phone: (407) 678-5600   *Calendar:* Qtr. plan
Inst. Accred.: ACICS (1982/2004)

Auburndale Campus
298 Havendale Blvd., Ste. 109, Auburndale 33823
Phone: (863) 967-8822

Deland Campus
1199 South Woodland Blvd., Deland 32720-7415
Phone: (386) 734-3303

Full Sail Real World Education
3300 University Blvd., Winter Park 32792-7429
Type: Private, proprietary, two-year
Degrees: A   *Enroll:* 4,328
URL: http://www.fullsail.com
Phone: (407) 679-0100
Inst. Accred.: ACCSCT (1986/2003)

Gulf Coast College
3910 U.S. Hwy. 301 North, Ste. 200, Tampa 33619-1290
Type: Private, proprietary, two-year
Degrees: A   *Enroll:* 133
URL: http://www.gulfcoastcollege.com
Phone: (813) 620-1446   *Calendar:* Qtr. plan
Inst. Accred.: ACICS (1996/2004)

Gulf Coast Community College
5230 West U.S. Hwy. 98, Panama City 32401-1058
Type: Public, state-related, two-year
System: Florida State Department of Education, Division
of Community Colleges
Degrees: A   *Enroll:* 3,527
URL: http://www.gulfcoast.edu
Phone: (850) 769-1551   *Calendar:* Sem. plan
Inst. Accred.: SACS (1962/2000)
Prog. Accred.: Culinary Education, Dental Assisting,
Dental Hygiene, EMT (Paramedic), Nursing, Physical
Therapy Assisting, Radiography

High-Tech Institute—Orlando
3710 Maguire Blvd., Orlando 32803
Type: Private, proprietary, two-year
System: High-Tech Institute
Degrees: A
URL: http://www.hightechinstitute.edu
Phone: (407) 893-7400
Inst. Accred.: ACCSCT (1998/2003)

Hillsborough Community College
PO Box 30030, Tampa 33630-3030
Type: Public, state, two-year
System: Florida State Department of Education, Division
of Community Colleges
Degrees: A   *Enroll:* 12,042
URL: http://www.hccfl.edu
Phone: (813) 253-7000   *Calendar:* Sem. plan
Inst. Accred.: SACS (1971/1996)
Prog. Accred.: Culinary Education, Dental Assisting,
Diagnostic Medical Sonography, EMT (Paramedic),
Nuclear Medicine Technology, Nursing, Ophthalmic Lab
Technology, Opticianry, Radiation Therapy, Radiography,
Respiratory Therapy

Hobe Sound Bible College
11298 SE Gomez Ave., Hobe Sound 33475
Type: Private, independent, four-year
Degrees: A, B   *Enroll:* 112
URL: http://www.hsbc.edu
Phone: (772) 546-5534   *Calendar:* Sem. plan
Inst. Accred.: ABHE (1986/1997)

IMPAC University
900 West Marion Ave., Punta Gorda 33950
Type: Private, proprietary, four-year
Degrees: M
URL: http://www.impacu.edu
Phone: (941) 639-7512
Inst. Accred.: DETC (2004)

Indian River Community College
3209 Virginia Ave., Fort Pierce 34981-5596
Type: Public, local, two-year
System: Florida State Department of Education, Division
of Community Colleges
Degrees: A *Enroll:* 7,288
URL: http://www.ircc.edu
Phone: (772) 462-4700 *Calendar:* Sem. plan
Inst. Accred.: SACS (1965/2003)
Prog. Accred.: Clinical Lab Technology, Dental Assisting,
Dental Hygiene, Dental Laboratory Technology, EMT
(Paramedic), Medical Assisting (AMA), Nursing, Physical
Therapy Assisting, Radiography, Respiratory Therapy

International Academy of Design and Technology
5225 Memorial Hwy., Tampa 33634-7350
Type: Private, proprietary, four-year
System: Career Education Corporation
Degrees: A, B *Enroll:* 1,799
URL: http://www.academy.edu
Phone: (813) 881-0007
Inst. Accred.: ACICS (1990/2005)
Prog. Accred.: Interior Design

Orlando Campus
5959 Lake Ellenor Dr., Orlando 32809
Phone: (407) 857-2300

International College
2655 Northbrooke Dr., Naples 34119-7932
Type: Private, independent, four-year
Degrees: A, B, M *Enroll:* 1,198
URL: http://www.internationalcollege.edu
Phone: (239) 513-1122 *Calendar:* Tri. plan
Inst. Accred.: SACS (1998/2003)
Prog. Accred.: Health Information Technician

Fort Myers Campus
Ste. 120, 8695 College Pkwy., Fort Myers 33919
Phone: (941) 482-0019
Prog. Accred.: Health Information Technician, Medical
Assisting (CAAHEP)

ITT Technical Institute
1400 South International Pkwy., Lake Mary 32746
Type: Private, proprietary, four-year
System: ITT Educational Services, Inc.
Degrees: A, B *Enroll:* 406
URL: http://www.itt-tech.edu
Phone: (407) 660-2900 *Calendar:* Qtr. plan
Inst. Accred.: ACICS (1999/2004)

ITT Technical Institute
4809 Memorial Hwy., Tampa 33634-7350
Type: Private, proprietary, four-year
System: ITT Educational Services, Inc.
Degrees: A, B *Enroll:* 546
URL: http://www.itt-tech.edu
Phone: (813) 885-2244 *Calendar:* Qtr. plan
Inst. Accred.: ACICS (1999/2004)

Bensalem Area Campus
3330 Tillman Dr., Bensalem, PA 19020
Phone: (215) 244-8871

Duluth Area Campus
10700 Abbotts Bridge Rd., Ste. 190, Duluth, GA 30097
Phone: (678) 957-8510

Jacksonville Campus
6600 Youngerman Circle, Ste. 10, Jacksonville 32244
Phone: (904) 573-9100

Kennesaw Campus
1000 Cobb Place Blvd., NW, Kennesaw, GA 30144-
3685
Phone: (770) 426-2300

Miami Campus
7955 NW 12th St., Ste. 119, Miami 33126
Phone: (305) 477-3080

Richmond Campus
300 Gateway Centre Pkwy., Richmond, VA 23235
Phone: (804) 330-4992

Springfield Campus
7300 Boston Blvd., Springfield, VA 22153
Phone: (703) 440-9535

Jacksonville University
2800 University Blvd. North, Jacksonville 32211
Type: Private, independent, four-year
Degrees: B, M *Enroll:* 2,416
URL: http://www.ju.edu
Phone: (904) 256-8000 *Calendar:* Sem. plan
Inst. Accred.: SACS (1950/2003)
Prog. Accred.: Dance, Music, Nursing, Orthodontic and
Dentofacial Orthopedics

Jones College
5353 Arlington Expressway, Jacksonville 32211-5588
Type: Private, independent, four-year
Degrees: A, B *Enroll:* 408
URL: http://www.jones.edu
Phone: (904) 743-1122 *Calendar:* Sem. plan
Inst. Accred.: ACICS (1957/2002)

Miami Campus
11430 North Kendall Dr., Ste. 200, Miami 33176
Phone: (305) 275-9996

West Campus
1195 Edgewood Ave., South, Jacksonville 32205
Phone: (904) 743-1122

Keiser Career College
6812 Forest Hill Blvd., Ste. D-1, Greenacres 33413
Type: Private, proprietary, two-year
Degrees: A
URL: http://www.keisercareer.edu
Phone: (561) 433-2330   *Calendar:* Sem. plan
Inst. Accred.: ACCSCT (2003)
Prog. Accred.: Medical Assisting (ABHES)

Miami Lakes Campus
17395 NW 57th Ave., Miami Lakes 33015
Phone: (305) 820-5003
Prog. Accred.: Medical Assisting (ABHES)

St. Petersburg Campus
11208 Danka Blvd., Ste. A, St. Petersburg 33716
Phone: (727) 576-6500

Keiser College
1500 NW 49th St., Fort Lauderdale 33309-3779
Type: Private, proprietary, four-year
Degrees: A, B   *Enroll:* 4,094
URL: http://www.keisercollege.edu
Phone: (954) 776-4456   *Calendar:* Sem. plan
Inst. Accred.: SACS (1991/1997)
Prog. Accred.: Clinical Lab Technology, Medical Assisting
  (ABHES), Medical Assisting (AMA), Medical Laboratory
  Technology, Occupational Therapy Assisting, Physical
  Therapy Assisting, Radiography

Daytona Beach Campus
1800 Business Park Blvd., Daytona Beach 32114
Phone: (386) 274-5060
Prog. Accred.: Radiography

Jacksonville Campus
6700 Southpoint Pkwy., Ste. 400, Jacksonville 32216
Phone: (904) 296-3440

Kendall Campus
8505 Mills Dr., Miami 33183
Phone: (305) 596-2226

Lakeland Campus
3515 Aviation Dr., Lakeland 33811
Phone: (863) 701-7789

Melbourne Campus
900 South Babcock St., Melbourne 32901
Phone: (321) 409-4800
Prog. Accred.: Medical Assisting (ABHES), Occupational
  Therapy Assisting

Online Campus
Phone: (954) 351-4040

Orlando Campus
5600 Lake Underhill Rd., Orlando 32807
Phone: (407) 273-5800

Pembroke Pines Campus
12520 Pines Blvd., Pembroke Pines 33027
Phone: (954) 431-4300

Port St. Lucie Campus
9468 South US 1, Port St. Lucie 34592
Phone: (772) 398-9990
Prog. Accred.: Medical Assisting (ABHES)

Sarasota Campus
6151 Lake Osprey Dr., Sarasota 34240
Phone: (941) 907-3900
Prog. Accred.: Medical Assisting (ABHES), Radiography

Tallahassee Campus
1700 Halstead Blvd., Building 2, Tallahassee 32308
Phone: (850) 906-9494
Prog. Accred.: Culinary Education, Medical Assisting
  (ABHES)

West Palm Beach Campus
2085 Vista Pkwy., West Palm Beach 33411
Phone: (561) 471-6000

Key College
225 East Dania Beach Blvd., Dania Beach 33004
Type: Private, proprietary, two-year
Degrees: A   *Enroll:* 104
URL: http://www.keycollege.edu
Phone: (954) 923-4440
Inst. Accred.: ACICS (1985/2003)

Knox Theological Seminary
5554 North Federal Hwy., Fort Lauderdale 33308
Type: Private, Presbyterian Church in America, four-year
Degrees: M, D
URL: http://www.knoxseminary.org
Phone: (954) 771-0376   *Calendar:* Sem. plan
Inst. Accred.: ATS (2005)

Lake City Community College
149 SE College Place, Lake City 32025-2006
Type: Public, state, two-year
System: Florida State Department of Education, Division
  of Community Colleges
Degrees: A   *Enroll:* 1,694
URL: http://www.lakecitycc.edu
Phone: (386) 752-1822   *Calendar:* Sem. plan
Inst. Accred.: SACS (1966/2000)
Prog. Accred.: Clinical Lab Technology, EMT (Paramedic),
  Nursing, Physical Therapy Assisting

Lake-Sumter Community College
9501 U.S. Hwy. 441, Leesburg 34788-8751
Type: Public, state/local, two-year
System: Florida State Department of Education, Division
  of Community Colleges
Degrees: A   *Enroll:* 1,797
URL: http://www.lscc.edu
Phone: (352) 787-3747   *Calendar:* Sem. plan
Inst. Accred.: SACS (1966/2000)

Le Cordon Bleu College of Culinary Arts— Miami
3221 Enterprise Way, Miramar 33025
Type: Private, proprietary, two-year
Degrees: A
URL: http://www.miamiculinary.com
Phone: (954) 438-8882
Inst. Accred.: ACCSCT (2004)

Lynn University
3601 North Military Trail, Boca Raton 33431
Type: Private, independent, four-year
Degrees: A, B, M, D   *Enroll:* 1,884
URL: http://www.lynn.edu
Phone: (561) 237-7000   *Calendar:* Sem. plan
Inst. Accred.: SACS (1967/2001)
Prog. Accred.: Dance, Music

Manatee Community College
PO Box 1849, Bradenton 34206
Type: Public, state/local, two-year
System: Florida State Department of Education, Division
  of Community Colleges
Degrees: A   *Enroll:* 5,408
URL: http://www.mccfl.edu
Phone: (941) 752-5000   *Calendar:* Sem. plan
Inst. Accred.: SACS (1963/2005)
Prog. Accred.: Dental Hygiene, Nursing, Occupational
  Therapy Assisting, Physical Therapy Assisting,
  Radiography, Respiratory Therapy

Miami International University of Art and Design
1501 Biscayne Blvd., Miami 33132
Type: Private, proprietary, four-year
System: Education Management Corporation
Degrees: A, B, M   *Enroll:* 1,197
URL: http://www.ifac.edu
Phone: (305) 373-4684   *Calendar:* Sem. plan
Inst. Accred.: SACS (1979/2002)
Prog. Accred.: Interior Design

Miami-Dade College
300 NE 2nd Ave., Miami 33132
Type: Public, state/local, four-year
System: Florida State Department of Education, Division
  of Community Colleges
Degrees: A, B   *Enroll:* 36,134
URL: http://www.mdc.edu
Phone: (305) 237-3131   *Calendar:* Sem. plan
Inst. Accred.: SACS (1965/2005)
Prog. Accred.: Clinical Lab Technology, Dental Hygiene,
  Diagnostic Medical Sonography, EMT (Paramedic),
  Funeral Service Education (Mortuary Science), Health
  Information Technician, Nursing, Optometric Technician,
  Physical Therapy Assisting, Physician Assistant,
  Radiography, Respiratory Therapy, Respiratory Therapy
  Technology

Hialeah Campus
1780 West 49th St., Hialeah 33012
Phone: (305) 237-8700

Homestead Campus
500 College Terrace, Homestead 33030-6009
Phone: (305) 237-5555

InterAmerican Campus
627 Southwest 27th Ave., Miami 33135
Phone: (305) 237-6500

Kendall Campus
11011 SW 104 St., Miami 33176
Phone: (305) 237-2500

Medical Center Campus
950 NW 20th St., Miami 33127
Phone: (305) 237-4141
Prog. Accred.: Dental Hygiene, Histologic Technology,
  Midwifery Education, Opticianry, Radiation Therapy,
  Radiography

North Campus
11380 NW 27th Ave., Miami 33167-3495
Phone: (305) 237-8500

National School of Technology
111 NW 183rd St., 2nd Flr., Miami 33169
Type: Private, proprietary, two-year
System: Corinthian Colleges, Inc
Degrees: A   *Enroll:* 1,563
URL: http://www.nst.cc
Phone: (305) 949-9500
Inst. Accred.: ABHES (1978/2002)
Prog. Accred.: Medical Assisting (ABHES), Surgical
  Technology

National School of Technology
9020 SW 137th Ave., Miami 33186
Type: Private, proprietary, two-year
System: Corinthian Colleges, Inc
Degrees: A   *Enroll:* 1,754
URL: http://www.nst.cc
Phone: (305) 386-9900
Inst. Accred.: ABHES (1994/2002)
Prog. Accred.: Medical Assisting (ABHES), Surgical
  Technology

Ft. Lauderdale Campus
1040 Bayview Dr., Ft. Lauderdale 33304
Phone: (954) 630-0066
Prog. Accred: Medical Assisting (ABHES)

Hialeah Campus
4410 West 16th Ave., 2nd Flr., Hialeah 33012-7628
Phone: (305) 558-9500
Prog. Accred: Medical Assisting (ABHES), Surgical
  Technology

New College of Florida
5700 North Tamiami Trail, Sarasota 34243-2197
Type: Public, state, four-year
Degrees: B   *Enroll:* 670
URL: http://www.ncf.edu
Phone: (941) 359-4700   *Calendar:* 4-1-4 plan
Inst. Accred.: SACS (2004)

New England Institute of Technology at Palm Beach
2410 Metrocentre Blvd., West Palm Beach 33407
Type: Private, proprietary, two-year
Degrees: A　　　　　　　　　　　　　*Enroll:* 1,238
URL: http://www.newenglandtech.com
Phone: (561) 842-8324　　　　　*Calendar:* Qtr. plan
Inst. Accred.: ACICS (2003)
Prog. Accred.: Culinary Education, Medical Assisting (CAAHEP)

New World School of the Arts
300 Northeast Second Ave., Miami 33132
Type: Public, joint partnership of Miami-Dade College and Universi, four-year
Degrees: A, B
URL: http://www.mdcc.edu/nwsa
Phone: (305) 237-3135　　　　　*Calendar:* Sem. plan
Inst. Accred.: SACS (1993/2003, *Indirect accreditation through University of Florida, Gainesville, FL and Miami-Dade College, Miami, FL*)
Prog. Accred.: Art, Dance, Music, Theatre

North Florida Community College
1000 Turner Davis Dr., Madison 32340-1698
Type: Public, state, two-year
System: Florida State Department of Education, Division of Community Colleges
Degrees: A　　　　　　　　　　　　*Enroll:* 741
URL: http://www.nfcc.edu
Phone: (850) 973-1600　　　　　*Calendar:* Sem. plan
Inst. Accred.: SACS (1963/2005)

Nova Southeastern University
3301 College Ave., Fort Lauderdale 33314
Type: Private, independent, four-year
Degrees: B, M, P, D　　　　　　　*Enroll:* 15,278
URL: http://www.nova.edu
Phone: (954) 262-7300　　　　　*Calendar:* Sem. plan
Inst. Accred.: SACS (1971/1998)
Prog. Accred.: Advanced Education in General Dentistry, Audiology, Clinical Psychology, Combined Prosthodontics, Dentistry, Endodontics, General Dentistry, Law, Marriage and Family Therapy, Occupational Therapy, Optometric Residency, Optometry, Oral and Maxillofacial Surgery, Orthodontic and Dentofacial Orthopedics, Osteopathy, Pediatric Dentistry, Periodontics, Pharmacy, Physical Therapy, Physician Assistant, Psychology Internship, Public Health, Speech-Language Pathology

Okaloosa-Walton College
100 College Blvd., Niceville 32578-1295
Type: Public, state/local, two-year
System: Florida State Department of Education, Division of Community Colleges
Degrees: A　　　　　　　　　　　　*Enroll:* 4,110
URL: http://www.owc.edu
Phone: (850) 678-5111　　　　　*Calendar:* Sem. plan
Inst. Accred.: SACS (1967/2001)

Orlando Culinary Academy
8511 Commodity Circle, Ste. 100, Orlando 32819
Type: Private, independent, two-year
System: Career Education Corporation
Degrees: A
URL: http://www.orlandoculinary.com
Phone: (407) 888-4000
Inst. Accred.: ACICS (2003/2005)
Prog. Accred.: Culinary Education

Palm Beach Atlantic University
901 South Flagler Dr., PO Box 24708, West Palm Beach 33416-4708
Type: Private, interdenominational, four-year
Degrees: A, B, M, P, D　　　　　*Enroll:* 2,755
URL: http://www.pba.edu
Phone: (561) 803-2000　　　　　*Calendar:* Sem. plan
Inst. Accred.: SACS (1972/1998)
Prog. Accred.: Music, Pharmacy

Orlando Campus
4700 Millenia Blvd., Ste. 100, Orlando 32839
Phone: (407) 226-5955

Palm Beach Community College
4200 Congress Ave., Lake Worth 33461-4796
Type: Public, local, two-year
System: Florida State Department of Education, Division of Community Colleges
Degrees: A　　　　　　　　　　　　*Enroll:* 12,037
URL: http://www.pbcc.edu
Phone: (561) 868-3350　　　　　*Calendar:* Sem. plan
Inst. Accred.: SACS (1942/2001)
Prog. Accred.: Dental Assisting, Dental Hygiene, EMT (Paramedic), Montessori Teacher Education, Nursing, Radiography, Respiratory Therapy, Respiratory Therapy Technology

Eissey Campus
3160 PGA Blvd., Palm Beach Gardens 33410
Phone: (561) 868-3350
Prog. Accred: Radiography

Glades Campus
1977 College Dr., Belle Glade 33430
Phone: (561) 868-3350

South Campus
3000 Saint Lucie Ave., Boca Raton 33431
Phone: (561) 868-3350

Pasco-Hernando Community College
10230 Ridge Rd., New Port Richey 34654-5199
Type: Public, state/local, two-year
System: Florida State Department of Education, Division
of Community Colleges
Degrees: A *Enroll:* 3,801
URL: http://www.phcc.edu
Phone: (727) 847-2727 *Calendar:* Sem. plan
Inst. Accred.: SACS (1974/1999)
Prog. Accred.: Dental Hygiene, EMT (Paramedic), Nursing

East Campus
36727 Blanton Rd., Dade City 33523-7599
Phone: (352) 567-6701

North Campus
11415 Ponce de Leon Blvd., Brooksville 34601-8698
Phone: (352) 796-6726

Pensacola Junior College
1000 College Blvd., Pensacola 32504-8998
Type: Public, state/local, two-year
System: Florida State Department of Education, Division
of Community Colleges
Degrees: A *Enroll:* 6,703
URL: http://www.pjc.edu
Phone: (850) 484-1000 *Calendar:* Sem. plan
Inst. Accred.: SACS (1956/1997)
Prog. Accred.: Culinary Education, Dental Assisting,
Dental Hygiene, EMT (Paramedic), Health Information
Technician, Medical Assisting (AMA), Physical Therapy
Assisting, Radiography, Respiratory Therapy

Milton Campus
5988 Hwy. 90, Milton 32583
Phone: (904) 484-4400

Warrington Campus
5555 Hwy. 98 West, Pensacola 32507
Phone: (904) 484-2230
Prog. Accred: Radiography

Polk Community College
999 Ave. H, NE, Winter Haven 33881-4299
Type: Public, local, two-year
System: Florida State Department of Education, Division
of Community Colleges
Degrees: A *Enroll:* 3,703
URL: http://www.polk.edu
Phone: (863) 297-1000 *Calendar:* Sem. plan
Inst. Accred.: SACS (1967/2001)
Prog. Accred.: EMT (Paramedic), Health Information
Technician, Nursing, Occupational Therapy Assisting,
Physical Therapy Assisting, Radiography

Professional Training Center
13926 SW 47th St., Miami 33175
Type: Private, proprietary, two-year
Degrees: A
URL: http://www.ptcmatt.com
Phone: (305) 220-4120
Inst. Accred.: ABHES (1998/2005)
Prog. Accred.: Radiography

Remington College—Tampa
2410 East Busch Blvd., Tampa 33612-8410
Type: Private, proprietary, four-year
System: Education America, Inc.
Degrees: A, B *Enroll:* 856
URL: http://www.remingtoncollege.edu
Phone: (813) 935-5700 *Calendar:* Qtr. plan
Inst. Accred.: ACCSCT (1968/2002)

Fort Worth Campus
300 East Loop 820, Fort Worth, TX 76112-1225
Phone: (817) 451-0017

Jacksonville Campus
7011 A. C. Skinner Pkwy., Ste. 140, Jacksonville
32256
Phone: (904) 296-3435

Largo Campus
8550 Ulmerton Rd., Unit 100, Largo 33771-3842
Phone: (727) 532-1999

Ringling School of Art and Design
2700 North Tamiami Trail, Sarasota 34234-5895
Type: Private, independent, four-year
Degrees: B *Enroll:* 973
URL: http://www.rsad.edu
Phone: (941) 351-5100 *Calendar:* Sem. plan
Inst. Accred.: SACS (1979/1995)
Prog. Accred.: Art, Interior Design

Rollins College
1000 Holt Ave., Winter Park 32789-4499
Type: Private, independent, four-year
Degrees: A, B, M *Enroll:* 3,232
URL: http://www.rollins.edu
Phone: (407) 646-2000 *Calendar:* Sem. plan
Inst. Accred.: SACS (1927/2005)
Prog. Accred.: Business (AACSB), Counseling, Music

Saint John Vianney College Seminary
2900 SW 87th Ave., Miami 33165-3244
Type: Private, Roman Catholic Church, four-year
Degrees: B *Enroll:* 55
URL: http://www.sjvcs.edu
Phone: (305) 223-4561 *Calendar:* Sem. plan
Inst. Accred.: SACS (1970/1996)

Saint Johns River Community College
5001 St. Johns Ave., Palatka 32177-3897
Type: Public, state/local, two-year
System: Florida State Department of Education, Division
of Community Colleges
Degrees: A *Enroll:* 2,588
URL: http://www.sjrcc.edu
Phone: (386) 312-4200 *Calendar:* Tri. plan
Inst. Accred.: SACS (1963/2003)

Saint Leo University
MC 2187, PO Box 6665, St. Leo 33574-6665
Type: Private, Roman Catholic Church, four-year
Degrees: A, B, M   *Enroll:* 9,088
URL: http://www.saintleo.edu
Phone: (352) 588-8200   *Calendar:* Sem. plan
Inst. Accred.: SACS (1967/2002)
Prog. Accred.: Social Work

Saint Petersburg College
PO Box 13489, St. Petersburg 33733-3489
Type: Public, local, four-year
System: Florida State Department of Education, Division
of Community Colleges
Degrees: A, B   *Enroll:* 14,459
URL: http://www.spjc.edu
Phone: (727) 341-3600   *Calendar:* Sem. plan
Inst. Accred.: SACS (1931/2000)
Prog. Accred.: Clinical Lab Technology, Dental Hygiene,
EMT (Paramedic), Funeral Service Education (Mortuary
Science), Health Information Technician, Nursing,
Physical Therapy Assisting, Respiratory Therapy,
Veterinary Technology

Saint Thomas University
16400 NW 32nd Ave., Miami 33054
Type: Private, Roman Catholic Church, four-year
Degrees: B, M, D   *Enroll:* 2,164
URL: http://www.stu.edu
Phone: (305) 625-6000   *Calendar:* Sem. plan
Inst. Accred.: SACS (1968/2003)
Prog. Accred.: Law

Saint Vincent de Paul Regional Seminary
10701 South Military Trail, Boynton Beach 33436-4899
Type: Private, Roman Catholic Church, four-year
Degrees: M   *Enroll:* 79
URL: http://www.svdp.edu
Phone: (561) 732-4424   *Calendar:* Sem. plan
Inst. Accred.: ATS (1984/1999), SACS (1968/2000)

Sanford-Brown Institute—Jacksonville
10255 Fortune Pkwy., Ste. 501, Jacksonville 32256
Type: Private, proprietary, two-year
System: Career Education Corporation
Degrees: A   *Enroll:* 570
URL: http://www.sbjacksonville.com
Phone: (904) 363-6221
Inst. Accred.: ABHES (1993/2004), ACICS (1999/2004)
Prog. Accred.: Medical Assisting (ABHES), Surgical
Technology

Iselin Campus
675 U.S. Route 1, 2nd Flr., Iselin, NJ 08830
Phone: (732) 634-1131
Prog. Accred: Medical Assisting (ABHES), Surgical
Technology

Tampa Campus
5701 East Hillsborough Ave., Tampa 33610
Phone: (813) 621-0072
Prog. Accred: Cardiovascular Technology, Medical
Assisting (ABHES), Surgical Technology

Santa Fe Community College
3000 NW 83rd St., Gainesville 32606-6200
Type: Public, local, two-year
System: Florida State Department of Education, Division
of Community Colleges
Degrees: A   *Enroll:* 8,764
URL: http://www.sfcc.edu
Phone: (352) 395-5000   *Calendar:* Sem. plan
Inst. Accred.: SACS (1968/2002)
Prog. Accred.: Construction Education, Dental Assisting,
Dental Hygiene, EMT (Paramedic), Nuclear Medicine
Technology, Nursing, Practical Nursing, Radiography,
Respiratory Therapy, Surgical Technology

Schiller International University
453 Edgewater Dr., Dunedin 34698-7532
Type: Private, proprietary, four-year
Degrees: A, B, M   *Enroll:* 149
URL: http://www.schiller.edu
Phone: (727) 736-5082   *Calendar:* Sem. plan
Inst. Accred.: ACICS (1983/2003)

Engelberg, Switzerland Campus
Dortstrasse 40, Engelberg, Switzerland 6390
Phone: 011 41 41 639 74 74

Heidelberg, Germany Campus
Bergstrasse 106, Heidelberg, Germany 69124
Phone: 011 49 62 21 4 58 10

The Leysin, Switzerland Campus
The American College of Switzerland, Leysin,
Switzerland CH-1854
Phone: 011 41 24 493 03 09

London, England Campus
Royal Waterloo House, 51-55 Waterloo Rd., London,
United Kingdom SE1 8TX
Phone: 011 44 20 7928-1372

Madrid, Spain Campus
Edificio Columina, San Bernardo 97-99, Madrid, Spain
28015
Phone: 011 34 91 448-2488

Paris, France Campus
32 Blvd. de Vaugirard, Paris, France 75015
Phone: 011 33 1 45 38 56 01

Strasbourg, France Campus
Chateau Pourtales, 161 rue Melanie, Strasbourg,
France 67000
Phone: 011 33 3 88 45 84 62

Saint Petersburg Theological Seminary
10830 Navajo Dr., St. Petersburg 33708-3116
Type: Private, interdenominational, four-year
Degrees: B, M, D   *Enroll:* 46
URL: http://www.sptseminary.edu
Phone: (727) 399-0276   *Calendar:* Sem. plan
Inst. Accred.: TRACS (2003)

Seminole Community College
100 Weldon Blvd., Sanford 32773-6199
Type: Public, local, two-year
System: Florida State Department of Education, Division
of Community Colleges
Degrees: A   *Enroll:* 7,131
URL: http://www.scc-fl.edu
Phone: (407) 328-4722   *Calendar:* Sem. plan
Inst. Accred.: SACS (1969/2003)
Prog. Accred.: EMT (Paramedic), Interior Design, Medical
Assisting (AMA), Nursing, Physical Therapy Assisting,
Respiratory Therapy

South Florida Community College
600 West College Dr., Avon Park 33825-9356
Type: Public, local, two-year
System: Florida State Department of Education, Division
of Community Colleges
Degrees: A   *Enroll:* 1,556
URL: http://www.southflorida.edu
Phone: (863) 453-6661   *Calendar:* Sem. plan
Inst. Accred.: SACS (1968/2002)
Prog. Accred.: Dental Assisting, Dental Hygiene

Southeastern University
1000 Longfellow Blvd., Lakeland 33801
Type: Private, Assemblies of God, four-year
Degrees: B, M   *Enroll:* 1,590
URL: http://www.seuniversity.edu
Phone: (863) 667-5000   *Calendar:* Sem. plan
Inst. Accred.: SACS (1986/2001)

Southwest Florida College
1685 Medical Ln., Fort Myers 33907
Type: Private, independent, two-year
Degrees: A   *Enroll:* 1,721
URL: http://www.swfc.edu
Phone: (239) 939-4766   *Calendar:* Qtr. plan
Inst. Accred.: ACICS (1984/2003)
Prog. Accred.: Medical Assisting (ABHES), Surgical
Technology

Tampa Campus
3910 Riga Blvd., Tampa 33619
Phone: (813) 630-4401
Prog. Accred.: Medical Assisting (ABHES), Surgical
Technology

Stetson University
421 North Woodland Blvd., DeLand 32720
Type: Private, Southern Baptist Church, four-year
Degrees: B, M, P, D   *Enroll:* 3,135
URL: http://www.stetson.edu
Phone: (386) 822-7000   *Calendar:* Sem. plan
Inst. Accred.: SACS (1932/2001)
Prog. Accred.: Accounting, Athletic Training, Business
(AACSB), Counseling, Law, Music, Teacher Education
(NCATE)

Tallahassee Community College
444 Appleyard Dr., Tallahassee 32304-2895
Type: Public, state/local, two-year
System: Florida State Department of Education, Division
of Community Colleges
Degrees: A   *Enroll:* 8,122
URL: http://www.tcc.fl.edu
Phone: (850) 201-6200   *Calendar:* Sem. plan
Inst. Accred.: SACS (1969/2005)
Prog. Accred.: Dental Assisting, Dental Hygiene, EMT
(Paramedic), Respiratory Therapy

Pat Thomas Law Enforcement Academy
85 Academy Dr., Havana 32333
Phone: (850) 539-4002

Talmudic College of Florida
1910 Alton Rd., Miami Beach 33139
Type: Private, independent, four-year
Degrees: B, M, P, D   *Enroll:* 40
Phone: (305) 534-7050   *Calendar:* Sem. plan
Inst. Accred.: AARTS (1977/1999)

Trinity Baptist College
800 Hammond Blvd., Jacksonville 32221
Type: Private, independent, four-year
Degrees: A, B, M   *Enroll:* 365
URL: http://www.tbc.edu
Phone: (904) 596-2400   *Calendar:* Sem. plan
Inst. Accred.: TRACS (1997/2002)

Trinity College of Florida
2430 Welbilt Blvd., Trinity 34655-4401
Type: Private, nondenominational, four-year
Degrees: A, B   *Enroll:* 150
URL: http://www.trinitycollege.edu
Phone: (727) 376-6911   *Calendar:* Sem. plan
Inst. Accred.: ABHE (1996/2002)

Universidad FLET
14540 SW 136th St., Ste. 202, Miami 33186
Type: Private, independent, four-year
Degrees: B, M
URL: http://www.flet.edu
Phone: (305) 378-8700
Inst. Accred.: DETC (2003)

University of Central Florida
4000 Central Florida Blvd., Orlando 32816-0002
Type: Public, state, four-year
System: Florida Board of Education, Division of Colleges
and Universities
Degrees: A, B, M, P, D   *Enroll:* 33,640
URL: http://www.ucf.edu
Phone: (407) 823-2000   *Calendar:* Sem. plan
Inst. Accred.: SACS (1970/1995)
Prog. Accred.: Accounting, Business (AACSB), Clinical Lab
Scientist, Clinical Psychology, Computer Science,
Counseling, Engineering (aerospace, civil, computer,
electrical, environmental/sanitary, industrial,
mechanical), Engineering Technology (electrical,
general), English Language Education, Health
Information Administration, Health Services
Administration, Music, Nursing, Nursing Education,
Physical Therapy, Public Administration, Radiography,
Respiratory Therapy, Social Work, Speech-Language
Pathology, Teacher Education (NCATE)

University of Florida
PO Box 113150, Gainesville 32611-3150
Type: Public, state, four-year
System: Florida Board of Education, Division of Colleges
and Universities
Degrees: A, B, M, P, D   *Enroll:* 44,382
URL: http://www.ufl.edu
Phone: (352) 392-3261   *Calendar:* Sem. plan
Inst. Accred.: SACS (1913/2003)
Prog. Accred.: Accounting, Applied Science
(surveying/geomatics), Art, Athletic Training, Audiology,
Business (AACSB), Clinical Psychology, Combined
Prosthodontics, Construction Education, Counseling,
Counseling Psychology, Dental Public Health, Dentistry,
Dietetics (internship), Endodontics, Engineering
(aerospace, agricultural, chemical, civil, computer,
electrical, engineering physics/science,
environmental/sanitary, industrial, materials,
mechanical, nuclear, ocean), Forestry, Health Services
Administration, Interior Design, Journalism, Landscape
Architecture, Law, Medicine, Music, Nurse (Midwifery),
Nursing, Nursing Education, Occupational Therapy,
Ophthalmic Medical Technology, Oral and Maxillofacial
Pathology, Oral and Maxillofacial Surgery, Orthodontic
and Dentofacial Orthopedics, Pediatric Dentistry,
Periodontics, Pharmacy, Physical Therapy, Physician
Assistant, Planning, Psychology Internship, Recreation
and Leisure Services, Rehabilitation Counseling, School
Psychology, Speech-Language Pathology, Teacher
Education (NCATE), Theatre, Veterinary Medicine

Shands Jacksonville Medical Center
655 West 8th St., Jacksonville 32209
Phone: (352) 265-0111
Prog. Accred: Advanced Education in General
Dentistry, Clinical Lab Scientist, Clinical Pastoral
Education, Oral and Maxillofacial Surgery,
Radiography

University of Miami
PO Box 248006, Coral Gables 33124-4600
Type: Private, independent, four-year
Degrees: B, M, D   *Enroll:* 14,202
URL: http://www.miami.edu
Phone: (305) 284-2211   *Calendar:* Sem. plan
Inst. Accred.: SACS (1940/1997)
Prog. Accred.: Accounting, Business (AACSB), Clinical
Pastoral Education, Clinical Psychology, Counseling
Psychology, Engineering (architectural, bioengineering,
civil, computer, electrical, environmental/sanitary,
industrial, manufacturing, mechanical), English
Language Education, General Practice Residency,
Health Services Administration, Journalism, Law,
Medicine, Music, Nuclear Medicine Technology, Nurse
(Midwifery), Nursing, Oral and Maxillofacial Surgery,
Physical Therapy, Psychology Internship, Public Health,
Teacher Education (NCATE)

University of North Florida
4567 St. John's Bluff Rd. South, Jacksonville 32224
Type: Public, state, four-year
System: Florida Board of Education, Division of Colleges
and Universities
Degrees: B, M, D   *Enroll:* 10,872
URL: http://www.unf.edu
Phone: (904) 620-1000   *Calendar:* Sem. plan
Inst. Accred.: SACS (1974/1999)
Prog. Accred.: Accounting, Athletic Training, Business
(AACSB), Computer Science, Construction Education,
Counseling, Cytotechnology, Dietetics (internship),
Engineering (civil, electrical, mechanical), Health
Services Administration, Music, Nursing, Nursing
Education, Physical Therapy, Public Administration,
Rehabilitation Counseling, Teacher Education (NCATE)

University of South Florida
4202 East Fowler Ave., Tampa 33620
Type: Public, state, four-year
System: Florida Board of Education, Division of Colleges
and Universities
Degrees: A, B, M, P, D   *Enroll:* 31,363
URL: http://www.usf.edu
Phone: (813) 974-2011   *Calendar:* Sem. plan
Inst. Accred.: SACS (1965/2005)
Prog. Accred.: Accounting, Applied Science (industrial
hygiene), Art, Audiology, Business (AACSB), Clinical
Psychology, Computer Science, Engineering (chemical,
civil, computer, electrical, industrial, mechanical),
English Language Education, Journalism, Librarianship,
Medicine, Music, Nursing, Nursing Education, Physical
Therapy, Psychology Internship, Public Administration,
Public Health, Rehabilitation Counseling, School
Psychology, Social Work, Speech-Language Pathology,
Teacher Education (NCATE), Theatre

Lakeland Campus
3433 Winter Lake Rd., Lakeland 33803
Phone: (863) 667-7000

Saint Petersburg Campus
140 7th Ave. South, St. Petersburg 33701
Phone: (727) 553-4873
Prog. Accred: Journalism

Sarasota Campus
5700 North Tamiami Trail, Sarasota 34243-2197
Phone: (941) 359-4210

University of St. Augustine for Health Sciences
One University Blvd., St. Augustine 32086-5783
Type: Private, proprietary, four-year
Degrees: M, P   *FTE Enroll:* 380
URL: http://www.usa.edu
Phone: (904) 826-0084   *Calendar:* Sem. plan
Inst. Accred.: DETC (1993/2003)
Prog. Accred.: Occupational Therapy, Physical Therapy

University of Tampa
401 West Kennedy Blvd., Tampa 33606-1490
Type: Private, independent, four-year
Degrees: A, B, M   *Enroll:* 4,111
URL: http://www.ut.edu
Phone: (813) 253-3333   *Calendar:* Sem. plan
Inst. Accred.: SACS (1951/2005)
Prog. Accred.: Business (AACSB), Music, Nursing

University of West Florida
11000 University Pkwy., Pensacola 32514-5750
Type: Public, state, four-year
System: Florida Board of Education, Division of Colleges
and Universities
Degrees: A, B, M, D   *Enroll:* 7,320
URL: http://www.uwf.edu
Phone: (850) 474-2000   *Calendar:* Sem. plan
Inst. Accred.: SACS (1969/2005)
Prog. Accred.: Business (AACSB), Clinical Lab Scientist,
Music, Nursing, Nursing Education, Public
Administration, Social Work, Teacher Education (NCATE)

Valencia Community College
PO Box 3028, Orlando 32802-3028
Type: Public, state, two-year
System: Florida State Department of Education, Division
of Community Colleges
Degrees: A   *Enroll:* 17,183
URL: http://valenciacc.edu
Phone: (407) 299-5000   *Calendar:* Sem. plan
Inst. Accred.: SACS (1969/2003)
Prog. Accred.: Dental Hygiene, Diagnostic Medical
Sonography, EMT (Paramedic), Nursing, Radiography,
Respiratory Therapy

East Campus
701 North Econlockhatchee Trail, Orlando 32825
Phone: (407) 299-5000

West Campus
1800 South Kirkman Rd., Orlando 32811
Phone: (407) 299-5000

Winter Park Campus
850 West Morse Blvd., Winter Park 32789
Phone: (407) 299-5000

Virginia College at Pensacola
19 West Garden St., Pensacola 32501
Type: Private, proprietary, two-year
Degrees: A
URL: http://www.vc.edu
Phone: (850) 436-8444
Inst. Accred.: ACICS (2002)

Mobile Campus
2970 Cottage Hill Rd., Mobile, AL 36606
Phone: (251) 343-7227

Warner Southern College
13895 U.S. Hwy. 27, Lake Wales 33859-8797
Type: Private, Church of God, four-year
Degrees: A, B, M   *Enroll:* 888
URL: http://www.warner.edu
Phone: (863) 638-1426   *Calendar:* Sem. plan
Inst. Accred.: SACS (1977/2002, Warning)

Webber International University
PO Box 96, 1201 North Scenic Hwy., Babson Park 33827
Type: Private, independent, four-year
Degrees: A, B, M   *Enroll:* 609
URL: http://www.webber.edu
Phone: (863) 638-1431   *Calendar:* Sem. plan
Inst. Accred.: SACS (1969/1997)

Webster College—Ocala
2221 Southwest 19th Ave. Rd., Ocala 34474
Type: Private, proprietary, four-year
Degrees: A, B
URL: http://www.webstercollege.edu
Phone: (352) 629-1941   *Calendar:* Qtr. plan
Inst. Accred.: ACICS (1968/1999)

Fairmont Campus
102 Benoni Ave., Fairmont, WV 26554
Phone: (304) 363-8824

Holiday Campus
2127 Grand Blvd., Holiday 34691
Phone: (727) 942-0069

Yeshiva Gedolah Rabbinical College
1140 Alton Rd., Miami Beach 33139
Type: Private, independent, four-year
Degrees: B, M   *Enroll:* 128
Phone: (305) 653-8770   *Calendar:* Sem. plan
Inst. Accred.: AARTS (1997/2004)

GEORGIA

Abraham Baldwin Agricultural College
2802 Moore Hwy., Tifton 31794
Type: Public, state, two-year
System: Board of Regents of the University System of
Georgia
Degrees: A   *Enroll:* 2,452
URL: http://www.abac.peachnet.edu
Phone: (229) 386-3230   *Calendar:* Sem. plan
Inst. Accred.: SACS (1953/1996)
Prog. Accred.: Nursing

Agnes Scott College
141 East College Ave., Decatur 30030
Type: Private, Presbyterian Church (USA), four-year
Degrees: B, M   *Enroll:* 891
URL: http://www.agnesscott.edu
Phone: (404) 471-6000   *Calendar:* Sem. plan
Inst. Accred.: SACS (1907/2004)

Albany State University
504 College Dr., Albany 31705-2794
Type: Public, state, four-year
System: Board of Regents of the University System of
Georgia
Degrees: B, M, P   *Enroll:* 3,118
URL: http://asuweb.asurams.edu
Phone: (229) 430-4600   *Calendar:* Sem. plan
Inst. Accred.: SACS (1951/1998)
Prog. Accred.: Business (AACSB), Business (ACBSP),
Nursing, Social Work, Teacher Education (NCATE)

Albany Technical College
1704 South Slappey Blvd., Albany 31701
Type: Public, state, two-year
System: Georgia Department of Technical and Adult
Education
Degrees: A   *Enroll:* 1,917
URL: http://www.albanytech.edu
Phone: (229) 430-3500   *Calendar:* Qtr. plan
Inst. Accred.: COE (1974/2000), SACS (2005)
Prog. Accred.: Dental Assisting, Medical Assisting (AMA),
Radiography, Surgical Technology

Early County Campus
Highway 27 North Bypass, Blakely 31723
Phone: (229) 724-3500

Altamaha Technical College
1777 West Cherry St., Jesup 31545
Type: Public, state, two-year
System: Georgia Department of Technical and Adult
Education
Degrees: A
URL: http://www.altamahatech.org
Phone: (912) 427-5800   *Calendar:* Qtr. plan
Inst. Accred.: COE (1992/2003)

Appling Technical Education Center
1334 Golden Isles Pkwy. West, Baxley 31514
Phone: (912) 427-5800

Jeff Davis Community School
677 Douglas Hwy., Hazlehurst 31539
Phone: (912) 379-0041

The American InterContinental University
6600 Peachtree-Dunwoody Rd., 500 Embassy Row,
Atlanta 30328-1649
Type: Private, proprietary, four-year
System: Career Education Corporation
Degrees: A, B, M   *Enroll:* 6,019
URL: http://www.aiuniv.edu
Phone: (404) 965-5700   *Calendar:* Qtr. plan
Inst. Accred.: SACS (1987/2002, Probation)
Prog. Accred.: Interior Design

American InterContinental University Online
5550 Prairie Stone Pkwy., Hoffman Estates, IL 60192
Phone: (877) 701-3800

Buckhead Campus
3330 Peachtree Rd., NE, Atlanta 30326-1016
Phone: (404) 965-5712

Dubai Campus
PO Box 28282, Dubai, United Arab Emirates
Phone: 011 971 4 388 883

Houston Campus
9999 Richmond Ave., Houston, TX 77042
Phone: (800) 524-3995

London Campus
110 Marylebone High St., London, United Kingdom
W1M 3DB
Phone: 011-44-071 486-1772

Los Angeles Campus
12655 West Jefferson Blvd., Los Angeles, CA 90066-
7008
Phone: (310) 302-2000
Prog. Accred: Interior Design

Weston/Ft. Lauderdale Campus
2250 North Commerce Parway, Ste. 100, Weston, FL
33326
Phone: (954) 835-0939

Andrew College
413 College St., Cuthbert 31740
Type: Private, United Methodist Church, two-year
Degrees: A   *Enroll:* 321
URL: http://www.andrewcollege.edu
Phone: (229) 732-2171   *Calendar:* Sem. plan
Inst. Accred.: SACS (1927/1995)

Appalachian Technical College
100 Campus Dr., Jasper 30143
Type: Public, state, two-year
System: Georgia Department of Technical and Adult
  Education
Degrees: A   *Enroll:* 564
URL: http://www.apptec.org
Phone: (706) 253-4500
Inst. Accred.: COE (1971/2003)

Argosy University Atlanta
990 Hammond Dr., Ste. 1100, Atlanta 30328
Type: Private, proprietary, four-year
System: Argosy University
Degrees: M, D
URL: http://www.argosyu.edu
Phone: (770) 671-1200   *Calendar:* Tri. plan
Inst. Accred.: NCA-HLC (1981/2001, *Indirect accreditation
  through Argosy University, Chicago, IL*)
Prog. Accred.: Clinical Psychology

Armstrong Atlantic State University
11935 Abercorn St., Savannah 31419-1997
Type: Public, state, four-year
System: Board of Regents of the University System of
  Georgia
Degrees: A, B, M   *Enroll:* 4,862
URL: http://www.armstrong.edu
Phone: (912) 927-5211   *Calendar:* Sem. plan
Inst. Accred.: SACS (1940/2002)
Prog. Accred.: Clinical Lab Scientist, Computer Science,
  Dental Hygiene, Music, Nursing, Nursing Education,
  Physical Therapy, Public Health, Radiation Therapy,
  Radiography, Respiratory Therapy, Teacher Education
  (NCATE)

The Art Institute of Atlanta
6600 Peachtree-Dunwoody Rd., 100 Embassy Row,
Atlanta 30328
Type: Private, proprietary, four-year
System: Education Management Corporation
Degrees: A, B   *Enroll:* 2,474
URL: http://www.aia.artinstitute.edu
Phone: (770) 394-8300   *Calendar:* Qtr. plan
Inst. Accred.: SACS (1985/2000)
Prog. Accred.: Culinary Education, Interior Design

The Art Institute of Washington
1820 North Fort Myer Dr., Arlington, VA 22209-1802
Phone: (703) 358-9550
Prog. Accred: Culinary Education

Ashworth College
430 Technology Pkwy., Norcross 30092-3406
Type: Private, proprietary, four-year
Degrees: A, M
URL: http://www.ashworthcollege.com
Phone: (770) 729-8400
Inst. Accred.: DETC (2000/2002)

Athens Technical College
800 U.S. Hwy. 29 North, Athens 30601-1500
Type: Public, state, two-year
System: Georgia Department of Technical and Adult
  Education
Degrees: A   *Enroll:* 1,716
URL: http://www.athenstech.edu
Phone: (706) 355-5000   *Calendar:* Qtr. plan
Inst. Accred.: SACS (1988/2003)
Prog. Accred.: Business (ACBSP), Dental Hygiene,
  Nursing, Physical Therapy Assisting, Radiography,
  Respiratory Therapy, Respiratory Therapy Technology,
  Surgical Technology

Atlanta Christian College
2605 Ben Hill Rd., East Point 30344
Type: Private, Christian Churches/Churches of Christ,
  four-year
Degrees: A, B   *Enroll:* 348
URL: http://www.acc.edu
Phone: (404) 761-8861   *Calendar:* Sem. plan
Inst. Accred.: SACS (1990/1995)
Prog. Accred.: Teacher Education (NCATE)

Atlanta College of Art
1280 Peachtree St., NE, Atlanta 30309
Type: Private, independent, four-year
Degrees: B   *Enroll:* 309
URL: http://www.aca.edu
Phone: (404) 733-5001   *Calendar:* Sem. plan
Inst. Accred.: SACS (1969/2002)
Prog. Accred.: Art

Atlanta Metropolitan College
1630 Metropolitan Pkwy., SW, Atlanta 30310
Type: Public, state, two-year
System: Board of Regents of the University System of
  Georgia
Degrees: A   *Enroll:* 1,192
URL: http://www.atlm.peachnet.edu
Phone: (404) 756-4000   *Calendar:* Sem. plan
Inst. Accred.: SACS (1976/2001)
Prog. Accred.: Business (ACBSP)

Atlanta Technical College
1560 Metropolitan Ave., SW, Atlanta 30310
Type: Public, state, two-year
System: Georgia Department of Technical and Adult
  Education
Degrees: A   *Enroll:* 2,335
URL: http://www.atlantatech.org
Phone: (404) 756-3700   *Calendar:* Qtr. plan
Inst. Accred.: COE (1971/2003)
Prog. Accred.: Clinical Lab Technology, Dental Assisting,
  Dental Laboratory Technology, Medical Assisting
  (CAAHEP)

Delta Airlines Campus
Hartfield International Airport, Atlanta 30310
Phone: (404) 758-5591

Augusta State University
2500 Walton Way, Augusta 30904-2200
Type: Public, state, four-year
System: Board of Regents of the University System of
Georgia
Degrees: A, B, M, P   *Enroll:* 4,703
URL: http://www.aug.edu
Phone: (706) 737-1400   *Calendar:* Sem. plan
Inst. Accred.: SACS (1926/2001)
Prog. Accred.: Art, Business (AACSB), Music, Nursing,
Teacher Education (NCATE)

Augusta Technical College
3200 Augusta Tech Dr., Augusta 30906
Type: Public, state, two-year
System: Georgia Department of Technical and Adult
Education
Degrees: A   *Enroll:* 2,902
URL: http://www.augustatech.edu
Phone: (706) 771-4000   *Calendar:* Qtr. plan
Inst. Accred.: SACS (1988/2003)
Prog. Accred.: Cardiovascular Technology, Dental
Assisting, Engineering Technology (electrical,
mechanical), Medical Assisting (AMA), Occupational
Therapy Assisting, Practical Nursing, Respiratory
Therapy, Surgical Technology

Thompson McDuffie Campus
388 Tech Dr., NW, Thompson 30824
Phone: (706) 595-0166

Bainbridge College
2500 East Shotwell St., Bainbridge 31717
Type: Public, state, two-year
System: Board of Regents of the University System of
Georgia
Degrees: A   *Enroll:* 1,283
URL: http://www.bainbridge.edu
Phone: (229) 248-2500   *Calendar:* Sem. plan
Inst. Accred.: SACS (1975/2000)

Bauder College
384 Northyards Blvd. NW, Ste. 190, Atlanta 30313
Type: Private, proprietary, two-year
System: Kaplan Higher Education Corporation
Degrees: A   *Enroll:* 318
URL: http://www.bauder.edu
Phone: (404) 237-7573   *Calendar:* Qtr. plan
Inst. Accred.: SACS (1985/2000)

Beacon University
6003 North Veterans Pkwy., PO Box 8766, Columbus
31909
Type: Private, interdenominational, four-year
Degrees: A, B, M   *Enroll:* 174
URL: http://www.beacon.edu
Phone: (706) 323-5364   *Calendar:* Sem. plan
Inst. Accred.: TRACS (2000)

Berry College
PO Box 490039, Mount Berry 30149-0039
Type: Private, independent, four-year
Degrees: B, M, P   *Enroll:* 1,939
URL: http://www.berry.edu
Phone: (706) 232-5374   *Calendar:* Sem. plan
Inst. Accred.: SACS (1957/1998)
Prog. Accred.: Business (AACSB), Music, Teacher
Education (NCATE)

Beulah Heights Bible College
892 Berne St., SE, Atlanta 30316-1873
Type: Private, Pentacostal Church of Christ, four-year
Degrees: A, B   *Enroll:* 416
URL: http://www.beulah.org
Phone: (404) 627-2681   *Calendar:* Sem. plan
Inst. Accred.: ABHE (1999/2003), TRACS (1997/2002)

Brenau University
One Centennial Circle, Gainesville 30501
Type: Private, independent, four-year
Degrees: B, M, P   *Enroll:* 1,492
URL: http://www.brenau.edu
Phone: (770) 534-6299   *Calendar:* Sem. plan
Inst. Accred.: SACS (1947/2001)
Prog. Accred.: Dance, Interior Design, Nursing,
Occupational Therapy

Brewton-Parker College
Highway 280, Mount Vernon 30445-0197
Type: Private, Georgia Baptist Convention, four-year
Degrees: A, B   *Enroll:* 960
URL: http://www.bpc.edu
Phone: (912) 583-2241   *Calendar:* Sem. plan
Inst. Accred.: SACS (1962/2002)
Prog. Accred.: Music

Brown Mackie College—Atlanta
4975 Jimmy Carter Blvd., Ste. 600, Norcross 30093
Type: Private, proprietary, two-year
System: Education Management Corporation
Degrees: A   *Enroll:* 134
URL: http://www.brownmackie.edu
Phone: (770) 638-0121   *Calendar:* Sem. plan
Inst. Accred.: ACICS (2003)

Central Georgia Technical College
3300 Macon Tech Dr., Macon 31206
Type: Public, state, two-year
System: Georgia Department of Technical and Adult
Education
Degrees: A   *Enroll:* 3,704
URL: http://www.cgtcollege.org
Phone: (478) 757-3400   *Calendar:* Qtr. plan
Inst. Accred.: SACS (1999/2005)
Prog. Accred.: Clinical Lab Technology, Dental Hygiene,
Respiratory Therapy

Milledgeville Campus
54 Hwy. 22 West, PO Box 1009, Milledgeville 31206
Phone: (478) 445-2300

Chattahoochee Technical College
980 South Cobb Dr., Marietta 30060
Type: Public, state, two-year
System: Georgia Department of Technical and Adult
  Education
Degrees: A   *Enroll:* 2,303
URL: http://www.chattcollege.com
Phone: (770) 528-4500   *Calendar:* Qtr. plan
Inst. Accred.: SACS (1988/2003)
Prog. Accred.: Business (ACBSP), Culinary Education,
  Engineering Technology (biomedical, computer,
  electrical), Surgical Technology

Clark Atlanta University
223 James P. Brawley Dr., Atlanta 30314
Type: Private, United Methodist Church, four-year
Degrees: B, M, D   *Enroll:* 4,537
URL: http://www.cau.edu
Phone: (404) 880-8000   *Calendar:* Sem. plan
Inst. Accred.: SACS (1990/1995)
Prog. Accred.: Business (AACSB), Health Information
  Administration, Librarianship, Public Administration,
  Social Work, Teacher Education (NCATE)

Clayton State University
5900 North Lee St., Morrow 30260-0285
Type: Public, state, four-year
System: Board of Regents of the University System of
  Georgia
Degrees: A, B   *Enroll:* 3,869
URL: http://www.clayton.edu
Phone: (770) 961-3400   *Calendar:* Sem. plan
Inst. Accred.: SACS (1971/2004)
Prog. Accred.: Business (AACSB), Dental Hygiene,
  Nursing, Nursing Education, Teacher Education (NCATE)

Coastal Georgia Community College
3700 Altama Ave., Brunswick 31520-3644
Type: Public, state, two-year
System: Board of Regents of the University System of
  Georgia
Degrees: A   *Enroll:* 1,557
URL: http://www.cgcc.edu
Phone: (912) 264-7235   *Calendar:* Sem. plan
Inst. Accred.: SACS (1967/2001)
Prog. Accred.: Clinical Lab Technology, Nursing,
  Radiography, Surgical Technology

Columbia Theological Seminary
701 Columbia Dr., PO Box 520, Decatur 30031
Type: Private, Presbyterian Church (USA), four-year
Degrees: M, D   *Enroll:* 254
URL: http://www.ctsnet.edu
Phone: (404) 378-8821   *Calendar:* 4-1-4 plan
Inst. Accred.: ATS (1938/2003), SACS (1983/2003)

Columbus State University
4225 University Ave., Columbus 31907-5645
Type: Public, state, four-year
System: Board of Regents of the University System of
  Georgia
Degrees: A, B, M, P   *Enroll:* 5,299
URL: http://www.colstate.edu
Phone: (706) 568-2001   *Calendar:* Sem. plan
Inst. Accred.: SACS (1963/1995)
Prog. Accred.: Art, Business (AACSB), Counseling, Dental
  Hygiene, Music, Nursing, Occupational Therapy, Teacher
  Education (NCATE), Theatre

Columbus Technical College
928 Manchester Expressway, Columbus 31904-6572
Type: Public, state, two-year
System: Georgia Department of Technical and Adult
  Education
Degrees: A   *Enroll:* 2,063
URL: http://www.columbustech.edu
Phone: (706) 649-1800   *Calendar:* Qtr. plan
Inst. Accred.: SACS (1990/2005)
Prog. Accred.: Dental Hygiene, Medical Assisting (AMA),
  Radiography, Surgical Technology

Coosa Valley Technical College
1 Maurice Culberson Dr., Rome 30161-6757
Type: Public, state, two-year
System: Georgia Department of Technical and Adult
  Education
Degrees: A   *Enroll:* 1,404
URL: http://www.coosavalleytech.edu
Phone: (706) 295-6963   *Calendar:* Qtr. plan
Inst. Accred.: COE (1972/2004)
Prog. Accred.: Medical Assisting (AMA), Radiography,
  Respiratory Therapy Technology

Calhoun/Gordon County Campus
1151 Hwy. 53 Spur, Calhoun 30701
Phone: (706) 295-6927

Polk County Campus
466 Brock Rd., Rockmart 30153
Phone: (770) 684-5696

Covenant College
14049 Scenic Hwy., Lookout Mountain 30750
Type: Private, Reformed Presbyterian Church, four-year
Degrees: A, B, M   *Enroll:* 1,230
URL: http://www.covenant.edu
Phone: (706) 820-1560   *Calendar:* Sem. plan
Inst. Accred.: SACS (1971/1996, Warning)

Dalton State College
213 North College Dr., Dalton 30720-3797
Type: Public, state, four-year
System: Board of Regents of the University System of
Georgia
Degrees: A, B   *Enroll:* 2,765
URL: http://www.daltonstate.edu
Phone: (706) 272-4436   *Calendar:* Sem. plan
Inst. Accred.: SACS (1969/2003)
Prog. Accred.: Clinical Lab Technology, Medical Assisting
(AMA), Nursing, Phlebotomy, Radiography

Darton College
2400 Gillionville Rd., Albany 31707-3098
Type: Public, state, two-year
System: Board of Regents of the University System of
Georgia
Degrees: A   *Enroll:* 2,592
URL: http://www.darton.edu
Phone: (229) 430-6740   *Calendar:* Sem. plan
Inst. Accred.: SACS (1968/2003)
Prog. Accred.: Clinical Lab Technology, Dental Hygiene,
Health Information Technician, Nursing, Occupational
Therapy Assisting, Physical Therapy Assisting,
Respiratory Therapy

DeKalb Technical College
495 North Indian Creek Dr., Clarkston 30021
Type: Public, state, two-year
System: Georgia Department of Technical and Adult
Education
Degrees: A   *Enroll:* 3,079
URL: http://www.dekalbtech.org
Phone: (404) 297-9522   *Calendar:* Qtr. plan
Inst. Accred.: SACS (1967/2002)
Prog. Accred.: Clinical Lab Technology, Engineering
Technology (electrical), Medical Assisting (AMA),
Opticianry, Surgical Technology

DeVry University Georgia
250 North Arcadia Ave., Decatur 30030-2198
Type: Private, proprietary, four-year
System: DeVry University
Degrees: A, B, M   *Enroll:* 3,931
URL: http://www.devry.edu/decatur
Phone: (404) 292-7900   *Calendar:* Sem. plan
Inst. Accred.: NCA-HLC (2002, *Indirect accreditation
through DeVry University, Oakbrook Terrace, IL*)
Prog. Accred.: Engineering Technology (electrical)

Alpharetta Campus
2555 Northwinds Pkwy., Alpharetta 30004
Phone: (770) 521-4900

East Central Technical College
667 Perry House Rd., PO Box 1069, Fitzgerald 31750
Type: Public, state, two-year
System: Georgia Department of Technical and Adult
Education
Degrees: A   *Enroll:* 912
URL: http://www.ecti.org
Phone: (229) 468-2000   *Calendar:* Qtr. plan
Inst. Accred.: COE (1973/2000)

Coffeee County/Douglas Campus
706 West Baker Hwy., Douglas 31533
Phone: (229) 389-4303

East Georgia College
131 College Circle, Swainsboro 30401
Type: Public, state, two-year
System: Board of Regents of the University System of
Georgia
Degrees: A   *Enroll:* 1,049
URL: http://www.ega.peachnet.edu
Phone: (478) 289-2000   *Calendar:* Sem. plan
Inst. Accred.: SACS (1975/2000)

Emmanuel College
PO Box 129, Franklin Springs 30639
Type: Private, International Pentecostal Holiness Church,
four-year
Degrees: A, B   *Enroll:* 678
URL: http://www.emmanuelcollege.edu
Phone: (706) 245-7226   *Calendar:* Sem. plan
Inst. Accred.: SACS (1967/1997)

Emory University
Atlanta 30322
Type: Private, United Methodist Church, four-year
Degrees: A, B, M, P, D   *Enroll:* 11,113
URL: http://www.emory.edu
Phone: (404) 727-6123   *Calendar:* Sem. plan
Inst. Accred.: ATS (1938/2003), SACS (1917/2003)
Prog. Accred.: Anesthesiologist Assisting, Business
(AACSB), Clinical Pastoral Education, Clinical
Psychology, Dietetics (internship), Law, Medicine,
Music, Nurse (Midwifery), Nursing, Nursing Education,
Ophthalmic Medical Technology, Oral and Maxillofacial
Pathology, Oral and Maxillofacial Surgery, Physical
Therapy, Physician Assistant, Psychology Internship,
Public Health, Radiography, Teacher Education (NCATE)

Flint River Technical College
1533 Hwy. 19, South, PO Box 1089, Thomaston 30286-
4752
Type: Public, state, two-year
System: Georgia Department of Technical and Adult
Education
Degrees: A   *Enroll:* 671
URL: http://www.flint.tec.ga.us
Phone: (706) 646-6144   *Calendar:* Qtr. plan
Inst. Accred.: COE (1973/2003)

Fort Valley State University
1005 State University Dr., Fort Valley 31030-4313
Type: Public, state, four-year
System: Board of Regents of the University System of Georgia
Degrees: A, B, M, P   *Enroll:* 2,237
URL: http://www.fvsu.edu
Phone: (478) 825-6211   *Calendar:* Sem. plan
Inst. Accred.: SACS (1951/2000)
Prog. Accred.: Engineering Technology (electrical), Family and Consumer Science, Montessori Teacher Education, Rehabilitation Counseling, Teacher Education (NCATE), Veterinary Technology

Gainesville College
PO Box 1358, Gainesville 30503-1358
Type: Public, state, two-year
System: Board of Regents of the University System of Georgia
Degrees: A   *Enroll:* 3,880
URL: http://www.gc.peachnet.edu
Phone: (770) 718-3639   *Calendar:* Sem. plan
Inst. Accred.: SACS (1968/2002)
Prog. Accred.: Business (ACBSP), Dental Assisting

Georgia Aviation and Technical College
71 Airport Rd., Eastman 31023
Type: Public, state, two-year
System: Georgia Department of Technical and Adult Education
Degrees: A
URL: http://www.gavtc.org
Phone: (478) 374-6402   *Calendar:* Qtr. plan
Inst. Accred.: COE (2001/2002)

Georgia College and State University
Milledgeville 31061-0490
Type: Public, state, four-year
System: Board of Regents of the University System of Georgia
Degrees: A, B, M, P   *Enroll:* 4,845
URL: http://www.gcsu.edu
Phone: (478) 445-5004   *Calendar:* Sem. plan
Inst. Accred.: SACS (1925/2004)
Prog. Accred.: Business (AACSB), Music, Nursing, Public Administration, Teacher Education (NCATE)

Georgia Highlands College
PO Box 1864, Rome 30162-1864
Type: Public, state, two-year
System: Board of Regents of the University System of Georgia
Degrees: A   *Enroll:* 2,139
URL: http://www.floyd.edu
Phone: (706) 802-5000   *Calendar:* Sem. plan
Inst. Accred.: SACS (1972/1997)
Prog. Accred.: Dental Hygiene, Nursing

Cartersville Campus
5441 Hwy. 20, NE, Cartersville 30121
Phone: (678) 872-8000

Georgia Institute of Technology
225 North Ave., NW, Atlanta 30332-0325
Type: Public, state, four-year
System: Board of Regents of the University System of Georgia
Degrees: B, M, D   *Enroll:* 15,605
URL: http://www.gatech.edu
Phone: (404) 894-2000   *Calendar:* Sem. plan
Inst. Accred.: SACS (1923/2004)
Prog. Accred.: Art, Business (AACSB), Computer Science, Construction Education, Engineering (aerospace, chemical, civil, computer, electrical, environmental/sanitary, industrial, materials, mechanical, nuclear, textile), Planning

Institute of Paper Science and Technology at Georgia Tech
500 10th St., N.W., Atlanta 30318
Phone: (404) 894-5700

Georgia Medical Institute
1706 Northeast Expressway, Atlanta 30329
Type: Private, proprietary, two-year
System: Corinthian Colleges, Inc
Degrees: A
URL: http://georgia-med.com
Phone: (404) 327-8787
Inst. Accred.: ACCSCT (2000/2005)

Georgia Military College
201 East Greene St., Milledgeville 31061-3398
Type: Public, local, two-year
Degrees: A   *Enroll:* 938
URL: http://www.gmc.cc.ga.us
Phone: (478) 445-2700   *Calendar:* Qtr. plan
Inst. Accred.: SACS (1940/1996)

Georgia Perimeter College
3251 Panthersville Rd., Decatur 30034
Type: Public, state, two-year
System: Board of Regents of the University System of Georgia
Degrees: A   *Enroll:* 12,052
URL: http://www.gpc.edu
Phone: (404) 244-5090   *Calendar:* Sem. plan
Inst. Accred.: SACS (1967/2002)

Clarkston Campus
555 North Indian Creek Dr., Clarkston 30021-2396
Phone: (404) 299-4000

Dunwwody Campus
2101 Womack Rd., Dunwoody 30338-4497
Phone: (770) 551-3000
Prog. Accred: Dental Hygiene

Gwinnett University Center
1000 University Center Ln., Lawrenceville 30043
Phone: (678) 407-5000

Georgia Southern University
PO Box 8033, Statesboro 30460-8033
Type: Public, state, four-year
System: Board of Regents of the University System of Georgia
Degrees: A, B, M, P, D   *Enroll:* 13,936
URL: http://www.gasou.edu
Phone: (912) 681-5611   *Calendar:* Sem. plan
Inst. Accred.: SACS (1935/2005)
Prog. Accred.: Accounting, Art, Business (AACSB), Computer Science, Construction Education, Engineering Technology (civil/construction, electrical, industrial, mechanical), Industrial Technology, Interior Design, Music, Nursing, Nursing Education, Public Administration, Recreation and Leisure Services, Teacher Education (NCATE)

Georgia Southwestern State University
800 Wheatley St., Americus 31709-4693
Type: Public, state, four-year
System: Board of Regents of the University System of Georgia
Degrees: A, B, M, P   *Enroll:* 1,914
URL: http://www.gsw.edu
Phone: (229) 928-1273   *Calendar:* Sem. plan
Inst. Accred.: SACS (1932/2003)
Prog. Accred.: Business (AACSB), Nursing, Teacher Education (NCATE)

Georgia State University
University Plaza, Atlanta 30303-3083
Type: Public, state, four-year
System: Board of Regents of the University System of Georgia
Degrees: A, B, M, P, D   *Enroll:* 21,748
URL: http://www.gsu.edu
Phone: (404) 651-2000   *Calendar:* Sem. plan
Inst. Accred.: SACS (1952/1998)
Prog. Accred.: Accounting, Art, Business (AACSB), Clinical Psychology, Counseling, Counseling Psychology, Dietetics (internship), Health Services Administration, Law, Music, Nursing, Physical Therapy, Psychology Internship, Public Administration, Rehabilitation Counseling, Respiratory Therapy, Respiratory Therapy Technology, School Psychology, Social Work, Speech-Language Pathology, Teacher Education (NCATE)

Gordon College
419 College Dr., Barnesville 30204
Type: Public, state, two-year
System: Board of Regents of the University System of Georgia
Degrees: A   *Enroll:* 2,627
URL: http://www.gdn.edu
Phone: (770) 358-5000   *Calendar:* Sem. plan
Inst. Accred.: SACS (1941/1996)
Prog. Accred.: Nursing

Griffin Technical College
501 Varsity Rd., Griffin 30223
Type: Public, state, two-year
System: Georgia Department of Technical and Adult Education
Degrees: A   *Enroll:* 2,104
URL: http://www.griffintech.edu
Phone: (770) 228-7348   *Calendar:* Qtr. plan
Inst. Accred.: COE (1971/2003), SACS (1998/2003)
Prog. Accred.: Radiography

Gupton-Jones College of Funeral Service
5141 Snapfinger Woods Dr., Decatur 30035-4022
Type: Private, independent, two-year
Degrees: A   *Enroll:* 221
URL: http://www.gupton-jones.edu
Phone: (770) 593-2257   *Calendar:* Qtr. plan
Inst. Accred.: ABFSE (1965/2000)

Gwinnett College
4230 Hwy. 29, Ste. 11, Liburn 30047
Type: Private, proprietary, two-year
Degrees: A
URL: http://www.gwinnettcollege.com
Phone: (770) 381-7200   *Calendar:* Qtr. plan
Inst. Accred.: ACICS (1988/2002)

Gwinnett Technical College
5150 Sugarloaf Pkwy., Lawrenceville 30043-5702
Type: Public, local, two-year
System: Georgia Department of Technical and Adult Education
Degrees: A   *Enroll:* 2,666
URL: http://www.gwinnetttech.edu
Phone: (770) 962-7580   *Calendar:* Qtr. plan
Inst. Accred.: SACS (1991/1997)
Prog. Accred.: Dental Assisting, Dental Laboratory Technology, Industrial Technology, Medical Assisting (AMA), Physical Therapy Assisting, Radiography, Respiratory Therapy Technology, Surgical Technology, Veterinary Technology

Heart of Georgia Technical College
560 Pinehill Rd., Dublin 31021-8896
Type: Public, state, two-year
System: Georgia Department of Technical and Adult Education
Degrees: A   *Enroll:* 628
URL: http://www.hgtc.org
Phone: (478) 275-6590   *Calendar:* Qtr. plan
Inst. Accred.: COE (1986/2003)
Prog. Accred.: Medical Assisting (AMA), Radiography, Respiratory Therapy Technology

Herzing College
3355 Lenox Rd., Ste. 100, Atlanta 30326
Type: Private, proprietary, four-year
System: Herzing College Corporate Offices
Degrees: A, B   *Enroll:* 220
URL: http://www.herzing.edu
Phone: (404) 816-4533   *Calendar:* Qtr. plan
Inst. Accred.: NCA-HLC (2004, *Indirect accreditation through Herzing College Corporate Offices, Milwaukee, WI*)

New Orleans Campus
2400 Veterans Blvd., Ste. 410, Kenner, LA 70062
Phone: (504) 733-0074

Winter Park Campus
1595 South Semoran Blvd., Winter Park, FL 32792
Phone: (407) 478-0500

Interactive College of Technology
5303 New Peachtree Rd., Chamblee 30341
Type: Private, proprietary, two-year
Degrees: A   *Enroll:* 234
Phone: (770) 216-2960
Inst. Accred.: COE (1989/2000)

College Park Campus
1580 South Lake Pkwy., Ste. C, Morrow 30260
Phone: (770) 960-1298

Florence Campus
11 Spiral Dr., Ste. 8, Florence, KY 41042
Phone: (859) 282-8989

Interdenominational Theological Center
700 Martin Luther King Jr. Dr., SW, Atlanta 30314-4143
Type: Private, interdenominational, four-year
Degrees: M, D   *Enroll:* 339
URL: http://www.itc.edu
Phone: (404) 527-7700   *Calendar:* Sem. plan
Inst. Accred.: ATS (1960/2001), SACS (1984/2001)

Kennesaw State University
1000 Chastain Rd., Kennesaw 30144-5591
Type: Public, state, four-year
System: Board of Regents of the University System of Georgia
Degrees: A, B, M   *Enroll:* 13,304
URL: http://www.kennesaw.edu
Phone: (770) 423-6000   *Calendar:* Sem. plan
Inst. Accred.: SACS (1968/1996)
Prog. Accred.: Accounting, Art, Business (AACSB), Cytogenetic Technology, Music, Nursing, Nursing Education, Teacher Education (NCATE), Theatre

LaGrange College
601 Broad St., LaGrange 30240-2999
Type: Private, United Methodist Church, four-year
Degrees: A, B, M   *Enroll:* 942
URL: http://www.lgc.edu
Phone: (706) 880-8000   *Calendar:* 4-1-4 plan
Inst. Accred.: SACS (1946/2002)
Prog. Accred.: Business (ACBSP), Nursing

Lanier Technical College
2990 Landrum Education Dr., Oakwood 30566
Type: Public, state, two-year
System: Georgia Department of Technical and Adult Education
Degrees: A   *Enroll:* 1,773
URL: http://www.laniertech.org
Phone: (770) 531-6300   *Calendar:* Qtr. plan
Inst. Accred.: COE (1972/2003)
Prog. Accred.: Clinical Lab Technology, Dental Assisting, Dental Hygiene, Medical Assisting (CAAHEP)

Forsyth Campus
7745 Majors Rd., Cumming 30028-6508
Phone: (770) 781-6800

Life University
1269 Barclay Circle, Marietta 30060
Type: Private, independent, four-year
Degrees: B, M, D   *Enroll:* 1,100
URL: http://www.life.edu
Phone: (770) 426-2600   *Calendar:* Qtr. plan
Inst. Accred.: SACS (1986/2004)
Prog. Accred.: Chiropractic Education

Luther Rice Bible College and Seminary
3038 Evans Mill Rd., Lithonia 30038
Type: Private, Southern Baptist Church, four-year
Degrees: B, M, D
URL: http://www.lrs.edu
Phone: (770) 484-1204   *Calendar:* Sem. plan
Inst. Accred.: TRACS (1988/1995)

Macon State College
100 College Station Dr., Macon 31206-5144
Type: Public, state, four-year
System: Board of Regents of the University System of Georgia
Degrees: A, B   *Enroll:* 3,481
URL: http://www.maconstate.edu
Phone: (478) 471-2700   *Calendar:* Sem. plan
Inst. Accred.: SACS (1970/2002)
Prog. Accred.: Dental Hygiene, Health Information Technician, Nursing, Respiratory Therapy

Medical College of Georgia
1120 15th St., Augusta 30912
Type: Public, state, four-year
System: Board of Regents of the University System of Georgia
Degrees: A, B, M, D   *Enroll:* 1,964
URL: http://www.mcg.edu
Phone: (706) 721-0211   *Calendar:* Sem. plan
Inst. Accred.: SACS (1973/2000)
Prog. Accred.: Clinical Lab Scientist, Combined Prosthodontics, Dental Hygiene, Dentistry, Diagnostic Medical Sonography, Endodontics, General Practice Residency, Health Information Administration, Medical Illustration, Medicine, Nuclear Medicine Technology, Nurse Anesthesia Education, Nursing, Occupational Therapy, Oral and Maxillofacial Surgery, Orthodontic and Dentofacial Orthopedics, Pediatric Dentistry, Periodontics, Physical Therapy, Physician Assistant, Prosthodontics, Psychology Internship, Radiation Therapy, Radiography, Respiratory Therapy

Mercer University
1400 Coleman Ave., Macon 31207
Type: Private, Georgia Baptist Convention, four-year
Degrees: B, M, P, D   *Enroll:* 6,185
URL: http://www.mercer.edu
Phone: (478) 301-2700   *Calendar:* Sem. plan
Inst. Accred.: SACS (1911/2005)
Prog. Accred.: Business (AACSB), Computer Science, Engineering (general), Engineering Technology (industrial), Law, Marriage and Family Therapy, Medicine, Music

Cecil B. Day Campus
3001 Mercer University Dr., Atlanta 30341
Phone: (678) 547-6000
Prog. Accred: Business (AACSB), Nursing Education, Pharmacy

Georgia Baptist College of Nursing of Mercer University
3001 Mercer University Dr., Atlanta 30341
Phone: (678) 547-6799
Prog. Accred: Nursing, Nursing Education

Middle Georgia College
1100 Second St., SE, Cochran 31014
Type: Public, state, two-year
System: Board of Regents of the University System of Georgia
Degrees: A   *Enroll:* 1,888
URL: http://www.mgc.peachnet.edu
Phone: (478) 934-6221   *Calendar:* Sem. plan
Inst. Accred.: SACS (1933/1999)
Prog. Accred.: Nursing, Occupational Therapy Assisting, Physical Therapy Assisting

Middle Georgia Technical College
80 Cohen Walker Dr., Warner Robins 31088
Type: Public, state, two-year
System: Georgia Department of Technical and Adult Education
Degrees: A
URL: http://www.middlegatech.edu
Phone: (478) 988-6800   *Calendar:* Qtr. plan
Inst. Accred.: COE (1978/2005)
Prog. Accred.: Dental Assisting, Dental Hygiene, Nuclear Medicine Technology, Radiography

Robbins Air Force Base Campus
Robbins Air Force Museum, Robbins Air Force Base 31099
Phone: (912) 929-6849

Morehouse College
830 Westview Dr., SW, Atlanta 30314
Type: Private, independent, four-year
Degrees: B   *Enroll:* 2,772
URL: http://www.morehouse.edu
Phone: (404) 681-2800   *Calendar:* Sem. plan
Inst. Accred.: SACS (1932/1998)
Prog. Accred.: Business (AACSB)

Morehouse School of Medicine
720 Westview Dr., SW, Atlanta 30310-1495
Type: Private, independent, four-year
Degrees: D   *Enroll:* 227
URL: http://www.msm.edu
Phone: (404) 752-1500   *Calendar:* Sem. plan
Inst. Accred.: SACS (1986/2001)
Prog. Accred.: Medicine, Public Health

Moultrie Technical College
361 Industrial Dr., Moultrie 31768
Type: Public, state, two-year
System: Georgia Department of Technical and Adult Education
Degrees: A   *Enroll:* 1,272
URL: http://www.moultrietech.org
Phone: (229) 891-7000   *Calendar:* Tri. plan
Inst. Accred.: COE (1974/2001)
Prog. Accred.: Radiography

Tiftarea Campus
52 Tech Dr., Tifton 31794
Phone: (229) 391-2600

Turner County Campus
222 Rock House Rd., Ashburn 31714
Phone: (229) 567-2045

North Georgia College and State University
32 College Circle, Dahlonega 30597
Type: Public, state, four-year
System: Board of Regents of the University System of
Georgia
Degrees: A, B, M, P   *Enroll:* 3,758
URL: http://www.ngcsu.edu
Phone: (706) 864-1400   *Calendar:* Sem. plan
Inst. Accred.: SACS (1935/1998)
Prog. Accred.: Business (AACSB), Business (ACBSP),
Nursing, Physical Therapy, Teacher Education (NCATE)

North Georgia Technical College
PO Box 65, 1500 Hwy. 197, North, Clarkesville 30523
Type: Public, state, two-year
System: Georgia Department of Technical and Adult
Education
Degrees: A   *Enroll:* 1,380
URL: http://www.ngtcollege.org
Phone: (706) 754-7700   *Calendar:* Qtr. plan
Inst. Accred.: COE (1972/2004)
Prog. Accred.: Clinical Lab Technology, Medical Assisting
(CAAHEP)

Blairsville Campus
434 Meeks Ave., Blairsville 30512
Phone: (706) 781-2300

North Metro Technical College
5198 Ross Rd., Acworth 30102
Type: Public, state, two-year
System: Georgia Department of Technical and Adult
Education
Degrees: A
URL: http://www.northmetro.tec.ga.us
Phone: (770) 975-4000   *Calendar:* Qtr. plan
Inst. Accred.: COE (1991/2003)
Prog. Accred.: Radiography

Northwestern Technical College
265 Bicentennial Trail, PO Box 569, Rock Spring 30739
Type: Public, state, two-year
System: Georgia Department of Technical and Adult
Education
Degrees: A   *Enroll:* 1,155
URL: http://www.nwtcollege.org
Phone: (706) 764-3510   *Calendar:* Qtr. plan
Inst. Accred.: SACS (1997/2002)
Prog. Accred.: Medical Assisting (AMA), Occupational
Therapy Assisting

Ogeechee Technical College
One Joe Kennedy Blvd., Statesboro 30458-8049
Type: Public, state, two-year
System: Georgia Department of Technical and Adult
Education
Degrees: A   *Enroll:* 1,416
URL: http://www.ogeecheetech.edu
Phone: (912) 681-5500   *Calendar:* Qtr. plan
Inst. Accred.: COE (1992/2004)
Prog. Accred.: Dental Assisting, Funeral Service
Education (Mortuary Science), Medical Assisting (AMA),
Opticianry, Radiography, Surgical Technology

Oglethorpe University
4484 Peachtree Rd., NE, Atlanta 30319-2797
Type: Private, independent, four-year
Degrees: B, M   *Enroll:* 903
URL: http://www.oglethorpe.edu
Phone: (404) 261-1441   *Calendar:* Sem. plan
Inst. Accred.: SACS (1950/1996)

Okefenokee Technical College
1701 Carswell Ave., Waycross 31503
Type: Public, state/local, two-year
System: Georgia Department of Technical and Adult
Education
Degrees: A   *Enroll:* 898
URL: http://www.okefenokeetech.edu
Phone: (912) 287-6584   *Calendar:* Qtr. plan
Inst. Accred.: COE (1972/2003)
Prog. Accred.: Clinical Lab Technology, Radiography,
Respiratory Therapy Technology, Surgical Technology

Alma Education Center
416 W. 12th St., Alma 31510
Phone: (912) 632-0951

Paine College
1235 15th St., Augusta 30901-3182
Type: Private, United Methodist Church, four-year
Degrees: B   *Enroll:* 903
URL: http://www.paine.edu
Phone: (706) 821-8200   *Calendar:* Sem. plan
Inst. Accred.: SACS (1944/2001)
Prog. Accred.: Business (ACBSP)

Piedmont College
PO Box 10, Demorest 30535
Type: Private, independent, four-year
Degrees: B, M   *Enroll:* 1,601
URL: http://www.piedmont.edu
Phone: (706) 778-3000   *Calendar:* Sem. plan
Inst. Accred.: SACS (1965/1996)
Prog. Accred.: Business (ACBSP)

Psychological Studies Institute
2055 Mount Paran Rd., NW, McCarty Bldg., Atlanta
30327
Type: Private, independent, four-year
Degrees: M
URL: http://www.psy.edu
Phone: (404) 233-3949   *Calendar:* Sem. plan
Inst. Accred.: SACS (2003)

Chattanooga Campus
1815 McCallie Ave., Chattanooga, TN 37404-3026
Phone: (423) 266-4574

Reinhardt College
7300 Reinhardt College Circle, Waleska 30183-2981
Type: Private, United Methodist Church, four-year
Degrees: A, B   *Enroll:* 998
URL: http://www.reinhardt.edu
Phone: (770) 720-5600   *Calendar:* Sem. plan
Inst. Accred.: SACS (1953/1999)

Sandersville Technical College
PO Box 6179, Sandersville 31082
Type: Public, state, two-year
System: Georgia Department of Technical and Adult
Education
Degrees: A
URL: http://www.sandersvilletech.org
Phone: (912) 553-2060   *Calendar:* Sem. plan
Inst. Accred.: COE (1999/2005)

Sanford-Brown Institute—Atlanta
1140 Hammond Dr., Ste. A-1150, Atlanta 30328
Type: Private, proprietary, two-year
System: Career Education Corporation
Degrees: A   *Enroll:* 1,185
URL: http://www.sb-atlanta.com
Phone: (770) 350-0009
Inst. Accred.: ABHES (1990/2002), ACICS (2004)

Cleveland Campus
17535 Rosbough Dr., Ste. 100, Middleburg Heights,
OH 44130
Phone: (440) 239-9640
Prog. Accred: Medical Assisting (ABHES)

Houston Campus
10500 Forum Place Dr., Ste. 200, Houston, TX 77036
Phone: (713) 779-1110
Prog. Accred: Medical Assisting (ABHES), Medical
Laboratory Technology, Surgical Technology

Houston North Loop Campus
2627 Northloop West, Ste. 100, Houston, TX 77008
Phone: (713) 863-0429
Prog. Accred: Medical Assisting (ABHES), Surgical
Technology

Landover Campus
8401 Corporate Dr., Ste. 500, Landover, MD 20785
Phone: (301) 918-8221
Prog. Accred: Medical Assisting (ABHES)

Lauderdale Lakes Campus
4780 North State Rd. 7, Building E, Ste. 100,
Lauderdale Lakes, FL 33319
Phone: (954) 733-8900
Prog. Accred: Medical Assisting (ABHES), Surgical
Technology

New York Campus
120 East 16th St., 2nd Flr., New York, NY 10003
Phone: (212) 460-8567
Prog. Accred: Medical Assisting (ABHES)

Philadelphia Campus
3600 Horizon Blvd., Ste. GL-1, Trevose, PA 19053
Phone: (215) 244-4906
Prog. Accred: Medical Assisting (ABHES)

The Savannah College of Art and Design
PO Box 3146, Savannah 31402-3146
Type: Private, independent, four-year
Degrees: B, M   *Enroll:* 5,822
URL: http://www.scad.edu
Phone: (912) 525-5100   *Calendar:* Qtr. plan
Inst. Accred.: SACS (1983/1999)

Savannah River College
2528 Center West Pkwy., Building A, Augusta 30909
Type: Private, proprietary, two-year
Degrees: A
URL: http://savannahrivercollege.edu
Phone: (706) 738-5046
Inst. Accred.: ACICS (1976/1999)

Savannah State University
State College Branch, PO Box 20449, Savannah 31404
Type: Public, state, four-year
System: Board of Regents of the University System of
Georgia
Degrees: B, M   *Enroll:* 2,478
URL: http://www.savstate.edu
Phone: (912) 356-2187   *Calendar:* Sem. plan
Inst. Accred.: SACS (1951/2001)
Prog. Accred.: Business (AACSB), Engineering Technology
(civil/construction, electrical, mechanical), Social Work

Savannah Technical College
5717 White Bluff Rd., Savannah 31405-5521
Type: Public, state, two-year
System: Georgia Department of Technical and Adult
Education
Degrees: A   *Enroll:* 2,295
URL: http://www.savtec.org
Phone: (912) 351-6362   *Calendar:* Qtr. plan
Inst. Accred.: SACS (1991/1997, Warning)
Prog. Accred.: Culinary Education, Dental Assisting,
Engineering Technology (electrical), Medical Assisting
(AMA), Practical Nursing, Surgical Technology

Shorter College
315 Shorter Ave., Rome 30165-4298
Type: Private, Georgia Baptist Convention, four-year
Degrees: B, M   *Enroll:* 2,383
URL: http://www.shorter.edu
Phone: (706) 291-2121   *Calendar:* Sem. plan
Inst. Accred.: SACS (1923/2002)
Prog. Accred.: Music

South Georgia College
100 West College Park Dr., Douglas 31533-5098
Type: Public, state, two-year
System: Board of Regents of the University System of Georgia
Degrees: A   *Enroll:* 982
URL: http://www.sga.edu
Phone: (912) 389-4510   *Calendar:* Sem. plan
Inst. Accred.: SACS (1934/1997)
Prog. Accred.: Nursing

South Georgia Technical College
1583 Southerfield Rd., Americus 31709-8104
Type: Public, state, two-year
System: Georgia Department of Technical and Adult Education
Degrees: A   *Enroll:* 1,161
URL: http://www.sgatech.org
Phone: (229) 931-2394   *Calendar:* Qtr. plan
Inst. Accred.: COE (1973/2005)
Prog. Accred.: Medical Assisting (CAAHEP)

Cordele Campus
402 Midway Rd., Cordele 31015
Phone: (229) 931-2150

South University
709 Mall Blvd., Savannah 31406
Type: Private, proprietary, four-year
System: Education Management Corporation
Degrees: A, B, M   *Enroll:* 541
URL: http://www.southuniversity.cdu
Phone: (912) 201-8000   *Calendar:* Qtr. plan
Inst. Accred.: SACS (1985/2000)
Prog. Accred.: Medical Assisting (AMA), Pharmacy, Physical Therapy Assisting, Physician Assistant

Columbia Campus
PO Box 1196, 3810 Main St., Columbia, SC 29203
Phone: (803) 799-9082

Montgomery Campus
5355 Vaughn Rd., Montgomery, AL 36116
Phone: (334) 263-1013
Prog. Accred: Medical Assisting (AMA), Physical Therapy Assisting

West Palm Beach Campus
1760 North Congress Ave., West Palm Beach, FL 33409-5178
Phone: (561) 697-9200
Prog. Accred: Medical Assisting (AMA), Nursing Education, Physical Therapy Assisting

Southeastern Technical College
3001 East First St., Vidalia 30474
Type: Public, state, two-year
System: Georgia Department of Technical and Adult Education
Degrees: A
URL: http://www.southeasterntech.edu
Phone: (912) 538-3100   *Calendar:* Qtr. plan
Inst. Accred.: COE (1992/2003)
Prog. Accred.: Radiography

Glennville Campus
211 S. Tillman St., Glennville 30427
Phone: (912) 654-5276

Southern Polytechnic State University
1100 South Marietta Pkwy., Marietta 30060-2896
Type: Public, state, four-year
System: Board of Regents of the University System of Georgia
Degrees: A, B, M   *Enroll:* 2,818
URL: http://www.spsu.edu
Phone: (770) 528-7200   *Calendar:* Sem. plan
Inst. Accred.: SACS (1964/1998)
Prog. Accred.: Business (ACBSP), Construction Education, Engineering Technology (apparel, civil/construction, computer, electrical, industrial, mechanical, telecommunications)

Southwest Georgia Technical College
15689 US Hwy. 19 North, Thomasville 31792
Type: Public, state, two-year
System: Georgia Department of Technical and Adult Education
Degrees: A   *Enroll:* 717
URL: http://www.swgtc.net
Phone: (229) 225-4096   *Calendar:* Qtr. plan
Inst. Accred.: SACS (1997/2002)
Prog. Accred.: Clinical Lab Technology, Medical Assisting (AMA), Radiography, Respiratory Therapy, Surgical Technology

Spelman College
350 Spelman Ln., SW, Atlanta 30314-4399
Type: Private, independent, four-year
Degrees: B   *Enroll:* 2,013
URL: http://www.spelman.edu
Phone: (404) 681-3643   *Calendar:* Sem. plan
Inst. Accred.: SACS (1932/2000)
Prog. Accred.: Music, Teacher Education (NCATE)

Swainsboro Technical College
346 Kite Rd., Swainsboro 30401
Type: Public, state, two-year
System: Georgia Department of Technical and Adult Education
Degrees: A   *Enroll:* 422
URL: http://www.swainsboro.tec.ga.us
Phone: (478) 289-2200   *Calendar:* Qtr. plan
Inst. Accred.: COE (1973/2005)
Prog. Accred.: Medical Assisting (CAAHEP)

Thomas University
1501 Millpond Rd., Thomasville 31792
Type: Private, independent, four-year
Degrees: A, B, M   *Enroll:* 629
URL: http://www.thomasu.edu
Phone: (229) 226-1621   *Calendar:* Sem. plan
Inst. Accred.: SACS (1984/1995)
Prog. Accred.: Nursing, Social Work

Toccoa Falls College
PO Box 800777, Toccoa Falls 30598
Type: Private, Christian and Missionary Alliance, four-year
Degrees: A, B   *Enroll:* 803
URL: http://www.tfc.edu
Phone: (706) 886-6831   *Calendar:* Sem. plan
Inst. Accred.: ABHE (1957/1998), SACS (1983/2001)
Prog. Accred.: Music

Epworth Campus
PO Box 539, Epworth 30541
Phone: (706) 492-5921

Truett McConnell College
100 Alumni Dr., Cleveland 30528
Type: Private, Georgia Baptist Convention, four-year
Degrees: A, B   *Enroll:* 363
URL: http://www.truett.edu
Phone: (706) 865-2134   *Calendar:* Sem. plan
Inst. Accred.: SACS (1966/2000)
Prog. Accred.: Music

The University of Georgia
436 East Broad St., Athens 30602
Type: Public, state, four-year
System: Board of Regents of the University System of Georgia
Degrees: A, B, M, P, D   *Enroll:* 30,841
URL: http://www.uga.edu
Phone: (706) 542-3000   *Calendar:* Sem. plan
Inst. Accred.: SACS (1909/2001)
Prog. Accred.: Accounting, Art, Audiology, Business (AACSB), Clinical Psychology, Counseling, Counseling Psychology, Engineering (agricultural, bioengineering), Family and Consumer Science, Forestry, Interior Design, Journalism, Landscape Architecture, Law, Marriage and Family Therapy, Music, Pharmacy, Public Administration, Recreation and Leisure Services, Rehabilitation Counseling, School Psychology, Social Work, Speech-Language Pathology, Teacher Education (NCATE), Theatre, Veterinary Medicine

University of West Georgia
1600 Maple St., Carrollton 30118-0001
Type: Public, state, four-year
System: Board of Regents of the University System of Georgia
Degrees: A, B, M, P, D   *Enroll:* 8,332
URL: http://www.westga.edu
Phone: (770) 839-5000   *Calendar:* Sem. plan
Inst. Accred.: SACS (1936/2003)
Prog. Accred.: Accounting, Art, Business (AACSB), Computer Science, Counseling, Music, Nursing, Nursing Education, Public Administration, Teacher Education (NCATE), Theatre

Valdosta State University
1500 North Patterson St., Valdosta 31698
Type: Public, state, four-year
System: Board of Regents of the University System of Georgia
Degrees: A, B, M, P, D   *Enroll:* 8,669
URL: http://www.valdosta.edu
Phone: (229) 333-5800   *Calendar:* Sem. plan
Inst. Accred.: SACS (1929/2000)
Prog. Accred.: Art, Business (AACSB), Dental Hygiene, Marriage and Family Therapy, Music, Nursing, Nursing Education, Public Administration, Social Work, Speech-Language Pathology, Teacher Education (NCATE), Theatre

Valdosta Technical College
4089 Val-Tech Rd., PO Box 928, Valdosta 31603-0928
Type: Public, state, two-year
System: Georgia Department of Technical and Adult Education
Degrees: A   *Enroll:* 1,461
URL: http://www.valdostatech.org
Phone: (229) 333-2100   *Calendar:* Qtr. plan
Inst. Accred.: COE (1974/2002)
Prog. Accred.: Athletic Training, Dental Assisting, Dental Hygiene, Medical Assisting (AMA), Radiography

Waycross College
2001 South Georgia Pkwy., Waycross 31503-9248
Type: Public, state, two-year
System: Board of Regents of the University System of Georgia
Degrees: A   *Enroll:* 615
URL: http://www.waycross.edu
Phone: (912) 285-6133   *Calendar:* Sem. plan
Inst. Accred.: SACS (1978/2003)

Wesleyan College
4760 Forsyth Rd., Macon 31210-4462
Type: Private, United Methodist Church, four-year
Degrees: B, M   *Enroll:* 642
URL: http://www.wesleyancollege.edu
Phone: (478) 477-1110   *Calendar:* Sem. plan
Inst. Accred.: SACS (1919/2005)
Prog. Accred.: Music

West Central Technical College
176 Murphy Campus Blvd., Waco 30182
Type: Public, state, two-year
System: Georgia Department of Technical and Adult
  Education
Degrees: A   *Enroll:* 1,154
URL: http://www.westcentraltech.edu
Phone: (770) 537-6000   *Calendar:* Qtr. plan
Inst. Accred.: SACS (1998/2003)

Carroll Campus
997 South Hwy. 16, Carrollton 30116
Phone: (770) 836-6800

Douglas Campus
4600 Timber Ridge Dr., Douglasville 30135
Phone: (770) 947-7200
Prog. Accred: Dental Hygiene, Medical Assisting
  (AMA), Radiography

Newman Campus
160 Martin Luther King, Jr. Dr., Newman 30263
Phone: (678) 423-2000
Prog. Accred: Dental Hygiene

West Georgia Technical College
303 Fort Dr., LaGrange 30240
Type: Public, state, two-year
System: Georgia Department of Technical and Adult
  Education
Degrees: A   *Enroll:* 1,179
URL: http://www.westgatech.edu
Phone: (706) 845-4323   *Calendar:* Qtr. plan
Inst. Accred.: COE (1973/2005)
Prog. Accred.: Medical Assisting (AMA), Radiography

Young Harris College
PO Box 68, 1 College St., Young Harris 30582
Type: Private, United Methodist Church, two-year
Degrees: A   *Enroll:* 587
URL: http://www.yhc.edu
Phone: (706) 379-3111   *Calendar:* Sem. plan
Inst. Accred.: SACS (1938/2001)
Prog. Accred.: Music

GUAM

Guam Community College
PO Box 23069, Guam Main Facility, Barrigada 96921
Type: Public, state/local, two-year
Degrees: A   *Enroll:* 799
URL: http://www.guamcc.net
Phone: (671) 735-4422   *Calendar:* Sem. plan
Inst. Accred.: WASC-JR. (1979/2000)

Pacific Islands Bible College
PO Box 22619, Guam Main Facility, Barrigada 96921-2619
Type: Private, Evangelical Church, four-year
Degrees: A, B
URL: http://www.pibc-edu.org
Phone: (671) 734-1812   *Calendar:* Sem. plan
Inst. Accred.: TRACS (2004)

University of Guam
UOG Station, Mangilao 96923
Type: Public, state, four-year
Degrees: A, B, M   *Enroll:* 2,384
URL: http://www.uog.edu
Phone: (671) 735-2975   *Calendar:* Sem. plan
Inst. Accred.: WASC-SR. (1963/2002)
Prog. Accred.: Business (AACSB), Nursing, Social Work

HAWAII

Argosy University Hawai'i
400 Pacific Tower, 1001 Bishop St., Honolulu 96813
Type: Private, proprietary, four-year
System: Argosy University
Degrees: M, D
URL: http://www.argosyu.edu
Phone: (808) 536-5555   *Calendar:* Tri. plan
Inst. Accred.: NCA-HLC (1981/2001, *Indirect accreditation through Argosy University, Chicago, IL*)
Prog. Accred.: Clinical Psychology

Babel University
Professional School of Translation
1720 Ala Moana Blvd., Tradewinds, Ste. A5, Honolulu 96815-1302
Type: Private, proprietary, four-year
Degrees: M
URL: http://www.babel-unv.org
Phone: (808) 946-3773
Inst. Accred.: DETC (2002)

Brigham Young University—Hawaii Campus
55-220 Kulanui St., A152 ASB, Laie 96762-1266
Type: Public, The Church of Jesus Christ of Latter-day Saints, four-year
Degrees: A, B   *Enroll:* 2,538
URL: http://www.byuh.edu
Phone: (808) 293-3211   *Calendar:* 4-4-x plan
Inst. Accred.: WASC-SR. (1959/1996)
Prog. Accred.: Business (AACSB), Social Work

Chaminade University of Honolulu
3140 Waialae Ave., Honolulu 96816-1578
Type: Private, Roman Catholic Church, four-year
Degrees: A, B, M   *Enroll:* 2,223
URL: http://www.chaminade.edu
Phone: (808) 735-4711   *Calendar:* Sem. plan
Inst. Accred.: WASC-SR. (1960/2002)
Prog. Accred.: Montessori Teacher Education

Hawaii Business College
33 South King St., Honolulu 96813-4316
Type: Private, proprietary, two-year
Degrees: A   *Enroll:* 328
URL: http://www.hbc.edu
Phone: (808) 524-4014
Inst. Accred.: ACICS (1976/2001)

Hawaii Community College
200 West Kawili St., Hilo 96720-4091
Type: Public, state, two-year
System: University of Hawaii System
Degrees: A   *Enroll:* 1,531
URL: http://www.hawcc.hawaii.edu
Phone: (808) 974-7611   *Calendar:* Sem. plan
Inst. Accred.: WASC-JR. (1973/2001, Warning)
Prog. Accred.: Culinary Education, English Language Education, Nursing

Hawaii Pacific University
1166 Fort St. Mall, Honolulu 96813
Type: Private, independent, four-year
Degrees: A, B, M   *Enroll:* 5,722
URL: http://www.hpu.edu
Phone: (808) 544-0200   *Calendar:* Sem. plan
Inst. Accred.: WASC-SR. (1973/2005)
Prog. Accred.: Social Work

Windward Hawaii Loa Campus
45-045 Kamehameha Hwy., Kaneohe 96744
Phone: (808) 235-3641
Prog. Accred: Nursing

Hawaii Technology Institute
629 Pohukaina St., Honolulu 96813
Type: Private, proprietary, two-year
Degrees: A
URL: http://www.hti.edu
Phone: (808) 522-2700
Inst. Accred.: ACCSCT (2000/2005, Probation)

Hawaii Tokai International College
2241 Kapiolani Blvd., Honolulu 96826
Type: Private, independent, two-year
Degrees: A
URL: http://www.tokai.edu
Phone: (808) 983-4100   *Calendar:* Qtr. plan
Inst. Accred.: WASC-JR. (1994/2000)

Heald College—Honolulu
1500 Kapiolani Blvd., Ste. 201, Honolulu 96814
Type: Private, independent, two-year
System: Heald Colleges
Degrees: A   *Enroll:* 982
URL: http://www.heald.edu
Phone: (808) 955-1500   *Calendar:* Qtr. plan
Inst. Accred.: WASC-JR. (1983/2000)

Honolulu Community College
874 Dillingham Blvd., Honolulu 96817
Type: Public, state, two-year
System: University of Hawaii System
Degrees: A   *Enroll:* 2,534
URL: http://honolulu.hawaii.edu
Phone: (808) 845-9225   *Calendar:* Sem. plan
Inst. Accred.: WASC-JR. (1970/2001, Warning)

Institute of Clinical Acupuncture and Oriental Medicine
1270 Queen Emma St., Auite 400, Honolulu 96813
Type: Private, proprietary, four-year
Degrees: M
URL: http://www.orientalmedschool.com
Phone: (808) 521-2288   *Calendar:* Sem. plan
Inst. Accred.: ACAOM (2002)

International College and Graduate School
20 Dowsett Ave., Honolulu 96817
Type: Private, nondenominational, four-year
Degrees: B, M   *Enroll:* 42
URL: http://www.icgshawaii.org
Phone: (808) 595-4247   *Calendar:* Sem. plan
Inst. Accred.: TRACS (1994/2000, Warning)

Kapi'olani Community College
4303 Diamond Head Rd., Honolulu 96816
Type: Public, state, two-year
System: University of Hawaii System
Degrees: A   *Enroll:* 4,472
URL: http://www.kcc.hawaii.edu
Phone: (808) 734-9000   *Calendar:* Sem. plan
Inst. Accred.: WASC-JR. (1970/2001)
Prog. Accred.: Clinical Lab Technology, Culinary
Education, Medical Assisting (AMA), Nursing,
Occupational Therapy Assisting, Phlebotomy, Physical
Therapy Assisting, Radiography, Respiratory Therapy

Kaua'i Community College
University of Hawaii, 3-1901 Kaumaiali, Lihue 96766
Type: Public, state, two-year
System: University of Hawaii System
Degrees: A   *Enroll:* 701
URL: http://www.kauaicc.hawaii.edu
Phone: (808) 245-8311   *Calendar:* Sem. plan
Inst. Accred.: WASC-JR. (1971/2001)
Prog. Accred.: Nursing

Leeward Community College
96-045 Ala Ike, Pearl City 96782
Type: Public, state, two-year
System: University of Hawaii System
Degrees: A   *Enroll:* 3,896
URL: http://www.lcc.hawaii.edu
Phone: (808) 455-0011   *Calendar:* Sem. plan
Inst. Accred.: WASC-JR. (1971/2001)
Prog. Accred.: Culinary Education

Maui Community College
310 West Kaahumanu Ave., Kahului 96732
Type: Public, state, two-year
System: University of Hawaii System
Degrees: A   *Enroll:* 1,755
URL: http://www.maui.hawaii.edu
Phone: (808) 984-3500   *Calendar:* Sem. plan
Inst. Accred.: WASC-JR. (1980/2001)
Prog. Accred.: Culinary Education, Nursing

Traditional Chinese Medicine College of Hawaii
65-1206 Mamalohoa Hwy., Building 3, Ste. 9, Kamuela
96743
Type: Private, proprietary, four-year
Degrees: M
URL: http://www.ilhawaii.net/~chinese
Phone: (808) 885-9226
Inst. Accred.: ACAOM (2002)

TransPacific Hawaii College
5257 Kalanianaole Hwy., Honolulu 96821
Type: Private, independent, two-year
Degrees: A
URL: http://www.transpacific.org
Phone: (808) 377-5402   *Calendar:* Sem. plan
Inst. Accred.: WASC-JR. (1985/2002)

University of Hawaii at Hilo
200 West Kawili St., Hilo 96720
Type: Public, state, four-year
System: University of Hawaii System
Degrees: A, B, M   *Enroll:* 2,897
URL: http://www.uhh.hawaii.edu
Phone: (808) 974-7414   *Calendar:* Sem. plan
Inst. Accred.: WASC-SR. (1976/2004)
Prog. Accred.: Business (AACSB), Nursing

University of Hawaii at Manoa
2444 Dole St., Bachman Hall, Honolulu 96844
Type: Public, state, four-year
System: University of Hawaii System
Degrees: A, B, M, P, D   *Enroll:* 16,562
URL: http://www.uhm.hawaii.edu
Phone: (808) 956-8111   *Calendar:* Sem. plan
Inst. Accred.: WASC-SR. (1952/2005)
Prog. Accred.: Audiology, Business (AACSB), Clinical Lab
Scientist, Clinical Psychology, Counseling, Dental
Hygiene, Engineering (bioengineering, civil, electrical,
mechanical, ocean), Law, Librarianship, Medicine,
Music, Nursing, Nursing Education, Planning,
Psychology Internship, Public Health, Rehabilitation
Counseling, Social Work, Speech-Language Pathology,
Teacher Education (NCATE)

University of Hawaii at West Oahu
96-129 Ala Ike, Pearl City 96782
Type: Public, state, four-year
System: University of Hawaii System
Degrees: B   *Enroll:* 524
URL: http://www.uhwo.hawaii.edu
Phone: (808) 454-4750   *Calendar:* Sem. plan
Inst. Accred.: WASC-SR. (1981/2005)

Windward Community College
45-720 Keaahala Rd., Kaneohe 96744
Type: Public, state, two-year
System: University of Hawaii System
Degrees: A   *Enroll:* 1,187
URL: http://www.wcc.hawaii.edu
Phone: (808) 235-7400   *Calendar:* Sem. plan
Inst. Accred.: WASC-JR. (1977/2001, Warning)

World Medicine Institute
1110 University Ave., Ste. 308, Honolulu 96826
Type: Private, proprietary, four-year
Degrees: M   *Enroll:* 28
URL: http://www.acupuncture-hi.com
Phone: (808) 949-1050   *Calendar:* Sem. plan
Inst. Accred.: ACAOM (1991/2002)

IDAHO

Albertson College of Idaho
2112 Cleveland Blvd., Caldwell 83605
Type: Private, independent, four-year
Degrees: B, M *Enroll:* 808
URL: http://www.albertson.edu
Phone: (208) 459-5011 *Calendar:* 4-1-4 plan
Inst. Accred.: NWCCU (1922/1999)

Apollo College—Boise
1200 North Liberty Rd., Boise 83704
Type: Private, proprietary, two-year
System: U.S. Education Corporation
Degrees: A
URL: http://www.apolloboise.com
Phone: (208) 377-8080
Inst. Accred.: ABHES (1982/2005)
Prog. Accred.: Dental Assisting, Dental Hygiene, Medical
  Assisting (ABHES)

Boise Bible College
8695 West Marigold St., Boise 83714-1220
Type: Private, Christian Churches/Churches of Christ,
  four-year
Degrees: A, B *Enroll:* 99
URL: http://www.boisebible.edu
Phone: (208) 376-7731 *Calendar:* Sem. plan
Inst. Accred.: ABHE (1988/1999)

Boise State University
1910 University Dr., Boise 83725
Type: Public, state, four-year
System: State Board of Education and Board of Regents
  of the University of Idaho
Degrees: A, B, M, D *Enroll:* 13,868
URL: http://www.boisestate.edu
Phone: (208) 426-1011 *Calendar:* Sem. plan
Inst. Accred.: NWCCU (1941/1999)
Prog. Accred.: Accounting, Art, Athletic Training, Business
  (AACSB), Computer Science, Construction Education,
  Counseling, Culinary Education, Dental Assisting,
  Engineering (civil, electrical, mechanical), Health
  Information Technician, Music, Nursing, Public
  Administration, Radiography, Respiratory Therapy,
  Respiratory Therapy Technology, Social Work, Surgical
  Technology, Teacher Education (NCATE), Theatre

Brigham Young University—Idaho
525 South Center, Rexburg 83460
Type: Private, The Church of Jesus Christ of Latter-day
  Saints, four-year
Degrees: A, B *Enroll:* 10,599
URL: http://www.byui.edu
Phone: (208) 496-2011 *Calendar:* Sem. plan
Inst. Accred.: NWCCU (1936/2004)
Prog. Accred.: Engineering Technology (electrical,
  manufacturing), Interior Design, Music, Nursing

College of Southern Idaho
315 Falls Ave., PO Box 1238, Twin Falls 83303-1238
Type: Public, local, two-year
System: State Board of Education and Board of Regents
  of the University of Idaho
Degrees: A *Enroll:* 4,350
URL: http://www.csi.edu
Phone: (208) 733-9554 *Calendar:* Sem. plan
Inst. Accred.: NWCCU (1968/2005)
Prog. Accred.: Medical Assisting (AMA), Nursing,
  Radiography, Veterinary Technology

Eastern Idaho Technical College
1600 South 25th East, Idaho Falls 83404-5788
Type: Public, state, two-year
System: State Board of Education and Board of Regents
  of the University of Idaho
Degrees: A *Enroll:* 552
URL: http://www.eitc.edu
Phone: (208) 524-3000 *Calendar:* Sem. plan
Inst. Accred.: NWCCU (1982/2002)
Prog. Accred.: Medical Assisting (CAAHEP)

Idaho State University
921 South Eighth Ave., Pocatello 83209
Type: Public, state, four-year
System: State Board of Education and Board of Regents
  of the University of Idaho
Degrees: A, B, M, P, D *Enroll:* 10,789
URL: http://www.isu.edu
Phone: (208) 282-0211 *Calendar:* Sem. plan
Inst. Accred.: NWCCU (1923/1999)
Prog. Accred.: Accounting, Advanced Education in
  General Dentistry, Applied Science (occupational health
  and safety), Audiology, Business (AACSB), Clinical Lab
  Scientist, Clinical Psychology, Counseling, Culinary
  Education, Dental Hygiene, Dental Laboratory
  Technology, Dietetics (Internship), Engineering (civil,
  electrical, general, mechanical), Health Information
  Technician, Medical Assisting (AMA), Music, Nursing,
  Nursing Education, Occupational Therapy, Pharmacy,
  Physical Therapy, Physical Therapy Assisting, Physician
  Assistant, Public Health, Social Work, Speech-Language
  Pathology, Teacher Education (NCATE)

ITT Technical Institute
12302 West Explorer Dr., Boise 83713
Type: Private, proprietary, four-year
System: ITT Educational Services, Inc.
Degrees: A, B   *Enroll:* 357
URL: http://www.itt-tech.edu
Phone: (208) 322-8844   *Calendar:* Qtr. plan
Inst. Accred.: ACICS (1999/2004)

Albany Campus
13 Airline Dr., Albany, NY 12205
Phone: (518) 452-9300

Owings Mills Campus
11301 Red Run Blvd., Owings Mills, MD 21117
Phone: (443) 394-7115

Lewis-Clark State College
500 8th Ave., Lewiston 83501
Type: Public, state, four-year
System: State Board of Education and Board of Regents
of the University of Idaho
Degrees: A, B   *Enroll:* 2,746
URL: http://www.lcsc.edu
Phone: (208) 792-5272   *Calendar:* Sem. plan
Inst. Accred.: NWCCU (1964/2003)
Prog. Accred.: Nursing, Nursing Education, Social Work,
Teacher Education (NCATE)

North Idaho College
1000 West Garden Ave., Coeur d'Alene 83814
Type: Public, local, two-year
System: State Board of Education and Board of Regents
of the University of Idaho
Degrees: A   *Enroll:* 3,318
URL: http://www.nic.edu
Phone: (208) 769-3300   *Calendar:* Sem. plan
Inst. Accred.: NWCCU (1947/2003)
Prog. Accred.: Nursing

Northwest Nazarene University
623 Holly St., Nampa 83686-5897
Type: Private, Church of the Nazarene, four-year
Degrees: A, B, M   *Enroll:* 1,436
URL: http://www.nnu.edu
Phone: (208) 467-8011   *Calendar:* Sem. plan
Inst. Accred.: NWCCU (1930/2001)
Prog. Accred.: Business (ACBSP), Counseling, Music,
Nursing Education, Social Work, Teacher Education
(NCATE)

University of Idaho
Moscow 83844-3151
Type: Public, state, four-year
System: State Board of Education and Board of Regents
of the University of Idaho
Degrees: B, M, D   *Enroll:* 11,042
URL: http://www.uidaho.edu
Phone: (208) 885-6111   *Calendar:* Sem. plan
Inst. Accred.: NWCCU (1918/1999)
Prog. Accred.: Accounting, Art, Business (AACSB),
Computer Science, Counseling, Dietetics (coordinated),
Engineering (agricultural, bioengineering, chemical,
civil, computer, electrical, geological/geophysical,
mechanical, metallurgical, mining), Forestry, Landscape
Architecture, Law, Music, Recreation and Leisure
Services, Rehabilitation Counseling, Teacher Education
(NCATE)

ILLINOIS

Adler School of Professional Psychology
65 East Wacker Place, Ste. 2100, Chicago 60601
Type: Private, independent, four-year
Degrees: M, D   *Enroll:* 214
URL: http://www.adler.edu
Phone: (312) 201-5900   *Calendar:* Sem. plan
Inst. Accred.: NCA-HLC (1978/2002)
Prog. Accred.: Clinical Psychology

American Academy of Art
332 South Michigan Ave., #300, Chicago 60604-4302
Type: Private, proprietary, four-year
Degrees: A, B   *Enroll:* 290
URL: http://www.aaart.edu
Phone: (312) 461-0600   *Calendar:* Sem. plan
Inst. Accred.: ACCSCT (1974/2004)

Argosy University Chicago
Two First National Plaza, 20 South Clark St., Chicago 60603
Type: Private, proprietary, four-year
System: Argosy University
Degrees: M, D   *Enroll:* 575
URL: http://www.argosyu.edu
Phone: (312) 201-0200   *Calendar:* Tri. plan
Inst. Accred.: NCA-HLC (1981/2001, *Indirect accreditation through Argosy University, Chicago, IL*)
Prog. Accred.: Clinical Psychology

Argosy University Schaumburg
1000 North Plaza Dr., Ste. 100, Schaumburg 60173
Type: Private, proprietary, four-year
System: Argosy University
Degrees: M, D
URL: http://www.argosy.edu
Phone: (847) 290-7400   *Calendar:* Tri. plan
Inst. Accred.: NCA-HLC (1981/2001, *Indirect accreditation through Argosy University, Chicago, IL*)
Prog. Accred.: Clinical Psychology

Augustana College
639 38th St., Rock Island 61201
Type: Private, Evangelical Lutheran Church in America, four-year
Degrees: B   *Enroll:* 2,290
URL: http://www.augustana.edu
Phone: (309) 794-7000   *Calendar:* Qtr. plan
Inst. Accred.: NCA-HLC (1913/1996)
Prog. Accred.: Music, Teacher Education (NCATE)

Aurora University
347 South Gladstone Ave., Aurora 60506-4892
Type: Private, independent, four-year
Degrees: B, M, D   *Enroll:* 2,604
URL: http://www.aurora.edu
Phone: (630) 892-6431   *Calendar:* Tri. plan
Inst. Accred.: NCA-HLC (1938/2003)
Prog. Accred.: Business (ACBSP), Nursing, Nursing Education, Recreation and Leisure Services, Social Work

New College of Aurora University
University Ctr., 14 N. Sheridan Rd., Waukegan 60085
Phone: (708) 662-0100

School of Nursing/Chicago Campus
300 North Michigan, Ste. 300, Chicago 60601
Phone: (312) 357-1080

Wisconsin Campus
PO Box 51687, New Berlin, WI 53151
Phone: (414) 789-6260

Barat College of DePaul University
700 East Westleigh Rd., Lake Forest 60045
Type: Private, Roman Catholic Church, four-year
Degrees: B, M   *Enroll:* 103
URL: http://www.barat.edu
Phone: (847) 234-3000   *Calendar:* Sem. plan
Inst. Accred.: NCA-HLC (1943/2003)
Prog. Accred.: Nursing

Benedictine University
5700 College Rd., Lisle 60532
Type: Private, Roman Catholic Church, four-year
Degrees: A, B, M, D   *Enroll:* 2,160
URL: http://www.ben.edu
Phone: (630) 829-6005   *Calendar:* Sem. plan
Inst. Accred.: NCA-HLC (1958/1996)
Prog. Accred.: Dietetics (internship), Nursing

Black Hawk College
6600 34th Ave., Moline 61265
Type: Public, local, two-year
System: Illinois Community College Board
Degrees: A   *Enroll:* 4,158
URL: http://www.bhc.edu
Phone: (309) 796-1311   *Calendar:* Sem. plan
Inst. Accred.: NCA-HLC (1986/2003)
Prog. Accred.: Medical Assisting (AMA), Nursing, Occupational Therapy Assisting, Physical Therapy Assisting

Blackburn College
700 College Ave., Carlinville 62626
Type: Private, United Presbyterian Church, four-year
Degrees: B   *Enroll:* 605
URL: http://www.blackburn.edu
Phone: (217) 854-3231   *Calendar:* Sem. plan
Inst. Accred.: NCA-HLC (1918/2001)

Blessing-Rieman College of Nursing
Broadway at 11th St., PO Box 7005, Quincy 62305-7005
Type: Private, independent, four-year
Degrees: B   *Enroll:* 163
URL: http://www.brcn.edu
Phone: (217) 228-5520   *Calendar:* Sem. plan
Inst. Accred.: NCA-HLC (2003)
Prog. Accred.: Clinical Lab Scientist, Nursing, Nursing
  Education

Bradley University
1501 West Bradley Ave., Peoria 61625
Type: Private, independent, four-year
Degrees: B, M, D   *Enroll:* 5,532
URL: http://www.bradley.edu
Phone: (309) 676-7611   *Calendar:* Sem. plan
Inst. Accred.: NCA-HLC (1913/2001)
Prog. Accred.: Accounting, Art, Business (AACSB),
  Construction Education, Counseling, Engineering (civil,
  electrical, industrial, manufacturing, mechanical),
  Engineering Technology (manufacturing), Music, Nurse
  Anesthesia Education, Nursing, Physical Therapy, Social
  Work, Teacher Education (NCATE), Theatre

Cardean University
111 North Canal St., Ste. 455, Chicago 60606-7204
Type: Private, proprietary, four-year
Degrees: M   *Enroll:* 860
URL: http://www.cardean.edu
Phone: (312) 669-8000   *Calendar:* Sem. plan
Inst. Accred.: DETC (2000)

Career Colleges of Chicago
11 East Adams St., Chicago 60603
Type: Private, proprietary, two-year
Degrees: A   *Enroll:* 35
URL: http://www.careerchi.com
Phone: (312) 895-6300   *Calendar:* Qtr. plan
Inst. Accred.: ACICS (1968/2004, Probation)

Carl Sandburg College
2400 Tom L. Wilson Blvd., Galesburg 61401
Type: Public, state/local, two-year
System: Illinois Community College Board
Degrees: A   *Enroll:* 2,164
URL: http://www.sandburg.edu
Phone: (309) 344-2518   *Calendar:* Sem. plan
Inst. Accred.: NCA-HLC (1974/2001)
Prog. Accred.: Dental Hygiene, Funeral Service Education
  (Mortuary Science), Radiography

Bushnell Extension Campus
380 East Main St., Bushnell 61422
Phone: (309) 772-2177

Carthage Campus
305 Sandburg Dr., Carthage 62321
Phone: (217) 357-3129

Catholic Theological Union
5401 South Cornell Ave., Chicago 60615-5698
Type: Private, Roman Catholic Church, four-year
Degrees: M, D   *Enroll:* 382
URL: http://www.ctu.edu
Phone: (773) 324-8000   *Calendar:* Qtr. plan
Inst. Accred.: ATS (1972/2001), NCA-HLC (1972/2002)

The Chicago School of Professional Psychology
325 North Wells St., Chicago 60610
Type: Private, independent, four-year
Degrees: M, D   *Enroll:* 627
URL: http://www.csopp.edu
Phone: (312) 786-9443   *Calendar:* Sem. plan
Inst. Accred.: NCA-HLC (1984/2001)
Prog. Accred.: Clinical Psychology

Chicago State University
9501 South King Dr., Chicago 60628-1598
Type: Public, state, four-year
System: Illinois Board of Higher Education
Degrees: B, M, D   *Enroll:* 4,910
URL: http://www.csu.edu
Phone: (773) 995-2000   *Calendar:* Sem. plan
Inst. Accred.: NCA-HLC (1941/2003)
Prog. Accred.: Business (AACSB), Counseling, Health
  Information Administration, Music, Nursing,
  Occupational Therapy, Social Work, Teacher Education
  (NCATE)

Chicago Theological Seminary
5757 South University Ave., Chicago 60637
Type: Private, United Church of Christ, four-year
Degrees: M, D   *Enroll:* 140
URL: http://www.ctschicago.edu
Phone: (773) 752-5757   *Calendar:* Qtr. plan
Inst. Accred.: ATS (1938/1996), NCA-HLC (1982/1997)

Christian Life College
400 East Gregory St., Mount Prospect 60056-2522
Type: Private, independent Pentacostal/Charismatic, four-
  year
Degrees: B   *Enroll:* 70
URL: http://www.christianlifecollege.edu
Phone: (847) 259-1840   *Calendar:* Sem. plan
Inst. Accred.: TRACS (2002)

City Colleges of Chicago—
Harold Washington College
30 East Lake St., Chicago 60601
Type: Public, state/local, two-year
System: City Colleges of Chicago
Degrees: A   *Enroll:* 4,925
URL: http://hwashington.ccc.edu
Phone: (312) 553-5600   *Calendar:* Sem. plan
Inst. Accred.: NCA-HLC (1967/1998)
Prog. Accred.: Business (ACBSP)

City Colleges of Chicago—
Harry S Truman College
1145 West Wilson Ave., Chicago 60640
Type: Public, state/local, two-year
System: City Colleges of Chicago
Degrees: A   *Enroll:* 6,596
URL: http://www.trumancollege.cc
Phone: (773) 907-4700   *Calendar:* Sem. plan
Inst. Accred.: NCA-HLC (1967/2000)
Prog. Accred.: Health Information Technician, Nursing

City Colleges of Chicago—
Kennedy-King College
6800 South Wentworth Ave., Chicago 60621
Type: Public, state/local, two-year
System: City Colleges of Chicago
Degrees: A   *Enroll:* 4,277
URL: http://kennedyking.ccc.edu
Phone: (773) 602-5000   *Calendar:* Sem. plan
Inst. Accred.: NCA-HLC (1967/1996)
Prog. Accred.: Dental Hygiene, Nursing

City Colleges of Chicago—Malcolm X College
1900 West Van Buren St., Chicago 60612
Type: Public, state/local, two-year
System: City Colleges of Chicago
Degrees: A   *Enroll:* 5,399
URL: http://malcolmx.ccc.edu
Phone: (312) 850-7000   *Calendar:* Sem. plan
Inst. Accred.: NCA-HLC (1967/1998)
Prog. Accred.: Clinical Lab Technology, Funeral Service
   Education (Mortuary Science), Nursing, Physician
   Assistant, Radiography, Surgical Technology

City Colleges of Chicago—Olive-Harvey College
10001 South Woodlawn Ave., Chicago 60628-1645
Type: Public, state/local, two-year
System: City Colleges of Chicago
Degrees: A   *Enroll:* 4,273
URL: http://oliveharvey.ccc.edu
Phone: (773) 291-6100   *Calendar:* Sem. plan
Inst. Accred.: NCA-HLC (1967/2000)

City Colleges of Chicago—
Richard J. Daley College
7500 South Pulaski Rd., Chicago 60652
Type: Public, state/local, two-year
System: City Colleges of Chicago
Degrees: A   *Enroll:* 6,154
URL: http://daley.ccc.edu
Phone: (773) 838-7500   *Calendar:* Sem. plan
Inst. Accred.: NCA-HLC (1967/2001)
Prog. Accred.: Nursing

City Colleges of Chicago—
Wilbur Wright College
4300 North Narragansett Ave., Chicago 60634
Type: Public, state/local, two-year
System: City Colleges of Chicago
Degrees: A   *Enroll:* 6,184
URL: http://wright.ccc.edu
Phone: (773) 777-7900   *Calendar:* Sem. plan
Inst. Accred.: NCA-HLC (1967/2002)
Prog. Accred.: Business (ACBSP), Occupational Therapy
   Assisting, Radiography

College of DuPage
425 Fawell Blvd., Glen Ellyn 60137
Type: Public, state/local, two-year
System: Illinois Community College Board
Degrees: A   *Enroll:* 17,056
URL: http://www.cod.edu
Phone: (630) 942-2800   *Calendar:* Qtr. plan
Inst. Accred.: NCA-HLC (1932/2004)
Prog. Accred.: Culinary Education, Dental Hygiene, Health
   Information Technician, Nuclear Medicine Technology,
   Nursing, Physical Therapy Assisting, Radiography,
   Respiratory Therapy, Respiratory Therapy Technology

College of Lake County
19351 West Washington St., Grayslake 60030
Type: Public, state/local, two-year
System: Illinois Community College Board
Degrees: A   *Enroll:* 8,035
URL: http://www.clcillinois.edu
Phone: (847) 223-6601   *Calendar:* Sem. plan
Inst. Accred.: NCA-HLC (1974/1996)
Prog. Accred.: Clinical Lab Technology, Dental Hygiene,
   Health Information Technician, Nursing, Phlebotomy,
   Radiography

Lakeshore Campus
111 N. Genesee St., Waukegan
Phone: (847) 623-8686

The College of Office Technology
1520 Division St., Chicago 60622
Type: Private, proprietary, two-year
Degrees: A   *Enroll:* 625
URL: http://www.cotedu.com
Phone: (773) 278-0042
Inst. Accred.: ACICS (1986/2003)

Columbia College Chicago
600 South Michigan Ave., Chicago 60605
Type: Private, independent, four-year
Degrees: B, M   *Enroll:* 8,831
URL: http://www.colum.edu
Phone: (312) 344-7202   *Calendar:* Sem. plan
Inst. Accred.: NCA-HLC (1974/1999)
Prog. Accred.: Interior Design

Concordia University River Forest
7400 Augusta St., River Forest 60305
Type: Private, Lutheran Church-Missouri Synod, four-year
System: Concordia University System
Degrees: B, M, D   *Enroll:* 1,316
URL: http://www.curf.edu
Phone: (708) 771-8300   *Calendar:* Sem. plan
Inst. Accred.: NCA-HLC (1950/2002)
Prog. Accred.: Counseling, Music, Teacher Education
   (NCATE)

Cooking and Hospitality Institute of Chicago
361 West Chestnut St., Chicago 60610-3050
Type: Private, proprietary, two-year
System: Career Education Corporation
Degrees: A   *Enroll:* 945
URL: http://www.chic.edu
Phone: (312) 944-0884   *Calendar:* Sem. plan
Inst. Accred.: ACCSCT (1986/2002), NCA-HLC (2003)
Prog. Accred.: Culinary Education

Danville Area Community College
2000 East Main St., Danville 61832
Type: Public, state/local, two-year
System: Illinois Community College Board
Degrees: A   *Enroll:* 1,774
URL: http://www.dacc.edu
Phone: (217) 443-1811   *Calendar:* Sem. plan
Inst. Accred.: NCA-HLC (1967/1999)
Prog. Accred.: Radiography

DePaul University
1 East Jackson Blvd., Chicago 60604
Type: Private, Roman Catholic Church, four-year
Degrees: B, M, P, D   *Enroll:* 18,909
URL: http://www.depaul.edu
Phone: (312) 362-8300   *Calendar:* Qtr. plan
Inst. Accred.: NCA-HLC (1925/1997)
Prog. Accred.: Accounting, Business (AACSB), Clinical
   Psychology, Law, Music, Nurse Anesthesia Education,
   Nursing, Nursing Education, Teacher Education (NCATE)

DeVry University Chicago
3300 North Campbell Ave., Chicago 60618-5994
Type: Private, proprietary, four-year
System: DeVry University
Degrees: A, B, M   *Enroll:* 8,625
URL: http://www.devry.edu/chicago
Phone: (773) 929-8500   *Calendar:* Sem. plan
Inst. Accred.: NCA-HLC (2002, *Indirect accreditation
   through DeVry University, Oakbrook Terrace, IL*)
Prog. Accred.: Engineering Technology (electrical)

DeVry University DuPage
1221 North Swift Rd., Addison 60101-6106
Type: Private, proprietary, four-year
System: DeVry University
Degrees: A, B, M   *FTE Enroll:* 2,980
URL: http://www.devry.edu/addison
Phone: (630) 953-1300   *Calendar:* Sem. plan
Inst. Accred.: NCA-HLC (2002, *Indirect accreditation
   through DeVry University, Oakbrook Terrace, IL*)
Prog. Accred.: Engineering Technology (electrical)

Tinley Park Campus
18624 West Creek Dr., Tinley Park 60477-6243
Phone: (708) 342-3300

Dominican University
7900 West Division St., River Forest 60305
Type: Private, Roman Catholic Church, four-year
Degrees: B, M   *Enroll:* 1,954
URL: http://www.dom.edu
Phone: (708) 366-2490   *Calendar:* Sem. plan
Inst. Accred.: NCA-HLC (1919/2005)
Prog. Accred.: Business (ACBSP), Librarianship

Dr. William M. Scholl College of Podiatric Medicine
3333 Green Bay Rd., North Chicago 60064
Type: Private, independent, four-year
Degrees: B, D   *Enroll:* 263
URL: http://www.rosalindfranklin.edu/scpm
Phone: (847) 578-8400   *Calendar:* Sem. plan
Inst. Accred.: NCA-HLC (1985/2000)
Prog. Accred.: Podiatry

East-West University
816 South Michigan Ave., Chicago 60605
Type: Private, independent, four-year
Degrees: A, B   *Enroll:* 993
URL: http://www.eastwest.edu
Phone: (312) 939-0111   *Calendar:* Qtr. plan
Inst. Accred.: NCA-HLC (1983/2002)

Eastern Illinois University
600 Lincoln Ave., Charleston 61920
Type: Public, state, four-year
System: Illinois Board of Higher Education
Degrees: B, M, P   *Enroll:* 10,298
URL: http://www.eiu.edu
Phone: (217) 581-5000   *Calendar:* Sem. plan
Inst. Accred.: NCA-HLC (1915/2005)
Prog. Accred.: Accounting, Art, Athletic Training, Business
   (AACSB), Counseling, Dietetics (internship), Family and
   Consumer Science, Industrial Technology, Journalism,
   Music, Recreation and Leisure Services, Speech-
   Language Pathology, Teacher Education (NCATE)

Elgin Community College
1700 Spartan Dr., Elgin 60123
Type: Public, state/local, two-year
System: Illinois Community College Board
Degrees: A *Enroll:* 5,644
Phone: (847) 697-1000 *Calendar:* Sem. plan
Inst. Accred.: NCA-HLC (1968/1996)
Prog. Accred.: Clinical Lab Technology, Culinary
Education, Dental Assisting, Nursing, Physical Therapy
Assisting, Surgical Technology

Elmhurst College
190 Prospect Ave., Elmhurst 60126-3296
Type: Private, United Church of Christ, four-year
Degrees: B, M *Enroll:* 2,272
URL: http://www.elmhurst.edu
Phone: (630) 617-3500 *Calendar:* 4-1-4 plan
Inst. Accred.: NCA-HLC (1924/1999)
Prog. Accred.: Nursing, Nursing Education, Teacher
Education (NCATE)

Erikson Institute
420 North Wabash Ave., Chicago 60611-5627
Type: Private, independent, four-year
Degrees: B, M, P, D *Enroll:* 132
URL: http://www.erikson.edu
Phone: (312) 755-2250 *Calendar:* Tri. plan
Inst. Accred.: NCA-HLC (2000/2005)

Eureka College
300 East College Ave., Eureka 61530-1500
Type: Private, Disciples of Christ, four-year
Degrees: B *Enroll:* 480
URL: http://www.eureka.edu
Phone: (309) 467-3721 *Calendar:* Sem. plan
Inst. Accred.: NCA-HLC (1924/2004)

Fox College
4201 West 93rd St., Oak Lawn 60453
Type: Private, proprietary, two-year
Degrees: A
URL: http://www.foxcollege.edu
Phone: (708) 636-7700 *Calendar:* Sem. plan
Inst. Accred.: ACICS (1987/2005)

Frontier Community College
2 Frontier Dr., Fairfield 62837
Type: Public, state/local, two-year
System: Illinois Eastern Community Colleges System
Degrees: A *Enroll:* 779
URL: http://www.iecc.edu/fcc
Phone: (618) 842-3711 *Calendar:* Sem. plan
Inst. Accred.: NCA-HLC (1984/1995, *Indirect accreditation
through Illinois Eastern Community Colleges System,
Olney, IL*)
Prog. Accred.: Nursing

Garrett-Evangelical Theological Seminary
2121 Sheridan Rd., Evanston 60201
Type: Private, United Methodist Church, four-year
Degrees: M, D *Enroll:* 215
URL: http://www.garrett.northwestern.edu
Phone: (847) 866-3900 *Calendar:* Qtr. plan
Inst. Accred.: ATS (1938/1998), NCA-HLC (1974/1999)

Gem City College
700 State St., Quincy 62301
Type: Private, proprietary, two-year
Degrees: A *Enroll:* 42
URL: http://www.gemcitycollege.com
Phone: (217) 222-0391
Inst. Accred.: ACICS (1954/2004)

Governors State University
One University Pkwy., University Park 60466
Type: Public, state, four-year
System: Illinois Board of Higher Education
Degrees: B, M *Enroll:* 3,001
URL: http://www.govst.edu
Phone: (708) 534-5000 *Calendar:* Tri. plan
Inst. Accred.: NCA-HLC (1975/2000)
Prog. Accred.: Business (ACBSP), Counseling, Health
Services Administration, Nursing, Occupational Therapy,
Physical Therapy, Public Administration, Social Work,
Speech-Language Pathology

Greenville College
315 East College Ave., PO Box 159, Greenville 62246
Type: Private, Free Methodist Church, four-year
Degrees: B, M *Enroll:* 1,257
URL: http://www.greenville.edu
Phone: (618) 664-1840 *Calendar:* 4-1-4 plan
Inst. Accred.: NCA-HLC (1948/2001)

Harrington College of Design
200 West Madison, Second Flr., Chicago 60606-3433
Type: Private, proprietary, four-year
System: Career Education Corporation
Degrees: A, B *Enroll:* 928
URL: http://www.interiordesign.edu
Phone: (312) 939-4975 *Calendar:* Sem. plan
Inst. Accred.: NASAD (1994/2002), ACICS (2004)
Prog. Accred.: Interior Design

Heartland Community College
1500 West Raab Rd., Normal 61761
Type: Public, state/local, two-year
System: Illinois Community College Board
Degrees: A *Enroll:* 2,850
URL: http://www.hcc.cc.il.us
Phone: (309) 268-8100 *Calendar:* Sem. plan
Inst. Accred.: NCA-HLC (1994/1999)
Prog. Accred.: Nursing

Hebrew Theological College
7135 North Carpenter Rd., Skokie 60077
Type: Private, independent, four-year
Degrees: B   *Enroll:* 330
URL: http://www.htcnet.edu
Phone: (847) 982-2500   *Calendar:* Sem. plan
Inst. Accred.: NCA-HLC (1997/2002)

Highland Community College
2998 West Pearl City Rd., Freeport 61032
Type: Public, state/local, two-year
System: Illinois Community College Board
Degrees: A   *Enroll:* 1,588
URL: http://www.highland.edu
Phone: (815) 235-6121   *Calendar:* Sem. plan
Inst. Accred.: NCA-HLC (1973/1996)

Illinois Central College
One College Dr., East Peoria 61635
Type: Public, state/local, two-year
System: Illinois Community College Board
Degrees: A   *Enroll:* 7,059
URL: http://www.icc.edu
Phone: (309) 694-5422   *Calendar:* Sem. plan
Inst. Accred.: NCA-HLC (1972/2002)
Prog. Accred.: Clinical Lab Technology, Dental Hygiene,
  Music, Nursing, Occupational Therapy Assisting,
  Physical Therapy Assisting, Practical Nursing,
  Radiography, Respiratory Therapy, Surgical Technology

Illinois College
1101 West College St., Jacksonville 62650
Type: Private, Presbyterian Church (USA), four-year
Degrees: B   *Enroll:* 1,008
URL: http://www.ic.edu
Phone: (217) 245-3000   *Calendar:* Sem. plan
Inst. Accred.: NCA-HLC (1913/2005)

Illinois College of Optometry
3241 South Michigan Ave., Chicago 60616
Type: Private, independent, four-year
Degrees: M, P   *Enroll:* 606
URL: http://www.ico.edu
Phone: (312) 225-1700   *Calendar:* Qtr. plan
Inst. Accred.: NCA-HLC (1969/1999)
Prog. Accred.: Optometric Residency, Optometry

The Illinois Institute of Art
350 North Orleans St., Ste. 136, Chicago 60654
Type: Private, proprietary, four-year
System: Education Management Corporation
Degrees: A, B   *Enroll:* 1,818
URL: http://www.ilic.artinstitutes.edu
Phone: (312) 280-3500   *Calendar:* Qtr. plan
Inst. Accred.: ACCSCT (1975/2002), NCA-HLC (2004)
Prog. Accred.: Culinary Education, Interior Design

Schaumburg Campus
1000 Plaza Dr., Ste. 100, Schaumburg 60173-4913
Phone: (847) 619-3450
Prog. Accred: Interior Design

Illinois Institute of Technology
300 South Federal St., Chicago 60616-3793
Type: Private, independent, four-year
Degrees: B, M, D   *Enroll:* 4,968
URL: http://www.iit.edu
Phone: (312) 567-3000   *Calendar:* Sem. plan
Inst. Accred.: NCA-HLC (1941/1997)
Prog. Accred.: Business (AACSB), Clinical Psychology,
  Computer Science, Engineering (aerospace,
  architectural, chemical, civil, computer, electrical,
  materials, mechanical, metallurgical), Law,
  Rehabilitation Counseling

Daniel F. and Ada L. Rice Campus
201 East Loop Rd., Wheaton 60187-8489
Phone: (708) 682-6000

Illinois State University
1000 Illinois State University, Normal 61790-1000
Type: Public, state, four-year
System: Illinois Board of Higher Education
Degrees: B, M, P, D   *Enroll:* 19,059
URL: http://www.ilstu.edu
Phone: (309) 438-2111   *Calendar:* Sem. plan
Inst. Accred.: NCA-HLC (1913/2005)
Prog. Accred.: Accounting, Art, Audiology, Business
  (AACSB), Clinical Lab Scientist, Computer Science,
  Construction Education, Dietetics (internship), Family
  and Consumer Science, Health Information
  Administration, Industrial Technology, Interior Design,
  Music, Nursing, Nursing Education, Psychology
  Internship, Recreation and Leisure Services, School
  Psychology, Social Work, Speech-Language Pathology,
  Teacher Education (NCATE), Theatre

Mennonite College of Nursing
Campus Box 58, Normal 61790-5810
Phone: (309) 438-2174

Illinois Valley Community College
815 North Orlando Smith Ave., Oglesby 61348
Type: Public, state/local, two-year
System: Illinois Community College Board
Degrees: A   *Enroll:* 2,538
Phone: (815) 224-2720   *Calendar:* Sem. plan
Inst. Accred.: NCA-HLC (1929/1998)
Prog. Accred.: Dental Assisting, Nursing

Illinois Wesleyan University
PO Box 2900, Bloomington 61702
Type: Private, United Methodist Church, four-year
Degrees: B   *Enroll:* 2,102
URL: http://www.iwu.edu
Phone: (309) 556-1000   *Calendar:* 4-1-4 plan
Inst. Accred.: NCA-HLC (1916/2003)
Prog. Accred.: Music, Nursing, Nursing Education

Institute for Clinical Social Work, Inc.
180 North Michigan Ave., Ste. 1605, Chicago 60601-7454
Type: Private, independent, four-year
Degrees: D *Enroll:* 67
URL: http://icsw.edu
Phone: (312) 726-8480 *Calendar:* Sem. plan
Inst. Accred.: NCA-HLC (1994/1999)

International Academy of Design and Technology
One North State St., Ste. 400, Chicago 60602-3300
Type: Private, proprietary, four-year
System: Career Education Corporation
Degrees: A, B *Enroll:* 2,645
URL: http://www.iadtchicago.edu
Phone: (312) 980-9200 *Calendar:* Qtr. plan
Inst. Accred.: ACICS (1981/2002)
Prog. Accred.: Interior Design

Schaumburg Campus
915 National Pkwy., Schaumburg 60173
Phone: (312) 980-9200

John A. Logan College
700 Logan College Rd., Carterville 62918
Type: Public, state/local, two-year
System: Illinois Community College Board
Degrees: A *Enroll:* 3,884
URL: http://www.jal.cc.il.us
Phone: (618) 985-3741 *Calendar:* Sem. plan
Inst. Accred.: NCA-HLC (1972/1997)
Prog. Accred.: Construction Education, Dental Assisting, Dental Hygiene

The John Marshall Law School
315 South Plymouth Ct., Chicago 60604
Type: Private, independent, four-year
Degrees: M, P *Enroll:* 1,287
URL: http://www.jmls.edu
Phone: (312) 427-2737 *Calendar:* Sem. plan
Inst. Accred.: NCA-HLC (2000)
Prog. Accred.: Law

John Wood Community College
1301 South 48th St., Quincy 62305
Type: Public, state/local, two-year
System: Illinois Community College Board
Degrees: A *Enroll:* 1,601
URL: http://www.jwcc.edu
Phone: (217) 224-6500 *Calendar:* Sem. plan
Inst. Accred.: NCA-HLC (1980/2003)

Joliet Junior College
1215 Houbolt Rd., Joliet 60431-8938
Type: Public, state/local, two-year
System: Illinois Community College Board
Degrees: A *Enroll:* 7,404
URL: http://www.jjc.edu
Phone: (815) 729-9020 *Calendar:* Sem. plan
Inst. Accred.: NCA-HLC (1917/2002)
Prog. Accred.: Business (ACBSP), Culinary Education, Music, Nursing, Veterinary Technology

Judson College
1151 North State St., Elgin 60123
Type: Private, American Baptist Church, four-year
Degrees: B, M *Enroll:* 1,012
URL: http://www.judsoncollege.edu
Phone: (847) 695-2500 *Calendar:* 4-1-4 plan
Inst. Accred.: NCA-HLC (1973/2001)

Kankakee Community College
PO Box 888, 817 River Rd., Kankakee 60901
Type: Public, state/local, two-year
System: Illinois Community College Board
Degrees: A *Enroll:* 2,001
URL: http://www.kankakee.edu
Phone: (815) 802-8100 *Calendar:* Sem. plan
Inst. Accred.: NCA-HLC (1974/2004)
Prog. Accred.: Clinical Lab Technology, Respiratory Therapy

Kaskaskia College
27210 College Rd., Centralia 62801
Type: Public, state/local, two-year
System: Illinois Community College Board
Degrees: A *Enroll:* 2,975
URL: http://www.kaskaskia.edu
Phone: (618) 545-3000 *Calendar:* Sem. plan
Inst. Accred.: NCA-HLC (1964/1999)
Prog. Accred.: Dental Assisting, Nursing, Physical Therapy Assisting, Radiography, Respiratory Therapy Technology

Keller Graduate School of Management of DeVry University
One Tower Ln., Oakbrook Terrace 60181-4624
Type: Private, proprietary, four-year
System: DeVry University
Degrees: M *FTE Enroll:* 1,242
URL: http://www.keller.edu
Phone: (630) 574-1960 *Calendar:* Qtr. plan
Inst. Accred.: NCA-HLC (2002, *Indirect accreditation through DeVry University, Oakbrook Terrace, IL*)

Alpharetta Center Campus
2555 Northwinds Pkwy., Alpharetta, GA 30004-2231
Phone: (770) 521-0118

Atlanta Perimeter Center
Two Ravinia Dr., Atlanta, GA 30346-2104
Phone: (770) 671-1744

Chicago/Loop Center
225 West Washington St., Chicago 60606-3418
Phone: (312) 372-4900

Crystal City Center
Crystal Gateway Three, 1215 Jefferson Davis Hwy., Arlington, VA 22202-4337
Phone: (703) 415-0600

Decatur Center
250 North Arcadia Ave., Decatur, GA 30030-2198
Phone: (404) 298-9444

Keller Graduate School *(continued)*

Denver/Interlocken Campus
12202 Airport Way, Ste. 190, Broomfield, CO 80021

East Valley Center Campus
1201 South Alma School Rd., Ste. 5450, Mesa, AZ 85210
Phone: (480) 827-1511

Elgin Center
385 Airport Rd., Elgin 60123-9341
Phone: (847) 622-1135

Kansas City Downtown Campus
City Center Square, 1100 Main St., Kansas City, MO 64105-2112
Phone: (816) 221-1300

Kansas City South Campus
11224 Holmes Rd., Kansas City, MO 64131
Phone: (816) 941-0367

Manhattan Center
120 West 45th St., New York, NY 10036
Phone: (212) 556-0002

McLean Center Campus
1751 Pinnacle Dr., McLean, VA 22102-3832
Phone: (703) 556-9669

Miami Center
200 South Biscayne Blvd., Ste. 500, Miami, FL 33131-5351
Phone: (786) 425-1113

Milwaukee Center Campus
330 East Kilbourn Ave., Milwaukee, WI 53202-3141
Phone: (414) 278-7677

North Suburban Center Campus
Tri-State International Office Center, Building 25, Ste. 130, Lincolnshire 60069-4460
Phone: (847) 940-7768

Northwest Suburban Center Campus
1051 Perimeter Dr., Schaumburg 60173-5009
Phone: (847) 330-0040

Orlando North Center
1800 Pembrook Dr., Ste. 160, Orlando, FL 32810-6303
Phone: (407) 659-0900

Phoenix/Northwest Center Campus
2149 West Dunlap Ave., Phoenix, AZ 85021
Phone: (602) 870-0117

Ponoma Center
901 Corporate Center Dr., Ponoma, CA 91768-2642
Phone: (909) 865-0402

Saint Louis/Downtown Campus
1010 Market St., St. Louis, MO 63101-2000
Phone: (314) 542-4222

Saint Louis West Center Campus
1801 Park 270 Dr., Ste. 260, St. Louis, MO 63146-4020
Phone: (314) 542-4222

San Diego Center Campus
2655 Camino Del Rio North, Ste. 201, San Diego, CA 92108-1633
Phone: (619) 683-2446

Scottsdale Center
9201 East Mountain View Rd., Ste. 115, Scottsdale, AZ 85258-5140
Phone: (480) 657-3223

Seattle Center
500 108th Ave., NE, Bellevue, WA 98004
Phone: (425) 455-2242

South Suburban Center Campus
15255 South 94th Ave., Orland Park 60462-3823
Phone: (708) 460-9580

Tampa Bay Center Campus
3030 North Rocky Point Dr. West, Tampa, FL 33607-5901
Phone: (813) 288-8994

Waukesha Center Campus
20935 Swenson Dr., Waukesha, WI 53186
Phone: (414) 798-9889

West Suburban Center Campus
6200 Route 53, Lisle 60532-3198
Phone: (630) 969-6624

Kendall College
900 North Branch St., Chicago 60622
Type: Private, independent, four-year
Degrees: A, B   *Enroll:* 522
URL: http://www.kendall.edu
Phone: (752) 752-2000   *Calendar:* Qtr. plan
Inst. Accred.: NCA-HLC (1962/2005)
Prog. Accred.: Culinary Education

Kishwaukee College
21193 Malta Rd., Malta 60150
Type: Public, state/local, two-year
System: Illinois Community College Board
Degrees: A   *Enroll:* 2,599
URL: http://www.kishwaukeecollege.edu
Phone: (815) 825-2086   *Calendar:* Sem. plan
Inst. Accred.: NCA-HLC (1974/1999)
Prog. Accred.: Massage Therapy, Radiography, Respiratory Therapy Technology

Knowledge Systems Institute
3420 Main St., Skokie 60076
Type: Private, proprietary, four-year
Degrees: M   *Enroll:* 57
URL: http://www.ksi.edu
Phone: (847) 679-3135   *Calendar:* Sem. plan
Inst. Accred.: NCA-HLC (1991/2001)

Knox College
2 East South St., Galesburg 61401
Type: Private, independent, four-year
Degrees: B   *Enroll:* 1,114
URL: http://www.knox.edu
Phone: (309) 341-7000   *Calendar:* Tri. plan
Inst. Accred.: NCA-HLC (1913/2000)

Lake Forest College
555 North Sheridan Rd., Lake Forest 60045-2399
Type: Private, United Presbyterian Church, four-year
Degrees: B, M   *Enroll:* 1,337
URL: http://www.lakeforest.edu
Phone: (847) 234-3100   *Calendar:* Sem. plan
Inst. Accred.: NCA-HLC (1913/1997)

Lake Forest Graduate School of Management
1905 West Field Ct., Lake Forest 60045
Type: Private, independent, four-year
Degrees: M   *Enroll:* 316
URL: http://www.lfgsm.edu
Phone: (847) 234-5005   *Calendar:* Qtr. plan
Inst. Accred.: NCA-HLC (1978/2003)

Chicago Campus
176 West Jackson Blvd., Chicago 60604
Phone: (312) 435-5330

Schaumburg Campus
1295 East Algonquin Rd., Schaumburg 60196
Phone: (847) 576-1212

Lake Land College
5001 Lake Land Blvd., Mattoon 61938
Type: Public, state/local, two-year
System: Illinois Community College Board
Degrees: A   *Enroll:* 4,598
URL: http://www.lakelandcollege.edu
Phone: (217) 234-5253   *Calendar:* Sem. plan
Inst. Accred.: NCA-HLC (1973/2005)
Prog. Accred.: Dental Hygiene, Nursing, Physical Therapy
  Assisting, Practical Nursing

Lakeview College of Nursing
903 North Logan Ave., Danville 61832
Type: Private, independent, four-year
Degrees: B   *Enroll:* 79
URL: http://www.lakeviewcol.edu
Phone: (217) 443-5238   *Calendar:* Sem. plan
Inst. Accred.: NCA-HLC (1995/2001)
Prog. Accred.: Nursing, Nursing Education

Lewis and Clark Community College
5800 Godfrey Rd., Godfrey 62035
Type: Public, state/local, two-year
System: Illinois Community College Board
Degrees: A   *Enroll:* 3,999
URL: http://www.lc.edu
Phone: (618) 466-3411   *Calendar:* Sem. plan
Inst. Accred.: NCA-HLC (1971/2003)
Prog. Accred.: Clinical Lab Technology, Dental Assisting,
  Dental Hygiene, Nursing, Occupational Therapy
  Assisting

Lewis University
One University Pkwy., Romeoville 60446-2298
Type: Private, Roman Catholic Church, four-year
Degrees: A, B, M, P   *Enroll:* 3,150
URL: http://www.lewisu.edu
Phone: (815) 838-0500   *Calendar:* Sem. plan
Inst. Accred.: NCA-HLC (1963/1997)
Prog. Accred.: Nursing, Nursing Education, Teacher
  Education (NCATE)

Lexington College
310 South Peoria St., Ste. 512, Chicago 60607-3534
Type: Private, independent, four-year
Degrees: A, B   *Enroll:* 42
URL: http://www.lexingtoncollege.edu
Phone: (312) 226-6294   *Calendar:* Sem. plan
Inst. Accred.: NCA-HLC (1993/2003)

Lincoln Christian College and Seminary
100 Campus View Dr., Lincoln 62656-2167
Type: Private, Christian Churches/Churches of Christ,
  four-year
Degrees: A, B, M   *Enroll:* 872
URL: http://www.lccs.edu
Phone: (217) 732-3168   *Calendar:* Sem. plan
Inst. Accred.: ABHE (1954/1996), ATS (1991/1996), NCA-
  HLC (1991/1996)

Lincoln College
300 Keokuk St., Lincoln 62656
Type: Private, state/local, two-year
Degrees: A   *Enroll:* 1,148
URL: http://www.lincolncollege.edu
Phone: (217) 732-3155   *Calendar:* Sem. plan
Inst. Accred.: NCA-HLC (1929/2004)

Lincoln College at Normal
715 West Raab Rd., Normal 61761
Phone: (309) 452-0500

Lincoln Land Community College
5250 Shepard Rd., PO Box 19256, Springfield 62794-
9256
Type: Public, local, two-year
System: Illinois Community College Board
Degrees: A   *Enroll:* 4,241
URL: http://www.llcc.edu
Phone: (217) 786-2200   *Calendar:* Sem. plan
Inst. Accred.: NCA-HLC (1973/2003)
Prog. Accred.: Nursing, Occupational Therapy Assisting,
  Radiography, Respiratory Therapy

Lincoln Trail College
11220 State Hwy. 1, Robinson 62454
Type: Public, state/local, two-year
System: Illinois Eastern Community Colleges System
Degrees: A   *Enroll:* 750
URL: http://www.iecc.cc.il.us/ltc
Phone: (618) 544-8657   *Calendar:* Sem. plan
Inst. Accred.: NCA-HLC (1984/1995, *Indirect accreditation
  through Illinois Eastern Community Colleges System,
  Olney, IL*)
Prog. Accred.: Nursing

Loyola University of Chicago
820 North Michigan Ave., Chicago 60611
Type: Private, Roman Catholic Church, four-year
Degrees: B, M, D   *Enroll:* 11,465
URL: http://www.luc.edu
Phone: (312) 915-6000   *Calendar:* Sem. plan
Inst. Accred.: ATS (2000), NCA-HLC (1921/2005)
Prog. Accred.: Accounting, Business (AACSB), Clinical
  Pastoral Education, Clinical Psychology, Combined
  Prosthodontics, Counseling Psychology, Dietetics
  (internship), EMT (Paramedic), General Practice
  Residency, Law, Medicine, Nursing, Nursing Education,
  Oral and Maxillofacial Surgery, Social Work, Theatre

Lake Shore Campus
6525 N. Sheridan Rd., Chicago 60626
Phone: (773) 274-3000

Mallinckrodt Campus
1041 Ridge Rd., Wilmette 60091
Phone: (847) 853-3000

Medical Center
2160 South First Ave., Maywood 60153
Phone: (708) 216-9000
Prog. Accred: General Practice Residency, Oral and
  Maxillofacial Surgery

Lutheran School of Theology at Chicago
1100 East 55th St., Chicago 60615-5199
Type: Private, Lutheran Church in America, four-year
Degrees: M, D   *Enroll:* 255
URL: http://www.lstc.edu
Phone: (773) 753-0700   *Calendar:* Qtr. plan
Inst. Accred.: ATS (1945/1997), NCA-HLC (1982/1997)

MacCormac College
29 East Madison St., Chicago 60602-4405
Type: Private, independent, two-year
Degrees: A   *Enroll:* 246
URL: http://www.maccormac.edu
Phone: (312) 922-1884   *Calendar:* Sem. plan
Inst. Accred.: NCA-HLC (1979/2005)

Elmhurst Campus
615 N. West Ave., Elmhurst 60126
Phone: (708) 941-1200

MacMurray College
447 East College Ave., Jacksonville 62650-2590
Type: Private, United Methodist Church, four-year
Degrees: A, B   *Enroll:* 638
URL: http://www.mac.edu
Phone: (217) 479-7025   *Calendar:* 4-1-4 plan
Inst. Accred.: NCA-HLC (1921/2003)
Prog. Accred.: Nursing, Nursing Education, Social Work

McCormick Theological Seminary
5460 South University Ave., Chicago 60615
Type: Private, Presbyterian Church (USA), four-year
Degrees: M, D   *Enroll:* 286
URL: http://www.mccormick.edu
Phone: (773) 947-6300   *Calendar:* Qtr. plan
Inst. Accred.: ATS (1938/1996), NCA-HLC (1982/1997)

McHenry County College
8900 U.S. Hwy. 14, Crystal Lake 60012-2761
Type: Public, state/local, two-year
System: Illinois Community College Board
Degrees: A   *Enroll:* 3,355
URL: http://www.mchenry.edu
Phone: (815) 455-3700   *Calendar:* Sem. plan
Inst. Accred.: NCA-HLC (1976/2002)
Prog. Accred.: Massage Therapy

McKendree College
701 College Rd., Lebanon 62254-1299
Type: Private, United Methodist Church, four-year
Degrees: A, B, M   *Enroll:* 1,779
URL: http://www.mckendree.edu
Phone: (618) 537-4481   *Calendar:* Sem. plan
Inst. Accred.: NCA-HLC (1970/1999)
Prog. Accred.: Nursing

Louisville Campus
11850 Commonwealth Dr., Jeffersontown, KY 40299
Phone: (502) 266-6696

Radcliff Campus
1635 West Lincoln Trail Blvd., Radcliff, KY 40160
Phone: (270) 351-5003

Scott AFB Center
375 MSS/DPE, 604 Tyler St., Rm. 73, Scott AFB
62225-5420
Phone: (618) 256-2006

Meadville Lombard Theological School
5701 South Woodlawn Ave., Chicago 60637
Type: Private, Unitarian Universalist Church, four-year
Degrees: M, D   *Enroll:* 82
URL: http://www.meadville.edu
Phone: (773) 256-3000   *Calendar:* Qtr. plan
Inst. Accred.: ATS (1940/2003)

Midstate College
411 W. North Moor Rd., Peoria 61614
Type: Private, independent, four-year
Degrees: A, B   *Enroll:* 315
URL: http://www.midstate.edu
Phone: (309) 692-4092   *Calendar:* Qtr. plan
Inst. Accred.: NCA-HLC (1982/2003)
Prog. Accred.: Medical Assisting (CAAHEP)

Carthage Campus
30 South Washington, Carthage 62321
Phone: (217) 357-6626

Midwestern University
555 31st St., Downers Grove 60515
Type: Private, independent, four-year
Degrees: B, M, P, D   *Enroll:* 1,658
URL: http://www.midwestern.edu
Phone: (630) 969-4400   *Calendar:* Qtr. plan
Inst. Accred.: NCA-HLC (1993/1998)
Prog. Accred.: Computer Science, Occupational Therapy,
   Osteopathy, Pharmacy, Physical Therapy, Physician
   Assistant

Glendale Campus
19555 North 59th Ave., Glendale, AZ 85308
Phone: (623) 572-3200
Prog. Accred: Occupational Therapy, Osteopathy,
   Pharmacy, Physician Assistant

Millikin University
1184 West Main St., Decatur 62522
Type: Private, United Presbyterian Church, four-year
Degrees: B, M   *Enroll:* 2,578
URL: http://www.millikin.edu
Phone: (217) 424-6211   *Calendar:* Sem. plan
Inst. Accred.: NCA-HLC (1914/1997)
Prog. Accred.: Music, Nursing, Nursing Education

Monmouth College
700 East Broadway, Monmouth 61462
Type: Private, Presbyterian Church (USA), four-year
Degrees: B   *Enroll:* 1,158
URL: http://www.monm.edu
Phone: (309) 457-2311   *Calendar:* Sem. plan
Inst. Accred.: NCA-HLC (1913/1998)

Moody Bible Institute
820 North LaSalle Dr., Chicago 60610-3214
Type: Private, interdenominational, four-year
Degrees: B, M   *Enroll:* 1,636
URL: http://www.moody.edu
Phone: (312) 329-4000   *Calendar:* Sem. plan
Inst. Accred.: ABHE (1951/2005), NCA-HLC (1989/1995)
Prog. Accred.: Music

Moraine Valley Community College
10900 South 88th Ave., Palos Hills 60465
Type: Public, state/local, two-year
System: Illinois Community College Board
Degrees: A   *Enroll:* 9,436
URL: http://www.morainevalley.edu
Phone: (708) 974-4300   *Calendar:* Sem. plan
Inst. Accred.: NCA-HLC (1975/1996)
Prog. Accred.: Clinical Lab Technology, Health Information
   Technician, Nursing, Phlebotomy, Radiography,
   Respiratory Therapy

Morrison Institute of Technology
701 Portland Ave., PO Box 410, Morrison 61270-0410
Type: Private, independent, two-year
Degrees: A   *Enroll:* 143
URL: http://www.morrison.tec.il.us
Phone: (815) 772-7218   *Calendar:* Sem. plan
Inst. Accred.: COE (2000)
Prog. Accred.: Engineering Technology (general)

Morton College
3801 South Central Ave., Cicero 60804
Type: Public, state/local, two-year
System: Illinois Community College Board
Degrees: A   *Enroll:* 2,325
URL: http://www.morton.edu
Phone: (708) 656-8000   *Calendar:* Sem. plan
Inst. Accred.: NCA-HLC (1927/2004, Warning)
Prog. Accred.: Dental Assisting, Massage Therapy,
   Physical Therapy Assisting

National University of Health Sciences
200 East Roosevelt Rd., Lombard 60148
Type: Private, independent, four-year
Degrees: B, D   *Enroll:* 450
URL: http://www.nuhs.edu
Phone: (630) 629-2000   *Calendar:* Tri. plan
Inst. Accred.: NCA-HLC (1981/1996)
Prog. Accred.: Chiropractic Education, Massage Therapy

National-Louis University
122 South Michigan Ave., Chicago 60603-6191
Type: Private, independent, four-year
Degrees: B, M, P, D   *Enroll:* 5,030
URL: http://www.nl.edu
Phone: (312) 621-9650   *Calendar:* Qtr. plan
Inst. Accred.: NCA-HLC (1946/2001)
Prog. Accred.: Clinical Lab Scientist, Radiation Therapy, Respiratory Therapy, Teacher Education (NCATE)

Atlanta Academic Center Campus
Blackstone Center, 1777 N.E. Expressway, Ste. 250, Atlanta, GA 30329
Phone: (404) 633-1223

Chicago Campus
18 South Michigan Ave., Chicago 60603
Phone: (312) 621-9650

Elgin Facility Campus
400 Federation Place, Elgin 60123
Phone: (708) 695-6070

Evanston Campus
2840 Sheridan Rd., Evanston 60201-1796
Phone: (708) 475-1100

Heidelberg Academic Center Campus
Rohrbacher Strasse 47, Heidelberg, Germany 69115
Phone: 011-49-6221-29025

Milwaukee/Beloit Academic Center Campus
325 North Corporate Dr., Ste. 200, Brookfield, WI 53045-5861
Phone: (414) 792-3699

Northern Virginia/Washington, DC Academic Center Campus
8000 Westpark Dr., Ste. 125, McLean, VA 22102
Phone: (703) 749-3000

St. Louis Academic Center Campus
12412 Powerscourt Dr., Ste. LL20, St. Louis, MO 63131
Phone: (314) 822-2110

Tampa Academic Center Campus
4890 West Kennedy Blvd., Ste. 145, Tampa, FL 33609
Phone: (813) 286-8087

Wheaton Campus
200 South Naperville Rd., Wheaton 60187
Phone: (708) 668-3838

Wheeling Campus
1000 Capitol Dr., Wheeling 60090
Phone: (708) 465-0575

North Central College
30 North Brainard St., PO Box 3063, Naperville 60566-7063
Type: Private, United Methodist Church, four-year
Degrees: B, M   *Enroll:* 2,094
URL: http://www.noctrl.edu
Phone: (630) 637-5100   *Calendar:* Tri. plan
Inst. Accred.: NCA-HLC (1914/2000)

North Park University
3225 West Foster Ave., Chicago 60625
Type: Private, Evangelical Covenant Church, four-year
Degrees: B, M, D   *Enroll:* 2,027
URL: http://www.northpark.edu
Phone: (773) 244-6200   *Calendar:* Sem. plan
Inst. Accred.: ATS (1963/1996), NCA-HLC (1926/2001)
Prog. Accred.: Music, Nursing, Nursing Education

Northeastern Illinois University
5500 North St. Louis Ave., Chicago 60625
Type: Public, state, four-year
System: Illinois Board of Higher Education
Degrees: B, M   *Enroll:* 7,924
URL: http://www.neiu.edu
Phone: (773) 583-4050   *Calendar:* Tri. plan
Inst. Accred.: NCA-HLC (1961/2001)
Prog. Accred.: Business (AACSB), Counseling, Social Work, Teacher Education (NCATE)

Northern Illinois University
DeKalb 60115
Type: Public, state, four-year
System: Illinois Board of Higher Education
Degrees: B, M, P, D   *Enroll:* 21,186
URL: http://www.niu.edu
Phone: (815) 753-1000   *Calendar:* Sem. plan
Inst. Accred.: NCA-HLC (1915/2004)
Prog. Accred.: Accounting, Art, Athletic Training, Audiology, Business (AACSB), Clinical Lab Scientist, Clinical Psychology, Counseling, Dietetics (internship), Engineering (electrical, industrial, mechanical), Industrial Technology, Law, Marriage and Family Therapy, Music, Nursing, Nursing Education, Physical Therapy, Psychology Internship, Public Administration, Public Health, Rehabilitation Counseling, Speech-Language Pathology, Teacher Education (NCATE), Theatre

Northern Seminary
660 East Butterfield Rd., Lombard 60148
Type: Private, American Baptist Churches in the USA, four-year
Degrees: M, P, D   *FTE Enroll:* 214
URL: http://www.seminary.edu
Phone: (630) 620-2100   *Calendar:* Qtr. plan
Inst. Accred.: ATS (1968/1997), NCA-HLC (1947/1998)

Northwestern Business College
9700 West Higgins Rd., Ste. 750, Rosemont 60018
Type: Private, proprietary, two-year
Degrees: A   *Enroll:* 790
URL: http://www.northwesternbc.edu
Phone: (773) 777-4220   *Calendar:* Qtr. plan
Inst. Accred.: NCA-HLC (1997/2002)
Prog. Accred.: Business (ACBSP), Medical Assisting
  (CAAHEP)

Southwestern Campus
8020 West 87th St., Hickory Hills 60457
Phone: (708) 430-0990

Northwestern University
633 Clark St., Evanston 60208
Type: Private, independent, four-year
Degrees: B, M, D   *Enroll:* 15,592
URL: http://www.northwestern.edu
Phone: (847) 491-3741   *Calendar:* Qtr. plan
Inst. Accred.: NCA-HLC (1913/2005)
Prog. Accred.: Audiology, Business (AACSB), Clinical
  Psychology, Combined Prosthodontics, Counseling
  Psychology, Endodontics, Engineering (bioengineering,
  chemical, civil, computer, electrical,
  environmental/sanitary, industrial, manufacturing,
  materials, mechanical), General Dentistry, Health
  Services Administration, Journalism, Law, Marriage and
  Family Therapy, Medicine, Music, Oral and Maxillofacial
  Surgery, Orthodontic and Dentofacial Orthopedics,
  Orthotist/Prothetist, Pediatric Dentistry, Periodontics,
  Physical Therapy, Psychology Internship, Public Health,
  Speech-Language Pathology, Theatre

Oakton Community College
1600 East Golf Rd., Des Plaines 60016
Type: Public, state/local, two-year
System: Illinois Community College Board
Degrees: A   *Enroll:* 6,132
URL: http://www.oakton.edu
Phone: (847) 635-1600   *Calendar:* Sem. plan
Inst. Accred.: NCA-HLC (1976/1998)
Prog. Accred.: Clinical Lab Technology, Health Information
  Technician, Nursing, Physical Therapy Assisting

Ray Hartstein Campus
7701 North Lincoln Ave., Skokie 60077
Phone: (847) 635-1400

Olivet Nazarene University
One University Ave., Bourbonnais 60914
Type: Private, Church of the Nazarene, four-year
Degrees: B, M   *Enroll:* 3,007
URL: http://www.olivet.edu
Phone: (815) 939-5011   *Calendar:* Sem. plan
Inst. Accred.: NCA-HLC (1956/2005)
Prog. Accred.: Engineering (general), Music, Nursing,
  Nursing Education, Social Work

Olney Central College
305 North West St., Olney 62450
Type: Public, state/local, two-year
System: Illinois Eastern Community Colleges System
Degrees: A   *Enroll:* 1,134
URL: http://www.iecc.edu/occ
Phone: (618) 395-7777   *Calendar:* Sem. plan
Inst. Accred.: NCA-HLC (1984/1995, *Indirect accreditation*
  through Illinois Eastern Community Colleges System,
  Olney, IL)
Prog. Accred.: Nursing, Radiography

OSF Saint Francis Medical Center
530 NE Glen Oak Ave., Peoria 61637
Type: Private, Roman Catholic Church, four-year
Degrees: B, M   *Enroll:* 190
URL: http://www.osfsaintfrancis.org
Phone: (309) 655-2323   *Calendar:* Sem. plan
Inst. Accred.: NCA-HLC (1991/2001)
Prog. Accred.: Clinical Lab Scientist, Histologic
  Technology, Nursing, Radiography

Parkland College
2400 West Bradley Ave., Champaign 61821
Type: Public, state/local, two-year
System: Illinois Community College Board
Degrees: A   *Enroll:* 6,212
URL: http://www.parkland.edu
Phone: (217) 351-2200   *Calendar:* Sem. plan
Inst. Accred.: NCA-HLC (1972/2003)
Prog. Accred.: Dental Hygiene, Nursing, Occupational
  Therapy Assisting, Practical Nursing, Radiography,
  Respiratory Therapy, Surgical Technology, Veterinary
  Technology

Prairie State College
202 South Halsted St., Chicago Heights 60411
Type: Public, state/local, two-year
System: Illinois Community College Board
Degrees: A   *Enroll:* 2,979
URL: http://www.prairie.cc.il.us/
Phone: (708) 709-3500   *Calendar:* Sem. plan
Inst. Accred.: NCA-HLC (1965/1999)
Prog. Accred.: Dental Hygiene, Nursing

Principia College
1 Maybeck Place, Elsah 62028
Type: Private, independent, four-year
Degrees: B   *Enroll:* 548
URL: http://www.prin.edu/college
Phone: (618) 374-2131   *Calendar:* Qtr. plan
Inst. Accred.: NCA-HLC (1923/1995)

Quincy University
1800 College Ave., Quincy 62301
Type: Private, Roman Catholic Church, four-year
Degrees: B, M   *Enroll:* 1,104
URL: http://www.quincy.edu
Phone: (217) 222-8020   *Calendar:* Sem. plan
Inst. Accred.: NCA-HLC (1954/2002)
Prog. Accred.: Music, Nursing Education

Rend Lake College
468 N. Ken Gray Pkwy., Ina 62846
Type: Public, state/local, two-year
System: Illinois Community College Board
Degrees: A   *Enroll:* 2,257
URL: http://www.rlc.edu
Phone: (618) 437-5321   *Calendar:* Sem. plan
Inst. Accred.: NCA-HLC (1969/1999)
Prog. Accred.: Health Information Technician

Richland Community College
One College Park, Decatur 62521
Type: Public, state/local, two-year
System: Illinois Community College Board
Degrees: A   *Enroll:* 1,917
URL: http://www.richland.edu
Phone: (217) 875-7200   *Calendar:* Sem. plan
Inst. Accred.: NCA-HLC (1978/2003)
Prog. Accred.: Nursing, Surgical Technology

Robert Morris College
401 South State St., Chicago 60605
Type: Private, independent, four-year
Degrees: A, B   *Enroll:* 4,865
URL: http://www.robertmorris.edu
Phone: (312) 935-6600   *Calendar:* Qtr. plan
Inst. Accred.: NCA-HLC (1986/2001)
Prog. Accred.: Health Information Technician, Medical
  Assisting (CAAHEP)

Rock Valley College
3301 North Mulford Rd., Rockford 61114-5699
Type: Public, state/local, two-year
System: Illinois Community College Board
Degrees: A   *Enroll:* 5,331
URL: http://www.rockvalleycollege.edu
Phone: (815) 921-7821   *Calendar:* Sem. plan
Inst. Accred.: NCA-HLC (1971/2004)
Prog. Accred.: Dental Hygiene, Respiratory Therapy

Rockford Business College
730 North Church St., Rockford 61103
Type: Private, proprietary, two-year
System: American Higher Education Development
  Corporation
Degrees: A   *Enroll:* 367
URL: http://www.rbcsuccess.com
Phone: (815) 965-8616   *Calendar:* Qtr. plan
Inst. Accred.: ACICS (1968/2003)
Prog. Accred.: Medical Assisting (CAAHEP)

Rockford College
5050 East State St., Rockford 61108-2393
Type: Private, independent, four-year
Degrees: B, M   *Enroll:* 1,075
URL: http://www.rockford.edu
Phone: (815) 226-4010   *Calendar:* Sem. plan
Inst. Accred.: NCA-HLC (1913/2001)
Prog. Accred.: Nursing

Roosevelt University
430 South Michigan Ave., Chicago 60605
Type: Private, independent, four-year
Degrees: B, M, D   *Enroll:* 4,547
URL: http://www.roosevelt.edu
Phone: (312) 341-3500   *Calendar:* Sem. plan
Inst. Accred.: NCA-HLC (1946/1996)
Prog. Accred.: Business (ACBSP), Clinical Psychology,
  Counseling, Music, Teacher Education (NCATE)

Albert A. Robin Campus
1400 North Roosevelt Blvd., Schaumburg 60173-4348
Phone: (847) 619-5300

The Rosalind Franklin University of Medicine and Science
3333 Green Bay Rd., North Chicago 60064
Type: Private, independent, four-year
Degrees: B, M, D   *Enroll:* 1,335
URL: http://www.rosalindfranklin.edu
Phone: (847) 578-3000   *Calendar:* Qtr. plan
Inst. Accred.: NCA-HLC (1980/1998)
Prog. Accred.: Clinical Lab Scientist, Clinical Psychology,
  Immunology, Medicine, Nursing, Pathologists' Assistant,
  Phlebotomy, Physical Therapy, Physician Assistant

Rush University
1653 W. Congress Pkwy., Chicago 60612
Type: Private, independent, four-year
Degrees: B, M, D   *Enroll:* 1,045
URL: http://www.rushu.rush.edu
Phone: (312) 942-7120   *Calendar:* Qtr. plan
Inst. Accred.: NCA-HLC (1974/1998)
Prog. Accred.: Audiology, Clinical Lab Scientist, Health
  Services Administration, Medicine, Nurse Anesthesia
  Education, Nursing, Nursing Education, Occupational
  Therapy, Perfusion, Speech-Language Pathology

Saint Anthony College of Nursing
5658 East State St., Rockford 61108-2468
Type: Private, Roman Catholic Church, four-year
Degrees: B   *Enroll:* 91
URL: http://www.sacn.edu
Phone: (815) 395-5091   *Calendar:* Sem. plan
Inst. Accred.: NCA-HLC (1994/1999)
Prog. Accred.: Nursing, Nursing Education

Saint Augustine College
1333-45 West Argyle St., Chicago 60640
Type: Private, independent, four-year
Degrees: A, B   *Enroll:* 1,531
URL: http://www.staugustinecollege.edu
Phone: (773) 878-8756   *Calendar:* Sem. plan
Inst. Accred.: NCA-HLC (1987/1999)
Prog. Accred.: Respiratory Therapy, Respiratory Therapy
  Technology

Saint John's College
421 North Ninth St., Springfield 62702
Type: Private, independent, four-year
Degrees: B   *Enroll:* 61
URL: http://www.st-johns.org/education/schools/nursing
Phone: (217) 525-5628   *Calendar:* Sem. plan
Inst. Accred.: NCA-HLC (1995/2000)
Prog. Accred.: Clinical Lab Scientist, Nursing

Saint Xavier University
3700 West 103rd St., Chicago 60655
Type: Private, Roman Catholic Church, four-year
Degrees: B, M   *Enroll:* 3,739
URL: http://www.sxu.edu
Phone: (773) 298-3000   *Calendar:* Sem. plan
Inst. Accred.: NCA-HLC (1937/1998)
Prog. Accred.: Business (ACBSP), Music, Nursing, Nursing
   Education, Speech-Language Pathology, Teacher
   Education (NCATE)

Sauk Valley Community College
173 Illinois Route 2, Dixon 61021
Type: Public, state/local, two-year
System: Illinois Community College Board
Degrees: A   *Enroll:* 1,611
URL: http://www.svcc.edu
Phone: (815) 288-5511   *Calendar:* Sem. plan
Inst. Accred.: NCA-HLC (1972/2002)
Prog. Accred.: Clinical Lab Technology, Radiography

The School of the Art Institute of Chicago
37 South Wabash Ave., Chicago 60603
Type: Private, independent, four-year
Degrees: B, M   *Enroll:* 2,451
URL: http://www.artic.edu/saic/saichome.html
Phone: (312) 899-5219   *Calendar:* Sem. plan
Inst. Accred.: NCA-HLC (1936/2003)
Prog. Accred.: Art

Seabury-Western Theological Seminary
2122 Sheridan Rd., Evanston 60201-2938
Type: Private, Episcopal Church, four-year
Degrees: M, D   *Enroll:* 109
URL: http://www.seabury.edu
Phone: (847) 328-9300   *Calendar:* Qtr. plan
Inst. Accred.: ATS (1938/1998), NCA-HLC (1981/1998)

Shawnee Community College
8364 Shawnee College Rd., Ullin 62992-9725
Type: Public, state/local, two-year
System: Illinois Community College Board
Degrees: A   *Enroll:* 1,361
URL: http://www.shawnee.edu
Phone: (618) 634-2242   *Calendar:* Sem. plan
Inst. Accred.: NCA-HLC (1974/2005)

Shimer College
438 North Sheridan Rd., Waukegan 60085
Type: Private, independent, four-year
Degrees: B   *Enroll:* 123
URL: http://www.shimer.edu
Phone: (847) 623-8400   *Calendar:* Sem. plan
Inst. Accred.: NCA-HLC (1991/2001)

South Suburban College of Cook County
15800 South State St., South Holland 60473
Type: Public, state/local, two-year
System: Illinois Community College Board
Degrees: A   *Enroll:* 4,201
URL: http://www.southsuburbancollege.edu
Phone: (708) 596-2000   *Calendar:* Sem. plan
Inst. Accred.: NCA-HLC (1933/1999)
Prog. Accred.: Diagnostic Medical Sonography, Music,
   Nursing, Occupational Therapy Assisting, Phlebotomy,
   Practical Nursing, Radiography

Southeastern Illinois College
3575 College Rd., Harrisburg 62946
Type: Public, state/local, two-year
System: Illinois Community College Board
Degrees: A   *Enroll:* 1,731
URL: http://www.sic.edu
Phone: (618) 252-6376   *Calendar:* Sem. plan
Inst. Accred.: NCA-HLC (1976/1998)
Prog. Accred.: Health Information Technician, Nursing

Southern Illinois University Carbondale
Carbondale 62901-4304
Type: Public, state, four-year
System: Southern Illinois University System
Degrees: A, B, M, D   *Enroll:* 18,697
URL: http://www.siuc.edu
Phone: (618) 453-2121   *Calendar:* Sem. plan
Inst. Accred.: NCA-HLC (1913/1999)
Prog. Accred.: Accounting, Art, Athletic Training, Business
   (AACSB), Clinical Psychology, Counseling, Counseling
   Psychology, Dental Hygiene, Dental Laboratory
   Technology, Dietetics (internship), Engineering (civil,
   computer, electrical, mechanical, mining), Engineering
   Technology (electrical, mechanical), Forestry, Funeral
   Service Education (Mortuary Science), Industrial
   Technology, Interior Design, Journalism, Law, Medicine,
   Music, Physical Therapy Assisting, Physician Assistant,
   Psychology Internship, Public Administration,
   Radiography, Recreation and Leisure Services,
   Rehabilitation Counseling, Respiratory Therapy, Social
   Work, Speech-Language Pathology, Teacher Education
   (NCATE), Theatre

Southern Illinois University at Carbondale in Niigata
439-1, Oaza Nagahashikami, Nakajo, Kitakanbara,
Niigata, Japan 959-26
Phone: 011-81-254-43-6205

Southern Illinois University Edwardsville
SIUE Campus Box 1151, Edwardsville 62026-1151
Type: Public, state, four-year
System: Southern Illinois University System
Degrees: B, M, P, D   *Enroll:* 11,143
URL: http://www.siue.edu
Phone: (618) 650-2000   *Calendar:* Sem. plan
Inst. Accred.: NCA-HLC (1969/2005)
Prog. Accred.: Accounting, Business (AACSB), Computer
   Science, Construction Education, Dental Hygiene,
   Dental Laboratory Technology, Dentistry, Engineering
   (civil, computer, electrical, industrial, mechanical),
   General Dentistry, General Practice Residency,
   Journalism, Music, Nurse Anesthesia Education,
   Nursing, Nursing Education, Public Administration,
   Social Work, Speech-Language Pathology, Teacher
   Education (NCATE)

Southwestern Illinois College
2500 Carlyle Rd., Belleville 62221
Type: Public, state/local, two-year
System: Illinois Community College Board
Degrees: A   *Enroll:* 8,468
URL: http://www.swic.edu
Phone: (618) 235-2700   *Calendar:* Sem. plan
Inst. Accred.: NCA-HLC (1961/1999)
Prog. Accred.: Clinical Lab Technology, Culinary
   Education, Health Information Technician, Medical
   Assisting (AMA), Nursing, Physical Therapy Assisting,
   Radiography, Respiratory Therapy Technology

Red Bud Campus
500 West South Fourth St., Red Bud 62278
Phone: (618) 282-6682

Spertus Institute of Jewish Studies
618 South Michigan Ave., Chicago 60605
Type: Private, independent, four-year
Degrees: M, D   *Enroll:* 107
URL: http://www.spertus.edu
Phone: (312) 922-9012   *Calendar:* Qtr. plan
Inst. Accred.: NCA-HLC (1971/1998)

Spoon River College
23235 North County 22, Canton 61520
Type: Public, state/local, two-year
System: Illinois Community College Board
Degrees: A   *Enroll:* 1,400
URL: http://www.spoonrivercollege.edu
Phone: (309) 647-4645   *Calendar:* Sem. plan
Inst. Accred.: NCA-HLC (1977/2002)

Springfield College in Illinois
1500 North Fifth St., Springfield 62702
Type: Private, Roman Catholic Church, two-year
Degrees: A   *Enroll:* 337
URL: http://www.sci.edu
Phone: (217) 525-1420   *Calendar:* Sem. plan
Inst. Accred.: NCA-HLC (1933/1996)

Taylor Business Institute
200 North Michigan Ave., Ste. 301, Chicago 60601-5908
Type: Private, proprietary, two-year
Degrees: A   *Enroll:* 298
URL: http://www.tbiil.edu
Phone: (312) 236-6400
Inst. Accred.: ACICS (1973/2001)

Telshe Yeshiva-Chicago
3535 West Foster Ave., Chicago 60625
Type: Private, independent, four-year
Degrees: Rabbinic   *Enroll:* 72
Phone: (773) 463-7738   *Calendar:* Sem. plan
Inst. Accred.: AARTS (1976/2002)

Trinity Christian College
6601 West College Dr., Palos Heights 60463
Type: Private, Christian Reformed, four-year
Degrees: B   *Enroll:* 1,123
URL: http://www.trnty.edu
Phone: (708) 597-3000   *Calendar:* Sem. plan
Inst. Accred.: NCA-HLC (1976/2001)
Prog. Accred.: Business (ACBSP), Nursing, Nursing
   Education

Trinity College of Nursing and Health Sciences School
2701 17th St., Rock Island 61201
Type: Private, independent, four-year
Degrees: A, B   *Enroll:* 105
URL: http://www.trinitycollegeqc.edu
Phone: (309) 779-7700   *Calendar:* Sem. plan
Inst. Accred.: NCA-HLC (1996/2003)
Prog. Accred.: Nursing Education, Radiography

Trinity International University
2065 Half Day Rd., Deerfield 60015
Type: Private, Evangelical Free Church of America, four-year
Degrees: B, M, D   *Enroll:* 2,049
URL: http://www.tiu.edu
Phone: (847) 945-8800   *Calendar:* Sem. plan
Inst. Accred.: ATS (1973/1999), NCA-HLC (1996)

South Florida Campus
500 N.E. First Ave., PO Box 019674, Miami, FL 33101
Phone: (305) 577-4600

Trinity Law School
2200 North Grand Ave., Santa Ana, CA 92705
Phone: (714) 836-7500

Triton College
2000 Fifth Ave., River Grove 60171
Type: Public, local, two-year
System: Illinois Community College Board
Degrees: A   *Enroll:* 7,451
URL: http://www.triton.edu
Phone: (708) 456-0300   *Calendar:* Sem. plan
Inst. Accred.: NCA-HLC (1972/1999)
Prog. Accred.: Dental Laboratory Technology, Diagnostic
   Medical Sonography, Nuclear Medicine Technology,
   Nursing, Ophthalmic Medical Technology, Practical Nursing,
   Radiography, Respiratory Therapy, Surgical Technology

University of Chicago
5801 South Ellis Ave., Chicago 60637
Type: Private, independent, four-year
Degrees: B, M, D   *Enroll:* 12,715
URL: http://www.uchicago.edu
Phone: (773) 702-1234   *Calendar:* Qtr. plan
Inst. Accred.: ATS (1938/2002), NCA-HLC (1913/1996)
Prog. Accred.: Accounting, Business (AACSB), Clinical
Pastoral Education, General Practice Residency, Law,
Maxillofacial Prosthetics, Medicine, Oral and
Maxillofacial Surgery, Psychology Internship, Social
Work

Graduate School of Business
1101 East 58th St., Chicago 60637
Phone: (773) 702-7743

University of Illinois at Chicago
601 South Morgan St., M/C 102, Chicago 60607-7128
Type: Public, state, four-year
System: University of Illinois Central Office
Degrees: B, M, P, D   *Enroll:* 22,648
URL: http://www.uic.edu
Phone: (312) 996-7000   *Calendar:* Sem. plan
Inst. Accred.: NCA-HLC (1970/1997)
Prog. Accred.: Accounting, Applied Science (industrial
hygiene), Art, Blood Bank Technology, Business
(AACSB), Clinical Lab Scientist, Clinical Psychology,
Combined Prosthodontics, Computer Science, Dentistry,
Dietetics (coordinated), Endodontics, Engineering
(bioengineering, chemical, civil, computer, electrical,
industrial, mechanical), English Language Education,
General Practice Residency, Health Information
Administration, Medical Illustration, Medicine, Nurse
(Midwifery), Nursing, Nursing Education, Occupational
Therapy, Oral and Maxillofacial Surgery, Orthodontic
and Dentofacial Orthopedics, Pediatric Dentistry,
Periodontics, Pharmacy, Physical Therapy, Planning,
Psychology Internship, Public Administration, Public
Health, Social Work

College of Medicine at Peoria
1 Illini Dr., PO Box 1649, Peoria 62656
Phone: (309) 671-3000

College of Medicine at Rockford
1601 Parkview Ave., Rockford 61107
Phone: (815) 395-0600

University of Illinois at Springfield
PO Box 19243, Springfield 62794-9243
Type: Public, state, four-year
System: University of Illinois Central Office
Degrees: B, M, D   *Enroll:* 2,937
URL: http://www.uis.edu
Phone: (217) 206-6600   *Calendar:* Sem. plan
Inst. Accred.: NCA-HLC (1975/2001)
Prog. Accred.: Business (AACSB), Clinical Lab Scientist,
Counseling, Nursing, Social Work

University of Illinois at Urbana-Champaign
601 East John St., Champaign 61820
Type: Public, state, four-year
System: University of Illinois Central Office
Degrees: B, M, D   *Enroll:* 38,229
URL: http://www.uiuc.edu
Phone: (217) 333-1000   *Calendar:* Sem. plan
Inst. Accred.: NCA-HLC (1913/1999)
Prog. Accred.: Accounting, Art, Athletic Training,
Audiology, Business (AACSB), Clinical Psychology,
Computer Science, Counseling Psychology, Dance,
Dietetics (internship), Engineering (aerospace,
agricultural, chemical, civil, computer, electrical,
engineering mechanics, general, industrial, materials,
mechanical, nuclear), Forestry, Journalism, Landscape
Architecture, Law, Librarianship, Music, Planning,
Psychology Internship, Recreation and Leisure Services,
Rehabilitation Counseling, Social Work, Speech-
Language Pathology, Theatre, Veterinary Medicine

University of Saint Francis
500 North Wilcox St., Joliet 60435
Type: Private, Roman Catholic Church, four-year
Degrees: B, M   *Enroll:* 2,516
URL: http://www.stfrancis.edu
Phone: (815) 740-3360   *Calendar:* Sem. plan
Inst. Accred.: NCA-HLC (1938/1999)
Prog. Accred.: Nursing Education, Recreation and Leisure
Services, Social Work

Albuquerque Campus
4401 Silver Ave., SE, Albuquerque, NM 87108
Phone: (505) 266-5565
Prog. Accred: Physician Assistant

Saint Joseph College of Nursing
290 North Springfield Ave., Joliet 60435
Phone: (815) 741-7132
Prog. Accred: Nursing

University of Saint Mary of the Lake Mundelein Seminary
1000 East Maple, Mundelein 60060
Type: Private, Roman Catholic Church, four-year
Degrees: M, D   *Enroll:* 228
URL: http://www.usml.edu
Phone: (847) 566-6401   *Calendar:* Sem. plan
Inst. Accred.: ATS (1972/2002)

VanderCook College of Music
3140 South Federal St., Chicago 60616
Type: Private, independent, four-year
Degrees: B, M   *Enroll:* 135
URL: http://www.vandercook.edu
Phone: (312) 225-6288   *Calendar:* Sem. plan
Inst. Accred.: NCA-HLC (1971/2003)
Prog. Accred.: Music

Wabash Valley College
2200 College Dr., Mount Carmel 62863
Type: Public, state/local, two-year
System: Illinois Eastern Community Colleges System
Degrees: A *Enroll:* 1,810
URL: http://www.iecc.edu/wvc
Phone: (618) 262-8641 *Calendar:* Sem. plan
Inst. Accred.: NCA-HLC (1984/1995, *Indirect accreditation through Illinois Eastern Community Colleges System, Olney, IL)*
Prog. Accred.: Nursing

Waubonsee Community College
Illinois Route 47 at Waubonsee Dr., Sugar Grove 60554
Type: Public, state/local, two-year
System: Illinois Community College Board
Degrees: A *Enroll:* 4,399
URL: http://www.waubonsee.edu
Phone: (630) 466-7900 *Calendar:* Sem. plan
Inst. Accred.: NCA-HLC (1972/1996)

West Suburban College of Nursing
3 Erie St., Oak Park 60302
Type: Private, independent, four-year
Degrees: B *Enroll:* 92
URL: http://www.wscn.curf.edu
Phone: (708) 763-6530 *Calendar:* Sem. plan
Inst. Accred.: NCA-HLC (1986/1995)
Prog. Accred.: Nursing, Nursing Education

Western Illinois University
One University Circle, Macomb 61455-1390
Type: Public, state, four-year
System: Illinois Board of Higher Education
Degrees: B, M, P *Enroll:* 11,722
URL: http://www.wiu.edu
Phone: (309) 298-1414 *Calendar:* Sem. plan
Inst. Accred.: NCA-HLC (1913/2001)
Prog. Accred.: Accounting, Athletic Training, Audiology, Business (AACSB), Counseling, English Language Education, Music, Recreation and Leisure Services, Social Work, Speech-Language Pathology, Teacher Education (NCATE)

Westwood College—DuPage
7155 Janes Ave., Woodridge 60517
Type: Private, proprietary, four-year
Degrees: A, B
URL: http://www.westwood.edu
Phone: (630) 434-8244
Inst. Accred.: ACICS (1992/2001)

Atlanta Midtown Campus
1100 Spring St., Atlanta, GA 30309
Phone: (404) 745-9096

Fort Worth Campus
4232 North Freeway, Fort Worth, TX 76137
Phone: (817) 547-9600

Westwood College—O'Hare Airport
8501 West Higgins Rd., Ste. 100, Chicago 60631
Type: Private, proprietary, four-year
Degrees: A, B
URL: http://www.westwoodcollege.com
Phone: (773) 380-6800
Inst. Accred.: ACICS (1985/2004)

Atlanta Northlake Campus
2220 Parklake Dr., NE, Atlanta, GA 30345
Phone: (404) 962-2999

Wheaton College
501 College Ave., Wheaton 60187
Type: Private, interdenominational, four-year
Degrees: B, M, D *Enroll:* 2,757
URL: http://www.wheaton.edu
Phone: (630) 752-5000 *Calendar:* Sem. plan
Inst. Accred.: NCA-HLC (1913/2004)
Prog. Accred.: Clinical Psychology, Music, Teacher Education (NCATE)

William Rainey Harper College
1200 West Algonquin Rd., Palatine 60067-7398
Type: Public, state/local, two-year
System: Illinois Community College Board
Degrees: A *Enroll:* 8,644
URL: http://www.harpercollege.edu
Phone: (847) 925-6000 *Calendar:* Sem. plan
Inst. Accred.: NCA-HLC (1971/1998)
Prog. Accred.: Business (ACBSP), Dental Hygiene, English Language Education, Medical Assisting (AMA), Music, Nursing

Worsham College of Mortuary Science
495 Northgate Pkwy., Wheeling 60090-2646
Type: Private, proprietary, two-year
Degrees: A
URL: http://www.worshamcollege.com
Phone: (847) 808-8444 *Calendar:* 12-mos. pr
Inst. Accred.: ABFSE (1952/2001)

INDIANA

Ancilla College
PO Box 1, Union Rd., Donaldson 46513
Type: Private, Roman Catholic Church, two-year
Degrees: A   *Enroll:* 469
URL: http://www.ancilla.edu
Phone: (574) 936-8898   *Calendar:* Sem. plan
Inst. Accred.: NCA-HLC (1973/1998)

Anderson University
1100 East Fifth St., Anderson 46012-3495
Type: Private, Church of God, four-year
Degrees: A, B, M, D   *Enroll:* 2,274
URL: http://www.anderson.edu
Phone: (765) 649-9071   *Calendar:* Sem. plan
Inst. Accred.: ATS (1965/1999), NCA-HLC (1946/2001)
Prog. Accred.: Athletic Training, Business (ACBSP), Music, Nursing, Social Work, Teacher Education (NCATE)

Associated Mennonite Biblical Seminary
3003 Benham Ave., Elkhart 46517-1999
Type: Private, Mennonite Church, four-year
Degrees: M   *Enroll:* 122
URL: http://www.ambs.edu
Phone: (574) 295-3726   *Calendar:* 4-1-4 plan
Inst. Accred.: ATS (1958/1999), NCA-HLC (1974/1999)

Aviation Institute of Maintenance Training Academy
7251 West McCarty St., Indianapolis 46241-1445
Type: Private, proprietary, two-year
Degrees: A   *Enroll:* 142
URL: http://www.aviationtraining.net
Phone: (317) 243-4519   *Calendar:* Sem. plan
Inst. Accred.: ACCSCT (1996/2001)

Ball State University
2000 University Ave., Muncie 47306
Type: Public, state, four-year
System: Indiana Commission for Higher Education
Degrees: A, B, M, P, D   *Enroll:* 18,564
URL: http://www.bsu.edu
Phone: (765) 289-1241   *Calendar:* Sem. plan
Inst. Accred.: NCA-HLC (1925/2004)
Prog. Accred.: Accounting, Art, Athletic Training, Audiology, Business (AACSB), Counseling, Counseling Psychology, Dietetics (internship), Engineering Technology (manufacturing), Journalism, Landscape Architecture, Music, Nursing, Planning, Psychology Internship, Radiation Therapy, Radiography, School Psychology, Social Work, Speech-Language Pathology, Teacher Education (NCATE), Theatre

Bethany Theological Seminary
615 National Rd. West, Richmond 47374-4019
Type: Private, Church of the Brethren, four-year
Degrees: M, D   *Enroll:* 65
URL: http://www.bethanyseminary.edu
Phone: (765) 983-1800   *Calendar:* Sem. plan
Inst. Accred.: ATS (1940/1996), NCA-HLC (1971/1997)

Bethel College
1001 West McKinley Ave., Mishawaka 46545
Type: Private, Missionnary Church, four-year
Degrees: A, B, M   *Enroll:* 1,523
URL: http://www.bethelcollege.edu
Phone: (219) 259-8511   *Calendar:* Sem. plan
Inst. Accred.: NCA-HLC (1971/1998)
Prog. Accred.: Nursing, Teacher Education (NCATE)

Brown Mackie College—Merrillville
1000 East 80th Place, Ste. 101 North, Merrillville 46410-4388
Type: Private, proprietary, two-year
System: Education Management Corporation
Degrees: A   *Enroll:* 454
URL: http://www.brownmackie.edu
Phone: (219) 769-3321   *Calendar:* Qtr. plan
Inst. Accred.: ACICS (1978/2005)
Prog. Accred.: Medical Assisting (ABHES)

Michigan City Campus
325 East US Hwy. 20, Michigan City 46350
Phone: (219) 877-3100
Prog. Accred.: Medical Assisting (ABHES)

Moline Campus
1527 47th Ave., Moline, IL 61265
Phone: (309) 762-2100

Brown Mackie College—South Bend
1030 East Jefferson Blvd., South Bend 46617
Type: Private, proprietary, two-year
System: Education Management Corporation
Degrees: A   *Enroll:* 513
URL: http://www.brownmackie.edu
Phone: (574) 237-0774   *Calendar:* Qtr. plan
Inst. Accred.: ACICS (1960/2003)
Prog. Accred.: Medical Assisting (AMA), Occupational Therapy Assisting, Physical Therapy Assisting

Denver Campus
1200 Lincoln St., Denver, CO 80203
Phone: (303) 248-2700

Fort Wayne Campus
4422 East State Blvd., Fort Wayne 46815
Phone: (260) 484-4400
Prog. Accred: Medical Assisting (AMA), Occupational Therapy Assisting

Butler University
4600 Sunset Ave., Indianapolis 46208
Type: Private, independent, four-year
Degrees: A, B, M, P, D   *Enroll:* 4,049
URL: http://www.butler.edu
Phone: (317) 940-8000   *Calendar:* Sem. plan
Inst. Accred.: NCA-HLC (1915/2003)
Prog. Accred.: Business (AACSB), Counseling, Dance, Music, Pharmacy, Physician Assistant, Psychology Internship, Teacher Education (NCATE), Theatre

Calumet College of Saint Joseph
2400 New York Ave., Whiting 46394
Type: Private, Roman Catholic Church, four-year
Degrees: A, B *Enroll:* 793
URL: http://www.ccsj.edu
Phone: (219) 473-7770 *Calendar:* Sem. plan
Inst. Accred.: NCA-HLC (1968/2001)

Christian Theological Seminary
1000 West 42nd St., PO Box 88267, Indianapolis 46208-3301
Type: Private, Christian Churches/Disciples of Christ, four-year
Degrees: M, D *Enroll:* 199
Phone: (317) 924-1331 *Calendar:* Sem. plan
Inst. Accred.: ATS (1944/1998), NCA-HLC (1973/1998)
Prog. Accred.: Marriage and Family Therapy

College of Court Reporting, Inc.
111 West 10th St., Ste. 111, Hobart 46342
Type: Private, proprietary, two-year
Degrees: A *Enroll:* 35
URL: http://www.ccredu.com
Phone: (219) 942-1459 *Calendar:* Sem. plan
Inst. Accred.: ACICS (1989/2001)

Concordia Theological Seminary
6600 North Clinton St., Fort Wayne 46825-4996
Type: Private, Lutheran Church—Missouri Synod, four-year
System: Concordia University System
Degrees: M, D *Enroll:* 351
URL: http://www.ctsfw.edu
Phone: (260) 452-2100 *Calendar:* Qtr. plan
Inst. Accred.: ATS (1968/2003), NCA-HLC (1981/2003)

Crossroads Bible College
601 North Shortridge Rd., Indianapolis 46219
Type: Private, independent, four-year
Degrees: A, B
URL: http://www.crossroads.edu
Phone: (317) 352-8736 *Calendar:* Sem. plan
Inst. Accred.: ABHE (1999/2005)

DePauw University
313 South Locust St., Greencastle 46135
Type: Private, United Methodist Church, four-year
Degrees: B *Enroll:* 2,341
URL: http://www.depauw.edu
Phone: (765) 658-4800 *Calendar:* 4-1-4 plan
Inst. Accred.: NCA-HLC (1915/1998)
Prog. Accred.: Athletic Training, Music, Teacher Education (NCATE)

Earlham College
801 National Rd. West, Richmond 47374-4095
Type: Private, independent, four-year
Degrees: B, M *Enroll:* 1,218
URL: http://www.earlham.edu
Phone: (765) 983-1200 *Calendar:* Sem. plan
Inst. Accred.: ATS (1973/1996), NCA-HLC (1915/2004)

Franklin College
101 Branigin Blvd., Franklin 46131-2623
Type: Private, American Baptist Churches (USA), four-year
Degrees: B *Enroll:* 1,005
URL: http://www.franklincollege.edu
Phone: (317) 738-8000 *Calendar:* 4-1-4 plan
Inst. Accred.: NCA-HLC (1915/2002)
Prog. Accred.: Teacher Education (NCATE)

Goshen College
1700 South Main St., Goshen 46526
Type: Private, Mennonite Church, four-year
Degrees: B *Enroll:* 856
URL: http://www.goshen.edu
Phone: (574) 535-7000 *Calendar:* 4-1-4 plan
Inst. Accred.: NCA-HLC (1941/2005)
Prog. Accred.: Nursing, Nursing Education, Social Work, Teacher Education (NCATE)

Grace College and Seminary
200 Seminary Dr., Winona Lake 46590
Type: Private, Fellowship of Grace Brethren Churches, four-year
Degrees: A, B, M, D *Enroll:* 1,097
URL: http://www.grace.edu
Phone: (800) 544-7223 *Calendar:* Sem. plan
Inst. Accred.: NCA-HLC (1994/1999)
Prog. Accred.: Counseling, Music, Social Work

Hanover College
PO Box 108, Hanover 47243-0108
Type: Private, Presbyterian Church (USA), four-year
Degrees: B *Enroll:* 992
URL: http://www.hanover.edu
Phone: (812) 866-7000 *Calendar:* 4-1-4 plan
Inst. Accred.: NCA-HLC (1915/2000)
Prog. Accred.: Teacher Education (NCATE)

Holy Cross College
54515 State Rd. 933 North, PO Box 308, Notre Dame 46556
Type: Private, Holy-Cross Brothers-Midwest, two-year
Degrees: A *Enroll:* 479
Phone: (219) 239-8400 *Calendar:* Sem. plan
Inst. Accred.: NCA-HLC (1987/1997)

Huntington College
2303 College Ave., Huntington 46750
Type: Private, United Brethren in Christ, four-year
Degrees: A, B, M *Enroll:* 886
Phone: (260) 356-6000 *Calendar:* 4-1-4 plan
Inst. Accred.: NCA-HLC (1961/2004)
Prog. Accred.: Music, Teacher Education (NCATE)

Indiana Business College
411 West Riggin Rd., Muncie 47303
Type: Private, proprietary, two-year
Degrees: A *Enroll:* 280
URL: http://www.indianabusinesscollege.com
Phone: (765) 288-8681
Inst. Accred.: ACICS (1989/2004)

Indiana Business College
550 East Washington St., Indianapolis 46204
Type: Private, proprietary, two-year
Degrees: A   *Enroll:* 710
URL: http://www.indianabusinesscollege.com
Phone: (317) 375-8000
Inst. Accred.: ACICS (1980/2004)

Anderson Campus
140 East 53rd St., Anderson 46013
Phone: (765) 644-7414

Columbus Campus
2222 Poshard Dr., Columbus 47203
Phone: (812) 379-9000

Evansville Campus
4601 Theater Dr., Evansville 47715
Phone: (812) 476-6000
Prog. Accred: Medical Assisting (CAAHEP)

Fort Wayne Campus
6413 North Clinton St., Ft. Wayne 46825
Phone: (219) 471-7667

Indianapolis Medical Division Campus
8150 Brookville Rd., Indianapolis 46239
Phone: (317) 783-5100
Prog. Accred: Medical Assisting (CAAHEP)

Indianapolis Northwest Campus
6300 Technology Center Dr., Indianapolis 46278
Phone: (317) 873-6500

Lafayette Campus
2 Executive Dr., Lafayette 47905
Phone: (765) 447-9550

Marion Campus
830 North Miller Ave., Marion 46952
Phone: (765) 662-7497

Terre Haute Campus
3175 South Third St., Terre Haute 47802
Phone: (812) 232-4458

Indiana Institute of Technology
1600 East Washington Blvd., Fort Wayne 46803
Type: Private, proprietary, four-year
Degrees: A, B, M   *Enroll:* 2,390
URL: http://www.indianatech.edu
Phone: (800) 937-2448   *Calendar:* Sem. plan
Inst. Accred.: NCA-HLC (1962/1996)
Prog. Accred.: Engineering (electrical, mechanical)

Indiana State University
200 North Seventh St., Terre Haute 47809
Type: Public, state, four-year
System: Indiana Commission for Higher Education
Degrees: A, B, M, P, D   *Enroll:* 9,943
URL: http://www.indstate.edu
Phone: (812) 237-6311   *Calendar:* Sem. plan
Inst. Accred.: NCA-HLC (1915/2000)
Prog. Accred.: Art, Athletic Training, Business (AACSB),
   Clinical Psychology, Construction Education,
   Counseling, Counseling Psychology, Dietetics
   (coordinated), Electronic Technology, English Language
   Education, Family and Consumer Science, Industrial
   Technology, Manufacturing Technology, Marriage and
   Family Therapy, Mechanical Technology, Music,
   Nursing, Recreation and Leisure Services, School
   Psychology, Social Work, Speech-Language Pathology,
   Teacher Education (NCATE)

Indiana University Bloomington
107 South Indiana Ave., Bloomington 47405-7000
Type: Public, state, four-year
System: Indiana University System
Degrees: A, B, M, P, D   *Enroll:* 35,667
URL: http://www.iub.edu
Phone: (812) 855-4848   *Calendar:* Sem. plan
Inst. Accred.: NCA-HLC (1913/1997)
Prog. Accred.: Accounting, Art, Athletic Training,
   Audiology, Business (AACSB), Clinical Psychology,
   Counseling, Counseling Psychology, Interior Design,
   Journalism, Law, Librarianship, Music, Opticianry,
   Optometric Residency, Optometric Technician,
   Optometry, Psychology Internship, Public
   Administration, Public Health, Recreation and Leisure
   Services, School Psychology, Social Work, Speech-
   Language Pathology, Teacher Education (NCATE),
   Theatre

Indiana University East
2325 North Chester Blvd., Richmond 47374
Type: Public, state, four-year
System: Indiana University System
Degrees: A, B   *Enroll:* 1,804
URL: http://www.iue.edu
Phone: (317) 973-8200   *Calendar:* Sem. plan
Inst. Accred.: NCA-HLC (1971/2002)
Prog. Accred.: Business (ACBSP), Nursing, Social Work,
   Teacher Education (NCATE)

Indiana University Kokomo
PO Box 9003, 2300 South Washington St., Kokomo
46904-9003
Type: Public, state, four-year
System: Indiana University System
Degrees: A, B, M   *Enroll:* 2,047
URL: http://www.iuk.edu
Phone: (765) 453-2000   *Calendar:* Sem. plan
Inst. Accred.: NCA-HLC (1969/1999)
Prog. Accred.: Business (AACSB), Nursing, Nursing
   Education, Radiography, Teacher Education (NCATE)

Indiana University Northwest
3400 Broadway, Gary 46408
Type: Public, state, four-year
System: Indiana University System
Degrees: A, B, M   *Enroll:* 3,530
URL: http://www.iun.edu
Phone: (219) 980-6500   *Calendar:* Sem. plan
Inst. Accred.: NCA-HLC (1969/2003)
Prog. Accred.: Clinical Lab Technology, Dental Assisting, Dental Hygiene, Health Information Technician, Nursing, Nursing Education, Phlebotomy, Public Administration, Radiation Therapy, Radiography, Respiratory Therapy, Social Work, Teacher Education (NCATE)

Indiana University South Bend
1700 Mishawaka Ave., PO Box 7111, South Bend 46634
Type: Public, state, four-year
System: Indiana University System
Degrees: A, B, M   *Enroll:* 5,064
URL: http://www.iusb.edu
Phone: (574) 520-4872   *Calendar:* Sem. plan
Inst. Accred.: NCA-HLC (1969/2001)
Prog. Accred.: Business (AACSB), Dental Assisting, Dental Hygiene, Montessori Teacher Education, Nursing, Nursing Education, Public Administration, Radiation Therapy, Radiography, Social Work, Teacher Education (NCATE)

Indiana University Southeast
4201 Grant Line Rd., New Albany 47150
Type: Public, state, four-year
System: Indiana University System
Degrees: A, B, M   *Enroll:* 4,451
URL: http://www.ius.edu
Phone: (812) 941-2333   *Calendar:* Sem. plan
Inst. Accred.: NCA-HLC (1969/2000)
Prog. Accred.: Business (AACSB), Nursing, Nursing Education, Teacher Education (NCATE)

Indiana University-Purdue University Fort Wayne
2101 Coliseum Blvd. East, Fort Wayne 46805-1499
Type: Public, state, four-year
System: Indiana University System
Degrees: A, B, M   *Enroll:* 8,574
URL: http://www.ipfw.edu
Phone: (260) 481-6100   *Calendar:* Sem. plan
Inst. Accred.: NCA-HLC (1974/2001)
Prog. Accred.: Business (AACSB), Computer Science, Dental Assisting, Dental Hygiene, Dental Laboratory Technology, Engineering (architectural, electrical, mechanical), Engineering Technology (architectural, civil/construction, electrical, industrial, mechanical), Health Information Technician, Music, Nursing, Public Administration, Teacher Education (NCATE)

Indiana University-Purdue University Indianapolis
355 North Lansing St., Indianapolis 46202
Type: Public, state, four-year
System: Indiana University System
Degrees: A, B, M, D   *Enroll:* 21,955
URL: http://www.iupui.edu
Phone: (317) 274-5555   *Calendar:* Sem. plan
Inst. Accred.: NCA-HLC (1971/2003)
Prog. Accred.: Art, Clinical Lab Scientist, Clinical Psychology, Combined Prosthodontic/Maxillofacial Prosthetics, Combined Prosthodontics, Computer Science, Cytotechnology, Dental Assisting, Dental Hygiene, Dentistry, Dietetics (internship), Endodontics, Engineering (architectural, electrical, mechanical), Engineering Technology (civil/construction, computer, electrical, mechanical), General Practice Residency, Health Information Technician, Health Services Administration, Histologic Technology, Law, Medicine, Nuclear Medicine Technology, Nursing, Nursing Education, Occupational Therapy, Oral and Maxillofacial Pathology, Oral and Maxillofacial Surgery, Orthodontic and Dentofacial Orthopedics, Pediatric Dentistry, Periodontics, Physical Therapy, Psychology Internship, Public Administration, Public Health, Radiation Therapy, Radiography, Respiratory Therapy, Social Work

Indiana University-Purdue University Columbus
4601 Central Ave., Columbus 47203
Phone: (812) 348-7311

Indiana Wesleyan University
4201 South Washington St., Marion 46953
Type: Private, The Wesleyan Church, four-year
Degrees: A, B, M   *Enroll:* 9,474
URL: http://www.indwes.edu
Phone: (765) 674-6901   *Calendar:* Sem. plan
Inst. Accred.: NCA-HLC (1966/2000)
Prog. Accred.: Counseling, Music, Nursing, Nursing Education, Social Work, Teacher Education (NCATE)

International Business College
5699 Coventry Ln., Fort Wayne 46804
Type: Private, proprietary, four-year
Degrees: A, B   *Enroll:* 495
URL: http://www.ibcfortwayne.edu
Phone: (260) 459-4500
Inst. Accred.: ACICS (1953/2003)
Prog. Accred.: Medical Assisting (CAAHEP)

International Business College
7205 Shadeland Station, Indianapolis 46256
Type: Private, proprietary, two-year
Degrees: A   *Enroll:* 317
URL: http://www.ibcindianapolis.edu
Phone: (317) 813-2300
Inst. Accred.: ACICS (1988/2000)
Prog. Accred.: Medical Assisting (CAAHEP)

ITT Technical Institute
9511 Angola Ct., Indianapolis 46268-1119
Type: Private, proprietary, four-year
System: ITT Educational Services, Inc.
Degrees: A, B   *Enroll:* 978
URL: http://www.itt-tech.edu
Phone: (317) 875-8640   *Calendar:* Qtr. plan
Inst. Accred.: ACICS (1999/2003)

ITT Technical Institute
4919 Coldwater Rd., Fort Wayne 46825-5532
Type: Private, proprietary, four-year
System: ITT Educational Services, Inc.
Degrees: A, B   *Enroll:* 454
URL: http://www.itt-tech.edu
Phone: (260) 484-4107   *Calendar:* Qtr. plan
Inst. Accred.: ACICS (1999/2004)

ITT Technical Institute
10999 Stahl Rd., Newburgh 47630
Type: Private, proprietary, four-year
System: ITT Educational Services, Inc.
Degrees: A, B   *Enroll:* 363
URL: http://www.itt-tech.edu
Phone: (812) 858-1600   *Calendar:* Qtr. plan
Inst. Accred.: ACICS (1999/2003)

Arnold Campus
1930 Meyer Drury Dr., Arnold, MO 63010
Phone: (636) 464-6600

Austin Campus
6330 Hwy. 290 East, Ste. 150, Austin, TX 78723
Phone: (512) 467-6800

Burr Ridge Campus
7040 High Grove Blvd., Burr Ridge, IL 60527
Phone: (630) 455-6470

Fort Lauderdale Campus
3401 South University Dr., Fort Lauderdale, FL 33328
Phone: (954) 476-9300

Houston North Campus
15621 Blue Ash Dr., Ste. 160, Houston, TX 77090-5821
Phone: (281) 873-0512

Houston West Campus
2950 South Gessner Rd., Houston, TX 77063-3751
Phone: (713) 952-2294

Louisville Campus
10509 Timberwood Circle, Louisville, KY 40223
Phone: (502) 327-7424

Mechanicsburg Area Campus
5020 Louise Dr., Mechanicsburg, PA 17055
Phone: (717) 691-9263

Mount Prospect Campus
1401 Freehanville Dr., Mount Prospect, IL 60056
Phone: (847) 375-8800

Norfolk Campus
863 Glenrock Rd., Ste. 100, Norfolk, VA 23502-3701
Phone: (757) 466-1260

Norwood Campus
333 Providence Hwy., Route 1, Norwood, MA 02062
Phone: (781) 278-7200

Troy Campus
1522 East Big Beaver Rd., Troy, MI 48083-1905
Phone: (248) 524-1800

Woburn Campus
10 Forbes Rd., Woburn, MA 01801-2103
Phone: (781) 937-8324

Ivy Tech Community College of Indiana—Bloomington
200 Daniels Way, Bloomington 47404
Type: Public, state, two-year
System: Ivy Tech Community College of Indiana—Central Office
Degrees: A   *FTE Enroll:* 1,700
URL: http://www.bloomington.ivytech.edu/ivytech
Phone: (812) 332-1559   *Calendar:* Sem. plan
Inst. Accred.: NCA-HLC (1995, *Indirect accreditation through Ivy Tech Community College of Indiana—Central Indiana, Indianapolis, IN*)
Prog. Accred.: Business (ACBSP), Nursing

Ivy Tech Community College of Indiana—Central Indiana
One West 26th St., PO Box 1763, Indianapolis 46206-1763
Type: Public, state, two-year
System: Ivy Tech Community College of Indiana—Central Office
Degrees: A   *Enroll:* 5,044
URL: http://www.ivytech.edu/indianapolis
Phone: (317) 921-4882   *Calendar:* Sem. plan
Inst. Accred.: NCA-HLC (1995)
Prog. Accred.: Business (ACBSP), Culinary Education, Design Technology, Electronic Technology, Industrial Technology, Manufacturing Technology, Medical Assisting (AMA), Nursing, Practical Nursing, Radiography, Respiratory Therapy, Surgical Technology

Ivy Tech Community College of Indiana—Columbus
4475 Central Ave., Columbus 47203-1868
Type: Public, state, two-year
System: Ivy Tech Community College of Indiana—Central Office
Degrees: A   *Enroll:* 889
URL: http://www.ivytech.edu/columbus
Phone: (812) 372-9925   *Calendar:* Sem. plan
Inst. Accred.: NCA-HLC (1995, *Indirect accreditation through Ivy Tech Community College of Indiana—Central Indiana, Indianapolis, IN*)
Prog. Accred.: Business (ACBSP), Dental Assisting, Medical Assisting (CAAHEP)

Ivy Tech Community College of Indiana—East Central

4301 South Cowan Rd., Muncie 47302-9448
Type: Public, state, two-year
System: Ivy Tech Community College of Indiana—Central Office
Degrees: A *Enroll:* 3,467
URL: http://www.ivytech.edu/eastcentral
Phone: (765) 289-2291 *Calendar:* Sem. plan
Inst. Accred.: NCA-HLC (1995, *Indirect accreditation through Ivy Tech Community College of Indiana—Central Indiana, Indianapolis, IN*)
Prog. Accred.: Business (ACBSP), Medical Assisting (AMA), Physical Therapy Assisting

Anderson Campus

104 West 53rd St., Anderson 46013-1502
Phone: (765) 643-7133
Prog. Accred: Medical Assisting (CAAHEP)

Marion Campus

1015 E. 3rd St., Marion 46952
Phone: (765) 662-9843
Prog. Accred: Radiography

Ivy Tech Community College of Indiana—Kokomo

1815 East Morgan St., Kokomo 46903-1373
Type: Public, state, two-year
System: Ivy Tech Community College of Indiana—Central Office
Degrees: A *Enroll:* 1,406
URL: http://www.ivytech.edu/kokomo
Phone: (765) 459-0561 *Calendar:* Sem. plan
Inst. Accred.: NCA-HLC (1995, *Indirect accreditation through Ivy Tech Community College of Indiana—Central Indiana, Indianapolis, IN*)
Prog. Accred.: Business (ACBSP), Medical Assisting (CAAHEP)

Logansport Campus

3001 East Market St., Ste. 7, Logansport 46947-2152
Phone: (219) 753-5101

Wabash Campus

277 North Thorne St., Wabash 46992
Phone: (260) 563-8828

Ivy Tech Community College of Indiana—Lafayette

PO Box 6299, 3101 S. Creasy Ln., Lafayette 47903-6299
Type: Public, state, two-year
System: Ivy Tech Community College of Indiana—Central Office
Degrees: A *Enroll:* 3,044
URL: http://www.laf.ivytech.edu
Phone: (765) 772-9100 *Calendar:* Sem. plan
Inst. Accred.: NCA-HLC (1995, *Indirect accreditation through Ivy Tech Community College of Indiana—Central Indiana, Indianapolis, IN*)
Prog. Accred.: Business (ACBSP), Dental Assisting, Medical Assisting (AMA), Nursing, Respiratory Therapy, Surgical Technology

Ivy Tech Community College of Indiana—Madison

590 Ivy Tech Dr., Madison 47250-1881
Type: Public, state, two-year
System: Ivy Tech Community College of Indiana—Central Office
Degrees: A *Enroll:* 898
URL: http://www.ivytech.edu/madison
Phone: (812) 265-2580 *Calendar:* Sem. plan
Inst. Accred.: NCA-HLC (1995, *Indirect accreditation through Ivy Tech Community College of Indiana—Central Indiana, Indianapolis, IN*)
Prog. Accred.: Business (ACBSP), Medical Assisting (CAAHEP)

Lawrenceburg Campus

500 Industrial Dr., Lawrenceburg 47025
Phone: (812) 537-4010

Ivy Tech Community College of Indiana—North Central

220 Dean Johnson Blvd., South Bend 46601-3415
Type: Public, state, two-year
System: Ivy Tech Community College of Indiana—Central Office
Degrees: A *Enroll:* 2,296
URL: http://www.ivytech.edu/northcentral
Phone: (574) 289-7001 *Calendar:* Sem. plan
Inst. Accred.: NCA-HLC (1995, *Indirect accreditation through Ivy Tech Community College of Indiana—Central Indiana, Indianapolis, IN*)
Prog. Accred.: Business (ACBSP), Clinical Lab Technology, Culinary Education, Nursing, Phlebotomy

Elkhart Campus

2521 Industrial Pkwy., Elkhart 46516-5430
Phone: (219) 293-4657

Warsaw Campus

850 East Smith St., Warsaw 46580-4546
Phone: (219) 267-5428

Ivy Tech Community College of Indiana—Northeast

3800 North Anthony Blvd., Fort Wayne 46805-1489
Type: Public, state, two-year
System: Ivy Tech Community College of Indiana—Central Office
Degrees: A *Enroll:* 2,840
URL: http://www.ivytech.edu/fortwayne
Phone: (260) 480-4220 *Calendar:* Sem. plan
Inst. Accred.: NCA-HLC (1995, *Indirect accreditation through Ivy Tech Community College of Indiana—Central Indiana, Indianapolis, IN*)
Prog. Accred.: Business (ACBSP), Construction Technology, Culinary Education, Electronic Technology, Industrial Technology, Manufacturing Technology, Medical Assisting (AMA), Respiratory Therapy

Ivy Tech Community College of Indiana—Northwest
1440 East 35th Ave., Gary 46409-1499
Type: Public, state, two-year
System: Ivy Tech Community College of Indiana—Central Office
Degrees: A   *Enroll:* 2,939
URL: http://www.gary.ivytech.edu
Phone: (219) 981-1111   *Calendar:* Sem. plan
Inst. Accred.: NCA-HLC (1995, *Indirect accreditation through Ivy Tech Community College of Indiana—Central Indiana, Indianapolis, IN*)
Prog. Accred.: Business (ACBSP), Culinary Education, Physical Therapy Assisting

East Chicago Campus
410 Columbus Dr., East Chicago 46312-2714
Phone: (219) 392-3600
Prog. Accred: Funeral Service Education (Mortuary Science)

Michigan City Campus
3714 Franklin, Michigan City 46360
Phone: (219) 879-9137

Valpariso Campus
2401 Valley Dr., Valparaiso 46383-2520
Phone: (219) 464-8514
Prog. Accred: Medical Assisting (AMA), Practical Nursing, Respiratory Therapy Technology, Surgical Technology

Ivy Tech Community College of Indiana—Richmond
2325 Chester Blvd., Richmond 47374
Type: Public, state, two-year
System: Ivy Tech Community College of Indiana—Central Office
Degrees: A   *Enroll:* 800
URL: http://www.ivytech.edu/richmond
Phone: (317) 966-2656   *Calendar:* Sem. plan
Inst. Accred.: NCA-HLC (1995, *Indirect accreditation through Ivy Tech Community College of Indiana—Central Indiana, Indianapolis, IN*)
Prog. Accred.: Business (ACBSP), Construction Technology, Electronic Technology, Industrial Technology, Manufacturing Technology, Medical Assisting (AMA), Nursing

Ivy Tech Community College of Indiana—Sellersburg
8204 Hwy. 311, Sellersburg 47172
Type: Public, state, two-year
System: Ivy Tech Community College of Indiana—Central Office
Degrees: A   *Enroll:* 1,523
URL: http://www.ivytech.edu/sellersburg
Phone: (812) 246-3301   *Calendar:* Sem. plan
Inst. Accred.: NCA-HLC (1995, *Indirect accreditation through Ivy Tech Community College of Indiana—Central Indiana, Indianapolis, IN*)
Prog. Accred.: Business (ACBSP), Design Technology, Electronic Technology, Industrial Technology, Manufacturing Technology, Medical Assisting (CAAHEP)

Ivy Tech Community College of Indiana—Southwest
3501 First Ave., Evansville 47710-3398
Type: Public, state, two-year
System: Ivy Tech Community College of Indiana—Central Office
Degrees: A   *Enroll:* 2,373
URL: http://www.ivytech.edu/evansville
Phone: (812) 426-2865   *Calendar:* Sem. plan
Inst. Accred.: NCA-HLC (1995, *Indirect accreditation through Ivy Tech Community College of Indiana—Central Indiana, Indianapolis, IN*)
Prog. Accred.: Business (ACBSP), Design Technology, EMT (Paramedic), Electronic Technology, Industrial Technology, Manufacturing Technology, Medical Assisting (AMA), Nursing, Practical Nursing, Surgical Technology

Ivy Tech Community College of Indiana—Wabash Valley
7999 U.S. Hwy. 41, Terre Haute 47802-4898
Type: Public, state, two-year
System: Ivy Tech Community College of Indiana—Central Office
Degrees: A   *Enroll:* 2,641
URL: http://ivytech7.cc.in.us
Phone: (812) 299-1121   *Calendar:* Sem. plan
Inst. Accred.: NCA-HLC (1995, *Indirect accreditation through Ivy Tech Community College of Indiana—Central Indiana, Indianapolis, IN*)
Prog. Accred.: Business (ACBSP), Clinical Lab Technology, Design Technology, Electronic Technology, Industrial Technology, Manufacturing Technology, Medical Assisting (AMA), Radiography

Lincoln Technical Institute
7225 Winton Dr., Building 128, Indianapolis 46268
Type: Private, proprietary, two-year
System: Lincoln Educational Services
Degrees: A   *Enroll:* 1,181
URL: http://www.lincolntech.com
Phone: (317) 632-5553
Inst. Accred.: ACCSCT (1968/2002)

Accredited Degree-Granting Institutions

Manchester College
604 East College Ave., North Manchester 46962
Type: Private, Church of the Brethren, four-year
Degrees: A, B, M   *Enroll:* 1,141
URL: http://www.manchester.edu
Phone: (260) 982-5000   *Calendar:* 4-1-4 plan
Inst. Accred.: NCA-HLC (1932/2003)
Prog. Accred.: Social Work, Teacher Education (NCATE)

Marian College
3200 Cold Spring Rd., Indianapolis 46222-1997
Type: Private, Roman Catholic Church, four-year
Degrees: A, B   *Enroll:* 1,251
URL: http://www.marian.edu
Phone: (317) 955-6000   *Calendar:* Sem. plan
Inst. Accred.: NCA-HLC (1956/1996)
Prog. Accred.: Dietetics (coordinated), Nursing, Nursing
Education, Teacher Education (NCATE)

Martin University
2171 Avondale Place, Indianapolis 46218
Type: Private, independent, four-year
Degrees: B, M   *Enroll:* 396
URL: http://www.martin.edu
Phone: (317) 543-3237   *Calendar:* Sem. plan
Inst. Accred.: NCA-HLC (1987/2002)

Mid-America College of Funeral Service
3111 Hamburg Pike, Jeffersonville 47130
Type: Private, independent, four-year
Degrees: A, B   *Enroll:* 61
URL: http://www.mid-america.edu
Phone: (812) 288-8878   *Calendar:* Qtr. plan
Inst. Accred.: ABFSE (1967/2002)

Mid-America Reformed Seminary
229 Seminary Dr., Dyer 46311
Type: Private, Reformed and Presbyterian churches, four-
year
Degrees: M
URL: http://www.midamerica.edu
Phone: (219) 864-2400   *Calendar:* Sem. plan
Inst. Accred.: TRACS (2005)

Oakland City University
143 North Lucretia St., Oakland City 47660
Type: Private, General Baptist Church, four-year
Degrees: A, B, M   *Enroll:* 1,446
URL: http://www.oak.edu
Phone: (812) 749-1222   *Calendar:* Sem. plan
Inst. Accred.: NCA-HLC (1977/2004)
Prog. Accred.: Teacher Education (NCATE)

Professional Careers Institute
7302 Woodland Dr., Indianapolis 46278-1736
Type: Private, proprietary, two-year
System: Kaplan Higher Education Corporation
Degrees: A   *Enroll:* 590
URL: http://www.pcicareers.com
Phone: (317) 299-6001
Inst. Accred.: ACCSCT (1970/2002)
Prog. Accred.: Dental Assisting, Medical Assisting
(CAAHEP)

Purdue University
West Lafayette 47907
Type: Public, state, four-year
System: Purdue University System
Degrees: A, B, M, P, D   *Enroll:* 37,287
URL: http://www.purdue.edu
Phone: (765) 494-4600   *Calendar:* Sem. plan
Inst. Accred.: NCA-HLC (1913/2000)
Prog. Accred.: Applied Science (industrial hygiene),
Athletic Training, Audiology, Business (AACSB), Clinical
Psychology, Construction Education, Counseling,
Counseling Psychology, Dietetics (coordinated),
Engineering (aerospace, agricultural, chemical, civil,
computer, construction, electrical,
environmental/sanitary, food process, industrial,
materials, mechanical, nuclear, surveying), Engineering
Technology (computer, electrical, mechanical), Forestry,
Industrial Technology, Interior Design, Landscape
Architecture, Marriage and Family Therapy, Nursing,
Nursing Education, Pharmacy, Psychology Internship,
Speech-Language Pathology, Teacher Education
(NCATE), Theatre, Veterinary Medicine, Veterinary
Technology

School of Technology at Kokomo
2300 South Washington St., Kokomo 46904-9003
Phone: (765) 455-9339
Prog. Accred: Engineering Technology (electrical)

School of Technology at New Albany
4201 Grant Line Rd., New Albany 47150-6405
Phone: (812) 941-2353
Prog. Accred: Engineering Technology (mechanical)

School of Technology at South Bend/Elkhart
1733 Northside Blvd., PO Box 711, South Bend
46634-7111
Phone: (219) 237-4180

School of Technology at Versailles
901 West U.S. 50, Versailles 47042-9198
Phone: (812) 689-7040

Purdue University Calumet
2200 169th St., Hammond 46323
Type: Public, state, four-year
System: Purdue University System
Degrees: A, B   *Enroll:* 6,508
URL: http://www.calumet.purdue.edu
Phone: (219) 989-2993   *Calendar:* Sem. plan
Inst. Accred.: NCA-HLC (1969/1997)
Prog. Accred.: Engineering (computer, electrical,
mechanical), Engineering Technology (architectural,
civil/construction, electrical, industrial, manufacturing,
mechanical), Marriage and Family Therapy, Nursing,
Teacher Education (NCATE)

Purdue University North Central
1401 South U.S. Hwy. 421, Westville 46391-9528
Type: Public, state, four-year
System: Purdue University System
Degrees: A, B   *Enroll:* 2,610
URL: http://www.pnc.edu
Phone: (219) 785-5200   *Calendar:* Sem. plan
Inst. Accred.: NCA-HLC (1971/2001)
Prog. Accred.: Business (ACBSP), Engineering Technology
  (civil/construction, electrical, industrial, mechanical),
  Nursing

Rose-Hulman Institute of Technology
5500 Wabash Ave., Box 20, Terre Haute 47803
Type: Private, independent, four-year
Degrees: B, M   *Enroll:* 1,802
URL: http://www.rose-hulman.edu
Phone: (812) 877-8000   *Calendar:* Qtr. plan
Inst. Accred.: NCA-HLC (1916/2002)
Prog. Accred.: Engineering (chemical, civil, computer,
  electrical, mechanical)

Saint Joseph's College
U.S. Hwy. 231, Rensselaer 47978
Type: Private, Roman Catholic Church, four-year
Degrees: A, B, M   *Enroll:* 903
URL: http://www.saintjoe.edu
Phone: (219) 866-6000   *Calendar:* Sem. plan
Inst. Accred.: NCA-HLC (1932/2002)
Prog. Accred.: Teacher Education (NCATE)

Saint Mary's College
Notre Dame 46556
Type: Private, Roman Catholic Church, four-year
Degrees: B   *Enroll:* 1,453
URL: http://www.saintmarys.edu
Phone: (574) 284-4000   *Calendar:* Sem. plan
Inst. Accred.: NCA-HLC (1922/1996)
Prog. Accred.: Art, Music, Nursing, Social Work, Teacher
  Education (NCATE)

Saint Mary-of-the-Woods College
St. Mary's Rd., St. Mary-of-the-Woods 47876
Type: Private, Roman Catholic Church, four-year
Degrees: A, B, M   *Enroll:* 942
URL: http://www.smwc.edu
Phone: (812) 535-5151   *Calendar:* Sem. plan
Inst. Accred.: NCA-HLC (1919/2005)
Prog. Accred.: Music, Teacher Education (NCATE)

Saint Meinrad School of Theology
One Hill Dr., St. Meinrad 47577
Type: Private, Roman Catholic Church, four-year
Degrees: M   *Enroll:* 110
URL: http://www.saintmeinrad.edu
Phone: (812) 357-6611   *Calendar:* 4-1-4 plan
Inst. Accred.: ATS (1968/2003), NCA-HLC (1979/2004)

Sawyer College, Inc.
7833 Indianapolis Blvd., Hammond 46324
Type: Private, proprietary, two-year
System: Kaplan Higher Education Corporation
Degrees: A   *Enroll:* 206
URL: http://www.sawyercollege.edu
Phone: (219) 844-0100   *Calendar:* Qtr. plan
Inst. Accred.: ACICS (1982/2004)

Merrillville Campus
3803 East Lincoln Hwy., Merrillville 46410
Phone: (800) 964-0218

Taylor University
236 West Reade Ave., Upland 46989
Type: Private, independent, four-year
Degrees: A, B   *Enroll:* 1,814
URL: http://www.taylor.edu
Phone: (765) 998-2751   *Calendar:* 4-1-4 plan
Inst. Accred.: NCA-HLC (1947/1997)
Prog. Accred.: Music, Social Work, Teacher Education
  (NCATE)

Fort Wayne Campus
1025 West Rudisill Blvd., Fort Wayne 46807
Phone: (219) 456-2111

Tri-State University
One University Ave., Angola 46703
Type: Private, independent, four-year
Degrees: A, B   *Enroll:* 1,096
URL: http://www.tristate.edu
Phone: (260) 665-4100   *Calendar:* Sem. plan
Inst. Accred.: NCA-HLC (1966/1996)
Prog. Accred.: Engineering (chemical, civil, electrical,
  mechanical)

University of Evansville
1800 Lincoln Ave., Evansville 47722
Type: Private, United Methodist Church, four-year
Degrees: A, B, M   *Enroll:* 2,373
URL: http://www.evansville.edu
Phone: (800) 423-8633   *Calendar:* Sem. plan
Inst. Accred.: NCA-HLC (1931/1996)
Prog. Accred.: Engineering (civil, computer, electrical,
  mechanical), Music, Nursing, Physical Therapy, Physical
  Therapy Assisting, Teacher Education (NCATE)

The University of Indianapolis
1400 East Hanna Ave., Indianapolis 46227-3697
Type: Private, United Methodist Church, four-year
Degrees: A, B, M, D   *Enroll:* 3,071
URL: http://www.uindy.edu
Phone: (317) 788-3368
Inst. Accred.: NCA-HLC (1947/1998)
Prog. Accred.: Business (ACBSP), Clinical Psychology,
Music, Nursing, Nursing Education, Occupational
Therapy, Physical Therapy, Physical Therapy Assisting,
Social Work, Teacher Education (NCATE)

Indianapolis International Campus
29, Voulis St., Syntagma Sq., Athens, Greece 105 57
Phone: 30 132 39740

Intercollege Campus
17 Heroes Ave., PO Box 4005, Nicosia, Cyprus
Phone: 011 35 723 57735

University of Notre Dame
Notre Dame 46556
Type: Private, Roman Catholic Church, four-year
Degrees: B, M, P, D   *Enroll:* 11,244
URL: http://www.nd.edu
Phone: (574) 631-5000   *Calendar:* Sem. plan
Inst. Accred.: ATS (1977/2003), NCA-HLC (1913/2004)
Prog. Accred.: Accounting, Art, Business (AACSB),
Counseling Psychology, Engineering (aerospace,
chemical, civil, computer, electrical, mechanical), Law,
Psychology Internship

University of Saint Francis
2701 Spring St., Fort Wayne 46808
Type: Private, Roman Catholic Church, four-year
Degrees: A, B, M   *Enroll:* 1,512
URL: http://www.sf.edu
Phone: (219) 434-3100   *Calendar:* Sem. plan
Inst. Accred.: NCA-HLC (1957/1996)
Prog. Accred.: Art, Nursing, Nursing Education, Physical
Therapy Assisting, Physician Assistant, Radiography,
Social Work, Teacher Education (NCATE)

University of Southern Indiana
8600 University Blvd., Evansville 47712
Type: Public, state, four-year
System: Indiana Commission for Higher Education
Degrees: A, B, M   *Enroll:* 8,383
URL: http://www.usi.edu
Phone: (812) 464-8600   *Calendar:* Sem. plan
Inst. Accred.: NCA-HLC (1974/1997)
Prog. Accred.: Accounting, Business (AACSB), Dental
Assisting, Dental Hygiene, Engineering Technology
(civil/construction, electrical, mechanical), Journalism,
Nursing, Nursing Education, Occupational Therapy,
Occupational Therapy Assisting, Radiography,
Respiratory Therapy, Social Work, Teacher Education
(NCATE)

Valparaiso University
U.S. Hwy. 30, Valparaiso 46383
Type: Private, Lutheran Church, four-year
Degrees: A, B, M, D   *Enroll:* 3,611
URL: http://www.valpo.edu
Phone: (219) 464-5000   *Calendar:* Sem. plan
Inst. Accred.: NCA-HLC (1929/1998)
Prog. Accred.: Business (AACSB), Engineering (civil,
electrical, mechanical), Law, Music, Nursing, Nursing
Education, Social Work, Teacher Education (NCATE)

Vincennes University
1002 North First St., Vincennes 47591-5201
Type: Public, state, two-year
System: Indiana Commission for Higher Education
Degrees: A   *Enroll:* 5,972
URL: http://www.vinu.edu
Phone: (800) 742-9198   *Calendar:* Sem. plan
Inst. Accred.: NCA-HLC (1958/2001)
Prog. Accred.: Art, Business (ACBSP), Funeral Service
Education (Mortuary Science), Health Information
Technician, Nursing, Physical Therapy Assisting,
Practical Nursing, Respiratory Therapy, Surgical
Technology, Theatre

Wabash College
301 West Wabash Ave., PO Box 352, Crawfordsville
47933
Type: Private, independent, four-year
Degrees: B   *Enroll:* 859
URL: http://www.wabash.edu
Phone: (765) 361-6100   *Calendar:* Sem. plan
Inst. Accred.: NCA-HLC (1913/2003)
Prog. Accred.: Teacher Education (NCATE)

IOWA

AIB College of Business
2500 Fleur Dr., Des Moines 50321-1799
Type: Private, independent, two-year
Degrees: A   *Enroll:* 825
URL: http://www.aib.edu
Phone: (515) 244-4221   *Calendar:* Qtr. plan
Inst. Accred.: NCA-HLC (1986/1999)

Allen College
1825 Logan Ave., Waterloo 50703
Type: Private, independent, four-year
Degrees: A, B, M   *Enroll:* 269
URL: http://www.allencollege.edu
Phone: (319) 226-3000   *Calendar:* Sem. plan
Inst. Accred.: NCA-HLC (1995/1998)
Prog. Accred.: Nursing, Radiography

The Ashford University
400 North Bluff Blvd., PO Box 2967, Clinton 52733
Type: Private, Roman Catholic Church, four-year
Degrees: A, B   *Enroll:* 486
URL: http://www.ashford.edu
Phone: (866) 974-5700   *Calendar:* Sem. plan
Inst. Accred.: NCA-HLC (1950/1996)

Briar Cliff University
3303 Rebecca St., PO Box 2100, Sioux City 51104
Type: Private, Roman Catholic Church, four-year
Degrees: A, B, M   *Enroll:* 954
URL: http://www.briarcliff.edu
Phone: (712) 279-5321   *Calendar:* Tri. plan
Inst. Accred.: NCA-HLC (1945/2005)
Prog. Accred.: Nursing, Social Work

Buena Vista University
610 West Fourth St., Storm Lake 50588
Type: Private, Presbyterian Church (USA), four-year
Degrees: B, M   *Enroll:* 2,620
URL: http://www.bvu.edu
Phone: (712) 749-2103   *Calendar:* 4-1-4 plan
Inst. Accred.: NCA-HLC (1952/2001)
Prog. Accred.: Social Work

Central College
812 University St., Pella 50219-1902
Type: Private, Reformed Church in America, four-year
Degrees: B   *Enroll:* 1,517
URL: http://www.central.edu
Phone: (641) 628-5269   *Calendar:* Sem. plan
Inst. Accred.: NCA-HLC (1942/2004)
Prog. Accred.: Music

Clarke College
1550 Clarke Dr., Dubuque 52001
Type: Private, Roman Catholic Church, four-year
Degrees: A, B, M   *Enroll:* 957
URL: http://www.clarke.edu
Phone: (319) 588-6300   *Calendar:* Sem. plan
Inst. Accred.: NCA-HLC (1918/2004)
Prog. Accred.: Music, Nursing, Nursing Education,
    Physical Therapy, Social Work

Clinton Community College
1000 Lincoln Blvd., Clinton 52732
Type: Public, state/local, two-year
System: Eastern Iowa Community College District
Degrees: A   *FTE Enroll:* 612
URL: http://www.eicc.edu/ccc
Phone: (563) 244-7001   *Calendar:* Qtr. plan
Inst. Accred.: NCA-HLC (1983/2003, *Indirect accreditation
    through Eastern Iowa Community College District,
    Davenport, IA*)

Coe College
1220 First Ave., NE, Cedar Rapids 52402
Type: Private, Iowa Presbyterian Synod, four-year
Degrees: B, M   *Enroll:* 1,232
URL: http://www.coe.edu
Phone: (319) 399-8000   *Calendar:* 4-1-4 plan
Inst. Accred.: NCA-HLC (1913/1999)
Prog. Accred.: Music, Nursing, Nursing Education

Cornell College
600 First St. West, Mount Vernon 52314-1098
Type: Private, United Methodist Church, four-year
Degrees: B   *Enroll:* 1,110
URL: http://www.cornellcollege.edu
Phone: (319) 895-4000
Inst. Accred.: NCA-HLC (1913/2003)

Des Moines Area Community College

2006 South Ankeny Blvd., Ankeny 50021
Type: Public, state/local, two-year
System: Iowa Department of Education, Division of
Community Colleges and Workforce Preparation
Degrees: A   *Enroll:* 8,593
URL: http://www.dmacc.edu
Phone: (515) 964-6200   *Calendar:* Sem. plan
Inst. Accred.: NCA-HLC (1974/1996)
Prog. Accred.: Clinical Lab Technology, Culinary
Education, Dental Assisting, Dental Hygiene, Funeral
Service Education (Mortuary Science), Medical Assisting
(AMA), Nursing, Practical Nursing, Respiratory Therapy

Boone Campus

1125 Hancock Dr., Boone 50036
Phone: (515) 432-7203

Carroll Campus

906 North Grant Rd., Carroll 51401
Phone: (712) 792-1755

Newton Polytechnic Campus

600 North 2nd Ave., Newton 50208
Phone: (515) 791-3622

Urban Campus

1100 7th St., Des Moines 50314-2597
Phone: (515) 244-4226
Prog. Accred: Funeral Service Education (Mortuary
Science)

Des Moines University—Osteopathic Medical Center

3200 Grand Ave., Des Moines 50312
Type: Private, independent, four-year
Degrees: B, M, D   *Enroll:* 1,122
URL: http://www.dmu.edu
Phone: (515) 271-1400
Inst. Accred.: NCA-HLC (1986/2002)
Prog. Accred.: Osteopathy, Physical Therapy, Physician
Assistant, Podiatry, Public Health

Divine Word College

102 Jacoby Dr., SW, Epworth 52045
Type: Private, Roman Catholic Church, four-year
Degrees: A, B   *Enroll:* 84
URL: http://www.dwci.edu
Phone: (563) 876-3353   *Calendar:* Sem. plan
Inst. Accred.: NCA-HLC (1970/1996)

Dordt College

498 4th Ave., NE, Sioux Center 51250-1697
Type: Private, Christian Reformed Church, four-year
Degrees: A, B, M   *Enroll:* 1,282
URL: http://www.dordt.edu
Phone: (712) 722-6000   *Calendar:* Sem. plan
Inst. Accred.: NCA-HLC (1969/2002)
Prog. Accred.: Engineering (general), Social Work

Drake University

2507 University Ave., Des Moines 50311
Type: Private, independent, four-year
Degrees: B, M, P, D   *Enroll:* 4,347
URL: http://www.drake.edu
Phone: (515) 271-2191   *Calendar:* Sem. plan
Inst. Accred.: NCA-HLC (1913/1998)
Prog. Accred.: Accounting, Art, Business (AACSB),
Journalism, Law, Music, Nursing, Pharmacy,
Rehabilitation Counseling

Ellsworth Community College

1100 College Ave., Iowa Falls 50126
Type: Public, state/local, two-year
System: Iowa Valley Community College District
Degrees: A   *FTE Enroll:* 795
URL: http://iavalley.cc.ia.us/ecc
Phone: (641) 648-4611   *Calendar:* Sem. plan
Inst. Accred.: NCA-HLC (1963/2002, *Indirect accreditation
through Iowa Valley Community College District,
Marshalltown, IA*)

Emmaus Bible College

2570 Asbury Rd., Dubuque 52001-3096
Type: Private, nondenominational, four-year
Degrees: A, B   *Enroll:* 253
URL: http://www.emmaus.edu
Phone: (563) 588-8000   *Calendar:* Sem. plan
Inst. Accred.: ABHE (1986/1997)

Faith Baptist Bible College

1900 NW Fourth St., Ankeny 50021-2152
Type: Private, General Association of Regular Baptist
Churches, four-year
Degrees: A, B, M   *Enroll:* 450
URL: http://www.faith.edu
Phone: (515) 964-0601   *Calendar:* Sem. plan
Inst. Accred.: ABHE (1969/2002), NCA-HLC (1996/2001)

Graceland University

1 University Place, Lamoni 50140-1641
Type: Private, Community of Christ, four-year
Degrees: B, M   *Enroll:* 1,768
URL: http://www.graceland.edu
Phone: (641) 784-5000   *Calendar:* 4-1-4 plan
Inst. Accred.: NCA-HLC (1920/1997)
Prog. Accred.: Nursing, Nursing Education, Teacher
Education (NCATE)

Independence Campus

1401 West Truman Rd., Independence, MO 64050
Phone: (816) 833 0524
Prog. Accred: Nursing Education

Grand View College

1200 Grandview Ave., Des Moines 50316
Type: Private, Evangelical Lutheran Church in America,
four-year
Degrees: A, B   *Enroll:* 1,358
URL: http://www.gvc.edu
Phone: (515) 263-2800   *Calendar:* Sem. plan
Inst. Accred.: NCA-HLC (1959/2005)
Prog. Accred.: Nursing, Nursing Education

Grinnell College
1121 Park Ave., Grinnell 50112
Type: Private, independent, four-year
Degrees: B   *Enroll:* 1,500
URL: http://www.grinnell.edu
Phone: (641) 269-4000   *Calendar:* Sem. plan
Inst. Accred.: NCA-HLC (1913/1999)

Hamilton College—Cedar Rapids
3165 Edgewood Pkwy., SW, Cedar Rapids 52404
Type: Private, proprietary, four-year
System: Kaplan Higher Education Corporation
Degrees: A, B   *Enroll:* 614
URL: http://www.hamilton-cr.com
Phone: (319) 363-0481   *Calendar:* Qtr. plan
Inst. Accred.: NCA-HLC (1996/2001)

Cedar Falls Campus
7009 Nordic Dr., Cedar Falls 50613
Phone: (319) 277-0220

Des Moines Campus
4655 121st St., Urbandale 50323
Phone: (515) 727-2100
Prog. Accred: Medical Assisting (CAAHEP)

Lincoln Campus
PO Box 82826, 1821 K St., Lincoln, NE 68501-2826
Phone: (402) 474-5315
Prog. Accred: Medical Assisting (CAAHEP)

Mason City Campus
100 First St., NW, Mason City 50401
Phone: (641) 423-2530

Omaha Campus
3350 North 90th St., Omaha, NE 68134
Phone: (402) 572-8500
Prog. Accred: Medical Assisting (CAAHEP)

Hamilton Technical College
1011 East 53rd St., Davenport 52807-2616
Type: Private, proprietary, four-year
Degrees: A, B   *Enroll:* 220
URL: http://www.hamiltontechcollege.com
Phone: (319) 386-3570   *Calendar:* Sem. plan
Inst. Accred.: ACCSCT (1974/2005)

Hawkeye Community College
1501 East Orange Rd., Waterloo 50701-9014
Type: Public, state/local, two-year
System: Iowa Department of Education, Division of
Community Colleges and Workforce Preparation
Degrees: A   *Enroll:* 4,047
URL: http://www.hawkeyecollege.edu
Phone: (319) 296-4201   *Calendar:* Sem. plan
Inst. Accred.: NCA-HLC (1975/1995)
Prog. Accred.: Clinical Lab Technology, Dental Assisting,
Dental Hygiene

Indian Hills Community College
525 Grandview Ave., Ottumwa 52501
Type: Public, state/local, two-year
System: Iowa Department of Education, Division of
Community Colleges and Workforce Preparation
Degrees: A   *Enroll:* 3,020
URL: http://www.ihcc.cc.ia.us
Phone: (641) 683-5111   *Calendar:* Qtr. plan
Inst. Accred.: NCA-HLC (1980/2001)
Prog. Accred.: Culinary Education, Health Information
Technician, Physical Therapy Assisting, Radiography

Centerville Campus
721 North First St., Centerville 52544
Phone: (641) 856-2143

Iowa Central Community College
330 Ave. M, Fort Dodge 50501
Type: Public, state/local, two-year
System: Iowa Department of Education, Division of
Community Colleges and Workforce Preparation
Degrees: A   *Enroll:* 3,406
URL: http://www.iccc.cc.ia.us
Phone: (515) 576-7201   *Calendar:* Sem. plan
Inst. Accred.: NCA-HLC (1974/2001)
Prog. Accred.: Clinical Lab Technology, Medical Assisting
(AMA), Nursing, Radiography

Iowa Lakes Community College
19 South 7th St., Estherville 51334
Type: Public, state/local, two-year
System: Iowa Department of Education, Division of
Community Colleges and Workforce Preparation
Degrees: A   *Enroll:* 1,955
URL: http://www.iowalakes.edu
Phone: (712) 362-2604   *Calendar:* Sem. plan
Inst. Accred.: NCA-HLC (1976/1998)

Emmetsburg Campus
3200 College Dr., Emmettsburg 50536
Phone: (712) 852-3554

Spencer Campus
Gateway North Shopping Center, Spencer 51301
Phone: (712) 262-7141
Prog. Accred: Medical Assisting (CAAHEP)

Iowa State University

117 Beardshear Hall, Ames 50011-2035
Type: Public, state, four-year
System: Board of Regents, State of Iowa
Degrees: B, M, P, D   *Enroll:* 25,150
URL: http://www.iastate.edu
Phone: (515) 294-4111   *Calendar:* Sem. plan
Inst. Accred.: NCA-HLC (1916/1996)
Prog. Accred.: Accounting, Business (AACSB), Computer
Science, Counseling Psychology, Dietetics (internship),
Engineering (aerospace, agricultural, chemical, civil,
computer, construction, electrical, industrial, materials,
mechanical), Family and Consumer Science, Forestry,
Industrial Technology, Interior Design, Journalism,
Landscape Architecture, Marriage and Family Therapy,
Music, Planning, Psychology Internship, Veterinary
Medicine

Iowa Valley Community College District

3702 South Center St., Marshalltown 50158
Type: Public, state/local, two-year
System: Iowa Department of Education, Division of
Community Colleges and Workforce Preparation
Degrees: A
URL: http://www.iavalley.cc.ia.us
Phone: (515) 752-4643   *Calendar:* Sem. plan
Inst. Accred.: NCA-HLC (1996)

Iowa Wesleyan College

601 North Main St., Mount Pleasant 52641
Type: Private, United Methodist Church, four-year
Degrees: B   *Enroll:* 619
URL: http://www.iwc.edu
Phone: (319) 385-8021   *Calendar:* 4-1-4 plan
Inst. Accred.: NCA-HLC (1916/2001)
Prog. Accred.: Nursing

Iowa Western Community College

2700 College Rd., Council Bluffs 51501
Type: Public, state/local, two-year
System: Iowa Department of Education, Division of
Community Colleges and Workforce Preparation
Degrees: A   *Enroll:* 3,087
URL: http://www.iwcc.edu
Phone: (712) 325-3200   *Calendar:* Sem. plan
Inst. Accred.: NCA-HLC (1975/2000)
Prog. Accred.: Culinary Education, Dental Assisting,
Dental Hygiene, Engineering Technology (architectural,
civil/construction, electrical), Medical Assisting
(CAAHEP)

Kaplan University

1801 East Kimberly Rd., Ste. 1, Davenport 52807
Type: Private, proprietary, four-year
System: Kaplan Higher Education Corporation
Degrees: A, B, M   *Enroll:* 4,610
URL: http://www.kaplan.edu
Phone: (563) 355-3500   *Calendar:* Qtr. plan
Inst. Accred.: NCA-HLC (1997/2003)
Prog. Accred.: Medical Assisting (CAAHEP)

Kirkwood Community College

6301 Kirkwood Blvd., SW, PO Box 2068, Cedar Rapids
52406-2068
Type: Public, state/local, two-year
System: Iowa Department of Education, Division of
Community Colleges and Workforce Preparation
Degrees: A   *Enroll:* 10,571
URL: http://www.kirkwood.edu
Phone: (319) 398-5411   *Calendar:* Sem. plan
Inst. Accred.: NCA-HLC (1970/2000)
Prog. Accred.: Business (ACBSP), Culinary Education,
Dental Assisting, Dental Hygiene, Dental Laboratory
Technology, Electroneurodiagnostic Technology, Health
Information Technician, Medical Assisting (AMA),
Occupational Therapy Assisting, Physical Therapy
Assisting, Respiratory Therapy, Surgical Technology,
Veterinary Technology

Loras College

1450 Alta Vista, Dubuque 52004-0178
Type: Private, Roman Catholic Church, four-year
Degrees: A, B, M   *Enroll:* 1,642
URL: http://www.loras.edu
Phone: (563) 588-7103   *Calendar:* Sem. plan
Inst. Accred.: NCA-HLC (1917/2000)
Prog. Accred.: Social Work

Luther College

700 College Dr., Decorah 52101-1045
Type: Private, Evangelic Lutheran Church in America,
four-year
Degrees: B   *Enroll:* 2,527
URL: http://www.luther.edu
Phone: (319) 387-2000   *Calendar:* 4-1-4 plan
Inst. Accred.: NCA-HLC (1915/1999)
Prog. Accred.: Music, Nursing, Nursing Education, Social
Work, Teacher Education (NCATE)

Maharishi University of Management

1000 North Fourth St., DB 1113, Fairfield 52557-1113
Type: Private, independent, four-year
Degrees: A, B, M, D   *Enroll:* 693
URL: http://www.mum.edu
Phone: (641) 472-1110   *Calendar:* Sem. plan
Inst. Accred.: NCA-HLC (1980/2000)

Marshalltown Community College

3700 South Center St., Marshalltown 50158
Type: Public, state/local, two-year
System: Iowa Valley Community College District
Degrees: A   *Enroll:* 1,077
URL: http://www.iavalley.cc.ia.us/mcc
Phone: (641) 752-7106   *Calendar:* Sem. plan
Inst. Accred.: NCA-HLC (1966/2002, *Indirect accreditation
through Iowa Valley Community College District,
Marshalltown, IA*)
Prog. Accred.: Dental Assisting, Medical Assisting (AMA),
Surgical Technology

Mercy College of Health Sciences
928 6th Ave., Des Moines 50309-1239
Type: Private, Religious Sisters of Mercy, four-year
Degrees: A, B   *Enroll:* 464
URL: http://www.mchs.edu
Phone: (515) 643-6601   *Calendar:* Sem. plan
Inst. Accred.: NCA-HLC (1999/2004)
Prog. Accred.: Clinical Lab Scientist, Cytotechnology,
   Diagnostic Medical Sonography, EMT (Paramedic),
   Nursing Education, Radiography, Surgical Technology

Morningside College
1501 Morningside Ave., Sioux City 51106
Type: Private, United Methodist Church, four-year
Degrees: B, M   *Enroll:* 988
URL: http://www.morningside.edu
Phone: (712) 274-5000   *Calendar:* Sem. plan
Inst. Accred.: NCA-HLC (1913/2004)
Prog. Accred.: Music, Nursing, Teacher Education (NCATE)

Mount Mercy College
1330 Elmhurst Dr., NE, Cedar Rapids 52402
Type: Private, Roman Catholic Church, four-year
Degrees: B   *Enroll:* 1,171
URL: http://www2.mtmercy.edu
Phone: (319) 363-1323   *Calendar:* 4-1-4 plan
Inst. Accred.: NCA-HLC (1932/2003)
Prog. Accred.: Nursing, Nursing Education, Social Work

Muscatine Community College
152 Colorado St., Muscatine 52761
Type: Public, state/local, two-year
System: Eastern Iowa Community College District
Degrees: A   *FTE Enroll:* 639
URL: http://www.eicc.edu/mcc
Phone: (563) 288-6001   *Calendar:* Qtr. plan
Inst. Accred.: NCA-HLC (1983/2003, *Indirect accreditation
   through Eastern Iowa Community College District,
   Davenport, IA*)

North Iowa Area Community College
500 College Dr., Mason City 50401
Type: Public, state/local, two-year
System: Iowa Department of Education, Division of
   Community Colleges and Workforce Preparation
Degrees: A   *Enroll:* 2,132
URL: http://www.niacc.cc.ia.us
Phone: (515) 422-4000   *Calendar:* Sem. plan
Inst. Accred.: NCA-HLC (1919/2004)
Prog. Accred.: Electronic Technology, Mechanical
   Technology, Medical Assisting (AMA), Nursing, Physical
   Therapy Assisting

Northeast Iowa Community College
PO Box 400, Calmar 52132-0400
Type: Public, state/local, two-year
System: Iowa Department of Education, Division of
   Community Colleges and Workforce Preparation
Degrees: A   *Enroll:* 3,044
URL: http://www.nicc.edu
Phone: (800) 728-2256   *Calendar:* Sem. plan
Inst. Accred.: NCA-HLC (1977/1998)
Prog. Accred.: Health Information Technician,
   Radiography, Respiratory Therapy

Peosta Campus
10250 Sundown Rd., Peosta 52068
Phone: (563) 556-5110
Prog. Accred: Dental Assisting, Radiography

Northwest Iowa Community College
603 West Park St., Sheldon 51201
Type: Public, state/local, two-year
System: Iowa Department of Education, Division of
   Community Colleges and Workforce Preparation
Degrees: A   *Enroll:* 716
URL: http://www.nwicc.edu
Phone: (712) 324-5061   *Calendar:* Sem. plan
Inst. Accred.: NCA-HLC (1980/2005)
Prog. Accred.: Health Information Technician

Northwestern College
101 7th St., SW, Orange City 51041
Type: Private, Reformed Church in America, four-year
Degrees: A, B   *Enroll:* 1,248
URL: http://www.nwciowa.edu
Phone: (712) 737-7000   *Calendar:* Sem. plan
Inst. Accred.: NCA-HLC (1953/1996)
Prog. Accred.: Social Work, Teacher Education (NCATE)

Palmer College of Chiropractic
1000 Brady St., Davenport 52803-5287
Type: Private, independent, four-year
System: Palmer Chiropractic University System
Degrees: A, B, M, D   *Enroll:* 1,838
URL: http://www.palmer.edu
Phone: (563) 884-5656   *Calendar:* Tri. plan
Inst. Accred.: NCA-HLC (1984/1999)
Prog. Accred.: Chiropractic Education

Florida Campus
4705 South Clyde Morris Blvd., Port Orange, FL
32129-4103
Phone: (386) 763-2709

Saint Ambrose University
518 West Locust St., Davenport 52803
Type: Private, Roman Catholic Church, four-year
Degrees: B, M, D   *Enroll:* 2,755
URL: http://www.sau.edu
Phone: (563) 333-6213   *Calendar:* Sem. plan
Inst. Accred.: NCA-HLC (1927/1998)
Prog. Accred.: Business (ACBSP), Engineering (industrial),
   Nursing Education, Occupational Therapy, Physical
   Therapy, Social Work

Saint Luke's College
2720 Stone Park Blvd., PO Box 2000, Sioux City 51104
Type: Private, independent, two-year
Degrees: A   *Enroll:* 116
URL: http://www.stlukescollege.com
Phone: (712) 279-3149   *Calendar:* Sem. plan
Inst. Accred.: NCA-HLC (1997/2001)
Prog. Accred.: Clinical Lab Scientist, Clinical Pastoral
    Education, Nursing, Radiography

Scott Community College
500 Belmont Rd., Bettendorf 52722
Type: Public, state/local, two-year
System: Eastern Iowa Community College District
Degrees: A   *FTE Enroll:* 3,402
URL: http://www.eicc.edu/scc
Phone: (563) 441-4001   *Calendar:* Qtr. plan
Inst. Accred.: NCA-HLC (1983/2003, *Indirect accreditation
    through Eastern Iowa Community College District,
    Davenport, IA*)
Prog. Accred.: Dental Assisting, Electroneurodiagnostic
    Technology, Radiography

Simpson College
701 North C St., Indianola 50125
Type: Private, independent, four-year
Degrees: B   *Enroll:* 1,633
URL: http://www.simpson.edu
Phone: (515) 961-6251   *Calendar:* Sem. plan
Inst. Accred.: NCA-HLC (1913/1996)
Prog. Accred.: Music

Southeastern Community College
PO Box 180, 1500 West Agency Rd., West Burlington
52655-0180
Type: Public, state/local, two-year
System: Iowa Department of Education, Division of
    Community Colleges and Workforce Preparation
Degrees: A   *Enroll:* 2,394
URL: http://www.scciowa.edu
Phone: (319) 752-2731   *Calendar:* Sem. plan
Inst. Accred.: NCA-HLC (1974/1999)
Prog. Accred.: Medical Assisting (CAAHEP)

South Campus
335 Messenger Rd., Keokuk 52632-6007
Phone: (319) 524-3221

Southwestern Community College
1501 Townline St., PO Box 458, Creston 50801
Type: Public, state/local, two-year
System: Iowa Department of Education, Division of
    Community Colleges and Workforce Preparation
Degrees: A   *Enroll:* 932
URL: http://www.southwesterncc.edu
Phone: (641) 782-7081   *Calendar:* Sem. plan
Inst. Accred.: NCA-HLC (1974/1996)

University of Dubuque
2000 University Ave., Dubuque 52001-5050
Type: Private, Presbyterian Church (USA), four-year
Degrees: A, B, M, D   *Enroll:* 1,163
URL: http://www.dbq.edu
Phone: (319) 589-3223   *Calendar:* Sem. plan
Inst. Accred.: ATS (1944/1999), NCA-HLC (1921/1989)

University of Iowa
101 Jessup Hall, Iowa City 52242-1316
Type: Public, state, four-year
System: Board of Regents, State of Iowa
Degrees: B, M, P, D   *Enroll:* 26,102
URL: http://www.uiowa.edu
Phone: (319) 335-3500   *Calendar:* Sem. plan
Inst. Accred.: NCA-HLC (1913/1998)
Prog. Accred.: Accounting, Advanced Education in
    General Dentistry, Applied Science (industrial hygiene),
    Athletic Training, Audiology, Business (AACSB), Clinical
    Lab Scientist, Clinical Pastoral Education, Clinical
    Psychology, Combined Prosthodontics, Counseling,
    Counseling Psychology, Dental Public Health, Dentistry,
    Diagnostic Medical Sonography, Dietetics (internship),
    Endodontics, Engineering (bioengineering, chemical,
    civil, electrical, industrial, mechanical), English
    Language Education, General Dentistry, General
    Practice Residency, Health Services Administration,
    Journalism, Law, Librarianship, Medicine, Music,
    Nuclear Medicine Technology, Nurse Anesthesia
    Education, Nursing, Nursing Education, Oral and
    Maxillofacial Pathology, Oral and Maxillofacial
    Radiology, Oral and Maxillofacial Surgery, Orthodontic
    and Dentofacial Orthopedics, Pediatric Dentistry,
    Perfusion, Periodontics, Pharmacy, Physical Therapy,
    Physician Assistant, Planning, Psychology Internship,
    Public Health, Radiation Therapy, Radiography,
    Recreation and Leisure Services, Rehabilitation
    Counseling, School Psychology, Social Work, Speech-
    Language Pathology, Theatre

University of Northern Iowa
1227 West 27th St., Cedar Falls 50614
Type: Public, state, four-year
System: Board of Regents, State of Iowa
Degrees: B, M, P, D   *Enroll:* 12,055
URL: http://www.uni.edu
Phone: (319) 273-2311   *Calendar:* Sem. plan
Inst. Accred.: NCA-HLC (1913/2001)
Prog. Accred.: Art, Audiology, Business (AACSB),
    Construction Technology, Counseling, Industrial
    Technology, Manufacturing Technology, Music,
    Recreation and Leisure Services, Social Work, Speech-
    Language Pathology

Upper Iowa University
PO Box 1857, 605 Washington St., Fayette 52142
Type: Private, independent, four-year
Degrees: A, B, M   *Enroll:* 3,273
URL: http://www.uiu.edu
Phone: (563) 425-5200   *Calendar:* Sem. plan
Inst. Accred.: NCA-HLC (1913/1999)

Vatterott College—Des Moines
6100 Thornton Ave., Ste. 290, Des Moines 50321
Type: Private, proprietary, two-year
Degrees: A   *Enroll:* 155
URL: http://www.vatterott-college.com
Phone: (515) 309-9000   *Calendar:* Sem. plan
Inst. Accred.: ACCSCT (1999/2004)
Prog. Accred.: Medical Assisting (ABHES)

Saint Joseph Campus
3131 Frederick Blvd., St. Joseph, MO 64501
Phone: (816) 364-5399

Vennard College
2300 8th Ave. East, PO Box 29, University Park 52595-
0029
Type: Private, independent, four-year
Degrees: A, B   *Enroll:* 97
URL: http://www.vennard.edu
Phone: (515) 673-8391   *Calendar:* Sem. plan
Inst. Accred.: ABHE (1997/2002)

Waldorf College
106 South Sixth St., Forest City 50436
Type: Private, Lutheran Church, four-year
Degrees: A, B   *Enroll:* 526
URL: http://www.waldorf.edu
Phone: (641) 582-2450   *Calendar:* Sem. plan
Inst. Accred.: NCA-HLC (1948/2001)

Wartburg College
222 9th St., N.W., Waverly 50677-1003
Type: Private, Lutheran Church, four-year
Degrees: B   *Enroll:* 1,732
URL: http://www.wartburg.edu
Phone: (319) 352-8200
Inst. Accred.: NCA-HLC (1948/1997)
Prog. Accred.: Music, Social Work, Teacher Education
   (NCATE)

Wartburg Theological Seminary
333 Wartburg Place, PO Box 5004, Dubuque 52004-5004
Type: Private, Evangelic Lutheran Church in America,
   four-year
Degrees: M   *Enroll:* 185
Phone: (319) 589-0200   *Calendar:* 4-1-4 plan
Inst. Accred.: ATS (1944/1998), NCA-HLC (1976/1998)

Western Iowa Tech Community College
4647 Stone Ave., PO Box 5199, Sioux City 51102-5199
Type: Public, state/local, two-year
System: Iowa Department of Education, Division of
   Community Colleges and Workforce Preparation
Degrees: A   *Enroll:* 3,129
URL: http://www.witcc.edu
Phone: (712) 274-6400   *Calendar:* Sem. plan
Inst. Accred.: NCA-HLC (1977/2002)
Prog. Accred.: Dental Assisting, Nursing, Physical Therapy
   Assisting, Practical Nursing, Surgical Technology

Cherokee Campus
228-1/2 West Main, Cherokee 51012
Phone: (712) 225-0238

Denison Campus
11 North 35th St., Denison 51142
Phone: (712) 263-3419

William Penn University
201 Trueblood Ave., Oskaloosa 52577
Type: Private, Society of Friends, four-year
Degrees: A, B   *Enroll:* 1,364
URL: http://www.wmpenn.edu
Phone: (614) 673-1001   *Calendar:* Sem. plan
Inst. Accred.: NCA-HLC (1913/2001)

KANSAS

Allen County Community College
1801 North Cottonwood, Iola 66749
Type: Public, state/local, two-year
System: Kansas Board of Regents
Degrees: A   *Enroll:* 1,422
URL: http://www.allencc.edu
Phone: (620) 365-5116   *Calendar:* Sem. plan
Inst. Accred.: NCA-HLC (1974/1999)

Burlingame Campus
PO Box 66, 100 Bloomquist Dr., Burlingame 66413-0066
Phone: (785) 654-2416

Baker University
618 Eighth St., PO Box 65, Baldwin City 66006-0065
Type: Private, United Methodist Church, four-year
Degrees: A, B, M   *Enroll:* 866
URL: http://www.bakeru.edu
Phone: (785) 594-6451   *Calendar:* 4-1-4 plan
Inst. Accred.: NCA-HLC (1913/2002)
Prog. Accred.: Business (ACBSP), Music, Nursing, Teacher Education (NCATE)

School of Nursing Campus
Stormont-Vail Medical Center, 1500 Southwest 10th St., Topeka 66604-1353
Phone: (913) 354-5850
Prog. Accred: Nursing Education

School of Professional and Graduate Studies—Overland
8001 College Blvd., Ste. 100, Overland Park 66210
Phone: (913) 491-4432

School of Professional and Graduate Studies—Wichita
3450 North Rock Rd., #400, Wichita 67206
Phone: (316) 636-2322

Barclay College
607 North Kingman, PO Box 288, Haviland 67059-0288
Type: Private, Evangelical Friends International, four-year
Degrees: A, B   *Enroll:* 176
URL: http://www.barclaycollege.edu
Phone: (620) 862-5252   *Calendar:* Sem. plan
Inst. Accred.: ABHE (1975/1997)

Barton County Community College
243 NE 30th Rd., Great Bend 67530-9283
Type: Public, state/local, two-year
System: Kansas Board of Regents
Degrees: A   *Enroll:* 1,583
URL: http://www.bartonccc.edu
Phone: (620) 792-2701   *Calendar:* Sem. plan
Inst. Accred.: NCA-HLC (1974/2003)
Prog. Accred.: Clinical Lab Technology, Nursing

Benedictine College
1020 North Second St., Atchison 66002
Type: Private, Roman Catholic Church, four-year
Degrees: A, B, M   *Enroll:* 1,137
URL: http://www.benedictine.edu
Phone: (913) 367-5340   *Calendar:* Sem. plan
Inst. Accred.: NCA-HLC (1971/2000)
Prog. Accred.: Music, Teacher Education (NCATE)

Bethany College
421 North First St., Lindsborg 67456-1897
Type: Private, Evangelical Lutheran Church in America, four-year
Degrees: B   *Enroll:* 599
URL: http://www.bethanylb.edu
Phone: (785) 227-3311   *Calendar:* 4-1-4 plan
Inst. Accred.: NCA-HLC (1932/2001)
Prog. Accred.: Music, Social Work, Teacher Education (NCATE)

Bethel College
300 East 27th St., North Newton 67117
Type: Private, General Conference Mennonite Church, four-year
Degrees: B   *Enroll:* 449
URL: http://www.bethelks.edu
Phone: (316) 283-2500   *Calendar:* 4-1-4 plan
Inst. Accred.: NCA-HLC (1938/1999)
Prog. Accred.: Nursing, Nursing Education, Social Work

The Brown Mackie College
2106 South 9th St., Salina 67401
Type: Private, proprietary, two-year
System: Education Management Corporation
Degrees: A   *Enroll:* 351
URL: http://www.brownmackie.edu
Phone: (913) 825-5422   *Calendar:* Sem. plan
Inst. Accred.: NCA-HLC (1980/2001)

Kansas City Campus
9705 Lenexa Dr., Lenexa 66215
Phone: (913) 768-1900

Los Angeles Campus
2900 31st St., Santa Monica, CA 90405
Phone: (866) 505-0332

Orange County Campus
3601 West Sunflower Ave., Santa Ana, CA 92704
Phone: (866) 505-0334

Butler County Community College
901 South Haverhill Rd., El Dorado 67042
Type: Public, state/local, two-year
System: Kansas Board of Regents
Degrees: A   *Enroll:* 5,200
URL: http://www.butlercc.edu
Phone: (316) 312-2222   *Calendar:* Sem. plan
Inst. Accred.: NCA-HLC (1970/2000)
Prog. Accred.: Nursing

Central Baptist Theological Seminary
741 North 31st St., Kansas City 66102-3964
Type: Private, American Baptist Churches (USA),
  Cooperative Baptis, four-year
Degrees: M   *Enroll:* 80
URL: http://www.cbts.edu
Phone: (913) 371-5313   *Calendar:* Sem. plan
Inst. Accred.: ATS (1962/2001), NCA-HLC (1979/2001,
  Warning)

Central Christian College of Kansas
1200 South Main St., PO Box 1403, McPherson 67460
Type: Private, Free Methodist Church, four-year
Degrees: A, B   *Enroll:* 308
URL: http://www.centralcollege.edu
Phone: (620) 241-0723   *Calendar:* 4-1-4 plan
Inst. Accred.: NCA-HLC (1975/2004)

Cloud County Community College
2221 Campus Dr., PO Box 1002, Concordia 66901-1002
Type: Public, state/local, two-year
System: Kansas Board of Regents
Degrees: A   *Enroll:* 1,590
URL: http://www.cloud.edu
Phone: (800) 729-5101   *Calendar:* Sem. plan
Inst. Accred.: NCA-HLC (1977/2001)
Prog. Accred.: Nursing, Practical Nursing

Coffeyville Community College
400 West 11th St., Coffeyville 67337-5064
Type: Public, state/local, two-year
System: Kansas Board of Regents
Degrees: A   *Enroll:* 1,035
URL: http://www.coffeyville.edu
Phone: (620) 251-7700   *Calendar:* Sem. plan
Inst. Accred.: NCA-HLC (1972/2005)

Technical Campus
600 Roosevelt St., Coffeyville 67337-3421
Phone: (621) 251-3910

Colby Community College
1255 South Range, Colby 67701
Type: Public, state/local, two-year
System: Kansas Board of Regents
Degrees: A   *Enroll:* 1,183
URL: http://www.colbycc.edu
Phone: (785) 462-3984   *Calendar:* Sem. plan
Inst. Accred.: NCA-HLC (1972/2005)
Prog. Accred.: Dental Hygiene, Nursing, Physical Therapy
  Assisting, Veterinary Technology

Cowley County Community College
125 South Second St., PO Box 1147, Arkansas City
67005-1147
Type: Public, state/local, two-year
System: Kansas Board of Regents
Degrees: A   *Enroll:* 3,064
URL: http://www.cowley.edu
Phone: (620) 442-0430   *Calendar:* Sem. plan
Inst. Accred.: NCA-HLC (1975/2000)

Dodge City Community College
2501 North 14th St., Dodge City 67801
Type: Public, state/local, two-year
System: Kansas Board of Regents
Degrees: A   *Enroll:* 1,171
Phone: (800) 262-4565   *Calendar:* Sem. plan
Inst. Accred.: NCA-HLC (1966/1997)
Prog. Accred.: Health Information Technician, Nursing,
  Practical Nursing

Donnelly College
608 North 18th St., Kansas City 66102
Type: Private, Roman Catholic Church, two-year
Degrees: A   *Enroll:* 450
Phone: (913) 621-8747   *Calendar:* Sem. plan
Inst. Accred.: NCA-HLC (1958/1996)

Emporia State University
1200 Commercial St., Emporia 66801-5087
Type: Public, state, four-year
System: Kansas Board of Regents
Degrees: B, M, P, D   *Enroll:* 4,924
URL: http://www.emporia.edu
Phone: (620) 341-1200   *Calendar:* Sem. plan
Inst. Accred.: NCA-HLC (1915/2005)
Prog. Accred.: Athletic Training, Business (AACSB),
  Counseling, Librarianship, Music, Nursing,
  Rehabilitation Counseling, Teacher Education (NCATE)

Flint Hills Technical College
3301 West 18th Ave., Emporia 66801
Type: Public, state/local, two-year
System: Kansas Board of Regents
Degrees: A   *Enroll:* 276
URL: http://www.fhtc.kansas.net
Phone: (316) 341-2300   *Calendar:* Sem. plan
Inst. Accred.: COE (2003)
Prog. Accred.: Dental Assisting

Fort Hays State University
600 Park St., Hays 67601
Type: Public, state, four-year
System: Kansas Board of Regents
Degrees: A, B, M, P   *Enroll:* 5,614
URL: http://www.fhsu.edu
Phone: (785) 628-4000   *Calendar:* Sem. plan
Inst. Accred.: NCA-HLC (1915/2002)
Prog. Accred.: Music, Nursing, Nursing Education,
  Radiography, Social Work, Speech-Language Pathology,
  Teacher Education (NCATE)

Fort Scott Community College
2108 South Horton St., Fort Scott 66701
Type: Public, state/local, two-year
System: Kansas Board of Regents
Degrees: A   *Enroll:* 1,192
URL: http://www.fortscott.edu
Phone: (620) 223-2700   *Calendar:* Sem. plan
Inst. Accred.: NCA-HLC (1976/2003)
Prog. Accred.: Nursing

Friends University
2100 University Ave., Wichita 67213
Type: Private, independent, four-year
Degrees: A, B, M   *Enroll:* 2,577
URL: http://www.friends.edu
Phone: (316) 261-5800   *Calendar:* Sem. plan
Inst. Accred.: NCA-HLC (1915/2001)
Prog. Accred.: Marriage and Family Therapy, Music,
   Teacher Education (NCATE)

Mission Campus
Foxridge Tower, 5700 Broadmoor, Ste. 1020, Mission
66202
Phone: (913) 236-9191
Prog. Accred: Marriage and Family Therapy

Garden City Community College
801 Campus Dr., Garden City 67846
Type: Public, state/local, two-year
System: Kansas Board of Regents
Degrees: A   *Enroll:* 1,337
URL: http://www.gcccks.edu
Phone: (800) 658-1696   *Calendar:* Sem. plan
Inst. Accred.: NCA-HLC (1975/2005)
Prog. Accred.: Nursing

Haskell Indian Nations University
155 Indian Ave., Lawrence 66046-4800
Type: Public, tribal, four-year
Degrees: A, B   *Enroll:* 882
URL: http://www.haskell.edu
Phone: (785) 749-8404   *Calendar:* Sem. plan
Inst. Accred.: NCA-HLC (1979/2005)

Hesston College
PO Box 3000, 325 South College Dr., Hesston 67062
Type: Private, Mennonite Church, two-year
Degrees: A   *Enroll:* 414
URL: http://www.hesston.edu
Phone: (620) 327-4221   *Calendar:* Sem. plan
Inst. Accred.: NCA-HLC (1964/2001)
Prog. Accred.: Nursing

Highland Community College
606 West Main St., Highland 66035-4165
Type: Public, state/local, two-year
System: Kansas Board of Regents
Degrees: A   *Enroll:* 1,661
URL: http://www.highlandcc.edu
Phone: (785) 442-6000   *Calendar:* Sem. plan
Inst. Accred.: NCA-HLC (1977/1999)

Hutchinson Community College
1300 North Plum St., Hutchinson 67501
Type: Public, state/local, two-year
System: Kansas Board of Regents
Degrees: A   *Enroll:* 2,833
URL: http://www.hutchcc.edu
Phone: (620) 665-3500   *Calendar:* Sem. plan
Inst. Accred.: NCA-HLC (1960/2004)
Prog. Accred.: Health Information Technician, Nursing,
   Practical Nursing, Radiography

Independence Community College
Independence 67301
Type: Public, state/local, two-year
System: Kansas Board of Regents
Degrees: A   *Enroll:* 799
URL: http://www.indycc.edu
Phone: (620) 331-4100   *Calendar:* Sem. plan
Inst. Accred.: NCA-HLC (1957/1998)

Johnson County Community College
12345 College Blvd., Overland Park 66210-1299
Type: Public, state/local, two-year
System: Kansas Board of Regents
Degrees: A   *Enroll:* 10,269
URL: http://www.jccc.net
Phone: (913) 469-8500   *Calendar:* Sem. plan
Inst. Accred.: NCA-HLC (1975/1997)
Prog. Accred.: Business (ACBSP), Culinary Education,
   Dental Hygiene, EMT (Paramedic), Nursing, Respiratory
   Therapy

Kansas City Kansas Community College
7250 State Ave., Kansas City 66112
Type: Public, state/local, two-year
System: Kansas Board of Regents
Degrees: A   *Enroll:* 3,118
URL: http://www.kckcc.edu
Phone: (913) 334-1100   *Calendar:* Sem. plan
Inst. Accred.: NCA-HLC (1951/1996)
Prog. Accred.: Business (ACBSP), Funeral Service
   Education (Mortuary Science), Nursing, Physical
   Therapy Assisting, Respiratory Therapy, Respiratory
   Therapy Technology

Kansas State University
Manhattan 66506-0113
Type: Public, state, four-year
System: Kansas Board of Regents
Degrees: A, B, M, D   *Enroll:* 19,986
URL: http://www.ksu.edu
Phone: (785) 532-6011   *Calendar:* Sem. plan
Inst. Accred.: NCA-HLC (1916/2002)
Prog. Accred.: Accounting, Art, Athletic Training, Business
   (AACSB), Computer Science, Construction Education,
   Counseling, Dietetics (coordinated), Engineering
   (agricultural, architectural, chemical, civil, computer,
   electrical, industrial, manufacturing, mechanical),
   Interior Architecture, Interior Design, Journalism,
   Landscape Architecture, Marriage and Family Therapy,
   Music, Planning, Psychology Internship, Public
   Administration, Recreation and Leisure Services, Social
   Work, Speech-Language Pathology, Teacher Education
   (NCATE), Theatre, Veterinary Medicine

College of Technology and Aviation
2409 Scanlan Ave., Salina 67401-8196
Phone: (913) 825-0275
Prog. Accred: Engineering Technology
   (civil/construction, computer, electrical,
   environmental/sanitary, mechanical)

Kansas Wesleyan University
100 East Claflin Ave., Salina 67401-6146
Type: Private, United Methodist Church, four-year
Degrees: A, B, M　　　　　　　　　　*Enroll:* 678
URL: http://www.kwu.edu
Phone: (785) 827-5541　　　　*Calendar:* Sem. plan
Inst. Accred.: NCA-HLC (1916/1997)
Prog. Accred.: Nursing

Labette Community College
200 South 14th St., Parsons 67357
Type: Public, state/local, two-year
System: Kansas Board of Regents
Degrees: A　　　　　　　　　　　*Enroll:* 753
URL: http://www.labette.edu
Phone: (620) 421-6700　　　　*Calendar:* Sem. plan
Inst. Accred.: NCA-HLC (1976/1996)
Prog. Accred.: Nursing, Radiography, Respiratory Therapy

Manhattan Christian College
1415 Anderson Ave., Manhattan 66502-4081
Type: Private, Christian Churches/Churches of Christ,
　four-year
Degrees: A, B　　　　　　　　　　*Enroll:* 287
URL: http://www.mccks.edu
Phone: (785) 539-3571　　　　*Calendar:* Sem. plan
Inst. Accred.: ABHE (1948/1997), NCA-HLC (2000/2005)

McPherson College
1600 East Euclid St., McPherson 67460-3847
Type: Private, Church of the Brethren, four-year
Degrees: A, B　　　　　　　　　　*Enroll:* 399
URL: http://www.mcpherson.edu
Phone: (620) 241-0731　　　　*Calendar:* 4-1-4 plan
Inst. Accred.: NCA-HLC (1921/2005)

MidAmerica Nazarene University
2030 East College Way, Olathe 66062-1899
Type: Private, Church of the Nazarene, four-year
Degrees: A, B, M　　　　　　　　　*Enroll:* 1,679
URL: http://www.mnu.edu
Phone: (913) 791-3750　　　　*Calendar:* Sem. plan
Inst. Accred.: NCA-HLC (1974/1999)
Prog. Accred.: Music, Nursing, Nursing Education

European Nazarene College
Junkerstrasse 68-70, B¸singen, Switzerland 8238
Phone: 011 49 7734-80900

Neosho County Community College
800 West 14th St., Chanute 66720
Type: Public, state/local, two-year
System: Kansas Board of Regents
Degrees: A　　　　　　　　　　　*Enroll:* 1,016
URL: http://www.neosho.edu
Phone: (620) 431-2820　　　　*Calendar:* Sem. plan
Inst. Accred.: NCA-HLC (1976/1996)
Prog. Accred.: Business (ACBSP), Nursing

Newman University
3100 McCormick Ave., Wichita 67213-2097
Type: Private, Roman Catholic Church, four-year
Degrees: A, B, M　　　　　　　　　*Enroll:* 1,537
URL: http://www.newmanu.edu
Phone: (316) 942-4291　　　　*Calendar:* Sem. plan
Inst. Accred.: NCA-HLC (1967/1997)
Prog. Accred.: Nurse Anesthesia Education, Nursing,
　Nursing Education, Radiography, Respiratory Therapy,
　Social Work

North Central Kansas Technical College
PO Box 507, Beloit 67420
Type: Public, state, two-year
Degrees: A　　　　　　　　　　　*Enroll:* 470
URL: http://www.ncktc.tec.ks.us
Phone: (785) 738-2276　　　　*Calendar:* Sem. plan
Inst. Accred.: NCA-HLC (1981/2002)
Prog. Accred.: Practical Nursing

Hays Campus
2205 Wheatland, Hays 67601
Phone: (913) 625-2437

Northeast Kansas Technical College
1501 west Riley St., Atchison 66002
Type: Public, state, two-year
Degrees: A
URL: http://www.nektc.net
Phone: (913) 367-6204　　　　*Calendar:* Sem. plan
Inst. Accred.: COE (2002)

Northwest Kansas Technical College
1209 Harrison St., Goodland 67211
Type: Public, state, two-year
Degrees: A
URL: http://www.nwktc.org
Phone: (785) 899-3641
Inst. Accred.: COE (2001)

Ottawa University
1001 South Cedar St., Ottawa 66067-3399
Type: Private, American Baptist Churches, USA, four-year
Degrees: B, M　　　　　　　　　　*Enroll:* 521
URL: http://www.ottawa.edu
Phone: (785) 242-5200　　　　*Calendar:* Sem. plan
Inst. Accred.: NCA-HLC (1914/2004)
Prog. Accred.: Teacher Education (NCATE)

Kansas City Campus
10865 Grandview, Bldg. 20, Overland Park 66210
Phone: (913) 451-1431

Milwaukee Campus
300 North Corporate Dr., Ste. 110, Brookfield, WI
53045
Phone: (414) 879-0200

Phoenix Campus
2340 West Mission Ln., Phoenix, AZ 85021
Phone: (602) 371-1188

Pittsburg State University
1701 South Broadway, Pittsburg 66762
Type: Public, state, four-year
System: Kansas Board of Regents
Degrees: A, B, M, P   *Enroll:* 5,912
URL: http://www.pittstate.edu
Phone: (316) 231-7000   *Calendar:* Sem. plan
Inst. Accred.: NCA-HLC (1915/2003)
Prog. Accred.: Business (AACSB), Counseling, Engineering
  Technology (civil/construction, electrical,
  manufacturing, mechanical, plastics), Music, Nursing,
  Nursing Education, Social Work, Teacher Education
  (NCATE)

Pratt Community College
348 NE SR 61, Pratt 67124
Type: Public, state/local, two-year
System: Kansas Board of Regents
Degrees: A   *Enroll:* 928
URL: http://www.prattcc.edu
Phone: (620) 672-9800   *Calendar:* Sem. plan
Inst. Accred.: NCA-HLC (1976/2005)
Prog. Accred.: Business (ACBSP), Nursing

Seward County Community College
1801 North Kansas St., Box 1137, Liberal 67901
Type: Public, state/local, two-year
System: Kansas Board of Regents
Degrees: A   *Enroll:* 1,159
URL: http://www.sccc.edu
Phone: (620) 624-1951   *Calendar:* Sem. plan
Inst. Accred.: NCA-HLC (1975/2000)
Prog. Accred.: Business (ACBSP), Clinical Lab Technology,
  Nursing, Practical Nursing, Respiratory Therapy,
  Respiratory Therapy Technology, Surgical Technology

Southwestern College
100 College St., Winfield 67156-2499
Type: Private, United Methodist Church, four-year
Degrees: B, M   *Enroll:* 1,016
URL: http://www.sckans.edu
Phone: (620) 229-6223   *Calendar:* Sem. plan
Inst. Accred.: NCA-HLC (1918/2001)
Prog. Accred.: Music, Nursing, Nursing Education

Sterling College
Cooper at Broadway, PO Box 98, Sterling 67579
Type: Private, Presbyterian Church (USA), four-year
Degrees: B   *Enroll:* 457
URL: http://www.sterling.edu
Phone: (316) 278-2173   *Calendar:* 4-1-4 plan
Inst. Accred.: NCA-HLC (1928/1999)

Tabor College
400 South Jefferson St., Hillsboro 67063
Type: Private, Conference of the Mennonite Brethren
  Church of Nor, four-year
Degrees: A, B, M   *Enroll:* 465
URL: http://www.tabor.edu
Phone: (620) 947-3121   *Calendar:* 4-1-4 plan
Inst. Accred.: NCA-HLC (1965/1999)
Prog. Accred.: Music, Nursing Education

Wichita Campus
7348 West 21st St. North, Ste. 117, Wichita 67205-1765
Phone: (316) 729-6333

United States Army Command and General Staff College
1 Reynolds Ave., Bldg. 111, Fort Leavenworth 66027-1352
Type: Public, federal, four-year
Degrees: M   *FTE Enroll:* 1,108
URL: http://www.cgsc.army.mil
Phone: (913) 684-3097   *Calendar:* Tri. plan
Inst. Accred.: NCA-HLC (1976/1995)

University of Kansas
230 Strong Hall, Lawrence 66045
Type: Public, state, four-year
System: Kansas Board of Regents
Degrees: B, M, P, D   *Enroll:* 23,262
URL: http://www.ku.edu
Phone: (785) 864-2700   *Calendar:* Sem. plan
Inst. Accred.: NCA-HLC (1913/2005)
Prog. Accred.: Accounting, Art, Audiology, Business
  (AACSB), Clinical Psychology, Computer Science,
  Counseling Psychology, Engineering (aerospace,
  architectural, chemical, civil, computer, electrical,
  engineering physics/science, mechanical, petroleum),
  English Language Education, Health Services
  Administration, Journalism, Law, Music, Pharmacy,
  Planning, Psychology Internship, Public Administration,
  School Psychology, Social Work, Speech-Language
  Pathology, Teacher Education (NCATE)

Edwards Campus
12600 Quivira Rd., Overland 66213
Phone: (913) 897-8400

The School of Medicine—Wichita
1010 N. Kansas, Wichita 67214-3199
Phone: (316) 293-2600
Prog. Accred: Public Health

University of Kansas Medical Center
3901 Rainbow Blvd., Kansas City 66160
Phone: (913) 588-1401
Prog. Accred: Clinical Lab Scientist, Cytotechnology,
  Dietetics (internship), Health Information
  Administration, Medicine, Nuclear Medicine
  Technology, Nurse (Midwifery), Nurse Anesthesia
  Education, Nursing, Nursing Education, Occupational
  Therapy, Physical Therapy, Respiratory Therapy

University of Saint Mary
4100 South 4th St., Leavenworth 66048
Type: Private, Roman Catholic Church, four-year
Degrees: A, B, M   *Enroll:* 592
URL: http://www.smcks.edu
Phone: (913) 758-6102   *Calendar:* Sem. plan
Inst. Accred.: NCA-HLC (1928/1997)
Prog. Accred.: Teacher Education (NCATE)

Washburn University
17th and College St.s, Topeka 66621
Type: Public, state/local, four-year
Degrees: A, B, M, D   *Enroll:* 5,531
URL: http://www.washburn.edu
Phone: (785) 670-1010   *Calendar:* Sem. plan
Inst. Accred.: NCA-HLC (1913/1998)
Prog. Accred.: Art, Business (AACSB), Health Information
   Technician, Law, Music, Nursing, Nursing Education,
   Physical Therapy Assisting, Radiation Therapy,
   Radiography, Respiratory Therapy, Respiratory Therapy
   Technology, Social Work, Teacher Education (NCATE)

Wichita State University
1845 Fairmont St., Wichita 67260-0001
Type: Public, state, four-year
System: Kansas Board of Regents
Degrees: A, B, M, P, D   *Enroll:* 10,790
URL: http://www.wichita.edu
Phone: (800) 362-2594   *Calendar:* Sem. plan
Inst. Accred.: NCA-HLC (1927/2001)
Prog. Accred.: Accounting, Audiology, Business (AACSB),
   Clinical Lab Scientist, Clinical Psychology, Dance,
   Dental Hygiene, Engineering (aerospace, computer,
   electrical, industrial, manufacturing, mechanical),
   Music, Nursing, Nursing Education, Physician Assistant,
   Psychology Internship, Public Health, Social Work,
   Speech-Language Pathology, Teacher Education
   (NCATE)

KENTUCKY

Alice Lloyd College
100 Purpose Rd., Pippa Passes 41844-8884
Type: Private, independent, four-year
Degrees: B *Enroll:* 604
URL: http://www.alc.edu
Phone: (606) 368-2101 *Calendar:* Sem. plan
Inst. Accred.: SACS (1952/1997)

Asbury College
One Macklem Dr., Wilmore 40390-1198
Type: Private, independent, four-year
Degrees: B, M *Enroll:* 1,192
URL: http://www.asbury.edu
Phone: (859) 858-3511 *Calendar:* Sem. plan
Inst. Accred.: SACS (1940/1999)
Prog. Accred.: Music, Social Work

Asbury Theological Seminary
204 North Lexington Ave., Wilmore 40390-1199
Type: Private, interdenominational, four-year
Degrees: M, D *Enroll:* 1,197
URL: http://www.asburyseminary.edu
Phone: (859) 858-3581 *Calendar:* 4-1-4 plan
Inst. Accred.: ATS (1960/2005), SACS (1984/2005)

Florida Campus
8401 Velencia College Ln., Orlando, FL 32825
Phone: (407) 482-7564

Ashland Community and Technical College
1400 College Dr., Ashland 41101-3683
Type: Public, state, two-year
System: Ashland Community and Technical College
District
Degrees: A *Enroll:* 1,712
URL: http://www.ashland.kctcs.edu
Phone: (606) 329-2999 *Calendar:* Sem. plan
Inst. Accred.: SACS (1952/2001)
Prog. Accred.: Business (ACBSP)

Roberts Drive Campus
4818 Roberts Dr., Ashland 41102-9046
Phone: (606) 928-6427

Beckfield College
16 Spiral Dr., Florence 41042
Type: Private, proprietary, four-year
Degrees: A, B *Enroll:* 327
URL: http://www.beckfieldcollege.com
Phone: (859) 371-9393 *Calendar:* Qtr. plan
Inst. Accred.: ACICS (1993/2002)

Bellarmine University
2001 Newburg Rd., Louisville 40205-0671
Type: Private, Roman Catholic Church, four-year
Degrees: A, B, M *Enroll:* 2,339
URL: http://www.bellarmine.edu
Phone: (502) 452-8000 *Calendar:* Sem. plan
Inst. Accred.: SACS (1956/1998)
Prog. Accred.: Clinical Lab Scientist, Nursing, Nursing
Education, Physical Therapy Assisting, Teacher
Education (NCATE)

Berea College
Berea 40404
Type: Private, independent, four-year
Degrees: B *Enroll:* 1,532
URL: http://www.berea.edu
Phone: (859) 985-3000 *Calendar:* 4-1-4 plan
Inst. Accred.: SACS (1926/1995)
Prog. Accred.: Nursing, Nursing Education, Teacher
Education (NCATE)

Big Sandy Community and Technical College
One Bert T. Combs Dr., Prestonsburg 41653
Type: Public, state, two-year
System: Big Sandy Community and Technical College
District
Degrees: A *Enroll:* 2,054
URL: http://www.bigsandy.kctcs.edu
Phone: (606) 886-3863 *Calendar:* Sem. plan
Inst. Accred.: SACS (1971/2001)
Prog. Accred.: Dental Hygiene

Mayo Campus
513 Third St., Paintsville 41240
Phone: (606) 789-5321
Prog. Accred: Respiratory Therapy Technology

Pikeville Campus
120 South River Fill Dr., Pikeville 41501
Phone: (606) 218-2060

Bluegrass Community and Technical College
Oswald Bldg., Cooper Dr., Lexington 40506-0235
Type: Public, state, two-year
System: Bluegrass Community and Technical College
District
Degrees: A *Enroll:* 6,524
URL: http://www.bluegrass.kctcs.edu
Phone: (859) 257-4872 *Calendar:* Sem. plan
Inst. Accred.: SACS (1965/2001)
Prog. Accred.: Dental Hygiene, Dental Laboratory
Technology, Nursing, Respiratory Therapy

Anderson Campus
1500 Bypass North, US 127, Lawrenceburg 40342
Phone: (502) 839-8488

Central Campus
308 Vo-Tech Rd., Lexington 40511-2626
Phone: (859) 246-2400
Prog. Accred: Clinical Lab Technology, Dental
Assisting, Medical Assisting (AMA), Radiography,
Respiratory Therapy Technology, Surgical Technology

Danville Campus
59 Corporate Dr., Danville 40422
Phone: (859) 239-7030

Bowling Green Technical College
1845 Loop Dr., Bowling Green 42101-9202
Type: Public, state, two-year
System: Bowling Green Community and Technical
College District
Degrees: A
URL: http://www.bowlinggreen.kctcs.edu
Phone: (270) 901-1000   *Calendar:* Sem. plan
Inst. Accred.: COE (1972/2004)
Prog. Accred.: Dental Assisting, Radiography, Respiratory
Therapy Technology, Surgical Technology

Glasgow Health Campus
129 State St., Glasgow 42141
Phone: (502) 651-5673

Glasgow Technology Campus
500 Hilltopper Way, Glasgow 42141
Phone: (270) 659-6900

Kentucky Advanced Technology Institute
1127 Morgantown Rd., Bowling Green 42101-9202
Phone: (270) 746-7807

Brescia University
717 Frederica St., Owensboro 42301-3023
Type: Private, Roman Catholic Church, four-year
Degrees: A, B, M   *Enroll:* 585
URL: http://www.brescia.edu
Phone: (270) 685-3131   *Calendar:* Sem. plan
Inst. Accred.: SACS (1957/1999)
Prog. Accred.: Social Work

Brown Mackie College—Louisville
300 High Rise Dr., Louisville 40213
Type: Private, proprietary, two-year
System: Education Management Corporation
Degrees: A   *Enroll:* 350
URL: http://www.brownmackie.edu
Phone: (502) 968-7191   *Calendar:* Sem. plan
Inst. Accred.: ACICS (2000/2004)

Hopkinsville Campus
4001 Ft. Campbell Blvd., Hopkinsville 42240
Phone: (270) 886-1302

Campbellsville University
1 University Dr., Campbellsville 42718
Type: Private, Southern Baptist Church, four-year
Degrees: A, B, M   *Enroll:* 1,515
URL: http://www.campbellsville.edu
Phone: (270) 789-5000   *Calendar:* Sem. plan
Inst. Accred.: SACS (1963/2004)
Prog. Accred.: Music, Social Work

Centre College
600 West Walnut St., Danville 40422-1394
Type: Private, independent, four-year
Degrees: B   *Enroll:* 1,059
URL: http://www.centre.edu
Phone: (859) 238-5200   *Calendar:* 4-1-4 plan
Inst. Accred.: SACS (1904/1995)

Clear Creek Baptist Bible College
300 Clear Creek Rd., Pineville 40977-9754
Type: Private, Kentucky Baptist Convention, four-year
Degrees: A, B   *Enroll:* 166
URL: http://www.ccbbc.edu
Phone: (606) 337-3196   *Calendar:* Sem. plan
Inst. Accred.: ABHE (1986/1997), SACS (1999/2005)

Daymar College
3361 Buckland Square, Owensboro 42301
Type: Private, proprietary, two-year
Degrees: A   *Enroll:* 378
URL: http://www.daymarcollege.edu
Phone: (270) 926-4040   *Calendar:* Qtr. plan
Inst. Accred.: ACICS (1969/2004)

Louisville Campus
4400 Breakenridge Ln., Ste. 415, Louisville 40219
Phone: (502) 495-1040

Newport Campus
76 Carothers Rd., Newport 41071
Phone: (859) 291-0800

Decker College of Business Technology
9721 Ormsby Station Rd., Ste. 100, Louisville 40223
Type: Private, proprietary, two-year
Degrees: A
URL: http://www.deckercollege.com
Phone: (502) 327-6462   *Calendar:* Qtr. plan
Inst. Accred.: COE (1992/2004)

Eastern Kentucky University
521 Lancaster Ave., Richmond 40475-3102
Type: Public, state, four-year
System: Kentucky Council on Postsecondary Education
Degrees: A, B, M, P   *Enroll:* 12,885
URL: http://www.eku.edu
Phone: (859) 622-1000   *Calendar:* Sem. plan
Inst. Accred.: SACS (1928/1996)
Prog. Accred.: Athletic Training, Business (AACSB),
  Clinical Lab Scientist, Clinical Lab Technology,
  Computer Science, Construction Education, Counseling,
  Dietetics (internship), EMT (Paramedic), Electronic
  Technology, Health Information Administration, Health
  Information Technician, Industrial Technology, Medical
  Assisting (AMA), Music, Nursing, Nursing Education,
  Occupational Therapy, Public Administration, Recreation
  and Leisure Services, Social Work, Speech-Language
  Pathology, Teacher Education (NCATE)

Elizabethtown Community and Technical College
600 College St. Rd., Elizabethtown 42701
Type: Public, state, two-year
System: Elizabethtown Community and Technical College
  District
Degrees: A   *Enroll:* 2,306
URL: http://www.elizabethtown.kctcs.edu
Phone: (270) 769-2371   *Calendar:* Sem. plan
Inst. Accred.: SACS (1964/2001)
Prog. Accred.: Dental Hygiene, Nursing, Radiography

Frontier School of Midwifery and Family Nursing
195 School St., Hyden 41749
Type: Private, independent, four-year
Degrees: M   *FTE Enroll:* 190
URL: http://www.midwives.org
Phone: (606) 672-2312
Inst. Accred.: SACS (2004)
Prog. Accred.: Nurse (Midwifery)

The Galen College of Nursing
612 South Fourth St., Ste. 400, Louisville 40202
Type: Private, proprietary, four-year
Degrees: A, B
URL: http://www.galened.com
Phone: (502) 580-3660   *Calendar:* Sem. plan
Inst. Accred.: COE (1983/2004)

Saint Petersburg Campus
9549 Koger Blvd., Gadsden Bldg. #100, St.
Petersburg, FL 33702
Phone: (813) 577-1497

San Antonio Campus
6800 Park Ten Blvd., Ste. 160, South, San Antonio, TX
78213
Phone: (210) 733-3056

Gateway Community and Technical College
1025 Amsterdam Rd., Covington 41011
Type: Public, state, two-year
System: Gateway Community and Technical College
  District
Degrees: A
URL: http://www.gateway.kctcs.edu
Phone: (859) 292-3930   *Calendar:* Sem. plan
Inst. Accred.: COE (1973/1999)

Edgewood Campus
790 Thomas More Pkwy., Edgewood 41017
Phone: (606) 341-5200

Highland Heights Campus
90 Campbell Dr., Highland Heights 41076
Phone: (859) 441-2010

Georgetown College
400 East College St., Georgetown 40324
Type: Private, Southern Baptist Church, four-year
Degrees: B, M   *Enroll:* 1,451
URL: http://www.georgetowncollege.edu
Phone: (502) 863-8000   *Calendar:* Sem. plan
Inst. Accred.: SACS (1919/2002, Probation)

Hazard Community and Technical College
One Community College Dr., Hazard 41701
Type: Public, state, two-year
System: Hazard Community and Technical College
  District
Degrees: A   *Enroll:* 2,568
URL: http://www.hazcc.kctcs.edu
Phone: (606) 436-5721   *Calendar:* Sem. plan
Inst. Accred.: SACS (2002)
Prog. Accred.: Clinical Lab Technology, Physical Therapy
  Assisting, Radiography

Knott County Area Technology Center
1996 Hwy. 160, South, Hindman 41822
Phone: (606) 785-5350

Lee County Area Technology Center
PO Box B, 960 Center St., Beattyville 41311
Phone: (606) 464-5018

Lees College Campus
601 Jefferson Ave., Jackson 41339
Phone: (606) 666-7521

Leslie County Area Technology Center
PO Box 902, 175 Eagle Ln., Hyden 41749
Phone: (606) 672-2859

Letcher County Area Technology Center
185 Circle Dr., Whitesburg 41858
Phone: (606) 633-5053

Technical Campus
101 Vo-Tech Dr., Hazard 41701
Phone: (606) 435-6101

Henderson Community College
2660 South Green St., Henderson 42420
Type: Public, state, two-year
System: Henderson Community and Technical College
  District
Degrees: A   *Enroll:* 1,093
URL: http://www.hencc.kctcs.edu
Phone: (502) 827-1867   *Calendar:* Sem. plan
Inst. Accred.: SACS (1971/2001)
Prog. Accred.: Clinical Lab Technology, Dental Hygiene,
  Nursing

Hopkinsville Community College
PO Box 2100, Hopkinsville 42241-2100
Type: Public, state, two-year
System: Hopkinsville Community and Technical College
  District
Degrees: A   *Enroll:* 2,015
URL: http://www.hopcc.kctcs.edu
Phone: (270) 886-3921   *Calendar:* Sem. plan
Inst. Accred.: SACS (1971/2001)

Jefferson Community and Technical College
109 East Broadway, Louisville 40202-2005
Type: Public, state, two-year
System: Jefferson Community and Technical College
  District
Degrees: A   *Enroll:* 5,719
URL: http://www.jefferson.kctcs.edu
Phone: (502) 213-5333   *Calendar:* Sem. plan
Inst. Accred.: SACS (1971/2002)
Prog. Accred.: Culinary Education, Nuclear Medicine
  Technology, Nursing, Occupational Therapy Assisting,
  Physical Therapy Assisting, Radiography, Respiratory
  Therapy

Technical Campus
727 West Chestnut St., Louisville 40203-2071
Phone: (502) 213-4200
Prog. Accred: Medical Assisting (CAAHEP)

Kentucky Christian University
100 Academic Pkwy., Grayson 41143-2205
Type: Private, Chiristian Churches and Churches of
  Christ, four-year
Degrees: A, B, M   *Enroll:* 542
URL: http://www.kcu.edu
Phone: (606) 474-3000   *Calendar:* Sem. plan
Inst. Accred.: SACS (1984/1999)
Prog. Accred.: Nursing Education, Social Work

Kentucky Mountain Bible College
855 Kentucky Hwy. 541, Vancleve 41385
Type: Private, Kentucky Mountain Holiness Association,
  four-year
Degrees: A, B   *Enroll:* 62
URL: http://www.kmbc.edu
Phone: (606) 666-5000   *Calendar:* Sem. plan
Inst. Accred.: ABHE (1994/1999)

Kentucky State University
400 East Main St., Frankfort 40601
Type: Public, state, four-year
System: Kentucky Council on Postsecondary Education
Degrees: A, B, M   *Enroll:* 1,960
URL: http://www.kysu.edu
Phone: (502) 227-6000   *Calendar:* Sem. plan
Inst. Accred.: SACS (1939/1999)
Prog. Accred.: Business (ACBSP), Music, Nursing, Public
  Administration, Social Work, Teacher Education (NCATE)

Kentucky Wesleyan College
3000 Frederica St., PO Box 1039, Owensboro 42302
Type: Private, United Methodist Church, four-year
Degrees: A, B   *Enroll:* 588
URL: http://www.kwc.edu
Phone: (270) 926-3111   *Calendar:* Sem. plan
Inst. Accred.: SACS (1948/1998)

Lexington Theological Seminary
631 South Limestone St., Lexington 40508
Type: Private, Disciples of Christ, four-year
Degrees: M, D   *Enroll:* 77
URL: http://www.lextheo.edu
Phone: (859) 252-0361   *Calendar:* Sem. plan
Inst. Accred.: ATS (1938/1995), SACS (1984/1995)

Lindsey Wilson College
210 Lindsey Wilson St., Columbia 42728
Type: Private, Louisville Conference of the Methodist
  Church, four-year
Degrees: A, B, M   *Enroll:* 1,561
URL: http://www.lindsey.edu
Phone: (270) 384-2126   *Calendar:* Sem. plan
Inst. Accred.: SACS (1951/2003)
Prog. Accred.: Counseling

Louisville Presbyterian Theological Seminary
1044 Alta Vista Rd., Louisville 40205
Type: Private, Presbyterian Church (USA), four-year
Degrees: M, D   *Enroll:* 144
URL: http://www.lpts.edu
Phone: (502) 895-3411   *Calendar:* 4-1-4 plan
Inst. Accred.: ATS (1938/1999), SACS (1973/1999)
Prog. Accred.: Marriage and Family Therapy

Louisville Technical Institute
3901 Atkinson Dr., Louisville 40218-4528
Type: Private, proprietary, two-year
System: Sullivan Colleges System
Degrees: A   *Enroll:* 578
URL: http://www.louisvilletech.edu
Phone: (502) 456-6509   *Calendar:* Qtr. plan
Inst. Accred.: ACICS (2000/2004)

Madisonville Community College
2000 College Dr., Madisonville 42431
Type: Public, state, two-year
System: Madisonville Community and Technical College
District
Degrees: A   *Enroll:* 2,201
URL: http://www.madcc.kctcs.edu
Phone: (270) 821-2250   *Calendar:* Sem. plan
Inst. Accred.: SACS (1971/2001)
Prog. Accred.: Nursing, Physical Therapy Assisting

Health Campus
750 North Laffoon St., Madisonville 42431
Phone: (270) 824-7552
Prog. Accred: Occupational Therapy Assisting,
Radiography

Technical Campus
150 School Ave., Madisonville 42431
Phone: (270) 824-7544

Maysville Community and Technical College
1755 US 68, Maysville 41056
Type: Public, state, two-year
System: Maysville Community and Technical College
District
Degrees: A   *Enroll:* 1,159
URL: http://www.maycc.kctcs.edu
Phone: (606) 759-7141   *Calendar:* Sem. plan
Inst. Accred.: SACS (1971/2001)

Eastern Kentucky Campus
319 Webster Ave., Cynthiana 41031
Phone: (859) 234-8626

Rowan Campus
609 Viking Dr., Morehead 40351
Phone: (606) 783-1538
Prog. Accred: Respiratory Therapy Technology

Mid-Continent University
99 Powell Rd. East, Mayfield 42066
Type: Private, Baptist Church, four-year
Degrees: B   *Enroll:* 634
URL: http://www.midcontinent.edu
Phone: (270) 247-8521   *Calendar:* Sem. plan
Inst. Accred.: SACS (1987/2002)

Midway College
512 East Stephens St., Midway 40347-1120
Type: Private, Disciples of Christ Church, four-year
Degrees: A, B   *Enroll:* 913
URL: http://www.midway.edu
Phone: (859) 846-4421   *Calendar:* Sem. plan
Inst. Accred.: SACS (1949/2005)
Prog. Accred.: Nursing

Morehead State University
150 University Blvd., Morehead 40351-1689
Type: Public, state, four-year
System: Kentucky Council on Postsecondary Education
Degrees: A, B, M, P   *Enroll:* 7,897
URL: http://www.morehead-st.edu
Phone: (606) 783-2221   *Calendar:* Sem. plan
Inst. Accred.: SACS (1930/2000)
Prog. Accred.: Business (AACSB), Industrial Technology,
Music, Nursing, Nursing Education, Phlebotomy,
Radiography, Social Work, Teacher Education (NCATE),
Veterinary Technology

Murray State University
PO Box 9, Murray 42071
Type: Public, state, four-year
System: Kentucky Council on Postsecondary Education
Degrees: A, B, M, P   *Enroll:* 8,444
URL: http://www.murraystate.edu
Phone: (270) 762-3011   *Calendar:* Sem. plan
Inst. Accred.: SACS (1928/2004)
Prog. Accred.: Applied Science (occupational health and
safety), Art, Business (AACSB), Counseling, Engineering
(engineering physics/science), Engineering Technology
(civil/construction, manufacturing), Journalism, Music,
Nurse Anesthesia Education, Nursing, Social Work,
Speech-Language Pathology, Teacher Education
(NCATE), Veterinary Technology

National College of Business and Technology—Lexington Campus
628 East Main St., Lexington 40508
Type: Private, proprietary, two-year
Degrees: A   *Enroll:* 439
URL: http://www.ncbt.edu
Phone: (859) 253-0621   *Calendar:* Qtr. plan
Inst. Accred.: ACICS (1970/2002)
Prog. Accred.: Health Information Technician, Medical
Assisting (CAAHEP)

Cincinnati Campus
6871 Steger Dr., Cincinnati, OH 45237
Phone: (513) 761-1291

Danville Campus
115 East Lexington Ave., Danville 40422
Phone: (859) 236-6991

Dayton Area Campus
1837 Woodman Center Dr., Kettering, OH 45420
Phone: (937) 299-9450

Florence Campus
7627 Ewing Blvd., Florence 41042
Phone: (859) 525-6510
Prog. Accred: Medical Assisting (CAAHEP)

Indianapolis Campus
6060 Castleway West Dr., Indianapolis, IN 46250
Phone: (317) 578-7353

Knoxville Campus
8415 Kingston Pike, Knoxville, TN 37919
Phone: (865) 539-2011

Louisville Campus
4205 Dixie Hwy., Louisville 40216
Phone: (502) 447-7634
Prog. Accred: Health Information Technician, Medical
  Assisting (CAAHEP)

Nashville Campus
3748 Nolensville Pike, Nashville, TN 37211
Phone: (615) 333-3344
Prog. Accred: Medical Assisting (CAAHEP)

Pikeville Campus
288 South Mayo Trail, Ste. 2, Pikeville 41501
Phone: (606) 432-5477
Prog. Accred: Medical Assisting (CAAHEP)

Richmond Campus
139 South Killarney Ln., Richmond 40475
Phone: (859) 623-8956
Prog. Accred: Medical Assisting (CAAHEP)

Northern Kentucky University
Nunn Dr., Highland Heights 41099
Type: Public, state, four-year
System: Kentucky Council on Postsecondary Education
Degrees: A, B, M, D   *Enroll:* 11,324
URL: http://www.nku.edu
Phone: (859) 572-5220   *Calendar:* Sem. plan
Inst. Accred.: SACS (1973/1998)
Prog. Accred.: Business (AACSB), Construction Education,
  Engineering Technology (electrical, manufacturing),
  Law, Music, Nursing, Radiography, Respiratory Therapy,
  Social Work, Teacher Education (NCATE)

Owensboro Community and Technical College
4800 New Hartford Rd., Owensboro 42303
Type: Public, state/local, two-year
System: Owensboro Community and Technical College
  District
Degrees: A   *Enroll:* 1,947
URL: http://www.owensboro.kctcs.edu
Phone: (270) 686-4400   *Calendar:* Sem. plan
Inst. Accred.: SACS (2003)
Prog. Accred.: Nursing, Radiography

Daviess County Extension
1901 Southeastern Pkwy., Owensboro 42303-1677
Phone: (502) 687-7620

Frederica Street Campus
1501 Frederica St., Owensboro 42301
Phone: (270) 687-7255

Ohio County Technology Center
1406 S. Main St., Hartford 42347
Phone: (270) 274-9612

Paducah Technical College
509 South 30th St., Paducah 42002-4181
Type: Private, proprietary, two-year
Degrees: A   *Enroll:* 123
URL: http://www.ptc-ky.com
Phone: (270) 444-9676   *Calendar:* Sem. plan
Inst. Accred.: ACCSCT (1968/1999)

Lexington Electronics Institute
Clays Mill Shopping Center, 3340 Holwyn Rd.,
  Lexington 40503-9938
Phone: (606) 223-9608

Pikeville College
147 Sycamore St., Pikeville 41501
Type: Private, United Presbyterian Church, four-year
Degrees: A, B, D   *Enroll:* 987
URL: http://www.pc.edu
Phone: (606) 218-5250   *Calendar:* Sem. plan
Inst. Accred.: SACS (1931/2002)
Prog. Accred.: Clinical Lab Scientist, Osteopathy

Saint Catharine College
2735 Bardstown Rd., St. Catharine 40061
Type: Private, Roman Catholic Church, two-year
Degrees: A   *Enroll:* 553
URL: http://www.sccky.edu
Phone: (859) 336-5082   *Calendar:* Sem. plan
Inst. Accred.: SACS (1957/1998)

Somerset Community College
808 Monticello St., Somerset 42501
Type: Public, state, two-year
System: Somerset Community and Technical College
  District
Degrees: A   *Enroll:* 2,715
URL: http://www.somcc.kctcs.edu
Phone: (606) 679-8501   *Calendar:* Sem. plan
Inst. Accred.: SACS (1971/2001)
Prog. Accred.: Clinical Lab Technology, Nursing, Physical
  Therapy Assisting, Radiography

Laurel South Campus
235 South Laurel Rd., London 40744
Phone: (606) 864-7311

Southeast Kentucky Community and Technical College
700 College Rd., Cumberland 40823-1099
Type: Public, state, two-year
System: Southeast Kentucky Community and Technical College District
Degrees: A   *Enroll:* 2,748
URL: http://www.secc.kctcs.edu
Phone: (606) 589-2145   *Calendar:* Sem. plan
Inst. Accred.: SACS (1971/2001)
Prog. Accred.: Nursing, Respiratory Therapy, Respiratory Therapy Technology

Harlan Campus
164 Ballpark Rd., Harlan 40831
Phone: (606) 573-1506

Middlesboro Campus
1305 Chichester Ave., Middlesboro 40965-2265
Phone: (606) 242-2145

Pineville Campus
US 25E, PO Box 187, Pineville 40977
Phone: (606) 337-3106
Prog. Accred: Clinical Lab Technology, Radiography, Respiratory Therapy Technology

The Southern Baptist Theological Seminary
2825 Lexington Rd., Louisville 40280-2899
Type: Private, Southern Baptist Church, four-year
Degrees: A, B, M, D   *Enroll:* 2,337
URL: http://www.sbts.edu
Phone: (502) 897-4011   *Calendar:* Sem. plan
Inst. Accred.: ATS (1938/2002), SACS (1968/2003)
Prog. Accred.: Music

Spalding University
851 South Fourth St., Louisville 40203
Type: Private, Roman Catholic Church, four-year
Degrees: A, B, M, P, D   *Enroll:* 1,311
URL: http://www.spalding.edu
Phone: (502) 585-9911   *Calendar:* Sem. plan
Inst. Accred.: SACS (1938/1996)
Prog. Accred.: Clinical Psychology, Dietetics (internship), Montessori Teacher Education, Nursing, Nursing Education, Occupational Therapy, Social Work, Teacher Education (NCATE)

Spencerian College
4627 Dixie Hwy., Louisville 40216
Type: Private, independent, two-year
System: Sullivan Colleges System
Degrees: A   *Enroll:* 1,218
URL: http://www.spencerian.edu
Phone: (502) 447-1000   *Calendar:* Qtr. plan
Inst. Accred.: ACICS (1954/2004)
Prog. Accred.: Medical Assisting (ABHES), Medical Assisting (AMA), Radiography

Lexington Campus
2355 Harrodsburg Rd., Lexington 40504
Phone: (859) 223-9608

Sullivan University
3101 Bardstown Rd., Louisville 40205
Type: Private, proprietary, four-year
System: Sullivan Colleges System
Degrees: A, B, M   *Enroll:* 4,040
URL: http://www.sullivan.edu
Phone: (502) 456-6504   *Calendar:* Qtr. plan
Inst. Accred.: SACS (1979/2005)
Prog. Accred.: Culinary Education

Fort Knox Campus
PO Box 998, Fort Knox 40121-0998
Phone: (502) 942-8500

Lexington Campus
2355 Harrodsburg Rd., Lexington 40504
Phone: (859) 276-4357
Prog. Accred: Medical Assisting (CAAHEP)

Thomas More College
333 Thomas More Pkwy., Crestview Hills 41017-3495
Type: Private, Roman Catholic Church, four-year
Degrees: A, B, M   *Enroll:* 1,319
URL: http://www.thomasmore.edu
Phone: (859) 341-5800   *Calendar:* Sem. plan
Inst. Accred.: SACS (1959/2002, Warning)
Prog. Accred.: Nursing

Transylvania University
300 North Broadway, Lexington 40508-1797
Type: Private, Christian Church/Disciples of Christ, four-year
Degrees: B   *Enroll:* 1,127
URL: http://www.transy.edu
Phone: (859) 233-8300   *Calendar:* 4-1-4 plan
Inst. Accred.: SACS (1915/2002)
Prog. Accred.: Teacher Education (NCATE)

Union College
310 College St., Barbourville 40906
Type: Private, United Methodist Church, four-year
Degrees: A, B, M   *Enroll:* 737
URL: http://www.unionky.edu
Phone: (606) 546-4151   *Calendar:* Sem. plan
Inst. Accred.: SACS (1932/2005)

University of Kentucky

Lexington 40506
Type: Public, state, four-year
System: University of Kentucky
Degrees: A, B, M, P, D   *Enroll:* 22,525
URL: http://www.uky.edu
Phone: (859) 257-9000   *Calendar:* Sem. plan
Inst. Accred.: SACS (1915/2002)
Prog. Accred.: Accounting, Business (AACSB), Clinical Lab
  Scientist, Clinical Pastoral Education, Clinical
  Psychology, Counseling Psychology, Dentistry, Dietetics
  (coordinated), Dietetics (internship), Engineering
  (agricultural, chemical, civil, electrical, materials,
  mechanical, mining), Family and Consumer Science,
  Forestry, General Practice Residency, Health Services
  Administration, Interior Design, Journalism, Landscape
  Architecture, Law, Librarianship, Marriage and Family
  Therapy, Medicine, Music, Nursing, Nursing Education,
  Oral and Maxillofacial Surgery, Orthodontic and
  Dentofacial Orthopedics, Pediatric Dentistry,
  Periodontics, Pharmacy, Physical Therapy, Physician
  Assistant, Public Administration, Radiation Therapy,
  Rehabilitation Counseling, School Psychology, Social
  Work, Speech-Language Pathology, Teacher Education
  (NCATE)

University of Louisville

2301 South Third St., Louisville 40292-0001
Type: Public, state, four-year
System: Kentucky Council on Postsecondary Education
Degrees: A, B, M, P, D   *Enroll:* 16,637
URL: http://www.louisville.edu
Phone: (502) 852-5555   *Calendar:* Sem. plan
Inst. Accred.: SACS (1915/1997)
Prog. Accred.: Accounting, Advanced Education in
  General Dentistry, Audiology, Business (AACSB), Clinical
  Lab Scientist, Clinical Pastoral Education, Clinical
  Psychology, Combined Prosthodontics, Computer
  Science, Counseling Psychology, Cytotechnology, Dental
  Hygiene, Dentistry, Diagnostic Medical Sonography,
  Endodontics, Engineering (chemical, civil, computer,
  electrical, industrial, mechanical), General Dentistry,
  General Practice Residency, Interior Design, Law,
  Marriage and Family Therapy, Medicine, Music,
  Nursing, Nursing Education, Oral and Maxillofacial
  Surgery, Orthodontic and Dentofacial Orthopedics,
  Periodontics, Prosthodontics, Psychology Internship,
  Public Administration, Radiation Therapy, Radiography,
  Respiratory Therapy, Social Work, Speech-Language
  Pathology, Teacher Education (NCATE)

University of the Cumberlands

6191 College Station Dr., Williamsburg 40769
Type: Private, Kentucky Baptist (SBC), four-year
Degrees: A, B, M   *Enroll:* 1,502
URL: http://www.cumberlandcollege.edu
Phone: (606) 549-2200   *Calendar:* Sem. plan
Inst. Accred.: SACS (1964/1995)

West Kentucky Community and Technical College

4810 Alben Barkley Dr., PO Box 7380, Paducah 42002-7380
Type: Public, state, two-year
System: West Kentucky Community and Technical
  College District
Degrees: A   *Enroll:* 2,025
URL: http://www.westkentucky.kctcs.edu
Phone: (270) 554-9200   *Calendar:* Sem. plan
Inst. Accred.: SACS (1953/2001)
Prog. Accred.: Nursing, Physical Therapy Assisting,
  Radiography

Paducah Area Technology Center

2400 Adams St., Paducah 42001
Phone: (502) 443-6592

Western Kentucky University

One Big Red Way, Bowling Green 42101-3576
Type: Public, state, four-year
System: Kentucky Council on Postsecondary Education
Degrees: A, B, M, P   *Enroll:* 15,546
URL: http://www.wku.edu
Phone: (270) 745-0111   *Calendar:* Sem. plan
Inst. Accred.: SACS (1926/2005)
Prog. Accred.: Art, Business (AACSB), Computer Science,
  Dental Hygiene, Engineering Technology
  (civil/construction, electrical, mechanical), Health
  Information Technician, Industrial Technology,
  Journalism, Music, Nursing, Nursing Education, Public
  Health, Recreation and Leisure Services, Social Work,
  Speech-Language Pathology, Teacher Education
  (NCATE)

LOUISIANA

Baton Rouge Community College
5310 Florida Blvd., Baton Rouge 70806
Type: Public, state, two-year
System: Louisiana Community and Technical College
  System
Degrees: A
URL: http://www.brcc.cc.la.us
Phone: (225) 216-8700   *Calendar:* Sem. plan
Inst. Accred.: SACS (2004)

Baton Rouge School of Computers
10425 Plaza Americana, Baton Rouge 70816
Type: Private, proprietary, two-year
Degrees: A   *Enroll:* 111
URL: http://www.brsc.net
Phone: (225) 923-2525
Inst. Accred.: ACCSCT (1982/2002)

Blue Cliff College
3501 Severn Ave., Ste. 20, Metairie 70002
Type: Private, proprietary, two-year
Degrees: A
URL: http://www.bluecliffcollege.com
Phone: (504) 456-3141   *Calendar:* Qtr. plan
Inst. Accred.: ACCSCT (1998/2003)

Gulfport Campus
942 East Beach Blvd., Gulfport, MS 39507
Phone: (228) 896-9727

Lafayette Campus
100 Asma Blvd., Ste. 350, Lafayette 70508
Phone: (337) 269-0620

Shreveport Campus
200 North Thomas Dr., Ste. A, Shreveport 71107
Phone: (318) 425-7941

Bossier Parish Community College
2719 Airline Dr. at I-220, Bossier City 71111
Type: Public, state/local, two-year
System: Louisiana Community and Technical College
  System
Degrees: A   *Enroll:* 2,914
URL: http://www.bpcc.edu
Phone: (318) 746-9851   *Calendar:* Sem. plan
Inst. Accred.: SACS (1983/1998)
Prog. Accred.: Culinary Education, Phlebotomy, Physical
  Therapy Assisting, Respiratory Therapy, Respiratory
  Therapy Technology, Surgical Technology

Camelot College
2618 Wooddale Blvd., Ste. A, Baton Rouge 70805
Type: Private, proprietary, two-year
Degrees: A   *Enroll:* 317
URL: http://www.camelotcollege.com
Phone: (225) 928-3005
Inst. Accred.: ACICS (1991/2003)

Cameron College
2740 Canal St., New Orleans 70119
Type: Private, proprietary, two-year
Degrees: A   *Enroll:* 189
URL: http://www.cameroncollege.com
Phone: (504) 821-5881
Inst. Accred.: COE (1982/2002)

Career Technical College
2319 Louisville Ave., Monroe 71201
Type: Private, proprietary, two-year
Degrees: A
URL: http://www.careertc.com
Phone: (318) 323-2889
Inst. Accred.: COE (1989/2000)

Shreveport Campus
1227 Shreveport-Barksdale Hwy., Shreveport 71005-
2405
Phone: (877) 266-7250

Centenary College of Louisiana
PO Box 41188, Shreveport 71134-1188
Type: Private, United Methodist Church, four-year
Degrees: B, M   *Enroll:* 897
URL: http://www.centenary.edu
Phone: (318) 869-5011   *Calendar:* Sem. plan
Inst. Accred.: SACS (1925/1997)
Prog. Accred.: Music

Delgado Community College
501 City Park Ave., New Orleans 70119-4399
Type: Public, state/local, two-year
System: Louisiana Community and Technical College
  System
Degrees: A   *Enroll:* 10,439
URL: http://www.dcc.edu
Phone: (504) 483-4114   *Calendar:* Sem. plan
Inst. Accred.: SACS (1971/1996)
Prog. Accred.: Business (ACBSP), Clinical Lab Technology,
  Culinary Education, Engineering Technology (electrical),
  Funeral Service Education (Mortuary Science), Health
  Information Technician, Nuclear Medicine Technology,
  Nursing, Occupational Therapy Assisting, Phlebotomy,
  Physical Therapy Assisting, Radiation Therapy,
  Radiography, Respiratory Therapy, Respiratory Therapy
  Technology, Surgical Technology

West Bank Campus
2600 General Meyer Ave., New Orleans 70114-3095
Phone: (504) 361-6444

Delta College of Arts and Technology
7380 Exchange Place, Baton Rouge 70806-3851
Type: Private, proprietary, two-year
Degrees: A   *Enroll:* 411
URL: http://www.deltacollege.com
Phone: (225) 928-7770
Inst. Accred.: ACCSCT (1987/2002)

Delta School of Business and Technology
517 Broad St., Lake Charles 70601
Type: Private, proprietary, two-year
Degrees: A   *Enroll:* 464
Phone: (318) 439-5765
Inst. Accred.: ACICS (1976/2002)

Dillard University
2601 Gentilly Blvd., New Orleans 70122
Type: Private, United Methodist Church, four-year
Degrees: B   *Enroll:* 2,167
URL: http://www.dillard.edu
Phone: (504) 283-8822   *Calendar:* Sem. plan
Inst. Accred.: SACS (1938/1999)
Prog. Accred.: Nursing

Elaine P. Nunez Community College
3710 Paris Rd., Chalmette 70043
Type: Public, state, two-year
System: Louisiana Community and Technical College
  System
Degrees: A   *FTE Enroll:* 1,207
URL: http://www.nunez.edu
Phone: (504) 680-2240   *Calendar:* Sem. plan
Inst. Accred.: SACS (1992/1997)

New Orleans Campus
901 Delery St., New Orleans 70117
Phone: (504) 278-7440

Port Sulphur Campus
PO Drawer 944, Port Sulphur 70083
Phone: (504) 564-2701

Grambling State University
PO Drawer 607, Grambling 71245
Type: Public, state, four-year
System: University of Louisiana System
Degrees: A, B, M, P, D   *Enroll:* 4,348
URL: http://www.gram.edu
Phone: (318) 247-6117   *Calendar:* Sem. plan
Inst. Accred.: SACS (1949/2000, Probation)
Prog. Accred.: Business (AACSB), Computer Science,
  Engineering Technology (electrical, mechanical
  drafting/design), Journalism, Music, Nursing, Public
  Administration, Recreation and Leisure Services, Social
  Work, Teacher Education (NCATE), Theatre

Gretna Career College Training Institute
1415 Whitney Ave., Gretna 70053-5835
Type: Private, proprietary, two-year
Degrees: A
URL: http://gretnacareercollege.com
Phone: (504) 366-5409
Inst. Accred.: ACCSCT (1993/2003)

L.E. Fletcher Technical Community College
301 St. Charles St., PO Box 5033, Houma 70361-5033
Type: Public, state, two-year
System: Louisiana Community and Technical College
  System
Degrees: A   *Enroll:* 395
URL: http://www.lefletcher.edu
Phone: (985) 857-3655   *Calendar:* Sem. plan
Inst. Accred.: COE (1975/2001)

Louisiana College
1140 College Dr., Pineville 71359
Type: Private, Southern Baptist Church, four-year
Degrees: A, B   *Enroll:* 1,038
URL: http://www.lacollege.edu
Phone: (318) 487-7011   *Calendar:* Sem. plan
Inst. Accred.: SACS (1923/2001, Probation)
Prog. Accred.: Business (ACBSP), Nursing, Nursing
  Education, Social Work

Louisiana State University and Agricultural and Mechanical College
Baton Rouge 70803
Type: Public, state, four-year
System: Louisiana State University System
Degrees: B, M, P, D   *Enroll:* 29,426
URL: http://www.lsu.edu
Phone: (225) 578-3202   *Calendar:* Sem. plan
Inst. Accred.: SACS (1913/2004)
Prog. Accred.: Art, Audiology, Business (AACSB), Clinical
  Psychology, Construction Education, Counseling,
  Dietetics (internship), Engineering (bioengineering,
  chemical, civil, computer, electrical,
  environmental/sanitary, industrial, mechanical,
  petroleum), Family and Consumer Science, Forestry,
  Interior Design, Journalism, Landscape Architecture,
  Law, Librarianship, Music, School Psychology, Social
  Work, Speech-Language Pathology, Teacher Education
  (NCATE), Veterinary Medicine

Louisiana State University at Alexandria
8100 Hwy. 71 South, Alexandria 71302-9121
Type: Public, state, four-year
System: Louisiana State University System
Degrees: A, B   *Enroll:* 2,131
URL: http://www.lsua.edu
Phone: (318) 445-3672   *Calendar:* Sem. plan
Inst. Accred.: SACS (1960/2005)
Prog. Accred.: Clinical Lab Technology, Nursing

Louisiana State University at Eunice
PO Box 1129, Eunice 70535
Type: Public, state, two-year
System: Louisiana State University System
Degrees: A   *Enroll:* 2,339
URL: http://www.lsue.edu
Phone: (337) 457-7311   *Calendar:* Sem. plan
Inst. Accred.: SACS (1967/2004)
Prog. Accred.: Nursing, Radiography, Respiratory Therapy
  Technology

Louisiana State University Health Sciences Center in New Orleans
433 Bolivar St., New Orleans 70112-2223
Type: Public, state, four-year
System: Louisiana State University System
Degrees: A, B, M, D   *Enroll:* 2,699
URL: http://www.lsuhsc.edu
Phone: (504) 568-4808   *Calendar:* Sem. plan
Inst. Accred.: SACS (1931/2005)
Prog. Accred.: Advanced Education in General Dentistry, Audiology, Clinical Lab Scientist, Combined Prosthodontics, Dental Hygiene, Dental Laboratory Technology, Dentistry, Endodontics, General Dentistry, General Practice Residency, Maxillofacial Prosthetics, Medicine, Nursing, Nursing Education, Occupational Therapy, Ophthalmic Medical Technology, Oral and Maxillofacial Surgery, Orthodontic and Dentofacial Orthopedics, Pediatric Dentistry, Periodontics, Physical Therapy, Prosthodontics, Psychology Internship, Public Health, Rehabilitation Counseling, Respiratory Therapy, Speech-Language Pathology

Louisiana State University in Shreveport
One University Place, Shreveport 71115-2399
Type: Public, state, four-year
System: Louisiana State University System
Degrees: B, M, P   *Enroll:* 3,364
URL: http://www.lsus.edu
Phone: (318) 797-5000   *Calendar:* Sem. plan
Inst. Accred.: SACS (1975/2005)
Prog. Accred.: Business (AACSB), Computer Science, Medicine, Physical Therapy, Physician Assistant, Teacher Education (NCATE)

Health Sciences Center—Shreveport
1501 Kings Hwy., Shreveport 71130
Phone: (318) 675-5000
Prog. Accred: Occupational Therapy

Louisiana Tech University
PO Box 3168, Tech Station, Ruston 71272
Type: Public, state, four-year
System: University of Louisiana System
Degrees: A, B, M, P, D   *Enroll:* 10,201
URL: http://www.latech.edu
Phone: (318) 257-0211   *Calendar:* Qtr. plan
Inst. Accred.: SACS (1927/1995)
Prog. Accred.: Accounting, Art, Audiology, Business (AACSB), Computer Science, Dietetics (internship), Engineering (bioengineering, chemical, civil, electrical, industrial, mechanical), Engineering Technology (civil/construction, electrical), Family and Consumer Science, Forestry, Health Information Administration, Health Information Technician, Interior Design, Music, Nursing, Speech-Language Pathology, Teacher Education (NCATE)

Louisiana Technical College—Acadian Campus
1933 West Hutchinson Ave., Crowley 70526
Type: Public, state
System: Louisiana Technical College System
Degrees: A   *Enroll:* 190
URL: http://www.acadiancampus.net
Phone: (337) 788-7521   *Calendar:* Sem. plan
Inst. Accred.: COE (1976/2003)

Louisiana Technical College—Alexandria Campus
4311 South MacArthur Dr., PO Box 5698, Alexandria 71307-5698
Type: Public, state, two-year
System: Louisiana Technical College System
Degrees: A   *Enroll:* 174
URL: http://www.alexandriacampus.com
Phone: (318) 487-5439   *Calendar:* Sem. plan
Inst. Accred.: COE (1976/2003)

Louisiana Technical College—Ascension Campus
9697 Airline Hwy., Sorrento 70778-3007
Type: Public, state, two-year
System: Louisiana Technical College System
Degrees: A   *Enroll:* 153
URL: http://www.ascensioncampus.edu
Phone: (225) 675-5398   *Calendar:* Sem. plan
Inst. Accred.: COE (1982/2004)

Louisiana Technical College—Avoyelles Campus
508 Choupique St., PO Box 307, Cottonport 71327
Type: Public, state, two-year
System: Louisiana Technical College System
Degrees: A   *Enroll:* 322
URL: http://www.avoyellescampus.com
Phone: (318) 876-2401   *Calendar:* Sem. plan
Inst. Accred.: COE (1979/2003)

Hessmer Extension Center
4137 East School St., Hessmer 71341
Phone: (318) 563-8685

Louisiana Technical College—Bastrop Campus
729 Kammell St., PO Box 1120, Bastrop 71221-1120
Type: Public, state, two-year
System: Louisiana Technical College System
Degrees: A   *Enroll:* 240
URL: http://www.ltc.edu/bastrop
Phone: (318) 283-0836   *Calendar:* Sem. plan
Inst. Accred.: COE (1981/2000)

Louisiana Technical College—Baton Rouge Campus
3250 North Acadian Thruway, Baton Rouge 70805
Type: Public, state, two-year
System: Louisiana Technical College System
Degrees: A   *Enroll:* 755
URL: http://www.brti.tec.la.us
Phone: (225) 359-9204   *Calendar:* Sem. plan
Inst. Accred.: COE (1973/2003)
Prog. Accred.: Culinary Education

J.M. Frazier Campus
555 Julia St., Baton Rouge 70802
Phone: (225) 342-5850

Louisiana Technical College—Charles B. Coreil Campus
1124 Vocational Dr., Ward 1, Industrial Park, Ville Platte 70586-0296
Type: Public, state, two-year
System: Louisiana Technical College System
Degrees: A   *Enroll:* 166
URL: http://www.cbcoreilcampus.net
Phone: (318) 363-2197   *Calendar:* Qtr. plan
Inst. Accred.: COE (1981/2004)

Louisiana Technical College—Delta-Ouachita Campus
609 Vocational Pkwy., West Ouachita Industrial Park, West Monroe 71292-9064
Type: Public, state, two-year
System: Louisiana Technical College System
Degrees: A   *Enroll:* 383
URL: http://www.delta.tec.la.us
Phone: (318) 397-6100   *Calendar:* Qtr. plan
Inst. Accred.: COE (1976/2003)

Louisiana Technical College—Evangeline Campus
600 South Martin Luther King, Jr. Dr., PO Box 68, St. Martinville 70582
Type: Public, state, two-year
System: Louisiana Technical College System
Degrees: A   *Enroll:* 154
URL: http://www.ltc.edu/evangeline
Phone: (318) 394-6466   *Calendar:* Sem. plan
Inst. Accred.: COE (1974/2000)

St. Martindale Campus
Main and Martin St., St. Martinsville 70517
Phone: (337) 394-6466

Louisiana Technical College—Florida Parishes Campus
137 College St., PO Box 1300, Greensburg 70441
Type: Public, state, two-year
System: Louisiana Technical College System
Degrees: A   *Enroll:* 203
URL: http://www.floridaparishescampus.com
Phone: (225) 222-4251   *Calendar:* Qtr. plan
Inst. Accred.: COE (1977/2003)

Louisiana Technical College—Folkes Campus
3337 Hwy. 10, PO Box 808, Jackson 70748
Type: Public, state, two-year
System: Louisiana Technical College System
Degrees: A   *Enroll:* 126
URL: http://www.ltc.edu/folkes
Phone: (225) 634-2636   *Calendar:* Qtr. plan
Inst. Accred.: COE (1981/2005)

Jackson Center
Dixon Correctional Facility, PO Box 788, 5568 Hwy. 68, Jackson 70748
Phone: (504) 342-6661

Louisiana Technical College—Gulf Area Campus
1115 Clover St., PO Box 878, Abbeville 70511-0878
Type: Public, state, two-year
System: Louisiana Technical College System
Degrees: A   *Enroll:* 269
URL: http://www.gulfareacampus.net
Phone: (337) 893-4984
Inst. Accred.: COE (1975/2002)

Louisiana Technical College—Hammond Area Campus
111 Pride Ave., PO Box 489, Hammond 70404-0489
Type: Public, state, two-year
System: Louisiana Technical College System
Degrees: A   *Enroll:* 182
URL: http://www.ltc.edu/hammond
Phone: (985) 543-4120   *Calendar:* Sem. plan
Inst. Accred.: COE (1975/2002)

Louisiana Technical College—Huey P. Long Campus
303 South Jones St., Winnfield 71483
Type: Public, state
System: Louisiana Technical College System
Degrees: A   *Enroll:* 196
URL: http://www.theltc.net/hueyplong
Phone: (318) 628-3815   *Calendar:* Sem. plan
Inst. Accred.: COE (1977/1999)

Rod Brady Campus
521 East Bradford Sreet, Jena 71342
Phone: (318) 992-2910

Louisiana Technical College—Jefferson Campus
5200 Blair Dr., Metairie 70001
Type: Public, state, two-year
System: Louisiana Technical College System
Degrees: A   *Enroll:* 117
URL: http://www.jeffersoncampus.com
Phone: (504) 736-7020   *Calendar:* Qtr. plan
Inst. Accred.: COE (1975/2000)

Louisiana Technical College—Jumonville Memorial Campus
605 Hospital Rd., New Roads 70760-2628
Type: Public, state, two-year
System: Louisiana Technical College System
Degrees: A   *Enroll:* 197
URL: http://www.ltc.edu/jumonville
Phone: (225) 638-8613   *Calendar:* Sem. plan
Inst. Accred.: COE (1976/2003)

Angola Correctional Facility
Loiusiana State Penitentiary, General Delivery, Angola 70712
Phone: (504) 655-4411

Hunt Correctional Center
Hunt Correctional Center, PO Box 40, St. Gabriel 70776
Phone: (504) 642-3306

Louisiana Correctional Center
Louisiana Correctional Inst. for Women, PO Box 40, St. Gabriel 70776
Phone: (504) 642-5529

Louisiana Technical College—Lafayette Campus
1101 Bertrand Dr., PO Box 4909, Lafayette 70506
Type: Public, state, two-year
System: Louisiana Technical College System
Degrees: A   *Enroll:* 756
URL: http://www.lafayettecampus.net
Phone: (337) 262-5962   *Calendar:* Sem. plan
Inst. Accred.: COE (1981/2003)
Prog. Accred.: Clinical Lab Technology, Culinary Education, Surgical Technology

Louisiana Technical College—LaFourche Campus
1425 Tiger Dr., PO Box 1831, Thibodaux 70302-1831
Type: Public, state, two-year
System: Louisiana Technical College System
Degrees: A   *Enroll:* 206
URL: http://www.ltc.edu/lafourche
Phone: (985) 447-0924   *Calendar:* Sem. plan
Inst. Accred.: COE (1988/2005)

Louisiana Technical College—Lamar Salter Campus
15014 Lake Charles Hwy., Leesville 71446
Type: Public, state, two-year
System: Louisiana Technical College System
Degrees: A   *Enroll:* 328
URL: http://www.ltc.edu/lamarsalter
Phone: (337) 537-3135   *Calendar:* Qtr. plan
Inst. Accred.: COE (1983/1999)

Louisiana Technical College—Mansfield Campus
943 Oxford Rd., PO Box 1236, Mansfield 71052
Type: Public, state, two-year
System: Louisiana Technical College System
Degrees: A   *Enroll:* 112
URL: http://www.ltc.edu/mansfield
Phone: (318) 872-2243   *Calendar:* Sem. plan
Inst. Accred.: COE (1993/2005)

Coushatta Center
PO Box 1236, Mansfield 71052
Phone: (337) 932-7014

Louisiana Technical College—Morgan Smith Campus
1230 North Main St., PO Box 1327, Jennings 70546-1327
Type: Public, state, two-year
System: Louisiana Technical College System
Degrees: A   *Enroll:* 88
URL: http://www.ltc.edu/morgansmith
Phone: (337) 824-4811   *Calendar:* Sem. plan
Inst. Accred.: COE (1976/2003)

Louisiana Technical College—Natchitoches Campus
6587 Hwy. 1 Bypass, PO Box 657, Natchitoches 71458-0657
Type: Public, state, two-year
System: Louisiana Technical College System
Degrees: A   *Enroll:* 301
URL: http://www.ltc.edu/natchitoches
Phone: (318) 357-3162   *Calendar:* Sem. plan
Inst. Accred.: COE (1982/2004)

David Wade Facility
670 Bell Hill Rd., Homer 71040
Phone: (518) 927-9631

Louisiana Technical College—North Central Campus
605 West Boundary, PO Box 548, Farmerville 71241-0548
Type: Public, state, two-year
System: Louisiana Technical College System
Degrees: A   *Enroll:* 93
URL: http://www.ltc.edu/northcentral
Phone: (318) 368-3179   *Calendar:* Sem. plan
Inst. Accred.: COE (1979/2005)

Louisiana Technical College—Northeast Louisiana Campus
1710 Warren St., Winnsboro 71295
Type: Public, state, two-year
System: Louisiana Technical College System
Degrees: A   *Enroll:* 178
URL: http://www.ltcnortheast.com
Phone: (318) 435-2163   *Calendar:* Sem. plan
Inst. Accred.: COE (1976/2004)

Louisiana Technical College— Northwest Louisiana Campus

814 Constable St., PO Box 835, Minden 71058-0835
Type: Public, state, two-year
System: Louisiana Technical College System
Degrees: A   *Enroll:* 572
URL: http://www.ltc.edu/northwest
Phone: (318) 371-3035   *Calendar:* Qtr. plan
Inst. Accred.: COE (1975/2001)

Homer Campus

3001 Minden Rd., PO Box 509, Homer 71040-0509
Phone: (318) 927-2034

Springhill Campus

102 1st St., NE, Springhill 71075
Phone: (518) 371-3035

Louisiana Technical College—Oakdale Campus

117 Hwy. 1152, PO Drawer EM, Oakdale 71463
Type: Public, state, two-year
System: Louisiana Technical College System
Degrees: A   *Enroll:* 242
URL: http://www.ltc.edu/oakdale
Phone: (318) 335-3944   *Calendar:* Qtr. plan
Inst. Accred.: COE (1983/2003)

Louisiana Technical College—River Parishes Campus

181 Regala Park Rd., PO Drawer AQ, Reserve 70084
Type: Public, state, two-year
System: Louisiana Technical College System
Degrees: A   *Enroll:* 263
URL: http://www.ltc.edu/riverparishes
Phone: (985) 536-4418   *Calendar:* Qtr. plan
Inst. Accred.: COE (1984/2001)

Louisiana Technical College—Ruston Campus

1010 James St., PO Box 1070, Ruston 71270-1070
Type: Public, state, two-year
System: Louisiana Technical College System
Degrees: A
URL: http://www.ltc.edu/ruston
Phone: (318) 251-4145   *Calendar:* Sem. plan
Inst. Accred.: COE (1982/2000)
Prog. Accred.: Counseling Psychology

Louisiana Technical College—Sabine Valley Campus

1255 Fisher Rd., PO Box 790, Many 71449
Type: Public, state, two-year
System: Louisiana Technical College System
Degrees: A   *Enroll:* 121
URL: http://www.sabinevalleycampus.com
Phone: (318) 256-4101   *Calendar:* Sem. plan
Inst. Accred.: COE (1977/2005)

Louisiana Technical College— Shelby M. Jackson Campus

2100 E.E. Wallace Blvd., PO Box 1465, Ferriday 71334
Type: Public, state, two-year
System: Louisiana Technical College System
Degrees: A   *Enroll:* 146
URL: http://www.ltc.edu/smjackson
Phone: (318) 757-6501   *Calendar:* Qtr. plan
Inst. Accred.: COE (1980/2001)

Louisiana Technical College—Shreveport-Bossier Campus

2010 North Market St., PO Box 78527, Shreveport 71137-8527
Type: Public, state
System: Louisiana Technical College System
Degrees: A   *Enroll:* 690
URL: http://www.shreveportcampus.com
Phone: (318) 676-7811   *Calendar:* Sem. plan
Inst. Accred.: COE (1976/2003)
Prog. Accred.: Culinary Education

Louisiana Technical College—Sidney N. Collier Campus

3727 Louisa St., New Orleans 70126
Type: Public, state, two-year
System: Louisiana Technical College System
Degrees: A   *Enroll:* 330
URL: http://www.sidneyncolliercampus.com
Phone: (504) 942-8333   *Calendar:* Sem. plan
Inst. Accred.: COE (1977/2005)

Louisiana Technical College—Slidell Campus

1000 Canulette Rd., PO Box 827, Slidell 70459-0827
Type: Public, state, two-year
System: Louisiana Technical College System
Degrees: A   *Enroll:* 209
URL: http://www.slidellcampus.com
Phone: (985) 646-6430
Inst. Accred.: COE (1974/2000)
Prog. Accred.: Culinary Education

Louisiana Technical College—Sullivan Campus

1710 Sullivan Dr., Bogalusa 70427
Type: Public, state, two-year
System: Louisiana Technical College System
Degrees: A   *Enroll:* 561
URL: http://www.ltc.edu/sullivan
Phone: (985) 732-6640   *Calendar:* Sem. plan
Inst. Accred.: COE (1970/1999)

Louisiana Technical College—T.H. Harris Campus

322 East South St., Opelousas 70570-6114
Type: Public, state, two-year
System: Louisiana Technical College System
Degrees: A   *Enroll:* 520
URL: http://www.ltc.edu/thharris
Phone: (337) 948-0239   *Calendar:* Qtr. plan
Inst. Accred.: COE (1970/2002)

Louisiana Technical College—Tallulah Campus
Old Hwy. 65 South, PO Box 1740, Tallulah 71284-1740
Type: Public, state, two-year
System: Louisiana Technical College System
Degrees: A
URL: http://www.ltc.edu/tallulah
Phone: (318) 574-4820   *Calendar:* Sem. plan
Inst. Accred.: COE (1980/2001)

Margaret Surles Center
Highway 883-1, PO Box 368, Lake Providence 71254
Phone: (318) 559-0239

Louisiana Technical College—Teche Area Campus
609 Ember Dr., PO Box 11057, New Iberia 70562-1057
Type: Public, state, two-year
System: Louisiana Technical College System
Degrees: A   *Enroll:* 380
URL: http://www.techeareacampus.net
Phone: (337) 373-0011   *Calendar:* Sem. plan
Inst. Accred.: COE (1976/2003)

Louisiana Technical College—West Jefferson Campus
475 Manhattan Blvd., Harvey 70058
Type: Public, state, two-year
System: Louisiana Technical College System
Degrees: A   *Enroll:* 242
URL: http://www.westjeffcampus.com
Phone: (504) 361-6464   *Calendar:* Sem. plan
Inst. Accred.: COE (1982/1999)
Prog. Accred.: Respiratory Therapy Technology

Louisiana Technical College—Westside Campus
59125 Bayou Rd., PO Box 733, Plaquemine 70765-0733
Type: Public, state
System: Louisiana Technical College System
Degrees: C
URL: http://www.ltc.edu/westside
Phone: (225) 342-8228   *Calendar:* Sem. plan
Inst. Accred.: COE (1974/2005)

Louisiana Technical College—Young Memorial Campus
900 Youngs Rd., PO Box 2148, Morgan City 70381
Type: Public, state, two-year
System: Louisiana Technical College System
Degrees: A
URL: http://www.ltc.edu/youngmemorial
Phone: (985) 380-2436   *Calendar:* Qtr. plan
Inst. Accred.: COE (1976/2003)

Franklin Campus
1401 A Cynthia St., Franklin 70538
Phone: (337) 828-1448

Loyola University New Orleans
6363 St. Charles Ave., New Orleans 70118
Type: Private, Roman Catholic Church, four-year
Degrees: B, M, D   *Enroll:* 4,675
URL: http://www.loyno.edu
Phone: (504) 865-2011   *Calendar:* Sem. plan
Inst. Accred.: SACS (1929/1995)
Prog. Accred.: Accounting, Business (AACSB), Counseling, Law, Music, Nursing

McNeese State University
4100 Ryan St., Lake Charles 70609
Type: Public, state, four-year
System: University of Louisiana System
Degrees: A, B, M, P   *Enroll:* 7,171
URL: http://www.mcneese.edu
Phone: (337) 475-5000   *Calendar:* Sem. plan
Inst. Accred.: SACS (1954/1996)
Prog. Accred.: Business (AACSB), Clinical Lab Scientist, Computer Science, Dietetics (internship), Engineering (general), Engineering Technology (electrical, instrumentation, process/piping design), Family and Consumer Science, Journalism, Music, Nursing, Radiography, Teacher Education (NCATE)

New Orleans Baptist Theological Seminary
3939 Gentilly Blvd., New Orleans 70126-4858
Type: Private, Southern Baptist Church, four-year
Degrees: A, B, M, D   *Enroll:* 1,878
URL: http://www.nobts.edu
Phone: (504) 282-4455   *Calendar:* Sem. plan
Inst. Accred.: ATS (1954/1996), SACS (1965/1996)
Prog. Accred.: Music

Nicholls State University
Thibodaux 70310
Type: Public, state, four-year
System: University of Louisiana System
Degrees: A, B, M, P   *Enroll:* 6,145
URL: http://www.nicholls.edu
Phone: (985) 446-8111   *Calendar:* Sem. plan
Inst. Accred.: SACS (1964/1995)
Prog. Accred.: Accounting, Art, Business (AACSB), Computer Science, Cytotechnology, EMT (Paramedic), Family and Consumer Science, Journalism, Music, Nursing, Nursing Education, Respiratory Therapy, Respiratory Therapy Technology, Teacher Education (NCATE)

Northwestern State University
College Ave., Natchitoches 71497
Type: Public, state, four-year
System: University of Louisiana System
Degrees: A, B, M, P, D   *Enroll:* 8,523
URL: http://www.nsula.edu
Phone: (318) 357-6361   *Calendar:* Sem. plan
Inst. Accred.: SACS (1941/1996)
Prog. Accred.: Art, Business (AACSB), Counseling,
Engineering Technology (electrical, industrial), Family
and Consumer Science, Industrial Technology,
Journalism, Music, Nursing, Nursing Education,
Radiography, Social Work, Teacher Education (NCATE),
Theatre, Veterinary Technology

College of Nursing at Shreveport
1800 Line Ave., Shreveport 71101
Phone: (318) 677-3100
Prog. Accred: Radiography

Notre Dame Seminary
2901 South Carrollton Ave., New Orleans 70118-4391
Type: Private, Roman Catholic Church, four-year
Degrees: M   *Enroll:* 125
URL: http://www.notredameseminary.edu
Phone: (504) 866-7426   *Calendar:* Sem. plan
Inst. Accred.: ATS (1979/1995), SACS (1951/1996)

Our Lady of Holy Cross College
4123 Woodland Dr., New Orleans 70131-7399
Type: Private, Roman Catholic Church, four-year
Degrees: A, B, M   *Enroll:* 1,094
URL: http://www.olhcc.edu
Phone: (504) 394-7744   *Calendar:* Sem. plan
Inst. Accred.: SACS (1972/1996)
Prog. Accred.: Counseling, Nursing, Radiography,
Respiratory Therapy, Respiratory Therapy Technology

Our Lady of the Lake College
7434 Perkins Rd., Baton Rouge 70808-4380
Type: Private, Roman Catholic Church, four-year
Degrees: A, B, M   *Enroll:* 1,065
URL: http://www.ololcollege.edu
Phone: (225) 768-1700   *Calendar:* Sem. plan
Inst. Accred.: SACS (1994/1999)
Prog. Accred.: Clinical Lab Scientist, Clinical Lab
Technology, Nursing, Physical Therapy Assisting,
Radiography, Surgical Technology

Remington College—Lafayette
303 Rue Louis XIV, Lafayette 70508
Type: Private, proprietary, two-year
System: Education America, Inc.
Degrees: A   *Enroll:* 452
URL: http://www.remingtoncollege.edu
Phone: (337) 981-4010   *Calendar:* Qtr. plan
Inst. Accred.: ACICS (1988/2001)

Baton Rouge Campus
1900 North Lobdell Ave., Baton Rouge 70806-1725
Phone: (225) 922-3990

Remington College—New Orleans
321 Veterans Blvd., Metairie 70005
Type: Private, proprietary, two-year
System: Education America, Inc.
Degrees: A   *Enroll:* 405
URL: http://www.remingtoncollege.edu
Phone: (504) 831-8889   *Calendar:* Qtr. plan
Inst. Accred.: ACCSCT (1976/2003)

River Parishes Community College
9697 Airline Hwy., PO Box 310, Sorrento 70778
Type: Public, state, two-year
System: Louisiana Community and Technical College
System
Degrees: A
URL: http://rpcc.cc.la.us
Phone: (225) 675-8270   *Calendar:* Sem. plan
Inst. Accred.: SACS (2004)

Saint Joseph Seminary College
75376 River Rd., St. Benedict 70457-9990
Type: Private, Roman Catholic Church, four-year
Degrees: B   *Enroll:* 112
URL: http://www.stjosephabbey.org
Phone: (985) 892-1800   *Calendar:* Sem. plan
Inst. Accred.: SACS (1956/2003)

Southeastern Louisiana University
SLU 10784, Hammond 70402-0001
Type: Public, state, four-year
System: University of Louisiana System
Degrees: A, B, M, P   *Enroll:* 13,382
URL: http://www.selu.edu
Phone: (985) 549-2000   *Calendar:* Sem. plan
Inst. Accred.: SACS (1946/2005)
Prog. Accred.: Accounting, Business (AACSB), Computer
Science, Counseling, Industrial Technology, Music,
Nursing, Social Work, Speech-Language Pathology,
Teacher Education (NCATE)

Southern University and Agricultural and Mechanical College at Baton Rouge
PO Box 9374, Baton Rouge 70813
Type: Public, state, four-year
System: Southern University System
Degrees: A, B, M, P, D   *Enroll:* 8,033
URL: http://www.subr.edu
Phone: (225) 771-4500   *Calendar:* Sem. plan
Inst. Accred.: SACS (1938/2000)
Prog. Accred.: Business (AACSB), Computer Science,
Dietetics (internship), Engineering (civil, electrical,
mechanical), Engineering Technology (electrical), Family
and Consumer Science, Journalism, Law (ABA only),
Music, Nursing, Nursing Education, Public
Administration, Rehabilitation Counseling, Social Work,
Speech-Language Pathology, Teacher Education
(NCATE)

Southern University at New Orleans
6400 Press Dr., New Orleans 70126
Type: Public, state, four-year
System: Southern University System
Degrees: A, B, M   *Enroll:* 2,869
URL: http://www.suno.edu
Phone: (504) 286-5000   *Calendar:* Sem. plan
Inst. Accred.: SACS (1970/2000)
Prog. Accred.: Social Work

Southern University at Shreveport
3050 Martin Luther King, Jr. Dr., Shreveport 71107
Type: Public, state, two-year
System: Southern University System
Degrees: A   *Enroll:* 1,799
URL: http://www.susla.edu
Phone: (318) 674-3300   *Calendar:* Sem. plan
Inst. Accred.: SACS (1975/2000)
Prog. Accred.: Clinical Lab Technology, Dental Hygiene,
   Health Information Technician, Radiography, Respiratory
   Therapy, Surgical Technology

Southwest University
2200 Veterans Blvd., Kenner 70062
Type: Private, independent, four-year
Degrees: A, B, M
URL: http://www.southwest.edu
Phone: (504) 468-2900
Inst. Accred.: DETC (2004)

Sowela Technical Community College
3820 Bennet Johnston Ave., PO Box 16950, Lake
Charles 70615
Type: Public, state, two-year
System: Louisiana Community and Technical College
   System
Degrees: A   *Enroll:* 1,203
URL: http://www.sowela.edu
Phone: (337) 491-2688   *Calendar:* Sem. plan
Inst. Accred.: COE (1971/2004)

Tulane University
6823 St. Charles Ave., New Orleans 70118
Type: Private, independent, four-year
Degrees: B, M, D   *Enroll:* 10,935
URL: http://www.tulane.edu
Phone: (504) 865-5000   *Calendar:* Sem. plan
Inst. Accred.: SACS (1903/2001)
Prog. Accred.: Applied Science (industrial hygiene),
   Business (AACSB), Computer Science, Dietetics
   (internship), Engineering (bioengineering, chemical,
   civil, electrical, environmental/sanitary, mechanical),
   Health Services Administration, Law, Medicine,
   Psychology Internship, Public Health, School
   Psychology, Social Work

The University of Louisiana at Lafayette
PO Drawer 41008, Lafayette 70504
Type: Public, state, four-year
System: University of Louisiana System
Degrees: A, B, M, D   *Enroll:* 14,172
URL: http://www.louisiana.edu
Phone: (337) 482-1000   *Calendar:* Sem. plan
Inst. Accred.: SACS (1925/2000)
Prog. Accred.: Art, Business (AACSB), Computer Science,
   Dietetics (internship), EMT (Paramedic), Engineering
   (chemical, civil, electrical, mechanical, petroleum),
   Family and Consumer Science, Health Information
   Administration, Industrial Technology, Interior Design,
   Journalism, Music, Nursing, Speech-Language
   Pathology, Teacher Education (NCATE)

The University of Louisiana at Monroe
700 University Ave., Monroe 71209
Type: Public, state, four-year
System: University of Louisiana System
Degrees: A, B, M, P, D   *Enroll:* 7,400
URL: http://www.ulm.edu
Phone: (318) 342-1000   *Calendar:* Sem. plan
Inst. Accred.: SACS (1955/1999)
Prog. Accred.: Accounting, Business (AACSB), Computer
   Science, Construction Education, Counseling, Dental
   Hygiene, Family and Consumer Science, Journalism,
   Marriage and Family Therapy, Music, Nursing, Nursing
   Education, Occupational Therapy, Occupational Therapy
   Assisting, Pharmacy, Radiography, Social Work, Speech-
   Language Pathology, Teacher Education (NCATE)

University of New Orleans
Lakefront, 2000 Lakeshore Dr., New Orleans 70148
Type: Public, state, four-year
System: Louisiana State University System
Degrees: A, B, M, D   *Enroll:* 13,586
URL: http://www.uno.edu
Phone: (504) 280-6000   *Calendar:* Sem. plan
Inst. Accred.: SACS (1958/2005)
Prog. Accred.: Accounting, Art, Business (AACSB),
   Computer Science, Counseling, Engineering (civil,
   electrical, mechanical, naval architecture/marine),
   Music, Planning, Teacher Education (NCATE), Theatre

Xavier University of Louisiana
1 Drexel Dr., New Orleans 70125-1098
Type: Private, Roman Catholic Church, four-year
Degrees: B, M, P, D   *Enroll:* 3,767
URL: http://www.xula.edu
Phone: (504) 486-7411   *Calendar:* Sem. plan
Inst. Accred.: SACS (1938/2000)
Prog. Accred.: Business (ACBSP), Music, Nurse
   Anesthesia Education, Pharmacy, Teacher Education
   (NCATE)

MAINE

Andover College
901 Washington Ave., Portland 04103-2791
Type: Private, proprietary, two-year
System: Kaplan Higher Education Corporation
Degrees: A   *Enroll:* 556
URL: http://www.andovercollege.edu
Phone: (207) 774-6126   *Calendar:* Sem. plan
Inst. Accred.: NEASC-CTCI (1998)

Lewiston Campus
475 Lisbon St., Lewiston 04240
Phone: (207) 333-3300

Bangor Theological Seminary
300 Union St., Bangor 04401
Type: Private, United Church of Christ, four-year
Degrees: M, D   *Enroll:* 72
URL: http://www.bts.edu
Phone: (207) 942-6781   *Calendar:* Sem. plan
Inst. Accred.: ATS (1974/1998), NEASC-CIHE (1968/1998)

Portland Campus
159 State St., Portland 04102
Phone: (207) 774-5212

Bates College
2 Andrews Rd., Lewiston 04240-6047
Type: Private, independent, four-year
Degrees: B   *Enroll:* 1,746
URL: http://www.bates.edu
Phone: (207) 786-6255   *Calendar:* Sem. plan
Inst. Accred.: NEASC-CIHE (1929/2000)

Beal College
99 Farm Rd., Bangor 04401
Type: Private, independent, two-year
Degrees: A   *Enroll:* 272
URL: http://www.bealcollege.edu
Phone: (207) 947-4591
Inst. Accred.: ACICS (1966/2001)
Prog. Accred.: Medical Assisting (CAAHEP)

Bowdoin College
5700 College Station, Brunswick 04011-8448
Type: Private, independent, four-year
Degrees: B   *Enroll:* 1,643
URL: http://www.bowdoin.edu
Phone: (207) 725-3000   *Calendar:* Sem. plan
Inst. Accred.: NEASC-CIHE (1929/1996)

Central Maine Community College
1250 Turner St., Auburn 04210-6498
Type: Public, state, two-year
System: Maine Community College System
Degrees: A   *Enroll:* 1,192
URL: http://www.cmcc.edu
Phone: (207) 755-5100   *Calendar:* Sem. plan
Inst. Accred.: NEASC-CIHE (2003)
Prog. Accred.: Applied Science (occupational health and
   safety), Business (ACBSP), Clinical Lab Technology,
   Engineering Technology (civil/construction), Nursing

Central Maine Medical Center School of Nursing
70 Middle St., Lewiston 04240
Type: Private, independent, two-year
Degrees: A   *Enroll:* 67
URL: http://www.cmmcson.edu
Phone: (207) 795-2840   *Calendar:* Sem. plan
Inst. Accred.: NEASC-CTCI (1978/2000)
Prog. Accred.: Nursing

Colby College
4000 Mayflower Hill, Waterville 04901-8840
Type: Private, independent, four-year
Degrees: B   *Enroll:* 1,768
URL: http://www.colby.edu
Phone: (207) 872-3000   *Calendar:* 4-1-4 plan
Inst. Accred.: NEASC-CIHE (1929/1997)

College of the Atlantic
105 Eden St., Bar Harbor 04609-1198
Type: Private, independent, four-year
Degrees: B, M   *Enroll:* 283
URL: http://www.coa.edu
Phone: (207) 288-5015   *Calendar:* Tri. plan
Inst. Accred.: NEASC-CIHE (1976/1997)

Eastern Maine Community College
354 Hogan Rd., Bangor 04401-4280
Type: Public, state, two-year
System: Maine Community College System
Degrees: A   *Enroll:* 1,317
URL: http://www.emcc.org
Phone: (207) 941-4600   *Calendar:* Sem. plan
Inst. Accred.: NEASC-CIHE (2004)
Prog. Accred.: Nursing, Radiography

Husson College
One College Circle, Bangor 04401-2999
Type: Private, independent, four-year
Degrees: A, B, M   *Enroll:* 1,527
URL: http://www.husson.edu
Phone: (207) 941-7000   *Calendar:* Sem. plan
Inst. Accred.: NEASC-CIHE (1974/2003)
Prog. Accred.: Medical Assisting (AMA), Nursing, Nursing
   Education, Occupational Therapy, Physical Therapy

Kennebec Valley Community College
92 Western Ave., Fairfield 04937-1367
Type: Public, state, two-year
System: Maine Community College System
Degrees: A   *Enroll:* 975
URL: http://www.kvcc.me.edu
Phone: (207) 453-5000   *Calendar:* Sem. plan
Inst. Accred.: NEASC-CIHE (2003)
Prog. Accred.: Business (ACBSP), Health Information
  Technician, Medical Assisting (AMA), Nursing,
  Occupational Therapy Assisting, Physical Therapy
  Assisting, Respiratory Therapy

Maine College of Art
97 Spring St., Portland 04101-3987
Type: Private, independent, four-year
Degrees: B, M   *Enroll:* 450
URL: http://www.meca.edu
Phone: (207) 775-3052   *Calendar:* Sem. plan
Inst. Accred.: NEASC-CIHE (1978/2005)
Prog. Accred.: Art

Maine Maritime Academy
Castine 04420-0001
Type: Public, state, four-year
Degrees: B, M   *Enroll:* 753
URL: http://www.mainemaritime.edu
Phone: (207) 326-4311   *Calendar:* Sem. plan
Inst. Accred.: NEASC-CIHE (1971/1996)
Prog. Accred.: Business (AACSB), Engineering (naval
  architecture/marine), Engineering Technology (naval
  architecture/marine)

New England School of Communications
One College Circle, Bangor 04401-2999
Type: Private, independent, four-year
Degrees: A, B   *Enroll:* 138
URL: http://www.nescom.edu
Phone: (207) 947-3987   *Calendar:* Sem. plan
Inst. Accred.: ACCSCT (1986/2004)

Northern Maine Community College
33 Edgemont Dr., Presque Isle 04769-2099
Type: Public, state, two-year
System: Maine Community College System
Degrees: A   *Enroll:* 766
URL: http://www.nmtc.net
Phone: (207) 768-2700   *Calendar:* Sem. plan
Inst. Accred.: NEASC-CIHE (2003)
Prog. Accred.: Business (ACBSP), Nursing

Saint Joseph's College of Maine
278 Whites Bridge Rd., Standish 04084-5263
Type: Private, Roman Catholic Church, four-year
Degrees: B, M   *Enroll:* 2,095
URL: http://www.sjcme.edu
Phone: (207) 892-6766
Inst. Accred.: NEASC-CIHE (1961/2001)
Prog. Accred.: Nursing, Nursing Education

Southern Maine Community College
2 Fort Rd., South Portland 04106
Type: Public, state, two-year
System: Maine Community College System
Degrees: A   *Enroll:* 2,319
URL: http://www.smtc.net
Phone: (207) 741-5501   *Calendar:* Sem. plan
Inst. Accred.: NEASC-CIHE (2003)
Prog. Accred.: Nursing, Radiation Therapy, Radiography,
  Respiratory Therapy

Thomas College
180 West River Rd., Waterville 04901-5097
Type: Private, independent, four-year
Degrees: A, B, M   *Enroll:* 657
URL: http://www.thomas.edu
Phone: (207) 859-1111   *Calendar:* Sem. plan
Inst. Accred.: NEASC-CIHE (1969/2003)

Unity College
90 Quaker Hill Rd., Unity 04988
Type: Private, independent, four-year
Degrees: A, B   *Enroll:* 479
URL: http://www.unity.edu
Phone: (207) 948-3131   *Calendar:* Sem. plan
Inst. Accred.: NEASC-CIHE (1974/2002)

University of Maine
Orono 04469-0001
Type: Public, state, four-year
System: University of Maine System
Degrees: A, B, M, D   *Enroll:* 9,510
URL: http://www.umaine.edu
Phone: (207) 581-1110   *Calendar:* Sem. plan
Inst. Accred.: NEASC-CIHE (1929/1999)
Prog. Accred.: Business (AACSB), Clinical Psychology,
  Computer Science, Dental Assisting, Dental Hygiene,
  Dietetics (internship), Engineering (bioengineering,
  chemical, civil, computer, electrical, engineering
  physics/science, mechanical, surveying), Engineering
  Technology (civil/construction, electrical, mechanical),
  Forestry, Health Information Technician, Music, Nursing,
  Nursing Education, Psychology Internship, Public
  Administration, Social Work, Speech-Language
  Pathology, Teacher Education (NCATE)

University of Maine at Augusta
46 University Dr., Augusta 04330-9410
Type: Public, state, four-year
System: University of Maine System
Degrees: A, B   *Enroll:* 3,406
URL: http://www.uma.maine.edu
Phone: (207) 621-3000   *Calendar:* Sem. plan
Inst. Accred.: NEASC-CIHE (1973/2005)
Prog. Accred.: Clinical Lab Technology, Nursing

University College of Bangor
216 Texas Ave., Bangor 04401-4324
Phone: (207) 581-6182
Prog. Accred: Dental Assisting, Dental Hygiene,
  Veterinary Technology

University of Maine at Farmington
111 South St., Farmington 04938-1911
Type: Public, state, four-year
System: University of Maine System
Degrees: B   *Enroll:* 2,240
URL: http://www.umf.maine.edu
Phone: (207) 778-7000   *Calendar:* Sem. plan
Inst. Accred.: NEASC-CIHE (1958/2002)
Prog. Accred.: Teacher Education (NCATE)

University of Maine at Fort Kent
23 University Dr., Fort Kent 04743-1292
Type: Public, state, four-year
System: University of Maine System
Degrees: A, B   *Enroll:* 775
URL: http://www.umfk.maine.edu
Phone: (207) 834-7500   *Calendar:* Sem. plan
Inst. Accred.: NEASC-CIHE (1970/2005)
Prog. Accred.: Nursing, Nursing Education

University of Maine at Machias
9 O'Brien Ave., Machias 04654-1397
Type: Public, state, four-year
System: University of Maine System
Degrees: A, B   *Enroll:* 874
URL: http://www.umm.maine.edu
Phone: (207) 255-1200   *Calendar:* Sem. plan
Inst. Accred.: NEASC-CIHE (1970/2004)
Prog. Accred.: Recreation and Leisure Services

University of Maine at Presque Isle
181 Main St., Presque Isle 04769-2888
Type: Public, state, four-year
System: University of Maine System
Degrees: A, B   *Enroll:* 1,267
URL: http://www.umpi.maine.edu
Phone: (207) 768-9400   *Calendar:* Sem. plan
Inst. Accred.: NEASC-CIHE (1968/2003)
Prog. Accred.: Clinical Lab Technology, Recreation and
Leisure Services, Social Work

University of New England
11 Hills Beach Rd., Biddeford 04005-9988
Type: Private, independent, four-year
Degrees: A, B, M, D   *Enroll:* 2,555
URL: http://www.une.edu
Phone: (207) 283-0171   *Calendar:* Sem. plan
Inst. Accred.: NEASC-CIHE (1966/1997)
Prog. Accred.: Dental Hygiene, Nurse Anesthesia
Education, Nursing, Occupational Therapy, Osteopathy,
Physical Therapy, Physician Assistant, Social Work

Westbrook College
716 Stevens Ave., Portland 04103
Phone: (207) 797-7261
Prog. Accred: Dental Hygiene, Nursing

University of Southern Maine
96 Falmouth St., Portland 04104-9300
Type: Public, state, four-year
System: University of Maine System
Degrees: A, B, M, D   *Enroll:* 7,898
URL: http://www.usm.maine.edu
Phone: (207) 780-4141   *Calendar:* Sem. plan
Inst. Accred.: NEASC-CIHE (1960/2001)
Prog. Accred.: Art, Business (AACSB), Computer Science,
Counseling, Engineering (electrical), Health Services
Administration, Industrial Technology, Law, Music,
Nursing, Nursing Education, Public Administration,
Rehabilitation Counseling, Social Work, Teacher
Education (NCATE)

Lewiston-Auburn College
51 Westminster St., Lewiston 04240
Phone: (207) 783-4860
Prog. Accred: Occupational Therapy

Washington County Community College
RRI, Box 22C, Calais 04619-9704
Type: Public, state, two-year
System: Maine Community College System
Degrees: A   *Enroll:* 365
URL: http://www.wccc.me.edu
Phone: (207) 454-1000   *Calendar:* Sem. plan
Inst. Accred.: NEASC-CIHE (2004)

York County Community College
112 College Dr., Wells 04090-0529
Type: Public, state, two-year
System: Maine Community College System
Degrees: A   *Enroll:* 512
URL: http://www.yccc.edu
Phone: (207) 646-9282   *Calendar:* Sem. plan
Inst. Accred.: NEASC-CIHE (2004)

MARYLAND

Allegany College of Maryland
12401 Willowbrook Rd., Southeast, Cumberland 21502
Type: Public, local, two-year
System: Maryland Higher Education Commission
Degrees: A   *Enroll:* 2,584
URL: http://www.allegany.edu
Phone: (301) 784-5000   *Calendar:* Sem. plan
Inst. Accred.: MSA-CHE (1965/2005)
Prog. Accred.: Clinical Lab Technology, Dental Hygiene,
   Massage Therapy, Occupational Therapy Assisting,
   Physical Therapy Assisting, Radiography, Respiratory
   Therapy

Bedford County Campus
18 North River Ln., Everett, PA 15537
Phone: (814) 652-9528

Somerset County Campus
6022 Glades Pike, Ste. 100, Somerset, PA 15501-
4300
Phone: (814) 445-9848

Anne Arundel Community College
101 College Pkwy., Arnold 21012
Type: Public, state/local, two-year
System: Maryland Higher Education Commission
Degrees: A   *Enroll:* 7,973
URL: http://www.aacc.edu
Phone: (410) 647-7100   *Calendar:* Sem. plan
Inst. Accred.: MSA-CHE (1968/2004)
Prog. Accred.: Culinary Education, Nursing, Physical
   Therapy Assisting, Physician Assistant, Radiography

Baltimore City Community College
2901 Liberty Heights Ave., Baltimore 21215
Type: Public, state, two-year
System: Maryland Higher Education Commission
Degrees: A   *Enroll:* 4,040
URL: http://www.bccc.edu
Phone: (410) 462-8000   *Calendar:* Sem. plan
Inst. Accred.: MSA-CHE (1963/2003)
Prog. Accred.: Business (ACBSP), Dental Hygiene, Health
   Information Technician, Physical Therapy Assisting

Harbor Campus
600 East Lombard St., Baltimore 21202
Phone: (410) 333-8348

Baltimore Hebrew University
5800 Park Heights Ave., Baltimore 21215
Type: Private, independent, four-year
Degrees: A, B, M, D   *Enroll:* 82
URL: http://www.bhu.edu
Phone: (410) 578-6900   *Calendar:* Sem. plan
Inst. Accred.: MSA-CHE (1974/2005)

Baltimore International College
17 Commerce St., Baltimore 21202
Type: Private, independent, four-year
Degrees: A, B   *Enroll:* 547
URL: http://www.bic.edu
Phone: (410) 752-4710   *Calendar:* Sem. plan
Inst. Accred.: MSA-CHE (1996/2002)

Bowie State University
14000 Jericho Park Rd., Bowie 20715-9465
Type: Public, state, four-year
System: University System of Maryland
Degrees: B, M, D   *Enroll:* 4,204
URL: http://www.bowiestate.edu
Phone: (301) 860-4000   *Calendar:* Sem. plan
Inst. Accred.: MSA-CHE (1961/2001)
Prog. Accred.: Business (ACBSP), Computer Science,
   Nursing, Social Work, Teacher Education (NCATE)

Capital Bible Seminary
6511 Princess Garden Pkwy., Lanham 20706
Type: Private, independent, four-year
Degrees: A, B, M, P   *Enroll:* 444
URL: http://www.bible.edu/cbs
Phone: (301) 552-1400   *Calendar:* Sem. plan
Inst. Accred.: ATS (1998/2002)

Capitol College
11301 Springfield Rd., Laurel 20708
Type: Private, independent, four-year
Degrees: A, B, M   *Enroll:* 441
URL: http://www.capitol-college.edu
Phone: (301) 369-2800   *Calendar:* Sem. plan
Inst. Accred.: MSA-CHE (1976/2001)
Prog. Accred.: Engineering (electrical), Engineering
   Technology (computer, electrical, telecommunications)

Carroll Community College
1601 Washington Rd., Westminster 21157-6913
Type: Public, local, two-year
System: Maryland Higher Education Commission
Degrees: A   *Enroll:* 1,877
URL: http://www.carrollcc.edu
Phone: (410) 386-8000   *Calendar:* Sem. plan
Inst. Accred.: MSA-CHE (1996/2001)
Prog. Accred.: Physical Therapy Assisting

Cecil Community College
One Seahawk Dr., North East 21901-1999
Type: Public, state/local, two-year
System: Maryland Higher Education Commission
Degrees: A   *Enroll:* 999
URL: http://cecilcc.edu
Phone: (410) 287-1000   *Calendar:* Sem. plan
Inst. Accred.: MSA-CHE (1974/2005)
Prog. Accred.: Nursing

Chesapeake College
PO Box 8, Wye Mills 21679-0008
Type: Public, state/local, two-year
System: Maryland Higher Education Commission
Degrees: A   *Enroll:* 1,388
URL: http://www.chesapeake.edu
Phone: (410) 822-5400   *Calendar:* Sem. plan
Inst. Accred.: MSA-CHE (1970/2005)
Prog. Accred.: Radiography, Surgical Technology

College of Notre Dame of Maryland
4701 North Charles St., Baltimore 21210
Type: Private, Roman Catholic Church, four-year
Degrees: B, M   *Enroll:* 1,607
URL: http://www.ndm.edu
Phone: (410) 435-0100   *Calendar:* Sem. plan
Inst. Accred.: MSA-CHE (1925/2002)
Prog. Accred.: Nursing, Teacher Education (NCATE)

The College of Southern Maryland
8730 Mitchell Rd., PO Box 910, La Plata 20646-0910
Type: Public, state, two-year
System: Maryland Higher Education Commission
Degrees: A   *Enroll:* 4,129
URL: http://www.csmd.edu
Phone: (301) 934-2251   *Calendar:* Sem. plan
Inst. Accred.: MSA-CHE (1969/2004)
Prog. Accred.: Business (ACBSP), Nursing, Practical
  Nursing

Columbia Union College
7600 Flower Ave., Takoma Park 20912
Type: Private, Seventh-Day Adventist Church, four-year
Degrees: A, B, M   *Enroll:* 927
URL: http://www.cuc.edu
Phone: (301) 891-4000   *Calendar:* Sem. plan
Inst. Accred.: MSA-CHE (1942/2002)
Prog. Accred.: Nursing, Respiratory Therapy

The Community College of Baltimore County
800 South Rolling Rd., Baltimore 21228-5381
Type: Public, state/local, two-year
Degrees: A   *FTE Enroll:* 10,331
URL: http://www.ccbcmd.edu
Phone: (410) 869-1212   *Calendar:* Sem. plan
Inst. Accred.: MSA-CHE (1966/2002)
Prog. Accred.: Funeral Service Education (Mortuary
  Science), Music, Nursing, Occupational Therapy
  Assisting, Radiography, Theatre, Veterinary Technology

Dundalk Campus
7200 Sollers Point Rd., Dundalk 21222-4692
Phone: (410) 282-6700

Essex Campus
7201 Rossville Blvd., Baltimore 21237-3899
Phone: (410) 682-6000
Prog. Accred: Physician Assistant, Radiation Therapy,
  Radiography, Respiratory Therapy

Coppin State University
2500 West North Ave., Baltimore 21216-3698
Type: Public, state, four-year
System: University System of Maryland
Degrees: B, M   *Enroll:* 2,944
URL: http://www.coppin.edu
Phone: (410) 951-3000   *Calendar:* Sem. plan
Inst. Accred.: MSA-CHE (1962/2003)
Prog. Accred.: Nursing, Rehabilitation Counseling, Social
  Work, Teacher Education (NCATE)

Frederick Community College
7932 Opossumtown Pike, Frederick 21702-2097
Type: Public, state/local, two-year
System: Maryland Higher Education Commission
Degrees: A   *Enroll:* 2,780
URL: http://www.frederick.edu
Phone: (301) 846-2400   *Calendar:* Sem. plan
Inst. Accred.: MSA-CHE (1971/2001)
Prog. Accred.: Respiratory Therapy, Surgical Technology

Frostburg State University
101 Braddock Rd., Frostburg 21532-1099
Type: Public, state, four-year
System: University System of Maryland
Degrees: B, M   *Enroll:* 4,870
URL: http://www.frostburg.edu
Phone: (301) 687-4000   *Calendar:* Sem. plan
Inst. Accred.: MSA-CHE (1953/2001)
Prog. Accred.: Business (AACSB), Engineering (electrical,
  mechanical), Recreation and Leisure Services, Social
  Work, Teacher Education (NCATE)

Garrett College
PO Box 151, 687 Mosser Rd., McHenry 21541
Type: Public, state/local, two-year
System: Maryland Higher Education Commission
Degrees: A   *Enroll:* 457
URL: http://www.garrettcollege.edu
Phone: (301) 387-3000   *Calendar:* Sem. plan
Inst. Accred.: MSA-CHE (1975/2003)

Goucher College
1021 Dulaney Valley Rd., Baltimore 21204-2794
Type: Private, independent, four-year
Degrees: B, M   *Enroll:* 1,738
URL: http://www.goucher.edu
Phone: (410) 337-6000   *Calendar:* Sem. plan
Inst. Accred.: MSA-CHE (1921/1999)

Griggs University
12501 Old Columbia Pike, PO Box 4437, Silver Spring
20914-4437
Type: Private, Seventh-Day Adventist, four-year
Degrees: A, B, M
URL: http://www.griggs.edu
Phone: (301) 680-6570   *Calendar:* Sem. plan
Inst. Accred.: DETC (1967/2003)

Accredited Degree-Granting Institutions

Hagerstown Business College
18618 Crestwood Dr., Hagerstown 21742
Type: Private, proprietary, two-year
System: Kaplan Higher Education Corporation
Degrees: A   *Enroll:* 834
URL: http://www.hagerstownbusinesscol.org
Phone: (301) 739-2670   *Calendar:* Qtr. plan
Inst. Accred.: ACICS (1968/2002)
Prog. Accred.: Health Information Technician, Medical Assisting (AMA), Phlebotomy

Frederick Campus
5301 Buckeystown Pike, Ste. 150, Frederick 21704
Phone: (301) 682-4882

Hagerstown Community College
11400 Robinwood Dr., Hagerstown 21740-6590
Type: Public, state/local, two-year
System: Maryland Higher Education Commission
Degrees: A   *Enroll:* 1,829
URL: http://www.hagerstowncc.edu
Phone: (301) 790-2800   *Calendar:* Sem. plan
Inst. Accred.: MSA-CHE (1968/1999)
Prog. Accred.: Radiography

Harford Community College
401 Thomas Run Rd., Bel Air 21015-1698
Type: Public, state/local, two-year
System: Maryland Higher Education Commission
Degrees: A   *Enroll:* 3,113
URL: http://www.harford.edu
Phone: (410) 836-4000   *Calendar:* Sem. plan
Inst. Accred.: MSA-CHE (1967/2002)
Prog. Accred.: Histologic Technology, Nursing

Hood College
401 Rosemont Ave., Frederick 21701-8575
Type: Private, independent, four-year
Degrees: B, M   *Enroll:* 1,160
URL: http://www.hood.edu
Phone: (301) 663-3131   *Calendar:* Sem. plan
Inst. Accred.: MSA-CHE (1922/2002, Warning)
Prog. Accred.: Social Work

Howard Community College
10901 Little Patuxent Pkwy., Columbia 21044
Type: Public, state/local, two-year
System: Maryland Higher Education Commission
Degrees: A   *Enroll:* 3,670
URL: http://www.howardcc.edu
Phone: (410) 772-4800   *Calendar:* Sem. plan
Inst. Accred.: MSA-CHE (1975/2001)
Prog. Accred.: Cardiovascular Technology, Nursing, Practical Nursing

Johns Hopkins University
3400 North Charles St., Baltimore 21218
Type: Private, independent, four-year
Degrees: B, M, P, D   *Enroll:* 13,420
URL: http://www.jhu.edu
Phone: (410) 516-8000   *Calendar:* Sem. plan
Inst. Accred.: MSA-CHE (1921/2004)
Prog. Accred.: Applied Science (industrial hygiene), Blood Bank Technology, Clinical Pastoral Education, Cytotechnology, Diagnostic Medical Sonography, Engineering (bioengineering, chemical, civil, computer, electrical, engineering mechanics, materials, mechanical), Health Services Administration, Medical Illustration, Medicine, Nuclear Medicine Technology, Nursing, Nursing Education, Perfusion, Psychology Internship, Public Health

Columbia Center Campus
6740 Alexander Bell Dr., Columbia 21046
Phone: (410) 290-1777

The Paul H. Nitze School of Advanced International Studies
1740 Massachusetts Ave., NW, Washington, DC 20036
Phone: (202) 663-5600

Peabody Institute of the Johns Hopkins University
One East Mount Vernon Place, Baltimore 21202-2397
Phone: (410) 659-8150
Prog. Accred: Music

Loyola College in Maryland
4501 North Charles St., Baltimore 21210-2699
Type: Private, Roman Catholic Church, four-year
Degrees: B, M, D   *Enroll:* 4,751
URL: http://www.loyola.edu
Phone: (410) 617-2000   *Calendar:* Sem. plan
Inst. Accred.: MSA-CHE (1931/2005)
Prog. Accred.: Accounting, Business (AACSB), Clinical Psychology, Computer Science, Counseling, Engineering (electrical, engineering physics/science), Speech-Language Pathology

Maple Springs Baptist Bible College and Seminary
4130 Belt Rd., Capitol Heights 20743
Type: Private, Baptist Church, four-year
Degrees: A, B, M, D
URL: http://www.msbbcs.edu
Phone: (301) 736- 3631   *Calendar:* Sem. plan
Inst. Accred.: TRACS (2000/2004)

The Maryland Institute College of Art
1300 West Mount Royal Ave., Baltimore 21217
Type: Private, independent, four-year
Degrees: B, M   *Enroll:* 1,620
URL: http://www.mica.edu
Phone: (410) 669-9200   *Calendar:* Sem. plan
Inst. Accred.: MSA-CHE (1967/1998)
Prog. Accred.: Art

McDaniel College
2 College Hill, Westminster 21157
Type: Private, independent, four-year
Degrees: B, M   *Enroll:* 2,395
URL: http://www.mcdaniel.edu
Phone: (410) 848-7000   *Calendar:* Sem. plan
Inst. Accred.: MSA-CHE (1922/2003)
Prog. Accred.: Social Work

Montgomery College—Germantown Campus
20200 Observation Dr., Germantown 20876
Type: Public, local, two-year
System: Montgomery College
Degrees: A   *FTE Enroll:* 1,810
URL: http://www.montgomerycollege.edu
Phone: (301) 353-7700   *Calendar:* Sem. plan
Inst. Accred.: MSA-CHE (1980/2003)

Montgomery College—Rockville Campus
51 Mannakee St., Rcokville 20850
Type: Public, local, two-year
System: Montgomery College
Degrees: A   *Enroll:* 12,468
URL: http://www.montgomerycollege.edu
Phone: (301) 279-5000   *Calendar:* Sem. plan
Inst. Accred.: MSA-CHE (1968/2003)
Prog. Accred.: Diagnostic Medical Sonography, Health
    Information Technician, Music, Radiography

Montgomery College—Takoma Park Campus
7600 Takoma Ave., Takoma Park 20912
Type: Public, state/local, two-year
System: Montgomery College
Degrees: A   *FTE Enroll:* 2,279
URL: http://www.montgomerycollege.edu
Phone: (301) 650-1300   *Calendar:* Sem. plan
Inst. Accred.: MSA-CHE (1950/2003)
Prog. Accred.: Nursing, Physical Therapy Assisting,
    Radiography

The School of Art and Design at Montgomery College
10500 Georgia Ave., Silver Spring 20902
Phone: (301) 649-4454

Morgan State University
1700 East Cold Spring Ln., Baltimore 21251
Type: Public, state, four-year
System: Maryland Higher Education Commission
Degrees: B, M, D   *Enroll:* 6,010
URL: http://www.morgan.edu
Phone: (443) 885-3333   *Calendar:* Sem. plan
Inst. Accred.: MSA-CHE (1925/2003)
Prog. Accred.: Accounting, Business (AACSB), Clinical Lab
    Scientist, Engineering (civil, electrical, industrial),
    Landscape Architecture, Music, Planning, Social Work,
    Teacher Education (NCATE)

Mount Saint Mary's University
16300 Old Emmitsburg Rd., Emmitsburg 21727-7797
Type: Private, Roman Catholic Church, four-year
Degrees: B, M, P   *Enroll:* 1,780
URL: http://www.msmary.edu
Phone: (301) 447-6122   *Calendar:* Sem. plan
Inst. Accred.: ATS (1987/2005), MSA-CHE (1922/2005)

National Labor College
10000 New Hampshire Ave., Silver Spring 20903
Type: Private, independent, four-year
Degrees: B
URL: http://www.georgemeany.org
Phone: (301) 431-6400   *Calendar:* Sem. plan
Inst. Accred.: MSA-CHE (2004)

Ner Israel Rabbinical College
400 Mount Wilson Ln., Baltimore 21208
Type: Private, independent, four-year
Degrees: B, M, D   *Enroll:* 551
Phone: (410) 484-7200   *Calendar:* Sem. plan
Inst. Accred.: AARTS (1974/2004)

Prince George's Community College
301 Largo Rd., Largo 20774
Type: Public, state/local, two-year
System: Maryland Higher Education Commission
Degrees: A   *Enroll:* 6,445
URL: http://www.pgcc.edu
Phone: (301) 336-6000   *Calendar:* Sem. plan
Inst. Accred.: MSA-CHE (1969/2005)
Prog. Accred.: Engineering Technology (electrical), Health
    Information Technician, Nuclear Medicine Technology,
    Nursing, Radiography, Respiratory Therapy

Saint John's College
60 College Ave., PO Box 2800, Annapolis 21404
Type: Private, independent, four-year
Degrees: B, M   *Enroll:* 554
URL: http://www.sjca.edu
Phone: (410) 263-2371   *Calendar:* Sem. plan
Inst. Accred.: MSA-CHE (1923/1999), AALE (2004)

Saint Mary's College of Maryland
18952 East Fisher Rd., St. Mary's City 20686-3001
Type: Public, state, four-year
System: Maryland Higher Education Commission
Degrees: B, M   *Enroll:* 1,853
URL: http://www.smcm.edu
Phone: (240) 895-2000   *Calendar:* Sem. plan
Inst. Accred.: MSA-CHE (1959/2005)
Prog. Accred.: Music

Saint Mary's Seminary and University
5400 Roland Ave., Baltimore 21210
Type: Private, Roman Catholic Church, four-year
Degrees: B, M, P   *Enroll:* 167
URL: http://www.stmarys.edu
Phone: (410) 864-4000   *Calendar:* Sem. plan
Inst. Accred.: ATS (1971/2001), MSA-CHE (1951/2001)

Salisbury University
1101 Camden Ave., Salisbury 21801-6837
Type: Public, state, four-year
System: University System of Maryland
Degrees: B, M   *Enroll:* 6,064
URL: http://www.salisbury.edu
Phone: (410) 543-6000   *Calendar:* Sem. plan
Inst. Accred.: MSA-CHE (1956/2001)
Prog. Accred.: Athletic Training, Business (AACSB),
  Clinical Lab Scientist, Nursing, Nursing Education,
  Respiratory Therapy, Social Work, Teacher Education
  (NCATE)

Sojourner-Douglass College
500 North Caroline St., Baltimore 21205
Type: Private, independent, four-year
Degrees: B, M   *Enroll:* 933
URL: http://www.sdc.edu
Phone: (410) 276-0306   *Calendar:* Tri. plan
Inst. Accred.: MSA-CHE (1980/2001)

Nassau Campus
Pilot House, 2nd Flr., Nassau, Bahamas
Phone: 011 12423948570

Tai Sophia Institute
7750 Monteplier Rd., Laurel 20723
Type: Private, independent, four-year
Degrees: M   *Enroll:* 280
URL: http://www.tai.edu
Phone: (410) 888-9048   *Calendar:* Tri. plan
Inst. Accred.: ACAOM (1985/2000)

TESST College of Technology
1520 South Caton Ave., Baltimore 21227-1063
Type: Private, proprietary, two-year
Degrees: A
URL: http://www.tesstcollege.com
Phone: (410) 644-6400   *Calendar:* Qtr. plan
Inst. Accred.: ACCSCT (1973/2001)

TESST College of Technology
4600 Powder Mill Rd., Beltsville 20705
Type: Private, proprietary, two-year
Degrees: A
URL: http://www.tesstcollege.com
Phone: (301) 937-8448   *Calendar:* Qtr. plan
Inst. Accred.: ACCSCT (1975/2003)

TESST College of Technology
803 Glen Eagles Ct., Towson 21286
Type: Private, proprietary, two-year
Degrees: A   *Enroll:* 418
URL: http://www.tesstcollege.com
Phone: (410) 296-5350   *Calendar:* Qtr. plan
Inst. Accred.: ACCSCT (2000/2005)

Towson University
8000 York Rd., Towson 21252-0001
Type: Public, state, four-year
System: University System of Maryland
Degrees: B, M, D   *Enroll:* 14,503
URL: http://www.towson.edu
Phone: (410) 704-2000   *Calendar:* 4-1-4 plan
Inst. Accred.: MSA-CHE (1949/2005)
Prog. Accred.: Accounting, Athletic Training, Audiology,
  Business (AACSB), Computer Science, Dance, Music,
  Nursing, Nursing Education, Occupational Therapy,
  Psychology Internship, Speech-LanguagePathology,
  Teacher Education (NCATE), Theatre

Uniformed Services University of the Health Sciences
4301 Jones Bridge Rd., Bethesda 20814-4799
Type: Public, federal, four-year
Degrees: M, P, D   *FTE Enroll:* 835
URL: http://www.usuhs.mil
Phone: (301) 295-3050   *Calendar:* Sem. plan
Inst. Accred.: MSA-CHE (1984/2003)
Prog. Accred.: Applied Science (industrial hygiene),
  Clinical Psychology, Medicine, Nurse Anesthesia
  Education, Nursing, Nursing Education, Public Health

United States Naval Academy
121 Blake Rd., Annapolis 21402-5000
Type: Public, federal, four-year
Degrees: B   *Enroll:* 4,335
URL: http://www.usna.edu
Phone: (410) 293-1000   *Calendar:* Sem. plan
Inst. Accred.: MSA-CHE (1947/2001)
Prog. Accred.: Computer Science, Engineering
  (aerospace, electrical, mechanical, naval
  architecture/marine, ocean, systems)

University of Baltimore
1420 North Charles St., Baltimore 21201
Type: Public, state, four-year
System: University System of Maryland
Degrees: B, M, P, D   *Enroll:* 3,458
URL: http://www.ubalt.edu
Phone: (410) 837-4200   *Calendar:* Sem. plan
Inst. Accred.: MSA-CHE (1971/2002)
Prog. Accred.: Business (AACSB), Law, Public
  Administration

University of Maryland Baltimore
520 West Lombard St., Baltimore 21201-1627
Type: Public, state, four-year
System: University System of Maryland
Degrees: B, M, P, D   *Enroll:* 4,806
URL: http://www.umaryland.edu
Phone: (410) 706-3100   *Calendar:* 4-1-4 plan
Inst. Accred.: MSA-CHE (1921/2001)
Prog. Accred.: Advanced Education in General Dentistry,
  Clinical Lab Scientist, Combined Prosthodontics, Dental
  Hygiene, Dentistry, Dietetics (internship), EMT
  (Paramedic), Endodontics, General Dentistry, General
  Practice Residency, Law, Medicine, Nurse (Midwifery),
  Nursing, Oral and Maxillofacial Pathology, Oral and
  Maxillofacial Surgery, Orthodontic and Dentofacial
  Orthopedics, Pathologists' Assistant, Pediatric Dentistry,
  Periodontics, Pharmacy, Physical Therapy,
  Prosthodontics, Social Work

The University of Maryland Baltimore County
1000 Hilltop Circle, Baltimore 21250
Type: Public, state, four-year
System: University System of Maryland
Degrees: B, M, D   *Enroll:* 10,106
URL: http://www.umbc.edu
Phone: (410) 455-1000   *Calendar:* 4-1-4 plan
Inst. Accred.: MSA-CHE (1966/2001)
Prog. Accred.: Clinical Psychology, Computer Science,
  Diagnostic Medical Sonography, EMT (Paramedic),
  Engineering (chemical, computer, mechanical),
  Psychology Internship, Public Administration, Social
  Work, Teacher Education (NCATE)

University of Maryland College Park
College Park 20742
Type: Public, state, four-year
System: University System of Maryland
Degrees: B, M, P, D   *Enroll:* 31,722
URL: http://www.umcp.umd.edu
Phone: (301) 405-1000   *Calendar:* Sem. plan
Inst. Accred.: MSA-CHE (1921/2002)
Prog. Accred.: Audiology, Business (AACSB), Clinical
  Psychology, Counseling, Counseling Psychology,
  Engineering (aerospace, agricultural, chemical, civil,
  computer, electrical, fire protection, general, materials,
  mechanical, nuclear), Journalism, Landscape
  Architecture, Librarianship, Marriage and Family
  Therapy, Music, Planning, Psychology Internship, Public
  Health, Rehabilitation Counseling, School Psychology,
  Speech-Language Pathology, Teacher Education
  (NCATE), Teacher Education (TEAC), Theatre

University of Maryland Eastern Shore
1 Backbone Rd., Princess Anne 21853
Type: Public, state, four-year
System: University System of Maryland
Degrees: B, M, D   *Enroll:* 3,467
URL: http://www.umes.edu
Phone: (410) 651-2200   *Calendar:* Sem. plan
Inst. Accred.: MSA-CHE (1937/2001)
Prog. Accred.: Construction Education, Physical Therapy,
  Physician Assistant

University of Maryland University College
3501 University Blvd. East, College Park 20783
Type: Public, state, four-year
System: University System of Maryland
Degrees: A, B, M, D   *Enroll:* 11,802
URL: http://www.umuc.edu
Phone: (301) 985-7000   *Calendar:* Sem. plan
Inst. Accred.: MSA-CHE (1946/2001)

Villa Julie College
1525 Green Spring Valley Rd., Stevenson 21153
Type: Private, independent, four-year
Degrees: A, B, M   *Enroll:* 2,315
URL: http://www.vjc.edu
Phone: (410) 486-7000   *Calendar:* Sem. plan
Inst. Accred.: MSA-CHE (1962/2003)
Prog. Accred.: Clinical Lab Technology, Nursing

Washington Bible College
6511 Princess Garden Pkwy., Lanham 20706-3538
Type: Private, independent, four-year
Degrees: A, B, M, P   *Enroll:* 444
URL: http://www.bible.edu
Phone: (301) 552-1400   *Calendar:* Sem. plan
Inst. Accred.: ABHE (1962/2002)

Washington College
300 Washington Ave., Chestertown 21620-1197
Type: Private, independent, four-year
Degrees: B, M   *Enroll:* 1,394
URL: http://www.washcoll.edu
Phone: (410) 778-2800   *Calendar:* Sem. plan
Inst. Accred.: MSA-CHE (1925/2004)

Wor-Wic Community College
32000 Campus Dr., Salisbury 21804
Type: Public, state/local, two-year
System: Maryland Higher Education Commission
Degrees: A   *Enroll:* 1,607
URL: http://www.worwic.edu
Phone: (410) 334-2800   *Calendar:* Sem. plan
Inst. Accred.: MSA-CHE (1980/2005)
Prog. Accred.: Radiography

MASSACHUSETTS

American International College
1000 State St., Springfield 01109-3155
Type: Private, independent, four-year
Degrees: B, M, D   *Enroll:* 1,337
URL: http://www.aic.edu
Phone: (413) 737-7000   *Calendar:* Sem. plan
Inst. Accred.: NEASC-CIHE (1933/1999)
Prog. Accred.: Nursing, Occupational Therapy, Physical
  Therapy

Amherst College
PO Box 5000, Amherst 01002-5000
Type: Private, independent, four-year
Degrees: B   *Enroll:* 1,618
URL: http://www.amherst.edu
Phone: (413) 542-2000   *Calendar:* Sem. plan
Inst. Accred.: NEASC-CIHE (1929/1988)

Andover Newton Theological School
210 Herrick Rd., Newton Centre 02459-2243
Type: Private, independent, four-year
Degrees: M, D   *Enroll:* 377
URL: http://www.ants.edu
Phone: (617) 964-1100   *Calendar:* Sem. plan
Inst. Accred.: ATS (1938/1998), NEASC-CIHE (1978/1998)

Anna Maria College
Box 32 Sunset Ln., Paxton 01612-1198
Type: Private, Roman Catholic Church, four-year
Degrees: A, B, M   *Enroll:* 835
URL: http://www.annamaria.edu
Phone: (508) 849-3300   *Calendar:* 4-1-4 plan
Inst. Accred.: NEASC-CIHE (1955/1998)
Prog. Accred.: Music, Nursing, Social Work

Assumption College
500 Salisbury St., Worcester 01615-0005
Type: Private, Roman Catholic Church, four-year
Degrees: A, B, M   *Enroll:* 2,454
URL: http://www.assumption.edu
Phone: (508) 767-7000   *Calendar:* Sem. plan
Inst. Accred.: NEASC-CIHE (1949/2001)
Prog. Accred.: Rehabilitation Counseling

Atlantic Union College
PO Box 1000, 338 Main St., South Lancaster 01561-
1000
Type: Private, Seventh-Day Adventist Church, four-year
Degrees: A, B, M   *Enroll:* 465
URL: http://www.atlanticuc.edu
Phone: (978) 368-2000   *Calendar:* Sem. plan
Inst. Accred.: NEASC-CIHE (1945/1998)
Prog. Accred.: Music, Nursing, Social Work

Babson College
231 Forest St., Babson Park 02457-0310
Type: Private, independent, four-year
Degrees: B, M   *Enroll:* 2,601
URL: http://www.babson.edu
Phone: (781) 235-1200   *Calendar:* Sem. plan
Inst. Accred.: NEASC-CIHE (1950/2001)
Prog. Accred.: Business (AACSB)

Bay Path College
588 Longmeadow St., Longmeadow 01106-2292
Type: Private, independent, four-year
Degrees: A, B, M   *Enroll:* 1,168
URL: http://www.baypath.edu
Phone: (413) 567-1000   *Calendar:* Sem. plan
Inst. Accred.: NEASC-CIHE (1965/1996)
Prog. Accred.: Occupational Therapy

Bay State College
122 Commonwealth Ave., Boston 02116-2975
Type: Private, independent, four-year
Degrees: A, B   *Enroll:* 629
URL: http://www.baystate.edu
Phone: (617) 236-8000   *Calendar:* Sem. plan
Inst. Accred.: NEASC-CTCI (1989/1998)
Prog. Accred.: Medical Assisting (ABHES), Physical
  Therapy Assisting

Becker College
61 Sever St., PO Box 15071, Worcester 01609
Type: Private, independent, four-year
Degrees: A, B   *Enroll:* 1,078
URL: http://www.beckercollege.edu
Phone: (508) 791-9241   *Calendar:* Sem. plan
Inst. Accred.: NEASC-CIHE (1976/1997)
Prog. Accred.: Nursing, Physical Therapy Assisting

Leicester Campus
3 Paxton St., Leicester 01524
Phone: (508) 791-9241
Prog. Accred: Veterinary Technology

Benjamin Franklin Institute of Technology
41 Berkeley St., Boston 02116-6296
Type: Private, independent, four-year
Degrees: A, B   *Enroll:* 266
URL: http://www.bfit.edu
Phone: (617) 423-4630   *Calendar:* Sem. plan
Inst. Accred.: NEASC-CTCI (1970/2000)
Prog. Accred.: Engineering Technology (computer,
  electrical, mechanical)

Bentley College
175 Forest St., Waltham 02452-4705
Type: Private, independent, four-year
Degrees: A, B, M   *Enroll:* 4,844
URL: http://www.bentley.edu
Phone: (781) 891-2000   *Calendar:* Sem. plan
Inst. Accred.: NEASC-CIHE (1966/2002)
Prog. Accred.: Accounting, Business (AACSB)

Berklee College of Music
1140 Boylston St., Boston 02215-3693
Type: Private, independent, four-year
Degrees: B   *Enroll:* 3,799
URL: http://www.berklee.edu
Phone: (617) 266-1400   *Calendar:* Sem. plan
Inst. Accred.: NEASC-CIHE (1973/2003)

Berkshire Community College
West St., Pittsfield 01201-5786
Type: Public, state, two-year
System: Massachusetts Board of Higher Education
Degrees: A   *Enroll:* 1,380
URL: http://www.berkshirecc.edu
Phone: (413) 499-4660   *Calendar:* Sem. plan
Inst. Accred.: NEASC-CIHE (1964/1999)
Prog. Accred.: Nursing, Physical Therapy Assisting,
    Respiratory Therapy

Blessed John XXIII National Seminary
558 South Ave., Weston 02193-2699
Type: Private, Roman Catholic Church, four-year
Degrees: M   *Enroll:* 69
URL: http://www.blessedjohnxxiii.edu
Phone: (781) 899-5500   *Calendar:* Sem. plan
Inst. Accred.: ATS (1983/1998)

The Boston Architectural Center
320 Newbury St., Boston 02115-2795
Type: Private, independent, four-year
Degrees: B, M   *Enroll:* 854
URL: http://www.the-bac.edu
Phone: (617) 262-5000   *Calendar:* Sem. plan
Inst. Accred.: NEASC-CIHE (1991/1996)
Prog. Accred.: Interior Design

Boston Baptist College
950 Metropolitan Ave., Boston 02136
Type: Private, Baptist Church, four-year
Degrees: A, B   *Enroll:* 110
URL: http://www.boston.edu
Phone: (617) 364-3510   *Calendar:* Sem. plan
Inst. Accred.: TRACS (1996/2001)

Boston College
140 Commonwealth Ave., Chestnut Hill 02467-3934
Type: Private, Roman Catholic Church, four-year
Degrees: B, M, D   *Enroll:* 12,265
URL: http://www.bc.edu
Phone: (617) 552-8000   *Calendar:* Sem. plan
Inst. Accred.: NEASC-CIHE (1935/1997)
Prog. Accred.: Business (AACSB), Counseling Psychology,
    Law, Nursing, Nursing Education, Social Work, Teacher
    Education (NCATE)

The Boston Conservatory
8 The Fenway, Boston 02215
Type: Private, independent, four-year
Degrees: B, M   *Enroll:* 530
URL: http://www.bostonconservancy.edu
Phone: (617) 536-6340   *Calendar:* Sem. plan
Inst. Accred.: NEASC-CIHE (1968/1999)
Prog. Accred.: Music

Boston Graduate School of Psychoanalysis
1581 Beacon St., Brookline 02446-4602
Type: Private, independent, four-year
Degrees: M, D   *Enroll:* 76
URL: http://www.bgsp.edu
Phone: (617) 277-3915   *Calendar:* Sem. plan
Inst. Accred.: NEASC-CIHE (1996/2001)

Boston University
One Sherborne St., Boston 02215
Type: Private, independent, four-year
Degrees: B, M, D   *Enroll:* 25,963
URL: http://www.bu.edu
Phone: (617) 353-2000   *Calendar:* Sem. plan
Inst. Accred.: ATS (1938/2001), NEASC-CIHE (1929/1999)
Prog. Accred.: Advanced Education in General Dentistry,
    Athletic Training, Audiology, Business (AACSB), Clinical
    Psychology, Combined Prosthodontics, Dental Public
    Health, Dentistry, Dietetics (internship), Endodontics,
    Engineering (aerospace, bioengineering, computer,
    electrical, manufacturing, mechanical), English
    Language Education, General Dentistry, Health Services
    Administration, Law, Medicine, Music, Nurse
    (Midwifery), Occupational Therapy, Oral and
    Maxillofacial Pathology, Oral and Maxillofacial Surgery,
    Orthodontic and Dentofacial Orthopedics, Pediatric
    Dentistry, Periodontics, Physical Therapy, Psychology
    Internship, Public Health, Rehabilitation Counseling,
    Social Work, Speech-Language Pathology

Brandeis University
415 South St., Waltham 02454-9110
Type: Private, independent, four-year
Degrees: B, M, D   *Enroll:* 4,671
URL: http://www.brandeis.edu
Phone: (781) 736-2000   *Calendar:* Sem. plan
Inst. Accred.: NEASC-CIHE (1953/1996)

Bridgewater State College
Bridgewater 02325-0001
Type: Public, state, four-year
System: Massachusetts Board of Higher Education
Degrees: B, M   *Enroll:* 7,722
URL: http://www.bridgew.edu
Phone: (508) 531-1200   *Calendar:* Sem. plan
Inst. Accred.: NEASC-CIHE (1953/2002)
Prog. Accred.: Athletic Training, Social Work, Teacher
    Education (NCATE)

Bristol Community College
777 Elsbree St., Fall River 02720-7395
Type: Public, state, two-year
System: Massachusetts Board of Higher Education
Degrees: A   *Enroll:* 4,156
URL: http://www.bristol.mass.edu
Phone: (508) 678-2811   *Calendar:* Sem. plan
Inst. Accred.: NEASC-CIHE (1970/2004)
Prog. Accred.: Clinical Lab Technology, Dental Hygiene,
    Health Information Technician, Nursing, Occupational
    Therapy Assisting

Bunker Hill Community College
250 New Rutherford Ave., Boston 02129-2991
Type: Public, state, two-year
System: Massachusetts Board of Higher Education
Degrees: A   *Enroll:* 4,195
URL: http://www.bhcc.mass.edu
Phone: (617) 228-2000   *Calendar:* Sem. plan
Inst. Accred.: NEASC-CIHE (1976/2000)
Prog. Accred.: Diagnostic Medical Sonography, Nuclear Medicine Technology, Nursing, Radiography

Chelsea Campus
175 Hawthorne St., Bellingham Square, Chelsea 02150-2917
Phone: (617) 228-2101
Prog. Accred: Surgical Technology

Cambridge College
1000 Massachusetts Ave., Cambridge 02138-5304
Type: Private, independent, four-year
Degrees: B, M   *Enroll:* 1,990
URL: http://www.cambridgecollege.edu
Phone: (617) 868-1000   *Calendar:* Sem. plan
Inst. Accred.: NEASC-CIHE (1981/2005)

Chesapeake Campus
1403 Greenbrier Pkwy., The Oracle Bldg., Ste. 300, Chesapeake, VA 23320
Phone: (757) 424-0333

Springfield Campus
570 Cottage St., Springfield 01104
Phone: (413) 747-0204

Cape Cod Community College
2240 Iyanough Rd., West Barnstable 02668-1599
Type: Public, state, two-year
System: Massachusetts Board of Higher Education
Degrees: A   *Enroll:* 2,469
URL: http://www.capecod.mass.edu
Phone: (508) 362-2131   *Calendar:* Sem. plan
Inst. Accred.: NEASC-CIHE (1967/1998)
Prog. Accred.: Dental Hygiene, Nursing

Caritas Laboure College
2120 Dorchester Ave., Boston 02124-5698
Type: Private, Roman Catholic Church, two-year
Degrees: A   *Enroll:* 226
URL: http://www.laboure.edu
Phone: (617) 296-8300   *Calendar:* Sem. plan
Inst. Accred.: NEASC-CTCI (1975/1995)
Prog. Accred.: Electroneurodiagnostic Technology, Health Information Technician, Nursing, Radiation Therapy

Clark University
950 Main St., Worcester 01610-1477
Type: Private, independent, four-year
Degrees: B, M, D   *Enroll:* 2,766
URL: http://www.clarku.edu
Phone: (508) 793-7711   *Calendar:* Sem. plan
Inst. Accred.: NEASC-CIHE (1929/2005)
Prog. Accred.: Business (AACSB), Clinical Psychology

College of Our Lady of the Elms
291 Springfield St., Chicopee 01013-2839
Type: Private, Roman Catholic Church, four-year
Degrees: B, M   *Enroll:* 735
URL: http://www.elms.edu
Phone: (413) 594-2761   *Calendar:* Sem. plan
Inst. Accred.: NEASC-CIHE (1942/2003)
Prog. Accred.: Nursing, Nursing Education, Social Work

College of the Holy Cross
One College St., Worcester 01610-2395
Type: Private, Roman Catholic Church, four-year
Degrees: B   *Enroll:* 2,758
URL: http://www.holycross.edu
Phone: (508) 793-2011   *Calendar:* Sem. plan
Inst. Accred.: NEASC-CIHE (1930/2000)
Prog. Accred.: Theatre

Conway School of Landscape Design
PO Box 179, Conway 01341-0179
Type: Private, independent, four-year
Degrees: M   *Enroll:* 16
URL: http://www.csld.edu
Phone: (413) 369-4044   *Calendar:* Tri. plan
Inst. Accred.: NEASC-CIHE (1989/2005)

Curry College
1071 Blue Hill Ave., Milton 02186-2395
Type: Private, independent, four-year
Degrees: B, M   *Enroll:* 2,041
URL: http://www.curry.edu
Phone: (617) 333-0500   *Calendar:* Sem. plan
Inst. Accred.: NEASC-CIHE (1970/2002)
Prog. Accred.: Nursing, Nursing Education

Dean College
99 Main St., Franklin 02038-1994
Type: Private, independent, four-year
Degrees: A, B   *Enroll:* 1,052
URL: http://www.dean.edu
Phone: (508) 528-9100   *Calendar:* Sem. plan
Inst. Accred.: NEASC-CIHE (1957/1996)

Eastern Nazarene College
23 East Elm Ave., Quincy 02170-2999
Type: Private, Church of the Nazarene, four-year
Degrees: A, B, M   *Enroll:* 1,150
URL: http://www.enc.edu
Phone: (617) 745-3000   *Calendar:* 4-1-4 plan
Inst. Accred.: NEASC-CIHE (1943/2000)
Prog. Accred.: Social Work

Emerson College
100 Beacon St., Boston 02116-1596
Type: Private, independent, four-year
Degrees: B, M, D   *Enroll:* 3,984
URL: http://www.emerson.edu
Phone: (617) 824-8500   *Calendar:* Sem. plan
Inst. Accred.: NEASC-CIHE (1950/2002)
Prog. Accred.: Speech-Language Pathology

European Institute for International Communication
Brusselsestraat 84, Maastricht, Netherlands 6211 PH
Phone: 011 31 (043) 25 82 82

Emmanuel College
400 The Fenway, Boston 02115-5798
Type: Private, Roman Catholic Church, four-year
Degrees: B, M   *Enroll:* 1,479
URL: http://www.emmanuel.edu
Phone: (617) 277-9430   *Calendar:* Sem. plan
Inst. Accred.: NEASC-CIHE (1933/2002)
Prog. Accred.: Clinical Pastoral Education (ACPEI),
Nursing, Nursing Education

Endicott College
376 Hale St., Beverly 01915-2098
Type: Private, independent, four-year
Degrees: A, B, M   *Enroll:* 1,772
URL: http://www.endicott.edu
Phone: (978) 927-0585   *Calendar:* Sem. plan
Inst. Accred.: NEASC-CIHE (1952/1997)
Prog. Accred.: Athletic Training, Interior Design, Nursing

Episcopal Divinity School
99 Brattle St., Cambridge 02138
Type: Private, Episcopal Church, four-year
Degrees: M, D   *Enroll:* 70
URL: http://www.episdivschool.edu
Phone: (617) 868-3450   *Calendar:* Sem. plan
Inst. Accred.: ATS (1938/1998)

FINE Mortuary College
150 Kerry Place, Norwood 02062
Type: Private, independent, two-year
Degrees: A
URL: http://www.fine-ne.com
Phone: (781) 762-1211   *Calendar:* Qtr. plan
Inst. Accred.: ABFSE (1969/2004)

Fisher College
118 Beacon St., Boston 02116-1500
Type: Private, independent, four-year
Degrees: A, B   *Enroll:* 1,064
URL: http://www.fisher.edu
Phone: (617) 236-8800   *Calendar:* Sem. plan
Inst. Accred.: NEASC-CIHE (1970/2000)
Prog. Accred.: Health Information Technician

Fitchburg State College
160 Pearl St., Fitchburg 01420-2697
Type: Public, state, four-year
System: Massachusetts Board of Higher Education
Degrees: B, M   *Enroll:* 3,645
URL: http://www.fsc.edu
Phone: (978) 345-2151   *Calendar:* Sem. plan
Inst. Accred.: NEASC-CIHE (1953/2002)
Prog. Accred.: Clinical Lab Scientist, Nursing, Nursing
Education, Teacher Education (NCATE)

Framingham State College
100 State St., PO Box 9101, Framingham 01701-9101
Type: Public, state, four-year
System: Massachusetts Board of Higher Education
Degrees: B, M   *Enroll:* 4,361
URL: http://www.framingham.edu
Phone: (508) 626-1220   *Calendar:* Sem. plan
Inst. Accred.: NEASC-CIHE (1950/2004)
Prog. Accred.: Dietetics (coordinated), Nursing

Gibbs College of Boston, Inc.
126 Newbury St., Boston 02116-2904
Type: Private, proprietary, two-year
System: Career Education Corporation
Degrees: A   *Enroll:* 855
URL: http://www.gibbsboston.com
Phone: (617) 578-7100   *Calendar:* Qtr. plan
Inst. Accred.: ACICS (1967/2005)

Gordon College
255 Grapevine Rd., Wenham 01984-1899
Type: Private, independent, four-year
Degrees: B, M   *Enroll:* 1,632
URL: http://www.gordon.edu
Phone: (978) 927-2300   *Calendar:* Sem. plan
Inst. Accred.: NEASC-CIHE (1961/2002)
Prog. Accred.: Music, Social Work

Gordon-Conwell Theological Seminary
130 Essex St., South Hamilton 01982-2317
Type: Private, independent, four-year
Degrees: M, D   *Enroll:* 1,213
URL: http://www.gordonconwell.edu
Phone: (978) 468-7111   *Calendar:* Sem. plan
Inst. Accred.: ATS (1964/2005), NEASC-CIHE (1985/2005)

Center for Urban Ministerial Education
363 South Huntington Ave., Boston 02130
Phone: (617) 983-9393

Charlotte Campus
9401-N Southern Pine Blvd., Charlotte, NC 28273-5596
Phone: (704) 527-9909

Greenfield Community College
One College Dr., Greenfield 01301-9734
Type: Public, state, two-year
System: Massachusetts Board of Higher Education
Degrees: A   *Enroll:* 1,457
URL: http://www.gcc.mass.edu
Phone: (413) 775-1000   *Calendar:* Sem. plan
Inst. Accred.: NEASC-CIHE (1966/2000)
Prog. Accred.: Massage Therapy, Nursing

Hampshire College
893 West St., Amherst 01002
Type: Private, independent, four-year
Degrees: B   *Enroll:* 1,334
URL: http://www.hampshire.edu
Phone: (413) 549-4600   *Calendar:* 4-1-4 plan
Inst. Accred.: NEASC-CIHE (1974/1997)

Harvard University
Massachusetts Hall, Cambridge 02138-3800
Type: Private, independent, four-year
Degrees: A, B, M, D   *Enroll:* 21,257
URL: http://www.harvard.edu
Phone: (617) 495-1000   *Calendar:* Sem. plan
Inst. Accred.: ATS (1940/2002), NEASC-CIHE (1929/1997)
Prog. Accred.: Advanced Education in General Dentistry,
Applied Science (industrial hygiene), Business (AACSB),
Combined Prosthodontics, Dental Public Health,
Dentistry, Endodontics, Engineering (engineering
physics/science), General Dentistry, Landscape
Architecture, Law, Medicine, Oral and Maxillofacial
Pathology, Orthodontic and Dentofacial Orthopedics,
Pediatric Dentistry, Periodontics, Planning, Psychology
Internship, Public Health

Harvard School of Public Health
677 Huntington Ave., Boston 02115
Phone: (617) 432-1000
Prog. Accred: Applied Science (industrial hygiene)

Radcliffe Institute for Advanced Study
10 Garden St., Cambridge 02138
Phone: (617) 495-8601

Hebrew College
160 Herrick Rd., Newton Centre 02459
Type: Private, independent, four-year
Degrees: B, M   *Enroll:* 81
URL: http://www.hebrewcollege.org
Phone: (617) 559-8600   *Calendar:* Sem. plan
Inst. Accred.: NEASC-CIHE (1955/1998)

Hellenic College/Holy Cross Greek Orthodox School of Theology
50 Goddard Ave., Brookline 02445-7496
Type: Private, Greek Orthodox Church, four-year
Degrees: B, M   *Enroll:* 252
URL: http://www.hchc.edu
Phone: (617) 731-3500   *Calendar:* Sem. plan
Inst. Accred.: ATS (1974/2001), NEASC-CIHE (1974/2001)

Holyoke Community College
303 Homestead Ave., Holyoke 01040-1099
Type: Public, state, two-year
System: Massachusetts Board of Higher Education
Degrees: A   *Enroll:* 4,257
URL: http://www.hcc.mass.edu
Phone: (413) 538-7000   *Calendar:* Sem. plan
Inst. Accred.: NEASC-CIHE (1970/2000)
Prog. Accred.: Business (ACBSP), Culinary Education,
Music, Nursing, Ophthalmic Lab Technology, Opticianry,
Radiography, Veterinary Technology

Hult International Business School
One Education St., Cambridge 02141
Type: Private, proprietary, four-year
Degrees: M   *FTE Enroll:* 59
URL: http://www.hult.edu
Phone: (617) 746 1990   *Calendar:* Tri. plan
Inst. Accred.: NEASC-CIHE (1976/1997)

Lasell College
1844 Commonwealth Ave., Newton 02466-2716
Type: Private, independent, four-year
Degrees: A, B, M   *Enroll:* 1,074
URL: http://www.lasell.edu
Phone: (617) 243-2000   *Calendar:* Sem. plan
Inst. Accred.: NEASC-CIHE (1932/2002)

Lesley University
29 Everett St., Cambridge 02138-2790
Type: Private, independent, four-year
Degrees: A, B, M, D   *Enroll:* 3,444
URL: http://www.lesley.edu
Phone: (617) 868-9600   *Calendar:* Sem. plan
Inst. Accred.: NEASC-CIHE (1952/2005)

The Art Institute of Boston at Lesley University
700 Beacon St., Boston 02215
Phone: (617) 585-6600
Prog. Accred: Art

Longy School of Music
One Follen St., Cambridge 02138-3599
Type: Private, independent, four-year
Degrees: M   *Enroll:* 157
URL: http://www.longy.edu
Phone: (617) 876-0956
Inst. Accred.: NEASC-CIHE (1995/2001)
Prog. Accred.: Music

Marian Court College
35 Little's Point Rd., Swampscott 01907
Type: Private, Roman Catholic Church, two-year
Degrees: A   *Enroll:* 249
URL: http://www.mariancourt.edu
Phone: (781) 595-6768   *Calendar:* Sem. plan
Inst. Accred.: NEASC-CIHE (2004)

Massachusetts Bay Community College
50 Oakland St., Wellesley Hills 02481-5357
Type: Public, state, two-year
System: Massachusetts Board of Higher Education
Degrees: A   *Enroll:* 3,456
URL: http://www.massbay.edu
Phone: (781) 239-3000   *Calendar:* Sem. plan
Inst. Accred.: NEASC-CIHE (1967/2005)
Prog. Accred.: Nursing, Physical Therapy Assisting,
   Radiography, Respiratory Therapy, Respiratory Therapy
   Technology

Massachusetts College of Art
621 Huntington Ave., Boston 02115-5882
Type: Public, state, four-year
System: Massachusetts Board of Higher Education
Degrees: B, M   *Enroll:* 1,669
URL: http://www.massart.edu
Phone: (617) 879-7000   *Calendar:* Sem. plan
Inst. Accred.: NEASC-CIHE (1954/2005)
Prog. Accred.: Art

Massachusetts College of Liberal Arts
375 Church St., North Adams 01247-4100
Type: Public, state, four-year
System: Massachusetts Board of Higher Education
Degrees: B, M   *Enroll:* 1,435
URL: http://www.mcla.mass.edu
Phone: (413) 662-5000   *Calendar:* Sem. plan
Inst. Accred.: NEASC-CIHE (1953/2003)

Massachusetts College of Pharmacy and Health Sciences
179 Longwood Ave., Boston 02115-5896
Type: Private, independent, four-year
Degrees: A, B, M, P, D   *Enroll:* 2,308
URL: http://www.mcp.edu
Phone: (617) 732-2800   *Calendar:* Sem. plan
Inst. Accred.: NEASC-CIHE (1974/1997)
Prog. Accred.: Dental Hygiene, Nuclear Medicine
   Technology, Nursing, Pharmacy, Physician Assistant,
   Radiation Therapy, Radiography

Manchester Center for Health Sciences
1528 Elm St., Manchester, NH 03101
Phone: (800) 225-5506
Prog. Accred: Physician Assistant

Worcester Campus
19 Foster St., Worcester 01608
Phone: (508) 890-8855
Prog. Accred: Pharmacy

Massachusetts Institute of Technology
77 Massachusetts Ave., Cambridge 02139-4307
Type: Private, independent, four-year
Degrees: B, M, D   *Enroll:* 10,129
URL: http://www.mit.edu
Phone: (617) 253-1000   *Calendar:* 4-1-4 plan
Inst. Accred.: NEASC-CIHE (1929/1999)
Prog. Accred.: Business (AACSB), Computer Science,
   Engineering (aerospace, chemical, civil, computer,
   electrical, environmental/sanitary, materials,
   mechanical, nuclear, ocean), Planning

Massachusetts Maritime Academy
101 Academy Dr., Buzzards Bay 02532-3400
Type: Public, state, four-year
System: Massachusetts Board of Higher Education
Degrees: B, M   *Enroll:* 900
URL: http://www.mma.mass.edu
Phone: (508) 830-5000   *Calendar:* Sem. plan
Inst. Accred.: NEASC-CIHE (1974/2001)

Massachusetts School of Law
500 Federal St., Andover 01810-1094
Type: Private, independent, four-year
Degrees: D   *Enroll:* 423
URL: http://www.mslaw.edu
Phone: (978) 681-0800   *Calendar:* Sem. plan
Inst. Accred.: NEASC-CIHE (1997/2002)

Massachusetts School of Professional Psychology
221 Rivermoor St., Boston 02132-4935
Type: Private, independent, four-year
Degrees: D   *Enroll:* 159
URL: http://www.mspp.edu
Phone: (617) 327-6777   *Calendar:* Sem. plan
Inst. Accred.: NEASC-CIHE (1984/2002)
Prog. Accred.: Clinical Psychology

Massasoit Community College
One Massasoit Blvd., Brockton 02402
Type: Public, state, two-year
System: Massachusetts Board of Higher Education
Degrees: A   *Enroll:* 4,397
URL: http://www.massasoit.mass.edu
Phone: (508) 588-9100   *Calendar:* Sem. plan
Inst. Accred.: NEASC-CIHE (1971/1996)
Prog. Accred.: Medical Assisting (AMA), Nursing,
   Radiography, Respiratory Therapy

Canton Campus
900 Randolph St., Canton 02021
Phone: (781) 821-2222
Prog. Accred: Dental Assisting

Merrimack College
315 Turnpike St., North Andover 01845-5800
Type: Private, Roman Catholic Church, four-year
Degrees: A, B, M   *Enroll:* 2,137
URL: http://www.merrimack.edu
Phone: (978) 837-5000   *Calendar:* Sem. plan
Inst. Accred.: NEASC-CIHE (1953/2001)
Prog. Accred.: Business (AACSB), Engineering (civil, electrical)

MGH Institute of Health Professions
36 First Ave., Charlestown Navy Yard, Boston 02129-4557
Type: Private, independent, four-year
Degrees: M, D   *Enroll:* 451
URL: http://www.mghihp.edu
Phone: (617) 726-2947   *Calendar:* Sem. plan
Inst. Accred.: NEASC-CIHE (1985/2000)
Prog. Accred.: Nursing, Physical Therapy, Speech-Language Pathology

Middlesex Community College
590 Springs Rd., Bedford 01730-1197
Type: Public, state, two-year
System: Massachusetts Board of Higher Education
Degrees: A   *Enroll:* 5,176
URL: http://www.middlesex.mass.edu
Phone: (781) 280-3200   *Calendar:* Sem. plan
Inst. Accred.: NEASC-CIHE (1973/2004)
Prog. Accred.: Diagnostic Medical Sonography, Nursing, Radiography

Lowell Campus
Kearney Square, Lowell 01852
Phone: (508) 656-3200
Prog. Accred: Dental Assisting, Dental Hygiene, Dental Laboratory Technology, Medical Assisting (CAAHEP)

Montserrat College of Art
23 Essex St., Box 26, Beverly 01915-4508
Type: Private, independent, four-year
Degrees: B   *Enroll:* 371
URL: http://www.montserrat.edu
Phone: (978) 922-8222   *Calendar:* Sem. plan
Inst. Accred.: NEASC-CIHE (1995/2001)
Prog. Accred.: Art

Mount Holyoke College
50 College St., South Hadley 01075
Type: Private, independent, four-year
Degrees: B, M   *Enroll:* 2,116
URL: http://www.mtholyoke.edu
Phone: (413) 538-2000   *Calendar:* 4-1-4 plan
Inst. Accred.: NEASC-CIHE (1929/1997)

Mount Ida College
777 Dedham St., Newton Centre 02159-3310
Type: Private, independent, four-year
Degrees: A, B   *Enroll:* 1,194
URL: http://www.mountida.edu
Phone: (617) 928-4500   *Calendar:* Sem. plan
Inst. Accred.: NEASC-CIHE (1970/1997)
Prog. Accred.: Art, Dental Hygiene, Funeral Service Education (Mortuary Science), Interior Design, Veterinary Technology

Mount Wachusett Community College
444 Green St., Gardner 01440-1000
Type: Public, state, two-year
System: Massachusetts Board of Higher Education
Degrees: A   *Enroll:* 2,560
URL: http://www.mwcc.mass.edu
Phone: (978) 632-6600   *Calendar:* Sem. plan
Inst. Accred.: NEASC-CIHE (1968/2002)
Prog. Accred.: Medical Assisting (AMA), Nursing, Physical Therapy Assisting

The National Graduate School
186 Jones Rd., Falmouth 02540
Type: Private, independent, four-year
Degrees: M
URL: http://www.ngs.edu
Phone: (800) 838-2580
Inst. Accred.: NEASC-CIHE (1998/2001)

The New England College of Finance
10 High St., Ste. 204, Boston 02110
Type: Private, independent, two-year
Degrees: A   *FTE Enroll:* 293
URL: http://www.finance.edu
Phone: (617) 951-2350   *Calendar:* Sem. plan
Inst. Accred.: NEASC-CTCI (1985/1996)

New England College of Optometry
424 Beacon St., Boston 02115-1129
Type: Private, independent, four-year
Degrees: B, M, P, D   *Enroll:* 411
URL: http://www.ne-optometry.edu
Phone: (617) 266-2030   *Calendar:* Sem. plan
Inst. Accred.: NEASC-CIHE (1976/2003)
Prog. Accred.: Optometric Residency, Optometry

New England Conservatory of Music
290 Huntington Ave., Boston 02115-5018
Type: Private, independent, four-year
Degrees: B, M, D   *Enroll:* 746
URL: http://www.newenglandconservatory.edu
Phone: (617) 585-1100   *Calendar:* Sem. plan
Inst. Accred.: NEASC-CIHE (1951/1998)
Prog. Accred.: Music

The New England Institute of Art
10 Brookline Place West, Brookline 02445
Type: Private, independent, four-year
System: Education Management Corporation
Degrees: A, B   *Enroll:* 865
URL: http://www.aine.artinstitute.edu
Phone: (617) 739-1700   *Calendar:* Sem. plan
Inst. Accred.: NEASC-CIHE (2004)

New England School of Acupuncture
40 Belmont St., Watertown 02472
Type: Private, proprietary, four-year
Degrees: M   *Enroll:* 216
URL: http://www.nesa.edu
Phone: (617) 926-1788   *Calendar:* Sem. plan
Inst. Accred.: ACAOM (1988/2003)

Newbury College
129 Fisher Ave., Brookline 02445-5796
Type: Private, independent, four-year
Degrees: A, B   *Enroll:* 894
URL: http://www.newbury.edu
Phone: (617) 730-7034   *Calendar:* Sem. plan
Inst. Accred.: NEASC-CIHE (2000/2005)
Prog. Accred.: Interior Design

Nichols College
PO Box 5000, Dudley 01571
Type: Private, independent, four-year
Degrees: A, B, M   *Enroll:* 1,228
URL: http://www.nichols.edu
Phone: (508) 943-1560   *Calendar:* Sem. plan
Inst. Accred.: NEASC-CIHE (1965/2004)

North Shore Community College
1 Ferncroft Rd., Danvers 01923-0840
Type: Public, state/local, two-year
System: Massachusetts Board of Higher Education
Degrees: A   *Enroll:* 3,946
URL: http://www.nscc.mass.edu
Phone: (978) 762-4000   *Calendar:* Sem. plan
Inst. Accred.: NEASC-CIHE (1969/1999)
Prog. Accred.: Medical Assisting (AMA), Nursing,
  Occupational Therapy Assisting, Physical Therapy
  Assisting, Radiography, Respiratory Therapy, Surgical
  Technology

Essex Agricultural and Technical Institute
562 Maple St., Hathorne 01937
Phone: (978) 762-4000

Northeastern University
360 Huntington Ave., Boston 02115-0195
Type: Private, independent, four-year
Degrees: A, B, M, P, D   *Enroll:* 19,512
URL: http://www.northeastern.edu
Phone: (617) 373-2000   *Calendar:* Qtr. plan
Inst. Accred.: NEASC-CIHE (1940/1998)
Prog. Accred.: Athletic Training, Audiology, Business
  (AACSB), Clinical Lab Scientist, Clinical Lab Technology,
  Combined Professional-Scientific Psychology, Computer
  Science, Engineering (chemical, civil, electrical,

industrial, mechanical), Engineering Technology
  (electrical, mechanical), Health Information
  Administration, Law, Nurse Anesthesia Education,
  Nursing, Nursing Education, Perfusion, Pharmacy,
  Physical Therapy, Physician Assistant, Public
  Administration, Radiography, Rehabilitation Counseling,
  Respiratory Therapy, Speech-Language Pathology

Northern Essex Community College
100 Elliott Way, Haverhill 01830-2399
Type: Public, state, two-year
System: Massachusetts Board of Higher Education
Degrees: A   *Enroll:* 3,615
URL: http://www.necc.mass.edu
Phone: (978) 556-3000   *Calendar:* Sem. plan
Inst. Accred.: NEASC-CIHE (1969/2000)
Prog. Accred.: Health Information Technician, Medical
  Assisting (AMA), Nursing, Practical Nursing,
  Radiography, Respiratory Therapy, Respiratory Therapy
  Technology

Lawrence Campus
45 Franklin St., Lawrence 01841
Phone: (978) 556-3000
Prog. Accred: Dental Assisting, Radiography

Pine Manor College
400 Heath St., Chestnut Hill 02467-2332
Type: Private, independent, four-year
Degrees: A, B, M   *Enroll:* 480
URL: http://www.pmc.edu
Phone: (617) 731-7000   *Calendar:* Sem. plan
Inst. Accred.: NEASC-CIHE (1939/2003)

Quincy College
34 Coddington St., Quincy 02169-4501
Type: Public, local, two-year
Degrees: A   *Enroll:* 2,570
URL: http://www.quincycollege.edu
Phone: (617) 984-1600   *Calendar:* Sem. plan
Inst. Accred.: NEASC-CIHE (1980/1996)
Prog. Accred.: Nursing, Practical Nursing, Surgical
  Technology

Quinsigamond Community College
670 West Boylston St., Worcester 01606-2092
Type: Public, state, two-year
System: Massachusetts Board of Higher Education
Degrees: A   *Enroll:* 4,107
URL: http://www.qcc.edu
Phone: (508) 853-2300   *Calendar:* Sem. plan
Inst. Accred.: NEASC-CIHE (1967/2003)
Prog. Accred.: Dental Assisting, Dental Hygiene, Nursing,
  Occupational Therapy Assisting, Radiography,
  Respiratory Therapy, Surgical Technology

Regis College
235 Wellesley St., Weston 02493-1571
Type: Private, Roman Catholic Church, four-year
Degrees: B, M   *Enroll:* 839
URL: http://www.regiscollege.edu
Phone: (781) 768-7000   *Calendar:* Sem. plan
Inst. Accred.: NEASC-CIHE (1933/1996)
Prog. Accred.: Nursing, Social Work

Roxbury Community College
1234 Columbus Ave., Roxbury Crossing 02120-3400
Type: Public, state, two-year
System: Massachusetts Board of Higher Education
Degrees: A   *Enroll:* 1,414
URL: http://www.rcc.mass.edu
Phone: (617) 427-0060   *Calendar:* Sem. plan
Inst. Accred.: NEASC-CIHE (1981/2005)
Prog. Accred.: Nursing

Saint John's Seminary
127 Lake St., Brighton 02135-3898
Type: Private, Roman Catholic Church, four-year
Degrees: B, M, P   *Enroll:* 62
URL: http://www.sjs.edu
Phone: (617) 254-2610   *Calendar:* Sem. plan
Inst. Accred.: ATS (1970/2000), NEASC-CIHE (1969/2000)

Salem State College
352 Lafayette St., Salem 01970-5353
Type: Public, state, four-year
System: Massachusetts Board of Higher Education
Degrees: B, M   *Enroll:* 6,579
URL: http://www.salemstate.edu
Phone: (978) 542-6000   *Calendar:* Sem. plan
Inst. Accred.: NEASC-CIHE (1953/2001)
Prog. Accred.: Art, Athletic Training, Computer Science,
   Nuclear Medicine Technology, Nursing, Nursing
   Education, Occupational Therapy, Social Work, Teacher
   Education (NCATE), Theatre

School of the Museum of Fine Arts, Boston
230 The Fenway, Boston 02115-9975
Type: Private, independent, four-year
Degrees: B, M   *Enroll:* 848
URL: http://www.smfa.edu
Phone: (617) 267-6100   *Calendar:* Sem. plan
Inst. Accred.: NASAD (1948/2004)

Simmons College
300 The Fenway, Boston 02115-5898
Type: Private, independent, four-year
Degrees: B, M, D   *Enroll:* 2,860
URL: http://www.simmons.edu
Phone: (617) 521-2000   *Calendar:* Sem. plan
Inst. Accred.: NEASC-CIHE (1929/2000)
Prog. Accred.: Business (AACSB), Dietetics (internship),
   Health Services Administration, Librarianship, Nursing,
   Physical Therapy, Social Work

Simon's Rock College of Bard
84 Alford Rd., Great Barrington 01230-9072
Type: Private, independent, four-year
Degrees: A, B   *Enroll:* 395
URL: http://www.simons-rock.edu
Phone: (413) 528-0771   *Calendar:* Sem. plan
Inst. Accred.: NEASC-CIHE (1974/1996)

Smith College
Northampton 01063-0001
Type: Private, independent, four-year
Degrees: B, M, D   *Enroll:* 3,114
URL: http://www.smith.edu
Phone: (413) 584-2700   *Calendar:* Sem. plan
Inst. Accred.: NEASC-CIHE (1929/1997)
Prog. Accred.: Social Work

Southern New England School of Law
333 Faunce Corner Rd., North Dartmouth 02747-1252
Type: Private, independent, four-year
Degrees: D   *Enroll:* 212
URL: http://www.snesl.edu
Phone: (508) 998-9600
Inst. Accred.: NEASC-CIHE (1995/2000)

Springfield College
263 Alder St., Springfield 01109-3788
Type: Private, independent, four-year
Degrees: B, M, D   *Enroll:* 4,554
URL: http://www.spfldcol.edu
Phone: (413) 748-3000   *Calendar:* Sem. plan
Inst. Accred.: NEASC-CIHE (1930/2000)
Prog. Accred.: Athletic Training, Occupational Therapy,
   Physical Therapy, Physician Assistant, Recreation and
   Leisure Services, Rehabilitation Counseling, Social Work

Springfield Technical Community College
One Armory Square, Springfield 01105-1296
Type: Public, state, two-year
System: Massachusetts Board of Higher Education
Degrees: A   *Enroll:* 3,956
URL: http://www.stcc.edu
Phone: (413) 781-7822   *Calendar:* Sem. plan
Inst. Accred.: NEASC-CIHE (1971/2001)
Prog. Accred.: Clinical Assistant, Clinical Lab Technology,
   Dental Assisting, Dental Hygiene, Diagnostic Medical
   Sonography, Massage Therapy, Medical Assisting
   (AMA), Nuclear Medicine Technology, Nursing,
   Occupational Therapy Assisting, Physical Therapy
   Assisting, Radiography, Respiratory Therapy, Surgical
   Technology

Stonehill College
Washington St., Easton 02357-6110
Type: Private, Roman Catholic Church, four-year
Degrees: B, M   *Enroll:* 2,372
URL: http://www.stonehill.edu
Phone: (508) 565-1000   *Calendar:* Sem. plan
Inst. Accred.: NEASC-CIHE (1959/1999)

Suffolk University
8 Ashburton Place, Bsoton 02108-2701
Type: Private, independent, four-year
Degrees: A, B, M, P, D   *Enroll:* 6,109
URL: http://www.suffolk.edu
Phone: (617) 573-8000   *Calendar:* Sem. plan
Inst. Accred.: NEASC-CIHE (1952/2002)
Prog. Accred.: Accounting, Business (AACSB), Clinical
   Psychology, Law, Psychology Internship, Public
   Administration, Radiation Therapy

New England School of Art and Design at Suffolk University
81 Arlington St., Boston 02116
Phone: (617) 573-8785
Prog. Accred: Art, Interior Design

Tufts University
Medford 02155
Type: Private, independent, four-year
Degrees: B, M, P, D   *Enroll:* 8,897
URL: http://www.tufts.edu
Phone: (617) 628-5000   *Calendar:* Sem. plan
Inst. Accred.: NEASC-CIHE (1929/2003)
Prog. Accred.: Combined Prosthodontics, Dentistry,
   Dietetics (internship), Endodontics, Engineering
   (chemical, civil, computer, electrical,
   environmental/sanitary, mechanical), General Practice
   Residency, Medicine, Occupational Therapy, Oral and
   Maxillofacial Surgery, Orthodontic and Dentofacial
   Orthopedics, Pediatric Dentistry, Periodontics,
   Psychology Internship, Public Health, Veterinary
   Medicine

University of Massachusetts Amherst
Whitmore Bldg., 181 President Dr., Amherst 01003-0001
Type: Public, state, four-year
System: University of Massachusetts
Degrees: A, B, M, P, D   *Enroll:* 21,378
URL: http://www.umass.edu
Phone: (413) 545-0111   *Calendar:* Sem. plan
Inst. Accred.: NEASC-CIHE (1932/1998)
Prog. Accred.: Accounting, Audiology, Business (AACSB),
   Clinical Psychology, Dietetics (internship), Engineering
   (civil, computer, electrical, environmental/sanitary,
   industrial, manufacturing, mechanical), Forestry, Interior
   Design, Landscape Architecture, Music, Nursing, Nursing
   Education, Planning, Psychology Internship, Public
   Administration, Public Health, School Psychology,
   Speech-Language Pathology, Teacher Education (NCATE)

University of Massachusetts Boston
100 Morrisey Blvd., Boston 02125-3393
Type: Public, state, four-year
System: University of Massachusetts
Degrees: B, M, D   *Enroll:* 8,799
URL: http://www.umb.edu
Phone: (617) 287-5000   *Calendar:* Sem. plan
Inst. Accred.: NEASC-CIHE (1972/2005)
Prog. Accred.: Business (AACSB), Clinical Psychology,
   Marriage and Family Therapy, Nursing, Nursing
   Education, Rehabilitation Counseling

University of Massachusetts Dartmouth
285 Old Westport Rd., North Dartmouth 02747-2300
Type: Public, state, four-year
System: University of Massachusetts
Degrees: B, M, D   *Enroll:* 7,200
URL: http://www.umassd.edu
Phone: (508) 999-8000   *Calendar:* Sem. plan
Inst. Accred.: NEASC-CIHE (1964/2000)
Prog. Accred.: Art, Business (AACSB), Clinical Lab
   Scientist, Computer Science, Engineering (civil,
   computer, electrical, mechanical), Nursing

University of Massachusetts Lowell
One University Ave., Lowell 01854-9985
Type: Public, state, four-year
System: University of Massachusetts
Degrees: A, B, M, D   *Enroll:* 8,590
URL: http://www.uml.edu
Phone: (978) 934-4000   *Calendar:* Sem. plan
Inst. Accred.: NEASC-CIHE (1975/2003)
Prog. Accred.: Applied Science (industrial hygiene), Art,
   Business (AACSB), Clinical Lab Scientist, Computer
   Science, Engineering (chemical, civil, electrical,
   mechanical, nuclear, plastics), Engineering Technology
   (civil/construction, electrical, mechanical), Music,
   Nursing, Nursing Education, Physical Therapy, Teacher
   Education (NCATE)

University of Massachusetts Medical School
55 Lake Ave., North, Worcester 01605-0001
Type: Public, state, four-year
System: University of Massachusetts
Degrees: P, D   *Enroll:* 773
URL: http://www.umassmed.edu
Phone: (508) 856-8989   *Calendar:* Sem. plan
Inst. Accred.: NEASC-CIHE (1997/2002)
Prog. Accred.: Clinical Pastoral Education (ACPEI),
   Medicine, Nuclear Medicine Technology, Nursing,
   Nursing Education, Radiation Therapy

Urban College of Boston
178 Tremont St., Boston 02111-1093
Type: Private, independent, two-year
Degrees: A   *Enroll:* 251
URL: http://www.urbancollege.edu
Phone: (617) 292-4723   *Calendar:* Sem. plan
Inst. Accred.: NEASC-CIHE (2001)

Wellesley College
106 Central St., Wellesley 02481-8203
Type: Private, independent, four-year
Degrees: B   *Enroll:* 2,256
URL: http://www.wellesley.edu
Phone: (781) 283-1000   *Calendar:* Sem. plan
Inst. Accred.: NEASC-CIHE (1929/1999)

Wentworth Institute of Technology
550 Huntington Ave., Boston 02115-5998
Type: Private, independent, four-year
Degrees: A, B   *Enroll:* 3,125
URL: http://www.wit.edu
Phone: (617) 989-4590   *Calendar:* Sem. plan
Inst. Accred.: NEASC-CIHE (1967/2001)
Prog. Accred.: Construction Education, Engineering
Technology (architectural, civil/construction, computer,
electrical, electromechanical, environmental/sanitary,
manufacturing, mechanical), Interior Design

Western New England College
1215 Wilbraham Rd., Springfield 01119-2684
Type: Private, independent, four-year
Degrees: B, M, P, D   *Enroll:* 3,347
URL: http://www.wnec.edu
Phone: (413) 782-3111   *Calendar:* Sem. plan
Inst. Accred.: NEASC-CIHE (1965/2002)
Prog. Accred.: Business (AACSB), Engineering (electrical,
industrial, mechanical), Law, Social Work

Westfield State College
PO Box 1630, Westfield 01086-1630
Type: Public, state, four-year
System: Massachusetts Board of Higher Education
Degrees: B, M   *Enroll:* 4,235
URL: http://www.wsc.ma.edu
Phone: (413) 572-5300   *Calendar:* Sem. plan
Inst. Accred.: NEASC-CIHE (1957/2002)
Prog. Accred.: Athletic Training, Social Work

Weston Jesuit School of Theology
3 Phillips Place, Cambridge 02138-3495
Type: Private, Roman Catholic Church, four-year
Degrees: M   *Enroll:* 155
URL: http://www.wjst.edu
Phone: (617) 492-1960   *Calendar:* Sem. plan
Inst. Accred.: ATS (1968/1998)

Wheaton College
26 East Main St., Norton 02766-2322
Type: Private, independent, four-year
Degrees: B   *Enroll:* 1,553
URL: http://www.wheatonma.edu
Phone: (508) 285-7722   *Calendar:* Sem. plan
Inst. Accred.: NEASC-CIHE (1929/1999)

Wheelock College
200 The Riverway, Boston 02215-4176
Type: Private, independent, four-year
Degrees: A, B, M   *Enroll:* 820
URL: http://www.wheelock.edu
Phone: (617) 734-5200   *Calendar:* Sem. plan
Inst. Accred.: NEASC-CIHE (1950/2004)
Prog. Accred.: Social Work, Teacher Education (NCATE)

Williams College
PO Box 687, Williamstown 01267
Type: Private, independent, four-year
Degrees: B, M   *Enroll:* 2,072
URL: http://www.williams.edu
Phone: (413) 597-3131   *Calendar:* 4-1-4 plan
Inst. Accred.: NEASC-CIHE (1929/1997)

Woods Hole Oceanographic Institution
Education Off., Clark Laboratory, MS #31, 360 Woods
Hole Rd., Woods Hole 02543-1522
Type: Private, independent, four-year
Degrees: D
URL: http://www.whoi.edu
Phone: (508) 289-2000
Inst. Accred.: NEASC-CIHE (2001)

Worcester Polytechnic Institute
100 Institute Rd., Worcester 01609-2280
Type: Private, independent, four-year
Degrees: B, M, D   *Enroll:* 3,409
URL: http://www.wpi.edu
Phone: (508) 831-5000   *Calendar:* Sem. plan
Inst. Accred.: NEASC-CIHE (1937/2001)
Prog. Accred.: Business (AACSB), Computer Science,
Engineering (bioengineering, chemical, civil, electrical,
industrial, manufacturing, mechanical)

Worcester State College
486 Chandler St., Worcester 01602-2597
Type: Public, state, four-year
System: Massachusetts Board of Higher Education
Degrees: B, M   *Enroll:* 4,070
URL: http://www.worcester.edu
Phone: (508) 793-8000   *Calendar:* Sem. plan
Inst. Accred.: NEASC-CIHE (1957/2002)
Prog. Accred.: Nursing, Occupational Therapy, Speech-
Language Pathology

MICHIGAN

Adrian College
110 South Madison St., Adrian 49221
Type: Private, United Methodist Church, four-year
Degrees: A, B *Enroll:* 1,002
URL: http://www.adrian.edu
Phone: (517) 265-5161 *Calendar:* Sem. plan
Inst. Accred.: NCA-HLC (1916/1999)

Albion College
611 East Porter St., Albion 49224
Type: Private, United Methodist Church, four-year
Degrees: B *Enroll:* 1,716
URL: http://www.albion.edu
Phone: (517) 629-0210 *Calendar:* Sem. plan
Inst. Accred.: NCA-HLC (1915/2001)
Prog. Accred.: Music

Alma College
614 West Superior St., Alma 48801
Type: Private, United Presbyterian Church, four-year
Degrees: B *Enroll:* 1,265
URL: http://www.alma.edu
Phone: (989) 463-7111 *Calendar:* 4-4-x plan
Inst. Accred.: NCA-HLC (1916/2000)
Prog. Accred.: Music

Alpena Community College
666 Johnson St., Alpena 49707-1495
Type: Public, state/local, two-year
System: Michigan Department of Education
Degrees: A *Enroll:* 1,304
URL: http://www.alpenacc.edu
Phone: (989) 356-9021 *Calendar:* Sem. plan
Inst. Accred.: NCA-HLC (1963/1998)
Prog. Accred.: Business (ACBSP), Medical Assisting
  (CAAHEP)

Huron Shores Campus
5800 Skeel Ave., Oscoda 48750-1587
Phone: (517) 739-1449

Andrews University
US 31 North, Berrien Springs 49104-1500
Type: Private, Seventh-Day Adventist Church, four-year
Degrees: A, B, M, P, D *Enroll:* 2,460
URL: http://www.andrews.edu
Phone: (269) 471-7771 *Calendar:* Qtr. plan
Inst. Accred.: ATS (1970/1999), NCA-HLC (1922/1999)
Prog. Accred.: Clinical Lab Scientist, Counseling, Music,
  Nursing, Physical Therapy, Social Work, Teacher
  Education (NCATE)

Aquinas College
1607 Robinson Rd., SE, Grand Rapids 49506-1799
Type: Private, Roman Catholic Church, four-year
Degrees: A, B, M *Enroll:* 1,921
URL: http://www.aquinas.edu
Phone: (616) 632-8900 *Calendar:* Sem. plan
Inst. Accred.: NCA-HLC (1946/2004)

Ave Maria School of Law
3475 Plymouth Rd., Ann Arbor 48105-2550
Type: Private, Roman Catholic Church, four-year
Degrees: P
URL: http://www.avemarialaw.edu
Phone: (734) 827-8040 *Calendar:* Sem. plan
Inst. Accred.: ABA (2005)

Baker College Business and Corporate Services
1050 West Bristol Rd., Flint 48507-5508
Type: Private, proprietary, four-year
System: Baker College System
Degrees: A, B, M *Enroll:* 282
URL: https://www.baker.edu
Phone: (810) 766-4242 *Calendar:* Qtr. plan
Inst. Accred.: NCA-HLC (1985/2000, *Indirect accreditation
  through Baker College System, Flint, MI*)

Baker College Center for Graduate Studies
1116 West Bristol Rd., Flint 48507-9843
Type: Private, proprietary, four-year
System: Baker College System
Degrees: M *Enroll:* 2,287
URL: http://www.baker.edu
Phone: (810) 766-4390 *Calendar:* Qtr. plan
Inst. Accred.: NCA-HLC (1985/2000, *Indirect accreditation
  through Baker College System, Flint, MI*)

Baker College of Allen Park
4500 Enterprise Dr., Allen Park 48101
Type: Private, proprietary, four-year
Degrees: A, B
URL: https://www.baker.edu
Phone: (313) 425-3700 *Calendar:* Qtr. plan
Inst. Accred.: NCA-HLC (1985/2002, *Indirect accreditation
  through Baker College System, Flint, MI*)

Baker College of Auburn Hills
1500 University Dr., Auburn Hills 48326-2642
Type: Private, proprietary, four-year
System: Baker College System
Degrees: A, B, M *Enroll:* 2,258
URL: http://www.baker.edu
Phone: (248) 340-0600 *Calendar:* Qtr. plan
Inst. Accred.: NCA-HLC (1985/2000, *Indirect accreditation
  through Baker College System, Flint, MI*)
Prog. Accred.: Medical Assisting (CAAHEP)

Baker College of Cadillac
9600 East 13th St., Cadillac 49601-9600
Type: Private, proprietary, four-year
System: Baker College System
Degrees: A, B *Enroll:* 1,062
URL: http://www.baker.edu
Phone: (231) 775-8458 *Calendar:* Qtr. plan
Inst. Accred.: NCA-HLC (1985/2000, *Indirect accreditation
  through Baker College System, Flint, MI*)
Prog. Accred.: Medical Assisting (CAAHEP)

Baker College of Clinton Township
34950 Little Mack Ave., Clinton Township 48035-6611
Type: Private, proprietary, four-year
System: Baker College System
Degrees: A, B   *Enroll:* 3,336
URL: http://www.baker.edu
Phone: (810) 791-6610   *Calendar:* Qtr. plan
Inst. Accred.: NCA-HLC (1985/2000, *Indirect accreditation
   through Baker College System, Flint, MI*)
Prog. Accred.: Health Information Technician, Medical
   Assisting (AMA), Surgical Technology

Baker College of Flint
1050 West Bristol Rd., Flint 48507-5508
Type: Private, proprietary, four-year
System: Baker College System
Degrees: A, B, M   *Enroll:* 4,194
URL: http://www.baker.edu
Phone: (810) 766-4000   *Calendar:* Qtr. plan
Inst. Accred.: NCA-HLC (1985/2000, *Indirect accreditation
   through Baker College System, Flint, MI*)
Prog. Accred.: Engineering (mechanical), Health
   Information Administration, Medical Assisting (AMA),
   Occupational Therapy, Physical Therapy Assisting,
   Surgical Technology

Baker College of Jackson
2800 Springport Rd., Jackson 49202-1299
Type: Private, proprietary, four-year
System: Baker College System
Degrees: A, B   *FTE Enroll:* 250
URL: http://www.baker.edu
Phone: (517) 788-7800   *Calendar:* Qtr. plan
Inst. Accred.: NCA-HLC (1985/2000, *Indirect accreditation
   through Baker College System, Flint, MI*)
Prog. Accred.: Medical Assisting (AMA), Radiation Therapy

Baker College of Muskegon
1903 Marquette Ave., Muskegon 49442-3404
Type: Private, proprietary, four-year
System: Baker College System
Degrees: A, B, M   *Enroll:* 3,185
URL: http://www.baker.edu
Phone: (231) 777-5200   *Calendar:* Qtr. plan
Inst. Accred.: NCA-HLC (1985/200, *Indirect accreditation
   through Baker College System, Flint, MI*)
Prog. Accred.: Culinary Education, Medical Assisting
   (AMA), Occupational Therapy Assisting, Physical
   Therapy Assisting, Surgical Technology

Baker College of Owosso
1020 South Washington St., Owosso 48867-4400
Type: Private, proprietary, four-year
System: Baker College System
Degrees: A, B, M   *Enroll:* 1,984
URL: http://www.baker.edu
Phone: (989) 729-3350   *Calendar:* Qtr. plan
Inst. Accred.: NCA-HLC (1985/2000, *Indirect accreditation
   through Baker College System, Flint, MI*)
Prog. Accred.: Clinical Lab Scientist, Clinical Lab
   Technology, Medical Assisting (AMA), Phlebotomy,
   Radiation Therapy, Radiography

Baker College of Port Huron
3403 Lapeer Rd., Port Huron 48060-2597
Type: Private, proprietary, four-year
System: Baker College System
Degrees: A, B   *Enroll:* 1,076
URL: http://www.baker.edu
Phone: (810) 985-7000   *Calendar:* Qtr. plan
Inst. Accred.: NCA-HLC (1985/2000, *Indirect accreditation
   through Baker College System, Flint, MI*)
Prog. Accred.: Dental Hygiene, Medical Assisting
   (CAAHEP)

Baker College Online
1116 West Bristol Rd., Flint 48507
Type: Private, proprietary, four-year
Degrees: A, B, M
URL: https://www.baker.edu
Phone: (810) 766-4390
Inst. Accred.: NCA-HLC (1985/2000, *Indirect accreditation
   through Baker College System, Flint, MI*)

Bay de Noc Community College
2001 North Lincoln Rd., Escanaba 49829-2511
Type: Public, state/local, two-year
System: Michigan Department of Education
Degrees: A   *Enroll:* 1,799
URL: http://www.baydenoc.cc.mi.us
Phone: (906) 786-5802   *Calendar:* Sem. plan
Inst. Accred.: NCA-HLC (1976/2001)

Bay Mills Community College
12214 West Lakeshore Dr., Brimley 49715
Type: Public, Bay Mills Indian Community, two-year
System: American Indian Higher Education Consortium
Degrees: A   *Enroll:* 246
URL: http://www.bmcc.edu
Phone: (906) 248-3354   *Calendar:* Sem. plan
Inst. Accred.: NCA-HLC (1995/1998)

Calvin College
3201 Burton St., SE, Grand Rapids 49546
Type: Private, Christian Reformed Church, four-year
Degrees: B, M   *Enroll:* 4,185
URL: http://www.calvin.edu
Phone: (616) 526-6000   *Calendar:* 4-1-4 plan
Inst. Accred.: NCA-HLC (1930/2005)
Prog. Accred.: Computer Science, Engineering (general),
   Music, Nursing, Nursing Education, Social Work,
   Teacher Education (NCATE)

Calvin Theological Seminary
3233 Burton St., SE, Grand Rapids 49546
Type: Private, Christian Reformed Church, four-year
Degrees: M, D   *Enroll:* 239
URL: http://www.calvinseminary.edu
Phone: (616) 957-6036   *Calendar:* Qtr. plan
Inst. Accred.: ATS (1944/1998)

Center for Humanistic Studies
26811 Orchard Lake Rd., Farmington Hills 48334-4512
Type: Private, independent, four-year
Degrees: M, P, D   *Enroll:* 82
URL: http://www.humanpsych.edu
Phone: (248) 476-1122   *Calendar:* Sem. plan
Inst. Accred.: NCA-HLC (1984/1997)

Central Michigan University
106 Warriner Hall, Mount Pleasant 48859
Type: Public, state, four-year
System: Michigan Department of Education
Degrees: B, M, P, D   *Enroll:* 22,407
URL: http://www.cmich.edu
Phone: (989) 774-4000   *Calendar:* Sem. plan
Inst. Accred.: NCA-HLC (1915/1996)
Prog. Accred.: Accounting, Athletic Training, Audiology,
   Business (AACSB), Clinical Psychology, Dietetics
   (internship), Journalism, Music, Physical Therapy,
   Physician Assistant, Recreation and Leisure Services,
   School Psychology, Social Work, Speech-Language
   Pathology

Charles Stewart Mott Community College
1401 East Ct. St., Flint 48503
Type: Public, local, two-year
System: Michigan Department of Education
Degrees: A   *Enroll:* 5,709
URL: http://www.mcc.edu
Phone: (810) 762-0200   *Calendar:* Sem. plan
Inst. Accred.: NCA-HLC (1926/2000)
Prog. Accred.: Dental Assisting, Dental Hygiene, Nursing,
   Occupational Therapy Assisting, Physical Therapy
   Assisting, Respiratory Therapy

Southern Lakes Campus
2100 West Thompson Rd., Fenton 48430-9798
Phone: (810) 750-8585

Cleary University
3601 Plymouth Rd., Ann Arbor 48105
Type: Private, independent, four-year
Degrees: A, B, M   *Enroll:* 547
URL: http://www.cleary.edu
Phone: (734) 332-4477   *Calendar:* Qtr. plan
Inst. Accred.: NCA-HLC (1988/1997)

Livingston Campus
3750 Cleary Dr., Howell 49943
Phone: (517) 548-3670

The College for Creative Studies
245 East Kirby St., Detroit 48202-4013
Type: Private, independent, four-year
Degrees: B   *Enroll:* 1,117
URL: http://www.ccscad.edu
Phone: (313) 664-7400   *Calendar:* Sem. plan
Inst. Accred.: NCA-HLC (1977/1996)
Prog. Accred.: Art

Concordia University, Ann Arbor
4090 Geddes Rd., Ann Arbor 48105
Type: Private, Lutheran Church-Missouri Synod, four-year
System: Concordia University System
Degrees: A, B, M   *Enroll:* 435
URL: http://www.cuaa.edu
Phone: (734) 995-7300   *Calendar:* Sem. plan
Inst. Accred.: NCA-HLC (1968/2001)
Prog. Accred.: Teacher Education (NCATE)

Cornerstone University
1001 East Beltline Ave., NE, Grand Rapids 49505
Type: Private, Baptist Church, four-year
Degrees: A, B, M, D   *Enroll:* 1,960
URL: http://www.cornerstone.edu
Phone: (616) 949-5300   *Calendar:* Sem. plan
Inst. Accred.: ATS (2002), NCA-HLC (1977/2002)
Prog. Accred.: Music, Social Work

Cranbrook Academy of Art
39221 Woodward Ave., PO Box 801, Bloomfield Hills
48303-0801
Type: Private, proprietary, four-year
Degrees: M   *Enroll:* 150
URL: http://www.cranbrook.edu/art
Phone: (248) 645-3300   *Calendar:* Sem. plan
Inst. Accred.: NCA-HLC (1960/1999)
Prog. Accred.: Art

Davenport University
415 East Fulton St., Grand Rapids 49503
Type: Private, independent, four-year
Degrees: A, B, M   *Enroll:* 1,420
URL: http://www.davenport.edu
Phone: (616) 451-3511   *Calendar:* Qtr. plan
Inst. Accred.: NCA-HLC (1976/2004)
Prog. Accred.: Medical Assisting (CAAHEP)

Bad Axe Campus
150 Nugent Rd., Bad Axe 48413
Phone: (989) 269-9288

Bay City Campus
3930 Traxler Ct., Bay City 48706
Phone: (517) 686-1572

Caro Campus
1231 Cleaver Rd., Caro 48723
Phone: (989) 673-5857
Prog. Accred: Medical Assisting (CAAHEP)

Dearborn Campus
4801 Oakman Blvd., Dearborn 48126
Phone: (313) 581-4400

Flint Campus
3488 North Jennings Rd., Flint 48504
Phone: (810) 789-2200

Granger Campus
7121 Grape Rd., Granger, IN 46530
Phone: (219) 277-8447
Prog. Accred: Medical Assisting (ABHES)

Davenport University *(continued)*

Holland Campus
643 South Waverly Rd., Holland 49423
Phone: (616) 395-4600

Kalamazoo Campus
4123 West Main St., Kalamazoo 49006
Phone: (269) 382-2835
Prog. Accred: Medical Assisting (CAAHEP)

Lansing Campus
220 East Kalamazoo St., Lansing 48933
Phone: (517) 484-2600
Prog. Accred: Medical Assisting (CAAHEP)

Merrillville Campus
8200 Georgia St., Merrillville, IN 46410
Phone: (219) 769-5556
Prog. Accred: Medical Assisting (ABHES)

Midland Campus
3555 East Patrick Rd., Midland 48642
Phone: (989) 835-5578
Prog. Accred: Medical Assisting (CAAHEP)

Saginaw Campus
5300 Bay Rd., Saginaw 48604
Phone: (517) 755-3444
Prog. Accred: Medical Assisting (CAAHEP)

Warren Campus
27500 Dequindre Rd., Warren 48092-5209
Phone: (586) 558-8700

Delta College
1961 Delta Dr., University Center 48710
Type: Public, state/local, two-year
System: Michigan Department of Education
Degrees: A   *Enroll:* 6,031
URL: http://www.delta.edu
Phone: (517) 686-9000   *Calendar:* Sem. plan
Inst. Accred.: NCA-HLC (1968/2004)
Prog. Accred.: Dental Assisting, Dental Hygiene,
Engineering Technology (mechanical), Nursing, Physical
Therapy Assisting, Radiography, Respiratory Therapy,
Surgical Technology

Eastern Michigan University
Ypsilanti 48197-2207
Type: Public, state, four-year
System: Michigan Department of Education
Degrees: B, M, P, D   *Enroll:* 18,426
URL: http://www.emich.edu
Phone: (734) 487-1849   *Calendar:* Sem. plan
Inst. Accred.: NCA-HLC (1915/2001)
Prog. Accred.: Athletic Training, Aviation Technology,
Business (AACSB), Clinical Lab Scientist, Construction
Education, Counseling, Dietetics (coordinated),
Industrial Technology, Interior Design, Manufacturing
Technology, Music, Nursing, Nursing Education,
Occupational Therapy, Planning, Public Administration,
Recreation and Leisure Services, Social Work, Speech-
Language Pathology, Teacher Education (NCATE)

Ecumenical Theological Seminary
2930 Woodward Ave., Detroit 48201
Type: Private, interdenominational, four-year
Degrees: B, M, D
URL: http://www.etseminary.org
Phone: (313) 831-5200   *Calendar:* Qtr. plan
Inst. Accred.: ATS (2005)

Ferris State University
Big Rapids 49307
Type: Public, state, four-year
System: Michigan Department of Education
Degrees: A, B, M, P, D   *Enroll:* 10,229
URL: http://www.ferris.edu
Phone: (231) 591-2000   *Calendar:* Sem. plan
Inst. Accred.: NCA-HLC (1959/2001)
Prog. Accred.: Clinical Lab Scientist, Clinical Lab
Technology, Construction Education, Dental Hygiene,
Engineering (surveying), Engineering Technology
(electrical, mechanical), Health Information
Administration, Health Information Technician, Nuclear
Medicine Technology, Nursing, Optometric Residency,
Optometry, Pharmacy, Radiography, Recreation and
Leisure Services, Respiratory Therapy, Social Work

Kendall College of Art and Design of Ferris State University
17 Fountain St., Grand Rapids 49503-3102
Phone: (616) 451.2787
Prog. Accred: Art, Interior Design

Northern Michigan Regional Center
1701 Front St., Traverse City 49684-3061
Phone: (616) 922-1734

Southeast Michigan Regional Center
1401 East Ct. St., Flint 48503-2018
Phone: (810) 762-0461

Southwest Michigan Regional Center
Applied Technology Center, 151 Fountain Northeast,
Grand Rapids 49503-3263
Phone: (616) 771-3770

Finlandia University
601 Quincy St., Hancock 49930-1882
Type: Private, Evangelic Lutheran Church in America,
four-year
Degrees: A, B   *Enroll:* 492
URL: http://www.finlandia.edu
Phone: (800) 682-7604   *Calendar:* Tri. plan
Inst. Accred.: NCA-HLC (1969/2000)
Prog. Accred.: Physical Therapy Assisting

Glen Oaks Community College
62249 Shimmel Rd., Centreville 49032
Type: Public, state/local, two-year
System: Michigan Department of Education
Degrees: A   *Enroll:* 1,012
URL: http://www.glenoaks.edu
Phone: (269) 467-9945   *Calendar:* Sem. plan
Inst. Accred.: NCA-HLC (1975/2003)

Gogebic Community College
E-4946 Jackson Rd., Ironwood 49938
Type: Public, local, two-year
System: Michigan Department of Education
Degrees: A   *Enroll:* 728
URL: http://www.gogebic.edu
Phone: (906) 932-4231   *Calendar:* Sem. plan
Inst. Accred.: NCA-HLC (1949/2002)

Grace Bible College
1011 Aldon St. SW, Wyoming 49509
Type: Private, Grace Gospel Fellowship, four-year
Degrees: A, B   *Enroll:* 148
URL: http://www.gbcol.edu
Phone: (616) 538-2330   *Calendar:* Sem. plan
Inst. Accred.: ABHE (1964/2005), NCA-HLC (1990/2000)

Grand Rapids Community College
143 Bostwick St., NE, Grand Rapids 49503-3263
Type: Public, state/local, two-year
System: Michigan Department of Education
Degrees: A   *Enroll:* 8,706
URL: http://www.grcc.edu
Phone: (616) 234-4000   *Calendar:* Sem. plan
Inst. Accred.: NCA-HLC (1917/2001)
Prog. Accred.: Culinary Education, Dental Assisting,
Dental Hygiene, Music, Nursing, Occupational Therapy
Assisting, Practical Nursing, Radiography

Grand Valley State University
One Campus Dr., Allendale 49401
Type: Public, state, four-year
System: Michigan Department of Education
Degrees: B, M   *Enroll:* 17,917
URL: http://www.gvsu.edu
Phone: (616) 331-5000   *Calendar:* Sem. plan
Inst. Accred.: NCA-HLC (1968/1999)
Prog. Accred.: Accounting, Art, Athletic Training, Business
(AACSB), Engineering (general, manufacturing,
mechanical), Music, Nursing, Nursing Education,
Occupational Therapy, Physical Therapy, Physician
Assistant, Psychology Internship, Public Administration,
Social Work, Teacher Education (NCATE)

Grand Rapids Campus
301 West Fulton St., Grand Rapids 49504
Prog. Accred: Nursing Education, Radiation Therapy

Great Lakes Christian College
6211 West Willow Hwy., Lansing 48917-1299
Type: Private, Christian Churches/Churches of Christ,
four-year
Degrees: A, B   *Enroll:* 188
URL: http://www.glcc.edu
Phone: (517) 321-0242   *Calendar:* Sem. plan
Inst. Accred.: ABHE (1977/1998), NCA-HLC (2003)

Henry Ford Community College
5101 Evergreen Rd., Dearborn 48128-1495
Type: Public, state/local, two-year
System: Michigan Department of Education
Degrees: A   *Enroll:* 7,384
URL: http://www.hfcc.edu
Phone: (313) 271-2750   *Calendar:* Sem. plan
Inst. Accred.: NCA-HLC (1949/2005)
Prog. Accred.: Culinary Education, Health Information
Technician, Medical Assisting (AMA), Nursing, Physical
Therapy Assisting, Radiography, Respiratory Therapy,
Surgical Technology

Hillsdale College
33 East College Ave., Hillsdale 49242
Type: Private, independent, four-year
Degrees: B   *FTE Enroll:* 1,175
URL: http://www.hillsdale.edu
Phone: (517) 437-7341   *Calendar:* Sem. plan
Inst. Accred.: NCA-HLC (1915/1998)

Hope College
141 East 12th St., PO Box 9000, Holland 49422-9000
Type: Private, Reformed Church in America, four-year
Degrees: B   *Enroll:* 3,001
URL: http://www.hope.edu
Phone: (616) 395-7000   *Calendar:* Sem. plan
Inst. Accred.: NCA-HLC (1915/2004)
Prog. Accred.: Art, Athletic Training, Dance, Engineering
(general), Music, Nursing, Nursing Education, Social
Work, Teacher Education (NCATE), Theatre

International Academy of Design and Technology
1850 Research Dr., Troy 48083
Type: Private, proprietary, two-year
Degrees: A
URL: http://www.iadtdetroit.com
Phone: (248) 526-1700
Inst. Accred.: ACICS (2003)

ITT Technical Institute
4020 Sparks Dr., SE, Grand Rapids 49546
Type: Private, proprietary, two-year
System: ITT Educational Services, Inc.
Degrees: A   *Enroll:* 573
URL: http://www.itt-tech.edu
Phone: (616) 956-1060   *Calendar:* Qtr. plan
Inst. Accred.: ACICS (1999/2005)

Buffalo Campus
2295 Millersport Hwy., PO Box 327, Getzville, NY
14068
Phone: (716) 689-2200

Canton Campus
1905 South Haggerty Rd., Canton 48188-2025
Phone: (734) 397-7800

Matteson Campus
600 Holiday Plaza Dr., Matteson, IL 60443
Phone: (708) 747-2571

Jackson Community College
2111 Emmons Rd., Jackson 49201
Type: Public, state/local, two-year
System: Michigan Department of Education
Degrees: A   *Enroll:* 3,350
URL: http://www.jackson.cc.mi.us
Phone: (517) 787-0800   *Calendar:* Sem. plan
Inst. Accred.: NCA-HLC (1933/1996)
Prog. Accred.: Business (ACBSP), Diagnostic Medical Sonography, Medical Assisting (AMA), Radiography

Kalamazoo College
1200 Academy St., Kalamazoo 49006-3295
Type: Private, American Baptist Church, four-year
Degrees: B   *Enroll:* 1,280
URL: http://www.kzoo.edu
Phone: (616) 337-7000   *Calendar:* Tri. plan
Inst. Accred.: NCA-HLC (1915/2003)

Kalamazoo Valley Community College
6767 West O Ave., PO Box 4070, Kalamazoo 49003-4070
Type: Public, state/local, two-year
System: Michigan Department of Education
Degrees: A   *Enroll:* 5,997
URL: http://www.kvcc.edu
Phone: (616) 372-5000   *Calendar:* Sem. plan
Inst. Accred.: NCA-HLC (1972/1996)
Prog. Accred.: Dental Hygiene, Medical Assisting (AMA), Respiratory Therapy, Surgical Technology

Arcadia Commons Campus
202 North Rose St., Kalamazoo 49003-4070
Phone: (616) 373-7800

Kellogg Community College
450 North Ave., Battle Creek 49017-3397
Type: Public, state/local, two-year
System: Michigan Department of Education
Degrees: A   *Enroll:* 3,070
URL: http://www.kellogg.edu
Phone: (269) 965-3931   *Calendar:* Sem. plan
Inst. Accred.: NCA-HLC (1965/2002)
Prog. Accred.: Clinical Lab Technology, Dental Hygiene, Physical Therapy Assisting, Radiography

Kettering University
1700 West Third Ave., Flint 48504-4898
Type: Private, independent, four-year
Degrees: B, M   *Enroll:* 2,780
URL: http://www.kettering.edu
Phone: (810) 762-9500   *Calendar:* Sem. plan
Inst. Accred.: NCA-HLC (1962/1997)
Prog. Accred.: Business (ACBSP), Engineering (computer, electrical, industrial, manufacturing, mechanical)

Kirtland Community College
10775 North St. Helen Rd., Roscommon 48653
Type: Public, state/local, two-year
System: Michigan Department of Education
Degrees: A   *Enroll:* 1,048
URL: http://www.kirtland.edu
Phone: (989) 275-5000   *Calendar:* Sem. plan
Inst. Accred.: NCA-HLC (1976/1999)
Prog. Accred.: Medical Assisting (CAAHEP)

Lake Michigan College
2755 East Napier St., Benton Harbor 49022
Type: Public, state/local, two-year
System: Michigan Department of Education
Degrees: A   *Enroll:* 2,048
URL: http://www.lakemichigancollege.edu
Phone: (269) 927-8100   *Calendar:* Sem. plan
Inst. Accred.: NCA-HLC (1962/1999)
Prog. Accred.: Dental Assisting, Dental Hygiene, Nursing, Radiography

Lake Superior State University
650 West Easterday Ave., Sault Sainte Marie 49783
Type: Public, state, four-year
System: Michigan Department of Education
Degrees: A, B, M   *Enroll:* 2,789
URL: http://www.lssu.edu
Phone: (906) 632-6841   *Calendar:* Sem. plan
Inst. Accred.: NCA-HLC (1968/2001)
Prog. Accred.: Nursing, Recreation and Leisure Services

Lansing Community College
PO Box 40010, Lansing 48901-7210
Type: Public, state/local, two-year
System: Michigan Department of Education
Degrees: A   *Enroll:* 10,113
URL: http://www.lansing.cc.mi.us
Phone: (517) 483-1265   *Calendar:* Sem. plan
Inst. Accred.: NCA-HLC (1964/2004)
Prog. Accred.: Dental Assisting, Dental Hygiene, EMT (Paramedic), Histologic Technology, Medical Assisting (AMA), Nursing, Radiography, Surgical Technology

Lawrence Technological University
21000 West Ten Mile Rd., Ste. M351, Southfield 48075-1058
Type: Private, independent, four-year
Degrees: A, B, M, D   *Enroll:* 2,671
URL: http://www.ltu.edu
Phone: (248) 204-2000   *Calendar:* Sem. plan
Inst. Accred.: NCA-HLC (1967/2001)
Prog. Accred.: Art, Business (ACBSP), Engineering (civil, electrical, mechanical), Interior Design

Lewis College of Business
17370 Meyers Rd., Detroit 48235
Type: Private, proprietary, two-year
Degrees: A   *Enroll:* 242
URL: http://www.lewiscollege.edu
Phone: (313) 862-6300   *Calendar:* Sem. plan
Inst. Accred.: NCA-HLC (1978/2001)

Macomb Community College
14500 East Twelve Mile Rd., Warren 48093-3896
Type: Public, state/local, two-year
System: Michigan Department of Education
Degrees: A   *Enroll:* 11,633
URL: http://www.macomb.edu
Phone: (586) 445-7999   *Calendar:* Sem. plan
Inst. Accred.: NCA-HLC (1970/1997)
Prog. Accred.: Culinary Education, Medical Assisting
  (AMA), Nursing, Physical Therapy Assisting, Respiratory
  Therapy, Veterinary Technology

Center Campus
44575 Garfield Rd., Clinton Township 48038-1139
Phone: (810) 445-7999
Prog. Accred: Occupational Therapy Assisting

Madonna University
36600 Schoolcraft Rd., Livonia 48150
Type: Private, Roman Catholic Church, four-year
Degrees: A, B, M   *Enroll:* 2,630
URL: http://www.madonna.edu
Phone: (800) 852-5315   *Calendar:* Sem. plan
Inst. Accred.: NCA-HLC (1959/1998)
Prog. Accred.: Nursing, Social Work, Teacher Education
  (NCATE)

Orchard Lake Center
3535 Indian Trail, Orchard Lake 48324
Phone: (248) 682-1885

Marygrove College
8425 West McNichols Rd., Detroit 48221
Type: Private, Sisters, Servants of the Immaculate Heart
  of Mary, four-year
Degrees: A, B, M   *Enroll:* 5,283
URL: http://www.marygrove.edu
Phone: (313) 864-8000   *Calendar:* Sem. plan
Inst. Accred.: NCA-HLC (1926/1997)
Prog. Accred.: Radiography, Respiratory Therapy, Social
  Work, Teacher Education (NCATE)

Michigan Jewish Institute
25401 Coolidge Hwy., Oak Park 48237-1304
Type: Private, independent, four-year
Degrees: A, B   *Enroll:* 35
URL: http://www.mji.edu
Phone: (248) 414-6900   *Calendar:* Sem. plan
Inst. Accred.: ACICS (1998/2001)

Michigan State University
450 Administration Bldg., East Lansing 48824
Type: Public, state, four-year
System: Michigan Department of Education
Degrees: B, M, P, D   *Enroll:* 40,501
URL: http://www.msu.edu
Phone: (517) 355-1855   *Calendar:* Sem. plan
Inst. Accred.: NCA-HLC (1915/1996)
Prog. Accred.: Accounting, Audiology, Business (AACSB),
  Clinical Lab Scientist, Clinical Psychology, Construction
  Education, Counseling Psychology, Engineering
  (agricultural, chemical, civil, computer, electrical,
  materials, mechanical), English Language Education,
  Forestry, Interior Design, Journalism, Landscape
  Architecture, Marriage and Family Therapy, Medicine,
  Music, Nursing, Nursing Education, Osteopathy,
  Planning, Psychology Internship, Public Administration,
  Recreation and Leisure Services, Rehabilitation
  Counseling, School Psychology, Social Work, Speech-
  Language Pathology, Veterinary Medicine, Veterinary
  Technology

Detroit College of Law
364 Law College Bldg., East Lansing 48824-1300
Phone: (517) 432-6800
Prog. Accred: Law

James Madison College
368 South Case Hall, East Lansing 48825
Phone: (517) 353-6750
Prog. Accred: Liberal Education

Michigan Technological University
1400 Townsend Dr., Houghton 49931
Type: Public, state, four-year
System: Michigan Department of Education
Degrees: A, B, M, D   *Enroll:* 5,931
URL: http://www.mtu.edu
Phone: (906) 487-1885   *Calendar:* Qtr. plan
Inst. Accred.: NCA-HLC (1928/1998)
Prog. Accred.: Applied Science (surveying/geomatics),
  Business (AACSB), Engineering (chemical, civil,
  electrical, environmental/sanitary, general,
  geological/geophysical, materials, mechanical, mineral,
  mining), Engineering Technology (chemical,
  civil/construction, electrical, electromechanical,
  mechanical), Forestry

Michigan Theological Seminary
41550 East Ann Arbor Trail, Plymouth 48170
Type: Private, nondenominational, four-year
Degrees: B, M, D   *Enroll:* 117
URL: http://www.mts.edu
Phone: (734) 207-9581   *Calendar:* Sem. plan
Inst. Accred.: TRACS (1998/2003, Warning)

Mid Michigan Community College
1375 South Clare Ave., Harrison 48625
Type: Public, state/local, two-year
System: Michigan Department of Education
Degrees: A   *Enroll:* 1,909
URL: http://www.midmich.edu
Phone: (989) 386-6622   *Calendar:* Sem. plan
Inst. Accred.: NCA-HLC (1974/2003)
Prog. Accred.: Medical Assisting (AMA), Radiography

Monroe County Community College
1555 South Raisinville Rd., Monroe 48161-9746
Type: Public, local, two-year
System: Michigan Department of Education
Degrees: A   *Enroll:* 2,321
URL: http://www.monroeccc.edu
Phone: (734) 242-7300   *Calendar:* Sem. plan
Inst. Accred.: NCA-HLC (1972/2000)
Prog. Accred.: Culinary Education, Nursing, Respiratory
Therapy, Respiratory Therapy Technology

Montcalm Community College
2800 College Dr., Sidney 48885-9723
Type: Public, state/local, two-year
System: Michigan Department of Education
Degrees: A   *Enroll:* 959
URL: http://www.montcalm.edu
Phone: (989) 328-2111   *Calendar:* Sem. plan
Inst. Accred.: NCA-HLC (1974/1996)

Muskegon Community College
221 South Quarterline Rd., Muskegon 49442
Type: Public, state/local, two-year
System: Michigan Department of Education
Degrees: A   *Enroll:* 2,916
URL: http://muskegoncc.edu
Phone: (231) 773-9131   *Calendar:* Sem. plan
Inst. Accred.: NCA-HLC (1929/2001)
Prog. Accred.: Respiratory Therapy, Respiratory Therapy
Technology

North Central Michigan College
1515 Howard St., Petoskey 49770
Type: Public, state/local, two-year
System: Michigan Department of Education
Degrees: A   *Enroll:* 1,368
URL: http://www.ncmich.edu
Phone: (231) 348-6600   *Calendar:* Sem. plan
Inst. Accred.: NCA-HLC (1972/2005)

Northern Michigan University
1401 Presque Isle Ave., Marquette 49855
Type: Public, state, four-year
System: Michigan Department of Education
Degrees: A, B, M, P   *Enroll:* 8,364
URL: http://www.nmu.edu
Phone: (906) 227-1000   *Calendar:* Sem. plan
Inst. Accred.: NCA-HLC (1916/2000)
Prog. Accred.: Business (AACSB), Clinical Assistant,
Clinical Lab Scientist, Clinical Lab Technology,
Cytogenetic Technology, Industrial Technology, Music,
Nursing, Nursing Education, Social Work, Speech-
Language Pathology, Surgical Technology, Teacher
Education (NCATE)

Northwestern Michigan College
1701 East Front St., Traverse City 49686-3061
Type: Public, state/local, two-year
System: Michigan Department of Education
Degrees: A   *Enroll:* 2,694
URL: http://www.nmc.edu
Phone: (231) 922-1000   *Calendar:* Sem. plan
Inst. Accred.: NCA-HLC (1961/2000)
Prog. Accred.: Business (ACBSP), Culinary Education,
Dental Assisting, Medical Assisting (CAAHEP)

Northwood University
4000 Whiting Dr., Midland 48640-2398
Type: Private, independent, four-year
Degrees: A, B, M   *Enroll:* 2,879
URL: http://www.northwood.edu
Phone: (517) 837-4200   *Calendar:* Tri. plan
Inst. Accred.: NCA-HLC (1974/1996)

Florida Campus
2600 North Military Trail, West Palm Beach, FL 33409-
2911
Phone: (561) 478-5500

Texas Campus
1114 West FM 1382, Cedar Hill, TX 75104
Phone: (972) 291-1541

University College
4000 Whiting Dr., Midland 48640
Phone: (989) 837-4455

Oakland Community College
2480 Opdyke Rd., Bloomfield Hills 48304-2266
Type: Public, state/local, two-year
System: Michigan Department of Education
Degrees: A *Enroll:* 12,897
URL: http://www.oaklandcc.edu
Phone: (248) 341-2000 *Calendar:* Sem. plan
Inst. Accred.: NCA-HLC (1971/1998)
Prog. Accred.: Diagnostic Medical Sonography,
Radiography, Respiratory Therapy

Auburn Hills Campus
2900 Featherstone Rd., Auburn Hills 48326
Phone: (248) 232-4100

Highland Lakes Campus
7350 Cooley Lake Rd., Waterford 48327-4187
Phone: (248) 942-3100
Prog. Accred: Dental Hygiene, Medical Assisting
(AMA), Nursing

Orchard Ridge Campus
27055 Orchard Lake Rd., Farmington Hills 48334
Phone: (248) 522-3400
Prog. Accred: Culinary Education

Royal Oak Campus
739 South Washington, Royal Oak 48067-3898
Phone: (248) 246-2400

Southfield Campus
22322 Rutland Dr., Southfield 48075-4793
Phone: (248) 233-2700
Prog. Accred: Radiography

Oakland University
Rochester 48309-4401
Type: Public, state, four-year
System: Michigan Department of Education
Degrees: B, M, P, D *Enroll:* 12,779
URL: http://www3.oakland.edu
Phone: (248) 370-2100 *Calendar:* Sem. plan
Inst. Accred.: NCA-HLC (1966/2001)
Prog. Accred.: Accounting, Business (AACSB), Computer
Science, Counseling, Dance, Engineering (computer,
electrical, manufacturing, mechanical, systems), Music,
Nurse Anesthesia Education, Nursing, Nursing
Education, Physical Therapy, Public Administration,
Teacher Education (NCATE), Theatre

Olivet College
320 South Main St., Olivet 40976
Type: Private, United Church of Christ, four-year
Degrees: B, M *Enroll:* 1,004
URL: http://www.olivetcollege.edu
Phone: (616) 749-7000 *Calendar:* Sem. plan
Inst. Accred.: NCA-HLC (1913/2000)

Reformed Bible College
3333 East Beltline Ave., NE, Grand Rapids 49525-9749
Type: Private, independent, four-year
Degrees: A, B *Enroll:* 261
URL: http://www.reformed.edu
Phone: (616) 222-3000 *Calendar:* Sem. plan
Inst. Accred.: ABHE (1964/2005), NCA-HLC (1995/2005)

Rochester College
800 West Avon Rd., Rochester Hills 48307
Type: Private, Churches of Christ, four-year
Degrees: A, B *Enroll:* 753
URL: http://www.rc.edu
Phone: (248) 218-2000 *Calendar:* Sem. plan
Inst. Accred.: NCA-HLC (1974/1996)

Sacred Heart Major Seminary
2701 Chicago Blvd., Detroit 48206
Type: Private, Roman Catholic Church, four-year
Degrees: A, B, M *Enroll:* 192
URL: http://www.shmsonline.org
Phone: (313) 883-8501 *Calendar:* Sem. plan
Inst. Accred.: ATS (1991/2004), NCA-HLC (1960/2004)

Saginaw Valley State University
7400 Bay Rd., University Center 48710
Type: Public, state, four-year
System: Michigan Department of Education
Degrees: B, M, P *Enroll:* 6,993
URL: http://www.svsu.edu
Phone: (989) 964-4000 *Calendar:* Sem. plan
Inst. Accred.: NCA-HLC (1970/2004)
Prog. Accred.: Business (AACSB), Engineering (electrical,
mechanical), Nursing, Nursing Education, Occupational
Therapy, Social Work, Teacher Education (NCATE)

Saint Clair County Community College
323 Erie St., PO Box 5015, Port Huron 48061-5015
Type: Public, local, two-year
System: Michigan Department of Education
Degrees: A *Enroll:* 2,689
URL: http://www.sc4.edu
Phone: (810) 984-3881 *Calendar:* Sem. plan
Inst. Accred.: NCA-HLC (1930/1997)

Schoolcraft College
18600 Haggerty Rd., Livonia 48152-2696
Type: Public, state/local, two-year
System: Michigan Department of Education
Degrees: A *Enroll:* 5,692
URL: http://www.schoolcraft.edu
Phone: (734) 462-4400 *Calendar:* Sem. plan
Inst. Accred.: NCA-HLC (1968/2001)
Prog. Accred.: Health Information Technician, Medical
Assisting (CAAHEP)

Siena Heights University
1247 East Siena Heights Dr., Adrian 49221
Type: Private, Roman Catholic Church, four-year
Degrees: A, B, M   *Enroll:* 1,430
URL: http://www.sienahts.edu
Phone: (517) 263-0731   *Calendar:* Sem. plan
Inst. Accred.: NCA-HLC (1940/2001)
Prog. Accred.: Art

Southwestern Michigan College
58900 Cherry Grove Rd., Dowagiac 49047-9793
Type: Public, state, two-year
System: Michigan Department of Education
Degrees: A   *Enroll:* 1,705
URL: http://www.swmich.edu
Phone: (269) 782-1000   *Calendar:* Sem. plan
Inst. Accred.: NCA-HLC (1971/2001)

Spring Arbor University
106 E. Main St., Spring Arbor 49283
Type: Private, Free Methodist Church of North America,
  four-year
Degrees: A, B, M   *Enroll:* 3,017
URL: http://www.arbor.edu
Phone: (517) 750-1200   *Calendar:* Sem. plan
Inst. Accred.: NCA-HLC (1960/1998)
Prog. Accred.: Nursing, Nursing Education, Social Work,
  Teacher Education (NCATE)

SS. Cyril and Methodius Seminary
3535 Indian Trail, Orchard Lake 48324
Type: Private, Roman Catholic Church, four-year
Degrees: M   *FTE Enroll:* 82
URL: http://www.sscms.edu
Phone: (248) 683-0310   *Calendar:* Sem. plan
Inst. Accred.: ATS (1995/1999)

Thomas M. Cooley Law School
300 South Capitol Ave., Lansing 48933
Type: Private, independent, four-year
Degrees: P   *Enroll:* 1,448
URL: http://www.cooley.edu
Phone: (517) 371-5140   *Calendar:* Sem. plan
Inst. Accred.: NCA-HLC (2001)
Prog. Accred.: Law (ABA only)

University of Detroit Mercy
4001 West McNichols Rd., PO Box 19900, Detroit 48219-0900
Type: Private, Sisters of Mercy and Society of Jesus,
  four-year
Degrees: A, B, M, P, D   *Enroll:* 4,066
URL: http://www.udmercy.edu
Phone: (313) 993-1000   *Calendar:* Sem. plan
Inst. Accred.: NCA-HLC (1931/1997)
Prog. Accred.: Business (AACSB), Clinical Psychology,
  Counseling, Dental Hygiene, Dentistry, Endodontics,
  Engineering (chemical, civil, electrical, mechanical),
  Law, Nurse Anesthesia Education, Nursing, Nursing
  Education, Orthodontic and Dentofacial Orthopedics,
  Physician Assistant, Social Work

University of Michigan
2074 Fleming Administration Bldg., Ann Arbor 48109-1340
Type: Public, state, four-year
System: Michigan Department of Education
Degrees: B, M, P, D   *Enroll:* 37,075
URL: http://www.umich.edu
Phone: (734) 764-1817   *Calendar:* Tri. plan
Inst. Accred.: NCA-HLC (1913/2000)
Prog. Accred.: Advanced Education in General Dentistry,
  Applied Science (occupational health and safety), Art,
  Business (AACSB), Clinical Psychology, Combined
  Prosthodontics, Computer Science, Dental Hygiene,
  Dental Public Health, Dentistry, Dietetics (internship),
  Endodontics, Engineering (aerospace, chemical, civil,
  computer, electrical, industrial, materials, mechanical,
  naval architecture/marine, nuclear), Forestry, General
  Dentistry, General Practice Residency, Health Services
  Administration, Landscape Architecture, Law,
  Librarianship, Medical Illustration, Medicine, Music,
  Nurse (Midwifery), Nursing, Nursing Education, Oral and
  Maxillofacial Surgery, Orthodontic and Dentofacial
  Orthopedics, Pediatric Dentistry, Periodontics,
  Pharmacy, Planning, Prosthodontics, Psychology
  Internship, Public Health, Social Work

University of Michigan—Dearborn
4901 Evergreen Rd., Dearborn 48128-1491
Type: Public, state, four-year
System: Michigan Department of Education
Degrees: B, M   *Enroll:* 5,946
URL: http://www.umd.umich.edu
Phone: (313) 593-5000   *Calendar:* Sem. plan
Inst. Accred.: NCA-HLC (1970/2003)
Prog. Accred.: Business (AACSB), Computer Science,
  Engineering (computer, electrical, industrial,
  manufacturing, mechanical)

University of Michigan—Flint
303 East Kearsley, Flint 48502-1950
Type: Public, state, four-year
System: Michigan Department of Education
Degrees: B, M   *Enroll:* 4,546
URL: http://www.flint.umich.edu
Phone: (810) 762-3000   *Calendar:* Sem. plan
Inst. Accred.: NCA-HLC (1970/2000)
Prog. Accred.: Business (AACSB), Music, Nurse
  Anesthesia Education, Nursing, Nursing Education,
  Physical Therapy, Radiation Therapy, Social Work

Walsh College of Accountancy and Business Administration
3838 Livernois Rd., PO Box 7006, Troy 48007-7006
Type: Private, proprietary, four-year
Degrees: B, M   *Enroll:* 1,339
URL: http://www.walshcollege.edu
Phone: (248) 689-8282   *Calendar:* Tri. plan
Inst. Accred.: NCA-HLC (1975/2001)

Novi Campus
41700 Gardenbrook, Novi 48375-1320
Phone: (810) 349-5454

Port Huron Campus
Bayview Office Bldg., 805-B 10th Ave., Port Huron 48060
Phone: (810) 984-4444

University Center Campus
Macomb Community College, 44575 Garfield Rd., Clinton Township 48038-1139
Phone: (810) 263-6630

Washtenaw Community College
4800 East Huron River Dr., PO Box D-1, Ann Arbor 48106-1610
Type: Public, local, two-year
System: Michigan Department of Education
Degrees: A   *Enroll:* 6,332
URL: http://www.wccnet.edu
Phone: (734) 973-3300   *Calendar:* Sem. plan
Inst. Accred.: NCA-HLC (1973/2000)
Prog. Accred.: Business (ACBSP), Construction Education, Culinary Education, Dental Assisting, Nursing, Radiography, Respiratory Therapy, Surgical Technology

Wayne County Community College District
801 West Fort St., Detroit 48226-3010
Type: Public, state/local, two-year
System: Michigan Department of Education
Degrees: A   *Enroll:* 5,857
URL: http://www.wccc.edu
Phone: (313) 496-2500   *Calendar:* Sem. plan
Inst. Accred.: NCA-HLC (1976/1999)
Prog. Accred.: Occupational Therapy Assisting, Respiratory Therapy, Respiratory Therapy Technology, Veterinary Technology

Downriver Campus
21000 Northline Rd., Taylor 48180
Phone: (734) 946-3500

Downtown Campus
1001 West Fort St., Detroit 48226
Phone: (313) 496-2758

Eastern Campus
5901 Connor St., Detroit 48213-3457
Phone: (313) 922-3311

Northwest Campus
8551 Greenfield Rd., Detroit 48228
Phone: (313) 943-4000
Prog. Accred: Dental Assisting, Dental Hygiene

Western Campus
9555 Haggerty Rd., Belleville 48111
Phone: (734) 699 7008

Wayne State University
656 West Kirby, Detroit 48202
Type: Public, state, four-year
System: Michigan Department of Education
Degrees: B, M, P, D   *Enroll:* 22,911
URL: http://www.wayne.edu
Phone: (313) 577-2424   *Calendar:* Sem. plan
Inst. Accred.: NCA-HLC (1915/1997)
Prog. Accred.: Applied Science (occupational health and safety), Audiology, Business (AACSB), Clinical Lab Scientist, Clinical Psychology, Counseling, Dance, Dietetics (coordinated), Engineering (chemical, civil, electrical, industrial, mechanical), Engineering Technology (electrical, mechanical), Funeral Service Education (Mortuary Science), Law, Librarianship, Medicine, Music, Nurse Anesthesia Education, Nursing, Nursing Education, Occupational Therapy, Pathologists' Assistant, Pharmacy, Physical Therapy, Physician Assistant, Planning, Psychology Internship, Public Administration, Radiation Therapy, Rehabilitation Counseling, Social Work, Speech-Language Pathology, Teacher Education (NCATE), Theatre

Detroit Medical Center University Laboratories
4201 St. Antoine Blvd., Detroit 48201-2194
Phone: (313) 993-0482
Prog. Accred: Clinical Lab Scientist, Histologic Technology

West Shore Community College
3000 North Stiles Rd., PO Box 277, Scottville 49454-0277
Type: Public, state/local, two-year
System: Michigan Department of Education
Degrees: A   *Enroll:* 795
URL: http://www.westshore.edu
Phone: (231) 845-6211   *Calendar:* Sem. plan
Inst. Accred.: NCA-HLC (1974/1996)

Western Michigan University
1903 West Michigan Ave., Kalamazoo 49008-5130
Type: Public, state, four-year
System: Michigan Department of Education
Degrees: B, M, P, D   *Enroll:* 24,223
URL: http://www.wmich.edu
Phone: (616) 387-2351   *Calendar:* Sem. plan
Inst. Accred.: NCA-HLC (1915/2000)
Prog. Accred.: Accounting, Art, Audiology, Business
  (AACSB), Clinical Psychology, Computer Science,
  Counseling, Counseling Psychology, Dance, Dietetics
  (internship), Engineering (aerospace, chemical,
  computer, construction, electrical, industrial,
  mechanical, paper), Engineering Technology (general
  drafting/design, manufacturing), English Language
  Education, Interior Design, Music, Nursing, Nursing
  Education, Occupational Therapy, Physician Assistant,
  Psychology Internship, Public Administration,
  Rehabilitation Counseling, Social Work, Speech-
  Language Pathology, Teacher Education (NCATE),
  Theatre

Battle Creek Regional Center/Kendall Center
50 West Jackson St., Battle Creek 49017
Phone: (616) 965-5380

Grand Rapids Regional Center
2333 East Beltline, SE, Grand Rapids 49546
Phone: (616) 771-9470

Lansing Regional Center
300 North Washington Square, Ste. 200, Lansing 48933
Phone: (517) 372-8114

Muskegon Regional Center
221 South Quarterline Rd., Muskegon 49442
Phone: (616) 777-0500

Southwest Regional Center
2510 Lakeview Ave., St. Joseph 49085
Phone: (616) 983-1968

Western Theological Seminary
101 East 13th St., Holland 49423
Type: Private, Reformed Church in America, four-year
Degrees: M, D   *Enroll:* 164
URL: http://www.westernsem.edu
Phone: (616) 392-8555   *Calendar:* Sem. plan
Inst. Accred.: ATS (1940/2003)

Yeshiva Beth Yehuda-Yeshiva Gedolah of Greater Detroit
24600 Greenfield St., Oak Park 48237
Type: Private, independent, four-year
Degrees: B, M, P, D   *Enroll:* 41
Phone: (248) 968-3360   *Calendar:* Sem. plan
Inst. Accred.: AARTS (1986/2002)

MINNESOTA

Academy College
1101 East 78th St., Ste. 100, Minneapolis 55420
Type: Private, proprietary, four-year
Degrees: A, B
URL: http://www.academycollege.edu
Phone: (952) 851-0066   *Calendar:* Qtr. plan
Inst. Accred.: ACICS (1976/2003)

Adler Graduate School
1001 Hwy. 7, Ste. 311, Hopkins 55305
Type: Private, independent, four-year
Degrees: M   *Enroll:* 72
URL: http://www.alfredadler.edu
Phone: (952) 988-4170   *Calendar:* Qtr. plan
Inst. Accred.: NCA-HLC (1991/2001)

Alexandria Technical College
1601 Jefferson St., Alexandria 56308
Type: Public, state/local, two-year
System: Minnesota State Colleges and Universities
Degrees: A   *Enroll:* 1,872
URL: http://web.alextech.edu
Phone: (320) 762-0221   *Calendar:* Sem. plan
Inst. Accred.: NCA-HLC (1980/2004)
Prog. Accred.: Clinical Lab Technology, Interior Design

American Academy of Acupuncture and Oriental Medicine
1925 West County Rd. B2, Roseville 55113
Type: Private, proprietary, four-year
Degrees: M
URL: http://www.aaaom.org
Phone: (651) 631-0204   *Calendar:* Tri. plan
Inst. Accred.: ACAOM (2003)

Anoka Technical College
1355 West Hwy. 10, Anoka 55303
Type: Private, state, two-year
System: Minnesota State Colleges and Universities
Degrees: A   *Enroll:* 1,417
URL: http://www.anokatech.edu
Phone: (763) 576-4700   *Calendar:* Sem. plan
Inst. Accred.: NCA-HLC (1999/2004)
Prog. Accred.: Health Information Technician, Medical
  Assisting (AMA), Occupational Therapy Assisting,
  Practical Nursing, Surgical Technology

Anoka-Ramsey Community College
11200 Mississippi Blvd. NW, Coon Rapids 55433-3499
Type: Public, state, two-year
System: Minnesota State Colleges and Universities
Degrees: A   *Enroll:* 4,445
URL: http://www.anokaramsey.mnscu.edu
Phone: (763) 427-2600   *Calendar:* Sem. plan
Inst. Accred.: NCA-HLC (1975/1997)
Prog. Accred.: Nursing, Physical Therapy Assisting

Cambridge Campus
300 Polk St. South, Cambridge 55008
Phone: (763) 689-7000

Argosy University Twin Cities
1515 Central Pkwy., Eagan 55121
Type: Private, proprietary, four-year
System: Argosy University
Degrees: A, B, M, D   *Enroll:* 1,031
URL: http://www.argosyu.edu
Phone: (952) 921-9500   *Calendar:* Tri. plan
Inst. Accred.: NCA-HLC (1981/2001, *Indirect accreditation
  through Argosy University, Chicago, IL*)
Prog. Accred.: Clinical Lab Technology, Clinical
  Psychology, Dental Hygiene, Histologic Technology,
  Medical Assisting (AMA), Radiation Therapy,
  Radiography, Veterinary Technology

Duluth Learning Center
512 Lonsdale Bldg., 302 West Superior St., Duluth
55802
Phone: (218) 723-8470

Art Institutes International—Minnesota
15 South 9th St., Minneapolis 55402-3137
Type: Private, proprietary, four-year
System: Education Management Corporation
Degrees: A, B   *Enroll:* 1,027
URL: http://www.aim.artinstitutes.edu
Phone: (612) 332-3361   *Calendar:* Qtr. plan
Inst. Accred.: ACICS (1971/2003)
Prog. Accred.: Culinary Education

Augsburg College
2211 Riverside Ave., Minneapolis 55454
Type: Private, Evangelic Lutheran Church in America,
  four-year
Degrees: B, M   *Enroll:* 2,787
URL: http://www.augsburg.edu
Phone: (612) 330-1000   *Calendar:* 4-1-4 plan
Inst. Accred.: NCA-HLC (1954/1997)
Prog. Accred.: Music, Nursing, Nursing Education,
  Physician Assistant, Social Work, Teacher Education
  (NCATE)

Bemidji State University
1500 Birchmont Dr., NE, Bemidji 56601-2699
Type: Public, state, four-year
System: Minnesota State Colleges and Universities
Degrees: A, B, M   *Enroll:* 4,073
URL: http://www.bemidji.msus.edu
Phone: (218) 755-2000   *Calendar:* Sem. plan
Inst. Accred.: NCA-HLC (1943/2000)
Prog. Accred.: Music, Nursing, Nursing Education, Social
  Work, Teacher Education (NCATE)

Bethany Lutheran College
700 Luther Dr., Mankato 56001
Type: Private, Evangelic Lutheran Synod, four-year
Degrees: A, B   *Enroll:* 442
URL: http://www.blc.edu
Phone: (507) 344-7000   *Calendar:* Sem. plan
Inst. Accred.: NCA-HLC (1974/1999)

Bethel Seminary of Bethel University
3949 Bethel Dr., St. Paul 55112
Type: Private, Baptist General Conference, four-year
Degrees: M, D   *Enroll:* 554
URL: http://www.bethel.edu/seminary
Phone: (651) 638-6180   *Calendar:* Qtr. plan
Inst. Accred.: ATS (1966/2001)

Pennsylvania Campus
1605 North Limekin Pike, Dresher, PA 19025
Phone: (215) 641-4801

San Diego Campus
6116 Arosa St., San Diego, CA 92115-3902
Phone: (619) 582-8188

Bethel University
3900 Bethel Dr., St. Paul 55112
Type: Private, Baptist General Conference, four-year
Degrees: A, B, M, D   *Enroll:* 2,949
URL: http://www.bethel.edu
Phone: (651) 638-6400   *Calendar:* Sem. plan
Inst. Accred.: NCA-HLC (1959/2000)
Prog. Accred.: Nursing, Nursing Education, Social Work,
  Teacher Education (NCATE)

Brown College
1440 Northland Dr., Mendota Heights 55120
Type: Private, proprietary, four-year
System: Career Education Corporation
Degrees: A, B   *Enroll:* 1,671
URL: http://www.browncollege.edu
Phone: (651) 905-3400
Inst. Accred.: ACCSCT (1967/2002)
Prog. Accred.: Culinary Education

The Capella University
222 South 9th St., Ste. 2000, Minneapolis 55401
Type: Private, proprietary, four-year
Degrees: B, M, D   *Enroll:* 4,909
URL: http://www.capellauniversity.edu
Phone: (888) 227-3552   *Calendar:* Qtr. plan
Inst. Accred.: NCA-HLC (1997)
Prog. Accred.: Counseling

Carleton College
One North College St., Northfield 55057
Type: Private, independent, four-year
Degrees: B   *Enroll:* 1,930
URL: http://www.carleton.edu
Phone: (507) 646-4334   *Calendar:* Tri. plan
Inst. Accred.: NCA-HLC (1913/1999)

Central Lakes College
501 West College Dr., Brainerd 56401-3900
Type: Public, state, two-year
System: Minnesota State Colleges and Universities
Degrees: A   *Enroll:* 2,328
URL: http://www.clcmn.edu
Phone: (218) 855-8053   *Calendar:* Sem. plan
Inst. Accred.: NCA-HLC (1977/2003)
Prog. Accred.: Dental Assisting

Staples Campus
1830 Airport Rd., Staples 56479
Phone: (218) 894-5100

Century College
3300 Century Ave. North, White Bear Lake 55110-5655
Type: Public, state, two-year
System: Minnesota State Colleges and Universities
Degrees: A   *FTE Enroll:* 3,000
URL: http://www.century.mnscu.edu
Phone: (651) 779-3200   *Calendar:* Qtr. plan
Inst. Accred.: NCA-HLC (1974/2001)
Prog. Accred.: Dental Assisting, Dental Hygiene, Dental
  Laboratory Technology, EMT (Paramedic), Medical
  Assisting (AMA), Radiography

College of Saint Benedict
37 South College Ave., St. Joseph 56374
Type: Private, Roman Catholic Church, four-year
Degrees: B   *Enroll:* 2,020
URL: http://www.csbsju.edu
Phone: (320) 363-5505
Inst. Accred.: NCA-HLC (1933/1999)
Prog. Accred.: Dietetics (coordinated), Music, Nursing,
  Nursing Education, Social Work, Teacher Education
  (NCATE)

College of Saint Catherine
2004 Randolph Ave., St. Paul 55105
Type: Private, Roman Catholic Church, four-year
Degrees: A, B, M   *Enroll:* 3,740
URL: http://www.stkate.edu
Phone: (651) 690-6000   *Calendar:* 4-1-4 plan
Inst. Accred.: NCA-HLC (1916/2003)
Prog. Accred.: Diagnostic Medical Sonography, Health
  Information Technician, Montessori Teacher Education,
  Music, Nursing, Occupational Therapy, Phlebotomy,
  Radiography, Respiratory Therapy, Social Work, Teacher
  Education (NCATE)

Minneapolis Campus
601 25th Ave. South, Minneapolis 55454-1494
Phone: (651) 690-7800
Prog. Accred: Nursing, Occupational Therapy
  Assisting, Physical Therapy, Physical Therapy
  Assisting

The College of Saint Scholastica
1200 Kenwood Ave., Duluth 55811
Type: Private, Roman Catholic Church, four-year
Degrees: B, M   *Enroll:* 2,568
URL: http://www.css.edu
Phone: (800) 447-5444   *Calendar:* Sem. plan
Inst. Accred.: NCA-HLC (1931/2001)
Prog. Accred.: Clinical Lab Scientist, Health Information
   Administration, Nursing, Occupational Therapy, Physical
   Therapy, Social Work

College of Visual Arts
344 Summit Ave., St. Paul 55102-2199
Type: Private, independent, four-year
Degrees: B   *Enroll:* 198
URL: http://www.cva.edu
Phone: (651) 224-3416   *Calendar:* Sem. plan
Inst. Accred.: NCA-HLC (1998/2003)

Concordia College
901 South 8th St., Moorhead 56562
Type: Private, Evangelical Lutheran Church in America,
   four-year
Degrees: B   *Enroll:* 2,801
URL: http://www.cord.edu
Phone: (218) 299-4000   *Calendar:* Sem. plan
Inst. Accred.: NCA-HLC (1927/2004)
Prog. Accred.: Dietetics (internship), Music, Nursing,
   Nursing Education, Social Work, Teacher Education
   (NCATE)

Concordia University Saint Paul
275 North Syndicate St., St. Paul 55104
Type: Private, Lutheran Church-Missouri Synod, four-year
System: Concordia University System
Degrees: A, B, M   *Enroll:* 1,908
URL: http://www.csp.edu
Phone: (651) 641-8278   *Calendar:* Sem. plan
Inst. Accred.: NCA-HLC (1959/1998)
Prog. Accred.: Teacher Education (NCATE)

Crossroads College
920 Mayowood Rd., SW, Rochester 55902
Type: Private, Christian Churches/Churches of Christ,
   four-year
Degrees: A, B   *Enroll:* 121
URL: http://www.crossroadscollege.edu
Phone: (507) 288-4563   *Calendar:* Sem. plan
Inst. Accred.: ABHE (1948/2004)

Crown College
8700 College View Dr., Saint Bonifacius 55375
Type: Private, Christian and Missionary Alliance, four-year
Degrees: A, B, M   *Enroll:* 877
URL: http://www.crown.edu
Phone: (952) 446-4100   *Calendar:* Sem. plan
Inst. Accred.: ABHE (1950/2002), NCA-HLC (1980/2002)

Dakota County Technical College
1300 145th St. East, Rosemount 55068
Type: Public, state/local, two-year
System: Minnesota State Colleges and Universities
Degrees: A   *Enroll:* 2,038
URL: http://www.dctc.mnscu.edu
Phone: (651) 423-8000   *Calendar:* Sem. plan
Inst. Accred.: NCA-HLC (1996/2001)
Prog. Accred.: Dental Assisting, Interior Design, Medical
   Assisting (AMA), Practical Nursing

Duluth Business University
4724 Mike Colalillo Dr., Duluth 55807
Type: Private, proprietary, two-year
Degrees: A   *Enroll:* 280
URL: http://www.dbumn.com
Phone: (218) 722-4000   *Calendar:* Qtr. plan
Inst. Accred.: ACICS (1970/2003)
Prog. Accred.: Dental Assisting, Medical Assisting
   (CAAHEP)

Dunwoody College of Technology
818 Dunwoody Blvd., Minneapolis 55403-1192
Type: Private, independent, two-year
Degrees: A   *Enroll:* 1,527
URL: http://www.dunwoody.edu
Phone: (612) 374-5800   *Calendar:* Qtr. plan
Inst. Accred.: NCA-HLC (1998)

Fond du Lac Tribal and Community College
2101 14th St., Cloquet 55720
Type: Public, tribal, two-year
System: Minnesota State Colleges and Universities
Degrees: A   *Enroll:* 1,131
URL: http://www.fdltcc.edu
Phone: (218) 879-0800   *Calendar:* Sem. plan
Inst. Accred.: NCA-HLC (1997/1999)

Globe College
7166 Tenth St. North, Oakdale 55128-5939
Type: Private, proprietary, four-year
Degrees: A, B   *Enroll:* 657
URL: http://www.globecollege.com
Phone: (651) 730-5100   *Calendar:* Qtr. plan
Inst. Accred.: ACICS (1953/2001, Probation)
Prog. Accred.: Medical Assisting (CAAHEP)

Gustavus Adolphus College
800 West College Ave., St. Peter 56082
Type: Private, Evangelical Lutheran Church in America,
   four-year
Degrees: B   *Enroll:* 2,563
URL: http://www.gustavus.edu
Phone: (507) 933-8000   *Calendar:* 4-1-4 plan
Inst. Accred.: NCA-HLC (1915/2003)
Prog. Accred.: Athletic Training, Music, Nursing, Nursing
   Education, Teacher Education (NCATE)

Hamline University
1536 Hewitt Ave., St. Paul 55104
Type: Private, United Methodist Church, four-year
Degrees: B, M, D   *Enroll:* 3,483
URL: http://www.hamline.edu
Phone: (651) 523-2800   *Calendar:* 4-1-4 plan
Inst. Accred.: NCA-HLC (1914/1998)
Prog. Accred.: Law, Music, Teacher Education (NCATE)

Hennepin Technical College
9000 Brooklyn Blvd., Brooklyn Park 55445-2399
Type: Public, state/local, two-year
System: Minnesota State Colleges and Universities
Degrees: A   *Enroll:* 3,293
URL: http://www.hennepintech.edu
Phone: (763) 425-3800   *Calendar:* Sem. plan
Inst. Accred.: NCA-HLC (1999)
Prog. Accred.: Culinary Education, Dental Assisting,
    Practical Nursing

Eden Prairie Campus
9200 Flying Cloud Dr., Eden Prairie 55347
Phone: (952) 944-2222
Prog. Accred.: Culinary Education, Dental Assisting

Herzing College—Lakeland Medical-Dental Academy
5700 West Broadway, Crystal 55428
Type: Private, proprietary, four-year
System: Herzing College Corporate Offices
Degrees: A, B
URL: http://www.herzing.edu
Phone: (763) 535-3000   *Calendar:* Sem. plan
Inst. Accred.: NCA-HLC (2004, *Indirect accreditation
    through Herzing College Corporate Offices, Milwaukee,
    WI*)
Prog. Accred.: Clinical Lab Technology, Dental Assisting,
    Dental Hygiene, Medical Assisting (CAAHEP)

Hibbing Community College
1515 East 25th St., Hibbing 55746-3354
Type: Public, state, two-year
System: Northeast Higher Education District
Degrees: A   *Enroll:* 1,454
URL: http://www.hcc.mnscu.edu
Phone: (218) 262-7200   *Calendar:* Sem. plan
Inst. Accred.: NCA-HLC (1997/2000)
Prog. Accred.: Clinical Lab Technology, Dental Assisting

Inver Hills Community College
2500 80th St., East, Inver Grove Heights 55076-3224
Type: Public, state, two-year
System: Minnesota State Colleges and Universities
Degrees: A   *Enroll:* 3,152
URL: http://www.inverhills.edu
Phone: (651) 450-8500   *Calendar:* Qtr. plan
Inst. Accred.: NCA-HLC (1976/1998)
Prog. Accred.: Nursing

Itasca Community College
1851 East Hwy. 169, Grand Rapids 55744-3361
Type: Public, state/local, two-year
System: Northeast Higher Education District
Degrees: A   *Enroll:* 933
URL: http://www.itascacc.edu
Phone: (218) 327-4460   *Calendar:* Sem. plan
Inst. Accred.: NCA-HLC (1997/1999)

Lake Superior College
2101 Trinity Rd., Duluth 55811-3399
Type: Public, state, two-year
System: Minnesota State Colleges and Universities
Degrees: A   *Enroll:* 3,114
URL: http://www.lsc.mnscu.edu
Phone: (218) 733-7600   *Calendar:* Sem. plan
Inst. Accred.: NCA-HLC (1998)
Prog. Accred.: Clinical Lab Technology, Dental Hygiene,
    Physical Therapy Assisting, Radiography, Respiratory
    Therapy, Surgical Technology

Le Cordon Bleu College of Culinary Arts— Minneapolis/St. Paul
1408 Northland Dr., Ste. 102, Mendota Heights 55120
Type: Private, proprietary, two-year
Degrees: A
Phone: (651) 675-4700
Inst. Accred.: ACCSCT (2005)

Leech Lake Tribal College
PO Box 180, Cass Lake 56633-0180
Type: Public, tribal, two-year
System: American Indian Higher Education Consortium
Degrees: A   *Enroll:* 133
URL: http://www.leechlaketribalcollege.org
Phone: (218) 335-4200   *Calendar:* Qtr. plan
Inst. Accred.: NCA-CASI (1993/2005)

Luther Seminary
2481 Como Ave., St. Paul 55108
Type: Private, Evangelical Lutheran Church in America,
    four-year
Degrees: M, D   *Enroll:* 648
URL: http://www.luthersem.edu
Phone: (651) 641-3456   *Calendar:* 4-1-4 plan
Inst. Accred.: ATS (1944/2004), NCA-HLC (1979/2005)

Macalester College
1600 Grand Ave., St. Paul 55105-1899
Type: Private, Presbyterian Church (USA), four-year
Degrees: B   *Enroll:* 1,854
URL: http://www.macalester.edu
Phone: (651) 696-6000   *Calendar:* Sem. plan
Inst. Accred.: NCA-HLC (1913/1996)

Martin Luther College
1995 Luther Ct., New Ulm 56073
Type: Private, Evangelical Lutheran Synod, four-year
Degrees: B　　　　　　　　　　　　*Enroll:* 1,014
URL: http://www.mlc-wels.edu
Phone: (507) 354-8221　　　　*Calendar:* Sem. plan
Inst. Accred.: NCA-HLC (1995/1999)

Mayo Graduate School
200 First St., SW, Rochester 55905
Type: Private, independent, four-year
System: Mayo Clinic College of Medicine
Degrees: M, D　　　　　　　　　*Enroll:* 232
URL: http://www.mayo.edu/mgs
Phone: (507) 284-2511　　　　*Calendar:* Sem. plan
Inst. Accred.: NCA-HLC (1984/1999, *Indirect accreditation through Mayo Clinic College of Medicine, Rochester, MN)*
Prog. Accred.: Combined Prosthodontic/Maxillofacial Prosthetics, Cytotechnology, Diagnostic Medical Sonography, Medicine, Nuclear Medicine Technology, Nurse Anesthesia Education, Oral and Maxillofacial Surgery, Orthodontic and Dentofacial Orthopedics, Periodontics, Physical Therapy

Mayo Medical School
200 First St., SW, Rochester 55905
Type: Private, independent, four-year
System: Mayo Clinic College of Medicine
Degrees: D　　　　　　　　　　*Enroll:* 171
URL: http://www.mayo.edu/mms
Phone: (507) 284-3671
Inst. Accred.: NCA-HLC (1984/1999, *Indirect accreditation through Mayo Clinic College of Medicine, Rochester, MN)*

Mayo School of Health Sciences
200 First St., SW, Rochester 55905
Type: Private, independent, four-year
System: Mayo Clinic College of Medicine
Degrees: A, M　　　　　　　　　*Enroll:* 316
URL: http://www.mayo.edu/mshs
Phone: (507) 284-3678
Inst. Accred.: NCA-HLC (1984/1999, *Indirect accreditation through Mayo Clinic College of Medicine, Rochester, MN)*
Prog. Accred.: Combined Prosthodontic/Maxillofacial Prosthetics, Oral and Maxillofacial Surgery, Orthodontic and Dentofacial Orthopedics, Periodontics, Radiation Therapy, Radiography

Mayo Clinic—Jacksonville
4500 San Pablo Rd., Jacksonville, FL 32224
Phone: (904) 953-8663
Prog. Accred: Radiography

McNally Smith College of Music
19 Exchange St. East, Saint Paul 55101-2220
Type: Private, proprietary, two-year
Degrees: A
URL: http://www.mcnallysmith.edu
Phone: (651) 291-0177　　　　*Calendar:* Sem. plan
Inst. Accred.: NASM (1989/1996)

Mesabi Range Community and Technical College
1001 West Chestnut St., Virginia 55792
Type: Public, state/local, two-year
System: Northeast Higher Education District
Degrees: A　　　　　　　　　　*Enroll:* 1,182
URL: http://www.mesabirange.mnscu.edu
Phone: (218) 749-7700　　　　*Calendar:* Qtr. plan
Inst. Accred.: NCA-HLC (2001)

Eveleth Campus
1100 Industrial Park Dr., PO Box 0648, Eveleth 55734-0648
Phone: (218) 744-3095

Metropolitan State University
700 East 7th St., St. Paul 55106-5000
Type: Public, state, four-year
System: Minnesota State Colleges and Universities
Degrees: B, M　　　　　　　　　*Enroll:* 3,878
URL: http://www.metrostate.edu
Phone: (651) 793-1212　　　　*Calendar:* Sem. plan
Inst. Accred.: NCA-HLC (1975/1995)
Prog. Accred.: Nursing, Nursing Education, Social Work

Minneapolis Campus
730 Hennepin Ave., Minneapolis 55403
Phone: (651) 772-7777

Minneapolis Business College
1711 West County Rd. B, Roseville 55113
Type: Private, proprietary, two-year
Degrees: A　　　　　　　　　　*Enroll:* 366
URL: http://www.minneapolisbusinesscollege.edu
Phone: (651) 636-7406
Inst. Accred.: ACICS (1962/2000)
Prog. Accred.: Medical Assisting (CAAHEP)

Minneapolis College of Art and Design
2501 Stevens Ave. South, Minneapolis 55404
Type: Private, independent, four-year
Degrees: B, M　　　　　　　　　*Enroll:* 628
URL: http://www.mcad.edu
Phone: (612) 874-3700　　　　*Calendar:* Sem. plan
Inst. Accred.: NCA-HLC (1960/1995)
Prog. Accred.: Art

Minneapolis Community and Technical College

1501 Hennepin Ave., Minneapolis 55403-1779
Type: Public, state/local, two-year
System: Minnesota State Colleges and Universities
Degrees: A   *Enroll:* 4,632
URL: http://www.mctc.mnscu.edu
Phone: (612) 341-7000   *Calendar:* Sem. plan
Inst. Accred.: NCA-HLC (1977/2003)
Prog. Accred.: Dental Assisting, Nursing, Practical Nursing

Minnesota Institute of Technologies

7300 France Ave., South, Ste. 100, Minneapolis 55435
Type: Private, proprietary, two-year
Degrees: A
Phone: (952) 831-2960
Inst. Accred.: ACICS (2003)

Minnesota School of Business

1401 West 76th St., Richfield 55423
Type: Private, proprietary, four-year
Degrees: A, B   *Enroll:* 573
URL: http://www.msbcollege.com
Phone: (612) 861-2000   *Calendar:* Qtr. plan
Inst. Accred.: ACICS (1953/2002)
Prog. Accred.: Medical Assisting (CAAHEP)

Brooklyn Center Campus

5910 Shingle Creek Pkwy., Brooklyn Center 55430
Phone: (763) 566-7777
Prog. Accred: Dental Assisting, Medical Assisting
(CAAHEP)

Plymouth Campus

1455 County Rd. 101 North, Plymouth 55447
Phone: (763) 476-2000

Rochester Campus

2521 Pennington Dr., NW, Rochester 55901
Phone: (507)536-9500

Saint Cloud Campus

1201 2nd St. South, Waite Park 56387
Phone: (320) 257-2000

Shakopee Campus

1200 Shakopee Town Square, Shakopee 55379
Phone: (952) 345-1200

Minnesota State College-Southeast Technical

1250 Homer Rd., PO Box 409, Winona 55987-0409
Type: Public, state/local, two-year
System: Minnesota State Colleges and Universities
Degrees: A
URL: http://www.southeastmn.edu
Phone: (507) 453-2700   *Calendar:* Sem. plan
Inst. Accred.: NCA-HLC (1995/2001)

Red Wing Campus

308 Pioneer Rd. and Hwy. 58, Red Wing 55066
Phone: (651) 385-6300

Minnesota State Community and Technical College

1414 College Way, Fergus Falls 56537-1009
Type: Public, state, two-year
System: Minnesota State Colleges and Universities
Degrees: A   *Enroll:* 1,299
URL: http://www.minnesota.edu
Phone: (218) 739-7500   *Calendar:* Sem. plan
Inst. Accred.: NCA-HLC (1972/2003)
Prog. Accred.: Clinical Lab Technology, Histologic
Technology

Detroit Lakes Campus

900 Hwy. 34 East, Detroit Lakes 56601-2698
Phone: (218) 846-7444

Moorhead Campus

1900 28th Ave. South, Moorhead 56560-4899
Phone: (218) 236-6277
Prog. Accred: Dental Assisting, Dental Hygiene, Health
Information Technician

Wadena Campus

405 SW Colfax, PO Box 56, Wadena 56482-0566
Phone: (218) 631-3530

Minnesota State University Moorhead

1104 7th Ave. South, Moorhead 56563
Type: Public, state, four-year
System: Minnesota State Colleges and Universities
Degrees: A, B, M, P   *Enroll:* 6,903
URL: http://www.mnstate.edu
Phone: (218) 236-2011   *Calendar:* Sem. plan
Inst. Accred.: NCA-HLC (1916/2000)
Prog. Accred.: Art, Business (AACSB), Construction
Education, Construction Technology, Counseling,
Industrial Technology, Music, Nursing, Nursing
Education, Social Work, Speech-Language Pathology,
Teacher Education (NCATE)

Minnesota State University—Mankato

309 Wigley Administration Center, Mankato 56001
Type: Public, state, four-year
System: Minnesota State Colleges and Universities
Degrees: A, B, M, P   *Enroll:* 12,653
URL: http://www.mankato.msus.edu
Phone: (507) 389-2463   *Calendar:* Sem. plan
Inst. Accred.: NCA-HLC (1916/2000)
Prog. Accred.: Art, Athletic Training, Business (AACSB),
Counseling, Dental Hygiene, Engineering (civil,
electrical, mechanical), Engineering Technology
(automotive, electrical, manufacturing), Music, Nursing,
Nursing Education, Recreation and Leisure Services,
Rehabilitation Counseling, Social Work, Speech-
Language Pathology, Teacher Education (NCATE)

Minnesota West Community and Technical College—Granite Falls
1593 11th Ave., Granite Falls 56241
Type: Public, state/local, two-year
System: Minnesota State Colleges and Universities
Degrees: A   *Enroll:* 2,038
URL: http://www.mnwest.edu
Phone: (320) 564-4511   *Calendar:* Sem. plan
Inst. Accred.: NCA-HLC (1997/2002)
Prog. Accred.: Dental Assisting, Medical Assisting (CAAHEP)

Canby Campus
1011 1st St. West, Canby 56220
Phone: (507) 223-7252
Prog. Accred: Dental Assisting

Jackson Campus
401 West St., Jackson 56143
Phone: (507) 847-3320

Pipestone Campus
1314 North Hiawatha, PO Box 250, Pipestone 56164-0250
Phone: (507) 825-5471
Prog. Accred: Clinical Lab Technology

Worthington Campus
1450 College Way, Worthington 56187-3024
Phone: (507) 372-2107

Normandale Community College
9700 France Ave. South, Bloomington 55431-4309
Type: Public, state/local, two-year
System: Minnesota State Colleges and Universities
Degrees: A   *Enroll:* 5,417
URL: http://www.normandale.mnscu.edu
Phone: (952) 487-8200   *Calendar:* Sem. plan
Inst. Accred.: NCA-HLC (1973/2001)
Prog. Accred.: Dental Assisting, Dental Hygiene, Music, Nursing

North Central University
910 Elliot Ave. South, Minneapolis 55404
Type: Private, Assemblies of God, four-year
Degrees: A, B   *Enroll:* 1,160
URL: http://www.northcentral.edu
Phone: (612) 343-4400   *Calendar:* Sem. plan
Inst. Accred.: NCA-HLC (1986/1998)

North Hennepin Community College
7411 85th Ave. North, Brooklyn Park 55445-2231
Type: Public, state, two-year
System: Minnesota State Colleges and Universities
Degrees: A   *Enroll:* 3,817
URL: http://www.nhcc.mnscu.edu
Phone: (763) 424-0702   *Calendar:* Sem. plan
Inst. Accred.: NCA-HLC (1972/2004)
Prog. Accred.: Business (ACBSP), Clinical Lab Technology, Nursing

Northland Community and Technical College
1101 Hwy. 1 East, Thief River Falls 56701-2598
Type: Public, state, two-year
System: Minnesota State Colleges and Universities
Degrees: A   *Enroll:* 1,389
URL: http://www.northlandcollege.edu
Phone: (218) 681-0845   *Calendar:* Sem. plan
Inst. Accred.: NCA-HLC (1976/2000)

East Grand Forks Campus
2022 Central Ave., NE, East Grand Forks 56721-2702
Phone: (218) 773-3441
Prog. Accred: Cardiovascular Technology, Clinical Lab Technology, EMT (Paramedic), Medical Assisting (AMA), Occupational Therapy Assisting, Radiography, Respiratory Therapy, Respiratory Therapy Technology, Surgical Technology

Northwest Technical College
905 Grant Ave., SE, Bemidji 56601
Type: Public, state, two-year
System: Minnesota State Colleges and Universities
Degrees: A   *Enroll:* 4,570
URL: http://www.ntcmn.edu
Phone: (218) 755-4280   *Calendar:* Qtr. plan
Inst. Accred.: NCA-HLC (1995)
Prog. Accred.: Dental Assisting

Northwestern College
3003 Snelling Ave. North, Saint Paul 55113-1598
Type: Private, independent, four-year
Degrees: A, B   *Enroll:* 2,222
URL: http://www.nwc.edu
Phone: (651) 631-5100   *Calendar:* Qtr. plan
Inst. Accred.: NCA-HLC (1978/1999)
Prog. Accred.: Music

Northwestern Health Sciences University
2501 West 84th St., Bloomington 55431-1599
Type: Private, proprietary, four-year
Degrees: B, M, P   *Enroll:* 761
URL: http://www.nwhealth.edu
Phone: (952) 888-4777   *Calendar:* Tri. plan
Inst. Accred.: NCA-HLC (1988/2001)
Prog. Accred.: Chiropractic Education, Massage Therapy

Minnesota Institute of Acupuncture and Oriental Medicine
2501 West 84th St., Bloomington 55431
Phone: (952) 885-5435
Prog. Accred: Acupuncture

NTI School of CAD Technology
11995 Singletree Ln., Eden Prairie 55344-5351
Type: Private, two-year
Degrees: A   *Enroll:* 82
URL: http://www.nw-ti.com
Phone: (952) 944-0080   *Calendar:* Sem. plan
Inst. Accred.: ACCSCT (1972/2001)

Oak Hills Christian College
1600 Oak Hills Rd., SW, Bemidji 56601-8826
Type: Private, interdenominational, four-year
Degrees: A, B   *Enroll:* 163
URL: http://www.oakhills.edu
Phone: (218) 751-8670   *Calendar:* Sem. plan
Inst. Accred.: ABHE (1990/1996)

Pillsbury Baptist Bible College
315 South Grove Ave., Owatonna 55060-3068
Type: Private, Minnesota Baptist State Convention, four-year
Degrees: A, B   *Enroll:* 173
URL: http://www.pillsbury.edu
Phone: (507) 451-2710   *Calendar:* Sem. plan
Inst. Accred.: ABHE (2005)

Pine Technical College
900 4th St., SE, Pine City 55063
Type: Public, state/local, two-year
System: Minnesota State Colleges and Universities
Degrees: A   *Enroll:* 430
URL: http://www.pinetech.edu
Phone: (320) 629-5100   *Calendar:* Sem. plan
Inst. Accred.: NCA-HLC (1994/1999)

Rainy River Community College
1501 Hwy. 71, International Falls 56649-2187
Type: Public, state/local, two-year
System: Northeast Higher Education District
Degrees: A   *Enroll:* 304
URL: http://www.rrcc.mnscu.edu
Phone: (218) 254-7976   *Calendar:* Sem. plan
Inst. Accred.: NCA-HLC (1997)

San Diego Campus
7650 Mission Valley Rd., San Diego, CA 92108
Phone: (866) 505-0333

Rasmussen College—Eagan Campus
3500 Federal Dr., Eagan 55122-1346
Type: Private, proprietary, two-year
System: Rasmussen College Systems Office
Degrees: A   *Enroll:* 308
URL: http://www.rasmussen.edu
Phone: (651) 687-9000   *Calendar:* Qtr. plan
Inst. Accred.: NCA-HLC (1995/2004, *Indirect accreditation through Rasmussen College Systems, Roseville, MN*)

Rasmussen College—Mankato Campus
501 Holly Ln., Mankato 56001-6803
Type: Private, proprietary, two-year
System: Rasmussen College Systems Office
Degrees: A   *Enroll:* 264
URL: http://www.rasmussen.edu
Phone: (507) 625-6556   *Calendar:* Qtr. plan
Inst. Accred.: NCA-HLC (1995/2004, *Indirect accreditation through Rasmussen College Systems, Roseville, MN*)

Boise Campus
5551 Bloom St., Boise, ID 83703
Phone: (208) 853-6074

Rasmussen College—Minnetonka Campus
12450 Wayzata Blvd., Ste. 315, Minnetonka 55305-1928
Type: Private, proprietary, two-year
System: Rasmussen College Systems Office
Degrees: A   *Enroll:* 245
URL: http://www.rasmussen.edu
Phone: (952) 545-2000   *Calendar:* Qtr. plan
Inst. Accred.: NCA-HLC (1995/2004, *Indirect accreditation through Rasmussen College Systems, Roseville, MN*)
Prog. Accred.: Health Information Technician

Rasmussen College—St. Cloud Campus
226 Park Ave. South, St. Cloud 56303-3713
Type: Private, proprietary, two-year
System: Rasmussen College Systems Office
Degrees: A   *Enroll:* 315
URL: http://www.rasmussen.edu
Phone: (320) 251-5600   *Calendar:* Qtr. plan
Inst. Accred.: NCA-HLC (1995/2004, *Indirect accreditation through Rasmussen College Systems, Roseville, MN*)

Ridgewater College
PO Box 1097, 2101 15th Ave., NW, Wilmar 56201
Type: Public, state, two-year
System: Minnesota State Colleges and Universities
Degrees: A   *FTE Enroll:* 970
URL: http://www.ridgewater.mnscu.edu
Phone: (320) 235-5114   *Calendar:* Sem. plan
Inst. Accred.: NCA-HLC (1996)
Prog. Accred.: Health Information Technician, Medical Assisting (AMA), Nursing

Hutchinson Campus
2 Century Ave., SE, Hutchinson 55350
Phone: (320) 587-3636
Prog. Accred.: Practical Nursing, Veterinary Technology

Riverland Community College—Austin
1900 8th Ave., NW, Austin 55912-1407
Type: Public, state, two-year
System: Minnesota State Colleges and Universities
Degrees: A   *Enroll:* 2,522
URL: http://www.riverland.edu
Phone: (507) 433-0600   *Calendar:* Sem. plan
Inst. Accred.: NCA-HLC (1996)
Prog. Accred.: Nursing, Radiography

Albert Lea Campus
2200 Tech Dr., Albert Lea 56007-3499
Phone: (507) 379-3300
Prog. Accred.: Dental Assisting

Rochester Community and Technical College
851 30th Ave., SE, Rochester 55904-4999
Type: Public, state, two-year
System: Minnesota State Colleges and Universities
Degrees: A   *Enroll:* 4,146
URL: http://www.rctc.edu
Phone: (507) 285-7210   *Calendar:* Sem. plan
Inst. Accred.: NCA-HLC (1923/2001)
Prog. Accred.: Dental Assisting, Dental Hygiene, Medical Assisting (AMA), Nursing, Practical Nursing, Respiratory Therapy, Surgical Technology

Saint Cloud State University
720 Fourth Ave. South, St. Cloud 56301-4498
Type: Public, state, four-year
System: Minnesota State Colleges and Universities
Degrees: A, B, M, P   *Enroll:* 13,906
URL: http://www.stcloudstate.edu
Phone: (320) 255-0121   *Calendar:* Sem. plan
Inst. Accred.: NCA-HLC (1915/1997)
Prog. Accred.: Art, Business (AACSB), Computer Science, Counseling, Engineering (electrical, manufacturing, mechanical), Journalism, Music, Rehabilitation Counseling, Social Work, Speech-Language Pathology, Teacher Education (NCATE), Theatre

Akita Campus
193-2 Oku-Tsubakidai, Yuwa-Machi, Akita, Japan 010-12
Phone: (651) 649-5758

Saint Cloud Technical College
1540 Northway Dr., St. Cloud 56303-1240
Type: Public, state, two-year
System: Minnesota State Colleges and Universities
Degrees: A   *Enroll:* 2,539
URL: http://www.sctc.edu
Phone: (320) 654-5017   *Calendar:* Sem. plan
Inst. Accred.: NCA-HLC (1985/1997)
Prog. Accred.: Dental Assisting, Dental Hygiene, Practical Nursing, Surgical Technology

Saint John's University
PO Box 7155, Collegeville 56321
Type: Private, Roman Catholic Church, four-year
Degrees: B, M   *Enroll:* 1,995
URL: http://www.csbsju.edu
Phone: (320) 363-2882   *Calendar:* Sem. plan
Inst. Accred.: ATS (1969/1998), NCA-HLC (1950/1999)
Prog. Accred.: Nursing Education, Social Work

Saint Mary's University of Minnesota
700 Terrace Heights, Winona 55987-1399
Type: Private, Roman Catholic Church, four-year
Degrees: B, M   *Enroll:* 3,049
URL: http://www.smumn.edu
Phone: (507) 457-4430   *Calendar:* Sem. plan
Inst. Accred.: NCA-HLC (1934/1997)
Prog. Accred.: Nuclear Medicine Technology, Nurse Anesthesia Education

Twin Cities Campus
2500 Park Ave., Minneapolis 55404-4403
Phone: (800) 328-4827

Saint Olaf College
1520 St. Olaf Ave., Northfield 55057
Type: Private, Evangelical Lutheran Church in America, four-year
Degrees: B   *Enroll:* 2,955
URL: http://www.stolaf.edu
Phone: (507) 646-2222   *Calendar:* 4-1-4 plan
Inst. Accred.: NCA-HLC (1915/2004)
Prog. Accred.: Dance, Music, Nursing, Nursing Education, Social Work, Teacher Education (NCATE), Theatre

Saint Paul College—A Community and Technical College
235 Marshall Ave., St. Paul 55102
Type: Public, state, two-year
System: Minnesota State Colleges and Universities
Degrees: A   *Enroll:* 2,676
URL: http://www.sptc.mnscu.edu
Phone: (651) 221-1335   *Calendar:* Sem. plan
Inst. Accred.: NCA-HLC (1983/2003)
Prog. Accred.: Clinical Lab Technology, Culinary Education, Practical Nursing, Respiratory Therapy

South Central College—Mankato
1920 Lee Blvd., North Mankato 56003
Type: Public, state, two-year
System: Minnesota State Colleges and Universities
Degrees: A   *Enroll:* 2,279
URL: http://www.sctc.mnscu.edu
Phone: (507) 389-7200   *Calendar:* Sem. plan
Inst. Accred.: NCA-HLC (1995/2000)
Prog. Accred.: Dental Assisting

Faribault Campus
1225 SW Third St., Faribault 55021
Phone: (507) 334-3965
Prog. Accred: Clinical Lab Technology

Southwest Minnesota State University
1501 State St., Marshall 56258
Type: Public, state, four-year
System: Minnesota State Colleges and Universities
Degrees: A, B, M   *Enroll:* 3,872
URL: http://www.southwest.msus.edu
Phone: (507) 537-6272   *Calendar:* Sem. plan
Inst. Accred.: NCA-HLC (1972/2004)
Prog. Accred.: Music, Social Work

United Theological Seminary of the Twin Cities
3000 Fifth St., N.W., New Brighton 55112
Type: Private, United Church of Christ, four-year
Degrees: M, D   *Enroll:* 132
URL: http://www.unitedseminary-mn.org
Phone: (651) 633-4311   *Calendar:* 4-1-4 plan
Inst. Accred.: ATS (1966/2002), NCA-HLC (1977/2002)

University of Minnesota—Crookston
2900 University Ave., Crookston 56716
Type: Public, state, four-year
System: University of Minnesota System
Degrees: A, B   *Enroll:* 1,583
URL: http://www.crk.umn.edu
Phone: (218) 281-6510   *Calendar:* Sem. plan
Inst. Accred.: NCA-HLC (1971/1995)

University of Minnesota—Duluth
515 Darland Admin. Bldg., 10 University Dr., Duluth
55812
Type: Public, state, four-year
System: University of Minnesota System
Degrees: B, M   *Enroll:* 9,233
URL: http://www.d.umn.edu
Phone: (218) 726-7106   *Calendar:* Qtr. plan
Inst. Accred.: NCA-HLC (1968/1998)
Prog. Accred.: Business (AACSB), Computer Science,
   Counseling, Engineering (chemical, computer,
   industrial), Medicine, Music, Social Work, Speech-
   Language Pathology, Teacher Education (NCATE)

University of Minnesota—Morris
600 East Fourth St., Morris 56267
Type: Public, state, four-year
System: University of Minnesota System
Degrees: B   *Enroll:* 1,781
URL: http://www.mrs.umn.edu
Phone: (320) 589-2211   *Calendar:* Qtr. plan
Inst. Accred.: NCA-HLC (1970/2000)
Prog. Accred.: Teacher Education (NCATE)

University of Minnesota—Twin Cities
100 Church St., SE, Minneapolis 55455-0213
Type: Public, state, four-year
System: University of Minnesota System
Degrees: B, M, P, D   *Enroll:* 40,567
URL: http://www.umn.edu
Phone: (612) 625-5000   *Calendar:* Sem. plan
Inst. Accred.: NCA-HLC (1913/1996)
Prog. Accred.: Accounting, Advanced Education in
   General Dentistry, Applied Science (industrial hygiene),
   Audiology, Clinical Lab Scientist, Clinical Psychology,
   Combined Prosthodontics, Counseling Psychology,
   Dance, Dental Hygiene, Dentistry, Dietetics
   (coordinated), Dietetics (internship), Endodontics,
   Engineering (aerospace, agricultural, chemical, civil,
   computer, electrical, geological/geophysical, materials,
   mechanical), Forestry, Funeral Service Education
   (Mortuary Science), General Dentistry, General Practice
   Residency, Health Services Administration, Interior
   Design, Journalism, Landscape Architecture, Law,
   Marriage and Family Therapy, Medicine, Music, Nurse
   (Midwifery), Nurse Anesthesia Education, Nursing,
   Nursing Education, Occupational Therapy, Oral and
   Maxillofacial Pathology, Oral and Maxillofacial Surgery,
   Orthodontic and Dentofacial Orthopedics, Pediatric
   Dentistry, Perfusion, Periodontics, Pharmacy, Physical
   Therapy, Planning, Psychology Internship, Public Health,
   Radiography, Recreation and Leisure Services, School
   Psychology, Social Work, Speech-Language Pathology,
   Teacher Education (NCATE), Theatre, Veterinary
   Medicine

University of Saint Thomas
2115 Summit Ave., St. Paul 55105
Type: Private, Roman Catholic Church, four-year
Degrees: B, M, P, D   *Enroll:* 7,700
URL: http://www.stthomas.edu
Phone: (651) 962-5000   *Calendar:* 4-1-4 plan
Inst. Accred.: ATS (1974/2003), NCA-HLC (1916/2004)
Prog. Accred.: Engineering (manufacturing, mechanical),
   Health Services Administration, Law (ABA only), Music,
   Psychology Internship, Social Work, Teacher Education
   (NCATE)

Gainey Conference Center
RR2 Box 1, Owatonna 55060
Phone: (612) 962-4444

The Meeting Point Campus
1107 Hazeltine Blvd., Chaska 55318
Phone: (612) 448-8800

Minneapolis Campus
1000 LaSalle Ave., Ste. 201, Minneapolis 55403
Phone: (612) 962-4000
Prog. Accred: Counseling Psychology

Vermilion Community College
1900 East Camp St., Ely 55731-1918
Type: Public, state/local, two-year
System: Northeast Higher Education District
Degrees: A   *Enroll:* 682
URL: http://www.vcc.edu
Phone: (218) 365-7200   *Calendar:* Sem. plan
Inst. Accred.: NCA-HLC (2001)

Walden University
155 South Fifth Ave., Minneapolis 55401
Type: Private, proprietary, four-year
Degrees: M, D   *Enroll:* 7,748
URL: http://www.waldenu.edu
Phone: (866) 925-3364   *Calendar:* Qtr. plan
Inst. Accred.: NCA-HLC (1990/1999)

William Mitchell College of Law
875 Summit Ave., St. Paul 55105
Type: Private, independent, four-year
Degrees: P   *Enroll:* 873
URL: http://www.wmitchell.edu
Phone: (651) 227-9171   *Calendar:* Sem. plan
Inst. Accred.: ABA (1938/1998)

Winona State University
PO Box 5838, Winona 55987
Type: Public, state, four-year
System: Minnesota State Colleges and Universities
Degrees: A, B, M, P   *Enroll:* 7,414
URL: http://www.winona.edu
Phone: (507) 457-5000   *Calendar:* Sem. plan
Inst. Accred.: NCA-HLC (1913/2002)
Prog. Accred.: Athletic Training, Business (AACSB),
  Counseling, Engineering (materials), Music, Nursing,
  Nursing Education, Social Work, Teacher Education
  (NCATE), Theatre

Rochester Center Campus
Highway 14 East, 859 30th Ave., SE, Rochester 55904
Phone: (507) 285-7100
Prog. Accred: Counseling

MISSISSIPPI

Alcorn State University
1000 ASU Dr. 359, Alcorn State 39096-7510
Type: Public, state, four-year
System: Mississippi Board of Trustees of State
Institutions of Higher Learning
Degrees: A, B, M, P   *Enroll:* 2,822
URL: http://www.alcorn.edu
Phone: (601) 877-6100   *Calendar:* Sem. plan
Inst. Accred.: SACS (1948/2001)
Prog. Accred.: Business (AACSB), Family and Consumer
Science, Industrial Technology, Music, Nursing, Teacher
Education (NCATE)

Belhaven College
1500 Peachtree St., Jackson 39202
Type: Private, Presbyterian Church (USA), four-year
Degrees: B, M   *Enroll:* 2,285
URL: http://www.belhaven.edu
Phone: (601) 968-5928   *Calendar:* Sem. plan
Inst. Accred.: SACS (1946/1997)
Prog. Accred.: Art, Music

Blue Mountain College
PO Box 160, Blue Mountain 38610
Type: Private, Southern Baptist Church, four-year
Degrees: B   *Enroll:* 372
URL: http://www.bmc.edu
Phone: (662) 685-4771   *Calendar:* Sem. plan
Inst. Accred.: SACS (1927/2005)

Coahoma Community College
3240 Friars Point Rd., Clarksdale 38614
Type: Public, state/local, two-year
System: Mississippi State Board for Community and
Junior Colleges
Degrees: A   *Enroll:* 1,718
URL: http://www.coahomacc.edu
Phone: (662) 627-2571   *Calendar:* Sem. plan
Inst. Accred.: SACS (1975/2000)

Copiah-Lincoln Community College
PO Box 649, Wesson 39191
Type: Public, state, two-year
System: Mississippi State Board for Community and
Junior Colleges
Degrees: A   *Enroll:* 1,675
URL: http://www.colin.edu
Phone: (601) 643-5101   *Calendar:* Sem. plan
Inst. Accred.: SACS (1936/2005)
Prog. Accred.: Clinical Lab Technology, Nursing,
Radiography, Respiratory Therapy, Respiratory Therapy
Technology

Delta State University
Highway 8 West, Cleveland 38733
Type: Public, state, four-year
System: Mississippi Board of Trustees of State
Institutions of Higher Learning
Degrees: A, B, M, D   *Enroll:* 3,207
URL: http://www.deltastate.edu
Phone: (662) 846-3000   *Calendar:* Sem. plan
Inst. Accred.: SACS (1930/2004)
Prog. Accred.: Art, Business (ACBSP), Counseling, Family
and Consumer Science, Music, Nursing, Nursing
Education, Social Work, Teacher Education (NCATE)

East Central Community College
PO Box 129, Decatur 39327-0129
Type: Public, state/local, two-year
System: Mississippi State Board for Community and
Junior Colleges
Degrees: A   *Enroll:* 2,146
URL: http://www.eccc.edu
Phone: (601) 635-2111   *Calendar:* Sem. plan
Inst. Accred.: SACS (1939/2001)
Prog. Accred.: Nursing

East Mississippi Community College
PO Box 158, Scooba 39358
Type: Public, state/local, two-year
System: Mississippi State Board for Community and
Junior Colleges
Degrees: A   *Enroll:* 3,063
URL: http://www.eastms.edu
Phone: (662) 974-4600   *Calendar:* Sem. plan
Inst. Accred.: SACS (1949/1996)
Prog. Accred.: Funeral Service Education (Mortuary
Science)

Hinds Community College
PO Box 1100, 505 East Main St., Raymond 39154-1100
Type: Public, state/local, two-year
System: Mississippi State Board for Community and
Junior Colleges
Degrees: A   *Enroll:* 8,090
URL: http://www.hindscc.edu
Phone: (601) 857-5261   *Calendar:* Sem. plan
Inst. Accred.: SACS (1928/1996)
Prog. Accred.: Clinical Lab Technology, Dental Assisting,
Health Information Technician, Medical Assisting (AMA),
Nursing, Physical Therapy Assisting, Respiratory
Therapy, Respiratory Therapy Technology, Surgical
Technology, Veterinary Technology

Jackson Campus (Academic/Technical Center)
3925 Sunset Dr., Jackson 39213-5899
Phone: (601) 366-1405

Nursing/Allied Health Center
1750 Chadwick Dr., Jackson 39204-3490
Phone: (601) 372-6507
Prog. Accred: Dental Assisting

Rankin Campus
3805 Hwy. 80 East, Pearl 39208-4295
Phone: (601) 932-5237

Raymond Campus
505 East Main St., Raymond 39154-9799
Phone: (601) 352-3011
Prog. Accred: Radiography

Utica Campus
Highway 18 West, Utica 39175-9599
Phone: (601) 885-6062

Vicksburg-Warren County Branch
1624 Hwy. 27, Vicksburg 39180-8699
Phone: (601) 638-0600

Holmes Community College
PO Box 369, Goodman 39079
Type: Public, local, two-year
System: Mississippi State Board for Community and
  Junior Colleges
Degrees: A   *Enroll:* 3,049
URL: http://www.holmescc.edu
Phone: (662) 472-2312   *Calendar:* Sem. plan
Inst. Accred.: SACS (1934/1995)
Prog. Accred.: Funeral Service Education (Mortuary
  Science), Nursing

Ridgeland Campus
412 W. Ridgeland Ave., Ridgeland 39157
Phone: (801) 856-5400
Prog. Accred: Occupational Therapy Assisting

Itawamba Community College
602 West Hill St., Fulton 38843
Type: Public, state/local, two-year
System: Mississippi State Board for Community and
  Junior Colleges
Degrees: A   *Enroll:* 3,769
URL: http://www.iccms.edu
Phone: (662) 862-8000   *Calendar:* Sem. plan
Inst. Accred.: SACS (1955/1998)
Prog. Accred.: EMT (Paramedic), Health Information
  Technician, Nursing, Physical Therapy Assisting,
  Radiography, Respiratory Therapy, Respiratory Therapy
  Technology

Jackson State University
1400 J.R. Lynch St., Jackson 39217
Type: Public, state, four-year
System: Mississippi Board of Trustees of State
  Institutions of Higher Learning
Degrees: B, M, P, D   *Enroll:* 6,720
URL: http://www.jsums.edu
Phone: (601) 979-2121   *Calendar:* Sem. plan
Inst. Accred.: SACS (1948/2001)
Prog. Accred.: Art, Business (AACSB), Clinical Psychology,
  Computer Science, Industrial Technology, Journalism,
  Music, Public Administration, Rehabilitation Counseling,
  Social Work, Speech-Language Pathology, Teacher
  Education (NCATE)

Jones County Junior College
900 Ct. St., Ellisville 39437
Type: Public, state/local, two-year
System: Mississippi State Board for Community and
  Junior Colleges
Degrees: A   *Enroll:* 4,467
URL: http://www.jcjc.edu
Phone: (601) 477-4000   *Calendar:* Sem. plan
Inst. Accred.: SACS (1940/1997)
Prog. Accred.: Business (ACBSP), EMT (Paramedic),
  Nursing, Radiography

Magnolia Bible College
PO Box 1109, 822 South Huntington, Kosciusko 39090-
1109
Type: Private, nondenominational, four-year
Degrees: B   *Enroll:* 40
URL: http://www.magnolia.edu
Phone: (622) 289-2896   *Calendar:* Sem. plan
Inst. Accred.: SACS (1990/2005)

Meridian Community College
910 Hwy. 19 North, Meridian 39307
Type: Public, state/local, two-year
System: Mississippi State Board for Community and
  Junior Colleges
Degrees: A   *Enroll:* 2,971
URL: http://www.mcc.cc.ms.us
Phone: (601) 483-8241   *Calendar:* Sem. plan
Inst. Accred.: SACS (1942/2001)
Prog. Accred.: Clinical Lab Technology, Dental Hygiene,
  Health Information Technician, Nursing, Physical
  Therapy Assisting, Practical Nursing, Radiography,
  Respiratory Therapy Technology

Millsaps College
1701 North State St., Jackson 39210
Type: Private, United Methodist Church, four-year
Degrees: B, M   *Enroll:* 1,146
URL: http://www.millsaps.edu
Phone: (601) 974-1000   *Calendar:* Sem. plan
Inst. Accred.: SACS (1912/2002)
Prog. Accred.: Business (AACSB), Teacher Education
  (NCATE)

Mississippi College
PO Box 4001, Clinton 39058
Type: Private, Southern Baptist Church, four-year
Degrees: B, M, P, D   *Enroll:* 2,961
URL: http://www.mc.edu
Phone: (601) 925-3000   *Calendar:* Sem. plan
Inst. Accred.: SACS (1922/2003)
Prog. Accred.: Business (AACSB), Business (ACBSP),
  Counseling, Law, Music, Nursing, Social Work, Teacher
  Education (NCATE)

Mississippi Delta Community College
PO Box 668, Moorhead 38761
Type: Public, state/local, two-year
System: Mississippi State Board for Community and
Junior Colleges
Degrees: A   *Enroll:* 3,052
URL: http://www.msdelta.edu
Phone: (662) 246-6322   *Calendar:* Sem. plan
Inst. Accred.: SACS (1930/1997)
Prog. Accred.: Clinical Lab Technology, Dental Hygiene,
Nursing, Radiography

Mississippi Gulf Coast Community College
PO Box 609, Perkinston 39573
Type: Public, state/local, two-year
System: Mississippi State Board for Community and
Junior Colleges
Degrees: A   *Enroll:* 7,662
URL: http://www.mgccc.edu
Phone: (601) 928-5211   *Calendar:* Sem. plan
Inst. Accred.: SACS (1929/1999)
Prog. Accred.: Clinical Lab Technology, EMT (Paramedic),
Funeral Service Education (Mortuary Science), Nursing,
Practical Nursing, Radiography, Respiratory Therapy

Jackson County Campus
PO Box 100, Gautier 39553
Phone: (228) 497-9602
Prog. Accred: Radiography

Jefferson Davis Campus
2226 Switzer Rd., Gulfport 39507
Phone: (228) 896-3355

Mississippi State University
PO Box 5325, Mississippi State 39762-5325
Type: Public, state, four-year
System: Mississippi Board of Trustees of State
Institutions of Higher Learning
Degrees: B, M, P, D   *Enroll:* 14,153
URL: http://www.msstate.edu
Phone: (662) 325-2323   *Calendar:* Sem. plan
Inst. Accred.: SACS (1926/2003)
Prog. Accred.: Accounting, Art, Business (AACSB),
Computer Science, Counseling, Dietetics (internship),
Engineering (aerospace, agricultural, bioengineering,
chemical, civil, computer, electrical, industrial,
mechanical), Family and Consumer Science, Forestry,
Interior Design, Landscape Architecture, Music, Public
Administration, Rehabilitation Counseling, School
Psychology, Social Work, Teacher Education (NCATE),
Veterinary Medicine

Meridian Campus
1000 Hwy. 19 North, Meridian 39307
Phone: (601) 484-0144
Prog. Accred: Social Work

Mississippi University for Women
1100 College St., Columbus 39701-5800
Type: Public, state, four-year
System: Mississippi Board of Trustees of State
Institutions of Higher Learning
Degrees: A, B, M   *Enroll:* 1,768
URL: http://www.muw.edu
Phone: (662) 329-4750   *Calendar:* Sem. plan
Inst. Accred.: SACS (1921/2003)
Prog. Accred.: Art, Business (ACBSP), Music, Nursing,
Nursing Education, Speech-Language Pathology,
Teacher Education (NCATE)

Mississippi Valley State University
14000 Hwy. 82 West, Itta Bena 38941-1400
Type: Public, state, four-year
System: Mississippi Board of Trustees of State
Institutions of Higher Learning
Degrees: B, M   *Enroll:* 3,030
URL: http://www.mvsu.edu
Phone: (662) 254-3997   *Calendar:* Sem. plan
Inst. Accred.: SACS (1968/2002)
Prog. Accred.: Art, Business (ACBSP), Industrial
Technology, Music, Social Work, Teacher Education
(NCATE)

Northeast Mississippi Community College
101 Cunningham Blvd., Booneville 38829
Type: Public, state/local, two-year
System: Mississippi State Board for Community and
Junior Colleges
Degrees: A   *Enroll:* 2,927
URL: http://www.nemcc.edu
Phone: (662) 728-7751   *Calendar:* Sem. plan
Inst. Accred.: SACS (1956/2000)
Prog. Accred.: Clinical Lab Technology, Dental Hygiene,
Medical Assisting (AMA), Nursing, Radiography,
Respiratory Therapy, Respiratory Therapy Technology

Northwest Mississippi Community College
4975 Hwy. 51 North, Senatobia 38668
Type: Public, state, two-year
System: Mississippi State Board for Community and
Junior Colleges
Degrees: A   *Enroll:* 5,039
URL: http://www.northwestms.edu
Phone: (662) 562-3200   *Calendar:* Sem. plan
Inst. Accred.: SACS (1953/1997)
Prog. Accred.: EMT (Paramedic), Funeral Service
Education (Mortuary Science), Nursing

Southaven Campus
5197 W.E. Ross Pkwy., Southaven 38671
Phone: (662) 342-1570
Prog. Accred: Respiratory Therapy

Pearl River Community College
101 Hwy. 11 North, Poplarville 39470-2201
Type: Public, state/local, two-year
System: Mississippi State Board for Community and
Junior Colleges
Degrees: A   *Enroll:* 2,853
URL: http://www.prcc.edu
Phone: (601) 403-1000   *Calendar:* Sem. plan
Inst. Accred.: SACS (1929/1995)
Prog. Accred.: Clinical Lab Technology, Dental Assisting,
Dental Hygiene, Nursing, Respiratory Therapy
Technology, Surgical Technology

Hattiesburg Campus
5448 US Hwy. 495, Hattiesburg 39401
Phone: (601) 795-6801
Prog. Accred: Dental Assisting, Dental Hygiene,
Occupational Therapy Assisting, Physical Therapy
Assisting, Radiography, Respiratory Therapy
Technology, Surgical Technology

Reformed Theological Seminary
5422 Clinton Blvd., Jackson 39209-3099
Type: Private, independent, four-year
Degrees: M, D   *FTE Enroll:* 160
URL: http://www.rts.edu
Phone: (601) 923-1600   *Calendar:* Sem. plan
Inst. Accred.: ATS (1977/2001), SACS (1977/2003)
Prog. Accred.: Marriage and Family Therapy

Charlotte Campus
2101 Carmel Rd., Charlotte, NC 28226
Phone: (704) 366-5066

Orlando Campus
1231 Reformation Dr., Oviedo, FL 32765
Phone: (407) 366-9493

Rust College
150 East Rust Ave., Holly Springs 38635
Type: Private, United Methodist Church, four-year
Degrees: A, B   *Enroll:* 870
URL: http://www.rustcollege.edu
Phone: (662) 252-8000   *Calendar:* Sem. plan
Inst. Accred.: SACS (1970/2004)
Prog. Accred.: Social Work

Southeastern Baptist College
4229 Hwy. 15 North, Laurel 39440-1096
Type: Private, Baptist Missionary Association, four-year
Degrees: A, B   *Enroll:* 82
URL: http://www.southeasternbaptist.edu
Phone: (601) 426-6346   *Calendar:* Sem. plan
Inst. Accred.: ABHE (1988/1999)

Southwest Mississippi Community College
College Dr., Summit 39666-9704
Type: Public, local, two-year
System: Mississippi State Board for Community and
Junior Colleges
Degrees: A   *Enroll:* 1,800
URL: http://www.smcc.edu
Phone: (601) 276-2000   *Calendar:* Sem. plan
Inst. Accred.: SACS (1958/2000)
Prog. Accred.: EMT (Paramedic), Nursing

Tougaloo College
500 West County Line Rd., Tougaloo 39174
Type: Private, United Church of Christ, four-year
Degrees: A, B   *Enroll:* 905
URL: http://www.tougaloo.edu
Phone: (601) 977-7700   *Calendar:* Sem. plan
Inst. Accred.: SACS (1953/2001)

University of Mississippi
PO Box 1848, University 38677-1848
Type: Public, state, four-year
System: Mississippi Board of Trustees of State
Institutions of Higher Learning
Degrees: B, M, P, D   *Enroll:* 12,613
URL: http://www.olemiss.edu
Phone: (662) 915-7211   *Calendar:* Sem. plan
Inst. Accred.: SACS (1895/1999)
Prog. Accred.: Accounting, Art, Audiology, Business
(AACSB), Clinical Psychology, Computer Science,
Counseling, Engineering (chemical, civil, electrical,
geological/geophysical, mechanical), Family and
Consumer Science, Journalism, Law, Music, Nursing,
Pharmacy, Psychology Internship, Social Work, Speech-
Language Pathology, Teacher Education (NCATE)

University of Mississippi Medical Center
2500 North State St., Jackson 39216-4500
Type: Public, state, four-year
System: Mississippi Board of Trustees of State
Institutions of Higher Learning
Degrees: B, M, D   *Enroll:* 1,691
URL: http://www.umc.edu
Phone: (601) 984-1000   *Calendar:* Qtr. plan
Inst. Accred.: SACS (1991/2001)
Prog. Accred.: Advanced Education in General Dentistry,
Clinical Lab Scientist, Cytotechnology, Dental Hygiene,
Dentistry, EMT (Paramedic), General Dentistry, General
Practice Residency, Health Information Administration,
Medicine, Nuclear Medicine Technology, Nursing
Education, Occupational Therapy, Pediatric Dentistry,
Physical Therapy, Radiography

The University of Southern Mississippi
118 College Dr., Hattiesburg 39406-0001
Type: Public, state, four-year
System: Mississippi Board of Trustees of State
 Institutions of Higher Learning
Degrees: B, M, P, D   *Enroll:* 12,739
URL: http://www.usm.edu
Phone: (601) 266-7011   *Calendar:* Sem. plan
Inst. Accred.: SACS (1929/1995, Probation)
Prog. Accred.: Accounting, Art, Athletic Training,
 Audiology, Business (AACSB), Clinical Lab Scientist,
 Clinical Psychology, Computer Science, Construction
 Education, Counseling, Counseling Psychology, Dance,
 Dietetics (internship), Engineering Technology
 (architectural, civil/construction, computer, electrical,
 industrial), English Language Education, Family and
 Consumer Science, Interior Design, Journalism,
 Librarianship, Marriage and Family Therapy, Music,
 Nursing, Nursing Education, Psychology Internship,
 Public Health, Recreation and Leisure Services, School
 Psychology, Social Work, Speech-Language Pathology,
 Teacher Education (NCATE), Theatre

Gulf Park Campus
East Beach Blvd., Long Beach 39560
Phone: (601) 865-4500

Wesley Biblical Seminary
787 East Northside Dr., PO Box 9938, Jackson 39286
Type: Private, multidenominational, four-year
Degrees: M   *Enroll:* 80
URL: http://www.wbs.edu
Phone: (601) 366-8880   *Calendar:* Sem. plan
Inst. Accred.: ATS (1991/2004)

Wesley College
111 Wesley Circle, PO Box 1070, Florence 39073-0070
Type: Private, Congregational Methodist Church, four-
 year
Degrees: B   *Enroll:* 74
URL: http://www.wesleycollege.edu
Phone: (800) 748-9972   *Calendar:* Sem. plan
Inst. Accred.: ABHE (1979/2001)

William Carey College
498 Tuscan Ave., Hattiesburg 39401-5499
Type: Private, Southern Baptist Church, four-year
Degrees: B, M, P   *Enroll:* 2,208
URL: http://www.wmcarey.edu
Phone: (601) 582-5051   *Calendar:* Tri. plan
Inst. Accred.: SACS (1958/1999)
Prog. Accred.: Music, Nursing

MISSOURI

A.T. Still University of Health Sciences
800 West Jefferson St., Kirksville 63501-1497
Type: Private, independent, four-year
Degrees: M, D   *Enroll:* 1,231
URL: http://www.atsu.edu
Phone: (660) 626-2121   *Calendar:* Qtr. plan
Inst. Accred.: NCA-HLC (1994/1999)
Prog. Accred.: Dentistry, Osteopathy

The Arizona School of Health Sciences
5850 East Still Circle, Mesa, AZ 85206-3618
Phone: (480) 219-6000
Prog. Accred: Occupational Therapy, Physical Therapy,
   Physician Assistant

Allied College
13723 Riverport Dr., Ste. 103, Maryland Heights 63073
Type: Private, proprietary, two-year
System: High-Tech Institute
Degrees: A
URL: http://www.alliedcollege.edu
Phone: (314) 739-4450
Inst. Accred.: ABHES (1985/2005)
Prog. Accred.: Dental Assisting, Medical Assisting
   (ABHES), Surgical Technology

Cambridge College Campus
4145 SW Watson Ave., Beaverton, OR 97005
Phone: (503) 646-6000
Prog. Accred: Medical Assisting (ABHES), Surgical
   Technology

Fenton Campus
645 Gravois Bluffs Blvd., Fenton 63026
Phone: (636) 326-7343
Prog. Accred: Medical Assisting (ABHES)

Aquinas Institute of Theology
3642 Lindell Blvd., St. Louis 63108-3396
Type: Private, Roman Catholic Church, four-year
Degrees: M, D   *Enroll:* 181
URL: http://www.ai.edu
Phone: (314) 977-3882   *Calendar:* Sem. plan
Inst. Accred.: ATS (1968/1996), NCA-HLC (1964/1996)

Assemblies of God Theological Seminary
1435 North Glenstone Ave., Springfield 65802-2131
Type: Private, Assemblies of God, four-year
Degrees: M, D   *Enroll:* 345
URL: http://www.agts.edu
Phone: (417) 268-1010   *Calendar:* Sem. plan
Inst. Accred.: ATS (1992/2001), NCA-HLC (1978/2001)

Avila University
11901 Wornall Rd., Kansas City 64145
Type: Private, Roman Catholic Church, four-year
Degrees: B, M   *Enroll:* 1,340
URL: http://www.avila.edu
Phone: (816) 942-8400   *Calendar:* Sem. plan
Inst. Accred.: NCA-HLC (1946/1998)
Prog. Accred.: Nursing, Nursing Education, Radiography,
   Social Work

Baptist Bible College
628 East Kearney St., Springfield 65803-3498
Type: Private, Baptist Bible Fellowship International, four-
   year
Degrees: A, B, M   *Enroll:* 657
URL: http://www.bbcnet.edu
Phone: (417) 268-6060   *Calendar:* Sem. plan
Inst. Accred.: ABHE (1978/1999)

Barnes-Jewish College of Nursing and Allied Health
306 South Kingshighway Blvd., MS 90 30-625, St. Louis
63110-1091
Type: Private, independent, four-year
Degrees: A, B, M   *Enroll:* 458
URL: http://barnesjewishcollege.edu
Phone: (314) 454-7055   *Calendar:* Sem. plan
Inst. Accred.: NCA-HLC (1995/2000)
Prog. Accred.: Clinical Lab Scientist, Cytotechnology,
   Nursing, Nursing Education, Radiation Therapy

Blue River Community College—Blue Springs Campus
1501 West Jefferson St., Blue Springs 64015
Type: Public, state/local, two-year
System: Metropolitan Community College District
Degrees: A
URL:
   http://www.kcmetro.cc.mo.us/blueriver/brhome.html
Phone: (816) 655-6000   *Calendar:* Sem. plan
Inst. Accred.: NCA-HLC (1986/1996, *Indirect accreditation
   through Metropolitan Community College District,
   Kansas City, MO*)

Blue River Community College—Independence Campus
20301 East 78 Hwy., Independence 64057
Type: Public, state/local, two-year
System: Metropolitan Community College District
Degrees: A
URL:
   http://www.kcmetro.cc.mo.us/blueriver/brhome.html
Phone: (816) 220-6550   *Calendar:* Qtr. plan
Inst. Accred.: NCA-HLC (1986/1996, *Indirect accreditation
   through Metropolitan Community College District,
   Kansas City, MO*)

Bryan College—Springfield
237 South Florence Ave., Springfield 65806-2507
Type: Private, proprietary, two-year
Degrees: A
URL: http://www.bryancareercolleges.com
Phone: (417) 862-5700
Inst. Accred.: ACICS (1991/2000)

Calvary Bible College and Theological Seminary
15800 Calvary Rd., Kansas City 64147-1341
Type: Private, interdenominational, four-year
Degrees: A, B, M   *Enroll:* 257
URL: http://www.calvary.edu
Phone: (816) 322-0110   *Calendar:* Sem. plan
Inst. Accred.: ABHE (1961/2001), NCA-HLC (2003)

Central Bible College
3000 North Grant Ave., Springfield 65803-1096
Type: Private, Assemblies of God Church, four-year
Degrees: A, B   *Enroll:* 771
URL: http://www.cbcag.edu
Phone: (417) 833-2551   *Calendar:* Sem. plan
Inst. Accred.: ABHE (1948/1996)

Central Christian College of the Bible
911 East Urbandale Dr., Moberly 65270
Type: Private, Christian Churches/Churches of Christ, four-year
Degrees: A, B   *Enroll:* 260
URL: http://cccb.edu
Phone: (660) 263-3900   *Calendar:* Sem. plan
Inst. Accred.: ABHE (1982/2003)

Central Methodist University
411 Central Methodist Square, Fayette 65248
Type: Private, United Methodist Church, four-year
Degrees: A, B, M   *Enroll:* 1,467
URL: http://www.cmc.edu
Phone: (660) 248-3391   *Calendar:* Sem. plan
Inst. Accred.: NCA-HLC (1913/1998)
Prog. Accred.: Music

Central Missouri State University
PO Box 800, Warrensburg 64093
Type: Public, state, four-year
System: Missouri Coordinating Board for Higher Education
Degrees: A, B, M, P   *Enroll:* 8,627
URL: http://www.cmsu.edu
Phone: (660) 543-4111   *Calendar:* Sem. plan
Inst. Accred.: NCA-HLC (1915/2004)
Prog. Accred.: Accounting, Applied Science (industrial hygiene, occupational health and safety), Art, Audiology, Business (AACSB), Construction Education, Construction Technology, Electronic Technology, Industrial Technology, Music, Nursing, Nursing Education, Social Work, Speech-Language Pathology, Teacher Education (NCATE)

Cleveland Chiropractic College
6401 Rockhill Rd., Kansas City 64131
Type: Private, independent, four-year
Degrees: B, P, D   *Enroll:* 473
URL: http://www.clevelandchiropractic.edu
Phone: (800) 467-2252   *Calendar:* Tri. plan
Inst. Accred.: NCA-HLC (1984/1997)
Prog. Accred.: Chiropractic Education

Los Angeles Campus
590 North Vermont Ave., Los Angeles, CA 90004
Phone: (323) 660-6166
Prog. Accred: Chiropractic Education

College of the Ozarks
PO Box 17, Point Lookout 65726
Type: Private, Presbyterian Church, four-year
Degrees: B   *Enroll:* 1,305
Phone: (800) 222-0525   *Calendar:* Sem. plan
Inst. Accred.: NCA-HLC (1961/2001)

Columbia College
1001 Rogers St., Columbia 65216
Type: Private, Disciples of Christ, four-year
Degrees: A, B, M   *Enroll:* 7,782
URL: http://www.ccis.edu
Phone: (573) 875-8700   *Calendar:* Sem. plan
Inst. Accred.: NCA-HLC (1918/2003)
Prog. Accred.: Nursing, Social Work

Orlando Campus
2600 Technology Dr., Ste. 100, Orlando, FL 32804
Phone: (407) 293-9911

Conception Seminary College
PO Box 502, Conception 64433
Type: Private, Roman Catholic Church, four-year
Degrees: B   *Enroll:* 94
URL: http://www.conception.edu
Phone: (660) 944-2218   *Calendar:* Sem. plan
Inst. Accred.: NCA-HLC (1960/2004)

Concorde Career College
3239 Broadway Blvd., Kansas City 64111-2407
Type: Private, proprietary, two-year
Degrees: A   *Enroll:* 500
URL: http://www.concordecareercolleges.com
Phone: (816) 531-5223
Inst. Accred.: ACCSCT (1986/2001)
Prog. Accred.: Dental Assisting, Medical Assisting (AMA), Respiratory Therapy, Respiratory Therapy Technology

Concordia Seminary
801 DeMun Ave., St. Louis 63105
Type: Private, Lutheran Church-Missouri Synod, four-year
System: Concordia University System
Degrees: M, D   *Enroll:* 641
URL: http://www.csl.edu
Phone: (314) 505-7000   *Calendar:* Qtr. plan
Inst. Accred.: ATS (1963/2003), NCA-HLC (1978/2004)

Cottey College
1000 West Austin St., Nevada 64772
Type: Private, PEO Sisterhood, two-year
Degrees: A   *Enroll:* 285
URL: http://www.cottey.edu
Phone: (417) 667-8181   *Calendar:* Sem. plan
Inst. Accred.: NCA-HLC (1918/2003)
Prog. Accred.: Music

Covenant Theological Seminary
12330 Conway Rd., St. Louis 63141
Type: Private, Presbyterian Church in America, four-year
Degrees: M, D   *Enroll:* 547
Phone: (314) 434-4044   *Calendar:* 4-1-4 plan
Inst. Accred.: ATS (1983/1998), NCA-HLC (1973/1998)

Crowder College
601 Laclede Ave., Neosho 64850
Type: Public, state/local, two-year
System: Missouri Coordinating Board for Higher
Education
Degrees: A   *Enroll:* 1,794
URL: http://www.crowder.edu
Phone: (417) 451-3226   *Calendar:* Sem. plan
Inst. Accred.: NCA-HLC (1977/2002)
Prog. Accred.: Design Technology, Electronic Technology,
Industrial Technology

Culver-Stockton College
One College Hill, Canton 63435
Type: Private, Christian Church/Disciples of Christ, four-
year
Degrees: B   *Enroll:* 794
URL: http://www.culver.edu
Phone: (217) 231-6000   *Calendar:* Sem. plan
Inst. Accred.: NCA-HLC (1924/2002)
Prog. Accred.: Music, Nursing Education

Deaconess College of Nursing
6150 Oakland Ave., St. Louis 63139
Type: Private, proprietary, four-year
System: DeVry University
Degrees: A, B   *Enroll:* 74
URL: http://www.deaconess.edu
Phone: (314) 768-3044   *Calendar:* Sem. plan
Inst. Accred.: NCA-HLC (1985/1997)
Prog. Accred.: Nursing, Nursing Education

DeVry University Kansas City
11224 Holmes Rd., Kansas City 64131
Type: Private, proprietary, four-year
System: DeVry University
Degrees: A, B, M   *Enroll:* 1,741
URL: http://www.devry.edu/kansascity
Phone: (816) 941-0430   *Calendar:* Sem. plan
Inst. Accred.: NCA-HLC (2002, *Indirect accreditation
through DeVry University, Oakbrook Terrace, IL*)
Prog. Accred.: Engineering Technology (computer)

Drury University
900 North Benton Ave., Springfield 65802
Type: Private, independent, four-year
Degrees: A, B, M   *Enroll:* 3,520
URL: http://www.drury.edu
Phone: (417) 873-7879   *Calendar:* Sem. plan
Inst. Accred.: NCA-HLC (1915/2001)
Prog. Accred.: Business (ACBSP), Music, Teacher
Education (NCATE)

Fort Leonard Wood Campus
Truman Education Center, Building 499, Fort Leonard
Wood 65473
Phone: (314) 873-7399

East Central College
1964 Prairie Dell Rd., Union 63084
Type: Public, state/local, two-year
System: Missouri Coordinating Board for Higher
Education
Degrees: A   *Enroll:* 2,096
URL: http://www.eastcentral.edu
Phone: (636) 583-5193   *Calendar:* Sem. plan
Inst. Accred.: NCA-HLC (1976/2000)
Prog. Accred.: Culinary Education, Dental Assisting

Eden Theological Seminary
475 East Lockwood Ave., St. Louis 63119-3192
Type: Private, United Church of Christ, four-year
Degrees: M, D   *Enroll:* 170
URL: http://www.eden.edu
Phone: (314) 918-2627   *Calendar:* 4-1-4 plan
Inst. Accred.: ATS (1938/1998), NCA-HLC (1973/1999)

Evangel University
1111 North Glenstone Ave., Springfield 65802
Type: Private, General Council of the Assemblies of God,
four-year
Degrees: A, B, M   *Enroll:* 1,781
Phone: (417) 865-2811   *Calendar:* Sem. plan
Inst. Accred.: NCA-HLC (1965/1998)
Prog. Accred.: Music, Social Work, Teacher Education
(NCATE)

Fontbonne University
6800 Wydown Blvd., St. Louis 63105
Type: Private, Roman Catholic Church, four-year
Degrees: B, M   *Enroll:* 2,000
URL: http://www.fontbonne.edu
Phone: (314) 889-1419   *Calendar:* Sem. plan
Inst. Accred.: NCA-HLC (1926/2000)
Prog. Accred.: Speech-Language Pathology

Forest Institute of Professional Psychology
2885 West Battlefield, Springfield 65807
Type: Private, independent, four-year
Degrees: M, D   *Enroll:* 205
URL: http://www.forestinstitute.org
Phone: (417) 823-3477
Inst. Accred.: NCA-HLC (1983/2004)
Prog. Accred.: Clinical Psychology, Marriage and Family
Therapy

Global University
1211 South Glenstone Ave., Springfield 65804
Type: Private, Asemblies of God, four-year
Degrees: A, B, M   *FTE Enroll:* 1,200
URL: http://www.globaluniversity.edu
Phone: (417) 862-9533
Inst. Accred.: DETC (2000/2005)

Grantham University
7200 Northwest 86th St., Kansas City 64153
Type: Private, proprietary, four-year
Degrees: A, B, M   *FTE Enroll:* 450
URL: http://www.grantham.edu
Phone: (800) 955-2527
Inst. Accred.: DETC (1961/2000)

Hannibal-LaGrange College
2800 Palmyra Rd., Hannibal 63401
Type: Private, Missouri Baptist Convention, four-year
Degrees: A, B   *Enroll:* 887
URL: http://www.hlg.edu
Phone: (573) 221-3675   *Calendar:* Sem. plan
Inst. Accred.: NCA-HLC (1958/2005)
Prog. Accred.: Nursing

Harris-Stowe State College
3026 Laclede Ave., St. Louis 63103
Type: Public, state, four-year
System: Missouri Coordinating Board for Higher
   Education
Degrees: B   *Enroll:* 1,124
URL: http://www.hssc.edu
Phone: (314) 340-3366   *Calendar:* Sem. plan
Inst. Accred.: NCA-HLC (1924/2001)
Prog. Accred.: Business (ACBSP), Teacher Education
   (NCATE)

Hickey College
940 West Port Plaza Dr., St. Louis 63146
Type: Private, proprietary, two-year
Degrees: A   *Enroll:* 421
URL: http://www.hickeycollege.edu
Phone: (314) 434-2212
Inst. Accred.: ACICS (1971/2001)

High-Tech Institute—Kansas City
9001 State Line Rd., Kansas City 66101
Type: Private, proprietary, two-year
Degrees: A
URL: http://www.hightechinstitute.edu
Phone: (816) 444-4300
Inst. Accred.: ACCSCT (2005)

ICI University
1211 South Glenstone Ave., Springfield 65804
Type: Private, Assemblies of God, four-year
Degrees: A, B, M   *FTE Enroll:* 1,109
URL: http://www.globaluniversity.edu
Phone: (417) 862-9533
Inst. Accred.: DETC (1977/2000)

IHM Health Studies Center
2500 Abbott Place, St. Louis 63143-2636
Type: Private, independent, two-year
Degrees: A
URL: http://www.ihmhealthstudies.com
Phone: (314) 768-1234
Inst. Accred.: ABHES (1992/2005)
Prog. Accred.: EMT (Paramedic)

ITT Technical Institute
13505 Lakefront Dr., Earth City 63045-1416
Type: Private, proprietary, four-year
System: ITT Educational Services, Inc.
Degrees: A, B   *Enroll:* 563
URL: http://www.itt-tech.edu
Phone: (314) 298-7800   *Calendar:* Qtr. plan
Inst. Accred.: ACICS (1999/2004)

Memphis Area Campus
7260 Goodlett Farms Pkwy., Cordova, TN 38016
Phone: (901) 381-0200

Omaha Campus
9814 M St., Omaha, NE 68127-2056
Phone: (402) 331-2900

Warrensville Heights Campus
4700 Richmond Rd., Warrensville Heights, OH 44128
Phone: (216) 896-6500

Jefferson College
1000 Viking Dr., Hillsboro 63050-1000
Type: Public, state/local, two-year
System: Missouri Coordinating Board for Higher
   Education
Degrees: A   *Enroll:* 2,810
URL: http://www.jeffco.edu
Phone: (636) 797-3000   *Calendar:* Sem. plan
Inst. Accred.: NCA-HLC (1969/1999)
Prog. Accred.: Veterinary Technology

Kansas City Art Institute
4415 Warwick Blvd., Kansas City 64111
Type: Private, independent, four-year
Degrees: B   *Enroll:* 576
URL: http://www.kcai.edu
Phone: (816) 472-4852   *Calendar:* Sem. plan
Inst. Accred.: NCA-HLC (1964/2001)
Prog. Accred.: Art

The Kansas City University of Medicine and Biosciences
1750 Independence Blvd., Kansas City 64106-1453
Type: Private, independent, four-year
Degrees: D   *Enroll:* 909
URL: http://www.uhs.edu
Phone: (816) 283-2000   *Calendar:* Sem. plan
Inst. Accred.: NCA-HLC (1998)
Prog. Accred.: Osteopathy

Kenrick-Glennon Seminary
5200 Glennon Dr., St. Louis 63119-4399
Type: Private, Roman Catholic Church, four-year
Degrees: M   *Enroll:* 65
URL: http://www.kenrick.edu
Phone: (314) 792-6100   *Calendar:* Sem. plan
Inst. Accred.: ATS (1973/1999), NCA-HLC (1973/2004)

L'Ecole Culinaire
9811 South Forty Dr., Saint Louis 63124-1103
Type: Private, proprietary, two-year
Degrees: A
URL: http://www.lecoleculinaire.com
Phone: (314) 587-2433
Inst. Accred.: ACCSCT (2004)

Lester L. Cox College of Nursing and Health Sciences
1423 North Jefferson Ave., Springfield 65802
Type: Private, independent, four-year
Degrees: A, B   *Enroll:* 362
URL: http://www.coxcollege.edu
Phone: (417) 269-3424   *Calendar:* Sem. plan
Inst. Accred.: NCA-HLC (2000/2005)
Prog. Accred.: Nursing, Nursing Education

Lincoln University
820 Chestnut St., Jefferson City 65101
Type: Public, state, four-year
System: Missouri Coordinating Board for Higher Education
Degrees: A, B, M   *Enroll:* 2,418
URL: http://www.lincolnu.edu
Phone: (573) 681-5000   *Calendar:* Sem. plan
Inst. Accred.: NCA-HLC (1926/2003)
Prog. Accred.: Business (ACBSP), Music, Nursing, Teacher Education (NCATE)

Lindenwood University
209 South Kingshighway Blvd., Saint Charles 63301-1695
Type: Private, United Presbyterian Church, four-year
Degrees: B, M, P   *Enroll:* 6,249
URL: http://www.lindenwood.edu
Phone: (636) 949-2000
Inst. Accred.: NCA-HLC (1918/2004)

Linn State Technical College
One Technology Dr., Linn 65051
Type: Public, state, two-year
Degrees: A   *Enroll:* 813
URL: http://www.linnstate.edu
Phone: (573) 897-3603   *Calendar:* Sem. plan
Inst. Accred.: NCA-HLC (2000/2005)
Prog. Accred.: Aviation Technology, Design Technology, Electronic Technology, Industrial Technology, Manufacturing Technology, Mechanical Technology, Physical Therapy Assisting

Logan University
1851 Schoettler Rd., PO Box 1065, Chesterfield 63006-1065
Type: Private, independent, four-year
Degrees: B, P, D   *Enroll:* 1,090
URL: http://www.logan.edu
Phone: (636) 227-2100   *Calendar:* Tri. plan
Inst. Accred.: NCA-HLC (1987/2002)
Prog. Accred.: Chiropractic Education

Longview Community College
500 Longview Rd., Lee's Summit 64081
Type: Public, state/local, two-year
System: Metropolitan Community College District
Degrees: A   *Enroll:* 3,476
URL: http://www.kcmetro.edu
Phone: (816) 672-2000   *Calendar:* Sem. plan
Inst. Accred.: NCA-HLC (1986/1996, *Indirect accreditation through Metropolitan Community College District, Kansas City, MO*)

Maple Woods Community College
2601 North East Barry Rd., Kansas City 64156-1299
Type: Public, state/local, two-year
System: Metropolitan Community College District
Degrees: A   *Enroll:* 2,935
URL: http://www.kcmetro.cc.mo.us/maplewoods
Phone: (816) 437-3000   *Calendar:* Sem. plan
Inst. Accred.: NCA-HLC (1986/1996, *Indirect accreditation through Metropolitan Community College District, Kansas City, MO*)
Prog. Accred.: Veterinary Technology

Maryville University of St. Louis
13550 Conway Rd., St. Louis 63141-7299
Type: Private, independent, four-year
Degrees: B, M   *Enroll:* 2,331
URL: http://www.maryville.edu
Phone: (314) 529-9300   *Calendar:* Sem. plan
Inst. Accred.: NCA-HLC (1941/2005)
Prog. Accred.: Art, Business (ACBSP), Interior Design, Music, Nursing, Nursing Education, Occupational Therapy, Physical Therapy, Rehabilitation Counseling, Teacher Education (NCATE)

Messenger College
PO Box 4050, 300 East 50th St., Joplin 64803
Type: Private, Pentecostal Church of God, four-year
Degrees: A, B   *Enroll:* 90
URL: http://www.messengercollege.edu
Phone: (417) 624-7070   *Calendar:* Sem. plan
Inst. Accred.: TRACS (1998/2003)

Metro Business College
1732 North Kingshighway Blvd., Cape Girardeau 63701
Type: Private, proprietary, two-year
Degrees: A   *Enroll:* 402
URL: http://www.metrobusinesscollege.edu
Phone: (573) 334-9181   *Calendar:* Qtr. plan
Inst. Accred.: ACICS (1979/2003)

Jefferson City Campus
1407 Southwest Blvd., Jefferson City 65109
Phone: (573) 635-6600

Rolla Campus
1202 East Hwy. 72, Rolla 65401
Phone: (573) 364-8464

Midwest Institute for Medical Assistants
10910 Manchester Rd., Kirkwood 63122
Type: Private, proprietary, two-year
Degrees: A
URL: http://www.midwestinstitute.com
Phone: (314) 965-8363
Inst. Accred.: ABHES (1978/2002)
Prog. Accred.: Medical Assisting (ABHES)

Earth City Campus
4260 Shoreline Dr., Earth City 63045
Phone: (314) 344-3334
Prog. Accred: Medical Assisting (ABHES)

Midwest Theological Seminary
PO Box 365, 851 Parr Rd., Wentzville 63385
Type: Private, International Evangelical Association, four-year
Degrees: B, M, D
URL: http://www.midwest.edu
Phone: (636) 327-4645   *Calendar:* Sem. plan
Inst. Accred.: TRACS (2004)

Midwestern Baptist Theological Seminary
5001 North Oak St. Trafficway, Kansas City 64118
Type: Private, Southern Baptist Convention, four-year
Degrees: A, M, D   *Enroll:* 348
URL: http://www.mbts.edu
Phone: (816) 414-3700   *Calendar:* Qtr. plan
Inst. Accred.: ATS (1964/2002), NCA-HLC (1971/2003)

Mineral Area College
5270 Flat River Rd., PO Box 1000, Park Hills 63601
Type: Public, state/local, two-year
System: Missouri Coordinating Board for Higher Education
Degrees: A   *Enroll:* 2,082
URL: http://www.mineralarea.edu
Phone: (573) 431-4593   *Calendar:* Sem. plan
Inst. Accred.: NCA-HLC (1971/1998)
Prog. Accred.: Dental Assisting

Missouri Baptist University
One College Park Dr., St. Louis 63141-8660
Type: Private, Southern Baptist Church, four-year
Degrees: A, B, M   *Enroll:* 2,189
URL: http://www.mobap.edu
Phone: (314) 434-1115   *Calendar:* Sem. plan
Inst. Accred.: NCA-HLC (1978/1997)
Prog. Accred.: Music

Missouri College
10121 Manchester Rd., St. Louis 63122-1583
Type: Private, proprietary, two-year
System: Career Education Corporation
Degrees: A   *Enroll:* 818
URL: http://www.missouricollege.com
Phone: (314) 821-7700
Inst. Accred.: ACCSCT (1970/2001)
Prog. Accred.: Dental Assisting

Missouri Southern State University
3950 East Newman Rd., Joplin 64801-1595
Type: Public, state, four-year
System: Missouri Coordinating Board for Higher Education
Degrees: A, B, M, D   *Enroll:* 4,289
URL: http://www.mssu.edu
Phone: (417) 625-9500   *Calendar:* Sem. plan
Inst. Accred.: NCA-HLC (1949/1998)
Prog. Accred.: Business (ACBSP), Dental Hygiene, Engineering Technology (general drafting/design), Nursing, Radiography, Respiratory Therapy, Respiratory Therapy Technology, Teacher Education (NCATE)

Missouri State University
901 South National Ave., Springfield 65804
Type: Public, state, four-year
System: Missouri Coordinating Board for Higher Education
Degrees: A, B, M, P   *Enroll:* 15,605
URL: http://www.missouristate.edu
Phone: (417) 836-8500   *Calendar:* Sem. plan
Inst. Accred.: NCA-HLC (1915/1996)
Prog. Accred.: Accounting, Athletic Training, Audiology, Business (AACSB), Computer Science, Construction Education, Family and Consumer Science, Industrial Technology, Music, Nursing, Nursing Education, Physical Therapy, Physician Assistant, Public Administration, Recreation and Leisure Services, Social Work, Speech-Language Pathology, Teacher Education (NCATE), Theatre

Missouri State University—West Plains
128 Garfield Ave., West Plains 65775
Type: Public, state, two-year
System: Missouri Coordinating Board for Higher Education
Degrees: A   *Enroll:* 1,185
URL: http://www.wp.missouristate.edu
Phone: (417) 255-7900   *Calendar:* Sem. plan
Inst. Accred.: NCA-HLC (1994/2004)

Missouri Tech
1167 Corporate Lake Dr., St. Louis 63132-2907
Type: Private, proprietary, four-year
Degrees: A, B   *Enroll:* 113
URL: http://www.motech.edu
Phone: (314) 569-3600   *Calendar:* Sem. plan
Inst. Accred.: ACCSCT (1985/2000)

Missouri Valley College
500 East College Dr., Marshall 65340
Type: Private, Presbyterian Church (USA), four-year
Degrees: A, B   *Enroll:* 1,476
URL: http://www.moval.edu
Phone: (660) 831-4000   *Calendar:* 4-1-4 plan
Inst. Accred.: NCA-HLC (1916/2004)

Missouri Western State University
4525 Downs Dr., St. Joseph 64507-2294
Type: Public, state, four-year
System: Missouri Coordinating Board for Higher
    Education
Degrees: A, B   *Enroll:* 4,198
URL: http://www.missouriwestern.edu
Phone: (816) 271-4237   *Calendar:* Sem. plan
Inst. Accred.: NCA-HLC (1923/2000)
Prog. Accred.: Engineering Technology (civil/construction,
    electrical), Health Information Technician, Music,
    Nursing, Nursing Education, Physical Therapy Assisting,
    Social Work, Teacher Education (NCATE)

Moberly Area Community College
101 College Ave., Moberly 65270-1304
Type: Public, state/local, two-year
System: Missouri Coordinating Board for Higher
    Education
Degrees: A   *Enroll:* 2,366
URL: http://www.macc.edu
Phone: (660) 263-4110   *Calendar:* Sem. plan
Inst. Accred.: NCA-HLC (1980/2002)

Nazarene Theological Seminary
1700 East Meyer Blvd., Kansas City 64131-1246
Type: Private, Church of the Nazarene, four-year
Degrees: M, D   *Enroll:* 287
URL: http://www.nts.edu
Phone: (816) 333-6254   *Calendar:* Sem. plan
Inst. Accred.: ATS (1970/2000)

North Central Missouri College
1301 Main St., Trenton 64683
Type: Public, state/local, two-year
System: Missouri Coordinating Board for Higher
    Education
Degrees: A   *Enroll:* 1,010
URL: http://www.ncmc.cc.mo.us
Phone: (660) 359-3948   *Calendar:* Sem. plan
Inst. Accred.: NCA-HLC (1983/2002)

Northwest Missouri State University
800 University Dr., Maryville 64468-6001
Type: Public, state, four-year
System: Missouri Coordinating Board for Higher
    Education
Degrees: B, M, P   *Enroll:* 5,593
URL: http://www.nwmissouri.edu
Phone: (660) 562-1110   *Calendar:* Sem. plan
Inst. Accred.: NCA-HLC (1921/1998)
Prog. Accred.: Business (ACBSP), Family and Consumer
    Science, Music, Teacher Education (NCATE)

Ozark Christian College
1111 North Main St., Joplin 64801-4804
Type: Private, Christian Churches/Churches of Christ,
    four-year
Degrees: A, B   *Enroll:* 760
URL: http://www.occ.edu
Phone: (417) 624-2518   *Calendar:* Sem. plan
Inst. Accred.: ABHE (1988/1999)

Ozarks Technical Community College
PO Box 5958, Springfield 65801
Type: Public, local, two-year
System: Missouri Coordinating Board for Higher
    Education
Degrees: A   *Enroll:* 5,661
URL: http://www.otc.edu
Phone: (417) 895-7000   *Calendar:* Sem. plan
Inst. Accred.: NCA-HLC (1996/2001)
Prog. Accred.: Construction Technology, Culinary
    Education, Dental Assisting, Dental Hygiene, Design
    Technology, Health Information Technician, Industrial
    Technology, Manufacturing Technology, Occupational
    Therapy Assisting, Physical Therapy Assisting,
    Respiratory Therapy, Surgical Technology

Park University
8700 NW River Park Dr., Parkville 64152
Type: Private, Church of Latter-Day Saints, four-year
Degrees: A, B, M   *Enroll:* 5,380
URL: http://www.park.edu
Phone: (816) 741-2000   *Calendar:* Sem. plan
Inst. Accred.: NCA-HLC (1913/2005)
Prog. Accred.: Nursing

Ford Motor Company On-Site Program
Kansas City Assembly Plant, PO Box 11009, Kansas
City 64119
Phone: (816) 459-1138

Graduate School of Religion Campus
PO Box 1059, Independence 64051-1059
Phone: (816) 833-1000

Independence Campus
2200 South 291 Hwy., Independence 64057
Phone: (816) 252-9065

MetroPark Campus
934 Wyandotte St., Kansas City 64105-1630
Phone: (816) 842-6182

Patricia Stevens College
300 North 4th St., St. Louis 63102
Type: Private, proprietary, two-year
Degrees: A   *Enroll:* 140
URL: http://www.patriciastevenscollege.edu
Phone: (314) 421-0949   *Calendar:* Qtr. plan
Inst. Accred.: ACICS (1968/2004)

Penn Valley Community College
3201 South West Trafficway, Kansas City 64111
Type: Public, state/local, two-year
System: Metropolitan Community College District
Degrees: A   *Enroll:* 2,546
URL: http://www.kcmetro.cc.mo.us/pennvalley
Phone: (816) 759-4000   *Calendar:* Sem. plan
Inst. Accred.: NCA-HLC (1986/1996, *Indirect accreditation through Metropolitan Community College District, Kansas City, MO)*
Prog. Accred.: Dental Assisting, EMT (Paramedic), Health Information Technician, Nursing, Occupational Therapy Assisting, Physical Therapy Assisting, Practical Nursing, Radiography, Surgical Technology

Pinnacle Career Institute
15329 Kensington Ave., Kansas City 64147-1212
Type: Private, proprietary, two-year
Degrees: A   *Enroll:* 206
URL: http://www.pcitraining.com
Phone: (816) 331-5700   *Calendar:* Qtr. plan
Inst. Accred.: ACCSCT (1971/2001)

Ranken Technical College
4431 Finney Ave., St. Louis 63113
Type: Private, independent, four-year
Degrees: A, B   *Enroll:* 1,267
URL: http://www.ranken.edu
Phone: (314) 371-0233   *Calendar:* Sem. plan
Inst. Accred.: NCA-HLC (1989/1999)

Research College of Nursing
2300 East Meyer Blvd., Kansas City 64132
Type: Private, independent, four-year
Degrees: B, M   *Enroll:* 184
URL: http://www.researchcollege.edu
Phone: (816) 276-4721   *Calendar:* Sem. plan
Inst. Accred.: NCA-HLC (1987/2002)
Prog. Accred.: Nursing, Nursing Education

Rockhurst University
1100 Rockhurst Rd., Kansas City 64110
Type: Private, Roman Catholic Church, four-year
Degrees: B, M   *Enroll:* 1,910
URL: http://www.rockhurst.edu
Phone: (816) 501-4250   *Calendar:* Sem. plan
Inst. Accred.: NCA-HLC (1934/2003)
Prog. Accred.: Business (AACSB), Nursing, Occupational Therapy, Physical Therapy, Speech-Language Pathology

Saint Charles Community College
4601 Mid Rivers Mall Dr., St. Peters 63376
Type: Public, state/local, two-year
System: Missouri Coordinating Board for Higher Education
Degrees: A   *Enroll:* 4,338
URL: http://www.stchas.edu
Phone: (636) 922-8000   *Calendar:* Sem. plan
Inst. Accred.: NCA-HLC (1991/2002)
Prog. Accred.: Health Information Technician, Nursing, Occupational Therapy Assisting

Saint Louis Christian College
1360 Grandview Dr., Florissant 63033-6499
Type: Private, independent, four-year
Degrees: A, B   *Enroll:* 171
URL: http://www.slcconline.edu
Phone: (314) 837-6777   *Calendar:* Sem. plan
Inst. Accred.: ABHE (1977/1998)

Saint Louis College of Health Careers
909 South Taylor Ave., St. Louis 63110-1511
Type: Private, proprietary, two-year
Degrees: A
URL: http://www.stlouiscollege.com
Phone: (314) 652-0300
Inst. Accred.: ABHES (1986/2001)
Prog. Accred.: Medical Assisting (ABHES)

County Campus
1297 North Hwy. Dr., Fenton 63026
Phone: (636) 529-0000
Prog. Accred: Medical Assisting (ABHES)

Saint Louis College of Pharmacy
4588 Parkview Place, St. Louis 63110
Type: Private, independent, four-year
Degrees: B, M, P, D   *Enroll:* 753
URL: http://www.stlcop.edu
Phone: (314) 367-8700   *Calendar:* Sem. plan
Inst. Accred.: NCA-HLC (1967/2002)
Prog. Accred.: Pharmacy

Saint Louis Community College at Florissant Valley
3400 Pershall Rd., St. Louis 63135
Type: Public, state/local, two-year
System: Saint Louis Community College District
Degrees: A   *Enroll:* 4,227
URL: http://www.stlcc.cc.mo.us/fv
Phone: (314) 595-4200   *Calendar:* Sem. plan
Inst. Accred.: NCA-HLC (1988/1998, *Indirect accreditation through Saint Louis Community College District, St. Louis, MO)*
Prog. Accred.: Art, Engineering Technology (electrical, mechanical), Nursing

Saint Louis Community College at Forest Park
5600 Oakland Ave., St. Louis 63110
Type: Public, state/local, two-year
System: Saint Louis Community College District
Degrees: A   *Enroll:* 4,226
URL: http://www.stlcc.edu
Phone: (314) 644-9100   *Calendar:* Sem. plan
Inst. Accred.: NCA-HLC (1988/1998, *Indirect accreditation through Saint Louis Community College District, St. Louis, MO)*
Prog. Accred.: Clinical Lab Technology, Culinary Education, Dental Assisting, Dental Hygiene, Diagnostic Medical Sonography, Funeral Service Education (Mortuary Science), Nursing, Radiography, Respiratory Therapy, Surgical Technology

Saint Louis Community College at Meramec
11333 Big Bend Blvd., St. Louis 63122
Type: Public, state/local, two-year
System: Saint Louis Community College District
Degrees: A   *Enroll:* 8,040
URL: http://www.stlcc.cc.mo.us/mc
Phone: (314) 984-7500   *Calendar:* Sem. plan
Inst. Accred.: NCA-HLC (1988/1998, *Indirect accreditation through Saint Louis Community College District, St. Louis, MO)*
Prog. Accred.: Art, Nursing, Occupational Therapy Assisting, Physical Therapy Assisting

Saint Louis University
221 North Grand Blvd., St. Louis 63103-2097
Type: Private, Society of Jesus, four-year
Degrees: A, B, M, P, D   *Enroll:* 10,850
URL: http://www.slu.edu
Phone: (314) 977-2222   *Calendar:* Sem. plan
Inst. Accred.: NCA-HLC (1916/2002)
Prog. Accred.: Business (AACSB), Clinical Lab Scientist, Clinical Pastoral Education (ACPEI), Clinical Psychology, Dietetics (internship), Endodontics, Engineering (aerospace, electrical, mechanical), Health Information Administration, Health Services Administration, Law, Medicine, Nuclear Medicine Technology, Nursing, Nursing Education, Occupational Therapy, Orthodontic and Dentofacial Orthopedics, Periodontics, Physical Therapy, Physician Assistant, Public Administration, Public Health, Social Work, Speech-Language Pathology, Teacher Education (NCATE)

Parks College
Falling Springs Rd., Cahokia, IL 62206
Phone: (618) 337-7500

Saint Luke's College
4426 Wornall Rd., Kansas City 64111
Type: Private, independent, four-year
Degrees: B   *Enroll:* 95
URL: http://www.saintlukescollege.edu
Phone: (816) 932-2233   *Calendar:* Sem. plan
Inst. Accred.: NCA-HLC (1994/1999)
Prog. Accred.: Nursing Education

Saint Paul School of Theology
5123 Truman Rd., Kansas City 64127
Type: Private, United Methodist Church, four-year
Degrees: M, D   *Enroll:* 231
URL: http://www.spst.edu
Phone: (816) 483-9600
Inst. Accred.: ATS (1964/2001), NCA-HLC (1976/2002)

Sanford-Brown College—Fenton
1203 Smizer Mill Rd., Fenton 63026
Type: Private, proprietary, four-year
System: Career Education Corporation
Degrees: A, B   *Enroll:* 438
URL: http://www.sbcfenton.com
Phone: (636) 349-4900   *Calendar:* Sem. plan
Inst. Accred.: ACICS (1982/2001)
Prog. Accred.: Radiography

Hazelwood Campus
75 Village Square, Hazelwood 63042
Phone: (314) 731-1101
Prog. Accred: Medical Assisting (ABHES), Occupational Therapy Assisting, Respiratory Therapy, Respiratory Therapy Technology

Saint Charles Campus
3555 Franks Dr., St. Charles 63301
Phone: (314) 724-7100

Southeast Missouri Hospital College of Nursing and Health Sciences
1819 Broadway, Cape Girardeau 63701
Type: Private, independent, four-year
Degrees: A, P   *Enroll:* 68
URL: http://www.southeastmissourihospital.com/college
Phone: (573) 334-4822
Inst. Accred.: NCA-HLC (2005)
Prog. Accred.: Clinical Lab Scientist, Radiography

Southeast Missouri State University
One University Plaza, Cape Girardeau 63701
Type: Public, state, four-year
System: Missouri Coordinating Board for Higher Education
Degrees: A, B, M, P   *Enroll:* 7,873
URL: http://www.semo.edu
Phone: (573) 651-2222   *Calendar:* Sem. plan
Inst. Accred.: NCA-HLC (1915/2001)
Prog. Accred.: Athletic Training, Business (AACSB), Counseling, Dietetics (internship), Engineering (engineering physics/science), Industrial Technology, Journalism, Music, Nursing, Nursing Education, Recreation and Leisure Services, Social Work, Speech-Language Pathology, Teacher Education (NCATE)

Southwest Baptist University
1600 University Ave., Bolivar 65613-2496
Type: Private, Southern Baptist Church, four-year
Degrees: A, B, M   *Enroll:* 2,548
URL: http://www.sbuniv.edu
Phone: (417) 328-5281   *Calendar:* Sem. plan
Inst. Accred.: NCA-HLC (1957/1996)
Prog. Accred.: Business (ACBSP), Music, Nursing,
  Physical Therapy

Springfield College
1010 West Sunshine St., Springfield 65807
Type: Private, proprietary, two-year
System: Corinthian Colleges, Inc
Degrees: A   *Enroll:* 462
URL: http://www.springfield-college.com
Phone: (417) 864-7220   *Calendar:* Qtr. plan
Inst. Accred.: ACICS (1981/2005)
Prog. Accred.: Medical Assisting (CAAHEP)

Rancho Cucamonga Campus
9616 Archibald Ave., Ste. 100, Rancho Cucamonga,
CA 91730
Phone: (909) 484-4311

State Fair Community College
3201 West 16th St., Sedalia 65301-2199
Type: Public, state/local, two-year
System: Missouri Coordinating Board for Higher
  Education
Degrees: A   *Enroll:* 2,261
URL: http://sfcc.cc.mo.us
Phone: (660) 530-5800   *Calendar:* Sem. plan
Inst. Accred.: NCA-HLC (1977/1999)
Prog. Accred.: Construction Education, Industrial
  Technology, Manufacturing Technology, Radiography

Stephens College
1200 East Broadway, Columbia 65215
Type: Private, independent, four-year
Degrees: A, B, M   *Enroll:* 550
URL: http://www.stephens.edu
Phone: (573) 442-2211   *Calendar:* Sem. plan
Inst. Accred.: NCA-HLC (1918/1998)
Prog. Accred.: Health Information Administration

Three Rivers Community College
2080 Three Rivers Blvd., Poplar Bluff 63901
Type: Public, state/local, two-year
System: Missouri Coordinating Board for Higher
  Education
Degrees: A   *Enroll:* 2,179
URL: http://www.trcc.cc.mo.us
Phone: (573) 840-9600   *Calendar:* Sem. plan
Inst. Accred.: NCA-HLC (1974/1998)
Prog. Accred.: Business (ACBSP), Clinical Lab Technology,
  Nursing, Surgical Technology

Truman State University
100 East Normal St., Kirksville 63501-4221
Type: Public, state, four-year
System: Missouri Coordinating Board for Higher
  Education
Degrees: B, M   *Enroll:* 5,634
URL: http://www.truman.edu
Phone: (660) 785-4000   *Calendar:* Sem. plan
Inst. Accred.: NCA-HLC (1914/2005)
Prog. Accred.: Accounting, Business (AACSB), Counseling,
  Music, Nursing, Nursing Education, Speech-Language
  Pathology, Teacher Education (NCATE)

University of Missouri—Columbia
105 Jesse Hall, Columbia 65211
Type: Public, state, four-year
System: University of Missouri System
Degrees: B, M, P, D   *Enroll:* 24,219
URL: http://www.missouri.edu
Phone: (573) 882-2121   *Calendar:* Sem. plan
Inst. Accred.: NCA-HLC (1913/2005)
Prog. Accred.: Accounting, Business (AACSB), Clinical
  Psychology, Counseling Psychology, Dietetics
  (coordinated), Engineering (bioengineering, chemical,
  civil, computer, electrical, industrial, mechanical),
  Forestry, Health Services Administration, Interior
  Design, Journalism, Law, Librarianship, Medicine,
  Music, Nuclear Medicine Technology, Nurse (Midwifery),
  Nursing, Nursing Education, Occupational Therapy,
  Physical Therapy, Psychology Internship, Public
  Administration, Radiography, Recreation and Leisure
  Services, Rehabilitation Counseling, Respiratory
  Therapy, School Psychology, Social Work, Speech-
  Language Pathology, Veterinary Medicine

University of Missouri—Kansas City
5100 Rockhill Rd., Kansas City 64110
Type: Public, state, four-year
System: University of Missouri System
Degrees: B, M, P, D   *Enroll:* 10,171
URL: http://www.umkc.edu
Phone: (816) 235-1000   *Calendar:* Sem. plan
Inst. Accred.: NCA-HLC (1938/1999)
Prog. Accred.: Advanced Education in General Dentistry,
  Business (AACSB), Clinical Psychology, Combined
  Prosthodontics, Counseling Psychology, Dental Hygiene,
  Dentistry, Endodontics, Engineering (civil, electrical,
  mechanical), General Dentistry, General Practice
  Residency, Law, Maxillofacial Prosthetics, Medicine,
  Music, Nursing, Nursing Education, Oral and
  Maxillofacial Radiology, Oral and Maxillofacial Surgery,
  Orthodontic and Dentofacial Orthopedics, Pediatric
  Dentistry, Periodontics, Pharmacy, Psychology
  Internship, Public Administration, Social Work, Teacher
  Education (NCATE), Theatre

University of Missouri—Rolla
206 Parker Hall, Rolla 65409-0470
Type: Public, state, four-year
System: University of Missouri System
Degrees: B, M, D   *Enroll:* 4,876
URL: http://www.umr.edu
Phone: (573) 341-4111   *Calendar:* Sem. plan
Inst. Accred.: NCA-HLC (1913/1999)
Prog. Accred.: Computer Science, Engineering
  (aerospace, ceramic, chemical, civil, computer,
  electrical, engineering management,
  geological/geophysical, mechanical, metallurgical,
  mining, nuclear, petroleum)

University of Missouri—St. Louis
8001 Natural Bridge Rd., St. Louis 63121
Type: Public, state, four-year
System: University of Missouri System
Degrees: B, M, D   *Enroll:* 10,008
URL: http://www.umsl.edu
Phone: (314) 516-5000   *Calendar:* Sem. plan
Inst. Accred.: NCA-HLC (1960/1999)
Prog. Accred.: Accounting, Business (AACSB), Clinical
  Psychology, Counseling, Engineering (civil, electrical,
  mechanical), Music, Nursing, Nursing Education,
  Optometric Residency, Optometry, Public
  Administration, Social Work, Teacher Education (NCATE)

Vatterott College
3925 Industrial Dr., St. Ann 63074-1807
Type: Private, proprietary, four-year
Degrees: A, B   *Enroll:* 535
URL: http://www.vatterott-college.edu
Phone: (314) 428-5900   *Calendar:* Sem. plan
Inst. Accred.: ACCSCT (1982/2003)

Cleveland Campus
5025 E. Royalton Rd., Broadview Heights, OH 44147
Phone: (440) 526-1660

Joplin Campus
5898 North Main St., Joplin 64801
Phone: (417) 781-5633

Kansas City Campus
8955 East 38th Terrace, Kansas City 64129
Phone: (816) 861-1000

Memphis Campus
6152 Macon Rd., Memphis, TN 38134
Phone: (901) 761-5730

O'Fallon Campus
927 East Terra Ln., O'Fallon 63366
Phone: (636) 978-7488

Springfield Campus
3850 South Campbell Ave., Springfield 65807-5340
Phone: (417) 831-8116

Sunset Hills (St. Louis) Campus
12970 Maurer Industrial Dr., Sunset Hills 63127-1516
Phone: (314) 843-4200

Tulsa Campus
555 South Memorial Dr., Tulsa, OK 74112
Phone: (918) 835-8288

Wichita Campus
3639 North Comotara St., Wichita, KS 67226
Phone: (316) 634-0066

Washington University in St. Louis
One Brookings Dr., Box 1192, St. Louis 63130
Type: Private, independent, four-year
Degrees: B, M, D   *Enroll:* 11,455
URL: http://www.wustl.edu
Phone: (314) 935-5000   *Calendar:* Sem. plan
Inst. Accred.: NCA-HLC (1913/2004)
Prog. Accred.: Art, Audiology, Business (AACSB), Clinical
  Psychology, Engineering (chemical, civil, computer,
  electrical, mechanical, systems), Health Services
  Administration, Law, Medicine, Occupational Therapy,
  Physical Therapy, Social Work, Teacher Education (NCATE)

Webster University
470 East Lockwood Ave., St. Louis 63119-3194
Type: Private, independent, four-year
Degrees: B, M, P, D   *Enroll:* 11,444
URL: http://www.webster.edu
Phone: (314) 968-6900   *Calendar:* Sem. plan
Inst. Accred.: NCA-HLC (1925/1998)
Prog. Accred.: Music, Nursing

Wentworth Military Academy and Junior College
1880 Washington Ave., Lexington 64067
Type: Private, independent, two-year
Degrees: A   *Enroll:* 375
URL: http://www.wma1880.org
Phone: (660) 259-2221   *Calendar:* Sem. plan
Inst. Accred.: NCA-HLC (1930/2002)

Westminster College
501 Westminster Ave., Fulton 65251-1299
Type: Private, independent, four-year
Degrees: B   *Enroll:* 809
URL: http://www.westminster-mo.edu
Phone: (573) 642-3361   *Calendar:* Sem. plan
Inst. Accred.: NCA-HLC (1913/2005)

William Jewell College
500 College Hill, Liberty 64068
Type: Private, Missouri Baptist Convention, four-year
Degrees: B   *Enroll:* 1,362
URL: http://www.jewell.edu
Phone: (816) 781-7700   *Calendar:* Sem. plan
Inst. Accred.: NCA-HLC (1915/2001)
Prog. Accred.: Music, Nursing, Nursing Education

William Woods University
One University Ave., Fulton 65251
Type: Private, independent, four-year
Degrees: A, B, M   *Enroll:* 1,453
URL: http://www.wmwoods.edu
Phone: (573) 642-2251   *Calendar:* Sem. plan
Inst. Accred.: NCA-HLC (1919/1997)
Prog. Accred.: Social Work

MONTANA

Blackfeet Community College
PO Box 819, Browning 59417
Type: Public, tribal, two-year
System: American Indian Higher Education Consortium
Degrees: A   _Enroll:_ 491
URL: http://www.bfcc.org
Phone: (406) 338-7755   _Calendar:_ Qtr. plan
Inst. Accred.: NWCCU (1985/2001)

Carroll College
1601 North Benton Ave., Helena 59625
Type: Private, Roman Catholic Church, four-year
Degrees: B   _Enroll:_ 1,301
URL: http://www.carroll.edu
Phone: (406) 447-4300   _Calendar:_ Sem. plan
Inst. Accred.: NWCCU (1949/2000)
Prog. Accred.: Engineering (civil), Nursing, Nursing
  Education

Chief Dull Knife College
PO Box 98, One College Dr., Lame Deer 59043-0098
Type: Public, tribal, two-year
System: American Indian Higher Education Consortium
Degrees: A   _Enroll:_ 214
URL: http://www.cdkc.edu
Phone: (406) 477-6215   _Calendar:_ Sem. plan
Inst. Accred.: NWCCU (1996/2005)

Dawson Community College
300 College Dr., Box 421, Glendive 59330-0421
Type: Public, state/local, two-year
System: Montana University System
Degrees: A   _Enroll:_ 376
URL: http://www.dawson.edu
Phone: (406) 377-3396   _Calendar:_ Sem. plan
Inst. Accred.: NWCCU (1969/2004)

Flathead Valley Community College
777 Grandview Dr., Kalispell 59901-2699
Type: Public, state/local, two-year
System: Montana University System
Degrees: A   _Enroll:_ 1,533
URL: http://www.fvcc.edu
Phone: (406) 756-3822   _Calendar:_ Sem. plan
Inst. Accred.: NWCCU (1970/2004)
Prog. Accred.: Medical Assisting (CAAHEP)

Fort Belknap College
PO Box 159, Harlem 59526-0159
Type: Public, tribal, two-year
System: American Indian Higher Education Consortium
Degrees: A   _Enroll:_ 147
URL: http://www.fortbelknap.cc.mt.us
Phone: (406) 353-2607   _Calendar:_ Qtr. plan
Inst. Accred.: NWCCU (1993/2003)

Fort Peck Community College
PO Box 398, Poplar 59255
Type: Public, tribal, two-year
System: American Indian Higher Education Consortium
Degrees: A   _Enroll:_ 315
URL: http://www.fpcc.edu
Phone: (406) 768-5551   _Calendar:_ Sem. plan
Inst. Accred.: NWCCU (1991/2001)

Little Big Horn College
1 Forest Ln., Crow Agency 59022
Type: Public, tribal, two-year
System: American Indian Higher Education Consortium
Degrees: A   _Enroll:_ 309
URL: http://www.lbhc.cc.mt.us
Phone: (406) 638-3104   _Calendar:_ Sem. plan
Inst. Accred.: NWCCU (1990/2005)

Miles Community College
2715 Dickinson, Miles City 59301-4799
Type: Public, state/local, two-year
System: Montana University System
Degrees: A   _Enroll:_ 458
URL: http://www.milescc.edu
Phone: (406) 234-3031   _Calendar:_ Sem. plan
Inst. Accred.: NWCCU (1971/2001)
Prog. Accred.: Nursing

Montana State University College of Technology—Great Falls
2100 16th Ave., South, Great Falls 59406-6010
Type: Public, state, two-year
System: Montana University System
Degrees: A   _Enroll:_ 967
URL: http://www.msugf.edu
Phone: (406) 771-4300   _Calendar:_ Sem. plan
Inst. Accred.: NWCCU (1979/2005)
Prog. Accred.: Dental Assisting, Dental Hygiene, Health
  Information Technician, Medical Assisting (AMA),
  Respiratory Therapy

Montana State University—Billings
1500 North 30th St., Billings 59101-0298
Type: Public, state, four-year
System: Montana University System
Degrees: A, B, M   _Enroll:_ 3,270
URL: http://www.msubillings.edu
Phone: (406) 657-2011   _Calendar:_ Sem. plan
Inst. Accred.: NWCCU (1932/2001)
Prog. Accred.: Art, Business (AACSB), Music,
  Rehabilitation Counseling, Teacher Education (NCATE)

College of Technology Campus
3803 Central Ave., Billings 59102
Phone: (406) 656-4445

Montana State University—Bozeman
PO Box 17200, Bozeman 59717-2000
Type: Public, state, four-year
System: Montana University System
Degrees: B, M, D   *Enroll:* 10,637
URL: http://www.montana.edu
Phone: (406) 994-0211   *Calendar:* Sem. plan
Inst. Accred.: NWCCU (1932/2001)
Prog. Accred.: Art, Computer Science, Counseling,
  Engineering (chemical, civil, computer, electrical,
  industrial, mechanical), Engineering Technology
  (civil/construction, mechanical), Family and Consumer
  Science, Music, Nursing, Nursing Education, Psychology
  Internship, Teacher Education (NCATE)

Montana State University—Northern
PO Box 7751, Havre 59501-7751
Type: Public, state, four-year
System: Montana University System
Degrees: A, B, M   *Enroll:* 1,266
URL: http://www.msun.edu
Phone: (406) 265-3700   *Calendar:* Sem. plan
Inst. Accred.: NWCCU (1932/1999)
Prog. Accred.: Engineering Technology (civil/construction,
  electrical), Nursing

Montana Tech of The University of Montana
1300 West Park St., Butte 59701-8997
Type: Public, state, four-year
System: Montana University System
Degrees: A, B, M   *Enroll:* 1,724
URL: http://www.mtech.edu
Phone: (406) 496-4101   *Calendar:* Sem. plan
Inst. Accred.: NWCCU (1932/2005)
Prog. Accred.: Applied Science (industrial hygiene),
  Computer Science, Engineering (environmental/sanitary,
  general, geological/geophysical, metallurgical, mining,
  petroleum)

College of Technology
25 Basin Creek Rd., Butte 59701
Phone: (406) 494-2894

Rocky Mountain College
1511 Poly Dr., Billings 59102-1796
Type: Private, interdenominational, four-year
Degrees: A, B   *Enroll:* 902
URL: http://www.rocky.edu
Phone: (406) 657-1000   *Calendar:* Sem. plan
Inst. Accred.: NWCCU (1949/2002)
Prog. Accred.: Physician Assistant

Salish Kootenai College
PO Box 117, Pablo 59855
Type: Public, tribal, four-year
System: American Indian Higher Education Consortium
Degrees: A, B   *Enroll:* 810
URL: http://www.skc.edu
Phone: (406) 675-4800   *Calendar:* Qtr. plan
Inst. Accred.: NWCCU (1984/2005)
Prog. Accred.: Dental Assisting, Health Information
  Technician, Nursing

Stone Child College
RRI, Box 1082, Box Elder 59521-9796
Type: Public, tribal, two-year
System: American Indian Higher Education Consortium
Degrees: A   *Enroll:* 275
URL: http://www.montana.edu/wwwscc
Phone: (406) 395-4313   *Calendar:* Sem. plan
Inst. Accred.: NWCCU (1993/2005)

University of Great Falls
1301 20th St., Great Falls 59405-4996
Type: Private, Roman Catholic Church, four-year
Degrees: B, M   *Enroll:* 622
URL: http://www.ugf.edu
Phone: (406) 761-8210   *Calendar:* Sem. plan
Inst. Accred.: NWCCU (1935/2004)

The University of Montana
32 Campus Dr., Missoula 59812
Type: Public, state, four-year
System: Montana University System
Degrees: A, B, M, P, D   *Enroll:* 11,936
URL: http://www.umt.edu
Phone: (406) 243-0211   *Calendar:* Sem. plan
Inst. Accred.: NWCCU (1932/2005)
Prog. Accred.: Accounting, Art, Business (AACSB), Clinical
  Psychology, Computer Science, Forestry, Journalism,
  Law, Music, Pharmacy, Physical Therapy, Recreation
  and Leisure Services, Social Work, Teacher Education
  (NCATE), Theatre

The University of Montana— College of Technology
909 South Ave., West, Missoula 59801
Type: Public, state, two-year
Degrees: A
URL: http://www.cte.umt.edu
Phone: (406) 243-7811   *Calendar:* Sem. plan
Inst. Accred.: NWCCU (1977/2004)
Prog. Accred.: Athletic Training, Culinary Education,
  Surgical Technology

The University of Montana— Helena College of Technology
1115 North Roberts St., Helena 59601
Type: Public, state, two-year
System: Montana University System
Degrees: A   *Enroll:* 689
URL: http://www.umh.umontana.edu
Phone: (406) 444-6800   *Calendar:* Sem. plan
Inst. Accred.: NWCCU (1977/2002)

University of Montana—Western
710 South Atlantic St., Dillon 59725-3598
Type: Public, state, four-year
System: Montana University System
Degrees: A, B   *Enroll:* 974
URL: http://www.umwestern.edu
Phone: (406) 683-7011   *Calendar:* Sem. plan
Inst. Accred.: NWCCU (1932/2005)
Prog. Accred.: Teacher Education (NCATE)

NEBRASKA

Bellevue University
1000 Galvin Rd. South, Bellevue 68005
Type: Private, independent, four-year
Degrees: B, M   *Enroll:* 3,889
URL: http://www.bellevue.edu
Phone: (402) 293-2000   *Calendar:* Sem. plan
Inst. Accred.: NCA-HLC (1977/2002)

Central Community College
PO Box 4903, Grand Island 68802-4903
Type: Public, state, two-year
System: Nebraska State College System
Degrees: A   *Enroll:* 3,611
URL: http://www.cccneb.edu
Phone: (308) 398-4222   *Calendar:* Sem. plan
Inst. Accred.: NCA-HLC (1980/1995)
Prog. Accred.: Health Information Technician, Medical
Assisting (AMA), Nursing

Columbus Campus
PO Box 1027, 4500 63rd St., Columbus 68602-1027
Phone: (402) 564-7132

Grand Island Campus
PO Box 4903, Grand Island 68802-4903
Phone: (308) 384-5220

Hastings Campus
PO Box 1024, Hastings 68901-1024
Phone: (402) 463-9811
Prog. Accred: Dental Assisting, Dental Hygiene, Dental
Laboratory Technology

Chadron State College
1000 Main St., Chadron 69337-2690
Type: Public, state, four-year
System: Nebraska State College System
Degrees: A, B, M, P   *Enroll:* 2,162
URL: http://www.csc.edu
Phone: (308) 432-6000   *Calendar:* Sem. plan
Inst. Accred.: NCA-HLC (1915/1997)
Prog. Accred.: Business (ACBSP), Social Work, Teacher
Education (NCATE)

Clarkson College
101 South 42nd St., Omaha 68131
Type: Private, Episcopal Church, four-year
Degrees: A, B, M   *Enroll:* 420
URL: http://www.clarksoncollege.edu
Phone: (402) 552-3394   *Calendar:* Sem. plan
Inst. Accred.: NCA-HLC (1984/1999)
Prog. Accred.: Nursing, Physical Therapy Assisting,
Radiography

College of Saint Mary
1901 South 72nd St., Omaha 68124
Type: Private, Roman Catholic Church, four-year
Degrees: A, B   *Enroll:* 725
URL: http://www.csm.edu
Phone: (402) 399-2400   *Calendar:* Sem. plan
Inst. Accred.: NCA-HLC (1958/2001)
Prog. Accred.: Dental Hygiene, Health Information
Administration, Health Information Technician, Nursing,
Occupational Therapy, Radiation Therapy

Concordia University
800 North Columbia Ave., Seward 68434
Type: Private, Lutheran Church-Missouri Synod, four-year
System: Concordia University System
Degrees: B, M   *Enroll:* 1,150
URL: http://www.cune.edu
Phone: (402) 643-3651   *Calendar:* Sem. plan
Inst. Accred.: NCA-HLC (1953/1998)
Prog. Accred.: Music, Teacher Education (NCATE)

The Creative Center
10850 Emmet St. South East, Omaha 68164
Type: Private, prorpeitary, two-year
Degrees: A
URL: http://www.thecreativecenter.com
Phone: (402) 898-1000   *Calendar:* Qtr. plan
Inst. Accred.: ACCSCT (1996/2002)

Creighton University
2500 California Plaza, Omaha 68178
Type: Private, Roman Catholic Church, four-year
Degrees: A, B, M, P, D   *Enroll:* 6,077
URL: http://www.creighton.edu
Phone: (402) 280-2700   *Calendar:* Sem. plan
Inst. Accred.: NCA-HLC (1916/1997)
Prog. Accred.: Accounting, Business (AACSB), Dentistry,
EMT (Paramedic), Law, Medicine, Nursing, Nursing
Education, Occupational Therapy, Pharmacy, Physical
Therapy, Social Work, Teacher Education (NCATE)

Dana College
2848 College Dr., Blair 68008
Type: Private, Evangelic Lutheran Church in America,
four-year
Degrees: B   *Enroll:* 570
URL: http://www.dana.edu
Phone: (402) 426-9000   *Calendar:* 4-1-4 plan
Inst. Accred.: NCA-HLC (1958/2002)
Prog. Accred.: Business (ACBSP), Social Work, Teacher
Education (NCATE)

Doane College
1014 Boswell Ave., Crete 68333
Type: Private, United Church of Christ, four-year
Degrees: B, M   *Enroll:* 1,864
URL: http://www.doane.edu
Phone: (402) 826-2161   *Calendar:* 4-1-4 plan
Inst. Accred.: NCA-HLC (1913/2002)
Prog. Accred.: Business (ACBSP), Teacher Education
   (NCATE)

Grand Island Campus
180 West US Hwy. 34, Grand Island 68801-7279
Phone: (308) 398-0800

Lincoln Campus
303 North 52nd St., Lincoln 68504
Phone: (402) 466-4774

Grace University
1311 South Ninth St., Omaha 68108
Type: Private, independent, four-year
Degrees: A, B, M   *Enroll:* 481
URL: http://www.graceu.edu
Phone: (402) 449-2800   *Calendar:* Sem. plan
Inst. Accred.: ABHE (1948/1995), NCA-HLC (1994/1999)

Hastings College
710 North Turner Ave., Hastings 68901-7621
Type: Private, Presbyterian Church (USA), four-year
Degrees: B, M   *Enroll:* 1,096
URL: http://www.hastings.edu
Phone: (402) 463-2402   *Calendar:* 4-1-4 plan
Inst. Accred.: NCA-HLC (1916/2005)
Prog. Accred.: Music, Teacher Education (NCATE)

Little Priest Tribal College
601 East College Dr., Winnebago 68071
Type: Public, tribal, two-year
System: American Indian Higher Education Consortium
Degrees: A   *Enroll:* 92
URL: http://www.lptc.bia.edu
Phone: (402) 878-2380   *Calendar:* Sem. plan
Inst. Accred.: NCA-HLC (1998/2003)

McCook Community College
1205 East Third St., McCook 69001
Type: Public, state/local, two-year
System: Mid-Plains Community College Area
Degrees: A   *FTE Enroll:* 523
URL: http://www.mpcca.cc.ne.us
Phone: (308) 345-6303   *Calendar:* Sem. plan
Inst. Accred.: NCA-HLC (1986/2004, *Indirect accreditation
   through Mid-Plains Community College Area, North
   Platte, NE*)
Prog. Accred.: Dental Assisting

Metropolitan Community College
PO Box 3777, Omaha 68103-0777
Type: Public, state/local, two-year
System: Nebraska State College System
Degrees: A   *Enroll:* 7,406
URL: http://www.mccneb.edu
Phone: (402) 457-2000   *Calendar:* Qtr. plan
Inst. Accred.: NCA-HLC (1979/2003)
Prog. Accred.: Business (ACBSP), Culinary Education,
   Dental Assisting, Nursing, Respiratory Therapy, Surgical
   Technology

Mid-Plains Community College
601 West State Farm Rd., North Platte 69101
Type: Public, state/local, two-year
System: Mid-Plains Community College Area
Degrees: A   *FTE Enroll:* 1,113
URL: http://www.mpcca.cc.ne.us
Phone: (308) 535-3600   *Calendar:* Sem. plan
Inst. Accred.: NCA-HLC (1986/2004, *Indirect accreditation
   through Mid-Plains Community College Area, North
   Platte, NE*)
Prog. Accred.: Clinical Lab Technology, Dental Assisting,
   Nursing, Practical Nursing

Mid-Plains Community College—North
1101 Halligan Dr., North Platte 69101
Type: Public, state/local, two-year
System: Mid-Plains Community College Area
Degrees: A
URL: http://www.mpcca.cc.ne.us
Phone: (308) 535-3600   *Calendar:* Sem. plan
Inst. Accred.: NCA-HLC (1986/2004, *Indirect accreditation
   through Mid-Plains Community College Area, North
   Platte, NE*)

Midland Lutheran College
900 Clarkson St., Fremont 68025
Type: Private, Evangelical Lutheran Church in America,
   four-year
Degrees: A, B   *Enroll:* 932
URL: http://www.mlc.edu
Phone: (402) 941-6001   *Calendar:* 4-1-4 plan
Inst. Accred.: NCA-HLC (1947/1999)
Prog. Accred.: Nursing

Myotherapy Institute
6020 South 58th St., Bldg. D, Lincoln 68516
Type: Private, proprietary, two-year
Degrees: A   *Enroll:* 48
Phone: (402) 421-7410
Inst. Accred.: ACCSCT (1998/2001)

Nebraska Christian College
1800 Syracuse Ave., Norfolk 68701-2458
Type: Private, Christian Churches/Churches of Christ,
   four-year
Degrees: A, B   *Enroll:* 151
URL: http://www.nechristian.edu
Phone: (402) 379-5000   *Calendar:* Sem. plan
Inst. Accred.: ABHE (1985/1996)

Nebraska College of Technical Agriculture
Rural Route 3, Box 23A, 404 East 7th St., Curtis 69025-9502
Type: Private, independent, two-year
Degrees: A   *Enroll:* 204
URL: http://www.ncta.unl.edu
Phone: (308) 367-4124   *Calendar:* Sem. plan
Inst. Accred.: NCA-HLC (2004)
Prog. Accred.: Veterinary Technology

Nebraska Indian Community College
PO Box 428, Macy 68039
Type: Public, tribal, two-year
System: American Indian Higher Education Consortium
Degrees: A   *Enroll:* 128
URL: http://www.thenicc.edu
Phone: (402) 837-5078   *Calendar:* Sem. plan
Inst. Accred.: NCA-HLC (1986/2005)

Nebraska Methodist College
8501 West Dodge Rd., Omaha 68114-3403
Type: Private, United Methodist Church, four-year
Degrees: A, B, M   *Enroll:* 364
URL: http://www.methodistcollege.edu
Phone: (402) 354-4879   *Calendar:* Sem. plan
Inst. Accred.: NCA-HLC (1989/2003)
Prog. Accred.: Diagnostic Medical Sonography, Nursing, Nursing Education, Respiratory Therapy

Nebraska Wesleyan University
5000 St. Paul Ave., Lincoln 68504-2796
Type: Private, United Methodist Church, four-year
Degrees: B, M   *Enroll:* 1,652
URL: http://www.nebrwesleyan.edu
Phone: (402) 466-2371   *Calendar:* Sem. plan
Inst. Accred.: NCA-HLC (1914/2000)
Prog. Accred.: Business (ACBSP), Music, Nursing, Social Work, Teacher Education (NCATE)

Northeast Community College
801 East Benjamin Ave., PO Box 469, Norfolk 68702-0469
Type: Public, state/local, two-year
System: Nebraska State College System
Degrees: A   *Enroll:* 2,884
URL: http://www.northeastcollege.com
Phone: (402) 371-2020   *Calendar:* Sem. plan
Inst. Accred.: NCA-HLC (1979/2004)
Prog. Accred.: Nursing, Physical Therapy Assisting, Veterinary Technology

Peru State College
600 Hoyt St., PO Box 10, Peru 68421-0010
Type: Public, state, four-year
System: Nebraska State College System
Degrees: B, M   *Enroll:* 1,198
URL: http://www.peru.edu
Phone: (402) 872-3815   *Calendar:* Sem. plan
Inst. Accred.: NCA-HLC (1915/2002)
Prog. Accred.: Teacher Education (NCATE)

Southeast Community College
8800 O St., Lincoln 68520-1299
Type: Public, state/local, two-year
System: Nebraska State College System
Degrees: A   *Enroll:* 6,761
URL: http://www.southeast.edu
Phone: (402) 471-3333   *Calendar:* Qtr. plan
Inst. Accred.: NCA-HLC (1983/2003)
Prog. Accred.: Business (ACBSP), Clinical Lab Technology, Culinary Education, Dental Assisting, Medical Assisting (AMA), Nursing, Practical Nursing, Radiography, Respiratory Therapy, Surgical Technology

Union College
3800 South 48th St., Lincoln 68506
Type: Private, Seventh-Day Adventist Church, four-year
Degrees: A, B   *Enroll:* 836
URL: http://www.ucollege.edu
Phone: (402) 486-2500   *Calendar:* Sem. plan
Inst. Accred.: NCA-HLC (1923/2000)
Prog. Accred.: Nursing, Nursing Education, Physician Assistant, Social Work, Teacher Education (NCATE)

University of Nebraska at Kearney
905 West 25th St., Kearney 68849-0601
Type: Public, state, four-year
System: University of Nebraska Central Administration
Degrees: B, M, P   *Enroll:* 5,537
URL: http://www.unk.edu
Phone: (308) 865-8441   *Calendar:* Sem. plan
Inst. Accred.: NCA-HLC (1916/2004)
Prog. Accred.: Business (AACSB), Construction Technology, Counseling, Industrial Technology, Music, Social Work, Speech-Language Pathology, Teacher Education (NCATE)

University of Nebraska at Omaha
60th and Dodge, Omaha 68182-0108
Type: Public, state, four-year
System: University of Nebraska Central Administration
Degrees: B, M, P, D   *Enroll:* 10,818
URL: http://www.unomaha.edu
Phone: (402) 554-2800   *Calendar:* Sem. plan
Inst. Accred.: NCA-HLC (1939/1997)
Prog. Accred.: Art, Business (AACSB), Computer Science, Counseling, Engineering (civil, computer, electrical), Engineering Technology (civil/construction, electrical, manufacturing), Music, Public Administration, Social Work, Speech-Language Pathology, Teacher Education (NCATE)

University of Nebraska Medical Center
987020 Nebraska Medical Center, Omaha 68198-7020
Type: Public, state, four-year
System: University of Nebraska Central Administration
Degrees: B, M, P, D   *Enroll:* 2,596
URL: http://www.unmc.edu
Phone: (402) 559-4000   *Calendar:* Sem. plan
Inst. Accred.: NCA-HLC (1913/1997)
Prog. Accred.: Clinical Lab Scientist, Cytotechnology, Diagnostic Medical Sonography, Dietetics (internship), Medicine, Nuclear Medicine Technology, Nursing, Nursing Education, Perfusion, Pharmacy, Physical Therapy, Physician Assistant, Radiation Therapy, Radiography

University of Nebraska—Lincoln
201 Canfield Admin. Bldg., 14th and R St.s, Lincoln 68588-0419
Type: Public, state, four-year
System: University of Nebraska Central Administration
Degrees: A, B, M, P, D   *Enroll:* 20,235
URL: http://www.unl.edu
Phone: (402) 472-7211   *Calendar:* Sem. plan
Inst. Accred.: NCA-HLC (1913/2000)
Prog. Accred.: Accounting, Art, Audiology, Business (AACSB), Clinical Psychology, Combined Prosthodontics, Construction Education, Counseling Psychology, Dental Hygiene, Dentistry, Dietetics (internship), Endodontics, Engineering (agricultural, bioengineering, chemical, civil, computer, electrical, industrial, mechanical), Engineering Technology (civil/construction, electrical, manufacturing), Family and Consumer Science, General Dentistry, General Practice Residency, Interior Design, Journalism, Law, Marriage and Family Therapy, Music, Oral and Maxillofacial Surgery, Orthodontic and Dentofacial Orthopedics, Pediatric Dentistry, Periodontics, Planning, School Psychology, Speech-Language Pathology, Teacher Education (NCATE), Theatre

Vatterott College—Spring Valley
11818 I St., Omaha 68137
Type: Private, proprietary, two-year
Degrees: A
URL: http://www.vatterott-college.com
Phone: (402) 891-9411   *Calendar:* Sem. plan
Inst. Accred.: ACCSCT (1986/2001)
Prog. Accred.: Dental Assisting, Medical Assisting (ABHES), Medical Assisting (AMA), Veterinary Technology

Wayne State College
1111 Main St., Wayne 68787-1923
Type: Public, state, four-year
System: Nebraska State College System
Degrees: B, M, P   *Enroll:* 2,871
URL: http://www.wsc.edu
Phone: (402) 375-7000   *Calendar:* Sem. plan
Inst. Accred.: NCA-HLC (1917/2002)
Prog. Accred.: Teacher Education (NCATE)

Western Nebraska Community College
1601 East 27th St., NE, Scottsbluff 69361
Type: Public, state/local, two-year
System: Nebraska State College System
Degrees: A   *Enroll:* 1,549
URL: http://wncc.net
Phone: (308) 635-3606   *Calendar:* Sem. plan
Inst. Accred.: NCA-HLC (1988/2000)
Prog. Accred.: Health Information Technician, Practical Nursing

York College
1125 East 8th St., York 68467-2699
Type: Private, Church of Christ, four-year
Degrees: A, B   *Enroll:* 443
URL: http://www.york.edu
Phone: (732) 363-5600   *Calendar:* Sem. plan
Inst. Accred.: NCA-HLC (1970/2004)

NEVADA

The Art Institute of Las Vegas
2350 Corporate Circle, Henderson 89074
Type: Private, proprietary, four-year
System: Education Management Corporation
Degrees: A, B
URL: http://www.ailv.aii.edu
Phone: (702) 369-9944   *Calendar:* Qtr. plan
Inst. Accred.: ACCSCT (1992/2002)

Career College of Northern Nevada
1195-A Corporate Blvd., Reno 89502-2331
Type: Private, proprietary, two-year
Degrees: A   *Enroll:* 345
URL: http://www.ccnn4u.com
Phone: (775) 856-2266
Inst. Accred.: ACCSCT (1989/2003)

Community College of Southern Nevada
6375 W. Charleston Blvd., North Las Vegas 89030
Type: Public, state, two-year
System: Nevada System of Higher Education
Degrees: A   *Enroll:* 16,698
URL: http://www.ccsn.edu
Phone: (702) 651-5600   *Calendar:* Sem. plan
Inst. Accred.: NWCCU (1975/2002)
Prog. Accred.: Clinical Lab Technology, Culinary
  Education, Health Information Technician, Nursing,
  Opticianry, Physical Therapy Assisting, Practical Nursing

Cheyenne Campus
3200 East Cheyenne Ave., North Las Vegas 89030
Phone: (702) 651- 4002
Prog. Accred: Dental Assisting, Dental Hygiene

Henderson Campus
700 College Dr., Henderson 89015
Phone: (702) 651-3162

West Charleston Campus
6375 West Charleston Blvd., W1A, Las Vegas 89146
Phone: (702) 651-5000
Prog. Accred: Dental Assisting, Occupational Therapy
  Assisting

Great Basin College
1500 College Pkwy., Elko 89801
Type: Public, state, four-year
System: Nevada System of Higher Education
Degrees: A, B   *Enroll:* 1,422
URL: http://www.gbcnv.edu
Phone: (775) 738-8493   *Calendar:* Sem. plan
Inst. Accred.: NWCCU (1974/2005)
Prog. Accred.: Nursing

Heritage College
3315 Spring Mountain Rd., Ste. 7, Las Vegas 89102
Type: Private, proprietary, two-year
System: Kaplan Higher Education Corporation
Degrees: A
URL: http://www.heritagecollege.com
Phone: (702) 368-2338
Inst. Accred.: ACCSCT (1991/2004)
Prog. Accred.: Medical Assisting (ABHES), Medical
  Assisting (CAAHEP)

High-Tech Institute—Las Vegas
2320 South Rancho Dr., Las Vegas 89102
Type: Private, proprietary, two-year
System: High-Tech Institute
Degrees: A
URL: http://www.hightechinstitute.edu
Phone: (702) 385-6700
Inst. Accred.: ACCSCT (2002/2004)

International Academy of Design and Technology
2495 Village View Dr., Henderson 89074
Type: Private, proprietary, two-year
System: Career Education Corporation
Degrees: A
URL: http://www.iadtvegas.com
Phone: (866) 400-4238
Inst. Accred.: ACICS (2003)

Las Vegas College
4100 West Flamingo Rd., Ste. 2100, Las Vegas 89103
Type: Private, proprietary, two-year
System: Corinthian Colleges, Inc
Degrees: A   *Enroll:* 546
URL: http://lasvegas-college.com
Phone: (702) 368-6200   *Calendar:* Qtr. plan
Inst. Accred.: ACICS (1983/2005)

Henderson Campus
170 North Stephanie St., First Flr., Henderson 89014
Phone: (702) 567-1920

Le Cordon Bleu College of Culinary Arts—Las Vegas
1451 Center Crossing Rd., Las Vegas 89144
Type: Private, proprietary, two-year
Degrees: A
URL: http://www.vegasculinary.com
Phone: (702) 365-7690
Inst. Accred.: ACCSCT (2003)

Morrison University
10315 Professional Circle, Ste. 201, Reno 89521
Type: Private, proprietary, four-year
Degrees: A, B   *Enroll:* 95
URL: http://www.morrison.northface.edu
Phone: (775) 850-0700   *Calendar:* Qtr. plan
Inst. Accred.: ACICS (1990/2005)

Northface University
10701 South River Front Pkwy., Ste. 300, South
Jordan, UT 84095
Phone: (801) 733-2800

Sierra Nevada College
999 Tahoe Blvd., Incline Village 89451
Type: Private, independent, four-year
Degrees: B   *Enroll:* 403
URL: http://www.sierranevada.edu
Phone: (775) 831-1314   *Calendar:* Sem. plan
Inst. Accred.: NWCCU (1977/2004)

Truckee Meadows Community College
7000 Dandini Blvd., Reno 89512
Type: Public, state, two-year
System: Nevada System of Higher Education
Degrees: A   *Enroll:* 5,160
URL: http://www.tmcc.edu
Phone: (775) 673-7000   *Calendar:* Sem. plan
Inst. Accred.: NWCCU (1980/2000)
Prog. Accred.: Culinary Education, Dental Assisting,
   Dental Hygiene, Nursing, Radiography

University of Nevada, Las Vegas
PO Box 451002, 4505 Maryland Pkwy., Las Vegas
89154-1002
Type: Public, state, four-year
System: Nevada System of Higher Education
Degrees: A, B, M, D   *Enroll:* 19,329
URL: http://www.unlv.edu
Phone: (702) 895-3011   *Calendar:* Sem. plan
Inst. Accred.: NWCCU (1964/2005)
Prog. Accred.: Accounting, Art, Athletic Training, Business
   (AACSB), Clinical Lab Scientist, Computer Science,
   Construction Education, Counseling, Dentistry,
   Engineering (civil, electrical, mechanical), Interior
   Design, Kinesiotherapy, Landscape Architecture, Law,
   Music, Nuclear Medicine Technology, Nursing, Physical
   Therapy, Public Administration, Radiography, Social
   Work, Teacher Education (NCATE), Theatre

University of Nevada, Reno
Reno 89557
Type: Public, state, four-year
System: Nevada System of Higher Education
Degrees: A, B, M, D   *Enroll:* 12,632
URL: http://www.unr.edu
Phone: (775) 784-1110   *Calendar:* Sem. plan
Inst. Accred.: NWCCU (1938/2005)
Prog. Accred.: Accounting, Business (AACSB), Clinical
   Psychology, Computer Science, Counseling, Dietetics
   (internship), Engineering (chemical, civil, electrical,
   environmental/sanitary, geological/geophysical,
   mechanical, mining), General Practice Residency,
   Journalism, Medicine, Music, Nuclear Medicine
   Technology, Nursing, Nursing Education, Social Work,
   Speech-Language Pathology, Teacher Education
   (NCATE)

Western Nevada Community College
2201 West College Pkwy., Carson City 89703-7399
Type: Public, state, two-year
System: Nevada System of Higher Education
Degrees: A   *Enroll:* 2,173
URL: http://www.wncc.edu
Phone: (775) 445-3000   *Calendar:* Sem. plan
Inst. Accred.: NWCCU (1975/2005)
Prog. Accred.: Nursing

NEW HAMPSHIRE

Chester College of New England
40 Chester St., Chester 03036-4331
Type: Private, independent, four-year
Degrees: A, B   *Enroll:* 167
URL: http://www.chestercollege.edu
Phone: (603) 887-4401   *Calendar:* Sem. plan
Inst. Accred.: NEASC-CIHE (1975/2003)

Colby-Sawyer College
100 Main St., New London 03257-4648
Type: Private, independent, four-year
Degrees: A, B   *Enroll:* 964
URL: http://www.colby-sawyer.edu
Phone: (603) 526-3000   *Calendar:* Sem. plan
Inst. Accred.: NEASC-CIHE (1933/2005)
Prog. Accred.: Athletic Training, Nursing, Nursing
    Education

Daniel Webster College
20 University Dr., Nashua 03063-1300
Type: Private, independent, four-year
Degrees: A, B, M   *Enroll:* 988
URL: http://www.dwc.edu
Phone: (603) 577-6000   *Calendar:* Sem. plan
Inst. Accred.: NEASC-CIHE (1972/1996)

Dartmouth College
Hanover 03755-4030
Type: Private, independent, four-year
Degrees: B, M, P, D   *Enroll:* 5,595
URL: http://www.dartmouth.edu
Phone: (603) 646-1110   *Calendar:* Qtr. plan
Inst. Accred.: NEASC-CIHE (1929/1999)
Prog. Accred.: Business (AACSB), Engineering (general),
    Medicine, Psychology Internship, Public Health, Theatre

Franklin Pierce College
College Rd., Rindge 03461-0060
Type: Private, independent, four-year
Degrees: B, M   *Enroll:* 1,579
URL: http://www.fpc.edu
Phone: (603) 899-4000   *Calendar:* Sem. plan
Inst. Accred.: NEASC-CIHE (1968/1998)
Prog. Accred.: Physical Therapy

Franklin Pierce Law Center
2 White St., Concord 03301-4197
Type: Private, independent, four-year
Degrees: P, D   *Enroll:* 455
URL: http://www.fplc.edu
Phone: (603) 228-1541   *Calendar:* Sem. plan
Inst. Accred.: NEASC-CIHE (2000/2005)
Prog. Accred.: Law (ABA only)

Granite State College
8 Old Suncook Rd., Concord 03301
Type: Public, state, four-year
System: University System of New Hampshire
Degrees: A, B   *Enroll:* 770
URL: http://www.granite.edu
Phone: (603) 228-3000   *Calendar:* Sem. plan
Inst. Accred.: NEASC-CIHE (1980/2005)

Hesser College
3 Sundial Ave., Manchester 03103-7245
Type: Private, proprietary, four-year
System: Kaplan Higher Education Corporation
Degrees: A, B   *Enroll:* 2,437
URL: http://www.hesser.edu
Phone: (603) 668-6660   *Calendar:* Sem. plan
Inst. Accred.: NEASC-CTCI (1985/1995)
Prog. Accred.: Medical Assisting (AMA), Physical Therapy
    Assisting

Concord Campus
25 Hall St., Ste. 104, Concord 03301
Phone: (603) 225-9200

Nashua Campus
410 Amherst St., Nashua 03063
Phone: (603) 883-0404

Portsmouth Campus
170 Commerce Way, Portsmouth 03801
Phone: (603) 436-5300

Salem Campus
1A Keewaydin Dr., Salem 03079
Phone: (603) 898-3480

Keene State College
229 Main St., Keene 03435-0002
Type: Public, state, four-year
System: University System of New Hampshire
Degrees: A, B, M   *Enroll:* 4,473
URL: http://www.keene.edu
Phone: (603) 352-1909   *Calendar:* Sem. plan
Inst. Accred.: NEASC-CIHE (1949/2000)
Prog. Accred.: Athletic Training, Dietetics (internship),
    Music, Teacher Education (NCATE)

McIntosh College
23 Cataract Ave., Dover 03820-3990
Type: Private, proprietary, two-year
System: Career Education Corporation
Degrees: A   *Enroll:* 1,274
URL: http://www.mcintoshcollege.edu
Phone: (603) 742-1234
Inst. Accred.: NEASC-CTCI (1988/1998)

New England College
7 Main St., Henniker 03242-3244
Type: Private, independent, four-year
Degrees: B, M   *Enroll:* 997
URL: http://www.nec.edu
Phone: (603) 428-2211   *Calendar:* Sem. plan
Inst. Accred.: NEASC-CIHE (1967/2004)

New Hampshire Community Technical College—Berlin
2020 Riverside Dr., Berlin 03570-3799
Type: Public, state, two-year
System: New Hampshire Community Technical College System
Degrees: A   *Enroll:* 1,169
URL: http://www.berlin.nhctc.edu
Phone: (603) 752-1113   *Calendar:* Sem. plan
Inst. Accred.: NEASC-CIHE (2003)

New Hampshire Community Technical College—Claremont
One College Dr., Claremont 03743-9707
Type: Public, state, two-year
Degrees: A   *FTE Enroll:* 400
URL: http://www.claremont.nhctc.edu
Phone: (603) 542-7744   *Calendar:* Sem. plan
Inst. Accred.: NEASC-CIHE (2002)
Prog. Accred.: Clinical Lab Technology, Medical Assisting (AMA), Nursing, Occupational Therapy Assisting, Physical Therapy Assisting, Respiratory Therapy

New Hampshire Community Technical College—Laconia
379 Prescott Hill Rd., Laconia 03246
Type: Public, state, two-year
Degrees: A   *FTE Enroll:* 550
URL: http://www.laconia.nhctc.edu
Phone: (603) 524-3207   *Calendar:* Sem. plan
Inst. Accred.: NEASC-CIHE (2003)

New Hampshire Community Technical College—Manchester
1066 Front St., Manchester 03102-8518
Type: Public, state, two-year
System: New Hampshire Community Technical College System
Degrees: A   *Enroll:* 2,215
URL: http://ms.nhctc.edu
Phone: (603) 668-6706   *Calendar:* Sem. plan
Inst. Accred.: NEASC-CIHE (2002)
Prog. Accred.: Business (ACBSP), Medical Assisting (AMA), Nursing

New Hampshire Community Technical College—Nashua
505 Amherst St., Nashua 03063-1092
Type: Public, state, two-year
System: New Hampshire Community Technical College System
Degrees: A   *Enroll:* 1,799
URL: http://www.nashua.nhctc.edu
Phone: (603) 882-6923   *Calendar:* Sem. plan
Inst. Accred.: NEASC-CIHE (2002)
Prog. Accred.: Engineering Technology (computer)

New Hampshire Community Technical College—Stratham
277 Portsmouth Ave., Stratham 03885-2297
Type: Public, state, two-year
Degrees: A   *FTE Enroll:* 616
URL: http://ms.nhctc.edu
Phone: (603) 772-1194   *Calendar:* Sem. plan
Inst. Accred.: NEASC-CIHE (2002)
Prog. Accred.: Surgical Technology, Veterinary Technology

New Hampshire Technical Institute
11 Institute Dr., Concord 03301-7412
Type: Public, state, two-year
System: New Hampshire Community Technical College System
Degrees: A   *Enroll:* 2,237
URL: http://www.nhti.edu
Phone: (603) 271-6484   *Calendar:* Sem. plan
Inst. Accred.: NEASC-CIHE (2001)
Prog. Accred.: Dental Assisting, Dental Hygiene, EMT (Paramedic), Engineering Technology (architectural, computer, electrical, manufacturing, mechanical), Nursing, Radiation Therapy, Radiography

Plymouth State University
17 High St., Plymouth 03264-1595
Type: Public, state, four-year
System: University System of New Hampshire
Degrees: A, B, M   *Enroll:* 4,192
URL: http://www.plymouth.edu
Phone: (603) 535-5000   *Calendar:* Sem. plan
Inst. Accred.: NEASC-CIHE (1955/2003)
Prog. Accred.: Athletic Training, Business (ACBSP), Social Work, Teacher Education (NCATE)

Rivier College
420 Main St., Nashua 03060-5086
Type: Private, Roman Catholic Church, four-year
Degrees: A, B, M   *Enroll:* 1,495
URL: http://www.rivier.edu
Phone: (603) 888-1311   *Calendar:* Sem. plan
Inst. Accred.: NEASC-CIHE (1948/2002)
Prog. Accred.: Nursing

Saint Anselm College
100 St. Anselm Dr., Manchester 03102-1310
Type: Private, Roman Catholic Church, four-year
Degrees: A, B   *Enroll:* 1,966
URL: http://www.anselm.edu
Phone: (603) 641-7000   *Calendar:* Sem. plan
Inst. Accred.: NEASC-CIHE (1941/1999)
Prog. Accred.: Nursing, Nursing Education

Southern New Hampshire University
2500 North River Rd., Manchester 03106-1045
Type: Private, independent, four-year
Degrees: A, B, M, D   *Enroll:* 4,491
URL: http://www.snhu.edu
Phone: (603) 668-2211   *Calendar:* Sem. plan
Inst. Accred.: NEASC-CIHE (1973/2001)
Prog. Accred.: Business (ACBSP), Culinary Education

The Thomas More College of Liberal Arts
6 Manchester St., Merrimack 03054-4805
Type: Private, Roman Catholic Church, four-year
Degrees: B   *Enroll:* 88
URL: http://www.thomasmorecollege.edu
Phone: (603) 880-8308   *Calendar:* Sem. plan
Inst. Accred.: NEASC-CIHE (1996/2001), AALE (2000)

University of New Hampshire
Main St., Durham 03824-3529
Type: Public, state, four-year
System: University System of New Hampshire
Degrees: A, B, M, D   *Enroll:* 13,433
URL: http://www.unh.edu
Phone: (603) 862-1234   *Calendar:* Sem. plan
Inst. Accred.: NEASC-CIHE (1929/2003)
Prog. Accred.: Athletic Training, Business (AACSB), Clinical Lab Scientist, Computer Science, Dietetics (internship), Engineering (chemical, civil, electrical, environmental/sanitary, mechanical), Engineering Technology (electrical, mechanical), Forestry, Marriage and Family Therapy, Music, Nursing, Nursing Education, Occupational Therapy, Psychology Internship, Recreation and Leisure Services, Social Work, Speech-Language Pathology

Manchester Campus
400 Commercial St., Manchester 03101-1113
Phone: (603) 641-4321

NEW JERSEY

Assumption College for Sisters
350 Bernardsville Rd., Mendham 07945-0800
Type: Private, Roman Catholic Church, two-year
Degrees: A   *Enroll:* 24
URL: http://www.acscollegeforsisters.org
Phone: (973) 543-6528   *Calendar:* Sem. plan
Inst. Accred.: MSA-CHE (1965/2005)

Atlantic Cape Community College
5100 Black Horse Pike, Mays Landing 08330-2699
Type: Public, state/local, two-year
System: New Jersey Commission on Higher Education
Degrees: A   *Enroll:* 3,869
URL: http://www.atlantic.edu
Phone: (609) 343-4900   *Calendar:* Sem. plan
Inst. Accred.: MSA-CHE (1971/2001)
Prog. Accred.: Dental Assisting, Nursing

Bergen Community College
400 Paramus Rd., Paramus 07652-1595
Type: Public, state/local, two-year
System: New Jersey Commission on Higher Education
Degrees: A   *Enroll:* 9,285
URL: http://www.bergen.edu
Phone: (201) 447-7100   *Calendar:* Sem. plan
Inst. Accred.: MSA-CHE (1972/2001)
Prog. Accred.: Clinical Lab Technology, Dental Hygiene,
   Diagnostic Medical Sonography, Medical Assisting
   (AMA), Nursing, Physical Therapy Assisting,
   Radiography, Respiratory Therapy, Surgical Technology,
   Veterinary Technology

Berkeley College—Garret Mountain Campus
44 Rifle Camp Rd., West Paterson 07424
Type: Private, proprietary, four-year
System: Berkeley College of New York and New Jersey
Degrees: A, B   *Enroll:* 1,988
URL: http://www.berkeleycollege.edu
Phone: (973) 278-5400   *Calendar:* Qtr. plan
Inst. Accred.: MSA-CHE (1983/2001)
Prog. Accred.: Business (ACBSP)

Bergen Campus
64 East Midland Ave., Paramus 07652-2931
Phone: (201) 652-0388

Woodbridge Campus
430 Rahway Ave., Woodbridge 07095
Phone: (732) 750-1800

Beth Medrash Govoha
617 Sixth St., Lakewood 08701
Type: Private, independent, four-year
Degrees: B, M   *Enroll:* 3,789
Phone: (732) 367-1060   *Calendar:* Sem. plan
Inst. Accred.: AARTS (1974/2005)

Bloomfield College
467 Franklin St., Bloomfield 07003
Type: Private, Presbyterian Church (USA), four-year
Degrees: B   *Enroll:* 1,785
URL: http://www.bloomfield.edu
Phone: (973) 748-9000   *Calendar:* Sem. plan
Inst. Accred.: MSA-CHE (1960/2002)
Prog. Accred.: Nursing, Nursing Education

Brookdale Community College
765 Newman Springs Rd., Lincroft 07738
Type: Public, local, two-year
System: New Jersey Commission on Higher Education
Degrees: A   *Enroll:* 8,648
URL: http://www.brookdalecc.edu
Phone: (732) 842-1900   *Calendar:* 4-4-x plan
Inst. Accred.: MSA-CHE (1972/2003)
Prog. Accred.: Clinical Lab Technology, Nursing,
   Radiography, Respiratory Therapy

Burlington County College
County Route 530, Pemberton 08068-1599
Type: Public, state/local, two-year
System: New Jersey Commission on Higher Education
Degrees: A   *Enroll:* 4,790
URL: http://www.bcc.edu
Phone: (609) 894-9311   *Calendar:* Sem. plan
Inst. Accred.: MSA-CHE (1972/1999)
Prog. Accred.: Clinical Lab Technology, Engineering
   Technology (electrical), Health Information Technician,
   Nursing, Radiography

Caldwell College
9 Ryerson Ave., Caldwell 07006-6195
Type: Private, Roman Catholic Church, four-year
Degrees: B, M   *Enroll:* 1,575
URL: http://www.caldwell.edu
Phone: (973) 618-3000   *Calendar:* Sem. plan
Inst. Accred.: MSA-CHE (1952/2005)

Camden County College
PO Box 200, Blackwood 08012
Type: Public, state/local, two-year
System: New Jersey Commission on Higher Education
Degrees: A   *Enroll:* 9,886
URL: http://www.camdencc.edu
Phone: (856) 277-7200   *Calendar:* Sem. plan
Inst. Accred.: MSA-CHE (1972/2002)
Prog. Accred.: Clinical Lab Technology, Dental Assisting,
   Dental Hygiene, Opticianry, Veterinary Technology

Camden Campus
Seventh and Cooper St.s, Camden 08102
Phone: (609) 338-1817

Centenary College
400 Jefferson St., Hackettstown 07840
Type: Private, independent, four-year
Degrees: A, B, M   *Enroll:* 1,787
URL: http://www.centenarycollege.edu
Phone: (908) 852-1400   *Calendar:* Sem. plan
Inst. Accred.: MSA-CHE (1932/2005)

The College of New Jersey
PO Box 7718, Ewing 08628-0718
Type: Public, state, four-year
System: New Jersey Commission on Higher Education
Degrees: B, M   *Enroll:* 6,193
URL: http://www.tcnj.edu
Phone: (609) 771-1855   *Calendar:* Sem. plan
Inst. Accred.: MSA-CHE (1939/2005)
Prog. Accred.: Audiology, Business (AACSB), Computer
  Science, Counseling, Engineering (engineering
  physics/science), Music, Nursing, Nursing Education,
  Speech-Language Pathology, Teacher Education
  (NCATE)

College of Saint Elizabeth
2 Convent Rd., Morristown 07960-6989
Type: Private, Roman Catholic Church, four-year
Degrees: B, M   *Enroll:* 1,176
URL: http://www.cse.edu
Phone: (973) 290-4000   *Calendar:* Sem. plan
Inst. Accred.: MSA-CHE (1921/2005)
Prog. Accred.: Dietetics (internship), Nursing

County College of Morris
214 Center Grove Rd., Randolph 07869-2086
Type: Public, state/local, two-year
System: New Jersey Commission on Higher Education
Degrees: A   *Enroll:* 5,712
URL: http://www.ccm.edu
Phone: (973) 328-5000   *Calendar:* Sem. plan
Inst. Accred.: MSA-CHE (1972/2003)
Prog. Accred.: Business (ACBSP), Clinical Lab Technology,
  Engineering Technology (electrical, mechanical),
  Nursing, Phlebotomy, Radiography

Cumberland County College
3322 College Dr., PO Box 1500, Vineland 08362-1500
Type: Public, state/local, two-year
System: New Jersey Commission on Higher Education
Degrees: A   *Enroll:* 2,060
URL: http://www.cccnj.edu
Phone: (609) 691-8600   *Calendar:* Sem. plan
Inst. Accred.: MSA-CHE (1970/2001)
Prog. Accred.: Nursing, Radiography

DeVry College of Technology—North Brunswick
630 U.S. Hwy. One, North Brunswick 08902-3362
Type: Private, proprietary, four-year
System: DeVry University
Degrees: A, B   *Enroll:* 1,969
URL: http://www.devry.edu/northbrunswick
Phone: (732) 435-4880   *Calendar:* Sem. plan
Inst. Accred.: NCA-HLC (2002, *Indirect accreditation
  through DeVry University, Oakbrook Terrace, IL*)

Drew University
36 Madison Ave., Madison 07940
Type: Private, independent, four-year
Degrees: B, M, P, D   *Enroll:* 2,212
URL: http://www.drew.edu
Phone: (973) 408-3000   *Calendar:* 4-1-4 plan
Inst. Accred.: ATS (1938/2001), MSA-CHE (1932/2001)

Essex County College
303 University Ave., Newark 07102
Type: Public, state/local, two-year
System: New Jersey Commission on Higher Education
Degrees: A   *Enroll:* 6,329
URL: http://www.essex.edu
Phone: (973) 877-3000   *Calendar:* Sem. plan
Inst. Accred.: MSA-CHE (1974/2001)
Prog. Accred.: Engineering Technology (civil/construction,
  manufacturing), Nursing, Opticianry, Physical Therapy
  Assisting, Radiography

West Essex Campus
730 Bloomfield Ave., West Caldwell 07006
Phone: (201) 228-3970

Fairleigh Dickinson University
1000 River Rd., Teaneck 07666-1996
Type: Private, independent, four-year
Degrees: A, B, M, D   *Enroll:* 4,479
URL: http://www.fdu.edu
Phone: (201) 692-2000   *Calendar:* Sem. plan
Inst. Accred.: MSA-CHE (1948/2001)
Prog. Accred.: Business (AACSB), Computer Science,
  Engineering (electrical), Engineering Technology
  (civil/construction, electrical, mechanical), Nursing
  Education

Florham-Madison Campus
285 Madison Ave., Madison 07940
Phone: (201) 593-8500

Felician College
262 South Main St., Lodi 07644
Type: Private, Roman Catholic Church, four-year
Degrees: A, B, M   *Enroll:* 1,190
URL: http://www.felician.edu
Phone: (201) 559-6000   *Calendar:* Sem. plan
Inst. Accred.: MSA-CHE (1974/2005)
Prog. Accred.: Clinical Lab Technology, Nursing, Nursing
  Education

Georgian Court University
900 Lakewood Ave., Lakewood 08701-2697
Type: Private, Roman Catholic Church, four-year
Degrees: B, M   *Enroll:* 1,989
URL: http://www.georgian.edu
Phone: (732) 364-2200   *Calendar:* Sem. plan
Inst. Accred.: MSA-CHE (1922/1999)
Prog. Accred.: Business (ACBSP), Social Work

Gibbs College
630 West Mount Pleasant Ave., Route 10, Livingston 07039
Type: Private, proprietary, two-year
System: Career Education Corporation
Degrees: A   *Enroll:* 1,651
URL: http://www.gibbsnj.edu
Phone: (973) 369-1360   *Calendar:* Sem. plan
Inst. Accred.: ACICS (1967/2004)

Piscataway Campus
180 Centennial Ave., Piscataway 08854
Phone: (732) 885-1580

Gloucester County College
1400 Tanyard Rd., Sewell 08080
Type: Public, state/local, two-year
System: New Jersey Commission on Higher Education
Degrees: A   *Enroll:* 3,843
URL: http://www.gccnj.edu
Phone: (856) 468-5000   *Calendar:* 4-1-4 plan
Inst. Accred.: MSA-CHE (1973/2003)
Prog. Accred.: Diagnostic Medical Sonography, Nuclear Medicine Technology, Nursing, Respiratory Therapy Technology

Hudson County Community College
25 Journal Square, Jersey City 07307
Type: Public, state/local, two-year
System: New Jersey Commission on Higher Education
Degrees: A   *Enroll:* 4,842
URL: http://www.hccc.edu
Phone: (201) 714-2186   *Calendar:* Sem. plan
Inst. Accred.: MSA-CHE (1981/2002)
Prog. Accred.: Culinary Education, Engineering Technology (electrical), Health Information Technician

Immaculate Conception Seminary
400 South Orange Ave., South Orange 07079
Type: Private, Roman Catholic Church, four-year
Degrees: M   *FTE Enroll:* 141
URL: http://theology.shu.edu
Phone: (973) 761-9575   *Calendar:* Sem. plan
Inst. Accred.: ATS (1977/2004)

Kean University
1000 Morris Ave., Union 07083-7131
Type: Public, state, four-year
System: New Jersey Commission on Higher Education
Degrees: B, M   *Enroll:* 9,885
URL: http://www.kean.edu
Phone: (908) 527-2000   *Calendar:* Sem. plan
Inst. Accred.: MSA-CHE (1960/2001)
Prog. Accred.: Art, Athletic Training, Counseling, Health Information Administration, Industrial Technology, Interior Design, Music, Nursing, Occupational Therapy, Public Administration, Social Work, Speech-Language Pathology, Teacher Education (NCATE), Theatre

Mercer County Community College
1200 Old Trenton Rd., PO Box B, Trenton 08690-0182
Type: Public, state/local, two-year
System: New Jersey Commission on Higher Education
Degrees: A   *Enroll:* 5,306
URL: http://www.mccc.edu
Phone: (609) 586-4800   *Calendar:* Sem. plan
Inst. Accred.: MSA-CHE (1967/2005)
Prog. Accred.: Clinical Lab Technology, Funeral Service Education (Mortuary Science), Nursing, Physical Therapy Assisting, Radiography

James Kerney Campus
North Broad and Academy St.s, Trenton 08690
Phone: (609) 586-4800

Metropolitan Learning Institute
104-70 Queens Blvd., Ste. 307, Forest Hills 11375
Type: Private, independent, two-year
Degrees: A   *Enroll:* 7,731
URL: http://www.gettraining.org
Phone: (718) 896-2685
Inst. Accred.: COE (2004)

Middlesex County College
2600 Woodbridge Ave., Edison 08818-3050
Type: Public, state/local, two-year
System: New Jersey Commission on Higher Education
Degrees: A   *Enroll:* 7,731
URL: http://www.middlesexcc.edu
Phone: (732) 548-6000   *Calendar:* Sem. plan
Inst. Accred.: MSA-CHE (1970/2000)
Prog. Accred.: Clinical Lab Technology, Dental Hygiene, Engineering Technology (civil/construction, electrical, mechanical), Nursing, Radiography

Monmouth University
400 Cedar Ave., West Long Branch 07764-1898
Type: Private, independent, four-year
Degrees: A, B, M   *Enroll:* 5,108
URL: http://www.monmouth.edu
Phone: (732) 571-3400   *Calendar:* Sem. plan
Inst. Accred.: MSA-CHE (1952/2001)
Prog. Accred.: Business (AACSB), Nursing, Nursing Education, Social Work

Montclair State University
1 University Ave., Upper Montclair 07043-1624
Type: Public, state, four-year
System: New Jersey Commission on Higher Education
Degrees: B, M, D   *Enroll:* 11,837
URL: http://www.montclair.edu
Phone: (973) 655-4000   *Calendar:* Sem. plan
Inst. Accred.: MSA-CHE (1937/2002)
Prog. Accred.: Art, Business (AACSB), Computer Science, Dance, Family and Consumer Science, Music, Recreation and Leisure Services, Speech-Language Pathology, Teacher Education (NCATE), Theatre

New Brunswick Theological Seminary
17 Seminary Place, New Brunswick 08901-1196
Type: Private, Reformed Church in America, four-year
Degrees: M   *Enroll:* 141
URL: http://www.nbts.edu
Phone: (732) 247-5241   *Calendar:* Sem. plan
Inst. Accred.: ATS (1938/1996)

New Jersey City University
2039 Kennedy Blvd., Jersey City 07305-1597
Type: Public, state, four-year
System: New Jersey Commission on Higher Education
Degrees: B, M   *Enroll:* 6,246
URL: http://www.njcu.edu
Phone: (201) 200-2000   *Calendar:* Sem. plan
Inst. Accred.: MSA-CHE (1959/2005)
Prog. Accred.: Art, Business (ACBSP), Music, Nursing,
    Teacher Education (NCATE)

New Jersey Institute of Technology
University Heights, Newark 07102-1982
Type: Public, state, four-year
System: New Jersey Commission on Higher Education
Degrees: B, M, D   *Enroll:* 6,744
URL: http://www.njit.edu
Phone: (973) 596-3000   *Calendar:* Sem. plan
Inst. Accred.: MSA-CHE (1934/2002)
Prog. Accred.: Business (AACSB), Computer Science,
    Engineering (chemical, civil, computer, electrical,
    industrial, mechanical), Engineering Technology
    (civil/construction, electrical, manufacturing,
    mechanical, surveying), Public Health

Mount Laurel Campus
Technology and Eng. Ctr., 3331 Route 38, Mount
Laurel 08054
Phone: (800) 222-6548

Ocean County College
College Dr., Toms River 08754-2001
Type: Public, state/local, two-year
System: New Jersey Commission on Higher Education
Degrees: A   *Enroll:* 5,355
URL: http://www.ocean.edu
Phone: (732) 255-0400   *Calendar:* Sem. plan
Inst. Accred.: MSA-CHE (1969/2004)
Prog. Accred.: Histologic Technology

Passaic County Community College
One College Blvd., Paterson 07509-1179
Type: Public, state/local, two-year
System: New Jersey Commission on Higher Education
Degrees: A   *Enroll:* 3,410
URL: http://www.pccc.edu
Phone: (973) 684-6888   *Calendar:* Sem. plan
Inst. Accred.: MSA-CHE (1978/2004)
Prog. Accred.: Health Information Technician, Nursing,
    Radiography, Respiratory Therapy

Princeton Theological Seminary
PO Box 821, Princeton 08542-0803
Type: Private, Presbyterian Church (USA), four-year
Degrees: M, P, D   *Enroll:* 703
URL: http://www.ptsem.edu
Phone: (609) 921-8300   *Calendar:* Sem. plan
Inst. Accred.: ATS (1938/1997), MSA-CHE (1968/2003)

Princeton University
Princeton 08544-0015
Type: Private, independent, four-year
Degrees: B, M, D   *Enroll:* 6,688
URL: http://www.princeton.edu
Phone: (609) 258-3000   *Calendar:* Sem. plan
Inst. Accred.: MSA-CHE (1921/2004)
Prog. Accred.: Engineering (aerospace, chemical, civil,
    electrical, engineering physics/science, mechanical)

Rabbi Jacob Joseph School
One Plainfield Ave., Edison 08817
Type: Private, independent, four-year
Degrees: B   *Enroll:* 53
Phone: (732) 985-6533   *Calendar:* Sem. plan
Inst. Accred.: AARTS (1991/2002)

Rabbinical College of America
226 Sussex Ave., Morristown 07960
Type: Private, independent, four-year
Degrees: B   *Enroll:* 234
Phone: (973) 267-9404   *Calendar:* Sem. plan
Inst. Accred.: AARTS (1979/2004)

Ramapo College of New Jersey
505 Ramapo Valley Rd., Mahwah 07430-1680
Type: Public, state, four-year
System: New Jersey Commission on Higher Education
Degrees: B, M   *Enroll:* 4,641
URL: http://www.ramapo.edu
Phone: (201) 684-7500   *Calendar:* Sem. plan
Inst. Accred.: MSA-CHE (1975/2005)
Prog. Accred.: Business (AACSB), Social Work

Raritan Valley Community College
PO Box 3300, Somerville 08876
Type: Public, state/local, two-year
System: New Jersey Commission on Higher Education
Degrees: A   *Enroll:* 3,847
URL: http://www.raritan.edu
Phone: (908) 526-1200   *Calendar:* Sem. plan
Inst. Accred.: MSA-CHE (1972/2002)
Prog. Accred.: Nursing, Ophthalmic Lab Technology,
    Opticianry

Richard Stockton College of New Jersey
Jimme Leeds Rd., PO Box 195, Pomona 08240-0195
Type: Public, state, four-year
System: New Jersey Commission on Higher Education
Degrees: B, M   *Enroll:* 6,067
URL: http://www2.stockton.edu
Phone: (609) 652-1776   *Calendar:* Sem. plan
Inst. Accred.: MSA-CHE (1975/2002)
Prog. Accred.: Nursing, Nursing Education, Occupational
Therapy, Physical Therapy, Social Work

Rider University
2083 Lawrenceville Rd., Lawrenceville 08648-3099
Type: Private, independent, four-year
Degrees: A, B, M   *Enroll:* 4,457
URL: http://www.rider.edu
Phone: (609) 896-5000   *Calendar:* Sem. plan
Inst. Accred.: MSA-CHE (1955/2001)
Prog. Accred.: Accounting, Business (AACSB), Counseling,
Teacher Education (NCATE)

Westminster Choir College
101 Walnut Ln., Princeton 08540
Phone: (609) 921-7100
Prog. Accred: Music

Rowan University
201 Mullica Hill Rd., Glassboro 08028-1701
Type: Public, state, four-year
System: New Jersey Commission on Higher Education
Degrees: B, M, D   *Enroll:* 8,052
URL: http://www.rowan.edu
Phone: (856) 256-4000   *Calendar:* Sem. plan
Inst. Accred.: MSA-CHE (1958/1999)
Prog. Accred.: Art, Business (AACSB), Computer Science,
Engineering (chemical, civil, electrical, mechanical),
Music, Teacher Education (NCATE), Theatre

Camden Campus
One Broadway, Camden 08102
Phone: (609) 757-2857

Rutgers, The State University of New Jersey Camden Campus
Armitage Hall, 311 North 5th St., Camden 08102-1461
Type: Public, state, four-year
System: Rutgers, The State University of New Jersey
Central Office
Degrees: B, M, P, D   *Enroll:* 4,508
URL: http://www.camden.rutgers.edu
Phone: (856) 225-6095   *Calendar:* Sem. plan
Inst. Accred.: MSA-CHE (1921/2003, *Indirect
accreditation through Rutgers, The State University of
New Jersey New Brunswick Campus, New Brunswick,
NJ*)
Prog. Accred.: Business (AACSB), Law, Nursing, Nursing
Education, Physical Therapy, Public Administration,
Social Work

Rutgers, The State University of New Jersey New Brunswick Campus
83 Somerset St., Old Queens Bldg., New Brunswick
08901-1281
Type: Public, state, four-year
System: Rutgers, The State University of New Jersey
Central Office
Degrees: B, M, P, D   *Enroll:* 31,234
URL: http://www.rutgers.edu
Phone: (732) 932-4636   *Calendar:* Sem. plan
Inst. Accred.: MSA-CHE (1921/2003)
Prog. Accred.: Clinical Psychology, Dance, Engineering
(agricultural, ceramic, chemical, civil, electrical,
industrial, mechanical), Landscape Architecture,
Librarianship, Music, Orthotist/Prothetist, Pharmacy,
Planning, Public Health, School Psychology, Social Work

Douglass College
125 George St., New Brunswick 08901
Phone: (732) 932-9721

Rutgers, The State University of New Jersey Newark Campus
15 Washington St., Newark 07102
Type: Public, state, four-year
System: Rutgers, The State University of New Jersey
Central Office
Degrees: B, M, P, D   *Enroll:* 8,051
URL: http://www.newark.rutgers.edu
Phone: (973) 648-1766   *Calendar:* Sem. plan
Inst. Accred.: MSA-CHE (1921/2003, *Indirect
accreditation through Rutgers, The State University of
New Jersey New Brunswick Campus, New Brunswick,
NJ*)
Prog. Accred.: Accounting, Business (AACSB), Law,
Nursing, Nursing Education, Public Administration,
Social Work

Saint Peter's College
2641 Kennedy Blvd., Jersey City 07306-5997
Type: Private, Roman Catholic Church, four-year
Degrees: A, B, M   *Enroll:* 2,314
URL: http://www.spc.edu
Phone: (201) 915-9000   *Calendar:* Sem. plan
Inst. Accred.: MSA-CHE (1935/2003)
Prog. Accred.: Nursing

Englewood Cliffs Campus
Hudson Terrace, Englewood Cliffs 07632
Phone: (201) 568-7730
Prog. Accred: Nursing Education

Salem Community College
460 Hollywood Ave., Carneys Point 08069-2799
Type: Public, state/local, two-year
System: New Jersey Commission on Higher Education
Degrees: A   *Enroll:* 743
URL: http://www.salemcc.edu
Phone: (856) 299-2100   *Calendar:* Sem. plan
Inst. Accred.: MSA-CHE (1979/2005)

Seton Hall University
400 South Orange Ave., South Orange 07079
Type: Private, Roman Catholic Church, four-year
Degrees: B, M, P, D   *Enroll:* 7,866
URL: http://www.shu.edu
Phone: (973) 761-9000   *Calendar:* Sem. plan
Inst. Accred.: MSA-CHE (1932/2004)
Prog. Accred.: Audiology, Business (AACSB), Counseling
Psychology, Marriage and Family Therapy, Nursing,
Nursing Education, Occupational Therapy, Oral and
Maxillofacial Surgery, Physical Therapy, Physician
Assistant, Public Administration, Social Work, Speech-
Language Pathology

School of Law Campus
One Newark Center, Newark 07102-5210
Phone: (201) 642-8500
Prog. Accred: Law

Somerset Christian College
10 Liberty Square, Zarephath 08890
Type: Private, Pillar of Fire, International, two-year
Degrees: A
URL: http://www.somersetchristian.edu
Phone: (732) 356-1595   *Calendar:* Sem. plan
Inst. Accred.: ABHE (2002)

Somerset County Technology Institute
PO Box 6350, North Bridge St. and Vogt Dr., Bridgewater
08807
Type: Public, state/local, two-year
Degrees: A
URL: http://www.scti.org
Phone: (908) 526-8900   *Calendar:* Sem. plan
Inst. Accred.: COE (2003)

Stevens Institute of Technology
Castle Point on the Hudson, Hoboken 07030
Type: Private, independent, four-year
Degrees: B, M, D   *Enroll:* 3,213
URL: http://www.stevens-tech.edu
Phone: (201) 216-5100   *Calendar:* Sem. plan
Inst. Accred.: MSA-CHE (1927/2003)
Prog. Accred.: Computer Science, Engineering (chemical,
civil, computer, electrical, engineering management,
engineering physics/science, environmental/sanitary,
general, mechanical, metallurgical)

Sussex County Community College
One College Ave., Newton 07860-9937
Type: Public, state/local, two-year
System: New Jersey Commission on Higher Education
Degrees: A   *Enroll:* 1,866
URL: http://www.sussex.edu
Phone: (973) 300-2100   *Calendar:* Sem. plan
Inst. Accred.: MSA-CHE (1993/2003)
Prog. Accred.: Medical Assisting (CAAHEP)

Talmudical Academy of New Jersey
Route 524, Adelphia 07710
Type: Private, independent, four-year
Degrees: B   *Enroll:* 32
Phone: (732) 431-1600   *Calendar:* Sem. plan
Inst. Accred.: AARTS (1980/2001)

Thomas Edison State College
101 West State St., Trenton 08608-1176
Type: Public, state, four-year
System: New Jersey Commission on Higher Education
Degrees: A, B, M   *Enroll:* 4,120
URL: http://www.tesc.edu
Phone: (609) 984-1100   *Calendar:* Sem. plan
Inst. Accred.: MSA-CHE (1977/2002)
Prog. Accred.: Nursing

Union County College
1033 Springfield Ave., Cranford 07016
Type: Public, state/local, two-year
System: New Jersey Commission on Higher Education
Degrees: A   *Enroll:* 7,098
URL: http://www.ucc.edu
Phone: (908) 709-7000   *Calendar:* Sem. plan
Inst. Accred.: MSA-CHE (1957/2002)
Prog. Accred.: Physical Therapy Assisting, Respiratory
Therapy

Elizabeth Campus
12 West Jersey St., Elizabeth 07206
Phone: (908) 965-6000

Plainfield Campus
232 East Second St., Plainfield 07060
Phone: (908) 412-3550
Prog. Accred: Practical Nursing

University of Medicine and Dentistry of New Jersey
65 Bergen St., Newark 07107-3001
Type: Public, state, four-year
System: New Jersey Commission on Higher Education
Degrees: A, B, M, P, D   *Enroll:* 4,191
URL: http://www.umdnj.edu
Phone: (973) 972-4300   *Calendar:* Sem. plan
Inst. Accred.: MSA-CHE (1979/2000)
Prog. Accred.: Advanced Education in General Dentistry, Clinical Lab Scientist, Clinical Lab Technology, Combined Prosthodontics, Cytotechnology, Dentistry, Diagnostic Medical Sonography, Dietetics (coordinated), Dietetics (internship), Endodontics, General Practice Residency, Nuclear Medicine Technology, Nurse (Midwifery), Nurse Anesthesia Education, Nursing, Oral and Maxillofacial Surgery, Orthotist/Prothetist, Osteopathy, Pediatric Dentistry, Periodontics, Phlebotomy, Physical Therapy, Psychology Internship, Radiography, Respiratory Therapy, Surgical Technology

Graduate School of Biomedical Sciences
185 South Orange Ave., Newark 07103
Phone: (973) 972-4511

New Jersey Dental School
110 Bergen St., Newark 07103
Phone: (973) 972-4300
Prog. Accred: Combined Prosthodontics, Dental Assisting, Dental Hygiene, Dentistry, Endodontics, General Dentistry, General Practice Residency, Oral and Maxillofacial Surgery, Orthodontic and Dentofacial Orthopedics, Pediatric Dentistry, Periodontics

New Jersey Medical School
185 South Orange Ave., Newark 07103
Phone: (973) 972-4539
Prog. Accred: Medicine

New Jersey School of Osteopathic Medicine
406 East Laurel Rd., Stratford 08084-1350
Phone: (856) 566-6995

Robert Wood Johnson Medical School
671 Hoes Ln., Piscataway 08854
Phone: (732) 235-5600
Prog. Accred: Clinical Pastoral Education (ACPEI), General Practice Residency, Medicine, Physician Assistant, Psychology Internship, Public Health

School of Health-Related Professions
65 Bergen St., Newark 07107
Phone: (973) 972-5453
Prog. Accred: Dental Assisting, Dental Hygiene

School of Nursing
30 Bergen St., Administrative Complex Bldg. One, Newark 07107
Phone: (973) 972-4322

School of Public Health
170 Frelinghuysen Rd., Rm.236, Piscataway 08854
Phone: (732) 445-0199

Warren County Community College
475 Route 57 West, Box 55A, Washington 07882-4343
Type: Public, state/local, two-year
System: New Jersey Commission on Higher Education
Degrees: A   *Enroll:* 689
URL: http://www.warren.edu
Phone: (908) 835-9222   *Calendar:* Sem. plan
Inst. Accred.: MSA-CHE (1993/2003)
Prog. Accred.: Medical Assisting (CAAHEP)

William Paterson University of New Jersey
300 Pompton Rd., Wayne 07470-2152
Type: Public, state, four-year
System: New Jersey Commission on Higher Education
Degrees: B, M   *Enroll:* 9,084
URL: http://www.wpunj.edu
Phone: (973) 720-2000   *Calendar:* Sem. plan
Inst. Accred.: MSA-CHE (1958/2001)
Prog. Accred.: Athletic Training, Business (AACSB), Counseling, Music, Nursing, Nursing Education, Speech-Language Pathology, Teacher Education (NCATE)

NEW MEXICO

Albuquerque Technical Vocational Institute
525 Buena Vista Dr., SE, Albuquerque 87106
Type: Public, state/local, two-year
System: New Mexico Commission on Higher Education
Degrees: A   *Enroll:* 11,790
URL: http://www.tvi.edu
Phone: (505) 224-3000   *Calendar:* Tri. plan
Inst. Accred.: NCA-HLC (1978/2003)
Prog. Accred.: Business (ACBSP), Clinical Lab Technology, Construction Education, Culinary Education, Dental Assisting, Engineering Technology (electrical, general drafting/design, mechanical drafting/design), Nursing, Practical Nursing, Respiratory Therapy

Clovis Community College
417 Schepps Blvd., Clovis 88101
Type: Public, state, two-year
System: New Mexico Commission on Higher Education
Degrees: A   *Enroll:* 1,787
URL: http://www.clovis.edu
Phone: (505) 769-2811   *Calendar:* Sem. plan
Inst. Accred.: NCA-HLC (1987/2002)
Prog. Accred.: Nursing, Radiography

The College of Santa Fe
1600 St. Michael's Dr., Santa Fe 87501
Type: Private, Christian Brothers, four-year
Degrees: A, B, M   *Enroll:* 1,188
URL: http://www.csf.edu
Phone: (505) 473-6133   *Calendar:* Sem. plan
Inst. Accred.: NCA-HLC (1965/2001)

College of the Southwest
6610 Lovington Hwy., Hobbs 88240
Type: Private, independent, four-year
Degrees: B, M   *Enroll:* 667
URL: http://www.csw.edu
Phone: (800) 530-4400   *Calendar:* Sem. plan
Inst. Accred.: NCA-HLC (1980/2003)

Crownpoint Institute of Technology
PO Box 849, Crownpoint 87313
Type: Private, tribal, two-year
System: American Indian Higher Education Consortium
Degrees: A
URL: http://crownpointtech.org
Phone: (505) 786-4100   *Calendar:* Sem. plan
Inst. Accred.: NCA-HLC (2005)

Eastern New Mexico University
Campus Station #1, Portales 88130
Type: Public, state, four-year
System: New Mexico Commission on Higher Education
Degrees: A, B, M   *Enroll:* 3,048
URL: http://www.enmu.edu
Phone: (505) 562-2121   *Calendar:* Sem. plan
Inst. Accred.: NCA-HLC (1947/1997)
Prog. Accred.: Business (ACBSP), Music, Nursing, Speech-Language Pathology, Teacher Education (NCATE)

Eastern New Mexico University—Roswell
PO Box 6000, Roswell 88202
Type: Public, state, two-year
System: New Mexico Commission on Higher Education
Degrees: A   *Enroll:* 2,394
URL: http://www.roswell.enmu.edu
Phone: (505) 624-7000   *Calendar:* Sem. plan
Inst. Accred.: NCA-HLC (1971/2002)
Prog. Accred.: EMT (Paramedic), Medical Assisting (AMA), Nursing, Occupational Therapy Assisting

Institute of American Indian and Alaskan Native Culture and Arts Development
83 Avon Rd., Santa Fe 87504
Type: Public, federal, four-year
System: American Indian Higher Education Consortium
Degrees: A, B   *Enroll:* 146
URL: http://www.iaiancad.org
Phone: (505) 988-6463   *Calendar:* Sem. plan
Inst. Accred.: NCA-HLC (1984/2004)
Prog. Accred.: Art

Luna Community College
366 Luna Dr., Las Vegas 87701
Type: Public, state/local, two-year
System: New Mexico Commission on Higher Education
Degrees: A   *Enroll:* 957
URL: http://www.lvti.cc.nm.us
Phone: (505) 454-2500   *Calendar:* Sem. plan
Inst. Accred.: NCA-HLC (1982/2005)

Mesalands Community College
911 South 10th St., Tucumcari 88401
Type: Public, state, two-year
Degrees: A   *Enroll:* 319
URL: http://www.mesalands.edu
Phone: (505) 461-4413   *Calendar:* Sem. plan
Inst. Accred.: NCA-HLC (1999/2004)

Metropolitan College—Albuquerque Campus
8100 Mountain Rd., NE, Ste. 210, Albuquerque 87110-4129
Type: Private, proprietary, four-year
System: Wyandotte Collegiate Systems
Degrees: A, B   *Enroll:* 202
URL: http://www.metropolitancollege.edu
Phone: (505) 888-3400   *Calendar:* Tri. plan
Inst. Accred.: ACCSCT (1993/2000)

Kansas City College
800 101st Terrace, Sute 100, Kansas City, MO 64131
Phone: (816) 444-2232

National College of Midwifery
#209 State Rd. 240, Taos 87571
Type: Private, independent, four-year
Degrees: A, B, M, D
URL: http://www.midwiferycollege.org
Phone: (505) 758-1216   *Calendar:* Sem. plan
Inst. Accred.: MEAC (2001)

New Mexico Highlands University
PO Box 9000, Las Vegas 87701
Type: Public, state, four-year
System: New Mexico Commission on Higher Education
Degrees: A, B, M   *Enroll:* 2,297
URL: http://www.nmhu.edu
Phone: (877) 850-9064   *Calendar:* Sem. plan
Inst. Accred.: NCA-HLC (1926/2001)
Prog. Accred.: Business (ACBSP), Social Work, Teacher
   Education (NCATE)

New Mexico Institute of Mining and Technology
801 Leroy Place, Socorro 87801
Type: Public, state, four-year
System: New Mexico Commission on Higher Education
Degrees: A, B, M, D   *Enroll:* 1,529
URL: http://www.nmt.edu
Phone: (505) 835-5600   *Calendar:* Sem. plan
Inst. Accred.: NCA-HLC (1949/2005)
Prog. Accred.: Engineering (chemical, electrical,
   environmental/sanitary, materials, mechanical, mineral,
   petroleum)

New Mexico Junior College
5317 Lovington Hwy., Hobbs 88240
Type: Public, state/local, two-year
System: New Mexico Commission on Higher Education
Degrees: A   *Enroll:* 1,517
URL: http://www.nmjc.edu
Phone: (505) 392-4510   *Calendar:* Sem. plan
Inst. Accred.: NCA-HLC (1970/1996)
Prog. Accred.: Nursing

New Mexico Military Institute
101 West College Blvd., Roswell 88201
Type: Public, state, two-year
System: New Mexico Commission on Higher Education
Degrees: A   *Enroll:* 408
URL: http://www.nmmi.edu
Phone: (505) 622-6250   *Calendar:* Sem. plan
Inst. Accred.: NCA-HLC (1938/2001)

New Mexico State University
PO Box 30001, Las Cruces 88003-8001
Type: Public, state, four-year
System: New Mexico Commission on Higher Education
Degrees: A, B, M, P, D   *Enroll:* 13,712
URL: http://www.nmsu.edu
Phone: (505) 646-2035   *Calendar:* Sem. plan
Inst. Accred.: NCA-HLC (1926/1998)
Prog. Accred.: Accounting, Applied Science
   (surveying/geomatics), Business (AACSB), Counseling,
   Counseling Psychology, Engineering (agricultural,
   chemical, civil, electrical, geological/geophysical,
   industrial, mechanical, surveying), Engineering
   Technology (bioengineering, civil/construction,
   mechanical), Journalism, Music, Nursing, Nursing
   Education, Public Administration, Public Health, Social
   Work, Speech-Language Pathology, Teacher Education
   (NCATE), Teacher Education (TEAC)

Doña Ana Branch Community College
Box 30001, 3400 South Epina St., Las Cruces 88003
Phone: (505) 527-7500
Prog. Accred: Athletic Training, Nursing, Radiography

Grants Campus
1500 North Third St., Grants 87020
Phone: (505) 287-6678

New Mexico State University at Alamogordo
2400 North Scenic Dr., Alamogordo 88310
Type: Public, state, two-year
Degrees: A   *Enroll:* 1,112
URL: http://alamo.nmsu.edu
Phone: (505) 439-3600   *Calendar:* Sem. plan
Inst. Accred.: NCA-HLC (1973/2003)
Prog. Accred.: Clinical Lab Technology, Nursing

New Mexico State University at Carlsbad
1500 University Dr., Carlsbad 88220
Type: Public, state, two-year
Degrees: A   *Enroll:* 799
URL: http://cavern.nmsu.edu
Phone: (505) 234-9200   *Calendar:* Sem. plan
Inst. Accred.: NCA-HLC (1980/2002)
Prog. Accred.: Nursing

Northern New Mexico College
921 Paseo de Onate, Espanola 87532
Type: Public, state/local, four-year
System: New Mexico Commission on Higher Education
Degrees: A, B   *Enroll:* 1,133
URL: http://nnmcc.edu
Phone: (505) 747-2100   *Calendar:* Sem. plan
Inst. Accred.: NCA-HLC (1982/2004)
Prog. Accred.: Business (ACBSP), Radiography

Saint John's College
1160 Camino Cruz Blanca, Santa Fe 87505-4599
Type: Private, independent, four-year
Degrees: B, M   *Enroll:* 533
URL: http://www.sjcsf.edu
Phone: (505) 984-6000   *Calendar:* Sem. plan
Inst. Accred.: NCA-HLC (1969/1999)

San Juan College
4601 College Blvd., Farmington 87402
Type: Public, local, two-year
System: New Mexico Commission on Higher Education
Degrees: A   *Enroll:* 3,385
URL: http://www.sanjuancollege.edu
Phone: (505) 326-3311   *Calendar:* Sem. plan
Inst. Accred.: NCA-HLC (1973/1994)
Prog. Accred.: Business (ACBSP), Dental Assisting, Dental
   Hygiene, Engineering Technology (mechanical
   drafting/design), Nursing, Physical Therapy Assisting

Santa Fe Community College
6401 Richards Ave., Santa Fe 87508
Type: Public, state, two-year
System: New Mexico Commission on Higher Education
Degrees: A   *Enroll:* 1,998
URL: http://www.sfccnm.edu
Phone: (505) 428-1000   *Calendar:* Sem. plan
Inst. Accred.: NCA-HLC (1988/2003)
Prog. Accred.: Dental Assisting, Nursing

Southwest Acupuncture College
2960 Rodeo Park Dr. West, Santa Fe 87505
Type: Private, proprietary, four-year
Degrees: M   *Enroll:* 84
URL: http://www.acupuncturecollege.edu
Phone: (505) 438-8884   *Calendar:* Tri. plan
Inst. Accred.: ACAOM (1989/2004)

Albuquerque Campus
7801 Academy Rd., NE, North Towne Bldg., Ste. 1,
Albuquerque 87109-3191
Phone: (505) 888-8898
Prog. Accred: Acupuncture

Boulder Campus
6658 Gunpark Dr., Boulder, CO 80301
Phone: (303) 581-9955
Prog. Accred: Acupuncture

Southwestern College
PO Box 4788, Santa Fe 87502
Type: Private, independent, four-year
Degrees: M   *Enroll:* 111
URL: http://www.swc.edu
Phone: (505) 471-5756   *Calendar:* Qtr. plan
Inst. Accred.: NCA-HLC (1996/2001)

Southwestern Indian Polytechnic Institute
9169 Coors Rd., NW, Box 10146, Albuquerque 87184
Type: Public, tribal, two-year
System: American Indian Higher Education Consortium
Degrees: A   *Enroll:* 798
URL: http://www.sipi.bia.edu
Phone: (505) 346-4766   *Calendar:* Tri. plan
Inst. Accred.: NCA-HLC (1975/2000)
Prog. Accred.: Opticianry

The University of New Mexico
One University of New Mexico, Albuquerque 87131-1001
Type: Public, state, four-year
System: New Mexico Commission on Higher Education
Degrees: A, B, M, P, D   *Enroll:* 20,682
URL: http://www.unm.edu
Phone: (505) 277-0111   *Calendar:* Sem. plan
Inst. Accred.: NCA-HLC (1922/1999)
Prog. Accred.: Accounting, Athletic Training, Audiology,
   Clinical Lab Scientist, Clinical Psychology, Computer
   Science, Construction Education, Counseling, Dance,
   Dental Hygiene, Dietetics (internship), EMT (Paramedic),
   Engineering (chemical, civil, computer, construction,
   electrical, mechanical, nuclear), General Dentistry, Law,
   Medicine, Music, Nurse (Midwifery), Nursing, Nursing
   Education, Occupational Therapy, Pharmacy, Physical
   Therapy, Physician Assistant, Planning, Psychology
   Internship, Public Administration, Public Health,
   Radiography, Speech-Language Pathology, Teacher
   Education (NCATE), Theatre

Gallup Campus
200 College Rd., Gallup 87301
Phone: (505) 843-7783
Prog. Accred: Clinical Lab Technology, Dental
   Assisting, Health Information Technician, Nursing

Los Alamos Campus
4000 University Dr., Los Alamos 87544
Phone: (505) 867-2379

Taos Education Center Campus
115 Civic Plaza Dr., Taos 87571
Phone: (505) 758-7667

Valencia Campus
280 La Entrada, Los Lunas 87031
Phone: (505) 865-1639

Western New Mexico University
PO Box 680, 1000 West College Ave., Silver City 88062
Type: Public, state, four-year
System: New Mexico Commission on Higher Education
Degrees: A, B, M   *Enroll:* 2,161
URL: http://www.wnmu.edu
Phone: (800) 222-9668   *Calendar:* Sem. plan
Inst. Accred.: NCA-HLC (1926/1997)
Prog. Accred.: Business (ACBSP), Nursing, Occupational
   Therapy Assisting, Social Work, Teacher Education
   (NCATE)

NEW YORK

Adelphi University
1 South Ave., Garden City 11530
Type: Private, independent, four-year
Degrees: A, B, M, D   *Enroll:* 5,424
URL: http://www.adelphi.edu
Phone: (516) 877-3000   *Calendar:* Sem. plan
Inst. Accred.: MSA-CHE (1921/1999)
Prog. Accred.: Audiology, Business (AACSB), Clinical
   Psychology, Nursing, Nursing Education, Social Work,
   Speech-Language Pathology

Adirondack Community College
640 Bay Rd., Queensbury 12804
Type: Public, state/local, two-year
System: State University of New York Office of
   Community Colleges
Degrees: A   *Enroll:* 2,518
URL: http://www.sunyacc.edu
Phone: (518) 743-2200   *Calendar:* Sem. plan
Inst. Accred.: MSA-CHE (1972/2003)
Prog. Accred.: Health Information Technician

Albany College of Pharmacy of Union University
106 New Scotland Ave., Albany 12208
Type: Private, independent, four-year
System: Union University
Degrees: B, P   *Enroll:* 882
URL: http://www.acp.edu
Phone: (518) 445-7200   *Calendar:* Sem. plan
Inst. Accred.: MSA-CHE (1921/1999)
Prog. Accred.: Pharmacy

Albany Law School
80 New Scotland Ave., Albany 12208
Type: Private, independent, four-year
System: Union University
Degrees: M, P, D   *Enroll:* 770
URL: http://www.als.edu
Phone: (518) 445-2311   *Calendar:* Sem. plan
Inst. Accred.: ABA (1930/2000)
Prog. Accred.: Law

Albany Medical College
47 New Scotland Ave., MC-34, Albany 12208
Type: Private, independent, four-year
System: Union University
Degrees: M, P, D   *Enroll:* 651
URL: http://www.amc.edu
Phone: (518) 262-6008
Inst. Accred.: MSA-CHE (1921/2005)
Prog. Accred.: Cytotechnology, General Practice
   Residency, Medicine, Nurse Anesthesia Education,
   Physician Assistant

Alfred University
One Saxon Dr., Alfred 14802-1205
Type: Private, independent, four-year
System: State University of New York System Office
Degrees: B, M, D   *Enroll:* 2,229
URL: http://www.alfred.edu
Phone: (607) 871-2111   *Calendar:* Sem. plan
Inst. Accred.: MSA-CHE (1921/2004)
Prog. Accred.: Business (AACSB), Construction Education,
   Engineering (ceramic, electrical, materials, mechanical)

New York State College of Ceramics at Alfred University
2 Pine St., Alfred 14802-1296
Phone: (607) 871-2411
Prog. Accred: Art

American Academy McAllister Institute of Funeral Service, Inc.
450 West 56th St., New York 10019
Type: Private, independent, two-year
Degrees: A   *Enroll:* 123
URL: http://www.a-a-m-i.org
Phone: (212) 757-1190   *Calendar:* Sem. plan
Inst. Accred.: ABFSE (1964/1999)

American Academy of Dramatic Arts
120 Madison Ave., New York 10016
Type: Private, independent, two-year
Degrees: A   *Enroll:* 241
URL: http://www.aada.org
Phone: (212) 686-9244
Inst. Accred.: MSA-CHE (1983/2005), NYBOR
   (1972/2001)
Prog. Accred.: Theatre

The Art Institute of New York City
75 Varick St., 16th Flr., New York 10013-1917
Type: Private, proprietary, two-year
System: Education Management Corporation
Degrees: A
URL: http://www.ainyc.artinstitutes.edu
Phone: (212) 226-5500   *Calendar:* Sem. plan
Inst. Accred.: ACICS (1999/2002)
Prog. Accred.: Culinary Education

ASA Institute, The College of Advanced Technology
151 Lawrence St., Brooklyn 11201
Type: Private, independent, two-year
Degrees: A
URL: http://www.asa-institute.com
Phone: (718) 522-9073
Inst. Accred.: ACICS (1992/2002)
Prog. Accred.: Medical Assisting (CAAHEP)

Bank Street College of Education
610 West 112th St., New York 10025
Type: Private, independent, four-year
Degrees: M   *Enroll:* 599
URL: http://www.bankstreet.edu
Phone: (212) 875-4400   *Calendar:* Sem. plan
Inst. Accred.: MSA-CHE (1960/2005)
Prog. Accred.: Teacher Education (NCATE)

Bard College
Annandale-on-Hudson 12504
Type: Private, independent, four-year
Degrees: B, M, D   *Enroll:* 1,776
URL: http://www.bard.edu
Phone: (845) 758-6822   *Calendar:* Sem. plan
Inst. Accred.: MSA-CHE (1922/2002)

Barnard College
3009 Broadway, New York 10027-6598
Type: Private, independent, four-year
Degrees: B   *Enroll:* 2,251
URL: http://www.barnard.edu
Phone: (212) 854-5262   *Calendar:* Sem. plan
Inst. Accred.: MSA-CHE (1921/2001)
Prog. Accred.: Dance

Berkeley College of New York City
3 East 43rd St., New York 10017
Type: Private, proprietary, four-year
System: Berkeley College of New York and New Jersey
Degrees: A, B   *Enroll:* 1,758
URL: http://www.berkeleycollege.edu
Phone: (212) 986-4343   *Calendar:* Qtr. plan
Inst. Accred.: MSA-CHE (1993/2003)

Westchester Campus
99 Church St., White Plains 10601
Phone: (914) 694-1122

Beth HaMedrash Shaarei Yosher
4102 16th Ave., Brooklyn 11204
Type: Private, independent, four-year
Degrees: Talmudic   *Enroll:* 133
Phone: (718) 854-2290   *Calendar:* Sem. plan
Inst. Accred.: AARTS (1982/2001)

Beth HaTalmud Rabbinical College
2127 82nd St., Brooklyn 11214
Type: Private, independent, four-year
Degrees: Talmudic   *Enroll:* 92
Phone: (718) 259-2525   *Calendar:* Sem. plan
Inst. Accred.: AARTS (1978/2002)

Bexley Hall Seminary
26 Broadway, Rochester 14607-1704
Type: Private, Episcopal Church, four-year
Degrees: M, D
URL: http://www.bexley.edu
Phone: (716) 340-9550   *Calendar:* Sem. plan
Inst. Accred.: ATS (1952/2003)

Columbus Campus
583 Sheridan Ave., Columbus, OH 43209-2325
Phone: (614) 231-309

Boricua College
3755 Broadway, New York 10032
Type: Private, independent, four-year
Degrees: A, B, M   *Enroll:* 1,264
URL: http://www.boricuacollege.edu
Phone: (212) 694-1000   *Calendar:* Sem. plan
Inst. Accred.: MSA-CHE (1980/2004)

Bramson ORT College
69-30 Austin St., Forest Hills 11375-4222
Type: Private, independent, two-year
Degrees: A   *Enroll:* 437
URL: http://www.bramsonort.org
Phone: (716) 261-5800   *Calendar:* Sem. plan
Inst. Accred.: NYBOR (1979/2002)

Bensonhurst Campus
5815 20th Ave., Brooklyn 11230
Phone: (718) 259-5300

Briarcliffe College
1055 Stewart Ave., Bethpage 11714-3545
Type: Private, proprietary, four-year
System: Career Education Corporation
Degrees: A, B   *Enroll:* 2,504
URL: http://www.bcbeth.com
Phone: (516) 918-3600   *Calendar:* Sem. plan
Inst. Accred.: MSA-CHE (1996/2001)

Patchogue Campus
10 Lake St., Patchogue 11772
Phone: (516) 654-5300

Bryant and Stratton
2340 North Forest Rd., Getzville 14068
Type: Private, proprietary, four-year
System: Bryant and Stratton
Degrees: A, B
URL: http://www.bryantstratton.edu
Phone: (716) 250-7500   *Calendar:* Sem. plan
Inst. Accred.: MSA-CHE (2002)

Bryant and Stratton College—Albany Campus
1259 Central Ave., Albany 12205-5230
Type: Private, proprietary, two-year
System: Bryant and Stratton
Degrees: A　　　　　　　　　　　　　　*Enroll:* 350
URL: http://www.bryantstratton.edu
Phone: (518) 437-1802　　　　　　*Calendar:* Sem. plan
Inst. Accred.: MSA-CHE (2002, *Indirect accreditation through Bryant and Stratton, Getzville, NY*)
Prog. Accred.: Medical Assisting (CAAHEP)

Bryant and Stratton College—Buffalo
465 Main St., Ste. 400, Buffalo 14203-1795
Type: Private, proprietary, two-year
System: Bryant and Stratton
Degrees: A　　　　　　　　　　　　　　*Enroll:* 532
URL: http://www.bryantstratton.edu
Phone: (716) 884-9120　　　　　　*Calendar:* Sem. plan
Inst. Accred.: MSA-CHE (2002, *Indirect accreditation through Bryant and Stratton, Getzville, NY*)
Prog. Accred.: Medical Assisting (CAAHEP)

Amherst Campus
Audubon Business Center, 40 Hazelwood Dr., Amherst 14228
Phone: (716) 691-0012

Southtowns Campus
Sterling Park, 200 Red Tail, Orchard Park 14127-1562
Phone: (716) 677-9500

Bryant and Stratton College—Greece Campus
150 Bellwood Dr., Rochester 14606
Type: Private, proprietary, two-year
System: Bryant and Stratton
Degrees: A　　　　　　　　　　　　　　*Enroll:* 170
URL: http://www.bryantstratton.edu
Phone: (585) 720-0660　　　　　　*Calendar:* Sem. plan
Inst. Accred.: MSA-CHE (2002, *Indirect accreditation through Bryant and Stratton, Getzville, NY*)

Henrietta Campus
1225 Jefferson Rd., Rochester 14623-5627
Phone: (585) 292-5627
Prog. Accred: Medical Assisting (CAAHEP)

Bryant and Stratton College—Syracuse
953 James St., Syracuse 13203-2502
Type: Private, proprietary, two-year
System: Bryant and Stratton
Degrees: A　　　　　　　　　　　　　　*Enroll:* 513
URL: http://www.bryantstratton.edu
Phone: (315) 472-6603　　　　　　*Calendar:* Sem. plan
Inst. Accred.: MSA-CHE (2002, *Indirect accreditation through Bryant and Stratton, Getzville, NY*)
Prog. Accred.: Medical Assisting (CAAHEP)

Syracuse North Campus
8687 Carling Rd., Liverpool 13090-1315
Phone: (315) 652-6500

Canisius College
2001 Main St., Buffalo 14208-1908
Type: Private, independent, four-year
Degrees: A, B, M　　　　　　　　　　*Enroll:* 4,327
URL: http://www.canisius.edu
Phone: (716) 883-7000　　　　　　*Calendar:* Sem. plan
Inst. Accred.: MSA-CHE (1921/2005)
Prog. Accred.: Athletic Training, Business (AACSB)

Cayuga County Community College
197 Franklin St., Auburn 13021-3099
Type: Public, state/local, two-year
System: State University of New York Office of Community Colleges
Degrees: A　　　　　　　　　　　　　　*Enroll:* 2,643
URL: http://www.cayuga-cc.edu
Phone: (315) 255-1743　　　　　　*Calendar:* Sem. plan
Inst. Accred.: MSA-CHE (1965/2001)
Prog. Accred.: Nursing

Cazenovia College
22 Sullivan St., Cazenovia 13035-1084
Type: Private, independent, four-year
Degrees: A, B　　　　　　　　　　　　*Enroll:* 879
URL: http://www.cazenovia.edu
Phone: (800) 655-3210　　　　　　*Calendar:* Sem. plan
Inst. Accred.: MSA-CHE (1961/2003)

Central Yeshiva Tomchei Tmimim-Lubavitch
841-853 Ocean Pkwy., Brooklyn 11230
Type: Private, independent, four-year
Degrees: Rabbinic, Talmudic　　　　*Enroll:* 600
Phone: (718) 434-0784　　　　　　*Calendar:* Sem. plan
Inst. Accred.: AARTS (1976/2000)

Christ the King Seminary
711 Knox Rd., PO Box 607, East Aurora 14052-0607
Type: Private, Roman Catholic Church, four-year
Degrees: M, P　　　　　　　　　　　　*Enroll:* 51
URL: http://www.cks.edu
Phone: (716) 652-8900　　　　　　*Calendar:* Sem. plan
Inst. Accred.: ATS (1977/2002), MSA-CHE (1974/2003)

The City University of New York
Bernard M. Baruch College
One Bernard Baruch Way, New York 10010
Type: Public, state/local, four-year
System: City University of New York System
Degrees: B, M　　　　　　　　　　　　*Enroll:* 11,853
URL: http://www.baruch.cuny.edu
Phone: (646) 312-2000　　　　　　*Calendar:* Sem. plan
Inst. Accred.: MSA-CHE (1968/2005)
Prog. Accred.: Accounting, Business (AACSB), Health Services Administration, Public Administration

City University of New York
Borough of Manhattan Community College
199 Chambers St., New York 10007
Type: Public, state/local, two-year
System: City University of New York System
Degrees: A *Enroll:* 13,628
URL: http://www.bmcc.cuny.edu
Phone: (212) 220-8000 *Calendar:* Sem. plan
Inst. Accred.: MSA-CHE (1964/2003)
Prog. Accred.: EMT (Paramedic), Health Information
Technician, Nursing, Respiratory Therapy

City University of New York
Bronx Community College
West 181st St. and University Ave., Bronx 10453
Type: Public, state/local, two-year
System: City University of New York System
Degrees: A *Enroll:* 5,808
URL: http://www.bcc.cuny.edu
Phone: (718) 289-5100 *Calendar:* Sem. plan
Inst. Accred.: MSA-CHE (1961/1999)
Prog. Accred.: Business (ACBSP), Engineering Technology
(electrical), Nuclear Medicine Technology, Nursing,
Radiography

City University of New York
Brooklyn College
2900 Bedford Ave., Brooklyn 11210-2889
Type: Public, state/local, four-year
System: City University of New York System
Degrees: B, M *Enroll:* 10,936
URL: http://www.brooklyn.cuny.edu
Phone: (718) 951-5000 *Calendar:* Sem. plan
Inst. Accred.: MSA-CHE (1933/1999)
Prog. Accred.: Audiology, Public Health, Speech-
Language Pathology

City University of New York
City College
160 Convent Ave. at 138th St., New York 10031-9198
Type: Public, state/local, four-year
System: City University of New York System
Degrees: B, M *Enroll:* 8,576
URL: http://www1.ccny.cuny.edu
Phone: (212) 650-7000 *Calendar:* Sem. plan
Inst. Accred.: MSA-CHE (1921/2003)
Prog. Accred.: Clinical Psychology, Computer Science,
Engineering (chemical, civil, electrical, mechanical),
Landscape Architecture, Physician Assistant

City University of New York
College of Staten Island
2800 Victory Blvd., Staten Island 10314
Type: Public, state/local, four-year
System: City University of New York System
Degrees: A, B, M *Enroll:* 9,351
URL: http://www.csi.cuny.edu
Phone: (718) 982-2000 *Calendar:* Sem. plan
Inst. Accred.: MSA-CHE (1963/2001)
Prog. Accred.: Computer Science, Engineering
(engineering physics/science), Engineering Technology
(electrical), Nursing, Physical Therapy, Social Work

Sunnyside Campus
715 Ocean Terrace, Staten Island 10301
Phone: (718) 390-7664

City University of New York
Graduate Center
365 5th Ave., New York 10016-4309
Type: Public, state, four-year
System: City University of New York System
Degrees: M, D *Enroll:* 3,738
URL: http://www.gc.cuny.edu
Phone: (212) 817-7000 *Calendar:* Sem. plan
Inst. Accred.: MSA-CHE (1961/2005)
Prog. Accred.: School Psychology

City University of New York
Herbert H. Lehman College
250 Bedford Park Blvd. West, Bronx 10468
Type: Public, state/local, four-year
System: City University of New York System
Degrees: B, M *Enroll:* 6,635
URL: http://www.lehman.cuny.edu
Phone: (718) 960-8000 *Calendar:* Sem. plan
Inst. Accred.: MSA-CHE (1968/1999)
Prog. Accred.: Audiology, Dietetics (internship), Nursing,
Nursing Education, Social Work, Speech-Language
Pathology

City University of New York
Hostos Community College
500 Grand Concourse, Bronx 10451-5323
Type: Public, state/local, two-year
System: City University of New York System
Degrees: A *Enroll:* 3,010
URL: http://www.hostos.cuny.edu
Phone: (718) 518-4444 *Calendar:* Sem. plan
Inst. Accred.: MSA-CHE (1974/2002)
Prog. Accred.: Dental Hygiene, Radiography

City University of New York Hunter College
695 Park Ave., New York 10021-5085
Type: Public, state/local, four-year
System: City University of New York System
Degrees: B, M　　　　　　　　　　　　*Enroll:* 15,031
URL: http://www.hunter.cuny.edu
Phone: (212) 772-4000　　　　　*Calendar:* Sem. plan
Inst. Accred.: MSA-CHE (1921/1998)
Prog. Accred.: Applied Science (occupational health and safety), Audiology, Dietetics (internship), Nursing, Nursing Education, Physical Therapy, Planning, Public Health, Rehabilitation Counseling, Social Work, Speech-Language Pathology

City University of New York
John Jay College of Criminal Justice
899 10th Ave., New York 10019
Type: Public, state/local, four-year
System: City University of New York System
Degrees: A, B, M　　　　　　　　　　*Enroll:* 10,462
URL: http://www.jjay.cuny.edu
Phone: (212) 237-8800　　　　*Calendar:* Sem. plan
Inst. Accred.: MSA-CHE (1965/2003)
Prog. Accred.: Public Administration

City University of New York
Kingsborough Community College
2001 Oriental Blvd., Brooklyn 11235
Type: Public, state/local, two-year
System: City University of New York System
Degrees: A　　　　　　　　　　　　*Enroll:* 9,986
URL: http://www.kbcc.cuny.edu
Phone: (718) 368-5000　　　　*Calendar:* Sem. plan
Inst. Accred.: MSA-CHE (1964/2001)
Prog. Accred.: Nursing, Physical Therapy Assisting

City University of New York
La Guardia Community College
31-10 Thomson Ave., Long Island City 11101-3083
Type: Public, state/local, two-year
System: City University of New York System
Degrees: A　　　　　　　　　　　　*Enroll:* 9,180
URL: http://www.lagcc.cuny.edu
Phone: (718) 482-7200　　　　*Calendar:* Sem. plan
Inst. Accred.: MSA-CHE (1974/2002)
Prog. Accred.: Nursing, Occupational Therapy Assisting, Physical Therapy Assisting, Veterinary Technology

City University of New York
Medgar Evers College
1650 Bedford Ave., Brooklyn 11225-2010
Type: Public, state/local, four-year
System: City University of New York System
Degrees: A, B　　　　　　　　　　　*Enroll:* 3,455
URL: http://www.mec.cuny.edu
Phone: (718) 270-4900　　　　*Calendar:* Sem. plan
Inst. Accred.: MSA-CHE (1976/2002)
Prog. Accred.: Business (ACBSP), Nursing

City University of New York
New York City College of Technology
300 Jay St., Brooklyn 11201-1909
Type: Public, state/local, four-year
System: City University of New York System
Degrees: A, B　　　　　　　　　　　*Enroll:* 8,799
URL: http://www.citytech.cuny.edu
Phone: (718) 260-5000　　　　*Calendar:* Sem. plan
Inst. Accred.: MSA-CHE (1957/2002)
Prog. Accred.: Construction Education, Dental Hygiene, Dental Laboratory Technology, Engineering Technology (civil/construction, computer, electrical, electromechanical, mechanical, telecommunications), Nursing, Opticianry, Radiography

City University of New York Queens College
65-30 Kissena Blvd., Flushing 11367-1597
Type: Public, state/local, four-year
System: City University of New York System
Degrees: B, M, P　　　　　　　　　*Enroll:* 11,805
URL: http://www.qc.edu
Phone: (718) 997-5000　　　　*Calendar:* Sem. plan
Inst. Accred.: MSA-CHE (1941/2002)
Prog. Accred.: Dietetics (internship), Family and Consumer Science, Law (ABA only), Librarianship, Speech-Language Pathology

City University School of Law at Queens College
65-21 Main St., Flushing 11367
Phone: (718) 575-4200
Prog. Accred.: Law

City University of New York
Queensborough Community College
222-05 56th Ave., Bayside 11364-1497
Type: Public, state/local, two-year
System: City University of New York System
Degrees: A　　　　　　　　　　　　*Enroll:* 8,282
URL: http://www.qcc.cuny.edu
Phone: (718) 631-6262　　　　*Calendar:* Sem. plan
Inst. Accred.: MSA-CHE (1963/1999)
Prog. Accred.: Business (ACBSP), Engineering Technology (computer, electrical, mechanical), Nursing

City University of New York York College
94-20 Guy R. Brewer Blvd., Jamaica 11451-0001
Type: Public, state/local, four-year
System: City University of New York System
Degrees: B　　　　　　　　　　　　*Enroll:* 4,326
URL: http://www.york.cuny.edu
Phone: (718) 262-2000　　　　*Calendar:* Sem. plan
Inst. Accred.: MSA-CHE (1967/2003)
Prog. Accred.: Nursing, Occupational Therapy, Social Work

Clarkson University
Potsdam 13699-5500
Type: Private, independent, four-year
Degrees: B, M, D   *Enroll:* 3,068
URL: http://www.clarkson.edu
Phone: (315) 268-6400   *Calendar:* Sem. plan
Inst. Accred.: MSA-CHE (1927/2003)
Prog. Accred.: Business (AACSB), Engineering (aerospace, chemical, civil, computer, electrical, mechanical), Physical Therapy

Clinton Community College
136 Clinton Point Dr., Plattsburgh 12901-9573
Type: Public, state/local, two-year
System: State University of New York Office of Community Colleges
Degrees: A   *Enroll:* 1,645
URL: http://clintoncc.suny.edu
Phone: (518) 562-4200   *Calendar:* Sem. plan
Inst. Accred.: MSA-CHE (1975/2002)
Prog. Accred.: Nursing

Cold Spring Harbor Laboratory
PO Box 100, One Bungtown Rd., Cold Spring Harbor 11724-0100
Type: Private, independent, four-year
Degrees: D
URL: http://www.cshl.org
Phone: (516) 367-8397
Inst. Accred.: NYBOR (1998/2001)

Colgate Rochester Crozer Divinity School
1100 South Goodman St., Rochester 14620
Type: Private, independent, four-year
Degrees: M, D   *Enroll:* 101
URL: http://www.crcds.edu
Phone: (716) 271-1320   *Calendar:* Sem. plan
Inst. Accred.: ATS (1938/2003)

Colgate University
13 Oak Dr., Hamilton 13346-1366
Type: Private, independent, four-year
Degrees: B, M   *Enroll:* 2,782
URL: http://www.colgate.edu
Phone: (315) 228-1000   *Calendar:* Sem. plan
Inst. Accred.: MSA-CHE (1921/2003)

College of Mount Saint Vincent
6301 Riverdale Ave., Riverdale 10471
Type: Private, independent, four-year
Degrees: A, B, M   *Enroll:* 1,328
URL: http://www.cmsv.edu
Phone: (718) 405-3200   *Calendar:* Sem. plan
Inst. Accred.: MSA-CHE (1921/2002)
Prog. Accred.: Business (ACBSP), Nursing, Nursing Education

The College of New Rochelle
29 Castle Place, New Rochelle 10805-2339
Type: Private, independent, four-year
Degrees: B, M   *Enroll:* 5,351
URL: http://www.cnr.edu
Phone: (914) 632-5300   *Calendar:* Sem. plan
Inst. Accred.: MSA-CHE (1921/2002)
Prog. Accred.: Nursing, Nursing Education, Social Work

Brooklyn Campus
1368 Fulton St., Brooklyn 11216
Phone: (718) 638-2500

Co-op City Campus
755 Co-Op City Blvd., Bronx 10475
Phone: (718) 320-0300

DC 37 Campus
125 Barclay St., New York 10007
Phone: (212) 815-1710

New York Theological Seminary Campus
5 West 29th St., 7th Flr., New York 10001
Phone: (212) 689-6208

Rosa Parks Campus
144 West 125th St., New York 10024
Phone: (212) 662-7500

South Bronx Campus
332 East 149th St., Bronx 10451
Phone: (718) 665-1310

The College of Saint Rose
432 Western Ave., Albany 12203-1490
Type: Private, independent, four-year
Degrees: B, M   *Enroll:* 3,795
URL: http://www.strose.edu
Phone: (518) 454-5111   *Calendar:* Sem. plan
Inst. Accred.: MSA-CHE (1928/2004)
Prog. Accred.: Art, Business (ACBSP), Music, Social Work, Speech-Language Pathology

The College of Westchester
PO Box 710, 325 Central Park Ave., White Plains 10602
Type: Private, independent, two-year
Degrees: A   *Enroll:* 940
URL: http://www.wbi.org
Phone: (914) 948-4442   *Calendar:* Qtr. plan
Inst. Accred.: MSA-CHE (2003)

Columbia University in the City of New York
2960 Broadway, New York 10027-6902
Type: Private, independent, four-year
Degrees: B, M, P, D   *Enroll:* 19,467
URL: http://www.columbia.edu
Phone: (212) 854-1754   *Calendar:* Sem. plan
Inst. Accred.: MSA-CHE (1921/2001)
Prog. Accred.: Advanced Education in General Dentistry,
Business (AACSB), Combined Prosthodontic/Maxillofacial
Prosthetics, Combined Prosthodontics, Dental Assisting,
Dentistry, Dietetics (internship), Endodontics,
Engineering (chemical, civil, electrical, environmental/
sanitary, industrial, mechanical), General Dentistry,
Journalism, Law, Maxillofacial Prosthetics, Medicine,
Nurse (Midwifery), Nurse Anesthesia Education, Nursing,
Occupational Therapy, Orthodontic and Dentofacial
Orthopedics, Pediatric Dentistry, Periodontics, Physical
Therapy, Planning, Public Health, Social Work

Columbia-Greene Community College
4400 Route 23, Hudson 12534-9447
Type: Public, state, two-year
System: State University of New York Office of
Community Colleges
Degrees: A   *Enroll:* 1,211
URL: http://www.sunycgcc.edu
Phone: (518) 828-4181   *Calendar:* Sem. plan
Inst. Accred.: MSA-CHE (1975/2001)
Prog. Accred.: Nursing

Concordia College New York
171 White Plains Rd., Bronxville 10708-1998
Type: Private, Lutheran Church-Missouri Synod, four-year
System: Concordia University System
Degrees: A, B   *Enroll:* 598
URL: http://www.concordia-ny.edu
Phone: (914) 337-9300   *Calendar:* Sem. plan
Inst. Accred.: MSA-CHE (1941/2001)
Prog. Accred.: Social Work

The Cooper Union for the Advancement of Science and Art
30 Cooper Square, New York 10003
Type: Private, independent, four-year
Degrees: B, M   *Enroll:* 932
URL: http://www.cooper.edu
Phone: (212) 353-4100   *Calendar:* Sem. plan
Inst. Accred.: MSA-CHE (1946/2003)
Prog. Accred.: Art, Engineering (chemical, civil, electrical,
mechanical)

Cornell University
Ithaca 14853
Type: Private, independent, four-year
Degrees: B, M, P, D   *Enroll:* 19,595
URL: http://www.cornell.edu
Phone: (607) 255-2000   *Calendar:* Sem. plan
Inst. Accred.: MSA-CHE (1921/2001)
Prog. Accred.: Business (AACSB), Dietetics (internship),
Engineering (bioengineering, chemical, civil, electrical,
engineering management, engineering physics/science,
materials, mechanical), Health Services Administration,
Interior Design, Landscape Architecture, Law, Medical
Assisting (AMA), Medicine, Physician Assistant,
Planning, Psychology Internship, Surgeon Assisting,
Veterinary Medicine

College of Agriculture and Life Sciences
260 Roberts Hall, Ithaca 14853
Phone: (607) 255-2036

New York State College of Human Ecology
Ithaca 14853-4401
Phone: (607) 255-2138

New York State College of Veterinary Medicine
Ithaca 14853-6401
Phone: (607) 253-3700

New York State School of Industrial and Labor Relations
Ithaca 14853-1296
Phone: (607) 255-2222

Weill Cornell Campus
1300 York Ave., New York 10021-4805
Phone: (914) 682-9100
Prog. Accred: Clinical Pastoral Education (ACPEI),
General Practice Residency, Oral and Maxillofacial
Surgery

Corning Community College
1 Academic Dr., Corning 14830
Type: Public, state/local, two-year
System: State University of New York Office of
Community Colleges
Degrees: A   *Enroll:* 3,294
URL: http://www.corning-cc.edu
Phone: (607) 962-9222   *Calendar:* Sem. plan
Inst. Accred.: MSA-CHE (1964/2005)
Prog. Accred.: Nursing

Culinary Institute of America
1946 Campus Dr., Hyde Park 12538-1499
Type: Private, independent, four-year
Degrees: A, B   *Enroll:* 2,451
URL: http://www.ciachef.edu
Phone: (845) 452-9600
Inst. Accred.: ACCSCT (1983/2004), MSA-CHE (2002)

The Greystone Campus
2555 Main St., St. Helena, CA 94754-9504
Phone: (914) 452-9600

D'Youville College
320 Porter Ave., Buffalo 14201-1084
Type: Private, independent, four-year
Degrees: B, M, P, D   *Enroll:* 2,115
URL: http://www.dyc.edu
Phone: (716) 881-3200   *Calendar:* Sem. plan
Inst. Accred.: MSA-CHE (1928/2005)
Prog. Accred.: Dietetics (coordinated), Nursing, Nursing
Education, Occupational Therapy, Physical Therapy,
Physician Assistant

Daemen College
4380 Main St., Amherst 14226-3592
Type: Private, independent, four-year
Degrees: B, M, P, D   *Enroll:* 1,886
URL: http://www.daemen.edu
Phone: (716) 839-3600   *Calendar:* Sem. plan
Inst. Accred.: MSA-CHE (1956/2001)
Prog. Accred.: Nursing, Physical Therapy, Physician
Assistant, Social Work

Darkei No'am Rabbinical College
2822 Ave. J, Brooklyn 11210
Type: Private, independent, four-year
Degrees: Rabbinic   *Enroll:* 57
Phone: (718) 338-6464   *Calendar:* Sem. plan
Inst. Accred.: AARTS (1983/2000)

Davis College
400 Riverside Dr., Johnson City 13790
Type: Private, independent, four-year
Degrees: A, B   *Enroll:* 308
URL: http://www.davisny.edu
Phone: (607) 729-1581   *Calendar:* Sem. plan
Inst. Accred.: ABHE (1985/1996), MSA-CHE (2005)

DeVry Institute of Technology
3020 Thomson Ave., Long Island City 11101-3051
Type: Private, proprietary, four-year
System: DeVry University
Degrees: A, B   *Enroll:* 1,621
URL: http://www.ny.devry.edu
Phone: (718) 269-4200   *Calendar:* Sem. plan
Inst. Accred.: NCA-HLC (2002, *Indirect accreditation
through DeVry University, Oakbrook Terrace, IL*)

Dominican College of Blauvelt
470 Western Hwy., Orangeburg 10956
Type: Private, independent, four-year
Degrees: A, B, M   *Enroll:* 1,114
URL: http://www.dc.edu
Phone: (845) 359-7800   *Calendar:* Sem. plan
Inst. Accred.: MSA-CHE (1972/2002)
Prog. Accred.: Nursing, Nursing Education, Occupational
Therapy, Physical Therapy, Social Work

Dowling College
Idle Hour Blvd., Oakdale 11769-1999
Type: Private, independent, four-year
Degrees: B, M, D   *Enroll:* 4,319
URL: http://www.dowling.edu
Phone: (631) 244-3000   *Calendar:* 4-1-4 plan
Inst. Accred.: MSA-CHE (1971/2003)

Dutchess Community College
53 Pendell Rd., Poughkeepsie 12601-1595
Type: Public, state/local, two-year
System: State University of New York Office of
Community Colleges
Degrees: A   *Enroll:* 5,125
URL: http://www.sunydutchess.edu
Phone: (845) 431-8000   *Calendar:* Sem. plan
Inst. Accred.: MSA-CHE (1964/2005)
Prog. Accred.: Clinical Lab Technology, Nursing

Fishkill Campus
Southern Dutchess Extension Site, Blodgett House,
Fishkill 12524
Phone: (914) 896-5775

Poughkeepsie Campus
Martha Lawrence Extension Site, Spackenhill Rd.,
Poughkeepsie 12603
Phone: (914) 462-0063

Southern Dutchess Extention Site
Hollowbrook Park, Bldg. # 4, Myers Corners Rd.,
Wappingers Falls 12590
Phone: (914) 298-0755

Elmira Business Institute
Langdon Plaza, 303 North Main St., Elmira 14901
Type: Private, proprietary, two-year
Degrees: A
URL: http://www.ebi-college.com
Phone: (607) 733-7177   *Calendar:* Sem. plan
Inst. Accred.: ACICS (1969/2004)

Vestal Campus
Vestal Executive Park, 4100 Vestal Rd., Vestal 13850
Phone: (607) 729-8915

Elmira College
One Park Place, Elmira 14901
Type: Private, independent, four-year
Degrees: A, B, M   *Enroll:* 1,476
URL: http://www.elmira.edu
Phone: (607) 735-1800
Inst. Accred.: MSA-CHE (1921/2000)
Prog. Accred.: Nursing

Erie Community College City Campus
121 Ellicott St., Buffalo 14203
Type: Public, state/local, two-year
System: State University of New York Office of
Community Colleges
Degrees: A   *Enroll:* 1,751
URL: http://www.ecc.edu
Phone: (716) 851-1200   *Calendar:* Sem. plan
Inst. Accred.: MSA-CHE (1981/2001, Probation)
Prog. Accred.: Business (ACBSP), Health Information
Technician, Medical Assisting (AMA), Nursing, Radiation
Therapy, Respiratory Therapy

Orchard Park Campus
S-4041 Southwestern Blvd., Orchard Park 14127-
2199
Phone: (716) 648-5400
Prog. Accred: Dental Laboratory Technology

Williamsville Campus
6205 Main St., Williamsville 14221-7095
Phone: (716) 634-0800
Prog. Accred: Clinical Lab Technology, Dental Hygiene,
Engineering Technology (civil/construction, electrical,
mechanical), Health Information Technician, Medical
Assisting (AMA), Occupational Therapy Assisting,
Ophthalmic Lab Technology, Opticianry, Respiratory
Therapy

Excelsior College
7 Columbia Circle, Albany 12203-5159
Type: Private, independent, four-year
Degrees: A, B, M   *Enroll:* 10,317
URL: http://www.excelsior.edu
Phone: (518) 464-8500
Inst. Accred.: MSA-CHE (1977/2002)
Prog. Accred.: Engineering Technology (electrical,
nuclear), Nursing

Fashion Institute of Technology
Seventh Ave. at 27th St., New York 10001-5992
Type: Public, state/local, four-year
System: State University of New York Office of
Community Colleges
Degrees: A, B, M   *Enroll:* 8,296
URL: http://www.fitnyc.suny.edu
Phone: (212) 217-7999   *Calendar:* Sem. plan
Inst. Accred.: MSA-CHE (1957/2002)
Prog. Accred.: Art, Interior Design

Finger Lakes Community College
4355 Lake Shore Dr., Canandaigua 14424
Type: Public, state/local, two-year
System: State University of New York Office of
Community Colleges
Degrees: A   *Enroll:* 3,268
URL: http://www.flcc.edu
Phone: (585) 394-3500   *Calendar:* Sem. plan
Inst. Accred.: MSA-CHE (1977/2002)
Prog. Accred.: Nursing

Five Towns College
305 North Service Rd., Dix Hills 11746-5871
Type: Private, proprietary, four-year
Degrees: A, B, M   *Enroll:* 1,098
URL: http://www.fivetowns.edu
Phone: (631) 424-7000   *Calendar:* Sem. plan
Inst. Accred.: MSA-CHE (1988/2001)

Fordham University
441 East Fordham Rd., Bronx 10458
Type: Private, independent, four-year
Degrees: B, M, P, D   *Enroll:* 11,930
URL: http://www.fordham.edu
Phone: (718) 817-1000   *Calendar:* Sem. plan
Inst. Accred.: MSA-CHE (1921/2000)
Prog. Accred.: Business (AACSB), Clinical Psychology,
Counseling Psychology, Law, School Psychology, Social
Work, Teacher Education (NCATE)

Marymount College of Fordham University
100 Marymount Ave., Tarrytown 10591-3796
Phone: (914) 631-3200
Prog. Accred: Social Work

Fulton-Montgomery Community College
2805 State Hwy. 67, Johnstown 12095-3790
Type: Public, state/local, two-year
System: State University of New York Office of
Community Colleges
Degrees: A   *Enroll:* 1,561
URL: http://www.fmcc.suny.edu
Phone: (518) 762-4651   *Calendar:* Sem. plan
Inst. Accred.: MSA-CHE (1969/2001)

The General Theological Seminary
175 Ninth Ave., New York 10011-4977
Type: Private, Episcopal Church, four-year
Degrees: M, D   *Enroll:* 148
URL: http://www.gts.edu
Phone: (212) 243-5150   *Calendar:* Sem. plan
Inst. Accred.: ATS (1938/2004)

Genesee Community College
One College Rd., Batavia 14020-9704
Type: Public, state/local, two-year
System: State University of New York Office of
Community Colleges
Degrees: A   *Enroll:* 3,859
URL: http://www.genesee.suny.edu
Phone: (585) 343-0055   *Calendar:* Sem. plan
Inst. Accred.: MSA-CHE (1971/2002)
Prog. Accred.: Nursing, Occupational Therapy Assisting,
Physical Therapy Assisting, Respiratory Therapy

Globe Institute of Technology
291 Broadway, Second Flr., New York 10007-1814
Type: Private, proprietary, four-year
Degrees: A, B   *Enroll:* 818
URL: http://www.globe.edu
Phone: (212) 349-4330   *Calendar:* Sem. plan
Inst. Accred.: NYBOR (1996/2002)

The Graduate College of Union University
Lamont House, 807 Union St., Schenectady 12308
Type: Private, independent, four-year
System: Union University
Degrees: M
URL: http://www.gcuu.edu
Phone: (518) 388-6148   *Calendar:* Tri. plan
Inst. Accred.: NYBOR (2004)

Graduate School of Figurative Art of the New York Academy of Art
111 Franklin St., New York 10013-2911
Type: Private, independent, four-year
Degrees: M
URL: http://www.nyaa.edu/gschool.html
Phone: (212) 966-0300   *Calendar:* Sem. plan
Inst. Accred.: NYBOR (1989/2002)

Hamilton College
198 College Hill Rd., Clinton 13323
Type: Private, independent, four-year
Degrees: B   *Enroll:* 1,784
URL: http://www.hamilton.edu
Phone: (315) 859-4011   *Calendar:* 4-1-4 plan
Inst. Accred.: MSA-CHE (1921/2001)

Hartwick College
One Hartwick Dr., PO Box 4040, Oneonta 13820-4020
Type: Private, independent, four-year
Degrees: B   *Enroll:* 1,433
URL: http://www.hartwick.edu
Phone: (607) 431-4000   *Calendar:* 4-1-4 plan
Inst. Accred.: MSA-CHE (1949/1999)
Prog. Accred.: Art, Music, Nursing, Nursing Education

Hebrew Union College—Jewish Institute of Religion
One West Fourth St., New York 10012-1186
Type: Private, Union for Reform Judaism, four-year
System: Hebrew Union College—Jewish Institute of Religion Central Office
Degrees: M, P, D   *Enroll:* 136
URL: http://www.huc.edu
Phone: (212) 674-5300   *Calendar:* Sem. plan
Inst. Accred.: MSA-CHE (1960/2002)

Helene Fuld College of Nursing
1879 Madison Ave., New York 10035
Type: Private, independent, two-year
Degrees: A   *Enroll:* 224
URL: http://www.helenefuld.edu
Phone: (212) 423-2700   *Calendar:* Qtr. plan
Inst. Accred.: MSA-CHE (1988/2003)
Prog. Accred.: Nursing

Herkimer County Community College
Reservoir Rd., Herkimer 13350-9987
Type: Public, state/local, two-year
System: State University of New York Office of Community Colleges
Degrees: A   *Enroll:* 2,563
URL: http://www.hccc.suny.edu
Phone: (315) 866-0300   *Calendar:* Sem. plan
Inst. Accred.: MSA-CHE (1972/2003)
Prog. Accred.: Physical Therapy Assisting

Hilbert College
5200 South Park Ave., Hamburg 14075-1597
Type: Private, independent, four-year
Degrees: A, B   *Enroll:* 855
URL: http://www.hilbert.edu
Phone: (716) 649-7900   *Calendar:* Sem. plan
Inst. Accred.: MSA-CHE (1976/2001)

Hobart and William Smith Colleges
337 Pulteney St., Geneva 14456
Type: Private, independent, four-year
Degrees: B, M   *Enroll:* 1,869
URL: http://www.hws.edu
Phone: (315) 781-3000   *Calendar:* Sem. plan
Inst. Accred.: MSA-CHE (1921/2004)

Hofstra University
100 Hofstra University, Hempstead 11549
Type: Private, independent, four-year
Degrees: A, B, M, P, D   *Enroll:* 11,595
URL: http://www.hofstra.edu
Phone: (516) 463-6600   *Calendar:* Sem. plan
Inst. Accred.: MSA-CHE (1940/1999)
Prog. Accred.: Accounting, Athletic Training, Audiology, Business (AACSB), Combined Professional-Scientific Psychology, Engineering (electrical, engineering physics/science, mechanical), Journalism, Law, Physician Assistant, Rehabilitation Counseling, School Psychology, Speech-Language Pathology, Teacher Education (NCATE)

Houghton College
One Willard Ave., Houghton 14744
Type: Private, Wesleyan Church, four-year
Degrees: A, B, M   *Enroll:* 1,407
URL: http://www.houghton.edu
Phone: (585) 567-9200   *Calendar:* Sem. plan
Inst. Accred.: MSA-CHE (1935/2005)
Prog. Accred.: Music

Buffalo Suburban Campus
910 Union Rd., West Seneca 14224
Phone: (716) 674-6363

Hudson Valley Community College
80 Vandenburgh Ave., Troy 12180
Type: Public, state/local, two-year
System: State University of New York Office of
   Community Colleges
Degrees: A   *Enroll:* 8,138
URL: http://www.hvcc.edu
Phone: (518) 629-4822   *Calendar:* Sem. plan
Inst. Accred.: MSA-CHE (1969/2004)
Prog. Accred.: Clinical Lab Technology, Construction
   Education, Dental Hygiene, Diagnostic Medical
   Sonography, Engineering Technology (civil/construction,
   electrical, mechanical), Funeral Service Education
   (Mortuary Science), Nursing, Radiography, Respiratory
   Therapy

Institute of Design and Construction
141 Willoughby St., Brooklyn 11210-1919
Type: Private, independent, two-year
Degrees: A   *Enroll:* 147
Phone: (718) 855-3661
Inst. Accred.: NYBOR (1972/2001)

Interboro Institute
450 West 56th St., New York 10019-3697
Type: Private, proprietary, two-year
Degrees: A   *Enroll:* 2,508
URL: http://www.interboro.com
Phone: (212) 399-0091   *Calendar:* Tri. plan
Inst. Accred.: NYBOR (1972/2001)
Prog. Accred.: Ophthalmic Lab Technology, Opticianry

Iona College
715 North Ave., New Rochelle 10801-1890
Type: Private, independent, four-year
Degrees: B, M   *Enroll:* 3,593
URL: http://www.iona.edu
Phone: (914) 633-2000   *Calendar:* Sem. plan
Inst. Accred.: MSA-CHE (1952/2003)
Prog. Accred.: Business (AACSB), Journalism, Marriage
   and Family Therapy, Nursing, Practical Nursing, Social
   Work

Manhattan Campus
425 West 33rd St., New York 10001
Phone: (212) 714-9444

Rockland Campus
One Dutch Hill Rd., Orangeburg 10962
Phone: (914) 359-2252

Ithaca College
300 Job Hall, Ithaca 14850-7001
Type: Private, independent, four-year
Degrees: B, M, D   *Enroll:* 6,396
URL: http://www.ithaca.edu
Phone: (607) 274-3011   *Calendar:* Sem. plan
Inst. Accred.: MSA-CHE (1955/2002)
Prog. Accred.: Athletic Training, Audiology, Business
   (AACSB), Music, Occupational Therapy, Physical
   Therapy, Recreation and Leisure Services, Speech-
   Language Pathology, Theatre

Jamestown Business College
PO Box 429, 7 Fairmont Ave., Jamestown 14702-0429
Type: Private, proprietary, two-year
Degrees: A   *Enroll:* 323
URL: http://www.jbcny.org
Phone: (716) 664-5100   *Calendar:* Qtr. plan
Inst. Accred.: MSA-CHE (2001)

Jamestown Community College
525 Falconer St., PO Box 20, Jamestown 14702-0020
Type: Public, state/local, two-year
System: State University of New York Office of
   Community Colleges
Degrees: A   *Enroll:* 2,898
URL: http://www.sunyjcc.edu
Phone: (716) 665-5220   *Calendar:* Sem. plan
Inst. Accred.: MSA-CHE (1956/2001)
Prog. Accred.: Nursing, Occupational Therapy Assisting

Cattaraugus County Campus
244 North Union St., Olean 14760
Phone: (716) 372-1661

Jefferson Community College
1220 Coffeen St., Watertown 13601
Type: Public, state/local, two-year
System: State University of New York Office of
   Community Colleges
Degrees: A   *Enroll:* 2,410
URL: http://www.sunyjefferson.edu
Phone: (315) 786-2200   *Calendar:* Sem. plan
Inst. Accred.: MSA-CHE (1969/2000)
Prog. Accred.: Nursing

The Jewish Theological Seminary
3080 Broadway, New York 10027-4649
Type: Private, independent, four-year
Degrees: B, M, P, D   *Enroll:* 539
URL: http://www.jtsa.edu
Phone: (212) 678-8000   *Calendar:* Sem. plan
Inst. Accred.: MSA-CHE (1954/2001)

The Juilliard School
60 Lincoln Center Plaza, New York 10023-6588
Type: Private, independent, four-year
Degrees: B, M, D   *Enroll:* 888
URL: http://www.juilliard.edu
Phone: (212) 799-5000   *Calendar:* Sem. plan
Inst. Accred.: MSA-CHE (1956/2003)

Katharine Gibbs School
50 West 40th St., First Flr., New York 10138-1347
Type: Private, proprietary, two-year
System: Career Education Corporation
Degrees: A   *Enroll:* 3,432
URL: http://www.gibbsny.com
Phone: (212) 867-9300
Inst. Accred.: ACICS (1967/2004)

Katharine Gibbs School
320 South Service Rd., Melville 11747
Type: Private, proprietary, two-year
System: Career Education Corporation
Degrees: A   *Enroll:* 837
URL: http://www.gibbsmelville.edu
Phone: (631) 293-2460   *Calendar:* Qtr. plan
Inst. Accred.: ACICS (1973/2003)

Norristown Campus
2501 Monroe Blvd., Norristown, PA 19403
Phone: (610) 676-0500

Kehilath Yakov Rabbinical Seminary
638 Bedford Avneue, Brooklyn 11211-8007
Type: Private, independent, four-year
Degrees: Rabbinic   *Enroll:* 105
Phone: (718) 963-3940   *Calendar:* Sem. plan
Inst. Accred.: AARTS (1980/2002)

Keuka College
141 Central Ave., Keuka Park 14478
Type: Private, independent, four-year
Degrees: B, M   *Enroll:* 1,216
URL: http://www.keuka.edu
Phone: (315) 279-5000   *Calendar:* Sem. plan
Inst. Accred.: MSA-CHE (1927/2003)
Prog. Accred.: Nursing, Occupational Therapy, Social
Work

The King's College
Empire State Bldg., 350 Fifth Ave., Ste. 1500, New York
10118
Type: Private, independent, four-year
Degrees: A, B   *FTE Enroll:* 392
URL: http://www.tkc.edu
Phone: (212) 659-7200   *Calendar:* Sem. plan
Inst. Accred.: NYBOR (1999)

Kol Yaakov Torah Center
29 West Maple Ave., PO Box 402, Monsey 10952
Type: Private, independent, four-year
Degrees: Rabbinic   *Enroll:* 17
Phone: (845) 425-3863   *Calendar:* Sem. plan
Inst. Accred.: AARTS (1984/2003)

Laboratory Institute of Merchandising
12 East 53rd St., New York 10022
Type: Private, proprietary, four-year
Degrees: A, B   *Enroll:* 488
URL: http://www.limcollege.edu
Phone: (212) 752-1530   *Calendar:* Sem. plan
Inst. Accred.: MSA-CHE (1977/2002)

Le Moyne College
1419 Salt Springs Rd., Syracuse 13214
Type: Private, independent, four-year
Degrees: B, M   *Enroll:* 2,761
URL: http://www.lemoyne.edu
Phone: (315) 445-4100   *Calendar:* Sem. plan
Inst. Accred.: MSA-CHE (1953/2001)
Prog. Accred.: Physician Assistant

Long Island Business Institute
6500 Jericho Turnpike, Commack 11725
Type: Private, proprietary, two-year
Degrees: A
URL: http://www.libi.edu
Phone: (631) 499-7100   *Calendar:* Qtr. plan
Inst. Accred.: ACICS (1978/2002)

Flushing Campus
37-12 Prince St., Flushing 11354
Phone: (718) 939-5100

Long Island University
700 Northern Blvd., Brookville 11548-1326
Type: Private, independent, four-year
Degrees: A, B, M, P, D   *FTE Enroll:* 12,975
URL: http://www.liu.edu
Phone: (516) 299-2501   *Calendar:* Sem. plan
Inst. Accred.: MSA-CHE (1955/2003)
Prog. Accred.: Business (AACSB), Dietetics (internship),
Librarianship, Radiography, Respiratory Therapy,
Speech-Language Pathology

Brentwood Campus
100 Second Ave., Brentwood 11717
Phone: (631) 273-5112

Brooklyn Campus
One University Plaza, Brooklyn 11201
Phone: (718) 488-1000
Prog. Accred: Clinical Psychology, Nursing, Nursing
Education, Occupational Therapy, Pharmacy, Physical
Therapy, Physician Assistant, Respiratory Therapy,
Social Work, Speech-Language Pathology

C.W. Post Campus
720 Northern Blvd., Brookville 11548-1300
Phone: (516) 299-2000
Prog. Accred: Business (AACSB), Clinical Lab Scientist,
Clinical Psychology, Counseling, Health Information
Administration, Nursing, Nursing Education, Public
Administration, Radiography, Social Work

Rockland Campus
70 Route 340, Orangeburg 10962
Phone: (845) 359-7200

Southampton Campus
239 Montauk Hwy, Southampton 11968
Phone: (631) 283-4000

Westchester Campus
735 Anderson Hill Rd., Purchase 10577-1400
Phone: (800) 472-3548

Machzikei Hadath Rabbinical College
5407 16th Ave., Brooklyn 11204
Type: Private, independent, four-year
Degrees: Talmudic   *Enroll:* 153
Phone: (718) 854-8777   *Calendar:* Sem. plan
Inst. Accred.: AARTS (1980/2003)

Manhattan College
Manhattan College Pkwy., Bronx 10471
Type: Private, independent, four-year
Degrees: B, M   *Enroll:* 2,928
URL: http://www.manhattan.edu
Phone: (718) 862-8000   *Calendar:* Sem. plan
Inst. Accred.: MSA-CHE (1921/2002)
Prog. Accred.: Engineering (chemical, civil, computer, electrical, environmental/sanitary, mechanical), Nuclear Medicine Technology

Manhattan School of Music
120 Claremont Ave., New York 10027-4698
Type: Private, independent, four-year
Degrees: B, M, D   *Enroll:* 802
URL: http://www.msmnyc.edu
Phone: (212) 749-2802   *Calendar:* Sem. plan
Inst. Accred.: MSA-CHE (1956/2003)

Manhattanville College
2900 Purchase St., Purchase 10577-2132
Type: Private, independent, four-year
Degrees: B, M   *Enroll:* 2,070
URL: http://www.mville.edu
Phone: (914) 694-2200   *Calendar:* Sem. plan
Inst. Accred.: MSA-CHE (1926/2000)

Maria College of Albany
700 New Scotland Ave., Albany 12208-1798
Type: Private, independent, two-year
Degrees: A   *Enroll:* 424
URL: http://www.mariacollege.edu
Phone: (518) 438-3111   *Calendar:* 4-1-4 plan
Inst. Accred.: MSA-CHE (1973/2003)
Prog. Accred.: Nursing, Occupational Therapy Assisting

Marist College
3399 North Rd., Poughkeepsie 12601-1387
Type: Private, independent, four-year
Degrees: B, M   *Enroll:* 4,828
URL: http://www.marist.edu
Phone: (845) 575-3000   *Calendar:* Sem. plan
Inst. Accred.: MSA-CHE (1964/2003)
Prog. Accred.: Business (AACSB), Clinical Lab Scientist, Social Work

Marymount Manhattan College
221 East 71st St., New York 10021-4597
Type: Private, independent, four-year
Degrees: B   *Enroll:* 1,829
URL: http://marymount.mmm.edu
Phone: (212) 517-0400   *Calendar:* Sem. plan
Inst. Accred.: MSA-CHE (1961/2002)

Medaille College
18 Agassiz Circle, Buffalo 14214-2695
Type: Private, independent, four-year
Degrees: A, B, M   *Enroll:* 2,092
URL: http://www.medaille.edu
Phone: (716) 884-3281   *Calendar:* Sem. plan
Inst. Accred.: MSA-CHE (1951/2003)
Prog. Accred.: Veterinary Technology

Amherst Campus ACCEI Program
400 Essjay Rd., Ste. 100, Center Pointe Corporate park, Williamsville 14221
Phone: (719) 631-1061

Mercy College
555 Broadway, Dobbs Ferry 10522-1189
Type: Private, independent, four-year
Degrees: A, B, M   *Enroll:* 7,072
URL: http://www.mercy.edu
Phone: (914) 693-4500   *Calendar:* Sem. plan
Inst. Accred.: MSA-CHE (1968/2004)
Prog. Accred.: Acupuncture, Nursing, Nursing Education, Occupational Therapy, Occupational Therapy Assisting, Physical Therapy, Physical Therapy Assisting, Physician Assistant, Social Work, Speech-Language Pathology, Veterinary Technology

Bronx Campus
50 Antin Place, Bronx 10462
Phone: (212) 798-8952

White Plains Campus
Martine Ave. and South Broadway, White Plains 10601
Phone: (914) 948-3666

Yorktown Campus
2651 Stang Blvd., Yorktown Heights 10598
Phone: (914) 245-6100

Mesivta of Eastern Parkway Rabbinical Seminary
510 Dahill Rd., Brooklyn 11218
Type: Private, independent, four-year
Degrees: Talmudic   *Enroll:* 53
Phone: (718) 438-1002   *Calendar:* Sem. plan
Inst. Accred.: AARTS (1980/2004)

Mesivta Tifereth Jerusalem of America
141 East Broadway, New York 10002
Type: Private, independent, four-year
Degrees: Talmudic   *Enroll:* 74
Phone: (212) 964-2830   *Calendar:* Sem. plan
Inst. Accred.: AARTS (1979/2000)

Mesivta Torah Vodaath Seminary
425 East 9th St., Brooklyn 11218
Type: Private, independent, four-year
Degrees: Talmudic   *Enroll:* 339
Phone: (718) 941-8000   *Calendar:* Sem. plan
Inst. Accred.: AARTS (1976/2000)

Metropolitan College of New York
75 Varick St., New York 10013-1919
Type: Private, independent, four-year
Degrees: A, B, M   *Enroll:* 1,565
URL: http://www.metropolitan.edu
Phone: (212) 343-1234   *Calendar:* Sem. plan
Inst. Accred.: MSA-CHE (1984/1999)

Mildred Elley
800 New Loudon Rd., Ste. 5120, Latham 12110
Type: Private, proprietary, two-year
Degrees: A   *Enroll:* 410
URL: http://www.mildred-elley.edu
Phone: (518) 786-0855   *Calendar:* Sem. plan
Inst. Accred.: ACICS (1982/2004)

Pittsfield Campus
St. Lukes Square, 505 East St., Pittsfield, MA 01201
Phone: (413) 499-8618

Mirrer Yeshiva
1795 Ocean Pkwy., Brooklyn 11223
Type: Private, independent, four-year
Degrees: Talmudic   *Enroll:* 338
Phone: (718) 645-0536   *Calendar:* Sem. plan
Inst. Accred.: AARTS (1975/2001)

Mohawk Valley Community College
1101 Sherman Dr., Utica 13501-5394
Type: Public, state/local, two-year
System: State University of New York Office of
   Community Colleges
Degrees: A   *Enroll:* 4,523
URL: http://www.mvcc.edu
Phone: (315) 792-5400   *Calendar:* Sem. plan
Inst. Accred.: MSA-CHE (1960/2003)
Prog. Accred.: Engineering Technology (civil/construction,
   electrical, mechanical, surveying), Health Information
   Technician, Nursing, Respiratory Therapy, Respiratory
   Therapy Technology

Rome Campus
1101 Floyd Ave., Rome 13440
Phone: (315) 339-3470

Molloy College
1000 Hempstead Ave., Rockville Centre 11571-5002
Type: Private, independent, four-year
Degrees: A, B, M   *Enroll:* 2,218
URL: http://www.molloy.edu
Phone: (516) 678-5000   *Calendar:* 4-1-4 plan
Inst. Accred.: MSA-CHE (1967/2004)
Prog. Accred.: Cardiovascular Technology, Health
   Information Technician, Nuclear Medicine Technology,
   Nursing, Nursing Education, Respiratory Therapy, Social
   Work

Monroe College
2501 Jerome Ave., Bronx 10468
Type: Private, independent, four-year
Degrees: A, B, M   *Enroll:* 3,701
URL: http://www.monroecollege.edu
Phone: (718) 933-6700   *Calendar:* Sem. plan
Inst. Accred.: MSA-CHE (1990/2005)

New Rochelle Campus
434 Main St., New Rochelle 10801
Phone: (914) 632-5400

Monroe Community College
1000 East Henrietta Rd., Rochester 14623
Type: Public, state/local, two-year
System: State University of New York Office of
   Community Colleges
Degrees: A   *Enroll:* 11,815
URL: http://www.monroecc.edu
Phone: (585) 292-2000   *Calendar:* Sem. plan
Inst. Accred.: MSA-CHE (1965/2001)
Prog. Accred.: Dental Assisting, Dental Hygiene,
   Engineering Technology (electrical), Health Information
   Technician, Nursing, Radiography

Damon City Center
228 East Main St., Rochester 14604
Phone: (716) 262-1610

Mount Saint Mary College
330 Powell Ave., Newburgh 12550
Type: Private, independent, four-year
Degrees: B, M   *Enroll:* 2,035
URL: http://www.msmc.edu
Phone: (845) 561-0800   *Calendar:* Sem. plan
Inst. Accred.: MSA-CHE (1968/2002)
Prog. Accred.: Nursing, Nursing Education

Nassau Community College
1 Education Dr., Garden City 11530
Type: Public, state/local, two-year
System: State University of New York Office of
   Community Colleges
Degrees: A   *Enroll:* 15,717
URL: http://www.ncc.edu
Phone: (516) 572-7205   *Calendar:* Sem. plan
Inst. Accred.: MSA-CHE (1967/2004)
Prog. Accred.: Engineering Technology (civil/construction,
   electrical), Funeral Service Education (Mortuary
   Science), Music, Nursing, Physical Therapy Assisting,
   Radiation Therapy, Radiography, Respiratory Therapy,
   Surgical Technology

Nazareth College of Rochester
4245 East Ave., Rochester 14618-3790
Type: Private, independent, four-year
Degrees: B, M   *Enroll:* 2,472
URL: http://www.naz.edu
Phone: (585) 389-2525   *Calendar:* Sem. plan
Inst. Accred.: MSA-CHE (1930/2001)
Prog. Accred.: Music, Nursing, Nursing Education,
   Physical Therapy, Social Work, Speech-Language
   Pathology

The New School
66 West 12th St., New York 10011
Type: Private, independent, four-year
Degrees: A, B, M, D   *Enroll:* 6,870
URL: http://www.newschool.edu
Phone: (212) 229-5600   *Calendar:* Sem. plan
Inst. Accred.: MSA-CHE (1960/2003)
Prog. Accred.: Clinical Psychology, Public Administration

Parsons School of Design—New York
66 Fifth Ave., New York 10011
Phone: (212) 229-8950
Prog. Accred: Art

Parsons School of Design—Paris, France
14 Rue Letellier, Paris, France 75015
Phone: 011 33 145 77 39 66

New York Career Institute
11 Park Place, New York 10007
Type: Private, proprietary, two-year
Degrees: A   *Enroll:* 552
URL: http://www.nyci.com
Phone: (212) 962-0002
Inst. Accred.: NYBOR (1982/2002)

New York Chiropractic College
2360 State Route 89, Seneca Falls 13148-0800
Type: Private, independent, four-year
Degrees: P   *Enroll:* 741
URL: http://www.nycc.edu
Phone: (315) 568-3000   *Calendar:* Tri. plan
Inst. Accred.: MSA-CHE (1985/2005)
Prog. Accred.: Chiropractic Education

New York College of Podiatric Medicine
53 East 124th St., New York 10035
Type: Private, independent, four-year
Degrees: P   *Enroll:* 291
URL: http://www.nycpm.edu
Phone: (212) 410-8000   *Calendar:* Sem. plan
Inst. Accred.: APMA (1923/2003)

New York Institute of Technology— Old Westbury
Northern Blvd., Old Westbury 11568-0170
Type: Private, independent, four-year
Degrees: A, B, M, P   *Enroll:* 4,892
URL: http://www.nyit.edu
Phone: (516) 686-7516   *Calendar:* Sem. plan
Inst. Accred.: MSA-CHE (1969/2003)
Prog. Accred.: Dietetics (internship), Engineering
  (electrical, mechanical), Engineering Technology
  (electrical, mechanical), Interior Design, Occupational
  Therapy, Osteopathy, Physical Therapy, Physician
  Assistant

Central Islip Campus
PO Box 9029, Central Islip 11722-9029
Phone: (516) 348-3000
Prog. Accred: Culinary Education

Manhattan Campus
1855 Broadway, New York 10023-7692
Phone: (212) 399-8300
Prog. Accred: Engineering (electrical), Engineering
  Technology (electrical)

New York Medical College
Administration Bldg., Valhalla 10595
Type: Private, independent, four-year
Degrees: M, P, D   *Enroll:* 1,113
URL: http://www.nymc.edu
Phone: (914) 594-4000
Inst. Accred.: MSA-CHE (1995/2005)
Prog. Accred.: Cytotechnology, General Practice
  Residency, Medicine, Oral and Maxillofacial Surgery,
  Physical Therapy, Public Health, Speech-Language
  Pathology

New York School of Interior Design
170 70th St., New York 10021-5110
Type: Private, independent, four-year
Degrees: A, B, M   *Enroll:* 364
URL: http://www.nysid.edu
Phone: (212) 472-1500   *Calendar:* 4-1-4 plan
Inst. Accred.: NASAD (1996/2002)
Prog. Accred.: Interior Design

New York Theological Seminary
475 Riverside Dr., Ste. 500, New York 10115
Type: Private, interdenominational, four-year
Degrees: M, D   *Enroll:* 234
URL: http://www.nyts.edu
Phone: (212) 870-1211   *Calendar:* Sem. plan
Inst. Accred.: ATS (1958/2004)

New York University
70 Washington Square South, New York 10012
Type: Private, independent, four-year
Degrees: A, B, M, P, D   *Enroll:* 32,299
URL: http://www.nyu.edu
Phone: (212) 998-1212   *Calendar:* Sem. plan
Inst. Accred.: MSA-CHE (1921/1999)
Prog. Accred.: Accounting, Advanced Education in
General Dentistry, Business (AACSB), Clinical Pastoral
Education (ACPEI), Clinical Psychology, Combined
Prosthodontics, Counseling Psychology, Dental
Assisting, Dental Hygiene, Dentistry, Diagnostic Medical
Sonography, Dietetics (internship), Endodontics, General
Dentistry, Health Services Administration, Journalism,
Law, Medicine, Montessori Teacher Education, Nurse
(Midwifery), Nursing, Occupational Therapy, Oral and
Maxillofacial Surgery, Orthodontic and Dentofacial
Orthopedics, Pediatric Dentistry, Periodontics, Physical
Therapy, Physical Therapy Assisting, Planning,
Psychology Internship, Public Administration, Public
Health, Rehabilitation Counseling, Respiratory Therapy,
School Psychology, Social Work, Speech-Language
Pathology, Surgical Technology

Ehrenkranz School of Social Work
125 Route 340, Room 208 The Village, Sparkill 10976
Phone: (845) 359-6084

Medical School Campus
One Gustave L. Levy Place, New York 10029-6574
Phone: (212) 241-6500
Prog. Accred: General Practice Residency, Medicine,
Oral and Maxillofacial Surgery

Stern School of Business
2900 Purchase St., Purchase 10577
Phone: (914) 323-5333

Niagara County Community College
3111 Saunders Settlement Rd., Sanborn 14132-9460
Type: Public, state/local, two-year
System: State University of New York Office of
Community Colleges
Degrees: A   *Enroll:* 3,984
URL: http://www.niagaracc.suny.edu
Phone: (716) 614-6222   *Calendar:* Sem. plan
Inst. Accred.: MSA-CHE (1970/2001)
Prog. Accred.: Electroneurodiagnostic Technology,
Medical Assisting (AMA), Nursing, Physical Therapy
Assisting, Radiography, Surgical Technology

Niagara University
Niagara University 14109-9999
Type: Private, independent, four-year
Degrees: A, B, M   *Enroll:* 3,273
URL: http://www.niagara.edu
Phone: (716) 285-1212   *Calendar:* Sem. plan
Inst. Accred.: MSA-CHE (1922/2002)
Prog. Accred.: Business (AACSB), Nursing, Social Work,
Teacher Education (NCATE)

North Country Community College
20 Winona Ave., PO Box 89, Saranac Lake 12983
Type: Public, state/local, two-year
System: State University of New York Office of
Community Colleges
Degrees: A   *Enroll:* 1,095
URL: http://www.nccc.edu
Phone: (518) 891-2915   *Calendar:* Sem. plan
Inst. Accred.: MSA-CHE (1975/2005)
Prog. Accred.: Radiography

Malone Campus
College Ave., Malone 12953
Phone: (518) 483-4550

Ticonderoga Campus
Montcalm St., Ticonderoga 12883
Phone: (518) 585-4454

North Shore Long Island Jewish Graduate School of Molecular Medicine
350 Community Dr., Manhasset 11030-3828
Type: Private, independent, four-year
Degrees: D
URL: http://www.northshorelij.com
Phone: (718) 470-7553   *Calendar:* Sem. plan
Inst. Accred.: NYBOR (1994/2002)

Northeastern Seminary
2265 Westside Dr., Rochester 14624
Type: Private, independent, four-year
Degrees: M
URL: http://www.nes.edu
Phone: (585) 594-6800   *Calendar:* Sem. plan
Inst. Accred.: NYBOR (1998/2002)
Prog. Accred.: Graduate Scoial Work

Nyack College
One South Blvd., Nyack 10960-3698
Type: Private, Christian Church Missionary Alliance, four-year
Degrees: A, B, M, P   *Enroll:* 2,354
URL: http://www.nyackcollege.edu
Phone: (845) 358-1710   *Calendar:* Sem. plan
Inst. Accred.: ATS (1990/2000), MSA-CHE (1962/2005)
Prog. Accred.: Music

Alliance Theological Seminary
350 North Highland Ave., Nyack 10960-1416
Phone: (845) 353-2020

Manhattan Center Campus
335 Broadway, New York 10013
Phone: (212) 625-0500

Ohr HaMeir Theological Seminary
Furnace Woods Rd., PO Box 2130, Cortland Manor 10567
Type: Private, independent, four-year
Degrees: Talmudic   *Enroll:* 81
Phone: (914) 736-1500   *Calendar:* Sem. plan
Inst. Accred.: AARTS (1979/2001)

Ohr Somayach-Tanenbaum Educational Center
PO Box 334, Monsey 10952
Type: Private, independent, four-year
Degrees: Talmudic　　　　　*Enroll:* 125
URL: http://www.ohrsomayach.edu
Phone: (845) 425-1370　　　　　*Calendar:* Tri. plan
Inst. Accred.: AARTS (1984/2003)

Olean Business Institute
301 North Union St., Olean 14760
Type: Private, proprietary, two-year
Degrees: A　　　　　*Enroll:* 102
URL: http://www.oleanbusinessinstitute.net
Phone: (716) 372-7978　　　　　*Calendar:* Sem. plan
Inst. Accred.: ACICS (1969/1999)

Onondaga Community College
4941 Onondaga Rd., Syracuse 13215
Type: Public, state/local, two-year
System: State University of New York Office of
　Community Colleges
Degrees: A　　　　　*Enroll:* 5,892
URL: http://www.sunyocc.edu
Phone: (315) 498-2622　　　　　*Calendar:* Sem. plan
Inst. Accred.: MSA-CHE (1972/2003)
Prog. Accred.: Dental Hygiene, Engineering Technology
　(computer, electrical), Health Information Technician,
　Nursing, Physical Therapy Assisting, Respiratory
　Therapy, Respiratory Therapy Technology, Surgical
　Technology

Orange County Community College
115 South St., Middletown 10940
Type: Public, state/local, two-year
System: State University of New York Office of
　Community Colleges
Degrees: A　　　　　*Enroll:* 4,055
URL: http://www.sunyorange.edu
Phone: (845) 344-6222　　　　　*Calendar:* Sem. plan
Inst. Accred.: MSA-CHE (1962/2004)
Prog. Accred.: Business (ACBSP), Clinical Lab Technology,
　Dental Hygiene, Nursing, Occupational Therapy
　Assisting, Phlebotomy, Physical Therapy Assisting,
　Radiography

Pace University
One Pace Plaza, New York 10038
Type: Private, independent, four-year
Degrees: A, B, M, P, D　　　　　*Enroll:* 10,468
URL: http://www.pace.edu
Phone: (212) 346-1200　　　　　*Calendar:* Sem. plan
Inst. Accred.: MSA-CHE (1957/2003)
Prog. Accred.: Business (AACSB), Combined Professional-
　Scientific Psychology, Computer Science, Nursing
　Education, Physician Assistant, Psychology Internship

Pleasantville/Briarcliff Campus
861 Bedford Rd., Pleasantville 10570
Phone: (914) 773-3200
Prog. Accred: Nursing, Nursing Education

White Plains Campus
78 North Broadway, White Plains 10603
Phone: (914) 422-4000
Prog. Accred: Law

Pacific College of Oriental Medicine—New York
915 Broadway, 3rd Flr., New York 10010
Type: Private, proprietary, four-year
Degrees: M
URL: http://www.pacificcollege.edu
Phone: (212) 982-3456
Inst. Accred.: ACAOM (1995/2004)

Paul Smith's College of Arts and Sciences
PO Box 265, Paul Smiths 12970-0265
Type: Private, independent, four-year
Degrees: A, B　　　　　*Enroll:* 846
URL: http://www.paulsmiths.edu
Phone: (518) 327-6231　　　　　*Calendar:* Tri. plan
Inst. Accred.: MSA-CHE (1977/2003)
Prog. Accred.: Culinary Education, Engineering
　Technology (surveying)

Plaza College
74-09 37th Ave., Jackson Heights 11372-6340
Type: Private, proprietary, two-year
Degrees: A　　　　　*Enroll:* 747
URL: http://www.plazacollege.edu
Phone: (718) 779-1430　　　　　*Calendar:* Qtr. plan
Inst. Accred.: MSA-CHE (2002), NYBOR (1982/2002)

Polytechnic University
6 MetroTech Center, Brooklyn 11201
Type: Private, independent, four-year
Degrees: B, M, D　　　　　*Enroll:* 2,343
URL: http://www.poly.edu
Phone: (718) 260-3600　　　　　*Calendar:* Sem. plan
Inst. Accred.: MSA-CHE (1927/2003)
Prog. Accred.: Computer Science, Engineering (chemical,
　civil, computer, electrical, mechanical)

Long Island Center
Route 110, Farmingdale 11735
Phone: (516) 755-4400

Westchester Graduate Center
36 Saw Mill River Rd., Hawthorne 10532
Phone: (914) 347-6940

Pratt Institute
200 Willoughby Ave., Brooklyn 11205
Type: Private, independent, four-year
Degrees: A, B, M　　　　　*Enroll:* 4,204
URL: http://www.pratt.edu
Phone: (718) 636-3600　　　　　*Calendar:* Sem. plan
Inst. Accred.: MSA-CHE (1950/2005)
Prog. Accred.: Art, Interior Design, Librarianship, Planning

Professional Business College
125 Canal St., New York 10002
Type: Private, proprietary, two-year
Degrees: A
Phone: (212) 226-7300
Inst. Accred.: ACICS (1985/2004)

Rabbi Isaac Elchanan Theological Seminary
2540 Amsterdam Ave., New York 10033
Type: Private, independent, four-year
Degrees: P   *FTE Enroll:* 209
Phone: (212) 960-5344   *Calendar:* Sem. plan
Inst. Accred.: NYBOR (1973/2002)

Rabbinical Academy Mesivta Rabbi Chaim Berlin
1593 Coney Island Ave., Brooklyn 11230
Type: Private, independent, four-year
Degrees: Talmudic   *Enroll:* 364
Phone: (718) 377-0777   *Calendar:* Sem. plan
Inst. Accred.: AARTS (1975/1998)

Rabbinical College Beth Shraga
28 Saddle River Rd., Monsey 10952
Type: Private, independent, four-year
Degrees: Talmudic   *Enroll:* 33
Phone: (845) 356-1980   *Calendar:* Sem. plan
Inst. Accred.: AARTS (1978/2001)

Rabbinical College Bobover Yeshiva B'nei Zion
1577 48th St., Brooklyn 11219
Type: Private, independent, four-year
Degrees: Rabbinic, Talmudic   *Enroll:* 296
Phone: (718) 438-2018   *Calendar:* Sem. plan
Inst. Accred.: AARTS (1979/2001)

Rabbinical College Ch'san Sofer
1876 50th St., Brooklyn 11204
Type: Private, independent, four-year
Degrees: Talmudic   *Enroll:* 153
Phone: (718) 236-1171   *Calendar:* Sem. plan
Inst. Accred.: AARTS (1979/2003)

Rabbinical College of Long Island
205 West Beech St., PO Box 630, Long Beach 11561
Type: Private, independent, four-year
Degrees: Talmudic   *Enroll:* 136
Phone: (516) 255-4700   *Calendar:* Sem. plan
Inst. Accred.: AARTS (1979/2001)

Rabbinical College of Ohr Shimon Yisroel
215-217 Hewes St., Brooklyn 11211
Type: Private, independent, four-year
Degrees: Talmudic   *Enroll:* 158
Phone: (718) 855-4095   *Calendar:* Sem. plan
Inst. Accred.: AARTS (1992/2002)

Rabbinical Seminary Adas Yereim
185 Wilson St., Brooklyn 11211
Type: Private, independent, four-year
Degrees: Talmudic   *Enroll:* 84
Phone: (718) 388-1751   *Calendar:* Sem. plan
Inst. Accred.: AARTS (1979/2001)

Rabbinical Seminary M'kor Chaim
1571 55th St., Brooklyn 11219
Type: Private, independent, four-year
Degrees: Talmudic   *Enroll:* 48
Phone: (718) 851-0183   *Calendar:* Sem. plan
Inst. Accred.: AARTS (1979/2004)

Rabbinical Seminary of America
76-01 147th St., Flushing 11367
Type: Private, independent, four-year
Degrees: Talmudic   *Enroll:* 466
Phone: (718) 268-4700   *Calendar:* Sem. plan
Inst. Accred.: AARTS (1975/2005)

Rensselaer Polytechnic Institute
110 Eighth St., Troy 12180-3590
Type: Private, independent, four-year
Degrees: B, M, D   *Enroll:* 6,710
URL: http://www.rpi.edu
Phone: (518) 276-6000   *Calendar:* Sem. plan
Inst. Accred.: MSA-CHE (1927/2001)
Prog. Accred.: Business (AACSB), Engineering (aerospace, bioengineering, chemical, civil, computer, electrical, engineering physics/science, environmental/sanitary, industrial, materials, mechanical, nuclear)

Roberts Wesleyan College
2301 Westside Dr., Rochester 14624-1997
Type: Private, independent, four-year
Degrees: A, B, M, D   *Enroll:* 1,590
URL: http://www.roberts.edu
Phone: (585) 594-6000   *Calendar:* Sem. plan
Inst. Accred.: MSA-CHE (1963/2001)
Prog. Accred.: Art, Music, Nursing, Social Work

Rochester Business Institute
1630 Portland Ave., Rochester 14621
Type: Private, proprietary, two-year
System: Corinthian Colleges, Inc
Degrees: A   *Enroll:* 1,275
URL: http://rochester-institute.com
Phone: (585) 266-0430   *Calendar:* Qtr. plan
Inst. Accred.: ACICS (1966/2001)

Everest College—Arlington
2801 East Division St., Ste. 250, Arlington, TX 76011
Phone: (817) 652-7790

Rochester Institute of Technology
One Lomb Memorial Dr., Rochester 14623-5603
Type: Private, independent, four-year
Degrees: A, B, M, D   *Enroll:* 12,863
URL: http://www.rit.edu
Phone: (585) 475-2411   *Calendar:* Qtr. plan
Inst. Accred.: MSA-CHE (1958/2002)
Prog. Accred.: Art, Business (AACSB), Computer Science, Diagnostic Medical Sonography, Dietetics (coordinated), Engineering (computer, electrical, industrial, mechanical), Engineering Technology (automation-robotic technology, civil/construction, computer, electrical, electromechanical, manufacturing, mechanical, telecommunications), Interior Design, Nuclear Medicine Technology, Physician Assistant, Social Work

American College of Management and Technology
C`ira Caric`a 4, Dubrovnik, Croatia 20000
Phone: 011 38520435555

National Technical Institute for the Deaf
Lyndon Baines Johnson Bldg., 52 Lomd Memorial Dr., Rochester 14623-5604
Phone: (716) 475-6700
Prog. Accred: Art

U.S. Business School in Prague
Jose Marti 2, Prague, Czech Republic 16200
Phone: (716) 475-7784

Rockefeller University
1230 York Ave., New York 10021
Type: Private, independent, four-year
Degrees: M, D   *Enroll:* 176
URL: http://www.rockefeller.edu
Phone: (212) 327-8000
Inst. Accred.: NYBOR (1954/2002)

The Sage Colleges
45 Ferry St., Troy 12180
Type: Private, independent, four-year
Degrees: A, B, M, D   *Enroll:* 914
URL: http://www.sage.edu
Phone: (518) 244-2644   *Calendar:* Sem. plan
Inst. Accred.: MSA-CHE (1928/2005)
Prog. Accred.: Dietetics (internship), Nursing, Nursing Education, Occupational Therapy, Physical Therapy, Teacher Education (NCATE)

Russell Sage College
45 Ferry St., Troy 12180
Phone: (518) 244-2000

Sage College of Albany
140 New Scotland Ave., Albany 12208
Phone: (518) 244-2000
Prog. Accred: Art

Saint Bernard's School of Theology and Ministry
1100 South Goodman St., Rochester 14620
Type: Private, Roman Catholic Church, four-year
Degrees: M   *Enroll:* 68
URL: http://www.stbernards.edu
Phone: (585) 271-3657   *Calendar:* Sem. plan
Inst. Accred.: ATS (1970/2003)

Saint Bonaventure University
St. Bonaventure 14778
Type: Private, Roman Catholic Church, four-year
Degrees: B, M   *Enroll:* 2,585
URL: http://www.sbu.edu
Phone: (716) 375-2000   *Calendar:* Sem. plan
Inst. Accred.: MSA-CHE (1924/1999)
Prog. Accred.: Business (AACSB), Liberal Education, Teacher Education (NCATE)

Saint Elizabeth College of Nursing
2215 Genesee St., Utica 13501-5998
Type: Private, independent, two-year
Degrees: A   *Enroll:* 163
URL: http://www.stemc.org/college/edu.php
Phone: (315) 798-8144   *Calendar:* Sem. plan
Inst. Accred.: MSA-CHE (2005)

Saint Francis College
180 Remsen St., Brooklyn Heights 11201
Type: Private, independent, four-year
Degrees: A, B   *Enroll:* 2,117
URL: http://www.stfranciscollege.edu
Phone: (718) 522-2300   *Calendar:* Sem. plan
Inst. Accred.: MSA-CHE (1959/1999)
Prog. Accred.: Nursing Education

Saint John Fisher College
3690 East Ave., Rochester 14618
Type: Private, independent, four-year
Degrees: B, M   *Enroll:* 2,652
URL: http://www.sjfc.edu
Phone: (585) 385-8000   *Calendar:* Sem. plan
Inst. Accred.: MSA-CHE (1957/2001)
Prog. Accred.: Business (AACSB), Nursing, Nursing Education

Saint John's University
8000 Utopia Pkwy., Jamaica 11439-0001
Type: Private, Roman Catholic Church, four-year
Degrees: A, B, M, P, D   *Enroll:* 16,098
URL: http://new.stjohns.edu
Phone: (718) 990-6161   *Calendar:* Sem. plan
Inst. Accred.: MSA-CHE (1921/2001)
Prog. Accred.: Accounting, Art, Audiology, Business
  (AACSB), Clinical Psychology, Counseling, Law,
  Librarianship, Pharmacy, Speech-Language Pathology

Manhattan Campus
101 Murray St., New York 10007
Phone: (212) 962-4111

Staten Island Campus
300 Howard Ave., Staten Island 10301
Phone: (718) 390-4500
Prog. Accred: Counseling

Saint Joseph's College
245 Clinton Ave., Brooklyn 11205-3688
Type: Private, independent, four-year
Degrees: B, M   *Enroll:* 856
URL: http://www.sjcny.edu
Phone: (718) 636-6800   *Calendar:* Sem. plan
Inst. Accred.: MSA-CHE (1928/2003)
Prog. Accred.: Nursing

Suffolk Campus
155 Roe Blvd., Patchogue 11772
Phone: (631) 447-3200

Saint Joseph's Seminary
Dunwoodie, 201 Seminary Ave., Yonkers 10704
Type: Private, Roman Catholic Church, four-year
Degrees: M, P   *Enroll:* 98
URL: http://www.ny-
  archdiocese.org/pastoral/seminary.cfm
Phone: (914) 968-6200   *Calendar:* Qtr. plan
Inst. Accred.: ATS (1973/2004), MSA-CHE (1961/2005)

Saint Lawrence University
23 Romoda Dr., Canton 13617
Type: Private, independent, four-year
Degrees: B, M   *Enroll:* 2,199
URL: http://www.stlawu.edu
Phone: (315) 229-5011
Inst. Accred.: MSA-CHE (1921/2003)

Saint Thomas Aquinas College
125 Route 340, Sparkill 10976-1050
Type: Private, independent, four-year
Degrees: A, B, M   *Enroll:* 1,811
URL: http://www.stac.edu
Phone: (845) 398-4000   *Calendar:* 4-1-4 plan
Inst. Accred.: MSA-CHE (1972/2002)

Saint Vladimir's Orthodox Theological Seminary
575 Scarsdale Rd., Crestwood 10707
Type: Private, Orthodox Church in America, four-year
Degrees: M, D   *Enroll:* 77
URL: http://www.svots.edu
Phone: (914) 961-8313   *Calendar:* Sem. plan
Inst. Accred.: ATS (1973/2003)

Salvation Army School for Officer Training
201 Lafayette Ave., Suffern 10901
Type: Private, independent, two-year
Degrees: A
URL: http://www1.salvationarmy.org/use/www_use_
  sfot.nsf
Phone: (845) 357-3501   *Calendar:* Qtr. plan
Inst. Accred.: NYBOR (2005)

Sarah Lawrence College
One Meadway, Bronxville 10708
Type: Private, independent, four-year
Degrees: B, M   *Enroll:* 1,517
URL: http://www.slc.edu
Phone: (914) 337-0700   *Calendar:* Sem. plan
Inst. Accred.: MSA-CHE (1937/2002)

Schenectady County Community College
78 Washington Ave., Schenectady 12305
Type: Public, state/local, two-year
System: State University of New York Office of
  Community Colleges
Degrees: A   *Enroll:* 2,753
URL: http://www.sunysccc.edu
Phone: (518) 381-1200   *Calendar:* Sem. plan
Inst. Accred.: MSA-CHE (1974/1999)
Prog. Accred.: Business (ACBSP), Culinary Education,
  Music

School of Visual Arts
209 East 23rd St., New York 10010
Type: Private, proprietary, four-year
Degrees: B, M   *Enroll:* 3,253
URL: http://www.schoolofvisualarts.edu
Phone: (212) 592-2000   *Calendar:* Sem. plan
Inst. Accred.: MSA-CHE (1978/2002)
Prog. Accred.: Art, Interior Design

Seminary of the Immaculate Conception
440 West Neck Rd., Huntington 11743
Type: Private, Roman Catholic Church, four-year
Degrees: M, P, D   *Enroll:* 81
URL: http://www.icseminary.edu
Phone: (631) 423-0483   *Calendar:* Sem. plan
Inst. Accred.: ATS (1976/2001), MSA-CHE (1976/2001)

Sh'or Yoshuv Rabbinical College
1 Cedar Lawn Ave., Lawrence 11559
Type: Private, independent, four-year
Degrees: Talmudic   *Enroll:* 158
Phone: (516) 239-9002   *Calendar:* Sem. plan
Inst. Accred.: AARTS (1979/1999)

Siena College
515 Loudon Rd., Loudonville 12211-1462
Type: Private, independent, four-year
Degrees: B, M   *Enroll:* 3,164
URL: http://www.sienna.edu
Phone: (518) 783-2300   *Calendar:* Sem. plan
Inst. Accred.: MSA-CHE (1943/1999)
Prog. Accred.: Business (AACSB), Social Work

Simmons Institute of Funeral Service
1828 South Ave., Syracuse 13207
Type: Private, independent, two-year
Degrees: A   *Enroll:* 19
URL: http://www.simmonsinstitute.com
Phone: (315) 475-5142   *Calendar:* Sem. plan
Inst. Accred.: ABFSE (2000)

Skidmore College
815 North Broadway, Saratoga Springs 12866-1632
Type: Private, independent, four-year
Degrees: B, M   *Enroll:* 2,403
URL: http://www.skidmore.edu
Phone: (518) 580-5000   *Calendar:* Sem. plan
Inst. Accred.: MSA-CHE (1925/2001)
Prog. Accred.: Art, Social Work

State University of New York at Albany
1400 Washington Ave., Albany 12222
Type: Public, state, four-year
System: State University of New York System Office
Degrees: B, M, D   *Enroll:* 14,534
URL: http://www.albany.edu
Phone: (518) 442-3300   *Calendar:* Sem. plan
Inst. Accred.: MSA-CHE (1938/2005)
Prog. Accred.: Accounting, Business (AACSB), Clinical
Psychology, Counseling Psychology, Dental Public
Health, Librarianship, Planning, Public Administration,
Public Health, Rehabilitation Counseling, School
Psychology, Social Work

State University of New York at Binghamton
Vestal Pkwy., East, PO Box 6000, Binghamton 13902-6000
Type: Public, state, four-year
System: State University of New York System Office
Degrees: B, M, D   *Enroll:* 12,405
URL: http://www.binghamton.edu
Phone: (607) 777-2000   *Calendar:* Sem. plan
Inst. Accred.: MSA-CHE (1952/2001)
Prog. Accred.: Business (AACSB), Clinical Psychology,
Computer Science, Engineering (computer, electrical,
mechanical), Engineering Technology (welding), Music,
Nursing Education

State University of New York at Buffalo
Capen Hall, Buffalo 14260
Type: Public, state, four-year
System: State University of New York System Office
Degrees: A, B, M, P, D   *Enroll:* 24,084
URL: http://www.buffalo.edu
Phone: (716) 645-2000   *Calendar:* Sem. plan
Inst. Accred.: MSA-CHE (1921/2004)
Prog. Accred.: Accounting, Advanced Education in
General Dentistry, Art, Audiology, Clinical Psychology,
Combined Professional-Scientific Psychology, Combined
Prosthodontics, Dental Assisting, Dentistry, Endodontics,
Engineering (aerospace, chemical, civil, computer,
electrical, environmental/sanitary, industrial,
mechanical), English Language Education, General
Dentistry, General Practice Residency, Law,
Librarianship, Medicine, Nurse Anesthesia Education,
Nursing, Nursing Education, Occupational Therapy, Oral
and Maxillofacial Pathology, Oral and Maxillofacial
Surgery, Orthodontic and Dentofacial Orthopedics,
Pediatric Dentistry, Periodontics, Pharmacy, Physical
Therapy, Planning, Psychology Internship, Rehabilitation
Counseling, Social Work, Speech-Language Pathology

State University of New York at New Paltz
75 South Manheim Blvd., New Paltz 12561
Type: Public, state, four-year
System: State University of New York System Office
Degrees: B, M   *Enroll:* 6,685
URL: http://www.newpaltz.edu
Phone: (845) 257-2121   *Calendar:* Sem. plan
Inst. Accred.: MSA-CHE (1950/2001)
Prog. Accred.: Art, Audiology, Computer Science,
Engineering (computer, electrical), Music, Nursing,
Nursing Education, Speech-Language Pathology,
Theatre

State University of New York at Stony Brook
Stony Brook 11794-1401
Type: Public, state, four-year
System: State University of New York System Office
Degrees: B, M, P, D   *Enroll:* 19,068
URL: http://www.stonybrook.edu
Phone: (631) 689-6000   *Calendar:* Sem. plan
Inst. Accred.: MSA-CHE (1957/2004)
Prog. Accred.: Advanced Education in General Dentistry,
Clinical Lab Scientist, Clinical Psychology,
Cytotechnology, Dentistry, Dietetics (internship),
Endodontics, Engineering (computer, electrical,
engineering physics/science, mechanical), General
Dentistry, General Practice Residency, Medicine, Nurse
(Midwifery), Nursing, Nursing Education, Occupational
Therapy, Orthodontic and Dentofacial Orthopedics,
Periodontics, Physical Therapy, Physician Assistant,
Psychology Internship, Radiation Therapy, Respiratory
Therapy, Social Work

State University of New York
Broome Community College
Upper Front St., PO Box 1017, Binghamton 13902-1017
Type: Public, state/local, two-year
System: State University of New York Office of
  Community Colleges
Degrees: A   *Enroll:* 4,940
URL: http://www.sunybroome.edu
Phone: (607) 778-5000   *Calendar:* Sem. plan
Inst. Accred.: MSA-CHE (1960/2005)
Prog. Accred.: Clinical Lab Technology, Dental Hygiene,
  Engineering Technology (civil/construction, electrical,
  mechanical), Health Information Technician, Medical
  Assisting (AMA), Nursing, Physical Therapy Assisting,
  Radiography

State University of New York
College at Brockport
350 New Campus Dr., Brockport 14420
Type: Public, state, four-year
System: State University of New York System Office
Degrees: B, M   *Enroll:* 7,357
URL: http://www.brockport.edu
Phone: (585) 395-2211   *Calendar:* Sem. plan
Inst. Accred.: MSA-CHE (1952/2002)
Prog. Accred.: Business (AACSB), Computer Science,
  Counseling, Dance, Nursing, Nursing Education, Public
  Administration, Recreation and Leisure Services, Social
  Work

State University of New York
College at Buffalo
1300 Elmwood Ave., Buffalo 14222-1095
Type: Public, state, four-year
System: State University of New York System Office
Degrees: B, M   *Enroll:* 9,361
URL: http://www.buffalostate.edu
Phone: (716) 878-4000   *Calendar:* Sem. plan
Inst. Accred.: MSA-CHE (1948/2003)
Prog. Accred.: Audiology, Clinical Lab Scientist, Dietetics
  (coordinated), Engineering Technology (electrical,
  mechanical), Industrial Technology, Interior Design,
  Nuclear Medicine Technology, Social Work, Speech-
  Language Pathology, Teacher Education (NCATE)

State University of New York
College at Cortland
PO Box 2000, Cortland 13045
Type: Public, state, four-year
System: State University of New York System Office
Degrees: B, M   *Enroll:* 6,369
URL: http://www.cortland.edu
Phone: (607) 753-2201   *Calendar:* Sem. plan
Inst. Accred.: MSA-CHE (1949/2002)
Prog. Accred.: Athletic Training, Recreation and Leisure
  Services

State University of New York
College at Fredonia
280 Central Ave., Fredonia 14063
Type: Public, state, four-year
System: State University of New York System Office
Degrees: B, M   *Enroll:* 4,983
URL: http://www.fredonia.edu
Phone: (716) 673-3111   *Calendar:* Sem. plan
Inst. Accred.: MSA-CHE (1952/2005)
Prog. Accred.: Audiology, Music, Social Work, Speech-
  Language Pathology, Theatre

State University of New York
College at Geneseo
One College Circle, Geneseo 14454
Type: Public, state, four-year
System: State University of New York System Office
Degrees: B, M   *Enroll:* 5,369
URL: http://www.geneseo.edu
Phone: (585) 245-5501   *Calendar:* Sem. plan
Inst. Accred.: MSA-CHE (1952/2002)
Prog. Accred.: Business (AACSB), Speech-Language
  Pathology

State University of New York
College at Old Westbury
PO Box 210, Old Westbury 11568-0210
Type: Public, state, four-year
System: State University of New York System Office
Degrees: B, M   *Enroll:* 2,772
URL: http://www.oldwestbury.edu
Phone: (516) 876-3000   *Calendar:* Sem. plan
Inst. Accred.: MSA-CHE (1976/2001)

State University of New York
College at Oneonta
Ravine Pkwy., Oneonta 13820-4015
Type: Public, state, four-year
System: State University of New York System Office
Degrees: B, M   *Enroll:* 5,529
URL: http://www.oneonta.edu
Phone: (607) 436-3500   *Calendar:* Sem. plan
Inst. Accred.: MSA-CHE (1949/2003)
Prog. Accred.: Business (AACSB), Family and Consumer
  Science, Teacher Education (NCATE)

State University of New York
College at Oswego
7060 State Route 104, Oswego 13126
Type: Public, state, four-year
System: State University of New York System Office
Degrees: B, M   *Enroll:* 7,522
URL: http://www.oswego.edu
Phone: (315) 312-2500   *Calendar:* Sem. plan
Inst. Accred.: MSA-CHE (1950/2002)
Prog. Accred.: Business (AACSB), Music, Teacher
  Education (NCATE)

State University of New York
College at Plattsburgh
101 Broad St., Plattsburgh 12901-2681
Type: Public, state, four-year
System: State University of New York System Office
Degrees: B, M   *Enroll:* 5,552
URL: http://www.plattsburgh.edu
Phone: (518) 564-2000   *Calendar:* Sem. plan
Inst. Accred.: MSA-CHE (1952/2002)
Prog. Accred.: Business (AACSB), Counseling, Nursing, Nursing Education, Social Work, Speech-Language Pathology

State University of New York
College at Potsdam
44 Pierrepont Ave., Potsdam 13676-2294
Type: Public, state, four-year
System: State University of New York System Office
Degrees: B, M   *Enroll:* 4,045
URL: http://www.potsdam.edu
Phone: (315) 267-2000   *Calendar:* Sem. plan
Inst. Accred.: MSA-CHE (1952/2002)
Prog. Accred.: Music

State University of New York
College at Purchase
735 Anderson Hill Rd., Purchase 10577-1400
Type: Public, state, four-year
System: State University of New York System Office
Degrees: B, M   *Enroll:* 4,028
URL: http://www.purchase.edu
Phone: (914) 251-6000   *Calendar:* Sem. plan
Inst. Accred.: MSA-CHE (1976/2002)
Prog. Accred.: Art, Music

State University of New York
College of Agriculture and Technology
at Cobleskill
Cobleskill 12043
Type: Public, state, four-year
System: State University of New York System Office
Degrees: A, B   *Enroll:* 2,409
URL: http://www.cobleskill.edu
Phone: (518) 255-5111   *Calendar:* Sem. plan
Inst. Accred.: MSA-CHE (1952/2001)
Prog. Accred.: Culinary Education, Histologic Technology

State University of New York
College of Agriculture and Technology
at Morrisville
PO Box 901, Morrisville 13408
Type: Public, state, four-year
System: State University of New York System Office
Degrees: A, B, D   *Enroll:* 3,001
URL: http://www.morrisville.edu
Phone: (315) 684-6000   *Calendar:* Sem. plan
Inst. Accred.: MSA-CHE (1952/2002)
Prog. Accred.: Business (ACBSP), Engineering Technology (electrical, mechanical), Nursing

State University of New York
College of Environmental Science and Forestry
One Forestry Dr., Syracuse 13210-2778
Type: Public, state, four-year
System: State University of New York System Office
Degrees: A, B, M, D   *Enroll:* 1,699
URL: http://www.esf.edu
Phone: (315) 470-6500   *Calendar:* Sem. plan
Inst. Accred.: MSA-CHE (1952/2002)
Prog. Accred.: Construction Education, Engineering (forest, paper), Forestry, Landscape Architecture

State University of New York
College of Optometry
33 West 42nd St., New York 10010
Type: Public, state, four-year
System: State University of New York System Office
Degrees: M, P, D   *Enroll:* 291
URL: http://www.sunyopt.edu
Phone: (212) 780-4900   *Calendar:* Qtr. plan
Inst. Accred.: MSA-CHE (1976/2003)
Prog. Accred.: Optometric Residency, Optometry

State University of New York
College of Technology at Alfred
Alfred 14802-1196
Type: Public, state, four-year
System: State University of New York System Office
Degrees: A, B   *Enroll:* 3,232
URL: http://www.alfredstate.edu
Phone: (607) 587-4111   *Calendar:* Sem. plan
Inst. Accred.: MSA-CHE (1952/2005)
Prog. Accred.: Clinical Lab Technology, Construction Education, Engineering Technology (agricultural, civil/construction, computer, electrical, electromechanical, general drafting/design, mechanical, surveying), Health Information Technician, Nursing, Veterinary Technology

Wellsville Campus
Wellsville 14895
Phone: (607) 587-3105

State University of New York
College of Technology at Canton
34 Cornell Dr., Canton 13617
Type: Public, state, four-year
System: State University of New York System Office
Degrees: A, B   *Enroll:* 2,300
URL: http://www.canton.edu
Phone: (315) 386-7011   *Calendar:* Sem. plan
Inst. Accred.: MSA-CHE (1952/2003)
Prog. Accred.: Clinical Lab Technology, Engineering Technology (air conditioning, civil/construction, electrical, mechanical), Funeral Service Education (Mortuary Science), Nursing, Occupational Therapy Assisting, Physical Therapy Assisting, Veterinary Technology

State University of New York
College of Technology at Delhi
2 Main St., Delhi 13753
Type: Public, state, four-year
System: State University of New York System Office
Degrees: A, B   *Enroll:* 2,141
URL: http://www.delhi.edu
Phone: (607) 746-4000   *Calendar:* Sem. plan
Inst. Accred.: MSA-CHE (1952/2002)
Prog. Accred.: Construction Education, Culinary
  Education, Veterinary Technology

State University of New York
College of Technology at Farmingdale
2350 Broadhollow Rd., Farmingdale 11735-1021
Type: Public, state, four-year
System: State University of New York System Office
Degrees: A, B   *Enroll:* 4,574
URL: http://www.farmingdale.edu
Phone: (631) 420-2000   *Calendar:* Sem. plan
Inst. Accred.: MSA-CHE (1952/2001)
Prog. Accred.: Clinical Lab Technology, Dental Hygiene,
  Engineering Technology (automotive, civil/construction,
  computer, electrical, manufacturing, mechanical),
  Nursing

State University of New York
Empire State College
One Union Ave., Saratoga Springs 12866
Type: Public, state, four-year
System: State University of New York System Office
Degrees: A, B, M   *Enroll:* 5,616
URL: http://www.esc.edu
Phone: (518) 587-2100
Inst. Accred.: MSA-CHE (1974/2005)

Central New York Regional Center
219 Walton St., Syracuse 13202-1226
Phone: (315) 472-5730

Collegewide Programs Campus
28 Union Ave., Saratoga Springs 12866-4309
Phone: (518) 587-2100

Genessee Valley Regional Center
8 Prince St., Rochester 14607
Phone: (716) 244-3641

Hudson Valley Regional Center
200 North Central Ave., Hartsdale 10530
Phone: (914) 948-6206

Long Island Regional Center
Trainor House, PO Box 130, 223 Store Hill Rd., Old
Westbury 11568
Phone: (516) 997-4700

Metropolitan Regional Center
225 Varick St., New York 10014-4382
Phone: (212) 647-7800

Niagara Frontier Center
Market Archade, 3rd Flr., 617 Main St., Buffalo 14203
Phone: (716) 853-7700

Northeast Center
845 Central Ave., Albany 12206
Phone: (518) 485-5964

State University of New York
Health Science Center at Brooklyn
450 Clarkson Ave., Box 1, Brooklyn 11203
Type: Public, state, four-year
System: State University of New York System Office
Degrees: B, M, P, D   *Enroll:* 1,297
URL: http://www.downstate.edu
Phone: (718) 270-1000   *Calendar:* Sem. plan
Inst. Accred.: MSA-CHE (1952/2001)
Prog. Accred.: Diagnostic Medical Sonography, Health
  Information Administration, Medicine, Nurse
  (Midwifery), Nurse Anesthesia Education, Nursing,
  Nursing Education, Occupational Therapy, Physical
  Therapy, Physician Assistant, Radiography

State University of New York
Institute of Technology at Utica/Rome
PO Box 3050, Utica 13504-3050
Type: Public, state, four-year
System: State University of New York System Office
Degrees: B, M   *Enroll:* 1,945
URL: http://www.sunyit.edu
Phone: (315) 792-7100   *Calendar:* Sem. plan
Inst. Accred.: MSA-CHE (1979/2005)
Prog. Accred.: Business (AACSB), Engineering Technology
  (civil/construction, computer, electrical, industrial,
  mechanical), Health Information Administration, Nursing

State University of New York
Maritime College
6 Pennyfield Ave., Bronx 10465
Type: Public, state, four-year
System: State University of New York System Office
Degrees: A, B, M   *Enroll:* 1,064
URL: http://www.sunymaritime.edu
Phone: (718) 409-7200   *Calendar:* Sem. plan
Inst. Accred.: MSA-CHE (1952/2002)
Prog. Accred.: Engineering (naval architecture/marine)

State University of New York
Rockland Community College
145 College Rd., Suffern 10901
Type: Public, state/local, two-year
System: State University of New York Office of
  Community Colleges
Degrees: A   *Enroll:* 4,613
URL: http://www.sunyrockland.edu
Phone: (845) 574-4000   *Calendar:* Sem. plan
Inst. Accred.: MSA-CHE (1968/2000)
Prog. Accred.: Health Information Technician, Nursing,
  Occupational Therapy Assisting, Respiratory Therapy

Haverstraw Learning Center
36-39 Main St., Haberstraw 10927
Phone: (914) 942-0624

Nyack Learning Center
92-94 Main St., Nyack 10960
Phone: (914) 358-9392

Spring Valley Learning Center
185 North Main St., Spring Valley 10977
Phone: (914) 352-5535

State University of New York
Upstate Medical University
750 East Adams St., Syracuse 13210
Type: Public, state, four-year
System: State University of New York System Office
Degrees: A, B, M, P, D   *Enroll:* 1,034
URL: http://www.upstate.edu
Phone: (315) 464-5540   *Calendar:* Sem. plan
Inst. Accred.: MSA-CHE (1952/1999)
Prog. Accred.: Clinical Lab Scientist, Cytotechnology, EMT
  (Paramedic), General Practice Residency, Medicine,
  Nursing, Nursing Education, Perfusion, Physical
  Therapy, Psychology Internship, Radiation Therapy,
  Radiography, Respiratory Therapy

Suffolk County Community College—
Ammerman Campus
533 College Rd., NFL37, Selden 11784
Type: Public, state/local, two-year
System: Suffolk County Community College Central
  Administration
Degrees: A   *Enroll:* 6,963
URL: http://www.sunysuffolk.edu
Phone: (631) 451-4110   *Calendar:* Sem. plan
Inst. Accred.: MSA-CHE (1966/2002)
Prog. Accred.: Nursing, Physical Therapy Assisting

Eastern Campus
121 Speonk-Riverhead Rd., Riverhead 11901-3499
Phone: (631) 548-2500
Prog. Accred: Interior Design

Grant Campus
Crooked Hill Rd., Brentwood 11717
Phone: (631) 851-6700
Prog. Accred: Medical Assisting (AMA), Nursing,
  Occupational Therapy Assisting, Veterinary
  Technology

Sullivan County Community College
112 College Rd., Loch Sheldrake 12759-5151
Type: Public, state/local, two-year
System: State University of New York Office of
  Community Colleges
Degrees: A   *Enroll:* 1,421
URL: http://www.sullivan.suny.edu
Phone: (845) 434-5750   *Calendar:* Sem. plan
Inst. Accred.: MSA-CHE (1968/2002)
Prog. Accred.: Business (ACBSP), Culinary Education,
  Nursing

Sunbridge College
285 Hungry Hollow Rd., Spring Valley 10977-6398
Type: Private, independent, four-year
Degrees: M   *Enroll:* 37
URL: http://www.sunbridge.edu
Phone: (845) 425-0055   *Calendar:* Sem. plan
Inst. Accred.: NYBOR (1991/2002)

The Swedish Institute: School of Acupuncture
and Massage Therapy
226 West 26th St., PO Box 11130, New York 10001
Type: Private, proprietary, four-year
Degrees: A, M   *Enroll:* 485
URL: http://www.swedishinstitute.org
Phone: (212) 924-5900   *Calendar:* Sem. plan
Inst. Accred.: ACCSCT (1981/2004)
Prog. Accred.: Acupuncture

Syracuse University
300 Tolley, Syracuse 13244-1100
Type: Private, independent, four-year
Degrees: A, B, M, P, D   *Enroll:* 16,743
URL: http://www.syr.edu
Phone: (315) 443-1870   *Calendar:* Sem. plan
Inst. Accred.: MSA-CHE (1921/2003)
Prog. Accred.: Art, Audiology, Business (AACSB), Clinical
  Psychology, Computer Science, Counseling, Dietetics
  (coordinated), Dietetics (internship), Engineering
  (aerospace, bioengineering, chemical, civil, computer,
  electrical, environmental/sanitary, mechanical), Interior
  Architecture, Interior Design, Journalism, Law,
  Librarianship, Marriage and Family Therapy, Music,
  Nursing, Public Administration, Rehabilitation
  Counseling, School Psychology, Social Work, Speech-
  Language Pathology

Talmudical Institute of Upstate New York
769 Park Ave., Rochester 14607
Type: Private, independent, four-year
Degrees: Talmudic   *Enroll:* 13
Phone: (585) 473-2810   *Calendar:* Sem. plan
Inst. Accred.: AARTS (1984/2000)

Talmudical Seminary Oholei Torah
667 Eastern Pkwy., Brooklyn 11213
Type: Private, independent, four-year
Degrees: Talmudic   *Enroll:* 315
Phone: (718) 774-5050   *Calendar:* Sem. plan
Inst. Accred.: AARTS (1979/2005)

Taylor Business Institute
23 West 17th St., 7th Flr., New York 10011-5501
Type: Private, proprietary, two-year
Degrees: A   *Enroll:* 925
URL: http://www.tbiglobal.com
Phone: (800) 959-9999   *Calendar:* Sem. plan
Inst. Accred.: ACICS (1962/2001)

Teachers College of Columbia University
525 West 120th St., New York 10027-6413
Type: Private, independent, four-year
Degrees: M, D   *Enroll:* 3,511
URL: http://www.tc.columbia.edu
Phone: (212) 678-3000   *Calendar:* Sem. plan
Inst. Accred.: MSA-CHE (1921/2001)
Prog. Accred.: Clinical Psychology, Counseling
Psychology, Nursing, School Psychology, Speech-
Language Pathology

Technical Career Institute, Inc.
320 West 31st St., New York 10001-2789
Type: Private, proprietary, two-year
Degrees: A   *Enroll:* 2,968
URL: http://www.tcicollege.net
Phone: (212) 594-4000   *Calendar:* Sem. plan
Inst. Accred.: MSA-CHE (2005), NYBOR (1972/2002)
Prog. Accred.: Engineering Technology (electrical)

Tompkins Cortland Community College
PO Box 139, Dryden 13053-0139
Type: Public, state/local, two-year
System: State University of New York Office of
Community Colleges
Degrees: A   *Enroll:* 2,503
URL: http://www.sunytccc.edu
Phone: (607) 844-8211   *Calendar:* Sem. plan
Inst. Accred.: MSA-CHE (1973/2003)
Prog. Accred.: Nursing

Torah Temimah Talmudical Seminary
507 Ocean Pkwy., Brooklyn 11218
Type: Private, independent, four-year
Degrees: Talmudic   *Enroll:* 192
Phone: (718) 853-8500   *Calendar:* Sem. plan
Inst. Accred.: AARTS (1981/1999)

Touro College
27 West 23rd St., 7th Flr., New York 10010
Type: Private, independent, four-year
Degrees: A, B, M, P, D   *Enroll:* 13,990
URL: http://www.touro.edu
Phone: (212) 463-0400   *Calendar:* Sem. plan
Inst. Accred.: MSA-CHE (1976/2004, Probation)
Prog. Accred.: Acupuncture, Occupational Therapy,
Occupational Therapy Assisting, Physical Therapy,
Physician Assistant, Speech-Language Pathology

Harlem Campus
27-33 West 23rd St., New York 10010
Phone: (212) 463-0400

School of Health Sciences
1700 Union Blvd., Bay Shore 11706
Phone: (631) 665-1600
Prog. Accred: Occupational Therapy, Physician
Assistant

Touro Law Center
300 Nassau Rd., Huntington 11743
Phone: (613) 421-2244 x312
Prog. Accred: Law (ABA only)

Touro University
College of Osteopathic Medicine
874 American Pacific Dr., Henderson, NV 89014
Phone: (702) 777-8687
Prog. Accred: Occupational Therapy, Physician
Assistant

Tri-State College of Acupuncture
80 8th Ave., 4th Flr., New York 10011
Type: Private, proprietary, four-year
Degrees: M
URL: http://www.tsca.edu
Phone: (212) 242-2255   *Calendar:* Sem. plan
Inst. Accred.: ACAOM (1993/2003)

Trocaire College
360 Choate Ave, Buffalo 14220
Type: Private, independent, two-year
Degrees: A   *Enroll:* 757
URL: http://www.trocaire.edu
Phone: (716) 826-1200   *Calendar:* Sem. plan
Inst. Accred.: MSA-CHE (1974/1999)
Prog. Accred.: Health Information Technician, Medical
Assisting (AMA), Nursing, Phlebotomy, Radiography,
Surgical Technology

U.T.A. Mesivta of Kiryas Joel
PO Box 2009, 9 Nicholsberg Rd., Monroe 10950-8509
Type: Private, independent, four-year
Degrees: Rabbinic   *FTE Enroll:* 717
Phone: (845) 783-9901   *Calendar:* Sem. plan
Inst. Accred.: AARTS (2003)

Ulster County Community College
Cottekill Rd., Stone Ridge 12484
Type: Public, state/local, two-year
System: State University of New York Office of
Community Colleges
Degrees: A   *Enroll:* 2,020
URL: http://www.sunyulster.edu
Phone: (845) 687-5000   *Calendar:* Sem. plan
Inst. Accred.: MSA-CHE (1971/2001)
Prog. Accred.: Nursing

Unification Theological Seminary
30 Seminary Dr., Barrytown 12507
Type: Private, Unification Church, four-year
Degrees: M, P   *Enroll:* 124
URL: http://www.uts.edu
Phone: (845) 752-3100   *Calendar:* Tri. plan
Inst. Accred.: MSA-CHE (1996/2003, Warning)

Union College
Schenectady 12308
Type: Private, independent, four-year
System: Union University
Degrees: B, M   *Enroll:* 2,423
URL: http://www.union.edu
Phone: (518) 388-6000   *Calendar:* Tri. plan
Inst. Accred.: MSA-CHE (1921/2005)
Prog. Accred.: Business (AACSB), Engineering (civil, computer, electrical, mechanical), Health Services Administration

Union Theological Seminary
3041 Broadway, New York 10027-5710
Type: Private, independent, four-year
Degrees: M, P, D   *Enroll:* 170
URL: http://www.uts.columbia.edu
Phone: (212) 662-7100   *Calendar:* Sem. plan
Inst. Accred.: ATS (1938/1998), MSA-CHE (1967/1999)

United States Merchant Marine Academy
300 Steamboat Rd., Kings Point 11024-1699
Type: Public, federal, four-year
Degrees: B, M   *Enroll:* 952
URL: http://www.usmma.edu
Phone: (516) 773-5000   *Calendar:* Tri. plan
Inst. Accred.: MSA-CHE (1949/2000)
Prog. Accred.: Engineering (naval architecture/marine)

United States Military Academy
West Point 10996-5000
Type: Public, federal, four-year
Degrees: B   *Enroll:* 4,209
URL: http://www.usma.edu
Phone: (914) 938-4200   *Calendar:* Sem. plan
Inst. Accred.: MSA-CHE (1949/2005)
Prog. Accred.: Computer Science, Engineering (civil, electrical, engineering management, environmental/sanitary, mechanical, systems)

United Talmudical Seminary
45C Williamsburg St., West, Brooklyn 11211-7984
Type: Private, independent, four-year
Degrees: Rabbinic   *Enroll:* 1,678
Phone: (718) 963-9770   *Calendar:* Sem. plan
Inst. Accred.: AARTS (1979/2001)

University of Rochester
Rochester 14627
Type: Private, independent, four-year
Degrees: B, M, P, D   *Enroll:* 7,665
URL: http://www.rochester.edu
Phone: (585) 275-2121   *Calendar:* Sem. plan
Inst. Accred.: MSA-CHE (1921/2004)
Prog. Accred.: Advanced Education in General Dentistry, Business (AACSB), Clinical Pastoral Education (ACPEI), Clinical Psychology, Combined Prosthodontics, Counseling, Engineering (bioengineering, chemical, electrical, mechanical), General Dentistry, General Practice Residency, Marriage and Family Therapy, Medicine, Microbiology, Music, Nursing, Oral and Maxillofacial Surgery, Orthodontic and Dentofacial Orthopedics, Pediatric Dentistry, Periodontics, Psychology Internship, Public Health

Utica College
1600 Burrstone Rd., Utica 13502-4892
Type: Private, independent, four-year
Degrees: B, M   *Enroll:* 2,161
URL: http://www.utica.edu
Phone: (315) 792-3111   *Calendar:* Sem. plan
Inst. Accred.: MSA-CHE (1946/2003)
Prog. Accred.: Nursing, Occupational Therapy, Physical Therapy

Utica School of Commerce
201 Bleecker St., Utica 13501-2280
Type: Private, proprietary, two-year
Degrees: A   *Enroll:* 298
URL: http://www.uscny.com
Phone: (315) 733-2307   *Calendar:* Sem. plan
Inst. Accred.: NYBOR (1972/2001)

Canastota Campus
PO Box 462, Route 5, Canastota 13032-0462
Phone: (315) 697-8200

Oneonta Campus
17 Elm St., Oneonta 138201828
Phone: (607) 432-7003

Vassar College
124 Raymond Ave., Poughkeepsie 12604-0002
Type: Private, independent, four-year
Degrees: B, M   *Enroll:* 2,414
URL: http://www.vassar.edu
Phone: (845) 437-7000   *Calendar:* Sem. plan
Inst. Accred.: MSA-CHE (1921/1999)

Vaughn College of Aeronautics and Technology
86-01 23rd Ave., Flushing 11369
Type: Private, independent, four-year
Degrees: A, B   *Enroll:* 1,129
URL: http://www.aero.edu
Phone: (718) 429-6600   *Calendar:* Sem. plan
Inst. Accred.: MSA-CHE (1969/2002)
Prog. Accred.: Engineering Technology (aerospace)

Villa Maria College of Buffalo
240 Pine Ridge Rd., Buffalo 14225-3999
Type: Private, independent, four-year
Degrees: A, B   *Enroll:* 384
URL: http://www.villa.edu
Phone: (716) 896-0700   *Calendar:* Sem. plan
Inst. Accred.: MSA-CHE (1972/2003)
Prog. Accred.: Interior Design, Physical Therapy Assisting

Wagner College
One Campus Rd., Staten Island 10301
Type: Private, independent, four-year
Degrees: B, M   *Enroll:* 2,061
URL: http://www.wagner.edu
Phone: (718) 390-3100   *Calendar:* Sem. plan
Inst. Accred.: MSA-CHE (1931/2001)
Prog. Accred.: Business (ACBSP), Nursing, Physician
   Assistant

Webb Institute
298 Crescent Beach Rd., Glen Cove 11542-1398
Type: Private, independent, four-year
Degrees: B   *Enroll:* 72
URL: http://www.webb-institute.edu
Phone: (516) 671-2277   *Calendar:* Sem. plan
Inst. Accred.: MSA-CHE (1950/2005)
Prog. Accred.: Engineering (naval architecture/marine)

Wells College
170 Main St., Aurora 13026-0500
Type: Private, independent, four-year
Degrees: B   *Enroll:* 403
URL: http://www.wells.edu
Phone: (315) 364-3265   *Calendar:* Sem. plan
Inst. Accred.: MSA-CHE (1921/1999)

Westchester Community College
75 Grasslands Rd., Valhalla 10595-1698
Type: Public, state/local, two-year
System: State University of New York Office of
   Community Colleges
Degrees: A   *Enroll:* 7,542
URL: http://www.sunywcc.edu
Phone: (914) 785-6600   *Calendar:* Sem. plan
Inst. Accred.: MSA-CHE (1970/2005)
Prog. Accred.: Radiography, Respiratory Therapy

Wood Tobe-Coburn School
8 East 40th St., New York 10016-0190
Type: Private, proprietary, two-year
Degrees: A   *Enroll:* 438
URL: http://www.woodtobecoburn.edu
Phone: (212) 686-9040   *Calendar:* Sem. plan
Inst. Accred.: NYBOR (1972/2002)
Prog. Accred.: Medical Assisting (CAAHEP)

Yeshiva and Kolel Bais Medrosh Elyon
73 Main St., Monsey 10952
Type: Private, independent, four-year
Degrees: Talmudic   *FTE Enroll:* 42
Phone: (845) 356-7064   *Calendar:* Sem. plan
Inst. Accred.: AARTS (1989/2004)

Yeshiva and Kollel Harbotzas Torah
1049 East 15th St., Brooklyn 11230
Type: Private, independent, four-year
Degrees: Talmudic   *Enroll:* 40
Phone: (718) 692-0208   *Calendar:* Sem. plan
Inst. Accred.: AARTS (1985/2005)

Yeshiva D'Monsey Rabbinical College
2 Roman Blvd., Monsey 10952
Type: Private, independent, four-year
Degrees: Talmudic   *FTE Enroll:* 96
Phone: (845) 426-3276   *Calendar:* Sem. plan
Inst. Accred.: AARTS (2003)

Yeshiva Derech Chaim
1573 39th St., Brooklyn 11218
Type: Private, independent, four-year
Degrees: Talmudic   *Enroll:* 174
Phone: (718) 438-5476   *Calendar:* Sem. plan
Inst. Accred.: AARTS (1984/2005)

Yeshiva Gedolah Imrei Yosef D'Spinka
1466 56th St., Brooklyn 11219
Type: Private, independent, four-year
Degrees: Talmudic   *Enroll:* 186
Phone: (718) 851-1600   *Calendar:* Sem. plan
Inst. Accred.: AARTS (1989/2005)

Yeshiva Karlin Stolin Beth Aaron V'Israel Rabbinical Institute
1818 54th St., Brooklyn 11204
Type: Private, independent, four-year
Degrees: Talmudic   *Enroll:* 96
Phone: (718) 232-7800   *Calendar:* Sem. plan
Inst. Accred.: AARTS (1975/2002)

Yeshiva Mikdash Melech
1326 Ocean Pkwy., Brooklyn 11230-5655
Type: Private, independent, four-year
Degrees: Rabbinic   *Enroll:* 87
Phone: (718) 339-1090   *Calendar:* Sem. plan
Inst. Accred.: AARTS (1984/2005)

Yeshiva of Nitra—Rabbinical College Yeshiva Farm Settlement
Pines Bridge Rd., Mount Kisco 10549
Type: Private, independent, four-year
Degrees: Rabbinic, Talmudic   *Enroll:* 200
Phone: (718) 387-0422   *Calendar:* Sem. plan
Inst. Accred.: AARTS (1980/2001)

Yeshiva of the Telshe Alumni
4904 Independence Ave., Riverdale 10471
Type: Private, independent, four-year
Degrees: Talmudic   *Enroll:* 126
Phone: (718) 601-3523   *Calendar:* Sem. plan
Inst. Accred.: AARTS (1995/2003)

Yeshiva Shaar HaTorah Talmudic Research Institute
83-96 117th St., Kew Gardens 11415
Type: Private, independent, four-year
Degrees: Rabbinic, Talmudic　　　　　　　*Enroll:* 130
Phone: (718) 846-1940　　　　　　*Calendar:* Sem. plan
Inst. Accred.: AARTS (1984/2002)

Yeshiva Shaarei Torah of Rockland
91 West Carlton Rd., Suffern 10901-4013
Type: Private, independent, four-year
Degrees: Talmudic　　　　　　　　*FTE Enroll:* 45
Phone: (845) 352-3431　　　　　　*Calendar:* Sem. plan
Inst. Accred.: AARTS (2000/2004)

Yeshiva University
500 West 185th St., New York 10033-3299
Type: Private, independent, four-year
Degrees: A, B, M, P, D　　　　　　　*Enroll:* 5,636
URL: http://www.yu.edu
Phone: (212) 960-5400　　　　　*Calendar:* Sem. plan
Inst. Accred.: MSA-CHE (1948/2002)
Prog. Accred.: Clinical Psychology, Combined Professional-Scientific Psychology, Combined Prosthodontics, General Practice Residency, Law, Medicine, Oral and Maxillofacial Surgery, Orthodontic and Dentofacial Orthopedics, Pediatric Dentistry, School Psychology, Social Work

Yeshiva Zichron Aryeh
100 Cedarhurst Ave., Cedarhurst 11516-2158
Type: Private, independent, four-year
Degrees: Talmudic　　　　　　　*FTE Enroll:* 30
Phone: (516) 295-5700　　　　*Calendar:* Sem. plan
Inst. Accred.: AARTS (2004)

Yeshivas Novominsk
1569 47th St., Brooklyn 11219
Type: Private, independent, four-year
Degrees: Talmudic　　　　　　　*Enroll:* 123
Phone: (718) 438-2727　　　　*Calendar:* Sem. plan
Inst. Accred.: AARTS (1992/2005)

Yeshivath Viznitz
15 Elyon Rd., Monsey 10952
Type: Private, independent, four-year
Degrees: Rabbinic　　　　　　　*Enroll:* 454
Phone: (845) 356-1010　　　　*Calendar:* Sem. plan
Inst. Accred.: AARTS (1980/2002)

Yeshivath Zichron Moshe
Laurel Park Rd., South Fallsburg 12779
Type: Private, independent, four-year
Degrees: Talmudic　　　　　　　*Enroll:* 184
Phone: (845) 434-5240　　　　*Calendar:* Sem. plan
Inst. Accred.: AARTS (1979/2000)

NORTH CAROLINA

Alamance Community College
PO Box 8000, Graham 27253-8000
Type: Public, state/local, two-year
System: North Carolina Community College System
Degrees: A   *Enroll:* 2,657
URL: http://www.alamancecc.edu
Phone: (336) 578-2002   *Calendar:* Sem. plan
Inst. Accred.: SACS (1969/2003)
Prog. Accred.: Clinical Lab Technology, Culinary
    Education, Dental Assisting

Apex School of Theology
5104 Revere Rd., Durham 27713
Type: Private, nondenominational, four-year
Degrees: B, M
URL: http://www.apexsot.org
Phone: (919) 572-1625   *Calendar:* Sem. plan
Inst. Accred.: TRACS (2004)

Appalachian State University
Boone 28608
Type: Public, state, four-year
System: University of North Carolina System
Degrees: B, M, P, D   *Enroll:* 13,201
URL: http://www.appstate.edu
Phone: (828) 262-2000   *Calendar:* Sem. plan
Inst. Accred.: SACS (1942/2002)
Prog. Accred.: Art, Athletic Training, Business (AACSB),
    Computer Science, Counseling, Dietetics (internship),
    Family and Consumer Science, Marriage and Family
    Therapy, Music, Public Administration, Recreation and
    Leisure Services, Social Work, Speech-Language
    Pathology, Teacher Education (NCATE), Theatre

The Art Institute of Charlotte
Three LakePointe Plaza, 2110 Water Ridge Pkwy.,
Charlotte 28217
Type: Private, proprietary, four-year
System: Education Management Corporation
Degrees: A, B
URL: http://www.aich.artinstitutes.edu
Phone: (704) 357-8020   *Calendar:* Qtr. plan
Inst. Accred.: ACICS (1978/2003)

Asheville-Buncombe Technical Community College
340 Victoria Rd., Asheville 28801
Type: Public, state/local, two-year
System: North Carolina Community College System
Degrees: A   *Enroll:* 3,371
URL: http://www.abtech.edu
Phone: (828) 254-1921   *Calendar:* Sem. plan
Inst. Accred.: SACS (1969/2004)
Prog. Accred.: Clinical Lab Technology, Culinary
    Education, Dental Assisting, Dental Hygiene,
    Phlebotomy, Radiography

Barton College
College Station, Wilson 27893
Type: Private, Christian Church/Disciples of Christ, four-
    year
Degrees: B   *Enroll:* 1,043
URL: http://www.barton.edu
Phone: (252) 399-6300   *Calendar:* Sem. plan
Inst. Accred.: SACS (1955/1998)
Prog. Accred.: Nursing, Social Work, Teacher Education
    (NCATE)

Beaufort County Community College
PO Box 1069, Washington 27889
Type: Public, state/local, two-year
System: North Carolina Community College System
Degrees: A   *Enroll:* 1,056
URL: http://www.beaufortccc.edu
Phone: (252) 946-6194   *Calendar:* Sem. plan
Inst. Accred.: SACS (1973/1998)
Prog. Accred.: Clinical Lab Technology

Belmont Abbey College
100 Belmont-Mount Holly Rd., Belmont 28012-1802
Type: Private, Roman Catholic Church, four-year
Degrees: B, M   *Enroll:* 803
URL: http://www.belmontabbeycollege.edu
Phone: (704) 825-6700   *Calendar:* Sem. plan
Inst. Accred.: SACS (1957/1999)
Prog. Accred.: Teacher Education (NCATE)

Bennett College
900 East Washington St., Greensboro 27401-3239
Type: Private, United Methodist Church, four-year
Degrees: B   *Enroll:* 427
URL: http://www.bennett.edu
Phone: (336) 273-4431   *Calendar:* Sem. plan
Inst. Accred.: SACS (1935/1999, Probation)
Prog. Accred.: Social Work, Teacher Education (NCATE)

Bladen Community College
PO Box 266, Dublin 28332-0266
Type: Public, state, two-year
System: North Carolina Community College System
Degrees: A   *Enroll:* 1,032
URL: http://www.bladen.cc.nc.us
Phone: (910) 862-2164   *Calendar:* Sem. plan
Inst. Accred.: SACS (1976/2002)

Blue Ridge Community College
College Dr., Flat Rock 28731-7756
Type: Public, state/local, two-year
System: North Carolina Community College System
Degrees: A   *Enroll:* 1,272
URL: http://www.blueridge.edu
Phone: (828) 694-1700   *Calendar:* Sem. plan
Inst. Accred.: SACS (1973/1998)
Prog. Accred.: Surgical Technology

Brevard College
400 North Broad St., Brevard 28712-3306
Type: Private, United Methodist Church, four-year
Degrees: A, B   *Enroll:* 580
URL: http://www.brevard.edu
Phone: (828) 883-8292   *Calendar:* Sem. plan
Inst. Accred.: SACS (1949/2001)
Prog. Accred.: Music

Brunswick Community College
PO Box 30, Supply 28462
Type: Public, state, two-year
System: North Carolina Community College System
Degrees: A   *Enroll:* 734
URL: http://www.brunswickcc.edu
Phone: (910) 755-7300   *Calendar:* Sem. plan
Inst. Accred.: SACS (1983/1998)
Prog. Accred.: Phlebotomy

Cabarrus College of Health Sciences
401 Medical Park Dr., Concord 28025-3959
Type: Private, independent, four-year
Degrees: A, B   *Enroll:* 206
URL: http://www.cabarruscollege.edu
Phone: (704) 783-1555   *Calendar:* Sem. plan
Inst. Accred.: SACS (1995/2000)
Prog. Accred.: Medical Assisting (AMA), Nursing, Nursing
   Education, Occupational Therapy Assisting, Surgical
   Technology

Caldwell Community College and Technical Institute
2855 Hickory Blvd., Hudson 28638
Type: Public, state/local, two-year
System: North Carolina Community College System
Degrees: A   *Enroll:* 2,390
URL: http://www.cccti.edu
Phone: (828) 726-2200   *Calendar:* Sem. plan
Inst. Accred.: SACS (1969/1996)
Prog. Accred.: Diagnostic Medical Sonography, Nuclear
   Medicine Technology, Physical Therapy Assisting,
   Radiography

Campbell University
PO Box 127, Buies Creek 27506-0127
Type: Private, Southern Baptist Church, four-year
Degrees: B, M, P, D   *Enroll:* 5,332
URL: http://www.campbell.edu
Phone: (910) 893-1200   *Calendar:* Sem. plan
Inst. Accred.: SACS (1941/2000)
Prog. Accred.: Law (ABA only), Pharmacy, Social Work,
   Teacher Education (NCATE)

Cape Fear Community College
411 North Front St., Wilmington 28401-3993
Type: Public, state/local, two-year
System: North Carolina Community College System
Degrees: A   *Enroll:* 4,783
URL: http://www.cfcc.edu
Phone: (910) 362-7000   *Calendar:* Sem. plan
Inst. Accred.: SACS (1971/1996)
Prog. Accred.: Dental Assisting, Dental Hygiene, Nursing,
   Occupational Therapy Assisting, Phlebotomy,
   Radiography

Carolinas College of Health Sciences
PO Box 32861, 1200 Blythe Blvd., Charlotte 28232-2861
Type: Public, state-related, two-year
Degrees: A   *FTE Enroll:* 7
URL: http://www.carolinascollege.edu
Phone: (704) 355-5043   *Calendar:* Sem. plan
Inst. Accred.: SACS (1995/2000)
Prog. Accred.: Clinical Lab Scientist, Clinical Pastoral
   Education (ACPEI), General Practice Residency, Nursing,
   Phlebotomy, Radiography, Surgical Technology

Carteret Community College
3505 Arendell St., Morehead City 28557-2989
Type: Public, state/local, two-year
System: North Carolina Community College System
Degrees: A   *Enroll:* 1,028
URL: http://www.carteret.edu
Phone: (252) 222-6000   *Calendar:* Sem. plan
Inst. Accred.: SACS (1974/1999)
Prog. Accred.: Medical Assisting (AMA), Phlebotomy,
   Radiography, Respiratory Therapy Technology

Catawba College
2300 West Innes St., Salisbury 28144
Type: Private, United Church of Christ, four-year
Degrees: B, M   *Enroll:* 1,421
URL: http://www.catawba.edu
Phone: (704) 637-4111   *Calendar:* Sem. plan
Inst. Accred.: SACS (1928/1995)
Prog. Accred.: Athletic Training, Teacher Education
   (NCATE)

Catawba Valley Community College
2550 Hwy. 70 SE, Hickory 28602-9699
Type: Public, state/local, two-year
System: North Carolina Community College System
Degrees: A   *Enroll:* 3,010
URL: http://www.cvcc.edu
Phone: (828) 327-7000   *Calendar:* Sem. plan
Inst. Accred.: SACS (1969/1994, Warning)
Prog. Accred.: Business (ACBSP), Dental Hygiene, EMT
   (Paramedic), Health Information Technician, Nursing,
   Respiratory Therapy, Surgical Technology

Central Carolina Community College
1105 Kelly Dr., Sanford 27330
Type: Public, state/local, two-year
System: North Carolina Community College System
Degrees: A   *Enroll:* 2,817
URL: http://www.cccc.edu
Phone: (919) 775-5401   *Calendar:* Sem. plan
Inst. Accred.: SACS (1972/1997)
Prog. Accred.: Medical Assisting (AMA), Veterinary
   Technology

Central Piedmont Community College
PO Box 35009, Charlotte 28235-5009
Type: Public, state/local, two-year
System: North Carolina Community College System
Degrees: A   *Enroll:* 9,254
URL: http://www.cpcc.edu
Phone: (704) 330-2722   *Calendar:* Sem. plan
Inst. Accred.: SACS (1969/2003)
Prog. Accred.: Clinical Lab Technology, Cytotechnology,
   Dental Assisting, Dental Hygiene, Engineering
   Technology (computer, electrical, manufacturing,
   mechanical), Health Information Technician, Medical
   Assisting (AMA), Physical Therapy Assisting, Respiratory
   Therapy

Chowan College
200 Jones Dr., Murfreesboro 27855
Type: Private, Southern Baptist Church, four-year
Degrees: A, B   *Enroll:* 764
URL: http://www.chowan.edu
Phone: (252) 398-6500   *Calendar:* Sem. plan
Inst. Accred.: SACS (1956/1998)
Prog. Accred.: Music, Teacher Education (NCATE)

Cleveland Community College
137 South Post Rd., Shelby 28152
Type: Public, state/local, two-year
System: North Carolina Community College System
Degrees: A   *Enroll:* 1,665
URL: http://www.clevelandcommunitycollege.edu
Phone: (704) 484-4000   *Calendar:* Sem. plan
Inst. Accred.: SACS (1975/2001)
Prog. Accred.: Radiography

Coastal Carolina Community College
444 Western Blvd., Jacksonville 28546-6899
Type: Public, state/local, two-year
System: North Carolina Community College System
Degrees: A   *Enroll:* 2,809
URL: http://www.coastalcarolina.edu
Phone: (910) 455-1221   *Calendar:* Sem. plan
Inst. Accred.: SACS (1972/1997)
Prog. Accred.: Clinical Lab Technology, Dental Assisting,
   Dental Hygiene, Surgical Technology

College of The Albemarle
PO Box 2327, Elizabeth City 27906-2327
Type: Public, state/local, two-year
System: North Carolina Community College System
Degrees: A   *Enroll:* 1,400
URL: http://www.albemarle.edu
Phone: (252) 335-0821   *Calendar:* Sem. plan
Inst. Accred.: SACS (1968/2003)
Prog. Accred.: Nursing

Craven Community College
800 College Ct., New Bern 28562
Type: Public, state/local, two-year
System: North Carolina Community College System
Degrees: A   *Enroll:* 1,692
URL: http://www.cravencc.edu
Phone: (252) 638-4131   *Calendar:* Sem. plan
Inst. Accred.: SACS (1971/1996)

Davidson College
Davidson 28035
Type: Private, Presbyterian Church (USA), four-year
Degrees: B   *Enroll:* 1,711
URL: http://www.davidson.edu
Phone: (704) 894-2000   *Calendar:* Sem. plan
Inst. Accred.: SACS (1917/1996)
Prog. Accred.: Teacher Education (NCATE)

Davidson County Community College
PO Box 1287, Lexington 27293-1287
Type: Public, state/local, two-year
System: North Carolina Community College System
Degrees: A   *Enroll:* 1,765
URL: http://www.davidsonccc.edu
Phone: (336) 249-8186   *Calendar:* Sem. plan
Inst. Accred.: SACS (1968/2002)
Prog. Accred.: Clinical Lab Technology, Engineering
   Technology (electrical), Health Information Technician,
   Medical Assisting (AMA), Nursing

Duke University
207 Allen Bldg., Box 90001, Durham 27708
Type: Private, independent, four-year
Degrees: A, B, M, D   *Enroll:* 12,013
URL: http://www.duke.edu
Phone: (919) 684-8111   *Calendar:* Sem. plan
Inst. Accred.: ATS (1938/2005), SACS (1895/1998)
Prog. Accred.: Business (AACSB), Clinical Lab Scientist,
   Clinical Pastoral Education (ACPEI), Clinical Psychology,
   Engineering (bioengineering, civil, computer, electrical,
   mechanical), Forestry, Health Services Administration,
   Law, Medicine, Nursing, Nursing Education, Ophthalmic
   Medical Technology, Pathologists' Assistant, Physical
   Therapy, Physician Assistant, Psychology Internship,
   Teacher Education (NCATE)

Durham Technical Community College
1637 Lawson St., Durham 27703-5023
Type: Public, state/local, two-year
System: North Carolina Community College System
Degrees: A   *Enroll:* 2,909
URL: http://www.durhamtech.edu
Phone: (919) 686-3300   *Calendar:* Sem. plan
Inst. Accred.: SACS (1971/1996)
Prog. Accred.: Dental Laboratory Technology,
   Occupational Therapy Assisting, Opticianry, Respiratory
   Therapy, Respiratory Therapy Technology

East Carolina University
East Fifth St., Greenville 27858-4353
Type: Public, state, four-year
System: University of North Carolina System
Degrees: B, M, P, D   *Enroll:* 19,013
URL: http://www.ecu.edu
Phone: (252) 328-6131   *Calendar:* Sem. plan
Inst. Accred.: SACS (1927/2002)
Prog. Accred.: Art, Athletic Training, Audiology, Business
   (AACSB), Clinical Lab Scientist, Construction Education,
   Design Technology, Dietetics (internship), Electronic
   Technology, General Practice Residency, Health
   Information Administration, Industrial Technology,
   Interior Design, Manufacturing Technology, Marriage
   and Family Therapy, Medicine, Music, Nurse
   (Midwifery), Nursing, Occupational Therapy, Physical
   Therapy, Physician Assistant, Public Administration,
   Recreation and Leisure Services, Rehabilitation
   Counseling, Social Work, Speech-Language Pathology,
   Teacher Education (NCATE)

Edgecombe Community College
2009 West Wilson St., Tarboro 27886
Type: Public, state/local, two-year
System: North Carolina Community College System
Degrees: A   *Enroll:* 1,520
URL: http://www.edgecombe.edu
Phone: (252) 823-5166   *Calendar:* Sem. plan
Inst. Accred.: SACS (1973/1998)
Prog. Accred.: Health Information Technician, Medical
   Assisting (AMA), Radiography, Respiratory Therapy,
   Respiratory Therapy Technology

Elizabeth City State University
1704 Weeksville Rd., Elizabeth City 27909
Type: Public, state, four-year
System: University of North Carolina System
Degrees: B, M   *Enroll:* 2,077
URL: http://www.ecsu.edu
Phone: (252) 335-3400   *Calendar:* Sem. plan
Inst. Accred.: SACS (1947/2001)
Prog. Accred.: Industrial Technology, Teacher Education
   (NCATE)

Elon University
2700 Campus Box, Elon 27244-2010
Type: Private, United Church of Christ, four-year
Degrees: B, M, D   *Enroll:* 4,456
URL: http://www.elon.edu
Phone: (336) 278-2000   *Calendar:* Sem. plan
Inst. Accred.: SACS (1947/2002)
Prog. Accred.: Athletic Training, Business (AACSB),
   Physical Therapy, Teacher Education (NCATE)

Fayetteville State University
1200 Murchison Rd., Newbold Station, Fayetteville
28301-4298
Type: Public, state, four-year
System: University of North Carolina System
Degrees: A, B, M, D   *Enroll:* 4,368
URL: http://www.uncfsu.edu
Phone: (910) 672-1111   *Calendar:* Sem. plan
Inst. Accred.: SACS (1947/2001)
Prog. Accred.: Business (AACSB), Nursing Education,
   Teacher Education (NCATE)

Fayetteville Technical Community College
PO Box 35236, 2201 Hull Rd., Fayetteville 28303-0236
Type: Public, state, two-year
System: North Carolina Community College System
Degrees: A   *Enroll:* 6,388
URL: http://www.faytechcc.edu
Phone: (910) 678-8400   *Calendar:* Sem. plan
Inst. Accred.: SACS (1967/2001)
Prog. Accred.: Dental Assisting, Dental Hygiene,
   Engineering Technology (civil/construction, electrical),
   Funeral Service Education (Mortuary Science), Nursing,
   Phlebotomy, Physical Therapy Assisting, Radiography,
   Respiratory Therapy, Surgical Technology

Forsyth Technical Community College
2100 Silas Creek Pkwy., Winston-Salem 27103
Type: Public, state, two-year
System: North Carolina Community College System
Degrees: A   *Enroll:* 4,292
URL: http://www.forsythtech.edu
Phone: (336) 723-0371   *Calendar:* Sem. plan
Inst. Accred.: SACS (1968/2002)
Prog. Accred.: Dental Assisting, Diagnostic Medical
   Sonography, Engineering Technology (electrical),
   Medical Assisting (AMA), Nuclear Medicine Technology,
   Radiation Therapy, Radiography, Respiratory Therapy

Gardner-Webb University
PO Box 897, Boiling Springs 28017
Type: Private, Southern Baptist Church, four-year
Degrees: A, B, M, D   *Enroll:* 3,042
URL: http://www.gardner-webb.edu
Phone: (704) 406-2361   *Calendar:* Sem. plan
Inst. Accred.: ATS (1998/2000), SACS (1948/1996)
Prog. Accred.: Music, Nursing, Teacher Education (NCATE)

Gaston College

201 Hwy. 321 South, Dallas 28034-1499
Type: Public, state/local, two-year
System: North Carolina Community College System
Degrees: A   *Enroll:* 3,089
URL: http://www.gaston.edu
Phone: (704) 922-6200   *Calendar:* Sem. plan
Inst. Accred.: SACS (1967/2001)
Prog. Accred.: Engineering Technology (civil/construction,
electrical, industrial, mechanical), Medical Assisting
(AMA), Veterinary Technology

Greensboro College

815 West Market St., Greensboro 27401-1875
Type: Private, United Methodist Church, four-year
Degrees: B, M   *Enroll:* 1,018
URL: http://www.gborocollege.edu
Phone: (336) 272-7102   *Calendar:* Sem. plan
Inst. Accred.: SACS (1926/2005)
Prog. Accred.: Music, Teacher Education (NCATE)

Guilford College

5800 West Friendly Ave., Greensboro 27410
Type: Private, Religious Society of Friends (Quaker), four-
year
Degrees: A, B   *Enroll:* 1,878
URL: http://www.guilford.edu
Phone: (336) 316-2000   *Calendar:* Sem. plan
Inst. Accred.: SACS (1926/1996)
Prog. Accred.: Teacher Education (NCATE)

Guilford Technical Community College

PO Box 309, Jamestown 27282
Type: Public, state, two-year
System: North Carolina Community College System
Degrees: A   *Enroll:* 6,118
URL: http://www.gtcc.edu
Phone: (336) 334-4822   *Calendar:* Sem. plan
Inst. Accred.: SACS (1969/2005)
Prog. Accred.: Culinary Education, Dental Assisting,
Dental Hygiene, Medical Assisting (AMA), Physical
Therapy Assisting, Surgical Technology

Halifax Community College

PO Drawer 809, Weldon 27890
Type: Public, state/local, two-year
System: North Carolina Community College System
Degrees: A   *Enroll:* 1,207
URL: http://www.halifaxcc.edu
Phone: (252) 536-2551   *Calendar:* Sem. plan
Inst. Accred.: SACS (1975/2000)
Prog. Accred.: Clinical Lab Technology, Phlebotomy

Haywood Community College

185 Freedlander Dr., Clyde 28721
Type: Public, state, two-year
System: North Carolina Community College System
Degrees: A   *Enroll:* 1,200
URL: http://www.haywood.edu
Phone: (828) 627-2821   *Calendar:* Sem. plan
Inst. Accred.: SACS (1973/1998)
Prog. Accred.: Medical Assisting (CAAHEP)

Heritage Bible College

PO Box 1628, 1747 Bud Hawkins Rd., Dunn 28335-1628
Type: Private, Penticostal Free Will Baptist Church, four-
year
Degrees: A, B   *Enroll:* 90
URL: http://www.heritagebiblecollege.org
Phone: (910) 892-3178   *Calendar:* Sem. plan
Inst. Accred.: TRACS (1998/2003)

High Point University

833 Montlieu Ave., High Point 27262
Type: Private, United Methodist Church, four-year
Degrees: B, M   *Enroll:* 2,655
URL: http://www.highpoint.edu
Phone: (336) 841-9000   *Calendar:* Sem. plan
Inst. Accred.: SACS (1951/1995)
Prog. Accred.: Athletic Training, Teacher Education
(NCATE)

Hood Theological Seminary

800 West Thomas St., Salisbury 28144
Type: Private, African Methodist Episcopal Zion Church,
four-year
Degrees: M
URL: http://www.hoodseminary.edu
Phone: (704) 636-7611
Inst. Accred.: ATS (1998)

Isothermal Community College

PO Box 804, Spindale 28160-0804
Type: Public, state/local, two-year
System: North Carolina Community College System
Degrees: A   *Enroll:* 1,314
URL: http://www.isothermal.edu
Phone: (828) 286-3636   *Calendar:* Sem. plan
Inst. Accred.: SACS (1970/1995)

James Sprunt Community College

PO Box 398, Kenansville 28349-0398
Type: Public, state, two-year
System: North Carolina Community College System
Degrees: A   *Enroll:* 973
URL: http://www.sprunt.com
Phone: (910) 296-2400   *Calendar:* Sem. plan
Inst. Accred.: SACS (1973/1998)
Prog. Accred.: Medical Assisting (AMA), Phlebotomy

John Wesley College

2314 North Centennial St., High Point 27265-3197
Type: Private, independent, four-year
Degrees: A, B   *Enroll:* 124
URL: http://www.johnwesley.edu
Phone: (336) 889-2262   *Calendar:* Sem. plan
Inst. Accred.: ABHE (1982/2003)

Johnson C. Smith University
100 Beatties Ford Rd., Charlotte 28216
Type: Private, independent, four-year
Degrees: B *Enroll:* 1,428
URL: http://www.jcsu.edu
Phone: (704) 378-1000 *Calendar:* Sem. plan
Inst. Accred.: SACS (1933/1996)
Prog. Accred.: Business (ACBSP), Social Work, Teacher
Education (NCATE)

Johnston Community College
PO Box 2350, Smithfield 27577-2350
Type: Public, state/local, two-year
System: North Carolina Community College System
Degrees: A *Enroll:* 2,378
URL: http://www.johnstoncc.edu
Phone: (919) 934-3051 *Calendar:* Sem. plan
Inst. Accred.: SACS (1977/2002)
Prog. Accred.: Radiography

King's College
322 Lamar Ave., Charlotte 28204
Type: Private, proprietary, two-year
Degrees: A *FTE Enroll:* 385
URL: http://www.kingscollegecharlotte.edu
Phone: (704) 372-0266 *Calendar:* Qtr. plan
Inst. Accred.: ACICS (1954/2004)
Prog. Accred.: Medical Assisting (CAAHEP)

Lees-McRae College
PO Box 128, Banner Elk 28604
Type: Private, United Presbyterian Church (USA), four-
year
Degrees: A, B *Enroll:* 916
URL: http://www.lmc.edu
Phone: (828) 898-5241 *Calendar:* Sem. plan
Inst. Accred.: SACS (1953/2005, Probation)
Prog. Accred.: Nursing Education, Teacher Education
(NCATE)

Lenoir Community College
PO Box 188, Kinston 28502-0188
Type: Public, state/local, two-year
System: North Carolina Community College System
Degrees: A *Enroll:* 1,702
URL: http://www.lenoircc.edu
Phone: (252) 527-6223 *Calendar:* Sem. plan
Inst. Accred.: SACS (1968/2003)
Prog. Accred.: Medical Assisting (AMA), Surgical
Technology

Lenoir-Rhyne College
625 7th Ave., NE, Hickory 28601
Type: Private, North Carolina Synod of Evangelical
Lutheran Churc, four-year
Degrees: B, M *Enroll:* 1,378
URL: http://www.lrc.edu
Phone: (828) 328-1741 *Calendar:* Sem. plan
Inst. Accred.: SACS (1928/2002, Probation)
Prog. Accred.: Athletic Training, Business (ACBSP),
Nursing, Nursing Education, Occupational Therapy,
Teacher Education (NCATE)

Livingstone College
701 West Monroe St., Salisbury 28144
Type: Private, African Methodist Episcopal Zion Church,
four-year
Degrees: B *Enroll:* 989
URL: http://www.livingstone.edu
Phone: (704) 216-6000 *Calendar:* Sem. plan
Inst. Accred.: SACS (1944/2001)
Prog. Accred.: Social Work, Teacher Education (NCATE)

Louisburg College
501 North Main St., Louisburg 27549
Type: Private, North Carolina Conference of the Methodist
Church, two-year
Degrees: A *Enroll:* 495
URL: http://www.louisburg.edu
Phone: (919) 496-2521 *Calendar:* Sem. plan
Inst. Accred.: SACS (1952/1996, Warning)

Mars Hill College
100 Athletic St., Mars Hill 28754
Type: Private, Southern Baptist Church, four-year
Degrees: B *Enroll:* 1,203
URL: http://www.mhc.edu
Phone: (828) 689-1111 *Calendar:* Sem. plan
Inst. Accred.: SACS (1926/2001)
Prog. Accred.: Music, Social Work, Teacher Education
(NCATE), Theatre

Martin Community College
1161 Kehukee Park Rd., Williamston 27892-8307
Type: Public, state/local, two-year
System: North Carolina Community College System
Degrees: A *Enroll:* 575
URL: http://www.martincc.edu
Phone: (252) 792-1521 *Calendar:* Sem. plan
Inst. Accred.: SACS (1972/1998)
Prog. Accred.: Dental Assisting, Medical Assisting (AMA),
Physical Therapy Assisting

Mayland Community College
PO Box 547, Spruce Pine 28777
Type: Public, state/local, two-year
System: North Carolina Community College System
Degrees: A *Enroll:* 819
URL: http://www.mayland.edu
Phone: (828) 765-7351 *Calendar:* Sem. plan
Inst. Accred.: SACS (1978/2005)

McDowell Technical Community College
54 College Dr., Marion 28752-8728
Type: Public, state/local, two-year
System: North Carolina Community College System
Degrees: A *Enroll:* 787
URL: http://www.mcdowelltech.edu
Phone: (828) 652-6021 *Calendar:* Sem. plan
Inst. Accred.: SACS (1975/2000)

Meredith College
3800 Hillsborough St., Raleigh 27607-5298
Type: Private, independent, four-year
Degrees: B, M   *Enroll:* 1,804
URL: http://www.meredith.edu
Phone: (919) 760-8600   *Calendar:* Sem. plan
Inst. Accred.: SACS (1921/2000)
Prog. Accred.: Dietetics (internship), Interior Design, Music, Social Work, Teacher Education (NCATE)

Methodist College
5400 Ramsey St., Fayetteville 28311-1420
Type: Private, United Methodist Church, four-year
Degrees: A, B, M   *Enroll:* 1,918
URL: http://www.methodist.edu
Phone: (919) 630-7000   *Calendar:* Sem. plan
Inst. Accred.: SACS (1966/1999)
Prog. Accred.: Business (ACBSP), Physician Assistant, Social Work, Teacher Education (NCATE)

Mitchell Community College
500 West Broad St., Statesville 28677
Type: Public, state, two-year
System: North Carolina Community College System
Degrees: A   *Enroll:* 1,413
URL: http://www.mitchellcc.edu
Phone: (704) 878-3200   *Calendar:* Sem. plan
Inst. Accred.: SACS (1955/1997)
Prog. Accred.: Medical Assisting (CAAHEP)

Montgomery Community College
1011 Page St., Troy 27371-8387
Type: Public, state/local, two-year
System: North Carolina Community College System
Degrees: A   *Enroll:* 592
URL: http://www.montgomery.edu
Phone: (910) 576-6222   *Calendar:* Sem. plan
Inst. Accred.: SACS (1978/2003)
Prog. Accred.: Medical Assisting (CAAHEP)

Montreat College
PO Box 1267, Montreat 28757
Type: Private, Presbyterian Church (USA), four-year
Degrees: A, B, M   *Enroll:* 1,005
URL: http://www.montreat.edu
Phone: (828) 669-8011   *Calendar:* Sem. plan
Inst. Accred.: SACS (1960/2000)
Prog. Accred.: Teacher Education (NCATE)

Mount Olive College
634 Henderson St., Mount Olive 28365
Type: Private, Convention of Original Free Will Baptists, four-year
Degrees: A, B   *Enroll:* 2,041
URL: http://www.mountolivecollege.edu
Phone: (919) 658-2502   *Calendar:* Sem. plan
Inst. Accred.: SACS (1960/2001)

Nash Community College
PO Box 7488, Rocky Mount 27804-0488
Type: Public, state/local, two-year
System: North Carolina Community College System
Degrees: A   *Enroll:* 1,462
URL: http://www.nashcc.edu
Phone: (252) 443-4011   *Calendar:* Sem. plan
Inst. Accred.: SACS (1976/2001)
Prog. Accred.: Phlebotomy, Physical Therapy Assisting

North Carolina Agricultural and Technical State University
1601 East Market St., Greensboro 27411
Type: Public, state, four-year
System: University of North Carolina System
Degrees: B, M, D   *Enroll:* 9,107
URL: http://www.ncat.edu
Phone: (336) 334-7500   *Calendar:* Sem. plan
Inst. Accred.: SACS (1936/2000)
Prog. Accred.: Accounting, Business (AACSB), Computer Science, Construction Education, Construction Technology, Counseling, Electronic Technology, Engineering (agricultural, architectural, chemical, civil, electrical, environmental/sanitary, industrial, mechanical), Family and Consumer Science, Industrial Technology, Journalism, Landscape Architecture, Manufacturing Technology, Music, Nursing, Social Work, Teacher Education (NCATE), Theatre

North Carolina Central University
1801 Fayetteville St., Durham 27707
Type: Public, state, four-year
System: University of North Carolina System
Degrees: B, M, D   *Enroll:* 5,872
URL: http://www.nccu.edu
Phone: (919) 560-6100   *Calendar:* Sem. plan
Inst. Accred.: SACS (1938/1999)
Prog. Accred.: Business (AACSB), Business (ACBSP), Dietetics (internship), Law (ABA only), Librarianship, Nursing, Recreation and Leisure Services, Social Work, Speech-Language Pathology, Teacher Education (NCATE), Theatre

North Carolina School of the Arts
1533 South Main St., Winston-Salem 27127-2738
Type: Public, state, four-year
System: University of North Carolina System
Degrees: B, M   *Enroll:* 785
URL: http://www.ncarts.edu
Phone: (336) 770-3399   *Calendar:* Tri. plan
Inst. Accred.: SACS (1970/1995)

North Carolina State University
Campus Box 7001, Raleigh 27695-7001
Type: Public, state, four-year
System: University of North Carolina System
Degrees: A, B, M, D   *Enroll:* 25,386
URL: http://www.ncsu.edu
Phone: (919) 515-2011   *Calendar:* Sem. plan
Inst. Accred.: SACS (1928/2004)
Prog. Accred.: Art, Business (AACSB), Computer Science,
  Counseling, Engineering (aerospace, agricultural,
  chemical, civil, computer, construction, electrical,
  environmental/sanitary, industrial, materials,
  mechanical, nuclear, textile), Forestry, Landscape
  Architecture, Public Administration, Recreation and
  Leisure Services, School Psychology, Social Work,
  Teacher Education (NCATE), Veterinary Medicine

North Carolina Wesleyan College
3400 North Wesleyan Blvd., Rocky Mount 27804-9906
Type: Private, United Methodist Church, four-year
Degrees: B   *Enroll:* 1,308
URL: http://www.ncwc.edu
Phone: (252) 985-5100   *Calendar:* 4-1-4 plan
Inst. Accred.: SACS (1966/2002)
Prog. Accred.: Teacher Education (NCATE)

Pamlico Community College
PO Box 185, Grantsboro 28529
Type: Public, state/local, two-year
System: North Carolina Community College System
Degrees: A   *Enroll:* 226
URL: http://www.pamlico.cc.nc.us
Phone: (252) 249-1851   *Calendar:* Sem. plan
Inst. Accred.: SACS (1977/2002)

Peace College
15 East Peace St., Raleigh 27604-1194
Type: Private, Presbyterian Church (USA), four-year
Degrees: A, B   *Enroll:* 680
URL: http://www.peace.edu
Phone: (919) 508-2000   *Calendar:* Sem. plan
Inst. Accred.: SACS (1947/2001)

Pfeiffer University
PO Box 960, Misenheimer 28109-0960
Type: Private, United Methodist Church, four-year
Degrees: B, M   *Enroll:* 1,474
URL: http://www.pfeiffer.edu
Phone: (704) 463-1360   *Calendar:* Sem. plan
Inst. Accred.: SACS (1942/2002)
Prog. Accred.: Music, Teacher Education (NCATE)

Charlotte Campus
4701 Park Rd., Charlotte 28209
Phone: (704) 521-9116

Triangle Campus
5001 South Miami Blvd., Ste. 118, Durham 27703
Phone: (919) 941-2920

Piedmont Baptist College
716 Franklin St., Winston-Salem 27101-5133
Type: Private, independent, four-year
Degrees: A, B, M   *Enroll:* 228
URL: http://www.pbc.edu
Phone: (336) 725-8344   *Calendar:* Sem. plan
Inst. Accred.: TRACS (1994/2000)

Piedmont Community College
PO Box 1197, Roxboro 27573
Type: Public, state/local, two-year
System: North Carolina Community College System
Degrees: A   *Enroll:* 1,233
URL: http://www.piedmontcc.edu
Phone: (336) 599-1181   *Calendar:* Sem. plan
Inst. Accred.: SACS (1977/2002)

Pitt Community College
PO Drawer 7007, Greenville 27835-7007
Type: Public, state, two-year
System: North Carolina Community College System
Degrees: A   *Enroll:* 4,073
URL: http://www.pittcc.edu
Phone: (252) 321-4200   *Calendar:* Sem. plan
Inst. Accred.: SACS (1969/2003)
Prog. Accred.: Diagnostic Medical Sonography, Health
  Information Technician, Medical Assisting (AMA),
  Occupational Therapy Assisting, Radiation Therapy,
  Radiography, Respiratory Therapy

Queens University of Charlotte
1900 Selwyn Ave., Charlotte 28274
Type: Private, Presbyterian Church (USA), four-year
Degrees: B, M   *Enroll:* 1,386
URL: http://www.queens.edu
Phone: (704) 337-2200   *Calendar:* Sem. plan
Inst. Accred.: SACS (1932/2001)
Prog. Accred.: Business (AACSB), Business (ACBSP),
  Music, Nursing, Nursing Education, Teacher Education
  (NCATE)

Randolph Community College
PO Box 1009, Asheboro 27204-1009
Type: Public, state/local, two-year
System: North Carolina Community College System
Degrees: A   *Enroll:* 1,421
URL: http://www.randolph.edu
Phone: (336) 633-0200   *Calendar:* Sem. plan
Inst. Accred.: SACS (1974/1999)
Prog. Accred.: Nursing

Richmond Community College
PO Box 1189, Hamlet 28345
Type: Public, state/local, two-year
System: North Carolina Community College System
Degrees: A   *Enroll:* 1,159
URL: http://www.richmondcc.edu
Phone: (910) 582-7000   *Calendar:* Sem. plan
Inst. Accred.: SACS (1969/2003)

Roanoke Bible College

715 North Poindexter St., Elizabeth City 27909-4054
Type: Private, Christian Churches/Churches of Christ,
four-year
Degrees: A, B   *Enroll:* 170
URL: http://www.roanokebible.edu
Phone: (252) 334-2070   *Calendar:* Sem. plan
Inst. Accred.: ABHE (1979/2000), SACS (1999/2005)

Roanoke-Chowan Community College

109 Community College Rd., Ahoskie 27910
Type: Public, state/local, two-year
System: North Carolina Community College System
Degrees: A   *Enroll:* 666
URL: http://www.roanokechowan.edu
Phone: (252) 862-1200   *Calendar:* Sem. plan
Inst. Accred.: SACS (1976/2002)

Robeson Community College

PO Box 1420, Lumberton 28359
Type: Public, state/local, two-year
System: North Carolina Community College System
Degrees: A   *Enroll:* 1,578
URL: http://www.robeson.cc.nc.us
Phone: (910) 738-7101   *Calendar:* Sem. plan
Inst. Accred.: SACS (1975/2001)
Prog. Accred.: Respiratory Therapy

Rockingham Community College

PO Box 38, Wentworth 27375-0038
Type: Public, state/local, two-year
System: North Carolina Community College System
Degrees: A   *Enroll:* 1,389
URL: http://www.rockinghamcc.edu
Phone: (336) 342-4261   *Calendar:* Sem. plan
Inst. Accred.: SACS (1968/2003)
Prog. Accred.: Phlebotomy, Surgical Technology

Rowan-Cabarrus Community College

PO Box 1595, Salisbury 28145-1595
Type: Public, state, two-year
System: North Carolina Community College System
Degrees: A   *Enroll:* 3,244
URL: http://www.rowancabarrus.edu
Phone: (704) 637-0760   *Calendar:* Sem. plan
Inst. Accred.: SACS (1970/1995)
Prog. Accred.: Dental Assisting, Nursing, Radiography

Saint Andrews Presbyterian College

1700 Dogwood Mile, Laurinburg 28352
Type: Private, Presbyterian Church (USA), four-year
Degrees: B   *Enroll:* 655
URL: http://www.sapc.edu
Phone: (910) 277-5000   *Calendar:* Sem. plan
Inst. Accred.: SACS (1961/2000, Warning)
Prog. Accred.: Teacher Education (NCATE)

Saint Augustine's College

1315 Oakwood Ave., Raleigh 27610-2298
Type: Private, Episcopal Church, four-year
Degrees: B   *Enroll:* 1,582
URL: http://www.st-aug.edu
Phone: (919) 516-4000   *Calendar:* Sem. plan
Inst. Accred.: SACS (1942/2002)
Prog. Accred.: Teacher Education (NCATE)

Salem College

Salem Station, PO Box 10548, Winston-Salem 27108-
0548
Type: Private, independent, four-year
Degrees: B, M   *Enroll:* 878
URL: http://www.salem.edu
Phone: (336) 721-2600   *Calendar:* 4-1-4 plan
Inst. Accred.: SACS (1922/2000)
Prog. Accred.: Music, Teacher Education (NCATE)

Sampson Community College

PO Box 318, Highway 24 West, Clinton 28329-0318
Type: Public, state/local, two-year
System: North Carolina Community College System
Degrees: A   *Enroll:* 977
URL: http://www.sampsoncc.edu
Phone: (910) 592-8081   *Calendar:* Sem. plan
Inst. Accred.: SACS (1977/2003)

Sandhills Community College

3395 Airport Rd., Pinehurst 28374
Type: Public, state/local, two-year
System: North Carolina Community College System
Degrees: A   *Enroll:* 2,371
URL: http://www.sandhills.edu
Phone: (910) 695-6185   *Calendar:* Sem. plan
Inst. Accred.: SACS (1968/2003)
Prog. Accred.: Clinical Lab Technology, Radiography,
Respiratory Therapy, Surgical Technology

School of Communication Arts

3000 Wakefield Crossing Dr., Raleigh 27614
Type: Private, proprietary, two-year
Degrees: A
URL: http://www.higherdigital.com
Phone: (919) 488-8500   *Calendar:* Qtr. plan
Inst. Accred.: COE (1994/2000)

Shaw University

118 East South St., Raleigh 27601
Type: Private, Baptist Church, four-year
Degrees: A, B, M   *Enroll:* 2,394
URL: http://www.shawuniversity.edu
Phone: (919) 546-8200   *Calendar:* Sem. plan
Inst. Accred.: ATS (1997/1999), SACS (1943/2002)
Prog. Accred.: Kinesiotherapy, Teacher Education (NCATE)

South College
1567 Patton Ave., Asheville 28806-1748
Type: Private, proprietary, two-year
Degrees: A   *Enroll:* 98
URL: http://www.southcollegenc.com
Phone: (828) 252-2486   *Calendar:* Sem. plan
Inst. Accred.: ACICS (1971/2000)
Prog. Accred.: Medical Assisting (CAAHEP)

South Piedmont Community College
PO Box 126, Polkton 28135
Type: Public, state/local, two-year
System: North Carolina Community College System
Degrees: A   *Enroll:* 1,088
URL: http://www.spcc.edu
Phone: (704) 272-7635   *Calendar:* Sem. plan
Inst. Accred.: SACS (1977/2003)
Prog. Accred.: Health Information Technician, Medical
Assisting (CAAHEP)

The Southeastern Baptist Theological Seminary
PO Box 1889, Wake Forest 27588-1889
Type: Private, Southern Baptist Church, four-year
Degrees: A, B, M, D   *Enroll:* 1,579
URL: http://www.sebts.edu
Phone: (919) 761-2100   *Calendar:* Sem. plan
Inst. Accred.: ATS (1958/2001), SACS (1978/2002)

Southeastern Community College
PO Box 151, Whiteville 28472
Type: Public, state, two-year
System: North Carolina Community College System
Degrees: A   *Enroll:* 1,372
URL: http://www.southeastern.cc.nc.us
Phone: (910) 642-7141   *Calendar:* Sem. plan
Inst. Accred.: SACS (1967/2001)
Prog. Accred.: Clinical Lab Technology

Southern Evangelical Seminary
3000 Tilley Morris Rd., Matthews 28104
Type: Private, nondenominational, four-year
Degrees: B, M
URL: http://www.ses.edu
Phone: (704) 847-5600   *Calendar:* Sem. plan
Inst. Accred.: TRACS (2001)

Southwestern Community College
447 College Dr., Sylva 28779
Type: Public, state/local, two-year
System: North Carolina Community College System
Degrees: A   *Enroll:* 1,240
URL: http://www.southwesterncc.edu
Phone: (828) 586-4091   *Calendar:* Sem. plan
Inst. Accred.: SACS (1971/1996)
Prog. Accred.: Clinical Lab Technology,
Electroneurodiagnostic Technology, Health Information
Technician, Phlebotomy, Physical Therapy Assisting,
Radiography, Respiratory Therapy

Stanly Community College
141 College Dr., Albemarle 28001
Type: Public, state/local, two-year
System: North Carolina Community College System
Degrees: A   *Enroll:* 1,269
URL: http://www.stanly.edu
Phone: (704) 982-0121   *Calendar:* Sem. plan
Inst. Accred.: SACS (1979/2005)
Prog. Accred.: Medical Assisting (AMA), Phlebotomy,
Respiratory Therapy

Surry Community College
630 South Main St., PO Box 304, Dobson 27017
Type: Public, state/local, two-year
System: North Carolina Community College System
Degrees: A   *Enroll:* 2,184
URL: http://www.surry.edu
Phone: (336) 386-8121   *Calendar:* Sem. plan
Inst. Accred.: SACS (1969/2004)

Tri-County Community College
4600 East Hwy. 64, Murphy 28906
Type: Public, state, two-year
System: North Carolina Community College System
Degrees: A   *Enroll:* 739
URL: http://www.tricountycc.edu
Phone: (828) 837-6810   *Calendar:* Sem. plan
Inst. Accred.: SACS (1975/2000)

The University of North Carolina at Asheville
One University Heights, Asheville 28804-8503
Type: Public, state, four-year
System: University of North Carolina System
Degrees: B, M   *Enroll:* 3,018
URL: http://www.unca.edu
Phone: (828) 251-6600   *Calendar:* Sem. plan
Inst. Accred.: SACS (1958/2002)
Prog. Accred.: Business (AACSB), Teacher Education
(NCATE)

The University of North Carolina at Chapel Hill
Chapel Hill 27599
Type: Public, state, four-year
System: University of North Carolina System
Degrees: B, M, P, D   *Enroll:* 23,588
URL: http://www.unc.edu
Phone: (919) 962-2211   *Calendar:* Sem. plan
Inst. Accred.: SACS (1895/1995)
Prog. Accred.: Advanced Education in General Dentistry, Applied Science (industrial hygiene), Athletic Training, Audiology, Business (AACSB), Clinical Lab Scientist, Clinical Pastoral Education (ACPEI), Clinical Psychology, Combined Prosthodontics, Counseling, Cytotechnology, Dental Assisting, Dental Hygiene, Dentistry, Dietetics (coordinated), Endodontics, Engineering (environmental/sanitary), General Dentistry, General Practice Residency, Health Services Administration, Immunology, Journalism, Law, Librarianship, Medicine, Microbiology, Nuclear Medicine Technology, Nursing, Nursing Education, Occupational Therapy, Oral and Maxillofacial Pathology, Oral and Maxillofacial Radiology, Oral and Maxillofacial Surgery, Orthodontic and Dentofacial Orthopedics, Pediatric Dentistry, Periodontics, Pharmacy, Physical Therapy, Planning, Psychology Internship, Public Administration, Public Health, Radiation Therapy, Radiography, Recreation and Leisure Services, Rehabilitation Counseling, School Psychology, Social Work, Speech-Language Pathology, Teacher Education (NCATE)

The University of North Carolina at Charlotte
9201 University City Blvd., Charlotte 28223-0007
Type: Public, state, four-year
System: University of North Carolina System
Degrees: B, M, P, D   *Enroll:* 15,672
URL: http://www.uncc.edu
Phone: (704) 687-2000   *Calendar:* Sem. plan
Inst. Accred.: SACS (1957/2002)
Prog. Accred.: Accounting, Business (AACSB), Counseling, Engineering (civil, computer, electrical, mechanical), Engineering Technology (civil/construction, electrical, mechanical), Nurse Anesthesia Education, Nursing, Nursing Education, Psychology Internship, Public Administration, Social Work, Teacher Education (NCATE)

The University of North Carolina at Greensboro
PO Box 26170, Greensboro 27402
Type: Public, state, four-year
System: University of North Carolina System
Degrees: B, M, P, D   *Enroll:* 12,213
URL: http://www.uncg.edu
Phone: (336) 334-5000   *Calendar:* Sem. plan
Inst. Accred.: SACS (1921/2003)
Prog. Accred.: Accounting, Audiology, Business (AACSB), Clinical Psychology, Computer Science, Counseling, Dance, Dietetics (internship), English Language Education, Interior Design, Librarianship, Music, Nurse Anesthesia Education, Nursing, Nursing Education, Public Administration, Public Health, Recreation and Leisure Services, Social Work, Speech-Language Pathology, Teacher Education (NCATE), Theatre

The University of North Carolina at Pembroke
PO Box 1510, One University Dr., Pembroke 28372-1510
Type: Public, state, four-year
System: University of North Carolina System
Degrees: B, M   *Enroll:* 3,893
URL: http://www.uncp.edu
Phone: (910) 521-6000   *Calendar:* Sem. plan
Inst. Accred.: SACS (1951/2000)
Prog. Accred.: Music, Nursing, Nursing Education, Social Work, Teacher Education (NCATE)

The University of North Carolina at Wilmington
601 South College Rd., Wilmington 28403-3297
Type: Public, state, four-year
System: University of North Carolina System
Degrees: B, M, D   *Enroll:* 10,062
URL: http://www.uncwil.edu
Phone: (910) 962-3000   *Calendar:* Sem. plan
Inst. Accred.: SACS (1952/2002)
Prog. Accred.: Business (AACSB), Music, Nursing, Recreation and Leisure Services, Social Work, Teacher Education (NCATE)

Vance-Granville Community College
PO Box 917, Henderson 27536
Type: Public, state-related, two-year
System: North Carolina Community College System
Degrees: A   *Enroll:* 2,727
URL: http://www.vgcc.edu
Phone: (252) 492-2061   *Calendar:* Sem. plan
Inst. Accred.: SACS (1977/2003)
Prog. Accred.: Radiography

Wake Forest University
PO Box 7373, Reynolds Station, Winston-Salem 27109
Type: Private, independent, four-year
Degrees: B, M, D   *Enroll:* 6,275
URL: http://www.wfu.edu
Phone: (336) 758-5000   *Calendar:* Sem. plan
Inst. Accred.: ATS (2005), SACS (1921/1997)
Prog. Accred.: Accounting, Business (AACSB), Clinical Lab Scientist, Clinical Pastoral Education (ACPEI), Counseling, General Practice Residency, Law, Medicine, Physician Assistant, Teacher Education (NCATE)

Wake Technical Community College
9101 Fayetteville Rd., Raleigh 27603-5696
Type: Public, state/local, two-year
System: North Carolina Community College System
Degrees: A   *Enroll:* 6,332
URL: http://www.waketech.edu
Phone: (919) 662-3400   *Calendar:* Sem. plan
Inst. Accred.: SACS (1970/2005, Warning)
Prog. Accred.: Clinical Lab Technology, Dental Assisting, Dental Hygiene, Engineering Technology (automated systems, civil/construction, computer, electrical, mechanical), Medical Assisting (AMA), Phlebotomy, Radiography

Warren Wilson College
PO Box 9000, Asheville 28815-9000
Type: Private, independent, four-year
Degrees: B, M   *Enroll:* 842
URL: http://www.warren-wilson.edu
Phone: (828) 298-3325   *Calendar:* Sem. plan
Inst. Accred.: SACS (1952/2005)
Prog. Accred.: Social Work, Teacher Education (NCATE)

Wayne Community College
Box 8002, Goldsboro 27533-8002
Type: Public, state/local, two-year
System: North Carolina Community College System
Degrees: A   *Enroll:* 2,156
URL: http://www.waynecc.edu
Phone: (919) 735-5151   *Calendar:* Sem. plan
Inst. Accred.: SACS (1970/1995)
Prog. Accred.: Dental Assisting, Dental Hygiene, Medical
   Assisting (CAAHEP)

Western Carolina University
1 University Dr., Cullowhee 28723
Type: Public, state, four-year
System: University of North Carolina System
Degrees: B, M, P, D   *Enroll:* 6,434
URL: http://www.wcu.edu
Phone: (828) 227-7211   *Calendar:* Sem. plan
Inst. Accred.: SACS (1946/1996)
Prog. Accred.: Accounting, Business (AACSB), Clinical Lab
   Scientist, Counseling, Dietetics (internship), EMT
   (Paramedic), Engineering Technology (electrical,
   manufacturing), Family and Consumer Science, Health
   Information Administration, Interior Design, Music,
   Nursing, Nursing Education, Physical Therapy, Social
   Work, Speech-Language Pathology, Teacher Education
   (NCATE)

Western Piedmont Community College
1001 Burkemont Ave., Morganton 28655
Type: Public, state, two-year
System: North Carolina Community College System
Degrees: A   *Enroll:* 1,910
URL: http://www.wpcc.edu
Phone: (828) 438-6000   *Calendar:* Sem. plan
Inst. Accred.: SACS (1968/2003)
Prog. Accred.: Clinical Lab Technology, Dental Assisting,
   Medical Assisting (AMA), Nursing

Wilkes Community College
PO Box 120, Wilkesboro 28697-0120
Type: Public, state, two-year
System: North Carolina Community College System
Degrees: A   *Enroll:* 1,943
URL: http://www.wilkescc.edu
Phone: (336) 838-6100   *Calendar:* Sem. plan
Inst. Accred.: SACS (1970/1995)
Prog. Accred.: Dental Assisting, Medical Assisting
   (CAAHEP)

Wilson Technical Community College
PO Box 4305, 902 Herring Ave, Wilson 27893
Type: Public, state, two-year
System: North Carolina Community College System
Degrees: A   *Enroll:* 1,352
URL: http://www.wilsontech.edu
Phone: (252) 291-1195   *Calendar:* Sem. plan
Inst. Accred.: SACS (1969/2005)

Wingate University
315 East Wilson St., Wingate 28174-0159
Type: Private, Southern Baptist Church, four-year
Degrees: A, B, M, D   *Enroll:* 1,398
URL: http://www.wingate.edu
Phone: (704) 233-8000   *Calendar:* Sem. plan
Inst. Accred.: SACS (1951/1995)
Prog. Accred.: Athletic Training, Business (ACBSP), Music,
   Pharmacy, Teacher Education (NCATE)

Winston-Salem State University
601 Martin Luther King, Jr. Dr., Winston-Salem 27110
Type: Public, state, four-year
System: University of North Carolina System
Degrees: B, M   *Enroll:* 3,673
URL: http://www.wssu.edu
Phone: (336) 750-2000   *Calendar:* Sem. plan
Inst. Accred.: SACS (1947/2001)
Prog. Accred.: Business (AACSB), Clinical Lab Scientist,
   Computer Science, Music, Nursing, Nursing Education,
   Occupational Therapy, Physical Therapy, Recreation and
   Leisure Services, Teacher Education (NCATE)

NORTH DAKOTA

Aaker's Business College
4012 19th Ave., SW, Fargo 58103
Type: Private, proprietary, two-year
Degrees: A   *Enroll:* 327
URL: http://www.aakers.com
Phone: (701) 277-3889   *Calendar:* Qtr. plan
Inst. Accred.: ACICS (1966/2002)

Bismarck Campus
1701 East Century Ave., Bismarck 58503-0658
Phone: (701) 530-9600

Bismarck State College
1500 Edwards Ave., PO Box 5587, Bismarck 58506-5587
Type: Public, state, two-year
System: North Dakota University System
Degrees: A   *Enroll:* 2,671
Phone: (701) 224-5400   *Calendar:* Sem. plan
Inst. Accred.: NCA-HLC (1966/1998)
Prog. Accred.: Clinical Lab Technology, Phlebotomy

Cankdeska Cikana Community College
PO Box 269, 214 1st Ave., Fort Totten 58335
Type: Public, tribal, two-year
System: American Indian Higher Education Consortium
Degrees: A   *Enroll:* 140
URL: http://www.littlehoop.cc
Phone: (701) 766-4415   *Calendar:* Sem. plan
Inst. Accred.: NCA-HLC (1990/1998)

Dickinson State University
291 Campus Dr., Dickinson 58601-4896
Type: Public, state, four-year
System: North Dakota University System
Degrees: A, B   *Enroll:* 2,023
URL: http://www.dsu.nodak.edu
Phone: (800) 227-2507   *Calendar:* Sem. plan
Inst. Accred.: NCA-HLC (1928/2005)
Prog. Accred.: Nursing, Practical Nursing, Teacher
   Education (NCATE)

Fort Berthold Community College
PO Box 490, 220 8th Ave., New Town 58763
Type: Public, tribal, two-year
System: American Indian Higher Education Consortium
Degrees: A   *Enroll:* 219
URL: http://www.fbcc.bia.edu
Phone: (701) 627-4738   *Calendar:* Sem. plan
Inst. Accred.: NCA-HLC (1988/1996)

Jamestown College
6000 College Ln., Jamestown 58405
Type: Private, United Presbyterian Church, four-year
Degrees: B   *Enroll:* 1,113
URL: http://www.jc.edu
Phone: (701) 252-3467   *Calendar:* Sem. plan
Inst. Accred.: NCA-HLC (1920/2001)
Prog. Accred.: Nursing

Lake Region State College
1801 North College Dr., Devils Lake 58301-1598
Type: Public, state, two-year
System: North Dakota University System
Degrees: A   *Enroll:* 763
Phone: (701) 662-1500   *Calendar:* Sem. plan
Inst. Accred.: NCA-HLC (1974/2001)

Mayville State University
330 3rd St., NE, Mayville 58257-1299
Type: Public, state, four-year
System: North Dakota University System
Degrees: A, B   *Enroll:* 695
URL: http://www.mayvillestate.edu
Phone: (701) 788-4754   *Calendar:* Sem. plan
Inst. Accred.: NCA-HLC (1917/1996)
Prog. Accred.: Teacher Education (NCATE)

Medcenter One Health Systems
300 North 7th St., Bismarck 58501
Type: Private, independent, four-year
Degrees: B   *Enroll:* 80
URL: http://www.medcenterone.com
Phone: (701) 323-6000   *Calendar:* Sem. plan
Inst. Accred.: NCA-HLC (1990/1996)
Prog. Accred.: Nursing, Radiography

Minot State University
500 University Ave., West, Minot 58707-0001
Type: Public, state, four-year
System: North Dakota University System
Degrees: A, B, M, P, D   *Enroll:* 3,091
URL: http://www.minotstateu.edu
Phone: (701) 858-3000   *Calendar:* Sem. plan
Inst. Accred.: NCA-HLC (1917/1998)
Prog. Accred.: Audiology, Music, Nursing, Social Work,
   Speech-Language Pathology, Teacher Education
   (NCATE)

Minot State University—Bottineau
105 Simrall Blvd., Bottineau 58318-1198
Type: Public, state, two-year
System: North Dakota University System
Degrees: A   *Enroll:* 466
URL: http://www.misu-b.nodak.edu
Phone: (701) 228-2277   *Calendar:* Sem. plan
Inst. Accred.: NCA-HLC (1971/2001)

North Dakota State College of Science
800 North 6th St., Wahpeton 58076-0002
Type: Public, state, two-year
System: North Dakota University System
Degrees: A   *Enroll:* 2,127
URL: http://www.ndscs.nodak.edu
Phone: (701) 671-2221   *Calendar:* Sem. plan
Inst. Accred.: NCA-HLC (1971/2001)
Prog. Accred.: Dental Assisting, Dental Hygiene, Health
   Information Technician, Nursing, Occupational Therapy
   Assisting, Practical Nursing

North Dakota State University
1301 12th Ave. North, Fargo 58105
Type: Public, state, four-year
System: North Dakota University System
Degrees: B, M, P, D   *Enroll:* 10,292
URL: http://www.ndsu.nodak.edu
Phone: (701) 231-8011   *Calendar:* Sem. plan
Inst. Accred.: NCA-HLC (1915/1996)
Prog. Accred.: Art, Athletic Training, Business (AACSB),
  Computer Science, Construction Education, Counseling,
  Dietetics (coordinated), Dietetics (internship),
  Engineering (agricultural, civil, construction, electrical,
  industrial, manufacturing, mechanical), Interior Design,
  Landscape Architecture, Marriage and Family Therapy,
  Music, Nursing, Nursing Education, Pharmacy,
  Respiratory Therapy, Teacher Education (NCATE),
  Theatre, Veterinary Technology

Sitting Bull College
1341 92nd St., Box 4, Fort Yates 58538
Type: Public, Standing Rock Sioux Tribe, two-year
System: American Indian Higher Education Consortium
Degrees: A   *Enroll:* 256
URL: http://www.sittingbull.edu
Phone: (701) 854-3861   *Calendar:* Sem. plan
Inst. Accred.: NCA-HLC (1984/2004)

Trinity Bible College
50 6th Ave. South, Ellendale 58436-7150
Type: Private, Assemblies of God Church, four-year
Degrees: A, B   *Enroll:* 287
URL: http://www.trinitybiblecollege.edu
Phone: (701) 349-3621   *Calendar:* Sem. plan
Inst. Accred.: ABHE (1980/2001), NCA-HLC (1991/1995)

Turtle Mountain Community College
PO Box 340, Belcourt 58316
Type: Private, tribal, four-year
System: American Indian Higher Education Consortium
Degrees: A, B   *Enroll:* 719
URL: http://www.tm.edu
Phone: (701) 477-5605   *Calendar:* Sem. plan
Inst. Accred.: NCA-HLC (1984/2004)

United Tribes Technical College
3315 University Dr., Bismarck 58504
Type: Private, tribal, two-year
System: American Indian Higher Education Consortium
Degrees: A   *Enroll:* 425
URL: http://www.uttc.edu
Phone: (701) 255-3285   *Calendar:* Sem. plan
Inst. Accred.: NCA-HLC (1982/2001)
Prog. Accred.: Health Information Technician, Practical
  Nursing

University of Mary
7500 University Dr., Bismarck 58504
Type: Private, Roman Catholic Church, four-year
Degrees: A, B, M   *Enroll:* 2,400
URL: http://www.umary.edu
Phone: (701) 255-7500   *Calendar:* Sem. plan
Inst. Accred.: NCA-HLC (1969/2003)
Prog. Accred.: Athletic Training, Nursing, Nursing
  Education, Occupational Therapy, Physical Therapy,
  Respiratory Therapy, Social Work

University of North Dakota
Box 8193, University Station, Grand Forks 58202-8193
Type: Public, state, four-year
System: North Dakota University System
Degrees: B, M, P, D   *Enroll:* 11,691
URL: http://www.und.nodak.edu
Phone: (701) 777-2011   *Calendar:* Sem. plan
Inst. Accred.: NCA-HLC (1913/2004)
Prog. Accred.: Art, Athletic Training, Business (AACSB),
  Clinical Lab Scientist, Clinical Psychology, Computer
  Science, Counseling Psychology, Cytotechnology,
  Dietetics (coordinated), Engineering (chemical, civil,
  electrical, geological/geophysical, mechanical),
  Industrial Technology, Law, Medicine, Music, Nurse
  Anesthesia Education, Nursing, Nursing Education,
  Occupational Therapy, Physical Therapy, Physician
  Assistant, Social Work, Speech-Language Pathology,
  Teacher Education (NCATE), Theatre

Valley City State University
101 College St. SW, Valley City 58072-4195
Type: Public, state, four-year
System: North Dakota University System
Degrees: B   *Enroll:* 844
URL: http://www.vcsu.edu
Phone: (800) 532-8641   *Calendar:* Sem. plan
Inst. Accred.: NCA-HLC (1915/2002)
Prog. Accred.: Music, Teacher Education (NCATE)

Williston State College
PO Box 1326, 1410 University Ave., Williston 58802-
1326
Type: Public, state, two-year
System: North Dakota University System
Degrees: A   *Enroll:* 693
URL: http://www.wsc.nodak.edu
Phone: (701) 774-4200   *Calendar:* Sem. plan
Inst. Accred.: NCA-HLC (1972/2000)
Prog. Accred.: Physical Therapy Assisting

OHIO

Academy of Court Reporting
2044 Euclid Aveneue, Cleveland 44115
Type: Private, proprietary, two-year
Degrees: A   *Enroll:* 306
URL: http://www.acr.edu
Phone: (216) 861-3222
Inst. Accred.: ACICS (1980/2002)

Akron Campus
2930 West Market St., Akron 44313
Phone: (330) 867-4030

Cincinnati Campus
830 Main St., Cincinnati 45202
Phone: (513) 723-0551

Clawson Campus
1330 West 14 Mile Rd., Clawson, MI 48017
Phone: (248) 353-4880

Columbus Campus
630 East Broad St., Columbus 43215
Phone: (614) 221-7770

Pittsburgh Campus
239 Fourth Ave., Pittsburgh, PA 15222
Phone: (412) 535-0560

Air Force Institute of Technology
Hobson Way, Building 642, Wright-Patterson AFB 45433-7765
Type: Public, federal, four-year
System: Air University
Degrees: M, D   *FTE Enroll:* 538
URL: http://www.afit.edu
Phone: (937) 255-2321   *Calendar:* Qtr. plan
Inst. Accred.: NCA-HLC (1960/2001)
Prog. Accred.: Engineering (aerospace, computer, electrical, engineering management, nuclear, systems)

Allegheny Wesleyan College
2161 Woodsdale Rd., Salem 44460
Type: Private, Wesleyan Church, four-year
Degrees: B   *Enroll:* 36
URL: http://www.awc.edu
Phone: (330) 337-6403   *Calendar:* Sem. plan
Inst. Accred.: ABHE (2004)

Antioch University
150 East South College St., Yellow Springs 45387
Type: Private, independent, four-year
Degrees: B, M, D   *Enroll:* 593
URL: http://www.antioch.edu
Phone: (937) 769-1340
Inst. Accred.: NCA-HLC (1927/2003)

Antioch College
795 Livermore St., Yellow Springs 45387
Phone: (513) 767-7331

Antioch New England Graduate School
40 Avon St., Keene, NH 03431-3516
Phone: (603) 357-3122
Prog. Accred.: Clinical Psychology, Marriage and Family Therapy

Antioch Southern California—Los Angeles
13274 Fiji Way, Marina del Rey, CA 90292
Phone: (310) 578-1080

Antioch Southern California—Santa Barbara
801 Garden St., Santa Barbara, CA 93101
Phone: (805) 962-8179

Antioch University McGregor
800 Livermore St., Yellow Springs 45387
Phone: (937) 767-6321

Antioch University Seattle
2607 Second Ave., Seattle, WA 98121
Phone: (206) 441-5352

Antonelli College
124 East Seventh St., Cincinnati 45202-2592
Type: Private, proprietary, two-year
Degrees: A   *Enroll:* 288
URL: http://www.antonellic.com
Phone: (513) 241-4338   *Calendar:* Qtr. plan
Inst. Accred.: ACCSCT (1975/2001)

Hattiesburg Campus
1500 North 31st Ave., Hattiesburg, MS 39401
Phone: (601) 583-4100

Jackson Campus
2323 Lakeland Dr., Jackson, MS 39208
Phone: (601) 362-9991

Art Academy of Cincinnati
1212 Jackson St., Cincinnati 45202
Type: Private, independent, four-year
Degrees: A, B, M   *Enroll:* 185
URL: http://www.artacademy.edu
Phone: (513) 562 6262   *Calendar:* Sem. plan
Inst. Accred.: NCA-HLC (1990/2002)
Prog. Accred.: Art

The Art Institute of Cincinnati
1171 East Kemper Rd., Cincinnati 45246
Type: Private, independent, two-year
Degrees: A   *Enroll:* 97
URL: http://www.theartinstituteofcincinnati.com
Phone: (513) 751-1206   *Calendar:* Qtr. plan
Inst. Accred.: ACCSCT (1979/2003)

The Art Institute of Ohio—Cincinnati
1011 Glendale Rd., Cincinnati 45215
Type: Private, proprietary, two-year
Degrees: A
URL: http://www.aioc.artinstitutes.edu
Phone: (513) 771-2821
Inst. Accred.: ACICS (2004)

Ashland Theological Seminary
910 Center St., Ashland 44805
Type: Private, independent, four-year
Degrees: M, D
URL: http://www.ashland.edu/seminary/home.html
Phone: (419) 289-5161   *Calendar:* Sem. plan
Inst. Accred.: ATS (1969/1998)

Ashland University
401 College Ave., Ashland 44805
Type: Private, Brethren Church, four-year
Degrees: A, B, M, D   *Enroll:* 5,220
URL: http://www.ashland.edu
Phone: (419) 289-4142   *Calendar:* Sem. plan
Inst. Accred.: NCA-HLC (1930/1998)
Prog. Accred.: Business (ACBSP), Music, Nursing, Nursing
   Education, Social Work, Teacher Education (NCATE)

The Athenaeum of Ohio
6616 Beechmont Ave., Cincinnati 45230-2091
Type: Private, Roman Catholic Archdiocese of Cincinnati,
   four-year
Degrees: M   *Enroll:* 215
URL: http://www.mtsm.org
Phone: (513) 231-2223   *Calendar:* Qtr. plan
Inst. Accred.: ATS (1972/2002), NCA-HLC (1959/2003)

ATS Institute of Technology
230 Alpha Park, Highland Heights 44143
Type: Private, proprietary, two-year
Degrees: A
URL: http://www.atsinstitute.com
Phone: (440) 449-1700   *Calendar:* Qtr. plan
Inst. Accred.: ACICS (2000/2003)

Baldwin-Wallace College
275 Eastland Rd., Berea 44017-2088
Type: Private, United Methodist Church, four-year
Degrees: B, M   *Enroll:* 3,935
URL: http://www.bw.edu
Phone: (440) 826-2900   *Calendar:* Sem. plan
Inst. Accred.: NCA-HLC (1913/1998)
Prog. Accred.: Music, Teacher Education (NCATE)

Belmont Technical College
120 Fox-Shannon Place, St. Clairsville 43950-9735
Type: Public, state, two-year
System: Ohio Board of Regents
Degrees: A   *Enroll:* 1,369
URL: http://www.btc.edu
Phone: (740) 695-9500   *Calendar:* Qtr. plan
Inst. Accred.: NCA-HLC (1978/1996)
Prog. Accred.: Medical Assisting (CAAHEP)

Bluffton University
1 University Dr., Bluffton 45817
Type: Private, General Conference Mennonite, four-year
Degrees: B, M   *Enroll:* 1,056
URL: http://www.bluffton.edu
Phone: (419) 358-3000   *Calendar:* Qtr. plan
Inst. Accred.: NCA-HLC (1953/1999)
Prog. Accred.: Music, Social Work

Bohecker College
326 East Main St., Ravenna 44266-3136
Type: Private, proprietary, two-year
Degrees: A   *Enroll:* 269
URL: http://www.boheckers.com
Phone: (330) 297-7319
Inst. Accred.: ACICS (1985/2001)

Bowling Green State University
Bowling Green 43403-0001
Type: Public, state, four-year
System: Ohio Board of Regents
Degrees: A, B, M, P, D   *Enroll:* 16,966
URL: http://www.bgsu.edu
Phone: (419) 372-2531   *Calendar:* Sem. plan
Inst. Accred.: NCA-HLC (1916/2003)
Prog. Accred.: Accounting, Art, Aviation Technology,
   Business (AACSB), Clinical Lab Scientist, Clinical
   Psychology, Construction Education, Construction
   Technology, Design Technology, Dietetics (internship),
   Electronic Technology, Health Information Technician,
   Journalism, Manufacturing Technology, Mechanical
   Technology, Music, Public Health, Recreation and
   Leisure Services, Rehabilitation Counseling, Respiratory
   Therapy, Social Work, Speech-Language Pathology,
   Teacher Education (NCATE), Theatre

Firelands College
901 Rye Beach Rd., Huron 44839
Phone: (419) 433-5560

Bradford School
2469 Stelzer Rd., Columbus 43219
Type: Private, proprietary, two-year
Degrees: A   *Enroll:* 312
URL: http://www.bradfordschoolcolumbus.edu
Phone: (614) 416-6200   *Calendar:* Qtr. plan
Inst. Accred.: ACICS (1960/2000)
Prog. Accred.: Medical Assisting (CAAHEP)

Brown Mackie College—Cincinnati
1011 Glendale-Milford Rd., Cincinnati 45215-1107
Type: Private, proprietary, two-year
System: Education Management Corporation
Degrees: A   *FTE Enroll:* 1,200
URL: http://www.brownmackie.edu
Phone: (513) 771-2424   *Calendar:* Qtr. plan
Inst. Accred.: ACICS (1964/2005)
Prog. Accred.: Medical Assisting (CAAHEP)

Akron Campus
2791 Mogadore Rd., Akron 44312
Phone: (330) 733-8766
Prog. Accred: Medical Assisting (CAAHEP)

Dallas Campus
1500 Eastgate Dr., Garland, TX 75041
Phone: (972) 279-4446

Fort Worth Campus
301 NE Loop 820, Hurst, TX 76053
Phone: (817) 589-0505

North Canton Campus
1320 West Maple St., NW, North Canton 44720-2854
Phone: (330) 494-1214

Northern Kentucky Campus
309 Buttermilk Pike, Fort Mitchell, KY 41017
Phone: (859) 341-5627

Brown Mackie College—Findlay
1700 Fostoria Ave., Ste. 100, Findlay 45840
Type: Private, proprietary, two-year
System: Education Management Corporation
Degrees: A   *Enroll:* 499
URL: http://www.brownmackie.edu
Phone: (419) 423-2211   *Calendar:* Qtr. plan
Inst. Accred.: ACICS (1989/2003)

Bryant and Stratton College—Cleveland Downtown Campus
1700 East 13th St., Cleveland 44114-3203
Type: Private, proprietary, four-year
System: Bryant and Stratton
Degrees: A, B   *Enroll:* 196
URL: http://www.bryantstratton.edu
Phone: (216) 771-1700   *Calendar:* Qtr. plan
Inst. Accred.: MSA-CHE (2002, *Indirect accreditation through Bryant and Stratton, Getzville, NY*)

Bryant and Stratton College—Cleveland West Campus
12955 Snow Rd., Parma 44130-1013
Type: Private, proprietary, four-year
System: Bryant and Stratton
Degrees: A, B   *Enroll:* 167
URL: http://www.bryantstratton.edu
Phone: (216) 265-3151   *Calendar:* Qtr. plan
Inst. Accred.: MSA-CHE (2002, *Indirect accreditation through Bryant and Stratton, Getzville, NY*)
Prog. Accred.: Medical Assisting (CAAHEP)

Willoughby Hills Campus
27557 Chardon Rd., Willoughby Hills 44092
Phone: (440) 944-6800

Capital University
2199 East Main St., Columbus 43209
Type: Private, Evangelic Lutheran Church in America, four-year
Degrees: B, M, D   *Enroll:* 3,315
URL: http://www.capital.edu
Phone: (800) 289-6289   *Calendar:* Sem. plan
Inst. Accred.: NCA-HLC (1921/2004)
Prog. Accred.: Athletic Training, Business (ACBSP), Law, Music, Nursing, Nursing Education, Social Work, Teacher Education (NCATE)

Case Western Reserve University
10900 Euclid Ave., Cleveland 44106-7001
Type: Private, independent, four-year
Degrees: B, M, D   *Enroll:* 7,888
URL: http://www.cwru.edu
Phone: (800) 444-6984   *Calendar:* Sem. plan
Inst. Accred.: NCA-HLC (1913/2005)
Prog. Accred.: Accounting, Advanced Education in General Dentistry, Anesthesiologist Assisting, Business (AACSB), Clinical Psychology, Computer Science, Dentistry, Dietetics (internship), Endodontics, Engineering (aerospace, bioengineering, chemical, civil, computer, electrical, engineering physics/science, materials, mechanical, polymer, systems), General Dentistry, Law, Medicine, Music, Nurse (Midwifery), Nurse Anesthesia Education, Nursing, Oral and Maxillofacial Surgery, Orthodontic and Dentofacial Orthopedics, Pediatric Dentistry, Periodontics, Social Work, Speech-Language Pathology

Cedarville University
251 North Main St., Box 601, Cedarville 45314-0601
Type: Private, Baptist Church, four-year
Degrees: A, B, M, D   *Enroll:* 2,902
URL: http://www.cedarville.edu
Phone: (800) 766-2211   *Calendar:* Qtr. plan
Inst. Accred.: NCA-HLC (1975/1997)
Prog. Accred.: Business (AACSB), Engineering (electrical, mechanical), Nursing, Nursing Education, Social Work

Central Ohio Technical College
1179 University Dr., Newark 43055-1767
Type: Public, state/local, two-year
System: Ohio Board of Regents
Degrees: A   *Enroll:* 1,633
URL: http://www.cotc.edu
Phone: (740) 366-1351   *Calendar:* Qtr. plan
Inst. Accred.: NCA-HLC (1975/1998)
Prog. Accred.: Diagnostic Medical Sonography, Nursing,
  Radiography

Central State University
PO Box 1004, 1400 Brush Row Rd., Wilberforce 45384-
1004
Type: Public, state, four-year
System: Ohio Board of Regents
Degrees: B, M   *Enroll:* 1,540
URL: http://www.centralstate.edu
Phone: (937) 376-6011   *Calendar:* Qtr. plan
Inst. Accred.: NCA-HLC (1949/2003)
Prog. Accred.: Engineering (manufacturing), Music

Chatfield College
20918 State Route 251, St. Martin 45118
Type: Private, Roman Catholic Church, two-year
Degrees: A   *FTE Enroll:* 151
URL: http://www.chatfield.edu
Phone: (513) 875-3344   *Calendar:* Sem. plan
Inst. Accred.: NCA-HLC (1971/2001)

Cincinnati Christian University
2700 Glenway Ave., Cincinnati 45204
Type: Private, Christian Churches/Churches of Christ,
  four-year
Degrees: A, B, M, P   *Enroll:* 734
URL: http://www.cincybible.edu
Phone: (513) 244-8100   *Calendar:* Sem. plan
Inst. Accred.: ABHE (1966/2005), ATS (2004), NCA-HLC
  (1989/2004)

Cincinnati College of Mortuary Science
645 West North Bend Rd., Cincinnati 45224
Type: Private, independent, four-year
Degrees: A, B   *Enroll:* 122
URL: http://www.ccms.edu
Phone: (513) 761-2020   *Calendar:* Qtr. plan
Inst. Accred.: NCA-HLC (1982/2001)
Prog. Accred.: Funeral Service Education (Mortuary
  Science)

Cincinnati State Technical and Community College
3520 Central Pkwy., Cincinnati 45223-2690
Type: Public, state, two-year
System: Ohio Board of Regents
Degrees: A   *Enroll:* 4,561
URL: http://www.cincinnatistate.edu
Phone: (513) 569-1500
Inst. Accred.: NCA-HLC (1976/2001)
Prog. Accred.: Clinical Lab Technology, Construction
  Education, Culinary Education, Engineering Technology
  (bioengineering, civil/construction, computer, electrical,
  electromechanical, environmental/sanitary,
  mechanical), Health Information Technician, Medical
  Assisting (AMA), Nursing, Occupational Therapy
  Assisting, Respiratory Therapy, Surgical Technology

Circleville Bible College
1476 Lancaster Pike, Circleville 43113
Type: Private, Churches of Christ in Christian Union, four-
  year
Degrees: A, B   *Enroll:* 313
URL: http://www.biblecollege.edu
Phone: (740) 474-8896   *Calendar:* Sem. plan
Inst. Accred.: ABHE (1976/1997), NCA-HLC (2005)

Clark State Community College
570 East Leffel Ln., PO Box 570, Springfield 45505-4795
Type: Public, state, two-year
System: Ohio Board of Regents
Degrees: A   *Enroll:* 2,003
URL: http://www.clarkstate.edu
Phone: (937) 325-0691   *Calendar:* Qtr. plan
Inst. Accred.: NCA-HLC (1974/1999)
Prog. Accred.: Clinical Lab Technology, Nursing, Physical
  Therapy Assisting

Cleveland Institute of Art
11141 East Blvd., Cleveland 44106
Type: Private, independent, four-year
Degrees: B, M   *Enroll:* 607
URL: http://www.cia.edu
Phone: (216) 421-7000   *Calendar:* Sem. plan
Inst. Accred.: NCA-HLC (1970/2001)
Prog. Accred.: Art

Cleveland Institute of Electronics, Inc.
1776 East 17th St., Cleveland 44114
Type: Private, proprietary, two-year
Degrees: A   *FTE Enroll:* 1,826
URL: http://www.cie-wc.edu
Phone: (216) 781-9400
Inst. Accred.: DETC (1956/2003)

Cleveland Institute of Music
11021 East Blvd., Cleveland 44106
Type: Private, independent, four-year
Degrees: B, M, D   *Enroll:* 412
URL: http://www.cim.edu
Phone: (216) 791-5000   *Calendar:* Sem. plan
Inst. Accred.: NCA-HLC (1980/2005)
Prog. Accred.: Music

Cleveland State University

2121 Euclid Ave., Cleveland 44115-2214
Type: Public, state, four-year
System: Ohio Board of Regents
Degrees: B, M, P, D   *Enroll:* 11,740
URL: http://www.csuohio.edu
Phone: (216) 687-2000   *Calendar:* Sem. plan
Inst. Accred.: NCA-HLC (1940/2001)
Prog. Accred.: Accounting, Business (AACSB), Counseling,
   Engineering (chemical, civil, electrical, industrial,
   mechanical), Engineering Technology (electrical), Health
   Services Administration, Law, Music, Nursing, Nursing
   Education, Occupational Therapy, Physical Therapy,
   Planning, Public Administration, Public Health, Social
   Work, Speech-Language Pathology, Teacher Education
   (NCATE)

College of Art Advertising

4343 Bridgetown Rd., Cincinnati 45211-4427
Type: Private, proprietary, two-year
Degrees: A   *Enroll:* 26
URL: http://www.collegeofartadvertising.com
Phone: (513) 574-1010   *Calendar:* Qtr. plan
Inst. Accred.: ACCSCT (1984/1998)

College of Mount Saint Joseph

5701 Delhi Rd., Cincinnati 45233
Type: Private, Roman Catholic Church, four-year
Degrees: A, B, M   *Enroll:* 1,618
URL: http://www.msj.edu
Phone: (513) 244-4200   *Calendar:* Sem. plan
Inst. Accred.: NCA-HLC (1932/1996)
Prog. Accred.: Music, Nursing, Physical Therapy, Social
   Work

The College of Wooster

1189 Beall Ave., Wooster 44691
Type: Private, independent, four-year
Degrees: B   *Enroll:* 1,851
URL: http://www.wooster.edu
Phone: (330) 263-2311   *Calendar:* Sem. plan
Inst. Accred.: NCA-HLC (1915/2003)
Prog. Accred.: Music

Columbus College of Art and Design

107 North Ninth St., Columbus 43215
Type: Private, independent, four-year
Degrees: B   *Enroll:* 1,425
URL: http://www.ccad.edu
Phone: (614) 224-9101   *Calendar:* Sem. plan
Inst. Accred.: NCA-HLC (1986/2001)
Prog. Accred.: Art, Interior Design

Columbus State Community College

550 East Spring St., PO Box 1609, Columbus 43216
Type: Public, state, two-year
System: Ohio Board of Regents
Degrees: A   *Enroll:* 13,868
URL: http://www.cscc.edu
Phone: (614) 287-2400   *Calendar:* Qtr. plan
Inst. Accred.: NCA-HLC (1973/2000)
Prog. Accred.: Business (ACBSP), Clinical Lab Technology,
   Construction Education, Culinary Education, Dental
   Hygiene, Dental Laboratory Technology, EMT
   (Paramedic), Engineering Technology (electrical), Health
   Information Technician, Histologic Technology, Medical
   Assisting (AMA), Nursing, Phlebotomy, Radiography,
   Respiratory Therapy, Respiratory Therapy Technology,
   Veterinary Technology

Cuyahoga Community College

700 Carnegie Ave., Cleveland 44115-2878
Type: Public, state/local, two-year
System: Ohio Board of Regents
Degrees: A   *Enroll:* 13,485
URL: http://www.tri-c.edu
Phone: (216) 987-6000   *Calendar:* Sem. plan
Inst. Accred.: NCA-HLC (1979/2000)
Prog. Accred.: Business (ACBSP), Cardiovascular
   Technology, Health Information Technician, Medical
   Assisting (AMA), Phlebotomy, Physician Assistant,
   Radiography, Respiratory Therapy

Corporate Campus

25425 Center Ridge Rd., Westlake 44145-4122
Phone: (866) 806-2677

Eastern Campus

4250 Richmond Rd., Highland Hills 44122
Phone: (216) 987-2000

Metropolitan Campus

2900 Community College Ave., Cleveland 44115
Phone: (216) 987-4000
Prog. Accred: Culinary Education, Dental Assisting,
   Dental Hygiene, Nursing, Occupational Therapy
   Assisting, Physical Therapy Assisting

Western Campus

11000 West Pleasant Valley Rd., Parma 44130
Phone: (216) 987-5000
Prog. Accred: Nuclear Medicine Technology, Nursing,
   Radiography, Veterinary Technology

David N. Myers University

112 Prospect Ave., SE, Cleveland 44115
Type: Private, independent, four-year
Degrees: A, B, M   *Enroll:* 759
URL: http://www.dnmyers.edu
Phone: (216) 696-9000   *Calendar:* Sem. plan
Inst. Accred.: NCA-HLC (1978/2005)

Davis College
4747 Monroe St., Toledo 43623
Type: Private, proprietary, two-year
Degrees: A   *Enroll:* 278
URL: http://www.daviscollege.edu
Phone: (419) 473-2700   *Calendar:* Qtr. plan
Inst. Accred.: NCA-HLC (1991/1999)
Prog. Accred.: Medical Assisting (CAAHEP)

The Defiance College
701 North Clinton St., Defiance 43512
Type: Private, United Church of Christ, four-year
Degrees: A, B, M   *Enroll:* 848
URL: http://www.defiance.edu
Phone: (419) 784-4010   *Calendar:* Sem. plan
Inst. Accred.: NCA-HLC (1916/2003)
Prog. Accred.: Social Work

Denison University
1 Main St., Granville 43023
Type: Private, independent, four-year
Degrees: B   *Enroll:* 2,211
URL: http://www.denison.edu
Phone: (740) 587-0810   *Calendar:* Sem. plan
Inst. Accred.: NCA-HLC (1913/2000)

DeVry University Columbus
1350 Alum Creek Dr., Columbus 43209-2705
Type: Private, proprietary, four-year
System: DeVry University
Degrees: A, B, M   *Enroll:* 2,752
URL: http://www.devry.edu/columbus
Phone: (614) 253-7291   *Calendar:* Sem. plan
Inst. Accred.: NCA-HLC (2002, *Indirect accreditation
    through DeVry University, Oakbrook Terrace, IL*)
Prog. Accred.: Engineering Technology (computer)

Edison State Community College
1973 Edison Dr., Piqua 45356-9253
Type: Public, state, two-year
System: Ohio Board of Regents
Degrees: A   *Enroll:* 1,828
URL: http://www.edisonohio.edu
Phone: (937) 778-8600   *Calendar:* Sem. plan
Inst. Accred.: NCA-HLC (1981/2004)
Prog. Accred.: Nursing

EduTek College
3855 Fishcreek Rroad, Stow 44224
Type: Private, proprietary, two-year
Degrees: A
URL: http://www.edutekcollege.com
Phone: (330) 677-4667   *Calendar:* Qtr. plan
Inst. Accred.: ACICS (2004)

ETI Technical College of Niles
2076-86 Youngstown-Warren Rd., Niles 44446-4398
Type: Private, proprietary, two-year
Degrees: A
URL: http://www.eticollege.edu
Phone: (330) 652-9919
Inst. Accred.: ACCSCT (1992/2001)

Franciscan University of Steubenville
1235 University Blvd., Steubenville 43952
Type: Private, Roman Catholic Church, four-year
Degrees: A, B, M   *Enroll:* 2,025
URL: http://www.franciscan.edu
Phone: (740) 283-3771   *Calendar:* Sem. plan
Inst. Accred.: NCA-HLC (1960/2005)
Prog. Accred.: Nursing

Franklin University
201 South Grant Ave., Columbus 43215
Type: Private, independent, four-year
Degrees: A, B, M   *Enroll:* 4,096
URL: http://www.franklin.edu
Phone: (614) 341-6237   *Calendar:* Tri. plan
Inst. Accred.: NCA-HLC (1976/2001)
Prog. Accred.: Nursing

Gallipolis Career College
1176 Jackson Pike, Ste. 312, Gallipolis 45631
Type: Private, proprietary, two-year
Degrees: A   *Enroll:* 156
URL: http://www.gallipoliscareercollege.com
Phone: (740) 446-4367   *Calendar:* Qtr. plan
Inst. Accred.: ACICS (1989/2002)

God's Bible School and College
1810 Young St., Cincinnati 45210-1599
Type: Private, interdenominational, four-year
Degrees: A, B   *Enroll:* 226
URL: http://www.gbs.edu
Phone: (513) 721-7944   *Calendar:* Sem. plan
Inst. Accred.: ABHE (1986/1997)

Hebrew Union College—Jewish Institute of Religion
3101 Clifton Ave., Cincinnati 45220
Type: Private, Union for Reform Judaism, four-year
System: Hebrew Union College—Jewish Institute of
    Religion Central Office
Degrees: M, P, D   *Enroll:* 120
URL: http://www.huc.edu
Phone: (513) 221-1875   *Calendar:* Sem. plan
Inst. Accred.: NCA-HLC (1960/2002)

Heidelberg College
310 East Market St., Tiffin 44883
Type: Private, United Church of Christ, four-year
Degrees: B, M   *Enroll:* 1,126
URL: http://www.heidelberg.edu
Phone: (419) 448-2000   *Calendar:* Sem. plan
Inst. Accred.: NCA-HLC (1913/2005)
Prog. Accred.: Music

Hiram College
PO Box 67, Hiram 44234
Type: Private, independent, four-year
Degrees: B, M   *Enroll:* 978
URL: http://www.hiram.edu
Phone: (330) 569-3211   *Calendar:* Sem. plan
Inst. Accred.: NCA-HLC (1914/2000)
Prog. Accred.: Music

Hocking College
3301 Hocking Pkwy., Nelsonville 45764-9704
Type: Public, state, two-year
System: Ohio Board of Regents
Degrees: A   *Enroll:* 3,716
URL: http://www.hocking.edu
Phone: (740) 753-3591   *Calendar:* Qtr. plan
Inst. Accred.: NCA-HLC (1976/2002)
Prog. Accred.: Business (ACBSP), Culinary Education, Engineering Technology (ceramic), Health Information Technician, Medical Assisting (AMA), Nursing, Physical Therapy Assisting, Practical Nursing

Hondros College
4140 Executive Pkwy., Westerville 43081
Type: Private, proprietary, two-year
Degrees: A   *FTE Enroll:* 240
URL: http://www.hondroscollege.com
Phone: (614) 508-7277
Inst. Accred.: ACICS (1990/2004)

Dayton Campus
1810 Successful Dr., Fairborn 45324
Phone: (937) 879-1940

ITT Technical Institute
3325 Stop Eight Rd., Dayton 45414-9915
Type: Private, proprietary, two-year
System: ITT Educational Services, Inc.
Degrees: A   *Enroll:* 473
URL: http://www.itt-tech.edu
Phone: (937) 454-2267   *Calendar:* Qtr. plan
Inst. Accred.: ACICS (1999/2004)

ITT Technical Institute
1030 North Meridian Rd., Youngstown 44509-4098
Type: Private, proprietary, two-year
System: ITT Educational Services, Inc.
Degrees: A   *Enroll:* 502
URL: http://www.itt-tech.edu
Phone: (330) 270-1600   *Calendar:* Qtr. plan
Inst. Accred.: ACICS (1977/2001)

Pittsburgh Area Campus
10 Pkwy. Center, Pittsburgh, PA 15220-3801
Phone: (412) 937-9150

Monroeville Area Campus
105 Mall Blvd., Ste. 200 East, Monroeville, PA 15146
Phone: (412) 856-5920

Strongsville Campus
14955 Sprague Rd., Strongsville 44136
Phone: (440) 234-9091

James A. Rhodes State College
4240 Campus Dr., Lima 45804-3597
Type: Public, state, two-year
System: Ohio Board of Regents
Degrees: A   *Enroll:* 1,895
URL: http://www.rhodesstate.edu
Phone: (419) 995-8000   *Calendar:* Qtr. plan
Inst. Accred.: NCA-HLC (1979/2002)
Prog. Accred.: Business (ACBSP), Dental Hygiene, Engineering Technology (electrical, mechanical), Nursing, Occupational Therapy Assisting, Physical Therapy Assisting, Radiography, Respiratory Therapy

Jefferson Community College
4000 Sunset Blvd., Steubenville 43952-3594
Type: Public, state, two-year
System: Ohio Board of Regents
Degrees: A   *Enroll:* 1,104
URL: http://ns3.jeffersoncc.org/jcc
Phone: (740) 264-5591   *Calendar:* Sem. plan
Inst. Accred.: NCA-HLC (1973/1997)
Prog. Accred.: Clinical Lab Technology, Dental Assisting, Medical Assisting (AMA), Radiography, Respiratory Therapy

John Carroll University
20700 North Park Blvd., University Heights 44118
Type: Private, Roman Catholic Church, four-year
Degrees: B, M   *Enroll:* 3,769
URL: http://www.jcu.edu
Phone: (216) 397-1886   *Calendar:* Sem. plan
Inst. Accred.: NCA-HLC (1922/2004)
Prog. Accred.: Accounting, Business (AACSB), Counseling, Teacher Education (NCATE)

Kent State University
PO Box 5190, Kent 44242-0001
Type: Public, state, four-year
System: Ohio Board of Regents
Degrees: A, B, M, P, D   *Enroll:* 20,537
URL: http://www.kent.edu
Phone: (330) 672-3000   *Calendar:* Sem. plan
Inst. Accred.: NCA-HLC (1915/2004)
Prog. Accred.: Art, Audiology, Business (AACSB), Business (ACBSP), Clinical Psychology, Counseling, Dance, Interior Design, Journalism, Librarianship, Music, Nursing, Nursing Education, Public Administration, Public Health, Radiography, Recreation and Leisure Services, Rehabilitation Counseling, School Psychology, Speech-Language Pathology, Teacher Education (NCATE), Theatre

Ashtabula Campus
3325 West 13th St., Ashtabula 44004
Phone: (216) 964-3322
Prog. Accred: Business (ACBSP), Nursing, Physical Therapy Assisting

East Liverpool Campus
400 East Fourth St., East Liverpool 43920
Phone: (216) 385-3805
Prog. Accred: Business (ACBSP), Nursing,
  Occupational Therapy Assisting, Physical Therapy
  Assisting

Geauga Campus
14111 Claridon-Troy Rd., Burton Township 44021
Phone: (216) 834-4187
Prog. Accred: Business (ACBSP)

Salem Campus
2491 State Route 45 South, Salem 44460
Phone: (216) 332-0361
Prog. Accred: Business (ACBSP), Radiography

Stark Campus
6000 Frank Ave., N.W., Canton 44720
Phone: (330) 499-9600

Trumbull Campus
4314 Mahoning Ave., N.W., Warren 44483
Phone: (216) 678-4281
Prog. Accred: Business (ACBSP)

Tuscarawas Campus
University Dr., N.E., New Philadelphia 44663
Phone: (330) 339-3391
Prog. Accred: Business (ACBSP), Engineering
  Technology (electrical, mechanical), Nursing

Kenyon College
Gambier 43022-9623
Type: Private, Episcopal Church, four-year
Degrees: B   *Enroll:* 1,601
URL: http://www.kenyon.edu
Phone: (740) 427-5000   *Calendar:* Sem. plan
Inst. Accred.: NCA-HLC (1913/2001)

Kettering College of Medical Arts
3737 Southern Blvd., Kettering 45429
Type: Private, Seventh-Day Adventist Church, four-year
Degrees: A, B   *Enroll:* 505
URL: http://www.kcma.edu
Phone: (937) 296-7201   *Calendar:* Sem. plan
Inst. Accred.: NCA-HLC (1974/2001)
Prog. Accred.: Clinical Pastoral Education (ACPEI),
  Diagnostic Medical Sonography, Nursing, Physician
  Assistant, Radiography, Respiratory Therapy

Lake Erie College
391 West Washington St., Painesville 44077
Type: Private, independent, four-year
Degrees: B, M   *Enroll:* 747
URL: http://www.lec.edu
Phone: (440) 296-1856   *Calendar:* Sem. plan
Inst. Accred.: NCA-HLC (1913/1999)

Lakeland Community College
7700 Clocktower Dr., Kirtland 44094-5198
Type: Public, state/local, two-year
System: Ohio Board of Regents
Degrees: A   *Enroll:* 4,957
URL: http://www.lakelandcc.edu
Phone: (440) 953-7000   *Calendar:* Sem. plan
Inst. Accred.: NCA-HLC (1973/2000)
Prog. Accred.: Clinical Lab Technology, Dental Hygiene,
  Engineering Technology (civil/construction, electrical,
  mechanical), Nursing, Ophthalmic Medical Technology,
  Radiography, Respiratory Therapy

Laura and Alvin Siegal College of Judaic Studies
26500 Shaker Blvd., Beachwood 44122
Type: Private, independent, four-year
Degrees: B, M   *Enroll:* 70
URL: http://www.siegalcollege.edu
Phone: (216) 464-4050   *Calendar:* Sem. plan
Inst. Accred.: NCA-HLC (1988/2003)

Lorain County Community College
1005 North Abbe Rd., Elyria 44035-1691
Type: Public, state/local, two-year
System: Ohio Board of Regents
Degrees: A   *Enroll:* 5,439
URL: http://www.lorainccc.edu
Phone: (440) 365-5222   *Calendar:* Sem. plan
Inst. Accred.: NCA-HLC (1971/2004)
Prog. Accred.: Clinical Lab Technology, Dental Hygiene,
  Diagnostic Medical Sonography, Medical Assisting
  (AMA), Nursing, Phlebotomy, Physical Therapy Assisting,
  Practical Nursing, Radiography, Surgical Technology

Lourdes College
6832 Convent Blvd., Sylvania 43560
Type: Private, Roman Catholic Church, four-year
Degrees: A, B   *Enroll:* 818
URL: http://www.lourdes.edu
Phone: (419) 885-3211   *Calendar:* Sem. plan
Inst. Accred.: NCA-HLC (1964/1997)
Prog. Accred.: Nursing, Nursing Education, Social Work

Malone College
5115 25th St., NW, Canton 44709
Type: Private, Evangelical Church Eastern Region, four-year
Degrees: B, M   *Enroll:* 1,883
URL: http://www.malone.edu
Phone: (330) 471-8100   *Calendar:* Sem. plan
Inst. Accred.: NCA-HLC (1964/2004)
Prog. Accred.: Nursing, Nursing Education, Social Work

Marietta College
215 5th St., Marietta 45750
Type: Private, independent, four-year
Degrees: A, B, M   *Enroll:* 1,246
URL: http://www.marietta.edu
Phone: (740) 376-4643   *Calendar:* Sem. plan
Inst. Accred.: NCA-HLC (1913/1997)
Prog. Accred.: Athletic Training, Engineering (petroleum),
  Physician Assistant

Marion Technical College
1467 Mount Vernon Ave., Marion 43302-5694
Type: Public, state, two-year
System: Ohio Board of Regents
Degrees: A   *Enroll:* 1,352
URL: http://www.mtc.edu
Phone: (614) 389-4636   *Calendar:* Qtr. plan
Inst. Accred.: NCA-HLC (1977/2001)
Prog. Accred.: Clinical Lab Technology, Medical Assisting
(AMA), Nursing, Phlebotomy, Physical Therapy Assisting,
Radiography

MedCentral College of Nursing
335 Glessner Ave., Mansfield 44903
Type: Private, independent, four-year
Degrees: B
URL: http://www.medcentral.edu
Phone: (419) 520-2600   *Calendar:* Sem. plan
Inst. Accred.: NCA-HLC (2003)
Prog. Accred.: Nursing Education

Medical University of Ohio
3000 Arlington Ave., Toledo 43614
Type: Public, state, four-year
System: Ohio Board of Regents
Degrees: M, D   *Enroll:* 912
URL: http://www.meduohio.edu
Phone: (419) 383-4000   *Calendar:* Sem. plan
Inst. Accred.: NCA-HLC (1980/2001)
Prog. Accred.: Applied Science (occupational health and
safety), General Practice Residency, Medicine, Nursing,
Nursing Education, Occupational Therapy, Physical
Therapy, Physician Assistant, Psychology Internship,
Public Health

Mercy College of Northwest Ohio
2221 Madison Ave., Toledo 43624-1132
Type: Private, independent, four-year
Degrees: A, B   *Enroll:* 395
URL: http://www.mercycollege.edu
Phone: (419) 251-1313   *Calendar:* Sem. plan
Inst. Accred.: NCA-HLC (1995, 2000)
Prog. Accred.: Clinical Lab Technology, Health Information
Technician, Nursing, Radiography

Methodist Theological School in Ohio
PO Box 8004, 3081 Columbus Pike, Delaware 43015-
8004
Type: Private, United Methodist Church, four-year
Degrees: M   *Enroll:* 201
Phone: (740) 363-1146   *Calendar:* Qtr. plan
Inst. Accred.: ATS (1965/1998), NCA-HLC (1976/1999)

Miami University
501 East High St., Oxford 45056
Type: Public, state, four-year
System: Ohio Board of Regents
Degrees: A, B, M, P, D   *Enroll:* 16,190
URL: http://www.muohio.edu
Phone: (513) 529-1809   *Calendar:* Sem. plan
Inst. Accred.: NCA-HLC (1913/2005)
Prog. Accred.: Accounting, Art, Athletic Training,
Audiology, Business (AACSB), Clinical Psychology,
Engineering (manufacturing, paper), Engineering
Technology (electrical, mechanical), Music, Nursing,
Psychology Internship, Social Work, Speech-Language
Pathology, Teacher Education (NCATE), Theatre

Hamilton Campus
1601 Peck Blvd., Hamilton 45011
Phone: (513) 863-8833
Prog. Accred: Nursing

Middletown Campus
4200 East University Blvd., Middletown 45042
Phone: (513) 424-4444
Prog. Accred: Nursing

Miami-Jacobs College
110 North Patterson, Dayton 45402
Type: Private, independent, two-year
Degrees: A   *Enroll:* 332
URL: http://www.miamijacobs.edu
Phone: (937) 461-5174   *Calendar:* Qtr. plan
Inst. Accred.: ACICS (1957/2005)
Prog. Accred.: Medical Assisting (CAAHEP)

Mount Carmel College of Nursing
127 South Davis Ave., Columbus 43222
Type: Private, Sisters of the Holy Cross, four-year
Degrees: B   *Enroll:* 480
Phone: (614) 225-5800   *Calendar:* Sem. plan
Inst. Accred.: NCA-HLC (1994/1999)
Prog. Accred.: Dietetics (internship), Nursing

Mount Union College
1972 Clark Ave., Alliance 44601
Type: Private, United Methodist Church, four-year
Degrees: B   *Enroll:* 2,234
URL: http://www.muc.edu
Phone: (330) 821-5320   *Calendar:* Sem. plan
Inst. Accred.: NCA-HLC (1913/2002)
Prog. Accred.: Athletic Training, Music

Mount Vernon Nazarene University
800 Martinsburg Rd., Mount Vernon 43050-5000
Type: Private, Church of the Nazarene, four-year
Degrees: A, B, M   *Enroll:* 2,138
URL: http://www.mvnu.edu
Phone: (740) 392-6868   *Calendar:* 4-1-4 plan
Inst. Accred.: NCA-HLC (1972/2001)

Muskingum College
163 Stormont St., New Concord 43762
Type: Private, Presbyterian Church (USA), four-year
Degrees: B, M   *Enroll:* 1,827
URL: http://www.muskingum.edu
Phone: (740) 826-8211   *Calendar:* Sem. plan
Inst. Accred.: NCA-HLC (1919/2003)
Prog. Accred.: Music

North Central State College
2441 Kenwood Circle, PO Box 698, Mansfield 44901-0698
Type: Public, state, two-year
System: Ohio Board of Regents
Degrees: A   *Enroll:* 2,398
URL: http://www.ncstatecollege.edu
Phone: (419) 755-4800   *Calendar:* Qtr. plan
Inst. Accred.: NCA-HLC (1976/1998)
Prog. Accred.: Business (ACBSP), Nursing, Physical
  Therapy Assisting, Radiography, Respiratory Therapy

Northeastern Ohio Universities College of Medicine
4209 State Route 44, Rootstown 44272-0095
Type: Public, state, four-year
System: Ohio Board of Regents
Degrees: D   *Enroll:* 430
URL: http://www.neoucom.edu
Phone: (330) 325-2511   *Calendar:* Sem. plan
Inst. Accred.: NCA-HLC (1998/2003)
Prog. Accred.: Medicine, Psychology Internship, Public
  Health

Northwest State Community College
22600 State Route 34, Archbold 43502
Type: Public, state, two-year
System: Ohio Board of Regents
Degrees: A   *Enroll:* 1,855
URL: http://www.northweststate.edu
Phone: (419) 267-5511   *Calendar:* Sem. plan
Inst. Accred.: NCA-HLC (1977/1996)
Prog. Accred.: Business (ACBSP), Engineering Technology
  (electrical), Nursing

Notre Dame College
4545 College Rd., South Euclid 44121
Type: Private, Roman Catholic Church, four-year
Degrees: A, B, M   *Enroll:* 587
URL: http://www.notredamecollege.edu
Phone: (216) 381-1680   *Calendar:* Sem. plan
Inst. Accred.: NCA-HLC (1931/2001)

Oberlin College
101 North Professor St., Oberlin 44074-1075
Type: Private, independent, four-year
Degrees: B, M   *Enroll:* 2,862
URL: http://www.oberlin.edu
Phone: (440) 775-8400   *Calendar:* 4-1-4 plan
Inst. Accred.: NCA-HLC (1913/1998)
Prog. Accred.: Music

Ohio Business College
1907 North Ridge Rd., Lorain 44055
Type: Private, proprietary, two-year
Degrees: A   *Enroll:* 324
URL: http://www.ohiobusinesscollege.edu
Phone: (888) 514-3126
Inst. Accred.: ACICS (1980/2002)

Sandusky Campus
4020 Milan Rd., Sandusky 44870
Phone: (419) 627-8345

Ohio College of Podiatric Medicine
10515 Carnegie Ave., Cleveland 44106
Type: Private, independent, four-year
Degrees: D   *Enroll:* 228
URL: http://www.ocpm.edu
Phone: (216) 231-3300   *Calendar:* Sem. plan
Inst. Accred.: NCA-HLC (1987/2003)
Prog. Accred.: Podiatry

Ohio Dominican University
1216 Sunbury Rd., Columbus 43219
Type: Private, Roman Catholic Church, four-year
Degrees: A, B   *Enroll:* 2,161
URL: http://www.ohiodominican.edu
Phone: (614) 251-4690   *Calendar:* Sem. plan
Inst. Accred.: NCA-HLC (1934/1998)

Ohio Institute of Photography and Technology
2029 Edgefield Rd., Dayton 45439-1984
Type: Private, proprietary, two-year
System: Kaplan Higher Education Corporation
Degrees: A   *Enroll:* 615
URL: http://www.iopt.com
Phone: (937) 294-6155   *Calendar:* Sem. plan
Inst. Accred.: ACCSCT (1976/2000)
Prog. Accred.: Medical Assisting (CAAHEP)

Ohio Northern University
525 South Main St., Ada 45810
Type: Private, United Methodist Church, four-year
Degrees: B, P, D   *Enroll:* 3,334
URL: http://www.onu.edu
Phone: (419) 772-2000   *Calendar:* Qtr. plan
Inst. Accred.: NCA-HLC (1958/2005)
Prog. Accred.: Athletic Training, Business (AACSB),
  Engineering (civil, computer, electrical, mechanical),
  Law, Music, Pharmacy, Teacher Education (NCATE)

The Ohio State University
205 Bricker Hall, 190 North Oval Dr., Columbus 43210-1357
Type: Public, state, four-year
System: Ohio Board of Regents
Degrees: A, B, M, P, D   *Enroll:* 46,249
URL: http://www.osu.edu
Phone: (614) 292-6446   *Calendar:* Qtr. plan
Inst. Accred.: NCA-HLC (1913/1997)
Prog. Accred.: Accounting, Applied Science (surveying/geomatics), Art, Audiology, Blood Bank Technology, Business (AACSB), Clinical Lab Scientist, Clinical Pastoral Education (ACPEI), Clinical Psychology, Combined Prosthodontics, Computer Science, Counseling Psychology, Dance, Dental Hygiene, Dentistry, Dietetics (coordinated), Dietetics (internship), Endodontics, Engineering (aerospace, agricultural, ceramic, chemical, civil, computer, electrical, environmental/sanitary, industrial, materials, mechanical, metallurgical, welding), Forestry, General Dentistry, General Practice Residency, Health Information Administration, Health Services Administration, Interior Design, Landscape Architecture, Law, Marriage and Family Therapy, Medicine, Music, Nuclear Medicine Technology, Nurse (Midwifery), Nursing, Nursing Education, Occupational Therapy, Optometric Residency, Optometry, Oral and Maxillofacial Pathology, Oral and Maxillofacial Surgery, Orthodontic and Dentofacial Orthopedics, Pathologists' Assistant, Pediatric Dentistry, Perfusion, Periodontics, Pharmacy, Physical Therapy, Planning, Psychology Internship, Public Administration, Public Health, Radiography, Radiation Therapy, Rehabilitation Counseling, Respiratory Therapy, Social Work, Speech-Language Pathology, Teacher Education (NCATE), Theatre, Veterinary Medicine

Lima Campus
4240 Campus Dr., Lima 45804
Phone: (419) 221-1641

Mansfield Campus
1680 University Dr., Mansfield 44906
Phone: (419) 755-4011

Marion Campus
1465 Mount Vernon Ave., Marion 43302-5695
Phone: (740) 389-6786

Newark Campus
1179 University Dr., Newark 43055-1797
Phone: (614) 366-3321

The Ohio State University—Agricultural Technical Institute
1328 Dover Rd., Wooster 44691
Type: Public, state, two-year
Degrees: A   *Enroll:* 764
URL: http://www.ati.ohio-state.edu
Phone: (330) 264-3911   *Calendar:* Qtr. plan
Inst. Accred.: NCA-HLC (1978/2003)

Ohio University
Athens 45701-2979
Type: Public, state, four-year
System: Ohio Board of Regents
Degrees: A, B, M, D   *Enroll:* 19,354
URL: http://www.ohiou.edu
Phone: (740) 593-1000   *Calendar:* Qtr. plan
Inst. Accred.: NCA-HLC (1913/2001)
Prog. Accred.: Accounting, Applied Science (industrial hygiene), Athletic Training, Audiology, Business (AACSB), Clinical Psychology, Computer Science, Counseling, Dance, Engineering (chemical, civil, electrical, industrial, mechanical), Family and Consumer Science, Industrial Technology, Interior Design, Journalism, Music, Nursing, Nursing Education, Osteopathy, Physical Therapy, Recreation and Leisure Services, Rehabilitation Counseling, Social Work, Speech-Language Pathology, Teacher Education (NCATE), Theatre

Chillicothe Campus
571 West 5th St., Chillicothe 45601
Phone: (614) 774-7200

Eastern Campus
National Rd., West St., St. Clairsville 43950
Phone: (614) 695-1720

Lancaster Campus
1570 Granville Pike, Lancaster 43130
Phone: (614) 654-6711

Southern Campus
1804 Liberty Ave., Ironton 43701
Phone: (614) 533-4600

Zanesville Campus
1425 Neward Rd., Zanesville 43701
Phone: (614) 453-0762
Prog. Accred: Nursing

Ohio Valley College of Technology
PO Box 7000, 16808 St. Clair Ave., East Liverpool 43920
Type: Private, proprietary, two-year
Degrees: A   *Enroll:* 122
URL: http://www.ohiovalleytech.com
Phone: (330) 385-1070
Inst. Accred.: ACICS (1985/2005)
Prog. Accred.: Medical Assisting (CAAHEP)

Ohio Wesleyan University
61 South Sandusky St., Delaware 43015
Type: Private, United Methodist Church, four-year
Degrees: B   *Enroll:* 1,914
URL: http://web.owu.edu
Phone: (740) 368-2000   *Calendar:* Sem. plan
Inst. Accred.: NCA-HLC (1913/1999)
Prog. Accred.: Music

Otterbein College
One Otterbein College, Westerville 43081
Type: Private, United Methodist Church, four-year
Degrees: B, M   *Enroll:* 2,448
URL: http://www.otterbein.edu
Phone: (614) 890-3000   *Calendar:* Qtr. plan
Inst. Accred.: NCA-HLC (1913/2005)
Prog. Accred.: Music, Nursing, Nursing Education,
  Teacher Education (NCATE), Theatre

Owens Community College
PO Box 10000, Toledo 43699-1947
Type: Public, state, two-year
System: Ohio Board of Regents
Degrees: A   *Enroll:* 10,524
URL: http://www.owens.edu
Phone: (419) 661-7000   *Calendar:* Sem. plan
Inst. Accred.: NCA-HLC (1976/2001)
Prog. Accred.: Business (ACBSP), Dental Hygiene,
  Diagnostic Medical Sonography, Engineering
  Technology (architectural, mechanical), Nursing,
  Occupational Therapy Assisting, Physical Therapy
  Assisting, Radiography, Surgical Technology

Findlay Campus
300 Davis St., Findlay 45840-3600
Phone: (567) 429-3604

Payne Theological Seminary
1230 Wilberforce Clifton Rd., Wilberforce 45384
Type: Private, African Methodist Episcopal Church, four-year
Degrees: M   *Enroll:* 88
URL: http://www.payne.edu
Phone: (937) 376-2946
Inst. Accred.: ATS (1995/1998)

Pontifical College Josephinum
7625 North High St., Columbus 43235
Type: Private, Roman Catholic Church, four-year
Degrees: B, M   *Enroll:* 147
URL: http://www.pcj.edu
Phone: (614) 885-5585   *Calendar:* Sem. plan
Inst. Accred.: ATS (1970/2001), NCA-HLC (1977/2001)

Professional Skills Institute
20 Arco Dr., Toledo 43607
Type: Private, proprietary, two-year
Degrees: A   *Enroll:* 231
URL: http://www.proskills.com
Phone: (419) 531-9610   *Calendar:* Qtr. plan
Inst. Accred.: ABHES (1986/2003)
Prog. Accred.: Medical Assisting (AMA), Physical Therapy
  Assisting

Santa Barbara Campus
4213 State St., Ste. 302, Santa Barbara, CA 93110
Phone: (805) 683-1902

Rabbinical College of Telshe
28400 Euclid Ave., Wickliffe 44092-2523
Type: Private, independent, four-year
Degrees: M, D   *Enroll:* 64
Phone: (440) 943-5300   *Calendar:* Sem. plan
Inst. Accred.: AARTS (1974/1998)

Remington College—Cleveland
14445 Broadway Ave., Cleveland 44125
Type: Private, proprietary, two-year
System: Education America, Inc.
Degrees: A
URL: http://www.remingtoncollege.edu
Phone: (216) 475-7520   *Calendar:* Qtr. plan
Inst. Accred.: ACCSCT (1990/2000)

Cleveland West Campus
26350 Brookpark Rd., North Olmstead 44070
Phone: (440) 777-2560

RETS Tech Center
555 East Alex-Bell Rd., Centerville 45459
Type: Private, proprietary, two-year
Degrees: A   *Enroll:* 599
URL: http://retstechcenter.com
Phone: (937) 433-3410   *Calendar:* Sem. plan
Inst. Accred.: ACCSCT (1974/2003)
Prog. Accred.: Medical Assisting (CAAHEP)

Rosedale Bible College
2270 Rosedale Rd., Irwin 43029-9501
Type: Private, Conservative Mennonite Conference, two-year
Degrees: A
URL: http://www.rosedale.edu
Phone: (740) 857-1311
Inst. Accred.: ABHE (2002)

Saint Mary Seminary and Graduate School of Theology
28700 Euclid Ave., Wickliffe 44092-2585
Type: Private, Roman Catholic Church, four-year
Degrees: M, D   *Enroll:* 80
URL: http://www.stmarysem.edu
Phone: (440) 943-7600   *Calendar:* Sem. plan
Inst. Accred.: ATS (1970/2005), NCA-HLC (1981/1996)

School of Advertising Art
1725 East David Rd., Dayton 45440-1612
Type: Private, proprietary, two-year
Degrees: A   *Enroll:* 121
URL: http://www.saacollege.com
Phone: (937) 294-0592
Inst. Accred.: ACCSCT (1988/2003)

Shawnee State University
940 Second St., Portsmouth 45662-4303
Type: Public, state, four-year
System: Ohio Board of Regents
Degrees: A, B   *Enroll:* 3,308
URL: http://www.shawnee.edu
Phone: (740) 354-3205   *Calendar:* Qtr. plan
Inst. Accred.: NCA-HLC (1975/1998)
Prog. Accred.: Clinical Lab Scientist, Clinical Lab
  Technology, Dental Hygiene, Occupational Therapy,
  Occupational Therapy Assisting, Physical Therapy
  Assisting, Radiography, Respiratory Therapy, Teacher
  Education (NCATE)

Sinclair Community College
444 West Third St., Dayton 45402-1460
Type: Public, state/local, two-year
System: Ohio Board of Regents
Degrees: A   *Enroll:* 11,618
URL: http://www.sinclair.edu
Phone: (937) 226-2500   *Calendar:* Qtr. plan
Inst. Accred.: NCA-HLC (1970/1998)
Prog. Accred.: Art, Business (ACBSP), Culinary Education,
  Dental Hygiene, Engineering Technology
  (civil/construction, electrical, industrial, mechanical,
  quality technology), Health Information Technician,
  Industrial Technology, Medical Assisting (AMA), Music,
  Nursing, Occupational Therapy Assisting, Physical
  Therapy Assisting, Radiography, Respiratory Therapy,
  Surgical Technology

Southeastern Business College
1855 Western Ave., Chillicothe 45601
Type: Private, proprietary, two-year
Degrees: A   *Enroll:* 81
URL: http://www.careersohio.com
Phone: (740) 774-6300   *Calendar:* Qtr. plan
Inst. Accred.: ACICS (1976/2002)

Jackson Campus
504 McCarty Ln., Jackson 45640
Phone: (740) 286-1554

Lancaster Campus
1522 Sheridan Dr., Lancaster 43130
Phone: (740) 687-6126

New Boston Campus
3879 Rhodes Ave., New Boston 45662
Phone: (740) 456-4124

Southern State Community College
100 Hobart Dr., Hillsboro 45133-9487
Type: Public, state, two-year
System: Ohio Board of Regents
Degrees: A   *Enroll:* 1,560
URL: http://www.sscc.edu
Phone: (937) 393-3431   *Calendar:* Qtr. plan
Inst. Accred.: NCA-HLC (1981/1996)
Prog. Accred.: Medical Assisting (AMA), Nursing

Southwestern College
111 West First St., Ste. 1140, Dayton 45402
Type: Private, proprietary, two-year
System: Lincoln Educational Services
Degrees: A   *Enroll:* 222
URL: http://www.swcollege.net
Phone: (937) 224-0061   *Calendar:* Qtr. plan
Inst. Accred.: ACICS (1978/2001)

Florence Campus
8095 Connector Dr., Florence, KY 41042-1466
Phone: (859) 282-9999

Franklin Campus
201 East Second St., Franklin 45005
Phone: (937) 746-6633

Tri-County Campus
149 Northland Blvd., Cincinnati 45246
Phone: (513) 874-0432

Vine Street Campus
632 Vine St., Ste. 200, Cincinnati 45202
Phone: (513) 421-3212

Stark State College of Technology
6200 Frank Ave., NW, Canton 44720-7299
Type: Public, state, two-year
System: Ohio Board of Regents
Degrees: A   *Enroll:* 3,158
URL: http://www.starkstate.edu
Phone: (330) 494-6170   *Calendar:* Sem. plan
Inst. Accred.: NCA-HLC (1976/2001)
Prog. Accred.: Clinical Lab Technology, Dental Hygiene,
  Engineering Technology (civil/construction, electrical,
  mechanical, mechanical drafting/design), Health
  Information Technician, Medical Assisting (AMA),
  Nursing, Occupational Therapy Assisting, Physical
  Therapy Assisting, Respiratory Therapy

Stautzenberger College
5355 Southwyck Blvd., Toledo 43614
Type: Private, proprietary, two-year
System: American Higher Education Development
  Corporation
Degrees: A   *Enroll:* 582
URL: http://www.stautzen.com
Phone: (419) 866-0261   *Calendar:* Qtr. plan
Inst. Accred.: ACICS (1962/2001)
Prog. Accred.: Medical Assisting (AMA), Veterinary
  Technology

Technology Education College
2745 Winchester Pike, Columbus 43232
Type: Private, proprietary, two-year
System: Kaplan Higher Education Corporation
Degrees: A   *Enroll:* 456
URL: http://www.teccollege.com
Phone: (614) 456-4600
Inst. Accred.: ACCSCT (1980/2000)

Terra State Community College
2830 Napoleon Rd., Fremont 43420-9670
Type: Public, state, two-year
System: Ohio Board of Regents
Degrees: A   *Enroll:* 1,570
URL: http://www.terra.edu
Phone: (419) 334-8400   *Calendar:* Qtr. plan
Inst. Accred.: NCA-HLC (1975/1997)

Tiffin University
155 Miami St., Tiffin 44883
Type: Private, independent, four-year
Degrees: A, B, M   *Enroll:* 1,226
URL: http://www.tiffin.edu
Phone: (419) 447-6442   *Calendar:* Sem. plan
Inst. Accred.: NCA-HLC (1985/2000)
Prog. Accred.: Business (ACBSP)

Tri-State Bible College
PO Box 445, 506 Margaret St., South Point 45680
Type: Private, independent, four-year
Degrees: A, B   *Enroll:* 27
URL: http://www.tsbc.edu
Phone: (740) 377-2520   *Calendar:* Sem. plan
Inst. Accred.: ABHE (2004)

Trinity Lutheran Seminary
2199 East Main St., Columbus 43209-2334
Type: Private, Evangelical Lutheran Church in America, four-year
Degrees: M   *Enroll:* 165
URL: http://www.trinitylutheranseminary.edu
Phone: (614) 235-4136   *Calendar:* Sem. plan
Inst. Accred.: ATS (1940/2002), NCA-HLC (1978/2002)

Trumbull Business College
3200 Ridge Rd., Warren 44484
Type: Private, proprietary, two-year
Degrees: A   *Enroll:* 410
URL: http://www.tbc-trumbullbusiness.com
Phone: (330) 369-3200
Inst. Accred.: ACICS (1976/2000)

The Union Institute and University
440 East McMillan St., Cincinnati 45206-1947
Type: Private, independent, four-year
Degrees: B, D   *Enroll:* 2,621
URL: http://www.tui.edu
Phone: (513) 861-6400   *Calendar:* Sem. plan
Inst. Accred.: NCA-HLC (1985/2000, Warning)

Vermont College
College St., Montpelier, VT 05602
Phone: (800) 336-6794

United Theological Seminary
1810 Harvard Blvd., Dayton 45406
Type: Private, The United Methodist Church, four-year
Degrees: M, D   *Enroll:* 302
URL: http://www.united.edu
Phone: (937) 278-5817   *Calendar:* Sem. plan
Inst. Accred.: ATS (1938/2001), NCA-HLC (1975/2002, Warning)

The University of Akron
302 East Buchtel Common, Akron 44325-4702
Type: Public, state, four-year
System: Ohio Board of Regents
Degrees: A, B, M, D   *Enroll:* 18,400
URL: http://www.uakron.edu
Phone: (330) 972-7111   *Calendar:* Sem. plan
Inst. Accred.: NCA-HLC (1914/2003)
Prog. Accred.: Accounting, Art, Audiology, Business (AACSB), Business (ACBSP), Counseling, Counseling Psychology, Dance, Dietetics (coordinated), Engineering (bioengineering, chemical, civil, computer, electrical, mechanical, polymer), Engineering Technology (civil/construction, electrical, mechanical, surveying), Family and Consumer Science, Interior Design, Law, Marriage and Family Therapy, Medical Assisting (AMA), Music, Nurse Anesthesia Education, Nursing, Psychology Internship, Public Administration, Public Health, Respiratory Therapy, Social Work, Speech-Language Pathology, Surgical Technology, Teacher Education (NCATE)

University of Akron—Wayne College
1901 Smucker Rd., Orrville 44667
Type: Public, state, two-year
System: Ohio Board of Regents
Degrees: A   *Enroll:* 1,114
URL: http://www.wayne.uakron.edu
Phone: (330) 683-2010   *Calendar:* Sem. plan
Inst. Accred.: NCA-HLC (1972/2001)

University of Cincinnati
PO Box 210063, Cincinnati 45221-0063
Type: Public, state, four-year
System: Ohio Board of Regents
Degrees: A, B, M, P, D   *Enroll:* 23,075
URL: http://www.uc.edu
Phone: (513) 556-6000   *Calendar:* Qtr. plan
Inst. Accred.: NCA-HLC (1913/1999)
Prog. Accred.: Applied Science (industrial hygiene), Art, Athletic Training, Audiology, Blood Bank Technology, Business (AACSB), Clinical Lab Scientist, Clinical Psychology, Construction Education, Counseling, Dance, Dental Hygiene, EMT (Paramedic), Engineering (aerospace, chemical, civil, computer, electrical, engineering mechanics, environmental/sanitary, industrial, materials, mechanical), Engineering Technology (architectural, civil/construction, electrical, manufacturing, mechanical), Interior Design, Law, Medicine, Music, Nuclear Medicine Technology, Nurse (Midwifery), Nurse Anesthesia Education, Nursing, Nursing Education, Oral and Maxillofacial Surgery, Pharmacy, Physical Therapy, Physical Therapy Assisting, Planning, Psychology Internship, Radiography, Social Work, Speech-Language Pathology, Teacher Education (NCATE), Theatre

College-Conservatory of Music
PO Box 210236, Cincinnati 45221-9988
Phone: (513) 556-2595
Prog. Accred: Music

University of Cincinnati—Clermont College
4200 Clermont College Dr., Batavia 45103
Type: Public, state, two-year
System: Ohio Board of Regents
Degrees: A   *Enroll:* 1,929
Phone: (513) 732-5200   *Calendar:* Qtr. plan
Inst. Accred.: NCA-HLC (1978/1996)

University of Cincinnati—Raymond Walters College
9555 Plainfield Rd., Cincinnati 45236-1096
Type: Public, state, four-year
System: Ohio Board of Regents
Degrees: A, B   *Enroll:* 2,852
URL: http://www.rwc.uc.edu
Phone: (513) 745-5600   *Calendar:* Qtr. plan
Inst. Accred.: NCA-HLC (1969/1999)
Prog. Accred.: Dental Hygiene, Nursing, Radiation
   Therapy, Radiography, Veterinary Technology

University of Dayton
300 College Park Ave., Dayton 45469-1624
Type: Private, Society of Mary, four-year
Degrees: B, M, P, D   *Enroll:* 9,017
URL: http://www.udayton.edu
Phone: (937) 229-1000   *Calendar:* Tri. plan
Inst. Accred.: NCA-HLC (1928/1998)
Prog. Accred.: Accounting, Business (AACSB),
   Engineering (chemical, civil, computer, electrical,
   mechanical), Engineering Technology (electrical,
   industrial, manufacturing, mechanical), Law, Music,
   Teacher Education (NCATE), Teacher Education (TEAC)

University of Findlay
1000 North Main St., Findlay 45840
Type: Private, Churches of God, General Conference, four-
   year
Degrees: A, B, M   *Enroll:* 3,659
URL: http://www.findlay.edu
Phone: (419) 424-8313   *Calendar:* Sem. plan
Inst. Accred.: NCA-HLC (1933/2004)
Prog. Accred.: Nuclear Medicine Technology,
   Occupational Therapy, Physical Therapy, Physician
   Assistant, Social Work, Teacher Education (NCATE)

University of Northwestern Ohio
1441 North Cable Rd., Lima 45805
Type: Private, independent, four-year
Degrees: A, B   *Enroll:* 2,486
URL: http://www.unoh.edu
Phone: (419) 227-3141   *Calendar:* Qtr. plan
Inst. Accred.: NCA-HLC (1987/1996)
Prog. Accred.: Business (ACBSP), Medical Assisting
   (CAAHEP)

University of Rio Grande and Rio Grande Community College
East College Ave., PO Box 500, Rio Grande 45674
Type: Private, independent, four-year
Degrees: A, B, M   *Enroll:* 1,715
URL: http://www.rio.edu
Phone: (740) 245-5353   *Calendar:* Qtr. plan
Inst. Accred.: NCA-HLC (1969/1995)
Prog. Accred.: Clinical Lab Technology, Nursing, Social
   Work

University of Toledo
2801 West Bancroft St., Toledo 43606-3390
Type: Public, state, four-year
System: Ohio Board of Regents
Degrees: A, B, M, P, D   *Enroll:* 17,482
URL: http://www.utoledo.edu
Phone: (419) 530-4636   *Calendar:* Sem. plan
Inst. Accred.: NCA-HLC (1922/2002)
Prog. Accred.: Art, Athletic Training, Business (AACSB),
   Cardiovascular Technology, Clinical Psychology,
   Computer Science, Counseling, Engineering
   (bioengineering, chemical, civil, computer, electrical,
   industrial, mechanical), Engineering Technology
   (civil/construction, computer, electrical, mechanical),
   Law, Medical Assisting (AMA), Music, Nursing,
   Pharmacy, Public Administration, Public Health,
   Recreation and Leisure Services, Respiratory Therapy,
   Respiratory Therapy Technology, Social Work, Speech-
   Language Pathology, Teacher Education (NCATE)

Urbana University
579 College Way, Urbana 43078
Type: Private, Swedenborgian, four-year
Degrees: A, B, M   *Enroll:* 1,136
URL: http://www.urbana.edu
Phone: (937) 484-1301   *Calendar:* Sem. plan
Inst. Accred.: NCA-HLC (1975/2001)
Prog. Accred.: Nursing Education

Ursuline College
2550 Lander Rd., Pepper Pike 44124
Type: Private, Roman Catholic Church, four-year
Degrees: B, M   *Enroll:* 1,006
URL: http://www.ursuline.edu
Phone: (440) 449-4200   *Calendar:* Sem. plan
Inst. Accred.: NCA-HLC (1931/2002)
Prog. Accred.: Nursing, Nursing Education, Social Work

Virginia Marti College of Art and Design
PO Box 580, 11724 Detroit Ave., Lakewood 44107
Type: Private, independent, two-year
Degrees: A   *Enroll:* 218
URL: http://www.virginiamarticollege.com
Phone: (216) 221-8584   *Calendar:* Qtr. plan
Inst. Accred.: ACCSCT (1975/2002)

Walsh University
2020 Easton St., NW, Canton 44720
Type: Private, Roman Catholic Church, four-year
Degrees: A, B, M *Enroll:* 1,458
URL: http://www.walsh.edu
Phone: (330) 499-7090 *Calendar:* Sem. plan
Inst. Accred.: NCA-HLC (1970/2000)
Prog. Accred.: Nursing, Physical Therapy

Washington State Community College
710 Colegate Dr., Marietta 45750-9803
Type: Public, state, two-year
System: Ohio Board of Regents
Degrees: A *Enroll:* 1,582
URL: http://www.wscc.edu
Phone: (740) 374-8716 *Calendar:* Qtr. plan
Inst. Accred.: NCA-HLC (1979/1995)
Prog. Accred.: Clinical Lab Technology, Physical Therapy
Assisting, Respiratory Therapy

Wilberforce University
1055 North Bickett Rd., PO Box 1001, Wilberforce
45384-1001
Type: Private, African Methodist Episcopal Church, four-year
Degrees: B, M *Enroll:* 1,171
URL: http://www.wilberforce.edu
Phone: (937) 376-2911 *Calendar:* Tri. plan
Inst. Accred.: NCA-HLC (1939/1999)

Wilmington College
251 Ludovic St., PO Box 1185, Wilmington 45177
Type: Private, Religious Society of Friends (Quaker), four-year
Degrees: B *Enroll:* 1,560
URL: http://www.wilmington.edu
Phone: (937) 382-6661 *Calendar:* Sem. plan
Inst. Accred.: NCA-HLC (1944/2004)
Prog. Accred.: Athletic Training

Eastgate Campus
4360 Ferguson Dr., Cincinnati 45245
Phone: (513) 943-3600

Tri-County Campus
1 Triangle Park Dr., Cincinnati 45246
Phone: (513) 772-7516

Winebrenner Theological Seminary
950 N. Main St., Findlay 45840-3652
Type: Private, Churches of God, General Conference, four-year
Degrees: M, D *Enroll:* 79
URL: http://www.winebrenner.edu
Phone: (419) 422-4824 *Calendar:* 4-1-4 plan
Inst. Accred.: ATS (1991/2004), NCA-HLC (1986/2005)

Wittenberg University
PO Box 720, Springfield 45501-0720
Type: Private, Evangelic Church in America, four-year
Degrees: B, M *Enroll:* 2,149
URL: http://www.wittenberg.edu
Phone: (937) 327-6231 *Calendar:* Sem. plan
Inst. Accred.: NCA-HLC (1916/1997)
Prog. Accred.: Music

Wright State University
3640 Colonel Glenn Hwy., Dayton 45435-0001
Type: Public, state, four-year
System: Ohio Board of Regents
Degrees: A, B, M, P, D *Enroll:* 12,795
URL: http://www.wright.edu
Phone: (937) 775-3333 *Calendar:* Qtr. plan
Inst. Accred.: NCA-HLC (1968/1996)
Prog. Accred.: Accounting, Business (AACSB), Clinical Lab
Scientist, Clinical Psychology, Computer Science,
Counseling, Engineering (bioengineering, computer,
electrical, engineering physics/science, industrial,
materials, mechanical), Medicine, Music, Nursing,
Nursing Education, Psychology Internship,
Rehabilitation Counseling, Social Work, Teacher
Education (NCATE)

Lake Campus
7600 State Route 703, Celina 45822
Phone: (419) 586-2365

Xavier University
3800 Victory Pkwy., Cincinnati 45207
Type: Private, Roman Catholic Church, four-year
Degrees: A, B, M, D *Enroll:* 5,010
URL: http://www.xu.edu
Phone: (513) 745-3000 *Calendar:* Sem. plan
Inst. Accred.: NCA-HLC (1925/1999)
Prog. Accred.: Athletic Training, Business (AACSB),
Clinical Psychology, Health Services Administration,
Montessori Teacher Education, Nursing, Nursing
Education, Occupational Therapy, Radiography, Social
Work

Youngstown State University
One University Plaza, Youngstown 44555-3101
Type: Public, state, four-year
System: Ohio Board of Regents
Degrees: A, B, M, D *Enroll:* 10,828
URL: http://www.ysu.edu
Phone: (330) 742-3000 *Calendar:* Qtr. plan
Inst. Accred.: NCA-HLC (1945/1998)
Prog. Accred.: Art, Business (AACSB), Clinical Lab
Technology, Counseling, Dental Hygiene, Dietetics
(coordinated), EMT (Paramedic), Engineering (chemical,
civil, electrical, industrial, mechanical), Engineering
Technology (civil/construction, electrical, mechanical),
Histologic Technology, Medical Assisting (AMA), Music,
Nurse Anesthesia Education, Nursing, Physical Therapy,
Public Health, Respiratory Therapy, Social Work,
Teacher Education (NCATE), Theatre

Zane State College
1555 Newark Rd., Zanesville 43701-2694
Type: Public, state, two-year
System: Ohio Board of Regents
Degrees: A   *Enroll:* 1,164
URL: http://www.zanestate.edu
Phone: (740) 454-2501   *Calendar:* Qtr. plan
Inst. Accred.: NCA-HLC (1975/1998)
Prog. Accred.: Clinical Lab Technology, Culinary
  Education, Engineering Technology (electrical), Medical
  Assisting (AMA), Occupational Therapy Assisting,
  Phlebotomy, Physical Therapy Assisting, Radiography

OKLAHOMA

Bacone College
2299 Old Bacone Rd., Muskogee 74403-1597
Type: Private, American Baptist Church, four-year
Degrees: A, B   *Enroll:* 785
URL: http://www.bacone.edu
Phone: (918) 683-4581   *Calendar:* 4-1-4 plan
Inst. Accred.: NCA-HLC (1965/2005)
Prog. Accred.: Nursing, Radiography

Cameron University
2800 West Gore Blvd., Lawton 73505-6377
Type: Public, state, four-year
System: Oklahoma State Regents for Higher Education
Degrees: A, B, M   *Enroll:* 4,194
URL: http://www.cameron.edu
Phone: (580) 581-2200   *Calendar:* Sem. plan
Inst. Accred.: NCA-HLC (1962/2001)
Prog. Accred.: Business (ACBSP), Music, Teacher
  Education (NCATE)

Carl Albert State College
1507 South McKenna, Poteau 74953-5208
Type: Public, state, two-year
System: Oklahoma State Regents for Higher Education
Degrees: A   *Enroll:* 2,044
URL: http://www.carlalbert.edu
Phone: (918) 647-8660   *Calendar:* Sem. plan
Inst. Accred.: NCA-HLC (1978/2003)
Prog. Accred.: Business (ACBSP), Nursing, Physical
  Therapy Assisting, Radiography

Sallisaw Campus
PO Box 1437, Sallisaw 77495
Phone: (918) 775-6977

Connors State College
Route 1, Box 1000, Warner 74469
Type: Public, state, two-year
System: Oklahoma State Regents for Higher Education
Degrees: A   *Enroll:* 1,676
URL: http://www.connorsstate.edu
Phone: (918) 463-2931   *Calendar:* Sem. plan
Inst. Accred.: NCA-HLC (1963/2000)
Prog. Accred.: Nursing

Muskogee Campus
201 Ct. St., Muskogee 74401
Phone: (918) 687-6747

East Central University
1100 East 14th St., Ada 74820-6999
Type: Public, state, four-year
System: Oklahoma State Regents for Higher Education
Degrees: B, M   *Enroll:* 3,732
URL: http://www.ecok.edu
Phone: (928) 428-8322   *Calendar:* Sem. plan
Inst. Accred.: NCA-HLC (1922/2002)
Prog. Accred.: Business (ACBSP), Health Information
  Administration, Music, Nursing, Rehabilitation
  Counseling, Social Work, Teacher Education (NCATE)

Eastern Oklahoma State College
1301 West Main St., Wilburton 74578-4999
Type: Public, state, two-year
System: Oklahoma State Regents for Higher Education
Degrees: A   *Enroll:* 2,291
URL: http://www.eosc.edu
Phone: (918) 465-2361   *Calendar:* Sem. plan
Inst. Accred.: NCA-HLC (1954/1996)
Prog. Accred.: Nursing

Heritage College Hair Design
7100 I-35 Services Rd., Ste. 7118, Oklahoma City 73149
Type: Private, proprietary, two-year
Degrees: A
URL: http://www.heritage-education.com
Phone: (405) 631-3399
Inst. Accred.: ACCSCT (1994/2002)

Hillsdale Free Will Baptist College
PO Box 7208, Moore 73153-1208
Type: Private, Free Will Baptist Church, four-year
Degrees: A, B, M   *Enroll:* 236
URL: http://www.hc.edu
Phone: (405) 912-9000   *Calendar:* Sem. plan
Inst. Accred.: TRACS (1999/2004)

Langston University
PO Box 907, Langston 73050-0907
Type: Public, state, four-year
System: Oklahoma State Regents for Higher Education
Degrees: A, B, M   *Enroll:* 2,563
URL: http://www.lunet.edu
Phone: (405) 466-3207   *Calendar:* Sem. plan
Inst. Accred.: NCA-HLC (1948/1997)
Prog. Accred.: Business (ACBSP), Nursing, Physical
  Therapy, Teacher Education (NCATE)

Metropolitan College
10820 East 45th St., Ste. B-101, Tulsa 74146
Type: Private, proprietary, four-year
System: Wyandotte Collegiate Systems
Degrees: A, B
URL: http://www.metropolitancollege.edu
Phone: (918) 627-9300   *Calendar:* Tri. plan
Inst. Accred.: ACCSCT (1991/2005)

Metropolitan College—Oklahoma City Campus
1900 NW Expressway #R302, Oklahoma City 73118
Type: Private, proprietary, four-year
System: Wyandotte Collegiate Systems
Degrees: A, B
URL: http://www.metropolitancollege.edu
Phone: (405) 843-1000
Inst. Accred.: ACCSCT (1992/2005)

Mid-America Christian University
3500 SW 119th St., Oklahoma City 73170
Type: Private, Church of God, four-year
Degrees: A, B   *Enroll:* 594
URL: http://www.macu.edu
Phone: (405) 691-3800   *Calendar:* Sem. plan
Inst. Accred.: NCA-HLC (1985/2002)

Murray State College
1 Murray Campus St., Tishomingo 73460-3137
Type: Public, state, two-year
System: Oklahoma State Regents for Higher Education
Degrees: A   *Enroll:* 1,409
URL: http://www.mscok.edu
Phone: (580) 371-2371   *Calendar:* Sem. plan
Inst. Accred.: NCA-HLC (1964/2004)
Prog. Accred.: Nursing, Physical Therapy Assisting,
    Veterinary Technology

Northeastern Oklahoma A&M College
200 I St. NE, Miami 74354
Type: Public, state, two-year
System: Oklahoma State Regents for Higher Education
Degrees: A   *Enroll:* 1,631
URL: http://www.neoam.edu
Phone: (918) 542-8441   *Calendar:* Sem. plan
Inst. Accred.: NCA-HLC (1925/1997)
Prog. Accred.: Clinical Lab Technology, Medical Assisting
    (AMA), Nursing, Physical Therapy Assisting, Surgical
    Technology

Northeastern State University
601 North Grand, Tahlequah 74464-2399
Type: Public, state, four-year
System: Oklahoma State Regents for Higher Education
Degrees: B, M, D   *Enroll:* 7,783
URL: http://www.nsuok.edu
Phone: (918) 456-5511   *Calendar:* Sem. plan
Inst. Accred.: NCA-HLC (1922/2002)
Prog. Accred.: Business (ACBSP), Music, Nursing,
    Optometric Residency, Optometry, Social Work, Speech-
    Language Pathology, Teacher Education (NCATE)

Muskogee Campus
PO Box 549, Muskogee 74402-0549
Phone: (918) 683-0641

Northern Oklahoma College
PO Box 310, 1220 East Grand, Tonkawa 74653-0310
Type: Public, state, two-year
System: Oklahoma State Regents for Higher Education
Degrees: A   *Enroll:* 2,598
URL: http://www.north-ok.edu
Phone: (580) 628-6200   *Calendar:* Sem. plan
Inst. Accred.: NCA-HLC (1948/1998)
Prog. Accred.: Nursing

Northwestern Oklahoma State University
709 Oklahoma Blvd., Alva 73717-2799
Type: Public, state, four-year
System: Oklahoma State Regents for Higher Education
Degrees: B, M   *Enroll:* 1,763
URL: http://www.nwalva.edu
Phone: (580) 327-1700   *Calendar:* Sem. plan
Inst. Accred.: NCA-HLC (1922/2004)
Prog. Accred.: Nursing, Teacher Education (NCATE)

Enid Campus
2929 East Randolph, Enid 73701
Phone: (580) 213-3101

Woodward Campus
High Plains Technical Center, 3921 34th St.,
Woodward 73801
Phone: (405) 256-0047

Oklahoma Baptist University
500 West University, Shawnee 74801
Type: Private, Southern Baptist Church, four-year
Degrees: A, B, M   *Enroll:* 1,612
URL: http://www.okbu.edu
Phone: (405) 275-2850   *Calendar:* Sem. plan
Inst. Accred.: NCA-HLC (1952/1998)
Prog. Accred.: Business (ACBSP), Music, Nursing, Teacher
    Education (NCATE)

Oklahoma Christian University
PO Box 11000, Oklahoma City 73136-1100
Type: Private, independent, four-year
Degrees: B, M   *Enroll:* 1,514
URL: http://www.oc.edu
Phone: (405) 425-5000   *Calendar:* Tri. plan
Inst. Accred.: NCA-HLC (1966/1996)
Prog. Accred.: Business (ACBSP), Engineering (electrical,
    mechanical), Music, Teacher Education (NCATE)

Cascade College
9101 East Burnside St., Portland, OR 97216-1515
Phone: (503) 257-1365

Oklahoma City Community College
7777 South May Ave., Oklahoma City 73159-4444
Type: Public, state/local, two-year
System: Oklahoma State Regents for Higher Education
Degrees: A   *Enroll:* 7,275
Phone: (405) 682-1611   *Calendar:* Sem. plan
Inst. Accred.: NCA-HLC (1977/2002)
Prog. Accred.: EMT (Paramedic), Nursing, Occupational
    Therapy Assisting, Physical Therapy Assisting

Oklahoma City University
2501 North Blackwelder Ave., Oklahoma City 73106
Type: Private, United Methodist Church, four-year
Degrees: B, M, D   *Enroll:* 3,225
URL: http://www.okcu.edu
Phone: (405) 521-5000   *Calendar:* Sem. plan
Inst. Accred.: NCA-HLC (1951/2002)
Prog. Accred.: Business (ACBSP), Law, Montessori
    Teacher Education, Music, Nursing

Oklahoma Panhandle State University
323 West Eagle Blvd., PO Box 430, Goodwell 73939
Type: Public, state, four-year
System: Oklahoma State Regents for Higher Education
Degrees: A, B   *Enroll:* 1,030
URL: http://www.opsu.edu
Phone: (580) 349-2611   *Calendar:* Sem. plan
Inst. Accred.: NCA-HLC (1926/2001)

Oklahoma State University
107 Whitehurst Hall, Stillwater 74078-0004
Type: Public, state, four-year
System: Oklahoma State Regents for Higher Education
Degrees: B, M, P, D   *Enroll:* 20,590
URL: http://www.okstate.edu
Phone: (405) 744-5000   *Calendar:* Sem. plan
Inst. Accred.: NCA-HLC (1916/1996)
Prog. Accred.: Accounting, Business (AACSB), Clinical
Psychology, Counseling Psychology, Dietetics
(internship), Engineering (aerospace, agricultural,
bioengineering, chemical, civil, electrical, industrial,
mechanical), Engineering Technology (civil/construction,
electrical, fire protection/safety, mechanical), Forestry,
Interior Design, Journalism, Landscape Architecture,
Marriage and Family Therapy, Music, Recreation and
Leisure Services, School Psychology, Speech-Language
Pathology, Teacher Education (NCATE), Theatre,
Veterinary Medicine

College of Osteopathic Medicine
1111 West 17th St., Tulsa 74107
Phone: (918) 582-1972
Prog. Accred: Osteopathy

Tulsa Campus
700 N. Greenwood Ave., Tulsa 74106-0203
Phone: (918) 586-0703

Oklahoma State University—Oklahoma City
900 North Portland Ave., Oklahoma City 73107
Type: Public, state, two-year
Degrees: A   *Enroll:* 3,178
URL: http://www.osuokc.edu
Phone: (405) 947-4421   *Calendar:* Sem. plan
Inst. Accred.: NCA-HLC (1975/2000)
Prog. Accred.: Nursing

Oklahoma State University—Okmulgee
1801 East Fourth St., Okmulgee 74447-3901
Type: Public, state, four-year
Degrees: A, B   *Enroll:* 2,111
URL: http://www.osu-okmulgee.edu
Phone: (918) 293-4636   *Calendar:* Tri. plan
Inst. Accred.: NCA-HLC (1975/2000)

Oklahoma Wesleyan University
2201 Silver Lake Rd., Bartlesville 74006
Type: Private, Wesleyan Church, four-year
Degrees: A, B   *Enroll:* 655
URL: http://www.okwu.edu
Phone: (918) 335-6200   *Calendar:* Sem. plan
Inst. Accred.: NCA-HLC (1978/2004)
Prog. Accred.: Nursing, Nursing Education

Oral Roberts University
7777 South Lewis Ave., Tulsa 74171
Type: Private, interdenominational, four-year
Degrees: B, M, D   *Enroll:* 3,667
URL: http://www.oru.edu
Phone: (918) 495-6161   *Calendar:* Sem. plan
Inst. Accred.: ATS (1980/1998), NCA-HLC (1971/1998)
Prog. Accred.: Engineering (general), English Language
Education, Music, Nursing, Social Work, Teacher
Education (NCATE)

Phillips Theological Seminary
901 North Mingo Rd., Tulsa 74116-5612
Type: Private, Christian Church (Disciples of Christ), four-
year
Degrees: M, D   *Enroll:* 151
URL: http://www.ptstulsa.edu
Phone: (918) 610-8303   *Calendar:* Sem. plan
Inst. Accred.: ATS (1952/1999), NCA-HLC (1992/1999)

Platt College
3801 South Sheridan, Tulsa 74145-1132
Type: Private, proprietary, two-year
Degrees: A
URL: http://www.plattcollege.org
Phone: (918) 663-9000
Inst. Accred.: ACCSCT (1985/2001)

Central Oklahoma City Campus
309 South Ann Arbor, Oklahoma City 73128
Phone: (405) 946-7799

Lawton Campus
112 Southwest Eleventh St., Lawton 73501
Phone: (580) 355-4416

Oklahoma City North Campus
2727 West Memorial Rd., Oklahoma City 73134
Phone: (405) 749-2433
Prog. Accred: Culinary Education

Redlands Community College
1300 South Country Club Rd., El Reno 73036-5304
Type: Public, state/local, two-year
System: Oklahoma State Regents for Higher Education
Degrees: A   *Enroll:* 1,378
URL: http://www.redlandscc.edu
Phone: (405) 262-2552   *Calendar:* Sem. plan
Inst. Accred.: NCA-HLC (1978/2002)
Prog. Accred.: Nursing

Rogers State University
1701 W. Will Rogers Blvd., Claremore 74017-3252
Type: Public, state, four-year
Degrees: A, B   *Enroll:* 2,557
URL: http://www.rsu.edu
Phone: (918) 343-7500   *Calendar:* Sem. plan
Inst. Accred.: NCA-HLC (1950/2000)
Prog. Accred.: Nursing

Rose State College
6420 South East 15th St., Midwest City 73110-2799
Type: Public, state, two-year
System: Oklahoma State Regents for Higher Education
Degrees: A   *Enroll:* 5,189
URL: http://www.rose.edu
Phone: (405) 733-7311   *Calendar:* Sem. plan
Inst. Accred.: NCA-HLC (1975/1998)
Prog. Accred.: Clinical Lab Technology, Dental Assisting,
   Dental Hygiene, Health Information Technician, Nursing,
   Radiography, Respiratory Therapy

Saint Gregory's University
1900 West MacArthur, Shawnee 74801
Type: Private, Roman Catholic Church, four-year
Degrees: A, B   *Enroll:* 604
URL: http://www.stgregorys.edu
Phone: (405) 878-5100   *Calendar:* Sem. plan
Inst. Accred.: NCA-HLC (1969/2001)

Seminole State College
PO Box 351, Seminole 74818-0351
Type: Public, state, two-year
System: Oklahoma State Regents for Higher Education
Degrees: A   *Enroll:* 1,570
URL: http://www.ssc.cc.ok.us
Phone: (405) 382-9950   *Calendar:* Sem. plan
Inst. Accred.: NCA-HLC (1975/2000)
Prog. Accred.: Clinical Lab Technology, Nursing

Southeastern Oklahoma State University
PO Box 4236, Durant 74701-0609
Type: Public, state, four-year
System: Oklahoma State Regents for Higher Education
Degrees: B, M   *Enroll:* 3,504
URL: http://www.sosu.edu
Phone: (580) 745-2500   *Calendar:* Sem. plan
Inst. Accred.: NCA-HLC (1922/2004)
Prog. Accred.: Business (ACBSP), Music, Teacher
   Education (NCATE)

Southern Nazarene University
6729 NW 39th Expressway, Bethany 73008
Type: Private, Church of the Nazarene, four-year
Degrees: A, B, M   *Enroll:* 2,102
URL: http://www.snu.edu
Phone: (405) 789-6400   *Calendar:* Sem. plan
Inst. Accred.: NCA-HLC (1956/2000)
Prog. Accred.: Music, Nursing, Nursing Education,
   Teacher Education (NCATE)

Southwestern Christian University
PO Box 340, Bethany 73008-0340
Type: Private, International Pentecostal Holiness Church,
   four-year
Degrees: A, B, M   *Enroll:* 217
URL: http://www.swcu.edu
Phone: (405) 789-7661   *Calendar:* Sem. plan
Inst. Accred.: NCA-HLC (1973/2004)

Southwestern Oklahoma State University
100 Campus Dr., Weatherford 73096-3098
Type: Public, state, four-year
System: Oklahoma State Regents for Higher Education
Degrees: A, B, M, P, D   *Enroll:* 4,728
URL: http://www.swosu.edu
Phone: (580) 772-6611   *Calendar:* Sem. plan
Inst. Accred.: NCA-HLC (1922/2001)
Prog. Accred.: Business (ACBSP), Engineering Technology
   (manufacturing), Health Information Administration,
   Music, Nursing, Pharmacy, Radiography, Social Work,
   Teacher Education (NCATE)

Sayre Campus
409 East Mississippi, Sayre 73662
Phone: (405) 928-5533
Prog. Accred: Medical Laboratory Technology, Physical
   Therapy Assisting, Radiography

Spartan College of Aeronautics and Technology
8820 East Pine St., PO Box 582833, Tulsa 74158-2833
Type: Private, proprietary, four-year
Degrees: A, B   *Enroll:* 1,267
URL: http://www.spartan.edu
Phone: (918) 836-6886   *Calendar:* Sem. plan
Inst. Accred.: ACCSCT (1969/2003)

Tulsa Community College
6111 East Skelly Dr., Rm. 200, Tulsa 74135-6198
Type: Public, state, two-year
System: Oklahoma State Regents for Higher Education
Degrees: A   *Enroll:* 9,841
URL: http://www.tulsacc.edu
Phone: (918) 595-7000   *Calendar:* Sem. plan
Inst. Accred.: NCA-HLC (1974/1999)
Prog. Accred.: Clinical Lab Technology, Dental Hygiene,
   Health Information Technician, Medical Assisting (AMA),
   Nursing, Phlebotomy, Physical Therapy Assisting,
   Radiography, Respiratory Therapy, Respiratory Therapy
   Technology, Veterinary Technology

Metro Campus
909 South Boston Ave., Tulsa 74119-2095
Phone: (918) 595-7224
Prog. Accred: Occupational Therapy Assisting,
   Radiography

Northeast Campus
3727 East Apache St., Tulsa 74115-3151
Phone: (918) 595-7524

Southeast Campus
10300 East 81st St., Tulsa 74133-4513
Phone: (918) 595-7724

West Campus
7505 West 41st St., Tulsa 74107-8633
Phone: (918) 595-8100

University of Central Oklahoma
100 North University Dr., Edmond 73034-0170
Type: Public, state, four-year
System: Oklahoma State Regents for Higher Education
Degrees: B, M   *Enroll:* 11,900
URL: http://www.ucok.edu
Phone: (405) 341-2980   *Calendar:* Sem. plan
Inst. Accred.: NCA-HLC (1921/2003)
Prog. Accred.: Business (ACBSP), Dietetics (internship),
  Funeral Service Education (Mortuary Science), Music,
  Nursing, Speech-Language Pathology, Teacher
  Education (NCATE)

University of Oklahoma
660 Parrington Oval, Room 104, Norman 73019-0390
Type: Public, state, four-year
System: Oklahoma State Regents for Higher Education
Degrees: B, M, D   *Enroll:* 23,013
URL: http://www.ou.edu
Phone: (405) 325-0311   *Calendar:* Sem. plan
Inst. Accred.: NCA-HLC (1913/2002)
Prog. Accred.: Accounting, Business (AACSB), Computer
  Science, Construction Education, Counseling
  Psychology, Engineering (aerospace, chemical, civil,
  computer, electrical, engineering physics/science,
  environmental/sanitary, general, industrial, mechanical,
  petroleum), Health Services Administration, Interior
  Design, Journalism, Landscape Architecture, Law,
  Librarianship, Music, Planning, Social Work, Teacher
  Education (NCATE), Theatre

College of Medicine
City Plaza West, Ste. 200, 5310 31st, Tulsa 74135-
5027
Phone: (918) 838-4600
Prog. Accred: Occupational Therapy

Health Sciences Center
PO Box 26901, 1000 Stanton L. Young Blvd.,
Oklahoma City 73126-0901
Phone: (405) 271-4000
Prog. Accred: Advanced Education in General
  Dentistry, Applied Science (industrial hygiene),
  Audiology, Combined Prosthodontics, Dental
  Hygiene, Dentistry, Diagnostic Medical Sonography,
  Dietetics (coordinated), Dietetics (internship),
  Engineering (environmental/sanitary), General
  Dentistry, Medicine, Nuclear Medicine Technology,
  Nursing, Occupational Therapy, Oral and
  Maxillofacial Surgery, Orthodontic and Dentofacial
  Orthopedics, Periodontics, Pharmacy, Physical
  Therapy, Physician Assistant, Psychology Internship,
  Public Health, Radiation Therapy, Radiography,
  Speech-Language Pathology

University of Science and Arts of Oklahoma
1727 West Alabama Ave., Chickasha 73018-5322
Type: Public, state, four-year
System: Oklahoma State Regents for Higher Education
Degrees: B   *Enroll:* 1,220
URL: http://www.usao.edu
Phone: (405) 224-3140   *Calendar:* Tri. plan
Inst. Accred.: NCA-HLC (1920/1999)
Prog. Accred.: Music, Teacher Education (NCATE)

University of Tulsa
600 South College Ave., Tulsa 74104
Type: Private, United Presbyterian Church (USA), four-
  year
Degrees: B, M, D   *Enroll:* 3,697
URL: http://www.utulsa.edu
Phone: (918) 631-2000   *Calendar:* Sem. plan
Inst. Accred.: NCA-HLC (1929/2001)
Prog. Accred.: Athletic Training, Business (AACSB),
  Clinical Psychology, Computer Science, Engineering
  (chemical, electrical, engineering physics/science,
  mechanical, petroleum), Law, Music, Nursing, Speech-
  Language Pathology, Teacher Education (NCATE)

Western Oklahoma State College
2801 North Main St., Altus 73521-1397
Type: Public, state, two-year
System: Oklahoma State Regents for Higher Education
Degrees: A   *Enroll:* 1,310
URL: http://www.wosc.edu
Phone: (580) 477-2000   *Calendar:* Sem. plan
Inst. Accred.: NCA-HLC (1976/1998)
Prog. Accred.: Nursing, Radiography

OREGON

Apollo College—Portland Campus
2004 Lloyd Center, 3rd Flr., Portland 97232
Type: Private, proprietary, two-year
System: U.S. Education Corporation
Degrees: A
URL: http://www.apollocollege.com
Phone: (503) 761-6100
Inst. Accred.: ABHES (1985/2002)
Prog. Accred.: Medical Assisting (ABHES)

Spokane Campus
10102 East Knox Rd., Ste. 200, Spokane, WA 99206
Phone: (509) 532-8888
Prog. Accred: Medical Assisting (ABHES), Radiography

The Art Institute of Portland
1122 NW Davis St., Portland 97209-2911
Type: Private, proprietary, four-year
System: Education Management Corporation
Degrees: A, B   *Enroll:* 1,122
URL: http://www.aipd.aii.edu
Phone: (503) 228-6528   *Calendar:* Qtr. plan
Inst. Accred.: NWCCU (1977/2001)

Blue Mountain Community College
PO Box 100, Pendleton 97801
Type: Public, state/local, two-year
System: Department of Community Colleges and
  Workforce Development
Degrees: A   *Enroll:* 1,142
URL: http://www.bluecc.edu
Phone: (541) 276-1260   *Calendar:* Qtr. plan
Inst. Accred.: NWCCU (1968/1999)
Prog. Accred.: Dental Assisting, Engineering Technology
  (electrical)

Central Oregon Community College
2600 NW College Way, Bend 97701-5998
Type: Public, state/local, two-year
System: Department of Community Colleges and
  Workforce Development
Degrees: A   *Enroll:* 2,324
URL: http://www.cocc.edu
Phone: (541) 383-7700   *Calendar:* Qtr. plan
Inst. Accred.: NWCCU (1966/2004)
Prog. Accred.: Culinary Education, Dental Assisting,
  Health Information Technician

Chemeketa Community College
PO Box 14007, Salem 97309-7070
Type: Public, local, two-year
System: Department of Community Colleges and
  Workforce Development
Degrees: A   *Enroll:* 5,892
URL: http://www.chemeketa.edu
Phone: (503) 399-5000   *Calendar:* Qtr. plan
Inst. Accred.: NWCCU (1972/2001)
Prog. Accred.: Dental Assisting, EMT (Paramedic),
  Medical Assisting (AMA), Nursing

Clackamas Community College
19600 South Molalla Ave., Oregon City 97045-8980
Type: Public, state/local, two-year
System: Department of Community Colleges and
  Workforce Development
Degrees: A   *Enroll:* 4,086
URL: http://www.clackamas.edu
Phone: (503) 657-6958   *Calendar:* Qtr. plan
Inst. Accred.: NWCCU (1971/2001)
Prog. Accred.: Medical Assisting (AMA), Nursing

Clatsop Community College
1653 Jerome Ave., Astoria 97103
Type: Public, state/local, two-year
System: Department of Community Colleges and
  Workforce Development
Degrees: A   *Enroll:* 788
URL: http://www.clatsopcc.edu
Phone: (503) 325-0910   *Calendar:* Qtr. plan
Inst. Accred.: NWCCU (1965/1996)

Concordia University Portland
2811 NE Holman St., Portland 97211-6099
Type: Private, Lutheran Church-Missouri Synod, four-year
System: Concordia University System
Degrees: A, B, M   *Enroll:* 1,048
URL: http://www.cu-portland.edu
Phone: (503) 288-9371   *Calendar:* Sem. plan
Inst. Accred.: NWCCU (1962/2003)

Corban College
5000 Deer Park Dr., SE, Salem 97301-9330
Type: Private, General Association of Regular Baptist
  Churches, four-year
Degrees: A, B   *Enroll:* 665
URL: http://www.corban.edu
Phone: (503) 581-8600   *Calendar:* Sem. plan
Inst. Accred.: NWCCU (1971/2001)

Eastern Oregon University
One University Blvd., Le Grande 97850-2807
Type: Public, state, four-year
System: Oregon University System
Degrees: A, B, M   *Enroll:* 2,515
URL: http://www.eou.edu
Phone: (541) 962-3672   *Calendar:* Qtr. plan
Inst. Accred.: NWCCU (1931/2001)

Eugene Bible College
2155 Bailey Hill Rd., Eugene 97405-1194
Type: Private, Open Bible Standard Churches, four-year
Degrees: B   *Enroll:* 152
URL: http://www.ebc.edu
Phone: (541) 485-1780   *Calendar:* Qtr. plan
Inst. Accred.: ABHE (1983/2004)

George Fox University
414 North Meridian St., Newberg 97132-2697
Type: Private, The Religious Society of Friends, four-year
Degrees: B, M, D   *Enroll:* 2,216
URL: http://www.georgefox.edu
Phone: (503) 538-8383   *Calendar:* Sem. plan
Inst. Accred.: ATS (1974/2001), NWCCU (1959/2004)
Prog. Accred.: Clinical Psychology, Music, Social Work

Portland Center
PO Box 23939, Portland 97281-3939
Phone: (503) 639-0559

Heald College—Portland
625 SW Broadway, Ste. 201, Portland 97205
Type: Private, independent, two-year
System: Heald Colleges
Degrees: A
URL: http://www.heald.edu
Phone: (503) 229-0492   *Calendar:* Qtr. plan
Inst. Accred.: WASC-JR. (1996)

ITT Technical Institute
6035 NE 78th Ct., Portland 97218
Type: Private, proprietary, four-year
System: ITT Educational Services, Inc.
Degrees: A, B   *Enroll:* 525
URL: http://www.itt-tech.edu
Phone: (503) 255-6500   *Calendar:* Qtr. plan
Inst. Accred.: ACICS (1999/2004)

Klamath Community College
7390 South 6th St., Klamath Falls 97603-7121
Type: Public, state/local, two-year
Degrees: A   *Enroll:* 629
URL: http://www.klamathcc.edu
Phone: (541) 882-3521   *Calendar:* Qtr. plan
Inst. Accred.: NWCCU (2004)

Lane Community College
4000 East 30th Ave., Eugene 97405
Type: Public, local, two-year
System: Department of Community Colleges and
  Workforce Development
Degrees: A   *Enroll:* 6,210
URL: http://www.lanecc.edu
Phone: (541) 463-3000   *Calendar:* Qtr. plan
Inst. Accred.: NWCCU (1968/1999)
Prog. Accred.: Culinary Education, Dental Assisting,
  Dental Hygiene, Medical Assisting (AMA), Nursing,
  Respiratory Therapy

Lewis and Clark College
0615 South West Palatine Hill Rd., Portland 97219-7899
Type: Private, independent, four-year
Degrees: B, M   *Enroll:* 2,802
URL: http://www.lclark.edu
Phone: (503) 768-7000   *Calendar:* Sem. plan
Inst. Accred.: NWCCU (1943/2003)
Prog. Accred.: Law

Linfield College
900 SE Baker St., McMinnville 97128-6894
Type: Private, American Baptist Church, four-year
Degrees: B, M   *Enroll:* 1,629
URL: http://www.linfield.edu
Phone: (503) 883-2200   *Calendar:* 4-1-4 plan
Inst. Accred.: NWCCU (1928/1999)
Prog. Accred.: Music, Nursing

Portland Campus
2215 NW Northrup St., Portland 97210-2932
Phone: (503) 413-8481

Linn-Benton Community College
6500 Pacific Blvd. SW, Albany 97321
Type: Public, local, two-year
System: Department of Community Colleges and
  Workforce Development
Degrees: A   *Enroll:* 3,815
URL: http://www.linnbenton.edu
Phone: (541) 917-4811   *Calendar:* Qtr. plan
Inst. Accred.: NWCCU (1972/1999)
Prog. Accred.: Dental Assisting, Medical Assisting (AMA),
  Nursing

Marylhurst University
PO Box 261, Marylhurst 97036
Type: Private, Roman Catholic Church, four-year
Degrees: B, M   *Enroll:* 660
URL: http://www.marylhurst.edu
Phone: (503) 636-8141   *Calendar:* Qtr. plan
Inst. Accred.: NWCCU (1977/2001)
Prog. Accred.: Music

Mount Angel Seminary
One Abbey Dr., St. Benedict 97373
Type: Private, Roman Catholic Church, four-year
Degrees: B, M   *Enroll:* 161
URL: http://www.mtangel.edu
Phone: (503) 845-3951   *Calendar:* Sem. plan
Inst. Accred.: ATS (1978/1996), NWCCU (1929/2003)

Mount Hood Community College
26000 South East Stark St., Gresham 97030
Type: Public, local, two-year
System: Department of Community Colleges and
  Workforce Development
Degrees: A   *Enroll:* 4,723
URL: http://www.mhcc.edu
Phone: (503) 491-7161   *Calendar:* Qtr. plan
Inst. Accred.: NWCCU (1972/1999)
Prog. Accred.: Dental Hygiene, Funeral Service Education
  (Mortuary Science), Medical Assisting (AMA), Nursing,
  Physical Therapy Assisting, Respiratory Therapy,
  Surgical Technology

Multnomah Bible College

8435 NE Glisan St., Portland 97220-5814
Type: Private, independent, four-year
Degrees: B, M   *Enroll:* 687
URL: http://www.multnomah.edu
Phone: (503) 255-0332   *Calendar:* Sem. plan
Inst. Accred.: ABHE (1953/2004), ATS (1996/2003)

National College of Naturopathic Medicine

049 Southwest Porter St., Portland 97201
Type: Private, proprietary, four-year
Degrees: M, D   *Enroll:* 572
URL: http://www.ncnm.edu
Phone: (503) 552-1702   *Calendar:* Qtr. plan
Inst. Accred.: NWCCU (2004)
Prog. Accred.: Acupuncture, Naturopathic Medicine

Northwest Christian College

828 East 11th Ave., Eugene 97401-3745
Type: Private, Disciples of Christ Church, four-year
Degrees: A, B, M   *Enroll:* 441
URL: http://www.nwcc.edu
Phone: (541) 343-1641   *Calendar:* Sem. plan
Inst. Accred.: NWCCU (1962/2001)

Oregon College of Art and Craft

8245 SW Barnes Rd., Portland 97225
Type: Private, independent, four-year
Degrees: B
URL: http://www.ocac.edu
Phone: (503) 297-5544   *Calendar:* Sem. plan
Inst. Accred.: NASAD (1989/2002)

Oregon College of Oriental Medicine

10525 SE Cherry Blossom Dr., Portland 97216
Type: Private, proprietary, four-year
Degrees: M   *Enroll:* 232
URL: http://www.ocom.edu
Phone: (503) 253-3443   *Calendar:* Qtr. plan
Inst. Accred.: ACAOM (1989/2004)

Oregon Health and Science University

3181 South West Sam Jackson Park Rd., Portland
97201-3098
Type: Public, state, four-year
System: Oregon University System
Degrees: A, B, M, D   *Enroll:* 2,000
URL: http://www.ohsu.edu
Phone: (503) 494-8311   *Calendar:* Qtr. plan
Inst. Accred.: NWCCU (1980/2005)
Prog. Accred.: Clinical Lab Scientist, Dental Hygiene,
   Dentistry, Dietetics (internship), EMT (Paramedic),
   Endodontics, General Practice Residency, Medicine,
   Nurse (Midwifery), Nursing, Nursing Education, Oral and
   Maxillofacial Surgery, Orthodontic and Dentofacial
   Orthopedics, Pediatric Dentistry, Periodontics, Physician
   Assistant, Psychology Internship, Public Health,
   Radiation Therapy

Oregon Graduate Institute
School of Science and Engineering at
Oregon Health and Science University

PO Box 91000, 20000 N.W. Walker Rd., Beaverton
97006
Phone: (503) 748-1121

Oregon Institute of Technology

3201 Campus Dr., Klamath Falls 97601-8801
Type: Public, state, four-year
System: Oregon University System
Degrees: A, B   *Enroll:* 2,525
URL: http://www.oit.edu
Phone: (541) 885-1100   *Calendar:* Qtr. plan
Inst. Accred.: NWCCU (1962/2002)
Prog. Accred.: Applied Science (surveying/geomatics),
   Clinical Lab Scientist, Dental Hygiene, Engineering
   Technology (computer, electrical, manufacturing,
   mechanical, surveying), Nuclear Medicine Technology,
   Radiography

Oregon State University

Corvallis 97331-2128
Type: Public, state, four-year
System: Oregon University System
Degrees: B, M, P, D   *Enroll:* 17,433
URL: http://oregonstate.edu
Phone: (541) 737-0912   *Calendar:* Qtr. plan
Inst. Accred.: NWCCU (1924/2004)
Prog. Accred.: Accounting, Athletic Training, Business
   (AACSB), Computer Science, Construction Education,
   Counseling, Engineering (chemical, civil, computer,
   electrical, environmental/sanitary, forest, industrial,
   manufacturing, mechanical, nuclear), Family and
   Consumer Science, Forestry, Pharmacy, Public Health,
   Teacher Education (NCATE), Veterinary Medicine

Pacific Northwest College of Art
1241 NW Johnson Ave., Portland 97209-3023
Type: Private, independent, four-year
Degrees: B   *Enroll:* 283
URL: http://www.pnca.edu
Phone: (503) 226-4391   *Calendar:* Sem. plan
Inst. Accred.: NWCCU (1961/2000)
Prog. Accred.: Art

Pacific University
2043 College Way, Forest Grove 97116
Type: Private, United Church of Christ, four-year
Degrees: B, M, D   *Enroll:* 2,236
URL: http://www.pacificu.edu
Phone: (503) 357-6151   *Calendar:* Sem. plan
Inst. Accred.: NWCCU (1929/1999)
Prog. Accred.: Clinical Psychology, Music, Occupational
   Therapy, Optometric Residency, Optometry, Physical
   Therapy, Physician Assistant

Pioneer Pacific College
27501 Southwest Pkwy. Ave., Wilsonville 97070
Type: Private, proprietary, two-year
Degrees: A   *Enroll:* 760
URL: http://www.pioneerpacificcollege.com
Phone: (503) 682-3903
Inst. Accred.: ACICS (1995/2002)

Springfield Campus
3800 Sports Way, Springfield 97477
Phone: (541) 684-4644

Portland Community College
PO Box 19000, Portland 97280-0990
Type: Public, state/local, two-year
System: Department of Community Colleges and
   Workforce Development
Degrees: A   *Enroll:* 13,289
URL: http://www.pcc.edu
Phone: (503) 977-4329   *Calendar:* Qtr. plan
Inst. Accred.: NWCCU (1970/2005)
Prog. Accred.: Clinical Lab Technology, Dental Assisting,
   Dental Hygiene, Dental Laboratory Technology, Health
   Information Technician, Medical Assisting (AMA),
   Nursing, Ophthalmic Medical Technology, Radiography,
   Veterinary Technology

Portland State University
PO Box 751, Portland 97207-0751
Type: Public, state, four-year
System: Oregon University System
Degrees: B, M, D   *Enroll:* 16,759
URL: http://www.pdx.edu
Phone: (503) 725-3000   *Calendar:* Qtr. plan
Inst. Accred.: NWCCU (1955/2000)
Prog. Accred.: Accounting, Art, Audiology, Business
   (AACSB), Computer Science, Counseling, Engineering
   (civil, computer, electrical, mechanical), Music,
   Planning, Public Administration, Public Health,
   Rehabilitation Counseling, Social Work, Speech-
   Language Pathology, Teacher Education (NCATE)

Reed College
3203 SE Woodstock Blvd., Portland 97202-8199
Type: Private, independent, four-year
Degrees: B, M   *Enroll:* 1,295
URL: http://www.reed.edu
Phone: (503) 771-1112   *Calendar:* Sem. plan
Inst. Accred.: NWCCU (1920/1999)

Rogue Community College
3345 Redwood Hwy., Grants Pass 97527
Type: Public, local, two-year
System: Department of Community Colleges and
   Workforce Development
Degrees: A   *Enroll:* 2,679
URL: http://www.roguecc.edu
Phone: (541) 956-7500   *Calendar:* Qtr. plan
Inst. Accred.: NWCCU (1976/2001)
Prog. Accred.: Nursing, Respiratory Therapy

Southern Oregon University
1250 Siskiyou Blvd., Ashland 97520
Type: Public, state, four-year
System: Oregon University System
Degrees: B, M   *Enroll:* 4,582
URL: http://www.sou.edu
Phone: (541) 552-7672   *Calendar:* Qtr. plan
Inst. Accred.: NWCCU (1928/2004)
Prog. Accred.: Counseling, Music

Southwestern Oregon Community College
1988 Newmark Ave., Coos Bay 97420
Type: Public, state/local, two-year
System: Department of Community Colleges and
   Workforce Development
Degrees: A   *Enroll:* 1,267
URL: http://www.socc.edu
Phone: (541) 888-2525   *Calendar:* Qtr. plan
Inst. Accred.: NWCCU (1966/2004)

Treasure Valley Community College
650 College Blvd., Ontario 97914
Type: Public, local, two-year
System: Department of Community Colleges and
   Workforce Development
Degrees: A   *Enroll:* 1,505
URL: http://www.tvcc.cc.or.us
Phone: (541) 881-8822   *Calendar:* Qtr. plan
Inst. Accred.: NWCCU (1966/2000)

Umpqua Community College
1140 College Rd., PO Box 967, Roseburg 97470
Type: Public, state/local, two-year
System: Department of Community Colleges and
   Workforce Development
Degrees: A   *Enroll:* 995
URL: http://www.umpqua.edu
Phone: (541) 440-4600   *Calendar:* Qtr. plan
Inst. Accred.: NWCCU (1970/2000)
Prog. Accred.: Nursing

University of Oregon
Eugene 97403-1226
Type: Public, state, four-year
System: Oregon University System
Degrees: B, M, D   *Enroll:* 18,416
URL: http://www.uoregon.edu
Phone: (541) 346-3036   *Calendar:* Qtr. plan
Inst. Accred.: NWCCU (1918/2002)
Prog. Accred.: Accounting, Art, Business (AACSB), Clinical
  Psychology, Counseling Psychology, English Language
  Education, Interior Design, Journalism, Landscape
  Architecture, Law, Marriage and Family Therapy, Music,
  Planning, Psychology Internship, Public Administration,
  School Psychology, Speech-Language Pathology

University of Portland
5000 North Willamette Blvd., Portland 97203
Type: Private, Roman Catholic Church, four-year
Degrees: B, M   *Enroll:* 2,956
URL: http://www.up.edu
Phone: (503) 943-8000   *Calendar:* Sem. plan
Inst. Accred.: NWCCU (1931/2001)
Prog. Accred.: Business (AACSB), Computer Science,
  Engineering (civil, electrical, mechanical), Music,
  Nursing, Nursing Education, Teacher Education (NCATE),
  Theatre

Warner Pacific College
2219 S.E. 68th Ave., Portland 97215
Type: Private, Church of God, four-year
Degrees: A, B, M   *Enroll:* 461
URL: http://www.warnerpacific.edu
Phone: (503) 517-1000   *Calendar:* Sem. plan
Inst. Accred.: NWCCU (1961/2002)

Western Business College
425 SW Washington St., Portland 97204
Type: Private, proprietary, two-year
System: Corinthian Colleges, Inc
Degrees: A   *Enroll:* 761
URL: http://www.western-college.com
Phone: (503) 222-3225   *Calendar:* Qtr. plan
Inst. Accred.: ACICS (1969/2001)
Prog. Accred.: Medical Assisting (CAAHEP)

Everest College—Dallas
6060 North Central Expressway, Ste. 101, Dallas, TX
75206
Phone: (214) 234-4850

Vancouver Campus
120 Northeast 136th Ave., Ste. 130, Vancouver, WA
98684
Phone: (360) 254-3282

Western Culinary Institute
921 SW Morrison St., Ste. 400, Portland 97205
Type: Private, proprietary, two-year
System: Career Education Corporation
Degrees: A
URL: http://www.westernculinary.com
Phone: (503) 223-2245
Inst. Accred.: ACCSCT (1990/2002)
Prog. Accred.: Culinary Education

Le Cordon Bleu College of Culinary Arts
1927 Lakeside Pkwy., Tucker, GA 30084
Phone: (770) 938-4711

Western Oregon University
345 North Monmouth Ave., Monmouth 97361
Type: Public, state, four-year
System: Oregon University System
Degrees: A, B, M   *Enroll:* 4,492
URL: http://www.wou.edu
Phone: (503) 838-8000   *Calendar:* Qtr. plan
Inst. Accred.: NWCCU (1924/2002)
Prog. Accred.: Music, Rehabilitation Counseling

Western Seminary
5511 S.E. Hawthorne Blvd., Portland 97215
Type: Private, independent, four-year
Degrees: M, D   *Enroll:* 306
URL: http://www.westernseminary.edu
Phone: (503) 517-1800   *Calendar:* Tri. plan
Inst. Accred.: ATS (1991/2000), NWCCU (1969/2005)

Western States Chiropractic College
2900 NE 132nd Ave., Portland 97230
Type: Private, independent, four-year
Degrees: B, D   *Enroll:* 372
URL: http://www.wschiro.edu
Phone: (503) 256-3180   *Calendar:* Qtr. plan
Inst. Accred.: NWCCU (1986/2001)
Prog. Accred.: Chiropractic Education

Willamette University
900 State St., Salem 97301
Type: Private, independent, four-year
Degrees: B, M   *Enroll:* 2,530
URL: http://www.willamette.edu
Phone: (503) 370-6300   *Calendar:* Sem. plan
Inst. Accred.: NWCCU (1924/2001)
Prog. Accred.: Business (AACSB), Law, Music, Public
  Administration

PENNSYLVANIA

Albright College
13th and Bern St.s, PO Box 15234, Reading 19612-5234
Type: Private, United Methodist Church, four-year
Degrees: B, M   *Enroll:* 2,044
URL: http://www.albright.edu
Phone: (610) 921-2381   *Calendar:* 4-1-4 plan
Inst. Accred.: MSA-CHE (1926/2001)

Allegheny College
520 North Main St., Meadville 16335
Type: Private, independent, four-year
Degrees: B   *Enroll:* 1,825
URL: http://www.alleg.edu
Phone: (814) 332-3100   *Calendar:* Sem. plan
Inst. Accred.: MSA-CHE (1921/2004)

Allied Medical and Technical Institute
166 Slocum St., Forty Fort 18704
Type: Private, proprietary, two-year
Degrees: A
URL: http://www.alliedteched.com
Phone: (570) 288-8400
Inst. Accred.: ACCSCT (1995/2001)

Alvernia College
400 Saint Bernadine St., Reading 19607
Type: Private, Roman Catholic Church, four-year
Degrees: A, B, M   *Enroll:* 1,823
URL: http://www.alvernia.edu
Phone: (610) 796-8200   *Calendar:* Sem. plan
Inst. Accred.: MSA-CHE (1967/2005)
Prog. Accred.: Nursing, Nursing Education, Occupational
  Therapy, Social Work

The American College
270 Bryn Mawr Ave., Bryn Mawr 19010
Type: Private, independent, four-year
Degrees: M   *Enroll:* 337
URL: http://www.theamericancollege.edu
Phone: (610) 526-1000   *Calendar:* Qtr. plan
Inst. Accred.: MSA-CHE (1978/2003)

Antonelli Institute
300 Montgomery Ave., Erdenheim 19038
Type: Private, proprietary, two-year
Degrees: A   *Enroll:* 192
URL: http://www.antonelli.org
Phone: (215) 836-2222   *Calendar:* Sem. plan
Inst. Accred.: ACCSCT (1975/2003)

Arcadia University
450 South Easton Rd., Glenside 19038-3295
Type: Private, independent, four-year
Degrees: B, M, P, D   *Enroll:* 2,445
URL: http://www.arcadia.edu
Phone: (215) 572-2900   *Calendar:* Sem. plan
Inst. Accred.: MSA-CHE (1946/1999)
Prog. Accred.: Art, Physical Therapy, Physician Assistant

The Art Institute of Philadelphia
1622 Chestnut St., Philadelphia 19103-5198
Type: Private, proprietary, four-year
System: Education Management Corporation
Degrees: A, B   *Enroll:* 2,539
URL: http://www.aiph.aii.edu
Phone: (215) 567-7080   *Calendar:* Qtr. plan
Inst. Accred.: ACICS (2000/2002)
Prog. Accred.: Culinary Education

The Art Institute of Pittsburgh
420 Blvd. of the Allies, Pittsburgh 15219-1328
Type: Private, proprietary, four-year
System: Education Management Corporation
Degrees: A, B   *Enroll:* 2,611
URL: http://www.aip.aii.edu
Phone: (412) 291-6200   *Calendar:* Qtr. plan
Inst. Accred.: ACICS (2000/2003)
Prog. Accred.: Culinary Education

The Art Institute of California—Los Angeles
2900 31st St., Santa Monica, CA 90405-3035
Phone: (310) 752-4700

Baptist Bible College and Seminary
538 Venard Rd., PO Box 800, Clarks Summit 18411-1297
Type: Private, independent, four-year
Degrees: A, B, M, D   *Enroll:* 830
URL: http://www.bbc.edu
Phone: (570) 586-2400   *Calendar:* Sem. plan
Inst. Accred.: ABHE (1968/1996), MSA-CHE (1984/2005)

Berean Institute
1901 West Girard Ave., Philadelphia 19130-1599
Type: Private, proprietary, two-year
Degrees: A   *Enroll:* 186
URL: http://www.bereaninstitute.org
Phone: (215) 763-4833   *Calendar:* Sem. plan
Inst. Accred.: ACCSCT (2002)

Berks Technical Institute
2205 Ridgewood Rd., Wyomissing 19610
Type: Private, proprietary, two-year
Degrees: A   *Enroll:* 597
URL: http://www.berkstechnical.com
Phone: (610) 372-1722
Inst. Accred.: ACCSCT (1984/2004)
Prog. Accred.: Medical Assisting (CAAHEP)

Biblical Theological Seminary
200 North Main St., Hatfield 19440
Type: Private, independent, four-year
Degrees: M, P, D   *Enroll:* 213
URL: http://www.biblical.edu
Phone: (215) 368-5000   *Calendar:* Sem. plan
Inst. Accred.: ATS (1996/1999), MSA-CHE (1990/2000)

Bidwell Training Center
1815 Metropolitan St., Pittsburgh 15233-2234
Type: Private, proprietary, two-year
Degrees: A
URL: http://www.bidwell-training.org
Phone: (412) 323-4000
Inst. Accred.: ACCSCT (1993/2001)

Bloomsburg University of Pennsylvania
400 East 2nd St., Bloomsburg 17815
Type: Public, state, four-year
System: Pennsylvania State System of Higher Education
Degrees: A, B, M, D   *Enroll:* 7,673
URL: http://www.bloomu.edu
Phone: (570) 389-4000   *Calendar:* Sem. plan
Inst. Accred.: MSA-CHE (1950/1999)
Prog. Accred.: Audiology, Nursing, Nursing Education, Social Work, Speech-Language Pathology, Teacher Education (NCATE)

Bradford School
707 Grant St., Gulf Tower, Pittsburgh 15219
Type: Private, proprietary, two-year
Degrees: A   *Enroll:* 384
URL: http://www.bradfordpittsburgh.edu
Phone: (412) 391-6710
Inst. Accred.: ACICS (1970/2005)
Prog. Accred.: Medical Assisting (CAAHEP)

Bradley Academy for the Visual Arts
1409 Williams Rd., York 17402-9012
Type: Private, proprietary, two-year
System: Education Management Corporation
Degrees: A   *Enroll:* 389
URL: http://www.bradleyacademy.edu
Phone: (717) 755-2300   *Calendar:* Sem. plan
Inst. Accred.: ACCSCT (1983/2004)

Bryn Athyn College of the New Church
PO Box 717, 2895 College Dr., Bryn Athyn 19009-0717
Type: Private, The New Church/General Church of the New Jersusale, four-year
Degrees: A, B, M, P   *Enroll:* 137
URL: http://www.brynathyn.edu
Phone: (215) 947-4200   *Calendar:* Tri. plan
Inst. Accred.: MSA-CHE (1952/2003)

Bryn Mawr College
101 North Merion Ave., Bryn Mawr 19010-2899
Type: Private, independent, four-year
Degrees: B, M, D   *Enroll:* 1,633
URL: http://www.brynmawr.edu
Phone: (610) 526-5000   *Calendar:* Sem. plan
Inst. Accred.: MSA-CHE (1921/1999)
Prog. Accred.: Social Work

Bucknell University
Lewisburg 17837-2086
Type: Private, independent, four-year
Degrees: B, M   *Enroll:* 3,600
URL: http://www.bucknell.edu
Phone: (570) 577-2000   *Calendar:* Sem. plan
Inst. Accred.: MSA-CHE (1921/2004)
Prog. Accred.: Computer Science, Engineering (chemical, civil, computer, electrical, mechanical), Music

Bucks County Community College
275 Swamp Rd., Newtown 18940-4106
Type: Public, state/local, two-year
Degrees: A   *Enroll:* 6,086
URL: http://www.bucks.edu
Phone: (215) 968-8000   *Calendar:* Sem. plan
Inst. Accred.: MSA-CHE (1968/2002)
Prog. Accred.: Art, Business (ACBSP), Medical Assisting (AMA), Music, Nursing, Radiography

Business Institute of Pennsylvania
335 Boyd Dr., Sharon 16146
Type: Private, proprietary, two-year
Degrees: A
URL: http://www.biop.edu
Phone: (724) 983-0700
Inst. Accred.: ACICS (1977/2002)

Butler County Community College
College Dr., Oak Hills, PO Box 1203, Butler 16003-1203
Type: Public, state/local, two-year
Degrees: A   *Enroll:* 2,517
URL: http://www.bc3.org
Phone: (724) 287-8711   *Calendar:* Sem. plan
Inst. Accred.: MSA-CHE (1971/2001)
Prog. Accred.: Business (ACBSP), Industrial Technology, Medical Assisting (AMA), Nursing, Physical Therapy Assisting

Cabrini College
610 King of Prussia Rd., Radnor 19087-3698
Type: Private, Roman Catholic Church, four-year
Degrees: B, M   *Enroll:* 1,742
URL: http://www.cabrini.edu
Phone: (610) 902-8100   *Calendar:* Sem. plan
Inst. Accred.: MSA-CHE (1965/2005)
Prog. Accred.: Social Work

California University of Pennsylvania
250 University Ave., California 15419-1394
Type: Public, state, four-year
System: Pennsylvania State System of Higher Education
Degrees: A, B, M   *Enroll:* 5,670
URL: http://www.cup.edu
Phone: (724) 938-4000   *Calendar:* Sem. plan
Inst. Accred.: MSA-CHE (1951/2005)
Prog. Accred.: Athletic Training, Engineering Technology (electrical), Nursing, Nursing Education, Physical Therapy Assisting, Social Work, Speech-Language Pathology, Teacher Education (NCATE)

Cambria-Rowe Business College
221 Central Ave., Johnstown 15902
Type: Private, proprietary, two-year
Degrees: A   *Enroll:* 240
URL: http://www.crbc.net
Phone: (814) 536-5168   *Calendar:* Qtr. plan
Inst. Accred.: ACICS (1959/2005)

Indiana Campus
422 South 13th St., Indiana 15701
Phone: (724) 463-0222

Career Training Academy
950 Fifth Ave., New Kensington 15068-6301
Type: Private, proprietary, two-year
Degrees: A   *Enroll:* 68
URL: http://www.careerta.com
Phone: (724) 337-1000
Inst. Accred.: ACCSCT (1987/1996)
Prog. Accred.: Massage Therapy, Medical Assisting
   (CAAHEP)

Monroeville Campus
Expo Mart-105 Mall Blvd., Ste. 300-W, Monroeville
15146
Phone: (412) 372-3900
Prog. Accred: Massage Therapy, Medical Assisting
   (CAAHEP)

Pittsburgh Campus
1500 Northway Mall, Ste. 200, Pittsburgh 15237
Phone: (412) 367-4000
Prog. Accred: Massage Therapy

Carlow University
3333 Fifth Ave., Pittsburgh 15213-3165
Type: Private, Roman Catholic Church, four-year
Degrees: B, M   *Enroll:* 1,542
URL: http://www.carlow.edu
Phone: (412) 578-6000   *Calendar:* Sem. plan
Inst. Accred.: MSA-CHE (1935/2001)
Prog. Accred.: Nursing, Nursing Education, Social Work

Carnegie Mellon University
5000 Forbes Ave., Pittsburgh 15213
Type: Private, independent, four-year
Degrees: B, M, D   *Enroll:* 8,841
URL: http://www.cmu.edu
Phone: (412) 268-2000   *Calendar:* Sem. plan
Inst. Accred.: MSA-CHE (1921/2003)
Prog. Accred.: Art, Business (AACSB), Engineering
   (chemical, civil, electrical, general, materials,
   mechanical), Music, Public Administration

Cedar Crest College
100 College Dr., Allentown 18104-6196
Type: Private, United Church of Christ, four-year
Degrees: B, M   *Enroll:* 1,228
URL: http://www.cedarcrest.edu
Phone: (610) 437-4471   *Calendar:* Sem. plan
Inst. Accred.: MSA-CHE (1944/2004)
Prog. Accred.: Nuclear Medicine Technology, Nursing,
   Social Work

Central Pennsylvania College
College Hill Rd., Summerdale 17093-0309
Type: Private, proprietary, two-year
Degrees: A   *Enroll:* 739
URL: http://www.centralpenn.edu
Phone: (717) 732-0702   *Calendar:* Qtr. plan
Inst. Accred.: MSA-CHE (1977/2003)
Prog. Accred.: Medical Assisting (AMA), Physical Therapy
   Assisting

Chatham College
Woodland Rd., Pittsburgh 15232
Type: Private, independent, four-year
Degrees: B, M, D   *Enroll:* 929
URL: http://www.chatham.edu
Phone: (412) 365-1100   *Calendar:* 4-1-4 plan
Inst. Accred.: MSA-CHE (1924/2002)
Prog. Accred.: Occupational Therapy, Physical Therapy,
   Physician Assistant, Social Work

Chestnut Hill College
9601 Germantown Ave., Philadelphia 19118-2963
Type: Private, Roman Catholic Church, four-year
Degrees: A, B, M, D   *Enroll:* 1,050
URL: http://www.chc.edu
Phone: (215) 248-7000   *Calendar:* Sem. plan
Inst. Accred.: MSA-CHE (1930/2003)
Prog. Accred.: Clinical Psychology, Montessori Teacher
   Education

Cheyney University of Pennsylvania
1837 University Circle, PO Box 200, Cheyney 19319-
0200
Type: Public, state, four-year
System: Pennsylvania State System of Higher Education
Degrees: B, M   *Enroll:* 1,367
URL: http://www.cheyney.edu
Phone: (610) 399-2000   *Calendar:* Sem. plan
Inst. Accred.: MSA-CHE (1951/2001)
Prog. Accred.: Teacher Education (NCATE)

CHI Institute
520 St. Rd., Southampton 18966-3787
Type: Private, proprietary, two-year
System: Kaplan Higher Education Corporation
Degrees: A   *Enroll:* 559
URL: http://www.chitraining.com
Phone: (215) 357-5100
Inst. Accred.: ACCSCT (1985/2004)

Career Centers of Texas—Fort Worth
2001 Beach St., Ste. 201, Fort Worth, TX 76103
Phone: (817) 413-2000

RETS Campus
1991 Sproul Rd., Ste. 42, Lawrence Park Shopping
Center, Broomall 19008
Phone: (610) 359-7630

The Cittone Institute—Center City
3600 Market St., Philadelphia 19104-2684
Type: Private, proprietary, two-year
System: Lincoln Educational Services
Degrees: A
URL: http://www.cittone.com
Phone: (215) 382-1553
Inst. Accred.: ACICS (1985/2001)

Clarion University of Pennsylvania
840 Wood St., Clarion 16214
Type: Public, state, four-year
System: Pennsylvania State System of Higher Education
Degrees: A, B, M   *Enroll:* 5,884
URL: http://www.clarion.edu
Phone: (814) 393-2000   *Calendar:* Sem. plan
Inst. Accred.: MSA-CHE (1948/2002)
Prog. Accred.: Art, Business (AACSB), Librarianship,
  Music, Speech-Language Pathology, Teacher Education
  (NCATE)

Venango Campus
West First St., Oil City 16301
Phone: (814) 676-6591
Prog. Accred: Nursing

College Misericordia
301 Lake St., Dallas 18612-1098
Type: Private, Roman Catholic Church, four-year
Degrees: A, B, M, D   *Enroll:* 1,672
URL: http://www.misericordia.edu
Phone: (570) 674-6400   *Calendar:* Sem. plan
Inst. Accred.: MSA-CHE (1935/2004)
Prog. Accred.: Nursing, Nursing Education, Occupational
  Therapy, Physical Therapy, Radiography, Social Work

Commonwealth Technical Institute
727 Goucher St., Johnstown 15905-3092
Type: Private, proprietary, two-year
Degrees: A
URL: http://www.hgac.org
Phone: (814) 255-8200
Inst. Accred.: ACCSCT (1987/2002)
Prog. Accred.: Dental Assisting

Community College of Allegheny County
Allegheny Campus
800 Allegheny Ave., Pittsburgh 15233
Type: Public, state /local, two-year
System: Community Colleges of Allegheny County
  College Office
Degrees: A   *Enroll:* 11,626
URL: http://www.ccac.edu/about/allegheny
Phone: (412) 237-2525   *Calendar:* Sem. plan
Inst. Accred.: MSA-CHE (1970/2000, Warning, *Indirect
  accreditation through Community Colleges of Allegheny
  County College Office, Pittsburgh, PA*)
Prog. Accred.: Health Information Technician, Medical
  Assisting (AMA), Nuclear Medicine Technology, Nursing,
  Radiation Therapy, Respiratory Therapy

Community College of Allegheny County
Boyce Campus
595 Beatty Rd., Monroeville 15146
Type: Public, state/local, two-year
System: Community Colleges of Allegheny County
  College Office
Degrees: A   *FTE Enroll:* 16,257
URL: http://www.ccac.edu/about/boyce
Phone: (724) 327-1327   *Calendar:* Sem. plan
Inst. Accred.: MSA-CHE (1970/2000, Warning, *Indirect
  accreditation through Community Colleges of Allegheny
  County College Office, Pittsburgh, PA*)
Prog. Accred.: Diagnostic Medical Sonography,
  Occupational Therapy Assisting, Physical Therapy
  Assisting, Radiography, Surgical Technology

Community College of Allegheny County
North Campus
8701 Perry Hwy., Pittsburgh 15237
Type: Public, state/local, two-year
System: Community Colleges of Allegheny County
  College Office
Degrees: A   *Enroll:* 11,626
URL: http://www.ccac.edu/about/north
Phone: (412) 931-8500   *Calendar:* Sem. plan
Inst. Accred.: MSA-CHE (1970/2000, Warning, *Indirect
  accreditation through Community Colleges of Allegheny
  County College Office, Pittsburgh, PA*)

Community College of Allegheny County
South Campus
1750 Clairton Rd. (Route 885), West Mifflin 15122-3097
Type: Public, state /local, two-year
System: Community Colleges of Allegheny County
  College Office
Degrees: A   *FTE Enroll:* 4,400
URL: http://www.ccac.edu
Phone: (412) 469-1100   *Calendar:* Sem. plan
Inst. Accred.: MSA-CHE (1970/2000, Warning, *Indirect
  accreditation through Community Colleges of Allegheny
  County College Office, Pittsburgh, PA*)
Prog. Accred.: Clinical Lab Technology

Community College of Beaver County
One Campus Dr., Monaca 15061-2588
Type: Public, state/local, two-year
Degrees: A   *Enroll:* 1,693
URL: http://www.ccbc.edu
Phone: (724) 775-8561   *Calendar:* Sem. plan
Inst. Accred.: MSA-CHE (1972/2004)
Prog. Accred.: Clinical Lab Technology, Nursing,
  Phlebotomy

Community College of Philadelphia
1700 Spring Garden St., Philadelphia 19130-3991
Type: Public, state/local, two-year
Degrees: A   *Enroll:* 10,967
URL: http://www.ccp.edu
Phone: (215) 751-8000   *Calendar:* Sem. plan
Inst. Accred.: MSA-CHE (1968/2004)
Prog. Accred.: Clinical Lab Technology, Dental Assisting,
   Dental Hygiene, Health Information Technician, Medical
   Assisting (AMA), Nursing, Phlebotomy, Radiography,
   Respiratory Therapy

Consolidated School of Business
2124 Ambassador Circle, Lancaster 17603
Type: Private, proprietary, two-year
Degrees: A   *Enroll:* 174
URL: http://www.csb.edu
Phone: (717) 394-6211
Inst. Accred.: ACICS (1987/2002)

Consolidated School of Business
1605 Clugston Rd., York 17404
Type: Private, proprietary, two-year
Degrees: A   *Enroll:* 171
URL: http://www.csb.edu
Phone: (717) 764-9950
Inst. Accred.: ACICS (1984/2003)

The Curtis Institute of Music
1726 Locust St., Philadelphia 19103
Type: Private, independent, four-year
Degrees: B, M   *Enroll:* 161
URL: http://www.curtis.edu
Phone: (215) 893-5252   *Calendar:* Sem. plan
Inst. Accred.: MSA-CHE (1993/2003)
Prog. Accred.: Music

Dean Institute of Technology
1501 West Liberty Ave., Pittsburgh 15226-1197
Type: Private, proprietary, two-year
Degrees: A   *Enroll:* 99
URL: hhttp://www.deantech.edu
Phone: (412) 531-4433   *Calendar:* Qtr. plan
Inst. Accred.: ACCSCT (1969/2005)

Delaware County Community College
901 South Media Line Rd., Media 19063
Type: Public, state/local, two-year
Degrees: A   *Enroll:* 6,393
URL: http://www.dccc.edu
Phone: (610) 359-5000   *Calendar:* Sem. plan
Inst. Accred.: MSA-CHE (1970/2001)
Prog. Accred.: Medical Assisting (AMA), Nursing, Surgical
   Technology

Delaware Valley College of Science and Agriculture
700 East Butler Ave., Doylestown 18901-2697
Type: Private, independent, four-year
Degrees: A, B, M   *Enroll:* 1,669
URL: http://www.devalcol.edu
Phone: (215) 345-1500   *Calendar:* Sem. plan
Inst. Accred.: MSA-CHE (1962/2003)

DeSales University
2755 Station Ave., Center Valley 18034-9568
Type: Private, Roman Catholic Church, four-year
Degrees: B, M   *Enroll:* 2,180
URL: http://www.desales.edu
Phone: (610) 282-1100   *Calendar:* Sem. plan
Inst. Accred.: MSA-CHE (1970/2003)
Prog. Accred.: Business (ACBSP), Nursing, Physician
   Assistant

DeVry University Philadelphia
1140 Virginia Dr., Fort Washington 19034
Type: Private, proprietary, four-year
System: DeVry University
Degrees: A, B, M
URL: http://www.devry.edu/fortwashington
Phone: (215) 591-5700   *Calendar:* Sem. plan
Inst. Accred.: NCA-HLC (2002, *Indirect accreditation
   through DeVry University, Oakbrook Terrace, IL*)

Dickinson College
PO Box 1773, Carlisle 17013-2896
Type: Private, independent, four-year
Degrees: B   *Enroll:* 2,255
URL: http://www.dickinson.edu
Phone: (717) 243-5121   *Calendar:* Sem. plan
Inst. Accred.: MSA-CHE (1921/2002)

Douglas Education Center
130 Seventh St., Monessen 15062
Type: Private, proprietary, two-year
Degrees: A   *Enroll:* 195
URL: http://www.douglas-school.com
Phone: (724) 684-3684   *Calendar:* Sem. plan
Inst. Accred.: ACICS (1977/2004)

Drexel University
3141 Chestnut St., Philadelphia 19104
Type: Private, independent, four-year
Degrees: B, M, D   *Enroll:* 13,966
URL: http://www.drexel.edu
Phone: (215) 895-2000   *Calendar:* Qtr. plan
Inst. Accred.: MSA-CHE (1927/2002)
Prog. Accred.: Art, Business (AACSB), Clinical Psychology,
   Computer Science, Engineering (architectural,
   bioengineering, chemical, civil, computer, electrical,
   environmental/sanitary, materials, mechanical), English
   Language Education, Interior Design, Librarianship,
   Nursing Education

Center City Hahnemann Campus
245 North 15th St., Philadelphia 19102-1192
Phone: (215) 762-8900
Prog. Accred: General Practice Residency, Marriage
   and Family Therapy, Medicine, Nurse Anesthesia
   Education, Nursing, Oral and Maxillofacial Surgery,
   Perfusion, Physical Therapy Assisting, Physician
   Assistant, Radiography

DuBois Business College
One Beaver Dr., DuBois 15801
Type: Private, proprietary, two-year
Degrees: A   *Enroll:* 254
URL: http://www.dbcollege.com
Phone: (814) 371-6920   *Calendar:* Qtr. plan
Inst. Accred.: ACICS (1954/2001)

Huntingdon Campus
1001 Moore St., Huntingdon 16652
Phone: (814) 641-0440

Oil City Campus
701 East Third St., Oil City 16301
Phone: (814) 677-1322

Duff's Business Institute
100 Forbes Ave., Ste. 1200, Pittsburgh 15222
Type: Private, proprietary, two-year
System: Corinthian Colleges, Inc
Degrees: A   *Enroll:* 946
URL: http://www.duffs-institute.com
Phone: (412) 261-4520   *Calendar:* Qtr. plan
Inst. Accred.: ACICS (1961/2005)
Prog. Accred.: Medical Assisting (CAAHEP)

Duquesne University
600 Forbes Ave., Pittsburgh 15282
Type: Private, Roman Catholic Church, four-year
Degrees: B, M, P, D   *Enroll:* 8,587
URL: http://www.duq.edu
Phone: (412) 396-6000   *Calendar:* Sem. plan
Inst. Accred.: MSA-CHE (1935/2003)
Prog. Accred.: Athletic Training, Business (AACSB),
Clinical Psychology, Counseling, English Language
Education, Health Information Administration, Law,
Music, Nursing, Nursing Education, Occupational
Therapy, Perfusion, Pharmacy, Physical Therapy,
Physician Assistant, Speech-Language Pathology

East Stroudsburg University of Pennsylvania
200 Prospect St., East Stroudsburg 18301-2999
Type: Public, state, four-year
System: Pennsylvania State System of Higher Education
Degrees: A, B, M   *Enroll:* 5,416
URL: http://www.esu.edu
Phone: (570) 422-3545   *Calendar:* Sem. plan
Inst. Accred.: MSA-CHE (1950/2002)
Prog. Accred.: Athletic Training, Nursing, Public Health,
Recreation and Leisure Services, Speech-Language
Pathology, Teacher Education (NCATE)

Eastern University
1300 Eagle Rd., St. Davids 19087-3696
Type: Private, American Baptist Churches in the USA,
four-year
Degrees: A, B, M   *Enroll:* 2,824
URL: http://www.eastern.edu
Phone: (610) 341-5800
Inst. Accred.: MSA-CHE (1954/2002)
Prog. Accred.: Nursing, Nursing Education, Social Work

Edinboro University of Pennsylvania
Edinboro 16444
Type: Public, state, four-year
System: Pennsylvania State System of Higher Education
Degrees: A, B, M   *Enroll:* 7,203
URL: http://www.edinboro.edu
Phone: (814) 732-2000   *Calendar:* Sem. plan
Inst. Accred.: MSA-CHE (1949/2003)
Prog. Accred.: Business (ACBSP), Counseling, Dietetics
(coordinated), Music, Nursing, Nursing Education,
Rehabilitation Counseling, Social Work, Speech-
Language Pathology, Teacher Education (NCATE)

Elizabethtown College
One Alpha Dr., Elizabethtown 17022-2298
Type: Private, Church of the Brethren, four-year
Degrees: A, B, M   *Enroll:* 1,860
URL: http://www.etown.edu
Phone: (717) 361-1000   *Calendar:* Sem. plan
Inst. Accred.: MSA-CHE (1948/1999)
Prog. Accred.: Business (ACBSP), Music, Occupational
Therapy, Social Work

Erie Business Center
246 West Ninth St., Erie 16501
Type: Private, proprietary, two-year
Degrees: A   *Enroll:* 380
URL: http://www.eriebc.com
Phone: (814) 456-7504
Inst. Accred.: ACICS (1952/2000)

New Castle Campus
170 Cascade Galleria, New Castle 16101
Phone: (724) 658-9066

Erie Institute of Technology
5539 Peach St., Erie 16509-2603
Type: Private, proprietary, two-year
Degrees: A   *Enroll:* 184
URL: http://www.erieit.org
Phone: (814) 868-9900
Inst. Accred.: ACCSCT (1979/2002, Probation)

Evangelical School of Theology
121 South College St., Myerstown 17067
Type: Private, Evangelical Congregational Church, four-
year
Degrees: M, P   *Enroll:* 86
URL: http://www.evangelical.edu
Phone: (717) 866-5775   *Calendar:* Sem. plan
Inst. Accred.: ATS (1987/2000), MSA-CHE (1984/2001)

Franklin and Marshall College
PO Box 3003, Lancaster 17604-3003
Type: Private, independent, four-year
Degrees: B   *Enroll:* 1,899
URL: http://www.fandm.edu
Phone: (717) 291-3911   *Calendar:* Sem. plan
Inst. Accred.: MSA-CHE (1921/1999)

Gannon University
109 University Square, Erie 16541-0001
Type: Private, Roman Catholic Church, four-year
Degrees: A, B, M, D   *Enroll:* 2,868
URL: http://www.gannon.edu
Phone: (814) 871-7000   *Calendar:* Sem. plan
Inst. Accred.: MSA-CHE (1951/2003)
Prog. Accred.: Business (ACBSP), Dietetics (coordinated),
  Engineering (electrical, mechanical), Nurse Anesthesia
  Education, Nursing, Nursing Education, Occupational
  Therapy, Physical Therapy, Physician Assistant,
  Radiography, Respiratory Therapy, Social Work

Geneva College
3200 College Ave., Beaver Falls 15010
Type: Private, Reformed Presbyterian Church of North
  America, four-year
Degrees: A, B, M   *Enroll:* 1,965
URL: http://www.geneva.edu
Phone: (724) 846-5100   *Calendar:* Sem. plan
Inst. Accred.: MSA-CHE (1922/2003)
Prog. Accred.: Business (ACBSP), Engineering (general)

Gettysburg College
300 North Washington St., Gettysburg 17325-1486
Type: Private, Evangelic Lutheran Church, four-year
Degrees: B   *Enroll:* 2,400
URL: http://www.gettysburg.edu
Phone: (717) 337-6000   *Calendar:* Sem. plan
Inst. Accred.: MSA-CHE (1921/2004)

Gratz College
7605 Old York Rd., Melrose Park 19027
Type: Private, independent, four-year
Degrees: B, M   *Enroll:* 245
URL: http://www.gratzcollege.edu
Phone: (215) 635-7300   *Calendar:* Sem. plan
Inst. Accred.: MSA-CHE (1967/2002)

Grove City College
100 Campus Dr., Grove City 16127-2104
Type: Private, independent, four-year
Degrees: B, M   *Enroll:* 2,293
URL: http://www.gcc.edu
Phone: (724) 458-2000   *Calendar:* Sem. plan
Inst. Accred.: MSA-CHE (1922/2003)
Prog. Accred.: Engineering (electrical, mechanical)

Gwynedd-Mercy College
1325 Sumneytown Pike, PO Box 901, Gwynedd Valley
19437-0901
Type: Private, Roman Catholic Church, four-year
Degrees: A, B, M   *Enroll:* 1,805
URL: http://www.gmc.edu
Phone: (215) 646-7300   *Calendar:* Sem. plan
Inst. Accred.: MSA-CHE (1958/2001)
Prog. Accred.: Cardiovascular Technology, Health
  Information Administration, Health Information
  Technician, Nursing, Radiation Therapy, Respiratory
  Therapy, Respiratory Therapy Technology

Center for Lifelong Learning
1250 Virginia Pike, Fort Washington 19034-3206
Phone: (877) 499-6333

Harcum College
750 Montgomery Ave., Bryn Mawr 19010
Type: Private, independent, two-year
Degrees: A   *Enroll:* 436
URL: http://www.harcum.edu
Phone: (610) 525-4100   *Calendar:* Sem. plan
Inst. Accred.: MSA-CHE (1970/2000)
Prog. Accred.: Clinical Lab Technology, Dental Assisting,
  Dental Hygiene, Physical Therapy Assisting, Veterinary
  Technology

Harrisburg Area Community College
One HACC Dr., Harrisburg 17110-2999
Type: Public, state/local, two-year
Degrees: A   *Enroll:* 5,651
URL: http://www.hacc.edu
Phone: (717) 780-2300   *Calendar:* Sem. plan
Inst. Accred.: MSA-CHE (1967/2002)
Prog. Accred.: Business (ACBSP), Clinical Lab Technology,
  Dental Assisting, Dental Hygiene, EMT (Paramedic),
  Nursing, Practical Nursing, Respiratory Therapy

Gettysburg Campus
705 Old Harrisburg Rd., Ste. 2, Gettysburg 17325
Phone: (717) 337-3855

Lancaster Campus
1008 New Holland Ave., Lancaster 17604
Phone: (717) 293-5000

Lebanon Campus
735 Cumberland St., Lebanon 17042
Phone: (717) 270-4222

Harrisburg Institute of Trade and Technology
1519 West Harrisburg Pike, Middletown 17057-4851
Type: Private, proprietary, two-year
Degrees: A   *Enroll:* 84
Phone: (717) 944-2731
Inst. Accred.: ACCSCT (1967/2004, Probation)

Haverford College
370 Lancaster Ave., Haverford 19041-1392
Type: Private, independent, four-year
Degrees: B   *Enroll:* 1,163
URL: http://www.haverford.edu
Phone: (610) 896-1000   *Calendar:* Sem. plan
Inst. Accred.: MSA-CHE (1921/1999)

Holy Family University
Grant and Frankford Ave.s, Philadelphia 19114-2094
Type: Private, Roman Catholic Church, four-year
Degrees: A, B, M   *Enroll:* 1,909
URL: http://www.holyfamily.edu
Phone: (215) 637-7700   *Calendar:* Sem. plan
Inst. Accred.: MSA-CHE (1961/2001)
Prog. Accred.: Nursing, Nursing Education, Radiography

Hussian School of Art
1118 Market St., Philadelphia 19107-3679
Type: Private, independent, two-year
Degrees: A   *Enroll:* 138
URL: http://www.hussianart.edu
Phone: (215) 981-0900   *Calendar:* Sem. plan
Inst. Accred.: ACCSCT (1972/2000)

ICM School of Business and Medical Careers
10 Wood St., Pittsburgh 15222
Type: Private, proprietary, two-year
System: Kaplan Higher Education Corporation
Degrees: A   *Enroll:* 954
URL: http://www.icmschool.com
Phone: (800) 441-5222
Inst. Accred.: ACICS (1967/2003)
Prog. Accred.: Medical Assisting (AMA), Occupational
Therapy Assisting

Immaculata University
1145 King Rd., Immaculata 19345
Type: Private, Roman Catholic Church, four-year
Degrees: A, B, M, D   *Enroll:* 1,660
URL: http://www.immaculata.edu
Phone: (610) 647-4400   *Calendar:* Sem. plan
Inst. Accred.: MSA-CHE (1928/2004)
Prog. Accred.: Clinical Psychology, Dietetics (internship),
Music, Nursing, Nursing Education

Indiana University of Pennsylvania
Sutton Hall, Indiana 15705
Type: Public, state, four-year
System: Pennsylvania State System of Higher Education
Degrees: A, B, M, D   *Enroll:* 12,709
URL: http://www.iup.edu
Phone: (724) 357-2100   *Calendar:* Sem. plan
Inst. Accred.: MSA-CHE (1941/2001)
Prog. Accred.: Applied Science (occupational health and
safety), Business (AACSB), Clinical Psychology, Dietetics
(internship), Music, Nursing, Nursing Education,
Respiratory Therapy, Speech-Language Pathology,
Teacher Education (NCATE), Theatre

Armstrong County Campus
Kittanning 16201
Phone: (814) 543-1078

Punxsutawney Campus
125 South Gilpin St., Punxsutawney 15767
Phone: (814) 938-6711
Prog. Accred: Culinary Education

Information Computer Systems Institute
2201 Hangar Place, Ste. 200, Allentown 18103-9504
Type: Private, proprietary, two-year
Degrees: A   *Enroll:* 37
URL: http://www.icsinstitute.com
Phone: (610) 264-8029
Inst. Accred.: ACCSCT (1984/2004)

International Academy of Design and Technology
555 Grant St., Fulton Bldg., Pittsburgh 15219
Type: Private, proprietary, two-year
System: Career Education Corporation
Degrees: A   *Enroll:* 470
URL: http://www.iadtpitt.com
Phone: (412) 391-4197
Inst. Accred.: ACICS (1971/2001)

Fairmont Campus
2000 Green River Dr., Fairmont, WV 26554
Phone: (304) 534-5677

Johnson College
3427 North Main Ave., Scranton 18508-1495
Type: Private, independent, two-year
Degrees: A   *Enroll:* 357
URL: http://www.johnson.edu
Phone: (570) 342-6404   *Calendar:* Sem. plan
Inst. Accred.: ACCSCT (1979/2003)
Prog. Accred.: Radiography, Veterinary Technology

Juniata College
1700 Moore St., Huntingdon 16652-2119
Type: Private, independent, four-year
Degrees: B   *Enroll:* 1,361
URL: http://www.juniata.edu
Phone: (814) 641-3000   *Calendar:* Sem. plan
Inst. Accred.: MSA-CHE (1922/2003)
Prog. Accred.: Social Work

Keystone College
One College Green, La Plume 18440-0200
Type: Private, independent, four-year
Degrees: A, B   *Enroll:* 1,227
URL: http://www.keystone.edu
Phone: (570) 945-5141   *Calendar:* Sem. plan
Inst. Accred.: MSA-CHE (1936/2003)

King's College
133 North River St., Wilkes-Barre 18711
Type: Private, Roman Catholic Church, four-year
Degrees: A, B, M   *Enroll:* 1,963
URL: http://www.kings.edu
Phone: (570) 208-5900   *Calendar:* Sem. plan
Inst. Accred.: MSA-CHE (1955/2004)
Prog. Accred.: Business (AACSB), Health Services
  Administration, Physician Assistant

Kutztown University of Pennsylvania
15200 Kutztown Rd., Kutztown 19530-0730
Type: Public, state, four-year
System: Pennsylvania State System of Higher Education
Degrees: B, M   *Enroll:* 8,069
URL: http://www.kutztown.edu
Phone: (610) 683-4000   *Calendar:* Sem. plan
Inst. Accred.: MSA-CHE (1944/2003)
Prog. Accred.: Art, Music, Nursing, Social Work, Teacher
  Education (NCATE)

La Roche College
9000 Babcock Blvd., Pittsburgh 15237-5828
Type: Private, Roman Catholic Church, four-year
Degrees: A, B, M   *Enroll:* 1,472
URL: http://www.laroche.edu
Phone: (412) 536-1272   *Calendar:* Sem. plan
Inst. Accred.: MSA-CHE (1973/2004)
Prog. Accred.: Art, Business (ACBSP), Interior Design,
  Nurse Anesthesia Education, Nursing

La Salle University
1900 West Olney Ave., Philadelphia 19141
Type: Private, Roman Catholic Church, four-year
Degrees: A, B, M, D   *Enroll:* 4,538
URL: http://www.lasalle.edu
Phone: (215) 951-1000   *Calendar:* Sem. plan
Inst. Accred.: MSA-CHE (1930/2001)
Prog. Accred.: Business (AACSB), Clinical Psychology,
  Nurse Anesthesia Education, Nursing, Nursing
  Education, Social Work

Lackawanna College
501 Vine St., Scranton 18509
Type: Private, independent, two-year
Degrees: A   *Enroll:* 893
URL: http://www.lackawanna.edu
Phone: (570) 961-7810   *Calendar:* 4-1-4 plan
Inst. Accred.: MSA-CHE (1973/2005)

Hazleton Center
226 West Broad St., Hazleton 18201
Phone: (717) 459-1573

Honesdale Center
627 Main St., Honesdale 18431
Phone: (717) 253-5408

Towanda Center
201 Main St., Towanda 18848
Phone: (717) 265-3449

Lafayette College
High St., Easton 18042-1768
Type: Private, independent, four-year
Degrees: B   *Enroll:* 2,242
URL: http://www.lafayette.edu
Phone: (610) 330-5000   *Calendar:* Sem. plan
Inst. Accred.: MSA-CHE (1921/2003)
Prog. Accred.: Computer Science, Engineering (chemical,
  civil, computer, electrical, mechanical)

Lancaster Bible College and Graduate School
901 Eden Rd., PO Box 83403, Lancaster 17608-3403
Type: Private, independent, four-year
Degrees: A, B, M   *Enroll:* 689
URL: http://www.lbc.edu
Phone: (717) 569-7071   *Calendar:* Sem. plan
Inst. Accred.: ABHE (1964/1998), MSA-CHE (1982/2002)

Lancaster Theological Seminary
555 West James St., Lancaster 17603-2897
Type: Private, United Church of Christ, four-year
Degrees: M, P, D   *Enroll:* 139
URL: http://www.lts.org
Phone: (717) 393-0654
Inst. Accred.: ATS (1938/2004), MSA-CHE (1978/2004)

Lansdale School of Business
201 Church Rd., North Wales 19454
Type: Private, proprietary, two-year
Degrees: A   *Enroll:* 305
URL: http://www.lsbonline.com
Phone: (215) 699-5700
Inst. Accred.: ACICS (1967/2004)

Laurel Business Institute
11-15 Penn St., PO Box 877, Uniontown 15401
Type: Private, proprietary, two-year
Degrees: A   *Enroll:* 290
URL: http://www.laurelbusiness.net
Phone: (724) 439-4900
Inst. Accred.: ACICS (1987/2003)
Prog. Accred.: Medical Assisting (CAAHEP)

Lebanon Valley College
101 North College Ave., Annville 17003-1400
Type: Private, United Methodist Church, four-year
Degrees: A, B, M   *Enroll:* 1,676
URL: http://www.lvc.edu
Phone: (717) 867-6100   *Calendar:* Sem. plan
Inst. Accred.: MSA-CHE (1922/2002)
Prog. Accred.: Music

Lehigh Carbon Community College
4525 Education Park Dr., Schnecksville 18078-2598
Type: Public, state/local, two-year
Degrees: A   *Enroll:* 3,699
URL: http://www.lccc.edu
Phone: (610) 799-2121   *Calendar:* Sem. plan
Inst. Accred.: MSA-CHE (1972/2003)
Prog. Accred.: Business (ACBSP), Health Information
  Technician, Medical Assisting (AMA), Nursing,
  Occupational Therapy Assisting, Physical Therapy
  Assisting, Practical Nursing, Respiratory Therapy,
  Veterinary Technology

Lehigh University
27 Memorial Dr. West, Bethlehem 18015-3094
Type: Private, independent, four-year
Degrees: B, M, D   *Enroll:* 5,992
URL: http://www.lehigh.edu
Phone: (610) 758-3000   *Calendar:* Sem. plan
Inst. Accred.: MSA-CHE (1921/2003)
Prog. Accred.: Accounting, Business (AACSB), Computer
  Science, Counseling Psychology, Engineering (chemical,
  civil, computer, electrical, industrial, materials,
  mechanical), School Psychology, Theatre

Lehigh Valley College
2809 East Saucon Valley Rd., Center Valley 18034
Type: Private, proprietary, two-year
System: Career Education Corporation
Degrees: A   *Enroll:* 1,408
URL: http://www.lehighvalley.edu
Phone: (610) 791-5100   *Calendar:* Sem. plan
Inst. Accred.: ACICS (1968/2004)

Lincoln Technical Institute
9191 Torresdale Ave., Philadelphia 19136
Type: Private, proprietary, two-year
System: Lincoln Educational Services
Degrees: A   *Enroll:* 592
URL: http://www.lincolntech.com
Phone: (215) 335-0800
Inst. Accred.: ACCSCT (1969/2003)

Lincoln Technical Institute
5151 Tilghman St., Allentown 18104-3298
Type: Private, proprietary, two-year
System: Lincoln Educational Services
Degrees: A   *Enroll:* 405
URL: http://www.lincolntech.com
Phone: (610) 398-5300
Inst. Accred.: ACCSCT (1967/2002)

Lincoln University
PO Box 179, Lincoln University 19352-0999
Type: Public, independent, four-year
Degrees: B, M   *Enroll:* 1,826
URL: http://www.lincoln.edu
Phone: (610) 932-8300   *Calendar:* Sem. plan
Inst. Accred.: MSA-CHE (1922/2003)
Prog. Accred.: Recreation and Leisure Services

Lock Haven University of Pennsylvania
401 North Fairview St., Lock Haven 17745-2390
Type: Public, state, four-year
System: Pennsylvania State System of Higher Education
Degrees: A, B, M   *Enroll:* 4,591
URL: http://www.lhup.edu
Phone: (570) 893-2011   *Calendar:* Sem. plan
Inst. Accred.: MSA-CHE (1949/2005)
Prog. Accred.: Athletic Training, Nursing, Physician
  Assistant, Social Work, Teacher Education (NCATE)

Clearfield Campus
119 Byres St., Clearfield 16830
Phone: (814) 765-0619

Lutheran Theological Seminary at Gettysburg
61 Seminary Ridge, Gettysburg 17325-1795
Type: Private, Evangelical Lutheran Church in America,
  four-year
Degrees: M, P   *Enroll:* 215
URL: http://www.ltsg.edu
Phone: (717) 334-6286   *Calendar:* 4-1-4 plan
Inst. Accred.: ATS (1938/2000), MSA-CHE (1971/2001)

The Lutheran Theological Seminary at Philadelphia
7301 Germantown Ave., Philadelphia 19119
Type: Private, Evangelical Lutheran Church in America,
  four-year
Degrees: M, P, D   *Enroll:* 214
URL: http://www.ltsp.edu
Phone: (215) 248-4616
Inst. Accred.: ATS (1938/2002), MSA-CHE (1971/2002)

Luzerne County Community College
1333 South Prospect St., Nanticoke 18634
Type: Public, local, two-year
Degrees: A   *Enroll:* 4,024
URL: http://www.luzerne.edu
Phone: (570) 740-0200   *Calendar:* Sem. plan
Inst. Accred.: MSA-CHE (1975/2001)
Prog. Accred.: Dental Assisting, Dental Hygiene, Nursing

Lycoming College
700 College Place, Williamsport 17701
Type: Private, United Methodist Church, four-year
Degrees: B   *Enroll:* 1,393
URL: http://www.lycoming.edu
Phone: (570) 321-4000   *Calendar:* Sem. plan
Inst. Accred.: MSA-CHE (1934/2001)
Prog. Accred.: Business (ACBSP), Nursing

Manor College
700 Fox Chase Rd., Jenkintown 19046
Type: Private, Ukrainian Catholic Church, two-year
Degrees: A   *Enroll:* 605
URL: http://www.manor.edu
Phone: (215) 885-2360   *Calendar:* Sem. plan
Inst. Accred.: MSA-CHE (1967/2003)
Prog. Accred.: Clinical Lab Technology, Dental Assisting, Dental Hygiene, Veterinary Technology

Mansfield University of Pennsylvania
Mansfield 16933
Type: Public, state, four-year
System: Pennsylvania State System of Higher Education
Degrees: A, B, M   *Enroll:* 3,188
URL: http://www.mansfield.edu
Phone: (570) 662-4000   *Calendar:* Sem. plan
Inst. Accred.: MSA-CHE (1942/2002)
Prog. Accred.: Music, Nursing, Radiography, Respiratory Therapy, Social Work, Teacher Education (NCATE)

Marywood University
2300 Adams Ave., Scranton 18509
Type: Private, Roman Catholic Church, four-year
Degrees: A, B, M, D   *Enroll:* 2,441
URL: http://www.marywood.edu
Phone: (570) 348-6211   *Calendar:* Sem. plan
Inst. Accred.: MSA-CHE (1921/2001)
Prog. Accred.: Art, Business (ACBSP), Counseling, Dietetics (coordinated), Dietetics (internship), Music, Nursing, Physician Assistant, Social Work, Speech-Language Pathology, Teacher Education (NCATE)

McCann School of Business and Technology—Pottsville
2650 Woodglen Rd., Pottsville 17901
Type: Private, proprietary, two-year
Degrees: A
URL: http://www.mccannschool.com
Phone: (570) 773-1820   *Calendar:* Qtr. plan
Inst. Accred.: ACICS (1962/2001)

Mahanoy City Campus
47 South Main St., Mahanoy City 17948-2698
Phone: (570) 773-1820

Scranton Campus
222 Mulberry St., Third Flr., Scranton 18503
Phone: (570) 969-4330

Sunbury Campus
225 Market St., Third Flr., Sunbury 17801
Phone: (570) 286-3058

Median School of Allied Health Careers
125 Seventh St., Pittsburgh 15222-3400
Type: Private, proprietary, two-year
Degrees: A   *Enroll:* 338
URL: http://www.medianschool.edu
Phone: (412) 391-7021   *Calendar:* Qtr. plan
Inst. Accred.: ACCSCT (1970/2004)
Prog. Accred.: Dental Assisting, Medical Assisting (CAAHEP)

Mercyhurst College
501 East 38th St., Erie 16546
Type: Private, Roman Catholic Church, four-year
Degrees: A, B, M   *Enroll:* 3,482
URL: http://www.mercyhurst.edu
Phone: (814) 824-2000   *Calendar:* Tri. plan
Inst. Accred.: MSA-CHE (1931/2003)
Prog. Accred.: Athletic Training, Dietetics (coordinated), Music, Physical Therapy Assisting, Social Work

North East Campus
16 West Division St., North East 16428
Phone: (814) 725-6100

Messiah College
One College Ave., Grantham 17027
Type: Private, Brethren in Christ Church, four-year
Degrees: B   *Enroll:* 2,917
URL: http://www.messiah.edu
Phone: (717) 766-2511   *Calendar:* Sem. plan
Inst. Accred.: MSA-CHE (1963/2003)
Prog. Accred.: Art, Athletic Training, Engineering (general), Music, Nursing, Social Work

City Campus
2026 North Broad St., Philadelphia 19121
Phone: (215) 769-2526

Metropolitan Career Center and Computer Technology Institute
100 South Broad St., #830, Land Title Bldg., Philadelphia 19110
Type: Private, independent, two-year
Degrees: A
URL: http://www.metropolitancareercenter.org
Phone: (215) 568-9215   *Calendar:* Sem. plan
Inst. Accred.: ACCSCT (1999/2002)

Millersville University of Pennsylvania
PO Box 1002, Millersville 17551-0302
Type: Public, state, four-year
System: Pennsylvania State System of Higher Education
Degrees: A, B, M   *Enroll:* 6,927
URL: http://muweb.millersville.edu
Phone: (717) 872-3024   *Calendar:* 4-1-4 plan
Inst. Accred.: MSA-CHE (1950/2005)
Prog. Accred.: Applied Science (occupational health and safety), Business (ACBSP), Computer Science, Industrial Technology, Music, Nursing, Respiratory Therapy, Social Work, Teacher Education (NCATE)

Montgomery County Community College
340 DeKalb Pike, Blue Bell 19422
Type: Public, state/local, two-year
Degrees: A   *Enroll:* 6,508
URL: http://www.mc3.edu
Phone: (215) 641-6300   *Calendar:* Sem. plan
Inst. Accred.: MSA-CHE (1970/2005)
Prog. Accred.: Clinical Lab Technology, Dental Hygiene, Nursing, Phlebotomy

West Campus
101 College Dr., Pottstown 19464
Phone: (610) 718-1800
Prog. Accred: Radiography

Moore College of Art and Design
The Pkwy. at 20th St., Philadelphia 19103
Type: Private, independent, four-year
Degrees: B   *Enroll:* 627
URL: http://www.moore.edu
Phone: (215) 568-4515   *Calendar:* Sem. plan
Inst. Accred.: MSA-CHE (1958/2002)
Prog. Accred.: Art, Interior Design

Moravian College
1200 Main St., Bethlehem 18018-6650
Type: Private, Moravian Church, four-year
Degrees: B, M, P   *Enroll:* 1,774
URL: http://www.moravian.edu
Phone: (610) 861-1300   *Calendar:* Sem. plan
Inst. Accred.: ATS (1954/1998), MSA-CHE (1922/2003)
Prog. Accred.: Music, Nursing, Nursing Education

Moravian Theological Seminary
1200 Main St., Bethleham 18018
Phone: (610) 861-1516

Mount Aloysius College
7373 Admiral Peary Hwy., Cresson 16630-1999
Type: Private, Roman Catholic Church, four-year
Degrees: A, B, M   *Enroll:* 1,250
URL: http://www.mtaloy.edu
Phone: (814) 886-4131   *Calendar:* Sem. plan
Inst. Accred.: MSA-CHE (1943/2000)
Prog. Accred.: Medical Assisting (AMA), Nursing, Occupational Therapy Assisting, Physical Therapy Assisting, Surgical Technology

Muhlenberg College
2400 Chew St., Allentown 18104
Type: Private, Evangelical Lutheran Church in America, four-year
Degrees: A, B   *Enroll:* 2,354
URL: http://www.muhlenberg.edu
Phone: (484) 664-3100   *Calendar:* Sem. plan
Inst. Accred.: MSA-CHE (1921/2001)

Neumann College
One Neumann Dr., Aston 19014-1298
Type: Private, Sisters of St. Francis of Philadelphia, four-year
Degrees: A, B, M   *Enroll:* 2,077
URL: http://www.neumann.edu
Phone: (610) 558-5616   *Calendar:* Sem. plan
Inst. Accred.: MSA-CHE (1972/2001)
Prog. Accred.: Clinical Lab Scientist, Nursing, Physical Therapy

New Castle School of Trades
New Castle Youngstown Rd., Route 422, R.D. 1, Pulaski 16143-9721
Type: Private, proprietary, two-year
Degrees: A   *Enroll:* 369
URL: http://www.ncstrades.com
Phone: (724) 964-8811
Inst. Accred.: ACCSCT (1973/2005)

Newport Business Institute
941 West Third St., Williamsport 17701
Type: Private, proprietary, two-year
Degrees: A   *Enroll:* 111
URL: http://www.nbi.edu
Phone: (570) 326-2869   *Calendar:* Qtr. plan
Inst. Accred.: ACICS (1955/2004)

Newport Business Institute
945 Greensburg Rd., Lower Burrell 15068
Type: Private, proprietary, two-year
Degrees: A   *Enroll:* 88
URL: http://www.nbi.edu
Phone: (724) 339-7542   *Calendar:* Qtr. plan
Inst. Accred.: ACICS (1965/2002)

Northampton County Area Community College
3835 Green Pond Rd., Bethlehem 18017
Type: Public, state/local, two-year
Degrees: A   *Enroll:* 3,935
URL: http://www.northampton.edu
Phone: (610) 861-5300   *Calendar:* Sem. plan
Inst. Accred.: MSA-CHE (1970/2005)
Prog. Accred.: Business (ACBSP), Dental Hygiene, Funeral Service Education (Mortuary Science), Nursing, Practical Nursing, Radiography

Monroe County Branch Campus
PO Box 639, Tannersville 18372
Phone: (570) 620-9221

Oakbridge Academy of Arts
1250 Greensburg Rd., Lower Burrell 15068
Type: Private, proprietary, two-year
Degrees: A   *Enroll:* 89
URL: http://oakbridgeacademy.com
Phone: (724) 335-5336   *Calendar:* Qtr. plan
Inst. Accred.: ACCSCT (1980/2002)

Orleans Technical Institute
1845 Walnut St., Ste. 700, Philadelphia 19103-4707
Type: Private, independent, two-year
Degrees: A
URL: http://www.orleanstech.org
Phone: (215) 854-1853
Inst. Accred.: ACCSCT (1981/2005)

Pace Institute
606 Ct. St., Reading 19601
Type: Private, proprietary, two-year
Degrees: A   *Enroll:* 310
URL: http://www.paceinstitute.edu
Phone: (610) 375-1212
Inst. Accred.: ACICS (1984/2002)

The Palmer Theological Seminary
6 E. Lancaster Ave., Wynnewood 19096-3494
Type: Private, American Baptist Churches, U.S.A., four-year
Degrees: M, P, D   *Enroll:* 335
URL: http://www.palmerseminary.edu
Phone: (610) 896-5000   *Calendar:* 4-1-4 plan
Inst. Accred.: ATS (1954/2005)

Peirce College
1420 Pine St., Philadelphia 19102
Type: Private, independent, four-year
Degrees: A, B   *Enroll:* 1,081
URL: http://www.peirce.edu
Phone: (215) 545-6400   *Calendar:* Sem. plan
Inst. Accred.: MSA-CHE (1971/2001)
Prog. Accred.: Business (ACBSP)

Penn Commercial, Inc.
242 Oak Spring Rd., Washington 15301
Type: Private, proprietary, two-year
Degrees: A   *Enroll:* 342
URL: http://www.penn-commercial.com
Phone: (724) 222-5330   *Calendar:* Sem. plan
Inst. Accred.: ACICS (1960/2003)
Prog. Accred.: Medical Assisting (CAAHEP)

Penn Foster Career School
925 Oak St., Scranton 18515
Type: Private, proprietary, two-year
Degrees: A   *FTE Enroll:* 1,705
URL: http://www.pennfoster.edu
Phone: (570) 342-7701   *Calendar:* Sem. plan
Inst. Accred.: DETC (1974/2004)

Pennco Tech
3815 Otter St., Bristol 19007-3696
Type: Private, proprietary, two-year
Degrees: A   *Enroll:* 304
Phone: (215) 824-3200
Inst. Accred.: ACCSCT (1969/2002)

Pennsylvania Academy of the Fine Arts
118 North Broad St., Philadelphia 19102
Type: Private, independent, four-year
Degrees: M   *Enroll:* 250
URL: http://www.pafa.edu
Phone: (215) 972-7600   *Calendar:* Sem. plan
Inst. Accred.: NASAD (1979/1995)

Pennsylvania College of Art and Design
204 North Prince St., Lancaster 17603
Type: Private, independent, four-year
Degrees: B
URL: http://www.psad.org
Phone: (717) 396-7833   *Calendar:* Sem. plan
Inst. Accred.: NASAD (1984/1995)

Pennsylvania College of Optometry
8360 Old York Rd., Elkins Park 19027
Type: Private, independent, four-year
Degrees: B, M, P   *Enroll:* 632
URL: http://www.pco.edu
Phone: (215) 780-1400   *Calendar:* Qtr. plan
Inst. Accred.: MSA-CHE (1954/2005)
Prog. Accred.: Optometric Residency, Optometry

Pennsylvania College of Technology
One College Ave., Williamsport 17701
Type: Public, state, four-year
Degrees: A, B   *Enroll:* 5,625
URL: http://www.pct.edu
Phone: (570) 326-3761   *Calendar:* Sem. plan
Inst. Accred.: MSA-CHE (1970/2002)
Prog. Accred.: Construction Education, Culinary Education, Dental Hygiene, Engineering Technology (civil/construction, plastics, surveying), Nursing, Occupational Therapy Assisting, Physician Assistant, Radiography

North Campus
Mansfield Rd., Wellsboro 16901
Phone: (717) 724-7703

Pennsylvania Culinary Institute
717 Liberty Ave., Pittsburgh 15222-3500
Type: Private, proprietary, two-year
System: Career Education Corporation
Degrees: A   *Enroll:* 1,523
URL: http://www.pci.edu
Phone: (412) 566-2433
Inst. Accred.: ACCSCT (1990/2005)
Prog. Accred.: Culinary Education

Pennsylvania Highlands Community College
PO Box 68, Johnson 15907-0068
Type: Public, state/local, two-year
Degrees: A   *Enroll:* 840
URL: http://www.pennhighlands.edu
Phone: (814) 532-5300   *Calendar:* Sem. plan
Inst. Accred.: MSA-CHE (2002)

Pennsylvania Institute of Technology
800 Manchester Ave., Media 19063
Type: Private, independent, two-year
Degrees: A   *Enroll:* 213
URL: http://www.pit.edu
Phone: (610) 892-1500   *Calendar:* Sem. plan
Inst. Accred.: MSA-CHE (1983/2001)

The Pennsylvania State University
201 Old Main, University Park 16804-3000
Type: Public, state, four-year
Degrees: A, B, M, P, D   *Enroll:* 39,911
URL: http://www.psu.edu
Phone: (814) 865-4700   *Calendar:* Sem. plan
Inst. Accred.: MSA-CHE (1921/2005)
Prog. Accred.: Accounting, Applied Science (industrial hygiene), Art, Athletic Training, Audiology, Business (AACSB), Clinical Psychology, Counseling, Counseling Psychology, Engineering (aerospace, agricultural, architectural, chemical, civil, computer, electrical, engineering physics/science, environmental/sanitary, industrial, materials, mechanical, metallurgical, mineral, mining, nuclear, petroleum), Forestry, Health Services Administration, Journalism, Landscape Architecture, Music, Nursing, Nursing Education, Psychology Internship, Recreation and Leisure Services, Rehabilitation Counseling, School Psychology, Speech-Language Pathology, Teacher Education (NCATE), Theatre

Altoona Campus
3000 Ivyside Park, Ste. 1, Altoona 16601-3760
Phone: (724)773-3500
Prog. Accred: Engineering Technology (electrical, electromechanical, mechanical)

Beaver Campus
Brodhead Rd., Monaca 15061
Phone: (412) 773-3500
Prog. Accred: Engineering Technology (electrical)

Berks Campus
Tulpehocken Rd., PO Box 7009, Reading 19610-6009
Phone: (610) 320-4800
Prog. Accred: Engineering Technology (electrical, electromechanical, mechanical), Occupational Therapy Assisting

Delaware County Campus
25 Yearsley Mill Rd., Media 19063-5596
Phone: (610) 892-1350

Dickinson School of Law
150 South College St., Carlisle 17013
Phone: (717) 243-4611
Prog. Accred: Law

DuBois Campus
College Place, DuBois 15801
Phone: (814) 375-4700
Prog. Accred: Engineering Technology (electrical, mechanical), Occupational Therapy Assisting, Physical Therapy Assisting

Erie Campus
Station Rd., Erie 16563-0101
Phone: (814) 898-6000
Prog. Accred: Business (AACSB), Engineering (computer, electrical, mechanical), Engineering Technology (electrical, mechanical, plastics)

Fayette Campus
PO Box 519, Route 119 North, Uniontown 15401
Phone: (724) 430-4100
Prog. Accred: Engineering Technology (architectural, electrical)

Great Valley Graduate Center
30 East Swedesford Rd., Malvern 19355
Phone: (610) 648-3200

Harrisburg Campus
777 West Harrisburg Pike, Middletown 17057-4898
Phone: (717) 948-6000
Prog. Accred: Business (AACSB), Engineering (electrical, environmental/sanitary), Engineering Technology (civil/construction, electrical, environmental/sanitary, mechanical), Public Administration

Hazleton Campus
Highacres, Hazleton 18201
Phone: (717) 450-3000
Prog. Accred: Clinical Lab Technology, Engineering Technology (electrical, mechanical), Physical Therapy Assisting

Hershey Medical Center
The Milton S. Hershey Medical Center, 500 University Dr., PO Box 850, Hershey 17033
Phone: (717) 531-8521
Prog. Accred: Clinical Pastoral Education (ACPEI), Medicine

Lehigh Valley Campus
8380 Mohr Ln., Fogelsville 18051-9999
Phone: (610) 285-5000

McKeesport Campus
4000 University Dr., McKeesport 15132
Phone: (412) 675-9000

Mont Alto Campus
Campus Dr., Mont Alto 17237-9703
Phone: (717) 749-6000
Prog. Accred: Occupational Therapy Assisting, Physical Therapy Assisting

New Kensington Campus
3550 Seventh St. Rd., New Kensington 15068-1798
Phone: (724) 339-5466
Prog. Accred: Clinical Lab Technology, Engineering Technology (bioengineering, electrical, electromechanical, mechanical), Radiography

Ogontz Campus
1600 Woodland Rd., Abington 19001-3990
Phone: (215) 881-7300

Schuylkill Campus
200 University Dr., Schuylkill Haven 17972-2208
Phone: (717) 385-6000
Prog. Accred: Engineering Technology (electrical),
   Radiography

Shenango Campus
147 Shenango Ave., Sharon 16146
Phone: (724) 983-5800
Prog. Accred: Engineering Technology (mechanical),
   Physical Therapy Assisting

Wilkes-Barre Campus
PO Box PSU, Lehman 18627
Phone: (717) 675-2171
Prog. Accred: Applied Science (surveying/geomatics),
   Engineering Technology (electrical, surveying,
   telecommunications)

Worthington-Scranton Campus
120 Ridge View Dr., Dunmore 18512
Phone: (570) 963-2500
Prog. Accred: Engineering Technology (architectural)

York Campus
1031 Edgecomb Ave., York 17403
Phone: (717) 771-4000
Prog. Accred: Engineering Technology (electrical,
   mechanical)

Philadelphia Biblical University
200 Manor Ave., Langhorne 19047-2990
Type: Private, interdenominational, four-year
Degrees: A, B, M, P   *Enroll:* 1,071
URL: http://www.pbu.edu
Phone: (215) 752-5800   *Calendar:* Sem. plan
Inst. Accred.: ABHE (1950/1996), MSA-CHE (1967/2005)
Prog. Accred.: Music, Social Work

New Jersey Campus
PO Box 19, Liberty Corner, NJ 07938
Phone: (908) 604-2707

Wisconsin Wilderness Campus
HC 60, Box 60, Cable, WI 54821
Phone: (715) 798-3525

Philadelphia College of Osteopathic Medicine
4170 City Ave., Philadelphia 19131
Type: Private, independent, four-year
Degrees: M, P, D   *Enroll:* 1,563
URL: http://www.pcom.edu
Phone: (215) 871-6100   *Calendar:* Tri. plan
Inst. Accred.: MSA-CHE (1999/2004)
Prog. Accred.: Clinical Psychology, Osteopathy, Physician
   Assistant

Philadelphia University
Schoolhouse Ln. and Henry Ave., Philadelphia 19144
Type: Private, independent, four-year
Degrees: A, B, M, D   *Enroll:* 2,654
URL: http://www.philau.edu
Phone: (215) 951-2700   *Calendar:* Sem. plan
Inst. Accred.: MSA-CHE (1995/2001)
Prog. Accred.: Engineering (textile), Interior Design,
   Occupational Therapy, Physician Assistant

Pittsburgh Institute of Aeronautics
PO Box 10897, Pittsburgh 15236-0897
Type: Private, proprietary, two-year
Degrees: A   *Enroll:* 496
Phone: (412) 466-9011   *Calendar:* Qtr. plan
Inst. Accred.: ACCSCT (1970/2004)

Pittsburgh Institute of Mortuary Science
5808 Baum Blvd., Pittsburgh 15206
Type: Private, independent, two-year
Degrees: A   *Enroll:* 117
URL: http://www.p-i-m-s.com
Phone: (412) 362-8500   *Calendar:* Tri. plan
Inst. Accred.: ABFSE (1962/1997)

Pittsburgh Technical Institute
1111 McKee Rd., Oakdale 15071-3205
Type: Private, proprietary, two-year
Degrees: A   *FTE Enroll:* 1,120
URL: http://www.pittsburghtechnical.com
Phone: (412) 809-5100
Inst. Accred.: MSA-CHE (2002)

Pittsburgh Center
635 Smithfield St., Pittsburgh 15222
Phone: (412) 809-5100

Pittsburgh Theological Seminary
616 North Highland Ave., Pittsburgh 15206
Type: Private, Presbyterian Church (USA), four-year
Degrees: M, P, D   *Enroll:* 330
URL: http://www.pts.edu
Phone: (412) 362-5610   *Calendar:* Qtr. plan
Inst. Accred.: ATS (1938/2002), MSA-CHE (1970/2003)

The PJA School
7900 West Chester Pike, Upper Darby 19082-1926
Type: Private, proprietary, two-year
Degrees: A
URL: http://www.pjaschool.com
Phone: (610) 789-6700
Inst. Accred.: ACCSCT (1985/2001)

Point Park University
201 Wood St., Pittsburgh 15222
Type: Private, independent, four-year
Degrees: A, B, M   *Enroll:* 2,577
URL: http://www.pointpark.edu
Phone: (412) 391-4100   *Calendar:* Sem. plan
Inst. Accred.: MSA-CHE (1968/2001)
Prog. Accred.: Dance, Engineering Technology
   (civil/construction, electrical, mechanical), Respiratory
   Therapy Technology

Reading Area Community College
PO Box 1706, Reading 19603-1706
Type: Public, state/local, two-year
Degrees: A   *Enroll:* 2,445
URL: http://www.racc.edu
Phone: (610) 372-4721   *Calendar:* Tri. plan
Inst. Accred.: MSA-CHE (1979/2003)
Prog. Accred.: Clinical Lab Technology, Nursing, Practical
Nursing, Respiratory Therapy, Respiratory Therapy
Technology

Reconstructionist Rabbinical College
1299 Church Rd., Wyncote 19095
Type: Private, independent, four-year
Degrees: M, P, D   *Enroll:* 71
URL: http://www.rrc.edu
Phone: (215) 576-0800   *Calendar:* Sem. plan
Inst. Accred.: MSA-CHE (1990/2005)

Reformed Presbyterian Theological Seminary
7418 Penn Ave., Pittsburgh 15208
Type: Private, Reformed Presbyterian Church of North
America, four-year
Degrees: M   *Enroll:* 49
URL: http://www.rpts.edu
Phone: (412) 731-8690   *Calendar:* Sem. plan
Inst. Accred.: ATS (1994/1997)

The Restaurant School at Walnut Hill College
4207 Walnut St., Philadelphia 19104-3518
Type: Private, proprietary, four-year
Degrees: A, B   *Enroll:* 620
URL: http://www.therestaurantschool.com
Phone: (215) 222-4200
Inst. Accred.: ACCSCT (1982/2003)

Robert Morris University
6001 University Blvd., Moon Township 15108-1189
Type: Private, independent, four-year
Degrees: A, B, M, D   *Enroll:* 3,550
URL: http://www.rmu.edu
Phone: (412) 262-8200   *Calendar:* Sem. plan
Inst. Accred.: MSA-CHE (1968/2002)
Prog. Accred.: Business (AACSB), Engineering (general,
manufacturing), Nursing Education, Radiography

Pittsburgh Campus
600 Fifth Ave., Pittsburgh 15219
Phone: (412) 227-6800
Prog. Accred: Radiography

Rosedale Technical Institute
4634 Browns Hill Rd., Pittsburgh 15217-2919
Type: Private, proprietary, two-year
Degrees: A   *Enroll:* 175
URL: http://rosedaletech.org
Phone: (412) 521-6200   *Calendar:* Qtr. plan
Inst. Accred.: ACCSCT (1974/2001)

Rosemont College
1400 Montgomery Ave., Rosemont 19010-1699
Type: Private, Society of the Holy Child Jesus, four-year
Degrees: B, M   *Enroll:* 696
URL: http://www.rosemont.edu
Phone: (610) 527-0200
Inst. Accred.: MSA-CHE (1930/2005)

Saint Charles Borromeo Seminary
100 East Wynnewood Rd., Wynnewood 19096-3099
Type: Private, Roman Catholic Church, four-year
Degrees: B, M, P   *Enroll:* 267
URL: http://www.scs.edu
Phone: (610) 667-3394   *Calendar:* Sem. plan
Inst. Accred.: ATS (1970/1998), MSA-CHE (1971/1999)

Saint Francis University
PO Box 600, Loretto 15940
Type: Private, Roman Catholic Church, four-year
Degrees: A, B, M   *Enroll:* 1,556
URL: http://www.sfcpa.edu
Phone: (814) 472-3000   *Calendar:* Sem. plan
Inst. Accred.: MSA-CHE (1939/2001)
Prog. Accred.: Nursing, Nursing Education, Occupational
Therapy, Physical Therapy, Physician Assistant, Social
Work

Saint Joseph's University
5600 City Line Ave., Philadelphia 19131
Type: Private, Roman Catholic Church, four-year
Degrees: A, B, M, D   *Enroll:* 5,579
URL: http://www.sju.edu
Phone: (610) 660-1000   *Calendar:* Sem. plan
Inst. Accred.: MSA-CHE (1922/2004)
Prog. Accred.: Accounting, Business (AACSB), Nurse
Anesthesia Education

Saint Tikhon's Orthodox Theological Seminary
St. Tikhon's Rd., PO Box 130, South Canaan 18459-0130
Type: Private, Russian Orthodox Greek Catholic Church,
four-year
Degrees: M
URL: http://www.stots.edu
Phone: (570) 937-4411   *Calendar:* Sem. plan
Inst. Accred.: ATS (2004)

Saint Vincent College and Seminary
300 Fraser Purchase Rd., Latrobe 15650-2690
Type: Private, Roman Catholic Church, four-year
Degrees: B, M, P   *Enroll:* 1,372
URL: http://www.stvincent.edu
Phone: (724) 539-9761   *Calendar:* Sem. plan
Inst. Accred.: ATS (1984/1998), MSA-CHE (1921/2003)
Prog. Accred.: Business (ACBSP)

Schuylkill Institute of Business and Technology
171 Red Horse Rd., Pottsville 17901-8898
Type: Private, proprietary, two-year
Degrees: A   *Enroll:* 105
URL: http://www.sibtechnical.com
Phone: (570) 622-4835
Inst. Accred.: ACICS (1980/2002)

Seton Hill University
One Seton Hill Dr., Greensburg 15601
Type: Private, Roman Catholic Church, four-year
Degrees: B, M   *Enroll:* 1,301
URL: http://www.setonhill.edu
Phone: (724) 834-2200   *Calendar:* Sem. plan
Inst. Accred.: MSA-CHE (1921/2002)
Prog. Accred.: Dietetics (coordinated), Marriage and
   Family Therapy, Music, Physician Assistant, Social Work

Shippensburg University of Pennsylvania
1871 Old Main Dr., Shippensburg 17257-2299
Type: Public, state, four-year
System: Pennsylvania State System of Higher Education
Degrees: B, M   *Enroll:* 6,929
URL: http://www.ship.edu
Phone: (717) 477-7447   *Calendar:* Sem. plan
Inst. Accred.: MSA-CHE (1939/1999)
Prog. Accred.: Business (AACSB), Counseling, Social
   Work, Teacher Education (NCATE)

Slippery Rock University of Pennsylvania
1 Morrow Way, Slippery Rock 16057-1383
Type: Public, state, four-year
System: Pennsylvania State System of Higher Education
Degrees: B, M, D   *Enroll:* 7,144
URL: http://www.sru.edu
Phone: (724) 738-9000   *Calendar:* Sem. plan
Inst. Accred.: MSA-CHE (1943/2001)
Prog. Accred.: Athletic Training, Business (ACBSP),
   Counseling, Dance, Music, Nursing, Physical Therapy,
   Social Work, Teacher Education (NCATE)

South Hills School of Business and Technology
480 Waupelani Dr., State College 16801-4516
Type: Private, proprietary, two-year
Degrees: A   *Enroll:* 722
URL: http://www.southhills.edu
Phone: (814) 234-7755   *Calendar:* Qtr. plan
Inst. Accred.: ACICS (1976/2004)
Prog. Accred.: Health Information Technician

Altoona Campus
508 58th St., Altoona 16602
Phone: (814) 944-6134

Lewistown Campus
124 East Market St., Lewistown 17044
Phone: (717) 248-8140

Philipsburg Campus
200 Shady Ln., Philipsburg 16866
Phone: (814) 342-7427

Susquehanna University
514 University Ave., Selinsgrove 17870-1025
Type: Private, Evangelical Lutheran Church, four-year
Degrees: A, B   *Enroll:* 1,954
URL: http://www.susqu.edu
Phone: (570) 374-0101   *Calendar:* Sem. plan
Inst. Accred.: MSA-CHE (1930/2004)
Prog. Accred.: Business (AACSB), Music

Swarthmore College
500 College Ave., Swarthmore 19081
Type: Private, Religious Society of Friends (Quakers),
   four-year
Degrees: B, M   *Enroll:* 1,492
URL: http://www.swarthmore.edu
Phone: (610) 328-8000   *Calendar:* Sem. plan
Inst. Accred.: MSA-CHE (1921/1999)
Prog. Accred.: Engineering (general)

Talmudical Yeshiva of Philadelphia
6063 Drexel Rd., Philadelphia 19131
Type: Private, independent, four-year
Degrees: Rabbinic, Talmudic   *Enroll:* 86
Phone: (215) 473-1212   *Calendar:* Sem. plan
Inst. Accred.: AARTS (1975/2001)

Temple University
1801 North Broad St., Philadelphia 19122
Type: Private, state-related, four-year
Degrees: A, B, M, P, D   *Enroll:* 27,397
URL: http://www.temple.edu
Phone: (215) 204-7000   *Calendar:* Sem. plan
Inst. Accred.: MSA-CHE (1921/2005)
Prog. Accred.: Advanced Education in General Dentistry,
Art, Athletic Training, Audiology, Business (AACSB),
Clinical Psychology, Combined Prosthodontics,
Counseling Psychology, Dance, Dentistry, Endodontics,
Engineering (civil, electrical, mechanical), Engineering
Technology (civil/construction, electrical,
environmental/sanitary, general, mechanical), General
Dentistry, Health Information Administration, Health
Services Administration, Journalism, Landscape
Architecture, Law, Medicine, Music, Nurse Anesthesia
Education, Nursing, Nursing Education, Occupational
Therapy, Oral and Maxillofacial Surgery, Orthodontic
and Dentofacial Orthopedics, Pediatric Dentistry,
Periodontics, Pharmacy, Physical Therapy, Psychology
Internship, Public Health, Recreation and Leisure
Services, School Psychology, Social Work, Speech-
Language Pathology, Teacher Education (NCATE),
Theatre

Ambler Campus
580 Meeting House Rd., Ambler 19002-3999
Phone: (215) 283-1201

Center City Campus
1616 Walnut St., Philadelphia 19103
Phone: (215) 204-1500

Harrisburg Center
223 Walnut St., Harrisburg 17101
Phone: (717) 232-6400

Japan Campus
2-2 Minami Osewaw, Hachioji-shi, Tokyo, Japan 192-
03
Phone: [011] 81-426-77-5116

Rome Campus
Lungotevere Arnaldo da Brescia, 15, Rome, Italy
00196
Phone: [011] 39-6-320-2808

School of Podiatric Medicine
8th and Race St.s, Philadelphia 19107
Phone: (215) 629-0300
Prog. Accred: Podiatry

Thaddeus Stevens College of Technology
750 East King St., Lancaster 17602
Type: Public, state, two-year
Degrees: A   *Enroll:* 646
URL: http://www.stevenstech.org
Phone: (717) 299-7730   *Calendar:* Sem. plan
Inst. Accred.: MSA-CHE (1991/2002)

Thiel College
75 College Ave., Greenville 16125
Type: Private, Evangelial Lutheran Church in America,
four-year
Degrees: A, B   *Enroll:* 1,214
URL: http://www.thiel.edu
Phone: (724) 589-2000   *Calendar:* Sem. plan
Inst. Accred.: MSA-CHE (1922/2002)
Prog. Accred.: Nursing

Thomas Jefferson University
1020 Walnut St., Philadelphia 19107
Type: Private, independent, four-year
Degrees: A, B, M, P, D   *Enroll:* 1,918
URL: http://www.tju.edu
Phone: (215) 955-6000   *Calendar:* Sem. plan
Inst. Accred.: MSA-CHE (1976/2004)
Prog. Accred.: Clinical Lab Scientist, Clinical Pastoral
Education (ACPEI), Cytogenetic Technology,
Cytotechnology, Diagnostic Medical Sonography,
Medicine, Nursing, Nursing Education, Occupational
Therapy, Oral and Maxillofacial Surgery, Physical
Therapy, Radiography

Thompson Institute
5650 Derry St., Harrisburg 17111-4112
Type: Private, proprietary, two-year
System: Kaplan Higher Education Corporation
Degrees: A   *Enroll:* 404
URL: http://www.thompson.edu
Phone: (717) 564-4112   *Calendar:* Qtr. plan
Inst. Accred.: ACICS (1962/2002)

Chambersburg Campus
2593 Philadelphia Ave., Chambersburg 17201
Phone: (717) 709-9400

Philadelphia Campus
University City Science Center, 3010 Market St.,
Philadelphia 19104
Phone: (215) 594-4000
Prog. Accred: Medical Assisting (CAAHEP)

Tri-State Business Institute
5757 West 26th St., Erie 16506
Type: Private, proprietary, two-year
Degrees: A   *Enroll:* 295
URL: http://www.tsbi.org
Phone: (814) 838-7673
Inst. Accred.: ACICS (1990/2003)
Prog. Accred.: Medical Assisting (ABHES)

Triangle Tech
1940 Perrysville Ave., Pittsburgh 15214-3897
Type: Private, proprietary, two-year
Degrees: A   *Enroll:* 415
URL: http://www.triangle-tech.com
Phone: (412) 359-1000
Inst. Accred.: ACCSCT (1970/2003)

Triangle Tech
222 Pittsburgh St., Ste. A, Greensburg 15601
Type: Private, proprietary, two-year
Degrees: A   *Enroll:* 264
URL: http://www.triangle-tech.com
Phone: (724) 832-1050
Inst. Accred.: ACCSCT (1979/2003)

Triangle Tech
PO Box 551, DuBois 15801-9990
Type: Private, proprietary, two-year
Degrees: A   *Enroll:* 291
URL: http://www.triangle-tech.com
Phone: (814) 371-2090
Inst. Accred.: ACCSCT (1981/2003)

Triangle Tech
2000 Liberty St., Erie 16502-9987
Type: Private, proprietary, two-year
Degrees: A   *Enroll:* 167
URL: http://www.triangle-tech.com
Phone: (814) 453-6016
Inst. Accred.: ACCSCT (1978/2002)

Business Careers Institute
222 East Pittsburg St., Greensburg 15601-2394
Phone: (412) 834-1258

Business Careers Institute
1940 Perryville Ave., Pittsburgh 15214-3826
Phone: (412) 359-9000

Triangle Tech—Sunbury
RR #1, Box 51, Route 890, Sunbury 17801
Type: Private, proprietary, two-year
Degrees: A
URL: http://www.triangle-tech.com
Phone: (570) 988-0700
Inst. Accred.: ACCSCT (2002/2004)

Trinity Episcopal School for Ministry
311 Eleventh St., Ambridge 15003
Type: Private, Episcopal Church, four-year
Degrees: M   *Enroll:* 235
URL: http://www.tesm.edu
Phone: (724) 266-3838   *Calendar:* Sem. plan
Inst. Accred.: ATS (1985/1996)

United States Army War College
122 Forbes Ave., Carlisle 17013
Type: Public, federal, four-year
Degrees: M
URL: http://carlisle-www.army.mil
Phone: (717) 245-4101
Inst. Accred.: MSA-CHE (2004)

University of Pennsylvania
3451 Walnut St., Philadelphia 19104
Type: Private, independent, four-year
Degrees: A, B, M, P, D   *Enroll:* 20,675
URL: http://www.upenn.edu
Phone: (215) 898-5000   *Calendar:* Sem. plan
Inst. Accred.: MSA-CHE (1921/1999)
Prog. Accred.: Advanced Education in General Dentistry, Business (AACSB), Clinical Pastoral Education (ACPEI), Clinical Psychology, Combined Professional-Scientific Psychology, Dentistry, Endodontics, Engineering (bioengineering, chemical, civil, computer, electrical, materials, mechanical, systems), English Language Education, General Dentistry, General Practice Residency, Health Services Administration, Landscape Architecture, Law, Medicine, Microbiology, Nurse (Midwifery), Nursing, Oral and Maxillofacial Surgery, Orthodontic and Dentofacial Orthopedics, Pediatric Dentistry, Periodontics, Planning, Practical Nursing, Psychology Internship, Radiography, Social Work, Veterinary Medicine

University of Pittsburgh
4200 Fifth Ave., Pittsburgh 15260
Type: Public, state-related, four-year
Degrees: A, B, M, P, D   *Enroll:* 23,552
URL: http://www.pitt.edu
Phone: (412) 624-4200   *Calendar:* Sem. plan
Inst. Accred.: MSA-CHE (1921/2002)
Prog. Accred.: Advanced Education in General Dentistry,
Athletic Training, Audiology, Business (AACSB),
Combined Prosthodontics, Counseling, Cytotechnology,
Dental Hygiene, Dental Public Health, Dentistry,
Dietetics (coordinated), Endodontics, Engineering
(bioengineering, chemical, civil, computer, electrical,
engineering physics/science, industrial, materials,
mechanical, metallurgical), English Language
Education, General Dentistry, Health Information
Administration, Health Services Administration, Law,
Librarianship, Maxillofacial Prosthetics, Medicine, Nurse
Anesthesia Education, Nursing, Nursing Education,
Occupational Therapy, Oral and Maxillofacial Surgery,
Orthodontic and Dentofacial Orthopedics, Pediatric
Dentistry, Periodontics, Pharmacy, Physical Therapy,
Psychology Internship, Public Administration, Public
Health, Social Work, Speech-Language Pathology,
Theatre

Bradford Campus
300 Campus Dr., Bradford 16701
Phone: (814) 362-7500
Prog. Accred: Nursing

Greensburg Campus
1150 Mount Pleasant Rd., Greensburg 15601
Phone: (724) 837-7040

Johnstown Campus
450 Schoolhouse Rd., Johnstown 15904
Phone: (814) 269-7000
Prog. Accred: Engineering Technology
(civil/construction, electrical, mechanical),
Respiratory Therapy

Titusville Campus
504 East Main St., Titusville 16354
Phone: (814) 827-4400
Prog. Accred: Physical Therapy Assisting

University of Pittsburgh Medical Center Northwest
100 Fairfield Dr., Seneca 16346
Phone: (814) 676-7600
Prog. Accred: Radiography

University of Pittsburgh Medical Center Presbyterian
200 Lothrop St., Pittsburgh 15213-2582
Phone: (412) 647-2345
Prog. Accred: Radiography

University of Scranton
800 Linden St., Scranton 18510-4501
Type: Private, Roman Catholic Church, four-year
Degrees: A, B, M   *Enroll:* 4,265
URL: http://www.uofs.edu
Phone: (570) 941-7500   *Calendar:* Sem. plan
Inst. Accred.: MSA-CHE (1927/2003)
Prog. Accred.: Business (AACSB), Computer Science,
Counseling, Health Services Administration, Nurse
Anesthesia Education, Nursing, Nursing Education,
Occupational Therapy, Physical Therapy, Rehabilitation
Counseling, Teacher Education (NCATE)

University of the Arts
320 South Broad St., Philadelphia 19102
Type: Private, independent, four-year
Degrees: B, M   *Enroll:* 2,074
URL: http://www.uarts.edu
Phone: (215) 717-6000   *Calendar:* Sem. plan
Inst. Accred.: MSA-CHE (1969/1999)
Prog. Accred.: Art, Music

University of the Sciences in Philadelphia
600 South 43rd St., Philadelphia 19104-4495
Type: Private, independent, four-year
Degrees: B, M, P, D   *Enroll:* 2,448
URL: http://www.usip.edu
Phone: (215) 596-8800   *Calendar:* Sem. plan
Inst. Accred.: MSA-CHE (1962/2003)
Prog. Accred.: Occupational Therapy, Pharmacy, Physical
Therapy

Ursinus College
Box 1000, Collegeville 19426-1000
Type: Private, independent, four-year
Degrees: A, B   *Enroll:* 1,475
URL: http://www.ursinus.edu
Phone: (610) 489-3000   *Calendar:* Sem. plan
Inst. Accred.: MSA-CHE (1921/1999)

Valley Forge Christian College
1401 Charlestown Rd., Phoenixville 19460-2399
Type: Private, Assemblies of God Church, four-year
Degrees: B   *Enroll:* 821
URL: http://www.vfcc.edu
Phone: (610) 935-0450   *Calendar:* Sem. plan
Inst. Accred.: MSA-CHE (2002)

Valley Forge Military College
1001 Eagle Rd., Wayne 19087-3695
Type: Private, independent, two-year
Degrees: A   *Enroll:* 228
URL: http://www.vfmac.edu
Phone: (610) 989-1200   *Calendar:* Sem. plan
Inst. Accred.: MSA-CHE (1954/2000)

Villanova University
800 Lancaster Ave., Villanova 19085-1699
Type: Private, Roman Catholic Church, four-year
Degrees: A, B, M, P, D   *Enroll:* 8,952
URL: http://www.villanova.edu
Phone: (610) 519-4500   *Calendar:* Sem. plan
Inst. Accred.: MSA-CHE (1921/2001)
Prog. Accred.: Accounting, Business (AACSB), Computer
Science, Engineering (chemical, civil, computer,
electrical, mechanical), Law, Nurse Anesthesia
Education, Nursing, Nursing Education

Washington and Jefferson College
60 South Lincoln St., Washington 15301-4801
Type: Private, independent, four-year
Degrees: A, B   *Enroll:* 1,224
URL: http://www.washjeff.edu
Phone: (724) 222-4400   *Calendar:* 4-1-4 plan
Inst. Accred.: MSA-CHE (1921/1999)

Waynesburg College
51 West College St., Waynesburg 15370
Type: Private, Presbyterian Church (USA), four-year
Degrees: A, B, M   *Enroll:* 1,526
URL: http://www.waynesburg.edu
Phone: (724) 627-8191   *Calendar:* Sem. plan
Inst. Accred.: MSA-CHE (1950/2000)
Prog. Accred.: Athletic Training, Nursing, Nursing
Education

West Chester University of Pennsylvania
South High St., West Chester 19383
Type: Public, state, four-year
System: Pennsylvania State System of Higher Education
Degrees: B, M   *Enroll:* 10,875
URL: http://www.wcupa.edu
Phone: (610) 436-1000   *Calendar:* Sem. plan
Inst. Accred.: MSA-CHE (1946/2001)
Prog. Accred.: Athletic Training, Business (AACSB), Music,
Nursing, Nursing Education, Public Health, Respiratory
Therapy, Social Work, Speech-Language Pathology,
Teacher Education (NCATE)

Western School of Health and Business Careers
421 Seventh Ave., Pittsburgh 15219
Type: Private, proprietary, two-year
System: Career Education Corporation
Degrees: A
URL: http://www.westernschoolpitt.com
Phone: (412) 281-2600
Inst. Accred.: ACCSCT (1986/2001)
Prog. Accred.: Medical Assisting (ABHES), Radiography,
Respiratory Therapy

Monroeville Campus
One Monroeville Center, Ste. 250, Route 22 and 3824
Northern Pike, Monroeville 15146-2142
Phone: (412) 373-6400
Prog. Accred: Medical Assisting (ABHES)

Westminster College
319 South Market St., New Wilmington 16172-0001
Type: Private, Presbyterian Church, four-year
Degrees: B, M   *Enroll:* 1,522
URL: http://www.westminster.edu
Phone: (724) 946-8761   *Calendar:* Sem. plan
Inst. Accred.: MSA-CHE (1921/2001)
Prog. Accred.: Music

Westminster Theological Seminary
960 West Church Rd., Glenside 19038
Type: Private, interdenominational, four-year
Degrees: M, P, D   *Enroll:* 540
URL: http://www.wts.edu
Phone: (215) 887-5511   *Calendar:* Sem. plan
Inst. Accred.: ATS (1986/2001), MSA-CHE (1954/2002)

Westmoreland County Community College
400 Armbrust Rd., Youngwood 15697-1895
Type: Public, state/local, two-year
Degrees: A   *Enroll:* 3,809
URL: http://www.wccc-pa.edu
Phone: (724) 925-4001   *Calendar:* Sem. plan
Inst. Accred.: MSA-CHE (1978/2003)
Prog. Accred.: Culinary Education, Dental Assisting,
Dental Hygiene

Widener University
One University Place, Chester 19013-5792
Type: Private, independent, four-year
Degrees: A, B, M, P, D   *Enroll:* 3,276
URL: http://www.widener.edu
Phone: (610) 499-4100   *Calendar:* Sem. plan
Inst. Accred.: MSA-CHE (1954/2001)
Prog. Accred.: Business (AACSB), Clinical Psychology,
Engineering (chemical, civil, electrical, mechanical),
Health Services Administration, Nursing, Physical
Therapy, Psychology Internship, Social Work

Harrisburg Campus
3800 Vartan Way, Harrisburg 17110-9450
Phone: (717) 541-3900
Prog. Accred: Law (ABA only)

School of Law Campus
4601 Concord Pike, PO Box 7474, Wilmington, DE
19803-0474
Phone: (302) 477-2100
Prog. Accred: Law

Wilkes University
170 South Franklin St., PO Box 111, Wilkes-Barre 18766-
0001
Type: Private, independent, four-year
Degrees: B, M, P   *Enroll:* 3,013
URL: http://www.wilkes.edu
Phone: (570) 408-5000   *Calendar:* Sem. plan
Inst. Accred.: MSA-CHE (1937/2005)
Prog. Accred.: Business (ACBSP), Engineering (electrical,
environmental/sanitary, mechanical), Nursing, Nursing
Education, Pharmacy

The Williamson Free School of Mechanical Trades
106 South New Middletown Rd., Media 19063-5299
Type: Private, independent, two-year
Degrees: A   *FTE Enroll:* 250
URL: http://www.williamsonschool.org
Phone: (610) 566-1776   *Calendar:* Sem. plan
Inst. Accred.: ACCSCT (1970/2003)

Wilson College
1015 Philadelphia Ave., Chambersburg 17201-1285
Type: Private, Presbyterian Church, four-year
Degrees: A, B   *Enroll:* 551
URL: http://www.wilson.edu
Phone: (717) 264-4141   *Calendar:* 4-1-4 plan
Inst. Accred.: MSA-CHE (1922/2003)
Prog. Accred.: Veterinary Technology

Winner Institute of Arts and Sciences
One Winner Place, Transfer 16154
Type: Private, proprietary, two-year
Degrees: A
URL: http://www.winner-institute.com
Phone: (724) 646-2433
Inst. Accred.: COE (2003)
Prog. Accred.: Culinary Education

WyoTech—Blairsville
500 Innovation Dr., Blairsville 15717
Type: Private, proprietary, two-year
Degrees: A
URL: http://www.wyotech.com
Phone: (724) 459-9500
Inst. Accred.: ACCSCT (2001/2003)

Yeshiva Beth Moshe
930 Hickory St., PO Box 1141, Scranton 18505
Type: Private, independent, four-year
Degrees: Talmudic   *Enroll:* 47
Phone: (570) 346-1747   *Calendar:* Sem. plan
Inst. Accred.: AARTS (1976/2000)

York College of Pennsylvania
Country Club Rd., York 17405-7199
Type: Private, independent, four-year
Degrees: A, B, M   *Enroll:* 4,749
URL: http://www.ycp.edu
Phone: (717) 846-7788   *Calendar:* Sem. plan
Inst. Accred.: MSA-CHE (1959/2001)
Prog. Accred.: Business (ACBSP), Engineering
   (mechanical), Nursing, Recreation and Leisure Services,
   Respiratory Therapy, Respiratory Therapy Technology

York Technical Institute
1405 Williams Rd., York 17402-9017
Type: Private, proprietary, two-year
Degrees: A   *Enroll:* 1,297
URL: http://www.yti.edu
Phone: (717) 757-1100   *Calendar:* Qtr. plan
Inst. Accred.: ACCSCT (1979/2001)

Lancaster Campus
3050 Hempland Rd., Lancaster 17601
   Phone: (717) 295-1135

Yorktowne Business Institute
West Seventh Ave., York 17404
Type: Private, proprietary, two-year
Degrees: A   *Enroll:* 334
URL: http://www.ybi.edu
Phone: (717) 846-5000
Inst. Accred.: ACICS (1979/2003)

PUERTO RICO

American University of Puerto Rico
PO Box 2037, Bayamon 00960-2037
Type: Private, independent, four-year
Degrees: A, B, M   *Enroll:* 1,519
URL: http://www.aupr.edu
Phone: (787) 620-2040   *Calendar:* Sem. plan
Inst. Accred.: MSA-CHE (1982/2002)

Manati Campus
PO Box 1082, Manati 00701
Phone: (809) 854-2835

Atlantic College
PO Box 3918, Guaynabo 00970
Type: Private, independent, four-year
Degrees: A, B   *Enroll:* 594
URL: http://www.atlanticcollege-pr.com
Phone: (787) 720-1022   *Calendar:* Tri. plan
Inst. Accred.: ACICS (1987/2005)

Bayamon Central University
PO Box 1725, Bayamon 00960-1725
Type: Private, Roman Catholic Church, four-year
Degrees: A, B, M   *Enroll:* 2,993
URL: http://www.ucb.edu.pr
Phone: (787) 786-3030   *Calendar:* Sem. plan
Inst. Accred.: MSA-CHE (1971/2005)

Caribbean University
Box 493, Road 167, Km 21.2, Ave. Comerio, Bayamon
00960-0493
Type: Private, independent, four-year
Degrees: A, B, M   *Enroll:* 1,318
URL: http://www.caribbean.edu
Phone: (787) 780-0070   *Calendar:* Sem. plan
Inst. Accred.: MSA-CHE (1977/2001)

Carlos Albizu University—San Juan Campus
PO Box 9023711, 151 Tanca St., Old San Juan, San Juan
00902-3711
Type: Private, independent, four-year
System: Carlos Albizu—Central Administration
Degrees: B, M, D   *Enroll:* 644
URL: http://www.albizu.edu
Phone: (787) 725-6500   *Calendar:* Sem. plan
Inst. Accred.: MSA-CHE (1974/2005)
Prog. Accred.: Clinical Psychology

Centro de Estudios Avanzados de Puerto Rico y El Caribe
PO Box 9023970, San Juan 00902-3970
Type: Private, independent, four-year
Degrees: M, D   *FTE Enroll:* 609
Phone: (787) 723-4481   *Calendar:* Sem. plan
Inst. Accred.: MSA-CHE (1982/2003)

Colegio Biblico Pentecostal de Puerto Rico
Road 848 Km. 0.5 Entrada Los Marquez, PO Box 901,
Saint Just 00978-0901
Type: Private, Church of God, four-year
Degrees: B   *Enroll:* 165
URL: http://www.cbp.edu
Phone: (787) 761-0640   *Calendar:* Sem. plan
Inst. Accred.: ABHE (1990/1996)

Colegio Pentecostal Mizpa
PO Box 20966, San Juan 00928-0966
Type: Private, Pentecostal Church of God, four-year
Degrees: A, B
URL: http://www.colmizpa.edu
Phone: (787) 720-4476   *Calendar:* Sem. plan
Inst. Accred.: ABHE (1997/2001)

Columbia Center University
PO Box 8517, Caguas 00726
Type: Private, proprietary, four-year
Degrees: A, B, M   *Enroll:* 604
URL: http://www.columbiaco.edu
Phone: (787) 743-4041   *Calendar:* Sem. plan
Inst. Accred.: ACICS (1976/2001)

Yauco Campus
PO Box 3060, Yauco 00698-3060
Phone: (787) 856-0845

Conservatory of Music of Puerto Rico
350 Rafael Lamar St., San Juan 00918-2127
Type: Public, independent, four-year
Degrees: B   *Enroll:* 244
URL: http://www.cmpr.edu
Phone: (787) 751-0160   *Calendar:* Sem. plan
Inst. Accred.: MSA-CHE (1975/2001)
Prog. Accred.: Music

Dominican Study Center of the Caribbean
Apartado Postal 1968, Bayamon 00960-1968
Type: Private, Roman Catholic Church, four-year
Degrees: M
URL: http://www.cedocpr.org
Phone: (787) 787-1826
Inst. Accred.: ATS (2005)

Electronic Data Processing College
560 Ponce De Leon Ave., Hato Rey 00919
Type: Private, proprietary, four-year
Degrees: A, B, M   *Enroll:* 878
URL: http://www.edpcollege.com
Phone: (787) 765-3560   *Calendar:* Sem. plan
Inst. Accred.: ACICS (1976/2002)

San Sebastian Campus
48 Betances St., PO Box 1674, San Sebastian 00685
Phone: (787) 896-2137

Escuela de Artes Plasticas de Puerto Rico
PO Box 9021112, San Juan 00902-1112
Type: Public, state, four-year
Degrees: B   *Enroll:* 368
URL: http://www.eap.gobierno.pr
Phone: (787) 725-8120   *Calendar:* Sem. plan
Inst. Accred.: MSA-CHE (1997/2002)

Evangelical Seminary of Puerto Rico
776 Ponce de Leon Ave., San Juan 00925-2207
Type: Private, interdenominational, four-year
Degrees: M, P   *Enroll:* 74
URL: http://www.seminarioevangelicopr.org
Phone: (787) 763-6700   *Calendar:* Sem. plan
Inst. Accred.: ATS (1982/1997), MSA-CHE (1995/2005)

Huertas Junior College
PO Box 8429, Caguas 00726
Type: Private, proprietary, two-year
Degrees: A   *Enroll:* 1,374
URL: http://www.huertasjrcollege.org
Phone: (787) 743-1242   *Calendar:* Tri. plan
Inst. Accred.: ACICS (1977/2005)
Prog. Accred.: Health Information Technician

Humacao Community College
PO Box 9139, Humacao 00792
Type: Private, independent, two-year
Degrees: A   *Enroll:* 385
Phone: (787) 852-1430   *Calendar:* Tri. plan
Inst. Accred.: ACICS (1979/2000)

Fajardo Campus
PO Box 1185, Gerrido Morales No. 52, Fajardo 00738
Phone: (809) 863-5210

Instituto Comercial de Puerto Rico Junior College
558 Munoz Riviera Ave., PO Box 190304, San Juan 00919-0304
Type: Private, proprietary, two-year
Degrees: A   *Enroll:* 389
URL: http://www.icprjc.edu
Phone: (787) 753-6335   *Calendar:* Tri. plan
Inst. Accred.: MSA-CHE (1985/2002)

Arecibo Campus
Road 2, KM 80.4, San Daniel Box 1606, Arecibo 00614-0067
Phone: (787) 878-0524

Mayaguez Campus
Mendez Vigo No. 55, PO Box 1108, Mayaguez 00708-1108
Phone: (809) 832-2250

McKinley Street Campus
McKinley St. 80 West, Mayaguez 00681-1108
Phone: (787) 832-6000

Inter American University of Puerto Rico Aguadilla Campus
Call Box 20000, Road 459 Int. 463, Aguadilla 00605-2000
Type: Private, independent, four-year
System: Inter American University of Puerto Rico Central Office of the System
Degrees: A, B, M   *Enroll:* 3,822
URL: http://www.interaguadilla.edu
Phone: (787) 891-0925   *Calendar:* Sem. plan
Inst. Accred.: MSA-CHE (1957/2003)

Inter American University of Puerto Rico Arecibo Campus
PO Box 4050, Arecibo 00614-4050
Type: Private, independent, four-year
System: Inter American University of Puerto Rico Central Office of the System
Degrees: A, B, M   *Enroll:* 3,945
URL: http://www.arecibo.inter.edu
Phone: (787) 878-5475   *Calendar:* Sem. plan
Inst. Accred.: MSA-CHE (1957/2003)
Prog. Accred.: Nurse Anesthesia Education, Social Work

Inter American University of Puerto Rico Barranquitas Campus
PO Box 517, Barranquitas 00794-0517
Type: Private, independent, four-year
System: Inter American University of Puerto Rico Central Office of the System
Degrees: A, B   *Enroll:* 2,058
URL: http://www.br.inter.edu
Phone: (787) 857-4040   *Calendar:* Sem. plan
Inst. Accred.: MSA-CHE (1957/2003)

Inter American University of Puerto Rico Bayamon Campus
500 Rd. Dr., John Will Harris, Bayamon 00957
Type: Private, independent, four-year
System: Inter American University of Puerto Rico Central Office of the System
Degrees: A, B   *Enroll:* 4,732
URL: http://www.bc.inter.edu
Phone: (787) 279-1912   *Calendar:* Sem. plan
Inst. Accred.: MSA-CHE (1960/2003)

Inter American University of Puerto Rico Fajardo Campus
Call Box 70003, Fajardo 00738-7003
Type: Private, independent, four-year
System: Inter American University of Puerto Rico Central Office of the System
Degrees: A, B   *Enroll:* 1,903
URL: http://www.fajardo.inter.edu
Phone: (787) 863-2390   *Calendar:* Sem. plan
Inst. Accred.: MSA-CHE (1961/2003)

Inter American University of Puerto Rico
Guayama Campus
PO Box 10004, Guayama 00785
Type: Private, independent, four-year
System: Inter American University of Puerto Rico Central
Office of the System
Degrees: A, B, M   *Enroll:* 2,027
URL: http://guayama.inter.edu
Phone: (787) 864-2222   *Calendar:* Sem. plan
Inst. Accred.: MSA-CHE (1957/2003)

Inter American University of Puerto Rico
Metropolitan Campus
PO Box 191293, San Juan 00919-1293
Type: Private, indepenednt, four-year
System: Inter American University of Puerto Rico Central
Office of the System
Degrees: A, B, M, P, D   *Enroll:* 7,677
URL: http://www.metro.inter.edu
Phone: (787) 250-1912   *Calendar:* Sem. plan
Inst. Accred.: MSA-CHE (1960/2003)
Prog. Accred.: Clinical Lab Scientist, Nursing, Optometry,
Social Work

Inter American University of Puerto Rico
Ponce Campus
Road #1 Km 123.2 Interior, Mercedita Ponce 00715
Type: Private, independent, four-year
System: Inter American University of Puerto Rico Central
Office of the System
Degrees: A, B   *Enroll:* 4,624
URL: http://ponce.inter.edu
Phone: (787) 284-1912   *Calendar:* Sem. plan
Inst. Accred.: MSA-CHE (1962/2003)

Inter American University of Puerto Rico
San German Campus
PO Box 5100, San German 00683
Type: Private, independent, four-year
System: Inter American University of Puerto Rico Central
Office of the System
Degrees: A, B, M, D
URL: http://www.sg.inter.edu
Phone: (787) 264-1912   *Calendar:* Sem. plan
Inst. Accred.: MSA-CHE (1944/2003)
Prog. Accred.: Clinical Lab Scientist, Health Information
Technician

Inter American University of Puerto Rico
School of Law
PO Box 70351, San Juan 00936-8351
Type: Private, independent, four-year
System: Inter American University of Puerto Rico Central
Office of the System
Degrees: P   *Enroll:* 667
URL: http://www.derecho.inter.edu
Phone: (787) 751-1912   *Calendar:* Sem. plan
Inst. Accred.: MSA-CHE (1961/2003)
Prog. Accred.: Law (ABA only)

Inter American University of Puerto Rico
School of Optometry
118 Eleanor Roosevelt St., Hato Ray 00919
Type: Private, independent, four-year
System: Inter American University of Puerto Rico Central
Office of the System
Degrees: P   *Enroll:* 166
URL: http://www.optonet.inter.edu
Phone: (787) 765-1915   *Calendar:* Sem. plan
Inst. Accred.: MSA-CHE (1981/2003)

International Junior College
PO Box 19828, San Juan 00910-1828
Type: Private, proprietary, two-year
Degrees: A   *Enroll:* 182
Phone: (787) 724-5858
Inst. Accred.: ACICS (1984/2005)

Caguas Campus
Calle Baldorioty #1, Bayamon 00961
Phone: (787) 746-3777

Humacao Campus
Calle Dr. Carreras #6, Ste. 414, Humacao 00791
Phone: (787) 850-0055

Ponce Campus
57 Estrella St., PO Box 1284, Ponce 00731
Phone: (787) 844-5325

John Dewey College
427 Ave Barbosa, San Juan 00923-1524
Type: Private, proprietary, four-year
Degrees: B
URL: http://www.johndeweycollege.com
Phone: (787) 753-0039
Inst. Accred.: ACICS (1994/2004)

Bayamon Campus
Carr. #2, Km 15.9 Bo. Hato Tejas, Bayamon 00959
Phone: (787) 778-1200

Carolina Campus
Carr. #3, Km 11 lote 7, Carolina Industrial Park,
Carolina 00986
Phone: (787) 769-1515

National College of Business and Technology
Ramos Bldg., Hwy. No. 2, PO Box 2036, Bayamon 00960
Type: Private, proprietary, four-year
Degrees: A, B   *Enroll:* 2,159
URL: http://www.nationalcollegepr.edu
Phone: (787) 780-5134   *Calendar:* Tri. plan
Inst. Accred.: ACICS (1983/2001)

Arecibo Campus
PO Box 4035, Arecibo 00614
Phone: (787) 879-5044

Rio Grande Campus
State Rd. #3 Km.22.1, Barrio Cienaga, Rio Grande
00745
Phone: (787) 780-5134

Ponce Paramedical College
PO Box 800106, Coto Laurel 00780-0106
Type: Private, independent, two-year
Degrees: A
URL: http://ponce.library.net
Phone: (787) 848-1589
Inst. Accred.: ACCSCT (1987/2003)
Prog. Accred.: Respiratory Therapy Technology

Ponce School of Medicine
PO Box 7004, Ponce 00732
Type: Private, independent, four-year
Degrees: P, D   *Enroll:* 445
URL: http://www.psm.edu
Phone: (787) 840-2575   *Calendar:* Sem. plan
Inst. Accred.: MSA-CHE (2003)
Prog. Accred.: Clinical Psychology, Medicine

Pontifical Catholic University of Puerto Rico—Arecibo Campus
PO Box 144045, Arecibo 00614-4045
Type: Private, Roman Catholic Church, four-year
Degrees: A, B, M   *Enroll:* 702
URL: http://www.pucpr.edu
Phone: (787) 881-1212   *Calendar:* Sem. plan
Inst. Accred.: MSA-CHE (1981/1998)

Pontifical Catholic University of Puerto Rico—Guayama Campus
5 South Palmer St., Guayama 00784
Type: Private, Roman Catholic Church, four-year
Degrees: A, B   *FTE Enroll:* 352
URL: http://www.pucpr.edu
Phone: (787) 864-0550   *Calendar:* Sem. plan
Inst. Accred.: MSA-CHE (1962/1998)

Pontifical Catholic University of Puerto Rico—Mayaguez Campus
482 South Post St., PO Box 1326, Mayaguez 00681
Type: Private, Roman Catholic Church, four-year
Degrees: A, B, M   *Enroll:* 1,608
URL: http://www.pucpr.edu
Phone: (787) 834-5151   *Calendar:* Sem. plan
Inst. Accred.: MSA-CHE (1962/2004)

Pontifical Catholic University of Puerto Rico—Ponce Campus
2250 Avenida las Americas, Ste. 564, Ponce 00717-0777
Type: Private, Roman Catholic Church, four-year
Degrees: A, B, M, P, D   *Enroll:* 6,303
URL: http://www.pucpr.edu
Phone: (787) 841-2000   *Calendar:* Sem. plan
Inst. Accred.: MSA-CHE (1953/2004)
Prog. Accred.: Clinical Lab Scientist, Law (ABA only), Nursing, Social Work

Seminario Major San Juan Bautista
PO Box 11714, San Juan 00922-1714
Phone: (787) 783-0645

Puerto Rico Technical Junior College
Avenida Ponce de Leon No. 703, Hato Rey 00917
Type: Private, proprietary, two-year
Degrees: A   *Enroll:* 285
Phone: (787) 751-0133
Inst. Accred.: ACCSCT (1992/2002, Probation)

Mayaguez Campus
Calle Santiago R. Palmer #15 Est, Mayaguez 00680
Phone: (787) 832-2762

Ramirez College of Business and Technology
PO Box 195460, San Juan 00910-5460
Type: Private, proprietary, two-year
Degrees: A   *Enroll:* 423
Phone: (787) 831-3755   *Calendar:* Tri. plan
Inst. Accred.: ACICS (1975/2001)

Mayaguez Campus
61 Pilar Defillo Avenida, Mayaguez 00680
Phone: (787) 831-3755

San Juan Bautista School of Medicine
PO Box 4968, Luis Munoz Marin Ave., Caguas 00726-4968
Type: Private, independent, four-year
Degrees: P   *Enroll:* 156
URL: http://www.sanjuanbautista.edu
Phone: (787) 743-3038   *Calendar:* Sem. plan
Inst. Accred.: MSA-CHE (2004)

Universal Technology College of Puerto Rico
Apartado 1955, Victoria Station, Aguadilla 00605
Type: Private, proprietary, two-year
Degrees: A
URL: http://www.unitecpr.net
Phone: (787) 882-2065   *Calendar:* Qtr. plan
Inst. Accred.: ACCSCT (2000)

Universidad Adventista de las Antillas
PO Box 118, Mayaguez 00681
Type: Private, Seventh-Day Adventist Church, four-year
Degrees: A, B, M   *Enroll:* 809
URL: http://www.uaa.edu
Phone: (787) 834-9595   *Calendar:* Sem. plan
Inst. Accred.: MSA-CHE (1978/2003)
Prog. Accred.: Health Information Technician, Respiratory Therapy

Universidad Central del Caribe
PO Box 60327, Bayamon 00960-6032
Type: Private, independent, four-year
Degrees: M, P   *Enroll:* 353
URL: http://www.uccaribe.edu
Phone: (787) 798-3001   *Calendar:* Sem. plan
Inst. Accred.: MSA-CHE (2003)
Prog. Accred.: Medicine, Radiography

Universidad del Este
PO Box 2010, Carolina 00983-2010
Type: Private, independent, four-year
System: Sistema Universitario Ana G. Mendez Central
   Office
Degrees: A, B, M   *Enroll:* 8,332
URL: http://www.suagm.edu/une
Phone: (787) 257-7373   *Calendar:* Sem. plan
Inst. Accred.: MSA-CHE (1959/2005)
Prog. Accred.: Health Information Technician

Universidad del Turabo
Box 3030, Gurabo 00778-3030
Type: Private, independent, four-year
System: Sistema Universitario Ana G. Mendez Central
   Office
Degrees: A, B, M, D   *Enroll:* 10,763
URL: http://www.suagm.edu/ut
Phone: (787) 743-7979   *Calendar:* Sem. plan
Inst. Accred.: MSA-CHE (1974/2005)
Prog. Accred.: Nursing Education

Universidad Metropolitana
Box 21150, Rio Piedras 00928-1150
Type: Private, independent, four-year
System: Sistema Universitario Ana G. Mendez Central
   Office
Degrees: A, B, M   *Enroll:* 7,513
URL: http://www.suagm.edu/umet
Phone: (787) 766-1717   *Calendar:* Sem. plan
Inst. Accred.: MSA-CHE (1980/2002)
Prog. Accred.: Nursing, Respiratory Therapy

Universidad Politecnica de Puerto Rico
Box 192017, San Juan 00919-2017
Type: Private, independent, four-year
Degrees: B, M   *Enroll:* 4,049
URL: http://www.pupr.edu
Phone: (787) 622-8000   *Calendar:* Tri. plan
Inst. Accred.: MSA-CHE (1985/2005)
Prog. Accred.: Engineering (civil, electrical,
   environmental/sanitary, industrial, mechanical)

Polytechnic University of the Americas
PO Box 526223, Miami, FL 33152-6223
Phone: (305) 418-4220

University College of San Juan
180 Jose Oliver St., Urban Tres Monijitas, San Juan
00918
Type: Public, state/local, four-year
Degrees: A, B   *Enroll:* 810
URL: http://www.cunisanjuan.edu
Phone: (787) 250-7111   *Calendar:* Sem. plan
Inst. Accred.: MSA-CHE (1978/2002)
Prog. Accred.: Nursing

University of Puerto Rico at Aguadilla
PO Box 250160, Aguadilla 00604-0160
Type: Public, state, four-year
System: University of Puerto Rico Central Administration
Degrees: A, B   *Enroll:* 3,086
URL: http://www.cuna.upr.edu
Phone: (787) 890-2681   *Calendar:* Sem. plan
Inst. Accred.: MSA-CHE (1976/2001)

University of Puerto Rico at Arecibo
PO Box 4010, Arecibo 00614-4010
Type: Public, state, four-year
System: University of Puerto Rico Central Administration
Degrees: A, B   *Enroll:* 4,103
URL: http://www.upra.edu
Phone: (787) 878-2831   *Calendar:* Sem. plan
Inst. Accred.: MSA-CHE (1967/1999, Warning)
Prog. Accred.: Nursing

University of Puerto Rico at Bayamon
#170 Call.174 Parque Industria Minillas, Bayamon
00959-1919
Type: Public, state, four-year
System: University of Puerto Rico Central Administration
Degrees: A, B   *Enroll:* 4,592
URL: http://www.uprb.edu
Phone: (787) 786-2885   *Calendar:* Sem. plan
Inst. Accred.: MSA-CHE (1960/2001)

University of Puerto Rico at Carolina
PO Box 4800, Carolina 00984-4800
Type: Public, state, four-year
System: University of Puerto Rico Central Administration
Degrees: A, B   *Enroll:* 3,587
URL: http://www.upr.clu.edu
Phone: (787) 257-0000   *Calendar:* Tri. plan
Inst. Accred.: MSA-CHE (1978/2001)

University of Puerto Rico at Cayey
205 Antonio R. Barcelo Ave., Cayey 00736
Type: Public, state, four-year
System: University of Puerto Rico Central Administration
Degrees: A, B   *Enroll:* 3,753
URL: http://www.cayey.upr.edu
Phone: (787) 738-2161   *Calendar:* Sem. plan
Inst. Accred.: MSA-CHE (1967/2005)

University of Puerto Rico at Humacao
CUH Station, 100 Rd. 908, Humacao 00791-4300
Type: Public, state, four-year
System: University of Puerto Rico Central Administration
Degrees: A, B   *Enroll:* 3,983
URL: http://www.uprh.edu
Phone: (787) 850-0000   *Calendar:* Sem. plan
Inst. Accred.: MSA-CHE (1962/2000)
Prog. Accred.: Nursing, Occupational Therapy,
   Occupational Therapy Assisting, Physical Therapy
   Assisting, Social Work

University of Puerto Rico at Mayaguez
PO Box 9000, Mayaguez 00681
Type: Public, state, four-year
System: University of Puerto Rico Central Administration
Degrees: A, B, M, D   *Enroll:* 11,417
URL: http://www.uprm.edu
Phone: (787) 832-4040   *Calendar:* Sem. plan
Inst. Accred.: MSA-CHE (1946/2005)
Prog. Accred.: Engineering (chemical, civil, computer,
   electrical, industrial, mechanical), Nursing

University of Puerto Rico at Ponce
PO Box 7186, Ponce 00732
Type: Public, state, four-year
System: University of Puerto Rico Central Administration
Degrees: A, B   *Enroll:* 3,431
URL: http://www.upr-ponce.upr.edu
Phone: (787) 844-8181   *Calendar:* Sem. plan
Inst. Accred.: MSA-CHE (1970/2005)
Prog. Accred.: Physical Therapy Assisting

University of Puerto Rico at Rio Piedras
PO Box 23300, San Juan 00931-3300
Type: Public, state, four-year
System: University of Puerto Rico Central Administration
Degrees: B, M, P, D   *Enroll:* 18,238
URL: http://www.rrp.upr.edu
Phone: (787) 764-0000   *Calendar:* Sem. plan
Inst. Accred.: MSA-CHE (1946/2005)
Prog. Accred.: Law, Librarianship, Oral and Maxillofacial
   Surgery, Planning, Rehabilitation Counseling, Social
   Work

University of Puerto Rico at Utuado
PO Box 2500, Utuado 00641
Type: Public, state, four-year
System: University of Puerto Rico Central Administration
Degrees: A, B   *Enroll:* 1,543
URL: http://upr-utuado.upr.clu.edu
Phone: (787) 894-2828   *Calendar:* Sem. plan
Inst. Accred.: MSA-CHE (1986/2001)

University of Puerto Rico—Medical Sciences Campus
PO Box 365067, San Juan 00936-5067
Type: Public, state, four-year
System: University of Puerto Rico Central Administration
Degrees: A, B, M, P, D   *Enroll:* 2,194
URL: http://www.rcm.upr.edu
Phone: (787) 758-2525   *Calendar:* Sem. plan
Inst. Accred.: MSA-CHE (1949/2001)
Prog. Accred.: Clinical Lab Scientist, Combined
   Prosthodontics, Cytotechnology, Dental Assisting, Dental
   Hygiene, Dentistry, Dietetics (internship), General
   Practice Residency, Health Information Administration,
   Health Services Administration, Medicine, Nuclear
   Medicine Technology, Nurse (Midwifery), Nurse
   Anesthesia Education, Nursing, Nursing Education,
   Occupational Therapy, Ophthalmic Medical Technology,
   Oral and Maxillofacial Surgery, Orthodontic and
   Dentofacial Orthopedics, Pediatric Dentistry, Pharmacy,
   Physical Therapy, Public Health, Radiography,
   Respiratory Therapy, Veterinary Technology

University of the Sacred Heart
Box 12383, San Juan 00914-0383
Type: Private, Roman Catholic Church, four-year
Degrees: A, B, M   *Enroll:* 4,025
URL: http://www.sagrado.edu
Phone: (787) 728-1515   *Calendar:* Sem. plan
Inst. Accred.: MSA-CHE (1950/2003)
Prog. Accred.: Clinical Lab Scientist, Nursing, Social Work

RHODE ISLAND

Brown University
Providence 02912
Type: Private, independent, four-year
Degrees: B, M, P, D*Enroll:* 7,649
URL: http://www.brown.edu
Phone: (401) 863-1000*Calendar:* Sem. plan
Inst. Accred.: NEASC-CIHE (1929/1998)
Prog. Accred.: Engineering (chemical, civil, electrical, materials, mechanical), Medicine, Psychology Internship, Public Health

Bryant University
1150 Douglas Pike, Smithfield 02917-1284
Type: Private, independent, four-year
Degrees: A, B, M*Enroll:* 3,051
URL: http://www.bryant.edu
Phone: (401) 232-6000*Calendar:* Sem. plan
Inst. Accred.: NEASC-CIHE (1964/2000)
Prog. Accred.: Business (AACSB)

Community College of Rhode Island
400 East Ave., Warwick 02886-1807
Type: Public, state, two-year
System: Rhode Island Board of Governors for Higher Education
Degrees: A*Enroll:* 9,220
URL: http://www.ccri.edu
Phone: (401) 825-1000*Calendar:* Sem. plan
Inst. Accred.: NEASC-CIHE (1969/2004)
Prog. Accred.: Business (ACBSP), Clinical Lab Technology, Dental Assisting, Dental Hygiene, Massage Therapy, Nursing, Occupational Therapy Assisting, Physical Therapy Assisting, Practical Nursing, Respiratory Therapy

Flanagan Campus
1762 Louisquisset Pike, Lincoln 02865-4585
Phone: (401) 333-7000
Prog. Accred: Radiography

Liston Campus
One Hilton St., Providence 02905-2304
Phone: (401) 455-6000

Johnson and Wales University
8 Abbott Park Place, Providence 02903-3703
Type: Private, independent, four-year
Degrees: A, B, M, P, D*Enroll:* 9,169
URL: http://www.jwu.edu
Phone: (401) 598-1000*Calendar:* Qtr. plan
Inst. Accred.: NEASC-CIHE (1993/1998)

Charleston Campus
701 East Bay St., Charleston, SC 29403-5000
Phone: (843) 727-3000

Charlotte Campus
801 West Trade St., Charlotte, NC 28202-1122
Phone: (980) 598-1000

Denver Campus
7150 Montview Blvd., Denver, CO 80220
Phone: (303) 256-9300

Norfolk Campus
2428 Almeda Ave., Ste. 316, Norfolk, VA 23513
Phone: (757) 853-3508

North Miami Campus
1701 NE 127th St., North Miami, FL 33181
Phone: (305) 892-7000

Naval War College
686 Cushing Rd., Newport 02841-1207
Type: Public, federal, four-year
Degrees: M
URL: http://www.nwc.navy.mil
Phone: (401) 841-3089*Calendar:* Tri. plan
Inst. Accred.: NEASC-CIHE (1989/2004)

New England Institute of Technology
2500 Post Rd., Warwick 02886-2266
Type: Private, independent, four-year
Degrees: A, B*Enroll:* 2,558
URL: http://www.neit.edu
Phone: (401) 467-7744*Calendar:* Qtr. plan
Inst. Accred.: NEASC-CIHE (2005)
Prog. Accred.: Occupational Therapy Assisting, Surgical Technology

Providence College
Providence 02918-0002
Type: Private, Roman Catholic Church, four-year
Degrees: B, M, D*Enroll:* 4,358
URL: http://www.providence.edu
Phone: (401) 865-1000*Calendar:* Sem. plan
Inst. Accred.: NEASC-CIHE (1933/1997)
Prog. Accred.: Social Work

Rhode Island College
600 Mount Pleasant Ave., Providence 02908-1991
Type: Public, state, four-year
System: Rhode Island Board of Governors for Higher Education
Degrees: B, M, D*Enroll:* 6,679
URL: http://www.ric.edu
Phone: (401) 456-8000*Calendar:* Sem. plan
Inst. Accred.: NEASC-CIHE (1958/2000)
Prog. Accred.: Art, Music, Nursing, Social Work, Teacher Education (NCATE)

Rhode Island School of Design
2 College St., Providence 02903
Type: Private, independent, four-year
Degrees: B, M*Enroll:* 2,294
URL: http://www.risd.edu
Phone: (401) 454-6100*Calendar:* Sem. plan
Inst. Accred.: NEASC-CIHE (1949/1996)
Prog. Accred.: Art, Landscape Architecture

Roger Williams University
One Old Ferry Rd., Bristol 02809-2921
Type: Private, independent, four-year
Degrees: A, B, M, P   *Enroll:* 3,786
URL: http://www.rwu.edu
Phone: (401) 253-1040   *Calendar:* Sem. plan
Inst. Accred.: NEASC-CIHE (1972/1996)
Prog. Accred.: Business (AACSB), Construction Education,
  Engineering (environmental/sanitary, general), Law
  (ABA only)

Salve Regina University
100 Ochre Point Ave., Newport 02840-4192
Type: Private, Roman Catholic Church, four-year
Degrees: A, B, M, D   *Enroll:* 2,120
URL: http://www.salve.edu
Phone: (401) 847-6650   *Calendar:* Sem. plan
Inst. Accred.: NEASC-CIHE (1956/2001)
Prog. Accred.: Art, Nursing, Social Work

University of Rhode Island
75 Lower College Rd., Ste. 7, Kingston 02881-1966
Type: Public, state, four-year
System: Rhode Island Board of Governors for Higher
  Education
Degrees: A, B, M, P, D   *Enroll:* 12,473
URL: http://www.uri.edu
Phone: (401) 874-1000   *Calendar:* Sem. plan
Inst. Accred.: NEASC-CIHE (1930/1997)
Prog. Accred.: Accounting, Audiology, Business (AACSB),
  Clinical Psychology, Dental Hygiene, Dietetics
  (internship), Engineering (chemical, civil, computer,
  electrical, industrial, manufacturing, mechanical,
  ocean), Landscape Architecture, Librarianship, Marriage
  and Family Therapy, Music, Nurse (Midwifery), Nursing,
  Nursing Education, Pharmacy, Physical Therapy,
  Planning, School Psychology, Speech-Language
  Pathology, Teacher Education (NCATE)

Zion Bible College
27 Middle Hwy., Barrington 02806
Type: Private, Assemblies of God Church, four-year
Degrees: B   *Enroll:* 275
URL: http://www.zbi.edu
Phone: (401) 246-0900   *Calendar:* Sem. plan
Inst. Accred.: ABHE (2001)

SOUTH CAROLINA

Aiken Technical College
PO Box 696, Aiken 29802-0696
Type: Public, state, two-year
System: South Carolina State Board for Technical and
  Comprehensive Education
Degrees: A   *Enroll:* 1,676
URL: http://www.atc.edu
Phone: (803) 593-9231   *Calendar:* Sem. plan
Inst. Accred.: SACS (1975/2001)
Prog. Accred.: Business (ACBSP), Dental Assisting,
  Engineering Technology (electrical), Radiography

Allen University
1530 Harden St., Columbia 29204
Type: Private, African Methodist Episcopal Church, four-
  year
Degrees: B   *Enroll:* 557
URL: http://www.allenuniversity.edu
Phone: (803) 254-4165   *Calendar:* Sem. plan
Inst. Accred.: SACS (1992/1997)

Anderson University
316 Blvd., Anderson 29621
Type: Private, Southern Baptist Convention, four-year
Degrees: A, B, M   *Enroll:* 1,413
URL: http://www.anderson-college.edu
Phone: (864) 231-2000   *Calendar:* Sem. plan
Inst. Accred.: SACS (1959/1998)
Prog. Accred.: Business (ACBSP), Music, Teacher
  Education (NCATE)

Benedict College
1600 Harden St., Columbia 29204
Type: Private, independent, four-year
Degrees: B   *Enroll:* 2,783
URL: http://bchome.benedict.edu
Phone: (803) 256-4220   *Calendar:* Sem. plan
Inst. Accred.: SACS (1946/2001)
Prog. Accred.: Social Work

Central Carolina Technical College
506 North Guignard Dr., Sumter 29150-2499
Type: Public, state, two-year
System: South Carolina State Board for Technical and
  Comprehensive Education
Degrees: A   *Enroll:* 1,750
URL: http://www.cctech.edu
Phone: (803) 778-1961   *Calendar:* Sem. plan
Inst. Accred.: SACS (1970/1995)
Prog. Accred.: Business (ACBSP), Engineering Technology
  (civil/construction), Nursing, Surgical Technology

Charleston Southern University
PO Box 118087, 9200 University Blvd., Charleston
29423-8087
Type: Private, Southern Baptist Church, four-year
Degrees: A, B, M   *Enroll:* 2,467
URL: http://www.csuniv.edu
Phone: (843) 863-7000   *Calendar:* 4-1-4 plan
Inst. Accred.: SACS (1970/1995)
Prog. Accred.: Music

The Citadel
171 Moultrie St., Charleston 29409
Type: Public, state, four-year
Degrees: B, M, P   *Enroll:* 2,757
URL: http://www.citadel.edu
Phone: (843) 953-5000   *Calendar:* Sem. plan
Inst. Accred.: SACS (1924/2004)
Prog. Accred.: Business (AACSB), Engineering (civil,
  electrical), Teacher Education (NCATE)

Claflin University
400 Magnolia St., Orangeburg 29115
Type: Private, United Methodist Church, four-year
Degrees: B, M   *Enroll:* 1,530
URL: http://www.claflin.edu
Phone: (803) 535-5000   *Calendar:* Sem. plan
Inst. Accred.: SACS (1947/2001)
Prog. Accred.: Business (ACBSP)

Clemson University
201 Sikes Hall, Clemson 29634
Type: Public, state, four-year
Degrees: B, M, P, D   *Enroll:* 15,634
URL: http://www.clemson.edu
Phone: (864) 656-3311   *Calendar:* Sem. plan
Inst. Accred.: SACS (1927/2002)
Prog. Accred.: Accounting, Art, Business (AACSB),
  Computer Science, Construction Education, Counseling,
  Engineering (agricultural, ceramic, chemical, civil,
  computer, electrical, industrial, materials, mechanical),
  Forestry, Landscape Architecture, Nursing, Nursing
  Education, Planning, Recreation and Leisure Services,
  Teacher Education (NCATE)

Clinton Junior College
1029 Crawford Rd., Rock Hill 29730-5153
Type: Private, African Methodist Episcopal Zion Church,
  two-year
Degrees: A   *Enroll:* 95
URL: http://www.clintonjrcollege.org
Phone: (803) 327-7402   *Calendar:* Sem. plan
Inst. Accred.: TRACS (2000)

Coastal Carolina University
PO Box 261954, Conway 29528
Type: Public, state, four-year
Degrees: A, B, M   *Enroll:* 5,683
URL: http://www.coastal.edu
Phone: (843) 347-3161   *Calendar:* Sem. plan
Inst. Accred.: SACS (1976/2001)
Prog. Accred.: Art, Business (AACSB), Teacher Education
  (NCATE)

Coker College
300 East College Ave., Hartsville 29550
Type: Private, independent, four-year
Degrees: B   *Enroll:* 991
URL: http://www.coker.edu
Phone: (843) 383-8000   *Calendar:* Sem. plan
Inst. Accred.: SACS (1923/2005)
Prog. Accred.: Music

College of Charleston
66 George St., Charleston 29424
Type: Public, state, four-year
Degrees: B, M   *Enroll:* 10,094
URL: http://www.cofc.edu
Phone: (843) 953-5507   *Calendar:* Sem. plan
Inst. Accred.: SACS (1916/1996)
Prog. Accred.: Accounting, Business (AACSB), Computer
  Science, Music, Public Administration, Teacher
  Education (NCATE)

Columbia College
1301 Columbia College Dr., Columbia 29203
Type: Private, United Methodist Church, four-year
Degrees: B, M   *Enroll:* 1,313
URL: http://www.colacoll.edu
Phone: (803) 786-3871   *Calendar:* Sem. plan
Inst. Accred.: SACS (1938/2001)
Prog. Accred.: Art, Dance, Music, Social Work, Teacher
  Education (NCATE)

Columbia International University
7435 Monticello Rd., PO Box 3122, Columbia 29230-
3122
Type: Private, independent, four-year
Degrees: A, B, M, D   *Enroll:* 854
URL: http://www.ciu.edu
Phone: (803) 754-4100   *Calendar:* Sem. plan
Inst. Accred.: ABHE (1948/2004), ATS (1985/1998), SACS
  (1982/1998)

Converse College
580 East Main St., Spartanburg 29302-0006
Type: Private, independent, four-year
Degrees: B, M, P   *Enroll:* 1,113
URL: http://www.converse.edu
Phone: (864) 596-9000   *Calendar:* Sem. plan
Inst. Accred.: SACS (1912/1996)
Prog. Accred.: Marriage and Family Therapy, Music

Denmark Technical College
500 Solomon Blatt Blvd., PO Box 327, Denmark 29042-
0327
Type: Public, state, two-year
System: South Carolina State Board for Technical and
  Comprehensive Education
Degrees: A   *Enroll:* 1,202
URL: http://www.denmarktech.edu
Phone: (803) 793-5100   *Calendar:* Sem. plan
Inst. Accred.: SACS (1979/2005)
Prog. Accred.: Business (ACBSP), Engineering Technology
  (electromechanical)

Erskine College
2 Washington St., Due West 29639
Type: Private, Presbyterian Church (USA), four-year
Degrees: A, B, M, D   *Enroll:* 803
URL: http://www.erskine.edu
Phone: (864) 379-2131   *Calendar:* 4-1-4 plan
Inst. Accred.: ATS (1981/2001), SACS (1925/2002)

Florence-Darlington Technical College
PO Box 100548, Florence 29501-0548
Type: Public, state, two-year
System: South Carolina State Board for Technical and
  Comprehensive Education
Degrees: A   *Enroll:* 2,819
URL: http://www.fdtc.edu
Phone: (843) 661-8324   *Calendar:* Sem. plan
Inst. Accred.: SACS (1970/1995)
Prog. Accred.: Business (ACBSP), Clinical Lab Technology,
  Cosmetology, Dental Assisting, Dental Hygiene,
  Engineering Technology (civil/construction, electrical,
  general drafting/design), Health Information Technician,
  Nursing, Practical Nursing, Radiography, Respiratory
  Therapy, Respiratory Therapy Technology, Surgical
  Technology

Forrest Junior College
601 East River St., Anderson 29624
Type: Private, proprietary, two-year
Degrees: A   *Enroll:* 163
URL: http://www.forrestcollege.com
Phone: (864) 225-7653   *Calendar:* Qtr. plan
Inst. Accred.: ACICS (1972/2004)
Prog. Accred.: Medical Assisting (CAAHEP)

Francis Marion University
PO Box 100547, Florence 29501-0547
Type: Public, state, four-year
Degrees: A, B, M   *Enroll:* 3,164
URL: http://www.fmarion.edu
Phone: (843) 661-1362   *Calendar:* Sem. plan
Inst. Accred.: SACS (1972/1997)
Prog. Accred.: Art, Business (AACSB), Teacher Education
  (NCATE), Theatre

Furman University

3300 Poinsett Hwy., Greenville 29613
Type: Private, independent, four-year
Degrees: B, M   *Enroll:* 2,986
URL: http://www.furman.edu
Phone: (864) 294-2000   *Calendar:* 3-3 plan
Inst. Accred.: SACS (1924/1997)
Prog. Accred.: Music, Teacher Education (NCATE)

Greenville Technical College

PO Box 5616, Greenville 29606-5616
Type: Public, state, two-year
System: South Carolina State Board for Technical and
   Comprehensive Education
Degrees: A   *Enroll:* 7,254
URL: http://www.greenvilletech.com
Phone: (864) 250-8000   *Calendar:* Sem. plan
Inst. Accred.: SACS (1968/2002)
Prog. Accred.: Business (ACBSP), Clinical Lab Technology,
   Culinary Education, Dental Assisting, Dental Hygiene,
   EMT (Paramedic), Engineering Technology
   (architectural, civil/construction, electrical, general
   drafting/design, mechanical, surveying), Health
   Information Technician, Medical Assisting (AMA),
   Nursing, Occupational Therapy Assisting, Physical
   Therapy Assisting, Practical Nursing, Radiography,
   Respiratory Therapy, Respiratory Therapy Technology,
   Surgical Technology

Horry-Georgetown Technical College

PO Box 261966, Conway 29528
Type: Public, state, two-year
System: South Carolina State Board for Technical and
   Comprehensive Education
Degrees: A   *Enroll:* 3,351
URL: http://www.hgtc.edu
Phone: (843) 347-3186   *Calendar:* Sem. plan
Inst. Accred.: SACS (1972/1998)
Prog. Accred.: Business (ACBSP), Culinary Education,
   Dental Assisting, Dental Hygiene, Engineering
   Technology (civil/construction, electrical), Nursing,
   Radiography

Lander University

320 Stanley Ave., Greenwood 29649-2099
Type: Public, state, four-year
Degrees: B, M   *Enroll:* 2,544
URL: http://www.lander.edu
Phone: (864) 388-8000   *Calendar:* Sem. plan
Inst. Accred.: SACS (1952/1996)
Prog. Accred.: Art, Business (AACSB), Music, Nursing,
   Teacher Education (NCATE), Theatre

Limestone College

1115 College Dr., Gaffney 29340-3799
Type: Private, independent, four-year
Degrees: B   *Enroll:* 2,086
URL: http://www.limestone.edu
Phone: (864) 489-7151   *Calendar:* Sem. plan
Inst. Accred.: SACS (1928/1999)
Prog. Accred.: Music, Social Work

Lutheran Theological Southern Seminary

4201 North Main St., Columbia 29203
Type: Private, Evangelical Lutheran Church, four-year
Degrees: M, D   *Enroll:* 162
URL: http://www.ltss.edu
Phone: (803) 786-5150   *Calendar:* Sem. plan
Inst. Accred.: ATS (1944/2003), SACS (1983/2003, Warning)

Medical University of South Carolina

171 Ashley Ave., Charleston 29425
Type: Public, state, four-year
Degrees: B, M, P, D   *Enroll:* 2,134
URL: http://www.musc.edu
Phone: (843) 792-2300   *Calendar:* Sem. plan
Inst. Accred.: SACS (1971/1996)
Prog. Accred.: Advanced Education in General Dentistry,
   Cytotechnology, Dental Public Health, Dentistry,
   Dietetics (internship), General Dentistry, Health Services
   Administration, Medicine, Nurse (Midwifery), Nurse
   Anesthesia Education, Nursing, Nursing Education,
   Occupational Therapy, Oral and Maxillofacial Surgery,
   Pediatric Dentistry, Perfusion, Periodontics, Pharmacy,
   Physical Therapy, Physician Assistant, Psychology
   Internship, Speech-Language Pathology

Midlands Technical College

PO Box 2408, Columbia 29202
Type: Public, state, two-year
System: South Carolina State Board for Technical and
   Comprehensive Education
Degrees: A   *Enroll:* 6,896
URL: http://www.midlandstech.edu
Phone: (803) 738-1400   *Calendar:* Sem. plan
Inst. Accred.: SACS (1974/1999)
Prog. Accred.: Business (ACBSP), Clinical Lab Technology,
   Dental Assisting, Dental Hygiene, Engineering
   Technology (architectural, civil/construction, electrical),
   Health Information Technician, Medical Assisting (AMA),
   Nuclear Medicine Technology, Nursing, Physical Therapy
   Assisting, Practical Nursing, Radiography, Respiratory
   Therapy, Respiratory Therapy Technology, Surgical
   Technology

Morris College

100 West College St., Sumter 29150-3599
Type: Private, Baptist Educational and Missionary
   Convention of South Carolina, four-year
Degrees: B   *Enroll:* 995
URL: http://www.morris.edu
Phone: (803) 934-3200   *Calendar:* Sem. plan
Inst. Accred.: SACS (1978/2002)

Newberry College

2100 College St., Newberry 29108
Type: Private, Evangelical Lutheran Church of America,
   four-year
Degrees: B   *Enroll:* 728
URL: http://www.newberry.edu
Phone: (803) 276-5010   *Calendar:* Sem. plan
Inst. Accred.: SACS (1936/2002)
Prog. Accred.: Music, Teacher Education (NCATE),
   Veterinary Technology

North Greenville College
PO Box 1892, Tigerville 29688-1892
Type: Private, Southern Baptist Church, four-year
Degrees: A, B *Enroll:* 1,542
URL: http://www.ngc.edu
Phone: (864) 977-7000 *Calendar:* Sem. plan
Inst. Accred.: SACS (1957/1999)

Northeastern Technical College
1201 Chesterfield Hwy., Cheraw 29520-1007
Type: Public, state, two-year
System: South Carolina State Board for Technical and
Comprehensive Education
Degrees: A *Enroll:* 750
URL: http://www.northeasterntech.org
Phone: (843) 921-6900 *Calendar:* Sem. plan
Inst. Accred.: SACS (1973/1998)

Orangeburg-Calhoun Technical College
3250 St. Matthews Rd., NE, Orangeburg 29118
Type: Public, state/local, two-year
System: South Carolina State Board for Technical and
Comprehensive Education
Degrees: A *Enroll:* 1,753
URL: http://www.octech.edu
Phone: (803) 536-0311 *Calendar:* Sem. plan
Inst. Accred.: SACS (1970/1995)
Prog. Accred.: Business (ACBSP), Clinical Lab Technology,
Engineering Technology (electrical), Medical Assisting
(AMA), Nursing, Practical Nursing, Radiography,
Respiratory Therapy Technology

Piedmont Technical College
PO Box 1467, 620 North Emerald Rd., Greenwood
29648-1467
Type: Public, state, two-year
System: South Carolina State Board for Technical and
Comprehensive Education
Degrees: A *Enroll:* 3,049
URL: http://www.ptc.edu
Phone: (864) 941-8324 *Calendar:* Sem. plan
Inst. Accred.: SACS (1972/1997)
Prog. Accred.: Business (ACBSP), Engineering Technology
(electrical, general drafting/design), Funeral Service
Education (Mortuary Science), Radiography, Respiratory
Therapy, Respiratory Therapy Technology, Surgical
Technology

Presbyterian College
503 South Broad St., Clinton 29325
Type: Private, Presbyterian Church (USA), four-year
Degrees: B *Enroll:* 1,158
URL: http://www.presby.edu
Phone: (864) 833-2820 *Calendar:* Sem. plan
Inst. Accred.: SACS (1949/1996)
Prog. Accred.: Business (ACBSP), Teacher Education
(NCATE)

Sherman College of Straight Chiropractic
PO Box 1452, 2020 Springfield Rd., Spartanburg 29304
Type: Private, independent, four-year
Degrees: P, D *Enroll:* 423
URL: http://www.sherman.edu
Phone: (864) 578-8770 *Calendar:* Qtr. plan
Inst. Accred.: SACS (2002)
Prog. Accred.: Chiropractic Education

South Carolina State University
300 College Ave., NE, Orangeburg 29117-0001
Type: Public, state, four-year
Degrees: B, M, P, D *Enroll:* 3,868
URL: http://www.scsu.edu
Phone: (803) 536-7000 *Calendar:* Sem. plan
Inst. Accred.: SACS (1941/2000)
Prog. Accred.: Business (AACSB), Computer Science,
Engineering Technology (civil/construction, electrical,
industrial, mechanical), Family and Consumer Science,
Music, Rehabilitation Counseling, Social Work, Speech-
Language Pathology, Teacher Education (NCATE)

Southern Methodist College
PO Box 1027, 541 Broughton St., Orangeburg 29116-
1027
Type: Private, Southern Methodist Church, four-year
Degrees: A, B *Enroll:* 85
URL: http://www.southernmethodistcollege.org
Phone: (803) 534-7826 *Calendar:* Sem. plan
Inst. Accred.: TRACS (2002, Warning)

Southern Wesleyan University
PO Box 1020, 907 Wesleyan Dr., Central 29630-1020
Type: Private, Wesleyan Church, four-year
Degrees: A, B, M *Enroll:* 2,341
URL: http://www.swu.edu
Phone: (864) 644-5000 *Calendar:* Sem. plan
Inst. Accred.: SACS (1973/1999)

Spartanburg Methodist College
1200 Textile Rd., Spartanburg 29301-0009
Type: Private, United Methodist Church, two-year
Degrees: A *Enroll:* 711
URL: http://www.smcsc.edu
Phone: (864) 587-4000 *Calendar:* Sem. plan
Inst. Accred.: SACS (1957/1998)

Spartanburg Technical College
PO Box 4386, Spartanburg 29305
Type: Public, state, two-year
System: South Carolina State Board for Technical and
Comprehensive Education
Degrees: A *Enroll:* 2,823
URL: http://www.stcsc.edu
Phone: (864) 591-3600 *Calendar:* Sem. plan
Inst. Accred.: SACS (1970/1995)
Prog. Accred.: Business (ACBSP), Clinical Lab Technology,
Culinary Education, Dental Hygiene, Engineering
Technology (civil/construction, electrical, mechanical),
Medical Assisting (AMA), Radiation Therapy,
Radiography, Respiratory Therapy, Respiratory Therapy
Technology, Surgical Technology

Technical College of the Lowcountry
921 Ribaut Rd., PO Box 1288, Beaufort 29901
Type: Public, state, two-year
System: South Carolina State Board for Technical and
  Comprehensive Education
Degrees: A   *Enroll:* 1,060
URL: http://www.tcl.edu
Phone: (843) 525-8324   *Calendar:* Sem. plan
Inst. Accred.: SACS (1978/2004)
Prog. Accred.: Business (ACBSP), Cosmetology, Nursing,
  Practical Nursing, Radiography

Tri-County Technical College
PO Box 587, 7900 Hwy. 76, Pendleton 29670
Type: Public, state, two-year
System: South Carolina State Board for Technical and
  Comprehensive Education
Degrees: A   *Enroll:* 3,040
URL: http://www.tctc.edu
Phone: (864) 646-8361   *Calendar:* Sem. plan
Inst. Accred.: SACS (1971/1996)
Prog. Accred.: Business (ACBSP), Clinical Lab Technology,
  Dental Assisting, Engineering Technology (electrical,
  general, instrumentation), Nursing, Surgical Technology,
  Veterinary Technology

Trident Technical College
PO Box 118067, Charleston 29423-8067
Type: Public, state, two-year
System: South Carolina State Board for Technical and
  Comprehensive Education
Degrees: A   *Enroll:* 7,391
URL: http://www.tridenttech.edu
Phone: (843) 574-6111   *Calendar:* Sem. plan
Inst. Accred.: SACS (1974/2000)
Prog. Accred.: Business (ACBSP), Clinical Lab Technology,
  Cosmetology, Culinary Education, Dental Assisting,
  Dental Hygiene, Engineering Technology
  (civil/construction, electrical, mechanical), Medical
  Assisting (AMA), Nursing, Occupational Therapy
  Assisting, Physical Therapy Assisting, Radiography,
  Respiratory Therapy, Veterinary Technology

University of South Carolina—Aiken
471 University Pkwy., Aiken 29801
Type: Public, state, four-year
System: University of South Carolina Central Office
Degrees: A, B, M   *Enroll:* 2,753
URL: http://www.usca.sc.edu
Phone: (803) 648-6851   *Calendar:* Sem. plan
Inst. Accred.: SACS (1977/2001)
Prog. Accred.: Business (AACSB), Nursing, Teacher
  Education (NCATE)

University of South Carolina—Beaufort
801 Carteret St., Beaufort 29902
Type: Public, state, two-year
System: University of South Carolina Central Office
Degrees: A   *Enroll:* 752
URL: http://www.sc.edu/beaufort
Phone: (843) 521-4100   *Calendar:* Sem. plan
Inst. Accred.: SACS (2004)

University of South Carolina—Columbia
Columbia 29208
Type: Public, state, four-year
System: University of South Carolina Central Office
Degrees: A, B, M, P, D   *Enroll:* 21,771
URL: http://www.sc.edu
Phone: (803) 777-7000   *Calendar:* Sem. plan
Inst. Accred.: SACS (1917/2001)
Prog. Accred.: Accounting, Applied Science (industrial
  hygiene), Art, Athletic Training, Business (AACSB),
  Clinical Psychology, Computer Science, Counseling,
  Engineering (chemical, civil, computer, electrical,
  mechanical), English Language Education, Health
  Services Administration, Journalism, Law, Librarianship,
  Medicine, Music, Nurse Anesthesia Education, Nursing,
  Nursing Education, Pharmacy, Physical Therapy,
  Psychology Internship, Public Administration, Public
  Health, Rehabilitation Counseling, School Psychology,
  Social Work, Speech-Language Pathology, Teacher
  Education (NCATE), Theatre

Lancaster Campus
PO Box 889, Lancaster 29721-0889
Phone: (803) 285-7471
Prog. Accred: Business (ACBSP)

University of South Carolina—Salkehatchie
PO Box 617, Allendale 29810-0617
Phone: (803) 584-3446

University of South Carolina—Sumter
200 Miller Rd., Sumter 29150-2498
Phone: (803) 775-6341

University of South Carolina—Union
PO Drawer 729, Union 29379-0729
Phone: (864) 429-8728

University of South Carolina—Upstate
800 University Way, Spartanburg 29303
Type: Public, state, four-year
System: University of South Carolina Central Office
Degrees: A, B, M   *Enroll:* 3,869
URL: http://www.uscs.edu
Phone: (864) 503-5000   *Calendar:* Sem. plan
Inst. Accred.: SACS (1976/2001)
Prog. Accred.: Business (AACSB), Computer Science,
  Nursing, Teacher Education (NCATE)

Voorhees College
PO Box 678, 1411 Voorhees Rd., Denmark 29042
Type: Private, Protestant Episcopal Church, four-year
Degrees: A, B   *Enroll:* 853
URL: http://www.voorhees.edu
Phone: (803) 793-3351   *Calendar:* Sem. plan
Inst. Accred.: SACS (1946/2003)
Prog. Accred.: Business (ACBSP)

Williamsburg Technical College

601 Martin Luther King, Jr. Ave., Kingstree 29556-4192
Type: Public, state, two-year
System: South Carolina State Board for Technical and
  Comprehensive Education
Degrees: A   *Enroll:* 378
URL: http://www.williamsburgtech.com
Phone: (843) 354-2021   *Calendar:* Sem. plan
Inst. Accred.: SACS (1977/2002)
Prog. Accred.: Business (ACBSP)

Winthrop University

701 Oakland Ave., Rock Hill 29733
Type: Public, state, four-year
Degrees: B, M, P   *Enroll:* 5,539
URL: http://www.winthrop.edu
Phone: (803) 323-2211   *Calendar:* Sem. plan
Inst. Accred.: SACS (1923/2001)
Prog. Accred.: Art, Business (AACSB), Computer Science,
  Counseling, Dance, Dietetics (internship), Interior
  Design, Journalism, Music, Social Work, Teacher
  Education (NCATE), Theatre

Wofford College

429 North Church St., Spartanburg 29303-3663
Type: Private, United Methodist Church, four-year
Degrees: B   *Enroll:* 1,148
URL: http://www.wofford.edu
Phone: (864) 597-4000   *Calendar:* 4-1-4 plan
Inst. Accred.: SACS (1917/1996)

York Technical College

452 South Anderson Rd., Rock Hill 29730
Type: Public, state, two-year
System: South Carolina State Board for Technical and
  Comprehensive Education
Degrees: A   *Enroll:* 2,747
URL: http://newweb.yorktech.com
Phone: (803) 327-8000   *Calendar:* Sem. plan
Inst. Accred.: SACS (1970/1995)
Prog. Accred.: Business (ACBSP), Clinical Lab Technology,
  Dental Assisting, Dental Hygiene, Engineering
  Technology (computer, electrical, mechanical,
  mechanical drafting/design), Nursing, Radiography

SOUTH DAKOTA

Augustana College
2001 South Summit Ave., Sioux Falls 57197
Type: Private, Evangelical Lutheran Church in America,
  four-year
Degrees: B, M   *Enroll:* 1,749
URL: http://www.augie.edu
Phone: (605) 274-0770   *Calendar:* 4-1-4 plan
Inst. Accred.: NCA-HLC (1931/2002)
Prog. Accred.: Athletic Training, Music, Nursing, Nursing
  Education, Social Work, Teacher Education (NCATE)

Black Hills State University
1200 University Ave., Spearfish 57799-9500
Type: Public, state, four-year
System: South Dakota Board of Regents
Degrees: A, B, M   *Enroll:* 3,221
URL: http://www.bhsu.edu
Phone: (605) 642-6011   *Calendar:* Sem. plan
Inst. Accred.: NCA-HLC (1928/2003)
Prog. Accred.: Music, Teacher Education (NCATE)

Dakota State University
820 North Washington Ave., Madison 57042-1799
Type: Public, state, four-year
System: South Dakota Board of Regents
Degrees: A, B, M   *Enroll:* 1,679
URL: http://www.dsu.edu
Phone: (605) 256-5111   *Calendar:* Sem. plan
Inst. Accred.: NCA-HLC (1920/2001)
Prog. Accred.: Business (ACBSP), Health Information
  Administration, Health Information Technician,
  Respiratory Therapy, Teacher Education (NCATE)

Dakota Wesleyan University
1200 West University Ave., Mitchell 57301
Type: Private, United Methodist Church, four-year
Degrees: A, B   *Enroll:* 709
URL: http://www.dwu.edu
Phone: (605) 995-2600   *Calendar:* Sem. plan
Inst. Accred.: NCA-HLC (1916/1997)
Prog. Accred.: Nursing

Kilian Community College
300 East 6th St., Sioux Falls 57103-7020
Type: Private, independent, two-year
Degrees: A   *Enroll:* 256
URL: http://www.kilian.edu
Phone: (605) 221-3100   *Calendar:* Sem. plan
Inst. Accred.: NCA-HLC (1986/2001)

Lake Area Technical Institute
230 11th St., NE, PO Box 730, Watertown 57201
Type: Public, state/local, two-year
Degrees: A   *Enroll:* 935
URL: http://lati.tec.sd.us
Phone: (800) 657-4344   *Calendar:* Sem. plan
Inst. Accred.: NCA-HLC (1980/1997)
Prog. Accred.: Clinical Lab Technology, Dental Assisting,
  Medical Assisting (AMA), Occupational Therapy
  Assisting, Physical Therapy Assisting, Practical Nursing

Mitchell Technical Institute
821 North Capital St., Mitchell 57301
Type: Public, state/local, two-year
Degrees: A   *Enroll:* 756
URL: http://mti.tec.sd.us
Phone: (605) 995-3024   *Calendar:* Sem. plan
Inst. Accred.: NCA-HLC (1980/2001)
Prog. Accred.: Clinical Lab Technology, Medical Assisting
  (AMA), Radiography

Mount Marty College
1105 West Eighth St., Yankton 57078
Type: Private, Roman Catholic Church, four-year
Degrees: A, B, M   *Enroll:* 953
URL: http://www.mtmc.edu
Phone: (605) 668-1514   *Calendar:* Sem. plan
Inst. Accred.: NCA-HLC (1961/2003)
Prog. Accred.: Nurse Anesthesia Education, Nursing

National American University
321 Kansas City St., Rapid City 57701
Type: Private, proprietary, four-year
Degrees: A, B, M   *Enroll:* 995
URL: http://www.national.edu
Phone: (605) 394-4800   *Calendar:* Qtr. plan
Inst. Accred.: NCA-HLC (1985/1998)
Prog. Accred.: Health Information Technician, Medical
Assisting (AMA), Veterinary Technology

Albuquerque Campus
1202 Pennsylvania Ave., NW, Albuquerque, NM 87110
Phone: (505) 265-7517

Brooklyn Center Campus
6120 Earle Brown Dr., Ste. 100, Brooklyn Center, MN
55430
Phone: (866) 628-6387

Colorado Springs Campus
2577 North Chelton, Colorado Springs, CO 80909
Phone: (719) 471-4205

Denver Campus
1325 South Colorado Blvd., #100, Denver, CO 80222
Phone: (303) 758-6700

Ellsworth AFB Extension Campus
PO Box 1780, Rapid City 57709
Phone: (605) 923-5856

Kansas City Campus
Blue Ridge Mall, 4200 Blue Ridge Blvd., Kansas City,
MO 64133
Phone: (816) 353-4554

Mall of America Campus
W 112 West Market, Bloomington, MN 55425
Phone: (952) 883-0439

Roseville Campus
1500 West Hwy. 36, Roseville, MN 55113-4035
Phone: (651) 582-0536

Sioux Falls Campus
3109 South Kiwanis Ave., Sioux Falls 57105
Phone: (605) 334-5430

North American Baptist Seminary
1525 South Grange Ave., Sioux Falls 57105-1599
Type: Private, North America Baptist Conference, four-
year
Degrees: M, D   *Enroll:* 100
URL: http://www.nabs.edu
Phone: (605) 336-6588   *Calendar:* 4-1-4 plan
Inst. Accred.: ATS (1968/2004), NCA-HLC (1979/2004)

Northern State University
1200 South Jay St., Aberdeen 57401
Type: Public, state, four-year
System: South Dakota Board of Regents
Degrees: A, B, M   *Enroll:* 2,212
URL: http://www.northern.edu
Phone: (605) 626-3000   *Calendar:* Sem. plan
Inst. Accred.: NCA-HLC (1918/1997)
Prog. Accred.: Business (AACSB), Music, Teacher
Education (NCATE)

Oglala Lakota College
PO Box 490, Piya Wiconi Rd., Kyle 57752
Type: Public, tribal, four-year
System: American Indian Higher Education Consortium
Degrees: A, B, M   *Enroll:* 1,036
URL: http://www.olc.edu
Phone: (605) 455-2321   *Calendar:* Sem. plan
Inst. Accred.: NCA-HLC (1983/2003)

Presentation College
1500 North Main St., Aberdeen 57401
Type: Private, Roman Catholic Church, four-year
Degrees: A, B   *Enroll:* 507
URL: http://www.presentation.edu
Phone: (605) 225-1634   *Calendar:* Sem. plan
Inst. Accred.: NCA-HLC (1971/1999)
Prog. Accred.: Clinical Lab Technology, Nursing,
Radiography, Social Work, Surgical Technology

Fairmont Campus
714 Victoria St., Fairmont, MN 56031
Phone: (507) 235-4658

Lakota Campus
PO Box 1070, Eagle Butte 57625
Phone: (605) 964-4071

Si Tanka University
PO Box 220, 435 North Elm St., Eagle Butte 57625
Type: Public, tribal, two-year
System: American Indian Higher Education Consortium
Degrees: A
URL: http://www.sitanka.edu
Phone: (605) 964-8011   *Calendar:* Sem. plan
Inst. Accred.: NCA-HLC (2000/2004, Warning)

Sinte Gleska University
PO Box 105, 150 East Second St., Mission 57555-0105
Type: Public, Rosebud Sioux Tribe, four-year
System: American Indian Higher Education Consortium
Degrees: A, B, M   *Enroll:* 621
URL: http://sinte.indian.com
Phone: (605) 747-2263   *Calendar:* Sem. plan
Inst. Accred.: NCA-HLC (1983/2003)

Sisseton-Wahpeton Community College
PO Box 689, Old Agency, Agency Village 57262-0689
Type: Public, Sisseton Wahpeton Sioux Tribe, two-year
System: American Indian Higher Education Consortium
Degrees: A   *Enroll:* 205
URL: http://www.swcc.cc.sd.us
Phone: (605) 698-3966   *Calendar:* Sem. plan
Inst. Accred.: NCA-HLC (1990/1999)

South Dakota School of Mines and Technology
501 East St. Joseph St., Rapid City 57701-3995
Type: Public, state, four-year
System: South Dakota Board of Regents
Degrees: A, B, M, D   *Enroll:* 2,123
URL: http://www.sdsmt.edu
Phone: (605) 394-2400   *Calendar:* Sem. plan
Inst. Accred.: NCA-HLC (1925/1996)
Prog. Accred.: Computer Science, Engineering (chemical,
   civil, computer, electrical, geological/geophysical,
   industrial, mechanical, metallurgical, mining)

South Dakota State University
Box 2201, Brookings 57007
Type: Public, state, four-year
System: South Dakota Board of Regents
Degrees: A, B, M, P, D   *Enroll:* 8,819
URL: http://www.sdstate.edu
Phone: (605) 688-4151   *Calendar:* Sem. plan
Inst. Accred.: NCA-HLC (1916/2001)
Prog. Accred.: Athletic Training, Counseling, Engineering
   (agricultural, civil, electrical, mechanical), Family and
   Consumer Science, Journalism, Music, Nursing, Nursing
   Education, Pharmacy, Teacher Education (NCATE)

Southeast Technical Institute
2320 North Career Ave., Sioux Falls 57107
Type: Public, state/local, two-year
Degrees: A   *Enroll:* 1,994
URL: http://www.southeasttech.com
Phone: (605) 367-7624   *Calendar:* Sem. plan
Inst. Accred.: NCA-HLC (1981/2003)
Prog. Accred.: Cardiovascular Technology, Nuclear
   Medicine Technology, Surgical Technology

University of Sioux Falls
1101 West 22nd St., Sioux Falls 57105-1699
Type: Private, American Baptist Churches in the USA,
   four-year
Degrees: A, B, M   *Enroll:* 1,207
Phone: (605) 331-5000   *Calendar:* 4-1-4 plan
Inst. Accred.: NCA-HLC (1931/2002)
Prog. Accred.: Social Work, Teacher Education (NCATE)

The University of South Dakota
414 East Clark St., Vermillion 57069-2390
Type: Public, state, four-year
System: South Dakota Board of Regents
Degrees: A, B, M, P, D   *Enroll:* 6,314
URL: http://www.usd.edu
Phone: (605) 677-5276   *Calendar:* Sem. plan
Inst. Accred.: NCA-HLC (1913/2001)
Prog. Accred.: Art, Audiology, Business (AACSB), Clinical
   Psychology, Counseling, Dental Hygiene, Journalism,
   Law, Medicine, Music, Nursing, Occupational Therapy,
   Physical Therapy, Physician Assistant, Public
   Administration, Social Work, Speech-Language
   Pathology, Teacher Education (NCATE), Theatre

Western Dakota Technical Institute
800 Mickelson Dr., Rapid City 57701-4178
Type: Public, local, two-year
Degrees: A   *Enroll:* 854
URL: http://www.westerndakotatech.org
Phone: (605) 394-4034   *Calendar:* Sem. plan
Inst. Accred.: NCA-HLC (1983/2003)
Prog. Accred.: Phlebotomy

TENNESSEE

American Baptist College
1800 Baptist World Center Dr., Nashville 37207-4994
Type: Private, National Baptist/Southern Baptist
  Conventions, four-year
Degrees: A, B *Enroll:* 105
URL: http://www.abcnash.edu
Phone: (615) 256-1463 *Calendar:* Sem. plan
Inst. Accred.: ABHE (1971/2003)

Aquinas College
4210 Harding Rd., Nashville 37205
Type: Private, Roman Catholic Church, four-year
Degrees: A, B *Enroll:* 736
URL: http://www.aquinas-tn.edu
Phone: (615) 297-7545 *Calendar:* Sem. plan
Inst. Accred.: SACS (1971/2001)
Prog. Accred.: Nursing

Austin Peay State University
601 College St., Clarksville 37040
Type: Public, state, four-year
System: Tennessee Board of Regents
Degrees: A, B, M, P *Enroll:* 6,314
URL: http://www.apsu.edu
Phone: (931) 221-7011 *Calendar:* Sem. plan
Inst. Accred.: SACS (1947/2004)
Prog. Accred.: Art, Clinical Lab Scientist, Music, Nursing,
  Social Work, Teacher Education (NCATE)

Baptist Memorial College of Health Sciences
1003 Monroe Ave., Memphis 38104
Type: Private, independent, four-year
Degrees: A, B *Enroll:* 638
URL: http://www.bchs.edu
Phone: (901) 572-2468 *Calendar:* Sem. plan
Inst. Accred.: SACS (1999/2005)
Prog. Accred.: Diagnostic Medical Sonography, Nuclear
  Medicine Technology, Nursing Education, Radiation
  Therapy, Radiography, Respiratory Therapy Technology

Belmont University
1900 Belmont Blvd., Nashville 37212-3757
Type: Private, Southern Baptist Church, four-year
Degrees: A, B, M, D *Enroll:* 3,198
URL: http://www.belmont.edu
Phone: (615) 460-6000 *Calendar:* Sem. plan
Inst. Accred.: SACS (1959/2000)
Prog. Accred.: Accounting, Business (AACSB), Music,
  Nursing, Nursing Education, Occupational Therapy,
  Physical Therapy, Social Work, Teacher Education
  (NCATE)

Bethel College
325 Cherry St., McKenzie 38201
Type: Private, West Tennessee Synod, four-year
Degrees: B, M *Enroll:* 1,126
URL: http://www.bethel-college.edu
Phone: (731) 352-4000 *Calendar:* Sem. plan
Inst. Accred.: SACS (1952/2000)
Prog. Accred.: Physician Assistant

Bryan College
PO Box 7000, Dayton 37321
Type: Private, independent, four-year
Degrees: A, B *Enroll:* 570
URL: http://www.bryan.edu
Phone: (423) 775-2041 *Calendar:* Sem. plan
Inst. Accred.: SACS (1969/2004)

Carson-Newman College
1646 Russell Ave., PO Box 557, Jefferson City 37760
Type: Private, Southern Baptist Church, four-year
Degrees: B, M *Enroll:* 1,967
URL: http://www.cn.edu
Phone: (865) 471-2000 *Calendar:* Sem. plan
Inst. Accred.: SACS (1927/2003)
Prog. Accred.: Art, Family and Consumer Science, Music,
  Nursing, Nursing Education, Teacher Education (NCATE)

Chattanooga State Technical Community College
4501 Amnicola Hwy., Chattanooga 37406
Type: Public, state, two-year
System: Tennessee Board of Regents
Degrees: A *Enroll:* 5,220
URL: http://www.chattanoogastate.edu
Phone: (423) 697-4400 *Calendar:* Sem. plan
Inst. Accred.: SACS (1967/2001)
Prog. Accred.: Dental Assisting, Dental Hygiene,
  Diagnostic Medical Sonography, EMT (Paramedic),
  Engineering Technology (automated systems,
  civil/construction, computer, mechanical), Health
  Information Technician, Medical Assisting (AMA),
  Nuclear Medicine Technology, Nursing, Physical Therapy
  Assisting, Radiation Therapy, Radiography, Respiratory
  Therapy, Surgical Technology

Christian Brothers University
650 East Pkwy. South, Memphis 38104
Type: Private, Roman Catholic Church, four-year
Degrees: A, B, M *Enroll:* 1,522
URL: http://www.cbu.edu
Phone: (901) 321-3000 *Calendar:* Sem. plan
Inst. Accred.: SACS (1958/2000)
Prog. Accred.: Business (AACSB), Engineering (chemical,
  civil, electrical, mechanical)

The Church of God Theological Seminary
900 Walker St., NE, Cleveland 37320-3330
Type: Private, Church of God, four-year
Degrees: M, D *Enroll:* 210
URL: http://www.cogts.edu
Phone: (423) 478-1131 *Calendar:* 4-1-4 plan
Inst. Accred.: ATS (1989/1999), SACS (1984/1999)

Cleveland State Community College
PO Box 3570, Cleveland 37312-3570
Type: Public, state, two-year
System: Tennessee Board of Regents
Degrees: A   *Enroll:* 2,206
URL: http://www.clevelandstatecc.edu
Phone: (423) 472-7141   *Calendar:* Sem. plan
Inst. Accred.: SACS (1969/2004)
Prog. Accred.: Industrial Technology, Medical Assisting
   (AMA), Nursing

Columbia State Community College
PO Box 1315, Columbia 38402-1315
Type: Public, state, two-year
System: Tennessee Board of Regents
Degrees: A   *Enroll:* 3,158
URL: http://www.coscc.cc.tn.us
Phone: (931) 540-2722   *Calendar:* Sem. plan
Inst. Accred.: SACS (1968/2003)
Prog. Accred.: EMT (Paramedic), Nursing, Radiography,
   Respiratory Therapy, Veterinary Technology

Concorde Career College
5100 Poplar Ave., Ste. 132, Memphis 38137
Type: Private, proprietary, two-year
Degrees: A
URL: http://www.concordecareercolleges.com
Phone: (901) 761-9494
Inst. Accred.: COE (1980/2000)
Prog. Accred.: Dental Assisting

Crichton College
255 North Highland St., Memphis 38111-4745
Type: Private, independent, four-year
Degrees: B   *Enroll:* 792
URL: http://www.crichton.edu
Phone: (901) 320-9700   *Calendar:* Sem. plan
Inst. Accred.: SACS (1986/2001)

Cumberland University
One Cumberland Square, Lebanon 37087-3554
Type: Private, independent, four-year
Degrees: A, B, M   *Enroll:* 1,043
URL: http://www.cumberland.edu
Phone: (615) 444-2562   *Calendar:* Sem. plan
Inst. Accred.: SACS (1962/2000)
Prog. Accred.: Business (ACBSP), Nursing

Draughons Junior College
340 Plus Park at Pavilion Blvd., Nashville 37217
Type: Private, proprietary, two-year
Degrees: A   *Enroll:* 996
URL: http://www.draughons.edu
Phone: (615) 361-7555   *Calendar:* Qtr. plan
Inst. Accred.: ACICS (1954/2001)

Bowling Green Campus
2421 Fitzgerald Industrial Dr., Bowling Green, KY
42101
Phone: (270) 843-6750

Clarksville Campus
1860 Wilma Rudolph Blvd., Clarksville 37040
Phone: (931) 552-7600

Murfreesboro Campus
1237 Commerce Park Dr., Murfreesboro 37130
Phone: (615) 217-9347

Dyersburg State Community College
1510 Lake Rd., Dyersburg 38024
Type: Public, state, two-year
System: Tennessee Board of Regents
Degrees: A   *Enroll:* 1,873
URL: http://www.dscc.edu
Phone: (731) 286-3200   *Calendar:* Sem. plan
Inst. Accred.: SACS (1971/1996)
Prog. Accred.: Nursing

East Tennessee State University
807 University Pkwy., Johnson City 37614-0000
Type: Public, state, four-year
System: Tennessee Board of Regents
Degrees: A, B, M, P, D   *Enroll:* 10,061
URL: http://www.etsu.edu
Phone: (423) 439-1000   *Calendar:* Sem. plan
Inst. Accred.: SACS (1927/2002)
Prog. Accred.: Accounting, Applied Science
   (surveying/geomatics), Art, Audiology, Business
   (AACSB), Clinical Lab Technology, Computer Science,
   Counseling, Dental Assisting, Dental Hygiene, Dental
   Laboratory Technology, Dietetics (internship),
   Engineering Technology (civil/construction, electrical),
   Journalism, Medical Assisting (AMA), Medicine, Music,
   Nursing, Physical Therapy, Public Health, Radiography,
   Respiratory Therapy, Respiratory Therapy Technology,
   Social Work, Speech-Language Pathology, Teacher
   Education (NCATE)

Electronic Computer Programming College
3805 Brainerd Rd., Chattanooga 37411-3798
Type: Private, proprietary, two-year
Degrees: A   *Enroll:* 158
URL: http://www.ecpconline.com
Phone: (423) 624-0077
Inst. Accred.: ACCSCT (1982/2004)

Emmanuel School of Religion
One Walker Dr., Johnson City 37601
Type: Private, Christian Churches/Churches of Christ,
four-year
Degrees: M, D   *Enroll:* 124
URL: http://www.esr.edu
Phone: (423) 926-1186   *Calendar:* Sem. plan
Inst. Accred.: ATS (1981/1996), SACS (1986/1996)

Fisk University
1000 17th Ave. North, Nashville 37208-3051
Type: Private, independent, four-year
Degrees: B, M   *Enroll:* 854
URL: http://www.fisk.edu
Phone: (615) 329-8500   *Calendar:* Sem. plan
Inst. Accred.: SACS (1930/1999)
Prog. Accred.: Business (ACBSP), Music

Fountainhead College of Technology
3202 Tazewell Pike, Knoxville 37918-2530
Type: Private, proprietary, four-year
Degrees: A, B   *Enroll:* 149
URL: http://www.fountainheadcollege.edu
Phone: (865) 688-9422   *Calendar:* Qtr. plan
Inst. Accred.: ACCSCT (1967/2002)

Free Will Baptist Bible College
3606 West End Ave., PO Box 50117, Nashville 37205-
0117
Type: Private, National Association of Free Will Baptist
Churches, four-year
Degrees: A, B   *Enroll:* 317
URL: http://www.fwbbc.edu
Phone: (615) 844-5000   *Calendar:* Sem. plan
Inst. Accred.: ABHE (1958/1999), SACS (1996/2002)

Freed-Hardeman University
158 East Main St., Henderson 38340
Type: Private, Church of Christ, four-year
Degrees: B, M   *Enroll:* 1,685
URL: http://www.fhu.edu
Phone: (731) 989-6000   *Calendar:* Sem. plan
Inst. Accred.: SACS (1956/2001)
Prog. Accred.: Business (ACBSP), Social Work, Teacher
Education (NCATE)

Harding University Graduate School of Religion
1000 Cherry Rd., Memphis 38117-5499
Type: Private, Churches of Christ, four-year
Degrees: M, D   *Enroll:* 118
URL: http://www.hugsr.edu
Phone: (901) 761-1356   *Calendar:* Sem. plan
Inst. Accred.: ATS (1995/1997), NCA-HLC (1954/1995,
Indirect accreditation through Harding University,
Searcy, AR)

High-Tech Institute—Memphis
5866 Shelby Oaks Circle, Ste. 100, Memphis 38134
Type: Private, proprietary, two-year
System: High-Tech Institute
Degrees: A
URL: http://www.hightechinstitute.edu
Phone: (901) 432-3800
Inst. Accred.: ACCSCT (2003)
Prog. Accred.: Surgical Technology

High-Tech Institute—Nashville
560 Royal Pkwy., Nashville 37214
Type: Private, proprietary, two-year
System: High-Tech Institute
Degrees: A
URL: http://www.hightechinstitute.edu
Phone: (615) 902-9705
Inst. Accred.: ACCSCT (1999/2004)
Prog. Accred.: Surgical Technology

Hiwassee College
225 Hiwassee College Dr., Madisonville 37354
Type: Private, United Methodist Church, two-year
Degrees: A   *Enroll:* 375
URL: http://www.hiwassee.edu
Phone: (423) 442-2001   *Calendar:* Sem. plan
Inst. Accred.: SACS (1958/2000, Probation)

Huntington College of Health Sciences
1204 Kenesaw Ave., Knoxville 37919-7736
Type: Private, proprietary, four-year
Degrees: A, M
URL: http://hchs.edu
Phone: (865) 524-8079
Inst. Accred.: DETC (1989/2000)

ITT Technical Institute
10208 Technology Dr., Knoxville 37932
Type: Private, proprietary, four-year
System: ITT Educational Services, Inc.
Degrees: A, B   *Enroll:* 554
URL: http://www.itt-tech.edu
Phone: (865) 671-2800   *Calendar:* Qtr. plan
Inst. Accred.: ACICS (1999/2004)

Birmingham Campus
6270 Park South Dr., Bessemer, AL 35022
Phone: (205) 497-5700

Chantilly Campus
14420 Albemarle Point Place, Ste. 100, Chantilly, VA
20151
Phone: (703) 263-2541

Cincinnati Campus
4750 Wesley Ave., Norwood, OH 45212
Phone: (513) 531-8300

Greenville Campus
One Marcus Dr., Ste. 402, Greenville, SC 29615-4818
Phone: (864) 288-0777

Richardson Campus
2101 Waterview Pkwy., Richardson, TX 75080
Phone: (972) 690-9100

ITT Technical Institute
2845 Elm Hill Pike, Nashville 37214-3717
Type: Private, proprietary, four-year
System: ITT Educational Services, Inc.
Degrees: A, B   *Enroll:* 682
URL: http://www.itt-tech.edu
Phone: (615) 889-8700   *Calendar:* Qtr. plan
Inst. Accred.: ACICS (1999/2003)

Jackson State Community College
2046 North Pkwy., Jackson 38301-3797
Type: Public, state, two-year
System: Tennessee Board of Regents
Degrees: A   *Enroll:* 2,803
URL: http://www.jscc.edu
Phone: (731) 424-3520   *Calendar:* Sem. plan
Inst. Accred.: SACS (1969/1994)
Prog. Accred.: Business (ACBSP), Clinical Lab Technology,
  EMT (Paramedic), Industrial Technology, Nursing,
  Physical Therapy Assisting, Radiography, Respiratory
  Therapy

John A. Gupton College
1616 Church St., Nashville 37203
Type: Private, independent, two-year
Degrees: A   *Enroll:* 87
URL: http://www.guptoncollege.com
Phone: (615) 327-3927   *Calendar:* Sem. plan
Inst. Accred.: SACS (1971/1996)
Prog. Accred.: Funeral Service Education (Mortuary
  Science)

Johnson Bible College
7900 Johnson Dr., Knoxville 37998-0001
Type: Private, Christian Churches/Churches of Christ,
  four-year
Degrees: A, B, M   *Enroll:* 788
URL: http://www.jbc.edu
Phone: (865) 573-4517   *Calendar:* Sem. plan
Inst. Accred.: ABHE (1970/1996), SACS (1979/1995)

King College
1350 King College Rd., Bristol 37620-2699
Type: Private, Presbyterian Church (USA), four-year
Degrees: B, M   *Enroll:* 648
URL: http://www.king.edu
Phone: (423) 968-1187   *Calendar:* 4-1-4 plan
Inst. Accred.: SACS (1947/1998)
Prog. Accred.: Nursing Education

Lambuth University
705 Lambuth Blvd., Jackson 38301
Type: Private, United Methodist Church, four-year
Degrees: B   *Enroll:* 800
URL: http://www.lambuth.edu
Phone: (731) 425-2500   *Calendar:* Sem. plan
Inst. Accred.: SACS (1954/1999)
Prog. Accred.: Business (ACBSP)

Lane College
545 Lane Ave., Jackson 38301-4598
Type: Private, Christian Methodist Episcopal Church, four-
  year
Degrees: B   *Enroll:* 943
URL: http://www.lanecollege.edu
Phone: (731) 426-7500   *Calendar:* Sem. plan
Inst. Accred.: SACS (1949/2002)

Lee University
1120 North Ocoee St., PO Box 3450, Cleveland 37320-
3450
Type: Private, Church of God, four-year
Degrees: B, M   *Enroll:* 3,513
URL: http://www.leeuniversity.edu
Phone: (423) 614-8000   *Calendar:* Sem. plan
Inst. Accred.: SACS (1960/1994)
Prog. Accred.: Music

LeMoyne-Owen College
807 Walker Ave., Memphis 38126
Type: Private, United Church of Christ, four-year
Degrees: B, M   *Enroll:* 710
URL: http://www.lemoyne-owen.edu
Phone: (901) 774-9090   *Calendar:* Sem. plan
Inst. Accred.: SACS (1939/1993, Warning)

Lincoln Memorial University
6965 Cumberland Gap Pkwy., Harrogate 37752
Type: Private, independent, four-year
Degrees: A, B, M   *Enroll:* 2,068
URL: http://www.lmunet.edu
Phone: (423) 869-3611   *Calendar:* Sem. plan
Inst. Accred.: SACS (1936/2000)
Prog. Accred.: Clinical Lab Scientist, Nursing, Social
  Work, Veterinary Technology

Lipscomb University
3901 Granny White Pike, Nashville 37204-3951
Type: Private, Churches of Christ, four-year
Degrees: B, M   *Enroll:* 2,396
URL: http://www.lipscomb.edu
Phone: (615) 269-1000   *Calendar:* Sem. plan
Inst. Accred.: SACS (1954/1996)
Prog. Accred.: Athletic Training, Business (ACBSP), Music,
  Social Work, Teacher Education (NCATE)

Martin Methodist College
433 West Madison St., Pulaski 38478
Type: Private, United Methodist Church, four-year
Degrees: A, B   *Enroll:* 510
URL: http://www.martinmethodist.edu
Phone: (931) 363-9804   *Calendar:* Sem. plan
Inst. Accred.: SACS (1952/1999)

Maryville College
502 East Lamar Alexander Pkwy., Maryville 37804-5907
Type: Private, Presbyterian Church (USA), four-year
Degrees: B   *Enroll:* 1,036
URL: http://www.maryvillecollege.edu
Phone: (865) 981-8000   *Calendar:* Sem. plan
Inst. Accred.: SACS (1922/2003)
Prog. Accred.: Music

MedVance Institute
1065 East Tenth St., Cookeville 38501
Type: Private, proprietary, two-year
Degrees: A   *Enroll:* 88
URL: http://www.medvance.edu
Phone: (931) 526-3660   *Calendar:* Qtr. plan
Inst. Accred.: COE (1988/2004)
Prog. Accred.: Clinical Lab Technology, Radiography

Miami Campus
9035 Sunset Dr., Ste. 200, Miami, FL 33173
Phone: (305) 596-5553

West Palm Beach Campus
1630†Congress Ave., Palm Beach, FL 33461
Phone: (561) 304-3466

Meharry Medical College
1005 D.B. Todd Blvd., Nashville 37208
Type: Private, United Methodist Church, four-year
Degrees: M, D   *Enroll:* 723
URL: http://mmc.edu
Phone: (615) 327-6111   *Calendar:* Sem. plan
Inst. Accred.: SACS (1972/1997)
Prog. Accred.: Dental Hygiene, Dentistry, General Practice
  Residency, Medicine, Oral and Maxillofacial Surgery

Memphis College of Art
Overton Park, 1930 Poplar Ave., Memphis 38104-2764
Type: Private, independent, four-year
Degrees: B, M   *Enroll:* 319
URL: http://www.mca.edu
Phone: (901) 272-5100   *Calendar:* Sem. plan
Inst. Accred.: SACS (1963/2002)
Prog. Accred.: Art

Memphis Theological Seminary
168 East Pkwy. South, Memphis 38104-4340
Type: Private, Cumberland Presbyterian Church, four-year
Degrees: M, D   *Enroll:* 252
URL: http://www.mtscampus.edu
Phone: (901) 458-8232   *Calendar:* Sem. plan
Inst. Accred.: ATS (1973/1998), SACS (1988/1998)

Mid-America Baptist Theological Seminary
PO Box 381528, Germantown 38183-1528
Type: Private, independent, four-year
Degrees: A, M, D   *FTE Enroll:* 284
URL: http://www.mabts.edu
Phone: (901) 751-8453   *Calendar:* Sem. plan
Inst. Accred.: SACS (1981/1996)

Middle Tennessee School of Anesthesia
PO Box 6414, Madison 37116
Type: Private, independent, four-year
Degrees: M   *Enroll:* 140
URL: http://www.mtsa.edu
Phone: (615) 868-6503   *Calendar:* Qtr. plan
Inst. Accred.: SACS (1994/1999)
Prog. Accred.: Nurse Anesthesia Education

Middle Tennessee State University
1301 East Main St., Murfreesboro 37132
Type: Public, state, four-year
System: Tennessee Board of Regents
Degrees: A, B, M, P, D   *Enroll:* 19,018
URL: http://www.mtsu.edu
Phone: (615) 898-2300   *Calendar:* Sem. plan
Inst. Accred.: SACS (1928/1995)
Prog. Accred.: Accounting, Business (AACSB), Computer
  Science, Counseling, Engineering Technology
  (computer, electromechanical, manufacturing), Family
  and Consumer Science, Industrial Technology, Interior
  Design, Journalism, Music, Nursing, Nursing Education,
  Recreation and Leisure Services, Social Work, Teacher
  Education (NCATE)

Miller-Motte Technical College
1820 Business Park Dr., Clarksville 37040-0415
Type: Private, proprietary, four-year
Degrees: A, B   *Enroll:* 106
URL: http://www.miller-
  motte.com/clarksvillewelcome.html
Phone: (931) 553-0071   *Calendar:* Qtr. plan
Inst. Accred.: ACICS (1989/2003)
Prog. Accred.: Medical Assisting (CAAHEP)

Cary Campus
2205 Walnut St., Cary, NC 27511
Phone: (888) 286-9961

Charleston Campus
8085 Rivers Ave., Ste. E, Charleston, SC 29406
Phone: (843) 574-0101

Chattanooga Campus
6020 Shallowford Rd., Ste.100, Chattanooga 37421
Phone: (423) 510-9675

Goodlettsville Campus
801 Spice Park North, Goodlettsville 37072-1870
Phone: (615) 859-8090

Wilmington Campus
5000 Market St., Wilmington, NC 28405
Phone: (910) 392-4660
Prog. Accred: Medical Assisting (CAAHEP)

Milligan College
PO Box 50, Milligan College 37682
Type: Private, independent, four-year
Degrees: A, B, M   *Enroll:* 805
URL: http://www.milligan.edu
Phone: (423) 461-8700   *Calendar:* Sem. plan
Inst. Accred.: SACS (1960/2002)
Prog. Accred.: Nursing Education, Occupational Therapy,
  Teacher Education (NCATE)

Motlow State Community College
PO Box 8500, Lynchburg 37352-8500
Type: Public, state, two-year
System: Tennessee Board of Regents
Degrees: A   *Enroll:* 2,476
URL: http://www.mscc.edu
Phone: (931) 393-1500   *Calendar:* Sem. plan
Inst. Accred.: SACS (1971/1996)
Prog. Accred.: Business (ACBSP), Nursing

Nashville Auto Diesel College
1524 Gallatin Rd., Nashville 37206-3298
Type: Private, proprietary, two-year
Degrees: A   *Enroll:* 1,565
Phone: (615) 226-3990
Inst. Accred.: ACCSCT (1967/2002)

Nashville State Community College
120 White Bridge Rd., Nashville 37209-4515
Type: Public, state, two-year
System: Tennessee Board of Regents
Degrees: A   *Enroll:* 3,730
URL: http://www.nscc.edu
Phone: (615) 353-3333   *Calendar:* Sem. plan
Inst. Accred.: SACS (1972/1997)
Prog. Accred.: Business (ACBSP), Engineering Technology
   (architectural, civil/construction, electrical),
   Occupational Therapy Assisting, Surgical Technology

North Central Institute
168 Jack Miller Blvd., Clarksville 37042-4810
Type: Private, proprietary, two-year
Degrees: A   *Enroll:* 103
URL: http://www.nci.edu
Phone: (931) 431-9700
Inst. Accred.: COE (1992/2003)

Northeast State Technical Community College
PO Box 246, 2425 Hwy. 75, Blountville 37617-0246
Type: Public, state, two-year
System: Tennessee Board of Regents
Degrees: A   *Enroll:* 3,309
URL: http://www.nstcc.cc.tn.us
Phone: (423) 323-3191   *Calendar:* Sem. plan
Inst. Accred.: SACS (1984/2000)
Prog. Accred.: Business (ACBSP), EMT (Paramedic)

Nossi College of Art
907 Rivergate Pkwy., Ste. E6, Goodlettsville 37072-2319
Type: Private, independent, four-year
Degrees: A, B   *Enroll:* 225
URL: http://www.nossi.com
Phone: (615) 851-1088   *Calendar:* Sem. plan
Inst. Accred.: ACCSCT (1988/2004)

O'More College of Design
423 South Margin St., PO Box 908, Franklin 37065-0908
Type: Private, professional, four-year
Degrees: B   *Enroll:* 113
Phone: (615) 794-4254   *Calendar:* Sem. plan
Inst. Accred.: ACCSCT (1994/2004)
Prog. Accred.: Interior Design

Pellissippi State Technical Community College
10915 Hardin Valley Rd., PO Box 22990, Knoxville 37933
Type: Public, state, two-year
System: Tennessee Board of Regents
Degrees: A   *Enroll:* 5,162
URL: http://www.pstcc.edu
Phone: (865) 694-6400   *Calendar:* Sem. plan
Inst. Accred.: SACS (1977/2002)
Prog. Accred.: Business (ACBSP), Engineering Technology
   (chemical, civil/construction, computer, electrical,
   mechanical)

Rhodes College
2000 North Pkwy., Memphis 38112-1690
Type: Private, Presbyterian Church (USA), four-year
Degrees: B, M   *Enroll:* 1,544
URL: http://www.rhodes.edu
Phone: (901) 843-3000   *Calendar:* Sem. plan
Inst. Accred.: SACS (1911/1999)

Roane State Community College
276 Patton Ln., Harriman 37748-5011
Type: Public, state, two-year
System: Tennessee Board of Regents
Degrees: A   *Enroll:* 3,781
URL: http://www.roanestate.edu
Phone: (865) 354-3000   *Calendar:* Sem. plan
Inst. Accred.: SACS (1974/2000)
Prog. Accred.: Business (ACBSP), Dental Hygiene, EMT
   (Paramedic), Health Information Technician, Massage
   Therapy, Nursing, Occupational Therapy Assisting,
   Opticianry, Physical Therapy Assisting, Radiography,
   Respiratory Therapy

South College
720 North Fifth Ave., Knoxville 37917
Type: Private, proprietary, four-year
Degrees: A, B   *Enroll:* 443
URL: http://www.southcollegetn.edu
Phone: (865) 524-3043   *Calendar:* Qtr. plan
Inst. Accred.: SACS (2000, Warning)
Prog. Accred.: Medical Assisting (AMA), Occupational
   Therapy Assisting, Physical Therapy Assisting,
   Radiography

Southeastern Career College
2416 21st Ave. South, Ste. 300, Nashville 37212
Type: Private, proprietary, two-year
System: Kaplan Higher Education Corporation
Degrees: A
URL: http://www.southeasterncareercollege.co
Phone: (615) 269-9900
Inst. Accred.: COE (1985/2002)

Southern Adventist University
PO Box 370, Collegedale 37315-0370
Type: Private, Seventh-Day Adventist Church, four-year
Degrees: A, B, M   *Enroll:* 2,051
URL: http://www.southern.edu
Phone: (423) 238-2111   *Calendar:* Sem. plan
Inst. Accred.: SACS (1950/2002)
Prog. Accred.: Music, Nursing, Social Work, Teacher
   Education (NCATE)

Southern College of Optometry
1245 Madison Ave., Memphis 38104
Type: Private, independent, four-year
Degrees: D   *Enroll:* 461
URL: http://www.sco.edu
Phone: (901) 722-3200   *Calendar:* Qtr. plan
Inst. Accred.: SACS (1967/2002)
Prog. Accred.: Optometric Residency, Optometry

Southwest Tennessee Community College
5983 Macon Cove, Memphis 38134-7693
Type: Public, state, two-year
System: Tennessee Board of Regents
Degrees: A   *Enroll:* 7,538
URL: http://www.southwest.tn.edu
Phone: (901) 333-4986   *Calendar:* Sem. plan
Inst. Accred.: SACS (2000/2005)
Prog. Accred.: Business (ACBSP), Clinical Lab Technology,
  EMT (Paramedic), Nursing, Phlebotomy, Physical
  Therapy Assisting, Radiography

Macon Cove Campus
5983 Macon Cove, Memphis 38134-7693
Phone: (901) 333-4111
Prog. Accred: Engineering Technology (architectural,
  bioengineering, chemical, civil/construction,
  computer, electrical, industrial, mechanical,
  telecommunications)

Temple Baptist Seminary
1815 Union Ave., Chattanooga 37404
Type: Private, Southern Baptist Church, four-year
Degrees: M, D   *FTE Enroll:* 73
URL: http://www.templebaptistseminary.edu
Phone: (423) 493-4221   *Calendar:* Sem. plan
Inst. Accred.: TRACS (2000)

Tennessee State University
3500 John Merritt Blvd., Nashville 37209-1561
Type: Public, state, four-year
System: Tennessee Board of Regents
Degrees: A, B, M, P, D   *Enroll:* 7,523
URL: http://www.tnstate.edu
Phone: (615) 963-5000   *Calendar:* Sem. plan
Inst. Accred.: SACS (1946/2000)
Prog. Accred.: Art, Business (AACSB), Clinical Lab
  Scientist, Counseling Psychology, Dental Hygiene,
  Engineering (architectural, civil, electrical, mechanical),
  Family and Consumer Science, Health Information
  Administration, Music, Nursing, Occupational Therapy,
  Physical Therapy, Public Administration, Respiratory
  Therapy, Social Work, Speech-Language Pathology,
  Teacher Education (NCATE)

Tennessee Technological University
North Dixie Ave., Campus Box 5007, Cookeville 38505
Type: Public, state, four-year
System: Tennessee Board of Regents
Degrees: A, B, M, P, D   *Enroll:* 7,765
URL: http://www.tntech.edu
Phone: (931) 372-3101   *Calendar:* Sem. plan
Inst. Accred.: SACS (1939/1995)
Prog. Accred.: Accounting, Art, Business (AACSB),
  Engineering (chemical, civil, computer, electrical,
  industrial, mechanical), Industrial Technology, Music,
  Nursing, Nursing Education, Teacher Education (NCATE)

Tennessee Temple University
1815 Union Ave., Chattanooga 37404-3587
Type: Private, independent Baptist Church, four-year
Degrees: A, B, M   *Enroll:* 479
URL: http://www.tntemple.edu
Phone: (423) 493-4100   *Calendar:* Sem. plan
Inst. Accred.: TRACS (2000)

Tennessee Wesleyan College
PO Box 40, Athens 37371-0040
Type: Private, United Methodist Church, four-year
Degrees: B   *Enroll:* 704
URL: http://www.twcnet.edu
Phone: (423) 745-7504   *Calendar:* Sem. plan
Inst. Accred.: SACS (1926/2000)
Prog. Accred.: Nursing Education

Trevecca Nazarene University
333 Murfreesboro Rd., Nashville 37210
Type: Private, Church of the Nazarene, four-year
Degrees: A, B, M, D   *Enroll:* 1,674
URL: http://www.trevecca.edu
Phone: (615) 248-1200   *Calendar:* Sem. plan
Inst. Accred.: SACS (1969/2003)
Prog. Accred.: Music, Physician Assistant

Tusculum College
PO Box 5048, Greeneville 37743
Type: Private, Presbyterian Church (USA), four-year
Degrees: B, M   *Enroll:* 2,122
URL: http://www.tusculum.edu
Phone: (423) 636-7300   *Calendar:* Sem. plan
Inst. Accred.: SACS (1926/2003)
Prog. Accred.: Liberal Education

Union University
1050 Union University Dr., Jackson 38305
Type: Private, Tennessee Baptist Convention, four-year
Degrees: A, B, M, D   *Enroll:* 2,445
URL: http://www.uu.edu
Phone: (731) 668-1818   *Calendar:* Sem. plan
Inst. Accred.: SACS (1948/1996)
Prog. Accred.: Art, Music, Nursing Education, Social Work,
  Teacher Education (NCATE)

The University of Memphis
Memphis 38152
Type: Public, state, four-year
System: Tennessee Board of Regents
Degrees: B, M, P, D   *Enroll:* 15,996
URL: http://www.memphis.edu
Phone: (901) 678-2000   *Calendar:* Sem. plan
Inst. Accred.: SACS (1927/1994)
Prog. Accred.: Accounting, Art, Audiology, Business
(AACSB), Clinical Psychology, Counseling, Counseling
Psychology, Dietetics (internship), Engineering (civil,
computer, electrical, mechanical), Engineering
Technology (computer, electrical, manufacturing),
Family and Consumer Science, Health Services
Administration, Interior Design, Journalism, Law, Music,
Nursing, Nursing Education, Planning, Psychology
Internship, Public Administration, Rehabilitation
Counseling, Social Work, Speech-Language Pathology,
Teacher Education (NCATE), Theatre

The University of Tennessee
800 Andy Holt Tower, Knoxville 37996-0150
Type: Public, state, four-year
System: University of Tennessee System
Degrees: B, M, P, D   *Enroll:* 24,853
URL: http://www.tennessee.edu
Phone: (865) 974-1000   *Calendar:* Sem. plan
Inst. Accred.: SACS (1897/2000)
Prog. Accred.: Accounting, Art, Audiology, Business
(AACSB), Clinical Lab Scientist, Clinical Pastoral
Education (ACPEI), Clinical Psychology, Counseling,
Counseling Psychology, Dietetics (internship),
Engineering (aerospace, bioengineering, chemical, civil,
computer, electrical, engineering physics/science,
industrial, materials, mechanical, nuclear), Family and
Consumer Science, Forestry, General Practice
Residency, Interior Design, Journalism, Law,
Librarianship, Music, Nuclear Medicine Technology,
Nursing, Nursing Education, Oral and Maxillofacial
Surgery, Planning, Psychology Internship, Public Health,
Radiography, Recreation and Leisure Services,
Rehabilitation Counseling, School Psychology, Social
Work, Speech-Language Pathology, Teacher Education
(NCATE), Veterinary Medicine

Health Science Center
800 Madison Ave., Memphis 38163
Phone: (901) 448-5500
Prog. Accred: Advanced Education in General
Dentistry, Clinical Lab Scientist, Combined
Prosthodontics, Cytotechnology, Dental Hygiene,
Dentistry, General Dentistry, Health Information
Administration, Medicine, Nurse Anesthesia
Education, Nursing, Nursing Education, Occupational
Therapy, Oral and Maxillofacial Surgery, Orthodontic
and Dentofacial Orthopedics, Pediatric Dentistry,
Periodontics, Pharmacy, Physical Therapy,
Psychology Internship, Social Work

The University of Tennessee at Chattanooga
615 McCallie Ave., Chattanooga 37403-2598
Type: Public, state, four-year
System: University of Tennessee System
Degrees: B, M, P, D   *Enroll:* 7,258
URL: http://www.utc.edu
Phone: (423) 425-4111   *Calendar:* Sem. plan
Inst. Accred.: SACS (1910/2002)
Prog. Accred.: Art, Business (AACSB), Computer Science,
Counseling, Engineering (electrical, general,
mechanical), Journalism, Music, Nurse Anesthesia
Education, Nursing, Nursing Education, Physical
Therapy, Public Administration, Social Work, Teacher
Education (NCATE)

The University of Tennessee at Martin
University St., Martin 38238
Type: Public, state, four-year
System: University of Tennessee System
Degrees: A, B, M   *Enroll:* 5,076
URL: http://www.utm.edu
Phone: (731) 587-7000   *Calendar:* Sem. plan
Inst. Accred.: SACS (1951/2002)
Prog. Accred.: Business (AACSB), Dietetics (internship),
Engineering (general), Family and Consumer Science,
Journalism, Music, Nursing, Social Work, Teacher
Education (NCATE)

The University of the South
735 University Ave., Sewanee 37383-1000
Type: Private, Prostestant Episcopal Church, four-year
Degrees: B, M, D   *Enroll:* 1,466
URL: http://www.sewanee.edu
Phone: (931) 598-1000   *Calendar:* Sem. plan
Inst. Accred.: ATS (1958/2005), SACS (1895/1995)

Vanderbilt University
2201 West End Ave., Nashville 37240
Type: Private, interdenominational, four-year
Degrees: B, M, P, D   *Enroll:* 10,831
URL: http://www.vanderbilt.edu
Phone: (615) 322-7311   *Calendar:* Sem. plan
Inst. Accred.: ATS (1938/2005), SACS (1895/1996)
Prog. Accred.: Audiology, Business (AACSB), Clinical Lab
Scientist, Clinical Psychology, Computer Science,
Counseling, Dietetics (internship), Engineering
(bioengineering, chemical, civil, computer, electrical,
mechanical), General Practice Residency, Law,
Medicine, Music, Nuclear Medicine Technology, Nurse
(Midwifery), Nursing, Oral and Maxillofacial Surgery,
Orthodontic and Dentofacial Orthopedics, Perfusion,
Psychology Internship, Radiation Therapy, Speech-
Language Pathology, Teacher Education (NCATE)

Volunteer State Community College
1480 Nashville Pike, Gallatin 37066-3188
Type: Public, state, two-year
System: Tennessee Board of Regents
Degrees: A   *Enroll:* 4,568
URL: http://www.volstate.edu
Phone: (615) 452-8600   *Calendar:* Sem. plan
Inst. Accred.: SACS (1973/1999)
Prog. Accred.: Business (ACBSP), Dental Assisting, EMT
  (Paramedic), Health Information Technician, Physical
  Therapy Assisting, Radiography, Respiratory Therapy,
  Respiratory Therapy Technology

Walters State Community College
500 South Davy Crockett Pkwy., Morristown 37813-6899
Type: Public, state, two-year
System: Tennessee Board of Regents
Degrees: A   *Enroll:* 4,240
URL: http://www.ws.edu
Phone: (423) 585-2600   *Calendar:* Sem. plan
Inst. Accred.: SACS (1972/1997)
Prog. Accred.: Business (ACBSP), Culinary Education,
  EMT (Paramedic), Industrial Technology, Nursing,
  Physical Therapy Assisting, Respiratory Therapy
  Technology

Watkins College of Art and Design
2298 MetroCenter Blvd., Nashville 37228
Type: Private, independent, four-year
Degrees: A, B   *Enroll:* 252
URL: http://www.watkins.edu
Phone: (615) 383-4848   *Calendar:* Sem. plan
Inst. Accred.: NASAD (1996/2002)
Prog. Accred.: Interior Design

West Tennessee Business College
1186 Hwy. 45 By-Pass, Jackson 38301-1668
Type: Private, proprietary, two-year
Degrees: A
URL: http://www.wtbc.com
Phone: (731) 668-7240   *Calendar:* Tri. plan
Inst. Accred.: ACICS (1953/2004)
Prog. Accred.: Medical Assisting (CAAHEP)

Williamson Christian College
200 Seaboard Ln., Franklin 37067
Type: Private, interdenominational, four-year
Degrees: A, B
URL: http://www.williamsoncc.edu
Phone: (615) 771-7821   *Calendar:* Sem. plan
Inst. Accred.: TRACS (2002)

TEXAS

Abilene Christian University
Abilene 79699
Type: Private, Church of Christ, four-year
Degrees: A, B, M, D   *Enroll:* 4,342
URL: http://www.acu.edu
Phone: (325) 674-2000   *Calendar:* Sem. plan
Inst. Accred.: ATS (2002), SACS (1951/2001)
Prog. Accred.: Business (AACSB), Interior Design,
   Journalism, Marriage and Family Therapy, Music,
   Nursing Education, Social Work, Speech-Language
   Pathology

The Academy of Health Care Professions
1900 North Loop West, Ste. 100, Houston 77018
Type: Private, proprietary, two-year
Degrees: A
URL: http://www.academyofhealth.com
Phone: (713) 425-3100
Inst. Accred.: ABHES (1999/2005)

Austin Campus
6505 Airport Blvd., Ste. 102, Austin 78752
Phone: (512) 892-2835
Prog. Accred: Medical Assisting (ABHES)

Southwest Campus
8313 Southwest Freeway, Ste. 300, Houston 77074
Phone: (713) 470-2427
Prog. Accred: Medical Assisting (ABHES), Surgical
   Technology

Academy of Oriental Medicine at Austin
2700 West Anderson Ln., Ste. 204, Austin 78757
Type: Private, proprietary, four-year
Degrees: M   *Enroll:* 162
URL: http://www.aoma.edu
Phone: (512) 454-1188
Inst. Accred.: ACAOM (1996/2004)

Alvin Community College
3110 Mustang Rd., Alvin 77511-4898
Type: Public, local, two-year
Degrees: A   *Enroll:* 2,358
URL: http://www.alvin.cc.tn.us
Phone: (281) 756-3500   *Calendar:* Sem. plan
Inst. Accred.: SACS (1959/2000)
Prog. Accred.: Nursing, Respiratory Therapy, Respiratory
   Therapy Technology

Amarillo College
PO Box 447, Amarillo 79178
Type: Public, state/local, two-year
Degrees: A   *Enroll:* 5,718
URL: http://www.actx.edu
Phone: (806) 371-5000   *Calendar:* Sem. plan
Inst. Accred.: SACS (1933/2002)
Prog. Accred.: Clinical Lab Technology, Dental Hygiene,
   Engineering Technology (electrical), Funeral Service
   Education (Mortuary Science), Music, Nuclear Medicine
   Technology, Nursing, Occupational Therapy Assisting,
   Physical Therapy Assisting, Radiation Therapy,
   Radiography, Respiratory Therapy, Surgical Technology

Amarillo Technical Center
PO Box 11197, Amarillo 79111
Phone: (806) 335-2316

Amberton University
1700 Eastgate Dr., Garland 75041
Type: Private, independent, four-year
Degrees: B, M   *Enroll:* 675
URL: http://www.amberton.edu
Phone: (972) 279-6511   *Calendar:* Qtr. plan
Inst. Accred.: SACS (1981/1997)

American College of Acupuncture and Oriental Medicine
9100 Park West Dr., Houston 77063
Type: Private, proprietary, four-year
Degrees: M   *Enroll:* 137
URL: http://www.acaom.edu
Phone: (713) 780-9777   *Calendar:* Sem. plan
Inst. Accred.: ACAOM (1996/2003)

Angelina College
PO Box 1768, Lufkin 75902
Type: Public, state/local, two-year
Degrees: A   *Enroll:* 3,096
URL: http://www.angelina.edu
Phone: (936) 639-1301   *Calendar:* Sem. plan
Inst. Accred.: SACS (1970/1995)
Prog. Accred.: Radiography, Respiratory Therapy

Angelo State University
2601 West Ave. North, San Angelo 76909
Type: Public, state, four-year
System: Texas State University System
Degrees: A, B, M   *Enroll:* 5,247
URL: http://www.angelo.edu
Phone: (325) 942-2073   *Calendar:* Sem. plan
Inst. Accred.: SACS (1936/2002)
Prog. Accred.: Business (ACBSP), Music, Nursing,
   Physical Therapy

Argosy University Dallas
One NorthPark, Ste. 315, 8950 North Central Expressway, Dallas 75231
Type: Private, proprietary, four-year
System: Argosy University
Degrees: M, D
URL: http://www.argosyu.edu
Phone: (214) 890-9900   *Calendar:* Tri. plan
Inst. Accred.: NCA-HLC (1981/2001, *Indirect accreditation through Argosy University, Chicago, IL*)

Arlington Baptist College
3001 West Division St., Arlington 76012-3497
Type: Private, World Baptist Fellowship, four-year
Degrees: B   *FTE Enroll:* 163
URL: http://www.abconline.edu
Phone: (817) 461-8741   *Calendar:* Sem. plan
Inst. Accred.: ABHE (1981/2002)

The Art Institute of Dallas
Two North Park, 8080 Park Ln. #100, Dallas 75231-9959
Type: Private, proprietary, four-year
System: Education Management Corporation
Degrees: A, B   *Enroll:* 1,177
URL: http://www.aid.edu
Phone: (214) 692-8080   *Calendar:* Qtr. plan
Inst. Accred.: SACS (1998/2003)
Prog. Accred.: Culinary Education

The Art Institute of Houston
1900 Yorktown St., Houston 77056
Type: Private, proprietary, four-year
System: Education Management Corporation
Degrees: A, B   *Enroll:* 1,288
URL: http://www.artinstitutes.edu/houston
Phone: (713) 623-2040   *Calendar:* Qtr. plan
Inst. Accred.: SACS (2000/2005)
Prog. Accred.: Culinary Education, Interior Design

ATI Career Training Center
10003 Technology Blvd. West, Dallas 75220
Type: Private, proprietary, two-year
Degrees: A
URL: http://www.aticareertraining.com
Phone: (972) 263-4284
Inst. Accred.: ACCSCT (1986/2005)

The Austin Business College
2101 I-35 South, 3rd Flr., Austin 78741
Type: Private, proprietary, two-year
Degrees: A   *Enroll:* 282
URL: http://www.abctx.edu
Phone: (512) 447-9415
Inst. Accred.: ACICS (1978/2001)

Austin College
900 North Grand Ave., Sherman 75090-4440
Type: Private, Presbyterian Church (USA), four-year
Degrees: B, M   *Enroll:* 1,322
URL: http://www.austincollege.edu
Phone: (903) 813-2000   *Calendar:* 4-1-4 plan
Inst. Accred.: SACS (1947/1999)

Austin Community College
5930 Middle Fiskville Rd., Austin 78752-4390
Type: Public, state/local, two-year
Degrees: A   *Enroll:* 15,746
URL: http://www.austincc.edu
Phone: (512) 223-7000   *Calendar:* Sem. plan
Inst. Accred.: SACS (1978/2004)
Prog. Accred.: Clinical Lab Technology, Culinary Education, Diagnostic Medical Sonography, EMT (Paramedic), Nursing, Occupational Therapy Assisting, Phlebotomy, Physical Therapy Assisting, Practical Nursing, Surgical Technology

Cypress Creek Campus
1555 Cypress Creek Rd.., Austin 78702
Phone: (512) 223-2000

Eastview Campus
3401 Webberville Rd., Cedar Park 78613
Phone: (512) 223-5100
Prog. Accred: Radiography

Northridge Campus
11928 Stinehollow Dr., Austin 78758
Phone: (512) 223-4000

Pinnacle Campus
7748 Hwy. 290 West, Austin 78786
Phone: (512) 223-8001
Prog. Accred: Business (ACBSP)

Rio Grande Campus
1212 Rio Grande St., Austin 78701
Phone: (512) 223-3000

Riverside Campus
1020 Grove Blvd., Austin 78741
Phone: (512) 223-6000

Austin Graduate School of Theology
1909 University Ave., Austin 78705
Type: Private, Church of Christ, four-year
Degrees: B, M   *Enroll:* 34
URL: http://www.austingrad.edu
Phone: (512) 476-2772   *Calendar:* Sem. plan
Inst. Accred.: SACS (1987/2003)

Austin Presbyterian Theological Seminary
100 East 27th St., Austin 78705-5797
Type: Private, Presbyterian Church (USA), four-year
Degrees: M, D   *Enroll:* 204
URL: http://www.austinseminary.edu
Phone: (512) 472-6736   *Calendar:* 4-1-4 plan
Inst. Accred.: ATS (1940/1999), SACS (1973/1999)

Baptist Health System
School of Health Professions
730 North Main Ave., Ste. 212, San Antonio 78205
Type: Private, independent, two-year
Degrees: A
URL: http://www.baptistschools.com
Phone: (210) 297-9636
Inst. Accred.: ABHES (2005)
Prog. Accred.: Surgical Technology

Baptist Missionary Association Theological Seminary
1530 East Pine St., Jacksonville 75766-5407
Type: Private, Baptist Missionary Association of America, four-year
Degrees: A, B, M   *Enroll:* 60
URL: http://www.bmats.edu
Phone: (903) 586-2501   *Calendar:* Sem. plan
Inst. Accred.: SACS (1986/2001)

Baptist University of the Americas
8019 South Pan Am Expressway, San Antonio 78224-1397
Type: Private, Southern Baptist Church, four-year
Degrees: B
URL: http://www.hbts.org
Phone: (210) 924-4338   *Calendar:* Sem. plan
Inst. Accred.: ABHE (2003)

Baylor College of Medicine
One Baylor Plaza, Houston 77030-3498
Type: Private, independent, four-year
Degrees: M, D   *Enroll:* 1,287
URL: http://www.bcm.tmc.edu
Phone: (713) 798-4951   *Calendar:* Qtr. plan
Inst. Accred.: SACS (1970/1995)
Prog. Accred.: Clinical Pastoral Education (ACPEI), Medicine, Microbiology, Nurse (Midwifery), Nurse Anesthesia Education, Physician Assistant, Psychology Internship

Baylor University
Waco 76798
Type: Private, Southern Baptist Church, four-year
Degrees: B, M, D   *Enroll:* 13,408
URL: http://www.baylor.edu
Phone: (254) 710-1011   *Calendar:* Sem. plan
Inst. Accred.: SACS (1914/1996)
Prog. Accred.: Accounting, Business (AACSB), Clinical Psychology, Computer Science, Engineering (electrical, general, mechanical), Family and Consumer Science, Health Services Administration, Interior Design, Journalism, Law, Liberal Education, Montessori Teacher Education, Music, Nurse (Midwifery), Nursing, Nursing Education, Social Work, Speech-Language Pathology, Teacher Education (NCATE), Theatre

Blinn College
902 College Ave., Brenham 77833
Type: Public, state/local, two-year
Degrees: A   *Enroll:* 9,654
URL: http://www.blinn.edu
Phone: (979) 830-4000   *Calendar:* Sem. plan
Inst. Accred.: SACS (1950/2005)
Prog. Accred.: Nursing, Physical Therapy Assisting, Radiography

Bryan Campus
PO Box 6030, 423 Blinn Blvd., Bryan 77805-6030
Phone: (979) 209-7200
Prog. Accred: Dental Hygiene

Border Institute of Technology
9611 Acer Ave., El Paso 79925-6744
Type: Private, proprietary, two-year
Degrees: A   *Enroll:* 159
URL: http://info.bitelp.edu
Phone: (915) 593-7328
Inst. Accred.: ACCSCT (1975/2003)

Brazosport College
500 College Dr., Lake Jackson 77566
Type: Public, state/local, four-year
Degrees: A, B   *Enroll:* 1,847
URL: http://www.brazosport.edu
Phone: (979) 230-3000   *Calendar:* Sem. plan
Inst. Accred.: SACS (1970/1995)

Brookhaven College
3939 Valley View Ln., Dallas 75244-4997
Type: Public, state/local, two-year
System: Dallas County Community College District
Degrees: A   *Enroll:* 5,674
URL: http://www.brookhavencollege.edu
Phone: (972) 860-4700   *Calendar:* Sem. plan
Inst. Accred.: SACS (1979/2003)

Cedar Valley College
3030 North Dallas Ave., Lancaster 75134
Type: Public, state/local, two-year
System: Dallas County Community College District
Degrees: A   *Enroll:* 2,452
URL: http://www.cedarvalleycollege.edu
Phone: (972) 860-8200   *Calendar:* Sem. plan
Inst. Accred.: SACS (1979/2003)
Prog. Accred.: Veterinary Technology

Center for Advanced Legal Studies
3910 Kirby Dr., Ste. 200, Houston 77098
Type: Private, proprietary, two-year
Degrees: A   *Enroll:* 224
URL: http://www.paralegalpeople.com
Phone: (713) 529-2778
Inst. Accred.: COE (1989/2001)

Central Texas College
PO Box 1800, Killeen 76540-1800
Type: Public, state, two-year
Degrees: A   *Enroll:* 7,723
URL: http://www.ctcd.edu
Phone: (254) 526-7161   *Calendar:* Sem. plan
Inst. Accred.: SACS (1969/2005)
Prog. Accred.: Clinical Lab Technology, Nursing

Cisco Junior College
101 College Heights, Cisco 76437
Type: Public, state, two-year
Degrees: A   *Enroll:* 1,944
URL: http://www.cisco.cc.tx.us
Phone: (254) 442-2567   *Calendar:* Sem. plan
Inst. Accred.: SACS (1958/1999)
Prog. Accred.: Medical Assisting (AMA), Practical Nursing

Clarendon College
PO Box 968, Clarendon 79226
Type: Public, state/local, two-year
Degrees: A   *Enroll:* 598
URL: http://www.clarendoncollege.edu
Phone: (806) 874-3571   *Calendar:* Sem. plan
Inst. Accred.: SACS (1970/1995)

Coastal Bend College
3800 Charco Rd., Beeville 78102
Type: Public, state/local, two-year
Degrees: A   *Enroll:* 2,371
URL: http://vct.coastalbend.edu
Phone: (361) 358-2838   *Calendar:* Sem. plan
Inst. Accred.: SACS (1969/1994, Probation)
Prog. Accred.: Dental Hygiene, Health Information
  Technician

College of Biblical Studies—Houston
7000 Regency Square Blvd., Ste. 110, Houston 77036-3211
Type: Private, independent, four-year
Degrees: A, B   *Enroll:* 790
URL: http://www.cbshouston.edu
Phone: (713) 785-5995   *Calendar:* Sem. plan
Inst. Accred.: ABHE (1999/2004)

The College of Saint Thomas Moore
3020 Lubbock Ave., Fort Worth 76109-2322
Type: Private, Roman Catholic Church, four-year
Degrees: A, B   *Enroll:* 17
URL: http://www.cstm.edu
Phone: (817) 923-8459   *Calendar:* Sem. plan
Inst. Accred.: SACS (1994/1999)

College of the Mainland
1200 Amburn Rd., Texas City 77591
Type: Public, local, two-year
Degrees: A   *Enroll:* 2,300
URL: http://www.com.edu
Phone: (409) 938-1211   *Calendar:* Sem. plan
Inst. Accred.: SACS (1969/2003)
Prog. Accred.: EMT (Paramedic), Nursing

Collin County Community College District
4800 Preston Park Blvd., Plano 75093
Type: Public, state/local, two-year
Degrees: A   *Enroll:* 9,963
URL: http://www.cccd.edu
Phone: (972) 881-5790   *Calendar:* Sem. plan
Inst. Accred.: SACS (1989/1994, Warning)
Prog. Accred.: Nursing, Phlebotomy, Respiratory Therapy

Central Park Campus
PO Box 8001, 2200 West University Dr., McKinney 75069-8001
Phone: (972) 548-6790
Prog. Accred: Dental Hygiene

Commonwealth Institute of Funeral Service
415 Barren Springs Dr., Houston 77090
Type: Private, independent, two-year
Degrees: A   *Enroll:* 147
URL: http://www.commonwealthinst.org
Phone: (281) 873-0262   *Calendar:* Qtr. plan
Inst. Accred.: ABFSE (1961/1996)

Computer Career Center
6101 Montana Ave., El Paso 79925
Type: Private, proprietary, two-year
Degrees: A   *Enroll:* 414
URL: http://www.computercareercenter.com
Phone: (915) 779-8031   *Calendar:* Sem. plan
Inst. Accred.: COE (1989/2000)
Prog. Accred.: Medical Assisting (ABHES), Medical
  Assisting (CAAHEP)

Concordia University at Austin
3400 I.H. 35 North, Austin 78705
Type: Private, Lutheran Church-Missouri Synrd, four-year
System: Concordia University System
Degrees: A, B, M   *Enroll:* 892
URL: http://www.concordia.edu
Phone: (512) 486-2000   *Calendar:* Sem. plan
Inst. Accred.: SACS (1968/1998)

Court Reporting Institute of Dallas
8585 North Stemmons Freeway, Ste. 200, North, Dallas 75247
Type: Private, proprietary, two-year
Degrees: A
URL: http://www.crid.com
Phone: (214) 350-9722
Inst. Accred.: ACICS (1986/2004)

Court Reporting Institute of Houston
13101 Northwest Freeway, Ste. 100, Houston 77040
Phone: (713) 996-8300

The Criswell College
4010 Gaston Ave., Dallas 75246-1537
Type: Private, First Baptist Church of Dallas, four-year
Degrees: A, B, M   *FTE Enroll:* 283
URL: http://www.criswell.edu
Phone: (214) 821-5433   *Calendar:* Sem. plan
Inst. Accred.: SACS (1985/2002, Warning)

Dallas Baptist University
3000 Mountain Creek Pkwy., Dallas 75211-9299
Type: Private, Baptist General Convention of Texas, four-year
Degrees: A, B, M, D　　　　　　*Enroll:* 3,081
URL: http://www.dbu.edu
Phone: (214) 333-7100　　*Calendar:* 4-1-4 plan
Inst. Accred.: SACS (1959/1998)
Prog. Accred.: Business (ACBSP), Music

Dallas Christian College
2700 Christian Pkwy., Dallas 75234-7299
Type: Private, Christian Churches/Churches of Christ, four-year
Degrees: B　　　　　　　　*Enroll:* 265
URL: http://www.dallas.edu
Phone: (972) 241-3371　　*Calendar:* Sem. plan
Inst. Accred.: ABHE (1978/1999)

Dallas Theological Seminary
3909 Swiss Ave., Dallas 75204
Type: Private, interdenominational, four-year
Degrees: M, D　　　　　　*Enroll:* 1,341
URL: http://www.dts.edu
Phone: (214) 824-3094　　*Calendar:* Sem. plan
Inst. Accred.: ATS (1994/2003), SACS (1969/2003)

Del Mar College
101 Baldwin Blvd., Corpus Christi 78404-3897
Type: Public, state/local, two-year
Degrees: A　　　　　　　*Enroll:* 6,343
URL: http://www.delmar.edu
Phone: (361) 698-1200　　*Calendar:* Sem. plan
Inst. Accred.: SACS (1946/2000)
Prog. Accred.: Art, Clinical Lab Technology, Culinary Education, Dental Assisting, Dental Hygiene, Diagnostic Medical Sonography, Engineering Technology (electrical), Music, Nursing, Occupational Therapy Assisting, Physical Therapy Assisting, Radiography, Respiratory Therapy, Respiratory Therapy Technology, Surgical Technology, Theatre

DeVry University Irving
4800 Regent Blvd., Irving 75063-2440
Type: Private, proprietary, four-year
System: DeVry University
Degrees: A, B, M　　　　　*Enroll:* 2,254
URL: http://www.devry.edu/irving
Phone: (972) 929-6777　　*Calendar:* Sem. plan
Inst. Accred.: NCA-HLC (2002, *Indirect accreditation through DeVry University, Oakbrook Terrace, IL*)
Prog. Accred.: Engineering Technology (computer)

Houston Campus
11125 Equity Dr., Houston 77041
Phone: (866) 703-3879

East Texas Baptist University
1209 North Grove Ave., Marshall 75670-1498
Type: Private, Baptist General Convention of Texas, four-year
Degrees: A, B　　　　　　*Enroll:* 1,257
URL: http://www.etbu.edu
Phone: (903) 935-7963　　*Calendar:* 4-1-4 plan
Inst. Accred.: SACS (1957/1998)
Prog. Accred.: Music, Nursing, Nursing Education

Eastfield College
3737 Motley Dr., Mesquite 75150-2099
Type: Public, state/local, two-year
System: Dallas County Community College District
Degrees: A　　　　　　　*Enroll:* 6,103
URL: http://www.eastfieldcollege.edu
Phone: (972) 860-7100　　*Calendar:* Sem. plan
Inst. Accred.: SACS (1972/2003, Warning)

El Centro College
Main and Lamar St.s, Dallas 75202-3604
Type: Public, state/local, two-year
System: Dallas County Community College District
Degrees: A　　　　　　　*Enroll:* 3,016
URL: http://www.elcentrocollege.edu
Phone: (214) 860-2037　　*Calendar:* Sem. plan
Inst. Accred.: SACS (1968/2003)
Prog. Accred.: Cardiovascular Technology, Clinical Lab Technology, Culinary Education, Diagnostic Medical Sonography, Interior Design, Medical Assisting (AMA), Nursing, Practical Nursing, Radiography, Respiratory Therapy, Surgical Technology

El Paso County Community College District
PO Box 20500, El Paso 79998-0500
Type: Public, local, two-year
Degrees: A　　　　　　　*Enroll:* 15,297
URL: http://www.epcc.edu
Phone: (915) 831-2000　　*Calendar:* Sem. plan
Inst. Accred.: SACS (1978/1994)
Prog. Accred.: Clinical Lab Technology, Dental Assisting, Dental Hygiene, Diagnostic Medical Sonography, Health Information Technician, Medical Assisting (AMA), Nursing, Ophthalmic Lab Technology, Opticianry, Physical Therapy Assisting, Radiography, Respiratory Therapy, Surgical Technology

The Episcopal Theological Seminary of the Southwest
PO Box 2247, 606 Rathervue Place, Austin 78768-2247
Type: Private, Episcopal Church, four-year
Degrees: M　　　　　　　*Enroll:* 88
URL: http://www.etss.edu
Phone: (512) 472-4133　　*Calendar:* Sem. plan
Inst. Accred.: ATS (1958/2004), SACS (1983/1993, Warning)
Prog. Accred.: Clinical Pastoral Education (ACPEI)

Frank Phillips College
PO Box 5118, Borger 79008-5118
Type: Public, local, two-year
Degrees: A   *Enroll:* 660
URL: http://www.fpc.cc.tx.us
Phone: (806) 457-4200   *Calendar:* Sem. plan
Inst. Accred.: SACS (1958/1999)

Galveston College
4015 Ave. Q, Galveston 77550
Type: Public, state/local, two-year
Degrees: A   *Enroll:* 1,284
URL: http://www.gc.edu
Phone: (409) 763-6551   *Calendar:* Sem. plan
Inst. Accred.: SACS (1969/2005)
Prog. Accred.: Nuclear Medicine Technology, Nursing,
Radiation Therapy, Radiography

Grayson County College
6101 Grayson Dr., Denison 75020
Type: Public, state/local, two-year
Degrees: A   *Enroll:* 2,413
URL: http://www.grayson.edu
Phone: (903) 465-6030   *Calendar:* Sem. plan
Inst. Accred.: SACS (1967/2001)
Prog. Accred.: Clinical Lab Technology, Dental Assisting,
Nursing

Hallmark Institute of Aeronautics
8901 Wetmore Rd., San Antonio 78216
Type: Private, proprietary, two-year
Degrees: A
URL: http://www.hallmarkinstitute.com
Phone: (210) 826-1000
Inst. Accred.: ACCSCT (1973/2001)

Hallmark Institute of Technology
10401 IH 10 West, San Antonio 78216-1737
Type: Private, proprietary, two-year
Degrees: A   *Enroll:* 790
URL: http://www.hallmarkinstitute.com
Phone: (210) 690-9000
Inst. Accred.: ACCSCT (1971/2004)

Hardin-Simmons University
2200 Hickory St., Abilene 79698
Type: Private, Baptist General Convention of Texas, four-
year
Degrees: A, B, M, D   *Enroll:* 2,054
URL: http://www.hsutx.edu
Phone: (915) 670-1000   *Calendar:* Sem. plan
Inst. Accred.: SACS (1927/1997)
Prog. Accred.: Business (ACBSP), Music, Nursing
Education, Physical Therapy, Social Work

Hill College
112 Lamar Dr., Hillsboro 76645
Type: Public, local, two-year
Degrees: A   *Enroll:* 1,259
URL: http://www.hillcollege.edu
Phone: (254) 582-2555   *Calendar:* Sem. plan
Inst. Accred.: SACS (1966/2000)

Houston Baptist University
7502 Fondren Rd., Houston 77074-3298
Type: Private, Southern Baptist Church, four-year
Degrees: A, B, M   *Enroll:* 2,053
URL: http://www.hbu.edu
Phone: (281) 649-3000   *Calendar:* Qtr. plan
Inst. Accred.: SACS (1968/2002)
Prog. Accred.: Nursing

Houston Community College
PO Box 667517, Houston 77266-7517
Type: Public, state, two-year
System: Texas Higher Education Coordinating Board
Degrees: A   *Enroll:* 20,779
URL: http://www.hccs.edu
Phone: (713) 718-2000   *Calendar:* Sem. plan
Inst. Accred.: SACS (1977/2002)
Prog. Accred.: Clinical Lab Technology, Dental Assisting,
EMT (Paramedic), Health Information Technician,
Histologic Technology, Interior Design, Medical Assisting
(AMA), Nuclear Medicine Technology, Physical Therapy
Assisting, Radiography, Respiratory Therapy,
Respiratory Therapy Technology, Surgical Technology

Central Campus
1300 Holman Ave., Houston 77004
Phone: (713) 718-6000
Prog. Accred: Health Information Technician, Interior
Design, Nuclear Medicine Technology, Respiratory
Therapy, Respiratory Therapy Technology, Surgical
Technology

College Without Walls
4310 Dunlavy St., Houston 77270
Phone: (713) 868-0799

Northeast Campus
4638 Airline Dr., PO Box 7849, Houston 77270-7849
Phone: (713) 694-5384
Prog. Accred: Engineering Technology (electrical)

Northwest Campus
16360 Park Ten Place, Houston 77084
Phone: (713) 718-5500

Southeast Campus
6815 Rustic St., Houston 77012
Phone: (713) 641-2725
Prog. Accred: Occupational Therapy Assisting

Southwest Campus
5407 Gulfton St., Houston 77081
Phone: (713) 661-4589

Houston Graduate School of Theology
1311 Holman, Ste. 200, Houston 77004
Type: Private, Religious Society of Friends, four-year
Degrees: M, D   *FTE Enroll:* 72
URL: http://www.hgst.edu
Phone: (713) 942-9505   *Calendar:* Sem. plan
Inst. Accred.: ATS (1997/2000)

Howard College
1001 Birdwell Ln., Big Spring 79720
Type: Public, state/local, two-year
System: Howard County Junior College District
Degrees: A   *Enroll:* 1,632
URL: http://www.howardcollege.edu
Phone: (432) 264-5000   *Calendar:* Sem. plan
Inst. Accred.: SACS (1955/1996)
Prog. Accred.: Dental Hygiene, Health Information
  Technician, Nursing, Respiratory Therapy Technology

Howard Payne University
1000 Fisk Ave., Brownwood 76801
Type: Private, Southern Baptist Church, four-year
Degrees: A, B   *Enroll:* 1,200
URL: http://www.hputx.edu
Phone: (325) 649-8020   *Calendar:* Sem. plan
Inst. Accred.: SACS (1948/2004)
Prog. Accred.: Music, Social Work

Huston-Tillotson University
900 Chicon St., Austin 78702-2795
Type: Private, United Methodist/United Church of Christ,
  four-year
Degrees: B   *Enroll:* 596
URL: http://www.htu.edu
Phone: (512) 505-3000   *Calendar:* Sem. plan
Inst. Accred.: SACS (1943/2002)

International Business College
5700 Cromo Dr., El Paso 79912
Type: Private, proprietary, two-year
Degrees: A
URL: http://www.ibcelpaso.com
Phone: (915) 842-0422
Inst. Accred.: ACICS (1969/2004)

International Business College
4630 50th St., Ste. 100, Lubbock 79414
Type: Private, proprietary, two-year
Degrees: A
URL: http://www.ibclubbock.com
Phone: (806) 797-1933
Inst. Accred.: ACICS (1987/2004)

Denton Campus
2006 West University Dr., Denton 76201
Phone: (940) 380-0024

McKinney Campus
901 North McDonald St., Building 7, Ste. 702,
McKinney 75069-2169
Phone: (972) 548-0774

Midland Campus
3305 Andrews Hwy., Midland 79703
Phone: (915) 694-7584

Sherman Campus
4107 North Texoma Pkwy., Sherman 75090
Phone: (903) 893-6604

Zaragosa Campus
1155 North Zaragosa Rd., El Paso 79907
Phone: (915) 859-0422

ITT Technical Institute
551 Ryan Plaza Dr., Arlington 76011
Type: Private, proprietary, two-year
System: ITT Educational Services, Inc.
Degrees: A   *Enroll:* 508
URL: http://www.itt-tech.edu
Phone: (817) 794-5100   *Calendar:* Qtr. plan
Inst. Accred.: ACICS (1999/2004)

ITT Technical Institute
5700 Northwest Pkwy., San Antonio 78249-3303
Type: Private, proprietary, two-year
System: ITT Educational Services, Inc.
Degrees: A   *Enroll:* 770
URL: http://www.itt-tech.edu
Phone: (210) 694-4612   *Calendar:* Qtr. plan
Inst. Accred.: ACICS (1999/2004)

Houston South Campus
2222 Bay Area Blvd., Houston 77058
Phone: (281) 486-2630

Jacksonville College
105 B.J. Albritton Dr., Jacksonville 75766-4759
Type: Private, Baptist Missionary Association of Texas,
  two-year
Degrees: A   *Enroll:* 273
URL: http://www.jacksonville-college.edu
Phone: (903) 586-2518   *Calendar:* Sem. plan
Inst. Accred.: SACS (1974/1999)

Jarvis Christian College
PO Box 1470, Hawkins 75765-1470
Type: Private, Disciples of Christ, four-year
Degrees: A, B   *Enroll:* 648
URL: http://www.jarvis.edu
Phone: (903) 769-5700   *Calendar:* Sem. plan
Inst. Accred.: SACS (1967/2003)
Prog. Accred.: Business (ACBSP)

KD Studio
2600 Stemmons Freeway, No. 117, Dallas 75207
Type: Private, independent, two-year
Degrees: A   *Enroll:* 157
URL: http://www.kdstudio.com
Phone: (214) 638-0484   *Calendar:* Sem. plan
Inst. Accred.: NAST (1988/2003)

Kilgore College
1100 Broadway Blvd., Kilgore 75662
Type: Public, local, two-year
Degrees: A   *Enroll:* 3,435
URL: http://www.kilgore.cc.tx.us
Phone: (903) 984-8531   *Calendar:* Sem. plan
Inst. Accred.: SACS (1939/1999)
Prog. Accred.: Clinical Lab Technology, Medical Assisting
  (AMA), Nursing, Physical Therapy Assisting,
  Radiography, Surgical Technology

Lamar Institute of Technology
PO Box 10043, Beaumont 77710
Type: Public, state, two-year
System: Texas State University System
Degrees: A
URL: http://www.theinstitute.lamar.edu
Phone: (409) 880-8321   *Calendar:* Sem. plan
Inst. Accred.: SACS (2000/2005)
Prog. Accred.: Radiography

Lamar State College—Orange
410 Front St., Orange 77630
Type: Public, state, two-year
System: Texas State University System
Degrees: A   *Enroll:* 1,233
URL: http://www.orange.lamar.edu
Phone: (409) 883-7750   *Calendar:* Sem. plan
Inst. Accred.: SACS (1989/2005)
Prog. Accred.: Clinical Lab Technology, Dental Assisting

Lamar State College—Port Arthur
1500 Procter St., Port Arthur 77640
Type: Public, state, two-year
System: Texas State University System
Degrees: A   *Enroll:* 1,515
URL: http://www.pa.lamar.edu
Phone: (409) 983-4921   *Calendar:* Sem. plan
Inst. Accred.: SACS (1988/2003)
Prog. Accred.: Business (ACBSP)

Lamar University
4400 MLK Blvd., PO Box 100009, Beaumont 77710
Type: Public, state, four-year
System: Texas State University System
Degrees: A, B, M, D   *Enroll:* 8,322
URL: http://www.lamar.edu
Phone: (409) 880-7011   *Calendar:* Sem. plan
Inst. Accred.: SACS (1955/1998)
Prog. Accred.: Audiology, Business (AACSB), Computer
  Science, Culinary Education, Dental Hygiene,
  Engineering (chemical, civil, electrical, industrial,
  mechanical), Music, Nursing, Radiography, Respiratory
  Therapy, Respiratory Therapy Technology, Social Work,
  Speech-Language Pathology

Laredo Community College
West End Washington St., Laredo 78040-4395
Type: Public, state/local, two-year
Degrees: A   *Enroll:* 4,798
URL: http://www.laredo.edu
Phone: (956) 722-0521   *Calendar:* Sem. plan
Inst. Accred.: SACS (1957/1999)
Prog. Accred.: Clinical Lab Technology, Nursing,
  Occupational Therapy Assisting, Physical Therapy
  Assisting, Radiography

Lee College
PO Box 818, Baytown 77522-0818
Type: Public, state/local, two-year
Degrees: A   *Enroll:* 3,485
URL: http://www.lee.edu
Phone: (281) 427-5611   *Calendar:* Sem. plan
Inst. Accred.: SACS (1948/1995)
Prog. Accred.: EMT (Paramedic), Health Information
  Technician, Nursing

LeTourneau University
2100 Mobberly Ave., PO Box 7001, Longview 75607-
7001
Type: Private, independent, four-year
Degrees: A, B, M   *Enroll:* 2,219
URL: http://www.letu.edu
Phone: (903) 233-3000   *Calendar:* Sem. plan
Inst. Accred.: SACS (1970/1995)
Prog. Accred.: Engineering (general), Engineering
  Technology (electrical)

Lon Morris College
800 College Ave., Jacksonville 75766-2900
Type: Private, Texas Annual Conference of The United
  Methodist Church, two-year
Degrees: A   *Enroll:* 411
URL: http://www.lonmorris.edu
Phone: (903) 589-4000   *Calendar:* Sem. plan
Inst. Accred.: SACS (1927/1994, Warning)

Lubbock Christian University
5601 19th St., Lubbock 79407-2099
Type: Private, Church of Christ, four-year
Degrees: A, B, M   *Enroll:* 1,588
URL: http://www.lcu.edu
Phone: (806) 796-8800   *Calendar:* Sem. plan
Inst. Accred.: SACS (1963/1998)
Prog. Accred.: Nursing, Social Work

McLennan Community College
1400 College Dr., Waco 76708
Type: Public, state/local, two-year
Degrees: A   *Enroll:* 4,410
URL: http://www.mclennan.edu
Phone: (254) 299-8000   *Calendar:* Sem. plan
Inst. Accred.: SACS (1968/2002)
Prog. Accred.: Clinical Lab Technology, Health Information
  Technician, Nursing, Physical Therapy Assisting,
  Radiography, Respiratory Therapy, Respiratory Therapy
  Technology

McMurry University
South 14th St. and Sayles Blvd., Abilene 79697
Type: Private, United Methodist Church, four-year
Degrees: A, B   *Enroll:* 1,245
URL: http://www.mcm.edu
Phone: (915) 793-3800   *Calendar:* Sem. plan
Inst. Accred.: SACS (1949/1999, Probation)
Prog. Accred.: Nursing Education

Midland College
3600 North Garfield St., Midland 79705
Type: Public, local, four-year
Degrees: A, B   *Enroll:* 3,188
URL: http://www.midland.edu
Phone: (432) 685-4500   *Calendar:* Sem. plan
Inst. Accred.: SACS (1975/2001)
Prog. Accred.: Health Information Technician, Nursing,
  Radiography, Respiratory Therapy, Respiratory Therapy
  Technology, Veterinary Technology

Midwestern State University
3410 Taft Blvd., Wichita Falls 76308-2099
Type: Public, state, four-year
Degrees: A, B, M   *Enroll:* 5,040
URL: http://www.mwsu.edu
Phone: (940) 397-4000   *Calendar:* Sem. plan
Inst. Accred.: SACS (1950/2002)
Prog. Accred.: Business (ACBSP), Dental Hygiene,
  Engineering Technology (manufacturing), Music,
  Nursing, Nursing Education, Radiography, Respiratory
  Therapy, Social Work

Mountain View College
4849 West Illinois Ave., Dallas 75211-6599
Type: Public, state/local, two-year
System: Dallas County Community College District
Degrees: A   *Enroll:* 3,399
URL: http://www.mountainviewcollege.edu
Phone: (214) 860-8700   *Calendar:* Sem. plan
Inst. Accred.: SACS (1972/2003)
Prog. Accred.: Health Information Technician, Medical
  Assisting (CAAHEP)

MTI College of Business and Technology
7277 Regency Square Blvd., Houston 77036-3163
Type: Private, proprietary, two-year
Degrees: A   *Enroll:* 795
URL: http://www.mtitexas.com
Phone: (713) 974-7181   *Calendar:* Sem. plan
Inst. Accred.: ACCSCT (1983/2001)

Houston Campus
1275 Space Park Dr., Houston 77058
Phone: (281) 333-3363

Navarro College
3200 West Seventh Ave., Corsicana 75110
Type: Public, local, two-year
Degrees: A   *Enroll:* 3,911
URL: http://www.navarrocollege.edu
Phone: (903) 874-6501   *Calendar:* Sem. plan
Inst. Accred.: SACS (1954/1995)
Prog. Accred.: Nursing, Occupational Therapy Assisting

North Central Texas College
1525 West California St., Gainesville 76240-4699
Type: Public, state/local, two-year
Degrees: A   *Enroll:* 3,953
URL: http://www.nctc.edu
Phone: (940) 668-7731   *Calendar:* Sem. plan
Inst. Accred.: SACS (1961/2001)
Prog. Accred.: Health Information Technician, Nursing

North Harris Montgomery Community College District

5000 Research Forest Dr., The Woodlands 77381-4399
Type: Public, state/local, two-year
System: Texas Higher Education Coordinating Board
Degrees: A   *Enroll:* 19,266
URL: http://www.nhmccd.edu
Phone: (832) 813-6500   *Calendar:* Sem. plan
Inst. Accred.: SACS (1976/2001)
Prog. Accred.: Montessori Teacher Education, Nursing

Cy-Fair College

14955 NW Freeway, Houston 77040
Phone: (832) 782-5000

Kingwood College

20000 Kingwood Dr., Kingwood 77339
Phone: (281) 312-1600
Prog. Accred: Occupational Therapy Assisting,
Respiratory Therapy

Montgomery College

3200 College Park Dr., Conroe 77384
Phone: (409) 273-7000
Prog. Accred: Physical Therapy Assisting, Radiography

North Harris College

2700 W.W. Thorne Dr., Houston 77073
Phone: (281) 618-5400
Prog. Accred: English Language Education

Tomball College

30555 Tomball Pkwy., Tomball 77375-4036
Phone: (281) 351-3300
Prog. Accred: Occupational Therapy Assisting,
Veterinary Technology

North Lake College

5001 North MacArthur Blvd., Irving 75038-3899
Type: Public, state/local, two-year
System: Dallas County Community College District
Degrees: A   *Enroll:* 4,686
URL: http://www.northlakecollege.edu
Phone: (972) 273-3000   *Calendar:* Sem. plan
Inst. Accred.: SACS (1979/2003)
Prog. Accred.: Construction Education

Northeast Texas Community College

PO Box 1307, Mount Pleasant 75456-1307
Type: Public, local, two-year
Degrees: A   *Enroll:* 1,471
URL: http://www.ntcc.edu
Phone: (903) 572-1911   *Calendar:* Sem. plan
Inst. Accred.: SACS (1987/2002)

Northwest Vista College

3535 North Ellison Dr., San Antonio 78251
Type: Public, state, two-year
System: Alamo Community College District
Degrees: A   *Enroll:* 4,626
URL: http://www.accd.edu/nvc
Phone: (210) 348-2000   *Calendar:* Sem. plan
Inst. Accred.: SACS (2001)

Oblate School of Theology

285 Oblate Dr., San Antonio 78216-6693
Type: Private, Roman Catholic Church, four-year
Degrees: M, D   *Enroll:* 152
URL: http://www.ost.edu
Phone: (210) 341-1366   *Calendar:* Sem. plan
Inst. Accred.: ATS (1982/1999), SACS (1968/1999)

Odessa College

201 West University Blvd., Odessa 79764-7127
Type: Public, local, two-year
Degrees: A   *Enroll:* 2,707
URL: http://www.odessa.edu
Phone: (915) 335-6400   *Calendar:* Sem. plan
Inst. Accred.: SACS (1952/2002)
Prog. Accred.: Clinical Lab Technology, Music, Nursing,
Physical Therapy Assisting, Radiography, Respiratory
Therapy, Respiratory Therapy Technology, Surgical
Technology

Our Lady of the Lake University

411 SW 24th St., San Antonio 78207-4689
Type: Private, Roman Catholic Church, four-year
Degrees: B, M, D   *Enroll:* 2,196
URL: http://www.ollusa.edu
Phone: (210) 434-6711   *Calendar:* Sem. plan
Inst. Accred.: SACS (1923/2002)
Prog. Accred.: Business (ACBSP), Counseling Psychology,
Social Work, Speech-Language Pathology

Palo Alto College

1400 West Villaret Blvd., San Antonio 78224-2499
Type: Public, local, two-year
System: Alamo Community College District
Degrees: A   *Enroll:* 4,476
URL: http://www.accd.edu/pac
Phone: (210) 921-5000   *Calendar:* Sem. plan
Inst. Accred.: SACS (1987/2002)
Prog. Accred.: Veterinary Technology

Panola College

1109 West Panola St., Carthage 75633
Type: Public, local, two-year
Degrees: A   *Enroll:* 1,147
URL: http://www.panola.edu
Phone: (903) 693-2000   *Calendar:* Sem. plan
Inst. Accred.: SACS (1960/2000)
Prog. Accred.: Health Information Technician,
Occupational Therapy Assisting

Paris Junior College

2400 Clarksville St., Paris 75460
Type: Public, state/local, two-year
Degrees: A   *Enroll:* 2,599
URL: http://www.parisjc.edu
Phone: (903) 785-7661   *Calendar:* Sem. plan
Inst. Accred.: SACS (1934/2002)
Prog. Accred.: Nursing

Parker College of Chiropractic
2500 Walnut Hill Ln., Dallas 75229-5668
Type: Private, independent, four-year
Degrees: B, D   *Enroll:* 751
URL: http://www.parkercc.edu
Phone: (972) 438-6932   *Calendar:* Tri. plan
Inst. Accred.: SACS (1987/2002)
Prog. Accred.: Chiropractic Education

Paul Quinn College
3837 Simpson Stuart Rd., Dallas 75241
Type: Private, African Methodist Episcopal Church, four-
year
Degrees: B   *Enroll:* 792
URL: http://www.pqc.edu
Phone: (214) 376-1000   *Calendar:* Sem. plan
Inst. Accred.: SACS (1972/1997)

Prairie View A&M University
PO Box 188, Prairie View 77446-0188
Type: Public, state, four-year
System: Texas A&M University System
Degrees: B, M, D   *Enroll:* 6,742
URL: http://www.pvamu.edu
Phone: (936) 857-3311   *Calendar:* Sem. plan
Inst. Accred.: SACS (1934/2003)
Prog. Accred.: Business (AACSB), Computer Science,
Dietetics (internship), Engineering (chemical, civil,
electrical, mechanical), Engineering Technology
(computer, electrical), Nursing, Social Work, Teacher
Education (NCATE)

Ranger College
College Circle, Ranger 76470-3298
Type: Public, local, two-year
Degrees: A   *Enroll:* 553
URL: http://www.ranger.cc.tx.us
Phone: (254) 647-3234   *Calendar:* Sem. plan
Inst. Accred.: SACS (1968/2002)

Remington College—Dallas
1800 Eastgate Dr., Garland 75041-5513
Type: Private, proprietary, two-year
Degrees: A
URL: http://www.remingtoncollege.edu
Phone: (972) 686-7878   *Calendar:* Qtr. plan
Inst. Accred.: ACICS (1989/2003)

Remington College—Houston
3110 Hayes Rd., Ste. 380, Houston 77082
Type: Private, proprietary, two-year
System: Education America, Inc.
Degrees: A
URL: http://www.remingtoncollege.edu
Phone: (281) 899-1240   *Calendar:* Qtr. plan
Inst. Accred.: ACCSCT (1990/2004)

Richland College
12800 Abrams Rd., Dallas 75243-2199
Type: Public, state/local, two-year
System: Dallas County Community College District
Degrees: A   *Enroll:* 7,790
URL: http://www.richlandcollege.edu
Phone: (972) 238-6106   *Calendar:* Sem. plan
Inst. Accred.: SACS (1974/2002)
Prog. Accred.: Health Information Technician, Medical
Assisting (CAAHEP)

Rio Grande Bible Institute
4300 South Business Hwy. 281, Edinburg 78539
Type: Private, interdenominational, four-year
Degrees: B
URL: http://www.riogrande.edu
Phone: (956) 380-8100   *Calendar:* Sem. plan
Inst. Accred.: ABHE (1999/2004)

Saint Edward's University
3001 South Congress Ave., Austin 78704-6489
Type: Private, Roman Catholic Church, four-year
Degrees: B, M   *Enroll:* 3,324
URL: http://www.stedwards.edu
Phone: (512) 448-8400   *Calendar:* Sem. plan
Inst. Accred.: SACS (1958/1996)
Prog. Accred.: Social Work

Saint Mary's University
One Camino Santa Maria, San Antonio 78228-8572
Type: Private, Roman Catholic Church, four-year
Degrees: B, M, D   *Enroll:* 3,636
URL: http://www.stmarytx.edu
Phone: (210) 436-3011   *Calendar:* Sem. plan
Inst. Accred.: SACS (1949/1994, Warning)
Prog. Accred.: Business (AACSB), Counseling, Engineering
(electrical, industrial), Law, Marriage and Family
Therapy, Music

Saint Philip's College
1801 Martin Luther King Dr., San Antonio 78203
Type: Public, local, two-year
System: Alamo Community College District
Degrees: A   *Enroll:* 5,960
URL: http://www.accd.edu/spc
Phone: (210) 531-3500   *Calendar:* Sem. plan
Inst. Accred.: SACS (1951/1995)
Prog. Accred.: Clinical Lab Technology, Culinary
Education, Health Information Technician, Occupational
Therapy Assisting, Physical Therapy Assisting, Practical
Nursing, Radiography, Respiratory Therapy, Respiratory
Therapy Technology, Surgical Technology

Sam Houston State University
1803 Ave. I, Huntsville 77341
Type: Public, state, four-year
System: Texas State University System
Degrees: B, M, D   *Enroll:* 11,457
URL: http://www.shsu.edu
Phone: (936) 294-1111   *Calendar:* Sem. plan
Inst. Accred.: SACS (1925/1999)
Prog. Accred.: Business (AACSB), Music, Teacher
Education (NCATE)

San Antonio College
1300 San Pedro Ave., San Antonio 78212-4299
Type: Public, state/local, two-year
System: Alamo Community College District
Degrees: A   *Enroll:* 12,352
URL: http://www.accd.edu/sac
Phone: (210) 733-2000   *Calendar:* Sem. plan
Inst. Accred.: SACS (1952/1995)
Prog. Accred.: Dental Assisting, Funeral Service
  Education (Mortuary Science), Medical Assisting (AMA),
  Nursing

San Jacinto College Central
8060 Spencer Hwy., PO Box 2007, Pasadena 77501-
2007
Type: Public, local, two-year
System: San Jacinto College District
Degrees: A
URL: http://www.sjcd.edu
Phone: (281) 476-1501   *Calendar:* Sem. plan
Inst. Accred.: SACS (1966/1999, *Indirect accreditation
  through San Jacinto College District, Pasadena, TX*)
Prog. Accred.: Radiography

San Jacinto College North
5800 Uvalde Rd., Houston 77049-4599
Type: Public, local, two-year
System: San Jacinto College District
Degrees: A
URL: http://www.sjcd.edu
Phone: (281) 458-4050   *Calendar:* Sem. plan
Inst. Accred.: SACS (1966/1999, *Indirect accreditation
  through San Jacinto College District, Pasadena, TX*)
Prog. Accred.: Health Information Administration

San Jacinto College South
1373 Beamer Rd., Houston 77089-6099
Type: Public, local, two-year
System: San Jacinto College District
Degrees: A
URL: http://www.sjcd.edu
Phone: (281) 484-1900   *Calendar:* Sem. plan
Inst. Accred.: SACS (1966/1999, *Indirect accreditation
  through San Jacinto College District, Pasadena, TX*)
Prog. Accred.: Physical Therapy Assisting

Schreiner University
2100 Memorial Blvd., Kerrville 78028
Type: Private, Presbyterian Church (USA), four-year
Degrees: A, B, M   *Enroll:* 728
URL: http://www.schreiner.edu
Phone: (830) 896-5411   *Calendar:* Sem. plan
Inst. Accred.: SACS (1934/2000)

South Plains College
1401 South College Ave., Levelland 79336
Type: Public, state, two-year
Degrees: A   *Enroll:* 6,232
URL: http://www.southplainscollege.edu
Phone: (806) 894-9611   *Calendar:* Sem. plan
Inst. Accred.: SACS (1963/2003)
Prog. Accred.: Health Information Technician, Nursing,
  Radiography, Respiratory Therapy, Respiratory Therapy
  Technology, Surgical Technology

South Texas College
PO Box 9701, McAllen 78502-9701
Type: Public, state, four-year
Degrees: A, B   *Enroll:* 9,000
URL: http://www.southtexascollege.edu
Phone: (956) 631-4922   *Calendar:* Sem. plan
Inst. Accred.: SACS (1995/2000)
Prog. Accred.: Health Information Technician,
  Occupational Therapy Assisting, Physical Therapy
  Assisting

South Texas College of Law
1303 San Jacinto St., Houston 77002-7000
Type: Private, independent, four-year
Degrees: P   *Enroll:* 1,134
URL: http://www.stcl.edu
Phone: (713) 659-8040   *Calendar:* Sem. plan
Inst. Accred.: ABA (1959/2001)

Southern Methodist University
6425 Boaz St., Dallas 75275
Type: Private, United Methodist Church, four-year
Degrees: B, M, D   *Enroll:* 9,214
URL: http://www.smu.edu
Phone: (214) 768-2000   *Calendar:* Sem. plan
Inst. Accred.: ATS (1938/2000), SACS (1921/2000)
Prog. Accred.: Business (AACSB), Computer Science,
  Dance, Engineering (computer, electrical,
  environmental/sanitary, mechanical), Law, Music,
  Theatre

Southwest Institute of Technology
5424 Hwy. 290 West, Ste. 200, Austin 78735-8800
Type: Private, proprietary, two-year
Degrees: A   *Enroll:* 78
URL: http://www.swse.net
Phone: (512) 892-2640
Inst. Accred.: ACCSCT (1978/1996)

Southwest Texas Junior College
2401 Garner Field Rd., Uvalde 78801-6297
Type: Public, local, two-year
Degrees: A   *Enroll:* 2,960
URL: http://www.swtjc.edu
Phone: (830) 278-4401   *Calendar:* Sem. plan
Inst. Accred.: SACS (1964/1995)

Southwestern Adventist University
PO Box 567, Keene 76059
Type: Private, Seventh-Day Adventist Church, four-year
Degrees: A, B, M   *Enroll:* 796
URL: http://www.swau.edu
Phone: (817) 645-3921   *Calendar:* Sem. plan
Inst. Accred.: SACS (1958/1995)
Prog. Accred.: Nursing, Social Work

Southwestern Assemblies of God University
1200 Sycamore St., Waxahachie 75165-2397
Type: Private, Assemblies of God Church, four-year
Degrees: A, B, M   *Enroll:* 1,473
URL: http://www.sagu.edu
Phone: (972) 937-4010   *Calendar:* Sem. plan
Inst. Accred.: SACS (1968/2002)

Southwestern Baptist Theological Seminary
2001 West Seminary Dr., Fort Worth 76115-1153
Type: Private, Southern Baptist Convention, four-year
Degrees: M, D   *Enroll:* 1,985
URL: http://www.swbts.edu
Phone: (817) 923-1921   *Calendar:* Sem. plan
Inst. Accred.: ATS (1944/2001), SACS (1969/2001)
Prog. Accred.: Music

Southwestern Christian College
PO Box 10, Terrell 75160
Type: Private, Church of Christ, four-year
Degrees: A, B   *Enroll:* 213
URL: http://www.swcc.edu
Phone: (972) 524-3341   *Calendar:* Sem. plan
Inst. Accred.: SACS (1973/2001)

Southwestern University
1001 East University Ave., PO Box 770, Georgetown
78627-0770
Type: Private, United Methodist Church, four-year
Degrees: B   *Enroll:* 1,248
URL: http://www.southwestern.edu
Phone: (512) 863-6511   *Calendar:* Sem. plan
Inst. Accred.: SACS (1915/2002)
Prog. Accred.: Athletic Training, Music

Stephen F. Austin State University
PO Box 6078, SFA Station, Nacogdoches 75962
Type: Public, state, four-year
Degrees: B, M, D   *Enroll:* 9,943
URL: http://www.sfasu.edu
Phone: (936) 468-2011   *Calendar:* Sem. plan
Inst. Accred.: SACS (1927/2000)
Prog. Accred.: Art, Business (AACSB), Computer Science,
Counseling, Family and Consumer Science, Forestry,
Interior Design, Music, Nursing, Rehabilitation
Counseling, Social Work, Speech-Language Pathology,
Teacher Education (NCATE), Theatre

Sul Ross State University
Highway 90, Alpine 79832
Type: Public, state, four-year
System: Texas State University System
Degrees: A, B, M   *Enroll:* 2,276
URL: http://www.sulross.edu
Phone: (432) 837-8011   *Calendar:* Sem. plan
Inst. Accred.: SACS (1929/1998)
Prog. Accred.: Business (ACBSP), Veterinary Technology

Rio Grande College—Del Rio Campus
205 Wildcat Dr., Del Rio 78840
Phone: (830) 768-4065

Rio Grande College—Eagle Pass Campus
Route 3, PO Box 1200, Eagle Pass 78852
Phone: (830) 758-5005

Rio Grande College—Uvalde Campus
400 Sul Ross Dr., Uvalde 78801
Phone: (830) 279-3001

Tarleton State University
1333 West Washington St., Stephenville 76401-4168
Type: Public, state, four-year
System: Texas A&M University System
Degrees: A, B, M, D   *Enroll:* 7,179
URL: http://www.tarleton.edu
Phone: (254) 968-9000   *Calendar:* Sem. plan
Inst. Accred.: SACS (1926/2000)
Prog. Accred.: Business (ACBSP), Clinical Lab Scientist,
Music, Nursing Education, Social Work

Central Texas Campus
1901 South Clear Creek Rd., Kileen 76549-4111
Phone: (254) 519-5435

Tarrant County College District
1500 Houston St., Fort Worth 76102-6599
Type: Public, state/local, two-year
System: Texas Higher Education Coordinating Board
Degrees: A   *Enroll:* 18,933
URL: http://www.tccd.edu
Phone: (817) 515-5100   *Calendar:* Sem. plan
Inst. Accred.: SACS (1969/2003)
Prog. Accred.: Dental Hygiene, EMT (Paramedic), Health
   Information Technician, Nursing, Physical Therapy
   Assisting, Radiography, Respiratory Therapy, Surgical
   Technology

Northeast Campus
828 Harwood Rd., Hurst 76054
Phone: (817) 515-6100
Prog. Accred: Dental Hygiene, Radiography

Northwest Campus
4801 Marine Creek Pkwy., Fort Worth 76179
Phone: (817) 515-7100

South Campus
5301 Campus Dr., Fort Worth 76119
Phone: (817) 515-4100

Southeast Campus
2100 Southeast Pkwy., Arlington 76018
Phone: (817) 515-5100

Temple College
2600 South First St., Temple 76504-7435
Type: Public, local, two-year
Degrees: A   *Enroll:* 2,312
URL: http://www.templejc.edu
Phone: (254) 298-8282   *Calendar:* Sem. plan
Inst. Accred.: SACS (1959/2000)
Prog. Accred.: Clinical Lab Technology, Dental Hygiene,
   Nursing, Respiratory Therapy, Surgical Technology

Texarkana College
2500 North Robison Rd., Texarkana 75501
Type: Public, local, two-year
Degrees: A   *Enroll:* 2,741
URL: http://www.texarkanacollege.edu
Phone: (903) 838-4541   *Calendar:* Sem. plan
Inst. Accred.: SACS (1931/1995)
Prog. Accred.: Nursing

Texas A&M International University
5201 University Blvd., Laredo 78041-1900
Type: Public, state, four-year
System: Texas A&M University System
Degrees: A, B, M, D   *Enroll:* 2,944
URL: http://www.tamiu.edu
Phone: (956) 326-2001   *Calendar:* Sem. plan
Inst. Accred.: SACS (1970/1995)
Prog. Accred.: Business (AACSB)

Texas A&M University
1246 TAMU, College Station 77843-1246
Type: Public, state, four-year
System: Texas A&M University System
Degrees: B, M, D   *Enroll:* 41,555
URL: http://www.tamu.edu
Phone: (979) 845-3211   *Calendar:* Sem. plan
Inst. Accred.: SACS (1924/2002)
Prog. Accred.: Accounting, Business (AACSB), Clinical
   Psychology, Computer Science, Construction Education,
   Counseling Psychology, Dietetics (internship),
   Engineering (aerospace, agricultural, bioengineering,
   chemical, civil, computer, electrical, industrial,
   mechanical, nuclear, ocean, petroleum, radiological
   health), Engineering Technology (electrical,
   manufacturing, mechanical, telecommunications),
   English Language Education, Forestry, Journalism,
   Landscape Architecture, Medicine, Planning,
   Psychology Internship, Recreation and Leisure Services,
   School Psychology, Teacher Education (NCATE),
   Veterinary Medicine

Galveston Campus
PO Box 1675, Galveston 77553
Phone: (409) 740-4400
Prog. Accred: Engineering (naval architecture/marine)

Texas A&M University at Qatar
Education City, Doha, Qatar
Phone: (740) 492-7368

The Texas A&M University System Health Science Center
301 Tarrow St., John B. Connally Bldg., MS 1361, College
Station 77840-7896
Type: Public, state, four-year
System: Texas A&M University System
Degrees: B, M, D   *Enroll:* 1,044
URL: http://tamushsc.tamu.edu
Phone: (979) 458-7200   *Calendar:* Sem. plan
Inst. Accred.: SACS (1999/2002)
Prog. Accred.: Public Health

The Baylor College of Dentistry
PO Box 660677, Dallas 75266-0677
Phone: (214) 828-8100
Prog. Accred: Advanced Education in General
   Dentistry, Combined Prosthodontics, Dental Hygiene,
   Dental Public Health, Dentistry, Dietetics (internship),
   Endodontics, General Dentistry, General Practice
   Residency, Oral and Maxillofacial Pathology, Oral and
   Maxillofacial Surgery, Orthodontic and Dentofacial
   Orthopedics, Pediatric Dentistry, Periodontics

Texas A&M University—Commerce
PO Box 3011, 2600 South Neal, Commerce 75429-3011
Type: Public, state, four-year
System: Texas A&M University System
Degrees: B, M, D   *Enroll:* 5,888
URL: http://www.tamu-commerce.edu
Phone: (903) 886-5000   *Calendar:* Sem. plan
Inst. Accred.: SACS (1925/2003)
Prog. Accred.: Business (AACSB), Counseling, Industrial
Technology, Music, Social Work

Texas A&M University—Corpus Christi
6300 Ocean Dr., Corpus Christi 78412-5599
Type: Public, state, four-year
System: Texas A&M University System
Degrees: A, B, M, D   *Enroll:* 6,237
URL: http://www.tamucc.edu
Phone: (361) 825-5700   *Calendar:* Sem. plan
Inst. Accred.: SACS (1975/2000)
Prog. Accred.: Applied Science (surveying/geomatics),
Business (AACSB), Clinical Lab Scientist, Counseling,
Engineering Technology (instrumentation, mechanical),
Music, Nursing, Nursing Education

Texas A&M University—Kingsville
700 University Blvd., MSC 101, Kingsville 78363-8202
Type: Public, state, four-year
System: Texas A&M University System
Degrees: B, M, D   *Enroll:* 5,461
URL: http://www.tamuk.edu
Phone: (361) 593-2111   *Calendar:* Sem. plan
Inst. Accred.: SACS (1933/1995)
Prog. Accred.: Business (AACSB), Business (ACBSP),
Dietetics (internship), Engineering (chemical, civil,
electrical, mechanical, petroleum), Industrial
Technology, Music, Social Work, Speech-Language
Pathology

Texas A&M University—Texarkana
PO Box 5518, 2600 North Robison Rd., Texarkana
75505-5518
Type: Public, state, four-year
System: Texas A&M University System
Degrees: B, M   *Enroll:* 903
URL: http://www.tamut.edu
Phone: (903) 223-3000   *Calendar:* Sem. plan
Inst. Accred.: SACS (1979/1995)
Prog. Accred.: Nursing Education

Texas Chiropractic College
5912 Spencer Hwy., Pasadena 77505-1699
Type: Private, independent, four-year
Degrees: B, D   *Enroll:* 586
URL: http://www.txchiro.edu
Phone: (281) 487-1170   *Calendar:* Tri. plan
Inst. Accred.: SACS (1984/1999)
Prog. Accred.: Chiropractic Education

Texas Christian University
2800 South University Dr., Fort Worth 76129
Type: Private, Christian Church/Disciples of Christ, four-
year
Degrees: B, M, D   *Enroll:* 7,499
URL: http://www.tcu.edu
Phone: (817) 257-7000   *Calendar:* Sem. plan
Inst. Accred.: ATS (1942/2000), SACS (1922/2003,
Warning)
Prog. Accred.: Accounting, Athletic Training, Business
(AACSB), Computer Science, Dietetics (coordinated),
Engineering (general), Interior Design, Journalism,
Music, Nursing, Nursing Education, Social Work,
Speech-Language Pathology

Texas College
2404 North Grand Ave., Tyler 75702
Type: Private, Christian Methodist Episcopal Church, four-
year
Degrees: A, B   *Enroll:* 1,012
URL: http://www.texascollege.edu
Phone: (903) 593-8311   *Calendar:* Sem. plan
Inst. Accred.: SACS (2001, Probation)

Texas College of Traditional Chinese Medicine
4005 Manchaca Rd., Ste. 200, Austin 78704
Type: Private, proprietary, four-year
Degrees: M   *Enroll:* 98
URL: http://www.texastcm.edu
Phone: (512) 444-8082   *Calendar:* Tri. plan
Inst. Accred.: ACAOM (1996/2000)

Texas Culinary Academy
11400 Burnett Rd., Ste. 2100, Austin 78752
Type: Private, proprietary, two-year
System: Career Education Corporation
Degrees: A   *Enroll:* 496
URL: http://www.txca.com
Phone: (512) 339-2665
Inst. Accred.: ACICS (2005), COE (1990/2002)
Prog. Accred.: Culinary Education

Texas Lutheran University
1000 West Court St., Seguin 78155-5999
Type: Private, Evangelical Lutheran Church in America,
four-year
Degrees: A, B   *Enroll:* 1,343
URL: http://www.tlu.edu
Phone: (830) 372-8000   *Calendar:* Sem. plan
Inst. Accred.: SACS (1940/1998)
Prog. Accred.: Business (ACBSP), Social Work, Teacher
Education (TEAC)

Texas Southern University
3100 Cleburne St., Houston 77004
Type: Public, state, four-year
Degrees: B, M, P, D   *Enroll:* 9,861
URL: http://www.tsu.edu
Phone: (713) 313-7011   *Calendar:* Sem. plan
Inst. Accred.: SACS (1948/2000)
Prog. Accred.: Aviation Technology, Business (AACSB),
Clinical Lab Scientist, Health Information
Administration, Industrial Technology, Law (ABA only),
Pharmacy, Respiratory Therapy, Social Work

Texas State Technical College—Marshall
2400 East End Blvd., South, Marshall 75672
Type: Public, state, two-year
System: Texas State Technical College System
Degrees: A
URL: http://www.marshall.tstc.edu
Phone: (903) 935-1010   *Calendar:* Sem. plan
Inst. Accred.: SACS (2002)

Texas State Technical College—Harlingen
1902 North Loop 499, Harlingen 78550-3697
Type: Public, state, two-year
System: Texas State Technical College System
Degrees: A   *Enroll:* 2,501
URL: http://www.harlingen.tstc.edu
Phone: (956) 364-4000   *Calendar:* Sem. plan
Inst. Accred.: SACS (1971/2005)
Prog. Accred.: Dental Assisting, Dental Hygiene, Health
Information Technician

Texas State Technical College—Waco
3801 Campus Dr., Waco 76705
Type: Public, state, two-year
System: Texas State Technical College System
Degrees: A   *Enroll:* 3,488
URL: http://www.waco.tstc.edu
Phone: (254) 799-3611   *Calendar:* Sem. plan
Inst. Accred.: SACS (1968/2003)
Prog. Accred.: Dental Assisting, Health Information
Technician

Texas State Technical College—West Texas at Sweetwater
300 College Dr., Sweetwater 79556-3697
Type: Public, state, two-year
System: Texas State Technical College System
Degrees: A   *Enroll:* 1,489
URL: http://www.westtexas.tstc.edu
Phone: (915) 235-7300   *Calendar:* Sem. plan
Inst. Accred.: SACS (1979/2005)

Texas State University—San Marcos
601 University Dr., San Marcos 78666-4616
Type: Public, state, four-year
System: Texas State University System
Degrees: B, M, D   *Enroll:* 22,005
URL: http://www.txstate.edu
Phone: (512) 245-2111   *Calendar:* Sem. plan
Inst. Accred.: SACS (1925/1999)
Prog. Accred.: Athletic Training, Business (AACSB),
Clinical Lab Scientist, Computer Science, Counseling,
Dietetics (internship), Family and Consumer Science,
Health Information Administration, Health Services
Administration, Interior Design, Journalism, Music,
Physical Therapy, Public Administration, Radiation
Therapy, Recreation and Leisure Services, Respiratory
Therapy, Respiratory Therapy Technology, Social Work,
Speech-Language Pathology

Texas Tech University
PO Box 42005, Lubbock 79409-2005
Type: Public, state, four-year
System: Texas Tech University System
Degrees: B, M, D   *Enroll:* 26,043
URL: http://www.texastech.edu
Phone: (806) 742-2011   *Calendar:* Sem. plan
Inst. Accred.: SACS (1928/1994)
Prog. Accred.: Accounting, Art, Audiology, Business
(AACSB), Clinical Psychology, Counseling, Counseling
Psychology, Dietetics (internship), Engineering
(chemical, civil, computer, electrical, engineering
physics/science, environmental/sanitary, industrial,
mechanical, petroleum), Engineering Technology
(civil/construction, electrical, mechanical), Family and
Consumer Science, Health Services Administration,
Interior Design, Journalism, Landscape Architecture,
Law, Marriage and Family Therapy, Music, Psychology
Internship, Public Administration, Social Work, Speech-
Language Pathology, Teacher Education (NCATE)

Texas Tech University Health Sciences Center
3601 Fourth St., Lubbock 79430
Type: Public, state, four-year
System: Texas Tech University System
Degrees: B, M, P, D   *Enroll:* 1,889
URL: http://www.ttuhsc.edu
Phone: (806) 743-3111   *Calendar:* Sem. plan
Inst. Accred.: SACS (2004)
Prog. Accred.: Clinical Lab Scientist, Diagnostic Molecular
Scientist, EMT (Paramedic), Medicine, Nursing, Nursing
Education, Physical Therapy

Amarillo Campus
1400 Wallace Blvd., Amarillo 79106
Phone: (806) 354-5411
Prog. Accred: Pharmacy

Odessa Campus
800 West 4th St., Odessa 79763
Phone: (915) 335-5111
Prog. Accred: Physician Assistant

Texas Wesleyan University
1201 Wesleyan St., Fort Worth 76105-1536
Type: Private, United Methodist Church, four-year
Degrees: B, M, D   *Enroll:* 2,204
URL: http://www.txwesleyan.edu
Phone: (817) 531-4444   *Calendar:* Sem. plan
Inst. Accred.: SACS (1949/2003)
Prog. Accred.: Law (ABA only), Music, Nurse Anesthesia
  Education

Texas Woman's University
PO Box 425587, Denton 76204-5587
Type: Public, state, four-year
Degrees: B, M, D   *Enroll:* 7,007
URL: http://www.twu.edu
Phone: (940) 898-2000   *Calendar:* Sem. plan
Inst. Accred.: SACS (1923/2003)
Prog. Accred.: Business (AACSB), Counseling, Counseling
  Psychology, Dance, Dental Hygiene, Dietetics
  (internship), Health Services Administration,
  Librarianship, Music, Nursing, Occupational Therapy,
  Physical Therapy, Psychology Internship, Social Work,
  Speech-Language Pathology

Dallas/Presbyterian Campus
8194 Walnut Hill Ln., Dallas 75231-4365
Phone: (214) 706-2350
Prog. Accred: Occupational Therapy

Houston Institute of Health Sciences
1140 M.D. Anderson Blvd., Houston 77030-2897
Phone: (713) 794-2331
Prog. Accred: Occupational Therapy

Trinity University
One Trinity Place, San Antonio 78212-7200
Type: Private, Presbyterian Church (USA), four-year
Degrees: B, M   *Enroll:* 2,608
URL: http://www.trinity.edu
Phone: (210) 999-7011   *Calendar:* Sem. plan
Inst. Accred.: SACS (1946/1997)
Prog. Accred.: Business (AACSB), Engineering
  (engineering physics/science), Health Services
  Administration, Music, Teacher Education (NCATE)

Trinity Valley Community College
500 South Prairieville St., Athens 75751
Type: Public, state/local, two-year
Degrees: A   *Enroll:* 3,505
URL: http://www.tvcc.edu
Phone: (903) 675-6200   *Calendar:* Sem. plan
Inst. Accred.: SACS (1952/1996)
Prog. Accred.: Nursing, Surgical Technology

Anderson County Campus
Highway 19 North at 287, PO Box 2530, Palestine
75802
Phone: (903) 729-0256

Health Science Center
800 Hwy. 243, Kaufman 75142-1861
Phone: (972) 932-4309

Kaufman County Campus
PO Box 668, Terrell 75160
Phone: (972) 563-9573

Tyler Junior College
PO Box 9020, Tyler 75711
Type: Public, state/local, two-year
Degrees: A   *Enroll:* 3,670
URL: http://www.tjc.edu
Phone: (903) 510-2200   *Calendar:* Sem. plan
Inst. Accred.: SACS (1931/2000)
Prog. Accred.: Clinical Lab Technology, Dental Hygiene,
  Diagnostic Medical Sonography, Health Information
  Technician, Ophthalmic Lab Technology, Opticianry,
  Radiography, Respiratory Therapy

The University of Dallas
1845 East Northgate Dr., Irving 75062-4799
Type: Private, Roman Catholic Church, four-year
Degrees: B, M, D   *Enroll:* 2,121
URL: http://www.udallas.edu
Phone: (972) 721-5000   *Calendar:* Sem. plan
Inst. Accred.: SACS (1963/2004), AALE (1997)

University of Houston
4800 Calhoun Rd., Houston 77204
Type: Public, state, four-year
System: University of Houston System
Degrees: B, M, P, D   *Enroll:* 28,267
URL: http://www.uh.edu
Phone: (713) 743-1000   *Calendar:* Sem. plan
Inst. Accred.: SACS (1954/1997)
Prog. Accred.: Accounting, Business (AACSB), Clinical
  Psychology, Computer Science, Counseling Psychology,
  Dietetics (internship), Engineering (chemical, civil,
  electrical, industrial, mechanical), Engineering
  Technology (civil/construction, computer, electrical,
  mechanical), Law, Music, Optometric Residency,
  Optometry, Pharmacy, Psychology Internship, Social
  Work, Speech-Language Pathology, Teacher Education
  (NCATE)

University of Houston—Clear Lake
2700 Bay Area Blvd., Houston 77058-1098
Type: Public, state, four-year
System: University of Houston System
Degrees: B, M   *Enroll:* 4,955
URL: http://www.cl.uh.edu
Phone: (281) 283-7600   *Calendar:* Sem. plan
Inst. Accred.: SACS (1976/2002)
Prog. Accred.: Accounting, Business (AACSB), Computer
Science, Engineering (computer), Health Services
Administration, Marriage and Family Therapy, Teacher
Education (NCATE)

University of Houston—Downtown
One Main St., Houston 77002
Type: Public, state, four-year
System: University of Houston System
Degrees: B, M   *Enroll:* 7,801
URL: http://www.dt.uh.edu
Phone: (713) 221-8000   *Calendar:* Sem. plan
Inst. Accred.: SACS (1976/1995)
Prog. Accred.: Business (AACSB), Engineering Technology
(civil/construction, instrumentation, process/piping
design)

University of Houston—Victoria
3007 North Ben Wilson, Victoria 77901-4450
Type: Public, state, four-year
System: University of Houston System
Degrees: B, M   *Enroll:* 1,361
URL: http://www.vic.uh.edu
Phone: (361) 570-4848   *Calendar:* Sem. plan
Inst. Accred.: SACS (1978/2003)
Prog. Accred.: Business (AACSB)

University of Mary Hardin-Baylor
900 College St., Belton 76513-2599
Type: Private, Southern Baptist Church, four-year
Degrees: B, M   *Enroll:* 2,387
URL: http://www.umhb.edu
Phone: (254) 295-8642   *Calendar:* Sem. plan
Inst. Accred.: SACS (1926/2003)
Prog. Accred.: Counseling, Nursing, Nursing Education,
Social Work

University of North Texas
PO Box 311425, Denton 76203-1425
Type: Public, state, four-year
System: University of North Texas System
Degrees: B, M, D   *Enroll:* 24,980
URL: http://www.unt.edu
Phone: (940) 565-2000   *Calendar:* Sem. plan
Inst. Accred.: SACS (1925/1995)
Prog. Accred.: Accounting, Audiology, Business (AACSB),
Clinical Psychology, Computer Science, Counseling,
Counseling Psychology, Engineering Technology
(electrical, manufacturing, mechanical, nuclear), English
Language Education, Interior Design, Journalism,
Librarianship, Music, Public Administration, Recreation
and Leisure Services, Rehabilitation Counseling, Social
Work, Speech-Language Pathology, Teacher Education
(NCATE)

University of North Texas Health Science Center at Fort Worth
3500 Camp Bowie Blvd., Fort Worth 76107-2699
Type: Public, state, four-year
System: University of North Texas System
Degrees: D   *Enroll:* 891
URL: http://www.hsc.unt.edu
Phone: (817) 735-2000   *Calendar:* Sem. plan
Inst. Accred.: SACS (1995/2000)
Prog. Accred.: Osteopathy, Physician Assistant, Public
Health

University of Saint Thomas
3800 Montrose Blvd., Houston 77006-4696
Type: Private, Roman Catholic Church, four-year
Degrees: B, M, D   *Enroll:* 2,870
URL: http://www.stthom.edu
Phone: (713) 522-7911   *Calendar:* Sem. plan
Inst. Accred.: ATS (1990/1998), SACS (1954/2005)
Prog. Accred.: Business (ACBSP)

The University of Texas at Arlington
Box 19088, Arlington 76019-0088
Type: Public, state, four-year
System: University of Texas System
Degrees: B, M, D   *Enroll:* 19,783
URL: http://www.uta.edu
Phone: (817) 272-2011   *Calendar:* Sem. plan
Inst. Accred.: SACS (1964/1997)
Prog. Accred.: Accounting, Business (AACSB), Computer
Science, Engineering (aerospace, civil, computer,
electrical, industrial, mechanical), Interior Design,
Landscape Architecture, Music, Nursing, Planning,
Public Administration, Social Work

The University of Texas at Austin
Austin 78712-1026
Type: Public, state, four-year
System: University of Texas System
Degrees: B, M, P, D   *Enroll:* 48,397
URL: http://www.utexas.edu
Phone: (512) 471-3434   *Calendar:* Sem. plan
Inst. Accred.: SACS (1901/1998)
Prog. Accred.: Accounting, Art, Audiology, Business
(AACSB), Clinical Psychology, Counseling Psychology,
Dance, Dietetics (coordinated), Engineering (aerospace,
architectural, chemical, civil, computer, electrical,
environmental/sanitary, geological/geophysical,
mechanical, petroleum), Interior Design, Journalism,
Law, Librarianship, Music, Nursing, Nursing Education,
Pharmacy, Planning, Psychology Internship, Public
Administration, Rehabilitation Counseling, School
Psychology, Social Work, Speech-Language Pathology,
Theatre

The University of Texas at Brownsville/Texas Southmost College
80 Fort Brown, Brownsville 78520
Type: Public, state, four-year
System: University of Texas System
Degrees: A, B, M   *Enroll:* 7,091
URL: http://www.utb.edu
Phone: (956) 544-8200   *Calendar:* Sem. plan
Inst. Accred.: SACS (1995/1998)
Prog. Accred.: Business (AACSB), Clinical Lab Technology, Nursing, Radiography, Respiratory Therapy, Respiratory Therapy Technology

The University of Texas at Dallas
PO Box 830688, Richardson 75083-0688
Type: Public, state, four-year
System: University of Texas System
Degrees: B, M, D   *Enroll:* 10,247
URL: http://www.utdallas.edu
Phone: (972) 883-2111   *Calendar:* Sem. plan
Inst. Accred.: SACS (1972/1998)
Prog. Accred.: Accounting, Audiology, Business (AACSB), Engineering (electrical, textile), Public Administration, Speech-Language Pathology

The University of Texas at El Paso
500 West University Ave., El Paso 79968-0500
Type: Public, state, four-year
System: University of Texas System
Degrees: B, M, D   *Enroll:* 14,573
URL: http://www.utep.edu
Phone: (915) 747-5000   *Calendar:* Sem. plan
Inst. Accred.: SACS (1936/1996)
Prog. Accred.: Accounting, Business (AACSB), Clinical Lab Scientist, Computer Science, Engineering (civil, electrical, industrial, mechanical, metallurgical), Music, Nurse (Midwifery), Nursing, Nursing Education, Occupational Therapy, Physical Therapy, Public Administration, Social Work, Speech-Language Pathology

The University of Texas at San Antonio
6900 North Loop 1604 West, San Antonio 78249-0617
Type: Public, state, four-year
System: University of Texas System
Degrees: B, M, D   *Enroll:* 19,812
URL: http://www.utsa.edu/
Phone: (210) 458-4011   *Calendar:* Sem. plan
Inst. Accred.: SACS (1974/2000)
Prog. Accred.: Accounting, Art, Business (AACSB), Engineering (civil, electrical, mechanical), Histologic Technology, Interior Design, Music, Nursing

The University of Texas at Tyler
3900 University Blvd., Tyler 75799
Type: Public, state, four-year
System: University of Texas System
Degrees: B, M   *Enroll:* 3,612
URL: http://www.uttyler.edu
Phone: (903) 566-7000   *Calendar:* Sem. plan
Inst. Accred.: SACS (1974/2000)
Prog. Accred.: Business (AACSB), Clinical Lab Scientist, Engineering (electrical, mechanical), Industrial Technology, Nursing, Nursing Education

The University of Texas Health Science Center at Houston
PO Box 20036, Houston 77225
Type: Public, state, four-year
System: University of Texas System
Degrees: B, M, D   *Enroll:* 2,785
URL: http://www.uth.tmc.edu
Phone: (713) 500-3000   *Calendar:* Sem. plan
Inst. Accred.: SACS (1973/2000)
Prog. Accred.: Advanced Education in General Dentistry, Applied Science (industrial hygiene), Clinical Lab Scientist, Clinical Pastoral Education (ACPEI), Combined Prosthodontics, Cytogenetic Technology, Cytotechnology, Dental Hygiene, Dental Public Health, Dentistry, Dietetics (internship), Endodontics, General Dentistry, General Practice Residency, Histologic Technology, Maxillofacial Prosthetics, Medicine, Nurse Anesthesia Education, Nursing, Nursing Education, Oral and Maxillofacial Pathology, Oral and Maxillofacial Surgery, Orthodontic and Dentofacial Orthopedics, Pediatric Dentistry, Periodontics, Psychology Internship, Public Health, Radiation Therapy

The University of Texas Health Science Center at San Antonio
7703 Floyd Curl Dr., San Antonio 78229-3900
Type: Public, state, four-year
System: University of Texas System
Degrees: B, M, D   *Enroll:* 2,493
URL: http://www.uthscsa.edu
Phone: (210) 567-7000   *Calendar:* Sem. plan
Inst. Accred.: SACS (1973/1998)
Prog. Accred.: Advanced Education in General Dentistry, Blood Bank Technology, Clinical Lab Scientist, Combined Prosthodontics, Cytogenetic Technology, Dental Hygiene, Dental Laboratory Technology, Dental Public Health, Dentistry, EMT (Paramedic), Endodontics, General Practice Residency, Medicine, Nursing, Nursing Education, Occupational Therapy, Oral and Maxillofacial Pathology, Oral and Maxillofacial Radiology, Oral and Maxillofacial Surgery, Orthodontic and Dentofacial Orthopedics, Pediatric Dentistry, Periodontics, Physical Therapy, Physician Assistant, Prosthodontics, Psychology Internship, Respiratory Therapy, Respiratory Therapy Technology

The University of Texas Medical Branch at Galveston
301 University Blvd., Galveston 77555-0129
Type: Public, state, four-year
System: University of Texas System
Degrees: B, M, D   *Enroll:* 1,754
URL: http://www.utmb.edu
Phone: (409) 772-1011   *Calendar:* Sem. plan
Inst. Accred.: SACS (1973/1998)
Prog. Accred.: Blood Bank Technology, Clinical Lab Scientist, Health Information Administration, Medicine, Microbiology, Nurse (Midwifery), Nursing, Nursing Education, Occupational Therapy, Oral and Maxillofacial Surgery, Physical Therapy, Physician Assistant, Public Health, Respiratory Therapy

The University of Texas of the Permian Basin
4901 East University Blvd., Odessa 79762-0001
Type: Public, state, four-year
System: University of Texas System
Degrees: B, M   *Enroll:* 2,286
URL: http://www.utpb.edu
Phone: (432) 552-2020   *Calendar:* Sem. plan
Inst. Accred.: SACS (1975/2000)
Prog. Accred.: Business (AACSB)

The University of Texas Southwestern Medical Center at Dallas
5323 Harry Hines Blvd., Dallas 75390-9082
Type: Public, state, four-year
System: University of Texas System
Degrees: B, M, D   *Enroll:* 1,617
URL: http://www.utsouthwestern.edu
Phone: (214) 648-3111   *Calendar:* Sem. plan
Inst. Accred.: SACS (1973/1998)
Prog. Accred.: Blood Bank Technology, Clinical Lab Scientist, Clinical Pastoral Education (ACPEI), Clinical Psychology, Dietetics (coordinated), EMT (Paramedic), Medical Illustration, Medicine, Nurse (Midwifery), Nurse Practitioner, Oral and Maxillofacial Surgery, Physical Therapy, Physician Assistant, Psychology Internship, Rehabilitation Counseling

The University of Texas—Pan American
1201 West University Dr., Edinburg 78539-2999
Type: Public, state, four-year
System: University of Texas System
Degrees: A, B, M, D   *Enroll:* 12,403
URL: http://www.panam.edu
Phone: (956) 381-2011   *Calendar:* Sem. plan
Inst. Accred.: SACS (1956/1996)
Prog. Accred.: Business (AACSB), Clinical Lab Scientist, Computer Science, Dietetics (coordinated), Engineering (electrical, manufacturing, mechanical), Nursing, Nursing Education, Occupational Therapy, Physician Assistant, Social Work, Speech-Language Pathology, Theatre

University of the Incarnate Word
4301 Broadway, San Antonio 78209-6397
Type: Private, Roman Catholic Church, four-year
Degrees: B, M, D   *Enroll:* 2,994
URL: http://www.uiw.edu
Phone: (210) 829-6500   *Calendar:* Sem. plan
Inst. Accred.: SACS (1925/1995)
Prog. Accred.: Business (ACBSP), Dietetics (internship), Nuclear Medicine Technology, Nursing, Nursing Education, Theatre

Vernon College
4400 College Dr., Vernon 76384-4092
Type: Public, state/local, two-year
Degrees: A   *Enroll:* 1,464
URL: http://www.vernoncollege.edu
Phone: (940) 552-6291   *Calendar:* Sem. plan
Inst. Accred.: SACS (1974/1999)

The Victoria College
2200 East Red River St., Victoria 77901-4494
Type: Public, local, two-year
Degrees: A   *Enroll:* 2,476
URL: http://www.victoriacollege.edu
Phone: (361) 573-3291   *Calendar:* Sem. plan
Inst. Accred.: SACS (1951/2003)
Prog. Accred.: Clinical Lab Technology, Nursing, Respiratory Therapy, Respiratory Therapy Technology

Wade College
PO Box 586343, Dallas 75258
Type: Private, proprietary, two-year
Degrees: A   *Enroll:* 229
URL: http://www.wadecollege.com
Phone: (214) 637-3530   *Calendar:* Tri. plan
Inst. Accred.: SACS (1985/2000)

Wayland Baptist University
1900 West Seventh St., Plainview 79072
Type: Private, Baptist General Convention of Texas, four-year
Degrees: A, B, M   *Enroll:* 3,065
URL: http://www.wbu.edu
Phone: (806) 296-5521   *Calendar:* Sem. plan
Inst. Accred.: SACS (1956/1998)
Prog. Accred.: Music

Weatherford College
225 College Park Dr., Weatherford 76086
Type: Public, local, two-year
Degrees: A   *Enroll:* 2,699
URL: http://www.wc.edu
Phone: (817) 594-5471   *Calendar:* Sem. plan
Inst. Accred.: SACS (1956/2001)

West Texas A&M University
PO Box 60999, Canyon 79016-0001
Type: Public, state, four-year
System: Texas A&M University System
Degrees: B, M, D   *Enroll:* 5,605
URL: http://www.wtamu.edu
Phone: (806) 651-2000   *Calendar:* Sem. plan
Inst. Accred.: SACS (1925/1995)
Prog. Accred.: Business (ACBSP), Music, Nursing, Nursing Education, Social Work, Speech-Language Pathology

Western Technical Institute
1000 Texas Ave., El Paso 79901-1536
Type: Private, proprietary, two-year
Degrees: A   *Enroll:* 334
URL: http://www.wti-ep.com
Phone: (915) 532-3737
Inst. Accred.: ACCSCT (1978/2001)
Prog. Accred.: Medical Assisting (CAAHEP)

Diana Drive Campus
9451 Diana Dr., El Paso 79924
Phone: (915) 566-9621

Western Texas College
6200 South College Ave., Snyder 79549-9599
Type: Public, state/local, two-year
Degrees: A   *Enroll:* 874
URL: http://www.wtc.edu
Phone: (915) 573-8511   *Calendar:* Sem. plan
Inst. Accred.: SACS (1973/1998)

Wharton County Junior College
911 Boling Hwy., Wharton 77488
Type: Public, local, two-year
Degrees: A   *Enroll:* 3,808
URL: http://www.wcjc.edu
Phone: (979) 532-4560   *Calendar:* Sem. plan
Inst. Accred.: SACS (1951/1998)
Prog. Accred.: Clinical Lab Technology, Dental Hygiene, EMT (Paramedic), Health Information Technician, Physical Therapy Assisting, Radiography

Wiley College
711 Wiley Ave., Marshall 75670
Type: Private, United Methodist Church, four-year
Degrees: A, B   *Enroll:* 700
URL: http://www.wileyc.edu
Phone: (903) 927-3300   *Calendar:* Sem. plan
Inst. Accred.: SACS (1933/2003)

William Marsh Rice University
PO Box 1892, Houston 77251-1892
Type: Private, independent, four-year
Degrees: B, M, D   *Enroll:* 4,760
URL: http://www.rice.edu
Phone: (713) 348-0000   *Calendar:* Sem. plan
Inst. Accred.: SACS (1914/1995)
Prog. Accred.: Business (AACSB), Engineering (chemical, civil, electrical, mechanical)

UTAH

Brigham Young University
Provo 84602
Type: Private, The Church of Jesus Christ of Latter-day Saints, four-year
Degrees: A, B, M, D   *Enroll:* 30,296
URL: http://www.byu.edu
Phone: (801) 378-4636   *Calendar:* Tri. plan
Inst. Accred.: NWCCU (1923/2001)
Prog. Accred.: Accounting, Art, Athletic Training, Audiology, Business (AACSB), Clinical Lab Scientist, Clinical Psychology, Computer Science, Construction Education, Counseling, Counseling Psychology, Dance, Engineering (chemical, civil, computer, electrical, mechanical), Engineering Technology (electrical, manufacturing), Journalism, Law, Marriage and Family Therapy, Music, Nursing, Psychology Internship, Public Administration, Recreation and Leisure Services, Social Work, Speech-Language Pathology, Teacher Education (NCATE), Theatre, Veterinary Technology

Careers Unlimited
1176 South 1480 West, Orem 84058
Type: Private, proprietary, two-year
Degrees: A
Phone: (801) 426-8234
Inst. Accred.: ACCSCT (2005)

College of Eastern Utah
451 East 400 North, Price 84501-2699
Type: Public, state, two-year
System: Utah System of Higher Education
Degrees: A   *Enroll:* 1,876
URL: http://www.ceu.edu
Phone: (435) 637-2120   *Calendar:* Sem. plan
Inst. Accred.: NWCCU (1945/2003)
Prog. Accred.: Nursing

San Juan Campus
639 West 100 South, Blanding 84511
Phone: (435)678-2201

Dixie State College of Utah
225 South 700 East, St. George 84770-3876
Type: Public, state, four-year
System: Utah System of Higher Education
Degrees: A, B   *Enroll:* 5,079
URL: http://www.dixie.edu
Phone: (435) 652-7505   *Calendar:* Sem. plan
Inst. Accred.: NWCCU (1945/2004)
Prog. Accred.: Dental Hygiene, Nursing

Independence University
5295 South Commerce Dr., Ste. G-50, Salt Lake City 84107
Type: Private, proprietary, four-year
Degrees: A, B, M   *Enroll:* 81
URL: http://www.cchs.edu
Phone: (801) 290-3280   *Calendar:* Sem. plan
Inst. Accred.: DETC (1981/2002)
Prog. Accred.: Respiratory Therapy, Respiratory Therapy Technology

ITT Technical Institute
920 West LeVoy Dr., Murray 84123-2500
Type: Private, proprietary, four-year
System: ITT Educational Services, Inc.
Degrees: A, B   *Enroll:* 464
URL: http://www.itt-tech.edu
Phone: (801) 263-3313   *Calendar:* Qtr. plan
Inst. Accred.: ACICS (1999/2004)

Henderson Campus
168 North Gibson Rd., Henderson, NV 89104
Phone: (702) 558-5404

King of Prussia Campus
760 Moore Rd., King of Prussia, PA 19406-1212
Phone: (610) 491-8004

Latter-Day Saints Business College
411 East South Temple St., Salt Lake City 84111
Type: Private, The Church of Jesus Christ of Latter-day Saints, two-year
Degrees: A   *Enroll:* 1,078
URL: http://www.ldsbc.edu
Phone: (801) 524-8100   *Calendar:* Sem. plan
Inst. Accred.: NWCCU (1977/1997)
Prog. Accred.: Medical Assisting (CAAHEP)

Midwives College of Utah
560 South State St., Ste. B2, Orem 84058
Type: Private, independent, four-year
Degrees: A, B, M
URL: http://www.midwifery.edu
Phone: (801) 764-9068   *Calendar:* Sem. plan
Inst. Accred.: MEAC (1996/2001)

Mountain West College
3280 West 3500 South, West Valley City 84119
Type: Private, proprietary, two-year
System: Corinthian Colleges, Inc
Degrees: A   *Enroll:* 621
URL: http://www.mwcollege.com
Phone: (801) 840-4800
Inst. Accred.: ACICS (1985/2001)
Prog. Accred.: Medical Assisting (CAAHEP)

Everest College—Ft. Worth
5237 North Riverside Dr., Ste. 100, Ft. Worth, TX 76137
Phone: (817) 838-3000

Provo College
1450 West 820 North, Provo 84601
Type: Private, proprietary, two-year
Degrees: A   *Enroll:* 372
URL: http://www.provocollege.com
Phone: (801) 375-1861
Inst. Accred.: ACCSCT (1986/2003)
Prog. Accred.: Dental Assisting, Physical Therapy
  Assisting

Salt Lake Community College
400 South Redwood Rd., PO Box 30808, Salt Lake City
84130-0808
Type: Public, state, two-year
System: Utah System of Higher Education
Degrees: A   *Enroll:* 13,745
URL: http://www.slcc.edu
Phone: (801) 957-4111   *Calendar:* Sem. plan
Inst. Accred.: NWCCU (1969/1999)
Prog. Accred.: Business (ACBSP), Clinical Lab Technology,
  Culinary Education, Dental Hygiene, Medical Assisting
  (AMA), Nursing, Occupational Therapy Assisting,
  Physical Therapy Assisting, Practical Nursing,
  Radiography, Surgical Technology

South City Campus
1575 State State St., Salt Lake City 84115
Phone: (801) 957-3413
Prog. Accred: Radiography

Snow College
150 East College Ave., Ephraim 84627-1299
Type: Public, state, two-year
System: Utah System of Higher Education
Degrees: A   *Enroll:* 2,528
URL: http://www.snow.edu
Phone: (435) 283-7000   *Calendar:* Sem. plan
Inst. Accred.: NWCCU (1953/2004)
Prog. Accred.: Music

Richfield Campus
200 South 800 West, Richfield 84701
Phone: (435) 896-8202

Southern Utah University
351 West Center, Administration Bldg., Cedar City 84720
Type: Public, state, four-year
System: Utah System of Higher Education
Degrees: A, B, M   *Enroll:* 5,035
URL: http://www.suu.edu
Phone: (435) 586-7700   *Calendar:* Sem. plan
Inst. Accred.: NWCCU (1933/2001)
Prog. Accred.: Business (AACSB), Business (ACBSP),
  Music

Stevens-Henager College
PO Box 9428, 1350 West 1890 South, Ogden 84401
Type: Private, proprietary, four-year
Degrees: A, B   *Enroll:* 433
URL: http://www.stevenshenager.edu
Phone: (801) 394-7791   *Calendar:* Sem. plan
Inst. Accred.: ACCSCT (2002)

Murray Campus
635 West 5300 South, Murray 84123
Phone: (801) 262-7600

Providence Campus
169 North Spring Creek Pkwy., Ste. 210, Providence
84332
Phone: (435) 713-4777

Provo Campus
25 East 1700 South, Provo 84606-6157
Phone: (801) 375-5455

University of Utah
201 South Presidents Circle, Ste. 203, Salt Lake City
84112-9008
Type: Public, state, four-year
System: Utah System of Higher Education
Degrees: A, B, M, P, D   *Enroll:* 23,125
URL: http://www.utah.edu
Phone: (801) 581-7200   *Calendar:* Sem. plan
Inst. Accred.: NWCCU (1933/2001)
Prog. Accred.: Accounting, Applied Science (industrial
  hygiene), Audiology, Business (AACSB), Clinical Lab
  Scientist, Clinical Psychology, Counseling Psychology,
  Cytotechnology, Dietetics (coordinated), Engineering
  (chemical, civil, computer, electrical,
  geological/geophysical, materials, mechanical,
  metallurgical, mining), English Language Education,
  General Dentistry, General Practice Residency,
  Journalism, Law, Medicine, Microbiology, Music,
  Nuclear Medicine Technology, Nurse (Midwifery),
  Nursing, Nursing Education, Occupational Therapy,
  Pharmacy, Physical Therapy, Physician Assistant,
  Psychology Internship, Public Administration, Public
  Health, Recreation and Leisure Services, School
  Psychology, Social Work, Speech-Language Pathology

The Utah Career College
1902 West 7800 South, West Jordan 84088
Type: Private, proprietary, two-year
Degrees: A   *Enroll:* 300
URL: http://www.utahcollege.com
Phone: (801) 975-7000   *Calendar:* Qtr. plan
Inst. Accred.: ACCSCT (1973/2003)
Prog. Accred.: Medical Assisting (CAAHEP)

Utah State University
Logan 84322
Type: Public, state, four-year
System: Utah System of Higher Education
Degrees: A, B, M, D   *Enroll:* 13,922
URL: http://www.usu.edu
Phone: (435) 797-1157   *Calendar:* Sem. plan
Inst. Accred.: NWCCU (1924/2000)
Prog. Accred.: Accounting, Applied Science (industrial hygiene), Audiology, Business (AACSB), Combined Professional-Scientific Psychology, Computer Science, Dietetics (coordinated), Engineering (agricultural, civil, computer, electrical, environmental/sanitary, mechanical), English Language Education, Forestry, Interior Design, Landscape Architecture, Marriage and Family Therapy, Music, Psychology Internship, Recreation and Leisure Services, Rehabilitation Counseling, Social Work, Speech-Language Pathology, Teacher Education (NCATE)

Utah Valley State College
800 West University Pkwy., Orem 84058-5999
Type: Public, state/local, four-year
System: Utah System of Higher Education
Degrees: A, B   *Enroll:* 17,048
URL: http://www.uvsc.edu
Phone: (801) 863-8000   *Calendar:* Sem. plan
Inst. Accred.: NWCCU (1969/2005)
Prog. Accred.: Business (AACSB), Computer Science, Dental Hygiene, Engineering Technology (electrical), Nursing

Weber State University
1001 University Circle, Ogden 84408-1001
Type: Public, state, four-year
System: Utah System of Higher Education
Degrees: A, B, M   *Enroll:* 14,211
URL: http://www.weber.edu
Phone: (801) 626-6000   *Calendar:* Sem. plan
Inst. Accred.: NWCCU (1932/1999)
Prog. Accred.: Accounting, Business (AACSB), Clinical Lab Scientist, Clinical Lab Technology, Construction Education, Dental Hygiene, EMT (Paramedic), Engineering Technology (computer, electrical, manufacturing, mechanical), Health Information Administration, Health Information Technician, Music, Nursing, Practical Nursing, Respiratory Therapy, Respiratory Therapy Technology, Social Work, Teacher Education (NCATE)

Western Governors University
4001 South 700 East, Ste. 700, Salt Lake City 84107-2533
Type: Private, independent, four-year
Degrees: A, B, M   *Enroll:* 1,366
URL: http://www.wgu.edu
Phone: (801) 274-3280
Inst. Accred.: DETC (2001), NWCCU (2003), NCA-HLC (2003), WASC-SR. (2003)

Westminster College
1840 South 1300 East, Salt Lake City 84105
Type: Private, independent, four-year
Degrees: B, M   *Enroll:* 2,133
URL: http://www.westminstercollege.edu
Phone: (801) 488-7651   *Calendar:* Sem. plan
Inst. Accred.: NWCCU (1936/2005)
Prog. Accred.: Business (ACBSP), Nursing Education

VERMONT

Bennington College
One College Dr., Bennington 05201-6003
Type: Private, independent, four-year
Degrees: B, M   *Enroll:* 718
URL: http://www.bennington.edu
Phone: (802) 442-5401   *Calendar:* Sem. plan
Inst. Accred.: NEASC-CIHE (1935/1999)

Burlington College
95 North Ave., Burlington 05401-8477
Type: Private, independent, four-year
Degrees: A, B   *Enroll:* 166
URL: http://www.burlcol.edu
Phone: (802) 862-9616   *Calendar:* Sem. plan
Inst. Accred.: NEASC-CIHE (1982/1997)

Castleton State College
86 Seminary St., Castleton 05735
Type: Public, state, four-year
System: Vermont State Colleges
Degrees: A, B, M   *Enroll:* 1,663
URL: http://www.csc.vsc.edu
Phone: (802) 468-5611   *Calendar:* Sem. plan
Inst. Accred.: NEASC-CIHE (1960/2001)
Prog. Accred.: Nursing, Social Work

Champlain College
163 South Willard St., Burlington 05402-0670
Type: Private, independent, four-year
Degrees: A, B, M   *Enroll:* 2,027
URL: http://www.champlain.edu
Phone: (802) 860-2700   *Calendar:* Sem. plan
Inst. Accred.: NEASC-CIHE (1972/2005)
Prog. Accred.: Radiography, Respiratory Therapy

College of Saint Joseph
71 Clement Rd., Rutland 05701-3899
Type: Private, Roman Catholic Church, four-year
Degrees: A, B, M   *Enroll:* 378
URL: http://www.csj.edu
Phone: (802) 773-5900   *Calendar:* Sem. plan
Inst. Accred.: NEASC-CIHE (1972/2005)

Community College of Vermont
PO Box 120, Waterbury 05676-0120
Type: Public, state, two-year
System: Vermont State Colleges
Degrees: A   *Enroll:* 2,330
URL: http://www.ccv.edu
Phone: (802) 241-3535   *Calendar:* Sem. plan
Inst. Accred.: NEASC-CIHE (1975/2002)

Goddard College
123 Pitkin Rd., Plainfield 05667-9432
Type: Private, independent, four-year
Degrees: B, M   *Enroll:* 497
URL: http://www.goddard.edu
Phone: (802) 454-8311   *Calendar:* Sem. plan
Inst. Accred.: NEASC-CIHE (1959/2002)

Green Mountain College
1 College Circle, Poultney 05764-1199
Type: Private, independent, four-year
Degrees: B   *Enroll:* 590
URL: http://www.greenmtn.edu
Phone: (802) 287-8000   *Calendar:* Sem. plan
Inst. Accred.: NEASC-CIHE (1934/1997)
Prog. Accred.: Recreation and Leisure Services

Johnson State College
337 College Hill, Johnson 05656-9464
Type: Public, state, four-year
System: Vermont State Colleges
Degrees: A, B, M   *Enroll:* 1,392
URL: http://www.jsc.vsc.edu
Phone: (802) 635-2356   *Calendar:* Sem. plan
Inst. Accred.: NEASC-CIHE (1961/2005)

Landmark College
River Rd. South, Putney 05346
Type: Private, independent, two-year
Degrees: A   *Enroll:* 327
URL: http://www.landmarkcollege.org
Phone: (802) 387-4767   *Calendar:* Sem. plan
Inst. Accred.: NEASC-CIHE (1991/1996)

Lyndon State College
1001 College Rd., PO Box 919, Lyndonville 05851-0919
Type: Public, state, four-year
System: Vermont State Colleges
Degrees: A, B, M   *Enroll:* 1,252
URL: http://www.lsc.vsc.edu
Phone: (802) 626-6200   *Calendar:* Sem. plan
Inst. Accred.: NEASC-CIHE (1965/2000)
Prog. Accred.: Recreation and Leisure Services

Marlboro College
PO Box A, Marlboro 05344-9999
Type: Private, independent, four-year
Degrees: B, M   *Enroll:* 326
URL: http://www.marlboro.edu
Phone: (802) 257-4333   *Calendar:* Sem. plan
Inst. Accred.: NEASC-CIHE (1965/2004)

Middlebury College
Middlebury 05753-6200
Type: Private, independent, four-year
Degrees: B, M, D   *Enroll:* 2,409
URL: http://www.middlebury.edu
Phone: (802) 443-5000   *Calendar:* 4-1-4 plan
Inst. Accred.: NEASC-CIHE (1929/1999)

New England Culinary Institute
250 Main St., Montpelier 05602-9720
Type: Private, proprietary, four-year
Degrees: A, B   *Enroll:* 156
URL: http://www.neculinary.com
Phone: (802) 223-6324   *Calendar:* Sem. plan
Inst. Accred.: ACCSCT (1984/2000)

Essex Campus
48 1/2 park St., Essex Junction 05452
Phone: (802) 872-3400

Paraquita Bay Campus
PO Box 3097, Road Town, Tortola, Virgin Islands
(British)
Phone: 011 284 1494 4994

Norwich University
158 Harmon Dr., Northfield 05663
Type: Private, independent, four-year
Degrees: A, B, M   *Enroll:* 2,127
URL: http://www.norwich.edu
Phone: (802) 485-2000   *Calendar:* Sem. plan
Inst. Accred.: NEASC-CIHE (1933/2000)
Prog. Accred.: Business (ACBSP), Engineering (civil,
   electrical, mechanical), Nursing

Saint Michael's College
One Winooski Park, Colchester 05439-0001
Type: Private, Roman Catholic Church, four-year
Degrees: B, M   *Enroll:* 2,180
URL: http://www.smcvt.edu
Phone: (802) 654-2000   *Calendar:* Sem. plan
Inst. Accred.: NEASC-CIHE (1939/2000)

School for International Training
PO Box 676, Brattleboro 05301-0676
Type: Private, independent, four-year
Degrees: B, M   *Enroll:* 319
URL: http://www.sit.edu
Phone: (802) 257-7751   *Calendar:* Sem. plan
Inst. Accred.: NEASC-CIHE (1974/2002)

Southern Vermont College
Monument Rd., Bennington 05201-2128
Type: Private, independent, four-year
Degrees: A, B   *Enroll:* 378
URL: http://www.svc.edu
Phone: (802) 442-5427   *Calendar:* Sem. plan
Inst. Accred.: NEASC-CIHE (1979/1999)
Prog. Accred.: Nursing

Sterling College
PO Box 72, Craftsbury Common 05827-0072
Type: Private, independent, four-year
Degrees: A, B   *Enroll:* 98
URL: http://www.sterlingcollege.edu
Phone: (802) 586-7711   *Calendar:* Sem. plan
Inst. Accred.: NEASC-CTCI (1987/1997)

University of Vermont
85 South Prospect St., Burlington 05405-0160
Type: Public, state, four-year
Degrees: A, B, M, P, D   *Enroll:* 9,611
URL: http://www.uvm.edu
Phone: (802) 656-3131   *Calendar:* Sem. plan
Inst. Accred.: NEASC-CIHE (1929/1999)
Prog. Accred.: Athletic Training, Business (AACSB),
   Clinical Lab Scientist, Clinical Psychology, Counseling,
   Dental Hygiene, Engineering (civil, electrical,
   mechanical), Forestry, Medicine, Nuclear Medicine
   Technology, Nursing, Nursing Education, Physical
   Therapy, Radiation Therapy, Social Work, Speech-
   Language Pathology, Teacher Education (NCATE)

Vermont Law School
Chelsea St., PO Box 96, South Royalton 05068-0096
Type: Private, independent, four-year
Degrees: M, P, D   *Enroll:* 582
URL: http://www.vermontlaw.edu
Phone: (802) 763-8303   *Calendar:* Sem. plan
Inst. Accred.: NEASC-CIHE (1980/2005)
Prog. Accred.: Law

Vermont Technical College
PO Box 500, Randolph Center 05061-0500
Type: Public, state, four-year
System: Vermont State Colleges
Degrees: A, B   *Enroll:* 1,022
URL: http://www.vtc.vsc.edu
Phone: (802) 728-1000   *Calendar:* Sem. plan
Inst. Accred.: NEASC-CTCI (1970/2000)
Prog. Accred.: Engineering Technology (architectural,
   civil/construction, computer, electrical, mechanical),
   Practical Nursing, Veterinary Technology

Thompson School of Practical Nursing
30 Maple St., Brattleboro 05301
Phone: (802) 254-5570
Prog. Accred: Practical Nursing

Woodbury College
660 Elm St., Montpelier 05602
Type: Private, independent, four-year
Degrees: A, B   *Enroll:* 140
URL: http://www.woodbury-college.edu
Phone: (802) 229-0516   *Calendar:* Tri. plan
Inst. Accred.: NEASC-CIHE (2004)

VIRGIN ISLANDS

University of the Virgin Islands
#2 John Brewers Bay, St. Thomas 00802-9990
Type: Public, state, four-year
Degrees: A, B, M   *Enroll:* 1,051
URL: http://www.uvi.edu
Phone: (340) 776-9200   *Calendar:* Sem. plan
Inst. Accred.: MSA-CHE (1971/2002)
Prog. Accred.: Nursing

Saint Croix Campus
RR2, Box 10,000, Kingshill, St. Croix 00850-9781
Phone: (340) 778-1620

VIRGINIA

Advanced Technology Institute
5700 Southern Blvd., Ste. 100, Virginia Beach 23462
Type: Private, proprietary, two-year
Degrees: A
URL: http://www.auto.edu
Phone: (757) 490-1241
Inst. Accred.: ACCSCT (1996/2001)

Applied Career Training, Inc.
1100 Wilson Blvd., Ste. M780, Arlington 22209
Type: Private, proprietary, two-year
Degrees: A
URL: http://www.actcollege.edu
Phone: (703) 527-6660
Inst. Accred.: ABHES (1997/2001)
Prog. Accred.: Medical Assisting (ABHES)

Alexandria Campus
6118 Franconia Rd., Second Flr., Alexandria 22310
Phone: (703) 719-0700
Prog. Accred: Medical Assisting (ABHES)

Manassas Campus
8870 Rixlew Ln., Ste. 201, Manassas 20109
Phone: (703) 365-9286
Prog. Accred: Medical Assisting (ABHES)

Argosy University Washington, DC
1550 Wilson Blvd., Arlington 22209
Type: Private, proprietary, four-year
System: Argosy University
Degrees: M, D
URL: http://www.argosyu.edu
Phone: (703) 526-5800   *Calendar:* Tri. plan
Inst. Accred.: NCA-HLC (1981/2001, *Indirect accreditation through Argosy University, Chicago, IL*)
Prog. Accred.: Clinical Psychology

Atlantic University
215 67th St., Virginia Beach 23451-2061
Type: Private, proprietary, four-year
Degrees: M   *Enroll:* 46
URL: http://www.atlanticuniv.edu
Phone: (757) 631-8101   *Calendar:* Sem. plan
Inst. Accred.: DETC (1994/2004)

Averett University
420 West Main St., Danville 24541
Type: Private, independent, four-year
Degrees: B, M   *Enroll:* 2,038
URL: http://www.averett.edu
Phone: (804) 791-5600   *Calendar:* Sem. plan
Inst. Accred.: SACS (1928/1998)

Baptist Theological Seminary at Richmond
3400 Brook Rd., Richmond 23227
Type: Private, Cooperative Baptist Fellowship, four-year
Degrees: M   *Enroll:* 197
URL: http://www.btsr.edu
Phone: (804) 355-8135
Inst. Accred.: ATS (1997/2001)

Beta Tech
7914 Midlothian Turnpike, Richmond 23236
Type: Private, proprietary, two-year
Degrees: A
URL: http://www.tidetech.com
Phone: (804) 330-0111
Inst. Accred.: ACCSCT (1994/2004)

Richmond West Campus
7001 West Broad St., Richmond 23294
Phone: (804) 672-2300

Blue Ridge Community College
Box 80, Weyers Cave 24486
Type: Public, state, two-year
System: Virginia Community College System
Degrees: A   *Enroll:* 2,142
URL: http://www.brcc.edu
Phone: (540) 234-9261   *Calendar:* Sem. plan
Inst. Accred.: SACS (1969/2005)
Prog. Accred.: Nursing, Veterinary Technology

Bluefield College
3000 College Dr., Bluefield 24605
Type: Private, Southern Baptist Church, four-year
Degrees: A, B   *Enroll:* 688
URL: http://www.bluefield.edu
Phone: (276) 326-3682   *Calendar:* Sem. plan
Inst. Accred.: SACS (1949/2003)

Bridgewater College
402 East College St., Bridgewater 22812-1599
Type: Private, Church of Brethren, four-year
Degrees: B   *Enroll:* 1,387
URL: http://www.bridgewater.edu
Phone: (540) 828-8000   *Calendar:* 4-1-4 plan
Inst. Accred.: SACS (1925/2001)

Bryant and Stratton College—Virginia Beach Campus
301 Centre Pointe Dr., Virginia Beach 23462-4417
Type: Private, proprietary, four-year
System: Bryant and Stratton
Degrees: A, B   *Enroll:* 319
URL: http://www.commonwealthcollege.com/
Phone: (757) 499-7900   *Calendar:* Tri. plan
Inst. Accred.: MSA-CHE (2002, *Indirect accreditation through Bryant and Stratton, Getzville, NY*)
Prog. Accred.: Medical Assisting (CAAHEP)

Richmond Campus
8141 Hull St. Rd., Richmond 23235-6411
Phone: (804) 745-2444
Prog. Accred: Medical Assisting (CAAHEP)

The Catholic Distance University
120 East Colonial Hwy., Hamilton 20158-9012
Type: Private, independent, four-year
Degrees: B, M
URL: http://www.cdu.edu
Phone: (540) 338-2700
Inst. Accred.: DETC (1986/2001)

Central Virginia Community College
3506 Wards Rd., Lynchburg 24502-2498
Type: Public, state, two-year
System: Virginia Community College System
Degrees: A   *Enroll:* 2,305
URL: http://www.cvcc.vccs.edu
Phone: (434) 832-7600   *Calendar:* Sem. plan
Inst. Accred.: SACS (1969/2004)
Prog. Accred.: Radiography

The Christendom College
134 Christendom Dr., Front Royal 22630
Type: Private, Roman Catholic Church, four-year
Degrees: A, B, M   *FTE Enroll:* 312
URL: http://www.christendom.edu
Phone: (540) 636-2900   *Calendar:* Sem. plan
Inst. Accred.: SACS (1987/2002, Warning)

The Notre Dame Graduate School
4407 Sano St., Alexandria 22312
Phone: (703) 658-4304

Christopher Newport University
One University Place, Newport News 23606-2998
Type: Public, state, four-year
System: State Council of Higher Education for Virginia
Degrees: B, M   *Enroll:* 4,385
URL: http://www.cnu.edu
Phone: (757) 594-7000   *Calendar:* Sem. plan
Inst. Accred.: SACS (1971/1996)
Prog. Accred.: Engineering (computer), Music, Nursing Education, Social Work

The College of William and Mary
PO Box 8795, Williamsburg 23187-8795
Type: Public, state, four-year
System: College of William and Mary Central Office
Degrees: A, B, M, D   *Enroll:* 7,396
URL: http://www.wm.edu
Phone: (757) 221-4000   *Calendar:* Sem. plan
Inst. Accred.: SACS (1921/1995)
Prog. Accred.: Accounting, Business (AACSB), Clinical Psychology, Counseling, Law, Teacher Education (NCATE)

Dabney S. Lancaster Community College
PO Box 1000, Clifton Forge 24422-1000
Type: Public, state, two-year
System: Virginia Community College System
Degrees: A   *Enroll:* 758
URL: http://www.dl.vccs.edu
Phone: (540) 863-2800   *Calendar:* Sem. plan
Inst. Accred.: SACS (1969/2004)
Prog. Accred.: Nursing

Danville Community College
1008 South Main St., Danville 24541
Type: Public, state, two-year
System: Virginia Community College System
Degrees: A   *Enroll:* 2,280
URL: http://www.dcc.vccs.edu
Phone: (434) 797-2222   *Calendar:* Sem. plan
Inst. Accred.: SACS (1970/1995)

DeVry University Crystal City
2450 Crystal Dr., Arlington 22202
Type: Private, proprietary, four-year
System: DeVry University
Degrees: A, B, M
URL: http://www.devry.edu/arlington
Phone: (866) 338-7932   *Calendar:* Sem. plan
Inst. Accred.: NCA-HLC (2002, *Indirect accreditation through DeVry University, Oakbrook Terrace, IL*)

Eastern Mennonite University
1200 Park Rd., Harrisonburg 22802-2462
Type: Private, Mennonite Church, four-year
Degrees: A, B, M   *Enroll:* 1,138
URL: http://www.emu.edu
Phone: (540) 432-4000   *Calendar:* Sem. plan
Inst. Accred.: ATS (1986/1999), SACS (1959/2000)
Prog. Accred.: Counseling, Nursing, Social Work, Teacher Education (NCATE)

Eastern Shore Community College
29300 Lankford Hwy., Melfa 23410
Type: Public, state, two-year
System: Virginia Community College System
Degrees: A   *Enroll:* 444
URL: http://www.es.vccs.edu
Phone: (757) 787-5900   *Calendar:* Sem. plan
Inst. Accred.: SACS (1973/1998)

Eastern Virginia Medical School
PO Box 1980, Norfolk 23501-1980
Type: Private, independent, four-year
Degrees: M, D   *Enroll:* 621
URL: http://www.evms.edu
Phone: (757) 446-5600   *Calendar:* Sem. plan
Inst. Accred.: SACS (1984/1999)
Prog. Accred.: Clinical Psychology, Medicine, Physician
   Assistant, Psychology Internship, Public Health

ECPI College of Technology
5555 Greenwich Rd., Virginia Beach 23462
Type: Private, proprietary, four-year
Degrees: A, B   *Enroll:* 3,208
URL: http://www.ecpi.edu
Phone: (757) 671-7171   *Calendar:* Sem. plan
Inst. Accred.: SACS (1998/2003)

Charlotte Campus
1121 Wood Ridge Center Dr., Ste. 150, Charlotte, NC
28217-1986
Phone: (704) 357-0077

Dulles Campus
21020 Dulles Town Center, Dulles 20166
Phone: (703) 421-9191

Greensboro Campus
7015-G Albert Pick Rd., Greensboro, NC 27409-9654
Phone: (910) 665-1400

Greenville Campus
15 Brendan Way, Ste. 120, Greenville, SC 29615
Phone: (864) 288-2828

Mansasas Campus
10021 Balls Ford Rd., Manassas 20109
Phone: (703) 330-5300

Newport News Campus
1001 Omni Blvd., Ste. 100, Newport News 23606
Phone: (757) 838-9191

ECPI Technical College
800 Moorefield Park Dr., Richmond 23236-3659
Type: Private, proprietary, two-year
Degrees: A   *Enroll:* 1,167
URL: http://www.ecpitech.edu
Phone: (804) 330-5533   *Calendar:* Sem. plan
Inst. Accred.: ACCSCT (1986/2002)

ECPI Technical College
5234 Airport Rd. NW, Roanoke 24012-1603
Type: Private, proprietary, two-year
Degrees: A   *Enroll:* 353
URL: http://www.ecpitech.edu
Phone: (540) 563-8000   *Calendar:* Sem. plan
Inst. Accred.: ACCSCT (1986/2002)

Glen Allen Campus
4305 Cox Rd., Glen Allen 23060
Phone: (804) 934-0100

Emory and Henry College
PO Box 947, Emory 24327
Type: Private, United Methodist Church, four-year
Degrees: B, M   *Enroll:* 885
URL: http://www.ehc.edu
Phone: (276) 944-4121   *Calendar:* Sem. plan
Inst. Accred.: SACS (1925/1996)

Ferrum College
PO Box 1000, Ferrum 24088
Type: Private, United Methodist Church, four-year
Degrees: A, B   *Enroll:* 933
URL: http://www.ferrum.edu
Phone: (540) 365-2121   *Calendar:* Sem. plan
Inst. Accred.: SACS (1960/2002)
Prog. Accred.: Recreation and Leisure Services, Social
   Work

George Mason University
4400 University Dr., Fairfax 22030-4444
Type: Public, state, four-year
System: State Council of Higher Education for Virginia
Degrees: B, M, D   *Enroll:* 19,981
URL: http://www.gmu.edu
Phone: (703) 993-1000   *Calendar:* Sem. plan
Inst. Accred.: SACS (1972/2001)
Prog. Accred.: Accounting, Business (AACSB), Clinical
   Psychology, Computer Science, Engineering (civil,
   computer, electrical, systems), Law, Music, Nursing,
   Nursing Education, Public Administration, Social Work,
   Teacher Education (NCATE)

Germanna Community College
2130 Germanna Hwy., Locust Grove 22508-2102
Type: Public, state, two-year
System: Virginia Community College System
Degrees: A   *Enroll:* 2,390
URL: http://www.gcc.vccs.edu
Phone: (540) 727-3000   *Calendar:* Sem. plan
Inst. Accred.: SACS (1972/1997)
Prog. Accred.: Nursing

Gibbs College—Vienna
1980 Gallows Rd., Vienna 22182
Type: Private, proprietary, four-year
System: Career Education Corporation
Degrees: A, B
URL: http://www.gibbsva.edu
Phone: (703) 556-8888   *Calendar:* Qtr. plan
Inst. Accred.: ACICS (1969/2002)

Hampden-Sydney College
PO Box 128, Hampden-Sydney 23943
Type: Private, Presbyterian Church (USA), four-year
Degrees: B   *Enroll:* 1,035
URL: http://www.hsc.edu
Phone: (434) 223-6000   *Calendar:* Sem. plan
Inst. Accred.: SACS (1919/1996)

Hampton University
East Queen St., Hampton 23668
Type: Private, independent, four-year
Degrees: B, M, P, D   *Enroll:* 5,352
URL: http://www.hamptonu.edu
Phone: (757) 727-5000   *Calendar:* Sem. plan
Inst. Accred.: SACS (1932/1998)
Prog. Accred.: Computer Science, Engineering (chemical,
electrical), Journalism, Music, Nursing, Nursing
Education, Pharmacy, Physical Therapy, Recreation and
Leisure Services, Speech-Language Pathology, Teacher
Education (NCATE)

Hollins University
PO Box 9688, Roanoke 24020
Type: Private, independent, four-year
Degrees: B, M   *Enroll:* 935
URL: http://www.hollins.edu
Phone: (540) 362-6000   *Calendar:* 4-1-4 plan
Inst. Accred.: SACS (1932/1996)
Prog. Accred.: Teacher Education (TEAC)

J. Sargeant Reynolds Community College
PO Box 85622, Richmond 23285-5622
Type: Public, state, two-year
System: Virginia Community College System
Degrees: A   *Enroll:* 5,588
URL: http://www.jsr.vccs.edu
Phone: (804) 371-3000   *Calendar:* Sem. plan
Inst. Accred.: SACS (1974/1999)
Prog. Accred.: Clinical Lab Technology, Dental Assisting,
Dental Laboratory Technology, Nursing, Opticianry,
Respiratory Therapy, Respiratory Therapy Technology

James Madison University
800 South Main St., Harrisonburg 22807
Type: Public, state, four-year
System: State Council of Higher Education for Virginia
Degrees: B, M, P, D   *Enroll:* 15,339
URL: http://www.jmu.edu
Phone: (540) 568-6211   *Calendar:* Sem. plan
Inst. Accred.: SACS (1927/2002)
Prog. Accred.: Accounting, Art, Athletic Training,
Audiology, Business (AACSB), Combined Professional-
Scientific Psychology, Counseling, Dance, Dietetics
(internship), Interior Design, Music, Nursing, Nursing
Education, Occupational Therapy, Physician Assistant,
Social Work, Speech-Language Pathology, Teacher
Education (NCATE), Theatre

Jefferson College of Health Sciences
PO Box 13186, 920 Jefferson St., Roanoke 24031-3186
Type: Private, independent, four-year
Degrees: A, B, M   *Enroll:* 491
URL: http://www.chs.edu
Phone: (540) 985-8483   *Calendar:* Sem. plan
Inst. Accred.: SACS (1986/2000)
Prog. Accred.: EMT (Paramedic), Nursing, Nursing
Education, Occupational Therapy, Occupational Therapy
Assisting, Phlebotomy, Physical Therapy Assisting,
Physician Assistant, Respiratory Therapy

John Tyler Community College
13101 Jefferson Davis Hwy., Chester 23831-5399
Type: Public, state, two-year
System: Virginia Community College System
Degrees: A   *Enroll:* 2,981
URL: http://www.jtcc.edu
Phone: (804) 796-4000   *Calendar:* Sem. plan
Inst. Accred.: SACS (1969/2002)
Prog. Accred.: Funeral Service Education (Mortuary
Science), Nursing

The Judge Advocate General's School
600 Massie Rd., Charlottesville 22903-1781
Type: Public, federal, four-year
Degrees: M, P
URL: http://www.jagcnet.army.mil/tjagsa
Phone: (434) 972-6300   *Calendar:* Qtr. plan
Inst. Accred.: ABA (1958/2000)

Liberty University
1971 University Blvd., Lynchburg 24502
Type: Private, independent, four-year
Degrees: A, B, M, D   *Enroll:* 7,722
URL: http://www.liberty.edu
Phone: (434) 582-2000   *Calendar:* Sem. plan
Inst. Accred.: SACS (1980/1997), TRACS (1984/2000)
Prog. Accred.: Nursing, Nursing Education

Longwood University
201 High St., Farmville 23909-1898
Type: Public, state, four-year
System: State Council of Higher Education for Virginia
Degrees: B, M   *Enroll:* 3,854
URL: http://www.longwood.edu
Phone: (434) 395-2000   *Calendar:* Sem. plan
Inst. Accred.: SACS (1927/2003)
Prog. Accred.: Business (AACSB), Music, Recreation and
Leisure Services, Social Work, Teacher Education
(NCATE), Theatre

Lord Fairfax Community College
PO Box 47, 173 Skirmisher Ln., Middletown 22645
Type: Public, state, two-year
System: Virginia Community College System
Degrees: A   *Enroll:* 2,685
URL: http://www.lf.vccs.edu
Phone: (540) 868-7000   *Calendar:* Sem. plan
Inst. Accred.: SACS (1972/1997)

Lynchburg College
1501 Lakeside Dr., Lynchburg 24501-3199
Type: Private, Disciples of Christ, four-year
Degrees: B, M   *Enroll:* 1,856
URL: http://www.lynchburg.edu
Phone: (434) 544-8100   *Calendar:* Sem. plan
Inst. Accred.: SACS (1927/2003)
Prog. Accred.: Business (AACSB), Counseling, Nursing,
Nursing Education

Mary Baldwin College
Frederick and New St., Staunton 24401
Type: Private, Presbyterian Church (USA), four-year
Degrees: B, M   *Enroll:* 1,404
URL: http://www.mbc.edu
Phone: (540) 887-7000   *Calendar:* Sem. plan
Inst. Accred.: SACS (1931/1997)

Marymount University
2807 North Glebe Rd., Arlington 22207-4299
Type: Private, Roman Catholic Church, four-year
Degrees: A, B, M   *Enroll:* 2,849
URL: http://www.marymount.edu
Phone: (703) 522-5600   *Calendar:* Sem. plan
Inst. Accred.: SACS (1958/1998)
Prog. Accred.: Business (ACBSP), Counseling, Health Services Administration, Interior Design, Nursing, Physical Therapy, Teacher Education (NCATE)

Medical Careers Institute
1001 Omi Blvd., Ste. 200, Newport News 23606
Type: Private, proprietary, two-year
Degrees: A
URL: http://www.medicalcareersinstitute.com
Phone: (757) 873-2423
Inst. Accred.: COE (1983/2003)
Prog. Accred.: Medical Assisting (CAAHEP)

Richmond Campus
800 Moorefield Park Dr., Richmond 23606
Phone: (804) 521-0400

Virginia Beach Campus
5501 Greenwich Rd., Virginia Beach 23462
Phone: (757) 497-8400

Mountain Empire Community College
3441 Mountain Empire Rd., Big Stone Gap 24219
Type: Public, state, two-year
System: Virginia Community College System
Degrees: A   *Enroll:* 1,792
URL: http://www.me.vccs.edu
Phone: (276) 523-2400   *Calendar:* Sem. plan
Inst. Accred.: SACS (1974/1999)
Prog. Accred.: Respiratory Therapy, Respiratory Therapy Technology

National College of Business and Technology
1813 East Main St., Salem 24153
Type: Private, proprietary, four-year
Degrees: A, B   *Enroll:* 694
URL: http://www.ncbt.edu
Phone: (540) 986-1800   *Calendar:* Qtr. plan
Inst. Accred.: ACICS (1954/2002)
Prog. Accred.: Medical Assisting (CAAHEP)

Bluefield Campus
100 Logan St., PO Box 629, Bluefield 24605
Phone: (276) 326-3621
Prog. Accred: Medical Assisting (CAAHEP)

Charlottesville Campus
1819 Emmet St., Charlottesville 22901
Phone: (434) 295-0136
Prog. Accred: Medical Assisting (CAAHEP)

Danville Campus
336 Old Riverside Dr., Danville 24541-3454
Phone: (434) 793-6822
Prog. Accred: Medical Assisting (CAAHEP)

Harrisonburg Campus
51-B Burgess Rd., Harrisonburg 22801
Phone: (540) 432-0943
Prog. Accred: Medical Assisting (CAAHEP)

Lynchburg Campus
104 Candlewood Ct., Lynchburg 24502
Phone: (434) 239-3500
Prog. Accred: Medical Assisting (CAAHEP)

Martinsville Campus
10 Church St., Martinsville 24114
Phone: (276) 632-5621

Tri-Cities Campus
1328 Hwy. 11 West, Bristol, TN 37620
Phone: (423) 878-4440
Prog. Accred: Medical Assisting (CAAHEP)

New River Community College
PO Box 1127, Dublin 24084
Type: Public, state, two-year
System: Virginia Community College System
Degrees: A   *Enroll:* 2,690
URL: http://www.nr.vccs.edu
Phone: (540) 674-3600   *Calendar:* Sem. plan
Inst. Accred.: SACS (1972/1997)
Prog. Accred.: Nursing

Norfolk State University
700 Park Ave., Norfolk 23504
Type: Public, state, four-year
System: State Council of Higher Education for Virginia
Degrees: A, B, M, D   *Enroll:* 5,812
URL: http://www.nsu.edu
Phone: (757) 823-8600   *Calendar:* Sem. plan
Inst. Accred.: SACS (1969/1998)
Prog. Accred.: Business (AACSB), Clinical Lab Scientist, Clinical Psychology, Computer Science, Construction Technology, Design Technology, Electronic Technology, Funeral Service Education (Mortuary Science), Industrial Technology, Journalism, Music, Nursing, Social Work, Teacher Education (NCATE)

Northern Virginia Community College
4001 Wakefield Chapel Rd., Annandale 22003
Type: Public, state, two-year
System: Virginia Community College System
Degrees: A *Enroll:* 20,869
URL: http://www.nvcc.edu
Phone: (703) 323-3000 *Calendar:* Sem. plan
Inst. Accred.: SACS (1968/2002)
Prog. Accred.: Clinical Lab Technology, Dental Hygiene,
EMT (Paramedic), Health Information Technician,
Nursing, Physical Therapy Assisting, Radiography,
Respiratory Therapy, Veterinary Technology

Alexandria Campus
3001 North Beauregard St., Alexandria 22311
Phone: (703) 845-6200

Annandale Campus
8333 Little River Turnpike, Annandale 22003
Phone: (703) 323-3010

Loudoun Campus
1000 Harry Flood Byrd Hwy., Sterling 22170
Phone: (703) 450-2500

Manassas Campus
6901 Sudley Rd., Manassas 22110
Phone: (703) 257-6600

Woodbridge Campus
15200 Neabsco Mills Rd., Woodbridge 22191
Phone: (703) 878-5700

Old Dominion University
5215 Hampton Blvd., Norfolk 23529
Type: Public, state, four-year
System: State Council of Higher Education for Virginia
Degrees: B, M, P, D *Enroll:* 14,883
URL: http://www.odu.edu
Phone: (757) 683-3000 *Calendar:* Sem. plan
Inst. Accred.: SACS (1961/2002)
Prog. Accred.: Accounting, Art, Business (AACSB), Clinical
Lab Scientist, Clinical Psychology, Counseling,
Cytotechnology, Dental Assisting, Dental Hygiene,
Engineering (civil, computer, electrical,
environmental/sanitary, mechanical), Engineering
Technology (civil/construction, electrical, mechanical),
Music, Nuclear Medicine Technology, Nurse Anesthesia
Education, Nursing, Nursing Education, Ophthalmic
Medical Technology, Physical Therapy, Public
Administration, Public Health, Recreation and Leisure
Services, Speech-Language Pathology, Teacher
Education (NCATE), Theatre

Patrick Henry Community College
PO Box 5311, Martinsville 24115
Type: Public, state, two-year
System: Virginia Community College System
Degrees: A *Enroll:* 2,057
URL: http://www.ph.vccs.edu
Phone: (276) 656-0202 *Calendar:* Sem. plan
Inst. Accred.: SACS (1972/1997)
Prog. Accred.: Nursing

Paul D. Camp Community College
100 North College Dr., PO Box 737, Franklin 23851
Type: Public, state, two-year
System: Virginia Community College System
Degrees: A *Enroll:* 809
URL: http://www.pc.vccs.edu
Phone: (757) 569-6700 *Calendar:* Sem. plan
Inst. Accred.: SACS (1973/1998)

Piedmont Virginia Community College
501 College Dr., Charlottesville 22902-7589
Type: Public, state, two-year
System: Virginia Community College System
Degrees: A *Enroll:* 2,203
URL: http://www.pvcc.edu
Phone: (434) 977-3900 *Calendar:* Sem. plan
Inst. Accred.: SACS (1974/1999)
Prog. Accred.: Nursing

Protestant Episcopal Theological Seminary in Virginia
3737 Seminary Rd., Alexandria 22304
Type: Private, Episcopal Church, four-year
Degrees: M, D *FTE Enroll:* 111
URL: http://www.vts.edu
Phone: (703) 370-6600 *Calendar:* Sem. plan
Inst. Accred.: ATS (1938/2003)

Radford University
East Main St., Radford 24142
Type: Public, state, four-year
System: State Council of Higher Education for Virginia
Degrees: B, M, P *Enroll:* 8,565
URL: http://www.radford.edu
Phone: (540) 831-5000 *Calendar:* Sem. plan
Inst. Accred.: SACS (1928/2002)
Prog. Accred.: Audiology, Business (AACSB), Computer
Science, Counseling, Music, Nursing, Recreation and
Leisure Services, Social Work, Speech-Language
Pathology, Teacher Education (NCATE), Theatre

Randolph-Macon College
PO Box 5005, Ashland 23005-5505
Type: Private, United Methodist Church, four-year
Degrees: B *Enroll:* 1,097
URL: http://www.rmc.edu
Phone: (804) 752-7200 *Calendar:* 4-1-4 plan
Inst. Accred.: SACS (1904/1997)

Randolph-Macon Woman's College
2500 Rivermont Ave., Lynchburg 24503-1526
Type: Private, United Methodist Church, four-year
Degrees: B *Enroll:* 718
URL: http://www.rmwc.edu
Phone: (434) 947-8000 *Calendar:* Sem. plan
Inst. Accred.: SACS (1902/2000)

Rappahannock Community College
12745 College Dr., Glenns 23149-2616
Type: Public, state, two-year
System: Virginia Community College System
Degrees: A   *Enroll:* 1,337
URL: http://www.rcc.vccs.edu
Phone: (804) 758-6700   *Calendar:* Sem. plan
Inst. Accred.: SACS (1973/1998)

Regent University
1000 Regent University Dr., ADM 154, Virginia Beach
23464-9801
Type: Private, independent, four-year
Degrees: B, M, D   *Enroll:* 2,204
URL: http://www.regent.edu
Phone: (757) 226-4000   *Calendar:* Sem. plan
Inst. Accred.: ATS (1993/1997), SACS (1984/1999)
Prog. Accred.: Clinical Psychology, Counseling, Law (ABA
   only)

Richard Bland College
11301 Johnson Rd., Petersburg 23805
Type: Public, state, two-year
System: College of William and Mary Central Office
Degrees: A   *Enroll:* 969
URL: http://www.rbc.edu
Phone: (804) 862-6100   *Calendar:* Sem. plan
Inst. Accred.: SACS (1961/1998)

Roanoke College
221 College Ln., Salem 24153-3794
Type: Private, Evangelical Lutheran Church in America,
   four-year
Degrees: B   *Enroll:* 1,822
URL: http://www.roanoke.edu
Phone: (540) 375-2500   *Calendar:* Sem. plan
Inst. Accred.: SACS (1927/2001)
Prog. Accred.: Business (ACBSP)

Saint Paul's College
115 College Dr., Lawrenceville 23868
Type: Private, Episcopal Church, four-year
Degrees: B   *Enroll:* 451
URL: http://www.saintpauls.edu
Phone: (434) 848-3111   *Calendar:* Sem. plan
Inst. Accred.: SACS (1950/2000)

Shenandoah University
1460 University Dr., Winchester 22601
Type: Private, United Methodist Church, four-year
Degrees: A, B, M, P, D   *Enroll:* 2,327
URL: http://www.su.edu
Phone: (540) 665-4500   *Calendar:* Sem. plan
Inst. Accred.: SACS (1973/1999)
Prog. Accred.: Business (AACSB), Music, Nurse
   (Midwifery), Nursing, Nursing Education, Occupational
   Therapy, Pharmacy, Physical Therapy, Physician
   Assistant, Respiratory Therapy

Southern Virginia University
One College Hill Dr., Buena Vista 24416
Type: Private, independent, two-year
Degrees: A   *Enroll:* 524
URL: http://www.southernvirginia.edu
Phone: (540) 261-8400   *Calendar:* Sem. plan
Inst. Accred.: AALE (2003)

Southside Virginia Community College
109 Campus Dr., Alberta 23821
Type: Public, state, two-year
System: Virginia Community College System
Degrees: A   *Enroll:* 2,604
URL: http://www.sv.vccs.edu
Phone: (434) 949-1000   *Calendar:* Sem. plan
Inst. Accred.: SACS (1972/1997)

Southwest Virginia Community College
PO Box SVCC, Richlands 24641
Type: Public, state, two-year
System: Virginia Community College System
Degrees: A   *Enroll:* 2,465
URL: http://www.sw.vccs.edu
Phone: (540) 964-2555   *Calendar:* Sem. plan
Inst. Accred.: SACS (1970/1995)
Prog. Accred.: Diagnostic Medical Sonography, Nursing,
   Occupational Therapy Assisting, Radiography,
   Respiratory Therapy

Stratford University
7777 Leesburg Pike, Falls Church 22043
Type: Private, proprietary, four-year
Degrees: A, B, M
URL: http://www.stratford.edu
Phone: (703) 821-8570   *Calendar:* Qtr. plan
Inst. Accred.: ACICS (2003, Probation)
Prog. Accred.: Culinary Education

Woodbridge Campus
13576 Minneville Rd., Woodbridge 22192
Phone: (703) 897-1982

Sweet Briar College
PO Box C, Sweet Briar 24595
Type: Private, independent, four-year
Degrees: B   *Enroll:* 680
URL: http://www.sbc.edu
Phone: (434) 381-6100   *Calendar:* Sem. plan
Inst. Accred.: SACS (1920/2001)

Thomas Nelson Community College
99 Thomas Nelson Dr., PO Box 9407, Hampton 23670
Type: Public, state, two-year
System: Virginia Community College System
Degrees: A   *Enroll:* 4,546
URL: http://www.tncc.vccs.edu
Phone: (757) 825-2700   *Calendar:* Sem. plan
Inst. Accred.: SACS (1970/1995)
Prog. Accred.: Clinical Lab Technology, Nursing

Tidewater Community College
121 College Place, Norfolk 23510-1907
Type: Public, state, two-year
System: Virginia Community College System
Degrees: A   *Enroll:* 12,957
URL: http://www.tcc.edu
Phone: (757) 822-1000   *Calendar:* Sem. plan
Inst. Accred.: SACS (1971/1996)
Prog. Accred.: Culinary Education, Diagnostic Medical
   Sonography, Health Information Technician, Nursing,
   Radiography, Respiratory Therapy, Respiratory Therapy
   Technology

Chesapeake Campus
1428 Cedar Rd., Chesapeake 23322-7199
Phone: (757) 822-5100

Portsmouth Campus
7000 College Dr., Portsmouth 23703-6158
Phone: (757) 822-2124

Virginia Beach Campus
1700 College Crescent, Virginia Beach 23456
Phone: (757) 822-7100
Prog. Accred: Occupational Therapy Assisting,
   Physical Therapy Assisting, Radiography

Tidewater Tech
2697 Dean Dr., Ste. 100, Virginia Beach 23452-9835
Type: Private, proprietary, two-year
Degrees: A   *Enroll:* 247
URL: http://www.tidetech.com/student/tidewater.html
Phone: (757) 340-2121
Inst. Accred.: ACCSCT (1986/2002)
Prog. Accred.: Medical Assisting (CAAHEP)

Chesapeake Campus
932 B Ventures Way, Ste. 310, Chesapeake 23320
Phone: (757) 549-2121

Norfolk Campus
7020 North Military Hwy., Norfolk 23518-4202
Phone: (757) 853-2121
Prog. Accred: Dental Assisting

Peninsula Campus
616 Denbigh Blvd., Newport News 23402
Phone: (757) 874-2121
Prog. Accred: Dental Assisting

Union Theological Seminary and Presbyterian School of Christian Education
3401 Brook Rd., Richmond 23227
Type: Private, Presbyterian Church (USA), four-year
Degrees: M, D   *Enroll:* 314
URL: http://www.union-psce.edu
Phone: (804) 355-0671   *Calendar:* Sem. plan
Inst. Accred.: ATS (1938/2002), SACS (1997/2002)

United States Marine Corps University
2076 South St., Quantico 22134-5067
Type: Public, federal, four-year
Degrees: A, B, M
URL: http://www.mcu.usmc.mil
Phone: (703) 784-2105   *Calendar:* Sem. plan
Inst. Accred.: SACS (1999/2005)

University of Management and Technology
1901 North Fort Meyer Dr., Ste. 700, Arlington 22209-1609
Type: Private, proprietary, four-year
Degrees: A, B, M
URL: http://www.umtweb.edu
Phone: (703) 516-0035
Inst. Accred.: DETC (2002)

University of Mary Washington
1301 College Ave., Fredericksburg 22401-5358
Type: Public, state, four-year
System: State Council of Higher Education for Virginia
Degrees: B, M   *Enroll:* 4,100
URL: http://www.umw.edu
Phone: (540) 654-1000   *Calendar:* Sem. plan
Inst. Accred.: SACS (1930/2003)
Prog. Accred.: Music

James Monroe Center for Graduate and Professional Studies
121 University Blvd., Fredericksburg 22406
Phone: (540) 286-8000

University of Northern Virginia
10021 Balls Ford Rd., Manassas 20109
Type: Private, proprietary, four-year
Degrees: B, M   *FTE Enroll:* 434
URL: http://www.unva.edu
Phone: (703) 392-0771   *Calendar:* Qtr. plan
Inst. Accred.: ACICS (2003)

University of Richmond
28 Westhampton Way, Richmond 23173
Type: Private, independent, four-year
Degrees: A, B, M, D   *Enroll:* 3,896
URL: http://www.richmond.edu
Phone: (804) 289-8000   *Calendar:* Sem. plan
Inst. Accred.: SACS (1910/1998)
Prog. Accred.: Accounting, Business (AACSB), Law, Music

University of Virginia
PO Box 400224, Charlottesville 22904-4224
Type: Public, state, four-year
System: University of Virginia Central Office
Degrees: B, M, P, D *Enroll:* 20,416
URL: http://www.virginia.edu
Phone: (434) 924-0311 *Calendar:* Sem. plan
Inst. Accred.: SACS (1904/1996)
Prog. Accred.: Accounting, Audiology, Business (AACSB),
Clinical Pastoral Education (ACPEI), Clinical Psychology,
Counseling, Dietetics (internship), Engineering
(aerospace, chemical, civil, computer, electrical,
mechanical, systems), General Practice Residency,
Landscape Architecture, Law, Medicine, Nursing,
Planning, Psychology Internship, Radiography, Speech-
Language Pathology, Teacher Education (NCATE),
Teacher Education (TEAC), Theatre

The University of Virginia's College at Wise
One College Ave., Wise 24293
Type: Public, state, four-year
System: State Council of Higher Education for Virginia
Degrees: B *Enroll:* 1,500
URL: http://www.uvawise.edu
Phone: (276) 328-0100 *Calendar:* Sem. plan
Inst. Accred.: SACS (1970/1995)
Prog. Accred.: Nursing, Nursing Education

Virginia Commonwealth University
PO Box 842512, Richmond 23284-2512
Type: Public, state, four-year
System: State Council of Higher Education for Virginia
Degrees: A, B, M, P, D *Enroll:* 21,222
URL: http://www.vcu.edu
Phone: (804) 828-0100 *Calendar:* Sem. plan
Inst. Accred.: SACS (1953/2004)
Prog. Accred.: Accounting, Advanced Education in
General Dentistry, Art, Business (AACSB), Clinical Lab
Scientist, Clinical Pastoral Education (ACPEI), Clinical
Psychology, Combined Prosthodontics, Computer
Science, Counseling Psychology, Dance, Dental
Hygiene, Dentistry, Endodontics, Engineering
(bioengineering, chemical, electrical, mechanical),
General Dentistry, General Practice Residency, Health
Services Administration, Interior Design, Medicine,
Music, Nuclear Medicine Technology, Nurse Anesthesia
Education, Nursing, Occupational Therapy, Oral and
Maxillofacial Surgery, Orthodontic and Dentofacial
Orthopedics, Pediatric Dentistry, Periodontics,
Pharmacy, Physical Therapy, Planning, Psychology
Internship, Public Administration, Public Health,
Radiation Therapy, Radiography, Recreation and Leisure
Services, Rehabilitation Counseling, Social Work,
Teacher Education (NCATE), Theatre

Virginia Commonwealth University School of the Arts in Qatar
PO Box 8095, Doha, Qatar
Phone: 011 974 492-7200

Virginia Highlands Community College
PO Box 828, Abingdon 24212-0828
Type: Public, state, two-year
System: Virginia Community College System
Degrees: A *Enroll:* 1,435
URL: http://www.vh.vccs.edu
Phone: (276) 739-2400 *Calendar:* Sem. plan
Inst. Accred.: SACS (1972/1997)
Prog. Accred.: Nursing

Virginia Intermont College
1013 Moore St., Bristol 24201
Type: Private, Southern Baptist Church, four-year
Degrees: A, B *Enroll:* 1,028
URL: http://www.vic.edu
Phone: (276) 669-6101 *Calendar:* Sem. plan
Inst. Accred.: SACS (1925/1997)
Prog. Accred.: Social Work

Virginia Military Institute
Smith Hall, Lexington 24450
Type: Public, state, four-year
System: State Council of Higher Education for Virginia
Degrees: B *Enroll:* 1,333
URL: http://www.vmi.edu
Phone: (540) 464-7000 *Calendar:* Sem. plan
Inst. Accred.: SACS (1926/1996)
Prog. Accred.: Engineering (civil, electrical, mechanical)

Virginia Polytechnic Institute and State University
210 Burruss Hall, Blacksburg 24061-0131
Type: Public, state, four-year
System: State Council of Higher Education for Virginia
Degrees: A, B, M, D *Enroll:* 25,902
URL: http://www.vt.edu
Phone: (540) 231-6000 *Calendar:* Sem. plan
Inst. Accred.: SACS (1923/1998)
Prog. Accred.: Accounting, Art, Business (AACSB), Clinical
Psychology, Computer Science, Construction Education,
Counseling, Dietetics (internship), Engineering
(aerospace, agricultural, chemical, civil, computer,
electrical, engineering mechanics,
environmental/sanitary, industrial, materials,
mechanical, mining, ocean), English Language
Education, Family and Consumer Science, Forestry,
Interior Design, Landscape Architecture, Marriage and
Family Therapy, Planning, Psychology Internship, Public
Administration, Teacher Education (NCATE), Theatre,
Veterinary Medicine

Northern Virginia Graduate Center
7054 Haycock Rd., Falls Church 22043-2311
Phone: (703) 538-8324
Prog. Accred: Marriage and Family Therapy

Virginia State University
1 Hayden Dr., Box 9001, Petersburg 23806
Type: Public, state, four-year
System: State Council of Higher Education for Virginia
Degrees: B, M, D   *Enroll:* 4,220
URL: http://www.vsu.edu
Phone: (804) 524-5000   *Calendar:* Sem. plan
Inst. Accred.: SACS (1933/1998)
Prog. Accred.: Art, Dietetics (internship), Engineering Technology (electrical, mechanical), Music, Social Work, Teacher Education (NCATE)

Virginia Union University
1500 North Lombardy St., Richmond 23220-1711
Type: Private, Baptist Church, four-year
Degrees: B, M, D   *Enroll:* 1,896
URL: http://www.vuu.edu
Phone: (804) 257-5600   *Calendar:* Sem. plan
Inst. Accred.: ATS (1971/1997), SACS (1935/2000, Warning)
Prog. Accred.: Business (ACBSP), Social Work, Teacher Education (NCATE)

Virginia Wesleyan College
1584 Wesleyan Dr., Norfolk 23502-5599
Type: Private, United Methodist Church, four-year
Degrees: B   *Enroll:* 1,251
URL: http://www.vwc.edu
Phone: (757) 455-3200   *Calendar:* Sem. plan
Inst. Accred.: SACS (1970/1995)
Prog. Accred.: Recreation and Leisure Services

Virginia Western Community College
3095 Colonial Ave., SW, PO Box 14007, Roanoke 24038-4007
Type: Public, state, two-year
System: Virginia Community College System
Degrees: A   *Enroll:* 4,141
URL: http://www.vw.vccs.edu
Phone: (540) 857-7311   *Calendar:* Sem. plan
Inst. Accred.: SACS (1969/2003)
Prog. Accred.: Business (ACBSP), Dental Hygiene, Nursing, Radiography

Washington and Lee University
Washington St., Lexington 24450-0303
Type: Private, independent, four-year
Degrees: B, D   *Enroll:* 2,135
URL: http://www2.wlu.edu
Phone: (540) 463-8400
Inst. Accred.: SACS (1895/1999)
Prog. Accred.: Business (AACSB), Journalism, Law

World College
Lake Shores Plaza, 5193 Shore Dr., Ste. 105, Virginia Beach 23455-2500
Type: Private, proprietary, four-year
Degrees: B
URL: http://www.cie-wc.edu
Phone: (757) 464-4600
Inst. Accred.: DETC (1993/2003)

Wytheville Community College
1000 East Main St., Wytheville 24382
Type: Public, state, two-year
System: Virginia Community College System
Degrees: A   *Enroll:* 1,641
URL: http://www.wcc.vccs.edu
Phone: (276) 223-4700   *Calendar:* Sem. plan
Inst. Accred.: SACS (1970/1995)
Prog. Accred.: Clinical Lab Technology, Dental Assisting, Dental Hygiene, Nursing, Physical Therapy Assisting

WASHINGTON

Argosy University Seattle
1019 8th Ave. North, Seattle 98109
Type: Private, proprietary, four-year
System: Argosy University
Degrees: M, D
URL: http://www.argosyu.edu
Phone: (206) 283-4500   *Calendar:* Tri. plan
Inst. Accred.: NCA-HLC (1981/2001, *Indirect accreditation through Argosy University, Chicago, IL)*

The Art Institute of Seattle
2323 Elliott Ave., Seattle 98121-1633
Type: Private, proprietary, two-year
System: Education Management Corporation
Degrees: A   *Enroll:* 2,117
URL: http://www.ais.edu
Phone: (206) 448-0900   *Calendar:* Qtr. plan
Inst. Accred.: ACCSCT (1983/1999), NWCCU (1999/2001)
Prog. Accred.: Culinary Education

Bakke Graduate University
1013 8th Ave., Seattle 98104
Type: Private, nondenominational, four-year
Degrees: M
URL: http://www.bgu.edu
Phone: (206) 264-9100   *Calendar:* Sem. plan
Inst. Accred.: TRACS (1994/2004)

Bastyr University
14500 Juanita Dr. NE, Kenmore 98028-4995
Type: Private, independent, four-year
Degrees: B, M, D   *Enroll:* 1,046
URL: http://www.bastyr.edu
Phone: (425) 823-1300   *Calendar:* Qtr. plan
Inst. Accred.: NWCCU (1989/2004)
Prog. Accred.: Acupuncture, Dietetics (internship), Naturopathic Medicine

Bates Technical College
1101 South Yakima Ave., Tacoma 98405-4895
Type: Public, state, two-year
System: Washington State Board for Community and Technical Colleges
Degrees: A   *Enroll:* 3,844
URL: http://www.bates.ctc.edu
Phone: (253) 680-7000   *Calendar:* Qtr. plan
Inst. Accred.: NWCCU (1988/2001)
Prog. Accred.: Dental Assisting, Dental Laboratory Technology

Bellevue Community College
3000 Landerholm Circle, SE, Bellevue 98007-6484
Type: Public, state/local, two-year
System: Washington State Board for Community and Technical Colleges
Degrees: A   *Enroll:* 7,926
URL: http://www.bcc.ctc.edu
Phone: (425) 564-2305   *Calendar:* Qtr. plan
Inst. Accred.: NWCCU (1970/2000)
Prog. Accred.: Diagnostic Medical Sonography, Nuclear Medicine Technology, Nursing, Radiation Therapy, Radiography

Bellingham Technical College
3028 Lindbergh Ave., Bellingham 98225-1599
Type: Public, state/local, two-year
System: Washington State Board for Community and Technical Colleges
Degrees: A   *Enroll:* 1,488
URL: http://www.beltc.ctc.edu
Phone: (360) 738-3105   *Calendar:* Qtr. plan
Inst. Accred.: NWCCU (1999)
Prog. Accred.: Culinary Education, Dental Assisting, EMT (Paramedic)

Big Bend Community College
7662 Chanute St., Moses Lake 98837-3299
Type: Public, state, two-year
System: Washington State Board for Community and Technical Colleges
Degrees: A   *Enroll:* 1,567
URL: http://www.bbcc.ctc.edu
Phone: (509) 762-5351   *Calendar:* Qtr. plan
Inst. Accred.: NWCCU (1965/1997)

Central Washington University
400 East 8th Ave., Ellensburg 98926-7501
Type: Public, state, four-year
System: Washington Higher Education Coordinating Board
Degrees: B, M   *Enroll:* 9,044
URL: http://www.cwu.edu
Phone: (509) 963-1111   *Calendar:* Qtr. plan
Inst. Accred.: NWCCU (1918/2001)
Prog. Accred.: Business (AACSB), Clinical Lab Scientist, Construction Education, Dietetics (internship), EMT (Paramedic), Engineering Technology (electrical, mechanical), Music, Recreation and Leisure Services, Teacher Education (NCATE)

Centralia College
600 West Locust, Centralia 98531
Type: Public, state, two-year
System: Washington State Board for Community and Technical Colleges
Degrees: A   *Enroll:* 2,310
URL: http://www.centralia.ctc.edu
Phone: (360) 736-9391   *Calendar:* Qtr. plan
Inst. Accred.: NWCCU (1948/2000)

City University

11900 NE First St., Bellevue 98005
Type: Private, independent, four-year
Degrees: A, B, M   *Enroll:* 2,885
URL: http://www.cityu.edu
Phone: (425) 637-1010   *Calendar:* Qtr. plan
Inst. Accred.: NWCCU (1978/200)

Clark College

1800 East McLoughlin Blvd., Vancouver 98663
Type: Public, state, two-year
System: Washington State Board for Community and
  Technical Colleges
Degrees: A   *Enroll:* 6,298
URL: http://www.clark.edu
Phone: (360) 992-2000   *Calendar:* Qtr. plan
Inst. Accred.: NWCCU (1948/2000)
Prog. Accred.: Dental Hygiene, Medical Assisting (AMA),
  Nursing

Clover Park Technical College

4500 Steilacoom Blvd., SW, Lakewood 98499
Type: Public, state, two-year
System: Washington State Board for Community and
  Technical Colleges
Degrees: A
URL: http://www.cptc.edu
Phone: (253) 589-5800   *Calendar:* Qtr. plan
Inst. Accred.: NWCCU (1999)
Prog. Accred.: Clinical Lab Technology, Dental Assisting

Columbia Basin College

2600 North 20th Ave., Pasco 99301-3397
Type: Public, state, two-year
System: Washington State Board for Community and
  Technical Colleges
Degrees: A   *Enroll:* 3,879
URL: http://www.cbc2.org
Phone: (509) 547-0511   *Calendar:* Qtr. plan
Inst. Accred.: NWCCU (1960/2004)
Prog. Accred.: Dental Hygiene, EMT (Paramedic)

Cornish College of the Arts

1000 Lenora St., Seattle 98121
Type: Private, independent, four-year
Degrees: B   *Enroll:* 681
URL: http://www.cornish.edu
Phone: (206) 726-5151   *Calendar:* Sem. plan
Inst. Accred.: NWCCU (1977/1997)
Prog. Accred.: Art

Crown College

8739 South Hosmer St., Tacoma 98444
Type: Private, proprietary, four-year
Degrees: A, B   *Enroll:* 318
URL: http://www.crowncollege.edu
Phone: (253) 531-3123   *Calendar:* Sem. plan
Inst. Accred.: ACCSCT (1979/2002)

DeVry University Seattle

3600 South 344th Way, Federal Way 98001
Type: Private, proprietary, four-year
Degrees: A, B, M
URL: http://www.devry.edu/federalway
Phone: (877) 923-3879   *Calendar:* Sem. plan
Inst. Accred.: NCA-HLC (2002, *Indirect accreditation*
  through DeVry University, Oakbrook Terrace, IL)

DigiPen Institute of Technology

5001 150th Ave., NE, Redmond 98052
Type: Private, proprietary, four-year
Degrees: A, B
URL: http://www.digipen.edu
Phone: (425) 558-0299   *Calendar:* Sem. plan
Inst. Accred.: ACCSCT (2002)

Eastern Washington University

526 5th St., Cheney 99004-2424
Type: Public, state, four-year
System: Washington Higher Education Coordinating
  Board
Degrees: B, M   *Enroll:* 9,145
URL: http://www.ewu.edu
Phone: (509) 359-6200   *Calendar:* Qtr. plan
Inst. Accred.: NWCCU (1919/2003)
Prog. Accred.: Business (AACSB), Computer Science,
  Counseling, Dental Hygiene, Engineering Technology
  (computer, mechanical), English Language Education,
  Music, Nursing, Occupational Therapy, Physical
  Therapy, Planning, Recreation and Leisure Services,
  Social Work, Speech-Language Pathology, Teacher
  Education (NCATE)

Edmonds Community College

20000 68th Ave. West, Lynnwood 98036
Type: Public, state/local, two-year
System: Washington State Board for Community and
  Technical Colleges
Degrees: A   *Enroll:* 5,331
URL: http://www.edcc.edu
Phone: (425) 640-1500   *Calendar:* Qtr. plan
Inst. Accred.: NWCCU (1973/2003)

Everett Community College

2000 Tower St., Everett 98201-1352
Type: Public, state, two-year
System: Washington State Board for Community and
  Technical Colleges
Degrees: A   *Enroll:* 4,229
URL: http://www.evcc.ctc.edu
Phone: (425) 388-9100   *Calendar:* Qtr. plan
Inst. Accred.: NWCCU (1948/2005)
Prog. Accred.: Medical Assisting (AMA), Nursing

Evergreen State College
2700 Evergreen Pkwy., Olympia 98505-0005
Type: Public, state, four-year
System: Washington Higher Education Coordinating
  Board
Degrees: B, M   *Enroll:* 3,952
URL: http://www.evergreen.edu
Phone: (360) 866-6000   *Calendar:* Qtr. plan
Inst. Accred.: NWCCU (1974/2001)

Faith Evangelical Lutheran Seminary
3504 North Pearl St., Tacoma 98407
Type: Private, Conservative Lutheran Association, four-
  year
Degrees: B, M
URL: http://www.faithseminary.edu
Phone: (253) 752-2020   *Calendar:* Qtr. plan
Inst. Accred.: TRACS (2001)

Gonzaga University
502 East Boone Ave., Spokane 99258-0001
Type: Private, Roman Catholic Church, four-year
Degrees: B, M, D   *Enroll:* 4,843
URL: http://www.gonzaga.edu
Phone: (509) 328-4220   *Calendar:* Sem. plan
Inst. Accred.: ATS (1999), NWCCU (1927/2004)
Prog. Accred.: Business (AACSB), Engineering (civil,
  computer, electrical, mechanical), English Language
  Education, Law, Nurse Anesthesia Education, Nursing,
  Nursing Education, Teacher Education (NCATE)

Grays Harbor College
1620 Edward P. Smith Dr., Aberdeen 98520
Type: Public, state/local, two-year
System: Washington State Board for Community and
  Technical Colleges
Degrees: A   *Enroll:* 1,593
URL: http://www.ghc.ctc.edu
Phone: (360) 532-9020   *Calendar:* Qtr. plan
Inst. Accred.: NWCCU (1948/2003)
Prog. Accred.: Nursing

Green River Community College
12401 SE 320th St., Auburn 98002-3699
Type: Public, state, two-year
System: Washington State Board for Community and
  Technical Colleges
Degrees: A   *Enroll:* 4,802
URL: http://www.greenriver.edu
Phone: (253) 833-9111   *Calendar:* Qtr. plan
Inst. Accred.: NWCCU (1967/2005)
Prog. Accred.: Occupational Therapy Assisting, Physical
  Therapy Assisting

Henry Cogswell College
3002 Colby Ave., Everett 98201
Type: Private, independent, four-year
Degrees: B   *Enroll:* 198
URL: http://www.henrycogswell.edu
Phone: (425) 258-3351   *Calendar:* Tri. plan
Inst. Accred.: NWCCU (1998/2001)
Prog. Accred.: Engineering (electrical, mechanical),
  Engineering Technology (mechanical)

Heritage University
3240 Fort Rd., Toppenish 98948
Type: Private, Roman Catholic Church, four-year
Degrees: A, B, M   *Enroll:* 978
URL: http://www.heritage.edu
Phone: (509) 865-8500   *Calendar:* Sem. plan
Inst. Accred.: NWCCU (1986/2001)
Prog. Accred.: Social Work

Highline Community College
PO Box 98000, Des Moines 98198-9800
Type: Public, state, two-year
System: Washington State Board for Community and
  Technical Colleges
Degrees: A   *Enroll:* 4,342
URL: http://www.highline.edu
Phone: (206) 878-3710   *Calendar:* Qtr. plan
Inst. Accred.: NWCCU (1965/2003)
Prog. Accred.: Dental Assisting, Medical Assisting (AMA),
  Nursing, Respiratory Therapy

International Academy of Design and Technology—Seattle
645 Andover Park West, Seattle 98188
Type: Private, proprietary, four-year
System: Career Education Corporation
Degrees: A, B
URL: http://www.iadtseattle.com
Inst. Accred.: ACICS (2005)

ITT Technical Institute
12720 Gateway Dr., Ste. 100, Seattle 98168-3334
Type: Private, proprietary, four-year
System: ITT Educational Services, Inc.
Degrees: A, B   *Enroll:* 428
URL: http://www.itt-tech.edu
Phone: (206) 244-3300   *Calendar:* Qtr. plan
Inst. Accred.: ACICS (1999/2004)

ITT Technical Institute
North 1050 Argonne Rd., Spokane 99212-2610
Type: Private, proprietary, four-year
System: ITT Educational Services, Inc.
Degrees: A, B   *Enroll:* 402
URL: http://www.itt-tech.edu
Phone: (509) 926-2900   *Calendar:* Qtr. plan
Inst. Accred.: ACICS (1999/2003)

Bothell Area Campus
2525 223rd St., SE, Bothell 98021
Phone: (425) 485-0303

Columbus Area Campus
3781 Park Mill Run Dr., Hilliard, OH 43026
Phone: (614) 771-4888

Lake Washington Technical College
11605 132nd Ave., NE, Kirkland 98034-8506
Type: Public, state, two-year
System: Washington State Board for Community and
Technical Colleges
Degrees: A   *Enroll:* 2,469
URL: http://www.lwtc.ctc.edu
Phone: (425) 739-8100   *Calendar:* Qtr. plan
Inst. Accred.: NWCCU (1981/2001)
Prog. Accred.: Culinary Education, Dental Assisting,
Dental Hygiene, Medical Assisting (CAAHEP)

Lower Columbia College
1600 Maple St., PO Box 3010, Longview 98632-0310
Type: Public, state, two-year
System: Washington State Board for Community and
Technical Colleges
Degrees: A   *Enroll:* 2,316
URL: http://www.lcc.ctc.edu
Phone: (360) 442-2000   *Calendar:* Qtr. plan
Inst. Accred.: NWCCU (1948/2000)
Prog. Accred.: Medical Assisting (AMA), Nursing

Mars Hill Graduate School
2525 220th St. SE, Ste. 100, Bothell 98021
Type: Private, inter-denominational, four-year
Degrees: M
URL: http://www.mhgs.edu
Phone: (425) 415-0505   *Calendar:* Tri. plan
Inst. Accred.: TRACS (2001)

North Seattle Community College
9600 College Way North, Seattle 98103
Type: Public, state/local, two-year
System: Seattle Community College District
Degrees: A   *Enroll:* 3,631
URL: http://www.northseattle.edu
Phone: (206) 527-3600   *Calendar:* Qtr. plan
Inst. Accred.: NWCCU (1973/2004)
Prog. Accred.: Culinary Education, Medical Assisting
(CAAHEP)

Northwest Aviation College
506 23rd NE, Auburn 98002
Type: Private, proprietary, two-year
Degrees: A
URL: http://www.afsnac.com
Phone: (253) 854-4960   *Calendar:* Qtr. plan
Inst. Accred.: ACCSCT (1995/2000)

Northwest Baptist Seminary
4301 North Stevens St., Tacoma 98407
Type: Private, independent, four-year
Degrees: M   *Enroll:* 48
URL: http://www.nbs.edu
Phone: (253) 759-6104   *Calendar:* Qtr. plan
Inst. Accred.: TRACS (1999/2003)

Northwest College of Art
16464 State Hwy. 305, Poulsbo 98370-0932
Type: Private, independent, four-year
Degrees: B   *Enroll:* 135
URL: http://www.nca.edu
Phone: (360) 779-9993   *Calendar:* Sem. plan
Inst. Accred.: ACCSCT (1989/2004)

Northwest Indian College
2522 Kwina Rd., Bellingham 98226
Type: Private, tribal, two-year
System: American Indian Higher Education Consortium
Degrees: A   *Enroll:* 417
URL: http://www.nwic.edu
Phone: (360) 676-2772   *Calendar:* Qtr. plan
Inst. Accred.: NWCCU (1993/2001)

Northwest University
PO Box 579, 5520 108th Ave., NE, Kirkland 98083
Type: Private, Northwest Council of the Assemblies of
God, four-year
Degrees: A, B, M   *Enroll:* 1,101
URL: http://www.northwestu.edu
Phone: (425) 822-8266   *Calendar:* Sem. plan
Inst. Accred.: NWCCU (1973/2004)
Prog. Accred.: Nursing Education

Olympic College
1600 Chester Ave., Bremerton 98337-1699
Type: Public, state, two-year
System: Washington State Board for Community and
Technical Colleges
Degrees: A   *Enroll:* 4,307
URL: http://www.olympic.edu
Phone: (360) 792-6050   *Calendar:* Qtr. plan
Inst. Accred.: NWCCU (1948/2001)
Prog. Accred.: Culinary Education, Medical Assisting
(AMA), Nursing

Pacific Lutheran University
Tacoma 98447-0003
Type: Private, Evangelical Lutheran Church in America,
four-year
Degrees: B, M   *Enroll:* 3,244
URL: http://www.plu.edu
Phone: (253) 535-6900   *Calendar:* Sem. plan
Inst. Accred.: NWCCU (1936/2003)
Prog. Accred.: Accounting, Business (AACSB), Computer
Science, Marriage and Family Therapy, Music, Nursing,
Nursing Education, Social Work, Teacher Education
(NCATE)

Peninsula College
1502 East Lauridsen Blvd., Port Angeles 98362
Type: Public, state/local, two-year
System: Washington State Board for Community and
Technical Colleges
Degrees: A   *Enroll:* 2,306
URL: http://www.pc.ctc.edu
Phone: (360) 452-9277   *Calendar:* Qtr. plan
Inst. Accred.: NWCCU (1965/2002)

Pierce College
1601 39th Ave., SE, Puyallup 98374-2222
Type: Public, state, two-year
Degrees: A   *Enroll:* 4,405
URL: http://www.pierce.ctc.edu
Phone: (253) 964-6500   *Calendar:* Qtr. plan
Inst. Accred.: NWCCU (1972/2001)
Prog. Accred.: Dental Hygiene, Veterinary Technology

Tacoma Campus
9401 Farwest Dr., Southwest, Tacoma 98498
Phone: (253) 964-6500
Prog. Accred: Dental Hygiene

Puget Sound Christian College
PO Box 13108, 1618 Hewitt Ave., Everett 98206-3108
Type: Private, Christian Churches/Churches of Christ,
four-year
Degrees: A, B   *Enroll:* 134
URL: http://www.pscc.edu
Phone: (425) 257-3090   *Calendar:* Sem. plan
Inst. Accred.: ABHE (1979/1999, Probation)

Renton Technical College
3000 NE Fourth St., Renton 98056-4195
Type: Public, state, two-year
System: Washington State Board for Community and
Technical Colleges
Degrees: A   *Enroll:* 2,449
URL: http://www.renton-tc.ctc.edu
Phone: (425) 235-2352   *Calendar:* Qtr. plan
Inst. Accred.: NWCCU (1978/1998)
Prog. Accred.: Culinary Education, Dental Assisting,
Medical Assisting (AMA), Surgical Technology

Saint Martin's University
5300 Pacific Ave. Southeast, Lacey 98513
Type: Private, Roman Catholic Church, four-year
Degrees: A, B, M   *Enroll:* 1,105
URL: http://www.stmartin.edu
Phone: (360) 438-4307   *Calendar:* Sem. plan
Inst. Accred.: NWCCU (1933/2004)
Prog. Accred.: Engineering (civil, mechanical), Nursing

Seattle Central Community College
1701 Broadway, Seattle 98122
Type: Public, state, two-year
System: Seattle Community College District
Degrees: A   *Enroll:* 4,953
URL: http://www.seattlecentral.edu
Phone: (206) 587-3800   *Calendar:* Qtr. plan
Inst. Accred.: NWCCU (1970/2005)
Prog. Accred.: Culinary Education, Nursing, Opticianry,
Respiratory Therapy, Surgical Technology

Seattle Vocational Institute
2120 South Jackson St., Seattle 98144
Phone: (206) 587-4950
Prog. Accred: Dental Assisting

Seattle Institute of Oriental Medicine
916 NE 65th St., Ste. B, Seattle 98115
Type: Private, proprietary, four-year
Degrees: M
URL: http://www.siom.com
Phone: (206) 517-4541
Inst. Accred.: ACAOM (1998/2001)

Seattle Pacific University
3307 Third Ave. West, Seattle 98119-1997
Type: Private, Free Methodist Church, four-year
Degrees: B, M, D   *Enroll:* 3,208
URL: http://www.spu.edu
Phone: (206) 281-2800   *Calendar:* Qtr. plan
Inst. Accred.: NWCCU (1933/2002)
Prog. Accred.: Business (AACSB), Engineering (electrical),
Marriage and Family Therapy, Music, Nursing, Nursing
Education, Teacher Education (NCATE)

Seattle University
900 Broadway, Seattle 98122
Type: Private, Roman Catholic Church, four-year
Degrees: B, M, D   *Enroll:* 5,552
URL: http://www.seattleu.edu
Phone: (206) 296-6000   *Calendar:* Qtr. plan
Inst. Accred.: ATS (1993/2000), NWCCU (1935/2005)
Prog. Accred.: Accounting, Business (AACSB), Diagnostic
Medical Sonography, Engineering (civil, electrical,
mechanical), Law, Montessori Teacher Education,
Nursing, Nursing Education, Teacher Education (NCATE)

Shoreline Community College
16101 Greenwood Ave. North, Seattle 98133
Type: Public, state/local, two-year
System: Washington State Board for Community and
  Technical Colleges
Degrees: A   *Enroll:* 4,811
URL: http://www.shoreline.edu
Phone: (206) 546-4552   *Calendar:* Qtr. plan
Inst. Accred.: NWCCU (1966/2004)
Prog. Accred.: Clinical Lab Technology, Dental Hygiene,
  Health Information Technician, Nursing

Skagit Valley College
2405 East College Way, Mount Vernon 98273-5899
Type: Public, state, two-year
System: Washington State Board for Community and
  Technical Colleges
Degrees: A   *Enroll:* 3,882
URL: http://www.skagit.edu
Phone: (360) 416-7600   *Calendar:* Qtr. plan
Inst. Accred.: NWCCU (1948/2004)
Prog. Accred.: Culinary Education, Nursing

Whidbey Island Campus
1900 SE Pioneer Way, Oak Harbor 98277-3099
Phone: (360) 675-6656

South Puget Sound Community College
2011 Mottman Rd., SW, Olympia 98512-6292
Type: Public, state, two-year
System: Washington State Board for Community and
  Technical Colleges
Degrees: A   *Enroll:* 3,316
URL: http://www.spscc.ctc.edu
Phone: (360) 754-7711   *Calendar:* Qtr. plan
Inst. Accred.: NWCCU (1975/2003)
Prog. Accred.: Culinary Education, Dental Assisting,
  Medical Assisting (AMA), Nursing

South Seattle Community College
6000 16th Ave., S.W., Seattle 98106
Type: Public, state, two-year
System: Seattle Community College District
Degrees: A   *Enroll:* 3,419
URL: http://southseattle.edu
Phone: (206) 764-5300   *Calendar:* Qtr. plan
Inst. Accred.: NWCCU (1975/2000)
Prog. Accred.: Culinary Education

Spokane Community College
1810 North Greene St., Spokane 99217-5499
Type: Public, state/local, two-year
System: Community Colleges of Spokane
Degrees: A   *Enroll:* 5,678
URL: http://www.scc.spokane.edu
Phone: (509) 533-7000   *Calendar:* Qtr. plan
Inst. Accred.: NWCCU (1967/2005)
Prog. Accred.: Cardiovascular Technology, Culinary
  Education, Dental Assisting, Dental Hygiene, EMT
  (Paramedic), Health Information Technician, Nursing,
  Optometric Technician, Respiratory Therapy, Surgical
  Technology

Spokane Falls Community College
3410 West Ft. George Wright Dr., Spokane 99224-5288
Type: Public, state/local, two-year
System: Community Colleges of Spokane
Degrees: A   *Enroll:* 6,611
URL: http://www.spokanefalls.edu
Phone: (509) 533-3500   *Calendar:* Qtr. plan
Inst. Accred.: NWCCU (1967/2005)
Prog. Accred.: Physical Therapy Assisting

Tacoma Community College
6501 South 19th St., Tacoma 98466
Type: Public, state, two-year
System: Washington State Board for Community and
  Technical Colleges
Degrees: A   *Enroll:* 4,699
URL: http://www.tacoma.ctc.edu
Phone: (253) 566-5000   *Calendar:* Qtr. plan
Inst. Accred.: NWCCU (1967/2004)
Prog. Accred.: EMT (Paramedic), Health Information
  Technician, Nursing, Radiography, Respiratory Therapy

Trinity Lutheran College
4221 228th Ave. Southeast, Issaquah 98029-9299
Type: Private, independent, four-year
Degrees: A, B   *Enroll:* 141
URL: http://www.tlc.edu
Phone: (425) 392-0400   *Calendar:* Qtr. plan
Inst. Accred.: NWCCU (1982/2005)

University of Puget Sound
1500 North Warner, Tacoma 98416
Type: Private, independent, four-year
Degrees: B, M, D   *Enroll:* 2,677
URL: http://www.ups.edu
Phone: (253) 879-3207   *Calendar:* Sem. plan
Inst. Accred.: NWCCU (1923/2004)
Prog. Accred.: Music, Occupational Therapy, Physical
  Therapy, Teacher Education (NCATE)

University of Washington
Box 351230, Seattle 98195
Type: Public, state, four-year
System: Washington Higher Education Coordinating
 Board
Degrees: B, M, P, D *Enroll:* 35,294
URL: http://www.washington.edu
Phone: (206) 543-6616 *Calendar:* Qtr. plan
Inst. Accred.: NWCCU (1918/2003)
Prog. Accred.: Accounting, Applied Science (industrial
 hygiene), Audiology, Business (AACSB), Clinical Lab
 Scientist, Clinical Psychology, Combined
 Prosthodontics, Construction Education, Cytotechnology,
 Dentistry, Dietetics (internship), EMT (Paramedic),
 Endodontics, Engineering (aerospace, chemical, civil,
 computer, electrical, forest, industrial, materials,
 mechanical, paper), English Language Education,
 Forestry, General Practice Residency, Health Information
 Administration, Health Services Administration,
 Journalism, Landscape Architecture, Law, Librarianship,
 Medicine, Microbiology, Music, Nurse (Midwifery),
 Nursing, Nursing Education, Occupational Therapy, Oral
 and Maxillofacial Surgery, Orthodontic and Dentofacial
 Orthopedics, Orthotist/Prothetist, Pediatric Dentistry,
 Periodontics, Pharmacy, Physical Therapy, Physician
 Assistant, Planning, Psychology Internship, Public
 Health, School Psychology, Social Work, Speech-
 Language Pathology, Teacher Education (NCATE)

Bothell Campus
PO Box 35800, 18115 Campus Way, NE, Bothell
98011-8246
Phone: (425) 352-5000

Tacoma Campus
1103 A St., Tacoma 98402
Phone: (253) 692-4000

Walla Walla College
204 South College Ave., College Place 99324-1198
Type: Private, Seventh-Day Adventist Church, four-year
Degrees: A, B, M *Enroll:* 1,816
URL: http://www.wwc.edu
Phone: (509) 527-2615 *Calendar:* Qtr. plan
Inst. Accred.: NWCCU (1932/2004)
Prog. Accred.: Business (ACBSP), Engineering (general),
 Music, Nursing, Social Work

Walla Walla Community College
500 Tausick Way, Walla Walla 99362
Type: Public, state, two-year
System: Washington State Board for Community and
 Technical Colleges
Degrees: A *Enroll:* 3,220
URL: http://www.wwcc.edu
Phone: (509) 522-2500 *Calendar:* Qtr. plan
Inst. Accred.: NWCCU (1969/2000)
Prog. Accred.: Engineering Technology
 (civil/construction), Nursing

Washington State University
PO Box 641048, Pullman 99164-1048
Type: Public, state, four-year
System: Washington Higher Education Coordinating
 Board
Degrees: B, M, P, D *Enroll:* 20,196
URL: http://www.wsu.edu
Phone: (509) 335-3564 *Calendar:* Sem. plan
Inst. Accred.: NWCCU (1918/2004)
Prog. Accred.: Accounting, Athletic Training, Audiology,
 Business (AACSB), Clinical Psychology, Computer
 Science, Construction Education, Counseling
 Psychology, Dietetics (coordinated), Engineering
 (agricultural, chemical, civil, computer, electrical,
 manufacturing, materials, mechanical), English
 Language Education, Forestry, Interior Design,
 Landscape Architecture, Music, Nursing, Pharmacy,
 Psychology Internship, Recreation and Leisure Services,
 Speech-Language Pathology, Teacher Education
 (NCATE), Veterinary Medicine

Spokane Campus
310 North Riverpoint Blvd., Spokane 99202
Phone: (509) 358-7500
Prog. Accred: Health Services Administration

Tri-Cities Campus
2710 University Dr., Richland 99352-1643
Phone: (509) 372-7250

Vancouver Campus
14204 NE Salmon Creek Ave., Vancouver 98686-9600
Phone: (360) 546-9788

Wenatchee Valley College
1300 Fifth St., Wenatchee 98801
Type: Public, state, two-year
System: Washington State Board for Community and
 Technical Colleges
Degrees: A *Enroll:* 2,359
URL: http://www.wvc.edu
Phone: (509) 682-6800 *Calendar:* Qtr. plan
Inst. Accred.: NWCCU (1948/2003)
Prog. Accred.: Clinical Lab Technology, Medical Assisting
 (AMA), Nursing, Radiography

Western Washington University
516 High St., Bellingham 98225-9033
Type: Public, state, four-year
System: Washington Higher Education Coordinating
 Board
Degrees: B, M *Enroll:* 12,920
URL: http://www.wwu.edu
Phone: (360) 650-3480 *Calendar:* Qtr. plan
Inst. Accred.: NWCCU (1921/2003)
Prog. Accred.: Art, Audiology, Business (AACSB),
 Computer Science, Counseling, Engineering Technology
 (electrical, manufacturing, plastics), Music, Recreation
 and Leisure Services, Speech-Language Pathology,
 Teacher Education (NCATE)

Whatcom Community College
237 West Kellogg Rd., Bellingham 98226
Type: Public, state, two-year
System: Washington State Board for Community and
  Technical Colleges
Degrees: A   *Enroll:* 2,869
URL: http://www.whatcom.ctc.edu
Phone: (360) 676-2170   *Calendar:* Qtr. plan
Inst. Accred.: NWCCU (1976/2001)
Prog. Accred.: Medical Assisting (AMA), Physical Therapy
  Assisting

Whitman College
345 Boyer Ave., Walla Walla 99362
Type: Private, independent, four-year
Degrees: B   *Enroll:* 1,430
URL: http://www.whitman.edu
Phone: (509) 527-5111   *Calendar:* Sem. plan
Inst. Accred.: NWCCU (1918/1997)

Whitworth College
300 West Hawthorne Rd., Spokane 99251-0001
Type: Private, Presbyterian Church (USA), four-year
Degrees: B, M   *Enroll:* 2,132
URL: http://www.whitworth.edu
Phone: (509) 777-1000   *Calendar:* 4-1-4 plan
Inst. Accred.: NWCCU (1933/2001)
Prog. Accred.: Athletic Training, Music, Nursing, Teacher
  Education (NCATE)

Yakima Valley Community College
PO Box 22520, Yakima 98907-2520
Type: Public, state, two-year
System: Washington State Board for Community and
  Technical Colleges
Degrees: A   *Enroll:* 3,466
URL: http://www.yvcc.edu
Phone: (509) 574-4600   *Calendar:* Qtr. plan
Inst. Accred.: NWCCU (1948/2001)
Prog. Accred.: Dental Hygiene, Nursing, Radiography,
  Veterinary Technology

WEST VIRGINIA

Alderson-Broaddus College
College Hill, Philippi 26416
Type: Private, American Baptist Churches (USA), four-year
Degrees: A, B, M   *Enroll:* 730
URL: http://blue.ab.edu
Phone: (304) 457-1700   *Calendar:* Sem. plan
Inst. Accred.: NCA-HLC (1959/2003)
Prog. Accred.: Nursing, Physician Assistant, Teacher
  Education (NCATE)

American Military University
111 West Congress St., Charles Town 25414
Type: Private, proprietary, four-year
System: American Public University System
Degrees: A, B, M   *FTE Enroll:* 308
URL: http://www.apus.edu
Phone: (304) 724-3700   *Calendar:* Sem. plan
Inst. Accred.: DETC (1995/2004, *Indirect accreditation
  through American Public University System, Charles
  Town, WV)*

American Public University
111 West Congress St., Charles Town 25414
Type: Private, proprietary, four-year
System: American Public University System
Degrees: A, B, M
URL: http://www.apus.edu
Phone: (304) 724-3700   *Calendar:* Sem. plan
Inst. Accred.: DETC (2002/2004, *Indirect accreditation
  through American Public University System, Charles
  Town, WV)*

Appalachian Bible College
5701 Robert C. Byrd Dr., Bradley 25818
Type: Private, independent, four-year
Degrees: A, B, M   *Enroll:* 271
URL: http://www.abc.edu
Phone: (304) 877-6428   *Calendar:* Sem. plan
Inst. Accred.: ABHE (1967/1999), NCA-HLC (2000/2005)

Bethany College
Bethany 26032
Type: Private, Christian Church Disciples of Christ, four-
  year
Degrees: B   *Enroll:* 896
URL: http://www.bethanywv.edu
Phone: (304) 829-7000   *Calendar:* 4-1-4 plan
Inst. Accred.: NCA-HLC (1926/1999)
Prog. Accred.: Social Work, Teacher Education (NCATE)

Bluefield State College
219 Rock St., Bluefield 24701
Type: Public, state, four-year
System: West Virginia Higher Education Policy
  Commission
Degrees: A, B   *Enroll:* 2,838
URL: http://www.bluefieldstate.edu
Phone: (304) 327-4000   *Calendar:* Sem. plan
Inst. Accred.: NCA-HLC (1951/2002)
Prog. Accred.: Business (ACBSP), Engineering (civil),
  Engineering Technology (architectural, electrical,
  mechanical), Nursing Education, Radiography, Teacher
  Education (NCATE)

Greenbrier Community College Center
Drawer 151, Lewisburg 24901
Phone: (304) 645-3303

Community and Technical College at West Virginia University Institute of Technology
208 Davis Hall, Montgomery 25136
Type: Public, state, two-year
Degrees: A
URL: http://ctc.wvutech.edu
Phone: (304) 442-3149   *Calendar:* Sem. plan
Inst. Accred.: NCA-HLC (2004)

Community and Technical College of Shepherd
400 West Stephen St., Martinsburg 25401
Type: Public, state, two-year
Degrees: A
URL: http://www.shepherd.edu/ctcweb
Phone: (304) 260-4380   *Calendar:* Sem. plan
Inst. Accred.: NCA-HLC (2005)

Concord University
PO Box 1000, Athens 24712-1000
Type: Public, state, four-year
System: West Virginia Higher Education Policy
  Commission
Degrees: A, B   *Enroll:* 2,505
URL: http://www.concord.edu
Phone: (304) 384-3115   *Calendar:* Sem. plan
Inst. Accred.: NCA-HLC (1931/1998)
Prog. Accred.: Social Work, Teacher Education (NCATE)

Davis and Elkins College
100 Campus Dr., Elkins 26241
Type: Private, Presbyterian Church (USA), four-year
Degrees: A, B   *Enroll:* 591
URL: http://www.davisandelkins.edu
Phone: (304) 637-1900   *Calendar:* Sem. plan
Inst. Accred.: NCA-HLC (1946/2000)
Prog. Accred.: Nursing, Theatre

Eastern West Virginia Community and Technical College
1929 State Rd. 55†, Moorefield 26836
Type: Public, state, two-year
System: Community and Technical College System of West Virginia
Degrees: A
URL: http://www.eastern.wvnet.edu
Phone: (304) 434-8000   *Calendar:* Sem. plan
Inst. Accred.: NCA-HLC (1971/2004, *Indirect accreditation through Southern West Virginia Community and Technical College, Mount Gay, WV*)

Fairmont State Community and Technical College
1201 Locust Ave., Fairmont 26554
Type: Public, state, two-year
Degrees: A
URL: http://www.fscwv.edu/fsctc
Phone: (304) 367-4000   *Calendar:* Sem. plan
Inst. Accred.: NCA-HLC (2003)
Prog. Accred.: Physical Therapy Assisting

Fairmont State University
1201 Locust Ave., Fairmont 26554
Type: Public, state, four-year
System: West Virginia Higher Education Policy Commission
Degrees: A, B, M   *Enroll:* 3,600
URL: http://www.fairmontstate.edu
Phone: (304) 367-4000   *Calendar:* Sem. plan
Inst. Accred.: NCA-HLC (1928/2003)
Prog. Accred.: Business (ACBSP), Clinical Lab Technology, Engineering Technology (civil/construction, electrical, mechanical, mechanical drafting/design), Health Information Technician, Nursing, Nursing Education, Teacher Education (NCATE), Veterinary Technology

Glenville State College
200 High St., Glenville 26351
Type: Public, state, four-year
System: West Virginia Higher Education Policy Commission
Degrees: A, B   *Enroll:* 1,276
URL: http://www.glenville.edu
Phone: (304) 462-7361   *Calendar:* Sem. plan
Inst. Accred.: NCA-HLC (1949/2003)
Prog. Accred.: Teacher Education (NCATE)

Huntington Junior College
900 Fifth Ave., Huntington 25701
Type: Private, proprietary, two-year
Degrees: A   *Enroll:* 767
URL: http://www.huntingtonjuniorcollege.com
Phone: (304) 697-7550   *Calendar:* Qtr. plan
Inst. Accred.: NCA-HLC (1997/2002)
Prog. Accred.: Medical Assisting (CAAHEP)

Marshall Community and Technical College
One John Marshall Dr., Huntington 25755-2700
Type: Public, state, two-year
System: Community and Technical College System of West Virginia
Degrees: A
URL: http://www.marshall.edu/ctc
Phone: (304) 696-6282   *Calendar:* Sem. plan
Inst. Accred.: NCA-HLC (2003)
Prog. Accred.: Business (ACBSP), Engineering Technology (manufacturing)

Marshall University
One John Marshall Dr., Huntington 25755
Type: Public, state, four-year
System: West Virginia Higher Education Policy Commission
Degrees: A, B, M, P, D   *Enroll:* 13,158
URL: http://www.marshall.edu
Phone: (304) 696-2301   *Calendar:* Sem. plan
Inst. Accred.: NCA-HLC (1928/2001)
Prog. Accred.: Applied Science (occupational health and safety), Athletic Training, Business (AACSB), Clinical Lab Scientist, Clinical Lab Technology, Dietetics (internship), Health Information Technician, Journalism, Medicine, Music, Nursing, Physical Therapy Assisting, Recreation and Leisure Services, Social Work, Speech-Language Pathology, Teacher Education (NCATE)

Graduate College Campus
100 Angus E. Peyton Dr., South Charleston 25303-1600
Phone: (800) 642-9842
Prog. Accred: Nurse Anesthesia Education

Mountain State College
Spring at 16th St., Parkersburg 26101
Type: Private, proprietary, two-year
Degrees: A   *Enroll:* 133
URL: http://www.mountainstate.org
Phone: (304) 485-5487   *Calendar:* Qtr. plan
Inst. Accred.: ACICS (1950/2005)

The Mountain State University
PO Box 9003, Beckley 25802
Type: Private, independent, four-year
Degrees: A, B, M   *Enroll:* 3,457
URL: http://www.mountainstate.edu
Phone: (304) 253-7351   *Calendar:* Sem. plan
Inst. Accred.: NCA-HLC (1981/2001)
Prog. Accred.: Culinary Education, Diagnostic Medical Sonography, Medical Assisting (AMA), Nursing, Occupational Therapy Assisting, Physical Therapy Assisting, Physician Assistant, Radiography, Respiratory Therapy, Social Work

National Institute of Technology—Cross Lanes
5514 Big Tyler Rd., Cross Lanes 25313-9998
Type: Private, proprietary, two-year
System: Corinthian Colleges, Inc
Degrees: A   *Enroll:* 573
URL: http://www.nitschools.com
Phone: (304) 776-6290
Inst. Accred.: ACCSCT (1971/2001)

New River Community and Technical College
167 Dye Dr., Beckley 25801
Type: Public, state, two-year
Degrees: A
URL: http://www.nrctc.edu
Phone: (304) 255-5812   *Calendar:* Sem. plan
Inst. Accred.: NCA-HLC (2005)

Ohio Valley University
One Campus View Dr., Vienna 26105-8000
Type: Private, Churches of Christ, four-year
Degrees: A, B   *Enroll:* 502
URL: http://www.ovu.edu
Phone: (304) 865-6000   *Calendar:* Sem. plan
Inst. Accred.: NCA-HLC (1978/2003)

Potomac State College of West Virginia University
101 Fort Ave., Keyser 26726
Type: Public, state, four-year
System: West Virginia Higher Education Policy Commission
Degrees: A, B   *Enroll:* 1,005
URL: http://www.potomacstatecollege.edu
Phone: (304) 788-6800   *Calendar:* Sem. plan
Inst. Accred.: NCA-HLC (1926/2004)

Salem International University
PO Box 500, Salem 26426
Type: Private, independent, four-year
Degrees: A, B, M   *Enroll:* 478
URL: http://www.salemiu.edu
Phone: (304) 782-5234   *Calendar:* Sem. plan
Inst. Accred.: NCA-HLC (1963/2005)

Shepherd University
PO Box 3210, Shepherdstown 25443-3210
Type: Public, state, four-year
System: West Virginia Higher Education Policy Commission
Degrees: A, B   *Enroll:* 3,817
URL: http://www.shepherd.edu
Phone: (304) 876-5000   *Calendar:* Sem. plan
Inst. Accred.: NCA-HLC (1950/2002)
Prog. Accred.: Music, Nursing, Social Work, Teacher Education (NCATE)

Southern West Virginia Community and Technical College
Dempsey Branch Rd., PO Box 2900, Mount Gay 25637
Type: Public, state, two-year
System: Community and Technical College System of West Virginia
Degrees: A   *Enroll:* 1,838
URL: http://www.southern.wvnet.edu
Phone: (304) 792-7098   *Calendar:* Sem. plan
Inst. Accred.: NCA-HLC (1971/2004)
Prog. Accred.: Clinical Lab Technology, Nursing, Radiography

The University of Charleston
2300 MacCorkle Ave., Charleston 25304
Type: Private, independent, four-year
Degrees: A, B, M   *Enroll:* 915
URL: http://www.ucwv.edu
Phone: (304) 357-4800   *Calendar:* Sem. plan
Inst. Accred.: NCA-HLC (1958/2005)
Prog. Accred.: Athletic Training, Nursing, Radiography, Respiratory Therapy, Teacher Education (NCATE)

Valley College of Technology—Beckley
713 South Oakwood Ave., Beckley 25801
Type: Private, proprietary, two-year
Degrees: A
URL: http://www.vct.edu
Phone: (304) 252-9547   *Calendar:* Sem. plan
Inst. Accred.: ACCET (1992/2005)

Valley College of Technology—Princeton
616 Harrison St., Princeton 24740
Type: Private, proprietary, two-year
Degrees: A
URL: http://www.vct.edu
Phone: (304) 425-2323   *Calendar:* Sem. plan
Inst. Accred.: ACCET (1992/2005)

West Liberty State College
PO Box 295, West Liberty 26074
Type: Public, state, four-year
System: West Virginia Higher Education Policy Commission
Degrees: A, B   *Enroll:* 2,302
URL: http://www.wlsc.wvnet.edu
Phone: (304) 336-8000   *Calendar:* Sem. plan
Inst. Accred.: NCA-HLC (1942/1998)
Prog. Accred.: Clinical Lab Scientist, Dental Hygiene, Music, Nursing, Teacher Education (NCATE)

West Virginia Business College
1052 Main St., Wheeling 26003
Type: Private, proprietary, two-year
Degrees: A   *FTE Enroll:* 23
URL: http://www.wvbusinesscollege.com
Phone: (304) 232-0631   *Calendar:* Sem. plan
Inst. Accred.: ACICS (1990/2003)

Nutter Fort Campus
116 Pennsylvania Ave., Nutter Fort 26301
Phone: (304) 624-7695

West Virginia Junior College
1000 Virginia St., East, Charleston 25301
Type: Private, proprietary, two-year
Degrees: A   *Enroll:* 224
URL: http://www.wvjc.edu
Phone: (304) 345-2820   *Calendar:* Qtr. plan
Inst. Accred.: ACICS (1971/2000)

Bridgeport Campus
176 Thompson Dr., Bridgeport 26330
Phone: (304) 842-4007

West Virginia Junior College at Morgantown
148 Willey St., Morgantown 26505
Type: Private, proprietary, two-year
Degrees: A   *Enroll:* 176
URL: http://www.wvjcmorgantown.edu
Phone: (304) 296-8282   *Calendar:* Qtr. plan
Inst. Accred.: ACICS (1953/2000)

West Virginia Career Institute
Mount Braddock Rd., Uniontown, PA 15401
Phone: (724) 437-4600

West Virginia Northern Community College
1704 Market St., College Square, Wheeling 26003
Type: Public, state, two-year
System: Community and Technical College System of
  West Virginia
Degrees: A   *Enroll:* 1,789
URL: http://www.northern.wvnet.edu
Phone: (304) 233-5900   *Calendar:* Sem. plan
Inst. Accred.: NCA-HLC (1972/2003)
Prog. Accred.: Clinical Lab Technology, Culinary
  Education, Health Information Technician, Nursing,
  Respiratory Therapy, Surgical Technology

West Virginia State Community and Technical College
PO Box 1000, Campus Box 183, Institute 25112-1000
Type: Public, state, two-year
Degrees: A
URL: http://www.wvsc.edu
Phone: (304) 766-3000   *Calendar:* Sem. plan
Inst. Accred.: NCA-HLC (2004)

West Virginia State University
PO Box 1000, Institute 25112
Type: Public, state, four-year
System: West Virginia Higher Education Policy
  Commission
Degrees: A, B   *Enroll:* 3,969
URL: http://www.wvsc.edu
Phone: (304) 766-3000   *Calendar:* Sem. plan
Inst. Accred.: NCA-HLC (1927/2005)
Prog. Accred.: Engineering Technology (electrical),
  Nuclear Medicine Technology, Recreation and Leisure
  Services, Social Work, Teacher Education (NCATE)

West Virginia University
PO Box 6201, Morgantown 26506-6201
Type: Public, state, four-year
System: West Virginia Higher Education Policy
  Commission
Degrees: B, M, P, D   *Enroll:* 22,132
URL: http://www.wvu.edu
Phone: (304) 293-0111   *Calendar:* Sem. plan
Inst. Accred.: NCA-HLC (1926/2004)
Prog. Accred.: Accounting, Advanced Education in
  General Dentistry, Applied Science (industrial hygiene,
  occupational health and safety), Art, Athletic Training,
  Audiology, Business (AACSB), Clinical Lab Scientist,
  Clinical Pastoral Education (ACPEI), Clinical Psychology,
  Combined Prosthodontics, Counseling, Counseling
  Psychology, Dental Hygiene, Dentistry, Diagnostic
  Medical Sonography, Dietetics (internship), Endodontics,
  Engineering (aerospace, chemical, civil, computer,
  electrical, industrial, mechanical, mining, petroleum),
  Forestry, General Dentistry, Interior Design, Journalism,
  Landscape Architecture, Law, Medicine, Music, Nuclear
  Medicine Technology, Nursing, Nursing Education,
  Occupational Therapy, Oral and Maxillofacial Surgery,
  Orthodontic and Dentofacial Orthopedics, Pharmacy,
  Physical Therapy, Psychology Internship, Public
  Administration, Public Health, Radiation Therapy,
  Radiography, Recreation and Leisure Services,
  Rehabilitation Counseling, Social Work, Speech-
  Language Pathology, Teacher Education (NCATE),
  Theatre

Charleston Medical Center
3110 MacCorkle Ave., SE, Charleston 25304-1299
Phone: (304) 347-1209
Prog. Accred: Advanced Education in General
  Dentistry, Cytotechnology, General Practice
  Residency

West Virginia University at Parkersburg
300 Campus Dr., Parkersburg 26104
Type: Public, state, four-year
System: West Virginia Higher Education Policy
  Commission
Degrees: A, B   *Enroll:* 2,777
URL: http://www.wvup.edu
Phone: (304) 424-8200   *Calendar:* Sem. plan
Inst. Accred.: NCA-HLC (1971/2004)
Prog. Accred.: Nursing, Teacher Education (NCATE)

West Virginia University Institute of Technology
405 Fayette Pike, Montgomery 25136
Type: Public, state, four-year
System: West Virginia Higher Education Policy
  Commission
Degrees: A, B, M   *Enroll:* 2,029
URL: http://www.wvutech.edu
Phone: (888) 554-8324   *Calendar:* Sem. plan
Inst. Accred.: NCA-HLC (1956/2000)
Prog. Accred.: Dental Hygiene, Engineering (chemical,
  civil, electrical, mechanical), Engineering Technology
  (civil/construction, electrical, mechanical, mechanical
  drafting/design), Nursing

West Virginia Wesleyan College
59 College Ave., Buckhannon 26201
Type: Private, Methodist Episcopal Church, four-year
Degrees: B, M   *Enroll:* 1,591
URL: http://www.wvwc.edu
Phone: (304) 473-8000   *Calendar:* 4-1-4 plan
Inst. Accred.: NCA-HLC (1927/2000)
Prog. Accred.: Athletic Training, Music, Nursing, Teacher
  Education (NCATE)

Wheeling Jesuit University
316 Washington Ave., Wheeling 26003
Type: Private, Roman Catholic Church, four-year
Degrees: B, M   *Enroll:* 1,292
URL: http://www.wju.edu
Phone: (304) 243-2000   *Calendar:* Sem. plan
Inst. Accred.: NCA-HLC (1962/2001)
Prog. Accred.: Nuclear Medicine Technology, Nursing,
  Nursing Education, Physical Therapy, Respiratory
  Therapy

WISCONSIN

Alverno College
3401 South 39th St., PO Box 343922, Milwaukee 53215
Type: Private, Roman Catholic Church, four-year
Degrees: A, B, M   *Enroll:* 1,577
URL: http://www.alverno.edu
Phone: (414) 382-6000   *Calendar:* Sem. plan
Inst. Accred.: NCA-HLC (1951/1997)
Prog. Accred.: Music, Nursing, Nursing Education,
  Teacher Education (NCATE)

Bellin College of Nursing
725 South Webster Ave., PO Box 23400, Green Bay
54305-3400
Type: Private, independent, four-year
Degrees: B   *Enroll:* 184
URL: http://www.bcon.edu
Phone: (920) 433-3560   *Calendar:* 4-1-4 plan
Inst. Accred.: NCA-HLC (1989/2004)
Prog. Accred.: Nursing, Nursing Education

Beloit College
700 College St., Beloit 53511
Type: Private, independent, four-year
Degrees: B   *Enroll:* 1,293
URL: http://www.beloit.edu
Phone: (608) 363-2000   *Calendar:* Sem. plan
Inst. Accred.: NCA-HLC (1913/1997)

Blackhawk Technical College
PO Box 5009, 6004 Praire Rd., Janesville 53547-5009
Type: Public, state/local, two-year
System: Wisconsin Technical College System Board
Degrees: A   *Enroll:* 1,627
URL: http://www.blackhawk.edu
Phone: (608) 758-6900   *Calendar:* Sem. plan
Inst. Accred.: NCA-HLC (1978/2000)
Prog. Accred.: Culinary Education, Dental Assisting,
  Medical Assisting (AMA), Nursing, Physical Therapy
  Assisting, Radiography

Bryant and Stratton College—Milwaukee Campus
310 West Wisconsin Ave., Ste. 500, Milwaukee 53203
Type: Private, proprietary, four-year
System: Bryant and Stratton
Degrees: A, B   *Enroll:* 553
URL: http://www.bryantstratton.edu
Phone: (414) 276-5200   *Calendar:* Qtr. plan
Inst. Accred.: MSA-CHE (2002, *Indirect accreditation
  through Bryant and Stratton, Getzville, NY*)
Prog. Accred.: Medical Assisting (CAAHEP)

Cardinal Stritch University
6801 North Yates Rd., Milwaukee 53217-3985
Type: Private, Roman Catholic Church, four-year
Degrees: A, B, M, D   *Enroll:* 5,467
URL: http://www.stritch.edu
Phone: (414) 410-4000   *Calendar:* Sem. plan
Inst. Accred.: NCA-HLC (1953/2004)
Prog. Accred.: Business (ACBSP), Nursing, Nursing
  Education, Teacher Education (NCATE)

Edina Campus
3300 Edinborough Way, Ste. 505, Edina, MN 55435
Phone: (612) 835-6418

Madison Campus
8071 Excelsior Dr., Madison 53717
Phone: (608) 831-2722

Carroll College
100 North East Ave., Waukesha 53186
Type: Private, Presbyterian Church (USA), four-year
Degrees: B, M   *Enroll:* 2,438
URL: http://www.cc.edu
Phone: (262) 547-1211   *Calendar:* Sem. plan
Inst. Accred.: NCA-HLC (1913/1998)
Prog. Accred.: Nursing, Nursing Education, Physical
  Therapy, Social Work

Carthage College
2001 Alford Park Dr., Kenosha 53140-1994
Type: Private, Evangelic Lutheran Church of America,
  four-year
Degrees: B, M   *Enroll:* 2,220
URL: http://www.carthage.edu
Phone: (262) 551-8500   *Calendar:* 4-1-4 plan
Inst. Accred.: NCA-HLC (1916/2005)
Prog. Accred.: Music, Social Work

Chippewa Valley Technical College
620 West Clairemont Ave., Eau Claire 54701
Type: Public, state/local, two-year
System: Wisconsin Technical College System Board
Degrees: A   *Enroll:* 3,299
URL: http://www.cvtc.edu
Phone: (715) 833-6200   *Calendar:* Sem. plan
Inst. Accred.: NCA-HLC (1973/2003)
Prog. Accred.: Clinical Lab Technology, Diagnostic
  Medical Sonography, Health Information Technician,
  Nursing, Radiography

College of the Menominee Nation
Highway 47-55, PO Box 1179, Keshena 54135
Type: Public, tribal, two-year
System: American Indian Higher Education Consortium
Degrees: A   *Enroll:* 322
URL: http://www.menominee.edu
Phone: (715) 799-5600   *Calendar:* Sem. plan
Inst. Accred.: NCA-HLC (1998/2003)

Columbia College of Nursing
2121 East Newport Ave., Milwaukee 53211
Type: Private, independent, four-year
System: Columbia Saint Mary's
Degrees: B   *FTE Enroll:* 286
URL: http://www.ccon.edu
Phone: (414) 961-3530   *Calendar:* Sem. plan
Inst. Accred.: NCA-HLC (1988/2003)
Prog. Accred.: Nursing

Concordia University Wisconsin
12800 North Lake Shore Dr., Mequon 53097-2402
Type: Private, Lutheran Church—Missouri Synod, four-year
System: Concordia University System
Degrees: A, B, M   *Enroll:* 3,762
URL: http://www.cuw.edu
Phone: (262) 243-5700   *Calendar:* 4-1-4 plan
Inst. Accred.: NCA-HLC (1964/2003)
Prog. Accred.: Medical Assisting (AMA), Nursing, Nursing Education, Occupational Therapy, Physical Therapy, Social Work

Edgewood College
1000 Edgewood College Dr., Madison 53711
Type: Private, Roman Catholic Church, four-year
Degrees: A, B, M, D   *Enroll:* 1,879
URL: http://www.edgewood.edu
Phone: (800) 444-4861   *Calendar:* 4-1-4 plan
Inst. Accred.: NCA-HLC (1958/1998)
Prog. Accred.: Nursing, Nursing Education, Teacher Education (NCATE)

Fox Valley Technical College
1825 North Bluemound Dr., PO Box 2277, Appleton 54912-2277
Type: Public, state/local, two-year
System: Wisconsin Technical College System Board
Degrees: A   *Enroll:* 3,877
URL: http://www.foxvalley.tec.wi.us
Phone: (920) 735-5600   *Calendar:* Sem. plan
Inst. Accred.: NCA-HLC (1974/1996)
Prog. Accred.: Culinary Education, Dental Assisting, Nursing, Occupational Therapy Assisting

Gateway Technical College
3520 30th Ave., Kenosha 53144-1690
Type: Public, state/local, two-year
System: Wisconsin Technical College System Board
Degrees: A   *Enroll:* 3,332
URL: http://www.gtc.edu
Phone: (262) 656-6900   *Calendar:* Sem. plan
Inst. Accred.: NCA-HLC (1970/2000)
Prog. Accred.: Dental Assisting, Health Information Technician, Medical Assisting (AMA), Nursing, Physical Therapy Assisting, Surgical Technology

Elkhorn Campus
400 County Rd. H, Elkhorn 53121-2046
Phone: (262) 741-8200
Prog. Accred: Medical Assisting (CAAHEP)

Herzing College—Madison Campus
5218 E Terrace Dr., Madison 53718-8340
Type: Private, proprietary, two-year
System: Herzing College Corporate Offices
Degrees: A   *Enroll:* 510
URL: http://www.herzing.edu
Phone: (608) 249-6611   *Calendar:* Sem. plan
Inst. Accred.: ACCSCT (1970/2004), NCA-HLC (2004, Indirect accreditation through Herzing College Corporate Offices, Milwaukee, WI)

ITT Technical Institute
6300 West Layton Ave., Greenfield 53220-4612
Type: Private, proprietary, four-year
System: ITT Educational Services, Inc.
Degrees: A, B   *Enroll:* 531
URL: http://www.itt-tech.edu
Phone: (414) 282-9494   *Calendar:* Qtr. plan
Inst. Accred.: ACICS (1999/2004)

Eden Prairie Campus
8911 Columbine Rd., Eden Prairie, MN 55347
Phone: (952) 914-5300

Green Bay Campus
470 Security Blvd., Green Bay 54313
Phone: (920) 662-9000

Lac Courte Oreilles Ojibwa Community College
13466 West Trepania Rd., Hayward 54843
Type: Public, tribal, two-year
System: American Indian Higher Education Consortium
Degrees: A   *Enroll:* 402
URL: http://www.lco-college.edu
Phone: (715) 634-4790   *Calendar:* Sem. plan
Inst. Accred.: NCA-HLC (1993/2004)
Prog. Accred.: Medical Assisting (CAAHEP)

Lakeland College
PO Box 359, Sheboygan 53082-0359
Type: Private, United Church of Christ, four-year
Degrees: A, B, M   *Enroll:* 2,338
URL: http://www.lakeland.edu
Phone: (920) 565-2111   *Calendar:* 4-1-4 plan
Inst. Accred.: NCA-HLC (1961/2002)

Lakeshore Technical College
1290 North Ave., Cleveland 53015
Type: Public, state/local, two-year
System: Wisconsin Technical College System Board
Degrees: A   *Enroll:* 1,566
URL: http://www.gotoltc.com
Phone: (920) 693-1000   *Calendar:* Sem. plan
Inst. Accred.: NCA-HLC (1977/2002)
Prog. Accred.: Dental Assisting, Medical Assisting (AMA), Nursing, Radiography

Lawrence University
PO Box 599, Appleton 54912
Type: Private, independent, four-year
Degrees: B   *Enroll:* 1,368
URL: http://www.lawrence.edu
Phone: (920) 832-7000   *Calendar:* Qtr. plan
Inst. Accred.: NCA-HLC (1913/1999)
Prog. Accred.: Music

Madison Area Technical College
3550 Anderson St., Madison 53704
Type: Public, state/local, two-year
System: Wisconsin Technical College System Board
Degrees: A   *Enroll:* 8,048
URL: http://matcmadison.edu
Phone: (608) 246-6100   *Calendar:* Sem. plan
Inst. Accred.: NCA-HLC (1969/2003)
Prog. Accred.: Clinical Lab Technology, Culinary
Education, Dental Assisting, Dental Hygiene, Medical
Assisting (AMA), Nursing, Occupational Therapy
Assisting, Optometric Technician, Practical Nursing,
Radiography, Respiratory Therapy, Surgical Technology,
Veterinary Technology

Marantha Baptist Bible College
745 West Main St., PO Box 438, Watertown 53094
Type: Private, independent Baptist, four-year
Degrees: A, B, M   *Enroll:* 802
URL: http://www.mbbc.edu
Phone: (920) 261-9300   *Calendar:* Sem. plan
Inst. Accred.: NCA-HLC (1993/1998)

Marian College of Fond du Lac
45 South National Ave., Fond du Lac 54935
Type: Private, Roman Catholic Church, four-year
Degrees: B, M   *Enroll:* 1,846
URL: http://www.mariancollege.edu
Phone: (920) 923-7600   *Calendar:* Sem. plan
Inst. Accred.: NCA-HLC (1960/1996)
Prog. Accred.: Nursing, Nursing Education, Social Work,
Teacher Education (NCATE)

Marquette University
PO Box 1881, 615 North 11th St., Milwaukee 53201-
1881
Type: Private, Roman Catholic Church, four-year
Degrees: A, B, M, P, D   *Enroll:* 10,168
URL: http://www.mu.edu
Phone: (414) 288-7223   *Calendar:* Sem. plan
Inst. Accred.: NCA-HLC (1922/2004)
Prog. Accred.: Accounting, Advanced Education in
General Dentistry, Business (AACSB), Clinical Lab
Scientist, Clinical Psychology, Combined
Prosthodontics, Counseling Psychology, Dental Hygiene,
Dentistry, Endodontics, Engineering (bioengineering,
civil, computer, electrical, industrial, mechanical),
General Dentistry, Journalism, Law, Nurse (Midwifery),
Nursing, Nursing Education, Orthodontic and
Dentofacial Orthopedics, Physical Therapy, Physician
Assistant, Speech-Language Pathology, Teacher
Education (NCATE)

Medical College of Wisconsin
8701 Watertown Plank Rd., Milwaukee 53226
Type: Private, independent, four-year
Degrees: M, D   *Enroll:* 1,088
URL: http://www.mcw.edu
Phone: (414) 456-8296   *Calendar:* Qtr. plan
Inst. Accred.: NCA-HLC (1922/1997)
Prog. Accred.: Medicine, Oral and Maxillofacial Surgery,
Public Health

Mid-State Technical College
500 32nd St. North, Wisconsin Rapids 54494
Type: Public, state, two-year
System: Wisconsin Technical College System Board
Degrees: A   *Enroll:* 1,781
URL: http://www.mstc.edu
Phone: (715) 422-5300   *Calendar:* Sem. plan
Inst. Accred.: NCA-HLC (1979/1994)
Prog. Accred.: Medical Assisting (AMA), Nursing,
Respiratory Therapy, Surgical Technology

Marshfield Campus
2600 West 5th St., Marshfield 54449
Phone: (715) 387-2538

Stevens Point Campus
933 Michigan Ave., Stevens Point 54481
Phone: (715) 344-3063
Prog. Accred.: Medical Assisting (AMA), Phlebotomy

Midwest College of Oriental Medicine—Wisconsin
6226 Bankers Rd., Racine 53403
Type: Private, proprietary, four-year
Degrees: M   *Enroll:* 95
URL: http://www.acupuncture.edu/midwest
Phone: (262) 554-2010   *Calendar:* Qtr. plan
Inst. Accred.: ACAOM (1993/2001)

Chicago Campus
4334 North Hazel St., Ste. 206, Chicago, IL 60613-
1429
Phone: (773) 975-1295

Milwaukee Area Technical College
700 West State St., Milwaukee 53233
Type: Public, state/local, two-year
System: Wisconsin Technical College System Board
Degrees: A   *Enroll:* 9,715
URL: http://www.matc.edu
Phone: (414) 297-6600   *Calendar:* Sem. plan
Inst. Accred.: NCA-HLC (1959/1999)
Prog. Accred.: Clinical Lab Technology, Culinary
Education, Dental Hygiene, Dental Laboratory
Technology, Funeral Service Education (Mortuary
Science), Medical Assisting (AMA), Nursing,
Occupational Therapy Assisting, Opticianry, Phlebotomy,
Physical Therapy Assisting, Practical Nursing,
Radiography, Respiratory Therapy, Surgical Technology

Milwaukee Institute of Art and Design
273 East Erie St., Milwaukee 53202
Type: Private, independent, four-year
Degrees: B *Enroll:* 598
URL: http://www.miad.edu
Phone: (414) 276-7889 *Calendar:* Sem. plan
Inst. Accred.: NCA-HLC (1987/2000)
Prog. Accred.: Art

Milwaukee School of Engineering
1025 North Broadway, Milwaukee 53202-3109
Type: Private, independent, four-year
Degrees: A, B, M *Enroll:* 2,036
URL: http://www.msoe.edu
Phone: (414) 277-7300 *Calendar:* Qtr. plan
Inst. Accred.: NCA-HLC (1971/2005)
Prog. Accred.: Construction Education, Engineering
(architectural, bioengineering, computer, electrical,
industrial, mechanical), Engineering Technology
(electrical, mechanical), Nursing Education

Moraine Park Technical College
235 North National Ave., PO Box 1940, Fond Du Lac
54936-1940
Type: Public, state/local, two-year
System: Wisconsin Technical College System Board
Degrees: A *Enroll:* 3,343
URL: http://www.moraine.tec.wi.us
Phone: (920) 929-8611 *Calendar:* Sem. plan
Inst. Accred.: NCA-HLC (1975/1995)
Prog. Accred.: Culinary Education, Health Information
Technician, Nursing, Practical Nursing

Mount Mary College
2900 North Menomonee River Pkwy., Milwaukee 53222
Type: Private, School Sisters of Notre Dame, four-year
Degrees: B, M *Enroll:* 1,085
URL: http://www.mtmary.edu
Phone: (414) 258-4810 *Calendar:* Sem. plan
Inst. Accred.: NCA-HLC (1926/2003)
Prog. Accred.: Dietetics (coordinated), Dietetics
(internship), Interior Design, Occupational Therapy,
Social Work

Nashotah House
2777 Mission Rd., Nashotah 53058-9793
Type: Private, Episcopal Church, four-year
Degrees: M *Enroll:* 39
URL: http://www.nashotah.edu
Phone: (262) 646-6500 *Calendar:* Sem. plan
Inst. Accred.: ATS (1954/1999)

Nicolet Area Technical College
PO Box 518, County Hwy. G, Rhinelander 54501
Type: Public, state/local, two-year
System: Wisconsin Technical College System Board
Degrees: A *Enroll:* 964
URL: http://www.nicoletcollege.edu
Phone: (715) 365-4410 *Calendar:* Sem. plan
Inst. Accred.: NCA-HLC (1975/2005)
Prog. Accred.: Medical Assisting (AMA), Nursing

Northcentral Technical College
1000 West Campus Dr., Wausau 54401
Type: Public, local, two-year
System: Wisconsin Technical College System Board
Degrees: A *Enroll:* 2,101
URL: http://www.ntc.edu
Phone: (715) 675-3331 *Calendar:* Sem. plan
Inst. Accred.: NCA-HLC (1970/1999)
Prog. Accred.: Dental Hygiene, Nursing, Radiography,
Surgical Technology

Northeast Wisconsin Technical College
PO Box 19042, 2740 West Mason St., Green Bay 54307-
9042
Type: Public, state/local, two-year
System: Wisconsin Technical College System Board
Degrees: A *Enroll:* 5,694
URL: http://www.nwtc.edu
Phone: (920) 498-5500 *Calendar:* Sem. plan
Inst. Accred.: NCA-HLC (1976/2001)
Prog. Accred.: Clinical Lab Technology, Dental Assisting,
Dental Hygiene, Engineering Technology
(civil/construction), Health Information Technician,
Medical Assisting (AMA), Nursing, Physical Therapy
Assisting, Respiratory Therapy, Surgical Technology

Marinette Campus
1601 University Ave., Marinette 54143
Phone: (715) 735-9361

Sturgeon Bay Campus
229 North 14th Ave., Sturgeon Bay 54235-1317
Phone: (414) 743-2207

Northland College
1411 Ellis Ave., Ashland 54806
Type: Private, United Church of Christ, four-year
Degrees: B *Enroll:* 703
URL: http://www.northland.edu
Phone: (715) 682-1699
Inst. Accred.: NCA-HLC (1957/2001)

Ripon College
300 Seward St., PO Box 248, Ripon 54971
Type: Private, Associated Colleges of the Midwest, four-
year
Degrees: B *Enroll:* 986
URL: http://www.ripon.edu
Phone: (920) 748-8115 *Calendar:* Sem. plan
Inst. Accred.: NCA-HLC (1913/2000)

Sacred Heart School of Theology
PO Box 429, 7335 South Hwy. 100, Hales Corners
53130-0429
Type: Private, Roman Catholic Church, four-year
Degrees: M *Enroll:* 60
URL: http://www.shst.edu
Phone: (414) 425-8300 *Calendar:* Sem. plan
Inst. Accred.: ATS (1981/1999), NCA-HLC (1995/2000)

Saint Francis Seminary
3257 South Lake Dr., St. Francis 53235
Type: Private, Roman Catholic Church, four-year
Degrees: M   *Enroll:* 45
URL: http://www.sfc.edu
Phone: (414) 747-6400   *Calendar:* Sem. plan
Inst. Accred.: ATS (1975/2000), NCA-HLC (1963/2001)

Saint Norbert College
100 Grant St., De Pere 54115-2099
Type: Private, Roman Catholic Church, four-year
Degrees: B, M   *Enroll:* 2,064
URL: http://www.snc.edu
Phone: (920) 403-3181   *Calendar:* Sem. plan
Inst. Accred.: NCA-HLC (1934/2002)

Sanford-Brown College—Milwaukee
6737 West Washington St., Ste. 2355, West Allis 53214
Type: Private, proprietary, four-year
System: Career Education Corporation
Degrees: A, B
URL: http://sbcmilwaukee.com
Inst. Accred.: ACICS (2004)

Silver Lake College
2406 South Alverno Rd., Manitowoc 54220
Type: Private, Roman Catholic Church, four-year
Degrees: A, B, M   *Enroll:* 615
URL: http://www.sl.edu
Phone: (920) 236-4752   *Calendar:* Sem. plan
Inst. Accred.: NCA-HLC (1959/2001)
Prog. Accred.: Music

Southwest Wisconsin Technical College
1800 Bronson Blvd., Fennimore 53809
Type: Public, state/local, two-year
System: Wisconsin Technical College System Board
Degrees: A   *Enroll:* 1,407
URL: http://www.swtc.edu
Phone: (608) 822-3262   *Calendar:* Sem. plan
Inst. Accred.: NCA-HLC (1976/1996)
Prog. Accred.: Medical Assisting (AMA), Nursing, Practical
  Nursing

University of Wisconsin Colleges
780 Regent St., PO Box 8680, Madison 53708-8680
Type: Public, state, two-year
System: University of Wisconsin System
Degrees: A   *Enroll:* 9,747
URL: http://www.uwc.edu
Phone: (608) 262-1783   *Calendar:* Sem. plan
Inst. Accred.: NCA-HLC (1977/2003)
Prog. Accred.: Business (AACSB)

Baraboo-Sauk Campus
1006 Connie Rd., Baraboo 53913-1098
Phone: (608) 356-8351

Barron Campus
1800 College Dr., Rice Lake 54868-2497
Phone: (715) 234-8176

Fond du Lac Campus
400 Campus Dr., Fond du Lac 54935-2998
Phone: (920) 929-3600

Fox Valley Campus
1478 Midway Rd., PO Box 8002, Menasha 54952-8002
Phone: (920) 832-2600

Manitowoc Campus
705 Viebahn St., Manitowoc 54220-6699
Phone: (920) 683-4700

Marathon Campus
518 South Seventh Ave., Wausau 54401-9602
Phone: (715) 261-6100

Marinette Campus
750 West Bay Shore St., Marinette 54143-4300
Phone: (715) 735-4300

Marshfield-Wood County Campus
2000 West 5th St., Marshfield 54449-3310
Phone: (715) 389-6500

Richland Campus
Highway 14 West, Richland Center 53581-1399
Phone: (608) 647-6186

Rock County Campus
2909 Kellogg Ave., Janesville 53545-5699
Phone: (608) 758-6565

Sheboygan Campus
One University Dr., Sheboygan 53081-4789
Phone: (920) 459-6600

Washington County Campus
400 University Dr., West Bend 53095-3699
Phone: (262) 335-5200

Waukesha Campus
1500 University Dr., Waukesha 53188-2799
Phone: (262) 521-5200

University of Wisconsin—Eau Claire
105 Garfield Ave., PO Box 4004, Eau Claire 54702-4004
Type: Public, state, four-year
System: University of Wisconsin System
Degrees: A, B, M, D   *Enroll:* 9,857
URL: http://www.uwec.edu
Phone: (715) 836-2637   *Calendar:* Sem. plan
Inst. Accred.: NCA-HLC (1950/2000)
Prog. Accred.: Business (AACSB), Computer Science,
  Engineering (bioengineering), Journalism, Music,
  Nursing, Nursing Education, Social Work, Speech-
  Language Pathology

University of Wisconsin—Green Bay
2420 Nicolet Dr., Green Bay 54311-7001
Type: Public, state, four-year
System: University of Wisconsin System
Degrees: A, B, M   *Enroll:* 4,927
URL: http://www.uwgb.edu
Phone: (920) 465-2000   *Calendar:* Sem. plan
Inst. Accred.: NCA-HLC (1972/1998)
Prog. Accred.: Dietetics (internship), Music, Nursing, Nursing Education, Social Work

University of Wisconsin—La Crosse
1725 State St., La Crosse 54601
Type: Public, state, four-year
System: University of Wisconsin System
Degrees: A, B, M, D   *Enroll:* 8,541
URL: http://www.uwlax.edu
Phone: (608) 785-8000   *Calendar:* Sem. plan
Inst. Accred.: NCA-HLC (1928/1996)
Prog. Accred.: Athletic Training, Business (AACSB), Clinical Lab Scientist, Music, Nurse Anesthesia Education, Occupational Therapy, Physical Therapy, Physician Assistant, Public Health, Radiation Therapy, Recreation and Leisure Services, Teacher Education (NCATE)

University of Wisconsin—Madison
500 Lincoln Dr., Madison 53706
Type: Public, state, four-year
System: University of Wisconsin System
Degrees: B, M, P, D   *Enroll:* 38,081
URL: http://www.wisc.edu
Phone: (608) 262-1234   *Calendar:* Sem. plan
Inst. Accred.: NCA-HLC (1913/1999)
Prog. Accred.: Accounting, Art, Audiology, Business (AACSB), Clinical Lab Scientist, Clinical Psychology, Counseling Psychology, Diagnostic Medical Sonography, Dietetics (coordinated), Dietetics (internship), Engineering (agricultural, chemical, civil, computer, construction, electrical, engineering mechanics, geological/geophysical, industrial, materials, mechanical, nuclear), Forestry, Interior Design, Landscape Architecture, Law, Librarianship, Medicine, Music, Nursing, Nursing Education, Occupational Therapy, Pharmacy, Physical Therapy, Physician Assistant, Planning, Psychology Internship, Public Administration, Rehabilitation Counseling, School Psychology, Social Work, Speech-Language Pathology, Theatre, Veterinary Medicine

University of Wisconsin—Milwaukee
PO Box 413, Milwaukee 53201
Type: Public, state, four-year
System: University of Wisconsin System
Degrees: B, M, D   *Enroll:* 21,341
URL: http://www.uwm.edu
Phone: (414) 229-1122   *Calendar:* Sem. plan
Inst. Accred.: NCA-HLC (1969/2005)
Prog. Accred.: Business (AACSB), Clinical Lab Scientist, Clinical Psychology, Counseling Psychology, Engineering (civil, electrical, industrial, materials, mechanical), Health Information Administration, Librarianship, Music, Nursing, Nursing Education, Occupational Therapy, Planning, Public Administration, Rehabilitation Counseling, School Psychology, Social Work, Speech-Language Pathology

University of Wisconsin—Oshkosh
800 Algoma Blvd., Oshkosh 54901-8601
Type: Public, state, four-year
System: University of Wisconsin System
Degrees: A, B, M   *Enroll:* 9,734
URL: http://www.uwosh.edu
Phone: (920) 424-1234   *Calendar:* Sem. plan
Inst. Accred.: NCA-HLC (1915/1997)
Prog. Accred.: Audiology, Business (AACSB), Computer Science, Counseling, Journalism, Music, Nursing, Nursing Education, Social Work, Speech-Language Pathology, Teacher Education (NCATE)

University of Wisconsin—Parkside
900 Wood Rd., PO Box 2000, Kenosha 53141-2000
Type: Public, state, four-year
System: University of Wisconsin System
Degrees: B, M   *Enroll:* 4,126
URL: http://www.uwp.edu
Phone: (262) 595-2345   *Calendar:* Sem. plan
Inst. Accred.: NCA-HLC (1972/2003)
Prog. Accred.: Business (AACSB)

University of Wisconsin—Platteville
One University Plaza, Platteville 53818-3099
Type: Public, state, four-year
System: University of Wisconsin System
Degrees: A, B, M   *Enroll:* 5,500
URL: http://www.uwplatt.edu
Phone: (608) 342-1491   *Calendar:* Sem. plan
Inst. Accred.: NCA-HLC (1918/1997)
Prog. Accred.: Engineering (civil, electrical, engineering physics/science, environmental/sanitary, industrial, mechanical), Industrial Technology, Music, Teacher Education (NCATE)

University of Wisconsin—River Falls
410 South Third St., River Falls 54022-5001
Type: Public, state, four-year
System: University of Wisconsin System
Degrees: B, M, D   *Enroll:* 5,456
URL: http://www.uwrf.edu
Phone: (715) 425-3911   *Calendar:* Sem. plan
Inst. Accred.: NCA-HLC (1935/1998)
Prog. Accred.: Business (AACSB), Journalism, Music, Social Work, Speech-Language Pathology, Teacher Education (NCATE)

University of Wisconsin—Stevens Point
2100 Main St., Stevens Point 54481-3897
Type: Public, state, four-year
System: University of Wisconsin System
Degrees: A, B, M   *Enroll:* 8,245
URL: http://www.uwsp.edu
Phone: (715) 346-0123   *Calendar:* Sem. plan
Inst. Accred.: NCA-HLC (1916/1999)
Prog. Accred.: Art, Audiology, Clinical Lab Scientist,
   Dance, Forestry, Interior Design, Music, Speech-
   Language Pathology, Theatre

University of Wisconsin—Stout
1 Clock Tower Plaza, Menomonie 54751-0790
Type: Public, state, four-year
System: University of Wisconsin System
Degrees: B, M, P   *Enroll:* 7,261
URL: http://www.uwstout.edu
Phone: (715) 232-2441   *Calendar:* Sem. plan
Inst. Accred.: NCA-HLC (1928/1996)
Prog. Accred.: Art, Construction Education, Dietetics
   (internship), Engineering (manufacturing), Industrial
   Technology, Interior Design, Marriage and Family
   Therapy, Rehabilitation Counseling

University of Wisconsin—Superior
PO Box 2000, Belknap and Catlin, Superior 54880-4500
Type: Public, state, four-year
System: University of Wisconsin System
Degrees: A, B, M, P   *Enroll:* 2,441
URL: http://www.uwsuper.edu
Phone: (715) 394-8101   *Calendar:* Sem. plan
Inst. Accred.: NCA-HLC (1916/2003)
Prog. Accred.: Counseling, Music, Social Work

University of Wisconsin—Whitewater
800 West Main St., Whitewater 53190-1790
Type: Public, state, four-year
System: University of Wisconsin System
Degrees: A, B, M, P   *Enroll:* 9,716
URL: http://www.uww.edu
Phone: (262) 472-1234   *Calendar:* Sem. plan
Inst. Accred.: NCA-HLC (1915/1996)
Prog. Accred.: Business (AACSB), Counseling, Music,
   Social Work, Speech-Language Pathology, Teacher
   Education (NCATE), Theatre

Viterbo University
815 South Ninth St., La Crosse 54601
Type: Private, Franciscan Sisters, four-year
Degrees: B, M   *Enroll:* 1,926
URL: http://www.viterbo.edu
Phone: (608) 796-3000   *Calendar:* Sem. plan
Inst. Accred.: NCA-HLC (1954/1989)
Prog. Accred.: Dietetics (coordinated), Dietetics
   (internship), Music, Nursing, Nursing Education, Teacher
   Education (NCATE)

Waukesha County Technical College
800 Main St., Pewaukee 53072
Type: Public, state/local, two-year
System: Wisconsin Technical College System Board
Degrees: A   *Enroll:* 3,281
URL: http://www.wctc.edu
Phone: (262) 691-5566   *Calendar:* Sem. plan
Inst. Accred.: NCA-HLC (1975/2000)
Prog. Accred.: Culinary Education, Dental Hygiene,
   Medical Assisting (AMA), Nursing, Surgical Technology

Western Wisconsin Technical College
304 North Sixth St., La Crosse 54602
Type: Public, state/local, two-year
System: Wisconsin Technical College System Board
Degrees: A   *Enroll:* 3,165
URL: http://www.wwtc.edu
Phone: (608) 785-9200   *Calendar:* Sem. plan
Inst. Accred.: NCA-HLC (1972/2000)
Prog. Accred.: Clinical Lab Technology, Dental Assisting,
   Electroneurodiagnostic Technology, Health Information
   Technician, Medical Assisting (AMA), Nursing,
   Occupational Therapy Assisting, Physical Therapy
   Assisting, Radiography, Respiratory Therapy, Surgical
   Technology

Wisconsin Indianhead Technical College
505 Pine Ridge Rd., Shell Lake 54871
Type: Public, local, two-year
System: Wisconsin Technical College System Board
Degrees: A   *Enroll:* 2,313
URL: http://www.witc.edu
Phone: (715) 468-2815   *Calendar:* Sem. plan
Inst. Accred.: NCA-HLC (1979/2004)
Prog. Accred.: Medical Assisting (AMA), Nursing

Ashland Campus
2100 Beaser Ave., Ashland 54806
Phone: (715) 682-4591
Prog. Accred: Occupational Therapy Assisting

Wisconsin Lutheran College
8830 West Bluemond Rd., Milwaukee 53226
Type: Private, Wisconsin Evangelical Lutheran Synod,
   four-year
Degrees: B   *Enroll:* 685
Phone: (414) 443-8800   *Calendar:* Sem. plan
Inst. Accred.: NCA-HLC (1987/1997)

Wisconsin School of Professional Psychology
9120 West Hampton Ave., Ste. 212, Milwaukee 53225
Type: Private, professional, four-year
Degrees: M, D   *Enroll:* 27
Phone: (414) 464-9777   *Calendar:* Sem. plan
Inst. Accred.: NCA-HLC (1987/1995)

WYOMING

Casper College
125 College Dr., Casper 82601
Type: Public, local, two-year
System: Wyoming Community College Commission
Degrees: A   *Enroll:* 2,679
URL: http://www.caspercollege.edu
Phone: (307) 268-2110   *Calendar:* Sem. plan
Inst. Accred.: NCA-HLC (1960/1999)
Prog. Accred.: Art, Music, Nursing, Occupational Therapy, Occupational Therapy Assisting, Radiography, Theatre

Central Wyoming College
2660 Peck Ave., Riverton 82501
Type: Public, state/local, two-year
System: Wyoming Community College Commission
Degrees: A   *Enroll:* 1,143
URL: http://www.cwc.edu
Phone: (307) 855-2000   *Calendar:* Sem. plan
Inst. Accred.: NCA-HLC (1976/1996)
Prog. Accred.: Nursing, Surgical Technology

Eastern Wyoming College
3200 West C St., Torrington 82240
Type: Public, state/local, two-year
System: Wyoming Community College Commission
Degrees: A   *Enroll:* 831
URL: http://ewc.wy.edu
Phone: (800) 658-3195   *Calendar:* Sem. plan
Inst. Accred.: NCA-HLC (1976/2001)
Prog. Accred.: Veterinary Technology

Laramie County Community College
1400 East College Dr., Cheyenne 82007
Type: Public, state/local, two-year
System: Wyoming Community College Commission
Degrees: A   *Enroll:* 2,499
URL: http://www.lccc.wy.edu
Phone: (307) 778-5222   *Calendar:* Sem. plan
Inst. Accred.: NCA-HLC (1975/2000)
Prog. Accred.: Dental Assisting, Nursing, Practical Nursing, Radiography

Northern Wyoming Community College District—Sheridan
PO Box 1500, Sheridan 82801
Type: Public, state/local, two-year
System: Wyoming Community College Commission
Degrees: A   *Enroll:* 1,513
URL: http://www.sheridan.edu
Phone: (307) 674-6446   *Calendar:* Sem. plan
Inst. Accred.: NCA-HLC (1968/1988)
Prog. Accred.: Dental Assisting, Dental Hygiene, Nursing, Practical Nursing

Gillette Campus
720 West 8th St., Gillette 82716
Phone: (307) 674-6446

Northwest College
231 West Sixth St., Powell 82435
Type: Public, state/local, two-year
System: Wyoming Community College Commission
Degrees: A   *Enroll:* 1,311
URL: http://www.northwestcollege.edu
Phone: (307) 754-6000   *Calendar:* Sem. plan
Inst. Accred.: NCA-HLC (1964/2001)
Prog. Accred.: Music, Nursing, Practical Nursing

University of Wyoming
1000 East University Ave., Laramie 82071
Type: Public, state, four-year
Degrees: B, M, P, D   *Enroll:* 10,514
URL: http://www.uwyo.edu
Phone: (307) 766-4121   *Calendar:* Sem. plan
Inst. Accred.: NCA-HLC (1923/2000)
Prog. Accred.: Audiology, Business (AACSB), Clinical Psychology, Computer Science, Counseling, Engineering (architectural, chemical, civil, computer, electrical, mechanical), Law, Music, Nursing, Nursing Education, Pharmacy, Social Work, Speech-Language Pathology, Teacher Education (NCATE)

Western Wyoming Community College
2500 College Dr., Rock Springs 82901
Type: Public, state/local, two-year
System: Wyoming Community College Commission
Degrees: A   *Enroll:* 1,571
URL: http://www.wwcc.wy.edu
Phone: (307) 382-1600   *Calendar:* Sem. plan
Inst. Accred.: NCA-HLC (1976/2004)
Prog. Accred.: Nursing, Respiratory Therapy, Respiratory Therapy Technology

WyoTech
4373 North Third St., Laramie 82070
Type: Private, proprietary, two-year
System: Corinthian Colleges, Inc
Degrees: A   *Enroll:* 2,029
URL: http://www.wyotech.com
Phone: (307) 742-3776
Inst. Accred.: ACCSCT (1969/2004)

AUSTRALIA

Deakin University
Pigdons Rd., Geelong, VI, Australia 3217
Type: Private, independent, four-year
Degrees: B, M, P
URL: http://www.deakin.edu.au
Phone: 011 61 3 9244 5095
Inst. Accred.: DETC (2005)

Monash University
Wellington Rd., Clayton, VI, Australia 3800
Type: Private, state, four-year
Degrees: B, M, P
URL: http://www.monash.edu.au
Phone: 011 61 3 9902 6000   *Calendar:* Sem. plan
Inst. Accred.: DETC (2005)

BULGARIA

The American University in Bulgaria
Blagoevard, Bulgaria 2700
Type: Private, independent, four-year
Degrees: B, M
URL: http://www.aubg.bg
Phone: 011 359 73 888218
Inst. Accred.: NEASC-CIHE (2001)

CANADA

Acadia Divinity College
Wolfville, Canada B4P 2R6
Type: Private, Baptist Church, four-year
Degrees: M
URL: http://ace.acadiau.ca/divcol
Phone: (902) 585-2215   *Calendar:* Sem. plan
Inst. Accred.: ATS (1984/2000)

Alliance University College
630-833 4th Ave., SW, Calgary, Canada T2P 3TS
Type: Private, Christian and Missionary Alliance, four-year
Degrees: A, B, M, P
URL: http://www.auc-nuc.ca
Phone: (403) 410-2000   *Calendar:* Sem. plan
Inst. Accred.: ABHE (1961/2004), ATS (1989/2005)

Athabasca University
1 University Dr., Athabasca, Canada T9S 3A3
Type: Public, independent, four-year
Degrees: B, M
URL: http://www.athabascau.ca
Phone: (780) 675-6100   *Calendar:* Sem. plan
Inst. Accred.: MSA-CHE (2005)

Atlantic School of Theology
660 Francklyn St., Halifax, Canada B3H 3B5
Type: Private, interdenominational, four-year
Degrees: M
URL: http://astheology.ns.ca
Phone: (902) 423-6939   *Calendar:* Sem. plan
Inst. Accred.: ATS (1976/1998)

Bethany Bible College
26 Western St., Sussex, Canada E4E 1E6
Type: Private, Wesleyan Church, four-year
Degrees: B, D
URL: http://www.bethany-ca.edu
Phone: (506) 432-4400   *Calendar:* Sem. plan
Inst. Accred.: ABHE (1987/1998)

Bethany College
702 2nd St., East, Hepburn, Canada S0K 1Z0
Type: Private, Mennonite Brethren/Evangelical Mennonite Mission C, four-year
Degrees: B
URL: http://www.bethany.sk.ca
Phone: (306) 947-2175   *Calendar:* Sem. plan
Inst. Accred.: ABHE (1996/2005)

Briercrest Biblical Seminary
510 College Dr., Caronport, Canada S0H 0S0
Type: Private, nondenominational, four-year
Degrees: M
URL: http://www.briercrest.ca
Phone: (306) 765-3200
Inst. Accred.: ATS (1998)

Briercrest College
510 College Dr., Caronport, Canada S0H 0S0
Type: Private, interdenominational, four-year
Degrees: A, B, M
URL: http://www.briercrest.ca
Phone: (306) 756-3200   *Calendar:* Sem. plan
Inst. Accred.: ABHE (1976/1997)

Canadian College of Naturopathic Medicine
1255 Sheppard Ave. East, Toronto, Canada M2K 1E2
Type: Private, independent, four-year
Degrees: D
URL: http://www.ccnm.edu
Phone: (416) 498-1255
Inst. Accred.: CNME (2000)

Canadian Southern Baptist Seminary
200 Seminary View, Cochrane, Canada T4C 2G1
Type: Private, Canadian Convention of Southern Baptists, four-year
Degrees: M
URL: http://www.csbs.edu
Phone: (403) 932-6622   *Calendar:* Sem. plan
Inst. Accred.: ATS (2001)

Central Pentecostal College
1303 Jackson Ave., Saskatoon, Canada S7H 2M9
Type: Private, Pentecostal Assemblies of Canada, four-year
Degrees: B, M
URL: http://www.cpc-paoc.edu
Phone: (306) 374-6655   *Calendar:* Sem. plan
Inst. Accred.: ABHE (1997/2002)

Columbia Bible College

2940 Clearbook Rd., Abbotsford, Canada V2T 2Z8
Type: Private, Mennonite Brethren/Conference of
  Mennonites, four-year
Degrees: B
URL: http://www.columbiabc.edu
Phone: (604) 853-3358   *Calendar:* Sem. plan
Inst. Accred.: ABHE (1991/1997)

Concordia Lutheran Seminary

7040 Ada Rd., Edmonton, Canada T5B 4E3
Type: Private, Lutheran Church-Canada, four-year
Degrees: M
URL: http://www.concordiasem.ab.ca
Phone: (780) 474-1468
Inst. Accred.: ATS (1998)

DeVry Institute of Technology, Calgary

2700 3rd Ave. SE, Calgary, Canada T2A 7W4
Type: Private, proprietary, four-year
System: DeVry University
Degrees: A, B
URL: http://www.cal.devry.ca
Phone: (403) 235-3450   *Calendar:* Sem. plan
Inst. Accred.: NCA-HLC (2002, *Indirect accreditation
  through DeVry University, Oakbrook Terrace, IL*)

Edmonton Baptist Seminary

11525-23 Ave., Edmonton, Canada T6J 4T3
Type: Private, Baptist Church, four-year
Degrees: M
URL: http://www.nabcebs.ab.ca
Phone: (780) 431-5200   *Calendar:* Sem. plan
Inst. Accred.: ATS (1997)

Emmanuel Bible College

100 Fergus Ave., Kitchener, Canada N2A 2H2
Type: Private, Evangelical Missionary Church of Canada
  East, four-year
Degrees: B, D
URL: http://www.ebcollege.on.ca
Phone: (519) 894-8900   *Calendar:* Sem. plan
Inst. Accred.: ABHE (1982/2003)

Emmanuel College of Victoria University

75 Queen's Park Crescent, East, Toronto, Canada M5S
1K7
Type: Private, United Church of Canada, four-year
Degrees: M, D
URL: http://vicu.utoronto.ca/emmanuel
Phone: (416) 585-4539   *Calendar:* Sem. plan
Inst. Accred.: ATS (1938/2001)

Heritage College and Seminary

175 Holiday Inn Dr., Cambridge, Canada N3C 3T2
Type: Private, Fellowship of Evangelical Baptist Churches
  in Canada, four-year
Degrees: B, M
URL: http://www.heritage-theo.edu
Phone: (519) 651-2869   *Calendar:* Sem. plan
Inst. Accred.: ABHE (1996/2001), ATS (2005)

Huron University College
Faculty of Theology

1349 Western Rd., London, Canada N6G 1H3
Type: Private, Anglican Church of Canada, four-year
Degrees: M
URL: http://www.huronuc.on.ca/theology
Phone: (519) 438-7224   *Calendar:* Sem. plan
Inst. Accred.: ATS (1981/1995)

Joint Board of Theological Colleges

3473 University St., Montreal, Canada H3A 2A8
Type: Private, interdenominational, four-year
Degrees: M
URL: http://www.mcgill.ca/religiousstudies/joint-board
Phone: (514) 849-8511   *Calendar:* Sem. plan
Inst. Accred.: ATS (1989/2001)

Knox College

59 St. George St., Toronto, Canada M5S 2E6
Type: Private, Presbyterian Church in Canada, four-year
Degrees: M, D
URL: http://www.utoronto.ca/knox
Phone: (416) 978-4500   *Calendar:* Sem. plan
Inst. Accred.: ATS (1948/2001)

Lansbridge University

10 Knowledge Park Dr., Ste. 120, Fredericton, Canada
E3C 2M7
Type: Private, proprietary, four-year
Degrees: M
URL: http://www.lansbridge.com
Phone: (506) 443-0780
Inst. Accred.: DETC (2005)

Lutheran Theological Seminary

114 Seminary Crescent, Saskatoon, Canada S7N 0X3
Type: Private, Evangelical Lutheran Church, four-year
Degrees: M
URL: http://www.usask.ca/stu/luther
Phone: (306) 966-7850   *Calendar:* Sem. plan
Inst. Accred.: ATS (1976/1999)

Master's College and Seminary

3080 Younge St., Ste. 3040, Box 70, Toronto, Canada
M4N 3N1
Type: Private, Pentacostal Assemblies of Canada, four-
  year
Degrees: B, M
URL: http://www.mcs.edu
Phone: (416) 482-2224   *Calendar:* Sem. plan
Inst. Accred.: ABHE (1989/1995)

Greater Toronto Campus

2476 Argentia Rd., Missassuaga, Canada C5N 6M1
Phone: (905) 819-1936

McGill University
845 Sherbrooke St. West, Montreal, Canada H3A 2T5
Type: Private, interdenominational, four-year
Degrees: B, M, D
URL: http://www.mcgill.ca
Phone: (514) 398-4455   *Calendar:* Sem. plan
Inst. Accred.: ATS (1952/2001)
Prog. Accred.: Clinical Psychology, Counseling
  Psychology, Dentistry, General Practice Residency,
  Librarianship, Medicine, Oral and Maxillofacial Surgery,
  Psychology Internship, School Psychology

McMaster University
1280 Main St., West, Hamilton, Canada L8S 4L8
Type: Private, Union Baptist, four-year
Degrees: M, P, D
URL: http://www.mcmaster.ca
Phone: (905) 525-9140   *Calendar:* Sem. plan
Inst. Accred.: ATS (1954/1998)
Prog. Accred.: Medicine

Newman Theological College
15611 St. Albert Trail, Edmonton, Canada T6V 1H3
Type: Private, Roman Catholic Church, four-year
Degrees: M
URL: http://www.newman.edu
Phone: (403) 447-2993   *Calendar:* Sem. plan
Inst. Accred.: ATS (1992/1996)

Prairie Bible College
319 5th Ave. North, PO Box 4000, Three Hills, Canada
T0M 2N0
Type: Private, interdenominational, four-year
Degrees: A, B
URL: http://www.prairie.edu/biblecollege.htm
Phone: (403) 443-5511   *Calendar:* Sem. plan
Inst. Accred.: ABHE (1997/2002)

Providence College and Theological Seminary
Otterburne, Canada R0A 1G0
Type: Private, interdenominational, four-year
Degrees: B, M, P, D
URL: http://prov.ca
Phone: (204) 433-7488   *Calendar:* Sem. plan
Inst. Accred.: ABHE (1973/1994), ATS (1992/1997)

Queen's Theological College
Kingston, Canada K7L 3N6
Type: Private, United Church of Canada, four-year
Degrees: M
URL: http://www.queensu.ca/theology
Phone: (613) 545-2110   *Calendar:* Sem. plan
Inst. Accred.: ATS (1986/2001)

Regent College
5800 University Blvd., Vancouver, Canada V6T 2E4
Type: Private, interdenominational, four-year
Degrees: M
URL: http://www.regent-college.edu
Phone: (604) 224-3245   *Calendar:* Sem. plan
Inst. Accred.: ATS (1985/2000)

Regis College
15 St. Mary St., Toronto, Canada M4Y 2R5
Type: Private, Roman Catholic Church, four-year
Degrees: M, D
URL: http://www.utoronto.ca/regis
Phone: (416) 922-5474   *Calendar:* Sem. plan
Inst. Accred.: ATS (1970/2001)

Rocky Mountain College
4039 Brentwood Rd., NW, Calgary, Canada T2L 1L1
Type: Private, Missionary Church of Canada, four-year
Degrees: B
URL: http://www.rockymountaincollege.ca
Phone: (403) 284-5100   *Calendar:* Sem. plan
Inst. Accred.: ABHE (1989/1996)

Saint Andrew's College
1121 College Dr., Saskatoon, Canada S7N 0N3
Type: Public, United Church of Canada, four-year
Degrees: B, M
URL: http://www.usask.ca/stu/standrews/index.html
Phone: (306) 966-8970   *Calendar:* Sem. plan
Inst. Accred.: ATS (1996/2001)

Saint Augustine's Seminary of Toronto
2661 Kingston Rd., Toronto, Canada M1M 1M3
Type: Private, Roman Catholic Church, four-year
Degrees: M
URL: http://www.staugustines.on.ca
Phone: (416) 261-7207   *Calendar:* Sem. plan
Inst. Accred.: ATS (1980/2001)

Saint Peter's Seminary
1040 Waterloo St. North, London, Canada N6A 3Y1
Type: Private, Roman Catholic Church, four-year
Degrees: M
URL: http://www.stpetersseminary.ca
Phone: (519) 432-1824   *Calendar:* Sem. plan
Inst. Accred.: ATS (1986/2001)

Steinbach Bible College
50 PTH 12N, Steinbach, Canada R5G 1T4
Type: Private, Evangelical Mennonite Conference, four-
  year
Degrees: B
URL: http://www.sbcollege.mb.ca
Phone: (204) 326-6451
Inst. Accred.: ABHE (1991/1997)

Summit Pacific College
35235 Straiton Rd., Abbotsford, Canada V2S 7E7
Type: Private, Pentecostal Assemblies of Canada, four-
  year
Degrees: B
URL: http://www.summitpacific.ca
Phone: (604) 853-7491   *Calendar:* Sem. plan
Inst. Accred.: ABHE (1980/2001)

Taylor University College and Seminary
11525 23rd Ave., Edmonton, Canada T6J 4T3
Type: Private, North American Baptist Conference, four-year
Degrees: A, B, M, P, D
URL: http://www.taylor-edu.ca
Phone: (780) 431-5200   *Calendar:* Sem. plan
Inst. Accred.: ATS (1997/2002)

Toronto School of Theology
47 Queen's Park Crescent, East, Toronto, Canada M5S 2C3
Type: Private, interdenominational, four-year
Degrees: M, D
URL: http://www.tst.edu
Phone: (416) 978-4039   *Calendar:* Sem. plan
Inst. Accred.: ATS (1980/1997)

Trinity Western University
Fosmark Centre, 7600 Glover Rd., Langley, Canada V2Y 1Y1
Type: Private, Evangelical Free Churches of America, four-year
Degrees: B, M
URL: http://www.twu.ca
Phone: (604) 888-7511   *Calendar:* Sem. plan
Inst. Accred.: ATS (1997/2002)
Prog. Accred.: Counseling

Tyndale University College and Seminary
25 Ballyconnor Ct., Toronto, Canada M2M 4B3
Type: Private, interdenominational, four-year
Degrees: B, M, P
URL: http://www.tyndale-canada.edu
Phone: (416) 226-6380   *Calendar:* Sem. plan
Inst. Accred.: ABHE (1966/1999), ATS (1989/1998)

University of Saint Michael's College
81 St. Mary St., Toronto, Canada M5S 1J4
Type: Private, Roman Catholic Church, four-year
Degrees: M, D
URL: http://www.utoronto.ca/stmikes
Phone: (416) 926-7140   *Calendar:* Sem. plan
Inst. Accred.: ATS (1972/2001)

The University of Trinity College in the University of Toronto
6 Hoskin Ave., Toronto, Canada M5S 1H8
Type: Private, Anglican Church of Canada, four-year
Degrees: M, D
URL: http://www.trinity.utoronto.ca
Phone: (416) 978-2133   *Calendar:* Sem. plan
Inst. Accred.: ATS (1938/2002)

Vancouver School of Theology
6000 Iona Dr., Vancouver, Canada V6T 1L4
Type: Private, interdenominational, four-year
Degrees: M
URL: http://www.vst.edu
Phone: (604) 228-9031   *Calendar:* Sem. plan
Inst. Accred.: ATS (1976/2003)

Vanguard College
12140 103rd St., Edmonton, Canada T5G 2J9
Type: Private, Pentecostal Assemblies of Canada, four-year
Degrees: B
URL: http://www.vanguardcollege.com
Phone: (780) 452-0808   *Calendar:* Sem. plan
Inst. Accred.: ABHE (1997/2001)

Calgary Leadership Training Center
5810 2nd St., SW, Ste. 101, Calgary, Canada T2H 0H2
Phone: (403) 640-4988

Waterloo Lutheran Seminary
75 University Ave., West, Waterloo, Canada N2L 3C5
Type: Private, Evangelical Luthern Church, four-year
Degrees: M
URL: http://www.wlu.ca/~wwwsem
Phone: (519) 884-1970   *Calendar:* Sem. plan
Inst. Accred.: ATS (1982/1997)

William and Catherine Booth College
447 Webb Place, Winnipeg, Canada R3B 2P2
Type: Private, Salvation Army, four-year
Degrees: B
URL: http://www.wcbc-sa.edu
Phone: (204) 947-6701   *Calendar:* Sem. plan
Inst. Accred.: ABHE (1991/1997)

Wycliffe College
5 Hoskin Ave., Toronto, Canada M5S 1H7
Type: Private, Anglican Church of Canada, four-year
Degrees: M, D
URL: http://www.wycliffecollege.ca
Phone: (416) 946-3535   *Calendar:* Sem. plan
Inst. Accred.: ATS (1978/2001)

CAYMAN ISLANDS

International College of the Cayman Islands
PO Box 136 Savannah, Grand Cayman, Cayman Islands
Type: Private, proprietary, four-year
Degrees: A, B, M
URL: http://cayman.com.ky/pub/icci
Phone: (345) 947-1100   *Calendar:* Qtr. plan
Inst. Accred.: ACICS (1979/2001)

COSTA RICA

Instituto Centroamericano de Administracion de Empresas
Apartado Postal 960, Alajuela, Costa Rica 4040
Type: Private, independent, four-year
Degrees: M
URL: http://www.incae.ac.cr
Phone: 011 506 433 9908   *Calendar:* Tri. plan
Inst. Accred.: SACS (1994/1999)
Prog. Accred.: Business (AACSB)

EGYPT

The American University in Cairo
PO Box 2511, 113 Sharia Dasr El Aini, Cairo, Egypt
Type: Private, independent, four-year
Degrees: B, M   *FTE Enroll:* 563
URL: http://www.aucegypt.edu
Phone: 011 2 02 794 2964   *Calendar:* Sem. plan
Inst. Accred.: MSA-CHE (1982/2003)
Prog. Accred.: Computer Science, Engineering
(construction, mechanical)

FEDERATED STATES OF MICRONESIA

College of Micronesia-FSM
PO Box 159, Kolonia, Pohnpei, Micronesia, Federated
States 96941
Type: Public, state, two-year
Degrees: A   *Enroll:* 1,187
URL: http://www.comfsm.fm
Phone: (691) 320-2480   *Calendar:* Sem. plan
Inst. Accred.: WASC-JR. (1978/2004)

FRANCE

The American University of Paris
31 Ave. Bosquet, Paris, France 75007
Type: Private, independent, four-year
Degrees: B, M
URL: http://www.aup.edu
Phone: 011 33 1 40 62 06 00   *Calendar:* Sem. plan
Inst. Accred.: MSA-CHE (1973/2003)

GREECE

American College of Thessaloniki
PO Box 21021, Pylea, Thessaloniki, Greece 555 10
Type: Private, independent, four-year
Degrees: B
URL: http://www.act.edu
Phone: 011 2310 398 238
Inst. Accred.: NEASC-CIHE (1997/2002)

Deree College, The American College of Greece
6 Gravitas St., GR-153 42 Aghia Paraskevi, Athens,
Greece
Type: Private, independent, four-year
Degrees: A, B, M   *FTE Enroll:* 4,404
URL: http://www.acg.gr
Phone: 011 301 600-9800   *Calendar:* 4-1-4 plan
Inst. Accred.: NEASC-CIHE (1981/1996)

HUNGARY

Central European University
Nador Utca 9, Budapest, Hungary H-1051
Type: Private, independent, four-year
Degrees: B, M, D
URL: http://www.ceu.hu
Phone: 011 361327 3000
Inst. Accred.: MSA-CHE (2004)

IRELAND

American College Dublin
2 Merrion Square, Dublin, DU, Ireland 2
Type: Private, independent, four-year
Degrees: B
URL: http://www.amcd.edu
Phone: 011 353 1 676 8939   *Calendar:* Sem. plan
Inst. Accred.: ACICS (2004)

ITALY

American University of Rome
Via Pietro Roselli 4, Rome, Italy 00153
Type: Private, independent, four-year
Degrees: A, B
URL: http://www.aur.edu
Phone: 011 3906 5833 0919   *Calendar:* Sem. plan
Inst. Accred.: ACICS (1992/2003)

John Cabot University
Via Della Lungara 233, Rome, Italy 00165
Type: Private, independent, four-year
Degrees: A, B
URL: http://www.johncabot.edu
Phone: 011 39 0668 19121   *Calendar:* Sem. plan
Inst. Accred.: MSA-CHE (2003)

KENYA

United States International University—Africa
PO Box 14634, Thika Rd., Kasarani, Nairobi, Kenya
Type: Private, independent, four-year
System: Alliant International University
Degrees: B, M
URL: http://www.alliant.edu
Phone: 011 254 2 502532   *Calendar:* Sem. plan
Inst. Accred.: WASC-SR. (1977/1998, *Indirect
accreditation through Alliant International University,
San Francisco, CA*)

LEBANON

American University of Beirut
PO Box 11-0236, Beirut, Lebanon 1107 2020
Type: Private, independent, four-year
Degrees: B, M, P   *FTE Enroll:* 1
URL: http://www.aub.edu.lb
Phone: 011 9611-340460   *Calendar:* Sem. plan
Inst. Accred.: MSA-CHE (2004)

MARSHALL ISLANDS

College of the Marshall Islands
PO Box 1258, Majuro, Marshall Islands 96960
Type: Public, state, two-year
Degrees: A *Enroll:* 495
URL: http://www.cmiedu.net
Phone: (692) 625-3394 *Calendar:* Sem. plan
Inst. Accred.: WASC-JR. (1991/2003, Probation)

MEXICO

Alliant International University—Mexico City
Alvaro Obregon #110, Colonia Roma, Mexico City, Mexico
CP 06700
Type: Private, independent, four-year
System: Alliant International University
Degrees: A, B, M, D
URL: http://www.alliant.edu
Phone: 011 52 5 264 2187 *Calendar:* Sem. plan
Inst. Accred.: WASC-SR. (1977/1998, *Indirect
accreditation through Alliant International University,
San Francisco, CA*)

Instituto Tecnologico y de Estudios Superiores de Monterrey
Ave. Eugenio Garza Sada, 2501 Sur, Monterrey, Mexico
64849
Type: Private, independent, four-year
Degrees: B, M, D
URL: http://www.sistema.itesm.mx
Phone: 011 52 8 358 2000
Inst. Accred.: SACS (1950/1998)
Prog. Accred.: Business (AACSB)

Universidad de las Americas, A.C.
Calle de Puebla No. 223, Col. Roma, Mexico, Mexico
06700
Type: Private, independent, four-year
Degrees: B, M
URL: http://www.udla.mx
Phone: 011 52 5 209 9800 *Calendar:* Sem. plan
Inst. Accred.: SACS (1991/1997)

Universidad de las Americas—Puebla
Station Catarina Martir, Cholula, PU, Mexico 72820
Type: Private, independent, four-year
Degrees: B, M, D
URL: http://info.pue.udlap.mx
Phone: 011 52 222 229 2000 *Calendar:* Sem. plan
Inst. Accred.: SACS (1959/1994)

Universidad de Monterrey
Ave Ignacio Morones Prieto 4500 Pte., San Pedro Garza
Garcia, Mexico 66238
Type: Private, independent, four-year
Degrees: B, M
URL: http://www.udem.edu.mx
Phone: 011 81 8124 1000 *Calendar:* Sem. plan
Inst. Accred.: SACS (2001)

Westhill University
Domingo Garcia Ramos 56, Prados de la Montaña I,
Santa Fe, Mexico City, Mexico
Type: Private, independent, two-year
Degrees: A
URL: http://www.westhill.edu.mx
Phone: 011 5292-1729
Inst. Accred.: ACICS (2003/2004)

MONACO

International University of Monaco
2 Ave. Prince Héréditaire Albert, Stade Louis II, Entree B,
Monaco MC98000
Type: Private, independent, four-year
Degrees: B, M
URL: http://www.monaco.edu
Phone: 011 377 97 986 986 *Calendar:* Sem. plan
Inst. Accred.: ACICS (1996/2005)

NORTHERN MARIANA ISLANDS

Northern Marianas College
PO Box 1250, Saipan, CNMI, Northern Mariana Islands
96950
Type: Public, state, four-year
Degrees: A, B *Enroll:* 999
URL: http://www.nmcnet.edu
Phone: (670) 234-5498 *Calendar:* Sem. plan
Inst. Accred.: WASC-JR. (1985/2001), WASC-SR. (2001,
Warning)

SOUTH AFRICA

University of South Africa (UNISA)
PO Box 392, Unisa, Pretoria, South Africa 0003
Type: Private, proprietary, four-year
Degrees: A, B, M, P
URL: http://www.unisa.ac.za
Phone: 011 27 12 429 3111
Inst. Accred.: DETC (2002)

SWITZERLAND

Ecole Hoteliere de Lausanne
Le Chalet-a-Gobet, Luasanne, Switzerland CH 1000
Type: Private, proprietary, four-year
Degrees: A, B, M
URL: http://www.ehl.ch
Phone: 011 41 21 785 1111
Inst. Accred.: NEASC-CIHE (2003)

Franklin College Switzerland
Via Ponte Tresa 29, Sorengo, Switzerland CH 6924
Type: Private, independent, four-year
Degrees: A, B
URL: http://www.fc.edu
Phone: 011 41 91 993 0101　　　*Calendar:* Sem. plan
Inst. Accred.: MSA-CHE (1975/2005)

Glion Institute of Higher Education
Route de Glion 111, Glion-sur-Montreux, Switzerland 1823
Type: Private, proprietary, four-year
Degrees: A, B
URL: http://www.glion.ch/en
Phone: 011 41 021 966 35 35　　　*Calendar:* Sem. plan
Inst. Accred.: NEASC-CTCI (2001)

Les Roches School of Hotel Management
Bluche Crans-Montana, Valais, Switzerland CH-3975
Type: Private, proprietary, four-year
Degrees: A, B
URL: http://www.les-roches.ch
Phone: 011 41 27 485 96 00　　　*Calendar:* Sem. plan
Inst. Accred.: NEASC-CTCI (1991/2002)

UNITED ARAB EMIRATES

American University of Sharjah
PO Box 26666, Sharjah, United Arab Emirates
Type: Private, independent, four-year
Degrees: B, M
URL: http://www.ausharjah.edu
Phone: 011 971 6 515 1000　　　*Calendar:* Sem. plan
Inst. Accred.: MSA-CHE (2004)

UNITED KINGDOM

The Open University, UK
PO Box 75, Walton Hall, Milton Keynes, United Kingdom MK7 6AA
Type: Public, independent, four-year
Degrees: B, M, D
URL: http://www.open.ac.uk
Phone: 011 44 190 865-3788
Inst. Accred.: MSA-CHE (2005)

Rhodec International
35 East St., Brighton, E., United Kingdom BN1 1HL
Type: Private, proprietary, four-year
Degrees: A, B
URL: http://www.rhodec.edu
Phone: 011 44 0 1273 327476
Inst. Accred.: DETC (1998/2003)

Massachusetts Campus
59 Coddington St., Ste. 104, Quincy, MA 02169
Phone: (617) 472-4942

Richmond, The American International University in London
Queens Rd., Richmond, SU, United Kingdom TW10 6JP
Type: Private, independent, four-year
Degrees: A, B, M
URL: http://www.richmond.ac.uk
Phone: 011 44 20 83329000　　　*Calendar:* Sem. plan
Inst. Accred.: MSA-CHE (1981/2001)

University of Leicester's Centre for Labour Market Studies
7-9 Salisbury Rd., Leicester, United Kingdom LE1 7QR
Type: Private, independent, four-year
Degrees: M
URL: http://www.clms.le.ac.uk
Phone: 011 44 116-252-5950
Inst. Accred.: DETC (1997/2003)

Accredited Non–Degree-Granting Institutions

ALABAMA

Alabama State College of Barber Styling
9480 Pkwy. East, Birmingham 35215-8308
Type: Private, proprietary
Degrees: C
URL: http://www.alabamabarbercollege.com
Phone: (205) 836-2404
Inst. Accred.: ACCSCT (1990/2004)

16th Street Campus
1001 South 16th St., Birmingham 35205
Phone: (205) 933-7600

Blue Cliff School of Therapeutic Massage
3737 Government Blvd., Ste. 517, Mobile 36693
Type: Private, proprietary
Degrees: C
URL: http://www.bluecliffmassage.com
Phone: (251) 665-9900
Inst. Accred.: ACCSCT (2003)

Capps College
3590 Pleasant Valley Rd., Mobile 36609
Type: Private, proprietary
Degrees: C
URL: http://www.medcareers.net
Phone: (250) 650-0800
Inst. Accred.: ABHES (1986/2003)

Capps Medical Institute
6420 North 9th Ave., Pensacola, FL 32504
Phone: (850) 476-7607
Prog. Accred: Medical Assisting (ABHES)

Montgomery Campus
3736 Atlanta Hwy., Montgomery 36109
Phone: (334) 272-3857
Prog. Accred: Medical Assisting (ABHES)

Capps College—Foley
914 North McKenzie St., Foley 36535
Type: Private, proprietary
Degrees: C
URL: http://www.medcareers.net
Phone: (334) 970-1460
Inst. Accred.: ABHES (1998/2003)
Prog. Accred.: Medical Assisting (ABHES)

Dothan Campus
200 Vulcan Way, Dothan 36303
Phone: (334) 677-2852
Prog. Accred: Medical Assisting (ABHES)

Gadsden Business College
3225 Rainbow Dr., Ste. 246, Rainbow City 35906-5821
Type: Private, proprietary
Degrees: C
URL: http://www.gadsdenbusinesscollege.com
Phone: (256) 442-2805   *Calendar:* Qtr. plan
Inst. Accred.: ACICS (1962/2004)

Anniston Campus
PO Box 1559, 630 South Wilmer Ave., Anniston 36202-1559
Phone: (256) 237-7517

Gaither and Company Beauty College
414 East Willow St., Scottsboro 35768
Type: Private, proprietary
Degrees: C
Phone: (256) 259-1001
Inst. Accred.: NACCAS (1985/2003)

Leadership Development, Inc.
Dale Carnegie Training
300 Cahaba Park Circle, Ste. 118, Birmingham 35242
Type: Private, proprietary
Degrees: C
URL: http://www.birmingham.dale-carnegie.com
Phone: (205) 995-5059
Inst. Accred.: ACCET (1976/2001)

Montgomery Job Corps Center
1145 Air Base Blvd., Montgomery 36108
Type: Public, federal
Degrees: C
Phone: (334) 262-8883
Inst. Accred.: COE (2000)

Southeastern School of Cosmetology
26B Phillips Dr., Midfield 35228
Type: Private, proprietary
Degrees: C
Phone: (205) 925-0011
Inst. Accred.: COE (1999)

Southern Community College
205 South Main St., PO Box 830688, Tuskegee 36083
Type: Private, independent
Degrees: C
URL: http://www.southerncommunitycollege.org
Phone: (334) 727-5220
Inst. Accred.: COE (1983/2005)

United States Air Force Institute for Advanced Distributed Learning
50 South Turner Blvd., Maxwell AFB-Gunter Annex,
Montgomery 36118-5643
Type: Public, federal
System: Air University
Degrees: C
URL: http://www.maxwell.af.mil/au/afiadl
Phone: (334) 416-4252
Inst. Accred.: DETC (1975/2000)

United States Army Ordnance Munitions and Electronic Maintenance School
3300 Patton Rd., Building 3301, Redstone Arsenal
35897-6000
Type: Public, federal
Degrees: C
URL: http://omems.redstone.army.mil
Phone: (256) 876-3349
Inst. Accred.: COE (1976/2003)

ALASKA

Alaska Vocational Technical Center
809 Second Ave., PO Box 889, Seward 99664
Type: Public, state
Degrees: C
URL: http://www.avtec.alaska.edu
Phone: (907) 224-4159
Inst. Accred.: COE (1983/2003)
Prog. Accred.: Culinary Education

Career Academy
1415 East Tudor Rd., Anchorage 99507-1033
Type: Private, proprietary
Degrees: C
URL: http://www.careeracademy.net
Phone: (907) 563-7575
Inst. Accred.: ACCSCT (1987/2002)

Galena City Schools Post Secondary School
PO Box 359, Antoski Dr., Galena 99741
Type: Private, proprietary
Degrees: C
URL: http://postsec.galenaalaska.org
Phone: (907) 656-2053
Inst. Accred.: NACCAS (1988/2003)

ARIZONA

American Institute of Technology
440 South 54th Ave., Phoenix 85043-4729
Type: Private, proprietary
Degrees: C
URL: http://www.ait-schools.com
Phone: (602) 233-2222 *Calendar:* Qtr. plan
Inst. Accred.: ACCSCT (1985/2004)

North Las Vegas Campus
4610-A Vandenberg Dr., North Las Vegas, NV 89031
Phone: (702) 644-1234

Arizona Academy of Beauty, Inc.
5631 East Speedway Blvd., Tucson 85712
Type: Private, proprietary
Degrees: C
Phone: (520) 885-4120
Inst. Accred.: NACCAS (1971/2001)

Arizona Academy of Beauty—North Inc.
4046 North Oracle Rd., Tucson 85705
Type: Private, proprietary
Degrees: C
Phone: (520) 888-0170
Inst. Accred.: NACCAS (1974/2005)

Arizona College of Allied Health
4425 West Olive St., Ste. 300, Glendale 85302
Type: Private, proprietary
Degrees: C
URL: http://www.arizonacollege.edu
Phone: (602) 222-9300
Inst. Accred.: ABHES (1994/1998)

Artistic Beauty Colleges
1790 Route 66, Flagstaff 86004
Type: Private, proprietary
Degrees: C
URL: http://www.artisticbeautycolleges.com
Phone: (928) 774-7146
Inst. Accred.: NACCAS (1971/2003)

Chandler Campus
2978 North Alma School Rd., Stes. 1-3, Chandler 85224
Phone: (480) 855-7901

Prescott Campus
410 West Goodwin St., Prescott 86004
Phone: (520) 778-5064

Artistic Beauty Colleges—Glendale
10820 North 43rd Ave., Glendale 85257
Type: Private, proprietary
Degrees: C
URL: http://www.artisticbeautycolleges.com
Phone: (623) 937-2749
Inst. Accred.: NACCAS (1974/2005)

Phoenix North Central
402 East Greenway Pkwy., Stes. 21 & 28, Phoenix 85022
Phone: (602) 863-2101

Artistic Beauty Colleges—Phoenix
2727 West Glendale Ave., Ste. 200, Phoenix 85051
Type: Private, proprietary
Degrees: C
URL: http://www.artisticbeautycolleges.com
Phone: (602) 249-1262
Inst. Accred.: NACCAS (1982/2002)

Artistic Beauty Colleges—Scottsdale
7730 East McDowell Rd., Ste. 106, Scottsdale 85257
Type: Private, proprietary
Degrees: C
URL: http://www.artisticbeautycolleges.com
Phone: (480) 949-7557
Inst. Accred.: NACCAS (1975/2001)

Artistic Beauty Colleges—Tuscon
3030 East Speedway Blvd., Tucson 85716
Type: Private, proprietary
Degrees: C
URL: http://www.artisticbeautycolleges.com
Phone: (520) 327-6544
Inst. Accred.: NACCAS (1975/2003)

Tucson North Campus
4343 North Oracle Rd., Ste. I, Tucson 85705
Phone: (520) 888-3011

Astrological Institute
7501 East Oak St., Ste. 130, Scottsdale 85257
Type: Private, proprietary
Degrees: C
URL: http://www.primenet.com/astroin
Phone: (480) 423-9494
Inst. Accred.: ACCSCT (2001)

Carsten Institute of Hair and Beauty
3345 South Rural Rd., Tempe 85282
Type: Private, proprietary
Degrees: C
URL: http://www.carsteninstitute.com/
  institutestempe.html
Phone: (480) 491-0449
Inst. Accred.: NACCAS (1993/2001)

Charles of Italy Beauty College and School of Massage Therapy
1987 McCulloch Blvd., Ste. 205, Lake Havasu City 86403
Type: Private, proprietary
Degrees: C
URL: http://charlesofitaly.com
Phone: (928) 453-6666
Inst. Accred.: NACCAS (1984/2004)

Conservatory of Recording Arts & Sciences
2300 East Broadway Rd., Tempe 85282
Type: Private, independent
Degrees: C
URL: http://www.cras.org
Phone: (480) 858-9400
Inst. Accred.: ACCSCT (1990/2004)

Desert Institute of the Healing Arts
639 North Sixth Ave., Tucson 85705-8330
Type: Private, proprietary
Degrees: C
URL: http://www.desertinstitute.org
Phone: (520) 882-0899
Inst. Accred.: ACCSCT (1987/2001), CMTA (2001/2004)

DeVoe College of Beauty
750 East Barstow Dr., Sierra Vista 85635
Type: Private, proprietary
Degrees: C
Phone: (520) 458-8660
Inst. Accred.: NACCAS (1981/2001)

Earl's Academy of Beauty
2111 South Alma School Rd., Ste. 21, Mesa 85210
Type: Private, proprietary
Degrees: C
URL: http://www.earlsacademy.com
Phone: (480) 897-1688
Inst. Accred.: NACCAS (1972/2003)

Phoenix Campus
1107 East Bell Rd., Ste. 104, Phoenix 85022
Phone: (602) 443-0076

East Valley Institute of Technology
1601 West Main St., Mesa 85201
Type: Public, state/local
Degrees: C
URL: http://www.evit.com
Phone: (480) 461-4000
Inst. Accred.: NCA-CASI (1986/2004)

The Hair Academy of Safford
1550 West Thatcher Blvd., Safford 85546
Type: Private, proprietary
Degrees: C
Phone: (520) 428-0331
Inst. Accred.: NACCAS (1989/2004)

HDS Truck Driving Institute
6251 South Wilmont Rd., PO Box 17600, Tucson 85706
Type: Private, proprietary
Degrees: C
URL: http://www.hdsdrivers.com
Phone: (520) 721-5825
Inst. Accred.: ACCSCT (2000/2005)

International Academy of Beauty #6
3350 North Arizona Ave., Ste. 4, Chandler 85224
Type: Private, proprietary
Degrees: C
URL: http://www.intlacademy.biz
Phone: (480) 820-9422
Inst. Accred.: NACCAS (1972/2003)

Mesa Campus
42 North Stapley Dr., Mesa 85203
Phone: (480) 964-8675

Laun & Associates, Inc.
4105 North 20th St., Ste. 100, Phoenix 85016
Type: Private, proprietary
Degrees: C
URL: http://www.dalecarnegieaz.com
Phone: (602) 954-8044
Inst. Accred.: ACCET (1977/2004)

Maricopa Beauty College
515 West Western Ave., Avondale 85323
Type: Private, proprietary
Degrees: C
URL: http://www.maricopabeautycollege.com
Phone: (623) 932-4414
Inst. Accred.: NACCAS (1982/2002)

Motorcycle and Marine Mechanics Institute
2844 West Deer Valley Rd., Phoenix 85027-9951
Type: Private, proprietary
Degrees: C
URL: http://www.uticorp.com
Phone: (623) 869-9644
Inst. Accred.: ACCSCT (1979/2004)

Orlando Campus
9751 Delegates Dr., Orlando, FL 32837-9835
Phone: (407) 240-2422

Mundus Institute
2001 West Camelback, Ste. 400, Phoenix 85015
Type: Private, proprietary
Degrees: C
URL: http://www.mundusinstitute.com
Phone: (602) 246-7111
Inst. Accred.: ACCSCT (1989/2004)

Phoenix Therapeutic Massage College
609 North Scottsdale Rd., Scottsdale 85257
Type: Private, proprietary
Degrees: C
URL: http://www.ptmcaz.com
Phone: (480) 945-9461
Inst. Accred.: ACCET (1989/2001)

Flagstaff Campus
1000 North Humphreys St., Ste. 204, Flagstaff 86001-3125
Phone: (520) 213-0010

Phoenix Campus
9201 North 29th Ave., Ste. B-33, Phoenix 85051-3470
Phone: (602) 395-9494

Pima Medical Institute—Mesa
941 South Dobson Rd., Mesa 85202
Type: Private, proprietary
Degrees: C
URL: http://www.pmi.edu
Phone: (480) 644-0267
Inst. Accred.: ACCSCT (1973/2003)
Prog. Accred.: Medical Assisting (ABHES), Radiography, Respiratory Therapy, Respiratory Therapy Technology

Premier Training, Inc. Dale Carnegie Training
6121 East Broadway Blvd., Ste. 146, Tucson
Type: Private, proprietary
Degrees: C
URL: http://www.tucson.dalecarnegie.com
Phone: (520) 747-4664
Inst. Accred.: ACCET (1977/2004)

Quantum Helicopters
2370 South Airport Blvd., Chandler 85249
Type: Private, proprietary
Degrees: C
URL: http://www.quantumhelicopters.com
Phone: (480) 814-8118
Inst. Accred.: ACCSCT (2002)

Roberto-Venn School of Luthiery
4011 South 16th St., Phoenix 85040-1314
Type: Private, proprietary
Degrees: C
URL: http://www.roberto-venn.com
Phone: (602) 243-1179
Inst. Accred.: ACCSCT (1979/2004)

Sonoran Desert Institute
10245 East Via Linda, Ste. 102, Scottsdale 85258
Type: Private, proprietary
Degrees: C
URL: http://www.sonoranlearning.com
Phone: (480) 314-2102
Inst. Accred.: DETC (2004)

Southwest Institute of Healing Arts
1100 Apache Blvd., Tempe 85281
Type: Private, proprietary
Degrees: C
URL: http://www.swiha.org
Phone: (480) 994-9244
Inst. Accred.: ACCET (2003)

Toni & Guy Hairdressing Academy
7201 East Camelback Rd., Ste. 100, Scottsdale 85251
Type: Private, proprietary
Degrees: C
URL: http://www.toniguy.com
Phone: (480) 994-4222
Inst. Accred.: NACCAS (1988/2003)

Phoenix Campus
15210 South 50th St., Ste. 150, Phoenix 85044
Phone: (480) 940-5300

Tucson College
7310 East 22nd St., Tucson 85710
Type: Private, proprietary
Degrees: C
URL: http://tucsoncollege.com
Phone: (520) 296-3261
Inst. Accred.: ACICS (1966/2003)

Tucson College of Beauty
3955 North Flowing Wells, Tucson 85705
Type: Private, proprietary
Degrees: C
URL: http://www.tucsoncollegeofbeauty.com
Phone: (520)-887-8262
Inst. Accred.: NACCAS (2005)

Turning Point Beauty College, Inc.
1226 East Florence Blvd., Box #3, Casa Grande 85222
Type: Private, proprietary
Degrees: C
Phone: (520) 836-1476
Inst. Accred.: NACCAS (2003)

ARKANSAS

ABC Barber College
103 Brenda St., Hot Springs 71913
Type: Private, proprietary
Degrees: C
Phone: (501) 624-0885
Inst. Accred.: NACCAS (1997/2001)

Arkadelphia Beauty College
2708 Pine St., Arkadelphia 71923
Type: Private, proprietary
Degrees: C
Phone: (870) 246-6726
Inst. Accred.: NACCAS (1991/2001)

Arkansas Beauty School
5108 Baseline Rd., Little Rock 72209
Type: Private, proprietary
Degrees: C
Phone: (501) 562-5673
Inst. Accred.: NACCAS (1990/2005)

Arkansas Beauty School—Conway
1061 Markham St., Conway 72032
Type: Private, proprietary
Degrees: C
Phone: (501) 329-8303
Inst. Accred.: NACCAS (1990/2003)

Arthur's Beauty College
2000 North B St., Fort Smith 72901
Type: Private, proprietary
Degrees: C
Phone: (479) 783-3301
Inst. Accred.: NACCAS (1980/2005)

Arthur's Beauty College
2600 John Harden Dr., Jacksonville 72076
Type: Private, proprietary
Degrees: C
Phone: (501) 982-8987
Inst. Accred.: NACCAS (1987/2004)

> **Conway Campus**
> 2320 Washington Ave., Conway 72032
> *Phone:* (50) /329-7770

> **Pine Bluff Campus**
> 2710 Commerce Dr., Pine Bluff 71601
> *Phone:* (870) 534-0498

Askins Vo-Tech, Inc.
7716 Hwy. 271 South, Fort Smith 72908
Type: Private, proprietary
Degrees: C
Phone: (479) 646-4803
Inst. Accred.: ACCET (1995/2003)

Bee-Jay's Hairstyling Academy
1907 Hinson Loop Rd., Little Rock 72212
Type: Private, proprietary
Degrees: C
Phone: (501) 224-2442
Inst. Accred.: NACCAS (1978/2004)

> **Batesville Campus**
> 130 West Main St., Batesville 72501
> *Phone:* (501) 793-3898

Blytheville Academy of Cosmetology
100 East Main St., Blytheville 72315
Type: Private, proprietary
Degrees: C
Phone: (870) 763-6326
Inst. Accred.: NACCAS (1995/2001)

Career Academy of Hair Design
200 Holcomb St., Springdale 72764
Type: Private, proprietary
Degrees: C
Phone: (479) 756-6060
Inst. Accred.: NACCAS (1986/2001)

Cass Job Corps Center
21424 North Hwy. 23, Ozark 72949
Type: Public, federal
Degrees: C
URL: http://jobcorps.doleta.gov
Phone: (501) 667-3686
Inst. Accred.: COE (1998/2004)

Crowley's Ridge Technical Institute
1620 Newcastle Rd., Forrest City 72335
Type: Public, (local)
Degrees: C
URL: http://www.crti.tec.ar.us
Phone: (870) 633-5411   *Calendar:* Sem. plan
Inst. Accred.: COE (2003)

Deluxe Beauty School
1609 West 26th, Pine Bluff 71601
Type: Private, proprietary
Degrees: C
Phone: (870) 534-7609
Inst. Accred.: NACCAS (1994/2002)

Eastern College of Health Vocations
6423 Forbing Rd., Little Rock 72209
Type: Private, proprietary
Degrees: C
URL: http://www.echv.com
Phone: (501) 568-0211
Inst. Accred.: ABHES (1984/2003)
Prog. Accred.: Medical Assisting (ABHES)

Metairie Campus
3321 Hessmer Ave., Ste. 200, Metairie, LA 70002
Phone: (504) 885-3353
Prog. Accred: Medical Assisting (ABHES)

Shreveport Campus
9700 St. Vincent Ave., Shreveport, LA 71106
Phone: (318) 861-3246

Eaton Beauty Stylist College, Inc.
814 West Seventh St., Little Rock 72201
Type: Private, proprietary
Degrees: C
Phone: (501) 375-0211
Inst. Accred.: NACCAS (1995/2003)

Fayetteville Beauty College
2167-2177 West 6th St., Fayetteville 72701
Type: Private, proprietary
Degrees: C
Phone: (501) 442-5181
Inst. Accred.: NACCAS (1967/2004)

Hot Springs Beauty College
100 Cones Rd., Hot Springs 71901
Type: Private, proprietary
Degrees: C
Phone: (501) 624-0203
Inst. Accred.: NACCAS (1989/2004)

Jerry Wilson & Associates, Inc.
4 Shackleford Plaza, Ste. 100, Little Rock 72211
Type: Private, proprietary
Degrees: C
URL: http://www.arkansas.dalecarnegie.com
Phone: (501) 224-5000
Inst. Accred.: ACCET (1976/2001)

Lee's School of Cosmetology
2700 West Pershing Blvd., North Little Rock 72114
Type: Private, proprietary
Degrees: C
Phone: (501) 758-2800
Inst. Accred.: NACCAS (1987/2003)

Little Rock Job Corps Center
2020 Vance St., Little Rock 72206
Type: Public, federal
Degrees: C
URL: http://jobcorps.doleta.gov/centers
Phone: (501) 376-4600
Inst. Accred.: NCA-CASI (1995/2005)

Lynndale Fundamentals of Beauty School
1729 Champagnolle Rd., El Dorado 71730
Type: Private, proprietary
Degrees: C
Phone: (870) 863-3919
Inst. Accred.: NACCAS (2003)

Margaret's Hair Academy, Inc.
502 Tyler Rd., Russellville 72812
Type: Private, proprietary
Degrees: C
Phone: (479) 890-0215
Inst. Accred.: NACCAS (1998/2001)

Monticello Campus
305 East Gaines St., Monticello 71655
Phone: (870) 367-5533

Marsha Kay Beauty College
408 Hwy. 201 North, Mountain Home 72653-3164
Type: Private, proprietary
Degrees: C
Phone: (870) 425-7575
Inst. Accred.: NACCAS (1984/2004)

Mellie's Beauty College
311 1/2 South Sixteenth St., Fort Smith 72901
Type: Private, proprietary
Degrees: C
Phone: (479) 782-5059
Inst. Accred.: NACCAS (1972/2003)

Mena Cosmetology College
1310 Hwy. 71 North, Mena 71953
Type: Private, proprietary
Degrees: C
Phone: (479) 394-7272
Inst. Accred.: NACCAS (2005)

New Tyler Barber College
1221 East Seventh St., North Little Rock 72114-4973
Type: Private, proprietary
Degrees: C
Phone: (501) 375-0377
Inst. Accred.: ACCSCT (1984/2005)

Northwest Technical Institute
709 South Old Missouri Rd., Springdale 72764
Type: Private, proprietary
Degrees: C
Phone: (479) 751-8824
Inst. Accred.: COE (2003)

Professional Cosmetology Education Center
2027 North West Ave., El Dorado 71730
Type: Private, proprietary
Degrees: C
Phone: (870) 864-9292
Inst. Accred.: NACCAS (1982/2005)

Searcy Beauty College
1004 South Main St., Searcy 72143
Type: Private, proprietary
Degrees: C
Phone: (501) 268-6300
Inst. Accred.: NACCAS (1988/2003)

Southern Institute of Cosmetology
103 South Avalon St., West Memphis 72301
Type: Private, proprietary
Degrees: C
Phone: (870) 735-2800
Inst. Accred.: NACCAS (1986/2001)

Memphis Campus
3099 South Perkins, Memphis, TN 38118
Phone: (901) 363-3553

Thelma's Beauty Academy
2501 State St., Little Rock 72206
Type: Private, proprietary
Degrees: C
Phone: (501) 371-9253
Inst. Accred.: ACCSCT (2001)

Velvatex College of Beauty Culture
1520 Dr. Martin Luther King Jr. Dr., Little Rock 72202
Type: Private, proprietary
Degrees: C
Phone: (501) 372-9678
Inst. Accred.: NACCAS (1997/2005)

CALIFORNIA

Absolute Safety Training Paramedic Program
78 Table Mountain Blvd., Oroville 95965
Type: Private, proprietary
Degrees: C
Phone: (530) 934-7257
Inst. Accred.: ABHES (2005)

Academy Education Services
520 West Fifth St., Ste. #D, Oxnard 93030
Type: Private, proprietary
Degrees: C
URL: http://www.academyed.com
Phone: (805) 486-1102
Inst. Accred.: ACCSCT (2002)

Academy of Professional Careers
6160 Mission Gorge Rd., La Mesa 92120
Type: Private, proprietary
Degrees: C
URL: http://www.academyofhealthcareers.com/Academy
Phone: (619) 461-5100
Inst. Accred.: ACCET (1993/2005)

Amarillo Campus
2201 South Western, Stes. 102 & 103, Amarillo, TX 79109
Phone: (806) 353-3500

Boise Campus
8590 West Fairview Ave., Boise, ID 83704-8320
Phone: (208) 672-9500

Indio Campus
45-691 Monroe Ave., Indio 92201
Phone: (760) 347-5000

Academy of Radio and Television Broadcasting
16052 Beach Blvd., Ste. 263-N, Huntington Beach 92647
Type: Private, proprietary
Degrees: C
URL: http://www.arbradio.com
Phone: (714) 842-0100
Inst. Accred.: ACCET (1986/2002)

Phoenix Campus
4914 East McDowell Rd., Ste. 107, Phoenix, AZ 85008
Phone: (602) 267-8001

Academy Pacific Travel College
1777 North Vine St., Hollywood 90028-5218
Type: Private, proprietary
Degrees: C
URL: http://www.academypacific.com
Phone: (323) 462-3211
Inst. Accred.: ACCSCT (1973/2000)

Adelante Career Institute
14547 Titus St., Ste. 100, Van Nuys 91402
Type: Private, proprietary
Degrees: C
URL: http://www.adelantecareerinstitute.com
Phone: (818) 908-9912
Inst. Accred.: ACCET (1990/2005)

Adrian's Beauty College of Turlock
2253 Geer Rd., Turlock 95382
Type: Private, proprietary
Degrees: C
Phone: (209) 632-2233
Inst. Accred.: NACCAS (1986/2001)

Advance Beauty College
10121 Westminister Ave., Garden Grove 92843
Type: Public, proprietary
Degrees: C
Phone: (714) 530-2131
Inst. Accred.: NACCAS (2003)

Advanced Career Technologies Institute
2880 Sunrise Blvd., Ste. 232, Rancho Cordova 95742
Type: Private, proprietary
Degrees: C
URL: http://www.actech.org
Phone: (916) 635-3435
Inst. Accred.: ACCSCT (1999/2002)

Advanced College
8527 Alondra Blvd., Set. 143, Paramount 90723
Type: Private, proprietary
Degrees: C
URL: http://www.advancedcollege.net
Phone: (562) 408-6969
Inst. Accred.: COE (2003)

Advanced Training Associates, Inc.
1870 Joe Crosson Dr., El Cajon 92020
Type: Public, proprietary
Degrees: C
URL: http://www.advancedtraining.net
Phone: (619) 596-2766
Inst. Accred.: COE (2000)

AF International School of Languages, Inc
3625 Thousand Oaks Blvd., Westlake Village 91362
Type: Private, proprietary
Degrees: C
URL: http://www.afint.com
Phone: (805) 496-6694
Inst. Accred.: ACCET (2004)

Alameda Beauty College, Inc.
2318 Central Ave., Alameda 94501
Type: Private, proprietary
Degrees: C
Phone: (510) 523-1050
Inst. Accred.: NACCAS (1977/2004)

Alhambra Beauty College
200 West Main St., PO Box 7494, Alhambra 91802
Type: Private, proprietary
Degrees: C
Phone: (626) 282-7765
Inst. Accred.: NACCAS (1978/2003)

All American Career College
101 East Redlands Blvd., Ste. 247, Redlands 92373
Type: Private, proprietary
Degrees: C
Phone: (909) 792-5593
Inst. Accred.: COE (2003)

Allied Business Schools, Inc.
22952 Alcalde Dr., Ste. 150, Laguna Hills 92653
Type: Private, proprietary
Degrees: C
URL: http://www.alliedschools.com
Phone: (949) 598-0875
Inst. Accred.: DETC (2002)

Allied Schools
22952 Alcalde Dr., Laguna Hills 92653
Phone: (949) 598-0875

American Academy of English
530 Golden Gate Ave., San Francisco 94102
Type: Private, proprietary
Degrees: C
URL: http://www.aaesl.com
Phone: (415) 567-0189
Inst. Accred.: ACCET (2001/2004)

American Auto Institute
17522 Studebaker Rd., Cerritos 90703
Type: Private, proprietary
Degrees: C
URL: http://www.americanautoinstitute.com
Phone: (562) 403-2660
Inst. Accred.: ACCSCT (2005)

American Beauty College
16512 Bellflower Blvd., Bellflower 90706
Type: Private, proprietary
Degrees: C
Phone: (562) 866-0728
Inst. Accred.: NACCAS (1977/2002)

American Career College
4021 Rosewood Ave., Los Angeles 90004-2932
Type: Private, proprietary
Degrees: C
URL: http://www.americancareer.com
Phone: (323) 668-7555
Inst. Accred.: ABHES (1983/2005)

Norco Campus
3299 Horseless Carriage Rd., Ste. C, Norco 92860
Phone: (951) 739-0788
Prog. Accred: Medical Assisting (ABHES)

Orange County Campus
1200 North Magnolia Ave., Anaheim 92801
Phone: (714) 952-9066

American College of California
760 Market St., Ste. 1009, San Francisco 94102-2305
Type: Private, proprietary
Degrees: C
URL: http://www.acofca.com
Phone: (415) 677-9717
Inst. Accred.: ACCSCT (2004)

American College of Health Professions
700 East Redlands Blvd., No. U227, Redlands 92373
Type: Private, proprietary
Degrees: C
Phone: (909) 307-6022   *Calendar:* Qtr. plan
Inst. Accred.: ABHES (1996/2004)

Riverside Campus
3715 La Sierra Ave., Riverside 92505
Phone: (951) 637-6900
Prog. Accred: Medical Assisting (ABHES), Surgical
Technology

American College of Medical Technology
555 West Redondo Beach Blvd., Ste. 100, Gardena
90248
Type: Private, proprietary
Degrees: C
URL: http://www.acmt.ac
Phone: (310) 324-1000
Inst. Accred.: ACCSCT (1995/2002)

American English Academy
111 North Atlantic Blvd., Ste. 112, Monterey Park 91754
Type: Private, proprietary
Degrees: C
URL: http://www.aea-usa.com
Phone: (626) 457-2800
Inst. Accred.: ACCET (2005)

American Institute of Health Sciences
3501 Atlantic Ave., Long Beach 90807
Type: Private, independent
Degrees: C
URL: http://www.aihs.edu
Phone: (562) 988-2278
Inst. Accred.: ACICS (2004)

American Institute of Massage Therapy
1570 East Warner Ave., Ste. 200, Santa Ana 92705
Type: Private, proprietary
Degrees: C
URL: http://www.aimtinc.com
Phone: (714) 432-7879
Inst. Accred.: ABHES (2004)

American Medical Sciences Center— North Hollwood
5077 Lankershim Blvd., Ste. 201, North Hollywood 91601
Type: Private, proprietary
Degrees: C
Phone: (818) 763-9999
Inst. Accred.: ABHES (2002/2003)

Antelope Valley Medical College
44201 10th St. West, Lancaster 93534
Type: Private, independent
Degrees: C
URL: http://www.antelopevalleymedicalcollege.com
Phone: (661) 726-1911
Inst. Accred.: ABHES (2001/2005)
Prog. Accred.: Medical Assisting (ABHES)

Applied Professional Training, Inc.
6976 Mimosa Dr., PO Box 131717, Carlsbad 92013
Type: Private, proprietary
Degrees: C
URL: http://www.aptc.com
Phone: (800) 431-8488
Inst. Accred.: DETC (2003)

Asian American International Beauty College
7871 Westminster Blvd., Westminster 92683
Type: Private, proprietary
Degrees: C
Phone: (714) 891-0508
Inst. Accred.: NACCAS (1994/2002)

ASPECT International Language Schools
One West Victoria St., Santa Barbara 93101
Type: Private, proprietary
Degrees: C
URL: http://www.aspectworld.com
Phone: (805) 564-8330
Inst. Accred.: ACCET (1992/2001)

Chicago Campus
3424 South State St., Chicago, IL 60616
Phone: (312) 328-0262

Franklin Campus
99 Main St., Franklin, MA 02038
Phone: (508) 541-1776

La Jolla Campus
1111 Torrey Pines Rd., La Jolla 92037
Phone: (858) 551-5750

Orlando Campus
4000 Central Florida Blvd., PC 620, Rm. 102B, Orlando, FL 32837-7662
Phone: (407) 823-3183

Riverdale Campus
4513 Manhattan College Pkwy., de La Salle Hall, 4th Flr., Riverdale, NY 10471
Phone: (718) 549-4838

San Francisco Campus
530 Bush St., Ste. 500, San Francisco 94108
Phone: (415) 362-1588

Santa Barabra Campus
721 Cliff Dr., Building ECC #20, Santa Barbara 93109
Phone: (805) 966-1620

Whittier Campus
13509 Earlham Dr., PO Box 634, Whittier 90608
Phone: (562) 693-9023

Associated Technical College
1445 Sixth Ave., San Diego 92101-3245
Type: Private, proprietary
Degrees: C
URL: http://www.associatedtechcollege.com
Phone: (619) 234-2181
Inst. Accred.: ACCSCT (1984/2004)

Associated Technical College
1670 Wilshire Blvd., Los Angeles 90017-1690
Type: Private, proprietary
Degrees: C
URL: http://www.associatedtechcollege.com
Phone: (213) 353-1845
Inst. Accred.: ACCSCT (1969/2002)

Associated Technical College
1593 East Vista Way, Ste. C, Vista 92084
Type: Private, proprietary
Degrees: C
URL: http://www.associatedtechcollege.com
Phone: (760) 643-0505
Inst. Accred.: ACCSCT (1984/2001)

ATI College
12440 Firestone Blvd., Ste. 2001, Norwalk 90650
Type: Private, proprietary
Degrees: C
URL: http://www.adconsys.com
Phone: (562) 864-0506
Inst. Accred.: ACCSCT (2002)

Tustin Campus
17821 East 17th St., Ste. 120, Tustin 92780
Phone: (714) 730-7080

Avalon Beauty College
504 North Milipas St., Santa Barbara 93103
Type: Private, proprietary
Degrees: C
Phone: (805) 966-1931
Inst. Accred.: NACCAS (2001/2004)

Avance Beauty College
750 Beyer Way, Ste. B-D, San Diego 92154
Type: Private, proprietary
Degrees: C
Phone: (619) 575-1511
Inst. Accred.: NACCAS (1987/2002)

Bay Vista College of Beauty
1520 Plaza Blvd., National City 91950
Type: Private, proprietary
Degrees: C
URL: http://www.sandiegobeautyacademy.com
Phone: (619) 474-6607
Inst. Accred.: NACCAS (1974/2001)

Brandon College
25 Kearny St., 2nd Flr., San Francisco 94108
Type: Private, proprietary
Degrees: C
URL: http://www.brandoncollege.com
Phone: (415) 391-5711
Inst. Accred.: ACCET (2000)

Bridges Academy of Beauty
423 East Main St., Barstow 92311
Type: Private, proprietary
Degrees: C
URL: http://www.bridgesacademyofbeauty.com
Phone: (760) 256-0515
Inst. Accred.: NACCAS (2005)

Brownson Technical School
1110 Technology Circle, Ste. D, Anaheim 92805
Type: Private, proprietary
Degrees: C
URL: http://www.brownsontechnicalschool.com
Phone: (714) 774-9443
Inst. Accred.: ACCSCT (2002)

Bryan College of Court Reporting
2333 Beverly Blvd., Los Angeles 90057
Type: Private, proprietary
Degrees: C
URL: http://www.bryancollege.edu
Phone: (213) 484-8850
Inst. Accred.: ACICS (1975/2005)

Bryman College
217 Club Center, Ste. A, San Bernardino 92408
Type: Private, proprietary
System: Corinthian Colleges, Inc
Degrees: C
URL: http://www.bryman-college.com
Phone: (909) 777-3300   *Calendar:* Qtr. plan
Inst. Accred.: ACICS (1962/2001)

Bryman College—Anaheim
511 North Brookhurst, Ste. 300, Anaheim 92801
Type: Private, proprietary
System: Corinthian Colleges, Inc
Degrees: C
URL: http://www.cci.edu
Phone: (714) 953-6500
Inst. Accred.: ACCSCT (1973/2002)
Prog. Accred.: Medical Assisting (CAAHEP)

Bryman College—El Monte
3208 Rosemead Blvd., Ste. 100, El Monte 91731
Type: Private, proprietary
System: Corinthian Colleges, Inc
Degrees: C
URL: http://www.bryman-college.com
Phone: (626) 573-5470
Inst. Accred.: ACCSCT (1968/2004)
Prog. Accred.: Medical Assisting (CAAHEP)

Bryman College—Gardena
1045 W. Redondo Beach Blvd., Ste. 275, Gardena 90247
Type: Private, proprietary
System: Corinthian Colleges, Inc
Degrees: C
URL: http://www.bryman-college.com
Phone: (310) 527-7105
Inst. Accred.: ACCSCT (1973/2002)
Prog. Accred.: Medical Assisting (CAAHEP)

   Georgia Medical Institute
   1750 Beaver Ruin Rd., Ste. 500, Norcross, GA 30093
   Phone: (770) 921-1085

Bryman College—Hayward
22336 Main St., First Flr., Hayward 94541
Type: Private, proprietary
System: Corinthian Colleges, Inc
Degrees: C
URL: http://www.bryman-college.com
Phone: (510) 582-9500
Inst. Accred.: ACCSCT (1973/2001)

   New Orleans Campus
   1200 Elenwood Park Blvd., Ste. 600, New Orleans, LA 70123
   Phone: (504) 733-7117
   Prog. Accred: Medical Assisting (CAAHEP)

Bryman College—Los Angeles
3460 Wilshire Blvd., Ste. 500, Los Angeles 90010
Type: Private, proprietary
System: Corinthian Colleges, Inc
Degrees: C
URL: http://www.bryman-college.com
Phone: (213) 388-9950
Inst. Accred.: ACCSCT (1962/2002)
Prog. Accred.: Medical Assisting (CAAHEP)

Bryman College—Reseda
18040 Sherman Way, Ste. 400, Reseda 91335-4631
Type: Private, proprietary
System: Corinthian Colleges, Inc
Degrees: C
URL: http://www.bryman-college.com
Phone: (818) 774-0550
Inst. Accred.: ACCSCT (1974/2001)
Prog. Accred.: Medical Assisting (ABHES), Respiratory
  Therapy Technology

Bryman College—San Francisco
814 Mission St., Ste. 500, San Francisco 94103-9946
Type: Private, proprietary
System: Corinthian Colleges, Inc
Degrees: C
URL: http://www.bryman-college.com
Phone: (415) 777-2500
Inst. Accred.: ACCSCT (1972/2002)
Prog. Accred.: Medical Assisting (CAAHEP)

Olympia College—Chicago
247 South State St., Ste. 400, Chicago, IL 60604
Phone: (312) 913-1616

Bryman College—San Jose
1245 South Winchester Blvd., Ste. 102, San Jose 95128
Type: Private, proprietary
System: Corinthian Colleges, Inc
Degrees: C
URL: http://www.bryman-college.com
Phone: (408) 246-0859
Inst. Accred.: ACCSCT (1973/2003)

Bryman College—Torrance
1231 Cabrillo Ave., Ste. 201, Torrance 90501
Type: Private, proprietary
Degrees: C
URL: http://www.bryman-college.com
Phone: (310) 320-3200
Inst. Accred.: ACCSCT (2004)

California Beauty College
1115 Fifteenth St., Modesto 95354
Type: Private, proprietary
Degrees: C
Phone: (209) 524-5184
Inst. Accred.: NACCAS (1977/2001)

California Career College
7108 De Soto Ave., Ste. 207, Canoga Park 91303
Type: Private, proprietary
Degrees: C
Phone: (818) 710-1310
Inst. Accred.: ABHES (2004)

California Career School
1100 Technology Circle, Anaheim 92805-6329
Type: Private, proprietary
Degrees: C
URL: http://www.californiacareerschool.edu
Phone: (714) 635-6585
Inst. Accred.: ACCSCT (1994/2005)

California College of Vocational Careers
2822 F St., Ste. L, Bakersfield 93301
Type: Private, proprietary
Degrees: C
URL: http://www.californiacollegevc.com
Phone: (661) 323-6791
Inst. Accred.: ABHES (2002)

California Cosmetology College, San Jose, Inc.
955 Monroe St., Santa Clara 95050
Type: Private, proprietary
Degrees: C
URL: http://www.cacosmetologycollege.com
Phone: (408) 247-2200
Inst. Accred.: NACCAS (1976/2005)

California Hair Design Academy
8011 University Ave., Ste. A-2, La Meas 91941
Type: Private, proprietary
Degrees: C
Phone: (619) 461-8600
Inst. Accred.: NACCAS (1974/2001)

California Healing Arts College
12217 Santa Monica Blvd., Ste. 206, West Los Angeles
90025
Type: Private, proprietary
Degrees: C
Phone: (310) 826-7622
Inst. Accred.: ACCSCT (2002)

California Institute of the Healing Arts and Sciences
1111 Howe Ave., Ste. 150, Sacramento 95825
Type: Private, proprietary
Degrees: C
URL: http://www.californiainstitute.net
Phone: (916) 484-1700
Inst. Accred.: ACCET (2004)

California Learning Center
222 South Harbor Blvd., Ste. 200, Anaheim 92805
Type: Private, proprietary
Degrees: C
Phone: (714) 956-5656
Inst. Accred.: ACCSCT (2001)

California School of Culinary Arts
521 East Green St., Pasadena 91101
Type: Private, proprietary
System: Career Education Corporation
Degrees: C
URL: http://www.calchef.com
Phone: (626) 403-8490   *Calendar:* Sem. plan
Inst. Accred.: ACICS (1997/2000)

Kitchen Academy
6370 West Sunset Blvd., Hollywood 90028
Phone: (866) 548-2223

California School of Modern Sciences
291 South La Cienega, Ste. 200, Beverly Hills 90211
Type: Private, proprietary
Degrees: C
Phone: (310) 657-9495
Inst. Accred.: ABHES (1999/2002)

Cambridge Career College
990-A Klamath Ln., Yuba City 95993
Type: Private, proprietary
Degrees: C
URL: http://www.cambridge.edu
Phone: (530) 674-9199
Inst. Accred.: ACICS (2003)

Career Academy of Beauty—West Garden Grove
12471 Valley View Blvd., West Garden Grove 92845
Type: Private, proprietary
Degrees: C
URL: http://www.beautycareers.com
Phone: (704) 897-3010
Inst. Accred.: NACCAS (1977/2003)

Anaheim Campus
663 North Euclid, Anaheim 92801
Phone: (714) 776-8400

Career Care Institute
43770 15th St. West, Ste. 205, Lancaster 93534
Type: Private, proprietary
Degrees: C
URL: http://www.careercareinstitute.com
Phone: (661) 942-6204
Inst. Accred.: ABHES (2003/2005)

Ventura Campus
1730 South Victoria Ave., Ste. 230, Ventura 93003
Phone: (805) 477-0660
Prog. Accred: Medical Assisting (ABHES)

Career Colleges of America
5612 East Imperial Hwy., South Gate 90280
Type: Private, proprietary
Degrees: C
URL: http://www.careercolleges.org
Phone: (562) 861-8702
Inst. Accred.: ACCET (1999/2005)

San Bernardino Campus
184 Club Center Dr., San Bernardino 92408
Phone: (909) 876-0919

Career Networks Institute
3420 Bristol St., Ste. 209, Costa Mesa 92626
Type: Private, proprietary
Degrees: C
URL: http://www.cniworks.com
Phone: (714) 437-9697
Inst. Accred.: ABHES (1997/2001)

Casa Loma College
6850 Van Nuys Blvd., Ste. 318, Van Nuys 91405
Type: Private, independent
Degrees: C
URL: http://www.casalomacollege.com
Phone: (818) 785-2726
Inst. Accred.: ABHES (2002/2005)
Prog. Accred.: Medical Assisting (ABHES), Practical Nursing

Hawthorne Campus
12540 South Crenshaw Blvd., Hawthorne 90250
Phone: (310) 220-3111
Prog. Accred: Medical Assisting (ABHES)

CBD College
5724 West Third St., Ste. 314, Los Angeles 90036
Type: Private, proprietary
Degrees: C
URL: http://www.cbdcollege.com
Phone: (323) 937-7772
Inst. Accred.: ACCET (1997/2000)

Central for Information Technology
53690 Tomahawk Dr., Ste. 144, San Diego 92147
Type: Public, federal
Degrees: C
Phone: (619) 767-4177
Inst. Accred.: COE (2004)

Center for Seabees and Facilities Engineering
3502 Godspeed St., Ste. 2, Port Hueneme 93043
Type: Public, federal
Degrees: C
URL: https://www.npdc.navy.mil/csfe
Phone: (805) 982-3300
Inst. Accred.: COE (2004)

Central California School of Continuing Education
271 Ott St., Ste. 23, Corona 91720
Type: Private, proprietary
Degrees: C
URL: http://www.ccsce.org
Phone: (909) 549-0693
Inst. Accred.: ACCSCT (1992/2003)
Prog. Accred.: Radiography

Corona Campus
271 Ott St., Ste. 23, Corona 91720
Phone: (909) 549-0693

Central Coast College
480 South Main St., Salinas 93901
Type: Private, proprietary
Degrees: C
URL: http://www.centralcoastcollege.edu
Phone: (831) 424-6767
Inst. Accred.: ACCET (1989/2005)
Prog. Accred.: Medical Assisting (ABHES)

Champion Institute of Cosmetology
611 South Palm Canyon Dr., Ste. 22, Palm Springs 92264
Type: Private, proprietary
Degrees: C
Phone: (760) 322-2227
Inst. Accred.: NACCAS (2005)

Chase College
3580 Wilshire Blvd., 4th Flr., Los Angeles 90010
Type: Private, proprietary
Degrees: C
URL: http://chase.edu
Phone: (213) 365-1999
Inst. Accred.: ACCSCT (1998/2001)

Clarita Career College
27125 Sierra Hwy., Ste. 329, Canyon Country 91351
Type: Private, proprietary
Degrees: C
URL: http://www.claritacareercollege.com
Phone: (661) 252-1864
Inst. Accred.: ACCSCT (1998/2003)

Coachella Valley Technical Skills Center
35-325 Date Palm Dr., Suite 101, Cathedral City 92234
Type: Private, proprietary
Degrees: C
Phone: (760) 328-5554
Inst. Accred.: COE (2003)

Coastline Beauty College
10840 Warner Ave., Ste. 207, Fountain Valley 92708
Type: Private, proprietary
Degrees: C
URL: http://www.coastlinebeauty.com
Phone: (714) 963-4000
Inst. Accred.: NACCAS (2005)

Colleen O'Hara's Beauty Academy—Orange
102 North Glasselll St., Orange 92866
Type: Private, proprietary
Degrees: C
URL: http://www.colleenoharas.com
Phone: (714) 633-5950
Inst. Accred.: NACCAS (2000/2003)

Colleen O'Hara's Beauty Academy—Santa Ana
109 West 4th St., 2nd Flr., Santa Ana 92701
Type: Private, proprietary
Degrees: C
URL: http://www.colleenoharas.com
Phone: (714) 568-5399
Inst. Accred.: NACCAS (1990/2002)

Community Business School
3800 McHenry Ave., Ste. M, Modesto 95356
Type: Private, proprietary
Degrees: C
URL: http://www.communitybusinessschool.com
Phone: (209) 529-3648
Inst. Accred.: ACCSCT (2001)

Community Enhancement Services Adult Education Division
1335 North La Brea Ave., Ste. 3, Los Angeles 90028
Type: Private, independent
Degrees: C
Phone: (323) 850-4676
Inst. Accred.: ACCET (2002/2005)

Computer Training Institute
6250 Thornton Ave., Newark 94560
Type: Private, proprietary
Degrees: C
URL: http://www.itscti.net
Phone: (510) 742-9600
Inst. Accred.: ACCET (1999/2002)

Cynthia's Beauty Academy
4130 East Gage Ave., Bell 90201
Type: Private, proprietary
Degrees: C
Phone: (323) 560-2207
Inst. Accred.: NACCAS (1979/2005)

Dale Carnegie Training of Central California
7208 Darrin Ave., Bakersfield 93305
Type: Private, proprietary
Degrees: C
URL: http://www.centralcalif.dalecarnegie.com
Phone: (661) 393-5050
Inst. Accred.: ACCET (1983/2003)

Dale Carnegie Training of Los Angeles
1317 West Foothill Blvd., Ste. 235, Upland 91786
Type: Private, proprietary
Degrees: C
URL: http://www.dalecarnegie.com
Phone: (909) 931-3384
Inst. Accred.: ACCET (1979/2005)

Dale Carnegie Training of San Jose
274 East Hamilton, Ste. H, Campbell 95008
Type: Private, proprietary
Degrees: C
URL: http://www.DCTinfo.net
Phone: (408) 378-5244
Inst. Accred.: ACCET (1975/2001)

Design School of Cosmetology
715 24th St., Ste. E, Paso Robles 93446
Type: Private, proprietary
Degrees: C
Phone: (805) 237-8575
Inst. Accred.: NACCAS (2001/2004)

Diversified Language Institute
1670 Wilshire Blvd., Los Angeles 90017
Type: Private, proprietary
Degrees: C
URL: http://www.dliusa.com
Phone: (213) 353-1849
Inst. Accred.: ACCET (1986/2003)

Torrance Campus
3525 Lomita Blvd., Torrance 90505
Phone: (310) 530-4009

Diversified Language Institute—San Diego
1403 Sixth Ave., San Diego 92101
Type: Private, proprietary
Degrees: C
URL: http://www.dliusa.com
Phone: (619) 234-4354
Inst. Accred.: ACCET (2003)

DVS College
3325 Wilshire Blvd., Ste. 200, Los Angeles 90010
Type: Private, proprietary
Degrees: C
URL: http://www.dvusa.com
Phone: (213) 639-1470
Inst. Accred.: ABHES (2000/2005)

Montclair Campus
9740 Central Ave., Montclair 91763
Phone: (909) 447-6750
Prog. Accred: Medical Assisting (ABHES)

Eddie C. Snow & Associates, Inc.
304 Pendleton Way, Oakland 94621
Type: Private, proprietary
Degrees: C
URL: http://www.oakland.dale-carnegie.com
Phone: (510) 635-8598
Inst. Accred.: ACCET (1975/2005)

Edgewood College of California
4930 Earle Ave., Rosemead 91770
Type: Private, proprietary
Degrees: C
URL: http://www.edgewood-usa.com
Phone: (626) 291-5000
Inst. Accred.: COE (2004)

EdNet Career Institute, Inc.
6018 Variel Ave., Woodland Hills 91367
Type: Private, proprietary
Degrees: C
URL: http://www.ednet4u.com
Phone: (818) 702-8050
Inst. Accred.: ACCET (2000/2004)

Elegance International
1622 North Highland Ave., Hollywood 90028
Type: Private, proprietary
Degrees: C
URL: http://www.eleganceacademy.com
Phone: (323) 871-8318   *Calendar:* Sem. plan
Inst. Accred.: ACCSCT (1978/2004)

Elite Progressive School of Cosmetology
5522 Garfield Ave., Sacramento 95841
Type: Private, proprietary
Degrees: C
Phone: (916) 338-1885
Inst. Accred.: ACCSCT (2000/2005)

Emergency Training Services, Inc.
3050 Paul Sweet Rd., Santa Cruz 95065
Type: Private, proprietary
Degrees: C
URL: http://www.etsclassroom.com
Phone: (831) 476-8813
Inst. Accred.: ABHES (2003)

English Center for International Women
PO Box 9968, Mills College, 5000 MacArthur Blvd.,
Oakland 94613
Type: Private, independent
Degrees: C
URL: http://www.eciw.org
Phone: (510) 430-2234
Inst. Accred.: ACCET (1985/2005)

English Language Institute
760 Market St., #401-4, San Francisco 94102
Type: Private, proprietary
Degrees: C
URL: http://www.elisf.com
Phone: (415) 544-0311
Inst. Accred.: ACCET (1999/2005)

Market Street Campus
1177 Polk St., Ste. 200, San Francisco 94109
Phone: (415) 771-4070

Estes Institute of Cosmetology Arts and Sciences
324 East Main St., Visalia 93291
Type: Private, proprietary
Degrees: C
Phone: (209) 733-3617
Inst. Accred.: NACCAS (1980/2004)

Federico Beauty Institute
2100 Arden Way, Ste. 265, Sacramento 95825
Type: Private, proprietary
Degrees: C
URL: http://www.federicocollege.com
Phone: (916) 929-4242
Inst. Accred.: NACCAS (1967/2000)

FLS International
101 East Green St., Ste. 14, Pasadena 91105
Type: Private, proprietary
Degrees: C
URL: http://www.fls.net
Phone: (626) 795-2912
Inst. Accred.: ACCET (2000/2003)

Franklin Campus
99 Main St., Franklin, MA 02038
Phone: (626) 795-2912

Glendora Campus
1000 West Foothill Blvd., Glendora 91741
Phone: (626) 852-0075

Las Vegas Campus
6375 West Charleston Blvd., Las Vegas, NV 89146
Phone: (702) 651-5653

Lock Haven Campus
151 Susquehanna Ave., Lock Haven, PA 17745
Phone: (570) 893-8474

Oceanside Campus
One Barnard Dr., MiraCosta College, Oceanside 92056
Phone: (760) 795-6663

Oxnard Campus
4000 South Rose Ave., Oxnard 93030
Phone: (805) 986-8200

Saint George Campus
225 South 700 East, St. George, UT 84770
Phone: (435) 652-7758

Four-D College
1020 East Washington St., Colton 92324-4117
Type: Private, proprietary
Degrees: C
URL: http://www.4Dcollege.com
Phone: (909) 783-9331
Inst. Accred.: ABHES (1996/2003)

Fredrick and Charles Beauty College
831 F St., Eureka 95501
Type: Private, proprietary
Degrees: C
Phone: (707) 443-2733
Inst. Accred.: NACCAS (1976/2003)

Galen College of Medical and Dental Assistants
1325 North Wishon Ave., Fresno 93728-2381
Type: Private, proprietary
Degrees: C
URL: http://www.galencollege.com
Phone: (559) 264-9726
Inst. Accred.: ACCSCT (1974/2003)

Modesto Campus
1604 Ford Ave., Ste. 10, Modesto 95350-4665
Phone: (209) 527-5084

Visalia Campus
3908 West Caldwell, Ste. A, Visalia 93277
Phone: (559) 732-2217

Gemological Institute of America
The Robert Mouawad Campus, 5345 Armada Dr.,
Carlsbad 92008
Type: Private, proprietary
Degrees: C
URL: http://www.gia.edu
Phone: (760) 603-4000
Inst. Accred.: ACCSCT (1973/2001), DETC (1965/2003)

Manhattan Campus
580 Fifth Ave., New York, NY 10036-4794
Phone: (212) 944-5900

GEOS English Academy
949 South Coast Dr., Ste. 450, Costa Mesa 92626
Type: Private, proprietary
Degrees: C
URL: http://www.geos.net
Phone: (714) 662-7413
Inst. Accred.: ACCET (1999/2002)

Boston Campus
40 Ct. St., Ste. 402, Boston, MA 02108
Phone: (617) 277-4600

Honolulu Campus
2222 Kalakaua Ave., Ste. 601, Honolulu, HI 96815
Phone: (808) 924-7733

New York Campus
350 5th Ave., Ste. 612, New York, NY 10118
Phone: (646) 674-0001

San Francisco Campus
1 Sutter St., Ste. 400, San Francisco 94104-4921
Phone: (415) 392-6852

Torrance Campus
21515 Hawthorne Blvd., Ste. G120, Torrance 90503
Phone: (310) 792-7270

Glendale Career College
1015 Grandview Ave., Glendale 91201
Type: Private, proprietary
Degrees: C
URL: http://www.success.edu
Phone: (757) 446-2799
Inst. Accred.: ACCET (1988/2005)
Prog. Accred.: Medical Assisting (AMA), Surgical
  Technology

Nevada Career Institute—East Campus
3025 East Desert Inn Rd., Ste. A, Las Vegas, NV 89121
Phone: (702) 893-3300

Oceanside Campus
2204 El Camino Real, Ste. 315, Oceanside 92054-
6306
Phone: (760) 450-0340

Golden State College
3356 South Fairway St., Visalia 93277-8109
Type: Private, proprietary
Degrees: C
URL: http://www.goldenstatecollege.com
Phone: (559) 735-3818
Inst. Accred.: ACCET (1987/2001)

Fairfield Campus
934 Missouri St., Ste. K,L,Q, Fairfield 94585
Phone: (707) 425-2288

Hair California Beauty Academy
1110 North Tustin St., Orange 92867
Type: Private, proprietary
Degrees: C
Phone: (714) 633-7170
Inst. Accred.: NACCAS (2004)

Hair Masters University of Beauty
208-210 West Highland Ave., San Bernadino 92405
Type: Private, proprietary
Degrees: C
Phone: (909) 882-2987
Inst. Accred.: NACCAS (1979/2004)

Health Staff Training Institute
1505 East 17th St., #122, Santa Ana 92705
Type: Private, proprietary
Degrees: C
Phone: (714) 543-9828
Inst. Accred.: ABHES (1988/2001)

Riverside Campus
1115 Spruce St., Ste. E, Riverside 92507
Phone: (909) 955-9737

Healthy Hair Academy, Inc.
2648 West Imperial Hwy., Inglewood 90303
Type: Private, proprietary
Degrees: C
URL: http://www.healthyhairacademy.org
Phone: (310) 671-0614
Inst. Accred.: NACCAS (2005)

Heartwood Institute
220 Harmony Ln., Garberville 95542
Type: Private, proprietary
Degrees: C
URL: http://www.heartwoodinstitute.com
Phone: (707) 923-5000
Inst. Accred.: ACCET (1998/2001)

Hilltop Beauty School
6317 Mission St., Daly City 94014
Type: Private, proprietary
Degrees: C
URL: http://www.hilltopbeautyschool.com
Phone: (650) 756-2720
Inst. Accred.: NACCAS (1979/2004)

Hypnosis Motivation Institute
18607 Ventura Blvd., Ste. 310, Tarzana 91356
Type: Private, proprietary
Degrees: C
URL: http://www.hypnosismotivation.com
Phone: (800) 682-4464
Inst. Accred.: ACCET (1987/2001, Warning), DETC
  (1989/2003, Warning)

ICDC College
6363 Wilshire Blvd., Ste. 600, Los Angeles 90048
Type: Private, proprietary
Degrees: C
URL: http://www.learncareer.com
Phone: (323) 655-9100
Inst. Accred.: ACCSCT (1999/2004)

Huntington Park Campus
6330 Pacific Blvd., Ste. 200, Huntington Park 90255
Phone: (323) 277-1900

Lawndale Campus
4415 Redondo Beach Blvd., Lawndale 90260
Phone: (310) 793-4100

San Fernando Valley Campus
14545 Victory Blvd., Ste. 600, Van Nuys 91411
Phone: (818) 787-0007

Image Schools of Cosmetology, Inc.
2627 West Florida Ave., Hemet 92545
Type: Private, proprietary
Degrees: C
Phone: (909) 766-5759
Inst. Accred.: NACCAS (1999/2002)

Image Schools of Cosmetology, Inc.
13070 Palm Dr., Desert Hot Springs 92240
Type: Private, proprietary
Degrees: C
Phone: (760) 251-5373
Inst. Accred.: NACCAS (1999/2002)

Institute for Business & Technology
2400 Walsh Ave., Santa Clara 95050
Type: Private, proprietary
Degrees: C
URL: http://www.ibttech.com
Phone: (408) 727-1060
Inst. Accred.: ACCSCT (1979/2002)

Institute of Network Technology
2727 East Willow St., Signal Hill 90806
Type: Private, proprietary
Degrees: C
Phone: (562) 424-9200
Inst. Accred.: ACCSCT (2001, Probation)

Institute of Technology
731 West Shaw Ave., Clovis 93612
Type: Private, proprietary
Degrees: C
URL: http://www.it-colleges.com
Phone: (559) 297-4500
Inst. Accred.: ACCSCT (1991/2001)

Modesto Campus
5737 Stoddard Rd., Modesto 95356
Phone: (209) 545-3100

Roseville Campus
333 Sunrise Ave., Ste. 400, Roseville 95661
Phone: (800) 939-9005

Sacramento Campus
3695 Bleckely St., Sacramento 95655
Phone: (916) 363-4300

InterCoast Colleges
1631 North Bristol St., Ste. 200, Santa Ana 92706
Type: Private, proprietary
Degrees: C
URL: http://www.intercoastcolleges.com
Phone: (714) 560-6900   *Calendar:* Sem. plan
Inst. Accred.: ACCET (1988/2004)

Burbank Campus
401 South Glenoaks Blvd., Ste. 211, Burbank 91502
Phone: (818) 500-8400

Riverside Campus
1115 Spruce St., Ste. C, Riverside 92507
Phone: (909) 779-0700

West Covina Campus
1400 West Covina Pkwy., Second Flr., West Covina 91790-2731
Phone: (626) 337-6800

International Academy of Cosmetology
4085 Tweedy Blvd., South Gate 90280
Type: Private, proprietary
Degrees: C
URL: http://www.internationalacademyof cosmetology.com
Phone: (323) 249-0270
Inst. Accred.: NACCAS (2005)

International Center for American English
1012 Prospect St., #200, La Jolla 92037
Type: Private, proprietary
Degrees: C
URL: http://www.icae-lajolla.com
Phone: (858) 456-1212
Inst. Accred.: ACCET (1993/2001)

International Christian Education
3807 Wilshire Blvd., Ste. 730, Los Angeles 90010
Type: Private, proprietary
Degrees: C
Phone: (213) 368-0316
Inst. Accred.: ACCSCT (2001)

International School of Beauty, Inc.
72-261 State Hwy. 111, Ste. 121-B, Palm Desert 92260
Type: Private, proprietary
Degrees: C
URL: http://www.internationalschoolofbeauty.com
Phone: (760) 674-1624
Inst. Accred.: NACCAS (2005)

International School of Cosmetology, Inc.
13613 Hawthorne Blvd., Hawthorne 90250
Type: Private, proprietary
Degrees: C
Phone: (310) 973-7774
Inst. Accred.: NACCAS (1979/2002)

INTRAX English Institute
2226 Bush St., San Francisco 94115
Type: Private, proprietary
Degrees: C
URL: http://www.intraxenglish.com
Phone: (415) 434-1221
Inst. Accred.: ACCET (1996/2005)

Chicago Campus
174 North Michigan Ave., 2nd Flr., Chicago, IL 60601
Phone: (312) 236-3208

San Diego Campus
1250 Sixth Ave., Ste. 300A, San Diego 92101
Phone: (619) 702-6300

San Francisco Campus
551 Sutter St., San Francisco 94105
Phone: (415) 835-4766

Ivory Dental Technology College
13800 Beach Blvd., Westminster 92683
Type: Private, proprietary
Degrees: C
URL: http://www.ivorydentalcollege.com
Phone: (714) 899-2038
Inst. Accred.: ACCSCT (1998/2003)

James Albert School of Cosmetology
281 East 17th St., Costa Mesa 92627
Type: Private, proprietary
Degrees: C
Phone: (949) 642-0606
Inst. Accred.: NACCAS (1999/2002)

Anaheim Campus
2289 West Ball Rd., Anaheim 92804
Phone: (714) 774-8736

Je Boutique College of Beauty
1073 East Main St., El Cajon 92021
Type: Private, proprietary
Degrees: C
URL: http://www.sandiegobeautyacademy.com
Phone: (619) 442-3407
Inst. Accred.: NACCAS (1974/2001)

John Tracy Clinic
806 West Adams Blvd., Los Angeles 90007
Type: Private, proprietary
Degrees: C
URL: http://www.jtc.org
Phone: (213) 748-5481
Inst. Accred.: DETC (1965/2004)

John Wesley International Barber and Beauty College
717 Pine Ave., Long Beach 90813
Type: Private, proprietary
Degrees: C
URL: http://www.johnwesleybarberandbeauty.com
Phone: (562) 435-7060
Inst. Accred.: NACCAS (1994/2002)

Joint Intelligence Training Activity, Pacific
3955 North Harbor Dr., San Diego 92102-1031
Type: Public, federal
Degrees: C
URL: https://www.fitcpac.navy.mil
Phone: (619) 524-5814
Inst. Accred.: COE (2002)

Kensington College
2428 North Grand Ave., Ste. D, Santa Ana 92705-8708
Type: Private, proprietary
Degrees: C
Phone: (714) 542-8086
Inst. Accred.: ACICS (1998/2001)

Kim Anh Academy of Beauty
8528 Westminster Blvd., Westminster 92683
Type: Private, proprietary
Degrees: C
Phone: (714) 741-0700
Inst. Accred.: NACCAS (1998/2001)

Garden Grove Campus
12141 Brookhurst St., Ste. 101, Garden Grove 92840
Phone: (714) 741-0700

Ladera Career Paths Training Center
6820 La Tijera Blvd., Ste. 217, Los Angeles 90045
Type: Private, proprietary
Degrees: C
URL: http://www.laderacareerpathsinc.com
Phone: (310) 568-0244
Inst. Accred.: ACCSCT (2004)

Lake Forest Beauty College
23600 Rockfield Blvd., Ste. C-3, Lake Forest 92630
Type: Private, proprietary
Degrees: C
Phone: (949) 951-8883
Inst. Accred.: NACCAS (1983/2001)

Lancaster Beauty School
44646 North 10th St. West, Lancaster 93534
Type: Private, proprietary
Degrees: C
URL: http://www.lancasterbeautyschool.com
Phone: (661) 948-1672
Inst. Accred.: NACCAS (1975/2002)

Language Studies International
1706 Fifth Ave., 3rd Flr., San Diego 92101
Type: Private, proprietary
Degrees: C
URL: http://www.lsi.edu/englisch
Phone: (619) 234-2881
Inst. Accred.: ACCET (1997/2005)

Berkeley Campus
2015 Center St., Berkeley 94704
Phone: (510) 841-4695

Boston Campus
105 Beach St., Boston, MA 2111
Phone: (617) 542-3600

New York Campus
75 Varick St., New York, NY
Phone: (212) 965-9940

Learning Tree University
20916 Knapp St., Chatsworth 91311
Type: Private, proprietary
Degrees: C
URL: http://www.ltu.org
Phone: (818) 882-5599
Inst. Accred.: ACCET (1986/2004)

Costa Mesa Campus
265 Mccormick Ave., Costa Mesa 92626-3308
Phone: (714) 427-0588

Leicester School
1940 South Figueroa St., Los Angeles 90007
Type: Private, independent
Degrees: C
Phone: (213) 746-7666
Inst. Accred.: ACCSCT (1992/2004, Probation)

Liberty Training Institute
2706 Wilshire Blvd., 2nd Flr., Los Angeles 90057
Type: Private, proprietary
Degrees: C
URL: http://www.vocrehab.net/liberty
Phone: (213) 383-9545
Inst. Accred.: ACCSCT (2001)

Lola Beauty College
11883 Valley View St., Garden Grove 92645
Type: Private, proprietary
Degrees: C
Phone: (714) 894-3366
Inst. Accred.: NACCAS (1977/2002)

Los Angeles ORT Technical Institute
6435 Wilshire Blvd., Los Angeles 90048
Type: Private, independent
Degrees: C
URL: http://www.laort.com
Phone: (323) 966-5444
Inst. Accred.: ACCET (1988/1999)

Chicago Campus
3050 West Touhy Ave., Chicago, IL 60645
Phone: (773) 761-5900

Valley Campus
15130 Ventura Blvd., Ste. 250, Sherman Oaks 91403-2122
Phone: (818) 382-6000

Los Angeles Recording Workshop
6690 Sunset Blvd., Hollywood 90028
Type: Private, proprietary
Degrees: C
URL: http://www.recordingcareer.com
Phone: (323) 464-5200
Inst. Accred.: ACCET (1989/2001)

Lyle's Bakersfield College of Beauty
2935 F St., Bakersfield 93301
Type: Private, proprietary
Degrees: C
Phone: (661) 327-9784
Inst. Accred.: NACCAS (1975/2005)

Lyle's College of Beauty
6735 North First St., Ste. 112, Fresno 93710
Type: Private, proprietary
Degrees: C
Phone: (559) 431-6060
Inst. Accred.: NACCAS (1994/2002)

Lyle's Fresno College of Beauty
3125 West Shaw Ave., Fresno 93711
Type: Private, proprietary
Degrees: C
Phone: (559) 222-6060
Inst. Accred.: NACCAS (1974/2005)

Lytle's Redwood Empire Beauty College, Inc.
186 Wikiup Dr., Santa Rosa 95403
Type: Private, proprietary
Degrees: C
URL: http://www.lytles-rebc.com
Phone: (707) 545-8490
Inst. Accred.: NACCAS (1976/2002)

Madera Beauty College
200 West Olive Ave., Ste. A, Madera 93637
Type: Private, proprietary
Degrees: C
Phone: (559) 673-9201
Inst. Accred.: NACCAS (1977/2004)

Make-Up Designory
129 South San Fernando Blvd., Burbank 91502
Type: Private, proprietary
Degrees: C
URL: http://www.makeupschool.com
Phone: (818)729-9420
Inst. Accred.: ACCSCT (2003)

Manchester Beauty College
3756 North Blackstone Ave., Fresno 93726
Type: Private, proprietary
Degrees: C
Phone: (559) 224-4242
Inst. Accred.: NACCAS (1974/2005)

Maria Montessori Teacher Training Center
5331 Dent Ave., San Jose 95118
Type: Private, independent
Degrees: C
Phone: (408) 723-5140
Inst. Accred.: MACTE (2005)

Marian Health Careers Center
3325 Wilshire Blvd., Ste. 1010, Los Angeles 90010
Type: Private, proprietary
Degrees: C
URL: http://www.mariancollege-california.com
Phone: (213) 388-3566
Inst. Accred.: ABHES (1999/2002)

Van Nuys Campus
5900 North Sepulveda Blvd., Ste. 101, Van Nuys 91411
Phone: (818) 782-6163

Maric College—Anaheim
1360 South Anaheim Blvd., Anaheim 92805
Type: Private, proprietary
Degrees: C
URL: http://www.ceicollege.com
Phone: (714) 758-1500
Inst. Accred.: ACICS (1991/2005)

San Fernando Valley Campus
14355 Roscoe Blvd., Panorama City 91402
Phone: (818) 672-8907

Maric College—Bakersfield
1914 Wible Rd., Bakersfield 93304
Type: Private, proprietary
System: Kaplan Higher Education Corporation
Degrees: C
URL: http://www.mariccollege.edu
Phone: (866) 574-5550
Inst. Accred.: ACICS (2004)

Maric College—Los Angeles
3699 Wilshire Blvd., Ste. 420, Los Angeles 90010
Type: Private, proprietary
Degrees: C
URL: http://www.mariccollege.edu
Phone: (213) 351-2000
Inst. Accred.: ACCET (1994/2001)

Carson Campus
20700 Avalon Blvd., Ste. 210, Carson 90746
Phone: (310) 532-6328

East County Campus
6160 Mission Gorge Rd., Ste. 108, San Diego 92120
Phone: (619) 282-9000

Irwindale Campus
4900 Rivergrade Rd., Bldg. E, Irwindale 91706
Phone: (626) 338-8886

Palm Springs Campus
2475 East Tahquitz Canyon Way, Palm Springs 92262
Phone: (760) 327-4562

Pomona Campus
980 Corporate Center Dr., Pomona 91768-2643
Phone: (909) 865-9008

Riverside Campus
1635 Spruce St., Riverside 92507
Phone: (909) 276-1704

Maric College—Sacramento
4330 Watt Ave., Ste. 400, Sacramento 95660
Type: Private, proprietary
System: Kaplan Higher Education Corporation
Degrees: C   *Enroll:* 378
URL: http://www.californiacollege.com
Phone: (916) 649-8168   *Calendar:* Qtr. plan
Inst. Accred.: ACICS (1986/2004)

Maric College—Stockton
722 West March Ln., Stockton 95207
Type: Private, proprietary
System: Kaplan Higher Education Corporation
Degrees: C
URL: http://www.mariccollege.edu
Phone: (209) 462-8777   *Calendar:* Qtr. plan
Inst. Accred.: ACCSCT (2004)
Prog. Accred.: Medical Assisting (ABHES)

Marinello School of Beauty—City of Industry
1600 South Azusa Ave., Ste. 244, City of Industry 91748
Type: Private, proprietary
Degrees: C
URL: http://www.marinello.com
Phone: (626) 965-2532
Inst. Accred.: NACCAS (1975/2001)

Marinello School of Beauty—Eagle Rock
2700 Colorado Blvd., Eagle Rock Plaza, #266, Eagle Rock 90041
Type: Private, proprietary
Degrees: C
URL: http://www.marinello.com
Phone: (323) 254-6226
Inst. Accred.: NACCAS (1968/2004)

Marinello School of Beauty—East Los Angeles
1241 South Soto St., Ste. 101, Los Angeles 90023
Type: Private, proprietary
Degrees: C
URL: http://www.marinello.com
Phone: (323) 980-9253
Inst. Accred.: NACCAS (1968/2004)

Marinello School of Beauty—Huntington Beach
19022 Brookhurst St., Huntington Beach 92646
Type: Private, proprietary
Degrees: C
URL: http://www.marinello.com
Phone: (714) 962-8831
Inst. Accred.: NACCAS (2005)

Marinello School of Beauty—Inglewood
240 South Market St., Inglewood 90301
Type: Private, proprietary
Degrees: C
URL: http://www.marinello.com
Phone: (310) 674-8100
Inst. Accred.: NACCAS (1968/2004)

Marinello School of Beauty—Lake Forest
23635 El Toro Rd., Ste. K, Lake Forest 92630
Type: Private, proprietary
Degrees: C
URL: http://www.marinello.com
Phone: (949) 586-4900
Inst. Accred.: NACCAS (1976/2001)

Marinello School of Beauty—Moreno Valley
24741 Alessandro Blvd., Moreno Valley 92553
Type: Private, proprietary
Degrees: C
URL: http://www.marinello.com
Phone: (951) 247-2047
Inst. Accred.: NACCAS (1976/2005)

Marinello School of Beauty—North Hollywood
6219 Laurel Canyon Blvd., North Hollywood 91606
Type: Private, proprietary
Degrees: C
URL: http://www.marinello.com
Phone: (818) 980-1300
Inst. Accred.: NACCAS (1968/2005)

Marinello School of Beauty—Ontario
940 North Mountain Ave., Ontario 91762
Type: Private, proprietary
Degrees: C
URL: http://www.marinello.com
Phone: (909) 984-5884
Inst. Accred.: NACCAS (1972/2003)

Marinello School of Beauty—Paramount
8527 Alondra Blvd., Ste. 129, Paramount 90723
Type: Private, proprietary
Degrees: C
URL: http://www.marinello.com
Phone: (562) 531-1800
Inst. Accred.: NACCAS (1983/2001)

Marinello School of Beauty—Reseda
18442 Sherman Way, Reseda 91335
Type: Private, proprietary
Degrees: C
URL: http://www.marinello.com
Phone: (818) 881-2521
Inst. Accred.: NACCAS (1968/2005)

Marinello School of Beauty—San Bernadino
721 West 2nd St., Ste. E, San Bernardino 92410
Type: Private, proprietary
Degrees: C
URL: http://www.marinello.com
Phone: (909) 884-8747
Inst. Accred.: NACCAS (1968/2003)

Marinello School of Beauty—San Diego
1226 University Ave., San Diego 92103
Type: Private, proprietary
Degrees: C
URL: http://www.marinello.com
Phone: (619) 298-7187
Inst. Accred.: NACCAS (1968/2004)

Marinello School of Beauty—West Covina
118 Plaza Dr., West Covina 91790
Type: Private, proprietary
Degrees: C
URL: http://www.marinello.com
Phone: (626) 962-1021
Inst. Accred.: NACCAS (1968/2005)

Marinello School of Beauty—Whittier
6538 Greenleaf Ave., Whittier 90601
Type: Private, proprietary
Degrees: C
URL: http://www.marinello.com
Phone: (562) 698-0068
Inst. Accred.: NACCAS (1967/2002)

Marinello School of Beauty—Wilshire West
6111 Wilshire Blvd., Los Angeles 90048
Type: Private, proprietary
Degrees: C
URL: http://www.marinello.com
Phone: (323) 938-2005
Inst. Accred.: NACCAS (1968/2004)

MCed Career College
2002 North Gateway Blvd., Fresno 93727
Type: Private, proprietary
Degrees: C
URL: http://www.mced.com
Phone: (559) 456-0623
Inst. Accred.: ACCSCT (1994/2004)

Medical Institute
5170 Santa Monica Blvd., Los Angeles 90029
Type: Private, proprietary
Degrees: C
Phone: (323) 663-2700
Inst. Accred.: COE (2004)

Miss Marty's Hair Academy and Esthetics Institute
1087 Mission St., San Francisco 94103
Type: Private, proprietary
Degrees: C
URL: http://www.missmartys.com
Phone: (415) 227-4240
Inst. Accred.: NACCAS (1986/2002)

Modern Beauty Academy
699 South C St., Oxnard 93030
Type: Private, proprietary
Degrees: C
Phone: (541) 955-4741
Inst. Accred.: NACCAS (1972/2003)

Modern Technology School
1232 East Katella Ave., Anaheim 92805
Type: Private, proprietary
Degrees: C
Phone: (714) 978-7702
Inst. Accred.: ACCSCT (1988/2003)

Mojave Barber College
15505 7th St., Victorville 92392
Type: Private, proprietary
Degrees: C
URL: http://www.mojavebarbercollege.com
Phone: (760) 955-2934
Inst. Accred.: NACCAS (2005)

Moler Barber College
3500 Broadway St., Oakland 94611-5729
Type: Private, proprietary
Degrees: C
Phone: (510) 652-4177
Inst. Accred.: ACCSCT (1980/2001)

Montebello Beauty College
2201 West Whittier Blvd., Montebello 90640
Type: Private, proprietary
Degrees: C
Phone: (323) 727-7851
Inst. Accred.: NACCAS (1986/2004)

Monterey Park College
583 South Monterey Pass Rd., Monterey Park 91754
Type: Private, proprietary
Degrees: C
URL: http://www.montereyparkcollege.com
Phone: (626) 576-2444
Inst. Accred.: ACICS (1994/2003)

Stanton Campus
12362 Beach Blvd., Ste. 100, Stanton 90680-3900
Phone: (714) 901-9447

Walnut Campus
20265 Valley Blvd., Ste. F-1, Walnut 91789
Phone: (909) 598-1994

Montessori Institute of Advanced Studies
1101 Walpert St., Hayward 94541-6705
Type: Private, independent
Degrees: C
URL: http://www.montessori-training.com/MIAS.htm
Phone: (510) 581-3724
Inst. Accred.: MACTE (2001)

Montessori Teacher Edcuation Center— San Francisco Bay Area
16492 Foothill Blvd., San Leandro 94578
Type: Private, independent
Degrees: C
URL: http://www.montessoritec-sf.com
Phone: (510) 278-1115
Inst. Accred.: MACTE (1999)

Montessori Teachers College of San Diego
4544 Pocahontas Ave., San Diego 92117
Type: Public, independent
Degrees: C
URL: http://www.sandiego-ncme.org
Phone: (858) 270-9350
Inst. Accred.: MACTE (2001)

Montessori Western Teacher Training
6202 Cerulean Ave., Garden Grove 92845-2711
Type: Private, independent
Degrees: C
Phone: (714) 897-3833
Inst. Accred.: MACTE (2001)

MTI Business College of Stockton Inc.
6006 North El Dorado St., Stockton 95207-4349
Type: Private, proprietary
Degrees: C
URL: http://www.mtistockton.com
Phone: (209) 957-3030
Inst. Accred.: ACCSCT (1987/2004)

MTMA Schools, Inc.
1313 P St., Ste. 205, Fresno 93721
Type: Private, proprietary
Degrees: C
URL: http://www.mtmaschools.com
Phone: (559) 268-0938
Inst. Accred.: ACCET (2001/2005)

Mueller College of Holistic Massage Therapies
4607 Park Blvd., San Diego 92116-2630
Type: Private, proprietary
Degrees: C
URL: http://www.muellercollege.com
Phone: (619) 291-9811
Inst. Accred.: CMTA (2001/2004)

My-Le's Beauty College
5972 Stockton Blvd., Sacramento 95824
Type: Private, proprietary
Degrees: C
Phone: (916) 422-0223
Inst. Accred.: ACCSCT (1999/2004)

National Career Education
6060 Sunrise Vista Dr., Ste. 3000, Citrus Heights 95610-7053
Type: Private, proprietary
Degrees: C
URL: http://www.ncecollege.org
Phone: (916) 969-4900
Inst. Accred.: ACCSCT (1986/2005)

National Holistic Institute
5900 Hollis St., Ste. J, Emeryville
Type: Private, proprietary
Degrees: C
URL: http://www.nhimassage.com
Phone: (510) 547-6442
Inst. Accred.: ACCET (1987/2005)

National Institute of Technology—San Jose
235 Charcot Ave., San Jose 95131
Type: Private, proprietary
Degrees: C
URL: http://www.cci.edu
Phone: (408) 441-6990
Inst. Accred.: ACCET (1994/2003)

National Polytechnic College
2465 West Whittier Blvd., Ste. 201, Montebello 90640
Type: Private, proprietary
Degrees: C
Phone: (323) 728-9636
Inst. Accred.: ACCSCT (2003)

Newberry School of Beauty
16860 Devonshire St., Granada Hills 91344
Type: Private, proprietary
Degrees: C
Phone: (818) 366-3211
Inst. Accred.: NACCAS (1975/2001)

Newbridge College
1840 East 17th St., Santa Ana 92705
Type: Private, proprietary
Degrees: C
URL: http://newbridgecollege.edu
Phone: (714) 550-8000
Inst. Accred.: ACCSCT (1988/2001)
Prog. Accred.: Surgical Technology

North Adrian's Beauty College
124 Floyd Ave., Modesto 95350
Type: Private, proprietary
Degrees: C
Phone: (209) 526-2040
Inst. Accred.: NACCAS (1975/2005)

North-West College
2121 West Garvey Ave., West Covina 91790-2097
Type: Private, proprietary
Degrees: C
URL: http://www.northwestcollege.com
Phone: (626) 960-5046
Inst. Accred.: ACCSCT (1973/2004)

Glendale Campus
221 North Brand, Lower Level, Glendale 91205-1109
Phone: (818) 242-0205

Pasadena Campus
530 East Union Ave., Pasadena 91101-1744
Phone: (626) 796-5815

Pomona Campus
134 West Holt Ave., Pomona 91768-3199
Phone: (909) 623-1552

Riverside Campus
10020 Indiana Ave., Ste. 202, Second Flr., Riverside 92503
Phone: (951) 351-7750

NTMA Training Centers of Southern California
14926 Bloomfield Ave., Norwalk 90650
Type: Private, independent
Degrees: C
URL: http://www.ntmatrainingcenters.org
Phone: (562) 921-3722
Inst. Accred.: ACCSCT (2001)

Inland Empire Training Center
1717 South Grove Ave., Ontario 91761
Phone: (909) 947-9363

Orange County Training Center
3036 Enterprise St., Costa Mesa 92626
Phone: (714) 545-3202

Occupational Training Services
8799 Balboa Ave., Ste. 100, San Diego 92123
Type: Private, independent
Degrees: C
URL: http://www.ots-sdchc.org
Phone: (858) 560-0411
Inst. Accred.: ACCSCT (1997/2003 Probation)

Oceanside College of Beauty
1575 South Coast Hwy., Oceanside 92054
Type: Private, proprietary
Degrees: C
URL: http://www.ocb.edu
Phone: (760) 757-6161
Inst. Accred.: NACCAS (1976/2001)

OSULA Education Center
3921 Laurel Canyon Blvd., Studio City 91604
Type: Private, independent
Degrees: C
URL: http://www.osula.com
Phone: (818) 509-1484
Inst. Accred.: ACCET (2002)

Oxman College of San Francisco
375 3rd Ave., San Francisco 94118
Type: Private, proprietary
Degrees: C
URL: http://oxmancollege.com
Phone: (415) 751-6461
Inst. Accred.: COE (2004)

Los Angeles Campus
5250 West Century Blvd., Los Angeles 90045
Phone: (415) 751-6461

Pacific College
3160 Redhill Ave., Costa Mesa 92626
Type: Private, proprietary
Degrees: C
Phone: (714) 662-4402
Inst. Accred.: ACCSCT (1998/2003)

Palace Beauty College
1517 South Western Ave., Los Angeles 90006
Type: Private, proprietary
Degrees: C
URL: http://palacebeautycollege.com
Phone: (323) 731-2075
Inst. Accred.: NACCAS (2005)

Palomar Institute of Cosmetology
355 Via Vera Cruz #3, San Marcos 92069
Type: Private, proprietary
Degrees: C
URL: http://pic.edu
Phone: (760) 744-7900
Inst. Accred.: NACCAS (1985/2005)

Paris Beauty College
1950 East Market St., Concord 94520
Type: Private, proprietary
Degrees: C
URL: http://www.parisbeautycollege.com
Phone: (925) 685-7600
Inst. Accred.: NACCAS (1976/2003)

PCI College
17215 Studebaker Rd., Ste. 310, Cerritos 90703
Type: Private, proprietary
Degrees: C
URL: http://www.pci-ed.com
Phone: (562) 916-5055
Inst. Accred.: ACCSCT (2000/2005)

POLY Languages Institute
4201 Wilshire Blvd., Ste. 114, Los Angeles 90010
Type: Private, proprietary
Degrees: C
URL: http://www.polylanguages.com
Phone: (323) 933-9399
Inst. Accred.: ACCET (2000/2004)

Irvine Campus
4255 Campus Dr., Ste. A-200, Irvine 92612
Phone: (949) 737-7628

Pasadena Campus
350 South Lake Ave., Ste. 200, Pasadena 91101
Phone: (626) 499-4441

Poway Academy of Hair Design
13266 Poway Rd., Poway 92064
Type: Private, proprietary
Degrees: C
URL: http://www.sandiegobeautyacademy.com
Phone: (858) 748-1490
Inst. Accred.: NACCAS (1986/2004)

Premiere Career College
12901 Ramona Blvd., Ste. D, Irwindale 91706
Type: Private, proprietary
Degrees: C
URL: http://www.premcol.com
Phone: (626) 814-2080
Inst. Accred.: ACICS (1995/2004)
Prog. Accred.: Surgical Technology

Professional Institute of Beauty
10801 East Valley Mall, El Monte 91731
Type: Private, proprietary
Degrees: C
URL: http://www.pibschool.com
Phone: (626) 443-9401
Inst. Accred.: NACCAS (1975/2001)

Richard's Beauty College
200 North Euclid Ave., Ontario 91712
Type: Private, proprietary
Degrees: C
Phone: (909) 988-7584
Inst. Accred.: NACCAS (1971/2002)

Robert M. Scherer & Associates, Inc.
1787 Tribute Rd., Ste. K, Sacramento 95815
Type: Private, proprietary
Degrees: C
URL: http://www.sacramento.dalecarnegie.com
Phone: (916) 929-3911
Inst. Accred.: ACCET (1975/2001)

Rosemead Beauty School, Inc.
8531 East Valley Blvd., Rosemead 91770
Type: Private, proprietary
Degrees: C
Phone: (626) 286-2147
Inst. Accred.: NACCAS (1986/2001)

Ross Business Institute
229 East Palm Ave., 2nd Flr., Burbank 91502
Type: Private, proprietary
Degrees: C
URL: http://www.rbiworks.com
Phone: (818) 557-7677
Inst. Accred.: ACICS (1998/2001)

Royale College of Beauty
27485 Commerce Center Dr., Temecula 92590
Type: Private, proprietary
Degrees: C
URL: http://www.beautyschool.com/royale
Phone: (909) 676-0833
Inst. Accred.: NACCAS (1991/2001)

Saint Francis Career College
3630 East Imperial Hwy., Lynwood 90262
Type: Private, proprietary
Degrees: C
Phone: (310) 603-1830
Inst. Accred.: ACCSCT (1998/2003)

Saint Giles College
One Hallidie Plaza, Ste. 350, San Francisco 94102
Type: Private, independent
Degrees: C
URL: http://www.stgiles-usa.com
Phone: (415) 788-3552
Inst. Accred.: CEA (2002)

Salon Success Academy
107 North McKinley St., Ste. 109, Corona 92879
Type: Private, proprietary
Degrees: C
Phone: (909) 736-9725
Inst. Accred.: NACCAS (1976/2003)

San Fernando Beauty Academy, Inc.
8700 Van Nuys Blvd., Panorama City 91402
Type: Private, proprietary
Degrees: C
URL: http://www.sanfernandobeautyacademy.com
Phone: (818) 894-9550
Inst. Accred.: NACCAS (1974/2003)

Lancaster Campus
2733 West Ave. L, Lancaster 93536
Phone: (661) 718-8410

Santa Monica Montessori Institute
1909 Colorado Ave., Santa Monica 90404
Type: Private, independent
Degrees: C
Phone: (310) 829-3551
Inst. Accred.: MACTE (2000/2005)

Scandinavian Aviation Academy
8665 Gibbs Dr., Ste. 110, San Diego 92123
Type: Private, proprietary
Degrees: C
URL: http://www.scanavia.com
Phone: (858) 278-5770
Inst. Accred.: ACCET (1999/2005)

Sierra Academy of Aeronautics Technical Institute
Oakland International Airport, PO Box 2429, Oakland 94614-0429
Type: Private, proprietary
Degrees: C
URL: http://www.sierraacademy.com
Phone: (510) 568-6100
Inst. Accred.: ACCSCT (1987/2002)

Sierra College of Beauty
1340 West 18th St., Merced 95340
Type: Private, proprietary
Degrees: C
Phone: (209) 723-2989
Inst. Accred.: NACCAS (1988/2003)

Sierra Valley Business College
4747 North First St., Building D, Fresno 93726
Type: Private, proprietary
Degrees: C
Phone: (209) 222-0947
Inst. Accred.: ACICS (1981/2003)

Sound Master Recording Engineer School/Audio-Video Institute
10747 Magnolia Blvd., North Hollywood 91601
Type: Private, proprietary
Degrees: C
Phone: (323) 650-8000
Inst. Accred.: ACCET (1989/2005)

Stanbridge College
2041 Business Center Dr., Ste. 107, Irvine 92612
Type: Private, proprietary
Degrees: C
URL: http://www1.stanbridge.edu
Phone: (949) 794-9090
Inst. Accred.: ACCSCT (2004)

Summit Career College, Inc.
1250 East Cooley Dr., Colton 92324
Type: Private, proprietary
Degrees: C
URL: http://www.summitcollege.com
Phone: (909) 422-8950
Inst. Accred.: ACCET (1994/2005)

Anaheim Campus
1830 West Romneya Dr., Anaheim 92801-1833
Phone: (714) 635-6232

Thanh Le College, School of Cosmetology
12875 Chapman Ave., Garden Grove 92640
Type: Private, proprietary
Degrees: C
Phone: (714) 748-7019
Inst. Accred.: NACCAS (1983/2003)

Thomas J. Kiblen & Associates
3530 Atlantic Ave., Ste. 200, Long Beach 90807-4569
Type: Private, proprietary
Degrees: C
URL: http://www.longbeach.dalecarnegie.com
Phone: (562) 427-1040
Inst. Accred.: ACCET (1979/2005)

Thuy Princess Beauty College
252 East Second St., Pomona 91766
Type: Private, proprietary
Degrees: C
Phone: (909) 620-6893
Inst. Accred.: NACCAS (2005)

Transworld Schools
701 Sutter St., 2nd Flr., San Francisco 94109
Type: Private, proprietary
Degrees: C
URL: http://www.transworldschools.com
Phone: (415) 928-2835
Inst. Accred.: ACCET (2003)

Truck Marketing Institute
1090 Eugenia Place, Ste. 101, Carpinteria 93014-5000
Type: Private, proprietary
Degrees: C
URL: http://www.truckmarketinginstitute.com
Phone: (805) 684-4558
Inst. Accred.: DETC (1968/2005)

Tulare Beauty College
325 North Gateway Dr., Madera 93637
Type: Private, proprietary
Degrees: C
Phone: (209) 688-2901
Inst. Accred.: NACCAS (1974/2000)

United Beauty College, Inc.
10229 Lower Azusa Rd., Temple City 91780
Type: Private, proprietary
Degrees: C
URL: http://www.unitedbeautycollege.com
Phone: (626) 443-0900
Inst. Accred.: NACCAS (2001/2004)

United Education Institute
3020 Wilshire Blvd., Ste. 250, Los Angeles 90010
Type: Private, proprietary
Degrees: C
URL: http://www.uei-edu.com
Phone: (213) 427-3700
Inst. Accred.: ACCET (1988/2005)

Chula Vista Campus
310 Third Ave., Chula Vista 91910
Phone: (619) 409-4111

El Monte Campus
9330 Flair Dr., Ste. 100, El Monte 91731
Phone: (949) 794-9999

Huntington Park Capmus
6812 Pacific Blvd., Huntington Park 90255
Phone: (323) 277-8000

Ontario Campus
3380 Shelby St., Ste. 150, Ontario 91764
Phone: (909) 476-2424

San Bernardino Campus
295 East Caroline St., Ste. E, San Bernardino 92408
Phone: (909) 554-1999

San Diego Campus
1323 6th Ave., San Diego 92101
Phone: (619) 544-9800

Van Nuys Campus
7335 Van Nuys Blvd., Van Nuys 91405
Phone: (818) 756-1200

United Car and Truck Driving School
2425 Camino del Rio South, San Diego 92108
Type: Private, proprietary
Degrees: C
URL: http://www.drivetrucks.com
Phone: (619) 296-2020
Inst. Accred.: ACCSCT (2003)

Universal College of Beauty, Inc.— South Vermont Avenue
8619 South Vermont Ave., Los Angeles 90044
Type: Private, proprietary
Degrees: C
Phone: (323) 750-5750
Inst. Accred.: NACCAS (1975/2004)

Compton Campus
718 West Compton Blvd., Compton 90220
Phone: (310) 635-6969

Universal College of Beauty, Inc.— West 43rd Place
3419 West 43rd Place, Los Angeles 90008
Type: Private, proprietary
Degrees: C
Phone: (323) 298-0045
Inst. Accred.: NACCAS (1985/2004)

Valley Career College
878 Jackman St., El Cajon 92020
Type: Private, proprietary
Degrees: C
URL: http://www.valleycareercollege.com
Phone: (619) 593-5111   *Calendar:* Qtr. plan
Inst. Accred.: ACCET (1999/2002)

Victor Valley Beauty College
16515 Mojave Dr., Victorville 92392
Type: Private, proprietary
Degrees: C
URL: http://www.victorvalleybeautycollege.com
Phone: (760) 245-2522
Inst. Accred.: NACCAS (1976/2003)

Video Symphony EnterTraining, Inc.
731 North Hollywood Way, Burbank 91505-3183
Type: Private, proprietary
Degrees: C
URL: http://www.videosymphony.com
Phone: (818) 557-7200
Inst. Accred.: ACCET (2003)

Virginia Sewing Machines & School Center
1033 South Broadway St., Los Angeles 90015-4001
Type: Private, proprietary
Degrees: C
Phone: (213) 747-8292
Inst. Accred.: ACCET (1995/2003)

West Coast Ultrasound Institute
291 South La Cienega Blvd., Ste. 500, Beverly Hills
90211
Type: Private, proprietary
Degrees: C
URL: http://www.ultrasoundinstitute.com
Phone: (310) 289-5123
Inst. Accred.: ACCSCT (2001)

Westech College
500 West Mission Blvd., Pomona 91766-1532
Type: Private, proprietary
Degrees: C
URL: http://www.westech.edu
Phone: (909) 622-6486
Inst. Accred.: ACCSCT (1991/2003)

COLORADO

Academy of Beauty Culture
2992 North Ave., Grand Junction 81504
Type: Private, proprietary
Degrees: C
Phone: (970) 245-5570
Inst. Accred.: NACCAS (1981/2001)

Americana Beauty College II
3650 Austin Bluff Pkwy., Ste. 174, Colorado Springs 80918
Type: Private, proprietary
Degrees: C
URL: http://www.americanabeautycollege.com
Phone: (719) 598-4188
Inst. Accred.: NACCAS (1976/2003)

Artistic Beauty Colleges
3049-A West 74th Ave., Westminister 80030
Type: Private, proprietary
Degrees: C
URL: http://www.artisticbeautycolleges.com
Phone: (303) 428-5100
Inst. Accred.: NACCAS (1980/2005)

Aurora Campus
16800 East Mississippi Ave., Aurora 80017
Phone: (303) 745-6300

Littleton Campus
8996 West Bowles Ave., Stes. E-F, Littleton 80123
Phone: (303) 904-4400

Artistic Beauty Colleges—Denver
6520 Wadsworth Blvd., Ste. 209, Arvada 80003
Type: Private, proprietary
Degrees: C
URL: http://www.artisticbeautycolleges.com
Phone: (303) 455-0100
Inst. Accred.: NACCAS (1977/2002)

Artistic Beauty Colleges—Lakewood
1225 Wadsworth Blvd., Lakewood 80215
Type: Private, proprietary
Degrees: C
URL: http://www.artisticbeautycolleges.com
Phone: (303) 238-7501
Inst. Accred.: NACCAS (1972/2003)

Artistic Beauty Colleges—Thornton
3811 East 120th Ave., Thornton 80241
Type: Private, proprietary
Degrees: C
URL: http://www.artisticbeautycolleges.com
Phone: (303) 451-5808
Inst. Accred.: NACCAS (1981/2001)

At-Home Professions
2001 Lowe St., Fort Collins 80525
Type: Private, proprietary
Degrees: C
URL: http://www.ahpschools.com
Phone: (970) 225-6300
Inst. Accred.: DETC (2004)

Bridge Linguatec
915 South Colorado Blvd., Denver 80246
Type: Private, proprietary
Degrees: C
URL: http://www.bridgelinguatec.com
Phone: (303) 777-7783
Inst. Accred.: ACCET (1998/2004)

Center of Advanced Therapeutics
1212 South Broadway, Ste. 200, Denver 80210
Type: Private, proprietary
Degrees: C
URL: http://www.catinc.net
Phone: (303) 765-2201
Inst. Accred.: ACCSCT (2000/2005)

Colorado Institute of Taxidermy Training, Inc.
708 Royal Gorge Blvd., Canon City 81212
Type: Private, proprietary
Degrees: C
URL: http://www.coloinsttaxidermytrain.com
Phone: (719) 276-2883
Inst. Accred.: ACCSCT (2002)

Colorado School of English
331 14th St., Ste. 300, Denver 80202
Type: Private, proprietary
Degrees: C
URL: http://www.englishamerica.com
Phone: (720) 932-8900
Inst. Accred.: ACCET (1998/2004)

Corporate Change Catalysts
Dale Carnegie Training
5619 DTC Pkwy., Ste. 620, Greenwood Village 80111
Type: Private, proprietary
Degrees: C
URL: http://www.denver.dalecarnegie.com
Phone: (303) 964-8688
Inst. Accred.: ACCET (2004)

Culinary School of the Rockies
637 South Broadway, Ste. H, Boulder 80305
Type: Private, independent
Degrees: C
URL: http://www.cookingschoolrockies.com
Phone: (303) 494-7988
Inst. Accred.: ACCET (2002)

Cuttin Up Beauty Academy
8101 East Colfax Ave., Denver 80220
Type: Private, proprietary
Degrees: C
Phone: (303) 388-5700
Inst. Accred.: NACCAS (2005)

Delta-Montrose Technical College
1765 Hwy. 50, Delta 81416
Type: Public, state/local
Degrees: C
URL: http://www.dmavtc.edu
Phone: (970) 874-7671
Inst. Accred.: NCA-CASI (1977/2005)

Emily Griffith Opportunity School
1250 Welton St., Denver 80204
Type: Private, independent
Degrees: C
URL: http://www.egos-school.com
Phone: (303) 575-4700   *Calendar:* Sem. plan
Inst. Accred.: NCA-CASI (1926/2003)
Prog. Accred.: Dental Assisting, Medical Assisting
(CAAHEP)

Glenwood Beauty Academy
51241 Hwy. 6 & 24, West Glenwood Plaza, Ste. 1,
Glenwood Springs 81601
Type: Private, proprietary
Degrees: C
Phone: (970) 945-0485
Inst. Accred.: NACCAS (1984/2004)

Hair Dynamics Education Center
6464 South College Ave., Fort Collins 80525
Type: Private, proprietary
Degrees: C
Phone: (970) 223-9943
Inst. Accred.: NACCAS (1987/2002)

International Beauty Academy
1360 North Academy Blvd., Colorado Springs 80909
Type: Private, proprietary
Degrees: C
URL: http://www.csbeautyschools.com
Phone: (719) 597-1413
Inst. Accred.: NACCAS (1975/2000)

Language Consultants International, LLC
2055 South Oneida, Ste. 300, Denver 80224
Type: Private, proprietary
Degrees: C
URL: http://www.languageconsultants.org
Phone: (303) 756-0760
Inst. Accred.: ACCET (2000)

Massage Therapy Institute of Colorado
1441 York St., Ste. 301, Denver 80206-2127
Type: Private, proprietary
Degrees: C
URL: http://www.mtic-co.com
Phone: (303) 329-6345
Inst. Accred.: CMTA (2005)

MJM Institute of Cosmetology
1048 Independent Ave., Ste. A113, Grand Junction 81505
Type: Private, proprietary
Degrees: C
Phone: (970) 241-9060
Inst. Accred.: NACCAS (2001)

Ohio Center for Broadcasting—Colorado
5800 West Alameda Ave., Ste. A, Lakewood 80226
Type: Private, proprietary
Degrees: C
URL: http://www.beonair.com
Phone: (303) 937-7070
Inst. Accred.: ACCSCT (2001/2003)

San Juan Basin Technical College
33057 Hwy. 160, Mancos 81328
Type: Public, state/local
Degrees: C
URL: http://www.sjbtc.edu
Phone: (970) 565-8457   *Calendar:* Sem. plan
Inst. Accred.: NCA-CASI (1975/2005)

Spring Institute for Intercultural Learning
1610 Emerson St., Denver 80218
Type: Private, independent
Degrees: C
URL: http://www.spring-institute.org
Phone: (303) 863-0188
Inst. Accred.: ACCET (2001/2004)

Spring International Language Center, Inc.
5900 South Santa Fe Dr., Littleton 80120
Type: Private, proprietary
Degrees: C
URL: http://www.spring-usa.com
Phone: (303) 797-0100
Inst. Accred.: ACCET (2000/2005)

Denver Campus
900 Auraria Pkwy., Tivoli Bldg., #454, Auraria Higher
Education Center, Denver 80204
Phone: (303) 534-1616

Fayetteville Campus
300 Hotz Hall, University of Arkansas, Fayetteville, AR
72701
Phone: (479) 575-7600

T.H. Pickens Technical Center
500 Airport Blvd., Aurora 80011-9307
Type: Public, state/local
Degrees: C
URL: http://www.aps.k12.co.us/pickens
Phone: (303) 344-4910
Inst. Accred.: NCA-CASI (1975/2002)
Prog. Accred.: Dental Assisting, Respiratory Therapy
Technology

Technical Education College
2458 Waynoka Rd., Colorado Springs 80915
Type: Private, independent
Degrees: C
URL: http://www.technicaleducationcollege.com
Phone: (719) 597-8446
Inst. Accred.: NCA-CASI (2003)

Toni & Guy Hairdressing Academy
332 Main St., Colorado Springs 80911
Type: Private, proprietary
Degrees: C
Phone: (719) 390-9898
Inst. Accred.: ACCSCT (2001)

U.S. Career Institute
2001 Lowe St., Fort Collins 80525
Type: Private, proprietary
Degrees: C
URL: http://www.uscareerinstitute.com
Phone: (970) 207-4500
Inst. Accred.: DETC (2005)

Xenon International School of Hair Design III
2231 South Peoria St., Aurora 80014
Type: Private, proprietary
Degrees: C
URL: http://www.xenonintl.com
Phone: (303) 752-1560
Inst. Accred.: NACCAS (1990/2000)

CONNECTICUT

The Albert School
19 Hope St., Niantic 06357
Type: Private, proprietary
Degrees: C
URL: http://www.thealbertschool.com
Phone: (860) 739-2466
Inst. Accred.: NACCAS (2004)

American Academy of Cosmetology
109 South St., Danbury 6810
Type: Private, proprietary
Degrees: C
URL: http://www.americanacademyofcosmetology.com
Phone: (203) 744-0900
Inst. Accred.: NACCAS (1971/2004)

B. Dickson and Associates, LLC
21 Maple St., Naugatuck 06770
Type: Private, proprietary
Degrees: C
URL: http://www.westernct.dalecarnegie.com
Phone: (203) 723-9888
Inst. Accred.: ACCET (1975/2001)

Baran Institute of Technology
611 Day Hill Rd., Windsor 06095-0725
Type: Private, proprietary
Degrees: C
URL: http://www.baraninstitute.com
Phone: (800) 243-4242
Inst. Accred.: ACCSCT (1983/2003)

West Haven Campus
15 Kimberly Ave., West Haven 06516
Phone: (203) 934-7289

Branford Hall Career Institute
1 Summit Place, Branford 06405
Type: Private, proprietary
Degrees: C
URL: http://www.branfordhall.com
Phone: (203) 488-2525
Inst. Accred.: ACICS (1977/2002)
Prog. Accred.: Medical Assisting (CAAHEP)

Chicopee Campus
54 Center St., Chicopee, MA 01013
Phone: (413) 598-8300

Southington Campus
35 North Main St., Southington 06489
Phone: (860) 276-0600

Springfield Campus
112 Industry Ave., Springfield, MA 01104
Phone: (413) 781-2276
Prog. Accred.: Medical Assisting (ABHES)

Windsor Campus
995 Day Hill Rd., Windsor 06095
Phone: (860) 683-4900
Prog. Accred.: Medical Assisting (ABHES)

Brio Academy of Cosmetology
1000 Main St., East Hartford 06108-2220
Type: Private, proprietary
Degrees: C
URL: http://www.brioacademy.com
Phone: (860) 528-7178
Inst. Accred.: NACCAS (1971/2002)

Brio Academy of Cosmetology
1231 East Main St., Meriden 6450
Type: Private, proprietary
Degrees: C
URL: http://www.brioacademy.com
Phone: (203) 237-6683
Inst. Accred.: NACCAS (1975/2005)

Fairfield Campus
675 Kings Hwy. East, Fairfield 06824
Phone: (203) 331-0852

New Haven Campus
514 Orchard St., New Haven 06511
Phone: (203) 787-1264

Butler Business School
2710 North Ave., Bridgeport 06604
Type: Private, proprietary
Degrees: C
Phone: (203) 333-3601
Inst. Accred.: ACICS (1979/2001)

Connecticut Center for Massage Therapy
75 Kitts Ln., Newington 06111-3954
Type: Private, proprietary
Degrees: C
URL: http://www.ccmt.com
Phone: (860) 667-1886
Inst. Accred.: CMTA (1995/2005)

Groton Campus
1154 Poquonnock Rd., Groton 06340
Phone: (860) 446-2299
Prog. Accred.: Massage Therapy

Westport Campus
25 Sylvan Rd. South, Westport 06880
Phone: (877) 292-2268
Prog. Accred.: Massage Therapy

Connecticut Culinary Institute
230 Farmington Ave., Farmington 06032
Type: Private, proprietary
Degrees: C
URL: http://www.ctculinary.com
Phone: (860) 677-7869
Inst. Accred.: ACCSCT (1994/2004)
Prog. Accred.: Culinary Education

Suffield Campus
1760 Mapleton Ave., Suffield 06078
Phone: (860) 668-3500
Prog. Accred: Culinary Education

Connecticut Institute of Hair Design
1681 Meriden Rd., Wolcott 06716-3322
Type: Private, proprietary
Degrees: C
Phone: (203) 879-4247
Inst. Accred.: ACCSCT (1980/2004)

Connecticut School of Electronics
221 West Main St., Branford 06405-4049
Type: Private, proprietary
Degrees: C
URL: http://www.ctschoolofelectronics.com
Phone: (203) 624-2121　　　*Calendar:* Sem. plan
Inst. Accred.: ACCSCT (1968/2002)
Prog. Accred.: Medical Assisting (ABHES)

Connecticut Training Center
1137 Main St., East Hartford 06108-2236
Type: Private, independent
Degrees: C
URL: http://www.cttraining.org
Phone: (860) 291-9898
Inst. Accred.: ACICS (1998/2001)

Fox Institute of Business
99 South St., West Hartford 06110
Type: Private, proprietary
Degrees: C
URL: http://www.foxinstitute.com
Phone: (860) 947-2299　　　*Calendar:* Qtr. plan
Inst. Accred.: ACICS (1979/2001)
Prog. Accred.: Medical Assisting (CAAHEP)

Hartford Conservatory
834 Asylum Ave., Hartford 06105
Type: Private, independent
Degrees: C
URL: http://www.hartfordconservatory.org
Phone: (860) 246-2588　　　*Calendar:* Sem. plan
Inst. Accred.: NEASC-CTCI (1979/2005)

Industrial Management and Training Institute
233 Mill St., Waterbury 06706
Type: Private, proprietary
Degrees: C
URL: http://www.imtiusa.com
Phone: (203) 753-7910
Inst. Accred.: ACCSCT (1993/2004)

Leon Institute of Hair Design
111 Wall St., Bridgeport 6604
Type: Private, proprietary
Degrees: C
Phone: (203) 335-0364
Inst. Accred.: NACCAS (1975/2005)

M.J. Francoeur & Associates
8 Ellsworth Rd., West Hartford 6107
Type: Private, proprietary
Degrees: C
URL: http://www.hartford.dalecarnegie.com
Phone: (860) 232-6000
Inst. Accred.: ACCET (1978/2001)

New England Technical Institute of Connecticut
200 John Downey Dr., New Britain 06051-2904
Type: Private, proprietary
Degrees: C
URL: http://www.gonewenglandtech.com
Phone: (860) 225-8641
Inst. Accred.: ACCSCT (1983/2003)
Prog. Accred.: Medical Assisting (CAAHEP)

Center for Culinary Arts
8 Progress Dr., Shelton 06484
Phone: (203) 929-0592
Prog. Accred: Culinary Education

Hamden Campus
109 Sanford St., Hamden 06514
Phone: (203) 287-7300

New England Tractor Trailer Training School
32 Field Rd., Somers 06071-0326
Type: Private, proprietary
Degrees: C
URL: http://www.nettts.com
Phone: (860) 749-0711
Inst. Accred.: ACCSCT (1982/2003)

North Haven Academy
97 Washington Ave., North Haven 06473
Type: Private, proprietary
Degrees: C
URL: http://www.galmaracademy.com
Phone: (203) 985-0222
Inst. Accred.: NACCAS (1979/2004)

Nutmeg Conservatory for the Arts
58 Main St., Torrington 06790
Type: Private, independent
Degrees: C
URL: http://www.nutmegballet.org
Phone: (860) 482-4413
Inst. Accred.: NASD (1995/2002)

Porter and Chester Institute
670 Lordship Blvd., PO Box 364, Stratford 06615-7123
Type: Private, proprietary
Degrees: C
URL: http://www.porterchester.com
Phone: (203) 375-4463   *Calendar:* Qtr. plan
Inst. Accred.: ACCSCT (1972/2003)
Prog. Accred.: Medical Assisting (ABHES), Medical
  Assisting (CAAHEP)

Chicopee Campus
134 Dulong Circle, Chicopee, MA 01022
Phone: (413) 593-3339
Prog. Accred: Medical Assisting (CAAHEP)

Enfield Campus
138 Weymouth St., Enfield 06082-6028
Phone: (860) 741-2561
Prog. Accred: Dental Assisting

Watertown Campus
320 Sylvan Lake Rd., Watertown 06779-1400
Phone: (860) 274-9294
Prog. Accred: Medical Assisting (ABHES), Medical
  Assisting (CAAHEP)

Wethersfield Campus
125 Silas Deane Hwy., Wethersfield 06109-1238
Phone: (860) 529-2519
Prog. Accred: Medical Assisting (ABHES), Medical
  Assisting (CAAHEP)

Renasci Academy of Hair, Inc.
486 Bridgeport Ave., Milford 06460
Type: Private, proprietary
Degrees: C
URL: http://www.renasciacademy.com
Phone: (203) 878-4900
Inst. Accred.: NACCAS (1975/2004)

School of Dance Connecticut
Hartford Courant Arts Center, 224 Farmington Ave.,
Hartford 06105
Type: Private, independent
Degrees: C
URL: http://www.dancect.com
Phone: (860) 525-9396
Inst. Accred.: NASD (1982/1998)

Stone Academy
1315 Dixwell Ave., Hamden 06514
Type: Private, proprietary
Degrees: C
Phone: (203) 288-7474
Inst. Accred.: ACICS (1974/2001)
Prog. Accred.: Medical Assisting (CAAHEP)

Submarine Learning Center
PO Box 5029, Naval Submarine Base New London,
Groton 06349-5029
Type: Public, Federal
Degrees: C
URL: https://www.npdc.navy.mil/slc
Phone: (860) 694-1701
Inst. Accred.: COE (2004)

Westlawn Institute of Marine Technology
733 Summer St., Stamford 06901
Type: Private, proprietary
Degrees: C
URL: http://www.westlawn.org
Phone: (203) 359-0500
Inst. Accred.: DETC (1971/2002)

DELAWARE

Dawn Training Centre
3700 Lancaster Ave., Ste. 105, Wilmington 19805
Type: Private, proprietary
Degrees: C
URL: http://www.dawntrainingcentre.edu
Phone: (302) 575-1322
Inst. Accred.: ACCSCT (1990/2001)

Deep Muscle Therapy School
5317 Limestone Rd., Wilmington 19807
Type: Private, proprietary
Degrees: C
URL: http://www.dmtcmassage.com
Phone: (302) 239-1613
Inst. Accred.: ACCET (2000, Warning)

The Delaware Learning Institute of Cosmetology
Country Garden Business Center, Route 113, Ste. F2, Dagsboro 19939
Type: Private, proprietary
Degrees: C
URL: http://www.delawarecosmetology.com
Phone: (888) 663-1121
Inst. Accred.: NACCAS (2003)
Prog. Accred.: Massage Therapy

Delaware School of Hotel Management
3005 Philadelphia Pike, Claymont 19703
Type: Private, proprietary
Degrees: C
URL: http://www.delawareschoolofhotel.com
Phone: (302) 793-1101   *Calendar:* Sem. plan
Inst. Accred.: ACICS (2004)

Harrison Career Institute—Wilmington
631 West Newport Pike, Grayston Plaza, Wilmington 19804
Type: Private, proprietary
Degrees: C
URL: http://www.harrisoncareerinst.com
Phone: (302) 999-7827
Inst. Accred.: ACCSCT (1986/2002)

Allentown Campus
2102 Union Blvd., Allentown, PA 18103
Phone: (610) 434-9963

Montessori Institute for Teacher Education
PO Box 408, Yorklyn 19736
Type: Private, independent
Degrees: C
Phone: (610) 444-4643
Inst. Accred.: MACTE (1999)

The National Massage Therapy Institute
1601 Concord Pike, Stes. 82-84, Wilmington 19803
Type: Private, proprietary
Degrees: C
Phone: (888) 663-1121
Inst. Accred.: CMTA (2001/2005)

Schilling-Douglas School of Hair Design
70 Amstel Ave., Newark 19711
Type: Private, proprietary
Degrees: C
URL: http://www.schillingdouglas.com
Phone: (302) 737-5100
Inst. Accred.: NACCAS (1981/2001)

DISTRICT OF COLUMBIA

Bennett Career Institute, Inc.
700 Monroe St. NE, Washington 20017
Type: Private, proprietary
Degrees: C
Phone: (202) 526-1400
Inst. Accred.: NACCAS (1999/2002)

Career Blazers Learning Center of Washington
2131 K St. NW, Washington 20037
Type: Private, proprietary
Degrees: C
Phone: (202) 467-4223
Inst. Accred.: COE (2004)

Dudley Beauty College—Washington
2031 Rhode Island Ave., NE, Washington 20018
Type: Private, proprietary
Degrees: C
URL: http://www.dudleyq.com/Education
Phone: (202) 269-3666
Inst. Accred.: NACCAS (1984/2004)

Joint Military Intelligence Training Center, Defense
Defense Intelligence Agency, Bldg. 6000, Washington 20340-5100
Type: Public, federal
Degrees: C
URL: http://www.dia.mil
Phone: (202) 231-2800
Inst. Accred.: COE (2003)

Lado International College
2233 Wisconsin Ave., NW, Washington 20007
Type: Private, proprietary
Degrees: C
URL: http://www.lado.com
Phone: (202) 223-0023
Inst. Accred.: ACCET (1996/2002)

Arlington Campus
1550 Wilson Blvd., Garden Level, Arlington, VA 22209
Phone: (703) 524-1100

Silver Spring Campus
1400 Spring St., #250, Silver Spring, MD 20910
Phone: (301) 565-5236

Levine School of Music
1901 Mississippi Ave., SE, Washington 20020
Type: Public, independent
Degrees: C
URL: http://www.levineschool.org
Phone: (202) 686-8000   *Calendar:* Sem. plan
Inst. Accred.: NASM (1989/1995)

The National Conservatory of Dramatic Arts
1556 Wisconsin Ave., NW, Washington 20007-2758
Type: Private, independent
Degrees: C
URL: http://www.theconservatory.org
Phone: (202) 333-2202
Inst. Accred.: ACCSCT (1980/2003)

Potomac Massage Training Institute
5028 Wisconsin Ave., NW, Ste. LL, Washington 20016-4118
Type: Private, proprietary
Degrees: C
URL: http://www.pmti.org
Phone: (202) 686-7046
Inst. Accred.: CMTA (1999/2004)

Sanz School, Inc.
1720 I St., NW, Washington 20006
Type: Private, proprietary
Degrees: C
URL: http://www.sanzschool.com
Phone: (202) 872-4700
Inst. Accred.: ACCET (1988/2004)

Falls Church Campus
2930 Patrick Henry Dr., Falls Church, VA 22044
Phone: (703) 237-6200

Silver Spring Campus
8455 Colesville Rd., Silver Spring, MD 20910
Phone: (301) 608-2300

School of Tomorrow
810 5th St., NW, Washington 20001
Type: Private, proprietary
Degrees: C
URL: http://www.grm.org
Phone: (202) 789-1810
Inst. Accred.: ACCET (2000/2005)

Technical Learning Centers, Inc.
1012 14th Street NW, Ste.309, Washington 20005
Type: Private, proprietary
Degrees: C
URL: http://www.tlc-corp.com
Phone: (202) 393-7100
Inst. Accred.: ACCET (2003)

United States Marine Corps Institute
Washington Navy Yard, 912 Charles Poor St., SE, Washington 20391-5680
Type: Public, federal
Degrees: C
URL: http://www.mci.usmc.mil
Phone: (202) 685-7463
Inst. Accred.: DETC (1977/2003)

FLORIDA

A.M.I., Inc.
3042 West International Speedway Blvd., Daytona Beach 32124
Type: Private, proprietary
System: Corinthian Colleges, Inc
Degrees: C
URL: http://www.amiwrench.com
Phone: (386) 255-0295
Inst. Accred.: ACCET (1986/2002)

Academy for Practical Nursing and Health Occupations
5154 Okeechobee Blvd., Ste. 201, West Palm Beach 33417
Type: Private, independent
Degrees: C
Phone: (561) 683-1400
Inst. Accred.: COE (1999)

Academy of Cosmetology
4711 Babcock St., NE, Ste. 26, Palm Bay 32905
Type: Private, proprietary
Degrees: C
URL: http://www.raphaelsbeautyschool.com
Phone: (321) 951-0595
Inst. Accred.: NACCAS (1989/2004)

Academy of Cosmetology
2088 North Courtenay Pkwy., Merritt Island 32953
Type: Private, proprietary
Degrees: C
URL: http://www.raphaelsbeautyschool.com
Phone: (321) 452-8490
Inst. Accred.: NACCAS (1987/2002)

Academy of Healing Arts, Massage and Facial Skin Care
3141 South Military Trail, Lake Worth 33463-2113
Type: Private, proprietary
Degrees: C
URL: http://www.ahamassage.org
Phone: (561) 965-5550
Inst. Accred.: ACCSCT (1992/2003, Probation)

Advance Science Institute
3750 West 12th Ave., Hialeah 33012
Type: Private, proprietary
Degrees: C
Phone: (305) 827-5452
Inst. Accred.: ACCSCT (2003)

American Advanced Technicians Institute Corporation
6801 West 20th Ave., Hialeah 33014
Type: Private, proprietary
Degrees: C
URL: http://www.aationline.com
Phone: (305) 362-5519
Inst. Accred.: ACCET (2002)

American Institute of Beauty, Inc
13244 66th St. North, Largo 33773
Type: Private, proprietary
Degrees: C
URL: http://aibschool.com
Phone: (727) 532-2125
Inst. Accred.: NACCAS (2005)

American Institute of Massage Therapy
416 East Atlantic Blvd., Pompano Beach 33060
Type: Private, proprietary
Degrees: C
URL: http://www.aimt.com
Phone: (954) 781-2468
Inst. Accred.: ACCET (1986/2004)

Americare School of Nursing
7275 Estapona Circle, Fern Park 32730
Type: Private, proprietary
Degrees: C
URL: http://www.americareschoolofnursing.com
Phone: (407) 673-7406
Inst. Accred.: ABHES (1997/2001)
Prog. Accred.: Dental Assisting

   Saint Petersburg Campus
   5335 66th St. North, St. Petersburg 33709
   Phone: (727) 547-1822
   Prog. Accred: Medical Assisting (ABHES)

Ari-Ben Aviator
3800 St. Lucie Blvd., Ft. Pierce 34946
Type: Private, proprietary
Degrees: C
URL: http://www.aribenaviator.com
Phone: (561) 466-4822
Inst. Accred.: ACCSCT (1997/2001)

Artistic Nails and Beauty Academy
4951-A Adamo Dr., Tampa 33605
Type: Private, proprietary
Degrees: C
URL: http://www.artisticbeautyschool.com
Phone: (813) 654-4529
Inst. Accred.: NACCAS (2003)

ASM Beauty World Academy
6423 Stirling Rd., Davie 33314
Type: Private, proprietary
Degrees: C
Phone: (954) 966-5998
Inst. Accred.: NACCAS (1990/2005)

Atlantic Technical Center
4700 Coconut Creek Pkwy., Coconut Creek 33063
Type: Public, state
Degrees: C
URL: http://www.atlantictechcenter.com
Phone: (954) 977-2000
Inst. Accred.: COE (1978/2000)
Prog. Accred.: Culinary Education, Practical Nursing

Pompano Beach Campus
1400 NE 6th St., Pompano Beach 33060
Phone: (305) 786-7600

Audio Recording Technology Institute
4525 Vineland Rd., Ste. 201B, Orlando 32811
Type: Private, proprietary
Degrees: C
URL: http://www.audiocareer.com
Phone: (407) 423-2784
Inst. Accred.: ACCSCT (1999/2004)

The Beauty Institute, Inc.
2215 North Military Trail, #1, West Palm Beach 33409
Type: Private, proprietary
Degrees: C
Phone: (561) 688-0225
Inst. Accred.: NACCAS (2003)

Beauty Schools of America
1060 W. 49th St., Hialeah 33012
Type: Private, proprietary
Degrees: C
Phone: (305) 362-9003
Inst. Accred.: COE (1989/2001)

Miami Campus
1176 SW 67th Ave., Miami 33144
Phone: (305) 267-6604

Bene's International School of Beauty, Inc.
7127 U.S. Hwy. 19, New Port Richey 34652
Type: Private, proprietary
Degrees: C
URL: http://www.isbschool.com
Phone: (727) 848-8415
Inst. Accred.: NACCAS (1979/2005)

Bradenton Beauty & Barber Academy, Inc.
5505 Manatee Ave. West, Bradenton 34209
Type: Private, proprietary
Degrees: C
Phone: (941) 761-4400
Inst. Accred.: NACCAS (1982/2002)

Bradford-Union Area Vocational-Technical Center
609 North Orange St., Starke 32091
Type: Public, local
Degrees: C
URL: http://www.bradfordvotech.com
Phone: (966) 966-6760
Inst. Accred.: COE (1998/2003)

Cambridge Institute of Allied Health
1912 Boothe Circle, Ste. 200, Longwood 32750
Type: Private, proprietary
Degrees: C
Phone: (407) 265-8383
Inst. Accred.: ABHES (2003)
Prog. Accred.: Medical Assisting (ABHES)

Career Training Institute
2463 East Semoran Blvd., Apopka 32703
Type: Private, proprietary
Degrees: C
Phone: (407) 884-1816
Inst. Accred.: ACCSCT (1988/2002)

Center for Information Dominance Corry Station
640 Roberts Ave., Code CIS, Pensacola 32511-5138
Type: Public, federal
Degrees: C
URL: https://www.npdc.navy.mil/ceninfodom
Phone: (850) 452-6516
Inst. Accred.: COE (1975/2002)

Center for Naval Aviation Technical Training
230 Chevalier Field Ave., Pensacola 32508-5113
Type: Public, federal
Degrees: C
URL: https://www.cnet.navy.mil/cnet/nattc
Phone: (850) 452-9700
Inst. Accred.: COE (1976/2004)

Center for Explosive Ordnance Disposal and Diving
350 South Crag Rd., Panama City 32407-7016
Type: Public, federal
Degrees: C
URL: https://www.npdc.navy.mil/ceneoddive
Phone: (850) 235-5241
Inst. Accred.: COE (1983/2002)

Charlotte Vocational-Technical Center
18300 Toledo Blade Blvd., Port Charlotte 33948-3399
Type: Public, state
Degrees: C
URL: http://www.ccps.k12.fl.us/schools/techcenter
Phone: (941) 255-7500
Inst. Accred.: COE (1983/2205)
Prog. Accred.: Dental Assisting

Commercial Diving Academy
8137 North Main St., Jacksonville 32208
Type: Private, proprietary
Degrees: C
URL: http://www.commercialdivingacademy.com
Phone: (904) 766-7736
Inst. Accred.: ACCET (2005)

Compu-Med Vocational Careers
2900 West 12th Ave., 3rd Flr., Hialeah 33012
Type: Private, proprietary
Degrees: C
Phone: (305) 888-9200
Inst. Accred.: ACCSCT (1994/2004)

Compu-Med Vocational Careers
9738 SW 24th St., Miami 33165
Type: Private, proprietary
Degrees: C
Phone: (305) 553-2898
Inst. Accred.: ACCSCT (1999/2004)

Concorde Career Institute
7960 Arlington Expressway, Jacksonville 32211-7429
Type: Private, proprietary
Degrees: C
URL: http://www.concordecareercolleges.com
Phone: (904) 725-0525
Inst. Accred.: ACCSCT (1977/2004)

Concorde Career Institute
4000 North State Rd. 7, Ste. 100, Lauderdale Lakes 33319
Type: Private, proprietary
Degrees: C
URL: http://www.concordecareercolleges.com
Phone: (954) 731-8880
Inst. Accred.: ACCSCT (1983/2005)

Concorde Career Institute
4202 West Spruce St., Tampa 33607-4127
Type: Private, proprietary
Degrees: C
URL: http://www.concordecareercolleges.com
Phone: (813) 874-0094
Inst. Accred.: ACCSCT (1981/2004)

Coral Ridge Training School
2740 East Oakland Park Blvd., Ft. Lauderdale 33306
Type: Private, proprietary
Degrees: C
URL: http://www.geocities.com/crtrainingschool
Phone: (954) 561-2022
Inst. Accred.: COE (1996/2002)

CORE Institute
223 West Carolina St., Tallahassee 32301
Type: Private, proprietary
Degrees: C
URL: http://www.coreinstitute.com
Phone: (850) 222-8673
Inst. Accred.: CMTA (2004)
Prog. Accred.: Massage Therapy

Dade Medical Institute
3401 NW 7th St., Miami 33125
Type: Private, proprietary
Degrees: C
URL: http://www.dademedicalinstitute.com
Phone: (305) 644-1171
Inst. Accred.: ABHES (2003/2005)

David G. Erwin Technical Center
2010 East Hillsborough Ave., Tampa 33612
Type: Public, state
Degrees: C
Phone: (813) 231-1800
Inst. Accred.: COE (1981/2003)
Prog. Accred.: Clinical Lab Technology, Dental Assisting, Electroneurodiagnostic Technology, Medical Assisting (AMA), Respiratory Therapy Technology, Surgical Technology

Defense Equal Opportunity Management Institute
740 O'Malley Rd., MS 9121, Patrick Air Force Base 32925-3399
Type: Public, federal
Degrees: C
URL: http://www.patrick.af.mil/deomi/deomi.htm
Phone: (407) 494-6976
Inst. Accred.: COE (1983/1999)

Delta Connection Academy
2700 Flight Line Ave., Sanford 32773-9683
Type: Private, proprietary
Degrees: C　　　　　　　　　　　　　　*Enroll:* 365
URL: http://www.deltaconnectionacademy.com
Phone: (407) 330-7020
Inst. Accred.: ACCSCT (1995/2005)

Duwayne E. Keller & Associates, Inc.
12415 SW Sheri Ave., Ste. A, Lake Suzy 34269
Type: Private, proprietary
Degrees: C
URL: http://www.swflorida.dale-carnegie.com
Phone: (941) 766-7227
Inst. Accred.: ACCET (1976/2002)

Educating Hands School of Massage
120 SW 8th St., Miami 33130-3513
Type: Private, proprietary
Degrees: C
URL: http://www.educatinghands.com
Phone: (305) 285-6991
Inst. Accred.: CMTA (2004)

EduTech Centers
18850 U.S. Hwy. 19 North, Bldg. 5, Clearwater 34764
Type: Private, proprietary
Degrees: C
URL: http://www.edutechctr.com
Phone: (727) 535-0608
Inst. Accred.: COE (1991/2003)

The English Center
3501 SW 28 St., Miami 33133
Type: Public, local
Degrees: C
URL: http://www.tecmiami.com
Phone: (305) 445 7731
Inst. Accred.: COE (2004)

Embassy CES
301 East Las Olas Blvd., 6th Flr., Ft. Lauderdale 33301
Type: Private, proprietary
Degrees: C
URL: http://www.studygroup.com/embassyces
Phone: (954) 522-0081
Inst. Accred.: ACCET (1984/2002)

Boston Campus
Eager House, 49 Seminary Ave., Lasell College,
Newton, MA 2466
Phone: (617) 796-4303

Federal Way Campus
3600 South 344th Way, Federal Way, WA 98001

New York Campus
330 7th Ave., 5th & 6th Flrs., New York, NY 10001
Phone: (212) 629-7300

San Diego Campus
600 B St., Ste. 1700, San Diego, CA 92101
Phone: (619) 235-9222

San Francisco Campus
1462 Pine St., San Francisco, CA 94109
Phone: (415) 447-9014

West Hills Campus
22801 Roscoe Blvd., West Hills, CA 91304
Phone: (813) 731-8111

Westminster Campus
1870 West 122nd Ave., Westminster, CO 80234

FAA Center for Management Development
4500 Palm Coast Pkwy., SE, Palm Coast 32137
Type: Public, federal
Degrees: C
URL: http://www.faa.gov/ahr
Phone: (904) 446-7136
Inst. Accred.: COE (1989/2000)

Fashion Focus Hair Academy
2184 Gulf Gate Dr., Sarasota 34231
Type: Private, proprietary
Degrees: C
URL: http://www.dudleyq.com/cosmetology.html
Phone: (941) 921-4877
Inst. Accred.: NACCAS (1980/2003)

Federal Correctional Institution—Tallahassee
501 Capital Circle, NE, Tallahassee 32301-3572
Type: Public, federal
Degrees: C
URL: http://www.bop.gov/locations/institutions/
tal/index.jsp
Phone: (850) 878-2173
Inst. Accred.: COE (1985/2002)
Prog. Accred.: Psychology Internship

First Coast Technical Institute
2980 Collins Ave., St. Augustine 32095-1919
Type: Public, state-chartered
Degrees: C
URL: http://www.fcti.org
Phone: (904) 829-1010
Inst. Accred.: COE (1980/2002)
Prog. Accred.: Culinary Education, EMT (Paramedic)

Clay County Campus
4035 Reynolds Blvd., Bldg. 91, Green Cove Springs
32043-8360
Phone: (904) 824-4401

Putnam County Campus
820 Reid St., Ste. D, Palatka 32177
Phone: (904) 329-3550

FlightSafety Academy
Vero Beach Airport, PO Box 2708, Vero Beach 32961
Type: Private, proprietary
Degrees: C
URL: http://www.flightsafetyacademy.com
Phone: (561) 564-7600
Inst. Accred.: ACCSCT (1975/2003)

Florida Academy of Health and Beauty
2300 NW 9th Ave., Wilton Manors 33311
Type: Private, proprietary
Degrees: C
Phone: (954) 563-9098
Inst. Accred.: NACCAS (2003)

Florida Barber Academy
3269 North Federal Hwy., Pompano Beach 33064
Type: Private, proprietary
Degrees: C
Phone: (954) 428-8488
Inst. Accred.: COE (2001)

Florida Career Institute
4222 South Florida Ave., Lakeland 33813
Type: Private, proprietary
Degrees: C
URL: http://www.floridacareerinstitute.com
Phone: (863) 646-1400
Inst. Accred.: ACCET (1989/2004)
Prog. Accred.: Medical Assisting (CAAHEP)

Florida Education Institute
4790 NW 7th St., Suite 104, Miami 33126
Type: Private, proprietary
Degrees: C
Phone: (305) 444-1515
Inst. Accred.: COE (2001)

The Florida Institute of Animal Arts
3776 Howell Branch Rd., Winter Park 32792
Type: Private, proprietary
Degrees: C
URL: http://www.fifi-inc.com
Phone: (407) 657-8088
Inst. Accred.: ACCSCT (2001)

Florida Institute of Montessori Studies
1240 Banana River Dr., Indian Harbour Beach 32937-4105
Type: Private, independent
Degrees: C
URL: http://www.montessorischools.org
Phone: (321) 779-0031
Inst. Accred.: MACTE (1999/2002)

Florida Institute of Ultrasound, Inc.
8800 University Pkwy., Building A, #4, Pensacola 32514
Type: Private, proprietary
Degrees: C
URL: http://www.fiuonline.net
Phone: (850) 478-7611
Inst. Accred.: ABHES (1985/2002)

Florida Medical Training Institute
4400 West Sample Rd., Ste. 134, Coconut Creek 33073
Type: Private, proprietary
Degrees: C
URL: http://www.fmti.edu
Phone: (954) 979-6500
Inst. Accred.: ABHES (2003)

Florida Medical Training Institute
478 Ballard Dr., Melbourne 32935
Type: Private, proprietary
Degrees: C
URL: http://www.ems-training.com
Phone: (321) 751-9696
Inst. Accred.: ABHES (2003)

Miami Campus
7902 NW 36th St., Ste. 214-215, Miami 33166
Phone: (305) 715-0377

Orlando Campus
5575 South Semoran Blvd., Ste. 34-35, Orlando 32822
Phone: (407) 275-9660

Florida School of Massage
6421 SW 13th St., Gainesville 32608
Type: Private, proprietary
Degrees: C
URL: http://www.floridaschoolofmassage.com
Phone: (352) 378-7891
Inst. Accred.: CMTA (1999/2004)

Florida School of Traditional Midwifery
PO Box 5505, Gainesville 32627-5505
Type: Private, independent
Degrees: C
URL: http://www.fstmgainesville.com
Phone: (352) 338-0766   *Calendar:* Sem. plan
Inst. Accred.: MEAC (2000)

Folkner Training Associates, Inc.
8641 Baypine Rd., Ste. 2, Jacksonville 32256
Type: Private, proprietary
Degrees: C
URL: http://www.jacksonvill.dale-carnegie.com
Phone: (904) 443-2929
Inst. Accred.: ACCET (1978/2004)

Fontecha Institute
1305 West 49th St., Hialeah 33012
Type: Private, proprietary
Degrees: C
Phone: (305) 824-0600
Inst. Accred.: ACCSCT (2000/2002)

Fort Pierce Beauty Academy
3028 South U.S. 1, Fort Pierce 34982
Type: Private, proprietary
Degrees: C
Phone: (772) 464-4885
Inst. Accred.: NACCAS (1985/2000)

Beauty and Massage Institute
719 17th St., Vero Beach 32960
Phone: (772) 978-7178

Port Saint Lucie Beauty Academy
7644 South U.S. 1, Port St. Lucie 34983
Phone: (772) 340-3540

George Stone Vocational-Technical Center
2400 Longleaf Dr., Pensacola 32526-8922
Type: Public, state
Degrees: C
URL: http://www.gsconline.org
Phone: (850) 941-6200
Inst. Accred.: COE (1981/2003)

George T. Baker Aviation School
3275 NW 42nd Ave., Miami 33142
Type: Public, state
Degrees: C
Phone: (305) 871-3143
Inst. Accred.: COE (1978/2005)

Guadalupe Vocational Institute
2500 SW 107th Ave., Suite 29, Miami 33165-2492
Type: Private, proprietary
Degrees: C
Phone: (305) 559-7728
Inst. Accred.: COE (2002)

The Harid Conservatory
2285 Potomac Rd., Boca Raton 33431-5518
Type: Private, independent
Degrees: C
URL: http://www.harid.edu
Phone: (561) 997-2677
Inst. Accred.: NASD (1993/2004)

Health Opportunity Technical Center, Inc.
18441 NW 2nd Ave., Ste. 300, Miami 33169
Type: Private, proprietary
Degrees: C
Phone: (305) 249-2275
Inst. Accred.: ABHES (2005)

Helicopter Adventures
365 Golden Knights Blvd., Titusville 32780
Type: Private, proprietary
Degrees: C
URL: http://www.heli.com
Phone: (321) 385-2919
Inst. Accred.: ACCSCT (1994/2004)

Heliflight
2675 NW 56th St., Hanger 51, Fort Lauderdale 33309
Type: Private, proprietary
Degrees: C
Phone: (954) 771-6969
Inst. Accred.: ACCSCT (2001)

Henry W. Brewster Technical Center
2222 North Tampa St., Tampa 33602
Type: Public, state
Degrees: C
URL: http://www.brewstertech.org
Phone: (813) 276-5448
Inst. Accred.: COE (1989/2002)

Heritage Institute
4130 Salisbury Rd., Ste. 1100, Jacksonville 33216
Type: Private, proprietary
Degrees: C
URL: http://www.heritage-education.com
Phone: (904) 332-0910
Inst. Accred.: NACCAS (1991/1999)

Heritage Institute
6811 Palisades Park Ct., Fort Myers 33912
Type: Private, proprietary
Degrees: C
URL: http://www.heritage-education.com
Phone: (239) 936-5822
Inst. Accred.: NACCAS (1989/1999)

Hollywood Institute of Beauty Careers
2642 Hollywood Blvd., Hollywood 33020
Type: Private, proprietary
Degrees: C
Phone: (954) 922-5505
Inst. Accred.: NACCAS (2002/2005)

Humanities Center Institute of Allied Health/School of Massage
4045 Park Blvd., Pinellas Park 33718
Type: Private, proprietary
Degrees: C
URL: http://www.2touch.com
Phone: (727) 541-5200
Inst. Accred.: ACCSCT (1984/2005)

I.C.E. Beauty School and Spa Training Center
280 South State Rd. 434, Ste. 2045, Altamonte Springs 32714
Type: Private, proprietary
Degrees: C
Phone: (407) 862-4001
Inst. Accred.: NACCAS (2004)

Institute of Allied Medical Professions
Saint Mary's Hospital, 27 45th St., Ste. 302, West Palm Beach 33407
Type: Private, proprietary
Degrees: C
URL: http://www.iampny.com
Phone: (561) 841-1441
Inst. Accred.: ABHES (2005)

Saint Joseph's Hospital Campus
5673 Peachtree Dunwoody Rd., Ste. 450, Atlanta, GA 30342
Phone: (404) 255-4500

International Academy
2550 South Ridgewood Ave., South Daytona 32119
Type: Private, proprietary
Degrees: C
URL: http://www.iahd.net
Phone: (386) 767-4600
Inst. Accred.: NACCAS (1984/2004)

International Training Careers
7360 SW 24th St., Miami 33155
Type: Private, independent
Degrees: C
Phone: (305) 263-9696
Inst. Accred.: COE (2001)

Jacksonville Beauty Institute, Inc.
5045 Sontel Dr., Ste. 80, Jacksonville 32208
Type: Private, proprietary
Degrees: C
Phone: (904) 768-9001
Inst. Accred.: NACCAS (2001/2004)

Tampa Bay Beauty Institute
6211 East Hillsborough Ave., Tampa 33610
Phone: (813) 514-9100

Ken Roberts Corporation
4295 South Atlantic Ave., Wilbur by the Sea 32119
Type: Private, proprietary
Degrees: C
URL: http://www.centralflorida.dalecarnegie.com
Phone: (904) 767-6346
Inst. Accred.: ACCET (1976/2004)

La Belle Beauty Academy—Miami
2960 SW 8th St., Miami 33135
Type: Private, proprietary
Degrees: C
URL: http://www.beautyacademy.com
Phone: (305) 649-2800
Inst. Accred.: NACCAS (1988/2003)

La Belle Beauty School—Hialeah
775 West 49th St., Ste. 5, Hialeah 33012
Type: Private, proprietary
Degrees: C
URL: http://www.beautyacademy.com
Phone: (305) 558-0562
Inst. Accred.: NACCAS (1979/2003)

Lake Technical Center
2001 Kurt St., Eustis 32726
Type: Public, state
Degrees: C
URL: http://www.laketech.org
Phone: (352) 589-2250
Inst. Accred.: COE (1974/2000)
Prog. Accred.: EMT (Paramedic)

Kenneth Bragg Public Safety Complex
12900 Ln. Park Cutoff, Tavares 32778-9653
Phone: (352) 742-6463

The Langauge Academy
300 NE 3rd Ave., Ste. 100, Fort Lauderdale 33301
Type: Private, proprietary
Degrees: C
URL: http://www.languageacademy.com
Phone: (954) 462-8373
Inst. Accred.: ACCET (2002)

Language Exchange International
500 Spanish River Blvd., NE, Ste. 19, Boca Raton 11341
Type: Private, proprietary
Degrees: C
URL: http://www.languageexchange.com
Phone: (561) 368-3913
Inst. Accred.: ACCET (1989/2004)

Alexandria Campus
621 King St., 2nd Flr., Alexandria, VA 22314
Phone: (703) 299-0306

Lee County High Tech Center—Central
3800 Michigan Ave., Fort Myers 33916
Type: Public, state
Degrees: C
URL: http://www.lee.k12.fl.us/voc
Phone: (941) 334-4544
Inst. Accred.: COE (1978/2005)
Prog. Accred.: Medical Assisting (AMA), Surgical
Technology

Lee County High Tech Center—North
360 Santa Barbara Blvd. North, Cape Coral 33993
Type: Public, state
Degrees: C
URL: http://www.hightechnorth.com
Phone: (239) 574-4440
Inst. Accred.: COE (1996/2002)
Prog. Accred.: Surgical Technology

Levin School of Health Care
2206 West Atlantic Ave., Delray Beach 33445
Type: Private, proprietary
Degrees: C
URL: http://levinschoolofhealthcare.com
Phone: (561) 274-9663
Inst. Accred.: ACICS (2004)

Lindsey Hopkins Technical Education Center
750 NW 20th St., Miami 33127
Type: Public, state
Degrees: C
URL: http://www.dade.k12.fl.us/lindsey
Phone: (305) 324-6070
Inst. Accred.: COE (1972/2005)
Prog. Accred.: Dental Assisting, Dental Laboratory
Technology, Surgical Technology

Lively Area Vocational-Technical Center
500 North Appleyard Dr., Tallahassee 32304-2895
Type: Public, state
Degrees: C
URL: http://www.livelytech.com
Phone: (850) 487-7555
Inst. Accred.: COE (1977/2004)

Florida State Hospital Campus
HRS, District 2, Chattahoochee 32324
Phone: (850) 663-7202

Lively Aviation Center
3290 Capital Circle, SW, Tallahassee 32310
Phone: (850) 488-4161

Loraine's Academy, Inc.
1012 58th St. North, Tyrone Garden Center, St.
Petersburg 33710
Type: Private, proprietary
Degrees: C
URL: http://www.lorainesacademy.net
Phone: (727) 347-4247
Inst. Accred.: NACCAS (1968/2004)

Lorenzo Walker Institute of Technology
3702 Estey Ave., Naples 34104-4498
Type: Public, state
Degrees: C
URL: http://www.collier.k12.fl.us/lwit
Phone: (239) 430-6900
Inst. Accred.: COE (1980/2002)
Prog. Accred.: Dental Assisting, Medical Assisting (AMA),
Surgical Technology

Manatee Technical Institute
5603 34th St., West, Bradenton 34210-5297
Type: Public, state
Degrees: C
URL: http://www.manatee.k12.fl.us/sites/mti
Phone: (941) 751-7900
Inst. Accred.: COE (1980/2002)
Prog. Accred.: Cosmetology, Dental Assisting, EMT
(Paramedic)

Manhattan Hairstyling Academy
1906 West Platt St., Tampa 33606
Type: Private, proprietary
Degrees: C
URL: http://www.manhattanhairstylingacademy.com
Phone: (813) 837-2525
Inst. Accred.: NACCAS (1980/2001)

Manhattan Beauty School, Inc.
1720 16th St. North, St. Petersburg 33705
Phone: (727) 821-7575

Tampa Campus
2317 East Fletcher Ave., Tampa 33612
Phone: (813) 264-3535

Valrico Campus
Royal Oak Plaza, 3244 Lithia Pinecrest, #103-104,
Valrico 33594
Phone: (813) /258-0505

Manna School of Midwifery and Health Sciences
PO Drawer 2248, Bonita Springs 34133
Type: Private, independent
Degrees: C
Phone: (941) 992-1211
Inst. Accred.: MEAC (2000)

Margate School of Beauty
5281 Coconut Creek Pkwy., Coco Centre 33063
Type: Private, proprietary
Degrees: C
Phone: (954) 972-9630
Inst. Accred.: NACCAS (1980/2005)

Medical Career Institute of South Florida
802 South Dixie Hwy., Lake Worth 33460
Type: Private, proprietary
Degrees: C
URL: http://www.mcisf.com
Phone: (561) 493-5022
Inst. Accred.: COE (2004)

Melbourne Beauty School
686 North Wickham Rd., Melbourne 32935
Type: Private, proprietary
Degrees: C
Phone: (321) 259-0001
Inst. Accred.: NACCAS (1981/2005)

The Miami Ad School
955 Alton Rd., Miami Beach 33139
Type: Private, proprietary
Degrees: C
URL: http://www.adschool.edu
Phone: (305) 538-3193
Inst. Accred.: COE (1995/2001)

Minneapolis Campus
25 North 4th St., #201, Minneapolis, MN 55401
Phone: (612) 339-4089

Miami Job Corps Center
3050 NW 183rd St., Miami 33056-3536
Type: Public, federal
Degrees: C
URL: http://www.miamijobcorps.com
Phone: (305) 626-7800
Inst. Accred.: COE (1986/2003)

Miami Lakes Technical Education Center
5780 NW 158th St., Miami 33014
Type: Public, state
Degrees: C
URL: http://mlec.dadeschools.net
Phone: (305) 557-1100
Inst. Accred.: COE (1983/2005)

Montessori Teacher Traininig Institute
6050 SW 57th Ave., Miami 33143
Type: Private, independent
Degrees: C
URL: http://www.alexandermontessori.com/
mtti%20right.htm
Phone: (305) 665-6033
Inst. Accred.: MACTE (2001)

National Association of Photoshop Professionals
333 Douglas Rd. East, Oldsmar 34677
Type: Private, independent
Degrees: C
URL: http://www.photoshopuser.com
Phone: (813) 433-5000
Inst. Accred.: ACCET (2003)

National Aviation Academy
5770 Roosevelt Blvd., #105, Clearwater 33760
Type: Private, proprietary
Degrees: C
URL: http://www.naa.edu
Phone: (727) 531-2080
Inst. Accred.: COE (1991/2003)

National Training, Inc.
188 College Dr., PO Box 65789, Orange Park 32067-5789
Type: Private, proprietary
Degrees: C
URL: http://www.truckschool.com
Phone: (904) 272-4000
Inst. Accred.: DETC (1982/2003)

Truck Driving and Heavy Equipment Operating Training Site
SR 202, Green Cove Springs 32043
Phone: (904) 272-4000

New Concept Massage & Beauty School, Inc.
2022 SW 1st St., Miami 33135
Type: Private, proprietary
Degrees: C
Phone: (305) 642-3020
Inst. Accred.: NACCAS (2000/2003)

New Gate Center for Montessori Studies
5237 Ashton Rd., Sarasota 34233
Type: Private, independent
Degrees: C
URL: http://www.thenewgateschool.org
Phone: (941) 922-4949
Inst. Accred.: MACTE (2001)

New Professions Technical Institute
4100 West Flagler St., Miami 33134
Type: Private, proprietary
Degrees: C
URL: http://www.npti.com
Phone: (305) 461-2223
Inst. Accred.: ACCET (1997/2001)

New World Symphony
541 Lincoln Rd., Miami Beach 33139
Type: Private, independent
Degrees: C
URL: http://www.nws.org
Phone: (305) 673-3330
Inst. Accred.: NASM (1999/2004)

Normandy Beauty School of Jacksonville
5373 Lenox Ave., Jacksonville 32205
Type: Private, proprietary
Degrees: C
Phone: (904) 786-6250
Inst. Accred.: NACCAS (1979/2004)

North Florida Cosmetology Institute, Inc.
2424 Allen Rd., Tallahassee 32312
Type: Private, proprietary
Degrees: C
URL: http://www.cosmetologyinst.com
Phone: (850) 878-5269
Inst. Accred.: NACCAS (2001/2004)

North Florida Institute
560 Wells Rd., Orange Park 32073
Type: Private, proprietary
Degrees: C
Phone: (904) 269-7086
Inst. Accred.: ACICS (1999/2002)

Jacksonville Campus
5995-3 University Blvd. West, Jacksonville 32216
Phone: (904) 443-6300

Nouvelle Institute
3271 Northwest 7th St., Ste. 106, Miami 33125
Type: Private, proprietary
Degrees: C
Phone: (305) 643-3360
Inst. Accred.: NACCAS (1992/2005)

Hialeah Campus
500 West 49th St., Second Flr., Hialeah 33012
Phone: (305) 557-3017

Okaloosa Applied Technology Center
1976 Lewis Turner Blvd., Fort Walton Beach 32547
Type: Public, state
Degrees: C
URL: http://www.okaloosa.k12.fl.us/oatc
Phone: (850) 833-3500
Inst. Accred.: COE (1979/2000)

Orange Technical Education Center— Mid Florida Tech
2900 West Oak Ridge Rd., Orlando 32809
Type: Public, state
Degrees: C
URL: http://www.mft.ocps.net
Phone: (407) 855-5880
Inst. Accred.: COE (1974/2000)

Orange Technical Education Center— Orlando Tech
301 West Amelia St., Orlando 32801
Type: Public, state
Degrees: C
URL: http://www.orlandotech.ocps.net
Phone: (407) 246-7060
Inst. Accred.: COE (1983/1999)
Prog. Accred.: Dental Assisting, Surgical Technology

Orange Technical Education Center— Westside Tech
955 East Story Rd., Winter Garden 34787
Type: Public, state
Degrees: C
URL: http://www.westside.ocps.net
Phone: (407) 905-2001
Inst. Accred.: COE (1981/2003)

Orange Technical Education Center— Winter Park Tech
901 Webster Ave., Winter Park 32789
Type: Public, state
Degrees: C
URL: http://www.wpt.ocps.net
Phone: (407) 622-2900
Inst. Accred.: COE (1986/2005)
Prog. Accred.: Medical Assisting (CAAHEP)

Orlando Montessori Teacher Education Institute
PO Box 770298, Orlando 32877-0298
Type: Private, independent
Degrees: C
Phone: (407) 566-1561
Inst. Accred.: MACTE (1996/2003)

PC Professor of Boca Raton
7056 Beracasa Way, Boca Raton 33433
Type: Private, proprietary
Degrees: C
URL: http://www.pcprofessor.com
Phone: (561) 750-7879
Inst. Accred.: ACCSCT (2001)

PC Professor of West Palm Beach
6080 Okeechobee Blvd., Ste. 200, West Palm Beach 33417
Type: Private, proprietary
Degrees: C
URL: http://www.pcprofessor.com
Phone: (561) 684-3333
Inst. Accred.: ACCSCT (2001)

Pelican Flight Training Center
1601 SW 75th Ave., Pembroke Pines 33023
Type: Private, proprietary
Degrees: C
URL: http://www.pelican-airways.com
Phone: (954) 966-9750
Inst. Accred.: ACCSCT (2000/2003)

Phoenix East Aviation, Inc.
561 Pearl Harbor Dr., Daytona Beach 32114
Type: Private, proprietary
Degrees: C
URL: http://www.pea.com
Phone: (386) 258-0703
Inst. Accred.: ACCET (1995/2004)

Pinellas Technical Education Center—Clearwater Campus
6100 154th Ave., North, Clearwater 34620
Type: Public, state
Degrees: C
URL: http://www.ptecclw.pinellas.k12.fl.us
Phone: (727) 538-7167
Inst. Accred.: COE (1970/2002)
Prog. Accred.: Culinary Education

Clearwater Extension Campus
2735 Whitney Rd., Clearwater 33760-1610
Phone: (727) 538-7167

Pinellas County Jail
14400 49th St., North, Clearwater 34620
Phone: (813) 531-3531

Pinellas Technical Education Center—Saint Petersburg Campus
901 34th St., St. Petersburg 33711-2298
Type: Public, state
Degrees: C
URL: http://www.ptecclw.pinellas.k12.fl.us
Phone: (727) 893-2500
Inst. Accred.: COE (1975/1995)
Prog. Accred.: Dental Assisting, Medical Assisting (AMA), Respiratory Therapy Technology

The Poynter Institute for Media Studies
801 Third St., South, St. Petersburg 33701
Type: Private, proprietary
Degrees: C
URL: http://www.poynter.org
Phone: (727) 821-9494
Inst. Accred.: COE (1983/2005)

Praxis Institute
1850 SW 8th St., 4th Flr., Miami 33135
Type: Private, proprietary
Degrees: C
URL: http://www.thepraxisinstitute.com
Phone: (305) 642-4104
Inst. Accred.: COE (1994/2000)

Radford M. Locklin Technical Center
5330 Berryhill Rd., Milton 32571
Type: Public, state
Degrees: C
URL: http://www.santarosa.k12.fl.us/ltc
Phone: (850) 983-5700
Inst. Accred.: COE (1988/2005)

Regent Language Training U.S.A
1137 71st St., Miami Beach 33141
Type: Private, proprietary
Degrees: C
URL: http://www.regentusa.com
Phone: (305) 886-9290
Inst. Accred.: ACCET (1999/2002)

Rick J. Gallegos & Associates, Inc.
1408 North Westshore Blvd., Ste. 912, Tampa 33607
Type: Private, proprietary
Degrees: C
URL: http://www.tampabay.dale-carnegie.com
Phone: (813) 288-8778
Inst. Accred.: ACCET (1976/2001)

Ridge Vocational-Technical Center
7700 State Rd. 544, Winter Haven 33881
Type: Public, state
Degrees: C
URL: http://www.pcsb.k12.fl.us
Phone: (863) 419-3060
Inst. Accred.: COE (1982/2005)

Riverside Hairstyling Academy
3530 Beach Blvd., Jacksonville 32207
Type: Private, proprietary
Degrees: C
URL: http://www.riversidehair.com
Phone: (904) 398-0502
Inst. Accred.: NACCAS (1974/2004)

Robert Morgan Vocational-Technical Institute
18180 SW 122nd Ave., Miami 33177
Type: Public, state
Degrees: C
URL: http://www.dade.k12.fl.us/rmorgan
Phone: (305) 253-9920
Inst. Accred.: COE (1983/1999)
Prog. Accred.: Dental Assisting, Medical Assisting
(CAAHEP)

Community Habilitation Center
11450 Southwest 79th St., Miami 33173
Phone: (305) 279-7999

Haven Center
11300 SW 80 Terrace, Miami 33173
Phone: (305) 271-3232

Princeton Agribusiness Training Center
24315 South Dixie Hwy., Princeton 33030
Phone: (305) 279-7999

Ross Medical Education Center
2601 South Military Trail, Ste. 29, West Palm Beach
33415
Type: Private, proprietary
Degrees: C
URL: http://www.rossmedicaleducation.com
Phone: (561) 433-1288
Inst. Accred.: ACCSCT (1991/2003)
Prog. Accred.: Medical Assisting (ABHES)

Hollywood Campus
6847 Taft St., Hollywood 33024
Phone: (954) 963-0043
Prog. Accred: Medical Assisting (ABHES)

Sarasota County Technical Institute
4748 Beneva Rd., Sarasota 34233
Type: Public, state
Degrees: C   *Enroll:* 72
URL: http://www.careerscape.org/scti/scti_index.html
Phone: (941) 924-1365
Inst. Accred.: COE (1971/2003)
Prog. Accred.: EMT (Paramedic), Medical Assisting (AMA),
Practical Nursing, Surgical Technology

Sarasota School of Massage Therapy
1932 Ringling Blvd., Sarasota 34326
Type: Private, proprietary
Degrees: C
URL: http://www.sarasotamassageschool.com
Phone: (941) 957-0577
Inst. Accred.: COE (1994/2000)
Prog. Accred.: Massage Therapy

The School of Health Careers
3190 North State Rd. 7, Lauderdale Lakes 33319
Type: Private, proprietary
Degrees: C
Phone: (954) 777-0083
Inst. Accred.: ACCSCT (2002)

Sheridan Technical Center
5400 Sheridan St., Hollywood 33021
Type: Public, state
Degrees: C
URL: http://www.sheridantechnical.com
Phone: (954) 985-3220
Inst. Accred.: COE (1974/2000)
Prog. Accred.: Clinical Lab Technology, Culinary
Education, Practical Nursing, Surgical Technology

South Florida Institute of Technology
2141 South West 1st St., #104, Miami 33135
Type: Private, proprietary
Degrees: C
Phone: (305) 649-2050
Inst. Accred.: ACCSCT (2002)

South Florida Montessori Education Center
606 South Palmway, Lake Worth 33460
Type: Private, independent
Degrees: C
Phone: (561) 493-3093
Inst. Accred.: MACTE (2002)

Southeast Florida Institute, Inc.
2401 PGA Blvd., Ste. 196, Palm Beach Gardens 33410
Type: Private, proprietary
Degrees: C
URL: http://www.southflorida.dalecarnegie.com
Phone: (561) 624-3660
Inst. Accred.: ACCET (1976/2005)

Southeastern School of Neuromuscular and Massage Therapy, Inc.
9424 Baymeadows Rd., Ste. 200, Jacksonville 32256
Type: Private, proprietary
Degrees: C
URL: http://se-massage.com
Phone: (904) 448-9499   *Calendar:* Tri. plan
Inst. Accred.: ACCSCT (2001)

Southern Technical Institute
1819 North Semoran Blvd., Orlando 32807
Type: Private, proprietary
Degrees: C
URL: http://www.stiorlando.com
Phone: (407) 478-5300
Inst. Accred.: ACICS (2004)

Stenotype Institute of Jacksonville
3986 Blvd. Center Dr., Ste. 200, Jacksonville 32207-2819
Type: Private, independent
Degrees: C
URL: http://www.stenotypeinstitute.com
Phone: (904) 246-7466
Inst. Accred.: ACICS (1968/2001)

Orlando Campus
1636 West Oakridge Rd., Orlando 32809
Phone: (407) 816-5573

SunCoast II—The Tampa Bay School of Health/Suncoast School
2005 Pan Am Circle, Ste. 100, Tampa 33607
Type: Private, proprietary
Degrees: C
Phone: (813) 879-1500
Inst. Accred.: ACCSCT (1986/2001)

Sunstate Academy of Hair Design
4424 Bee Ridge Rd., Sarasota 34233-2502
Type: Private, proprietary
Degrees: C
Phone: (941) 377-4880
Inst. Accred.: ACCSCT (1983/2001)

Sunstate Academy of Hair Design
2418 Colonial Blvd., Fort Myers 33907-1415
Type: Private, proprietary
Degrees: C
Phone: (941) 278-1311
Inst. Accred.: ACCSCT (1988/2004)

Sunstate Academy of Hair Design
18453 U.S. Hwy. 19, Clearwater 33764
Type: Private, proprietary
Degrees: C
Phone: (727) 538-3827
Inst. Accred.: ACCSCT (1984/2004)

Suwanee-Hamilton Technical Center
415 Pinewood Dr., SW, Live Oak 32060
Type: Public, state
Degrees: C
Phone: (904) 364-2750
Inst. Accred.: COE (1973/2001)

TALK International
2455 East Sunrise Blvd., Ste. 200, Fort Lauderdale 33304
Type: Private, proprietary
Degrees: C
URL: http://www.talkinusa.com
Phone: (954) 565-8505
Inst. Accred.: ACCET (1999/2004)

Taylor Technical Institute
3233 Hwy. 19, South, Perry 32347
Type: Public, state
Degrees: C
URL: http://www.taylortech.org
Phone: (850) 838-2545
Inst. Accred.: COE (1993/2005)

Technical Career Institute
4299 NW 36th St., Ste. 300, Miami Springs 33166-7345
Type: Private, proprietary
Degrees: C
URL: http://www.technicalcareerinstitute.com
Phone: (305) 863-1818
Inst. Accred.: COE (1991/2001)

Technical Education Center-Osceola
501 Simpson Rd., Kissimmee 34744
Type: Public, state
Degrees: C
URL: http://www.teco.osceola.k12.fl.us
Phone: (407) 344-5080
Inst. Accred.: COE (1996/2002)

Tom P. Haney Technical Center
3016 Hwy. 77, Panama City 32444
Type: Public, state
Degrees: C
URL: http://www.bay.k12.fl.us/schools/htc
Phone: (850) 747-5500
Inst. Accred.: COE (1977/2004)
Prog. Accred.: Medical Assisting (CAAHEP)

Traviss Technical Center
3225 Winter Lake Rd., Lakeland 33803
Type: Public, state
Degrees: C
URL: http://www.pcsb.k12.fl.us/traviss
Phone: (863) 499-2700
Inst. Accred.: COE (1978/2000)
Prog. Accred.: Dental Assisting, Surgical Technology

Trendsetters Florida School of Beauty and Barbering
5337 Lenox Ave., Jacksonville 32205
Type: Private, proprietary
Degrees: C
Phone: (904) 764-9932
Inst. Accred.: NACCAS (2005)

Ultimate Medical Academy
1218 Ct. St., Ste. B, Clearwater 33756
Type: Private, proprietary
Degrees: C
URL: http://www.studymedical.com
Phone: (727) 446-8655
Inst. Accred.: ABHES (2000/2005)

Universal Beauty School
10720 West Flagler St., Miami 33174
Type: Private, proprietary
Degrees: C
URL: http://www.universalbeautyschool.com
Phone: (305) 485-7700
Inst. Accred.: COE (2004)

Washington-Holmes Area Vocational-Technical Center
757 Hoyt St., Chipley 32428
Type: Public, state
Degrees: C
URL: http://www.whtc.org
Phone: (850) 638-1180
Inst. Accred.: COE (1976/1997)

William T. McFatter Technical Center
6500 Nova Dr., Davie 33314
Type: Public, state
Degrees: C
URL: http://www.mcfattertech.com
Phone: (954) 370-8324
Inst. Accred.: COE (1989/2000)
Prog. Accred.: Dental Laboratory Technology, Practical
  Nursing

Davie Campus
Broward Fire Acad., 2600 SW 71 Terrace, Davie 33314
Phone: (954) 370-8324

Withlacoochee Technical Institute
1201 West Main St., Inverness 34450-4696
Type: Public, state
Degrees: C
URL: http://www.wtionline.cc
Phone: (352) 726-2430
Inst. Accred.: COE (1984/2000)

GEORGIA

Advanced Career Training
2 Executive Park West, Ste. 100, Atlanta 30329
Type: Private, proprietary
Degrees: C
URL: http://www.act-edu.com
Phone: (404) 321-2929
Inst. Accred.: ACCET (1987/2004)

Jacksonville Campus
7660 Phillips Hwy., Ste. 14, Jacksonville, FL 32256
Phone: (904) 737-6911

Riverdale Campus
7165 Georgia Hwy. 85, Riverdale 30274
Phone: (770) 991-9356

American Professional Institute
630 North Ave., Ste. J, Macon 31211
Type: Private, proprietary
Degrees: C
Phone: (478) 746-3243
Inst. Accred.: COE (1983/2002)

Arnold/Padrick's University of Cosmetology
4971 Courtney Dr., Forest Park 30297
Type: Private, proprietary
Degrees: C
Phone: (404) 361-5641
Inst. Accred.: NACCAS (1988/2003)

The Atlanta Ballet Centre for Dance Education
1400 West Peachtree St., NW, Atlanta 30309
Type: Private, independent
Degrees: C
URL: http://www.atlantaballet.com/new/fs_centre.htm
Phone: (404) 873-5811 ext 1
Inst. Accred.: NASD (2003)

Atlanta Institute of Music
5985 Financial Dr., Ste. 200, Norcross 30071
Type: Private, proprietary
Degrees: C
URL: http://www.aim-music.com
Phone: (770) 242-7717   *Calendar:* Qtr. plan
Inst. Accred.: COE (1994/2004)

Atlanta Job Corps Center
239 West Lake Ave., NW, Atlanta 30314
Type: Public, state
Degrees: C
URL: http://www.atljcc.org
Phone: (404) 794-9512
Inst. Accred.: COE (1985/2001)

Atlanta School of Massage
2 Dunwoody Park South, Atlanta 30338
Type: Private, proprietary
Degrees: C
URL: http://www.atlantaschoolofmassage.com
Phone: (770) 454-7167
Inst. Accred.: ACCSCT (1988/2003)

Aveda Institute Atlanta
3402 Piedmont Rd., Atlanta 30305
Type: Private, proprietary
Degrees: C
URL: http://www.avedainstitutes.com/atlanta.php
Phone: (404) 649-7119
Inst. Accred.: NACCAS (2004/2005)

Aviation Institute of Maintenance
500 Briscoe Blvd., Lawrenceville 30045
Type: Private, proprietary
Degrees: C
URL: http://www.aim-atlanta.com
Phone: (678) 377-5600
Inst. Accred.: ACCSCT (2000/2005)

Manassas Campus
9821 Godwin Dr., Manassas, VA 20110
Phone: (703) 257-5515

Virginia Beach Campus
1429 Miller Store Rd., Virginia Beach, VA 23455-3324
Phone: (757) 363-2121

Beauty College of America
1171 Main St., Forest Park 30050
Type: Private, proprietary
Degrees: C
Phone: (404) 361-4098
Inst. Accred.: NACCAS (1988/2003)

Brown College of Court Reporting and Medical Transcription
1740 Peachtree St., NW, Atlanta 30309
Type: Private, proprietary
Degrees: C
URL: http://www.browncollege.com
Phone: (404) 876-1227   *Calendar:* Qtr. plan
Inst. Accred.: COE (1984/2001)

Longview Campus
1125 Judson Plaza, #119, Longview, TX 75601-5120
Phone: (903) 757-4338

Cobb Beauty College
3096 Cherokee St., Kennesaw 30144
Type: Private, proprietary
Degrees: C
URL: http://www.cobbbeautycollege.com
Phone: (770) 424-6915
Inst. Accred.: COE (1993/2005)

Creative Circus
812 Lambert St., Atlanta 30324
Type: Private, proprietary
Degrees: C
URL: http://www.creativecircus.com
Phone: (404) 607-8880
Inst. Accred.: COE (1983/2005)

Empire Beauty School
425 Ernest Barrett Pkwy., Ste. H-2, Kennesaw 30144
Type: Private, proprietary
Degrees: C
URL: http://www.empirebeauty.com
Phone: (770) 419-2303
Inst. Accred.: NACCAS (1971/2003)

Empire Beauty School—Dunwoody
4719 Ashford-Dunwwody Rd., Ste. 205, Dunwoody 30338
Type: Private, proprietary
Degrees: C
URL: http://www.empirebeauty.com
Phone: (770) 671-1448
Inst. Accred.: NACCAS (1989/2004)

Empire Beauty School—Lawrenceville, GA
1455 Pleasant Rd., Ste. 105, Lawrenceville 30044
Type: Private, proprietary
Degrees: C
URL: http://www.empirebeauty.com
Phone: (704) 564-0725
Inst. Accred.: NACCAS (1975/2004)

Empire-Lackawanna Beauty School
425 Ernest-Barrett Pkwy., Ste. H-2, Town Center Plaza, Kennesaw 30144
Type: Private, proprietary
Degrees: C
URL: http://www.empirebeauty.com
Phone: (770) 419-2303
Inst. Accred.: NACCAS (1971/1998)

English for Internationals
575 Colonial Park Dr., Roswell 30075
Type: Private, proprietary
Degrees: C
URL: http://www.eng4intl.com
Phone: (770) 587-9640
Inst. Accred.: ACCET (2002)

ESL Instruction and Consulting, Inc.
3855 Presidential Pkwy., Atlanta 30340
Type: Private, proprietary
Degrees: C
URL: http://www.eslinstruction.com
Phone: (770) 457-7071
Inst. Accred.: ACCET (2003)

ETI Career Institute
1150 Lake Hearn Dr., Ste. 260, Atlanta 30342
Type: Private, proprietary
Degrees: C
URL: http://www.etimedicalschool.com
Phone: (404) 303-2929
Inst. Accred.: ACCSCT (1991/2001)

Jonesboro Campus
9500 South Main St., Jonesboro 30236
Phone: (770) 477-2799

Fayette Beauty Academy
386 North Glynn St., Fayetteville 30214
Type: Private, proprietary
Degrees: C
Phone: (770) 461-4669
Inst. Accred.: NACCAS (1999/2002)

Georgia Career Institute
1820 Hwy. 20, Ste. 200, Conyers 30013
Type: Private, proprietary
Degrees: C
URL: http://www.georgiacareerinstitute.com
Phone: (770) 922-7653
Inst. Accred.: COE (1990/2004)

Georgia Driving Academy
1449 V.F.W. Dr., SW, Conyers 30012
Type: Private, proprietary
Degrees: C
URL: http://www.gadrivingacademy.org
Phone: (770) 918-8501
Inst. Accred.: COE (1998/2004)

Georgia Institute of Cosmetology
3341 Lexington Hwy., Athens 30605
Type: Private, proprietary
Degrees: C
Phone: (706) 549-6003
Inst. Accred.: COE (1993/2003)

Georgia Medical Institute
101 Marietta St., NW, 6th Flr., Atlanta 30303
Type: Private, proprietary
System: Corinthian Colleges, Inc
Degrees: C
URL: http://www.georgia-med.com
Phone: (404) 525-1111
Inst. Accred.: ABHES (1985/2004)
Prog. Accred.: Medical Assisting (ABHES)

Marietta Campus
1600 Terrell Mill Rd., Ste. G, Marietta 30067
Phone: (770) 303-7997
Prog. Accred: Medical Assisting (ABHES), Surgical Technology

Jonesboro Campus
6431 Tara Blvd., Jonesboro 30236
Phone: (770) 603-0000
Prog. Accred: Medical Assisting (ABHES)

International City Beauty College
1859 Watson Blvd., Warner Robins 31093
Type: Private, proprietary
Degrees: C
URL: http://www.icbeauty.edu
Phone: (478) 923-0915
Inst. Accred.: NACCAS (1988/2003)

International School of Skin & Nailcare
5600 Roswell Rd., NE, Atlanta 30342
Type: Private, proprietary
Degrees: C
URL: http://www.skin-nails.com
Phone: (404) 843-1005
Inst. Accred.: COE (1987/2004)

Javelin Technical Training Center
4501 Circle 75, Suite C-3180, Atlanta 30359
Type: Private, proprietary
Degrees: C
URL: http://www.javelintraining.com
Phone: (770) 859-9779
Inst. Accred.: COE (2003)

Morrow Campus
1333 Mount Zion Rd., Morrow 30260
Phone: (770) 968-9155

Ke Vos Nik School of Hair Design, Inc.
400 West Moore St., Dublin 31021
Type: Private, proprietary
Degrees: C
Phone: (478) 275-7251
Inst. Accred.: NACCAS (2003)

Medix School
2108 Cobb Pkwy., Smyrna 30080
Type: Private, proprietary
Degrees: C
URL: http://www.medixschool.com
Phone: (770) 980-0002
Inst. Accred.: ABHES (1999/2005)
Prog. Accred.: Dental Assisting, Medical Assisting
(ABHES), Medical Assisting (CAAHEP)

Michael's School of Beauty
630 North Ave., Ste. J, Macon 31211
Type: Private, proprietary
Degrees: C
Phone: (478) 741-0030
Inst. Accred.: NACCAS (2003)

North Fulton Beauty College
408 South Atlanta St., Ste. 180, Roswell 30075
Type: Private, proprietary
Degrees: C
Phone: (770) 552-9570
Inst. Accred.: COE (1992/2005)

OmniTech Institute
4319 Covington Hwy., Suite 202, Decatur 30035
Type: Private, proprietary
Degrees: C
URL: http://www.omnitechinc.com
Phone: (404) 284-8121
Inst. Accred.: COE (2003)

Portfolio Center
125 Bennett St., NW, Atlanta 30308
Type: Private, proprietary
Degrees: C
URL: http://www.portfoliocenter.com
Phone: (404) 351-5055
Inst. Accred.: COE (1982/2004)

Powder Springs Beauty College
4114 Austell Powder Springs Rd., Powder Springs 30073
Type: Private, proprietary
Degrees: C
Phone: (770) 439-9432
Inst. Accred.: NACCAS (2000/2003)

Pro Way Hair School
6254 Memorial Dr., Stone Mountain 30083
Type: Private, proprietary
Degrees: C
Phone: (770) 879-6673
Inst. Accred.: COE (1993/2005)

Professional Career Development Institute
430 Technology Pkwy., Norcross 30092-3406
Type: Private, proprietary
Degrees: C
URL: http://www.pcdi.com
Phone: (770) 729-8400
Inst. Accred.: DETC (1993/2003)

National College of Appraisal and Property Management
430 Technology Pkwy., Norcross 30092
Phone: (770) 729-8400

Rising Spirit Institute of Natural Health
4536 Chamblee Dunwoody Rd., Ste. 250 , Atlanta 30338
Type: Private, proprietary
Degrees: C
URL: http://www.risingspiritinstitute.com
Phone: (770) 457-2021
Inst. Accred.: ACCSCT (1999/2004)

Rivertown School of Beauty
3750 Woodruff Rd., Columbus 31904
Type: Private
Degrees: C
Phone: (706) 653-9223
Inst. Accred.: COE (1994/2003)

Roffler-Moler Hairstyling College
1311 Roswell Rd, Marietta 30062
Type: Private, proprietary
Degrees: C
Phone: (770) 366-2838
Inst. Accred.: ACCSCT (1988/2005)

Roswell Road Campus
1311 Roswell Rd., Marietta 30062
Phone: (770) 565-3285

Ross Medical Education Center
2645 North Decatur Rd., Decatur 30033
Type: Private, proprietary
Degrees: C
URL: http://www.rossmedicaleducation.com
Phone: (404) 377-5744
Inst. Accred.: ABHES (1999/2005)
Prog. Accred.: Medical Assisting (ABHES)

Smyrna Campus
2534 Cobb Pkwy., Smyrna 30080
Phone: (770) 951-9255
Prog. Accred: Medical Assisting (ABHES)

Southeastern Beauty School—Midtown
PO Box 12483, 1826 Midtown Dr., Columbus 31907
Type: Private, proprietary
Degrees: C
Phone: (706) 687-1054
Inst. Accred.: NACCAS (1986/2004)

Southeastern Beauty School—North Lumpkin
3448 North Lumpkin Rd., Columbus 31903
Type: Private, proprietary
Degrees: C
Phone: (706) 687-1054
Inst. Accred.: NACCAS (1987/2005)

Turner Job Corps Center
2000 Schilling Ave., Albany 31705-1524
Type: Public, federal
Degrees: C
URL: http://www.turnerjobcorps.org
Phone: (800) 476-5627
Inst. Accred.: COE (1984/2004)

United States Army Infantry School
Building 4, Rm. 514, Ft. Benning 31905-5593
Type: Public, federal
Degrees: C
URL: http://www.benning.army.mil
Phone: (706) 545-5717
Inst. Accred.: COE (1999/2005)

United States Navy Supply Corps School
1425 Prince Ave., Athens 30606-2205
Type: Public, federal
Degrees: C
URL: http://www.nscs.com
Phone: (706) 354-7200
Inst. Accred.: COE (1981/2004)

Vogue Beauty School
3655 Macland Rd., Hiram 30141
Type: Private, proprietary
Degrees: C
Phone: (770) 943-6811
Inst. Accred.: COE (1995/2001)

Cartersville Campus
238 Nelson St., Bldg. 10, Cartersville 30120
Phone: (770) 943-6811

HAWAII

Center for Asia Pacific Exchange
1616 Makiki St., Honolulu 96822
Type: Public, independent
Degrees: C
URL: http://www.capealoha.org
Phone: (808) 942-8553
Inst. Accred.: ACCET (1998/2003)

Hawaii Institute of Hair Design
71 South Hotel St., Honolulu 96813-3112
Type: Private, proprietary
Degrees: C
Phone: (808) 533-6596
Inst. Accred.: ACCSCT (1978/2005)

Hollywood Beauty College
99-084 Kauhale St., Building A, Aiea 96701
Type: Private, proprietary
Degrees: C
URL: http://www.hollywoodbeautycollege.com
Phone: (808) 486-7255
Inst. Accred.: NACCAS (1973/2001)

Intercultural Communications College
1601 Kapiolani Blvd., Ste. 1000, Honolulu 96814
Type: Private, proprietary
Degrees: C
URL: http://www.gvenglish.com
Phone: (808) 946-2445
Inst. Accred.: ACCET (1996/2004)

James E. Varner & Associates, Inc.
Gentry Pacific Center, 560 North Nimitz Hwy., #112,
Honolulu 96817
Type: Private, proprietary
Degrees: C
URL: http://www.hawaii.dalecarnegie.com
Phone: (808) 536-1400
Inst. Accred.: ACCET (1975/2001)

Maui Academy of Cosmetology
55 Kaahumanu Ave., Unit K, Kahului 96732
Type: Private, proprietary
Degrees: C
Phone: (808) 893-0007
Inst. Accred.: NACCAS (2004)

Med-Assist School of Hawaii
33 South King St., Ste. 223, Honolulu 96813
Type: Private, proprietary
Degrees: C
Phone: (808) 524-3363
Inst. Accred.: ABHES (1984/2002)

New York Technical Institute of Hawaii
1375 Dillingham Blvd., Honolulu 96817-4415
Type: Private, proprietary
Degrees: C
Phone: (808) 841-5827
Inst. Accred.: ACCSCT (1990/2005 Probation)

Travel Institute of the Pacific
1314 South King St., Ste. 1164, Honolulu 96814-2004
Type: Private, proprietary
Degrees: C
Phone: (808) 591-2708
Inst. Accred.: ACCSCT (1990/20055)

IDAHO

Ballet Idaho Academy
501 South 8th St., Boise 83702
Type: Private, independent
Degrees: C
URL: http://www.balletidaho.org/academy.html
Phone: (208) 343-0556
Inst. Accred.: NASD (2003)

Career Beauty College
57 College Ave., Rexburg 83440
Type: Private, proprietary
Degrees: C
Phone: (208) 356-0222
Inst. Accred.: NACCAS (1982/2002)

Cosmetology School of Arts and Sciences
529 Overland Ave., Burley 83318
Type: Private, proprietary
Degrees: C
Phone: (208) 678-0741
Inst. Accred.: NACCAS (2003/2004)

The Headmasters School of Hair Design
317 East Coeur D'Alene Ave., Coeur D'Alene 83814
Type: Private, proprietary
Degrees: C
URL: http://www.headmastersschool.com
Phone: (208) 664-0541
Inst. Accred.: NACCAS (1985/2005)

Boise Campus
5823 West Franklin Rd., Boise 83709
Phone: (208) 429-8070

Headmasters School of Hair Design—Lewiston
602 Main St., Lewiston 83501
Type: Private, proprietary
Degrees: C
URL: http://www.headmastersschoolhairdesign.com
Phone: (208) 743-1512
Inst. Accred.: NACCAS (1986/2001)

Mr. Juan's College of Hair Design
586 Blue Lakes Blvd. North, Twin Falls 83301
Type: Private, proprietary
Degrees: C
Phone: (208) 733-7777
Inst. Accred.: NACCAS (1969/2005)

Mr. Leon's School of Hair Design
618 South Main St., Moscow 83843
Type: Private, proprietary
Degrees: C
Phone: (208) 882-2923
Inst. Accred.: NACCAS (1984/2004)

Lewiston Campus
205 10th St., Lewiston 83501
Phone: (208) 743-6822

Northwest Lineman College
7600 South Meridian Rd., Meridian 83642
Type: Private, proprietary
Degrees: C
URL: http://www.lineman.com
Phone: (208) 888-4817
Inst. Accred.: ACCSCT (2000/2005)

Razzle Dazzle College of Hair Design
214 Holly St., Nampa 83686-5163
Type: Private, proprietary
Degrees: C
URL: http://www.razzledazzlecollege.com
Phone: (208) 465-7660
Inst. Accred.: NACCAS (1988/2003)

Sage Technical Services
2845 West Seltice Way, Coeur d'Alene 83814
Type: Private, proprietary
Degrees: C
URL: http://www.sageschools.com
Phone: (208) 765-6346
Inst. Accred.: ACCSCT (1998/2003)

The School of Hairstyling
141 East Chubbuck Rd., Chubbuck 83202
Type: Private, proprietary
Degrees: C
Phone: (208) 232-9170
Inst. Accred.: NACCAS (1985/2005)

Scot Lewis Schools-Paul Mitchell Partner School—Boise
1270 South Vinnell Way, Boise 83709
Type: Private, proprietary
Degrees: C
URL: http://www.scotlewisschools.com
Phone: (208) 375-0190
Inst. Accred.: NACCAS (1989/2004)

ILLINOIS

Alvareita's College of Cosmetology
333 South Kansas St., Edwardsville 62025
Type: Private, proprietary
Degrees: C
Phone: (618) 656-2593
Inst. Accred.: NACCAS (1984/2004)

Belleville Campus
5400 West Main St., Belleville 62226
Phone: (618) 257-9193

Alvareita's College of Cosmetology—Godfrey Campus
3048 Godfrey Rd., Godfrey 62035
Type: Private, proprietary
Degrees: C
Phone: (618) 466-8952
Inst. Accred.: NACCAS (1986/2005)

American Career College of Hair Design. Inc.
7000 West Cermak Rd., Berwyn 60402
Type: Private, proprietary
Degrees: C
Phone: (708) 795-1500
Inst. Accred.: NACCAS (2002)

American Health Information Management Association
233 North Michigan Ave., Ste. 2150, Chicago 60601
Type: Private, proprietary
Degrees: C
URL: http://www.ahima.org
Phone: (312) 233-1184
Inst. Accred.: DETC (2003)

American Institute for Paralegal Studies
17W705 Butterfield Rd., Ste. A, Oakbrook 60181
Type: Private, proprietary
Degrees: C
URL: http://www.americanparalegal.edu
Phone: (630) 916-6680
Inst. Accred.: ACCET (1981/2005)

Beck Area Career Center
6137 Beck Rd., Red Bud 62278
Type: Public, state/local
Degrees: C
URL: http://www.schools.lth5.k12.il.us/beck
Phone: (618) 473-2222
Inst. Accred.: NCA-CASI (1977/2005)

Bell Mar Beauty College
5717 West Cermak Rd., Cicero 60650
Type: Private, proprietary
Degrees: C
Phone: (708) 863-6644
Inst. Accred.: NACCAS (1987/2002)

BIR Training Center—North
3601 West Devon Ave., Ste. 210, Chicago 60659
Type: Private, proprietary
Degrees: C
URL: http://birtraining.com
Phone: (773) 866-0111
Inst. Accred.: NCA-CASI (1997/2004)

Cain's Barber College
365 East 51st St., Chicago 60615-3510
Type: Private, proprietary
Degrees: C
URL: http://www.cainsbarbers.com
Phone: (773) 536-4441
Inst. Accred.: ACCSCT (1993/2001)

CALC, Institute of Technology
235A East Center Dr., Alton 62002
Type: Private, proprietary
Degrees: C
URL: http://www.calc4it.com
Phone: (618) 474-0616
Inst. Accred.: COE (2004)

Cameo Beauty Academy
9714 South Cicero Ave., Oak Lawn 60453
Type: Private, proprietary
Degrees: C
URL: http://www.caemeobeautyacademy.com
Phone: (708) 636-4660
Inst. Accred.: NACCAS (1992/2002)

Cannella School of Hair Design—Blue Island
12840 South Western Ave., Blue Island 60406
Type: Private, proprietary
Degrees: C
URL: http://www.cannellabeautyschools.com
Phone: (708) 388-4949
Inst. Accred.: NACCAS (1975/2005)

Cannella School of Hair Design—Elgin
117 West Chicago St., Elgin 60120
Type: Private, proprietary
Degrees: C
URL: http://www.cannellabeautyschools.com
Phone: (847) 742-6611
Inst. Accred.: NACCAS (1984/2003)

Cannella School of Hair Design—Elmhurst
191 North York Rd., Elmhurst 60126
Type: Private, proprietary
Degrees: C
URL: http://www.cannellabeautyschools.com
Phone: (630) 833-6118
Inst. Accred.: NACCAS (1982/2002)

Cannella School of Hair Design—South Archer
4269 South Archer Ave., Chicago 60632
Type: Private, proprietary
Degrees: C
URL: http://www.cannellabeautyschools.com
Phone: (773) 890-0412
Inst. Accred.: NACCAS (1986/2004)

West Belmont Campus
6000 West Belmont, Chicago 60653
Phone: (773) 283-8340

Cannella School of Hair Design—South Commercial
9012 South Commercial Ave., Chicago 60617-4303
Type: Private, proprietary
Degrees: C
URL: http://www.cannellabeautyschools.com
Phone: (773) 221-4700
Inst. Accred.: NACCAS (1969/2004)

Cannella School of Hair Design—West North Avenue
4217 West North Ave., Chicago 60639
Type: Private, proprietary
Degrees: C
URL: http://www.cannellabeautyschools.com
Phone: (773) 278-4477
Inst. Accred.: NACCAS (1984/2003)

Cannella School of Hair Design—West Roosevelt
5912 West Roosevelt Rd., Chicago 60650
Type: Private, proprietary
Degrees: C
URL: http://www.cannellabeautyschools.com
Phone: (773) 287-3400
Inst. Accred.: NACCAS (1981/2005)

Capital Area Career Center
12201 Toronto Rd., Springfield 62707
Type: Public, state/local
Degrees: C
URL: http://www.capital.tec.il.us
Phone: (217) 529-5431
Inst. Accred.: NCA-CASI (1998/2005)
Prog. Accred.: Practical Nursing

Capri Garfield Ridge School of Beauty Culture
2659 West 63rd St., Chicago 60629
Type: Private, proprietary
Degrees: C
URL: http://www.capribeautyschool.com
Phone: (773) 778-8161
Inst. Accred.: NACCAS (1976/2002)

Capri Oak Forest College of Beauty Culture
15815 Rob Roy Dr., Oak Forest 60452
Type: Private, proprietary
Degrees: C
URL: http://www.capribeautyschool.com
Phone: (708) 687-3020
Inst. Accred.: NACCAS (1976/2002)

Chicago School of Massage Therapy
17 North State St., 5th Flr., Chicago 60602
Type: Private, proprietary
Degrees: C
URL: http://www.csmt.com
Phone: (773) 477-9444
Inst. Accred.: CMTA (1999)

Chicago Urban League Computer Training Center
220 South State St., 11th Flr., Chicago 60604
Type: Private, independent
Degrees: C
URL: http://www.cul-chicago.org
Phone: (312) 692-0766
Inst. Accred.: ACCET (2000)

The Chubb Institute—Chicago
25 East Washington St., Chicago 60602
Type: Private, proprietary
System: High-Tech Institute
Degrees: C
URL: http://www.chubbinstitute.edu
Phone: (312) 821-7561   *Calendar:* Sem. plan
Inst. Accred.: ACCET (2001/2004)

Computer Systems Institute
318 West Adams St., Floor 10, Chicago 60606
Type: Private, proprietary
Degrees: C
URL: http://www.csinow.com
Phone: (312) 346-6774
Inst. Accred.: NCA-CASI (2004)

Computer Systems Institute
8930 Gross Point Rd., Skokie 60077
Type: Private, proprietary
Degrees: C
URL: http://www.csinow.com
Phone: (847) 967-5030
Inst. Accred.: NCA-CASI (1998/2004)

Concept College of Cosmetology
2500 Georgetown Rd., Danville 61832
Type: Private, proprietary
Degrees: C
URL: http://conceptcollege.com
Phone: (217) 442-9329
Inst. Accred.: NACCAS (1985/2003)

Urbana Campus
129 North Race St., Urbana 61801
Phone: (217) 344-7550

The Cosmetology and Spa Institute
4320 West Elm St., McHenry 60050
Type: Private, proprietary
Degrees: C
Phone: (815) 455-5900
Inst. Accred.: NACCAS (1980/2001)

The Cosmetology and Spa Institute
700 East Terra Cotta Ave., Crystal Lake 60014
Type: Private, proprietary
Degrees: C
Phone: (815) 455-5900
Inst. Accred.: NACCAS (1980/2001)

Coyne American Institute
1235 West Fullerton Ave., Chicago 60614-2102
Type: Private
Degrees: C
Phone: (773) 935-2520   *Calendar:* Qtr. plan
Inst. Accred.: ACCSCT (1968/1998)

Greenwich Village Campus
230 West Monroe St., Fourth Floor, Chicago 60606
Phone: (773) 935-2520

Designs for Lifelong Learning
1633 Westes #3, Chicago 60626
Type: Private, independent
Degrees: C
Phone: (773) 761-8750
Inst. Accred.: MACTE (2000)

Greenwich Village Campus
16 Cooper Square, New York, NY 10003-7110
Phone: (212) 590-2800

Nashville Campus
2404 West End Ave., Ste. 201, Nashville, TN 37203
Phone: (615) 321-5199

New Brunswick Campus
390 George St., 3rd Flr., New Brunswick, NJ 08901
Phone: (732) 628-0111

New Haven Campus
970 Chapel St., New Haven, CT 06510-1011
Phone: (203) 789-1169

The Don Adams Corporation
1333 Butterfield Rd., Ste. 140, Downers Grove 60515
Type: Private, proprietary
Degrees: C
URL: http://www.chicago.dalecarnegie.com
Phone: (630) 971-1900
Inst. Accred.: ACCET (1975/2001)

DuQuoin Beauty College
202 South Washington, DuQuoin 62832
Type: Private, proprietary
Degrees: C
Phone: (618) 542-5226
Inst. Accred.: NACCAS (1975/2005)

Trend Beauty College
Town and Country Center, Carbon Rd. #21, Marion 62959
Phone: (618) 997-3138

Educators of Beauty—La Salle
122 Wright St., La Salle 61301
Type: Private, proprietary
Degrees: C
URL: http://www.educatorsofbeauty.com
Phone: (815) 223-7326
Inst. Accred.: NACCAS (1970/2003)

Educators of Beauty—Sterling
211 East Third St., Sterling 61081
Type: Private, proprietary
Degrees: C
URL: http://www.educatorsofbeauty.com
Phone: (815) 625-0247
Inst. Accred.: NACCAS (1967/2005)

Rockford Campus
128 South Fifth St., Rockford 61104
Phone: (815) 969-7030

Empire Beauty School—Hanover Park
1166 West Lake St., Hanover Park 60103
Type: Private, proprietary
Degrees: C
URL: http://www.empirebeauty.com
Phone: (630) 830-6560
Inst. Accred.: NACCAS (1984/2002)

Environmental Technical Institute
1101 West Thorndale Ave., Itasca 60143-1334
Type: Private, proprietary
Degrees: C
URL: http://www.eticampus.com
Phone: (630) 285-9100
Inst. Accred.: ACCSCT (1988/2005)

Blue Island Campus
13010 South Division St., Blue Island 60406-2606
Phone: (708) 385-0707

European Healing Massage Therapy School
8707 Skokie Blvd., Ste. 106, Skokie 60077
Type: Private, proprietary
Degrees: C
URL: http://www.school-for-massage.com
Phone: (847) 673-7585
Inst. Accred.: ABHES (2003)

First Institute, Inc.
790 McHenry Ave., Crystal Lake 60014
Type: Private, proprietary
Degrees: C
URL: http://www.firstinstitute.com
Phone: (815) 459-3500
Inst. Accred.: ACCET (1988/2005)

Greater West Town Training Partnership
2021 West Fulton St., Ste. 204, Chicago 60612
Type: Private, proprietary
Degrees: C
Phone: (312) 563-9570
Inst. Accred.: ACCSCT (1999/2004)

The Hadley School for the Blind
700 Elm St., Winnetka 60093
Type: Private, independent
Degrees: C
URL: http://www.hadley-school.org
Phone: (847) 446-8111
Inst. Accred.: DETC (1958/2004)

Hair Professionals Academy of Cosmetology—Elgin
449 C Airport Blvd., Elgin 60123
Type: Private, proprietary
Degrees: C
URL: http://www.enzotestonespa.com/school.html
Phone: (847) 622-7871
Inst. Accred.: NACCAS (1984/2004)

Hair Professionals Academy of Cosmetology—Wheaton
1145 East Butterfield, Wheaton 60187
Type: Private, proprietary
Degrees: C
URL: http://www.enzotestonespa.com/school.html
Phone: (630) 653-6630
Inst. Accred.: NACCAS (1987/2002)

Naperville Skin Institute
1100 North Sherman Ave., Naperville 60563
Phone: (630) 369-7546

Hair Professionals Career College
10321 South Roberts Rd., Palos Hills 60465
Type: Private, proprietary
Degrees: C
URL: http://www.hairpros.edu/schools.html
Phone: (708) 430-1755
Inst. Accred.: NACCAS (1988/2003)

Hair Professionals Career College, Inc.—Sycamore
2245 Gateway Dr., Sycamore 60542
Type: Private, proprietary
Degrees: C
URL: http://www.hairpros.edu/schools.html
Phone: (815) 756-3596
Inst. Accred.: NACCAS (1986/2001)

Hair Professionals School of Cosmetology, Inc.—Oswego
5460 Route 34, Oswego 60543
Type: Private, proprietary
Degrees: C
URL: http://www.hairpros.edu/schools.html
Phone: (630) 554-2266
Inst. Accred.: NACCAS (1984/2004)

Hairmasters Institute of Cosmetology, Inc.
506 South McClun St., Bloomington 61701
Type: Private, proprietary
Degrees: C
Phone: (309) 828-1884
Inst. Accred.: NACCAS (1990/2005)

Illinois Center for Broadcasting
200 West 22nd St., Ste. 202, Lombard 60148
Type: Private, proprietary
Degrees: C
URL: http://www.beonair.com
Phone: (630) 916-1700
Inst. Accred.: ACCSCT (1993/2003)

Illinois School of Health Careers
220 South State St., Ste. 600, Chicago 60604
Type: Private, proprietary
Degrees: C
URL: http://www.ishc.edu
Phone: (312) 913-1230
Inst. Accred.: ABHES (1993/2002)
Prog. Accred.: Medical Assisting (ABHES)

Chicago O'Hare Airport Campus
8750 West Bryn Mawr Ave., Chicago 60631
Phone: (773) 444-0300

Illinois Welding School
5901 Washington St., Bartonville 61607
Type: Private, proprietary
Degrees: C
URL: http://www.illinoisweldingschool.com
Phone: (309) 633-0379
Inst. Accred.: ACCSCT (2001)

John Amico's School of Hair Design
15301 South Cicero Ave., Oak Forest 60452
Type: Private, proprietary
Degrees: C
Phone: (708) 687-7800
Inst. Accred.: NACCAS (1981/2004)

Kankakee Academy of Hair Design
100 East 115th St., Chicago 60629
Type: Private, proprietary
Degrees: C
Phone: (773) 468-8666
Inst. Accred.: NACCAS (1988/1998)

La' James International College—East Moline
485 42nd Ave., East Moline 61244
Type: Private, proprietary
Degrees: C
URL: http://www.lajames.net
Phone: (309) 755-1313
Inst. Accred.: NACCAS (1967/2004)

LaMont's International School of Cosmetology
60-64 East Elm St., Canton 61520
Type: Private, proprietary
Degrees: C
Phone: (309) 647-4224
Inst. Accred.: NACCAS (1976/1999)

Lincoln Technical Institute
8317 West North Ave., Melrose Park 60160
Type: Private, proprietary
System: Lincoln Educational Services
Degrees: C
URL: http://www.lincolntech.com
Phone: (708) 344-4700
Inst. Accred.: ACCSCT (1971/2004)

Mac Daniel's Beauty School
5228 North Clark St., Second Flr., Chicago 60640
Type: Private, proprietary
Degrees: C
Phone: (773) 561-2376
Inst. Accred.: NACCAS (1977/2003)

Midwest Institute of Massage Therapy
4715 West Main St., Belleville 62223
Type: Private, proprietary
Degrees: C
Phone: (618) 239-6468
Inst. Accred.: ABHES (2004)

Midwest Montessori Teacher Training Center
926 Noyes St., Evanston 60201
Type: Private, independent
Degrees: C
Phone: (847) 276-0405
Inst. Accred.: MACTE (2005)

Midwest Technical Institute
405 North Limit St., Lincoln 62656
Type: Private, proprietary
Degrees: C
URL: http://www.midwest-school.com
Phone: (217) 735-3105
Inst. Accred.: ACCSCT (1999/2004)

Montessori Education Centers Associated-Seton
5728 Virginia St., Clarendon Hills 60514
Type: Public, independent
Degrees: C
URL: http://www.meca-seton.com
Phone: (630) 654-0151
Inst. Accred.: MACTE (1999)

Mr. John's School of Cosmetology Esthetics and Nails
1745 East Eldorado, Decatur 62521
Type: Private, proprietary
Degrees: C
URL: http://www.mrjohns.com
Phone: (217) 423-8173
Inst. Accred.: NACCAS (1982/2002)

Mr. John's School of Cosmetology, Esthetics and Nails
111 Lincoln Square, Urbana 61820
Type: Private, proprietary
Degrees: C
URL: http://www.mrjohns.com
Phone: (217) 328-2590
Inst. Accred.: NACCAS (1987/2002)

Mr. John's School of Cosmetology, Esthetics and Nails
1429 South Main St., Jacksonville 62650
Type: Private, proprietary
Degrees: C
URL: http://www.mrjohns.com
Phone: (217) 243-1744
Inst. Accred.: NACCAS (2001/2004)

Ms. Robert's Academy of Beauty Culture
17-19 East Park Blvd., Villa Park 60181
Type: Private, proprietary
Degrees: C
Phone: (630) 941-3880
Inst. Accred.: NACCAS (1974/2003)

Hillsdale Campus
552 Mannheim Rd., Hillsdale 60162
Phone: (708) 649-9088

Music Institute of Chicago
300 Green Bay Rd., Winnetka 60093
Type: Private, independent
Degrees: C
URL: http://www.musicinst.com
Phone: (847) 446-3822   *Calendar:* Sem. plan
Inst. Accred.: NASM (1978/1995)

Niles School of Beauty Culture
8057 North Milwaukee Ave., Niles 60648
Type: Private, proprietary
Degrees: C
Phone: (847) 965-8061
Inst. Accred.: NACCAS (1987/2002)

Oehrlein School of Cosmetology, Inc.
100 Meadow Ave., East Peoria 61611
Type: Private, proprietary
Degrees: C
Phone: (309) 699-1561
Inst. Accred.: NACCAS (1985/2005)

Olympia College—Skokie
9811 Woods Dr., Skokie 60077
Type: Private, proprietary
System: Corinthian Colleges, Inc
Degrees: C
URL: http://www.olympia-college.com
Phone: (847) 470-0277   *Calendar:* Qtr. plan
Inst. Accred.: ACCSCT (1973/2005)

Burr Ridge Campus
6880 North Frontage Rd., Ste. 400, Burr Ridge 60527
Phone: (630) 920-1102

Pivot Point International Academy
1560 Sherman Ave., Annex, Evanston 60201
Type: Private, proprietary
Degrees: C
URL: http://www.pivot-point.com
Phone: (847) 866-0500
Inst. Accred.: NACCAS (1967/2004)

Bloomingdale Campus
144 C East Lake St., Bloomingdale 60108
Phone: (847) 985-5900

Cosmetology Research Center
3901 West Irving Park Rd., Chicago 60618
Phone: (773) 463-3121

Pivot Point the Masters
8215 Stephanie Dr., Huntsville, AL 35802
Phone: (256) 881-8587

Professional's Choice Hair Design Academy
2719 West Jefferson St., Joliet 60435
Type: Private, proprietary
Degrees: C
URL: http://www.pchairdesign.com
Phone: (815) 741-8224
Inst. Accred.: NACCAS (1985/2005)

Pyramid Career Institute
3051 North Lincoln Ave, Chicago 60657
Type: Private, proprietary
Degrees: C
Phone: (773) 975-9898
Inst. Accred.: ACCSCT (1996/2001)

Rosel School of Cosmetology
2444 West Devon, Chicago 60659
Type: Private, proprietary
Degrees: C
Phone: (773) 508-5600
Inst. Accred.: NACCAS (1992/2005)

S.J. Grant and Associates, Inc.
806 West Tailcreek Dr., Peoria 61615
Type: Private, proprietary
Degrees: C
URL: http://www.centralil.dale-carnegie.com
Phone: (309) 691-6808
Inst. Accred.: ACCET (1976/2002)

Sanford-Brown College—Collinsville
1101 Eastport Plaza Dr., Collinsville 62234
Type: Private, proprietary
System: Career Education Corporation
Degrees: C   *Enroll:* 276
URL: http://www.sbcollinsville.com
Phone: (618) 931-0300
Inst. Accred.: ACICS (1991/2002)
Prog. Accred.: Medical Assisting (ABHES)

Spanish Coalition for Jobs, Inc.
2011 West Pershing Rd., Chicago 60609
Type: Private, independent
Degrees: C
URL: http://www.scj-usa.org
Phone: (773) 247-0707
Inst. Accred.: ACICS (1994/2001)

Sparks College
131 South Morgan St., Shelbyville 62565
Type: Private, independent
Degrees: C
URL: http://www.sparkscollege.org
Phone: (217) 774-5112
Inst. Accred.: ACICS (1954/2002)

Trend Setters College of Cosmetology
605 East North St., Bradley 60915
Type: Private, proprietary
Degrees: C
URL: http://www.trendsetterscollege.com
Phone: (815) 932-5049
Inst. Accred.: NACCAS (1991/2005)

Mokena Campus
19031 Old La Grange Rd., Ste. 209, Mokena 60448
Phone: (708) 478-6907

Tri-County Beauty Academy
219 North State St., Litchfield 62056
Type: Private, proprietary
Degrees: C
Phone: (217) 324-9062
Inst. Accred.: NACCAS (1973/2004)

UCPA Employment & Training
106 North Wacker Dr., Chicago 60606
Type: Private, proprietary
Degrees: C
Phone: (312) 368-0380
Inst. Accred.: ACCSCT (2002)

University of Spa and Cosmetology Art
2913 West White Oaks Dr., Springfield 62704
Type: Private, proprietary
Degrees: C
URL: http://www.uscart.com
Phone: (217) 753-8990
Inst. Accred.: NACCAS (1979/2005)

Vatterott College—Quincy
501 North Third St., Quincy 62301-9990
Type: Private, proprietary
Degrees: C
URL: http://www.vatterott-college.com
Phone: (217) 224-0600   *Calendar:* Sem. plan
Inst. Accred.: ACCSCT (1977/2001)

Oklahoma City Campus
4629 NW 23rd St., Oklahoma City, OK 73112
Phone: (405) 945-0088

Vee's School of Beauty Culture
2701 State St., East St. Louis 62205
Type: Private, proprietary
Degrees: C
Phone: (618) 247-1751
Inst. Accred.: NACCAS (2001/2004)

Your School of Beauty Culture
116 East Pershing Rd., Chicago 60653
Type: Private, proprietary
Degrees: C
Phone: (773) 538-4886
Inst. Accred.: NACCAS (2003)

INDIANA

A Cut Above Beauty College
3810 East Southport Rd., Indianapolis 46237
Type: Private, proprietary
Degrees: C
URL: http://www.acutabovebeautyschool.com
Phone: (317) 781-0959
Inst. Accred.: NACCAS (1986/2001)

Alexandria School of Scientific Therapeutics, Inc.
809 South Harrison St., PO Box 287, Alexandria 46001
Type: Private, proprietary
Degrees: C
URL: http://www.assti.com
Phone: (765) 724-9152
Inst. Accred.: CMTA (1999/2005)

Apex Academy of Hair Design
333 Jackson St., Anderson 46016
Type: Private, proprietary
Degrees: C
Phone: (765) 642-7560
Inst. Accred.: NACCAS (1966/1998)

Charles D. Eubank & Associates, Inc.
747 Oak Hill Rd., Evansville
Type: Private, proprietary
Degrees: C
URL: http://www.southillinois.dale-carnegie.com
Phone: (812) 424-3253
Inst. Accred.: ACCET (1976/2002)

Creative Hair Styling Academy
2549 Hwy. Ave., Highland 46322
Type: Private, proprietary
Degrees: C
URL: http://www.creativehair.com
Phone: (219) 838-2004
Inst. Accred.: NACCAS (1973/2004)

David Demuth Institute of Cosmetology
#2 South West Fifth St., Richmond 47374
Type: Private, proprietary
Degrees: C
Phone: (765) 935-7964
Inst. Accred.: NACCAS (1997/2005)

Don Roberts Beauty School
1354 Lincoln Way, Valparaiso 46383
Type: Private, proprietary
Degrees: C
Phone: (219) 462-5189
Inst. Accred.: NACCAS (1978/2003)

Don Roberts School of Hair Design
152 East Route 30, Schererville 46375
Type: Private, proprietary
Degrees: C
Phone: (219) 864-1600
Inst. Accred.: NACCAS (1977/2003)

Evansville Tri-State Beauty College
4920 Tippecanoe Ave., Evansville 47715
Type: Private, proprietary
Degrees: C
Phone: (812) 479-6989
Inst. Accred.: NACCAS (1978/2004)

Hair Arts Academy
933 North Walnut St., Bloomington 47404
Type: Private, proprietary
Degrees: C
Phone: (812) 339-1117
Inst. Accred.: NACCAS (1989/2002)

Hair Fashions by Kaye Beauty College— Indianapolis
6346 East 82nd St., Indianapolis 46250
Type: Private, proprietary
Degrees: C
Phone: (317) 576-8000
Inst. Accred.: NACCAS (1986/2001)

Hair Fashions by Kaye Beauty College— Noblesville
1111 South 10th St., Noblesville 46060
Type: Private, proprietary
Degrees: C
Phone: (317) 773-6189
Inst. Accred.: NACCAS (1986/2001)

Hanes & Associates, Inc.
9296 Waldemar Rd., Indianapolis 46268
Type: Private, proprietary
Degrees: C
URL: http://www.centralindiana.dalecarnegie.com
Phone: (317) 875-4229
Inst. Accred.: ACCET (1976/2004)

Ideal Beauty Academy, Inc.
1401 Youngstown Rd., Jeffersonville 47130
Type: Private, proprietary
Degrees: C
Phone: (812) 282-1371
Inst. Accred.: NACCAS (2005)

J. Everett Light Career Center
1901 East 86 St., Indianapolis 46240
Type: Public, state/local
Degrees: C
URL: http://www.jelcc.com
Phone: (317) 259-5265
Inst. Accred.: NCA-CASI (1984/2005)

J. Michael Harrold Beauty Academy, Inc.
2232 Wabash Ave., Terre Haute 47807
Type: Private, proprietary
Degrees: C
URL: http://www.harroldbeautyacademy.com
Phone: (812) 232-8334
Inst. Accred.: NACCAS (1966/2004)

Knox Beauty College
320 East Culver Rd., Knox 46534
Type: Private, proprietary
Degrees: C
Phone: (574) 772-5500
Inst. Accred.: NACCAS (1986/2001)

Lafayette Beauty Academy, Inc.
833 Ferry St., Lafayette 47901
Type: Private, proprietary
Degrees: C
Phone: (765) 742-0068
Inst. Accred.: NACCAS (2000/2003)

The Masters of Cosmetology College, Inc.
1732 Bluffton Rd., Fort Wayne 46809
Type: Private, proprietary
Degrees: C
URL: http://www.mastersofcosmetology.com
Phone: (260) 747-6667
Inst. Accred.: NACCAS (1985/2005)

Merrillville Beauty College
48 West 67th Place, Merrillville 46410
Type: Private, proprietary
Degrees: C
URL: http://www.merrillvillebeautycollege.com
Phone: (219) 769-2232
Inst. Accred.: NACCAS (1968/2004)

Olympia College—Merrillville
707 East 80th Place, Ste. 200, Merrillville 46410
Type: Private, proprietary
System: Corinthian Colleges, Inc
Degrees: C
URL: http://www.olympia-college.com
Phone: (219) 756-6811
Inst. Accred.: ABHES (1995/2005)

> **Merrionette Park Campus**
> 11560 South Kedzie Ave., Merrionette Park, IL 60803
> *Phone:* (708) 239-0055

PJ's College of Cosmetology—Clarksville
1414 Blackiston Mill Rd., Clarksville 47129
Type: Private, proprietary
Degrees: C
URL: http://www.gotopjs.com
Phone: (812) 282-0459
Inst. Accred.: NACCAS (1983/2003)

PJ's College of Cosmetology—Richmond
115 North 9th St., Richmond 47374
Type: Private, proprietary
Degrees: C
URL: http://www.gotopjs.com
Phone: (765) 962-3005
Inst. Accred.: NACCAS (1984/2004)

Ravenscroft Beauty College
6110 Stellhorn Rd., Fort Wayne 46815
Type: Private, proprietary
Degrees: C
Phone: (260) 486-8868
Inst. Accred.: NACCAS (1978/2004)

Roger's Academy of Hair Design, Inc.
2903 Mount Vernon Ave., Evansville 47712
Type: Private, proprietary
Degrees: C
Phone: (812) 429-0110
Inst. Accred.: NACCAS (1986/2001)

Rudae's School of Beauty Culture
208 West Jefferson St., Kokomo 46901
Type: Private, proprietary
Degrees: C
URL: http://www.rudaes.com
Phone: (765) 459-4197
Inst. Accred.: NACCAS (1965/2003)

> **Fort Wayne Campus**
> 5317 Coldwater Rd., Coldwater Crossings, Fort Wayne 46825
> *Phone:* (260) 483-2466

Vincennes Beauty College
12 South Second St., Vincennes 47591
Type: Private, proprietary
Degrees: C
Phone: (812) 882-1086
Inst. Accred.: NACCAS (1971/2003)

IOWA

American College of Hairstyling—Cedar Rapids
1531 First Ave., SE, Cedar Rapids 52402-5123
Type: Private, proprietary
Degrees: C
Phone: (319) 362-1488
Inst. Accred.: ACCSCT (1977/2001)

American College of Hairstyling—Des Moines
603 East Sixth St., Des Moines 50309-5478
Type: Private, proprietary
Degrees: C
Phone: (515) 244-0971
Inst. Accred.: ACCSCT (1975/2005)

Bill Hill's College of Cosmetology
910 Ave. G, Fort Madison 52627
Type: Private, proprietary
Degrees: C
Phone: (319) 372-6248
Inst. Accred.: NACCAS (1984/2003)

Capri College
395 Main St., PO Box 873, Dubuque 52004-0873
Type: Private, proprietary
Degrees: C
URL: http://www.capricollege.com
Phone: (563) 588-2379
Inst. Accred.: ACCSCT (1990/2005)

Capri College
425 East 59th St., Davenport 52807-2622
Type: Private, proprietary
Degrees: C
URL: http://www.capricollege.com
Phone: (319) 388-6642
Inst. Accred.: ACCSCT (1994/2004)

Capri College
2945 Williams Pkwy., SW, Cedar Rapids 52404
Type: Private, proprietary
Degrees: C
URL: http://www.capricollege.com
Phone: (319) 364-1541
Inst. Accred.: ACCSCT (1994/2004)

Carlson College of Massage Therapy
11809 County Rd. X28, Stone City 52205
Type: Private, proprietary
Degrees: C
URL: http://www.carlsoncollege.com
Phone: (319) 462-3402
Inst. Accred.: CMTA (1999/2004)

College of Hair Design
722 Water St, Ste 201, Waterloo 50702-1834
Type: Private, proprietary
Degrees: C
Phone: (319) 232-9995
Inst. Accred.: ACCSCT (1989/2005)

Davenport Barber-Styling College
730 East Kimberly Rd., Davenport 52807
Type: Private, proprietary
Degrees: C
Phone: (319) 391-9950
Inst. Accred.: ACCSCT (1996/2001)

Dayton's School of Hair Design—Burlington
315 North Main St., Burlington 52601
Type: Private, proprietary
Degrees: C
Phone: (319) 752-3193
Inst. Accred.: NACCAS (1975/2005)

Dayton's School of Hair Design—Keokuk
23 South Second St., Keokuk 52632
Type: Private, proprietary
Degrees: C
Phone: (319) 524-6445
Inst. Accred.: NACCAS (1985/2005)

EQ School of Hair Design
536 West Broadway, Council Bluffs 51503
Type: Private, proprietary
Degrees: C
Phone: (712) 328-2613
Inst. Accred.: NACCAS (1972/2003)

The Faust Institute of Cosmetology
502 Erie St., PO Box 29, Storm Lake 50588
Type: Private, proprietary
Degrees: C
Phone: (712) 732-6571
Inst. Accred.: NACCAS (1984/2004)

Spirit Lake Campus
1543 18th St., Spirit Lake 51360
Phone: (712) 336-0512

Iowa School of Beauty—Des Moines
3305 70th St., Des Moines 50322
Type: Private, proprietary
Degrees: C
URL: http://www.iowaschoolofbeauty.com
Phone: (515) 278-9939
Inst. Accred.: NACCAS (1980/2000)

Iowa School of Beauty—Marshalltown
112 Nicholas Dr., Marshalltown 50158
Type: Private, proprietary
Degrees: C
URL: http://www.iowaschoolofbeauty.com
Phone: (515) 752-4223
Inst. Accred.: NACCAS (1985/2000)

Iowa School of Beauty—Ottumwa
609 West Second St., Ottumwa 52501
Type: Private, proprietary
Degrees: C
URL: http://www.iowaschoolofbeauty.com
Phone: (641) 684-6504
Inst. Accred.: NACCAS (1977/2003)

Iowa School of Beauty—Sioux City
2524 Glenn Ave., Sioux City 51106
Type: Private, proprietary
Degrees: C
URL: http://www.iowaschoolofbeauty.com
Phone: (712) 274-9733
Inst. Accred.: NACCAS (1972/2003)

La' James College of Hairstyling—Mason City
24 Second St., NE, Mason City 50401
Type: Private, proprietary
Degrees: C
URL: http://www.lajames.net
Phone: (641) 424-2161
Inst. Accred.: NACCAS (1974/2005)

La' James International College—Cedar Falls
6322 University Ave., Cedar Falls 50613
Type: Private, proprietary
Degrees: C
URL: http://www.lajames.net
Phone: (319) 277-2150
Inst. Accred.: NACCAS (1976/2003)

La' James International College—Davenport
3802 East 53rd St., Davenport 52807
Type: Private, proprietary
Degrees: C
URL: http://www.lajames.net
Phone: (563) 386-7700
Inst. Accred.: NACCAS (1980/2005)

La' James International College—Des Moines
8805 Chambery Boulvard, Johnston 50131
Type: Private, proprietary
Degrees: C
URL: http://www.lajames.net
Phone: (515) 278-2208
Inst. Accred.: NACCAS (1984/2004)

La' James International College—Fort Dodge
2419 5th Ave. South, Fort Dodge 50501
Type: Private, proprietary
Degrees: C
URL: http://www.lajames.net
Phone: (515) 576-3119
Inst. Accred.: NACCAS (1974/2005)

La' James International College—Iowa City
227 East Market St., Brewery Square, Iowa City 52240
Type: Private, proprietary
Degrees: C
URL: http://www.lajames.net
Phone: (319) 338-3926
Inst. Accred.: NACCAS (1965/2003)

The Salon Professional Academy
309 Kitty Hawk Dr., Ames 50010-8592
Type: Private, proprietary
Degrees: C
URL: http://www.pciames.com
Phone: (515) 232-7250
Inst. Accred.: NACCAS (1981/2001)

New Hope Campus
4411 Winnetka Ave. North, New Hope, MN 55446
Phone: (763) 536-0772

Total Look School of Cosmetology and Massage Therapy
806 West Third St., Cresco 52136
Type: Private, proprietary
Degrees: C
Phone: (563) 547-3624
Inst. Accred.: NACCAS (2001/2004)

KANSAS

Academy of Hair Design
115 South Fifth St., Salina 67401
Type: Private, proprietary
Degrees: C
Phone: (785) 825-8155
Inst. Accred.: NACCAS (1970/2003)

American Academy of Hair Design
901 SW 37th St., Topeka 66611
Type: Private, proprietary
Degrees: C
URL: http://www.aaahairdesign.com
Phone: (785) 267-5800
Inst. Accred.: NACCAS (1982/2002)

American Institute of Baking
1213 Bakers Way, Manhattan 66502
Type: Private, independent
Degrees: C
URL: http://www.aibonline.org
Phone: (785) 537-4750
Inst. Accred.: NCA-CASI (1985/2001)

BMSI Institute, LLC
8665 West 96th St., Ste. 300, Overland Park 66212
Type: Private, proprietary
Degrees: C
URL: http://www.bmsi-institute.com
Phone: (913) 649-3322   *Calendar:* Sem. plan
Inst. Accred.: CMTA (2004, Probation)

Bryan College—Topeka
1527 SW Fairlawn Rd., Topeka 66604
Type: Private, proprietary
Degrees: C
URL: http://www.bryancareercolleges.com
Phone: (785) 272-0889
Inst. Accred.: ACICS (1991/2000)

CB&T, Inc
5700 Broadmoor, #202, Mission 66202
Type: Private, proprietary
Degrees: C
URL: http://www.kansascity.dalecarnegie.com
Phone: (913) 831-9330
Inst. Accred.: ACCET (1976/2001)

Community College of Cosmetology
3602 Topeka Blvd., SW, Topeka 66611
Type: Private, proprietary
Degrees: C
URL: http://superiorbeautyschools.com
Phone: (785) 267-7701
Inst. Accred.: NACCAS (2000/2003)

Classic College of Hair Design
1675 South Rock Rd., Ste. 101, Wichita 67207
Phone: (316) 681-2288

Crum's Beauty College
512 Poyntz Ave., Manhattan 66502
Type: Private, proprietary
Degrees: C
URL: http://www.crumsbeautycollege.com
Phone: (785) 776-4794
Inst. Accred.: NACCAS (1967/2003)

Cutting Edge Hairstyling Academy
4327 State Ave., Kansas City 66102
Type: Private, proprietary
Degrees: C
URL: http://cuttingedge-kc.com
Phone: (913) 321-0214
Inst. Accred.: ACCSCT (1987/2004)

Shawnee Campus
12148 Shawnee Mission Pkwy., Shawnee 66216
Phone: (913) 962-0076

Hays Academy of Hair Design
119 West 10th St., Hays 67601
Type: Private, proprietary
Degrees: C
Phone: (785) 628-3981
Inst. Accred.: NACCAS (1984/2005)

Kansas City Kansas Area Technical School
2220 North 59th St., Kansas City 66104
Type: Public, state/local
Degrees: C
URL: http://www.kckats.com
Phone: (913) 627-4100
Inst. Accred.: NCA-CASI (1996/2002)

Kaw Area Technical School
5724 SW Huntoon St., Topeka 66604-2199
Type: Public, local
Degrees: C
URL: http://www.kats.tec.ks.us
Phone: (785) 273-7140   *Calendar:* Qtr. plan
Inst. Accred.: COE (2004)

LaBaron Hairdressing Academy— Overland Park
8119 Robinson St., Overland Park 66204
Type: Private, proprietary
Degrees: C
URL: http://www.labaronacademy.com
Phone: (913) 642-0077
Inst. Accred.: NACCAS (1986/2001)

Old Town Barber and Beauty College
1207 East Douglas Ave., Wichita 67211-1693
Type: Private, proprietary
Degrees: C
Phone: (316) 264-4891
Inst. Accred.: ACCSCT (1980/2001)

Pinnacle Career Institute—Lawrence
1601 West 23rd St., Ste. 200, Lawrence 66046
Type: Private, proprietary
Degrees: C
URL: http://www.pcitraining.edu
Phone: (785) 841-9640
Inst. Accred.: ACICS (1989/2002)

Salina Area Technical School
2562 Centennial Rd., Salina 67401
Type: Public, state/local
Degrees: C
URL: http://www.salinatech.com
Phone: (785) 309-3100   *Calendar:* Sem. plan
Inst. Accred.: NCA-CASI (1997/2004)
Prog. Accred.: Dental Assisting

Sidney's Hairdressing College, Inc.
916 East 4th Ave., Hutchinson 67501
Type: Private, proprietary
Degrees: C
URL: http://www.sidneyshair.com
Phone: (620) 662-5481
Inst. Accred.: NACCAS (2001/2004)

Southwest Kansas Technical School
2215 North Kansas Ave., Liberal 67901-2013
Type: Public, state/local
Degrees: C
URL: http://www.usd480.net/swkts
Phone: (620) 626-3819
Inst. Accred.: NCA-CASI (1983/2002)

Superior School of Hairstyling
1215 East Santa Fe, Olathe 66061
Type: Private, proprietary
Degrees: C
URL: http://superiorbeautyschools.com
Phone: (913) 782-4004
Inst. Accred.: NACCAS (1990/2005)

College of Hair Design
10324 Mastin St., Overland Park 66212
Phone: (913) 492-4114

Vernon's Kansas School of Cosmetology
2531 South Seneca St., Wichita 67217
Type: Private, proprietary
Degrees: C
URL: http://www.vksc.edu
Phone: (316) 265-2629
Inst. Accred.: NACCAS (1965/2005)

Wichita Area Technical College
301 South Grove St., Wichita 67211
Type: Private, proprietary
Degrees: C   *Enroll:* 1,052
URL: http://www.watc.edu
Phone: (316) 677-9282   *Calendar:* Sem. plan
Inst. Accred.: COE (1995/2001)
Prog. Accred.: Clinical Lab Technology, Medical Assisting
(AMA), Practical Nursing, Surgical Technology

Airport Campus
2021 South Eisenhower St., Wichita 67209-2848
Phone: (316) 973-9550

Central Campus
324 North Emporia St., Wichita 67202-2512
Phone: (316) 973-4340
Prog. Accred: Dental Assisting

Dunbar Campus
923 Cleveland St., Wichita 67214-3495
Phone: (316) 973-3150

Schweiter Camous
1400 George Washington Dr., Wichita 67211
Phone: (316) 973-0950

Seneca Campus
4141 North Seneca St., Wichita 67204-3103
Phone: (316) 973-1200

Wichita Technical Institute
942 South West St., Wichita 67213-1681
Type: Private, proprietary
Degrees: C
URL: http://www.wtielectronics.com
Phone: (316) 943-2241
Inst. Accred.: ACCSCT (1971/2004)
Prog. Accred.: Dental Assisting

Wichita Campus
1710 SW Topeka Blvd., Topeka 66612
Phone: (785) 354-4568

Wright Business School
8951 Metcalf Ave., Overland Park 66212
Type: Private, proprietary
Degrees: C
URL: http://www.wrightbusinessschool.edu
Phone: (913) 385-7700
Inst. Accred.: ACICS (1988/2004)

Oklahoma City Campus
2219 SW 74th St., Ste. 124, Oklahoma City, OK 73159
Phone: (405) 681-2300

Tulsa Campus
4908 South Sheridan Rd., Tulsa, OK 74145
Phone: (918) 628-7700

Xenon International School of Hair Design
3804 West Douglas Ave., Wichita 67203
Type: Private, proprietary
Degrees: C
URL: http://www.xenonintl.com
Phone: (316) 943-5516
Inst. Accred.: NACCAS (1989/2004)

KENTUCKY

Appalachian Beauty School
29100 Appalachian Plaza, US Hwy. 119 South, South Williamson 41503
Type: Private, proprietary
Degrees: C
Phone: (606) 237-6650
Inst. Accred.: NACCAS (1980/2005)

ATA Career Education
10180 Linn Station Rd., Ste. A-200, Louisville 40223
Type: Private, proprietary
Degrees: C
URL: http://www.ata.edu
Phone: (502) 371-8330
Inst. Accred.: ABHES (2005)

Saint Louis Campus
77 West Port Plaza, Ste. 100, St. Louis, MO 63146
Phone: (314) 469-3933

Barrett & Company School of Hair Design
973 Kimberly Square, Nicholasville 40356
Type: Private, proprietary
Degrees: C
Phone: (859) 885-9136
Inst. Accred.: COE (1987/2004)

Bellefonte Academy of Beauty
420 Belfont St., PO Box 40, Russell 41169
Type: Private, proprietary
Degrees: C
Phone: (606) 833-5446
Inst. Accred.: NACCAS (2003)

Carl D. Perkins Job Corps Center
478 Meadows Branch Rd., Prestonsburg 41653-1501
Type: Public, state
Degrees: C
Phone: (606) 886-1037
Inst. Accred.: COE (1985/2001)

Collins School of Cosmetology
111 West Chester Ave., PO Box 1370, Middlesboro 40965
Type: Private, proprietary
Degrees: C
Phone: (606) 248-3602
Inst. Accred.: NACCAS (1973/2003)

Donta School of Beauty Culture
515 West Oak St., Louisville 40203
Type: Private, proprietary
Degrees: C
Phone: (502) 583-1018
Inst. Accred.: NACCAS (1980/2005)

Earle C. Clements Job Corps Center
2302 US Hwy. 60 East, Morganfield 42437
Type: Public, federal
Degrees: C
Phone: (270) 389-2419
Inst. Accred.: COE (1983/2005)

Elizabethtown Beauty School
308 North Miles St., Elizabethtown 42701
Type: Private, proprietary
Degrees: C
Phone: (270) 765-2118
Inst. Accred.: NACCAS (1984/2004)

Ezell's Cosmetology School
504 Maple St., PO Box 1431, Murray 42071
Type: Private, proprietary
Degrees: C
Phone: (270) 753-4723
Inst. Accred.: NACCAS (2000/2003)

Federal Medical Center—Lexington
3301 Leestown Rd., Lexington 40511-8799
Type: Public, federal
Degrees: C
Phone: (859) 255-6812
Inst. Accred.: COE (2000)

The Hair Design School
7285 Turfway Rd., Florence 41042
Type: Private, proprietary
Degrees: C
URL: http://www.hairdesignschool.com
Phone: (859) 283-2690
Inst. Accred.: NACCAS (1975/2001)

The Hair Design School
1049 Bardstown Rd., Louisville 40204
Type: Private, proprietary
Degrees: C
URL: http://www.hairdesignschool.com
Phone: (502) 459-8150
Inst. Accred.: NACCAS (1980/2005)

The Hair Design School
5120 Dixie Hwy., Louisville 40216
Type: Private, proprietary
Degrees: C
URL: http://www.hairdesignschool.com
Phone: (502) 447-0111
Inst. Accred.: NACCAS (1975/2001)

The Hair Design School
151 Chenoweth Ln., Louisville 40207
Type: Private, proprietary
Degrees: C
URL: http://www.hairdesignschool.com
Phone: (502) 897-9401
Inst. Accred.: COE (1989/2002)

The Hair Design School
554 Westport Rd., Elizabethtown 42701
Type: Private, proprietary
Degrees: C
URL: http://www.hairdesignschool.com
Phone: (270) 765-3374
Inst. Accred.: NACCAS (1976/2001)

The Hair Design School—Louisville
5314 Bardstown Rd., Louisville 40291
Type: Private, proprietary
Degrees: C
URL: http://www.hairdesignschool.com
Phone: (502) 499-0070
Inst. Accred.: NACCAS (1975/2001)

Head's West Kentucky Beauty College
Briarwood Shopping Center, Madisonville 42431
Type: Private, proprietary
Degrees: C
Phone: (270) 825-3019
Inst. Accred.: NACCAS (1990/2005)

J & M Academy of Cosmetology, Inc.
110 A Brighton Park Blvd., Frankfort 40601
Type: Private, proprietary
Degrees: C
Phone: (502) 695-8001
Inst. Accred.: NACCAS (1986/2004)

Jenny Lea Academy of Cosmetology—Harlan
114 North Cumberland Ave., Harlan 40831
Type: Private, proprietary
Degrees: C
Phone: (606) 573-4276
Inst. Accred.: NACCAS (1984/2004)

**Jenny Lea Academy of Cosmetology—
Whitesburg**
74 Pkwy. Plaza Loop, Whitesburg 41858
Type: Private, proprietary
Degrees: C
Phone: (606) 633-8784
Inst. Accred.: NACCAS (1987/2005)

Kaufman Beauty School
701 East High St., Lexington 40502
Type: Private, proprietary
Degrees: C
URL: http://www.kaufmaneducation.com
Phone: (859) 266-2024
Inst. Accred.: NACCAS (1971/2003)

Motif Beauty Academy
23 West Lexington Ave., Winchester 40391
Type: Private, proprietary
Degrees: C
Phone: (859) 745-5886
Inst. Accred.: NACCAS (1993/2001)

Mr. Jim's Beauty College
1240 Carter Rd., Owensboro 42301
Type: Private, proprietary
Degrees: C
Phone: (270) 684-3505
Inst. Accred.: NACCAS (1994/2002)

Nu-Tek Academy of Beauty
153 Evans Dr., Mount Sterling 40353
Type: Private, proprietary
Degrees: C
Phone: (606) 498-4460
Inst. Accred.: COE (1990/2005)

Pat Wilson Beauty College, Inc.
326 North Main St., Henderson 42420
Type: Private, proprietary
Degrees: C
Phone: (270) 826-5195
Inst. Accred.: NACCAS (1985/2003)

PJ's College of Cosmetology
1901 Russellville Rd., Ste. 10, Bowling Green 42101
Type: Private, proprietary
Degrees: C
URL: http://www.gotopjs.com
Phone: (270) 842-8149
Inst. Accred.: COE (1986/2003)

PJ's College of Cosmetology
124 South Public Square, Glasgow 42141
Type: Private, proprietary
Degrees: C
URL: http://www.gotopjs.com
Phone: (270) 651-6553
Inst. Accred.: COE (1987/2004)

Greenfield Campus
1400 West Main St., Greenfield, IN 46140
Phone: (317) 462-9239

Indianapolis Campus
5539 South Madison St., Indianapolis, IN 46227
Phone: (317) 781-9600

Muncie Campus
2006 North Walnut St., Muncie, IN 47303
Phone: (765) 289-6144

Plainfield Campus
2026 Stafford Rd., Plainfield, IN 46168
Phone: (317) 839-2761

Regency School of Hair Design
567 North Lake Dr., Prestonsburg 41653
Type: Private, proprietary
Degrees: C
Phone: (606) 886-6457
Inst. Accred.: NACCAS (2003/2004)

Southeast School of Cosmetology
356 Manchester Square Center, PO Box 493, Manchester
40962
Type: Private, proprietary
Degrees: C
Phone: (606) 598-7901
Inst. Accred.: NACCAS (1988/2003)

Trend Setter's Academy of Beauty Culture
7283 Dixie Hwy., Louisville 40258
Type: Private, proprietary
Degrees: C
Phone: (502) 937-6704
Inst. Accred.: NACCAS (1981/2001)

Elizabethtown Campus
622 Westport Rd., Ste. B, Elizabethtown 42701
Phone: (270) 765-5243

William F. Lea & Associates, Inc.
4010 Dupont Circle, Ste. 581, Louisville 40207
Type: Private, proprietary
Degrees: C
URL: http://www.kentuckiana.dalecarnegie.com
Phone: (502) 893-2928
Inst. Accred.: ACCET (1998/2003)

LOUISIANA

Alexandria Academy of Beauty
2305 Rapides Ave., Alexandria 71301
Type: Private, proprietary
Degrees: C
Phone: (318) 442-7715
Inst. Accred.: NACCAS (1987/2002)

American School of Business
702 Professional Dr. North, Shreveport 71105
Type: Private, proprietary
Degrees: C
URL: http://www.americanschoolofbusiness.com
Phone: (318) 798-3333
Inst. Accred.: ACICS (1988/2004)

Ascension College
320 East Ascension St., Gonzales 70737
Type: Private, proprietary
Degrees: C
Phone: (225) 647-6609
Inst. Accred.: COE (1991/2000)

Aveda Institute
1355 Polders Ln., Covington 70434
Type: Private, proprietary
Degrees: C
URL: http://www.avedainstitutes.com
Phone: (985) 892-3826
Inst. Accred.: NACCAS (1988/2001)

Charlotte Campus
1520 South Blvd., Ste. 150, Charlotte, NC 28203
Phone: (704) 333-9940

Conroe Campus
1212 D. South Frazier, Conroe, TX 77301
Phone: (936) 539-6770

New Orleans Campus
3330 Veterans Blvd., Ste. A, Metairie 70002
Phone: (504) 454-1400

Aveda Institute Baton Rouge
2834 South Sherwood Forest Blvd., Baton Rouge 70816
Type: Private, proprietary
Degrees: C
URL: http://www.avedainstitutes.com
Phone: (225) 295-1435
Inst. Accred.: NACCAS (1981/2001)

Aveda Institute Lafayette
2922 Johnston St., Lafayette 70503
Type: Private, proprietary
Degrees: C
URL: http://www.avedainstitutes.com
Phone: (337) 233-0511
Inst. Accred.: NACCAS (1979/2001)

Ayers Institute
3010 Knight St., Ste. 300, Shreveport 71105
Type: Private, proprietary
Degrees: C
URL: http://www.ayersinstitute.com
Phone: (318) 868-3000
Inst. Accred.: COE (1995/2001)

Bastrop Beauty School No. 1
117 South Vine St., Bastrop 71220
Type: Private, proprietary
Degrees: C
Phone: (318) 281-8652
Inst. Accred.: NACCAS (1984/2004)

Baton Rouge College
2834 South Sherwood Forest Blvd., B-12, Baton Rouge
Type: Private, proprietary
Degrees: C
URL: http://www.brcollege.edu
Phone: (225) 292-5464
Inst. Accred.: ACCET (1989/2002)

Cassia Beauty College
6960 Martin Dr., Ste. 120, New Orleans 70126
Type: Private, proprietary
Degrees: C
Phone: (504) 244-3700
Inst. Accred.: NACCAS (2001/2003)

Cloyd's Beauty School No. 1
603 Natchitoches St., West Monroe 71291
Type: Private, proprietary
Degrees: C
Phone: (318) 322-5314
Inst. Accred.: NACCAS (1986/2001)

Cloyd's Beauty School No. 2
1311 Winnsboro Rd., Monroe 71201
Type: Private, proprietary
Degrees: C
Phone: (318) 322-5314
Inst. Accred.: COE (1991/2001)

Cloyd's Beauty School No. 3
2514 Ferrand St., PO Box 603, West Monroe 71294
Type: Private, proprietary
Degrees: C
Phone: (318) 322-5314
Inst. Accred.: COE (1991/2001)

Cosmetology Business and Management Institute
59 West Bank Expressway, Gretna 70053
Type: Private, proprietary
Degrees: C
Phone: (504) 362-1999
Inst. Accred.: NACCAS (1982/2001)

Cosmetology Training Center
2516 Johnston St., Lafayette 70503
Type: Private, proprietary
Degrees: C
Phone: (337) 237-6868
Inst. Accred.: NACCAS (1987/2002)

Court Reporting Institute of Louisiana, Inc.
2834 South Sherwood Forest Blvd., Ste. D-12, Baton Rouge 70816
Type: Private, proprietary
Degrees: C
URL: http://www.courtreportinginstituteoflouisiana.com
Phone: (225) 292-1950
Inst. Accred.: COE (2003)

Crescent Schools
209 North Broad St., New Orleans 70119
Type: Private, proprietary
Degrees: C
URL: http://www.crescentschools.com
Phone: (504) 822-3362
Inst. Accred.: ACCET (1990/2003)

Gulfport Campus
1205 25th Ave., Gulfport, MS 39501
Phone: (228) 822-2444

Las Vegas Campus
4180 South Sandhill Rd., Ste. B8/9, Las Vegas, NV 89121
Phone: (702) 458-9910

Culinary Institute of New Orleans
2100 Saint Charles Ave., New Orleans 70140
Type: Private, proprietary
Degrees: C
Phone: (504) 525-2433
Inst. Accred.: COE (1998/2005)

D-Jay's School of Beauty Arts & Sciences
5131 Government St., Baton Rouge 70806
Type: Private, proprietary
Degrees: C
Phone: (225) 926-2530
Inst. Accred.: NACCAS (1974/2003)

Delta College
2401 Hwy. 190 North, Covington 70433
Type: Private, proprietary
Degrees: C
URL: http://www.deltacollege.com
Phone: (225) 892-6651
Inst. Accred.: COE (1998/2004)

Demmon School of Beauty
1222 Ryan St., Lake Charles 70601
Type: Private, proprietary
Degrees: C
Phone: (337) 439-9265
Inst. Accred.: NACCAS (1967/2005)

Denham Springs Beauty College
923 Florida Ave., SE, Denham Springs 70726
Type: Private, proprietary
Degrees: C
Phone: (225) 665-6188
Inst. Accred.: COE (1989/2000)

Diesel Driving Academy
8136 Airline Hwy., Baton Rouge 70815
Type: Private, proprietary
Degrees: C
URL: http://www.dieseldrivingacademy.com
Phone: (225) 929-9990
Inst. Accred.: COE (1990/2004)

Diesel Driving Academy
4709 Greenwood Rd., PO Box 36949, Shreveport 71133-6949
Type: Private, proprietary
Degrees: C
URL: http://www.dieseldrivingacademy.com
Phone: (318) 636-6300
Inst. Accred.: COE (1982/2002)

New Orleans Campus
4100 Jourdan Rd., New Orleans 70126-5044
Phone: (800) 551-8900

Domestic Health Care Institute
4826 Jamestown Ave., Baton Rouge 70808
Type: Private, proprietary
Degrees: C
Phone: (225) 925-5312
Inst. Accred.: ABHES (1990/2005)

Franklin College of Court Reporting
1200 South Clearview Pkwy., Elmwood Center 1180, New Orleans 70123
Type: Private, proprietary
Degrees: C
Phone: (504) 734-1000
Inst. Accred.: COE (1990/2005)

Guy's Academy Hair, Skin, and Nails
1141 Shreveport-Barksdale Hwy., Shreveport 71105
Type: Private, proprietary
Degrees: C
URL: http://www.guysacademy.com
Phone: (318) 865-5591
Inst. Accred.: NACCAS (1988/2003)

ITI Technical College
13944 Airline Hwy., Baton Rouge 70817-5998
Type: Private, proprietary
Degrees: C   *Enroll:* 278
Phone: (225) 752-4233
Inst. Accred.: ACCSCT (1981/2005)

John Jay Beauty College
540 Robert E. Lee Blvd., New Orleans 70124
Type: Private, proprietary
Degrees: C
Phone: (504) 282-8128
Inst. Accred.: NACCAS (1966/2001)

Slidell Campus
3144 Pontchartrain Dr., Slidell 70458
Phone: (985) 643-0677

John Jay Kenner Academy
2844 Tennessee Ave., Kenner 70062
Type: Private, proprietary
Degrees: C
Phone: (504) 466-4561
Inst. Accred.: NACCAS (1983/2003)

Jonesville Beauty School
208 Westside Dr., Vidalia 71373
Type: Private, proprietary
Degrees: C
Phone: (318) 336-2377
Inst. Accred.: NACCAS (1997/2005)

Vidalia Beauty School
208 Westside Dr., Vidalia 71373
Phone: (318) 336-2377

King's Career College—Florida Boulevard Campus
3875 Florida Blvd., Baton Rouge 70806
Type: Private, proprietary
Degrees: C
Phone: (225) 387-5535
Inst. Accred.: ABHES (1999/2001)

King's Career College—Ocean Drive Campus
1771 North Lobdell Blvd., Baton Rouge 70806
Type: Private, proprietary
Degrees: C
Phone: (225) 644-4432
Inst. Accred.: ABHES (1999/2001)

Louisiana Academy of Beauty
550 East Laurel St., Eunice 70535
Type: Private, proprietary
Degrees: C
Phone: (337) 457-7627
Inst. Accred.: NACCAS (1987/2002)

Massage Therapy College of Baton Rouge
6160 Perkins Rd., Ste. 200, Baton Rouge 70808-4191
Type: Private, proprietary
Degrees: C
Phone: (225) 757-3770
Inst. Accred.: CMTA (1999)

Medical Training College
10525 Plaza Americana Dr., Baton Rouge 70816
Type: Private, proprietary
Degrees: C
Phone: (225) 926-5820
Inst. Accred.: COE (1998/2004)

MedVance Institute of Baton Rouge
9255 Interline Ave., Baton Rouge 70809
Type: Private, proprietary
Degrees: C
URL: http://www.medvance.edu
Phone: (225) 248-1015   *Calendar:* Qtr. plan
Inst. Accred.: ABHES (1995/2001)
Prog. Accred.: Radiography

Fort Lauderdale Campus
4850 West Oakland Park Blvd., Ste.235, Ft Lauderdale, FL 33313
Phone: (954) 587-7100
Prog. Accred: Medical Assisting (ABHES), Radiography, Surgical Technology

Nashville Campus
2400 Parman Place, Building B, Ste. 3, Nashville, TN 37203
Phone: (561) 832-3535
Prog. Accred: Medical Assisting (ABHES)

Stuart Campus
851 Johnson Ave., Stuart, FL 34994
Phone: (772) 221-9799
Prog. Accred: Medical Assisting (ABHES), Surgical Technology

Moler Beauty College—Canal Street
2940 Canal St., New Orleans 70119
Type: Private, proprietary
Degrees: C
Phone: (504) 821-8842
Inst. Accred.: NACCAS (1966/2002)

Moler Beauty College—Kenner
1919 Veterans Blvd., Ste. 100 70062
Type: Private, proprietary
Degrees: C
Phone: (504) 467-1888
Inst. Accred.: NACCAS (1982/2001)

Chef Menteur Highway Campus
4301 Chef Menteur Hwy., New Orleans 70126
Phone: (504) 282-2539

New Orleans Job Corps Center
3801 Hollygrove St., New Orleans 70118
Type: Public, federal
Degrees: C
Phone: (504) 486-0641
Inst. Accred.: COE (1995/2001)

Omega Institute of Cosmetology
229 South Hollywood Rd., Houma 70360
Type: Private, proprietary
Degrees: C
URL: http://www.omegainstitutes.com
Phone: (985) 876-9334
Inst. Accred.: NACCAS (2000/2003)

Opelousas School of Cosmetology, Inc
529 East Vine St., Opelousas 70570
Type: Private, proprietary
Degrees: C
Phone: (337) 942-6147
Inst. Accred.: NACCAS (1989/2004)

Pat Goins Beauty School
3138 Louisville Ave., Monroe 71201
Type: Private, proprietary
Degrees: C
Phone: (318) 322-2500
Inst. Accred.: NACCAS (1975/2005)

Pat Goins Benton Road Beauty School
1701 Old Minden Rd., Ste. 36, Bossier City 71111
Type: Private, proprietary
Degrees: C
Phone: (318) 746-7674
Inst. Accred.: NACCAS (1975/2005)

Pat Goins Ruston Beauty School
213 West Alabama St., Ruston 71270
Type: Private, proprietary
Degrees: C
Phone: (318) 255-2717
Inst. Accred.: NACCAS (1971/2005)

Pat Goins Shreveport Beauty School
6363 Hearne Ave., Ste. 106, Shreveport 71108
Type: Private, proprietary
Degrees: C
Phone: (318) 631-1833
Inst. Accred.: NACCAS (1979/2005)

Paul Phillips and Associates, Inc.
2540 Severn Ave., Ste. 211, Metairie 70002
Type: Private, proprietary
Degrees: C
URL: http://www.neworleans.dalecarnegie.com
Phone: (985) 727-4636
Inst. Accred.: ACCET (1978/2004)

Pineville Beauty School
1008 Main St., Pineville 71360
Type: Private, proprietary
Degrees: C
Phone: (318) 445-1040
Inst. Accred.: NACCAS (1985/2005)

Professional Chefs Institute of the South
5454 Bluebonnet Blvd., Baton Rouge 70809
Type: Private, proprietary
Degrees: C
Phone: (225) 291-5766
Inst. Accred.: ACICS (2004)

Ray's Faith Academy of Beauty Education
1064 East Worthey Rd., Gonzales 70737
Type: Private, proprietary
Degrees: C
Phone: (225) 644-2872
Inst. Accred.: NACCAS (2004)

Ronnie & Dorman's School of Hair Design
2002 Johnston St., Lafayette 70503
Type: Private, proprietary
Degrees: C
Phone: (337) 232-1806
Inst. Accred.: NACCAS (1975/2001)

Shreveport Job Corps Center
2815 Lillian St., Shreveport 71109
Type: Public, federal
Degrees: C
Phone: (318) 227-9331
Inst. Accred.: COE (1997/2003)

South Louisiana Beauty College
300 Howard Ave., Houma 70363
Type: Private, proprietary
Degrees: C
Phone: (504) 873-8978
Inst. Accred.: COE (1987/2004)

Stage One—Hair School, Inc.
209 West College St., Lake Charles 70605
Type: Private, proprietary
Degrees: C
URL: http://www.stage-one.org
Phone: (337) 474-0533
Inst. Accred.: NACCAS (1986/2004)

Stevenson's Academy of Hair Design
2039 Lapeyrouse St., New Orleans 70116
Type: Private, proprietary
Degrees: C
URL: http://www.stevensonsacademy.com
Phone: (504) 945-2312
Inst. Accred.: NACCAS (1978/2004)

> **West Bank Campus**
> 401 Opelousas St., New Orleans 70114
> *Phone:* (504) 945-2312

Unitech Training Academy
3470 NE Evangeline Thruway, Lafayette 70507
Type: Private, proprietary
Degrees: C
URL: http://www.unitechtraining.com
Phone: (337) 886-9540
Inst. Accred.: COE (2003)

Vanguard College of Cosmetology
740 Oak Harbor Blvd., Slidell 70458
Type: Private, proprietary
Degrees: C
Phone: (985) 643-2614
Inst. Accred.: NACCAS (1988/2003)

Winner Institute, Inc.
519 Kimmeridge Dr., PO Box 40188, Baton Rouge
Type: Private, proprietary
Degrees: C
URL: http://www.batonrouge.dalecarnegie.com
Phone: (225) 273-8447
Inst. Accred.: ACCET (1977/2004)

MAINE

Birthwise Midwifery School
66 South High St., Bridgton 04009
Type: Private, independent
Degrees: C
URL: http://wwwbirthwisemidwifery.org
Phone: (207) 647-5968   *Calendar:* Sem. plan
Inst. Accred.: MEAC (1998/2001)

Dale Carnegie Training of Maine
75 John Roberts Rd., Ste. B11, South Portland 04106
Type: Private, proprietary
Degrees: C
URL: http://www.maine.dalecarnegie.com
Phone: (207) 985-8111
Inst. Accred.: ACCET (1997/2002)

Downeast School of Massage
PO Box 24, 99 Moose Meadow Ln., Waldoboro 04572-0024
Type: Private, proprietary
Degrees: C
URL: http://www.downeastschoolofmassage.net
Phone: (207) 832-5531
Inst. Accred.: CMTA (2004)

Fuller Circles School for Therapeutic Massage
169 Rice Rips Rd., Oakland 04963
Type: Private, proprietary
Degrees: C
URL: http://www.fullercircles.com
Phone: (207) 877-5650
Inst. Accred.: ABHES (2002/2005)

The Landing School of Boat Building and Design
PO Box 1490, Kennebunkport 04046-1490
Type: Private, proprietary
Degrees: C
URL: http://www.landingschool.org
Phone: (207) 985-7976
Inst. Accred.: ACCSCT (1987/2004)

Mr. Bernard's School of Hair Fashion, Inc.
711 Lisbon St., PO Box 1163, Lewiston 4243
Type: Private, proprietary
Degrees: C
URL: http://www.bernardschoolofhair.com
Phone: (207) 783-7250
Inst. Accred.: NACCAS (1966/2003)

New Hampshire Institute for Therapeutic Arts
27 Sandy Creek Rd., Bridgton 04009
Type: Private, proprietary
Degrees: C
URL: http://www.nhita.com
Phone: (207) 647-3794
Inst. Accred.: CMTA (1999)

Hudson Campus
153 Lowell Rd., Hudson, NH 03051
Phone: (603) 882-3022

Northeast Montessori Institute
PO Box 68, Rockport 04856
Type: Private, independent
Degrees: C
Phone: (207) 236-6316
Inst. Accred.: MACTE (2001)

Beijing Campus
7 Sanlitun Beiziaojie, Beijing, China 100027
Phone: 011 86 10 6532 6713

Pierre's School of Cosmetology
319 Marginal Way, Ste. 2, Portland 4101
Type: Private, proprietary
Degrees: C
URL: http://www.pierresschool.com
Phone: (207) 774-9413
Inst. Accred.: NACCAS (1967/2002)

Caribou Campus
30 Skyway Dr., Syway Plaza, Caribou 4736
Phone: (207) 498-6067

Sanford Campus
913 Main St., Sanford 4073
Phone: (207) 490-1274

Pierre's School of Cosmetology—Bangor
635 Broadway, Bangor 4401
Type: Private, proprietary
Degrees: C
URL: http://www.pierresschool.com
Phone: (207) 942-0039
Inst. Accred.: NACCAS (1996/2004)

Waterville Campus
215 Kennedy Memorial Dr., Waterville 4901
Phone: (207) 873-0682

Seacoast Career Schools
One Eagle Dr., Ste. 1, Sanford 4073
Type: Private, proprietary
Degrees: C
URL: http://www.seacoastcareerschools.com
Phone: (207) 490-0509
Inst. Accred.: ACCET (1999/2002)

Manchester Campus
670 North Commercial St., Manchester, NH 03101
Phone: (603) 624-7222

Spa Tech Institute
1041 Brighton Ave., Portland 4102
Type: Private, proprietary
Degrees: C
URL: http://www.spatechinstitute.com
Phone: (207) 772-2591
Inst. Accred.: NACCAS (1979/2004)

Ipswich Campus
126 High St., Ipswich, MA 01938
Phone: (978) 356-0980

Plymouth Campus
59 Industrial Park Rd., Plymouth, MA 02360
Phone: (508) 747-3130

South Portland Campus
505 Country Club Rd., South Portland 04106
Phone: (207) 253-1579

Westboro Campus
227 Turnpike Rd., Ste. 1, Westboro, MA 01581
Phone: (508) 836-8864

Worldwide Language Resources, Inc.
449 Upton Rd., Andover 4216
Type: Private, proprietary
Degrees: C
URL: http://www.wwlr.com
Phone: (207) 392-1403
Inst. Accred.: ACCET (2000/2003)

MARYLAND

Aaron's Academy of Beauty
11690 Doolittle Dr., Waldorf 20602
Type: Private, proprietary
Degrees: C
Phone: (301) 645-3681
Inst. Accred.: NACCAS (1991/2001)

AccuTech Business Institute
5310 Spectrum Dr., Frederick 21703
Type: Private, proprietary
Degrees: C
URL: http://accutechtraining.com
Phone: (301) 694-0211
Inst. Accred.: ACICS (1987/2001)

Aesthetics Institute of Cosmetology
15958-C Shady Grove Rd., Gaithersburg
Type: Private, proprietary
Degrees: C
Phone: (301) 330-9252
Inst. Accred.: NACCAS (1992/2005)

American Beauty Academy
2518 University Blvd. West, Wheaton 20902
Type: Private, proprietary
Degrees: C
URL: http://www.americanbeautyacademy.org
Phone: (301) 949-3000
Inst. Accred.: NACCAS (1996/2004)

Baltimore Campus
4719 Harford Rd., Baltimore 21214
Phone: (410) 444-3100

Award Beauty School, Inc.
26 East Antietam St., Hagerstown 21740
Type: Private, proprietary
Degrees: C
Phone: (301) 733-4520
Inst. Accred.: NACCAS (1966/2002)

The Baltimore School of Massage
517 Progress Dr., Stes. A-L, Linthicum 21090
System: Steiner Education Group
Type: Private, proprietary
Degrees: C
URL: http://www.bsom.com
Phone: (410) 636-7929
Inst. Accred.: ACCSCT (1998/2003)
Prog. Accred.: Massage Therapy

York Campus
170 Redrock Rd., York, PA 17402
Phone: (717) 268-1881
Prog. Accred: Massage Therapy

Baltimore Studio of Hair Design, Inc.
318 North Howard St., Baltimore 21201
Type: Private, proprietary
Degrees: C
URL: http://www.baltimorestudio.net
Phone: (410) 539-1935
Inst. Accred.: NACCAS (1987/2002)

Blades School of Hair Design
22576 McArthur Blvd., PO Box 226, California 20619
Type: Private, proprietary
Degrees: C
Phone: (301) 862-9797
Inst. Accred.: NACCAS (1990/2003)

Brescook, LLC
2331 York Rd., Ste. 202, Timonium 21093
Type: Private, proprietary
Degrees: C
URL: http://www.baltimore.dale-carnegie.com
Phone: (410) 560-2188
Inst. Accred.: ACCET (1976/2002)

Harrisburg Campus
4813 Jonestown Rd., Ste. 206, Harrisburg, PA 17109
Phone: (717) 540-0801

Broadcasting Institute of Maryland
7200 Harford Rd., Baltimore 21234-7765
Type: Private, proprietary
Degrees: C
URL: http://www.bim.org
Phone: (410) 254-2770　　　　*Calendar:* Sem. plan
Inst. Accred.: ACCSCT (1980/2005)

Defense Information School
6500 Mapes Rd., Fort Meade 20755-5620
Type: Public, federal
Degrees: C
URL: http://www.dinfos.osd.mil
Phone: (301) 677-2173
Inst. Accred.: COE (1995/2004)

Defense Security Service Academy
938 Elkridge Landing Rd., Linthicum 21090
Type: Public, federal
Degrees: C
URL: http://www.dss.mil/training
Phone: (410) 865-2295
Inst. Accred.: COE (2004)

Del-Mar-Va Beauty Academy
111 Milford St., Salisbury 21801
Type: Private, proprietary
Degrees: C
Phone: (410) 742-7929
Inst. Accred.: NACCAS (1966/2004)

Diesel Institute of America
Route 40, PO Box 69, Grantsville 21536-0069
Type: Private, proprietary
Degrees: C
URL: http://www.dieselinstitute.com
Phone: (301) 895-5139
Inst. Accred.: ACCSCT (1988/2003)

English House
26 North Summit Ave., Gaithersburg 20877
Type: Private, proprietary
Degrees: C
URL: http://www.englishhouseusa.com
Phone: (301) 527-0600
Inst. Accred.: ACCET (2004)

Everest Institute
8757 Georgia Ave., Silver Spring 20910
Type: Private, proprietary
System: Corinthian Colleges, Inc
Degrees: C
URL: http://www.everest-institute.com
Phone: (301) 495-4400
Inst. Accred.: ACICS (2004)

Hair Academy, Inc.
8435 Annapolis Rd., New Carrolton 20784
Type: Private, proprietary
Degrees: C
Phone: (301) 459-2509
Inst. Accred.: NACCAS (1986/2001)

Hair Expressions Academy, Inc.
12450 Parklawn Dr., Rockville 20852
Type: Private, proprietary
Degrees: C
URL: http://www.hairex.com
Phone: (301) 984-8182
Inst. Accred.: NACCAS (2005)

Home Study International
12501 Old Columbia Pike, PO Box 4437, Silver Spring
20914-4437
Type: Private, proprietary
Degrees: C   *FTE Enroll:* 656
URL: http://www.hsi.edu
Phone: (301) 680-6570
Inst. Accred.: DETC (1967/2003)

Institute for Advanced Montessori Studies
13500 Layhill Rd., Silver Spring 20906-3299
Type: Private, independent
Degrees: C
URL: http://www.barrie.org/iams/iams.htm
Phone: (301) 871-6200 x266
Inst. Accred.: MACTE (2000)

International Beauty School—Bel Air
227 Archer St., Bel Air 21014
Type: Private, proprietary
Degrees: C
Phone: (410) 838-0845
Inst. Accred.: NACCAS (1984/2004)

International Beauty School—Cumberland
119 North Centre St., Cumberland 21502
Type: Private, proprietary
Degrees: C
Phone: (301) 777-3020
Inst. Accred.: NACCAS (1969/2004)

L'Academie de Cuisine
16006 Industrial Dr., Gaithersburg 20877-1414
Type: Private, proprietary
Degrees: C
URL: http://www.lacadamie.com
Phone: (301) 670-8670
Inst. Accred.: ACCET (1988/2002)

Bethesda Campus
5021 Wilson Ln., Bethesda 20814
Phone: (301) 986-9490

Lincoln Technical Institute
9325 Snowden River Pkwy., Columbia 21046
Type: Private, proprietary
System: Lincoln Educational Services
Degrees: C
URL: http://www.lincolntech.com
Phone: (410) 290-7100
Inst. Accred.: ACCSCT (1968/2002)

Maryland Beauty Academy
152 Chartley Dr., Chartley Park Shopping Center,
Reisterstown 21136
Type: Private, proprietary
Degrees: C
URL: http://www.baltimorestudio.net
Phone: (410) 517-0442
Inst. Accred.: NACCAS (1987/2002)

Maryland Beauty Academy of Essex, Inc.
505 Eastern Blvd., Baltimore 21221
Type: Private, proprietary
Degrees: C
URL: http://www.baltimorestudio.net
Phone: (410) 686-4477
Inst. Accred.: NACCAS (1986/2001)

Maryland Center for Montessori Studies
10807 Tony Dr., Lutherville 21093
Type: Private, independent
Degrees: C
Phone: (410) 321-8555
Inst. Accred.: MACTE (2000)

Medix School
700 York Rd., Towson 21204-2511
Type: Private, proprietary
Degrees: C
URL: http://www.medixschool.com
Phone: (410) 337-5155
Inst. Accred.: ABHES (1999/2002)
Prog. Accred.: Dental Assisting, Medical Assisting
  (ABHES), Medical Assisting (CAAHEP)

Montgomery Beauty School
8736 Arliss St., Silver Spring 20901
Type: Private, proprietary
Degrees: C
Phone: (301) 588-3570
Inst. Accred.: NACCAS (1986/2001)

Montgomery Montessori Institute
10500 Darnestown Rd., Rockville 20850
Type: Private, independent
Degrees: C
URL: http://www.montessori-mmi.com
Phone: (301) 279-2799
Inst. Accred.: MACTE (2001)

National Cryptologic School
9800 Savage Rd., Ste. 6801, S309, Fort Meade 20755-6000
Type: Public, federal
Degrees: C
Phone: (410) 859-6321
Inst. Accred.: COE (1990/2002)

Naval Medical Education and Training Command
8901 Wisconsin Ave., Bethesda 20889-5611
Type: Public, federal
Degrees: C
URL: http://nshs.med.navy.mil
Phone: (202) 762-3830
Inst. Accred.: COE (1984/2002)

New Creations Academy of Hair Design
3930 Bexley Place, Suitland 20746
Type: Private, proprietary
Degrees: C
Phone: (301) 899-9100
Inst. Accred.: NACCAS (1998/2004)

Omega Studio's School of Applied Recording Arts and Sciences
5609 Fishers Ln., Rockville 20852
Type: Private, proprietary
Degrees: C
URL: http://www.omegastudios.com
Phone: (301) 230-9100
Inst. Accred.: ACCSCT (2003)

Robert Paul Academy of Cosmetology Arts & Sciences
1811 York Rd., Timonium 21093
Type: Private, proprietary
Degrees: C
URL: http://www.robertpaulacademy.com
Phone: (410) 252-4244
Inst. Accred.: NACCAS (1986/2001)

United States Army Ordnance Center and School
Bldg. 3072, Rm. 217-C, Aberdeen Proving Ground 21005-5201
Type: Public, federal
Degrees: C
URL: http://www.goordinance.apg.army.mil
Phone: (410) 278-3642
Inst. Accred.: COE (1978/2005)

Washington Conservatory of Music, Inc.
5144 Massachusetts Ave., Bethesda 20816
Type: Private, independent
Degrees: C
URL: http://www.washingtonconservatory.com
Phone: (301) 320-2770   *Calendar:* Sem. plan
Inst. Accred.: NASM (1991/2003)

MASSACHUSETTS

Ailano School of Cosmetology
541 West St., Brockton 2301
Type: Private, proprietary
Degrees: C
URL: http://ailanoschool.com
Phone: (508) 583-5433
Inst. Accred.: NACCAS (1991/2001)

Anglo-Continental USA, Inc.
1972 Massachusetts Ave., Ste. 300, Cambridge 2140
Type: Private, proprietary
Degrees: C
URL: http://www.anglo-continental.com
Phone: (617) 491-2157
Inst. Accred.: ACCET (1991/2001)

Bancroft School of Massage Therapy
333 Shrewsbury St., Worcester 01604
Type: Private, proprietary
Degrees: C
URL: http://www.bancroftsmt.com
Phone: (508) 757-7923
Inst. Accred.: ACCSCT (1986/2002)

Bay State School of Technology
225 Turnpike St., Route 138, Canton 02021
Type: Private, proprietary
Degrees: C
URL: http://www.ultranet.com/bssanet
Phone: (781) 828-3434
Inst. Accred.: ACCSCT (1986/2002)

Blaine, The Beauty Career Schools—Boston
30 West St., Downtown Crossing, Boston 02111
Type: Private, proprietary
Degrees: C
URL: http://www.blainebeautyschools.com
Phone: (617) 266-2661
Inst. Accred.: NACCAS (1975/2001)

Hyannis Campus
18 Center St., Hyannis 2601
Phone: (508) 771-1680

Blaine, The Beauty Career Schools—Lowell
231 Central St., Lowell 1852
Type: Private, proprietary
Degrees: C
URL: http://www.blainebeautyschools.com
Phone: (978) 459-9959
Inst. Accred.: NACCAS (1978/2004)

Blaine, The Beauty Career Schools—Malden
347 Pleasant St., Malden 2148
Type: Private, proprietary
Degrees: C
URL: http://www.blainebeautyschools.com
Phone: (781) 397-7400
Inst. Accred.: NACCAS (1977/2004)

Blaine, The Beauty Career Schools—Waltham
314 Moody St., Waltham 2154
Type: Private, proprietary
Degrees: C
URL: http://www.blainebeautyschools.com
Phone: (781) 899-1500
Inst. Accred.: NACCAS (1977/2004)

Framingham Campus
624 Worcester Rd., Route 9, Framingham 01702
Phone: (508) 370-3700

Boston School of Modern Languages, Inc.
814 South St., Boston 02131
Type: Private, proprietary
Degrees: C
URL: http://www.studyenglish.com
Phone: (617) 325-2760
Inst. Accred.: ACCET (2004)

Bryman Institute—Brighton
1505 Commonwealth Ave., Brighton 02135
Type: Private, proprietary
System: Corinthian Colleges, Inc
Degrees: C
URL: http://www.bryman-institute.com
Phone: (617) 783-9955
Inst. Accred.: ACCSCT (1973/2001)

Bryman Institute—Chelsea
70 Everett Ave., Chelsea 02150
Type: Private, proprietary
System: Corinthian Colleges, Inc
Degrees: C
URL: http://www.bryman-institute.com
Phone: (617) 889-5999
Inst. Accred.: ACCSCT (2004)

Butera School of Art
111 Beacon St., Boston 02116-1597
Type: Private, proprietary
Degrees: C
URL: http://www.buteraschool.com
Phone: (617) 536-4623   *Calendar:* Sem. plan
Inst. Accred.: ACCSCT (1977/2005)

The Cambridge School of Culinary Arts
2020 Massachusetts Ave., Cambridge 02140-2124
Type: Private, proprietary
Degrees: C
URL: http://www.cambridgeculinary.com
Phone: (617) 354-2020
Inst. Accred.: ACCSCT (1989/2005)

Career Education Institute—Somerville
5 Middlesex Ave., Somerville 02145
Type: Private, proprietary
System: Lincoln Educational Services
Degrees: C
URL: http://www.computered.com
Phone: (617) 776-3500
Inst. Accred.: ACICS (1997/2004)

Lowell Campus
211 Plain St., Lowell 01852
Phone: (978) 458-4800

Norcross Campus
5675 Jimmy Carter Blvd., Ste. 100, Norcross, GA
30071
Phone: (678) 966-9411

Catherine E. Hinds Institute of Esthetics
300 Wildwood Ave., Woburn 01801
Type: Private, proprietary
Degrees: C
URL: http://catherinehinds.com
Phone: (781) 935-3344
Inst. Accred.: ACCSCT (1983/2003)

Olympia Avenue Campus
82 Olympia Ave., Woburn 01801
Phone: (617) 933-2501

EF International Language Schools, Inc.
200 Lake St., Brighton 02135-3104
Type: Private, proprietary
Degrees: C
URL: http://www.ef.com
Phone: (617) 619-1700
Inst. Accred.: ACCET (1986/2002)

California State University Campus
9757 Zelzah, Building 12, Saguaro Hall, Ste. 112,
Northridge, CA 91330-8363
Phone: (818) 772-0903

Corporate Center Campus
EF Corporate Center, One Education St., Cambridge
02141
Phone: (617) 619-1800

Evergreen State College Campus
Seminar Bldg., Rm. 4154, 2700 Evergreen Pkwy., NW,
Olympia, WA 98505
Phone: (360) 867-6423

Marymount College Campus
100 Marymount Ave., Ursula Hall, Tarrytown, NY
10591-3796
Phone: (914) 332-1072

Miami Beach Campus
2469 Collins Ave., Miami Beach, FL 33140

Mills College Campus
White Hall, 5000 MacArthur Blvd., Oakland, CA 94613
Phone: (510) 430-3209

San Diego Campus
10455 Pomerado Rd., M-4, San Diego, CA 92131
Phone: (619) 693-0771
Phone: (305) 674-6535

Santa Barbara Campus
1421 Chapala St., Santa Barbara, CA 93101
Phone: (805) 962-8680

Electrology Institute of New England
1501 Main St., Ste. 50, Tewksbury 01876
Type: Private, proprietary
Degrees: C
URL: http://www.electrologyinstitute.com
Phone: (978) 851-4444
Inst. Accred.: NACCAS (2004)

The Elizabeth Grady School of Esthetics
222 Boston Ave., Medford 2155
Type: Private, proprietary
Degrees: C
URL: http://www.elizabethgrady.com
Phone: (781) 391-9380
Inst. Accred.: NACCAS (1987/2002)

Hair In Motion Beauty Academy
73 Hamilton St., Worcester 1604
Type: Private, proprietary
Degrees: C
URL: http://hairmotion.net
Phone: (508) 756-6060
Inst. Accred.: NACCAS (1997/2005)

Hallmark Institute of Photography
PO Box 308, Turners Falls 01376-0308
Type: Private, proprietary
Degrees: C
URL: http://www.hallmark-institute.com
Phone: (413) 863-2478
Inst. Accred.: ACCSCT (1982/2005)

Henri's School of Hair Design
276 Water St., PO Box 2244, Fitchburg 1420
Type: Private, proprietary
Degrees: C
Phone: (978) 342-6061
Inst. Accred.: NACCAS (1969/2005)

International Language Institute of Massachusetts, Inc.
17 New South St., Northampton 01060
Type: Private, independent
Degrees: C
URL: http://www.languageschoolusa.org
Phone: (413) 586-7569
Inst. Accred.: ACCET (1982/2001)

Jolie Hair and Beauty Academy, Inc.
44 Sewall St., Ludlow 1056
Type: Private, proprietary
Degrees: C
Phone: (413) 589-074
Inst. Accred.: NACCAS (1997/2005)

Kay Harvey Hairdressing Academy
11 Central St., West Springfield 01089
Type: Private, proprietary
Degrees: C
URL: http://www.labaronacademy.com
Phone: (413) 732-7117
Inst. Accred.: NACCAS (1995/2000)

LaBaron Hairdressing Academy—Brockton
240 Liberty St., Brockton 2401
Type: Private, proprietary
Degrees: C
URL: http://www.labaronacademy.com
Phone: (508) 583-1700
Inst. Accred.: NACCAS (1978/2005)

LaBaron Hairdressing Academy—New Bedford
281 Union St., New Bedford 2074
Type: Private, proprietary
Degrees: C
URL: http://www.labaronacademy.com
Phone: (508) 996-6611
Inst. Accred.: NACCAS (1977/2003)

Learning Institute for Beauty Sciences—Boston
867 Boylston St., Boston 2116
Type: Private, proprietary
Degrees: C
URL: http://www.libsbeautyschool.com
Phone: (617) 424-6565
Inst. Accred.: NACCAS (1976/2002)

Learning Institute for Beauty Sciences—Malden
384 Main St., Malden 2148
Type: Private, proprietary
Degrees: C
URL: http://www.libsbeautyschool.com
Phone: (781) 324-3400
Inst. Accred.: NACCAS (1976/2002)

Lowell Academy Hairstyling Institute
136 Central St., Lowell 1852
Type: Private, proprietary
Degrees: C
URL: http://www.lahair.net
Phone: (978) 453-3235
Inst. Accred.: NACCAS (1966/2002)

Mansfield Beauty School—Quincy
200 Parkingway St., Quincy 2169
Type: Private, proprietary
Degrees: C
Phone: (617) 479-1090
Inst. Accred.: NACCAS (1974/2001)

Mansfield Beauty School—Springfield
266 Bridge St., Springfield 1103
Type: Private, proprietary
Degrees: C
Phone: (413) 788-7575
Inst. Accred.: NACCAS (1974/2001)

Massachusetts School of Barbering & Men's Hairstyling
1585 Hancock St, Quincy 02169-5058
Type: Private
Degrees: C
Phone: (617) 770-4444   *Calendar:* Sem. plan
Inst. Accred.: ACCSCT (1978/1995)

Medical Professional Institute
388 Pleasant St., Ste. 302, Malden 02148
Type: Private, proprietary
Degrees: C
URL: http://www.mpi.edu
Phone: (781) 397-6822
Inst. Accred.: ABHES (2002/2005)
Prog. Accred.: Medical Assisting (ABHES)

Muscular Therapy Institute
122 Rindge Ave., Cambridge 02140-2527
Type: Private, proprietary
Degrees: C
URL: http://www.mtiweb.edu
Phone: (617) 576-1300
Inst. Accred.: ACCET (1986/1999), CMTA (2004)

New England Hair Academy
492-500 Main St., Malden 02148-5105
Type: Private, proprietary
Degrees: C
Phone: (781) 324-6799
Inst. Accred.: ACCSCT (1979/2000)

Haverhill Campus
80 Merrimack St., Haverhill 01830
Phone: (978) 521-6500

The New England School of English
36 John F. Kennedy St., Cambridge 02138
Type: Private, proprietary
Degrees: C
URL: http://www.nese.com
Phone: (617) 864-7170
Inst. Accred.: ACCET (1998/2003)

New England School of Photography
537 Commonwealth Ave., Boston 02215-2005
Type: Private
Degrees: C
Phone: (617) 437-1868
Inst. Accred.: ACCSCT (1995)

North Bennet Street School
39 North Bennet St., Boston 02113-1998
Type: Private
Degrees: C
Phone: (617) 227-0155
Inst. Accred.: ACCSCT (1982/1999)

The Olin Center
342 Newbury St., Boston 02115
Type: Private, independent
Degrees: C
URL: http://www.olincenter.com
Phone: (617) 247-3033
Inst. Accred.: ACCET (2003)

Performance Training Associates, Inc.
135 Beaver St., Waltham 02452
Type: Private, proprietary
Degrees: C
URL: http://www.boston.dalecarnegie.com
Phone: (781) 894-2700
Inst. Accred.: ACCET (1977/2002)

RETS Electronic Schools
965 Commonwealth Ave., Boston 02215-1397
Type: Private
Degrees: C
Phone: (617) 783-1197
Inst. Accred.: ACCSCT (1974/1995)

Rob Roy Academy, Inc.—New Bedford
1872 Acushnet Ave., New Bedford 2746
Type: Private, proprietary
Degrees: C
URL: http://www.rob-roy.com
Phone: (508) 995-8711
Inst. Accred.: NACCAS (1985/2005)

Rob Roy Academy, Inc.—Taunton Campus
One School St., Taunton 2780
Type: Private, proprietary
Degrees: C
URL: http://www.rob-roy.com
Phone: (508) 822-1405
Inst. Accred.: NACCAS (1969/2002)

Rob Roy Academy, Inc.—Worcester
150 Pleasant St., Worcester 1609
Type: Private, proprietary
Degrees: C
URL: http://www.rob-roy.com
Phone: (508) 799-2111
Inst. Accred.: NACCAS (1981/2001)

Woonsocket Campus
800 Clinton St., Woonsocket, RI 02895
Phone: (401) 769-1777

Rob Roy Academy—Fall River Campus
260 South Main St., Fall River 2721
Type: Private, proprietary
Degrees: C
URL: http://www.rob-roy.com
Phone: (508) 672-4751
Inst. Accred.: NACCAS (1970/2002)

The Salter School
155 Ararat St., Worcester 01606-3450
Type: Private, proprietary
Degrees: C
URL: http://www.salterschool.com
Phone: (508) 853-1074   *Calendar:* Sem. plan
Inst. Accred.: ACICS (1953/2003)
Prog. Accred.: Medical Assisting (CAAHEP)

Fall River Campus
82 Hartwell St., Fall River 02720
Phone: (508) 730-2740

Malden Campus
2 Florence St., Malden 02148
Phone: (781) 324-5454

Tewksbury Campus
515 Woburn St., Tewksbury 01876
Phone: (978) 934-9009

Thoreau Language Institute
63 Melcher St., 2nd Flr., Boston 02210
Type: Private, proprietary
Degrees: C
URL: http://www.tli-english.com
Phone: (617) 426-2600
Inst. Accred.: ACCET (2000/2003)

Western Massachusetts Precision Institute
122 Doty Circle, West Springfield 01089
Type: Private, proprietary
Degrees: C
URL: http://www.wmpi.org
Phone: (413) 781-0166
Inst. Accred.: ACCSCT (1999)

WyoTech—Boston
150 Hanscom Dr., Bedford 01730
Type: Private, proprietary
System: Corinthian Colleges, Inc
Degrees: C
URL: http://www.wyotech.com
Phone: (781) 274-8448
Inst. Accred.: ACCSCT (1970/2002)

MICHIGAN

Adrian Beauty Academy, Inc.
329 1/2 East Maumee St., Adrian 49221
Type: Private, proprietary
Degrees: C
Phone: (517) 263-0000
Inst. Accred.: NACCAS (1977/2003)

Adrian Dominican Montessori Teacher Institute
1257 East Siena Heights Dr., Adrian 49221
Type: Private, independent
Degrees: C
URL: http://www.tc3net.com/admtei
Phone: (517) 266-3415
Inst. Accred.: MACTE (2000)

Ann Arbor Institute of Massage Therapy
180 Jackson Plaza, Ste. 100, Ann Arbor 48103
Type: Private, proprietary
Degrees: C
URL: http://www.aaimt.com
Phone: (734) 677-4430
Inst. Accred.: ACCSCT (2001), CMTA (2001)

Bayshire Beauty Academy
917 Saginaw St., Bay City 48708
Type: Private, proprietary
Degrees: C
Phone: (989) 894-2431
Inst. Accred.: NACCAS (1984/2004)

Blue Water College of Cosmetology
1871 Gratiot Blvd., Marysville 48080
Type: Private, proprietary
Degrees: C
Phone: (810) 364-9595
Inst. Accred.: NACCAS (2002/2005)

Booker Institute of Cosmetology
1989 Lakeshore Dr., Muskegon 49441
Type: Private, proprietary
Degrees: C
URL: http://www.bookerinstitute.com
Phone: (231) 759-9800
Inst. Accred.: NACCAS (2005)

CareerWorks Institute of Technology
1200 East McNichols, Highland Park 48203
Type: Private, proprietary
Degrees: C
Phone: (313) 867-3500
Inst. Accred.: ACCSCT (2001)

Carnegie Institute
550 Stephenson Hwy., Ste. 100, Troy 48083-1159
Type: Private, independent
Degrees: C
URL: http://www.carnegie-institute.com
Phone: (248) 589-1078   *Calendar:* Qtr. plan
Inst. Accred.: ACCSCT (1968/2003)
Prog. Accred.: Medical Assisting (CAAHEP)

Chic University of Cosmetology—Grand Rapids
1735 Four Mile Rd., NE, Grand Rapids 49525
Type: Private, proprietary
Degrees: C
URL: http://www.chicuniversity.com
Phone: (616) 363-9853
Inst. Accred.: NACCAS (1965/2003)

Standale Plaza Campus
455 Standale Plaza, NW, Grand Rapids 49544
Phone: (616) 735-9680

Chic University of Cosmetology—Portage
6136 South Westnedge Ave., Portage 49002
Type: Private, proprietary
Degrees: C
URL: http://www.chicuniversity.com
Phone: (269) 329-3333
Inst. Accred.: NACCAS (1985/2005)

Creative Hair School of Cosmetology
G-4439 Clio Rd., Flint 48504
Type: Private, proprietary
Degrees: C
Phone: (810) 787-4247
Inst. Accred.: NACCAS (2005)

David Pressley School of Cosmetology
1127 South Washington St., Royal Oak 48067
Type: Private, proprietary
Degrees: C
URL: http://www.davidpressleyschool.com
Phone: (248) 548-5090
Inst. Accred.: NACCAS (1965/2003)

Detroit Business Institute
23022 Greenfield Rd., Ste. LL28, Southfield 48075
Type: Private, proprietary
Degrees: C
Phone: (248) 552-6300   *Calendar:* Qtr. plan
Inst. Accred.: ACICS (1961/2001)

Detroit Business Institute—Downriver
19100 Fort St., Riverview 48192
Type: Private, proprietary
Degrees: C
URL: http://www.dbidownriver.com
Phone: (734) 479-0660   *Calendar:* Qtr. plan
Inst. Accred.: ACICS (1983/2001)

Dorsey Business School
15755 Northline Rd., Southgate 48195
Type: Private, proprietary
Degrees: C
URL: http://www.dorseyschools.com
Phone: (734) 285-5400 *Calendar:* Qtr. plan
Inst. Accred.: ACICS (1972/2002)

Madison Heights Campus
30821 Barrington Ave., Madison Heights 48071
Phone: (248) 588-9660

Roseville Campus
31542 Gratiot Ave., Roseville 48066
Phone: (586) 296-3225

Wayne-Westland Campus
34841 Veteran's Plaza, Wayne 48184
Phone: (734) 595-1540

Douglas J Aveda Institute
331 East Grand River Ave., East Lansing 48823
Type: Private, proprietary
Degrees: C
URL: http://douglasj.seal-server.com
Phone: (517) 333-9656
Inst. Accred.: NACCAS (1988/2003)

Ann Arbor Campus
333 Maynard St., Ann Arbor 48104
Phone: (734) 929-0453

Flint Institute of Barbering
3214 Flushing Rd., Flint 48504-4395
Type: Private, proprietary
Degrees: C
Phone: (810) 232-4711
Inst. Accred.: ACCSCT (1972/2005)

Focus: Hope Information Technologies Center
1400 Oakman Blvd., Detroit 48238
Type: Private, proprietary
Degrees: C
URL: http://www.focushope.edu
Phone: (313) 494-4888
Inst. Accred.: ACCET (2004)

Focus: Hope Machinist Training Institute
1200 Oakman Blvd., Detroit 48238
Type: Private, independent
Degrees: C
URL: http://www.focushope.edu
Phone: (313) 494-4200
Inst. Accred.: ACCET (1986/2001)

The Gallery College of Beauty
38132 South Gratiot Ave., Clinton Township 48036-3591
Type: Private, proprietary
Degrees: C
URL: http://www.gallerycollegeofbeauty.com
Phone: (586) 783-7358
Inst. Accred.: NACCAS (2005)

Great Lakes Academy of Hair Design
2950 Lapeer Rd., Port Huron 48060
Type: Private, proprietary
Degrees: C
URL: http://www.glahd.com
Phone: (810) 987-8118
Inst. Accred.: NACCAS (2004)

Health Enrichment Center
204 East Nepessing Rd., Lapeer 48446
Type: Private, proprietary
Degrees: C
Phone: (810) 667-9453
Inst. Accred.: ACCSCT (1995/2005)

Indianapolis Campus
6801 Lake Plaza Dr., Ste. A102, Indianapolis, IN 46220
Phone: (317) 841-1414

Hillsdale Beauty College
64 Waldron St., Hillsdale 49242
Type: Private, proprietary
Degrees: C
Phone: (517) 437-4670
Inst. Accred.: NACCAS (1989/2004)

Houghton Lake Institute of Cosmetology
5921 West Houghton Lake Dr., PO Box 669, Houghton Lake 48629
Type: Private, proprietary
Degrees: C
Phone: (989) 422-4573
Inst. Accred.: NACCAS (1994/2002)

Howell College of Cosmetology
2373 West Grand River, Howell 48843
Type: Private, proprietary
Degrees: C
Phone: (517) 546-4155
Inst. Accred.: NACCAS (1989/2004)

In Session, Arts of Cosmetology Beauty School
7212 Gratiot Rd., Ste. D, Saginaw 48609
Type: Private, proprietary
Degrees: C
Phone: (989) 781-6282
Inst. Accred.: NACCAS (2003)

Irene's Myomassology Institute
26061 Franklin Rd., Southfield 48034
Type: Private, proprietary
Degrees: C
URL: http://www.myomassology.com
Phone: (248) 350-1400
Inst. Accred.: ACCET (2001/2004)

K.S.A. Academy of Cosmetology
1505 Newton St., Jackson 49202
Type: Private, proprietary
Degrees: C
Phone: (517) 782-3569
Inst. Accred.: NACCAS (2000)

Lakewood School of Therapeutic Massage
1102 6th St., Port Huron 48060
Type: Private, proprietary
Degrees: C
URL: http://www.lakewoodschool.com
Phone: (810) 987-3959
Inst. Accred.: CMTA (2004)

Lawton School
20755 Greenfield, Ste. 300, Southfield 48075
Type: Private, proprietary
Degrees: C
Phone: (248) 569-7787
Inst. Accred.: ACCSCT (1988/2005)

M.J. Murphy Beauty College
201 West Broadway, Mt. Pleasant 48858
Type: Private, proprietary
Degrees: C
Phone: (989) 772-2339
Inst. Accred.: NACCAS (1976/2003)

Clare Campus
210 Wilcox Pkwy., Clare 48617
Phone: (989) 386-6151

Michigan Barber School, Inc.
8988-90 Grand River Ave., Detroit 48204-2244
Type: Private, proprietary
Degrees: C
Phone: (313) 894-2300
Inst. Accred.: ACCSCT (1986/2002)

Michigan Career and Technical Institute
11611 West Pine Lake Rd., Plainwell 49080
Type: Public, state
Degrees: C
URL: http://www.michigan.gov/mdcd
Phone: (269) 664-4461
Inst. Accred.: NCA-CASI (1999/2005)

Michigan College of Beauty—Monroe
15233 South Dixie Hwy., Monroe 48161
Type: Private, proprietary
Degrees: C
URL: http://www.michigancollegebeauty.com
Phone: (734) 241-8877
Inst. Accred.: NACCAS (1985/2005)

Michigan College of Beauty—Troy
3498 Rochester Rd., Troy 48083
Type: Private, proprietary
Degrees: C
URL: http://www.michigancollege.nv.switchboard.com
Phone: (248) 528-0303
Inst. Accred.: NACCAS (1977/2003)

Michigan College of Beauty—Waterford
5620 Dixie Hwy., Waterford 48329
Type: Private, proprietary
Degrees: C
Phone: (248) 623-9494
Inst. Accred.: NACCAS (1968/2004)

Michigan Institute of Aeronautics
Willow Run Airport, 47884 D St., Belleville 48111-1278
Type: Private, proprietary
Degrees: C
URL: http://www.mioa.com
Phone: (734) 483-3758
Inst. Accred.: ACCSCT (1976/2001)

Michigan Montessori Teacher Education Center
1263 South Adams Rd., Rochester Hills 48309
Type: Private, independent
Degrees: C
Phone: (248) 375-2800
Inst. Accred.: MACTE (2000)

Mr. Bela's School of Cosmetology
5580 East 12 Mile Rd., Warren 48092
Type: Private, proprietary
Degrees: C
URL: http://www.mrbelas.com
Phone: (586) 751-4000
Inst. Accred.: NACCAS (1980/2005)

Mr. David's School of Cosmetology, Ltd.
4000 South Saginaw St., Flint 48507
Type: Private, proprietary
Degrees: C
URL: http://www.mrdavids.com
Phone: (810) 762-7474
Inst. Accred.: NACCAS (1990/2001)

National Institute of Technology—Southfield
26111 Evergreen Rd., Ste. 201, Southfield 48076-4491
Type: Private, proprietary
System: Corinthian Colleges, Inc
Degrees: C
URL: http://www.nitschools.com
Phone: (248) 799-9933   *Calendar:* Qtr. plan
Inst. Accred.: ACCSCT (1970/2003)
Prog. Accred.: Medical Assisting (CAAHEP)

Austin Campus
9100 US Hwy 290 East, Building 1, Ste. 100, Austin, TX 78754
Phone: (512) 928-1933

Dearborn Campus
23400 Michigan Ave., Ste. 200, Dearborn 48124
Phone: (313) 562-4228

Detroit Campus
300 River Place Dr., Ste. 1000, Detroit 48207
Phone: (313) 567-5350

Northwestern Technological Institute
24567 Northwestern Hwy., Ste. 200, Southfield 48075
Type: Private, proprietary
Degrees: C
URL: http://www.northwesterntech.org
Phone: (248) 358-4006
Inst. Accred.: ACCSCT (1995/2005)

Nuvo College of Cosmetology
4236 Grand Have Rd., Norton Shores 49441
Type: Private, proprietary
Degrees: C
URL: http://www.nuvocollege.com
Phone: (231) 799-1500
Inst. Accred.: NACCAS (2005)

Olympia Career Training Institute
1750 Woodworth St., NE, Grand Rapids 49505
Type: Private, proprietary
System: Corinthian Colleges, Inc
Degrees: C
URL: http://www.olympia-institute.com
Phone: (616) 364-8464
Inst. Accred.: ABHES (1985/2005)
Prog. Accred.: Medical Assisting (ABHES), Surgical
　Technology

Kalamazoo Campus
5349 West Main St., Kalamazoo 49009
Phone: (269) 381-9616
Prog. Accred: Medical Assisting (ABHES)

P & A Scholars Beauty School, Inc.
12001 Grand River Ave., Ste. A, Detroit 48204
Type: Private, proprietary
Degrees: C
Phone: (313) 933-9393
Inst. Accred.: NACCAS (2005)

Ralph Nichols Group, Inc.
19500 Victor Pkwy., Ste. 275, Livonia
Type: Private, proprietary
Degrees: C
URL: http://www.michigan.dalecarnegie.com
Phone: (734) 953-1200
Inst. Accred.: ACCET (1975/2001)

Ross Medical Education Center
1036 Gilbert Rd., Flint 48532-3527
Type: Private, proprietary
Degrees: C
URL: http://www.rossmedicaleducation.com
Phone: (810) 230-1100
Inst. Accred.: ACCSCT (1978/2001)
Prog. Accred.: Medical Assisting (ABHES)

Ross Medical Education Center
913 West Holmes Rd., Ste. 260, Lansing 48910-4490
Type: Private, proprietary
Degrees: C
URL: http://www.rossmedicaleducation.com
Phone: (517) 887-0180
Inst. Accred.: ACCSCT (1982/2001)
Prog. Accred.: Medical Assisting (ABHES)

Ross Medical Education Center
27120 Dequindre Rd., Warren 48092
Type: Private, proprietary
Degrees: C
URL: http://www.rossmedicaleducation.com
Phone: (586) 574-0830
Inst. Accred.: ACCSCT (1981/2003)
Prog. Accred.: Medical Assisting (ABHES)

Ross Medical Education Center
5757 Whitmore Lake Rd., Ste. 800, Brighton 48116-1091
Type: Private, proprietary
Degrees: C
URL: http://www.rossmedicaleducation.com
Phone: (810) 227-0160
Inst. Accred.: ACCSCT (1986/2003)
Prog. Accred.: Medical Assisting (ABHES)

Ann Arbor Campus
4741 Washtenaw Ave., Ann Arbor 48108-1411
Phone: (734) 434-7320
Prog. Accred: Medical Assisting (ABHES)

Grand Rapids Campus
2035 28th St., SE, Ste. O, Grand Rapids 49508-1539
Phone: (616) 243-3070
Prog. Accred: Medical Assisting (ABHES)

Port Huron Campus
3568 Pine Grove Ave., Port Huron 48060
Phone: (810) 982-0454
Prog. Accred: Medical Assisting (ABHES)

Redford Campus
9327 Telegraph Rd., Redford 48239
Phone: (313) 794-6448
Prog. Accred: Medical Assisting (ABHES)

Roosevelt Park Campus
950 West Norton Ave., Roosevelt Park 49441-4156
Phone: (231) 730-9531
Prog. Accred: Medical Assisting (ABHES)

Saginaw Campus
4054 Bay Rd., Saginaw 48603-1201
Phone: (989) 793-9800
Prog. Accred: Medical Assisting (ABHES)

Sally Esser Beauty School
27201 West Warren St., Dearborn Heights 48127-1804
Type: Private, proprietary
Degrees: C
Phone: (313) 724-0404
Inst. Accred.: NACCAS (2005)

The School of Creative Hair Designs, Inc.
470 Marshall St., Fairfield Plaza, Coldwater 49036
Type: Private, proprietary
Degrees: C
URL: http://www.schoolofhair.com
Phone: (517) 279-2355
Inst. Accred.: NACCAS (1994/2002)

Sharp's Academy of Hairstyling
115 Main St., Flushing 48439
Type: Private, proprietary
Degrees: C
Phone: (810) 659-3348
Inst. Accred.: ACCSCT (1993/2003)

Grand Blanc Campus
8166 Holly Rd., Grand Blanc 48499
Phone: (810) 695-6742

Specs Howard School of Broadcast Arts Inc.
19900 West Nine Mile Rd., Southfield 48075-5273
Type: Private, proprietary
Degrees: C
URL: http://www.specshoward.edu
Phone: (248) 358-9000
Inst. Accred.: ACCSCT (1978/2005)

Taylortown School of Beauty
23015 Ecorse Rd., Taylor 48180
Type: Private, proprietary
Degrees: C
Phone: (313) 291-2177
Inst. Accred.: NACCAS (1982/2002)

Twin City Beauty College
2600 Lincoln Ave., St. Joseph 49085
Type: Private, proprietary
Degrees: C
URL: http://tcbeautycollege.com
Phone: (269) 428-2900
Inst. Accred.: NACCAS (1992/2002)

Michiana Beauty College
6323 University Commons, South Bend, IN 46635
Phone: (574) 271-1542

Traverse City Beauty College
1144 Boon St., Ste. D, Traverse City 49686
Phone: (231) 929-0710

U.P. Academy of Hair Design, Inc.
1625 Sheridan Rd., Escanaba 49829
Type: Private, proprietary
Degrees: C
Phone: (906) 786-5750
Inst. Accred.: NACCAS (2000/2003)

Virginia Farrell Beauty School—Ferndale
22925 Woodward Ave., Ferndale 48220
Type: Private, proprietary
Degrees: C
URL: http://www.virginiafarrell.com
Phone: (248) 398-4647
Inst. Accred.: NACCAS (1969/2001)

Virginia Farrell Beauty School—Livonia
33425 Five Mile Rd., Livonia 48154
Type: Private, proprietary
Degrees: C
URL: http://www.virginiafarrell.com
Phone: (734) 427-3970
Inst. Accred.: NACCAS (1987/2002)

Virginia Farrell Beauty School—St. Clair Shores
23620 Harper Ave., St. Clair Shores 48080
Type: Private, proprietary
Degrees: C
URL: http://www.virginiafarrell.com
Phone: (586) 775-6640
Inst. Accred.: NACCAS (1969/2001)

Virginia Farrell Beauty School—Westland
34580 Ford Rd., Westland 48185
Type: Private, proprietary
Degrees: C
URL: http://www.virginiafarrell.com
Phone: (734) 729-9220
Inst. Accred.: NACCAS (1973/2002)

Warren Woods Vocational Adult Education
13400 East 12 Mile Rd., Warren 48088-4036
Type: Public, state/local
Degrees: C
URL: http://www.warrenwoods.misd.net
Phone: (810) 439-4408
Inst. Accred.: NCA-CASI (2001/2005)

West Michigan College of Barbering and Beauty
3026 Lovers Ln., Kalamazoo 49001
Type: Private, proprietary
Degrees: C
Phone: (269) 381-4424
Inst. Accred.: NACCAS (1986/2002)

Wright Beauty Academy—Battle Creek
492 Capital Ave., SW, Battle Creek 49015
Type: Private, proprietary
Degrees: C
URL: http://www.wrightbeautyacademy.com
Phone: (269) 964-4016
Inst. Accred.: NACCAS (1973/2005)

Wright Beauty Academy—Portage
6666 Lovers Ln., Portage 49002
Type: Private, proprietary
Degrees: C
URL: http://www.wrightbeautyacademy.com
Phone: (269) 321-8708
Inst. Accred.: NACCAS (1971/2004)

MINNESOTA

American Indian Opportunities Industrial Center
1845 East Franklin Ave., Minneapolis 55404
Type: Public, independent
Degrees: C
URL: http://www.aioic.org
Phone: (612) 341-3358   *Calendar:* Qtr. plan
Inst. Accred.: NCA-CASI (1985/2004)

Art Instruction Schools
3400 Technology Dr., Minneapolis 55418
Type: Private, proprietary
Degrees: C
URL: http://www.artists-ais.com
Phone: (612) 362-5000
Inst. Accred.: DETC (1956/2000)

Aveda Institute, Inc.
400 Central Ave., Minneapolis 55414
Type: Private, proprietary
Degrees: C
Phone: (612) 378-7403
Inst. Accred.: NACCAS (1979/2001)

Bryman Institute—Eagan
1000 Blue Gentian Rd., Ste. 250, Eagan 55122
Type: Private, proprietary
System: Corinthian Colleges, Inc
Degrees: C
URL: http://www.bryman-institute.com
Phone: (651) 688-2145
Inst. Accred.: ACCSCT (2004)

Cosmetology Careers Unlimited—Duluth
121 West Superior St., Duluth 55802
Type: Private, proprietary
Degrees: C
URL: http://www.coscareers.com
Phone: (218) 722-7484
Inst. Accred.: NACCAS (1970/2002)

Cosmetology Careers Unlimited—Hibbing
110 East Howard St., Hibbing 55746
Type: Private, proprietary
Degrees: C
URL: http://www.coscareers.com
Phone: (218) 263-8354
Inst. Accred.: NACCAS (1975/2005)

East Metro Opportunities Industrialization Center
1919 University Ave., St. Paul 55104
Type: Public, state/local
Degrees: C
URL: http://www.eastmetrooic.org
Phone: (651) 291-5088
Inst. Accred.: NCA-CASI (1987/2004)

Global Language Institute, Inc.
1536 Hewitt Ave., St. Paul 55104
Type: Private, proprietary
Degrees: C
URL: http://www.gli.org
Phone: (651) 523-2934
Inst. Accred.: ACCET (1995/2001)

Herzing College—Minneapolis Drafting School Campus
5700 West Broadway, Minneapolis 55428-3548
Type: Private, proprietary
Degrees: C
URL: http://www.herzing.edu
Phone: (763) 535-8843   *Calendar:* Sem. plan
Inst. Accred.: NCA-HLC (2004, *Indirect accreditation through Herzing College Corporate Offices, Milwaukee, WI)*

Ing'enue Beauty School
1024 Center Ave., Moorhead 56560
Type: Private, proprietary
Degrees: C
Phone: (218) 236-7201
Inst. Accred.: NACCAS (1987/2002)

Minneapolis School of Massage and Bodywork
81 Lowry Ave., NE, Minneapolis 55418
Type: Private, proprietary
Degrees: C
Phone: (612) 788-8907
Inst. Accred.: ACCSCT (1994/2004)

Minnesota School of Cosmetology
7166 10th St. North, Oakdale 55128
Type: Private, proprietary
Degrees: C
URL: http://www.msccollege.edu
Phone: (651) 287-2180
Inst. Accred.: NACCAS (1983/2003)

Model College of Hair Design
201 Eighth Ave. South, St. Cloud 56301
Type: Private, proprietary
Degrees: C
URL: http://www.modelcollegeharidesign.com
Phone: (320) 253-4222
Inst. Accred.: NACCAS (1966/2003)

Montessori Training Center of Minnesota
683 Dodd Rd., St. Paul 55107
Type: Private, independent
Degrees: C
URL: http://www.mtcm.org
Phone: (651) 298-1120
Inst. Accred.: MACTE (1995/2004)

Norman & Associates
4938 Lincoln Dr., Edina 55436
Type: Private, proprietary
Degrees: C
URL: http://www.minnesota.dalecarnegie.com
Phone: (952) 935-0515
Inst. Accred.: ACCET (1976/2002)

Regency Beauty Institute
14350 Buck Hill Rd., Burnsville 55306
Type: Private, proprietary
Degrees: C
URL: http://www.regencybeauty.com
Phone: (952) 435-3882
Inst. Accred.: NACCAS (1977/2003)

Regency Beauty Institute
40 Hwy. 10, Blaine 55434
Type: Private, proprietary
Degrees: C
URL: http://www.regencybeauty.com
Phone: (763) 784-9102
Inst. Accred.: NACCAS (1971/2003)

Aurora-Naperville Campus
4374 East New York St., Aurora, IL 60504
Phone: (630) 723-5051

Darien-Downers Grove Campus
7411 South Cass Ave., Darien, IL 60651
Phone: (630) 824-4022

Madison Campus
2358 East Springs Dr., Ste. 300, Madison, WI 53704
Phone: (608) 819-0469

Maplewood Campus
3000 White Bear Ave. North, Maplewood 55109
Phone: (651) 773-3951

Saint Cloud Regency Beauty Academy
912 West St. Germain St., St. Cloud 56301
Phone: (320) 251-0500

Waite Park Campus
Market Place of Waite, 110 2nd St. South, Waite Park 56387
Phone: (320) 251-0500

Scot Lewis School-Paul Mitchell Partner School—Bloomington
9749 Lyndale Ave South, Bloomington 55420
Type: Private, proprietary
Degrees: C
URL: http://www.scotlewis.com
Phone: (952) 881-8662
Inst. Accred.: NACCAS (1968/2001)

Scot Lewis School-Paul Mitchell Partner School—Plymouth
4124 Lancaster Ln., Plymouth 55441
Type: Private, proprietary
Degrees: C
URL: http://www.scotlewis.com
Phone: (763) 551-0562
Inst. Accred.: NACCAS (1966/2001)

Saint Paul Campus
1905 Suburban Ave., St. Paul 55119
Phone: (651) 209-6930

Summit Academy OIC
935 Olson Memorial Hwy., Minneapolis 55405
Type: Public, state/local
Degrees: C
URL: http://www.saoic.org
Phone: (612) 377-0150
Inst. Accred.: NCA-CASI (1983/2005)

MISSISSIPPI

Academy of Hair Design
3905 Main St., Moss Point 39563
Type: Private, proprietary
Degrees: C
Phone: (228) 474-7007
Inst. Accred.: COE (1999/2000)

The Academy of Hair Design #1
2003-B South Commerce St., Grenada 38901
Type: Private, proprietary
Degrees: C
Phone: (662) 226-2462
Inst. Accred.: NACCAS (1978/2004)

The Academy of Hair Design #3
1815 Terry Rd., Jackson 39204
Phone: (601) 372-9800

The Academy of Hair Design #8
4031 Popps Ferry Rd., D'Iberville 39532
Phone: (228) 354-8282

The Academy of Hair Design #4
3167 Hwy 80 East, McLaurin Mart, Pearl 39280
Type: Private, proprietary
Degrees: C
Phone: (601) 939-4441
Inst. Accred.: NACCAS (1983/2003)

The Academy of Hair Design #6
Cloverleaf Mall D-4, 5912 U.S. Hwy. 49, Hattiesburg 39401
Type: Private, proprietary
Degrees: C
Phone: (601) 583-1290
Inst. Accred.: NACCAS (1983/2001)

Batesville Job Corps Center
821 Hwy. 51 South, Batesville 38606
Type: Public, federal
Degrees: C
Phone: (662) 563-4656
Inst. Accred.: COE (1989/2000)

Chris' Beauty College
1265 Pass Rd., Gulfport 39501
Type: Private, proprietary
Degrees: C
URL: http://www.chrisbeautycollege.com
Phone: (228) 864-2920
Inst. Accred.: NACCAS (1977/2003)

Creations College of Cosmetology
2419 West Main St., PO Box 2635, Tupelo 38803
Type: Private, proprietary
Degrees: C
Phone: (662) 844-9264
Inst. Accred.: NACCAS (1987/2002)

Delta Beauty College
697 Delta Plaza, Greenville 38701
Type: Private, proprietary
Degrees: C
Phone: (662) 332-0587
Inst. Accred.: NACCAS (1978/2003)

The Final Touch Beauty School
5700 North Hills St., Meridian 39307
Type: Private, proprietary
Degrees: C
Phone: (601) 485-7733
Inst. Accred.: NACCAS (1990/2005)

Foster's Cosmetology College
1813 Hwy. 15 North, PO Box 66, Ripley 38663
Type: Private, proprietary
Degrees: C
Phone: (662) 837-9334
Inst. Accred.: NACCAS (1983/2001)

Gibson's Barber and Beauty College
120 East Main St., PO Box 990, West Point 39773
Type: Private, proprietary
Degrees: C
Phone: (662) 494-5444
Inst. Accred.: NACCAS (1988/2003)

Gulfport Job Corps Center
3300 20th St., Gulfport 39501
Type: Public, federal
Degrees: C
URL: http://www.jobcorps-rci.com/gulfport.htm
Phone: (228) 864-9691
Inst. Accred.: COE (1985/2005)

Healing Touch School of Massage Therapy
4700 Hardy St., Ste. X, Hattiesburg 39402
Type: Private, proprietary
Degrees: C
URL: http://www.healingtouchms.com
Phone: (601) 261-0111
Inst. Accred.: ABHES (2004)

ICS The Wright Beauty College
2077 Hwy. 72 East—Annex, Corinth 38834
Type: Private, proprietary
Degrees: C
Phone: (662) 287-0944
Inst. Accred.: NACCAS (1986/2001)

J & J Hair Design College
116 East Franklin St., Carthage 39050
Type: Private, proprietary
Degrees: C
Phone: (601) 267-3678
Inst. Accred.: ACCSCT (1985/2004)

Senatobia Campus
562B West Main St., Senatobia 38668
Phone: (662) 562-8010

Magnolia College of Cosmetology
4725 I-55 North, Jackson 39206
Type: Private, proprietary
Degrees: C
URL: http://www.magnoliacollegeofcosmetology.com
Phone: (601) 362-6940
Inst. Accred.: NACCAS (1985/2005)

Mississippi College of Beauty Culture
732 Sawmill Rd., Laurel 39440
Type: Private, proprietary
Degrees: C
Phone: (601) 428-7127
Inst. Accred.: NACCAS (1976/2004)

Mississippi Job Corps Center
400 Harmony Rd., Crystal Springs 39059
Type: Public, federal
Degrees: C
Phone: (601) 892-3348
Inst. Accred.: COE (1984/2000)

Mississippi School of Therapeutic Massage
5120 Galaxie Dr., Jackson 39206
Type: Private, proprietary
Degrees: C
Phone: (601) 362-3624
Inst. Accred.: CMTA (1999/2004)

MISSOURI

Abbott Academy of Cosmetology Arts and Sciences
2101 Pkwy. Dr., St. Peters 63376
Type: Private, proprietary
Degrees: C
URL: http://www.missouribeauty.com
Phone: (636) 447-0100
Inst. Accred.: NACCAS (1985/2005)

Academy of Hair Design, Inc.
1832 South Glenstone Ave., # 4, Springfield 65804
Type: Private, proprietary
Degrees: C
Phone: (417) 881-3900
Inst. Accred.: NACCAS (2003/2004)

Advance Beauty College, Inc.
202 East Main St., Warrenton 63383-2006
Type: Private, proprietary
Degrees: C
Phone: (636) 456-1180
Inst. Accred.: NACCAS (2004)

American College of Hair Design, Inc.
125 Duke Rd., Sedalia 65301
Type: Private, proprietary
Degrees: C
URL: http://www.americancollegeofhairdesign.com
Phone: (660) 827-1270
Inst. Accred.: NACCAS (1999/2002)

Andrews Academy of Cosmetology
100 West Main, Sullivan 63080
Type: Private, proprietary
Degrees: C
Phone: (573) 468-3864
Inst. Accred.: NACCAS (2002/2005)

Aviation Institute of Maintenance
3130 Terrace St., Kansas City 64141
Type: Private, proprietary
Degrees: C
URL: http://www.tidetech.com
Phone: (816) 753-9920
Inst. Accred.: ACCSCT (2001)

Broadcast Center
2360 Hampton Ave., St. Louis 63139
Type: Private, proprietary
Degrees: C
URL: http://www.broadcastcenterinfo.com
Phone: (314) 647-8181
Inst. Accred.: ACCET (1990/2005)

Bryman College—Earth City
3420 Rider Trail South, Earth City 63045-1100
Type: Private, proprietary
System: Corinthian Colleges, Inc
Degrees: C
URL: http://bryman-college.com
Inst. Accred.: ACICS (2005)

C.J. Sealey & Associates, LLC
1869 Craig Park Ct., Ste. A, St. Louis 63146
Type: Private, proprietary
Degrees: C
URL: http://www.carnegiestl.com
Phone: (314) 439-8090
Inst. Accred.: ACCET (1999/2005)

Central College of Cosmetology
1012 Missouri Ave., St. Robert 65584
Type: Private, proprietary
Degrees: C
Phone: (573) 336-3888
Inst. Accred.: NACCAS (1991/2001)

Camdenton Campus
1159 North Hwy. 5, Camdenton 65020
Phone: (573) 346-7800

Chillicothe Beauty Academy
505 Elm St., Chillicothe 64601
Type: Private, proprietary
Degrees: C
URL: http://www.chillicothecosmetology.com
Phone: (660) 646-4198
Inst. Accred.: NACCAS (1975/2003)

Class Act I School of Cosmetology
512 Main St., Joplin 64801
Type: Private, proprietary
Degrees: C
URL: http://www.neoshobeautycollege.com
Phone: (417) 781-7070
Inst. Accred.: NACCAS (1994/2004)

Columbia Beauty Academy
1729 West Broadway, Ste. 5, Columbia 65203
Type: Private, proprietary
Degrees: C
Phone: (573) 445-6611
Inst. Accred.: NACCAS (1987/2005)

Cosmetology Concepts Institute
1611 Burlington St., Ste. A, Columbia 65202
Type: Private, proprietary
Degrees: C
Phone: (573) 449-7527
Inst. Accred.: NACCAS (1992/2002)

Diva's Unlimited Academy
9723 St. Charles Rock Rd., St. Louis 63114
Type: Private, proprietary
Degrees: C
Phone: (314) 428-3482
Inst. Accred.: NACCAS (2005)

Elaine Steven Beauty College, Inc.
10420 West Florissant, St. Louis 63136
Type: Private, proprietary
Degrees: C
URL: http://www.esbc.edu
Phone: (314) 868-8196
Inst. Accred.: NACCAS (1988/2003)

Grabber School of Hair Design
14557 Manchester Rd., Ballwin 63011
Type: Private, proprietary
Degrees: C
Phone: (636) 227-4440
Inst. Accred.: NACCAS (1988/2003)

The Hair Academy—110
110 North Franklin St., Kirksville 63501
Type: Private, proprietary
Degrees: C
Phone: (660) 665-1028
Inst. Accred.: NACCAS (2005)

Hannibal Career and Technical Center
4500 McMasters Ave., Hannibal 63401
Type: Public, state/local
Degrees: C
URL: http://www.hannibal.tec.mo.us
Phone: (573) 221-4430
Inst. Accred.: NCA-CASI (1991/2005)

House of Heavilin Beauty College—Blue Springs
1405 SW Smith St., Blue Springs 64015
Type: Private, proprietary
Degrees: C
URL: http://www.kc-hair.com
Phone: (816) 229-9000
Inst. Accred.: NACCAS (1979/2005)

House of Heavilin Beauty College—Grandview
12020 Blue Ridge Blvd., Grandview 64030
Type: Private, proprietary
Degrees: C
URL: http://www.kc-hair.com
Phone: (816) 767-8000
Inst. Accred.: NACCAS (1992/2003)

House of Heavilin Beauty College—Kansas City
5720 Troost Ave., Kansas City 64110
Type: Private, proprietary
Degrees: C
URL: http://www.kc-hair.com
Phone: (816) 523-2471
Inst. Accred.: NACCAS (1968/2004)

Independence College of Cosmetology
815 West 23rd St., Independence 64055
Type: Private, proprietary
Degrees: C
URL: http://www.hair-skin-nails.com
Phone: (816) 252-4247
Inst. Accred.: NACCAS (1966/2004)

Jacobs Facilities, Inc.
501 North Broadway, St. Louis 63102
Type: Private, proprietary
Degrees: C
URL: http://www.jacobs.com
Phone: (801) 978-9050
Inst. Accred.: ACCET (1996/2001)

Martinez School of Cosmetology
248 1/2 East Broadway, Excelsior Springs 64024
Type: Private, proprietary
Degrees: C
Phone: (816) 630-3900
Inst. Accred.: NACCAS (1989/2004)

Massage Therapy Training Institute
9140 Ward Pkwy., Ste. 100, Kansas City 64114
Type: Private, proprietary
Degrees: C
URL: http://www.mtti.net
Phone: (816) 523-9140
Inst. Accred.: ABHES (2004)

Merrell University of Beauty Arts and Science
1101-R Southwest Blvd., Jefferson City 65109
Type: Private, proprietary
Degrees: C
URL: http://www.merrelluniversity.edu
Phone: (573) 635-4433
Inst. Accred.: NACCAS (1987/2005)

Missouri College of Cosmetology and Esthetics
401 West Reed St., Moberly 65270
Phone: (660) 263-9600

Missouri Beauty Academy
224 East Columbia St., Farmington 63640
Type: Private, proprietary
Degrees: C
URL: http://www.missouribeauty.com
Phone: (573) 756-2730
Inst. Accred.: NACCAS (1984/2004)

Festus Campus
109 A Main St., Festus 63028
Phone: (636) 933-3627

Missouri College of Cosmetology North
2555 West Kearney St., Springfield 65803
Type: Private, proprietary
Degrees: C
URL: http://missouricosmo.com
Phone: (417) 866-2786
Inst. Accred.: NACCAS (2000/2003)

Missouri College of Cosmetology—Bolivar
1820 Springfield Rd., Bolivar 65613
Type: Private, proprietary
Degrees: C
URL: http://missouricosmo.com
Phone: (417) 326-3002
Inst. Accred.: NACCAS (2002/2005)

Missouri College of Cosmetology—South
3636 South Campbell Ave., Bolivar
Type: Private, proprietary
Degrees: C
URL: http://missouricosmo.com
Phone: (417) 887-6511
Inst. Accred.: NACCAS (2002/2005)

Missouri Montessori Teacher Education Program
1100 White Rd., Chesterfield 63017
Type: Private, independent
Degrees: C
URL: http://www.chesterfielddayschool.org/MOMTEP/
    index.html
Phone: (314) 469-6622
Inst. Accred.: MACTE (1999)

Missouri School of Barbering and Hairstyling
1125 North Hwy. 67, Florissant 63031
Type: Private, proprietary
Degrees: C
Phone: (314) 839-0310
Inst. Accred.: ACCSCT (1980/2005)

National Academy of Beauty Arts
157 Concord Plaza, St. Louis 63128
Type: Private, proprietary
Degrees: C
URL: http://www.nationalacademyofbeautyarts.com
Phone: (314) 842-3616
Inst. Accred.: NACCAS (1967/2005)

Crystal City Campus
26 Twin City Plaza, Crystal City 63019
Phone: (636) 931-7100

Neosho Beauty College
116 North Wood St., Neosho 64850
Type: Private, proprietary
Degrees: C
URL: http://www.neoshobeautycollege.com
Phone: (417) 451-7216
Inst. Accred.: NACCAS (1989/2004)

New Dimensions School of Hair Design
621 Kentucky Ave., Ste. 12, Joplin 64801
Type: Private, proprietary
Degrees: C
Phone: (417) 782-2875
Inst. Accred.: NACCAS (1993/2001)

Paris II Educational Center
6840 North Oak Trafficway, Gladstone 64118
Type: Private, proprietary
Degrees: C
URL: http://parisii.net
Phone: (816) 468-6666
Inst. Accred.: NACCAS (1987/2002)

Patsy & Rob's Academy of Beauty
18 Northwest Plaza, St. Ann 63074
Type: Private, proprietary
Degrees: C
URL: http://www.praob.edu
Phone: (314) 298-8808
Inst. Accred.: NACCAS (1988/2003)

Professional Massage Training Center
229 East Commercial St., Springfield 65803-2939
Type: Private, proprietary
Degrees: C
Phone: (417) 863-7682
Inst. Accred.: ACCSCT (2001)

Saint Charles School of Massage Therapy
2440 Executive Dr., Ste. 100, St. Charles 63303
Type: Private, proprietary
Degrees: C
Phone: (636) 498-0777
Inst. Accred.: CMTA (2003/2004)

Saint Louis Hair Academy, Inc.
3701 Kossuth Ave., St. Louis 63107
Type: Private, proprietary
Degrees: C
Phone: (314) 533-3125
Inst. Accred.: NACCAS (1992/2003)

Salem College of Hairstyling
1051 Kings Hwy., Ste. 1, Rolla 65401
Type: Private, proprietary
Degrees: C
Phone: (573) 368-3136
Inst. Accred.: NACCAS (1982/2002)

SEMO Hairstyling Academy
904 Broadway St., Cape Girardeau 63701
Type: Private, proprietary
Degrees: C
Phone: (573) 651-0333
Inst. Accred.: NACCAS (2004)

St. Louis Tech
9741 St. Charles Rock Rd., St. Louis 63114
Type: Private
Degrees: C
Phone: (314) 427-3600
Inst. Accred.: ACCSCT (1977/1988)

Stage One, The Hair School
904 Broadway, Cape Girardeau 63701
Type: Private, proprietary
Degrees: C
Phone: (573) 335-5078
Inst. Accred.: NACCAS (1971/1998)

Texas County Technical Institute
6915 South Hwy. 63, Houston 65483
Type: Private, independent
Degrees: C
URL: http://www.texascountytech.org
Phone: (417) 967-5466
Inst. Accred.: ACICS (2001/2005)

Bolivar Technical College
PO Box 314, Houston 65483

Branson Technical College
PO Box 314, Houston 65483
Phone: (417) 967-5466

MONTANA

Academy of Cosmetology
133 West Mendenhall, Bozeman 59715
Type: Private, proprietary
Degrees: C
URL: http://academycosmetology.com
Phone: (406) 587-1265
Inst. Accred.: NACCAS (1989/2004)

Academy of Nail and Skin & Hair, LLP
928 Broadwater Ave., Ste. C, Billings 59101
Type: Private, proprietary
Degrees: C
URL: http://www.academyofnailandskin.com
Phone: (406) 252-3232
Inst. Accred.: NACCAS (2003)

Big Sky Somatic Institute, LLC
1802 11th Ave., Helena 59601
Type: Private, proprietary
Degrees: C
URL: http://www.bigskysomatic.com
Phone: (406) 442-8998
Inst. Accred.: CMTA (2005)

Butte Academy of Beauty Culture, Inc.
303 West Park St., Butte 59701
Type: Private, proprietary
Degrees: C
Phone: (406) 723-8565
Inst. Accred.: NACCAS (1965/2003)

The College of Coiffure Art
1423 Wyoming Ave., Billings 59102
Type: Private, proprietary
Degrees: C
Phone: (406) 656-9114
Inst. Accred.: NACCAS (1974/2005)

Dahl's College of Beauty, Inc.
716 Central Ave., Great Falls 59401
Type: Private, proprietary
Degrees: C
Phone: (406) 454-3453
Inst. Accred.: NACCAS (1972/2003)

David L. Pals & Associates, Inc.
632 Luther Circle, PO Box 21502, Billings 59104
Type: Private, proprietary
Degrees: C
URL: http://www.montana.dalecarnegie.com
Phone: (406) 652-4442
Inst. Accred.: ACCET (1978/2004)

Health Works Institute
111 South Grand, Annex 3, Bozeman 59715
Type: Private, (prorpeiatry)
Degrees: C
URL: http://www.healthworksinstitute.com
Phone: (406) 582-1555
Inst. Accred.: CMTA (1999/2004)
Prog. Accred.: Massage Therapy

Modern Beauty School, Inc.
2700 Paxson Plaza, Ste. G, Missoula 59801
Type: Private, proprietary
Degrees: C
Phone: (406) 549-9608
Inst. Accred.: NACCAS (1997/2005)

Sage Technical Services
3044 Hesper Rd., Billings 59102
Type: Private, proprietary
Degrees: C
URL: http://www.sageschools.com
Phone: (406) 652-3030
Inst. Accred.: ACCSCT (1994/2002)

NEBRASKA

Alegent Health Immanuel Medical Center
6901 North 72nd St., Omaha 68122
Type: Private, independent
Degrees: C
URL: http://www.alegent.com
Phone: (402) 572-2121
Inst. Accred.: ABHES (2005)
Prog. Accred.: Clinical Pastoral Education, Medical
Assisting (ABHES)

Capitol School of Hairstyling and Esthetics
2819 South 125th Ave., Ste. 268, Omaha 68144
Type: Private, proprietary
Degrees: C
URL: http://www.capitollook.com
Phone: (402) 333-3329
Inst. Accred.: NACCAS (1988/2003)

College of Hair Design
304 South 11th St., Lincoln 68508-2199
Type: Private, proprietary
Degrees: C
Phone: (402) 477-4040   *Calendar:* Qtr. plan
Inst. Accred.: ACCSCT (1977/2004)

Joseph's College of Beauty—Beatrice
618 Count St., Beatrice 68310
Type: Private, proprietary
Degrees: C
URL: http://josephscollege.com
Phone: (402) 223-3588
Inst. Accred.: NACCAS (1973/2004)

Joseph's College of Beauty—Hastings
828 West 2nd St., Hastings 68901
Type: Private, proprietary
Degrees: C
URL: http://josephscollege.com
Phone: (402) 463-1357
Inst. Accred.: NACCAS (1973/2004)

> **Grand Island Campus**
> 305 West 3rd St., Grand Island 68801
> *Phone:* (308) 381-8848

Joseph's College of Beauty—Lincoln
2241 O St., Ste. 2, Lincoln 68510
Type: Private, proprietary
Degrees: C
URL: http://josephscollege.com
Phone: (402) 435-2333
Inst. Accred.: NACCAS (1973/2004)

> **Omaha Campus**
> 3724 Farnam St., Omaha 68131
> *Phone:* (402) 345-4152

Joseph's College of Beauty—Norfolk
202 Madison Ave., Norfolk 68701
Type: Private, proprietary
Degrees: C
URL: http://josephscollege.com
Phone: (402) 371-3358
Inst. Accred.: NACCAS (1968/2005)

Joseph's of Kearney, School of Hair Design
2213 Central Ave., Kearney 68847
Type: Private, proprietary
Degrees: C
URL: http://josephscollege.com
Phone: (402) 475-5385
Inst. Accred.: NACCAS (1983/2003)

La' James International College
1660 North Grant St., Fremont 68025
Type: Private, proprietary
Degrees: C
URL: http://www.bahnercollege.com
Phone: (402) 721-6500
Inst. Accred.: NACCAS (1966/2003)

Mid-America Montessori Teacher Training Center
10730 Pacific St., Ste. 234, Omaha 68114
Type: Private, independent
Degrees: C
Phone: (402) 393-1311
Inst. Accred.: MACTE (2001)

North Platte Beauty Academy
107 West Sixth St., North Platte 69101
Type: Private, proprietary
Degrees: C
Phone: (308) 532-4664
Inst. Accred.: NACCAS (1987/2002)

Omaha School of Massage Therapy
9748 Park Dr., Omaha 68128
Type: Private, proprietary
Degrees: C
URL: http://www.osmt.com
Phone: (402) 331-3694
Inst. Accred.: ACCSCT (1995/2005)

Universal College of Healing Arts
4922 Dodge St., Omaha 68137
Type: Private, proprietary
Degrees: C
URL: http://www.ucha.com
Phone: (402) 556-4456
Inst. Accred.: ABHES (2002)

Xenon International School of Hair Design II
8516 Park Dr., Omaha 68127
Type: Private, proprietary
Degrees: C
URL: http://www.xenonintl.com
Phone: (402) 393-2933
Inst. Accred.: NACCAS (1989/2004)

NEVADA

Academy of Hair Design
4445 West Charleston Blvd., Las Vegas 89102
Type: Private, proprietary
Degrees: C
URL: http://www.ahdvegas.com
Phone: (702) 878-1185
Inst. Accred.: NACCAS (1976/2005)

American Career Institute
2340 Paseo Del Prado, Ste. D-208, Las Vegas 89102
Type: Private, proprietary
Degrees: C
URL: http://www.acinst.com
Phone: (702) 222-3522
Inst. Accred.: DETC (2002)

Carson City Beauty Academy
2531 North Carson St., Carson City 89706
Type: Private, proprietary
Degrees: C
Phone: (775) 885-9977
Inst. Accred.: NACCAS (1992/2005)

Euphoria Institute of Beauty Arts and Sciences
9340 West Sahara Ave., Ste. 205, Las Vegas 89117
Type: Private, proprietary
Degrees: C
URL: http://www.euphoriainstitute.com
Phone: (702) 341-8111
Inst. Accred.: NACCAS (2004)

Expertise School of Beauty
902 West Owens Ave., Las Vegas 89106
Type: Private, proprietary
Degrees: C
Phone: (702) 636-8686
Inst. Accred.: NACCAS (2003)

Institute of Professional Careers
4472 South Eastern Ave., Las Vegas 89119
Type: Private, proprietary
Degrees: C
Phone: (702) 734-9900
Inst. Accred.: ACCSCT (2005)

J. R. Rodgers & Associates, Inc.
1100 East Sahara, Ste. 105, Las Vegas 89104
Type: Private, proprietary
Degrees: C
URL: http://www.nevada.dalecarnegie.com
Phone: (702) 735-2115
Inst. Accred.: ACCET (1979/2005)

Leadership Institute of Utah
1100 East Sahara, #105, Las Vegas 89104
Type: Private, proprietary
Degrees: C
URL: http://www.utah.dalecarnegie.com
Phone: (702) 735-2115
Inst. Accred.: ACCET (2002)

Marinello School of Beauty—Las Vegas
5001 East Bonanza Rd., Ste. 110, Las Vegas 89110
Type: Private, proprietary
Degrees: C
URL: http://www.marinello.com
Phone: (702) 431-6200
Inst. Accred.: NACCAS (1965/2003)

Henderson Campus
4451 East Sunset Rd., Ste. 14, Henderson 89014
Phone: (702) 450-9988

Northwest Health Careers
7398 Smoke Ranch Rd., Ste. 100, Las Vegas 89128
Type: Private, proprietary
Degrees: C
URL: http://www.northwesthealthcareers.com
Phone: (702) 254-7577
Inst. Accred.: ABHES (2003)
Prog. Accred.: Medical Assisting (ABHES)

Southern Nevada University of Cosmetology
3430 East Tropicana Ave., Ste. 40, Las Vegas 89121
Type: Private, proprietary
Degrees: C
Phone: (702) 458-6333
Inst. Accred.: NACCAS (1978/2003)

NEW HAMPSHIRE

Continental Academie of Hair Design—Hudson
102 Derry Rd., Hudson 03051
Type: Private, proprietary
Degrees: C
URL: http://continentalacademie.net
Phone: (603) 889-1614
Inst. Accred.: NACCAS (1976/2002)

Continental Academie of Hair Design—Manchester
228 Maple St., Manchester 03103
Type: Private, proprietary
Degrees: C
URL: http://continentalacademie.net
Phone: (603) 622-5851
Inst. Accred.: NACCAS (1972/2003)

Empire Beauty School #3
362 Route 108, Somersworth 3878
Type: Private, proprietary
Degrees: C
URL: http://www.empirebeauty.com
Phone: (603) 692-1515
Inst. Accred.: NACCAS (1981/2001)

Portsmouth Campus
2454 Lafayette Rd., Portsmouth 03801
Phone: (603) 433-6664

Empire Beauty School—Laconia
556 Main St., Laconia 3246
Type: Private, proprietary
Degrees: C
URL: http://www.empirebeauty.com
Phone: (603) 524-8777
Inst. Accred.: NACCAS (1977/2004)

Esthetics Institute at Concord Academy
20 South Main St., Concord 3301
Type: Private, proprietary
Degrees: C
URL: http://www.estheticsinstitute.net
Phone: (603) 224-2211
Inst. Accred.: NACCAS (1985/2005)

Keene Beauty Academy, Inc.
800 Park Ave., Keene 3431
Type: Private, proprietary
Degrees: C
URL: http://www.keenebeautyacademy.com
Phone: (603) 357-3736
Inst. Accred.: NACCAS (1983/2003)

Michael's School of Hair Design
73 South River Rd., Bedford Mall, Bedford 03110
Type: Private, proprietary
Degrees: C
URL: http://www.michaelsschool.com
Phone: (603) 668-4300
Inst. Accred.: NACCAS (1981/2001)

New England Montessori Teacher Education Center
30 Moose Club Rd., Goffstown 03045
Type: Private, independent
Degrees: C
Phone: (603) 641-5256
Inst. Accred.: MACTE (1999)

New England School of Hair Design, Inc.
12 Interchange Dr., West Lebanon 3784
Type: Private, proprietary
Degrees: C
URL: http://www.neschoolofhairdesign.com
Phone: (603) 298-5199
Inst. Accred.: NACCAS (1983/2003)

The New Hampshire Career Institute
17 Knight St., Concord 03301
Type: Private, independent
Degrees: C
URL: http://www.second-start.org
Phone: (603) 228-1341
Inst. Accred.: ACCET (1998/2004)

Portsmouth Beauty School of Hair Design
140 Congress St., Portsmouth 03801
Type: Private, proprietary
Degrees: C
Phone: (603) 436-5456
Inst. Accred.: NACCAS (1976/2002)

Russian & East European Partnerships, Inc.
33 Hyacinth Dr., Nashua 3062
Type: Private, proprietary
Degrees: C
URL: http://www.usereep.com
Phone: (603) 891-1650
Inst. Accred.: ACCET (2002)

Seacoast Center for Education
PO Box 323, Greenland 03840
Type: Private, independent
Degrees: C
URL: http://www.seacoastcenter.com
Phone: (603) 772-0181
Inst. Accred.: MACTE (1999)

Upper Valley Teacher Institute
One Ct. St., Ste. 210, Lebanon 03766
Type: Private, independent
Degrees: C
URL: http://www.uvti.org
Phone: (603) 448-6507   *Calendar:* Sem. plan
Inst. Accred.: NEASC-CTCI (1999)

NEW JERSEY

Academy of Massage Therapy
401 South Van Brunt St., Ste. 204, Englewood 07631
Type: Private, proprietary
Degrees: C
URL: http://www.massageschool.baweb.com
Phone: (201) 568-3220   *Calendar:* Sem. plan
Inst. Accred.: CMTA (1999/2004)

Allied Medical and Technical Institute
201 Willowbrook Blvd., 2nd Flr., Wayne 07470
Type: Private, proprietary
Degrees: C
URL: http://www.alliedteched.com
Phone: (973) 837-1818
Inst. Accred.: ACICS (1985/2005)

The Artistic Academy of Hair Design
Route 10 East, Powder Mill Plaza, Morris Plains 07950
Type: Private, proprietary
Degrees: C
URL: http://www.artisticacademy.com
Phone: (973) 656-1401
Inst. Accred.: NACCAS (1987/2002)

Avtech Institute of Technology
4500 New Brunswick Ave., Piscataway 08854
Type: Private, proprietary
Degrees: C
Phone: (732) 424-8008
Inst. Accred.: ACCSCT (2005)

Berdan Institute
201 Willowbrook Blvd., 2nd Flr., Wayne 07470
Type: Private, proprietary
Degrees: C
URL: http://www.berdaninstitute.com
Phone: (973) 837-1818
Inst. Accred.: ABHES (2002)
Prog. Accred.: Dental Assisting, Medical Assisting
  (ABHES), Medical Assisting (CAAHEP)

Bergen County Technical Schools
200 Hackensack Ave., Hackensack 07601
Type: Public, local
Degrees: C
URL: http://www.bergen.org/academy
Phone: (201) 343-6000
Inst. Accred.: COE (2005)

Berlitz International, Inc.
400 Alexander Park, Princeton 08540
Type: Private, proprietary
Degrees: C
URL: http://www.berlitz.com
Phone: (609) 514-3127
Inst. Accred.: ACCET (1984/2000)

Akron Campus
156 South Main St., Akron, OH 44308
Phone: (330) 762-0991

Atlanta Campus
Tower Place 200, Ste. 130, 3348 Peachtree Rd., NE,
Atlanta, GA 30326
Phone: (404) 261-5062

Austin Campus
8400 North MoPac, Ste. 302, Austin, TX 78759
Phone: (512) 343-0087

Baltimore Campus
1467 York Rd., Ste. 312, Baltimore, MD 21093
Phone: (410) 296-8365

Bellevue Campus
520 112th Ave., NE, Ste. 210, Bellevue, WA 98004
Phone: (425) 451-0162

Beverly Hills Campus
9454 Wilshire Blvd., Ste. 100, Beverly Hills, CA 91212
Phone: (310) 276-1101

Bingham Farms Campus
30700 Telegraph Rd., Ste. 1660, Bingham Center,
Bingham Farms, MI 48025
Phone: (248) 642-9335

Boston Campus
437 Boylston St., Boston, MA 02116
Phone: (617) 266-6858

Campbell Campus
Creekside Business Mall, 1475 South Bascom Ave.,
Campbell, CA 95008
Phone: (408) 377-9513

Charlotte Campus
5821 Fairview Rd., Ste. 202, Charlotte, NC 28209
Phone: (704) 554-8169

Chicago Campus
2 North Lasalle St., Ste. 1810, Chicago, IL 60602
Phone: (312) 782-6820

Cincinnati Campus
580 Walnut St., Plaza Level, Ste. 172-E, Cincinnati, OH
45202
Phone: (513) 381-4650

Berlitz International, Inc. *(continued)*

Cleveland Campus
1300 East Ninth St., Ste. 112, Bond Ct. Bldg.,
Cleveland, OH 44114
Phone: (216) 861-0950

Coral Gables Campus
2199 Ponce de Leon Blvd., Ste. 101, Coral Gables, FL
33134
Phone: (305) 444-7665

Costa Mesa Campus
3070 Bristol St., Ste. 150, Costa Mesa, CA 92626
Phone: (714) 557-3535

Dallas Campus
17194 Preston Rd., Ste. 207, Dallas, TX 75248
Phone: (972) 380-0404

Denver Campus
55 Madison St., #175, Denver, CO 80206
Phone: (303) 399-8686

Ft. Lauderdale Campus
2400 East Commercial Blvd., Ste. 100, Ft. Lauderdale,
FL 33308
Phone: (954) 491-9393

Houston Campus
520 Post Oak Blvd., Ste. 500, Houston, TX 77027
Phone: (713) 626-7844

Indianapolis Campus
8888 Keystone Crossing, Ste. 848, Indianapolis, IN
46240
Phone: (317) 844-4303

Miami Campus
777 Brickell Ave., Ste. 970, Sun Bank Bldg., Miami, FL
33131
Phone: (305) 371-3686

Mineola Campus
47 Mineola Blvd., Mineola, NY 11501
Phone: (516) 741-9220

Minneapolis Campus
6800 South France Ave., Ste. 190, Minneapolis, MN
55435
Phone: (952) 920-4100

New York Rector Street Campus
2 Rector St., New York, NY 10006
Phone: (212) 766-2388

New York West 51st Campus
40 West 51st St., New York, NY 10020
Phone: (212) 765-1000

Northbrook Campus
One Northbrook Place, 5 Revere Dr., Ste. 505,
Northbrook, IL 60062
Phone: (847) 509-0338

Oakbrook Campus
1200 Harger Rd., Ste. 722, Oakbrook, IL 60521
Phone: (630) 954-3822

Orange Campus
1835 Orangewood Ave., Ste. 102, Orange, CA 92668
Phone: (714) 935-0828

Pasadena Campus
600 South Lake Ave., Ste. 101, Pasadena, CA 91106
Phone: (626) 795-5888 .

Philadelphia Campus
1608 Walnut St., Philadelphia, PA 19103
Phone: (215) 735-8500

Phoenix Campus
3333 E. Camelback Rd., #160, Phoenix, AZ 85018
Phone: (602) 468-9494

Pittsburgh Campus
Penn Center West, Building 3, Ste. 400, Pittsburgh, PA
15222
Phone: (412) 494-9122

Princeton Campus
400 Alexander Park, Princeton 08540-6306
Phone: (609) 514-3400

Raleigh Campus
5974-A Six Forks Rd., Raleigh, NC 27609
Phone: (919) 848-1888

Ridgewood Campus
40 West Ridgewood Ave., Ste. 201, Ridgewood 07450
Phone: (201) 444-6400

Rochester Campus
36 Main St. West, Rochester, NY 14614
Phone: (716) 232-6424

Rockville Campus
11300 Rockville Pike, Ste. 911, Rockville, MD 20852
Phone: (301) 770-7551

Saint Louis Campus
200 South Hanley Rd., Ste. 208, St. Louis, MO 63105
Phone: (314) 721-1070

San Antonio Campus
5825 Callaghan Rd., Ste. 200, San Antonio, TX 78228
Phone: (210) 681-7050

San Diego Campus
Home Savings Bldg., 225 Broadway, Ste. 200, San
Diego, CA 92101
Phone: (619) 235-8344

San Francisco Campus
180 Montgomery St., Ste. 1580, San Francisco, CA
94104
Phone: (415) 986-6464

Santa Monica Campus
616 Santa Monica Blvd., Santa Monica, CA 90401
Phone: (310) 458-0330

Schaumburg Campus
1821 Walden Office Square, Ste. 230, Schaumburg, IL 60173
Phone: (847) 397-9422

Stamford Campus
350 Bedford St., Ste. 407, Stamford, CT 06901
Phone: (203) 324-9551

Summit Campus
47 Maple St., Summit 07901
Phone: (908) 277-0300

Torrance Campus
Park Del Amo, 2355 Crenshaw Blvd., Building A, Ste. 185, Torrance, CA 90501
Phone: (310) 328-7722

Vienna Campus
Tyson Ct.house Bldg., 2070 Chain Bridge Rd., Ste. 140, Vienna, VA 22182
Phone: (703) 883-0627

Walnut Creek Campus
1646 North California Blvd., Ste. P-112, Walnut Creek, CA 94596
Phone: (925) 935-1386

Washington, DC Campus
1050 Connecticut Ave., NW, Washington, DC 20036
Phone: (202) 331-1160

Wauwatosa Campus
2675 North Mayfair Rd., Ste. 204, Wauwatosa, WI 53226
Phone: (414) 454-2744

Wayne Campus
Sugartown Square, 230 Sugartown Rd., Ste. 103, Wayne, PA 19087
Phone: (610) 964-8404

Wellesley Hills Campus
40 Washington St., Wellesley Hills, MA 02181
Phone: (781) 237-2220

West Hartford Campus
61 South Main St., West Hartford, CT 06107
Phone: (860) 231-7310

Westport Campus
The Market Place, 125 Main St., Ste. 340, Westport, CT 06880
Phone: (203) 226-4223

White Plains Campus
One North Broadway, Rm. 15, White Plains, NY 10601
Phone: (914) 946-8389

Woodland Hills Campus
6300 Canoga Ave., Ste. 1002, Woodland Hills, CA 91367
Phone: (818) 999-1870

Brick Computer Science Institute
515 Hwy. 70, Brick 08723-4043
Type: Private, proprietary
Degrees: C
URL: http://www.brickcomputer.com
Phone: (732) 477-0975
Inst. Accred.: ACCSCT (1974/2002, Probation)

Brookside Business and Training Institute
25 Brookside Ave., Sussex 07461-2223
Type: Private, proprietary
Degrees: C
URL: http://www.bbti.edu
Phone: (973) 875-4445
Inst. Accred.: ACICS (2003)

Capri Institute of Hair Design—Bricktown
268 Brick Blvd., Bricktown 8723
Type: Private, proprietary
Degrees: C
URL: http://www.capriinstitute.com
Phone: (732) 920-3600
Inst. Accred.: NACCAS (1984/2004)

Capri Institute of Hair Design—Clifton
1595 Main Ave., Clifton 7011
Type: Private, proprietary
Degrees: C
URL: http://www.capriinstitute.com
Phone: (973) 772-4610
Inst. Accred.: NACCAS (1972/2003)

Capri Institute of Hair Design—Kenilworth
660 North Michigan Ave., Kenilworth 07033
Type: Private, proprietary
Degrees: C
URL: http://www.capriinstitute.com
Phone: (908) 964-1330
Inst. Accred.: NACCAS (1981/2005)

Roxbury Campus
Roxbury Mall, 45 Sunset Strip & Route 10 East, Succasunna 07876
Phone: (973) 584-9030

Capri Institute of Hair Design—Paramus
615 Winters Ave., Paramus 7652
Type: Private, proprietary
Degrees: C
URL: http://www.capriinstitute.com
Phone: (201) 599-0880
Inst. Accred.: NACCAS (1978/2005)

CareerWorks
601 Broad St., Ste. 300, Newrak 07102
Type: Private, proprietary
Degrees: C
Phone: (973) 623-3535
Inst. Accred.: ACCSCT (2001)

Central Career Schools
126 Corporate Blvd., South Plainfield 07080
Type: Private, proprietary
Degrees: C
URL: http://www.centralcareer.com
Phone: (908) 412-8600
Inst. Accred.: ACCSCT (1998/2003)

The Chubb Institute—Parsippany
8 Sylvan Way, First Flr., Parsippany 07054-0342
Type: Private, proprietary
System: High-Tech Institute
Degrees: C
URL: http://www.chubbinstitute.edu
Phone: (973) 682-4900
Inst. Accred.: ACCSCT (1972/2004)

Jersey City Campus
40 Journal Square, Jersey City 07306-4009
Phone: (201) 876-3800

The Cittone Institute
1697 Oak Tree Rd., Edison 08820-2896
Type: Private, proprietary
System: Lincoln Educational Services
Degrees: C
URL: http://www.cittone.com
Phone: (732) 548-8798
Inst. Accred.: ACICS (1975/2003)

Mount Laurel Campus
1000 Howard Blvd., Mount Laurel 08054-3414
Phone: (856) 722-9333

Northeast Campus
2180 Horing Rd., Philadelphia, PA 19116
Phone: (215) 969-0869

Paramus Campus
160 East Route 4 and Forest Ave., Paramus
Phone: (201) 845-6868

Plymouth Meeting Campus
One Plymouth Meeting, Ste. 300, Plymouth Meeting,
PA 19462
Phone: (610) 941-0319

Princeton Campus
100 Canal Pointe Blvd., Princeton 08540
Phone: (609) 520-8798

Concorde School of Hair Design, Inc.
1458 State Route 35, Ocean 07712
Type: Private, proprietary
Degrees: C
URL: http://www.concordeschools.com
Phone: (732) 493-1355
Inst. Accred.: NACCAS (1983/2003)

Bloomfield Campus
15 Ward St., Bloomfield 07003
Phone: (973) 680-0099

Divers Academy international
2500 South Broadway, Camden 08104-2431
Type: Private, proprietary
Degrees: C
URL: http://www.diversacademy.com
Phone: (856) 966-1871
Inst. Accred.: ACCSCT (1981/2002)

Dover Business College
East 81 Route 4 West, Paramus 07652
Type: Private, proprietary
Degrees: C
URL: http://www.doverbusinesscollege.org
Phone: (201) 843-8500   *Calendar:* Qtr. plan
Inst. Accred.: ACICS (1974/2002)
Prog. Accred.: Medical Assisting (CAAHEP)

Dover Campus
15 East Blackwell St., Dover 07801
Phone: (973) 366—6700
Prog. Accred: Medical Assisting (CAAHEP)

Eastern School of Acupuncture and Traditional Medicine
215 Glenridge Ave., Montclair 07042
Type: Private, proprietary
Degrees: C
URL: http://www.easternschool.com
Phone: (973) 746-8717
Inst. Accred.: ACAOM (2003)

ELS Language Centers
400 Alexander Park, Princeton 08540-6306
Type: Private, proprietary
Degrees: C
URL: http://www.els.edu
Phone: (609) 750-3510
Inst. Accred.: ACCET (1978/2004)

Culver City Campus
9000 Overland Ave., Culver City, CA 90230-3519
Phone: (310) 451-4544

Boston Campus
400 The Fenway, Boston, MA 02115-5798
Phone: (617) 731-3600

Charlotte Campus
2324 Wellesley Ave., Barnhardt Hall, Charlotte, NC
28207-2448
Phone: (704) 337-2364

Cleveland Campus
Case Western Reserve University, 10900 Euclid Ave.,
Stone Commons, Cleveland, OH 44106
Phone: (216) 368-2716

DeLand Campus
145 East Michigan Ave., Campus Box 8416, DeLand,
FL 32720-6306
Phone: (386) 736-6330

Denver Campus
7150 Montview Blvd., Foote Hall, Denver, CO 80220
Phone: (303) 256-9480

Garden City Campus
Adelphi University, South Ave., Linen Hall, Garden City,
NY 11530
Phone: (516) 877-3910

Goleta Campus
Francisco Torres Student Center, 6850 El Colegio Rd.,
Goleta, CA 93117
Phone: (805) 685-7878

Grand Rapids Campus
301 Michigan St. NE, 5th Flr., Rm. 546, Grand Rapids,
MI 49503
Phone: (616) 331-5720

Hayward Campus
25555 Hesperian Blvd., Building 1800, Rm. 1814A,
Hayward, CA 94545
Phone: (510) 723-6885

Houston Campus
4200 Montrose Blvd., Ste. 120, Houston, TX 77006
Phone: (713) 521-2030

Indianapolis Campus
Indiana University°Purdue University Indianapolis, 620
Union Dr., Rm. 242, Indianapolis, IN 46202
Phone: (317) 274-2371

Laramie Campus
406 South 21st St., Room 215, Laramie, WY 82071
Phone: (307) 766-3900

Louisville Campus
2001 Newburg Rd., Bonaventure Hall, Louisville, KY
40205
Phone: (502) 473-3357

Marietta Campus
1100 South Marietta Pkwy., Building D, Marietta, GA
30060-2896
Phone: (770) 528-4960

Melbourne Campus
Florida Institute of Technology, 150 West University
Blvd., Melbourne, FL 32901
Phone: (321) 727-3990

Miami Shores Campus
11300 Northeast Second Ave., Miami Shores, FL
33161-6695
Phone: (305) 899-3390

Nashville Campus
1900 Belmont Blvd., Nashville, TN 37212
Phone: (615) 460-6011

New York Campus
75 Varick St., 2nd Flr., New York, NY 10013-1919
Phone: (212) 431-9330

Oklahoma City Campus
Oklahoma City University, 1915 NW 24th St., Harris
Hall, Oklahoma City, OK 73106
Phone: (405) 525-3738

Orange Campus
Chapman University, 410 North Glassell St., Orange,
CA 92866
Phone: (714) 538-6800

Philadelphia Campus
St. Joseph's University, 5414 Overbrook Ave.,
Philadelphia, PA 19131
Phone: (215) 473-4430

Portland Campus
1881 Southwest Naito Pkwy., Ste. 150, Portland, OR
97201
Phone: (971) 544-1655

River Forest Campus
7900 West Division St., River Forest, IL 60305-1499
Phone: (704) 488-5010

Riverdale Campus
College of Mount Saint Vincent-Seton Hall, 6301
Riverdale Ave., Riverdale, NY 10471
Phone: (718) 796-6325

Ruston Campus
PO Box 3006, Ruston, LA 71272
Phone: (318) 257-2012

Saint Paul Campus
2115 Summit Ave., Mail CHC 203, St. Paul, MN
55105-1096
Phone: (651) 962-5990

Saint Petersburg Campus
Eckerd College, 4200 54th Ave., South, St. Petersburg,
FL 33711
Phone: (727) 864-7820

San Antonio Campus
4301 Broadway, CPO #498, San Antonio, TX 78209
Phone: (210) 283-5077

San Diego Campus
225 Broadway, Ste. 200, San Diego, CA 92101
Phone: (619) 233-5433

ELS Language Centers *(continued)*

San Francisco Campus
1825 Sacramento St., 3rd Flr., San Francisco, CA 94109
Phone: (415) 561-0438

San Rafael Campus
50 Acacia Ave., San Rafael, CA 94901-8008
Phone: (415) 485-3224

Santa Clarita Campus
26455 Rockwell Canyon Rd., Santa Clarita, CA 91355
Phone: (661) 362-5554

Seattle Campus
718 12th Ave., Seattle, WA 98122
Phone: (206) 623-1481

Teaneck Campus
1000 River Rd., Robinson Hall, 4th Flr., Teaneck 07666
Phone: (201) 907-0004

West Haven Campus
300 Orange Ave., Bethel Hall, West Haven, CT 06516-1916
Phone: (203) 931-3000

White Plains Campus
99 Church St., White Plains, NY 10601
Phone: (914) 948-0635

Empire Beauty School—Bordentown
610 Route 206, Bordentown 08505
Type: Private, proprietary
Degrees: C
URL: http://www.empirebeauty.com
Phone: (609) 392-4545
Inst. Accred.: NACCAS (1990/2004)

Empire Beauty School—Cherry Hill
2100 State Hwy. 38, Cherry Hill Plaza, Cherry Hill 8002
Type: Private, proprietary
Degrees: C
URL: http://www.empirebeauty.com
Phone: (856) 667-8326
Inst. Accred.: NACCAS (1983/2001)

Empire Beauty School—Laurel Springs
1305 Blackwood-Clemton Rd., Laurel Springs 8021
Type: Private, proprietary
Degrees: C
URL: http://www.empirebeauty.com
Phone: (856) 425-8100
Inst. Accred.: NACCAS (1979/2004)

Engine City Technical Institute
901 Hadley Rd., South Plainfield 07080
Type: Private, proprietary
Degrees: C
URL: http://www.enginecitytech.com
Phone: (800) 305-3487
Inst. Accred.: ACCSCT (1984/2004)

European Academy of Cosmetology, Inc.
1126 Morris Ave., Union 7083
Type: Private, proprietary
Degrees: C
URL: http://www.eachair.com
Phone: (908) 686-4422
Inst. Accred.: NACCAS (1983/2003)

G. Mitchell Hartman & Associates, Inc.
155 Route 46 West, Wayne Plaza II, Wayne 07470
Type: Private, proprietary
Degrees: C
URL: http://www.northernnj.dale-carnegie.com
Phone: (973) 890-0909
Inst. Accred.: ACCET (1977/2004)

Harris School of Business
1 Cherry Hill, 1 Mall Dr., Ste. 700, Cherry Hill 08002
Type: Private, proprietary
Degrees: C
URL: http://www.harrisschool.edu
Phone: (856) 662-5300
Inst. Accred.: ACICS (1978/2004)

Harrison Career Institute—Delran
4000 Route 130 North, Heritage Square Shoppping Center, Delran 08075
Type: Private, proprietary
Degrees: C
URL: http://www.harrisoncareerinst.com
Phone: (856) 764-8933
Inst. Accred.: ACCSCT (1987/2005 Probation)

Jersey City Campus
600 Pavonia Ave., Jersey City 07306
Phone: (201) 222-1700

Kingston Campus
844 West Market St., Kingston, PA 18704
Phone: (570) 331-2006

Scranton Campus
Greenridge Plaza, 1600 Nay Aug Ave., Scranton, PA 18509
Phone: (717) 963-0144

South Orange Campus
525 South Orange Ave., South Orange 07079
Phone: (973) 763-9484

Harrison Career Institute—Deptford
1450 Clements Bridge Rd., The Plaza Deptford, Deptford 08096
Type: Private, proprietary
Degrees: C
URL: http://www.harrisoncareerinst.com
Phone: (856) 384-2888
Inst. Accred.: ACCSCT (1982/2004 Probation)

Harrison Career Institute—Vineland
1386 South Delsea Dr., Vineland 08360-6210
Type: Private, proprietary
Degrees: C
URL: http://www.harrisoncareerinst.com
Phone: (856) 696-0500
Inst. Accred.: ACCSCT (1985/2005 Probation)

Oakhurst Campus
2105 Hwy. 35, Oakhurst 07712-7201
Phone: (732) 493-1660

Pittsburgh Campus
717 Liberty Ave., Ste. 800, Clark Bldg., 8th Flr., Pittsburgh, PA 15222
Phone: (856) 696-0500

Healing Hands Institute
41 Bergenline Ave., Westwood 07675
Type: Private, proprietary
Degrees: C
URL: http://www.healinghandsinstitute.com
Phone: (201) 722-0099
Inst. Accred.: CMTA (1999/2004)

Healthcare Training Institute
1969 Morris Ave., Union 07083
Type: Private, proprietary
Degrees: C
URL: http://www.healthcareti.com
Phone: (908) 851-7711
Inst. Accred.: ACCSCT (2003)

Helma Institute of Massage Therapy
101 Route 46 West, Saddle Brook 07663
Type: Private, proprietary
Degrees: C
URL: http://www.helma.com
Phone: (201) 226-0056
Inst. Accred.: ACCSCT (2001)

HoHoKus RETS—Nutley
103 Park Ave., Nutley 07110-3505
Type: Private, proprietary
Degrees: C
URL: http://www.hohokusrets.com
Phone: (973) 661-0600
Inst. Accred.: ACCSCT (1977/2002)

HoHoKus School of Business and Medical Sciences
10 South Franklin Turnpike, Ramsey 07446
Type: Private, proprietary
Degrees: C
URL: http://www.hohokus.com
Phone: (201) 327-8877
Inst. Accred.: ACICS (1976/2003)

HoHoKus-Hackensack School of Business and Medical Science
66 Moore St., Hackensack 07601
Type: Private, proprietary
Degrees: C
URL: http://www.hohokushackensack.com
Phone: (201) 488-9400   *Calendar:* Qtr. plan
Inst. Accred.: ACICS (1976/2000)

Hudson Electrical Institute, Inc.
905 Bergen Ave., Jersey City 07306
Type: Private, proprietary
Degrees: C
URL: http://www.hudsonelectricalinstitute.com
Phone: (201) 239-7600
Inst. Accred.: ACCET (2000/2003)

The Institute for Health Education
7 Spielman Rd., Fairfield 07004
Type: Private, proprietary
Degrees: C
URL: http://www.healthed-nj.com
Phone: (973) 808-1666   *Calendar:* Qtr. plan
Inst. Accred.: ACCSCT (1997/2002)
Prog. Accred.: Dental Assisting

Institute for Therapeutic Massage, Inc.
125 Wanaque Ave., Pompton Lakes 07442
Type: Private, proprietary
Degrees: C
URL: http://www.massageprogram.com
Phone: (973) 839-6131
Inst. Accred.: CMTA (1999)

Atlantic Mind Body Center
Morristown Memorial Hospital, 95 Mt. Kemble Ave., Morristown 07962
Phone: (973) 839-613

Tinton Falls Campus
1 Sheila Dr., Tinton Falls 07724
Phone: (732) 936-9111

UMDNJ Campus
University of Medicine and Dentistry of New Jersey, 150 Bergen St., Bergen 07103
Phone: (973) 839-6131

Institute of Logistical Management
315 West Broad St., PO Box 427, Burlington 08016
Type: Private, proprietary
Degrees: C
URL: http://www.logistics-edu.com
Phone: (609) 747-1515
Inst. Accred.: DETC (2001)

Joe Kubert School of Cartoon and Graphic Art
37 Myrtle Ave., Dover 07801-4054
Type: Private, proprietary
Degrees: C
Phone: (973) 361-1327   *Calendar:* Sem. plan
Inst. Accred.: ACCSCT (1980/2005)

Joy's School of Hair Design
44 Glenwood Ave., East Orange 7017
Type: Private, proprietary
Degrees: C
Phone: (973) 673-4141
Inst. Accred.: NACCAS (1999/2005)

KeySkills Learning, Inc.
50 Mount Prospect Ave., Clifton 07013
Type: Private, proprietary
Degrees: C
URL: http://www.keyskillslearning.com
Phone: (973) 778-8136
Inst. Accred.: ACCSCT (2000/2005)

Maywood Campus
99 Essex St., Maywood 07607
Phone: (201) 587-0221

Lincoln Technical Institute
2299 Vauxhall Rd., Union 07083-5032
Type: Private, proprietary
System: Lincoln Educational Services
Degrees: C
URL: http://www.lincolntech.com
Phone: (908) 964-7800
Inst. Accred.: ACCSCT (1967/2004)

Mahwah Campus
70 McKee Dr., Mahwah 07430
Phone: (201) 529-1414

Metro Auto Electronics Training Institute, Inc.
111 Market St., Kenilworth 07033
Type: Private, proprietary
Degrees: C
URL: http://www.metro-auto.com
Phone: (908) 245-5335
Inst. Accred.: ACCET (2002)

Micro Tech Training Center
3000 Kennedy Blvd., 3rd Flr., Jersey City 07306
Type: Private, proprietary
Degrees: C
URL: http://www.microtech.net
Phone: (201) 216-9901
Inst. Accred.: ACCSCT (1995/2005)

Micropower Computer Institute
1203 St. Georges Ave., Linden 07036
Type: Private, proprietary
Degrees: C
URL: http://www.mpow.com
Phone: (908) 587-9070
Inst. Accred.: COE (2003)

Hauppauge Campus
120 Commerce Dr., Hauppauge, NY 11788
Phone: (631) 656-2940

Manhattan Campus
243 West 30th St., 9th Flr., New York, NY 10001
Phone: (212) 279-2550

Mineola Campus
85 Willis Ave., Mineola, NY 11501
Phone: (516) 742-5913

Queens Campus
75-26 Broadway, Elmhurst, NY 11373
Phone: (718) 507-2663

West Haven Campus
300 Orange Ave., Buckman Hall, Rm. 232, West
Haven, CT 06516
Phone: (203) 479-4565

Monmouth County Vocational School
255 West End Ave., Long Branch 07740
Type: Public, local
Degrees: C
URL: http://www.mcvsd.org
Phone: (732) 431-7942   <I>Calendar: <P>Sem. plan
Inst. Accred.: COE (2003)

Morris County School of Technology
400 East Main St., Denville 07834
Type: Public, local
Degrees: C
URL: http://www.mcvts.org
Phone: (973) 627-4600
Inst. Accred.: COE (2004)

National Massage Therapy Institute
Washington Square West, 6712 Washington Ave., Ste.
302, Egg Harbor 08234
Type: Private, proprietary
Degrees: C
Phone: (609) 227-8363
Inst. Accred.: CMTA (1999/2005)

National Massage Therapy Institute
108-L Greentree Rd. & Black Horse Pike, Turnersville
08012
Type: Private, proprietary
Degrees: C
Phone: (856) 227-8363
Inst. Accred.: CMTA (1999/2005)

National Tax Training School
67 Ramapo Valley Rd., Ste. 102, Mahwah 07430
Type: Private, proprietary
Degrees: C
URL: http://nattax.com
Phone: (201) 684-0828
Inst. Accred.: DETC (1965/2003)

Natural Motion Institute of Hair Design
2800 Kennedy Blvd., Jersey City 7306
Type: Private, proprietary
Degrees: C
URL: http://www.natural-motion.com
Phone: (201) 659-0303
Inst. Accred.: NACCAS (1973/2001)

New Community Workforce Development Center
201 Bergen St., Newark 07103
Type: Private, independent
Degrees: C
URL: http://www.newcommunity.org/whatwedo_human
  dev-workforce.htm
Phone: (973) 824-6484
Inst. Accred.: COE (2002/2005)

New Horizons Beauty School
5518 Bergenline Ave., West New York 7093
Type: Private, proprietary
Degrees: C
Phone: (201) 866-4000
Inst. Accred.: NACCAS (1983/2001)

Ocean County Vocational Technical School
1299 Old Freehold Rd., Toms River 08753-4201
Type: Public, local
Degrees: C
URL: http://www.ocvts.org
Phone: (732) 473-3159
Inst. Accred.: COE (2004)

Brick Campus
350 Chambers Ridge Rd., Brick 08723
Phone: (732) 920-0050

Jackson Campus
850 Toms River Rd., Jackson 08527
Phone: (732) 928-3830

Lakehurst Campus
Hanger One NAVAIR, Lakehurst 08733
Phone: (732) 657-4000

Southern Ocean Campus
423 Wells Mill Rd., Route 532, Waretown 08758
Phone: (609) 693-3434

Omega Institute
7050 Route 38 East, Pennsauken 08109
Type: Private, proprietary
Degrees: C
URL: http://www.omegacareers.com
Phone: (856) 663-4299
Inst. Accred.: ACICS (1982/2004)
Prog. Accred.: Massage Therapy

P. B. Cosmetology Education Centre
110 Monmouth St., Gloucester 8030
Type: Private, proprietary
Degrees: C
URL: http://www.cosedcenter.com
Phone: (856) 456-4927
Inst. Accred.: NACCAS (1972/2003)

Parisian Beauty Academy
362 State St., Hackensack 7601
Type: Private, proprietary
Degrees: C
URL: http://www.parisianbeautyacademy.com
Phone: (201) 487-2203
Inst. Accred.: NACCAS (1965/2003)

PC AGE Career Institute—Newark
89 Market St., 3rd Flr., Newark 07102
Type: Private, proprietary
Degrees: C
URL: http://www.pcage.com
Phone: (973) 565-9800
Inst. Accred.: ACCET (2001/2005, Warning)

Edison Campus
3 Ethel Rd., Durham Center, Ste. 301, Edison 08817
Phone: (732) 287-3622

PC Tech Learning Center
2815 Kennedy Blvd., 3rd Flr., Jersey City 07306
Type: Private, proprietary
Degrees: C
URL: http://www.pctech2000.com
Phone: (201) 761-0038
Inst. Accred.: ACCET (2003)

Pennco Tech
PO Box 1427, Blackwood 08012-9961
Type: Private, proprietary
Degrees: C
Phone: (856) 232-0310
Inst. Accred.: ACCSCT (1980/2003)

Performance Training
1012 Cox Cro Rd., Toms River 08753
Type: Private, proprietary
Degrees: C
Phone: (732) 505-9119
Inst. Accred.: ACCSCT (2001)

Princeton Center for Teacher Education
487 Cherry Valley Rd., Princeton 08540
Type: Private, independent
Degrees: C
URL: http://www.pctemontessori.org
Phone: (609) 924-4594
Inst. Accred.: MACTE (1999)

Prism Career Institute
2 Sindoni Ln., Hammonton 08037
Type: Private, proprietary
Degrees: C
URL: http://www.prismcareerinstitute.com
Phone: (609) 561-4424
Inst. Accred.: ACCET (1988/2001)

Philadelphia Campus
8040 Roosevelt Blvd., Philadelphia, PA 19152
Phone: (215) 331-4600

Sewell Campus
150 Delsea Dr., Ste. 2, Sewell 08080
Phone: (856) 881-6555

Reignbow Beauty Academy, Inc.
312 State St., Perth Amboy 8861
Type: Private, proprietary
Degrees: C
URL: http://www.reignbowbeautyacademy.com
Phone: (732) 442-6007
Inst. Accred.: NACCAS (1974/2005)

Reignbow Hair Fashion Institute
121 Watchung Ave., North Plainfield 7060
Type: Private, proprietary
Degrees: C
URL: http://www.reignbowbeautyacademy.com
Phone: (908) 754-4247
Inst. Accred.: NACCAS (1987/2005)

Rizzieri Aveda School for Beauty and Wellness
6001 West Lincoln Dr., Marlton 8053
Type: Private, proprietary
Degrees: C
URL: http://www.rizzieri.com
Phone: (856) 985-8600
Inst. Accred.: NACCAS (1972/2004)

Roman Academy of Beauty Culture
431 Lafayette Ave., Hawthorne 7506
Type: Private, proprietary
Degrees: C
URL: http://www.romanacademy.com
Phone: (973) 423-2223
Inst. Accred.: NACCAS (1976/2002)

Shore Beauty School
103 West Washington Ave., Pleasantville 8232
Type: Private, proprietary
Degrees: C
URL: http://www.shorebeautyschool.com
Phone: (609) 645-3635
Inst. Accred.: NACCAS (1983/2003)

Software Sense Computer Learning Center ,Inc.
225 Route 46 West, Ste. 8, Totowa 07512
Type: Private, proprietary
Degrees: C
URL: http://www.softwaresensetraining.com
Phone: (973) 256-7493
Inst. Accred.: ACCET (2002)

Somerset School of Massage Therapy
180 Centennial Ave., Piscataway 08854
Type: Private, proprietary
Degrees: C
URL: http://www.ssmt.org
Phone: (732) 885-3400
Inst. Accred.: ACCET (2001), CMTA (2001/2004)

Wall Township Campus
1985 Hwy. 34, Wall Township 7719
Phone: (732) 282-0100

Southern New Jersey Technical School
1833 Glassboro Rd. (Rt. 322), Williamstown 08094
Type: Private, proprietary
Degrees: C
URL: http://www.snjts.com
Phone: (856) 442-0006
Inst. Accred.: ABHES (2004)

Willingboro Campus
429 John F Kennedy Way, Willingboro 08046
Phone: (609) 877-8600

Star Technical Institute—Stratford
43 South White Horse Pike, Stratford 08084
Type: Private, proprietary
Degrees: C
URL: http://www.startechinstitute.com
Phone: (856) 435-7827
Inst. Accred.: ACCSCT (1985/2005)

Lakewood Campus
1255 Route 70, Ste. 12N, Lakewood 08701-5918
Phone: (732) 901-9710

StenoTech Career Institute
20 Just Rd., Fairfield 07004-3490
Type: Private, proprietary
Degrees: C
URL: http://www.stenotechcareerinst.com
Phone: (973) 882-4875
Inst. Accred.: ACICS (1996/2001)

Piscataway Campus
262 Old New Brunswick Rd., Piscataway 08854
Phone: (732) 562-1200

The Stuart School
2400 Belmar Blvd., Wall 07719
Type: Private, proprietary
Degrees: C
URL: http://www.stuartschool.com
Phone: (732) 681-7200   *Calendar:* Sem. plan
Inst. Accred.: ACICS (1967/2003)

MedTech College
6602 East 75th St., Heritage Park 1, Indianapolis, IN 46250
Phone: (317) 845-0100

Success Unlimited, Inc.
1301 East Route 70, Cherry Hill 08034-2101
Type: Private, proprietary
Degrees: C
URL: http://www.southjersey.dalecarenegie.com
Phone: (856) 428-4243
Inst. Accred.: ACCET (1977/2003)

Target Training Center
50 South 21st St., Kenilworth 07033
Type: Private, proprietary
Degrees: C
URL: http://www.ttcenter.com
Phone: (908) 686-7055
Inst. Accred.: ACCSCT (2002)

Teterboro School of Aeronautics
80 Moonachie Ave., Teterboro Airport, Teterboro 07608-1083
Type: Private, proprietary
Degrees: C
URL: http://www.teterboroschool.com
Phone: (201) 288-6300
Inst. Accred.: ACCSCT (1973/2002)

Union County Vocational-Technical Schools
1776 Raritan Rd., Scotch Plains 07076
Type: Public, state/local
Degrees: C
URL: http://www.ucvts.tec.nj.us
Phone: (908) 889-8288
Inst. Accred.: COE (20003)

NEW MEXICO

Albuquerque Barber College
525 San Pedro Dr. NE, Ste. 100, Albuquerque 87108-1847
Type: Private, proprietary
Degrees: C
Phone: (505) 266-4900
Inst. Accred.: ACCSCT (1987/2005 Probation)

Business Skills Institute
1400 El Paseo Dr., Las Cruces 88001
Type: Private, proprietary
Degrees: C
URL: http://www.ibclubbock.com
Phone: (505) 526-5579
Inst. Accred.: ACICS (1987/2002)

El Paso Campus
8037 Lockheed Dr., El Paso, TX 79925-2400
Phone: (915) 845-7772

Crystal Mountain School of Massage Therapy
4775 Indian School Rd., NE, Ste. 102, Albuquerque 87110
Type: Private, proprietary
Degrees: C
URL: http://crystalmtnmassage.com
Phone: (505) 872-2030
Inst. Accred.: CMTA (2005)

DeWolff College of Hairstyling and Cosmetology
1500 Eubank Blvd. NE, Albuquerque 87112
Type: Private, proprietary
Degrees: C
URL: http://www/dewolffcollege.com
Phone: (505) 296-4100
Inst. Accred.: NACCAS (1972/2003)

Eddy County Beauty College
1115 West Mermod, Carlsbad 88220
Type: Private, proprietary
Degrees: C
Phone: (505) 885-4545
Inst. Accred.: NACCAS (1990/2000)

International Schools
301 Victory Ln., Sunland 88063
Type: Private, proprietary
Degrees: C
URL: http://www.internationalschools.com
Phone: (505) 589-1414
Inst. Accred.: ACCSCT (1990/2001)

Massage Therapy Training Institute
2701 West Picacho Ave., Ste. 4, Las Cruces 88007
Type: Private, proprietary
Degrees: C
URL: http://www.mtti.org
Phone: (505) 523-6811
Inst. Accred.: ABHES (2002/2005)

National Training Center
PO Box 18041, Kirtland AFB, Albuquerque 87185
Type: Public, federal
Degrees: C
URL: http://www.ntc.doe.gov
Phone: (505) 845-5170
Inst. Accred.: COE (2001)

New Mexico Aveda Institute de Bellas Artes
2614 Pennsylvania St., NE, Albuquerque 87110
Type: Private, proprietary
Degrees: C
URL: http://www.nmaveda.com
Phone: (505) 298-3357
Inst. Accred.: NACCAS (1998/2001)

Olympian University of Cosmetology
1810 East Tenth St., Alamogordo 88310
Type: Private, proprietary
Degrees: C
Phone: (505) 437-2221
Inst. Accred.: NACCAS (1976/2005)

Albuquerque Campus
800 Juan Tabo, NE, Ste. I-J, Albuquerque 87123
Phone: (505) 765-1044

Las Cruces Campus
1460 Missouri Ave., Ste. 5, Las Cruces 88005
Phone: (505) 523-7181

Mesquite Campus
3330 North Galloway Ave., Ste. 160, Mesquite, TX 75150
Phone: (972) 682-5333

Roswell Campus
108 South Union Ave., Roswell 88203
Phone: (505) 623-6331

Pima Medical Institute—Albuquerque
2301 San Pedro NE, Ste. D, Albuquerque 87110
Type: Private, proprietary
Degrees: C
Phone: (505) 881-1314
Inst. Accred.: ABHES (2001)

Ron L. Straughan & Associates, Inc.
4108 Alcazar, NE, Ste. B, Albuquerque 87109
Type: Private, proprietary
Degrees: C
URL: http://www.newmexico.dalecarnegie.com
Phone: (505) 296-0408
Inst. Accred.: ACCET (2000/2005)

Southwest Health Career Institute, Inc.
5981 Jefferson NE, Ste. A, Albuquerque 87109
Type: Private, proprietary
Degrees: C
URL: http://www.swhci.com
Phone: (505) 345-6800
Inst. Accred.: ABHES (1996/2002)

Universal Therapeutic Massage Institute
3410 Aztec Rd., NE, Albuquerque 87107
Type: Private, proprietary
Degrees: C
URL: http://www.utmi.com
Phone: (505) 888-0020
Inst. Accred.: ACCSCT (1999)

NEW YORK

Adirondack Beauty School
108 Dix Ave., Glens Falls 12801
Type: Private, proprietary
Degrees: C
Phone: (518) 745-1646
Inst. Accred.: NACCAS (1993/1999)

Allen School
163-18 Jamaica Ave., Jamaica 11432
Type: Private, independent
System: Allen School, Inc.
Degrees: C
Phone: (212) 686-0036
Inst. Accred.: COE (2005)

   Brooklyn Campus
   188 Montague St., Brooklyn 11201-3609
   Phone: (718) 243-1700

The Alvin Ailey American Dance Center
405 West 55th St., New York 10019
Type: Private, independent
Degrees: C
URL: http://www.alvinailey.org/aileyschool.asp
Phone: (212) 405-9000
Inst. Accred.: NASD (1982/2005)

American Ballet Center/Joffrey Ballet School
434 Ave. of the Americas, New York 10011
Type: Private, independent
Degrees: C
URL: http://www.joffreyballetschool.com
Phone: (212) 254-8520
Inst. Accred.: NASD (1982/2002)

American Barber Institute
252 West 29th St., New York 10001-5271
Type: Private, proprietary
Degrees: C
Phone: (212) 290-2289
Inst. Accred.: COE (1998/2005)

The American Musical and Dramatic Academy
2109 Broadway, New York 10023
Type: Private, independent
Degrees: C
URL: http://www.amda.edu
Phone: (212) 787-5300   *Calendar:* Sem. plan
Inst. Accred.: NAST (1984/1996)

   Los Angeles Campus
   6305 Yucca St., Los Angeles, CA 90028
   Phone: (323) 469-3300

Andrew Terranova & Associates, Inc.
2350 North Forest Rd., Getzville 14068
Type: Private, proprietary
Degrees: C
URL: http://www.dalecarnegiewny.com
Phone: (716) 688-8100
Inst. Accred.: ACCET (2000/2005)

Apex Technical School
635 Ave. of the Americas, New York 10011-2030
Type: Private, proprietary
Degrees: C
URL: http://www.apextechnical.com
Phone: (212) 645-3300
Inst. Accred.: ACCSCT (1968/2005)

Associated Beth Rivkah Schools
310 Crown St., Brooklyn 11225
Type: Private, independent
Degrees: C
Phone: (718) 735-0400
Inst. Accred.: ACCET (1990/2001)

Austin's School of Spa Technology
527 Central Ave., Albany 12206
Type: Private, proprietary
Degrees: C
URL: http://www.austin.edu
Phone: (518) 438-7879
Inst. Accred.: NACCAS (1967/1998)

Beauty School of Middletown, Inc.
225 Dolson Ave., Ste. 100, Middletown 10940
Type: Private, proprietary
Degrees: C
Phone: (914) 343-2171
Inst. Accred.: NACCAS (1974/2001)

   Hyde Park Campus
   Route 9, Hyde Park Mall, Hyde Park 12538
   Phone: (914) 229-6541

Berk Trade and Business School
312 West 36th St., New York 10018-6402
Type: Private, proprietary
Degrees: C
Phone: (212) 629-3736
Inst. Accred.: ACCSCT (1973/2001)

Branford Hall Career Institute—Bohemia
565 Johnson Ave., Bohemia 11716
Type: Private, proprietary
Degrees: C
URL: http://www.branfordhall.com
Phone: (631) 589-1222
Inst. Accred.: ACICS (1997/2002)

Buffalo Montessori Teacher Education Program
453 Parker Ave., Buffalo 14216
Type: Private, independent
Degrees: C
Phone: (716) 832-0042
Inst. Accred.: MACTE (1998/2005)

Business Informatics Center
134 South Central Ave., Valley Stream 11580-5431
Type: Private, proprietary
Degrees: C
Phone: (516) 561-0050
Inst. Accred.: ACCSCT (1988/2004)

Caliber Training Institute
500 Seventh Ave., 2nd & 3rd Floor, New York 10018
Type: Private, proprietary
Degrees: C
URL: http://www.caliberny.com
Phone: (212) 564-0500
Inst. Accred.: ACCSCT (1985/2005)

Capri Cosmetology Learning Center
251 West Route 59, Nanuet 10954
Type: Private, proprietary
Degrees: C
URL: http://www.caprinow.com
Phone: (845) 623-6339
Inst. Accred.: NACCAS (1976/1997)

Career and Educational Consultants
270 Flatbush Ave. Extension, Brooklyn 11201
Type: Private, proprietary
Degrees: C
Phone: (718) 858-8500
Inst. Accred.: ACCSCT (2000/2005)

Career Blazers, Inc.
290 Madison Ave., New York 10017
Type: Private, proprietary
Degrees: C
URL: http://www.careerblazers.com
Phone: (212) 725-7900
Inst. Accred.: ACCET (1985/2004)

Carsten Institute New York
22 East 17th St., Second Flr., New York 10003
Type: Private, proprietary
Degrees: C
URL: http://www.carsteninstitute.com
/institutesnewyork.html
Phone: (212) 675-4884
Inst. Accred.: NACCAS (2003)

Center for Montessori Teacher Education of New York
785 Mamaroneck Ave., White Plains, NY 10605
Type: Private, independent
Degrees: C
URL: http://www.cmteny.com
Phone: (914) 948-2501
Inst. Accred.: MACTE (2005)

Villa Montessori School
4535 North 28th St., Phoenix, AZ 85016
Phone: (602) 955-2210

The Village School for Children
865 East Glen Ave., Ridgewood, NJ 07450
Phone: (914) 948-2501

Centurion Professional Training
2619 East 16th St., Brooklyn 11235
Type: Private, proprietary
Degrees: C
URL: http://www.mycenturion.com
Phone: (718) 646-4507
Inst. Accred.: COE (2004)

Charles Stuart School of Locksmithing
1420 Kings Hwy., Brooklyn 11229
Type: Private, proprietary
Degrees: C
URL: http://www.charlesstuartschool.com
Phone: (718) 339-2640
Inst. Accred.: ACCSCT (1993/2004)

New Jersey School of Locksmithing
392 Summit Ave., Jersey City, NJ 07306
Phone: (201) 963-9688

Cheryl Fell's School of Business
2541 Military Rd., Niagara Falls 14304
Type: Private, proprietary
Degrees: C
Phone: (716) 297-2750
Inst. Accred.: ACICS (1981/2002)

The Chubb Institute—New York City
498 Seventh Ave., 17th Flr., New York 10019
Type: Private, proprietary
System: High-Tech Institute
Degrees: C
URL: http://www.chubbinstitute.edu
Phone: (212) 659-2116　　　　*Calendar:* Sem. plan
Inst. Accred.: ACCET (1999/2004)

The Chubb Institute—Westbury
1400 Old Country Rd., Westbury 11590
Type: Private, proprietary
System: High-Tech Institute
Degrees: C
URL: http://www.chubbinstitute.edu
Phone: (516) 997-1400　　　　*Calendar:* Sem. plan
Inst. Accred.: ACCET (2001/2004)

Circle in the Square Theatre School
1633 Broadway, New York 10019
Type: Private, independent
Degrees: C
URL: http://www.circlesquare.org
Phone: (212) 307-0388
Inst. Accred.: NAST (1979/2004)

Commercial Driver Training
600 Patton Ave., West Babylon 11704-1421
Type: Private, proprietaty
Degrees: C
URL: http://www.cdtschool.com
Phone: (845) 336-2300
Inst. Accred.: ACCSCT (1984/2002)

Computer Career Center
200 Garden City Plaza, Ste. 519, Garden City 11530
Type: Private, proprietary
Degrees: C
URL: http://www.ccctraining.net
Phone: (516) 877-1225
Inst. Accred.: ACICS (1992/2002)

Brooklyn Campus
340 Flatbush Ave. Extension, Brooklyn 11201
Phone: (718) 422-1212

Rego Park Campus
95-25 Queens Blvd., Ste. 600, Rego Park 11374
Phone: (718) 897-4868

Continental School of Beauty Culture, Ltd.
633 Jefferson Rd., Rochester 14623
Type: Private, proprietary
Degrees: C
Phone: (716) 272-8060
Inst. Accred.: NACCAS (1973/1999)

Continental School of Beauty Culture—Batavia
215 Main St., Batavia 14020
Type: Private, proprietary
Degrees: C
Phone: (716) 344-0886
Inst. Accred.: NACCAS (1985/2000)

Continental School of Beauty Culture—Buffalo
326 Kenmore Ave., Buffalo 4223
Type: Private, proprietary
Degrees: C
Phone: (716) 833-5016
Inst. Accred.: NACCAS (1973/1999)

Continental School of Beauty Culture—Olean
515 North Union St., Olean 14760
Type: Private, proprietary
Degrees: C
Phone: (716) 372-5095
Inst. Accred.: NACCAS (1990/2000)

Continental School of Beauty Culture— West Seneca
1050 Union Rd., Southgate Plaza, West Seneca 14224
Type: Private, proprietary
Degrees: C
Phone: (716) 675-8205
Inst. Accred.: NACCAS (1989/1999)

Cope Institute
225 Broadway, 2nd Flr., New York 10007
Type: Private, independent
Degrees: C
Phone: (212) 809-5935   *Calendar:* Qtr. plan
Inst. Accred.: ACICS (1981/2004)

Culinary Academy of Long Island
125 Michael Dr., Syosset 11791
Type: Private, proprietary
Degrees: C
URL: http://www.culinaryacademyli.com
Phone: (516) 364-4344
Inst. Accred.: ACCSCT (1999/2004)

Culinary Academy of New York Management School
154 West 14th St., New York 10011-7307
Type: Private
Degrees: C
URL: http://www.nyadi.com
Phone: (212) 675-6655   *Calendar:* Sem. plan
Inst. Accred.: ACCSCT (1973/2001)

Dale Carnegie & Associates, Inc.
290 Motor Pkwy., Hauppauge 11788-5105
Type: Private, proprietary
Degrees: C
URL: http://www.longisland.dalecarnegie.com
Phone: (631) 415-9336
Inst. Accred.: ACCET (1975/2001)

New York City Campus
780 Third Ave., 22nd Flr., New York 10017
Phone: (212) 750-4455

San Francisco Campus
465 California St., Ste. 830, San Francisco, CA 94104
Phone: (415) 394-3253

Dance Theatre of Harlem, Inc.
466 West 152nd St., New York 10031
Type: Private, independent
Degrees: C
URL: http://www.dancetheatreofharlem.com
Phone: (212) 690-2800
Inst. Accred.: NASD (1982/2005)

David Hochstein Memorial Music School
50 North Plymouth Ave., Rochester 14614
Type: Private, independent
Degrees: C
URL: http://www.hochstein.org
Phone: (585) 454-4596   *Calendar:* Qtr. plan
Inst. Accred.: NASM (1976/2003)

FEGS Trades and Business School
80 Vandam St., New York 10013
Type: Private, proprietary
Degrees: C
Phone: (212) 366-8400
Inst. Accred.: ACCSCT (1986/2005)

Brooklyn Campus
199 Jay St., Brooklyn 11201
Phone: (718) 448-0120

Franklin Career Institute
91 North Franklin St., Ste. 300, Hempstead 11550-3003
Type: Private, independent
Degrees: C
Phone: (516) 679-1616
Inst. Accred.: COE (2005)

French Culinary Institute
462 Broadway, New York 10013
Type: Private, proprietary
Degrees: C
URL: http://www.frenchculinary.com
Phone: (212) 219-8890
Inst. Accred.: ACCSCT (1985/2001)

Girl Scouts of the U.S.A.
420 Fifth Ave., New York 10018-2798
Type: Private, independent
Degrees: C
URL: http://www.girlscouts.org
Phone: (212) 852-8584
Inst. Accred.: ACCET (1980/2003)

Global Business Institute
1931 Mott Ave., Far Rockaway 11691
Type: Private, proprietary
Degrees: C
URL: http://www.gbi.org
Phone: (718) 327-2220
Inst. Accred.: ACICS (1984/2001)

New York City Campus
209 West 125th St., New York 10027
Phone: (212) 663-1500

Grace Institute of Business Technology
1090 Coney Island Ave., Brooklyn 11230
Type: Private, proprietary
Degrees: C
Phone: (718) 859-3900
Inst. Accred.: ACICS (1999/2001)

Hair Design Institute at Fifth Avenue
6711 Fifth Ave., Brooklyn 11220
Type: Private, proprietary
Degrees: C
URL: http://www.hairdesigninstitute.com
Phone: (718) 745-1000
Inst. Accred.: NACCAS (1979/1999)

Harlem School of Technology
215 West 25th St., New York 10027
Type: Private, proprietary
Degrees: C
Phone: (212) 932-2849
Inst. Accred.: ACCSCT (1998/2003)

Holy Trinity Orthodox Seminary
PO Box 36, Jordanville 13361-1919
Type: Private, independent
Degrees: C   *FTE Enroll:* 37
URL: http://www.hts.edu
Phone: (315) 858-0945   *Calendar:* Sem. plan
Inst. Accred.: NYBOR (1948/2002)

Hunter Business School
3601 Hempstead Turnpike, Levittown 11756
Type: Private, proprietary
Degrees: C
URL: http://www.hunterbusinessschool.com
Phone: (516) 796-1000
Inst. Accred.: ACICS (1982/2002)

Institute of Audio Research
64 University Place, New York 10003-4595
Type: Private, proprietary
Degrees: C
URL: http://www.audioschool.com
Phone: (212) 677-7590
Inst. Accred.: ACCSCT (1985/2001)

The Institute of Culinary Education
50 West 23rd St., New York 10010
Type: Private, proprietary
Degrees: C
URL: http://www.newyorkculinary.com
Phone: (212) 847-0711
Inst. Accred.: ACCSCT (2000/2005)

Island Drafting and Technical Institute
128 Broadway, Amityville 11701-2789
Type: Private, proprietary
Degrees: C
Phone: (516) 691-8733
Inst. Accred.: ACCSCT (1967/2004)

Jothi Montessori Academy
PO Box 7453, Freeport 11520
Type: Private, independent
Degrees: C
Phone: (516)546-5809
Inst. Accred.: MACTE (1998)

Kaplan Test Prep
888 Seventh Ave., 22nd Flr., New York 10106-0001
Type: Private, proprietary
Degrees: C
URL: http://www.kaplan.com
Phone: (212) 492-5800
Inst. Accred.: ACCET (1979/2002)

Akron Campus
59 E. Market St., 2nd Flr., Akron, OH 44308
Phone: (330) 384-9499

Albany Campus
Executive Park Dr., Stuyvesant Plaza, Albany 12203-3520
Phone: http://www.kaptest.c

Albuquerque Campus
2501 San Pedro Dr., NE, Ste. 203, Albuquerque, NM 87110-4131
Phone: (505) 884-8880

Allentown Campus
1926 Catasauqua Rd., Allentown, PA 18103
Phone: (610) 231-2065

Amherst, MA Campus
150 Fearing St., Ste. 1, Amherst, MA 01002
Phone: (413) 549-5780

Amherst, NY Campus
520 Lee Entrance, UB Commons, Ste. 201, Amherst 14228-2580
Phone: (716) 636-1882

Ann Arbor Campus
337 East Liberty St., Ann Arbor, MI 48104
Phone: (734) 662-3149

Arlington Campus
1100 North Glebe Rd., Ballston Plaza, 1st Flr., Arlington, VA 22201
Phone: (703) 552-5882

Athens Campus
225 North Lumpkin St., Athens, GA 30601-2801
Phone: (706) 353-3202

Atlanta Campus
3867 Roswell Rd., Ste. 200, Atlanta, GA 30342
Phone: (404) 365-9004

Austin Campus
811 West 24th St., University Towers, Austin, TX 78705-9965
Phone: (512) 472-8085

Baltimore Campus
733 West 40th St., Ste. 200, Baltimore, MD 21211
Phone: (410) 243-1456

Beachwood Campus
24700 Chagrin Boulevrad, Ste. 309, Beachwood, OH 44122-5360
Phone: (216) 831-2233

Berkeley Campus
150 Beckley Square, Berkeley, CA 94724
Phone: (510) 204-8980

Birmingham Campus
1900 28th Ave. South, Ste. 100, Birmingham, AL 35209-2604
Phone: (205) 879-1307

Blacksburg Campus
460 Turner St., Ste. 214, Blacksburg, VA 24060
Phone: (540) 552-8186

Bloomington Campus
421 East 3rd, Stes. 6-7, Bloomington, IN 47401-3601
Phone: (812) 339-0084

Boca Raton Campus
2900 North Military Trail, Ste. 150, Boca Raton, FL 33431-6308
Phone: (561) 997-6388

Boston Campus
One Congress St., Boston, MA 02116-5198
Phone: (617) 722-4180

Boulder Campus
1310 College Ave., Hilltop Bldg., Upper Level, Ste. 400, Boulder, CO 80302-7324
Phone: (303) 444-1683

Brooklyn Campus
1602 Kings Hwy., 3rd Flr., Brooklyn 11229-1208
Phone: (718) 336-5300

Bryn Mawr Campus
950 Haverford Rd., Lower Level, Bryn Mawr, PA 19010-3820
Phone: (610) 526-9744

Cambridge Campus
727 Massachusetts Ave., Cambridge, MA 02139-3303
Phone: (617) 964-8378

Central Park Campus
131 West 56th St., New York 10019-3894
Phone: (212) 977-8200

Champaign Campus
405 East Green St., Champaign, IL 61820-5702
Phone: (217) 367-0011

Chapel Hill Campus
308 West Rosemary St., Ste. 103, Chapel Hill, NC 27514
Phone: (919) 960-4600

Charleston Campus
1650 Sam Rittenberg Blvd., Charleston, SC 29407-5768
Phone: (843) 571-6080

Charlotte Campus
1515 Mockingbird Ln., Ste. 203, Charlotte, NC 28209
Phone: (704) 522-7600

Charlottesville Campus
1928 Arlington Blvd., Ste. 200, Charlottesville, VA 22903-1561
Phone: (804) 979-3001

Chicago/North Clark Campus
2828 North Clark St., 4th Flr., Chicago, IL 60657
Phone: (773) 764-5151

Chicago/West Randolph Campus
205 West Randolph St., Ste. 200, Chicago, IL 60606-1814
Phone: (312) 606-8905

Cincinnati Campus
4600 Montgomery Rd., Ste. 100, Cincinnati, OH 45212
Phone: (513) 731-8378

College Park Campus
College Park Shopping Center, 7338 Baltimore Ave., College Park, MD 20740
Phone: (301) 779-8136

College Station Campus
707 Texas Ave., Ste. 106-E, College Station, TX 77840-1917
Phone: (409) 696-7737

Columbia, MO Campus
1103 East Broadway, Ste. 200, Columbia, MO 65201-4909
Phone: (573) 443-8378

Columbia, SC Campus
1717 Gervais St., Columbia, SC 29201
Phone: (803) 256-0673

Columbus Campus
1778 North High St., 2nd Flr., Columbus, OH 43201
Phone: (614) 294-7035

Coral Gables Campus
1320 South Dixie Hwy., Ste. 100, Coral Gables, FL 33146-2911
Phone: (305) 284-0090

Dallas Campus
10500 Steppington St., Ste. 150, Dallas, TX 75230
Phone: (214) 265-9805

Davie Campus
3501 South University Dr., Ste. 1, Davie, FL 33328-2023
Phone: (954) 370-2500

Davis Campus
132 E St., Davis, CA 95616-4515
Phone: (916) 753-4800

Dayton Campus
3077 Kettering Blvd., Ste. 319, Dayton, OH 45435-1922
Phone: (937) 293-1725

Decatur Campus
1248 Clairmont Rd., Ste. 4-B, Decatur, GA 30030
Phone: (404) 321-0801

Denver Campus
720 South Colorado Blvd., Ste. 140-A, Denver, CO 80246
Phone: (303) 757-5400

Des Moines Campus
Highline Community College, 2400 South 240th St., MS25-516, Des Moines, IA 98198
Phone: (206) 870-3740

Downers Grove Campus
3130 Finley Rd., Ste. 500, Downers Grove, IL 60515
Phone: (630) 271-4410

Durham Campus
501 Washington St., South Park Office Center, Durham, NC 27701
Phone: (919) 956-7374

East Hanover Campus
188 Route 10 West, East Hanover, NJ 07936
Phone: (973) 884-3500

East Lansing Campus
333 Albert St., Ste. 214, East Lansing, MI 48823
Phone: (517) 332-2539

Encino Campus
17167 Ventura Blvd., Plaza De Oro, 2nd Level, Encino, CA 91316
Phone: (818) 382-2421

Eugene Campus
720 East 13th Ave., Ste. 303, Eugene, OR 97401
Phone: (541) 345-4420

Fayetteville Campus
7 Colt Square Dr., Ste. 4, Fayetteville, AR 72703-2842
Phone: (479) 521-8599

Flushing Campus
65-30 Kissena Blvd., Queens College Student Union, Flushing 11367-1575
Phone: (718) 575-2400

Fresno Campus
1630 East Shaw Ave., Ste. 140, Fresno, CA 93710
Phone: (559) 225-4203

Kaplan Test Prep *(continued)*

Ft. Worth Campus
1701 River Run Rd., Ste. 102, Ft. Worth, TX 76107
Phone: (817) 877-0024

Gainesville Campus
409 SW 2nd Ave., Gainesville, FL 32601-6225
Phone: (352) 377-0014

Garden City Campus
400 Garden City Plaza, Ste. 110, Garden City 11530-3336
Phone: (516) 248-1134

Goleta Campus
6464 Hollister Ave., Ste. 7, Goleta, CA 93117-3113
Phone: (805) 685-5767

Greenville Campus
216 South Pleasantburg Dr., University Center of Greenville, Greenville, SC 29607
Phone: (864) 250-8832

Highland Park Campus
1893 Sheridan Rd., Ste. 200, Highland Park, IL 60035-9906
Phone: (847) 433-7410

Honolulu Campus
1580 Makaloa St., Ste. 500, Honolulu, HI 96814
Phone: (808) 946-5600

Houston Campus
2500 Dunstan Rd., 5th Flr., Houston, TX 77005-2523
Phone: (713) 988-4700

Indianapolis Campus
9102 North Meridian St., Ste. 440, Indianapolis, IN 46260
Phone: (317) 571-1009

Iowa City Campus
325 East Washington St., Ste. 208, Iowa City, IA 52240-3923
Phone: (319) 338-2588

Irvine Campus
2646 Dupont Dr., Ste. 50, Irvine, CA 92612-1688
Phone: (949) 756-2950

Irvine Valley College Campus
5500 Irvine Center Dr., Irvine, CA 92620
Phone: (949) 651-1163

Ithaca Campus
409 College Ave., 3rd Flr., Ithaca 14850
Phone: (607) 277-3307

Kalamazoo Campus
151 South Rose St., Ste. 106, Kalamazoo, MI 49007
Phone: (616) 342-8333

Kensington Campus
11301 Rockville Pike, 3rd Flr., Kensington, MD 20895-1021
Phone: (301) 770-2843

Knoxville Campus
100 Concord St., Cherokee Place, Knoxville, TN 37919-2329
Phone: (423) 971-5455

Las Vegas Campus
4632 South Maryland Pkwy., Ste. 23, Las Vegas, NV 89119
Phone: (702) 798-5005

Lawrence Campus
1000 Massachusetts St., Lawrence, KS 66044
Phone: (785) 842-5442

Lexington Campus
1050 Chinoe Rd., Ste. 200, Lexington, KY 40502
Phone: (859) 269-1172

Lincoln Campus
1821 K St., Lincoln, NE 68508-1401
Phone: (314) 997-7791

Little Rock Campus
10220 West Markham, Ste. 220, Centre Mark Bldg., Little Rock, AR 72205-2185
Phone: (501) 224-1060

Los Angeles Campus
750 W 7th St., Garden Level, Ste. RG024, Los Angeles, CA 90017
Phone: (213) 896-1844

Louisville Campus
420 South Hurstbourne Pkwy., Ste. 204, Louisville, KY 40222
Phone: (502) 339-8021

Lubbock Campus
4620 50th St., Ste. 1, Lubbock, TX 79414-3508
Phone: (806) 795-0344

Madison Campus
315-B West Gorham St., Madison, WI 53703
Phone: (608) 255-0575

Marlton Campus
169 Route 73 South, Marlton Crossing, Marlton, NJ 08053
Phone: (856) 988-6306

Memphis Campus
4515 Popular Ave., Ste. 330, Memphis, TN 38117-7503
Phone: (901) 767-1861

Miami Campus
11900 Biscayne Blvd., First Flr., Miami, FL 33181
Phone: (305) 892-9019

Milwaukee Campus
316 North Milwaukee St., Ste. 210, Milwaukee, WI
53202-5803
Phone: (414) 277-9990

Montreal Campus
550 Sherbrooke Quest, Ste. 550, Montreal, QC,
Canada H3A 1B9
Phone: (514) 287-1896

Newton Centre Campus
792 Beacon St., Newton Centre, MA 02459-1963
Phone: (617) 332-8241

Norfolk Campus
861 Glenrock Rd., Circle East Bldg., Ste. 155, Norfolk,
VA 23502-3701
Phone: (757) 466-1100

Norman Campus
408 West Main St., Norman, OK 73069-1327
Phone: (405) 321-7362

Oklahoma City Campus
777 NW Grand Blvd., Ste. 100, Oklahoma City, OK
73118-6103
Phone: (405) 848-3922

Omaha Campus
1020 South 74th Plaza, Omaha, NE 68114
Phone: (402) 393-8570

Orlando Campus
3403 Technological Ave., Ste. 13, Orlando, FL 32817-
1478
Phone: (407) 273-7111

Oxford Campus
13-B East High St., Second Flr., Oxford, OH 45056
Phone: (513) 523-4429

Palo Alto Campus
299 California Ave., Ste. 210, Palo Alto, CA 94306
Phone: (650) 327-4040

Paramus Campus
10 Forest Ave., Paramus, NJ 07652
Phone: (201) 845-6652

Pasadena Campus
251 South Lake Ave., Ste. 130, Pasadena, CA 91101
Phone: (626) 584-9613

Philadelphia Campus
1528 Walnut St., First Flr., Philadelphia, PA 19102-
3615
Phone: (215) 546-3317

Pittsburgh Campus
130 North Bellefield Ave., Bellfield Professional Bldg.,
3rd Flr., Pittsburgh, PA 15213
Phone: (412) 621-4620

Portland Campus
The Galleria, Rm. 402, 600 SW 10th St., Portland, OR
97205-2733
Phone: (503) 222-5556

Providence Campus
144 Wayland Ave., Providence, RI 02906
Phone: (401) 521-3926

Provo Campus
Brigham's Landing, 1774 North University Pkwy., Ste.
22, Provo, UT 84604
Phone: (801) 375-9955

Reno Campus
1048 North Sierra, Unit A, Reno, NV 89503
Phone: (775) 329-1755

Richmond Campus
1601 Willow Lawn Dr., Ste. 109-C, The Shops at
Willow Lawn, Richmond, VA 23230-3023
Phone: (804) 285-3414

Ridgeland Campus
731 South Pear Orchard Rd., Ste. 32, Ridgeland, MS
39157-4802
Phone: (601) 957-0084

Riverside Campus
3637 Canyon Crest Dr., Ste. J-115, Riverside, CA
92507
Phone: (909) 683-2221

Rochester Campus
1544 Mount Hope Ave., Rochester 14620-4240
Phone: (716) 461-9320

Rutherford Campus
223 Montrose Ave., Rutherford, NJ 07070
Phone: (201) 964-0997

Sacramento Campus
955 University Ave., Sacramento, CA 95825
Phone: (916) 929-4402

Saint Paul Campus
2610 University Ave. West, St. Paul, MN 55114-1066
Phone: (651) 641-1200

Saint Petersburg Campus
1700 66th St. North, Ste. 103, St. Petersburg, FL
33710
Phone: (727) 381-8378

Salt Lake City Campus
515 South 700 East, Ste. 3-J, Salt Lake City, UT
84102-2801
Phone: (801) 363-4446

San Antonio Campus
8401 Datapoint Dr., Ste. B-100, San Antonio, TX
78229-2974
Phone: (210) 614-2924

Kaplan Test Prep *(continued)*

San Diego Campus
4350 Executive Dr., Ste. 305, San Diego, CA 92121
Phone: (858) 457-7595

San Francisco Campus
50 First St., Ste. 601, San Francisco, CA 94105-2405
Phone: (415) 905-9000

San Jose Campus
100 Park Center Plaza, Ste. 112, San Jose, CA 95113
Phone: (408) 275-0100

Santa Cruz Campus
740 Front St., Ste. 130, Santa Cruz, CA 95060
Phone: (831) 457-3900

Schaumburg Campus
1014 East Algonquin Rd., Ste. 114, Schaumburg, IL 60173
Phone: (847) 397-5630

Seattle Campus
4216 University Way, NE, Seattle, WA 98105
Phone: (206) 632-0634

Shawnee Mission Campus
5800 Foxridge Dr., Ste. 103, Shawnee Mission, KS 66202
Phone: (913) 262-8378

Shreveport Campus
106 East King's Hwy., Ste. 211, Shreveport, LA 71104
Phone: (318) 868-6400

South Bend Campus
1717 East South Bend Ave., South Bend, IN 46637-5639
Phone: (219) 272-4135

Stamford Campus
189 Bedford St., Stamford, CT 06901-1902
Phone: (203) 353-1466

State College, PA Campus
522 East College Ave., Ste. 201, State College, PA 16801-5585
Phone: (814) 238-1423

Staten Island Campus
2795 Richmond Ave., Pergament Shopping Center, Staten Island 10314-5857
Phone: (718) 477-6343

Syracuse Campus
720 University Ave., Ste. 206, Marshall Square Mall, Syracuse 13210-1791
Phone: (315) 472-3702

Tallahassee Campus
675 West Jefferson St., Tallahassee, FL 32304
Phone: (850) 224-3555

Tempe Campus
310 S. Mill Ave., Ste. A-103, Tempe, AZ 85281
Phone: (602) 967-2967

Temple Terrace Campus
5405 East Fowler Ave., Temple Terrace, FL 33617
Phone: (813) 899-2355

Toledo Campus
3450 West Central Ave., The Westgate Bldg., Ste. 102, Toledo, OH 43606-1403
Phone: (419) 536-3701

Toronto Campus
180 Bloor St. West, 4th Flr., Toronto, ON, Canada M5S 2V6
Phone: (416) 967-4733

Tulsa Campus
2865 East Skelly Dr., Ste. 228, Tulsa, OK 74105-6221
Phone: (918) 748-8065

Tuscon Campus
845 East University, Ste. 175, Tuscon, AZ 85719-5048
Phone: (502) 622-4256

Vancouver, BC Campus
1490 West Broadway Ave., 3rd Flr., Vancouver, BC, Canada V6H 1H5
Phone: (604) 734-8378

Vestal Campus
3951 Vestal Pkwy. East, Vestal 13850-2336
Phone: (607) 797-2302

Washington, DC Campus
2025 M St., NW, Kaplan Computer Lab Location, Washington, DC 20036
Phone: (202) 835-9745

West Hartford Campus
967-D Farmington Ave., West Hartford, CT 06107-2123
Phone: (860) 236-6851

Westwood Village Square Campus
1133 Westwood Blvd., Ste. 201, Westwood Village Square, Los Angeles, CA 90024
Phone: (310) 209-0554

White Plains Campus
220 East Post Rd., White Plains 10601-4903
Phone: (914) 948-7801

Wilmington Campus
4758-D Limestone Rd., Wilmington, DE 19808
Phone: (302) 992-0980

Winooski Campus
20 West Canal St., The Woolen Mill, Winooski, VT 05404-2131
Phone: (802) 655-3300

Winston-Salem Campus
100 Northgate Park Dr., Ste. 102, Winston-Salem, NC 27106-3226
Phone: (336) 759-9987

Worcester Campus
352 Belmont St., Route 9, Worcester, MA 01604
Phone: (508) 757-8378

Laban/Bartenieff Institute of Movement Studies, Inc.
520 8th Ave., Ste. 304, 3rd Flr., New York 10018-6507
Type: Private, independent
Degrees: C
URL: http://www.limsonline.org
Phone: (212) 477-4299
Inst. Accred.: NASD (1983/2004)

Learning Institute for Beauty Sciences— Astoria
38-15 Broadway, Astoria 11103
Type: Private, proprietary
Degrees: C
URL: http://www.libsbeautyschool.com
Phone: (718) 726-8383
Inst. Accred.: NACCAS (1986/2001)

Learning Institute for Beauty Sciences— Hauppauge
544 Route 111, Hauppauge 11788
Type: Private, proprietary
Degrees: C
URL: http://www.libsbeautyschool.com
Phone: (516) 724-0440
Inst. Accred.: NACCAS (1974/2000)

Learning Institute for Beauty Sciences— Hempstead
173 A Fulton Ave., Hempstead 11550
Type: Private, proprietary
Degrees: C
URL: http://www.libsbeautyschool.com
Phone: (516) 483-6259
Inst. Accred.: NACCAS (1975/2002)

Learning Institute for Beauty Sciences— Levittown
3272 Hempstead Turnpike, Levittown 11756
Type: Private, proprietary
Degrees: C
URL: http://www.libsbeautyschool.com
Phone: (516) 731-8300
Inst. Accred.: NACCAS (1973/2001)

Learning Institute for Beauty Sciences— New York
22 West 34th St., New York 10001
Type: Private, proprietary
Degrees: C
URL: http://www.libsbeautyschool.com
Phone: (212) 695-4555
Inst. Accred.: NACCAS (1981/2001)

Bensonhurst Campus
2384 86th St., Bensonhurst 11214
Phone: (718) 373-2400

Leon Studio One School of Hair Design
5221 Main St., Williamsville 14221
Type: Private, proprietary
Degrees: C
URL: http://www.leonstudionone.com
Phone: (716) 631-3878
Inst. Accred.: NACCAS (2001)

Lia Schorr Institute of Cosmetic Skin Care
686 Lexington Ave., New York 10022
Type: Private, proprietary
Degrees: C
Phone: (212) 486-9541
Inst. Accred.: NACCAS (2000)

Limón Dance Institute
611 Broadway, Ste. 905, New York 10012
Type: Private, independent
Degrees: C
URL: http://www.limon.org
Phone: (212) 777-3353
Inst. Accred.: NASD (2003)

Mandl School
254 West 54th St., New York 10019-5516
Type: Private, proprietary
Degrees: C
URL: http://mandlschool.com
Phone: (212) 247-3434
Inst. Accred.: ABHES (1987/2002)

Manhattan School of Computer Technology
42 Broadway, 22nd Flr., New York 10004-1638
Type: Private, proprietary
Degrees: C
URL: http://www.manhattanschool.com
Phone: (212) 349-9768
Inst. Accred.: ACICS (1996/2004)

MarJon School of Beauty Culture
1154 Niagara Falls Blvd., Tonawanda 14150
Type: Private, proprietary
Degrees: C
URL: http://www.marjonbeautyschool.com
Phone: (716) 836-6240
Inst. Accred.: NACCAS (1982/1997)

Martha Graham School of Contemporary Dance, Inc.
316 East 63rd St., New York 10021
Type: Private, independent
Degrees: C
URL: http://www.marthagrahamdance.org/school.htm
Phone: (212) 838-5886
Inst. Accred.: NASD (1982/2002)

Merce Cunningham Studio
55 Bethune St., New York 10014
Type: Private, independent
Degrees: C   *Enroll:* 32
URL: http://www.merce.org
Phone: (212) 691-9751
Inst. Accred.: NASD (1982/1996)

Merkaz Bnos Business School
54 Ave. O, Brooklyn 11204
Type: Private, proprietary
Degrees: C
URL: http://www.mbs-career.org
Phone: (718) 234-4000
Inst. Accred.: COE (2000)

Midway Paris Beauty School—Queens
54-40 Myrtle Ave., Ridgewood 11385
Type: Private, proprietary
Degrees: C
Phone: (718) 418-2790
Inst. Accred.: NACCAS (1975/2001)

Modern Welding School
1842 State St., Schenectady 12304
Type: Private, proprietary
Degrees: C
URL: http://www.modernwelding.com
Phone: (518) 374-1216
Inst. Accred.: ACCSCT (1984/2004)

Munson-Williams-Proctor Institute
310 Genesee St., Utica 13502
Type: Private, independent
Degrees: C
URL: http://www.mwpai.org
Phone: (315) 797-8260   *Calendar:* 24-mos. pr
Inst. Accred.: NASAD (1981/1993)

Music Conservatory of Westchester
216 Central Ave., White Plains 10606
Type: Private, independent
Degrees: C
URL: http://www.musicconservatory.org
Phone: (914) 761-3900
Inst. Accred.: NASM (1977/2004)

The Nail Academy
162-04 Jamaica Ave., 5th Flr., Jamaica 11432
Type: Private, proprietary
Degrees: C
Phone: (718) 297-6330
Inst. Accred.: ACCSCT (2003)

National Tractor Trailer School
PO Box 208, Liverpool 13088-0208
Type: Private, proprietary
Degrees: C
URL: http://www.ntts.edu
Phone: (315) 451-2430
Inst. Accred.: ACCSCT (1984/2004)

Buffalo Campus
175 Katherine St., Buffalo 14210-2007
Phone: (716) 849-6887

Natural Gourmet Cookery School
48 West 21st St., 2nd Flr., New York 10010
Type: Private, proprietary
Degrees: C
URL: http://www.naturalgourmetschool.com
Phone: (212) 645-5170
Inst. Accred.: ACCET (2000/2003)

Neighborhood Playhouse School of Theatre
340 East 54th St., New York 10022-5017
Type: Private, independent
Degrees: C
URL: http://www.the-neiplay.org
Phone: (212) 688-3770
Inst. Accred.: NAST (1994/2000)

New Age Training
500 8th Ave., 5th Flr., New York 10018
Type: Private, proprietary
Degrees: C
URL: http://www.newagetraining.com
Phone: (212) 947-7940
Inst. Accred.: ACCET (2005)

The New School of Radio and Television
50 Colvin Ave., Albany 12206-1106
Type: Private, proprietary
Degrees: C
URL: http://www.nsrt.org
Phone: (518) 438-7682
Inst. Accred.: ACCSCT (1981/2005)

New York Automotive and Diesel Institute
178-18 Liberty Ave., Jamaica 11433
Type: Private, proprietary
Degrees: C
URL: http://www.nyadi.com
Phone: (718) 361-1300
Inst. Accred.: ACCSCT (1999/2004)

New York Institute of English and Business
248 West 35th St., 2nd Flr., New York 10016
Type: Private, proprietary
Degrees: C
URL: http://www.nyieb.com
Phone: (212) 725-9400
Inst. Accred.: ACICS (1985/2001)

New York Institute of Massage
PO Box 645, 4701 Transit Rd., Buffalo 14231
Type: Private, proprietary
Degrees: C
URL: http://www.nyinstituteofmassage.com
Phone: (716) 633-0355
Inst. Accred.: ACCSCT (1999/2004)

New York International Beauty School, LTD
308-312 West 36th St.
5th and 6th Flrs., New York 10019
Type: Private, proprietary
Degrees: C
URL: http://www.nyibs.baweb.com
Phone: (212) 868-7171
Inst. Accred.: NACCAS (1992/1998)

New York Paralegal School
299 Broadway, Ste. 200, New York 10007
Type: Private, proprietary
Degrees: C
URL: http://www.nyparalegal.com
Phone: (212) 349-8800
Inst. Accred.: ACICS (1994/2001)

New York School for Medical and Dental Assistants
116-16 Queens Blvd., Forest Hills 11375-2330
Type: Private, proprietary
Degrees: C
Phone: (718) 793-2330
Inst. Accred.: ACCSCT (1973/2004)

Northern Westchester School of Hairdressing
19 Bank St., Peekskill 10566
Type: Private, proprietary
Degrees: C
Phone: (914) 739-8400
Inst. Accred.: NACCAS (1985/2000)

The Orlo School of Hair Design and Cosmetology
232 North Allen St., Albany 12206
Type: Private, proprietary
Degrees: C
Phone: (518) 459-7832
Inst. Accred.: NACCAS (1988/1998)

Phillips Hairstyling Institute
709 East Genesee St., Syracuse 13210
Type: Private, proprietary
Degrees: C
Phone: (315) 422-9656
Inst. Accred.: NACCAS (1974/1999)

R.L. Heron and Associates, Inc.
290 Elwood Davis Rd., Ste. 340, Liverpool 13088
Type: Private, proprietary
Degrees: C
URL: http://www.centralny.dalecarnegie.com
Phone: (315) 457-1300
Inst. Accred.: ACCET (1977/2002)

Ridley-Lowell Business and Technical Institute
116 Front St., Binghamton 13905
Type: Private, proprietary
Degrees: C
URL: http://www.ridley.edu
Phone: (607) 724-2941
Inst. Accred.: ACICS (1977/2004)
Prog. Accred.: Medical Assisting (CAAHEP)

Poughkeepsie Campus
26 South Hamilton St., Poughkeepsie 12601
Phone: (914) 471-0330

New London Campus
470 Bank St., New London, CT 06320
Phone: (860) 443-7441
Prog. Accred: Medical Assisting (CAAHEP)

SAE Institute of Technology
1293 Broadway, 9th Flr., Herald Sq., New York 10001
Type: Private, proprietary
Degrees: C
URL: http://www.saeny.com
Phone: (212) 944-9121
Inst. Accred.: ACCSCT (2005)

Sanford-Brown Institute—White Plains
333 Westchester Ave., First Flr., White Plains 10604
Type: Private, proprietary
System: Career Education Corporation
Degrees: C
URL: http://www.sbiwhiteplains.com
Phone: (914) 874-2500
Inst. Accred.: ABHES (1985/2002)

Springfield Campus
365 Cadwell Dr., First Flr., Springfield, MA 01104-1739
Phone: (413) 739-4700
Prog. Accred: Medical Assisting (ABHES)

School for Film and Television at Three of Us Studio
39 West 19th St., 12th Flr., New York 10011
Type: Private, independent
Degrees: C   *Enroll:* 181
URL: http://www.filmandtelevision.com
Phone: (212) 645-0030
Inst. Accred.: NAST (1995/2001)

Seminar L'Moros Bais Yaakov
4409 15th Ave., Brooklyn 11219
Type: Private, proprietary
Degrees: C
Phone: (718) 851-2900
Inst. Accred.: ACCET (1988/2003)

Sessions.edu
350 Seventh Ave., Ste. 1203, New York 10001
Type: Private, proprietary
Degrees: C
URL: http://www.sessions.edu
Phone: (212) 239-3080
Inst. Accred.: DETC (2001)

Shear Ego International School of Hair Design
525 Titus Ave., Rochester 14617
Type: Private, proprietary
Degrees: C
Phone: (585) 342-0070
Inst. Accred.: NACCAS (1989/1999)

Sotheby's Institute of Art
1334 York Ave., New York 10021
Type: Private, independent
Degrees: C
URL: http://search.sothebys.com/about/institute
Phone: (212) 894-1111
Inst. Accred.: NASAD (1989/1994)

Spanish-American Institute
215 West 43rd St., New York 10036-3913
Type: Private, proprietary
Degrees: C
URL: http://www.sai2000.org
Phone: (212) 840-7111
Inst. Accred.: ACICS (1986/2004)

Stella Adler Studio of Acting
31 West 27th St., Third Flr., New York 10001
Type: Private, independent
Degrees: C
URL: http://www.stellaadler.com
Phone: (212) 260-0525　　　　*Calendar:* Sem. plan
Inst. Accred.: NAST (1994/2003)

Studio Art Centers International
809 United Nations Plaza, c/o Institute of International Education, New York 10017-3580
Type: Private, proprietary
Degrees: C
URL: http://www.saci-florence.org
Phone: (212) 984-5548
Inst. Accred.: NASAD (1996/2002)

Studio Jewelers, Ltd.
32 East 31st St., New York 10016
Type: Private, proprietary
Degrees: C
URL: http://www.studiojewelersltd.com
Phone: (212) 686-1944
Inst. Accred.: ACCSCT (1999/2004)

Suburban Technical School
175 Fulton Ave., Sixth Flr., Hempstead 11550-3771
Type: Private, proprietary
Degrees: C
Phone: (516) 481-6660
Inst. Accred.: ACCSCT (1972/2004)

Training Solutions, Inc.
450 West 41st St., 6th Flr., New York 10036
Type: Private, proprietary
Degrees: C
URL: http://www.trainsol.com
Phone: (212) 947-3039
Inst. Accred.: ACICS (2000/2002)

Triple Cities School of Beauty Culture
5 Ct. St., Binghamton 13901
Type: Private, proprietary
Degrees: C
Phone: (607) 722-1279
Inst. Accred.: NACCAS (1974/2000)

Troy School of Beauty Culture
86 Congress St., Troy 12180
Type: Private, proprietary
Degrees: C
Phone: (518) 273-7741
Inst. Accred.: NACCAS (1974/1997)

U.S.A. Beauty School International, Inc.
87 Walker St., New York 10013
Type: Private, proprietary
Degrees: C
Phone: (212) 431-0505
Inst. Accred.: NACCAS (2002)

West Side Montessori School Teacher Education Program
309 west 92ns St., New York 10025-7213
Type: Public, independent
Degrees: C
URL: http://www.wsms1.org
Phone: (212) 662-8000
Inst. Accred.: MACTE (1996/2003)

Westchester School of Beauty Culture
6 Gramatan Ave., Mt. Vernon 10550
Type: Private, proprietary
Degrees: C
Phone: (914) 699-2344
Inst. Accred.: NACCAS (1974/2000)

Western Suffolk BOCES
152 Laurel Hill Rd., Northport 11764
Type: Public, state/local
Degrees: C
URL: http://www.wsboces.org
Phone: (631) 667-6000
Inst. Accred.: NACCAS (2002)
Prog. Accred.: Diagnostic Medical Sonography, Practical Nursing, Surgical Technology

Willsey Institute
120 Stuyvesant Place, Staten Island 10301
Type: Private, proprietary
Degrees: C
URL: http://www.willsey.org
Phone: (718) 442-5706
Inst. Accred.: ACCET (1997/2004)

Word of Life Bible Institute
PO Box 129, 4200 Glendale Rd., Pottersville 12860-0129
Type: Private, nondenominational
Degrees: C
URL: http://www.wol.org
Phone: (518) 494-4723　　　　　　*Calendar:* Qtr. plan
Inst. Accred.: TRACS (1997/2002)

NORTH CAROLINA

American Institute of Applied Science
100 Hunter Place, Youngsville 27596-9909
Type: Private, proprietary
Degrees: C
URL: http://www.aiasinc.com
Phone: (919) 554-2500
Inst. Accred.: DETC (1999/2004)

Anson College of Cosmetology
1217 East Carswell St., Wadesboro 28170
Type: Private, proprietary
Degrees: C
Phone: (704) 694-6677
Inst. Accred.: COE (1997/2003)

Body Therapy Institute
300 Southwind Rd., Siler City 27344
Type: Private, proprietary
Degrees: C
URL: http://www.bti.edu
Phone: (919) 663-3111
Inst. Accred.: CMTA (1999/2005)

Brookstone College of Business
8307 University Exec. Park Dr., Ste. 240, Charlotte 28262
Type: Private, proprietary
Degrees: C   *FTE Enroll:* 118
URL: http://www.brookstone.edu
Phone: (704) 547-8600   *Calendar:* Qtr. plan
Inst. Accred.: ACICS (1987/2000)

Greensboro Campus
7815 National Service Rd., Greensboro 27409
Phone: (336) 668-2627

Carolina Academy of Cosmetic Art and Science
284 East Garrison Blvd., Gastonia 28054
Type: Private, proprietary
Degrees: C
Phone: (704) 864-8723
Inst. Accred.: NACCAS (2003)

Carolina Beauty College
2001 East Wendover Ave., Greensboro 27405
Type: Private, proprietary
Degrees: C
Phone: (336) 379-9404
Inst. Accred.: COE (1984/2004)

Charlotte Campus
1904-B North Tryon St., Charlotte 28213
Phone: (704) 597-5641

Durham Campus
5106 North Roxboro Rd., Durham 22704
Phone: (919) 477-4014

Winston-Salem Campus
7736-C Northpoint Blvd., Winston-Salem 27106
Phone: (910) 759-7969

Cheveux School Hair Design and Hairport, Inc.
4781 Gum Branch Rd., Ste. #1, Jacksonville 28540
Type: Private, proprietary
Degrees: C
Phone: (910) 455-5767
Inst. Accred.: NACCAS (1988/2003)

The Cosmetology Institute of Beauty Arts and Science
807 Silas Creek Pkwy., Winston Salem 27127
Type: Private, proprietary
Degrees: C
Phone: (336) 773-1472
Inst. Accred.: NACCAS (1991/2001)

Dudley Beauty College—Charlotte
1950 John McDonald Ave., Charlotte 28216
Type: Private, proprietary
Degrees: C
URL: http://www.dudleyq.com/Education
Phone: (704) 392-2564
Inst. Accred.: NACCAS (1998/2001)

Dudley Cosmetology University
900 East Mountain St., Kernersville 27284
Type: Private, proprietary
Degrees: C
URL: http://www.dudleyq.com/cosmetology.html
Phone: (336) 996-2030
Inst. Accred.: NACCAS (1992/2003)

E. J. Taylor Corporation
4814 Fox Chase Rd., Greensboro 27410
Type: Private, proprietary
Degrees: C
URL: http://www.nc.dale-carnegie.com
Phone: (336) 292-6102
Inst. Accred.: ACCET (1978/2004)

Empire Beauty School—Matthew
11032 East Independence Blvd., Matthew 28105
Type: Private, proprietary
Degrees: C
URL: http://www.empirebeauty.com
Phone: (704) 845-8033
Inst. Accred.: NACCAS (1965/2002)

Concord Campus
10075 Weddington Rd. Extension, Concord 28027
Phone: (704) 979-3500

Fayetteville Beauty College
3442 Bragg Blvd., Fayetteville 28303
Type: Private, proprietary
Degrees: C
Phone: (910) 484-0227
Inst. Accred.: COE (1989/2005)

Hairstyling Institute of Charlotte
209-B South Kings Dr., Charlotte 28204-2621
Type: Private, proprietary
Degrees: C
URL: http://www.yp.bellsouth.com/sites/hairstyling
Phone: (704) 334-5511
Inst. Accred.: ACCSCT (1983/2004)

Hairstylist Academy, Inc.
113 East Water St., Statesville 28677
Type: Private, proprietary
Degrees: C
Phone: (704) 873-8805
Inst. Accred.: NACCAS (1988/1998)

LaShe' Beauty Academy
3117 Shannon Rd., Durham 27707
Type: Private, proprietary
Degrees: C
Phone: (919) 493-9557
Inst. Accred.: NACCAS (2003)

Leon's Beauty School
1410 West Lee St., Greensboro 27403
Type: Private, proprietary
Degrees: C
Phone: (336) 274-4601
Inst. Accred.: NACCAS (1966/2005)

Medical Arts Massage School
6541 Meridien Dr., Ste. 113, Raleigh 27612
Type: Private, proprietary
Degrees: C
URL: http://www.medicalmassage.org
Phone: (919) 783-9290
Inst. Accred.: ACCET (1998/2001, Warning)

Mitchell's Hairstyling Academy—Goldsboro
1021 North Spence Ave., Goldsboro 27534
Type: Private, proprietary
Degrees: C
Phone: (919) 778-8200
Inst. Accred.: NACCAS (1976/2002)

Mitchell's Hairstyling Academy—Greenville
426 Arlington Blvd., Greenville 27858
Type: Private, proprietary
Degrees: C
Phone: (252) 756-3050
Inst. Accred.: NACCAS (1978/2004)

Mitchell's Hairstyling Academy—Wilson
2620 Forest Hills Rd., Ste. A, Wilson 27893
Type: Private, proprietary
Degrees: C
Phone: (252) 243-3158
Inst. Accred.: NACCAS (1973/2003)

Raleigh Campus
1301 Buck Jones Rd., Raleigh 27606
Phone: (919) 469-5807

Montgomery's Hair Styling Academy
222 Tallywood Shopping Center, Fayetteville 28303
Type: Private, proprietary
Degrees: C
Phone: (910) 485-6310
Inst. Accred.: NACCAS (1973/2004)

Mr. David's School of Hair Design
4348 Market St., N-17, Wilmington 28403-1411
Type: Private, proprietary
Degrees: C
Phone: (910) 763-4418
Inst. Accred.: COE (1989/2002)

North Carolina Center for Montessori Teacher Education
4817 Johnson Pond Rd., Apex 27502
Type: Private, independent
Degrees: C
Phone: (919) 779-6671
Inst. Accred.: MACTE (2000)

Franklin Montessori School
10500 Darnestown Rd., Rockville, MD 20850
Phone: (301) 279-2799

**Oconaluftee Job Corps
Civilian Conservation Center**
502 Oconaluftee Job Corps Rd., Cherokee 28719
Type: Public, federal
Degrees: C
URL: http://www.angelfire.com/nc/oconalufteejobcorps
Phone: (828) 497-5411
Inst. Accred.: COE (1984/2000)

Pinnacle Institute of Cosmetology, Inc
461 Plaza Dr., Ste. C, Mooresville 28115
Type: Private, proprietary
Degrees: C
URL: http://www.pinnacleinst.com
Phone: (704) 235-0185
Inst. Accred.: NACCAS (2004)

Schenck Civilian Conservation Center
98 Schenck Dr., Pisgah Forest 28768
Type: Public, federal
Degrees: C
Phone: (828) 862-6100
Inst. Accred.: COE (1985/2004)

Southeastern School of Neuromuscular and Massage Therapy, Inc.
4 Woodlawn Green, Ste. 200, Charlotte 28217
Type: Private, proprietary
Degrees: C
URL: http://www.se-massage.com
Phone: (704) 527-4979　　　　*Calendar:* Tri. plan
Inst. Accred.: ACCSCT (2001)

Winston-Salem Barber School
1531 Silas Creek Pkwy., Winston-Salem 27127-3757
Type: Private
Degrees: C
Phone: (336) 724-1459
Inst. Accred.: ACCSCT (1990)

NORTH DAKOTA

The Headquarters Academy of Hair Design, Inc.
108 South Main St., Minot 58701
Type: Private, proprietary
Degrees: C
Phone: (701) 852-8329
Inst. Accred.: NACCAS (1985/2005)

Josef's School of Hair Design Inc.—Fargo
627 NP Ave., Fargo
Type: Private, proprietary
Degrees: C
URL: http://www.josefsschoolofhairdesign.com
Phone: (701) 235-0011
Inst. Accred.: NACCAS (1967/2003)

**Josef's School of Hair Design, Inc.—
Grand Forks**
2011 South Washington St., Grand Forks 58201
Type: Private, proprietary
Degrees: C
URL: http://www.josefsschoolofhairdesign.com
Phone: (701) 772-2728
Inst. Accred.: NACCAS (1972/2003)

Moler Barber College of Hairstyling
16 South Eighth St., Fargo 58103-1805
Type: Private, proprietary
Degrees: C
Phone: (701) 232-6773
Inst. Accred.: ACCSCT (1992/2002)

R.D. Hairstyling College, Inc.
124 North Fourth St., Bismarck 58501
Type: Private, proprietary
Degrees: C
Phone: (701) 223-8804
Inst. Accred.: NACCAS (1975/2001)

The Salon Professionals Academy Fargo, Inc.
1435 University Dr. South, Fargo 58103
Type: Private, proprietary
Degrees: C
Phone: (701) 478-1772
Inst. Accred.: NACCAS (2005)

OHIO

Adult and Continuing Education—Cleveland Extension
4600 Detroit Ave., Room 169, Cleveland 44102
Type: Public, state/local
Degrees: C
URL: http://www.cmsdnet.net/schools/other/
extensionhigh.htm
Phone: (216) 631-2885
Inst. Accred.: NCA-CASI (1994/2004)

Adult Center for Education
400 Richards Rd., Zanesville 43701
Type: Public, state/local
Degrees: C
URL: http://adultcentereducation.org
Phone: (740) 455-3111
Inst. Accred.: NCA-CASI (1974/2005)

Adult Community Education Full Service Center
1510 Clarendon Ave. NW, Room 4, Canton 44708
Type: Public, state/local
Degrees: C
URL: http://www.ccsdistrict.org/adult
Phone: (330) 438-2603   *Calendar:* Sem. plan
Inst. Accred.: NCA-CASI (1950/2004)

Adult Vocational Services
147 Park St., Akron 44308
Type: Public, state/local
Degrees: C
URL: http://www.akron.k12.oh.us/dept/776
Phone: (330) 761-1385
Inst. Accred.: NCA-CASI (1985/2004)

Akron Institute
1625 Portage Trail, Cuyahoga Falls 44223-2166
Type: Private, proprietary
System: Herzing College Corporate Offices
Degrees: C
URL: http://www.akroninstitute.com
Phone: (330) 928-3400   *Calendar:* Qtr. plan
Inst. Accred.: ACCSCT (1977/2004)
Prog. Accred.: Medical Assisting (CAAHEP)

Akron Machining Institute Inc.
2959 Barber Rd., Barberton 44203-1005
Type: Private, proprietary
Degrees: C
URL: http://www.akronmach.com
Phone: (330) 745-1111
Inst. Accred.: ACCSCT (1986/2001)

Alliance City Schools Career Centre
200 Glamorgan St., Alliance 44601
Type: Public, state/local
Degrees: C
URL: http://www.aviators.stark.k12.oh.us
Phone: (330) 821-2102   *Calendar:* Sem. plan
Inst. Accred.: NCA-CASI (1912/2005)

American Institute of Alternative Medicine
6685 Doubletree Ave., Columbus 43229
Type: Private, proprietary
Degrees: C
URL: http://www.aiam.net
Phone: (614) 825-6278
Inst. Accred.: ACCSCT (2000/2005)
Prog. Accred.: Acupuncture

American School of Technology
2100 Morse Rd., Building 4599, Columbus 43229-6665
Type: Private, proprietary
Degrees: C
URL: http://www.americanschooloftech.com
Phone: (614) 436-4820
Inst. Accred.: ACCSCT (1985/2003)

Apollo Career Center
3325 Shawnee Rd., Lima 45806-1497
Type: Public, state/local
Degrees: C
URL: http://www.apollocareercenter.com
Phone: (419) 998-2999
Inst. Accred.: NCA-CASI (1988/2004)

Ashland County-West Holmes Career Center
1783 State Route 60, Ashland 44805
Type: Public, state/local
Degrees: C
URL: http://www.acwhcc-jvs.k12.oh.us
Phone: (419) 289-3313
Inst. Accred.: NCA-CASI (1995/2005)
Prog. Accred.: Medical Assisting (CAAHEP)

Ashtabula County Joint Vocational Sschool
1565 State Route 167, Jefferson 44047
Type: Public, state/local
Degrees: C
URL: http://www.acjvs.org
Phone: (440) 576-6015   *Calendar:* Sem. plan
Inst. Accred.: NCA-CASI (1986/2005)

Auburn Career Center
8140 Auburn Rd., Concord Township 44077
Type: Public, state/local
Degrees: C
URL: http://www.auburn.k12.oh.us
Phone: (440) 357-7542
Inst. Accred.: NCA-CASI (1990/2005)

Aveda Fredric's Institute
4235 Muhlhauser Rd., Fairfield 45014
Type: Private, proprietary
Degrees: C
URL: http://www.fredrics.com
Phone: (513) 874-2226
Inst. Accred.: NACCAS (2003/2004)

Beatrice Academy of Beauty
10500 Cedar Ave., Cleveland 44106
Type: Private, proprietary
Degrees: C
Phone: (216) 421-2313
Inst. Accred.: NACCAS (1980/2003)

Brighton College
85 South Main St., Ste. G, Hudson 44326
Type: Private, proprietary
Degrees: C
URL: http://www.brightoncollege.edu
Phone: (330) 342-5579
Inst. Accred.: DETC (1986/2002)

Buckeye Career Center
545 University Dr. NE, New Philadelphia 44663-9439
Type: Public, state/local
Degrees: C
URL: http://web.bjvs.k12.oh.us
Phone: (330) 339-2288
Inst. Accred.: NCA-CASI (1988/2004)

Buckeye Hills Career Center
351 Buckeye Hills Rd., Rio Grande 45674
Type: Public, state/local
Degrees: C
URL: http://www.bhcc.k12.oh.us
Phone: (740) 245-5334
Inst. Accred.: NCA-CASI (1990/2005)

Butler Technology and Career Development Schools
3603 Hamilton-Middletown Rd., Fairfield Township 45011
Type: Public, state/local
Degrees: C
URL: http://www.butlertech.org/adult
Phone: (513) 868-6300
Inst. Accred.: NCA-CASI (1982/2005)

Career and Technology Centers of Licking County
222 Price Rd., Newark 43055
Type: Public, state/local
Degrees: C
URL: http://www.c-tec.edu/adults
Phone: (740) 366-3358
Inst. Accred.: NCA-CASI (1981/2004)

The Career Center Adult Technical Training
21740 State Route 676, Marietta 45750
Type: Public, state/local
Degrees: C
URL: http://www.mycareerschool.com
Phone: (740) 373-6283
Inst. Accred.: NCA-CASI (1988/2004)

Carnegie Institute of Integrative Medicine and Massotherapy
1292 Waterloo Rd., Suffield 44260
Type: Private, proprietary
Degrees: C
URL: http://www.cimassotherapy.org
Phone: (330) 630-1132
Inst. Accred.: ABHES (2002)
Prog. Accred.: Medical Assisting (ABHES)

Carousel Beauty College—Dayton
125 East Second St., Dayton 45402
Type: Private, proprietary
Degrees: C
URL: http://carouselbeauty.com
Phone: (937) 224-1454
Inst. Accred.: NACCAS (1974/2005)

Kettering Campus
3120 Woodman Dr., Kettering 45420
Phone: (937) 298-5752

Springfield Campus
1475 Upper Valley Pike, Room 956, Springfield 45504
Phone: (937) 323-0277

Carousel Beauty College—Middletown
633 South Breiel Blvd., Middletown 45044
Type: Private, proprietary
Degrees: C
URL: http://carouselbeauty.com
Phone: (513) 422-2962
Inst. Accred.: NACCAS (1975/2005)

Carousel of Miami Valley Beauty College
7809 Waynetown Blvd., Huber Heights 45424
Type: Private, proprietary
Degrees: C
URL: http://carouselbeauty.com
Phone: (937) 233-8818
Inst. Accred.: NACCAS (1975/2005)

Casal's De Spa and Salon
4030 Boardman-Canfield Rd., Canfield 44406
Type: Private, proprietary
Degrees: C
URL: http://www.casalsspa.com
Phone: (330) 533-6766
Inst. Accred.: NACCAS (1988/2003)

Center for Employment Training
540 East 105 St., Cleveland 44108
Type: Public, state/local
Degrees: C
URL: www.cetcleveland.com
Phone: (216) 851-1919 121
Inst. Accred.: NCA-CASI (2004)

Central School of Practical Nursing
3300 Chester Ave., Cleveland 44114
Type: Private, independent
Degrees: C
URL: http://www.cspnohio.org
Phone: (216) 391-8434
Inst. Accred.: ABHES (2004)
Prog. Accred.: Practical Nursing

Century School of Cosmetology, Inc.
434 Market St., Steubenville 43952
Type: Private, proprietary
Degrees: C
Phone: (740) 282-3312
Inst. Accred.: NACCAS (1978/2004)

Charmayne Beauty Academy
20880 Southgate Park Blvd., Maple Heights 44137
Type: Private, proprietary
Degrees: C
Phone: (216) 662-4090
Inst. Accred.: NACCAS (1975/1999)

Choffin Career and Technical Center
200 East Wood St., Youngstown 44503
Type: Public, state/local
Degrees: C
URL: http://www.youngstown.k12.oh.us/choffin
Phone: (330) 744-8710   *Calendar:* Sem. plan
Inst. Accred.: NCA-CASI (1990/2005)
Prog. Accred.: Dental Assisting, Practical Nursing,
  Surgical Technology

CIMS College
5340 East Main St., Stes. 204-209, Whitehall 43213
Type: Private, proprietary
Degrees: C
Phone: (614) 367-2467
Inst. Accred.: ACCET (1999/2003)

Cleveland Institute of Dental-Medical Assistants, Inc.
2450 Prospect Ave., 2nd Flr., Cleveland 44115-2285
Type: Private, proprietary
Degrees: C
URL: http://www.cidma.com
Phone: (216) 241-2930
Inst. Accred.: ACCSCT (1979/2001)

Lyndhurst Campus
5564 Mayfield Rd., Lyndhurst 44124-2928
Phone: (440) 473-6273

Mentor Campus
5733 Hopkins Rd., Mentor 44060-2035
Phone: (440) 946-9530

The Cleveland Music School Settlement
11125 Magnolia Dr., Cleveland 44106
Type: Private, independent
Degrees: C
URL: http://www.thecmss.org
Phone: (216) 421-5806   *Calendar:* Sem. plan
Inst. Accred.: NASM (2000)

Collins Career Center
11627 State Route 243, Chesapeake 45619
Type: Public, state/local
Degrees: C
URL: http://www.collins-cc.k12.oh.us
Phone: (740) 867-6641
Inst. Accred.: NCA-CASI (1982/2002)
Prog. Accred.: Phlebotomy

Columbiana County Career and Technical Center
9364 State Route 45, Lisbon 44432
Type: Public, state/local
Degrees: C
URL: http://www.columbianajvs.k12.oh.us
Phone: (330) 424-9561
Inst. Accred.: NCA-CASI (1982/2005)

Columbus Montessori Center/COMET
933 Hamlet St., Columbus 43201
Type: Private, independent
Degrees: C
Phone: (614) 291-8601
Inst. Accred.: MACTE (2000)

Columbus Montessori Teacher Education Program
979 South James Rd., Columbus 43227
Type: Private, independent
Degrees: C
Phone: (614) 231-3790
Inst. Accred.: MACTE (1995/2002)

Conservatory of Cosmetology
190 South Hamilton Rd., Columbus 43213
Type: Private, proprietary
Degrees: C
URL: http://coc.edu
Phone: (614) 860-9999
Inst. Accred.: NACCAS (2003/2005)

Creative Images—A Certified Matrix Design Academy
1076 Kauffman Ave., Fairborn 45324
Type: Private, proprietary
Degrees: C
Phone: (937) 878-9555
Inst. Accred.: NACCAS (1998/2001)

Dayton Campus
568 Miamisburg-Centerville Rd., Dayton 45459
Phone: (937) 433-1944

Cuyahoga Valley Career Center
8001 Brecksville Rd., Brecksville 44141
Type: Public, state/local
Degrees: C
URL: http://www.cvcc.k12.oh.us/cvccworks
Phone: (440) 526-5200
Inst. Accred.: NCA-CASI (1930/2005)

Dale Carnegie Training of Greater Cincinnati
4243 Hunt Rd., Ste. 100, Cincinnati 45242-6657
Type: Private, proprietary
Degrees: C
URL: http://www.cincinnati.dalecarnegie.com
Phone: (513) 984-4448
Inst. Accred.: ACCET (1977/2003)

Dale Carnegie Training of Northwest Ohio and Northern Indiana
580 Carol Ln., Perrysburg 43551
Type: Private, proprietary
Degrees: C
URL: http://www.nwohio.dalecarnegie.com
Phone: (419) 872-9040
Inst. Accred.: ACCET (1996/2001)

Dayton Barber College
28 West Fifth St., Dayton 45402
Type: Private, proprietary
Degrees: C
URL: http://www.daytonbarbercollege.com
Phone: (937) 222-9101
Inst. Accred.: NACCAS (1994/2002)

Defense Institute of Security Assistance Management
2475 K St., Bldg. 52, Wright-Patterson AFB 45433-7641
Type: Public, federal
Degrees: C
URL: http://disam.osd.mil
Phone: (937) 255-5850
Inst. Accred.: COE (2001)

Delaware Area Career Center
4565 Columbus Pike, Delawar 43015
Type: Public, state/local
Degrees: C
URL: http://www.delawarejvs.org
Phone: (740) 548-0708
Inst. Accred.: NCA-CASI (1988/2005)

Eastern Hills Academy of Hair Design
7681 Beechmont Ave., Cincinnati 45255
Type: Private, proprietary
Degrees: C
Phone: (513) 231-8621
Inst. Accred.: NACCAS (1977/2003)

Eastland Career Center—Adult Workforce Development Center
4300 Amalgamated Place, Groveport 43125
Type: Public, state/local
Degrees: C
URL: http://www.eastland.k12.oh.us
Phone: (614) 836-454   *Calendar:* Qtr. plan
Inst. Accred.: NCA-CASI (1987/2004)

EHOVE Career Center
316 West Mason Rd., Milan 44846
Type: Public, state/local
Degrees: C
URL: http://www.ehove-jvs.k12.oh.us
Phone: (419) 499-4663   *Calendar:* Qtr. plan
Inst. Accred.: NCA-CASI (1990/2004)
Prog. Accred.: Medical Assisting (CAAHEP)

Euclid Beauty College
22741 Shore Center Dr., Euclid 44123
Type: Private, proprietary
Degrees: C
Phone: (216) 261-2600
Inst. Accred.: NACCAS (2002/2005)

Fairfield Career Center
4000 Columbus-Lancaster Rd., Carroll 43112
Type: Public, state/local
Degrees: C
URL: http://www.eastland.k12.oh.us
Phone: (614) 837-9443   *Calendar:* Qtr. plan
Inst. Accred.: NCA-CASI (1989/2004)
Prog. Accred.: Medical Assisting (CAAHEP)

Fairview Academy
22610 Lorain Rd., Fairview Park 44126
Type: Private, proprietary
Degrees: C
Phone: (440) 734-5555
Inst. Accred.: NACCAS (1990/2003)

Four County Career Center
22900 State Route 34, Archbold 43502-9586
Type: Public, state/local
Degrees: C
URL: http://www.fourcounty.net
Phone: (419) 267-3331
Inst. Accred.: NCA-CASI (1975/2005)

Gerber Akron Beauty School
33 Shiawassee Ave., Fairlawn 44333
Type: Private, proprietary
Degrees: C
Phone: (330) 867-6200
Inst. Accred.: NACCAS (1965/2003)

Great Oaks Institute of Technology and Career Development—Diamond Oaks Campus
6375 Harrison Ave., Cincinnati 45247-7898
Type: Public, state/local
Degrees: C
URL: http://www.greatoaks.com
Phone: (513) 574-1300
Inst. Accred.: NCA-CASI (1981/2004)

Great Oaks Institute of Technology and Career Development—Laurel Oaks Campus
300 Oak Dr., Wilmington 45177
Type: Public, state/local
Degrees: C
URL: http://www.greatoaks.com
Phone: (937) 382-1411
Inst. Accred.: NCA-CASI (1981/2004)

Great Oaks Institute of Technology and Career Development—Live Oaks Campus
5956 Buckwheat Rd., Milford 45150
Type: Public, state/local
Degrees: C
URL: http://www.greatoaks.com
Phone: (513) 575-1900
Inst. Accred.: NCA-CASI (1981/2004)

Great Oaks Institute of Technology and Career Development—Scarlet Oaks Campus
3254 East Kemper Rd., Cincinnati 45241
Type: Public, state/local
Degrees: C
URL: http://www.greatoaks.com
Phone: (513) 771-8810
Inst. Accred.: NCA-CASI (1981/2004)
Prog. Accred.: Practical Nursing

Greene County Career Center
2960 West Enon Rd., Xenia 45385
Type: Public, state/local
Degrees: C
URL: http://www.greeneccc.com
Phone: (937) 372-6941
Inst. Accred.: NCA-CASI (1987/2005)

Hamrick Truck Driving School
1156 Medina Rd., Medina 44256-9615
Type: Private, proprietary
Degrees: C
URL: http://www.hamricktruck.com
Phone: (330) 239-2229
Inst. Accred.: ACCSCT (1987/2003)

HARDI Home Study Institute
1389 Dublin Rd., PO Box 16790, Columbus 43216
Type: Private, independent
Degrees: C
URL: http://www.hardinet.org
Phone: (614) 488-1835
Inst. Accred.: DETC (1969/2001)

Hobart Institute of Welding Technology
400 Trade Square East, Troy 45373-9989
Type: Private, proprietary
Degrees: C
URL: http://www.welding.org
Phone: (937) 332-5610
Inst. Accred.: ACCSCT (1972/2004)

Inner State Beauty School
5150 Mayfield Rd., Lyndhurst 44124
Type: Private, proprietary
Degrees: C
URL: http://www.innerstatebeautyschool.com
Phone: (440) 442-4500
Inst. Accred.: NACCAS (1987/2004)

Institute of Medical and Dental Technology
375 Glensprings Dr., Ste. 201, Cincinnati 45246
Type: Private, proprietary
Degrees: C
URL: http://www.imdtcareers.com
Phone: (513) 851-8500
Inst. Accred.: ABHES (1983/202)

Eastgate Boulevard Campus
4452 Eastgate Blvd., Ste. 209, Cincinnati 45245
Phone: (513) 753-5030

International Academy of Hair Design
8419 Colerain Ave., Cincinnati 45239
Type: Private, proprietary
Degrees: C
URL: http://www.mybeautycareer.com
Phone: (513) 741-4777
Inst. Accred.: NACCAS (1986/2001)

International College of Broadcasting
6 South Smithville Rd., Dayton 45431-1833
Type: Private
Degrees: C   *Enroll:* 92
URL: http://www.icbcollege.com
Phone: (937) 258-8251
Inst. Accred.: ACCSCT (1976/2003)

Knox County Career Center
306 Martinsburg Rd., Mount Vernon 43050
Type: Private, state/local
Degrees: C
URL: http://www.knoxcc.org
Phone: (740) 397-5820   *Calendar:* Sem. plan
Inst. Accred.: NCA-CASI (1986/2005)
Prog. Accred.: Medical Assisting (CAAHEP)

Ladies and Gentlemen Hair Stylists
8800 Mentor Ave., Mentor 44060
Type: Private, proprietary
Degrees: C
URL: http://ladiesgentlemen.com
Phone: (440) 255-5572
Inst. Accred.: NACCAS (2001/2004)

Lance Tyson & Associates
Dale Carnegie Training of Northeast Ohio
5350 Transportation Blvd., Ste. 14, Cleveland 44125
Type: Private, proprietary
Degrees: C
URL: http://www.cleveland.dalecarnegie.com
Phone: (216) 663-2500
Inst. Accred.: ACCET (1975/2004)

Lorain County Joint Vocational School
Adult Career Center
15181 State Route 58, Oberlin 44074
Type: Public, state/local
Degrees: C
URL: http://adult.lcjvs.com/adult
Phone: (440) 774-1051
Inst. Accred.: NCA-CASI (1988/2005)

Madison Adult Education
600 Esley Ln., Mansfield 44905
Type: Public, state/local
Degrees: C
URL: http://www.madison-richland.k12.oh.us/adulted
Phone: (419) 589-6363
Inst. Accred.: NCA-CASI (1961/2005)

Mahoning County Career and Technical Center
7300 North Palmyra Rd., Canfield 44406
Type: Public, state/local
Degrees: C
URL: http://www.mahoningctc.com
Phone: (330) 729-4100
Inst. Accred.: NCA-CASI (1988/2004)

Medina County Career Center
1101 West Liberty St., Medina 44256-9969
Type: Public, state/local
Degrees: C
URL: http://www.mccc-jvsd.org
Phone: (330) 725-8461
Inst. Accred.: NCA-CASI (1978/2004)
Prog. Accred.: Medical Assisting (CAAHEP)

Miami Valley Career Technology Center
6800 Hoke Rd., Clayton 45315
Type: Public, state/local
Degrees: C
URL: http://mvctc.com/mvctc/index.htm
Phone: (937) 854-6297
Inst. Accred.: NCA-CASI (1976/2004)

Michael W. Jones & Associates, Inc.
6029 Cleveland Ave., Columbus 43231
Type: Private, proprietary
Degrees: C
URL: http://www.columbus.dalecarnegie.com
Phone: (614) 523-1080
Inst. Accred.: ACCET (1977/2001)

Moler-Hollywood Beauty College
130 East 6th St., Cincinnati 45202
Type: Private, proprietary
Degrees: C
Phone: (513) 621-5262
Inst. Accred.: NACCAS (1975/2005)

Moler-Pickens Beauty College
5951-S Boymel Dr., Fairfield 45014
Type: Private, proprietary
Degrees: C
Phone: (513) 874-5116
Inst. Accred.: NACCAS (1985/2005)

Montessori Opportunities, Inc.
2381 Plymouth Ln., Cuyahoga Falls 44221-3642
Type: Private, independent
Degrees: C
Phone: (330) 929-5581
Inst. Accred.: MACTE (2005)

Moore Universite' of Hair Design, Inc.
7030 Reading Rd., Ste. 640, Cincinnati 45237
Type: Private, proprietary
Degrees: C
Phone: (513) 531-3100
Inst. Accred.: NACCAS (1971/2002)

National Beauty College—Canton
4642 Cleveland Ave., NW, Canton 44709
Type: Private, proprietary
Degrees: C
Phone: (330) 499-9444
Inst. Accred.: NACCAS (1965/2002)

National Institute of Massotherapy, Inc.
2110 Copley Rd., Akron 44320
Type: Private, proprietary
Degrees: C
URL: http://www.naturalhealers.com
Phone: (330) 867-1996
Inst. Accred.: ACCET (1999/2002)

National Institute of Technology—
Cuyahoga Falls
2545 Bailey Rd., First Flr., Cuyahoga Falls 44221-2949
Type: Private, proprietary
Degrees: C
URL: http://www.nationalinstituteoftechnology.org
Phone: (330) 923-9959 *Calendar:* Qtr. plan
Inst. Accred.: ACCSCT (1969/2003)

Nationwide Beauty Academy
5300 WestPointe Plaza Dr., Columbus 43228
Type: Private, proprietary
System: Salon Schools Group
Degrees: C
URL: http://www.salonschools.com
Phone: (614) 921-9101
Inst. Accred.: NACCAS (1968/2004)

North Education Center
100 Arcadia Ave., Columbus 43202
Type: Public, state/local
Degrees: C
URL: http://www.cpsadulted.org
Phone: (614) 365-6000
Inst. Accred.: NCA-CASI (1983/2004)

Northern Institute of Cosmetology
667-669 Broadway, Lorain 44052
Type: Private, proprietary
Degrees: C
Phone: (440) 244-4282
Inst. Accred.: NACCAS (1967/1998)

Ohio Academy of Holistic Health, Inc.
2380 Bellbrook Ave., Xenia 45385
Type: Private, proprietary
Degrees: C
URL: http://www.oahh.com
Phone: (937) 708-3232
Inst. Accred.: ACCET (2001/2005)

Ohio Center for Broadcasting
4790 Red Bank Expressway, No. 102, Cincinnati 45227-1509
Type: Private, proprietary
Degrees: C
URL: http://www.beonair.com
Phone: (513) 271-6060
Inst. Accred.: ACCSCT (1992/2003)

Ohio Center for Broadcasting
9000 Sweet Valley Dr., Valley View 44125
Type: Private, proprietary
Degrees: C
URL: http://www.beonair.com
Phone: (216) 447-9117
Inst. Accred.: ACCSCT (1991/2001)

Ohio College of Massotherapy
225 Heritage Woods Dr., Akron 44321
Type: Private, proprietary
Degrees: C
URL: http://www.ocm.edu
Phone: (330) 665-1084
Inst. Accred.: ACCSCT (1994/2004)

Ohio Hi Point Career Center
2280 State Route 540, Bellefontaine 43311
Type: Public, state/local
Degrees: C
URL: www.ohp.k12.oh.us
Phone: (937) 599-6275
Inst. Accred.: NCA-CASI (1984/2004)

Ohio Institute of Health Careers
1880 East Dublin-Granville Rd., Columbus 43229
Type: Private, proprietary
Degrees: C
URL: http://www.cpi-careers.com
Phone: (614) 891-5030
Inst. Accred.: ACCSCT (1985/2000)

Elyria Campus
639 Griswold Rd., Elyria 44035
Phone: (440) 324-2293

Ohio State Beauty Academy
57 Town Square, Lima 45801
Type: Private, proprietary
Degrees: C
URL: http://www.ohiostatebeauty.com
Phone: (419) 229-7896
Inst. Accred.: NACCAS (1969/2005)

Ohio State College of Barber Styling
4614 East Broad St., Columbus 43213
Type: Private, proprietary
Degrees: C
Phone: (614) 868-1015
Inst. Accred.: ACCSCT (1977/2004)

Ohio State School of Cosmetology—Columbus
3717 South High St., Columbus 43207
Type: Private, proprietary
System: Salon Schools Group
Degrees: C
URL: http://www.salonschools.com
Phone: (614) 491-0492
Inst. Accred.: NACCAS (1982/2002)

Ohio State School of Cosmetology—East
6320 East Livingston Ave., Reynoldsburg 43068
Type: Private, proprietary
System: Salon Schools Group
Degrees: C
URL: http://www.salonschools.com
Phone: (614) 868-1601
Inst. Accred.: NACCAS (1976/2005)

Ohio State School of Cosmetology—Northland
4390 Karl Rd., Columbus 43224
Type: Private, proprietary
System: Salon Schools Group
Degrees: C
URL: http://www.salonschools.com
Phone: (614) 263-1861
Inst. Accred.: NACCAS (1973/2004)

Ohio State School of Cosmetology—Westerville
5970 Westerville Rd., Westerville 43081
Type: Private, proprietary
System: Salon Schools Group
Degrees: C
URL: http://www.salonschools.com
Phone: (614) 890-3535
Inst. Accred.: NACCAS (1983/2003)

Ohio Technical College
1374 East 51st St., Cleveland 44103-1269
Type: Private, proprietary
Degrees: C
Phone: (216) 881-1700
Inst. Accred.: ACCSCT (1973/2001)

Oregon Career and Technology Center
5721 Seaman Rd., Oregon 43616
Type: Public, state/local
Degrees: C
URL: http://www.oregon.k12.oh.us/pages/adulted.html
Phone: (419) 697-3450
Inst. Accred.: NCA-CASI (1931/2004)

Paramount Beauty Academy
1745 11th St., Portsmouth 45662
Type: Private, proprietary
Degrees: C
URL: http://www.paramountbeautyacademy.com
Phone: (740) 353-2436
Inst. Accred.: NACCAS (1993/2001)

Penta Career Center
30095 Oregon Rd., Perrysburg 43551
Type: Public, state/local
Degrees: C
URL: http://www.pentacareercenter.org
Phone: (419) 661-6555
Inst. Accred.: NCA-CASI (1973/2005)

Pickaway-Ross Career and Technology Center
895 Crouse Chapel Rd., Chillicothe 45601
Type: Public, state/local
Degrees: C
URL: http://www.pickawayross.com/adulted/adulted.htm
Phone: (740) 642-1200
Inst. Accred.: NCA-CASI (1988/2003)

Pioneer Career and Technical Center
27 Ryan Rd., Shelby 44875
Type: Public, state/local
Degrees: C
URL: http://www.pctc.k12.oh.us
Phone: (419) 347-7744
Inst. Accred.: NCA-CASI (1981/2004)

Polaris Career Center
7285 Old Oak Blvd., Middleburg Heights 44130
Type: Public, state/local
Degrees: C
URL: http://www.polaris.edu
Phone: (440) 891-7750
Inst. Accred.: NCA-CASI (1985/2005)
Prog. Accred.: Dental Assisting

Portage Lakes Career Center
4401 Shriver Rd., Green 44232
Type: Public, state/local
Degrees: C
URL: http://www.plcc.k12.oh.us
Phone: (330) 896-8200
Inst. Accred.: NCA-CASI (1988/2004)

Quest Career College
6248 Pearl Rd., Parma Heights 44130
Type: Private, proprietary
Degrees: C
URL: http://www.computerquest.com
Phone: (440) 886-5544
Inst. Accred.: ACCET (2001/2004)

Raphael's Salem Beauty Academy
2445 West State St., Alliance 44601
Type: Private, proprietary
Degrees: C
Phone: (330) 823-3884
Inst. Accred.: NACCAS (1988/2003)

Raphael's School of Beauty Culture
1324 Youngstown Warren Rd., Niles 44446
Type: Private, proprietary
Degrees: C
Phone: (330) 652-1559
Inst. Accred.: NACCAS (1978/2004)

Raphael's School of Beauty Culture
5311 Market St., Boardman 44512
Type: Private, proprietary
Degrees: C
Phone: (330) 782-3395
Inst. Accred.: NACCAS (1991/2001)

Raphael's School of Beauty Culture, Inc.
3307 Center Rd., Brunswick 44212
Type: Private, proprietary
Degrees: C
Phone: (330) 225-0195
Inst. Accred.: NACCAS (1985/2005)

Riggs Le Mar Beauty College
2115 Front St., Cuyahoga Falls 44221
Type: Private, proprietary
Degrees: C
Phone: (330) 945-4045
Inst. Accred.: NACCAS (1965/2003)

Sandusky High School Adult Education
2130 Hayes Ave., sandusky 44870
Type: Public, state/local
Degrees: C
URL: http://webserver.sandusky.k12.mi.us
Phone: (419) 621-2743
Inst. Accred.: NCA-CASI (1994/2005)

Scioto County Joint Vocational School
951 Vern Riffe Dr., Lucasville 45648
Type: Public, state/local
Degrees: C
URL: http://www.scjvs.com
Phone: (740) 259-5526
Inst. Accred.: NCA-CASI (1986/2004)

The Spa School
5050 North High St., Columbus 43214
Type: Private, proprietary
System: Salon Schools Group
Degrees: C
URL: http://www.salonschools.com
Phone: (614) 888-0725
Inst. Accred.: NACCAS (1965/2003)

Springfield-Clark County Joint Vocational School
1901 Selma Rd., Springfield 45505
Type: Public, state/local
Degrees: C
URL: http://sccjvs.org
Phone: (937) 325-7368   *Calendar:* Sem. plan
Inst. Accred.: NCA-CASI (1973/2005)

TDDS Technical Institute
1688 North Princetown Rd., Lake Milton 44429
Type: Private, proprietary
Degrees: C
URL: http://www.tdds.edu
Phone: (330) 538-2216
Inst. Accred.: ACCSCT (1987/2003)

Tiffin Academy of Hair Design
104 East Market St., Tiffin 44883
Type: Private, proprietary
Degrees: C
URL: http://tiffinacademy.com
Phone: (419) 447-3117
Inst. Accred.: NACCAS (1966/2003)

Toledo Academy of Beauty Culture—North
5020 Lewis Ave., Toledo 43612
Type: Private, proprietary
Degrees: C
Phone: (419) 478-5325
Inst. Accred.: NACCAS (1985/2005)

Northwood Campus
2592 Woodville Rd., Northwood 43619
Phone: (419) 693-7257

Toledo Academy of Beauty Culture—South
1554 South Byrne Rd., Glenbyrne Center, Toledo 43614
Type: Private, proprietary
Degrees: C
Phone: (419) 381-7218
Inst. Accred.: NACCAS (1987/2002)

Toledo Public Schools Adult Education Center
3301 Upton Ave., Ellis Center, Toledo 43613
Type: Public, state/local
Degrees: C
URL: http://www.tps.org
Phone: (419) 671-8700
Inst. Accred.: NCA-CASI (1994/2004)

Total Technical Institute
8720 Brookpark Rd., Brooklyn, OH 44129
Type: Private, proprietary
System: Kaplan Higher Education Corporation
Degrees: C
URL: http://www.ttinst.com
Phone: (216) 485-0900
Inst. Accred.: ACCSCT (1984/2004)

Tri County Beauty College
155 Northland Blvd., Cincinnati 45246
Type: Private, proprietary
Degrees: C
Phone: (513) 671-8340
Inst. Accred.: NACCAS (1975/2003)

Tri-County Career Center
15676 State Route 691, Nelsonville 45764
Type: Public, state/local
Degrees: C
URL: http://www.tricountyhightech.com
Phone: (740) 753-3511
Inst. Accred.: NCA-CASI (1981/2004)

Tri-Rivers Career Center
2222 Marion-Mount Gilead Rd., Marion 43302
Type: Public, state/local
Degrees: C
URL: http://www.tririvers.com
Phone: (740) 389-4681
Inst. Accred.: NCA-CASI (1985/2004)

Tri-State College of Massotherapy
9159 Market St., Ste. 26, North Lima 44452
Type: Private, proprietary
Degrees: C
URL: http://tristatemasso.com
Phone: (330) 629-9998
Inst. Accred.: ACCSCT (2001)

Tri-State Semi Driver Training, Inc.
6690 Germantown Rd., Middletown 45042
Type: Private, proprietary
Degrees: C
URL: http://www.learn2drive.com
Phone: (513) 424-1237
Inst. Accred.: ACCET (1986/2002)

Trumbull Career and Technical Center
1776 Salt Springs Rd., Lordstown 44481
Type: Public, state/local
Degrees: C
URL: http://www.tctcadulttraining.org
Phone: (330) 824-2588
Inst. Accred.: NCA-CASI (1988/2005)

U.S. Grant Joint Vocational School
718 West Plane St., Bethel 45106
Type: Public, state/local
Degrees: C
URL: http://www.grantcareer.com
Phone: (513) 734-6222
Inst. Accred.: NCA-CASI (1992/2004)

Upper Valley Joint Vocational School
5 East State Route 36, Piqua 45356
Type: Public, state/local
Degrees: C
URL: http://www.uvjvs.org/adulted/atc/index.htm
Phone: (937) 778-1980 ext 2
Inst. Accred.: NCA-CASI (1977/2005)

Valley Beauty School
706 Wheeling Ave., Cambridge 43725
Type: Private, proprietary
Degrees: C
Phone: (740) 439-5559
Inst. Accred.: NACCAS (1990/2002)

Parkersburg Campus
707 Market St., Parkersburg, WV 26101
Phone: (304) 422-2226

Valley Beauty School—Zanesville
627 Main St., Zanesville 43701
Type: Private, proprietary
Degrees: C
Phone: (740) 452-6821
Inst. Accred.: NACCAS (1999/2002)

Vanguard-Sentinel Joint Vocational School District
1220 Cedar St., Ste. B, Fremont 43420
Type: Public, state/local
Degrees: C
URL: http://www.vscc.k12.oh.us/adulted.html
Phone: (419) 332-2626
Inst. Accred.: NCA-CASI (1995/2004)

Vantage Career Center
818 North Franklin St., Van Wert 45891-1304
Type: Public, state/local
Degrees: C
URL: http://www.vantagecareercenter.com
Phone: (419) 238-5411
Inst. Accred.: NCA-CASI (1993/2004)

Vocational Guidance Services
2239 East 55th St., Cleveland 44103
Type: Private, independent
Degrees: C
URL: http://www.vgsjob.org
Phone: (216) 881-6007
Inst. Accred.: NCA-CASI (2003)

Vogue Beauty Academy—Cleveland
2051 East 4th St., Cleveland 44115
Type: Private, proprietary
Degrees: C
Phone: (216) 621-5552
Inst. Accred.: NACCAS (1975/1999)

Vogue Beauty Academy—Cleveland Heights
13238 Cedar Rd., Cleveland Heights 44118
Type: Private, proprietary
Degrees: C
Phone: (216) 321-4465
Inst. Accred.: NACCAS (1975/1999)

Warren County Career Center
3525 North State Route 48, Lebanon 45036
Type: Public, state/local
Degrees: C
URL: http://www.wccareercenter.com
Phone: (513) 932-8145
Inst. Accred.: NCA-CASI (1983/2004)

Wayne County Career Center
518 West Prospect St., Smithville 44677
Type: Public, state/local
Degrees: C
URL: http://www.wayne-jvs.k12.oh.us
Phone: (330) 669-9611
Inst. Accred.: NCA-CASI (1977/2004)

Western Hills School of Beauty & Hair Design
6490 Glenway Ave., Cincinnati 45211
Type: Private, proprietary
Degrees: C
Phone: (513) 574-3818
Inst. Accred.: NACCAS (1977/2003)

Youngstown Centre of Massotherapy
14 Highland Ave., Struthers 44471
Type: Private, proprietary
Degrees: C
URL: http://www.yocm.com
Phone: (330) 755-1406
Inst. Accred.: ACCSCT (1999/2004)

OKLAHOMA

4-States Academy of Cosmetology
123 South Wilson St., Vinita 74301-3729
Type: Private, proprietary
Degrees: C
Phone: (918) 323-0002
Inst. Accred.: NACCAS (2005)

American Beauty Institute
2009 North Main St., McAlester 74501
Type: Private, proprietary
Degrees: C
URL: http://www.americanbeautyinstitutes.com
Phone: (918) 420-4247
Inst. Accred.: NACCAS (1988/2003)

American Broadcasting School
4511 SE 29th St., Oklahoma City 73115
Type: Private, proprietary
Degrees: C
URL: http://www.radioschool.com
Phone: (405) 672-6511
Inst. Accred.: ACCET (1990/2004)

Arlington Campus
712 North Watson Rd., Ste. 200, Arlington, TX 76011
Phone: (817) 695-2474

Garland Campus
1914 Pendleton Dr., Garland, TX 75041-4840
Phone: (972) 682-5500

Tulsa Campus
2843 East 51st St., Tulsa 74105-1701
Phone: (918) 293-9100

Autry Technology Center
1201 West Willow St., Enid 73703
Type: Public, state/local
Degrees: C
URL: http://www.autrytech.com
Phone: (580) 242-2750
Inst. Accred.: NCA-CASI (1992/2003)
Prog. Accred.: Practical Nursing, Radiography, Surgical Technology

Beauty Technical College
1600 East Downing St., Tahlequah 74465
Type: Private, proprietary
Degrees: C
Phone: (918) 456-9431
Inst. Accred.: NACCAS (1988/2003)

Broken Arrow Beauty College, Inc.
400 South Elm Place, Broken Arrow 74012
Type: Private, proprietary
Degrees: C
Phone: (918) 251-9660
Inst. Accred.: NACCAS (1983/2003)

Cosmetology Education Center
11122 East 71st St. South, Tulsa 74133
Phone: (918) 294-8627

Caddo-Kiowa Technology Center
PO Box 90, Ft. Cobb 73015
Type: Public, state/local
Degrees: C
URL: http://www.caddokiowa.com
Phone: (405) 643-5511
Inst. Accred.: NCA-CASI (1973/2004)
Prog. Accred.: Occupational Therapy Assisting, Practical Nursing

CC's Cosmetology College
11630 East 21st St. South, Tulsa 74129
Type: Private, proprietary
Degrees: C
URL: http://www.ccscosmetology.edu
Phone: (918) 234-9444
Inst. Accred.: NACCAS (1988/2003)

Oklahoma City Campus
4439 NW 50th St., Oklahoma City 73112
Phone: (918) 943-2300

Central State Beauty Academy
8494 NW Expressway, Oklahoma City 73162
Type: Private, proprietary
Degrees: C
Phone: (405) 722-4499
Inst. Accred.: NACCAS (1983/2003)

Central State Massage Academy
8494 NW Expressway, OKC Market Square, Oklahoma City 73162
Type: Private, proprietary
Degrees: C
URL: http://www.centralstatemassageacademy.com
Phone: (405) 722-4499
Inst. Accred.: NACCAS (2004)

Central Technology Center—Drumright
3 CT Circle, Drumright 74030
Type: Public, state/local
Degrees: C
URL: http://www.ctechok.org
Phone: (918) 352-2551
Inst. Accred.: NCA-CASI (1973/2005)
Prog. Accred.: Practical Nursing

Central Technology Center—Sapulpa
1720 South Main St., Sapulpa 74066
Type: Public, state/local
Degrees: C
URL: http://www.ctechok.org
Phone: (918) 224-9300
Inst. Accred.: NCA-CASI (1987/2000)

City College, Inc.
2620 South Service Rd., Moore 73160
Type: Private, proprietary
Degrees: C
URL: http://www.citycollegeinc.com
Phone: (405) 329-5627
Inst. Accred.: ACCET (1988/2001)

Claremore Beauty College
200 North Cherokee Ave., Claremore 74017
Type: Private, proprietary
Degrees: C
URL: http://claremorebeautycollege.com
Phone: (918) 341-4370
Inst. Accred.: NACCAS (1988/2003)

Community Care College
4242 South Sheridan Rd., Tulsa 74145-1119
Type: Private, proprietary
Degrees: C
URL: http://www.communitycarecollege.com
Phone: (918) 610-0027
Inst. Accred.: ABHES (1998/2001)

DeMarge College, Inc.
9301 South Western, Oklahoma City 73139
Type: Private, proprietary
Degrees: C
URL: http://www.demarge.edu
Phone: (405) 692-2900
Inst. Accred.: ACCET (1987/2002, Warning)

Oklahoma City Campus
1331 West Memorial Rd., Oklahoma City 73162
Phone: (405) 607-3050

Enid Beauty College, Inc.
1601 East Broadway, Enid 73701
Type: Private, proprietary
Degrees: C
Phone: (580) 237-6677
Inst. Accred.: NACCAS (1977/2004)

Eve's College of Hairstyling
912 C Ave., Lawton 73501
Type: Private, proprietary
Degrees: C
Phone: (580) 355-6620
Inst. Accred.: NACCAS (1968/2004)

Gordon Cooper Technology Center
One John C Bruton Blvd., Shawnee 74804
Type: Public, state/local
Degrees: C
URL: http://www.gctech.org
Phone: (405) 273-7493
Inst. Accred.: NCA-CASI (1972/2003)

Great Plains Technology Center
4500 West Lee Blvd., Lawton 73505
Type: Public, local
Degrees: C
URL: http://www.gptech.org
Phone: (580) 355-6371
Inst. Accred.: NCA-CASI (1973/2004)
Prog. Accred.: Practical Nursing, Radiography,
Respiratory Therapy Technology, Surgical Technology

Frederick Campus
2001 East Gladstone Ave., Frederick 73542-4645
Phone: (580) 335-5525

Grove Beauty College
63155 East 290 Rd., Grove 74345
Type: Private, proprietary
Degrees: C
Phone: (918) 787-5810
Inst. Accred.: NACCAS (2004)

Hollywood Cosmetology Center
PO Box 890488, Oklahoma City 73189
Type: Private, proprietary
Degrees: C
Phone: (405) 364-3375
Inst. Accred.: ACCSCT (1991/1997)

Indian Capital Technology Center
HC 61 Box 12, 401 Houser Rd., Sallisaw 74955
Type: Public, state/local
Degrees: C
URL: http://www.icavts.tec.ok.us
Phone: (918) 775-9119
Inst. Accred.: NCA-CASI (1994/2005)

Indian Capital Technology Center
2403 North 41st St. East, Muskogee 74403
Type: Public, state/local
Degrees: C
URL: http://www.icavts.tec.ok.us
Phone: (918) 687-6383
Inst. Accred.: NCA-CASI (1974/2005)
Prog. Accred.: Radiography

Indian Capital Technology Center
240 Vo-Tech Rd., Tahlequah 74464-3466
Type: Public, state/local
Degrees: C
URL: http://www.icavts.tec.ok.us
Phone: (918) 456-2594
Inst. Accred.: NCA-CASI (1994/2005)

Indian Capital Technology Center
Rural Route 4, Box 3320, Stilwell 74960
Type: Public, state/local
Degrees: C
URL: http://www.icavts.tec.ok.us
Phone: (918) 696-3111
Inst. Accred.: NCA-CASI (1994/2005)

Institute of Hair Design
1601 1/2 North Harrison St., Shawnee 74804
Type: Private, proprietary
Degrees: C
Phone: (405) 275-8000
Inst. Accred.: NACCAS (2003/2004)

Kiamichi Technology Center—Atoka
1301 West Liberty Rd., Atoka 74525
Type: Public, state/local
Degrees: C
URL: http://www.kiamichi-atoka.tec.ok.us
Phone: (580) 889-7321
Inst. Accred.: NCA-CASI (1982/2002)

Kiamichi Technology Center—Durant
810 Waldron Rd., Durant 74701
Type: Public, state/local
Degrees: C
URL: http://www.kiamichi-durant.tec.ok.us
Phone: (580) 924-7081
Inst. Accred.: NCA-CASI (1992/2002)

Kiamichi Technology Center—Hugo
107 South 15th St., Hugo 74743-4254
Type: Public, state/local
Degrees: C
URL: http://www.kiamichi-hugo.tec.ok.us
Phone: (580) 326-6491
Inst. Accred.: NCA-CASI (1973/2002)

Kiamichi Technology Center—Idabel
Rural Route 3 Box 177, Idabel 74745-9534
Type: Public, state/local
Degrees: C
URL: http://www.kiamichi-idabel.tec.ok.us
Phone: (580) 286-7555
Inst. Accred.: NCA-CASI (1984/2002)

Kiamichi Technology Center—McAlester
301 Kiamichi Dr., McAlester 74501
Type: Public, state/local
Degrees: C
URL: http://www.kiamichi-mcalester.tec.ok.us
Phone: (918) 426-0940
Inst. Accred.: NCA-CASI (1973/2002)

Kiamichi Technology Center—Poteau
1509 South McKenna St., Poteau 74953-5207
Type: Public, state/local
Degrees: C
URL: www.kiamichi-poteau.tec.ok.us
Phone: (918) 647-4525
Inst. Accred.: NCA-CASI (1973/2002)

Kiamichi Technology Center—Spiro
610 SW Third St., Spiro 74959
Type: Public, state/local
Degrees: C
URL: http://www.kiamichi-spiro.tec.ok.us
Phone: (918) 962-3722
Inst. Accred.: NCA-CASI (1996/2002)

Kiamichi Technology Center—Stigler
1410 Old Military Rd., Stigler 74462
Type: Public, state/local
Degrees: C
URL: http://www.kiamichi-stigler.tec.ok.us
Phone: (918) 967-2801
Inst. Accred.: NCA-CASI (1996/2002)

Kiamichi Technology Center—Talihina
Route 2, Box 1800, Talihina 74571
Type: Public, state/local
Degrees: C
URL: http://www.kiamichi-talihina.tec.ok.us
Phone: (918) 567-2264
Inst. Accred.: NCA-CASI (1987/2002)
Prog. Accred.: Practical Nursing

The Language Company
6801 South Western, Ste. 200, Oklahoma City 73139
Type: Private, proprietary
Degrees: C
URL: http://www.thelanguagecompany.com
Phone: (405) 636-1333
Inst. Accred.: ACCET (2000)

Edmond Language Institute
University of Central Oklahoma, 100 North University Dr., PO Box 341881, Edmond 73034
Phone: (405) 341-2125

Hays Language Institute
Fort Hays State University, 600 Picken Hall, Rm. 200, Hays, KS 67601
Phone: (785) 628-2121

Orlando English Instiute
Florida Mall Business Center, 1650 Sand Lake Rd., Ste. 100, Orlando, FL 32809
Phone: (407) 859-5444

Pennsylvania Language Institute
Widener University, One Unversity Place, Chester, PA 19013
Phone: (610) 499-4550

The Shawnee Language Institute
1900 West MacArthur Dr., Shawnee 74804
Phone: (405) 273-8229

South Bend English Institute
1720 Ruskin St., Ste. 100, South Bend, IN 46615
Phone: (219) 287-3622

Tahlequah Campus
622 North Lewis Ave., Tahlequah 74464-2303
Phone: (918) 456-5511 x4730

The Tulsa English Institute
3115 South Winston, Tulsa 74135
Phone: (918) 742-8855

Metro Technology Center—South Bryant
4901 South Bryant Ave., Oklahoma City 73129
Type: Private, proprietary
Degrees: C
URL: http://www.metrotech.org
Phone: (405) 605-4488
Inst. Accred.: NCA-CASI (2001)

Metro Technology Centers—Springlake
1900 Springlake Dr., Oklahoma City 73111-5240
Type: Private, proprietary
Degrees: C
URL: http://www.metrotech.org
Phone: (405) 605-4488
Inst. Accred.: NCA-CASI (1996/2001)
Prog. Accred.: Dental Assisting, Medical Assisting (AMA),
Practical Nursing, Radiography, Surgical Technology

Mid-America Technology Center
PO Box H, Wayne 73095-0210
Type: Public, state/local
Degrees: C
URL: http://www.matech.org
Phone: (405) 449-3391
Inst. Accred.: NCA-CASI (1972/2002)

Mid-Del Technology Center
1612 Maple Dr., Midwest City 73110
Type: Public, state/local
Degrees: C
URL: http://www.mid-del.tec.ok.us
Phone: (405) 739-1707
Inst. Accred.: NCA-CASI (2001/2003)

Moore-Norman Area Vocational Technical School
4701 12th Ave., NW, Norman 73069
Type: Public, state/local
Degrees: C
URL: http://mntechnology.com
Phone: (405) 364-5763
Inst. Accred.: NCA-CASI (2001)
Prog. Accred.: Practical Nursing

Northeast Technology Center
PO Box 825, Pryor 74362
Type: Public, state/local
Degrees: C
URL: http://www.netechcenters.com
Phone: (918) 825-55550
Inst. Accred.: NCA-CASI (1989/2004)
Prog. Accred.: Practical Nursing

Northeast Technology Center
19901 South Hwy. 69, Afton 74331
Type: Public, state/local
Degrees: C
URL: http://www.netechcenters.com
Phone: (918) 257-8324
Inst. Accred.: NCA-CASI (1989/2004)

Northeast Technology Center
PO Box 30, Kansas 74347
Type: Public, state/local
Degrees: C
URL: http://www.netechcenters.com
Phone: (918) 868-3535
Inst. Accred.: NCA-CASI (1998/2004)

Oklahoma Health Academy—Moore
1939 North Moore Ave., Moore 73160
Type: Private, proprietary
Degrees: C
Phone: (405) 912-2777
Inst. Accred.: ACCSCT (1999/2004)

Oklahoma Health Academy—Tulsa
2865 East Skelly Dr., Ste. 224, Tulsa 74105
Type: Private, proprietary
Degrees: C
Phone: (918) 748-9900
Inst. Accred.: ACCSCT (1999/2004)

Oklahoma School of Photography, Inc.
2306 North Moore Ave., Oklahoma City 73160
Type: Private, proprietary
Degrees: C
URL: http://www.photocareers.com
Phone: (405) 799-1411
Inst. Accred.: ACCET (1990/2004)

Ponca City Beauty College
122 North 1st St., Ponca City 74601
Type: Private, proprietary
Degrees: C
Phone: (580) 762-1470
Inst. Accred.: NACCAS (1994/2002)

Pontotoc Technology Center
601 West 33rd St., Ada 74820
Type: Public, state/local
Degrees: C
URL: http://www.pontotoc.com
Phone: (580) 310-2200
Inst. Accred.: NCA-CASI (2001/2004)

Poteau Beauty College
301 Turman St., Poteau 74953
Type: Private, proprietary
Degrees: C
Phone: (918) 647-4119
Inst. Accred.: NACCAS (1989/2004)

Pryor Beauty College
330 West Graham Ave., Pryor 74361
Type: Private, proprietary
Degrees: C
Phone: (918) 825-2795
Inst. Accred.: NACCAS (1998/2001)

Ron Moore & Associates
300 North Meridian, Ste. 110N, Oklahoma City 73107
Type: Private, proprietary
Degrees: C
URL: http://www.oklahoma.dalecarnegie.com
Phone: (405) 947-2111
Inst. Accred.: ACCET (1977/2005)

Sand Springs Beauty College
28 East Second St., Sand Springs 74063
Type: Private, proprietary
Degrees: C
URL: http://www.jenksbeautycollege.com
Phone: (918) 245-6627
Inst. Accred.: NACCAS (1981/2004)

Jenks Beauty College
535 West Main St., Jenks 74037
Phone: (918) 299-0901

School of Hair Design
1437 SE Washington, Idabel 74745
Type: Private, proprietary
Degrees: C
Phone: (580) 286-7840
Inst. Accred.: NACCAS (1993/1996)

Hugo Campus
116 West Jackson St., Hugo 74743
Phone: (580) 326-7068

Shawnee Beauty College
410 East Main St., Shawnee 74801
Type: Private, proprietary
Degrees: C
Phone: (405) 275-8698
Inst. Accred.: NACCAS (2000/2003)

Southern School of Beauty
40 West Main St., Durant 74701
Type: Private, proprietary
Degrees: C
Phone: (580) 924-1049
Inst. Accred.: NACCAS (1993/2001)

Stanton Beauty College
127 West Main St., Ada 74820
Phone: (580) 924-1049

State Barber & Hair Design College Inc.
2514 South Agnew Ave., Oklahoma City 73108-6220
Type: Private, proprietary
Degrees: C
Phone: (405) 631-8621
Inst. Accred.: ACCSCT (1987/2004)

Stillwater Beauty Academy
1684 Cimarron Plaza, Stillwater 74075
Type: Private, proprietary
Degrees: C
Phone: (405) 377-4100
Inst. Accred.: NACCAS (1990/2005)

Academy of Cosmetology
607 West Grand Ave., Chickasha 73018
Phone: (405) 377-4100

Technical Institute of Cosmetology Arts and Sciences
822 East 6th St., Tulsa 74120
Type: Private, proprietary
Degrees: C
Phone: (918) 660-8828
Inst. Accred.: NACCAS (1992/2002)

Tri County Technology Center
6101 Nowata Rd., Bartlesville 74006
Type: Public, state/local
Degrees: C
URL: http://www.tctc.org
Phone: (918) 331-3333
Inst. Accred.: NCA-CASI (1975/2005)
Prog. Accred.: Practical Nursing

Tulsa Technology Center—Broken Arrow
4600 South Olive Ave., Tulsa 74011-1706
Type: Public, state/local
System: Tulsa Technology Center
Degrees: C
URL: http://www.tulsatech.com
Phone: (918) 828-3000   *Calendar:* Qtr. plan
Inst. Accred.: NCA-CASI (1985/2003)

Tulsa Technology Center—Lemley
3420 South Memorial Dr., Tulsa 74145-1390
Type: Public, state/local
System: Tulsa Technology Center
Degrees: C
URL: http://www.tulsatech.com
Phone: (918) 828-1000   *Calendar:* Qtr. plan
Inst. Accred.: NCA-CASI (1972/2003)
Prog. Accred.: Practical Nursing, Radiography, Surgical Technology

Tulsa Technology Center—Peoria
3850 North Peoria Ave., Tulsa 74106-1619
Type: Public, state/local
System: Tulsa Technology Center
Degrees: C
URL: http://www.tulsatech.com
Phone: (918) 828-2000   *Calendar:* Qtr. plan
Inst. Accred.: NCA-CASI (1977/2003)

Tulsa Technology Center—Riverside

801 East 91st St., Tulsa 74132-4008
Type: Public, state/local
System: Tulsa Technology Center
Degrees: C
URL: http://www.tulsatech.com
Phone: (918) 828-4000   *Calendar:* Qtr. plan
Inst. Accred.: NCA-CASI (1992/2003)
Prog. Accred.: Radiography

Tulsa Welding School

2545 East 11th St., Tulsa 74107-3818
Type: Private, proprietary
Degrees: C
URL: http://www.tulsaweldingschool.com
Phone: (918) 587-6789
Inst. Accred.: ACCSCT (1970/2003)

Jacksonville Campus

3500 Southside Blvd., Jacksonville, FL 32216
Phone: (904) 646-9353

Virgil's Beauty College

111 South Ninth St., Muskogee 74401
Type: Private, proprietary
Degrees: C
Phone: (918) 682-9429
Inst. Accred.: NACCAS (1970/2001)

Wes Watkins Technology Center

7892 Hwy. 9, Wetumka 74883-9522
Type: Public, state/local
Degrees: C
URL: http://www.wwtech.org
Phone: (405) 452-5500   *Calendar:* Sem. plan
Inst. Accred.: NCA-CASI (2001/2005)
Prog. Accred.: Surgical Technology

Woodward Beauty College

502 Texas St., Woodward 73801
Type: Private, proprietary
Degrees: C
Phone: (580) 256-7520
Inst. Accred.: NACCAS (1987/2002)

Yukon Beauty College

1231 South 11th St., Yukon 73099
Type: Private, proprietary
Degrees: C
Phone: (405) 354-3172
Inst. Accred.: NACCAS (1988/2003)

OREGON

Abdill Career College
843 East Main St., Ste. 203, Medford 97504
Type: Private, proprietary
Degrees: C
URL: http://www.abdill.com
Phone: (541) 779-8384
Inst. Accred.: ACCSCT (2003)

Academy of Hair Design, Inc.
305 Ct. St., NE, Salem 97301
Type: Private, proprietary
Degrees: C
Phone: (503) 585-8122
Inst. Accred.: NACCAS (1972/2003)

Airman's Proficiency Center
3565 NE Cornell Rd., Hillsboro 97124
Type: Private, proprietary
Degrees: C
URL: http://www.hillsboro-aviation.com
Phone: (503) 648-2831
Inst. Accred.: ACCSCT (1992/2000)

Australasian College of Health Sciences
5940 SW Hood Ave., Portland 97239
Type: Private, independent
Degrees: C
URL: http://www.achs.edu
Phone: (503) 244-0726
Inst. Accred.: DETC (2003)

Beau Monde College of Hair Design
1221 SW 12th Ave., Portland 97205
Type: Private, proprietary
Degrees: C
URL: http://www.beaumondecollege.com
Phone: (503) 226-1427
Inst. Accred.: NACCAS (1980/2005)

Birthingway College of Midwifery
12113 SE Foster Rd., Portland 97266
Type: Private, independent
Degrees: C
URL: http://www.birthingway.org
Phone: (503) 760-3131
Inst. Accred.: MEAC (2001)

College of Cosmetology, Inc.
357 East Main St., Klamath Falls 97601
Type: Private, proprietary
Degrees: C
URL: http://www.collegeofcos.com
Phone: (541) 882-6644
Inst. Accred.: NACCAS (1977/2003)

College of Hair Design Careers
1684 Clay St., NE, Salem 97301
Type: Private, proprietary
Degrees: C
Phone: (503) 588-5888
Inst. Accred.: NACCAS (1986/2001)

College of Legal Arts
1411 SW Morrison St., Ste. 350, Portland 97205-1971
Type: Private, proprietary
Degrees: C
URL: http://www.collegeoflegalarts.com
Phone: (503) 223-5100
Inst. Accred.: ACICS (1978/2004)

Concorde Career Institute
1425 NE Irving St., Ste. 300, Portland 97232
Type: Private, proprietary
Degrees: C
URL: http://www.concordecareercolleges.com
Phone: (503) 281-4181
Inst. Accred.: ACCSCT (1969/2001)
Prog. Accred.: Dental Assisting, Medical Assisting (CAAHEP)

East-West College of the Healing Arts
525 NE Oregon St., Portland 97232
Type: Private, proprietary
Degrees: C
URL: http://www.eastwestcollege.com
Phone: (503) 231-1500
Inst. Accred.: CMTA (2001/2004, Probation)

Beaverton Campus
The Cedar Hills Shopping Center, 10226 SW Park Way, Beaverton 97225
Phone: (503) 297-3800
Prog. Accred: Massage Therapy

IITR Truck Driving School
15828 SE 114th St., Clackamas 97015
Type: Private, proprietary
Degrees: C
URL: http://www.iitr.net
Phone: (503) 657-8225
Inst. Accred.: ACCET (1986/2001)

Magee Brothers Beaverton School of Beauty
18295 SW Tualatin Valley Hwy., Ste. A, Aloha 97007
Type: Private, proprietary
Degrees: C
Phone: (503) 649-1388
Inst. Accred.: NACCAS (1988/2001)

Montessori Institute Northwest
4506 Southeast Belmont St., Lower Level, Portland 97215-1658
Type: Private, independent
Degrees: C
Phone: (503) 963-8992
Inst. Accred.: MACTE (1996)

Northwest College of Hair Design
8307 SE Monterey Ave., Clackamas 97266
Type: Private, proprietary
Degrees: C
URL: http://www.nwchd.com
Phone: (503) 659-2834
Inst. Accred.: NACCAS (1977/2003)

Hillsboro Campus
210 SE Fourth Ave., Hillsboro 97123
Phone: (503) 844-7320

Northwest Nannies Institute
11830 SW Kerr Pkwy., Ste. 100, Lake Oswego 97035
Type: Private, proprietary
Degrees: C
URL: http://www.nwnanny.com
Phone: (503) 245-5288
Inst. Accred.: ACCET (1988/2005)

Paul Mitchell The School
1180 Commercial St., Astoria 97103
Type: Private, proprietary
System: Paul Mitchell The School—Corporate Office
Degrees: C
URL: http://pmts.paulmitchelltheschool.com
Phone: (503) 325-3163
Inst. Accred.: NACCAS (1985/2003)

Phagans' Beauty College
142 SW Second St., Corvallis 97333
Type: Private, proprietary
Degrees: C
URL: http://www.phagans-schools.com
Phone: (541) 753-6466
Inst. Accred.: NACCAS (1975/2002)

Phagans' Central Oregon Beauty College
355 NE Second St., Bend 97701
Type: Private, proprietary
Degrees: C
URL: http://www.phagans-schools.com
Phone: (541) 382-6171
Inst. Accred.: NACCAS (1975/2002)

Phagans' Grants Pass College of Beauty
304 Agness Ave., Ste. F, Grants Pass 97526
Type: Private, proprietary
Degrees: C
URL: http://www.phagans-schools.com
Phone: (541) 479-6678
Inst. Accred.: NACCAS (1995/2003)

Phagans' Medford Beauty School
2366 Poplar Dr., Medford 97504
Type: Private, proprietary
Degrees: C
URL: http://www.phagans-schools.com
Phone: (541) 772-6155
Inst. Accred.: NACCAS (1967/2004)

Phagans' Newport Academy of Cosmetology Careers
158 East Olive St., Newport 97365
Type: Private, proprietary
Degrees: C
URL: http://www.phagans-schools.com
Phone: (541) 265-3083
Inst. Accred.: NACCAS (1991/2001)

Phagans' School of Beauty
622 Lancaster Dr. NE, Salem 97303
Type: Private, proprietary
Degrees: C
URL: http://www.phagans-schools.com
Phone: (503) 363-6800
Inst. Accred.: NACCAS (1975/2002)

Phagans' School of Hair Design
16550 SE McLoughlin Blvd., Milwaukie 97267
Type: Private, proprietary
Degrees: C
URL: http://www.phagans.com
Phone: (503) 652-2668
Inst. Accred.: NACCAS (1981/2001)

Phagans' School of Hair Design
1542 NE Weidler Ave., Portland 97232
Type: Private, proprietary
Degrees: C
URL: http://www.phagans.com
Phone: (503) 239-0838
Inst. Accred.: NACCAS (1977/2003)

Phagans' Tigard Beauty School
8820 SW Center St., Tigard 97223
Type: Private, proprietary
Degrees: C
URL: http://www.phagansnw.com
Phone: (503) 639-6107
Inst. Accred.: NACCAS (1976/2001)

Roseburg Beauty College, Inc.
700 SE Stephens St., Roseburg 97470
Type: Private, proprietary
Degrees: C
Phone: (541) 673-5533
Inst. Accred.: NACCAS (1986/2001)

Springfield College of Beauty
307 Q St., Springfield 97477
Type: Private, proprietary
Degrees: C
Phone: (541) 746-4473
Inst. Accred.: NACCAS (1966/2004)

Valley Medical College, Inc.
3886 Beverly St., Building I-16, Salem 97305
Type: Private, proprietary
Degrees: C
URL: http://www.valleymedicalcollege.com
Phone: (503) 363-9001
Inst. Accred.: ACCET (2001/2004)

PENNSYLVANIA

The Academy of Creative Hair Design
Narrows Mall, 252 West Side Mall, Kingston 18704
Type: Private, proprietary
Degrees: C
Phone: (570) 288-4574
Inst. Accred.: NACCAS (1984/2004)

Academy of Hair Design
1057 A North Church St., Hazleton 18202
Type: Private, proprietary
Degrees: C
Phone: (570) 459-5501
Inst. Accred.: NACCAS (1981/2001)

Academy of Medical Arts and Business
2301 Academy Dr., Harrisburg 17102-2944
Type: Private, proprietary
Degrees: C
URL: http://www.acadcampus.com
Phone: (717) 545-4747
Inst. Accred.: ACCSCT (1983/2001)

Academy of Vocal Arts
1920 Spruce St., Philadelphia 19103
Type: Private, independent
Degrees: C
URL: http://www.avaopera.com
Phone: (215) 735-1685
Inst. Accred.: NASM (2000)

All-State Career School
97 Second St., North Versailles 15137-1000
Type: Private, proprietary
Degrees: C
URL: http://www.allstatecareer.com
Phone: (412) 823-1818
Inst. Accred.: ACCSCT (1991/2005)

All-State Career School
501 Seminole St., Lester 19029-1827
Type: Private, proprietary
Degrees: C
URL: http://www.allstatecareer.com
Phone: (610) 521-1818
Inst. Accred.: ACCSCT (1987/2003)

> **Baltimore Campus**
> 2200 Broening Hwy., Ste. 160, Baltimore, MD 21224-6658
> *Phone:* (410) 631-1818

Allentown School of Cosmetology, Inc.
1921 Union Blvd., Allentown 18103
Type: Private, proprietary
Degrees: C
Phone: (610) 437-4626
Inst. Accred.: NACCAS (1980/2000)

Allied Medical and Technical Institute
517 Ash St., Scranton 18510-2903
Type: Private, proprietary
Degrees: C
URL: http://www.alliedteched.com
Phone: (570) 558-1818
Inst. Accred.: ACCSCT (1995/2001)

The Alternative Conjunction Clinic and School of Massage Therapy
716 State St., Lemoyne 17043
Type: Private, proprietary
Degrees: C
Phone: (717) 737-6001
Inst. Accred.: NACCAS (1999/2002)

Altoona Beauty School, Inc.
1528 Valley View Blvd., Altoona 16602
Type: Private, proprietary
Degrees: C
Phone: (814) 942-3141
Inst. Accred.: NACCAS (1984/1999)

Antonelli Medical and Professional Institute
1700 Industrial Hwy., Pottstown 19464-9250
Type: Private, proprietary
Degrees: C
Phone: (610) 323-7270
Inst. Accred.: ACCSCT (1989/2004)

Automotive Training Center
114 Pickering Way, Exton 19341-1310
Type: Private, proprietary
Degrees: C
URL: http://www.autotraining.com
Phone: (610) 363-6716
Inst. Accred.: ACCSCT (1973/2003)

Aviation Institute of Maintenance
3001 Grant Ave., Philadelphia 19114
Type: Private, proprietary
Degrees: C
URL: http://www.tidetech.com
Phone: (215) 676-7700
Inst. Accred.: ACCSCT (1994/2003)

Beaver Falls Beauty Academy
720 13th St., Beaver Falls 15010
Type: Private, proprietary
Degrees: C
Phone: (724) 843-7700
Inst. Accred.: NACCAS (1980/2001)

Blackstone Career Institute
218 Main St., PO Box 899, Emmaus 18049
Type: Private, proprietary
Degrees: C
URL: http://www.blackstone.edu
Phone: (610) 967-3323
Inst. Accred.: DETC (2005)

Bucks County School of Beauty Culture, Inc.
1761 Bustleton Pike, Feasterville
Type: Private, proprietary
Degrees: C
URL: http://www.bcsbc.com
Phone: (215) 322-0666
Inst. Accred.: NACCAS (1984/1999)

Butler Beauty School
233 South Main St., Butler 16001
Type: Private, proprietary
Degrees: C
Phone: (412) 287-0708
Inst. Accred.: NACCAS (1987/2002)

Center for Innovative Training and Education
714 Market St., Ste. 433, Philadelphia 19106
Type: Private, independent
Degrees: C
Phone: (215) 922-6555
Inst. Accred.: ACCSCT (1996/2005)

The Chubb Institute—Springfield
400 South State Rd., Marple Crossroads, Springfield
19064
Type: Private, proprietary
System: High-Tech Institute
Degrees: C   *FTE Enroll:* 195
URL: http://www.chubbinstitute.edu
Phone: (610) 338-2300   *Calendar:* Sem. plan
Inst. Accred.: ACICS (1968/2002)

Cherry Hill Campus
The Plaza at Cherry Hill, 2100 Route 38 and Mall Dr.,
Cherry Hill, NJ 08002
Phone: (856) 755-4800

North Brunswick Campus
651 US Route 1, North Brunswick, NJ 08902
Phone: (732) 448-2600

Clearfield Beauty
22 North Third St., Clearfield 16830
Type: Private, proprietary
Degrees: C
Phone: (814) 765-2022
Inst. Accred.: NACCAS (1987/2002)

Computer Learning Network
401 East Winding Hill Rd., Mechanicsburg 17055-4989
Type: Private, proprietary
Degrees: C
URL: http://www.clncamphill.com
Phone: (717) 761-1481
Inst. Accred.: ACCSCT (1985/2004)

Altoona Campus
2900 Fairway Dr., Altoona 16602-4457
Phone: (814) 944-5643

DCI Career Institute
One Data Plaza, 561 Wallace Run Rd., Beaver Falls
15010
Type: Private, proprietary
Degrees: C
URL: http://www.dcitraining.com
Phone: (724) 847-0152
Inst. Accred.: ACCET (1991/2004)

Delaware Valley Academy of Medical and Dental Assistants
3330 Grant Ave., Grant Academy Shopping Center,
Philadelphia 19114
Type: Private, proprietary
Degrees: C
URL: http://www.delawarevalleyacademy.com
Phone: (215) 676-1200
Inst. Accred.: ABHES (1986/2005)

DPT Business School
11000 Roosevelt Blvd., Ste. 200, Philadelphia 19116
Type: Private, proprietary
Degrees: C
URL: http://www.dptschools.com
Phone: (215) 637-8140
Inst. Accred.: ACCET (1990/2005)

Denver Campus
405 South Platte River Dr., Ste. 3A, Denver, CO 80223
Phone: (303) 744-3075

Philadelphia Center City Campus
125-27 North 4th St., Philadelphia 19106
Phone: (215) 627-8140

Education and Technology Institute
Rural Route 12, PO Box 213, Greensburg 15601
Type: Public, independent
Degrees: C
URL: http://www.privateindustrycouncil.com/eti.html
Phone: (724) 836-2600
Inst. Accred.: ACICS (2004)

Empire Beauty School, Inc.—Hanover
Clearview Shopping Center, Carlise St., Hanover 17331
Type: Private, proprietary
Degrees: C
URL: http://www.empirebeauty.com
Phone: (570) 633-6201
Inst. Accred.: NACCAS (1990/2005)

Monroeville Campus
The Plaza on Mall Blvd., Monroeville 15146
Phone: (412) 373-7727

Empire Beauty School—Center City Philadelphia
1522 Chestnut St., Philadelphia 19102
Type: Private, proprietary
Degrees: C
URL: http://www.empirebeauty.com
Phone: (215) 568-3980
Inst. Accred.: NACCAS (1967/2003)

Accredited Non–Degree-Granting Institutions

Empire Beauty School—Exton
454 West Lincoln Hwy., Exton 19341
Type: Private, proprietary
Degrees: C
URL: http://www.empirebeauty.com
Phone: (610) 594-6181
Inst. Accred.: NACCAS (1979/2005)

Empire Beauty School—Harrisburg
3941 Jonestown Rd., Harrisburg 17901
Type: Private, proprietary
Degrees: C
URL: http://www.empirebeauty.com
Phone: (570) 652-8500
Inst. Accred.: NACCAS (1967/2004)

Empire Beauty School—Lancaster
801 Columbia Ave., Wheatland Shopping Center,
Lancaster 17604
Type: Private, proprietary
Degrees: C
URL: http://www.empirebeauty.com
Phone: (570) 394-8561
Inst. Accred.: NACCAS (1972/2004)

Empire Beauty School—Lebanon
1776 Quentin Rd., Cedar Crest Square, Lebanon 17042
Type: Private, proprietary
Degrees: C
URL: http://www.empirebeauty.com
Phone: (570) 272-3323
Inst. Accred.: NACCAS (1973/2004)

Empire Beauty School—Moosic
3409 Birney Ave., Birney Mall, Moosic 18507
Type: Private, proprietary
Degrees: C
URL: http://www.empirebeauty.com
Phone: (570) 343-4730
Inst. Accred.: NACCAS (1971/2004)

Empire Beauty School—Northeast Philadelphia
Knights Rd. Shopping Center, 4026 Woodhaven Rd.,
Philadelphia 19154
Type: Private, proprietary
Degrees: C
URL: http://www.empirebeautyschools.com
Phone: (215) 637-3700
Inst. Accred.: NACCAS (1965/2003)

Empire Beauty School—Pottstown
141 High St., Pottstown 19464
Type: Private, proprietary
Degrees: C
URL: http://www.empirebeauty.com
Phone: (610) 327-1313
Inst. Accred.: NACCAS (1977/2003)

Empire Beauty School—Pottsville
324 North Centre St., Pottsville 17901
Type: Private, proprietary
Degrees: C
URL: http://www.empirebeauty.com
Phone: (570) 622-6060
Inst. Accred.: NACCAS (1975/2005)

Empire Beauty School—Reading
2302 North Fifth St., Reading 19605
Type: Private, proprietary
Degrees: C
URL: http://www.empirebeauty.com
Phone: (610) 372-2777
Inst. Accred.: NACCAS (1967/2004)

Midlothian Campus
10807 Hull St. Rd., Midlothian, VA 23112
Phone: (804) 745-9062

Empire Beauty School—Shamokin Dam
Orchard Hills Plaza, PO Box397, Shamokin Dam 17876
Type: Private, proprietary
Degrees: C
URL: http://www.empirebeauty.com
Phone: (570) 743-1410
Inst. Accred.: NACCAS (1972/2004)

Empire Beauty School—State College
208 West Hamilton St., State College 16801
Type: Private, proprietary
Degrees: C
URL: http://www.empirebeauty.com
Phone: (814) 238-1961
Inst. Accred.: NACCAS (1975/2005)

West Mifflin Campus
2393 Mountain View Dr., West Mifflin 15122
Phone: (412) 653-2870

Empire Beauty School—Warminster
435 York Rd., Warminster 18974
Type: Private, proprietary
Degrees: C
URL: http://www.empirebeauty.com
Phone: (215) 443-8446
Inst. Accred.: NACCAS (1981/2001)

Empire Beauty School—Whitehall
1634 MacArthur Rd., Whitehall 18052
Type: Private, proprietary
Degrees: C
URL: http://www.empirebeauty.com
Phone: (610) 776-8908
Inst. Accred.: NACCAS (1967/2004)

Owings Mills Campus
9616 Reisterstown Rd., Ste. 105, Owings Mills, MD
21117
Phone: (410) 581-2373

Empire Beauty School—Williamsport
1808 East Third St., Williamsport 17701
Type: Private, proprietary
Degrees: C
URL: http://www.empirebeauty.com
Phone: (570) 322-8243
Inst. Accred.: NACCAS (1971/2003)

Pittsburgh Campus
4768 McKnight Rd., Pittsburgh 15237
Phone: (412) 367-9704

Empire Beauty School—York
2592 Eastern Blvd., Kingston Square, York 17402
Type: Private, proprietary
Degrees: C
URL: http://www.empirebeauty.com
Phone: (717) 600-8111
Inst. Accred.: NACCAS (1972/2004)

Richmond Campus
9049 West Broad St., #3, West Broad Commons,
Richmond, VA 23294
Phone: (804) 270-2095

GECAC Training Institute
18 West 9th St., Erie 16501
Type: Private, state-related
Degrees: C
URL: http://www.gecac.org/gti.htm
Phone: (814) 459-5610
Inst. Accred.: ACICS (1996/1999)

Great Lakes Institute of Technology
5100 Peach St., Erie 16509
Type: Private, proprietary
Degrees: C
URL: http://www.glit.org
Phone: (814) 846-6666
Inst. Accred.: ACCSCT (1979/2002 Probation)

Greater Altoona Career and Technology Center
1500 Fourth Ave., Altoona 16602
Type: Public, state/local
Degrees: C
URL: http://www.gactc.com
Phone: (814) 946-8450
Inst. Accred.: COE (2003)
Prog. Accred.: Medical Assisting (CAAHEP)

Greater Johnstown Career and Technology Center
445 Schoolhouse Rd., Johnstown 15904-2998
Type: Public, state/local
Degrees: C
URL: http://www.gjctc.tec.pa.us
Phone: (814) 269-3874
Inst. Accred.: COE (2004)
Prog. Accred.: Practical Nursing, Respiratory Therapy Technology

Harrison Career Institute—Philadelphia
1619 Walnut St., Third Flr., Philadelphia 19103
Type: Private, proprietary
Degrees: C
URL: http://www.harrisoncareerinstitute.com
Phone: (215) 640-0177
Inst. Accred.: ACCSCT (1996/2001)

Lawrenceville Campus
2 Carnegie Rd., Lawrenceville, NJ 08648
Phone: (609) 406-1505

ICT: School of Welding
RR#1, Box 53, Sunbury 17801
Type: Private, proprietary
Degrees: C
Phone: (570) 286-5523
Inst. Accred.: ACCSCT (1981/2002)

Jean Madeline Aveda Institute
315A Bainbridge St., Philadelphia 19147
Type: Private, proprietary
Degrees: C
URL: http://www.jeanmadeline.com
Phone: (215) 238-9998
Inst. Accred.: NACCAS (1989/1997)

JNA Institute of Culinary Arts
1212 South Broad St., Philadelphia 19146
Type: Private, proprietary
Degrees: C
URL: http://www.culinaryarts.com
Phone: (215) 468-8800
Inst. Accred.: ACCSCT (1994/2005)

JR Rodgers and Associates, Inc.
20 Stanwix St., 5th Flr., Pittsburgh 15222
Type: Private, proprietary
Degrees: C
URL: http://www.centralpa.dalecarnegie.com
Phone: (814) 238-2677
Inst. Accred.: ACCET (1997/2001)

Kittanning Beauty School of Cosmetology Arts
120 Market St., Kittanning 16201
Type: Private, proprietary
Degrees: C
Phone: (724) 548-2031
Inst. Accred.: NACCAS (1990/2000)

L.T. International Beauty School
1238 Spring Garden St., Second Flr., Philadelphia 19123
Type: Private, proprietary
Degrees: C
Phone: (215) 922-4478
Inst. Accred.: NACCAS (1997/1999)

Lancaster County Career and Technology Center
1730 Hans-Herr Dr., Willow Street 17584-0527
Type: Public, local
Degrees: C
URL: http://www.lcctc.org
Phone: (717) 464-7050
Inst. Accred.: COE (2001)
Prog. Accred.: Practical Nursing

Lancaster School of Cosmetology, Inc.
50 Ranck Ave., Lancaster 17602
Type: Private, proprietary
Degrees: C
URL: http://www.lancasterschoolofcosmetology.com
Phone: (717) 299-0200
Inst. Accred.: NACCAS (1982/1997)

Lansdale School of Cosmetology, Inc.
215 West Main St., Lansdale 19446
Type: Private, proprietary
Degrees: C
Phone: (215) 362-2322
Inst. Accred.: NACCAS (1984/1999)

Leadership Institute, Inc.
5050 Tilghman St., Ste. 430, Allentown 18104
Type: Private, proprietary
Degrees: C
URL: http://www.dalecarnegie.com
Phone: (610) 783-6500
Inst. Accred.: ACCET (1977/2001)

Leadership Training Services, Inc.
National City Center, 20 Stanwix St., Fifth Flr., Pittsburgh 15222
Type: Private, proprietary
Degrees: C
URL: http://www.pittsburgh.dale-carnegie.com
Phone: (412) 471-3500
Inst. Accred.: ACCET (1975/2001)

LearnQuest
225 City Ave., Ste. 106, Bala Cynwyd 19004
Type: Private, proprietary
Degrees: C
URL: http://www.learnquest.com
Phone: (610) 206-0101
Inst. Accred.: ACCET (2000/2005)

Lebanon County Career and Technology Center
833 Metro Dr., Lebanon 17042
Type: Public, local
Degrees: C
URL: http://www.lcctc.k12.pa.us
Phone: (717) 273-8551
Inst. Accred.: COE (2001)
Prog. Accred.: Practical Nursing

Lebanon County Career School
18 East Weidman St., Lebanon 17046
Type: Private, proprietary
Degrees: C
URL: http://www.sageschools.com
Phone: (717) 274-8804
Inst. Accred.: ACCSCT (1998/2003)

Levittown Beauty Academy
4257 New Falls Rd., Levittown 19056
Type: Private, proprietary
Degrees: C
URL: http://www.levittownbeautyacademy.com
Phone: (215) 943-0298
Inst. Accred.: NACCAS (1978/1999)

Magnolia School
50 East Butler Pike, Ambler 19002
Type: Private, proprietary
Degrees: C
URL: http://www.ababeauty.com
Phone: (215) 643-5994
Inst. Accred.: NACCAS (1982/2001)

American Beauty Academy, Inc.
6912 Frankford Ave., Philadelphia 19135
Phone: (215) 331-1515

Mercer County Career Center
776 Greenville Rd., PO Box 152, Mercer 16137
Type: Public, state/local
Degrees: C
URL: http://www.mccc.onlinecommunity.com
Phone: (724) 662-3000
Inst. Accred.: COE (2003)

National Massage Therapy Institute
10050 Roosevelt Blvd., Philadelphia 19116
Type: Private, proprietary
Degrees: C
Phone: (215) 698-0702
Inst. Accred.: CMTA (1999/2005)

NAWCC School of Horology
514 Poplar St., Columbia 17512-2130
Type: Private, independent
Degrees: C
URL: http://www.nawcc.org
Phone: (717) 684-8261
Inst. Accred.: ACCSCT (1999/2005)

New Castle School of Beauty Culture
314 East Washington St., New Castle 16101
Type: Private, proprietary
Degrees: C
Phone: (724) 654-6611
Inst. Accred.: NACCAS (1975/2000)

North Central Industrial Technical Education Center
PO Box 488, Ridgeway 15853
Type: Private, proprietary
Degrees: C
URL: http://www.ncentral.com/itec
Phone: (814) 773-3162   *Calendar:* Tri. plan
Inst. Accred.: ACCSCT (1999/2004)

Orleans Technical Institute
1330 Rhawn St., Philadelphia 19111-2899
Type: Private, proprietary, two-year
Degrees: C
URL: http://www.orleanstech.org
Phone: (215) 728-4700
Inst. Accred.: ACCSCT (1981/2000)

Penn Foster Career School
925 Oak St., Scranton 18515
Type: Private, proprietary
Degrees: C
URL: http://www.pennfoster.edu
Phone: (570) 342-7701
Inst. Accred.: DETC (1956/2004)

Penn State Cosmetology Academy
2200 East State St., Hermitage 16148
Type: Private, proprietary
Degrees: C
Phone: (724) 347-4503
Inst. Accred.: NACCAS (1982/1997)

Pennsylvania Academy of Cosmetology Arts and Sciences—Dubois
19 North Brady St., Dubois 15801
Type: Private, proprietary
Degrees: C
URL: http://www.pacas.com
Phone: (814) 371-4151
Inst. Accred.: NACCAS (1979/2000)

Pennsylvania Academy of Cosmetology Arts and Sciences—Johnstown
2445 Bedford St., Johnstown 15904
Type: Private, proprietary
Degrees: C
URL: http://www.pacas.com
Phone: (814) 269-3444
Inst. Accred.: NACCAS (1979/2000)

The Pennsylvania Academy of Music
42 North Prince St., Lancaster 17603-3840
Type: Private, independent
URL: http://paacademymusic.com
Phone: (717) 399-9733   *Calendar:* Sem. plan
Inst. Accred.: NASM (2003)

Pennsylvania Gunsmith School
812 Ohio River Blvd., Pittsburgh 15202-2699
Type: Private, proprietary
Degrees: C
URL: http://www.pagunsmith.com
Phone: (412) 766-1812
Inst. Accred.: ACCSCT (1985/2002)

Pennsylvania Institute of Taxidermy
118 Industrial Park Rd., Ebensburg 15931-8947
Type: Private, proprietary
Degrees: C
URL: http://www.studytaxidermy.com
Phone: (814) 472-4510
Inst. Accred.: ACCSCT (1988/2004)

Pennsylvania School of Muscle Therapy, Ltd.
1173 Egypt Rd., PO Box 400, Oaks 19456-0400
Type: Private, proprietary
Degrees: C
URL: http://www.psmt.com
Phone: (610) 666-9060
Inst. Accred.: CMTA (1999/2004)

Pittsburgh Beauty Academy
415 Smithfield St., Pittsburgh 15222
Type: Private, proprietary
Degrees: C
Phone: (412) 471-0270
Inst. Accred.: NACCAS (1967/2000)

Pittsburgh Beauty Academy of New Kensington
851 Fifth Ave., New Kensington 15068
Phone: (724) 337-8500

Pittsburgh Beauty Academy of Charleroi
313 Fifth St., Charleroi 15022
Type: Private, proprietary
Degrees: C
Phone: (724) 483-3551
Inst. Accred.: NACCAS (1974/2001)

Pittsburgh Beauty Academy of Greensburg
1000 West Pittsburgh St., Ste. 5, Greensburg 15601
Type: Private, proprietary
Degrees: C
Phone: (724) 834-3188
Inst. Accred.: NACCAS (1974/2001)

Pittsburgh Fillmmakers' School of Film, Video and Photography
477 Melwood Ave., Pittsburgh 15213
Type: Private, independent
Degrees: C
URL: http://www.pghfilmmakers.org/school.html
Phone: (412) 681-5449
Inst. Accred.: NASAD (1999)

Princeton Information Technology Center
137 South Easton Rd., Glenside 19038
Type: Private, proprietary
Degrees: C
URL: http://www.princetonweb.com
Phone: (215) 576-7377
Inst. Accred.: ACCSCT (2003)

Pruonto's Hair Design Institute
705 12th St., Altoona 16602
Type: Private, proprietary
Degrees: C
Phone: (814) 944-4494
Inst. Accred.: NACCAS (1983/1998)

Punxy Beauty School of Cosmetology Arts and Science
222 North Findley St., Punxsutawney 15767
Type: Private, proprietary
Degrees: C
Phone: (814) 938-8811
Inst. Accred.: NACCAS (1990/2000)

Schuylkill Training and Technology Center
101 Technology Dr., Frackville 17931
Type: Public,(state/local
Degrees: C
URL: http://www.sttc.ptd.net
Phone: (570) 874-1034
Inst. Accred.: COE (2000)
Prog. Accred.: Practical Nursing

Settlement Music School
PO Box 63966, Philadelphia 19147-3966
Type: Private, independent
Degrees: C
URL: http://www.smsmusic.org
Phone: (215) 320-2600
Inst. Accred.: NASM (1989/1996)

Camden School of Musical Arts
531-35 Market St., Camden, NJ 08105
Phone: (856) 541-6375

Germantown Campus
6128 Germantown Ave., Philadelphia 19144
Phone: (215) 320-2610

Jenkintown Music School
515 Meetinghouse Rd., Jenkintown 19046
Phone: (215) 320-2630

Kardon-Northeast Campus
3745 Clarendon Ave., Philadelphia 19114
Phone: (215) 320-2620

Mary Louise Curtis Campus
416 Queen St., Philadelphia 19147
Phone: (215) 320-2600

West Philadelphia Campus
4910 Wynnefield Ave., Philadelphia 19131
Phone: (215) 320-2640

South Hills Beauty Academy
3269 West Liberty Ave., Pittsburgh 15216
Type: Private, proprietary
Degrees: C
Phone: (412) 561-3381
Inst. Accred.: NACCAS (1975/2002)

North Hills Beauty Academy
434 Perry Hwy., Pittsburgh 15229
Phone: (412) 931-8563

Springhouse Computer School
770 Pennsylvania Dr., Ste. 120, Exton 19341-1129
Type: Private, proprietary
Degrees: C
URL: http://www.springhouse.com
Phone: (610) 321-2090
Inst. Accred.: ACCET (2001/2004)

Star Technical Institute—Philadelphia
9121-49 Roosevelt Blvd., Philadelphia 19114
Type: Private, proprietary
Degrees: C
URL: http://www.startechinstitute.com
Phone: (215) 969-5877
Inst. Accred.: ACCSCT (1994/2005)

Edison Campus
1199 Amboy Ave., Tano Mall, Edison, NJ 08837
Phone: (732) 548-6012

Star Technical Institute—Upper Darby
1570 Garrett Rd., Upper Darby 19082
Type: Private, proprietary
Degrees: C
URL: http://www.startechinstitute.com
Phone: (610) 626-2700
Inst. Accred.: ACCSCT (1994/2004)

Egg Harbor Campus
3003 English Creek Ave., Unit 212, Egg Harbor, NJ 08234
Phone: (609) 407-2999

Stroudsburg School of Cosmetology
100 North Eighth St., Stroudsburg 18360
Type: Private, proprietary
Degrees: C
URL: http://www.asc-ssc.com
Phone: (570) 421-3387
Inst. Accred.: NACCAS (1982/2002)

Susquehanna Career and Technology Center
PO Box 100, Schoolhouse Rd., Dimmock 18816-0100
Type: Public, state/local
Degrees: C
Phone: (570) 278-9229
Inst. Accred.: COE (2001)

Synergy Healing Arts Center and Massage School
13593 Monterey Ln., Blue Ridge Summit 17214
Type: Private, proprietary
Degrees: C
URL: http://www.synergymassage.com
Phone: (717) 794-5778
Inst. Accred.: CMTA (2005)

Upper Bucks Institute of Aeronautics
2375 Milford Square Pike, Quakertown 18951
Type: Public, state/local
Degrees: C
URL: http://www.ubaero.org
Phone: (215) 536-6786
Inst. Accred.: COE (2003)

Venus Beauty School
1033 Chester Pike, Sharon Hill 19079
Type: Private, proprietary
Degrees: C
Phone: (610) 586-2500
Inst. Accred.: NACCAS (1976/1997)

Welder Training and Testing Institute
729 East Highland St., Allentown 18103-1263
Type: Private, proprietary
Degrees: C   *Enroll:* 22
URL: http://www.welderinstitute.com
Phone: (215) 437-9720
Inst. Accred.: ACCSCT (1973/2001)

PUERTO RICO

Academia Maison D'Esthetique
904 Ave. Ponce De Leon, Santurce 00907-3330
Type: Private, proprietary
Degrees: C
Phone: (787) 723-4672
Inst. Accred.: NACCAS (1987/1998)

Academia Serrant
8180 Concordia St., Ponce 00717-1568
Type: Private, proprietary
Degrees: C
URL: http://www.serrant.com
Phone: (787) 259-4900
Inst. Accred.: ACCSCT (1995/2002)

Academia Vocational Del Turabo
Campio Alonso #41, Caquas 00725
Type: Private, proprietary
Degrees: C
Phone: (787) 746-6634
Inst. Accred.: ACCSCT (1996/2005)

Advance Tech College
PO Box 6602, Sta. Rosa Unit, Bayamon 00961
Type: Private, proprietary
Degrees: C
Phone: (787) 785-6841
Inst. Accred.: ACCSCT (2003)

Aguadilla Technical College
PO Box 988, Manati 00674
Type: Private, independent
Degrees: C
Phone: (787) 891-6966
Inst. Accred.: ACCSCT (2003)

American Educational College
PO Box 62, Bayamon 00960
Type: Private, proprietary
Degrees: C
Phone: (787) 798-2970
Inst. Accred.: ACICS (1985/2001)

Toa Alta Campus
25 Munoz Rivera St., Toa Alta 00961
Phone: (787) 870-2552

Antilles School of Technical Careers
1851 & 1905 Ave Fernandez Juncos #1851, Santurce 00907
Type: Private, proprietary
Degrees: C
Phone: (787) 268-2244
Inst. Accred.: ABHES (1985/2001)
Prog. Accred.: Practical Nursing

ASPIRA, Inc. de Puerto Rico
8887 St., Km.11.19, San Anton, San Juan 00929-0132
Type: Private, proprietary
Degrees: C
URL: http://www.aspirapr.org
Phone: (787) 641-1985
Inst. Accred.: ACCET (2005)

Automeca Technical College
Carr #2, Km. 14, Bayamon 00960
Type: Private, proprietary
Degrees: C
URL: http://www.automeca.com
Phone: (787) 792-5915
Inst. Accred.: ACCET (1985/2004)

Aguadilla Campus
Parque Industrial La Montana Lot #14, Carretera #459, Km 0.9 Edificio #932, Aguadilla 00605
Phone: (787) 882-2828

Caguas Campus
Calle Munoz Rivera #69, Caguas 00725
Phone: (787) 746-3468

Automeca Technical College—Ponce
452 Calle Villa, Ponce 00731
Type: Private, proprietary
Degrees: C
URL: http://www.automeca.com
Phone: (787) 840-7880
Inst. Accred.: ACCET (1990/2005)

Caguas Institute of Mechanical Technology
Calle B, No. 39-40, Caguas W. Ind. Park, Caguas 00726
Type: Private, proprietary
Degrees: C
Phone: (787) 743-0484
Inst. Accred.: ACCET (1990/2004)

Bayamon Campus
Carr #174 KM 3.0 Sector, Industrial Minillas, Solar 51 Lomas Verd, Bayamon 00856

Mayaguez Campus
Calle Balboa No. 69-71, Caguas West Industrial Park, Mayaguez 00680
Phone: (787) 834-5225

Centro de Estudios Multidisciplinarios
1206 13th St., San Agustin, San Juan 00926
Type: Private, proprietary
Degrees: C
Phone: (787) 765-4210
Inst. Accred.: ACCSCT (1981/2001)

Humacao Campus
6 Dr. Vidal St., Humacao 00791
Phone: (787) 852-5530
Prog. Accred: Practical Nursing

Colegio de las Ciencias Artes y Television
Calle Drive Veve #51 esq Calle Degetau, Bayamon 00960
Type: Private, proprietary
Degrees: C
Phone: (787) 779-2500
Inst. Accred.: ACCSCT (1995/2005)

Colegio Mayor de Tecnologia
Calle Morse, Arroyo 00714
Type: Private, proprietary
Degrees: C
Phone: (787) 839-5266
Inst. Accred.: ACCSCT (1988/2004)

Colegio Tecnico Metropolitano
1251 Franklin D. Roosevelt Ave., Puerto Nuevo 00920
Type: Private, proprietary
Degrees: C
Phone: (787) 781-5140
Inst. Accred.: ACCSCT (1992/2002)

Colegio Tecnologico y Comercial de Puerto Rico
Calle Paz 165 Altos, Aguada 00602
Type: Private, proprietary
Degrees: C
Phone: (787) 868-2688
Inst. Accred.: ACICS (1990/2003)

D'Mart Institute
Centro Commercial San Cristobal, Ste. 202, Barranquitas 00974
Type: Private, proprietary
Degrees: C
Phone: (787) 857-7882
Inst. Accred.: ACCSCT (1991/2004)

EDIC College
Urb. Caguas Norte Calle 8 Esq. 5, PO Box 9120, Caguas 00725
Type: Private, proprietary
Degrees: C   *FTE Enroll:* 578
Phone: (787) 743-0855
Inst. Accred.: ACICS (1990/2002)

Educatinal Technical College
Calle Degetau No. 5, Esq. Betances, Bayamon 00961-6208
Type: Private, proprietary
Degrees: C
Phone: (787) 785-2388
Inst. Accred.: ACCSCT (1988/2004)

Coamo Campus
Calle Ramon Power #5, Coamo 00769
Phone: (787) 825-0379

Emma's Beauty Academy—Juana Diaz
Carr. 149 Barrio Amuelas, Sector Guanabanos, Juana Diaz 00795
Type: Private, proprietary
Degrees: C
Phone: (787) 837-0303
Inst. Accred.: NACCAS (1986/2000)

Emma's Beauty Academy—Mayaguez
Munoz Rivera #9 Oeste, Mayaguez 680
Type: Private, proprietary
Degrees: C
Phone: (787) 833-0980
Inst. Accred.: NACCAS (1979/2002)

Escuela de Peritos Electricistas de Isabel
PO Box 457, Avenida Aguadilla No. 242, Isabel 00662
Type: Private, proprietary
Degrees: C
Phone: (787) 872-1747
Inst. Accred.: ACCSCT (1993/2003)

Escuela Tecnica de Electricidad, Inc.
Calle Villa #190, Ponce 00730-4875
Type: Private, proprietary
Degrees: C
URL: http://www.etepr.edu
Phone: (787) 843-3588
Inst. Accred.: ACCET (1988/2002)

Fajardo Campus
Calle Antonio R Barcelo #6, Fajardo
Phone: (787) 801-5555

Rio Piedras Campus
Ave Campo Rico 767, Country Club, PO Box 29743, 65th Infantry Station, Rio Piedras 00924
Phone: (787) 750-1020

Globelle Technical Institute
Call Marginal #114, Urbanizacion Monte Carlo, Veja Baja 00693
Type: Private, proprietary
Degrees: C
Phone: (787) 858-0236
Inst. Accred.: ACCSCT (1995/1999)

Hispanic American College
Calle Almodovar #25 ESQ Corchado/Dr Barrera #28, Juncos 00777
Type: Private, proprietary
Degrees: C
Phone: (787) 769-4938
Inst. Accred.: ACCSCT (1997/2002)

Institucion Chaviano de Mayaguez
Calle Ramos Antonini, No. 116 Este, Mayaguez 00608-5045
Type: Private, independent
Degrees: C
Phone: (787) 833-2474
Inst. Accred.: ACCSCT (1987/2003)

Institute of Beauty Careers
1315 Ponce de Leon Ave., San Juan 907
Type: Private, proprietary
Degrees: C
Phone: (787) 878-2880
Inst. Accred.: NACCAS (1982/1997)

Manati Campus
Mc Kinley #21, Manati 674
Phone: (787) 854-0019

Instituto de Banca y Comercio
61 Ponce de Leon Ave., Hato Rey 00919
Type: Private, proprietary
Degrees: C
URL: http://www.ibanca.net
Phone: (787) 754-7120
Inst. Accred.: ACICS (1978/2002)

Caguas Campus
52 Ruiz Belvis St., Caguas 00725
Phone: (787) 745-9525

Cayey Campus
Calle José de Diego 164, Cayey 00736
Phone: (787) 738-5555

Fajardo Campus
Calle Muñoz Rivera 205, Fajardo 00738
Phone: (787) 860-6262

Guayama Campus
Calle Derkes 4, Guayama 00784
Phone: (787) 864-3220

Manati Campus
56 Carrera No 2, Manati 00674
Phone: (787) 854-6634

Mayaguez Campus
Calle Méndez Vigo (Este) 155, Mayaguez 00680
Phone: (787) 833-4748

Ponce Campus
Calle Ferrocarril 609, Ponce 00731
Phone: (787) 840-6119

Instituto de Educacion Tecnica Ocupacional "LaReine"
Avenida Colon No. 8A, Manati 00674
Type: Private, proprietary
Degrees: C
Phone: (787) 854-1119
Inst. Accred.: ACCSCT (1991/2001)

Aguadilla Campus
Mercedes Moreno St., #3, Aguadilla 00603
Phone: (787) 819-0222

Instituto de Educacion Vocacional
Carr. 159 km 13.4—HC-03 Box 17272, Corozal 00783
Type: Private, independent
Degrees: C
Phone: (787) 859-6823
Inst. Accred.: ACCSCT (1995/1999, Probation)

Morovis Campus
Calle Comercio, Esquina Betances, Morovis 00687
Phone: (787) 862-1100

Instituto Irma Valentin—Caguas
Calle Betances 39, Caquas 00726
Type: Private, proprietary
Degrees: C
Phone: (787) 703-2705
Inst. Accred.: ACCSCT (1995/2005)

Instituto Irma Valentin—Manati
Calle McKinley #52, Manati 00674
Type: Private, proprietary
Degrees: C
Phone: (787) 854-2316
Inst. Accred.: NACCAS (1993/2004)

Catano Campus
Avenida Barbosa #127, Catano 00674
Phone: (787) 275-2511

Moca Campus
Carr #2 Km 115.2 Bo. Aceitunas, Moca 00676
Phone: (787) 830-0694

Instituto Irma Valentin—Mayaguez
Calle Ernesto Ramos Antonini #12, Mayaguez 00680
Type: Private, proprietary
Degrees: C
Phone: (787) 834-4857
Inst. Accred.: NACCAS (1984/2004)

Aricebo Campus
Carretera #2 Km 78.6 Avenida Miramar, #1070 B Hato Arriba, Arecibo 00612
Phone: (787) 816-5862

Instituto Merlix
Calle Betances No. 24, Box 6241, Station 1, Bayamon 00961-9998
Type: Private, proprietary
Degrees: C
Phone: (787) 786-7035
Inst. Accred.: ACCSCT (1989/2001)

Instituto Postsecundario de Educación a Distancia
PO Box 8517, Carretera 183, Km.1.7, Caguas 00726-8517
Type: Private, independent
Degrees: C
URL: http://www.columbiaco.edu
Phone: (787) 743-4041
Inst. Accred.: DETC (2003)

Instituto Tecnologico Empresarial
22 Munoz Rivera Ave., Trujillo Alto 00976
Type: Private, proprietary
Degrees: C
Phone: (787) 748-5577
Inst. Accred.: ACICS (2002/2004)

Lares Campus
8 Calle Munoz Rivera, Lares 00669-2422
Phone: (787) 748-5577

International Technical College
104 Loaiza Cordero St., San Juan 00918
Type: Private, proprietary
Degrees: C
Phone: (787) 767-8389
Inst. Accred.: ACCSCT (1988/2004)

Liceo de Arte y Tecnologia
PO Box 192346, Hato Rey 00918-2346
Type: Private, proprietary
Degrees: C
URL: http://www.liceopr.com
Phone: (787) 759-9800
Inst. Accred.: ACCSCT (1978/2001)

Liceo de Arte, Disenos y Comercio
Calle Acosta No. 47-49, PO Box 1889, Caguas 00626-1889
Type: Private, proprietary
Degrees: C
Phone: (787) 743-7447
Inst. Accred.: ACCSCT (1990/2003)

MBTI Business Training Institute
1256 Ponce de Leon Ave., Santurce 00907
Type: Private, proprietary
Degrees: C
Phone: (787) 723-9403
Inst. Accred.: ACICS (1969/2002)

Aguadilla Campus
99 Progreso St., Aguadilla 00831
Phone: (787) 891-9403

Modern Hairstyling Institute—Arecibo
Vista Azul Shopping Center, Carr. 2, Km. 30.0 Marginal, Arecibo 612
Type: Private, proprietary
Degrees: C
Phone: (787) 816-2991
Inst. Accred.: NACCAS (1980/2003)

Modern Hairstyling Institute—Bayamon
Dr. Veve #57, Bayamon 960
Type: Private, proprietary
Degrees: C
Phone: (787) 778-0300
Inst. Accred.: ACCSCT (2004)

Modern Hairstyling Institute—Carolina
Avenue Fernandez Juncos # 60, 2nd Flr., Carolina 980
Type: Private, proprietary
Degrees: C
Phone: (787) 752-8383
Inst. Accred.: NACCAS (1980/2003)

Fajardo Campus
Celis Aguilera 51, Fajardo 648
Phone: (787) 863-9922

Monteclaro: Escuela de Hoteleria y Artes Servicios de Hospitalidad
PO Box 447, Palmer 00721
Type: Private, proprietary
Degrees: C
Phone: (787) 888-1135
Inst. Accred.: ACCSCT (1999/2004)

Politec Institute
Guadalupe St. #78, PO Box 335577, Ponce 00733-5577
Type: Private, proprietary
Degrees: C
Phone: (787) 843-0204
Inst. Accred.: ACCSCT (1999/2002)

Ponce Technical School, Inc.
Carretera #2 Avenida Mirimar #1070, Arecibo 00612
Type: Private, proprietary
Degrees: C
Phone: (787) 817-8734
Inst. Accred.: ABHES (1985/2001)

Professional Electrical School
Ramos Velez No. 3, PO Box 1797, Manati 00674-1797
Type: Private, proprietary
Degrees: C
Phone: (787) 854-4776
Inst. Accred.: ACCSCT (1993/2003)

Professional Technical Institution
PO Box 607061-BMS 491, Bayamon 00960
Type: Private, proprietary
Degrees: C
Phone: (787) 740-6810
Inst. Accred.: ACCSCT (1992/2002)

Puerto Rico Barber College
PO Box 985, Calle General Valero #300 (altos), Fajardo 00738
Type: Private, proprietary
Degrees: C
Phone: (787) 863-2970
Inst. Accred.: ACCSCT (1987/2005)

Rogie's School of Beauty Culture
1315 Ponce de Leon Ave., PO Box 19828, San Juan 910
Type: Private, proprietary
Degrees: C
Phone: (787) 722-2293
Inst. Accred.: NACCAS (1987/1999)

Caguas Campus
Paseo Gautier Benitez, # 26 Altos, Caguas 725
Phone: (787) 746-3797

Rosslyn Training Academy of Cosmetology, Inc.
Calle Paz #213, Aguada 00602
Type: Private, proprietary
Degrees: C
Phone: (787) 868-2902
Inst. Accred.: NACCAS (2002)

Star Career College
Degetau St. #19, Bayamon 961
Type: Private, proprietary
Degrees: C
Phone: (787) 740-7490
Inst. Accred.: NACCAS (1991/2001)

Teddy Ulmo Institute
Avenida Fernandez Juncos #1859, Segundo Piso,
Santurce 909
Type: Private, proprietary
Degrees: C
Phone: (787) 727-7313
Inst. Accred.: NACCAS (1980/1998)

Trinity College of Puerto Rico
PO Box 34360, Ponce 00734-4360
Type: Private, proprietary
Degrees: C
Phone: (787) 842-0000   *Calendar:* Qtr. plan
Inst. Accred.: ACICS (1994/2005)

Universal Career Counseling Center
1902 Fernandez Juncos Ave., Santruce 00909
Type: Private, proprietary
Degrees: C
Phone: (787) 728-7268
Inst. Accred.: ACCSCT (1999/2004)

Universal Career Counseling Center
McKinley #113 St., Manati 00674
Type: Private, proprietary
Degrees: C
Phone: (787) 728-7211
Inst. Accred.: ACCSCT (1999/2004)

Humacao Center
#6 Antonio Lopez St., Humacao 00791
Phone: (787) 728-7211

RHODE ISLAND

Arthur Angelo School of Cosmetology and Hair Design
151 Broadway, Providence 2903
Type: Private, proprietary
Degrees: C
URL: http://www.arthurangelo.com
Phone: (401) 272-4300
Inst. Accred.: NACCAS (1977/2003)

Career Education Institute—Lincoln
622 George Washington Hwy., Lincoln Mall, Lincoln 02865
Type: Private, proprietary
System: Lincoln Educational Services
Degrees: C
URL: http://www.computered.com
Phone: (401) 344-2430
Inst. Accred.: ACICS (1997/2005)

Brockton Campus
375 Westgate Dr., Brockton, MA 02401
Phone: (508) 941-0730

Henderson Campus
2290 Corporate Circle, Ste. 100, Henderson, NV 89014
Phone: (702) 269-7600

Marietta Campus
2359 Windy Hill Rd., Ste. 280, Marietta, GA 30067
Phone: (770) 226-0056

Gibbs College—Cranston
85 Garfield Ave., Cranston 02920
Type: Private, proprietary
System: Career Education Corporation
Degrees: C   *Enroll:* 579
URL: http://www.gibbsri.edu
Phone: (800) 614-2888   *Calendar:* Sem. plan
Inst. Accred.: ACICS (1967/2005)

International Yacht Restoration School
449 Thames St., Newport 02840
Type: Private, proprietary
Degrees: C
URL: http://www.iyrs.org
Phone: (401) 848-5777
Inst. Accred.: ACCSCT (2002)

IMEDIA
400 Westminster St., Providence 02903
Type: Private, independent
Degrees: C
URL: http://www.imedia-academy.org
Phone: (401) 383-1900
Inst. Accred.: ACCET (2005)

MotoRing Technical Training Institute
54 Water St., East Providence 02914
Type: Private, proprietary
Degrees: C
URL: http://www.mtti.tec.ri.us
Phone: (401) 434-4840
Inst. Accred.: ACCSCT (1995/2005)

New England Tractor Trailer Training School
600 Moshassuck Industrial Hwy., Pawtucket 02860
Type: Private, proprietary
Degrees: C
URL: http://www.nettts.com
Phone: (401) 725-1220
Inst. Accred.: ACCSCT (1985/2004)

Newport School of Hairdressing, Inc.—Pawtucket
226 Main St., Pawtucket 2860
Type: Private, proprietary
Degrees: C
Phone: (401) 725-6882
Inst. Accred.: NACCAS (1983/2004)

Sawyer School
101 Main St., Pawtucket 02860
Type: Private, proprietary
Degrees: C
Phone: (401) 726-3804
Inst. Accred.: ACICS (1975/2001)

Hamden Campus
1125 Dixwell Ave., Hamden, CT 06514
Phone: (203) 865-2900

Hartford Campus
141 Washington St., Hartford, CT 06106
Phone: (860) 247-4440

Narragansett Campus
Mariner Square, 140 Point Judith Rd., Unit 3a, Narragansett 02882
Phone: (401) 348-8383

New London Campus
PO Box 510, New London, CT 06320
Phone: (860) 439-0065

Providence Campus
550 Hartford Ave., Providence 02909
Phone: (401) 272-3280

Warwick Academy of Beauty Culture
1276 Bald Hill Rd., Ste. 100-110, Warwick 02886
Type: Private, proprietary
Degrees: C
Phone: (401) 826-2022
Inst. Accred.: NACCAS (1981/2001)

SOUTH CAROLINA

Academy of Cosmetology, Inc.
5117 Dorchester Rd., Charleston 29418
Type: Private, proprietary
Degrees: C
Phone: (843) 552-3241
Inst. Accred.: NACCAS (1993/2003)

Academy of Hair Technology
3715 East North St., Ste. F, Greenville 29615
Type: Private, proprietary
Degrees: C
Phone: (864) 322-0300
Inst. Accred.: NACCAS (1987/2001)

Bamberg Job Corps Center
200 South Carlisle St., PO Box 967, Bamberg 29003
Type: Public, federal
Degrees: C
Phone: (803) 245-5101
Inst. Accred.: COE (1994/2000)

Beta Tech
8088 Rivers Ave., North Charleston 29406
Type: Private, proprietary
Degrees: C
URL: http://www.tidetech.com
Phone: (843) 569-0889
Inst. Accred.: ACCSCT (1998/2003)

> **Columbia Campus**
> 6699 Two Notch Rd., Columbia 29223
> *Phone:* (803) 754-7544

Charleston Cosmetology Institute
8484 Dorchester Rd., Charleston 29420
Type: Private, proprietary
Degrees: C
Phone: (843) 552-3670
Inst. Accred.: COE (1986/2003)

Charleston School of Massage
778 Folly Rd., Charleston 29412
Type: Private, proprietary
Degrees: C
URL: http://www.charlestonmassage.com
Phone: (843) 762-7727
Inst. Accred.: ACCET (2001/2004)

Charzanne Beauty College
1549 Hwy. 72, East, Greenwood 29649
Type: Private, proprietary
Degrees: C
Phone: (864) 223-7321
Inst. Accred.: COE (1986/2001)

Columbia Beauty School
1824 Airport Blvd., Cayce 29033
Type: Private, proprietary
Degrees: C
Phone: (803) 796-5252
Inst. Accred.: NACCAS (1979/2004)

Dale Carnegie Training of South Carolina, LLC
4120 Colonel Vanderhorst Circle, Mt. Pleasant 29466
Type: Private, proprietary
Degrees: C
URL: http://www.sc.dalecarnegie.com
Phone: (843) 884-4848
Inst. Accred.: ACCET (1977/2004)

Department of Defense Polygraph Institute
7540 Pickens Ave., Fort Jackson 29207
Type: Public, federal
Degrees: C
URL: http://www.dodpoly.army.mil
Phone: (803) 751-9100   *Calendar:* 3-3 plan
Inst. Accred.: ACICS (2003)

Institute for Guided Studies
190 Battleship Rd., Camden, SC 29020
Type: Private, proprietary
Degrees: C
URL: http://www.igs-montessori.com
Phone: (803) 370-3041
Inst. Accred.: MACTE (2005)

Kenneth Shuler's School of Cosmetology
736 Martintown Rd., North Augusta 29841
Type: Private, proprietary
Degrees: C
Phone: (803) 278-1200
Inst. Accred.: NACCAS (1991/2001)

Kenneth Shulers School of Cosmetology, Nail Design
449 Saint Andrews Rd., Columbia 29210
Type: Private, proprietary
Degrees: C
Phone: (803) 772-6042
Inst. Accred.: NACCAS (1985/2000)

Lacy Cosmetology School
3084 Whiskey Rd., Aiken, 29803
Type: Private, proprietary
Degrees: C
URL: http://www.lacyschools.com
Phone: (803) 648-6181
Inst. Accred.: COE (2000)

Plaza School of Beauty Culture
946 Oakland Ave., Rock Hill 29730
Type: Private, proprietary
Degrees: C
Phone: (803) 328-5166
Inst. Accred.: NACCAS (1996/2002)

Southeastern School of Neuromuscular and Massage Therapy, Inc.
3007 Broad River Rd., Columbia 29210
Type: Private, proprietary
Degrees: C
URL: http://se-massage.com
Phone: (803) 798-8800   *Calendar:* Tri. plan
Inst. Accred.: ACCSCT (2002)

Southeastern School of Neuromuscular and Massage Therapy, Inc.
4600 Goer Dr., Ste. 105, North Charleston 29406
Type: Private, proprietary
Degrees: C
URL: http://charlotte.se-massage.com
Phone: (843) 747-1279   *Calendar:* Tri. plan
Inst. Accred.: ACCSCT (2001)

Strand College of Hair Design
423 79th Ave. West, Myrtle Beach 29572
Type: Private, proprietary
Degrees: C
Phone: (843) 449-1017
Inst. Accred.: NACCAS (1996/2004)

Sumter Beauty College
921 Carolina Ave., Sumter 29150-2871
Type: Private, proprietary
Degrees: C
Phone: (803) 773-7311
Inst. Accred.: COE (1988/2005)

Wackenhut Services, Inc.—Savannah River Site
Building 703-1B, Aiken 29802
Type: Private, proprietary
Degrees: C
URL: http://www.srs.gov/general/people/wackenhut/
   over.htm
Phone: (803) 952-7502
Inst. Accred.: COE (2000)

SOUTH DAKOTA

Black Hills Beauty College
623 Saint Joseph St., Rapid City 57701
Type: Private, proprietary
Degrees: C
Phone: (605) 342-0697
Inst. Accred.: NACCAS (1980/2005)

Headlines Academy, Inc.
508 Sixth St., Rapid City 57701
Type: Private, proprietary
Degrees: C
Phone: (605) 348-4247
Inst. Accred.: NACCAS (1985/2005)

Leadership Training Institute
3109 West 41st St., Ste. 101B, Sioux Falls 57105
Type: Private, proprietary
Degrees: C
URL: http://www.dalecarnegiesd.com
Phone: (605) 332-0699
Inst. Accred.: ACCET (1977/2004)

TENNESSEE

Arnold's Beauty School
1179 South Second St., Milan 38358
Type: Private, proprietary
Degrees: C
Phone: (901) 686-7351
Inst. Accred.: COE (1983/2005)

Diamond Council of America
3212 West End Ave., Ste. 202, Nashville 37203
Type: Private, proprietary
Degrees: C
URL: http://www.diamondcouncil.org
Phone: (615) 385-5301
Inst. Accred.: DETC (1984/2003)

Fayetteville Beauty School
201 South Main Ave., Fayetteville 37334
Type: Private, proprietary
Degrees: C
Phone: (931) 433-1305
Inst. Accred.: NACCAS (1989/2004)

Franklin Academy
633 Mimosa Dr., NW, Cleveland 37320
Type: Private, proprietary
Degrees: C
Phone: (423) 476-3742
Inst. Accred.: COE (1994/2001)

Glyn Ed Newton & Associates, Inc.
1321 Murfreesboro Rd., Ste. 311, Nashville 37217
Type: Private, proprietary
Degrees: C
URL: http://www.nashville.dalecarnegie.com
Phone: (615) 399-5101
Inst. Accred.: ACCET (1976/2005)

Institute for Therapeutic Massage and Movement
2501 McGavock Pike, Ste. 100, Nashville 37214
Type: Private, proprietary
Degrees: C
URL: http://www.itmm.info
Phone: (615) 360-8554
Inst. Accred.: CMTA (2004, Probation)

International Academy of Design and Technology—Nashville
1 Bridgestone Park, Nashville 37214
Type: Private, proprietary
System: Career Education Corporation
Degrees: C
URL: http://www.ladtnashville.com
  Calendar: Qtr. plan
Inst. Accred.: ACICS (2005)

International English Institute
1228 16th Ave. South, Nashville 37212
Type: Private, independent
Degrees: C
URL: http://www.eslnashville.org
Phone: (615) 327-1715
Inst. Accred.: CEA (2000)

Jacobs Creek Job Corps
Civilian Conservation Ctr., 984 Denton Valley Rd., Bristol 37620
Type: Private, federal
Degrees: C
Phone: (423) 878-4021
Inst. Accred.: COE (1997/2003)

Jon Nave University of Cosmetology, Inc.
5128 Charlotte Ave., Nashville 37209
Type: Private, proprietary
Degrees: C
Phone: (615) 383-2255
Inst. Accred.: NACCAS (1980/2000)

Knox International 2000 Beauty College
3641 Brainerd Rd., Ste. F & G, Chattanooga 37411
Type: Private, proprietary
Degrees: C
Phone: (423) 622-1515
Inst. Accred.: NACCAS (2003)

McCollum & Ross, The Hair School
1433 Hollywood Dr., Jackson 38301
Type: Private, proprietary
Degrees: C
URL: http://www.leadersinbeautyed.com
Phone: (901) 427-6642
Inst. Accred.: NACCAS (1989/2004)

Memphis Montessori Institute
8563 Fay Rd., Cordova 38018
Type: Private, independent
Degrees: C
Phone: (901) 751-2000
Inst. Accred.: MACTE (2005)

Middle Tennessee School of Cosmetology
868 A East 10th St., Cookeville 38501
Type: Private, proprietary
Degrees: C
Phone: (931) 526-8735
Inst. Accred.: COE (1994/2000)

Mister Wayne's School of Unisex Hair Design
170 South Willow Ave., Cookeville 38501
Type: Private, proprietary
Degrees: C
Phone: (931) 526-1478
Inst. Accred.: ACCSCT (1984/2004)

Montessori Educators International, Inc.
913 East Cumberland Dr., Louisville 37777
Type: Private, independent
Degrees: C
URL: http://www.korrnet.org/mei_inc
Phone: (865) 970-4322
Inst. Accred.: MACTE (2000)

Nashville College of Medical Careers
1556 Crestview Dr., Madison 37115
Type: Private, proprietary
Degrees: C
Phone: (615) 868-2963
Inst. Accred.: ACCSCT (1990/2005)

New Directions Hair Academy
3744 Old Hickory Blvd., Ste. A-2, Nashville 37209
Type: Private, proprietary
Degrees: C
Phone: (615) 353-8333
Inst. Accred.: NACCAS (1996/2004)

The Beauty Institute
568 Colonial Rd., Memphis 38117
Phone: (901) 761-1888

New Wave Hair Academy—Coleman Road
3250 Coleman Rd., Memphis 38128
Type: Private, proprietary
Degrees: C
URL: http://www.leadersinbeautyed.com
Phone: (901) 323-6100
Inst. Accred.: NACCAS (1987/2004)

New Wave Hair Academy— South Highland Street
804 South Highland St., Memphis 38111
Type: Private, proprietary
Degrees: C
URL: http://www.leadersinbeautyed.com
Phone: (901) 320-9283
Inst. Accred.: NACCAS (1989/2004)

Plaza Beauty School
4682 Spottswood Ave., Memphis 38117
Type: Private, proprietary
Degrees: C
Phone: (901) 761-4445
Inst. Accred.: NACCAS (1966/2003)

Queen City College
1594 Fort Campbell Blvd., Clarksville 37042
Type: Private, proprietary
Degrees: C
Phone: (931) 645-2361
Inst. Accred.: COE (1987/2004)

Reuben Allen College
120 Center Park Dr., Knoxville 37922
Type: Private, proprietary
Degrees: C
Phone: (865) 966-0400
Inst. Accred.: NACCAS (1976/2003)

Seminary Extension Independent Study Institute
901 Commerce St., Ste. 500, Nashville 37203-3631
Type: Private, independent
Degrees: C
URL: http://www.seminaryextension.org
Phone: (615) 242-2453
Inst. Accred.: DETC (1972/2003)

Stylemasters Beauty Academy
223 North Cumberland St., Lebanon 37087
Type: Private, proprietary
Degrees: C
URL: http://www.stylemasters.net
Phone: (615) 444-4908
Inst. Accred.: NACCAS (1991/2001)

Dalton Beauty College
505 Underwood St., Dalton, GA 30721
Phone: (706) 278-1300

Styles and Profiles Beauty College
119 South Second St., PO Box 402, Selmer 38375
Type: Private, proprietary
Degrees: C
Phone: (791) 645-9728
Inst. Accred.: ACCSCT (1996/2001)

Tennessee Academy of Cosmetology— East Shelby Drive
7020 East Shelby Dr., Ste. 104, Memphis 38125
Type: Private, proprietary
Degrees: C
Phone: (901) 757-4166
Inst. Accred.: NACCAS (1990/2000)

Tennessee Academy of Cosmetology— Highway 64
7041 Hwy. 64, Ste. 101, Memphis 38133
Type: Private, proprietary
Degrees: C
Phone: (901) 382-9085
Inst. Accred.: NACCAS (1987/2000)

Tennessee Career College
443 Donelson Pike, Nashville 37214
Type: Private, proprietary
Degrees: C
URL: http://www.tennesseecareercollege.com
Phone: (615) 874-0774
Inst. Accred.: ACCET (1999/2002)

Tennessee School of Beauty, Inc.
4704 Western Ave., Knoxville 37921
Type: Private, proprietary
Degrees: C
URL: http://www.tennesseeschoolofbeauty.com
Phone: (865) 588-7878
Inst. Accred.: NACCAS (1965/2001)

Tennessee School of Massage
556 Colonial Rd., Memphis 38117-4023
Type: Private, proprietary
Degrees: C
URL: http://www.tsom.net
Phone: (901) 843-2706
Inst. Accred.: CMTA (2001)

Tennessee Technology Center at Athens
1635 Vo-Tech Dr., PO Box 848, Athens 37303-0848
Type: Public, state
Degrees: C
URL: http://www.athens.tec.tn.us
Phone: (423) 744-2814
Inst. Accred.: COE (1971/2004)

Tennessee Technology Center at Covington
1600 Hwy. 51 South, PO Box 249, Covington 38019
Type: Public, state
Degrees: C
URL: http://www.covington.tec.tn.us
Phone: (901) 475-2526
Inst. Accred.: COE (1972/2004)

Tennessee Technology Center at Crossville
910 North Miller Ave., PO Box 2959, Crossville 38557
Type: Public, state
Degrees: C
URL: http://www.crossville.tec.tn.us
Phone: (931) 484-7502
Inst. Accred.: COE (1971/2004)
Prog. Accred.: Surgical Technology

Tennessee Technology Center at Crump
3070 Hwy. 64, West, PO Box 89, Crump 38327
Type: Public, state
Degrees: C
URL: http://www.crump.tec.tn.us
Phone: (901) 632-3393
Inst. Accred.: COE (1974/2005)

Tennessee Technology Center at Dickson
740 Hwy. 46, Dickson 37055
Type: Public, state
Degrees: C
URL: http://www.dickson.tec.tn.us
Phone: (615) 441-6220
Inst. Accred.: COE (1974/2000)
Prog. Accred.: Dental Assisting

Tennessee Technology Center at Elizabethton
426 Hwy.91, PO Box 789, Elizabethton 37644
Type: Public, state
Degrees: C
URL: http://www.elizabethton.tec.tn.us
Phone: (423) 543-0070
Inst. Accred.: COE (1973/2005)

Tennessee Technology Center at Harriman
1745 Harriman Hwy., PO Box 1109, Harriman 37748-1109
Type: Public, state
Degrees: C
URL: http://www.harriman.tec.tn.us
Phone: (856) 882-6703
Inst. Accred.: COE (1973/2005)

Tennessee Technology Center at Hartsville
716 McMurry Blvd., Hartsville 37074
Type: Public, state
Degrees: C
URL: http://www.hartsville.tec.tn.us
Phone: (615) 374-2147
Inst. Accred.: COE (1971/2004)

Tennessee Technology Center at Hohenwald
813 West Main St., Hohenwald 38462-2201
Type: Public, state
Degrees: C
URL: http://www.hohnenwald.tec.tn.us
Phone: (931) 796-5351
Inst. Accred.: COE (1972/2004)

Tennessee Technology Center at Jacksboro
265 Elkins Rd., PO Box 419, Jacksboro 37757
Type: Public, state
Degrees: C
URL: http://www.jacksboro.tec.tn.us
Phone: (423) 566-9629
Inst. Accred.: COE (1972/2004)

Tennessee Technology Center at Jackson
2468 Technology Center Dr., Jackson 38301
Type: Public, state
Degrees: C
URL: http://www.jackson.tec.tn.us
Phone: (901) 424-0691
Inst. Accred.: COE (1972/2004)
Prog. Accred.: Surgical Technology

Tennessee Technology Center at Knoxville
1100 Liberty St., Knoxville 37919
Type: Public, state
Degrees: C
URL: http://www.knoxville.tec.tn.us
Phone: (865) 546-5567
Inst. Accred.: COE (1971/2004)
Prog. Accred.: Dental Assisting, Surgical Technology

Tennessee Technology Center at Livingston
740 High Tech Dr., PO Box 219, Livingston 38570
Type: Public, state
Degrees: C
URL: http://www.livingston.tec.tn.us
Phone: (931) 823-5525
Inst. Accred.: COE (1971/2004)
Prog. Accred.: Medical Assisting (CAAHEP)

Tennessee Technology Center at McKenzie
16940 Highland Dr., PO Box 427, McKenzie 38201
Type: Public, state
Degrees: C
URL: http://www.mckenzie.tec.tn.us
Phone: (901) 352-5364
Inst. Accred.: COE (1971/2005)

Tennessee Technology Center at McMinnville
241 Vo-Tech Dr., McMinnville 37110
Type: Public, state
Degrees: C
URL: http://www.mcminnville.tec.tn.us
Phone: (931) 473-5587
Inst. Accred.: COE (1971/2005)

Tennessee Technology Center at Memphis
550 Alabama Ave., Memphis 38105-3604
Type: Public, state
Degrees: C
URL: http://www.memphis.tec.tn.us
Phone: (901) 543-6100
Inst. Accred.: COE (1970/2002)
Prog. Accred.: Dental Assisting, Respiratory Therapy
Technology, Surgical Technology

Aviation Maintenance Campus
3435 Tchulahoma Rd., Memphis 38116
Phone: (901) 345-1995

Tennessee Technology Center at Morristown
821 West Louise Ave., Morristown 37813-2094
Type: Public, state
Degrees: C
URL: http://www.morristown.tec.tn.us
Phone: (423) 586-5771
Inst. Accred.: COE (1971/2004)

Surgoinsville Campus
323 Phipps Bend Rd., Surgoinsville 37873
Phone: (423) 272-2100

Tennessee Technology Center at Murfreesboro
1303 Old Fort Pkwy., Murfreesboro 37129-3312
Type: Public, state
Degrees: C
URL: http://www.murfreesboro.tec.tn.us
Phone: (615) 898-8010
Inst. Accred.: COE (1980/2001)
Prog. Accred.: Dental Assisting

Tennessee Technology Center at Nashville
100 White Bridge Rd., Nashville 37209
Type: Public, state
Degrees: C
URL: http://www.nashville.tec.tn.us
Phone: (615) 741-1241
Inst. Accred.: COE (1972/2004)

Cockrill Ben Campus
Cockrill Ben Industrial Park, 7204 Cockrill Ben Rd.,
Nashville 37209
Phone: (615) 350-6224

Tennessee Technology Center at Newbern
340 Washington St., Newbern 38059
Type: Public, state
Degrees: C
URL: http://www.newbern.tec.tn.us
Phone: (731) 627-2511
Inst. Accred.: COE (1972/2004)

Tennessee Technology Center at Oneida/Huntsville
355 Scott High Dr., Huntsville 37756-4120
Type: Public, state
Degrees: C
URL: http://www.huntsville.tec.tn
Phone: (423) 663-4900
Inst. Accred.: COE (1973/2005)

Tennessee Technology Center at Paris
312 South Wilson St., Paris 38242
Type: Public, state
Degrees: C
URL: http://www.paris.tec.tn.us
Phone: (901) 644-7365
Inst. Accred.: COE (1974/2004)

Tennessee Technology Center at Pulaski
1233 East College St., PO Box 614, Pulaski 38478-0614
Type: Public, state
Degrees: C
URL: http://www.pulaski.tec.tn.us
Phone: (931) 424-4014
Inst. Accred.: COE (1973/2005)

Tennessee Technology Center at Ripley
North Industrial Park, 127 Industrial Dr., Ripley 38063
Type: Public, state
Degrees: C
URL: http://www.ripley.tec.tn.us
Phone: (731) 635-3368
Inst. Accred.: COE (1973/2005)

Tennessee Technology Center at Shelbyville
1405 Madison St., Shelbyville 37160
Type: Public, state
Degrees: C
URL: http://www.shelbyville.tec.tn.us
Phone: (931) 685-5013
Inst. Accred.: COE (1972/2005)

Tennessee Technology Center at Whiteville
1685 Hwy. 64, PO Box 489, Whiteville 38075
Type: Public, state
Degrees: C
URL: http://www.whiteville.tec.tn.us
Phone: (901) 254-8521
Inst. Accred.: COE (1980/2002)

Volunteer Beauty Academy of Lawrenceburg
5666 Nolensville Rd., Nashville 37211
Type: Private, proprietary
Degrees: C
Phone: (615) 331-9111
Inst. Accred.: NACCAS (1986/2001)

Volunteer Beauty Academy—Dyersburg
1057 A Vendell Rd., Dyersburg 38024
Type: Private, proprietary
Degrees: C
Phone: (901) 285-1453
Inst. Accred.: NACCAS (1984/2004)

Volunteer Beauty Academy—Madison
1791 North Gallatin Rd., Madison 37115
Type: Private, proprietary
Degrees: C
Phone: (615) 860-4200
Inst. Accred.: NACCAS (1984/2004)

William R. Moore College of Technology
1200 Poplar Ave., Memphis 38104
Type: Private, independent
Degrees: C
URL: http://www.williammoore.org
Phone: (901) 726-1977
Inst. Accred.: COE (1971/2003)

World Class University
3532 West Hamilton Rd., Nashville 37218
Type: Private, proprietary
Degrees: C
Phone: (615) 876-2527
Inst. Accred.: NACCAS (2002)

TEXAS

A New Beginning School of Massage
2525 Wallingwood Dr., Ste. 1501, Austin 78746
Type: Private, proprietary
Degrees: C
URL: http://www.nbegin.com
Phone: (512) 306-0975
Inst. Accred.: ACCSCT (2002)

Academy of Cosmetology
5416 Manchaca Rd., Austin 78745
Type: Private, proprietary
Degrees: C
Phone: (512) 444-2249
Inst. Accred.: NACCAS (2002/2005)

Academy of Hair Design
744 F. M. 1960 West, Ste. G, Houston 77090
Type: Private, proprietary
Degrees: C
Phone: (281) 893-0980
Inst. Accred.: NACCAS (1986/2001)

Academy of Hair Design, Inc.
3141 College St., Ste. A-10, Beaumont 77701
Type: Private, proprietary
Degrees: C
Phone: (409) 813-3100
Inst. Accred.: NACCAS (1997/2005)

Academy of Hair Design, Inc.
512 South Chestnut, Lufkin 75901
Type: Private, proprietary
Degrees: C
Phone: (409) 634-8440
Inst. Accred.: NACCAS (1997/2005)

Jasper Campus
348 Springhill St., Jasper 75951
Phone: (409) 384-8200

Advanced Barber College and Hair Design
2818 South International, FM 1015, Weslaco 78596
Type: Private, proprietary
Degrees: C
Phone: (956) 969-0341
Inst. Accred.: COE (1999/2003)

Aeronautical Institute of Technologies
2502 West Ledbetter Dr., Dallas 75233
Type: Private, proprietary
Degrees: C
URL: http://fixthatplane.com
Phone: (214) 333-9711
Inst. Accred.: ACCSCT (2001/2004)

AIMS Academy
1106 North Hwy. 360, Ste. 305, Grand Prairie 75050
Type: Private, proprietary
Degrees: C
URL: http://www.aimsacademy.com
Phone: (972) 988-3202
Inst. Accred.: COE (1990/2005)

Dallas Campus
3300 Oak Lawn Ave. Ste. 100, Dallas 75219
Phone: (214) 520-6848

Allied Career Center
1933 East Frankford Rd., Ste. 110, Carrollton 75007
Type: Private, proprietary
Degrees: C
URL: http://www.alliedcareercenter.com
Phone: (972) 939-5482
Inst. Accred.: ACCET (2005)

Dallas Campus
9330 Amberton Pkwy., Ste. 1395, Dallas 75243
Phone: (972) 939-5482

AmesEd
2880 LBJ Freeway, Ste. 406, Dallas 75234
Type: Private, proprietary
Degrees: C
Phone: (972) 241-4005
Inst. Accred.: COE (2003)

American Commercial College
402 Butternut St., Abilene 79602
Type: Private, proprietary
Degrees: C
URL: http://www.acc-careers.com
Phone: (915) 672-8495
Inst. Accred.: ACICS (1970/2004)

American Commercial College
2115 East Eighth St., Odessa 79761
Type: Private, proprietary
Degrees: C
URL: http://www.acc-careers.com
Phone: (915) 332-0768
Inst. Accred.: ACICS (1970/2002)

American Commercial College
3177 Executive Dr., San Angelo 76904
Type: Private, proprietary
Degrees: C
URL: http://www.acc-careers.com
Phone: (915) 942-6797
Inst. Accred.: ACICS (1976/2002)

American Commercial College
2007 34th St., Lubbock 79411
Type: Private, proprietary
Degrees: C
URL: http://www.acc-careers.com
Phone: (806) 747-4339
Inst. Accred.: ACICS (1982/2003)

Shreveport Campus
3014 Knight St., Shreveport, LA 71105
Phone: (318) 861-2112

Wichita Falls Campus
4317 Barnett Rd., Wichita Falls 76310
Phone: (940) 691-0454

Anamarc Educational Institute
3210 Dyer St., El Paso 79930-6230
Type: Private, proprietary
Degrees: C
URL: http://www.anamarc.com
Phone: (915) 351-8100
Inst. Accred.: ACICS (2003)

Arlington Career Institute
901 Ave. K., Grand Prairie 75050
Type: Private, proprietary
Degrees: C
URL: http://www.themetro.com/aci
Phone: (972) 647-1607
Inst. Accred.: ACCSCT (1987/2003)

Arlington Medical Institute
2301 North Collins, Ste. 100, Arlington 76011
Type: Private, proprietary
Degrees: C
Phone: (817) 265-0706
Inst. Accred.: ABHES (1996/2004)

Astrodome Dental Career Center
2646 South Loop West, Ste. 415, Houston 77054
Type: Private, proprietary
Degrees: C
URL: http://www.astrodomecareercenter.com
Phone: (713) 664-5300
Inst. Accred.: COE (2001)

ATI Career Training Center
235 NE Loop 820, Ste. 110, Hurst 76053-7396
Type: Private, proprietary
Degrees: C
URL: http://www.aticareertraining.edu
Phone: (817) 284-1141
Inst. Accred.: ACCSCT (1986/2005)

ATI Technical Training Center
6627 Maple Ave., Dallas 75235-9990
Type: Private, proprietary
Degrees: C
URL: http://www.aticareertraining.edu
Phone: (214) 352-2222
Inst. Accred.: ACCSCT (1975/1999)

Baldwin Beauty School
3005 South Lamar, Ste. 103, Austin 78704
Type: Private, proprietary
Degrees: C
Phone: (512) 441-6898
Inst. Accred.: NACCAS (1978/2004)

Burnet Road Campus
8440 Burnet Rd., Austin 78758
Phone: (512) 458-4127

Behold! Beauty Academy
9937 Homestead Rd., Houston 77016
Type: Private, proprietary
Degrees: C
Phone: (713) 635-5252
Inst. Accred.: NACCAS (2001)

Bilingual Education Institute
8989 Westheimer Rd., Ste. 110, PO Box 570596, Houston 77063
Type: Private, proprietary
Degrees: C
URL: http://www.aetas.com
Phone: (713) 789-4555
Inst. Accred.: ACCET (1997/2005)

Bradford School of Business
4669 Southwest Freeway, Ste. 300, Houston 77027
Type: Private, proprietary
Degrees: C
URL: http://www.bradfordschoolhouston.edu
Phone: (713) 629-8940
Inst. Accred.: ACICS (1980/2004)
Prog. Accred.: Medical Assisting (CAAHEP)

Capitol City Careers
5424 Hwy. 290 West, Ste. 200, Austin 78745
Type: Private, proprietary
Degrees: C
Phone: (512) 892-4270
Inst. Accred.: COE (1989/2004)

Capitol City Trade and Technical School
205 East Riverside Dr., Austin 78704
Type: Private, proprietary
Degrees: C
URL: http://www.capcitytradetech.com
Phone: (512) 444-3257
Inst. Accred.: COE (1979/2000)

Career Academy
32 Oaklawn Village, Texarkana 75501
Type: Private, proprietary
Degrees: C
Phone: (903) 832-1021
Inst. Accred.: COE (1988/2001)

Career Centers of Texas—El Paso
8360 Burnham Rd., Ste. 100, El Paso 79907
Type: Private, proprietary
System: Kaplan Higher Education Corporation
Degrees: C
URL: http://www.careercenters.edu
Phone: (915) 595-1935
Inst. Accred.: ACCSCT (1995/2003)
Prog. Accred.: Medical Assisting (CAAHEP)

Brownsville Campus
1900 North Expressway, Brownsville 78521
Phone: (956) 547-8200

Career Point Institute
485 Spencer Ln., San Antonio 78201
Type: Private, proprietary
Degrees: C
URL: http://www.career-point.org
Phone: (210) 732-3000
Inst. Accred.: ACICS (1988/2004)

Tulsa Campus
3138 South Garnett Rd., Tulsa, OK 74146-1933
Phone: (918) 622-4100

Career Quest
5430 Fredericksburg, Ste. 310, San Antonio 78229
Type: Private, proprietary
Degrees: C
Phone: (210) 366-2701
Inst. Accred.: COE (1999/2005)

Career Tech Institute
2715 Cornerstone Blvd., Edinburg 78539
Type: Private, proprietary
Degrees: C
Phone: (956) 687-8138
Inst. Accred.: ABHES (1998/2001)

Careers Unlimited
10058 Long Point, Houston 77055
Type: Private, proprietary
Degrees: C
Phone: (713) 464-0770
Inst. Accred.: ACCSCT (1994/2005)

Careers Unlimited
335 South Bonner St., Tyler 75702
Type: Private, proprietary
Degrees: C
Phone: (903) 593-4424
Inst. Accred.: ACCSCT (1993/2003)

Center of English Language
3434 Forest Ln., Dallas 75234
Type: Private, proprietary
Degrees: C
URL: http://www.english-classes.com
Phone: (214) 696-0027
Inst. Accred.: ACCET (2001/2005)

Central Texas Beauty College
2010 South 57th St., Temple 76501
Type: Private, proprietary
Degrees: C
Phone: (254) 773-9911
Inst. Accred.: NACCAS (1985/2000)

Central Texas Beauty College #2
1350 East Palm Valley Rd., Ste. A, Round Rock 78664
Type: Private, proprietary
Degrees: C
Phone: (512) 244-2235
Inst. Accred.: NACCAS (1977/2000)

Central Texas Commercial College
9400 North Central Expressway, Ste. 200, Dallas 75231-4347
Type: Private, proprietary
Degrees: C
Phone: (214) 368-3680
Inst. Accred.: ACICS (1971/2004)

Charles & Sue's School of Hair Design
1711 Briarcrest Dr., Bryan 77802
Type: Private, proprietary
Degrees: C
Phone: (979) 776-4375
Inst. Accred.: NACCAS (1976/2001)

Circle J Beauty School
1611-E Spencer, South Houston 77587
Type: Private, proprietary
Degrees: C
Phone: (713) 946-5055
Inst. Accred.: NACCAS (1990/2000)

Jackson Beauty School
223 West Main, Ste. C, League City 77573
Phone: (281) 332-6604

Computer Labs, Inc.
1462A Lionel Dr., El Paso 79936
Type: Private, proprietary
Degrees: C
URL: http://geocities.com/computerlabsinc
Phone: (915) 591-8899
Inst. Accred.: ACICS (2003)

Concorde Career Institute—Arlington
601 Ryan Plaza Dr., Ste. 200, Arlington 76011
Type: Private, proprietary
Degrees: C
URL: http://www.concordecareercolleges.com
Phone: (817) 261-1594
Inst. Accred.: ABHES (1998/2001)

Conlee's College of Cosmetology
402 Quinlan St., Kerrville 78028
Type: Private, proprietary
Degrees: C
Phone: (830) 896-2380
Inst. Accred.: NACCAS (1976/2000)

Coryell Cosmetology College
608 East Leon St., Galesville 76528-2036
Type: Private, proprietary
Degrees: C
Phone: (254) 248-1716
Inst. Accred.: COE (2000)

Cosmetology Career Center
8030 Spring Valley Rd., Dallas 75240
Type: Private, proprietary
Degrees: C
URL: http://www.cosmetologycareers.com
Phone: (972) 669-0494
Inst. Accred.: NACCAS (1976/2001)

Culinary Academy of Austin
2823 Hancock Dr., Austin 78731
Type: Private, proprietary
Degrees: C
URL: http://www.culinaryacademyofaustin.com
Phone: (512) 451-5743
Inst. Accred.: COE (2002)

Dallas Barber and Stylist College
8224 Park Ln., Suite 120, Dallas 75231
Type: Private, proprietary
Degrees: C
Phone: (214) 360-9570
Inst. Accred.: COE (2002)

Dallas Institute of Funeral Services
3909 South Buckner Blvd., Dallas 75227
Type: Private, independent
Degrees: C
URL: http://www.dallasinstitute.edu
Phone: (214) 388-5466   *Calendar:* Qtr. plan
Inst. Accred.: ABFSE (1947/2003)

Dallas Montessori Teacher Education Programs
5757 Samuell Blvd., Ste. 200, Dallas 75227
Type: Private, independent
Degrees: C
URL: http://www.dallasmontessori.com
Phone: (214) 388-0091
Inst. Accred.: MACTE (1998/2005)

David L. Carrasco Job Corps Center
11155 Gateway West, El Paso 79935
Type: Public, federal
Degrees: C
URL: http://www.jobcorpsworks.org
Phone: (915) 594-0022
Inst. Accred.: COE (1986/2005)

Defense Language Institute English Language Center
2235 Andrews Ave., Lackland AFB 78236-5514
Type: Public, federal
Degrees: C
URL: http://www.dlielc.org
Phone: (210) 671-3540
Inst. Accred.: CEA (2000)

English Language Specialists
2323 South Voss, Ste. 580, Houston 77057
Type: Private, proprietary
Degrees: C
URL: http://www.el-inc.com
Phone: (713) 977-7767
Inst. Accred.: ACCET (1998/2001)

Exposito School of Hair Design
3710 Mockingbird Ln., Amarillo 79109
Type: Private, proprietary
Degrees: C
Phone: (806) 355-9111
Inst. Accred.: NACCAS (1984/2004)

Faris Computer School
1119 Kent Ave., Nederland 77627
Type: Private, proprietary
Degrees: C
URL: http://setx.com/fcsweb
Phone: (409) 722-4072
Inst. Accred.: COE (1997/2003)

Fort Worth Beauty School
2820 Hemphill St., Fort Worth 76110
Type: Private, proprietary
Degrees: C
Phone: (817) 924-4280
Inst. Accred.: NACCAS (1978/2002)

Franklin Beauty School #2
4965 Martin Luther King Blvd., Houston 77021
Type: Private, proprietary
Degrees: C
Phone: (713) 645-9060
Inst. Accred.: NACCAS (1976/2003)

Gulf Coast Trades Center
143 Forest Service Rd., Ste. 233, New Waverly 77358
Type: Private, independent
Degrees: C
Phone: (409) 344-6677
Inst. Accred.: COE (1984/2000)

HandsOn Therapy School of Massage
1804 North Galloway Ave., Mesquite 75149-2294
Type: Private, proprietary
Degrees: C
URL: http://www.handsontherapyschools.com
Phone: (972) 285-6133
Inst. Accred.: ACCSCT (2005)

High-Tech Institute—Dallas
4250 North Beltline Rd., Irving 75038-4201
Type: Private, proprietary
System: High-Tech Institute
Degrees: C
URL: http://www.hightechinstitute.edu
Phone: (972) 871-2824
Inst. Accred.: ACCSCT (2000/2003)

House of Tutors Learning Centers USA, Inc
2400 Pearl St., Austin 78705
Type: Private, proprietary
Degrees: C
URL: http://www.houseoftutors.com
Phone: (512) 472-6996
Inst. Accred.: ACCET (2003)

Houston Ballet's Ben Stevenson Academy
1921 West Bell St., PO Box 130487, Houston 77219-0487
Type: Private, independent
Degrees: C
URL: http://www.houstonballet.org
Phone: (713) 523-6300 x201   *Calendar:* Sem. plan
Inst. Accred.: NASD (1985/2005)

Houston Montessori Center
9601 Katy Freeway, Ste. 350, Houston 77024-1330
Type: Private, independent
Degrees: C
URL: http://www.houstonmontessoricenter.org
Phone: (713) 465-7670
Inst. Accred.: MACTE (2001)

Houston Training Schools
709 Shotwell St., Houston 77020-4813
Type: Private, proprietary
Degrees: C
Phone: (713) 675-4300
Inst. Accred.: COE (1979/2005)

Gulf Freeway Campus
6969 Gulf Freeway, Ste. 200, Houston 77087
Phone: (713) 649-5050

Houston's Training and Education Center
7457 Harwin Dr., Suite 190, Houston 77036
Type: Private, proprietary
Degrees: C
URL: http://www.houston-tec.com
Phone: (713) 783-2221
Inst. Accred.: COE (2004)

ICC Technical Institute
3333 Fannin St., Ste. 203, Houston 77004
Type: Private, independent
Degrees: C
Phone: (713) 522-7799
Inst. Accred.: COE (1995/2002)

Institute of Cosmetology
7011 Harwin Dr., Ste. 100, Houston
Type: Private, proprietary
Degrees: C
Phone: (713) 783-9988
Inst. Accred.: NACCAS (1988/2003)

Inter-American Air Forces Academy
2431 Carswell Ave., Lackland AFB 78236-2247
Type: Public, federal
Degrees: C
URL: http://www.lackland.af.mil/iaafa
Phone: (210) 671-0215
Inst. Accred.: COE (2003)

Interactive Learning Systems
8585 North Stemmons Freeway, Ste. M-29, Dallas 75247
Type: Private, proprietary
Degrees: C
URL: http://www.ict-ils.edu
Phone: (214) 637-3377
Inst. Accred.: COE (1989/2004)

Houston Campus
6200 Hillcroft Ave., Houston 77081
Phone: (713) 782-5161

International Beauty College #3
1225 Beltline Rd., Ste. 7, Garland 75040
Type: Private, proprietary
Degrees: C
Phone: (972) 530-1103
Inst. Accred.: NACCAS (1987/2002)

International Beauty College #4
2716 West Irving Blvd., Irving 75061
Type: Private, proprietary
Degrees: C
Phone: (972) 255-1176
Inst. Accred.: NACCAS (1976/2005)

International Renowned Beauty Academy
3536 East Lancaster Ave., Fort Worth 76103
Type: Private, proprietary
Degrees: C
Phone: (817) 531-3716
Inst. Accred.: NACCAS (2002)

Iverson Institute of Court Reporting
1601 Ivy Ln., Arlington 76011
Type: Private, proprietary
Degrees: C
Phone: (817) 274-6465
Inst. Accred.: COE (1988/2005)

Jay's Technical Institute
10750 South Gessner, Houston 77071
Type: Private, proprietary
Degrees: C
Phone: (713) 772-2410
Inst. Accred.: COE (2002)

John M. Jennings and Associates, Inc.
16990 North Dallas Pkwy., Ste. 108, Dallas 75248-1926
Type: Private, proprietary
Degrees: C
URL: http://www.texas.dalecarnegie.com
Phone: (972) 702-9600
Inst. Accred.: ACCET (1996/2001)

Jones Beauty College
10909 Webb Chapel Rd., Ste. 129, Dallas 75229
Type: Private, proprietary
Degrees: C
Phone: (214) 956-0088
Inst. Accred.: NACCAS (1991/2001)

Jones Beauty College #2
311-A East Hwy. 303, Grand Prairie 75051
Phone: (214) 956-0088

Kussad Institute of Court Reporting
2800 South IH-35, Ste. 110, Austin 78704
Type: Private, proprietary
Degrees: C
Phone: (512) 443-7286
Inst. Accred.: COE (2001)

Language Plus, Inc.
4110 Rio Bravo, Ste. 202, El Paso 79902
Type: Private, proprietary
Degrees: C
URL: http://www.languageplus.com
Phone: (915) 544-8600
Inst. Accred.: ACCET (1998/2004)

Laredo Beauty College
3002 North Malinche Ave., Laredo 78043
Type: Private, proprietary
Degrees: C
Phone: (956) 723-2059
Inst. Accred.: NACCAS (1974/2000)

Leadership Excellence, Inc.
9100 Southwest Freeway, Ste. 200, Houston 77074
Type: Private, proprietary
Degrees: C
URL: http://www.houston.dalecarnegie.com
Phone: (713) 779-8080
Inst. Accred.: ACCET (1975/2005)

Leadership Training
1616 South Kentucky, Building A, Ste. 110, Amarillo 79102
Type: Private, proprietary
Degrees: C
URL: http://www.dalecarnegie.com
Phone: (806) 355-5033
Inst. Accred.: ACCET (1977/2003)

Lincoln Technical Institute
2501 East Arkansas Ln., Grand Prairie 75051-7206
Type: Private, proprietary
System: Lincoln Educational Services
Degrees: C
URL: http://www.lincolntech.com
Phone: (972) 660-5701
Inst. Accred.: ACCSCT (1968/2001)

Lubbock Hair Academy
2844 34th St., Lubbock 79410-3524
Type: Private, proprietary
Degrees: C
URL: http://www.lubbockhairacademy.com
Phone: (806) 795-0806
Inst. Accred.: COE (2000)

Lumberton Adult Educational Center
103 South LHS Dr., Lumberton 77657
Type: Public, local
Degrees: C
URL: http://www.lumberton.k12.tx.us
Phone: (409) 755-6254
Inst. Accred.: COE (2004)

Maternidad La Luz
1308 Magoffin St., El Paso 79901
Type: Private, independent
Degrees: C
Phone: (915) 532-5895
Inst. Accred.: MEAC (1999)

MedVance Institute of Houston
6220 Westpark Dr., Ste. 180, Houston 77057-7378
Type: Private, proprietary
Degrees: C
URL: http://www.medvance.edu
Phone: (713) 266-6594
Inst. Accred.: COE (1996/2000)
Prog. Accred.: Radiography

Metroplex Beauty School
519 North Galloway Ave., Mesquite 75149
Type: Private, proprietary
Degrees: C
Phone: (972) 288-5485
Inst. Accred.: NACCAS (1975/2002)

Mid Cities Barber College
411 Marshall Plaza, Grand Prairie 75050
Type: Private, proprietary
Degrees: C
Phone: (214) 642-1892
Inst. Accred.: ACCSCT (1994/2002)

Milan Institute of Cosmetology
2400 South East 27th, Amarillo 79103
Type: Private, proprietary
Degrees: C
URL: http://www.milaninstitute.edu
Phone: (806) 371-7600
Inst. Accred.: NACCAS (1976/2001)

Milan Institute of Cosmetology
Ingram Park Mall, 6151 NW Loop 410, Ste. 201, San Antonio 78238
Type: Private, proprietary
Degrees: C
URL: http://www.milaninstitute.edu
Phone: (210) 647-5100
Inst. Accred.: COE (1999/2005)

Mims Classic Beauty College
5121 Blanco Rd., San Antonio 78216
Type: Private, proprietary
Degrees: C
Phone: (210) 344-2041
Inst. Accred.: NACCAS (1989/2004)

MJ's Beauty Academy, Inc.
3939 South Polk St., Ste. 505, Dallas 75224
Type: Private, proprietary
Degrees: C
Phone: (214) 374-7500
Inst. Accred.: NACCAS (2001)

National Beauty College—Garland
149 West Kingsley, Ste. 230, Garland 75040
Type: Private, proprietary
Degrees: C
Phone: (972) 278-2020
Inst. Accred.: NACCAS (1996/1999)

National Institute of Technology—San Antonio
3622 Fredericksburg Rd., San Antonio 78201-3841
Type: Private, proprietary
System: Corinthian Colleges, Inc
Degrees: C   *Enroll:* 1,717
URL: http://www.nitschools.com
Phone: (210) 733-6000   *Calendar:* Qtr. plan
Inst. Accred.: ACCSCT (1969/2001)
Prog. Accred.: Medical Assisting (CAAHEP)

Bissonnet Campus
9700 Bissonnet St., Ste. 1400, Houston 77036-8014
Phone: (713) 772-4200

Galleria Campus
4150 Westheimer, Ste. 200, Houston 77027
Phone: (713) 629-1637

Greenspoint Campus
255 Northpoint, Ste. 100, Houston 77060
Phone: (281) 447-7037

Houston (Hobby) Campus
7151 Office City Dr., Houston 77087
Phone: (713) 645-7404

Neilson Beauty College, Inc.
416 West Jefferson Blvd., Dallas 75208
Type: Private, proprietary
Degrees: C
Phone: (214) 941-8756
Inst. Accred.: NACCAS (1975/2002)

North Texas Professional Career Institute
6200 Maple Ave., Dallas 75235
Type: Private, proprietary
Degrees: C
URL: http://www.ntpci.com
Phone: (214) 351-0223
Inst. Accred.: ABHES (1999/2001)

Northwest Educational Center
2860 Antoine, Houston 77092
Type: Private, proprietary
Degrees: C
Phone: (713) 680-2929
Inst. Accred.: COE (1998/2003)

The Ocean Corporation
10840 Rockley Rd., Houston 77099-3416
Type: Private, proprietary
Degrees: C
Phone: (281) 530-0202
Inst. Accred.: ACCSCT (1989/2005)

Ogle School of Hair Design—Ft. Worth
5063 Old Granbury Rd., Ft. Worth 76133
Type: Private, proprietary
Degrees: C
URL: http://www.ogleschool.com
Phone: (817) 294-2950
Inst. Accred.: NACCAS (1982/2002)

Dallas Campus
6333 East Mockingbird Ln., Ste. 201, Dallas 75214
Phone: (214) 821-0819

Ogle School of Hair Design—Hurst
720 Arcadia St., Apartment B, Hurst 76053
Type: Private, proprietary
Degrees: C
URL: http://www.ogleschool.com
Phone: (817) 284-9231
Inst. Accred.: NACCAS (1982/2002)

Ogle School of Hair, Skin & Nails
2200 West Park Row Dr., Ste. 106, Arlington 76013
Type: Private, proprietary
Degrees: C
URL: http://www.ogleschool.com
Phone: (817) 277-6341
Inst. Accred.: NACCAS (1975/2001)

PCI Health Training Center
8101 John Carpenter Freeway, Dallas 75247-4720
Type: Private, proprietary
Degrees: C
Phone: (214) 630-0568
Inst. Accred.: ACCSCT (1986/2002)

Pipo Academy of Hair Design
3000 Pershing Dr., El Paso 79903
Type: Private, proprietary
Degrees: C
Phone: (915) 565-3491
Inst. Accred.: NACCAS (1981/2004)

Polytechnic Institute
5206 Airline, Houston 77022-2929
Type: Private, proprietary
Degrees: C
Phone: (713) 694-6027
Inst. Accred.: ACCSCT (1990/2001)

Professional Careers Institute, Inc.
6666 Harwin Dr., Ste. 160, Houston 77036
Type: Private, proprietary
Degrees: C
URL: http://www.pcitraining.org
Phone: (713) 783-3999
Inst. Accred.: ACCET (2004)

Ronny J's Barber and Styling College
443 Bruton Terrace Ctr., Dallas 75227
Type: Private, proprietary
Degrees: C
Phone: (214) 275-7151
Inst. Accred.: NACCAS (2002)

Royal Beauty Careers
5020 F.M. 1960 West, Ste. A-12, Houston 77069-4611
Type: Private, proprietary
Degrees: C
URL: http://www.royalschools.com
Phone: (281) 580-2554
Inst. Accred.: COE (1994/2005)

S.W. School of Business & Technical Careers
272 Commercial St., Eagle Pass 78852
Type: Private, proprietary
Degrees: C
Phone: (210) 773-1373
Inst. Accred.: COE (1989/2001)

S.W. School of Business & Technical Careers
2402 San Pedro, San Antonio 78212
Type: Private, proprietary
Degrees: C
Phone: (210) 225-7287
Inst. Accred.: COE (1992/2004)

S.W. School of Business & Technical Careers
602 West Southcross Blvd., San Antonio 78221
Type: Private, proprietary
Degrees: C
Phone: (210) 921-0951
Inst. Accred.: COE (1982/2003)

Uvalde Campus
122 West North St., Uvalde 78801
Phone: (210) 278-4103

San Antonio Beauty College #3
4021 Naco Perrin Blvd., San Antonio 78217
Type: Private, proprietary
Degrees: C
Phone: (210) 654-9734
Inst. Accred.: NACCAS (1986/2001)

San Antonio Beauty College #4
2423 Jamar, Ste. 2, San Antonio 78226
Type: Private, proprietary
Degrees: C
Phone: (210) 433-7222
Inst. Accred.: NACCAS (1990/2000)

San Antonio College of Medical and Dental Assistants
4205 San Pedro Ave., San Antonio 78212-1899
Type: Private, proprietary
System: Kaplan Higher Education Corporation
Degrees: C
URL: http://www.sacmda.com
Phone: (210) 733-0777
Inst. Accred.: ACCSCT (1970/2003)
Prog. Accred.: Medical Assisting (CAAHEP)

Career Centers of Texas—Corpus Christi
1620 South Padre Island, Corpus Christi 78416
Phone: (361) 852-2900

McAllen Campus
3900 North 23rd St., McAllen 78501-6053
Phone: (956) 360-1499

Sanford-Brown Institute—Dallas
1250 Mockingbird Ln., Dallas 75247
Type: Private, proprietary
System: Career Education Corporation
Degrees: C
URL: http://www.sbdallas.com
Phone: (214) 638-6400
Inst. Accred.: ABHES (1993/2003)

Garden City Campus
711 Stewart Ave., 2nd Flr., Garden City, NY 11530
Phone: (516) 248-6060
Prog. Accred: Medical Assisting (ABHES)

School of Automotive Machinists
1911 Antoine Dr., Houston 77055-1803
Type: Private, proprietary
Degrees: C
Phone: (713) 683-3817
Inst. Accred.: ACCSCT (1991/2001)

Sebring Career Schools
7060 Bissonnet, Houston 77074
Type: Private, proprietary
Degrees: C
Phone: (713) 772-0702
Inst. Accred.: COE (1985/2002)

Barker Campus
6672 Hwy. 6, South, Houston 77413-0277
Phone: (713) 561-0592

Huntsville Campus
2212 Ave. I, Huntsville 77340
Phone: (409) 291-6299

Seguin Beauty School
102 East Ct. St., Seguin 78155
Type: Private, proprietary
Degrees: C
Phone: (830) 372-0935
Inst. Accred.: COE (1987/2004)

New Braunfels Campus
214 West San Antonio St., New Braunfels 78130
Phone: (830) 620-1301

South Texas Barber College
3917 Ayers St., Corpus Christi 78415
Type: Private, proprietary
Degrees: C
Phone: (361) 855-2297
Inst. Accred.: COE (2004)

South Texas Vo-Tech Institute—McAllen
2901 North 23rd St., Ste. B, McAllen 78501-6148
Type: Private, proprietary
Degrees: C
URL: http://www.stvt.net
Phone: (956) 631-1107
Inst. Accred.: COE (1982/2004)

South Texas Vo-Tech Institute—Weslaco
2419 East Haggar Ave., Weslaco 78596
Type: Private, proprietary
Degrees: C
URL: http://www.stvt.net
Phone: (956) 969-1564
Inst. Accred.: COE (1982/2004)

Southeastern Career Institute
5440 Harvest Hill Rd., Ste. 200, Dallas 75230
Type: Private, proprietary
System: Kaplan Higher Education Corporation
Degrees: C
URL: http://www.dallasparalegal.com
Phone: (972) 385-1446
Inst. Accred.: COE (1989/2002)

Southern Careers Institute
2301 South Congress Ave., Ste. #27, Austin 78704
Type: Private, proprietary
Degrees: C
URL: http://www.scitexas.com
Phone: (512) 448-4795
Inst. Accred.: COE (1991/2003)

Corpus Christi Campus
5333 Everhart Rd., Building C, Corpus Christi 78415
Phone: (512) 857-5700

Pharr Campus
1414 North Jackson Rd., Pharr 78577
Phone: (956) 687-1415

San Antonio Campus
1405 North Main # 100, San Antonio 78212
Phone: (210) 271-0096

Southern Educational Alliance
6420 Richmond Ave., Ste. 610, Houston 77057
Type: Private, proprietary
Degrees: C
URL: http://www.seainstantlearning.com
Phone: (713) 975-9642
Inst. Accred.: ABHES (2001)

Southwestern Montessori Training Center
PO Box 310947 NT Station, denton 76207
Type: Private, independent
Degrees: C
Phone: (940)566-1640
Inst. Accred.: MACTE (1996/2004)

Southwestern Professional Institute
3033 Chimney Rock, Ste. 200, Houston 77056
Type: Private, proprietary
Degrees: C
URL: http://www.spi-careers.com
Phone: (713) 781-5908
Inst. Accred.: COE (1999/2004)

Star College of Cosmetology—Nacogdoches
705 North University, Nacogdoches 75961
Type: Private, proprietary
Degrees: C
Phone: (936) 462-7232
Inst. Accred.: NACCAS (1988/2003)

Star College of Cosmetology—Tyler
520 East Front St., Tyler 75702
Type: Private, proprietary
Degrees: C
Phone: (903) 596-7860
Inst. Accred.: NACCAS (1991/2001)

Longview Campus
700 East Whaley, Longview 75601
Phone: (903) 758-8611

State Beauty Academy, Inc.
663 Oriole Blvd., Duncanville 75116
Type: Private, proprietary
Degrees: C
Phone: (972) 298-0100
Inst. Accred.: NACCAS (2001)

Stephenville Beauty College
951 South Lillian St., Stephenville 76401
Type: Private, proprietary
Degrees: C
Phone: (254) 968-2111
Inst. Accred.: NACCAS (1977/2002)

Sylvia's International School of Beauty
434 West Parker Rd., Houston 77091
Type: Public, proprietary
Degrees: C
URL: http://www.sylviasbeautyschool.com
Phone: (713) 697-1200
Inst. Accred.: COE (2000)

Texas Barber College and Hairstyling Schools
531 West Jefferson Blvd., Dallas 75208
Type: Private, proprietary
Degrees: C
Phone: (214) 943-7255
Inst. Accred.: COE (1988/2005)

Dallas Campus
2406 Gus Thomason Rd., Dallas 75228
Phone: (214) 324-2851

Richardson Campus
9275 Richmond Ave., Stes. 178-184, Houston 77063
Phone: (972) 644-4106

Texas Careers
1015 Jackson-Keller Rd., San Antonio 78213
Type: Private, proprietary
System: Kaplan Higher Education Corporation
Degrees: C
URL: http://www.texascareers.com
Phone: (210) 308-8584
Inst. Accred.: COE (1995/2001)

Laredo Campus
6410 McPherson Ave., Laredo 78041-6191
Phone: (956) 717-5909

Texas College of Cosmetology
117 Sayles Blvd., Abilene 79605
Type: Private, proprietary
Degrees: C
Phone: (915) 677-0532
Inst. Accred.: NACCAS (1990/2000)

Texas College of Cosmetology
918 North Chadbourne St., San Angelo 76903
Type: Private, proprietary
Degrees: C
Phone: (915) 677-0532
Inst. Accred.: COE (1994/2001)

Texas School of Business
711 East Airtex Dr., Houston 77073
Type: Private, proprietary
System: Kaplan Higher Education Corporation
Degrees: C
URL: http://www.tsb.edu
Phone: (281) 443-8900
Inst. Accred.: ACICS (1985/2001)
Prog. Accred.: Medical Assisting (CAAHEP)

East Houston Campus
12030 East Freeway, Houston 77029
Phone: (713) 455-8555

Friendswood Campus
3208 Farm Rd. 528, Friendswood 77546-8938
Phone: (281) 648-0880

Southwest Campus
6363 Richmond Ave., Ste. 300, Houston 77057
Phone: (713) 975-7527
Prog. Accred.: Medical Assisting (CAAHEP)

Texas Vocational Schools
1921 East Red River, Victoria 77901
Type: Private, proprietary
Degrees: C
URL: http://www.texasvocationalschools.com
Phone: (361) 575-4768
Inst. Accred.: COE (1983/2005)

Victoria Campus
201 East Rio Grande, Victoria 77901
Phone: (512) 575-4768

Touch of Class School of Cosmetology
5015 Weslet St., Ste. A, Greenville 75402
Type: Private, proprietary
Degrees: C
Phone: (903) 455-1144
Inst. Accred.: NACCAS (1998/2001)

Trend Barber College
7725 West Bellfort St., Houston 77071-2104
Type: Private, proprietary
Degrees: C
URL: http://www.trendbarbercollege.com/trend.htm
Phone: (713) 721-0000
Inst. Accred.: COE (2002)

Tri-State Cosmetology Institute— Doniphan Drive
3910 Doniphan Dr., Ste. C-E, El Paso 79922
Type: Private, proprietary
Degrees: C
URL: http://www.tristatecosmetology.com
Phone: (915) 585-8777
Inst. Accred.: NACCAS (1982/2002)

Tri-State Cosmetology Institute—Gateway East
6800 Gateway East, #4-A, El Paso 79915
Type: Private, proprietary
Degrees: C
URL: http://www.tristatecosmetology.com
Phone: (915) 778-1741
Inst. Accred.: NACCAS (1982/2002)

United States Army Medical Department Center and School
2250 Stanley Rd., Building 2840, Rm. 307, MCCS-HB, San Antonio 78234-6100
Type: Public, federal
Degrees: C
URL: http://www.cs.amedd.army.mil/deansoffice
Phone: (210) 221-7316
Inst. Accred.: COE (1983/2005)
Prog. Accred.: Dental Laboratory Technology, Occupational Therapy Assisting, Radiography, Respiratory Therapy Technology

Army Medical Equipment and Optician School
Aurora, CO 80045-7040
Phone: (303) 943-4107

School of Aviation Medicine
Fort Rucker, AL 36362-5377
Phone: (205) 558-7409

Universal Technical Institute
721 Lockhaven Dr., Houston 77073-5598
Type: Private, proprietary
Degrees: C   *Enroll:* 1,844
URL: http://www.uticorp.com
Phone: (281) 443-6262
Inst. Accred.: ACCSCT (1983/2004)

University of Cosmetology Arts & Sciences
8401 North 10th St., PO Box 720391, McAllen 78504
Type: Private, proprietary
Degrees: C
Phone: (956) 687-9444
Inst. Accred.: NACCAS (1978/2000)

Harlingen Campus
913 North Thirteenth St., Harlingen 78550
Phone: (956) 412-1212

Valley Grande Institute for Academic Studies
414 South Missouri St., Weslaco 78596
Type: Private, proprietary
Degrees: C
URL: http://www.valleygrandeinstitute.com
Phone: (956) 973-1945
Inst. Accred.: ABHES (2001)

Vanguard Institute of Technology
221 North 8th St., Edinburg 78539
Type: Private, proprietary
Degrees: C
Phone: (956) 787-4388
Inst. Accred.: COE (1990/2001)

Ed Carey Drive Campus
603 Ed Carey Dr., Harlingen 78550
Phone: (210) 428-4999

West Price Road Campus
1424 West Price Rd, #K, Harlingen 78550
Phone: (210) 472-6668

Velma B's Beauty Academy
1511 South Ewing Ave., Dallas 75216
Type: Private, proprietary
Degrees: C
Phone: (214) 942-1541
Inst. Accred.: NACCAS (1975/1998)

Victoria Beauty College
1508 North Laurent St., Victoria 77901
Type: Private, proprietary
Degrees: C
Phone: (361) 575-4526
Inst. Accred.: NACCAS (1989/1999)

UTAH

American Institute of Medical-Dental Technology
1675 North Freedom Blvd., Building 3, Provo 84604
Type: Private, proprietary
Degrees: C
URL: http://www.americaninstitute.edu
Phone: (801) 377-2900
Inst. Accred.: ABHES (1984/2003)
Prog. Accred.: Dental Assisting, Medical Assisting (ABHES), Medical Assisting (AMA), Surgical Technology

Draper Campus
12257 Business Park Dr., Draper 84020
Phone: (801) 816-1444
Prog. Accred: Dental Assisting

Bon Losee Academy of Hair Artistry
2230 North University Pkwy., Building #5, Provo 84604
Type: Private, proprietary
Degrees: C
URL: http://www.bonlosse.com
Phone: (801) 375-8000
Inst. Accred.: NACCAS (1989/2004)

Cameo College of Essential Beauty
1600 South State St., Salt Lake City 84115
Type: Private, proprietary
Degrees: C
URL: http://www.cameocollege.com
Phone: (801) 484-6173
Inst. Accred.: NACCAS (1994/2002)

Certified Careers Institute
1455 West 2200 South, Ste. 100, Salt Lake City 84119
Type: Private, proprietary
Degrees: C   *Enroll:* 35
URL: http://www.cciutah.edu
Phone: (801) 886-0771
Inst. Accred.: ACCSCT (1988/2005)

Clearfield Campus
775 South 2000 East, Clearfield 84015
Phone: (801) 774-9900

Chatterton, Inc
180 South 300 West, Ste. 315, Salt Lake City 84101
Type: Private, proprietary
Degrees: C
URL: http://www.utah.dalecarnegie.com
Phone: (801) 363-5294
Inst. Accred.: ACCET (1988/2001)

Color My Nails School of Nail Technology
85 East 7200 South, Midvale 84047
Type: Private, proprietary
Degrees: C
URL: http://www.colormynails.com
Phone: (801) 561-9112
Inst. Accred.: NACCAS (2004)

Dallas Roberts Academy of Hair Design
1700 North State St., Ste. 18, Provo 84604
Type: Private, proprietary
Degrees: C
URL: http://www.dallasroberts.com
Phone: (801) 375-1501
Inst. Accred.: NACCAS (2000/2003)

Eagle Gate College
5588 South Green St., Murray 84123
Type: Private, proprietary
Degrees: C
URL: http://www.eaglegatecollege.com
Phone: (801) 268-9271   *Calendar:* Qtr. plan
Inst. Accred.: ACICS (1981/2005)

Layton Campus
915 North 400 West, Layton 84041
Phone: (801) 546-7500

Salt Lake City Campus
405 South Main St., Ste. 130, Salt Lake City 84111
Phone: (801) 287-9640

Evan's Hairstyling College—Cedar City
169 North 100 West, Cedar City 84720
Type: Private, proprietary
Degrees: C
URL: http://www.evanscollege.com
Phone: (435) 586-4486
Inst. Accred.: NACCAS (1988/2003)

Evan's Hairstyling College—Orem
798 West 400 North, Orem 84057
Type: Private, proprietary
Degrees: C
URL: http://www.evanscollege.com
Phone: (801) 224-6034
Inst. Accred.: NACCAS (2001/2004)

Evan's Hairstyling College—St. George
955 East Tabernacle St., St. George 84770
Type: Private, proprietary
Degrees: C
URL: http://www.evanscollege.com
Phone: (435) 673-6128
Inst. Accred.: NACCAS (1988/2003)

Fran Brown College of Beauty
521 West 600 North, Layton 84041
Type: Private, proprietary
Degrees: C
URL: http://www.franschool.com
Phone: (801) 546-1377
Inst. Accred.: NACCAS (1988/2003)

Francois D. Hair Design Academy
111 West 9000 South, Sandy 84070
Type: Private, proprietary
Degrees: C
URL: http://www.francoisd.com
Phone: (801) 561-2244
Inst. Accred.: NACCAS (1994/2002)

Hairitage Hair Academy
900 South Bluff St., Ste. 9, St. George 84770
Type: Private, proprietary
Degrees: C
Phone: (435) 673-5233
Inst. Accred.: NACCAS (1994/2002)

Healing Mountain Massage School
455 South 300 East, Ste. 103, Salt Lake City 84111
Type: Private, proprietary
Degrees: C
URL: http://www.healingmountain.org
Phone: (801) 355-6300
Inst. Accred.: ABHES (2001)

International Institute of Hair Design
273 West 500 South 84010
Type: Private, proprietary
Degrees: C
Phone: (801) 295-2389
Inst. Accred.: NACCAS (1971/2000)

Taylorsville Campus
5536 South 1900 West, Taylorsville 84118
Phone: (801) 965-8121

Maximum Style Tec School of Cosmetology
130 South Main St., Ste. 230, Logan 84321
Type: Private, proprietary
Degrees: C
Phone: (435) 752-3599
Inst. Accred.: NACCAS (2004)

Myotherapy College of Utah
1174 East 2700 South, Ste. 19, Graystone Plaza, Salt Lake City 84106
Type: Private, proprietary
Degrees: C
URL: http://www.myomassage.net
Phone: (801) 484-7624
Inst. Accred.: ACCSCT (1992/2002)

New Horizons Beauty College
550 North Main St., Ste. 115, Logan 84321
Type: Private, proprietary
Degrees: C
Phone: (435) 753-9779
Inst. Accred.: NACCAS (1993/2001)

Ogden Institute of Massage Therapy
3500 Harrison Blvd., Ogden 84403
Type: Private, proprietary
Degrees: C
URL: http://www.oimt.net
Phone: (801) 627-8227
Inst. Accred.: ABHES (2002/2005)

Paul Mitchell The School
1969 East Murray Holiday Rd., Salt Lake City 84117
Type: Private, proprietary
System: Paul Mitchell The School—Corporate Office
Degrees: C
URL: http://pmts.paulmitchelltheschool.com
Phone: (801) 266-4693
Inst. Accred.: NACCAS (1988/2003)

Paul Mitchell The School
480 North 900 East, Provo 84606
Type: Private, proprietary
System: Paul Mitchell The School—Corporate Office
Degrees: C
URL: http://pmts.paulmitchelltheschool.com
Phone: (801) 374-5111
Inst. Accred.: NACCAS (1987/2001)

Casselberry Campus
1271 Semoran Boulvard, Ste. 131, Casselberry, FL 32707
Phone: (407) 677-7695

Cranston Campus
379 Atwood Ave., Cranston, RI 02920
Phone: (401) 946-9920

Paul Mitchell—The School
1534 Adams Ave., Costa Mesa, CA 92626
Phone: (714) 546-8786

Premier Hair Academy
4616 South 4000 West, West Valley 84120
Type: Private, proprietary
Degrees: C
Phone: (801) 966-8414
Inst. Accred.: NACCAS (1988/2003)

Prime Cut Academy of Hair and Nail Artistry
1050 East 200 North, PO Box 582, Roosevelt 84066
Type: Private, proprietary
Degrees: C
URL: http://www.primecutacademy.com
Phone: (435) 722-3099
Inst. Accred.: NACCAS (2005)

Renaissance School of Therapeutic Massage
566 West 1350 South, Ste. 100, Bountiful 84010
Type: Private, proprietary
Degrees: C
URL: http://www.renaissancemassageschool.com
Phone: (801)292-8515
Inst. Accred.: ABHES (2004)

Sherman Kendall's Academy of Beauty Arts and Science—Midvale
7353 South 900 East, Midvale 84047
Type: Private, proprietary
Degrees: C
URL: http://www.shermankendallsacademy.com
Phone: (801) 561-5610
Inst. Accred.: NACCAS (1976/2003)

Sherman Kendall's Academy of Beauty Arts and Science—Salt Lake City
2230 South 700 East, Salt Lake City 84106
Type: Private, proprietary
Degrees: C
URL: http://www.shermankendallsacademy.com
Phone: (801) 486-0101
Inst. Accred.: NACCAS (1973/2003)

The Skin Institute
992 North Westridge Dr., Building A, St. George 84770
Type: Private, proprietary
Degrees: C
Phone: (435) 673-7696
Inst. Accred.: NACCAS (2005)

Skin Works School of Advanced Skin Care
144 South 400 East, Salt Lake City 84111
Type: Private, proprietary
Degrees: C
Phone: (801) 530-0001
Inst. Accred.: COE (2003)

Stacey's Hands of Champions Beauty College, Inc.
3721 South 250 West, Ogden 84405
Type: Private, proprietary
Degrees: C
URL: http://www.staceyscollege.com
Phone: (801) 394-5718
Inst. Accred.: NACCAS (1987/2002)

Taylor Andrews Academy of Hair Design
9052 South 1510 West, West Jordan 84088-6577
Type: Private, proprietary
Degrees: C
URL: http://www.taylorandrew.com
Phone: (801) 748-2288
Inst. Accred.: NACCAS (2005)

Utah College of Massage Therapy
25 South 300 East, Salt Lake City
Type: Private, proprietary
Degrees: C
URL: http://www.ucmt.com
Phone: (801) 521-3330
Inst. Accred.: ACCET (1990/2001)

Aurora Campus
14104 East Exposition Ave., Aurora, CO 80019
Phone: (800) 617-3302

Denver School of Massage Therapy
8991 Harlan St., Ste. B, Westminster, CO 80031
Phone: (303) 426-5621

Las Vegas Campus
2381 East Windmill Ln., Ste. 14, Las Vegas, NV 89123
Phone: (702) 456-4325

Lindon Campus
135 South State St., Ste. 12, Lindon 84042
Phone: (801) 796-0300

Nevada School of Massage Therapy
2381 East Windmill Ln., Ste. 14, Las Vegas, NV 89123
Phone: (702) 456-4325

Phoenix Campus
9201 North 29th Ave., Ste. 35, Phoenix, AZ 85051-3436
Phone: (602) 331-4325

Tempe Campus
1409 West Southern Ave., Ste. 6, Tempe, AZ 85282
Phone: (480) 983-2222

VERMONT

National Midwifery Institute
PO Box 128, Bristol 05443-0128
Type: Private, proprietary
Degrees: C
URL: http://www.nationalmidwiferyinstitute.com
Phone: (802) 453-3332
Inst. Accred.: MEAC (2002)

O'Brien's Training Center
1475 Shelburne Rd., Ste. 200, South Burlington 5403
Type: Private, proprietary
Degrees: C
Phone: (802) 658-9591
Inst. Accred.: NACCAS (1966/2003)

Vermont College of Cosmetology
400 Cornerstone Dr., Williston 05495
Type: Private, proprietary
Degrees: C
URL: http://www.vtcollegeofcosmo.com
Phone: (802) 879-4811
Inst. Accred.: NACCAS (1972/2005)

Vermont Training Solutions, Inc.
23 Athens Dr., Essex 05452
Type: Private, proprietary
Degrees: C
URL: http://www.vts-dalecarnegie.com
Phone: (802) 879-7219
Inst. Accred.: ACCET (1998/2003)

VIRGINIA

AKS Massage School
462 Herndon Pkwy., Ste. 208, Herndon 20170
Type: Private, proprietary
Degrees: C
URL: http://www.aksmassageschool.com
Phone: (703) 464-0333
Inst. Accred.: ACCSCT (2003)

BarPalma Beauty Careers Academy
3535 Franklin Rd., SW, Unit D, Roanoke 24014
Type: Private, proprietary
Degrees: C
URL: http://www.atihollywood.com
Phone: (540) 343-0153
Inst. Accred.: COE (1989/2004)

Blue Ridge Job Corps Center
234 West Main St., Marion 24354
Type: Public, federal
Degrees: C
URL: http://www.blueridgejc.org
Phone: (276) 783-7221
Inst. Accred.: COE (2004)

The Braxton School of Business
3600 Broad St., Ste. 190, Richmond 23230
Type: Private, proprietary
Degrees: C
URL: http://www.thebraxtonschool.com
Phone: (804) 353-4458
Inst. Accred.: ACICS (1988/2000)

Cleveland Campus
8101 Euclid Ave., Cleveland, OH 44103-5059

Career Training Solutions
4343 Planck Rd., Ste. 115, Fredericksburg 22407
Type: Private, proprietary
Degrees: C
Phone: (540) 785-2000
Inst. Accred.: COE (2002)

Cayce/Reilly School of Massotherqapy
215 67th St., Virginia Beach 23451
Type: Private, proprietary
Degrees: C
URL: http://edgarcayce.org/health/crsm_index.html
Phone: (757) 457-7270
Inst. Accred.: CMTA (1999/2004)

Center for Naval Engineering
1534 Piersey St., Ste. 321, Norfolk 23511-2613
Type: Public, federal
Degrees: C
URL: https://www.npdc.navy.mil/cne/ftcnor
Phone: (757) 444-5332
Inst. Accred.: COE (2004)

Center for Naval Intelligence
2088 Regulus Ave., Virginia Beach 23461-2099
Type: Public, federal
Degrees: C
URL: https://www.npdc.navy.mil/cennavintel
Phone: (757) 492-0016
Inst. Accred.: COE (2000)

Center for Personal Development
2025 Tartar Ave., Virginia Beach 23461-1933
Type: Public, federal
Degrees: C
URL: https://www.npdc.navy.mil/cpd
Phone: (757) 492-0770
Inst. Accred.: COE (2004)

Center for Surface Combat Systems
5395 First St., Bldg. 1520, Dahlgren 22448
Type: Public, federal
Degrees: C
URL: https://www.npdc.navy.mil/cscs
Phone: (540)-653-1023
Inst. Accred.: COE (2004)

The Chubb Institute—Arlington Campus
1515 North Ct.house Rd., Ste. 610, Arlington 22201
Type: Private, proprietary
System: High-Tech Institute
Degrees: C
URL: http://www.chubbinstitute.edu
Phone: (703) 908-8300
Inst. Accred.: ACCET (2001/2004)

Colonial Heights Beauty Academy
3233-B Blvd., Colonial Heights 23834
Type: Private, proprietary
Degrees: C
Phone: (804) 526-6363
Inst. Accred.: NACCAS (1986/2004)

Crescent Cosmetology University
2312 West Mercury Blvd., Hampton 23666
Type: Private, proprietary
Degrees: C
Phone: (757) 826-4609
Inst. Accred.: NACCAS (2000)

Culpeper Cosmetology Training Center
509 South Main St., Culpeper 22701
Type: Private, proprietary
Degrees: C
Phone: (540) 727-8003
Inst. Accred.: NACCAS (2004)

Danville Regional Medical Center
142 South Main St., Danville 24541
Type: Private, independent
Degrees: C
URL: http://www.danvilleregional.org
Phone: (434) 799-4510
Inst. Accred.: ABHES (2002)
Prog. Accred.: Radiography

Defense Acquisition University
9820 Belvior Rd., Bldg. 202, Fort Belvior 22060-5565
Type: Public, federal
Degrees: C
URL: http://www.dau.mil
Phone: (703) 805-3360
Inst. Accred.: COE (2003)

Defense Commissary Agency
1300 E. Ave., Building 11200, Fort Lee 23801-1800
Type: Public, federal
Degrees: C
URL: http://www.deca.mil
Phone: (804) 734-8560
Inst. Accred.: COE (1995/2003)

Dickerson Beauty Academy
609 Keen St., Ste. 204, Danville 24540
Type: Private, proprietary
Degrees: C
Phone: (434) 793-0558
Inst. Accred.: NACCAS (2001)

Flatwoods Civilian Conservation Center
2803 Dungannon Rd., Coeburn 24230
Type: Public, federal
Degrees: C
Phone: (540) 395-3384
Inst. Accred.: COE (1989/2005)

Graham Webb International Academy of Hair
1621 North Kent St., Ste. 1617 LL, Rosslyn Plaza,
Arlington 22209
Type: Private, proprietary
Degrees: C
URL: http://www.grahamwebbacademyonline.com
Phone: (703) 243-9322
Inst. Accred.: NACCAS (1989/2004)

Heritage Institute
350 South Washington St., Falls Church 22046
Type: Private, proprietary
Degrees: C
Phone: (703) 532-5050
Inst. Accred.: ACCSCT (2002)

Heritage Institute
8255 Shopper's Square, Manassas 22110-5405
Type: Private, proprietary
Degrees: C
Phone: (703) 361-7775
Inst. Accred.: ACCSCT (1990/2005)

Hicks Academy of Beauty Culture
904 Loudoun Ave., Portsmouth 23707
Type: Private, proprietary
Degrees: C
Phone: (757) 399-2400
Inst. Accred.: NACCAS (1965/2002)

International Beauty School—Charlottesville
2024 Holiday Dr., Charlottesville 22901
Type: Private, proprietary
Degrees: C
Phone: (804) 296-0159
Inst. Accred.: NACCAS (1970/2002)

Kee Business College—Newport News
803 Dilligence Dr., Newport News 23606
Type: Private, proprietary
System: Corinthian Colleges, Inc
Degrees: C
URL: http://keecollege.com
Phone: (757) 873-1111   *Calendar:* Qtr. plan
Inst. Accred.: ACICS (1955/2004)
Prog. Accred.: Medical Assisting (CAAHEP)

Chesapeake Campus
Greenbriar Circle Corporate Center, 825 Greenbriar
Circle, Ste. 100, Chesapeake 23320-2637
Phone: (757) 361-3900

Lawrence-White Associates, Inc.
1320 Grandin Rd., Ste. B, Roanoke 24015
Type: Private, proprietary
Degrees: C
URL: http://www.swvirginia.dalecarnegie.com
Phone: (540) 772-1723
Inst. Accred.: ACCET (2000/2005)

Legends Institute
3225 Old Forest Rd., Ste. 5, Lynchburg 24501
Type: Private, proprietary
Degrees: C
Phone: (804) 385-7722
Inst. Accred.: NACCAS (1973/2002)

Miller-Motte Technical College
1011 Creekside Ln., Lynchburg 24502
Type: Private, proprietary
Degrees: C
URL: http://www.miller-
motte.com/lynchburgwelcome.html
Phone: (434) 239-5222   *Calendar:* Qtr. plan
Inst. Accred.: ACICS (1953/2004)
Prog. Accred.: Medical Assisting (CAAHEP)

National Court Reporters Association
8224 Old Ct.house Rd., Vienna 22182-3808
Type: Private, independent
Degrees: C
URL: http://www.ncraonline.org
Phone: (703) 556-6272
Inst. Accred.: ACCET (1982/2004)

National Geospatial-Intelligence College
5855 21st St., Ste. 101, Fort Belvior 22060-5921
Type: Public, federal
Degrees: C
URL: http://www.nima.mil
Phone: (703) 805) 3268
Inst. Accred.: COE (2001)

Bethesda Campus
4600 Sangamore Rd., Bethesda, MD 20816-5003

National Imagery and Analysis School
1200 First St., SE, Washington Navy Yard, Bldg. 213,
Washington, DC 20303-0001

National Massage Therapy Institute
803 West Broad St., Ste. 110, Falls Church 22046
Type: Private, proprietary
Degrees: C
Phone: (703) 237-3905
Inst. Accred.: CMTA (1999/2005)

Norfolk Skills Center
922 West 21st St., Norfolk 23517-1516
Type: Public, local
Degrees: C
URL: http://www.nps.k12.va.us/schools/skillscenter
Phone: (757) 628-3300
Inst. Accred.: COE (1988/2004)

Northrop Grumman
Newport News Apprentice School
4101 Washington Ave., Newport News 23607
Type: Private, proprietary
Degrees: C
URL: http://www.apprenticeschool.com
Phone: (757) 380-2000
Inst. Accred.: COE (1982/2004)

Old Dominion Job Corps Center
PO Box 278, 1073 Father Judge Rd., Monroe 24574
Type: Public, federal
Degrees: C
URL: http://www.odjcc.com
Phone: (434) 929-4081
Inst. Accred.: COE (2001)

RSHT Training Center
1601 Willow Lawn Dr., Ste. 320, Richmond 23230
Type: Private, proprietary
Degrees: C
URL: http://www.rsht-trainingcenter.com
Phone: (804) 288-1000
Inst. Accred.: COE (1999/2005)

Charlottesville Campus
702 Charlton Ave., Ste. A, Charlottesville 22902
Phone: (434) 245-0400

Rudy & Kelly Academy of Hair & Nails
5606-8 Princess Anne Rd., Virginia Beach 23462
Type: Private, proprietary
Degrees: C
Phone: (757) 473-0994
Inst. Accred.: NACCAS (2001/2004)

Sentara School of Health Professions
1441 Crossways Blvd., Crossways I, Ste. 105,
Chesapeake 23320
Type: Private, independent
Degrees: C
URL: http://www.sentara.com
Phone: (757) 388-2900
Inst. Accred.: ABHES (1999/2004)

Springfield Beauty Academy, Inc.
4223 Annandale Rd., Annandale 22003
Type: Private, proprietary
Degrees: C
Phone: (703) 256-5662
Inst. Accred.: NACCAS (1993/2001)

Staunton School of Cosmetology, Inc.
128 East Beverly St., Staunton 24401
Type: Private, proprietary
Degrees: C
URL: http://hairstylingschool.com
Phone: (540) 885-0808
Inst. Accred.: NACCAS (1969/2002)

Suffolk Beauty Academy
860 Portsmouth Blvd., Suffolk 23434
Type: Private, proprietary
Degrees: C
Phone: (757) 934-0656
Inst. Accred.: NACCAS (1987/2002)

TESST College of Technology
6315 Bren Mar Dr., Alexandria 22312
Type: Private, proprietary
Degrees: C
URL: http://www.tesstcollege.com
Phone: (703) 354-1005   *Calendar:* Qtr. plan
Inst. Accred.: ACCSCT (1986/2003)

Unified Industries Incorporated
6551 Loisdale Ct., Ste. 400, Springfield 22150-1854
Type: Private, proprietary
Degrees: C
URL: http://www.uii.com
Phone: (703) 922-9800
Inst. Accred.: ACCET (1983/1999)

National City Campus
2104 Wilson Ave., Ste. C, National City, CA 92050
Phone: (619) 474-3738

Norfolk Campus
2733-C Ayliff Rd., Norfolk
Phone: (757) 857-5523

The United States Army Institute for Professional Development
U.S. Army Training Support Center, Attn: ATIC-ITS, Fort Eustis 23604-5166
Type: Public, federal
Degrees: C
URL: http://www.atsc.army.mil/accp/dlsd.htm
Phone: (757) 878-3866
Inst. Accred.: DETC (1978/2003)

United States Army Logistics Management College
2401 Quarters Rd., Fort Lee 23801-1705
Type: Public, federal
Degrees: C
URL: http://www.almc.army.mil
Phone: (804) 765-4605
Inst. Accred.: COE (2002)

United States Army Management Staff College
5500 21st St., Fort Belvior 22060-5934
Type: Public, federal
Degrees: C
URL: http://www.amsc.belvoir.army.mil
Phone: (703) 805-4714
Inst. Accred.: COE (2002)

United States Army Quartermaster Center and School
1201 22nd St., Fort Lee 23801-1601
Type: Public, federal
Degrees: C
Phone: (804) 734-3458
Inst. Accred.: COE (1975/2004)

United States Army Transportation and Aviation Logistics School
ATSD-BD-S, Bldg. 705, Rm. 214, Fort Eustis 23604-5450
Type: Public, federal
Degrees: C
URL: http://www.eustis.army.mil
Phone: (757) 878-4802
Inst. Accred.: COE (1975/2004)

Virginia Center for Montessori Training
499 North Parham Rd., Richmond 23229
Type: Private, independent
Degrees: C
Phone: (804) 741-0040
Inst. Accred.: MACTE (1998)

Virginia School of Hair Design
101 West Queens Way, Hampton 23669
Type: Private, proprietary
Degrees: C
Phone: (757) 722-0211
Inst. Accred.: NACCAS (1967/2003)

Virginia School of Massage
2008 Morton Dr., Charlottesville 22903
Type: Private, proprietary
System: Steiner Education Group
Degrees: C
URL: http://www.vasom.com
Phone: (804) 293-4031
Inst. Accred.: ACCSCT (1998/2003)
Prog. Accred.: Massage Therapy

Virginia School of Technology
100 Constitution Dr., Ste. 101, Virginia Beach 23462
Type: Private, proprietary
Degrees: C
URL: http://www.vstsuccess.com
Phone: (757) 499-5447   *Calendar:* Qtr. plan
Inst. Accred.: ACICS (1986/2003)

Richmond Campus
1001 Boulders Pkwy., Ste. 305, Richmond 23225
Phone: (804) 323-1020

Wade Powell & Associates, Inc.
291 Independence Blvd., Ste. 515, Pembroke Four, Virginia Beach 23462-5473
Type: Private, proprietary
Degrees: C
URL: http://www.easternvirginia.dalecarnegie.com
Phone: (757) 490-1611
Inst. Accred.: ACCET (1975/2001)

Wards Corner Beauty Academy
7525 Tidewater Dr., Ste. 45, Norfolk 23505
Type: Private, proprietary
Degrees: C
Phone: (757) 583-3300
Inst. Accred.: NACCAS (1977/2003)

Virginia Beach Campus
103 South Witchduck Rd., Virginia Beach 23462
Phone: (757) 473-5555

Washington County Adult Skill Center
848 Thompson Dr., Abingdon 24210
Type: Public, state
Degrees: C
URL: http://www.wcs.k12.va.us
Phone: (276) 676-1948
Inst. Accred.: COE (1990/2002)

Woodrow Wilson Rehabilitation Center
Materials Management Division, Box W-146, PO Box 1500, Fishersville 22939-1500
Type: Public, state
Degrees: C
URL: http://www.wwrc.net
Phone: (540) 332-7265
Inst. Accred.: COE (1983/2005)

Wray K. Powell & Associates, Inc.
2800 North Parham Rd., Ste. 102, Richmond 23294
Type: Private, proprietary
Degrees: C
URL: http://www.centralvirginia.dalecarnegie.com
Phone: (804) 270-0020
Inst. Accred.: ACCET (2000/2005)

WASHINGTON

The Academy of Hair Design
208 South Wenatchee Ave., Wenatchee 98801
Type: Private, proprietary
Degrees: C
Phone: (509) 662-9082
Inst. Accred.: NACCAS (1987/2002)

ALPS Language School
216 Broadway East, Ste. 202, Seattle 98102
Type: Private, proprietary
Degrees: C
URL: http://www.enlishintheusa.com
Phone: (206) 720-6363
Inst. Accred.: ACCET (1995/2000)

Ashmead College
2111 North Northgate Way, Ste. 218, Seattle 98133
Type: Private, proprietary
System: Corinthian Colleges, Inc
Degrees: C
URL: http://cci.edu/ashmead
Phone: (206) 527-0807
Inst. Accred.: ACCET (1989/2004)

Everett Campus
3019 Colby Ave., Everett 98201
Phone: (425) 339-2678

Fife Campus
5005 Pacific Hwy. East, Ste. 20, Fife 98424
Phone: (253) 922-2967

Tigard Campus
9600 SW Oak, 4th Flr., Tigard, OR 97223
Phone: (503) 892-8100

Vancouver Campus
120 136th Ave., NE, Ste. 220, Vancouver 98684
Phone: (360) 885-3152

B.J.'s Beauty & Barber College
5239 South Tacoma Way, Tacoma 98409
Type: Private, proprietary
Degrees: C
Phone: (253) 473-4320
Inst. Accred.: NACCAS (1987/2005)

Puyallup Campus
12020 Meridian East, Ste. K, Puyallup 98373
Phone: (253) 848-1595

Bellevue Beauty School
14045 NE 20th St., Bellevue 98007
Type: Private, proprietary
Degrees: C
Phone: (425) 643-0270
Inst. Accred.: NACCAS (1979/2004)

Bellingham Beauty School, Inc.
211 West Holly St., Bellingham 98225
Type: Private, proprietary
Degrees: C
Phone: (360) 734-1090
Inst. Accred.: NACCAS (1976/2003)

Brenneke School of Massage
160 Roy St., Seattle 98109
Type: Private, proprietary
Degrees: C
URL: http://www.brennekeschool.com
Phone: (206) 282-1233
Inst. Accred.: ACCET (1992/2001), CMTA (1999/2005)
Prog. Accred.: Massage Therapy

Brian Utting School of Massage
900 Thomas St., Ste. 200, Seattle 98109
Type: Private, proprietary
Degrees: C
URL: http://www.busm.com
Phone: (206) 292-8055
Inst. Accred.: CMTA (2001)

Bryman College
3649 Frontage Rd., Port Orchard 98366
Type: Private, proprietary
System: Corinthian Colleges, Inc
Degrees: C
URL: http://bryman-college.com
Phone: (360) 473-1120
Inst. Accred.: ACICS (1979/1999)
Prog. Accred.: Medical Assisting (CAAHEP)

Everett Campus
906 Everett Mall Way, Ste. 600, Everett 98208
Phone: (425) 789-7960
Prog. Accred: Medical Assisting (CAAHEP)

Federal Way Campus
31919 Sixth Ave. South, Federal Way 98003
Phone: (253) 941-5800
Prog. Accred: Medical Assisting (CAAHEP)

Tacoma Campus
2156 Pacific Ave., Tacoma 98402
Phone: (253) 207-4000

Bryman College—Renton
981 Powell Ave., Ste. 200, Renton 98055
Type: Private, proprietary
System: Corinthian Colleges, Inc
Degrees: C
URL: http://www.cci.edu
Phone: (425) 255-3281
Inst. Accred.: ACCSCT (1989/2002)
Prog. Accred.: Medical Assisting (CAAHEP)

Lynwood Campus
19020 33rd Ave. West, Ste. 250, Lynnwood 98036
Phone: (425) 778-9894

Chetta's Academy of Hair and Nails, Inc.
221 South Peabody St., Port Angeles 98362
Type: Private, proprietary
Degrees: C
Phone: (360) 417-0388
Inst. Accred.: NACCAS (2002/2005)

Clare's Beauty College
104 North Fourth Ave., Pasco 99301
Type: Private, proprietary
Degrees: C
Phone: (509) 547-8871
Inst. Accred.: NACCAS (1991/2001)

Court Reporting Institute
929 North 130th St., Ste. 2, Seattle 98133
Type: Private, proprietary
Degrees: C
URL: http://www.cri.org
Phone: (206) 363-8300
Inst. Accred.: ACICS (1991/2004)

Boise Campus
1951 South Saturn Way, Ste. 120, Boise, ID 83709
Phone: (208) 322-8517

CRI Career Training—Tacoma
15 Oregon Ave., Ste. 40, Tacoma 98409
Phone: (253) 474-4744

San Diego Campus
1333 Camino del Rio South, San Diego, CA 92108
Phone: (619) 294-5700

Crace & Associates
325 118th Ave., SE, Ste. 104, Bellevue 98005
Type: Private, proprietary
Degrees: C
URL: http://www.washington,dalecarnegie.com
Phone: (425) 453-8822
Inst. Accred.: ACCET (1978/2004)

Divers Institute of Technology
PO Box 70667, 4315 11th Ave., NW, Seattle 98107-0667
Type: Private, proprietary
Degrees: C
URL: http://www.diveweb.com/dit
Phone: (206) 783-5542
Inst. Accred.: ACCSCT (1973/2005)

Emil Fries School of Piano Tuning and Technology
2510 East Evergreen Blvd., Vancouver 98661
Type: Private, proprietary
Degrees: C
URL: http://www.pianotuningschool.org
Phone: (360) 693-1511
Inst. Accred.: ACCSCT (1993/2004)

Evergreen Beauty and Barber College
802 SE Everett Mall Way, Ste. A, Everett 98208
Type: Private, propietary
Degrees: C
URL: http://www.evergreenbeautybarber.com
Phone: (425) 423-9186
Inst. Accred.: NACCAS (2004)

Gene Juarez Academy of Beauty
10715 8th Ave., NE, Seattle 98125
Type: Private, proprietary
Degrees: C
URL: http://www.genejuarez.com
Phone: (206) 368-0210
Inst. Accred.: NACCAS (1977/2003)

Federal Way Campus
2222 South 314th St., Federal Way 98003
Phone: (253) 839-6483

Glen Dow Academy of Hair Design, Inc.
309 West Riverside Ave., Spokane 99201
Type: Private, proprietary
Degrees: C
URL: http://www.glendow.com
Phone: (509) 624-3244
Inst. Accred.: NACCAS (1970/2001)

Greenwood Academy of Hair Design
8501 Greenwood North, Seattle 98103
Type: Private, proprietary
Degrees: C
Phone: (206) 782-0220
Inst. Accred.: NACCAS (1975/2002)

Interface Computer School
9921 North Nevada St., Nevada 99218
Type: Private, proprietary
Degrees: C
URL: http://www.interface-net.com
Phone: (509) 467-1727
Inst. Accred.: ACCET (1986/2003)

Central Spokane Campus
1118 North Washington St., Spokane 99201
Phone: (509) 323-0070

International Air Academy
2901 East Mill Plain Blvd., Vancouver 98661-4899
Type: Private, proprietary
Degrees: C
URL: http://www.airacademy.com
Phone: (360) 695-2500
Inst. Accred.: ACCSCT (1983/2003)

Ontario Campus
2980 Inland Empire Blvd., Ontario, CA 91764-4804
Phone: (909) 989-5222

Kirkland Beauty School
17311 140th Ave., NE, Woodinville 98072
Type: Private, proprietary
Degrees: C
Phone: (425) 487-0437
Inst. Accred.: NACCAS (1980/2005)

Milan Institute of Cosmetology
607 SE Everett Mall Way, Ste. 5, Everett 98208
Type: Private, proprietary
Degrees: C
URL: http://www.milaninstitute.edu
Phone: (425) 353-8193
Inst. Accred.: NACCAS (1978/2005)

Montessori Schools of Washington
1804 Puget Dr., Everett 98203
Type: Private, independent
Degrees: C
Phone: (425) 355-1311
Inst. Accred.: MACTE (1999)

Montessori Teacher Preparation of Washington
3410 South 272, Kent 98032
Type: Private, independent
Degrees: C
Phone: (253) 859-2262
Inst. Accred.: MACTE (1996/2005)

Northwest Hair Academy
615 South First St., Mount Vernon 98273
Type: Private, proprietary
Degrees: C
URL: http://www.northwesthairacademy.com
Phone: (360) 336-6553
Inst. Accred.: NACCAS (1986/2001)

  Everett Campus
  520 128th St., SW, Everett 98204
  Phone: (425) 710-0888

Northwest HVC/R Association and Training Center
811 East Sprague, Ste. 6, Spokane 99202
Type: Private, independent
Degrees: C
URL: http://www.inwhvac.org
Phone: (509) 747-8810
Inst. Accred.: COE (2000)

Northwest School of Wooden Boatbuilding
42 North Water St., Port Hadlock 98339
Type: Private, independent
Degrees: C
Phone: (360) 385-4948
Inst. Accred.: ACCSCT (1993/2003)

Pacific Northwest Ballet School
301 Mercer St., Seattle 98109
Type: Private, independent
Degrees: C
URL: http://www.pnb.org
Phone: (206) 441-2435
Inst. Accred.: NASD (1988/1995)

Perry Technical Institute
2011 West Washington Ave., Yakima 98903-1296
Type: Private, proprietary
Degrees: C
Phone: (509) 453-0374
Inst. Accred.: ACCSCT (1969/2001)

Phagans' Orchards Beauty School
10411 NE Fourth Plain Blvd., Ste. 109, Vancouver 98662
Type: Private, proprietary
Degrees: C
URL: http://www.phagansnw.com
Phone: (360) 254-9517
Inst. Accred.: NACCAS (1986/2001)

The Photographic Center Northwest
900 Twelfth Ave., Seattle 98122
Type: Private, independent
Degrees: C
URL: http://www.pcnw.org
Phone: (206) 720-7222   *Calendar:* 10-mos. pr
Inst. Accred.: NASAD (1996/2002)

Professional Beauty School
2105 West Lincoln Ave., Ste. 2, Yakima 98902
Type: Private, proprietary
Degrees: C
Phone: (509) 576-0966
Inst. Accred.: NACCAS (1994/2003)

  Sunnyside Campus
  214 South 6th St., Sunnyside 98944
  Phone: (509) 837-4040

Sakie International College of Cosmetology
2106 West Nob Hill Blvd., Ste. 104, Yakima 98902
Type: Private, proprietary
Degrees: C
Phone: (509) 457-2773
Inst. Accred.: NACCAS (2005)

Seattle Midwifery School
2524 16th Ave. South, #300, Seattle 98144-5104
Type: Private, independent
Degrees: C
URL: http://www.seattlemidwifery.org
Phone: (206) 322-8834   *Calendar:* Qtr. plan
Inst. Accred.: MEAC (1999)

Stylemasters College of Hair Design
1224 Commerce Ave., Longview 98632
Type: Private, proprietary
Degrees: C
URL: http://stylemasters.edu
Phone: (360) 636-2720
Inst. Accred.: NACCAS (1982/2002)

Total Cosmetology Training Center
5303 North Market St., Spokane 99207
Type: Private, proprietary
Degrees: C
Phone: (509) 487-5500
Inst. Accred.: NACCAS (2004)

Yakima Beauty School Beauty Works
602 North First St., Yakima 98901
Type: Private, proprietary
Degrees: C
URL: http://www.yakimabeautyschool.com
Phone: (509) 248-2288
Inst. Accred.: NACCAS (2005)

WEST VIRGINIA

Academy of Careers and Technology
390 Stanaford Rd., Beckley 25801
Type: Public, state/local
Degrees: C
URL: http://www.wvact.net
Phone: (304) 256-4615   *Calendar:* Sem. plan
Inst. Accred.: NCA-CASI (1980/2004)

APUS Center for Professional and Workforce Development
111 West Congress St., Charles Town 25414
Type: Private, proprietary
Degrees: C
URL: http://www.apustraining.com
Phone: (877) 468-6269
Inst. Accred.: DETC (2005)

Art and Science Institute of Cosmetology and Massage Therapy
33 Corey Rd., Fairmont 26554
Type: Private, proprietary
Degrees: C
Phone: (304) 363-2015
Inst. Accred.: NACCAS (2004)

Beckley Beauty Academy
109 South Fayette St., Beckley 25801
Type: Private, proprietary
Degrees: C
Phone: (304) 253-8326
Inst. Accred.: NACCAS (1977/2004)

Ben Franklin Career Center
500 28th St., Dunbar 25064
Type: Public, state/local
Degrees: C
URL: http://bfcc.kana.tec.wv.us
Phone: (304) 766-0369
Inst. Accred.: NCA-CASI (1974/2003)

Cabell County Career Technology Center
1035 Norway Ave., Huntington 25705
Type: Public, state/local
Degrees: C
URL: http://boe.cabe.k12.wv.us/ctc
Phone: (304) 528-5106
Inst. Accred.: NCA-CASI (1977/2004)

Carver Career and Technical Education Center
4799 Midland Dr., Charleston 25306
Type: Public, state/local
Degrees: C
URL: http://kcs.kana.k12.wv.us/carver
Phone: (304) 348-1965
Inst. Accred.: NCA-CASI (1973/2004)
Prog. Accred.: Respiratory Therapy

Charleston School of Beauty Culture
210 Capitol St., Charleston 25301
Type: Private, proprietary
Degrees: C
URL: http://www.csbcwv.com
Phone: (304) 346-9603
Inst. Accred.: NACCAS (1981/2003)

Clarksburg Beauty Academy
120 South Third St., Clarksburg 26301
Type: Private, proprietary
Degrees: C
URL: http://www.clarksburgbeautyacademy.com
Phone: (304) 624-6475
Inst. Accred.: NACCAS (1970/2001)

Fayette Plateau Vocational Technology Center
300 West Oyler Ave., Oak Hill 25901
Type: Public, state/local
Degrees: C
URL: http://boe.faye.k12.wv.us
Phone: (304) 469-2911
Inst. Accred.: NCA-CASI (1992/2004)

Fred W. Eberle Technical Center
Rural Route 5 Box 2, Buckhannon 26201-9102
Type: Public, state/local
Degrees: C
URL: http://fetc.upsh.tec.wv.us
Phone: (304) 472-1259
Inst. Accred.: NCA-CASI (1980/2003)

Garnet Career Center
422 Dickinson St., Charleston 25301
Type: Public, state/local
Degrees: C
URL: http://kcs.kana.k12.wv.us/garnet
Phone: (304) 348-6195
Inst. Accred.: NCA-CASI (1982/2004)
Prog. Accred.: Practical Nursing

Harpers Ferry Job Corps Center
237 Job Corp Rd., Harpers Ferry 25425
Type: Public, federal
Degrees: C
Phone: (304) 728-5772
Inst. Accred.: COE (2001)

Huntington School of Beauty Culture, Inc.
East Hills Mall, 5185 U.S. Route 60 East, Rm. 115, Huntington 25705
Type: Private, proprietary
Degrees: C
Phone: (304) 736-6289
Inst. Accred.: NACCAS (1971/2002)

> **Ashland School of Beauty Culture**
> 1653 Greenup Ave., Ashland, KY 41101
> *Phone:* (606) 329-8720

International Beauty School—Martinsburg
201 West King St., Martinsburg 25401
Type: Private, proprietary
Degrees: C
Phone: (304) 263-4929
Inst. Accred.: NACCAS (1969/2005)

James Rumsey Technical Institute
3274 Hedgesville Rd., Martinsburg 25401-0259
Type: Public, state/local
Degrees: C
URL: http://www.jamesrumsey.com
Phone: (304) 754-7925
Inst. Accred.: NCA-CASI (1975/2002)

John D Rockefeller IV Career Center
Rural Route 4 Box 500, New Cumberland 26047
Type: Public, state/local
Degrees: C
URL: http://jdrcc.hanc.tec.wv.us
Phone: (304) 564-3337
Inst. Accred.: NCA-CASI (2004)

McDowell County Vocational Technical Center
PO Drawer V, Welch 24801
Type: Public, state/local
Degrees: C
URL: http://boe.mcdo.k12.wv.us/votech
Phone: (304) 436-3488
Inst. Accred.: NCA-CASI (1984/2003)

Mercer County Technical Education Center
1397 Stafford Dr., Princeton 24740
Type: Public, state/local
Degrees: C
URL: http://mctec.merc.tec.wv.us
Phone: (304) 425-9551
Inst. Accred.: NCA-CASI (1982/2004)

Meredith Manor International Equestrian Centre
Route 1, Box 66, Waverly 26184
Type: Private, proprietary
Degrees: C
URL: http://www.meredithmanor.com
Phone: (304) 679-3128
Inst. Accred.: ACCET (1987/2000)

Mineral County Technical Center
600 Harley O Staggers Dr., Keyser 26726
Type: Public, state/local
Degrees: C
URL: http://mctc.mine.tec.wv.us
Phone: (304) 788-4240
Inst. Accred.: NCA-CASI (1977/2002)

Monongalia County Technical Education Center
1000 Mississippi St., Morgantown 26505
Type: Public, state/local
Degrees: C
URL: http://boe.mono.k12.wv.us/mtec
Phone: (304) 291-9240
Inst. Accred.: NCA-CASI (1973/2005)
Prog. Accred.: Surgical Technology

Morgantown Beauty College, Inc.
276 Walnut St., Morgantown 26505
Type: Private, proprietary
Degrees: C
Phone: (304) 292-8475
Inst. Accred.: NACCAS (1993/2001)

Mountain State School of Massage
601 50th St., Charleston 25304
Type: Private, proprietary
Degrees: C
URL: http://www.mtnstmassage.com
Phone: (304) 926-8822
Inst. Accred.: CMTA (2004)

Mountaineer Beauty College, Inc.
700 6th Ave., PO Box 547, St. Albans 25177
Type: Private, proprietary
Degrees: C
URL: http://www.webmbc.com
Phone: (304) 727-9999
Inst. Accred.: NACCAS (1993/2004)

North Central West Virginia Opportunities Industrialization Center
120 Jackson St., Fairmont 26554
Type: Public, state/local
Degrees: C
URL: http://www.oicwv.org
Phone: (304) 366-8142
Inst. Accred.: NCA-CASI (1988/2004)

Putnam Career and Technical Center
101 Roosevelt Blvd., Eleanor 25070
Type: Public, state/local
Degrees: C
URL: http://boe.putn.k12.wv.us/pctc
Phone: (304) 586-3494
Inst. Accred.: NCA-CASI (1974/2005)

Ralph R. Willis Vocational Technical Center
PO Box 1747, Logan 25601
Type: Public, state/local
Degrees: C
URL: http://www.williscareercenter.com
Phone: (304) 752-4687
Inst. Accred.: NCA-CASI (1986/2005)

Roane Jackson Technical Center
4800 Spencer Rd., Leroy 25252
Type: Public, state/local
Degrees: C
URL: http://boe.jack.k12.wv.us/RJTCpage/Index.html
Phone: (304) 372-7335
Inst. Accred.: NCA-CASI (1975/2002)

Scott College of Cosmetology
1502 Market St., Wheeling 26003
Type: Private, proprietary
Degrees: C
Phone: (304) 232-7798
Inst. Accred.: NACCAS (1978/2004)

Stanley Technical Institute
1644 Mileground, Morgantown 26505
Type: Private, proprietary
Degrees: C
URL: http://www.hrdfwv.org
Phone: (304) 296-8223
Inst. Accred.: NCA-CASI (1997/2005)

Clarksburg Campus
120 Linden Ave., Clarksburg 26301
Phone: (304) 296-8223

Hinton Campus
McCreery Center, 320 Ω Second Ave., Hinton 25951
Phone: (304) 466-4805

Parkersburg Campus
800 Camden Ave., Parkersburg 26101
Phone: (304) 296-8223

United Technical Center
Route 3 Box 43-C, Clarksburg 26301
Type: Public, state/local
Degrees: C
URL: http://www.wvonline.com/utc
Phone: (304) 624-3280
Inst. Accred.: NCA-CASI (1975/2003)

Valley College of Technology—Martinsburg
287 Aikens Center, Martinsburg 24501
Type: Private, proprietary
Degrees: C
URL: http://www.vct.edu
Phone: (304) 263-0979   *Calendar:* Sem. plan
Inst. Accred.: ACICS (1996/2004)

West Virginia Career and Technical Center
PO Box 1004, Institute 25112
Type: Public, state/local
Degrees: C
Phone: (304) 766-4700
Inst. Accred.: NCA-CASI (1984/2002)

WISCONSIN

**Blue Sky School of Professional Massage and
Therapeutic Bodywork**
220 Oak St., Manchester Mall, Grafton 53024
Type: Private, proprietary
Degrees: C
URL: http://www.blueskyedu.org
Phone: (262) 376-1011
Inst. Accred.: CMTA (2004, Probation)

DePere/Green Bay Campus
1640-A Fire Ln. Dr., Green Bay 54311
Phone: (920) 406-9770

Madison Campus
2122 Luann Ln., Madison 53713
Phone: (608) 270-5245

Gill-Tech Academy of Hair Design
423 West College Ave., Appleton 54911
Type: Private, proprietary
Degrees: C
URL: http://www.gill-tech.com
Phone: (920) 739-8684
Inst. Accred.: NACCAS (1987/2002)

Four Seasons Salon and Day Spa
West Ct. Mall, 128 West 8th St., Ste. 8, Monroe 53566
Type: Private, proprietary
Degrees: C
URL: http://www.hairdirections.com/schoolhome.htm
Phone: (608) 325-4007
Inst. Accred.: COE (2003)

The Institute of Beauty and Wellness
342 North Water St., Milwaukee 53202
Type: Private, proprietary
Degrees: C
URL: http://www.institutebw.com
Phone: (414) 227-2889
Inst. Accred.: NACCAS (2003)

J. R. Rodgers & Associates, Inc.
2300 North Mayfair Rd., Ste. 945, Wauwatosa 53226
Type: Private, proprietary
Degrees: C
URL: http://www.sewis.dalecarnegie.com
Phone: (414) 771-3200
Inst. Accred.: ACCET (2000/2005)

John Hines & Associates, Inc.
2225 Jeffery Blvd., Cumberland 54829
Type: Private, proprietary
Degrees: C
Phone: (715) 822-4585
Inst. Accred.: ACCET (1977/2001)

Lakeside School of Massage Therapy
1726 North First St., Ste. 100, Milwaukee 53212
Type: Private, proprietary
Degrees: C
URL: http://www.lakesideschoolmassage.org
Phone: (414) 372-4345
Inst. Accred.: CMTA (2001)

Madison Campus
6121 Odana Rd., Madison 53719
Phone: (608) 274-2484

Madison Cosmetology College
310 Westgate Mall, Madison 53711
Type: Private, proprietary
Degrees: C
URL: http://www.cosmetologycollege.com
Phone: (608) 271-4204
Inst. Accred.: NACCAS (1975/2001)

Madison Media Institute
2702 Agriculture Dr., Madison 53718
Type: Private, proprietary
Degrees: C
URL: http://www.madisonmedia.com
Phone: (608) 663-2000   *Calendar:* Sem. plan
Inst. Accred.: ACCSCT (1972/2004)

Martin's College of Cosmetology—Green Bay
2575 West Mason St., Green Bay 54304
Type: Private, proprietary
Degrees: C
URL: http://www.mcofc.com
Phone: (920) 494-1430
Inst. Accred.: NACCAS (1989/2004)

Martin's College of Cosmetology—Madison
6414 Odana Rd., Madison 53717
Type: Private, proprietary
Degrees: C
URL: http://www.mcofc.com
Phone: (608) 270-0188
Inst. Accred.: NACCAS (1985/2005)

Martin's College of Cosmetology—Manitowoc
1034 South 18th St., Manitowoc 54220
Type: Private, proprietary
Degrees: C
URL: http://www.mcofc.com
Phone: (920) 684-3028
Inst. Accred.: NACCAS (1986/2001)

Appleton Campus
525 North Westhill Blvd., Appleton 54914
Phone: (920) 832-8686

Meyer Uebelher Associates, LLC
1463 County Rd. X, Mosinee 54455
Type: Private, proprietary
Degrees: C
URL: http://www.cwdalecarnegie.com
Phone: (715) 693-5007
Inst. Accred.: ACCET (2004)

Montessori Institute of Milwaukee, Inc.
3195 S. Superior St., Ste. L 428, Milwaukee 53207
Type: Public, independent
Degrees: C
URL: http://www.montessori6-12ami.org
Phone: (414) 481-5050
Inst. Accred.: MACTE (1998/2005)

Professional Hair Design Academy
3408 Mall Dr., Eau Claire 54701
Type: Private, proprietary
Degrees: C
URL: http://www.phdacademy.com
Phone: (715) 835-2345
Inst. Accred.: NACCAS (1997/2000)

Scientific College of Beauty and Barbering
326 Pearl St., LaCrosse 54601
Type: Private, proprietary
Degrees: C
URL: http://www.lacrossebeautyschool.com
Phone: (608) 784-4702
Inst. Accred.: NACCAS (1976/2002)

Siebert Associates, Inc.
802 West Broadway, Ste. L-9, Madison 53713
Type: Private, proprietary
Degrees: C
URL: http://www.swwis.dalecarnegie.com
Phone: (608) 222-5363
Inst. Accred.: ACCET (1999/2004)

State College of Beauty Culture
120 Clark St., Wausau 54401
Type: Private, proprietary
Degrees: C
URL: http://www.statecollegeofbeauty.com
Phone: (715) 845-2888
Inst. Accred.: NACCAS (1971/2002)

Vici Beauty School
4111 South 108th St., Greenfield 53228
Type: Private, proprietary
Degrees: C
URL: http://www.vicibeautyschool.com
Phone: (414) 425-1700
Inst. Accred.: NACCAS (1985/2003)

Vici Beauty School
11010 West Hampton Ave., Milwaukee 53225
Type: Private, proprietary
Degrees: C
URL: http://www.vicibeautyschool.com
Phone: (414) 464-5002
Inst. Accred.: NACCAS (1972/2003)

Wisconsin College of Cosmetology, Inc.
2960 Allied St., Green Bay 54304
Type: Private, proprietary
Degrees: C
URL: http://www.wccgb.com
Phone: (920) 336-8888
Inst. Accred.: NACCAS (1970/2005)

Wisconsin Conservatory of Music, Inc.
1584 North Prospect Ave., Milwaukee 53202
Type: Private, independent
Degrees: C
URL: http://www.wcmusic.org
Phone: (414) 276-5760
Inst. Accred.: NASM (1928/1997)

Wisconsin English Second Language Institute
19 North Pinckney St., Madison 53703
Type: Private, independent
Degrees: C
URL: http://www.ies-ed.com/descriptions/wiscesl_inst
Phone: (608) 257-4300
Inst. Accred.: CEA (2000)

WYOMING

Business Skills Institute
336 Summit St., Evanston 82930
Type: Private, proprietary
Degrees: C
URL: http://www.llc-evanston.org/llc/bsi.htm
Phone: (307) 789-5742
Inst. Accred.: ACCET (1998/2004)

Cheeks International Academy of Beauty Culture
207 West 18th St., Cheyenne 82001
Type: Private, proprietary
Degrees: C
URL: http://www.cheeksusa.com
Phone: (307) 637-8700
Inst. Accred.: NACCAS (1982/2002)

> **Fort Collins Campus**
> 4025 South Mason St., Unit 5, Fort Collins, CO 80525
> *Phone:* (970) 226-1416

> **Greeley Campus**
> 2547-B 11th Ave., Greeley, CO 80631
> *Phone:* (970) 352-4500

CANADA

Angela Martin Montessori Training Center
4052 Wilkerson Rd., Victoria V8Z 5A5
Type: Private, independent
Degrees: C
URL: http://www.montessori.bc.ca/ammtc/ammtc.htm
Phone: (250) 479-4746
Inst. Accred.: MACTE (2000)

Canadian Montessori Academy Teacher Education Program
70 Fieldrow Street, Nepean, Ontario K2G 1G7
Type: Private, independent
Degrees: C
URL: http://www.montessori-academy.com
Phone: (613) 727-9427
Inst. Accred.: MACTE (2005)

Canadian Montessori Teacher Education Institute
4427-4 Bath Road, Amherstview, Ontario K7N 1A1
Type: Private, independent
Degrees: C
Phone: (416) 458-8970
Inst. Accred.: MACTE (2003)

ICT Kikkawa College
2340 Dundas St., West, Unit G-04, Toronto M6P 4A9
Type: Private, proprietary
Degrees: C
URL: http://www.ictschools.com
Phone: (416) 762-4857
Inst. Accred.: CMTA (2001/2004, Probation)

ICT Northumberland College
1888 Brunswick St., Halifax B3J 3J8
Type: Private, proprietary
Degrees: C
URL: http://www.ictschools.com
Phone: (902) 425-2869
Inst. Accred.: CMTA (2001, Probation)
Prog. Accred.: Massage Therapy

The Massage Therapy College of Manitoba, Inc.
692 Wolseley Ave., 2nd Flr., Winnipeg R3G 1C3
Type: Private, proprietary
Degrees: C
URL: http://www.massagetherapycollege.com
Phone: (204) 772-8999
Inst. Accred.: CMTA (1999/2004)

Toronto Montessori Institute
8569 Bayview Ave., Richmond Hill L4B 3M7
Type: Private, independent
Degrees: C
URL: http://www.tmi.edu
Phone: (905) 857-0953
Inst. Accred.: MACTE (2000)

Montessori House of Children
711 Waterloo St., London N6A 3WI
Phone: (519) 433-9121

Vancouver ECE and Montessori College
#600-1788 West Broadway, Vancouver V6J 1Y1
Type: Private, independent
Degrees: C
URL: http://www.vemc.ca
Phone: (604) 731-8869
Inst. Accred.: MACTE (2004)

Vancouver Training Institute Montessori Program
1580 West Broadway, Vancouver V6J 5K8
Type: Private, independent
Degrees: C
Phone: (604) 713-4723
Inst. Accred.: MACTE (2005)

DOMINICAN REPUBLIC

Montessori Training Center of Santo Domingo
Prol. Hatuey Esquina Olegario Tenares, Santa Domingo, Dominican Republic
Type: Private, independent
Degrees: C
Phone: (809) 530-1838
Inst. Accred.: MACTE (2000/2003)

ISRAEL

Montessori Advanced Education Center
No. 16 Pinchas Rozen St., Tel-Aviv 69512
Type: Private, independent
Degrees: C
URL: http://www.montessori-center.org
Phone: 011972 3 6494796
Inst. Accred.: MACTE (2005)

JAPAN

Babel University
1-6-1 Roppongi, Izumi Garden, 7F, Minato-ku, Tokyo, Japan 106-6007
Type: Private, proprietary
Degrees: C
URL: http://www.babel.co.jp
Phone: 011 81 3 6229 2433
Inst. Accred.: DETC (2002)

MEXICO

Centro de Entrenamiento Montessori
PO Box 145, Garza Garcia, Mexico 66230
Type: Private, independent
Degrees: C
URL: http://www.giga.com/~montsm/cem.htm
Phone: 011 52 8 336 5150
Inst. Accred.: MACTE (2000/2003)

REPUBLIC OF KOREA

Dr. Jun Institute of Montessori Education
320-9 Wol Gye 4 Dong, Seoul, Republic of Korea
Type: Private, independent
Degrees: C
Phone: 011 82 2 979 8294
Inst. Accred.: MACTE (2002)

Korean Institute for Montessori
621 Sang do Bldg., Sang-do, Il Dong, Dong Zak Ku, Seoul, Korea, Republic of
Type: Private, independent
Degrees: C
Phone: 011 82 2 825 6231
Inst. Accred.: MACTE (1996/2005)

Korean Montessori College
150 Hongik-dong, Sungdong-Gu, Seoul, Republic of Korea
Type: Private, independent
Degrees: C
Phone: 011 82 2 2295 2111
Inst. Accred.: MACTE (1996/2005)

SAUDI ARABIA

Saudi Arabian Oil Company Training and Career Development
Dhahran, Saudi Arabia 31311
Type: Private, proprietary
Degrees: C
URL: http://www.saudiaramco.com
Phone: 011 966 3874 6043
Inst. Accred.: ACCET (1993/2001)

Abqaiq Campus
Abqaiq, Saudi Arabia
Phone: 011 966 3874 6043

Al Hasa/Mubarraz Campus
Al Hasa/Mubarraz, Saudi Arabia
Phone: 011 966 3874 6043

Jeddah Campus
Jeddah, Saudi Arabia
Phone: 011 966 3874 6043

Ras Tanura Campus
Ras Tanura, Saudi Arabia
Phone: 011 966 3874 6043

Udhailiyah Campus
Udhailiyah, Saudi Arabia
Phone: 011 966 3874 6043

Yenbu Campus
Yenbu, Saudi Arabia
Phone: 011 966 3874 6043

Saudi Aramco Training and Career Development Center
Dhahran, Saudi Arabia 31311
Type: Private, proprietary
Degrees: C
URL: http://www.saudiaramco.com
Phone: 011 966 3874 6043
Inst. Accred.: ACCET (1993/2001)

Abqaiq Campus
Abqaiq, Saudi Arabia
Phone: 011 966 3874 6043

Al Hasa/Mubarraz Campus
Al Hasa/Mubarraz, Saudi Arabia
Phone: 011 966 3874 6043

Riyadh Campus
Riyadh, Saudi Arabia
Phone: 011 966 3874 6043

Udhailiyah Campus
Udhailiyah, Saudi Arabia
Phone: 011 966 3874 6043

Yenbu Campus
Yenbu, Saudi Arabia
Phone: 011 966 3874 6043

Jeddah Campus
Jeddah, Saudi Arabia
Phone: 011 966 3874 6043

Saudi Electricity Company—Eastern Region Branch
SECTI, PO Box 5190, Damman, Saudi Arabia
Type: Private, proprietary
Degrees: C
URL: http://www.sceco-east.com.sa/English/index.htm
Phone: 011 3 842-5222
Inst. Accred.: ACCET (2004)

SOUTH AFRICA

The College of Modern Montessori
PO Box 119, Linbro Park, South Africa 2065
Type: Private, independent
Degrees: C
URL: http://www.montessoriint.com
Phone: 011 27 11 608 1584
Inst. Accred.: MACTE (1995/2004)

> **Durban Campus**
> 67 Elizabeth Dr., Forest Hills, Durban 2065
> *Phone:* 011 27 11 608 1584

> **Stepping Stones Montessori School**
> Sigmouth Ave., Oranjezicht, Cape Town 2065
> *Phone:* 011 27 11 608 1584

SPAIN

Les Roches Marbella School of Hotel Management
Urbanización Las Lomas de Rio Verde, Carretera de Istán, Km. 1, Marbella, Spain E-29602
Type: Private, proprietary
Degrees: C
URL: http://www.lesroches.es
Phone: 011 34 95 276 41 45
Inst. Accred.: NEASC-CTCI (2004)

SWEDEN

IHM Business School
Warfvinges Vag 21, Box 30163, Stockholm, Sweden 104 25
Type: Private, proprietary
Degrees: C
URL: http://www.ihm.se
Phone: 011 46 8 657 0000
Inst. Accred.: NEASC-CTCI (2000)

> **Gotenberg Campus**
> Fabriksgatan 21-25, Box 5273, Gotenborg, Sweden 402 25
> *Phone:* 011 46 31 335 2000

> **Malmo Campus**
> Carlsgatatn 12C, Malmo, Sweden 211 20
> *Phone:* 011 46 40 601 2300

SWITZERLAND

Hotel Institute Montreux
Avenue des Alpes, Montreux, Switzerland CH-1820
Type: Private, proprietary
Degrees: C
URL: http://www.him.ch
Phone: 011 41 21 966 4646   *Calendar:* Sem. plan
Inst. Accred.: NEASC-CTCI (1996)

Institut Hotelier "Cesar Ritz"
Le Bouveret, Switzerland CH-1897
Type: Private, proprietary
Degrees: C
URL: http://www.ihcritz.ch
Phone: 011 41 24 481 8282   *Calendar:* Sem. plan
Inst. Accred.: NEASC-CTCI (1999)

TAIWAN

Trillium Montessori Teacher Education Institute of Taiwan
67, Lane 270, Chuing Yang Road, Chang Hua, Taiwan, R.O.C.
Type: Private, independent
Degrees: C
Phone: 011886 476 37377
Inst. Accred.: MACTE (2005)

TRINIDAD AND TOBAGO

Trinidad and Tobago College of Therapeutic Massage
68 Market St., Gopaul Lands, Marabella, Trinidad and Tobago
Type: Private, proprietary
Degrees: C
Phone: (868) 658-3907
Inst. Accred.: CMTA (2005)

UNITED KINGDOM

The Kent and Sussex Montessori Centre
Hoath Hall, Walnut Tree Cross, Chiddingstone Hoath, Edenbridge, KE, United Kingdom TN8 7DB
Type: Private, independent
Degrees: C
URL: http://www.montessoricentre.com
Phone: 011 44 1892 870740
Inst. Accred.: MACTE (1997/2002)

VENEZUELA

Centro Electronico de Idiomas y Computacion
Av. 11 con 78 Edif. Centro Electronico de Idiomas, Planta Baja, Maracaibo, Venezuela 4001
Type: Private, proprietary
Degrees: C
URL: http://www.centroelectronic.com
Phone: (261) 797-6089
Inst. Accred.: ACCET (2001/2005)

Accredited Programs at
Other Facilities

This section lists accredited programs offered at facilities that are independent of any affiliation or connection with an accredited institution of postsecondary education.

ALABAMA

Alabama Reference Laboratories/ LabSouth, Inc.
543 South Hull St., PO Box 4600, Montgomery 36103-4600
Type: Private, proprietary
Degrees: C
Phone: (205) 263-5745
Prog. Accred.: Clinical Lab Scientist

Baptist Health System of Alabama
800 Montclair Rd., Birmingham 35213-1984
Type: Private, proprietary
Degrees: C
URL: http://www.bhsala.com
Phone: (205) 592-1390
Prog. Accred.: Clinical Pastoral Education

Montclair Baptist Medical Center
800 Montclair Rd., Birmingham 35213-1984
Phone: (205) 592-1593
Prog. Accred: Clinical Pastoral Education

Princeton Baptist Medical Center
701 Princeton Ave., SW, Birmingham 35211-1303
Phone: (205) 783-3493
Prog. Accred: Clinical Pastoral Education

Baptist Medical Center South School of Medical Technology
PO Box 11010, 2105 East South Blvd., Montgomery 36116
Type: Private, independent
Degrees: C
URL: http://www.baptistfirst.org
Phone: (334) 288-2100
Prog. Accred.: Clinical Lab Scientist, Nuclear Medicine Technology, Radiography

Carraway Methodist Medical Center
1600 Carraway Blvd., Birmingham 35234-1913
Type: Private, independent
Degrees: C
URL: Carraway Methodist Medical Center
Phone: (205) 502-6000
Prog. Accred.: Clinical Pastoral Education, Radiography

DCH Regional Medical Center
809 University Blvd. East, Tuscaloosa 35401
Type: Private, independent
Degrees: C
URL: http://www.dchsystem.com
Phone: (205) 759-7111
Prog. Accred.: Radiography

Huntsville Hospital
101 Sivley Rd., Huntsville 35801
Type: Private, independent
Degrees: C
URL: http://www.hhsys.org
Phone: (256) 265-1000
Prog. Accred.: Radiography

Veterans Affairs Medical Center—Birmingham
700 South 19th St., Birmingham 35233
Type: Public, federal
Degrees: C
Prog. Accred.: General Practice Residency

ALASKA

Southcentral Foundation-Alaska Native Medical Center
315 Diplomacy Dr., Anchorage 99508
Type: Private, independent
Degrees: C
URL: http://www.southcentralfoundation.org
Prog. Accred.: General Practice Residency

ARIZONA

Arizona State Hospital
2500 East Van Buren St., Phoenix 85008-6037
Type: Public, state
Degrees: C
URL: http://www.azdhs.gov/azsh
Phone: (602) 244-1331
Prog. Accred.: Psychology Internship

Carl T. Hayden Veterans Affairs Medical Center
650 East Indian School Rd., Phoenix 85012-1892
Type: Public, federal
Degrees: C
URL: http://www.phoenix.med.va.gov
Phone: (602) 277-5551
Prog. Accred.: Psychology Internship

Good Samaritan Medical Center
1111 E McDowell Rd., PO 2989, Phoenix 85006-2612
Type: Private, proprietary
Degrees: C
Phone: (602) 239-4324
Prog. Accred.: Clinical Pastoral Education

Kino Community Hospital
2800 Kino Community Way, Tucson 85713
Type: Private, independent
Degrees: C
Prog. Accred.: General Practice Residency

Accredited Programs at Other Facilities

Phoenix Institute of Herbal Medicine and Acupuncture
301 East Bethany Home Rd., Ste. A-100, Phoenix 85012
Type: Private, proprietary, four-year
Degrees: M
URL: http://www.pihma.com
Phone: (602) 274-1885
Prog. Accred.: Acupuncture

Southern Arizona Psychology Internship Consortium
502 West 29th St., Tucson 85713-3394
Type: Private, independent
Degrees: C
URL: http://www.u.arizona.edu/~penn/sapic
Phone: (520) 838-3923
Prog. Accred.: Psychology Internship

Southern Arizona Veterans Affairs Health Care System
3601 South 6th Ave., Tucson 85723
Type: Public, federal
Degrees: C
URL: http://www.va.gov/678savahcs
Phone: (520) 792-1450
Prog. Accred.: Psychology Internship

University Medical Center
1501 North Campbell Ave., Tucson 85724
Type: Private, independent
Degrees: C
Phone: (520) 694-6826
Prog. Accred.: Clinical Pastoral Education

Yuma Regional Medical Center
2400 South Ave. A, Yuma 85364
Type: Private, proprietary
Degrees: C
URL: http://www.yumaregional.org
Phone: (520) 344-7002
Prog. Accred.: Clinical Pastoral Education

ARKANSAS

Baptist Health System, Nursing and Allied Health Schools
11900 Colonel Glenn Rd., Ste. 1000, Little Rock 72210-2820
Type: Private, independent
Degrees: C
URL: http://www.baptist-health.org
Phone: (501) 202-2000
Prog. Accred.: Clinical Lab Scientist, Histologic Technology, Radiography

Central Arkansas Radiation Therapy Institute
PO Box 55050, Little Rock 72215
Type: Private, independent
Degrees: C
URL: http://www.carti.com
Phone: (501) 664-8573
Prog. Accred.: Radiation Therapy

Central Arkansas Veterans Healthcare System
4300 West 7th St., Little Rock 72205-5484
Type: Private, federal
Degrees: C
URL: http://www1.va.gov/directory
Phone: (501) 257-1000
Prog. Accred.: Psychology Internship

Jefferson Regional Medical Center
1515 West 42nd Ave., Pine Bluff 71306-7004
Type: Private, proprietary
Degrees: C
URL: http://www.jrmc.org
Phone: (870) 541-7167
Prog. Accred.: Clinical Pastoral Education

Northwest Technical Institute
PO Box 2000, Springdale 72765-2000
Type: Private, proprietary
Degrees: C
Phone: (501) 751-8824
Prog. Accred.: Surgical Technology

Saint Vincent Infirmary Medical Center
Two St. Vincent Circle, Little Rock 72205
Type: Private, independent
Degrees: C
URL: https://www.stvincenthealth.com
Phone: (501) 552-3000
Prog. Accred.: Radiography

CALIFORNIA

1st Dental Battalion/NDC
13128 14th St., Camp Pendleton 92055-5221
Type: Public, federal
Degrees: C
URL: http://www.ndc.cpen.med.navy.mil
Phone: (760) 725-5578
Prog. Accred.: Advanced Education in General Dentistry

60th Medical Group
101 Bodin Circle, Travis AFB 94535-1800
Type: Public, federal
Degrees: C
URL: https://www.travis.af.mil/dgmc
Phone: (707) 423-7000
Prog. Accred.: Advanced Education in General Dentistry, Oral and Maxillofacial Surgery

Alta Bates Medical Center
2450 Ashby Ave, Berkeley
Type: Private, proprietary
Degrees: C
Phone: (510) 204-6730
Prog. Accred.: Clinical Pastoral Education

Arrowhead Regional Medical Center
400 North Pepper Ave., Colton 92324-1819
Type: Private, independent
Degrees: C
URL: http://www.co.san-bernardino.ca.us/armc
Phone: (909) 580-1000   *Calendar:* 24-mos. pr
Prog. Accred.: Radiography

Atascadero State Hospital
PO Box 7001, Atascadero 93423-7001
Type: Public, state
Degrees: C
URL: http://www.dmh.ca.gov/Statehospitals/Atascadero
Phone: (805) 468-2000
Prog. Accred.: Psychology Internship

California Department of Mental Health Vacaville Psychiatric Program
1600 California Dr., Vacaville 95696-2297
Type: Public, state
Degrees: C
URL: http://www.dmh.ca.gov/Statehospitals/Vacaville
Phone: (707) 449-6571
Prog. Accred.: Psychology Internship

California Pacific Medical Center
Institute for Health & Healing, PO Box 7999, San Francisco
Type: Private, independent
Degrees: C
Phone: (415) 600-3660
Prog. Accred.: Clinical Pastoral Education

Cedars Sinai Medical Center
8700 Beverly Blvd., Los Angeles 90048
Type: Private, proprietary
Degrees: C
Prog. Accred.: General Practice Residency

The Center for Urban Ministry
2859 El Cajon Blvd., Ste. 2A, San Diego
Type: Private, independent
Degrees: C
Phone: (619) 260-7118 x5122
Prog. Accred.: Clinical Pastoral Education

Children's Hospital of Orange County
455 South Main St., Orange 92868-3874
Type: Private, independent
Degrees: C
URL: http://www.choc.com
Phone: (714) 997-3000
Prog. Accred.: Psychology Internship

Community Reach Center
8931 Huron St., Thornton 80260
Type: Private, independent
Degrees: C
URL: http://www.adamsmentalhealth.org
Phone: (303) 853-3500
Prog. Accred.: Psychology Internship

The Crystal Cathedral
12141 Lewis St, Garden Grove
Type: Private, independent
Degrees: C
URL: http://www.crystalcathedral.org
Phone: (714) 971-4038
Prog. Accred.: Clinical Pastoral Education

Didi Hirsch Community Mental Health Center
4760 South Sepulveda Blvd., Culver City 90230-4888
Type: Private, independent
Degrees: C
URL: http://www.didihirsch.org
Phone: (310) 390-6612
Prog. Accred.: Psychology Internship

East Los Angeles Occupational Center
2100 Marengo St., Los Angeles 90033
Type: Private, proprietary
Degrees: C
Phone: (213) 223-1283
Prog. Accred.: Dental Assisting

Eisenhower Medical Center School of Medical Technology
39000 Bob Hope Dr., Rancho Mirage 92270-3202
Type: Private, proprietary
Degrees: C
URL: http://www.emc.org
Phone: (760) 773-4525
Prog. Accred.: Clinical Lab Scientist

Greater Long Beach Child Guidance Center
2801 Atlantic Ave., Long Beach 90801
Type: Private, independent
Degrees: C
URL: http://www.glbcgc.org
Phone: (562) 424-4227
Prog. Accred.: Psychology Internship

Hacienda La Puente Adult Education
15540 East Fairgrove Ave., La Puente 91744
Type: Public, local
Degrees: C
URL: http://www.hlpusd.k12.ca.us/hlpae
Phone: (818) 855-3138
Prog. Accred.: Dental Assisting, Respiratory Therapy Technology

The Help Group
13130 Burbank Blvd., Sherman Oaks 91401
Type: Private, independent
Degrees: C
URL: http://www.thehelpgroup.org
Phone: (877) 943-5747
Prog. Accred.: Psychology Internship

Highland General Hospital
1411 East 31st St., Oakland 94602
Type: Private, proprietary
Degrees: C
Prog. Accred.: Oral and Maxillofacial Surgery

Kaiser Permanente Los Angeles Medical Center
4700 Sunset Blvd., 5th and 6th Flrs, Los Angeles 90027-6082
Type: Private, independent
Degrees: C
URL: http://members.kaiserpermanente.org
Phone: (323) 783-2600
Prog. Accred.: Psychology Internship

Kaiser Permanente School of Allied Health Sciences
938 Marina Way South, Richmond 94804
Type: Private, independent
Degrees: C
URL: http://www.kpsahs.org
Phone: (510) 231-5000
Prog. Accred.: Nuclear Medicine Technology, Radiography

Kaiser Permanente Vista Medical Offices
780 Shadowridge Dr., Vista 92083
Type: Private, independent
Degrees: C
URL: http://members.kaiserpermanente.org
Phone: (760) 599-2350
Prog. Accred.: Psychology Internship

Loma Linda Veterans Affairs Healthcare System
11201 Benton St., Loma Linda 92357
Type: Public, federal
Degrees: C
URL: http://www.lom.med.va.gov
Phone: (909) 825-7084
Prog. Accred.: General Practice Residency, Psychology Internship

Los Angeles County Harbor-UCLA Medical Center
1000 West Carson St., Torrance 90502
Type: Private, independent
Degrees: C
URL: http://www.humc.edu
Phone: (310) 222-2345
Prog. Accred.: Nuclear Medicine Technology, Nurse Practitioner, Radiography

Los Angeles County-USC Medical Center
1200 North State St., Los Angeles 90033
Type: Public, independent
Degrees: C
Phone: (323) 226-2800
Prog. Accred.: General Practice Residency

Lucile Packard Children's Hospital
725 Welch Rd., Palo Alto 94304
Type: Private, independent
Degrees: C
URL: http://www.lpch.org
Phone: (650) 497-8000
Prog. Accred.: Psychology Internship

Methodist Hospital of Southern California
300 W Huntington Dr, PO Box 60016, Arcadia
Type: Private, independent
Degrees: C
Phone: (626) 574-3433
Prog. Accred.: Clinical Pastoral Education

Children's Hospital of Los Angeles
4650 West Sunset Blvd., Los Angeles 90027
Phone: (323) 669-2482
Prog. Accred: Clinical Pastoral Education, Psychology Internship

The Metropolitan Detention Center
535 North Alameda St., Los Angeles 90012
Type: Public, federal
Degrees: C
URL: http://www.bop.gov/locations/institutions/los/index.jsp
Phone: (213) 485-0439
Prog. Accred.: Psychology Internship

Metropolitan State Hospital
11401 Bloomfield Ave., Norwalk 90650
Type: Public, state
Degrees: C
URL: http://www.dmh.ca.gov/Statehospitals/Metro
Phone: (562) 863-7011
Prog. Accred.: Psychology Internship

Mills-Peninsula Health Services
1783 El Camino Real, Burlingame 94010
Type: Private, independent
Degrees: C
URL: http://www.mills-peninsula.org
Phone: (650) 696 5400
Prog. Accred.: Radiography

Mount Diablo Medical Center
2540 East St, Concord
Type: Private, independent
Degrees: C
URL: http://www.johnmuirmt.diablo.com
Phone: (925) 674-2133
Prog. Accred.: Clinical Pastoral Education

Naval Dental Center—San Diego
Naval Station Box 368147, San Diego 92136-5596
Type: Public, federal
Degrees: C
Prog. Accred.: General Dentistry

Naval Hospital—Camp Pendelton
Camp Pendleton 92055-5191
Type: Public, federal
Degrees: C
Prog. Accred.: General Practice Residency

Naval Medical Center—San Diego
34800 Bob Willson Dr., San Diego 92134-5001
Type: Public, federal
Degrees: C
URL: http://www-nmcsd.med.navy.mil
Phone: (619) 532-6400
Prog. Accred.: General Practice Residency, Oral and Maxillofacial Surgery, Psychology Internship

Naval School of Health Sciences
34101 Farenholt Ave., Bldg. 14, San Diego 92021-5291
Type: Public, federal
Degrees: C
URL: http://nshssd.med.navy.mil
Phone: (619) 532-9712
Prog. Accred.: Clinical Lab Technology, Dental Laboratory Technology, Nuclear Medicine Technology, Nurse Anesthesia Education, Radiation Therapy, Radiography

Pacific Clinics
909 South Fair Oaks Ave., Pasadena 91105
Type: Private, independent
Degrees: C
URL: http://www.pacificclinics.org
Phone: (626) 254-5000
Prog. Accred.: Psychology Internship

Richmond Area Multi-Services, Inc.
3626 Balboa St., San Francisco 94121
Type: Private, independent
Degrees: C
URL: http://www.ramsinc.org/ramshome.html
Phone: (415) 668-5955
Prog. Accred.: Psychology Internship

River Oak Center for Children
4330 Auburn Blvd., Ste. 2000, Sacramento 95841
Type: Private, independent
Degrees: C
URL: http://www.riveroak.org
Phone: (916) 609-5100
Prog. Accred.: Psychology Internship

Saint John's Child and Family Development Center
1339 20th St., Santa Monica 90404
Type: Private, independent
Degrees: C
Phone: (310) 829-8921
Prog. Accred.: Psychology Internship

Saint John's Regional Medical Center
1600 North Rose Ave., Oxnard 93030-3722
Type: Private, independent
Degrees: C
Phone: (805) 988-2815
Prog. Accred.: Clinical Pastoral Education

Saint Joseph Hospital
1100 West Stewart Dr., Orange 92868-5600
Type: Private, independent
Degrees: C
Phone: (714) 771-8137
Prog. Accred.: Clinical Pastoral Education

Providence Saint Joseph Hospital
501 South Buena Vista Streeet, Burbank 91505-4809
Phone: (818) 729-1245
Prog. Accred.: Clinical Pastoral Education

Saint Mary's Medical Center
450 Stanyan St., San Francisco 94117-1079
Type: Private, independent
Degrees: C
Phone: (415) 750-5718
Prog. Accred.: Clinical Pastoral Education

San Bernardino County Department of Behavioral Health
700 East Gilbert St., San Bernardino 92415
Type: Public, state
Degrees: C
URL: http://www.co.san-bernardino.ca.us/dbh
Phone: (909) 873-4478
Prog. Accred.: Psychology Internship

San Joaquin General Hospital
500 West Hospital Rd., French Camp 95231
Type: Private, independent
Degrees: C
URL: http://www.sjgeneralhospital.com
Phone: (209) 468-6000
Prog. Accred.: Radiography

Santa Barbara Cottage Hospital
PO Box 689, Santa Barbara 93102-0689
Type: Private, independent
Degrees: C
URL: http://www.cottagehealthsystem.org
Phone: (805) 682-7111
Prog. Accred.: Clinical Lab Scientist

Sharp Memorial Hospital
7901 Frost St., San Diego 92123-2701
Type: Private, proprietary
Degrees: C
URL: http://www.sharp.com/hospital/index.cfm?id=919
Phone: (858) 939-3400
Prog. Accred.: Clinical Pastoral Education, Psychology Internship

Sharp Mesa Vista Hospital
7850 Vista Hill Ave., San Diego 92123
Type: Private, proprietary
Degrees: C
URL: http://www.sharp.com/hospital/index.cfm?id=921
Phone: (858) 278-4110
Prog. Accred.: Psychology Internship

Shasta Community Mental Health Center
2640 Breslauer Way, Redding 96001
Type: Private, independent
Degrees: C
Phone: (530) 246-5710
Prog. Accred.: Psychology Internship

Simi Valley Adult School
3192 Los Angeles Ave., Simi Valley 93065
Type: Private, proprietary
Degrees: C
Phone: (805) 527-4840
Prog. Accred.: Respiratory Therapy Technology, Surgical Technology

South Baylo University
1126 North Brookhurst St., Anaheim 92801
Type: Private, proprietary, four-year
Degrees: M   *Enroll:* 450
URL: http://southbaylo.edu
Phone: (714) 533-1495   *Calendar:* Qtr. plan
Prog. Accred.: Acupuncture

> **Los Angeles Campus**
> 2727 West 6th St., Los Angeles 90015
> *Phone:* (213) 738-0712
> *Prog. Accred:* Acupuncture

South Coast Nuclear Medicine
229 West Pueblo St., Santa Barbara 93105
Type: Private, independent
Degrees: C
Phone: (805) 563-5744   *Calendar:* 12-mos. pr
Prog. Accred.: Nuclear Medicine Technology

Southern California Counseling Center
5615 West Pico Blvd., Los Angeles 90019
Type: Private, independent, four-year
Degrees: M
URL: http://www.sccc-la.org
Phone: (213) 937-1344
Prog. Accred.: Marriage and Family Therapy

Southern California Regional Occupational Center
2300 Crenshaw Blvd., Torrance 90501
Type: Public, state
Degrees: C
Phone: (310) 224-4200   *Calendar:* Sem. plan
Prog. Accred.: Medical Assisting (CAAHEP)

Southwestern University School of Law
675 South Westmoreland Ave., Los Angeles 90005
Type: Private, proprietary, four-year
Degrees: P   *Enroll:* 858
Phone: (213) 738-6710   *Calendar:* Sem. plan
Prog. Accred.: Law

Sutter Medical Center
2800 L St., Sacramento 95816-5616
Type: Private, proprietary
Degrees: C
Phone: (916) 733-8848
Prog. Accred.: Clinical Pastoral Education

Tri-City Mental Health Center
790 East Bonita Ave., Pomona 91767-1906
Type: Public, state/local
Degrees: C
URL: http://www.tricitymhs.org
Phone: (909) 623-6131
Prog. Accred.: Psychology Internship

University of East-West Medicine
970 West EL Camino Real, Sunnyvale 94087
Type: Private, proprietary, four-year
Degrees: M
URL: http://www.uewm.edu
Phone: (408) 733-1878   *Calendar:* Tri. plan
Prog. Accred.: Acupuncture

Veterans Affairs Greater Los Angeles Healthcare System
11301 Wilshire Blvd., West Los Angeles 90073
Type: Public, federal
Degrees: C
URL: http://www.gla.med.va.gov
Phone: (310) 478-3711
Prog. Accred.: Combined Prosthodontics, General Practice Residency, Periodontics, Psychology Internship

> **Los Angeles Ambulatory Care Center**
> 351 East Temple St., Los Angeles 90012
> *Phone:* (213) 253-2677
> *Prog. Accred:* Psychology Internship

> **Sepulveda Ambulatory Care Center**
> 16111 Plummer St., Sepulveda 91343
> *Phone:* (818) 891-7711
> *Prog. Accred:* General Practice Residency, Psychology Internship

Veterans Affairs Medical Center—Long Beach
5901 East 7th St., Long Beach 90822-5201
Type: Public, federal
Degrees: C
URL: http://www.long-beach.med.va.gov
Phone: (562) 826-8000
Prog. Accred.: Endodontics, General Practice Residency, Psychology Internship

Veterans Affairs Medical Center— San Francisco
4150 Clement St., San Francisco 94121
Type: Public, federal
Degrees: C
URL: http://www.sf.med.va.gov
Phone: 415) 221-4810
Prog. Accred.: General Practice Residency, Psychology Internship

Veterans Affairs Northern California Health Care System—Mare Island
201 Walnut Ave., Vallejo 94592
Type: Public, federal
Degrees: C
URL: http://www.va.gov/sta/guide
Phone: (707) 562-8200
Prog. Accred.: General Practice Residency

Veterans Affairs Northern California Health Care System—Martinez
150 Muir Rd., Martinez 94553
Type: Private, federal
URL: http://www1.va.gov/directory
Phone: (925) 372-2000
Prog. Accred.: Psychology Internship

Veterans Affairs Palo Alto Health Care System
3801 Miranda Ave., Palo Alto 94304
Type: Public, federal
Degrees: C
URL: http://www.palo-alto.med.va.gov
Phone: (650) 493-5000
Prog. Accred.: General Practice Residency, Psychology Internship

Veterans Affairs San Diego Healthcare System
3350 La Jolla Village Dr., San Diego 92161
Type: Public, federal
Degrees: C
URL: http://www.san-diego.med.va.gov
Phone: (858) 552-8585
Prog. Accred.: General Practice Residency

COLORADO

10th Medical Group/SGFL
4102 Pinion Dr., Ste. 3, USAF Academy 80840
Type: Public, federal
Degrees: C
URL: http://www.usafa.af.mil/sg
Phone: (719) 333-5111
Prog. Accred.: Advanced Education in General Dentistry

Aurora Mental Health Center
14301 East Hampden Ave., Aurora 80014
Type: Private, independent
Degrees: C
URL: http://www.aumhc.org
Phone: (303) 617-2300
Prog. Accred.: Psychology Internship

Centura Health CPE (System Center)
4231 West 16th Ave., Denver 80204-1335
Type: Private, proprietary
Degrees: C
Phone: (303) 595-2770
Prog. Accred.: Clinical Pastoral Education

Penrose-Saint Francis Health Services
825 East Pikes Peak Ave., Colorado Springs 80933-7021
Phone: (719) 776-8643
Prog. Accred: Clinical Pastoral Education

Porter Adventist Hospital
2525 South Downing St., Denver 80210-5817
Phone: (303) 778-5683
Prog. Accred: Clinical Pastoral Education

School of Clinical Laboratory Science
2215 North Cascade Ave., PO Box 7021, Colorado Springs 80933-7021
Phone: (719) 776-5221
Prog. Accred: Clinical Lab Scientist

The Children's Hospital
1056 East 19th Ave., Denver 80218
Type: Private, independent
Degrees: C
URL: http://www.tchden.org
Phone: (303) 861-8888
Prog. Accred.: Pediatric Dentistry, Psychology Internship

Colorado Mental Health Institute at Fort Logan
3520 West Oxford Ave., Denver 80236-3108
Type: Public, proprietary
Degrees: C
URL: http://www.cdhs.state.co.us/ohr/mhs/mif
Phone: (303) 866-7080
Prog. Accred.: Clinical Pastoral Education, Psychology Internship

Rocky Mountain Pastoral Care and Training Associates
PO Box 630, Littleton 80160-0630
Phone: (303) 918-9540
Prog. Accred: Clinical Pastoral Education

Samaritan Counseling and Education Center
PO Box 788, Colorado Springs 80901
Phone: (719) 471-2500 x3
Prog. Accred: Clinical Pastoral Education

Denver Family Institute
7200 East Hampden Ave., Ste. 301, Denver 80224-3021
Type: Private, proprietary
Degrees: C
Phone: (303) 756-3340   *Calendar:* Qtr. plan
Prog. Accred.: Marriage and Family Therapy

Denver Health Medical Center
777 Bannock St., Denver 80204
Type: Private, independent
Degrees: C
URL: http://www.denverhealth.org
Phone: (303) 436-6000
Prog. Accred.: General Practice Residency, Oral and Maxillofacial Surgery, Psychology Internship

Family Therapy/Play Therapy Institute
12101 East Second Ave., Aurora 80011-8328
Type: Private, independent
Degrees: C
URL: http://www.familyplaytherapy.net
Phone: (720) 859-0464
Prog. Accred.: Marriage and Family Therapy

HealthONE Center for Health Science Education
1719 East 19th Ave., Denver 80218
Type: Private, proprietary
Degrees: C
URL: http://www.health1.org/education
Phone: (303) 839-6740
Prog. Accred.: Clinical Lab Scientist, Radiography

The Medical Center of Aurora
1501 South Potomac St., Aurora 80012-5411
Type: Private, independent
Degrees: C
Phone: (303) 695-2900
Prog. Accred.: Clinical Pastoral Education

Swedish Medical Center
501 East Hampden Ave., Englewood 80110-2702
Phone: (303) 788-6233
Prog. Accred: Clinical Pastoral Education

Memorial Hospital
1400 East Boulder, Colorado Springs 80909
Type: Private, independent
Degrees: C
URL: http://www.memorialhospital.com
Phone: (719) 365-5000
Prog. Accred.: Radiography

Parkview Medical Center School of Medical Technology
400 West 16th St., Pueblo 81003-2781
Type: Private, proprietary
Degrees: C
URL: http://www.parkviewmc.com/Lab_SMT.htm
Phone: (719) 584-4429
Prog. Accred.: Clinical Lab Scientist

Planned Parenthood of the Rocky Mountains
950 Broadway, Denver 80202
Type: Public, independent
Degrees: C
Phone: (303) 321-7526
Prog. Accred.: Nurse Practitioner

Saint Anthony Central Hospital
4231 West 16th Ave., Denver 80204
Type: Private, independent
Degrees: C
URL: http://www.stanthonyhosp.org
Phone: (303) 629-3511
Prog. Accred.: Radiography

United States Army Dental Activity—Ft. Carson
Ft. Carson 80913-5207
Type: Public, federal
Degrees: C
Prog. Accred.: General Dentistry

Veterans Affairs Eastern Colorado Healthcare System
1055 Clermont St., Denver 80220
Type: Public, federal
Degrees: C
URL: http://www1.va.gov/directory
Phone: (303) 399-8020
Prog. Accred.: General Practice Residency, Psychology Internship

CONNECTICUT

Albert I. Prince Regional Vocational-Technical School
500 Bookfield St., Hartford 06106
Type: Private, proprietary
Degrees: C
Phone: (860) 951-7112
Prog. Accred.: Dental Assisting

Avery Heights
705 New Britain Ave., Hartford 06106-4039
Type: Private, proprietary
Degrees: C
Phone: (860) 527-9126 x 326
Prog. Accred.: Clinical Pastoral Education

Bridgeport Hospital
267 Grant St., PO Box 5000, Bridgeport 06610-2805
Type: Private, independent
Degrees: C
Phone: (203) 384-3881
Prog. Accred.: Clinical Pastoral Education

Connecticut Valley Psychology Internship
PO Box 351, Silver St., Middletown 06457
Type: Private, independent
Degrees: C
URL: http://www.dmhas.state.ct.us/RVS/PsychIntern.htm
Phone: (860) 262-5200
Prog. Accred.: Psychology Internship

Danbury Hospital
24 Hospital Ave., Danbury 06810-5988
Type: Private, proprietary
Degrees: C
URL: http://www.danhosp.org
Phone: (203) 797-7804
Prog. Accred.: Clinical Lab Scientist, General Practice
Residency, Radiography

Eli Whitney Regional Vocational-Technical School
71 Jones Rd., Hamden 06514
Type: Public, state/local
Degrees: C
Phone: (203) 397-4031
Prog. Accred.: Dental Assisting

Greater Hartford Clinical Psychology Internship Consortium
555 Willard Ave., Newington 06111
Type: Private, independent
Degrees: C
URL: http://www.avapl.org/training/Hartford
Phone: (860) 667-6760
Prog. Accred.: Psychology Internship

Griffin Hospital
130 Division St., Derby 06418
Type: Private, independent
Degrees: C
URL: http://www.griffinhealth.org
Phone: (203) 735-7421
Prog. Accred.: Clinical Pastoral Education

Hartford Hospital School of Allied Health
560 Hudson St., Hartford 06102
Type: Private, independent
Degrees: C
URL: http://www.harthosp.org/Education/ProfEd/
AlliedHealth/index.htm
Phone: (860) 545-2611
Prog. Accred.: Clinical Lab Scientist, Clinical Pastoral
Education, General Practice Residency, Histologic
Technology, Radiation Therapy, Radiography

Hospital of Saint Raphael
1450 Chapel St., New Haven 06511
Type: Private, independent
Degrees: C
URL: http://www.srhs.org
Phone: (203) 789-3245
Prog. Accred.: Clinical Pastoral Education, Oral and
Maxillofacial Surgery

The Institute of Living
400 Washington St., Hartford 06106
Type: Private, independent
Degrees: C
URL: http://www.instituteofliving.org
Phone: (800) 673-2411
Prog. Accred.: Psychology Internship

The John D. Thompson Hospice Institute
61 Burban Dr., Branford 06405-4003
Type: Private, proprietary
Degrees: C
URL: http://www.hospice.com
Phone: (203) 481-6231 x 200
Prog. Accred.: Clinical Pastoral Education

Masonic Geriatric Healthcare Center
22 Masonic Ave., PO Box 70, Wallingford 06492-0070
Type: Private, proprietary
Degrees: C
Phone: (203) 679-6259
Prog. Accred.: Clinical Pastoral Education

New Britain School of Nurse Anesthesia
100 Grand St., New Britain 06050
Type: Private, proprietary
Phone: (203) 224-5612
Prog. Accred.: Nurse Anesthesia Education

Saint Francis/Mount Sinai Hospital
140 Woodland St., Hartford 06105
Type: Private, independent
Degrees: C
Prog. Accred.: General Practice Residency

Saint Mary's Hospital
56 Franklin St., Waterbury 06706
Type: Private, proprietary
Degrees: C
URL: http://www.stmh.org
Phone: (203) 574-6000
Prog. Accred.: Clinical Lab Scientist, General Practice
Residency

Stamford Health System
30 Shelburne Rd., Stamford 06904-9317
Type: Private, independent
Degrees: C
URL: http://www.stamhealth.org
Phone: (203) 276-1000
Prog. Accred.: Clinical Pastoral Education, Radiography

Veterans Affairs Connecticut Healthcare System West Haven
950 Campbell Ave., West Haven 06516
Type: Public, federal
Degrees: C
URL: http://www.visn1.med.va.gov/vact
Phone: (203) 932-5711
Prog. Accred.: Psychology Internship

The Village for Families and Children, Inc.
1680 Albany Ave., Hartford 06105
Type: Private, independent
Degrees: C
URL: http://www.villageforchildren.org
Phone: (860) 236-4511
Prog. Accred.: Psychology Internship

Waterbury Hospital Health Center
64 Robbins St., Waterbury 6721
Type: Private, proprietary
Degrees: C
URL: http://www.waterburyhospital.com
Prog. Accred.: General Practice Residency

Windham Community Memorial Hospital
112 Mansfield Ave., Willimantic 06226
Type: Private, independent
Degrees: C
URL: http://www.wcmh.org
Phone: (860) 456-9116
Prog. Accred.: Radiography

Windham Regional Vocational-Technical School
210 Birch St., Willimantic 06226
Type: Public, state/local
Degrees: C
URL: http://www.cttech.org/windham/adult-ed
Phone: (860) 456-3879
Prog. Accred.: Dental Assisting

Yale-New Haven Hospital
20 York St., New Haven 06504
Type: Private, independent
Degrees: C
Phone: (203) 688-2151
Prog. Accred.: Clinical Pastoral Education, General
  Practice Residency

DELAWARE

Alfred I. duPont Hospital for Children
PO Box 269, Wilmington 19899
Type: Private, independent
Degrees: C
URL: http://www.nemours.org
Phone: (302) 651-4000
Prog. Accred.: Psychology Internship

Christiana Care Health Services
PO Box 1668, Wilmington 19899-1668
Type: Private, proprietary
Degrees: C
Phone: (302) 428-2780
Prog. Accred.: Clinical Pastoral Education

Medical Center of Delaware
501 W. 14th St., Box 1668, Wilmington 19899
Type: Private, proprietary
Degrees: C
Prog. Accred.: General Practice Residency, Oral and
  Maxillofacial Surgery

Terry Children's Psychiatric Center
10 Central Ave., New Castle 19720
Type: Private, independent
Degrees: C
Phone: (302) 577-4270
Prog. Accred.: Psychology Internship

DISTRICT OF COLUMBIA

11th Medical Group/SGD
260 Brookley Ave., Ste. 2-48, Bolling AFB 20032
Type: Public, federal
Degrees: C
URL: http://www.bolling.af.mil/orgs/mdg/index_mdg.htm
Phone: (202) 404-3619
Prog. Accred.: Advanced Education in General Dentistry

The Armed Forces Institute of Pathology
6825 16th St., NW, Washington 20306-6000
Type: Public, federal
Degrees: C
URL: http://www.afip.org
Phone: (202) 782-2100
Prog. Accred.: Histologic Technology

Baptist Senior Adult Ministries
1330 Massachusetts Ave., NW, Washington 20005-4155
Type: Private, independent
Degrees: C
URL: http://www.bsam.org
Phone: (202) 626-5770
Prog. Accred.: Clinical Pastoral Education

Bureau of Medicine & Surgery (U.S. Navy)
2300 E. St., NW, Building 2, Washington 20372-5300
Type: Public, federal
Degrees: C
URL: http://www.navymedicine.med.navy.mil
Phone: (202) 762-3830
Prog. Accred.: Radiography

Bethesda Campus
8901 Wisconsin Ave., Bethesda, MD 20889-5602
Phone: (301) 295-0064
Prog. Accred: Combined Prosthodontics, Endodontics,
  General Dentistry, Maxillofacial Prosthetics, Oral and
  Maxillofacial Pathology, Periodontics

Medical Center Bethesda Branch
8901 Wisconsin Ave., Bethesda, MD 20889-5611
Phone: (301) 295-1204
Prog. Accred: Cardiovascular Technology,
  Electroneurodiagnostic Technology, Nuclear Medicine
  Technology, Nurse Anesthesia Education

Portsmouth Campus
10001 Holcomb Rd., Portsmouth, VA 23708-5200
Phone: (804) 398-5032
Prog. Accred: Surgical Technology

San Diego Norman Scott Road Campus
4170 Norman Scott Rd., PO Box 368147, San Diego,
CA 92136-5597
Phone: (619) 556-7640
Prog. Accred: Dental Laboratory Technology

Tri-Service Optician School
Tri-Service Optician School, PO Box 160, Yorktown, VA 23691-0350
Phone: (804) 887-7329
Prog. Accred: Ophthalmic Lab Technology, Opticianry

Children's National Medical Center
111 Michigan Ave., NW, Washington 20010
Type: Private, independent
Degrees: C
URL: http://www.cnmc.org
Phone: (202) 884-5000
Prog. Accred.: Clinical Pastoral Education, Orthodontic and Dentofacial Orthopedics, Pediatric Dentistry, Psychology Internship

Commission on Mental Health Services
2700 ML King Ave., SE, Washington 20032
Type: Private, independent
Degrees: C
Prog. Accred.: General Practice Residency

District of Columbia School of Law
4250 Connecticut Ave., NW, Washington 20008
Type: Public, state, four-year
Degrees: P   *Enroll:* 183
URL: http://www.law.udc.edu
Phone: (202) 727-5225   *Calendar:* Sem. plan
Prog. Accred.: Law

Margaret Murray Washington Vocational School
27 0 St., NW, Washington 20001
Type: Public, state
Degrees: C
URL: http://www.k12.dc.us/schools/mmwashington/index2.htm
Phone: (202) 673-7224
Prog. Accred.: Dental Assisting, Practical Nursing

Saint Elizabeths Hospital
2700 Martin Luther King Jr. Dr., SE, Washington 20032-2601
Type: Public, city
Degrees: C
Phone: (202) 373-7035
Prog. Accred.: Clinical Pastoral Education

Sibley Memorial Hospital
5255 Loughboro Rd., NW, Washington 20016-2633
Type: Private, independent
Degrees: C
Phone: (202) 537-4084
Prog. Accred.: Clinical Pastoral Education

Walter Reed Army Medical Center
6900 Georgia Ave., Washington 20307
Type: Public, federal
Degrees: C
URL: http://www.wramc.amedd.army.mil
Phone: (202) 782-1104
Prog. Accred.: Clinical Lab Scientist, Clinical Pastoral Education, Psychology Internship

Washington DC Veterans Affairs Medical Center
50 Irving St., NW, Washington 20422
Type: Public, federal
Degrees: C
URL: http://www1.va.gov/washington
Phone: (202) 745-8000
Prog. Accred.: Psychology Internship

Washington Hospital Center
110 Irving St., NW, Washington 20010-2975
Type: Private, independent
Degrees: C
URL: http://www.whcenter.org
Phone: (202) 877-7000
Prog. Accred.: Clinical Lab Scientist, Clinical Pastoral Education, Oral and Maxillofacial Surgery, Radiography

FLORIDA

96th Medical Group/SGD
307 Boatner Rd., Ste. 114, Eglin AFB 32542-1391
Type: Public, proprietary
Degrees: C
URL: https://www.afms.mil/mtf96/dentalres/dentalres.htm
Phone: (850) 883-8242
Prog. Accred.: Advanced Education in General Dentistry

Baptist Health Care
1000 West Moreno St., Pensacola 32522-7500
Type: Private, proprietary
Degrees: C
Phone: (850) 469-2363
Prog. Accred.: Clinical Pastoral Education

Baptist Health Systems of South Florida
8900 North Kendall Dr., Miami 33176-2118
Type: Private, proprietary
Degrees: C
URL: http://www.baptisthealth.net
Phone: (305) 596-6577
Prog. Accred.: Clinical Pastoral Education

Bay Pines Veterans Affairs Medical Center
10,000 Bay Pines Blvd., Bay Pines 33744
Type: Public, federal
Degrees: C
URL: http://www.visn8.med.va.gov/baypines
Phone: (727) 398-6661
Prog. Accred.: Psychology Internship

Bayfront Medical Center
701 6th St., South, St. Petersburg 33701-4814
Type: Private, proprietary
Degrees: C
URL: http://www.bayfront.org
Phone: (727) 823-1234
Prog. Accred.: Clinical Lab Scientist

Bethesda Memorial Hospital
2815 South Seacrest Blvd., Boynton Beach 33435
Type: Private, independent
Degrees: C
URL: http://www.bethesdaweb.com
Phone: (561) 737-7733
Prog. Accred.: Radiography

Career Training Institute
3326 Edgewater Dr., Orlando 32804-6948
Type: Private, proprietary
Degrees: C
Phone: (407) 843-3984
Prog. Accred.: Medical Assisting (CAAHEP)

Winter Park Campus
114 South Semoran Blvd., Ste. 1, Winter Park 32790
Phone: (407) 673-8477

The Children's Psychiatric Center, Inc.
15490 NW 7th Ave., Ste. 200, Miami 33169-6231
Type: Private, independent
Degrees: C
URL: http://www.fostercaremiami.org
Phone: (305) 235-8105
Prog. Accred.: Psychology Internship

Citrus Health Network, Inc.
175 West 20th Ave., Hialeah 33012-5875
Type: Private, proprietary
Degrees: C
URL: http://www.citrushealth.org
Phone: (305) 825-0300
Prog. Accred.: Psychology Internship

Coastal Behavioral Healthcare, Inc.
PO Box 1599, Sarasota 34230
Type: Private, proprietary
Degrees: C
URL: http://www.coastalbh.org
Phone: (941) 927-8900
Prog. Accred.: Psychology Internship

Dragon Rises School of Oriental Medicine
703 North Waldo Rd., Ste. 200, Gainesville 32641
Type: Private, proprietary, four-year
Degrees: M
URL: http://www.dragonrises.net
Phone: (352) 371-2833   *Calendar:* Sem. plan
Prog. Accred.: Acupuncture

Flagler Career Institute
5340 North Federal Hwy., Ste. 104, Lighthouse Point
33064-7058
Type: Private, proprietary, two-year
Degrees: C, A   *FTE Enroll:* 158
Phone: (954) 525-3485   *Calendar:* Qtr. plan
Prog. Accred.: Respiratory Therapy, Respiratory Therapy
  Technology

Florida College of Integrative Medicine
7100 Lake Ellenor Dr., Orlando 32809
Type: Private, proprietary, four-year
Degrees: C, M
URL: http://www.fcim.edu
Phone: (407) 888-8689   *Calendar:* Sem. plan
Prog. Accred.: Acupuncture

Florida State Hospital
100 North Main St., Chattahoochee 32324
Type: Public, state
Degrees: C
URL: http://www.dcf.state.fl.us/institutions/fsh
Phone: (850) 663-7001
Prog. Accred.: Psychology Internship

Gainesville Family Institute
1031 N.W. 6th St., Ste. C-2, Gainesville 32601
Type: Private, independent
Degrees: C
Phone: (352) 376-5543   *Calendar:* Sem. plan
Prog. Accred.: Marriage and Family Therapy

Good Samaritan Medical Center
Flagler Dr. at Palm Beach Lakes Blvd., West Palm Beach
33402-3166
Type: Private, proprietary
Degrees: C
Phone: (561) 882-6047
Prog. Accred.: Clinical Pastoral Education

Halifax Medical Center
303 North Clyde Morris Blvd., Daytona Beach 32114
Type: Private, independent
Degrees: C
URL: http://www.hfch.org
Phone: (386) 254-4000
Prog. Accred.: Radiation Therapy, Radiography

Hope Hospice
9470 Healthpark Circle, Fort Myers 33908-3600
Type: Private, proprietary
Degrees: C
Phone: (941) 482-4673
Prog. Accred.: Clinical Pastoral Education

Jackson Memorial Hospital
1611 NW 12th Ave., Miami 33136-1094
Type: Private, independent
Degrees: C
URL: http://um-jmh.org
Phone: (305) 585-1111
Prog. Accred.: Psychology Internship, Radiography

James A. Haley Veterans Affairs Medical Center
13000 Bruce B. Downs Blvd., Tampa 33612
Type: Public, federal
Degrees: C
URL: http://www.visn8.med.va.gov/Tampa
Phone: (813) 972-2000
Prog. Accred.: Psychology Internship

Lakeland Regional Medical Center
1324 Lakeland Hills Blvd., Lakeland 33805
Type: Private, independent
Degrees: C
URL: http://www.lakelandcc.edu
Phone: (863) 687-1100
Prog. Accred.: Radiography

Malcom Randall Veterans Affairs Medical Center
1601 SW Archer Rd., Gainesville 32608-1197
Type: Public, federal
Degrees: C
URL: http://www.visn8.med.va.gov/nfsg
Phone: (352) 376-1611
Prog. Accred.: General Practice Residency, Psychology Internship

Martin Memorial Health Systems
PO Box 9010, Stuart 34995-9010
Type: Private, proprietary
Degrees: C
Phone: (561) 288-5873
Prog. Accred.: Clinical Pastoral Education

Miami Veterans Affairs Medical Center
1201 NW 16th St., Miami 33125
Type: Public, federal
Degrees: C
URL: http://www.visn8.med.va.gov/miami
Phone: (305) 575-7000
Prog. Accred.: General Practice Residency, Psychology Internship

Miami-Dade County Department of Human Services
11025 SW 84 St., Miami 33173
Type: Public, state/local
Degrees: C
URL: http://www.miamidade.gov/dhs
Phone: (305) 270-2930
Prog. Accred.: Psychology Internship

Mount Sinai Medical Center
4300 Alton Rd., Miami Beach 33140
Type: Private, independent
Degrees: C
URL: http://www.msmc.com
Phone: (305) 674-2980　　　　*Calendar:* 12-mos. pr
Prog. Accred.: Clinical Pastoral Education, Nuclear Medicine Technology

Naval Dental Center—Gulf Coast
161 Turner St., Ste. B, Pensacola 32508-5526
Type: Public, federal
Degrees: C
Phone: (850) 452-5600
Prog. Accred.: General Dentistry

Naval Dental Center—Jacksonville
Branch Dental Clinic, Box 74, Jacksonville 32234
Type: Public, federal
Degrees: C
URL: http://ndcse.med.navy.mil/branches/jacksonville.htm
Phone: (904) 542-3441
Prog. Accred.: General Dentistry

NCH Healthcare System
350 7th St., Naples 34102-5754
Type: Private, proprietary
Degrees: C
URL: http://www.nchhcs.org/cpe
Phone: (941) 436-5449
Prog. Accred.: Clinical Pastoral Education

North Technical Education Center
7071 Garden Rd., Riviera Beach 33404
Type: Public, state
Degrees: C
Phone: (561) 881-4601
Prog. Accred.: Medical Assisting (CAAHEP)

Northeast Florida State Hospital
7487 South State Rd. 121, Macclenny 32063-5451
Type: Public, state
Degrees: C
URL: http://www.dcf.state.fl.us/institutions/nefsh
Phone: (904) 259-6211
Prog. Accred.: Psychology Internship

Radiation Therapy School for Radiation Therapy
1419 SE 8th Terrace, Cape Coral 33990
Type: Private, proprietary
Degrees: C
URL: http://www.rtsx.com/school/index.htm
Phone: (239) 573-5972
Prog. Accred.: Radiation Therapy

Saint Vincent's Medical Center
1800 Barrs St., PO Box 2982, Jacksonville 32203-2982
Type: Private, independent
Degrees: C
URL: http://www.jaxhealth.com
Phone: (904) 308-7300
Prog. Accred.: Clinical Lab Scientist, Clinical Pastoral Education, Radiography

South Florida State Hospital
800 East Cypress Dr., Pembroke Pines 33025
Type: Private, independent
Degrees: C
URL: http://www.sfsh.org
Phone: (954) 392-3000
Prog. Accred.: Psychology Internship

Tampa General Hospital
PO Box 1289, Tampa 33601-1289
Type: Private, proprietary
Degrees: C
URL: http://www.tgh.org
Phone: (813) 844-7000
Prog. Accred.: Clinical Lab Scientist, Clinical Pastoral Education

Veterans Affairs Medical Center—West Palm Beach
7305 Military Trail, West Palm Beach 33410-6400
Type: Public, federal
Degrees: C
URL: http://www.va.gov/sta
Phone: (561) 882-8262
Prog. Accred.: General Practice Residency

West Boca Medical Center
21644 State Rd. 7, Boca Raton 33428
Type: Private, independent
Degrees: C
URL: http://www.westbocamedctr.com
Phone: (561) 488-8000
Prog. Accred.: Radiography

GEORGIA

Atlanta Medical Center
303 Pkwy. Dr. NE, Atlanta 30312
Type: Private, independent
Degrees: C
URL: http://www.atlantamedcenter.com
Phone: (404) 265-4000
Prog. Accred.: Radiography

Atlanta Veterans Affairs Medical Center
1670 Clairmont Rd., Decatur 30033-4004
Type: Public, federal
Degrees: C
URL: http://www1.va.gov/atlanta
Phone: (404) 329-2220
Prog. Accred.: Clinical Pastoral Education, Psychology Internship

The Center for Disease Control and Prevention
1600 Clifton Rd., MS/D20, Atlanta 30333
Type: Public, federal
Degrees: C
Phone: (404) 687-6641
Prog. Accred.: Dental Public Health

Covenant Counseling Institute
2219 Scenic Dr., Snellville 30078-3131
Type: Private, proprietary
Degrees: C
URL: http://www.covenantcounseling.org/cpe.htm
Phone: (770) 985-0837
Prog. Accred.: Clinical Pastoral Education

DeKalb Medical Center Decatur
2701 North Decatur Rd., Decatur 30033
Type: Public, local
Degrees: C
URL: http://www.dekalbmedicalcenter.org
Phone: (404) 501-1000
Prog. Accred.: Radiography

Department of Army Headquarters
Building 300, Fort Gordon 30905-5650
Type: Public, federal
Degrees: C
Phone: (706) 787-1025
Prog. Accred.: Clinical Pastoral Education

Dwight David Eisenhower Army Medical Center
300 Hospital Rd., Fort Gordon 30905-5650
Type: Public, federal
Degrees: C
URL: http://www.ddeamc.amedd.army.mil
Phone: (706) 787-5811
Prog. Accred.: Psychology Internship

Georgia Association for Pastoral Care
1814 Clairmont Rd., Decatur 30033-3405
Type: Private, proprietary
Degrees: C
Phone: (404) 616-4270
Prog. Accred.: Clinical Pastoral Education

Georgia Baptist Health Care System
100 Tenth St., NW, Ste. 700, Atlanta 30309
Type: Private, proprietary
Degrees: C
URL: http://www.gbhcs.org
Phone: (404) 253-3000
Prog. Accred.: Clinical Pastoral Education

Grady Memorial Hospital
80 Jesse Hill Jr. Dr., SE, PO Box 26095, Atlanta 30303
Type: Private, independent
Degrees: C
URL: http://www.gradyhealthsystem.org
Phone: (404) 616-4307
Prog. Accred.: Radiation Therapy, Radiography

The Marcus Institute
1920 Briarcliff Rd., Atlanta 30329
Type: Private, independent
Degrees: C
URL: http://www.marcus.org
Phone: (404) 419-4000
Prog. Accred.: Psychology Internship

Morris Brown College
643 Martin Luther King, Jr. Dr., NW, Atlanta 30314-4140
Type: Private, African Methodist Episcopal Church, four-year
Degrees: B   *FTE Enroll:* 2,700
URL: http://www.morrisbrown.edu
Phone: (404) 739-1000   *Calendar:* Sem. plan
Prog. Accred.: Teacher Education (NCATE)

Northern Atlanta Tri-Hospital CPE Center
5665 Peachtree Dunwoody Rd., NE, Atlanta 30342-1786
Type: Private, independent
Degrees: C
Phone: (404) 851-751
Prog. Accred.: Clinical Pastoral Education

Northwest Georgia Regional Hospital
1305 Redmond Circle, Rome 30165
Type: Public, state
Degrees: C
URL: http://www.nwgahealth.com/irsweb/n50pwkd8.htm
Phone: (706) 295-6011
Prog. Accred.: Psychology Internship

Saint Francis Hospital
2122 Machester Expressway, Columbus 31908-7000
Type: Private, independent
Degrees: C
Phone: (706) 596-4000
Prog. Accred.: Clinical Pastoral Education

Saint Luke's Hospital
435 Peachtree St., NE, Atlanta 30308-3228
Type: Private, independent
Degrees: C
Phone: (404) 876-6266
Prog. Accred.: Clinical Pastoral Education

Southern Regional Medical Center
11 Upper Riverdale Rd., Riverdale 30274-2615
Type: Private, proprietary
Degrees: C
Phone: (770) 991-8399
Prog. Accred.: Clinical Pastoral Education

United States Army Dental Activity—Ft Benning
Ft. Gordon 30905-5660
Type: Public, federal
Degrees: C
Prog. Accred.: Combined Prosthodontics, Oral and Maxillofacial Surgery, Periodontics

United States Army Dental Activity—Ft Bragg
PO Box 56100, Ft. Benning 31905-6100
Type: Public, federal
Degrees: C
Prog. Accred.: Endodontics, General Dentistry

United States Penitentiary Atlanta
601 McDonough Blvd. SE, Atlanta 30315-4423
Type: Public, federal
Degrees: C
URL: http://www.bop.gov/locations/institutions/atl
Prog. Accred.: Psychology Internship

University Hospital
1350 Walton Way, Augusta 30901-3599
Type: Private, independent
Degrees: C
URL: http://www.universityhealth.org
Phone: (706) 722-9011
Prog. Accred.: Radiography

HAWAII

Pacific Health Ministry
2229 North School St., Ste. 210, Honolulu 96819-2588
Type: Private, proprietary
Degrees: C
Phone: (808) 843-8198
Prog. Accred.: Clinical Pastoral Education

Queen's Medical Center
1301 Punchbowl St., Honolulu 96813
Type: Private, independent
Degrees: C
URL: http://www.queens.org
Phone: (808) 538.9011
Prog. Accred.: General Practice Residency

Tripler Army Medical Center
1 Jarrett White Rd., Honolulu 96859-5000
Type: Public, federal
Degrees: C
URL: http://www.tamc.amedd.army.mil
Phone: (808) 433-6661
Prog. Accred.: General Dentistry, Oral and Maxillofacial Surgery, Psychology Internship

Veterans Affairs Pacific Islands Healthcare System
459 Patterson Rd., Honolulu 96819-1522
Type: Public, federal
Degrees: C
URL: http://www.va.gov/hawaii
Phone: (808) 433-0600
Prog. Accred.: Psychology Internship

IDAHO

Saint Luke's Clinical Pastoral Education Center
190 East Bannock St., Boise 83712-6261
Type: Private, independent
Degrees: C
Phone: (208) 381-2100
Prog. Accred.: Clinical Pastoral Education

ILLINOIS

375th Medical Group/SGDDT
310 West Losey St., Scott AFB 62225-5252
Type: Public, federal
Degrees: C
Phone: (618) 256-7500
Prog. Accred.: Advanced Education in General Dentistry

ACTS Urban CPE Program
1164 East 58th St., Chicago 60637-1538
Type: Private, independent
Degrees: C
Phone: (773) 322-0266
Prog. Accred.: Clinical Pastoral Education

Advocate Bethany Hospital
3435 West Van Buren St., Chicago 60624
Type: Private, independent
System: Advocate Health Care System
Degrees: C
URL: http://www.advocatehealth.com/beth
Phone: (773) 265-7000
Prog. Accred.: Clinical Pastoral Education

Advocate Christ Medical Center
4440 West 95th St., Oak Lawn 60453
Type: Private, independent
System: Advocate Health Care System
Degrees: C
URL: http://www.advocatehealth.com/cmc
Phone: (708) 425-8000
Prog. Accred.: Psychology Internship

Advocate Christ Medical Center
4440 West 95th St., Oak Lawn 60453
Type: Private, independent
System: Advocate Health Care System
Degrees: C
URL: http://www.advocatehealth.com
Phone: (708) 425-8000
Prog. Accred.: Clinical Pastoral Education, General Practice Residency

Advocate Illinois Masonic Medical Center
836 West Wellington Ave., Chicago 60657
Phone: (773) 975-1600
Prog. Accred: Psychology Internship, Radiography

Advocate Good Samaritan Hospital
3815 Highland Ave., Downers Grove 60515
Type: Private, independent
System: Advocate Health Care System
Degrees: C
URL: http://www.advocatehealth.com/gsam
Phone: (630) 275-5900
Prog. Accred.: Clinical Pastoral Education

Advocate Good Shepherd Hospital
450 West Hwy. 22, Barrington 60010
Type: Private, independent
System: Advocate Health Care System
Degrees: C
URL: http://www.advocatehealth.com/gshp
Phone: (847) 381-0123
Prog. Accred.: Clinical Pastoral Education

Advocate Lutheran General Hospital
1775 Dempster St., Park Ridge 60068
Type: Private, independent
System: Advocate Health Care System
Degrees: C
URL: http://www.advocatehealth.com/luth
Phone: (847) 723-2210
Prog. Accred.: Clinical Pastoral Education

Advocate South Suburban Hospital
17800 South Kedzie Ave., Hazel Crest 60429
Type: Private, independent
System: Advocate Health Care System
Degrees: C
URL: http://www.advocatehealth.com/ssub
Phone: (708) 799-8000
Prog. Accred.: Clinical Pastoral Education

Advocate Trinity Hospital
2320 East 93rd St., Chicago 60617
Type: Private, independent
System: Advocate Health Care System
Degrees: C
URL: http://www.advocatehealth.com/trin
Phone: (773) 967-2000
Prog. Accred.: Clinical Pastoral Education, Radiography

Alexian Brothers Health System
600 Alexian Way, Elk Grove Village 60007-3370
Type: Private, proprietary
Degrees: C
Phone: (847) 981-3621
Prog. Accred.: Clinical Pastoral Education

Alexian Brothers (System Center)
4624 Landsdowne Ave., St. Louis, MO 63116-1523
Phone: (847) 981-3508
Prog. Accred: Clinical Pastoral Education

Alexian Village of Milwaukee
7979 West Glenbrook Rd., Milwaukee, WI 53223-1062
Phone: (414) 355-9300
Prog. Accred: Clinical Pastoral Education

Saint Francis Hospital-Resurrection Health Care
355 Ridge Ave., Evanston 60202-3328
Phone: (847) 316-4040
Prog. Accred: Clinical Pastoral Education, Radiography

Alexian Brothers Medical Center
800 Biesterfield Rd., Elk Grove Village 60007-3311
Type: Private, proprietary
Degrees: C
Phone: (847) 437-5500 x4744
Prog. Accred.: Clinical Pastoral Education

Addolorata Villa Gatellite
555 McHenry Rd., Wheeling 60090
Phone: (847) 808-6168
Prog. Accred: Clinical Pastoral Education

Allendale Association
PO Box 1088, Lake Villa 60046
Type: Private, independent
Degrees: C
URL: http://www.allendale4kids.org
Phone: (888) 255-3631
Prog. Accred.: Psychology Internship

Blessing Hospital
1005 Broadway, PO Box 7005, Quincy 62305-7005
Type: Private, independent
Degrees: C
URL: http://www.blessinghospital.org
Phone: (217) 223-1200
Prog. Accred.: Radiography

Bloomington-Normal School of Radiography
900 Franklin Ave., Normal 61761
Type: Private, independent
Degrees: C
URL: http://www.bnradiography.com
Phone: (309) 452-2834   *Calendar:* 24-mos. pr
Prog. Accred.: Radiography

BroMenn Healthcare
PO Box 2850, Bloomington 61702-2850
Type: Private, proprietary
Degrees: C
URL: http://www.BroMenn.com
Phone: (309) 454-1400
Prog. Accred.: Clinical Pastoral Education

Carle Foundation Hospital
611 West Park St., Urbana 61801
Type: Private, independent
Degrees: C
URL: http://www.carle.com
Phone: (217) 383-4510
Prog. Accred.: Clinical Pastoral Education, Oral and
  Maxillofacial Surgery

Cermak Health Services of Cook County
2800 South California Ave., Chicago 60608
Type: Public, state-affiliated
Degrees: C
URL: http://www.cookcountyresearch.net/cer.html
Phone: (773) 890-5641
Prog. Accred.: Psychology Internship

Chicago Area Christian Training Consortium
336 Gunderson Dr., Ste. B, Carol Stream 60188
Type: Private, independent
Degrees: C
URL: http://www.cactc.org
Phone: (630) 871-2100
Prog. Accred.: Psychology Internship

Chicago-Reed Mental Health Center
4200 North Oak Park Ave., Chicago 60634
Type: Private, independent
Degrees: C
Prog. Accred.: Psychology Internship

Children's Memorial Hospital
2300 Children's Plaza, Chicago 60614-3394
Type: Private, independent
Degrees: C
URL: http://www.childrensmemorial.org
Phone: (773) 880-4000
Prog. Accred.: Psychology Internship

Children's Memorial Medical Center
2300 Childrens Plaza, Chicago 60614-3394
Type: Private, independent
Degrees: C
URL: http://www.childrensmemorial.org
Phone: (773) 880-4000
Prog. Accred.: Pediatric Dentistry

Cook County Hospital
1835 West Harrison St., Chicago 60612
Type: Private, independent
Degrees: C
Prog. Accred.: Oral and Maxillofacial Surgery

Deaconess Hospital
600 Mary St., Evanston 47747-0001
Type: Private, independent
Degrees: C
Phone: (812) 450-2260
Prog. Accred.: Clinical Pastoral Education

Edward Hines, Jr. Veterans Affairs Hospital
5th Ave. & Roosevelt Rd., PO Box 5000, Hines 60141
Type: Public, federal
Degrees: C
URL: http://www.visn12.med.va.gov/hines
Phone: (708) 202-8387
Prog. Accred.: Clinical Lab Scientist, Nuclear Medicine
  Technology, Psychology Internship

Edward Hospital
801 South Washington St., Naperville 60540-7430
Type: Private, independent
Degrees: C
Phone: (630) 527-3564
Prog. Accred.: Clinical Pastoral Education

Elmhurst Memorial Hospital
200 Berteau Ave., Elmhurst 60126-2966
Type: Private, independent
Degrees: C
Phone: (630) 833-1400 x4496
Prog. Accred.: Clinical Pastoral Education

Evanston-Glenbrook Hospital
2650 Ridge Ave., Evanston 60201
Type: Private, independent
Degrees: C
Prog. Accred.: General Practice Residency

Jesse Brown Veterans Affairs Medical Center
820 South Damen Ave., Chicago 60612
Type: Public, federal
Degrees: C
URL: http://www.visn12.med.va.gov/chicago
Phone: (312) 569-8387
Prog. Accred.: Psychology Internship

Jewish Children's Bureau of Chicago
255 Revere Dr., Ste. 200, Northbrook 60062
Type: Private, independent
Degrees: C
URL: http://www.jcbchicago.org
Phone: (847) 412-4350
Prog. Accred.: Psychology Internship

La Rabida Children's Hospital
East 65th St. at Lake Michigan, Chicago 60649
Type: Private, independent
Degrees: C
URL: http://www.larabida.org
Phone: (773) 363-6700
Prog. Accred.: Psychology Internship

MacNeal Hospital
3249 Oak Park Ave., Berwyn 60402-3429
Type: Private, independent
Degrees: C
Phone: (708) 795-3107/8
Prog. Accred.: Clinical Pastoral Education

McDonough District Hospital
525 East Grant St., Macomb 61455
Type: Public, local
Degrees: C
URL: http://www.mdh.org
Phone: (309) 833-4101
Prog. Accred.: Radiography

The Menta Group
900 Jorie Blvd., Ste. 59, Oak Brook 60521
Type: Private, independent
Degrees: C
URL: http://www.thementagroup.org
Phone: (630) 907-2400
Prog. Accred.: Psychology Internship

Methodist Medical Center of Illinois
221 Glen Oak Ave., NE, Peoria 61636-0001
Type: Private, proprietary
Degrees: C
Phone: (309) 672-4879
Prog. Accred.: Clinical Pastoral Education

Midwestern Regional Medical Center
2501 Emmaus Ave., Zion 60099-2575
Type: Private, proprietary
Degrees: C
Phone: (847) 872-6260
Prog. Accred.: Clinical Pastoral Education

Naval Dental Center—Great Lakes
2730 Sampson Rd., Great Lakes 60088
Type: Public, federal
Degrees: C
URL: http://www.ntcgl.navy.mil/ndc/index.html
Phone: (847) 688-5650
Prog. Accred.: General Dentistry

Naval Hospital—Great Lakes
3001A Sixth St., Great Lakes 60088-2833
Type: Public, federal
Degrees: C
URL: https://greatlakes.med.navy.mil
Phone: (847) 688-4560
Prog. Accred.: General Practice Residency

North Chicago Veterans Affairs Medical Center
3001 Greenbay Rd., North Chicago 60064
Type: Public, federal
Degrees: C
URL: http://www.visn12.med.va.gov/northchicago
Phone: (847) 688-1900
Prog. Accred.: General Practice Residency, Psychology Internship

Northwest Community Healthcare
800 West Central Rd., Arlington Heights 60005-2349
Type: Private, proprietary
Degrees: C
Phone: (847) 618-4259
Prog. Accred.: Clinical Pastoral Education

Northwestern Memorial Hospital
251 East Huron St., Chicago 60611-2908
Type: Private, independent, four-year
Degrees: C, B
URL: http://www.nmh.org
Phone: (31) 926-2000
Prog. Accred.: Clinical Pastoral Education, General Practice Residency, Nuclear Medicine Technology, Radiation Therapy

Oak Forest Hospital
15900 South Cicero Ave., Oak Forest 60452
Type: Private, independent
Degrees: C
Phone: (708) 633-2000
Prog. Accred.: Psychology Internship

Rockford Memorial Hospital
2400 North Rockton Ave., Rockford 61103-3655
Type: Private, independent
Degrees: C
URL: http://www.rhsnet.org
Phone: (815) 971-5000
Prog. Accred.: Clinical Pastoral Education, Radiography

Rush-Presbyterian-Saint Luke's Medical Center
1725 West Harrison, Chicago 60612
Type: Private, independent
Degrees: C
URL: http://www.rush.edu
Phone: (312) 942-5000
Prog. Accred.: Clinical Pastoral Education, General Practice Residency, Psychology Internship

Evanston Northwestern Healthcare
2650 Ridge Ave., Evanston 60201-1718
Phone: (847) 570-2330
Prog. Accred: Clinical Pastoral Education, General Practice Residency

Lake Forest Hospital
660 North Westmoreland Rd., Lake Forest 60045-1659
Phone: (847) 535-6070
Prog. Accred: Clinical Pastoral Education

The Mather Foundation
820 Foster St., Evanston 60201-3212
Phone: (847) 492-5695
Prog. Accred: Clinical Pastoral Education

Saint Elizabeth's Hospital
211 South 3rd St., Belleville 62222
Type: Private, proprietary
Degrees: C
Phone: (618) 234-2120
Prog. Accred.: Clinical Lab Scientist

Swedish American Hospital
1401 East State St., Rockford 61104
Type: Private, independent
Degrees: C
URL: http://www.swedishamerican.org
Phone: (815) 968-4400
Prog. Accred.: Radiation Therapy, Radiography

Veterans Affairs Illiana Health Care System
1900 East Main St., Danville 61832-5198
Type: Public, federal
Degrees: C
URL: http://www1.va.gov/directory/guide/home.asp
Phone: (217) 554-3000
Prog. Accred.: Psychology Internship

Victory Health Services Inc.
1324 North Sheridan Rd., Waukegan 60085-2161
Type: Private, proprietary
Degrees: C
Phone: (847) 360-4014
Prog. Accred.: Clinical Pastoral Education

INDIANA

Ball Memorial Hospital
2401 University Ave., Muncie 47303
Type: Private, independent, two-year
Degrees: C, A
URL: http://www.cardinalhealthsystem.org
Phone: (765) 747-3111
Prog. Accred.: Clinical Lab Scientist, Radiography

The Center for Behavioral Health
645 South Rogers St., Bloomington 47403-2367
Type: Private, independent
Degrees: C
URL: http://www.the-center.org
Phone: (812) 339-1691
Prog. Accred.: Psychology Internship

Clarian Health Partners, Inc./Methodist Hospital
1701 North Senate Blvd., PO Box 1367, Indianapolis 46206-1367
Type: Private, independent
Degrees: C
URL: http://www.clarian.org
Phone: (317) 962-2000
Prog. Accred.: Clinical Lab Scientist, Clinical Pastoral Education, Electroneurodiagnostic Technology, Medical Assisting (ABHES), Physician Assistant, Radiation Therapy, Respiratory Therapy, Surgical Technology

Clarion Health Partners
PO Box 1367, Indianapolis 46206-1367
Type: Private, proprietary
Degrees: C
Phone: (317) 929-8611
Prog. Accred.: Clinical Pastoral Education

Columbus Regional Hospital
2400 East 17th St., Columbus 47201
Type: Private, independent
Degrees: C
URL: http://www.crh.org
Phone: (812) 379-4441
Prog. Accred.: Radiography

Community Hospital East
1500 North Ritter Ave., Indianapolis 46219
Type: Private, independent
Degrees: C
URL: http://ecommunity.com
Phone: (317) 355-1411
Prog. Accred.: Radiography

Fort Wayne School of Radiography
700 Broadway, Fort Wayne 46802-1402
Type: Private, independent
Degrees: C
Phone: (219) 425-3990   *Calendar:* 24-mos. pr
Prog. Accred.: Radiography

Good Samaritan Hospital
520 South 7th St., Vincennes 47591
Type: Private, independent
Degrees: C
URL: http://www.gshvin.org
Phone: (812) 882-5220
Prog. Accred.: Clinical Lab Scientist, Radiography

Hamilton Center Inc.
620 Eighth Ave., Terre Haute 47804
Type: Private, independent
Degrees: C
URL: http://www.hamiltoncenter.org
Phone: (812) 231-8320
Prog. Accred.: Psychology Internship

Hancock Regional Hospital
801 North State St., Greenfield 46140
Type: Private, independent
Degrees: C
URL: http://www.hmhhs.org
Phone: (317) 462-5544
Prog. Accred.: Radiography

Howard Community Hospital
3500 South Lafountain St., Kokomo 46904-9001
Type: Private, independent
Degrees: C
Phone: (765) 453-8579
Prog. Accred.: Clinical Pastoral Education

King's Daughters' Hospital and Health Service
One King's Daughters' Dr., PO Box 447, Madison 47250
Type: Private, independent
Degrees: C
URL: http://www.kingsdaughtershospital.org
Phone: (812) 265-5211
Prog. Accred.: Radiography

Larue D. Carter Memorial Hospital
2601 Cold Spring Rd., Indianapolis 46222-2202
Type: Public, state
Degrees: C
Phone: (317) 941-4004
Prog. Accred.: Clinical Pastoral Education

Lutheran Hospital of Indiana
7950 West Jefferson Blvd., Fort Wayne 46804-4160
Type: Private, independent
Degrees: C
Phone: (219) 435-7117
Prog. Accred.: Clinical Pastoral Education

Park Center, Inc.
909 East State Blvd., Fort Wayne 46805
Type: Private, independent
Degrees: C
URL: http://www.parkcenter.org
Phone: (260) 481-2700
Prog. Accred.: Psychology Internship

Parkview Hospital
2200 Randallia Dr., Fort Wayne 46805
Type: Private, independent
Degrees: C
URL: http://www.parkview.com
Phone: (219) 373-4000
Prog. Accred.: Clinical Lab Scientist

Porter Valparaiso Hospital
814 LaPorte Ave., Valparaiso 46383
Type: Private, independent
Degrees: C
URL: http://www.porterhealth.org
Phone: (219) 263-4600
Prog. Accred.: Radiography

Quinco Behavioral Health Systems
720 North Marr Rd., Columbus 47201
Type: Private, independent
Degrees: C
URL: http://www.quincobhs.org
Phone: (812) 348-7449
Prog. Accred.: Psychology Internship

Reid Hospital and Health Care Services
1401 Chester Blvd., Richmond 47374
Type: Private, independent
Degrees: C
URL: http://www.reidhosp.com
Phone: (765) 983-3000
Prog. Accred.: Radiography

Richard L. Roudebush Veterans Affairs Medical Center
1481 West Tenth St., Indianapolis 46202
Type: Public, federal
Degrees: C
URL: http://www1.va.gov/directory/guide/home.asp
Phone: (317) 554-0000
Prog. Accred.: Endodontics, General Practice Residency, Periodontics

Saint Francis Hospital and Health Centers
1600 Albany St., Beech Grove 46107-1593
Type: Private, independent
Degrees: C
URL: http://beechgrove.stfrancishospitals.org
Phone: (317) 787-3311
Prog. Accred.: Clinical Lab Scientist

Saint Joseph's Regional Medical Center
801 East La Salle Ave., South Bend 46617-2814
Type: Private, independent
Degrees: C
URL: http://www.sjmed.com
Phone: (219) 237-7249
Prog. Accred.: Clinical Pastoral Education

Saint Margaret Mercy Healthcare Center
5454 Hohman Ave., Hammond 46320
Type: Private, independent
Degrees: C
URL: http://www.smmhc.com
Phone: (219) 932-2300
Prog. Accred.: Clinical Lab Scientist

Saint Vincent Indianapolis Hospital
2001 East 86th St., Indianapolis 46240-0970
Type: Private, independent
Degrees: C
URL: http://www.indianapolis.stvincent.org
Phone: (317) 338-2345
Prog. Accred.: Clinical Pastoral Education, Radiography

Southlake Center for Mental Health
8555 Taft St., Merrillville 46410-6199
Type: Private, independent
Degrees: C
URL: http://www.southlakecenter.com
Phone: (219) 769-4005
Prog. Accred.: Psychology Internship

Tri-City Community Mental Health Center
3903 Indianapolis Blvd., East Chicago 46312-2555
Type: Private, independent
Degrees: C
URL: http://www.tricitycenter.org
Phone: (219) 392-6001
Prog. Accred.: Psychology Internship

IOWA

Blank Children's Hospital
1200 Pleasant St., Des Moines 50309-1406
Type: Private, independent
Degrees: C
URL: http://www.blankchildrens.org
Phone: (515) 241-5437
Prog. Accred.: Clinical Pastoral Education

Cherokee Mental Health Institute
1251 West Cedar Loop, Cherokee 51012-1512
Type: Private, independent
Degrees: C
Phone: (712) 225-6929
Prog. Accred.: Clinical Pastoral Education

Covenant Medical Center
3421 West Ninth St., Waterloo 50702
Type: Private, independent
Degrees: C
URL: http://www.covhealth.com
Phone: (319) 272-8000
Prog. Accred.: Radiography

Genesis Medical Center
1227 East Rusholme St., Davenport 52803-2459
Type: Private, proprietary
Degrees: C
Phone: (319) 326-4772
Prog. Accred.: Clinical Pastoral Education

Glenwood State Resource Center
711 South Vine St., Glenwood 51534-1927
Type: Private, independent
Degrees: C
Phone: (712) 527-2551
Prog. Accred.: Clinical Pastoral Education

Jennie Edmundson Hospital
933 East Pierce St., Council Bluffs 51503
Type: Private, independent
Degrees: C
URL: http://www.bestcare.org
Phone: (712) 396-6000
Prog. Accred.: Radiography

Mercy Medical Center North Iowa
1000 4th St. SW, Mason City 50401
Type: Private, independent
Degrees: C
URL: http://www.mercynorthiowa.com
Phone: (641) 422-7000
Prog. Accred.: Radiography

Mercy Medical Center Sioux City
801 Fifth St., Sioux City 51102
Type: Private, independent
Degrees: C
URL: http://www.mercysiouxcity.com
Phone: (712) 279-2010
Prog. Accred.: Clinical Lab Scientist

Mercy/St. Luke's School of Radiologic Technology
810 First Ave. NE, Cedar Rapids 52402
Type: Private, independent
Degrees: C
URL: http://www.mercycare.org/services/radiology/
school/index.aspx
Phone: (319) 369-7097
Prog. Accred.: Radiography

Saint Luke's Hospital School of Clinical Science
PO Box 3026, 1026 A Ave., NE, Cedar Rapids 52406
Type: Private, independent
Degrees: C
URL: http://www.crstlukes.com/lab/school.htm
Phone: (319) 369-7309
Prog. Accred.: Clinical Lab Scientist

Veterans Affairs Central Iowa Healthcare System—Knoxville Division
1515 West Pleasant St., Knoxville 50138
Type: Public, federal
Degrees: C
URL: http://www1.va.gov/directory/guide
Phone: (515) 699-5999
Prog. Accred.: Psychology Internship

KANSAS

Colmery-O'Neil Veterans Affairs Medical Center
2200 SW Gage Blvd., Topeka 66622
Type: Public, federal
Degrees: C
URL: http://www1.va.gov/directory/guide/home.asp
Phone: (785) 350-3111
Prog. Accred.: Clinical Pastoral Education

Counseling & Mediation Center, Inc.
334 North Topeka St., Wichita 67202-2400
Type: Private, proprietary
Degrees: C
URL: http://wwwcounselingandmediation.org
Phone: (316) 269-2322
Prog. Accred.: Clinical Pastoral Education

Dwight D. Eisenhower Veterans Affairs Medical Center
4101 South 4th St., Leavenworth 66048-5055
Type: Public, federal
Degrees: C
URL: http://www1.va.gov/directory/guide/home.asp
Phone: (913) 682-2000
Prog. Accred.: Psychology Internship

Family Service and Guidance Center of Topeka, Inc.
325 SW Frazier Ave., Topeka 66606-1963
Type: Private, independent
Degrees: C
URL: http://www.fsgctopeka.com
Phone: (785) 232-5005
Prog. Accred.: Psychology Internship

Osawatomie State Hospital
500 State Hospital Dr., Ste. 500, Osawatomie 66064-1813
Type: Private, state
Degrees: C
Prog. Accred.: Clinical Pastoral Education

Wesley Medical Center
550 North Hillside St., Wichita 67214-4910
Type: Private, federal
Degrees: C
URL: http://www.wesleymc.com
Phone: (316) 688-2310
Prog. Accred.: Clinical Pastoral Education

KENTUCKY

Baptist Hospital East
4000 Kresge Way, Louisville 40207-4605
Type: Private, independent
Degrees: C
Phone: (502) 897-8804
Prog. Accred.: Clinical Pastoral Education

Central Baptist Hospital
1740 Nicholasville Rd., Lexington 40503-1424
Type: Private, independent
Degrees: C
Phone: (859) 260-6575
Prog. Accred.: Clinical Pastoral Education

Federal Medical Center—Lexington
3301 Leestown Rd., Lexington 40511
Type: Public, federal
Degrees: C
URL: http://www.bop.gov/locations/institutions/lex
Phone: (859) 255-681
Prog. Accred.: Psychology Internship

Hazard ARH Regional Medical Center
102 Medical Center Dr., Hazard 41701-9421
Type: Private, independent
Degrees: C
URL: http://www.arh.org
Prog. Accred.: Psychology Internship

Hospice of the Bluegrass
2312 Alexandria Dr., Lexington 40504-3229
Type: Private, independent
Degrees: C
Prog. Accred.: Clinical Pastoral Education

Jefferson County Internship Consortium
914 East Broadway, Ste. 200, Louisville 40204
Type: Private, independent
Degrees: C
URL: http://www.sevencounties.org
Phone: (502) 587-8833
Prog. Accred.: Psychology Internship

King's Daughters Medical Center
2201 Lexington Ave., Ashland 41101
Type: Private, independent
Degrees: C
URL: http://www.kdmc.com
Phone: (606) 327-4000
Prog. Accred.: Radiography

Lexington Veterans Affairs Medical Center
1101 Veterans Dr., Lexington 40502-2236
Type: Public, federal
Degrees: C
URL: http://www1.va.gov/directory/guide/home.asp
Phone: (859) 233-4511
Prog. Accred.: Psychology Internship

Louisville CPE Cluster, Pastoral Counseling and Consultation Center
173 Sears Ave., Ste. 274, Louisville 40207-5062
Type: Private, independent
Degrees: C
Phone: (502) 893-1913
Prog. Accred.: Clinical Pastoral Education

Norton Healthcare
PO Box 35070, Louisville 40232-5070
Type: Private, proprietary
Degrees: C
Phone: (502) 629-3152
Prog. Accred.: Clinical Pastoral Education

Owensboro Mercy Health System
811 East Parrish Ave., Ownsboro 42303
Type: Private, independent
Degrees: C
URL: http://www.omhs.org
Phone: (270) 688-2000
Prog. Accred.: Clinical Lab Scientist

Rockcastle Area Technology Center
955 West Main St., Mount Vernon 40456
Type: Public, state
Degrees: C
URL: http://www.rockcastle.k12.ky.us/ratc.html
Phone: (606) 256-4346
Prog. Accred.: Respiratory Therapy Technology

Saint Elizabeth Medical Center
One Medical Village Dr., Edgewood 41017
Type: Private, independent
Degrees: C
URL: http://www.stelizabeth.com
Phone: (859) 344-2000
Prog. Accred.: Clinical Lab Scientist

Saint Joseph Healthcare
One Saint Joseph Dr., Lexington 40504
Type: Private, independent
Degrees: C
URL: http://www.sjhlex.org
Phone: (859) 313-1000
Prog. Accred.: Radiography

United States Army DENTAC—Ft. Campbell
Attn: MCDS-SEC-ED, Ft. Campbell
Type: Public, federal
Degrees: C
Prog. Accred.: General Dentistry

LOUISIANA

2nd Medical Group/SGDDT
1067 Twining Dr., Barksdale AFB 71110-2486
Type: Public, federal
Degrees: C
Phone: (318) 456-6000
Prog. Accred.: Advanced Education in General Dentistry

Alexandria Veterans Affairs Medical Center
PO Box 69004, Alexnadria 71306-9004
Type: Public, federal
Degrees: C
URL: http://www.alexandria.med.va.gov
Phone: (318) 473-0010
Prog. Accred.: Clinical Pastoral Education

Baton Rouge General
3600 Florida Blvd., Baton Rouge 70806
Type: Private, independent
Degrees: C
URL: http://www.brgeneral.org
Phone: (225) 387-7000
Prog. Accred.: Radiography

Lafayette General Medical Center
1214 Coolidge St., PO Box 52009, Lafayette 70503
Type: Private, independent
Degrees: C
URL: http://www.lafayettegeneral.com
Phone: (337) 289-7991
Prog. Accred.: Radiography

Lake Charles Memorial Hospital School of Medical Technology
1701 Oak Park Blvd., Lake Charles 70601
Type: Private, independent
Degrees: C
URL: http://www.lcmh.com
Phone: (337) 494-3196
Prog. Accred.: Clinical Lab Scientist

The McFarland Institute
1450 Poydras St., CNG Tower, Ste. 1550, New Orleans 70112-6010
Type: Private, independent
Degrees: C
URL: http://www.tmcfi.org
Phone: (504) 593-2320
Prog. Accred.: Clinical Pastoral Education

East Jefferson General Hospital
4200 Houma Blvd., Metairie 70006-2970
Phone: (504) 454-4340
Prog. Accred: Clinical Pastoral Education

Memorial Medical Center
2700 Napoleon Ave., New Orleans 70115-6914
Phone: (504) 897-5961
Prog. Accred: Clinical Pastoral Education

New Orleans Police Deptartment
715 South Broad St., New Orleans 70119-7416
Phone: (504) 827-3855
Prog. Accred: Clinical Pastoral Education

New Orleans Veterans Affairs Medical Center
1601 Perdido St., New Orleans 70146
Type: Public, federal
Degrees: C
Prog. Accred.: General Practice Residency, Psychology Internship

North Oaks Medical Center
15790 Paul Vega M.D. Dr., Hammond 70403
Type: Private, independent
Degrees: C
URL: http://www.northoaks.org
Phone: (985) 345-2700
Prog. Accred.: Radiography

Ochsner School of Allied Health Sciences
1516 Jefferson Hwy., New Orleans 70123-3335
Type: Private, independent
Degrees: C
URL: http://www.ochsner.org/allied-health
Phone: (504) 842-3267
Prog. Accred.: Diagnostic Medical Sonography, Radiography, Respiratory Therapy, Respiratory Therapy Technology

The Overton Brooks Veterans Affairs Medical Center
510 East Stoner Ave., Shreveport 71101-4295
Type: Public, federal
Degrees: C
URL: http://www.va.gov
Phone: (318) 221-8411
Prog. Accred.: Clinical Lab Scientist

Pinecrest Developmental Center
100 Pinecrest Dr., Pineville 71360
Type: Public, state
Degrees: C
Phone: (318) 641-2000
Prog. Accred.: Psychology Internship

Rapides Regional Medical Center
211 4th St., Box 30101, Alexandria 71301
Type: Private, independent
Degrees: C
URL: http://www.rapidesregional.com
Phone: (318) 473-3000
Prog. Accred.: Clinical Lab Scientist, Phlebotomy

Saint Francis Medical Center
309 Jackson St., PO Box 1901, Monroe 71201-7407
Type: Private, independent
Degrees: C
URL: http://www.stfran.com
Phone: (318) 327-4000
Prog. Accred.: Clinical Lab Scientist

MAINE

Central Maine Medical Center
300 Main St., Lewiston 04240
Type: Private, independent
Degrees: C
URL: http://www.cmmc.org
Phone: (207) 795-0111
Prog. Accred.: Clinical Pastoral Education, Nuclear Medicine Technology, Radiography

Eastern Maine Medical Center
489 State St., PO Box 404, Bangor 04401
Type: Private, independent
Degrees: C
URL: http://www.emh.org/emmc
Phone: (207) 973-7000
Prog. Accred.: Clinical Lab Scientist

Maine Medical Center
27 Bramhall St., Portland 04102-3134
Type: Private, independent
Degrees: C
Phone: (207) 871-2951
Prog. Accred.: Clinical Pastoral Education

MaineGeneral Medical Center
6 East Chestnut St., Augusta 04330-5717
Type: Private, independent
Degrees: C
URL: http://www.mainegeneral.org
Phone: (207) 872-4093
Prog. Accred.: Clinical Pastoral Education

Mercy Hospital
144 State St., Portland 04101-3776
Type: Private, independent
Degrees: C
URL: http://www.mercyhospital.com
Phone: (207) 879-3000
Prog. Accred.: Radiography

Togus Veterans Affairs Medical Center
1 VA Center, Augusta 04330
Type: Public, federal
Degrees: C
URL: http://www.visn1.med.va.gov/togus
Phone: (207) 623-8411
Prog. Accred.: Psychology Internship

MARYLAND

Asbury Methodist Village
201 Russell Ave., Gaithersburg 20877-2813
Type: Private, proprietary
Degrees: C
URL: http://www.asburg.org
Phone: (301) 216-4093
Prog. Accred.: Clinical Pastoral Education

Greater Baltimore Medical Center
6701 North Charles St., Baltimore 21204
Type: Private, independent
Degrees: C
URL: http://www.gbmc.org
Phone: (443) 849-2000
Prog. Accred.: Radiography

Holy Cross Hospital
1500 Forest Glen Rd., Silver Spring 20910
Type: Private, independent
Degrees: C
URL: http://www.holycrosshealth.org
Phone: (301) 754-7000
Prog. Accred.: Radiography

John L. Gildner Regional Institute for Children and Adolescents
15000 Broschart Rd., Rockville 20850
Type: Public, state
Degrees: C
Prog. Accred.: Psychology Internship

The Johns Hopkins Hospital
600 North Wolfe St., Baltimore 21287
Type: Private, independent
Degrees: C
URL: http://www.hopkinshospital.org
Phone: (410) 955-5000
Prog. Accred.: Radiography

Kennedy Krieger Institute
707 North Broadway, Baltimore 21205
Type: Private, independent
Degrees: C
URL: http://www.kennedykrieger.org
Phone: (443) 923-9200
Prog. Accred.: Psychology Internship

Maryland General Hospital
827 Linden Ave., Baltimore 21201
Type: Private, independent
Degrees: C
URL: http://www.marylandgeneral.org
Phone: (410) 225-8000
Prog. Accred.: Radiography

Memorial Hospital and Medical Center of Cumberland Maryland
600 Memorial Ave., Cumberland
Type: Private, independent
Degrees: C
Phone: (301) 723-4297
Prog. Accred.: Clinical Pastoral Education

Mercy Medical Center
301 Saint Paul Place, Baltimore 21202
Type: Private, independent
Degrees: C
URL: http://www.mercymed.com
Phone: (410) 332-9000
Prog. Accred.: General Practice Residency

National Capital Consortium
4301 Jones Bridge Rd., Bethesda 20814-4799
Type: Private, independent
Degrees: C
Prog. Accred.: Oral and Maxillofacial Surgery

National Institute-Dental and Craniofacial Research
Natcher Bldg., Bethesda 20892-6401
Type: Private, independent
Degrees: C
Prog. Accred.: Dental Public Health

National Institutes of Health Clinical Center
6100 Executive Blvd., Ste. 3C01, MSC-7511, Bethesda 20892-7511
Type: Public, federal
Degrees: C
URL: http://www.cc.nih.gov
Phone: (301) 496-2563
Prog. Accred.: Clinical Pastoral Education

National Naval Medical Center
8901 Wisconsin Ave., Bethesda 20889
Type: Public, federal
Degrees: C
URL: http://www.bethesda.med.navy.mil
Phone: (301) 295-4611
Prog. Accred.: General Practice Residency, Psychology Internship

Naval Dental School
8901 Wisconsin Ave., Bethesda 20889-5602
Type: Public, federal
Degrees: C
Prog. Accred.: Combined Prosthodontics, Endodontics, General Dentistry, Oral and Maxillofacial Pathology, Periodontics

Prince George's Hospital Center
3001 Hospital Dr., Cheverly 20785
Type: Private, independent
Degrees: C
Prog. Accred.: General Practice Residency

Saint Joseph's Medical Center
7601 Osler Dr., Towson 21204-7700
Type: Private, independent
Degrees: C
Phone: (410) 337-1109
Prog. Accred.: Clinical Pastoral Education

Shady Grove Adventist Hospital
9901 Medical Center Dr., Rockville 20850-3357
Type: Private, independent
Degrees: C
URL: http://www.adventisthealthcare.com/SGAH
Phone: (301) 279-6000
Prog. Accred.: Clinical Pastoral Education

Spring Grove Hospital Center
55 Wade Ave., Catonsville 21228
Type: Public, state
Degrees: C
URL: http://www.springgrove.com
Phone: (410) 402-6000
Prog. Accred.: Psychology Internship

Springfield Hospital Center
6655 Sykesville Rd., Sykesville 21784
Type: Public, state
Degrees: C
URL: http://www.dhmh.state.md.us/springfield
Phone: (410) 970-7000
Prog. Accred.: Psychology Internship

United States Army Dental Clinic Command
8472 Simonds St., Fort Meade 20755
Type: Public, federal
Degrees: C
Prog. Accred.: General Dentistry

Veterans Affairs Medical Center—Baltimore
10 North Greene St., Baltimore 21201
Type: Public, federal
Degrees: C
Prog. Accred.: General Practice Residency

Veterans Affairs Medical Center—Perry Point
Dental Service, Perry Point 21902
Type: Public, federal
Degrees: C
Prog. Accred.: Dental Public Health

Washington Adventist Hospital
7600 Carroll Ave., Takoma Park 20912
Type: Private, independent
Degrees: C
URL: http://www.adventisthealthcare.com/WAH
Phone: (301) 891-7600
Prog. Accred.: Radiography

MASSACHUSETTS

Baystate Medical Center
689 Chestnut St., Springfield 01199
Type: Private, indepenednt
Degrees: C
URL: http://www.baystatehealth.com/baystatemidwifery
Phone: (413) 794-4448
Prog. Accred.: Nurse (Midwifery)

Berkshire Medical Center
725 North St., Pittsfield 01201
Type: Private, independent
Degrees: C
URL: http://www.bhs1.org/medschool.html
Phone: (413) 447-2000
Prog. Accred.: Clinical Lab Scientist, Clinical Pastoral Education, Cytotechnology, General Practice Residency

Beth Israel Deaconess Medical Center
330 Brookline Ave., Boston 02215
Type: Private, independent
Degrees: C
URL: http://www.bidmc.harvard.edu
Phone: (617) 667-7000
Prog. Accred.: Clinical Pastoral Education

Beverly Hospital
85 Herrick St., Beverly 01915-1776
Type: Private, independent
Degrees: C
Phone: (978) 922-3000 x 279
Prog. Accred.: Clinical Pastoral Education

The Boston Christian Counseling Center
88 Tremont St., Bsoton 02108
Type: Private, independent
Degrees: C
URL: http://www.bcccenter.org
Phone: (617) 523-1543
Prog. Accred.: Clinical Pastoral Education

Boston Medical Center
One Boston Medical Center Place, Boston 02118-2908
Type: Private, independent
Degrees: C
URL: http://www.bmc.org
Phone: (617) 638-8000
Prog. Accred.: General Practice Residency, Psychology Internship

Brigham & Women's Hospital
75 Francis St., Boston 02115
Type: Private, independent
Degrees: C
URL: http://www.brighamandwomens.org
Phone: (617) 732-5500
Prog. Accred.: Clinical Pastoral Education, General Practice Residency

Campion Renewal CPE Center
319 Concord Rd., Easton 02493-1398
Type: Private, independent
Degrees: C
Phone: (781) 788-6800
Prog. Accred.: Clinical Pastoral Education

Charles H. McCann Technical School
70 Hodges Cross Rd., North Adams 01247
Type: Public, local
Degrees: C
URL: http://www.mccanntech.org
Phone: (413) 663-5383
Prog. Accred.: Dental Assisting

Edith Nourse Rogers Memorial Veterans Hospital
200 Springs Rd., Bedford 01730
Type: Public, federal
Degrees: C
URL: http://www.visn1.med.va.gov/bedford
Phone: (781) 275-7500
Prog. Accred.: Psychology Internship

HEALTHSOUTH New England
2 Rehabilitation Way, Woburn 01801-6003
Type: Private, proprietary
Degrees: C
Phone: (781) 935-5050 x1200
Prog. Accred.: Clinical Pastoral Education

Holy Family Hospital and Medical Center
70 East St., Methuen 01844-4597
Type: Private, independent
Degrees: C
Phone: (978) 687-0151 x 200
Prog. Accred.: Clinical Pastoral Education

Massachusetts General Hospital
35 Fruit St., Boston 02114
Type: Private, independent
Degrees: C
URL: http://www.mgh.harvard.edu
Phone: (617) 726-2000
Prog. Accred.: Oral and Maxillofacial Surgery

New England Baptist Hospital
125 Parker Hill Ave., Boston 02120-2847
Type: Private, independent
Degrees: C
Phone: (617) 754-5160
Prog. Accred.: Clinical Pastoral Education

New England School of Law
154 Stuart St., Boston 02116
Type: Private, independent, four-year
Degrees: P　　　　　　　　　　*Enroll:* 882
URL: http://www.nesl.edu
Phone: (617) 451-0010　　　　*Calendar:* Sem. plan
Prog. Accred.: Law

Saint Anne's Hospital
75 Middle St., Fall River 02721-1733
Type: Private, independent
Degrees: C
Phone: (508) 674-5600
Prog. Accred.: Clinical Pastoral Education

Saint Elizabeth's Medical Center
736 Cambridge St., Brighton 02135-2907
Type: Private, independent
Degrees: C
Phone: (617) 789-3228
Prog. Accred.: Clinical Pastoral Education

Saint Vincent Hospital at Worcester Medical Center
20 Worcester Center Blvd., Worcester 01604-4015
Type: Private, independent
Degrees: C
Phone: (508) 363-6246
Prog. Accred.: Clinical Pastoral Education

Southeastern Technical Institute
250 Foundry St., South Easton 02375
Type: Private, proprietary
Degrees: C
Phone: (508) 238-4374
Prog. Accred.: Dental Assisting, Medical Assisting
(CAAHEP)

Westborough State Hospital
PO Box 288, Westborough 01581
Type: Private, state
Degrees: C
Phone: (508) 366-4401
Prog. Accred.: Clinical Pastoral Education

MICHIGAN

Bronson Healthcare Group Inc.
252 East Lovell St., Kalamazoo 49007-5348
Type: Private, proprietary
Degrees: C
Phone: (616) 341-6171
Prog. Accred.: Clinical Pastoral Education

Children's Hospital of Michigan
3901 Beaubien St., Detroit 48201-2119
Type: Private, independent
Degrees: C
Phone: (313) 745-5391
Prog. Accred.: Clinical Pastoral Education

Covenant HealthCare
1447 North Harrison St., Saginaw 48602-4727
Type: Private, proprietary
Degrees: C
Phone: (517) 583-6526
Prog. Accred.: Clinical Pastoral Education

Detroit Institute of Ophthalmology
15415 East Jefferson Ave., Grosse Pointe Park 48230
Type: Private, proprietary
Degrees: C
Phone: (313) 824-4800
Prog. Accred.: Ophthalmic Medical Technology

Detroit Practical Nursing Center
20119 Wisconsin, Detroit 48221
Type: Public, local
Degrees: C
Phone: (313) 494-8184
Prog. Accred.: Practical Nursing

Detroit Receiving Hospital
4201 St. Antoine St., Detroit 48201
Type: Private, independent
Degrees: C
URL: http://www.drhuhc.org
Phone: (313) 745-3000
Prog. Accred.: Oral and Maxillofacial Surgery

Detroit-Macomb Hospital Corporation
7733 East Jefferson, Detroit 48214
Type: Private, proprietary
Degrees: C
Prog. Accred.: Oral and Maxillofacial Surgery

Grace Hospital
6701 West Outer Dr., Detroit 48235-2624
Type: Private, independent
Degrees: C
Phone: (313) 966-3452
Prog. Accred.: Clinical Pastoral Education

Henry Ford Hospital
1 Ford Place, Detroit 48202
Type: Private, independent
Degrees: C
URL: http://www.henryfordhealth.org
Phone: (800) 436-7936
Prog. Accred.: Oral and Maxillofacial Surgery, Radiation Therapy, Radiography

Hurley Medical Center
One Hurley Plaza, Flint 48503-5993
Type: Private, proprietary
Degrees: C
URL: http://www.hurleymc.com
Phone: (810) 257-9130
Prog. Accred.: Clinical Lab Scientist, Radiography

Interlochen Center for the Arts
PO Box 199, Interlochen 49643-0199
Type: Private, independent
Degrees: C
URL: http://www.interlochen.org
Phone: (231) 276-7200
Prog. Accred.: Music

JTPA School of Practical Nursing
735 Griswold, Detroit 48226
Type: Public, local
Degrees: C
Phone: (313) 596-7608
Prog. Accred.: Practical Nursing

Marquette General Health System
580 West College Ave., Marquette 49855
Type: Private, independent
Degrees: C
URL: http://www.mgh.org
Phone: (906) 228-9440
Prog. Accred.: Radiography

MEDRIGHT-Professional Medical Education
735 Trinway Dr., Troy 48098
Type: Private, proprietary
Degrees: C
Phone: (248) 952-5770
Prog. Accred.: Phlebotomy

Pine Rest Christian Mental Health Services
300 68th St., SE, PO Box 165, Grand Rapids 49548
Type: Private, proprietary
Degrees: C
Phone: (616) 281-6399
Prog. Accred.: Clinical Pastoral Education

Port Huron Hospital
1221 Pine Grove Ave., Port Huron 48060
Type: Private, independent
Degrees: C
URL: http://www.porthuronhosp.org
Phone: (810) 987-5000
Prog. Accred.: Radiography

Providence Hospital and Medical Centers
16001 West Nine Mile Rd., Southfield 48075
Type: Private, independepnt
Degrees: C
URL: http://www.realmedicine.org/Providence
Phone: (248) 849-3000
Prog. Accred.: Diagnostic Medical Sonography,
  Radiography

**Saint John Health System
School of Medical Technology**
19251 Mack Ave., Grosse Pointe Woods 48236
Type: Private, proprietary
Degrees: C
URL: http://www.stjohn.org
Phone: (313) 343-3508
Prog. Accred.: Clinical Lab Scientist

Saint John Hospital and Medical Center
22101 Moross Rd., Grosse Pointe 48236-2148
Type: Private, independent
Degrees: C
URL: http://www.realmedicine.org/StJohnHospital
Phone: (313) 343-4000
Prog. Accred.: Radiography

Saint Joseph Mercy Hospital-Oakland
900 Woodward Ave., Pontiac 48341-2985
Type: Private, independent
Degrees: C
Prog. Accred.: Oral and Maxillofacial Surgery

Sinai-Grace Hospital
6767 West Outer Dr., Detroit 48235
Type: Private, independent
Degrees: C
URL: http://www.sinaigrace.org
Phone: (313) 966-3300
Prog. Accred.: Clinical Pastoral Education, General
  Practice Residency, Radiography

Spectrum Health—Butterworth Campus
100 Michigan St., NE, MC56, Grand Rapids 49503-2560
Type: Private, proprietary
Degrees: C
URL: http://www.spectrum-health.org
Phone: (616) 391-1839
Prog. Accred.: Clinical Lab Scientist

Veterans Affairs Medical Center—Allen Park
4646 John R. St., Detroit 48201
Type: Public, federal
Degrees: C
Prog. Accred.: General Practice Residency

Veterans Affairs Medical Center—Ann Arbor
2215 Fuller Rd., Ann Arbor 48105
Type: Public, federal
Degrees: C
Prog. Accred.: General Practice Residency

Wedgwood Christian Youth and Family Services
3300 36th St., SE, PO Box 88007, Grand Rapids 49518-0007
Type: Private, independent
Degrees: C
Phone: (616) 831-5558
Prog. Accred.: Clinical Pastoral Education

William Beaumont Hospital Schools of Allied Health
3601 West Thirteen Mile Rd., Royal Oak 48073-6769
Type: Private, independent
Degrees: C
URL: http://www.beaumonthospitals.com
Phone: (248) 551-5135
Prog. Accred.: Clinical Lab Scientist, Clinical Pastoral Education, Histologic Technology, Nuclear Medicine Technology, Radiation Therapy, Radiography

MINNESOTA

Allina Hospitals and Clinics
800 East 28th St., Minneapolis 55417
Type: Private, independent
Degrees: C
URL: http://www.allina.com
Phone: (612) 863-4370
Prog. Accred.: Clinical Pastoral Education

Abbott Northwestern Hospital/Childrens's Hospitals and Clinics
800 East 28th St., Minneapolis 55407
Phone: (612) 863-4370
Prog. Accred: Clinical Pastoral Education

Mercy-Unity Hospitals and Convalescent Center
550 Osborne Rd., Fridley 55432
Phone: (612) 780-6000
Prog. Accred: Clinical Pastoral Education

United Hospital/Children's Hospital and Clinic
333 North Smith Ave., St. Paul 55102
Phone: (651) 241-8000
Prog. Accred: Clinical Pastoral Education

Fairview-University Medical Center
2450 Riverside Ave., Minneapolis 55454
Type: Private, independent
Degrees: C
URL: http://fairview-university.fairview.org
Phone: (612) 273-3000
Prog. Accred.: Clinical Pastoral Education, Radiation Therapy, Radiography

Good Samaritan Society
2177 Youngman Ave., Ste. 200, St. Paul 55116-3042
Type: Private, independent
Degrees: C
URL: http://www.good-sam.com
Phone: (651) 696-0314
Prog. Accred.: Clinical Pastoral Education

Kissimmee Good Samaritan
1550 Aldersgate Dr., Kissimmee, FL 34746-6599
Phone: (407) 933-3213
Prog. Accred: Clinical Pastoral Education

University Good Samaritan Center
22 27th Ave., SE, Minneapolis 55414-3198
Phone: (612) 673-6298
Prog. Accred: Clinical Pastoral Education

HealthEast
559 Capitol Blvd., St. Paul 55103-2101
Type: Private, proprietary
Degrees: C
URL: http://www.healtheast.org
Phone: (651) 232-2060
Prog. Accred.: Clinical Pastoral Education

Hennepin County Medical Center
701 Park Ave. South, Lab #812, Minneapolis 55415-1676
Type: Private, proprietary
Degrees: C
URL: http://www.hcmc.org
Phone: (612) 347-3009
Prog. Accred.: Clinical Lab Scientist, Clinical Pastoral Education, General Practice Residency

Medical Institute of Minnesota
5503 Green Valley Dr., Bloomington 55437-1003
Type: Private, independent
Degrees: C
URL: http://www.medicalinstitute.org
Phone: (952) 844-0064
Prog. Accred.: Dental Hygiene

Methodist Hospital
6500 Excelsior Blvd., St. Louis Park 55426
Type: Private, independent
Degrees: C
URL: http://www.parknicollet.com/methodist
Phone: (952) 993-5000
Prog. Accred.: Clinical Pastoral Education, Radiography

North Memorial Medical Center
3300 Oakdale Ave. North, Robbinsdale 55422-2900
Type: Private, independent
Degrees: C
URL: http://www.northmemorial.com
Phone: (763) 520-5200
Prog. Accred.: Clinical Pastoral Education, Radiography

Planned Parenthood of Minnesota/South Dakota
1200 Lagoon Ave., Minneapolis 55406
Type: Public, independent
Degrees: C
Phone: (612) 823-0612
Prog. Accred.: Nurse Practitioner

Rice Memorial Hospital
301 SW Becker Ave., Willmar 56201
Type: Private, independent
Degrees: C
URL: http://www.ricehospital.com
Phone: (320) 235-4543
Prog. Accred.: Radiography

Accredited Programs at Other Facilities

Rochester Methodist Hospital
201 West Center St., Rochester 55902
Type: Private, independent
Degrees: C
URL: http://www.mayoclinic.org/methodisthospital
Phone: (507) 266-7890
Prog. Accred.: Clinical Pastoral Education

Saint Cloud Hospital
1406 Sixth Ave. North, St. Cloud 56303
Type: Private, independent
Degrees: C
URL: http://www.centracare.com/sch
Phone: (320) 251-2700
Prog. Accred.: Radiography

Veterans Affairs Medical Center—Minneapolis
One Veterans Dr., Minneapolis 55417
Type: Public, federal
Degrees: C
URL: http://www.visn23.med.va.gov/Service-Areas/Minneapolis-VAMC.asp
Phone: (612) 725-2000
Prog. Accred.: General Practice Residency, Radiography

Veterans Affairs Medical Center—Saint Cloud
4801 18th St. North, Saint Cloud 56303-2015
Type: Public, federal
Degrees: C
Phone: (320) 255-6386
Prog. Accred.: Clinical Pastoral Education

MISSISSIPPI

81 Dental Squadron/SGDDT
606 Fisher St., Kessler AFB 39534-2513
Type: Public, federal
Degrees: C
URL: http://www.keesler.af.mil/dental1.html
Phone: (228) 377-1110
Prog. Accred.: Advanced Education in General Dentistry

Mississippi Baptist Medical Center
1225 North State St., PO Box 23668, Jackson 39202
Type: Private, proprietary
Degrees: C
Phone: (601) 968-3070
Prog. Accred.: Clinical Lab Scientist, Clinical Pastoral Education

Mississippi Consortium of Religion and Pastoral Care
1500 East Woodrow Wilson Dr., Jackson 39216-5119
Type: Private, independent
Degrees: C
Phone: (601) 364-1397
Prog. Accred.: Clinical Pastoral Education

North Mississippi Medical Center
830 South Gloster St., Tupelo 38801-4934
Type: Private, independent
Degrees: C
URL: http://www.nmhs.net/nmmc
Phone: (662) 841-3082
Prog. Accred.: Clinical Lab Scientist, Clinical Pastoral Education

Oral & Facial Surgical Center
300 Hospital Dr., Columbus 39701
Type: Private, independent
Degrees: C
Prog. Accred.: Oral and Maxillofacial Surgery

MISSOURI

Baptist Medical Center
6601 Rockhill Rd., Kansas City 64131-1118
Type: Private, independent
Degrees: C
Phone: (816) 276-7675
Prog. Accred.: Clinical Pastoral Education

Research Medical Center
2316 East Meyer Blvd., Kansas City 64132-1136
Phone: (816) 276-4120
Prog. Accred: Clinical Pastoral Education

Trinity Lutheran Hospital
3030 Baltimore Ave., Kansas City 64108-3404
Phone: (816) 751-3223
Prog. Accred: Clinical Pastoral Education

Barnes-Jewish Hospital
One Barnes-Jewish Hospital Plaza, St. Louis 63110
Type: Private, independent, four-year
Degrees: C, B, M
URL: http://www.barnesjewish.org
Phone: (314) 747-3000
Prog. Accred.: Clinical Pastoral Education, General Practice Residency, Nursing Education, Radiography

Boone Hospital Center
1600 East Broadway, Columbia 65201
Type: Private, independent
Degrees: C
URL: http://www.boone.org
Phone: (573) 815-6385
Prog. Accred.: Clinical Pastoral Education

Cape Girardeau Area Vocational-Technical School
301 North Clark St., Cape Girardeau 63701
Type: Public, local
Degrees: C
Phone: (573) 334-0826
Prog. Accred.: Respiratory Therapy Technology

Carondelet Health
1000 Carondelet Dr., Kansas City 64114-4673
Type: Private, proprietary
Degrees: C
URL: http://www.carondelethealth.org
Phone: (816) 942-4400
Prog. Accred.: Clinical Pastoral Education

Christian Hospital Northeast-Northwest Baptist Medical Center
1133 Dunn Rd., St. Louis 63136-6119
Type: Private, independent
System: Saint Louis Cluster
Degrees: C
Phone: (314) 653-5360
Prog. Accred.: Clinical Pastoral Education

Cox Medical Center South
3801 South National Ave., Springfield 65807
Type: Private, independent
Degrees: C
URL: http://www.coxhealth.com
Phone: (417) 269-6000
Prog. Accred.: Clinical Lab Scientist, Radiation Therapy, Radiography

Forest Park Hospital
6150 Oakland Ave., St. Louis 63139-3215
Type: Private, independent
Degrees: C
URL: https://securepublic.etenet.com/CWSContent/forestparkhospital
Phone: (314) 768-3003
Prog. Accred.: Clinical Pastoral Education

Heartland Health
5325 Faraon St., Saint Joseph 64506-3373
Type: Private, proprietary
Degrees: C
URL: http://www.heartland-health.com
Phone: (816) 271-6040
Prog. Accred.: Clinical Pastoral Education

Hillyard Technical Center
3434 Faraon St., St. Joseph 64506
Type: Private, proprietary
Degrees: C
URL: http://www.hillyardtech.com
Phone: (816) 671-4170
Prog. Accred.: Radiography

Lutheran Senior Services CPE
723 South Laclede Station Rd., St. Louis 63119-4911
Type: Private, independent
Degrees: C
Phone: (314) 968-5570 x2343
Prog. Accred.: Clinical Pastoral Education

Mineral Area Regional Medical Center
1212 Weber Rd., Farmington 63640
Type: Private, independent
Degrees: C
URL: http://marmc.org
Phone: (573) 756-4581
Prog. Accred.: Radiography

Nichols Career Center
605 Union St., Jefferson City 65101
Type: Public, local
Degrees: C
URL: http://www.jcps.k12.mo.us/education/school
Phone: (573) 659-3000
Prog. Accred.: Dental Assisting, Practical Nursing, Radiography

North Kansas City Hospital
2800 Clay Edwards Dr., North Kansas City 64116
Type: Private, independent
Degrees: C
URL: https://www.nkch.org
Phone: (816) 691-2000
Prog. Accred.: Clinical Lab Scientist

Research Medical Center
2316 East Meyer Blvd., Kansas City 64132-1199
Type: Private, independent
Degrees: C
URL: http://researchmedicalcenter.com
Phone: (816) 276-4000
Prog. Accred.: Nuclear Medicine Technology, Radiography

Rolla Technical Institute
1304 East Tenth St., Rolla 65401-3699
Type: Public, local
Degrees: C
URL: http://rolla.k12.mo.us/Rti/index.htm
Phone: (314) 364-3726   *Calendar:* Sem. plan
Prog. Accred.: Radiography, Respiratory Therapy Technology

Saint John's Mercy Medical Center
615 South New Ballas Rd., St. Louis 63141
Type: Private, independent
Degrees: C
URL: http://www.stjohnsmercy.org/sjmmc
Phone: (314) 251-6000
Prog. Accred.: General Practice Residency, Radiography

Saint John's Regional Health System
1235 East Cherokee St., Springfield 65804-2263
Type: Private, independent
Degrees: C
URL: http://www.stjohns.com
Phone: (417) 820-2000
Prog. Accred.: Radiography

Saint John's Regional Medical Center
2727 McClelland Blvd., Joplin 64804
Type: Private, independent
Degrees: C
URL: http://www.stj.com
Phone: (417) 625-2727
Prog. Accred.: Clinical Lab Scientist

Saint Luke's Hospital
4401 Wornall Rd., Kansas City 64111
Type: Private, independent
Degrees: C
URL: http://www.saint-lukes.org
Phone: (816) 932-2000
Prog. Accred.: Clinical Lab Scientist, Clinical Pastoral Education, Radiography

Veterans Affairs Medical Center—Asheville
4801 East Linwood Blvd., Kansas City 64128-2226
Type: Public, federal
Degrees: C
Phone: (816) 922-2180
Prog. Accred.: Clinical Pastoral Education

MONTANA

Benefis Healthcare—West Campus
500 15th Ave. South, Great Falls 59405
Type: Private, independent
Degrees: C
URL: http://www.benefis.org
Phone: (406) 445-5000
Prog. Accred.: Clinical Lab Scientist, Radiography

The Northern Rockies Clinical Pastoral Education Center, Inc.
PO Box 1164, Billings 59103-1164
Type: Private, independent
Degrees: C
Phone: (406) 248-3620
Prog. Accred.: Clinical Pastoral Education

NEBRASKA

55th Dental Squadron/SGD
2501 Capehart Rd., Ste. 1K47, Offutt AFB 68113-2160
Type: Public, federal
Degrees: C
URL: http://www.offutt.af.mil/55thWing/55mdg/dental
Phone: (402) 294-5712
Prog. Accred.: Advanced Education in General Dentistry

Alegent Health Bergan Mercy Medical Center
7500 Mercy Rd., Omaha 68124
Type: Private, independent
Degrees: C
URL: http://www.alegent.com
Phone: (402) 398-6060
Prog. Accred.: Radiography

Mary Lanning Memorial Hospital
715 North St. Joseph Ave., Hastings 68901
Type: Private, independent
Degrees: C
URL: http://www.mlmh.org
Phone: (402) 463-4521
Prog. Accred.: Radiography

Regional West Medical Center
4021 Ave. B, Scottsbluff 69361
Type: Private, independent
Degrees: C
URL: http://www.rwmc.net
Phone: (308) 635-3711
Prog. Accred.: Radiography

NEVADA

Nevada State College at Henderson
610 West Lake Mead Dr., Henderson 89015
Type: Public, state, four-year
Degrees: A, B
URL: http://www.nsc.nevada.edu
Phone: (702) 992-2000   *Calendar:* Sem. plan
Prog. Accred.: Nursing Education

University of Southern Nevada
11 Sunset Way, Henderson 89014-2333
Type: Private, independent, four-year
Degrees: M, D
URL: http://www.usn.edu
Phone: (702) 990-4433
Prog. Accred.: Pharmacy

NEW HAMPSHIRE

Dartmouth-Hitchcock Medical Center
1 Medical Center Dr., Lebanon 03756-0001
Type: Private, independent
Degrees: C
Phone: (603) 650-7939
Prog. Accred.: Clinical Pastoral Education

Elliot Hospital
1 Elliot Way, Manchester 03103-3502
Type: Private, independent
Degrees: C
Phone: (603) 663-2780
Prog. Accred.: Clinical Pastoral Education

Havenwood-Heritage Heights
33 Christian Ave., Concord 03301
Type: Private, proprietary
Degrees: C
URL: http://www.hhhinfo.com
Phone: (603) 229-1103
Prog. Accred.: Clinical Pastoral Education

Lebanon College
15 Hanover St., Lebanon 03766
Type: Private, independent, two-year
Degrees: A
URL: http://www.lebanoncollege.edu
Phone: (603) 448-2445
Prog. Accred.: Radiography

Veterans Affairs Medical Center—Manchester
718 Smyth Rd., Manchester 03104
Type: Public, federal
Degrees: C
URL: http://www.va.gov/sta
Phone: (603) 624-4366
Prog. Accred.: General Practice Residency

NEW JERSEY

Atlantic County Vocational Technical School
5080 Atlantic Ave., Mays Landing 08330
Type: Public, local
Degrees: C
URL: http://www.acvts.org
Phone: (609) 625-2249
Prog. Accred.: Dental Assisting

Boggs Center on Developmental Disabilities
PO Box 2688, University Affiliated Program of New
Jersey, New Brunswick 08903-2688
Type: Private, independent
Degrees: C
Phone: (732) 235-9304
Prog. Accred.: Clinical Pastoral Education

Cape May County Technical Institute
188 Crest Haven Rd., Cape May Courthouse 08210
Type: Public, local
Degrees: C
URL: http://www.capemaytech.com
Phone: (609) 465-3064　　　　　*Calendar:* Sem. plan
Prog. Accred.: Dental Assisting

Christ Hospital
176 Palisade Ave., Jersey City 07306-1121
Type: Private, independent
Degrees: C
Phone: (201) 795-8397
Prog. Accred.: Clinical Pastoral Education

Clara Maass Medical Center
1 Clara Maass Dr., Belleville 07109-3550
Type: Private, independent
System: Saint Barnabas Health Care System
Degrees: C
URL: http://www.sbhcs.com/hospitals/clara_maass
Phone: (973) 450-2066
Prog. Accred.: Clinical Pastoral Education

Cooper University Hospital
One Cooper Plaza, Camden 08103
Type: Private, independent
Degrees: C
URL: http://www.cooperhealth.org
Phone: (856) 342-2000
Prog. Accred.: Clinical Pastoral Education, Perfusion,
Radiation Therapy, Radiography

Cumberland County Technical Education Center
601 Bridgeton Ave., Bridgeton 08302
Type: Private, independent
Degrees: C
URL: http://www.cumberland.tec.nj.us
Phone: (856) 451-9000
Prog. Accred.: Dental Assisting

Englewood Hospital and Medical Center
350 Engle St., Englewood 07631
Type: Private, independent
Degrees: C
URL: http://www.englewoodhospital.com
Phone: (201) 894-3000
Prog. Accred.: Radiography

Hackensack University Medical Center
30 Prospect Ave., Hackensack 07601
Type: Private, independent
Degrees: C
URL: http://www.humed.com
Phone: (201) 996-2000
Prog. Accred.: General Practice Residency

Hudson Area School of Radiologic Technology
176 Palisade Ave., Jersey City 07006
Type: Private, independent
Degrees: C
URL: http://www.bayonnemedicalcenter.org/
schoolofradiology.html
Phone: (201) 795-8246
Prog. Accred.: Radiography

Jersey City Medical Center
50 Baldwin Ave., Jersey City 07304
Type: Private, independent
Degrees: C
URL: http://www.libertyhcs.org/liberty/jcmc/main.html
Phone: (201) 915-2507
Prog. Accred.: General Practice Residency

Jersey Shore University Medical Center
1945 Rte 33, Neptune 07753
Type: Private, independent
Degrees: C
URL: http://www.meridianhealth.com/jsmc.cfm
Phone: (732) 775-5500
Prog. Accred.: General Practice Residency

John F. Kennedy Medical Center
65 James St., Edison 08818-3059
Type: Private, independent
Degrees: C
URL: http://jfkmc.org
Phone: (732) 321-7000
Prog. Accred.: General Practice Residency

Mercer County Technical Schools Health Careers Center
1070 Klockner Rd., Trenton 08619
Type: Public, local
Degrees: C
URL: http://www.mctec.net/hcc.htm
Phone: (609) 587-7640
Prog. Accred.: Dental Assisting, Dental Hygiene

Monmouth Medical Center
300 Second Ave., Long Branch 07740
Type: Private, independent
System: Saint Barnabas Health Care System
Degrees: C
URL: http://www.sbhcs.com/hospitals/
monmouth_medical
Phone: (732) 222-5200
Prog. Accred.: General Practice Residency

Morristown Memorial Hospital
100 Madison Ave., Morristown 07962
Type: Private, independent
Degrees: C
URL: http://www.atlantichealth.org/cons/
hospitals/at_MMH
Phone: (973) 971-5000
Prog. Accred.: General Practice Residency

Mountainside Hospital
Bay & Highland Aves., Montclair 07042
Type: Private, independent
Degrees: C
URL: http://www.atlantichealth.org/cons/
hospitals/at_MSH/
Phone: (973) 429-6000
Prog. Accred.: General Practice Residency

Muhlenberg Regional Medical Center
Park Ave. and Randolph Rd., Plainfield 07061
Type: Private, independent
Degrees: C
URL: http://www.muhlenbergschools.org
Phone: (908) 668-2400   *Calendar:* Sem. plan
Prog. Accred.: Nuclear Medicine Technology, Radiation
Therapy, Radiography

Newark Beth Israel Medical Center
201 Lyons Ave. at Osborne Ave., Newark 07112
Type: Private, independent
System: Saint Barnabas Health Care System
Degrees: C
URL: http://www.sbhcs.com/hospitals/
newark_beth_israel
Phone: (973) 926-7000
Prog. Accred.: General Practice Residency

Overlook Hospital
PO Box 220, Summitt 07902-0220
Type: Private, independent
Degrees: C
URL: http://www.atlantichealth.org/cons/hospitals/at_OH
Phone: (908) 522-2000
Prog. Accred.: Clinical Pastoral Education, General
Practice Residency

Pascack Valley Hospital
250 Old Hook Rd., Westwood 07675
Type: Public, local
Degrees: C
URL: http://www.pvhospital.org
Phone: (201) 358-3000
Prog. Accred.: Radiography

Saint Barnabas Medical Center
94 Old Short Hills Rd., Livingston 07039
Type: Private, independent
Degrees: C
URL: http://www.sbhcs.com
Phone: (973) 322-5000
Prog. Accred.: Radiation Therapy

Saint Francis Medical Center
601 Hamilton Ave., Trenton 08629
Type: Private, independent
Degrees: C
URL: http://www.stfrancismedical.com
Phone: (609) 599-5000
Prog. Accred.: Radiography

Saint Joseph's Regional Medical Center
703 Main St., Paterson 07503
Type: Private, independent
Degrees: C
URL: http://www.stjosephshealth.org
Prog. Accred.: General Practice Residency

Shore Memorial Hospital
1 East New York Ave., Somers Point 08244-2387
Type: Private, independent
Degrees: C
URL: http://www.shorememorial.org
Phone: (609) 653-3500
Prog. Accred.: Radiography

Somerset Medical Center
110 Rehill Ave., Somerville 08876
Type: Private, independent
Degrees: C
URL: http://www.somersetmedicalcenter.com
Phone: (908) 685-2200
Prog. Accred.: Clinical Pastoral Education

Technical Institute of Camden County
343 Berlin-Cross Keys Rd., Sicklerville 08081-9709
Type: Private, local
Degrees: C
URL: http://www.ccts.tec.nj.us/ti
Phone: (856) 767-7000
Prog. Accred.: Dental Assisting, Medical Assisting (CAAHEP)

The Valley Hospital
223 North Van Dien Ave., Ridgewood 07450
Type: Private, independent
Degrees: C
URL: http://www.valleyhealth.com
Phone: (201) 447-8000
Prog. Accred.: Clinical Pastoral Education, Radiography

Veterans Affairs Medical Center-East Orange
385 Tremont Ave., East Orange 07018-1095
Type: Public, federal
Degrees: C
Prog. Accred.: General Practice Residency

West Jersey Health System
Camden 08104
Type: Private, proprietary
Degrees: C
Prog. Accred.: General Practice Residency

NEW MEXICO

Albuquerque Area Indian Health Service
5300 Homestead Rd., NE, Albuquerque 87110
Type: Public, federal
Degrees: C
URL: http://www.ihs.gov
Phone: (505) 248-4102
Prog. Accred.: Dental Public Health

Gallup Indian Medical Center
PO Box 1337, Gallup 87301
Type: Private, federal
Degrees: C
URL: http://www.ihs.gov
Phone: (505) 722-1000
Prog. Accred.: General Practice Residency, Optometric
Residency

Presbyterian Healthcare Services
1100 Central Ave SE, PO Box 26666, Albuquerque
Type: Private, proprietary
Degrees: C
URL: http://phs.org/facilities/pastoralcare/index.shtml
Phone: (505) 841-1191
Prog. Accred.: Clinical Pastoral Education

NEW YORK

Arnot-Ogden Medical Center
600 Roe Ave., Elmira 14905
Type: Private, independent
Degrees: C
URL: http://www.aomc.org
Phone: (607) 737-4100   *Calendar:* 24-mos. pr
Prog. Accred.: Radiography

Bellevue Hospital Center
First Ave. & 27th St., New York 10016
Type: Private, independent
Degrees: C
URL: http://www.med.nyu.edu/bellevue
Phone: (212) 562-4691
Prog. Accred.: Clinical Pastoral Education, Radiography

Beth Israel Medical Center
First Ave. at 16th St., New York 10003
Type: Private, independent
Degrees: C
URL: http://www.wehealnewyork.org/patients/
bimc_description.html
Phone: (212) 420-2759
Prog. Accred.: Clinical Pastoral Education

Blanton-Peale Institute
3 West 29th St., New York 10001-4597
Type: Private, nondenominational, four-year
Degrees: C, P
URL: http://www.blantonpeale.org
Phone: (212) 725-7850   *Calendar:* Sem. plan
Prog. Accred.: Marriage and Family Therapy

Bronx Lebanon Hospital Center
1650 Selwyn Ave., 10B, Bronx 10457
Type: Private, independent
Degrees: C
URL: http://www.bronx-leb.org
Phone: 718-992-7669
Prog. Accred.: General Practice Residency, Pediatric
Dentistry

The Brookdale University Hospital and Medical Center
One Brookdale Plaza, Brooklyn 11212
Type: Private, independent
Degrees: C
URL: http://www.brookdale.edu
Phone: (718) 240-6785
Prog. Accred.: Clinical Pastoral Education, General
Practice Residency, Pediatric Dentistry

Brooklyn Hospital Center
121 DeKalb Ave., Brooklyn 11201
Type: Private, independent
Degrees: C
URL: http://www.tbh.org
Phone: (718) 250-8258
Prog. Accred.: General Practice Residency, Oral and
Maxillofacial Surgery

Accredited Programs at Other Facilities

Brooklyn Law School
250 Joralemon St., Brooklyn 11201
Type: Private, independent, four-year
Degrees: P   *Enroll:* 1,341
URL: http://www.brooklaw.edu
Phone: (718) 625-2200   *Calendar:* Sem. plan
Prog. Accred.: Law

Calvary Hospital
1740 Eastchester Rd., Bronx 10461-2322
Type: Private, independent
Degrees: C
URL: http://www.calvaryhospital.org
Phone: (718) 518-2114
Prog. Accred.: Clinical Pastoral Education

Central Suffolk Hospital
1300 Roanoke Ave., Riverhead 11944
Type: Private, independent
Degrees: C
URL: http://www.centralsuffolkhospital.org
Phone: (631) 548-6000
Prog. Accred.: Radiography

Champlain Valley Physicians Hospital Medical Center
75 Beekman St., Plattsburgh 12901
Type: Private, independent
Degrees: C
URL: http://www.cvph.org
Phone: (518) 561-2000
Prog. Accred.: Radiography

Coler-Goldwater Specialty Hospital and Nursing Facility
One Main St., Roosevelt Island 10044
Type: Private, independent
Degrees: C
URL: http://www.nyc.gov/html/hhc/coler-goldwater/home.html
Phone: (212) 848-6000
Prog. Accred.: General Practice Residency

Eastern Suffolk School for Practical Nursing
350 Martha Ave., Bellport 11713
Type: Public, local
Degrees: C
Phone: (516) 286-6592
Prog. Accred.: Practical Nursing

Eger Health Care Center of Staten Island
140 Meisner Ave., Staten Island 10306-1200
Type: Private, independent
Degrees: C
URL: http://www.eger.org
Phone: (718) 979-1800
Prog. Accred.: Clinical Pastoral Education

Erie County Medical Center
462 Grider St., Buffalo 14215
Type: Private, independent
Degrees: C
URL: http://www.ecmc.edu
Phone: (716) 898-3000
Prog. Accred.: General Practice Residency

Faxton-Saint Luke's Healthcare
PO Box 479, Utica 13503
Type: Private, independent
Degrees: C
URL: http://www.faxtonstlukes.com
Phone: (315) 624-6000
Prog. Accred.: General Practice Residency, Radiography

Flushing Hospital Medical Center
4500 Parsons Blvd., Flushing 11355
Type: Private, independent
Degrees: C
URL: http://www.flushinghospital.org
Phone: (718) 670-5000
Prog. Accred.: General Practice Residency

Glens Falls Hospital
100 Park St., Glens Falls 12801
Type: Private, independent
Degrees: C
URL: https://www.glensfallshospital.org
Phone: (518) 926-1000
Prog. Accred.: Radiography

Harlem Hospital Center
506 Lenox Ave., New York 10037
Type: Private, independent
Degrees: C
URL: http://www.ci.nyc.ny.us/html/hhc/html/harlem.html
Phone: (212) 939-1000   *Calendar:* 24-mos. pr
Prog. Accred.: General Practice Residency, Oral and Maxillofacial Surgery, Radiography

The HealthCare Chaplaincy
315 East 62nd St., New York 10021-7767
Type: Private, independent
Degrees: C
URL: http://www.healthcarechaplaincy.org
Phone: (212) 644-1111
Prog. Accred.: Clinical Pastoral Education

The Jewish Institute for Pastoral Care
307 East 60th St., New York 10022-1505
Phone: (212) 644-1111 x265
Prog. Accred: Clinical Pastoral Education

Institute of Allied Medical Professions
Mount Sinai Medical Center, 1 Gustave Levy Place, New York 10029
Type: Private, proprietary
Degrees: C
URL: http://www.iampny.com
Phone: (212) 758-1410
Prog. Accred.: Nuclear Medicine Technology

Interfaith Medical Center
1545 Atlantic Ave., Brooklyn 11213
Type: Private, independent
Degrees: C
URL: http://www.interfaithmedical.com
Phone: (718) 613-4000
Prog. Accred.: General Practice Residency, Pediatric
Dentistry

Isabella G. Hart School of Practical Nursing
1425 Portland Ave., Rochester 14621
Type: Private, independent
Degrees: C
Phone: (716) 338-4784
Prog. Accred.: Practical Nursing

Jamaica Hospital Medical Center
8900 Van Wyck Expressway, Jamaica 11418
Type: Private, independent
Degrees: C
URL: http://www.jamaicahospital.org
Phone: (718) 206-6000
Prog. Accred.: General Practice Residency

Kings County Hospital
451 Clarkson Ave., Brooklyn 11203
Type: Private, independent
Degrees: C
URL: http://www.ci.nyc.ny.us/html/hhc/html/kings.html
Phone: (718) 245-3131
Prog. Accred.: General Practice Residency, Oral and
Maxillofacial Surgery

Kingsbrook Jewish Medical Center
585 Schnectady Ave., Brooklyn 11203
Type: Private, independent
Degrees: C
URL: http://www.kingsbrook.org
Phone: (718) 604-5000
Prog. Accred.: General Practice Residency

Lenox Hill Hospital
100 East 77th St., New York 10021
Type: Private, independent
Degrees: C
URL: http://www.lenoxhillhospital.org
Phone: (212) 434-2000
Prog. Accred.: Clinical Pastoral Education

Lincoln Medical and Mental Health Center
234 East 149th St., Bronx 10451
Type: Private, independent
Degrees: C
URL: http://www.ci.nyc.ny.us/html/hhc/html/lincoln.html
Phone: (718) 579-5000
Prog. Accred.: General Practice Residency

Long Island College Hospital
340 Henry St., Brooklyn 11201
Type: Private, independent
Degrees: C
URL: http://www.wehealny.org/patients/
lich_description.html
Phone: (718) 780-1000
Prog. Accred.: General Practice Residency, Radiography

Long Island Jewish Medical Center
270-05 76th Ave., New Hyde Park 11040
Type: Private, independent
Degrees: C
URL: http://www.lij.edu
Phone: (718) 470-7000
Prog. Accred.: General Practice Residency, Oral and
Maxillofacial Pathology, Oral and Maxillofacial Surgery,
Pediatric Dentistry

Lutheran Care Ministries Network, Inc.
110 Utica Rd., Clinton 13323
Type: Private, independent
Degrees: C
URL: http://www.lutherancare.org
Phone: (315) 853-5515
Prog. Accred.: Clinical Pastoral Education

Lutheran Medical Center
150-55th St., Brooklyn 11220
Type: Private, independent
Degrees: C
URL: http://www.lutheranmedicalcenter.com
Phone: (718) 630-7000
Prog. Accred.: General Dentistry, General Practice
Residency, Pediatric Dentistry

Lutheran Service Society of New York
6680 Main St., Williamsville 14231-1963
Type: Private, independent
Degrees: C
Phone: (716) 631-9212
Prog. Accred.: Clinical Pastoral Education

Maimonides Medical Center
4802 Tenth Ave., Brooklyn 11219
Type: Private, independent
Degrees: C
URL: http://www.maimonidesmed.org
Phone: (718) 283-6000
Prog. Accred.: General Practice Residency, Pediatric
Dentistry

Marion S. Whelan School of Practical Nursing
196-198 North St., Geneva 14456
Type: Private, independent
Degrees: C
Phone: (315) 789-4222
Prog. Accred.: Practical Nursing

Memorial Sloan-Kettering Cancer Center
1275 York Ave., New York 10021
Type: Private, independent
Degrees: C
URL: http://www.mskcc.org
Phone: (212) 639-2000
Prog. Accred.: Clinical Pastoral Education, Radiation Therapy

Mercy Medical Center
1000 North Village Ave., PO Box 9024, Rockville Centre 11571-9024
Type: Private, Diocese of Rockville Centre
Degrees: C
URL: http://mercymedicalcenter.chsli.org
Phone: (516) 705-2525
Prog. Accred.: Radiography

Montefiore Medical Center East Campus
1825 Eastchester Rd., Bronx 10461
Type: Private, independent
Degrees: C
URL: http://www.montefiore.org
Phone: (718) 904-2000
Prog. Accred.: General Practice Residency

Montefiore Medical Center West Campus
111 East 210th St., Bronx 10467
Type: Private, independent
Degrees: C
URL: http://www.montefiore.org
Phone: (718) 920-4321
Prog. Accred.: Combined Prosthodontics, General Practice Residency, Oral and Maxillofacial Surgery, Orthodontic and Dentofacial Orthopedics, Pediatric Dentistry, Radiation Therapy

Mount Sinai Hospital
100th St. & Madison Ave., New York 10029
Type: Private, independent
Degrees: C
Prog. Accred.: General Dentistry, Oral and Maxillofacial Surgery

Nassau BOCES
71 Clinton Rd., Garden City 11530
Type: Public, state/local
Degrees: C
URL: http://www.nassauboces.org
Phone: (516) 396-2500
Prog. Accred.: Practical Nursing

Nassau Technological Center
1196 Prospect Ave., Westbury 11590
Type: Private, proprietary
Degrees: C
Phone: (516) 997-5410
Prog. Accred.: Practical Nursing

Nassau University Medical Center
2201 Hempstead Turnpike, East Meadow 11554
Type: Private, independent
Degrees: C
URL: http://www.ncmc.edu
Phone: (516) 572 0123
Prog. Accred.: General Practice Residency, Oral and Maxillofacial Surgery

New York College of Health Professions
6801 Jericho Turnpike, Syosset 11791-4465
Type: Private, proprietary, four-year
Degrees: M
URL: http://www.nycollege.edu
Phone: (516) 364-0808   *Calendar:* Tri. plan
Prog. Accred.: Acupuncture

New York College of Traditional Chinese Medicine
155 First St., Mineola 11501
Type: Private, proprietary, four-year
Degrees: M
URL: http://www.nyicm.org
Phone: (516) 739-1545   *Calendar:* Sem. plan
Prog. Accred.: Acupuncture

The New York Hospital Queens
56-45 Main St., Flushing 11355
Type: Private, independent
Degrees: C
URL: http://www.nyhq.org
Phone: (718) 670-1231
Prog. Accred.: General Practice Residency, Oral and Maxillofacial Pathology

New York Law School
57 Worth St., New York 10013
Type: Private, independent, four-year
Degrees: P   *Enroll:* 1,416
URL: http://www.nyls.edu
Phone: (212) 431-2840   *Calendar:* Sem. plan
Prog. Accred.: Law

New York Methodist Hospital
506 Sixth St., Brooklyn 11215
Type: Private, independent
Degrees: C
URL: http://www.nym.org
Phone: (718) 780-3000
Prog. Accred.: Clinical Pastoral Education, General Practice Residency, Radiation Therapy, Radiography

New York Presbyterian Hospital—Columbia University
622 West 168th St., New York 10032
Type: Private, independent
Degrees: C
URL: http://www.nyp.org
Phone: (212) 305-2500
Prog. Accred.: Clinical Pastoral Education, General Dentistry, General Practice Residency, Oral and Maxillofacial Surgery, Pediatric Dentistry

New York State Department of Health
Empire State Plaza, Tower Bl, Albany
Type: Private, state
Degrees: C
Prog. Accred.: Dental Public Health

Nicholas H. Noyes Memorial Hospital
111 Clara Barton St., Dansville 14437
Type: Private, independent
Degrees: C
URL: http://www.noyes-health.org
Phone: (585) 335-6001
Prog. Accred.: Phlebotomy

North General Hospital
1879 Madison Ave., New York 10036
Type: Private, independent
Degrees: C
URL: http://www.northgeneral.org
Phone: (212) 423-4000
Prog. Accred.: Clinical Pastoral Education

North Shore University Hospital at Manhasset
300 Community Dr., Manhasset 11030
Type: Private, independent
Degrees: C
URL: http://www.northshorelij.com
Phone: (516) 562-0100
Prog. Accred.: General Practice Residency

Northport Veterans Affairs Medical Center
79 Middleville Rd., Northport 11768
Type: Public, federal
Degrees: C
URL: http://www1.va.gov/visns/visn03/nrptinfo.asp
Phone: (631) 261-4400   *Calendar:* 24-mos. pr
Prog. Accred.: Nuclear Medicine Technology, Optometry

Nyack Hospital
160 North Midland Ave., Nyack 10960
Type: Private, independent
Degrees: C
URL: http://www.nyackhospital.org
Phone: (845) 348-2000
Prog. Accred.: Clinical Pastoral Education

Peninsula Hospital Center
5115 Beach Channel Dr., Far Rockaway 11691
Type: Private, independent
Degrees: C
URL: http://www.peninsulahospital.org
Phone: (718) 734-2000
Prog. Accred.: General Practice Residency

Phillips Beth Israel School of Nursing
310 East 22nd St., New York 10010
Type: Private, independent, two-year
Degrees: A   *Enroll:* 70
URL: http://www.wehealnewyork.org/bischoolofnursing
Phone: (212) 614-6104   *Calendar:* Sem. plan
Prog. Accred.: Nursing

Queens Hospital Center
82-68 164th St., Jamaica 11432
Type: Private, independent
Degrees: C
URL: http://www.ci.nyc.ny.us/html/hhc/html/queens.html
Phone: (718) 883-3000
Prog. Accred.: General Practice Residency

Rochester General Hospital
1425 Portland Ave., Rochester 14621
Type: Private, independent
Degrees: C
URL: http://www.viahealth.org/rgh
Phone: (585) 922-4000
Prog. Accred.: Phlebotomy

Saint Barnabas Hospital
183rd St. and 3rd Ave., Bronx 10457
Type: Private, independent
Degrees: C
URL: http://www.stbarnabashospital.org
Phone: (718) 960-9000
Prog. Accred.: General Practice Residency, Oral and
    Maxillofacial Surgery, Pediatric Dentistry

Saint Charles Hospital
200 Belle Terre Rd., Port Jefferson 11777
Type: Private, independent
Degrees: C
URL: http://stcharleshospital.chsli.org
Phone: (631) 474-6000
Prog. Accred.: General Practice Residency

Saint Clare's Hospital
600 Mcclellan St., Schenectady 12304
Type: Private, independent
Degrees: C
URL: http://www.stclaresny.org
Prog. Accred.: General Practice Residency

Saint Elizabeth Medical Center
2209 Genesee St., Utica 13501
Type: Private, independent
Degrees: C
URL: http://www.stemc.org
Phone: (315) 798-8100
Prog. Accred.: Radiography

Saint Francis School of Practical Nursing
2221 West State St., Olean 14760
Type: Private, proprietary
Degrees: C
Phone: (716) 375-7316
Prog. Accred.: Practical Nursing

Saint James Mercy Health System
411 Canisteo St., Hornell 14843
Type: Private, independent
Degrees: C
URL: http://www.stjamesmercy.org
Phone: (607) 324-8000
Prog. Accred.: Radiography

Saint John's Episcopal Hospital South Shore
327 Beach 19th St., Far Rockaway 11691
Type: Private, proprietary
Degrees: C
URL: http://www.ehs.org/sshr
Phone: (718) 869-7000
Prog. Accred.: Clinical Pastoral Education

Saint Joseph's Hospital Health Center
301 Prospect Avebue, Syracuse 13203
Type: Private, independent
Degrees: C
URL: http://www.sjhsyr.org/nursing
Phone: (315) 448-5111
Prog. Accred.: General Practice Residency

Saint Joseph's Medical Center
127 South Broadway, Yonkers 10701
Type: Private, independent
Degrees: C
URL: http://www.saintjosephs.org
Phone: (914) 378-7000
Prog. Accred.: Radiography

Saint Luke's-Roosevelt Hospital Center
1111 Amsterdam Ave., New York 10025
Type: Private, independent
Degrees: C
URL: http://www.wehealny.org
Prog. Accred.: General Practice Residency, Oral and
Maxillofacial Surgery

Saint Peter's Hospital
315 South Manning Blvd., Albany 12208
Type: Private, independent
Degrees: C
URL: http://www.stpetershealthcare.org
Phone: (518) 525-1550
Prog. Accred.: General Practice Residency

Saint Vincent Catholic Medical Centers of New York
175-05 Horace Harding Expressway, Fresh Meadows 11365
Type: Private, independent, four-year
Degrees: C, B
URL: http://www.svcmc.org
Phone: (718) 357-0500　　　　　*Calendar:* Sem. plan
Prog. Accred.: Clinical Lab Scientist, Physician Assistant, Radiography

Mary Immaculate Hospital
88-25 153rd St., Jamaica 11432
Phone: (718) 558-7280
Prog. Accred: General Practice Residency, Oral and
Maxillofacial Surgery

Staten Island Campus
75 Vanderbilt Ave., Staten Island 10304-3850
Phone: (718) 354-5570
Prog. Accred: Physician Assistant

Saint Vincent's Hospital and Medical Center
153 West 11th St., New York 10011
Type: Private, independent
Degrees: C
URL: http://www.nucmedicine.com
Phone: (212) 604-8716　　　　　*Calendar:* 12-mos. pr
Prog. Accred.: Clinical Lab Scientist, Nuclear Medicine
Technology

Sisters of Charity Hospital
2157 Main St., Buffalo 14214
Type: Private, independent
Degrees: C
URL: http://www.chsbuffalo.org
Phone: (716) 862-1420
Prog. Accred.: Clinical Pastoral Education

South Nassau Communities Hospital
One Healthy Way, Oceanside 11572
Type: Private, independent
Degrees: C
URL: http://www.southnassau.org
Phone: (516) 632-4678
Prog. Accred.: Radiography

State University of New York Educational Opportunity Center
465 Washington St., Buffalo 14203
Type: Public, state
Degrees: C
Prog. Accred.: Dental Assisting

Staten Island University Hospital
475 Seaview Ave., Staten Island 10305
Type: Private, independent
Degrees: C
URL: http://www.siuh.edu
Phone: (718) 226-9000
Prog. Accred.: General Practice Residency

Strong Memorial Hospital
601 Elmwood Ave., Rochester 14642
Type: Private, independent
Degrees: C ˉ
URL: http://www.stronghealth.com
Phone: (585) 275-2100
Prog. Accred.: General Practice Residency, Oral and
Maxillofacial Surgery

Veterans Affairs Medical Center—Bath
Bath 14810
Type: Public, federal
Degrees: C
Prog. Accred.: General Dentistry

Veterans Affairs Medical Center—Brooklyn
800 Poly Place, Brooklyn 11209
Type: Public, federal
Degrees: C
Prog. Accred.: General Practice Residency

Veterans Affairs Medical Center—Buffalo
3495 Bailey Ave., Buffalo 14215
Type: Public, federal
Degrees: C
Prog. Accred.: Combined Prosthodontics, General Practice
Residency

Veterans Affairs Medical Center—
New York City
423 East 23rd St., New York 10010
Type: Public, federal
Degrees: C
Prog. Accred.: Combined Prosthodontics, Endodontics,
General Practice Residency, Periodontics

Veterans Affairs Medical Center—Northport
Middleville Rd., Northport 11768
Type: Public, federal
Degrees: C
Prog. Accred.: General Practice Residency

Veterans Affairs Medical Center—Stratton
113 Holland Ave., Albany 12208
Type: Public, federal
Degrees: C
Prog. Accred.: General Practice Residency

Veterans Affairs Medical Center—Castle Point
Castle Point 12511
Type: Public, federal
Degrees: C
Prog. Accred.: General Dentistry

Westchester County Medical Center
Macy Pavilion, Valhalla 10595
Type: Private, independent
Degrees: C
URL: http://www.wcmc.com
Prog. Accred.: General Practice Residency, Oral and
Maxillofacial Surgery

Winthrop University Hospital
259 1st St., Mineola
Type: Private, independent
Degrees: C
URL: http://www.winthrop.org
Phone: (516) 663-4749
Prog. Accred.: Clinical Pastoral Education, Radiography

Women's Christian Association Hospital
PO Box 840, Jamestown 14702-0840
Type: Private, independent
Degrees: C
URL: http://www.wcahospital.org
Phone: (716) 487-0141
Prog. Accred.: Clinical Lab Scientist, Radiography

Woodhull Medical and Mental Health Center
760 Broadway Ave., Brooklyn 11206
Type: Private, independent
Degrees: C
URL: http://www.ci.nyc.ny.us/html/hhc/html/
woodhull.html
Phone: (718) 963-8000
Prog. Accred.: General Practice Residency, Oral and
Maxillofacial Surgery

Wyckoff Heights Medical Center
374 Stockholm St., Brooklyn 11237
Type: Private, independent
Degrees: C
URL: http://www.wyckoffhospital.org
Phone: (718) 963-7272
Prog. Accred.: General Practice Residency

NORTH CAROLINA

2nd Dental Battalion-Naval Dental Center
315 Main Service Rd., Camp LeJeune 28542-2508
Type: Public, federal
Degrees: C
URL: http://ndc-cl-www.med.navy.mil
Phone: (910) 451-2775
Prog. Accred.: Advanced Education in General Dentistry

Alamance Regional Medical Center
PO Box 202, Burlington 27216
Type: Private, independent
Degrees: C
URL: http://www.armc.com
Phone: (336) 538-7000
Prog. Accred.: Clinical Pastoral Education

John Umstead Hospital
1003 12th St., Butner 27509
Type: Private, independent
Degrees: C
Phone: (919) 575-7211
Prog. Accred.: Clinical Pastoral Education

Maria Parham Hospital, Inc.
Ruin Creek Rd. at I-85, PO Drawer 59, Henderson 27536
Type: Private, proprietary
Degrees: C
Phone: (252) 438-1130
Prog. Accred.: Medical Laboratory Technology

The Moses H. Cone Memorial Hospital
1200 North Elm St., Greensboro 27401
Type: Private, independent
Degrees: C
URL: http://www.mosescone.com
Phone: (336) 832-7000
Prog. Accred.: Radiography

Nash Health Care Systems
Department of Pastoral Care, 2460 Curtis Ellis Dr, Rocky Mount
Type: Private, proprietary
Degrees: C
URL: http://www.nhcs.org
Phone: (252) 443-8770
Prog. Accred.: Clinical Pastoral Education

New Hanover Regional Medical Center
2131 South 17th St., Wilmington 28401
Type: Private, independent
Degrees: C
URL: http://www.nhrmc.org
Phone: (910) 343-7000
Prog. Accred.: Clinical Pastoral Education

North Carolina Baptist Hospitals
Chaplaincy and Pastoral Education, Medical Center Blvd., Winston Salem
Type: Private, independent
Degrees: C
URL: http://www.wfubmc.edu
Phone: (336) 716-3409
Prog. Accred.: Clinical Pastoral Education

North Carolina Division of Dental Health
PO Box 27687, Raleigh 27611-7687
Type: Private, state
Degrees: C
Prog. Accred.: Dental Public Health

Presbyterian Hospital
200 Hawthorne Ln., PO Box 33549, Charlotte 28233-3549
Type: Private, independent
Degrees: C
URL: http://www.presbyterian.org
Phone: (704) 384-4000
Prog. Accred.: Radiography

Rex Healthcare
4420 Lake Boone Trail, Raleigh 27607
Type: Private, proprietary
Degrees: C
URL: http://www.rexhealth.com
Phone: (919) 784-3100
Prog. Accred.: Clinical Pastoral Education

United States Army DENTAC—Ft. Bragg
Fort Bragg 28310-5000
Type: Public, federal
Degrees: C
Prog. Accred.: General Dentistry

Veterans Affairs Medical Center—Asheville
1100 Tunnel Rd., Asheville 28805-2043
Type: Public, federal
Degrees: C
URL: http://www.med.va.gov
Phone: (828) 299-2554
Prog. Accred.: Clinical Pastoral Education

Veterans Affairs Medical Center—Durham
508 Fulton St., Durham 27705-3875
Type: Public, federal
Degrees: C
URL: http://www.acpub.duke.edu
Phone: (919) 286-0411
Prog. Accred.: Clinical Pastoral Education

WakeMed
3000 New Bern Ave., Raleigh 27610-1231
Type: Private, proprietary
Degrees: C
URL: http://www.wakemed.org
Phone: (919) 350-8556
Prog. Accred.: Clinical Pastoral Education

Wilkes Regional Medical Center
1370 West D St., North Wilkesboro 28659
Type: Private, independent
Degrees: C
URL: http://www.wilkesregional.org
Phone: (336) 651-8100
Prog. Accred.: Radiography

NORTH DAKOTA

Altru Hospital
1200 South Columbia Rd., PO Box 6002, Grand Forsk 58201-4036
Type: Private, independent
Degrees: C
URL: http://www.altru.org
Phone: (701) 780-5300
Prog. Accred.: Clinical Pastoral Education

Meritcare Hospital
720 4th St. North, Fargo 58122
Type: Private, proprietary
Degrees: C
URL: http://www.meritcare.com
Phone: (701) 234-6000
Prog. Accred.: Clinical Pastoral Education, Radiography

North Dakota State Hospital
PO Box 476, Jamestown
Type: Private, state
Degrees: C
Phone: (701) 253-3746
Prog. Accred.: Clinical Pastoral Education

Trinity Hospital
407 3rd St. SE, Minot 58701
Type: Private, independent
Degrees: C
URL: http://trinity.minot.org
Phone: (701) 857-5000
Prog. Accred.: Clinical Pastoral Education, Radiography

OHIO

74th Dental Squadron/SGD
4881 Sugar Maple Dr., Wright-Patterson AFB 45433-5529
Type: Public, federal
Degrees: C
URL: http://wpmc1.wpafb.af.mil/pages/dental/74.htm
Phone: (937) 257-9575
Prog. Accred.: Advanced Education in General Dentistry

Akron General Medical Center
400 Wabash Ave., Akron 44307
Type: Private, independent
Degrees: C
URL: http://www.agmc.org
Phone: (330) 384-6411
Prog. Accred.: Clinical Pastoral Education

Akron School of Practical Nursing
619 Sumner St., Akron 44311
Type: Private, local
Degrees: C
URL: http://www.akronschools.com/site/community/adult-nursing.html
Phone: (330) 761-3255
Prog. Accred.: Practical Nursing

Aultman Hospital
2600 Sixth St., SW, Canton 44710
Type: Private, independent
Degrees: C
URL: http://www.aultman.com
Phone: (330) 452-9911
Prog. Accred.: Nuclear Medicine Technology, Radiation Therapy, Radiography

Children's Hospital Medical Center of Akron
One Perkins Square, Akron 44308
Type: Private, independent
Degrees: C
URL: http://www.akronchildrens.org
Phone: (330) 543-1000
Prog. Accred.: Radiography

The Christ Hospital
2139 Auburn Ave., Cincinnati 45219-2906
Type: Private, independent
Degrees: C
Phone: (513) 585-2265
Prog. Accred.: Clinical Pastoral Education

Cincinnati Children's Hospital Medical Center
3333 Burnet Ave., Cincinnati
Type: Private, independent
Degrees: C
URL: http://www.cincinnatichildrens.org
Phone: (513) 636-4200
Prog. Accred.: Clinical Pastoral Education, Pediatric Dentistry

The Cleveland Clinic
9500 Euclid Ave., Cleveland 44195
Type: Private, independent
System: Cleveland Clinic Health System
Degrees: C
URL: http://www.clevelandclinic.org
Phone: (216) 444-2200
Prog. Accred.: Clinical Pastoral Education, General Practice Residency, Radiation Therapy

Columbus Children's Hospital
700 Children's Dr., Columbus 43205
Type: Private, independent
Degrees: C
URL: http://www.childrenscolumbus.org
Phone: (614) 722-2000
Prog. Accred.: Clinical Pastoral Education

Council for Pastoral Education and Development
3130 North Dixie Hwy., Troy 45373-1337
Type: Private, independent
Degrees: C
Phone: (937) 440-7575
Prog. Accred.: Clinical Pastoral Education

Euclid Hospital
18901 Lake Shore Blvd., Euclid 44119
Type: Private, independent
System: Cleveland Clinic Health System
Degrees: C
URL: http://www.euclidhospital.org
Phone: (216) 531-9000
Prog. Accred.: Radiography

Firelands Regional Medical Center
1101 Decatur St., Sandusky 44870
Type: Private, independent
Degrees: C
URL: http://www.firelands.com
Phone: (419) 557-7400
Prog. Accred.: Radiography

Hannah E. Mullins School of Practical Nursing
1200 East Sixth St., Salem 44460-1757
Type: Public, local
Degrees: C
URL: http://www.salem.k12.oh.us/Mullins/Mullins.html
Phone: (330) 332-8940
Prog. Accred.: Practical Nursing

Health Alliance of Greater Cincinnati
3200 Burnett Ave., Cincinnati 45219
Type: Private, independent
Degrees: C
URL: http://www.health-alliance.com
Phone: (513) 585-6687
Prog. Accred.: Phlebotomy

Marietta Memorial Hospital
401 Matthew St., Marietta 45750
Type: Private, independent
Degrees: C
URL: http://www.mmhospital.org
Phone: (740) 374-1400
Prog. Accred.: Radiography

Marymount School of Practical Nursing
12300 McCracken Rd., Garfield Heights 44125
Type: Private, proprietary
Degrees: C
Phone: (216) 587-8160
Prog. Accred.: Practical Nursing

Maxillofacial & Facial Aesthetic Surgery
280 East Town St., Ste. C, Columbus 43215
Type: Private, independent
Degrees: C
Prog. Accred.: Oral and Maxillofacial Surgery

Mercy Medical Center
1320 Mercy Dr. NW, Canton 44708
Type: Private, independent
Degrees: C
URL: http://www.cantonmercy.com
Phone: (330) 489-1105
Prog. Accred.: Radiography

The MetroHealth Medical Center
2500 MetroHealth Dr., Cleveland 44109-1998
Type: Private, independent
Degrees: C
URL: http://www.metrohealth.org
Phone: (216) 778-7800
Prog. Accred.: General Dentistry, General Practice
Residency, Oral and Maxillofacial Surgery, Pediatric
Dentistry

Miami Valley Hospital
1 Wyoming St., Dayton 45409
Type: Private, independent
Degrees: C
URL: http://www.miamivalleyhospital.com
Phone: (937) 208-8000
Prog. Accred.: General Practice Residency

Mount Carmel Health System
793 West State St., Columbus 43222
Type: Private, proprietary
Degrees: C
URL: http://www.mountcarmelhealth.com
Phone: (614) 234-5000
Prog. Accred.: Clinical Pastoral Education

Riverside Methodist Hospital/Grant Medical Center
3535 Olentangy River Rd., Columbus 43214
Type: Private, independent
Degrees: C
URL: http://www.ohiohealth.com
Phone: (614) 566-5000
Prog. Accred.: Clinical Pastoral Education

Saint Elizabeth Health Center
1044 Belmont Ave., Youngstown 44501-1790
Type: Private, independent
Degrees: C
Phone: (330) 480-3266   *Calendar:* 24-mos. pr
Prog. Accred.: Nuclear Medicine Technology

Saint Elizabeth's Hospital Medical Center
1044 Belmont Ave., PO Box 1790, Youngstown 44501
Type: Private, independent
Degrees: C
Phone: (330) 746-2111
Prog. Accred.: General Practice Residency

Saint Luke's Medical Center
11311 Shaker Blvd., Cleveland 44101
Type: Private, independent
Degrees: C
URL: http://www.svch.net
Phone: (216) 368-7125
Prog. Accred.: General Practice Residency

Saint Vincent Mercy Medical Center
2213 Cherry St., Toledo 43608-2801
Type: Private, independent
Degrees: C
URL: http://www.mercyweb.org
Phone: (419) 251-3232
Prog. Accred.: Clinical Lab Scientist

Saint Vincent's Charity Hospital
2351 East 22nd St., Cleveland 44115
Type: Private, independent
Degrees: C
URL: http://www.svch.net
Phone: (216) 861-6200
Prog. Accred.: Clinical Pastoral Education

Spiritual Care and Education Center
915 North Reynolds Rd., Toledo 43615
Type: Private, independent
Degrees: C
URL: http://www.scec-cpe.org
Phone: (419) 536-9351
Prog. Accred.: Clinical Pastoral Education

TriHealth Good Samaritan Hospital
375 Dixmyth Ave., Cincinnati 45220-2489
Type: Private, independent
Degrees: C
URL: http://www.trihealth.com
Phone: (513) 872-1400
Prog. Accred.: Clinical Pastoral Education

Trumbull Memorial Hospital
1350 East Market St., Warren 44482
Type: Private, independent
Degrees: C
URL: http://www.forumhealth.com/tmh
Phone: (330) 841-9011
Prog. Accred.: Phlebotomy

Veterans Affairs Medical Center—Cleveland
10701 East Blvd., Cleveland 44106
Type: Public, federal
Degrees: C
Prog. Accred.: General Practice Residency

Veterans Affairs Medical Center—Dayton
4100 West 3rd St., Dayton 45428
Type: Public, federal
Degrees: C
Prog. Accred.: Clinical Pastoral Education, General
Practice Residency

Western Reserve Care System
345 Oak Hill Ave., Youngstown 44501
Type: Private, proprietary
Degrees: C
Prog. Accred.: General Practice Residency

OKLAHOMA

Canadian Valley Area Vocational Technical School
6505 East Hwy. 66, El Reno 73036
Type: Public, local
Degrees: C
Phone: (405) 422-2217
Prog. Accred.: Practical Nursing, Surgical Technology

Chisholm Trail Area Vocational Technical School
Route 1, Box 60, Omega 73764
Type: Public, local
Degrees: C
Phone: (405) 729-8324
Prog. Accred.: Practical Nursing

Francis Tuttle Vocational-Technical Center
12777 North Rockwell Ave., Oklahoma City 73142-2789
Type: Public, local
Degrees: C
URL: http://www.francistuttle.com
Phone: (405) 717-7799
Prog. Accred.: Medical Assisting (AMA), Practical Nursing, Respiratory Therapy, Respiratory Therapy Technology

Hillcrest Medical Center
1120 South Utica Ave., Tulsa 74104-4012
Type: Private, independent
Degrees: C
URL: http://www.hillcrest.com
Phone: (918) 579-6230
Prog. Accred.: Clinical Pastoral Education

Integris Baptist Medical Center
3300 NW Expressway, Oklahoma City 73112
Type: Private, independent
Degrees: C
URL: http://www.integris-health.com
Phone: (405) 949-3011
Prog. Accred.: Clinical Pastoral Education

Meridian Technology Center
1312 South Sangre St., Stillwater 74074
Type: Public, local
Degrees: C
URL: http://www.meridian-technology.com
Phone: (405) 377-3333　　　*Calendar:* Qtr. plan
Prog. Accred.: Practical Nursing, Radiography

Oklahoma Health Center at OU Medical Center
700 NE 13th St., Oklahoma City 73104
Type: Private, independent
Degrees: C
URL: http://www.oumedical.com
Phone: (405) 271-5186
Prog. Accred.: Clinical Pastoral Education, General
Practice Residency

Red River Area Vocational Technical School
PO Box 1087, Duncan 73533
Type: Public, local
Degrees: C
Phone: (405) 255-2903
Prog. Accred.: Practical Nursing, Surgical Technology

Saint Anthony Hospital
1000 North Lee St., Box 205, Oklahoma City 73101
Type: Private, independent
Degrees: C
URL: http://www.saintsok.com
Prog. Accred.: General Practice Residency

Saint Francis Hospital
6161 South Yale Ave., Tulsa 74136
Type: Private, independent
Degrees: C
URL: http://www.sfh-tulsa.com
Phone: (918) 494-2200
Prog. Accred.: Clinical Lab Scientist

Veterans Affairs Medical Center— Oklahoma City
921 NE 13th St., Oklahoma City 73104
Type: Public, federal
Degrees: C
Prog. Accred.: General Practice Residency

W. W. Hastings Indian Hospital
100 South Bliss, Tahlequah 74464
Type: Private, tribal
Degrees: C
Phone: (918) 458-3100
Prog. Accred.: General Practice Residency

Western Oklahoma Area Vocational Technical School
621 Sooner Dr., PO Box 1469, Burns Flat 73624
Type: Public, local
Degrees: C
Phone: (405) 562-3181
Prog. Accred.: Practical Nursing

OREGON

Legacy Emanuel Children's Hospital
2801 North Gantenbein Ave., Portland 97227
Type: Private, proprietary
Degrees: C
URL: http://www.legacyhealth.org
Phone: (503) 413-2200
Prog. Accred.: Clinical Pastoral Education

Oregon State Hospital
2600 Center St., NE, Salem 97310
Type: Private, independent
Degrees: C
URL: http://omhs.mhd.hr.state.or.us/osh
Phone: (503) 945-2800
Prog. Accred.: Clinical Pastoral Education

Providence Portland Medical Center
4805 NE Glisan St., Portland 97213
Type: Private, independent
Degrees: C
URL: http://www.providence.org
Phone: (503) 215-1111
Prog. Accred.: Clinical Pastoral Education

Veterans Affairs Medical Center—Portland
Portland 97207-1034
Type: Public, federal
Degrees: C
Phone: (503) 220-8262
Prog. Accred.: Clinical Pastoral Education, Combined Prosthodontics, General Practice Residency

Veterans Affairs Medical Center—Salem
617 Chemeketa St., NE, Salem 97301
Type: Public, federal, four-year
Degrees: P
Phone: (503) 362-9911
Prog. Accred.: Optometric Residency

PENNSYLVANIA

Abington Memorial Health Center—Schilling Campus
2500 Maryland Rd., Willow Grove 19090-1284
Type: Private, independent
Degrees: C
URL: http://www.amh.org
Phone: (215) 481-5526
Prog. Accred.: Radiography

Abington Memorial Hospital
1200 Old York Rd., Abington 19001
Type: Private, independent
Degrees: C
URL: http://www.amh.org
Phone: (215) 481-2000
Prog. Accred.: Clinical Pastoral Education, General Practice Residency

Albert Einstein Medical Center
5501 Old York Rd., Philadelphia 19141
Type: Private, independent
Degrees: C
URL: http://www.einstein.edu
Phone: (215) 456-7890
Prog. Accred.: Clinical Pastoral Education, Endodontics, General Practice Residency, Orthodontic and Dentofacial Orthopedics, Radiography

Allegheny General Hospital
320 East North Ave., Pittsburgh 15212
Type: Private, independent
Degrees: C
URL: http://www.allhealth.edu/agh
Phone: (412) 359-3131
Prog. Accred.: General Practice Residency, Oral and Maxillofacial Surgery

Armstrong County Memorial Hospital
One Nolte Dr., Kittanning 16201
Type: Private, independent
Degrees: C
URL: http://www.acmh.org
Phone: (724) 543-8500   *Calendar:* 24-mos. pr
Prog. Accred.: Radiography

Bradford Regional Medical Center
116 Interstate Pkwy., Bradford 16701
Type: Private, independent
Degrees: C
URL: http://www.brmc.com
Phone: (814) 368-4143
Prog. Accred.: Radiography

Center for Arts and Technology
1635 E. Lincoln Hwy., Coatesville 19320
Type: Public, local
Degrees: C
URL: http://www.cciu.org/pnp
Phone: (610) 384-1585
Prog. Accred.: Practical Nursing

Central Pennsylvania Institute of Science and Technology
540 North Harrison Rd., Pleasant Gap 16823
Type: Public, state/local
Degrees: C
URL: http://www.cpi.tec.pa.us
Phone: (814) 359-2582
Prog. Accred.: Practical Nursing

Children's Hospital of Pittsburgh
3705 Fifth Ave., Pittsburgh 15213
Type: Private, independent
Degrees: C
URL: http://www.chp.edu
Phone: (412) 692-5325
Prog. Accred.: Pediatric Dentistry

Clarion County Area Vocational Technical School
1976 Career Way, Shippenville 16254
Type: Public, local
Degrees: C
Phone: (814) 226-5857
Prog. Accred.: Practical Nursing

Clearfield County Area Vocational Technical School
RR #1, Box 5, Clearfield 16830
Type: Public, local
Degrees: C
Phone: (814) 765-4047
Prog. Accred.: Practical Nursing

Clearfield Hospital
809 Turnpike Ave., PO Box 992, Clearfield 16830
Type: Private, independent
Degrees: C
URL: http://www.clearfieldhosp.org
Phone: (814) 765-5341
Prog. Accred.: Radiography

Conemaugh Memorial Medical Center
1086 Franklin St., Johnstown 15905
Type: Private, independent
Degrees: C
URL: http://www.conemaugh.org
Phone: (814) 534-9000
Prog. Accred.: Histologic Technology, Radiography

Council for Relationahips
4025 Chestnut St., Philadelphia 19104
Type: Private, proprietary
Degrees: C
URL: http://www.councilforrelationships.org
Phone: (215) 382-6680
Prog. Accred.: Marriage and Family Therapy

Crawford County Area Vocational Technical School
860 Thurston Rd., Meadville 16335
Type: Public, local
Degrees: C
Phone: (814) 724-6028
Prog. Accred.: Practical Nursing

Crozer-Chester Medical Center
One Medical Center Blvd., Upland 19013
Type: Private, independent
Degrees: C
URL: http://www.crozer.org
Phone: (610) 447-2000
Prog. Accred.: Radiography

East Montgomery County Area Vocational Technical School
3075 Terwood Rd., Willow Grove 19090
Type: Public, local
Degrees: C
Phone: (215) 657-7087
Prog. Accred.: Practical Nursing

Fayette County Area Vocational Technical School
RD #2, Box 122A, Uniontown 15401
Type: Public, local
Degrees: C
Phone: (412) 437-2724
Prog. Accred.: Practical Nursing

Franklin County Area Vocational Technical School
2463 Loop Rd., Chambersberg 17201
Type: Public, local
Degrees: C
Phone: (717) 263-5667
Prog. Accred.: Practical Nursing

Geisinger Medical Center
100 North Academy Ave., Danville 17822
Type: Private, independent
Degrees: C
URL: http://www.geisinger.org
Phone: (570) 271-3700
Prog. Accred.: Clinical Pastoral Education, Radiography

Graduate Hospital
1800 Lombard St., Philadelphia 19146
Type: Private, independent
Degrees: C
URL: http://www.graduatehospital.com
Phone: (215) 893-2000
Prog. Accred.: General Practice Residency

Greene County Area Vocational Technical School
RD 2, Box 40, Waynesburg 15370
Type: Public, local
Degrees: C
Phone: (412) 627-3106
Prog. Accred.: Practical Nursing

Hazleton Area Vocational Technical School
1451 West 23rd St., Hazleton 18201
Type: Public, local
Degrees: C
Phone: (570) 459-3178
Prog. Accred.: Practical Nursing

Holy Spirit Hospital
503 North 21st St., Camp Hill 17011-2288
Type: Private, Roman Catholic Church
Degrees: C
URL: http://www.hsh.org
Phone: (717) 763-2100
Prog. Accred.: Radiography

Institute of Midwifery, Women and Health
Schoolhouse Ln. and Henry Ave., Philadelphia 19144
Type: Private, independent
Degrees: C
URL: http://www.instituteofmidwifery.org
Phone: (215) 951-2525
Prog. Accred.: Nurse (Midwifery)

Jameson Hospital
1211 Wilmington Ave., New Castle 16105
Type: Private, independent
Degrees: C
URL: http://www.jamesonhealthsystem.com
Phone: (724) 658-9001
Prog. Accred.: Radiography

Jameson Hospital
1000 South Mercer St., New Castle 16101
Type: Private, independent
Degrees: C
URL: http://www.jamesonhealthsystem.com
Phone: (724) 656-4134
Prog. Accred.: Nuclear Medicine Technology

Jeanes Hospital
7600 central Ave., Philadelphia 19111-2442
Type: Private, independent
Degrees: C
URL: http://www.jeanes.com
Phone: (215) 728-2036
Prog. Accred.: Clinical Pastoral Education

Jefferson County-Dubois Area Vocational Technical School
100 Jeff Tech Dr., Reynoldsville 15851
Type: Public, local
Degrees: C
Phone: (814) 653-8265
Prog. Accred.: Practical Nursing

Lackawanna County Area Vocational Technical School
3201 Rockwell Ave., Scranton 18508
Type: Public, local
Degrees: C
Phone: (717) 346-8728
Prog. Accred.: Practical Nursing

Lancaster General Hospital
555 North Duke St., PO Box 3555, Lancaster 17604-3555
Type: Private, independent
Degrees: C
URL: http://www.lha.org
Phone: (717) 290-5979
Prog. Accred.: Clinical Pastoral Education

Lancaster Cleft Palate Clinic
223 North Lime St., Lancaster 17602
Phone: (717) 394-3793
Prog. Accred: General Dentistry

Lawrence County Area Vocational Technical School
750 Phelps Way, New Castle 16101
Type: Public, local
Degrees: C
URL: http://www.lcvt.tec.pa.us
Phone: (412) 654-2810
Prog. Accred.: Practical Nursing

Lehigh Valley Hospital—17th and Chew Streets
PO Box 7017, 17th & Chew St., Allentown 18107
Type: Private, proprietary
Degrees: C
URL: http://www.lvh.org
Phone: (610) 402-8000
Prog. Accred.: General Practice Residency

Lehigh Valley Hospital—Cedar Crest and I-78
PO Box 689, Cedar Crest & I-78, Allentown 18105
Type: Private, proprietary
Degrees: C
URL: http://www.lvh.org
Phone: (610) 402-2273
Prog. Accred.: Clinical Pastoral Education

Lehigh Valley Hospital—Muhlenberg
2545 Schoenersville Rd., Bethlehem 18017
Type: Private, independent
Degrees: C
URL: http://www.lvhhn.org
Phone: (610) 402-2273
Prog. Accred.: General Practice Residency

Lenape Area Vocational Technical School
2215 Chaplin Ave., Ford City 16226
Type: Public, local
Degrees: C
URL: http://www.lenape.k12.pa.us
Phone: (724) 763-7116
Prog. Accred.: Practical Nursing

Monroe County Area Vocational Technical School
Laurel Lake Dr., PO Box 66, Bartonsville 18321
Type: Public, local
Degrees: C
Phone: (570) 629-6563
Prog. Accred.: Practical Nursing

Northern Tier Career Center
Rural Route 1, PO Box 157A, Towanda 18848-9731
Type: Public, local
Degrees: C
URL: http://www.ntccschool.org
Phone: (570) 265-8111
Prog. Accred.: Practical Nursing

Ohio Valley General Hospital
25 Heckel Rd., McKees Rocks 15136
Type: Private, independent, two-year
Degrees: A
URL: http://www.ohiovalleyhospital.org
Phone: (412) 777-6200
Prog. Accred.: Radiography

Parkway West Vocational Technical School
7101 Steubenville Pike, Oakdale 15071
Type: Public, local
Degrees: C
Phone: (412) 923-1772
Prog. Accred.: Practical Nursing

Philadelphia Child and Family Therapy Training Center
PO Box 4092, Philadelphia 19118-8092
Type: Private, proprietary
Degrees: C
URL: http://www.philafamily.com
Phone: (215) 242-0949
Prog. Accred.: Marriage and Family Therapy

Philhaven
283 South Butler Rd., PO Box 550, Mt. Gretna 17064
Type: Private, proprietary
Degrees: C
URL: http://www.philhaven.com
Phone: (717) 273-8871
Prog. Accred.: Clinical Pastoral Education

Phoebe Ministries
1925 Turner St., Allentown 18104
Type: Private, independent
Degrees: C
URL: http://www.phoebe.org
Phone: (610) 794-5119
Prog. Accred.: Clinical Pastoral Education

Planned Parenthood Federation of America
260 South Broad St., Philadelphia 19102
Type: Public, independent
Degrees: C
Phone: (215) 985-2628
Prog. Accred.: Nurse Practitioner

The Reading Hospital and Medical Center
Sixth Ave. and Spruce St., PO Box 16052, West Reading 19612-6052
Type: Private, independent
Degrees: C
URL: http://www.readinghospital.org
Phone: (610) 988-4357
Prog. Accred.: Clinical Pastoral Education, Radiography

Sacred Heart Hospital
421 Chew St., Allentown 18102
Type: Private, independent
Degrees: C
URL: http://www.shh.org
Phone: (610) 776-4500
Prog. Accred.: General Practice Residency

Saint Christopher's Hospital for Children
Erie Ave. at Front St., Philadelphia 19134
Type: Private, independent
Degrees: C
URL: http://www.stchristophershospital.com
Phone: (215) 427-5000
Prog. Accred.: Pediatric Dentistry, Radiography

Saint Francis Medical Center
45th at Penn Ave., Pittsburgh 15201
Type: Private, independent
Degrees: C
Prog. Accred.: Oral and Maxillofacial Surgery

Saint Joseph Medical Center
215 North Twelfth St., Reading 19603
Type: Private, independent
Degrees: C
URL: http://www.sjmcberks.org
Phone: (610) 378-2000
Prog. Accred.: General Practice Residency, Radiography

Saint Luke's Hospital
801 Ostrum St., Bethlehem 18015-1014
Type: Private, independent
Degrees: C
URL: http://www.slhn-lehighvalley.org
Phone: (610) 954-4000
Prog. Accred.: Clinical Pastoral Education

Saint Mary Medical Center
Langhorne-Newtown Rd., Langhorne 19047-1295
Type: Private, independent
Degrees: C
URL: http://www.stmaryhealthcare.org
Phone: (215) 938-3820
Prog. Accred.: Clinical Pastoral Education

School District of the City of Erie
2931 Harvard Rd., Erie 16508
Type: Public, local
Degrees: C
Phone: (814) 868-3345
Prog. Accred.: Practical Nursing

Sewickley Valley Hospital
720 Blackburn Rd., Sewickley 15143
Type: Private, independent
Degrees: C
URL: http://www.heritagevalley.org/Content/SVH/SVHHome.htm
Phone: (412) 741-6600
Prog. Accred.: Radiography

Sharon Regional Health System
740 East State State, Sharon 16146
Type: Private, independent
Degrees: C
URL: http://www.sharonregional.com
Phone: (724) 983-5518
Prog. Accred.: Radiography

Somerset County Area Vocational Technical School
Rd 5, Box 24A, Somerset 15501
Type: Public, local
Degrees: C
Phone: (814) 445-8522
Prog. Accred.: Medical Assisting (AMA), Practical Nursing

Susquehanna Health System
777 Rural Ave., Williamsport 17701
Type: Private, proprietary
Degrees: C
URL: http://www.shscares.org
Phone: (570) 321-2215
Prog. Accred.: Clinical Pastoral Education

Venango County Area Vocational Technical School
1 Voc-Tech Dr., Oil City 16301
Type: Public, local
Degrees: C
URL: http://www.vtc1.org
Phone: (814) 677-3097
Prog. Accred.: Practical Nursing

Veterans Affairs Medical Center—Philadelphia
University & Woodland Aves., Philadelphia 19104
Type: Public, federal
Degrees: C
Prog. Accred.: General Practice Residency

Veterans Affairs Medical Center—Wilkes-Barre
1111 East End Blvd., Wilkes-Barre 18711
Type: Public, federal
Degrees: C
Prog. Accred.: General Practice Residency

Veterans Affairs Pittsburgh Healthcare System
7180 Highland Dr., Pittsburgh 15206
Type: Private, federal
Degrees: C
Phone: (412) 365-5144
Prog. Accred.: Clinical Pastoral Education, General Practice Residency

The Washington Hospital
155 Wilson Ave., Washington 15301
Type: Private, independent
Degrees: C
URL: http://www.washingtonhospital.org
Phone: (724) 225-7000
Prog. Accred.: Radiography

WellSpan Health—York Hospital
1001 South George St., York 17405-7198
Type: Private, proprietary
Degrees: C
URL: http://www.wellspan.org
Phone: (717) 851-3500
Prog. Accred.: Clinical Pastoral Education, General Practice Residency

Western Area Vocational Technical School
RD #1 Box 178-A, Cannonsburg 15317
Type: Public, local
Degrees: C
Phone: (412) 746-2890
Prog. Accred.: Practical Nursing

The Western Pennsylvania Hospital
4800 Friendship Ave., Pittsburgh 15224
Type: Private, independent
Degrees: C
URL: http://www.asri.edu/wph
Phone: (412) 578-5000
Prog. Accred.: Clinical Pastoral Education

Wilkes-Barre Area Vocational Technical School
Box 1699 North End Station, Wilkes-Barre 18705
Type: Public, local
Degrees: C
Phone: (717) 822-6539
Prog. Accred.: Practical Nursing

Wilkes-Barre General Hospital
575 North River St., Wilkes-Barre 18764-0001
Type: Private, independent
Degrees: C
URL: http://www.wvhc.org
Phone: (570) 829-8111   *Calendar:* 12-mos. pr
Prog. Accred.: Nuclear Medicine Technology, Radiography

York County Area Vocational Technical School
2179 South Queen St., York 17402
Type: Public, local
Degrees: C
Phone: (717) 741-0820
Prog. Accred.: Practical Nursing

PUERTO RICO

Veterans Affairs Medical Center—San Juan
One Verterans Plaza, San Juan 00927-5800
Type: Public, federal
Degrees: C
URL: http://www.va.gov/sta
Phone: (809) 758-7575
Prog. Accred.: General Practice Residency

RHODE ISLAND

The Chaplaincy Center
Gerry House #36, 593 Eddy St., Providence 02903-4970
Type: Private, independent
Degrees: C
URL: http://www.chaplaincycenter.org
Phone: (401) 444-8356
Prog. Accred.: Clinical Pastoral Education

Naval Dental Center—Northeast
1173 Whipple St., Newport 02841
Type: Public, federal
Degrees: C
Prog. Accred.: General Dentistry

Rhode Island Hospital
593 Eddy St., Providence 02903
Type: Private, independent
Degrees: C
URL: http://www.lifespan.org/partners/rih
Phone: (401) 444-4000
Prog. Accred.: Radiography

SOUTH CAROLINA

Anderson Area Medical Center
800 North Fant St., Anderson 29621
Type: Private, independent
Degrees: C
URL: http://www.anmed.com
Phone: (864) 261-1000
Prog. Accred.: Radiography

Bon Secours Saint Francis Hospital
2095 Henry Tecklenburg Dr., Charleston 29414-5733
Type: Private, independent
Degrees: C
URL: http://www.carealliance.com
Phone: (843) 402-1000
Prog. Accred.: Clinical Pastoral Education

Midlands Area Program—South Carolina Department of Mental Health
Academy for Pastoral Education, PO Box 119, Columbia
Type: Private, independent
Degrees: C
Phone: (803) 898-2160
Prog. Accred.: Clinical Pastoral Education

Naval Dental Center—Parris Island
PO Box 19701, Parris Island 29905-9701
Type: Public, federal
Degrees: C
Prog. Accred.: General Dentistry

Palmetto Health Baptist Hospital
Taylor at Marion St.s, Columbia 29220
Type: Private, proprietary
Degrees: C
URL: http://www.palmettohealth.org
Phone: (803) 296-5010
Prog. Accred.: Clinical Pastoral Education

Palmetto Richland Memorial Hospital
Five Richland Medical Park, Columbia 29203
Type: Private, independent
Degrees: C
URL: http://www.palmettohealth.org
Phone: (803) 434-7000
Prog. Accred.: Clinical Pastoral Education, General Practice Residency

Patrick B. Harris Psychiatric Hospital
130 Hwy. 252, Anderson 29622
Type: Private, independent
Degrees: C
URL: http://www.patrickbharrispsychiatrichospital.com
Phone: (864) 231-2600
Prog. Accred.: Clinical Pastoral Education

Piedmont Area Program
South Carolina Department of MHA for Pastoral Education, Patrick B. Harris Hospital, Anderson
Type: Private, independent
Degrees: C
Phone: (864) 231-2616
Prog. Accred.: Clinical Pastoral Education

Self Regional Healthcare
1325 Spring St., Greenwood 29646
Type: Private, independent
Degrees: C
URL: http://www.selfmemorial.org
Phone: (864) 227-4150
Prog. Accred.: Clinical Pastoral Education

Spartanburg Regional Medical Center
101 East Wood St., Spartanburg 29303
Type: Private, independent
Degrees: C
URL: http://www.spartanburgregional.com
Phone: (864) 560-6000
Prog. Accred.: Clinical Pastoral Education

United States Army Dental Activity— Fort Jackson
45902 Strom Thurmond Blvd., Ft. Jackson 29207-5720
Type: Public, federal
Degrees: C
Prog. Accred.: General Dentistry

Watkins Pre-Release Center
1700 Saint Andrews Terrace Rd., Columbia 29210-5412
Type: Private, state
Degrees: C
Phone: (803) 896-2331
Prog. Accred.: Clinical Pastoral Education

WestGate Training and Consultation Network
167 Alabama St., Spartansburg 29302
Type: Private, proprietary
Degrees: C
Phone: (864) 583-1010   *Calendar:* Sem. plan
Prog. Accred.: Marriage and Family Therapy

SOUTH DAKOTA

Avera Health
3900 West Avera Dr., Sioux Falls 57108
Type: Private, independent
Degrees: C
URL: http://www.avera.org
Phone: (605) 322-4700
Prog. Accred.: Clinical Pastoral Education

Avera McKennan Hospital and University Health Center
800 East 21st Street, PO Box 5045, Sioux Falls 57117-5045
Type: Private, independent
Degrees: C
URL: http://www.averamckennan.com
Phone: (605) 322-8000   *Calendar:* 24-mos. pr
Prog. Accred.: Radiography

Avera Sacred Heart Hospital
501 Summit St., Yankton 57078
Type: Private, independent
Degrees: C
URL: http://www.averasacredheart.com
Phone: (605) 668-8000   *Calendar:* 24-mos. pr
Prog. Accred.: Radiography

Bethesda Christian Counseling Midwest, Inc.
231 South Phillips Ave., Ste. 350, Sioux Falls 57104-6317
Type: Private, independent
Degrees: C
Phone: (605) 334-3739
Prog. Accred.: Clinical Pastoral Education

Rapid City Regional Hospital
353 Fairmont Blvd., Rapid City 57701
Type: Private, independent
Degrees: C
URL: http://www.rcrh.org
Phone: (605) 719-1000
Prog. Accred.: Radiography

Sioux Valley Hospital
1305 West 18th St., Sioux Falls 57117-5039
Type: Private, independent
Degrees: C
URL: http://www.siouxvalley.org
Phone: (605) 333-1000
Prog. Accred.: Radiography

TENNESSEE

Chattanooga Association for Clinical Pastoral Care
975 East Third St., Chattanooga 37403
Type: Private, independent
Degrees: C
URL: http://www.cacpc.org
Phone: (423) 778-7177
Prog. Accred.: Clinical Pastoral Education

Fort Sanders School of Nursing
1915 White Ave., Knoxville 37916
Type: Private, proprietary
Degrees: C
Phone: (615) 541-1290
Prog. Accred.: Nursing

James H. Quillen Veterans Affairs Medical Center
PO Box 1058, Mountain Home 37684-1058
Type: Public, federal
Degrees: C
Phone: (423) 926-1171 x2432
Prog. Accred.: Clinical Pastoral Education

Johnson City Medical Center
400 North State of Franklin Rd., Johnson City 37604-6094
Type: Private, independent
Degrees: C
URL: http://www.msha.com/facilities/jcmc.htm
Phone: (423) 431-6111
Prog. Accred.: Clinical Pastoral Education

Methodist University Hospital
1265 Union Ave., Memphis 38104
Type: Private, independent
Degrees: C
URL: http://www.methodisthealth.org
Phone: (901) 516-7000
Prog. Accred.: Clinical Pastoral Education, Nuclear Medicine Technology, Radiography

Nashville General Hospital at Meharry
1818 Albion St., Nashville 37208
Type: Public, city-owned
Degrees: C
URL: http://www.nashville.gov/general_hospital/index.htm
Phone: (615) 341-4000
Prog. Accred.: Radiography

Tennessee Department of Health
425 5th Ave. North, Nashville 37247-5010
Type: Public, state
Degrees: C
Prog. Accred.: Dental Public Health

Veterans Affairs Medical Center—Memphis
1030 Jefferson Ave., Memphis 38104-2127
Type: Public, federal
Degrees: C
Phone: (901) 577-7326
Prog. Accred.: Clinical Pastoral Education

Veterans Affairs Middle Tennessee Healthcare System
1310 24th Ave. South, Nashville 37212-2637
Type: Public, federal
Degrees: C
Phone: (615) 327-5362
Prog. Accred.: Clinical Pastoral Education

TEXAS

82nd Medical Group
149 Hart St., Ste. 4, Sheppard AFB 76311-3477
Type: Public, federal
Degrees: C
URL: http://webp.sheppard.af.mil/publicsite/82mdg/
  default.htm
Phone: (940) 676-1847
Prog. Accred.: Advanced Education in General Dentistry

Abilene Intercollegiate School of Nursing
2149 Hickory, Abilene 79601
Type: Private, independent, four-year
Degrees: B
URL: http://www.aisn.edu
Phone: (325) 672-2441   *Calendar:* Sem. plan
Prog. Accred.: Nursing

Academy of Health Sciences
3151 Scott Rd., Ste. 1202, Attn: MCCSHMP, Fort Sam
Houston 78234-6138
Type: Public, federal
Degrees: C
URL: http://www.cs.amedd.army.mil
Phone: (210) 221-8004
Prog. Accred.: Physician Assistant

Baptist Medical Center
111 Dallas St., San Antonio 78205-1230
Type: Private, independent
Degrees: C
URL: http://www.baptisthealthsystem.org
Phone: (210) 297-7000
Prog. Accred.: Clinical Pastoral Education, Radiography

Baylor University Medical Center
3500 Gaston Ave., Dallas 75246
Type: Private, independent
Degrees: C
URL: http://www.baylorhealth.com
Phone: (214) 820-0111
Prog. Accred.: Nuclear Medicine Technology, Radiography

Ben Taub General Hospital
1504 Taub Loop, Houston 77030
Type: Public, local
Degrees: C
URL: http://www.hchdonline.com
Phone: (713) 873-2000
Prog. Accred.: Clinical Pastoral Education, Radiography

Brooke Army Medical Center
3151 Scott Rd., Fort Sam Houston 78234
Type: Public, federal
Degrees: C
URL: http://www.cs.amedd.army.mil
Phone: (210) 916-1105
Prog. Accred.: Clinical Pastoral Education, Optometric
  Residency, Radiography

Children's Medical Center of Dallas
1935 Motor St., Dallas 75235-7701
Type: Private, independent
Degrees: C
URL: http://www.childrens.com
Phone: (214) 456-2822
Prog. Accred.: Clinical Pastoral Education

CHRISTUS Saint Elizabeth Hospital
2830 Calder St., Beaumont 77702-1809
Type: Private, independent
Degrees: C
URL: http://www.christusste.org
Phone: (409) 892-7171
Prog. Accred.: Phlebotomy

CHRISTUS Spohn Hospital Corpus Christi—Memorial
2606 Hospital Blvd., Corpus Christi 78405
Type: Private, independent
Degrees: C
URL: http://www.christusspohn.org
Phone: (361) 902-4890
Prog. Accred.: Clinical Pastoral Education

Citizens Medical Center
2701 Hospital Dr., Victoria 77901
Type: Private, independent
Degrees: C
URL: http://www.citizensmedicalcenter.org
Phone: (361) 573-9181
Prog. Accred.: Radiography

Covenant Medical Center
3615 19th St., Lubbock 79410
Type: Private, independent
Degrees: C
URL: http://www.covenanthealth.org
Phone: (806) 725-1011
Prog. Accred.: Clinical Pastoral Education, Radiography

Department of Defense Dental Laboratory Technician Course
917 Missile Rd., Sheppard AFB 76311-2246
Type: Public, federal
Degrees: C
Prog. Accred.: Dental Laboratory Technology

Ecumenical Center for Religion and Health
8310 Ewing Halsell Dr., San Antonio 78229
Type: Private, independent
Degrees: C
URL: http://www.ecrh.org
Phone: (210) 616-0885
Prog. Accred.: Clinical Pastoral Education

Good Shepherd Medical Center
700 East Marshall Ave., Longview 75601
Type: Private, independent
Degrees: C
URL: http://www.gsmc.org
Phone: (903) 236-2636
Prog. Accred.: Clinical Pastoral Education

Harris Methodist Fort Worth Hospital
1301 Pennsylvania Ave., Fort Worth 76104
Type: Private, independent
Degrees: C
URL: http://www.texashealth.org
Phone: (817) 882-2000
Prog. Accred.: Clinical Pastoral Education

Hendrick Medical Center
1900 Pine St., Abilene 79601
Type: Private, Baptist General Convention of Texas
Degrees: C
URL: http://www.ehendrick.org
Phone: (325) 670-2000
Prog. Accred.: Radiography

JPS Institute for Health Career Development
2500 Circle Dr., Fort Worth 76119
Type: Private, independent
Degrees: C
URL: http://www.jpshealthnet.org
Phone: (817) 920-7340
Prog. Accred.: Radiography

Memorial Hermann Baptist Beaumont Hospital
3080 College St., Beaumont 77701
Type: Private, independent
Degrees: C
URL: http://www.memorialhermann.org
Phone: (409) 212-5000
Prog. Accred.: Radiography

Memorial Hermann Memorial City Hospital
921 Gessner Rd., Houston 77024
Type: Private, independent
Degrees: C
URL: http://www.memorialhermann.org
Phone: (713) 242-3000
Prog. Accred.: Radiography

Memorial Hermann Southwest Hospital
7600 Beechnut St., Houston 77074-4302
Type: Private, independent
Degrees: C
URL: http://www.memorialhermann.org
Phone: (713) 456-5000
Prog. Accred.: Clinical Pastoral Education

Methodist Dallas Medical Center
1441 North Beckley Ave., Dallas 75203-1201
Type: Private, independent
Degrees: C
URL: http://www.methodisthealthsystem.org
Phone: (214) 947-8181
Prog. Accred.: Clinical Pastoral Education

The Methodist Hospital
6565 Fannin St., Houston 77030
Type: Private, proprietary
Degrees: C
URL: http://www.methodisthealth.com
Phone: (713) 790-3333
Prog. Accred.: Clinical Pastoral Education

Methodist Hospital
7700 Floyd Curl Dr., San Antonio 78229
Type: Private, independent
Degrees: C
URL: http://mh.sahealth.com
Phone: (210) 575-4000
Prog. Accred.: Clinical Pastoral Education

Saint Joseph Regional Health Center
2801 Franciscan Dr., Bryan 77802
Type: Private, independent
Degrees: C
URL: http://www.st-joseph.org/sjrhc
Phone: (979) 776-3777
Prog. Accred.: Clinical Pastoral Education

Saint Luke's Episcopal Hospital
6720 Bertner Ave., Houston 77030-2604
Type: Private, independent
Degrees: C
URL: http://www.sleh.com
Phone: (832) 355-1000
Prog. Accred.: Clinical Pastoral Education

Scenic Mountain Medical Center
1601 West 11th Place, Big Spring 79720-9990
Type: Private, independent
Degrees: C
URL: http://www.smmccares.com
Phone: (432) 268-4885
Prog. Accred.: Radiography

Scott & White Clinic in Temple
2401 South 31st St., Temple 76508
Type: Private, independent
Degrees: C
URL: http://www.sw.org
Phone: (254) 724-2558
Prog. Accred.: Clinical Pastoral Education

South Texas Veterans HealthCare System
7400 Merton Minter St., San Antonio 78284-5700
Type: Public, federal
Degrees: C
Phone: (210) 699-2130
Prog. Accred.: Clinical Pastoral Education

Terrell State Hospital
1200 East Brin, Terrell 75160-9000
Type: Public, state
Degrees: C
URL: http://www.mhmr.state.tx.us
Phone: (972) 563-6452
Prog. Accred.: Clinical Pastoral Education

Texas International Education Consortium
1103 West 24th St., Austin 78705
Type: Private, independent
Degrees: C
URL: http://www.tiec.org
Phone: (512) 477-9283
Prog. Accred.: English Language Education

United States Air Force School of Health Care Sciences
917 Missile Rd., Sheppard AFB 76311-2246
Type: Public, federal
Degrees: C
Phone: (817) 676-4033
Prog. Accred.: Dental Assisting, Dental Laboratory
Technology, Optometric Technician, Radiography

United States Army DENTAC—WBAMC
5005 North Piedras St., El Paso
Type: Public, federal
Degrees: C
Prog. Accred.: Oral and Maxillofacial Surgery

United States Army—Dental Activities
Fort Hood 76544-6063
Type: Public, federal
Degrees: C
Prog. Accred.: General Dentistry

Valley Baptist Medical Center
2101 Pease St., Harlingen 78550
Type: Private, independent
Degrees: C
URL: http://www.vbmc.org
Phone: (956) 389-1100
Prog. Accred.: Clinical Pastoral Education

Veterans Affairs Medical Center—Dallas
4500 South Lancaster Rd., Dallas 75216
Type: Public, federal
Degrees: C
URL: http://www.va.gov/sta
Phone: (214) 742-8387
Prog. Accred.: Clinical Pastoral Education, Dental Public
Health, General Practice Residency

Veterans Affairs Medical Center—Houston
2002 Holcombe Blvd., Houston 77030
Type: Public, federal
Degrees: C
URL: http://www.va.gov/sta
Phone: (713) 791-1414
Prog. Accred.: Combined Prosthodontics, General Practice
Residency

Veterans Affairs Medical Center—San Antonio
7400 Merton Minter Blvd., San Antonio 78284
Type: Public, federal
Degrees: C
URL: http://www.va.gov/sta
Phone: (210) 617-5300
Prog. Accred.: General Dentistry

Veterans Affairs Medical Center—Temple
1901 S. 1st St., Temple 76504
Type: Public, federal
Degrees: C
URL: http://www.va.gov/sta
Phone: (254) 778-4811
Prog. Accred.: General Practice Residency

Wilford Hall Medical Center
2200 Berquist Dr., Ste. 1, Lackland AFB 78236-9908
Type: Public, federal
Degrees: C
URL: http://www.whmc.af.mil
Phone: (210) 292-7100
Prog. Accred.: Combined Prosthodontics, Endodontics,
Oral and Maxillofacial Surgery, Orthodontic and
Dentofacial Orthopedics, Pediatric Dentistry,
Periodontics

UTAH

Primary Children's Medical Center
100 North Medical Dr., Salt Lake City 84113
Type: Private, independent
Degrees: C
URL: http://www.ihc.com/xp/ihc/primary
Phone: (801) 588-2000
Prog. Accred.: Pediatric Dentistry

Saint Mark's Hospital
1250 East 3900 South, Salt Lake City 84123
Type: Private, independent
Degrees: C
URL: http://www.stmarkshospital.com
Phone: (801) 268-7111
Prog. Accred.: Clinical Pastoral Education

Veterans Affairs Medical Center— Salt Lake City
500 Foothill Dr., Salt Lake City 84148
Type: Public, federal
Degrees: C
Prog. Accred.: General Practice Residency

VERMONT

The Center for Technology, Essex
3 Educational Dr., Essex Junction 05452
Type: Public, local
Degrees: C
URL: http://www.go-cte.org
Phone: (802) 879-5558   *Calendar:* Qtr. plan
Prog. Accred.: Dental Assisting

Fletcher Allen Health Care
111 Colchester Ave., Burlington 05401
Type: Private, independent
Degrees: C
URL: http://www.fahc.org
Phone: (802) 847-2770
Prog. Accred.: Clinical Pastoral Education, General
Practice Residency

New England School of Radiologic Technology
Rutland Regional Medical Center, 160 Allen St., Rotland 05701
Type: Private, independent
Degrees: C
URL: http://www.rrmc.org/progandserv/radiology.html
Phone: (802) 775-7111
Prog. Accred.: Radiography

VIRGINIA

1st Dental Squadron/SGD
45 Pine St., Langley AFB 23665-5300
Type: Public, federal
Degrees: C
URL: http://www.langley.af.mil/1mg/1ds/
   community.shtml
Prog. Accred.: General Dentistry

Hampton Roads Joint CPE Center
100 Emancipation Dr., Hampton 23667-0001
Type: Private, independent
Degrees: C
URL: http://www.chaplain.med.va.gov
Phone: (757) 728-3181
Prog. Accred.: Clinical Pastoral Education

Mary Washington Hospital
1001 Sam Perry Blvd., Fredericksburg 22401
Type: Private, independent
Degrees: C
URL: http://www.medicorp.org/mwh
Phone: (540) 741-1100
Prog. Accred.: Radiography

Maryview Medical Center
3636 High St., Portsmouth 23707
Type: Private, independent
Degrees: C
URL: http://www.bonsecourshamptonroads.com
Phone: (757) 398-2200
Prog. Accred.: Clinical Pastoral Education

Naval Dental Clinic
1647 Taussig Blvd., Norfolk 23511-2896
Type: Public, federal
Degrees: C
Prog. Accred.: General Dentistry

Naval Medical Center—Portsmouth
620 John Paul Jones Circle, Portsmouth 23708-2197
Type: Public, federal
Degrees: C
URL: http://www-nmcp.med.navy.mil
Phone: (757) 953-5000
Prog. Accred.: General Dentistry, Oral and Maxillofacial
   Surgery

Naval School of Health Sciences
1001 Holcomb Rd., Portsmouth 23708-5200
Type: Public, federal
Degrees: C
URL: https://www-nshspts.med.navy.mil
Phone: (757) 953-5040   *Calendar:* 12-mos. pr
Prog. Accred.: Nuclear Medicine Technology, Radiography

Norfolk Technical Vocational Center
1330 North Military Hwy., Norfolk 23502
Type: Private, proprietary
Degrees: C
URL: http://www.nps.k12.va.us/schools/ntvc
Phone: (757) 892-3300
Prog. Accred.: Practical Nursing

Riverside Regional Medical Center
500 J. Clyde Morris Blvd., Newport News 23601
Type: Private, independent
Degrees: C
URL: http://www.riverside-online.com/rrmc
Phone: (757) 594-2000
Prog. Accred.: Clinical Pastoral Education, Radiography

Rockingham Memorial Hospital
235 Cantrell Ave., Harrisonburg 22801-3293
Type: Private, independent
Degrees: C
URL: http://www.rmhonline.com
Phone: (540) 433-4100
Prog. Accred.: Radiography

Saint Mary's Hospital
5801 Bremo Rd., Richmond 23226
Type: Private, independent
Degrees: C
URL: http://www.bonsecours.com/smh
Phone: (804) 285-2011
Prog. Accred.: Radiography

Southside Regional Medical Center
801 South Adams St., Petersburg 23803
Type: Private, independent
Degrees: C
URL: http://www.srmconline.com
Phone: (804) 862-5000
Prog. Accred.: Radiography

Veterans Affairs Medical Center—Hampton
Hampton 23667
Type: Public, federal
Degrees: C
Prog. Accred.: General Practice Residency

Veterans Affairs Medical Center—Hunter Holmes McGuire
1201 Broad Rock Blvd., Richmond 23249-0001
Type: Public, federal
Degrees: C
Phone: (804) 675-5085
Prog. Accred.: Clinical Pastoral Education

Winchester Medical Center, Inc.
1840 Amherst St., PO Box 3340, Winchester 22601
Type: Private, independent
Degrees: C
URL: http://www.valleyhealthlink.com
Phone: (540) 536-8000
Prog. Accred.: Radiography

WASHINGTON

Evergreen Health Care
12040 NE 128th St., Kirkland 98034
Type: Private, independent
Degrees: C
URL: http://www.evergreenhealthcare.org
Phone: (425) 899-1000
Prog. Accred.: Clinical Pastoral Education

Harborview Medical Center
325 Ninth Ave., Seattle 98104
Type: Private, independent
Degrees: C
URL: http://www.washington.edu/medicine/hmc
Phone: (206) 731-3000
Prog. Accred.: Clinical Pastoral Education

Intercollegiate College of Nursing
2917 West Fort George Wright Dr., Spokane 99224-5291
Type: Public, consortium, four-year
Degrees: B, M
URL: http://www.icne.wsu.edu
Phone: (509) 324-7360   *Calendar:* Sem. plan
Prog. Accred.: Nursing Education

Madigan Army Medical Center
Building 9040 Fitzsimmons Dr., Tacoma 98431
Type: Public, federal
Degrees: C
URL: http://www.mamc.amedd.army.mil/wrmc
Phone: (253) 968-1110
Prog. Accred.: Clinical Pastoral Education, General
  Dentistry, Oral and Maxillofacial Surgery

Naval Dental Center—Northwest
2240 Decatur Ave., Bremerton 98310
Type: Public, federal
Degrees: C
URL: http://www.ndcnw.navy.mil
Phone: (360) 476-3218
Prog. Accred.: General Dentistry

Providence Saint Peter Hospital
413 Lilly Rd. NE, Olympia 98506
Type: Private, independent
Degrees: C
URL: http://www.providence.org
Phone: (360) 491-948
Prog. Accred.: Clinical Pastoral Education

Sacred Heart Medical Center
101 West Eighth Ave., PO Box 2555, Spokane 99220
Type: Private, independent
Degrees: C
URL: http://www.shmc.org
Phone: (509) 474-3131
Prog. Accred.: Radiography

Saint Joseph Medical Center
1717 South J St., Tacoma 98405
Type: Private, independent
Degrees: C
URL: https://www.fhshealth.org/location/sjmc.asp
Phone: (253) 426-4101
Prog. Accred.: Clinical Pastoral Education

Spring Valley Montessori Teacher Education Program
36605 Pacific Hwy. South, Federal Way 98003
Type: Private, independent
Degrees: C
URL: http://www.springvalley.org
Phone: (253) 927-2557
Prog. Accred.: Montessori Teacher Education

Swedish Medical Center
747 Broadway, Seattle 98122-4307
Type: Private, independent
Degrees: C
URL: http://www.swedish.org
Phone: (206) 386-6000
Prog. Accred.: Clinical Pastoral Education

Tri-Cities Chaplaincy
2108 West Entiat Ave., Kennewick 99336
Type: Private, independent
Degrees: C
URL: http://www.tricitieschaplaincy.org
Phone: (509) 783-7416
Prog. Accred.: Clinical Pastoral Education

Veterans Affairs Puget Sound Health Care System
1660 South Columbian Way, Seattle 98108-1532
Type: Public, federal
Degrees: C
Phone: (206) 768-5210
Prog. Accred.: Clinical Pastoral Education

WEST VIRGINIA

B.M. Spurr School of Practical Nursing
800 Wheeling Ave., Glen Dale 26038
Type: Private, independent
Degrees: C
Phone: (304) 845-3211
Prog. Accred.: Practical Nursing

Cabell Huntington Hospital
1340 Hal Greer Blvd., Huntington 25701
Type: Private, independent
Degrees: C
URL: http://www.cabellhuntington.org
Phone: (304) 526-2000
Prog. Accred.: Clinical Pastoral Education

Ohio Valley Medical Center
2000 Eoff St., Wheeling 26003
Type: Private, independent
Degrees: C
URL: http://www.ohiovalleymedicalcenter.com
Phone: (304) 234-0123
Prog. Accred.: Radiography

Saint Mary's Medical Center
2900 First Ave., Huntington 25702
Type: Private, independent
Degrees: C
URL: http://www.st-marys.org
Phone: (304) 526-1234
Prog. Accred.: Radiography

United Hospital Center
3 Hospital Plaza, PO Box 1680, Clarksburg 26301
Type: Private, independent
Degrees: C
URL: http://www.uhcwv.org
Phone: (304) 624-2121
Prog. Accred.: Radiography

Veterans Affairs Medical Center—Martinsburg
Route 9, Martinsburg 25401
Type: Public, federal
Degrees: C
Phone: (304) 263-0811
Prog. Accred.: General Dentistry

West Virginia School of Osteopathic Medicine
400 North Lee St., Lewisburg 24901
Type: Public, state, four-year
System: West Virginia Higher Education Policy
  Commission
Degrees: P   *Enroll:* 337
URL: http://www.wvsom.edu
Phone: (304) 647-6238   *Calendar:* Sem. plan
Prog. Accred.: Osteopathy

Wheeling Hospital
1 Medical Park, Wheeling 26003
Type: Private, independent
Degrees: C
URL: http://www.wheelinghospital.com
Phone: (304) 243-3000
Prog. Accred.: Radiography

Wood County Vocational School
#1 Campusview Dr., Vienna 26105
Type: Public, local
Degrees: C
Phone: (304) 420-9501
Prog. Accred.: Practical Nursing

WISCONSIN

All Saints Healthcare—St. Mary's Campus
3801 Spring St., Racine 53405
Type: Private, independent
Degrees: C
URL: http://www.allsaintshealth.com
Phone: (262) 687-4011
Prog. Accred.: Radiography

Aurora Family Service
PO Box 080440, Milwaukee 53208-0440
Type: Private, proprietary
Degrees: C
URL: http://www.aurorahealthcare.org
Phone: (414) 342-4560
Prog. Accred.: Marriage and Family Therapy

Aurora Sinai Medical Center
945 North 12th St., Milwaukee 53233
Type: Private, independent
Degrees: C
URL: http://www.aurorahealthcare.org
Phone: (414) 219-2000
Prog. Accred.: Clinical Pastoral Education

Bellin School of Radiology
PO Box 23400, Green Bay 54301
Type: Private, independent
Degrees: C
URL: http://www.bellin.org/careers/radiology.shtml
Phone: (920) 433-3497
Prog. Accred.: Radiography

Children's Hospital of Wisconsin—Appleton
1825 Bluemound Dr., Appleton 54913
Type: Private, independent
Degrees: C
URL: http://www.foxvalley.tec.wi.us
Phone: (920) 735-5600
Prog. Accred.: Dental Assisting

Children's Hospital of Wisconsin—Milwaukee
9000 West Wisconsin Ave., PO Box 1997, Milwaukee
53201-1997
Type: Private, independent
Degrees: C
URL: http://www.chw.org/default.htm
Phone: (414) 266-2000
Prog. Accred.: Pediatric Dentistry

Columbia Hospital
2025 East Newport Ave., Milwaukee 53211
Type: Private, independent
System: Columbia Saint Mary's
Degrees: C
URL: http://columbia-stmarys.com
Phone: (414) 961-3300
Prog. Accred.: Radiography

Community Health Care Wausau Hospital
425 Pine Ridge Blvd., Wausau 54401
Type: Private, independent
Degrees: C
URL: http://www.chcsys.org/wausau_hospital
Phone: (715) 847-2118
Prog. Accred.: Clinical Pastoral Education

Froedtert and Medical College Health Services
9200 West Wisconsin Ave., Milwaukee 53226
Type: Private, independent, four-year
Degrees: C, B
URL: http://www.froedtert.com
Phone: (414) 805-3666
Prog. Accred.: Nuclear Medicine Technology, Radiography

Gundersen Lutheran Medical Center
1900 South Ave., La Crosse 54601
Type: Private, independent, four-year
Degrees: C, B
URL: http://www.gundluth.org
Phone: (608) 782-7300
Prog. Accred.: Clinical Pastoral Education, Nuclear
Medicine Technology, Oral and Maxillofacial Surgery

Luther Hospital
1221 Whipple St., PO Box 4105, Eau Claire 54702-4105
Type: Private, independent
Degrees: C
URL: http://www.mayohealthsystem.org
Phone: (715) 838-3311
Prog. Accred.: Clinical Pastoral Education

Lutheran Homes of Oshkosh
225 North Eagle St., Oshkosh 54902-4125
Type: Private, independent
Degrees: C
URL: http://www.lutheranhomes.com
Phone: (920) 235-4653
Prog. Accred.: Clinical Pastoral Education

MENDOTA Mental Health Institute
301 Troy Dr., Madison 53704-1521
Type: Public, state
Degrees: C
URL: http://www.dhfs.state.wi.us/MH_Mendota
Phone: (608) 301-1000
Prog. Accred.: Clinical Pastoral Education

Mercy Medical Center
500 South Oakwood Rd., Oshkosh 54904
Type: Private, independent
Degrees: C
URL: http://www.affinityhealth.org/object/
mmchospital.html
Phone: (920) 223-2000
Prog. Accred.: Radiography

Meriter Hospital
202 South Park St., Madison 53715
Type: Private, independent
Degrees: C
URL: http://www.meriter.com
Phone: (608) 267-6000
Prog. Accred.: Clinical Pastoral Education, General
Practice Residency

Saint Camillus Campus
10101 W. Wisconsin Ave., Milwaukee
Type: Private, independent
Degrees: C
Phone: (414) 259-6575
Prog. Accred.: Clinical Pastoral Education

Saint Joseph's Hospital of Marshfield
611 Saint Joseph Ave., Marshfield 54449
Type: Private, independent
Degrees: C
URL: http://www.stjosephs-marshfield.org
Phone: (715) 387-1713
Prog. Accred.: Histologic Technology, Nuclear Medicine
Technology, Radiography

Saint Luke's Medical Center
2900 West Oklahoma Ave., Milwaukee 53201-2901
Type: Private, independent
Degrees: C
URL: http://www.aurorahealthcare.org
Phone: (414) 649-6000
Prog. Accred.: Clinical Pastoral Education, Nuclear
Medicine Technology, Radiography

Saint Michael Hospital
2400 West Villard Ave., Milwaukee 53209
Type: Private, independent
Degrees: C
URL: http://www.covhealth.org
Phone: (414) 527-8000
Prog. Accred.: Radiography

Theda Clark Medical Center
130 Second St., PO Box 2021, Neenah 54956-2021
Type: Private, independent
Degrees: C
URL: http://www.thedacare.org
Phone: (920) 729-3100
Prog. Accred.: Radiography

University of Wisconsin Hospital and Clinics
600 Highland Ave., Madison 53792
Type: Private, independent
Degrees: C
URL: http://www.uwhealth.org
Phone: (608) 263-6400
Prog. Accred.: Radiography

Veterans Affairs Medical Center—Milwaukee
5000 West National Ave., Milwaukee 53295
Type: Public, federal
Degrees: C
URL: http://www.va.gov/sta
Phone: (414) 384-2000
Prog. Accred.: General Practice Residency

Village at Manor Park
3023 South 84th St., Milwaukee 53227-3703
Type: Private, independent
Degrees: C
URL: http://www.vmpcares.com
Phone: (414) 607-4100 x2355
Prog. Accred.: Clinical Pastoral Education

AUSTRALIA

MacQuarie University
New South Wales, NS, Australia 2109
Type: Public, four-year
Degrees: P
Phone: 011 61 2 9850 9380
Prog. Accred.: Chiropractic Education

Royal Melbourne Institute of Technology
PO Box 71, Bundoora, VI, Australia 3083
Type: Public, four-year
Degrees: P
Phone: 011 613 9468 2440
Prog. Accred.: Chiropractic Education

The University of New South Wales
Sydney, NS, Australia 2052
Type: Public, four-year
Degrees: M
URL: http://www.unsw.edu.au
Phone: 011 61 29 385 1000
Prog. Accred.: Business (AACSB)

CANADA

Algonquin College
Woodroffe Ave., Ottawa, Canada K2G 1V8
Type: Public, provincial
Degrees: C
URL: http://www.algonquincollege.com
Phone: (613) 727-4723
Prog. Accred.: Dental Hygiene, Interior Design

Argyle Institute of Human Relations
4114 Sherbrook St. West, 5th Flr., Montreal, Canada H3Z 1K9
Type: Private, independent
Degrees: C
URL: http://home.total.net/~argyle
Phone: (514) 931-5629   *Calendar:* Sem. plan
Prog. Accred.: Marriage and Family Therapy

Calgary Regional Health Authority
1213 4th St., SW, First Flr., Colonel Belcher Hospital, Calgary, Canada T2R 0X7
Type: Private, proprietary
Degrees: C
URL: http://www.crha-health.ab.ca
Phone: (403) 541-2104   *Calendar:* Sem. plan
Prog. Accred.: Marriage and Family Therapy

Camosun College
3100 Foul Bay Rd., Victoria, Canada V8P 5J2
Type: Public, independent, four-year
Degrees: A, B
URL: http://www.camosun.bc.ca
Phone: (250) 370-3000
Prog. Accred.: Dental Assisting, Dental Hygiene

Canadian Memorial Chiropractic College
1900 Bayview Ave., Toronto, Canada M4G 3E6
Type: Private, independent, four-year
Degrees: P
URL: http://www.cmcc.ca
Phone: (416) 482-2340
Prog. Accred.: Chiropractic Education

College of New Caledonia
3330 22nd Ave., Prince George, Canada V2N 1P8
Type: Public, independent, two-year
Degrees: C, A
URL: http://www.cnc.bc.ca
Phone: (250) 562 2131
Prog. Accred.: Dental Assisting, Dental Hygiene

College of the Rockies
2700 College Way, PO Box 8500, Cranbrook, Canada V1C 5L7
Type: Public, independent, four-year
Degrees: C, A, B
URL: http://www.cotr.bc.ca
Phone: (250) 489-2751
Prog. Accred.: Dental Assisting

Concordia University
1455 de Maisonneuve Blvd. West, Montreal, Canada H3G 1M8
Type: Private, independent, four-year
Degrees: A, B, M, D
URL: http://www.concordia.ca
Phone: (514) 848-2424   *Calendar:* Sem. plan
Prog. Accred.: Accounting, Business (AACSB), Clinical Psychology

Dalhousie University
Halifax, Canada B3H 3J5
Type: Private, independent, four-year
Degrees: B, M, P, D
URL: http://www.dalhousie.edu
Phone: (902) 424-2211   *Calendar:* Sem. plan
Prog. Accred.: Clinical Psychology, Combined Prosthodontics, Dental Hygiene, Dentistry, Health Services Administration, Librarianship, Medicine, Oral and Maxillofacial Surgery

Dawson College
2120 Sherbrooke St. East, Montreal, Canada H2K 1C1
Type: Private, independent
Degrees: C
URL: http://www.dawsoncollege.qc.ca
Phone: (514) 931-8371   *Calendar:* Sem. plan
Prog. Accred.: Interior Design

Douglas College
PO Box 2503, 700 Royal Ave., New Westminster, Canada V3L 5B2
Type: Public, provincial, two-year
Degrees: C, A
URL: http://www.douglas.bc.ca
Phone: (604) 527-5400   *Calendar:* Sem. plan
Prog. Accred.: Dental Assisting

Humber College of Applied Arts and Technology
205 Humber College Blvd., Toronto, Canada M9W 5L7
Type: Public, independent
Degrees: C
URL: http://www.humberc.on.ca
Phone: (416) 675-3111 *Calendar:* Tri. plan
Prog. Accred.: Funeral Service Education (Mortuary Science), Interior Design

Interfaith Pastoral Counseling Centre
151 Frederick St., 3rd Flr., Kitchener, Canada N2H 2M2
Type: Private, independent, four-year
Degrees: M
Phone: (519) 743-6781
Prog. Accred.: Marriage and Family Therapy

International Academy of Merchandising and Design—Toronto
31 Wellesley St., East, Toronto, Canada M4V 1G7
Type: Private, independent
Degrees: C
Phone: (416) 927-7811
Prog. Accred.: Interior Design

Jewish General Hospital
4333 Chemin de la Cote Ste. Catherine, Montreal, Canada H3T 1E4
Type: Private, proprietary
Degrees: C
Phone: (514) 340-8210
Prog. Accred.: Marriage and Family Therapy

Keewatin Community College
PO Box 3000, The Pas, Canada R9A 1M7
Type: Public, local, two-year
Degrees: C, A
URL: http://www.keewatincc.mb.ca
Phone: (204) 627-8500
Prog. Accred.: Dental Assisting

Kwantlen University College
12666 - 72nd Ave., Surrey, Canada V3W 2M8
Type: Public, provincial
Degrees: C
URL: http://www.kwantlen.bc.ca
Phone: (604) 599-2100 *Calendar:* Sem. plan
Prog. Accred.: Interior Design

Lakeland College
Bag 5100, Vermillion, Canada T0B 4M0
Type: Private, independent
Degrees: C
URL: http://www.lakelandc.ab.ca
Phone: (403) 853-8400 *Calendar:* Sem. plan
Prog. Accred.: Interior Design

Malaspina University-College
900 Fifth St., Nanaimo, Canada V9R 5S5
Type: Public, independent, four-year
Degrees: C, A, B, M
URL: http://www.mala.ca
Phone: (250) 753-324
Prog. Accred.: Dental Assisting

Memorial University of Newfoundland
St. John's, Canada A1C 5S7
Type: Public, four-year
Degrees: B, M, P, D
URL: http://www.mun.ca
Phone: (709) 737-8000 *Calendar:* Sem. plan
Prog. Accred.: Business (AACSB), Medicine

Michener Institute for Applied Health Sciences
222 St. Patrick St., Toronto, Canada M5T 1V4
Type: Private, independent
Degrees: C
URL: http://www.michener.on.ca
Phone: (416) 596-3101 *Calendar:* Sem. plan
Prog. Accred.: Acupuncture

Mount Royal College
4825 Mount Royal Gate SW, Calgary, Canada T3E 6K6
Type: Private, independent, four-year
Degrees: B
URL: http://www.mtroyal.ab.ca
Phone: (403) 440-6111 *Calendar:* Sem. plan
Prog. Accred.: Interior Design

Okanagan University College
3333 College Way, Kelowna, Canada V1V 1V7
Type: Public, independent, four-year
Degrees: C, B
URL: http://www.ouc.bc.ca
Phone: (250) 762-5445
Prog. Accred.: Dental Assisting

Northern Alberta Institute of Technology
11762 - 106th St., Edmonton, Canada T5G 2R1
Type: Private, independent
Degrees: C
URL: http://www.nait.ab.ca
Phone: (780) 471-7400
Prog. Accred.: Dental Assisting, Interior Design

Queen's University at Kingston
Kingston, Canada K7L 3N6
Type: Private, four-year
Degrees: M, D
URL: http://www.queensu.ca
Phone: (613) 545-2000 *Calendar:* Sem. plan
Prog. Accred.: Business (AACSB), Clinical Psychology, Medicine

Red River College
2055 Notre Dame Ave., Winnipeg, Canada R3H 0J9
Type: Public, local
Degrees: C
URL: http://www.rrc.mb.ca
Phone: (204) 632-2311
Prog. Accred.: Dental Assisting

Robertson College
265 Notre Dame Ave., Winnipeg, Canada R3B 1N9
Type: Private, independent
Degrees: C
URL: http://www.robertsoncollege.com
Phone: (204) 943-5661
Prog. Accred.: Dental Assisting

Ryerson University
350 Victoria St., Toronto, Canada M5B 2K3
Type: Private, independent, four-year
Degrees: B
URL: http://www.ryerson.ca
Phone: (416) 979-5000   *Calendar:* Sem. plan
Prog. Accred.: Interior Design

Saint Clair College of Applied Arts and Technology
2000 Talbot Rd. West, Windsor, Canada N9A 6S4
Type: Private, independent
Degrees: C
URL: http://www.stclairc.on.ca
Phone: (519) 966-1656
Prog. Accred.: Interior Design

Sheridan College
1430 Trfalgar Rd., Oakville, Canada L6H 2L1
Type: Private, independent
Degrees: C
URL: http://www.sheridanc.on.ca
Phone: (905) 845-9430 x2403
Prog. Accred.: Montessori Teacher Education

Simon Fraser University
Burnaby, Canada V5A 1S6
Type: Private, four-year
Degrees: C, A, B
URL: http://www.sfu.ca
Phone: (604) 291-3111   *Calendar:* Sem. plan
Prog. Accred.: Clinical Psychology

Southern Alberta Institute of Technology
1301 16th Ave., NW, Calgary, Canada T2M 0L4
Type: Private, independent
Degrees: C
URL: http://www.sait.ab.ca
Phone: (403) 284-7248
Prog. Accred.: Dental Assisting

Université de Montréal
Case Postal 6128, Succursale A, Montréal, Canada H3C 3J7
Type: Private, independent, four-year
Degrees: B, M, P, D
URL: http://www.umontreal.ca
Phone: (514) 343-6111   *Calendar:* Sem. plan
Prog. Accred.: Combined Prosthodontics, Dentistry, General Practice Residency, Health Services Administration, Landscape Architecture, Librarianship, Medicine, Optometry, Orthodontic and Dentofacial Orthopedics, Pediatric Dentistry, Planning, Veterinary Medicine

Université de Sherbrooke
2500 Blvd. de l'Universite, Sherbrooke, Canada J1K 2R1
Type: Private, four-year
Degrees: B, M, P, D
URL: http://www.usherbrooke.ca
Phone: (819) 821-7000   *Calendar:* Sem. plan
Prog. Accred.: Medicine

Université Laval
Cité Universitairé, Québec City, Canada G1K 7P4
Type: Private, independent, four-year
Degrees: B, M, P, D
URL: http://www.ulaval.ca
Phone: (418) 656-2131   *Calendar:* Sem. plan
Prog. Accred.: Business (AACSB), Dentistry, Endodontics, General Practice Residency, Medicine, Oral and Maxillofacial Surgery, Periodontics

University of British Columbia
6328 Memorial Rd., Vancouver, Canada V6T 1Z2
Type: Public, four-year
Degrees: B, M, P, D
URL: http://www.ubc.ca
Phone: (604) 822-5017   *Calendar:* Sem. plan
Prog. Accred.: Clinical Psychology, Dentistry, General Practice Residency, Landscape Architecture, Librarianship, Medicine, Oral and Maxillofacial Radiography, Periodontics, Planning, Psychology Internship

University of Calgary
2500 University Dr., NW, Calgary, Canada T2N 1N4
Type: Public, four-year
Degrees: B, M, P, D
URL: http://www.ucalgary.ca
Phone: (403) 220-5110   *Calendar:* Sem. plan
Prog. Accred.: Business (AACSB), Medicine

University of Guelph
Guelph, Canada N1G 2W1
Type: Public, provincial, four-year
Degrees: B, M
URL: http://www.uoguelph.ca
Phone: (519) 824-4120   *Calendar:* Sem. plan
Prog. Accred.: Landscape Architecture, Marriage and Family Therapy, Veterinary Medicine

University of Manitoba
Winnipeg, Canada R3T 2N2
Type: Public, independent, four-year
Degrees: B, M, P, D
URL: http://www.umanitoba.ca
Phone: (204) 474-8880   *Calendar:* Sem. plan
Prog. Accred.: Business (AACSB), Clinical Psychology, Dental Hygiene, Dentistry, Interior Design, Landscape Architecture, Medicine, Oral and Maxillofacial Surgery, Orthodontic and Dentofacial Orthopedics, Periodontics, Psychology Internship

University of New Brunswick

PO Box 4400, Fredericton, Canada E3B 5A3
Type: Private, independent
Degrees: B, M
URL: http://www.unb.ca
Phone: (506) 453-4666   *Calendar:* Tri. plan
Prog. Accred.: Clinical Psychology

University of Ottawa

Ottawa, Canada K1N 6N5
Type: Public, four-year
Degrees: B, M, P, D
Phone: (613) 562-5800   *Calendar:* Sem. plan
Prog. Accred.: Business (AACSB), Clinical Psychology,
  Medicine, Psychology Internship, Recreation and
  Leisure Services

University of Prince Edward Island

550 University Ave., Charlottetown, Canada C1A 4P3
Type: Private, four-year
Degrees: C, A, B
URL: http://www.upei.ca
Phone: (902) 566-0439   *Calendar:* Sem. plan
Prog. Accred.: Veterinary Medicine

University of Saskatchewan

Saskatoon, Canada S7N 0W0
Type: Public, four-year
Degrees: B, M, P, D
Phone: (306) 966-6766   *Calendar:* Sem. plan
Prog. Accred.: Clinical Psychology, Dentistry, Medicine,
  Veterinary Medicine

University of Toronto

Toronto, Canada M5S 1A1
Type: Public, provincial, four-year
Degrees: B, M, P, D
URL: http://www.utoronto.ca
Phone: (416) 978-2011   *Calendar:* Sem. plan
Prog. Accred.: Business (AACSB), Combined Professional-
  Scientific Psychology, Combined Prosthodontics, Dental
  Public Health, Dentistry, Endodontics, Health Services
  Administration, Landscape Architecture, Librarianship,
  Medicine, Oral and Maxillofacial Pathology, Oral and
  Maxillofacial Radiology, Oral and Maxillofacial Surgery,
  Orthodontic and Dentofacial Orthopedics, Pediatric
  Dentistry, Periodontics, Physical Therapy

University of Victoria

Victoria, Canada V8W 3P5
Type: Public, four-year
Degrees: B, M, D
URL: http://www.uvic.ca
Phone: (604) 721-7211   *Calendar:* Qtr. plan
Prog. Accred.: Clinical Psychology

University of Waterloo

University Ave., Waterloo, Canada N2L 3G1
Type: Public, four-year
Degrees: B, M, P
URL: http://www.uwaterloo.ca
Phone: (519) 888-4567   *Calendar:* Sem. plan
Prog. Accred.: Clinical Psychology, Optometry

University of Western Ontario

1151 Richmond St., Ste. 2, London, Canada N6A 5B8
Type: Private, independent, four-year
Degrees: B, M, P, D
URL: http://www.uwo.ca
Phone: (519) 679-2111   *Calendar:* Sem. plan
Prog. Accred.: Clinical Psychology, Dentistry,
  Librarianship, Medicine, Orthodontic and Dentofacial
  Orthopedics, Physical Therapy

University of Windsor

Windsor, Canada N9B 3P4
Type: Public, four-year
Degrees: B, M, P, D
Phone: (519) 253-4232   *Calendar:* Sem. plan
Prog. Accred.: Clinical Psychology

University of Winnipeg

515 Portage Ave., Winnipeg, Canada R3B 2E9
Type: Public, provincial
Degrees: B, M
URL: http://www.uwinnipeg.ca
Phone: (204) 786-9716
Prog. Accred.: Marriage and Family Therapy

Vancouver Community College

250 West Pender St., Vancouver, Canada V6B 1S9
Type: Public, local, two-year
Degrees: C, A
URL: http://www.vcc.bc.ca
Phone: (604) 871-7000
Prog. Accred.: Dental Assisting, Dental Hygiene

York University

4700 Keele St., Toronto, Canada M3J 1P3
Type: Public, independent, four-year
Degrees: B, M, D
URL: http://www.yorku.ca
Phone: (416) 736-2100   *Calendar:* Sem. plan
Prog. Accred.: Clinical Psychology

CHILE

Pontificia Universidad Catolica de Chile—School of Journalism

Avenue Jaime Guzman Errazuriz 3.300, Providencia,
Santiago, Chile
Type: Private, independent, four-year
Degrees: M
URL: http://www.per.puc.cl
Phone: 011 56-2-868-5033
Prog. Accred.: Business (AACSB), Journalism

FRANCE

Centre Europeén de Management Hôtelier International
52 Rue Saint Lazure, Paris, France 75009
Type: Private, independent, four-year
Degrees: B, M
URL: http://www.cmh-school.com
Phone: 011 33 01 45 26 59 28
Prog. Accred.: Business (ACBSP)

Ecole des Hautes Etudes Commerciales
14, Ave. de la porte Champerret, Paris, France CEDEX 17
Type: Private, independent, four-year
Degrees: M
URL: http://www.hec.fr
Phone: 011 33 1 4409 3400
Prog. Accred.: Business (AACSB)

Ecole Superieure des Sciences Economiques et Commerciales
CNIT - B.P. 230, Paris, France 92053
Type: Private, independent, four-year
Degrees: M
URL: http://www.essec.fr/eme
Phone: 011 33 1 4692 4900
Prog. Accred.: Business (AACSB)

Institute Francais de Chiropractic
44 Rue Duhesme, Paris, France 75018
Type: Public, four-year
Degrees: P
Phone: 011 (331) 42-598020
Prog. Accred.: Chiropractic Education

GERMANY

University of Mannheim
Presse-und Oeffentlichkeitsarbeit, Schloss, Mannheim, Germany 68131
Type: Public, independent, four-year
Degrees: M
URL: http://www.uni-mannheim.de
Phone: 011 49 621 181 1013
Prog. Accred.: Business (AACSB)

HONG KONG

The Chinese University of Hong Kong
Shatin, Hong Kong SAR
Type: Private, independent, four-year
Degrees: B, M
URL: http://www.cuhk.edu.hk
Phone: 011 852 2609 6000   *Calendar:* Qtr. plan
Prog. Accred.: Accounting, Business (AACSB)

Hong Kong University of Science and Technology
Clear Water Bay, Kowloon, Hong Kong SAR
Type: Public, independent, four-year
Degrees: B, M
URL: http://www.ust.hk
Phone: 011 852 2258 6000   *Calendar:* Sem. plan
Prog. Accred.: Accounting, Business (AACSB)

IRELAND

Liberties College
Bull Alley St., Dublin, Ireland 8
Type: Public, independent
Degrees: C
URL: http://homepage.eircom.net/~libertiescollege/public_html
Phone: 011 353 1 454 0044
Prog. Accred.: Montessori Teacher Education

University College Dublin
Belfield, DU, Ireland 4
Type: Public, Governing Council, four-year
Degrees: B
URL: http://www.ucd.ie
Phone: 011 353 1 716 7777   *Calendar:* Sem. plan
Prog. Accred.: Business (AACSB)

JAPAN

3rd Dental Battalion/NDC Okinawa
Unit 38450, FPO AP 96604-8450, Okinawa, Japan
Type: Public, federal
Degrees: C
URL: http://www.3fssg.usmc.mil/dentalbn/default.htm
Phone: 011 81 61 745 7157
Prog. Accred.: Advanced Education in General Dentistry

Keio University
2-15-45 Mita, Minato-ku, Tokyo, Japan 108-8345
Type: Private, Board of Councillors, four-year
Degrees: M
URL: http://www.keio.ac.jp
Phone: 011 81 3 3453 4511
Prog. Accred.: Business (AACSB)

United States Naval Dental Center Far East
PSC 475, Box 1, FPO AP 96350-1600, Yokosuka, Japan, Japan
Type: Private, federal
Degrees: C
URL: http://www.fe-dental.med.navy.mil
Phone: 011 81 6160 43 7144
Prog. Accred.: Advanced Education in General Dentistry

LEBANON

Lebanese American University
PO Box 13-5053, Beirut, Lebanon
Type: Private, independent, four-year
Degrees: P
URL: http://www.lau.edu.lb
Phone: 011 961 1 867 620
Prog. Accred.: Pharmacy

MEXICO

Autonomous Technical Institute of Mexico
Rio Honda 1, Tizapan, San Angel, Alvaro Obregon, Mexico 01000
Type: Private, state, four-year
Degrees: M
URL: http://www.itam.mx
Phone: 011 52 5 628 4000
Prog. Accred.: Business (AACSB)

NETHERLANDS

Erasmus University Rotterdam
Postbus 1738, Burgermeester Oudlaan 50, Rotterdam, Netherlands 3000 DR
Type: Private, independent, four-year
Degrees: M, D
URL: http://www.eur.nl
Phone: 011 31 10 408 1649   *Calendar:* Sem. plan
Prog. Accred.: Business (AACSB)

Maastricht University
Postbus 616, Maastricht, Netherlands 6200 MD
Type: Private, independent, four-year
Degrees: M, D
URL: http://www.unimaas.nl
Phone: 011 31 43 388 2222
Prog. Accred.: Business (AACSB)

Tilburg University
Warandelaan 2, PO Box 90153, Tilburg, Netherlands 5000 LE
Type: Public, state, four-year
Degrees: C, M
URL: http://www.tilburguniversity.nl
Phone: 011 31 13 466 9111
Prog. Accred.: Business (AACSB)

University of Utrecht
PO Box 80.163, 3508 TD, Utrecht, Netherlands
Type: Public, state, four-year
Degrees: P
URL: http://www.ruu.nl
Phone: 011 31 30 2531815
Prog. Accred.: Veterinary Medicine

NEW ZEALAND

Massey University—Palmerston North
Private Bag 11 222, Palmerston North, New Zealand
Type: Public, independent, four-year
Degrees: B, M, D
URL: http://palmerstonnorth.massey.ac.nz
Phone: 011 64 6 356 9099
Prog. Accred.: Veterinary Medicine

REPUBLIC OF KOREA

Seoul National University
San 56-1, Shillim-dong, Kwanak-gu, Seoul, Korea, Republic of 151-742
Type: Public, University Council, four-year
Degrees: B, M
URL: http://www.snu.ac.kr
Phone: 011 82 2 880 5114   *Calendar:* Sem. plan
Prog. Accred.: Business (AACSB)

SAUDI ARABIA

Yanbu Industrial College
PO Box 30426, Madinat Yanbu Al Sinaiyah, Saudi Arabia
Type: Private, independent, two-year
Degrees: A
URL: http://www.yic.edu.sa
Phone: 011 966-04-3946111
Prog. Accred.: Business (ACBSP)

SPAIN

Escuela Superior de Administracion y Direccion de Empresas
Avda. Pedralbes, 60-62, Barcelona, Spain 08034
Type: Public, independent, four-year
Degrees: M, D
URL: http://www.esade.es
Phone: 011 34 93 280 6162
Prog. Accred.: Business (AACSB)

Instituto de Empresa
Maria de Molina, 11, Madrid, Spain 28006
Type: Private, independent, four-year
Degrees: M
URL: http://www.ie.edu
Phone: 011 34 91 568 9600
Prog. Accred.: Business (AACSB)

SWITZERLAND

Business School Lausanne
Av. Dapples 38, PO Box 160, Lausanne, Switzerland CH-1001
Type: Private, independent, four-year
Degrees: B, M
URL: http://www.bsl-lausanne.ch
Phone: 011 41 21 619 06 06
Prog. Accred.: Business (ACBSP)

UNITED ARAB EMIRATES

Higher Colleges of Technology Abu Dhabi Men's College
PO Box 25035, Abu Dhabi, United Arab Emirates
Type: Private, independent, four-year
Degrees: A, B
URL: http://www.admc.hct.ac.ae
Phone: 011 02 445 1514
Prog. Accred.: Business (ACBSP)

Higher Colleges of Technology Abu Dhabi Women's College
PO Box 41012, Abu Dhabi, United Arab Emirates
Type: Private, independent, four-year
Degrees: A, B
URL: http://adw.hct.ac.ae
Phone: 011 02 6413839
Prog. Accred.: Business (ACBSP)

Higher Colleges of Technology Al Ain Men's College
PO Box 17155, Al Ain, United Arab Emirates
Type: Private, independent, four-year
Degrees: A, B
URL: http://aam.hct.ac.ae
Phone: 011 971-3-782088
Prog. Accred.: Business (ACBSP)

Higher Colleges of Technology Al Ain Women's College
PO Box 17258, Al Ain, United Arab Emirates
Type: Private, independent, four-year
Degrees: A, B
URL: http://aaw.hct.ac.ae
Phone: 011 03 782 0777
Prog. Accred.: Business (ACBSP)

Higher Colleges of Technology Dubai Men's College
PO Box 15825, Dubai, United Arab Emirates
Type: Private, independent, four-year
Degrees: A, B
URL: http://dbm.hct.ac.ae
Phone: 011 971-4-3260333
Prog. Accred.: Business (ACBSP)

Higher Colleges of Technology Dubai Women's College
PO Box 16062, Dubai, United Arab Emirates
Type: Private, independent, four-year
Degrees: A, B
URL: http://dwc.hct.ac.ae
Phone: 011 971 4 267 2929
Prog. Accred.: Business (ACBSP)

Higher Colleges of Technology Ras Al Khaimah Men's College
PO Box 4793, Ras Al Khaimah, United Arab Emirates
Type: Private, independent, four-year
Degrees: A, B
URL: http://rkm.hct.ac.ae
Phone: 011 07-2462999
Prog. Accred.: Business (ACBSP)

Higher Colleges of Technology Ras Al Khaimah Women's College
PO Box 4792, Ras Al Khaimah, United Arab Emirates
Type: Private, independent
URL: http://rkw.hct.ac.ae
Phone: 011 07-2210550
Prog. Accred.: Business (ACBSP)

Higher Colleges of Technology Sharjah Men's College
PO Box 7947, Sharjah, United Arab Emirates
Type: Private, independent, four-year
Degrees: A, B
URL: http://sjm.hct.ac.ae
Phone: 011 9716 5585333
Prog. Accred.: Business (ACBSP)

Sharjah Women's College
PO Box 7947, Sharjah, United Arab Emirates
Type: Private, independent, four-year
Degrees: A, B
URL: http://swcweb.sjwc.hct.ac.ae
Phone: 011 9716 5585333
Prog. Accred.: Business (ACBSP)

United Arab Emirates University
PO Box 15551, Al-Ain, United Arab Emirates
Type: Public, state, four-year
Degrees: B
URL: http://www.uaeu.ac.ae
Phone: 011 971 3 642 500
Prog. Accred.: Business (AACSB)

UNITED KINGDOM

Anglo-European College of Chiropractic
13-15 Parkwood Rd., Bournemouth, United Kingdom BH5 2DF
Type: Private, independent, four-year
Degrees: P
URL: http://www.aecc.ac.uk
Phone: 011 44 0 1202 436200
Prog. Accred.: Chiropractic Education

Ashridge University
Berkhamsted, HE, United Kingdom HP4 1NS
Type: Public, independent, four-year
Degrees: B, M
URL: http://www.ashridge.org.uk
Phone: 011 44 0 1442 843491
Prog. Accred.: Business (AACSB)

Accredited Programs at Other Facilities

Aston University
Aston Triangle, Birmingham, United Kingdom B4 7ET
Type: Public, four-year
Degrees: B
URL: http://www.aston.ac.uk
Phone: 011 44 0 121 359 361
Prog. Accred.: Business (AACSB)

Cranfield University
Cranfield, BE, United Kingdom MK43 0AL
Type: Public, four-year
Degrees: M
URL: http://www.cranfield.ac.uk
Phone: 011 44 1234 750 111
Prog. Accred.: Business (AACSB)

The Robert Gordon University
Schoolhill, Aberdeen, Scotland, United Kingdom AB10 1FR
Type: Private, independent, four-year
Degrees: M
URL: http://www.rgu.ac.uk
Prog. Accred.: Physical Therapy

The University of Edingurgh
Old College, South Bridge, Edinburgh, United Kingdom EH8 9YL
Type: Public, independent, four-year
Degrees: B, M, D
URL: http://www.ed.ac.uk
Phone: 011 44 0131 650 1000
Prog. Accred.: Veterinary Medicine

University of Glasgow
Glasgow, United Kingdom G12 8QQ
Type: Public, four-year
Degrees: B, M, D
URL: http://www.gla.ac.uk
Phone: 011 0141 339 8855
Prog. Accred.: Veterinary Medicine

University of London—External Programme
Senate House, University of London, Malet St., London, United Kingdom WC1E 7HU
Type: Private, independent, four-year
Degrees: C, B
URL: http://www.londonexternal.ac.uk
Phone: 011 44 0 20 7862 836
Prog. Accred.: Liberal Education

University of London—London Business School
Sussex Place, Regent's Park, London, United Kingdom NW1 4SA
Type: Public, independent, four-year
Degrees: M, D
URL: http://www.lbs.ac.uk
Phone: 011 44 20 7262 5050
Prog. Accred.: Business (AACSB)

University of London—Royal Veterinary College
Royal College St., London, United Kingdom NW1 0TU
Type: Public, independent, four-year
Degrees: P, D
URL: http://www.rvc.ac.uk
Phone: 011 44 20 7468 5000
Prog. Accred.: Veterinary Medicine

University of Manchester
Oxford Rd., Manchester, United Kingdom M13 9PL
Type: Public, independent, four-year
Degrees: B, M
URL: http://www.man.ac.uk
Phone: 011 44 161 275 2000
Prog. Accred.: Business (AACSB)

University of Ulster at Jordanstown
Shore Rd., Newtownabbey, AN, United Kingdom BT37 0QB
Type: Public, four-year
Degrees: M
URL: http://www.ulst.ac.uk/campus/jordanstown
Phone: 011 08 700 400 700   *Calendar:* Tri. plan
Prog. Accred.: Physical Therapy

University of Warwick
Heath Park, Cardiff, Wales, United Kingdom CF4 4XN
Type: Public, independent, four-year
Degrees: B, M, D
URL: http://www.uwcm.ac.uk
Phone: 011 44 29 2074 7747
Prog. Accred.: Business (AACSB)

Major Institutional Changes

ALABAMA

Bessemer State Technical College merged with Lawson State Community College and changed its name to T.A. Lawson State Community College--Bessemer (Summer 2005)

Douglas MacArthur State Technical College merged with Lurleen B. Wallace State Junior College and changed its name to Lurleen B. Wallace Community College—MacArthur Campus (Summer 2003)

Education America—Southeast College of Technology—Mobile AL changed its name to Remington College—Mobile (Winter 2003)

Enterprise State Junior College changed its name to Enterprise-Ozark Community College (Spring 2003)

Gadsden State Community College merged with Harry M. Ayers Technical College (Spring 2003)

Harry M. Ayers Technical College merged with Gadsden State Community College and changed its name to Gadsden State Community College—Ayers Campus (Spring 2003)

International Bible College changed its name to Heritage Christian University (Fall 2000)

John C. Calhoun State Community College changed its name to Calhoun Community College (Fall 1997)

John Moser & Associates, Inc. changed its name to Leadership Development, Inc. Dale Carnegie Training (Summer 2003)

Lawson State Community College merged with Bessemer State Technical College (Summer 2005)

Lurleen B. Wallace State Junior College merged with Douglas MacArthur State Technical College and changed its name to Lurleen B. Wallace Community College (Summer 2003)

Medical Institute changed its name to Capps College—Foley (Summer 1996)

School of Advanced Airpower Studies changed its name to School of Advanced Air and Space Studies (Summer 2003)

Troy State University changed its name to Troy University (Spring 2004)

Troy State University Dothan changed its name to Troy University Dothan (Spring 2004)

ARIZONA

Arizona Institute of Business and Technology changed its name to International Institute of the Americas (Summer 2003)

Arizona State University East changed its name to Arizona State University Polytechnic Campus (Summer 2005)

College of the Humanities and Sciences changed its name to College of the Humanities and Sciences Harrison Middleton University (Summer 2005)

Education America—Tempe Campus changed its name to Remington College—Tempe (Winter 2003)

High-Tech Institute (system) merged with Allied Medical College (Spring 2003)

Phoenix Career College changed its name to Long Technical College—East Valley (Winter 2004)

Safford College of Beauty changed its name to The Hair Academy of Safford (Summer 2005)

Success Development Group, Inc. changed its name to Premier Training, Inc. Dale Carnegie Training (Summer 2003)

Thunderbird, The American Graduate School of International Management changed its name to Thunderbird, The Garvin Graduate School of International Management (Spring 2004)

Universal Technical Institute merged with Clinton Technical Institute (Fall 1998)

University of Advancing Computer Technology changed its name to University of Advancing Technology (Winter 2003)

ARKANSAS

Arkansas Northeastern College merged with Cotton Boll Technical Institute (Summer 2003)

Arkansas Tech University merged with Arkansas Valley Technical College (Summer 2003)

Arkansas Valley Technical College merged with Arkansas Tech University and changed its name to Arkansas Tech University—Ozark (Summer 2003)

Cotton Boll Technical Institute merged with Arkansas Northeastern College and changed its name to Arkansas Northeastern College—Burdette Center (Summer 2003)

Education American-Southeast College of Technology—Little Rock changed its name to Remington College—Little Rock (Winter 2003)

Garland County Community College merged with Quapaw Technical Institute and changed its name to National Park Community College at Hot Springs (Summer 2003)

Mississippi County Community College changed its name to Arkansas Northeastern College (Summer 2003)

Petit Jean College changed its name to University of Arkansas Community College at Morrilton (Summer 2001)

Quapaw Technical Institute merged with Garland County Community College and closed (Summer 2003)

Remington College—Fayetteville closed (Summer 1998)

CALIFORNIA

Academy of Art College changed its name to Academy of Art University (Winter 2004)

Adcon Technical Institute changed its name to ATI College (Summer 2004)

Advanced College of Technology merged with College of Oceaneering (Spring 2004)

Alliant International University merged with Alliant University—San Diego Cornerstone Court (Summer 2001)

American College of Business closed (Fall 2002)

Andon College at Modesto changed its name to California College—Modesto (Fall 2002)

Andon College at Stockton changed its name to California College—Stockton (Fall 2002)

Armstrong University was removed from accredited status by its accreditor (Winter 2002)

Bethany College changed its name to Bethany University (Summer 2005)

Bonar & Associates, Inc. changed its name to Dale Carnegie Training of Los Angeles (Summer 2003)

California College of Arts and Crafts changed its name to California College of the Arts (Summer 2003)

California College of Communication was removed from accredited status by its accreditor (Winter 2004)

California College of Technology changed its name to Maric College—Sacramento (Winter 2004)

California College—Modesto changed its name to Maric College—Modesto (Winter 2004)

California College—Stockton changed its name to Maric College—Stockton (Winter 2004)

California Paramedical & Technical College closed (Fall 2003)

California School of Court Reporting changed its name to Sage College (Fall 2003)

California School of Medical Sciences changed its name to California School of Modern Sciences (Summer 2004)

California State University—Hayward changed its name to California State University—East Bay (Winter 2005)

Capital Area Vocational Center changed its name to Capital Area Career Center (Summer 2004)

Career Institute of San Diego Occupational Training Services changed its name to Occupational Training Services (Winter 2003)

CEI College changed its name to Maric College—Anaheim (Winter 2004)

Christian Heritage College changed its name to San Diego Christian College (Summer 2005)

College of Oceaneering merged with Advanced College of Technology and changed its name to National Polytechnic College of Engineering and Oceaneering (Spring 2004)

Commonwealth International University changed its name to Education America University (Winter 2000)

Computer Education Institute changed its name to Maric College (Spring 2004)

Computer Education Institute—San Marcos closed (Spring 2004)

Concord University School of Law changed its name to Concord Law School (Summer 2003)

Concorde Career Institute—Garden Grove changed its name to Concorde Career College—Garden Grove (Winter 2003)

Concorde Career Institute—North Hollywood changed its name to Concorde Career College—North Hollywood (Winter 2003)

Concorde Career Institute—San Bernardino changed its name to Concorde Career College—San Bernardino (Winter 2003)

Concorde Career Institute—San Diego changed its name to Concorde Career College—San Diego (Winter 2003)

Corinthian Schools, Inc.—Sawyer Campus-Sacramento closed (Summer 2000)

D-Q University was removed from accredited status by its accreditor (Summer 2005)

Dominican College of San Rafael changed its name to Dominican University of California (Spring 2000)

Donald Vocational School changed its name to DVS College (Summer 2003)

Education America University changed its name to Remington College—San Diego (Winter 2003)

Elegante Beauty College—City of Industry merged with Marinello School of Beauty and changed its name to Marinello School of Beauty—City of Industry (Summer 2004)

Elegante Beauty College—Lake Forest merged with Marinello School of Beauty and changed its name to Marinello School of Beauty—Lake Forest (Summer 2004)

Elegante Beauty College—Moreno merged with Marinello School of Beauty and changed its name to Marinello School of Beauty—Moreno Valley (Summer 2004)

Elegante Beauty College—Moreno merged with Marinello School of Beauty and changed its name to Marinello School of Beauty—Burbank (Summer 2004)

Fashion Careers of California College changed its name to Fashion Careers College (Summer 2003)

Federico College of Hairstyling changed its name to Federico Beauty Institute (Winter 2005)

Fielding Graduate Institute changed its name to Fielding Graduate University (Winter 2005)

Foundation College closed (Fall 1999)

Four-D Success Academy changed its name to Four-D College (Summer 2004)

Fremont-Newark Community College District changed its name to Ohlone Community College District (Summer 2003)

Heald College, School of Business—Sacramento changed its name to Heald College—Sacramento (Winter 2003)

Heald College, School of Business—Salinas changed its name to Heald College—Salinas (Winter 2003)

Heald College, School of Business—Santa Rosa changed its name to Heald College—Santa Rosa (Winter 2003)

Heald College, Schools of Business—Concord changed its name to Heald College—Concord (Winter 2003)

Heald College, Schools of Business—Fresno changed its name to Heald College—Fresno (Winter 2003)

Heald College, Schools of Business—Hayward changed its name to Heald College—Hayward (Winter 2003)

Heald College, Schools of Business—San Francisco changed its name to Heald College—San Francisco (Winter 2003)

Heald College, Schools of Business—San Jose changed its name to Heald College—San Jose (Winter 2003)

Heald College—Santa Rosa closed (Spring 2003)

Holy Names College changed its name to Holy Names university (Spring 2004)

Hsi Lai University changed its name to University of the West (Spring 2004)

ITT Technical Institute—Hayward closed (Winter 2004)

J. Paul Bagan & Associates changed its name to Dale Carnegie Training of San Jose (Summer 2003)

Keller Graduate School of Management—Irvine Center changed its name to DeVry University Irvine (Summer 2004)

Los Angeles College of Chiropractic changed its name to Southern California University of Health Sciences (Summer 2000)

Los Angeles College of Micro Technology was removed from accredited status by its accreditor (Fall 2003)

Masters Institute closed (Spring 2001)

Meiji College of Oriental Medicine changed its name to Acupuncture and Integrative Medicine College, Berkeley (Spring 2003)

Microcomputer Education Center changed its name to MCed Career Center (Winter 2004)

Miss Marty's School of Beauty & Hairstyling changed its name to Miss Marty's Hair Academy and Esthetics Institute (Summer 2005)

Modern Technology College changed its name to Maric College—North Hollywood (Winter 2004)

Northrop Rice Aviation Institute of Technology was removed from accredited status by its accreditor (Summer 2005)

Northwestern Technical College changed its name to Northwestern College (Fall 2003)

Paramount School of Beauty merged with Marinello School of Beauty and changed its name to Marinello School of Beauty—Paramount (Summer 2004)

Patten College changed its name to Patten University (Summer 2003)

Platt College changed its name to Western College of Southern California (Summer 2005)

Practical Schools changed its name to Westwood College of Technology—Long Beach (Summer 2003)

Professional Career Institute changed its name to PCI College (Summer 2005)

Rand Graduate School changed its name to Pardee Rand Graduate School (Fall 2003)

Richard's Beauty College merged with Marinello School of Beauty and changed its name to Marinello School of Beauty—Huntington Beach (Summer 2004)

Right Way Computer Training Centers was removed from accredited status by its accreditor (Summer 2003)

Saint John's Seminary College closed (Spring 2003)

Salvation Army College for Officers Training changed its name to Salvation Army Crestmont College (Summer 2000)

Salvation Army Crestmont College changed its name to Salvation Army College for Officer Training at Crestmont (Summer 2005)

San Fernando College of Law merged with University of West Los Angeles and changed its name to University of West Los Angeles—San Fernando Valley Campus (Summer 2002)

San Jose Christian College changed its name to William Jessup University (Winter 2004)

Sequoia Institute changed its name to WyoTech—Fremont (Summer 2004)

Simpson College changed its name to Simpson University (Fall 2004)

Skadron College changed its name to Bryman College (Fall 2002)

Software Advanced Technologies Institute was removed from accredited status at the request of the institution (Spring 2003)

Touro University College of Osteopathic Medicine changed its name to Touro University—California (Summer 2005)

Travel and Trade Career Institute closed (Fall 2005)

Travel University International was removed from accredited status by its accreditor (Spring 2005)

Riverside Community College changed its name to Riverside City College (Winter 2005)

University of West Los Angeles merged with San Fernando College of Law (Summer 2002)

Western Institute of Science and Health changed its name to Sonoma College (Winter 2004)

Westwood College of Technology—Anaheim changed its name to Westwood College—Anaheim (Winter 2005)

Westwood College of Technology—Inland Empire changed its name to Westwood College—Inland Empire (Winter 2005)

Westwood College of Technology—Long Beach changed its name to Westwood College—Long Beach (Winter 2005)

Westwood College of Technology—Los Angeles changed its name to Westwood College—Los Angeles (Winter 2005)

COLORADO

Boulder School of Massage Therapy changed its name to Boulder College of Massage Therapy (Fall 1997)

Concorde Career Institute—Aurora changed its name to Concorde Career College—Aurora (Winter 2003)

Education America—Colorado Springs Campus changed its name to Remington College—Colorado Springs (Winter 2003)

Education America—Denver Campus changed its name to Remington College—Denver (Winter 2003)

Institute for Nuclear Medical Education, Inc. was removed from accredited status by its accreditor (Winter 2005)

ISIM University changed its name to Aspen University (Spring 2003)

National Technological University merged with Walden University and changed its name to NTU School of Engineering and Applied Science at Walden University (Summer 2005)

Revans University—The University of Action Learning was removed from accredited status by its accreditor (Summer 2004)

University of Action Learning at Boulder changed its name to Revans University—The University of Action Learning (Summer 2003)

University of Colorado at Denver merged with University of Colorado Health Sciences Center (Summer 2004)

University of Colorado Health Sciences Center merged with University of Colorado at Denver and changed its name to University of Colorado at Denver and Health Sciences Center (Summer 2004)

University of Southern Colorado changed its name to Colorado State University—Pueblo (Summer 2003)

Walden University merged with National Technological University (Summer 2005)

Westwood College of Technology—Denver North changed its name to Westwood College—Denver North (Winter 2005)

Westwood College of Technology—Denver South changed its name to Westwood College—Denver South (Winter 2005)

CONNECTICUT

Beth Benjamin Academy of Connecticut changed its name to Bais Binyomin Academy (Summer 2005)

Connecticut Business Institute—New Haven closed (Winter 1999)

Connecticut Institute of Art closed (Winter 2001)

Connecticut Institute of Hair Design changed its name to Brio Academy of Cosmetology (Summer 2005)

Gal Mar Academy of Hairdressing changed its name to North Haven Academy (Summer 2005)

Goodwin Institute—Waterbury changed its name to Stone Academy—Waterbury (Summer 2002)

Huntington Institute closed (Fall 2001)

Naugatuck Valley Community-Technical College changed its name to Naugatuck Valley Community College (Summer 2000)

Teikyo Post University changed its name to Post University (Fall 2004)

Three Rivers Community-Technical College Mohegan Campus changed its name to Three Rivers Community College (Summer 2000)

Walker & Associates, Inc. changed its name to B. Dickson and Associates, LLC (Winter 2004)

DELAWARE

Delaware Learning Institute of Cosmetology changed its name to National Massage Therapy Institute (Summer 2005)

DISTRICT OF COLUMBIA

Bennett Beauty Institute, Inc. changed its name to Bennett Career Institute, Inc. (Summer 2005)

Fleet Business School closed (Summer 2001)

Trinity College changed its name to Trinity University (Fall 2004)

FLORIDA

Advanced/Basic Hair Design Training Center changed its name to Academy of Cosmetology (Winter 2005)

American College of Prehospital Medicine closed (Summer 2004)

American Dura Skin Care, Massage & Nail School changed its name to Praxis Institute (Spring 1996)

American College of Prehospital Medicine was removed from accredited status at the request of the institution (Spring 2004)

ATI Health Education Center changed its name to ATI College of Health (Summer 2005)

Atlantic Coast Institute changed its name to Key College (Winter 2003)

Cape Coral Beauty School was removed from accredited status by its accreditor (Spring 2005)

Chipola Junior College changed its name to Chipola College (Summer 2003)

Clinton Technical Institute—Motorcyle/Marine Mechanics Institute changed its name to Motorcycle and Marine Mechanics Institute (Summer 2001)

Comair Aviation Academy changed its name to Delta Connection Academy (Summer 2003)

Cooper Career Institute closed (Winter 2005)

Darlyne McGee's Academy of Cosmetology, Inc. changed its name to Academy of Cosmetology (Winter 2005)

Edison Community College changed its name to Edison College (Winter 2005)

Education America—Tampa Technical Institute changed its name to Remington College—Tampa (Winter 2003)

Education America-Tampa Technical Institute—Jacksonville Campus changed its name to Remington College—Jacksonville (Winter 2003)

Education American-Tampa Technical Institute—Pinellas Campus changed its name to Remington College—Largo (Winter 2003)

Everglades College changed its name to Everglades University (Winter 2004)

Florida Computer & Business School changed its name to Florida Career College (Spring 2003)

Florida Institute of Traditional Chinese Medicine was removed from accredited status by its accreditor (Fall 2002)

Florida Language Center was removed from accredited status by its accreditor (Spring 2004)

Florida Memorial College changed its name to Florida Memorial University (Summer 2004)

Herzing College—Melbourne Campus closed (Winter 2002)

Hi-Tech School of Miami closed (Winter 2005)

Institute of Career Education changed its name to Summit Institute (Spring 2003)

International Fine Arts College changed its name to Miami International University of Art and Design (Summer 2002)

International School of Beauty changed its name to Bene's International School of Beauty (Winter 2005)

Lake County Vocational Technical Center changed its name to Lake Technical Center (Summer 2002)

Learey Technical Center was removed from accredited status at the request of the institution (Winter 2003)

Lively Area Vocational-Technical Center—Lively Criminal Justice Training changed its name to Pat Thomas Law Enforcement Academy (Summer 1998)

Manatee Area Vocational-Technical Center changed its name to Manatee Technical Institute (Winter 1996)

Medical Career Center changed its name to Virginia College at Pensacola (Summer 2001)

Miami-Dade Community College changed its name to Miami-Dade College (Summer 2003)

Naval Air Technical Training Center changed its name to Center for Naval Aviation Technical Training (Winter 2005)

Naval Diving and Salvage Training Center changed its name to Center for Explosive Ordnance Disposal and Diving (Winter 2005)

Naval Technical Training Center changed its name to Center for Information Dominance (CID) (Winter 2005)

New College of University of South Florida changed its name to New College of Florida (Summer 2001)

Okaloosa-Walton Community College changed its name to Okaloosa-Walton College (Summer 2004)

Omni Technical School closed (Fall 2002)

Pelican Airways changed its name to Pelican Flight Training Center (Summer 2004)

PHD Hair Academy changed its name to Sunstate Academy of Hair Design (Winter 1997)

Piedmont Baptist College merged with Spurgeon Baptist Bible College (Spring 2004)

Prospect Hall School of Business closed (Winter 2004)

Southeastern College of the Assemblies of God changed its name to Southeastern University (Spring 2005)

Southern Technical Center closed (Winter 2000)

Spurgeon Baptist Bible College merged with Piedmont Baptist College and closed (Spring 2004)

Summit Institute closed (Summer 2004)

Suncoast Center for Natural Health/Suncoast School changed its name to SunCoast II—The Tampa Bay School of Health/Suncoast School (Summer 2003)

. SunCoast Institute of Technology closed (Summer 2002)

Ultrasound Diagnostic School—Jacksonville changed its name to Sanford-Brown Institute—Jacksonville (Fall 2003)

Ultrasound Diagnostic School—Tampa changed its name to Sanford-Brown Institute—Tampa (Fall 2003)

Ultrasound Diagnostic School—Lauderdale Lakes changed its name to Sanford-Brown Institute—Lauderdale Lakes (Fall 2003)

Ultrasound Diagnostic School—Trevose changed its name to Sanford-Brown Institute—Philadelphia (Fall 2003)

University of Sarasota changed its name to Argosy University (Fall 2001)

Webster College changed its name to Gulf Coast College (Winter 2005)

Webster Tech changed its name to Webster College (Spring 2003)

GEORGIA

Albany Technical Institute changed its name to Albany Technical College (Summer 2000)

Altamaha Technical Institute changed its name to Altamaha Technical College (Summer 2000)

Appalachian Technical Institute changed its name to Appalachian Technical College (Winter 2000)

Asher School of Business changed its name to Brown Mackie College—Atlanta (Fall 2004)

Atlanta Technical Institute changed its name to Chattahoochee Technical College (Summer 2000)

Augusta Technical Institute changed its name to Augusta Technical College (Summer 2000)

Beacon College and Graduate School changed its name to Beacon University (Fall 1997)

Chattahoochee Technical Institute changed its name to Chattahoochee Technical College (Summer 2000)

Clayton College & State University changed its name to Clayton State University (Spring 2005)

Columbus Technical Institute changed its name to Columbus Technical College (Summer 2000)

Coosa Valley Technical Institute changed its name to Coosa Valley Technical College (Summer 2000)

Dalton Beauty Inc. changed its name to Dalton Beauty College (Spring 2005)

East Central Technical Institute changed its name to East Central Technical College (Summer 2000)

Executive Travel Institute changed its name to ETI Career Institute (Summer 2005)

Flint River Technical Institute changed its name to Flint River Technical College (Summer 2000)

Floyd College changed its name to Georgia Highlands College (Summer 2005)

Georgia Institute of Technology merged with the Institute of Paper Science and Technology (Summer 2003)

Georgia School of Professional Psychology changed its name to Argosy University Atlanta (Fall 2001)

Gwinnett Technical Institute changed its name to Gwinnett Technical College (Summer 2000)

Heart of Georgia Technical Institute changed its name to Heart of Georgia Technical College (Summer 2000)

Heart of Georgia Technical Institute—Eastman Center changed its name to Georgia Aviation Technical College (Fall 2000)

Institute of Paper Science and Technology merged with Georgia Institute of Technology and changed its name to Institute of Paper Science and Technology at Georgia Tech (Summer 2003)

Kerr Business College changed its name to Savannah River College (Winter 2005)

Lanier Technical Institute changed its name to Lanier Technical College (Summer 2000)

Middle Georgia Technical Institute changed its name to Middle Georgia Technical College (Summer 2000)

Morris Brown College was removed from accredited status by its accreditor (Winter 2002)

Moultrie Area Technical Institute changed its name to Moultrie Technical College (Summer 2000)

NCPT closed (Summer 2003)

North Georgia Technical Institute changed its name to North Georgia Technical College (Summer 2000)

North Metro Technical Institute changed its name to North Metro Technical College (Summer 2000)

Northwestern Technical Institute changed its name to Northwestern Technical College (Summer 2000)

Ogeechee Technical Institute changed its name to Ogeechee Technical College (Summer 2000)

Okefenokee Technical Institute changed its name to Okefenokee Technical College (Summer 2000)

Pro-Way Hari School was removed from accredited status by its accreditor (Winter 2002)

Sandersville Regional Technical Institute changed its name to Sandersville Technical College (Summer 2000)

South College merged with Columbia Junior College and changed its name to South University (Fall 2001)

South Georgia Technical Institute changed its name to South Georgia Technical College (Summer 2000)

Southeastern Technical Institute changed its name to Southeastern Technical College (Summer 2000)
State University of West Georgia changed its name to University of West Georgia (Winter 2005)
Ultrasound Diagnostic School—Atlanta changed its name to Sanford-Brown Institute—Atlanta (Fall 2003)
Valdosta Technical Institute changed its name to Valdosta Technical College (Summer 2000)

HAWAII
American Schools of Professional Psychology merged with Argosy University and changed its name to Argosy University Honolulu (Fall 2001)
Argosy University Hawai'i changed its name to Argosy University Honolulu (Fall 2001)
Education America—Honolulu Campus changed its name to Remington College—Honolulu (Winter 2003)
Heald College, Schools of Business—Honolulu changed its name to Heald College—Honolulu (Winter 2003)
International Mid Pac Academy changed its name to International Mid Pac College (Summer 2003)
International Mid Pac College was removed from accredited status by its accreditor (Spring 2004)
Tai Hsuan Foundation College of Acupuncture and Herbal Medicine changed its name to World Medicine Institute (Spring 2005)

IDAHO
American Institute of Health Technology, Inc. changed its name to Apollo College—Boise (Winter 2005)
New Images Academy of Beauty changed its name to Scot Lewis School (Summer 2005)
Northwest Nazarene College changed its name to Northwest Nazarene University (Summer 2003)

ILLINOIS
Argosy University Chicago Northwest changed its name to Argosy University Schaumburg (Summer 2004)
Barat College merged with DePaul University and changed its name to Barat College of DePaul University (Summer 2001)
Chubb Institute—Villa Park closed (Winter 2004)
DePaul University merged with Barat College of DePaul University (Winter 2005)
Hanover Park College of Beauty Culture, Inc. changed its name to Empire Beauty School—Hanover Park (Fall 2004)
Harrington Institute of Interior Design changed its name to Harrington College of Design (Summer 2003)
Herman M. Finch University of Health Sciences/The Chicago Medical School changed its name to Rosalind Franklin University of Medicine and Science (Spring 2004)
La' James College of Hairstyling—East Moline changed its name to La' James International College—East Moline (Summer 2005)
Lincoln Technical Institute closed (Summer 2002)
Midwest School of Welding & Technology changed its name to Midwest Technical Institute (Summer 2002)
NAES College was removed from accredited status by its accreditor (Summer 2005)
Northern Baptist Theological Seminary changed its name to Northern Seminary (Spring 2005)
Westwood College of Technology—Chicago Loop changed its name to Westwood College—Chicago Loop (Winter 2005)
Westwood College of Technology—DuPage changed its name to Westwood College—DuPage (Winter 2005)
Westwood College of Technology—O'Hare changed its name to Westwood College—O'Hare Airport (Winter 2005)
Westwood College of Technology—River Oaks changed its name to Westwood College—River Oaks (Winter 2005)

INDIANA
American Trans Air Aviation Training Academy changed its name to Aviation Institute of Maintenance Training Academy (Winter 2004)
Apex School of Beauty Culture changed its name to Apex Academy of Hair Design (Summer 2005)
Commonwealth Business College changed its name to Brown Mackie College—Merrillville (Fall 2004)
Ivy Tech State College—Bloomington changed its name to Ivy Tech Community College of Indiana—Bloomington (Summer 2005)
Ivy Tech State College—Columbus changed its name to Ivy Tech Community College—Columbus (Summer 2005)
Ivy Tech State College—East Central changed its name to Ivy Tech Community College of Indiana—East Central (Summer 2005)
Ivy Tech State College—Kokomo changed its name to Ivy Tech Community College—Kokomo (Summer 2005)
Ivy Tech State College—Lafayette changed its name to Ivy Tech Community College—Lafayette (Summer 2005)

Ivy Tech State College—North Central changed its name to Ivy Tech Community College of Indiana—North Central (Summer 2005)

Ivy Tech State College—Northeast changed its name to Ivy Tech Community College of Indiana—Northeast (Summer 2005)

Ivy Tech State College—Sellersburg changed its name to Ivy Tech Community College—Sellersburg (Summer 2005)

Ivy Tech State College—Southeast changed its name to Ivy Tech Community College of Indiana—Madison (Summer 2005)

Ivy Tech State College—Southwest changed its name to Ivy Tech Community College of Indiana—Southwest (Summer 2005)

Ivy Tech State College—Wabash Valley changed its name to Ivy Tech Community College of Indiana—Wabash Valley (Summer 2005)

Ivy Tech State College—Whitewater changed its name to Ivy Tech Community College—Richmond (Summer 2005)

Michiana College changed its name to Brown Mackie College—South Bend (Fall 2004)

IOWA

Franciscan University changed its name to The Franciscan University of the Prairies (Summer 2004)

The Franciscan University of the Prairies changed its name to Ashford University (Spring 2005)

Kaplan College changed its name to Kaplan University (Summer 2004)

La' James College of Hairstyling—Cedar Falls changed its name to La' James International College—Cedar Falls (Summer 2005)

La' James College of Hairstyling—Davenport changed its name to La' James International College—Davenport (Summer 2005)

La' James College of Hairstyling—Des Moines changed its name to La' James International College—Des Moines (Summer 2005)

La' James College of Hairstyling—Fort Dodge changed its name to La' James International College—Fort Dodge (Summer 2005)

La' James College of Hairstyling—Iowa City changed its name to La' James International College—Iowa City (Summer 2005)

Mount St. Clare College changed its name to The Franciscan University (Winter 2003)

Professional Cosmetology Institute, Ltd. changed its name to Salon Professional Academy (Spring 2005)

KANSAS

Bryan Career College changed its name to Bryan College—Topeka (Summer 2002)

Coffeyville Community College merged with Southeast Kansas Technical School and changed its name to Coffeyville Community College/Area Technical School (Summer 2001)

Lawrence Career College changed its name to Pinnacle Career Institute—Lawrence (Summer 2003)

Remington College closed (Spring 1998)

Saint Mary College changed its name to University of Saint Mary (Summer 2003)

Southeast Kansas Technical School merged with Coffeyville Community College and changed its name to Coffeyville Community College/Area Technical School—Technical Campus (Summer 2001)

KENTUCKY

Ashland Community College merged with Ashland Technical College and changed its name to Ashland Community and Technical College (Winter 2003)

Ashland Technical College merged with Ashland Community College and changed its name to Ashland Community and Technical College—Roberts Drive Campus (Winter 2003)

Brescia College changed its name to Brescia University (Summer 1998)

Central Kentucky Technical College merged with Lexington Community College and changed its name to Bluegrass Community and Technical College—Central (Winter 2005)

Cumberland College changed its name to University of the Cumberlands (Summer 2005)

Elizabethtown Community College merged with Elizabethtown Technical College and changed its name to Elizabethtown Community and Technical College (Summer 2004)

Elizabethtown Technical College merged with Elizabethtown Community College and changed its name to Elizabethtown Community and Technical College (Summer 2004)

Hazard Community College changed its name to Hazard Community and Technical College (Summer 2003)

Health Institute of Louisville changed its name to Galen College of Nursing (Winter 2005)

Jefferson Community College merged with Jefferson Technical College and changed its name to Jefferson Community and Technical College (Summer 2005)

Jefferson Technical College merged with Jefferson Community College and changed its name to Jefferson Community and Technical College (Summer 2005)

Kentucky Christian College changed its name to Kentucky Christian University (Fall 2004)

Lexington Community College merged with Central Kentucky Technical College and changed its name to Bluegrass Community and Technical College—Cooper (Winter 2005)

Madisonville Health Technology Center changed its name to Madisonville Technical College (Fall 1998)

Madisonville Technical College merged with Madisonville Community College and changed its name to Madisonville Community College—Technical Campus (Winter 2002)

Mayo Technical College merged with Prestonsburg Community College and changed its name to Big Sandy Community and Technical College—Mayo Campus (Summer 2003)

Maysville Community College merged with Rowan Technical College and changed its name to Maysville Community and Technical College (Summer 2004)

Mid-Continent College changed its name to Mid-Continent University (Spring 2004)

National College of Business and Technology—Lexington Campus merged with Fugazzi College—Nashville (Summer 2001)

Muhlenberg Job Corps Center was removed from accredited status at the request of the institution (Spring 2003)

Owensboro Community College merged with Owensboro Technical College and changed its name to Owensboro Community and Technical College (Winter 2002)

Owensboro Technical College merged with Owensboro Community College and changed its name to Owensboro Community and Technical College—Frederica Street Campus (Winter 2002)

Paducah Community College merged with West Kentucky Technical College and changed its name to West Kentucky Community and Technical College (Summer 2003)

Prestonsburg Community College merged with Mayo Technical College and changed its name to Big Sandy Community and Technical College (Summer 2003)

RETS Institute of Technology changed its name to Brown Mackie College—Louisville (Fall 2004)

Rowan Technical College merged with Maysville Community College and changed its name to Maysville Community and Technical College—Rowan (Summer 2004)

Rowan Technical College—Eastern Kentucky Campus merged with Maysville Community College and changed its name to Maysville Community and Technical College—Licking Valley (Summer 2004)

Southeast Community College changed its name to Southeast Kentucky Community and Technical College (Winter 2001)

Toyota Manufacturing USA was removed from accredited status at the request of the institution (Spring 2003)

West Kentucky Technical College merged with Paducah Community College and changed its name to West Kentucky Community and Technical College (Summer 2003)

LOUISIANA

Academy of Creative Hair Design changed its name to Vanguard College of Cosmetology (Summer 2005)

Culinary Arts Institute of Louisiana closed (Fall 2002)

Education America-Remington College—Baton Rouge Campus changed its name to Remington College—Baton Rouge (Winter 2003)

Education America-Remington College—Lafayette Campus changed its name to Remington College—Lafayette (Winter 2003)

Education America-Southeast College of Technology—New Orleans changed its name to Remington College—New Orleans (Winter 2003)

Guy's Shreveport Academy of Cosmetology changed its name to Guy's Academy Hair, Skin, and Nails (Summer 2005)

Lockworks Academy of Hairdressing—Baton Rouge changed its name to Aveda Institute Baton Rouge (Summer 2005)

Lockworks Academy of Hairdressing—Lafayette changed its name to Aveda Institute Lafayette (Summer 2005)

Louisiana Hair Design College closed (Summer 1997)

Louisiana State University Medical Center changed its name to Louisiana State University Health Sciences Center (Summer 2000)

Louisiana Technical College—L.E. Fletcher Campus changed its name to L.E. Fletcher Technical Community College (Winter 2002)

Louisiana Technical College—Sowela Campus changed its name to Sowela Technical Community College (Winter 2002)

Moler Beauty College—Gretna changed its name to Cosmetology Business and Management Institute (Summer 2005)

MAINE

Central Maine Technical College changed its name to Central Maine Community College (Summer 2003)

Eastern Maine Technical College changed its name to Eastern Maine Community College (Spring 2003)

Headhunter Institute changed its name to Spa Tech Institute (Spring 2005)

Kennebec Valley Technical College changed its name to Kennebec Valley Community College (Summer 2003)

Maine Technical College System changed its name to Maine Community College System (Summer 2003)

Mid-State College closed (Fall 2003)

Northern Maine Technical College changed its name to Northern Maine Community College (Spring 2003)

Southern Maine Technical College changed its name to Southern Maine Community College (Summer 2003)

Stearns & Associates, Inc. changed its name to Dale Carnegie Training of Maine (Summer 2003)

Washington County Technical College changed its name to Washington County Community College (Winter 2002)

York County Technical College changed its name to York County Community College (Summer 2003)

MARYLAND

Coppin State College changed its name to Coppin State University (Spring 2004)

Gordon Phillips School of Beauty Culture—Baltimore closed (Summer 1997)

Maryland College of Art and Design merged with and changed its name to School of Art and Design at Montgomery College (Winter 2004)

Maryland Institute of Traditional Chinese Medicine was removed from accredited status by its accreditor (Fall 2002)

Mount Saint Mary's College and Seminary changed its name to Mount Saint Mary's University (Summer 2004)

National Labor College changed its name to National Labor College (Summer 2004)

Ultrasound Diagnostic School—Landover changed its name to Sanford-Brown Institute—Landover (Fall 2003)

MASSACHUSETTS

Arthur D. Little School of Management changed its name to Hult International Business School (Winter 2004)

Computer Processing Institute closed (Winter 1999)

Computer-Ed Institute changed its name to Career Education Institute—Somerville (Spring 2004)

Concord School of Management changed its name to Arthur D. Little School of Management (Winter 2003)

Dale Carnegie Systems, Inc. changed its name to Ralph Nichols Group, Inc. (Summer 2003)

East Coast Aero Tech changed its name to WyoTech—Boston (Summer 2004)

East Coast Aero Technical School changed its name to East Coast Aero Tech (Summer 2001)

Franklin Institute of Boston changed its name to Benjamin Franklin Institute of Technology (Winter 2001)

Harcourt Learning Direct changed its name to Education Direct (Spring 1999)

Katherine Gibbs School—Boston changed its name to Gibbs College of Boston, Inc. (Winter 2003)

Laboure College changed its name to Caritas Laboure College (Spring 2005)

Massachusetts Career Development Institute, Inc. was removed from accredited status by its accreditor (Summer 2004)

National Educational Institute—New England changed its name to Funeral Institute of the Northeast (Summer 1998)

New England Institute of Art & Communications changed its name to The New England Institute of Art (Summer 2003)

Northeast Institute of Industrial Technology closed (Winter 1998)

Pope John XXIII National Seminary changed its name to Blessed John XXIII National Seminary (Summer 2004)

Saint Hyacinth College and Seminary closed (Summer 2001)

School of Business and Technology changed its name to Massachusetts Career Development Institute, Inc. (Summer 2003)

Ultrasound Diagnostic School—Springfield changed its name to Sanford-Brown Institute—Springfield (Fall 2003)

MICHIGAN

Center for Creative Studies—College of Art and Design changed its name to College for Creative Studies (Summer 2001)

Davenport University—Central Region merged with Davenport University—Western Region and changed its name to Davenport University—Midland Campus (Spring 2003)

Davenport University—Eastern Region merged with Davenport University—Western Region and changed its name to Davenport University—Dearborn Campus (Spring 2003)

Davenport University—Western Region changed its name to Davenport University (Spring 2003)

Detroit Barber College, Inc. closed (Summer 2002)
Lansing Computer Institute was removed from accredited status by its accreditor (Summer 2001)
Madonna University merged with Saint Mary's College of Ave Maria University (Summer 2003)
Ross Business Institute—Clinton Township closed (Winter 1997)
Ross Medical Education Center—Detroit closed (Spring 1998)
Ross Medical Education Center—Taylor closed (Winter 1997)
Ross Medical Education Center—Waterford Campus closed (Winter 2000)
Saint Mary's College of Ave Maria University merged with Madonna University and changed its name to Madonna
    University Orchard Lake Center (Summer 2003)
SER Business and Technical Institute closed (Winter 2004)
Siena Heights College changed its name to Siena Heights University (Summer 1998)
Travel Education Institute closed (Winter 2003)
William Tyndale College closed (Winter 2004)

MINNESOTA
Alfred Adler Graduate School changed its name to Adler Graduate School (Summer 2004)
Anoka-Hennepin Technical College changed its name to Anoka Technical College (Summer 2003)
Bethel College merged with Bethel Seminary and changed its name to Bethel University (Summer 2004)
Bethel Seminary merged with Bethel College and changed its name to Bethel University (Summer 2004)
Century Community and Technical College changed its name to Century College (Fall 1996)
Dunwoody College of Technology merged with NEI College of Technology (Summer 2003)
Fergus Falls Community College changed its name to Minnesota State Community and Technical College (Summer 2003)
Mayo Foundation changed its name to Mayo Clinic College of Medicine (Fall 2003)
McConnell School closed (Spring 2002)
Medical Institute of Minnesota merged with Minnesota School of Professional Psychology and changed its name to
    Argosy University Twin Cities (Fall 2001)
Minnesota Bible College changed its name to Crossroads College (Fall 2002)
Minnesota Cosmetology Education Center, Inc. changed its name to Minnesota School of Cosmetology (Fall 2003)
Minnesota School of Professional Psychology merged with Medical Institute of Minnesota and closed (Fall 2001)
Musictech College changed its name to McNally Smith College of Music (Winter 2005)
NEI College of Technology merged with Dunwoody College of Technology and closed (Summer 2003)
North Central Bible College changed its name to North Central University (Fall 1998)
Northwest Technical Institute changed its name to NTI School of CAD Technology (Summer 2001)
Oliver Thein Beauty School changed its name to Regency Beauty Institute (Winter 2004)
Regency Beauty Academy changed its name to Regecny Beauty Institute (Winter 2005)
Rita's Moorhead Beauty College changed its name to Ing'enue Beauty School (Spring 2005)
RMD Computer, Inc. closed (Winter 2003)
Saint Paul Technical College changed its name to Saint Paul College—A Community and Technical College (Fall 2002)
South Central Technical College—Mankato changed its name to South Central College—Mankato (Spring 2005)
Southwest State University changed its name to Southwest Minnesota State University (Summer 2003)
Walden University merged with National Technological University (Summer 2005)

MISSISSIPPI
Mary Holmes College was removed from accredited status by its accreditor (Winter 2002)
Traxler School of Hair closed (Summer 1995)
Wood Institute closed (Spring 2003)

MISSOURI
Allied Medical College merged with High-Tech Institute (system) and changed its name to Allied College (Spring 2003)
Barnes College of Nursing merged with University of Missouri—St. Louis and changed its name to Barnes College of
    Nusring and Health Studies at the University of Missouri—St. Louis (Summer 2004)
Bryan Career College changed its name to Bryan College—Springfield (Summer 2002)
Central Methodist College changed its name to Central Methodist University (Spring 2004)

Concorde Career Institute—Kansas City changed its name to Concorde Career College—Kansas City (Summer 2005)

Dale Carnegie Training—St. Louis changed its name to C.J. Sealey & Associates, LLC (Summer 2003)

Electronics Institute changed its name to Pinnacle Career Institute (Winter 2002)

Jerry's School of Hairstyling, Inc. changed its name to Cosmetology Concepts Institute (Spring 2005)

Jewish Hospital College of Nursing and Allied Health changed its name to Barnes-Jewish College of Nursing and Allied Health (Winter 2005)

Missouri Southern State College changed its name to Missouri Southern State University-Joplin (Summer 2003)

Missouri Southern State University-Joplin changed its name to Missouri Southern State University (Summer 2005)

Missouri Western State College changed its name to Missouri Western State University (Summer 2005)

Sanford-Brown College—North Kansas City changed its name to Colorado Technical University—North Kansas City (Winter 2005)

Southwest Missouri State University changed its name to Missouri State University (Summer 2005)

University of Health Sciences changed its name to Kansas City University of Medicine and Biosciences (Summer 2004)

University of Missouri—St. Louis merged with Barnes College of Nursing (Summer 2004)

MONTANA

Helena College of Technology of the University of Montana changed its name to University of Montana—Helena College of Technology (Fall 2003)

Montana Tech of The University of Montana—Division of Technology changed its name to Montana Tech of the University of Montana—College of Technology (Summer 2000)

NEBRASKA

Bahner College of Hairstyling changed its name to La' James International College (Spring 2006)

Lincoln School of Commerce changed its name to Hamilton College—Lincoln (Winter 2004)

Nebraska College of Business changed its name to Hamilton College—Omaha (Winter 2004)

Vatterott College—Deerfield merged with Vatterott College—Spring Valley and closed (Winter 2004)

Vatterott College—Spring Valley merged with Vatterott College—Deerfield (Winter 2004)

NEVADA

Dahan Institute of Massage Studies closed (Summer 2003)

Nevada College of Pharmacy changed its name to University of Southern Nevada (Fall 2004)

Nevada Leadership Institute changed its name to J. R. Rodgers & Associates, Inc. (Summer 2003)

NEW HAMPSHIRE

College for Lifelong Learning changed its name to Granite State College (Spring 2005)

Concord Academy of Hair Design changed its name to Esthetics Institute at Concord Academy (Winter 2005)

New Hampshire College changed its name to Southern New Hampshire University (Winter 2001)

New Hampshire Community Technical College—Berlin/Laconia has split and changed its name to New Hampshire Community Technical College—Berlin and New Hampshire Community Technical College—Laconia (Summer 2005)

New Hampshire Community Technical College—Manchester/Stratham has split and changed its name to New Hampshire Community Technical College—Manchester and New Hampshire Community Technical College—Stratham (Summer 2005)

New Hampshire Community Technical College—Nashua/Claermont has split and changed its name to New Hampshire Community Technical College—Nashua and New Hampshire Community Technical College—Claremont (Summer 2005)

Plymouth State College changed its name to Plymouth State University (Summer 2003)

White Pines College changed its name to Chester College of New England (Summer 2001)

NEW JERSEY

Academy of Computer Careers changed its name to Prism Career Institute—Hammonton (Summer 2004)

Allied Medical and Technical Careers changed its name to Allied Medical and Technical Institute (Summer 2004)

American Business Academy changed its name to HoHoKus-Hackensack School of Business and Medical Science (Winter 2004)

Best Care Training Institute was removed from accredited status by its accreditor (Spring 2005)

Boardwalk and Marina Casino Dealers School closed (Summer 2001)

Business Training Institute changed its name to Allied Medical and Technical Institute (Summer 2004)

DeVry Institute of Technology—North Brunswick changed its name to DeVry College of Technology—North Brunswick (Summer 2001)

Divers Academy of the Eastern Seaboard changed its name to Divers Academy International (Fall 2002)

Drake College of Business closed (Summer 2004)

Georgian Court College changed its name to Georgian Court University (Winter 2004)

Gibbs College was removed from accredited status by its accreditor (Summer 2005)

McEllis Training Institute was removed from accredited status by its accreditor (Spring 2005)

Metropolitan Technical Institute closed (Fall 2002)

New Jersey Association of Colleges and Universities changed its name to Association of Independent Colleges and Universities in New Jersey (Winter 2001)

PC AGE Career Institute closed (Summer 2004)

Philadelphia School of Massage Therapy changed its name to National Massage Therapy Institute (Summer 2005)

Plaza School of Technology closed (Fall 1990)

RETS Institute-Nutley changed its name to HoHoKus RETS—Nutley (Summer 2005)

Rizzieri Institute changed its name to Rizzieri Aveda School for Beauty and Wellness (Summer 2005)

Stuart School of Business Administration changed its name to The Stuart School (Spring 2004)

Ultrasound Diagnostic School—Iselin changed its name to Sanford-Brown Institute—Iselin (Fall 2003)

Worldwide Educational Services closed (Fall 2003)

Worldwide Educational Services—Clifton closed (Summer 2003)

Worldwide Educational Services—Newark closed (Summer 2003)

Zaraphath Bible Institute changed its name to Somerset Christian College (Spring 2001)

NEW MEXICO

International Institute of Chinese Medicine was removed from accredited status by its accreditor (Spring 2003)

International Institute of Chinese Medicine closed (Summer 2003)

International Institute of Chinese Medicine—Albuquerque closed (Spring 2003)

Mesa Technical College changed its name to Mesalands Community College (Fall 2001)

Nonproliferation and National Security Institute changed its name to National Training Center (Summer 2004)

Northern New Mexico Community College changed its name to Northern New Mexico College (Spring 2005)

Parks College closed (Fall 2000)

NEW YORK

ASA Institute of Business and Computer Technology changed its name to ASA Institute, The College of Advanced Technology (Summer 2003)

Austin Beauty School changed its name to Austin's School of Spa Technology (Spring 2005)

College of Aeronautics changed its name to Vaughn College of Aeronautics and Technology (Fall 2004)

Columbia-Greene Beauty School, Inc. was removed from accredited status by its accreditor (Fall 2005)

Drake Business School—Queens Astoria Campus closed (Summer 2004)

Drake Business School—Staten Island Campus closed (Summer 2004)

Drake School of Manhattan closed (Summer 2004)

Drake School of the Bronx closed (Summer 2004)

Gamla College was removed from accredited status by its accreditor (Winter 2003)

Genesee Hospital closed (Spring 2001)

Globe Institute of Technology was removed from candidate status at the request of the institution (Summer 2005)

Graduate School and University Center changed its name to City University of New York Graduate Center (Fall 1999)

Helene Fuld School of Nursing changed its name to Helene Fuld College of Nursing (Winter 1996)

Island Medical Center closed (Winter 2004)

John Paul's Hair, Nails and Skin Care Institute was removed from accredited status by its accreditor (Fall 2005)

Mildred Elley Business School changed its name to Mildred Elley (Fall 1998)

Municipal Training Center—Kings was removed from candidate status by its accreditor (Fall 2002)

New School University changed its name to The New School (Summer 2005)

New York Food & Hotel Management School changed its name to Culinary Academy of New York Management School (Summer 2005)

New York Institute of Chinese Medicine changed its name to New York College of Traditional Chinese Medicine (Winter 2004)

Plaza Business Institute changed its name to Plaza College (Summer 2002)

Practical Bible College changed its name to Davis College (Summer 2004)

Professional Business Institute changed its name to Professional Business College (Winter 2005)

Ultrasound Diagnostic School—Garden City changed its name to Sanford-Brown Institute—Garden City (Fall 2003)

Ultrasound Diagnostic School—Elmsford changed its name to Sanford-Brown Institute—Elmsford (Fall 2003)

Ultrasound Diagnostic School—New York changed its name to Sanford-Brown Institute—New York (Fall 2003)

Westchester Business Institute changed its name to The College of Westchester (Fall 2003)

York College changed its name to City University of New York York College (Fall 2000)

NORTH CAROLINA

Barber-Scotia College was removed from accredited status by its accreditor (Summer 2004)

ECPI Technical College—Raleigh closed (Spring 2005)

Mitchell's Hairstyling Academy—Fayetteville changed its name to Montgomery's Hair Styling Academy (Summer 2005)

North Carolina State University merged with Institute of Textile Technology (Winter 2003)

Piedmont Baptist College merged with Spurgeon Baptist Bible College (Spring 2004)

Spurgeon Baptist Bible College merged with Piedmont Baptist College and closed (Spring 2004)

OHIO

Adams Group, LLC changed its name to Dale Carnegie Training of Northwest Ohio and Northern Indiana (Summer 2003)

AEC Southern Ohio College merged with ETI Technical College—North Canton (Spring 2002)

AEC Southern Ohio College changed its name to Brown Mackie College—Cincinnati (Fall 2004)

AEC Southern Ohio College—Findlay changed its name to Brown Mackie College—Findlay (Fall 2004)

Bluffton College changed its name to Bluffton University (Summer 2004)

Bohecker's Business College changed its name to Bohecker College (Summer 2001)

Brown Aveda Institute changed its name to Ladies and Gentlemen Hair Stylists (Winter 2005)

Cedarville College changed its name to Cedarville University (Fall 2000)

Choffin Career Center changed its name to Choffin Career and Technical Center (Summer 2004)

Cincinnati Bible College and Seminary changed its name to Cincinnati Christian University (Fall 2004)

Columbus Para-Professional Institute changed its name to Ohio Institute of Health Careers—Columbus (Summer 2002)

Computer Quest Technical Institute changed its name to Quest Career College (Spring 2004)

Ed W. Grooms & Associates, Inc. changed its name to Dale Carnegie Training of Greater Cincinnati (Winter 2004)

Education America-Remington College—Cleveland Campus changed its name to Remington College—Cleveland (Winter 2003)

ETI Technical College—North Canton merged with AEC Southern Ohio College and changed its name to AEC Southern Ohio College—North Canton (Spring 2002)

Hair Academy changed its name to Casal's De Spa and Salon (Winter 2005)

HTC Distance Education changed its name to Brighton College (Summer 2004)

John D. Langdon & Associates, Inc. changed its name to Lance Tyson & Associates Dale Carnegie Training of Northeast Ohio (Summer 2003)

Medical College of Ohio changed its name to Medical University of Ohio (Spring 2005)

Muskingum Area Technical College changed its name to Zane State College (Summer 2004)

NHRAW Home Study Institute changed its name to HARDI Home Study Institute (Winter 2003)

Omni Technical School closed (Fall 2002)

TDDS—Professional Training Center changed its name to TDDS Technical Institute (Summer 2004)

Virginia Marti College of Fashion and Art changed its name to Virginia Marti College of Art and Design (Summer 2003)

West Side Institute of Technology closed (Summer 2001)

OKLAHOMA
Advance Barber College School of Hair Design changed its name to Heritage College Hair Design (Spring 2003)

American Christian College and Seminary was removed from accredited status by its accreditor (Spring 2004)

Central Oklahoma Area Vocational-Technical Center changed its name to Central Technology Center—Drumright (Summer 2004)

Mid-America Bible College changed its name to Mid-America Christian University (Summer 2003)

Northeast Area Vocational Technical School changed its name to Northeast Technology Center (Summer 2003)

Spartan School of Aeronautics changed its name to Spartan College of Aeronautics and Technology (Summer 2004)

OREGON
Art Institutes International at Portland changed its name to Art Institute of Portland (Winter 2000)

Astoria Beauty College changed its name to Paul Mitchell The School (Summer 2005)

Australasian College of Herbal Sciences changed its name to Australasian College of Health Sciences (Fall 2003)

Australasian College of Herbal Studies changed its name to Australasian College of Herbal Sciences (Summer 2003)

Heald College, Schools of Business—Portland changed its name to Heald College—Portland (Winter 2003)

Valley Career College, Inc. changed its name to Valley Medical College, Inc. (Summer 2004)

Western Baptist College changed its name to Corban College (Summer 2005)

PENNSYLVANIA
Academy of Hair Design changed its name to Academy of Creative Hair Design (Summer 2005)

Allentown Business School changed its name to Lehigh Valley College (Winter 2005)

Allied Medical and Technical Careers changed its name to Allied Medical and Technical Institute (Summer 2004)

Ambler Beauty Academy, Inc. changed its name to Magnolia School (Spring 2005)

American Center for Technical Arts and Sciences was removed from accredited status by its accreditor (Spring 2005)

Cambria County Area Community College changed its name to Pennsylvania Highlands Community College (Summer 2004)

Carlow College changed its name to Carlow University (Summer 2004)

Center for Advanced Manufacturing and Technology closed (Fall 2004)

Center for Lactation Education was removed from accredited status at the request of the institution (Spring 2004)

Centre County Area Vocational Technical School changed its name to Central Pennsylvania Institute of Science and Technology (Summer 2004)

Churchman Business School closed (Winter 2004)

Conemaugh Valley Memorial Hospital changed its name to Conemaugh Memorial Medical Center (Summer 2004)

CSC Institute closed (Winter 2005)

Dale Carnegie Systems changed its name to JR Rodgers and Associates, Inc. (Winter 2004)

Eastern Baptist Theological Seminary changed its name to Palmer Theological Seminary (Summer 2005)

Education Direct changed its name to Penn Foster Career School (Winter 2005)

Education Direct Center for Degree Studies was removed from accredited status at the request of the institution (Summer 2005)

Electronic Institutes changed its name to Harrisburg Institute of Trade and Technology (Spring 2005)

Gordon Phillips School of Beauty Culture—Norristown closed (Spring 2003)

Gordon Phillips School of Beauty Culture—Philadelphia closed (Fall 1994)

Gordon Phillips School of Beauty Culture—Upper Darbby closed (Spring 2003)

Holy Family College changed its name to Holy Family University (Winter 2002)

Information Computer Systems Institute changed its name to Pennsylvania School of Business (Spring 2005)

MBF Center was removed from accredited status by its accreditor (Winter 2005)

North Montco Technical Career Center was removed from accredited status at the request of the institution (Spring 2003)

Penn Council for Relationships changed its name to Council for Relationahips (Summer 2004)

Pennsylvania Institute of Culinary Arts changed its name to Pennsylvania Culinary Institute (Summer 2004)

Pennsylvania Institute of Massage Therapy was removed from accredited status by its accreditor (Spring 2004)

Pennsylvania School of Art and Design changed its name to Pennsylvania College of Art and Design (Summer 2003)

Pennsylvania State University Allentown Campus changed its name to Pennsylvania State University—Lehigh Valley Campus (Summer 1997)

Pennsylvania State University Fayette Campus changed its name to Pennsylvania State University Fayette, The Eberly Campus (Spring 2004)

Pennsylvania State University Ogontz Campus changed its name to Pennsylvania State University Abington Campus (Summer 1997)

Philadelphia College of Bible changed its name to Philadelphia Biblical University (Winter 2001)

Philadelphia School of Massage Therapy changed its name to National Massage Therapy Institute (Summer 2005)

Point Park College changed its name to Point Park University (Fall 2003)

Saint Francis College changed its name to Saint Francis University (Winter 2001)

The Sawyer School closed (Winter 1999)

South Philadelphia Beauty Academy closed (Spring 2004)

Talent Academy closed (Winter 2005)

Thompson Education Direct changed its name to Penn Foster Career School (Winter 2005)

Westinghouse Electric Corporation closed (Spring 1998)

Wyoming Technical Institute—Blairsville changed its name to WyoTech—Blairsville (Summer 2002)

PUERTO RICO

American Business College closed (Fall 2002)

Columbia College changed its name to Columbia Center University (Summer 2002)

Instituto Vocational y Comercial, EDIC changed its name to EDIC College (Summer 2002)

Marugie Beauty and Technical College closed (Spring 2002)

National Fashion and Beauty College was removed from accredited status by its accreditor (Winter 2004)

Technological College of the Municipality of San Juan changed its name to University College of San Juan (Winter 2003)

RHODE ISLAND

Bryant College changed its name to Bryant University (Summer 2004)

Computer-Ed Institute changed its name to Career Education Institute—Lincoln (Spring 2004)

Elite Beauty Institute of Midland was removed from accredited status by its accreditor (Spring 2005)

Interfaith Health Care Ministries, Rhode Island Hospital changed its name to The Chaplaincy Center (Winter 2004)

Katharine Gibbs School changed its name to Gibbs College—Cranston (Summer 2004)

Newport School of Hairdressing, Inc.—Cranston changed its name to Paul Mitchell The School—Cranston (Summer 2005)

Rhode Island Beauty Academy closed (Winter 2003)

Zion Bible Institute changed its name to Zion Bible College (Summer 2005)

SOUTH CAROLINA

Anderson College changed its name to Anderson University (Winter 2006)

Columbia Junior College of Business changed its name to Columbia Junior College (Fall 1999)

Leadership Development, Inc. changed its name to Dale Carnegie Training of South Carolina, LLC (Summer 2003)

University of South Carolina—Spartanburg changed its name to University of South Carolina—Upstate (Summer 2004)

SOUTH DAKOTA

Si Tanka Huron University changed its name to Si Tanka University (Summer 2004)

Si Tanka University—Huron closed (Spring 2005)

TENNESSEE

Academy of Beauty Arts changed its name to Franklin Academy (Summer 2005)

Ambassador Institute of Travel closed (Spring 2001)

American Academy of Nutrition changed its name to Huntington College of Health Sciences (Summer 2005)

Church of God School of Theology changed its name to Church of God Theological Seminary (Summer 1998)

Concorde Career Institute—Memphis changed its name to Concorde Career College (Winter 2003)

Education America-Southeast College of Technology—Memphis changed its name to Remington College—Memphis (Winter 2003)

Methodist Healthcare—University Hospital changed its name to Methodist University Hospital (Summer 2002)

Nashville State Technical Institute changed its name to Nashville State Community College (Summer 2002)

Tennessee Institute of Electronics changed its name to Fountainhead College of Technology (Spring 2003)

TEXAS

Amarillo College of Hairdressing, Inc. changed its name to Milan Institute of Cosmetology (Spring 2005)

American Weld Testing School closed (Summer 2000)

ATI—American Trades Institutes changed its name to ATI—Technical Training Center (Summer 2003)

Cape Coral Beauty School was removed from accredited status by its accreditor (Fall 2005)

Career Point Business School changed its name to Career Point Institute (Summer 2003)

Central Texas Commercial College closed (Spring 2003)

Dallas College of Oriental Medicine closed (Winter 2005)

DSU Training Institute closed (Spring 2004)

Education America—Dallas Campus changed its name to Remington College—Dallas (Winter 2003)

Education America—Houston changed its name to Remington College—Houston (Winter 2003)

Education America-Tampa Technical Institute—Ft. Worth Campus changed its name to Remington College—Ft. Worth (Winter 2003)

Extended Home Health Education changed its name to Concorde Career Institute—Arlington (Winter 2003)

Hispanic Baptist Theological School changed its name to Baptist University of the Americas (Fall 2003)

Houston Allied Health Careers, Inc. closed (Summer 2005)

Houston Ballet Academy changed its name to Houston Ballet's Ben Stevenson Academy (Summer 2003)

Huston-Tillotson College changed its name to Huston-Tillotson University (Winter 2005)

Institute for Christian Studies changed its name to Austin Graduate School of Theology (Spring 2001)

International Aviation and Travel Academy closed (Spring 2003)

National Association Medical Staff Services was removed from accredited status by its accreditor (Summer 2004)

R. C. Leffke & Associates, Inc. changed its name to John M. Jennings and Associates, Inc. (Spring 2005)

Savant Training and Technology was removed from accredited status by its accreditor (Spring 2003)

Shirley Baker Career Institute closed (Summer 2002)

South Texas Community College changed its name to South Texas College (Summer 2004)

South Texas Vo-Tech Institute—Brownsville closed (Spring 2003)

Southwest School of Electronics changed its name to Southwest Institute of Technology (Summer 2002)

Southwest Texas State University changed its name to Texas State University—San Marcos (Fall 2003)

Southwestern Adventist College changed its name to Southwestern Adventist University (Summer 1996)

Texas Beauty College changed its name to Milan Institute of Cosmetology (Spring 2005)

Texas Career Institute closed (Winter 2005)

Ultrasound Diagnostic School—Dallas changed its name to Sanford-Brown Institute—Dallas (Fall 2003)

Valley Grande College of Health and Technology changed its name to Valley Grande Institute for Academic Studies (Fall 2001)

Westwood College of Aviation Technology—Houston changed its name to Westwood Aviation Institute—Houston (Winter 2005)

Westwood College of Technology—Dallas changed its name to Westwood College—Dallas (Winter 2005)

Westwood College of Technology—Fort Worth changed its name to Westwood College—Fort Worth (Winter 2005)

Westwood Institute of Technology—Houston South changed its name to Westwood College—Houston South (Winter 2005)

UTAH

Beau La Reine College of Beauty Culture was removed from accredited status by its accreditor (Summer 2005)

California College for Health Sciences changed its name to Independence University (Summer 2005)

Computer Services and Instruction, Inc. changed its name to CSI Career College (Summer 2005)

Davis Applied Technology Center changed its name to Davis Applied Technology College (Fall 2001)

Hairitage College of Beauty changed its name to Paul Mitchell The School (Summer 2005)

Ogden-Weber Applied Technology Center changed its name to Ogden-Weber Applied Technology College (Fall 2001)

Utah College of Midwifery changed its name to Midwives College of Utah (Fall 2004)

Von Curtis Academy of Hair Design changed its name to Paul Mitchell The School (Summer 2005)

VIRGINIA

American School of Professional Psychology—Virginia Campus merged with Argosy University and changed its name to Argosy University Washington, DC (Fall 2001)

Applied Career Training, Inc. changed its name to ACT College (Summer 2003)

ATI—Hollywood changed its name to BarPalma Beauty Careers Academy (Summer 2005)

Central School of Practical Nursing changed its name to Norfolk Technical Vocational Center (Winter 2003)

College of Health Sciences changed its name to Community Hospital of Roanoke Valley College of Health Sciences (Fall 2000)

Community Hospital of Roanoke Valley College of Health Sciences changed its name to Jefferson College of Health Sciences (Fall 2003)

Ghent Beauty Academy closed (Summer 2004)

Gibbs School changed its name to Gibbs College—Vienna (Fall 2002)

Indian River Beauty Academy closed (Winter 2004)

Institute of Textile Technology merged with North Carolina State University and closed (Winter 2003)

LIFE Bible College East closed (Spring 2004)

Mary Washington College changed its name to University of Mary Washington (Summer 2004)

National Imagery and Mapping College changed its name to National Geospatial-Intelligence College (Fall 2005)

Potomac Academy of Hair Design changed its name to Heritage Institute (Summer 2004)

Potomac Academy of Hair Design—Falls Church changed its name to Heritage Institute (Summer 2004)

Ralph's Virginia School of Cosmetology, Inc. changed its name to Legends Institute (Summer 2005)

Richmond School of Health and Technology changed its name to RSHT Training Center (Summer 2005)

United States Navy and Marine Corps Intelligence Training Center changed its name to Center for Naval Intelligence (Summer 2003)

Virginia Careers Academy closed (Spring 2001)

Virginia College—Salem closed (Fall 1997)

Virginia Learning Institute Massage Therapy School changed its name to National Massage Therapy Institute (Summer 2005)

WASHINGTON

American College of Professional Education closed (Summer 2000)

Business Career Training Institute closed (Spring 2005)

Business Computer Training Institute changed its name to Business Career Training Institute (Summer 2004)

Emil Fries Piano & Training center changed its name to Emil Fries School of Piano Tuning and Technology (Summer 2000)

Eton Technical Institute changed its name to Bryman College (Summer 2003)

Eton Technical Institute—Everett changed its name to Bryman College—Everett (Summer 2003)

Eton Technical Institute—Federal Way changed its name to Bryman College—Federal Way (Summer 2003)

Eton Technical Institute—Tacoma changed its name to Bryman College—Tacoma (Summer 2003)

Everett Beauty Academy changed its name to Milan Institute of Cosmetology (Spring 2005)

Heritage College changed its name to Heritage University (Summer 2004)

Inland Northwest Heating, Ventilation, and Air Conditioning Training Center changed its name to Northwest HVC/R Association and Training Center (Summer 2004)

Northwest College of the Assemblies of God changed its name to Northwest University (Winter 2005)

Northwest Institute of Acupuncture and Oriental Medicine closed (Summer 2002)

RCH Technical Institute closed (Winter 2000)

Saint Martin's College changed its name to Saint Martin's University (Summer 2005)

Trident Training Facility Bangor was removed from accredited status at the request of the institution (Fall 2004)

WEST VIRGINIA

American Community College closed (Winter 2004)

Concord College changed its name to Concord University (Summer 2004)

Fairmont State College changed its name to Fairmont State University (Spring 2004)

Huntington Junior College of Business changed its name to Huntington Junior College (Summer 2001)

Ohio Valley College changed its name to Ohio Valley University (Summer 2005)
Shepherd College changed its name to Shepherd University (Spring 2004)
West Virginia State College changed its name to West Virginia State University (Summer 2004)

WISCONSIN
Associated Training Services Corporation was removed from accredited status by its accreditor (Summer 2004)
Mary C. Gwin & Associates changed its name to J. R. Rodgers & Associates Dale Carnegie Systems (Summer 2003)
MBTI Business Training Institute closed (Spring 2002)

WYOMING
Wyoming Technical Institute changed its name to WyoTech (Summer 2002)

CANADA

Bethany Bible Institute changed its name to Bethany College (Winter 2003)

Canadian Bible College changed its name to Alliance University College (Winter 2004)

Canadian School of Management was removed from accredited status by its accreditor (Summer 2004)

DeVry Univeristy College of Technology—Toronto merged with RCC Institute of Technology and closed (Fall 2003)

Eastern Pentecostal Bible College changed its name to Master's College (Summer 2001)

Full Gospel Bible Institute changed its name to Full Gospel Bible College (Winter 2005)

Northwest Bible College changed its name to Vanguard College (Summer 2004)

Ryerson Polytechnic University changed its name to Ryerson University (Summer 2002)

Tyndale College and Seminary changed its name to Tyndale University College and Seminary (Summer 2003)

Western Christian College was removed from accredited status by its accreditor (Winter 2005)

Western Pentecostal Bible College changed its name to Summit Pacific College (Summer 2004)

GERMANY

University of Maryland University College—European Division closed (Summer 2002)

GREECE

The American University of Athens was removed from accredited status by its accreditor (Summer 2005)

College of Southeastern Europe changed its name to The American University of Athens (Winter 2004)

University of La Verne—Athens Campus closed (Fall 2004)

IRELAND

Institute of Public Administration was removed from accredited status at the request of the institution (Spring 2004)

MEXICO

Centro de Capacitacion Montessori was removed from accredited status by its accreditor (Fall 2005)

MONACO

University of Southern Europe changed its name to The International University of Monaco (Summer 2003)

UNITED KINGDOM

International Management Centres Association was removed from accredited status by its accreditor (Summer 2004)

Candidates for Accreditation

Candidate for Accreditation is a status of affiliation with a recognized accrediting organization which indicates that an institution has achieved initial recognition and is progressing toward, but has not been assured, accreditation.

The Candidate for Accreditation classification is designed for postsecondary institutions which may or may not be fully operative. In either case, the institution must provide evidence of sound planning, the resources to implement these plans, and appear to have the potential for attaining its goals within a reasonable time.

To be considered for Candidate for Accreditation status, the applicant must be a postsecondary education institution with the following characteristics:

(1) Have a charter and/or formal authority from an appropriate governmental agency to award a certificate, diploma, or degree.

(2) Have a governing board which includes representation reflecting the public interest.

(3) Have employed a chief administrative officer.

(4) Offer, or plan to offer, one or more educational programs of at least one academic year in length, or the equivalent at the postsecondary level, with clearly defined and published educational objectives, as well as a clear statement of the means for achieving them.

(5) Include general education at the postsecondary level as a prerequisite to or as an essential element in its principal educational programs.

(6) Have admission policies compatible with its stated objectives.

(7) Have developed a preliminary survey or evidence of basic planning for the development of the institution.

(8) Have established an adequate financial base of funding commitments and have available a summary of its latest audited financial statement.

ALABAMA

Huntsville Bible College
904 Oakwood Ave., Huntsville 35810
Type: Private, independent, four-year
Degrees: A, B
URL: http://www.huntsvillebiblecollege.com
Phone: (256) 539-0834   *Calendar:* Sem. plan
Inst. Accred.: ABHE (2003)

Selma University
1501 Lapsley St., Selma 36701
Type: Private, Baptist Church, four-year
System: Alabama Association of Independent Colleges
and Universities
Degrees: A, B, M   *FTE Enroll:* 183
Phone: (334) 872-2533   *Calendar:* Sem. plan
Inst. Accred.: ABHE (2005)

ARIZONA

Asian Institute of Medical Studies
3131 North Country Club, Ste. 100, Tucson 85716
Type: Private, proprietary, four-year
Degrees: M
URL: http://www.asianinstitute.edu
Phone: (520) 322-6330   *Calendar:* Qtr. plan
Inst. Accred.: ACAOM (2004)

Tohono O'odham Community College
PO Box 3129, Sells 85634
Type: Public, tribal, two-year
Degrees: A
URL: http://www.tocc.cc.az.us
Phone: (520) 383-8401   *Calendar:* Sem. plan
Inst. Accred.: NCA-HLC (2003)

CALIFORNIA

American University of Armenia
300 Lakeside Dr., Fourth Flr., Oakland 94612
Type: Private, independent, four-year
Degrees: M
URL: http://www.aua.am
Phone: (510) 987-9452   *Calendar:* Qtr. plan
Inst. Accred.: WASC-SR. (2001)

Bethesda Christian University
730 North Euclid St., Anaheim 92801
Type: Private, Full Gospel World Mission, four-year
Degrees: B, M
URL: http://www.bcu.edu
Phone: (714) 517-1945   *Calendar:* Sem. plan
Inst. Accred.: TRACS (2003)

California State University—Channel Islands
One University Dr., Camarillo 93012
Type: Public, state, four-year
System: California State University System
Degrees: B, M
URL: http://www.csuci.edu
Phone: (805) 383-8400   *Calendar:* Sem. plan
Inst. Accred.: WASC-SR. (2005)

Community Christian College
251 Tennessee St., Redlands 92373
Type: Private, nondenominational, two-year
Degrees: A
URL: http://www.cccollege.net
Phone: (909) 335-8863   *Calendar:* Qtr. plan
Inst. Accred.: TRACS (2004)

InterAmerican College
140 West 16th St., National City 91950-4413
Type: Private, independent, four-year
Degrees: B
URL: http://www.iacnc.edu
Phone: (619) 477-6310   *Calendar:* Sem. plan
Inst. Accred.: WASC-SR. (2005)

Intercultural Institute of California
1362 Post St., San Francisco 94109
Type: Private, independent, four-year
Degrees: M
URL: http://www.iic.edu
Phone: (415) 441-1884   *Calendar:* Sem. plan
Inst. Accred.: WASC-SR. (2002)

International Theological Seminary
3215-3225 North Tyler Ave., El Monte 91731
Type: Private, nondenominational, four-year
Degrees: M, D
URL: http://www.itsla.edu
Phone: (626) 448-0023   *Calendar:* Qtr. plan
Inst. Accred.: ATS (2004)

Loyola Marymount University
One LMU Dr., Los Angeles 90045-2659
Type: Private, Roman Catholic Church, four-year
Degrees: B, M, P, D   *Enroll:* 8,013
URL: http://www.lmu.edu
Phone: (310) 338-2700   *Calendar:* Sem. plan
Inst. Accred.: ATS (2004)

University of the West
1409 North Walnut Grove Ave., Rosemead 91770
Type: Private, independent, four-year
Degrees: B, M, D
URL: http://www.uwest.edu
Phone: (626) 571-8811   *Calendar:* Sem. plan
Inst. Accred.: WASC-SR. (2002)

West Hills Community College—Lemoore
555 College Ave., Lemoore 93425
Type: Public, state/local, two-year
System: West Hills Community College District
Degrees: A
URL: http://www.westhillscollege.com/lemoore
Phone: (559) 925-3000   *Calendar:* Sem. plan
Inst. Accred.: WASC-JR. (2004)

World Mission University
500 Shatto Place, Ste. 600, Los Angeles 90020
Type: Private, independent, four-year
Degrees: B, M
URL: http://www.wmu.edu
Phone: (213) 385-2322   *Calendar:* Sem. plan
Inst. Accred.: ABHE (2004)

COLORADO

Institute of Taoist Education and Acupuncture
608 Main St., Louisville 80027
Type: Public, proprietary, four-year
Degrees: M
URL: http://www.acupunctureschool.ws
Phone: (720) 890-8922   *Calendar:* Sem. plan
Inst. Accred.: ACAOM (2003)

DELAWARE

Delaware College of Art and Design
600 North Market St., Wilmington 19801
Type: Private, independent, two-year
Degrees: A
URL: http://www.dcad.edu
Phone: (302) 622-8000   *Calendar:* Sem. plan
Inst. Accred.: MSA-CHE (2003)

DISTRICT OF COLUMBIA

Institute of World Politics
1521 16th St., NW, Washington 20036-1423
Type: Private, independent, four-year
Degrees: M
URL: http://www.iwp.edu
Phone: (202) 462 2101   *Calendar:* Sem. plan
Inst. Accred.: MSA-CHE (2003)

Potomac College
4000 Chesapeake St., NW, Washington 20016
Type: Private, proprietary, four-year
Degrees: B   *Enroll:* 222
URL: http://www.potomac.edu
Phone: (202) 686-0876   *Calendar:* Sem. plan
Inst. Accred.: MSA-CHE (2001)

Northern Virginia Campus
1029 Herndon Pkwy., Herndon, VA 20170
Phone: (703) 709-5875

FLORIDA

Florida Center for Theological Studies
111 NE First St., 8th Flr., Miami 33132
Type: Private, interdenominational, four-year
Degrees: M
URL: http://www.sfcts.org
Phone: (305) 379-3777   *Calendar:* Qtr. plan
Inst. Accred.: ATS (2004)

Inter-American Adventist Theological Seminary
PO Box 830518, Miami 33283
Type: Private, Seventh-day Adventist, two-year
Degrees: A
Phone: (305) 403-4700   *Calendar:* Sem. plan
Inst. Accred.: ATS (2001)

GEORGIA

Atlanta Technical College
1560 Metropolitan Ave., SW, Atlanta 30310
Type: Public, state, two-year
System: Georgia Department of Technical & Adult
Education
Degrees: A   *Enroll:* 2,335
URL: http://www.atlantatech.org
Phone: (404) 756-3700   *Calendar:* Qtr. plan
Inst. Accred.: SACS (2004)

Delta Airlines Campus
Hartfield International Airport, Atlanta 30310
Phone: (404) 758-5591

Carver Bible College
437 Nelson St., SW, PO Box 4335, Atlanta 30302
Type: Private, independent, four-year
Degrees: A, B
URL: http://www.carverbiblecollege.edu
Phone: (404) 527-4520   *Calendar:* Sem. plan
Inst. Accred.: ABHE (2001)

John Marshall Law School—Atlanta
1422 West Peachtree St. NW, Atlanta 30309
Type: Private, independent, four-year
Degrees: P
URL: http://www.johnmarshall.edu
Phone: (404) 872-3593   *Calendar:* Sem. plan
Inst. Accred.: ABA (2005)

Mercer University

1400 Coleman Ave., Macon 31207
Type: Private, Georgia Baptist Convention, four-year
Degrees: B, M, P, D　　　　　　　　　　*Enroll:* 6,185
URL: http://www.mercer.edu
Phone: (478) 301-2700　　　　　*Calendar:* Sem. plan
Inst. Accred.: ATS (2002)

Cecil B. Day Campus

3001 Mercer University Dr., Atlanta 30341
Phone: (678) 547-6000

Georgia Baptist College of Nursing of Mercer University

3001 Mercer University Dr., Atlanta 30341
Phone: (678) 547-6799

North Metro Technical College

5198 Ross Rd., Acworth 30102
Type: Public, state, two-year
System: Georgia Department of Technical & Adult Education
Degrees: A
URL: http://www.northmetro.tec.ga.us
Phone: (770) 975-4000　　　　　*Calendar:* Qtr. plan
Inst. Accred.: SACS (2004)

Southeastern Technical College

3001 East First St., Vidalia 30474
Type: Public, state, two-year
System: Georgia Department of Technical & Adult Education
Degrees: A
URL: http://www.southeasterntech.edu
Phone: (912) 538-3100　　　　　*Calendar:* Qtr. plan
Inst. Accred.: SACS (2005)

Glennville Campus

211 S. Tillman St., Glennville 30427
Phone: (912) 654-5276

West Georgia Technical College

303 Fort Dr., LaGrange 30240
Type: Public, state, two-year
System: Georgia Department of Technical & Adult Education
Degrees: A　　　　　　　　　　　　*Enroll:* 1,179
URL: http://www.westgatech.edu
Phone: (706) 845-4323　　　　　*Calendar:* Qtr. plan
Inst. Accred.: SACS (2005)

IDAHO

New Saint Andrews College

405 South Main St., PO Box 9025, Moscow 83843
Type: Private, Christ Church/Confederation of Reformed Evangelicals, four-year
Degrees: A, B
URL: http://www.newstandrews.org
Phone: (208) 882-1566　　　　　*Calendar:* 4-1-4 plan
Inst. Accred.: TRACS (2002)

ILLINOIS

Toyota Technological Institute at Chicago

1427 East 60th St., Second Flr., Chicago 60637
Type: Private, proprietary, four-year
Degrees: M, D
URL: http://www.tti-c.org
Phone: (773) 834-2500　　　　　*Calendar:* Qtr. plan
Inst. Accred.: NCA-HLC (2005)

INDIANA

Trinity College of the Bible and Theological Seminary

4233 Medwel Dr., Newburgh 47630-0717
Type: Private, nondenominational, four-year
Degrees: A, B, M, D
URL: http://www.trinitysem.edu
Phone: (812) 853-0611
Inst. Accred.: NCA-HLC (2004)

IOWA

Emmaus Bible College

2570 Asbury Rd., Dubuque 52001-3096
Type: Private, nondenominational, four-year
Degrees: A, B　　　　　　　　　　　*Enroll:* 253
URL: http://www.emmaus.edu
Phone: (563) 588-8000　　　　　*Calendar:* Sem. plan
Inst. Accred.: NCA-HLC (2004)

KANSAS

Barclay College

607 North Kingman, PO Box 288, Haviland 67059-0288
Type: Private, Evangelical Friends International, four-year
Degrees: A, B　　　　　　　　　　　*Enroll:* 176
URL: http://www.barclaycollege.edu
Phone: (620) 862-5252　　　　　*Calendar:* Sem. plan
Inst. Accred.: NCA-HLC (2002)

Manhattan Area Technical College

3136 Dickens Ave., Manhattan 66503-2499
Type: Public, state/local, two-year
Degrees: A　　　　　　　　　　　　*Enroll:* 337
URL: http://www.matc.net
Phone: (785) 587-2800
Inst. Accred.: NCA-HLC (2002)

LOUISIANA

School of Urban Missions—New Orleans
PO Box 53344, New Orleans 70153-3344
Type: Private, nondenominational, two-year
Degrees: A
URL: http://www.sumonline.org
Phone: (504) 362-6364 *Calendar:* Tri. plan
Inst. Accred.: ABHE (2003)

Oakland Campus
PO Box 14145, Oakland, CA 94614
Phone: (510) 567-6174

South Louisiana Community College
105 Patriot Ave., Lafayette 70508
Type: Public, state/local, two-year
System: Louisiana Community and Technical College
System
Degrees: A
URL: http://www.slcc.cc.la.us
Phone: (337) 984-3684 *Calendar:* Sem. plan
Inst. Accred.: SACS (2004)

MARYLAND

Capital Bible Seminary
6511 Princess Garden Pkwy., Lanham 20706
Type: Private, independent, four-year
Degrees: A, B, M, P *Enroll:* 444
URL: http://www.bible.edu/cbs
Phone: (301) 552-1400 *Calendar:* Sem. plan
Inst. Accred.: MSA-CHE (2002)

Tai Sophia Institute
7750 Monteplier Rd., Laurel 20723
Type: Private, independent, four-year
Degrees: M *Enroll:* 280
URL: http://www.tai.edu
Phone: (410) 888-9048 *Calendar:* Tri. plan
Inst. Accred.: MSA-CHE (2001)

Washington Bible College
6511 Princess Garden Pkwy., Lanham 20706-3538
Type: Private, independent, four-year
Degrees: A, B, M, P *Enroll:* 444
URL: http://www.bible.edu
Phone: (301) 552-1400 *Calendar:* Sem. plan
Inst. Accred.: MSA-CHE (2002)

Yeshiva College of the Nation's Capital
1216 Arcola Ave., Silver Spring 20902
Type: Private, independent, four-year
Degrees: B *FTE Enroll:* 56
Phone: (301) 593-2534 *Calendar:* Sem. plan
Inst. Accred.: AARTS (2003)

MASSACHUSETTS

Franklin W. Olin College of Engineering
Olin Way, Needham 02492-1245
Type: Private, independent, four-year
Degrees: B
URL: http://www.olin.edu
Phone: (781) 292-2222 *Calendar:* Sem. plan
Inst. Accred.: NEASC-CIHE (2004)

Gibbs College of Boston, Inc.
126 Newbury St., Boston 02116-2904
Type: Private, proprietary, two-year
System: Career Education Corporation
Degrees: A *Enroll:* 855
URL: http://www.gibbsboston.com
Phone: (617) 578-7100 *Calendar:* Qtr. plan
Inst. Accred.: NEASC-CTCI (2002)

MICHIGAN

Ave Maria College
300 West Forest Ave., Ypsilanti 48197
Type: Private, Roman Catholic Church, four-year
Degrees: B *Enroll:* 300
URL: http://www.avemaria.edu
Phone: (734) 482-4519 *Calendar:* Sem. plan
Inst. Accred.: AALE (2000), NCA-HLC (2003)

Ave Maria College of the Americas
San Marcos, Nicaragua
Phone: 011 505 432 2312

Michigan Theological Seminary
41550 East Ann Arbor Trail, Plymouth 48170
Type: Private, nondenominational, four-year
Degrees: B, M, D *Enroll:* 117
URL: http://www.mts.edu
Phone: (734) 207-9581 *Calendar:* Sem. plan
Inst. Accred.: NCA-HLC (2003)

Saginaw Chippewa Tribal College
2274 Enterprise Dr., Mount Pleasant 48858
Type: Public, tribal, two-year
Degrees: A
URL: http://www.sagchip.org
Phone: (989) 775-4123 *Calendar:* Sem. plan
Inst. Accred.: NCA-HLC (2003)

MINNESOTA

Hazelden Graduate School of Addiction Studies
C03, PO Box 11, Center City 55012-0011
Type: Private, independent, four-year
Degrees: M
URL: http://www.hazelden.org
Phone: (651) 213-4000 *Calendar:* Sem. plan
Inst. Accred.: NCA-HLC (2005)

Leech Lake Tribal College
PO Box 180, Cass Lake 56633-0180
Type: Public, tribal, two-year
System: American Indian Higher Education Consortium
Degrees: A   *Enroll:* 133
URL: http://www.leechlaketribalcollege.org
Phone: (218) 335-4200   *Calendar:* Qtr. plan
Inst. Accred.: NCA-HLC (2002)

White Earth Tribal and Community College
PO Box 478, 202-210 South Main St., Mahnomen 56557
Type: Public, tribal, two-year
System: American Indian Higher Education Consortium
Degrees: A
URL: http://www.wetcc.org
Phone: (218) 935-0417   *Calendar:* Sem. plan
Inst. Accred.: NCA-HLC (2004)

MISSOURI

Baptist Bible College
628 East Kearney St., Springfield 65803-3498
Type: Private, Baptist Bible Fellowship International, four-year
Degrees: A, B, M   *Enroll:* 657
URL: http://www.bbcnet.edu
Phone: (417) 268-6060   *Calendar:* Sem. plan
Inst. Accred.: NCA-HLC (2001)

Central Bible College
3000 North Grant Ave., Springfield 65803-1096
Type: Private, Assemblies of God Church, four-year
Degrees: A, B   *Enroll:* 771
URL: http://www.cbcag.edu
Phone: (417) 833-2551   *Calendar:* Sem. plan
Inst. Accred.: NCA-HLC (2005)

Saint Louis Christian College
1360 Grandview Dr., Florissant 63033-6499
Type: Private, independent, four-year
Degrees: A, B   *Enroll:* 171
URL: http://www.slcconline.edu
Phone: (314) 837-6777   *Calendar:* Sem. plan
Inst. Accred.: NCA-HLC (2001)

NEW HAMPSHIRE

Magdalen College
511 Kearsarge Mountain Rd., Warner 03278
Type: Private, independent, four-year
Degrees: A, B
URL: http://www.magdalen.edu
Phone: (603) 456-2656   *Calendar:* Sem. plan
Inst. Accred.: AALE (2002)

New Hampshire Institute of Art
148 Concord St., Manchester 03104-4158
Type: Private, independent, four-year
Degrees: B
URL: http://www.nhia.edu
Phone: (603) 623-0313   *Calendar:* Sem. plan
Inst. Accred.: NASAD (2001)

NEW YORK

ASA Institute, The College of Advanced Technology
151 Lawrence St., Brooklyn 11201
Type: Private, independent, two-year
Degrees: A
URL: http://www.asa-institute.com
Phone: (718) 522-9073
Inst. Accred.: WASC-SR. (2005)

Beis Medrash Heichal Dovid
257 Beach 17th St., Far Rockaway 11691
Type: Private, independent, four-year
Degrees: Talmudic   *FTE Enroll:* 70
Phone: (718) 868-2300   *Calendar:* Sem. plan
Inst. Accred.: AARTS (2002)

The Graduate College of Union University
Lamont House, 807 Union St., Schenectady 12308
Type: Private, independent, four-year
System: Union University
Degrees: M
URL: http://www.gcuu.edu
Phone: (518) 388-6148   *Calendar:* Tri. plan
Inst. Accred.: MSA-CHE (2004)

Northeastern Seminary
2265 Westside Dr., Rochester 14624
Type: Private, independent, four-year
Degrees: M
URL: http://www.nes.edu
Phone: (585) 594-6800   *Calendar:* Sem. plan
Inst. Accred.: MSA-CHE (2003)

NORTH CAROLINA

Campbell University
PO Box 127, Buies Creek 27506-0127
Type: Private, Southern Baptist Church, four-year
Degrees: B, M, P, D   *Enroll:* 5,332
URL: http://www.campbell.edu
Phone: (910) 893-1200   *Calendar:* Sem. plan
Inst. Accred.: ATS (2001)

Carolina Evangelical Divinity School
1208 Eastchester Dr., Ste. 130, PO Box 5831, High Point 27262
Type: Private, Friends United Meeting, four-year
Degrees: M
URL: http://www.carolinadivinity.org/web/templates/ceds.aspx
Phone: (336) 889-2262   *Calendar:* Sem. plan
Inst. Accred.: TRACS (2004)

New Life Theological Seminary
PO Box 790106, Charlotte 28206-7901
Type: Private, independent, four-year
Degrees: B, M, D
URL: http://www.nlts.org
Phone: (704) 334-6882
Inst. Accred.: TRACS (2003)

Winston-Salem Bible College
4117 Northampton Dr., Winston-Salem 27105
Type: Private, Christian Churches/Churches of Christ, four-year
Degrees: A, B   *Enroll:* 21
URL: http://www.wsbc.edu
Phone: (336) 744-0900   *Calendar:* Sem. plan
Inst. Accred.: ABHE (2001)

OHIO

Good Samaritan College of Nursing and Health Science
375 Dixmyth Ave., Cincinnati 45220
Type: Private, independent, two-year
Degrees: A
URL: http://www.goodsamaritancollege.com
Phone: (513) 872-2743   *Calendar:* Sem. plan
Inst. Accred.: NCA-HLC (2004)

Temple Baptist College
11965 Kenn Rd., Cincinnati 45240
Type: Private, Baptist Church, four-year
Degrees: B
URL: http://www.templebaptistcollege.net
Phone: (513) 851-3800   *Calendar:* Qtr. plan
Inst. Accred.: TRACS (2002)

OKLAHOMA

Family of Faith College
30 Kinville Rd., Shawnee 74804
Type: Private, independent, four-year
Degrees: B
URL: http://www.familyoffaithcollege.com
Phone: (405) 273-5331   *Calendar:* Sem. plan
Inst. Accred.: ABHE (2002)

OREGON

Gutenberg College
1883 University St., Eugene 97403
Type: Private, independent, four-year
Degrees: B
URL: http://www.gutenberg.edu
Phone: (541) 683-5141   *Calendar:* Qtr. plan
Inst. Accred.: TRACS (2004)

Multnomah Bible College
8435 NE Glisan St., Portland 97220-5814
Type: Private, independent, four-year
Degrees: B, M   *Enroll:* 687
URL: http://www.multnomah.edu
Phone: (503) 255-0332   *Calendar:* Sem. plan
Inst. Accred.: NWCCU (2001)

PENNSYLVANIA

The Art Institute of Pittsburgh
420 Blvd. of the Allies, Pittsburgh 15219-1328
Type: Private, proprietary, four-year
System: Education Management Corporation
Degrees: A, B   *Enroll:* 2,611
URL: http://www.aip.aii.edu
Phone: (412) 291-6200   *Calendar:* Qtr. plan
Inst. Accred.: MSA-CHE (2003)

The Art Institute of California—Los Angeles
2900 31st St., Santa Monica, CA 90405-3035
Phone: (310) 752-4700

Calvary Baptist Theological Seminary
1380 South Valley Forge Rd., Lansdale 19446
Type: Private, Calvary Baptist Church, four-year
Degrees: M
URL: http://seminary.cbs.edu
Phone: (215) 368-7538 ext 1   *Calendar:* Sem. plan
Inst. Accred.: MSA-CHE (2004)

Lake Erie College of Osteopathic Medicine
1858 West Grandview Blvd., Erie 16509
Type: Private, independent, four-year
Degrees: B, P, D   *Enroll:* 1,038
URL: http://www.lecom.edu
Phone: (814) 866-6641   *Calendar:* Sem. plan
Inst. Accred.: MSA-CHE (2003)

Lancaster General College of Nursing and Health Sciences
PO Box 3555, 410 North Lime St., Lancaster 17604-3555
Type: Private, independent, two-year
Degrees: A
URL: http://www.lancastergeneral.org
Phone: (717) 544-4912   *Calendar:* 12-mos. pr
Inst. Accred.: MSA-CHE (2003)

Pennsylvania College of Art and Design
204 North Prince St., Lancaster 17603
Type: Private, independent, four-year
Degrees: B
URL: http://www.psad.org
Phone: (717) 396-7833　　*Calendar:* Sem. plan
Inst. Accred.: MSA-CHE (2004)

Won Institute of Graduate Studies
137 South Easton Rd., Glenside 19038
Type: Private, independent, four-year
Degrees: M
URL: http://www.woninstitute.org
Phone: (215) 884-8942
Inst. Accred.: MSA-CHE (2003)

PUERTO RICO

Columbia Center University
PO Box 8517, Caguas 00726
Type: Private, proprietary, four-year
Degrees: A, B, M　　*Enroll:* 604
URL: http://www.columbiaco.edu
Phone: (787) 743-4041　　*Calendar:* Sem. plan
Inst. Accred.: MSA-CHE (2002)

Yauco Campus
PO Box 3060, Yauco 00698-3060
Phone: (787) 856-0845

Electronic Data Processing College
560 Ponce De Leon Ave., Hato Rey 00919
Type: Private, proprietary, four-year
Degrees: A, B, M　　*Enroll:* 878
URL: http://www.edpcollege.com
Phone: (787) 765-3560　　*Calendar:* Sem. plan
Inst. Accred.: MSA-CHE (2001)

San Sebastian Campus
48 Betances St., PO Box 1674, San Sebastian 00685
Phone: (787) 896-2137

Huertas Junior College
PO Box 8429, Caguas 00726
Type: Private, proprietary, two-year
Degrees: A　　*Enroll:* 1,374
URL: http://www.huertasjrcollege.org
Phone: (787) 743-1242　　*Calendar:* Tri. plan
Inst. Accred.: MSA-CHE (2002)

SOUTH CAROLINA

Bob Jones University
1700 Wade Hampton Blvd., Greenville 29614
Type: Private, independent, four-year
Degrees: B, M, D
URL: http://www.bju.edu
Phone: (864) 242-5100　　*Calendar:* Sem. plan
Inst. Accred.: TRACS (2005)

W.L. Bonner Bible College
4430 Argent Ct., Columbia 29203
Type: Private, independent, four-year
Degrees: A, B
Phone: (803) 754-3950　　*Calendar:* Sem. plan
Inst. Accred.: ABHE (2004)

TENNESSEE

Oxford Graduate School
500 Oxford Dr., Dayton 37321-6736
Type: Private, independent, four-year
Degrees: M, D
URL: http://www.oxnet.com
Phone: (423) 775-6596　　*Calendar:* Sem. plan
Inst. Accred.: TRACS (2003)

Visbile School, Music and Worship Arts College
9817 Huff N Puff Rd., Lakeland 38002
Type: Private, independent, four-year
Degrees: B
URL: http://www.visibleschool.com
Phone: (901) 381-3939　　*Calendar:* Sem. plan
Inst. Accred.: TRACS (2005)

Williamson Christian College
200 Seaboard Ln., Franklin 37067
Type: Private, interdenominational, four-year
Degrees: A, B
URL: http://www.williamsoncc.edu
Phone: (615) 771-7821　　*Calendar:* Sem. plan
Inst. Accred.: ABHE (2003)

TEXAS

Baylor University
Waco 76798
Type: Private, Southern Baptist Church, four-year
Degrees: B, M, D　　*Enroll:* 13,408
URL: http://www.baylor.edu
Phone: (254) 710-1011　　*Calendar:* Sem. plan
Inst. Accred.: ATS (2001)

Graduate Institute of Applied Linguistics
7500 West Camp Wisdom Rd., Dallas 75236
Type: Private, independent, four-year
Degrees: M
URL: http://www.gial.edu
Phone: (972) 708-7340
Inst. Accred.: SACS (2003)

Hardin-Simmons University
2200 Hickory St., Abilene 79698
Type: Private, Baptist General Convention of Texas, four-year
Degrees: A, B, M, D　　*Enroll:* 2,054
URL: http://www.hsutx.edu
Phone: (915) 670-1000　　*Calendar:* Sem. plan
Inst. Accred.: ATS (2004)

UTAH

Bridgerland Applied Technology College
1301 North 600 West, Logan 84321
Type: Public, state, two-year
System: Utah College of Applied Technology
Degrees: A
URL: http://www.batc.tec.ut.us
Phone: (435) 753-6780
Inst. Accred.: COE (2003)

Davis Applied Technology College
550 East 300 South, Kaysville 84037
Type: Public, state, two-year
System: Utah College of Applied Technology
Degrees: A
URL: http://www.datc.net
Phone: (801) 593-2500
Inst. Accred.: COE (2003)

Mountainland Applied Technology College
987 South Geneva Rd., Orem 84058
Type: Public, state, two-year
System: Utah College of Applied Technology
Degrees: A
URL: http://www.mountainlandatc.org
Phone: (801) 863-7662
Inst. Accred.: COE (2003)

Ogden-Weber Applied Technology College
200 North Washington Blvd., Ogden 84404
Type: Public, state, two-year
System: Utah College of Applied Technology
Degrees: A
URL: http://www.owatc.com
Phone: (801) 627-8300
Inst. Accred.: COE (2003)

Rocky Mountain University of Health Professions
1662 West 820 North, Provo 84601
Type: Private, independent, four-year
Degrees: M, D
URL: http://www.rmuohp.edu
Phone: (801) 375-5125
Inst. Accred.: NWCCU (2005)

Salt Lake-Tooele Applied Technology College
1655 East 3300 South, Salt Lake City 84106
Type: Public, state, two-year
System: Utah College of Applied Technology
Degrees: A
URL: http://www.sltatc.org
Phone: (801) 493-8700
Inst. Accred.: COE (2003)

Uintah Basin Applied Technology College
1100 East Lagoon Sreet, Roosevelt 84066
Type: Public, state, two-year
System: Utah College of Applied Technology
Degrees: A
URL: http://www.ubatc.tec.ut.us
Phone: (435) 722-4523
Inst. Accred.: COE (2003)

VIRGINIA

Appalachian School of Law
PO Box 1825, Grundy 24614-2825
Type: Private, independent, four-year
Degrees: P   *Enroll:* 353
URL: http://www.asl.edu
Phone: (800) 895-7411   *Calendar:* Sem. plan
Inst. Accred.: ABA (2001)

Central Baptist Theological Seminary
2221 Centerville Turnpike, Virginia Beach 23464
Type: Private, Baptist Church, four-year
Degrees: M
URL: http://www.baptistseminary.edu
Phone: (757) 479-3706   *Calendar:* Sem. plan
Inst. Accred.: TRACS (2004)

The Institute for the Psychological Sciences
2001 Jefferson Davis Hwy., Ste. 102, Arlington 22202
Type: Private, independent, four-year
Degrees: M, D
URL: http://www.ipsciences.edu
Phone: (703) 416-1441   *Calendar:* Sem. plan
Inst. Accred.: SACS (2003)

The John Leland Center for Theological Studies
1301 North Hartford St., Arlington 22201
Type: Private, Baptist World Alliance, four-year
Degrees: M
URL: http://www.johnlelandcenter.edu
Phone: (703) 812-4757   *Calendar:* Sem. plan
Inst. Accred.: ATS (2004)

Patrick Henry College
One Patrick Henry Circle, Purcellville 20132-1776
Type: Private, independent, four-year
Degrees: B
URL: http://www.phc.edu
Phone: (540) 338-1776   *Calendar:* Sem. plan
Inst. Accred.: AALE (2002), TRACS (2003)

TAP—This Valley Works Center for Employment Training
108 North Jefferson St., Roanoke 24001
Type: Private, proprietary, two-year
Degrees: A
URL: http://www.taproanoke.org/services/tvw.html
Phone: (540) 767-6221
Inst. Accred.: COE (2001)

Virginia University of Lynchburg
2058 Garfield Ave., Lynchburg 24501
Type: Private, Baptist Church, four-year
Degrees: A, B, M, D
URL: http://vulonline.net
Phone: (434) 528-5276
Inst. Accred.: TRACS (2003)

WASHINGTON

Cascadia Community College
18345 Campus Way, NE, Bothell 98011
Type: Public, state/local, two-year
Degrees: A
URL: http://www.cascadia.ctc.edu
Phone: (425) 352-8000   *Calendar:* Qtr. plan
Inst. Accred.: NWCCU (2002)

WEST VIRGINIA

American Military University
111 West Congress St., Charles Town 25414
Type: Private, proprietary, four-year
System: American Public University System
Degrees: A, B, M   *FTE Enroll:* 308
URL: http://www.apus.edu
Phone: (304) 724-3700   *Calendar:* Sem. plan
Inst. Accred.: NCA-HLC (2004, *Indirect accreditation through American Public University System, Charles Town, WV*)

American Public University
111 West Congress St., Charles Town 25414
Type: Private, proprietary, four-year
System: American Public University System
Degrees: A, B, M
URL: http://www.apus.edu
Phone: (304) 724-3700   *Calendar:* Sem. plan
Inst. Accred.: NCA-HLC (2004)

WISCONSIN

Northland Baptist Bible College
W10085 Pike Plains Rd., Dunbar 54119
Type: Private, nondenominational, four-year
Degrees: B, M, D
URL: http://www.nbbc.edu
Phone: (715) 324-6900   *Calendar:* Sem. plan
Inst. Accred.: TRACS (2004)

BERMUDA

Bermuda College
PO Box PG 297, Paget, Bermuda PG BX
Type: Private, independent, two-year
Degrees: A
URL: http://www.bercol.bm
Phone: (441) 236-9000   *Calendar:* Sem. plan
Inst. Accred.: NEASC-CIHE (2005)

CANADA

Alberta Bible College
635 Northmount Dr., NW, Calgary, Canada T2K 3J6
Type: Private, Church of Christ, four-year
Degrees: B
URL: http://www.abc-ca.org
Phone: (403) 282-2994   *Calendar:* Sem. plan
Inst. Accred.: ABHE (2004)

Boucher Institute of Naturopathic Medicine
200-668 Carnarvon St., New Westminster, Canada V3M 5Y6
Type: Private, indepenednt, four-year
Degrees: D
URL: http://www.binm.org
Phone: (604) 777-9981
Inst. Accred.: CNME (2003)

Full Gospel Bible College
730-1st St., SE, Box 579, Eston, Canada S0L 1A0
Type: Private, independent, four-year
Degrees: A, B
URL: http://www.fgbi.sk.ca
Phone: (306) 962-3621   *Calendar:* Sem. plan
Inst. Accred.: ABHE (2004)

Prairie Bible College
319 5th Ave. North, PO Box 4000, Three Hills, Canada T0M 2N0
Type: Private, interdenominational, four-year
Degrees: A, B
URL: http://www.prairie.edu/biblecollege.htm
Phone: (403) 443-5511   *Calendar:* Sem. plan
Inst. Accred.: ATS (2001)

University of Alberta
Edmonton, Canada T6G 2E1
Type: Public, provincial, four-year
Degrees: B, M, P, D
URL: http://www.ualberta.ca
Phone: (780) 492-3111   *Calendar:* Sem. plan
Inst. Accred.: ATS (1998)

SWITZERLAND

International University in Geneva
ICC, Rte. De Pre-Bois 20, Geneva, Switzerland 1215
Type: Private, independent, four-year
Degrees: B, M
URL: http://www.iun.ch
Phone: 011 41 11 71 07110   *Calendar:* Tri. plan
Inst. Accred.: MSA-CHE (2002)

TAIWAN, PROVINCE OF CHINA

Christ's College
51 Tzu Chiang Rd., Tanshui Taipei, Taiwan, Province of China 25120
Type: Private, independent, four-year
Degrees: B
URL: http://www.christc.org.tw
Phone: 011 886 2 28097661
Inst. Accred.: TRACS (2003)

UNITED ARAB EMIRATES

Zayed University
PO Box 19282, Dubai, United Arab Emirates
Type: Private, state, four-year
Degrees: B, M
URL: http://www.zu.ac.ae
Phone: 011 97 714 264-8899
Inst. Accred.: MSA-CHE (2004)

UNITED KINGDOM

London Metropolitan University
166-220 Holloway Rd., London, United Kingdom N7 8DB
Type: Private, proprietary, four-year
Degrees: A, B, M, P, D
URL: http://www.londonmet.ac.uk
Phone: 011 44 0 20 7423 000
Inst. Accred.: MSA-CHE (2005)

ARIZONA

Eastern Arizona Academy of Cosmetology
1926 Thatcher Blvd., Safford 85546
Type: Private, proprietary
Degrees: C
Phone: (920) 348-8878
Inst. Accred.: NACCAS (2005)

ARKANSAS

Arkansas Aviation Technologies Center
4248 South School Ave., Fayetteville 72701
Type: Private, proprietary
Degrees: C
URL: http://www.arkansasaviation.org
Phone: (479) 443-2283
Inst. Accred.: COE (2002)

Blackwood Beauty School
2105 Hwy. 67 South, Pocahontas 72444
Type: Private, proprietary
Degrees: C
Phone: (870) 892-3879
Inst. Accred.: NACCAS (2005)

Crossett School of Cosmetology LLC
121 Pine St., Crossett 71635
Type: Private, proprietary
Degrees: C
Phone: (870) 304-2545
Inst. Accred.: NACCAS (2004)

Marks-to Beauty Academy
1614 Brentwood Dr., PO Box 7646, Pine Bluff 71611
Type: Private, proprietary
Degrees: C
Phone: (870) 535-4111
Inst. Accred.: NACCAS (2004)

CALIFORNIA

Academy of Esthetics and Cosmetology
13782-2 Foothill Blvd., Sylmar 91342
Type: Private, proprietary
Degrees: C
Phone: (818) 833-5502
Inst. Accred.: NACCAS (2004)

Borner's Barber College
4608 South Western Ave., Los Angeles 90062
Type: Private, proprietary
Degrees: C
URL: http://www.bornersbarbercollege.com
Phone: (323) 299-8133
Inst. Accred.: NACCAS (2005)

California Nurses Education Institute
68-860 Perez Rd., Ste. E, Cathedral City 92237
Type: Private, proprietary
Degrees: C
Phone: (760) 416-5955
Inst. Accred.: COE (2004)

Coachella Valley Beauty College
47120 Dune Palms Rd., Ste. D, LaQuinta 92553
Type: Private, proprietary
Degrees: C
Phone: (760) 772-5950
Inst. Accred.: NACCAS (2004)

College of Career Training
7220 Fair Oaks Blvd., Ste. A, Carmichael 95608
Type: Private, proprietary
Degrees: C
Phone: (916) 481-9001
Inst. Accred.: COE (2004)

Computer Services and Instruction, Inc.
190 South Orchard Ave., Ste. B-230, Vacaville 95688
Type: Private, proprietary
Degrees: C
URL: http://www.traincsi.com
Phone: (707) 455-0557
Inst. Accred.: COE (2002)

CSI Career Acadmy
611-K Orange Dr., Vacaville 95687
Type: Private, proprietary
Degrees: C
URL: http://www.traincsi.com
Phone: (707) 455-0557
Inst. Accred.: COE (2004)

First Beauty College
15436 Brookhurst St., Westminister 93683
Type: Private, proprietary
Degrees: C
Phone: (714) 775-1887
Inst. Accred.: NACCAS (2004)

First Beauty College
15436 Brookhurst St., Westminster 93683
Type: Private, proprietary
Degrees: C
Phone: (714) 775-1887
Inst. Accred.: NACCAS (2005)

GDS Institute
7916 Long Beach Blvd., South Gate 90280
Type: Private, proprietary
Degrees: C
Phone: (323) 585-5577
Inst. Accred.: COE (2004)

Glamour Beauty College
130 South Harbor Blvd., Santa Ana 92704
Type: Private, proprietary
Degrees: C
Phone: (714) 839-0808
Inst. Accred.: NACCAS (2004)

Gnomon School of Visual Effects
1015 North Cahuenga Blcd., Ste. 5430i, Hollywood 90038
Type: Private, proprietary
Degrees: C
Phone: (323) 466-6663
Inst. Accred.: COE (2004)

Los Angeles Music Academy
370 South Fair Oaks Ave., Pasadena 91105
Type: Private, independent
Degrees: C
URL: http://www.lamusicacademy.com
Phone: (626) 568-8850　　　　*Calendar:* Qtr. plan
Inst. Accred.: NASM (2003)

Inland Empire Training Center
1717 South Grove Ave., Ontario 91761
Phone: (909) 947-9363

Orange County Training Center
3036 Enterprise St., Costa Mesa 92626
Phone: (714) 545-3202

NTMA Training Centers of Southern California
14926 Bloomfield Ave., Norwalk 90650
Type: Private, proprietary
Degrees: C
URL: http://www.trainingcenters.org
Phone: (562) 921-3722
Inst. Accred.: COE (2003)

New Technology Training Institute
1100 North Brand Blvd., Ste. 200, Glendale 91202
Type: Private, proprietary
Degrees: C
URL: http://www.newtechtrain.com
Phone: (818) 247-0989
Inst. Accred.: COE (2005)

Palladium Technical Academy
10507 Valley Blvd., Ste. 806, El Monte 91731
Type: Private, proprietary
Degrees: C
URL: http://www.palladiumta.com
Phone: (626) 444-0880
Inst. Accred.: COE (2004)

World Vision College of Cosmetology, Inc.
1722 Broadway, Oakland 94612
Type: Private, proprietary
Degrees: C
Phone: (510) 645-5873
Inst. Accred.: NACCAS (2004)

CONNECTICUT

Academy Di Capelli School of Cosmetology
950 Yale Ave., Yale Plaza, Unit 20, Wallingford 06492
Type: Private, proprietary
Degrees: C
URL: http://www.academydicapelli.com
Phone: (203) 294-9496
Inst. Accred.: NACCAS (2004)

Branford Academy of Hair and Cosmetology
675 East Main St., Branford 06405
Type: Private, proprietary
Degrees: C
URL: http://www.branfordacademy.com
Phone: (203) 315-2985
Inst. Accred.: NACCAS (2005)

FLORIDA

Academy of Career Training
3501 West Vine St., #111, Kissimmee 34741
Type: Public, proprietary
Degrees: C
URL: http://academyofcareertraining.com
Phone: (417) 943-8777
Inst. Accred.: NACCAS (2004)

Academy of Professional Careers
114 South Semoran Blvd., Winter Park 32792
Type: Private, proprietary
Degrees: C
Phone: (407) 673-8477
Inst. Accred.: NACCAS (2004)

Aveda Institute
235 3rd St. South, St. Petersburg 33709
Type: Private, proprietary
Degrees: C
URL: http://avedaflorida.com
Phone: (727) 820-3162
Inst. Accred.: NACCAS (2004)

Bly's School of Cosmetology
1405 Northwest 6th St., Ste. 110-120, Gainesville 32601
Type: Private, proprietary
Degrees: C
Phone: (352) 371-5891
Inst. Accred.: NACCAS (2004)

Broward Career Institute
9143 Taft St., Pembroke Pines 33024
Type: Private, proprietary
Degrees: C
Phone: (954) 431-3636
Inst. Accred.: NACCAS (2005)

International B Naturale Beauty School, Inc.
3772 West Oakland Park Blvd., Lauderdale 33311-1152
Type: Private, proprietary
Degrees: C
Phone: (954) 733-4800
Inst. Accred.: NACCAS (2004)

New Dimension Academy of Beauty
4551 Gunn Hwy., Tampa 33624
Type: Private, proprietary
Degrees: C
Phone: (813) 264-9677
Inst. Accred.: COE (2004)

Professional Health Training Academy
1240-A SE Hwy. 484, Ocala 34480
Type: Private, proprietary
Degrees: C
Phone: (352) 245-4119
Inst. Accred.: COE (2004)

SABER
3990 West Flagler St., Ste. 100, Miami 33134
Type: Private, independent
Degrees: C
Phone: (305) 443-7601
Inst. Accred.: COE (2002)

Vocational Institute of Florida
1849 West Flagler St., Miami 33135
Type: Private, proprietary
Degrees: C
Phone: (305) 643-6111
Inst. Accred.: COE (2004)

GEORGIA

Brunswick Job Corps Center
4401 Glynco Parkway, Brunswick 31525
Type: Public, federal
Degrees: C
URL: http://www.insideregion3.org
Phone: (912) 264-8843
Inst. Accred.: COE (2005)

The Hair Schools
1999 Candler Rd., Decatur 30032
Type: Private, proprietary
Degrees: C
Phone: (404) 534-1213
Inst. Accred.: NACCAS (2004)

Institute for Medical Services Certification
3781 Presidential Pkwy., Atlanta 30340
Type: Private, proprietary
Degrees: C
URL: http://www.imsmedicalservices.com
Phone: (404) 299-3838
Inst. Accred.: COE (2003)

World Outreach Medical Institute
4650 Memorial Dr., Devatur 30032
Type: Private, proprietary
Degrees: C
URL: http://www.worldoutreachmi.com
Phone: (404) 229-1271
Inst. Accred.: COE (2003)

ILLINOIS

Aveda Institute Chicago
2828 North Clark St., Chicago 60657
Type: Private, proprietary
Degrees: C
URL: http://www.avedainstitutechicago.com
Phone: (773) 289-1560
Inst. Accred.: NACCAS (2004)

DROS School of Cosmetology
1919 Sherman Ave., North Chicago 60064
Type: Private, proprietary
Degrees: C
Phone: (847) 473-4908
Inst. Accred.: NACCAS (2004)

Josef Phillips Academy of Cosmetology
9 North Van Buren Ave., Freeport 61032
Type: Private, proprietary
Degrees: C
Phone: (815) 599-8500
Inst. Accred.: NACCAS (2004)

INDIANA

Moler Hairstyling College, Inc.
4393 West 5th Ave., Gary 46404
Type: Private, proprietary
Degrees: C
Phone: (219) 944-0960
Inst. Accred.: NACCAS (2004)

KENTUCKY

Employment Solutions-Center for Training and Employment
1165 Centre Pkwy., Ste. 120, Lexington 40517
Type: Private, independent
Degrees: C
URL: http://www.employmentsolutionsinc.org
Phone: (859) 272-5225
Inst. Accred.: COE (2004)

LOUISIANA

Alden's School of Cosmetology
4321 Airline Hwy., Baton Rouge 70805-1502
Type: Private, proprietary
Degrees: C
URL: http://www.aldensschoolofcosmetology.com
Phone: (225) 355-5776
Inst. Accred.: NACCAS (2004)

Mercy Educational Institute
10001 Lake Forest Blvd., Ste. 1104, New Orleans 70127
Type: Private, proprietary
Degrees: C
Phone: (504) 244-0444
Inst. Accred.: COE (2004)

Northshore Career College
18175 Old Covington Hwy., Hammond 70403
Type: Private, proprietary
Degrees: C
Phone: (985) 419-2050
Inst. Accred.: COE (2005)

MAINE

Capilo Institute
110 Western Ave., Augusta† 04330
Type: Private, proprietary
Degrees: C
URL: http://www.capilo.com
Phone: (207) 621-9941
Inst. Accred.: NACCAS (2004)

MARYLAND

The Fila Academy
6320 Ritchie Hwy., Glen Burnie 21061
Type: Private, propietary
Degrees: C
URL: http://www.filaacademy.com
Phone: (410) 789-9516
Inst. Accred.: NACCAS (2004)

MASSACHUSETTS

DiGrigoli School of Cosmetology, Inc.
1578 Riverdale St., West Springfield 01089
Type: Private, proprietary
Degrees: C
URL: http://www.digrigoli.com/school
Phone: (413) 827-0037
Inst. Accred.: NACCAS (2004)

Sullivan and Cogliano Training Centers
365 Westgate Dr., Brockton 02301
Type: Private, proprietary
Degrees: C
URL: http://www.sctrain.com
Phone: (508) 584-9909
Inst. Accred.: COE (2005)

MISSOURI

Loria's College of Cosmetology
1709 Highgrove Rd., Grandview 64030
Type: Private, proprietary
Degrees: C
Phone: (816) 965-0010
Inst. Accred.: NACCAS (2004)

Trend Setters School of Cosmetology, Inc.
1100 South Main St., Sikeston 63801
Type: Private, proprietary
Degrees: C
URL: http://www.trendsettersschool.com
Phone: (573) 481-0012
Inst. Accred.: NACCAS (2004)

NEVADA

The Academy of Healing Arts
901 Rancho Ln., Ste. 190, Las Vegas 89106
Type: Private, proprietary
Degrees: C
URL: http://www.academylv.com
Phone: (702) 671-4242
Inst. Accred.: COE (2004)

Prater Way College of Beauty, Inc.
1627 Prater Way, Sparks 89431
Type: Private, proprietary
Degrees: C
Phone: (775) 355-6677
Inst. Accred.: NACCAS (2004)

NEW JERSEY

Health Careers Center of Mercy County Technical Schools
1070 Klockner Rd., Trenton 08619
Type: Private, proprietary
Degrees: C
URL: http://www.mctec.net
Phone: (6609) 587-7640
Inst. Accred.: COE (2002)

New Concept Beauty School #2, Inc.
263 North Broad St., Elizabeth 07208
Type: Private, proprietary
Degrees: C
Phone: (908) 355-9595
Inst. Accred.: NACCAS (2004)

Onyx Beauty Academy Inc.
25 Broad Ave., Palisades Park 07650
Type: Private, proprietary
Degrees: C
Phone: (201) 943-7211
Inst. Accred.: NACCAS (2004)

NEW YORK

ACE Computer Training Center
109-19 72nd Rd., Ste. 4F, Forest Hill 11375
Type: Private, proprietary
Degrees: C
URL: http://www.aceedu.com
Phone: (718) 575-3223
Inst. Accred.: COE (2004)

Aveda Institute New York
233 Spring St., New York 10013
Type: Private, proprietary
Degrees: C
Phone: (212) 367-0321
Inst. Accred.: NACCAS (2004)

Beauty Salon School
426 Kings High Way, Brooklyn 11223
Type: Private, proprietary
Degrees: C
URL: http://www.beautysalonschool.com
Phone: (718) 998-9388
Inst. Accred.: NACCAS (2004)

Bronx Institute for Career Training and Development
962 Ogden Ave., 2nd Flr., Bronx 10452
Type: Private, proprietary
Degrees: C
Phone: (718) 681-3537
Inst. Accred.: COE (2004)

Hudson Valley School of Advanced Aesthetic Skin Care, Inc.
256 Main St., New Paltz 12561
Type: Private, proprietary
Degrees: C
URL: http://www.hvsaesthetics.com
Phone: (845) 255-0013
Inst. Accred.: NACCAS (2004)

Onondaga-Cortland-Madison BOCES
4500 Crown Rd., Liverpool 13090
Type: Public, local
Degrees: C
URL: http://www.ocmboces.org
Phone: (315) 433-2600   *Calendar:* Sem. plan
Inst. Accred.: COE (2002)

Center for New Careers
242 Port Watson St., Cortland 13045-2823

Roberts Business Institute
500 Eigth Ave., New York 10018
Type: Private, proprietary
Degrees: C
Phone: (212) 273-9774
Inst. Accred.: COE (2003)

NORTH CAROLINA

Asheboro Beauty School
736 South Fayetteville St., Asheboro 27203
Type: Private, proprietary
Degrees: C
Phone: (336) 629-9639
Inst. Accred.: NACCAS (2004)

Atlantic University of Chinese Medicine
PO Box 790, Mars Hill 28754
Type: Private, proprietary
Degrees: C
URL: http://www.aucm.com
Phone: (828) 689-1669   *Calendar:* Tri. plan
Inst. Accred.: ACAOM (2002)

Cosmetic Arts Center
2703 High Point Rd., Ste. E, Greensboro 27403
Type: Private, proprietary
Degrees: C
Phone: (336) 855-8882
Inst. Accred.: NACCAS (2004)

EnVisionary I-Care
11431 Hwy. 70 West, Ste. 5201, Clayton 27520
Type: Private, independent
Degrees: C
URL: http://envisionary.com
Phone: (919) 661-7773
Inst. Accred.: COE (2004)

Jung Tao School of Classical Chinese Medicine
207 Dale Adams Rd., Sugar Grove 28679
Type: Private, proprietary
Degrees: C
URL: http://www.jungtao.edu
Phone: (828) 297-4181   *Calendar:* 12-mos. pr
Inst. Accred.: ACAOM (2001)

OHIO

Cincinnati Job Corps Center
1409 Western Ave., Cincinnati 45214
Type: Public, federal
Degrees: C
URL: http://jobcorps.doleta.gov/centers/oh.cfm
Phone: (513) 651-2000
Inst. Accred.: NCA-CASI (2005)

The Cut Beauty School, Inc.
1007 Ivanhoe Rd., Cleveland 44110
Type: Private, proprietary
Degrees: C
Phone: (216) 458-0448
Inst. Accred.: NACCAS (2004)

Darnell Institute of Cosmetology
2930 Market St., Youngstown 44507
Type: Private, proprietary
Degrees: C
Phone: (330) 783-9759
Inst. Accred.: NACCAS (2005)

Designer's Beauty Academy School of Cosmetology
401 Market St., East Liverpool 43920
Type: Private, prorpietary
Degrees: C
Phone: (330) 385-9330
Inst. Accred.: NACCAS (2004)

OKLAHOMA

Arleen's Clinton Beauty Academy
502 South 13th St., Clinton 73601
Type: Private, proprietary
Degrees: C
Phone: (580) 323-6700
Inst. Accred.: NACCAS (2005)

Oklahoma Technology Institute
9801 Broadway Extension, Oklahoma City 73114
Type: Private, proprietary
Degrees: C
URL: http://www.freedomcareers.com
Phone: (405) 842-9400
Inst. Accred.: COE (2005)

Tulsa Job Corps Center
3781 Presidential Pkwy., Atlanta 30340
Type: Public, federal
Degrees: C
Phone: (918) 585-9111
Inst. Accred.: COE (2005)

PENNSYLVANIA

Bella Capelli Academy
151 Wyngate Dr., Monroeville 15146
Type: Private, proprietary
Degrees: C
URL: http://www.paulmitchelltheschool.com/partners/
bellacapelli.asp
Phone: (412) 373-6311
Inst. Accred.: NACCAS (2004)

Indiana Cosmetology Academy
441 Hamill Rd., Indiana 15701
Type: Public, state/local
Degrees: C
URL: http://www.ictc.ws/adulted/cosmo_acad.htm
Phone: (724) 349-6700
Inst. Accred.: NACCAS (2004)

International Beauty Academy, Inc.
6534-36 Caster Ave., Philadelphia 19149
Type: Private, proprietary
Degrees: C
Phone: (215) 288-9080
Inst. Accred.: NACCAS (2004)

Pa. Barber School
145 Steuben St., Pittsburgh 15220
Type: Private, proprietary
Degrees: C
Phone: (412) 921-5150
Inst. Accred.: NACCAS (2004)

PUERTO RICO

Conservatorio de Estudios Avanzados y Especializad
Avenida Luis Munoz Marin Q-27, Caguas 00725
Type: Private, proprietary
Degrees: C
Phone: (787) 743-1975
Inst. Accred.: NACCAS (2005)

RTP Hispanic American College
Ruiz Belvis #52-54, Second Flr., Caguas 00725
Type: Private, proprietary
Degrees: C
Phone: (787) 258-4851
Inst. Accred.: COE (2004)

World Training Academy, Inc.
M-4 F St., Urb. HermanasDavila, Bayamon 00959
Type: Private, proprietary
Degrees: C
Phone: (787) 740-7372
Inst. Accred.: NACCAS (2004)

RHODE ISLAND

Gibbs College—Cranston
85 Garfield Ave., Cranston 02920
Type: Private, proprietary
System: Career Education Corporation
Degrees: C   *Enroll:* 579
URL: http://www.gibbsri.edu
Phone: (800) 614-2888   *Calendar:* Sem. plan
Inst. Accred.: NEASC-CTCI (2001)

SOUTH CAROLINA

Betty's Career College of Cosmetology
311 South Hampton Ave., Johnsonville 29555
Type: Private, proprietary
Degrees: C
Phone: (843) 386-3346
Inst. Accred.: NACCAS (2005)

Contemporary Hair Care Institution Inc.
1701 Leesburg Rd., Columbia 29209
Type: Private, proprietary
Degrees: C
Phone: (803) 776-4101
Inst. Accred.: NACCAS (2005)

TENNESSEE

Austin's Beauty College, Inc
585 South Riverside Dr., Clarksville 37040-3107
Type: Private, proprietary
Degrees: C
Phone: (931) 647-6543
Inst. Accred.: NACCAS (2004)

The Barber College
70 Church St., Cleveland 37311
Type: Private, proprietary
Degrees: C
Phone: (423) 473-8355
Inst. Accred.: NACCAS (2004)

Buchanan Beauty College
925 Sevier St., Shelbyville 37160
Type: Private, proprietary
Degrees: C
Phone: (931) 684-4080
Inst. Accred.: NACCAS (2004)

Elite College of Cosmetology
459 North Main St., Lexington 38351
Type: Private, proprietary
Degrees: C
Phone: (731) 968-5400
Inst. Accred.: NACCAS (2004)

Ezp's College of Barbering
3983 Brainerd Rd., Chattanooga 37411
Type: Private, proprietary
Degrees: C
Phone: (423) 316-9936
Inst. Accred.: NACCAS (2005)

Institute of Hair Design, Inc.
205 Enterprise Dr., Adamsville 38310
Type: Private, proprietary
Degrees: C
URL: http://www.ihd4me.com
Phone: (731) 632-9533
Inst. Accred.: NACCAS (2004)

Last Minute Cut School of Barbering
2195 South Third St., Memphis 38116
Type: Private, proprietary
Degrees: C
Phone: (901) 774-9699
Inst. Accred.: NACCAS (2004)

Mason Academy of Cosmetology
12198 Main St., PO Box 581, Mason 38049
Type: Private, proprietary
Degrees: C
Phone: (901) 294-2590
Inst. Accred.: NACCAS (2004)

Nave Cosmetology Academy, Inc.
112 East James Campbell Blvd., Columbia 38401
Type: Private, proprietary
Degrees: C
Phone: (931) 388-7717
Inst. Accred.: NACCAS (2004)

New Concepts School of Cosmetology
1701-M South Lee Hwy., Cleveland 37311
Type: Private, proprietary
Degrees: C
Phone: (423) 478-3231
Inst. Accred.: NACCAS (2004)

Shear Academy
780 West Academy, Crossville 38555
Type: Private, proprietary
Degrees: C
Phone: (931) 456-5391
Inst. Accred.: NACCAS (2004)

TLC NuWave School of Cosmetology
283 Stone Crossing Dr., Clarksville 37042
Type: Private, proprietary
Degrees: C
URL: http://www.tlcnuwaveschcos.com
Phone: (931) 920-5551
Inst. Accred.: NACCAS (2004)

TEXAS

A & B Training Academy
6065 Hillcroft St., Ste. 309, Houston 77081
Type: Private, proprietary
Degrees: C
Phone: (713) 777-5245
Inst. Accred.: COE (2004)

Acres Home College of Barber Design
2306 Ferguson Way, Houston 77088
Type: Private, proprietary
Degrees: C
URL: http://www.acreshomecollegeofbarberdesign.com
Phone: (281) 931-5591
Inst. Accred.: NACCAS (2004)

Austin Cosmetology and Permanent Cosmetics Institute
2521 Rutland Dr., Ste. 500, Austin 78758
Type: Private, proprietary
Degrees: C
Phone: (512) 821-2259
Inst. Accred.: NACCAS (2004)

Bessemer Beauty College
9935 Bessemer St., Houston 77034-2701
Type: Private, proprietary
Degrees: C
Phone: (713) 944-6700
Inst. Accred.: NACCAS (2005)

Compu Tech Consultants
811 South Central Expressway, Ste. 500, Richardson 75080
Type: Private, proprietary
Degrees: C
URL: http://www.computechus.com
Phone: (972) 570-0404
Inst. Accred.: COE (2004)

Diamond's Barber College
2812 Miller Ave., Fort Worth 76105
Type: Private, proprietary
Degrees: C
Phone: (817) 534-6203
Inst. Accred.: NACCAS (2005)

Dorsey's Beauty Academy
506 West 19th St., Ste. 251, Houston 77008
Type: Private, proprietary
Degrees: C
Phone: (713) 864-1080
Inst. Accred.: NACCAS (2004)

Gulf States Careers
6118 Ave. L, Galveston 77551
Type: Private, prorpeitary
Degrees: C
Phone: (409) 744-0067
Inst. Accred.: COE (2004)

Hair Expressions Barber School
4027 Ayers St., Corpus Christi 78415-4641
Type: Private, proprietary
Degrees: C
Phone: (361) 225-1041
Inst. Accred.: NACCAS (2004)

International Academy of Cosmetology
4520 San Bernardo Ave., Gateway Shopping Center, # 4,
Laredo 78041-5766
Type: Private, proprietary
Degrees: C
Phone: (956) 725-9229
Inst. Accred.: NACCAS (2004)

Jenissa Beauty Academy
PO Box 203203, Austin 78720-3203
Type: Private, proprietary
Degrees: C
URL: http://www.jenissa.com
Phone: (512) 374-1755
Inst. Accred.: NACCAS (2004)

Mai-trix Beauty College
5999 West 34th St., Houston 77092
Type: Private, proprietary
Degrees: C
Phone: (713) 957-0050
Inst. Accred.: NACCAS (2004)

North West Beauty School
6770 Antoine Dr., Houston 77091-1208
Type: Private, proprietary
Degrees: C
Phone: (713) 263-8333
Inst. Accred.: NACCAS (2004)

The Woodhouse School of Wellness
103 South Glass St., Victoria 77901-8016
Type: Private, proprietary
Degrees: C
URL: http://www.woodhouseschool.com
Phone: (361) 575-9355
Inst. Accred.: NACCAS (2004)

UTAH

Alpha Hair Academy
4160 South 1785 West, Taylorsville 84119
Type: Private, proprietary
Degrees: C
Phone: (801) 955-8686
Inst. Accred.: NACCAS (2004)

Bio Kosmetique Institute of Aesthetics
11075 South† State St., Crescent Office Park, Ste. 21,
Sandy 84070
Type: Private, proprietary
Degrees: C
URL: http://www.biokosmetique.com
Phone: (801) 523-0395
Inst. Accred.: NACCAS (2004)

Capelli Institute of Hair
200 East State Rd., Pleasant Grove 84062
Type: Private, proprietary
Degrees: C
URL: http://capellihair.com
Phone: (801) 785-3113
Inst. Accred.: NACCAS (2005)

DeLeon Academy of Esthetics
385 West 600 North, Lindon 84042
Type: Private, proprietary
Degrees: C
URL: http://www.deleondayspa.com/academy.html
Phone: (801) 796-8111
Inst. Accred.: NACCAS (2004)

Dixie Applied Technology College
55 South 900 East, St. George 84770
Type: Public, state
System: Utah College of Applied Technology
Degrees: C
URL: http://www.dixieatc.org
Phone: (435) 652-7731
Inst. Accred.: COE (2003)

Hobble Creek School of Holistic Esthetics
730 East 300 South, Springville 84663
Type: Private, proprietary
Degrees: C
URL: http://sashealth.com/school_of_holistic_esthetics
Phone: (801) 491-9008
Inst. Accred.: NACCAS (2004)

Image Works Academy of Hair Design, Inc.
77 East 800 North, Spanish Fork 84660
Type: Private, proprietary
Degrees: C
Phone: (801) 798-0448
Inst. Accred.: NACCAS (2004)

Jean's Nails, Etc.
356 North 100 West, Provo 84601
Type: Private, proprietary
Degrees: C
Phone: (801) 377-8267
Inst. Accred.: COE (2004)

Mandalyn Academy, Inc.
1472 East 820 North, Orem 84097
Type: Private, proprietary
Degrees: C
Phone: (801) 762-0900
Inst. Accred.: NACCAS (2004)

Southeast Applied Technology College
375 South Carbon Ave., Price 84501
Type: Public, state
System: Utah College of Applied Technology
Degrees: C
URL: http://www.seatc.ceu.edu
Phone: (435) 613-1438
Inst. Accred.: COE (2003)

Southwest Applied Technology College
510 West 800 South, Cedar City 84720
Type: Public, state
System: Utah College of Applied Technology
Degrees: C
URL: http://www.swatc.tec.ut.us
Phone: (435) 586-2899
Inst. Accred.: COE (2003)

VIRGINIA

Ana Visage Academy
10130 Colvin Run Rd., Great Falls 22066
Type: Private, proprietary
Degrees: C
Phone: (703) 759-2200
Inst. Accred.: COE (2004)

Anointed Hands Christian Cosmetology School
18605 Jefferson Davis Hwy., Triangle 22172
Type: Private, proprietary
Degrees: C
Phone: (540) 720-3917
Inst. Accred.: NACCAS (2004)

Cosmopolitan Beauty and Barber School
4201 John Marr Dr., Ste. 206, Annandale 22003
Type: Private, proprietary
Degrees: C
Phone: (703) 354-5475
Inst. Accred.: NACCAS (2004)

Dominion School of Hair Design
7118 Hayes Shopping Center, Hayes 23072
Type: Private, proprietary
Degrees: C
URL: http://www.dominionschoolofhairdesign.com
Phone: (804) 684-9150
Inst. Accred.: NACCAS (2005)

Trojan Beauty and Barber College
21500 Chesterfield Ave., Ettrick 23803
Type: Private, proprietary
Degrees: C
Phone: (804) 524-9745
Inst. Accred.: NACCAS (2004)

WASHINGTON

Alpine College
10102 East Knox Ave., Ste. 100, Spokane Valley 99206
Type: Private, proprietary
Degrees: C
Phone: (509) 455-5054
Inst. Accred.: COE (2004)

Cascade Beauty College
17160-116th Ave. SE, Renton 98058
Type: Private, proprietary
Degrees: C
Phone: (425) 226-2457
Inst. Accred.: NACCAS (2004)

Lincoln Beauty School, Inc.
702 South 38th St., Tacoma 98418
Type: Private, proprietary
Degrees: C
Phone: (253) 473-0501
Inst. Accred.: NACCAS (2004)

WISCONSIN

Academy of Cosmetology
2310 West Ct. St., Janesville 53545
Type: Private, proprietary
Degrees: C
Phone: (608) 758-4810
Inst. Accred.: NACCAS (2004)

First Class Cosmetology School
322 State St., Beloit 53511
Type: Private, proprietary
Degrees: C
URL: http://www.firstclasscosmetologyschool.com
Phone: (608) 362-5216
Inst. Accred.: NACCAS (2004)

Visions in Hair Design Institute of Cosmetology
7213 West Burleigh St., Milwaukee 53210
Type: Private, proprietary
Degrees: C
Phone: (414) 445-5545
Inst. Accred.: NACCAS (2004)

CANADA

Nightingale Medical Institute
11111 Jasper Ave., Main Flr., Rm. 3C04, Edmonton,
Alberta T5K 0L4
Type: Private, independent
Degrees: C
URL: http://www.nightingaleacademy.com
Phone: (780) 482-8928
Inst. Accred.: COE (2004)

SWITZERLAND

**DCT International Hotel & Business
Management School**
Seestrasse, Vitznau, Switzerland CH 6354
Type: Private, independent
Degrees: C
URL: http://www.dct.ch
Phone: 011 41 41 418-0707
Inst. Accred.: NEASC-CTCI (2001)

Appendices

AN OVERVIEW OF U.S. ACCREDITATION

Accreditation is a process of external quality review used by higher education to scrutinize colleges, universities, and higher education programs for quality assurance and quality improvement. Accreditation in the United States is more than 100 years old, emerging from concerns to protect public health and safety and to serve the public interest.

In the United States, accreditation is carried out by private, nonprofit organizations designed for this specific purpose. External quality review of higher education is a non-governmental enterprise. In other countries, accreditation and quality assurance activities are typically carried out by government.

The United States accreditation structure is decentralized and complex, mirroring the decentralization and complexity of American higher education. The higher education enterprise is made up of approximately 6,900 accredited degree-granting and non–degree-granting institutions. These institutions may be public or private, two- or four-year, nonprofit or for-profit. They spend approximately $230 billion per year, enroll more than 15 million credit students, and employ approximately 2.7 million full- and part-time workers.

Accreditors review colleges and universities in 50 states and a number of other countries. They review many thousands of programs in a range of professions and specialties including, law, medicine, business, nursing, social work, pharmacy, arts, and journalism.

There are three types of accreditors:

Regional accreditors: Accredit public and private, nonprofit and for-profit, two- and four-year institutions. They conduct a comprehensive review of all institutional functions.

National accreditors: Accredit public and private, nonprofit and for-profit, frequently single-purpose institutions, including distance learning colleges and universities, private career institutions, and faith-based colleges and universities.

Specialized and professional accreditors: Accredit specific programs and schools including law schools, medical schools, engineering schools and programs, and health profession programs.

The Purpose of Accreditation

Accreditation serves the following purposes:

Ensuring quality. Accreditation is the primary means by which colleges, universities, and programs ensure quality to students and the public. Accredited status is a signal to students and the public that an institution or program meets at least minimal standards for its faculty, curriculum, student services, and libraries. Accredited status is conveyed only if institutions and programs provide evidence of fiscal stability.

Allowing access to federal funds. Accreditation is required for access to federal funds, such as student aid and other federal programs. The federal government and accreditors sustain a cooperative relationship whereby government relies on accreditors to confirm the quality of institutions and programs in which students enroll using federal student aid funds. Federal student aid funds are available to students only if the institution they are attending is accredited by a recognized accrediting organization. The United States awarded $70 billion in student grants and loans in 2002–2003.

Easing transfer. Accreditation is important to students for a smooth transfer of courses and programs among colleges, universities, and programs. Receiving institutions take note of whether or not the credits a student wishes to transfer have been earned at an accredited institution. Although accreditation is but one among several factors taken into account by receiving institutions, it is viewed carefully and is considered an important indicator of quality.

Engendering employer confidence. The accreditation status of an institution or program is important to employers when evaluating credentials of job applicants and when deciding whether to provide tuition support for current employees seeking additional education.

How Accreditation Operates

Accreditation of institutions and programs take place on a cycle that may range from every few years to as many as every ten years. Accreditation is ongoing—the initial earning of accreditation is not entry to indefinite accredited status. Periodic review is a fact of life for accredited institutions and programs. Self-accreditation is not an option.

An institution or program seeking accreditation must go through a number of steps stipulated by an accrediting organization. These steps involve a combination of several tasks: preparation of evidence of accomplishment by the institution or program; scrutiny of these materials, with a site visit by faculty and administrative peers; and action to determine accreditation status by the accrediting organizations.

The five key features of accreditation are:

Self-study: Institutions and programs prepare a written summary of performance based on accrediting organizations' standards.

Peer review: Accreditation review is conducted primarily by faculty and administrative peers in the profession. These colleagues review the self-study and serve on visiting teams that review institutions and programs after the self-study is completed. Peers comprise the majority of members of the accrediting commissions or boards that make judgments about accrediting status.

Site visit: Accrediting organizations normally send a visiting team to review an institution or program. The self-study provides the foundation for the team visit. Teams, in addition to the peers described above, may also include public members (nonacademics who have an interest in higher education). All team members are volunteers and are generally not compensated.

Action (judgment) by accrediting organization: Accrediting organizations have commissions that affirm accreditation for new institutions and programs, reaffirm accreditation for ongoing institutions and programs, and deny accreditation to institutions and programs.

Ongoing external review: Institutions and programs continue to be reviewed over time on cycles that range from every few years to every ten years. They normally prepare a self-study and undergo a site visit each time.

Holding Accreditors Accountable

Accreditors are accountable to the institutions and programs they accredit. They are accountable to the public and government who have invested heavily in higher education and expect quality. Accreditors also undertake an organizational self-assessment on a routine basis and are required to have internal complaint procedures.

Accreditors undergo a periodic external review of their organizations known as "recognition." Recognition is carried out either by another private organization, the Council for Higher Education Accreditation (CHEA), a national coordinating body for national, regional, and specialized accreditation, or the U.S. Department of Education (USDE). Although accreditation is strictly a nongovernmental activity, recognition is not.

As of 1998–99, nineteen (19) institutional accrediting organizations are or have been recognized by either CHEA or the USDE or both. These organizations accredit more than 6,900 institutions. Sixty-six (66) specialized accrediting organizations are or have been recognized and accredit more than 20,000 programs.

CHEA has five recognition standards by which it reviews accrediting organizations. The standards place primary emphasis on academic quality assurance and improvement for an institution or program. They require accreditors to advance academic quality, demonstrate accountability, encourage purposeful change and needed improvement, employ appropriate and fair procedures in decision making, and continually reassess accreditation practices.

CHEA accreditors are normally reviewed on a ten-year cycle with a five-year interim report. The review is carried out by the CHEA Committee on Recognition, a group of institutional representatives, accreditors, and public members who scrutinize accreditors for CHEA recognition eligibility, and review accreditors based on an accreditor self-study. The review may also include a site visit. The Committee on Recognition makes recommendations to the CHEA governing board to affirm or deny recognition to an accreditor.

The USDE recognition standards place primary emphasis on whether an institution or program is of sufficient quality to qualify for federal funds for student financial aid and other federal programs. These standards require accreditors to maintain criteria or standards in specific areas: student achievement, curricula, faculty, facilities (includes equipment and supplies), fiscal and administrative capacity, student support services, recruiting and admissions practices, measures of the degree and objectives of degrees or credentials offered, record of student complaints, and record of compliance with program responsibilities for student aid as required by the 1965 federal Higher Education Act (Title IV) as amended.

USDE recognition review normally takes place every five years. USDE staff conduct the review based on communication with the accreditor, a written report from the accreditor and, from time to time, a visit to the accreditor. USDE staff make recommendations to the National Advisory Committee on Institutional Quality and Integrity (NACIQI), an appointed group of educators and public members, to recognize or not recognize an accrediting organization. The committee, in turn, recommends action to the U.S. Secretary of Education.

USDE and CHEA recognize many of the same accrediting organizations, but not all. Accreditors seek USDE or CHEA recognition for different reasons. USDE recognition is required for accreditors whose institutions or programs seek eligibility for federal student aid funds. CHEA recognition confers an academic legitimacy on accrediting organizations, helping to solidify the place of these organizations and their institutions and programs in the national higher education community.

Adapted from *An Overview of U.S. Accreditation*, Judith S. Eaton. Available through the courtesy of the Council for Higher Education Accreditation (CHEA) and James JF Forest and Kevin Kinser, eds. *Higher Education in the United States: An Encyclopedia*. Santa Barbara, CA; ABC-CLIO. http://www.higher-ed.org/HEUS/

RECOGNIZED ACCREDITING ORGANIZATIONS

The accrediting activities of institutional and professional associations are periodically evaluated through a formal recognition process by either CHEA, USDE, or both. Specific standards of quality in the accreditation process are ensured through this recognition process.

Key to Accrediting Organizations

Regional Institutional Accrediting Organizations

MSA	Middle States Association of Colleges and Schools, Commission on Higher Education
NWCCU	Northwest Commission on Colleges and Universities
NCA-HLC	North Central Association of Colleges and Schools, Higher Learning Commission
NCA-CASI	North Central Association of Colleges and Schools, Commission on Accreditation and School Improvement, Board of Trustees
NEASC-CIHE	New England Association of Schools and Colleges, Inc., Commission on Institutions of Higher Education
NEASC-CTCI	New England Association of Schools and Colleges, Inc., Commission on Technical and Career Institutions
SACS	Southern Association of Colleges and School, Commission on Colleges
WASC-ACCJC	Western Association of Schools and Colleges, Accrediting Commission for Community and Junior Colleges
WASC-ACSCU	Western Association of Schools and Colleges, Accrediting Commission for Senior Colleges and Universities

National Private Career Accrediting Organizations

ABHES	Accrediting Bureau of Health Education Schools
ACCET	Accrediting Council for Continuing Education and Training
ACCSCT	Accrediting Commission for Career Schools and Colleges of Technology
ACICS	Accrediting Council for Independent Colleges and Schools
COE	Council on Occupational Education
DETC	Distance Education and Training Council Accrediting Commission
NACCAS	National Accrediting Commission for Cosmetology Arts and Sciences

National Faith-based Accrediting Organizations

ABHE	Association for Biblical Higher Education
AARTS	Association of Advanced Rabbinical and Talmudic Schools
ATS	Commission on Accrediting of the Association of Theological Schools
TRACS	Transnational Association of Christian Colleges and Schools

Professional and Specialized Accrediting Organizations

Some professional and specialized accrediting organizations are recognized to accredit entire institutions as well as programs at other accredited and/or non-accredited facilities.

AACSB	AACSB International-The Association to Advance Collegiate Schools of Business
AAFCS	American Association of Family and Consumer Sciences, Council for Accreditation
AALE	American Academy for Liberal Education
AAMFT	American Association for Marriage and Family Therapy, Commission on Accreditation for Marriage and Family Therapy Education
AANA	American Association of Nurse Anesthetists, Council on Accreditation of Nurse Anesthesia Educational Programs
ABA	American Bar Association, Council of the Section of Legal Education and Admissions to the Bar
ABET	Accreditation Board for Engineering and Technology, Inc.
ABFSE-CA	American Board of Funeral Service Education, Committee on Accreditation
ACAOM	Accreditation Commission for Acupuncture and Oriental Medicine
ACBSP	Association of Collegiate Business Schools and Programs
ACCE	American Council for Construction Education
ACEJMC	Accrediting Council on Education in Journalism and Mass Communication
ACF	American Culinary Federation, Inc., Accrediting Commission
ACNM	American College of Nurse-Midwives, Division of Accreditation
ACPE	Accreditation Council for Pharmacy Education
ACPEI	Association for Clinical Pastoral Education, Inc., Accreditation Commission
ADA-CADE	American Dietetic Association, Commission on Accreditation for Dietetics Education
ADA-CDA	American Dental Association, Commission on Dental Accreditation
ALA	American Library Association, Committee on Accreditation
AOA-COCA	American Osteopathic Association, Commission on Osteopathic College Accreditation
AOA-COE	American Optometric Association, Accreditation Council on Optometric Education
AOTA-ACOTE	American Occupational Therapy Association, Accreditation Council for Occupational Therapy Education
APA	American Psychological Association, Committee on Accreditation
APMA	American Podiatric Medical Association, Council on Podiatric Medical Education
APTA	American Physical Therapy Association, Commission on Accreditation in Physical Therapy Education
ARC-PA	Accreditation Review Commission on Education for the Physician Assistant, Inc.
ASHA	American Speech-Language-Hearing Association, Council on Academic Accreditation in Audiology and Speech-Language Pathology
ASLA	American Society of Landscape Architects, Landscape Architectural Accreditation Board
AVMA	American Veterinary Medical Association, Council on Education
CAA	Council on Aviation Accreditation
CAAHEP	Commission on Accreditation of Allied Health Education Programs
CACREP	Council for Accreditation of Counseling and Related Educational Programs
CAHME	Commission on Accreditation of Healthcare Management Education
CCE	Council on Chiropractic Education, Commission on Accreditation
CCNE	Commission on Collegiate Nursing Education
CEA	Commission on English Language Program Accreditation

CEPH ....Council on Education for Public Health
CIDA ....Council for Interior Design Accreditation *(formerly FIDER)*
CMTA.......................Commission on Massage Therapy Accreditation
CNME ....Council on Naturopathic Medical Education
COA ....Commission on Opticianry Accreditation
CORE ....Council on Rehabilitation Education, Commission on Standards and Accreditation
CSWE.......................Council on Social Work Education, Office of Social Work Accreditation
and Educational Excellence
JRCERT ....Joint Review Committee on Education in Radiologic Technology
JRCNMT....................Joint Review Committee on Educational Programs in Nuclear Medicine
Technology
LCME.......................Liaison Committee on Medical Education (even years)
LCME.......................Liaison Committee on Medical Education (odd years)
MACTE....................Montessori Accreditation Council for Teacher Education, Commission on
Accreditation
MEAC.......................Midwifery Education Accreditation Council
NAACLS ....National Accrediting Agency for Clinical Laboratory Science
NAIT.......................National Association of Industrial Technology
NASAD ....National Association of Schools of Art and Design
NASD ....National Association of Schools of Dance
NASM ....National Association of Schools of Music
NASPAA ....National Association of Schools of Public Affairs and Administration,
Commission on Peer Review and Accreditation
NAST ....National Association of Schools of Theatre
NCATE ....National Council for Accreditation of Teacher Education
NLNAC ....National League for Nursing Accreditation Commission, Inc.
NPWH ....National Association of Nurse Practitioners in Women's Health,
Council on Accreditation
NRPA/AALR ....National Recreation and Park Association/American Association for Leisure
and Recreation, Council on Accreditation
PAB ....Planning Accreditation Board *(formerly American Institute of Certified
Planners/Association of Collegiate Schools of Planning, Planning Accreditation
Board)*
SAF ....Society of American Foresters, Commission on Accreditation
TEAC ....Teacher Education Accreditation Council, Accreditation Committee

State-based Accrediting Organization

NYBOR.....................New York Board of Regents

Programs Accredited by Specialized and Professional Programmatic Accrediting Organizations

Accounting ....AACSB International-The Association to Advance Collegiate Schools of Business (AACSB)

Acupuncture ....Accreditation Commission for Acupuncture and Oriental Medicine (ACAOM)

Allied Health ....Commission on Accreditation of Allied Health Education Programs (CAAHEP)

Applied Science......................................Accreditation Board for Engineering and Technology, Inc. (ABET)

Art...National Association of Schools of Art and Design (NASAD)

Audiology...American Speech-Language-Hearing Association (ASHA)

Aviation ....Council on Aviation Accreditation (CAA)

Aviation Technology ....National Association of Industrial Technology (NAIT)

Business ....AACSB International-The Association to Advance Collegiate Schools of Business (AACSB)

                        also   Association of Collegiate Business Schools and Programs (ACBSP)

Chiropractic Education............................Council on Chiropractic Education (CCE)

Clinical Assistant ....National Accrediting Agency for Clinical Laboratory Science (NAACLS)

Clinical Lab Scientist ....National Accrediting Agency for Clinical Laboratory Science (NAACLS)

Clinical Lab Technology ....National Accrediting Agency for Clinical Laboratory Science (NAACLS)

Clinical Pastoral Education......................Association for Clinical Pastoral Education, Inc. (ACPEI)

Clinical Psychology ....American Psychological Association (APA)

Combined Professional-Scientific
  Psychology ....American Psychological Association (APA)

Community Health ....Council on Education for Public Health (CEPH)

Community Health/Preventative
  Medicine ....Council on Education for Public Health (CEPH)

Computer Science ....Accreditation Board for Engineering and Technology, Inc. (ABET)

Construction Education ....American Council for Construction Education (ACCE)

Construction Technology ....National Association of Industrial Technology (NAIT)

Counseling...Council for Accreditation of Counseling and Related Educational Programs (CACREP)

Counseling Psychology ....American Psychological Association (APA)

Culinary Education..................................American Culinary Federation, Inc. (ACF)

Cytogenetic Technology ....National Accrediting Agency for Clinical Laboratory Science (NAACLS)

Dance ....National Association of Schools of Dance (NASD)

Dentistry ....American Dental Association (ADA-CDA)

Design Technology..................................National Association of Industrial Technology (NAIT)

Diagnostic Molecular Scientist................National Accrediting Agency for Clinical Laboratory Science (NAACLS)

Dietetics ....American Dietetic Association (ADA-CADE)

Electronic Technology ....National Association of Industrial Technology (NAIT)

Engineering ....Accreditation Board for Engineering and Technology, Inc. (ABET)

Engineering Technology ....Accreditation Board for Engineering and Technology, Inc. (ABET)

English Language Education ....Commission on English Language Program Accreditation (CEA)

Family and Consumer Science................American Association of Family and Consumer Sciences (AAFCS)

Forestry ....Society of American Foresters (SAF)

Funeral Service Education ....American Board of Funeral Service Education (ABFSE-CA)

Graduate Social Work ....Council on Social Work Education (CSWE)

Health Services Administration ....Commission on Accreditation of Healthcare Management Education (CAHME)

Histologic Technology ....National Accrediting Agency for Clinical Laboratory Science (NAACLS)

Industrial Technology ....National Association of Industrial Technology (NAIT)

Interior Architecture...............................Council for Interior Design Accreditation (CIDA)

Interior Design..Council for Interior Design Accreditation (CIDA)

Journalism..Accrediting Council on Education in Journalism and Mass Communication (ACEJMC)

Landscape Architecture ....American Society of Landscape Architects (ASLA)

Law...American Bar Association (ABA)

Liberal Education....................................American Academy for Liberal Education (AALE)

Librarianship ....American Library Association (ALA)

Manufacturing Technology ....National Association of Industrial Technology (NAIT)

Marriage and Family Therapy ....American Association for Marriage and Family Therapy (AAMFT)

Massage Therapy ....Commission on Massage Therapy Accreditation (CMTA)

Medical Assisiting ....Accrediting Bureau of Health Education Schools (ABHES)
    also   Commission on Accreditation of Allied Health Education Programs (CAAHEP)

Medical Laboratory Technology ....Accrediting Bureau of Health Education Schools (ABHES)

Medicine ....Liaison Committee on Medical Education (LCME)

Midwifery Education ....Midwifery Education Accreditation Council (MEAC)

Montessori Teacher Education ....Montessori Accreditation Council for Teacher Education (MACTE)

Mortuary Science ....American Board of Funeral Service Education (ABFSE-CA)

Music ....National Association of Schools of Music (NASM)

Naturopathic Medicine............................Council on Naturopathic Medical Education (CNME)

Nuclear Medicine Technology ....Joint Review Committee on Educational Programs in Nuclear Medicine Technology (JRCNMT)

Nurse Anesthesia Education ....American Association of Nurse Anesthetists (AANA)

Nurse Practitioner ....National Association of Nurse Practitioners in Women's Health (NPWH)

Nurse-Midwifery ....American College of Nurse-Midwives (ACNM)

Nursing ....National League for Nursing Accreditation Commission, Inc. (NLNAC)

Nursing Education ....Commission on Collegiate Nursing Education (CCNE)

Occupational Therapy ....American Occupational Therapy Association (AOTA)

Occupational Therapy Assisting ....American Occupational Therapy Association (AOTA)

Ophthalmic Lab Technology.....................Commission on Opticianry Accreditation (COA)

Opticianry ....Commission on Opticianry Accreditation (COA)

Optometric Residency ....American Optometric Association (AOA-COE)

Optometric Technician ....American Optometric Association (AOA-COE)

Optometry ....American Optometric Association (AOA-COE)

Osteopathy ....American Osteopathic Association (AOA-COCA)

Pharmacy ....Accreditation Council for Pharmacy Education (ACPE)

Physical Therapy ....American Physical Therapy Association (APTA)

Physical Therapy Assisting......................American Physical Therapy Association (APTA)

Physician Assisting ....Accreditation Review Commission on Education for the Physician Assistant, Inc. (ARC-PA)

Planning ....Planning Accreditation Board (PAB)

Podiatry...American Podiatric Medical Association (APMA)

Practical Nursing ....National League for Nursing Accreditation Commission, Inc. (NLNAC)

Psychology Internship ....American Psychological Association (APA)

Public Administration ....National Association of Schools of Public Affairs and Administration (NASPAA)

Public Health ....Council on Education for Public Health (CEPH)

Radiation Therapy ....Joint Review Committee on Education in Radiologic Technology (JRCERT)

Radiography ....Joint Review Committee on Education in Radiologic Technology (JRCERT)

Recreation and Leisure Services ....National Recreation and Park Association/American Association for Leisure and Recreation (NRPA/AALR)

Rehabilitation Counseling ....Council on Rehabilitation Education (CORE)

School Psychology...................................American Psychological Association (APA)

Social Work ....Council on Social Work Education (CSWE)

Speech-Language Pathology ....American Speech-Language-Hearing Association (ASHA)

Surgeon Assisting ....Accreditation Review Commission on Education for the Physician Assistant, Inc. (ARC-PA)

              also Commission on Accreditation of Allied Health Education Programs (CAAHEP)

Teacher Education ....National Council for Accreditation of Teacher Education (NCATE)

              also Teacher Education Accreditation Council (TEAC)

Theater ....National Association of Schools of Theatre (NAST)

Veterinary Medicine.................................American Veterinary Medical Association (AVMA)

Veterinary Technology ....American Veterinary Medical Association (AVMA)

Detailed Description of Broad Program Categories

Some of the categories in the previous list contain subcategories within the same general field of study.
The following list details the subcategories appearing in this directory.

Allied Health ....Anesthesiologist Assisting, Athletic Training, Blood Bank
Technology, Cardiovascular Technology, Cytotechnology,
Diagnostic Medical Sonography, Electroneurodiagnostic
Technology, EMT-Paramedic, Kinesiotherapy, Medical Assisting,
Medical Illustration, Health Information Administration, Health
Information Technician, Ophthalmic Medical Technology,
Orthotist/Prothetist, Perfusion, Phlebotomy, Physician Assisting,
Radiation Therapy, Radiography, Respiratory Therapy, Respiratory
Therapy Technology, Surgeon Assisting, Surgical Technology

Applied Science.......................................Health Physics, Industrial Hygiene, Industrial Management,
Occupational Health and Safety, Surveying/Geomatics

Dentistry ....Advanced Education in General Dentistry, Combined
Prosthodontics, Combined Prosthodontic/Maxillofacial
Prosthetics, Dental Assisting, Dental Hygiene, Dental Laboratory
Technology, Dental Public Health, Endodontics, General Dentistry,
General Practice Residency, Maxillofacial Prosthetics, Oral and
Maxillofacial Pathology, Oral and Maxillofacial Radiology, Oral and
Maxillofacial Surgery, Orthodontic and Dentofacial Orthopedics,
Pediatric Dentistry, Periodontics, Prosthodontics

Engineering ....Aerospace, Agricultural, Architectural, Bioengineering, Ceramic,
Chemical, Civil, Computer, Construction, Electrical, Engineering
Management, Engineering Mechanics, Engineering
Physics/Science, Environmental/Sanitary, Fire Protection, Food
Process, Forest, General, Geological/Geophysical, Industrial,
Information Systems, Manufacturing, Materials, Mechanical,
Metallurgical, Micro/Nano-Engineering, Mineral, Mining, Naval
Architecture/Marine, Nuclear, Ocean, Optical/Optics, Paper,
Petroleum, Plastics, Polymer, Radiological Health, Software,
Surveying, Systems, Telecommunications, Textile, Transportation,
Welding

Engineering Technology ....Aerospace, Agricultural, Air Conditioning, Apparel, Architectural,
Automated Systems, Automation-Robotic Technology,
Automotive, Bioengineering, Biomedical, Ceramic, Chemical,
Civil/Construction, Computer, Electrical, Electromechanical,
Energy, Environmental/Sanitary, Facilities, Fire Protection/Safety,
General, General Drafting/Design, Industrial, Information
Systems, Instrumentation, Management, Manufacturing, Marine
Group, Mechanical, Mechanical Drafting/Design, Mining, Naval
Architecture/Marine, Nuclear, Operations Technology,
Optical/Optics, Packaging, Petroleum, Plastics, Process/Piping
Design, Quality Technology, Software, Surveying, Systems,
Telecommunications, Textile, Welding

National Private Career Accrediting Organizations

Accrediting Bureau of Health Education Schools (ABHES)
Board of Commissioners
Carol A. Moneymaker, Executive Director
7777 Leesburg Pike, Ste. 314N
Falls Church, VA 22043
(703) 917-9503, Fax: (703) 917-9504
http://www.abhes.org

Accrediting Commission of Career Schools and Colleges of Technology (ACCSCT)
Elise Scanlon, Executive Director
2101 Wilson Blvd., Ste. 302
Arlington, VA 22201
(703) 247-4212, Fax: (703) 247-4533
http://www.accsct.org

Accrediting Council for Continuing Education and Training (ACCET)
Roger J. Williams, Executive Director
1722 N Street, NW
Washington, DC 20036
(202) 955-1113, Fax: (202) 955-1118
http://www.accet.org

Accrediting Council for Independent Colleges and Schools (ACICS)
Sheryl Moody, Executive Director
750 First Street, NE, Ste. 980
Washington, DC 20002-4241
(202) 336-6780, Fax: (202) 842-2593
http://www.acics.org

Council on Occupational Education (COE)
Gary Puckett, Executive Director
41 Perimeter Ctr. E., NE, Ste. 640
Atlanta, GA 30346
(800) 917-2081, Fax: (770) 396-3790
www.council.org

Distance Education and Training Council Accrediting Commission (DETC)
Michael P. Lambert, Executive Director
1601 Eighteenth Street, NW
Washington, DC 20009-2529
(202) 234-5100, Fax: (202) 332-1386
http://www.detc.org

National Accrediting Commission on Cosmetology Arts and Sciences, Inc. (NACCAS)
Christopher Walck, Executive Director
4401 Ford Ave., Ste. 1300
Alexandria, VA 22302
(703) 600-7600, Fax: (703) 379-2200
http://www.naccas.org

National Faith-based Accrediting Organizations

Association for Biblical Higher Education (ABHE)
Commission on Accreditation
Larry McKinney, Executive Director
5575 S. Semoran Blvd., Ste. 26
Orlando, FL 32822-1781
(407) 207-0808, Fax: (407) 207-0840
http://www.abhe.org

Association of Advanced Rabbinical and Talmudic Schools (AARTS)
Bernard Fryshman, Executive Vice President
11 Broadway, Ste. 405
New York, NY 10004-1392
(212) 363-1991, Fax: (212) 533-5335

Commission on Accrediting of the Association of Theological Schools (ATS)
Daniel O. Aleshire, Executive Director
10 Summit Park Dr.
Pittsburgh, PA 15275-1103
(412) 788-6505, Fax: (412) 788-6510
http://www.ats.edu

Transnational Association of Christian Colleges and Schools (TRACS)
Accreditation Commission
Russell G. Fitzgerald, Executive Director
PO Box 328
Forest, VA 24551
(434) 525-9539, Fax: (434) 525-9538
http://www.tracs.org

Regional Institutional Accrediting Organizations

Middle States Association of Colleges and Schools (MSA-CHE)
Commission on Higher Education
Jean Avnet Morse, Executive Director
3624 Market Street
Philadelphia, PA 19104-2680
(267) 284-5000, Fax: (215) 662-5501
http://www.msache.org

New England Association of Schools and Colleges (NEASC-CIHE)
Commission on Institutions of Higher Education
Barbara Brittingham, Director
209 Burlington Rd.
Bedford, MA 01730-1433
(781) 271-0022, Fax: (781) 271-0950
http://www.neasc.org

New England Association of Schools and Colleges (NEASC-CTCI)
Commission on Technical and Career Institutions
Paul Bento, Director
209 Burlington Rd.
Bedford, MA 01730-1433
(781) 271-0022, Fax: (781) 271-0950
http://www.neasc.org

North Central Association of Colleges and Schools (NCA-HLC)
The Higher Learning Commission
Steven D. Crow, Executive Director
30 N. LaSalle Street, Ste. 2400
Chicago, IL 60602-2504
(312) 263-0456, Fax: (312) 263-7462
http://www.ncahigherlearningcommission.org

Northwest Commission on Colleges and Universities (NWCCU)
Sandra E. Elman, President
8060 165th Ave., NE, Ste. 100
Redmond, WA 98052
(425) 558-4224, Fax: (425) 376-0596
http://www.nwccu.org

Southern Association of Colleges and Schools (SACS)
Commission on Colleges
Belle S. Whelan, President
1866 Southern Lane
Decatur, GA 30033-4097
(404) 679-4500, Fax: (404) 679-4525
http://www.sacscoc.org

Western Association of Schools and Colleges (WASC-ACSCU)
Accrediting Commission for Senior Colleges and Universities
Ralph A. Wolff, Executive Director
985 Atlantic Ave., Ste. 100
Alameda, CA 94501
(510) 748-9001, Fax: (510) 748-9797
http://www.wascweb.org

Western Association of Schools and Colleges (WASC-ACCJC)
Accrediting Commission for Community and Junior Colleges
Barbara A. Beno, President
10 Commercial Blvd., Ste. 204
Novato, CA 94949-6175
(415) 506-0234, Fax: (415) 506-0238
http://www.accjc.org

State-based Accrediting Organization

New York State Board of Regents (NYBOR)
The Commissioner of Education
Richard Mills, Commissioner of Education
State Education Dept., The University of the State of New York
Albany, NY 12224
(518) 474-5844, Fax: (518) 474-4909
http://www.nysed.gov

Specialized and Professional Programmatic Accrediting Organizations

AACSB International-The Association to Advance Collegiate Schools of Business (AACSB)
Jerry E. Trapnell, Executive Vice-President and Chief Accreditation Officer
777 S. Harbour Island Blvd., Ste. 750
Tampa, FL 33602
(813) 769-6500, Fax: (813) 769-6559
http://www.aacsb.edu

Accreditation Board for Engineering and Technology, Inc. (ABET)
Applied Science Accreditation Commission (ASAC)
Computing Accreditation Commission (CAC)
Engineering Accreditation Commission (EAC)
Technology Accreditation Commission (TAC)
George D. Peterson, Executive Director
111 Market Place, Ste. 1050
Baltimore, MD 21202
(410) 347-7700, Fax: (410) 625-2238
http://www.abet.org

Accreditation Commission for Acupuncture and Oriental Medicine (ACAOM)
Dort S. Bigg, Executive Director
Maryland Trade Ctr. 3, 7501 Greenway Ctr. Dr., Ste. 820
Greenbelt, MD 20770
(301) 313-0855, Fax: (301) 313-0912
http://www.acaom.org

Accreditation Council for Pharmacy Education (ACPE)
Peter H. Vlasses, Executive Director
20 N. Clark Street, Ste. 2500
Chicago, IL 60602-5109
(312) 664-3575, Fax: (312) 664-4652
http://www.acpe-accredit.org

Accreditation Review Commission on Education for the Physician Assistant, Inc. (ARC-PA)
John E. McCarty, Executive Director
12000 Findley Rd., Ste. 240
Duluth, GA 30097
(770) 476-1224, Fax: (770) 476-1249
http://www.arc-pa.org

Accrediting Council on Education in Journalism and Mass Communication (ACEJMC)
Susanne Shaw, Executive Director
Stauffer-Flint Hall, 1435 Jayhawk Blvd.
Lawrence, KS 66045-7575
(785) 864-3986, Fax: (785) 864-5225
http://www.ukans.edu/~acejmc or
http://www.ku.edu/~acejmc

American Academy for Liberal Education (AALE)
Jeffrey D. Wallin, President
1710 Rhode Island Ave., NW, 4th Floor
Washington, DC 20036
(202) 452-8611, Fax: (202) 452-8620
http://www.aale.org

American Association for Marriage and Family Therapy (AAMFT)
Commission on Accreditation for Marriage and Family Therapy Education
Donald B. Kaveny, Director of Accreditation Services
112 S. Alfred Street
Alexandria, VA 22314-3061
(703) 838-9808, Fax: (703) 253-0508
http://www.aamft.org

American Association of Family and Consumer Sciences (AAFCS)
Council for Accreditation
Karen S. Tucker, Executive Director
1555 King Street
Alexandria, VA 22314
(703) 706-4600, Fax: (703) 706-4663
www.aafcs.org

American Association of Nurse Anesthetists (AANA)
Council on Accreditation of Nurse Anesthesia Educational Programs
Francis Gerbasi, Director of Accreditation and Education
222 S. Prospect Ave., Ste. 304
Park Ridge, IL 60068-4010
(847) 692-7050, Fax: (847) 692-7137
http://www.aana.com

American Bar Association (ABA)
Council of the Section of Legal Education and Admissions to the Bar
John A. Sebert, Consultant on Legal Education, ABA
321 N. Clark Street, 21st Floor
Chicago, IL 60610
(312) 988-6738, Fax: (312) 988-5681
http://www.abanet.org/legaled/approvedlawschools/approved.html

American Board of Funeral Service Education (ABFSE-CA)
Committee on Accreditation
Michael Smith, Executive Director
3432 Ashland Ave., Ste. U
St. Joseph, MO 64506
(816) 233-3747, Fax: (816) 233-3793
http://www.abfse.org

American College of Nurse-Midwives (ACNM)
Division of Accreditation
Deanne Williams, Executive Director
8403 Colesville Rd., Ste. 1550
Silver Spring, MD 20910-6374
(240) 485-1800, Fax: (240) 485-1818
http://www.midwife.org

American Council for Construction Education (ACCE)
Michael Holland, Executive Vice President
1717 N. Loop 1604 E., Ste. 320
San Antonio, TX 78232-1570
(210) 495-6161, Fax: (210) 495-6168
http://www.acce-hq.org

American Culinary Federation, Inc. (ACF)
Accrediting Commission
Candice Childers, Accreditation Program Coordinator
180 Ctr. Place Way Street
St. Augustine, FL 32095
(904) 824-4468, Fax: (904) 825-4758
http://www.acfchefs.org

American Dental Association (ADA-CDA)
Commission on Dental Accreditation
Laura Neumann, Director
211 E. Chicago Ave., 18th Floor
Chicago, IL 60611-2678
(312) 440-2940, Fax: (312) 440-2915
http://www.ada.org

American Dietetic Association (ADA-CADE)
Commission on Accreditation for Dietetics Education
Beverly E. Mitchell, Director
120 S. Riverside Plaza, Ste. 2000
Chicago, IL 60606-6995
(312) 899-4872, Fax: (312) 899-4817
http://www.eatright.org/cade

American Library Association (ALA)
Committee on Accreditation
Karen O'Brien, Acting Director
50 E. Huron Street, Office for Accreditation
Chicago, IL 60611
(800) 545-2433 x2435, Fax: (312) 280-2433
http://www.ala.org/accreditation.html

American Massage Therapy Association (CMTA)
Commission on Massage Therapy Accreditation
Ellen Bateman, Executive Director
1007 Church Street, Ste. 302
Evanston, IL 60201
(847) 869-5039, Fax: (847) 869-6739
http://www.comta.org

American Occupational Therapy Association (AOTA)
Accreditation Council for Occupational Therapy Education
Sue Graves, Senior Program Administrator in Accreditation
4720 Montgomery Lane, PO Box 31220
Bethesda, MD 20824-1220
(301) 652-6611, Fax: (301) 652-7711
http://www.aota.org

American Optometric Association (AOA-COE)
Accreditation Council on Optometric Education
Joyce Urbeck, Administrative Director
243 N. Lindbergh Blvd.
St. Louis, MO 63141-7881
(314) 991-4100, Fax: (314) 991-4101
http://www.aoanet.org

American Osteopathic Association (AOA-COCA)
Commission on Osteopathic College Accreditation
Konrad C. Miskowicz-Retz, Director, Department of Education
Department of Education, 142 E. Ontario Street
Chicago, IL 60611-2864
(312) 202-8096, Fax: (312) 202-8396
http://do-online.osteotech.org

American Physical Therapy Association (APTA)
Commission on Accreditation in Physical Therapy Education
Mary Jane Harris, Director
1111 N. Fairfax Street
Alexandria, VA 22314-3229
(703) 684-2782, Fax: (703) 684-7343
http://www.apta.org

American Podiatric Medical Association (APMA)
Council on Podiatric Medical Education
Alan R. Tinkleman, Director
9312 Old Georgetown Rd.
Bethesda, MD 20814-1612
(301) 581-9290, Fax: (301) 571-4903
http://www.apma.org/cpme

American Psychological Association (APA)
Committee on Accreditation
Susan F. Zlotlow, Director, Program Consultation and Accreditation
750 First Street, NE
Washington, DC 20002-4242
(202) 336-5979, Fax: (202) 336-5978
http://www.apa.org/ed/accred.html

American Society of Landscape Architects (ASLA)
Landscape Architectural Accreditation Board
Ronald C. Leighton, Accreditation Manager
636 I Street, NW
Washington, DC 20001-3736
(202) 898-2444, Fax: (202) 898-1185
http://www.asla.org

American Speech-Language-Hearing Association (ASHA)
Council on Academic Accreditation in Audiology and Speech-Language Pathology
Patrima L. Tice, Director of Credentialing
10801 Rockville Pike
Rockville, MD 20852
(301) 897-5700, Fax: (301) 571-0481
http://www.asha.org

American Veterinary Medical Association (AVMA)
Council on Education
Donald G. Simmons, Director of Education and Research
1931 N. Meacham Rd., Ste. 100
Schaumburg, IL 60173-4360
(847) 925-8070, Fax: (847) 925-1329
http://www.avma.org

Association for Clinical Pastoral Education, Inc. (ACPEI)
Accreditation Commission
Teresa E. Snorton, Executive Director
1549 Clairmont Rd., Ste. 103
Decatur, GA 30033-4611
(404) 320-1472, Fax: (404) 320-0849
http://www.acpe.edu

Association of Collegiate Business Schools and Programs (ACBSP)
Douglas Viehland, Executive Director
7007 College Blvd., Ste. 420
Overland Park, KS 66211
(913) 339-9356, Fax: (913) 339-6226
http://www.acbsp.org

Commission on Accreditation of Allied Health Education Programs (CAAHEP)
CHEA recognizes the Commission on Accreditation of Allied Health Education Programs (CAAHEP) as an umbrella agency for 17 review committees representing professional organizations collaborating in the accreditation of programs in the following areas of allied health. All questions concerning accreditation of these programs should be directed to CAAHEP at the address given. The review committees are:
- Accreditation Committee-Perfusion Education
- Accreditation Review Committee for the Anesthesiologists Assistant
- Accreditation Review Committee for the Medical Illustrator
- Accreditation Review Committee on Education in Surgical Technology
- Committee on Accreditation for Respiratory Care
- Committee on Accreditation for Education in Electroneurodiagnostic Technology
- Committee on Accreditation of Education for Polysomnographic Technologists
- Committee on Accreditation of Education Programs for Kinesiotherapy
- Committee on Accreditation for the Exercise Sciences
- Committee on Accreditation of Educational Programs for the Emergency Medical Services Professions
- Committee on Accreditation of Specialist in Blood Bank Technology Schools
- Curriculum Review Board of the American Association of Medical Assistants' Endowment
- Cytotechnology Programs Review Committee
- Joint Review Committee on Education in Cardiovascular Technology
- Joint Review Committee on Education in Diagnostic Medical Sonography
- Joint Review Committee on Educational Programs in Athletic Training
- National Commission on Orthotic and Prosthetic Education

Kathleen Megivern, Executive Director
1361 Park St.
Clearwater, FL 33756
(727) 210-2350, Fax: (727) 210-2354
http://www.caahep.org

Commission on Accreditation of Healthcare Management Education (CAHME)
John S. Lloyd, President/CEO
Pamela S. Jenness, Director of Accreditation Operations
2000 14th Street N., Ste. 780
Arlington, VA 22201
(703) 894-0960, Fax: (703) 894-0941
http://www.cahmeweb.org

Commission on Collegiate Nursing Education (CCNE)
Jennifer L. Butlin, Director
One Dupont Cir. NW, Ste. 530
Washington, DC 20036-1120
(202) 887-6791, Fax: (202) 887-8476
http://www.aacn.nche.edu/accreditation

Commission on English Language Program Accreditation (CEA)
Teresa O'Donnell, Executive Director
1725 Duke Street, Ste. 500
Alexandria, VA 22314-3457
(703) 519-2070, Fax: (703) 683-8099
http://www.cea-accredit.org

Commission on Opticianry Accreditation (COA)
Tamara A.L. Halstead, Director of Accreditation
PO Box 3073
Merrifield, VA 22116-3073
(703) 940-9134, Fax: (703) 940-9135
http://www.coaccreditation.com

Council for Accreditation of Counseling and Related Educational Programs (CACREP)
Carol L. Bobby, Executive Director
5999 Stevenson Ave.
Alexandria, VA 22304-3302
(703) 823-9800, Fax: (703) 823-1581
http://www.cacrep.org

Council for Interior Design Accreditation (CIDA)
Kayem Dunn, Executive Director
146 Monroe Ctr., NW, Ste. 1318
Grand Rapids, MI 49503-2822
(616) 458-0400, Fax: (616) 458-0460
http://www.accredit.id.org

Council on Aviation Accreditation (CAA)
Gary W. Kiteley, Executive Director
3410 Skyway Dr.
Auburn, AL 36830
(334) 844-2431, Fax: (334) 844-2432
http://www.caaaccreditation.org

Council on Chiropractic Education (CCE)
Commission on Accreditation
Martha S. O'Connor, Executive Vice President
8049 N. 85th Way
Scottsdale, AZ 85258-4321
(480) 443-8877, Fax: (480) 483-7333
http://www.cce-usa.org

Council on Education for Public Health (CEPH)
Laura Rasar King, Acting Executive Director
800 Eye Street, NW, Ste. 202
Washington, DC 20001-3710
(202) 789-1050, Fax: (202) 789-1895
http://www.ceph.org

Council on Naturopathic Medical Education (CNME)
Daniel Seitz, Executive Director
PO Box 323
Johnson, VT 05656
(802) 635-7090, Fax: (802) 635-7492
http://www.cnme.org

Council on Rehabilitation Education (CORE)
Commission on Standards and Accreditation
Donald C. Linkowski, Executive Director
1835 Rohlwing Rd., Ste. E
Rolling Meadows, IL 60008
(847) 394-1785, Fax: (847) 394-2108
http://www.core-rehab.org

Council on Social Work Education (CSWE)
Office of Social Work Accreditation and Educational Excellence
Dean Pierce, Director
1725 Duke Street, Ste. 500
Alexandria, VA 22314-3457
(703) 683-8080, Fax: (703) 683-8099
http://www.cswe.org

Joint Review Committee on Education in Radiologic Technology (JRCERT)
Joanne S. Greathouse, Chief Executive Officer
20 N. Wacker Dr., Ste. 2850
Chicago, IL 60606-2901
(312) 704-5300, Fax: (312) 704-5304
http://www.jrcert.org

Joint Review Committee on Educational Programs in Nuclear Medicine Technology (JRCNMT)
Elaine Cuklanz, Executive Director
PMB #418, 1 Second Ave. E., Ste. C
Polson, MT 59860-2320
(406) 883-0003, Fax: (406) 883-0022
http://www.jrcnmt.org

Liaison Committee on Medical Education (EVEN) (LCME)
Robert Eaglen, Assistant LCME Secretary
Association of American Medical Colleges, 2450 N Street, NW
Washington, DC 20037
(202) 828-0596, Fax: (202) 828-1125
http://www.lcme.org

Liaison Committee on Medical Education (ODD) (LCME)
Barbara Barzansky, Assistant LCME Secretary
American Medical Association, 515 N. State Street
Chicago, IL 60610
(312) 464-4933, Fax: (312) 464-5830
http://www.lcme.org

Midwifery Education Accreditation Council (MEAC)
Mary Ann Baul, Executive Director
20 E. Cherry Ave.
Flagstaff, AZ 86001-4607
(928) 214-0997, Fax: (928) 773-9694
http://www.meacschools.org

Montessori Accreditation Council for Teacher Education (MACTE)
Commission on Accreditation
Gretchen Warner, Executive Director
524 Main Street, Ste. 202
Racine, WI 53403
(262) 595-3335, Fax: (262) 595-3332
http://www.macte.org

National Accrediting Agency for Clinical Laboratory Science (NAACLS)
Olive M. Kimball, Chief Executive Officer
8410 W. Bryn Mawr Ave., Ste. 670
Chicago, IL 60631-3415
(773) 714-8880, Fax: (773) 714-8886
http://www.naacls.org

National Association of Industrial Technology (NAIT)
Rick Coscarelli, Executive Director
3300 Washtenaw Ave., Ste. 220
Ann Arbor, MI 48104-4200
(734) 677-0720, Fax: (734) 677-0046
http://www.nait.org

National Association of Nurse Practitioners in Women's Health (NPWH)
Council on Accreditation
Susan Wysocki, Executive Director
503 Capitol Court, NE, Ste. 300
Washington, DC 20005
(202) 543-9693, Fax: (202) 543-9858
http://www.npwh.org

National Association of Schools of Art and Design (NASAD)
Samuel Hope, Executive Director
11250 Roger Bacon Dr., Ste. 21
Reston, VA 20190
(703) 437-0700, Fax: (703) 437-6312
http://www.arts-accredit.org

National Association of Schools of Dance (NASD)
Samuel Hope, Executive Director
11250 Roger Bacon Dr., Ste. 21
Reston, VA 20190
(703) 437-0700, Fax: (703) 437-6312
http://www.arts-accredit.org

National Association of Schools of Music (NASM)
Samuel Hope, Executive Director
11250 Roger Bacon Dr., Ste. 21
Reston, VA 20190
(703) 437-0700, Fax: (703) 437-6312
http://www.arts-accredit.org

National Association of Schools of Public Affairs and Administration (NASPAA)
Commission on Peer Review and Accreditation
Jinla Byrne, Director of Accreditation
1120 G Street, NW, Ste. 730
Washington, DC 20005
(202) 628-8965, Fax: (202) 626-4978
http://www.naspaa.org

National Association of Schools of Theatre (NAST)
Samuel Hope, Executive Director
11250 Roger Bacon Dr., Ste. 21
Reston, VA 20190
(703) 437-0700, Fax: (703) 437-6312
http://www.arts-accredit.org

National Council for Accreditation of Teacher Education (NCATE)
Arthur E. Wise, President
2010 Massachusetts Ave, NW, Ste. 500
Washington, DC 20036-1023
(202) 466-7496, Fax: (202) 296-6620
http://www.ncate.org

National League for Nursing Accreditation Commission, Inc. (NLNAC)
Patricia R. Forni, Acting Executive Director and Chair
61 Broadway, 33rd Floor
New York, NY 10006
(212) 363-5555, Fax: (212) 812-0390
http://www.nlnac.org

National Recreation and Park Association/American Association for Leisure and Recreation (NRPA/AALR)
Council on Accreditation
Lori Klinedinst, Accreditation Coordinator
22377 Belmont Ridge Rd.
Ashburn, VA 20148-4501
(703) 858-0784, Fax: (703) 858-0794
http://www.nrpa.org

Planning Accreditation Board (PAB)
Shonagh Merits, Executive Director
122 South Michigan Ave., Ste. 1600
Chicago, IL 60603
(312) 334-1271, Fax: (312) 334-1273
http://www.netins.net/showcase/pab_fi66

Society of American Foresters (SAF)
Commission on Accreditation
Terry Clark, Associate Director of Science and Education
5400 Grosvenor Lane
Bethesda, MD 20814-2198
(301) 897-8720, Fax: (301) 897-3690
http://www.safnet.org

Teacher Education Accreditation Council (TEAC)
Accreditation Committee
Frank B. Murray, President
One Dupont Cir. NW, Ste. 320
Washington, DC 20036-0110
(202) 466-7236, Fax: (202) 466-7238
http://www.teac.org

Recognized and Participating Organizations 2005

This chart lists regional, faith-based, private career, and specialized accreditors that are or have been recognized by the Council for Higher Education Accreditation (CHEA) or the U.S. Department of Education (USDE) or both. Organizations identified by (●) are recognized; (—) indicates those not currently recognized. This symbol (O) identifies accrediting organizations that were formerly recognized.

CHEA-recognized organizations must meet CHEA eligibility standards (*www.chea.org/recognition/recognition.asp*). Accreditors exercise independent judgment about whether to seek CHEA recognition. For USDE recognition, accreditation from the organization is used by an institution or program to establish eligibility to participate in federal student aid or other federal programs (*www.ed.gov/about/offices/list/ope/index.html*). Some accreditors cannot be considered for USDE recognition because they do not provide access to federal funds. Other accreditors have chosen not to pursue USDE recognition.

Because CHEA affiliation and USDE recognition depend on a range of factors, readers are strongly cautioned against making judgments about the quality of an accrediting organization and its institutions and programs based solely on CHEA or USDE status. Additional inquiry is essential. If you have any questions about the CHEA affiliation or USDE recognition status of an accreditor, please contact the accrediting organization.

ACCREDITOR	CHEA-Recognized Organization	USDE-Recognized Organization
REGIONAL ACCREDITING ORGANIZATIONS		
Middle States Association of Colleges and Schools, Commission on Higher Education	●	●
New England Association of Schools and Colleges, Commission on Institutions of Higher Education	●	●
New England Association of Schools and Colleges, Commission on Technical and Career Institutions	●	●
North Central Association of Colleges and Schools, The Higher Learning Commission	●	●
Northwest Commission on Colleges and Universities	●	●
Southern Association of Colleges and Schools, Commission on Colleges	●	●
Western Association of Schools and Colleges, Accrediting Commission for Community and Junior Colleges	●	●
Western Association of Schools and Colleges, Accrediting Commission for Senior Colleges and Universities	●	●
PRIVATE CAREER ACCREDITING ORGANIZATIONS		
Accrediting Bureau of Health Education Schools	—	●
Accrediting Commission of Career Schools and Colleges of Technology	—	●
Accrediting Council for Continuing Education and Training	—	●
Accrediting Council for Independent Colleges and Schools	●	●
Council on Occupational Education	—	●
Distance Education and Training Council Accrediting Commission	●	●
National Accrediting Commission on Cosmetology Arts and Sciences, Inc.	—	●

Source: *2003 CHEA Almanac of External Quality Review.* Washington, DC: Council for Higher Education Accreditation, 2003, revised November 2005.

ACCREDITOR	CHEA-Recognized Organization	USDE-Recognized Organization
FAITH-BASED ACCREDITING ORGANIZATIONS		
Association for Biblical Higher Education, Commission on Accreditation	●	●
Association of Advanced Rabbinical and Talmudic Schools, Accreditation Commission	●	●
Commission on Accrediting of the Association of Theological Schools	●	●
Transnational Association of Christian Colleges and Schools, Accreditation Commission	●	●
SPECIALIZED AND PROFESSIONAL ACCREDITING ORGANIZATIONS		
AACSB International—The Association to Advance Collegiate Schools of Business	●	○
Accreditation Board for Engineering and Technology, Inc.	●	○
Accreditation Commission for Acupuncture and Oriental Medicine	—	●
Accreditation Council for Pharmacy Education	●	●
Accredition Review Commission on Education for the Physician Assistant, Inc.	●	—
Accrediting Council on Education in Journalism and Mass Communication	●	○
American Academy for Liberal Education	—	●
American Association for Marriage and Family Therapy, Commission on Accreditation for Marriage and Family Therapy Education	●	●
American Association of Family and Consumer Sciences, Council for Accreditation	●	—
American Association of Nurse Anesthetists, Council on Accreditation of Nurse Anesthesia Educational Programs	●	●
American Bar Association, Council of the Section of Legal Education and Admissions to the Bar	—	●
American Board of Funeral Service Education, Committee on Accreditation	●	●
American College of Nurse-Midwives, Division of Accreditation	—	●
American Council for Construction Education	●	○
American Counseling Association, Council for Accreditation of Counseling and Related Educational Programs	●	—
American Culinary Federation, Inc.	●	○
American Dental Association, Commission on Dental Accreditation	—	●
American Dietetic Association, Commission on Accreditation for Dietetics Education	●	●
American Library Association, Committee on Accreditation	●	○
American Occupational Therapy Association, Accreditation Council for Occupational Therapy Education	●	●
American Optometric Association, Accreditation Council on Optometric Education	●	●
American Osteopathic Association, Commission on Osteopathic College Accreditation	○	●
American Physical Therapy Association, Commission on Accreditation in Physical Therapy Education	●	●
American Podiatric Medical Association, Council on Podiatric Medical Education	●	●
American Psychological Association, Committee on Accreditation	●	●
American Society for Microbiology/American College of Microbiology	—	○

○ *Accreditors that were not recognized by CHEA or USDE in 2005–2006 but have been recognized in prior years.*

ACCREDITOR	CHEA-Recognized Organization	USDE-Recognized Organization
SPECIALIZED AND PROFESSIONAL ACCREDITING ORGANIZATIONS (Continued)		
American Society of Landscape Architects, Landscape Architectural Accreditation Board	●	○
American Speech-Language-Hearing Association, Council on Academic Accreditation in Audiology and Speech-Language Pathology	●	●
American Veterinary Medical Association, Council on Education	●	●
Association for Clinical Pastoral Education, Inc., Accreditation Commission	—	●
Association of Collegiate Business Schools and Programs	●	○
Commission on Accreditation of Allied Health Education Programs	●	○
Commission on Accreditation of Healthcare Management Education	●	●
Commission on Collegiate Nursing Education	●	●
Commission on English Language Program Accreditation	—	●
Commission on Massage Therapy Accreditation	—	●
Commission on Opticianry Accreditation	—	●
Council for Interior Design Education Accreditation	●	○
Council on Aviation Accreditation	●	—
Council on Chiropractic Education, Commission on Accreditation	●	●
Council on Education for Public Health	—	●
Council on Naturopathic Medical Education	—	●
Council on Rehabilitation Education, Commission on Standards and Accreditation	●	○
Council on Social Work Education, Office of Social Work Accreditation and Educational Excellence	●	○
Joint Review Committee on Education in Radiologic Technology	●	●
Joint Review Committee on Educational Programs in Nuclear Medicine Technology	●	●
Liaison Committee on Medical Education	●	●
Midwifery Education Accreditation Council	—	●
Montessori Accreditation Council for Teacher Education, Commission on Accreditation	—	●
National Accrediting Agency for Clinical Laboratory Sciences	●	●
National Architectural Accrediting Board, Inc.	—	○
National Association of Industrial Technology	●	○
National Association of Nurse Practitioners in Women's Health, Council on Accreditation	—	●
National Association of Schools of Art and Design	●	●
National Association of Schools of Dance	●	●
National Association of Schools of Music	●	●
National Association of Schools of Public Affairs and Administration, Commission on Peer Review and Accreditation	●	—

○ Accreditors that were not recognized by CHEA or USDE in 2005–2006 but have been recognized in prior years.

ACCREDITOR	CHEA-Recognized Organization	USDE-Recognized Organization
SPECIALIZED AND PROFESSIONAL ACCREDITING ORGANIZATIONS (*Continued*)		
National Association of Schools of Theatre	●	●
National Council for Accreditation of Teacher Education	●	●
National Environmental Health Science and Protection Accreditation Council	—	○
National League for Nursing, Accreditation Commission, Inc.	●	●
National Recreation and Park Association/American Association for Leisure and Recreation, Council on Accreditation	●	—
Planning Accreditation Board	●	—
Society of American Foresters	●	○
Teacher Education Accreditation Council	●	●
United States Catholic Conference, Commission on Certification and Accreditation	—	○

○ *Accreditors that were not recognized by CHEA or USDE in 2005–2006 but have been recognized in prior years.*

Other Recognized Accrediting Organizations

Two accrediting organizations recognized by the U.S. Department of Education are not included in the preceding chart developed by the Council for Higher Education Accreditation.

The *North Central Association of Colleges and Schools, Commission on Accreditation and School Improvement* accredits schools ranging from pre-kindergarten through postsecondary. Only the adult education, vocational, and non-degree granting postsecondary schools they evaulate are included in this directory.

The *New York Board of Regents* accredits postsecondary institutions only within the confines of the State of New York.

JOINT STATEMENT ON TRANSFER AND AWARD OF ACADEMIC CREDIT

The following set of guidelines has been developed by the three national associations whose member institutions are directly involved in the transfer and award of academic credit: the American Association of Collegiate Registrars and Admissions Officers, the American Council on Education, and the Council for Higher Education Accreditation. The need for such a statement came from an awareness of the growing complexity of transfer policies and practices, which have been brought about, in part, by the changing nature of postsecondary education. With increasing frequency, students are pursuing their education in a variety of institutional and extrainstitutional settings. Social equity and the intelligent use of resources require that validated learning be recognized wherever it takes place.

The statement is thus intended to serve as a guide for institutions developing or reviewing policies dealing with transfer, acceptance, and award of credit. "Transfer" as used here refers to the movement of students from one college, university, or other education provider to another and to the process by which credits representing educational experiences, courses, degrees, or credentials that are awarded by an education provider are accepted or not accepted by a receiving institution.

Basic Assumptions

This statement is directed to institutions of postsecondary education and others concerned with the transfer of academic credit among institutions and the award of academic credit for learning that takes place at another institution or education provider. Basic to this statement is the principle that each institution is responsible for determining its own policies and practices with regard to the transfer, acceptance, and award of credit. Institutions are encouraged to review their policies and practices periodically to assure that they accomplish the institutions' objectives and that they function in a manner that is fair and equitable to students. General statements of policy such as this one or others referred to, should be used as guides, not as substitutes, for institutional policies and practices.

Transfer and award of credit is a concept that increasingly involves transfer between dissimilar institutions and curricula and recognition of extrainstitutional learning, as well as transfer between institutions and curricula with similar characteristics. As their personal circumstances and educational objectives change, students seek to have their learning, wherever and however attained, recognized by institutions where they enroll for further study. It is important for reasons of social equity and educational effectiveness for all institutions to develop reasonable and definitive policies and procedures for acceptance of such learning experiences, as well as for the transfer of credits earned at another institution. Such policies and procedures should provide maximum consideration for the individual student who has changed institutions or objectives. It is the receiving institution's responsibility to provide reasonable and definitive policies and procedures for determining a student's knowledge in required subject areas. All sending institutions have a responsibility to furnish transcripts and other documents necessary for a receiving institution to judge the quality and quantity of the student's work. Institutions also have a responsibility to advise the student that the work reflected on the transcript may or may not be accepted by a receiving institution as bearing the same (or any) credits as those awarded by the provider institution, or that the credits awarded will be applicable to the academic credential the student is pursuing.

Interinstitutional Transfer of Credit

Transfer of credit from one institution to another involves at least three considerations:

(1) the educational quality of the learning experience which the student transfers;

(2) the comparability of the nature, content, and level of the learning experience to that offered by the receiving institution; and

(3) the appropriateness and applicability of the learning experience to the programs offered by the receiving institution, in light of the student's educational goals.

Accredited Institutions

Accreditation speaks primarily to the first of these considerations, serving as the basic indicator that an institution meets certain minimum standards. Users of accreditation are urged to give careful attention to the accreditation conferred by accrediting bodies recognized by the Council for Higher Education Accreditation (CHEA). CHEA has a formal process of recognition which requires that all accrediting bodies so recognized must meet the same standards. Under these standards, CHEA has recognized a number of accrediting bodies, including:

(1) regional accrediting commissions (which historically accredited the more traditional colleges and universities but which now accredit proprietary, vocational-technical, distance learning providers, and single-purpose institutions as well);

(2) national accrediting bodies that accredit various kinds of specialized institutions, including distance learning providers and freestanding professional schools; and

(3) professional organizations that accredit programs within multipurpose institutions.

Although accrediting agencies vary in the ways they are organized and in their statements of scope and mission, all accrediting bodies that meet CHEA's standards for recognition function to ensure that the institutions or programs they accredit have met generally accepted minimum standards for accreditation.

Accreditation thus affords reason for confidence in an institution's or a program's purposes, in the appropriateness of its resources and plans for carrying out these purposes, and in its effectiveness in accomplishing its goals, insofar as these things can be judged. Accreditation speaks to the probability, but does not guarantee, that students have met acceptable standards of educational accomplishment.

Comparability and Applicability

Comparability of the nature, content, and level of transfer credit and the appropriateness and applicability of the credit earned to programs offered by the receiving institution are as important in the evaluation process as the accreditation status of the institution at which the transfer credit was awarded. Since accreditation does not address these questions, this information must be obtained from catalogues and other materials and from direct contact between knowledgeable and experienced faculty and staff at both the receiving and sending institutions. When such considerations as comparability and appropriateness of credit are satisfied, however, the receiving institution should have reasonable confidence that students from accredited institutions are qualified to undertake the receiving institution's educational program. In its articulation and transfer policies, the institution should judge courses, programs, and other learning experiences on their learning outcomes and the existence of valid evaluation measures, including third-party expert review, and not on modes of delivery.

Admissions and Degree Purposes

At some institutions there may be differences between the acceptance of credit for admission purposes and the applicability of credit for degree purposes. A receiving institution may accept previous work, place a credit value on it, and enter it on the transcript. However, that previous work, because of its nature and not its inherent quality, may be determined to have no applicability to a specific degree to be pursued by the student. Institutions have a responsibility to make this distinction, and its implications, clear to students before they decide to enroll. This should be a matter of full disclosure, with the best interests of the student in mind. Institutions also should make every reasonable effort to reduce the gap between credits accepted and credits applied toward an educational credential.

Additional Criteria for Transfer Decisions

The following additional criteria are offered to assist institutions, accreditors, and higher education associations in future transfer decisions. These criteria are intended to sustain academic quality in an environment of more varied transfer, assure consistency of transfer practice, and encourage appropriate accountability about transfer policy and practice.

Balance in the Use of Accreditation Status in Transfer Decisions. Institutions and accreditors need to assure that transfer decisions are not made solely on the source of accreditation of a sending program or institution. While acknowledging that accreditation is an important factor, receiving institutions ought to make clear their institutional reasons for accepting or not accepting credits that students seek to transfer. Students should have reasonable explanations about how work offered for credit is or is not of sufficient quality when compared with the receiving institution and how work is or is not comparable with curricula and standards to meet degree requirements of the receiving institution.

Consistency. Institutions and accreditors need to reaffirm that the considerations that inform transfer decisions are applied consistently in the context of changing student attendance patterns (students likely to engage in more transfer) and emerging new providers of higher education (new sources of credits and experience to be evaluated). New providers and new attendance patterns increase the number and type of transfer issues that institutions will address—making consistency even more important in the future.

Accountability for Effective Public Communication. Institutions and accreditors need to assure that students and the public are fully and accurately informed about their respective transfer policies and practices. The public has a significant interest in higher education's effective management of transfer, especially in an environment of expanding access and mobility. Public funding is routinely provided to colleges and universities. This funding is accompanied by public expectations that the transfer process is built on a strong commitment to fairness and efficiency.

Commitment to Address Innovation. Institutions and accreditors need to be flexible and open in considering alternative approaches to managing transfer when these approaches will benefit students. Distance learning and other applications of technology generate alternative approaches to many functions of colleges and universities. Transfer is inevitably among these.

Foreign Institutions

In most cases, foreign institutions are chartered and authorized to grant degrees by their national governments, usually through a Ministry of Education or similar appropriate ministerial body. No other nation has a system comparable with voluntary accreditation as it exists in the United States. At an operational level, AACRAO's Office of International Education Services can assist institutions by providing general or specific guidelines on admission and placement of foreign students, or by providing evaluations of foreign educational credentials.

Evaluation of Extrainstitutional and Experiential Learning for Purposes
of Transfer and Award of Credit

Transfer and award of credit policies should encompass educational accomplishment attained in extrainstitutional settings. In deciding on the award of credit for extrainstitutional learning, institutions will find the services of the American Council on Education's Center for Adult Learning and Educational Credentials helpful. One of the Center's functions is to operate and foster programs to determine credit equivalencies for various modes of extrainstitutional learning. The Center maintains evaluation programs for formal courses offered by the military and civilian organizations such as business, corporations, government agencies, training providers, institutes, and labor unions. Evaluation services are also available for examination programs, for occupations with validated job proficiency evaluation systems, and for correspondence courses offered by schools accredited by the Distance Education and Training Council. The results are published in a Guide series. Another resource is the General Educational Development (GED) Testing Program, which provides a means for assessing high school equivalency.

For learning that has not been evaluated through the ACE evaluation processes, institutions are encouraged to explore the Council for Adult and Experiential Learning (CAEL) procedures and processes.

Uses of this Statement

Institutions are encouraged to use this statement as a basis for discussions in developing or reviewing institutional policies with regard to the transfer and award of credit. If the statement reflects an institution's policies, that institution may wish to use these guidelines to inform faculty, staff, and students.

It is also recommended that accrediting bodies reflect the essential precepts of this statement in their criteria.

Ratified on September 28, 2001, by:

- The American Association of Collegiate Registrars and Admissions Officers
- The American Council on Education
- The Council for Higher Education Accreditation

Institutional Index

Abbreviations Used in this Index

Acad ....Academy
Assoc ....Association
Bus ....Business
Ctr................................Center
Coll ....College
Comm ....Community
Dept.............................Department
Dist ....District
Edu ....Education
Grad.............................Graduate
Hosp ....Hospital
Inst ....Institute

Int'l ....International
Jr ....Junior
Med ....Medical
Mem ....Memorial
Prof..............................Professional
Reg ....Regional
Sch ....School
Sr..................................Senior
Tech.............................Technical
Techno ....Technology
Univ ....University

10th Med. Group/SGFL 657
11th Med. Group/SGD 660
1st Dental Battalion/NDC 652
1st Dental Squadron/SGD 706
2nd Dental Battalion-Naval Dental Ctr. 691
2nd Med. Group/SGDDT 673
375th Dental Squadron *(see 375th Med. Group/SGDDT)*
375th Med. Group/SGDDT 665
3rd Dental Battalion/NDC Okinawa 715
4-States Acad. of Cosmetology 586
55th Dental Squadron/SGD 682
60th Med. Group 652
74th Dental Squadron/SGD 693
81 Dental Squadron/SGDDT 680
82nd Dental Squadron *(see 82nd Med. Group)*
82nd Med. Group 703
96th Dental Squadron *(see 96th Med. Group/SGD)*
96th Med. Group/SGD 661

A

A & B Training Acad. 759
A Cut Above Beauty Coll. 505
A New Beginning Sch. of Massage 616
A&M Commerce *(see Texas A&M Univ—Commerce)*
A&M Corpus Christi *(see Texas A&M Univ—Corpus Christi)*
A&M Kingsville *(see Texas A&M Univ—Kingsville)*
A&M Texarkana *(see Texas A&M Univ—Texarkana)*
A.M.I., Inc. 479
A.R.T. Tech. Coll. *(see Hamilton Tech. Coll.)*
A.T. Still Univ. of Health Sciences 223
A.T.E.S. Tech. Sch. *(see Erie Inst. of Techno.)*
Aaker's Bus. Coll. 296
Aaron's Acad. of Beauty 521
AB Tech *(see Asheville-Buncombe Tech. Comm. Coll.)*
Abbie Bus. Inst. *(see AccuTech Bus. Inst.)*
Abbott Acad. of Cosmetology Arts & Sciences 537
Abbott Northwestern Hosp/Childrens's Hospitals & Clinics 679
ABC Barber Coll. 447
ABC Training Ctr., Inc. *(see Americare Sch. of Nursing)*
Abdill Career Coll. 592
Abilene Baptist Coll. *(see Hardin-Simmons Univ.)*

Abilene Christian Coll. *(see Abilene Christian Univ.)*
Abilene Christian Univ. 373
Abilene Intercollegiate Sch. of Nursing 703
Abington Mem. Health Ctr-Schilling Campus 696
Abington Mem. Hosp. 696 *(see also Abington Mem. Health Ctr—Schilling Campus)*
Abraham Baldwin Agricultural Coll. 98
Abraham Baldwin Coll. *(see Abraham Baldwin Agricultural Coll.)*
Absolute Safety Training Paramedic Program 450
Abu Dhabi Men's Coll. *(see Higher Colleges of Techno. Abu Dhabi Men's Coll.)*
Abu Dhabi Women's Coll. *(see Higher Colleges of Techno. Abu Dhabi Women's Coll.)*
ACA Coll. of Design *(see Art Inst. of Cincinnati)*
Academia Maison D'Esthetique 602
Academia Serrant 602
Academia Vocational Del Turabo 602
Academic Sixth Form Centre *(see Bermuda Coll.)*
Acad. Coll. 207
Acad. Di Capelli Sch. of Cosmetology 754
Acad. Edu. Ctr., Inc. *(see Acad. Coll.)*
Acad. Edu. Services 450
Acad. for Five Element Acupuncture 81
Acad. for Practical Nursing & Health Occupations 479
Acad. Hair Expressions *(see Hair Expressions Acad., Inc.)*
Acad. of Aeronautics *(see Vaughn Coll. of Aeronautics & Techno.)*
Acad. of American English *(see American English Acad.)*
Acad. of Art Coll. 722 *(see also Acad. of Art Univ.)*
Acad. of Art Univ. 29, 722
Acad. of Beauty Arts 736 *(see also Franklin Acad.)*
Acad. of Beauty by Patsy & Rob, The *(see Patsy & Rob's Acad. of Beauty)*
Acad. of Beauty Culture 471
Acad. of Bus. Coll. *(see Everest Coll.)*
Acad. of Career Training 754
Acad. of Careers & Techno. 640
Acad. of Chinese Culture & Health Sciences 29
Acad. of Chinese Healing Arts *(see East West Coll. of Natural Medicine)*

Acad. of Chinese Medicine *(see East West Coll. of Natural Medicine)*
Acad. of Computer Careers 732 *(see also Prism Career Inst.)*
Acad. of Cosmetology 479, 541, 590, 616, 725, 761 *(see also Stillwater Beauty Acad.)*
Acad. of Cosmetology Training *(see Acad. of Career Training)*
Acad. of Cosmetology, Inc. 608
Acad. of Court Reporting 298
Acad. of Creative Hair Design 729, 735 *(see also Vanguard Coll. of Cosmetology)*
Acad. of Creative Hair Design, The 594
Acad. of Esthetics & Cosmetology 753
Acad. of Flight Safety *(see FlightSafety Acad.)*
Acad. of Hair Design *(see Acad. of Creative Hair Design)*
Acad. of Hair Design #1, The 535
Acad. of Hair Design #3, The 535
Acad. of Hair Design #4, The 535
Acad. of Hair Design #6, The 535
Acad. of Hair Design #8, The 535
Acad. of Hair Design 509, 535, 543, 594, 616, 735
Acad. of Hair Design, Inc. 537, 592, 616
Acad. of Hair Design, The 636
Acad. of Hair Techno. 608
Acad. of Healing Arts, Massage & Facial Skin Care 479
Acad. of Healing Arts, The 756 *(see also Acad. of Healing Arts, Massage & Facial Skin Care)*
Acad. of Health Care Professions, The 373
Acad. of Health Sciences 703
Acad. of Healthy Hair *(see Healthy Hair Acad., Inc.)*
Acad. of Holistic Health, Inc. *(see Ohio Acad. of Holistic Health, Inc.)*
Acad. of Idaho *(see Idaho State Univ.)*
Acad. of Int'l. Design & Techno. *(see Int'l. Acad. of Design & Techno.)*
Acad. of Massage Therapy 545
Acad. of Med. Arts & Bus. 594
Acad. of Nail & Skin & Hair, LLP 541
Acad. of Nail & Skin Techno. *(see Acad. of Nail & Skin & Hair, LLP)*
Acad. of Nutrition *(see Huntington Coll. of Health Sciences)*
Acad. of Oriental Medicine at Austin 373
Acad. of Prof. Careers 450, 754
Acad. of Radio & Television Broadcasting 450

Acad. of Radio & Television Electronics *(see Hamilton Tech. Coll.)*

Acad. of Recording Arts & Sciences, The *(see Conservatory of Recording Arts & Sciences)*

Acad. of the Fine Arts of Pennsylvania *(see Pennsylvania Acad. of the Fine Arts)*

Acad. of the New Church Theological Sch. *(see Bryn Athyn Coll. of the New Church)*

Acad. of Vocal Arts 594

Acad. Pacific Bus. & Travel Coll. *(see Acad. Pacific Travel Coll.)*

Acad. Pacific Travel Coll. 450

Acadia Coll. *(see Acadia Divinity Coll.)*

Acadia Divinity Coll. 431

AccuTech Bus. Inst. 521

ACE Computer Training Ctr. 756

Acme Sch. of Die Design *(see ITT Tech. Inst.)*

Acres Home Coll. of Barber Design 759

ACT Coll. 738

ACTech Inst. *(see Advanced Career Technologies Inst.)*

Actors Conservatory of the Southwest *(see KD Studio)*

Actors Studio Drama Sch. *(see New Sch.)*

ACTS Urban CPE Program 665

Acupressure-Acupuncture Inst. *(see Acupuncture & Massage Coll.)*

Acupuncture & Integrative Medicine Coll., Berkeley 29, 732

Acupuncture & Massage Coll. 81

Acupuncture Sch. of New England *(see New England Sch. of Acupuncture)*

Ad Sch. of Miami *(see Miami Ad Sch.)*

Ada Clement Piano Sch. *(see San Francisco Conservatory of Music)*

Adams Associates *(see Dale Carnegie Training of Northwest Ohio & Northern Indiana)*

Adams Coll. *(see Adams State Coll.)*

Adams Comm. Mental Health Ctr. *(see Comm. Reach Ctr.)*

Adams Corporation *(see Don Adams Corporation)*

Adams Group, LLC 734 *(see also Dale Carnegie Training of Northwest Ohio & Northern Indiana)*

Adams State Coll. 64

Adas Yereim Rabbinical Seminary *(see Rabbinical Seminary Adas Yereim)*

Adcon Tech. Inst. 722

Addolorata Villa Gatellite 666

AddRan Christian Univ.. *(see Texas Christian Univ.)*

Addran Male & Female Acad. *(see Texas Christian Univ.)*

Adelante Career Inst. 450

Adelante Schools, Inc. *(see Adelante Career Inst.)*

Adelphi Coll. *(see Adelphi Univ.)*

Adelphi Suffolk Coll. *(see Dowling Coll.)*

Adelphi Univ. 255

Adirondack Beauty Sch. 558

Adirondack Coll. *(see Adirondack Comm. Coll.)*

Adirondack Comm. Coll. 255

Adler Grad. Sch. 207, 731

Adler Sch. of Prof. Psychology 117

Adolphus Coll. *(see Gustavus Adolphus Coll.)*

Adrian Beauty Acad., Inc. 528

Adrian Coll. 195

Adrian Dominican Montessori Teacher Inst. 528

Adrian's Beauty Coll. of Turlock 450

Adult & Continuing Edu-Cleveland Extension 576

Adult & Experiental Learning Sch. *(see Antioch Univ. McGregor)*

Adult Ctr. for Edu. 576

Adult Ctr. for Lifelong Learning *(see Buckeye Hills Career Ctr.)*

Adult Comm. Edu. Full Service Ctr. 576

Adult Educational Ctr. of Lumberton *(see Lumberton Adult Educational Ctr.)*

Adult Psychiatric Clinic *(see Park Ctr., Inc.)*

Adult Vocational Services 576

Advance Barber Coll. Sch. of Hair Design 735 *(see also Heritage Coll. Hair Design)*

Advance Beauty Coll. 450

Advance Beauty Coll., Inc. 537

Advance Science Inst. 479

Advance Tech Coll. 602

Advanced Barber Coll. & Hair Design 616

Advanced Career Technologies Inst. 450

Advanced Career Training 492 *(see also Advanced Coll. of Techno.)*

Advanced Coll. 450

Advanced Coll. of Techno. 49, 722

Advanced Distributed Learning Inst. *(see United States Air Force Inst. for Advanced Distributed Learning)*

Advanced Hair Tech *(see Cutting Edge Hairstyling Acad.)*

Advanced Int'l. Studies Sch. *(see Paul H. Nitze Sch. of Advanced Int'l. Studies)*

Advanced Job Training *(see Advanced Coll. of Techno.)*

Advanced Legal Studies Ctr. *(see Ctr. for Advanced Legal Studies)*

Advanced Software Analysis *(see ASA Inst., The Coll. of Advanced Techno.)*

Advanced Techno. Coll. *(see Advanced Coll. of Techno.)*

Advanced Techno. Inst. 400

Advanced Techno. Inst. of Kentucky *(see Kentucky Advanced Techno. Inst.)*

Advanced Theraputics Ctr. *(see Ctr. of Advanced Therapeutics)*

Advanced Training Associates, Inc. 450

Advanced/Basic Hair Design Training Ctr. 725 *(see also Acad. of Cosmetology)*

Adventist Health Sciences Ctr. *(see Loma Linda Univ.)*

Adventist HealthCare *(see Shady Grove Adventist Hosp.)*

Advertising Art Coll. *(see Coll. of Art Advertising)*

Advertising Art Sch. *(see Sch. of Advertising Art)*

Advertising Arts Coll. *(see Art Inst. of California—San Diego)*

Advocate Bethany Hosp. 666

Advocate Christ Med. Ctr. 666

Advocate Family Care Network *(see Advocate Christ Med. Ctr.)*

Advocate Good Samaritan Hosp. 666

Advocate Good Shepherd Hosp. 666

Advocate Health Care System *(see also Advocate Bethany Hosp., Advocate Christ Med. Ctr., Advocate Good Samaritan Hosp., Advocate Good Shepherd Hosp., Advocate Lutheran General Hosp., Advocate South Suburban Hosp., Advocate Trinity Hosp.)*

Advocate Illinois Masonic Med. Ctr. 666

Advocate Lutheran General Hosp. 666

Advocate South Suburban Hosp. 666

Advocate Trinity Hosp. 666

AEC Southern Ohio Coll. 734 *(see also Brown Mackie Coll—Cincinnati)*

AEC Southern Ohio Coll—Findlay 734 *(see also Brown Mackie Coll—Findlay)*

AEC Southern Ohio Coll—North Canton 734

Aeronautical Inst. of Technologies 616

Aeronautics Coll. *(see Vaughn Coll. of Aeronautics & Techno.)*

Aeronautics Inst. of Pittsburgh *(see Pittsburgh Inst. of Aeronautics)*

Aesthetics Inst. of Cosmetology 521
Aetas, Inc. *(see Bilingual Edu. Inst.)*
AF Int'l. Sch. of Languages, Inc 450
Affinity Health System *(see Mercy Med. Ctr.)*
Agnes Scott Coll. 98
Agricultural & Industrial State Normal Sch. *(see Tennessee State Univ.)*
Agricultural & Mechanical Coll. *(see North Carolina Agricultural & Tech. State Univ.)*
Agricultural & Mechanical Coll. of Alabama *(see Auburn Univ.)*
Agricultural & Mechanical Coll. of Texas *(see Prairie View A&M Univ., Texas A&M Univ.)*
Agricultural & Tech. Coll. at Farmingdale *(see State Univ. of New York Coll. of Techno. at Farmingdale)*
Agricultural & Tech. Coll. of North Carolina *(see North Carolina Agricultural & Tech. State Univ.)*
Agricultural Coll. of Colorado *(see Colorado State Univ.)*
Agricultural Coll. of Oregon *(see Oregon State Univ.)*
Agricultural Coll. of Pennsylvania *(see Pennsylvania State Univ.)*
Agricultural Coll. of the State of Michigan *(see Michigan State Univ.)*
Agricultural Coll. of the State of Montana *(see Montana State Univ—Bozeman)*
Agricultural Coll. of Utah *(see Utah State Univ.)*
Agricultural Tech. Inst. of Ohio State Univ. *(see Ohio State Univ—Agricultural Tech. Inst.)*
Agricultural, Mining, & Mechanical Arts Coll. *(see Univ. of California, Berkeley)*
Agriculture & Techno. Coll. at Cobleskill *(see State Univ. of New York Coll. of Agriculture & Techno. at Cobleskill)*
Agriculture & Techno. Coll. at Morrisville *(see State Univ. of New York Coll. of Agriculture & Techno. at Morrisville)*
Agriculture Coll. of Nebraska *(see Nebraska Coll. of Tech. Agriculture)*
Aguadilla Tech. Coll. 602
AIB Coll. of Bus. 145
AIBT Inst. *(see Int'l. Inst. of the Americas)*
AIBT Int'l. Inst. of the Americas *(see Int'l. Inst. of the Americas)*
Aiken Coll. *(see Aiken Tech. Coll.)*

Aiken Tech. Coll. 355
Aiken Tech. Edu. Ctr. *(see Aiken Tech. Coll.)*
Ailano Sch. of Cosmetology 524
Ailey American Dance Ctr. *(see Alvin Ailey American Dance Ctr.)*
Ailey Sch., The *(see Alvin Ailey American Dance Ctr.)*
AIM—Indianapolis *(see Aviation Inst. of Maintenance Training Acad.)*
AIM—Kansas City *(see Aviation Inst. of Maintenance)*
AIM—Lawrenceville *(see Aviation Inst. of Maintenance)*
AIM—Manassas *(see Aviation Inst. of Maintenance—Manassas)*
AIM—Philadelphia *(see Aviation Inst. of Maintenance)*
AIMS Acad. 616
Aims Comm. Coll. 64
AIM—Virginia Beach *(see Aviation Inst. of Maintenance—Virgina Beach)*
AIM—Washington, DC *(see Aviation Inst. of Maintenance—Manassas)*
Air Corps Engineering Sch. *(see Air Force Inst. of Techno.)*
Air Force Acad. *(see United States Air Force Acad.)*
Air Force Acad. Hosp. *(see 10th Med. Group/SGFL)*
Air Force Comm. Coll. *(see Comm. Coll. of the Air Force)*
Air Force Inst. of Techno. 298
Air Force Sch. of Health Care Sciences *(see United States Air Force Sch. of Health Care Sciences)*
Air Force Sch. of Health Sciences *(see Comm. Coll. of the Air Force Sch. of Health Sciences)*
Air Hostess Training Sch. *(see Acad. Pacific Travel Coll.)*
Air Sch. of Application *(see Air Force Inst. of Techno.)*
Air Univ. 3
Air Univ. Sch. of Air & Space Studies *(see Sch. of Advanced Air & Space Studies)*
Airman's Proficiency Ctr. 592
Air-Vu Sch. of Drawing *(see DeVry Univ. Denver)*
Akron Beauty Sch. *(see Gerber Akron Beauty Sch.)*
Akron Children's Hosp. *(see Children's Hosp. Med. Ctr. of Akron)*
Akron General Med. Ctr. 693
Akron Inst. 576
Akron Machining Inst. Inc. 576
Akron Med-Dental Inst. *(see Akron Inst.)*

Akron Public Schools *(see Adult Vocational Services)*
Akron Sch. of Practical Nursing 693
Akron Univ. *(see Univ. of Akron)*
AKS Massage Sch. 631
Al Ain Women's Coll. *(see Higher Colleges of Techno. Al Ain Women's Coll.)*
Al Collins Graphic Design Sch. *(see Collins Coll.)*
Alabama A&M Univ. *(see Alabama Agricultural & Mechanical Univ.)*
Alabama Agricultural & Mechanical Univ. 3
Alabama Aviation & Tech. Coll. *(see Enterprise-Ozark Comm. Coll., Enterprise-Ozark Comm. Coll. Aviation Campus, George C. Wallace State Comm. Coll—Dothan)*
Alabama Baptist Normal & Theological Sch. *(see Selma Univ.)*
Alabama Career Coll. *(see Virginia Coll.)*
Alabama Christian Coll. *(see Faulkner Univ.)*
Alabama Coll. of Barber Styling *(see Alabama State Coll. of Barber Styling)*
Alabama Conference Female Coll. *(see Huntingdon Coll.)*
Alabama Lutheran Acad. & Jr. Coll. *(see Concordia Coll. Selma)*
Alabama Polytechnic Inst. *(see Auburn Univ.)*
Alabama Reference Laboratories/LabSouth, Inc. 651
Alabama Southern Coll. *(see Alabama Southern Comm. Coll.)*
Alabama Southern Comm. Coll. 3
Alabama State Barber Coll. *(see Alabama State Coll. of Barber Styling)*
Alabama State Coll. *(see Alabama State Univ.)*
Alabama State Coll. for Negroes *(see Alabama State Univ.)*
Alabama State Coll. of Barber Styling 441
Alabama State Univ. 3
Alabama Tech. Coll. *(see Gadsden State Comm. Coll.)*
Alamance Comm. Coll. 284
Alamance Reg. Med. Ctr. 691
Alameda Beauty Coll., Inc. 450
Alameda Coll. *(see Coll. of Alameda)*
Alamogordo Branch Comm. Coll. *(see New Mexico State Univ. at Alamogordo)*
Alaska Bible Coll. 11
Alaska Coll. *(see Alaska Bible Coll.)*

Alaska Methodist Univ. *(see Alaska Pacific Univ.)*
Alaska Native Med. Ctr. *(see Southcentral Foundation-Alaska Native Med. Ctr.)*
Alaska Pacific Univ. 11
Alaska Vocational Tech. Ctr. 443
Alaska Vo-Tec Ctr. *(see Alaska Vocational Tech. Ctr.)*
Albany Area Vocational-Tech. Sch. *(see Albany Tech. Coll.)*
Albany Bible & Manual Training Inst. *(see Albany State Univ.)*
Albany Coll. of Pharmacy of Union Univ. 255
Albany Collegiate Inst. *(see Lewis & Clark Coll.)*
Albany Law Coll. *(see Albany Law Sch.)*
Albany Law Sch. 255
Albany Med. Coll. 255
Albany Med. Coll. of Union Univ. *(see Albany Med. Coll.)*
Albany Pharmacy Coll. *(see Albany Coll. of Pharmacy of Union Univ.)*
Albany State Coll. *(see Albany State Univ.)*
Albany State Univ. 98 *(see also State Univ. of New York at Albany)*
Albany Tech. Coll. 98, 726
Albany Tech. Inst. 726 *(see also Albany Tech. Coll.)*
Albany Univ. *(see State Univ. of New York at Albany)*
Albemarle Coll. *(see Coll. of The Albemarle)*
Albert Einstein Healthcare Network *(see Albert Einstein Med. Ctr.)*
Albert Einstein Med. Ctr. 696
Albert I. Prince Reg. Vocational-Tech. Sch. 658
Albert Sch. of Cosmetology *(see James Albert Sch. of Cosmetology)*
Albert Sch., The 474
Albert State Coll. *(see Carl Albert State Coll.)*
Alberta Bible Coll. 752
Alberta Univ. *(see Univ. of Alberta)*
Albertson Coll. of Idaho 115
Albertus Magnus Coll. 72
Albion Coll. 195
Albizu Univ—Miami Campus *(see Carlos Albizu Univ—Miami Campus)*
Albizu Univ—San Juan Campus *(see Carlos Albizu Univ—San Juan Campus)*
Albright Art Sch. *(see State Univ. of New York at Buffalo)*
Albright Coll. 325

Albuquerque Area Indian Health Service 685
Albuquerque Barber Coll. 556
Albuquerque Tech. Inst. *(see Albuquerque Tech. Vocational Inst.)*
Albuquerque Tech. Vocational Inst. 252
Alcorn A&M Coll. *(see Alcorn State Univ.)*
Alcorn Agricultural & Mechanical Coll. *(see Alcorn State Univ.)*
Alcorn State Univ. 218
Alcorn Univ. *(see Alcorn State Univ.)*
Alden's Cosmetology Sch. *(see Alden's Sch. of Cosmetology)*
Alden's Sch. of Cosmetology 755
Alderson Acad. & Jr. Coll. *(see Alderson-Broaddus Coll.)*
Alderson-Broaddus Coll. 418
Alegent Health Bergan Mercy Med. Ctr. 682
Alegent Health Immanuel Med. Ctr. 542
Alegent Health Sch. of Med. Assisiting *(see Alegent Health Immanuel Med. Ctr.)*
Alexander City State Jr. Coll. *(see Central Alabama Comm. Coll.)*
Alexander Inst. *(see Lon Morris Coll.)*
Alexandria Acad. of Beauty 515
Alexandria Coll. *(see Alexandria Tech. Coll.)*
Alexandria Sch. of Scientific Therapeutics, Inc. 505
Alexandria Tech. Coll. 207
Alexandria VA Med. Ctr. *(see Alexandria Veterans Affairs Med. Ctr.)*
Alexandria Veterans Affairs Med. Ctr. 673
Alexian Brothers (System Ctr.) 666
Alexian Brothers Health System 666
Alexian Brothers Med. Ctr. 666
Alexian Village of Milwaukee 666
Alfred Adler Grad. Sch. 731 *(see also Adler Grad. Sch.)*
Alfred Adler Inst. of Chicago *(see Adler Sch. of Prof. Psychology)*
Alfred Adler Inst. of Minnesota *(see Adler Grad. Sch.)*
Alfred Coll. of Techno. *(see State Univ. of New York Coll. of Techno. at Alfred)*
Alfred I. duPont Hosp. for Children 660
Alfred I. duPont Inst. *(see Alfred I. duPont Hosp. for Children)*
Alfred Select Sch. *(see Alfred Univ.)*

Alfred State Coll. *(see State Univ. of New York Coll. of Techno. at Alfred)*
Alfred Univ. 255
Alfred Univ—New York State Coll. of Ceramics *(see New York State Coll. of Ceramics at Alfred Univ.)*
Algonquin Coll. 711
Algonquin Coll. of Applied Arts & Techno. *(see Algonquin Coll.)*
Alhambra Beauty Coll. 451
Alice Lloyd Coll. 158
All American Career Coll. 451
All Saints Healthcare System *(see All Saints Healthcare—St. Mary's Campus)*
All Saints Healthcare—St. Mary's Campus 708
Allan Hancock Coll. 29
Allegany Coll. of Maryland 178
Allegany Comm. Coll. *(see Allegany Coll. of Maryland)*
Allegheny Coll. 325
Allegheny County Comm. Coll. Allegheny Campus *(see Comm. Coll. of Allegheny County Allegheny Campus)*
Allegheny County Comm. Coll. Boyce Campus *(see Comm. Coll. of Allegheny County Boyce Campus)*
Allegheny County Comm. Coll. North Campus *(see Comm. Coll. of Allegheny County North Campus)*
Allegheny County Comm. Coll. South Campus *(see Comm. Coll. of Allegheny County South Campus)*
Allegheny General Hosp. 696
Allegheny Wesleyan Coll. 298
Allen Coll. 145 *(see also Allen Univ.)*
Allen Coll. of Nursing *(see Allen Coll.)*
Allen County Comm. Coll. 152
Allen Health Systems, Inc. *(see Allen Coll.)*
Allen Mem. Hosp. Sch. of Nursing *(see Allen Coll.)*
Allen Mem. Sch. of Practical Nursing *(see Vermont Tech. Coll—Colchester)*
Allen Park VA Med. Ctr. *(see Veterans Affairs Med. Ctr—Allen Park)*
Allen Park Veterans Affairs Med. Ctr. *(see Veterans Affairs Med. Ctr—Allen Park)*
Allen Sch. 558
Allen Univ. 355
Allendale Assoc. 666
Allentown Bus. Sch. 735 *(see also Lehigh Valley Coll.)*
Allentown Coll. of St. Francis De Sales *(see DeSales Univ.)*

Allentown Sch. of Cosmetology, Inc. 594

Alliance Career Centre *(see Alliance City Schools Career Centre)*

Alliance City Schools Career Centre 576

Alliance Coll. *(see Alliance Univ. Coll.)*

Alliance Sch. of Theology & Missions *(see Alliance Theological Seminary)*

Alliance Seminary *(see Alliance Theological Seminary)*

Alliance Theological Seminary 270 *(see also Nyack Coll.)*

Alliance Univ. Coll. 431, 740

Alliant Int'l. Univ. 722

Alliant Int'l. Univ—Fresno 29

Alliant Int'l. Univ—Irvine 29

Alliant Int'l. Univ—Los Angeles 29

Alliant Int'l. Univ—Mexico City 436

Alliant Int'l. Univ—Nairobi *(see United States Int'l. Univ—Africa)*

Alliant Int'l. Univ—San Diego Cornerstone Court 29

Alliant Int'l. Univ—San Diego Scripps Ranch 29

Alliant Int'l. Univ—San Francisco Bay 29

Alliant Univ—Fresno *(see Alliant Int'l. Univ—Fresno)*

Alliant Univ—Los Angeles *(see Alliant Int'l. Univ—Los Angeles)*

Alliant Univ—San Diego *(see Alliant Int'l. Univ—San Diego Cornerstone Court)*

Alliant Univ—San Diego Cornerstone Court 722

Alliant Univ—San Francisco Bay *(see Alliant Int'l. Univ—San Francisco Bay)*

Allied Bus. Schools, Inc. 451

Allied Career Ctr. 616

Allied Coll. 223, 731

Allied Health Coll. of Arizona *(see Arizona Coll. of Allied Health)*

Allied Med. & Tech. Careers 732, 735 *(see also Allied Med. & Tech. Inst.)*

Allied Med. & Tech. Inst. 325, 545, 594, 732, 733, 735

Allied Med. Careers *(see Allied Med. & Tech. Inst.)*

Allied Med. Coll. 721, 731 *(see also Allied Coll.)*

Allied Schools 451

Allina Clinical Pastoral Edu. Ctr. *(see Allina Hospitals & Clinics)*

Allina Hospitals & Clinics 679

All-State Career Sch. 594

Allstate Vocational Training *(see Northwestern Technological Inst.)*

Alma Coll. 195

Al-Med Acad. *(see Allied Coll.)*

Alpena Coll. *(see Alpena Comm. Coll.)*

Alpena Comm. Coll. 195

Alpha Hair Acad. 760

Alpine Coll. 761

ALPS Educational Services, Inc. *(see ALPS Language Sch.)*

ALPS Language Sch. 636

Alta Bates Med. Ctr. 652

Altamaha Coll. *(see Altamaha Tech. Coll.)*

Altamaha Tech. Coll. 98, 726

Altamaha Tech. Inst. *(see Altamaha Tech. Coll.)*

Alternative Conjunction Clinic & Sch. of Massage Therapy, The 594

Altoona Beauty Sch., Inc. 594

Altoona Sch. of Commerce *(see South Hills Sch. of Bus. & Techno.)*

Altru Hosp. 692

Altus Jr. Coll. *(see Western Oklahoma State Coll.)*

Alvareita's Coll. of Cosmetology 498

Alvareita's Coll. of Cosmetology— Godfrey Campus 498

Alvernia Coll. 325

Alverno Coll. 423

Alverno Teachers Coll. *(see Alverno Coll.)*

Alvin Ailey American Dance Ctr., The 558

Alvin Coll. *(see Alvin Comm. Coll.)*

Alvin Comm. Coll. 373

Amarillo Coll. 373

Amarillo Coll. of Hairdressing, Inc. 737 *(see also Milan Inst. of Cosmetology)*

Amarillo Jr. Coll. *(see Amarillo Coll.)*

Amarillo Tech. Ctr. 373 *(see also Amarillo Coll.)*

Ambassador Inst. of Travel 736

Amber Univ. *(see Amberton Univ.)*

Amberton Univ. 373

Ambler Beauty Acad., Inc. 735 *(see also Magnolia Sch.)*

AMEDD Ctr. & Sch. *(see Brooke Army Med. Ctr., United States Army Med. Dept. Ctr. & Sch.)*

American Acad. McAllister Inst. of Funeral Service, Inc. 255

American Acad. of Acupuncture & Oriental Medicine 207

American Acad. of Acupuncture & Traditional Chinese Medicine *(see American Coll. of Acupuncture & Oriental Medicine)*

American Acad. of Art 117

American Acad. of Cosmetology 474

American Acad. of Dramatic Arts 255

American Acad. of Dramatic Arts West 29

American Acad. of English 451

American Acad. of Hair Design 509

American Acad. of Music & Drama *(see American Musical & Dramatic Acad.)*

American Acad. of Nutrition 736 *(see also Huntington Coll. of Health Sciences)*

American Acupuncture & Oriental Medicine Acad. *(see American Acad. of Acupuncture & Oriental Medicine)*

American Advanced Technicians Inst. Corporation 479

American Art Acad. *(see American Acad. of Art)*

American Auto Inst. 451

American Ballet Ctr/Joffrey Ballet Sch. 558

American Baptist Coll. 364

American Baptist Coll. of the Bible *(see American Baptist Coll.)*

American Baptist Seminary of the West 30

American Barber Coll. *(see Borner's Barber Coll.)*

American Barber Inst. 558

American Beauty Acad. 521 *(see also Magnolia Sch.)*

American Beauty Acad., Inc. 598

American Beauty Coll. 451

American Beauty Inst. 586 *(see also American Inst. of Beauty, Inc)*

American Broadcasting Sch. 586

American Bus. Acad. 732 *(see also HoHoKus-Hackensack Sch. of Bus. & Med. Science)*

American Bus. & Fashion Inst. *(see Art Inst. of Charlotte)*

American Bus. Coll. 736 *(see also American Univ. of Puerto Rico)*

American Career Coll. 451

American Career Coll. of Hair Design. Inc. 498

American Career Inst. 543

American Ctr. for Tech. Arts & Sciences 735

American Christian Coll. & Seminary 735

American Coll. 325 *(see also American InterContinental Univ., American InterContinental Univ— London, American InterContinental Univ—Los Angeles)*

American Coll. Dublin 435

American Coll. of Acupuncture & Oriental Medicine 373

American Coll. of Bus. 722

American Coll. of California 451
American Coll. of Computer & Information Sciences 3
American Coll. of Greece, The *(see Deree Coll., The American Coll. of Greece)*
American Coll. of Hair Design, Inc. 537
American Coll. of Hairstyling—Cedar Rapids 507
American Coll. of Hairstyling—Des Moines 507
American Coll. of Health Professions 451
American Coll. of Life Underwriters, The *(see American Coll.)*
American Coll. of Management & Techno. 273 *(see also Rochester Inst. of Techno.)*
American Coll. of Med. Techno. 451
American Coll. of Optics *(see American Career Coll.)*
American Coll. of Prehospital Medicine 725
American Coll. of Prof. Edu. 738
American Coll. of Switzerland, The *(see Schiller Int'l. Univ.)*
American Coll. of Thessaloniki 435
American Coll. of Traditional Chinese Medicine 30
American Commercial Coll. 616, 617
American Comm. Coll. 738
American Computer & Information Sciences Coll. *(see American Coll. of Computer & Information Sciences)*
American Conservatory Theater 30
American Diamond Council *(see Diamond Council of America)*
American Dramatic Arts Acad. *(see American Acad. of Dramatic Arts, American Acad. of Dramatic Arts West)*
American Dura Skin Care, Massage & Nail Sch. 725
American Educational Coll. 602
American English Acad. 451
American English Language Inst. *(see English Language Inst.)*
American Film Inst., The 30
American Flyers Coll. *(see Everglades Univ.)*
American Grad. Sch. of Int'l. Management, The *(see Thunderbird, The Garvin Grad. Sch. of Int'l. Management)*
American Grad. Sch. of Management 64
American Grad. Univ. 30
American Health Information Management Assoc. 498

American Health Science Univ. 64
American Health Sciences Inst. *(see American Inst. of Health Sciences)*
American Home Bible Inst. *(see Washington Bible Coll.)*
American Indian Arts Inst. *(see Inst. of American Indian & Alaskan Native Culture & Arts Development)*
American Indian Coll. of the Assemblies of God 14
American Indian OIC *(see American Indian Opportunities Industrial Ctr.)*
American Indian Opportunities Industrial Ctr. 533
American Indian Satellite Comm. Coll. *(see Nebraska Indian Comm. Coll.)*
American Inst. for Computer Sciences *(see American Coll. of Computer & Information Sciences)*
American Inst. for Paralegal Studies 498
American Inst. of Alternative Medicine 576
American Inst. of Applied Science 572
American Inst. of Baking 509
American Inst. of Beauty, Inc 479
American Inst. of Bus. *(see AIB Coll. of Bus.)*
American Inst. of Commerce *(see Kaplan Univ.)*
American Inst. of Commerce—Dallas *(see Remington Coll—Dallas)*
American Inst. of Drafting *(see York Tech. Inst.)*
American Inst. of Health Sciences 451
American Inst. of Health Techno., Inc. 727 *(see also Apollo Coll—Boise)*
American Inst. of Massage Therapy 452, 479
American Inst. of Med-Dental Techno. 627
American Inst. of Techno. 444
American InterContinental Univ. Online, The 98
American InterContinental Univ., The 98
American Int'l. Coll. 184
American Int'l. Univ. in London *(see Richmond, The American Int'l. Univ. in London)*
American L&L Edu., Inc. *(see American Acad. of English)*
American Language Kollege, Inc. *(see TALK Int'l.)*
American Med. Sciences Ctr—North Hollwood 452
American Med. Techno. Coll. *(see American Coll. of Med. Techno.)*

American Military Univ. 418, 751
American Motorcycle Inst. *(see A.M.I., Inc.)*
American Musical & Dramatic Acad., The 558
American Nutrition Acad. *(see Huntington Coll. of Health Sciences)*
American Prof. Inst. 492
American Public Univ. 418, 751
American Public Univ. System Ctr. for Prof. & Workforce Development *(see APUS Ctr. for Prof. & Workforce Development)*
American River Coll. 30
American River Jr. Coll. *(see American River Coll.)*
American Samoa Comm. Coll. 13
American Sch. of Bus. 515 *(see also American Commercial Coll.)*
American Sch. of Prof. Psychology *(see Argosy Univ. Hawai'i, Argosy Univ. San Francisco Bay Area)*
American Sch. of Prof. Psychology—Virginia Campus 738 *(see also Argosy Univ. Washington, DC)*
American Sch. of Techno. 576
American Sch. of X-Ray *(see American Coll. of Med. Techno.)*
American Schools of Prof. Psychology 727
American Trades Institutes *(see ATI Tech. Training Ctr.)*
American Traditional Chinese Medicine Coll. *(see American Coll. of Traditional Chinese Medicine)*
American Trans Air Aviation Training Acad. 727 *(see also Aviation Inst. of Maintenance Training Acad.)*
American Univ. 78
American Univ. in Bulgaria, The 431
American Univ. in Cairo, The 435
American Univ. in London *(see Richmond, The American Int'l. Univ. in London)*
American Univ. of Armenia 743
American Univ. of Athens, The 740
American Univ. of Beirut 435
American Univ. of Paris, The 435
American Univ. of Puerto Rico 347
American Univ. of Rome 435
American Univ. of Sharjah 437
American Weld Testing Sch. 737
Americana Beauty Coll. II 471
Americare Sch. of Nursing 479
AmesEd 616
Amherst Coll. 184
Amherst Collegiate Institution *(see Amherst Coll.)*
AMI Int'l. Training Ctr. *(see A.M.I., Inc.)*

Ana G. Mendez—Universidad Metropolitana *(see Universidad Metropolitana)*
Ana Visage Acad. 761
Anamarc Educational Inst. 617
Anatolia Coll. *(see American Coll. of Thessaloniki)*
Ancilla Coll. 135
Anderson Area Med. Ctr. 701
Anderson Bible Training Sch. *(see Anderson Univ.)*
Anderson Cancer Ctr. *(see Univ. of Texas Health Science Ctr. at Houston)*
Anderson Coll. 736 *(see also Anderson Univ.)*
Anderson Theological Seminary *(see Anderson Univ.)*
Anderson Univ. 135, 355, 736
Andon Coll. at Modesto 722 *(see also Maric Coll—Modesto)*
Andon Coll. at Stockton 722 *(see also Maric Coll—Stockton)*
Andover Coll. 175
Andover Inst. of Bus. *(see Andover Coll.)*
Andover Newton Theological Sch. 184
Andover Theological Seminary *(see Andover Newton Theological Sch.)*
Andrew Coll. 98
Andrew Female Coll. *(see Andrew Coll.)*
Andrew Jackson Univ. 3
Andrew Terranova & Associates, Inc. 558
Andrews Acad. of Cosmetology 537
Andrews Acad. of Hair Design *(see Taylor Andrews Acad. of Hair Design)*
Andrews Ctr. *(see Commonwealth Tech. Inst.)*
Andrews Univ. 195
Anesthesia Sch. of Middle Tennessee *(see Middle Tennessee Sch. of Anesthesia)*
Angela Martin Montessori Training Ctr. 646
Angelina Coll. 373
Angelo Sch. of Cosmetology & Hair Design *(see Arthur Angelo Sch. of Cosmetology & Hair Design)*
Angelo State Coll. *(see Angelo State Univ.)*
Angelo State Univ. 373
Angley Coll. 81
Anglo-Continental Boston, Inc. *(see Anglo-Continental USA, Inc.)*
Anglo-Continental USA, Inc. 524
Anglo-European Coll. of Chiropractic 717

Angola Correctional Facility 170 *(see also Louisiana Tech. Coll—Jumonville)*
Animal Arts Inst. of Florida *(see Florida Inst. of Animal Arts)*
AnMed Health *(see Anderson Area Med. Ctr.)*
Ann Arbor Inst. of Massage Therapy 528
Ann Arbor VA Med. Ctr. *(see Veterans Affairs Med. Ctr—Ann Arbor)*
Ann Arbor Veterans Affairs Med. Ctr. *(see Veterans Affairs Med. Ctr—Ann Arbor)*
Anna Maria Coll. 184
Annapolis *(see United States Naval Acad.)*
Anne Arundel Coll. *(see Anne Arundel Comm. Coll.)*
Anne Arundel Comm. Coll. 178
Anointed Hands Christian Cosmetology Sch. 761
Anoka Tech. Coll. 207, 731
Anoka-Hennepin Tech. Coll. 731 *(see also Anoka Tech. Coll.)*
Anoka-Ramsey Comm. Coll. 207
Anson Coll. of Cosmetology 572
Anson Comm. Coll. *(see South Piedmont Comm. Coll.)*
Antelope Valley Coll. 30 *(see also Antelope Valley Med. Coll.)*
Antelope Valley Med. Coll. 452
Anthem Coll. Online *(see High-Tech Inst—Phoenix)*
Antillean Adventist Univ. *(see Universidad Adventista de las Antillas)*
Antillean Coll. *(see Universidad Adventista de las Antillas)*
Antilles Sch. of Tech. Careers 602
Antioch Coll. 298 *(see also Antioch Univ.)*
Antioch New England Grad. Sch. 298 *(see also Antioch Univ.)*
Antioch Seattle *(see Antioch Univ—Seattle)*
Antioch Southern California—Los Angeles 298
Antioch Southern California—Santa Barbara 298
Antioch Univ. 298
Antioch Univ. McGregor 298 *(see also Antioch Univ.)*
Antioch Univ. Seattle 298 *(see also Antioch Univ.)*
Antioch Univ. Southern California *(see Antioch Univ.)*
Antonelli Art & Photography Inst. *(see Antonelli Inst.)*
Antonelli Coll. 298

Antonelli Inst. 325 *(see also Antonelli Coll.)*
Antonelli Inst. of Art & Photography *(see Antonelli Coll.)*
Antonelli Med. & Prof. Inst. 594
Apex Acad. of Hair Design 505, 727
Apex Sch. of Beauty Culture 727 *(see also Apex Acad. of Hair Design)*
Apex Sch. of Theology 284
Apex Tech. Sch. 558
Apex Theology Sch. *(see Apex Sch. of Theology)*
Apollo Career Ctr. 576
Apollo Coll. of Med. & Dental Assistants. *(see Apollo Coll—Mesa Campus)*
Apollo Coll. of Med-Dental Careers *(see Apollo Coll—Portland)*
Apollo Coll—Boise 115, 727
Apollo Coll—Phoenix Campus 14
Apollo Coll—Portland Campus 320
App State *(see Appalachian State Univ.)*
Appalachian Beauty Sch. 512
Appalachian Bible Coll. 418
Appalachian Coll. *(see Appalachian Bible Coll.)*
Appalachian Reg. Healthcare *(see Hazard ARH Reg. Med. Ctr.)*
Appalachian Sch. of Law 750
Appalachian State Teachers' Coll. *(see Appalachian State Univ.)*
Appalachian State Univ. 284
Appalachian Tech. Coll. 99, 726
Appalachian Tech. Inst. 726 *(see also Appalachian Tech. Coll.)*
Appalachian Training Sch. for Teachers *(see Appalachian State Univ.)*
Applied Career Training, Inc. 400, 738
Applied Career Training, Inc—Alexandria Campus *(see ACT Coll—Alexandria)*
Applied Prof. Training, Inc. 452
Appling Tech. Edu. Ctr. 98
Appraisal & Property Management Coll. *(see National Coll. of Appraisal & Property Management)*
Apprentice Sch—Newport News Shipbuilding *(see Northrop Grumman Newport News Apprentice Sch.)*
APUS Ctr. for Prof. & Workforce Development 640
Aquinas Coll. 195, 364 *(see also Saint Thomas Aquinas Coll., Thomas Aquinas Coll.)*
Aquinas Inst. of Philosophy & Theology *(see Aquinas Inst. of Theology)*

Aquinas Inst. of Theology 223
Aquinas Jr. Coll. *(see Aquinas Coll.)*
Aquinas Theology Inst. *(see Aquinas Inst. of Theology)*
Arapahoe Coll. *(see Arapahoe Comm. Coll.)*
Arapahoe Comm. Coll. 64
Arapahoe Jr. Coll. *(see Arapahoe Comm. Coll.)*
Arcadia Univ. 325
Architectural Ctr. of Boston *(see Boston Architectural Ctr.)*
Architecture Inst. of Southern California *(see Southern California Inst. of Architecture)*
Area One Vocational-Tech. Sch. *(see Northeast Iowa Comm. Coll.)*
Area Vocational Sch. for Alachua County *(see Santa Fe Comm. Coll.)*
Argosy Atlanta *(see Argosy Univ. Atlanta)*
Argosy Univ. 726, 727, 738
Argosy Univ. Atlanta 99, 726
Argosy Univ. Chicago 117
Argosy Univ. Chicago Northwest 727 *(see also Argosy Univ. Schaumburg)*
Argosy Univ. Coll. of Health Sciences *(see Argosy Univ. Twin Cities)*
Argosy Univ. Dallas 374
Argosy Univ. Hawai'i 113, 727
Argosy Univ. Honolulu 727 *(see also Argosy Univ. Hawai'i)*
Argosy Univ. Los Angeles *(see Argosy Univ. Orange County)*
Argosy Univ. Orange County 30
Argosy Univ. Phoenix 14
Argosy Univ. San Francisco Bay Area 30
Argosy Univ. Schaumburg 117, 727
Argosy Univ. Seattle 410
Argosy Univ. Tampa 81
Argosy Univ. Twin Cities 207, 731
Argosy Univ. Washington, DC 400, 738
Argyle Inst. of Human Relations 711
Ari-Ben Aviator 479
Arizona Acad. of Beauty, Inc. 444
Arizona Acad. of Beauty—North Inc. 444
Arizona Acupuncture & Oriental Medicine Sch. *(see Arizona Sch. of Acupuncture & Oriental Medicine)*
Arizona Automotive Inst. 14
Arizona Coll. *(see Arizona Coll. of Allied Health, Midwestern Univ—Glendale)*
Arizona Coll. of Allied Health 444
Arizona Coll. of Osteopathic Medicine *(see Midwestern Univ—Glendale)*

Arizona Dept. of Health Services *(see Arizona State Hosp.)*
Arizona Golf Acad. *(see Golf Acad. of Arizona)*
Arizona Inst. of Bus. & Techno. 721 *(see also Int'l. Inst. of the Americas)*
Arizona Int'l. Campus of The Univ. of Arizona *(see Arizona Int'l. Coll.)*
Arizona Int'l. Coll., The 21
Arizona Int'l. Univ. *(see Arizona Int'l. Coll.)*
Arizona Paralegal Training Program *(see Long Tech. Coll—East Valley)*
Arizona Sch. of Acupuncture & Oriental Medicine 14
Arizona Sch. of Dentistry & Oral Health *(see Arizona Sch. of Health Sciences)*
Arizona Sch. of Health Sciences *(see A.T. Still Univ. of Health Sciences)*
Arizona Sch. of Health Sciences, The 223
Arizona Sch. of Pharmacy Techno. *(see Arizona Coll. of Allied Health)*
Arizona Sch. of Prof. Psychology *(see Argosy Univ. Phoenix)*
Arizona State Coll. at Flagstaff *(see Northern Arizona Univ.)*
Arizona State Coll. at Tempe *(see Arizona State Univ.)*
Arizona State Hosp. 651
Arizona State Teachers Coll. at Tempe *(see Arizona State Univ.)*
Arizona State Univ. 14
Arizona State Univ. East 721 *(see also Arizona State Univ. Polytechnic Campus)*
Arizona State Univ. Polytechnic Campus 721
Arizona State Univ. West 14
Arizona Territorial Normal Sch. *(see Arizona State Univ.)*
Arizona Univ. *(see Univ. of Arizona)*
Arizona Western Coll. 15
Arkadelphia Beauty Coll. 447
Arkadelphia Methodist Coll. *(see Henderson State Univ.)*
Arkansas Aviation Technologies Ctr. 753
Arkansas Baptist Coll. 24
Arkansas Beauty Sch. 447
Arkansas Beauty Sch—Conway 447
Arkansas Christian Coll. *(see Harding Univ.)*
Arkansas City Jr. Coll. *(see Cowley County Comm. Coll.)*
Arkansas Coll. *(see Lyon Coll.)*
Arkansas Continental Beauty Coll. *(see Arthur's Beauty Coll.)*

Arkansas Industrial Univ. *(see Univ. of Arkansas at Fayetteville)*
Arkansas Mental Health Services Division *(see Univ. of Arkansas for Med. Sciences)*
Arkansas Northeastern Coll. 24, 721
Arkansas Northeastern Coll—Burdette Ctr. 721
Arkansas Polytechnic Coll. *(see Arkansas Tech Univ.)*
Arkansas State Coll—Beebe Campus *(see Arkansas State Univ—Beebe)*
Arkansas State Hosp., Division of Mental Health Services *(see Univ. of Arkansas for Med. Sciences)*
Arkansas State Normal Sch. *(see Univ. of Central Arkansas)*
Arkansas State Teachers Coll. *(see Univ. of Central Arkansas)*
Arkansas State Univ. 24
Arkansas State Univ. Mountain Home 24
Arkansas State Univ—Beebe 24
Arkansas State Univ—Newport 24
Arkansas Tech Univ. 24, 721
Arkansas Tech Univ—Ozark 721
Arkansas Univ. at Fort Smith *(see Univ. of Arkansas at Fort Smith)*
Arkansas Valley Tech. Coll. 721 *(see also Arkansas Tech Univ—Ozark)*
Arkansas Valley Tech. Inst. *(see Arkansas Tech Univ—Ozark)*
Arkansas Vocational-Tech. Sch. *(see Southeast Arkansas Coll.)*
Arleen's Beauty Acad. *(see Arleen's Clinton Beauty Acad.)*
Arleen's Clinton Beauty Acad. 758
Arlington Baptist Coll. 374
Arlington Career Inst. 617
Arlington Coll. *(see Azusa Pacific Univ.)*
Arlington Coll. *(see also Univ. of Texas at Arlington)*
Arlington Court Reporting Coll. *(see Arlington Career Inst.)*
Arlington Med. Inst. 617
Arlington State Coll. *(see Univ. of Texas at Arlington)*
Armed Forces Inst. of Pathology, The 660
Armenian American Univ. *(see American Univ. of Armenia)*
Armour Inst. *(see Illinois Inst. of Techno.)*
Armstrong Atlantic State Univ. 99
Armstrong County Mem. Hosp. 696
Armstrong State Coll. *(see Armstrong Atlantic State Univ.)*
Armstrong State Univ. *(see Armstrong Atlantic State Univ.)*

Armstrong Univ. 722
Army Acad. of Health Sciences *(see United States Army Med. Dept. Ctr. & Sch.)*
Army Air Force Inst. of Techno. *(see Air Force Inst. of Techno.)*
Army Air Forces Engineering Sch. *(see Air Force Inst. of Techno.)*
Army Baylor Univ. *(see Acad. of Health Sciences)*
Army Command & General Staff Coll. *(see United States Army Command & General Staff Coll.)*
Army DENTAC at Fort Bragg *(see United States Army DENTAC—Ft. Bragg)*
Army Dental Activity—Ft Benning *(see United States Army Dental Activity—Ft Benning)*
Army Dental Activity—Ft Bragg *(see United States Army Dental Activity—Ft Bragg)*
Army Dental Activity—Ft Jackson *(see United States Army Dental Activity—Ft Jackson)*
Army Dental Activity—Tripler *(see Tripler Army Med. Ctr.)*
Army Dental Clinic Command *(see United States Army Dental Clinic Command)*
Army Dept. Headqaurters *(see Dept. of Army Headquarters)*
Army Infantry Sch. *(see United States Army Infantry Sch.)*
Army Inst. for Prof. Development *(see United States Army Inst. for Prof. Development)*
Army Med. Dept. Schools *(see United States Army Med. Dept. Ctr. & Sch.)*
Army Med. Equipment & Optician Sch. 626 *(see also U.S. Army Med. Equipment & Optical Sch.)*
Army Med. Service Sch. *(see United States Army Med. Dept. Ctr. & Sch.)*
Army Ordnance Ctr. & Sch. *(see United States Army Ordnance Ctr. & Sch.)*
Army Ordnance Missile & Munitions Ctr. & Sch. *(see United States Army Ordnance Munitions & Electronic Maintenance Sch.)*
Army Polygraph Sch. *(see Dept. of Defense Polygraph Inst.)*
Army Quartermaster Ctr. & Sch. *(see United States Army Quartermaster Ctr. & Sch.)*

Army Transportation & Aviation Logistics Sch. *(see United States Army Transportation & Aviation Logistics Sch.)*
Army War Coll. *(see United States Army War Coll.)*
Army-Baylor Univ. Grad. Program in Health Care Administration *(see Baylor Univ.)*
Army—Dental Activities *(see United States Army—Dental Activities)*
Arnold Coll. *(see Univ. of Bridgeport)*
Arnold/Padrick's Univ. of Cosmetology 492
Arnold's Beauty Coll. *(see LaShe' Beauty Acad.)*
Arnold's Beauty Sch. 611
Arnot Health *(see Arnot-Ogden Med. Ctr.)*
Arnot-Ogden Med. Ctr. 685
Arrowhead Comm. Coll. *(see Fond du Lac Tribal & Comm. Coll.)*
Arrowhead Comm. Colleges *(see Mesabi Range Comm. & Tech. Coll.)*
Arrowhead Reg. Med. Ctr. 653
Art Acad. of Cincinnati 298
Art & Design Coll. of Maryland *(see Sch. of Art & Design at Montgomery Coll.)*
Art & Design Coll. of Pennsylvania *(see Pennsylvania Coll. of Art & Design)*
Art & Design Sch. of New England *(see New England Sch. of Art & Design at Suffolk Univ.)*
Art & Science Inst. of Cosmetology & Massage Therapy 640
Art Ctr. *(see Art Ctr. Design Coll., Art Ctr. Coll. of Design, Art Ctr. Design Coll., The)*
Art Ctr. Coll. of Design 30
Art Ctr. Design Coll. *(see Art Ctr. Coll. of Design, Art Ctr. Design Coll., The)*
Art Ctr. Design Coll., The 15
Art Coll. of Columbus *(see Columbus Coll. of Art & Design)*
Art Coll. of Maine *(see Maine Coll. of Art)*
Art Coll. of Massachusetts *(see Massachusetts Coll. of Art)*
Art Coll. of Memphis *(see Memphis Coll. of Art)*
Art Coll. of Savannah *(see Savannah Coll. of Art & Design)*
Art Coll. of the Pacific Northwest *(see Pacific Northwest Coll. of Art)*
Art Inst. of Atlanta, The 99
Art Inst. of Boston *(see Art Inst. of Boston at Lesley Univ.)*

Art Inst. of Boston at Lesley Univ., The 188
Art Inst. of California—Los Angeles 325 *(see also Art Inst. of Pittsburgh)*
Art Inst. of California—Orange County, The 64
Art Inst. of California—San Diego, The 30
Art Inst. of California—San Francisco, The 30
Art Inst. of Charlotte, The 284
Art Inst. of Chicago *(see Sch. of the Art Inst. of Chicago)*
Art Inst. of Cincinnati, The 298
Art Inst. of Cleveland *(see Cleveland Inst. of Art)*
Art Inst. of Colorado, The 64
Art Inst. of Dallas, The 374
Art Inst. of Fort Lauderdale, The 81
Art Inst. of Houston, The 374
Art Inst. of Illinois *(see Illinois Inst. of Art)*
Art Inst. of Kansas City *(see Kansas City Art Inst.)*
Art Inst. of Las Vegas, The 240
Art Inst. of Los Angeles *(see Art Inst. of California—Los Angeles, Art Inst. of Pittsburgh)*
Art Inst. of Milwaukee *(see Milwaukee Inst. of Art & Design)*
Art Inst. of Minnesota *(see Art Institutes Int'l—Minnesota)*
Art Inst. of New England *(see New England Inst. of Art)*
Art Inst. of New Hampshire *(see New Hampshire Inst. of Art)*
Art Inst. of New York City, The 255
Art Inst. of Ohio—Cincinnati, The 299
Art Inst. of Orange County *(see Art Inst. of California—Orange County)*
Art Inst. of Philadelphia, The 325
Art Inst. of Phoenix, The 64
Art Inst. of Pittsburgh, The 325, 748
Art Inst. of Portland, The 320, 735
Art Inst. of San Francisco *(see San Francisco Art Inst.)*
Art Inst. of Seattle, The 410
Art Inst. of Southern California, The *(see Laguna Coll. of Art & Design)*
Art Inst. of Washington, The 99 *(see also Art Inst. of Atlanta)*
Art Institutes Int'l. at Portland 735 *(see also Art Inst. of Portland)*
Art Institutes Int'l. at San Francisco, The *(see Art Inst. of California—San Francisco)*
Art Institutes Int'l—Minnesota 207
Art Instruction Schools 533

Art Sch. of Minneapolis *(see Minneapolis Coll. of Art & Design)*
Art Sch. of Northern New England *(see New Hampshire Inst. of Art)*
Arthur Angelo Sch. of Cosmetology & Hair Design 607
Arthur D. Little Management Edu. Inst., Inc. *(see Hult Int'l. Bus. Sch.)*
Arthur D. Little Sch. of Management 730 *(see also Hult Int'l. Bus. Sch.)*
Arthur G. James Cancer Hosp. *(see Ohio State Univ.)*
Arthur's Beauty Coll. 447
Artistic Acad. of Hair Design, The 545
Artistic Beauty Coll. *(see Georgia Career Inst.)*
Artistic Beauty Colleges 444, 471
Artistic Beauty Colleges—Denver 471
Artistic Beauty Colleges—Glendale 444
Artistic Beauty Colleges—Lakewood 471
Artistic Beauty Colleges—Phoenix 444
Artistic Beauty Colleges—Scottsdale 444
Artistic Beauty Colleges—Thornton 471
Artistic Beauty Colleges—Tuscon 444
Artistic Beauty Sch. *(see Artistic Beauty Colleges)*
Artistic Nails & Beauty Acad. 479
Arts & Crafts Society *(see Oregon Coll. of Art & Craft)*
Arts Coll. of California *(see California Coll. of the Arts)*
Arts Sch. of North Carolina *(see North Carolina Sch. of the Arts)*
ASA Inst. of Bus. & Computer Techno. 733 *(see also ASA Inst., The Coll. of Advanced Techno.)*
ASA Inst., The Coll. of Advanced Techno. 255, 733, 747
Asbury Coll. 158 *(see also Asbury Theological Seminary)*
Asbury Methodist Village 674
Asbury Seminary *(see Asbury Theological Seminary)*
Asbury Theological Seminary 158
Ascension Coll. 515
Ascension Health *(see Saint Vincent's Med. Ctr.)*
Asheboro Beauty Sch. 757
Asheboro Bus. Coll. *(see Brookstone Coll. of Bus.)*
Asher Sch. of Bus. 726 *(see also Brown Mackie Coll—Cincinnati)*
Asheville Farm Sch. *(see Warren Wilson Coll.)*

Asheville VA Med. Ctr. *(see Veterans Affairs Med. Ctr—Asheville)*
Asheville Veterans Affairs Med. Ctr. *(see Veterans Affairs Med. Ctr— Asheville)*
Asheville-Biltmore Coll. *(see Univ. of North Carolina at Asheville)*
Asheville-Buncombe Coll. *(see Asheville-Buncombe Tech. Comm. Coll.)*
Asheville-Buncombe Tech. Comm. Coll. 284
Ashford Univ., The 145, 728
Ashland Coll. *(see Ashland Univ.)*
Ashland Comm. & Tech. Coll. 158, 728
Ashland Comm. & Tech. Coll— Roberts Drive Campus 728
Ashland Comm. Coll. 728 *(see also Ashland Comm. & Tech. Coll.)*
Ashland County Career Ctr. *(see Ashland County-West Holmes Career Ctr.)*
Ashland County-West Holmes Career Ctr. 576
Ashland Sch. of Beauty Culture 640
Ashland Seminary *(see Ashland Theological Seminary)*
Ashland Tech. Coll. 728 *(see also Ashland Comm. & Tech. Coll.)*
Ashland Theological Seminary 299
Ashland Univ. 299
Ashmead Coll. 636
Ashmead Edu., Inc. *(see Ashmead Coll.)*
Ashmore Bus. Coll. *(see Brookstone Coll. of Bus.)*
Ashridge Univ. 717
Ashtabula County Joint Vocational School 576
Ashtabula County JVS *(see Ashtabula County Joint Vocational School)*
Ashworth Coll. 99
Asian American Int'l. Beauty Coll. 452
Asian Inst. of Med. Studies 743
Asian Med. Studies Inst. *(see Asian Inst. of Med. Studies)*
Askins Vo-Tech, Inc. 447
ASM Beauty World Acad. 479
Asnuntuck Coll. *(see Asnuntuck Comm. Coll.)*
Asnuntuck Comm. Coll. 72
Asnuntuck Comm-Tech. Coll. *(see Asnuntuck Comm. Coll.)*
ASPECT Edu., Inc. *(see ASPECT Int'l. Language Schools)*
ASPECT Int'l. Language Schools 452
Aspen Univ. 64, 724
ASPIRA, Inc. de Puerto Rico 602
Assemblies of God Coll. *(see Southwestern Assemblies of God Univ., Southeastern Univ.)*

Assemblies of God Grad. Sch. *(see Assemblies of God Theological Seminary)*
Assemblies of God Theological Seminary 223
Assemblies of God Univ. *(see Southwestern Assemblies of God Univ.)*
Assembly's Training Sch. for Lay Workers *(see Union Theological Seminary & Presbyterian Sch. of Christian Edu.)*
Assisi Jr. Coll. *(see Univ. of Saint Francis)*
Associated Beth Rivkah Schools 558
Associated Canadian Theological Schools *(see Trinity Western Univ.)*
Associated Charities *(see Family Service & Guidance Ctr. of Topeka, Inc.)*
Associated Mennonite Biblical Seminary 135
Associated Tech. Coll. 452
Associated Training Services Corporation 739
Assoc. of Independent Colleges & Universities in New Jersey 733
Assumption Coll. 184
Assumption Coll. for Sisters 245
Aston Univ. 718
Astoria Beauty Coll. 735 *(see also Paul Mitchell The Sch.)*
Astrodome Dental Career Ctr. 617
Astrological Inst. 444
ASU Mountain Home *(see Arkansas State Univ. Mountain Home)*
ASU West *(see Arizona State Univ. West)*
ATA Aviation Training Acad. *(see Aviation Inst. of Maintenance Training Acad.)*
ATA Career Edu. 512
Atascadero State Hosp. 653
ATC Training Ctr. *(see Automotive Training Ctr.)*
ATDS—Prairie Hill *(see ATDS—Prairie Hill Truck Driving Sch.)*
Athabasca Univ. 431
Athenaeum of Ohio, The 299
Athens American Univ. *(see American Univ. of Athens)*
Athens Area Tech. Inst. *(see Athens Tech. Coll.)*
Athens Coll. *(see Athens State Univ.)*
Athens Female Acad. *(see Athens State Univ.)*
Athens Female Coll. *(see Athens State Univ., Tennessee Wesleyan Coll.)*
Athens Female Inst. *(see Athens State Univ.)*

Athens Sch. of the Univ. of Chattanooga *(see Tennessee Wesleyan Coll.)*
Athens State Coll. *(see Athens State Univ.)*
Athens State Univ. 3
Athens Tech. Coll. 99
At-Home Professions 471
ATI Career Inst. *(see Stratford Univ.)*
ATI Career Training Ctr. 81, 374, 617 *(see also ATI Career Training Ctr. Electronic Campus)*
ATI Career Training Ctr. Electronic Campus *(see ATI Career Training Ctr.)*
ATI Coll. 452, 722
ATI Coll. of Health 81, 725
ATI Health Edu. Ctr. 725 *(see also ATI Coll. of Health)*
ATI Tech. Training Ctr. 617
ATI—American Trades Institutes 737 *(see also ATI Tech. Training Ctr.)*
ATI—Hollywood *(see BarPalma Beauty Careers Acad.)*
ATI-Hollywood 738
ATI—Tech. Training Ctr. 737 *(see also ATI Tech. Training Ctr.)*
Atlanta Area Tech. Sch. *(see Atlanta Tech. Coll.)*
Atlanta Art Inst. *(see Art Inst. of Atlanta)*
Atlanta Ballet Centre for Dance Edu., The 492
Atlanta Baptist Coll. *(see Interdenominational Theological Ctr.)*
Atlanta Baptist Seminary *(see Interdenominational Theological Ctr.)*
Atlanta Christian Coll. 99
Atlanta Clinical Coll. *(see Psychological Studies Inst.)*
Atlanta Coll. *(see Atlanta Coll. of Art, Atlanta Metropolitan Coll.)*
Atlanta Coll. of Art 99
Atlanta Coll. of Culinary Arts *(see Le Cordon Bleu Coll. of Culinary Arts—Atlanta, Western Culinary Inst.)*
Atlanta Inst. of Music 492
Atlanta Job Corps Ctr. 492
Atlanta Jr. Coll. *(see Atlanta Metropolitan Coll.)*
Atlanta Med. Ctr. 664
Atlanta Metropolitan Coll. 99
Atlanta Penitentiary *(see United States Penitentiary Atlanta)*
Atlanta Sch. of Massage 492
Atlanta Tech. Coll. 99, 744
Atlanta Tech. Inst. 726 *(see also Atlanta Tech. Coll.)*

Atlanta Univ. *(see Clark Atlanta Univ.)*
Atlanta VA Med. Ctr. *(see Atlanta Veterans Affairs Med. Ctr.)*
Atlanta Veterans Affairs Med. Ctr. 664
Atlantic Cape Comm. Coll. 245
Atlantic Coast Inst. 725 *(see also Key Coll.)*
Atlantic Coll. 347 *(see also Coll. of the Atlantic)*
Atlantic Comm. Coll. *(see Atlantic Cape Comm. Coll.)*
Atlantic County Comm. Coll. *(see Atlantic Cape Comm. Coll.)*
Atlantic County Vocational Sch. *(see Atlantic County Vocational Tech. Sch.)*
Atlantic County Vocational Tech. Sch. 683
Atlantic Culinary Acad. *(see McIntosh Coll.)*
Atlantic Health System *(see Morristown Mem. Hosp., Overlook Hosp.)*
Atlantic Inst. of Oriental Medicine 81
Atlantic Mind Body Ctr. 551
Atlantic Sch. of Theology 431
Atlantic Shores Healthcare, Inc. *(see South Florida State Hosp.)*
Atlantic States Chiropractic Inst. *(see New York Chiropractic Coll.)*
Atlantic Tech *(see Atlantic Tech. Ctr.)*
Atlantic Tech. Ctr. 480
Atlantic Union Coll. 184
Atlantic Univ. 400
Atlantic Univ. of Chinese Medicine 757
Atlantic Vocational-Tech. Ctr. *(see Atlantic Tech. Ctr.)*
ATS Inst. of Techno. 299
Auburn Career Ctr. 576
Auburn Flight Service, Inc. *(see Northwest Aviation Coll.)*
Auburn Univ. 3
Auburn Univ. at Montgomery 4
Auburn Vocational Sch. Dist. *(see Auburn Career Ctr.)*
Auburndale Female Seminary *(see Lasell Coll.)*
Audio Recording Techno. Inst. 480
Audio Research Inst. *(see Inst. of Audio Research)*
Audio-Video Inst. *(see Sound Master Recording Engineer Sch/Audio-Video Inst.)*
Audrey Cohen Coll. *(see Metropolitan Coll. of New York)*
Augsburg Coll. 207
Augsburg Theological Seminary *(see Luther Seminary)*
Augusta Area Tech. Sch. *(see Augusta Tech. Coll.)*

Augusta Area Vocational-Tech. Sch. *(see Augusta Tech. Coll.)*
Augusta Coll. *(see Augusta State Univ.)*
Augusta Inst. *(see Interdenominational Theological Ctr.)*
Augusta State Univ. 100
Augusta Tech. Coll. 100, 726
Augusta Tech. Inst. 726 *(see also Augusta Tech. Coll.)*
Augustana Coll. 117, 361
Augustana Theological Seminary *(see Lutheran Sch. of Theology at Chicago)*
Augustinian Coll. of Villanova *(see Villanova Univ.)*
Aultman Hosp. 693
Aurora Comm. Coll. *(see Comm. Coll. of Aurora)*
Aurora Family Service 708
Aurora Health Care *(see Aurora Family Service, Saint Luke's Med. Ctr.)*
Aurora Health Care, Inc. *(see Saint Luke's Med. Ctr.)*
Aurora Health Ctr—Airport *(see Saint Luke's Med. Ctr.)*
Aurora Mental Health Ctr. 657
Aurora Public Schools *(see T.H. Pickens Tech. Ctr.)*
Aurora Sinai Med. Ctr. 708
Aurora Univ. 117
Austin Acad. of Oriental Medicine *(see Acad. of Oriental Medicine at Austin)*
Austin Beauty Sch. 733 *(see also Austin's Sch. of Spa Techno.)*
Austin Bus. Coll., The 374
Austin Coll. 374 *(see also Austin Comm. Coll.)*
Austin Comm. Coll. 374 *(see also Riverland Comm. Coll—Austin)*
Austin Cosmetology & Permanent Cosmetics Inst. 759
Austin Cosmetology Inst. *(see Austin Cosmetology & Permanent Cosmetics Inst.)*
Austin Grad. Sch. of Theology 374, 737
Austin Oriental Medicine Acad. *(see Acad. of Oriental Medicine at Austin)*
Austin Peay Normal Sch. *(see Austin Peay State Univ.)*
Austin Peay State Coll. *(see Austin Peay State Univ.)*
Austin Peay State Univ. 364
Austin Presbyterian Theological Seminary 374
Austin Sch. of Theology *(see Austin Grad. Sch. of Theology)*

Austin Seminary *(see Austin Presbyterian Theological Seminary)*
Austin State Univ. *(see Stephen F. Austin State Univ.)*
Austin Theology Sch. *(see Austin Grad. Sch. of Theology)*
Austin's Beauty Coll., Inc 758
Austin's Sch. of Spa Techno. 558, 733
Australasian Coll. of Health Sciences 592, 735
Australasian Coll. of Herbal Studies 735
Australian Grad. Sch. of Management *(see Univ. of New South Wales)*
Auto Diesel Coll. of Nashville *(see Nashville Auto Diesel Coll.)*
Automeca Tech. Coll. 602
Automeca Tech. Coll—Ponce 602
Automotive Inst. of Arizona *(see Arizona Automotive Inst.)*
Automotive Machinists Sch. *(see Sch. of Automotive Machinists)*
Automotive Management Coll. *(see Coll. of Automotive Management)*
Automotive Training Ctr. 594
Autonomous Tech. Inst. of Mexico 715
Autry Area Vocational-Tech. Ctr. *(see Autry Techno. Ctr.)*
Autry Tech *(see Autry Techno. Ctr.)*
Autry Techno. Ctr. 586
Avalon Beauty Coll. 452
Avance Beauty Coll. 453
Ave Maria Coll. 746
Ave Maria Sch. of Law 195
Ave Maria Univ. *(see Ave Maria Coll.)*
Aveda Fredric's Inst. 576
Aveda Inst. 515, 754 *(see also Douglas J Aveda Inst.)*
Aveda Inst. Atlanta 492
Aveda Inst. Baton Rouge 515, 739
Aveda Inst. Chicago 755
Aveda Inst. de Bellas Artes *(see New Mexico Aveda Inst. de Bellas Artes)*
Aveda Inst. Lafayette 515, 729
Aveda Inst. New York 757
Aveda Inst., Inc. 533
Avera Health 701
Avera Health ACPE Ctr. *(see Avera Health)*
Avera McKennan Hosp. & Univ. Health Ctr. 702
Avera Sacred Heart Hosp. 702
Averett Coll. *(see Averett Univ.)*
Averett Univ. 400
Avery Heights 658
Aviation & Electronic Sch. of America 30
Aviation Inst. of Maintenance 492, 537, 594

Aviation Inst. of Maintenance Training Acad. 135, 727
Aviation Inst. of Maintenance—Indianapolis *(see Aviation Inst. of Maintenance Training Acad.)*
Aviation Maintenance Training, Inc. *(see Aeronautical Inst. of Technologies)*
Aviation Medicine Sch. *(see Sch. of Aviation Medicine)*
Aviation Techno. Division *(see Hallmark Inst. of Aeronautics)*
Avila Coll. *(see Avila Univ.)*
Avila Univ. 223
Avtech Inst. of Techno. 545
Avtech Techno. Inc. *(see Avtech Inst. of Techno.)*
Award Beauty Sch., Inc. 521
Awesome Kneading Sch. *(see AKS Massage Sch.)*
Axia Coll. *(see Western Int'l. Univ.)*
Ayers Inst. 515
Ayers Sch. of Bus., Inc. *(see Ayers Inst.)*
Ayers State Tech. Coll. *(see Gadsden State Comm. Coll.)*
Azusa Coll. *(see Azusa Pacific Univ.)*
Azusa Pacific Univ. 31

B

B Naturale Beauty Sch., Inc. *(see Int'l. B Naturale Beauty Sch., Inc.)*
B. Dickson & Associates, LLC 474, 724
B.I.R. Training Ctr. *(see BIR Training Ctr.)*
B.J.'s Beauty & Barber Coll. 636
B.M. Spurr Sch. of Practical Nursing 707
Babel Univ. 646
Babel Univ. Hawaii *(see Babel Univ. Prof. Sch. of Translation)*
Babel Univ. Prof. Sch. of Translation 113 *(see also Babel Univ.)*
Babel Univ. PST *(see Babel Univ. Prof. Sch. of Translation)*
Babson Coll. 184
Babson Inst. *(see Babson Coll.)*
Bacone Coll. 315
Bahamas Hotel Training Coll. *(see Bahamas Hotel Training Coll.)*
Bahner Coll. of Hairstyling 732 *(see also La' James Int'l. Coll.)*
Bailey Tech. Sch., Inc. *(see ITT Tech. Inst.)*
Bainbridge Coll. 100
Bais Binyomin Acad. 72, 724
Baker Aviation Sch. *(see George T. Baker Aviation Sch.)*

Baker Coll. Bus. & Corporate Services 195
Baker Coll. Ctr. for Grad. Studies 195
Baker Coll. Corporate Services *(see Baker Coll. Bus. & Corporate Services)*
Baker Coll. of Allen Park 195
Baker Coll. of Auburn Hills 195
Baker Coll. of Cadillac 195
Baker Coll. of Clinton Township 196
Baker Coll. of Flint 196
Baker Coll. of Jackson 196
Baker Coll. of Mount Clemens *(see Baker Coll. of Clinton Township)*
Baker Coll. of Muskegon 196
Baker Coll. of Owosso 196
Baker Coll. of Port Huron 196
Baker Coll. Online 196
Baker Sch. of Aviation *(see George T. Baker Aviation Sch.)*
Baker Sch. of Nursing *(see Baker Univ—Sch. of Nursing)*
Baker Sch. of Prof. & Grad. Studies *(see Baker Univ—Sch. of Prof. & Grad. Studies)*
Baker Univ. 152
Baker Univ—Sch. of Prof. & Grad. Studies *(see Baker Univ.)*
Bakersfield Coll. 31
Baking Inst. of America *(see American Inst. of Baking)*
Bakke Grad. Univ. 410
Bakke Univ. *(see Bakke Grad. Univ.)*
Baldwin Agricultural Coll. *(see Abraham Baldwin Agricultural Coll.)*
Baldwin Beauty Sch. 617
Baldwin Coll. *(see Mary Baldwin Coll.)*
Baldwin Inst. *(see Baldwin-Wallace Coll.)*
Baldwin Sch. *(see Macalester Coll.)*
Baldwin Univ. *(see Baldwin-Wallace Coll., Macalester Coll.)*
Baldwin-Wallace Coll. 299
Ball Mem. Hosp. 669
Ball State Univ. 135
Ballet Acad. of Idaho *(see Ballet Idaho Acad.)*
Ballet Idaho Acad. 497
Ballet Sch. of the Pacific Northwest *(see Pacific Northwest Ballet Sch.)*
Baltimore City Comm. Coll. 178
Baltimore Coll. *(see Baltimore Int'l. Coll.)*
Baltimore County Comm. Coll. *(see Comm. Coll. of Baltimore County)*
Baltimore Hebrew Univ. 178
Baltimore Int'l. Coll. 178
Baltimore Int'l. Culinary Coll. *(see Baltimore Int'l. Coll.)*

Baltimore Jr. Coll. *(see Baltimore City Comm. Coll.)*

Baltimore Massage Sch. *(see Baltimore Sch. of Massage)*

Baltimore Med. Coll. *(see Maryland General Hosp.)*

Baltimore Normal Sch. *(see Bowie State Univ.)*

Baltimore Sch. of Hair Design *(see Baltimore Studio of Hair Design, Inc.)*

Baltimore Sch. of Massage, The 521

Baltimore Studio of Hair Design, Inc. 521

Baltimore Univ. *(see Univ. of Baltimore)*

Baltimore VA Med. Ctr. *(see Veterans Affairs Med. Ctr—Baltimore)*

Baltimore Veterans Affairs Med. Ctr. *(see Veterans Affairs Med. Ctr— Baltimore)*

Bamberg Job Corps Ctr. 608

Bancroft Health Ctr. *(see Bancroft Sch. of Massage Therapy)*

Bancroft Massage Therapy Sch. *(see Bancroft Sch. of Massage Therapy)*

Bancroft Sch. of Massage Therapy 524

Bangor Comm. Coll. *(see Univ. of Maine at Augusta)*

Bangor Seminary *(see Bangor Theological Seminary)*

Bangor Theological Seminary 175

Bank Street Coll. of Edu. 256

Banking & Commerce Inst. *(see Instituto de Banca y Comercio)*

Baptist Bible Coll. 223, 747 *(see Baptist Bible Coll. & Seminary)*

Baptist Bible Coll. & Seminary 325

Baptist Bible Coll. East *(see Boston Baptist Coll.)*

Baptist Bible Coll. of Indianapolis *(see Crossroads Bible Coll.)*

Baptist Bible Coll. of Pennsylvania *(see Baptist Bible Coll. & Seminary)*

Baptist Bible Grad. Sch. of Theology *(see Baptist Bible Coll.)*

Baptist Bible Inst. *(see Baptist Coll. of Florida, New Orleans Baptist Theological Seminary)*

Baptist Bible Inst. of Grand Rapids *(see Cornerstone Univ.)*

Baptist Bible Seminary *(see Baptist Bible Coll. & Seminary)*

Baptist Coll. at McMinnville *(see Linfield Coll.)*

Baptist Coll. of Arkansas *(see Arkansas Baptist Coll.)*

Baptist Coll. of Florida, The 81

Baptist Coll. of Health Sciences *(see Baptist Mem. Coll. of Health Sciences)*

Baptist Coll. of Hillsdale *(see Hillsdale Free Will Baptist Coll.)*

Baptist Coll. of Houston *(see Houston Baptist Univ.)*

Baptist Coll. of Missouri *(see Missouri Baptist Univ.)*

Baptist Health *(see Baptist Med. Ctr. South Sch. of Med. Techno.)*

Baptist Health Care 661

Baptist Health Med. Ctr—Little Rock *(see Baptist Health System, Nursing & Allied Health Schools)*

Baptist Health System *(see Baptist Med. Ctr.)*

Baptist Health System of Alabama 651

Baptist Health System Sch. of Health Professions 375

Baptist Health System, Nursing & Allied Health Schools 652

Baptist Health Systems *(see Baptist Med. Ctr.)*

Baptist Health Systems of South Florida 661

Baptist Hosp. East 672

Baptist Hosp. of New England *(see New England Baptist Hosp.)*

Baptist Inst., The *(see Arkansas Baptist Coll.)*

Baptist Med. Ctr. 680, 703

Baptist Med. Ctr. South Sch. of Med. Techno. 651

Baptist Mem. Coll. of Health Sciences 364

Baptist Mem. Hosp. *(see Baptist Mem. Coll. of Health Sciences)*

Baptist Missionary Assoc. Theological Seminary 375

Baptist Missionary Training Sch. *(see Colgate Rochester Crozer Divinity Sch.)*

Baptist Seminary of North America *(see North American Baptist Seminary)*

Baptist Seminary of the Northwest *(see Northwest Baptist Seminary)*

Baptist Sr. Adult Ministries 660

Baptist Theological Seminary at Richmond 400

Baptist Theological Seminary of New Orleans *(see New Orleans Baptist Theological Seminary)*

Baptist Univ. of California *(see California Baptist Univ.)*

Baptist Univ. of Dallas *(see Dallas Baptist Univ.)*

Baptist Univ. of Houston *(see Houston Baptist Univ.)*

Baptist Univ. of Missouri *(see Missouri Baptist Univ.)*

Baptist Univ. of the Americas 375, 737

Baran Inst. of Techno. 474

Baran Techno. Inst. *(see Baran Inst. of Techno.)*

Barat Coll. 727

Barat Coll. of DePaul Univ. 117, 727

Barber Acad. of Bradenton *(see Bradenton Beauty & Barber Acad., Inc.)*

Barber Coll. of Albuquerque *(see Albuquerque Barber Coll.)*

Barber Coll. of Puerto Rico *(see Puerto Rico Barber Coll.)*

Barber Coll. of South Texas *(see South Texas Barber Coll.)*

Barber Coll. of West Michigan *(see West Michigan Coll. of Barbering & Beauty)*

Barber Coll., The 759

Barber Sch. of Michigan *(see Michigan Barber Sch., Inc.)*

Barber Sch. of Winston-Salem *(see Winston-Salem Barber Sch.)*

Barber-Scotia Coll. 734

Barboursville Seminary *(see Univ. of Charleston)*

Barclay Coll. 152, 745

Bard Coll. 256

Barnard Coll. 256

Barnes Coll. of Nursing 731, 732

Barnes Coll. of Nursing & Health Studies *(see Univ. of Missouri— St. Louis)*

Barnes Coll. of Nusring & Health Studies at the Univ. of Missouri— St. Louis 731

Barnes Jewish Hosp. *(see Barnes- Jewish Coll. of Nursing & Allied Health)*

Barnes Sch. of Anatomy, Sanitary Science & Embalming *(see Dallas Inst. of Funeral Services)*

Barnes-Jewish Coll. of Nursing & Allied Health 223, 732 *(see also Barnes-Jewish Hosp.)*

Barnes-Jewish Hosp. 680

Barnes-Jewish Hosp. at Washington Univ. Med. Ctr. *(see Barnes- Jewish Hosp.)*

BarPalma Beauty Careers Acad. 631, 738

Barre Sch. *(see Westfield State Coll.)*

Barrett & Company Sch. of Hair Design 512

Barrett Sch. of Hair Design *(see Barrett & Company Sch. of Hair Design)*

Barrington Coll. *(see Gordon Coll.)*

Barry Coll. *(see Barry Univ.)*

Barry Univ. 82

Barstow Acad. of Beauty *(see Bridges Acad. of Beauty)*

Barstow Coll. 31

Barstow Jr. Coll. *(see Barstow Coll.)*

Bartlesville Wesleyan Coll. *(see Oklahoma Wesleyan Univ.)*

Barton Coll. 284 *(see also Barton County Comm. Coll.)*

Barton County Coll. *(see Barton County Comm. Coll.)*

Barton County Comm. Coll. 152

Baruch Coll. *(see City Univ. of New York Bernard M. Baruch Coll.)*

Bassist Coll. *(see Art Inst. of Portland)*

Bastrop Beauty Sch. *(see Bastrop Beauty Sch. #1)*

Bastrop Beauty Sch. #1 515

Bastyr Coll. *(see Bastyr Univ.)*

Bastyr Univ. 410

Bates Coll. 175

Bates Tech. Coll. 410

Batesville Comm. Coll. *(see Univ. of Arkansas Comm. Coll. at Batesville)*

Batesville Job Corps Ctr. 535

Bath VA Med. Ctr. *(see Veterans Affairs Med. Ctr—Bath)*

Bath Veterans Affairs Med. Ctr. *(see Veterans Affairs Med. Ctr—Bath)*

Baton Rouge Coll. 515

Baton Rouge Comm. Coll. 166

Baton Rouge Dale Carnegie Training *(see Winner Inst., Inc.)*

Baton Rouge General 673

Baton Rouge Massage Therapy Coll. *(see Massage Therapy Coll. of Baton Rouge)*

Baton Rouge Sch. of Computers 166

Battle Creek Coll. *(see Andrews Univ.)*

Bauder Coll. 100

Bautista Sch. of Medicine *(see San Juan Bautista Sch. of Medicine)*

Bay City Jr. Coll. *(see Delta Coll.)*

Bay Coll. *(see Bay de Noc Comm. Coll.)*

Bay de Noc Coll. *(see Bay de Noc Comm. Coll.)*

Bay de Noc Comm. Coll. 196

Bay Med. Ctr. 82

Bay Mills Coll. *(see Bay Mills Comm. Coll.)*

Bay Mills Comm. Coll. 196

Bay Path Coll. 184

Bay Path Jr. Coll. *(see Bay Path Coll.)*

Bay Pines VA Med. Ctr. *(see Bay Pines Veterans Affairs Med. Ctr.)*

Bay Pines Veterans Affairs Med. Ctr. 661

Bay State Coll. 184

Bay State Sch. of Appliances *(see Bay State Sch. of Techno.)*

Bay State Sch. of Techno. 524

Bay Vista Coll. of Beauty 453

Bayamon Central Univ. 347

Bayamon Inst. of Modern Hairstyling *(see Modern Hairstyling Inst—Bayamon)*

Bayamon Modern Hairstyling Inst. *(see Modern Hairstyling Inst—Bayamon)*

Bayamon Univ. *(see Bayamon Central Univ.)*

Bayfront Med. Ctr. 661

Baylor Coll. of Dentistry *(see Texas A&M Univ. System Health Science Ctr.)*

Baylor Coll. of Medicine 375

Baylor Theological Seminary *(see Southwestern Baptist Theological Seminary)*

Baylor Univ. 375, 749

Baylor Univ. Coll. of Medicine *(see Baylor Coll. of Medicine)*

Baylor Univ. Med. Ctr. 703

Bayonne Med. Ctr. *(see Hudson Area Sch. of Radiologic Techno.)*

Bayshire Beauty Acad. 528

Bayside Automotive Tech. Training Ctr. *(see New York Automotive & Diesel Inst.)*

Baystate Med. Ctr. 676

BCRI Career Training *(see Court Reporting Inst., Court Reporting Inst—Boise)*

Beacom Coll. *(see Goldey-Beacom Coll.)*

Beacon Coll. 82

Beacon Coll. & Grad. Sch. 726 *(see also Beacon Univ.)*

Beacon Grad. Sch. *(see Beacon Univ.)*

Beacon Theological Seminary *(see Beacon Univ.)*

Beacon Univ. 100, 726

Beal Coll. 175

Beatrice Acad. of Beauty 577

Beau La Reine Coll. of Beauty Culture 737

Beau Monde Coll. of Hair Design 592

Beaufort Coll. *(see Univ. of South Carolina—Beaufort)*

Beaufort County Coll. *(see Beaufort County Comm. Coll.)*

Beaufort County Comm. Coll. 284

Beaufort Reg. Training Ctr. *(see Tech. Coll. of the Lowcountry)*

Beaufort Tech. Coll. *(see Tech. Coll. of the Lowcountry)*

Beaufort Tech. Edu. Ctr. *(see Tech. Coll. of the Lowcountry)*

Beaumont Hosp. *(see Mem. Hermann Baptist Beaumont Hosp.)*

Beaumont Hosp. Schools of Allied Health *(see William Beaumont Hosp. Schools of Allied Health)*

Beauty Acad. of Adrian *(see Adrian Beauty Acad., Inc.)*

Beauty Acad. of Alexandria *(see Alexandria Acad. of Beauty)*

Beauty Acad. of Bradenton *(see Bradenton Beauty & Barber Acad., Inc.)*

Beauty Acad. of Carson City *(see Carson City Beauty Acad.)*

Beauty Acad. of Chillicothe *(see Chillicothe Beauty Acad.)*

Beauty Acad. of Fort Pierce *(see Fort Pierce Beauty Acad.)*

Beauty Acad. of Keene *(see Keene Beauty Acad., Inc.)*

Beauty Acad. of Lafayette *(see Lafayette Beauty Acad., Inc.)*

Beauty Acad. of North Platte *(see North Platte Beauty Acad.)*

Beauty Acad. of San Fernando *(see San Fernando Beauty Acad., Inc.)*

Beauty Acad. of Warwick *(see Warwick Acad. of Beauty Culture)*

Beauty & Massage Inst. 483 *(see also Fort Pierce Beauty Acad.)*

Beauty Arts Acad. *(see Franklin Acad.)*

Beauty Careers Inst. *(see Inst. of Beauty Careers)*

Beauty Coll. of Alameda *(see Alameda Beauty Coll., Inc.)*

Beauty Coll. of Alhambra *(see Alhambra Beauty Coll.)*

Beauty Coll. of America 492

Beauty Coll. of Fayetteville *(see Fayetteville Beauty Coll.)*

Beauty Coll. of Grove *(see Grove Beauty Coll.)*

Beauty Coll. of Hot Springs *(see Hot Springs Beauty Coll.)*

Beauty Coll. of Knox *(see Knox Beauty Coll.)*

Beauty Coll. of Lake Forest *(see Lake Forest Beauty Coll.)*

Beauty Coll. of Madera *(see Madera Beauty Coll.)*

Beauty Coll. of Merrillville *(see Merrillville Beauty Coll.)*

Beauty Coll. of Montebello *(see Montebello Beauty Coll.)*

Beauty Coll. of North Fulton *(see North Fulton Beauty Coll.)*

Beauty Coll. of Oceanside *(see Oceanside Coll. of Beauty)*

Beauty Coll. of South Louisiana *(see South Louisiana Beauty Coll.)*

Beauty Coll. of Tucson *(see Tucson Coll. of Beauty)*

Beauty Coll. of West Michigan *(see West Michigan Coll. of Barbering & Beauty)*

Beauty Culture Acad. *(see Acad. of Beauty Culture)*

Beauty Inst. of Jacksonville *(see Jacksonville Beauty Inst., Inc.)*

Beauty Inst., Inc., The 480 *(see also Jacksonville Beauty Inst., Inc.*

Beauty Inst., The 612 (see also Jacksonville Beauty Inst., Inc.

Beauty Salon Sch. 757

Beauty Sch. of Arkansas *(see Arkansas Beauty Sch.)*

Beauty Sch. of Asheboro *(see Asheboro Beauty Sch.)*

Beauty Sch. of Lancaster *(see Lancaster Beauty Sch.)*

Beauty Sch. of Melbourne *(see Melbourne Beauty Sch.)*

Beauty Sch. of Middletown, Inc. 558

Beauty Sch. of Rosemead *(see Rosemead Beauty Sch., Inc.)*

Beauty Schools of America 480

Beauty Tech. Coll. 586

Beauty Works *(see Yakima Beauty Sch. Beauty Works)*

Beaver Coll. *(see Arcadia Univ., Comm. Coll. of Beaver County)*

Beaver County Comm. Coll. *(see Comm. Coll. of Beaver County)*

Beaver Falls Beauty Acad. 594

Beaverton Sch. of Beauty *(see Magee Brothers Beaverton Sch. of Beauty)*

Beck Area Career Ctr. 498

Beck Career Ctr. *(see Beck Area Career Ctr.)*

Becker Coll. 184

Becker's Bus. Coll. *(see Rockford Bus. Coll.)*

Beckfield Coll. 158 *(see also Daymar Coll.)*

Beckley Beauty Acad. 640

Beckley Coll. *(see Mountain State Univ.)*

Beckman Research Inst. *(see City of Hope National Med. Ctr.)*

Bedford VA Med. Ctr. *(see Edith Nourse Rogers Mem. Veterans Hosp.)*

Bedford Veterans Affairs Med. Ctr. *(see Edith Nourse Rogers Mem. Veterans Hosp.)*

Bee County Coll. *(see Coastal Bend Coll.)*

Bee-Jay's Hairstyling Acad. 447

Behavioral Health Ctr. *(see Ctr. for Behavioral Health)*

Behavioral Science Centers *(see Hypnosis Motivation Inst.)*

Behold! Beauty Acad. 617

Behrend Coll., The *(see Pennsylvania State Univ.)*

Beis Medrash Heichal Dovid 747

Bela's Sch. of Cosmetology *(see Mr. Bela's Sch. of Cosmetology)*

Belhaven Coll. 218

Belhaven Collegiate & Industrial Inst. *(see Belhaven Coll.)*

Bell Mar Beauty Coll. 498

Bella Capelli Acad. 758

Bellarmine Coll. *(see Bellarmine Univ.)*

Bellarmine Univ. 158

Bellefonte Acad. of Beauty 512

Belleville Area Coll. *(see Southwestern Illinois Coll.)*

Belleville Jr. Coll. *(see Southwestern Illinois Coll.)*

Bellevue Beauty Sch. 636

Bellevue Coll. *(see Bellevue Comm. Coll.)*

Bellevue Comm. Coll. 410

Bellevue Hosp. Ctr. 685

Bellevue Univ. 236

Bellin Coll. of Nursing 423

Bellin Health Systems *(see Bellin Sch. of Radiology)*

Bellin Mem. Hosp. Sch. of Nursing *(see Bellin Coll. of Nursing)*

Bellin Nursing Coll. *(see Bellin Coll. of Nursing)*

Bellin Sch. of Radiology 708

Bellingham Beauty Sch., Inc. 636

Bellingham Coll. *(see Bellingham Tech. Coll.)*

Bellingham Tech. Coll. 410

Bellingham Vocational Tech. Inst. *(see Bellingham Tech. Coll.)*

Belmont Abbey Coll. 284

Belmont Coll. *(see Belmont Univ.)*

Belmont Tech. Coll. 299

Belmont Tech. Inst. *(see Belmont Tech. Coll.)*

Belmont Univ. 364

Beloit Coll. 423

Bel-Rea Inst. of Animal Techno. 64

Bemidji Area Vocational Tech. Inst. *(see Northwest Tech. Coll.)*

Bemidji State Univ. 207

Bemidji Univ. *(see Bemidji State Univ.)*

Ben Franklin Career & Techno. Ctr. *(see Ben Franklin Career Ctr.)*

Ben Franklin Career Ctr. 640

Ben Hill-Irwin Tech. Inst. *(see East Central Tech. Coll.)*

Ben Stevenson Acad. of Ballet *(see Houston Ballet's Ben Stevenson Acad.)*

Ben Taub General Hosp. 703

Benedict Coll. *(see Tech. Coll. of the Lowcountry)*

Benedict Coll. 355

Benedict Inst. *(see Benedict Coll.)*

Benedictine Coll. 152 *(see also Benedictine Univ.)*

Benedictine Health System *(see City of Lakes Transitional Care Ctr.)*

Benedictine Univ. 117 *(see also Springfield Coll. in Illinois)*

Benedictine Univ. Springfield Coll. of Illinois *(see Springfield Coll. in Illinois)*

Benefis Healthcare—West Campus 682

Bene's Int'l. Sch. of Beauty 725

Bene's Int'l. Sch. of Beauty, Inc. 480

Benjamin Franklin Inst. of Techno. 184, 730

Benjamin Franklin Techno. Inst. *(see Benjamin Franklin Inst. of Techno.)*

Benjamin P. Cheney Acad. *(see Eastern Washington Univ.)*

Bennett Beauty Inst., Inc. 724 *(see also Bennett Career Inst., Inc.)*

Bennett Career Inst., Inc. 478, 724

Bennett Coll. 284

Bennett-Clarkson Hosp. *(see Rapid City Reg. Hosp.)*

Bennington Coll. 397

Bentley Coll. 184

Benton Harbor Comm. Coll. & Tech. Inst. *(see Lake Michigan Coll.)*

Benton Harbor Jr. Coll. *(see Lake Michigan Coll.)*

Berdan Inst. 545

Berdan Sch. for Med. Secretaries *(see Berdan Inst.)*

Berea Coll. 158

Berean Inst. 325

Berean Manual & Industrial Sch. *(see Berean Inst.)*

Berean Sch. of the Bible *(see Global Univ.)*

Berean Univ. *(see Global Univ.)*

Bergan Mercy Med. Ctr. *(see Alegent Health Bergan Mercy Med. Ctr.)*

Bergen Comm. Coll. 245

Bergen County Tech. Schools 545

Berk Trade & Bus. Sch. 558

Berkeley Baptist Divinity Sch. *(see American Baptist Seminary of the West)*

Berkeley Coll. of Acupuncture & Integrative Medicine *(see Acupuncture & Integrative Medicine Coll., Berkeley)*

Berkeley Coll. of New York City 256

Berkeley Coll—Garret Mountain Campus 245

Berkeley Divinity Sch. 72
Berkeley Divinity Sch. at Yale *(see Berkeley Divinity Sch.)*
Berkeley Learning Pavilion *(see Vista Comm. Coll.)*
Berkeley Sch. of New York, The *(see Berkeley Coll. of New York City)*
Berkeley Univ. *(see Univ. of California, Berkeley)*
Berkeley-Charleston-Dorchester Tech. Edu. Ctr. *(see Trident Tech. Coll.)*
Berklee Coll. of Music 185
Berklee Music Coll. *(see Berklee Coll. of Music)*
Berklee Sch. of Music *(see Berklee Coll. of Music)*
Berks Tech. Inst. 325
Berkshire Coll. *(see Berkshire Comm. Coll.)*
Berkshire Comm. Coll. 185
Berkshire Med. Ctr. 676
Berlitz Int'l., Inc. 545
Berlitz Language Centers *(see Berlitz Int'l., Inc.)*
Bermuda Coll. 752
Bermuda Hotel & Catering Coll. *(see Bermuda Coll.)*
Bermuda Tech. Inst. *(see Bermuda Coll.)*
Bernard M. Baruch Coll. *(see City Univ. of New York Bernard M. Baruch Coll.)*
Bernard's Sch. of Hair Fashion *(see Mr. Bernard's Sch. of Hair Fashion, Inc.)*
Berry Coll. 100
Berry Jr. Coll. *(see Berry Coll.)*
Bessemer Beauty Coll. 759
Bessemer State Tech. Coll. 721 *(see also T.A. Lawson State Comm. Coll.)*
Bessemer State Tech. Inst. *(see T.A. Lawson State Comm. Coll.)*
Bessemer Tech *(see T.A. Lawson State Comm. Coll.)*
Best Care Training Inst. 732
Beta Tech 400, 608
Beth Benjamin Acad. of Connecticut 724 *(see also Bais Binyomin Acad.)*
Beth HaMedrash Shaarei Yosher 256
Beth HaTalmud Rabbinical Coll. 256
Beth Israel Deaconess Med. Ctr. 676
Beth Israel Med. Ctr. 685
Beth Medrash Govoha 245
Beth Shraga Rabbinical Coll. *(see Rabbinical Coll. Beth Shraga)*
Bethany Acad. *(see Bethany Coll.)*
Bethany Bible Coll. 431
Bethany Bible Inst. 740 *(see also Bethany Coll.)*

Bethany Coll. 152, 418, 431, 722, 740 *(see also Bethany Bible Coll., Bethany Lutheran Coll., Bethany Univ.)*
Bethany Coll. of the Assemblies of God *(see Bethany Univ.)*
Bethany Hosp. *(see Advocate Bethany Hosp.)*
Bethany Ladies Coll. *(see Bethany Lutheran Coll.)*
Bethany Lutheran Coll. 207
Bethany Seminary *(see Bethany Theological Seminary)*
Bethany Theological Seminary 135
Bethany Univ. 31, 722
Bethel Bible Inst. *(see Central Pentecostal Coll.)*
Bethel Coll. & Seminary—San Diego Campus *(see Bethel Seminary San Diego)*
Bethel Coll. 135, 152, 364, 731 *(see also Bethel Univ.)*
Bethel Coll. & Seminary *(see Bethel Univ.)*
Beth-El Coll. of Nursing & Health Sciences *(see Univ. of Colorado at Colorado Springs)*
Bethel Seminary 731 *(see also Bethel Coll., Bethel Seminary of Bethel Univ., Bethel Univ.)*
Bethel Seminary of Bethel Univ. 208
Bethel Theological Seminary *(see Bethel Seminary of Bethel Univ.)*
Bethel Univ. 208, 731 *(see also Bethel Seminary of Bethel Univ.)*
Bethesda Christian Counseling Midwest, Inc. 702
Bethesda Christian Univ. 31, 743
Bethesda Healthcare System *(see Bethesda Mem. Hosp.)*
Bethesda Mem. Hosp. 662
Bethesda North Hosp. *(see TriHealth Good Samaritan Hosp.)*
Bethune-Cookman Coll. 82
Betty's Career Coll. of Cosmetology 758
Betty's Cosmetology Coll. *(see Betty's Career Coll. of Cosmetology)*
Beuaty Coll. of Lexington *(see Lexington Beauty Coll., Inc.)*
Beulah Heights Bible Coll. 100
Beulah Heights Coll. *(see Beulah Heights Bible Coll.)*
Beverly Hosp. 676
Bevill Coll. *(see Bevill State Comm. Coll.)*
Bevill State Comm. Coll. 4
Bexley Hall *(see Bexley Hall Seminary, Colgate Rochester Crozer Divinity Sch.)*

Bexley Hall Episcopal Seminary *(see Bexley Hall Seminary)*
Bexley Hall Seminary 256
Bible Baptist Seminary *(see Arlington Baptist Coll.)*
Bible Coll. of Alberta *(see Alberta Bible Coll.)*
Bible Coll. of Boise *(see Boise Bible Coll.)*
Bible Coll. of Cincinnati *(see Cincinnati Christian Univ.)*
Bible Coll. of Circleville *(see Circleville Bible Coll.)*
Bible Coll. of Eugene *(see Eugene Bible Coll.)*
Bible Coll. of Hobe Sound *(see Hobe Sound Bible Coll.)*
Bible Coll. of Lancaster *(see Lancaster Bible Coll. & Grad. Sch.)*
Bible Coll. of Southern California *(see Southern California Seminary)*
Bible Coll. of the Pacific Islands *(see Pacific Islands Bible Coll.)*
Bible Coll. of Winston—Salem *(see Winston-Salem Bible Coll.)*
Bible Inst. of Los Angeles *(see Biola Univ.)*
Bible Inst. of Pennsylvania *(see Philadelphia Biblical Univ.)*
Bible Inst. of Washington *(see Washington Bible Coll.)*
Bible Normal Sch. *(see Hartford Seminary)*
Bible Teachers' Coll. *(see New York Theological Seminary)*
Bible Teachers' Training Sch. *(see New York Theological Seminary)*
Biblical Sch. of Theology *(see Biblical Theological Seminary)*
Biblical Seminary *(see Biblical Theological Seminary)*
Biblical Seminary in New York, The *(see New York Theological Seminary)*
Biblical Theological Seminary 325
Bidwell Training Ctr. 326
Big Bend Coll. *(see Big Bend Comm. Coll.)*
Big Bend Comm. Coll. 410
Big Horn Coll. *(see Little Big Horn Coll.)*
Big Sandy Comm. & Tech. Coll. 158, 729
Big Sandy Comm. & Tech. Coll—Mayo Campus 729
Big Sky Somatic Inst., LLC 541
Bilingual Edu. Inst. 617
Bill Hill's Coll. of Cosmetology 507
Billings Vocational-Tech. Ctr. *(see Montana State Univ—Billings)*

Binghamton Commercial Coll. *(see Ridley-Lowell Bus. & Tech. Inst.)*
Binghamton State *(see State Univ. of New York at Binghamton)*
Binghamton Univ. *(see State Univ. of New York at Binghamton)*
Bio Kosmetique Inst. of Aesthetics 760
Biola Coll. *(see Biola Univ.)*
Biola Univ. 31
Biomedical Sciences Grad. Sch. *(see Univ. of Medicine & Dentistry of NJ Grad. Sch. of Biomedical Sciences)*
BIR Training Ctr—North 498
Birdwood Jr. Coll. *(see Thomas Univ.)*
Birmingham Coll. *(see Birmingham-Southern Coll.)*
Birmingham Sch. of the Bible *(see Southeastern Bible Coll.)*
Birmingham VA Med. Ctr. *(see Veterans Affairs Med. Ctr—Birmingham)*
Birmingham Veterans Affairs Med. Ctr. *(see Veterans Affairs Med. Ctr—Birmingham)*
Birmingham-Southern Coll. 4
Birthingway Coll. of Midwifery 592
Birthwise Midwifery Sch. 519
Biscayne Coll. *(see Saint Thomas Univ.)*
Bishop Clarkson Coll. of Nursing *(see Clarkson Coll.)*
Bishop Coll. *(see Bishop State Comm. Coll., Paul Quinn Coll.)*
Bishop Payne Divinity Sch., The *(see Protestant Episcopal Theological Seminary in Virginia)*
Bishop State Comm. Coll. 4
Bismarck Coll. *(see Bismarck State Coll.)*
Bismarck Hosp. *(see Medcenter One Health Systems)*
Bismarck State Coll. 296
Black Hawk Coll. 117
Black Hills Beauty Coll. 610
Black Hills State Coll. *(see Black Hills State Univ.)*
Black Hills State Univ. 361
Black Hills Teachers Coll. *(see Black Hills State Univ.)*
Black River Coll. *(see Black River Tech. Coll.)*
Black River Tech. Coll. 24
Black River Vocational Tech. Sch. *(see Black River Tech. Coll.)*
Blackburn Coll. 117
Blackburn Theological Seminary *(see Blackburn Coll.)*
Blackfeet Comm. Coll. 234
Blackhawk Tech. Coll. 423

Blackhawk Tech. Inst. *(see Blackhawk Tech. Coll.)*
Blackstone Career Inst. 594
Blackstone Inst. *(see Blackstone Career Inst.)*
Blackstone Sch. of Law *(see Blackstone Career Inst.)*
Blackwood Beauty Sch. 753
Bladen Comm. Coll. 284
Blades Sch. of Hair Design 521
Blaine, The Beauty Career Schools—Boston 524
Blaine, The Beauty Career Schools—Lowell 524
Blaine, The Beauty Career Schools—Malden 524
Blaine, The Beauty Career Schools—Waltham 524
Blair Coll. 64
Blair Jr. Coll. *(see Blair Coll.)*
Blair's Bus. Coll. *(see Blair Coll.)*
Bland Coll. *(see Richard Bland Coll.)*
Blank Children's Hosp. 671
Blanton-Peale Inst. 685
Blauvelt Coll. *(see Dominican Coll. of Blauvelt)*
Blessed John XXIII National Seminary 185, 730
Blessing Coll. of Nursing *(see Blessing-Rieman Coll. of Nursing)*
Blessing Hosp. 667 *(see also Blessing-Rieman Coll. of Nursing)*
Blessing Sch. of Nursing *(see Blessing-Rieman Coll. of Nursing)*
Blessing-Rieman Coll. of Nursing 118
Blinn Coll. 375
Blinn Mem. Coll. *(see Blinn Coll.)*
Bloomfield Coll. 245
Bloomfield Coll. & Seminary *(see Bloomfield Coll.)*
Bloomington-Normal Sch. of Radiography 667
Bloomsburg Literary Inst. *(see Bloomsburg Univ. of Pennsylvania)*
Bloomsburg Univ. of Pennsylvania 326
Blount Coll. *(see Univ. of Tennessee)*
Blue Cliff Coll. 166
Blue Cliff Sch. of Therapeutic Massage 441 *(see also Blue Cliff Coll.)*
Blue Hills Tech. Inst. *(see Massasoit Comm. Coll.)*
Blue Mountain Coll. 218 *(see also Blue Mountain Comm. Coll.)*
Blue Mountain Comm. Coll. 320
Blue Mountain Vocational-Tech. Sch. *(see Blue Mountain Comm. Coll.)*
Blue Ridge Coll. *(see Blue Ridge Comm. Coll.)*
Blue Ridge Comm. Coll. 284, 400

Blue Ridge Job Corps Ctr. 631
Blue River Comm. Coll—Blue Springs Campus 223
Blue River Comm. Coll—Independence Campus 223
Blue Sky Educational Foundation *(see Blue Sky Sch. of Prof. Massage & Therapeutic Bodywork)*
Blue Sky Sch. of Prof. Massage & Therapeutic Bodywork 643
Blue Water Coll. of Cosmetology 528
Bluefield Coll. 400
Bluefield State Coll. 418 *(see also Concord Univ.)*
Bluefield State Coll. New River Comm. & Tech. Coll. *(see New River Comm. & Tech. Coll.)*
Bluegras Hospice *(see Hospice of the Bluegrass)*
Bluegrass Coll. *(see Bluegrass Comm. & Tech. Coll.)*
Bluegrass Comm. & Tech. Coll. 158
Bluegrass Comm. & Tech. Coll. Dist. *(see Bluegrass Comm. & Tech. Coll—Central)*
Bluegrass Comm. & Tech. Coll—Central 728
Bluegrass Comm. & Tech. Coll—Cooper 729
Bluegrass Comm. Coll. *(see Bluegrass Comm. & Tech. Coll., Bluegrass Comm. & Tech. Coll—Central, Bluegrass Comm. & Tech. Coll—Cooper)*
Bluffton Coll. 734 *(see also Bluffton Univ.)*
Bluffton Univ. 299, 734
Bly's Sch. of Cosmetology 754
Blytheville Acad. of Cosmetology 447
BMA Seminary *(see Baptist Missionary Assoc. Theological Seminary)*
BMSI Inst., LLC 509
Boardwalk & Marina Casino Dealers Sch. 732
Bob Jones Coll. *(see Bob Jones Univ.)*
Bob Jones Univ. 749
Bobover Yeshiva B'nei Zion Rabbinical Coll. *(see Rabbinical Coll. Bobover Yeshiva B'nei Zion)*
Body Therapy Inst. 572
Bogan Jr. Coll. *(see City Colleges of Chicago—Richard J. Daley Coll.)*
Boggs Ctr. on Developmental Disabilities 683 *(see also Robert Wood Johnson Med. Sch., Univ. of Medicine & Dentistry of New Jersey)*
Bohecker Coll. 299, 734
Bohecker's Bus. Coll. 734 *(see also Bohecker Coll.)*

Boiling Springs Jr. Coll. *(see Gardner-Webb Univ.)*

Boise Bible Coll. 115

Boise Court Reporting Inst. *(see Court Reporting Inst—Boise)*

Boise Jr. Coll. *(see Boise State Univ.)*

Boise State Coll. *(see Boise State Univ.)*

Boise State Univ. 115

Bolivar Tech. Coll. 540 *(see also Texas County Tech. Inst.)*

Bon Losee Acad. of Hair Artistry 627

Bon Secours Hosp. *(see Bon Secours Saint Francis Hosp.)*

Bon Secours Saint Francis Hosp. 701

Bonar & Associates, Inc. 722 *(see also Dale Carnegie Training of Los Angeles)*

Bonebrake Theological Seminary *(see United Theological Seminary)*

Bonner Bible Coll. *(see W.L. Bonner Bible Coll.)*

Booker Inst. of Cosmetology 528

Booker T. Washington Jr. Coll. *(see Pensacola Jr. Coll.)*

Boone Hosp. Ctr. 680

Booth Coll. *(see William & Catherine Booth Coll.)*

Border Inst. of Techno. 375

Borger Jr. Coll. Dist. *(see Frank Phillips Coll.)*

Boricua Coll. 256

Borner's Barber Coll. 753

Borough of Manhattan Comm. Coll. *(see City Univ. of New York Borough of Manhattan Comm. Coll.)*

Bosco Tech *(see Don Bosco Tech. Inst.)*

Bosco Tech. Inst. *(see Don Bosco Tech. Inst.)*

Bossier Parish Comm. Coll. 166

Boston Architectural Ctr., The 185

Boston Art Inst. *(see Art Inst. of Boston at Lesley Univ.)*

Boston Baptist Coll. 185

Boston Ctr. for Modern Psychoanalytic Studies *(see Boston Grad. Sch. of Psychoanalysis)*

Boston Christian Counseling Ctr. of the Andover Newton Pastoral *(see Boston Christian Counseling Ctr.)*

Boston Christian Counseling Ctr., The 676

Boston City Hosp. *(see Boston Med. Ctr.)*

Boston Coll. 185 *(see also Boston Baptist Coll.)*

Boston Conservatory, The 185

Boston Dale Carnegie Training *(see Performance Training Associates, Inc.)*

Boston Grad. Sch. of Psychoanalysis 185

Boston Med. Ctr. 676

Boston Missionary Training Sch. *(see Gordon-Conwell Theological Seminary)*

Boston Museum of Fine Arts *(see Sch. of the Museum of Fine Arts, Boston)*

Boston Museum of Fine Arts Sch. *(see Sch. of the Museum of Fine Arts, Boston)*

Boston Normal Sch. *(see Univ. of Massachusetts Boston)*

Boston Sch. of English *(see Boston Sch. of Modern Languages, Inc.)*

Boston Sch. of Modern Languages, Inc. 524

Boston Sch. of Occupational Therapy *(see Tufts Univ.)*

Boston State Coll. *(see Univ. of Massachusetts Boston)*

Boston Univ. 185

Boston Urban Coll. *(see Urban Coll. of Boston)*

Boucher Inst. of Naturopathic Medicine 752

Boulder Coll. of Massage Therapy 64, 724

Boulder Sch. of Massage Therapy 724

Bouleder Univ. *(see Univ. of Colorado at Boulder)*

Bowdoin Coll. 175

Bowie State Coll. *(see Bowie State Univ.)*

Bowie State Univ. 178

Bowling Green Bus. Univ. *(see Western Kentucky Univ.)*

Bowling Green Coll. *(see Bowling Green Tech. Coll.)*

Bowling Green Reg. Techno. Ctr. *(see Bowling Green Tech. Coll.)*

Bowling Green State Univ. 299

Bowling Green Tech. Coll. 159

Boyce Bible Sch. *(see Southern Baptist Theological Seminary)*

Boyce Coll. *(see Southern Baptist Theological Seminary)*

Boyd Career Schools *(see Pittsburgh Tech. Inst.)*

Boyles Coll. *(see Hamilton Coll—Omaha)*

Bradenton Barber Acad., Inc. *(see Bradenton Beauty & Barber Acad., Inc.)*

Bradenton Beauty & Barber Acad., Inc. 480

Bradenton Beauty Acad., Inc. *(see Bradenton Beauty & Barber Acad., Inc.)*

Bradford County Area Vocational Tech. Sch. *(see Northern Tier Career Ctr.)*

Bradford Hosp. *(see Bradford Reg. Med. Ctr.)*

Bradford Reg. Med. Ctr. 696

Bradford Sch. 299, 326

Bradford Sch. of Bus. 617

Bradford-Union Area Vocational-Tech. Ctr. 480

Bradley Acad. for the Visual Arts 326

Bradley Polytechnic Inst. *(see Bradley Univ.)*

Bradley Univ. 118

Bradley Visual Arts Acad. *(see Bradley Acad. for the Visual Arts)*

Bradley Visual Arts Acad. *(see Bradley Acad. for the Visual Arts)*

Bragg Public Safety Complex *(see Kenneth Bragg Public Safety Complex, Lake Tech. Ctr.)*

Brainerd Comm. Coll. *(see Central Lakes Coll.)*

Brainerd Jr. Coll. *(see Central Lakes Coll.)*

Brainerd Staples Tech. Coll. *(see Central Lakes Coll.)*

Brainerd Tech. Inst. *(see Central Lakes Coll.)*

Bramson Coll. *(see Bramson ORT Coll.)*

Bramson ORT Coll. 256

Bramson ORT Tech. Inst. *(see Bramson ORT Coll.)*

Bramson ORT Trade Sch. *(see Bramson ORT Coll.)*

Brandeis Sch. of Law *(see Univ. of Louisville)*

Brandeis Univ. 185

Brandon Coll. 453

Branford Acad. of Hair & Cosmetology 754

Branford Cosmetology Acad. *(see Branford Acad. of Hair & Cosmetology)*

Branford Hall Career Inst. 474

Branford Hall Career Inst—Bohemia 558

Branford Hall Career Inst—Ronkonoma *(see Branford Hall Career Inst—Bohemia)*

Branson Tech. Coll. *(see Texas County Tech. Inst.)*

Branson Tech. Coll. 540

Brawley Jr. Coll. *(see Imperial Valley Coll.)*

Braxton Sch. *(see Braxton Sch. of Bus., The)*

Braxton Sch. of Bus., The 631

Brazosport Coll. 375

Brazosport Jr. Coll. *(see Brazosport Coll.)*

BRC Paralegal Studies *(see Baton Rouge Coll.)*

Breeden Sch. of Welding *(see Welder Training & Testing Inst.)*

Bremerton Bus. Coll. *(see Bryman Coll.)*

Brenau Coll. *(see Brenau Univ.)*

Brenau Univ. 100

Brenneke Massage Sch. *(see Brenneke Sch. of Massage)*

Brenneke Sch. of Massage 636

Brescia Coll. 728 *(see also Brescia Univ.)*

Brescia Univ. 159, 728

Brescook, LLC 521

Brevard Coll. 285 *(see also Brevard Comm. Coll.)*

Brevard Comm. Coll. 82

Brevard Inst. *(see Brevard Coll.)*

Brewer State Jr. Coll. *(see Bevill State Comm. Coll.)*

Brewster Tech. Ctr. *(see Henry W. Brewster Tech. Ctr.)*

Brewton-Parker Coll. 100

Brian Utting Sch. of Massage 636

Briar Cliff Coll. *(see Briar Cliff Univ.)*

Briar Cliff Univ. 145

Briarcliffe Coll. 256

Briarcliffe Sch., Inc. *(see Briarcliffe Coll.)*

Briarwood Coll. 72

Brick Computer Science Inst. 547

Brick Inst. *(see Brick Computer Science Inst.)*

Bridge Int'l. Sch. *(see Bridge Linguatec)*

Bridge Linguatec 471

Bridgeport Hosp. 658

Bridgeport Univ. *(see Univ. of Bridgeport)*

Bridgerland Applied Techno. Coll. 750

Bridgerland Coll. *(see Bridgerland Applied Techno. Coll.)*

Bridges Acad. of Beauty 453

Bridgewater Coll. 400 *(see also Bridgewater State Coll.)*

Bridgewater State Coll. 185

Bridgewater State Teacher's Coll. *(see Bridgewater State Coll.)*

Briercrest Bible Coll. *(see Briercrest Coll.)*

Briercrest Bible Inst. *(see Briercrest Coll.)*

Briercrest Biblical Seminary 431

Briercrest Coll. 431

Briercrest Family of Schools *(see Briercrest Biblical Seminary, Briercrest Coll.)*

Briercrest Seminary *(see Briercrest Biblical Seminary)*

Brigham & Women's Hosp. 676

Brigham Young Acad. *(see Brigham Young Univ.)*

Brigham Young Univ. 394

Brigham Young Univ—Hawaii Campus 113

Brigham Young Univ—Idaho 115

Brighton Coll. 577, 734

Brio Acad. of Cosmetology 474, 724

Bristol Comm. Coll. 185

British Columbia Univ. *(see Univ. of British Columbia)*

Broadcast Ctr. 537

Broadcast Services, Inc. *(see Broadcast Ctr.)*

Broadcasting Ctr. of Illinois *(see Illinois Ctr. for Broadcasting)*

Broadcasting Inst. of Maryland 521

Broaddus Coll. *(see Alderson-Broaddus Coll.)*

Brockport Coll. *(see State Univ. of New York Coll. at Brockport)*

Brockport Collegiate Inst. *(see State Univ. of New York Coll. at Brockport)*

Brockport State Normal Sch. *(see State Univ. of New York Coll. at Brockport)*

Brock's Hair Design Coll. *(see J & J Hair Design Coll.)*

Broken Arrow Beauty Coll., Inc. 586

BroMenn Healthcare 667

Bromenn Reg. Med. Ctr. *(see Bloomington-Normal Sch. of Radiography)*

Bronson Healthcare Group Inc. 677

Bronx Comm. Coll. *(see City Univ. of New York Bronx Comm. Coll.)*

Bronx Inst. for Career Training & Development 757

Bronx Lebanon Hosp. Ctr. 685

Brookdale Coll. *(see Brookdale Comm. Coll.)*

Brookdale Comm. Coll. 245

Brookdale Hosp. *(see Brookdale Univ. Hosp. & Med. Ctr.)*

Brookdale Med. Ctr. *(see Brookdale Univ. Hosp. & Med. Ctr.)*

Brookdale Univ. Hosp. & Med. Ctr., The 685

Brooke Army Med. Ctr. 703

Brookhaven Coll. 375

Brooklyn Coll. *(see City Univ. of New York Brooklyn Coll.)*

Brooklyn Collegiate & Polytechnic Inst. *(see Polytechnic Univ.)*

Brooklyn Hosp. Ctr. 685

Brooklyn Law Sch. 686

Brooklyn VA Med. Ctr. *(see Veterans Affairs Med. Ctr—Brooklyn)*

Brooklyn Veterans Affairs Med. Ctr. *(see Veterans Affairs Med. Ctr—Brooklyn)*

Brooks Coll. 31

Brooks Inst. of Photography 31

Brooks VA Med. Ctr. *(see Overton Brooks Veterans Affairs Med. Ctr.)*

Brooks Veterans Affairs Med. Ctr. *(see Overton Brooks Veterans Affairs Med. Ctr.)*

Brookside Bus. & Training Inst. 547

Brookside Inst. *(see Brookside Bus. & Training Inst.)*

Brookstone Coll. of Bus. 572

Broome County Tech. Inst. *(see State Univ. of New York Broome Comm. Coll.)*

Broome Tech. Comm. Coll. *(see State Univ. of New York Broome Comm. Coll.)*

Broward Career Inst. 754

Broward Coll. *(see Broward Comm. Coll., Florida Metropolitan Univ—Pompano Beach)*

Broward Comm. Coll. 82

Broward Comm. Coll. Aviation Inst. *(see Broward Comm. Coll.)*

Brown Aveda Inst. *(see Ladies & Gentlemen Hair Stylists)*

Brown Aveda Inst. 734

Brown Coll. 208 *(see also Brown Inst. of Court Reporting & Bus., Fran Brown Coll. of Beauty)*

Brown Coll. of Beauty *(see Fran Brown Coll. of Beauty)*

Brown Coll. of Court Reporting & Med. Transcription *(see Brown Inst. of Court Reporting & Bus.)*

Brown Coll. of Court Reporting & Med. Transcription 492

Brown Inst. *(see Brown Coll.)*

Brown Mackie Coll., The 152

Brown Mackie Coll—Atlanta 100, 726

Brown Mackie Coll—Cincinnati 300, 734

Brown Mackie Coll—Findlay 300, 734

Brown Mackie Coll—Louisville 159, 729

Brown Mackie Coll—Merrillville 135, 727

Brown Mackie Coll—Miami 82

Brown Mackie Coll—South Bend 135, 728

Brown Univ. 353 *(see also John Brown Univ.)*

Brown VA Med. Ctr. *(see Jesse Brown Veterans Affairs Med. Ctr.)*

Brown Veterans Affairs Med. Ctr. *(see Jesse Brown Veterans Affairs Med. Ctr.)*

Brown's Bus. Coll. of Commerce *(see Midstate Coll.)*

Brown's Rockford Bus. Coll. *(see Rockford Bus. Coll.)*

Brown's Sch. of Bus. *(see Blair Coll.)*

Brownson Tech. Sch. 453

Brunswick Coll. *(see Brunswick Comm. Coll., Coastal Georgia Comm. Coll.)*

Brunswick Comm. Coll. 285

Brunswick Job Corps Ctr. 755

Bryan Career Coll. 728, 731

Bryan Coll. 364 *(see also Bryan Coll. of Court Reporting)*

Bryan Coll. of Court Reporting 453

Bryan Coll—Springfield 224, 731

Bryan Coll—Topeka 509, 728

Bryan Travel Coll. *(see Bryan Coll—Springfield)*

Bryant & Stratton Bus. Inst. *(see Bryant & Stratton Coll—Greece Campus)*

Bryant & Stratton Coll. *(see Bryant & Stratton Coll—Cleveland Downtown Campus)*

Bryant & Stratton Coll—Parma *(see Bryant & Stratton Coll—Cleveland West Campus)*

Bryant & Stratton—Albany Campus *(see Bryant & Stratton Coll—Albany Campus)*

Bryant & Stratton—Amherst Campus *(see Bryant & Stratton Coll—Amherst)*

Bryant & Stratton—Buffalo Campus *(see Bryant & Stratton Coll—Buffalo)*

Bryant & Stratton—Greece Campus *(see Bryant & Stratton Coll—Greece Campus)*

Bryant & Stratton—Southtowns Campus *(see Bryant & Stratton Coll—Southtowns)*

Bryant & Stratton 256

Bryant & Stratton Coll—Albany Campus 257

Bryant & Stratton Coll—Buffalo 257

Bryant & Stratton Coll—Cleveland Downtown Campus 300

Bryant & Stratton Coll—Cleveland West Campus 300

Bryant & Stratton Coll—Greece Campus 257

Bryant & Stratton Coll—Milwaukee Campus 423

Bryant & Stratton Coll—Syracuse 257

Bryant & Stratton Coll—Virginia Beach Campus 401

Bryant Coll. 736 *(see also Bryant Univ.)*

Bryant Univ. 353, 736

Bryman Coll. 453, 636, 723, 738

Bryman Coll—Anaheim 453

Bryman Coll—Earth City 537

Bryman Coll—El Monte 453

Bryman Coll—Everett 738

Bryman Coll—Federal Way 738

Bryman Coll—Gardena 453

Bryman Coll—Hayward 453

Bryman Coll—Los Angeles 453

Bryman Coll—Ontario 31

Bryman Coll—Renton 636

Bryman Coll—Reseda 454

Bryman Coll—San Bernardino *(see Bryman Coll.)*

Bryman Coll—San Francisco 454

Bryman Coll—San Jose 454

Bryman Coll—South Robertson Boulevard *(see Bryman Coll—West Los Angeles)*

Bryman Coll—Tacoma 738

Bryman Coll—Torrance 454

Bryman Coll—West Los Angeles 31

Bryman Coll—Whittier 31

Bryman Inst—Brighton 524

Bryman Inst—Chelsea 524

Bryman Inst—Eagan 533

Bryman Sch., The 15

Bryman Sch—Tempe, The 15

Bryn Athyn Coll. of the New Church 326

Bryn Mawr Coll. 326

Buchanan Beauty Coll. 759

Buchtel Coll. *(see Univ. of Akron)*

Buckeye Career Ctr. 577

Buckeye Coll. of Massotherapy *(see Ohio Coll. of Massotherapy)*

Buckeye Hills Career Ctr. 577

Bucknell Univ. 326

Bucknell Univ. Jr. Coll. *(see Wilkes Univ.)*

Bucks County Coll. *(see Bucks County Comm. Coll.)*

Bucks County Comm. Coll. 326

Bucks County Sch. of Beauty Culture, Inc. 595

Buena Vista Coll. *(see Buena Vista Univ.)*

Buena Vista Univ. 145

Buffalo Dale Carnegie Training *(see Andrew Terranova & Associates, Inc.)*

Buffalo Male & Female Inst. *(see Milligan Coll.)*

Buffalo Montessori Teacher Edu. Program 559

Buffalo State Coll. *(see State Univ. of New York Coll. at Buffalo)*

Buffalo State Univ. *(see State Univ. of New York at Buffalo)*

Buffalo Univ. *(see State Univ. of New York at Buffalo)*

Buffalo VA Med. Ctr. *(see Veterans Affairs Med. Ctr—Buffalo)*

Buffalo Veterans Affairs Med. Ctr. *(see Veterans Affairs Med. Ctr—Buffalo)*

Buhl Hosp. *(see Sharon Reg. Health System)*

Buies Creek Acad. *(see Campbell Univ.)*

Buncombe County Jr. Coll. *(see Univ. of North Carolina at Asheville)*

Bunker Hill Coll. *(see Bunker Hill Comm. Coll.)*

Bunker Hill Comm. Coll. 186

Bureau of Educational Experiments *(see Bank Street Coll. of Edu.)*

Bureau of Medicine & Surgery (U.S. Navy) 660

Bureau of Medicine & Surgery Aerospace & Operational Medicine Inst. *(see Bureau of Medicine & Surgery Naval Operational Medicine Inst.)*

Bureau of Medicine & Surgery—Field Med. Service Sch. *(see Bureau of Medicine & Surgery—Field Med. Service Sch.)*

Bureau of Medicine & Surgery—Naval Hosp. Corps Sch. *(see Bureau of Medicine & Surgery—Naval Hosp. Corps Sch.)*

Bureau of Medicine & Surgery—Naval Undersea Med. Inst/Naval Sub Base *(see Bureau of Medicine & Surgery—Naval Undersea Med. Inst.)*

Bureau of Medicine & Surgery—Tri-Service Optician Sch. *(see Bureau of Medicine & Surgery—Naval Opthamalic Support & Training Activity)*

Burlington Bus. Coll. *(see Champlain Coll.)*

Burlington Coll. 397

Burlington Collegiate Inst. *(see Champlain Coll.)*

Burlington County Coll. 245

Bus. & Techno. Inst. *(see Inst. for Bus. & Techno.)*

Bus. & Med. Careers Inst. *(see Inst. of Bus. & Med. Careers)*

Bus. & Techno. Ctr. *(see Metropolitan Comm. Coll. Bus. & Techno. Coll.)*

Bus. & Techno. Coll. *(see Metropolitan Comm. Coll. Bus. & Techno. Coll.)*

Bus. & Techno. Inst. of Schuylkill *(see Schuylkill Inst. of Bus. & Techno.)*

Bus. Career Training Inst. 738

Bus. Careers Inst—Greensburg 343

Bus. Careers Inst—Pittsburgh 343

Bus. Coll. of Austin *(see Austin Bus. Coll.)*

Bus. Coll. of Dover *(see Dover Bus. Coll.)*

Bus. Coll. of Hawaii *(see Hawaii Bus. Coll.)*

Bus. Coll. of Indiana *(see Indiana Bus. Coll.)*

Bus. Coll. of Jamestown *(see Jamestown Bus. Coll.)*

Bus. Coll. of Minneapolis *(see Minneapolis Bus. Coll.)*

Bus. Coll. of Santa Barbara *(see Santa Barbara Bus. Coll.)*

Bus. Coll. of Sierra Valley *(see Sierra Valley Bus. Coll.)*

Bus. Coll. of Stockton *(see MTI Bus. Coll. of Stockton Inc.)*

Bus. Coll. of West Tennessee *(see West Tennessee Bus. Coll.)*

Bus. Coll. of West Virginia *(see West Virginia Bus. Coll.)*

Bus. Computer Training Inst. 738

Bus. Etcetera Inst. *(see Bus. Etcetera Inst.)*

Bus. Informatics Ctr. 559

Bus. Inst. of Detroit *(see Detroit Bus. Inst.)*

Bus. Inst. of Long Island *(see Long Island Bus. Inst.)*

Bus. Inst. of Newport *(see Newport Bus. Inst.)*

Bus. Inst. of Pennsylvania 326

Bus. Inst. of Rochester *(see Rochester Bus. Inst.)*

Bus. Sch. in Prague *(see Rochester Inst. of Techno.)*

Bus. Sch. Lausanne 716

Bus. Sch. of Allentown *(see Lehigh Valley Coll.)*

Bus. Sch. of Minnesota *(see Minnesota Sch. of Bus.)*

Bus. Sch. of Texas *(see Texas Sch. of Bus.)*

Bus. Skills Inst. 556, 645

Bus. Training Inst. 733 *(see also Allied Med. & Tech. Inst.)*

Bus. Univ. of Duluth *(see Duluth Bus. Univ.)*

Butera Sch. of Art 524

Butler Beauty Sch. 595

Butler Bus. Sch. 474

Butler Coll. *(see Butler County Comm. Coll.)*

Butler Comm. Coll. *(see Butler County Comm. Coll.)*

Butler County Comm. Coll. 152, 326

Butler County Comm. Jr. Coll. *(see Butler County Comm. Coll.)*

Butler Sch. of Bus. *(see Butler Bus. Sch.)*

Butler Tech *(see Butler Techno. & Career Development Schools)*

Butler Techno. & Career Development Schools 577

Butler Univ. 135

Butte Acad. of Beauty Culture, Inc. 541

Butte Coll. 32

Butte County Coll. *(see Butte Coll.)*

Butte Vocational-Tech. Ctr. *(see Montana Tech of The Univ. of Montana)*

Butte Vo-Tech *(see Montana Tech of The Univ. of Montana)*

BYU *(see Brigham Young Univ.)*

C

C.C. Choffin Vocational Ctr. *(see Choffin Career & Tech. Ctr.)*

C.J. Sealey & Associates, LLC 537, 732

Cabarrus Coll. of Health Sciences 285

Cabarrus Mem. Hosp. *(see Cabarrus Coll. of Health Sciences)*

Cabell County Career Techno. Ctr. 640

Cabell County Vocational Techno. Ctr. *(see Cabell County Career Techno. Ctr.)*

Cabell County Voc-Tech Ctr. *(see Cabell County Career Techno. Ctr.)*

Cabell Huntington Hosp. 708

Cabot Univ. *(see John Cabot Univ.)*

Cabrillo Coll. 32

Cabrini Coll. 326

Caddo-Kiowa Techno. Ctr. 586

Cadek Conservatory of Music *(see Univ. of Tennessee at Chattanooga)*

Caguas Inst. of Mechanical Techno. 602

Cain's Barber Coll. 498

Cal Maritime *(see California Maritime Acad.)*

Cal Poly *(see California Polytechnic State Univ—San Luis Obispo)*

Cal Poly *(see California State Polytechnic Univ—Pomona)*

Cal State East Bay *(see California State Univ—East Bay)*

Cal State San Bernardino *(see California State Univ—San Bernardino)*

Cal State—Bakersfield *(see California State Univ—Bakersfield)*

Cal State—Channel Islands *(see California State Univ—Channel Islands)*

Cal State—Chico *(see California State Univ—Chico)*

Cal State—Dominguez Hills *(see California State Univ—Dominguez Hills)*

Cal State—Fresno *(see California State Univ—Fresno)*

Cal State—Fullerton *(see California State Univ—Fullerton)*

Cal State—Hayward *(see California State Univ., East Bay)*

Cal State—L.A. *(see California State Univ—Los Angeles)*

Cal State—Long Beach *(see California State Univ—Long Beach)*

Cal State—Monterey Bay *(see California State Univ—Monterey Bay)*

Cal State—Northridge *(see California State Univ—Northridge)*

Cal State—Sacramento *(see California State Univ—Sacramento)*

Cal State—San Marcos *(see California State Univ—San Marcos)*

Cal State—Stanislaus *(see California State Univ—Stanislaus)*

CalArts *(see California Inst. of the Arts)*

CALC, Inst. of Techno. 498

Caldwell Coll. 245

Caldwell Comm. Coll. & Tech. Inst. 285

Caldwell Tech. Inst. *(see Caldwell Comm. Coll. & Tech. Inst.)*

Cale Chiropractic Coll. *(see Southern California Univ. of Health Sciences)*

Calgary Leadership Training Ctr. *(see Vanguard Coll.)*

Calgary Reg. Health Authority 711

Calgary Univ. *(see Univ. of Calgary)*

Calhoun Coll. *(see Calhoun Comm. Coll.)*

Calhoun Comm. Coll. 4, 721

Calhoun State Comm. Coll. *(see Calhoun Comm. Coll.)*

Caliber Training Inst. 559

California Acad. of Drafting *(see Inst. for Bus. & Techno.)*

California Acad. of Merchandising, Art & Design *(see Maric Coll—Sacramento)*

California Art Inst—San Francisco *(see Art Inst. of California—San Francisco)*

California Arts Coll. *(see California Coll. of the Arts)*
California Baptist Coll. *(see California Baptist Univ.)*
California Baptist Theological Seminary *(see American Baptist Seminary of the West)*
California Baptist Univ. 32
California Beauty Coll. 454
California Career Sch. 454
California Christian Coll. 32 *(see also Chapman Univ.)*
California Coast Univ. 32
California Coll. *(see American Baptist Seminary of the West)*
California Coll. for Health Sciences 737 *(see also Independence Univ.)*
California Coll. of Arts & Crafts 722 *(see also California Coll. of the Arts)*
California Coll. of Chiropractic *(see Southern California Univ. of Health Sciences)*
California Coll. of Communication 722
California Coll. of Fashion Careers *(see Fashion Careers Coll.)*
California Coll. of Natural Healing Arts *(see Southern California Univ. of Health Sciences)*
California Coll. of Podiatric Medicine at Samuel Merritt Coll. 53 *(see also Samuel Merritt Coll.)*
California Coll. of Techno. 722 *(see also Maric Coll—Sacramento)*
California Coll. of the Arts 32, 722
California Coll. of Vocational Careers 454
California Coll. San Diego 32
California Coll—Modesto 722 *(see also Maric Coll—Modesto)*
California Coll—Stockton 722 *(see also Maric Coll—Stockton)*
California Cosmetology Coll., San Jose, Inc. 454
California Culinary Acad. 32
California Culinary Arts Sch. *(see California Sch. of Culinary Arts)*
California Dept. of Mental Health *(see Patton State Hosp., California Dept. of Mental Health Vacaville Psychiatric Program)*
California Dept. of Mental Health Vacaville Psychiatric Program 653
California Design Coll. 32
California Dominican Univ. *(see Dominican Univ. of California)*
California Family Study Ctr. *(see Phillips Grad. Inst.)*

California Guild of Arts & Crafts *(see California Coll. of the Arts)*
California Hair Design Acad. 454
California Healing Arts Coll. 454
California Inst. of Integral Studies 32
California Inst. of Techno. 32
California Inst. of the Arts 32
California Inst. of the Healing Arts & Sciences 454
California Integral Studies Inst. *(see California Inst. of Integral Studies)*
California Intercultural Inst. *(see Intercultural Inst. of California)*
California Learning Ctr. 454
California Lutheran Coll. *(see California Lutheran Univ.)*
California Lutheran Univ. 33
California Maritime Acad. 33
California Mental Health System *(see Metropolitan State Hosp.)*
California National Univ. for Advanced Studies 33
California Nautical Sch. *(see California Maritime Acad.)*
California New Coll. *(see New Coll. of California)*
California Normal Sch. *(see California Univ. of Pennsylvania)*
California Nurses Edu. Inst. 753
California Pacific Med. Ctr. 653
California Paramedical & Tech. 722
California Polytechnic Sch. *(see California Polytechnic State Univ—San Luis Obispo)*
California Polytechnic State Univ—San Luis Obispo 33
California Sch. of Court Reporting 722 *(see also Sage Coll.)*
California Sch. of Culinary Arts 454
California Sch. of Design *(see San Francisco Art Inst.)*
California Sch. of Fine Arts *(see San Francisco Art Inst.)*
California Sch. of Med. Sciences 722 *(see also California Sch. of Modern Sciences)*
California Sch. of Modern Sciences 455, 722
California Sch. of Podiatric Medicine *(see California Coll. of Podiatric Medicine)*
California Sch. of Prof. Psychology—Fresno *(see Alliant Int'l. Univ—Fresno)*
California Sch. of Prof. Psychology—Los Angeles *(see Alliant Int'l. Univ—Los Angeles)*
California Sch. of Prof. Psychology—San Diego *(see Alliant Int'l. Univ—San Diego Cornerstone Court)*

California Sch. of Prof. Psychology—San Francisco Bay *(see Alliant Int'l. Univ—San Francisco Bay)*
California Seminary *(see California Univ. of Pennsylvania)*
California State Coll. *(see California Univ. of Pennsylvania)*
California State Coll. at Fullerton *(see California State Univ—Fullerton)*
California State Coll. at Los Angeles *(see California State Univ—Los Angeles)*
California State Coll. at Palos Verdes *(see California State Univ—Dominguez Hills)*
California State Coll., Fullerton *(see California State Univ—Fullerton)*
California State Normal Sch. *(see San Jose State Univ.)*
California State Polytechnic Coll. *(see California Polytechnic State Univ—San Luis Obispo)*
California State Polytechnic Coll—Kellogg-Voorhis *(see California State Polytechnic Univ—Pomona)*
California State Polytechnic Coll—Pomona *(see California State Polytechnic Univ—Pomona)*
California State Polytechnic Univ—Pomona 33
California State Teachers Coll. *(see California Univ. of Pennsylvania)*
California State Univ. of Engineering, Techno. & Marine Transportation *(see California Maritime Acad.)*
California State Univ., Humboldt *(see Humboldt State Univ.)*
California State Univ—Bakersfield 33
California State Univ—Channel Islands 743
California State Univ—Chico 33
California State Univ—Dominguez Hills 33
California State Univ—East Bay 33, 722
California State Univ—Fresno 34
California State Univ—Fullerton 34
California State Univ—Hayward 722 *(see also California State Univ., East Bay)*
California State Univ—Long Beach 34
California State Univ—Los Angeles 34
California State Univ—Monterey Bay 34
California State Univ—Northridge 34
California State Univ—Sacramento 34
California State Univ—San Bernardino 35
California State Univ—San Marcos 35
California State Univ—Stanislaus 35
California Univ. of Pennsylvania 326

California Wesleyan Coll. *(see Univ. of the Pacific)*
California Western Sch. of Law 35
California Western Univ. *(see Alliant Int'l. Univ—San Diego Scripps Ranch)*
CalTech *(see California Inst. of Techno.)*
Calumet Coll. *(see Calumet Coll. of Saint Joseph)*
Calumet Coll. of Saint Joseph 136
Calvary Baptist Theological Seminary 748
Calvary Bible Coll. *(see Calvary Bible Coll. & Theological Seminary)*
Calvary Bible Coll. & Theological Seminary 224
Calvary Hosp. 686
Calvary Seminary *(see Calvary Bible Coll. & Theological Seminary)*
Calvin Coll. 196 *(see also Calvin Theological Seminary)*
Calvin Jr. Coll. *(see Calvin Coll.)*
Calvin Seminary *(see Calvin Theological Seminary)*
Calvin Theological Seminary 196 *(see also Calvin Coll.)*
Cambria Coll. *(see Pennsylvania Highlands Comm. Coll.)*
Cambria Comm. Coll. *(see Pennsylvania Highlands Comm. Coll.)*
Cambria County Area Comm. Coll. 735 *(see also Pennsylvania Highlands Comm. Coll.)*
Cambria-Rowe Bus. Coll. 327
Cambridge Allied Health Inst. *(see Cambridge Inst. of Allied Health)*
Cambridge Career Coll. 455
Cambridge Coll. 65, 186
Cambridge Culinary Sch. *(see Cambridge Sch. of Culinary Arts)*
Cambridge Inst. of Allied Health 480
Cambridge Sch. of Culinary Arts, The 524
Camden County Coll. 245
Camden County Tech. Inst. *(see Tech. Inst. of Camden County)*
Camden Sch. of Musical Arts 600 *(see also Settlement Music Sch.)*
Camelot Career Coll. *(see Camelot Coll.)*
Camelot Coll. 166
Cameo Beauty Acad. 498
Cameo Beauty Coll. *(see Cameo Coll. of Essential Beauty)*
Cameo Coll. of Essential Beauty 627
Cameo Essential Beauty Coll. *(see Cameo Coll. of Essential Beauty)*
Cameron Coll. *(see Cameron Univ.)*
Cameron Coll. 166

Cameron Univ. 315
Camosun Coll. 711
Camp Coll. *(see Paul D. Camp Comm. Coll.)*
Camp Comm. Coll. *(see Paul D. Camp Comm. Coll.)*
Campbell Jr. Coll. *(see Campbell Univ.)*
Campbell Univ. 285, 747
Campbellsville Coll. *(see Campbellsville Univ.)*
Campbellsville Univ. 159
Campellsville Coll. *(see Campbellsville Univ.)*
Campion Renewal CPE Ctr. 676
Cañada Coll. 35
Canadian Bible Coll. 740 *(see also Alliance Univ. Coll.)*
Canadian Bible Coll/Canadian Theological Seminary *(see Alliance Univ. Coll.)*
Canadian Bible Inst. *(see Alliance Univ. Coll.)*
Canadian Coll. of Naturopathic Medicine 431
Canadian Mem. Chiropractic Coll. 711
Canadian Montessori Acad. Teacher Edu. Program 646
Canadian Montessori Teacher Edu. Inst. 646
Canadian Pentecostal Seminary East *(see Master's Coll. & Seminary)*
Canadian Sch. of Management 740
Canadian Southern Baptist Seminary 431
Canadian Theological Seminary *(see Alliance Univ. Coll.)*
Canadian Valley Area Vocational Tech. Sch. 695
Canadian Valley Tech. Sch. *(see Canadian Valley Area Vocational Tech. Sch.)*
Candler Sch. of Theology *(see Emory Univ.)*
Canisius Coll. 257
Cankdeska Cikana (Little Hoop) Coll. *(see Cankdeska Cikana Comm. Coll.)*
Cankdeska Cikana (Little Hoop) Comm. Coll. *(see Cankdeska Cikana Comm. Coll.)*
Cankdeska Cikana Coll. *(see Cankdeska Cikana Comm. Coll.)*
Cankdeska Cikana Comm. Coll. 296
Cannella Sch. of Hair Design—Blue Island 498
Cannella Sch. of Hair Design—Elgin 498
Cannella Sch. of Hair Design—Elmhurst 498

Cannella Sch. of Hair Design—South Archer 499
Cannella Sch. of Hair Design—South Commercial 499
Cannella Sch. of Hair Design—West North Avenue 499
Cannella Sch. of Hair Design—West Roosevelt 499
Canton Coll. of Techno. *(see State Univ. of New York Coll. of Techno. at Canton)*
Canton Comm. Coll. *(see Spoon River Coll.)*
Canton Mercy Hosp. *(see Mercy Med. Ctr.)*
Canyons Coll. *(see Coll. of the Canyons)*
CAPE *(see Ctr. for Asia Pacific Exchange)*
Cape Cod Coll. *(see Cape Cod Comm. Coll.)*
Cape Cod Comm. Coll. 186
Cape Coral Beauty Sch. 725, 737
Cape Fear Coll. *(see Cape Fear Comm. Coll.)*
Cape Fear Comm. Coll. 285
Cape Girardeau Area Vocational-Tech. Sch. 680
Cape Girardeau Career & Techno. Ctr. *(see Cape Girardeau Area Vocational-Tech. Sch.)*
Cape May County Tech. Inst. 683
Capella Univ., The 208
Capelli Hair Inst. *(see Capelli Inst. of Hair)*
Capelli Inst. of Hair 760
Capilo Inst. 756
Capilo Inst. of Skin, Hair & Nails *(see Capilo Inst.)*
Capital Area Career Ctr. 499, 722
Capital Area Sch. of Practical Nursing *(see Capital Area Career Ctr.)*
Capital Area Vocational Ctr. 722 *(see also Capital Area Career Ctr.)*
Capital Bible Seminary 178, 746 *(see also Washington Bible Coll.)*
Capital Coll. *(see Capital Comm. Coll., Pennsylvania State Univ.)*
Capital Comm. Coll. 72
Capital Comm-Tech. Coll. *(see Capital Comm. Coll.)*
Capital Culinary Inst. *(see Keiser Coll.)*
Capital Univ. 300
Capitol City Barber Coll. *(see Cutting Edge Hairstyling Acad.)*
Capitol City Careers 617
Capitol City Hair Design Coll. *(see Cutting Edge Hairstyling Acad.)*
Capitol City Trade & Tech. Sch. 617
Capitol Coll. 178

Capitol Inst. of Techno. *(see Capitol Coll.)*

Capitol Radio Engineering Inst. *(see Capitol Coll.)*

Capitol Sch. of Esthetics *(see Capitol Sch. of Hairstyling & Esthetics)*

Capitol Sch. of Hairstyling & Esthetics 542

Capitol Sch. of Hairstyling—West *(see Capitol Sch. of Hairstyling & Esthetics)*

Capps Coll. 441

Capps Coll—Foley 441, 721

Capps Coll—Pensacola *(see Capps Med. Inst.)*

Capri Coll. 507 *(see also Capri Oak Forest Coll. of Beauty Culture)*

Capri Coll. of Beauty Culture *(see Capri Oak Forest Coll. of Beauty Culture)*

Capri Cosmetology Coll. *(see Capri Coll.)*

Capri Cosmetology Learning Ctr. 559

Capri Garfield Ridge Sch. of Beauty Culture 499

Capri Inst. of Hair Design—Bricktown 547

Capri Inst. of Hair Design—Clifton 547

Capri Inst. of Hair Design—Kenilworth 547

Capri Inst. of Hair Design—Paramus 547

Capri Oak Forest Coll. of Beauty Culture 499

Capri Sch. of Beauty Culture *(see Capri Garfield Ridge Sch. of Beauty Culture)*

Caquas Central Colleges, Inc. *(see Caguas Central Coll.)*

Cardean Univ. 118

Cardinal Glennon Coll. *(see Kenrick-Glennon Seminary)*

Cardinal Stritch Univ. 423

Career Acad. 443, 617

Career Acad. of Beauty—West Garden Grove 455

Career Acad. of Hair Design 447

Career Advancement & Applied Tech. Training Division *(see Career Advancement & Applied Tech. Training Division)*

Career Alternatives Learning Ctr. *(see CALC, Inst. of Techno.)*

Career & Educational Consultants 559

Career & Tech. Ctr. of Putnam County *(see Putnam Career & Tech. Ctr.)*

Career & Tech. Ctr. of West Virginia *(see West Virginia Career & Tech. Ctr.)*

Career & Techno. Ctr. of Oregon *(see Oregon Career & Techno. Ctr.)*

Career & Techno. Centers of Licking County 577

Career Beauty Coll. 497

Career Blazers Learning Ctr. *(see Career Blazers, Inc., Career Blazers Learning Ctr. of Washington)*

Career Blazers Learning Ctr. of Washington 478

Career Blazers, Inc. 559 *(see also Career Blazers Learning Ctr. of Washington)*

Career Care Inst. 455

Career Ctr. Adult Tech. Training, The 577

Career Ctr. of Greene County *(see Greene County Career Ctr.)*

Career Ctr. of Knox County *(see Knox County Career Ctr.)*

Career Ctr. of Medina County *(see Medina County Career Ctr.)*

Career Ctr. of Portage Lakes *(see Portage Lakes Career Ctr.)*

Career Ctr. of Washington County *(see Career Ctr. Adult Tech. Training)*

Career Ctr. of Wayne County *(see Wayne County Career Ctr.)*

Career Centers of Texas—Corpus Christi 623

Career Centers of Texas—El Paso 618

Career Centers of Texas—Fort Worth 327

Career Coll. for Prof. Golfers *(see Prof. Golfers Career Coll.)*

Career Coll. of California *(see California Career Coll.)*

Career Coll. of Denver *(see Denver Career Coll.)*

Career Coll. of Glendale *(see Glendale Career Coll.)*

Career Coll. of Northern Nevada 240

Career Coll. of St. Francis *(see Saint Francis Career Coll.)*

Career Coll. of Tennessee *(see Tennessee Career Coll.)*

Career Coll. of Utah *(see Utah Career Coll.)*

Career Colleges of America 455

Career Colleges of Chicago 118

Career Edu. Inst—Lincoln 607, 736

Career Edu. Inst—Somerville 525, 730

Career Floral Design Inst. *(see Bryman Coll—Renton)*

Career Inst. of Florida *(see Florida Career Inst.)*

Career Inst. of Health & Techno. *(see Computer Career Ctr.)*

Career Inst. of Nevada *(see Glendale Career Coll.)*

Career Inst. of New York *(see New York Career Inst.)*

Career Inst. of San Diego Occupational Training Services 722 *(see also Occupational Training Services)*

Career Networks Inst. 455

Career Point Bus. Sch. 737 *(see also Career Point Inst.)*

Career Point Inst. 618, 737

Career Quest 618

Career Quest Learning Ctr. *(see Career Quest Computer Learning Ctr.)*

Career Quest, Inc. *(see Career Quest Computer Learning Ctr.)*

Career Sch. of California *(see California Career Sch.)*

Career Tech Inst. 618

Career Tech. Coll. 166

Career Techno. Ctr. of Cabell County *(see Cabell County Career Techno. Ctr.)*

Career Training Acad. 327

Career Training Coll. *(see Coll. of Career Training)*

Career Training Inst. 480, 662

Career Training Solutions 631

Career Training Specialists *(see Career Tech. Coll.)*

Career Works *(see CareerWorks)*

Careers Unlimited 394, 618

CareerWorks 548

CareerWorks Inst. of Techno. 528

Carey Coll. *(see William Carey Coll.)*

Caribbean Ctr. for Advanced Studies—Miami Inst. of Psychology *(see Carlos Albizu Univ—Miami Campus)*

Caribbean Ctr. for Advanced Studies—San Juan Campus *(see Carlos Albizu Univ—San Juan Campus)*

Caribbean Jr. Coll. *(see Caribbean Univ.)*

Caribbean Univ. 347

Caritas Christi Health Care System *(see Caritas Laboure Coll.)*

Caritas Laboure Coll. 186, 730

Carl Albert Jr. Coll. *(see Carl Albert State Coll.)*

Carl Albert State Coll. 315

Carl D. Perkins Job Corps Ctr. 512

Carl Sandburg Coll. 118

Carl T. Hayden Veterans Affairs Med. Ctr. 651

Carle Foundation Hosp. 667

Carleton Coll. 208

Carlisle Barracks *(see United States Army War Coll.)*
Carlos Albizu Univ—Miami Campus 82
Carlos Albizu Univ—San Juan Campus 347
Carlos Alejandro, North General Hosp. *(see North General Hosp.)*
Carlow Coll. 735 *(see also Carlow Univ.)*
Carlow Univ. 327, 735
Carlsbad Branch Comm. Coll. *(see New Mexico State Univ. at Carlsbad)*
Carlson Coll. of Massage Therapy 507
Carnegie Inst. 528
Carnegie Inst. of Integrative Medicine & Massotherapy 577
Carnegie Inst. of Techno. *(see Carnegie Mellon Univ.)*
Carnegie Mellon Univ. 327
Carnegie Tech. Schools *(see Carnegie Mellon Univ.)*
Carolina Acad. of Cosmetic Art & Science 572
Carolina Beauty Coll. 572
Carolina Evangelical Divinity Sch. 748
Carolina Inst. of Modern Hairstyling *(see Modern Hairstyling Inst— Carolina)*
Carolina Sch. of Commerce *(see Forrest Jr. Coll.)*
Carolinas Coll. of Health Sciences 285
Carolinas Golf Acad. *(see Golf Acad. of the Carolinas)*
Carolinas Health Sciences Coll. *(see Carolinas Coll. of Health Sciences)*
Carondelet Health 681
Carousel Beauty Coll. of Miami Valley *(see Carousel of Miami Valley Beauty Coll.)*
Carousel Beauty Coll—Dayton 577
Carousel Beauty Coll—Middletown 577
Carousel of Miami Valley Beauty Coll. 577
Carrasco Job Corps Ctr. *(see David L. Carrasco Job Corps Ctr.)*
Carraway Hosp. *(see Carraway Methodist Med. Ctr.)*
Carraway Med. Ctr. *(see Carraway Methodist Med. Ctr.)*
Carraway Methodist Med. Ctr. 651
Carrier Seminary *(see Clarion Univ. of Pennsylvania)*
Carrier State Normal Sch. *(see Clarion Univ. of Pennsylvania)*
Carroll Coll. 234, 4223
Carroll Comm. Coll. 178

Carroll Tech. Inst. *(see West Central Tech. Coll.)*
Carroll Univ. *(see John Carroll Univ.)*
Carson C. Peck Mem. Hosp. *(see New York Methodist Hosp.)*
Carson City Beauty Acad. 543
Carson Coll. *(see Carson-Newman Coll.)*
Carson-Newman Coll. 364
Carsten Inst. New York 559
Carsten Inst. of Hair & Beauty 444
Carteret Coll. *(see Carteret Comm. Coll.)*
Carteret Comm. Coll. 285
Carthage Coll. 423
CARTI *(see Central Arkansas Radiation Therapy Inst.)*
Carver Bible Coll. 744
Carver Career & Tech. Edu. Ctr. 640
Carver Coll. *(see Carver Bible Coll.)*
Carver State Tech. Coll. *(see Bishop State Comm. Coll—Carver)*
Carver Tech. Edu. Ctr. *(see Carver Career & Tech. Edu. Ctr.)*
Casa Loma Coll. 455
Casal Aveda Inst. *(see Casal's De Spa & Salon)*
Casal's De Spa & Salon 577, 734
Cascade Beauty Coll. 761
Cascade Coll. *(see Oklahoma Christian Univ.)*
Cascade Culinary Inst. *(see Central Oregon Comm. Coll.)*
Cascadia Comm. Coll. 751
Case Inst. of Techno. *(see Case Western Reserve Univ.)*
Case Sch. of Applied Science *(see Case Western Reserve Univ.)*
Case Western Reserve Univ. 300
Casey County Area Techno. Ctr. *(see Somerset Comm. Coll.)*
Casey Jones Sch. of Aeronautics *(see Vaughn Coll. of Aeronautics & Techno.)*
Casper Coll. 430
Cass Civilian Conservation Job Corp Ctr. *(see Cass Job Corps Ctr.)*
Cass Job Corps Ctr. 447
Cassia Beauty Coll. 515
Castle Point VA Med. Ctr. *(see Veterans Affairs Med. Ctr—Castle Point)*
Castle Point Veterans Affairs Med. Ctr. *(see Veterans Affairs Med. Ctr— Castle Point)*
Castleton State Coll. 397
Castleton Teacher's Coll. *(see Castleton State Coll.)*
Catawba Coll. 285
Catawba Valley Coll. *(see Catawba Valley Comm. Coll.)*

Catawba Valley Comm. Coll. 285
Cathedral Coll. *(see Gannon Univ.)*
Catherine Booth Bible Coll. *(see William & Catherine Booth Coll.)*
Catherine E. Hinds Inst. of Esthetics 525
Catherine Hinds Inst. *(see Catherine E. Hinds Inst. of Esthetics)*
Catherine Laboure Sch. of Nursing *(see Caritas Laboure Coll.)*
Cathilic Health Initiatives *(see Saint Joseph Healthcare)*
Catholepistimiad in Detroit *(see Univ. of Michigan)*
Catholic Coll. of Maine *(see Saint Joseph's Coll. of Maine)*
Catholic Distance Inst. *(see Catholic Distance Univ.)*
Catholic Distance Univ., The 401
Catholic Health East *(see Saint James Mercy Health System)*
Catholic Health Initiatives *(see Saint Joseph Med. Ctr.)*
Catholic Health Services of Long Island *(see Mercy Med. Ctr.)*
Catholic Health System *(see Sisters of Charity Hosp.)*
Catholic Med. Centers of New York *(see Saint Vincent Catholic Med. Centers of New York)*
Catholic Theological Union 118
Catholic Univ. of America Sch. of Theology & Religious Studies *(see Catholic Univ. of America)*
Catholic Univ. of America, The 78
Catholic Univ. of Puerto Rico—Arecibo *(see Pontifical Catholic Univ. of Puerto Rico Arecibo Campus)*
Catholic Univ. of Puerto Rico— Guayama *(see Pontifical Catholic Univ. of Puerto Rico—Guayama Campus)*
Catholic Univ. of Puerto Rico— Mayaguez *(see Pontifical Catholic Univ. of Puerto Rico—Mayaguez Campus)*
Catholic Univ. of Puerto Rico—Ponce *(see Pontifical Catholic Univ. of Puerto Rico—Ponce Campus)*
Catonsville Comm. Coll. *(see Comm. Coll. of Baltimore County)*
Cayce/Reilly Sch. of Massotherqapy 631
Cayman Islands Coll. *(see Int'l. Coll. of the Cayman Islands)*
Cayuga Comm. Coll. *(see Cayuga County Comm. Coll.)*
Cayuga County Comm. Coll. 257
Cazenovia Coll. 257
Cazenovia Coll. for Women *(see Cazenovia Coll.)*

Cazenovia Jr. Coll. *(see Cazenovia Coll.)*
Cazenovia Seminary *(see Cazenovia Coll.)*
CB&T, Inc 509
CBD Coll. 455
CBN Univ. *(see Regent Univ.)*
CC's Cosmetology Coll. 586
CDT Sch. *(see Commercial Driver Training)*
CE Sch. of Commerce *(see Hamilton Coll—Omaha)*
Cecil Coll. *(see Cecil Comm. Coll.)*
Cecil Comm. Coll. 178
Cecil County Coll. *(see Cecil Comm. Coll.)*
Cecils Coll. *(see South Coll.)*
Cedar Crest Coll. 327
Cedar Rapids Collegiate Inst. *(see Coe Coll.)*
Cedar Rapids Sch. of Hairstyling *(see American Coll. of Hairstyling— Cedar Rapids)*
Cedar Valley Coll. 375
Cedars Sinai Med. Ctr. 653
Cedarville Coll. 734 *(see also Cedarville Univ.)*
Cedarville Univ. 300, 734
CEI Coll. 722 *(see also Maric Coll— Anaheim)*
CENEODDIVE *(see Ctr. for Explosive Ordnance Disposal & Diving)*
CENINFOCOM *(see Ctr. for Information Dominance Corry Station)*
CENNAVINTEL *(see Ctr. for Naval Intelligence)*
Centenary Biblical Inst. *(see Morgan State Univ.)*
Centenary Coll. 246 *(see also Centenary Coll. of Louisiana)*
Centenary Coll. for Women *(see Centenary Coll.)*
Centenary Coll. of Louisiana 166
Centenary Collegiate Inst. *(see Centenary Coll.)*
Centenary Jr. Coll. *(see Centenary Coll.)*
Ctr. for Advanced Legal Studies 375
Ctr. for Advanced Manufacturing & Techno. 735
Ctr. for Advanced Studies of Puerto Rico & the Caribbean *(see Centro de Estudios Avanzados de Puerto Rico y El Caribe)*
Ctr. for Arts & Techno. 696
Ctr. for Asia Pacific Exchange 496
Ctr. for Behavioral Health, The 669
Ctr. for Creative Studies—Coll. of Art & Design 730 *(see Coll. for Creative Studies)*

Ctr. for Cryptology Training *(see Ctr. for Information Dominance Corry Station)*
Ctr. for Culinary Arts 475
Ctr. for Degree Studies *(see Penn Foster Career Sch.)*
Ctr. for Disease Control & Prevention, The 664
Ctr. for Employment Training 577
Ctr. for Englsih Studies *(see Embassy CES)*
Ctr. for Explosive Ordnance Disposal & Diving 480, 725
Ctr. for Humanistic Studies 197
Ctr. for Information Dominance (CID) 725
Ctr. for Information Dominance Corry Station 480
Ctr. for Innovative Training & Edu. 595
Ctr. for Labor Studies *(see National Labor Coll.)*
Ctr. for Lactation Edu. 735
Ctr. for Languages & Electronic Computation *(see Centro Electronico de Idiomas y Computacion)*
Ctr. for Lifelong Learning 331
Ctr. for Montessori Teacher Edu. of New York 559
Ctr. for Naval Aviation Tech. Training 480, 725
Ctr. for Naval Engineering 631
Ctr. for Naval Intelligence 631, 738
Ctr. for Personal Development 631
Ctr. for Seabees & Facilities Engineering 455
Ctr. for Surface Combat Systems 631
Ctr. for Techno., Essex, The 705
Ctr. for Theological Studies of Florida *(see Florida Ctr. for Theological Studies)*
Ctr. for Training in Bus. & Industry *(see Pinnacle Career Inst— Lawrence)*
Ctr. for Urban Ministerial Edu. 187 *(see also Ctr. for Urban Ministry, The; Gordon-Conwell Theological Seminary)*
Ctr. for Urban Ministry, The 653
Ctr. of Advanced Therapeutics 471
Ctr. of English Language 618
Ctr. of Excellence Long Island Ctr. *(see Dale Carnegie & Associates, Inc.)*
CentraCare Health System *(see Saint Cloud Hosp.)*
Central Acad. & Coll. *(see Central Christian Coll. of Kansas)*
Central Alabama Coll. *(see Central Alabama Comm. Coll.)*
Central Alabama Comm. Coll. 4
Central Arizona Coll. 15

Central Arkansas Radiation Therapy Inst. 652
Central Arkansas Univ. *(see Univ. of Central Arkansas)*
Central Arkansas VA Med. Ctr. *(see Central Arkansas Veterans Healthcare System)*
Central Arkansas Veterans Affairs Med. Ctr. *(see Central Arkansas Veterans Healthcare System)*
Central Arkansas Veterans Healthcare System 652
Central Baptist Coll. 24
Central Baptist Hosp. 672
Central Baptist Seminary *(see Central Baptist Theological Seminary, Heritage Coll. & Seminary)*
Central Baptist Theological Seminary 153, 750
Central Bible Coll. 224, 747
Central California Dale Carnegie Training *(see Dale Carnegie Training of Central California)*
Central California Psychology Internship Consortium *(see Alliant Int'l. Univ—Fresno)*
Central California Sch. of Continuing Edu. 455
Central Career Schools 548
Central Caribbean Univ. *(see Universidad Central del Caribe)*
Central Carolina Coll. *(see Central Carolina Comm. Coll.)*
Central Carolina Comm. Coll. 286
Central Carolina Tech. Coll. 355
Central Chiropractic Coll. *(see Cleveland Chiropractic Coll.)*
Central Christian Coll. *(see Central Christian Coll. of Kansas, Central Christian Coll. of the Bible)*
Central Christian Coll. of Kansas 153
Central Christian Coll. of the Bible 224
Central Coast Coll. 455
Central Coll. 145 *(see also Central Christian Coll. of Kansas)*
Central Coll. of Cosmetology 537
Central Coll. of The Free Methodist Church *(see Central Christian Coll. of Kansas)*
Central Collegiate Inst. *(see Hendrix Coll.)*
Central Comm. Coll. 236
Central Connecticut State Coll. *(see Central Connecticut State Univ.)*
Central Connecticut State Univ. 72
Central European Univ. 435
Central Florida Bible Coll. *(see Florida Christian Coll.)*
Central Florida Comm. Coll. 82
Central Florida Inst., Inc. 83

Central Florida Jr. Coll. *(see Central Florida Comm. Coll.)*
Central Florida Univ. *(see Univ. of Central Florida)*
Central for Information Techno. 455
Central Georgia Coll. *(see Central Georgia Tech. Coll.)*
Central Georgia Tech. Coll. 100
Central Illinois Coll. *(see Illinois Central Coll.)*
Central Indiana Dale Carnegie Training *(see Hanes & Associates, Inc.)*
Central Indiana Tech. Inst. *(see Ivy Tech Comm. Coll. of Indiana— Central Indiana)*
Central Inst. *(see DeVry Univ. Kansas City, Hendrix Coll.)*
Central Inst. of Techno. *(see DeVry Univ. Kansas City)*
Central Iowa VA Healthcare System *(see Veterans Affairs Central Iowa Healthcare System—Knoxville Division)*
Central Iowa Veterans Affairs Healthcare System *(see Veterans Affairs Central Iowa Healthcare System—Knoxville Division)*
Central Kentucky Coll. *(see Bluegrass Comm. & Tech. Coll—Central)*
Central Kentucky State Vocational- Tech. Sch. *(see Bluegrass Comm. & Tech. Coll—Central)*
Central Kentucky Tech. Coll. 728, 729 *(see also Bluegrass Comm. & Tech. Coll—Central)*
Central Kentucky Tech. Coll— Anderson Campus *(see Bluegrass Comm. & Tech. Coll—Anderson)*
Central Kentucky Tech. Coll—Danville Campus *(see Bluegrass Comm. & Tech. Coll—Danville)*
Central Lakes Coll. 208
Central Louisiana State Hosp. *(see Pinecrest Developmental Ctr.)*
Central Maine Coll. *(see Central Maine Comm. Coll.)*
Central Maine Comm. Coll. 175, 730
Central Maine Med. Ctr. 674
Central Maine Med. Ctr. Sch. of Nursing 175
Central Maine Sch. of Nuclear Medicine Techno. *(see Central Maine Med. Ctr.)*
Central Maine Tech. Coll. 730 *(see also Central Maine Comm. Coll.)*
Central Mennonite Coll. *(see Bluffton Univ.)*
Central Methodist Coll. 731 *(see also Central Methodist Univ.)*
Central Methodist Univ. 224, 731

Central Michigan Coll. *(see Central Michigan Univ.)*
Central Michigan Coll. of Edu. *(see Central Michigan Univ.)*
Central Michigan Normal Sch. *(see Central Michigan Univ.)*
Central Michigan Univ. 197
Central Missouri State Univ. 224
Central New York Dale Carnegie Training *(see R.L. Heron & Associates, Inc.)*
Central Ohio Dale Carnegie Training *(see Michael W. Jones & Associates, Inc.)*
Central Ohio Tech. Coll. 301
Central Oklahoma Area Vocational- Tech. Ctr. 735 *(see also Central Techno. Ctr—Drumright)*
Central Oklahoma Univ. *(see Univ. of Central Oklahoma)*
Central Oregon Coll. *(see Central Oregon Comm. Coll.)*
Central Oregon Comm. Coll. 320
Central Pennsylvania Coll. 327
Central Pennsylvania Inst. of Science & Techno. 696, 735
Central Pentecostal Coll. 431
Central Piedmont Comm. Coll. 286 *(see also Central Piedmont Comm. Coll.)*
Central Pilgrim Coll. *(see Oklahoma Wesleyan Univ.)*
Central Sch. of Practical Nursing 578, 738 *(see also Norfolk Tech. Vocational Ctr.)*
Central Seminary *(see Central Baptist Theological Seminary)*
Central State Beauty Acad. 586
Central State Coll. *(see Central State Univ., Univ. of Central Oklahoma)*
Central State Massage Acad. 586
Central State Normal Sch. *(see Lock Haven Univ. of Pennsylvania)*
Central State Teachers Coll. *(see Central Michigan Univ., Univ. of Central Oklahoma)*
Central State Univ. 301
Central Suffolk Hosp. 686
Central Tech—Drumright *(see Central Techno. Ctr—Drumright)*
Central Tech. Comm. Coll. *(see Central Comm. Coll.)*
Central Tech. Inst. *(see DeVry Univ. Kansas City)*
Central Techno. Ctr—Drumright 586, 735
Central Techno. Ctr—Sapulpa 587
Central Tech—Sapulpa *(see Central Techno. Ctr—Sapulpa)*
Central Texas Beauty Coll. #2 618
Central Texas Beauty Coll. 618

Central Texas Coll. 376
Central Texas Commercial Coll. 618, 737
Central Theological Seminary *(see Eden Theological Seminary)*
Central Univ. of North Carolina *(see North Carolina Central Univ.)*
Central Utah Vocational Sch. *(see Utah Valley State Coll.)*
Central Virginia Coll. *(see Central Virginia Comm. Coll.)*
Central Virginia Comm. Coll. 401
Central Virginia Dale Carnegie Training *(see Wray K. Powell & Associates, Inc.)*
Central Washington Coll. of Edu. *(see Central Washington Univ.)*
Central Washington State Coll. *(see Central Washington Univ.)*
Central Washington Univ. 410
Central Wesleyan Coll. *(see Southern Wesleyan Univ.)*
Central Wisconsin Dale Carnegie *(see Meyer Uebelher Associates, LLC)*
Central Wyoming Coll. 430
Central Yeshiva Tomchei Tmimim- Lubavitch 257
Centralia Coll. *(see Centralia Coll.)*
Centralia Coll. 410
Centre Coll. 159
Centre County Area Vocational Tech. Sch. 735 *(see also Central Pennsylvania Inst. of Science & Techno.)*
Centre Europeén de Management Hôtelier International 715
Centre for Dance Edu., The *(see Atlanta Ballet Centre for Dance Edu.)*
Centre for Labour Market Studies *(see Univ. of Leicester's Centre for Labour Market Studies)*
Centro de Capacitacion Montessori 740
Centro de Entrenamiento Montessori 647
Centro de Estudios Avanzados de Puerto Rico y El Caribe 347 *(see also Centro de Estudios Avanzados de Puerto Rico y El Caribe)*
Centro de Estudios de los Dominicos del Caribe *(see Dominican Study Ctr. of the Caribbean)*
Centro de Estudios Multidisciplinarios 602 *(see also Centro de Estudios Multidisciplinarios)*
Centro Electronico de Idiomas y Computacion 648

Centro Entrenamiento Montessori de Santo Domingo *(see Montessori Training Ctr. of Santo Domingo)*
Centura Health *(see Centura Health CPE (System Ctr.), Saint Anthony Central Hosp.)*
Centura Health CPE (System Ctr.) 657
Centurion Prof. Training 559
Century Coll. 208, 731
Century Comm. & Tech. Coll. 731 *(see also Century Coll.)*
Century Sch. of Cosmetology, Inc. 578
Cermak Health Services of Cook County 667
Cerritos Coll. 35
Cerro Coso Comm. Coll. 35
Certified Careers Inst. 627
Certified Tech. Edu. Ctr. Acad., Tech Inst. of Georgia *(see CTEC Acad., Tech Inst. of Georgia)*
Cesar Ritz *(see Int'l. Coll. of Hospitality Management Cesar Ritz)*
Cesar Ritz Hotel Management Inst. *(see Institut Hotelier Cesar Ritz)*
Chabot Coll. 35
Chabot Coll. Valley Campus *(see Las Positas Coll.)*
Chadron State Coll. 236
Chaffey Coll. 35
Chaffey Jr. Coll. of Agriculture *(see Chaffey Coll.)*
Chamberlayne Jr. Coll. *(see Mount Ida Coll.)*
Chaminade Coll. of Honolulu *(see Chaminade Univ. of Honolulu)*
Chaminade Univ. of Honolulu 113
Champaign Sch. of Beauty Culture *(see Mr. John's Sch. of Cosmetology, Esthetics & Nails)*
Champion Inst. of Cosmetology 456
Champlain Coll. 397
Champlain Valley Hosp. *(see Champlain Valley Physicians Hosp. Med. Ctr.)*
Champlain Valley Physicians Hosp. Med. Ctr. 686
Chandler Med. Ctr. *(see Univ. of Kentucky)*
Chandler-Gilbert Coll. *(see Chandler-Gilbert Comm. Coll.)*
Chandler-Gilbert Comm. Coll. 15
Chandler-Gilbert Edu. Ctr. *(see Chandler-Gilbert Comm. Coll.)*
Chaparral Career Coll. *(see Chaparral Coll.)*
Chaparral Coll. 15
Chaplaincy Ctr., The 700, 736
Chapman Sch. of Religious Studies *(see Oakland City Univ.)*

Chapman Seminary of Oakland City Univ. *(see Oakland City Univ.)*
Chapman Univ. 35
Charity Hosp. *(see Saint Vincent Infirmary Med. Ctr.)*
Charles & Sue's Sch. of Hair Design 618
Charles County Comm. Coll. *(see Coll. of Southern Maryland)*
Charles D. Eubank & Associates, Inc. 505
Charles F. Kettering Mem. Hosp. *(see Kettering Coll. of Med. Arts)*
Charles H. Mason Theological Seminary *(see Interdenominational Theological Ctr.)*
Charles H. McCann Tech. Sch. 676
Charles of Italy Beauty Coll. *(see Charles of Italy Beauty Coll. & Sch. of Massage Therapy)*
Charles of Italy Beauty Coll. & Sch. of Massage Therapy 445
Charles R. Drew Univ. of Medicine & Science 35
Charles Stewart Mott Comm. Coll. 197
Charles Stuart Sch. of Diamond Setting *(see Charles Stuart Sch. of Locksmithing)*
Charles Stuart Sch. of Locksmithing 559
Charleston Coll. *(see Coll. of Charleston)*
Charleston Cosmetology Inst. 608
Charleston Culinary Inst. *(see Trident Tech. Coll.)*
Charleston Med. Ctr. 421 *(see also West Virginia Univ.)*
Charleston Sch. of Beauty Culture 640
Charleston Sch. of Massage 608
Charleston Southern Univ. 355
Charleston Univ. *(see Univ. of Charleston)*
Charlotte Art Inst. *(see Art Inst. of Charlotte)*
Charlotte Ctr., The *(see Univ. of North Carolina at Charlotte)*
Charlotte Coll. *(see Univ. of North Carolina at Charlotte)*
Charlotte Female Inst. *(see Queens Univ. of Charlotte)*
Charlotte Hairstyling Inst. *(see Hairstyling Inst. of Charlotte)*
Charlotte Inst. of Art *(see Art Inst. of Charlotte)*
Charlotte Tech Ctr. *(see Charlotte Vocational-Tech. Ctr.)*
Charlotte Vocational-Tech. Ctr. 480
Charmayne Beauty Acad. 578
Charter Coll. 11

Charter Oak Coll. *(see Charter Oak State Coll.)*
Charter Oak State Coll. 72
Charzanne Beauty Coll. 608
Chase Coll. 456
Chatfield Coll. 301
Chatham Coll. 327
Chattahoochee Coll. *(see Chattahoochee Tech. Coll.)*
Chattahoochee Tech. Coll. 101, 726
Chattahoochee Tech. Inst. 726 *(see also Chattahoochee Tech. Coll.)*
Chattahoochee Valley Comm. Coll. 4
Chattanooga Assoc. for Clinical Pastoral Care 702
Chattanooga Bible Inst. *(see Psychological Studies Inst.)*
Chattanooga City Coll. *(see Univ. of Tennessee at Chattanooga)*
Chattanooga State Tech. Comm. Coll. 364
Chattanooga State Tech. Inst. *(see Chattanooga State Tech. Comm. Coll.)*
Chattanooga Univ. *(see Univ. of Tennessee at Chattanooga)*
Chatterton, Inc 627
Chauncey Sparks State Tech. Coll. *(see George C. Wallace State Comm. Coll.)*
Chaviano de Mayaguez Institucion *(see Institucion Chaviano de Mayaguez)*
Chaviano Institution of Mayaguez *(see Institucion Chaviano de Mayaguez)*
Cheeks Int'l. Acad. of Beauty Culture 645
Chemeketa Coll. *(see Chemeketa Comm. Coll.)*
Chemeketa Comm. Coll. 320
Cherokee Indian Normal Sch. of Robeson County *(see Univ. of North Carolina at Pembroke)*
Cherokee Mental Health Inst. 671
Cherokee Nation Sch. of Information Techno. *(see Bacone Coll.)*
Cherokee National Female Seminary *(see Northeastern State Univ.)*
Cheryl Fell's Sch. of Bus. 559
Chesapeake Coll. 179
Chester Coll. of New England 242, 732
Chester County Intermediate Unit *(see Ctr. for Arts & Techno.)*
Chester Hosp. *(see Crozer-Chester Med. Ctr.)*
Chester Inst. for Tech. Edu. *(see Porter & Chester Inst.)*
Chesterfield-Marlboro Tech. Coll. *(see Northeastern Tech. Coll.)*

Chestnut Hill Coll. 327

Chetta's Acad. of Hair & Nails, Inc. 637

Cheveux Sch. Hair Design & Hairport, Inc. 572

Cheyenne River Comm. Coll. *(see Si Tanka Univ.)*

Cheyney Univ. of Pennsylvania 327

CHI Inst. 327 *(see also Career Centers of Texas—Fort Worth)*

Chic Univ. of Cosmetology—Grand Rapids 528

Chic Univ. of Cosmetology—Portage 528

Chicago Area Christian Training Consortium 667

Chicago Aveda Inst. *(see Aveda Inst. Chicago)*

Chicago Career Colleges *(see Career Colleges of Chicago)*

Chicago Catholic Theological Union *(see Catholic Theological Union)*

Chicago Children's Hosp. *(see Children's Mem. Hosp.)*

Chicago Children's Mem. Hosp. *(see Children's Mem. Hosp.)*

Chicago Coll. of Commerce *(see Career Colleges of Chicago)*

Chicago Coll. of Osteopathic Medicine *(see Midwestern Univ.)*

Chicago Coll. of Pharmacy *(see Midwestern Univ.)*

Chicago Cooking & Hospitality Inst. *(see Cooking & Hospitality Inst. of Chicago)*

Chicago Dale Carnegie Training *(see Don Adams Corporation)*

Chicago Evangelistic Inst. *(see Vennard Coll.)*

Chicago Evangelization Society *(see Moody Bible Inst.)*

Chicago Home for Jewish Orphans *(see Jewish Children's Bureau of Chicago)*

Chicago Inst. of Cooking & Hospitality *(see Cooking & Hospitality Inst. of Chicago)*

Chicago Inst. of Music *(see Music Inst. of Chicago)*

Chicago Lutheran Sch. of Theology *(see Lutheran Sch. of Theology at Chicago)*

Chicago Lutheran Theological Seminary *(see Lutheran Sch. of Theology at Chicago)*

Chicago Med. Coll. *(see Northwestern Univ.)*

Chicago Med. Sch., The *(see Dr. William M. Scholl Coll. of Podiatric Medicine, Rosalind Franklin Univ. of Medicine & Science)*

Chicago Music Inst. *(see Music Inst. of Chicago)*

Chicago ORT Tech. Inst. *(see Zarem/Golde ORT Tech. Inst.)*

Chicago Sch. of Art *(see Sch. of the Art Inst. of Chicago)*

Chicago Sch. of Massage Therapy 499 *(see also McHenry County Coll.)*

Chicago Sch. of Prof. Psychology, The 118

Chicago Seminary *(see Chicago Theological Seminary)*

Chicago State Coll. *(see Chicago State Univ.)*

Chicago State Univ. 118

Chicago Teachers Coll. South *(see Chicago State Univ.)*

Chicago Telshe Yeshiva *(see Telshe Yeshiva-Chicago)*

Chicago Theological Seminary 118 *(see also Trinity Int'l. Univ.)*

Chicago Theological Union *(see Catholic Theological Union)*

Chicago Training Sch. *(see Garrett-Evangelical Theological Seminary)*

Chicago Univ. *(see Univ. of Chicago)*

Chicago Urban League Computer Training Ctr. 499

Chicago VA Med. Ctr. *(see Jesse Brown Veterans Affairs Med. Ctr.)*

Chicago Veterans Affairs Med. Ctr. *(see Jesse Brown Veterans Affairs Med. Ctr.)*

Chicago-Kent Coll. of Law *(see Illinois Inst. of Techno.)*

Chicago-Reed Mental Health Ctr. 667

Chico State Coll. *(see California State Univ—Chico)*

Chico State Teachers Coll. *(see California State Univ—Chico)*

Chief Dull Knife Coll. 234

Child Guidance Ctr. of Greater Long Beach *(see Greater Long Beach Child Guidance Ctr.)*

Childers Classical Inst. *(see Abilene Christian Univ.)*

Children's Hosp. *(see Columbus Children's Hosp.; Children's Hosp., The)*

Children's Hosp. & Rehabilitation Ctr. *(see Faxton-St. Luke's Healthcare)*

Children's Hosp. at Stanford *(see Lucile Packard Children's Hosp.)*

Children's Hosp. Med. Ctr. *(see Cincinnati Children's Hosp. Med. Ctr.)*

Children's Hosp. Med. Ctr. of Akron 693

Children's Hosp. National Med. Ctr. *(see Children's National Med. Ctr.)*

Children's Hosp. of Chicago *(see Children's Mem. Hosp.)*

Children's Hosp. of Cincinnati *(see Cincinnati Children's Hosp. Med. Ctr.)*

Children's Hosp. of Columbus *(see Columbus Children's Hosp.)*

Children's Hosp. of Los Angeles 654

Children's Hosp. of Michigan 677

Children's Hosp. of Orange County 653

Children's Hosp. of Pittsburgh 696

Children's Hosp. of Wisconsin—Appleton 708

Children's Hosp. of Wisconsin—Milwaukee 708

Children's Hosp., The 657

Children's Med. Ctr. of Dallas 703

Children's Mem. Hosp. 667

Children's Mem. Med. Ctr. 667

Children's National Med. Ctr. 661

Children's Psychiatric Ctr. *(see Children's Psychiatric Ctr., Inc., The; Terry Children's Psychiatric Ctr.)*

Children's Psychiatric Ctr., Inc., The 662

Children's Rehabilitation Inst. *(see Kennedy Krieger Inst.)*

Chillicothe Beauty Acad. 537

China Med. Univ. *(see China Int'l. Med. Univ.)*

Chinese Culture Acad. *(see Acad. of Chinese Culture & Health Sciences)*

Chinese Culture & Health Sciences Acad. *(see Acad. of Chinese Culture & Health Sciences)*

Chinese Medicine Inst. of New York *(see New York Coll. of Traditional Chinese Medicine)*

Chinese Univ. of Hong Kong, The 715

Chipola Coll. 83, 725

Chipola Jr. Coll. 725 *(see also Chipola Coll.)*

Chippewa Valley Tech. Coll. 423

Chiropractic Coll. of Los Angeles *(see Southern California Univ. of Health Sciences)*

Chiropractic Coll. of New York *(see New York Chiropractic Coll.)*

Chisholm Trail Area Vocational Tech. Sch. 695

Chisholm Trail Vo-Tech Sch. (see Chisholm Trail Area Vocational Tech. Sch.)

Choffin Career & Tech. Ctr. 578, 734

Choffin Career Ctr. 734 (see also Choffin Career & Tech. Ctr.)

Choffin Tech. Ctr. (see Choffin Career & Tech. Ctr.)

Chouinard Art Inst. (see California Inst. of the Arts)

Chowan Coll. 286

Chris' Beauty Coll. 535

Christ Hosp. 683, 693 (see also Advocate Christ Med. Ctr.)

Christ Med. Ctr. (see Advocate Christ Med. Ctr.)

Christ the King Seminary 257

Christendom Coll., The 401

Christian Brothers Coll. (see Christian Brothers Univ.)

Christian Brothers Jr. Coll. (see Christian Brothers Univ.)

Christian Brothers Univ. 364

Christian Coll. in Abilene (see Abilene Christian Univ.)

Christian Coll. of Atlanta (see Atlanta Christian Coll.)

Christian Coll. of California (see California Christian Coll.)

Christian Coll. of Dallas (see Dallas Christian Coll.)

Christian Coll. of Florida (see Florida Christian Coll.)

Christian Coll. of Kentucky (see Kentucky Christian Univ.)

Christian Coll. of Nebraska (see Nebraska Christian Coll.)

Christian Coll. of Saint Louis (see Saint Louis Christian Coll.)

Christian Coll. of the Puget Sound (see Puget Sound Christian Coll.)

Christian Counseling Ctr. of Boston (see Boston Christian Counseling Ctr.)

Christian Female Coll. (see Columbia Coll.)

Christian H. Buhl Hosp. (see Sharon Reg. Health System)

Christian Heritage Coll. 722 (see also San Diego Christian Coll.)

Christian Hosp. Northeast-Northwest Baptist Med. Ctr. 681

Christian Life Coll. 118

Christian Normal Inst. (see Kentucky Christian Univ.)

Christian Studies Inst. (see Austin Grad. Sch. of Theology)

Christian Theological Seminary 136

Christian Training Inst. (see Taylor Univ. Coll. & Seminary)

Christian Univ. (see Colorado Christian Univ., Culver-Stockton Coll., Kentucky Christian Univ., Texas Christian Univ.)

Christian Univ. of Colorado (see Colorado Christian Univ.)

Christian Univ. of Kentucky (see Kentucky Christian Univ.)

Christian Univ. of Texas (see Texas Christian Univ.)

Christian Workers Univ. (see Manhattan Christian Coll.)

Christiana Care Health Services 660

Christopher Newport Univ. 401

Christ's Coll. 752

CHRISTUS Saint Elizabeth Hosp. 703

CHRISTUS Spohn Hosp. Corpus Christi-Mem. 703

CHRISTUS Spohn Hosp. Mem. (see CHRISTUS Spohn Hosp. Corpus Christi—Mem.)

Ch'san Sofer Rabbinical Coll. (see Rabbinical Coll. Ch'san Sofer)

Chubb Inst—Arlington Campus, The 631

Chubb Inst—Chicago, The 499

Chubb Inst—New York City, The 559

Chubb Inst—Parsippany, The 548

Chubb Inst—Springfield, The 595

Chubb Inst—Villa Park 727

Chubb Inst—Westbury, The 559

Church Divinity Sch. of the Pacific 36

Church of God Sch. of Theology 736

Church of God Theological Seminary, The 364, 736

Churchman Bus. Sch. 735

CIMS Coll. 578

Cincinnati Acad. of Art (see Art Acad. of Cincinnati)

Cincinnati Art Acad. (see Art Acad. of Cincinnati)

Cincinnati Art Inst. (see Art Inst. of Cincinnati)

Cincinnati Bible Coll. & Seminary 734 (see also Cincinnati Christian Univ.)

Cincinnati Bible Inst. (see Cincinnati Christian Univ.)

Cincinnati Bible Seminary (see Cincinnati Christian Univ.)

Cincinnati Children's Hosp. Med. Ctr. 693

Cincinnati Christian Univ. 301, 734

Cincinnati Coll. (see Cincinnati Coll. of Mortuary Science, Univ. of Cincinnati)

Cincinnati Coll. of Mortuary Science 301

Cincinnati Conservatory of Music (see Univ. of Cincinnati)

Cincinnati Dale Carnegie Training (see Dale Carnegie Training of Greater Cincinnati)

Cincinnati Job Corps Ctr. 757

Cincinnati Sch. of Embalming (see Cincinnati Coll. of Mortuary Science)

Cincinnati State Coll. (see Cincinnati State Tech. & Comm. Coll.)

Cincinnati State Tech. & Comm. Coll. 301

Cincinnati Univ. (see Univ. of Cincinnati)

Circle in the Square Theatre Sch. 560

Circle J Beauty Sch. 618

Circleville Bible Coll. 301

Circleville Coll. (see Circleville Bible Coll.)

Cisco Jr. Coll. 376

Citadel, The 355

Citadel Bible Coll. (see Calvary Bible Coll. & Theological Seminary)

Citizens Med. Ctr. 703

Citrus Coll. 36

Citrus Health Network, Inc. 662

Cittone Inst., The 548

Cittone Inst—Ctr. City, The 328

City Coll. 83 (see also City Univ., City Univ. of New York City Coll.)

City Coll. of Colorado Springs (see Remington Coll—San Diego)

City Coll. of Fresno (see Fresno City Coll.)

City Coll. of Long Beach (see Long Beach City Coll.)

City Coll. of Los Angeles (see Los Angeles City Coll.)

City Coll. of New York, The (see City Univ. of New York City Coll.)

City Coll. of Pasadena (see Pasadena City Coll.)

City Coll. of Sacramento (see Sacramento City Coll.)

City Coll. of San Diego (see San Diego City Coll.)

City Coll. of San Francisco 36

City Coll. of San Jose (see San Jose City Coll.)

City Coll. of Santa Barbara (see Santa Barbara City Coll.)

City Coll. of the City Univ. of New York, The (see City Univ. of New York City Coll.)

City Coll. Orlando (see City Coll. Casselberry)

City Coll., Inc. 587

City Coll—Casselberry Campus (see City Coll. Casselberry)

City Colleges of Chicago—Harold Washington Coll. 118

City Colleges of Chicago—Harry S
Truman Coll. 119
City Colleges of Chicago—Kennedy-
King Coll. 119
City Colleges of Chicago—Malcolm X
Coll. 119
City Colleges of Chicago—Olive-
Harvey Coll. 119
City Colleges of Chicago—Richard J.
Daley Coll. 119
City Colleges of Chicago—Wilbur
Wright Coll. 119
City Hosp. *(see Univ. Hosp.)*
City of Erie Sch. Dist. *(see Sch. Dist.
of the City of Erie)*
City of Hope Grad. Sch. of Biological
Sciences *(see City of Hope
National Med. Ctr.)*
City of Hope National Med. Ctr. 36
City Tech *(see City Univ. of New York
New York City Coll. of Techno.)*
City Univ. 411 *(see also New Jersey
City Univ.)*
City Univ. of New Jersey *(see New
Jersey City Univ.)*
City Univ. of New York Bernard M.
Baruch Coll., The 257
City Univ. of New York Borough of
Manhattan Comm. Coll. 258
City Univ. of New York Bronx Comm.
Coll. 258
City Univ. of New York Brooklyn Coll.
258
City Univ. of New York City Coll. 258
City Univ. of New York Coll. of Staten
Island 258
City Univ. of New York Grad. Ctr. 258,
733
City Univ. of New York Grad. Sch. &
Univ. Ctr. *(see City Univ. of New
York Grad. Ctr.)*
City Univ. of New York Herbert H.
Lehman Coll. 258
City Univ. of New York Hostos Comm.
Coll. 258
City Univ. of New York Hunter Coll.
259
City Univ. of New York John Jay Coll.
of Criminal Justice 259
City Univ. of New York Kingsborough
Comm. Coll. 259
City Univ. of New York La Guardia
Comm. Coll. 259
City Univ. of New York Medgar Evers
Coll. 259
City Univ. of New York Mount Sinai
Sch. of Medicine *(see Mount
Sinai Sch. of Medicine)*
City Univ. of New York New York City
Coll. of Techno. 259

City Univ. of New York New York City
Tech. Coll. *(see City Univ. of New
York New York City Coll. of
Techno.)*
City Univ. of New York Queens Coll.
259
City Univ. of New York Queensborough
Comm. Coll. 259
City Univ. of New York York Coll. 259,
734
City Univ. Sch. of Law at Queens Coll.
259 *(see also City Univ. of New
York Queens Coll.)*
Clackamas Coll. *(see Clackamas
Comm. Coll.)*
Clackamas Comm. Coll. 320
Clackamas County Coll. *(see
Clackamas Comm. Coll.)*
Claflin Coll. *(see Claflin Univ.)*
Claflin Univ. 355
Clara Maass Med. Ctr. 683
Claremont Grad. Sch. *(see Claremont
Grad. Univ.)*
Claremont Grad. Univ., The 36
Claremont McKenna Coll. 36
Claremont Sch. of Theology 36
Claremont Theology Sch. *(see
Claremont Sch. of Theology)*
Claremont Univ. *(see Claremont Grad.
Univ.)*
Claremore Beauty Coll. 587
Claremore Jr. Coll. *(see Rogers State
Univ.)*
Clarendon Coll. 376
Clare's Beauty Coll. 637
Clarian Health Partners, Inc/Methodist
Hosp. 669
Clarion County Area Vocational Tech.
Sch. 697
Clarion County Vo-Tech Sch. *(see
Clarion County Area Vocational
Tech. Sch.)*
Clarion Health Partners 669
Clarion State Coll. *(see Clarion Univ. of
Pennsylvania)*
Clarion State Teachers Coll. *(see
Clarion Univ. of Pennsylvania)*
Clarion Univ. of Pennsylvania 328
Clarita Career Coll. 456
Clark Art Inst., The *(see Williams Coll.)*
Clark Atlanta Univ. 101
Clark Coll. 411 *(see also Clark State
Comm. Coll., Clark Univ.)*
Clark Comm. Coll. *(see Clark State
Comm. Coll.)*
Clark County Tech. Inst. *(see Clark
State Comm. Coll.)*
Clark F. Miller Sch. of Radiologic
Techno. *(see Central Maine Med.
Ctr.)*

Clark State Coll. *(see Clark State
Comm. Coll.)*
Clark State Comm. Coll. 301
Clark Tech. Coll. *(see Clark State
Comm. Coll.)*
Clark Univ. 186
Clarke Coll. 145
Clark's Bus. Coll. *(see Erie Bus. Ctr.)*
Clarksburg Beauty Acad. 640
Clarksburg Skills Training Ctr. *(see
Stanley Tech. Inst.)*
Clarkson Coll. 236
Clarkson Univ. 260
Class Act I Sch. of Cosmetology 537
Classic Coll. of Hair Design 509 *(see
also Comm. Coll. of Cosmetology)*
Classical Chinese Medicine Clinic *(see
National Coll. of Naturopathic
Medicine)*
Clatsop Coll. *(see Clatsop Comm.
Coll.)*
Clatsop Comm. Coll. 320
Clayton Coll. & State Univ. 726 *(see
also Clayton State Univ.)*
Clayton State Coll. *(see Clayton State
Univ.)*
Clayton State Univ. 101, 726
Clayton Univ. *(see Clayton State Univ.)*
Clear Creek Baptist Bible Coll. 159
Clear Creek Baptist Sch. *(see Clear
Creek Baptist Bible Coll.)*
Clear Creek Coll. *(see Clear Creek
Baptist Bible Coll.)*
Clear Creek Mountain Preacher's
Bible Sch. *(see Clear Creek
Baptist Bible Coll.)*
Clearfield Beauty 595
Clearfield County Area Vocational
Tech. Sch. 697
Clearfield County Vo-Tech Sch. *(see
Clearfield County Area Vocational
Tech. Sch.)*
Clearfield Hosp. 697
Clearwater Christian Coll. 83
Clearwater Coll. *(see Clearwater
Christian Coll.)*
Cleary Bus. Coll. *(see Cleary Univ.)*
Cleary Coll. *(see Cleary Univ.)*
Cleary Jr. Coll. *(see Cleary Univ.)*
Cleary Sch. of Penmanship, The *(see
Cleary Univ.)*
Cleary Univ. 197
Cleft Palate Clinic of Lancaster *(see
Lancaster Cleft Palate Clinic)*
Clements Job Corps Ctr. *(see Earle C.
Clements Job Corps Ctr.)*
Clemson Agricultural Coll. *(see
Clemson Univ.)*
Clemson Coll. *(see Clemson Univ.)*
Clemson Univ. 355

Clermont Coll. *(see Univ. of Cincinnati—Clermont Coll.)*

Cleveland Art Inst. *(see Cleveland Inst. of Art)*

Cleveland Bible Coll. *(see Malone Coll.)*

Cleveland Ctr. for Employment Training *(see Ctr. for Employment Training)*

Cleveland Chiropractic Coll. 224

Cleveland Clinic Foundation, The *(see Cleveland Clinic, The)*

Cleveland Clinic, The 693

Cleveland Coll. *(see Cleveland Comm. Coll., Laura & Alvin Siegal Coll. of Judaic Studies)*

Cleveland Coll. of Jewish Studies *(see Laura & Alvin Siegal Coll. of Judaic Studies)*

Cleveland Comm. Coll. 286 *(see also Cleveland State Comm. Coll.)*

Cleveland County Tech. Inst. *(see Cleveland Comm. Coll.)*

Cleveland Dental-Med. Assistants Inst. *(see Cleveland Inst. of Dental-Med. Assistants, Inc.)*

Cleveland Extension High Sch. *(see Adult & Continuing Edu— Cleveland Extension)*

Cleveland Inst. of Art 301

Cleveland Inst. of Dental-Med. Assistants, Inc. 578

Cleveland Inst. of Electronics, Inc. 301

Cleveland Inst. of Music 301

Cleveland Music Inst. *(see Cleveland Inst. of Music)*

Cleveland Music Sch. Settlement, The 578

Cleveland State Coll. *(see Cleveland State Comm. Coll.)*

Cleveland State Comm. Coll. 365

Cleveland State Univ. 302

Cleveland Tech. Coll. *(see Cleveland Comm. Coll.)*

Cleveland Univ. *(see Cleveland State Univ.)*

Cleveland VA Med. Ctr. *(see Veterans Affairs Med. Ctr—Cleveland)*

Cleveland Veterans Affairs Med. Ctr. *(see Veterans Affairs Med. Ctr— Cleveland)*

Clinch Valley Coll. of the Univ. of Virginia *(see Univ. of Virginia's Coll. at Wise)*

Clinical Acupuncture & Oriental Medicine Inst. *(see Inst. of Clinical Acupuncture & Oriental Medicine)*

Clinical Pastoral Edu. Ctr. of the Northern Rockies *(see Northern Rockies Clinical Pastoral Edu. Ctr., Inc.)*

Clinical Social Work Inst. *(see Inst. for Clinical Social Work, Inc.)*

Clinton Beauty Acad. *(see Arleen's Clinton Beauty Acad.)*

Clinton Coll. *(see Clinton Jr. Coll., Presbyterian Coll.)*

Clinton Comm. Coll. 145, 260

Clinton County Area Techno. Ctr. *(see Somerset Comm. Coll.)*

Clinton Jr. Coll. 355 *(see also Clinton Comm. Coll.)*

Clinton Tech. Inst. 721 *(see also Clinton Tech. Inst— Motorcycle/Marine Mechanics Inst., Motorcycle & Marine Mechanics Inst.)*

Clinton Tech. Inst—Motorcycle/Marine Mechanics Inst. 725

Cloud Coll. *(see Cloud County Comm. Coll.)*

Cloud County Coll. *(see Cloud County Comm. Coll.)*

Cloud County Comm. Coll. 153

Cloud County Jr. Coll. *(see Cloud County Comm. Coll.)*

Clover Park Coll. *(see Clover Park Tech. Coll.)*

Clover Park Comm. Coll. *(see Pierce Coll. Fort Steilacoom, Pierce Coll. Puyallup)*

Clover Park Tech. Coll. 411

Clovis Coll. *(see Clovis Comm. Coll.)*

Clovis Comm. Coll. 252

Cloyd's Beauty Sch. #1 515

Cloyd's Beauty Sch. No. 2 515

Cloyd's Beauty Sch. No. 3 515

CMHA Sch. of Nursing *(see Carolinas Coll. of Health Sciences)*

CNATT *(see Ctr. for Naval Aviation Tech. Training)*

Coachella Valley Beauty Coll. 753

Coachella Valley Tech. Skills Ctr. 456

Coahoma Coll. *(see Coahoma Comm. Coll.)*

Coahoma Comm. Coll. 218

Coalinga Jr. Coll. *(see West Hills Comm. Coll.)*

Coast Guard Acad. *(see United States Coast Guard Acad.)*

Coastal Behavioral Healthcare, Inc. 662

Coastal Bend Coll. 376

Coastal Bend Health Edu. Ctr. *(see Texas A&M Univ. System Health Science Ctr.)*

Coastal Carolina Coll. *(see Coastal Carolina Comm. Coll., Coastal Carolina Univ.)*

Coastal Carolina Comm. Coll. 286

Coastal Carolina Univ. 356

Coastal Georgia Comm. Coll. 101

Coastal Valley Coll. *(see Expression Coll. for Digital Arts)*

Coastline Beauty Coll. 456

Coastline Comm. Coll. 36

Cobb Beauty Coll. 492

Cobleskill Coll. of Agriculture & Techno. *(see State Univ. of New York Coll. of Agriculture & Techno. at Cobleskill)*

Cochise Coll. 15

Cochise Comm. Coll. *(see Cochise Coll.)*

Coconino Coll. *(see Coconino County Comm. Coll.)*

Coconino County Comm. Coll. 15

Coe Coll. 145

Coeur d'Alene Jr. Coll. *(see North Idaho Coll.)*

Coffeyville Area Tech. Sch. *(see Coffeyville Comm. Coll.)*

Coffeyville Comm. Coll. 153, 728

Coffeyville Comm. Coll/Area Tech. Sch. 728 *(see also Coffeyville Comm. Coll.)*

Coffeyville Comm. Coll/Area Tech. Sch—Tech. Campus 728

Coffeyville Comm. Jr. Coll. *(see Coffeyville Comm. Coll.)*

Cogswell Coll. *(see Henry Cogswell Coll., Cogswell Polytech. Coll.)*

Cogswell Coll. North *(see Henry Cogswell Coll.)*

Cogswell Polytech. Coll. 36

Cohen Coll. *(see Metropolitan Coll. of New York)*

Coker Coll. 356

Coker Coll. for Women *(see Coker Coll.)*

Colburn Sch. of Performing Arts, The 36

Colby Acad. *(see Colby-Sawyer Coll.)*

Colby Coll. 175 *(see also Colby Comm. Coll.)*

Colby Comm. Coll. 153

Colby Jr. Coll. *(see Colby-Sawyer Coll.)*

Colby-Sawyer Coll. 242

Cold Spring Harbor Laboratory 260

Colegio Biblico Pentecostal de Puerto Rico 347

Colegio de las Ciencias Artes y Television 603

Colegio Mayor de Tecnologia 603

Colegio Pentecostal Mizpa 347

Colegio Technologica de San Juan *(see Univ. Coll. of San Juan)*

Colegio Tecnico Metropolitano 603

Colegio Tecnologico y Comercial de Puerto Rico 603

Colegio Universitario de San Juan *(see Univ. Coll. of San Juan)*

Colegio Universitario del Este *(see Universidad del Este)*

Colegio Universitario Metropolitano *(see Universidad Metropolitana)*

Coleman Coll. 36

Coler-Goldwater Mem. Hosp. *(see Coler-Goldwater Specialty Hosp. & Nursing Facility)*

Coler-Goldwater Specialty Hosp. & Nursing Facility 686

Colgate Rochester Crozer Divinity Sch. 260

Colgate Rochester Divinity Sch. *(see Colgate Rochester Crozer Divinity Sch.)*

Colgate Rochester Divinity Sch/Bexley Hall/Crozer Theological Seminary *(see Colgate Rochester Crozer Divinity Sch.)*

Colgate Univ. 260

Colleen O'Hara's Beauty Acad—Orange 456

Colleen O'Hara's Beauty Acad—Santa Ana 456

Coll. America *(see CollegeAmerica)*

Coll. & Acad. of the Incarnate Word *(see Univ. of the Incarnate Word)*

Coll. at Brockport *(see State Univ. of New York Coll. at Brockport)*

Coll. at Buffalo *(see State Univ. of New York Coll. at Buffalo)*

Coll. at Cobleskill *(see State Univ. of New York Coll. of Agriculture & Techno. at Cobleskill)*

Coll. at Cortland *(see State Univ. of New York Coll. at Cortland)*

Coll. at Fredonia *(see State Univ. of New York Coll. at Fredonia)*

Coll. at Geneseo *(see State Univ. of New York Coll. at Geneseo)*

Coll. at Morrisville *(see State Univ. of New York Coll. of Agriculture & Techno. at Morrisville)*

Coll. at New Paltz *(see State Univ. of New York at New Paltz)*

Coll. at Old Westbury, The *(see State Univ. of New York Coll. at Old Westbury)*

Coll. at Oneonta *(see State Univ. of New York Coll. at Oneonta)*

Coll. at Oswego *(see State Univ. of New York Coll. at Oswego)*

Coll. at Plattsburgh *(see State Univ. of New York Coll. at Plattsburgh)*

Coll. at Potsdam *(see State Univ. of New York Coll. at Potsdam)*

Coll. at Purchase *(see State Univ. of New York Coll. at Purchase)*

Coll. at Wise *(see Univ. of Virginia's Coll. at Wise)*

Coll. Dept. of the Acad. of Holy Angels, The *(see Our Lady of Holy Cross Coll.)*

Coll. East Carolina *(see East Carolina Univ.)*

Coll. for Creative Studies, The 197, 730

Coll. for Financial Planning 65

Coll. for Lifelong Learning 732 *(see also Granite State Coll.)*

Coll. for Prof. Studies, The 83

Coll. Misericordia 328

Coll. of Acupuncture & Herbal Medicine *(see World Medicine Inst.)*

Coll. of Acupuncture & Integrative Medicine, Berkeley *(see Acupuncture & Integrative Medicine Coll., Berkeley)*

Coll. of Acupuncture & Oriental Medicine of Minnesota *(see Northwestern Health Sciences Univ.)*

Coll. of Adrian *(see Adrian Coll.)*

Coll. of Advanced Techno. *(see Advanced Coll. of Techno.)*

Coll. of Aeronautics 733 *(see also Vaughn Coll. of Aeronautics & Techno.)*

Coll. of Agriculture & Life Sciences 261

Coll. of Agriculture & Techno. at Cobleskill *(see State Univ. of New York Coll. of Agriculture & Techno. at Cobleskill)*

Coll. of Agriculture & Techno. at Morrisville *(see State Univ. of New York Coll. of Agriculture & Techno. at Morrisville)*

Coll. of Alameda 36

Coll. of Albion *(see Albion Coll.)*

Coll. of Alma *(see Alma Coll.)*

Coll. of Amarillo *(see Amarillo Coll.)*

Coll. of Antelope Valley *(see Antelope Valley Coll.)*

Coll. of Art Advertising 302

Coll. of Art & Design at Minneapolis *(see Minneapolis Coll. of Art & Design)*

Coll. of Associated Arts *(see Coll. of Visual Arts)*

Coll. of Bainbridge *(see Bainbridge Coll.)*

Coll. of Bakersfield *(see Bakersfield Coll.)*

Coll. of Barstow *(see Barstow Coll.)*

Coll. of Baton Rouge *(see Baton Rouge Coll.)*

Coll. of Beloit *(see Beloit Coll.)*

Coll. of Bennington *(see Bennington Coll.)*

Coll. of Berea *(see Berea Coll.)*

Coll. of Bermuda *(see Bermuda Coll.)*

Coll. of Biblical Studies—Houston 376

Coll. of Boston *(see Boston Coll.)*

Coll. of Brooklyn *(see City Univ. of New York Brooklyn Coll.)*

Coll. of Bryn Athyn *(see Bryn Athyn Coll. of the New Church)*

Coll. of Bryn Mawr *(see Bryn Mawr Coll.)*

Coll. of Burlington County *(see Burlington County Coll.)*

Coll. of Bus. & Techno. 83

Coll. of Butte County *(see Butte Coll.)*

Coll. of Caldwell *(see Caldwell Coll.)*

Coll. of California *(see Univ. of California, Berkeley)*

Coll. of Camden County *(see Camden County Coll.)*

Coll. of Career Training 753

Coll. of Castleton *(see Castleton State Coll.)*

Coll. of Cazenovia *(see Cazenovia Coll.)*

Coll. of Central Arizona *(see Central Arizona Coll.)*

Coll. of Central Georgia *(see Central Georgia Tech. Coll.)*

Coll. of Central Illinois *(see Illinois Central Coll.)*

Coll. of Central Iowa *(see Iowa Central Comm. Coll.)*

Coll. of Central Pennsylvania *(see Central Pennsylvania Coll.)*

Coll. of Central Texas *(see Central Texas Coll.)*

Coll. of Central Virginia *(see Central Virginia Comm. Coll.)*

Coll. of Central Wyoming *(see Central Wyoming Coll.)*

Coll. of Charleston 356

Coll. of Chinese Acupuncture, U.S. *(see Tai Sophia Inst.)*

Coll. of Chiropractic Physicians & Surgeons *(see Southern California Univ. of Health Sciences)*

Coll. of Cinema Arts & Television *(see Colegio de las Ciencias Artes y Television)*

Coll. of Clinton *(see Presbyterian Coll.)*

Coll. of Coiffure Art, The 541

Coll. of Connecticut *(see Connecticut Coll.)*

Coll. of Cosmetology, Inc. 592

Coll. of Court Reporting, Inc. 136
Coll. of Crowley's Ridge *(see Crowley's Ridge Coll.)*
Coll. of Culinary Arts of Atlanta *(see Le Cordon Bleu Coll. of Culinary Arts—Atlanta, Western Culinary Inst.)*
Coll. of Culinary Arts of Las Vegas *(see Le Cordon Bleu Coll. of Culinary Arts—Las Vegas)*
Coll. of Culinary Arts of Miami *(see Le Cordon Bleu Coll. of Culinary Arts—Miami)*
Coll. of Culinary Arts of Minneapolis/St. Paul *(see Le Cordon Bleu Coll. of Culinary Arts—Minneapolis/St. Paul)*
Coll. of Cumberland County *(see Cumberland County Coll.)*
Coll. of Cypress *(see Cypress Coll.)*
Coll. of DuPage 119
Coll. of East Georgia *(see East Georgia Coll.)*
Coll. of East Los Angeles *(see East Los Angeles Coll.)*
Coll. of Eastern Arizona *(see Eastern Arizona Coll.)*
Coll. of Eastern Oklahoma *(see Eastern Oklahoma State Coll.)*
Coll. of Eastern Utah 394
Coll. of Eastern Wyoming *(see Eastern Wyoming Coll.)*
Coll. of Edu. & Industrial Arts at Wilberforce *(see Central State Univ.)*
Coll. of Electronic Computer Programming *(see Electronic Computer Programming Coll.)*
Coll. of Electronic Data Processing *(see Electronic Data Processing Coll.)*
Coll. of Elizabethtown *(see Elizabethtown Coll.)*
Coll. of Elmhurst *(see Elmhurst Coll.)*
Coll. of Environmental Science & Forestry at Syracuse *(see State Univ. of New York Coll. of Environmental Science & Forestry)*
Coll. of Essex & Franklin, The *(see North Country Comm. Coll.)*
Coll. of Essex County *(see Essex County Coll.)*
Coll. of Framingham *(see Framingham State Coll.)*
Coll. of Galveston *(see Galveston Coll.)*
Coll. of Georgetown *(see Georgetown Coll.)*
Coll. of Gettysburg *(see Gettysburg Coll.)*

Coll. of Gloucester County *(see Gloucester County Coll.)*
Coll. of Great Falls *(see Univ. of Great Falls)*
Coll. of Greensboro *(see Greensboro Coll.)*
Coll. of Greenville *(see Greenville Coll.)*
Coll. of Grove City *(see Grove City Coll.)*
Coll. of Guilford County *(see Guilford Coll.)*
Coll. of Hair Design 507, 510, 542 *(see also Coll. of Hair Design Careers, Superior Sch. of Hairstyling)*
Coll. of Hair Design Careers 592
Coll. of Hampton Roads *(see Kee Bus. Coll—Newport News)*
Coll. of Hanover *(see Hanover Coll.)*
Coll. of Hastings *(see Hastings Coll.)*
Coll. of Health Professions of New York *(see New York Coll. of Health Professions)*
Coll. of Health Sciences 738 *(see also Jefferson Coll. of Health Sciences)*
Coll. of Hesston *(see Hesston Coll.)*
Coll. of Hillsdale *(see Hillsdale Coll.)*
Coll. of Hiram *(see Hiram Coll.)*
Coll. of Hobe Sound *(see Hobe Sound Bible Coll.)*
Coll. of Hospitality Management *(see Int'l. Coll. of Hospitality Management Cesar Ritz)*
Coll. of Houghton *(see Houghton Coll.)*
Coll. of Houston *(see Univ. of Houston)*
Coll. of Huntington *(see Huntington Jr. Coll.)*
Coll. of Idaho *(see Albertson Coll. of Idaho)*
Coll. of Industrial Arts *(see Texas Woman's Univ.)*
Coll. of Insurance *(see Saint John's Univ.)*
Coll. of Integrative Medicine of Florida *(see Florida Coll. of Integrative Medicine)*
Coll. of Irvine Valley *(see Irvine Valley Coll.)*
Coll. of Ithaca *(see Ithaca Coll.)*
Coll. of Jacksonville *(see Jacksonville Coll.)*
Coll. of Jamestown *(see Jamestown Coll.)*
Coll. of Jones County *(see Jones County Jr. Coll.)*
Coll. of Knox County *(see Knox Coll.)*
Coll. of Lake County 119
Coll. of Lake Erie *(see Lake Erie Coll.)*

Coll. of Lake Forest *(see Lake Forest Coll.)*
Coll. of Lake Michigan *(see Lake Michigan Coll.)*
Coll. of Las Vegas *(see Las Vegas Coll.)*
Coll. of Lebanon *(see Lebanon Coll.)*
Coll. of Legal Arts 592
Coll. of Lincoln *(see Lincoln Coll.)*
Coll. of Manhattan *(see Manhattan Coll.)*
Coll. of Marietta *(see Marietta Coll.)*
Coll. of Marin 37
Coll. of Marion *(see Marion Tech. Coll.)*
Coll. of Mary Washington *(see Univ. of Mary Washington)*
Coll. of Maryville *(see Maryville Coll.)*
Coll. of McHenry County *(see McHenry County Coll.)*
Coll. of Med. Training *(see Med. Training Coll.)*
Coll. of Medicine & Dentistry of New Jersey *(see Univ. of Medicine & Dentistry of New Jersey)*
Coll. of Medicine at Peoria 133 *(see also Univ. of Illinois at Chicago)*
Coll. of Medicine at Rockford 133 *(see also Univ. of Illinois at Chicago)*
Coll. of Medicine of Maryland *(see Univ. of Maryland Baltimore)*
Coll. of Merrimack Valley *(see Merrimack Coll.)*
Coll. of Micronesia-FSM 435
Coll. of Micronesia-Majuro *(see Coll. of the Marshall Islands)*
Coll. of Middlesex County *(see Middlesex County Coll.)*
Coll. of Midland *(see Midland Coll.)*
Coll. of Midway *(see Midway Coll.)*
Coll. of Mines & Metallurgy, El Paso *(see Univ. of Texas at El Paso)*
Coll. of Modern Montessori, The 648
Coll. of Modern Techno. *(see Maric Coll—North Hollywood)*
Coll. of Monmouth *(see Monmouth Coll.)*
Coll. of Moorpark *(see Moorpark Coll.)*
Coll. of Mount Saint Joseph 302
Coll. of Mount Saint Mary *(see Mount Saint Mary Coll.)*
Coll. of Mount Saint Vincent 260
Coll. of Music *(see Univ. of Cincinnati)*
Coll. of Muskegon *(see Muskegon Comm. Coll.)*
Coll. of New Brunswick *(see Univ. of New Brunswick)*
Coll. of New Caledonia 711
Coll. of New Engelberg *(see Conception Seminary Coll.)*
Coll. of New England *(see New England Coll.)*

Accredited Institutions of Postsecondary Education | 2005–2006

Coll. of New Jersey *(see Coll. of New Jersey, The; Princeton Univ.)*
Coll. of New Jersey, The 246
Coll. of New Rochelle, The 260
Coll. of New York City *(see City Univ. of New York City Coll.)*
Coll. of Newberry *(see Newberry Coll.)*
Coll. of North Arkansas *(see North Arkansas Coll.)*
Coll. of North Central Kansas *(see North Central Kansas Tech. Coll.)*
Coll. of North Central Michigan *(see North Central Michigan Coll.)*
Coll. of North Central Missouri *(see North Central Missouri Coll.)*
Coll. of North Idaho *(see North Idaho Coll.)*
Coll. of Northern Marianas *(see Northern Marianas Coll.)*
Coll. of Northern Oklahoma *(see Northern Oklahoma Coll.)*
Coll. of Northwestern Michigan *(see Northwestern Michigan Coll.)*
Coll. of Notre Dame of Maryland 179
Coll. of Nursing at Shreveport 173
Coll. of Nutrition *(see Huntington Coll. of Health Sciences)*
Coll. of Oberlin *(see Oberlin Coll.)*
Coll. of Ocean County *(see Ocean County Coll.)*
Coll. of Oceaneering 722 *(see also National Polytechnic Coll. of Engineering & Oceaneering)*
Coll. of Odessa *(see Odessa Coll.)*
Coll. of Office Techno., The 119
Coll. of Olney *(see Olney Central Coll.)*
Coll. of Oriental Medicine of Oregon *(see Oregon Coll. of Oriental Medicine)*
Coll. of Oriental Medicine of the Midwest *(see Midwest Coll. of Oriental Medicine—Wisconsin)*
Coll. of Osteopathic Medicine 317 *(see also Kansas City Univ. of Medicine & Biosciences)*
Coll. of Osteopathic Medicine & Surgery *(see Des Moines Univ— Osteopathic Med. Ctr.)*
Coll. of Osteopathic Medicine of Philadelphia *(see Philadelphia Coll. of Osteopathic Medicine)*
Coll. of Osteopathic Medicine of the Pacific *(see Western Univ. of Health Sciences)*
Coll. of Our Lady of Mercy, The *(see Saint Joseph's Coll. of Maine)*
Coll. of Our Lady of the Elms 186
Coll. of Oxnard *(see Oxnard Coll.)*
Coll. of Peru *(see Peru State Coll.)*
Coll. of Philadelphia *(see Univ. of Pennsylvania)*

Coll. of Phoenix *(see Phoenix Coll.)*
Coll. of Podiatric Medicine at Finch Univ. *(see Dr. William M. Scholl Coll. of Podiatric Medicine)*
Coll. of Podiatric Medicine of New York *(see New York Coll. of Podiatric Medicine)*
Coll. of Podiatric Medicine of Ohio *(see Ohio Coll. of Podiatric Medicine)*
Coll. of Porterville *(see Porterville Coll.)*
Coll. of Providence *(see Providence Coll.)*
Coll. of Provo *(see Provo Coll.)*
Coll. of Queens *(see City Univ. of New York Queens Coll.)*
Coll. of Quincy *(see Quincy Coll.)*
Coll. of Rhode Island *(see Brown Univ., Rhode Island Coll.)*
Coll. of Ripon *(see Ripon Coll.)*
Coll. of Rockford *(see Rockford Coll.)*
Coll. of Saint Anselm *(see Saint Anselm Coll.)*
Coll. of Saint Augustine *(see Saint Augustine Coll.)*
Coll. of Saint Benedict 208
Coll. of Saint Catherine 208 *(see also Saint Catharine Coll.)*
Coll. of Saint Elizabeth 246
Coll. of Saint Francis *(see Univ. of Saint Francis)*
Coll. of Saint John's *(see Saint John's Coll.)*
Coll. of Saint Joseph *(see Saint Joseph Coll.)*
Coll. of Saint Joseph 397
Coll. of Saint Luke *(see Saint Luke's Coll.)*
Coll. of Saint Mary *(see Coll. of Saint Mary)*
Coll. of Saint Mary 236 *(see also Ohio Dominican Univ.)*
Coll. of Saint Mary of the Springs *(see Ohio Dominican Univ.)*
Coll. of Saint Mary's of California *(see Saint Mary's Coll. of California)*
Coll. of Saint Paul's *(see Saint Paul's Coll.)*
Coll. of Saint Peter's *(see Saint Peter's Coll.)*
Coll. of Saint Petersburg *(see Saint Petersburg Coll.)*
Coll. of Saint Rose, The 260
Coll. of Saint Scholastica, The 209
Coll. of Saint Teresa *(see Avila Univ.)*
Coll. of Saint Thomas Moore, The 376
Coll. of Samuel Merritt *(see Samuel Merritt Coll.)*
Coll. of San Antonio *(see San Antonio Coll.)*

Coll. of San Bernardino Valley *(see San Bernardino Valley Coll.)*
Coll. of San Juan *(see San Juan Coll.)*
Coll. of San Mateo 37
Coll. of Santa Ana *(see Santa Ana Coll.)*
Coll. of Santa Fe, The 252
Coll. of Santa Monica *(see Santa Monica Coll.)*
Coll. of Science & Agriculture of the Delaware Valley *(see Delaware Valley Coll. of Science & Agriculture)*
Coll. of Sierra Nevada *(see Sierra Nevada Coll.)*
Coll. of Slippery Rock *(see Slippery Rock Univ. of Pennsylvania)*
Coll. of South Georgia *(see South Georgia Coll.)*
Coll. of South Texas *(see South Texas Coll.)*
Coll. of Southeast Arkansas *(see Southeast Arkansas Coll.)*
Coll. of Southeastern Europe 740 *(see also American Univ. of Athens)*
Coll. of Southeastern Illinois *(see Southeastern Illinois Coll.)*
Coll. of Southern Idaho 115
Coll. of Southern Maryland, The 179
Coll. of Southern Nevada *(see Comm. Coll. of Southern Nevada)*
Coll. of Southern Vermont *(see Southern Vermont Coll.)*
Coll. of Southwest Florida *(see Southwest Florida Coll.)*
Coll. of Southwest Texas *(see Southwest Texas Jr. Coll.)*
Coll. of Southwestern Illinois *(see Southwestern Illinois Coll.)*
Coll. of Southwestern Michigan *(see Southwestern Michigan Coll.)*
Coll. of Springfield *(see Springfield Coll.)*
Coll. of St. Joseph *(see Saint Joseph Coll.)*
Coll. of St. Olaf *(see Saint Olaf Coll.)*
Coll. of St. Petersburg *(see Saint Petersburg Coll.)*
Coll. of Staten Island *(see City Univ. of New York Coll. of Staten Island)*
Coll. of Steubenville *(see Franciscan Univ. of Steubenville)*
Coll. of Swarthmore *(see Swarthmore Coll.)*
Coll. of Tech. Agriculture—Curtis *(see Nebraska Coll. of Tech. Agriculture)*
Coll. of Techno. at Alfred *(see State Univ. of New York Coll. of Techno. at Alfred)*

Coll. of Techno. at Canton *(see State Univ. of New York Coll. of Techno. at Canton)*

Coll. of Techno. at Delhi *(see State Univ. of New York Coll. of Techno. at Delhi)*

Coll. of Techno. at Farmingdale *(see State Univ. of New York Coll. of Techno. at Farmingdale)*

Coll. of Techno. of the Univ. of Montana *(see Univ. of Montana— Coll. of Techno.)*

Coll. of the Adirondacks, The *(see Paul Smith's Coll. of Arts & Sciences)*

Coll. of The Albemarle 286

Coll. of the Atlantic 175

Coll. of the Bible, The *(see Lexington Theological Seminary, Phillips Theological Seminary)*

Coll. of the Canyons 37

Coll. of the Cayman Islands *(see Int'l. Coll. of the Cayman Islands)*

Coll. of the Desert 37

Coll. of the Divine Word *(see Divine Word Coll.)*

Coll. of the Everglades *(see Everglades Univ.)*

Coll. of the Holy Cross 186

Coll. of the Humanities & Sciences 721 *(see also Coll. of the Humanities & Sciences Harrison Middleton Univ.)*

Coll. of the Humanities & Sciences Harrison Middleton Univ. 16, 721

Coll. of the Mainland 376

Coll. of the Marshall Islands 436

Coll. of the Menominee Nation 423

Coll. of the Missouri Valley *(see Missouri Valley Coll.)*

Coll. of the Ozarks 224

Coll. of the Pacific *(see also San Joaquin Delta Coll., Univ. of the Pacific)*

Coll. of the Pacific Jr. Coll. *(see San Joaquin Delta Coll.)*

Coll. of the Redwoods 37

Coll. of the Rockies 711

Coll. of the Sequoias 37

Coll. of the Siskiyous 37

Coll. of the Southwest 252

Coll. of Traditional Chinese Medicine of Hawaii *(see Traditional Chinese Medicine Coll. of Hawaii)*

Coll. of Tyler *(see Tyler Jr. Coll.)*

Coll. of Union County *(see Union County Coll.)*

Coll. of Unity *(see Unity Coll.)*

Coll. of Utica *(see Utica Coll.)*

Coll. of Ventura *(see Ventura Coll.)*

Coll. of Vernon *(see Vernon Coll.)*

Coll. of Visual Arts 209

Coll. of Wayne *(see Wayne State Coll.)*

Coll. of Waynesburg *(see Waynesburg Coll.)*

Coll. of West Los Angeles *(see West Los Angeles Coll.)*

Coll. of Westchester, The 260, 734

Coll. of Western Arizona *(see Arizona Western Coll.)*

Coll. of Western Colorado *(see Western State Coll. of Colorado)*

Coll. of Western Iowa *(see Iowa Western Comm. Coll.)*

Coll. of Western Maryland *(see McDaniel Coll.)*

Coll. of Western Missouri *(see Missouri Western State Univ.)*

Coll. of Western New England *(see Western New England Coll.)*

Coll. of Western Oklahoma *(see Western Oklahoma State Coll.)*

Coll. of Western Texas *(see Western Texas Coll.)*

Coll. of Western Washington *(see Western Washington Univ.)*

Coll. of Wharton County *(see Wharton County Jr. Coll.)*

Coll. of William & Mary, Norfolk Division, The *(see Old Dominion Univ.)*

Coll. of William & Mary, The 401 *(see also Old Dominion Univ.)*

Coll. of Wilmington *(see Wilmington Coll.)*

Coll. of Wingate *(see Wingate Univ.)*

Coll. of Wooster, The 302

Coll. of Worcester *(see Worcester State Coll.)*

Coll. Settlement House *(see Settlement Music Sch.)*

Coll. Without Walls 378 *(see also Houston Comm. Coll.)*

CollegeAmerica 16

CollegeAmerica—Colorado Springs 65

CollegeAmerica—Denver 65

CollegeAmerica—Fort Collins 65

Coll-Conservatory of Music 311 *(see also Univ. of Cincinnati)*

Collegiate Sch. *(see Yale Univ.)*

Collier Tech. Inst. *(see Louisiana Tech. Coll—Sidney N. Collier Campus)*

Collin County Coll. *(see Collin County Comm. Coll. Dist.)*

Collin County Comm. Coll. Dist. 376

Collins Career Ctr. 578

Collins Coll. 16

Collins Sch. of Cosmetology 512

Colmery-O'Neil Veterans Affairs Med. Ctr. 671

Colonial Heights Beauty Acad. 631

Color My Nails Sch. of Nail Techno. 627

Colorado Aero Tech *(see Westwood Coll. of Aviation Tech—Denver)*

Colorado Agricultural Coll. *(see Colorado State Univ.)*

Colorado Art Inst. *(see Art Inst. of Colorado)*

Colorado Baptist Univ. *(see Colorado Christian Univ.)*

Colorado Christian Coll. *(see Colorado Christian Univ.)*

Colorado Christian Univ. 65

Colorado Coll. 65

Colorado Dept. of Human Services *(see Colorado Mental Health Inst. at Fort Logan)*

Colorado Healing Arts Sch. *(see Colorado Sch. of Healing Arts)*

Colorado Inst. Massage Therapy *(see Massage Therapy Inst. of Colorado)*

Colorado Inst. of Art *(see Art Inst. of Colorado)*

Colorado Inst. of Taxidermy Training, Inc. 471

Colorado Massage Therapy Inst. *(see Massage Therapy Inst. of Colorado)*

Colorado Mental Health Inst. at Fort Logan 657

Colorado Mines Sch. *(see Colorado Sch. of Mines)*

Colorado Mountain Coll. 65

Colorado Northwestern Comm. Coll. 65

Colorado Sch. of English 471

Colorado Sch. of Healing Arts 65

Colorado Sch. of Mines 66

Colorado Sch. of Prof. Psychology, The 66

Colorado Sch. of Trades 66

Colorado Sch. of Traditional Chinese Medicine 66

Colorado Springs Academic Ctr. *(see Colorado Sch. of Prof. Psychology)*

Colorado Springs Bible Coll. *(see Oklahoma Wesleyan Univ.)*

Colorado Springs Mem. Hosp. *(see Mem. Hosp.)*

Colorado State Coll. of Agriculture & Mechanic Arts *(see Fort Lewis Coll.)*

Colorado State Coll. of Edu. *(see Univ. of Northern Colorado)*

Colorado State Teachers Coll. *(see Univ. of Northern Colorado)*

Colorado State Univ. 66

Colorado State Univ—Pueblo 66, 724

Colorado Taxidermy Training Inst. *(see Colorado Inst. of Taxidermy Training, Inc.)*
Colorado Tech. Univ. 66
Colorado Tech. Univ—North Kansas City 732
Colorado Univ. at Boulder *(see Univ. of Colorado at Boulder)*
Colorado Univ. at Colorado Springs *(see Univ. of Colorado at Colorado Springs)*
Colorado Women's Coll. *(see Univ. of Denver)*
Colored Industrial & Agricultural Sch., The *(see Grambling State Univ.)*
Columbia Basin Coll. 411
Columbia Beauty Acad. 537
Columbia Beauty Sch. 608
Columbia Bible Coll. 432 *(see also Columbia Int'l. Univ.)*
Columbia Bible Sch. *(see Columbia Int'l. Univ.)*
Columbia Ctr. Univ. 347, 736, 749
Columbia Centro Universitario *(see Columbia Ctr. Univ.)*
Columbia Coll. 37, 224, 356, 736 *(see also Columbia Bible Coll., Columbia Ctr. Univ., Columbia Coll. Chicago, Columbia Coll. Hollywood, Columbia Coll. of Nursing, Columbia Univ. in the City of New York, Loras Coll., Pacific Lutheran Univ.)*
Columbia Coll. Chicago 119
Columbia Coll. Hollywood 37
Columbia Coll. of Nursing 424
Columbia Coll—Yauco *(see Columbia Ctr. Univ—Yauco)*
Columbia Commercial Coll. *(see South Univ.)*
Columbia Female Coll. *(see Columbia Coll.)*
Columbia Forest Ranger Sch. *(see Lake City Comm. Coll.)*
Columbia Hosp. 708
Columbia Inst. of Chiropractic *(see New York Chiropractic Coll.)*
Columbia Institution for the Instruction of the Deaf & Dumb & the Blind *(see Gallaudet Univ.)*
Columbia Int'l. Univ. 356
Columbia Jr. Coll. 726, 736 *(see also Columbia Coll., Columbia Union Coll., South Univ.)*
Columbia Jr. Coll. of Bus. 736
Columbia Nursing Coll. *(see Columbia Coll. of Nursing)*
Columbia Seminary *(see Columbia Theological Seminary)*
Columbia Southern Univ. 4

Columbia St. Mary's *(see Columbia Hosp.)*
Columbia State Comm. Coll. 365
Columbia Tech. Edu. Ctr. *(see Midlands Tech. Coll.)*
Columbia Theological Seminary 101
Columbia Union Coll. 179
Columbia Univ. *(see Columbia Univ. in the City of New York, Univ. of Portland)*
Columbia Univ. in the City of New York 261
Columbia Univ. Med. Ctr. *(see New York Presbyterian Hosp—Columbia Univ.)*
Columbia Univ. Teachers Coll. *(see Teachers Coll. of Columbia Univ.)*
Columbia-Greene Beauty Sch., Inc. 733
Columbia-Greene Comm. Coll. 261
Columbian Coll., The *(see George Washington Univ.)*
Columbian Univ. *(see George Washington Univ.)*
Columbiana County Career & Tech. Ctr. 578
Columbiana County Joint Vocational Sch. *(see Columbiana County Career & Tech. Ctr.)*
Columbiana County Vocational Sch. Dist. *(see Columbiana County Career & Tech. Ctr.)*
Columbus Area Vocational-Tech. Sch. *(see Columbus Tech. Coll.)*
Columbus Children's Hosp. 693
Columbus Coll. *(see Columbus Coll. of Art & Design, Columbus State Univ.)*
Columbus Coll. of Art & Design 302
Columbus Design Coll. *(see Columbus Coll. of Art & Design)*
Columbus Montessori Ctr/COMET 578
Columbus Montessori Teacher Edu. Program 578
Columbus Para-Prof. Inst. 734 *(see also Ohio Inst. of Health Careers)*
Columbus Public Schools Dept. of Adult & Comm. Edu. *(see North Edu. Ctr.)*
Columbus Reg. Hosp. 669
Columbus Sch. of Applied Electronics *(see DeVry Univ. Columbus)*
Columbus State Coll. *(see Columbus State Comm. Coll.)*
Columbus State Comm. Coll. 302
Columbus State Univ. 101
Columbus Tech *(see Columbus Tech. Coll.)*
Columbus Tech. Coll. 101, 726

Columbus Tech. Inst. 726 *(see also Columbus Tech. Coll., Ivy Tech Comm. Coll. of Indiana—Columbus)*
Colver Inst. *(see Virginia Union Univ.)*
Comair Aviation Acad. 725 *(see also Delta Connection Acad.)*
Commercial Coll. of Central Texas *(see Central Texas Commercial Coll.)*
Commercial Diving Acad. 480
Commercial Driver Training 560
Commission on Mental Health Services 661
Commonwealth Bus. Coll. 727 *(see also Brown Mackie Coll—Merrillville)*
Commonwealth Coll. *(see Bryant & Stratton Coll—Virginia Beach Campus, Commonwealth Coll. of Funeral Service)*
Commonwealth Coll. of Funeral Service *(see Commonwealth Inst. of Funeral Service)*
Commonwealth Inst. of Funeral Service 376
Commonwealth Int'l. Univ. 722 *(see also Remington Coll—San Diego)*
Commonwealth Tech. Inst. 328
Commonwealth Univ. of Virginia *(see Virginia Commonwealth Univ.)*
Communication Arts Sch. *(see Sch. of Communication Arts)*
Communication Electronics Sch. *(see Sch. of Communication Electronics)*
Communications Sch. of New England *(see New England Sch. of Communications)*
Comm. & Tech. Coll. at West Virginia Univ. Inst. of Techno. 418
Comm. & Tech. Coll. of Minneapolis *(see Minneapolis Comm. & Tech. Coll.)*
Comm. & Tech. Coll. of Minnesota *(see Minnesota State Comm. & Tech. Coll.)*
Comm. & Tech. Coll. of Shepherd 418
Comm. & Tech. Coll. of Southeast Kentucky *(see Southeast Kentucky Comm. & Tech. Coll.)*
Comm. & Tech. Coll. of West Virginia *(see West Virginia State Comm. & Tech. Coll.)*
Comm. Based Edu. & Development, Inc. *(see CBD Coll.)*
Comm. Bus. Sch. 456
Comm. Care Coll. 587
Comm. Christian Coll. 743
Comm. Coll. at Hope *(see Univ. of Arkansas Comm. Coll. at Hope)*

Comm. Coll. at Jacksonville *(see Florida Comm. Coll. at Jacksonville)*

Comm. Coll. at Jamestown *(see Jamestown Comm. Coll.)*

Comm. Coll. at Morrilton *(see Univ. of Arkansas Comm. Coll. at Morrilton)*

Comm. Coll. of Allegheny County Allegheny Campus 328

Comm. Coll. of Allegheny County Boyce Campus 328

Comm. Coll. of Allegheny County North Campus 328

Comm. Coll. of Allegheny County South Campus 328

Comm. Coll. of Allen County *(see Allen County Comm. Coll.)*

Comm. Coll. of Alpena *(see Alpena Comm. Coll.)*

Comm. Coll. of Alvin *(see Alvin Comm. Coll.)*

Comm. Coll. of American Samoa *(see American Samoa Comm. Coll.)*

Comm. Coll. of Anne Arundel County *(see Anne Arundel Comm. Coll.)*

Comm. Coll. of Atlantic County *(see Atlantic Cape Comm. Coll.)*

Comm. Coll. of Aurora 66

Comm. Coll. of Austin *(see Austin Comm. Coll.)*

Comm. Coll. of Baltimore City *(see Baltimore City Comm. Coll.)*

Comm. Coll. of Baltimore County, The 179

Comm. Coll. of Barton County *(see Barton County Comm. Coll.)*

Comm. Coll. of Beaufort County *(see Beaufort County Comm. Coll.)*

Comm. Coll. of Beaver County 328

Comm. Coll. of Bellevue *(see Bellevue Comm. Coll.)*

Comm. Coll. of Bossier Parish *(see Bossier Parish Comm. Coll.)*

Comm. Coll. of Broward *(see Broward Comm. Coll.)*

Comm. Coll. of Bucks County *(see Bucks County Comm. Coll.)*

Comm. Coll. of Butler County *(see Butler County Comm. Coll.)*

Comm. Coll. of Cambria County *(see Pennsylvania Highlands Comm. Coll.)*

Comm. Coll. of Cape Cod *(see Cape Cod Comm. Coll.)*

Comm. Coll. of Carroll County *(see Carroll Comm. Coll.)*

Comm. Coll. of Catawba Valley *(see Catawba Valley Comm. Coll.)*

Comm. Coll. of Cayuga County *(see Cayuga County Comm. Coll.)*

Comm. Coll. of Cecil County *(see Cecil Comm. Coll.)*

Comm. Coll. of Central Alabama *(see Central Alabama Comm. Coll.)*

Comm. Coll. of Central Carolina *(see Central Carolina Comm. Coll.)*

Comm. Coll. of Central Florida *(see Central Florida Comm. Coll.)*

Comm. Coll. of Central Iowa *(see Iowa Central Comm. Coll.)*

Comm. Coll. of Central Maine *(see Central Maine Comm. Coll.)*

Comm. Coll. of Central Oregon *(see Central Oregon Comm. Coll.)*

Comm. Coll. of Central Virginia *(see Central Virginia Comm. Coll.)*

Comm. Coll. of Clackamas County *(see Clackamas Comm. Coll.)*

Comm. Coll. of Cleveland *(see Cleveland State Comm. Coll.)*

Comm. Coll. of Cloud County *(see Cloud County Comm. Coll.)*

Comm. Coll. of Clovis *(see Clovis Comm. Coll.)*

Comm. Coll. of Coconino County *(see Coconino County Comm. Coll.)*

Comm. Coll. of Coffeyville *(see Coffeyville Comm. Coll.)*

Comm. Coll. of Colby *(see Colby Comm. Coll.)*

Comm. Coll. of Collin County *(see Collin County Comm. Coll. Dist.)*

Comm. Coll. of Compton *(see Compton Comm. Coll.)*

Comm. Coll. of Cosmetology 509

Comm. Coll. of Cowley County *(see Cowley County Comm. Coll.)*

Comm. Coll. of Danville *(see Danville Comm. Coll.)*

Comm. Coll. of Davidson County *(see Davidson County Comm. Coll.)*

Comm. Coll. of Daytona Beach *(see Daytona Beach Comm. Coll.)*

Comm. Coll. of Delaware County *(see Delaware County Comm. Coll.)*

Comm. Coll. of Denver 67 *(see also Red Rocks Comm. Coll.)*

Comm. Coll. of Denver Health Sciences Ctr. *(see Comm. Coll. of Denver—Lowry)*

Comm. Coll. of Dodge City *(see Dodge City Comm. Coll.)*

Comm. Coll. of Doña Ana County *(see New Mexico State Univ.)*

Comm. Coll. of Dutchess County *(see Dutchess Comm. Coll.)*

Comm. Coll. of Dyersburg *(see Dyersburg State Comm. Coll.)*

Comm. Coll. of East Arkansas *(see East Arkansas Comm. Coll.)*

Comm. Coll. of East Mississippi *(see East Mississippi Comm. Coll.)*

Comm. Coll. of Eastern Los Angeles County *(see Mount San Antonio Coll.)*

Comm. Coll. of Eastern Maine *(see Eastern Maine Comm. Coll.)*

Comm. Coll. of Eastern West Virginia *(see Eastern West Virginia Comm. & Tech. Coll.)*

Comm. Coll. of El Paso *(see El Paso County Comm. Coll. Dist.)*

Comm. Coll. of Elizabethtown *(see Elizabethtown Comm. & Tech. Coll.)*

Comm. Coll. of Erie County *(see Erie Comm. Coll. City Campus)*

Comm. Coll. of Everett *(see Everett Comm. Coll.)*

Comm. Coll. of Fayetteville *(see Fayetteville Tech. Comm. Coll.)*

Comm. Coll. of Fort Scott *(see Fort Scott Comm. Coll.)*

Comm. Coll. of Frederick *(see Frederick Comm. Coll.)*

Comm. Coll. of Garden City *(see Garden City Comm. Coll.)*

Comm. Coll. of Gila County *(see Eastern Arizona Coll.)*

Comm. Coll. of Glen Oaks *(see Glen Oaks Comm. Coll.)*

Comm. Coll. of Glendale *(see Glendale Comm. Coll.)*

Comm. Coll. of Grand Rapids *(see Grand Rapids Comm. Coll.)*

Comm. Coll. of Greenfield *(see Greenfield Comm. Coll.)*

Comm. Coll. of Guam *(see Guam Comm. Coll.)*

Comm. Coll. of Hagerstown *(see Hagerstown Comm. Coll.)*

Comm. Coll. of Harrisburg *(see Harrisburg Area Comm. Coll.)*

Comm. Coll. of Hawaii *(see Hawaii Comm. Coll.)*

Comm. Coll. of Herkimer County *(see Herkimer County Comm. Coll.)*

Comm. Coll. of Highland *(see Highland Comm. Coll.)*

Comm. Coll. of Holmes County *(see Holmes Comm. Coll.)*

Comm. Coll. of Holyoke *(see Holyoke Comm. Coll.)*

Comm. Coll. of Honolulu *(see Honolulu Comm. Coll.)*

Comm. Coll. of Houston *(see Houston Comm. Coll.)*

Comm. Coll. of Howard County *(see Howard Comm. Coll.)*

Comm. Coll. of Hudson County *(see Hudson County Comm. Coll.)*

Comm. Coll. of Hudson Valley *(see Hudson Valley Comm. Coll.)*

Comm. Coll. of Humacao *(see Humacao Comm. Coll.)*

Comm. Coll. of Hutchinson *(see Hutchinson Comm. Coll.)*

Comm. Coll. of Independence *(see Independence Comm. Coll.)*

Comm. Coll. of Jefferson County *(see Jefferson Comm. Coll.)*

Comm. Coll. of Johnson County *(see Johnson County Comm. Coll.)*

Comm. Coll. of Kalamazoo Valley *(see Kalamazoo Valley Comm. Coll.)*

Comm. Coll. of Kankakee County *(see Kankakee Comm. Coll.)*

Comm. Coll. of Kansas City Kansas *(see Kansas City Kansas Comm. Coll.)*

Comm. Coll. of Kingsborough *(see City Univ. of New York Kingsborough Comm. Coll.)*

Comm. Coll. of Klamath County *(see Klamath Comm. Coll.)*

Comm. Coll. of La Guardia *(see City Univ. of New York La Guardia Comm. Coll.)*

Comm. Coll. of Lake Tahoe *(see Lake Tahoe Comm. Coll.)*

Comm. Coll. of Lamar *(see Lamar Comm. Coll.)*

Comm. Coll. of Lansing *(see Lansing Comm. Coll.)*

Comm. Coll. of Laramie County *(see Laramie County Comm. Coll.)*

Comm. Coll. of Laredo *(see Laredo Comm. Coll.)*

Comm. Coll. of Lexington *(see Bluegrass Comm. & Tech. Coll.)*

Comm. Coll. of Lorain County *(see Lorain County Comm. Coll.)*

Comm. Coll. of Luzerne County *(see Luzerne County Comm. Coll.)*

Comm. Coll. of Macomb County *(see Macomb Comm. Coll.)*

Comm. Coll. of Madisonville *(see Madisonville Comm. Coll.)*

Comm. Coll. of Manatee County *(see Manatee Comm. Coll.)*

Comm. Coll. of Marshall County *(see Marshalltown Comm. Coll.)*

Comm. Coll. of Marshalltown *(see Marshalltown Comm. Coll.)*

Comm. Coll. of Massachusetts Bay *(see Massachusetts Bay Comm. Coll.)*

Comm. Coll. of Mercer County *(see Mercer County Comm. Coll.)*

Comm. Coll. of Meridian *(see Meridian Comm. Coll.)*

Comm. Coll. of Micronesia *(see Coll. of Micronesia-FSM)*

Comm. Coll. of Mid Michigan *(see Mid Michigan Comm. Coll.)*

Comm. Coll. of Middlesex *(see Middlesex Comm. Coll.)*

Comm. Coll. of Monroe County *(see Monroe County Comm. Coll.)*

Comm. Coll. of Montgomery County *(see Montgomery County Comm. Coll.)*

Comm. Coll. of Moraine Valley *(see Moraine Valley Comm. Coll.)*

Comm. Coll. of Muskegon *(see Muskegon Comm. Coll.)*

Comm. Coll. of Naugatuck Valley *(see Naugatuck Valley Comm. Coll.)*

Comm. Coll. of Neosho County *(see Neosho County Comm. Coll.)*

Comm. Coll. of Niagara County *(see Niagara County Comm. Coll.)*

Comm. Coll. of North Florida *(see North Florida Comm. Coll.)*

Comm. Coll. of North Iowa *(see North Iowa Area Comm. Coll.)*

Comm. Coll. of North Seattle *(see North Seattle Comm. Coll.)*

Comm. Coll. of Northampton County *(see Northampton County Area Comm. Coll.)*

Comm. Coll. of Northeast Alabama *(see Northeast Alabama Comm. Coll.)*

Comm. Coll. of Northeast Iowa *(see Northeast Iowa Comm. Coll.)*

Comm. Coll. of Northeast Mississippi *(see Northeast Mississippi Comm. Coll.)*

Comm. Coll. of Northeast Texas *(see Northeast Texas Comm. Coll.)*

Comm. Coll. of Northern Essex *(see Northern Essex Comm. Coll.)*

Comm. Coll. of Northern Maine *(see Northern Maine Comm. Coll.)*

Comm. Coll. of Northern New Mexico *(see Northern New Mexico Coll.)*

Comm. Coll. of Northern Virginia *(see Northern Virginia Comm. Coll.)*

Comm. Coll. of Northern West Virginia *(see West Virginia Northern Comm. Coll.)*

Comm. Coll. of Northern Wyoming *(see Northern Wyoming Comm. Coll. Dist—Sheridan)*

Comm. Coll. of Northwest Arkansas *(see NorthWest Arkansas Comm. Coll.)*

Comm. Coll. of Northwest Iowa *(see Northwest Iowa Comm. Coll.)*

Comm. Coll. of Northwest Mississippi *(see Northwest Mississippi Comm. Coll.)*

Comm. Coll. of Northwestern Colorado *(see Colorado Northwestern Comm. Coll.)*

Comm. Coll. of Northwestern Connecticut *(see Northwestern Connecticut Comm. Coll.)*

Comm. Coll. of Norwalk *(see Norwalk Comm. Coll.)*

Comm. Coll. of Oklahoma City *(see Oklahoma City Comm. Coll.)*

Comm. Coll. of Orange County *(see Orange County Comm. Coll.)*

Comm. Coll. of Palm Beach *(see Palm Beach Comm. Coll.)*

Comm. Coll. of Passaic County *(see Passaic County Comm. Coll.)*

Comm. Coll. of Philadelphia 329

Comm. Coll. of Pikes Peak *(see Pikes Peak Comm. Coll.)*

Comm. Coll. of Portland *(see Portland Comm. Coll.)*

Comm. Coll. of Pratt *(see Pratt Comm. Coll.)*

Comm. Coll. of Prince George's County *(see Prince George's Comm. Coll.)*

Comm. Coll. of Prince William Sound *(see Prince William Sound Comm. Coll.)*

Comm. Coll. of Rhode Island 353

Comm. Coll. of Rio Grande *(see Univ. of Rio Grande & Rio Grande Comm. Coll.)*

Comm. Coll. of Riverside *(see Riverside City Coll.)*

Comm. Coll. of Robeson County *(see Robeson Comm. Coll.)*

Comm. Coll. of Rockingham County *(see Rockingham Comm. Coll.)*

Comm. Coll. of Rockland *(see Rockland Comm. Coll.)*

Comm. Coll. of Roswell *(see Eastern New Mexico Univ—Roswell)*

Comm. Coll. of Roxbury *(see Roxbury Comm. Coll.)*

Comm. Coll. of Salt Lake City *(see Salt Lake Comm. Coll.)*

Comm. Coll. of Santa Fe *(see Santa Fe Comm. Coll.)*

Comm. Coll. of Schenectady County *(see Schenectady County Comm. Coll.)*

Comm. Coll. of Scottsdale *(see Scottsdale Comm. Coll.)*

Comm. Coll. of Seminole County *(see Seminole Comm. Coll.)*

Comm. Coll. of Seward County *(see Seward County Comm. Coll.)*

Comm. Coll. of Somerset *(see Somerset Comm. Coll.)*

Comm. Coll. of South Arkansas *(see South Arkansas Comm. Coll.)*

Comm. Coll. of South Florida *(see South Florida Comm. Coll.)*

Comm. Coll. of South Louisiana *(see South Louisiana Comm. Coll.)*

Comm. Coll. of South Seattle *(see South Seattle Comm. Coll.)*

Comm. Coll. of South Texas *(see South Texas Coll.)*

Comm. Coll. of Southern Alabama *(see Alabama Southern Comm. Coll.)*

Comm. Coll. of Southern Maine *(see Southern Maine Comm. Coll.)*

Comm. Coll. of Southern Nevada 240

Comm. Coll. of Southern West Virginia *(see Southern West Virginia Comm. & Tech. Coll.)*

Comm. Coll. of Southside Virginia *(see Southside Virginia Comm. Coll.)*

Comm. Coll. of Southwest Mississippi *(see Southwest Mississippi Comm. Coll.)*

Comm. Coll. of Southwest Tennessee *(see Southwest Tennessee Comm. Coll.)*

Comm. Coll. of Southwest Virginia *(see Southwest Virginia Comm. Coll.)*

Comm. Coll. of Southwestern Oregon *(see Southwestern Oregon Comm. Coll.)*

Comm. Coll. of Spokane *(see Spokane Comm. Coll.)*

Comm. Coll. of St. Clair County *(see Saint Clair County Comm. Coll.)*

Comm. Coll. of Suffolk County *(see Suffolk County Comm. Coll—Ammerman Campus)*

Comm. Coll. of Sullivan County *(see Sullivan County Comm. Coll.)*

Comm. Coll. of Sussex County *(see Sussex County Comm. Coll.)*

Comm. Coll. of Tacoma *(see Tacoma Comm. Coll.)*

Comm. Coll. of Tallahassee *(see Tallahassee Comm. Coll.)*

Comm. Coll. of the Air Force 3

Comm. Coll. of the Bronx *(see City Univ. of New York Bronx Comm. Coll.)*

Comm. Coll. of the Danville Area *(see Danville Area Comm. Coll.)*

Comm. Coll. of the Des Moines Area *(see Des Moines Area Comm. Coll.)*

Comm. Coll. of the Florida Keys *(see Florida Keys Comm. Coll.)*

Comm. Coll. of the Kennebec Valley *(see Kennebec Valley Comm. Coll.)*

Comm. Coll. of the Mississippi Delta *(see Mississippi Delta Comm. Coll.)*

Comm. Coll. of the Mohawk Valley *(see Mohawk Valley Comm. Coll.)*

Comm. Coll. of the Reading Area *(see Reading Area Comm. Coll.)*

Comm. Coll. of Tulsa *(see Tulsa Comm. Coll.)*

Comm. Coll. of Turtle Mountain *(see Turtle Mountain Comm. Coll.)*

Comm. Coll. of Ulster County *(see Ulster County Comm. Coll.)*

Comm. Coll. of Vermont 397

Comm. Coll. of Walla Walla *(see Walla Walla Comm. Coll.)*

Comm. Coll. of Warren County *(see Warren County Comm. Coll.)*

Comm. Coll. of Washington County *(see Washington County Comm. Coll., Washington State Comm. Coll.)*

Comm. Coll. of Wayne County *(see Wayne County Comm. Coll. Dist.)*

Comm. Coll. of Western Iowa *(see Iowa Western Comm. Coll., Western Iowa Tech Comm. Coll.)*

Comm. Coll. of Western Nebraska *(see Western Nebraska Comm. Coll.)*

Comm. Coll. of Western Nevada *(see Western Nevada Comm. Coll.)*

Comm. Coll. of Western Virginia *(see Virginia Western Comm. Coll.)*

Comm. Coll. of Western Wyoming *(see Western Wyoming Comm. Coll.)*

Comm. Coll. of Westmoreland County *(see Westmoreland County Comm. Coll.)*

Comm. Coll. of Yakima Valley *(see Yakima Valley Comm. Coll.)*

Comm. Coll. of York County *(see York County Comm. Coll.)*

Comm. Coll. Raritan Valley *(see Raritan Valley Comm. Coll.)*

Comm. Colleges of Baltimore County *(see Comm. Coll. of Baltimore County)*

Comm. Enhancement Services Adult Edu. Division 456

Comm. Habilitation Ctr. 489

Comm. Health Care Wausau Hosp. 709

Comm. Health Network Sch. of Radiologic Techno. *(see Comm. Hosp. East)*

Comm. Health Systems, Inc. *(see Southside Reg. Med. Ctr.)*

Comm. Hosp. East 669

Comm. Hosp. of Roanoke Valley Coll. of Health Sciences 738 *(see also Jefferson Coll. of Health Sciences)*

Comm. Mental Health Affiliate *(see Greater Hartford Clinical Psychology Internship Consortium)*

Comm. Music Sch. of Webster Univ. *(see Webster Univ.)*

Comm. Reach Ctr. 653

Comm. Sch. of Performing Arts, The *(see Colburn Sch. of Performing Arts)*

Compton Coll. *(see Compton Comm. Coll.)*

Compton Comm. Coll. 37

Compu Tech Consultants 759 *(see also CompuTech Consultants, Inc.)*

Compu-Med Vocational Careers 481

Computer Career Ctr. 376, 560

Computer Careers Acad. *(see Prism Career Inst.)*

Computer Edu. Inst. 722 *(see also Maric Coll—Palm Springs)*

Computer Edu. Inst—Los Angeles Campus *(see Maric Coll—Los Angeles)*

Computer Edu. Inst—San Marcos 722

Computer Edu. Services *(see Decker Coll. of Bus. Techno.)*

Computer Labs, Inc. 618

Computer Learning Ctr—Henderson *(see Career Edu. Inst—Henderson)*

Computer Learning Centers, Inc. *(see Cittone Inst—Ctr. City)*

Computer Learning Network 595

Computer Processing Inst. 730

Computer Quest Tech. Inst. 734 *(see also Quest Career Coll.)*

Computer Sch. of Baton Rouge *(see Baton Rouge Sch. of Computers)*

Computer Services & Instruction, Inc. 737, 753

Computer Systems Inst. 499

Computer Tech *(see Int'l. Acad. of Design & Techno.)*

Computer Techno. Inst. *(see Inst. of Computer Techno., Metropolitan Career Ctr. & Computer Techno. Inst.)*

Computer Techno. Sch. of Manhattan *(see Manhattan Sch. of Computer Techno.)*

Computer Training Acad. *(see National Inst. of Tech—San Jose)*

Computer Training Ctr. of the Chicago Urban League *(see Chicago Urban League Computer Training Ctr.)*
Computer Training Inst. 456
Computer-Ed Bus. Inst. *(see Career Edu. Inst—Lincoln, Career Edu. Inst—Somerville)*
Computer-Ed Inst. 730, 736 *(see also Career Edu. Inst—Lincoln, Career Edu. Inst—Somerville)*
Concept Coll. of Cosmetology 499
Conception Coll. *(see Conception Seminary Coll.)*
Conception Seminary Coll. 224
Concord Acad. of Hair Design 732 *(see also Esthetics Inst. at Concord Acad.)*
Concord Coll. 738 *(see also Concord Univ.)*
Concord Law Sch. 37, 722
Concord Sch. of Management 730 *(see also Hult Int'l. Bus. Sch.)*
Concord State Normal Sch. *(see Concord Univ.)*
Concord State Teachers Coll. *(see Concord Univ.)*
Concord Univ. 418, 738
Concord Univ. Sch. of Law 722 *(see also Concord Law Sch.)*
Concorde Arlington *(see Concorde Career Inst—Arlington)*
Concorde Aurora *(see Concorde Career Coll.)*
Concorde Career Coll. 37, 38, 67, 224, 365, 736
Concorde Career Coll—Aurora 724
Concorde Career Coll—Garden Grove 722
Concorde Career Coll—Kansas City 732
Concorde Career Coll—North Hollywood 722
Concorde Career Coll—San Bernardino 722
Concorde Career Coll—San Diego 722
Concorde Career Inst. 481, 592 *(see also Concorde Career Coll.)*
Concorde Career Inst—Arlington 618, 737
Concorde Career Inst—Aurora 724
Concorde Career Inst—Garden Grove 722
Concorde Career Inst—Kansas City 732
Concorde Career Inst—Memphis 736
Concorde Career Inst—North Hollywood 722
Concorde Career Inst—San Bernardino 722

Concorde Career Inst—San Diego 722
Concorde Garden Grove *(see Concorde Career Coll.)*
Concorde Jacksonville *(see Concorde Career Inst.)*
Concorde Kansas City *(see Concorde Career Coll.)*
Concorde Lauderdale Lakes *(see Concorde Career Inst.)*
Concorde Memphis *(see Concorde Career Coll.)*
Concorde North Hollywood *(see Concorde Career Coll.)*
Concorde Portland *(see Concorde Career Inst.)*
Concorde San Bernardino *(see Concorde Career Coll.)*
Concorde San Diego *(see Concorde Career Coll.)*
Concorde Sch. of Hair Design, Inc. 548
Concorde Tampa *(see Concorde Career Inst.)*
Concordia Coll. 209 *(see also Concordia Coll. New York, Concordia Coll. Selma, Concordia Univ., Concordia Univ., Ann Arbor, Concordia Univ. Portland, Concordia Univ. Saint Paul, Concordia Univ. Wisconsin)*
Concordia Coll. New York 261
Concordia Coll. of the Northwest *(see Concordia Univ. Portland)*
Concordia Coll. Selma 4
Concordia Jr. Coll. *(see Concordia Theological Seminary)*
Concordia Lutheran Coll. *(see Concordia Univ. at Austin)*
Concordia Lutheran Jr. Coll. *(see Concordia Univ., Ann Arbor)*
Concordia Lutheran Seminary 432
Concordia Seminary 224 *(see also Concordia Lutheran Seminary, Concordia Theological Seminary)*
Concordia Sr. Coll. *(see Concordia Theological Seminary)*
Concordia Theological Seminary 136
Concordia Univ. 236, 711 *(see also Concordia Univ., Ann Arbor, Concordia Univ. at Austin, Concordia Univ. Irvine, Concordia Univ. Portland, Concordia Univ. River Forest, Concordia Univ. Saint Paul)*
Concordia Univ. at Austin 376
Concordia Univ. Irvine 38
Concordia Univ. Portland 320
Concordia Univ. River Forest 120
Concordia Univ. Saint Paul 209
Concordia Univ. Wisconsin 424

Concordia Univ., Ann Arbor 197
Cone Hosp. *(see Moses H. Cone Mem. Hosp.)*
Conemaugh Health System *(see Conemaugh Mem. Med. Ctr.)*
Conemaugh Mem. Med. Ctr. 697, 735
Conemaugh Valley Mem. Hosp. 735 *(see also Conemaugh Mem. Med. Ctr.)*
Conlee's Coll. of Cosmetology 618
Connecticut Agricultural Coll. *(see Univ. of Connecticut)*
Connecticut Bus. Inst—New Haven 724
Connecticut Ctr. for Culinary Arts *(see New England Tech. Inst—Ctr. for Culinary Arts)*
Connecticut Ctr. for Massage Therapy 474
Connecticut Coll. 72 *(see also Quinnipiac Univ.)*
Connecticut Coll. of Commerce *(see Quinnipiac Univ.)*
Connecticut Culinary Inst. 475
Connecticut Dance Sch. *(see Sch. of Dance Connecticut)*
Connecticut Inst. of Art 724
Connecticut Inst. of Hair Design 475, 724 *(see also Brio Acad. of Cosmetology)*
Connecticut Sch. of Broadcasting *(see Illinois Ctr. for Broadcasting, Ohio Ctr. for Broadcasting)*
Connecticut Sch. of Electronics 475
Connecticut Sch. of Radio & Television *(see Connecticut Sch. of Electronics)*
Connecticut State Coll. *(see Univ. of Connecticut)*
Connecticut State Hosp. *(see Connecticut Valley Psychology Internship)*
Connecticut Training Ctr. 475
Connecticut Univ. *(see Univ. of Connecticut)*
Connecticut VA Healthcare System West Haven *(see Veterans Affairs Connecticut Healthcare System West Haven)*
Connecticut Valley Hosp. *(see Connecticut Valley Psychology Internship)*
Connecticut Valley Psychology Internship 658
Connecticut Veterans Affairs Healthcare System West Haven *(see Veterans Affairs Connecticut Healthcare System West Haven)*
Connors Coll. *(see Connors State Coll.)*

Connors Coll. of Agriculture & Applied Science *(see Connors State Coll.)*
Connors State Agricultural Coll. *(see Connors State Coll.)*
Connors State Coll. 315
Connors State Sch. of Agriculture *(see Connors State Coll.)*
Conservative Baptist Theological Seminary *(see Denver Seminary)*
Conservatorio de Estudios Avanzados y Especializad 758
Conservatorio de Música de Puerto Rico *(see Conservatory of Music of Puerto Rico)*
Conservatory of Advanced Studies *(see Conservatorio de Estudios Avanzados y Especializad)*
Conservatory of Boston *(see Boston Conservatory)*
Conservatory of Cosmetology 578
Conservatory of Hartford *(see Hartford Conservatory)*
Conservatory of Music of Puerto Rico 347
Conservatory of Music of San Francisco *(see San Francisco Conservatory of Music)*
Conservatory of Music of Wisconsin *(see Wisconsin Conservatory of Music, Inc.)*
Conservatory of Recording Arts & Sciences 445
Consolidated Sch. of Bus. 329
Consulting Ctr., The *(see Quinco Behavioral Health Systems)*
Contemporary Hair Care Institution Inc. 758
Continental Academie of Hair Design—Hudson 544
Continental Academie of Hair Design—Manchester 544
Continental Sch. of Beauty Culture, Ltd. 560
Continental Sch. of Beauty Culture—Batavia 560
Continental Sch. of Beauty Culture—Buffalo 560
Continental Sch. of Beauty Culture—Olean 560
Continental Sch. of Beauty Culture—West Seneca 560
Continuing Edu. Sch. of Central California *(see Central California Sch. of Continuing Edu.)*
Continuum Health Partners *(see Phillips Beth Israel Sch. of Nursing)*
Contra Costa Coll. 38
Converse Coll. 356
Conway Baptist Coll. *(see Central Baptist Coll.)*

Conway Sch. of Landscape Design 186
Conwell Sch. of Theology *(see Gordon-Conwell Theological Seminary)*
Cook County Bureau of Health Service *(see Cermak Health Services of Cook County)*
Cook County Dept. of Comm. Supervision & Intervention *(see Cermak Health Services of Cook County)*
Cook County Dept. of Corrections *(see Cermak Health Services of Cook County)*
Cook County Hosp. 667 *(see also Cermak Health Services of Cook County)*
Cooking & Hospitality Inst. of Chicago 120
Cookman Inst. *(see Bethune-Cookman Coll.)*
Cooley Law Sch. *(see Thomas M. Cooley Law Sch.)*
Cooper Career Inst. 725
Cooper Coll. *(see Sterling Coll.)*
Cooper Health System—Ctr. for Allied Health Edu. *(see Cooper Univ. Hosp.)*
Cooper Hosp. *(see Cooper Univ. Hosp.)*
Cooper Hosp/Univ. Med. Ctr. *(see Cooper Univ. Hosp.)*
Cooper Techno. Ctr. *(see Gordon Cooper Techno. Ctr.)*
Cooper Union for the Advancement of Science & Art, The 261
Cooper Univ. Hosp. 683 *(see also Cooper Univ. Hosp.)*
Coosa Valley Coll. *(see Coosa Valley Tech. Coll.)*
Coosa Valley Sch. of Nursing *(see Central Alabama Comm. Coll.)*
Coosa Valley Tech *(see Coosa Valley Tech. Coll.)*
Coosa Valley Tech. Coll. 101, 726
Coosa Valley Tech. Inst. 726 *(see also Coosa Valley Tech. Coll.)*
Coosa Valley Vocational-Tech. Sch. *(see Coosa Valley Tech. Coll.)*
Cope Inst. 560
Copiah-Lincoln Coll. *(see Copiah-Lincoln Comm. Coll.)*
Copiah-Lincoln Comm. Coll. 218
Copiah-Lincoln Jr. Coll. *(see Copiah-Lincoln Comm. Coll.)*
Copper Mountain Coll. 38
Coppin State Coll. 730 *(see also Coppin State Univ.)*
Coppin State Teachers Coll. *(see Coppin State Univ.)*
Coppin State Univ. 179, 730

Coppin Teachers Coll. *(see Coppin State Univ.)*
Coral Ridge Nurse's Assistant Training Sch. *(see Coral Ridge Training Sch.)*
Coral Ridge Training Sch. 481
Corban Coll. 320, 735
Corcoran Coll. *(see Corcoran Coll. of Art & Design)*
Corcoran Coll. of Art & Design 78
CORE Inst. 481
Coreil Tech. Inst. *(see Louisiana Tech. Coll—Charles B. Coreil Campus)*
Corinthian Schools, Inc-Sawyer Campus—Sacramento 722
Corinthian Schools, Inc—Skadron Coll. of Bus. *(see Bryman Coll.)*
Cornell Coll. 145
Cornell Univ. 261
Cornerstone Univ. 197
Corning Coll. *(see Corning Comm. Coll.)*
Corning Comm. Coll. 261
Cornish Coll. of the Arts 411
Cornish Inst. *(see Cornish Coll. of the Arts)*
Cornish Sch. *(see Cornish Coll. of the Arts)*
Corporate Change Catalysts Consortium of the West *(see Corporate Change Catalysts Dale Carnegie Training)*
Corporate Change Catalysts Dale Carnegie Training 471
Corpus Christi State Univ. *(see Texas A&M Univ—Corpus Christi)*
Cortland Coll. *(see State Univ. of New York Coll. at Cortland)*
Corvallis Acad. *(see Oregon State Univ.)*
Corvallis Agricultural Coll. *(see Oregon State Univ.)*
Corvallis Coll. *(see Oregon State Univ.)*
Corvallis Coll. & Oregon State Agricultural Coll. *(see Oregon State Univ.)*
Corvallis State Agricultural Coll. *(see Oregon State Univ.)*
Coryell Cosmetology Coll. 619
Cosmetic Arts Ctr. 757
Cosmetolgy Sch. of Crossett *(see Crossett Sch. of Cosmetology LLC)*
Cosmetology Acad. of Branford *(see Branford Acad. of Hair & Cosmetology)*
Cosmetology Acad. of Eastern Arizona *(see Eastern Arizona Acad. of Cosmetology)*
Cosmetology Acad. of Janesville *(see Acad. of Cosmetology)*

Cosmetology Acad. of Mason *(see Mason Acad. of Cosmetology)*

Cosmetology & Esthetics Acad. *(see Acad. of Esthetics & Cosmetology)*

Cosmetology & Spa Inst., The 499, 500

Cosmetology Bus. & Management Inst. 515, 729

Cosmetology Career Ctr. 619

Cosmetology Careers Unlimited— Duluth 533

Cosmetology Careers Unlimited— Hibbing 533

Cosmetology Coll. of Madison *(see Madison Cosmetology Coll.)*

Cosmetology Coll. of Mena *(see Mena Cosmetology Coll.)*

Cosmetology Concepts Inst. 537, 732

Cosmetology Edu. Ctr. 586

Cosmetology Inst. of Austin *(see Austin Cosmetology & Permanent Cosmetics Inst.)*

Cosmetology Inst. of Beauty Arts & Science, The 572

Cosmetology Inst. of Charleston *(see Charleston Cosmetology Inst.)*

Cosmetology Inst. of Georgia *(see Georgia Inst. of Cosmetology)*

Cosmetology Inst. of North Florida *(see North Florida Cosmetology Inst., Inc.)*

Cosmetology Research Ctr. *(see Pivot Point Int'l. Acad.)*

Cosmetology Research Ctr. 503

Cosmetology Sch. of Arts & Sciences 497

Cosmetology Training Ctr. 516

Cosmetology Univ. of Southern Nevada *(see Southern Nevada Univ. of Cosmetology)*

Cosmopolitan Beauty & Barber Sch. 761

Cossatot Comm. Coll. of the Univ. of Arkansas 25

Cossatot Tech. Coll. *(see Cossatot Comm. Coll. of the Univ. of Arkansas)*

Cosumnes River Coll. 38

Cottey Coll. 225

Cotton Boll Tech. Inst. 721 *(see also Arkansas Northeastern Coll.)*

Council for Pastoral Edu. & Development 693

Council for Relationahips 697, 735

Counseling & Mediation Ctr., Inc. 671

Counseling & Pyschological Services (CAPS) *(see Univ. of California, Davis)*

Counseling Ctr. of Southern California *(see Southern California Counseling Ctr.)*

Counterintelligence Field Activity *(see Dept. of Defense Polygraph Inst.)*

County Coll. of Morris 246

County of San Bernardino Dept. of Behavioral Health *(see San Bernardino County Dept. of Behavioral Health)*

County of San Bernardino Dept. of Mental Health *(see San Bernardino County Dept. of Behavioral Health)*

Court Reporting Acad. *(see Acad. of Court Reporting, Denver Acad. of Court Reporting)*

Court Reporting Acad. of Denver *(see Denver Acad. of Court Reporting)*

Court Reporting Coll. *(see Coll. of Court Reporting, Inc.)*

Court Reporting Inst. 637 *(see also Court Reporting Inst. of Dallas; Court Reporting Inst. of Louisiana, Inc.; Orleans Tech. Inst—Ctr. City)*

Court Reporting Inst. of Dallas 376

Court Reporting Inst. of Houston 376 *(see also Court Reporting Inst. of Dallas)*

Court Reporting Inst. of Louisiana, Inc. 516

Court Reporting Sch. of California *(see Sage Coll.)*

Covenant Coll. 101

Covenant Counseling Inst. 664

Covenant Health System *(see Covenant Med. Ctr.)*

Covenant HealthCare 677 *(see also Saint Michael Hosp.)*

Covenant Healthcare System *(see Saint Michael Hosp.)*

Covenant Med. Ctr. 671, 703

Covenant Seminary *(see Covenant Theological Seminary)*

Covenant Theological Seminary 225

Cowley Coll. *(see Cowley County Comm. Coll.)*

Cowley County Comm. Coll. & Area Vocational/Tech. Sch. *(see Cowley County Comm. Coll.)*

Cowley County Comm. Coll. 153

Cowley County Comm. Coll. & Area Vocational-Tech. Sch. *(see Cowley County Comm. Coll.)*

Cowley County Comm. Jr. Coll. *(see Cowley County Comm. Coll.)*

Cox Coll. of Nursing & Health Sciences *(see Lester L. Cox Coll. of Nursing & Health Sciences)*

Cox Med. Ctr. South 681

Cox South *(see Cox Med. Ctr. South)*

CoxHealth Sch. of Radiation Therapy *(see Cox Med. Ctr. South)*

CoxHealth South *(see Cox Med. Ctr. South)*

Coyne American Inst. 500

Coyne Sch. of Tech. Electricity *(see Mount Ida Coll.)*

Crace & Associates 637

Crace, Inc. *(see Crace & Associates)*

Crafton Hills Coll. 38

Cranbrook Acad. of Art 197

Crane Sch. of Music *(see State Univ. of New York Coll. at Potsdam)*

Cranfield Univ. 718

Craven Comm. Coll. 286

Craven County Tech. Inst. *(see Craven Comm. Coll.)*

Crawford County Area Vocational Tech. Sch. 697

Crawford County Vo-Tech Sch. *(see Crawford County Area Vocational Tech. Sch.)*

Creations Coll. of Cosmetology 535

Creative Ctr., The 236

Creative Circus 493

Creative Hair Sch. of Cosmetology 528

Creative Hair Styling Acad. 505

Creative Images Coll. of Beauty, Inc. *(see Creative Images–A Certified Matrix Design Acad.)*

Creative Images–A Certified Matrix Design Acad. 578

Creative Networking Concepts *(see Brookside Bus. & Training Inst.)*

Creative Studies Ctr. *(see Coll. for Creative Studies)*

Creative Studies Coll. *(see Coll. for Creative Studies)*

Creighton Univ. 236

Crescent City Sch. of Gaming & Bartending, Inc. *(see Crescent Schools)*

Crescent Cosmetology Univ. 631

Crescent Schools 516

Crest Computer Inst. *(see Intelisource)*

Crestmont Coll. *(see Salvation Army Coll. for Officer Training at Crestmont)*

CRI Career Training *(see Court Reporting Inst.)*

CRI Career Training—Tacoma 637

Crichton Coll. 365

Criswell Ctr. for Biblical Studies *(see Criswell Coll.)*

Criswell Coll., The 376

Croatan Normal Sch. *(see Univ. of North Carolina at Pembroke)*

Cross Lanes National Inst. of Techno. *(see National Inst. of Tech— Cross Lanes)*

Crossett Sch. of Cosmetology LLC 753
Crossroads Bible Coll. 136
Crossroads Coll. 209, 731 *(see also Crossroads Bible Coll.)*
Crowder Coll. 225
Crowley's Ridge Coll. 25
Crowley's Ridge Tech. Inst. 447
Crown Acad. *(see Crown Coll.)*
Crown Coll. 209, 411
Crownpoint Inst. of Techno. 252
Crozer Hosp. *(see Crozer-Chester Med. Ctr.)*
Crozer Theological Seminary *(see Colgate Rochester Crozer Divinity Sch.)*
Crozer-Chester Med. Ctr. 697
Crozer-Keystone Health System *(see Crozer-Chester Med. Ctr.)*
Cruise Career Training Inst. *(see Keiser Career Coll.)*
Crum's Beauty Coll. 509
Cryptologic Sch. *(see National Cryptologic Sch.)*
Crystal Cathedral, The 653
Crystal Mountain Sch. of Massage Therapy 556
CSC Inst. 735
CSI Career Acadmy 753
CSI Career Coll. 737
CSU—Monterey Bay *(see California State Univ—Monterey Bay)*
CSU—Sacramento *(see California State Univ—Sacramento)*
CSU—San Bernardino *(see California State Univ—San Bernardino)*
CSU—Stanislaus *(see California State Univ—Stanislaus)*
CTC Shepherd *(see Comm. & Tech. Coll. of Shepherd)*
C-TEC Adult Edu. Ctr. *(see Career & Techno. Centers of Licking County)*
CU Denver *(see Univ. of Colorado at Denver & Health Sciences Ctr.)*
CU—Colorado Springs *(see Univ. of Colorado at Colorado Springs)*
Cuesta Coll. 38
Culinard at Virginia Coll. 10
Culinary Acad. of Austin 619
Culinary Acad. of California *(see California Culinary Acad.)*
Culinary Acad. of Long Island 560
Culinary Acad. of New York Management Sch. 560, 734
Culinary Acad. of Orlando *(see Orlando Culinary Acad.)*
Culinary Acad. of Texas *(see Texas Culinary Acad.)*
Culinary Arts Inst. of Louisiana 729

Culinary Arts Sch. of California *(see California Sch. of Culinary Arts)*
Culinary Edu. Inst. *(see Inst. of Culinary Edu.)*
Culinary Inst. of America 261
Culinary Inst. of America—Graystone *(see Culinary Inst. of America—Greystone)*
Culinary Inst. of Charleston *(see Trident Tech. Coll.)*
Culinary Inst. of Connecticut *(see Connecticut Culinary Inst.)*
Culinary Inst. of Florida *(see New England Inst. of Techno. at Palm Beach)*
Culinary Inst. of Las Vegas *(see Art Inst. of Las Vegas)*
Culinary Inst. of New England *(see New England Culinary Inst.)*
Culinary Inst. of New Orleans 516
Culinary Inst. of Pennsylvania *(see Pennsylvania Culinary Inst.)*
Culinary Inst. of Portland *(see Western Culinary Inst.)*
Culinary Inst. of Scottsdale *(see Scottsdale Culinary Inst.)*
Culinary Sch. of the Rockies 471
Culpeper Cosmetology Training Ctr. 631
Culver-Stockton Coll. 225
Cumberland Coll. 728 *(see also Cumberland Univ., Univ. of the Cumberlands)*
Cumberland County Coll. 246
Cumberland County Tech. Edu. Ctr. 683
Cumberland Presbyterian Theological Seminary *(see Memphis Theological Seminary)*
Cumberland Sch. of Med. Techno. *(see MedVance Inst., MedVance Inst. of Baton Rouge)*
Cumberland Sch. of Techno. *(see MedVance Inst., MedVance Inst. of Baton Rouge)*
Cumberland Univ. 365
Cumberland Valley State Normal Sch. *(see Shippensburg Univ. of Pennsylvania)*
Cumberland Valley Tech. Coll. *(see Southeast Kentucky Comm. & Tech. Coll.)*
Cumberlands Univ. *(see Univ. of the Cumberlands)*
Cunningham Studio *(see Merce Cunningham Studio)*
CUNY Bernard M. Baruch Coll. *(see City Univ. of New York Bernard M. Baruch Coll.)*

CUNY Borough of Manhattan Comm. Coll. *(see City Univ. of New York Borough of Manhattan Comm. Coll.)*
CUNY Bronx Comm. Coll. *(see City Univ. of New York Bronx Comm. Coll.)*
CUNY Brooklyn Coll. *(see City Univ. of New York Brooklyn Coll.)*
CUNY City Coll. *(see City Univ. of New York City Coll.)*
CUNY Coll. of Criminal Justice *(see City Univ. of New York John Jay Coll. of Criminal Justice)*
CUNY Coll. of Techno. *(see City Univ. of New York New York City Coll. of Techno.)*
CUNY Grad. Ctr. *(see City Univ. of New York Grad. Ctr.)*
CUNY Grad. Sch. & Univ. Ctr. *(see City Univ. of New York Grad. Ctr.)*
CUNY Harlem *(see City Univ. of New York City Coll.)*
CUNY Herbert H. Lehman Coll. *(see City Univ. of New York Herbert H. Lehman Coll.)*
CUNY Hostos Comm. Coll. *(see City Univ. of New York Hostos Comm. Coll.)*
CUNY Hunter Coll. *(see City Univ. of New York Hunter Coll.)*
CUNY John Jay Coll. of Criminal Justice *(see City Univ. of New York John Jay Coll. of Criminal Justice)*
CUNY Kingsborough Comm. Coll. *(see City Univ. of New York Kingsborough Comm. Coll.)*
CUNY La Guardia Comm. Coll. *(see City Univ. of New York La Guardia Comm. Coll.)*
CUNY Lehman Coll. *(see City Univ. of New York Herbert H. Lehman Coll.)*
CUNY Manhattan Comm. Coll. *(see City Univ. of New York Borough of Manhattan Comm. Coll.)*
CUNY Medgar Evers Coll. *(see City Univ. of New York Medgar Evers Coll.)*
CUNY Mount Sinai Sch. of Medicine *(see Mount Sinai Sch. of Medicine)*
CUNY New York City Coll. of Techno. *(see City Univ. of New York New York City Coll. of Techno.)*
CUNY New York City Tech. Coll. *(see City Univ. of New York New York City Coll. of Techno.)*
CUNY Queens Coll. *(see City Univ. of New York Queens Coll.)*

CUNY Queensborough Comm. Coll. *(see City Univ. of New York Queensborough Comm. Coll.)*

CUNY Sch. of Law *(see City Univ. of New York Queens Coll.)*

CUNY Staten Island Coll. *(see City Univ. of New York Coll. of Staten Island)*

CUNY Techno. Coll. *(see City Univ. of New York New York City Coll. of Techno.)*

CUNY York Coll. *(see City Univ. of New York York Coll.)*

Curry Coll. 186

Curtis Acad. of Hair Design *(see Paul Mitchell The Sch.)*

Curtis Inst. of Music, The 329

Custer County Coll. *(see Miles Comm. Coll.)*

Custer County Jr. Coll. *(see Miles Comm. Coll.)*

Cut Above Beauty Coll. *(see A Cut Above Beauty Coll.)*

Cut Beauty Sch., Inc., The 757

Cuttin Up Beauty Acad. 472

Cutting Edge Acad. *(see Cutting Edge Hairstyling Acad.)*

Cutting Edge Hairstyling Acad. 509

Cuyahoga Comm. Coll. 302

Cuyahoga Valley Career Ctr. 579

Cuyahoga Valley Joint Vocational Sch. *(see Cuyahoga Valley Career Ctr.)*

Cuyamaca Coll. 38

Cy-Fair Coll. 382 *(see also North Harris Montgomery Comm. Coll. Dist.)*

Cynthia's Beauty Acad. 456

Cypress Coll. 38

Cypress-Fairbanks Coll. *(see North Harris Montgomery Comm. Coll. Dist.)*

Cyril & Methodius Seminary *(see SS. Cyril & Methodius Seminary)*

D

Dabney S. Lancaster Comm. Coll. 401

Dade County Jr. Coll. *(see Miami-Dade Coll.)*

Dade Med. Inst. 481

Daemen Coll. 262

Dahan Inst. of Massage Studies 732

Dahl's Coll. of Beauty, Inc. 541

Dakota County Coll. *(see Dakota County Tech. Coll.)*

Dakota County Tech. Coll. 209

Dakota State Coll. *(see Dakota State Univ.)*

Dakota State Univ. 361

Dakota Univ. *(see Dakota State Univ., Dakota Wesleyan Univ.)*

Dakota Wesleyan Univ. 361

Dale Carnegie *(see Andrew Terranova & Associates, Inc.; B. Dickson & Associates, LLC; Brescook, LLC; C.J. Sealey & Associates, LLC; CB&T, Inc; Charles D. Eubank & Associates, Inc.; Chatterton, Inc; Corporate Change Catalysts Dale Carnegie Training; Crace & Associates; Dale Carnegie Training of Central California; Dale Carnegie Training of Greater Cincinnati; Dale Carnegie Training of Los Angeles; Dale Carnegie Training of San Jose; Dale Carnegie Training of South Carolina, LLC; David L. Pals & Associates, Inc.; Don Adams Corporation; Duwayne E. Keller & Associates, Inc.; E. J. Taylor Corporation; Eddie C. Snow & Associates, Inc.; Folkner Training Associates, Inc.; G. Mitchell Hartman & Associates, Inc.; Glyn Ed Newton & Associates, Inc.; Hanes & Associates, Inc.; J. R. Rodgers & Associates, Inc.; James E. Varner & Associates, Inc.; Jerry Wilson & Associates, Inc.; John Hines & Associates, Inc.; John M. Jennings & Associates, Inc.; JR Rodgers & Associates, Inc.; Ken Roberts Corporation; Lance Tyson & Associates Dale Carnegie Training of Northeast Ohio; Laun & Associates, Inc.; Lawrence-White Associates, Inc.; Leadership Development, Inc. Dale Carnegie Training; Leadership Excellence, Inc.; Leadership Inst., Inc.; Leadership Training; Leadership Training Inst.; M.J. Francoeur & Associates; Meyer Uebelher Associates, LLC; Michael W. Jones & Associates, Inc.; Norman & Associates; Paul Phillips & Associates, Inc.; Performance Training Associates, Inc.; Premier Training, Inc. Dale Carnegie Training; R.L. Heron & Associates, Inc.; Ralph Nichols Group, Inc.; Rick J. Gallegos & Associates, Inc.; Robert M. Scherer & Associates, Inc.; Ron L. Straughan & Associates, Inc.; Ron Moore & Associates; S.J. Grant & Associates, Inc.; Siebert Associates, Inc.; Southeast Florida Inst., Inc.; Thomas J. Kiblen & Associates; Wade Powell & Associates, Inc.; William F. Lea & Associates, Inc.; Winner Inst., Inc.; Wray K. Powell & Associates, Inc.)*

Dale Carnegie & Associates, Inc. 560

Dale Carnegie Courses *(see Ron L. Straughan & Associates, Inc.)*

Dale Carnegie Systems 735 *(see also JR Rodgers & Associates, Inc.; Ralph Nichols Group, Inc.)*

Dale Carnegie Systems, Inc. 730 *(see also Ralph Nichols Group, Inc.)*

Dale Carnegie Training *(see CB&T, Inc; Leadership Training Services, Inc.)*

Dale Carnegie Training of Central California 456

Dale Carnegie Training of Greater Cincinnati 579, 734

Dale Carnegie Training of Los Angeles 456, 722

Dale Carnegie Training of Maine 519, 730

Dale Carnegie Training of Northwest Ohio & Northern Indiana 579, 734

Dale Carnegie Training of San Jose 456, 723

Dale Carnegie Training of South Carolina, LLC 608, 736

Dale Carnegie Training of Southern New Jersey *(see Success Unlimited, Inc.)*

Dale Carnegie Training—St. Louis 732 *(see also C.J. Sealey & Associates, LLC)*

Daley Coll. *(see City Colleges of Chicago—Richard J. Daley Coll.)*

Dalhousie Univ. 711

Dallas Art Inst. *(see Art Inst. of Dallas)*

Dallas Baptist Univ. 377

Dallas Barber & Stylist Coll. 619

Dallas Christian Coll. 377

Dallas Coll. *(see Dallas Christian Coll., Dallas Coll. of Oriental Medicine)*

Dallas Coll. of Oriental Medicine 737

Dallas Court Reporting Inst. *(see Court Reporting Inst. of Dallas)*

Dallas Grad. Sch. of Theology *(see Dallas Theological Seminary)*

Dallas Inst. of Art *(see Art Inst. of Dallas)*

Dallas Inst. of Funeral Services 619

Dallas Inst. of Mortuary Science *(see Dallas Inst. of Funeral Services, Gupton-Jones Coll. of Funeral Service)*

Dallas Methodist Hosp. *(see Methodist Dallas Med. Ctr.)*

Dallas Montessori Teacher Edu. Programs 619

Dallas Roberts Acad. of Hair Design 627
Dallas Sch. of Embalming *(see Dallas Inst. of Funeral Services)*
Dallas Seminary *(see Dallas Theological Seminary)*
Dallas Theological Seminary 377
Dallas Univ. *(see Dallas Baptist Univ., Univ. of Dallas)*
Dallas VA Med. Ctr. *(see Veterans Affairs Med. Ctr—Dallas, Veterans Affairs Med. Ctr—Houston)*
Dallas Veterans Affairs Med. Ctr. *(see Veterans Affairs Med. Ctr—Dallas, Veterans Affairs Med. Ctr—Houston)*
Dalton Beauty Coll. 612, 726 *(see also Stylemasters Beauty Acad.)*
Dalton Beauty Inc. 726 *(see also Dalton Beauty Coll.)*
Dalton Coll. *(see Dalton State Coll.)*
Dalton State Coll. 102
Dana Coll. 236
Danbury Hosp. 659
Danbury Hosp. Allied Health Programs *(see Danbury Hosp.)*
Dance Sch. of Connecticut *(see Sch. of Dance Connecticut)*
Dance Theatre of Harlem, Inc. 560
Daniel Webster Coll. 242
Danville Area Comm. Coll. 120
Danville Coll. *(see Danville Comm. Coll.)*
Danville Comm. Coll. 401 *(see also Danville Area Comm. Coll.)*
Danville Jr. Coll. *(see Danville Area Comm. Coll.)*
Danville Reg. Health System *(see Danville Reg. Med. Ctr.)*
Danville Reg. Med. Ctr. 632
Danville Sch. of Health Occupations *(see Bluegrass Comm. & Tech. Coll—Danville)*
Danville Theological Seminary *(see Louisville Presbyterian Theological Seminary)*
Darkei No'am Rabbinical Coll. 262
Darlyne McGee's Acad. of Cosmetology, Inc. 725 *(see also Acad. of Cosmetology)*
Darnell Inst. of Cosmetology 757
Dartmouth Coll. 242
Dartmouth-Hitchcock Med. Ctr. 682
Darton Coll. 102
Data Consultants Computer Ctr. *(see DCI Career Inst.)*
Data Inst. *(see Goodwin Coll.)*
Data Inst—Waterbury *(see Stone Acad—Waterbury)*

Data Processing Trainers, Inc. *(see DPT Bus. Sch.)*
Date Carnegie *(see Vermont Training Solutions, Inc.)*
Daughters Coll. *(see William Woods Univ.)*
Davenport Barber-Styling Coll. 507
Davenport Coll. of Bus. *(see Davenport Univ.)*
Davenport Univ. 197, 730
Davenport Univ—Central Region 730 *(see also Davenport Univ—Midland Campus)*
Davenport Univ—Dearborn Campus 730
Davenport Univ—Eastern Region 730 *(see also Davenport Univ—Dearborn Campus)*
Davenport Univ—Kalamazoo *(see Davenport Univ.)*
Davenport Univ—Midland Campus 730
Davenport Univ—Western Region 730 *(see also Davenport Univ.)*
David A. Clarke Sch. of Law *(see Dist. of Columbia Sch. of Law)*
David C. Lawrence & Associates, Inc. *(see Lawrence-White Associates, Inc.)*
David Demuth Inst. of Cosmetology 505
David G. Erwin Tech. Ctr. 481
David Grant USAF Med. Ctr. *(see 60th Med. Group)*
David Hochstein Mem. Music Sch. 560
David Hochstein Music Sch. Settlement *(see David Hochstein Mem. Music Sch.)*
David L. Carrasco Job Corps Ctr. 619
David L. Pals & Associates, Inc. 541
David Lipscomb Univ. *(see Lipscomb Univ.)*
David N. Myers Coll. *(see David N. Myers Univ.)*
David N. Myers Univ. 302
David Pressley Prof. Sch. of Cosmetology *(see David Pressley Sch. of Cosmetology)*
David Pressley Sch. of Cosmetology 528
David Wolcott Kendall Sch. of Art *(see Ferris State Univ.)*
David's Sch. of Cosmetology *(see Mr. David's Sch. of Cosmetology, Ltd.)*
David's Sch. of Hair Design *(see Mr. David's Sch. of Hair Design)*
Davidson Coll. 286
Davidson County Coll. *(see Davidson County Comm. Coll.)*
Davidson County Comm. Coll. 286

Davis & Elkins Coll. 418
Davis Applied Techno. Ctr. *(see Davis Applied Techno. Coll.)*
Davis Applied Techno. Coll. 737, 750
Davis Bus. Coll. *(see Davis Coll.)*
Davis Coll. 262, 303, 734 *(see also Davis & Elkins Coll., Davis Applied Techno. Coll.)*
Davis State Jr. Coll. *(see Jefferson Davis Comm. Coll.)*
Dawn Training Centre 477
Dawn Training Inst. *(see Dawn Training Centre)*
Dawson Coll. 711
Dawson Comm. Coll. 234
Dawson Tech. Inst. *(see City Colleges of Chicago—Kennedy-King Coll.)*
Daymar Coll. 159
Dayton Barber Coll. 579
Dayton Univ. *(see Univ. of Dayton)*
Dayton VA Med. Ctr. *(see Veterans Affairs Med. Ctr—Dayton)*
Dayton Veterans Affairs Med. Ctr. *(see Veterans Affairs Med. Ctr—Dayton)*
Daytona Beach Coll. *(see Daytona Beach Comm. Coll.)*
Daytona Beach Comm. Coll. 83
Daytona Beach Jr. Coll. *(see Daytona Beach Comm. Coll.)*
Daytona Educational & Industrial Training Sch. *(see Bethune-Cookman Coll.)*
Dayton's Sch. of Hair Design—Burlington 507
Dayton's Sch. of Hair Design—Keokuk 507
DC Law Sch. *(see Dist. of Columbia Sch. of Law)*
DC VA Med. Ctr. *(see Washington DC Veterans Affairs Med. Ctr.)*
DC Veterans Affairs Med. Ctr. *(see Washington DC Veterans Affairs Med. Ctr.)*
DCH Health System *(see DCH Reg. Med. Ctr.)*
DCH Reg. Med. Ctr. 651
DCI Career Inst. 595
DCT Int'l. Hotel & Bus. Management Sch. 762
DDI Health Careers *(see Comm. Care Coll.)*
De Anza Coll. 38
Deaconess Coll. of Nursing 225
Deaconess Hosp. 667
Deaconess Sanitarium Training Sch. *(see Bellin Coll. of Nursing)*
Deakin Univ. 431
Dean Coll. 186
Dean Inst. of Techno. 329
Dean Tech *(see Dean Inst. of Techno.)*

Decatur Sch. of Beauty Culture *(see Mr. John's Sch. of Cosmetology Esthetics & Nails)*

Decatur VA Med. Ctr. *(see Atlanta Veterans Affairs Med. Ctr.)*

Decatur Veterans Affairs Med. Ctr. *(see Atlanta Veterans Affairs Med. Ctr.)*

Decker Coll. of Bus. Techno. 159

Deep Muscle Therapy Ctr. *(see Deep Muscle Therapy Sch., Pennsylvania Sch. of Muscle Therapy, Ltd.)*

Deep Muscle Therapy Ctr. of Delaware *(see Deep Muscle Therapy Sch.)*

Deep Muscle Therapy Sch. 477

Deep Springs Coll. 39

Deets Pacific Bible Coll. *(see Point Loma Nazarene Univ.)*

Defense Acquisition Univ. 632

Defense Commissary Agency 632

Defense Contract Audit Agency *(see Defense Contract Audit Inst.)*

Defense Equal Opportunity Management Inst. 481

Defense Information Sch. 521

Defense Inst. of Security Assistance Management 579

Defense Intelligence Coll. *(see Joint Military Intelligence Coll.)*

Defense Intelligence Sch. *(see Joint Military Intelligence Coll.)*

Defense Language Inst. *(see Defense Language Inst. English Language Ctr., Defense Language Inst. Foreign Language Ctr.)*

Defense Language Inst. English Language Ctr. 619

Defense Language Inst. Foreign Language Ctr. 39

Defense Security Service Acad. 521

Defense Univ. *(see National Defense Univ.)*

Defiance Coll., The 303

Defiance Female Seminary *(see Defiance Coll.)*

DeForest Training Sch. *(see DeVry Univ. Chicago)*

DeKalb Coll. *(see Georgia Perimeter Coll.)*

DeKalb County Hosp. *(see DeKalb Med. Ctr. Decatur)*

DeKalb General Hosp. *(see DeKalb Med. Ctr. Decatur)*

DeKalb Med. Ctr. Decatur 664

DeKalb Tech. Coll. 102

Del Mar Coll. 377

DeLand Acad. *(see Stetson Univ.)*

Delaware Area Career Ctr. 579

Delaware Coll. *(see Delaware Coll. of Art & Design, Univ. of Delaware)*

Delaware Coll. of Art & Design 744

Delaware County Coll. *(see Delaware County Comm. Coll.)*

Delaware County Comm. Coll. 329

Delaware Dale Carnegie Training *(see Leadership Inst., Inc.)*

Delaware Joint Vocational Sch. *(see Delaware Area Career Ctr.)*

Delaware Learning Inst. of Cosmetology, The 477, 724

Delaware Med. Ctr. *(see Med. Ctr. of Delaware)*

Delaware Sch. of Hotel Management 477

Delaware State Coll. *(see Delaware State Univ.)*

Delaware State Univ. 77

Delaware Tech. & Comm. Coll—Jack F. Owens Campus 77

Delaware Tech. & Comm. Coll— Stanton/Wilmington Campus 77

Delaware Tech. & Comm. Coll—Terry Campus 77

Delaware Univ. *(see Univ. of Delaware)*

Delaware Valley Acad. of Med. & Dental Assistants 595

Delaware Valley Coll. of Science & Agriculture 329

Delaware Valley Dental Assistants Acad. *(see Delaware Valley Acad. of Med. & Dental Assistants)*

Delaware Valley Med. Assistants Acad. *(see Delaware Valley Acad. of Med. & Dental Assistants)*

Delaware's Land Grant Coll. *(see Univ. of Delaware)*

DeLeon Acad. of Esthetics 760

DeLeon Day Spa *(see DeLeon Acad. of Esthetics)*

Delgado Coll. *(see Delgado Comm. Coll.)*

Delgado Comm. Coll. 166

Delhi Coll. of Techno. *(see State Univ. of New York Coll. of Techno. at Delhi)*

Dell'Arte International Sch. of Physical Theater 39

Delmarva Beauty Acad. *(see Del-Mar-Va Beauty Acad.)*

Del-Mar-Va Beauty Acad. 521

Delta Beauty Coll. 535

Delta Coll—Baton Rouge *(see Delta Coll. of Arts & Techno.)*

Delta Coll. *(see San Joaquin Delta Coll.)*

Delta Coll. 198, 516

Delta Coll. of Arts & Techno. 166

Delta Connection Acad. 481, 725

Delta Jr. Coll. *(see Delta Coll.)*

Delta Sch. of Bus. & Techno. 167

Delta State Coll. *(see Delta State Univ.)*

Delta State Teachers Coll. *(see Delta State Univ.)*

Delta State Univ. 218

Delta Univ. *(see Delta State Univ.)*

Delta-Montrose Area Vocational-Tech. Ctr. *(see Delta-Montrose Tech. Coll.)*

Delta-Montrose Tech. Coll. 472

Deluxe Beauty Sch. 447

DeMarge Coll., Inc. 587

Demmon Sch. of Beauty 516

Demuth Inst. of Cosmetology *(see David Demuth Inst. of Cosmetology)*

Denham Springs Beauty Coll. 516

Denison Univ. 303

Denmark Area Trade Sch. *(see Denmark Tech. Coll.)*

Denmark Coll. *(see Denmark Tech. Coll.)*

Denmark Tech. Coll. 356

Denmark Tech. Edu. Ctr. *(see Denmark Tech. Coll.)*

Dental & Craniofacial Research *(see National Inst-Dental & Craniofacial Research)*

Dental Assistants Sch. of New York *(see New York Sch. for Med. & Dental Assistants)*

Dental Auxiliary Training Acad. *(see Southwest Health Career Inst., Inc.)*

Dental Directions, Inc. *(see Comm. Care Coll.)*

Dental Sch. of New Jersey *(see New Jersey Dental Sch.)*

Dental Studies Inst. *(see Inst. for Health Edu.)*

Denver Acad. of Court Reporting 67

Denver Automotive & Diesel Coll. 67

Denver Automotive Inst. *(see Denver Automotive & Diesel Coll.)*

Denver Aviation Inst. *(see Westwood Coll. of Aviation Tech—Denver)*

Denver Bible Coll. *(see Colorado Christian Univ.)*

Denver Bible Inst. *(see Colorado Christian Univ.)*

Denver Career Coll. 67

Denver Ctr. for the Performing Arts, The *(see National Theatre Conservatory)*

Denver Children's Hosp. *(see Children's Hosp.)*

Denver Comm. Coll. *(see Comm. Coll. of Denver)*

Denver Family Inst. 657

Denver General Hosp. *(see Denver Health Med. Ctr.)*

Denver Health & Hosp. Authority *(see Denver Health Med. Ctr.)*
Denver Health Med. Ctr. 658
Denver Inst. of Techno. *(see Westwood Coll—Denver North, Westwood Coll—Denver South)*
Denver Metropolitan Coll. *(see Metropolitan State Coll. of Denver)*
Denver Paralegal Inst. *(see Denver Career Coll.)*
Denver Sch. of Massage Therapy 629 *(see also Utah Coll. of Massage Therapy)*
Denver Seminary 67
Denver Tech. Coll. at Colorado Springs *(see DeVry Univ. Colorado Springs)*
Denver Tech. Coll. At Denver *(see DeVry Univ. Denver)*
Denver Univ. *(see Univ. of Denver)*
Dept. of Army Headquarters 664
Dept. of Defense Dental Laboratory Technician Course 703
Dept. of Defense Polygraph Inst. 608
Dept. of Veterans Affairs Med. Ctr— Memphis *(see Veterans Affairs Med. Ctr—Memphis)*
DePaul Univ. 120, 727
DePauw Univ. 136
Deree Coll., The American Coll. of Greece 435
Des Moines Area Comm. Coll. 146
Des Moines Coll. *(see Des Moines Area Comm. Coll.)*
Des Moines Still Coll. of Osteopathy & Surgery *(see Des Moines Univ— Osteopathic Med. Ctr.)*
Des Moines Univ—Osteopathic Med. Ctr. 146
Des Moines VA Med. Ctr. *(see Veterans Affairs Central Iowa Healthcare System—Knoxville Division)*
Des Moines Veterans Affairs Med. Ctr. *(see Veterans Affairs Central Iowa Healthcare System—Knoxville Division)*
DeSales Univ. 329
Desert Coll. *(see Coll. of the Desert)*
Desert Inst. of the Healing Arts 445
Design & Construction Inst. *(see Inst. of Design & Construction)*
Design Coll. of California *(see California Design Coll.)*
Design Coll. of Tucson *(see Tucson Design Coll.)*
Design Inst. *(see Art Inst. of Las Vegas, Design Inst. of San Diego)*
Design Inst. of San Diego 39
Design Sch. of Cosmetology 456

Designer's Beauty Acad. Sch. of Cosmetology 757
Designs for Lifelong Learning 500
Detroit Barber Coll., Inc. 731
Detroit Bus. Inst. 528
Detroit Bus. Inst—Downriver 528
Detroit Coll. of Bus. *(see Davenport Univ.)*
Detroit Coll. of Law 201 *(see also Michigan State Univ.)*
Detroit Inst. of Ophthalmology 677
Detroit Jr. Coll. *(see Wayne State Univ.)*
Detroit Med. Ctr. Univ. Laboratories 205 *(see also Wayne State Univ.)*
Detroit Med. Coll. *(see Wayne State Univ.)*
Detroit Normal Training Sch. *(see Wayne State Univ.)*
Detroit Practical Nursing Ctr. 677
Detroit Receiving Hosp. 677
Detroit Sinai Hosp. *(see Sinai-Grace Hosp.)*
Detroit-Macomb Hosp. Corporation 677
DeVoe Coll. of Beauty 445
DeVry Calgary *(see DeVry Inst. of Techno., Calgary)*
DeVry Coll. of Tech—North Brunswick 246, 733
DeVry Inst. of Techno. 262 *(see also DeVry Coll. of Techno.)*
DeVry Inst. of Techno. City of Industry *(see DeVry Univ. Pomona)*
DeVry Inst. of Techno. Denver *(see DeVry Univ. Denver)*
DeVry Inst. of Techno., Calgary 432
DeVry Inst. of Tech—Addison *(see DeVry Univ. DuPage)*
DeVry Inst. of Tech—Alpharetta *(see DeVry Univ. Alpharetta)*
DeVry Inst. of Tech—Chicago *(see DeVry Univ. Chicago)*
DeVry Inst. of Tech—Columbus *(see DeVry Univ. Columbus)*
DeVry Inst. of Tech—DuPage *(see DeVry Univ. DuPage)*
DeVry Inst. of Tech—Fremont *(see DeVry Univ. Fremont)*
DeVry Inst. of Tech—Georgia *(see DeVry Univ. Georgia)*
DeVry Inst. of Tech—Irving *(see DeVry Univ. Irving)*
DeVry Inst. of Tech—Kansas City *(see DeVry Univ. Kansas City)*
DeVry Inst. of Tech—Lombard *(see DeVry Univ. DuPage)*
DeVry Inst. of Tech—Long Beach *(see DeVry Univ. Long Beach)*
DeVry Inst. of Tech—Orlando *(see DeVry Univ. Orlando)*

DeVry Inst. of Tech—Phoenix *(see DeVry Univ. Phoenix)*
DeVry Inst. of Tech—Pomona *(see DeVry Univ. Pomona)*
DeVry Inst. of Tech—Tinley Park *(see DeVry Univ. Tinley Park)*
DeVry New York *(see DeVry Inst. of Techno.)*
DeVry Tech. Inst. *(see DeVry Univ. Chicago, DeVry Univ. Colorado Springs, DeVry Univ. Denver, DeVry Univ. West Hills)*
DeVry Tech. Inst. at Colorado Springs *(see DeVry Univ. Colorado Springs)*
DeVry Tech. Inst. at Denver *(see DeVry Univ. Denver)*
DeVry Tech. Inst—West Hills *(see DeVry Univ. West Hills)*
DeVry Univeristy Coll. of Tech— Toronto 740
DeVry Univ. Arlington *(see DeVry Univ. Crystal City)*
DeVry Univ. Calgary *(see DeVry Inst. of Techno., Calgary)*
DeVry Univ. Chicago 120
DeVry Univ. Columbus 303
DeVry Univ. Crystal City 401
DeVry Univ. DuPage 120
DeVry Univ. Federal Way *(see DeVry Univ. Seattle)*
DeVry Univ. Fort Washington *(see DeVry Univ. Philadelphia)*
DeVry Univ. Georgia 102
DeVry Univ. Grad. Sch. of Management *(see Keller Grad. Sch. of Management of DeVry Univ.)*
DeVry Univ. Irvine 39, 723
DeVry Univ. Irving 377
DeVry Univ. Kansas City 225
DeVry Univ. North Brunswick *(see DeVry Coll. of Tech—North Brunswick)*
DeVry Univ. Orlando 83
DeVry Univ. Philadelphia 329
DeVry Univ. Phoenix 16
DeVry Univ. Pomona 39
DeVry Univ. San Diego *(see Keller Grad. Sch. of Management San Diego Ctr.)*
DeVry Univ. Seattle 411
DeVry Univ. Southern California *(see DeVry Univ. Pomona)*
DeVry Univ. Westminster 67
Dewey Coll. *(see John Dewey Coll.)*
DeWolff Coll. of Hairstyling & Cosmetology 556
Diablo Valley Coll. 39
Diamond Council of America 611

Diamond Oaks Career Development Campus *(see Great Oaks Inst. of Techno. & Career Development—Diamond Oaks Campus)*
Diamond's Barber Coll. 759
Dickerson Beauty Acad. 632
Dickinson Bus. Sch. *(see Career Point Inst., Wright Bus. Sch.)*
Dickinson Coll. 329 *(see also Fairleigh Dickinson Univ.)*
Dickinson Normal Sch. *(see Dickinson State Univ.)*
Dickinson Sch. of Law 338 *(see also Pennsylvania State Univ.)*
Dickinson State Coll. *(see Dickinson State Univ.)*
Dickinson State Teachers Coll. *(see Dickinson State Univ.)*
Dickinson State Univ. 296
Dickinson Univ. *(see Fairleigh Dickinson Univ.)*
Dickson & Associates, LLC *(see B. Dickson & Associates, LLC)*
Didi Hirsch Comm. Mental Health Ctr. 653
Diesel Driving Acad. 516
Diesel Inst. of America 522
DigiPen Applied Computer Graphics Sch. *(see DigiPen Inst. of Techno.)*
DigiPen Inst. of Techno. 411
Digital Circus *(see Sch. of Communication Arts)*
DiGrigoli Sch. of Cosmetology, Inc. 756
Dillard Univ. 167
Diné Coll. 16
Diocese of Rockville Centre *(see Seminary of the Immaculate Conception)*
Direct Learning Systems, Inc. *(see Blackstone Career Inst.)*
Dist. of Columbia Sch. of Law 661
Dist. of Columbia Teachers Coll. *(see Univ. of the Dist. of Columbia)*
Dist. of Columbia Univ. *(see Univ. of the Dist. of Columbia)*
Dist. of Columbia Veterans Affairs Med. Ctr. *(see Washington DC Veterans Affairs Med. Ctr.)*
Diva's Unlimited Acad. 538
Divers Acad. international 548, 733
Divers Acad. of the Eastern Seaboard 733 *(see also Divers Acad. international)*
Divers Inst. of Techno. 637
Diversified Language Inst. 457
Diversified Language Inst—San Diego 457
Divine Word Coll. 146
Dixie Applied Techno. Coll. 760

Dixie Coll. *(see Dixie State Coll. of Utah, Tennessee Technological Univ.)*
Dixie Jr. Coll. *(see Dixie State Coll. of Utah)*
Dixie Normal Coll. *(see Dixie State Coll. of Utah)*
Dixie State Coll. of Utah 394
D-Jay's Sch. of Beauty Arts & Sciences 516
DLI Foreign Language Ctr. *(see Defense Language Inst. Foreign Language Ctr.)*
D'Mart Inst. 603
Doane Coll. 237
Doctor Martin Luther Coll. *(see Martin Luther Coll.)*
DoD Dental Laboratory Technician Course *(see Dept. of Defense Dental Laboratory Technician Course)*
Dodge City Coll. *(see Dodge City Comm. Coll.)*
Dodge City Comm. Coll. 153
Domestic Health Care Inst. 516
Domincan Coll. of San Rafael 722
Dominican Coll. of Blauvelt 262
Dominican Coll. of San Rafael *(see Dominican Univ. of California)*
Dominican House of Studies 78
Dominican Sch. of Philosophy & Theology 39
Dominican Study Ctr. of the Caribbean 347
Dominican Univ. 120
Dominican Univ. of California 39, 722
Dominion Sch. of Hair Design 761
Don Adams Corporation, The 500
Don Bosco Tech. Inst. 39
Don Roberts Beauty Sch. 505
Don Roberts Sch. of Hair Design 505
Doña Ana Branch Comm. Coll. 253 *(see also New Mexico State Univ.)*
Doña Ana Comm. Coll. *(see also New Mexico State Univ.)*
Donald Vocational Sch. 722 *(see also DVS Coll.)*
Dongguk Royal Univ. 39
Dongguk Univ. *(see Dongguk Royal Univ.)*
Donnelly Coll. 153
Donta Sch. of Beauty Culture 512
Dordt Coll. 146
Dorsey Bus. Sch. 529
Dorsey Sch., The *(see Dorsey Bus. Sch.)*
Dorsey's Beauty Acad. 760
Douglas Coll. 711
Douglas Edu. Ctr. 329
Douglas J Aveda Inst. 529

Douglas J Educational Ctr. *(see Douglas J Aveda Inst.)*
Douglas MacArthur State Tech. Coll. 721 *(see also Lurleen B. Wallace Comm. Coll.)*
Douglas Sch. of Bus. *(see Douglas Edu. Ctr.)*
Douglass Coll. 249 *(see also Rutgers, The State Univ. of New Jersey New Brunswick Campus; Sojourner-Douglass Coll.)*
Dover Bus. Coll. 548
Dover Tech. Sch. *(see Branford Hall Career Inst—Bohemia)*
Dowling Coll. 262
Downeast Sch. of Massage 519
Downstate Med. Ctr. *(see State Univ. of New York Health Science Ctr. at Brooklyn)*
DPT Bus. Sch. 595
D-Q Univ. 722
Dr. Jun Inst. of Montessori Edu. 647
Dr. Martin Luther Coll. *(see Martin Luther Coll.)*
Dr. S.S. Still Coll. of Osteopathy *(see Des Moines Univ—Osteopathic Med. Ctr.)*
Dr. William M. Scholl Coll. of Podiatric Medicine 120
Dr. William M. Scholl Coll. of Podiatric Medicine at Finch Univ. *(see Dr. William M. Scholl Coll. of Podiatric Medicine)*
Dr. William M. Scholl Coll. of Podiatric Medicine at Rosalind Franklin Univ. *(see Dr. William M. Scholl Coll. of Podiatric Medicine)*
Dragon Rises Sch. of Oriental Medicine 662
Drake Bus. Sch—Queens Astoria Campus 733
Drake Bus. Sch—Staten Island Campus 733
Drake Coll. of Bus. 733
Drake Coll. of Florida *(see Florida Metropolitan Univ—Pompano Beach)*
Drake Sch. of Manhatten 733
Drake Sch. of the Bronx 733
Drake State Tech. Coll. *(see J.F. Drake State Tech. Coll.)*
Drake Univ. 146
Draughon's Bus. Coll. *(see Draughons Jr. Coll.)*
Draughons Jr. Coll. *(see South Univ.)*
Draughons Jr. Coll. 365
Draughon's Practical Bus. Coll. *(see Draughons Jr. Coll., South Univ.)*
Drew Theological Seminary *(see Drew Univ.)*
Drew Univ. 246

Drew Univ. of Medicine & Science
(see Charles R. Drew Univ. of
Medicine & Science)
Drexel Inst. (see Drexel Univ.)
Drexel Univ. 329
Driving Acad. of Georgia (see Georgia
Driving Acad.)
DROS Sch. of Cosmetology 755
Druid City Hosp. (see DCH Reg. Med.
Ctr.)
Drury Coll. (see Drury Univ.)
Drury Univ. 225
DSU Training Inst. 737
Dubai Men's Coll. (see Higher
Colleges of Techno. Dubai Men's
Coll.)
Dubai Women's Coll. (see Higher
Colleges of Techno. Dubai
Women's Coll.)
Dubois Area Vocational Tech. Sch.
(see Jefferson County-Dubois
Area Vocational Tech. Sch.)
DuBois Bus. Coll. 330
DuBois Coll. of Bus. (see DuBois Bus.
Coll.)
Dubuque Coll. (see Loras Coll.)
Dubuque Univ. (see Univ. of Dubuque)
Dudley Beauty Coll—Charlotte 572
Dudley Beauty Coll—Washington 478
Dudley Beauty Sch. (see Dudley
Beauty Coll—Washington)
Dudley Cosmetology Univ. 572
Due West Female Coll. (see Erskine
Coll.)
Duff's Bus. Inst. 330
Duff's Iron City Coll. (see Duff's Bus.
Inst.)
Duff's Mercantile Coll. (see Duff's
Bus. Inst.)
Duke Divinity Sch. (see Duke Univ.)
Duke Univ. 286
Duke Univ. Divinity Sch. (see Duke
Univ.)
Dull Knife Mem. Coll. (see Chief Dull
Knife Coll.)
Duluth Area Inst. of Techno. (see Lake
Superior Coll.)
Duluth Area Vocational Tech. Inst. (see
Lake Superior Coll.)
Duluth Bus. Univ. 209
Duluth Comm. Coll. Ctr. (see Lake
Superior Coll.)
Duluth Tech. Coll. (see Lake Superior
Coll.)
Dundalk Comm. Coll. (see Comm.
Coll. of Baltimore County)
Dunwoody Coll. of Techno. 209, 731
Dunwoody Inst. (see Dunwoody Coll.
of Techno.)
duPont Children's Hosp. (see Alfred I.
duPont Hosp. for Children)

duPont Hosp. for Children (see Alfred
I. duPont Hosp. for Children)
duPont Inst. (see Alfred I. duPont
Hosp. for Children)
Duquesne Univ. 330
DuQuoin Beauty Coll. 500
Durham Coll. (see Durham Tech.
Comm. Coll.)
Durham State Normal Sch. (see North
Carolina Central Univ.)
Durham Tech. Coll. (see Durham Tech.
Comm. Coll.)
Durham Tech. Comm. Coll. 287
Durham VA Med. Ctr. (see Veterans
Affairs Med. Ctr—Durham)
Durham Veterans Affairs Med. Ctr.
(see Veterans Affairs Med. Ctr—
Durham)
Dutchess Coll. (see Dutchess Comm.
Coll.)
Dutchess Comm. Coll. 262
Duwayne E. Keller & Associates, Inc.
481
DVS Coll. 457, 722
Dwight D. Eisenhower Veterans Affairs
Med. Ctr. 672
Dwight David Eisenhower Army Med.
Ctr. 664
Dyersburg Coll. (see Dyersburg State
Comm. Coll.)
Dyersburg State Comm. Coll. 365
Dyke Coll. (see David N. Myers Univ.)
D'Youville Coll. 262

E

E. J. Taylor Corporation 572
E.I.N.E., Inc. (see Electrology Inst. of
New England)
Eagle Gate Coll. 627
Earle C. Clements Job Corps Ctr. 512
Earlham Coll. 136
Earlham Sch. of Religion (see Earlham
Coll.)
Earl's Acad. of Beauty 445
East Alabama Male Coll. (see Auburn
Univ.)
East Arkansas Coll. (see East
Arkansas Comm. Coll.)
East Arkansas Comm. Coll. 25
East Carolina Coll. (see East Carolina
Univ.)
East Carolina Univ. 287
East Central Coll. 225 (see also East
Central Comm. Coll.)
East Central Comm. Coll. 218
East Central Tech. Coll. 102, 726
East Central Tech. Inst. 726 (see also
East Central Tech. Coll., Ivy Tech
Comm. Coll. of Indiana—East
Central)

East Central Univ. 315
East Coast Aero Tech 730 (see also
WyoTech—Boston)
East Coast Aero Tech. Sch. 730 (see
also WyoTech—Boston)
East Florida Seminary (see Univ. of
Florida)
East Georgia Coll. 102
East Grand Forks Tech. Coll. (see
Northland Comm. & Tech. Coll.)
East Grand Forks Tech. Inst. (see
Northland Comm. & Tech. Coll.)
East Jefferson General Hosp. 673
East Kentucky Rural Psychology
Predoctoral Internship Program
(see Hazard ARH Reg. Med. Ctr.)
East Los Angeles Coll. 40
East Los Angeles Occupational Ctr.
653
East Metro OIC (see East Metro
Opportunities Industrialization
Ctr.)
East Metro Opportunities
Industrialization Ctr. 533
East Mississippi Coll. (see East
Mississippi Comm. Coll.)
East Mississippi Comm. Coll. 218
East Montgomery County Area
Vocational Tech. Sch. 697
East Montgomery County Vo-Tech
Sch. (see East Montgomery
County Area Vocational Tech.
Sch.)
East Orange VA Med. Ctr. (see
Veterans Affairs Med. Ctr—East
Orange)
East Orange Veterans Affairs Med. Ctr.
(see Veterans Affairs Med. Ctr—
East Orange)
East Stroudsburg Univ. of
Pennsylvania 330
East Tech (see EasTech)
East Tennessee State Coll. (see East
Tennessee State Univ.)
East Tennessee State Normal Sch.
(see East Tennessee State Univ.)
East Tennessee State Teachers Coll.
(see East Tennessee State Univ.)
East Tennessee State Univ. 365
East Tennessee Univ. (see East
Tennessee State Univ., Univ. of
Tennessee)
East Tennessee Wesleyan Coll. (see
Tennessee Wesleyan Coll.)
East Tennessee Wesleyan Univ. (see
Tennessee Wesleyan Coll., Univ.
of Tennessee at Chattanooga)
East Texas Baptist Univ. 377
East Texas Normal Coll. (see Texas
A&M Univ—Commerce)

East Texas State Teachers Coll. *(see Texas A&M Univ—Commerce)*
East Texas State Univ. *(see Texas A&M Univ—Commerce)*
East Texas State Univ. at Texarkana *(see Texas A&M Univ—Texarkana)*
East Texas Univ. *(see East Texas Baptist Univ.)*
East Valley Inst. of Techno. 445
East West Coll. *(see East West Coll. of Natural Medicine)*
East West Coll. of Natural Medicine 83
Eastcentral Tech. Inst. *(see Ivy Tech Comm. Coll. of Indiana—East Central)*
Eastern Acupuncture Sch. *(see Eastern Sch. of Acupuncture & Traditional Medicine)*
Eastern Arizona Acad. of Cosmetology 753
Eastern Arizona Coll. 16
Eastern Arizona Jr. Coll. *(see Eastern Arizona Coll.)*
Eastern Baptist Coll. *(see Eastern Univ.)*
Eastern Baptist Theological Seminary 735 *(see also Palmer Theological Seminary)*
Eastern Coll. *(see Eastern Univ.)*
Eastern Coll. of Health Vocations 448
Eastern Connecticut Coll. *(see Eastern Connecticut State Univ.)*
Eastern Connecticut State Coll. *(see Eastern Connecticut State Univ.)*
Eastern Connecticut State Univ. 72
Eastern Health Vocations Coll. *(see Eastern Coll. of Health Vocations)*
Eastern Hills Acad. of Hair Design 579
Eastern Idaho Coll. *(see Eastern Idaho Tech. Coll.)*
Eastern Idaho Tech. Coll. 115
Eastern Illinois Normal Sch. *(see Eastern Illinois Univ.)*
Eastern Illinois State Teachers Coll. *(see Eastern Illinois Univ.)*
Eastern Illinois Univ. 120
Eastern Kansas VA Healthcare System *(see Colmery-O'Neil Veterans Affairs Med. Ctr., Dwight D. Eisenhower Veterans Affairs Med. Ctr.)*
Eastern Kansas Veterans Affairs Healthcare System *(see Colmery-O'Neil Veterans Affairs Med. Ctr., Dwight D. Eisenhower Veterans)*
Eastern Kentucky Univ. 160
Eastern Los Angeles County Comm. Coll. *(see Mount San Antonio Coll.)*

Eastern Louisiana Mental Health System *(see Louisiana State Univ. Health Sciences Ctr. in New Orleans)*
Eastern Maine Coll. *(see Eastern Maine Comm. Coll.)*
Eastern Maine Comm. Coll. 175, 730
Eastern Maine Med. Ctr. 674
Eastern Maine Tech. Coll. 730 *(see also Eastern Maine Comm. Coll.)*
Eastern Maine Vocational Tech. Inst. *(see Eastern Maine Comm. Coll.)*
Eastern Mennonite Coll. & Seminary *(see Eastern Mennonite Univ.)*
Eastern Mennonite Sch. *(see Eastern Mennonite Univ.)*
Eastern Mennonite Univ. 401
Eastern Michigan Univ. 198
Eastern Montana Coll. *(see Montana State Univ—Billings)*
Eastern Nazarene Coll. 186
Eastern Nebraska Tech. Comm. Coll. *(see Metropolitan Comm. Coll.)*
Eastern New Mexico Univ. 252
Eastern New Mexico Univ—Clovis Campus *(see Clovis Comm. Coll.)*
Eastern New Mexico Univ—Roswell 252
Eastern Normal Coll. *(see Dakota State Univ.)*
Eastern Oklahoma State Coll. 315
Eastern Oregon State Coll. *(see Eastern Oregon Univ.)*
Eastern Oregon Univ. 320
Eastern Pentecostal Bible Coll. 740 *(see also Master's Coll. & Seminary)*
Eastern Sch. of Acupuncture & Traditional Medicine 548
Eastern Seminary *(see Palmer Theological Seminary)*
Eastern Shore Coll. *(see Eastern Shore Comm. Coll.)*
Eastern Shore Comm. Coll. 401
Eastern Suffolk Sch. for Practical Nursing 686
Eastern Univ. 330
Eastern Univ. Preparatory Sch. *(see Rogers State Univ.)*
Eastern Utah Coll. *(see Coll. of Eastern Utah)*
Eastern Virginia Dale Carnegie Training *(see Wade Powell & Associates, Inc.)*
Eastern Virginia Med. Sch. 402
Eastern Washington Coll. of Edu. *(see Eastern Washington Univ.)*
Eastern Washington State Coll. *(see Eastern Washington Univ.)*
Eastern Washington Univ. 411

Eastern West Virginia Comm. & Tech. Coll. 419
Eastern Wyoming Coll. 430
Eastfield Coll. 377
Eastland Career Ctr—Adult Workforce Development Ctr. 579
Eastland-Fairfield Career & Tech. Schools *(see Eastland Career Ctr—Adult Workforce Development Ctr., Fairfield Career Ctr.)*
Eastman Sch. of Music *(see Univ. of Rochester)*
East-West Coll. of the Healing Arts 592
East-West Univ. 120
Eaton Beauty Stylist Coll., Inc. 448
Eberle Tech. Ctr. *(see Fred W. Eberle Tech. Ctr.)*
Ecclesia Coll. 25
Eckerd Coll. 83
Eclectic Coll. of Chiropractic *(see Southern California Univ. of Health Sciences)*
Ecole des Hautes Etudes Commerciales 715
Ecole Hoteliere de Lausanne 436
Ecole ""Les Roches"" *(see "Les Roches" Sch. of Hotel Management)*
Ecole Superieure des Sciences Economiques et Commerciales 715 *(see also Ecole Superieure des Sciences Economiques et Commerciales)*
ECPI Coll. of Techno. 402
ECPI Computer Inst. *(see ECPI Coll. of Techno., ECPI Tech. Coll.)*
ECPI Tech. Coll. 402
ECPI Tech. Coll—Raleigh 734
Ecumenical Ctr. for Religion & Health 703
Ecumenical Theological Seminary 198
Ed W. Grooms & Associates, Inc. 734 *(see also Dale Carnegie Training of Greater Cincinnati)*
Ed Waters Coll. *(see Edward Waters Coll.)*
Eddie C. Snow & Associates, Inc. 457
Eddy County Beauty Coll. 556
eDecker *(see Decker Coll. of Bus. Techno.)*
Eden Seminary *(see Eden Theological Seminary)*
Eden Theological Seminary 225
Edgecombe Coll. *(see Edgecombe Comm. Coll.)*
Edgecombe Comm. Coll. 287
Edgewood Coll. 424 *(see also Edgewood Coll. of California)*
Edgewood Coll. of California 457

EDIC Coll. 603, 736

Edinboro Acad. *(see Edinboro Univ. of Pennsylvania)*

Edinboro State Coll. *(see Edinboro Univ. of Pennsylvania)*

Edinboro State Teachers Coll. *(see Edinboro Univ. of Pennsylvania)*

Edinboro Univ. of Pennsylvania 330

Edinburg Jr. Coll. *(see Univ. of Texas—Pan American)*

Edison Coll. *(see Edison State Comm. Coll., Thomas Edison State Coll.)*

Edison Coll. 84, 725

Edison Comm. Coll. 725 *(see also Edison Coll., Edison State Comm. Coll.)*

Edison State Coll. *(see Thomas Edison State Coll.)*

Edison State Comm. Coll. 303

Edison State General & Tech. Coll. *(see Edison State Comm. Coll.)*

Edison Tech. Sch. *(see Seattle Central Comm. Coll.)*

Edith Nourse Rogers Mem. Veterans Hosp. 676

Edith Nourse Rogers VA Med. Ctr. *(see Edith Nourse Rogers Mem. Veterans Hosp.)*

Edith Nourse Rogers Veterans Affairs Med. Ctr. *(see Edith Nourse Rogers Mem. Veterans Hosp.)*

Edmond Language Inst. 588

Edmonds Coll. *(see Edmonds Comm. Coll.)*

Edmonds Comm. Coll. 411

Edmonton Baptist Seminary 432

Edmonton Seminary *(see Edmonton Baptist Seminary)*

Edmundson Hosp. *(see Jennie Edmundson Hosp.)*

Edmundson Mem. Hosp. *(see Jennie Edmundson Hosp.)*

EdNet Career Inst., Inc. 457

EDP Coll. *(see Electronic Data Processing Coll.)*

Educatinal Tech. Coll. 603

Educating Hands Sch. of Massage 481

Edu. America Univ. 722 *(see also Remington Coll—San Diego)*

Edu. America—Colorado Springs Campus 724

Edu. America—Dallas Campus *(see Remington Coll—Dallas)*

Edu. America—Dallas Campus 737

Edu. America—Denver Campus 724

Edu. America—Honolulu Campus 727

Edu. America—Houston 737 *(see also Remington Coll—Houston)*

Edu. American-Southeast Coll. of Tech—Little Rock 721

Edu. American-Tampa Tech. Inst— Pinellas Campus 725

Edu. America-Remington Coll—Baton Rouge Campus 729

Edu. America-Remington Coll— Cleveland Campus 734 *(see also Remington Coll—Cleveland)*

Edu. America-Remington Coll— Lafayette Campus 729 *(see also Remington Coll—Lafayette)*

Edu. America-Southeast Coll. of Tech—Memphis 736

Edu. America—Southeast Coll. of Tech—Mobile AL *(see Remington Coll—Mobile)*

Edu. America-Southeast Coll. of Tech—Mobile AL 721

Edu. America-Southeast Coll. of Tech—New Orleans 729 *(see also Remington Coll—New Orleans)*

Edu. America—Tampa Tech. Inst. *(see Remington Coll—Tampa)*

Edu. America-Tampa Tech. Inst. 725

Edu. America-Tampa Tech. Inst—Ft. Worth Campus 737

Edu. America-Tampa Tech. Inst— Jacksonville Campus 725

Edu. America—Tempe Campus 721

Edu. & Techno. Inst. 595

Edu. Direct 730, 735 *(see also Penn Foster Career Sch.)*

Edu. Direct Ctr. for Degree Studies 735 *(see also Penn Foster Career Sch.)*

Educational Management Services, Inc. *(see Baton Rouge Coll.)*

Educators of Beauty—La Salle 500

Educators of Beauty—Sterling 500

Educorp Career Coll. *(see National Inst. of Tech—Long Beach)*

EduTech Centers 481

EduTek Coll. 303

Edward Hines, Jr. VA Hosp. *(see Edward Hines, Jr. Veterans Affairs Hosp.)*

Edward Hines, Jr. Veterans Affairs Hosp. 667

Edward Hosp. 667

Edward Waters Coll. 84

EF Int'l. Language Schools, Inc. 525

EF Int'l. Schools of English in Boston *(see EF Int'l. Language Schools, Inc.)*

Eger Health Care Ctr. of Staten Island 686

Eger Lutheran Homes & Services *(see Eger Health Care Ctr. of Staten Island)*

EHOVE Career Ctr. 579

EHOVE Ghrist Adult Career Ctr. *(see EHOVE Career Ctr.)*

Ehrenkranz Sch. of Social Work 270

Ehrenkranz Sch. of Social Work at Saint Thomas Aquinas Coll. *(see New York Univ.)*

Ehrenkranz Sch. of Social Work of New York Univ. *(see NYU Ehrenkranz Sch. of Social Work at St. Thomas Aquinas Coll.)*

Einstein Healthcare Network *(see Albert Einstein Med. Ctr.)*

Einstein Med. Ctr. *(see Albert Einstein Med. Ctr.)*

Einstein/Montefiore Med/West *(see Montefiore Med. Ctr. West Campus)*

Eisenhower Army Med. Ctr. *(see Dwight David Eisenhower Army Med. Ctr.)*

Eisenhower Med. Ctr. Sch. of Med. Techno. 653

Eisenhower Sch. of Med. Techno. *(see Eisenhower Med. Ctr. Sch. of Med. Techno.)*

Eisenhower VA Med. Ctr. *(see Dwight D. Eisenhower Veterans Affairs Med. Ctr.)*

Eisenhower Veterans Affairs Med. Ctr. *(see Dwight D. Eisenhower Veterans Affairs Med. Ctr.)*

El Camino Coll. 40

El Camino Comm. Coll. *(see El Camino Coll.)*

El Centro Coll. 377

El Paso Coll. *(see El Paso County Comm. Coll. Dist.)*

El Paso Comm. Coll. *(see El Paso County Comm. Coll. Dist., Pikes Peak Comm. Coll.)*

El Paso County Comm. Coll. Dist. 377

El Paso Jr. Coll. *(see Univ. of Texas at El Paso)*

Elaine Kersten Children's Ctr. *(see Jewish Children's Bureau of Chicago)*

Elaine P. Nunez Comm. Coll. 167

Elaine Steven Beauty Coll., Inc. 538

Elchanan Theological Seminary *(see Rabbi Isaac Elchanan Theological Seminary)*

Electrical Techno. Sch. *(see Escuela Tecnica de Electricidad, Inc.)*

Electrology Inst. of New England 525

Electronic Ctr. of Languages & Computation *(see Centro Electronico de Idiomas y Computacion)*

Electronic Computer Programming Coll. 365

Electronic Data Processing Coll. 347, 749
Electronic Inst. of Arizona *(see High-Tech Inst—Phoenix)*
Electronic Inst. of Techno., The *(see Tidewater Tech)*
Electronic Institutes 735 *(see also Harrisburg Inst. of Trade & Techno.)*
Electronic Techno. Inst. *(see Paducah Tech. Coll.)*
Electronics Inst. 732 *(see also Pinnacle Career Inst., Lexington Electronics Inst.)*
Electronics Inst. of Lexington *(see Lexington Electronics Inst.)*
Electronics Sch. of Connecticut *(see Connecticut Sch. of Electronics)*
Elegance Int'l. 457
Elegante Beauty Coll—Burbank *(see Marinello Sch. of Beauty—Burbank)*
Elegante Beauty Coll—City of Industry 722 *(see also Marinello Sch. of Beauty—City of Industry)*
Elegante Beauty Coll—Lake Forest 722 *(see also Marinello Sch. of Beauty—Lake Forest)*
Elegante Beauty Coll—Moreno 722 *(see also Marinello Sch. of Beauty—Moreno Valley)*
Elgin Coll. *(see Elgin Comm. Coll.)*
Elgin Comm. Coll. 121
Eli Whitney Reg. Vocational-Tech. Sch. 659
Eli Whitney Tech. High Sch. *(see Eli Whitney Reg. Vocational-Tech. Sch.)*
Elite Beauty Inst. of Midland 736
Elite Coll. of Cosmetology 759
Elite Progressive Sch. of Cosmetology 457
Elizabeth City Normal Sch. *(see Elizabeth City State Univ.)*
Elizabeth City State Coll. *(see Elizabeth City State Univ.)*
Elizabeth City State Teachers Coll. *(see Elizabeth City State Univ.)*
Elizabeth City State Univ. 287
Elizabeth Grady Sch. of Esthetics, The 525
Elizabeth M. Boggs Ctr. on Developmental Disabilities *(see Robert Wood Johnson Med. Sch., Univ. of Medicine & Dentistry of New Jersey)*
Elizabethtown Beauty Sch. 512
Elizabethtown Coll. 330 *(see also Elizabethtown Comm. & Tech. Coll.)*

Elizabethtown Comm. & Tech. Coll. 160, 728
Elizabethtown Comm. Coll. 728 *(see also Elizabethtown Comm. & Tech. Coll.)*
Elizabethtown Tech. Coll. 728
Elkhart Inst. *(see Goshen Coll.)*
Elkins Coll. *(see Davis & Elkins Coll.)*
Elko Comm. Coll. *(see Great Basin Coll.)*
Elley Bus. Sch. *(see Mildred Elley)*
Elliot Hosp. 682
Ellis Coll. of New York Inst. of Techno. *(see New York Inst. of Tech—Old Westbury)*
Ellsworth Coll. *(see Ellsworth Comm. Coll.)*
Ellsworth Comm. Coll. 146
Elmhurst Acad. & Jr. Coll. *(see Elmhurst Coll.)*
Elmhurst Coll. 121
Elmhurst Mem. Hosp. 667
Elmira Bus. & Shorthand Coll. *(see Elmira Bus. Inst.)*
Elmira Bus. Inst. 262
Elmira Coll. 262
Elms Coll. *(see Coll. of Our Lady of the Elms)*
Elon Univ. 287
ELS Language Centers 548
Ely State Jr. Coll. *(see Vermilion Comm. Coll.)*
Embassy CES 482
Embry-Riddle Aeronautical Univ. 84
Emergency Training Services, Inc. 457
Emerson Coll. 187
Emery Aviation Coll. *(see Emery Aviation Coll.)*
Emery Aviation Coll. 68
Emes Investment Corporation *(see Career Colleges of America)*
Emil Fries Piano & Training 738 *(see also Emil Fries Sch. of Piano Tuning & Techno.)*
Emil Fries Piano & Training Ctr. *(see Emil Fries Sch. of Piano Tuning & Techno.)*
Emil Fries Sch. of Piano Tuning & Techno. 637, 738
Emily Griffith Opportunity Sch. 472
Emmanuel Bible Coll. 69, 432
Emmanuel Coll. 102, 187 *(see also Emmanuel Bible Coll.)*
Emmanuel Coll. of Victoria Univ. 432
Emmanuel Missionary Coll. *(see Andrews Univ.)*
Emmanuel Sch. of Religion 366
Emma's Beauty Acad—Juana Diaz 603
Emma's Beauty Acad—Mayaguez 603

Emmaus Bible Coll. 146, 745
Emmaus Coll. *(see Emmaus Bible Coll.)*
Emmett Comm. Coll. *(see North Central Michigan Coll.)*
Emory & Henry Coll. 402
Emory Coll. *(see Emory Univ.)*
Emory Univ. 102
Emperor's Coll. *(see Emperor's Coll. of Traditional Oriental Medicine)*
Emperor's Coll. of Traditional Oriental Medicine 40
Empire Beauty Sch. #3 544
Empire Beauty Sch. 493
Empire Beauty Sch., Inc—Hanover 595
Empire Beauty Sch—Bordentown 550
Empire Beauty Sch—Ctr. City Philadelphia 595
Empire Beauty Sch—Cherry Hill 550
Empire Beauty Sch—Dunwoody 493
Empire Beauty Sch—Exton 596
Empire Beauty Sch—Hanover Park 500, 727
Empire Beauty Sch—Harrisburg 596
Empire Beauty Sch—Laconia 544
Empire Beauty Sch—Lancaster 596
Empire Beauty Sch—Laurel Springs 550
Empire Beauty Sch—Lawrenceville, GA 493
Empire Beauty Sch—Lebanon 596
Empire Beauty Sch—Matthew 572
Empire Beauty Sch—Moosic 596
Empire Beauty Sch—Northeast Philadelphia 596
Empire Beauty Sch—Pottstown 596
Empire Beauty Sch—Pottsville 596
Empire Beauty Sch—Reading 596
Empire Beauty Sch—Shamokin Dam 596
Empire Beauty Sch—State Coll. 596
Empire Beauty Sch—Warminster 596
Empire Beauty Sch—Whitehall 596
Empire Beauty Sch—Williamsport 597
Empire Beauty Sch—York 597
Empire Coll. 40
Empire State Coll. *(see State Univ. of New York Empire State Coll.)*
Empire-Lackawanna Beauty Sch. 493
Employment Solutions-Ctr. for Training & Employment 755
Employment Training Ctr. of Cleveland *(see Ctr. for Employment Training)*
Emporia Kansas State Coll. *(see Emporia State Univ.)*
Emporia State Univ. 153
Emporia Univ. *(see Emporia State Univ.)*
Endicott Coll. 187

Engine City Tech. Inst. 550
Engineering Sch. of Milwaukee *(see Milwaukee Sch. of Engineering)*
Englewood Hosp. & Med. Ctr. 683
English Ctr. for Int'l. Women 457
English Ctr., The 481
English for Internationals 493
English House 522
English Language Ctr. *(see Ctr. of English Language)*
English Language Inst. 457
English Language Specialists 619
Enid Beauty Coll., Inc. 587
Enterprise Comm. Coll. *(see Enterprise-Ozark Comm. Coll.)*
Enterprise State Jr. Coll. *(see Enterprise-Ozark Comm. Coll.)*
Enterprise State Jr. Coll. 721
Enterprise Technological Inst. *(see Instituto Tecnologico Empresarial)*
Enterprise-Ozark Comm. Coll. 5, 721
Environmental Science & Forestry Coll. *(see State Univ. of New York Coll. of Environmental Science & Forestry)*
Environmental Tech. Inst. 500
EnVisionary I-Care 757
Episcopal Divinity Sch. 187
Episcopal Health Services Inc. *(see Saint John's Episcopal Hosp. South Shore)*
Episcopal Seminary of the Southwest *(see Episcopal Theological Seminary of the Southwest)*
Episcopal Seminary of the West, The *(see Church Divinity Sch. of the Pacific)*
Episcopal Theological Sch. *(see Episcopal Divinity Sch.)*
Episcopal Theological Seminary of the Southwest, The 377
EQ Sch. of Hair Design 507
Erasmus Universiteit Rotterdam *(see Erasmus Univ. Rotterdam)*
Erasmus Univ. Rotterdam 716
Erie Bus. Ctr. 330
Erie Coll. of Osteopathic Medicine *(see Lake Erie Coll. of Osteopathic Medicine)*
Erie Comm. Coll. City Campus 263
Erie County Med. Ctr. 686
Erie County Tech. Inst. *(see Erie Comm. Coll. City Campus)*
Erie Inst. of Techno. 330
Erie, Huron, Ottawa Vocational Edu. Career Ctr. *(see EHOVE Career Ctr.)*
Erikson Inst. 121
Erskine Coll. 356
Erskine Theological Seminary *(see Erskine Coll.)*

Erwin Tech. Ctr. *(see David G. Erwin Tech. Ctr.)*
Escuela de Artes Plasticas de Puerto Rico 348
Escuela de Hoteleria y Artes Servicios de Hospitalidad *(see Monteclaro: Escuela de Hoteleria y Artes Servicios de Hospitalidad)*
Escuela de Peritos Electricistas de Isabel 603
Escuela Superior de Administracion y Direccion de Empresas 716
Escuela Tecnica de Electricidad, Inc. 603
Escuelas Leicester *(see Leicester Sch.)*
ESL Instruction & Consulting, Inc. 493
Esser Beauty Sch. *(see Sally Esser Beauty Sch.)*
Essex Agricultural & Tech. Inst. 191 *(see also North Shore Comm. Coll.)*
Essex Agricultural & Tech. Institution *(see North Shore Comm. Coll.)*
Essex Ctr. for Techno. *(see Ctr. for Techno., Essex)*
Essex Comm. Coll. *(see Comm. Coll. of Baltimore County)*
Essex County Coll. 246
Estes Inst. of Cosmetology Arts & Sciences 457
Estes Vocational Ctr. *(see Metro Techno. Ctr—South Bryant)*
Esthetics & Cosmetology Acad. *(see Acad. of Esthetics & Cosmetology)*
Esthetics Inst. at Concord Acad. 544, 732
Estrella Mountain Coll. *(see Estrella Mountain Comm. Coll.)*
Estrella Mountain Comm. Coll. 16
ETI Career Inst. 493, 726
ETI Med. Sch. *(see ETI Career Inst.)*
ETI Tech. Coll. *(see Brown Mackie Coll—Cincinnati, Bryant & Stratton Coll—Cleveland Downtown Campus, ETI Tech. Coll. of Niles, ETI Tech. Coll—North Canton)*
ETI Tech. Coll. of Niles 303
ETI Tech. Coll—North Canton 734
ETI Training Ctr. *(see ETI Tech. Coll. of Niles)*
Eton Bus. Coll. *(see Bryman Coll.)*
Eton Tech. Inst. 738 *(see also Bryman Coll.)*
Eton Tech. Inst—Everett 738
Eton Tech. Inst—Federal Way 738
Eton Tech. Inst—Tacoma 738

Eubank & Associates, Inc. *(see Charles D. Eubank & Associates, Inc.)*
Euclid Beauty Coll. 579
Euclid Hosp. 693
Eugene Bible Coll. 320
Eugene Divinity Sch. *(see Northwest Christian Coll.)*
Eugene Lang Coll. *(see New Sch.)*
Eugene Lang Coll. The New Sch. for Liberal Arts *(see New Sch.)*
Eugenio Maria De Hostos Comm. Coll. *(see City Univ. of New York Hostos Comm. Coll.)*
Euphoria Inst. of Beauty Arts & Sciences 543
Eureka Coll. 121
European Acad. of Cosmetology, Inc. 550
European Ctr. of Int'l. Hotel Management *(see Centre Europeén de Management Hôtelier Int'l.)*
European Healing Massage Therapy Sch. 500
European Inst. for Int'l. Communication 187
European Massage Therapy Sch. *(see European Healing Massage Therapy Sch.)*
European Nazarene Bible Coll. *(see European Nazarene Coll.)*
Evangel Coll. *(see Evangel Univ.)*
Evangel Univ. 225
Evangelical Christian Coll. *(see Messenger Coll.)*
Evangelical Free Church Bible Inst. & Seminary *(see Trinity Int'l. Univ.)*
Evangelical Lutheran Theological Seminary *(see Trinity Lutheran Seminary)*
Evangelical Sch. of Theology 330
Evangelical Seminary of Puerto Rico 348
Evangelical Theological Coll. *(see Dallas Theological Seminary)*
Evangelical Theological Seminary *(see Garrett-Evangelical Theological Seminary)*
Evan's Hairstyling Coll—Cedar City 627
Evan's Hairstyling Coll—Orem 627
Evan's Hairstyling Coll—St. George 627
Evanston Collegiate Inst. *(see Kendall Coll.)*
Evanston Northwestern Healthcare 668
Evanston-Glenbrook Hosp. 667 *(see also Evanston Northwestern Healthcare)*

Evansville Coll. *(see Univ. of Evansville)*
Evansville Tri-State Beauty Coll. 505
Evansville Univ. *(see Univ. of Evansville)*
Eveleth Jr. Coll. *(see Mesabi Range Comm. & Tech. Coll.)*
Everest Coll. 16
Everest Coll—Arlington 272 *(see also Rochester Bus. Inst.)*
Everest Coll—Dallas 324
Everest Coll—Ft. Worth 394 *(see also Mountain West Coll.)*
Everest Coll—Rancho Cucamonga *(see Springfield Coll.)*
Everest Inst. 522
Everett Beauty Acad. 738 *(see also Milan Inst. of Cosmetology)*
Everett Coll. *(see Everett Comm. Coll.)*
Everett Comm. Coll. 411
Everglades Coll. 725 *(see also Everglades Univ.)*
Everglades Univ. 84, 725
Evergreen Barber Coll. *(see Evergreen Beauty & Barber Coll.)*
Evergreen Beauty & Barber Coll. 637
Evergreen Health Care 707
Evergreen State Coll. 412 *(see also Evergreen State Coll.)*
Evergreen Valley Coll. 40
Evers Coll. *(see City Univ. of New York Medgar Evers Coll.)*
Eve's Coll. of Hairstyling 587
Excelsior Coll. 263
Executive 2000, Inc. *(see Stanbridge Coll.)*
Executive Travel Inst. 726 *(see also ETI Career Inst.)*
Expertise Sch. of Beauty 543
Exposito Sch. of Hair Design 619
Expression Coll. for Digital Arts 40
Expression Digital Arts Coll. *(see Expression Coll. for Digital Arts)*
Extended Home Health Edu. 737 *(see also Concorde Career Inst—Arlington)*
Ezell's Cosmetology Sch. 512
Ezp's Coll. of Barbering 759

F

FAA Ctr. for Management Development 482
FAA Management Development Ctr. *(see FAA Ctr. for Management Development)*
Fairfax Comm. Coll. *(see Lord Fairfax Comm. Coll.)*
Fairfield Career Ctr. 579
Fairfield Coll. *(see Fairfield Univ.)*
Fairfield Univ. 72

Fairleigh Dickinson Coll. *(see Fairleigh Dickinson Univ.)*
Fairleigh Dickinson Univ. 246
Fairmont Acad. of Design & Techno. *(see Int'l. Acad. of Design & Tech—Fairmont)*
Fairmont Coll. *(see Fairmont State Univ.)*
Fairmont State Coll. 738 *(see also Fairmont State Univ.)*
Fairmont State Comm. & Tech. Coll. 419
Fairmont State Normal Sch. *(see Fairmont State Univ.)*
Fairmont State Teachers Coll. *(see Fairmont State Univ.)*
Fairmont State Univ. 419, 738
Fairmount Coll. *(see Wichita State Univ.)*
Fairview Acad. 579
Fairview Clinical Pastoral Edu. Ctr. *(see Fairview-Univ. Med. Ctr.)*
Fairview Health Services *(see Fairview-Univ. Med. Ctr.)*
Fairview-Univ. Med. Ctr. 679
Faith Acad. of Beauty Edu. *(see Ray's Faith Acad. of Beauty Edu.)*
Faith Baptist Bible Coll. 146
Faith Baptist Bible Coll. & Seminary *(see Faith Baptist Bible Coll.)*
Faith Baptist Coll. *(see Faith Baptist Bible Coll.)*
Faith Bible Coll. *(see Faith Baptist Bible Coll.)*
Faith Coll. *(see Family of Faith Coll.)*
Faith Evangelical Lutheran Seminary 412
Faith Evangelical Seminary *(see Faith Evangelical Lutheran Seminary)*
Falmouth National Grad. Management Grad. Sch. *(see National Grad. Sch.)*
Family Inst. of Denver *(see Denver Family Inst.)*
Family of Faith Coll. 748
Family Service & Guidance Ctr. of Topeka, Inc. 672
Family Service of Milwaukee *(see Aurora Family Service)*
Family Service of Topeka *(see Family Service & Guidance Ctr. of Topeka, Inc.)*
Family Therapy Training Ctr. of Colorado, Inc. *(see Denver Family Inst.)*
Family Therapy Training Inst. *(see Aurora Family Service)*
Family Therapy/Play Therapy Inst. 658
Fanny Allen Mem. Sch. of Practical Nursing *(see Vermont Tech. Coll.)*

Fanny Jackson Coppin Normal Sch. *(see Coppin State Univ.)*
Faris Computer Sch. 619
Farmingdale Coll. of Techno. *(see State Univ. of New York Coll. of Techno. at Farmingdale)*
Farmingdale State Univ. of New York *(see State Univ. of New York Coll. of Techno. at Farmingdale)*
Farmington Normal Sch. *(see Univ. of Maine at Farmington)*
Farrell Beauty Sch. *(see Virginia Farrell Beauty Sch.)*
Fashion Careers Coll. 40, 722
Fashion Careers of California Coll. 722 *(see also Fashion Careers Coll.)*
Fashion Design & Merchandising Inst. *(see Fashion Inst. of Design & Merchandising)*
Fashion Focus Hair Acad. 482
Fashion Inst. of Design & Merchandising, The 40
Fashion Inst. of Techno. 263
Faulkner State Comm. Coll. *(see James H. Faulkner State Comm. Coll.)*
Faulkner State Jr. Coll. *(see James H. Faulkner State Comm. Coll.)*
Faulkner Univ. 5
Faust Inst. of Cosmetology, The 507
Faxton Hosp. *(see Faxton-St. Luke's Healthcare)*
Faxton-Saint Luke's Healthcare 686
Fayette Beauty Acad. 493
Fayette County Area Vocational Tech. Sch. 697
Fayette County Vo-Tech Sch. *(see Fayette County Area Vocational Tech. Sch.)*
Fayette Plateau Vocational Techno. Ctr. 640
Fayette Plateau Vo-Tech Ctr. *(see Fayette Plateau Vocational Techno. Ctr.)*
Fayetteville Beauty Coll. 448, 572
Fayetteville Beauty Sch. 611
Fayetteville Coll. *(see Fayetteville Tech. Comm. Coll.)*
Fayetteville Comm. Coll. *(see Fayetteville Tech. Comm. Coll.)*
Fayetteville State Coll. *(see Fayetteville State Univ.)*
Fayetteville State Teachers Coll. *(see Fayetteville State Univ.)*
Fayetteville State Univ. 287
Fayetteville Tech. Coll. *(see Fayetteville Tech. Comm. Coll.)*
Fayetteville Tech. Comm. Coll. 287
Feather River Coll. 40

Federal Aviation Administration Ctr. for Management Development *(see FAA Ctr. for Management Development)*

Federal Aviation Administration Management Development Ctr. *(see FAA Ctr. for Management Development)*

Federal Bureau of Prisons *(see Metropolitan Detention Ctr.)*

Federal City Coll. *(see Univ. of the Dist. of Columbia)*

Federal Correctional Institution—Tallahassee 482

Federal Med. Ctr—Lexington 512, 672

Federico Beauty Inst. 457, 722

Federico Coll. of Hairstyling 722 *(see also Federico Beauty Inst.)*

FEGS Trades & Bus. Sch. 561

Feinberg Sch. of Medicine *(see Northwestern Univ.)*

Felician Coll. 246

Fell's Sch. of Bus. *(see Cheryl Fell's Sch. of Bus.)*

Female Beneficent Society of Hartford *(see Village for Families & Children, Inc.)*

Fenger Coll. *(see City Colleges of Chicago—Olive-Harvey Coll.)*

Fergus Falls Comm. Coll. 731 *(see also Minnesota State Comm. & Tech. Coll.)*

Ferris Industrial Sch. *(see Ferris State Univ.)*

Ferris Inst. *(see Ferris State Univ.)*

Ferris State Coll. *(see Ferris State Univ.)*

Ferris State Univ. 198

Ferrum Coll. 402

Fielding Grad. Inst. 723 *(see also Fielding Grad. Univ.)*

Fielding Grad. Univ. 40, 723

Fielding Inst. *(see Fielding Grad. Univ.)*

Fielding Univ. *(see Fielding Grad. Univ.)*

Fila Acad., The 756

Fillmmakers' Sch. of Pittsburgh *(see Pittsburgh Fillmmakers' Sch. of Film, Video & Photography)*

Film & Television Sch. *(see Sch. for Film & Television at Three of Us Studio)*

Film Inst. of America *(see American Film Inst.)*

Final Touch Beauty Sch., The 535

Finance Coll. of New England *(see New England Coll. of Finance)*

Financial Planning Coll. *(see Coll. for Financial Planning)*

Finch Univ. *(see Rosalind Franklin Univ. of Medicine & Science)*

Finch Univ. Coll. of Podiatric Medicine *(see Dr. William M. Scholl Coll. of Podiatric Medicine)*

Finch Univ. of Health Sciences/The Chicago Med. Sch. *(see Rosalind Franklin Univ. of Medicine & Science)*

Findlay Coll. *(see Univ. of Findlay, Winebrenner Theological Seminary)*

Findlay Coll. Seminary *(see Winebrenner Theological Seminary)*

Findlay Univ. *(see Univ. of Findlay)*

FINE Mortuary Coll. 187

Finger Lakes Coll. *(see Finger Lakes Comm. Coll.)*

Finger Lakes Comm. Coll. 263

Finger Lakes Reg. Care System *(see Marion S. Whelan Sch. of Practical Nursing)*

Finlandia Univ. 198

Firelands Coll. 299 *(see also Bowling Green State Univ.)*

Firelands Reg. Med. Ctr. 693

First Beauty Coll. 753

First Class Cosmetology Sch. 761

First Coast Inst. *(see First Coast Tech. Inst.)*

First Coast Tech. Inst. 482

First Dist. Normal Sch. *(see Truman State Univ.)*

First Inst. of Podiatry *(see New York Coll. of Podiatric Medicine)*

First Inst., Inc. 500

First National Television Sch. *(see DeVry Univ. Kansas City)*

Fisher Coll. 187 *(see also Saint John Fisher Coll.)*

Fisk Univ. 366

Fitchburg Coll. *(see Fitchburg State Coll.)*

Fitchburg State Coll. 187

Five Branches Inst. Coll. of Traditional Chinese Medicine 40

Five Colleges (consortium) *(see Amherst Coll.)*

Five Element Acupuncture Acad. *(see Acad. for Five Element Acupuncture)*

Five Towns Coll. 263

Flagler Career Inst. 662

Flagler Coll. 84

Flat River Jr. Coll. *(see Mineral Area Coll.)*

Flathead Valley Comm. Coll. 234

Flathead Valley Comm. Coll. Reservation Extension Ctr. *(see Salish Kootenai Coll.)*

Flatwoods Civilian Conservation Ctr. 632

Fleet Bus. Sch. 724

Fletcher Allen Health Care 705

Fletcher Hills Bible Coll. *(see Southern California Seminary)*

Flight Safety Acad. *(see FlightSafety Acad.)*

FlightSafety Acad. 482

Flint Coll. *(see Univ. of Michigan—Flint)*

Flint Hills Coll. *(see Flint Hills Tech. Coll.)*

Flint Hills Tech. Coll. 153

Flint Hills Tech. Sch. *(see Flint Hills Tech. Coll.)*

Flint Inst. of Barbering 529

Flint Jr. Coll. *(see Charles Stewart Mott Comm. Coll.)*

Flint River Coll. *(see Flint River Tech. Coll.)*

Flint River Tech. Coll. 102, 726

Flint River Tech. Inst. 726 *(see also Flint River Tech. Coll.)*

Flora MacDonald Coll. *(see Saint Andrews Presbyterian Coll.)*

Florence State Coll. *(see Univ. of North Alabama)*

Florence State Teachers Coll. *(see Univ. of North Alabama)*

Florence State Univ. *(see Univ. of North Alabama)*

Florence Wesleyan Univ. *(see Univ. of North Alabama)*

Florence-Darlington Tech. Coll. 356

Florence-Darlington Tech. Edu. Ctr. *(see Florence-Darlington Tech. Coll.)*

Florida A&M Univ. *(see Florida Agricultural & Mechanical Univ.)*

Florida Acad. of Health & Beauty 482

Florida Agricultural & Mechanical Univ. 84

Florida Agricultural Coll. *(see Univ. of Florida)*

Florida Animal Arts Inst. *(see Florida Inst. of Animal Arts)*

Florida Atlantic Univ. 84

Florida Baptist Acad. *(see Florida Mem. Univ.)*

Florida Baptist Coll. *(see Baptist Coll. of Florida)*

Florida Baptist Inst. *(see Florida Mem. Univ.)*

Florida Baptist Theological Coll. *(see Baptist Coll. of Florida)*

Florida Barber Acad. 482

Florida Beacon Bible Coll. *(see Beacon Univ.)*

Florida Bible Inst. *(see Trinity Coll. of Florida)*

Florida Career Coll. 84, 725
Florida Career Inst. 482
Florida Ctr. for Theological Studies 744
Florida Christian Coll. 84
Florida Coastal Sch. of Law 85
Florida Coll. 85 *(see also Florida Coll. of Integrative Medicine, Florida Coll. of Natural Health)*
Florida Coll. of Integrative Medicine 662
Florida Coll. of Natural Health 85
Florida Comm. Coll. at Jacksonville 85
Florida Computer & Bus. Sch. 725 *(see also Florida Career Coll.)*
Florida Culinary Inst. *(see New England Inst. of Techno. at Palm Beach)*
Florida Edu. Inst. 482
Florida Gulf Coast Univ. 85
Florida Hosp. Coll. of Health Sciences 85
Florida Inst. in Tallahassee *(see Florida State Univ.)*
Florida Inst. of Animal Arts, The 482
Florida Inst. of Massage Therapy & Esthetics *(see Florida Coll. of Natural Health)*
Florida Inst. of Montessori Studies _ 483
Florida Inst. of Techno. 85
Florida Inst. of Traditional Chinese Medicine 725
Florida Inst. of Ultrasound, Inc. 483
Florida Int'l. Inst. *(see Florida National Coll.)*
Florida Int'l. Univ. 85
Florida Keys Comm. Coll. 86
Florida Language Ctr. 725
Florida Med. Training Inst. 483
Florida Mem. Coll. 725 *(see also Florida Mem. Univ.)*
Florida Mem. Univ. 86, 725
Florida Metropolitan Univ—Orange Park 86
Florida Metropolitan Univ—Orlando North 86
Florida Metropolitan Univ—Pinellas 86
Florida Metropolitan Univ—Pompano Beach 86
Florida Metropolitan Univ—Tampa 86
Florida Military & Collegiate Inst., The *(see Florida State Univ.)*
Florida National Coll. 86
Florida Normal & Industrial Mem. Coll. *(see Florida Mem. Univ.)*
Florida Programming & Educational Ctr., Inc. *(see Florida Career Coll.)*

Florida Sch. of Beauty & Barbering *(see Trendsetters Florida Sch. of Beauty & Barbering)*
Florida Sch. of Massage 483
Florida Sch. of Prof. Psychology *(see Argosy Univ. Tampa)*
Florida Sch. of Traditional Midwifery 483
Florida Southern Coll. 87
Florida State Coll. *(see Florida State Univ.)*
Florida State Coll. for Women *(see Florida State Univ.)*
Florida State Hosp. 662 *(see also Lively Area Vocational-Tech. Ctr.)*
Florida State Univ. 87
Florida Talmudic Coll. *(see Talmudic Coll. of Florida)*
Florida Tech *(see Univ. of Central Florida, Florida Tech. Coll.)*
Florida Tech. Coll. 87
Florida Technological Univ. *(see Univ. of Central Florida)*
Florida Ultrasound Inst. *(see Florida Inst. of Ultrasound, Inc.)*
Florida Univ. *(see Univ. of Florida)*
Florissant Valley Coll. *(see Saint Louis Comm. Coll. at Florissant Valley)*
Floyd Coll. 726 *(see also Georgia Highlands Coll.)*
Floyd County Coll. *(see Georgia Highlands Coll.)*
Floyd Jr. Coll. *(see Georgia Highlands Coll.)*
FLS Int'l. 458
FLS Language Centers, Inc. *(see FLS Int'l.)*
Flushing Hosp. Med. Ctr. 686
FMC Lexington *(see Federal Med. Ctr—Lexington)*
FMU—Brandon *(see Florida Metropolitan Univ—Brandon)*
FMU—Fort Lauderdale *(see Florida Metropolitan Univ—Pompano Beach)*
FMU—Lakeland *(see Florida Metropolitan Univ—Lakeland)*
FMU—Orange Park *(see Florida Metropolitan Univ—Orange Park)*
FMU—Orlando North *(see Florida Metropolitan Univ—Orlando North)*
FMU—Orlando South *(see Florida Metropolitan Univ—Orlando South)*
FMU—Pinellas *(see Florida Metropolitan Univ—Pinellas)*
FMU—Tampa *(see Florida Metropolitan Univ—Tampa)*
Focus: Hope Information Technologies Ctr. 529

Focus: Hope Machinist Training Inst. 529
Folkner Training Associates, Inc. 483
Folsom Lake Coll. 41
Fond du Lac Coll. *(see Fond du Lac Tribal & Comm. Coll.)*
Fond du Lac Tribal & Comm. Coll. 209
Fontbonne Coll. *(see Fontbonne Univ.)*
Fontbonne Univ. 225
Fontecha Inst. 483
Foothill Coll. 41
Ford Comm. Coll. *(see Henry Ford Comm. Coll.)*
Fordham Univ. 263
ForeFront Edu. Inc. *(see Illinois Sch. of Health Careers)*
Foreign Language Ctr. *(see Defense Language Inst. Foreign Language Ctr.)*
Forest Inst. of Prof. Psychology 225
Forest Inst. of Psychology *(see Forest Inst. of Prof. Psychology)*
Forest Park Coll. *(see Saint Louis Comm. Coll. at Forest Park)*
Forest Park Hosp. 681
Forrest Coll. *(see Forrest Jr. Coll.)*
Forrest Jr. Coll. 356
Forsyth Sch. for Dental Hygienists *(see Massachusetts Coll. of Pharmacy & Health Sciences)*
Forsyth Tech. Coll. *(see Forsyth Tech. Comm. Coll.)*
Forsyth Tech. Comm. Coll. 287
Forsyth Tech. Inst. *(see Forsyth Tech. Comm. Coll.)*
Fort Belknap Coll. 234
Fort Berthold Coll. *(see Fort Berthold Comm. Coll.)*
Fort Berthold Comm. Coll. 296
Fort Hays Kansas State Coll. *(see Fort Hays State Univ.)*
Fort Hays Kansas State Normal Sch. *(see Fort Hays State Univ.)*
Fort Hays State Univ. 153
Fort Kent State Coll. *(see Univ. of Maine at Fort Kent)*
Fort Kent State Teacher's Coll. *(see Univ. of Maine at Fort Kent)*
Fort Lauderdale Art Inst. *(see Art Inst. of Fort Lauderdale)*
Fort Lauderdale City Coll. *(see City Coll.)*
Fort Lauderdale Coll. *(see Florida Metropolitan Univ—Pompano Beach)*
Fort Lauderdale Inst. of Art *(see Art Inst. of Fort Lauderdale)*
Fort Lewis A&M Coll. *(see Fort Lewis Coll.)*
Fort Lewis Agricultural & Mechanical Coll. *(see Fort Lewis Coll.)*

Fort Lewis Coll. 67
Fort Peck Coll. *(see Fort Peck Comm. Coll.)*
Fort Peck Comm. Coll. 234
Fort Pierce Beauty Acad. 483
Fort Sanders Sch. of Nursing 702
Fort Scott Coll. *(see Fort Scott Comm. Coll.)*
Fort Scott Comm. Coll. 153
Fort Smith Jr. Coll. *(see Univ. of Arkansas at Fort Smith)*
Fort Steilacoom Comm. Coll. *(see Pierce Coll. Puyallup)*
Fort Valley High & Industrial Sch. *(see Fort Valley State Univ.)*
Fort Valley State Coll. *(see Fort Valley State Univ.)*
Fort Valley State Univ. 103
Fort Wayne Bible Coll. *(see Taylor Univ.)*
Fort Wayne Child Guidance Clinic *(see Park Ctr., Inc.)*
Fort Wayne Coll. of Medicine *(see Taylor Univ.)*
Fort Wayne Commercial Coll. *(see Brown Mackie Coll—Fort Wayne)*
Fort Wayne Female Coll. *(see Taylor Univ.)*
Fort Wayne Sch. of Radiography 669
Fort Worth Beauty Sch. 619
Fort Worth Hosp. *(see Harris Methodist Fort Worth Hosp.)*
Fort Wright Coll. *(see Heritage Univ.)*
Foster Estes Vocational Ctr. *(see Metro Techno. Ctr—South Bryant)*
Foster's Cosmetology Coll. 535
Foundation Coll. 723
Foundation Coll. San Diego 41
Foundation Opens *(see Fundación ABRE)*
Fountainhead Coll. of Techno. 366, 737
Four County Career Ctr. 579
Four Seasons Salon & Day Spa 643
Four-D Coll. 458, 723
Four-D Success Acad. 723 *(see also Four-D Coll.)*
Fox Coll. 121
Fox Inst. of Bus. 475
Fox Secretarial Coll. *(see Fox Coll.)*
Fox Univ. *(see George Fox Univ.)*
Fox Valley Tech. Coll. 424
Fox Valley Tech. Inst. *(see Fox Valley Tech. Coll.)*
Framingham Coll. *(see Framingham State Coll.)*
Framingham State Coll. 187
Fran Brown Coll. of Beauty 627
Francis Marion Univ. 356

Francis T. Nicholls Jr. Coll. of Louisiana State Univ. *(see Nicholls State Univ.)*
Francis T. Nicholls State Coll. *(see Nicholls State Univ.)*
Francis Tuttle Vocational-Tech. Ctr. 695
Francis Tuttle Vo-Tech Ctr. *(see Francis Tuttle Vocational-Tech. Ctr.)*
Franciscan Sch. of Theology 41
Franciscan Univ. 728
Franciscan Univ. of Steubenville 303
Franciscan Univ. of the Prairies, The 728
Franciscan Univ., The *728 (see also Ashford Univ.)*
Francoeur & Associates *(see M.J. Francoeur & Associates)*
Francois D. Hair Design Acad. 628
Frank Lloyd Wright Sch. of Architecture 16
Frank Phillips Coll. 378
Frank Wiggins Trade Sch. *(see Los Angeles Trade-Tech. Coll.)*
Franklin Acad. *(see Louisburg Coll.)*
Franklin Acad. 611, 736
Franklin & Marshall Coll. 330
Franklin Beauty Sch. #2 619
Franklin Career Ctr. *(see Ben Franklin Career Ctr.)*
Franklin Career Inst. 561
Franklin Coll. 136 *(see also Franklin Coll., Franklin Coll. of Court Reporting, Franklin Coll. Switzerland, Franklin & Marshall Coll., Franklin Univ.)*
Franklin Coll. of Court Reporting 516
Franklin Coll. of Indiana *(see Franklin Coll.)*
Franklin Coll. Switzerland 437
Franklin County Area Vocational Tech. Sch. 697
Franklin County Vo-Tech Sch. *(see Franklin County Area Vocational Tech. Sch.)*
Franklin Court Reporting Coll. *(see Franklin Coll. of Court Reporting)*
Franklin Inst. of Boston 730 *(see also Benjamin Franklin Inst. of Techno.)*
Franklin Inst. of Techno. *(see Benjamin Franklin Inst. of Techno.)*
Franklin Montessori Sch. 573
Franklin Pierce Coll. 242
Franklin Pierce Law Ctr. 242
Franklin Union *(see Benjamin Franklin Inst. of Techno.)*
Franklin Univ. 303

Franklin Univ. of Medicine & Science *(see Rosalind Franklin Univ. of Medicine & Science)*
Franklin W. Olin Coll. of Engineering 746
Fraser Univ. *(see Simon Fraser Univ.)*
Frazier Vocational-Tech. Sch. *(see Louisiana Tech. Coll—Baton Rouge Campus)*
Fred W. Eberle Tech. Ctr. 640
Frederick Coll. *(see Frederick Comm. Coll.)*
Frederick Comm. Coll. 179
Frederick S. Pardee Rand Grad. Sch. *(see Pardee Rand Grad. Sch.)*
Fredonia Acad. *(see State Univ. of New York Coll. at Fredonia)*
Fredonia Coll. *(see State Univ. of New York Coll. at Fredonia)*
Fredonia Normal & Training Sch. *(see State Univ. of New York Coll. at Fredonia)*
Fredonia State Coll. *(see State Univ. of New York Coll. at Fredonia)*
Fredrick & Charles Beauty Coll. 458
Fredric's Inst. *(see Aveda Fredric's Inst.)*
Free Will Baptist Bible Coll. 366
Freed-Hardeman Univ. 366
Fremont-Newark Comm. Coll. Dist. 723
French Broad Baptist Acad. *(see Mars Hill Coll.)*
French Culinary Inst. 561
Fresno City Coll. 41
Fresno Coll. *(see Fresno City Coll.)*
Fresno Inst. of Techno. *(see Inst. of Techno.)*
Fresno Jr. Coll. *(see Fresno City Coll.)*
Fresno Pacific Coll. *(see Fresno Pacific Univ.)*
Fresno Pacific Univ. 41
Fresno State *(see California State Univ—Fresno)*
Fresno State Normal Sch. *(see California State Univ—Fresno)*
Friends Bible Coll. *(see Barclay Coll.)*
Friends Coll. *(see George Fox Univ.)*
Friends Pacific Acad. *(see George Fox Univ.)*
Friends Univ. 154
Fries Sch. of Piano Tuning & Techno. *(see Emil Fries Sch. of Piano Tuning & Techno.)*
Froedtert & Med. Coll. Health Services 709
Front Range Comm. Coll. 68
Frontier Coll. *(see Frontier Comm. Coll.)*
Frontier Comm. Coll. 121

Frontier Grad. Sch. of Midwifery *(see Frontier Sch. of Midwifery & Family Nursing)*

Frontier Midwifery Sch. *(see Frontier Sch. of Midwifery & Family Nursing)*

Frontier Sch. of Midwifery & Family Nursing 160

Frostburg State Coll. *(see Frostburg State Univ.)*

Frostburg State Teachers Coll. *(see Frostburg State Univ.)*

Frostburg State Univ. 179

Frostburg Univ. *(see Frostburg State Univ.)*

Ft. Belknap Coll. *(see Fort Belknap Coll.)*

Ft. Berthold Coll. *(see Fort Berthold Comm. Coll.)*

Ft. Berthold Comm. Coll. *(see Fort Berthold Comm. Coll.)*

Ft. Hays Kansas State Coll. *(see Fort Hays State Univ.)*

Ft. Hays Kansas State Normal Sch. *(see Fort Hays State Univ.)*

Ft. Hays State Univ. *(see Fort Hays State Univ.)*

Ft. Kent State Coll. *(see Univ. of Maine at Fort Kent)*

Ft. Kent State Teacher's Coll. *(see Univ. of Maine at Fort Kent)*

Ft. Lewis A&M Coll. *(see Fort Lewis Coll.)*

Ft. Lewis Agricultural & Mechanical Coll. *(see Fort Lewis Coll.)*

Ft. Lewis Coll. *(see Fort Lewis Coll.)*

Ft. Peck Coll. *(see Fort Peck Comm. Coll.)*

Ft. Peck Comm. Coll. *(see Fort Peck Comm. Coll.)*

Ft. Pierce Beauty Acad. *(see Fort Pierce Beauty Acad.)*

Ft. Sanders Sch. of Nursing *(see Fort Sanders Sch. of Nursing)*

Ft. Scott Coll. *(see Fort Scott Comm. Coll.)*

Ft. Scott Comm. Coll. *(see Fort Scott Comm. Coll.)*

Ft. Smith Jr. Coll. *(see Univ. of Arkansas at Fort Smith)*

Ft. Wayne Bible Coll. *(see Taylor Univ.)*

Ft. Wayne Child Guidance Clinic *(see Park Ctr., Inc.)*

Ft. Wayne Coll. *(see Taylor Univ.)*

Ft. Wayne Coll. of Medicine *(see Taylor Univ.)*

Ft. Wayne Commercial Coll. *(see Brown Mackie Coll—Fort Wayne)*

Ft. Wayne Female Coll. *(see Taylor Univ.)*

Ft. Wayne Sch. of Radiography *(see Fort Wayne Sch. of Radiography)*

Ft. Worth Hosp. *(see Harris Methodist Fort Worth Hosp.)*

Fugazzi Coll—Nashville 729

Fuld Coll. of Nursing 733 *(see also Helene Fuld Coll. of Nursing)*

Fuld Sch. of Nursing *(see Helene Fuld Coll. of Nursing)*

Full Gospel Bible Coll. 740, 752

Full Gospel Bible Inst. 740 *(see also Full Gospel Bible Coll.)*

Full Sail Real World Edu. 87

Fuller Circles Sch. for Therapeutic Massage 519

Fuller Circles Therapeutic Massage Sch. *(see Fuller Circles Sch. for Therapeutic Massage)*

Fuller Seminary *(see Fuller Theological Seminary)*

Fuller Theological Seminary 41

Fullerton Coll. 41

Fullerton Jr. Coll. *(see Fullerton Coll.)*

Fulton-Montgomery Coll. *(see Fulton-Montgomery Comm. Coll.)*

Fulton-Montgomery Comm. Coll. 263

Fundacion ABRE 57 *(see also Southern California Seminary)*

Fundacion Universidad de las Americas - Puebla *(see Universidad de las Americas—Puebla)*

Fundamental Bible Inst. *(see Arlington Baptist Coll.)*

Funeral Inst. of the North East *(see FINE Mortuary Coll.)*

Funeral Inst. of the Northeast 730 *(see FINE Mortuary Coll.)*

Funeral Services Inst. of Dallas *(see Dallas Inst. of Funeral Services)*

Furman Univ. 357

G

G. Mitchell Hartman & Associates, Inc. 550

Gadsden Bus. Coll. 441

Gadsden Coll. *(see Gadsden State Comm. Coll.)*

Gadsden Comm. Coll. *(see Gadsden State Comm. Coll.)*

Gadsden State Comm. Coll. 5, 721

Gadsden State Jr. Coll. *(see Gadsden State Comm. Coll.)*

Gadsden State Tech. Inst. *(see Gadsden State Comm. Coll.)*

Gadseden State Comm. Coll—Ayers Campus 721

Gainesville Coll. 103

Gainesville Family Inst. 662

Gainesville Jr. Coll. *(see North Central Texas Coll.)*

Gainesville VA Med. Ctr. *(see Malcom Randall Veterans Affairs Med. Ctr.)*

Gainesville Veterans Affairs Med. Ctr. *(see Malcom Randall Veterans Affairs Med. Ctr.)*

Gaither & Company Beauty Coll. 441

Gaither, Inc. *(see Gaither & Company Beauty Coll.)*

Gal Mar Acad. of Hairdressing 724 *(see also North Haven Acad.)*

Galen Coll. of Med. & Dental Assistants 458

Galen Coll. of Nursing, The 160, 728

Galen Health Institutes, Inc. *(see Galen Coll. of Nursing)*

Galen Nursing Coll. *(see Galen Coll. of Nursing)*

Galena City Schools *(see Galena City Schools Post Secondary Sch.)*

Galena City Schools Post Secondary Sch. 443

Galena Interior Learning Acad. *(see Galena City Schools Post Secondary Sch.)*

Galena Interior Learning Acad. Adult Programs *(see Galena City Schools Post Secondary Sch.)*

Galena Tech. Ctr. *(see Galena City Schools Post Secondary Sch.)*

Gallaudet Coll. *(see Gallaudet Univ.)*

Gallaudet Univ. 78

Gallegos & Associates, Inc. *(see Rick J. Gallegos & Associates, Inc.)*

Gallery Coll. of Beauty, The 529

Gallia-Jackson-Vinton Joint Career-Tech. Sch. Dist. *(see Buckeye Hills Career Ctr.)*

Gallipolis Career Coll. 303

Gallup Indian Med. Ctr. 685

Galveston Coll. 378

Gamla Coll. 733

Gammon Sch. of Theology *(see Interdenominational Theological Ctr.)*

Gammon Theological Seminary *(see Interdenominational Theological Ctr.)*

Gannon Coll. *(see Gannon Univ.)*

Gannon Univ. 331

Garden City Coll. *(see Garden City Comm. Coll.)*

Garden City Comm. Coll. 154

Garden City Comm. Jr. Coll. *(see Garden City Comm. Coll.)*

Garden City Jr. Coll. *(see Garden City Comm. Coll.)*

Gardner-Webb Coll. *(see Gardner-Webb Univ.)*

Gardner-Webb Univ. 287

Garland County Comm. Coll. 721 *(see also National Park Comm. Coll. at Hot Springs)*
Garnet Career Ctr. 640
Garnet Career Ctr. Sch. of Practical Nursing *(see Garnet Career Ctr.)*
Garrett Biblical Inst. *(see Garrett-Evangelical Theological Seminary)*
Garrett Coll. 179
Garrett Comm. Coll. *(see Garrett Coll.)*
Garrett-Evangelical Theological Seminary 121
Garvin Grad. Sch. of Int'l. Management, The *(see Thunderbird, The Garvin Grad. Sch. of Int'l. Management)*
Gaston Coll. 288
Gateway Coll. *(see Gateway Comm. Coll., Gateway Comm. & Tech. Coll., Gateway Tech. Coll.)*
Gateway Comm. & Tech. Coll. 160
Gateway Comm. Coll. 16, 73
Gateway Comm.-Tech. Coll. *(see Gateway Comm. Coll.)*
Gateway Tech. Coll. 424 *(see also Gateway Comm. & Tech. Coll., Univ. of Arkansas Comm. Coll. at Batesville)*
Gavilan Coll. 41
GBMC HealthCare *(see Greater Baltimore Med. Ctr.)*
GDS Inst. 753
GECAC Training Inst. 597
Gedolah of Greater Detroit *(see Yeshiva Beth Yehuda-Yeshiva Gedolah of Greater Detroit)*
Geisinger Med. Ctr. 697
Gem City Coll. 121
Gem Inst. of America *(see Gemological Inst. of America)*
Gemological Inst. of America 458
Gene Juarez Acad. of Beauty 637
General Beadle State Coll. *(see Dakota State Univ.)*
General Hosp. of Denver *(see Denver Health Med. Ctr.)*
General Hosp. of Nashville *(see Nashville General Hosp. at Meharry)*
General Theological Seminary, The 263
Genesee Coll. *(see Genesee Comm. Coll.)*
Genesee Comm. Coll. 263 *(see also Charles Stewart Mott Comm. Coll.)*
Genesee Hosp. 733
Geneseo Coll. *(see State Univ. of New York Coll. at Geneseo)*
Genesis Med. Ctr. 671
Geneva Coll. 331

Geneva General Hosp. *(see Marion S. Whelan Sch. of Practical Nursing)*
Geneva Hall *(see Geneva Coll.)*
Geneva Int'l. Univ. *(see Int'l. Univ. in Geneva)*
Geneva Med. Coll. *(see State Univ. of New York Upstate Med. Univ.)*
Genung-Simmons Embalming Inst. *(see Simmons Inst. of Funeral Service)*
George C. Wallace State Comm. Coll—Dothan 5
George C. Wallace State Jr. Coll. & Tech. Inst. *(see George Corley Wallace State Comm. Coll—Selma)*
George C. Wallace State Tech. Jr. Coll. *(see George C. Wallace State Comm. Coll—Dothan)*
George C. Wallace State Tech. Trade Sch. *(see George C. Wallace State Comm. Coll—Dothan)*
George Corley Wallace State Comm. Coll—Selma 5
George Fox Coll. *(see George Fox Univ.)*
George Fox Univ. 321
George Mason Coll. *(see George Mason Univ.)*
George Mason Univ. 402
George Meany Ctr. for Labor Studies *(see National Labor Coll.)*
George Stone Vocational-Tech. Ctr. 483
George Stone Vo-Tech Ctr. *(see George Stone Vocational-Tech. Ctr.)*
George T. Baker Aviation Sch. 483
George T. Baker Sch. of Aviation *(see George T. Baker Aviation Sch.)*
George Washington Univ. 78
George Williams Coll. *(see Aurora Univ.)*
George Williams Univ. *(see Concordia Univ.)*
Georgetown Coll. 160 *(see also Georgetown Univ.)*
Georgetown Univ. 78
Georgia Assoc. for Pastoral Care 664
Georgia Aviation & Tech. Coll. 103
Georgia Aviation Coll. *(see Georgia Aviation & Tech. Coll.)*
Georgia Aviation Tech. Coll. 726
Georgia Baptist Coll. of Nursing *(see Georgia Baptist Coll. of Nursing of Mercer Univ.)*
Georgia Baptist Coll. of Nursing of Mercer Univ. 106
Georgia Baptist Female Seminary *(see Brenau Univ.)*

Georgia Baptist Health Care System 664
Georgia Career Inst. 493
Georgia Coll. *(see Georgia Coll. & State Univ.)*
Georgia Coll. & State Univ. 103
Georgia Driving Acad. 493
Georgia Highlands Coll. 103, 726
Georgia Inst. of Cosmetology 493
Georgia Inst. of Techno. 103, 726
Georgia Med. Coll. *(see Med. Coll. of Georgia)*
Georgia Med. Employment Preparatory Ctr. *(see Georgia Med. Inst.)*
Georgia Med. Inst. 103, 453, 493 *(see also Bryman Coll—Gardena)*
Georgia Military Coll. 103
Georgia Normal & Agricultural Coll. *(see Albany State Univ.)*
Georgia Normal & Industrial Coll. *(see Georgia Coll. & State Univ.)*
Georgia Perimeter Coll. 103
Georgia Sch. of Prof. Psychology 726 *(see also Argosy Univ. Atlanta)*
Georgia Southern Coll. *(see Georgia Southern Univ.)*
Georgia Southern Univ. 104
Georgia Southwestern Coll. *(see Georgia Southwestern State Univ.)*
Georgia Southwestern State Univ. 104
Georgia State Coll. for Women *(see Georgia Coll. & State Univ.)*
Georgia State Univ. 104 *(see also Georgia Coll. & State Univ.)*
Georgia State Women's Coll. *(see Valdosta State Univ.)*
Georgia Tech *(see Georgia Inst. of Techno.)*
Georgia Tech. Coll. *(see Georgia Aviation & Tech. Coll.)*
Georgia Univ. *(see Univ. of Georgia)*
Georgian Court Coll. 733 *(see also Georgian Court Univ.)*
Georgian Court Univ. 246, 733
GEOS English Acad. 458
GEOS New York Corporation *(see GEOS English Acad.)*
Gerber Akron Beauty Sch. 579
Gerber Beauty Sch. *(see Gerber Akron Beauty Sch.)*
German Evangelical Proseminary *(see Elmhurst Coll.)*
German Theological Seminary *(see Bloomfield Coll.)*
German Wallace Coll. *(see Baldwin-Wallace Coll.)*
Germanna Comm. Coll. 402
Gettysburg Coll. 331

Gettysburg Lutheran Theological Seminary *(see Lutheran Theological Seminary at Gettysburg)*

Ghent Beauty Acad. 738

Gibbs Boston *(see Gibbs Coll. of Boston, Inc.)*

Gibbs Coll. 73, 247, 733 *(see also Gibbs Coll. of Boston, Inc.; Gibbs Coll—Cranston; Gibbs Coll—Vienna)*

Gibbs Coll. Connecticut *(see Gibbs Coll.)*

Gibbs Coll. Livingston *(see Gibbs Coll.)*

Gibbs Coll. of Boston, Inc. 187, 730, 746

Gibbs Coll—Cranston 607, 736, 758

Gibbs Coll—Vienna 402, 738

Gibbs Jr. Coll. *(see Saint Petersburg Coll.)*

Gibbs Melville *(see Katharine Gibbs Sch.)*

Gibbs New York *(see Katharine Gibbs Sch.)*

Gibbs Sch. 738 *(see also Gibbs Coll. of Boston, Inc.; Gibbs Coll—Cranston; Gibbs Coll—Vienna; Katharine Gibbs Sch.)*

Gibson's Barber & Beauty Coll. 535

Gibson's Beauty Coll. *(see Gibson's Barber & Beauty Coll.)*

Gila Acad. *(see Eastern Arizona Coll.)*

Gila Coll. *(see Eastern Arizona Coll.)*

Gila Comm. Coll. *(see Eastern Arizona Coll.)*

Gila County Comm. Coll. *(see Eastern Arizona Coll.)*

Gila Jr. Coll. *(see Eastern Arizona Coll.)*

Gila Normal Coll. *(see Eastern Arizona Coll.)*

Gildner Reg. Inst. for Children & Adolescents *(see John L. Gildner Reg. Inst. for Children & Adolescents)*

Gill-Tech Acad. of Hair Design 643

Girl Scouts of the U.S.A. 561

Girls Industrial Coll. *(see Texas Woman's Univ.)*

Glad Tidings Bible Inst. *(see Bethany Univ.)*

Glamour Beauty Coll. 754

Glasgow Univ. *(see Univ. of Glasgow)*

Glassboro Normal Sch. *(see Rowan Univ.)*

Glassboro State Coll. *(see Rowan Univ.)*

Glen Dow Acad. of Hair Design, Inc. 637

Glen Oaks Coll. *(see Glen Oaks Comm. Coll.)*

Glen Oaks Comm. Coll. 198

Glendale Career Coll. 459

Glendale Career Schools, Inc. *(see Glendale Career Coll.)*

Glendale Coll. *(see Glendale Comm. Coll.)*

Glendale Comm. Coll. 16, 41

Glendale Jr. Coll. *(see Glendale Comm. Coll.)*

Glens Falls Hosp. 686

Glenville Hosp. *(see Euclid Hosp.)*

Glenville State Coll. 419

Glenville State Normal Sch. *(see Glenville State Coll.)*

Glenwood Beauty Acad. 472

Glenwood State Resource Ctr. 671

Glion Inst. of Higher Edu. 437

Global Bus. Inst. 561

Global Language Inst., Inc. 533

Global Univ. 226 *(see also ICI Univ.)*

Globe Coll. 209 *(see also Minnesota Sch. of Bus.)*

Globe Coll. of Bus. *(see Globe Coll.)*

Globe Inst. of Techno. 263, 733

Globe Techno. Inst. *(see Globe Inst. of Techno.)*

Globelle Tech. Inst. 603

Gloucester County Coll. 247

Glyn Ed Newton & Associates, Inc. 611

GMI Engineering & Management Inst. *(see Kettering Univ.)*

Gnomon Sch. of Visual Effects 754

Goddard Coll. 397 *(see also Union Inst. & Univ.)*

Goddard Jr. Coll. *(see Goddard Coll.)*

Goddard Sch. for Girls *(see Goddard Coll.)*

Goddard Seminary *(see Goddard Coll.)*

God's Bible Coll. *(see God's Bible Sch. & Coll.)*

God's Bible Sch. & Coll. 303

Gogebic Coll. *(see Gogebic Comm. Coll.)*

Gogebic Comm. Coll. 199

Going Places Travel Sch. *(see Newbridge Coll.)*

Golden Gate Baptist Theological Seminary 41

Golden Gate Seminary *(see Golden Gate Baptist Theological Seminary)*

Golden Gate Univ. 41

Golden State Bus. Coll. *(see Golden State Coll.)*

Golden State Coll. 459

Golden State Coll. of Chiropractic *(see Southern California Univ. of Health Sciences)*

Golden State Sch. *(see Golden State Coll.)*

Golden Valley Inst. *(see Toccoa Falls Coll.)*

Golden West Coll. 42

Goldey-Beacom Coll. 77

Goldsboro Industrial Edu. Ctr. *(see Wayne Comm. Coll.)*

Golf Acad. of Arizona, The 42

Golf Acad. of Carolinas, The 42

Golf Acad. of Hawaii, The 42

Golf Acad. of San Diego, The 42

Golf Acad. of the South, The 42

Gonzaga Coll. *(see Gonzaga Univ.)*

Gonzaga Univ. 412

Good Samaritan Coll. of Nursing & Health Science 748

Good Samaritan Hosp. 669 *(see also Advocate Good Samaritan Hosp., Good Samaritan Coll. of Nursing & Health Science)*

Good Samaritan Hosp. of Cincinnati *(see Good Samaritan Coll. of Nursing & Health Science)*

Good Samaritan Med. Ctr. 651, 662

Good Samaritan Nursing Coll. *(see Good Samaritan Coll. of Nursing & Health Science)*

Good Samaritan Society 679

Good Shepherd Hosp. *(see Advocate Good Shepherd Hosp.)*

Good Shepherd Med. Ctr. 703

Goodman Child & Adolescent Inst. *(see Jewish Children's Bureau of Chicago)*

Goodwin Coll. 73 *(see also Goodwin Inst—Milford, Stone Acad.)*

Goodwin Inst. 73

Goodwin Inst—Waterbury 724 *(see also Stone Acad—Waterbury)*

Gordon Coll. 104, 187

Gordon Cooper Techno. Ctr. 587

Gordon Divinity Sch. *(see Gordon-Conwell Theological Seminary)*

Gordon Inst. *(see Gordon Coll., Robert Gordon Univ.)*

Gordon Inst. of Techno. *(see Robert Gordon Univ.)*

Gordon Jr. Coll. *(see Gordon Coll.)*

Gordon Phillips Sch. of Beauty Culture—Baltimore 730

Gordon Phillips Sch. of Beauty Culture—Norristown 735

Gordon Phillips Sch. of Beauty Culture—Philadelphia 735

Gordon Phillips Sch. of Beauty Culture—Upper Darbby 735

Gordon Univ. *(see Robert Gordon Univ.)*

Gordon-Barrington Coll. *(see Gordon Coll.)*

Gordon-Conwell Theological Seminary 187

Gordon's Coll. *(see Robert Gordon Univ.)*

Gordon's Inst. of Techno. *(see Robert Gordon Univ.)*

Goshen Coll. 136

Gospel Rescue Ministries *(see Sch. of Tomorrow)*

Goss Military Acad. *(see New Mexico Military Inst.)*

Goucher Coll. 179

Gourmet Cookery Sch. *(see Natural Gourmet Cookery Sch.)*

Governors State Univ. 121

Governors Univ. *(see Governors State Univ.)*

Grabber Sch. of Hair Design 538

Grace Bible Coll. 199 *(see also Grace Univ.)*

Grace Coll. *(see Grace Coll. & Seminary, Grace Univ.)*

Grace Coll. & Seminary 136

Grace Coll. of the Bible *(see Grace Univ.)*

Grace Grad. Sch. *(see Grace Coll. & Seminary)*

Grace Hosp. 677

Grace Inst. of Bus. Techno. 561

Grace Theological Seminary *(see Grace Coll. & Seminary)*

Grace Univ. 237

Graceland Coll. *(see Graceland Univ.)*

Graceland Univ. 146

Grad. Ctr. of New York *(see City Univ. of New York Grad. Ctr.)*

Grad. Coll. of Marshall Univ. *(see Marshall Univ. Grad. Coll.)*

Grad. Coll. of Union Univ., The 264, 747

Grad. Hosp. 697

Grad. Inst. of Applied Linguistics 749

Grad. Research Ctr. of the Southwest *(see Univ. of Texas at Dallas)*

Grad. Sch. & Univ. Ctr. 733 *(see also City Univ. of New York Grad. Ctr.)*

Grad. Sch. of America *(see Capella Univ.)*

Grad. Sch. of Biomedical Sciences *(see Texas A&M Univ. System Health Science Ctr., Univ. of Medicine & Dentistry of New Jersey Grad. Sch. of Biomedical Sciences)*

Grad. Sch. of Figurative Art of the New York Acad. of Art 264

Grad. Sch. of Molecular Medicine *(see North Shore Long Island Jewish Grad. Sch. of Molecular Medicine)*

Grad. Seminary of Phillips Univ., The *(see Phillips Theological Seminary)*

Grad. Theological Union 42

Grad. Theology Sch. of Austin *(see Austin Grad. Sch. of Theology)*

Grad. Theology Sch. of Houston *(see Houston Grad. Sch. of Theology)*

Grady Health System *(see Grady Mem. Hosp.)*

Grady Mem. Hosp. 664

Grady Sch. of Esthetics *(see Elizabeth Grady Sch. of Esthetics)*

Graham Webb Acad. *(see Graham Webb Int'l. Acad. of Hair)*

Graham Webb Int'l. Acad. of Hair 632

Grambling Coll. of Louisiana *(see Grambling State Univ.)*

Grambling State Univ. 167

Grand Canyon Coll. *(see Grand Canyon Univ.)*

Grand Canyon Univ. 16

Grand Rapids Baptist Bible Coll. *(see Cornerstone Univ.)*

Grand Rapids Baptist Seminary *(see Cornerstone Univ.)*

Grand Rapids Coll. *(see Grand Rapids Comm. Coll.)*

Grand Rapids Comm. Coll. 199

Grand Rapids Educational Ctr. *(see Olympia Career Training Inst.)*

Grand Rapids Jr. Coll. *(see Grand Rapids Comm. Coll.)*

Grand Rapids Theological Seminary *(see Cornerstone Univ.)*

Grand Valley State Univ. 199

Grand Valley Univ. *(see Grand Valley State Univ.)*

Grand View Coll. 146

Grand View Seminary *(see Lutheran Sch. of Theology at Chicago)*

Granite State Coll. 242, 732

Grant & Associates, Inc. *(see S.J. Grant & Associates, Inc.)*

Grant Career Ctr. *(see U.S. Grant Joint Vocational Sch.)*

Grant Joint Vocational School *(see U.S. Grant Joint Vocational Sch.)*

Grant JVS *(see U.S. Grant Joint Vocational Sch.)*

Grant Med. Ctr. *(see Riverside Methodist Hosp/Grant Med. Ctr.)*

Grant Mem. Univ. *(see Tennessee Wesleyan Coll.)*

Grant Tech. Coll. *(see American River Coll.)*

Grant Union Jr. Coll. *(see American River Coll.)*

Grant Univ. *(see Univ. of Tennessee at Chattanooga)*

Grant/Riverside Methodist Hospitals *(see Riverside Methodist Hosp/Grant Med. Ctr.)*

Grantham Coll. of Engineering *(see Grantham Univ.)*

Grantham Univ. 226

Granville Coll. *(see Denison Univ.)*

Granville Literary & Theological Institution *(see Denison Univ.)*

Gratz Coll. 331

Grays Harbor Coll. 412

Grayson Coll. *(see Grayson County Coll.)*

Grayson County Coll. 378

Graysville Acad. *(see Southern Adventist Univ.)*

Great Basin Coll. 240

Great Falls Coll. of Edu. *(see Univ. of Great Falls)*

Great Falls Jr. Coll. for Women *(see Univ. of Great Falls)*

Great Falls Normal Sch. *(see Univ. of Great Falls)*

Great Falls Univ. *(see Univ. of Great Falls)*

Great Falls Vocational-Tech. Ctr. *(see Montana State Univ. Coll. of Tech—Great Falls)*

Great Lakes Acad. of Hair Design 529

Great Lakes Bible Coll. *(see Great Lakes Christian Coll.)*

Great Lakes Christian Coll. 199

Great Lakes Coll. *(see Davenport Univ.)*

Great Lakes Culinary Inst. *(see Northwestern Michigan Coll.)*

Great Lakes Inst. of Techno. 597

Great Lakes Jr. Coll. *(see Davenport Univ.)*

Great Lakes Maritime Acad. *(see Northwestern Michigan Coll.)*

Great Lakes Naval Hosp. *(see Naval Hosp—Great Lakes)*

Great Lakes Region of Ascension Health *(see Providence Hosp. & Med. Centers)*

Great Lakes Techno. Inst. *(see Great Lakes Inst. of Techno.)*

Great Oaks Inst. of Techno. & Career Development—Diamond Oaks Campus 580

Great Oaks Inst. of Techno. & Career Development—Laurel Oaks Campus 580

Great Oaks Inst. of Techno. & Career Development—Live Oaks Campus 580

Great Oaks Inst. of Techno. & Career Development—Scarlet Oaks Campus 580

Great Oaks Sch. of Practical Nursing *(see Great Oaks Inst. of Techno. & Career Development—Scarlet Oaks Campus)*

Great Plains Techno. Ctr. 587

Great Smoky Mountains Comm. Coll. *(see Walters State Comm. Coll.)*
Greater Altoona Career & Techno. Ctr. 597
Greater Baltimore Med. Ctr. 674
Greater Erie Anti-Poverty Action Committee Training Inst. *(see GECAC Training Inst.)*
Greater Erie Comm. Action Committee *(see GECAC Training Inst.)*
Greater Hartford Clinical Psychology Internship Consortium 659
Greater Hartford Comm. Coll. *(see Capital Comm. Coll.)*
Greater Johnstown Area Vocational-Tech. Sch. *(see Greater Johnstown Career & Techno. Ctr.)*
Greater Johnstown Career & Techno. Ctr. 597
Greater Long Beach Child Guidance Ctr. 653
Greater Los Angeles VA Healthcare System *(see Veterans Affairs Greater Los Angeles Healthcare System, Veterans Affairs Greater Los Angeles Healthcare System—Los Angeles, Veterans Affairs Greater Los Angeles Healthcare System—Sepulveda)*
Greater Los Angeles Veterans Affairs Healthcare System *(see Veterans Affairs Greater Los Angeles Healthcare System)*
Greater New Haven State Tech. Coll. *(see Gateway Comm. Coll.)*
Greater West Town Training Partnership 500
Green County Area Techno. Ctr. *(see Somerset Comm. Coll.)*
Green Mountain Coll. 397
Green River Coll. *(see Green River Comm. Coll.)*
Green River Comm. Coll. 412
Greenbrier Comm. Coll. Ctr. 418 *(see also Bluefield State Coll.)*
Greene County Area Vocational Tech. Sch. 697
Greene County Career Ctr. 580
Greene County Vo-Tech Sch. *(see Greene County Area Vocational Tech. Sch.)*
Greenfield Coll. *(see Greenfield Comm. Coll.)*
Greenfield Comm. Coll. 188
Greensboro Coll. 288
Greenville Coll. 121
Greenville Mem. Hosp. *(see Greenville Hosp. System)*
Greenville Tech *(see Greenville Tech. Coll.)*
Greenville Tech. Coll. 357

Greenville Woman's Coll. *(see Furman Univ.)*
Greenwood Acad. of Hair Design 637
Gretna Career Coll. Training Inst. 167
Greys Harbor Coll. *(see Grays Harbor Coll.)*
Griffin Hosp. 659
Griffin Tech *(see Griffin Tech. Coll.)*
Griffin Tech. Coll. 104
Griffin Tech. Inst. *(see Griffin Tech. Coll.)*
Griffin-Spalding County Area Vocational Tech. Sch. *(see Griffin Tech. Coll.)*
Griffith Opportunity Sch. *(see Emily Griffith Opportunity Sch.)*
Griggs Univ. 179
Grinnell Coll. 147
Grooms & Associates, Inc. *(see Dale Carnegie Training of Greater Cincinnati)*
Grossmont Coll. 42
Group Theatre, The *(see Stella Adler Studio of Acting)*
Groupe HEC *(see Ecole des Hautes Etudes Commerciales)*
Grove Beauty Coll. 587
Grove City Coll. 331
Grubbs Vocational Coll. *(see Univ. of Texas at Arlington)*
Guadalupe Vocational Inst. 483
Guam Comm. Coll. 112
Guam Univ. *(see Univ. of Guam)*
Guelph Univ. *(see Univ. of Guelph)*
Guilford Coll. 288
Guilford County Coll. *(see Guilford Coll.)*
Guilford Industrial Edu. Ctr. *(see Guilford Tech. Comm. Coll.)*
Guilford Tech. Comm. Coll. 288
Guilford Tech. Inst. *(see Guilford Tech. Comm. Coll.)*
Guitar Inst. of Techno., The *(see Musicians Inst.)*
Gulf Coast Bible Coll. *(see Mid-America Christian Univ.)*
Gulf Coast Coll. *(see Gulf Coast Comm. Coll.)*
Gulf Coast Coll. 87, 726
Gulf Coast Comm. Coll. 87
Gulf Coast Trades Ctr. 619
Gulf States Careers 760
Gulfport Job Corps Ctr. 535
Gundersen Lutheran Med. Ctr. 709
Gunsmith Sch. of Pennsylvania *(see Pennsylvania Gunsmith Sch.)*
Gupton Coll. *(see John A. Gupton Coll.)*
Gupton-Jones Coll. of Funeral Service 104

Gupton-Jones Coll. of Mortuary Science *(see Gupton-Jones Coll. of Funeral Service)*
Gupton-Jones Sch. of Embalming *(see Gupton-Jones Coll. of Funeral Service)*
Gustavus Adolphus Coll. 209
Gustavus Coll. *(see Gustavus Adolphus Coll.)*
Gutenberg Coll. 748
Guy's Acad. Hair, Skin, & Nails 516, 729
Guy's Beauty Sch. *(see Guy's Acad. Hair, Skin, & Nails)*
Guy's Shreveport Acad. of Cosmetology 729 *(see also Guy's Acad. Hair, Skin, & Nails)*
GW Univ. *(see George Washington Univ.)*
Gwin & Associates *(see J. R. Rodgers & Associates, Inc.)*
Gwinnett Coll. 104 *(see also Gwinnett Tech. Coll.)*
Gwinnett Tech. Coll. 104, 726
Gwinnett Tech. Inst. 726 *(see also Gwinnett Tech. Coll.)*
Gwinnett Univ. Ctr. 103 *(see also Georgia Perimeter Coll.)*
Gwynedd-Mercy Coll. 331

H

H. Councill Trenholm State Tech. Coll. 5
Hacienda La Puente Adult Edu. 653
Hackensack Med. Ctr. *(see Hackensack Univ. Med. Ctr.)*
Hackensack Univ. Med. Ctr. 683
Hadley Sch. for Blind, The 501
Hagerstown Bus. Coll. 180
Hagerstown Coll. *(see Hagerstown Comm. Coll.)*
Hagerstown Comm. Coll. 180
Hagerstown Jr. Coll. *(see Hagerstown Comm. Coll.)*
Hair Acad. 734 *(see also Casal's De Spa & Salon, New England Hair Acad.)*
Hair Acad. of New England *(see New England Hair Acad.)*
Hair Acad. of Safford, The 445, 721
Hair Acad., Inc. 522
Hair Acad-110, The 538
Hair Arts Acad. 505
Hair California Beauty Acad. 459
Hair Design Acad. of Tiffin *(see Tiffin Acad. of Hair Design)*
Hair Design Coll. *(see Coll. of Hair Design)*

Hair Design Inst. *(see Hair Design Inst. at Fifth Avenue; Inst. of Hair Design, Inc.)*
Hair Design Inst. at Fifth Avenue 561
Hair Design Inst. of Connecticut *(see Brio Acad. of Cosmetology, Connecticut Inst. of Hair Design)*
Hair Design Sch. *(see Euro Hair Design Inst.)*
Hair Design Sch. of New England *(see New England Sch. of Hair Design, Inc.)*
Hair Design Sch., The 512, 513 *(see also Euro Hair Design Inst.; New England Sch. of Hair Design, Inc.; Hair Design Sch—Louisville, The)*
Hair Design Sch—Louisville, The 513
Hair Dynamics Edu. Ctr. 472
Hair Expressions Acad., Inc. 522
Hair Expressions Barber Sch. 760
Hair Fashions by Kaye Beauty Coll—Indianapolis 505
Hair Fashions by Kaye Beauty Coll—Noblesville 505
Hair In Motion Beauty Acad. 525
Hair Masters Univ. of Beauty 459
Hair Professionals Acad. of Cosmetology—Elgin 501
Hair Professionals Acad. of Cosmetology—Wheaton 501
Hair Professionals Career Coll. 501 *(see also Hair Professionals Sch. of Cosmetology, Inc—Oswego; Hair Professionals Career Coll., Inc—Sycamore)*
Hair Professionals Career Coll., Inc—Sycamore 501
Hair Professionals Sch. of Cosmetology, Inc—Oswego 501
Hair Sch., Inc. *(see Stage One—Hair Sch., Inc.)*
Hair Schools, The 755
Hairitage Beauty Coll. *(see Paul Mitchell The Sch.)*
Hairitage Coll. of Beauty 737 *(see also Paul Mitchell The Sch.)*
Hairitage Hair Acad. 628
Hairmasters Inst. of Cosmetology, Inc. 501
Hairstyling Inst. of Charlotte 573
Hairstylist Acad., Inc. 573
Haley VA Med. Ctr. *(see James A. Haley Veterans Affairs Med. Ctr.)*
Haley Veterans Affairs Med. Ctr. *(see James A. Haley Veterans Affairs Med. Ctr.)*
Halifax Coll. *(see Halifax Comm. Coll.)*
Halifax Comm. Coll. 288
Halifax Med. Ctr. 662
Hallmark Aero-Tech *(see Hallmark Inst. of Techno.)*

Hallmark Inst. of Aeronautics 378
Hallmark Inst. of Photography 525
Hallmark Inst. of Techno. 378
Hall-Moody Inst. *(see Univ. of Tennessee at Martin)*
Hall-Moody Jr. Coll. of Martin *(see Union Univ.)*
Hamilton Bus. Coll. *(see Hamilton Coll—Cedar Rapids)*
Hamilton Ctr. Inc. 669
Hamilton Coll. 264
Hamilton Coll—Cedar Rapids 147
Hamilton Coll—Lincoln 732
Hamilton Coll—Omaha 732
Hamilton Inst. *(see Colgate Univ.)*
Hamilton Jr. Coll. *(see Hamilton Coll—Lincoln)*
Hamilton Tech. Coll. 147
Hamilton-Oneida Acad. *(see Hamilton Coll.)*
Hamline Univ. 210
Hamma Divinity Sch. *(see Wittenberg Univ.)*
Hamma Sch. of Theology *(see Trinity Lutheran Seminary)*
Hampden-Sydney Coll. 402
Hampshire Coll. 188
Hampstead Acad. *(see Mississippi Coll.)*
Hampton Jr. Coll. *(see Central Florida Comm. Coll.)*
Hampton Roads Joint CPE Ctr. 706
Hampton Univ. 403
Hampton VA Med. Ctr. *(see Veterans Affairs Med. Ctr—Hampton)*
Hampton Veterans Affairs Med. Ctr. *(see Veterans Affairs Med. Ctr—Hampton)*
Hamrick Sch. *(see Hamrick Truck Driving Sch.)*
Hamrick Truck Driving Sch. 580
Hancock Coll. *(see Allan Hancock Coll.)*
Hancock Mem. Hosp. *(see Hancock Reg. Hosp.)*
Hancock Reg. Hosp. 670
Hands of Champions Beauty Coll. *(see Stacey's Hands of Champions Beauty Coll., Inc.)*
Hands On Therapy Sch. of Massage *(see HandsOn Therapy Sch. of Massage)*
HandsOn Therapy Sch. of Massage 619
Hanes & Associates, Inc. 505
Haney Tech. Ctr. *(see Tom P. Haney Tech. Ctr.)*
Hannah E. Mullins Sch. of Practical Nursing 693
Hannibal Area Vocational-Tech. Sch. *(see Hannibal Career & Tech. Ctr.)*

Hannibal Career & Tech. Ctr. 538
Hannibal Coll. *(see Hannibal-LaGrange Coll.)*
Hannibal Vo-Tech Sch. *(see Hannibal Career & Tech. Ctr.)*
Hannibal-LaGrange Coll. 226
Hanover Acad. *(see Hanover Coll.)*
Hanover Coll. 136
Hanover Park Coll. of Beauty Culture, Inc. 727 *(see also Empire Beauty Sch—Hanover Park)*
Harbor Coll. of Los Angeles *(see Los Angeles Harbor Coll.)*
Harbor Med. Coll. *(see Bryman Coll—Torrance)*
Harborview Med. Ctr. 707
Harcourt Learning Direct 730 *(see also Penn Foster Career Sch.)*
Harcourt Learning Direct Ctr. for Degree Studies *(see Penn Foster Career Sch.)*
Harcum Coll. 331
Harcum Post Grad. Sch. *(see Harcum Coll.)*
HARDI Home Study Inst. 580, 734
Hardin Coll. *(see Midwestern State Univ.)*
Hardin Jr. Coll. *(see Midwestern State Univ.)*
Harding Coll. *(see Harding Univ.)*
Harding Univ. 25 *(see also Harding Univ. Grad. Sch. of Religion)*
Harding Univ. Grad. Sch. of Religion 366
Hardin-Simmons Univ. 378, 749
Harford Coll. *(see Harford Comm. Coll.)*
Harford Comm. Coll. 180
Harid Conservatory of Music, Inc. *(see Harid Conservatory)*
Harid Conservatory Sch. of Music at Lynn Univ. *(see Harid Conservatory)*
Harid Conservatory, The 483
Harlan State Vocational-Tech. Sch. *(see Southeast Kentucky Comm. & Tech. Coll.)*
Harlem Dance Theatre *(see Dance Theatre of Harlem, Inc.)*
Harlem Hosp. Ctr. 686
Harlem Sch. of Dance *(see Dance Theatre of Harlem, Inc.)*
Harlem Sch. of Techno. 561
Harlem Techno. Sch. *(see Harlem Sch. of Techno.)*
Harold Washington Coll. *(see City Colleges of Chicago—Harold Washington Coll.)*
Harper Coll. *(see Harding Univ., William Rainey Harper Coll.)*
Harpers Ferry Job Corps Ctr. 640

Harpur Coll. *(see State Univ. of New York at Binghamton)*
Harrington Coll. of Design 121, 727
Harrington Design Coll. *(see Harrington Coll. of Design)*
Harrington Inst. of Interior Design 727 *(see also Harrington Coll. of Design)*
Harris County Hosp. Dist. *(see Ben Taub General Hosp.)*
Harris Methodist Fort Worth Hosp. 704
Harris Methodist Health System *(see Harris Methodist Fort Worth Hosp.)*
Harris Psychiatric Hosp. *(see Patrick B. Harris Psychiatric Hosp.)*
Harris Sch. of Bus. 550
Harris Tech. Inst. *(see Louisiana Tech. Coll—T.H. Harris Campus)*
Harrisburg Area Comm. Coll. 331
Harrisburg Inst. of Trade & Techno. 331, 735
Harrison Career Inst—Delran 550
Harrison Career Inst—Deptford 551
Harrison Career Inst—Philadelphia 597
Harrison Career Inst—Vineland 551
Harrison Career Inst—Wilmington 477
Harrison Middleton Univ. *(see Coll. of the Humanities & Sciences Harrison Middleton Univ.)*
Harris-Stowe Coll. *(see Harris-Stowe State Coll.)*
Harris-Stowe State Coll. 226
Harrold Beauty Acad., Inc. *(see J. Michael Harrold Beauty Acad., Inc.)*
Harry M. Ayers State Tech. Coll. *(see Gadsden State Comm. Coll.)*
Harry M. Ayers Tech. Coll. 721
Harry S Truman Coll. *(see City Colleges of Chicago—Harry S Truman Coll.)*
Hart Sch. of Practical Nursing *(see Isabella G. Hart Sch. of Practical Nursing)*
Hartford Art Sch. *(see Univ. of Hartford)*
Hartford Ballet Sch. *(see Sch. of Dance Connecticut)*
Hartford Camerata Conservatory *(see Hartford Conservatory)*
Hartford Coll. for Women *(see Univ. of Hartford)*
Hartford Conservatory 475
Hartford Grad. Ctr. *(see Rensselaer Polytechnic Inst. at Hartford)*
Hartford Hosp. Mental Health Network *(see Inst. of Living)*
Hartford Hosp. Sch. of Allied Health 659

Hartford Sch. of Religious Edu., The *(see Hartford Seminary)*
Hartford Sch. of Religious Pedagogy *(see Hartford Seminary)*
Hartford Secretarial Sch. *(see Fox Inst. of Bus.)*
Hartford Seminary 73
Hartford State Tech. Coll. *(see Capital Comm. Coll.)*
Hartford State Tech. Coll. *(see Capital Comm. Coll.)*
Hartford Univ. *(see Univ. of Hartford)*
Hartman & Associates, Inc. *(see G. Mitchell Hartman & Associates, Inc.)*
Hartnell Coll. 42
Hartt Sch., The *(see Univ. of Hartford)*
Hartwick Coll. 264
Hartwick Seminary *(see Hartwick Coll.)*
Harvard Coll. *(see Harvard Univ.)*
Harvard Divinity Sch. *(see Harvard Univ.)*
Harvard Sch. of Public Health 188
Harvard Univ. 188
Harvey Mudd Coll. 42
Haskell Indian Jr. Coll. *(see Haskell Indian Nations Univ.)*
Haskell Indian Nations Univ. 154
Hastings Coll. 237
Hastings Coll. of the Law *(see Univ. of California, Hastings Coll. of the Law)*
Hastings Indian Hosp. *(see W. W. Hastings Indian Hosp.)*
Havenwood/Heritage Heights *(see Havenwood-Heritage Heights)*
Havenwood-Heritage Heights 682
Haverford Coll. 332
Hawaii Bus. Coll. 113
Hawaii Coll. *(see Hawaii Comm. Coll.)*
Hawaii Coll. of Traditional Chinese Medicine *(see Traditional Chinese Medicine Coll. of Hawaii)*
Hawaii Comm. Coll. 113
Hawaii Dale Carnegie Training *(see James E. Varner & Associates, Inc.)*
Hawaii Inst. of Hair Design 496
Hawaii Pacific Coll. *(see Hawaii Pacific Univ.)*
Hawaii Pacific Univ. 113
Hawaii Tech. Sch. *(see Hawaii Comm. Coll.)*
Hawaii Techno. Inst. 113
Hawaii Tokai Int'l. Coll. 113
Hawaii Vocational Sch. *(see Hawaii Comm. Coll.)*
Hawes Career Inst. *(see Michigan Inst. of Aeronautics)*

Hawkeye Coll. *(see Hawkeye Comm. Coll.)*
Hawkeye Comm. Coll. 147
Hawkeye Inst. of Techno. *(see Hawkeye Comm. Coll.)*
Hayden VA Med. Ctr. *(see Carl T. Hayden Veterans Affairs Med. Ctr.)*
Hayden Veterans Affairs Med. Ctr. *(see Carl T. Hayden Veterans Affairs Med. Ctr.)*
Hays Acad. of Hair Design 509
Hays Language Inst. 588
Haywood Comm. Coll. 288
Haywood Industrial Edu. Ctr. *(see Haywood Comm. Coll.)*
Hazard ARH Reg. Med. Ctr. 672
Hazard Comm. & Tech. Coll. 160, 728
Hazard Comm. Coll. 728 *(see also Hazard Comm. & Tech. Coll.)*
Hazard Reg. Med. Ctr. *(see Hazard ARH Reg. Med. Ctr.)*
Hazard State Vocational-Tech. Sch. *(see Hazard Comm. & Tech. Coll.)*
Hazard Tech. Coll. *(see Hazard Comm. & Tech. Coll.)*
Hazelden Grad. Sch. of Addiction Studies 746
Hazelden Inst. of Addiction Studies *(see Hazelden Grad. Sch. of Addiction Studies)*
Hazleton Area Vocational Tech. Sch. 697
Hazleton Vo-Tech Sch. *(see Hazleton Area Vocational Tech. Sch.)*
HCC Central Coll. *(see Houston Comm. Coll—Central)*
HCC Northeast *(see Houston Comm. Coll—Northeast)*
HCC Northwest *(see Houston Comm. Coll—Northwest)*
HCC Southwest *(see Houston Comm. Coll—Southwest)*
HCT Abu Dhabi Men's Coll. *(see Higher Colleges of Techno. Abu Dhabi Men's Coll.)*
HCT Abu Dhabi Women's Coll. *(see Higher Colleges of Techno. Abu Dhabi Women's Coll.)*
HCT Al Ain Men's Coll. *(see Higher Colleges of Techno. Al Ain Men's Coll.)*
HCT Al Ain Women's Coll. *(see Higher Colleges of Techno. Al Ain Women's Coll.)*
HCT Dubai Men's Coll. *(see Higher Colleges of Techno. Dubai Men's Coll.)*
HCT Dubai Women's Coll. *(see Higher Colleges of Techno. Dubai Women's Coll.)*

HCT Ras Al Khaimah Men's Coll. *(see Higher Colleges of Techno. Ras Al Khaimah Men's Coll.)*

HCT Ras Al Khaimah Women's Coll. *(see Higher Colleges of Techno. Ras Al Khaimah Women's Coll.)*

HCT Sharjah Men's Coll. *(see Higher Colleges of Techno. Sharjah Men's Coll.)*

HCT Sharjah Women's Coll. *(see Sharjah Women's Coll.)*

HDS Truck Driving Inst. 445

Headhunter II Sch. of Hair Design *(see Spa Tech Inst.)*

Headhunter Inst. 730 *(see also Spa Tech Inst.)*

Headlines Acad., Inc. 610

Headmasters Sch. of Hair Design, The 497

Headmasters Sch. of Hair Design— Lewiston 497

Headquarters Acad. of Hair Design, Inc., The 575

Head's Beauty Coll. of West Kentucky *(see Head's West Kentucky Beauty Coll.)*

Head's West Kentucky Beauty Coll. 513

Heald Bus. Coll—Concord *(see Heald Coll—Concord)*

Heald Bus. Coll—Fresno *(see Heald Coll—Fresno)*

Heald Bus. Coll—Hayward *(see Heald Coll—Hayward)*

Heald Bus. Coll—Honolulu *(see Heald Coll—Honolulu)*

Heald Bus. Coll—Sacramento *(see Heald Coll—Sacramento)*

Heald Bus. Coll—Salinas *(see Heald Coll—Salinas)*

Heald Bus. Coll—San Francisco *(see Heald Coll—San Francisco)*

Heald Bus. Coll—San Jose *(see Heald Coll—San Jose)*

Heald Bus. Coll—Stockton *(see Heald Coll—Stockton)*

Heald Coll., Sch. of Bus. & Tech— Sacramento *(see Heald Coll— Sacramento)*

Heald Coll., Sch. of Bus. & Tech— Salinas *(see Heald Coll—Salinas)*

Heald Coll., Sch. of Bus. & Tech— Stockton *(see Heald Coll., Sch. of Bus. & Tech—Stockton)*

Heald Coll., Sch. of Bus—Sacramento 723

Heald Coll., Sch. of Bus—Salinas 723

Heald Coll., Sch. of Bus—Santa Rosa 723

Heald Coll., Schools of Bus. & Tech— Concord *(see Heald Coll— Concord)*

Heald Coll., Schools of Bus. & Tech— Fresno *(see Heald Coll—Fresno)*

Heald Coll., Schools of Bus. & Tech— Hayward *(see Heald Coll— Hayward)*

Heald Coll., Schools of Bus. & Tech— Honolulu *(see Heald Coll— Honolulu)*

Heald Coll., Schools of Bus. & Tech— Portland *(see Heald Coll— Portland)*

Heald Coll., Schools of Bus. & Tech— Roseville *(see Heald Coll— Roseville)*

Heald Coll., Schools of Bus. & Tech— San Francisco *(see Heald Coll— San Francisco)*

Heald Coll., Schools of Bus. & Tech— San Jose *(see Heald Coll—San Jose)*

Heald Coll., Schools of Bus. & Tech— Stockton *(see Heald Coll— Stockton)*

Heald Coll., Schools of Bus—Concord 723

Heald Coll., Schools of Bus—Fresno 723

Heald Coll., Schools of Bus—Hayward 723

Heald Coll., Schools of Bus—Honolulu 727

Heald Coll., Schools of Bus—Portland 735

Heald Coll., Schools of Bus—San Francisco 723

Heald Coll., Schools of Bus—San Jose 723

Heald Coll—Concord 42, 723

Heald Coll—Fresno 42, 723

Heald Coll—Hayward 42, 723

Heald Coll—Honolulu 113, 727

Heald Coll—Portland 321, 735

Heald Coll—Roseville 42

Heald Coll—Sacramento 43, 723

Heald Coll—Salinas 43, 723

Heald Coll—San Francisco 43, 723

Heald Coll—San Jose 43, 723

Heald Coll—Santa Rosa 723

Heald Coll—Stockton 43

Heald Inst. of Tech—Milpitas *(see Heald Coll—San Jose)*

Heald Inst. of Tech—Sacramento *(see Heald Coll—Roseville)*

Heald Sch. of Bus. & Tech—Fresno *(see Heald Coll—Fresno)*

Heald Sch. of Bus. & Tech—Hayward *(see Heald Coll—Hayward)*

Heald Sch. of Bus. & Tech—Honolulu *(see Heald Coll—Honolulu)*

Heald Sch. of Bus. & Tech—Portland *(see Heald Coll—Portland)*

Heald Sch. of Bus. & Tech—Roseville *(see Heald Coll—Roseville)*

Heald Sch. of Bus. & Tech— Sacramento *(see Heald Coll— Sacramento)*

Heald Sch. of Bus. & Tech—Salinas *(see Heald Coll—Salinas)*

Heald Sch. of Bus. & Tech—San Francisco *(see Heald Coll—San Francisco)*

Heald Sch. of Bus. & Tech—San Jose *(see Heald Coll—San Jose)*

Heald Schools of Bus. & Tech— Concord *(see Heald Coll— Concord)*

Healdsburg Coll. *(see Pacific Union Coll.)*

Healing Arts Acad. *(see Acad. of Healing Arts, Massage & Facial Skin Care)*

Healing Arts Coll. of California *(see California Healing Arts Coll.)*

Healing Arts Inst. of Tennessee *(see Tennessee Inst. of Healing Arts)*

Healing Arts Inst. of the Desert *(see Desert Inst. of the Healing Arts)*

Healing Arts Sch. of Colorado *(see Colorado Sch. of Healing Arts)*

Healing Hands Inst. 551

Healing Mountain Massage Sch. 628

Healing Touch Massage Therapy Sch. *(see Healing Touch Sch. of Massage Therapy)*

Healing Touch Sch. of Massage Therapy 535

Health Acad. of Oklahoma *(see Oklahoma Health Acad—Moore, Oklahoma Health Acad—Tulsa)*

Health Alliance of Greater Cincinnati 693

Health Care Professions Acad. *(see Acad. of Health Care Professions)*

Health Care Training Ctr. *(see Career Tech Inst.)*

Health Careers Ctr. of Mercer County Tech. Schools *(see Mercer County Tech. Schools Health Careers Ctr.)*

Health Careers Ctr. of Mercy County Tech. Schools 756

Health Careers Sch. of Illinois *(see Illinois Sch. of Health Careers)*

Health Edu. Inst. *(see Inst. for Health Edu.)*

Health Enrichment Ctr. 529

Health Inst. of Louisville 728 *(see also Galen Coll. of Nursing)*

Health Opportunity Tech. Ctr., Inc. 484

Health Professions Coll. of New York *(see New York Coll. of Health Professions)*
Health Science Ctr. at Brooklyn *(see State Univ. of New York Health Science Ctr. at Brooklyn)*
Health Science Ctr. at Fort Worth *(see Univ. of North Texas Health Science Ctr. at Fort Worth)*
Health Science Ctr. at Syracuse *(see State Univ. of New York Upstate Med. Univ.)*
Health Science Ctr. of the Texas A&M Univ. System *(see Texas A&M Univ. System Health Science Ctr.)*
Health Science Ctr. of the Univ. of Tennessee *(see Univ. of Tennessee Health Science Ctr.)*
Health Science Univ. of the Uniformed Services *(see Uniformed Services Univ. of the Health Sciences)*
Health Sciences Ctr. at Stony Brook *(see State Univ. of New York at Stony Brook)*
Health Sciences Ctr. of Louisiana State Univ. *(see Louisiana State Univ. Health Sciences Ctr. in New Orleans)*
Health Sciences Ctr. of Texas Tech Univ. *(see Texas Tech Univ. Health Sciences Ctr.)*
Health Sciences Coll. of California *(see Independence Univ.)*
Health Sciences Coll. of Florida Hosp. *(see Florida Hosp. Coll. of Health Sciences)*
Health Sciences Univ. *(see Kansas City Univ. of Medicine & Biosciences, Southern California Univ. of Health Sciences)*
Health Sciences Univ. of Southern California *(see Southern California Univ. of Health Sciences)*
Health Staff Training Inst. 459
Health Techno. Ctr. *(see Bowling Green Tech. Coll—Glasgow Health Campus)*
Health Works Inst. 541
HealthCare Chaplaincy, The 686
Healthcare Edu. Coll. *(see Virginia Coll.)*
Healthcare Ministry of the Diocese of Rockville Centre *(see Mercy Med. Ctr.)*
Healthcare Training Inst. 551
HealthEast 679
HealthONE Ctr. for Health Science Edu. 658

Health-Related Professions Sch. *(see Sch. of Health-Related Professions)*
HEALTHSOUTH New England 676
Healthstaff Training Inst. *(see Health Staff Training Inst.)*
Healthy Hair Acad. Sch. of Barbering & Cosmetology Arts & Sciences *(see Healthy Hair Acad., Inc.)*
Healthy Hair Acad., Inc. 459
Heart of Georgia Coll. *(see Heart of Georgia Tech. Coll.)*
Heart of Georgia Tech. Coll. 104, 726
Heart of Georgia Tech. Inst. 726 *(see also Heart of Georgia Tech. Coll.)*
Heart of Georgia Tech. Inst—Eastman Ctr. 726 *(see also Georgia Aviation & Tech. Coll.)*
Heart of Georgia Tech. Sch. *(see Heart of Georgia Tech. Coll.)*
Heart of the Ozarks Tech. Comm. Coll. *(see Ozarks Tech. Comm. Coll.)*
Heartland Coll. *(see Heartland Comm. Coll.)*
Heartland Comm. Coll. 121
Heartland Health 681
Heartland Sch. of Bus. *(see Westwood Coll—DuPage)*
Heartwood Inst. 459
Heating, Air Conditioning & Refrigeration Distributors Int'l. (HARDI) *(see HARDI Home Study Inst.)*
Hebrew Coll. 188 *(see also Hebrew Theological Coll., Hebrew Union Coll—Jewish Inst. of Religion)*
Hebrew Theological Coll. 122
Hebrew Union Coll-Jewish Inst. of Religion 43, 264, 303
Hebrew Univ. of Baltimore *(see Baltimore Hebrew Univ.)*
Heidelberg Coll. 303
Helena Coll. of Techno. *(see Univ. of Montana—Helena Coll. of Techno.)*
Helena Coll. of Techno. of the Univ. of Montana 732 *(see also Univ. of Montana—Helena Coll. of Techno.)*
Helena Vocational-Tech. Ctr. *(see Univ. of Montana—Helena Coll. of Techno.)*
Helene Fuld Coll. of Nursing 264
Helene Fuld Sch. of Nursing 733 *(see also Helene Fuld Coll. of Nursing)*
Helicopter Adventures 484
Heliflight 484
Hellenic Coll/Holy Cross Greek Orthodox Sch. of Theology 188
Helma Inst. of Massage Therapy 551
Help Group, The 653

Henderson Coll. *(see Henderson State Univ.)*
Henderson Comm. Coll. 161
Henderson County Jr. Coll. *(see Trinity Valley Comm. Coll.)*
Henderson State Coll. *(see Henderson State Univ.)*
Henderson State Teachers Coll. *(see Henderson State Univ.)*
Henderson State Univ. 25
Henderson-Brown Coll. *(see Henderson State Univ.)*
Hendrick Health System *(see Hendrick Med. Ctr.)*
Hendrick Med. Ctr. 704
Hendrix Coll. 25
Hennepin Coll. *(see Hennepin Tech. Coll.)*
Hennepin County Med. Ctr. 679
Hennepin Tech. Coll. 210
Henri's Sch. of Hair Design 525
Henry Cogswell Coll. 412
Henry Comm. Coll. *(see Patrick Henry Comm. Coll.)*
Henry Ford Coll. *(see Henry Ford Comm. Coll.)*
Henry Ford Comm. Coll. 199
Henry Ford Health System *(see Henry Ford Hosp.)*
Henry Ford Hosp. 677
Henry Kendall Coll. *(see Univ. of Tulsa)*
Henry W. Brewster Tech. Ctr. 484
Herbert Bible Sch. *(see Bethany Coll.)*
Herbert H. Lehman Coll. *(see City Univ. of New York Herbert H. Lehman Coll.)*
Heritage Baptist Coll. *(see Heritage Coll. & Seminary)*
Heritage Bible Coll. 288
Heritage Christian Univ. 5, 721
Heritage Coll. 68, 240, 738 *(see also Heritage Coll. & Seminary, Heritage Coll. Hair Design, Heritage Univ.)*
Heritage Coll. & Seminary 432
Heritage Coll. Hair Design 315, 735
Heritage Coll. of Health Careers *(see Heritage Coll.)*
Heritage Inst. 484, 632, 738
Heritage Theological Seminary *(see Heritage Coll. & Seminary)*
Heritage Univ. 412, 738
Heritage Valley Health System *(see Sewickley Valley Hosp.)*
Herkimer Coll. *(see Herkimer County Comm. Coll.)*
Herkimer County Comm. Coll. 264
Herman M. Finch Univ. of Health Sciences/The Chicago Med. Sch. 727 *(see also Rosalind Franklin Univ. of Medicine & Science)*

Hermann Baptist Beaumont Hosp. *(see Mem. Hermann Baptist Beaumont Hosp.)*
Hermann Mem. City Hosp. *(see Mem. Hermann Mem. City Hosp.)*
Hermann Southwest Hosp. *(see Mem. Hermann Southwest Hosp.)*
Heron & Associates, Inc. *(see R.L. Heron & Associates, Inc.)*
Herron Sch. of Art *(see Indiana Univ-Purdue Univ. Indianapolis)*
Hershey Med. Ctr. 338 *(see also Pennsylvania State Univ.)*
Herzing Coll. 105
Herzing Coll. of Bus. & Techno. *(see Herzing Coll—Birmingham Campus)*
Herzing Coll. of Techno. *(see Herzing Coll—Madison Campus)*
Herzing Coll—Birmingham Campus 5
Herzing Coll—Crystal Campus *(see Herzing Coll—Lakeland Med-Dental Acad.)*
Herzing Coll—Lakeland Med-Dental Acad. 210
Herzing Coll—Madison Campus 424
Herzing Coll—Melbourne Campus 725
Herzing Coll—Minneapolis Drafting Sch. Campus 533
Herzing Inst. *(see Herzing Coll—Birmingham Campus)*
Hesperian Coll. *(see Chapman Univ.)*
Hesser Coll. 242
Hesston Coll. 154
Hibbing Area Vocational Tech. Inst. *(see Hibbing Comm. Coll.)*
Hibbing Comm. Coll. 210
Hibbing Jr. Coll. *(see Hibbing Comm. Coll.)*
Hibbing State Jr. Coll. *(see Hibbing Comm. Coll.)*
Hickey Coll. 226
Hicks Acad. of Beauty Culture 632
High Point Coll. *(see High Point Univ.)*
High Point Univ. 288
Higher Colleges of Techno. Abu Dhabi Men's Coll. 717
Higher Colleges of Techno. Abu Dhabi Women's Coll. 717
Higher Colleges of Techno. Al Ain Men's Coll. 717
Higher Colleges of Techno. Al Ain Women's Coll. 717
Higher Colleges of Techno. Dubai Men's Coll. 717
Higher Colleges of Techno. Dubai Women's Coll. 717
Higher Colleges of Techno. Ras Al Khaimah Men's Coll. 717

Higher Colleges of Techno. Ras Al Khaimah Women's Coll. 717
Higher Colleges of Techno. Sharjah Men's Coll. 717
Highland Acad. *(see Lenoir-Rhyne Coll.)*
Highland Coll. *(see Highland Comm. Coll., Lenoir-Rhyne Coll.)*
Highland Comm. Coll. 122, 154
Highland Comm. Jr. Coll. *(see Highland Comm. Coll.)*
Highland General Hosp. 653
Highland Univ. *(see Highland Comm. Coll.)*
Highlands Univ. *(see New Mexico Highlands Univ.)*
Highline Coll. *(see Highline Comm. Coll.)*
Highline Comm. Coll. 412
High-Tech Inst. 721, 731
High-Tech Inst—Dallas 619
High-Tech Inst—Kansas City 226
High-Tech Inst—Las Vegas 240
High-Tech Inst—Memphis 366
High-Tech Inst—Nashville 366
High-Tech Inst—Orlando 87
High-Tech Inst—Phoenix 17
High-Tech Inst—Sacramento 43
Hilbert Coll. 264
Hill Coll. 378
Hillcrest Health Service System *(see Hackensack Univ. Med. Ctr.)*
Hillcrest Med. Ctr. 695
Hill's Coll. of Cosmetology *(see Bill Hill's Coll. of Cosmetology)*
Hillsboro Aviation *(see Airman's Proficiency Ctr.)*
Hillsboro Coll. *(see Carthage Coll.)*
Hillsboro Jr. Coll. *(see Hill Coll.)*
Hillsborough Coll. *(see Hillsborough Comm. Coll.)*
Hillsborough Comm. Coll. 87
Hillsdale Baptist Coll. *(see Hillsdale Free Will Baptist Coll.)*
Hillsdale Beauty Coll. 529
Hillsdale Coll. 199 *(see also Hillsdale Free Will Baptist Coll.)*
Hillsdale Free Will Baptist Coll. 315
Hilltop Beauty Sch. 459
Hillyard Tech *(see Hillyard Tech. Ctr.)*
Hillyard Tech. Ctr. 681
Hillyer Coll. *(see Univ. of Hartford)*
Hinds Coll. *(see Hinds Comm. Coll.)*
Hinds Comm. Coll. 218
Hinds Esthetics Inst. *(see Catherine E. Hinds Inst. of Esthetics)*
Hinds Inst. of Esthetics *(see Catherine E. Hinds Inst. of Esthetics)*
Hines & Associates, Inc. *(see John Hines & Associates, Inc.)*

Hines VA Hosp. *(see Edward Hines, Jr. Veterans Affairs Hosp.)*
Hines Veterans Affairs Hosp. *(see Edward Hines, Jr. Veterans Affairs Hosp.)*
Hiram Coll. 303
Hiram G. Andrews Ctr. *(see Commonwealth Tech. Inst.)*
Hirsch Comm. Mental Health Ctr. *(see Didi Hirsch Comm. Mental Health Ctr.)*
Hispanic American Coll. 603
Hispanic Baptist Theological Sch. 737 *(see also Baptist Univ. of the Americas)*
Hispanic Univ. *(see National Hispanic Univ.)*
Hi-Tech Sch. of Miami 725 *(see also Coll. of Bus. & Techno.)*
Hiwassee Coll. 366
Hobart & William Smith Colleges 264
Hobart Coll. *(see Hobart & William Smith Colleges)*
Hobart Inst. of Welding Techno. 580
Hobart Welding Techno. Inst. *(see Hobart Inst. of Welding Techno.)*
Hobble Creek Sch. of Holistic Esthetics 760
Hobe Sound Bible Coll. 87
Hobe Sound Bible Inst. *(see Hobe Sound Bible Coll.)*
Hobe Sound Coll. *(see Hobe Sound Bible Coll.)*
Hochstein Mem. Music Sch. *(see David Hochstein Mem. Music Sch.)*
Hochstein Music Sch. *(see David Hochstein Mem. Music Sch.)*
Hochstein Sch. of Music & Dance *(see David Hochstein Mem. Music Sch.)*
Hochstim Sch. of Radiography *(see South Nassau Communities Hosp.)*
Hocking Coll. 304
Hocking Tech. Coll. *(see Hocking Coll.)*
Hofstra Univ. 264
HoHoKus Bus. Sch. *(see HoHoKus Sch. of Bus. & Med. Sciences)*
HoHoKus RETS—Nutley 551, 733
HoHoKus Sch. of Bus. & Med. Sciences 551
HoHoKus-Hackensack Sch. of Bus. & Med. Science 551, 732
Hoke Smith Tech. Inst. *(see Atlanta Tech. Coll.)*
Holiness Evangelistic Inst. *(see Oklahoma Wesleyan Univ.)*
Holistic Health Acad. of Ohio *(see Ohio Acad. of Holistic Health, Inc.)*
Holland Acad., The *(see Hope Coll.)*

Hollins Coll. *(see Hollins Univ.)*
Hollins Inst. *(see Hollins Univ.)*
Hollins Univ. 403
Hollywood Beauty Coll. 496 *(see also Moler-Hollywood Beauty Coll.)*
Hollywood Coll. of Chiropractic *(see Southern California Univ. of Health Sciences)*
Hollywood Cosmetology Ctr. 587
Hollywood Inst. of Beauty Careers 484
Holmes Coll. *(see Holmes Comm. Coll.)*
Holmes Comm. Coll. 219
Holmes Inst. 43
Holmes Jr. Coll. *(see Holmes Comm. Coll.)*
Holy Apostles Coll. & Seminary 73
Holy Apostles Seminary *(see Holy Apostles Coll. & Seminary)*
Holy Cross Greek Orthodox Sch. of Theology *(see Hellenic Coll/Holy Cross Greek Orthodox Sch. of Theology)*
Holy Cross Hosp. 674
Holy Cross Normal Sch. *(see Our Lady of Holy Cross Coll.)*
Holy Cross Theological Sch. *(see Hellenic Coll/Holy Cross Greek Orthodox Sch. of Theology)*
Holy Family Coll. 735 *(see also Holy Family Univ.)*
Holy Family Hosp. & Med. Ctr. 676
Holy Family Med. Ctr. *(see Holy Family Hosp. & Med. Ctr.)*
Holy Family Univ. 332, 735
Holy Name Tech. Sch. *(see Lewis Univ.)*
Holy Names Coll. 723 *(see also Heritage Univ., Holy Names Univ.)*
Holy Names Univ. 43, 723
Holy Spirit Health System *(see Holy Spirit Hosp.)*
Holy Spirit Hosp. 697
Holy Trinity Orthodox Seminary 561
Holy Trinity Seminary *(see Holy Trinity Orthodox Seminary)*
Holyoke Coll. *(see Holyoke Comm. Coll.)*
Holyoke Comm. Coll. 188
Holyoke Jr. Coll. *(see Holyoke Comm. Coll.)*
Home Study Int'l. 522
Hondros Career Centers *(see Hondros Coll.)*
Hondros Coll. 304
Hong Kong Science & Techno. Univ. *(see Hong Kong Univ. of Science & Techno.)*
Hong Kong Univ. of Science & Techno. 715

Honolulu Christian Coll. *(see Hawaii Pacific Univ.)*
Honolulu Coll. *(see Hawaii Pacific Univ., Honolulu Comm. Coll.)*
Honolulu Comm. Coll. 113
Honolulu Tech. Sch. *(see Honolulu Comm. Coll.)*
Honolulu VA Med. Ctr. *(see Veterans Affairs Pacific Islands Healthcare System)*
Honolulu Veterans Affairs Med. Ctr. *(see Veterans Affairs Pacific Islands Healthcare System)*
Honolulu Vocational Sch. *(see Honolulu Comm. Coll.)*
Honors Coll. of Florida *(see New Coll. of Florida)*
Hood Coll. 180
Hood Seminary *(see Hood Theological Seminary)*
Hood Theological Seminary 288
Hope Coll. 199
Hope Comm. Coll. *(see Univ. of Arkansas Comm. Coll. at Hope)*
Hope Hospice 662
Hope Int'l. Univ. 43
Hope Univ. *(see Hope Int'l. Univ.)*
Hopkins Hosp. *(see Johns Hopkins Hosp.)*
Hopkins Sch. of Medicine *(see Johns Hopkins Hosp.)*
Hopkins Tech. Edu. Ctr. *(see Lindsey Hopkins Tech. Edu. Ctr.)*
Hopkins Univ. *(see Johns Hopkins Univ.)*
Hopkinsville Comm. Coll. 161
Horizon Career Coll. *(see Olympia Coll—Merrillville)*
Horry-Georgetown Coll. *(see Horry-Georgetown Tech. Coll.)*
Horry-Georgetown Tech. Coll. 357
Horton Acad. *(see Acadia Divinity Coll.)*
Hospice of the Bluegrass 672
Hosp. Ctr. of Brooklyn *(see Brooklyn Hosp. Ctr.)*
Hosp. Ctr. of Harlem *(see Harlem Hosp. Ctr.)*
Hosp. Ctr. of Prince George's County *(see Prince George's Hosp. Ctr.)*
Hosp. Ctr. of Washington *(see Washington Hosp. Ctr.)*
Hosp. of Oak Forest *(see Oak Forest Hosp.)*
Hosp. of Port Huron *(see Port Huron Hosp.)*
Hosp. of Rockford *(see Rockford Mem. Hosp.)*
Hosp. of Saint Raphael 659
Hosp. of the Univ. of Pennsylvania *(see Univ. of Pennsylvania)*

Hospitality Training Ctr. *(see Brighton Coll.)*
Hostos Comm. Coll. *(see City Univ. of New York Hostos Comm. Coll.)*
Hot Springs Beauty Coll. 448
Hotel & Bus. Management Sch. *(see DCT Int'l. Hotel & Bus. Management Sch.)*
Hotel Inst. Cesar Ritz *(see Institut Hotelier Cesar Ritz)*
Hotel Inst. Montreux 648
Hotel Management Sch. "Les Roches" *(see "Les Roches" Sch. of Hotel Management)*
Hotel Management Sch. of Delaware *(see Delaware Sch. of Hotel Management)*
Hotel Sch. of Lausanne *(see Ecole Hoteliere de Lausanne)*
Houghton Coll. 264
Houghton Lake Inst. of Cosmetology 529
Housatonic Comm. Coll. 73
Housatonic Comm-Tech. Coll. *(see Housatonic Comm. Coll.)*
House of Heavilin Beauty Coll—Blue Springs 538
House of Heavilin Beauty Coll— Grandview 538
House of Heavilin Beauty Coll— Kansas City 538
House of Tutors Learning Centers USA, Inc 620
Houston Acad. of Ballet *(see Houston Ballet's Ben Stevenson Acad.)*
Houston Allied Health Careers, Inc. 737
Houston Area Vocational Ctr. *(see Middle Georgia Tech. Coll.)*
Houston Art Inst. *(see Art Inst. of Houston)*
Houston Aviation Inst. *(see Westwood Coll. of Aviation Tech—Denver)*
Houston Ballet Acad. 737 *(see also Houston Ballet's Ben Stevenson Acad.)*
Houston Ballet's Ben Stevenson Acad. 620, 737
Houston Baptist Coll. *(see Houston Baptist Univ.)*
Houston Baptist Univ. 378
Houston Coll. *(see Coll. of Biblical Studies—Houston, Houston Comm. Coll.)*
Houston Coll. of Biblical Studies *(see Coll. of Biblical Studies— Houston)*
Houston Comm. Coll. 378
Houston Comm. Coll. Central Coll. *(see Houston Comm. Coll— Central)*

Houston Comm. Coll. System *(see Houston Comm. Coll.)*

Houston Court Reporting Inst. *(see Court Reporting Inst. of Dallas, Court Reporting Inst. of Houston)*

Houston Dale Carnegie Training *(see Leadership Excellence, Inc.)*

Houston Grad. Sch. of Theology 378 *(see also Carolina Evangelical Divinity Sch.)*

Houston Grad. Theology Sch. *(see Houston Grad. Sch. of Theology)*

Houston Inst. of Art *(see Art Inst. of Houston)*

Houston Inst. of Health Sciences 389 *(see also Texas Woman's Univ.)*

Houston Mem. City Hosp. *(see Mem. Hermann Mem. City Hosp.)*

Houston Montessori Ctr. 620

Houston Sch. of Commercial Art *(see Art Inst. of Houston)*

Houston State Univ. *(see Sam Houston State Univ.)*

Houston Training Schools 620

Houston Univ. *(see Sam Houston State Univ., Univ. of Houston)*

Houston Veterans Affairs Med. Ctr. *(see Veterans Affairs Med. Ctr—Houston)*

Houston Vocational Ctr. *(see Middle Georgia Tech. Coll.)*

Houston's Training & Edu. Ctr. 620

Howard Coll. 379 *(see also Marion Military Inst., Samford Univ.)*

Howard Comm. Coll. 180 *(see also Howard Coll.)*

Howard Comm. Hosp. 670

Howard County Jr. Coll. *(see Howard Coll.)*

Howard English & Classical Sch. *(see Marion Military Inst.)*

Howard Payne Coll. *(see Howard Payne Univ.)*

Howard Payne Univ. 379

Howard Sch. in Fayetteville *(see Fayetteville State Univ.)*

Howard Sch. of Broadcast Arts *(see Specs Howard Sch. of Broadcast Arts, Inc.)*

Howard Univ. 78

Howell Coll. of Cosmetology 529

HRDE, Stanley Tech. Inst. *(see Stanley Tech. Inst.)*

Hsi Lai Univ. 723 *(see also Univ. of the West)*

HTC Distance Edu. 734 *(see also Brighton Coll.)*

Hub City Bible Inst. *(see Trinity Bible Coll.)*

Hudson Area Sch. of Radiologic Techno. 683

Hudson County Coll. *(see Hudson County Comm. Coll.)*

Hudson County Comm. Coll. 247

Hudson Electrical Inst., Inc. 551

Hudson Valley Coll. *(see Hudson Valley Comm. Coll.)*

Hudson Valley Comm. Coll. 265

Hudson Valley Sch. of Advanced Aesthetic Skin Care, Inc. 757

Huertas Coll. *(see Huertas Jr. Coll.)*

Huertas Jr. Coll. 348, 749

Hult Int'l. Bus. Sch. 188, 730

Humacao Coll. *(see Humacao Comm. Coll.)*

Humacao Comm. Coll. 348

Human Resource Development & Employment, Inc. *(see Stanley Tech. Inst.)*

Human Resource Development Foundation, Inc. *(see Stanley Tech. Inst.)*

Humana Health Institutes *(see Galen Coll. of Nursing)*

Humanistic Psychology Inst., The *(see Saybrook Grad. Sch. & Research Ctr.)*

Humanistic Studies Ctr. *(see Ctr. for Humanistic Studies)*

Humanities Ctr. Inst. of Allied Health/Sch. of Massage 484

Humanities Ctr., The *(see Humanities Ctr. Inst. of Allied Health/Sch. of Massage)*

Humber Coll. *(see Humber Coll. of Applied Arts & Techno.)*

Humber Coll. of Applied Arts & Techno. 712

Humboldt State Normal Sch. *(see Humboldt State Univ.)*

Humboldt State Univ. 43

Humphreys Coll. 43

Hunt Correctional Ctr. 170 *(see also Jumonville Mem. Tech. Inst.)*

Hunter Bus. & Tech. Programs *(see Hunter Bus. Sch.)*

Hunter Bus. Sch. 561

Hunter Coll. *(see City Univ. of New York Hunter Coll.)*

Hunter Coll. of The City of New York *(see City Univ. of New York Hunter Coll.)*

Hunter Holmes McGuire VA Med. Ctr. *(see Veterans Affairs Med. Ctr— Hunter Holmes McGuire)*

Hunter Holmes McGuire Veterans Affairs Med. Ctr. *(see Veterans Affairs Med. Ctr—Hunter Holmes McGuire)*

Huntingdon Coll. 5

Huntington Coll. 136 *(see also Huntington Jr. Coll., Huntington Coll. of Health Sciences)*

Huntington Coll. of Health Sciences 366, 736

Huntington Dental Techno. Coll. *(see Huntington Coll. of Dental Techno.)*

Huntington Hosp. *(see Cabell Huntington Hosp.)*

Huntington Inst. 724

Huntington Jr. Coll. 419, 738

Huntington Jr. Coll. of Bus. 738 *(see also Huntington Jr. Coll.)*

Huntington Sch. of Beauty Culture, Inc. 640

Huntsville Baptist Inst. *(see Huntsville Bible Coll.)*

Huntsville Bible Coll. 743

Huntsville Coll. *(see Huntsville Bible Coll.)*

Huntsville Hosp. 651

Huntsville Hosp. System *(see Huntsville Hosp.)*

Hurley Health Group *(see Hurley Med. Ctr.)*

Hurley Med. Ctr. 678

Huron Coll. *(see Huron Univ. Coll. Faculty of Theology)*

Huron Univ. *(see Huron Univ. Coll. Faculty of Theology, Si Tanka Univ.)*

Huron Univ. Coll. Faculty of Theology 432

Hussian Sch. of Art 332

Husson Coll. 175

Huston-Tillotson Coll. 737 *(see also Huston-Tillotson Univ.)*

Huston-Tillotson Univ. 379, 737

Hutchinson Coll. *(see Hutchinson Comm. Coll.)*

Hutchinson Comm. Coll. 154

Hutchinson Comm. Jr. Coll. *(see Hutchinson Comm. Coll.)*

Hutchinson Jr. Coll. *(see Hutchinson Comm. Coll.)*

Hutchinson-Willmar Reg. Tech. Coll. *(see Ridgewater Coll.)*

Hutchinson-Willmar Tech. Coll. *(see Ridgewater Coll.)*

Hypnosis Motivation Inst. 459

I

I.C.E. Beauty Sch. & Spa Training Ctr. 484

I.C.E. Spa Training Ctr. *(see I.C.E. Beauty Sch. & Spa Training Ctr.)*

IADT Fairmont *(see Int'l. Acad. of Design & Tech—Fairmont)*

IADT Nashville *(see Int'l. Acad. of Design & Tech—Nashville)*
IADT Pittsburgh *(see Int'l. Acad. of Design & Techno.)*
IADT Seattle *(see Int'l. Acad. of Design & Tech—Seattle)*
IADT Tampa *(see Int'l. Acad. of Design & Techno.)*
IAUPR Sch. of Law *(see Inter American Univ. of Puerto Rico Sch. of Law)*
IAUPR Sch. of Optometry *(see Inter American Univ. of Puerto Rico Sch. of Optometry)*
ICC Tech. Inst. 620
ICDC Coll. 459
ICE Beauty Sch. & Spa Training Ctr. *(see I.C.E. Beauty Sch. & Spa Training Ctr.)*
ICI Univ. 226
ICI Univ. Int'l. *(see Global Univ.)*
ICM Sch. of Bus. & Med. Careers 332
ICPR Jr. Coll. *(see Instituto Comercial de Puerto Rico Jr. Coll.)*
ICR Grad. Sch. 43
ICS Ctr. for Degree Studies *(see Penn Foster Career Sch.)*
ICS Inst. *(see Information Computer Systems Inst.)*
ICS Learning Systems *(see Penn Foster Career Sch.)*
ICS The Wright Beauty Coll. 535
ICT Coll. *(see Inst. of Computer Techno.)*
ICT Kikkawa Coll. 646
ICT Northumberland Coll. 646
ICT: Sch. of Welding 597
Idaho Ballet Acad. *(see Ballet Idaho Acad.)*
Idaho State Coll. *(see Idaho State Univ.)*
Idaho State Univ. 115
Idaho Tech. Inst. *(see Idaho State Univ.)*
Idaho Univ. *(see Idaho State Univ., Univ. of Idaho)*
Ideal Beauty Acad., Inc. 505
IHM Bus. Sch. 648
IHM Health Studies Ctr. 226
IITR Truck Driving Sch. 592
Iliff Sch. of Theology 68
Iliff Theology Sch. *(see Iliff Sch. of Theology)*
Ilisagvik Coll. 11
Illiana Health Care System *(see Veterans Affairs Illiana Health Care System)*
Illiana VA Health Care System *(see Veterans Affairs Illiana Health Care System)*

Illiana Veterans Affairs Health Care System *(see Veterans Affairs Illiana Health Care System)*
Illinois Art Inst. *(see Illinois Inst. of Art)*
Illinois Benedictine Coll. *(see Benedictine Univ.)*
Illinois Ctr. for Broadcasting 501
Illinois Central Coll. 122
Illinois Coll. 122
Illinois Coll. of Optometry 122
Illinois Conference Female Acad. *(see MacMurray Coll.)*
Illinois Dale Carnegie Training *(see S.J. Grant & Associates, Inc.)*
Illinois Female Coll. *(see MacMurray Coll.)*
Illinois Holiness Univ. *(see Olivet Nazarene Univ.)*
Illinois Industrial Univ. *(see Univ. of Illinois at Urbana-Champaign)*
Illinois Inst. *(see Illinois Inst. of Art, The; Illinois Inst. of Techno.; Wheaton Coll.)*
Illinois Inst. of Art, The 122
Illinois Inst. of Techno. 122
Illinois Liberal Inst. *(see Meadville Lombard Theological Sch.)*
Illinois Sch. of Health Careers 501
Illinois Sch. of Prof. Psychology—Chicago *(see Argosy Univ. Chicago)*
Illinois Sch. of Prof. Psychology—Rolling Meadows *(see Argosy Univ. Schaumburg)*
Illinois State Univ. 122 *(see also Carthage Coll.)*
Illinois Teachers Coll. Chicago South *(see Chicago State Univ.)*
Illinois Valley Coll. *(see Illinois Valley Comm. Coll.)*
Illinois Valley Comm. Coll. 122
Illinois Welding Sch. 501
Illinois Wesleyan Univ. 122
Image Schools of Cosmetology, Inc. 459
Image Works Acad. of Hair Design, Inc. 760
IMEDIA 607
Immaculata Coll. *(see Immaculata Univ.)*
Immaculata Univ. 332
Immaculate Conception Jr. Coll. *(see Felician Coll.)*
Immaculate Conception Jr. Coll. *(see Marian Coll.)*
Immaculate Conception Normal Sch. *(see Felician Coll.)*
Immaculate Conception Seminary 247 *(see also Seminary of the Immaculate Conception)*

Immaculate Conception Seminary of Seton Hall Univ. *(see Immaculate Conception Seminary)*
Immanuel Med. Ctr. *(see Alegent Health Immanuel Med. Ctr.)*
IMPAC Univ. 87
Imperial Valley Coll. 44
Improved Management Productivity & Control Univ. *(see IMPAC Univ.)*
In Session, Arts of Cosmetology Beauty Sch. 529
Incarnate Word Coll. *(see Univ. of the Incarnate Word)*
Incarnate Word Univ. *(see Univ. of the Incarnate Word)*
Independence Coll. *(see Independence Coll. of Cosmetology, Independence Comm. Coll.)*
Independence Coll. of Cosmetology 538
Independence Comm. Coll. 154
Independence Univ. 394, 737
Independent Baptist Church *(see Appalachian Bible Coll.)*
Independent Study Inst. *(see Seminary Extension Independent Study Inst.)*
Indian Capital Techno. Ctr. 587, 588
Indian Coll. of the Assemblies of God *(see American Indian Coll. of the Assemblies of God)*
Indian Health Service *(see Albuquerque Area Indian Health Service, Gallup Indian Med. Ctr.)*
Indian Hills Coll. *(see Indian Hills Comm. Coll.)*
Indian Hills Comm. Coll. 147
Indian Meridian Area Vocational-Tech. Sch. *(see Meridian Techno. Ctr.)*
Indian Meridian Voational-Tech. Ctr. *(see Meridian Techno. Ctr.)*
Indian Normal Sch. of Robeson County *(see Univ. of North Carolina at Pembroke)*
Indian River Beauty Acad. 738
Indian River Coll. *(see Indian River Comm. Coll.)*
Indian River Comm. Coll. 88
Indian Valley Coll. *(see Coll. of Marin)*
Indiana Asbury Univ. *(see DePauw Univ.)*
Indiana Bus. Coll. 136, 137
Indiana Coll. of Mortuary Science *(see Mid-America Coll. of Funeral Service)*
Indiana Cosmetology Acad. 758
Indiana County Techno. Ctr. *(see Indiana Cosmetology Acad.)*
Indiana Inst. of Techno. 137

Indiana Lutheran Hosp. *(see Lutheran Hosp. of Indiana)*
Indiana Normal Sch. *(see Indiana Univ. of Pennsylvania)*
Indiana Seminary *(see McCormick Theological Seminary)*
Indiana State Coll. *(see Indiana State Univ., Indiana Univ. of Pennsylvania)*
Indiana State Normal Sch. *(see Indiana State Univ.)*
Indiana State Teachers Coll. *(see Indiana State Univ.)*
Indiana State Univ. 137
Indiana State Univ—Evansville *(see Univ. of Southern Indiana)*
Indiana Tech *(see Indiana Inst. of Techno.)*
Indiana Tech. Coll. *(see Indiana Inst. of Techno.)*
Indiana Univ. Bloomington 137
Indiana Univ. East 137
Indiana Univ. Indianapolis *(see Indiana Univ-Purdue Univ. Indianapolis)*
Indiana Univ. Kokomo 137
Indiana Univ. Northwest 138
Indiana Univ. of Pennsylvania 332
Indiana Univ. Sch. of Medicine *(see Indiana Univ-Purdue Univ. Indianapolis)*
Indiana Univ. South Bend 138
Indiana Univ. Southeast 138
Indiana Univ-Purdue Univ. Columbus 138
Indiana Univ-Purdue Univ. Fort Wayne 138
Indiana Univ-Purdue Univ. Indianapolis 138
Indiana Vocational Tech. Coll. *(see Ivy Tech Comm. Coll. of Indiana— Central Indiana, Ivy Tech Comm. Coll. of Indiana—Columbus, Ivy Tech Comm. Coll. of Indiana— East Central, Ivy Tech Comm. Coll. of Indiana—Kokomo, Ivy Tech Comm. Coll. of Indiana— Lafayette, Ivy Tech Comm. Coll. of Indiana—Madison, Ivy Tech Comm. Coll. of Indiana—North Central, Ivy Tech Comm. Coll. of Indiana—Northeast, Ivy Tech Comm. Coll. of Indiana— Northwest, Ivy Tech Comm. Coll. of Indiana—Richmond, Ivy Tech Comm. Coll. of Indiana— Sellersburg, Ivy Tech Comm. Coll. of Indiana—Southwest, Ivy Tech Comm. Coll. of Indiana—Wabash Valley)*
Indiana Wesleyan Univ. 138

Indianapolis Univ. *(see Univ. of Indianapolis)*
Indianapolis VA Med. Ctr. *(see Richard L. Roudebush Veterans Affairs Med. Ctr.)*
Indianapolis Veterans Affairs Med. Ctr. *(see Richard L. Roudebush Veterans Affairs Med. Ctr.)*
Indianhead Tech. Coll. *(see Wisconsin Indianhead Tech. Coll.)*
Industrial Coll. of Yanbu *(see Yanbu Industrial Coll.)*
Industrial Inst. & Coll. *(see Mississippi Univ. for Women)*
Industrial Inst. of South Dakota *(see Northern State Univ.)*
Industrial Management & Training Inst. 475
Information Computer Systems Inst. 332, 735
Ing'enue Beauty Sch. 533, 731
Ingram State Tech. Coll. *(see J.F. Ingram State Tech. Coll.)*
Inland Empire Training Ctr. 466
Inland Northwest Heating, Ventilation, & Air Conditioning Training Ctr. 738 *(see also Northwest HVC/R Assoc. & Training Ctr.)*
Inland Northwest HVAC Training Ctr. *(see Northwest HVC/R Assoc. & Training Ctr.)*
Inner State Beauty Sch. 580
Inservicer's Coll. of Health Edu. *(see Olympia Coll—Merrillville)*
Instittue of Techno. at Utica/Rome *(see State Univ. of New York Inst. of Techno. at Utica/Rome)*
Institucion Chaviano de Mayaguez 603
Institut Hotelier Cesar Ritz 648
Inst. for Advanced Distributed Learning *(see United States Air Force Inst. for Advanced Distributed Learning)*
Inst. for Advanced Montessori Studies 522
Inst. for Bus. & Techno. 460
Inst. for Christian Studies 737 *(see also Austin Grad. Sch. of Theology)*
Inst. for Clinical Social Work, Inc. 123
Inst. for Creation Research *(see ICR Grad. Sch.)*
Inst. for Guided Studies 608
Inst. for Health Edu., The 551
Inst. for Med. Services Certification 755
Inst. for Nuclear Med. Edu., Inc. 724
Inst. for Prof. Development *(see United States Army Inst. for Prof. Development)*

Inst. for Psychological Sciences, The 750
Inst. for Therapeutic Massage & Movement 611
Inst. for Therapeutic Massage, Inc. 551
Inst. Francais de Chiropractic 715
Inst. of Aeronautical Technologies *(see Aeronautical Inst. of Technologies)*
Inst. of Agriculture & Natural Resources *(see Nebraska Coll. of Tech. Agriculture)*
Inst. of Allied Med. Professions 484, 686
Inst. of American Indian & Alaskan Native Culture & Arts Development 252
Inst. of American Indian Arts *(see Inst. of American Indian & Alaskan Native Culture & Arts Development)*
Inst. of Animal Arts of Florida *(see Florida Inst. of Animal Arts)*
Inst. of Audio Recording Techno. *(see Audio Recording Techno. Inst.)*
Inst. of Audio Research 561
Inst. of Banking & Commerce *(see Instituto de Banca y Comercio)*
Inst. of Beauty & Wellness, The 643
Inst. of Beauty Careers 604
Inst. of Biosciences & Techno. *(see Texas A&M Univ. System Health Science Ctr.)*
Inst. of Bus. & Med. Careers 68
Inst. of Bus. Skills *(see Bus. Skills Inst.)*
Inst. of Career Edu. 725
Inst. of Central Florida *(see Central Florida Inst., Inc.)*
Inst. of Chinese Medicine of New York *(see New York Coll. of Traditional Chinese Medicine)*
Inst. of Clinical Acupuncture & Oriental Medicine 113
Inst. of Computer Management *(see ICM Sch. of Bus. & Med. Careers)*
Inst. of Computer Techno. 44
Inst. of Computer Training *(see Computer Training Inst.)*
Inst. of Cosmetology 620
Inst. of Culinary Edu., The 561
Inst. of Dental-Med. Assistants of Cleveland *(see Cleveland Inst. of Dental-Med. Assistants, Inc.)*
Inst. of Design *(see Illinois Inst. of Techno., Inst. of Design & Construction)*
Inst. of Design & Construction 265
Inst. of Electronic Techno. *(see Paducah Tech. Coll.)*

Inst. of Entertainment Media Production *(see Video Symphony EnterTraining, Inc.)*
Inst. of Fashion Design & Merchandising *(see Fashion Inst. of Design & Merchandising)*
Inst. of Fashion Techno. *(see Fashion Inst. of Techno.)*
Inst. of Grad. Health Sciences *(see Univ. of St. Augustine for Health Sciences)*
Inst. of Hair Design 588
Inst. of Hair Design, Inc. 759
Inst. of Health Professions *(see MGH Inst. of Health Professions)*
Inst. of Hypnosis Motivation *(see Hypnosis Motivation Inst.)*
Inst. of Industrial Management & Training *(see Industrial Management & Training Inst.)*
Inst. of Living, The 659
Inst. of Logistical Management 552
Inst. of Med. & Dental Techno. 580 *(see also Long Tech. Coll.)*
Inst. of Midwifery, Women & Health 697
Inst. of Modern Art *(see Instituto del Arte Moderno)*
Inst. of Modern Hairstyling—Bayamon *(see Modern Hairstyling Inst— Bayamon)*
Inst. of Movement Studies *(see Laban/Bartenieff Inst. of Movement Studies, Inc.)*
Inst. of Muscular Therapy *(see Muscular Therapy Inst.)*
Inst. of Musical Art *(see Juilliard Sch.)*
Inst. of Myotherapy *(see Myotherapy Inst.)*
Inst. of Network Techno. 460
Inst. of North Florida *(see North Florida Inst.)*
Inst. of Open Edu. at Newton Coll. of the Sacred Heart *(see Cambridge Coll.)*
Inst. of Oriental Medicine of Seattle *(see Seattle Inst. of Oriental Medicine)*
Inst. of Paper Chemistry *(see Georgia Inst. of Techno., Inst. of Paper Science & Techno. at Georgia Tech)*
Inst. of Paper Science & Techno. 726 *(see also Inst. of Paper Science & Techno. at Georgia Tech)*
Inst. of Paper Science & Techno. at Georgia Tech 103, 726 *(see also Georgia Inst. of Techno.)*
Inst. of Physical Therapy *(see Univ. of St. Augustine for Health Sciences)*
Inst. of Prof. Careers 543

Inst. of Prof. Skills *(see Prof. Skills Inst.)*
Inst. of Psychological Studies *(see Psychological Studies Inst.)*
Inst. of Public Administration 740
Inst. of Specialized Training & Management *(see City Coll. Casselberry)*
Inst. of Taoist Edu. & Acupuncture 744
Inst. of Techno. 460
Inst. of Techno. at Utica/Rome *(see State Univ. of New York Inst. of Techno. at Utica/Rome)*
Inst. of Techno. of Northern Alberta *(see Northern Alberta Inst. of Techno.)*
Inst. of Textile Techno. 734, 738 *(see also North Carolina State Univ.)*
Inst. of Transpersonal Psychology 44
Inst. of World Politics 744
Instituto Centroamericano de Administracion de Empresas 434
Instituto Chaviano de Mayaguez *(see Institucion Chaviano de Mayaguez)*
Instituto Comercial de Puerto Rico Jr. Coll. 348
Instituto de Banca y Comercio 604
Instituto de Capacitacion Tecnica en Servicios de Hospitalidad Monteclaro *(see Monteclaro: Escuela de Hoteleria y Artes Servicios de Hospitalidad)*
Instituto de Cosmetologia y Estetica La Reine *(see Instituto de Educacion Tecnica Ocupacional LaReine)*
Instituto de Educacion Tecnica Ocupacional LaReine 604
Instituto de Educacion Vocacional 604
Instituto de Empresa 716
Instituto Irma Valentin—Caguas 604
Instituto Irma Valentin—Manati 604
Instituto Irma Valentin—Mayaguez 604
Instituto Merlix 604
Instituto Postsecundario de Educación a Distancia 604
Instituto Tecnologico Autonoma de Mexico *(see Autonomous Tech. Inst. of Mexico)*
Instituto Tecnologico Empresarial 605
Instituto Tecnologico y de Estudios Superiores de Monterrey 436
Instituto Vocational y Comercial, EDIC 736 *(see also EDIC Coll.)*
Insurance Coll. *(see Saint John's Univ.)*
Integrated Control Systems, Inc. *(see IMPAC Univ.)*
Integris Baptist Med. Ctr. 695

Intellitec Coll—Colorado Springs 68
Intellitec Coll—Grand Junction 68
Intellitec Med. Inst. 68
Intensive American English Inst. *(see House of Tutors Learning Centers USA, Inc)*
Inter American Coll. *(see InterAmerican Coll.)*
Inter American Univ. of Puerto Rico Aguadilla Campus 348
Inter American Univ. of Puerto Rico Arecibo Campus 348
Inter American Univ. of Puerto Rico Barranquitas Campus 348
Inter American Univ. of Puerto Rico Bayamon Campus 348
Inter American Univ. of Puerto Rico Fajardo Campus 348
Inter American Univ. of Puerto Rico Guayama Campus 349
Inter American Univ. of Puerto Rico Metropolitan Campus 349
Inter American Univ. of Puerto Rico Ponce Campus 349
Inter American Univ. of Puerto Rico San German Campus 349
Inter American Univ. of Puerto Rico Sch. of Law 349
Inter American Univ. of Puerto Rico Sch. of Optometry 349
Interactive Coll. of Techno. 105 *(see also Interactive Learning Systems)*
Interactive Learning Systems 620
Inter-American Adventist Theological Seminary 744
Inter-American Air Forces Acad. 620
InterAmerican Coll. 743
Interboro Inst. 265
InterCoast Colleges 460
Intercollegiate Coll. of Nursing 707
Intercultural Communications Coll. 496
Intercultural Inst. of California 743
Interdenominational Theological Ctr. 105
Interface Computer Sch. 637
Interfaith Health Care Ministries, Rhode Island Hosp. 736 *(see also Chaplaincy Ctr.)*
Interfaith Med. Ctr. 687
Interfaith Pastoral Counseling Centre 712
Interior Design Sch. of New York *(see New York Sch. of Interior Design)*
Interior Designers Inst. 44
Interlochen Ctr. for the Arts 678
Intermountain Bus. Coll. *(see Stevens-Henager Coll.)*
Intermountain Coll. of Court Reporting *(see Eagle Gate Coll.)*

Internatinal Sch. of Physical Theater of Dell'Arte *(see Dell'Arte Internatinal Sch. of Physical Theater)*
Int'l. 2000 Beauty Coll. *(see Knox Int'l. 2000 Beauty Coll.)*
Int'l. Acad. 484 *(see also Aspen Univ.)*
Int'l. Acad. of Beauty #6 445
Int'l. Acad. of Cosmetology 460, 760
Int'l. Acad. of Design *(see Int'l. Acad. of Design & Techno.)*
Int'l. Acad. of Design & Techno. 88, 123, 199, 240, 332
Int'l. Acad. of Design & Tech— Nashville 611
Int'l. Acad. of Design & Tech—Seattle 412
Int'l. Acad. of Hair Design 580 *(see also Int'l. Acad., Int'l. Acad. of Beauty #6)*
Int'l. Acad. of Merchandising & Design *(see Int'l. Acad. of Design & Techno.)*
Int'l. Acad. of Merchandising & Design—Toronto 712
Int'l. Air Acad. 637
Int'l. Aviation & Travel Acad. 737
Int'l. B Naturale Beauty Sch., Inc. 755
Int'l. Baptist Coll. 17
Int'l. Beauty Acad. 472
Int'l. Beauty Acad., Inc. 758
Int'l. Beauty Coll. #3 620
Int'l. Beauty Coll. #4 620
Int'l. Beauty Sch. *(see Int'l. Sch. of Beauty, Inc.)*
Int'l. Beauty Sch—Bel Air 522
Int'l. Beauty Sch—Charlottesville 632
Int'l. Beauty Sch—Cumberland 522
Int'l. Beauty Sch—Martinsburg 641
Int'l. Bible Coll. 721 *(see also Heritage Christian Univ.)*
Int'l. Broadcasting Coll. *(see Int'l. Coll. of Broadcasting)*
Int'l. Bus. Coll. 138, 379 *(see also Bus. Skills Inst.)*
Int'l. Ctr. for American English 460
Int'l. Christian Edu. 460
Int'l. City Beauty Coll. 494
Int'l. Coll. 88
Int'l. Coll. & Grad. Sch. 114
Int'l. Coll. of Baltimore *(see Baltimore Int'l. Coll.)*
Int'l. Coll. of Broadcasting 580
Int'l. Coll. of Hospitality Management Cesar Ritz 73
Int'l. Coll. of the Cayman Islands 434
Int'l. Cosmetology Research Ctr. *(see Pivot Point Int'l. Acad.)*
Int'l. Culinary Acad. *(see Pennsylvania Culinary Inst.)*

Int'l. Divers Acad. *(see Divers Acad. international)*
Int'l. English Inst. 611
Int'l. Fine Arts Coll. 725 *(see also Miami Int'l. Univ. of Art & Design)*
Int'l. Grad. Sch. *(see Int'l. Coll. & Grad. Sch.)*
Int'l. Import-Export Inst. 17
Int'l. Inst. of Chinese Medicine 733
Int'l. Inst. of Chinese Medicine— Albuquerque 733
Int'l. Inst. of Hair Design 628
Int'l. Inst. of the Americas 17, 721
Int'l. Inst. of Transportation Resource, Inc. (I.I.T.R.) *(see IITR Truck Driving Sch.)*
Int'l. Jr. Coll. 349
Int'l. Language Inst. of Massachusetts, Inc. 525
Int'l. Management Centres Assoc. 740
Int'l. Mid Pac Acad. 727
Int'l. Mid Pac Coll. 727
Int'l. Renowned Beauty Acad. 620
Int'l. Sch. of Beauty 725 *(see also Bene's Int'l. Sch. of Beauty, Inc.)*
Int'l. Sch. of Beauty, Inc. 460
Int'l. Sch. of Cosmetology, Inc. 460
Int'l. Sch. of Information Management *(see Aspen Univ.)*
Int'l. Schools 556
Int'l. Studio Art Centers *(see Studio Art Centers Int'l.)*
Int'l. Tech. Coll. 605
Int'l. Technological Univ. 44
Int'l. Theological Seminary 743
Int'l. Theology Sch. *(see Int'l. Sch. of Theology)*
Int'l. Training & Exchange *(see INTRAX English Inst.)*
Int'l. Training Careers 484
Int'l. Training Sch. *(see Sch. for Int'l. Training)*
Int'l. Univ. *(see Int'l. Univ. in Geneva, Int'l. Univ. of Monaco, Jones Int'l. Univ.)*
Int'l. Univ. in Geneva 752
Int'l. Univ. of Monaco 436, 740
Int'l. Yacht Restoration Sch. 607
Interservice *(see Acad. of Health Sciences)*
InTouch Bodywork Inst., Inc. *(see Massage Therapy Coll. of Baton Rouge)*
INTRAX English Inst. 460
INTRAX Int'l. Inst. *(see INTRAX English Inst.)*
Inver Hills Coll. *(see Inver Hills Comm. Coll.)*
Inver Hills Comm. Coll. 210
Iola Jr. Coll. *(see Allen County Comm. Coll.)*

Iona Coll. 265
Iowa Central Coll. *(see Iowa Central Comm. Coll.)*
Iowa Central Comm. Coll. 147
Iowa Coll. *(see Grinnell Coll.)*
Iowa Health Des Moines *(see Blank Children's Hosp.)*
Iowa Lakes Coll. *(see Iowa Lakes Comm. Coll.)*
Iowa Lakes Comm. Coll. 147
Iowa Methodist, Lutheran & Blank Children's Hosp. *(see Blank Children's Hosp.)*
Iowa Sch. of Barbering & Hairstyling *(see American Coll. of Hairstyling—Des Moines)*
Iowa Sch. of Beauty—Des Moines 507
Iowa Sch. of Beauty—Marshalltown 507
Iowa Sch. of Beauty—Ottumwa 508
Iowa Sch. of Beauty—Sioux City 508
Iowa State Normal Sch. *(see Univ. of Northern Iowa)*
Iowa State Teachers Coll. *(see Univ. of Northern Iowa)*
Iowa State Univ. 148
Iowa Valley Coll. *(see Iowa Valley Comm. Coll. Dist.)*
Iowa Valley Comm. Coll. *(see Iowa Valley Comm. Coll. Dist.)*
Iowa Valley Comm. Coll. Dist. 148
Iowa Wesleyan Coll. 148
Iowa Western Coll. *(see Iowa Western Comm. Coll.)*
Iowa Western Comm. Coll. 148
Irene's Myomassology Inst. 529
Iron City Commercial Coll. *(see Duff's Bus. Inst.)*
Ironwood Jr. Coll. *(see Gogebic Comm. Coll.)*
Irvine Valley Coll. 44
Isabella G. Hart Sch. of Practical Nursing 687
ISIM Univ. 724 *(see also Aspen Univ.)*
Island Drafting & Tech. Inst. 561
Island Med. Ctr. 733
Island Univ., The *(see Texas A&M Univ—Corpus Christi)*
Isothermal Coll. *(see Isothermal Comm. Coll.)*
Isothermal Comm. Coll. 288
Itasca Comm. Coll. 210
Itawamba Coll. *(see Itawamba Comm. Coll.)*
Itawamba Comm. Coll. 219
Ithaca Coll. 265
ITI Tech. Coll. 516
ITT Tech. Inst. 17, 44, 45, 68, 88, 116, 139, 199, 226, 304, 321, 366, 367, 379, 394, 412, 413, 424

ITT Tech. Inst—Hayward 723
IU Bloomington *(see Indiana Univ. Bloomington)*
IU East *(see Indiana Univ. East)*
IU Kokomo *(see Indiana Univ. Kokomo)*
IU Northwest *(see Indiana Univ. Northwest)*
IU South Bend *(see Indiana Univ. South Bend)*
IU Southeast *(see Indiana Univ. Southeast)*
IUPU Columbus *(see Indiana Univ-Purdue Univ. Columbus)*
IUPU Fort Wayne *(see Indiana Univ-Purdue Univ. Fort Wayne)*
IUPU Indianapolis *(see Indiana Univ-Purdue Univ. Indianapolis)*
Iverson Court Reporting Inst. *(see Iverson Inst. of Court Reporting)*
Iverson Inst. of Court Reporting 620
Ivory Dental Techno. Coll. 461
Ivy Tech Comm. Coll. of Indiana—Bloomington 139, 727
Ivy Tech Comm. Coll. of Indiana—Central Indiana 139
Ivy Tech Comm. Coll. of Indiana—Columbus 139
Ivy Tech Comm. Coll. of Indiana—East Central 140, 727
Ivy Tech Comm. Coll. of Indiana—East Chicago *(see Ivy Tech Comm. Coll. of Indiana—Northwest)*
Ivy Tech Comm. Coll. of Indiana—Elkhart *(see Ivy Tech Comm. Coll. of Indiana—North Central)*
Ivy Tech Comm. Coll. of Indiana—Evansville *(see Ivy Tech Comm. Coll. of Indiana—Southwest)*
Ivy Tech Comm. Coll. of Indiana—Fort Wayne *(see Ivy Tech Comm. Coll. of Indiana—Northeast)*
Ivy Tech Comm. Coll. of Indiana—Indianapolis *(see Ivy Tech Comm. Coll. of Indiana—Central Indiana)*
Ivy Tech Comm. Coll. of Indiana—Kokomo 140
Ivy Tech Comm. Coll. of Indiana—Lafayette 140
Ivy Tech Comm. Coll. of Indiana—Madison 140, 728
Ivy Tech Comm. Coll. of Indiana—Marion *(see Ivy Tech Comm. Coll. of Indiana—Northwest)*
Ivy Tech Comm. Coll. of Indiana—Michigan City *(see Ivy Tech Comm. Coll. of Indiana—Northwest)*
Ivy Tech Comm. Coll. of Indiana—Muncie *(see Ivy Tech Comm. Coll. of Indiana—East Central)*

Ivy Tech Comm. Coll. of Indiana—North Central 140, 728
Ivy Tech Comm. Coll. of Indiana—Northeast 140, 728
Ivy Tech Comm. Coll. of Indiana—Northwest 141
Ivy Tech Comm. Coll. of Indiana—Richmond 141
Ivy Tech Comm. Coll. of Indiana—Sellersburg 141
Ivy Tech Comm. Coll. of Indiana—South Bend *(see Ivy Tech Comm. Coll. of Indiana—North Central)*
Ivy Tech Comm. Coll. of Indiana—Southeast *(see Ivy Tech Comm. Coll. of Indiana—Madison)*
Ivy Tech Comm. Coll. of Indiana—Southwest 141, 728
Ivy Tech Comm. Coll. of Indiana—Valparaiso *(see Ivy Tech Comm. Coll. of Indiana—Northwest)*
Ivy Tech Comm. Coll. of Indiana—Wabash Valley 141, 728
Ivy Tech Comm. Coll. of Indiana—Warsaw *(see Ivy Tech Comm. Coll. of Indiana—North Central)*
Ivy Tech Comm. Coll—Columbus 727 *(see also Ivy Tech Comm. Coll. of Indiana—Columbus)*
Ivy Tech Comm. Coll—Kokomo 727 *(see also Ivy Tech Comm. Coll. of Indiana—Kokomo)*
Ivy Tech Comm. Coll—Lafayette 727 *(see also Ivy Tech Comm. Coll. of Indiana—Lafayette)*
Ivy Tech Comm. Coll—Northwest *(see Ivy Tech Comm. Coll. of Indiana—Northwest)*
Ivy Tech Comm. Coll—Richmond 728 *(see also Ivy Tech Comm. Coll. of Indiana—Richmond)*
Ivy Tech Comm. Coll—Sellersburg 728 *(see also Ivy Tech Comm. Coll. of Indiana—Sellersburg)*
Ivy Tech Comm. Coll—Southern Indiana *(see Ivy Tech Comm. Coll. of Indiana—Sellersburg)*
Ivy Tech Region 1 *(see Ivy Tech Comm. Coll. of Indiana—East Chicago, Ivy Tech Comm. Coll. of Indiana—Michigan City, Ivy Tech Comm. Coll. of Indiana—Northwest, Ivy Tech Comm. Coll. of Indiana—Valparaiso)*
Ivy Tech Region 2 *(see Ivy Tech Comm. Coll. of Indiana—Elkhart, Ivy Tech Comm. Coll. of Indiana—North Central, Ivy Tech Comm. Coll. of Indiana—Warsaw)*

Ivy Tech Region 3 *(see Ivy Tech Comm. Coll. of Indiana—Northeast)*
Ivy Tech Region 4 *(see Ivy Tech Comm. Coll. of Indiana—Lafayette)*
Ivy Tech Region 5 *(see Ivy Tech Comm. Coll. of Indiana—Kokomo, Ivy Tech Comm. Coll. of Indiana—Logansport, Ivy Tech Comm. Coll. of Indiana—Wabash)*
Ivy Tech Region 6 *(see Ivy Tech Comm. Coll. of Indiana—Anderson, Ivy Tech Comm. Coll. of Indiana—East Central, Ivy Tech Comm. Coll. of Indiana—Marion)*
Ivy Tech Region 7 *(see Ivy Tech Comm. Coll. of Indiana—Wabash Valley)*
Ivy Tech Region 8 *(see Ivy Tech Comm. Coll. of Indiana—Central Indiana)*
Ivy Tech Region 9 *(see Ivy Tech Comm. Coll. of Indiana—Richmond)*
Ivy Tech Region 10 *(see Ivy Tech Comm. Coll. of Indiana—Columbus)*
Ivy Tech Region 11 *(see Ivy Tech Comm. Coll. of Indiana—Lawrenceburg, Ivy Tech Comm. Coll. of Indiana—Madison)*
Ivy Tech Region 12 *(see Ivy Tech Comm. Coll. of Indiana—Southwest)*
Ivy Tech Region 13 *(see Ivy Tech Comm. Coll. of Indiana—Sellersburg)*
Ivy Tech Region 14 *(see Ivy Tech Comm. Coll. of Indiana—Bloomington)*
Ivy Tech State Coll—Bloomington 727 *(see also Ivy Tech Comm. Coll. of Indiana—Bloomington)*
Ivy Tech State Coll—Central Indiana *(see Ivy Tech Comm. Coll. of Indiana—Central Indiana)*
Ivy Tech State Coll—Columbus 727 *(see also Ivy Tech Comm. Coll. of Indiana—Columbus)*
Ivy Tech State Coll—Columbus/Bloomington *(see Ivy Tech Comm. Coll. of Indiana—Columbus)*
Ivy Tech State Coll—East Central 727 *(see also Ivy Tech Comm. Coll. of Indiana—East Central)*
Ivy Tech State Coll—Indianapolis *(see Ivy Tech Comm. Coll. of Indiana—Central Indiana)*

Ivy Tech State Coll—Kokomo 727
*(see also Ivy Tech Comm. Coll. of
Indiana—Kokomo)*
Ivy Tech State Coll—Lafayette 727
*(see also Ivy Tech Comm. Coll. of
Indiana—Lafayette)*
Ivy Tech State Coll—North Central
728 *(see also Ivy Tech Comm.
Coll. of Indiana—North Central)*
Ivy Tech State Coll—Northeast 728
*(see also Ivy Tech Comm. Coll. of
Indiana—Northeast)*
Ivy Tech State Coll—Northwest *(see
Ivy Tech Comm. Coll. of Indiana—
Northwest)*
Ivy Tech State Coll—Sellersburg 728
*(see also Ivy Tech Comm. Coll. of
Indiana—Sellersburg)*
Ivy Tech State Coll—Southeast 728
*(see also Ivy Tech Comm. Coll. of
Indiana—Madison)*
Ivy Tech State Coll—Southwest 728
*(see also Ivy Tech Comm. Coll. of
Indiana—Southwest)*
Ivy Tech State Coll—Wabash Valley
728
Ivy Tech State Coll—Whitewater 728
*(see also Ivy Tech Comm. Coll. of
Indiana—Richmond)*
Ivy Tech—Bloomington *(see Ivy Tech
Comm. Coll. of Indiana—
Bloomington)*
Ivy Tech—Columbus *(see Ivy Tech
Comm. Coll. of Indiana—
Columbus)*
Ivy Tech—East Central *(see Ivy Tech
Comm. Coll. of Indiana—East
Central)*
Ivy Tech—East Chicago *(see Ivy Tech
Comm. Coll. of Indiana—
Northwest)*
Ivy Tech—Elkhart *(see Ivy Tech
Comm. Coll. of Indiana—North
Central)*
Ivy Tech—Evansville *(see Ivy Tech
Comm. Coll. of Indiana—
Southwest)*
Ivy Tech—Fort Wayne *(see Ivy Tech
Comm. Coll. of Indiana—
Northeast)*
Ivy Tech—Gary *(see Ivy Tech Comm.
Coll. of Indiana—Northwest)*
Ivy Tech—Indianapolis *(see Ivy Tech
Comm. Coll. of Indiana—Central
Indiana)*
Ivy Tech—Kokomo *(see Ivy Tech
Comm. Coll. of Indiana—Kokomo)*
Ivy Tech—Lafayette *(see Ivy Tech
Comm. Coll. of Indiana—
Lafayette)*

Ivy Tech—Lawrenceburg *(see Ivy
Tech Comm. Coll. of Indiana—
Madison)*
Ivy Tech—Madison *(see Ivy Tech
Comm. Coll. of Indiana—
Madison)*
Ivy Tech—Michigan City *(see Ivy Tech
Comm. Coll. of Indiana—
Northwest)*
Ivy Tech—North Central *(see Ivy Tech
Comm. Coll. of Indiana—North
Central)*
Ivy Tech—Northwest *(see Ivy Tech
Comm. Coll. of Indiana—
Northwest)*
Ivy Tech—Richmond *(see Ivy Tech
Comm. Coll. of Indiana—
Richmond)*
Ivy Tech—Sellersburg *(see Ivy Tech
Comm. Coll. of Indiana—
Sellersburg)*
Ivy Tech—South Bend *(see Ivy Tech
Comm. Coll. of Indiana—North
Central)*
Ivy Tech—Southeast *(see Ivy Tech
Comm. Coll. of Indiana—
Madison)*
Ivy Tech—Southwest *(see Ivy Tech
Comm. Coll. of Indiana—
Southwest)*
Ivy Tech—Terre Haute *(see Ivy Tech
Comm. Coll. of Indiana—Wabash
Valley)*
Ivy Tech—Valparaiso *(see Ivy Tech
Comm. Coll. of Indiana—
Northwest)*
Ivy Tech—Wabash Valley *(see Ivy
Tech Comm. Coll. of Indiana—
Wabash Valley)*
Ivy Tech—Warsaw *(see Ivy Tech
Comm. Coll. of Indiana—North
Central)*
Ivy Tech—Whitewater *(see Ivy Tech
Comm. Coll. of Indiana—
Richmond)*

J

J & J Hair Design Coll. 536
J & M Acad. of Cosmetology, Inc. 513
J. Everett Light Career Ctr. 505
J. Michael Harrold Beauty Acad., Inc.
505
J. Paul Bagan & Associates 723 *(see
also Dale Carnegie Training of
San Jose)*
J. R. Rodgers & Associates Dale
Carnegie Systems 739
J. R. Rodgers & Associates, Inc. 543,
643, 732

J. Sargeant Reynolds Coll. *(see J.
Sargeant Reynolds Comm. Coll.)*
J. Sargeant Reynolds Comm. Coll. 403
J.F. Drake State Tech. Coll. 6 *(see also
J.F. Drake State Tech. Coll.)*
J.F. Ingram Comm. Coll. *(see J.F.
Ingram State Tech. Coll.)*
J.F. Ingram State Tech. Coll. 6 *(see
also J.F. Ingram State Tech. Coll.)*
J.H. Thompson Academies *(see Great
Lakes Inst. of Techno.)*
J.S. Green Collegiate Inst. *(see
Piedmont Coll.)*
Jackie Nell Executive Secretary Sch.
(see Austin Bus. Coll.)
Jackson Beauty Sch. 618
Jackson Coll. *(see Jackson Comm.
Coll., Jackson State Comm. Coll.,
Tufts Univ.)*
Jackson Comm. Coll. 200 *(see also
Jackson State Comm. Coll.)*
Jackson County Industrial Edu. Ctr.
(see Southwestern Comm. Coll.)
Jackson County Tech. Ctr. *(see Roane
Jackson Tech. Ctr.)*
Jackson Health System *(see Jackson
Mem. Hosp.)*
Jackson Male Acad. *(see Union Univ.)*
Jackson Mem. Hosp. 662
Jackson Sch. of Bus. *(see West
Tennessee Bus. Coll.)*
Jackson State Coll. *(see Jackson
State Comm. Coll.)*
Jackson State Comm. Coll. 367
Jackson State Univ. 219
Jackson Univ. *(see Andrew Jackson
Univ., Jackson State Univ.)*
Jacksonville Baptist Coll. *(see
Jacksonville Coll.)*
Jacksonville Beauty Inst., Inc. 484
Jacksonville Coll. 379 *(see also
Baptist Missionary Assoc.
Theological Seminary)*
Jacksonville Coll. Seminary *(see
Baptist Missionary Assoc.
Theological Seminary)*
Jacksonville Comm. Coll. *(see Florida
Comm. Coll. at Jacksonville)*
Jacksonville Dale Carnegie Training
*(see Folkner Training Associates,
Inc.)*
Jacksonville Female Acad. *(see Illinois
Coll.)*
Jacksonville Jr. Coll. *(see Jacksonville
Univ.)*
Jacksonville Med. Ctr. *(see Shands
Jacksonville Med. Ctr.)*
Jacksonville State Normal Sch. *(see
Jacksonville State Univ.)*
Jacksonville State Teachers Coll. *(see
Jacksonville State Univ.)*

Jacksonville State Univ. 6
Jacksonville Stenotype Inst. *(see Stenotype Inst. of Jacksonville)*
Jacksonville Univ. 88 *(see also Jacksonville State Univ.)*
Jacobi/Montefiore Hosp/East *(see Montefiore Med. Ctr. East Campus)*
Jacobs Creek Job Corps 611
Jacobs Facilities, Inc. 538
Jaffray Sch. of Missions *(see Alliance Theological Seminary)*
JAG Sch. *(see Judge Advocate General's Sch.)*
Jamaica Hosp. Med. Ctr. 687
Jamaica Med. Ctr. *(see Jamaica Hosp. Med. Ctr.)*
Jameat Alemarat Al Arabia Al Mutaheda *(see United Arab Emirates Univ.)*
James A. Haley VA Med. Ctr. *(see James A. Haley Veterans Affairs Med. Ctr.)*
James A. Haley Veterans Affairs Med. Ctr. 662
James A. Rhodes State Coll. 304
James Albert Sch. of Cosmetology 461
James & Carolyn McAfee Sch. of Theology *(see Mercer Univ.)*
James Cancer Hosp. *(see Ohio State Univ.)*
James Connally Tech. Inst. *(see Texas State Tech. Coll—Harlingen, Texas State Tech. Coll—West Texas at Sweetwater, Texas State Tech. Coll—Waco)*
James E. Varner & Associates, Inc. 496
James Graham Brown Cancer Ctr. *(see Univ. of Louisville)*
James H. Faulkner State Comm. Coll. 6 *(see also James H. Faulkner State Comm. Coll.)*
James H. Quillen Veterans Affairs Med. Ctr. 702
James King Coll. *(see King Coll.)*
James L. Walker Vocational-Tech. Ctr. *(see Lorenzo Walker Inst. of Techno.)*
James Madison Coll. 201 *(see also Michigan State Univ.)*
James Madison Coll. at Michigan State Univ. *(see Michigan State Univ.)*
James Madison Univ. 403
James Monroe Ctr. for Grad. & Prof. Studies 407 *(see also Univ. of Mary Washington)*
James Rumsey Tech. Inst. 641

James Sprunt Coll. *(see James Sprunt Comm. Coll.)*
James Sprunt Comm. Coll. 288
Jameson Health System *(see Jameson Hosp.)*
Jameson Hosp. 698
Jameson Mem. Hosp. *(see Jameson Hosp.)*
Jamestown Bus. Coll. 265
Jamestown Coll. 296 *(see also Jamestown Comm. Coll.)*
Jamestown Coll—New York *(see Jamestown Comm. Coll.)*
Jamestown Comm. Coll. 265
Janesville Acad. of Cosmetology *(see Acad. of Cosmetology)*
Jarvis Christian Coll. 380
Jarvis Coll. *(see Jarvis Christian Coll.)*
Jasper County Jr. Coll. *(see Missouri Southern State Univ.)*
Javelin Tech. Training Ctr. 494
Jay Coll. of Criminal Justice *(see City Univ. of New York John Jay Coll. of Criminal Justice)*
Jay's Tech. Inst. 620
Je Boutique Coll. of Beauty 461
Jean Madeline Aveda Inst. 597
Jean Madeline Edu. Ctr. for Cosmetology *(see Jean Madeline Aveda Inst.)*
Jeanes Hosp. 698
Jean's Nails, Etc. 761
Jefferson Coll. 226 *(see also Jefferson Comm. Coll., Jefferson State Comm. Coll., Washington & Jefferson Coll.)*
Jefferson Coll. of Health Sciences 403, 738
Jefferson Comm. & Tech. Coll. 161, 729
Jefferson Comm. Coll. 265, 304, 729 *(see also Jefferson Comm. & Tech. Coll., Jefferson State Comm. Coll.)*
Jefferson Comm. Tech. Colleges *(see Jefferson Comm. & Tech. Coll.)*
Jefferson County Internship Consortium 672
Jefferson County State Vocational-Tech. Sch. *(see Jefferson Comm. & Tech. Coll.)*
Jefferson County State Vocational-Tech. Sch. & Manpower Skills Ctr. *(see Jefferson Comm. & Tech. Coll.)*
Jefferson County Tech. Inst. *(see Jefferson Comm. Coll.)*
Jefferson County-Dubois Area Vocational Tech. Sch. 698
Jefferson Davis Comm. Coll. 6

Jefferson Law Sch. *(see Thomas Jefferson Sch. of Law)*
Jefferson Med. Coll. *(see Thomas Jefferson Univ.)*
Jefferson Reg. Med. Ctr. 652
Jefferson Sch. of Law *(see Thomas Jefferson Sch. of Law)*
Jefferson State Coll. *(see Jefferson State Comm. Coll.)*
Jefferson State Comm. Coll. 6
Jefferson Tech. Coll. 729 *(see also Jefferson Comm. Coll., Jefferson Comm. & Tech. Coll.)*
Jefferson Univ. *(see Thomas Jefferson Univ.)*
Jenissa Beauty Acad. 760
Jenkintown Music Sch. 600 *(see also Settlement Music Sch.)*
Jenks Beauty Coll. 590 *(see also Sand Springs Beauty Coll.)*
Jennie Edmundson Hosp. 671
Jennie Edmundson Mem. Hosp. *(see Jennie Edmundson Hosp.)*
Jenny Lea Acad. of Cosmetology—Harlan 513
Jenny Lea Acad. of Cosmetology—Whitesburg 513
Jerry L. Pettis Mem. Veterans Affairs Hosp. *(see Loma Linda Veterans Affairs Healthcare System)*
Jerry Wilson & Associates, Inc. 448
Jerry's Sch. of Hairstyling, Inc. 732 *(see also Cosmetology Concepts Inst.)*
Jersey City Med. Ctr. 683
Jersey City State Coll. *(see New Jersey City Univ.)*
Jersey Sch. of Locksmithing *(see New Jersey Sch. of Locksmithing)*
Jersey Shore Med. Ctr. *(see Jersey Shore Univ. Med. Ctr.)*
Jersey Shore Univ. Med. Ctr. 683
Jesse Brown VA Med. Ctr. *(see Jesse Brown Veterans Affairs Med. Ctr.)*
Jesse Brown Veterans Affairs Med. Ctr. 667
Jessup Univ. *(see William Jessup Univ.)*
Jesuit Comm. Santa Clara Univ. *(see Santa Clara Univ.)*
Jesuit Sch. of Theology at Berkeley 45
Jesus Coll. *(see Macalester Coll.)*
Jewell Coll. *(see William Jewell Coll.)*
Jewish Children's Bureau of Chicago 668
Jewish General Hosp. 712
Jewish Hosp. Coll. of Nursing & Allied Health 732 *(see also Barnes-Jewish Coll. of Nursing & Allied Health)*

Jewish Inst. for Pastoral Care, The 686
Jewish Inst. of Michigan *(see Michigan Jewish Inst.)*
Jewish Inst. of Religion *(see Hebrew Union Coll—Jewish Inst. of Religion)*
Jewish Seminary of America *(see Jewish Theological Seminary)*
Jewish Seminary of America *(see Jewish Theological Seminary)*
Jewish Theological Seminary, The 265
JFK Med. Ctr. *(see John F. Kennedy Med. Ctr.)*
JFK Univ. *(see John F. Kennedy Univ.)*
JNA Culinary Inst. *(see JNA Inst. of Culinary Arts)*
JNA Inst. of Culinary Arts 597
Job Corps Ctr. of Atlanta *(see Atlanta Job Corps Ctr.)*
Job Corps Ctr. of Bamberg *(see Bamberg Job Corps Ctr.)*
Job Corps Ctr. of Batesville *(see Batesville Job Corps Ctr.)*
Job Corps Ctr. of Cincinnati *(see Cincinnati Job Corps Ctr.)*
Job Corps Ctr. of Denison *(see Denison Job Corps Ctr.)*
Job Corps Ctr. of Gulfport *(see Gulfport Job Corps Ctr.)*
Job Corps Ctr. of Miami *(see Miami Job Corps Ctr.)*
Job Corps Ctr. of Shreveport *(see Shreveport Job Corps Ctr.)*
Joe Kubert Sch. of Cartoon & Graphic Art 552
Joffrey Ballet Sch. *(see American Ballet Ctr/Joffrey Ballet Sch.)*
John A. Gupton Coll. 367
John A. Logan Coll. 123
John Amico's Sch. of Hair Design 501
John B. Stetson Univ. *(see Stetson Univ.)*
John Bastyr Coll. of Naturopathic Medicine *(see Bastyr Univ.)*
John Brown Coll. & Acad. *(see John Brown Univ.)*
John Brown Univ. 25 *(see also John Brown Univ.)*
John C. Calhoun State Comm. Coll. 721 *(see also Calhoun Comm. Coll.)*
John Cabot Univ. 435
John Calvin Jr. Coll. *(see Calvin Coll.)*
John Carroll Univ. 304
John D Rockefeller IV Career Ctr. 641
John D. Langdon & Associates, Inc. 734 *(see also Lance Tyson & Associates Dale Carnegie Training of Northeast Ohio)*

John D. Thompson Hospice Inst., The 659
John Dewey Coll. 349
John E. Brown Coll. *(see John Brown Univ.)*
John E. Brown Coll. & Acad. *(see John Brown Univ.)*
John F. Kennedy Med. Ctr. 684
John F. Kennedy Univ. 45
John Fisher Coll. *(see Saint John Fisher Coll.)*
John G. Hondros Acad. of Real Estate *(see Hondros Coll.)*
John Hines & Associates, Inc. 643
John Jay Beauty Coll. 517
John Jay Coll. of Criminal Justice *(see City Univ. of New York John Jay Coll. of Criminal Justice)*
John Jay Kenner Acad. 517
John L. Gildner Reg. Inst. for Children & Adolescents 674
John L. McClellan Mem. Veterans Hosp. *(see Central Arkansas Veterans Healthcare System)*
John Leland Ctr. for Theological Studies, The 750
John M. Jennings & Associates, Inc. 620, 737
John M. Patterson State Tech. Coll. *(see Trenholm State Tech. Coll.)*
John Marshall Law Sch., The 123
John Marshall Law Sch—Atlanta 744
John McNeese Jr. Coll. *(see McNeese State Univ.)*
John Moser & Associates, Inc. 721 *(see also Leadership Development, Inc. Dale Carnegie Training)*
John Paul's Hair, Nails & Skin Care Inst. 733
John R. Pelham Tech-Trade Sch. *(see T.A. Lawson State Comm. Coll.)*
John Rodgers & Associates, Inc. *(see JR Rodgers & Associates, Inc.)*
John Tarleton Agricultural Coll. *(see Tarleton State Univ.)*
John Tracy Clinic 461
John Tyler Coll. *(see John Tyler Comm. Coll.)*
John Tyler Comm. Coll. 403
John Umstead Hosp. 691
John Wesley Barber & Beauty Coll. *(see John Wesley Int'l. Barber & Beauty Coll.)*
John Wesley Coll. 288
John Wesley Int'l. Barber & Beauty Coll. 461
John Wood Coll. *(see John Wood Comm. Coll.)*
John Wood Comm. Coll. 123
Johns Hopkins Hosp., The 675

Johns Hopkins Sch. of Medicine *(see Johns Hopkins Hosp.)*
Johns Hopkins Univ. 180
Johns Hopkins Univ. Peabody Inst. *(see Peabody Inst. of the Johns Hopkins Univ.)*
Johnson & Wales Univ. 353
Johnson Bible Coll. 367
Johnson C. Smith Theological Seminary *(see Interdenominational Theological Ctr.)*
Johnson C. Smith Univ. 289
Johnson City Med. Ctr. 702
Johnson Civilian Conservation Ctr. *(see Lyndon B. Johnson Civilian Conservation Ctr.)*
Johnson Coll. 332 *(see also Johnson Bible Coll., Johnson County Comm. Coll., Johnson State Coll.)*
Johnson Comm. Health Ctr. *(see Ben Taub General Hosp.)*
Johnson County Coll. *(see Johnson County Comm. Coll.)*
Johnson County Comm. Coll. 154
Johnson Female Seminary *(see Anderson Univ.)*
Johnson Jr. Coll. *(see Lake-Sumter Comm. Coll.)*
Johnson Med. Sch. *(see Robert Wood Johnson Med. Sch., Univ. of Medicine & Dentistry of New Jersey)*
Johnson Normal Sch. *(see Johnson State Coll.)*
Johnson Sch. of Techno. *(see Johnson Coll.)*
Johnson State Coll. 397
Johnson State Teachers Coll. *(see Johnson State Coll.)*
Johnson Tech. Inst. *(see Johnson Coll.)*
Johnson Trade Sch. *(see Johnson Coll.)*
Johnston Coll. *(see Johnston Comm. Coll.)*
Johnston Comm. Coll. 289
Johnston County Tech. Inst. *(see Johnston Comm. Coll.)*
Johnston Tech. Coll. *(see Johnston Comm. Coll.)*
Johnston Tech. Inst. *(see Johnston Comm. Coll.)*
Joint Board of Theological Colleges 432
Joint Coll. of Military Intelligence *(see Joint Military Intelligence Coll.)*
Joint Intelligence Training Activity, Pacific 461
Joint Military Intelligence Coll. 79

Joint Military Intelligence Training Ctr., Defense 478
Joint Vocational Sch. of Medina County *(see Medina County Career Ctr.)*
Joint Vocational Sch. of Scioto County *(see Scioto County Joint Vocational Sch.)*
Joint Vocational Sch. of Springfield-Clark County *(see Springfield-Clark County Joint Vocational Sch.)*
Joint Vocational Schoolof Mahoning County *(see Mahoning County Career & Tech. Ctr.)*
Joint Vocational Sch. of Ashtabula County *(see Ashtabula County Joint Vocational Sch.)*
Jolie Hair & Beauty Acad., Inc. 525
Joliet Coll. *(see Joliet Jr. Coll.)*
Joliet Jr. Coll. 123
Jon Nave Cosmetology Acad. *(see Nave Cosmetology Acad., Inc.)*
Jon Nave Univ. of Cosmetology, Inc. 611
Jones & Associates, Inc. *(see Michael W. Jones & Associates, Inc.)*
Jones Beauty Coll. #2 621
Jones Beauty Coll. 621
Jones Coll. 88 *(see also Bob Jones Univ., Florida Metropolitan Univ—Orlando North)*
Jones County Coll. *(see Jones County Jr. Coll.)*
Jones County Jr. Coll. 219
Jones Int'l. Univ. 68
Jones Univ. *(see Bob Jones Univ., Jones Int'l. Univ.)*
Jonesville Beauty Sch. 517
Joplin Jr. Coll. *(see Missouri Southern State Univ.)*
José Limón Dance Inst. *(see Limón Dance Inst.)*
Josef Phillips Acad. of Cosmetology 755
Josef's Sch. of Hair Design Inc—Fargo 575
Josef's Sch. of Hair Design, Inc—Grand Forks 575
Joseph C. Laney Trade & Tech. Inst. *(see Laney Coll.)*
Joseph Sch. *(see Rabbi Jacob Joseph Sch.)*
Joseph's Coll. of Beauty *(see Joseph's of Kearney, Sch. of Hair Design)*
Joseph's Coll. of Beauty—Beatrice 542
Joseph's Coll. of Beauty—Hastings 542
Joseph's Coll. of Beauty—Lincoln 542
Joseph's Coll. of Beauty—Norfolk 542

Joseph's of Kearney, Sch. of Hair Design 542
Jothi Montessori Acad. 561
Joy's Sch. of Hair Design 552
JPS Health Ctr—South Campus *(see JPS Inst. for Health Career Development)*
JPS Health Network *(see JPS Inst. for Health Career Development)*
JPS Inst. for Health Career Development 704
JR Rodgers & Associates, Inc. 597, 735
JTPA Sch. of Practical Nursing 678
Juan Roberto Guitar Works *(see Roberto-Venn Sch. of Luthiery)*
Judaism Univ. *(see Univ. of Judaism)*
Judge Advocate General's Sch., The 403
Judson Coll. 6, 123
Juilliard Grad. Sch. *(see Juilliard Sch.)*
Juilliard Sch. of Music *(see Juilliard Sch.)*
Juilliard Sch., The 265
Jung Tao Sch. of Classical Chinese Medicine 757
Juniata Coll. 332
Jr. Agricultural Sch. of Central Arkansas *(see Arkansas State Univ—Beebe)*
Jr. Agriculture Coll. of Central Arkansas *(see Arkansas State Univ—Beebe)*
Jr. Coll. of Connecticut *(see Univ. of Bridgeport)*
Jr. Coll. of Joliet *(see Joliet Jr. Coll.)*
Jr. Coll. of Jones County *(see Jones County Jr. Coll.)*
Jr. Coll. of Modesto *(see Modesto Jr. Coll.)*
Jr. Coll. of Pensacola *(see Pensacola Jr. Coll.)*
Jr. Coll. of Puerto Rico *(see Puerto Rico Tech. Jr. Coll.)*
Jr. Coll. of Santa Rosa *(see Santa Rosa Jr. Coll.)*
Jr. Coll. of Southeastern Colorado *(see Lamar Comm. Coll.)*
Jr. Coll. of Tyler *(see Tyler Jr. Coll.)*
Jr. Coll. of West Virginia *(see West Virginia Jr. Coll.)*
Jr. Coll. of Wharton County *(see Wharton County Jr. Coll.)*

K

K.S.A. Acad. of Cosmetology 529
Kaiser Permanente Los Angeles Med. Ctr. 654

Kaiser Permanente Med. Care Program *(see Kaiser Permanente Los Angeles Med. Ctr., Kaiser Permanente Sch. of Allied Health Sciences, Kaiser Permanente Vista Med. Offices)*
Kaiser Permanente Sch. of Allied Health Sciences 654
Kaiser Permanente Vista Med. Offices 654
Kalamazoo Branch of the Univ. of Michigan *(see Kalamazoo Coll.)*
Kalamazoo Coll. 200
Kalamazoo Literary Inst. *(see Kalamazoo Coll.)*
Kalamazoo Valley Coll. *(see Kalamazoo Valley Comm. Coll.)*
Kalamazoo Valley Comm. Coll. 200
Kanawha Jr. Coll. *(see Univ. of Charleston)*
Kanawha Valley Career Ctr. *(see Garnet Career Ctr.)*
Kankakee Acad. of Hair Design 501
Kankakee Coll. *(see Kankakee Comm. Coll.)*
Kankakee Comm. Coll. 123
Kankakee County Coll. *(see Kankakee Comm. Coll.)*
Kansai Gaidai Hawaii Coll. *(see TransPacific Hawaii Coll.)*
Kansas Central Bible Training Sch. *(see Barclay Coll.)*
Kansas Central Christian Coll. *(see Central Christian Coll. of Kansas)*
Kansas City Area Tech. Sch. *(see Kansas City Kansas Area Tech. Sch.)*
Kansas City Art Inst. 226
Kansas City Bible Coll. *(see Calvary Bible Coll. & Theological Seminary)*
Kansas City Coll. 252 *(see also Kansas City Coll., Kansas City Kansas Comm. Coll., Metropolitan Coll—Albuquerque Campus)*
Kansas City Coll. of Legal Studies *(see Kansas City Coll., Metropolitan Coll—Albuquerque Campus)*
Kansas City Comm. Coll. *(see Kansas City Kansas Comm. Coll.)*
Kansas City Dale Carnegie Training *(see CB&T, Inc)*
Kansas City Kansas Area Tech. Sch. 509
Kansas City Kansas Coll. *(see Kansas City Kansas Comm. Coll.)*
Kansas City Kansas Comm. Coll. 154
Kansas City Kansas Jr. Coll. *(see Kansas City Kansas Comm. Coll.)*
Kansas City Univ. of Medicine & Biosciences, The 226, 732

Kansas City Vo-Tech *(see Kansas City Kansas Area Tech. Sch.)*

Kansas Coll. of Techno. *(see Kansas State Univ.)*

Kansas Coll. of Techno. *(see Kansas State Univ.)*

Kansas Newman Coll. *(see Newman Univ.)*

Kansas Sch. of Hairstyling *(see Old Town Barber & Beauty Coll.)*

Kansas State Normal Sch. *(see Emporia State Univ.)*

Kansas State Teachers Coll. *(see Emporia State Univ.)*

Kansas State Teachers Coll. of Hays *(see Fort Hays State Univ.)*

Kansas State Univ., The 154 *(see also Univ. of Kansas)*

Kansas Univ. *(see Kansas State Univ., The; Univ. of Kansas)*

Kansas Wesleyan Univ. 155

Kapi`olani Coll. *(see Kapi'olani Comm. Coll.)*

Kapi`olani Tech. Sch. *(see Kapi'olani Comm. Coll.)*

Kapi'olani Comm. Coll. 114

Kaplan Coll. *(see Kaplan Univ.)*

Kaplan Coll. 728

Kaplan Test Prep 562

Kaplan Univ. 148, 728

Kaskaskia Coll. 123

Katharine Gibbs Sch. 265, 266, 736 *(see also Gibbs Coll.; Gibbs Coll. of Boston, Inc.; Gibbs Coll— Farmington; Gibbs Coll—Vienna; Gibbs Coll—Cranston; Gibbs Coll—Farmington)*

Katharine Gibbs Sch., Long Island *(see Katharine Gibbs Sch.)*

Katharine Gibbs Sch—Boston *730 (see also Gibbs Coll. of Boston, Inc.)*

Katherine Hamilton Mental Health Ctr. *(see Hamilton Ctr. Inc.)*

Katholieke Universiteit Brabant te Tilburg *(see Tilburg Univ.)*

Kaua`i Coll. *(see Kaua'i Comm. Coll.)*

Kaua`i Vocational Sch. *(see Kaua'i Comm. Coll.)*

Kauai Coll. *(see Kaua'i Comm. Coll.)*

Kauai Comm. Coll. *(see Kaua'i Comm. Coll.)*

Kaua'i Comm. Coll. 114

Kaufman Beauty Sch. 513

Kaw Area Tech. Sch. 509

Kay Harvey Hairdressing Acad. 526

Kaye Beauty Coll. *(see Hair Fashions by Kaye Beauty Coll— Indianapolis, Hair Fashions by Kaye Beauty Coll—Noblesville)*

Kayenta Indian Med. Ctr. *(see Southern California Coll. of Optometry)*

KD Studio 380

Ke Vos Nik Sch. of Hair Design, Inc. 494

Kean Coll. of New Jersey *(see Kean Univ.)*

Kean Univ. 247

Kearney State Coll. *(see Univ. of Nebraska at Kearney)*

Keatchie Female Coll. *(see Louisiana Coll.)*

Keck Grad. Inst. of Applied Life Science 45

Kee Bus. Coll—Newport News 632

Keene Beauty Acad., Inc. 544

Keene Coll. *(see Keene State Coll.)*

Keene Industrial Acad. *(see Southwestern Adventist Univ.)*

Keene State Coll. 242

Keewatin Comm. Coll. 712

Kehilath Yakov Rabbinical Seminary 266

Keio Gijuku Daigaku *(see Keio Univ.)*

Keio Univ. 715

Keiser Career Coll. 89

Keiser Career Inst. *(see Keiser Career Coll.)*

Keiser Coll. 89

Keiser Coll. of Techno. *(see Keiser Coll.)*

Keist Bus. Coll. *(see Thomas Coll.)*

Keller & Associates, Inc. *(see Duwayne E. Keller & Associates, Inc.)*

Keller Grad. Sch. of Management *(see DeVry Univ., Keller Grad. Sch. of Management of DeVry Univ.)*

Keller Grad. Sch. of Management of DeVry Univ. 123 *(see also DeVry Univ. Fremont, DeVry Univ. Long Beach)*

Keller Grad. Sch. of Management— Irvine Ctr. 723

Keller Management Sch. *(see Keller Grad. Sch. of Management of DeVry Univ.)*

Keller Sch. of Management *(see Keller Grad. Sch. of Management of DeVry Univ.)*

Kellogg Coll. *(see Kellogg Comm. Coll.)*

Kellogg Comm. Coll. 200

Ken Roberts Corporation 484

Kenai Coll. *(see Kenai Peninsula Coll.)*

Kenai Peninsula Coll. 11

Kendall Coll. 124

Kendall Coll. of Art & Design *(see Ferris State Univ.)*

Kendall Coll. of Art & Design of Ferris State Univ. 198 *(see also Ferris State Univ.)*

Kendall Coll. of Design *(see Ferris State Univ.)*

Kendall Sch. of Art *(see Ferris State Univ.)*

Kendall Sch. of Design *(see Ferris State Univ.)*

Kennebec Valley Coll. *(see Kennebec Valley Comm. Coll.)*

Kennebec Valley Comm. Coll. 176, 730

Kennebec Valley Tech. Coll. 730 *(see also Kennebec Valley Comm. Coll.)*

Kennedy Inst. *(see Kennedy Krieger Inst.)*

Kennedy Krieger Inst. 675

Kennedy Med. Ctr. *(see John F. Kennedy Med. Ctr.)*

Kennedy Univ. *(see John F. Kennedy Univ.)*

Kennedy-King Coll. *(see City Colleges of Chicago—Kennedy-King Coll.)*

Kennesaw Coll. *(see Kennesaw State Univ.)*

Kennesaw Jr. Coll. *(see Kennesaw State Univ.)*

Kennesaw State Coll. *(see Kennesaw State Univ.)*

Kennesaw State Univ. 105

Kenneth Bragg Public Safety Complex 485 *(see also Lake Tech. Ctr.)*

Kenneth Shuler's Sch. of Cosmetology 608

Kenneth Shulers Sch. of Cosmetology, Nail Design 608

Kenrick Sch. of Theology *(see Kenrick-Glennon Seminary)*

Kenrick-Glennon Seminary 227

Kensington Coll. 461

Kent & Sussex Montessori Centre, The 648

Kent State Coll. *(see Kent State Univ.)*

Kent State Normal Coll. *(see Kent State Univ.)*

Kent State Normal Sch. *(see Kent State Univ.)*

Kent State Univ. 304

Kentucky Advanced Techno. Ctr. *(see Kentucky Advanced Techno. Inst.)*

Kentucky Career Inst. *(see Beckfield Coll., Daymar Coll.)*

Kentucky Christian Coll. 729 *(see also Kentucky Christian Univ.)*

Kentucky Christian Univ. 161, 729

Kentucky Coll. of Bus. *(see National Coll. of Bus. & Techno.)*

Kentucky Inst. of Advanced Techno. *(see Kentucky Advanced Techno. Inst.)*
Kentucky Mountain Bible Coll. 161
Kentucky Mountain Coll. *(see Kentucky Mountain Bible Coll.)*
Kentucky Sch. of Mortuary Science, The *(see Mid-America Coll. of Funeral Service)*
Kentucky State Univ. 161
Kentucky Tech *(see Jefferson Comm. & Tech. Coll.)*
Kentucky Tech—Ashland State Vocational Tech. Sch. *(see Ashland Comm. & Tech. Coll.)*
Kentucky Tech—Jefferson State Vocational-Tech. Ctr. *(see Jefferson Comm. & Tech. Coll.)*
Kentucky Tech—Owensboro Campus *(see Owensboro Comm. & Tech. Coll.)*
Kentucky Tech—Somerset Reg. Techno. Ctr. *(see Somerset Comm. Coll.)*
Kentucky Univ. Coll. of Agriculture & Mechanical Arts *(see Univ. of Kentucky)*
Kentucky Univ. Sch. of Biblical Literature & Moral Sciences *(see Lexington Theological Seminary)*
Kentucky Wesleyan Coll. 161
Kenyon Coll. 305
Kettering Coll. of Med. Arts 305
Kettering Med. Ctr. *(see Kettering Coll. of Med. Arts)*
Kettering Univ. 200
Keuka Coll. 266
Key Coll. 89, 725
KeySkills Learning, Inc. 552
Keystone Coll. 333
Keystone Sch. *(see Chubb Inst— Springfield)*
Kiamichi Area Vocational-Tech. Sch— Atoka *(see Kiamichi Techno. Ctr—Atoka)*
Kiamichi Area Vocational-Tech. Sch— Durant *(see Kiamichi Techno. Ctr—Durant)*
Kiamichi Area Vocational-Tech. Sch— Hugo *(see Kiamichi Techno. Ctr— Hugo)*
Kiamichi Area Vocational-Tech. Sch— Idabel *(see Kiamichi Techno. Ctr—Idabel)*
Kiamichi Area Vocational-Tech. Sch— McAlester *(see Kiamichi Techno. Ctr—McAlester)*
Kiamichi Area Vocational-Tech. Sch— Poteau *(see Kiamichi Techno. Ctr—Poteau)*

Kiamichi Area Vocational-Tech. Sch— Spiro *(see Kiamichi Techno. Ctr— Spiro)*
Kiamichi Area Vocational-Tech. Sch— Stigler *(see Kiamichi Techno. Ctr—Stigler)*
Kiamichi Area Vocational-Tech. Sch— Talihina *(see Kiamichi Techno. Ctr—Talihina)*
Kiamichi Area Vo-Tech—Atoka *(see Kiamichi Techno. Ctr—Atoka)*
Kiamichi Area Vo-Tech—Durant *(see Kiamichi Techno. Ctr—Durant)*
Kiamichi Area Vo-Tech—Hugo *(see Kiamichi Techno. Ctr—Hugo)*
Kiamichi Area Vo-Tech—Idabel *(see Kiamichi Techno. Ctr—Idabel)*
Kiamichi Area Vo-Tech—McAlester *(see Kiamichi Techno. Ctr— McAlester)*
Kiamichi Area Vo-Tech—Poteau *(see Kiamichi Techno. Ctr—Poteau)*
Kiamichi Area Vo-Tech—Spiro *(see Kiamichi Techno. Ctr—Spiro)*
Kiamichi Area Vo-Tech—Stigler *(see Kiamichi Techno. Ctr—Stigler)*
Kiamichi Area Vo-Tech—Talihina *(see Kiamichi Techno. Ctr—Talihina)*
Kiamichi Techno. Ctr—Atoka 588
Kiamichi Techno. Ctr—Durant 588
Kiamichi Techno. Ctr—Hugo 588
Kiamichi Techno. Ctr—Idabel 588
Kiamichi Techno. Ctr—McAlester 588
Kiamichi Techno. Ctr—Poteau 588
Kiamichi Techno. Ctr—Spiro 588
Kiamichi Techno. Ctr—Stigler 588
Kiamichi Techno. Ctr—Talihina 588
Kiblen & Associates *(see Thomas J. Kiblen & Associates)*
Kilgore Coll. 380
Kilian Comm. Coll. 361
Kim Anh Acad. of Beauty 461
KIMC Investments, L.P. *(see MedVance Inst.)*
King Beauty Careers *(see Royal Beauty Careers)*
King Coll. 367
King's Career Coll—Florida Boulevard Campus 517
King's Career Coll—Ocean Drive Campus 517
King's Coll. *(see Columbia Univ. in the City of New York; King's Coll., The; King's Coll. & Seminary, The; Univ. of Toronto)*
King's Coll. & Seminary, The 45
King's Coll., Charlotte *(see King's Coll.)*
King's Coll., New York *(see King's Coll.)*
King's Coll., The 266, 289, 333

Kings County Hosp. 687
Kings County Hosp. Downstate Med. Ctr. *(see Kings County Hosp.)*
King's Daughters' Hosp. & Health Service 670
King's Daughters Med. Ctr. 672
Kings River Comm. Coll. *(see Reedley Coll.)*
King's Seminary, The *(see King's Coll. & Seminary)*
Kingsborough Comm. Coll. *(see City Univ. of New York Kingsborough Comm. Coll.)*
Kingsbrook Jewish Med. Ctr. 687
Kingsbury Acad. in Ocala *(see Univ. of Florida)*
Kingwood Coll. 382 *(see also North Harris Montgomery Comm. Coll. Dist.)*
Kino Comm. Hosp. 651
Kirkland Beauty Sch. 638
Kirksville Coll. of Osteopathic Medicine *(see A.T. Still Univ. of Health Sciences)*
Kirkwood Comm. Coll. 148
Kirtland Coll. *(see Kirtland Comm. Coll.)*
Kirtland Comm. Coll. 200
Kishwaukee Coll. 124
Kissimmee Good Samaritan 679 *(see also Kissimmee Good Samaritan Retirement Village)*
Kitchen Acad. 454 *(see also California Sch. of Culinary Arts)*
Kittanning Beauty Sch. of Cosmetology Arts 597
Klamath Coll. *(see Klamath Comm. Coll.)*
Klamath Comm. Coll. 321
Klein Sch. of Optics *(see New England Coll. of Optometry)*
Knott County Area Techno. Ctr. 160
Knowledge Systems Inst. 124
Knox Beauty Coll. 506 *(see also Knox Int'l. 2000 Beauty Coll.)*
Knox Coll. 125, 432
Knox County Career Ctr. 580
Knox Int'l. 2000 Beauty Coll. 611
Knox Theological Seminary 89
Knoxville Bus. Coll. *(see South Coll.)*
Knoxville VA Med. Ctr. *(see Veterans Affairs Central Iowa Healthcare System—Knoxville Division)*
Knoxville Veterans Affairs Med. Ctr. *(see Veterans Affairs Central Iowa Healthcare System—Knoxville Division)*
Kodiak Coll. 11
Kokomo Tech. Inst. *(see Ivy Tech Comm. Coll. of Indiana—Kokomo)*
Kol Yaakov Torah Ctr. 266

Kootenai Coll. *(see Salish Kootenai Coll.)*
Korean Inst. for Montessori 647
Korean Montessori Coll. 647
Krolak Bus. Inst. *(see Las Vegas Coll.)*
K-State *(see Kansas State Univ.)*
K-State at Salina *(see Kansas State Univ.)*
Kubert Sch. of Cartoon & Graphic Art *(see Joe Kubert Sch. of Cartoon & Graphic Art)*
Kussad Inst. of Court Reporting 621
Kutztown Univ. of Pennsylvania 333
Kwantlen Univ. Coll. 712
K-Wes, LLC *(see Phoenix Therapeutic Massage Coll.)*

L

L.A Mission Coll. *(see Los Angeles Mission Coll.)*
L.A. County Coll. of Nursing *(see Los Angeles County Coll. of Nursing & Allied Health)*
L.A. Harbor Coll. *(see Los Angeles Harbor Coll.)*
L.A. Music Acad. *(see Los Angeles Music Acad.)*
L.A. ORT Tech. Inst. *(see Los Angeles ORT Tech. Inst.)*
L.A. Pierce Coll. *(see Los Angeles Pierce Coll.)*
L.A. Recording Sch. *(see Los Angeles Recording Workshop)*
L.A. Recording Workshop *(see Los Angeles Recording Workshop)*
L.A. Southwest Coll. *(see Los Angeles Southwest Coll.)*
L.A. Trade Tech *(see Los Angeles Trade-Tech. Coll.)*
L.A. Trade-Tech. Coll. *(see Los Angeles Trade-Tech. Coll.)*
L.A. Valley Coll. *(see Los Angeles Valley Coll.)*
L.E. Fletcher Tech. Comm. Coll. 167, 729
L.T. Int'l. Beauty Sch. 597
La Belle Beauty Acad—Miami 484
La Belle Beauty Sch—Hialeah 485
La Crosse Normal Sch. *(see Univ. of Wisconsin—La Crosse)*
La Crosse State Teachers Coll. *(see Univ. of Wisconsin—La Crosse)*
La Frontera Ctr., Inc *(see Southern Arizona Psychology Internship Consortium)*
La Grange Coll. *(see Hannibal-LaGrange Coll.)*
La Guardia Coll. *(see City Univ. of New York La Guardia Comm. Coll.)*

La Guardia Comm. Coll. *(see City Univ. of New York La Guardia Comm. Coll.)*
La' James Coll. of Hairstyling—Cedar Falls 728 *(see also La' James Int'l. Coll—Cedar Falls)*
La' James Coll. of Hairstyling—Davenport 728 *(see also La' James Int'l. Coll—Davenport)*
La' James Coll. of Hairstyling—Des Moines 728 *(see also La' James Int'l. Coll—Des Moines)*
La' James Coll. of Hairstyling—East Moline 727 *(see also La' James Int'l. Coll—East Moline)*
La' James Coll. of Hairstyling—Fort Dodge 728 *(see also La' James Int'l. Coll—Fort Dodge)*
La' James Coll. of Hairstyling—Iowa City 728 *(see also La' James Int'l. Coll—Iowa City)*
La' James Coll. of Hairstyling—Mason City 508
La' James Int'l. Coll. 542, 732
La' James Int'l. Coll—Cedar Falls 508, 728
La' James Int'l. Coll—Davenport 508, 728
La' James Int'l. Coll—Des Moines 508, 728
La' James Int'l. Coll—East Moline 501, 727
La' James Int'l. Coll—Fort Dodge 508, 728
La' James Int'l. Coll—Iowa City 508, 728
La Jolla Acad. of Advertising Arts *(see Art Inst. of California—San Diego)*
La Rabida Children's Hosp. 668
La Roche Coll. 333
La Salle Univ. 333
La Sierra Univ. 45
La Verne Coll. *(see Univ. of La Verne)*
La Verne Univ. *(see Univ. of La Verne)*
Laban/Bartenieff Inst. of Movement Studies, Inc. 567
LaBaron Hairdressing Acad—Brockton 526
LaBaron Hairdressing Acad—New Bedford 526
LaBaron Hairdressing Acad—Overland Park 509
Labette Coll. *(see Labette Comm. Coll.)*
Labette Comm. Coll. 155
Labette Comm. Jr. Coll. *(see Labette Comm. Coll.)*
Laboratory Inst. of Merchandising 266
Laboratory Merchandising Inst. *(see Laboratory Inst. of Merchandising)*

Laboure Coll. *(see Caritas Laboure Coll.)*
Laboure Coll. 730
Lac Courte Oreilles Ojibwa Comm. Coll. 424
L'Academie de Cuisine 522
LaCarm Sch. of Cosmetology *(see Pro Way Hair Sch.)*
Lackawanna Coll. 333
Lackawanna County Area Vocational Tech. Sch. 698
Lackawanna County Vo-Tech Sch. *(see Lackawanna County Area Vocational Tech. Sch.)*
Lackawanna Jr. Coll. *(see Lackawanna Coll.)*
LaCrosse Beauty Sch. *(see Scientific Coll. of Beauty & Barbering)*
Lacy Cosmetology Sch. 608
Ladera Career Paths Training Ctr. 461
Ladera Career Paths, Inc. *(see Ladera Career Paths Training Ctr.)*
Ladies & Gentlemen Hair Stylists 580, 734
Lado Enterprises, Inc. *(see Lado Int'l. Coll.)*
Lado Int'l. Coll. 478
Lady of the Elms Coll. *(see Coll. of Our Lady of the Elms)*
Lady of the Lake Coll. *(see Our Lady of the Lake Coll.)*
Lady of the Lake Univ. *(see Our Lady of the Lake Univ.)*
Lafayette Beauty Acad., Inc. 506
Lafayette Coll. 333
Lafayette General Med. Ctr. 673
Lafayette Tech. Inst. *(see Ivy Tech Comm. Coll. of Indiana—Lafayette)*
LaGrange Coll. 105 *(see also Univ. of North Alabama)*
LaGrange Cosmetology Sch. *(see Rivertown Sch. of Beauty)*
Laguna Beach Sch. of Art *(see Laguna Coll. of Art & Design)*
Laguna Coll. of Art & Design 45
Lake Area Tech *(see Lake Area Tech. Inst.)*
Lake Area Tech. Inst. 361
Lake Charles Hosp. *(see Lake Charles Mem. Hosp. Sch. of Med. Techno.)*
Lake Charles Jr. Coll. *(see McNeese State Univ.)*
Lake Charles Mem. Hosp. Sch. of Med. Techno. 673
Lake City Coll. *(see Lake City Comm. Coll.)*
Lake City Comm. Coll. 89
Lake City Jr. Coll. *(see Lake City Comm. Coll.)*

Lake County Area Vocational—Tech. Ctr. *(see Lake Tech. Ctr.)*
Lake County Coll. *(see Coll. of Lake County)*
Lake County Joint Vocational Sch. *(see Auburn Career Ctr.)*
Lake County Vocational Tech. Ctr. 725 *(see also Lake Tech. Ctr.)*
Lake Erie Coll. 305
Lake Erie Coll. of Osteopathic Medicine 748
Lake Forest Acad. *(see Lake Forest Coll.)*
Lake Forest Beauty Coll. 461
Lake Forest Coll. 125
Lake Forest Grad. Sch. of Management 125
Lake Forest Hosp. 669
Lake Forest Management Sch. *(see Lake Forest Grad. Sch. of Management)*
Lake Land Coll. 125 *(see also Lakeland Coll.)*
Lake Michigan Coll. 200
Lake Region Coll. *(see Lake Region State Coll.)*
Lake Region State Coll. 296
Lake Superior Coll. 210
Lake Superior State Univ. 200
Lake Tahoe Coll. *(see Lake Tahoe Comm. Coll.)*
Lake Tahoe Comm. Coll. 45
Lake Tech. Ctr. 485, 725
Lake Washington Coll. *(see Lake Washington Tech. Coll.)*
Lake Washington Tech. Coll. 413
Lake Washington Vocational Tech. Inst. *(see Lake Washington Tech. Coll.)*
Lakeland Coll. 424, 712 *(see also Lake Land Coll., Lakeland Comm. Coll.)*
Lakeland Comm. Coll. 305
Lakeland Hosp. *(see Lakeland Reg. Med. Ctr.)*
Lakeland Med. Ctr. *(see Lakeland Reg. Med. Ctr.)*
Lakeland Med-Dental Acad. *(see Herzing Coll—Lakeland Med-Dental Acad.)*
Lakeland Reg. Med. Ctr. 663
Lakeshore Coll. *(see Lakeshore Tech. Coll.)*
Lakeshore Tech *(see Lakeshore Tech. Coll.)*
Lakeshore Tech. Coll. 424
Lakeside Sch. of Massage Therapy 643
Lake-Sumter Coll. *(see Lake-Sumter Comm. Coll.)*
Lake-Sumter Comm. Coll. 89

Lake-Sumter Jr. Coll. *(see Lake-Sumter Comm. Coll.)*
Lakeview Coll. of Nursing 125
Lakeview Nursing Coll. *(see Lakeview Coll. of Nursing)*
Lakewood Comm. Coll. *(see Century Coll.)*
Lakewood Park Bible Sch. *(see Trinity Bible Coll.)*
Lakewood Sch. of Therapeutic Massage 530
Lakota Higher Edu. Ctr. *(see Oglala Lakota Coll.)*
Lamar Coll. *(see Lamar Comm. Coll., Lamar Univ.)*
Lamar Coll—Orange *(see Lamar State Coll—Orange)*
Lamar Coll—Port Arthur *(see Lamar State Coll—Port Arthur)*
Lamar Comm. Coll. 69
Lamar Hosp. *(see Univ. Hosp.)*
Lamar Inst. of Techno. 380
Lamar Jr. Coll. *(see Lamar Comm. Coll.)*
Lamar Sch. of Vocations *(see Lamar Inst. of Techno.)*
Lamar State Coll. of Techno. *(see Lamar Univ.)*
Lamar State Coll—Orange 380
Lamar State Coll—Port Arthur 380
Lamar Univ. 380
Lamar Univ. at Orange *(see Lamar State Coll—Orange)*
Lamar Univ. at Port Arthur *(see Lamar State Coll—Port Arthur)*
Lamar Univ—Inst. of Techno. *(see Lamar Inst. of Techno.)*
Lambuth Coll. *(see Lambuth Univ.)*
Lambuth Univ. 367
LaMont's Int'l. Sch. of Cosmetology 501
Lamson Coll. 17
Lamson Jr. Coll. *(see Lamson Coll.)*
Lancaster Beauty Sch. 461
Lancaster Bible Coll. & Grad. Sch. 333
Lancaster Bible Grad. Sch. *(see Lancaster Bible Coll. & Grad. Sch.)*
Lancaster Cleft Palate Clinic 698
Lancaster Coll. *(see Dabney S. Lancaster Comm. Coll., Lancaster Bible Coll. & Grad. Sch.)*
Lancaster Coll. of the Bible *(see Lancaster Bible Coll. & Grad. Sch.)*
Lancaster Comm. Coll. *(see Dabney S. Lancaster Comm. Coll.)*
Lancaster County Area Vocational Tech. Sch. *(see Lancaster County Career & Techno. Ctr.)*

Lancaster County Career & Techno. Ctr. 598
Lancaster County Normal Sch. *(see Millersville Univ. of Pennsylvania)*
Lancaster County Vo-Tech Sch. *(see Lancaster County Career & Techno. Ctr.)*
Lancaster General Coll. of Nursing & Health Sciences 748
Lancaster General Hosp. 698 *(see also Lancaster Cleft Palate Clinic)*
Lancaster Jr. Coll. *(see Atlantic Union Coll.)*
Lancaster Sch. of Cosmetology, Inc. 598
Lancaster Theological Seminary 333
Lance Tyson & Associates Dale Carnegie Training of Northeast Ohio 581, 734
Lander Coll. *(see Lander Univ.)*
Lander Univ. 357
Landig Coll. of Mortuary Science *(see Commonwealth Inst. of Funeral Service)*
Landing Sch. of Boat Building & Design, The 519
Landmark Coll. 397
Landmark Sch. *(see Landmark Coll.)*
Landscape Design Sch. of Conway *(see Conway Sch. of Landscape Design)*
Lane Coll. 367 *(see also Lane Comm. Coll.)*
Lane Comm. Coll. 321
Lane Inst. *(see Lane Coll.)*
Lane Theological Seminary *(see McCormick Theological Seminary)*
Laney Coll. 45
Laney Trade & Tech. Inst. *(see Laney Coll.)*
Langauge Acad., The 485
Langdon & Associates, Inc. *(see Lance Tyson & Associates Dale Carnegie Training of Northeast Ohio)*
Langston Univ. 315
Language Company, The 588
Language Consultants Int'l., LLC 472
Language Exchange Int'l. 485
Language Exchange, Inc. *(see Language Exchange Int'l.)*
Language Plus & Language Unlimited *(see Language Plus, Inc.)*
Language Plus, Inc. 621
Language Studies Int'l. 461
Language Unlimited *(see Language Plus, Inc.)*
Lanier Coll. *(see Lanier Tech. Coll.)*
Lanier Tech. Coll. 105, 726

Lanier Tech. Inst. 726 *(see also Lanier Tech. Coll.)*
Lanning Hosp. *(see Mary Lanning Mem. Hosp.)*
Lanning Mem. Hosp. *(see Mary Lanning Mem. Hosp.)*
Lansbridge Univ. 432
Lansdale Sch. of Bus. 333
Lansdale Sch. of Cosmetology, Inc. 598
Lansing Coll. *(see Lansing Comm. Coll.)*
Lansing Comm. Coll. 200
Lansing Computer Inst. 731
LaPorte Bus. Coll. *(see Brown Mackie Coll—Merrillville)*
Laramie Coll. *(see Laramie County Comm. Coll.)*
Laramie Comm. Coll. *(see Laramie County Comm. Coll.)*
Laramie County Coll. *(see Laramie County Comm. Coll.)*
Laramie County Comm. Coll. 430
Laredo Beauty Coll. 621
Laredo Coll. *(see Laredo Comm. Coll.)*
Laredo Comm. Coll. 380
Laredo Jr. Coll. *(see Laredo Comm. Coll.)*
Laredo State Univ. *(see Texas A&M Int'l. Univ.)*
LaRoche Coll. *(see La Roche Coll.)*
Larson Coll. *(see Quinnipiac Univ.)*
Larue D. Carter Mem. Hosp. 670
Las Cruces Coll. *(see New Mexico State Univ. at Alamogordo)*
Las Positas Coll. 45
Las Vegas Art Inst. *(see Art Inst. of Las Vegas)*
Las Vegas Bus. Coll. *(see Las Vegas Coll.)*
Las Vegas Coll. 240 *(see also Regis Univ.)*
Las Vegas Coll. of Culinary Arts *(see Le Cordon Bleu Coll. of Culinary Arts—Las Vegas)*
Las Vegas Culinary Arts Sch. *(see Le Cordon Bleu Coll. of Culinary Arts—Las Vegas)*
Las Vegas Culinary Inst. *(see Art Inst. of Las Vegas)*
LaSalle Univ. *(see La Salle Univ.)*
Lasell Coll. 188
Lasell Female Seminary *(see Lasell Coll.)*
Lasell Jr. Coll. *(see Lasell Coll.)*
LaShe' Beauty Acad. 573
Lassen Coll. 45
Lassen Comm. Coll. *(see Lassen Coll.)*
Lassen Jr. Coll. *(see Lassen Coll.)*
Last Minute Cut Sch. of Barbering 759

Latter-day Saint Acad. *(see Eastern Arizona Coll.)*
Latter-Day Saints Bus. Coll. 394
Laun & Associates, Inc. 445
Laura & Alvin Siegal Coll. of Judaic Studies 305
Laurel Bus. Inst. 333
Laurel County State Vocational-Tech. Sch. *(see Somerset Comm. Coll.)*
Laurel Oaks Career Development Campus *(see Great Oaks Inst. of Techno. & Career Development—Laurel Oaks Campus)*
Laurel Tech. Coll. *(see Somerset Comm. Coll.)*
Laurel Tech. Coll-Cumberland Valley Campus *(see Southeast Kentucky Comm. & Tech. Coll.)*
Laurentian Comm. & Tech. Coll. Dist—Mesabi Range, Virginia *(see Mesabi Range Comm. & Tech. Coll.)*
Laurentian Comm. Coll. Dist. *(see Vermilion Comm. Coll.)*
Lausanne Hotel Sch. *(see Ecole Hoteliere de Lausanne)*
Laval Univ. *(see Université Laval)*
LaVerne Coll. *(see Univ. of La Verne)*
LaVerne Univ. *(see Univ. of La Verne)*
Law Coll. of South Texas *(see South Texas Coll. of Law)*
Law Sch. of Albany *(see Albany Law Sch.)*
Law Sch. of Brooklyn *(see Brooklyn Law Sch.)*
Law Sch. of New England *(see New England Sch. of Law)*
Law Sch. of New York *(see New York Law Sch.)*
Law Sch. of Southern New England *(see Southern New England Sch. of Law)*
Law Sch. of Vermont *(see Vermont Law Sch.)*
Lawrence Career Coll. 728 *(see also Pinnacle Career Inst—Lawrence)*
Lawrence Coll. *(see Lawrence Univ., Sarah Lawrence Coll.)*
Lawrence County Area Vocational Tech. Sch. 698
Lawrence County Career & Tech. Ctr. *(see Lawrence County Area Vocational Tech. Sch.)*
Lawrence County Joint Vocational Sch. Dist. *(see Collins Career Ctr.)*
Lawrence County Vo-Tech Sch. *(see Lawrence County Area Vocational Tech. Sch.)*
Lawrence Inst. of Techno. *(see Lawrence Technological Univ.)*
Lawrence Technological Univ. 200

Lawrence Univ. 425
Lawrence-White Associates, Inc. 632
Lawson Coll. *(see T.A. Lawson State Comm. Coll.)*
Lawson Comm. Coll. *(see T.A. Lawson State Comm. Coll.)*
Lawson State Coll. *(see T.A. Lawson State Comm. Coll.)*
Lawson State Comm. Coll. 721 *(see also T.A. Lawson State Comm. Coll.)*
Lawton Sch. 530
LBW Coll. *(see Lurleen B. Wallace Comm. Coll.)*
LDS Bus. Coll. *(see Latter-Day Saints Bus. Coll.)*
Le Cordon Bleu Coll. of Culinary Arts 324
Le Cordon Bleu Coll. of Culinary Arts—Atlanta *(see Western Culinary Inst.)*
Le Cordon Bleu Coll. of Culinary Arts—Las Vegas 240
Le Cordon Bleu Coll. of Culinary Arts—Miami 90
Le Cordon Bleu Coll. of Culinary Arts—Minneapolis/St. Paul 210
Le Cordon Bleu Culinary Program at Brown Coll. *(see Le Cordon Bleu Coll. of Culinary Arts—Minneapolis/St. Paul)*
Le Cordon Bleu of Atlanta *(see Le Cordon Bleu Coll. of Culinary Arts—Atlanta, Western Culinary Inst.)*
Le Cordon Bleu of Las Vegas *(see Le Cordon Bleu Coll. of Culinary Arts—Las Vegas)*
Le Cordon Bleu of Miami *(see Le Cordon Bleu Coll. of Culinary Arts—Miami)*
Le Cordon Bleu of Minneapolis/St. Paul *(see Le Cordon Bleu Coll. of Culinary Arts—Minneapolis/St. Paul)*
Le Cordon Bleu of Orlando *(see Orlando Culinary Acad.)*
Le Mar Beauty Coll. *(see Riggs Le Mar Beauty Coll.)*
Le Moyne Coll. 266
Lea & Associates, Inc. *(see William F. Lea & Associates, Inc.)*
Lea Acad. of Cosmetology *(see Jenny Lea Acad. of Cosmetology—Harlan, Jenny Lea Acad. of Cosmetology—Whitesburg)*
Leadership Development, Inc. 736 *(see also Dale Carnegie Training of South Carolina, LLC)*
Leadership Development, Inc. Dale Carnegie Training 441, 721

Leadership Excellence, Inc. 621
Leadership Inst. of Utah 543 *(see also J. R. Rodgers & Associates, Inc.)*
Leadership Inst., Inc. 598
Leadership Institution of Georgia, The *(see North Georgia Coll. & State Univ.)*
Leadership Training 621
Leadership Training Inst. 610
Leadership Training Services, Inc. 598
Learey Tech. Ctr. 725
Learning Ctr. of California *(see California Learning Ctr.)*
Learning Inst. for Beauty Sciences—Astoria 567
Learning Inst. for Beauty Sciences—Boston 526
Learning Inst. for Beauty Sciences—Hauppauge 567
Learning Inst. for Beauty Sciences—Hempstead 567
Learning Inst. for Beauty Sciences—Levittown 567
Learning Inst. for Beauty Sciences—Malden 526
Learning Inst. for Beauty Sciences—New York 567
Learning Tree Univ. 462
LearnQuest 598
Leavenworth VA Med. Ctr. *(see Dwight D. Eisenhower Veterans Affairs Med. Ctr.)*
Leavenworth Veterans Affairs Med. Ctr. *(see Dwight D. Eisenhower Veterans Affairs Med. Ctr.)*
Lebanese American Univ. 716 *(see also Lebanese American Univ.)*
Lebanon Coll. 683
Lebanon County Area Vocational Tech. Sch. *(see Lebanon County Career & Techno. Ctr.)*
Lebanon County Career & Techno. Ctr. 598
Lebanon County Career Sch. 598
Lebanon County Vo-Tech Sch. *(see Lebanon County Career & Techno. Ctr.)*
Lebanon Valley Coll. 334
LeChef Coll. of Hospitality Careers *(see Texas Culinary Acad.)*
L'Ecole Culinaire 227
L'École de Cuisine *(see York Tech. Inst.)*
LeCordon Bleu Coll. of Culinary Arts *(see Brown Coll.)*
Lee Coll. 380 *(see also Lee Univ., Maric Coll—Anaheim)*
Lee County Area Techno. Ctr. 160
Lee County High Tech Ctr—Central 485
Lee County High Tech Ctr—North 485

Lee County Vocational High Tech Ctr. *(see Lee County High Tech Ctr.)*
Lee Univ. 367 *(see also Washington & Lee Univ.)*
Leech Lake Coll. *(see Leech Lake Tribal Coll.)*
Leech Lake Tribal Coll. 210, 747
Lees Coll. 160 *(see also Hazard Comm. & Tech. Coll.)*
Lee's Sch. of Cosmetology 448
Lees-McRae Coll. 289
Lees-McRae Inst. *(see Lees-McRae Coll.)*
Leeward Coll. *(see Leeward Comm. Coll.)*
Leeward Comm. Coll. 114
Leffke & Associates, Inc. *(see John M. Jennings & Associates, Inc.)*
Legacy Emanuel Children's Hosp. 696
Legacy Health System *(see Legacy Emanuel Children's Hosp.)*
Legal Arts Coll. *(see Coll. of Legal Arts)*
Legends Inst. 632, 738
Lehigh Carbon Coll. *(see Lehigh Carbon Comm. Coll.)*
Lehigh Carbon Comm. Coll. 334
Lehigh Data Processing Inst. *(see Berks Tech. Inst.)*
Lehigh Univ. 334
Lehigh Valley Coll. 334, 735
Lehigh Valley Hosp—17th & Chew Streets 698
Lehigh Valley Hosp—Cedar Crest & I-78 698
Lehigh Valley Hosp—Muhlenberg 698
Lehman Coll. *(see City Univ. of New York Herbert H. Lehman Coll.)*
Leicester Sch. 462
Leland Ctr. for Theological Studies *(see John Leland Ctr. for Theological Studies)*
LeMoyne Coll. *(see Le Moyne Coll.)*
LeMoyne-Owen Coll. 367
Lenape Area Vocational Tech. Sch. 698
Lenape Tech *(see Lenape Area Vocational Tech. Sch.)*
Lenape Vo-Tech Sch. *(see Lenape Area Vocational Tech. Sch.)*
Lenoir Coll. *(see Lenoir Comm. Coll., Lenoir-Rhyne Coll.)*
Lenoir Comm. Coll. 289
Lenoir County Industrial Educational Ctr. *(see Lenoir Comm. Coll.)*
Lenoir-Rhyne Coll. 289
Lenox Hill Hosp. 687
Leon Inst. of Hair Design 475
Leon Studio One Sch. of Hair Design 567
Leon's Beauty Sch. 573

Leon's Hair Training Acad. *(see Career Acad. of Hair Design)*
"Les Roches" Hotel & Tourism Sch. *(see "Les Roches" Sch. of Hotel Management)*
"Les Roches" Hotel Management Sch. *(see "Les Roches" Sch. of Hotel Management)*
"Les Roches" Int'l. Sch. *(see "Les Roches" Sch. of Hotel Management)*
"Les Roches" Marbella Sch. of Hotel Management 648
"Les Roches" Sch. of Hotel Management 437 *(see also "Les Roches" Marbella Sch. of Hotel Management)*
"Les Roches" Swiss Hotel Assoc. Sch. of Hotel Management *(see "Les Roches" Marbella Sch. of Hotel Management)*
Lesley Coll. *(see Lesley Univ.)*
Lesley Univ. 188
Leslie County Area Techno. Ctr. 160
Lester L. Cox Coll. of Nursing & Health Sciences 227
Letcher County Area Techno. Ctr. 160
LeTourneau Univ. 380
Levin Sch. of Health Care 485
Levine Music Sch. *(see Levine Sch. of Music)*
Levine Sch. of Music 478
Levittown Beauty Acad. 598
Lewis & Clark Coll. 321 *(see also Lewis & Clark Comm. Coll.)*
Lewis & Clark Comm. Coll. 125
Lewis Coll. of Bus. 200
Lewis Coll. of Science & Techno. *(see Lewis Univ.)*
Lewis Holy Name Tech. Sch. *(see Lewis Univ.)*
Lewis Inst. *(see Illinois Inst. of Techno.)*
Lewis Univ. 125
Lewis-Clark Coll. *(see Lewis-Clark State Coll.)*
Lewis-Clark State Coll. 116
Lewiston-Auburn Coll. 177 *(see also Univ. of Southern Maine)*
Lexington Coll. 125 *(see also Bluegrass Comm. & Tech. Coll.)*
Lexington Comm. Coll. 728, 729 *(see also Bluegrass Comm. & Tech. Coll.)*
Lexington Electronics Inst. 163
Lexington Inst. of Hospitality Careers *(see Lexington Coll.)*
Lexington Seminary *(see Lexington Theological Seminary)*
Lexington Theological Seminary 161

Lexington VA Med. Ctr. *(see Lexington Veterans Affairs Med. Ctr.)*
Lexington Veterans Affairs Med. Ctr. 672
Lia Schorr Inst. of Cosmetic Skin Care 567
Liberal Arts Coll. of Massachusetts *(see Massachusetts Coll. of Liberal Arts)*
Liberties Coll. 715
Liberty Seminary *(see Liberty Univ.)*
Liberty Training Inst. 462
Liberty Univ. 403
Liceo de Arte y Tecnologia 605
Liceo de Arte, Disenos y Comercio 605
Licking County Career & Techno. Centers *(see Career & Techno. Centers of Licking County)*
LIFE Bible Coll. *(see LIFE Pacific Coll.)*
LIFE Bible Coll. East 738
Life Chiropractic Coll. *(see Life Univ.)*
Life Chiropractic Coll. West 45
Life Coll. *(see Life Univ.)*
LIFE Pacific Coll. 45
Life Univ. 105
Lifelong Learning Ctr. *(see Bus. Skills Inst.)*
Lifelong Learning Coll. *(see Granite State Coll.)*
Light Career Ctr. *(see J. Everett Light Career Ctr.)*
Lima Tech. Coll. *(see James A. Rhodes State Coll.)*
Limestone Coll. 357
Limón Dance Inst. 567
Limon Inst. *(see Limón Dance Inst.)*
Lincoln Beauty Sch., Inc. 761
Lincoln Bible Inst. *(see Lincoln Christian Coll. & Seminary)*
Lincoln Christian Coll. & Seminary 125
Lincoln Christian Seminary *(see Lincoln Christian Coll. & Seminary)*
Lincoln Coll. 125 *(see also Lincoln Trail Coll., Washburn Univ.)*
Lincoln Coll. at Normal 125
Lincoln Inst. *(see Lincoln Univ.)*
Lincoln Land Coll. *(see Lincoln Land Comm. Coll.)*
Lincoln Land Comm. Coll. 125
Lincoln Med. & Mental Health Ctr. 687
Lincoln Mem. Univ. 367
Lincoln Normal Sch. at Marion *(see Alabama State Univ.)*
Lincoln Parish Training Sch. *(see Grambling State Univ.)*
Lincoln Sch. of Commerce 732 *(see also Hamilton Coll—Cedar Rapids)*

Lincoln Tech *(see Lincoln Tech. Inst.)*
Lincoln Tech. Inst. 141, 334, 502, 522, 621, 727
Lincoln Trail Coll. 125
Lincoln Univ. 45, 227, 334
Linda Vista Baptist Bible Coll. & Seminary *(see Southern California Seminary)*
Lindenwood Coll. *(see Lindenwood Univ.)*
Lindenwood Univ. 227
Lindsey Hopkins Tech. Edu. Ctr. 485
Lindsey Wilson Coll. 161
Lindsey Wilson Jr. Coll. *(see Lindsey Wilson Coll.)*
Lindsey Wilson Training Sch. *(see Lindsey Wilson Coll.)*
Linfield Coll. 321
Linn Coll. *(see Linn State Tech. Coll.)*
Linn State Tech. Coll. 227
Linn-Benton Coll. *(see Linn-Benton Comm. Coll.)*
Linn-Benton Comm. Coll. 321
Lipscomb Univ. 367
Literary & Bible Training Sch. for Christian Workers *(see Trevecca Nazarene Univ.)*
Literary & Theological Inst. of the Lutheran Church of the Far West, The *(see Carthage Coll.)*
Little Big Horn Coll. 234
Little Hoop Comm. Coll. *(see Cankdeska Cikana Comm. Coll.)*
Little Priest Coll. *(see Little Priest Tribal Coll.)*
Little Priest Tribal Coll. 237
Little Rock Coll. of Techno. *(see Remington Coll—Little Rock)*
Little Rock Infirmary *(see Saint Vincent Infirmary Med. Ctr.)*
Little Rock Job Corps Ctr. 448
Little Rock Jr. Coll. *(see Univ. of Arkansas at Little Rock)*
Little Rock Univ. *(see Univ. of Arkansas at Little Rock)*
Little Sch. of Management *(see Hult Int'l. Bus. Sch.)*
Live Oaks Career Development Campus *(see Great Oaks Inst. of Techno. & Career Development— Live Oaks Campus)*
Lively Area Vocational-Tech. Ctr. 485
Lively Area Vo-Tech Ctr. *(see Lively Area Vocational-Tech. Ctr.)*
Lively Aviation Ctr. 485 *(see also Lively Area Vocational Tech. Ctr.)*
Lively Criminal Justice Training 725
Lively Vo-Tech Ctr. *(see Lively Area Vocational-Tech. Ctr.)*

Livingston Female Acad. & State Normal Coll. *(see Univ. of West Alabama)*
Livingston State Coll. *(see Univ. of West Alabama)*
Livingston Univ. *(see Univ. of West Alabama)*
Livingstone Coll. 289
Lloyd Coll. *(see Alice Lloyd Coll.)*
Lock Haven Univ. of Pennsylvania 334
Locklin Tech. Ctr. *(see Radford M. Locklin Tech. Ctr.)*
Lockworks Academie of Hairdressing—Baton Rouge *(see Aveda Inst. Baton Rouge)*
Lockworks Academie of Hairdressing—Lafayette *(see Aveda Inst. Lafayette)*
Lockworks Acad. of Hairdressing— Baton Rouge 729
Lockworks Acad. of Hairdressing— Lafayette 729
Logan Coll. *(see John A. Logan Coll.)*
Logan Coll. of Chiropractic *(see Logan Univ.)*
Logan Univ. 227
Logistical Management Inst. *(see Inst. of Logistical Management)*
Logos Evangelical Seminary 46
Logsdon Sch. of Theology *(see Hardin-Simmons Univ.)*
Lola Beauty Coll. 462
Loma Linda Univ. 46
Loma Linda Veterans Affairs Healthcare System 654
Lombard Coll. *(see Meadville Lombard Theological Sch.)*
Lon Morris Coll. 380
London Baptist Bible Coll. & Seminary *(see Heritage Coll. & Seminary)*
London Guildhall Univ. *(see London Metropolitan Univ.)*
London Metropolitan Univ. 752
Long Beach City Coll. 46
Long Beach Coll. *(see Long Beach City Coll.)*
Long Beach Mem. Med. Ctr. *(see Greater Long Beach Child Guidance Ctr.)*
Long Beach VA Med. Ctr. *(see Veterans Affairs Med. Ctr—Long Beach)*
Long Beach Veterans Affairs Med. Ctr. *(see Veterans Affairs Med. Ctr— Long Beach)*
Long Island Agricultural & Tech. Inst. *(see State Univ. of New York Coll. of Techno. at Farmingdale)*
Long Island Bus. Inst. 266

Long Island Coll. Hosp. 687 *(see also State Univ. of New York Health Science Ctr. at Brooklyn)*

Long Island Coll. of Medicine *(see State Univ. of New York Health Science Ctr. at Brooklyn)*

Long Island Culinary Acad. *(see Culinary Acad. of Long Island)*

Long Island Dale Carnegie Training *(see Dale Carnegie & Associates, Inc.)*

Long Island Hosp. *(see Long Island Coll. Hosp.)*

Long Island Jewish Med. Ctr. 687

Long Island Rabbinical Coll. *(see Rabbinical Coll. of Long Island)*

Long Island Univ. 266

Long Island Univ. Coll. of Podiatry *(see New York Coll. of Podiatric Medicine)*

Long Med. Coll. *(see Long Tech. Coll.)*

Long Med. Inst. *(see Long Tech. Coll.)*

Long Tech. Coll. 17

Long Tech. Coll—East Valley 17, 721

Long Tech. Inst. *(see Louisiana Tech. Coll—Huey P. Long Campus)*

Longmire's Bus. Coll. *(see Bryman Coll.)*

Longview Coll. *(see Longview Comm. Coll.)*

Longview Comm. Coll. 227

Longwood Coll. *(see Longwood Univ.)*

Longwood Univ. 403

Longy Sch. of Music 188

Loop Coll. *(see City Colleges of Chicago—Harold Washington Coll.)*

Lorain County Coll. *(see Lorain County Comm. Coll.)*

Lorain County Comm. Coll. 305

Lorain County Joint Vocational Sch. Adult Career Ctr. 581

Lorain County JVS Adult Career Ctr. *(see Lorain County Joint Vocational Sch. Adult Career Ctr.)*

Lorain Sch. of Techno. *(see Lorain County Comm. Coll.)*

Loraine's Acad., Inc. 485

Loras Coll. 148

Lord Fairfax Coll. *(see Lord Fairfax Comm. Coll.)*

Lord Fairfax Comm. Coll. 403

Lordsburg Coll. *(see Univ. of La Verne)*

Lorenzo Walker Inst. of Techno. 485

Loretto Heights Coll. *(see Teikyo Loretto Heights Univ.)*

Loria's Coll. of Cosmetology 756

Los Angeles Ambulatory Care Ctr. 656 *(see also Veterans Affairs Greater Los Angeles Healthcare System—Los Angeles)*

Los Angeles Art Inst. *(see Art Inst. of California—Los Angeles, Art Inst. of Pittsburgh)*

Los Angeles Aviation Inst. *(see Westwood Coll. of Aviation Tech—Los Angeles)*

Los Angeles Children's Hosp. *(see Children's Hosp. of Los Angeles)*

Los Angeles City Coll. 46

Los Angeles Coll. *(see Loyola Marymount Univ., Southern California Univ. of Health Sciences)*

Los Angeles Coll. of Chiropractic 723 *(see also Southern California Univ. of Health Sciences)*

Los Angeles Coll. of Micro Techno. 723

Los Angeles Coll. of Nursing *(see Los Angeles County Coll. of Nursing & Allied Health)*

Los Angeles Colleges of Med. & Dental Assistants *(see Bryman Inst—Brighton)*

Los Angeles Conservatory of Music *(see California Inst. of the Arts)*

Los Angeles County Coll. of Nursing & Allied Health 46

Los Angeles County Harbor-UCLA Med. Ctr. 654

Los Angeles County Med. Ctr. Sch. of Nursing *(see Los Angeles County Coll. of Nursing & Allied Health)*

Los Angeles County-USC Med. Ctr. 654

Los Angeles Harbor Coll. 46

Los Angeles Inst. of Art *(see Art Inst. of Pittsburgh)*

Los Angeles Jr. Coll. *(see Los Angeles City Coll.)*

Los Angeles Med. Inst. *(see Med. Inst.)*

Los Angeles Metropolitan Detention Ctr. *(see Metropolitan Detention Ctr.)*

Los Angeles Mission Coll. 46

Los Angeles Music Acad. 754

Los Angeles ORT Tech. Inst. 462

Los Angeles Pacific Coll. *(see Azusa Pacific Univ.)*

Los Angeles Pierce Coll. 46

Los Angeles Recording Sch. *(see Los Angeles Recording Workshop)*

Los Angeles Recording Workshop 462

Los Angeles Southwest Coll. 46

Los Angeles State Coll. *(see California State Univ—Los Angeles)*

Los Angeles State Coll. of Applied Arts & Sciences *(see California State Univ—Los Angeles)*

Los Angeles State Coll. of Applied Arts & Sciences—San Fernando Valley *(see California State Univ—Northridge)*

Los Angeles Trade-Tech. Coll. 46

Los Angeles Valley Coll. 46

Los Medanos Coll. 47

Louis D. Brandeis Sch. of Law *(see Univ. of Louisville)*

Louisburg Coll. 289

Louisburg Female Acad. *(see Louisburg Coll.)*

Louisburg Female Coll. *(see Louisburg Coll.)*

Louise Harkey Sch. of Nursing *(see Cabarrus Coll. of Health Sciences)*

Louise Salinger Acad. of Fashion *(see Art Inst. of California—San Francisco)*

Louisiana A&M Coll. *(see Louisiana State Univ. & Agricultural & Mechanical Coll.)*

Louisiana Acad. of Beauty 517

Louisiana Agricultural & Mechanical Coll. *(see Louisiana State Univ. & Agricultural & Mechanical Coll.)*

Louisiana Art Inst. *(see Delta Coll. of Arts & Techno.)*

Louisiana Coll. 167

Louisiana Correctional Ctr. 170 *(see also Jumonville Mem. Tech. Inst.)*

Louisiana Culinary Arts Inst. *(see Culinary Arts Inst. of Louisiana)*

Louisiana Hair Design Coll. 729

Louisiana Negro Normal & Industrial Inst. *(see Grambling State Univ.)*

Louisiana State Normal Sch. *(see Northwestern State Univ.)*

Louisiana State Univ. & Agricultural & Mechanical Coll. 167

Louisiana State Univ. at Alexandria 167

Louisiana State Univ. at Eunice 167

Louisiana State Univ. Health Sciences Ctr. 729 *(see also Louisiana State Univ. Health Sciences Ctr. in New Orleans)*

Louisiana State Univ. Health Sciences Ctr. in New Orleans 168

Louisiana State Univ. in New Orleans *(see Univ. of New Orleans)*

Louisiana State Univ. in Shreveport 168

Louisiana State Univ. Med. Ctr. 729 *(see also Louisiana State Univ. Health Sciences Ctr. in New Orleans)*

Louisiana Tech Univ. 168

Louisiana Tech. Coll—Acadian Campus 168

Louisiana Tech. Coll—Alexandria Campus 168

Louisiana Tech. Coll—Ascension Campus 168

Louisiana Tech. Coll—Avoyelles Campus 168

Louisiana Tech. Coll—Bastrop Campus 168

Louisiana Tech. Coll—Baton Rouge Campus 169

Louisiana Tech. Coll—Charles B. Coreil Campus 169

Louisiana Tech. Coll—Delta-Ouachita Campus 169

Louisiana Tech. Coll—Evangeline Campus 169

Louisiana Tech. Coll—Florida Parishes Campus 169

Louisiana Tech. Coll—Folkes Campus 169

Louisiana Tech. Coll—Gulf Area Campus 169

Louisiana Tech. Coll—Hammond Area Campus 169

Louisiana Tech. Coll—Huey P. Long Campus 169

Louisiana Tech. Coll—Jefferson Campus 169

Louisiana Tech. Coll—Jumonville Mem. Campus 170

Louisiana Tech. Coll—L.E. Fletcher Campus 729 *(see also L.E. Fletcher Tech. Comm. Coll.)*

Louisiana Tech. Coll—Lafayette Campus 170

Louisiana Tech. Coll—LaFourche Campus 170

Louisiana Tech. Coll—Lamar Salter Campus 170

Louisiana Tech. Coll—Mansfield Campus 170

Louisiana Tech. Coll—Morgan Smith Campus 170

Louisiana Tech. Coll—Natchitoches Campus 170

Louisiana Tech. Coll—North Central Campus 170

Louisiana Tech. Coll—Northeast Louisiana Campus 170

Louisiana Tech. Coll—Northwest Louisiana Campus 171

Louisiana Tech. Coll—Oakdale Campus 171

Louisiana Tech. Coll—River Parishes Campus 171

Louisiana Tech. Coll—Ruston Campus 171

Louisiana Tech. Coll—Sabine Valley Campus 171

Louisiana Tech. Coll—Shelby M. Jackson Campus 171

Louisiana Tech. Coll—Shreveport-Bossier Campus 171

Louisiana Tech. Coll—Sidney N. Collier Campus 171

Louisiana Tech. Coll—Slidell Campus 171

Louisiana Tech. Coll—South Louisiana Campus *(see L.E. Fletcher Tech. Comm. Coll.)*

Louisiana Tech. Coll—Sowela Campus 729 *(see also Sowela Tech. Comm. Coll.)*

Louisiana Tech. Coll—Sullivan Campus 171

Louisiana Tech. Coll—T.H. Harris Campus 171

Louisiana Tech. Coll—Tallulah Campus 172

Louisiana Tech. Coll—Teche Area Campus 172

Louisiana Tech. Coll—West Jefferson Campus 172

Louisiana Tech. Coll—Westside Campus 172

Louisiana Tech. Coll—Young Mem. Campus 172

Louisville CPE Cluster, Pastoral Counseling & Consultation Ctr. 672

Louisville Dale Carnegie Training *(see William F. Lea & Associates, Inc.)*

Louisville Presbyterian Theological Seminary 161

Louisville Seminary *(see Louisville Presbyterian Theological Seminary)*

Louisville Tech *(see Louisville Tech. Inst.)*

Louisville Tech. Inst. 161

Louisville Univ. *(see Univ. of Louisville)*

Lourdes Coll. 305

Lourdes Jr. Coll. *(see Lourdes Coll.)*

Lowcountry Tech. Coll. *(see Tech. Coll. of the Lowcountry)*

Lowell Acad. Hairstyling Inst. 526

Lowell Normal Sch. *(see Univ. of Massachusetts Lowell)*

Lowell Sch. of Bus. *(see Ridley-Lowell Bus. & Tech. Inst.)*

Lowell State Coll. *(see Univ. of Massachusetts Lowell)*

Lowell Technological Inst. *(see Univ. of Massachusetts Lowell)*

Lowell Textile Inst. *(see Univ. of Massachusetts Lowell)*

Lowell's Commercial Coll. *(see Ridley-Lowell Bus. & Tech. Inst.)*

Lower Columbia Coll. 413

Lowthian Coll. *(see Art Institutes Int'l—Minnesota)*

Loyola Coll. *(see Concordia Univ., Loyola Coll. in Maryland, Loyola Marymount Univ.)*

Loyola Coll. in Maryland 180

Loyola Coll. of Los Angeles *(see Loyola Marymount Univ.)*

Loyola Marymount Univ. 47, 743

Loyola Univ. *(see Loyola Marymount Univ., Loyola Univ. New Orleans, Loyola Univ. of Chicago, Loyola Univ. of Chicago—Med. Ctr.)*

Loyola Univ. Med. Ctr. *(see Loyola Univ. of Chicago—Med. Ctr.)*

Loyola Univ. New Orleans 172

Loyola Univ. of Chicago 126

Loyola Univ. of Chicago—Lake Shore Campus *(see Loyola Univ. of Chicago—Lake Shore Campus)*

Loyola Univ. of Chicago—Mallinckrodt Campus *(see Loyola Univ. of Chicago—Mallinckrodt Campus)*

LSU Alexandria *(see Louisiana State Univ. at Alexandria)*

LSU Eunice *(see Louisiana State Univ. at Eunice)*

LSU Health Sciences Ctr., New Orleans *(see Louisiana State Univ. Health Sciences Ctr. in New Orleans)*

LSU Shreveport *(see Louisiana State Univ. in Shreveport)*

Lubbock Christian Univ. 381

Lubbock Hair Acad. 621

Lucile Packard Children's Hosp. 654

Lumberton Adult Educational Ctr. 621

Luna Area Vocational Tech. Sch. *(see Luna Comm. Coll.)*

Luna Coll. *(see Luna Comm. Coll.)*

Luna Comm. Coll. 252

Luna Vocational Tech. Inst. *(see Luna Comm. Coll.)*

Lurleen B. Wallace Comm. Coll. 6, 721

Lurleen B. Wallace Comm. Coll—MacArthur Campus 721

Lurleen B. Wallace State Jr. Coll. 721 *(see also Lurleen B. Wallace Comm. Coll.)*

Luther Coll. 148

Luther Hosp. 709

Luther Northwestern Theological Seminary *(see Luther Seminary)*

Luther Rice Bible Coll. & Seminary 105

Luther Rice Seminary *(see Luther Rice Bible Coll. & Seminary)*

Luther Seminary 210

Luther Theological Seminary *(see Luther Seminary)*

Lutheran Bible Inst. of Seattle *(see Trinity Lutheran Coll.)*

Lutheran Care Ministries Network, Inc. 687

Lutheran Coll. & Seminary *(see Lutheran Theological Seminary)*

Lutheran Coll. of Wisconsin *(see Wisconsin Lutheran Coll.)*

Lutheran General Hosp. *(see Advocate Lutheran General Hosp.)*

Lutheran HealthCare *(see Lutheran Med. Ctr.)*

Lutheran Homes of Oshkosh 709

Lutheran Hosp. of Indiana 670

Lutheran Jr. Coll. *(see Midland Lutheran Coll.)*

Lutheran Med. Ctr. 687

Lutheran Normal Sch. *(see Augustana Coll.)*

Lutheran Sch. of Theology at Chicago 126

Lutheran Seminary at Philadelphia *(see Lutheran Theological Seminary at Philadelphia)*

Lutheran Sr. Services CPE 681

Lutheran Service Society of New York 687

Lutheran Southern Seminary *(see Lutheran Theological Southern Seminary)*

Lutheran Theological Seminary 432

Lutheran Theological Seminary at Gettysburg 334

Lutheran Theological Seminary at Philadelphia, The 334

Lutheran Theological Southern Seminary 357

Lutheran Univ. of Texas *(see Texas Lutheran Univ.)*

Luzerne Coll. *(see Luzerne County Comm. Coll.)*

Luzerne County Coll. *(see Luzerne County Comm. Coll.)*

Luzerne County Comm. Coll. 334

Lyceum of Art & Techno. *(see Liceo de Arte y Tecnologia)*

Lyceum of Art, Design & Commerce *(see Liceo de Arte, Disenos y Comercio)*

Lyceum Theatre Sch. of Acting, The *(see American Acad. of Dramatic Arts)*

Lycoming Coll. 334

Lyle's Bakersfield Coll. of Beauty 462

Lyle's Coll. of Beauty 462 *(see also Lyle's Bakersfield Coll. of Beauty, Lyle's Fresno Coll. of Beauty)*

Lyle's Coll. of Beauty of Bakersfield *(see Lyle's Bakersfield Coll. of Beauty)*

Lyle's Coll. of Beauty of Fresno *(see Lyle's Fresno Coll. of Beauty)*

Lyle's Fresno Coll. of Beauty 462

Lyme Acad. Coll. of Fine Arts 73

Lyme Coll. of Fine Arts *(see Lyme Acad. Coll. of Fine Arts)*

Lynchburg Coll. 403

Lyndon B. Johnson Civilian Conservation Ctr. *(see Lyndon B. Johnson Civilian Conservation Ctr.)*

Lyndon B. Johnson Comm. Health Ctr. *(see Ben Taub General Hosp.)*

Lyndon Coll. *(see Lyndon State Coll.)*

Lyndon State Coll. 397

Lynn Univ. 90

Lynndale Fundamentals of Beauty Sch. 448

Lyon Coll. 25

Lytle's Beauty Coll. *(see Lytle's Redwood Empire Beauty Coll., Inc.)*

Lytle's Redwood Empire Beauty Coll., Inc. 462

M

M & M Word Processing Inst. *(see Remington Coll—Houston)*

M. D. Anderson Cancer Ctr. *(see Univ. of Texas Health Science Ctr. at Houston)*

M. M. Washington Vocational Sch. *(see Margaret Murray Washington Vocational Sch.)*

M.J. Francoeur & Associates 475

M.J. Lewi Coll. of Podiatry *(see New York Coll. of Podiatric Medicine)*

M.J. Murphy Beauty Coll. 530

Maastricht Univ. 716

Mac Daniel's Beauty Sch. 502

Macalester Coll. 210

MacArthur Coll. *(see Lurleen B. Wallace Comm. Coll.)*

MacArthur State Tech. Coll. *(see Lurleen B. Wallace Comm. Coll.)*

MacCormac Bus. Coll. *(see MacCormac Coll.)*

MacCormac Coll. 126

MacCormac Jr. Coll. *(see MacCormac Coll.)*

MacCormac Sch. *(see MacCormac Coll.)*

Machining Inst. of Akron *(see Akron Machining Inst. Inc.)*

Machzikei Hadath Rabbinical Coll. 266

Maclay Coll. of Theology *(see Claremont Sch. of Theology)*

MacMurray Coll. 126

MacNeal Hosp. 668

Macomb Coll. *(see Macomb Comm. Coll.)*

Macomb Comm. Coll. 201

Macomb Culinary Inst. *(see Macomb Comm. Coll.)*

Macon Beauty Sch. *(see American Prof. Inst.)*

Macon Coll. *(see Macon State Coll.)*

Macon State Coll. 105

Macon Tech. Inst. *(see Central Georgia Tech. Coll.)*

MacQuarie Univ. 711

MacQuarie Univ—Dept. of Chiropractic *(see MacQuarie Univ.)*

Madawaska Training Sch. *(see Univ. of Maine at Fort Kent)*

Madera Beauty Coll. 462

Madigan Army Med. Ctr. 707

Madison Adult Edu. 581

Madison Area Tech. Coll. 425

Madison Coll. *(see James Madison Univ.)*

Madison Cosmetology Coll. 643

Madison Hosp. Sch. of Anesthesia *(see Middle Tennessee Sch. of Anesthesia)*

Madison Media Inst. 643

Madison Normal Coll. *(see Dakota State Univ.)*

Madison Tech *(see Madison Area Tech. Coll.)*

Madison Tech. Coll. *(see Madison Area Tech. Coll.)*

Madison Univ. *(see Colgate Univ., James Madison Univ.)*

Madisonville Comm. Coll. 162, 729

Madisonville Comm. Coll—Tech. Campus 729

Madisonville Health Occupations Sch. *(see Madisonville Comm. Coll.)*

Madisonville Health Techno. Ctr. 729

Madisonville State Vocational-Tech. Sch. *(see Madisonville Comm. Coll.)*

Madisonville Tech. Coll. 729 *(see also Madisonville Comm. Coll.)*

Madonna Coll. *(see Madonna Univ.)*

Madonna Univ. 201, 731

Madonna Univ. Orchard Lake Ctr. 731

Magdalen Coll. 747

Magee Brothers Beaverton Sch. of Beauty 592

Magnolia Bible Coll. 219

Magnolia Coll. *(see Magnolia Bible Coll.)*

Magnolia Coll. of Cosmetology 536

Magnolia Sch. 598, 735

Magnus Coll. *(see Albertus Magnus Coll.)*

Maharishi Int'l. Univ. *(see Maharishi Univ. of Management)*

Maharishi Univ. of Management 148

Mahoning County Career & Tech. Ctr. 581
Mahoning County Joint Vocational Sch. *(see Mahoning County Career & Tech. Ctr.)*
Mahoning County JVS *(see Mahoning County Career & Tech. Ctr.)*
Mailman Ctr. for Child Development *(see Univ. of Miami)*
Maimonides Med. Ctr. 687
Maine Coll. of Agriculture & the Mechanic Arts *(see Univ. of Maine)*
Maine Coll. of Art 176
Maine Comm. Coll. System 730
Maine Dale Carnegie Training *(see Dale Carnegie Training of Maine)*
Maine Law Sch. *(see Univ. of Southern Maine)*
Maine Maritime Acad. 176
Maine Med. Ctr. 674
Maine Sch. of Commerce *(see Husson Coll.)*
Maine State Seminary *(see Bates Coll.)*
Maine Tech. Coll. System 730
Maine Vocational Tech. Inst. *(see Southern Maine Comm. Coll.)*
MaineGeneral Med. Ctr. 674
Mainland Coll. *(see Coll. of the Mainland)*
Maison D'Esthetique Acad. *(see Academia Maison D'Esthetique)*
Mai-trix Beauty Coll. 760
Make-Up Designory 462
Malaspina Univ-Coll. 712
Malcolm X Coll. *(see City Colleges of Chicago—Malcolm X Coll.)*
Malcom Randall VA Med. Ctr. *(see Malcom Randall Veterans Affairs Med. Ctr.)*
Malcom Randall Veterans Affairs Med. Ctr. 663
Malone Coll. 305
Management & Techno. Univ. *(see Univ. of Management & Techno.)*
Management Training & Marketing Associates *(see MTMA Schools, Inc.)*
Manatee Area Vocational-Tech. Ctr. 725
Manatee Coll. *(see Manatee Comm. Coll.)*
Manatee Comm. Coll. 90
Manatee Tech. Inst. 485, 725
Manchester Beauty Coll. 462
Manchester Ctr. for Health Sciences 189
Manchester Coll. 142 *(see also Manchester Comm. Coll.)*
Manchester Comm. Coll. 73

Manchester Comm-Tech. Coll. *(see Manchester Comm. Coll.)*
Manchester Inst. of Arts & Sciences *(see New Hampshire Inst. of Art)*
Manchester Univ. *(see Univ. of Manchester)*
Manchester VA Med. Ctr. *(see Veterans Affairs Med. Ctr— Manchester)*
Manchester Veterans Affairs Med. Ctr. *(see Veterans Affairs Med. Ctr— Manchester)*
Mandalyn Acad., Inc. 761
Mandl Sch. 567
Mandl Sch. for Med. & Dental Assistants *(see Mandl Sch.)*
Mandl Sch. for Med. Office Assistants *(see Mandl Sch.)*
Manhattan Area Coll. *(see Manhattan Area Tech. Coll.)*
Manhattan Area Tech. Coll. 745 *(see also Manhattan Area Tech. Coll.)*
Manhattan Area Vocational -Tech. Sch. *(see Manhattan Area Tech. Coll.)*
Manhattan Beauty Sch., Inc. 486 *(see also Manhattan Hairstyling Acad.)*
Manhattan Bible Coll. *(see Manhattan Christian Coll.)*
Manhattan Christian Coll. 155
Manhattan Coll. 267
Manhattan Comm. Coll. *(see City Univ. of New York Borough of Manhattan Comm. Coll.)*
Manhattan Hairstyling Acad. 486
Manhattan Sch. of Computer Techno. 567
Manhattan Sch. of Music 267
Manhattanville Coll. 267
Manitoba Coll. of Massage Therapy, The *(see Massage Therapy Coll. of Manitoba, Inc.)*
Manitoba Univ. *(see Univ. of Manitoba)*
Mankato Normal Sch. *(see Minnesota State Univ—Mankato)*
Mankato State Coll. *(see Minnesota State Univ—Mankato)*
Mankato State Teachers Coll. *(see Minnesota State Univ—Mankato)*
Mankato State Univ. *(see Minnesota State Univ—Mankato)*
Manna Sch. of Midwifery & Health Sciences 486
Mannes Coll. of Music *(see New Sch.)*
Mannes Coll. The New Sch. for Music *(see New Sch.)*
Mannheim Univ. *(see Univ. of Mannheim)*
Manor Coll. 335

Manor Int'l. Equestrian Centre *(see Meredith Manor Int'l. Equestrian Centre)*
Manor Jr. Coll. *(see Manor Coll.)*
Mansfield Beauty Sch—Quincy 526
Mansfield Beauty Sch—Springfield 526
Mansfield Bus. Coll. *(see Beta Tech)*
Mansfield Sch. of Techno. *(see North Central State Coll.)*
Mansfield Univ. of Pennsylvania 335
Manual Training Sch. *(see Univ. of Toledo)*
Maple Springs Baptist Bible Coll. & Seminary 180
Maple Springs Coll. *(see Maple Springs Baptist Bible Coll. & Seminary)*
Maple Springs Seminary *(see Maple Springs Baptist Bible Coll. & Seminary)*
Maple Woods Coll. *(see Maple Woods Comm. Coll.)*
Maple Woods Comm. Coll. 227
Marantha Baptist Bible Coll. 425
Marantha Coll. *(see Marantha Baptist Bible Coll.)*
Marcus Inst., The 664
Mare Island Outpatient Clinic *(see Veterans Affairs Northern California Health Care System— Mare Island)*
Mare Island VA Med. Ctr. *(see Veterans Affairs Northern California Health Care System— Mare Island)*
Mare Island Veterans Affairs Med. Ctr. *(see Veterans Affairs Northern California Health Care System— Mare Island)*
Margaret Murray Washington Vocational Sch. 661
Margaret's Hair Acad., Inc. 448
Margate Sch. of Beauty 486
Maria Coll. of Albany 267
Maria Montessori Teacher Training Ctr. 462
Maria Parham Hosp., Inc. 691
Marian Coll. 142 *(see also Marian Health Careers Ctr., Marist Coll.)*
Marian Coll. of Fond du Lac 425
Marian Court Coll. 188
Marian Court Jr. Coll. *(see Marian Court Coll.)*
Marian Health Careers Ctr. 463
Marian Health Ctr. *(see Mercy Med. Ctr. Sioux City)*
Maric Coll. 47, 722
Maric Coll. of Med. Careers *(see Maric Coll.)*

Maric Coll. Sch. of X-ray *(see Maric Coll—North Hollywood)*
Maric Coll—Anaheim 463
Maric Coll—Anaheim 722
Maric Coll—Bakersfield 463
Maric Coll—Los Angeles 463
Maric Coll—Modesto 47, 722
Maric Coll—North Hollywood 47, 723
Maric Coll—Sacramento 463, 722
Maric Coll—Stockton 463, 722
Maric Learning Systems *(see Maric Coll—Los Angeles)*
Maricopa Beauty Coll. 445
Maricopa Comm. Colleges—Estrella Mountain Comm. Coll. *(see Estrella Mountain Comm. Coll.)*
Maricopa Comm. Colleges—Glendale Comm. Coll. *(see Glendale Comm. Coll.)*
Maricopa Comm. Colleges—Mesa Comm. Coll. *(see Mesa Comm. Coll.)*
Maricopa Comm. Colleges—Paradise Valley Comm. Coll. *(see Paradise Valley Comm. Coll.)*
Maricopa Comm. Colleges—Phoenix Coll. *(see Phoenix Coll.)*
Maricopa Comm. Colleges—Scottsdale Comm. Coll. *(see Scottsdale Comm. Coll.)*
Maricpoa Comm. Colleges—Chandler-Gilbert Comm. Coll. *(see Chandler-Gilbert Comm. Coll.)*
Maricpoa Comm. Colleges—Gateway Comm. Coll. *(see Gateway Comm. Coll.)*
Maricpoa Comm. Colleges—Rio Salado Comm. Coll. *(see Rio Salado Comm. Coll.)*
Maricpoa Comm. Colleges—South Mountain Comm. Coll. *(see South Mountain Comm. Coll.)*
Marietta Coll. 305
Marietta Hosp. *(see Marietta Mem. Hosp.)*
Marietta Mem. Hosp. 694
Marietta-Cobb Area Vocational Tech. Sch. *(see Chattahoochee Tech. Coll.)*
Marin Coll. *(see Coll. of Marin)*
Marin Comm. Coll. *(see Coll. of Marin)*
Marin Jr. Coll. *(see Coll. of Marin)*
Marine Corps Inst. *(see United States Marine Corps Inst.)*
Marine Corps Univ. *(see United States Marine Corps Univ.)*
Marine Mechanics Inst. *(see Motorcycle & Marine Mechanics Inst.)*
Marinello Sch. of Beauty 722, 723

Marinello Sch. of Beauty—Burbank 722
Marinello Sch. of Beauty—City of Industry 463, 722
Marinello Sch. of Beauty—Colorado Boulevard *(see Marinello Sch. of Beauty—Eagle Rock)*
Marinello Sch. of Beauty—Eagle Rock 463
Marinello Sch. of Beauty—East Los Angeles 463
Marinello Sch. of Beauty—Huntington Beach 463, 723
Marinello Sch. of Beauty—Inglewood 464
Marinello Sch. of Beauty—Lake Forest 464, 722
Marinello Sch. of Beauty—Las Vegas 543
Marinello Sch. of Beauty—Moreno Valley 464, 722
Marinello Sch. of Beauty—North Hollywood 464
Marinello Sch. of Beauty—Ontario 464
Marinello Sch. of Beauty—Paramount 464, 723
Marinello Sch. of Beauty—Reseda 464
Marinello Sch. of Beauty—San Bernadino 464
Marinello Sch. of Beauty—San Diego 464
Marinello Sch. of Beauty—South Broadway *(see Marinello Sch. of Beauty—East Los Angeles)*
Marinello Sch. of Beauty—West Covina 464
Marinello Sch. of Beauty—Whittier 464
Marinello Sch. of Beauty—Wilshire West 464
Marinello-Eastern Hills Acad. of Hair Design *(see Eastern Hills Acad. of Hair Design)*
Marion Coll. *(see Indiana Wesleyan Univ., Marion Tech. Coll.)*
Marion Inst. *(see Marion Military Inst.)*
Marion Military Inst. 6
Marion Normal Coll. *(see Indiana Wesleyan Univ.)*
Marion Normal Inst. *(see Indiana Wesleyan Univ.)*
Marion S. Whelan Sch. of Practical Nursing 687
Marion Tech. Coll. 306
Marion Univ. *(see Francis Marion Univ.)*
Marist Coll. 267
Maritime Acad. of California *(see California Maritime Acad.)*

Maritime Acad. of Maine *(see Maine Maritime Acad.)*
Maritime Acad. of Massachusetts *(see Massachusetts Maritime Acad.)*
Maritime Coll. *(see State Univ. of New York Maritime Coll.)*
MarJon Sch. of Beauty Culture 567
Mark Hopkins Inst. of Art *(see San Francisco Art Inst.)*
Mark S. Norman & Associates, Inc. *(see C.J. Sealey & Associates, LLC)*
Marks-to Beauty Acad. 753
Marlboro Coll. 397
Marquette City Hosp. *(see Marquette General Health System)*
Marquette Coll. *(see Marquette Univ.)*
Marquette General Health System 678
Marquette General Hosp. *(see Marquette General Health System)*
Marquette Univ. 425
Marriage Council *(see Council for Relationahips)*
Mars Hill Coll. 289
Mars Hill Grad. Sch. 413
Mars Hill Sch. *(see Mars Hill Grad. Sch.)*
Marsha Kay Beauty Coll. 448
Marshall Acad. *(see Marshall Univ.)*
Marshall Coll. *(see Franklin & Marshall Coll., Marshall Comm. & Tech. Coll.)*
Marshall Coll. State Normal Sch. *(see Marshall Univ.)*
Marshall Comm. & Tech. Coll. 419
Marshall Comm. Coll. *(see Marshall Comm. & Tech. Coll.)*
Marshall County Comm. Coll. *(see Marshalltown Comm. Coll.)*
Marshall Islands Coll. *(see Coll. of the Marshall Islands)*
Marshall Law Sch. *(see John Marshall Law Sch.)*
Marshall Univ. 419
Marshalls Theological Coll. *(see Pacific Islands Bible Coll.)*
Marshalltown Comm. Coll. 148
Marshalltown Jr. Coll. *(see Marshalltown Comm. Coll.)*
Martha Graham Sch. of Contemporary Dance, Inc. 568
Marti Coll. of Fashion & Art *(see Virginia Marti Coll. of Art & Design)*
Martin Ctr. Coll. *(see Martin Univ.)*
Martin Coll. *(see Martin Comm. Coll.)*
Martin Comm. Coll. 289
Martin Luther Coll. 211
Martin Mem. Health Systems 663
Martin Methodist Coll. 367

Martin Tech. Inst. *(see Martin Comm. Coll.)*

Martin Univ. 142

Martinez Sch. of Cosmetology 538

Martinez VA Outpatient Clinic *(see Veterans Affairs Northern California Health Care System— Martinez)*

Martinez Veterans Affairs Outpatient Clinic *(see Veterans Affairs Northern California Health Care System—Martinez)*

Martin's Coll. of Cosmetology—Green Bay 643

Martin's Coll. of Cosmetology— Madison 643

Martin's Coll. of Cosmetology— Manitowoc 643

Martinsburg VA Med. Ctr. *(see Veterans Affairs Med. Ctr— Martinsburg)*

Martinsburg Veterans Affairs Med. Ctr. *(see Veterans Affairs Med. Ctr— Martinsburg)*

Marugie Beauty & Tech. Coll. 736

Mary Baldwin Coll. 404

Mary C. Gwin & Associates 739 *(see also J. R. Rodgers & Associates, Inc.)*

Mary Coll. *(see Univ. of Mary)*

Mary Hardin-Baylor Univ. *(see Univ. of Mary Hardin-Baylor)*

Mary Holmes Coll. 731

Mary Immaculate Hosp. 690

Mary Karl Vocational Sch. *(see Daytona Beach Comm. Coll.)*

Mary Lanning Mem. Hosp. 682

Mary Univ. *(see Univ. of Mary)*

Mary Washington Coll. 738 *(see also Univ. of Mary Washington)*

Mary Washington Hosp. 706

Marygrove Coll. 201

Maryland Art & Design Coll. *(see Sch. of Art & Design at Montgomery Coll.)*

Maryland Beauty Acad. 522

Maryland Beauty Acad. of Essex, Inc. 522

Maryland Broadcasting Inst. *(see Broadcasting Inst. of Maryland)*

Maryland Ctr. for Montessori Studies 522

Maryland Coll. of Art *(see Maryland Inst. Coll. of Art, Sch. of Art & Design at Montgomery Coll.)*

Maryland Coll. of Art & Design 730 *(see also Sch. of Art & Design at Montgomery Coll.)*

Maryland General Hosp. 675

Maryland Inst. Coll. of Art, The 180

Maryland Inst. for the Promotion of the Mechanic Arts *(see Maryland Inst. Coll. of Art)*

Maryland Inst. of Art *(see Maryland Inst. Coll. of Art)*

Maryland Inst. of Traditional Chinese Medicine 730

Maryland Med. Secretarial Sch. *(see Hagerstown Bus. Coll.)*

Maryland Normal & Industrial Sch. at Bowie *(see Bowie State Univ.)*

Maryland Normal Sch. #3 *(see Bowie State Univ.)*

Maryland State Normal Sch. *(see Towson Univ.)*

Maryland State Normal Sch. No. 2 at Frostburg *(see Frostburg State Univ.)*

Maryland State Teachers Coll. at Bowie *(see Bowie State Univ.)*

Maryland State Teachers Coll. at Towson *(see Towson Univ.)*

Marylhurst Univ. 321

Marymount Coll. 47 *(see also Loyola Marymount Univ., Marymount Coll. of Fordham Univ.)*

Marymount Coll. of Fordham Univ. 263 *(see also Fordham Univ.)*

Marymount Coll. of Manhattan *(see Marymount Manhattan Coll.)*

Marymount Manhattan Coll. 267

Marymount Sch. of Practical Nursing 694

Marymount Univ. 404

Maryview Med. Ctr. 706

Maryville Coll. 367

Maryville Univ. of St. Louis 227

Marywood Coll. *(see Marywood Univ.)*

Marywood Univ. 335

Mason Acad. of Cosmetology 759

Mason County Techno. Ctr. *(see Maysville Comm. & Tech. Coll.)*

Mason Univ. *(see George Mason Univ.)*

Masonic Geriatric Healthcare Ctr. 659

Massachusetts Agricultural Coll. *(see Univ. of Massachusetts Boston)*

Massachusetts Bay Coll. *(see Massachusetts Bay Comm. Coll.)*

Massachusetts Bay Comm. Coll. 189

Massachusetts Career Development Inst., Inc. 730

Massachusetts Coll. of Art 189

Massachusetts Coll. of Embalming *(see Mount Ida Coll.)*

Massachusetts Coll. of Liberal Arts 189

Massachusetts Coll. of Optometry *(see New England Coll. of Optometry)*

Massachusetts Coll. of Pharmacy & Allied Health Sciences *(see Massachusetts Coll. of Pharmacy & Health Sciences)*

Massachusetts Coll. of Pharmacy & Health Sciences 189

Massachusetts Communications Coll. *(see New England Inst. of Art)*

Massachusetts General Hosp. 676 *(see also MGH Inst. of Health Professions)*

Massachusetts General Hosp. Inst. of Health Professions *(see MGH Inst. of Health Professions)*

Massachusetts Inst. of Techno. 189

Massachusetts Int'l. Language Inst. *(see Int'l. Language Inst. of Massachusetts, Inc.)*

Massachusetts Law Sch. *(see Massachusetts Sch. of Law)*

Massachusetts Maritime Acad. 189

Massachusetts Nautical Sch. *(see Massachusetts Maritime Acad.)*

Massachusetts Nautical Training Sch. *(see Massachusetts Maritime Acad.)*

Massachusetts Normal Art Sch. *(see Massachusetts Coll. of Art)*

Massachusetts Pharmacy Coll. *(see Massachusetts Coll. of Pharmacy & Health Sciences)*

Massachusetts Sch. of Barbering & Men's Hairstyling 526

Massachusetts Sch. of Law 189

Massachusetts Sch. of Optometry *(see New England Coll. of Optometry)*

Massachusetts Sch. of Prof. Psychology 189

Massachusetts State Coll. *(see Univ. of Massachusetts Amherst)*

Massachusetts Univ. Med. Sch. *(see Univ. of Massachusetts Med. Sch.)*

Massage Acad. of Central State *(see Central State Massage Acad.)*

Massage Away, Inc. Sch. of Therapy *(see American Inst. of Alternative Medicine)*

Massage Inst. of New York *(see New York Inst. of Massage)*

Massage Sch. of Atlanta *(see Atlanta Sch. of Massage)*

Massage Sch. of Charleston *(see Charleston Sch. of Massage)*

Massage Sch. of Florida *(see Florida Sch. of Massage)*

Massage Sch. of Virginia *(see Virginia Sch. of Massage)*

Massage Therapy Acad. *(see Acad. of Massage Therapy)*

Massage Therapy Ctr. of Connecticut *(see Connecticut Ctr. for Massage Therapy)*

Massage Therapy Coll. of Baton Rouge 517

Massage Therapy Coll. of Boulder *(see Boulder Coll. of Massage Therapy)*

Massage Therapy Coll. of Manitoba, Inc., The 646

Massage Therapy Coll. of Utah *(see Utah Coll. of Massage Therapy)*

Massage Therapy Inst. of Ann Arbor *(see Ann Arbor Inst. of Massage Therapy)*

Massage Therapy Inst. of Colorado 472

Massage Therapy Inst. of Ogden *(see Ogden Inst. of Massage Therapy)*

Massage Therapy Inst. of the Midwest *(see Midwest Inst. of Massage Therapy)*

Massage Therapy Sch. of Chicago *(see Chicago Sch. of Massage Therapy)*

Massage Therapy Sch. of Denver *(see Denver Sch. of Massage Therapy)*

Massage Therapy Sch. of Omaha *(see Omaha Sch. of Massage Therapy)*

Massage Therapy Sch. of Philadelphia *(see National Massage Therapy Inst.)*

Massage Therapy Sch. of Sarasota *(see Sarasota Sch. of Massage Therapy)*

Massage Therapy Training Inst. 538, 556

MassArt *(see Massachusetts Coll. of Art)*

Massasoit Coll. *(see Massasoit Comm. Coll.)*

Massasoit Comm. Coll. 189

MassBay Comm. Coll. *(see Massachusetts Bay Comm. Coll.)*

Massey Bus. Coll. *(see Art Inst. of Atlanta)*

Massey Coll. of Bus. & Techno. *(see Herzing Coll.)*

Massey Univ—Palmerston North 716

Massotherapy Centre of Youngstown *(see Youngstown Centre of Massotherapy)*

Massotherapy Coll. of Ohio *(see Ohio Coll. of Massotherapy)*

Massotherapy Inst. *(see National Inst. of Massotherapy, Inc.)*

Master's Coll. 740

Master's Coll. & Seminary, The 47, 432

Masters Inst. 723

Masters of Cosmetology Coll., Inc., The 506

Master's Seminary *(see Master's Coll. & Seminary)*

Matanuska-Susitna Coll. 11

Maternidad La Luz 621

Mather Foundation, The 669

Mather Jr. Coll. *(see Tech. Coll. of the Lowcountry)*

Mather Sch., The *(see Tech. Coll. of the Lowcountry)*

Matrix Beauty Coll. *(see Mai-trix Beauty Coll.)*

Mat-Su Coll. *(see Matanuska-Susitna Coll.)*

Mattatuck Comm Coll. *(see Naugatuck Valley Comm. Coll.)*

Maui Acad. of Cosmetology 496

Maui Coll. *(see Maui Comm. Coll.)*

Maui Comm. Coll. 114

Maui Tech. Sch. *(see Maui Comm. Coll.)*

Maui Vocational Sch. *(see Maui Comm. Coll.)*

Maxillofacial & Facial Aesthetic Surgery 694

Maxim's Beauty Acad. *(see Regency Beauty Inst.)*

Maximum Style Tec Sch. of Cosmetology 628

Mayfair Coll. *(see City Colleges of Chicago—Harry S Truman Coll.)*

Mayland Coll. *(see Mayland Comm. Coll.)*

Mayland Comm. Coll. 289

Mayo Clinic Coll. of Medicine 731 *(see also Mayo Grad. Sch., Mayo Sch. of Health Sciences)*

Mayo Clinic—Jacksonville 211

Mayo Foundation 731

Mayo Grad. Sch. 211

Mayo Med. Sch. 211

Mayo Reg. Techno. Ctr. *(see Big Sandy Comm. & Tech. Coll— Mayo Campus)*

Mayo Sch. of Health Sciences 211

Mayo Sch. of Health-Related Sciences *(see Mayo Sch. of Health Sciences)*

Mayo Tech. Coll. 729 *(see also Big Sandy Comm. & Tech. Coll— Mayo Campus)*

Mayo Tech. Coll—Pikeville *(see Big Sandy Comm. & Tech. Coll— Pikeville Campus)*

Maysville Coll. *(see Maysville Comm. & Tech. Coll.)*

Maysville Comm. & Tech. Coll. 162, 729

Maysville Comm. & Tech. Coll— Licking Valley 729

Maysville Comm. & Tech. Coll— Rowan 729

Maysville Comm. Coll. 729 *(see also Maysville Comm. & Tech. Coll.)*

Mayville State Univ. *(see Mayville State Univ.)*

Mayville State Univ. 296

MBTI Bus. Training Inst. 605, 739

MBTI Training *(see MBTI Bus. Training Inst.)*

McAfee Sch. of Theology *(see Mercer Univ.)*

McAllister Inst. of Funeral Service, Inc. *(see American Acad. McAllister Inst. of Funeral Service, Inc.)*

McCann Sch. of Bus. & Techno-Pottsville 335

McCann Sch. of Bus—Pottsville *(see McCann Sch. of Bus. & Tech— Pottsville)*

McCann Tech *(see Charles H. McCann Tech. Sch.)*

McCann Tech. Sch. *(see Charles H. McCann Tech. Sch.)*

McClellan Mem. Veterans Hosp. *(see Central Arkansas Veterans Healthcare System)*

McCollum & Ross, The Hair Sch. 611

McComb Female Inst. *(see Belhaven Coll.)*

McConnell Coll. *(see Truett McConnell Coll.)*

McConnell Sch. 731

McCook Comm. Coll. 237 *(see also Mid-Plains Comm. Coll.)*

McCook Jr. Coll. *(see McCook Comm. Coll., Mid-Plains Comm. Coll.)*

McCormick Theological Seminary 126

McDaniel Coll. 181

McDonough County Hosp. Dist. *(see McDonough Dist. Hosp.)*

McDonough Dist. Hosp. 668

McDonough Hosp. *(see McDonough Dist. Hosp.)*

McDowell Coll. *(see McDowell Tech. Comm. Coll.)*

McDowell Comm. Coll. *(see McDowell Tech. Comm. Coll.)*

McDowell County Vocational Tech. Ctr. 641

McDowell County Voc-Tech Ctr. *(see McDowell County Vocational Tech. Ctr.)*

McDowell Tech. Coll. *(see McDowell Tech. Comm. Coll.)*

McDowell Tech. Comm. Coll. 289

MCed Career Ctr. 723

MCed Career Coll. 464

Mced Coll. *(see MCed Career Coll.)*

McEllis Training Inst. 733

McFarland Inst., The 673

McFatter Tech. Ctr. *(see William T. McFatter Tech. Ctr.)*

McFatter Vocational-Tech. Ctr. *(see William T. McFatter Tech. Ctr.)*

McGarvey Bible Coll. *(see Cincinnati Christian Univ.)*

McGee's Acad. of Cosmetology, Inc. *(see Acad. of Cosmetology)*

McGeorge Sch. of Law *(see Univ. of the Pacific)*

McGill Univ. 433

McGill Univ. Faculty of Religious Studies *(see McGill Univ.)*

McGregor Sch. of Antioch Univ. *(see Antioch Univ. McGregor)*

McHenry County Coll. 126

McIntosh Coll. 242

McKees Rocks General Hosp. *(see Ohio Valley General Hosp.)*

McKendree Coll. 126

McKenna Coll. *(see Claremont McKenna Coll.)*

McKennan Hosp. *(see Avera McKennan Hosp. & Univ. Health Ctr.)*

McKenzie Coll. *(see Southwestern Univ.)*

McKenzie Study Ctr. *(see Gutenberg Coll.)*

McLennan Coll. *(see McLennan Comm. Coll.)*

McLennan Comm. Coll. 381

McMaster Univ. 433

McMinnville Coll. *(see Linfield Coll.)*

McMurry Univ. 381

McNally Smith Coll. of Music 211, 731

McNeese State Coll. *(see McNeese State Univ.)*

McNeese State Univ. 172

MCP Hahnemann Univ. *(see Drexel Univ.)*

McPherson Coll. 155

Meadville Lombard Theological Sch. 126

Meadville Theological Sch. *(see Meadville Lombard Theological Sch.)*

Meany Ctr. for Labor Studies *(see National Labor Coll.)*

Mechanical Techno. Inst. of Caguas *(see Caguas Inst. of Mechanical Techno.)*

Med Tech Coll. *(see MedTech Coll., Stuart Sch.)*

Medaille Coll. 267

Med-Assist Sch. of Hawaii 496

Medcenter One Coll. of Nursing *(see Medcenter One Health Systems)*

Medcenter One Health Systems 296

Medcenter One Hosp. *(see Medcenter One Health Systems)*

MedCentral Coll. of Nursing 306

Median Sch. of Allied Health Careers 335

Med. & Dental Assistants Coll. of San Antonio *(see San Antonio Coll. of Med. & Dental Assistants)*

Med. & Dental Assistants Sch. of New York *(see New York Sch. for Med. & Dental Assistants)*

Med. & Dental Techno. Inst. of Cincinnati *(see Inst. of Med. & Dental Techno.)*

Med. & Dental Univ. of New Jersey *(see Univ. of Medicine & Dentistry of New Jersey)*

Med. Arts & Bus. Acad. *(see Acad. of Med. Arts & Bus.)*

Med. Arts Massage Sch. 573

Med. Assistants Sch. of New York *(see New York Sch. for Med. & Dental Assistants)*

Med. Career Ctr. 725 *(see also Virginia Coll. at Pensacola)*

Med. Career Inst. of South Florida 486

Med. Careers Acad. *(see MedVance Inst. of Baton Rouge)*

Med. Careers Coll. of Nashville *(see Nashville Coll. of Med. Careers)*

Med. Careers Inst. 404

Med. Careers Training Ctr. *(see Inst. of Bus. & Med. Careers)*

Med. Ctr. of Atlanta *(see Atlanta Med. Ctr.)*

Med. Ctr. of Aurora, The 658

Med. Ctr. of Boston *(see Boston Med. Ctr.)*

Med. Ctr. of Delaware 660

Med. Ctr. of Eastern Maine *(see Eastern Maine Med. Ctr.)*

Med. Ctr. of Erie County *(see Erie County Med. Ctr.)*

Med. Ctr. of North Mississippi *(see North Mississippi Med. Ctr.)*

Med. Ctr. of the Univ. of Mississippi *(see Univ. of Mississippi Med. Ctr.)*

Med. Ctr. of Westchester County *(see Westchester County Med. Ctr.)*

Med. Ctr. Ohio Valley *(see Ohio Valley Med. Ctr.)*

Med. Centers of the Mountains, The *(see Hazard ARH Reg. Med. Ctr.)*

Med. Coll. of Albany *(see Albany Med. Coll.)*

Med. Coll. of Georgia 106 *(see also Columbus State Univ.)*

Med. Coll. of Hampton Roads *(see Eastern Virginia Med. Sch.)*

Med. Coll. of Louisiana *(see Tulane Univ.)*

Med. Coll. of New York *(see New York Med. Coll.)*

Med. Coll. of Ohio 734 *(see also Med. Univ. of Ohio)*

Med. Coll. of Pennsylvania & Hahnemann Univ. *(see Drexel Univ.)*

Med. Coll. of South Carolina *(see Med. Univ. of South Carolina)*

Med. Coll. of Virginia *(see Virginia Commonwealth Univ.)*

Med. Coll. of Wisconsin 425

Med. Electronic Data Systems *(see Ladera Career Paths Training Ctr.)*

Med. Field Service Sch. *(see United States Army Med. Dept. Ctr. & Sch.)*

Med. Inst. 464, 721 *(see also Capps Coll—Foley)*

Med. Inst. of Arlington *(see Arlington Med. Inst.)*

Med. Inst. of Georgia *(see Georgia Med. Inst., Med. Coll. of Georgia)*

Med. Inst. of Los Angeles *(see Med. Inst.)*

Med. Inst. of Minnesota 679, 731

Med. Isntitute of Minnesota *(see Argosy Univ. Twin Cities)*

Med. Prof. Inst. 526

Med. Sch. of Eastern Virginia *(see Eastern Virginia Med. Sch.)*

Med. Sch. of New Jersey *(see New Jersey Med. Sch.)*

Med. Sch. of Ponce *(see Ponce Sch. of Medicine)*

Med. Sch. of the Univ. of Massachusetts *(see Univ. of Massachusetts Med. Sch.)*

Med. Sciences Campus of the Univ. of Puerto Rico *(see Univ. of Puerto Rico—Med. Sciences Campus)*

Med. Training Coll. 517

Med. Training Inst. of Florida *(see Florida Med. Training Inst.)*

Med. Univ. of Ohio 306, 734

Med. Univ. of South Carolina 357

MediCorp Health System *(see Mary Washington Hosp.)*

Medina Bus. Inst. *(see Medina County Career Ctr.)*

Medina County Career Ctr. 581

Medina County Joint Vocational Sch. *(see Medina County Career Ctr.)*

Medina County JVS *(see Medina County Career Ctr.)*

Medix Sch. 494, 522 *(see also Berdan Inst.)*

MEDRIGHT-Prof. Med. Edu. 678

MedStar Health System *(see Washington Hosp. Ctr.)*

MedTech Coll. 555 *(see also Stuart Sch.)*
MedVance Inst. 368
MedVance Inst. of Baton Rouge 517
MedVance Inst. of Houston 621
Meharry Coll. *(see Meharry Med. Coll.)*
Meharry Med. Coll. 368
Meiji Coll. of Oriental Medicine 723 *(see also Acupuncture & Integrative Medicine Coll., Berkeley)*
Melbourne Beauty Sch. 486
Mellie's Beauty Coll. 448
Mem. City Hosp. of Houston *(see Mem. Hermann Mem. City Hosp.)*
Mem. Hermann Baptist Beaumont Hosp. 704
Mem. Hermann Mem. City Hosp. 704
Mem. Hermann Southwest Hosp. 704
Mem. Hosp. 658
Mem. Hosp. & Med. Ctr. of Cumberland Maryland 675
Mem. Hosp. of Elmhurst *(see Elmhurst Mem. Hosp.)*
Mem. Med. Ctr. 673
Mem. Sloan-Kettering Cancer Ctr. 688
Mem. Univ. of Newfoundland 712
Memphis Art Coll. *(see Memphis Coll. of Art)*
Memphis Coll. of Art 368
Memphis Conference Female Inst. *(see Lambuth Univ.)*
Memphis Montessori Inst. 611
Memphis Seminary *(see Memphis Theological Seminary)*
Memphis State Coll. *(see Univ. of Memphis)*
Memphis State Tech. Inst. *(see Southwest Tennessee Comm. Coll.)*
Memphis State Univ. *(see Univ. of Memphis)*
Memphis Theological Seminary 368
Memphis Univ. *(see Univ. of Memphis)*
Memphis VA Med. Ctr. *(see Veterans Affairs Med. Ctr.—Memphis)*
Memphis Veterans Affairs Med. Ctr. *(see Veterans Affairs Med. Ctr.—Memphis)*
Mena Cosmetology Coll. 448
Mendocino Coll. 47
MENDOTA Mental Health Inst. 709
Menlo Coll. 47
Menlo Jr. Coll. *(see Menlo Coll.)*
Mennonite Brethren Biblical Seminary 47
Mennonite Coll. of Nursing 122 *(see also Illinois State Univ.)*
Mennonite Seminary *(see Associated Mennonite Biblical Seminary)*

Menominee Coll. *(see Coll. of the Menominee Nation)*
Menominee Nation Coll. *(see Coll. of the Menominee Nation)*
Menta Group, The 668
Mental Health Ctr. at Fort Wayne *(see Park Ctr., Inc.)*
Mental Health Ctr. of Aurora *(see Aurora Mental Health Ctr.)*
Mental Health Ctr. of Shasta *(see Shasta Comm. Mental Health Ctr.)*
Mental Health Inst. of Colorado *(see Colorado Mental Health Inst. at Fort Logan)*
Mental Health Services Commission *(see Commission on Mental Health Services)*
Merce Cunningham Studio 568
Merced Coll. 47
Mercer Comm. Coll. *(see Mercer County Comm. Coll.)*
Mercer County Career Ctr. 598
Mercer County Coll. *(see Mercer County Comm. Coll.)*
Mercer County Comm. Coll. 247
Mercer County Health Careers Ctr. *(see Mercer County Tech. Schools Health Careers Ctr.)*
Mercer County Tech. Ctr. *(see Mercer County Tech. Edu. Ctr.)*
Mercer County Tech. Edu. Ctr. 641
Mercer County Tech. Schools Health Careers Ctr. 684
Mercer Univ. 106, 745
Mercer Univ. Coll. of Nursing *(see Georgia Baptist Coll. of Nursing of Mercer Univ.)*
Merchant Marine Acad. *(see United States Merchant Marine Acad.)*
Mercy Coll. 267
Mercy Coll. of Detroit *(see Univ. of Detroit Mercy)*
Mercy Coll. of Health Sciences 149
Mercy Coll. of Northwest Ohio 306
Mercy Coll. of Ohio *(see Mercy Coll. of Northwest Ohio)*
Mercy Educational Inst. 756
Mercy Health Network *(see Mercy Med. Ctr. Sioux City)*
Mercy Health System of Maine *(see Mercy Hosp.)*
Mercy Healthcare Ctr. *(see Saint Margaret Mercy Healthcare Ctr.)*
Mercy Hosp. 674 *(see also Mercy Med. Ctr.)*
Mercy Hosp. Training Sch. *(see Mercy Coll. of Health Sciences)*
Mercy Med. Ctr. 675, 688, 694, 709 *(see also Mercy/St. Luke's Sch. of Radiologic Techno.)*
Mercy Med. Ctr. North Iowa 671

Mercy Med. Ctr. Sioux City 671
Mercy Sch. of Nursing *(see Mercy Coll. of Northwest Ohio)*
Mercy/St. Luke's Sch. of Radiologic Techno. 671
Mercyhurst Coll. 335
Mercy-Unity Hospitals & Convalescent Ctr. 679
Meredith Coll. 290
Meredith Manor Int'l. Equestrian Centre 641
Meridian Coll. *(see Meridian Comm. Coll.)*
Meridian Comm. Coll. 219
Meridian Health System *(see Jersey Shore Univ. Med. Ctr.)*
Meridian Tech *(see Meridian Techno. Ctr.)*
Meridian Techno. Ctr. 695
Meritcare Health System *(see Meritcare Hosp.)*
Meritcare Hosp. 692
Meritcare Med. Ctr. *(see Meritcare Hosp.)*
Meriter Hosp. 709
Merkaz Bnos Bus. Sch. 568
Merlix Prof. & Tech. Inst. *(see Instituto Merlix)*
Mermac Coll. *(see Saint Louis Comm. Coll. at Meramec)*
Merrell Univ. of Beauty Arts & Science 538
Merrill-Palmer Inst. *(see Ctr. for Humanistic Studies)*
Merrillville Beauty Coll. 506
Merrimack Coll. 190
Merrimack Valley Coll. *(see Univ. of New Hampshire, Univ. of New Hampshire at Manchester)*
Merritt Coll. 47 *(see also Samuel Merritt Coll.)*
Mesa Coll. *(see Mesa Comm. Coll., Mesa State Coll., San Diego Mesa Coll.)*
Mesa Coll. of San Diego *(see San Diego Mesa Coll.)*
Mesa Comm. Coll. 17
Mesa State Coll. 69
Mesa Tech. Coll. 733 *(see also Mesalands Comm. Coll.)*
Mesabi Range Comm. & Tech. Coll. 211
Mesabi State Jr. Coll. *(see Mesabi Range Comm. & Tech. Coll.)*
Mesalands Coll. *(see Mesalands Comm. Coll.)*
Mesalands Comm. Coll. 252, 733
Mesivta of Eastern Parkway Rabbinical Seminary 267
Mesivta Tifereth Jerusalem of America 267

Mesivta Torah Vodaath Seminary 267
Messenger Coll. 227
Messiah Bible Coll. *(see Messiah Coll.)*
Messiah Bible Sch. *(see Messiah Coll.)*
Messiah Coll. 335
Messiah Missionary Training Home *(see Messiah Coll.)*
Methodist Coll. 290
Methodist Coll. of Spartanburg *(see Spartanburg Methodist Coll.)*
Methodist Dallas Med. Ctr. 704
Methodist Episcopal Hosp. of Brooklyn *(see New York Methodist Hosp.)*
Methodist Health Care System *(see Methodist Hosp.)*
Methodist Health System *(see)*
Methodist Healthcare—Univ. Hosp. 736
Methodist Hosp. 679, 704 *(see also Clarian Health Partners, Inc/Methodist Hosp.)*
Methodist Hosp. of Minnesota *(see Methodist Hosp.)*
Methodist Hosp. of Southern California 654
Methodist Hospitals of Dallas *(see Methodist Dallas Med. Ctr.)*
Methodist Med. Ctr. of Illinois 668
Methodist Theological Sch. in Ohio 306 *(see also Methodist Theological Sch. in Ohio)*
Methodist Univ. Hosp. 702, 736
Metro Auto Electronics Training Inst., Inc. 552
Metro Bus. Coll. 228
Metro Techno. Ctr—South Bryant 589
Metro Techno. Centers—Springlake 589
MetroHealth Med. Ctr., The 694
MetroHealth System *(see MetroHealth Med. Ctr., The)*
Metroplex Beauty Sch. 621
Metropolitan Career Ctr. & Computer Techno. Inst. 335
Metropolitan Coll. 315
Metropolitan Coll. of Court Reporting *(see Metropolitan Coll—Albuquerque Campus, Metropolitan Coll—Oklahoma City Campus, Metropolitan Coll—Phoenix Campus)*
Metropolitan Coll. of Legal Studies *(see Metropolitan Coll.)*
Metropolitan Coll. of New York 268
Metropolitan Coll—Albuquerque Campus 252
Metropolitan Coll—Oklahoma City Campus 315

Metropolitan Coll—Phoenix Campus 18
Metropolitan Comm. Coll. 237 *(see also Blue Ridge Comm. Coll., Longview Comm. Coll., Maple Woods Comm. Coll., Penn Valley Comm. Coll.)*
Metropolitan Computer Techno. Inst. *(see Metropolitan Career Ctr. & Computer Techno. Inst.)*
Metropolitan Detention Ctr., The 654
Metropolitan Learning Inst. 247
Metropolitan London Univ. *(see London Metropolitan Univ.)*
Metropolitan Sch. Dist. of Washington Township *(see J. Everett Light Career Ctr.)*
Metropolitan State Coll. of Denver 69
Metropolitan State Hosp. 654
Metropolitan State Univ. 211
Metropolitan Tech. Comm. Coll. *(see Metropolitan Comm. Coll.)*
Metropolitan Tech. Inst. 733
Metropolitan Univ. *(see Universidad Metropolitana)*
Metropolitan Univ. Coll. *(see Universidad Metropolitana)*
Meyer Uebelher Associates, LLC 644
MGH Inst. of Health Professions 190
Miami Ad Sch., The 486
Miami Coll. of Culinary Arts *(see Le Cordon Bleu Coll. of Culinary Arts—Miami)*
Miami Dade Dept. of Human Services *(see Miami-Dade County Dept. of Human Services)*
Miami Inst. of Psychology *(see Carlos Albizu Univ—Miami Campus)*
Miami Int'l. Univ. of Art & Design 90, 725
Miami Job Corps Ctr. 486
Miami Lakes Tech. Edu. Ctr. 486
Miami Of Ohio *(see Miami Univ.)*
Miami Sch. of Mines *(see Northeastern Oklahoma A&M Coll.)*
Miami Univ. 306 *(see also Univ. of Miami)*
Miami Univ. of Art & Design *(see Miami Int'l. Univ. of Art & Design)*
Miami VA Med. Ctr. *(see Miami Veterans Affairs Med. Ctr.)*
Miami Valley Career Techno. Ctr. 581
Miami Valley Hosp. 694
Miami Veterans Affairs Med. Ctr. 663
Miami-Dade Coll. 90, 725
Miami-Dade Comm. Coll. 725 *(see also Miami-Dade Coll.)*
Miami-Dade Comm. Coll. Med. Ctr. *(see Miami-Dade Coll. Med. Ctr.)*

Miami-Dade Comm. Coll., Hialeah Campus *(see Miami-Dade Coll., Hialeah)*
Miami-Dade Comm. Coll., North Campus *(see Miami-Dade Coll., North)*
Miami-Dade Comm. Coll—InterAmerican Campus *(see Miami-Dade Coll., InterAmerican)*
Miami-Dade Comm. Coll—Kendall *(see Miami-Dade Coll., Kendall)*
Miami-Dade County Dept. of Human Services 663
Miami-Dade Jr. Coll. *(see Miami-Dade Coll.)*
Miami-Jacobs Career Coll. *(see Miami-Jacobs Coll.)*
Miami-Jacobs Coll. 306
Michael D. Norman & Associates, Inc. *(see Norman & Associates)*
Michael W. Jones & Associates, Inc. 581
Michael's Sch. of Beauty 494
Michael's Sch. of Hair Design 544
Michener Inst. for Applied Health Sciences 712
Michiana Beauty Coll. 532 *(see also Twin City Beauty Coll.)*
Michiana Coll. 728 *(see also Brown Mackie Coll—South Bend)*
Michigan Aeronautics Inst. *(see Michigan Inst. of Aeronautics)*
Michigan Agricultural Coll. *(see Michigan State Univ.)*
Michigan & Huron Inst., the *(see Kalamazoo Coll.)*
Michigan Barber Sch., Inc. 530
Michigan Career & Tech. Inst. 530
Michigan Central Coll. *(see Hillsdale Coll.)*
Michigan Christian Coll. *(see Rochester Coll.)*
Michigan Coll. of Beauty—Monroe 530
Michigan Coll. of Beauty—Troy 530
Michigan Coll. of Beauty—Waterford 530
Michigan Coll. of Edu. *(see Northern Michigan Univ.)*
Michigan Dale Carnegie Training *(see Ralph Nichols Group, Inc.)*
Michigan Inst. of Aeronautics 530
Michigan Jewish Inst. 201
Michigan Montessori Teacher Edu. Ctr. 530
Michigan Seminary *(see Michigan Theological Seminary)*
Michigan State Coll. of Agriculture & Applied Science *(see Michigan State Univ.)*
Michigan State Univ. 201

Michigan State Univ. Oakland *(see Oakland Univ.)*
Michigan State Univ. of Agriculture & Applied Science *(see Michigan State Univ.)*
Michigan Tech *(see Michigan Technological Univ.)*
Michigan Technological Univ. 201
Michigan Theological Coll. *(see Michigan Theological Seminary)*
Michigan Theological Seminary 201, 746
Michigan Univ. *(see Univ. of Michigan)*
Michigan Veterans Vocational Sch. *(see Michigan Career & Tech. Inst.)*
Micro Tech Training Ctr. 552
Microcomputer Edu. Ctr. 723 *(see also MCed Career Coll.)*
Microcomputer Techno. Inst. *(see MTI Coll. of Bus. & Techno.)*
Micronesia Coll. *(see Coll. of Micronesia-FSM)*
Micronesia Comm. Coll. *(see Coll. of Micronesia-FSM)*
Micronesian Inst. of Biblical Studies *(see Pacific Islands Bible Coll.)*
Micropower Computer Inst. 552
Mid Cities Barber Coll. 621
Mid Florida Tech *(see Orange Tech. Edu. Ctr—Mid Florida Tech)*
Mid Michigan Coll. *(see Mid Michigan Comm. Coll.)*
Mid Michigan Comm. Coll. 202
Mid-America Baptist Theological Seminary 368
Mid-America Bible Coll. 735 *(see also Mid-America Christian Univ.)*
Mid-America Christian Univ. 316, 735
Mid-America Coll. of Funeral Service 142
Mid-America Montessori Teacher Training Ctr. 542
MidAmerica Nazarene Coll. *(see MidAmerica Nazarene Univ.)*
MidAmerica Nazarene Univ. 155
Mid-America Reformed Seminary 142
Mid-America Seminary *(see Mid-America Baptist Theological Seminary)*
Mid-America Techno. Ctr. 589
MidAmerica Univ. *(see MidAmerica Nazarene Univ.)*
Mid-America Univ. *(see Mid-America Christian Univ.)*
Mid-Continent Baptist Bible Coll. *(see Mid-Continent Univ.)*
Mid-Continent Coll. 729 *(see also Mid-Continent Univ.)*
Mid-Continent Univ. 162, 729

Mid-Del Area Vocational-Tech. Sch. *(see Mid-Del Techno. Ctr.)*
Mid-Del Area Vo-Tech *(see Mid-Del Techno. Ctr.)*
Mid-Del Lewis Eubanks Area Vocational-Tech. Sch. *(see Mid-Del Techno. Ctr.)*
Mid-Del Lewis Eubanks Area Vo-Tech *(see Mid-Del Techno. Ctr.)*
Mid-Del Lewis Eubanks Techno. Ctr. *(see Mid-Del Techno. Ctr.)*
Mid-Del Techno. Ctr. 589
Mid-Del Vocational-Tech. Ctr. *(see Mid-Del Techno. Ctr.)*
Middle Georgia Coll. 106 *(see also Middle Georgia Tech. Coll.)*
Middle Georgia Tech. Coll. 106, 726
Middle Georgia Tech. Inst. 726 *(see also Middle Georgia Tech. Coll.)*
Middle Tennessee Sch. of Anesthesia 368
Middle Tennessee Sch. of Cosmetology 611 *(see also Middle Tennessee Sch. of Cosmetology)*
Middle Tennessee State Coll. *(see Middle Tennessee State Univ.)*
Middle Tennessee State Normal Sch. *(see Middle Tennessee State Univ.)*
Middle Tennessee State Univ. 368
Middlebury Coll. 397
Middlesex Coll. *(see Middlesex Comm. Coll., Middlesex County Coll.)*
Middlesex Comm. Coll. 73, 190
Middlesex County Coll. 247
Mid-East Career & Techno. Centers *(see Adult Ctr. for Edu.)*
Midland Coll. 381 *(see also Midland Lutheran Coll.)*
Midland Lutheran Coll. 237
Midland Radio & Television Sch. *(see DeVry Univ. Kansas City)*
Midlands Area Program-South Carolina Dept. of Mental Health 701
Midlands Tech. Coll. 357
Midlands Tech. Edu. Ctr. *(see Midlands Tech. Coll.)*
Mid-Plains Comm. Coll. 237
Mid-Plains Comm. Coll. Area *(see McCook Comm. Coll.)*
Mid-Plains Comm. Coll/Vo-Tech Campus *(see Mid-Plains Comm. Coll—North)*
Mid-Plains Comm. Coll—North 237
Mid-Plains Vocational Tech. Coll. *(see Mid-Plains Comm. Coll.)*
Mid-South Bible Coll. *(see Crichton Coll.)*

Mid-South Comm. Coll. 25
Mid-State Coll. *(see Mid-State Tech. Coll.)*
Midstate Coll. 126
Mid-State Coll. 730
Mid-State Tech. Coll. 425
Midway Coll. 162
Midway Paris Beauty Sch—Queens 568
Midway Sch. of Massage *(see East-West Coll. of the Healing Arts)*
Midwest Bible Coll. *(see Calvary Bible Coll. & Theological Seminary)*
Midwest Ctr. for the Study of Oriental Medicine *(see Midwest Coll. of Oriental Medicine—Wisconsin)*
Midwest Christian Coll. *(see Ozark Christian Coll.)*
Midwest Coll. of Oriental Medicine—Wisconsin 425
Midwest Inst. for Med. Assistants 228
Midwest Inst. of Massage Therapy 502
Midwest Med. Assistants Inst. *(see Midwest Inst. for Med. Assistants)*
Midwest Montessori Teacher Training Ctr. 502
Midwest Oriental Medicine Coll. *(see Midwest Coll. of Oriental Medicine—Wisconsin)*
Midwest Oriental Medicine Coll. *(see Midwest Coll. of Oriental Medicine—Wisconsin)*
Midwest Sch. of Welding & Techno. 727 *(see also Midwest Tech. Inst.)*
Midwest Seminary *(see Midwest Theological Seminary)*
Midwest Tech. Inst. 502, 727
Midwest Theological Seminary 228
Midwestern Baptist Seminary *(see Midwestern Baptist Theological Seminary)*
Midwestern Baptist Theological Seminary 228
Midwestern Reg. Med. Ctr. 668
Midwestern State Univ. 381
Midwestern Univ. 127 *(see also Midwestern State Univ.)*
Midwifery Coll. of Utah *(see Midwives Coll. of Utah)*
Midwifery Sch. of Seattle *(see Seattle Midwifery Sch.)*
Midwifery, Women & Health Inst. *(see Inst. of Midwifery, Women & Health)*
Midwives Coll. of Utah 394, 737
Milan Inst. of Cosmetology 621, 638, 737, 738
Mildred Elley 268, 733
Mildred Elley Bus. Sch. 733

Miles Coll. 6 *(see also Miles Comm. Coll.)*
Miles Comm. Coll. 234
Military Acad. *(see United States Military Acad.)*
Military Coll. of Georgia, The *(see Georgia Military Coll., North Georgia Coll. & State Univ.)*
Military Coll. of South Carolina, The *(see Citadel)*
Military Inst. of New Mexico *(see New Mexico Military Inst.)*
Miller Sch. of Medicine *(see Jackson Mem. Hosp.)*
Miller Sch. of Radiologic Techno. *(see Central Maine Med. Ctr.)*
Miller-Motte Bus. Coll. *(see Miller-Motte Tech. Coll.)*
Miller-Motte Tech. Coll. 368, 632
Millersville Coll. *(see Millersville Univ. of Pennsylvania)*
Millersville State Coll. *(see Millersville Univ. of Pennsylvania)*
Millersville State Teacher's Coll. *(see Millersville Univ. of Pennsylvania)*
Millersville Univ. of Pennsylvania 335
Milligan Coll. 368
Millikin Univ. 127
Mills Coll. 47
Mills Mem. Hosp. *(see Mills-Peninsula Health Services)*
Millsaps Coll. 219
Mills-Peninsula Health Services 654
Milton & Carroll Petrie Division of Beth Israel Med. Ctr. *(see Beth Israel Med. Ctr.)*
Milton S. Hershey Med. Ctr. *(see Pennsylvania State Univ.)*
Miltonvale Wesleyan Coll. *(see Oklahoma Wesleyan Univ.)*
Milwaukee Area Tech. Coll. 425
Milwaukee Art & Design Inst. *(see Milwaukee Inst. of Art & Design)*
Milwaukee Engineering Sch. *(see Milwaukee Sch. of Engineering)*
Milwaukee Inst. of Art & Design 426
Milwaukee Inst. of Techno. *(see Milwaukee Area Tech. Coll.)*
Milwaukee Sch. of Engineering 426
Milwaukee Tech. Coll. *(see Milwaukee Area Tech. Coll.)*
Milwaukee VA Med. Ctr. *(see Veterans Affairs Med. Ctr—Milwaukee)*
Milwaukee Veterans Affairs Med. Ctr. *(see Veterans Affairs Med. Ctr—Milwaukee)*
Mims Classic Beauty Coll. 622
Mineral Area Coll. 228
Mineral Area Hosp. *(see Mineral Area Reg. Med. Ctr.)*
Mineral Area Reg. Med. Ctr. 681

Mineral County Tech. Ctr. 641
Mineral Tech. Ctr. *(see Mineral County Tech. Ctr.)*
Mines & Techno. Sch. of South Dakota *(see South Dakota Sch. of Mines & Techno.)*
Mining Inst. of New Mexico *(see New Mexico Inst. of Mining & Techno.)*
Minister's Inst. *(see Arkansas Baptist Coll.)*
Minneapolis Ad Sch. *(see Miami Ad Sch., Miami Ad Sch. Minneapolis)*
Minneapolis Bible Coll. *(see Crossroads Coll.)*
Minneapolis Bible Univ. *(see Crossroads Coll.)*
Minneapolis Bus. Coll. 211
Minneapolis Coll. of Art & Design 211
Minneapolis Coll. of Culinary Arts *(see Le Cordon Bleu Coll. of Culinary Arts—Minneapolis/St. Paul)*
Minneapolis Coll. of Design *(see Minneapolis Coll. of Art & Design)*
Minneapolis Comm. & Tech. Coll. 212
Minneapolis Comm. Coll. *(see Minneapolis Comm. & Tech. Coll.)*
Minneapolis Drafting Sch. *(see Herzing Coll—Minneapolis Drafting Sch.)*
Minneapolis Massage Sch. *(see Minneapolis Sch. of Massage & Bodywork)*
Minneapolis Sch. of Art *(see Minneapolis Coll. of Art & Design)*
Minneapolis Sch. of Massage & Bodywork 533
Minneapolis VA Med. Ctr. *(see Veterans Affairs Med. Ctr— Minneapolis)*
Minneapolis Veterans Affairs Med. Ctr. *(see Veterans Affairs Med. Ctr— Minneapolis)*
Minnesota Acad. *(see Pillsbury Baptist Bible Coll.)*
Minnesota Adlerian Society *(see Adler Grad. Sch.)*
Minnesota Art Inst. *(see Art Institutes Int'l—Minnesota)*
Minnesota Bible Coll. 731 *(see also Crossroads Coll.)*
Minnesota Central Univ. *(see Pillsbury Baptist Bible Coll.)*
Minnesota Coll. of Acupuncture & Oriental Med. *(see Northwestern Health Sciences Univ.)*
Minnesota Cosmetology Edu. Ctr., Inc. 731 *(see also Minnesota Sch. of Cosmetology)*
Minnesota Dale Carnegie Training *(see Norman & Associates)*

Minnesota Inst. of Acupuncture & Herbal Studies *(see Minnesota Inst. of Acupuncture & Oriental Medicine)*
Minnesota Inst. of Acupuncture & Oriental Medicine 213 *(see also Northwestern Health Sciences Univ.)*
Minnesota Inst. of Art *(see Art Institutes Int'l—Minnesota)*
Minnesota Inst. of Technologies 212
Minnesota Med. Inst. *(see Med. Inst. of Minnesota)*
Minnesota Methodist Hosp. *(see Methodist Hosp.)*
Minnesota Montessori Training Ctr. *(see Montessori Training Ctr. of Minnesota)*
Minnesota Riverland Tech. Coll. *(see South Central Coll—Mankato)*
Minnesota Riverland Tech. Coll— Austin *(see Riverland Comm. Coll—Austin)*
Minnesota Sch. of Bus. 212 *(see also Globe Coll.)*
Minnesota Sch. of Cosmetology 533, 731
Minnesota Sch. of Prof. Psychology 731 *(see also Argosy Univ. Twin Cities)*
Minnesota State Coll—Southeast Tech. 212
Minnesota State Comm. & Tech. Coll. 212, 731
Minnesota State Univ. Moorhead 212
Minnesota State Univ—Mankato 212
Minnesota Tech. Coll. *(see Minnesota State Coll-Southeast Tech.)*
Minnesota Tech. Inst. *(see Minnesota State Coll-Southeast Tech.)*
Minnesota West Comm. & Tech. Coll—Granite Falls 213
Minot State Univ. 296
Minot State Univ—Bottineau 296
Mira Costa Coll. 48
MiraCosta Coll. *(see Mira Costa Coll.)*
Miramar Coll. *(see San Diego Miramar Coll.)*
Mirrer Yeshiva 268
Misericordia Coll. *(see Coll. Misericordia)*
Miss Marty's Beauty Sch. *(see Miss Marty's Hair Acad. & Esthetics Inst.)*
Miss Marty's Hair Acad. & Esthetics Inst. 464, 723
Miss Marty's Sch. of Beauty & Hairstyling 723 *(see also Miss Marty's Hair Acad. & Esthetics Inst.)*

Miss Wade's Fashion Merchandising Coll. *(see Wade Coll.)*
Mission Coll. of Los Angeles *(see Los Angeles Mission Coll.)*
Mission Coll. 48 *(see also Los Angeles Mission Coll.)*
Mission House *(see Lakeland Coll.)*
Mission House Seminary *(see United Theological Seminary of the Twin Cities)*
Mission Institution *(see Blinn Coll.)*
Missionary Training Inst. *(see Nyack Coll.)*
Missionshaus *(see Lakeland Coll.)*
Mississippi Acad. *(see Mississippi Coll.)*
Mississippi Baptist Med. Ctr. 680
Mississippi Coll. 219
Mississippi Coll. of Beauty Culture 536
Mississippi Consortium of Religion & Pastoral Care 680
Mississippi County Coll. *(see Arkansas Northeastern Coll.)*
Mississippi County Comm. Coll. 721 *(see also Arkansas Northeastern Coll.)*
Mississippi Delta Coll. *(see Mississippi Delta Comm. Coll.)*
Mississippi Delta Comm. Coll. 220
Mississippi Gulf Coast Coll. *(see Mississippi Gulf Coast Comm. Coll.)*
Mississippi Gulf Coast Comm. Coll. 220
Mississippi Job Corps Ctr. 536
Mississippi Normal Coll. *(see Univ. of Southern Mississippi)*
Mississippi Sch. of Therapeutic Massage 536
Mississippi Southern Coll. *(see Univ. of Southern Mississippi)*
Mississippi State Coll. for Women *(see Mississippi Univ. for Women)*
Mississippi State Univ. 220
Mississippi Synodical Coll. *(see Belhaven Coll.)*
Mississippi Univ. for Women 220
Mississippi Valley State Coll. *(see Mississippi Valley State Univ.)*
Mississippi Valley State Univ. 220
Mississippi Vocational Coll. *(see Mississippi Valley State Univ.)*
Mississippi Women's Univ. *(see Mississippi Univ. for Women)*
Missoula Vocational-Tech. Ctr. *(see Univ. of Montana—Coll. of Techno.)*
Missouri Baptist Coll. *(see Missouri Baptist Univ.)*
Missouri Baptist Univ. 228

Missouri Beauty Acad. 538
Missouri Coll. 228
Missouri Coll. of Cosmetology & Esthetics 538 *(see also Merrell Univ. of Beauty Arts & Science)*
Missouri Coll. of Cosmetology North 538
Missouri Coll. of Cosmetology—Bolivar 539
Missouri Coll. of Cosmetology—South 539
Missouri Inst. of Techno. *(see DeVry Univ. Kansas City)*
Missouri Montessori Teacher Edu. Program 539
Missouri Sch. for Doctors' Assistants *(see Missouri Coll.)*
Missouri Sch. of Barbering & Hairstyling 539
Missouri Sch. of Mines & Metallurgy *(see Univ. of Missouri—Rolla)*
Missouri Southern State Coll. 732 *(see also Missouri Southern State Univ.)*
Missouri Southern State Univ. 228, 732
Missouri Southern State Univ—Joplin 732
Missouri Southern Univ. *(see Missouri Southern State Univ.)*
Missouri State Univ. 228, 732
Missouri State Univ—West Plains 228
Missouri Tech 229
Missouri Tech. Sch. *(see Missouri Tech)*
Missouri Valley Coll. 229
Missouri Western State Coll. 732 *(see also Missouri Western State Univ.)*
Missouri Western State Univ. 229, 732
Mister Wayne's Sch. of Unisex Hair Design 611
MIT *(see Massachusetts Inst. of Techno.)*
Mitchell Coll. 74 *(see also Mitchell Comm. Coll.)*
Mitchell Coll. of Law *(see William Mitchell Coll. of Law)*
Mitchell Comm. Coll. 290
Mitchell Jr. Coll. *(see Pfeiffer Univ.)*
Mitchell Tech *(see Mitchell Tech. Inst.)*
Mitchell Tech. Inst. 361
Mitchell's Hairstyling Acad—Fayetteville 734 *(see also Montgomery's Hair Styling Acad.)*
Mitchell's Hairstyling Acad—Goldsboro 573
Mitchell's Hairstyling Acad—Greenville 573
Mitchell's Hairstyling Acad—Wilson 573

Mizpa Pentacostal Coll. *(see Colegio Pentecostal Mizpa)*
Mizzou *(see Univ. of Missouri—Columbia)*
MJM Inst. of Cosmetology 472
MJ's Beauty Acad., Inc. 622
M'kor Chaim Rabbinical Seminary *(see Rabbinical Seminary M'kor Chaim)*
Moats & Associates, Inc. *(see CB&T, Inc)*
Moberly Area Comm. Coll. 229
Moberly Coll. *(see Moberly Area Comm. Coll.)*
Mobile Campus of Techno. *(see Remington Coll—Mobile)*
Mobile State Jr. Coll. *(see Bishop State Comm. Coll.)*
Mobile Univ. *(see Univ. of Mobile)*
Model Coll. of Hair Design 533
Modern Beauty Acad. 464
Modern Beauty Sch., Inc. 541
Modern Bus. Sch. *(see Parks Coll.)*
Modern Hairstyling Inst—Arecibo 605
Modern Hairstyling Inst—Bayamon 605
Modern Hairstyling Inst—Carolina 605
Modern Techno. Coll. 723 *(see also Maric Coll—North Hollywood)*
Modern Techno. Sch. 465
Modern Welding Sch. 568
Moderncare, Inc. *(see Texas Careers)*
Modesto Coll. *(see Modesto Jr. Coll.)*
Modesto Jr. Coll. 48
Mohave Comm. Coll. 18
Mohawk Valley Coll. *(see Mohawk Valley Comm. Coll.)*
Mohawk Valley Comm. Coll. 268
Mohawk Valley Network *(see Faxton-St. Luke's Healthcare)*
Mohegan Comm. Coll. *(see Three Rivers Comm. Coll.)*
Mojave Barber Coll. 465
Moler Barber Coll. 465
Moler Barber Coll. of Hairstyling 575
Moler Beauty Coll—Canal Street 517
Moler Beauty Coll—Gretna 729 *(see also Cosmetology Bus. & Management Inst.)*
Moler Beauty Coll—Kenner 517
Moler Coll. of Hairstyling *(see Moler Hairstyling Coll., Inc.)*
Moler Hairstyling Coll., Inc. 755
Moler-Hollywood Beauty Coll. 581
Moler-Pickens Beauty Coll. 581
Molloy Catholic Coll. for Women *(see Molloy Coll.)*
Molloy Coll. 268
Monaco Univ. *(see Int'l. Univ. of Monaco)*

Monash Univ. 431
Monmouth Coll. 127 *(see also Monmouth Univ.)*
Monmouth County Vocational Sch. 552
Monmouth Jr. Coll. *(see Monmouth Univ.)*
Monmouth Med. Ctr. 684
Monmouth Univ. 247
Monongalia County Tech. Ctr. *(see Monongalia County Tech. Edu. Ctr.)*
Monongalia County Tech. Edu. Ctr. 641
Monroe Area Vocational-Tech. Sch. *(see Albany Tech. Coll.)*
Monroe Ctr. for Grad. & Prof. Studies *(see Univ. of Mary Washington)*
Monroe Coll. 268 *(see also Monroe Comm. Coll.)*
Monroe Coll. New Rochelle Campus *(see Monroe Coll. New Rochelle Campus)*
Monroe Comm. Coll. 268
Monroe County Area Vocational Tech. Sch. 698
Monroe County Coll. *(see Monroe County Comm. Coll.)*
Monroe County Comm. Coll. 202
Monroe County Vo-Tech Sch. *(see Monroe County Area Vocational Tech. Sch.)*
Monroe Sch. of Bus. *(see Monroe Coll.)*
Monroe Univ. *(see Univ. of Louisiana at Monroe)*
Monroeville Sch. of Bus. *(see Bus. Careers Inst.)*
Montana Agricultural Coll. *(see Montana State Univ—Bozeman)*
Montana Coll. of Agriculture & Mechanic Arts, The *(see Montana State Univ—Bozeman)*
Montana Coll. of Mineral Science & Techno. (see Montana Tech of The Univ. of Montana)*
Montana Dale Carnegie Training *(see David L. Pals & Associates, Inc.)*
Montana State Coll. *(see Montana State Univ—Bozeman)*
Montana State Normal Coll. *(see Univ. of Montana—Western)*
Montana State Sch. of Mines *(see Montana Tech of The Univ. of Montana)*
Montana State Univ. *(see Montana State Univ—Bozeman)*
Montana State Univ. Coll. of Tech— Great Falls 234
Montana State Univ—Billings 234
Montana State Univ—Bozeman 235

Montana State Univ—Northern 235
Montana Tech of The Univ. of Montana 235
Montana Tech of the Univ. of Montana—Coll. of Techno. 732
Montana Tech of The Univ. of Montana—Division of Techno. 732
Montana Univ. *(see Univ. of Montana)*
Montcalm Comm. Coll. 202
Montclair Baptist Med. Ctr. 651
Montclair Coll. *(see Montclair State Univ.)*
Montclair State Teachers Coll. *(see Montclair State Univ.)*
Montclair State Univ. 247
Montebello Beauty Coll. 465
Monteclaro: Escuela de Hoteleria y Artes Servicios de Hospitalidad 605
Monteclaro: Sch. of Hotel & Hospitality Arts *(see Monteclaro: Escuela de Hoteleria y Artes Servicios de Hospitalidad)*
Montefiore Med. Ctr. East Campus 688
Montefiore Med. Ctr. Weiler/Einstein Division *(see Montefiore Med. Ctr. East Campus)*
Montefiore Med. Ctr. West Campus 688
Monterey Inst. of Int'l. Studies 48
Monterey Int'l. Studies Inst. *(see Monterey Inst. of Int'l. Studies)*
Monterey Park Coll. 465
Monterey Peninsula Coll. 48
Monterrey Univ. *(see Universidad de Monterrey)*
Montessori Advanced Edu. Ctr. 646
Montessori Edu. Centers Associated-Seton 502
Montessori Edu. Inst/Pacific Northwest *(see Seattle Univ.)*
Montessori Educators Int'l., Inc. 612
Montessori House of Children 646
Montessori Inst. for Teacher Edu. 477
Montessori Inst. Northwest 592
Montessori Inst. of Advanced Studies 465
Montessori Inst. of Milwaukee, Inc. 644
Montessori Opportunities, Inc. 581
Montessori Schools of Washington 638
Montessori Teacher Edcuation Ctr—San Francisco Bay Area 465
Montessori Teacher Preparation of Washington 638
Montessori Teacher Traininig Inst. 486
Montessori Teachers Coll. of San Diego 465

Montessori Training Ctr. of Minnesota 533
Montessori Training Ctr. of Santo Domingo 646
Montessori Western Teacher Training 465
Montevallo Univ. *(see Univ. of Montevallo)*
Montgomery Beauty Sch. 523
Montgomery Bible Sch. *(see Faulkner Univ.)*
Montgomery Coll. 382 *(see also Montgomery County Comm. Coll., North Harris Montgomery Comm. Coll. Dist., Sch. of Art & Design at Montgomery Coll.)*
Montgomery Coll. Sch. of Art & Design *(see Sch. of Art & Design at Montgomery Coll.)*
Montgomery Coll—Germantown Campus 181
Montgomery Coll—Rockville Campus 181
Montgomery Coll—Takoma Park Campus 181
Montgomery Comm. Coll. 290
Montgomery County Coll. *(see Montgomery County Comm. Coll.)*
Montgomery County Coll. of Maryland *(see Montgomery Coll—Takoma Park Campus)*
Montgomery County Comm. Coll. 336
Montgomery Job Corps Ctr. 441
Montgomery Montessori Inst. 523
Montgomery Preparatory Sch. *(see West Virginia Univ. Inst. of Techno.)*
Montgomery Tech. Coll. *(see Montgomery Comm. Coll.)*
Montgomery Tech. Inst. *(see Montgomery Comm. Coll.)*
Montgomery's Hair Styling Acad. 573, 734
Montreal Sch. of Theology *(see Joint Board of Theological Colleges)*
Montreal Univ. *(see Université de Montréal)*
Montreat Coll. 290
Montreat Normal Sch. *(see Montreat Coll.)*
Montreux Hotel Inst. *(see Hotel Inst. Montreux)*
Montserrat Coll. of Art 190
Montserrat Sch. of Visual Art *(see Montserrat Coll. of Art)*
Moody Bible Inst. 127
Moody Inst. *(see Moody Bible Inst.)*
Moore & Associates *(see Ron Moore & Associates)*
Moore Art & Design Coll. *(see Moore Coll. of Art & Design)*

Moore Coll. of Art & Design 336

Moore Coll. of Techno. *(see William R. Moore Coll. of Techno.)*

Moore Sch. of Techno. *(see William R. Moore Coll. of Techno.)*

Moore Universite' of Hair Design, Inc. 581

Moored Associates Beauty Schools *(see Twin City Beauty Coll.)*

Moore-Norman Area Vocational Tech. Sch. 589

Moore-Norman Area Vo-Tech Sch. *(see Moore-Norman Area Vocational Tech. Sch.)*

Moores Hill Coll. *(see Univ. of Evansville)*

Moorhead State Univ. *(see Minnesota State Univ. Moorhead)*

Moorhead Univ. *(see Minnesota State Univ. Moorhead)*

Moorpark Coll. 48

Moraine Park Tech. Coll. 426

Moraine Valley Coll. *(see Moraine Valley Comm. Coll.)*

Moraine Valley Comm. Coll. 127

Morales Acad. *(see Academia Morales)*

Moravian Coll. 336

Moravian Seminary *(see Moravian Coll.)*

Moravian Theological Seminary 336 *(see also Moravian Coll.)*

More Coll. *(see Thomas More Coll., Thomas More Coll. of Liberal Arts)*

More Coll. of Liberal Arts *(see Thomas More Coll. of Liberal Arts)*

Morehead Normal Sch. *(see Morehead State Univ.)*

Morehead State Coll. *(see Morehead State Univ.)*

Morehead State Univ. 162

Morehouse Coll. 106

Morehouse Coll. & Sch. of Religion *(see Interdenominational Theological Ctr.)*

Morehouse Med. Sch. *(see Morehouse Sch. of Medicine)*

Morehouse Sch. of Medicine 106

Morgan Bus. Coll. *(see Thomas Coll.)*

Morgan Coll. *(see Morgan Comm. Coll., Morgan State Univ.)*

Morgan Comm. Coll. 69

Morgan County Jr. Coll. *(see Morgan Comm. Coll.)*

Morgan State Univ. 181

Morgan Vocational-Tech. Inst. *(see Robert Morgan Vocational-Tech. Inst.)*

Morgan Vo-Tech Inst. *(see Robert Morgan Vocational-Tech. Inst.)*

Morgan-Thomas Bus. Coll. *(see Thomas Coll.)*

Morgantown Beauty Coll., Inc. 641

Morgantown Skills Training Ctr. *(see Stanley Tech. Inst.)*

Morningside Coll. 149

Morrilton Comm. Coll. *(see Univ. of Arkansas Comm. Coll. at Morrilton)*

Morris Brown Coll. 664, 726

Morris Coll. 357 *(see also Lon Morris Coll., Robert Morris Coll., Robert Morris Univ.)*

Morris County Coll. *(see County Coll. of Morris)*

Morris County Sch. of Techno. 552

Morris Harvey Coll. *(see Univ. of Charleston)*

Morris Univ. *(see Robert Morris Univ.)*

Morrison Coll. *(see Morrison Univ.)*

Morrison Inst. of Techno. 127

Morrison Univ. 241 *(see also Northface Univ.)*

Morristown Mem. Hosp. 684 *(see also Inst. for Therapeutic Massage, Inc.)*

Morrisville Coll. of Agriculture & Techno. *(see State Univ. of New York Coll. of Agriculture & Techno. at Morrisville)*

Morrisville State Coll. *(see State Univ. of New York Coll. of Agriculture & Techno. at Morrisville)*

Morton Coll. 127

Mortuary Science Coll. of Cincinnati *(see Cincinnati Coll. of Mortuary Science)*

Moses Cone Health System *(see Moses H. Cone Mem. Hosp.)*

Moses Cone Hosp. *(see Moses H. Cone Mem. Hosp.)*

Moses Division of Montefiore Med. Ctr. *(see Montefiore Med. Ctr. West Campus)*

Moses H. Cone Mem. Hosp., The 691

Mossy Creek Coll. *(see Carson-Newman Coll.)*

Motif Beauty Acad. 513

Motlow Coll. *(see Motlow State Comm. Coll.)*

Motlow Comm. Coll. *(see Motlow State Comm. Coll.)*

Motlow State Comm. Coll. 369

Motorcycle & Marine Mechanics Inst. 445, 725

Motorcycle Mechanics Inst. *(see Motorcycle & Marine Mechanics Inst.)*

MotoRing Inst. *(see MotoRing Tech. Training Inst.)*

MotoRing Tech. Training Inst. 607

Mott Comm. Coll. *(see Charles Stewart Mott Comm. Coll.)*

Moultrie Area Tech. Inst. 726 *(see also Moultrie Tech. Coll.)*

Moultrie Coll. *(see Moultrie Tech. Coll.)*

Moultrie Tech. Coll. 106, 726

Moultrie Vocational-Tech. Sch. *(see Moultrie Tech. Coll.)*

Mount Allen Jr. Coll. *(see Mount Olive Coll.)*

Mount Aloysius Coll. 336

Mount Aloysius Jr. Coll. *(see Mount Aloysius Coll.)*

Mount Angel Seminary 321

Mount Carmel Coll. of Nursing 306

Mount Carmel Health System 694

Mount Carmel West Campus *(see Mount Carmel Health System)*

Mount Diablo Med. Ctr. 654

Mount Holyoke Coll. 190

Mount Hood Coll. *(see Mount Hood Comm. Coll.)*

Mount Hood Comm. Coll. 321

Mount Ida Coll. 190

Mount Lebanon Univ. *(see Louisiana Coll.)*

Mount Marty Coll. 361

Mount Mary Coll. 426

Mount Mercy Coll. *(see Carlow Univ.)*

Mount Mercy Coll. 149

Mount Morris Coll. *(see Manchester Coll.)*

Mount Olive Coll. 290

Mount Olive Jr. Coll. *(see Mount Olive Coll.)*

Mount Royal Coll. 712

Mount SAC *(see Mount San Antonio Coll.)*

Mount Saint Agnes Coll. *(see Loyola Coll. in Maryland)*

Mount Saint Bernard Coll. *(see Loras Coll.)*

Mount Saint Charles Coll. *(see Carroll Coll.)*

Mount Saint Clare Coll. 728 *(see also Ashford Univ.)*

Mount Saint Joseph Acad. & Coll. *(see Clarke Coll.)*

Mount Saint Joseph Coll. *(see Chestnut Hill Coll., Coll. of Mount Saint Joseph)*

Mount Saint Joseph Jr. Coll. for Women *(see Brescia Univ.)*

Mount Saint Joseph Teachers Coll. *(see Medaille Coll.)*

Mount Saint Mary Coll. 268

Mount Saint Mary Seminary *(see Athenaeum of Ohio)*

Mount Saint Mary's Coll. 48

Mount Saint Mary's Coll. & Seminary 730 *(see also Mount Saint Mary's Univ.)*

Mount Saint Mary's of the West *(see Athenaeum of Ohio)*

Mount Saint Mary's Univ. 181, 730

Mount Saint Vincent Coll. *(see Coll. of Mount Saint Vincent)*

Mount San Antonio Coll. 48

Mount San Jacinto Coll. 48

Mount Sierra Coll. 48

Mount Sinai Hosp. 688 *(see also Mount Sinai Sch. of Medicine, Saint Francis/Mount Sinai Hosp.)*

Mount Sinai Med. Ctr. 663 *(see also Inst. of Allied Med. Professions)*

Mount Sinai Sch. of Medicine *(see Mount Sinai Sch. of Medicine)*

Mount Union Coll. 306

Mount Vernon Beauty Sch. *(see Northwest Hair Acad.)*

Mount Vernon Coll. & Seminary *(see George Washington Univ.)*

Mount Vernon Comm. Coll. *(see Rend Lake Coll.)*

Mount Vernon Nazarene Coll. *(see Mount Vernon Nazarene Univ.)*

Mount Vernon Nazarene Univ. 306

Mount Vernon Univ. *(see Mount Vernon Nazarene Univ.)*

Mount Wachusett Coll. *(see Mount Wachusett Comm. Coll.)*

Mount Wachusett Comm. Coll. 190

Mountain Empire Coll. *(see Mountain Empire Comm. Coll.)*

Mountain Empire Comm. Coll. 404

Mountain Home Tech. Coll. *(see Arkansas State Univ. Mountain Home)*

Mountain Home Univ. *(see Arkansas State Univ. Mountain Home)*

Mountain Retreat Assoc. *(see Montreat Coll.)*

Mountain State Coll. 419

Mountain State Massage Sch. *(see Mountain State Sch. of Massage)*

Mountain State Sch. of Massage 641

Mountain State Univ., The 419

Mountain View Bible Coll. *(see Rocky Mountain Coll.)*

Mountain View Coll. 381

Mountain West Coll. 394

Mountaineer Beauty Coll., Inc. 641

Mountainland Applied Techno. Coll. 750

Mountainside Hosp. 684

Mountainwest Coll. of Bus. & Techno. *(see Mountain West Coll.)*

Mountainwest Computer Sch. *(see Mountain West Coll.)*

Mr. Bela's Sch. of Cosmetology 530

Mr. Bernard's Sch. of Hair Fashion, Inc. 519

Mr. David's Sch. of Cosmetology, Ltd. 530

Mr. David's Sch. of Hair Design 573

Mr. Jim's Beauty Coll. 513

Mr. Jim's Coll. of Cosmetology *(see Mr. Jim's Beauty Coll.)*

Mr. John's Sch. of Cosmetology *(see Mr. John's Sch. of Cosmetology, Esthetics & Nails)*

Mr. John's Sch. of Cosmetology & Nails *(see Mr. John's Sch. of Cosmetology, Esthetics & Nails)*

Mr. John's Sch. of Cosmetology, Esthetics & Nails 502

Mr. Juan's Coll. of Hair Design 497

Mr. Leon's Sch. of Hair Design 497

Ms. Robert's Acad. of Beauty Culture 502

MSU Detroit Coll. of Law *(see Michigan State Univ. Detroit Coll. of Law)*

Mt. Allen Jr. Coll. *(see Mount Olive Coll.)*

Mt. Aloysius Coll. *(see Mount Aloysius Coll.)*

Mt. Aloysius Jr. Coll. *(see Mount Aloysius Coll.)*

Mt. Angel Seminary *(see Mount Angel Seminary)*

Mt. Carmel Coll. of Nursing *(see Mount Carmel Coll. of Nursing)*

Mt. Carmel Health System *(see Mount Carmel Health System)*

Mt. Holyoke Coll. *(see Mount Holyoke Coll.)*

Mt. Hood Coll. *(see Mount Hood Comm. Coll.)*

Mt. Hood Comm. Coll. *(see Mount Hood Comm. Coll.)*

Mt. Lebanon Univ. *(see Louisiana Coll.)*

Mt. Mary Coll. *(see Mount Mary Coll.)*

Mt. Mercy Coll. *(see Carlow Univ., Mount Mercy Coll.)*

Mt. Olive Coll. *(see Mount Olive Coll.)*

Mt. Olive Jr. Coll. *(see Mount Olive Coll.)*

Mt. SAC *(see Mount San Antonio Coll.)*

Mt. Saint Charles Coll. *(see Carroll Coll.)*

Mt. Saint Joseph Coll. *(see Chestnut Hill Coll.)*

Mt. Saint Joseph Jr. Coll. for Women *(see Brescia Univ.)*

Mt. Saint Joseph Teachers Coll. *(see Medaille Coll.)*

Mt. Saint Mary Coll. *(see Mount Saint Mary Coll.)*

Mt. Saint Mary's Seminary *(see Mount Saint Mary's Univ.)*

Mt. Saint Vincent Coll. *(see Coll. of Mount Saint Vincent)*

Mt. San Antonio Coll. *(see Mount San Antonio Coll.)*

Mt. Sinai Hosp. *(see Saint Francis/Mount Sinai Hosp.)*

Mt. Sinai Med. Ctr. *(see Inst. of Allied Med. Professions)*

Mt. Sinai Med. Ctr. of Florida *(see Mount Sinai Med. Ctr.)*

Mt. St. Joseph Coll. *(see Chestnut Hill Coll., Coll. of Mount St. Joseph)*

Mt. St. Joseph Jr. Coll. for Women *(see Brescia Univ.)*

Mt. St. Joseph Teachers Coll. *(see Medaille Coll.)*

Mt. St. Mary Coll. *(see Mount Saint Mary Coll.)*

Mt. St. Mary's Univ. *(see Mount Saint Mary's Univ.)*

Mt. St. Vincent Coll. *(see Coll. of Mount Saint Vincent)*

Mt. Union Coll. *(see Mount Union Coll.)*

Mt. Vernon Coll. *(see George Washington Univ. at Mt. Vernon Collge)*

Mt. Vernon Comm. Coll. *(see Rend Lake Coll.)*

Mt. Vernon Nazarene Univ. *(see Mount Vernon Nazarene Univ.)*

Mt. Vernon Univ. *(see Mount Vernon Nazarene Univ.)*

Mt. Wachusett Coll. *(see Mount Wachusett Comm. Coll.)*

Mt. Wachusett Comm. Coll. *(see Mount Wachusett Comm. Coll.)*

MTI Bus. Coll. of Stockton Inc. 465

MTI Coll. of Bus. & Techno. 48, 381

MTI Western Bus. Coll. *(see MTI Coll. of Bus. & Techno.)*

MTMA Schools, Inc. 465

Mudd Coll. *(see Harvey Mudd Coll.)*

Mueller Coll. of Holistic Massage Therapies 465

Muhlenberg Coll. 336

Muhlenberg Hosp. Ctr. *(see Lehigh Valley Hosp—Muhlenberg)*

Muhlenberg Job Corps Ctr. 729

Muhlenberg Reg. Med. Ctr. 684 *(see also Lehigh Valley Hosp—Muhlenberg)*

Mullins Sch. of Practical Nursing *(see Hannah E. Mullins Sch. of Practical Nursing)*

Multnomah Bible Coll. 322, 748

Multnomah Biblical Seminary *(see Multnomah Bible Coll.)*

Multnomah Coll. *(see Multnomah Bible Coll.)*
Multnomah Grad. Sch. of Ministry *(see Multnomah Bible Coll.)*
Multnomah Sch. of the Bible *(see Multnomah Bible Coll.)*
Mundelein Coll. *(see Loyola Univ. of Chicago)*
Mundelein Seminary *(see Univ. of Saint Mary of the Lake Mundelein Seminary)*
Mundus Inst. 445
Municipal Training Ctr—Kings 733
Municipal Univ. of Omaha *(see Univ. of Nebraska at Omaha)*
Municipal Univ. of Wichita, The *(see Wichita State Univ.)*
Munson-Williams-Proctor Inst. 568
Murray Coll. *(see Murray State Coll.)*
Murray State Coll. 316
Murray State Univ. 162
Murray Univ. *(see Murray State Univ.)*
Muscatine Comm. Coll. 149
Muscatine Jr. Coll. *(see Muscatine Comm. Coll.)*
Muscogee Area Vocational-Tech. Sch. *(see Columbus Tech. Coll.)*
Muscular Therapy Inst. 526
Museum Art Sch. of the Portland Art Assoc. *(see Pacific Northwest Coll. of Art)*
Museum of American Folk Art Folk Art Inst. *(see Folk Art Inst. of the Museum of American Folk Art)*
Music Acad. of Los Angeles *(see Los Angeles Music Acad.)*
Music Acad. of Pennsylvania, The *(see Pennsylvania Acad. of Music)*
Music & Worship Arts Coll. *(see Visbile Sch., Music & Worship Arts Coll.)*
Music Ctr. of the North Shore *(see Music Inst. of Chicago)*
Music Conservatory of San Francisco *(see San Francisco Conservatory of Music)*
Music Conservatory of Washington *(see Washington Conservatory of Music, Inc.)*
Music Conservatory of Westchester 568
Music Conservatory of Wisconsin *(see Wisconsin Conservatory of Music, Inc.)*
Music Inst. of Atlanta *(see Atlanta Inst. of Music)*
Music Inst. of Chicago 502
Music Inst. of Cleveland *(see Cleveland Inst. of Music)*
Music Sch. of Manhattan *(see Manhattan Sch. of Music)*

Music Tech *(see McNally Smith Coll. of Music)*
Musical & Dramatic Acad. of America *(see American Musical & Dramatic Acad.)*
Musicians Inst. 48
Musictech Coll. 731 *(see also McNally Smith Coll. of Music)*
Muskegon Coll. *(see Muskegon Comm. Coll.)*
Muskegon Comm. Coll. 202
Muskegon Jr. Coll. *(see Muskegon Comm. Coll.)*
Muskingum Acad. *(see Marietta Coll.)*
Muskingum Area Tech. Coll. 734 *(see also Zane State Coll.)*
Muskingum Area Tech. Inst. *(see Zane State Coll.)*
Muskingum Coll. 307
Myers Univ. *(see David N. Myers Univ.)*
My-Le's Beauty Coll. 465
Myndall Cain Beauty Sch. *(see Regency Beauty Inst.)*
Myotherapy Coll. of Utah 628
Myotherapy Inst. 237 *(see also Myotherapy Coll. of Utah)*
Myotherapy Inst. of Utah *(see Myotherapy Coll. of Utah)*

N

Nacogdoches Univ. *(see Stephen F. Austin State Univ.)*
NAES Coll. 727
Nail Acad., The 568
Nancy Taylor Secretarial Sch. *(see Taylor Bus. Inst.)*
Napa Coll. *(see Napa Valley Coll.)*
Napa Valley Coll. 49
Naperville Skin Inst. 501 *(see also Hair Professionals Acad. of Cosmetology—Wheaton)*
Naropa Coll. *(see Naropa Univ.)*
Naropa Univ., The 69
NASCAR Tech. Inst. 20
Nash Coll. *(see Nash Comm. Coll.)*
Nash Comm. Coll. 290
Nash Health Care Systems 692
Nashotah House 426
Nashville Auto Diesel Coll. 369
Nashville Bible Coll. *(see Lipscomb Univ.)*
Nashville Coll. *(see Nashville Coll. of Med. Careers)*
Nashville Coll. of Med. Careers 612
Nashville Dale Carnegie Training *(see Glyn Ed Newton & Associates, Inc.)*
Nashville General Hosp. at Meharry 702

Nashville Hosp. *(see Nashville General Hosp. at Meharry)*
Nashville State Comm. Coll. 369, 737
Nashville State Tech. Inst. 737 *(see also Nashville State Comm. Coll.)*
Nassau Board of Cooperative Educational Services *(see Nassau BOCES)*
Nassau BOCES 688
Nassau Coll. *(see Nassau Comm. Coll.)*
Nassau Comm. Coll. 268
Nassau County Med. Ctr. *(see Nassau Univ. Med. Ctr.)*
Nassau Health Care Corporation *(see Nassau Univ. Med. Ctr.)*
Nassau Technological Ctr. 688 *(see also Nassau BOCES, Nassau Technological Ctr.)*
Nassau Univ. Med. Ctr. 688
National Acad. of Beauty Arts 539
National American Univ. 362
National Assoc. Med. Staff Services 737
National Assoc. of Photoshop Professionals 486
National Aviation Acad. 486
National Beauty Coll—Canton 581
National Beauty Coll—Garland 622
National Bus. Coll. *(see National Coll. of Bus. & Techno.)*
National Capital Consortium 675
National Career Edu. 465
National Ctr. for Hospitality Studies *(see Sullivan Univ.)*
National Ctr. for Montessori Edu. — New England *(see New England Montessori Teacher Edu. Ctr.)*
National Coll. *(see Florida Coll. of Integrative Medicine, Gallaudet Univ., National American Univ., National Coll. of Appraisal & Property Managemen, National Coll. of Bus. & Techno., National Coll. of Naturopathic Medicine, National Coll. of Midwifery, National-Louis Univ., National Univ. of Health Sciences)*
National Coll. for the Deaf & Dumb *(see Gallaudet Univ.)*
National Coll. of Appraisal & Property Management 494
National Coll. of Bus. & Techno. 349, 404
National Coll. of Bus. & Tech— Lexington Campus 162, 729
National Coll. of Chiropractic *(see National Univ. of Health Sciences)*
National Coll. of Edu. *(see National-Louis Univ.)*
National Coll. of Midwifery 252

National Coll. of Naturopathic Medicine 322

National Coll. of Oriental Medicine *(see Florida Coll. of Integrative Medicine)*

National Conservatory of Dramatic Arts, The 478

National Court Reporters Assoc. 632

National Cryptologic Sch. 523

National Deaf-Mute Coll. *(see Gallaudet Univ.)*

National Defense Univ. 79

National Dramatic Arts Conservatory *(see National Conservatory of Dramatic Arts)*

National Edu. Ctr. Allentown Campus *(see Lehigh Valley Coll.)*

National Edu. Ctr. Skadron Campus *(see Bryman Coll.)*

National Edu. Ctr. Thompson Campus *(see Thompson Inst.)*

National Edu. Ctr., Tampa Tech. Inst. *(see Remington Coll—Tampa)*

National Edu. Ctr—Arizona Automotive Inst. *(see Arizona Automotive Inst.)*

National Edu. Ctr—Brown Inst. Campus *(see Brown Coll.)*

National Edu. Ctr—Bryman *(see Bryman Coll—Anaheim, Bryman Coll—El Monte, Bryman Coll—Gardena, Bryman Coll—Hayward, Bryman Coll—Los Angeles, Bryman Coll—Reseda, Bryman Inst—Brighton)*

National Edu. Ctr—Bryman Campus *(see Bryman Coll—San Francisco)*

National Edu. Ctr—Kee Bus. Coll. *(see Kee Bus. Coll—Newport News)*

National Edu. Ctr—National Inst. of Techno. Campus *(see National Inst. of Tech—Cuyahoga Falls)*

National Edu. Ctr—Philadelphia *(see Thompson Inst.)*

National Edu. Ctr—RETS Campus *(see HoHoKus RETS—Nutley)*

National Edu. Ctr—Skadron Coll. of Bus. *(see Bryman Coll.)*

National Edu. Corporation—Spartan Sch. of Aeronautics *(see Spartan Coll. of Aeronautics & Techno.)*

National Educational Inst—New England 730

National Electronics Inst. *(see Brown Mackie Coll—North Canton)*

National Fashion & Beauty Coll. 736

National Geospatial-Intelligence Coll. 633, 738

National Grad. Sch. of Quality Management *(see National Grad. Sch., The)*

National Grad. Sch., The 190

National Health Sciences Univ. *(see National Univ. of Health Sciences)*

National Hispanic Univ., The 49

National Holistic Inst. 465

National Imagery & Analysis Sch. 633

National Imagery & Mapping Coll. 738 *(see also National Geospatial-Intelligence Coll.)*

National Inst. of Massotherapy, Inc. 581

National Inst. of Oriental Medicine *(see Florida Coll. of Integrative Medicine)*

National Inst. of Techno. *(see Olympia Coll—Skokie)*

National Inst. of Tech—Cross Lanes 420

National Inst. of Tech—Cuyahoga Falls 581

National Inst. of Tech—Long Beach 49

National Inst. of Tech—San Antonio 622

National Inst. of Tech—San Jose 466

National Inst. of Tech—Southfield 530

National Inst-Dental & Craniofacial Research 675

National Institutes of Health Clinical Ctr. 675

National Labor Coll. 181, 730

National Labor Coll—George Meany Campus *(see National Labor Coll.)*

National Legal Secretarial Sch. *(see Hagerstown Bus. Coll.)*

National Massage Therapy Inst., The 477, 552, 598, 633, 724, 733, 736, 738

National Midwifery Coll. *(see National Coll. of Midwifery)*

National Midwifery Inst. 630

National Naturopathic Medicine Coll. *(see National Coll. of Naturopathic Medicine)*

National Naval Med. Ctr. 675

National Park Coll. at Hot Springs *(see National Park Comm. Coll. at Hot Springs)*

National Park Comm. Coll. at Hot Springs 25, 721

National Polytechnic Coll. 466

National Polytechnic Coll. of Engineering & Oceaneering 49, 722 *(see also Advanced Coll. of Techno.)*

National Radio Inst. *(see Sonoran Desert Inst.)*

National Radio Sch. *(see ETI Tech. Coll. of Niles)*

National Religious Training Sch. *(see North Carolina Central Univ.)*

National Sch. of Bus. *(see National American Univ.)*

National Sch. of Health Techno., Inc. *(see National Sch. of Techno.)*

National Sch. of Techno. 90

National Tax Training Sch. 553

National Tech. Inst. for the Deaf 273 *(see also Rochester Inst. of Techno.)*

National Technological Univ. 724, 731 *(see also NTU Sch. of Engineering & Applied Science, Walden Univ.)*

National Theatre Conservatory 69

National Tooling & Machining Assoc. *(see NTMA Training Centers of Southern California)*

National Tractor Trailer Sch. 568

National Training Ctr. 556, 733

National Training Sch. *(see North Carolina Central Univ.)*

National Training, Inc. 486

National Univ. 49

National Univ. for Advanced Studies *(see California National Univ. for Advanced Studies)*

National Univ. of Health Sciences 127

National Univ. of Ireland, Dublin *(see Univ. Coll. Dublin)*

National-Louis Univ. 128

Nationwide Beauty Acad. 582

Natural Gourmet Cookery Corporation *(see Natural Gourmet Cookery Sch.)*

Natural Gourmet Cookery Sch. 568

Natural Health Ctr. Clinic *(see National Coll. of Naturopathic Medicine)*

Natural Motion Inst. of Hair Design 553

Naugatuck Valley Coll. *(see Naugatuck Valley Comm. Coll.)*

Naugatuck Valley Comm. Coll. 74, 724

Naugatuck Valley Comm—Tech. Coll. 724

Navajo Area Indian Health Service *(see Southern California Coll. of Optometry)*

Navajo Comm. Coll. *(see Diné Coll.)*

Navajo County Comm. Coll. Dist. *(see Northland Pioneer Coll.)*

Navajo Skills Ctr. *(see Crownpoint Inst. of Techno.)*

Naval Acad. *(see United States Naval Acad.)*

Naval Air Tech. Training Ctr. 725 *(see also Ctr. for Naval Aviation Tech. Training)*

Naval Construction Training Ctr. *(see Ctr. for Seabees & Facilities Engineering)*
Naval Dental Ctr—Great Lakes 668
Naval Dental Ctr—Gulf Coast 663
Naval Dental Ctr—Jacksonville 663
Naval Dental Ctr—Northeast 700
Naval Dental Ctr—Northwest 707
Naval Dental Ctr—Parris Island 701
Naval Dental Ctr—San Diego 654
Naval Dental Clinic 706
Naval Dental Sch. 675
Naval Diving & Salvage Training Ctr. 725 *(see also Ctr. for Explosive Ordnance Disposal & Diving)*
Naval Hosp—Camp Pendelton 654
Naval Hosp—Great Lakes 668
Naval Med. Ctr. *(see National Naval Med. Ctr.)*
Naval Med. Ctr—Portsmouth 706
Naval Med. Ctr—San Diego 655
Naval Med. Edu. & Training Command 523
Naval Postgraduate Sch. *(see United States Naval Postgraduate Sch.)*
Naval Sch. *(see Naval Sch. of Health Sciences, United States Naval Acad.)*
Naval Sch. of Health Sciences 655, 706
Naval Surface Warfare Training Ctr. *(see Ctr. for Surface Combat Systems)*
Naval Tech. Training Ctr. 725 *(see also Ctr. for Information Dominance Corry Station)*
Naval Tech. Training Ctr., Corry Station *(see Ctr. for Information Dominance Corry Station)*
Naval War Coll. 353
Navarro Coll. 381
Navarro Jr. Coll. *(see Navarro Coll.)*
NAVCONSTRACEN *(see Ctr. for Seabees & Facilities Engineering)*
Nave Cosmetology Acad., Inc. 759
Navy & Marine Corps Intelligence Training Ctr. *(see Ctr. for Naval Intelligence)*
Navy Supply Corps Sch. *(see United States Navy Supply Corps Sch.)*
NAWCC Sch. of Horology 598
Nazarene Bible Coll. 69
Nazarene Coll. *(see Nazarene Bible Coll.)*
Nazarene Indian Bible Coll. *(see Nazarene Indian Bible Coll.)*
Nazarene Seminary *(see Nazarene Theological Seminary)*
Nazarene Theological Seminary 229
Nazarene Univ. *(see Alliance Univ. Coll., Point Loma Nazarene Univ.)*

Nazarene Univ. Coll. *(see Alliance Univ. Coll.)*
Nazareth Coll. of Rochester 268
NC State Univ. *(see North Carolina State Univ.)*
NCH Healthcare System 663
NCPT 726
Nebraska Christian Coll. 237
Nebraska Coll. *(see Hamilton Coll—Cedar Rapids, Nebraska Methodist Coll.)*
Nebraska Coll. of Bus. 732 *(see Hamilton Coll—Cedar Rapids)*
Nebraska Coll. of Tech. Agriculture 238
Nebraska Indian Coll. *(see Nebraska Indian Comm. Coll.)*
Nebraska Indian Comm. Coll. 238
Nebraska Med. Ctr., The *(see Univ. of Nebraska Med. Ctr.)*
Nebraska Methodist Coll. 238
Nebraska Methodist Coll. of Nursing & Allied Health *(see Nebraska Methodist Coll.)*
Nebraska Normal Coll. of Wayne *(see Wayne State Coll.)*
Nebraska State Normal Sch. at Kearney *(see Univ. of Nebraska at Kearney)*
Nebraska State Teachers Coll. at Kearney *(see Univ. of Nebraska at Kearney)*
Nebraska Wesleyan Univ. 238
Nebraska Western Coll. *(see Western Nebraska Comm. Coll.)*
NEC-Spartan Sch. of Aeronautics *(see Spartan Coll. of Aeronautics & Techno.)*
NEI Ctr. at Dunwoody Coll. of Techno. *(see Dunwoody Coll. of Techno.)*
NEI Coll. of Techno. 731 *(see also Dunwoody Coll. of Techno.)*
Neighborhood Music Sch. *(see Manhattan Sch. of Music)*
Neighborhood Playhouse Sch. of Theatre 568
Neilson Beauty Coll., Inc. 622
Nell Inst. *(see Austin Bus. Coll.)*
Nelson Coll. *(see Thomas Nelson Comm. Coll.)*
Nelson Comm. Coll. *(see Thomas Nelson Comm. Coll.)*
Neosho Beauty Coll. 539
Neosho Coll. *(see Neosho County Comm. Coll.)*
Neosho County Comm. Coll. 155
NEOUCOM *(see Northeastern Ohio Universities Coll. of Medicine)*
Ner Israel Rabbinical Coll. 181
Nettleton Bus. Coll. *(see Hamilton Coll—Omaha)*

Network Techno. Inst. *(see Inst. of Network Techno.)*
Neumann Coll. 336
Nevada Bus. Inst. *(see Morrison Univ.)*
Nevada Career Inst. *(see Glendale Career Coll.)*
Nevada Career Inst—East Campus 459
Nevada Coll. *(see Nevada State Coll. at Henderson, Univ. of Southern Nevada)*
Nevada Coll. of Pharmacy 732 *(see also Univ. of Southern Nevada)*
Nevada Comm. Coll. *(see Great Basin Coll.)*
Nevada Dale Carnegie Training *(see J. R. Rodgers & Associates, Inc.)*
Nevada Leadership Inst. 732 *(see also J. R. Rodgers & Associates, Inc.)*
Nevada Sch. of Massage Therapy 629 *(see also Utah Coll. of Massage Therapy)*
Nevada Southern Univ. *(see Univ. of Nevada, Las Vegas)*
Nevada State Coll. *(see Nevada State Coll. at Henderson)*
Nevada State Coll. at Henderson 682
New Age Training 568
New Britain General Hosp. *(see Greater Hartford Clinical Psychology Internship Consortium)*
New Britain Normal Sch. *(see Central Connecticut State Univ.)*
New Britain Sch. of Nurse Anesthesia 659
New Brunswick Seminary *(see New Brunswick Theological Seminary)*
New Brunswick Theological Seminary 248
New Brunswick Univ. *(see Univ. of New Brunswick)*
New Castle Sch. of Beauty Culture 598
New Castle Sch. of Trades 336
New Ctr. for Wholistic Health Edu. & Research *(see New York Coll. of Health Professions)*
New Church Acad. *(see Bryn Athyn Coll. of the New Church)*
New Coll. of Aurora Univ. 117
New Coll. of California 49
New Coll. of Florida 90, 725
New Coll. of the Univ. of South Florida *(see New Coll. of Florida)*
New Coll. of Univ. of South Florida 725
New Comm. Coll. of Baltimore *(see Baltimore City Comm. Coll.)*
New Comm. Workforce Development Ctr. 553

New Concept Beauty Sch. #2, Inc. 756
New Concept Beauty Sch., Inc. *(see New Concept Massage & Beauty Sch., Inc.)*
New Concept Massage & Beauty Sch., Inc. 486
New Concepts Sch. of Cosmetology 759
New Creations Acad. of Hair Design 523
New Danville Masonic Female Acad. *(see Lon Morris Coll.)*
New Dimension Acad. of Beauty 755
New Dimensions Sch. of Hair Design 539
New Directions Hair Acad. 612
New Engelberg Abbey of the Immaculate Conception *(see Conception Seminary Coll.)*
New England Acupuncture Sch. *(see New England Sch. of Acupuncture)*
New England Aeronautical Inst. *(see Daniel Webster Coll.)*
New England Art Inst. *(see New England Inst. of Art)*
New England Baptist Hosp. 677
New England Coll. 243
New England Coll. of Finance, The 190
New England Coll. of Optometry 190
New England Coll. of Osteopathic Medicine *(see Univ. of New England)*
New England Conservatory of Music 190
New England Culinary Inst. 398
New England Culinary Inst. at Essex *(see New England Culinary Inst. at Essex)*
New England Electrology Inst. *(see Electrology Inst. of New England)*
New England Finance Coll. *(see New England Coll. of Finance)*
New England Hair Acad. 526
New England Inst. of Art & Communications 730 *(see also New England Inst. of Art)*
New England Inst. of Art, The 191, 730
New England Inst. of Electrology *(see Electrology Inst. of New England)*
New England Inst. of Funeral Service Edu. *(see Mount Ida Coll.)*
New England Inst. of Techno. 353
New England Inst. of Techno. at Palm Beach 91
New England Montessori Teacher Edu. Ctr. 544

New England Music Conservatory *(see New England Conservatory of Music)*
New England Sch. of Acupuncture 191
New England Sch. of Art & Design *(see Suffolk Univ.)*
New England Sch. of Art & Design at Suffolk Univ. 193
New England Sch. of Communications 176
New England Sch. of English, The 526
New England Sch. of Hair Design, Inc. 544
New England Sch. of Law 677
New England Sch. of Photography 526
New England Sch. of Radiologic Techno. 706
New England Tech *(see New England Inst. of Techno., New England Tech. Inst. of Connecticut)*
New England Tech at Palm Beach *(see New England Inst. of Techno. at Palm Beach)*
New England Tech. Inst. of Connecticut 475
New England Tractor Trailer Training Sch. 475, 607
New England Tractor Trailer Training Sch. of Connecticut *(see New England Tractor Trailer Training Sch.)*
New England Tractor Trailer Training Sch. of Rhode Island *(see New England Tractor Trailer Training Sch.)*
New England Univ. *(see Univ. of New England)*
New Gate Ctr. for Montessori Studies 487
New Hampshire Career Inst., The 544
New Hampshire Coll. 732 *(see also Southern New Hampshire Univ.)*
New Hampshire Comm. Coll.—Berlin *(see New Hampshire Comm. Tech. Coll—Berlin)*
New Hampshire Comm. Coll.—Manchester *(see New Hampshire Comm. Tech. Coll—Manchester)*
New Hampshire Comm. Coll.—Nashua *(see New Hampshire Comm. Tech. Coll—Nashua)*
New Hampshire Comm. Tech. Coll—Berlin 243, 732
New Hampshire Comm. Tech. Coll—Berlin/Laconia 732 *(see also New Hampshire Comm. Tech. Coll—Berlin, New Hampshire Comm. Tech. Coll—Laconia)*

New Hampshire Comm. Tech. Coll—Claremont 243, 732
New Hampshire Comm. Tech. Coll—Laconia 243, 732
New Hampshire Comm. Tech. Coll—Manchester 243, 732
New Hampshire Comm. Tech. Coll—Manchester/Stratham 732 *(see also New Hampshire Comm. Tech. Coll—Manchester, New Hampshire Comm. Tech. Coll—Stratham)*
New Hampshire Comm. Tech. Coll—Nashua 243, 732
New Hampshire Comm. Tech. Coll—Nashua/Claermont 732 *(see New Hampshire Comm. Tech. Coll—Claremont, New Hampshire Comm. Tech. Coll—Nashua)*
New Hampshire Comm. Tech. Coll—Stratham 243, 732
New Hampshire Inst. for Therapeutic Arts 519
New Hampshire Inst. of Art 747
New Hampshire Technica Coll—Berlin *(see New Hampshire Comm. Tech. Coll—Berlin)*
New Hampshire Tech. Coll—Claremont *(see New Hampshire Comm. Tech. Coll—Claremont, New Hampshire Comm. Tech. Coll—Nashua)*
New Hampshire Tech. Coll—Laconia *(see New Hampshire Comm. Tech. Coll—Berlin, New Hampshire Comm. Tech. Coll—Laconia)*
New Hampshire Tech. Coll—Manchester *(see New Hampshire Comm. Tech. Coll—Manchester)*
New Hampshire Tech. Coll—Nashua *(see New Hampshire Comm. Tech. Coll—Nashua)*
New Hampshire Tech. Inst. 243
New Hampshire Univ. *(see Univ. of New Hampshire)*
New Hanover Reg. Med. Ctr. 692
New Haven Coll. *(see Univ. of New Haven)*
New Haven Hosp. *(see Yale-New Haven Hosp.)*
New Haven State Teachers Coll. *(see Southern Connecticut State Univ.)*
New Haven Univ. *(see Univ. of New Haven)*
New Haven YMCA Jr. Coll. *(see Univ. of New Haven)*
New Horizons Beauty Coll. 628
New Horizons Beauty Sch. 553
New Horizons Computer Learning Ctr. *(see Northwestern Coll.)*

New Images Acad. of Beauty 727 *(see also Scot Lewis Schools-Paul Mitchell Partner Sch—Boise)*

New Jersey Assoc. of Colleges & Universities 733

New Jersey City Univ. 248

New Jersey Coll. *(see Coll. of New Jersey; Douglass Coll.; Rutgers, The State Univ. of New Jersey New Brunswick Campus; Univ. of Medicine & Dentistry of New Jersey)*

New Jersey Coll. for Women *(see Douglass Coll.; Rutgers, The State Univ. of New Jersey New Brunswick Campus)*

New Jersey Coll. of Medicine & Dentistry *(see Univ. of Medicine & Dentistry of New Jersey)*

New Jersey Dental Sch. 251 *(see also Univ. of Medicine & Dentistry of New Jersey)*

New Jersey Inst. of Techno. 248

New Jersey Locksmithing Sch. *(see New Jersey Sch. of Locksmithing)*

New Jersey Med. & Dental Univ. *(see Univ. of Medicine & Dentistry of New Jersey)*

New Jersey Med. Sch. 251 *(see also Univ. of Medicine & Dentistry of New Jersey)*

New Jersey Sch. of Locksmithing 559 *(see also Charles Stuart Sch. of Locksmithing)*

New Jersey Sch. of Osteopathic Medicine 251 *(see also Univ. of Medicine & Dentistry of New Jersey)*

New Jersey State Normal Sch. *(see Coll. of New Jersey, New Jersey City Univ., William Paterson Univ. of New Jersey)*

New Jersey State Normal Sch. at Paterson *(see William Paterson Univ. of New Jersey)*

New Jersey State Teachers Coll. *(see Coll. of New Jersey, New Jersey City Univ.)*

New Jersey State Teachers Coll. & State Normal Sch. at Trenton *(see Coll. of New Jersey)*

New Jersey State Teachers Coll. at Glassboro *(see Rowan Univ.)*

New Jersey State Teacher's Coll. at Paterson *(see William Paterson Univ. of New Jersey)*

New Jersey Talmudical Acad. *(see Talmudical Acad. of New Jersey)*

New Kensington Commercial Sch. *(see Newport Bus. Inst.)*

New Life Inst., Inc. Sch. of Massage Therapy *(see Rising Spirit Inst. of Natural Health)*

New Life Theological Seminary 748

New London Acad. *(see Colby-Sawyer Coll.)*

New Mexico Aveda Inst. de Bellas Artes 556

New Mexico Coll. *(see New Mexico Jr. Coll., New Mexico State Univ.)*

New Mexico Coll. of Agriculture & Mechanic Arts *(see New Mexico State Univ.)*

New Mexico Highlands Univ. 253

New Mexico Inst. of Mining & Techno. 253

New Mexico Jr. Coll. 253

New Mexico Military Inst. 253

New Mexico Normal Sch. *(see Western New Mexico Univ.)*

New Mexico Sch. of Mines *(see New Mexico Inst. of Mining & Techno.)*

New Mexico State Teachers' Coll. *(see Western New Mexico Univ.)*

New Mexico State Univ. 253

New Mexico State Univ. at Alamogordo 253

New Mexico State Univ. at Carlsbad 253

New Mexico State Univ—San Juan Campus *(see San Juan Coll.)*

New Mexico Tech *(see New Mexico Inst. of Mining & Techno.)*

New Mexico Tech. Vocational Sch. *(see Northern New Mexico Coll.)*

New Mexico Univ. *(see Univ. of New Mexico)*

New Mexicos L&-Grant Coll. *(see New Mexico State Univ.)*

New Orleans Baptist Bible Inst. *(see New Orleans Baptist Theological Seminary)*

New Orleans Baptist Seminary *(see New Orleans Baptist Theological Seminary)*

New Orleans Baptist Theological Seminary 172

New Orleans Culinary Inst. *(see Culinary Inst. of New Orleans)*

New Orleans Dale Carnegie Training *(see Paul Phillips & Associates, Inc.)*

New Orleans Job Corps Ctr. 517

New Orleans Police Deptartment 673

New Orleans Sch. of Urban Missions *(see Sch. of Urban Missions— New Orleans)*

New Orleans Seminary *(see New Orleans Baptist Theological Seminary)*

New Orleans Univ. *(see Dillard Univ., Univ. of New Orleans)*

New Orleans VA Med. Ctr. *(see New Orleans Veterans Affairs Med. Ctr.)*

New Orleans Veterans Affairs Med. Ctr. 673

New Paltz Acad. *(see State Univ. of New York at New Paltz)*

New Paltz Coll. *(see State Univ. of New York at New Paltz)*

New Professions Tech. Inst. 487

New River Coll. *(see New River Comm. & Tech. Coll.)*

New River Comm. & Tech. Coll. 420

New River Comm. Coll. 404 *(see also New River Comm. & Tech. Coll.)*

New River State Coll. *(see West Virginia Univ. Inst. of Techno.)*

New River State Sch. *(see West Virginia Univ. Inst. of Techno.)*

New Rochelle Coll. *(see Coll. of New Rochelle)*

New Saint Andrews Coll. 745

New Sch. for Social Research *(see New Sch.)*

New Sch. of Contemporary Radio *(see New Sch. of Radio & Television)*

New Sch. of Radio & Television, The 568

New Sch. Univ. 733 *(see also New Sch., The)*

New Sch., The 269, 733

New South Wales Univ. *(see Univ. of New South Wales)*

New Techno. Training Inst. 754

New Tyler Barber Coll. 448

New Wave Hair Acad—Coleman Road 612

New Wave Hair Acad—South Highland Street 612

New Whatcom Normal Sch. *(see Western Washington Univ.)*

New World Sch. of the Arts 91

New World Symphony 487

New York Acad. of Art Grad. Sch. *(see Grad. Sch. of Figurative Art of the New York Acad. of Art)*

New York Automotive & Diesel Inst. 568

New York Aveda Inst. *(see Aveda Inst. New York)*

New York Career Inst. 269

New York Ctr. for Montessori Teacher Edu. *(see Ctr. for Montessori Teacher Edu/NY)*

New York Chiropractic Coll. 269

New York City Art Inst. *(see Art Inst. of New York City)*

New York City Coll. *(see City Univ. of New York City Coll.)*

New York City Coll. of Techno. *(see City Univ. of New York New York City Coll. of Techno.)*

New York City Inst. of Art *(see Art Inst. of New York City)*

New York City VA Med. Ctr. *(see Veterans Affairs Med. Ctr—New York City)*

New York City Veterans Affairs Med. Ctr. *(see Veterans Affairs Med. Ctr—New York City)*

New York Coll. for Wholistic Health Edu. & Research *(see New York Coll. of Health Professions)*

New York Coll. of Health Professions 688

New York Coll. of Podiatric Medicine 269

New York Coll. of Traditional Chinese Medicine 688, 734

New York Culinary Acad. *(see Culinary Acad. of New York Management Sch.)*

New York Dental Assistants Sch. *(see New York Sch. for Med. & Dental Assistants)*

New York Diesel Inst. *(see New York Automotive & Diesel Inst.)*

New York Food & Hotel Management Sch. 734 *(see also Culinary Acad. of New York Management Sch.)*

New York Grad. Ctr. *(see City Univ. of New York Grad. Ctr.)*

New York Hosp. Queens, The 688

New York Inst. of Bus. Techno. *(see New York Inst. of English & Bus.)*

New York Inst. of Chinese Medicine 734 *(see also New York Coll. of Traditional Chinese Medicine)*

New York Inst. of Dietetics *(see Culinary Acad. of New York Management Sch.)*

New York Inst. of English & Bus. 568

New York Inst. of Massage 569

New York Inst. of Tech—Old Westbury 269

New York Inst. of Word Processing *(see New York Inst. of English & Bus.)*

New York Interior Design Sch. *(see New York Sch. of Interior Design)*

New York Int'l. Beauty Sch., LTD 569

New York Law Sch. 688

New York Massage Inst. *(see New York Inst. of Massage)*

New York Med. Assistants Sch. *(see New York Sch. for Med. & Dental Assistants)*

New York Med. Ctr. of Queens *(see New York Hosp. Queens)*

New York Med. Coll. 269

New York Methodist Hosp. 688

New York Optometry Coll. *(see State Univ. of New York Coll. of Optometry)*

New York Paralegal Sch. 569

New York Presbyterian Hosp— Columbia Presbyterian Campus *(see New York Presbyterian Hosp—Columbia Univ.)*

New York Presbyterian Hosp— Columbia Univ. 688

New York Presbyterian Hosp— Columbia Univ. Med. Ctr. *(see New York Presbyterian Hosp— Columbia Univ.)*

New York Restaurant Sch. *(see Art Inst. of New York City)*

New York Sch. for Med. & Dental Assistants 569

New York Sch. for Med/Dental Assistants *(see New York Sch. for Med. & Dental Assistants)*

New York Sch. for the Training of Teachers *(see Teachers Coll. of Columbia Univ.)*

New York Sch. of Chiropody *(see New York Coll. of Podiatric Medicine)*

New York Sch. of Interior Design 269

New York State Agricultural & Tech. Coll. at Alfred *(see Alfred Univ.)*

New York State Coll. of Agriculture & Life Sciences *(see Cornell Univ.)*

New York State Coll. of Ceramics at Alfred Univ. 255 *(see also Alfred Univ., New York State Coll. of Ceramics at Alfred Univ.)*

New York State Coll. of Human Ecology 261 *(see also Cornell Univ.)*

New York State Coll. of Veterinary Medicine 261 *(see also Cornell Univ.)*

New York State Dept. of Health 689 *(see also State Univ. of New York at Albany)*

New York State Inst. of Applied Arts & Sciences *(see State Univ. of New York Broome Comm. Coll., Westchester Comm. Coll.)*

New York State Inst. of Applied Arts & Sciences at Binghamton *(see State Univ. of New York Broome Comm. Coll.)*

New York State Sch. of Industrial & Labor Relations 261 *(see also Cornell Univ.)*

New York Tech. Inst. of Hawaii 496

New York Techno. Inst. *(see New York Inst. of Tech—Old Westbury)*

New York Theological Seminary 260, 269 *(see also Coll. of New Rochelle New York Theological Seminary Campus)*

New York Univ. 270

Newark Beth Israel Med. Ctr. 684

Newark Coll. *(see New Jersey Inst. of Techno., Univ. of Delaware)*

Newark Coll. of Engineering *(see New Jersey Inst. of Techno.)*

Newark Tech. Sch. *(see New Jersey Inst. of Techno.)*

Newberry Coll. 357

Newberry Sch. of Beauty 466

Newbridge Coll. 466

Newbury Coll. 191

Newcomb Coll. *(see Tulane Univ.)*

Newfoundland Mem. Univ. *(see Mem. Univ. of Newfoundland)*

Newman Coll. *(see Carson-Newman Coll., Newman Theological Coll., Newman Univ.)*

Newman Theological Coll. 433

Newman Univ. 155

Newport Bus. Inst. 336

Newport News Shipbuilding Apprentice Sch. *(see Northrop Grumman Newport News Apprentice Sch.)*

Newport Sch. of Hairdressing, Inc— Cranston 736 *(see also Paul Mitchell The Sch.)*

Newport Sch. of Hairdressing, Inc— Pawtucket 607

Newport Univ. *(see Christopher Newport Univ.)*

Newschool of Architecture *(see NewSchool of Architecture & Design)*

NewSchool of Architecture & Design 49

Newton & Associates, Inc. *(see Glyn Ed Newton & Associates, Inc.)*

Newton Coll. of the Sacred Heart *(see Boston Coll.)*

Newton Theological Institution *(see Andover Newton Theological Sch.)*

NHCTC—Berlin *(see New Hampshire Comm. Tech. Coll—Berlin)*

NHCTC—Claremont *(see New Hampshire Comm. Tech. Coll— Claremont)*

NHCTC—Laconia *(see New Hampshire Comm. Tech. Coll— Laconia)*

NHCTC—Nashua *(see New Hampshire Comm. Tech. Coll— Nashua)*

NHCTC—Stratham *(see New Hampshire Comm. Tech. Coll—Stratham)*

NHRAW Home Study Inst. *(see HARDI Home Study Inst.)*

Niagara Comm. Coll. *(see Niagara County Comm. Coll.)*

Niagara County Coll. *(see Niagara County Comm. Coll.)*

Niagara County Comm. Coll. 270

Niagara Univ. 270

Nicholas H. Noyes Mem. Hosp. 689

Nicholls Jr. Coll. *(see Nicholls State Univ.)*

Nicholls State Coll. *(see Nicholls State Univ.)*

Nicholls State Univ. 172

Nichols Acad. *(see Nichols Coll.)*

Nichols Career Ctr. 681

Nichols Coll. 191

Nichols Jr. Coll. *(see Nichols Coll.)*

Nick Randazzo Vocational Training Inst. *(see Gretna Career Coll. Training Inst.)*

Nicolet Area Tech. Coll. 426

Nicolet Coll. *(see Nicolet Area Tech. Coll.)*

Nicolet Tech. Coll. *(see Nicolet Area Tech. Coll.)*

Nightingale Med. Inst. 762

Niles Coll. of Loyola Univ. *(see Univ. of Saint Mary of the Lake Mundelein Seminary)*

Niles Sch. of Beauty Culture 502

Nitze Sch. of Advanced Int'l. Studies *(see Paul H. Nitze Sch. of Advanced Int'l. Studies)*

Nonproliferation & National Security Inst. 733 *(see also National Training Ctr.)*

Norfolk General Hosp. *(see Sentara Sch. of Health Professions)*

Norfolk Polytechnic Coll. *(see Norfolk State Univ.)*

Norfolk Skills Ctr. 633

Norfolk State Coll. *(see Norfolk State Univ.)*

Norfolk State Univ. 404

Norfolk Tech. Ctr. *(see Norfolk Tech. Vocational Ctr.)*

Norfolk Tech. Vocational Ctr. 706, 738

Norfolk Unit of Virginia Union Univ. *(see Norfolk State Univ.)*

Norfolk Univ. *(see Norfolk State Univ.)*

Norfolk Vocational Ctr. *(see Norfolk Tech. Vocational Ctr.)*

Normal Sch. for Colored Students *(see Alabama State Univ.)*

Normal Sch. of Arizona *(see Arizona State Univ.)*

Norman & Associates 534

Norman & Esther Allen Touro Coll. of Liberal Arts & Sciences *(see Michigan Jewish Inst.)*

Norman Vocational Tech. Sch. *(see Moore-Norman Area Vocational Tech. Sch.)*

Normandale Coll. *(see Normandale Comm. Coll.)*

Normandale Comm. Coll. 213

Normandy Beauty Sch. of Jacksonville 487

North Adams State Coll. *(see Massachusetts Coll. of Liberal Arts)*

North Adrian's Beauty Coll. 466

North Adult Edu. Ctr. *(see North Edu. Ctr.)*

North Alabama Univ. *(see Univ. of North Alabama)*

North American Baptist Coll. *(see Taylor Univ. Coll. & Seminary)*

North American Baptist Seminary 362

North American Heating, Refrigeration, & Air-Conditioning Wholesalers Associat *(see HARDI Home Study Inst.)*

North Arkansas Coll. 25

North Arkansas Comm/Tech. Coll. *(see North Arkansas Coll.)*

North Bennet Street Sch. 526

North Carolina A&T State Univ. *(see North Carolina Agricultural & Tech. State Univ.)*

North Carolina Agricultural & Tech. State Univ. 290

North Carolina Baptist Hosp. *(see Wake Forest Univ.)*

North Carolina Baptist Hospitals 692

North Carolina Ctr. for Montessori Teacher Edu. 573

North Carolina Central Univ. 290

North Carolina Coll. at Durham *(see North Carolina Central Univ.)*

North Carolina Coll. for Negroes *(see North Carolina Central Univ.)*

North Carolina Coll. for Women *(see Univ. of North Carolina at Greensboro)*

North Carolina Dale Carnegie Training *(see E. J. Taylor Corporation)*

North Carolina Division of Dental Health 692

North Carolina Sch. of the Arts 290

North Carolina State Univ. 291, 734, 738

North Carolina Univ. at Chapel Hill *(see Univ. of North Carolina at Chapel Hill)*

North Carolina Univ. at Greensboro *(see Univ. of North Carolina at Greensboro)*

North Carolina Univ. at Pembroke *(see Univ. of North Carolina at Pembroke)*

North Carolina Wesleyan Coll. 291

North Central Bible Coll. 731 *(see also North Central Univ.)*

North Central Bible Inst. *(see North Central Univ.)*

North Central Christian Coll. *(see Rochester Coll.)*

North Central Coll. 128 *(see also North Central State Coll.)*

North Central Industrial Tech. Edu. Ctr. 599 *(see also North Central Industrial Tech. Edu. Ctr.)*

North Central Inst. 369

North Central Kansas Area Vocational-Tech. Sch. *(see North Central Kansas Tech. Coll.)*

North Central Kansas Tech. Coll. 155

North Central Michigan Coll. 202

North Central Missouri Coll. 229

North Central State Coll. 307

North Central Texas Coll. 381

North Central Univ. 213, 731

North Central West Virginia OIC *(see North Central West Virginia Opportunities Industrialization Ctr.)*

North Central West Virginia Opportunities Industrialization Ctr. 641

North Chicago VA Med. Ctr. *(see North Chicago Veterans Affairs Med. Ctr.)*

North Chicago Veterans Affairs Med. Ctr. 668

North Country Coll. *(see North Country Comm. Coll.)*

North Country Comm. Coll. 270

North Dakota State Coll. of Science 296

North Dakota State Hosp. 692

North Dakota State Sch. of Science *(see North Dakota State Coll. of Science)*

North Dakota State Univ. 297

North Dakota State Univ—Bottineau *(see Minot State Univ—Bottineau)*

North Dakota State Univ—Bottineau Branch & Inst. of Forestry *(see Minot State Univ—Bottineau)*

North Dakota Univ. *(see Univ. of North Dakota)*

North East Funeral Inst. *(see FINE Mortuary Coll.)*

North Edu. Ctr. 582

North Face Learning Inc. *(see Northface Univ.)*

North Florida Coll. *(see North Florida Comm. Coll.)*

North Florida Comm. Coll. 91

North Florida Cosmetology Inst., Inc. 487

North Florida Inst. 487

North Florida Jr. Coll. *(see North Florida Comm. Coll.)*

North Florida South Georgia Veterans Health System *(see Malcom Randall Veterans Affairs Med. Ctr.)*

North Florida Univ. *(see Univ. of North Florida)*

North Fulton Beauty Coll. 494

North General Hosp. 689 *(see also Helene Fuld Coll. of Nursing)*

North Georgia Coll. *(see North Georgia Coll. & State Univ., North Georgia Tech. Coll.)*

North Georgia Coll. & State Univ. 107

North Georgia State Univ. *(see North Georgia Coll. & State Univ.)*

North Georgia Tech. Coll. 107, 726

North Georgia Tech. Inst. 726 *(see also North Georgia Tech. Coll.)*

North Greenville Baptist Acad. *(see North Greenville Coll.)*

North Greenville Coll. 358

North Greenville Jr. Coll. *(see North Greenville Coll.)*

North Harris Coll. 382 *(see also North Harris Montgomery Comm. Coll. Dist.)*

North Harris Montgomery Comm. Coll. Dist. 382

North Haven Acad. 475, 724

North Hennepin Coll. *(see North Hennepin Comm. Coll.)*

North Hennepin Comm. Coll. 213

North Hills Beauty Acad. 600

North Idaho Coll. 116

North Idaho Jr. Coll. *(see North Idaho Coll.)*

North Iowa Area Coll. *(see North Iowa Area Comm. Coll.)*

North Iowa Area Comm. Coll. 149

North Iowa Med. Ctr. *(see Mercy Med. Ctr. North Iowa)*

North Iowa Mercy Health Ctr. *(see Mercy Med. Ctr. North Iowa)*

North Kansas City Hosp. 681

North Kansas Hosp. *(see North Kansas City Hosp.)*

North Lake Coll. 382

North Mem. Health Care *(see North Mem. Med. Ctr.)*

North Mem. Hosp. *(see North Mem. Med. Ctr.)*

North Mem. Med. Ctr. 679

North Metro Coll. *(see North Metro Tech. Coll.)*

North Metro Tech *(see North Metro Tech. Coll.)*

North Metro Tech. Coll. 107, 726, 745

North Metro Tech. Inst. 726 *(see also North Metro Tech. Coll.)*

North Mississippi Med. Ctr. 680

North Missouri Normal Sch. & Commercial Coll. *(see Truman State Univ.)*

North Montco Tech. Career Ctr. 735

North Oaks Health System *(see North Oaks Med. Ctr.)*

North Oaks Hosp. *(see North Oaks Med. Ctr.)*

North Oaks Med. Ctr. 673

North Park Theological Seminary *(see North Park Univ.)*

North Park Univ. 128

North Peralta Comm. Coll. *(see Vista Comm. Coll.)*

North Platte Beauty Acad. 542

North Platte Comm. Coll. South Campus *(see Mid-Plains Comm. Coll.)*

North Platte Jr. Coll. *(see McCook Comm. Coll., Mid-Plains Comm. Coll.)*

North Seattle Coll. *(see North Seattle Comm. Coll.)*

North Seattle Comm. Coll. 413

North Shore Coll. *(see North Shore Comm. Coll.)*

North Shore Comm. Coll. 191

North Shore Long Island Jewish Grad. Sch. of Molecular Medicine 270

North Shore Univ. Hosp. at Manhasset 689

North Shore-LIJ Research Inst. *(see North Shore Long Island Jewish Grad. Sch. of Molecular Medicine)*

North Tech. Edu. Ctr. 663

North Texas Agricultural Coll. *(see Univ. of Texas at Arlington)*

North Texas Career Inst. *(see North Texas Prof. Career Inst.)*

North Texas Health Science Ctr. at Fort Worth *(see Univ. of North Texas Health Science Ctr. at Fort Worth)*

North Texas Normal Coll. *(see Univ. of North Texas)*

North Texas Prof. Career Inst. 622

North Texas State Coll. *(see Univ. of North Texas)*

North Texas State Normal Coll. *(see Univ. of North Texas)*

North Texas State Teachers Coll. *(see Univ. of North Texas)*

North Texas State Univ. *(see Univ. of North Texas)*

North Texas Univ. *(see Univ. of North Texas)*

North West Art Ctr. *(see Northwest Coll. of Art)*

North West Beauty Sch. 760

North West Coll. of Art *(see Northwest Coll. of Art)*

North West Iowa Coll. *(see Northwest Iowa Comm. Coll.)*

North West Iowa Comm. Coll. *(see Northwest Iowa Comm. Coll.)*

North West Iowa Tech. Coll. *(see Northwest Iowa Comm. Coll.)*

North West Mississippi Coll. *(see Northwest Mississippi Comm. Coll.)*

North West Mississippi Comm. Coll. *(see Northwest Mississippi Comm. Coll.)*

North West Mississippi Jr. Coll. *(see Northwest Mississippi Comm. Coll.)*

North West Nannies Inst. *(see Northwest Nannies Inst.)*

Northampton Coll. *(see Northampton County Area Comm. Coll.)*

Northampton Comm. Coll. *(see Northampton County Area Comm. Coll.)*

Northampton County Area Comm. Coll. 336

Northampton County Coll. *(see Northampton County Area Comm. Coll.)*

Northark Coll. *(see North Arkansas Coll.)*

Northcentral Coll. *(see North Central State Coll., Northcentral Tech. Coll.)*

Northcentral State Coll. *(see North Central State Coll.)*

Northcentral Techical Inst. *(see Colby Comm. Coll.)*

Northcentral Tech. Coll. 426

Northcentral Tech. Inst. *(see Ivy Tech Comm. Coll. of Indiana—North Central)*

Northcentral Univ. 18

Northeast Alabama Coll. *(see Northeast Alabama Comm. Coll.)*

Northeast Alabama Comm. Coll. 7

Northeast Alabama State Comm. Coll. *(see Northeast Alabama Comm. Coll.)*

Northeast Area Vocational Tech. Sch. 735 *(see also Northeast Techno. Ctr.)*

Northeast Area Vo-Tech Sch. *(see Northeast Techno. Ctr.)*

Northeast Bible Coll. *(see Valley Forge Christian Coll.)*

Northeast Coll. of Communications *(see New England Inst. of Art)*

Northeast Comm. Coll. 238
Northeast Florida State Hosp. 663
Northeast Funeral Inst. *(see FINE Mortuary Coll.)*
Northeast Inst. of Industrial Techno. 730
Northeast Iowa Coll. *(see Northeast Iowa Comm. Coll.)*
Northeast Iowa Comm. Coll. 149
Northeast Kansas Coll. *(see Northeast Kansas Tech. Coll.)*
Northeast Kansas Tech. Coll. 155
Northeast Louisiana Univ. *(see Univ. of Louisiana at Monroe)*
NorthEast Med. Ctr. *(see Cabarrus Coll. of Health Sciences)*
Northeast Metro Tech. Coll. *(see Century Coll.)*
Northeast Mississippi Coll. *(see Northeast Mississippi Comm. Coll.)*
Northeast Mississippi Comm. Coll. 220
Northeast Missouri State Coll. *(see Truman State Univ.)*
Northeast Missouri State Teachers Coll. *(see Truman State Univ.)*
Northeast Missouri State Univ. *(see Truman State Univ.)*
Northeast Montessori Inst. 519 *(see also Endicott Coll.)*
Northeast Nebraska Tech. Coll. *(see Northeast Comm. Coll.)*
Northeast Ohio Dale Carnegie Training *(see Lance Tyson & Associates Dale Carnegie Training of Northeast Ohio)*
Northeast State Coll. *(see Northeast State Tech. Comm. Coll.)*
Northeast State Comm. Coll. *(see Northeast State Tech. Comm. Coll.)*
Northeast State Tech. Coll. *(see Northeast State Tech. Comm. Coll.)*
Northeast State Tech. Comm. Coll. 369
Northeast Tech. Inst. *(see Ivy Tech Comm. Coll. of Indiana—Northeast)*
Northeast Techno. Ctr. 589, 735
Northeast Texas Coll. *(see Northeast Texas Comm. Coll.)*
Northeast Texas Comm. Coll. 382
Northeast Wisconsin Coll. *(see Northeast Wisconsin Tech. Coll.)*
Northeast Wisconsin Tech. Coll. 426
Northeastern Bible Coll. *(see King's Coll.)*
Northeastern Christian Jr. Coll. *(see Ohio Valley Univ.)*

Northeastern Coll. *(see Northeastern Jr. Coll., Northeastern Tech. Coll., Northeastern Univ.)*
Northeastern Illinois Univ. 128
Northeastern Inst. of Biblical Studies *(see King's Coll.)*
Northeastern Jr. Coll. 69
Northeastern Ohio Universities Coll. of Medicine 307
Northeastern Oklahoma A&M Coll. 316
Northeastern Oklahoma Agricultural & Mechanical Coll. *(see Northeastern Oklahoma A&M Coll.)*
Northeastern Oklahoma Jr. Coll. *(see Northeastern Oklahoma A&M Coll.)*
Northeastern Seminary 270, 747
Northeastern Seminary at Roberts Wesleyan Coll. 747
Northeastern State Univ. 316
Northeastern Tech. Coll. 358
Northeastern Univ. 191
Northern Alberta Inst. of Techno. 712
Northern Arizona Coll. of Health Careers *(see CollegeAmerica)*
Northern Arizona Normal Sch. *(see Northern Arizona Univ.)*
Northern Arizona State Teachers Coll. *(see Northern Arizona Univ.)*
Northern Arizona Univ. 18
Northern Atlanta Tri-Hosp. CPE Ctr. 665
Northern Baptist Theological Seminary 727 *(see also Northern Seminary)*
Northern Branch State Normal Sch. of California *(see California State Univ—Chico)*
Northern California VA Health Care System *(see Veterans Affairs Northern California Health Care System—Mare Island, Veterans Affairs Northern California Health Care System—Martinez)*
Northern California Veterans Affairs Health Care System *(see Veterans Affairs Northern California Health Care System—Mare Island, Veterans Affairs Northern California Health Care System—Martinez)*
Northern Campbell County Vocational-Tech. Sch. *(see Gateway Comm. & Tech. Coll.)*
Northern Colorado Univ. *(see Univ. of Northern Colorado)*
Northern Essex Coll. *(see Northern Essex Comm. Coll.)*
Northern Essex Comm. Coll. 191
Northern Illinois Univ. 128

Northern Inst. of Cosmetology 582
Northern Iowa Univ. *(see Univ. of Northern Iowa)*
Northern Kentucky Health Occupations Ctr. *(see Gateway Comm. & Tech. Coll.)*
Northern Kentucky State Vocational-Tech. Sch. *(see Gateway Comm. & Tech. Coll.)*
Northern Kentucky Tech. Coll. *(see Gateway Comm. & Tech. Coll.)*
Northern Kentucky Univ. 163
Northern Maine Coll. *(see Northern Maine Comm. Coll.)*
Northern Maine Comm. Coll. 176, 730
Northern Maine Tech. Coll. 730 *(see also Northern Maine Comm. Coll.)*
Northern Marianas Coll. 436
Northern Michigan Coll. *(see Northern Michigan Univ.)*
Northern Michigan State Teachers Coll. *(see Northern Michigan Univ.)*
Northern Michigan Univ. 202
Northern Montana Coll. *(see Montana State Univ—Northern)*
Northern Nevada Career Coll. *(see Career Coll. of Northern Nevada)*
Northern Nevada Comm. Coll. *(see Great Basin Coll.)*
Northern New Jersey Dale Carnegie Training *(see G. Mitchell Hartman & Associates, Inc.)*
Northern New Mexico Coll. 253, 733
Northern New Mexico Comm. Coll. 733 *(see also Northern New Mexico Coll.)*
Northern Normal & Industrial Sch. *(see Northern State Univ.)*
Northern Oklahoma Coll. 316
Northern Rockies Clinical Pastoral Edu. Ctr., Inc., The 682
Northern Seminary 128, 727
Northern State Coll. *(see Northern State Univ.)*
Northern State Normal Sch. *(see Northern Michigan Univ.)*
Northern State Teachers Coll. *(see Northern State Univ.)*
Northern State Univ. 362
Northern Tier Career Ctr. 698
Northern Virginia Comm. Coll. 405
Northern Virginia Grad. Ctr. 408 *(see also Virginia Polytechnic Inst. & State Univ.)*
Northern Westchester Sch. of Hairdressing 569
Northern Wyoming Coll—Gillette *(see Northern Wyoming Comm. Coll. Dist—Gillette)*

Northern Wyoming Coll—Sheridan *(see Northern Wyoming Comm. Coll. Dist—Sheridan)*
Northern Wyoming Comm. Coll. Dist—Sheridan 430
Northface Univ. 241 *(see also Morrison Univ.)*
Northfield Coll. *(see Carleton Coll.)*
Northland Baptist Bible Coll. 751
Northland Baptist Bible Inst. *(see Northland Baptist Bible Coll.)*
Northland Coll. *(see Northland Comm. & Tech. Coll.)*
Northland Comm. Coll. 426
Northland Comm. & Tech. Coll. 213
Northland Pioneer Coll. 18
Northpark Univ. *(see North Park Univ.)*
Northport VA Med. Ctr. *(see Veterans Affairs Med. Ctr—Northport)*
Northport Veterans Affairs Med. Ctr. *(see Veterans Affairs Med. Ctr—Northport)*
Northport Veterans Affairs Med. Ctr. 689
Northrop Grumman Newport News Apprentice Sch. 633
Northrop Rice Aviation Inst. of Techno. 723
Northrop Rice Inst. *(see Northrop Rice Aviation Inst. of Techno.)*
Northshore Career Coll. 756
Northwest Alabama Comm. Coll. *(see Northwest-Shoals Comm. Coll.)*
NorthWest Arkansas Coll. *(see NorthWest Arkansas Comm. Coll.)*
NorthWest Arkansas Comm. Coll. 26
Northwest Art Ctr. *(see Northwest Coll. of Art)*
Northwest Aviation Coll. 413
Northwest Baptist Seminary 413
Northwest Beauty Sch. *(see North West Beauty Sch.)*
Northwest Bible Coll. 740 *(see also Northwest Univ., Vanguard Coll.)*
Northwest Bible Inst. *(see Northwest Univ.)*
Northwest Christian Coll. 322
Northwest Coll. 430 *(see also Northwest Christian Coll., Northwest State Comm. Coll., Northwest Tech. Coll., Northwest Univ.)*
North-West Coll. 466
North-West Coll. Dental Assistants *(see North-West Coll.)*
Northwest Coll. of Art 413
Northwest Coll. of Hair Design 593
North-West Coll. of Med. & Dental Assistants *(see North-West Coll.)*

Northwest Coll. of the Assemblies of God 738 *(see also Northwest Univ.)*
Northwest Comm. Coll. *(see Northwest Coll., Northwest State Comm. Coll.)*
Northwest Comm. Healthcare 668
Northwest Dade Ctr., Inc. *(see Citrus Health Network, Inc.)*
Northwest Educational Ctr. 622
Northwest Georgia Reg. Hosp. 665
Northwest Grad. Ministry Sch. *(see Bakke Grad. Univ.)*
Northwest Grad. Sch. of Ministry *(see Bakke Grad. Univ.)*
Northwest Hair Acad. 638
Northwest Hair Acad., Mount Vernon *(see Northwest Hair Acad.)*
Northwest Health Careers 543
Northwest HVC/R Assoc. & Training Ctr. 638, 738
Northwest Indian Coll. 413
Northwest Inst. of Acupuncture & Oriental Medicine 738
Northwest Iowa Coll. *(see Northwest Iowa Comm. Coll.)*
Northwest Iowa Comm. Coll. 149
Northwest Iowa Tech. Coll. *(see Northwest Iowa Comm. Coll.)*
Northwest Kansas Tech. Coll. 155
Northwest Lineman Coll. 497
Northwest Mississippi Coll. *(see Northwest Mississippi Comm. Coll.)*
Northwest Mississippi Comm. Coll. 220
Northwest Mississippi Jr. Coll. *(see Northwest Mississippi Comm. Coll.)*
Northwest Missouri State Univ. 229
Northwest Missouri Univ. *(see Northwest Missouri State Univ.)*
Northwest Nannies Incorporated *(see Northwest Nannies Inst.)*
Northwest Nannies Inst. 593
Northwest Nazarene Coll. 727 *(see also Northwest Nazarene Univ.)*
Northwest Nazarene Univ. 116, 727
Northwest Ohio & Northern Indiana Dale Carnegie Training *(see Dale Carnegie Training of Northwest Ohio & Northern Indiana)*
Northwest Photographic Ctr. *(see Photographic Ctr. Northwest)*
Northwest Sch. of Wooden Boatbuilding 638
Northwest Seminary *(see Northwest Baptist Seminary)*
Northwest State Coll. *(see Northwest State Comm. Coll.)*
Northwest State Comm. Coll. 307

Northwest Tech. Coll. 213 *(see also Minnesota State Comm. & Tech. Coll., Northland Comm. & Tech. Coll.)*
Northwest Tech. Coll—Detroit Lakes *(see Minnesota State Comm. & Tech. Coll—Detroit Lakes)*
Northwest Tech. Coll—Moorhead *(see Minnesota State Comm. & Tech. Coll—Moorhead)*
Northwest Tech. Coll—Wadena *(see Minnesota State Comm. & Tech. Coll—Wadena)*
Northwest Tech. Inst. 448, 652, 731 *(see also Ivy Tech Comm. Coll. of Indiana—Northwest, NTI Sch. of CAD Techno.)*
Northwest Univ. 413, 738
Northwest Vista Coll. 382
Northwestern Bible & Missionary Sch. *(see Northwestern Coll.)*
Northwestern Bus. Coll. 129
Northwestern Coll. *(see Univ. of Northwestern Ohio)*
North-Western Coll. *(see North Central Coll.)*
Northwestern Coll. 49, 149, 213, 723 *(see also Martin Luther Coll.)*
Northwestern Coll. of Chiropractic *(see Northwestern Health Sciences Univ.)*
Northwestern Colorado Comm. Coll. *(see Colorado Northwestern Comm. Coll.)*
Northwestern Connecticut Coll. *(see Northwestern Connecticut Comm. Coll.)*
Northwestern Connecticut Comm. Coll. 74
Northwestern Electronics Inst. *(see Dunwoody Coll. of Techno.)*
Northwestern Health Sciences Univ. 213
Northwestern Inst. of Techno. *(see Northwestern Technological Inst.)*
Northwestern Lutheran Theological Seminary *(see Luther Seminary)*
Northwestern Mem. Hosp. 668
Northwestern Michigan Coll. 202
Northwestern Ohio Normal Sch. *(see Ohio Northern Univ.)*
Northwestern Ohio Univ. *(see Univ. of Northwestern Ohio)*
Northwestern Oklahoma State Univ. 316
Northwestern Oklahoma Univ. *(see Northwestern Oklahoma State Univ.)*
Northwestern Polytechnic Univ. 49
Northwestern State Univ. 173

Northwestern Tech. Coll. 107, 723, 726 *(see also Northwestern Coll.)*
Northwestern Tech. Inst. 726 *(see also Northwestern Tech. Coll.)*
Northwestern Technological Inst. 530
Northwestern Univ. 129
Northwestern Univ. Med. Sch. *(see Northwestern Univ.)*
Northwest-Shoals Comm. Coll. 7
Northwood Univ. 202
Norton Healthcare 672
Norwalk Coll. *(see Norwalk Comm. Coll.)*
Norwalk Comm. Coll. 74
Norwalk Comm-Tech. Coll. *(see Norwalk Comm. Coll.)*
Norwalk Seminary *(see Baldwin-Wallace Coll.)*
Norwalk State Tech. Coll. *(see Norwalk Comm. Coll.)*
Norwegian-Danish Sch. *(see Trinity Int'l. Univ.)*
Norwich Coll. *(see Norwich Univ.)*
Norwich Univ. 398
Nossi Coll. of Art 369
Notre Dame Coll. 307 *(see also Notre Dame de Namur Univ.)*
Notre Dame Coll. of Maryland *(see Coll. of Notre Dame of Maryland)*
Notre Dame de Namur Univ. 49
Notre Dame Grad. Sch., The 401 *(see also Christendom Coll.)*
Notre Dame Inst. *(see Notre Dame Grad. Sch. of Christendom Coll.)*
Notre Dame Seminary 173
Notre Dame Univ. *(see Univ. of Notre Dame)*
Nouvelle Inst. 487
Nova Southeastern Univ. 91
NTI Sch. of CAD Techno. 213, 731
NTMA Training Centers of Southern California 466, 754
NTU Sch. of Engineering & Applied Science at Walden Univ. 724 *(see also Walden Univ.)*
Nunez Comm. Coll. *(see Elaine P. Nunez Comm. Coll.)*
Nunnelley State Tech. Coll. *(see Central Alabama Comm. Coll.)*
Nurse Anesthesia Sch. of New Britain Sch. *(see New Britain Sch. of Nurse Anesthesia)*
Nursing Sch. of Central Maine *(see Central Maine Med. Ctr. Sch. of Nursing)*
Nu-Tek Acad. of Beauty 513
Nu-Tek Beauty Acad. *(see Nu-Tek Acad. of Beauty)*
Nutmeg Ballet *(see Nutmeg Conservatory for the Arts)*
Nutmeg Conservatory for the Arts 475

Nuvo Coll. of Cosmetology 531
NuWave Sch. of Cosmetology *(see TLC NuWave Sch. of Cosmetology)*
Nyack Coll. 270
Nyack Hosp. 689
Nyack Missionary Coll. *(see Nyack Coll.)*
NYS Coll. of Agriculture & Life Sciences *(see Cornell Univ.)*
NYS Coll. of Human Ecology *(see Cornell Univ.)*
NYS Coll. of Veterinary Medicine *(see Cornell Univ.)*
NYS Sch. of Industrial & Labor Relations *(see Cornell Univ.)*

O

O Street Vocational Sch. *(see Margaret Murray Washington Vocational Sch.)*
O.T. Autry Area Vocational-Tech. Ctr. *(see Autry Techno. Ctr.)*
Oak Forest Hosp. 668
Oak Hills Bible Coll. *(see Oak Hills Christian Coll.)*
Oak Hills Bible Inst. *(see Oak Hills Christian Coll.)*
Oak Hills Christian Coll. 214
Oak Hills Christian Training Sch. *(see Oak Hills Christian Coll.)*
Oak Hills Coll. *(see Oak Hills Christian Coll.)*
Oakbridge Acad. of Arts 336
Oakland Bible Inst. *(see Patten Univ.)*
Oakland City Coll. *(see Oakland City Univ.)*
Oakland City Univ. 142
Oakland Comm. Coll. 203
Oakland Univ. 203
Oakton Coll. *(see Oakton Comm. Coll.)*
Oakton Comm. Coll. 129
Oakwood Coll. 7
Oakwood Inst. *(see Eden Theological Seminary)*
Oberlin Coll. 307
Oberlin Collegiate Inst. *(see Oberlin Coll.)*
Oberlin Conservatory of Music *(see Oberlin Coll.)*
Oblate Sch. of Theology 382
O'Brien's Training Ctr. 630
OC Tech *(see Orangeburg-Calhoun Tech. Coll.)*
Occidental Coll. 49
Occupational Ctr. of East Los Angeles *(see East Los Angeles Occupational Ctr.)*
Occupational Training Services 466, 722

Ocean Corporation, The 622
Ocean County Coll. 248
Ocean County Vocational Tech. Sch. 553
Oceaneering Coll. *(see National Polytechnic Coll. of Engineering & Oceaneering)*
Oceanside Coll. of Beauty 466
Oceanside-Carlsbad Jr. Coll. *(see Mira Costa Coll.)*
Ochsner Clinic Foundation *(see Ochsner Sch. of Allied Health Sciences, Our Lady of Holy Cross Coll.)*
Ochsner Clinic Foundation Sch. of Allied Health Sciences *(see Ochsner Sch. of Allied Health Sciences)*
Ochsner Sch. of Allied Health Sciences 673
Oconaluftee Civilian Conservation Ctr. *(see Oconaluftee Job Corps Civilian Conservation Ctr.)*
Oconaluftee Job Corps Civilian Conservation Ctr. 573
Odessa Coll. 382
Oehrlein Sch. of Cosmetology, Inc. 502
Office Techno. Coll. *(see Coll. of Office Techno.)*
Ogden Inst. of Massage Therapy 628
Ogden-Weber Applied Techno. Ctr. 737 *(see also Ogden-Weber Applied Techno. Coll.)*
Ogden-Weber Applied Techno. Coll. 737, 750
Ogden-Weber Coll. *(see Ogden-Weber Applied Techno. Coll.)*
Ogeechee Coll. *(see Ogeechee Tech. Coll.)*
Ogeechee Tech. Coll. 107, 726
Ogeechee Tech. Inst. 726 *(see also Ogeechee Tech. Coll.)*
Oglala Coll. *(see Oglala Lakota Coll.)*
Oglala Lakota Coll. 362
Oglala Sioux Comm. Coll. *(see Oglala Lakota Coll.)*
Ogle Sch. of Hair Design—Ft. Worth 622
Ogle Sch. of Hair Design—Hurst 622
Ogle Sch. of Hair, Skin & Nails 622
Oglethorpe Univ. 107
O'Hara's Beauty Acad—Orange *(see Colleen O'Hara's Beauty Acad—Orange)*
O'Hara's Beauty Acad—Santa Ana *(see Colleen O'Hara's Beauty Acad—Santa Ana)*
Ohio Acad. of Holistic Health, Inc. 582
Ohio Agricultural & Mechanical Coll. *(see Ohio State Univ.)*

Ohio Art Inst. *(see Art Inst. of Ohio—Cincinnati)*

Ohio Broadcasting Ctr. *(see Ohio Ctr. for Broadcasting)*

Ohio Bus. Coll. 307

Ohio Ctr. for Broadcasting 582

Ohio Ctr. for Broadcasting—Colorado 472

Ohio Coll. of Chiropody, The *(see Ohio Coll. of Podiatric Medicine)*

Ohio Coll. of Massotherapy 582

Ohio Coll. of Podiatric Medicine 307

Ohio County Techno. Ctr. 163 *(see also Ohio County Techno. Ctr.)*

Ohio Dominican Coll. *(see Ohio Dominican Univ.)*

Ohio Dominican Univ. 307

Ohio Hi Point Adult & Continuing Edu. *(see Ohio Hi Point Career Ctr.)*

Ohio Hi Point Adult Edu. Ctr. *(see Ohio Hi Point Career Ctr.)*

Ohio Hi Point Career Ctr. 582

Ohio Inst. of Art *(see Art Inst. of Ohio—Cincinnati)*

Ohio Inst. of Health Careers 582

Ohio Inst. of Health Careers—Columbus 734

Ohio Inst. of Photography & Techno. 307

Ohio Inst. of Techno. *(see DeVry Univ. Columbus)*

Ohio Med. Coll. *(see Med. Univ. of Ohio)*

Ohio Med. Uninversity *(see Med. Univ. of Ohio)*

Ohio Normal Univ. *(see Ohio Northern Univ.)*

Ohio Northern Univ. 307

Ohio Photography Inst. *(see Ohio Inst. of Photography & Techno.)*

Ohio Real Estate Preparatory Sch., The *(see Hondros Coll.)*

Ohio Sch. of Court Reporting *(see CIMS Coll.)*

Ohio State Barber Coll. *(see Ohio State Coll. of Barber Styling)*

Ohio State Barber Styling Coll. *(see Ohio State Coll. of Barber Styling)*

Ohio State Beauty Acad. 582

Ohio State Coll. of Barber Styling 582

Ohio State Sch. of Cosmetology—Columbus 582

Ohio State Sch. of Cosmetology—East 582

Ohio State Sch. of Cosmetology—Northland 582

Ohio State Sch. of Cosmetology—Westerville 583

Ohio State Univ., The 308

Ohio State Univ—Agricultural Tech. Inst., The 308

Ohio Tech. Coll. 583 *(see also DeVry Univ. Columbus)*

Ohio Truck Driving Sch. *(see Hamrick Truck Driving Sch.)*

Ohio Univ. 308

Ohio VA Healthcare System *(see Veterans Affairs Med. Ctr—Dayton)*

Ohio Valley Bus. Coll. *(see Ohio Valley Coll. of Techno.)*

Ohio Valley Coll. 739 *(see also Ohio Valley Univ.)*

Ohio Valley Coll. of Techno. 308

Ohio Valley General Hosp. 698

Ohio Valley Med. Ctr. 708

Ohio Valley Univ. 420, 739

Ohio Veterans Affairs Healthcare System *(see Veterans Affairs Med. Ctr—Dayton)*

Ohio Wesleyan Univ. 308

Ohlone Coll. 49

Ohlone Comm. Coll. Dist. 723

Oholei Torah Talmudical Seminary *(see Talmudical Seminary Oholei Torah)*

Ohr HaMeir Theological Seminary 270

Ohr Shimon Yisroel Rabbinical Coll. *(see Rabbinical Coll. of Ohr Shimon Yisroel)*

Ohr Somayach-Monsey *(see Ohr Somayach-Tanenbaum Educational Ctr.)*

Ohr Somayach-Tanenbaum Educational Ctr. 271

OIC Training Acad. *(see North Central West Virginia Opportunities Industrialization Ctr.)*

Okalhoma Coll. of Liberal Arts *(see Univ. of Science & Arts of Oklahoma)*

Okaloosa Applied Techno. Ctr. 487

Okaloosa-Walton Coll. 91, 725

Okaloosa-Walton Comm. Coll. 725 *(see also Okaloosa-Walton Coll.)*

Okanagan Univ. Coll. 712

Okefenokee Coll. *(see Okefenokee Tech. Coll.)*

Okefenokee Tech. Coll. 107, 726

Okefenokee Tech. Inst. 726 *(see also Okefenokee Tech. Coll.)*

Oklahoma Baptist Univ. 316

Oklahoma Christian Univ. 316 *(see also Cascade Coll.)*

Oklahoma Christian Univ. of Science & Arts *(see Oklahoma Christian Univ.)*

Oklahoma City Coll. *(see Oklahoma City Comm. Coll.)*

Oklahoma City Comm. Coll. 316

Oklahoma City Univ. 316

Oklahoma City VA Med. Ctr. *(see Veterans Affairs Med. Ctr—Oklahoma City)*

Oklahoma City Veterans Affairs Med. Ctr. *(see Veterans Affairs Med. Ctr—Oklahoma City)*

Oklahoma Coll. for Women *(see Univ. of Science & Arts of Oklahoma)*

Oklahoma Dale Carnegie Training *(see Ron Moore & Associates)*

Oklahoma Health Acad. *(see Oklahoma Health Acad—Moore, Oklahoma Health Acad—Tulsa)*

Oklahoma Health Acad—Moore 589

Oklahoma Health Acad—Tulsa 589

Oklahoma Health Ctr. at OU Med. Ctr. 695

Oklahoma Military Acad. *(see Rogers State Univ.)*

Oklahoma Panhandle State Coll. of Agricultural & Applied Science *(see Oklahoma Panhandle State Univ.)*

Oklahoma Panhandle State Univ. 317

Oklahoma Sch. of Mines & Metallurgy *(see Eastern Oklahoma State Coll.)*

Oklahoma Sch. of Photography, Inc. 589

Oklahoma State Univ. 317

Oklahoma State Univ. Coll. of Osteopathic Medicine *(see Oklahoma State Univ. Ctr. for Health Sciences)*

Oklahoma State Univ. Tech. Inst. *(see Oklahoma State Univ—Oklahoma City)*

Oklahoma State Univ—Oklahoma City 317

Oklahoma State Univ—Okmulgee 317

Oklahoma Techno. Ctr. *(see Metro Techno. Ctr—South Bryant, Metro Techno. Centers—Springlake)*

Oklahoma Techno. Inst. 758

Oklahoma Univ. *(see Oklahoma State Univ., Univ. of Oklahoma)*

Oklahoma Wesleyan Univ. 317

Old Dominion Job Corps Ctr. 633

Old Dominion Univ. 405

Old Texas Coll. of Osteopathic Medicine *(see Univ. of North Texas Health Science Ctr. at Fort Worth)*

Old Town Barber & Beauty Coll. 509

Old Town Beauty Coll. *(see Old Town Barber & Beauty Coll.)*

Old Westbury Coll. *(see State Univ. of New York Coll. at Old Westbury)*

Olean Bus. Inst. 271

Olin & Preston Inst. *(see Virginia Polytechnic Inst. & State Univ.)*

Olin Ctr. for Int'l. Study *(see Olin Ctr.)*
Olin Ctr., The 527
Olive-Harvey Coll. *(see City Colleges of Chicago—Olive-Harvey Coll.)*
Oliver Thein Beauty Sch. 731 *(see also Regency Beauty Inst.)*
Olivet Coll. 203
Olivet Inst. *(see Olivet Coll.)*
Olivet Nazarene Univ. 129
Olivet Univ. *(see Olivet Nazarene Univ.)*
Olney Central Coll. 129
Olney Coll. *(see Olney Central Coll.)*
Olympia Career Training Inst. 531
Olympia Coll—Chicago 454 *(see also Bryman Coll—San Francisco)*
Olympia Coll—Merrillville 506
Olympia Coll—Skokie 502
Olympia Inst. *(see Olympia Career Training Inst.)*
Olympia Tech. Comm. Coll. *(see South Puget Sound Comm. Coll.)*
Olympia Vocational Tech. Inst. *(see South Puget Sound Comm. Coll.)*
Olympian Univ. of Cosmetology 556
Olympic Coll. 413
Olympic Jr. Coll. *(see Olympic Coll.)*
Omaha Baptist Bible Coll. *(see Faith Baptist Bible Coll.)*
Omaha Baptist Bible Inst. *(see Faith Baptist Bible Coll.)*
Omaha Bible Inst. *(see Faith Baptist Bible Coll.)*
Omaha Coll. of Health Careers *(see Vatterott Coll—Spring Valley)*
Omaha Med. Coll. *(see Univ. of Nebraska Med. Ctr.)*
Omaha Nebraska Tech. Comm. Coll. *(see Metropolitan Comm. Coll.)*
Omaha Sch. of Massage Therapy 542
Omega Inst. 553
Omega Inst. of Cosmetology 517
Omega Studio's Sch. of Applied Recording Arts & Sciences 523
Omni Tech. Sch. 725, 734
OmniTech Inst. 494
O'More Coll. of Design 369
O'More Design Coll. *(see O'More Coll. of Design)*
Oneonta Coll. *(see State Univ. of New York Coll. at Oneonta)*
Onondaga Coll. *(see Onondaga Comm. Coll.)*
Onondaga Comm. Coll. 271
Onondaga-Cortland-Madison BOCES 757
Ontario Agricultural Coll. & Experimental Farm *(see Univ. of Guelph)*
Ontario Bible Coll. *(see Tyndale Univ. Coll. & Seminary)*

Ontario Coll. of Naturopathic Medicine, The *(see Canadian Coll. of Naturopathic Medicine)*
Ontario Inst. for Studies in Edu. *(see Univ. of Toronto)*
Ontario Pentecostal Bible Sch. *(see Master's Coll. & Seminary)*
Ontario Sch. of Agriculture *(see Univ. of Guelph)*
Onyx Beauty Acad. Inc. 756
Opelousas Sch. of Cosmetology, Inc 518
Open Bible Coll. *(see Eugene Bible Coll.)*
Open Univ., UK, The 437
Ophthalmology Inst. of Detroit *(see Detroit Inst. of Ophthalmology)*
Opthalmis Support & Training *(see Opthalmis Support & Training)*
Optometry Coll. of Illinois *(see Illinois Coll. of Optometry)*
Optometry Coll. of Pennsylvania *(see Pennsylvania Coll. of Optometry)*
Oral & Facial Surgical Ctr. 680
Oral Roberts Univ. 317
Orange Coast Coll. 50
Orange County Art Inst. *(see Art Inst. of California—Orange County)*
Orange County Children's Hosp. *(see Children's Hosp. of Orange County)*
Orange County Coll. *(see Orange County Comm. Coll.)*
Orange County Coll. of Court Reporting *(see South Coast Coll.)*
Orange County Comm. Coll. 271
Orange County State Coll. *(see California State Univ—Fullerton)*
Orange County Training Ctr. 466
Orange State Coll. *(see California State Univ—Fullerton)*
Orange Tech. Edu. Ctr—Mid Florida Tech 487
Orange Tech. Edu. Ctr—Orlando Tech 487
Orange Tech. Edu. Ctr—Westside Tech 487
Orange Tech. Edu. Ctr—Winter Park Tech 487
Orangeburg-Calhoun Tech. Coll. 358
Orangeburg-Calhoun Tech. Edu. Ctr. *(see Orangeburg-Calhoun Tech. Coll.)*
Orchard Lakes Schools *(see SS. Cyril & Methodius Seminary)*
Orchard Lakes Seminary *(see SS. Cyril & Methodius Seminary)*
Oregon Agricultural Coll. *(see Oregon State Univ.)*
Oregon Art & Craft Coll. *(see Oregon Coll. of Art & Craft)*

Oregon Career & Techno. Ctr. 583
Oregon Coast Culinary Inst. *(see Southwestern Oregon Comm. Coll.)*
Oregon Coll. of Art & Craft 322
Oregon Coll. of Oriental Medicine 322
Oregon Grad. Inst. Sch. of Science & Engineering at Oregon Health & Science Univ. 322 *(see also Oregon Health & Science Univ.)*
Oregon Health & Science Univ. 322
Oregon Health Sciences Univ. *(see Oregon Health & Science Univ.)*
Oregon Inst. *(see Oregon Inst. of Techno., Willamette Univ.)*
Oregon Inst. of Techno. 322
Oregon Sch. of Arts & Crafts *(see Oregon Coll. of Art & Craft)*
Oregon State Agricultural Coll. *(see Oregon State Univ.)*
Oregon State Coll. *(see Oregon State Univ.)*
Oregon State Hosp. 696
Oregon State Univ. 322
Oregon Univ. *(see Oregon State Univ., Univ. of Oregon)*
Oregon Univ. of Health & Science *(see Oregon Health & Science Univ.)*
Oriental Medicine Acad. of Austin *(see Acad. of Oriental Medicine at Austin)*
Oriental Medicine Coll. of Oregon *(see Oregon Coll. of Oriental Medicine)*
Oriental Medicine Coll. of Santa Barbara *(see Santa Barbara Coll. of Oriental Medicine)*
Oriental Medicine Coll. of the Midwest *(see Midwest Coll. of Oriental Medicine—Wisconsin)*
Oriental Medicine Inst. of Seattle *(see Seattle Inst. of Oriental Medicine)*
Oriental Sch. of Embalming *(see Mount Ida Coll.)*
Orlando Coll. *(see Florida Metropolitan Univ—Orlando North)*
Orlando Culinary Acad. 91
Orlando Dale Carnegie Training *(see Ken Roberts Corporation)*
Orlando English Instiute 588
Orlando Montessori Teacher Edu. Inst. 487
Orlando Tech *(see Orange Tech. Edu. Ctr—Orlando Tech)*
Orleans Seminary *(see Central Christian Coll. of Kansas)*
Orleans Tech. Inst. 337, 599
Orlo Sch. of Hair Design & Cosmetology, The 569
ORT Tech. Inst. of Los Angeles *(see Los Angeles ORT Tech. Inst.)*

Osaka Sangyo Univ., Los Angeles *(see OSULA Edu. Ctr.)*
Osawatomie State Hosp. 672
Oscar Rose Jr. Coll. *(see Rose State Coll.)*
OSF Saint Francis Med. Ctr. 129
Oshkosh State Nomal Sch. *(see Univ. of Wisconsin—Oshkosh)*
Oshkosh State Teachers Coll. *(see Univ. of Wisconsin—Oshkosh)*
Osteopathic Med. Ctr. of Des Moines Univ. *(see Des Moines Univ—Osteopathic Med. Ctr.)*
Osteopathic Med. Coll. *(see Oklahoma State Univ. Ctr. for Health Sciences)*
Osteopathic Medicine Coll. of Lake Erie Coll. *(see Lake Erie Coll. of Osteopathic Medicine)*
Osteopathic Medicine Sch. of New Jersey *(see New Jersey Sch. of Osteopathic Medicine)*
OSU Okmulgee *(see Oklahoma State Univ—Okmulgee)*
OSULA Edu. Ctr. 466
Oswego Coll. *(see State Univ. of New York Coll. at Oswego)*
Otero Jr. Coll. 69
Otis Coll. of Art & Design 50
Ottawa Univ. 155 *(see also Univ. of Ottawa)*
Otterbein Coll. 309
Ottumwa Heights Coll. *(see Indian Hills Comm. Coll.)*
Ouachita Baptist Coll. *(see Ouachita Baptist Univ.)*
Ouachita Baptist Univ. 26
Ouachita Tech. Coll. 26
Ouachita Univ. *(see Ouachita Baptist Univ.)*
Ouachita Vocational Tech. Sch. *(see Ouachita Tech. Coll.)*
Our Lady of Angels Coll. *(see Neumann Coll.)*
Our Lady of Grace Coll. *(see Briar Cliff Univ.)*
Our Lady of Holy Cross Coll. 173
Our Lady of the Elms Coll. *(see Coll. of Our Lady of the Elms)*
Our Lady of the Lake Coll. 173
Our Lady of the Lake Univ. 382
Overlook Hosp. 684
Overton Brooks VA Med. Ctr. *(see Overton Brooks Veterans Affairs Med. Ctr.)*
Overton Brooks Veterans Affairs Med. Ctr., The 674
Owens Coll. *(see Owens Comm. Coll.)*
Owens Comm. Coll. 309
Owens Tech. Coll. *(see Owens Comm. Coll.)*

Owensboro Coll. *(see Owensboro Comm. & Tech. Coll.)*
Owensboro Comm. & Tech. Coll. 163, 729
Owensboro Comm. & Tech. Coll— Frederica Street Campus 729
Owensboro Comm. Coll. 729 *(see also Owensboro Comm. & Tech. Coll.)*
Owensboro Jr. Coll. of Bus. *(see Daymar Coll.)*
Owensboro Mercy Health System 672
Owensboro Tech. Coll. 729 *(see also Owensboro Comm. & Tech. Coll.)*
Oxford Grad. Sch. 749
Oxman Coll. of San Francisco 466
Oxnard Coll. 50
Ozark Bible Coll. *(see Ozark Christian Coll.)*
Ozark Christian Coll. 229
Ozark Coll. *(see Ozark Christian Coll.)*
Ozark Comm. Coll. *(see Enterprise-Ozark Comm. Coll.)*
Ozarka Coll. 26
Ozarka Tech. Coll. *(see Ozarka Coll.)*
Ozarka Vocational-Tech. Sch. *(see Ozarka Coll.)*
Ozarks Coll. *(see Coll. of the Ozarks, Ozarks Tech. Comm. Coll.)*
Ozarks Comm. Coll. *(see Ozarks Tech. Comm. Coll.)*
Ozarks Tech. Comm. Coll. 229

P

P & A Scholars Beauty Sch., Inc. 531
P. B. Cosmetology Edu. Centre 553
Pa. Barber Sch. 758
Pace Coll. *(see Pace Univ.)*
Pace Inst. 337 *(see also Pace Univ.)*
Pace Sch. of Accountancy *(see Pace Univ.)*
Pace Univ. 271
Pace Univ. Sch. of Law *(see Pace Univ. White Plains Campus)*
Pacific Bible Coll. *(see Azusa Pacific Univ., Point Loma Nazarene Univ., Warner Pacific Coll.)*
Pacific Bible Inst. *(see Fresno Pacific Univ.)*
Pacific Christian Coll. *(see Hope Int'l. Univ.)*
Pacific Church Divinity Sch. *(see Church Divinity Sch. of the Pacific)*
Pacific Clinics 655
Pacific Coast Baptist Theological Seminary *(see American Baptist Seminary of the West)*
Pacific Coll. 466
Pacific Coll. of Chiropractic *(see Western States Chiropractic Coll.)*

Pacific Coll. of Oriental Medicine 50
Pacific Coll. of Oriental Medicine— New York 271
Pacific Grad. Sch. of Psychology 50
Pacific Health Ministry 665
Pacific Islands Bible Coll. 112
Pacific Islands VA Healthcare System *(see Veterans Affairs Pacific Islands Healthcare System)*
Pacific Islands Veterans Affairs Healthcare System *(see Veterans Affairs Pacific Islands Healthcare System)*
Pacific Lutheran Coll. *(see Pacific Lutheran Univ.)*
Pacific Lutheran Seminary *(see Pacific Lutheran Theological Seminary)*
Pacific Lutheran Theological Seminary 50
Pacific Lutheran Univ. 414
Pacific Northwest Ballet Sch. 638
Pacific Northwest Coll. of Art 323
Pacific Oaks Coll. 50
Pacific Oriental Coll. of Medicine *(see Pacific Coll. of Oriental Medicine)*
Pacific Sch. of Religion 50
Pacific States Chiropractic Coll. *(see Life Chiropractic Coll. West)*
Pacific States Univ. 50
Pacific Theological Seminary *(see Pacific Sch. of Religion)*
Pacific Travel Inst. *(see Travel Inst. of the Pacific)*
Pacific Travel Sch. *(see Pacific Travel Trade Sch.)*
Pacific Union Coll. 50
Pacific Univ. 323 *(see also Univ. of the Pacific)*
Pacifica Grad. Inst. 50
Pacifica Inst. *(see Pacifica Grad. Inst.)*
Packard Children's Hosp. *(see Lucile Packard Children's Hosp.)*
Padrick's Univ. of Cosmetology *(see Arnold/Padrick's Univ. of Cosmetology)*
Paducah Area Techno. Ctr. 165
Paducah Coll. *(see Paducah Tech. Coll.)*
Paducah Comm. Coll. 729 *(see also West Kentucky Comm. & Tech. Coll.)*
Paducah Jr. Coll. *(see West Kentucky Comm. & Tech. Coll.)*
Paducah Tech. Coll. 163
Paier Coll. of Art 74
Paine Coll. 107
Palace Beauty Coll. 467
Palladium Tech. Acad. 754
Palm Beach Atlantic Coll. *(see Palm Beach Atlantic Univ.)*
Palm Beach Atlantic Univ. 91

Palm Beach Coll. *(see Palm Beach Comm. Coll.)*
Palm Beach Comm. Coll. 91
Palmer Coll. *(see Midlands Tech. Coll., Trident Tech. Coll.)*
Palmer Coll. of Chiropractic 149
Palmer Coll. of Chiropractic—West 50
Palmer Sch. & Cure *(see Palmer Coll. of Chiropractic)*
Palmer Theological Seminary, The 337, 735
Palmetto Health Alliance *(see Palmetto Health Baptist Hosp.)*
Palmetto Health Baptist Hosp. 701
Palmetto Richland Mem. Hosp. 701
Palo Alto Coll. 382
Palo Alto VA Med. Ctr. *(see Veterans Affairs Palo Alto Health Care System)*
Palo Alto Veterans Affairs Med. Ctr. *(see Veterans Affairs Palo Alto Health Care System)*
Palo Verde Coll. 50
Palo Verde Comm. Coll. *(see Palo Verde Coll.)*
Palo Verde Jr. Coll. *(see Palo Verde Coll.)*
Palomar Coll. 51
Palomar Comm. Coll. *(see Palomar Coll.)*
Palomar Inst. of Cosmetology 467
Pals & Associates, Inc. *(see David L. Pals & Associates, Inc.)*
Pamlico Comm. Coll. 291
Pan American Coll. *(see Univ. of Texas—Pan American)*
Pan American Univ. *(see Univ. of Texas—Pan American)*
Panhandle Agricultural & Mechanical Coll. *(see Oklahoma Panhandle State Univ.)*
Pan-Handle Agricultural Inst. *(see Oklahoma Panhandle State Univ.)*
Panhandle State Univ. *(see Oklahoma Panhandle State Univ.)*
Panola Coll. 382
Paper Science & Techno. Inst. *(see Georgia Inst. of Techno., Inst. of Paper Science & Techno. at Georgia Tech)*
Paradise Valley Coll. *(see Paradise Valley Comm. Coll.)*
Paradise Valley Comm. Coll. 18
Paralegal Inst., Inc., The 18
Paralegal Sch. of New York *(see New York Paralegal Sch.)*
Paramedical Coll. of Ponce *(see Ponce Paramedical Coll.)*
Paramount Beauty Acad. 583

Paramount Sch. of Beauty 723 *(see also Marinello Sch. of Beauty—Paramount)*
Pardee Rand Grad. Sch. 51, 723
Parham Hosp. *(see Maria Parham Hosp., Inc.)*
Paris Beauty Coll. 467
Paris Coll. *(see Paris Jr. Coll.)*
Paris II Educational Ctr. 539
Paris Jr. Coll. 382
Parisian Beauty Acad. 553
Park Ctr., Inc. 670
Park Coll. *(see Park Univ.)*
Park Hosp. *(see Mercy Med. Ctr. North Iowa)*
Park Nicollet Health Services *(see Methodist Hosp.)*
Park Univ. 229
Parker Chiropractic Coll. *(see Parker Coll. of Chiropractic)*
Parker Coll. of Chiropractic 383
Parkersburg Branch of West Virginia Univ. *(see West Virginia Univ. at Parkersburg)*
Parkersburg Comm. Coll. *(see West Virginia Univ. at Parkersburg)*
Parkland Coll. 129
Parks Coll. 69, 231, 733 *(see also Saint Louis Univ.)*
Parks Hosp. *(see Glens Falls Hosp.)*
Parks Jr. Coll. *(see Parks Coll.)*
Parks Sch. of Bus. Administration *(see Parks Coll.)*
Parkview Hosp. 670
Parkview Med. Ctr. Sch. of Med. Techno. 658
Parkway West Vocational Tech. Sch. 698
Parkway West Vo-Tech Sch. *(see Parkway West Vocational Tech. Sch.)*
Parma Sch. of Practical Nursing *(see Cuyahoga Valley Career Ctr.)*
Parsons Jr. Coll. *(see Labette Comm. Coll.)*
Parsons New York *(see New Sch., Parsons Sch. of Design—New York)*
Parsons Paris *(see New Sch., Parsons Sch. of Design—Paris, France)*
Parsons Sch. of Design *(see New Sch.)*
Parsons Sch. of Design—New York 269
Parsons Sch. of Design—Paris, France 269
Parsons The New Sch. for Design *(see New Sch.)*
Partners Healthcare System *(see Brigham & Women's Hosp.)*

Partners in ESL, Inc. *(see Colorado Sch. of English)*
Pasadena City Coll. 51
Pasadena Coll. *(see Pasadena City Coll., Point Loma Nazarene Univ.)*
Pasadena Jr. Coll. *(see Pasadena City Coll.)*
Pasadena Univ. *(see Point Loma Nazarene Univ.)*
Pascack Valley Hosp. 684
Pasco-Hernando Coll. *(see Pasco-Hernando Comm. Coll.)*
Pasco-Hernando Comm. Coll. 92
Passaic Coll. *(see Passaic County Comm. Coll.)*
Passaic Comm. Coll. *(see Passaic County Comm. Coll.)*
Passaic County Coll. *(see Passaic County Comm. Coll.)*
Passaic County Comm. Coll. 248
Pastoral Edu. & Development Council *(see Council for Pastoral Edu. & Development)*
Pastoral Union of Connecticut *(see Hartford Seminary)*
Pat Goins Beauty Sch. 518
Pat Goins Benton Road Beauty Sch. 518
Pat Goins Ruston Beauty Sch. 518
Pat Goins Shreveport Beauty Sch. 518
Pat Thomas Law Enforcement Acad. 94, 725
Pat Wilson Beauty Coll., Inc. 513
Paterson City Normal Sch. *(see William Paterson Univ. of New Jersey)*
Paterson Coll. of New Jersey *(see William Paterson Univ. of New Jersey)*
Paterson State Coll. *(see William Paterson Univ. of New Jersey)*
Paterson Univ. *(see William Paterson Univ. of New Jersey)*
Patricia Stevens Coll. 230
Patrick B. Harris Hosp. *(see Patrick B. Harris Psychiatric Hosp.)*
Patrick B. Harris Psychiatric Hosp. 701
Patrick Henry Coll. 750 *(see also Patrick Henry Comm. Coll.)*
Patrick Henry Comm. Coll. 405
Patsy & Rob's Acad. of Beauty 539
Patten Coll. 723 *(see also Patten Univ.)*
Patten Univ. 51, 723
Patterson State Tech. Coll. *(see Trenholm State Tech. Coll.)*
Paul Acad. of Cosmetology Arts & Sciences *(see Robert Paul Acad. of Cosmetology Arts & Sciences)*

Paul D. Camp Coll. *(see Paul D. Camp Comm. Coll.)*
Paul D. Camp Comm. Coll. 405
Paul DiGrigoli Sch. of Cosmotology *(see DiGrigoli Sch. of Cosmotology, Inc.)*
Paul H. Nitze Sch. of Advanced Int'l. Studies, The 180
Paul Mitchell Partner Sch. *(see Bella Capelli Acad., North Haven Acad., Scot Lewis Sch-Paul Mitchell Partner Sch—Bloomington, Scot Lewis Sch-Paul Mitchell Partner Sch—Plymouth, Scot Lewis Schools-Paul Mitchell Partner Sch—Boise)*
Paul Mitchell Sch. *(see Paul Mitchell The Sch.)*
Paul Mitchell The Sch. 593, 628, 735, 737
Paul Mitchell The Sch—Cranston 736
Paul Mitchell-The Sch. 628
Paul Phillips & Associates, Inc. 518
Paul Quinn Coll. 383
Paul Smith's Coll. of Arts & Sciences 271
Payne Coll. *(see Howard Payne Univ.)*
Payne Theological Seminary 309
Payne Univ. *(see Howard Payne Univ.)*
PC AGE Career Inst. 733
PC AGE Career Inst—Newark 553
PC Professor of Boca Raton 487
PC Professor of West Palm Beach 488
PC Tech Learning Ctr. 553
PCDI *(see Prof. Career Development Inst.)*
PCI Coll. 467, 723
PCI Health Training Ctr. 622
PCI Houston *(see Prof. Careers Inst., Inc.)*
PCI Indianapolis *(see Prof. Careers Inst.)*
Peabody Inst. of the Johns Hopkins Univ. 180
Peace Coll. 291
Peagasus Edu., Inc. *(see Learning Tree Univ.)*
Pearl River Coll. *(see Pearl River Comm. Coll.)*
Pearl River Comm. Coll. 221
Peirce Coll. 337
Pelican Airways 725 *(see also Pelican Flight Training Ctr.)*
Pelican Flight Training Ctr. 488, 725
Pellissippi State Tech. Comm. Coll. 369
Pembroke State Coll. *(see Univ. of North Carolina at Pembroke)*
Pembroke State Coll. for Indians *(see Univ. of North Carolina at Pembroke)*

Pembroke State Univ. *(see Univ. of North Carolina at Pembroke)*
Peninsula Coll. 414
Peninsula Hosp. & Med. Ctr. *(see Mills-Peninsula Health Services)*
Peninsula Hosp. Ctr. 689
Peninsula Med. Ctr. *(see Mills-Peninsula Health Services)*
Penn *(see Univ. of Pennsylvania)*
Penn Coll. *(see Pennsylvania Coll. of Techno., William Penn Univ.)*
Penn Commercial Bus. & Techno. Sch. *(see Penn Commercial, Inc.)*
Penn Commercial, Inc. 337
Penn Council for Relationships 735 *(see also Council for Relationahips)*
Penn Foster Career Sch. 337, 599, 735, 736
Penn Morton Coll. *(see Widener Univ.)*
Penn State *(see Pennsylvania State Univ.)*
Penn State Altoona *(see Pennsylvania State Univ.)*
Penn State Beaver *(see Pennsylvania State Univ.)*
Penn State Berks *(see Pennsylvania State Univ.)*
Penn State Cosmetology Acad. 599
Penn State Delaware County *(see Pennsylvania State Univ.)*
Penn State DuBois *(see Pennsylvania State Univ.)*
Penn State Erie *(see Pennsylvania State Univ.)*
Penn State Great Valley Grad. Ctr. *(see Pennsylvania State Univ.)*
Penn State Harrisburg *(see Pennsylvania State Univ.)*
Penn State Hazleton *(see Pennsylvania State Univ.)*
Penn State Lehigh Valley *(see Pennsylvania State Univ.)*
Penn State McKeesport *(see Pennsylvania State Univ.)*
Penn State Mont Alto *(see Pennsylvania State Univ.)*
Penn State New Kensington *(see Pennsylvania State Univ.)*
Penn State Schuylkill *(see Pennsylvania State Univ.)*
Penn State Shenango *(see Pennsylvania State Univ.)*
Penn State Wilkes-Barre *(see Pennsylvania State Univ.)*
Penn State Worthington-Scranton *(see Pennsylvania State Univ.)*
Penn State Wyomissing Ctr. *(see Pennsylvania State Univ.)*
Penn State York *(see Pennsylvania State Univ.)*

Penn State, The Eberly Campus *(see Pennsylvania State Univ.)*
Penn Univ. *(see William Penn Univ.)*
Penn Valley Coll. *(see Penn Valley Comm. Coll.)*
Penn Valley Comm. Coll. 230
Pennco Tech 337, 553
Pennsylvania Acad. of Cosmetology Arts & Sciences—Dubois 599
Pennsylvania Acad. of Cosmetology Arts & Sciences—Johnstown 599
Pennsylvania Acad. of Music, The 599
Pennsylvania Acad. of the Fine Arts 337
Pennsylvania Barber Sch. *(see Pa. Barber Sch.)*
Pennsylvania Bus. Inst. *(see Bus. Inst. of Pennsylvania)*
Pennsylvania Coll. for Women *(see Chatham Coll.)*
Pennsylvania Coll. of Art & Design 337, 735, 749
Pennsylvania Coll. of Optometry 337
Pennsylvania Coll. of Podiatric Medicine *(see Temple Univ.)*
Pennsylvania Coll. of Techno. 337
Pennsylvania Council for Relationships *(see Council for Relationahips)*
Pennsylvania Culinary Inst. 337, 735
Pennsylvania Female Coll. *(see Chatham Coll.)*
Pennsylvania Fine Arts Acad. *(see Pennsylvania Acad. of the Fine Arts)*
Pennsylvania Gunsmith Sch. 599
Pennsylvania Highlands Coll. *(see Pennsylvania Highlands Comm. Coll.)*
Pennsylvania Highlands Comm. Coll. 337, 735
Pennsylvania Inst. of Bus. *(see Bus. Inst. of Pennsylvania)*
Pennsylvania Inst. of Culinary Arts 735 *(see also Pennsylvania Culinary Inst.)*
Pennsylvania Inst. of Massage Therapy 735
Pennsylvania Inst. of Taxidermy 599
Pennsylvania Inst. of Techno. 338
Pennsylvania Language Inst. 588
Pennsylvania Military Acad. *(see Widener Univ.)*
Pennsylvania Military Coll. *(see Widener Univ.)*
Pennsylvania Museum & Sch. of Industrial Art *(see Univ. of the Arts)*
Pennsylvania Music Acad., The *(see Pennsylvania Acad. of Music)*

Accredited Institutions of Postsecondary Education | 2005–2006

Pennsylvania Optometry Coll. *(see Pennsylvania Coll. of Optometry)*
Pennsylvania Sch. of Art & Design 735 *(see also Pennsylvania Coll. of Art & Design)*
Pennsylvania Sch. of Bus. 735
Pennsylvania Sch. of Muscle Therapy, Ltd. 599
Pennsylvania Sch. of the Arts *(see Pennsylvania Coll. of Art & Design)*
Pennsylvania State Coll., The *(see Pennsylvania State Univ.)*
Pennsylvania State Forest Acad. *(see Pennsylvania State Univ.)*
Pennsylvania State Univ. Abington Campus 736
Pennsylvania State Univ. Allentown Campus 736
Pennsylvania State Univ. Dickinson Sch. of Law *(see Dickinson Sch. of Law of The Pennsylvania State Univ.)*
Pennsylvania State Univ. Fayette Campus 736
Pennsylvania State Univ. Fayette, The Eberly Campus 736
Pennsylvania State Univ. Ogontz Campus 736
Pennsylvania State Univ., The 338
Pennsylvania State Univ—Lehigh Valley Campus 736
Pennsylvania Techno. Coll. *(see Pennsylvania Coll. of Techno.)*
Penrose-Saint Francis Health Services 657
Pensacola Coll. *(see Pensacola Jr. Coll.)*
Pensacola Jr. Coll. 92
Penta Career Ctr. 583
Penta Career Ctr. Adult & Continuing Edu. *(see Penta Career Ctr.)*
Penta County Vocational Sch. *(see Penta Career Ctr.)*
Pentacostal Bible Coll. of Puerto Rico *(see Colegio Biblico Pentecostal de Puerto Rico)*
People's Bible Sch. *(see John Wesley Coll.)*
Pepperdine Coll. *(see Pepperdine Univ.)*
Pepperdine Univ. 51
Peralta Coll. for Non-Traditional Study *(see Vista Comm. Coll.)*
Performance Training 553
Performance Training Associates, Inc. 527
Perkins Comprehensive Rehabilitation Ctr. *(see Carl D. Perkins Comprehensive Rehabilitation Ctr.)*

Perkins Job Corps Ctr. *(see Carl D. Perkins Job Corps Ctr.)*
Perry Point VA Med. Ctr. *(see Veterans Affairs Med. Ctr—Perry Point)*
Perry Point Veterans Affairs Med. Ctr. *(see Veterans Affairs Med. Ctr—Perry Point)*
Perry Tech. Inst. 638
Peru Coll. *(see Peru State Coll.)*
Peru State Coll. 238
Peter Kump's New York Cooking Sch. *(see Inst. of Culinary Edu.)*
Petit Jean Coll. 721
Pettis Mem. Veterans Affairs Hosp. *(see Loma Linda Veterans Affairs Healthcare System)*
Pfeiffer Coll. *(see Pfeiffer Univ.)*
Pfeiffer Jr. Coll. *(see Pfeiffer Univ.)*
Pfeiffer Univ. 291
Phagans' Beauty Coll. 593
Phagans' Central Oregon Beauty Coll. 593
Phagans' Grants Pass Coll. of Beauty 593
Phagans' Medford Beauty Sch. 593
Phagans' Newport Acad. of Cosmetology Careers 593
Phagans' Orchards Beauty Sch. 638
Phagans' Sch. of Beauty 593
Phagans' Sch. of Hair Design 593
Phagans' Schools Northwest *(see Phagans' Tigard Beauty Sch.)*
Phagans' Tigard Beauty Sch. 593
Pharmacy Coll. of Albany *(see Albany Coll. of Pharmacy of Union Univ.)*
Pharmacy Coll. of Nevada *(see Univ. of Southern Nevada)*
PHD Hair Acad. 725
Philadelphia Art Inst. *(see Art Inst. of Philadelphia)*
Philadelphia Bible Inst. *(see Philadelphia Biblical Univ.)*
Philadelphia Biblical Univ. 339, 736
Philadelphia Child & Family Therapy Training Ctr. 699
Philadelphia Coll. & Infirmary of Osteopathy *(see Philadelphia Coll. of Osteopathic Medicine)*
Philadelphia Coll. of Art *(see Univ. of the Arts)*
Philadelphia Coll. of Bible 736 *(see also Philadelphia Biblical Univ.)*
Philadelphia Coll. of Osteopathic Medicine 339
Philadelphia Coll. of Pharmacy *(see Univ. of the Sciences in Philadelphia)*
Philadelphia Coll. of Textiles & Science *(see Philadelphia Univ.)*
Philadelphia Comm. Coll. *(see Comm. Coll. of Philadelphia)*

Philadelphia Divinity Sch. *(see Episcopal Divinity Sch.)*
Philadelphia Inst. of Art *(see Art Inst. of Philadelphia)*
Philadelphia Lutheran Seminary *(see Lutheran Theological Seminary at Philadelphia)*
Philadelphia Marriage Counse, The *(see Council for Relationahips)*
Philadelphia Museum Sch. of Art *(see Univ. of the Arts)*
Philadelphia Musical Acad. *(see Univ. of the Arts)*
Philadelphia Osteopathy Coll. *(see Philadelphia Coll. of Osteopathic Medicine)*
Philadelphia Pharmacy Coll. *(see Univ. of the Sciences in Philadelphia)*
Philadelphia Sch. of Design for Women *(see Moore Coll. of Art & Design)*
Philadelphia Sch. of Massage Therapy 733, 736 *(see also National Massage Therapy Inst.)*
Philadelphia Sch. of the Bible *(see Philadelphia Biblical Univ.)*
Philadelphia Sciences Univ. *(see Univ. of the Sciences in Philadelphia)*
Philadelphia Textile Inst. *(see Philadelphia Univ.)*
Philadelphia Textile Sch. *(see Philadelphia Univ.)*
Philadelphia Univ. 339
Philadelphia VA Med. Ctr. *(see Veterans Affairs Med. Ctr— Philadelphia)*
Philadelphia Veterans Affairs Med. Ctr. *(see Veterans Affairs Med. Ctr— Philadelphia)*
Philander Smith Coll. 26
Philhaven 699
Phillips & Associates, Inc. *(see Paul Phillips & Associates, Inc.)*
Phillips Beth Israel Sch. of Nursing 689
Phillips Bus. Coll. *(see Miller-Motte Tech. Coll.)*
Phillips Coll. *(see Frank Phillips Coll., Las Vegas Coll.)*
Phillips Comm. Coll. of the Univ. of Arkansas 26
Phillips Grad. Inst. 51
Phillips Grad. Seminary *(see Phillips Theological Seminary)*
Phillips Hairstyling Inst. 569
Phillips Inst. *(see Phillips Grad. Inst.)*
Phillips Jr. Coll. *(see Mountain West Coll.)*
Phillips Sch. of Theology *(see Interdenominational Theological Ctr.)*

Phillips Seminary *(see Phillips Theological Seminary)*
Phillips Theological Seminary 317
Phoebe Ministries 699
Phoenix Art Inst. *(see Art Inst. of Phoenix)*
Phoenix Career Coll. *(see Long Tech. Coll—East Valley)*
Phoenix Career Coll. 721
Phoenix Coll. 18
Phoenix East Aviation, Inc. 488
Phoenix Inst. *(see Art Inst. of Phoenix, Phoenix Inst. of Herbal Medicine & Acupuncture)*
Phoenix Inst. of Art *(see Art Inst. of Phoenix)*
Phoenix Inst. of Herbal Medicine & Acupuncture 652
Phoenix Jr. Coll. *(see Mesa Comm. Coll., Phoenix Coll.)*
Phoenix Seminary *(see Phoenix Seminary)*
Phoenix Seminary 18
Phoenix Therapeutic Massage Coll. 446
Photographic Ctr. Northwest, The 638
Photography & Techno. Inst. of Ohio *(see Ohio Inst. of Photography & Techno.)*
Photography Sch. of New England *(see New England Sch. of Photography)*
Photography Sch. of Oklahoma *(see Oklahoma Sch. of Photography, Inc.)*
Photoshop Users Assoc. *(see National Assoc. of Photoshop Professionals)*
Physical Theater Sch. *(see Dell'Arte Internatinal Sch. of Physical Theater)*
Pickaway-Ross Career & Techno. Ctr. 583
Pickaway-Ross Vocational Ctr. *(see Pickaway-Ross Career & Techno. Ctr.)*
Pickens Beauty Coll. *(see Moler-Pickens Beauty Coll.)*
Pickens Tech *(see T.H. Pickens Tech. Ctr.)*
Pickens Tech. Ctr. *(see T.H. Pickens Tech. Ctr.)*
Picower Inst. for Med. Research *(see North Shore Long Island Jewish Grad. Sch. of Molecular Medicine)*
Piedmont Area Program 701
Piedmont Baptist Coll. 291, 725, 734
Piedmont Bible Coll. *(see Piedmont Baptist Coll.)*

Piedmont Coll. 107 *(see also Piedmont Baptist Coll., Piedmont Comm. Coll., Piedmont Tech. Coll.)*
Piedmont Comm. Coll. 291
Piedmont Tech. Coll. 358
Piedmont Tech. Edu. Ctr. *(see Piedmont Tech. Coll.)*
Piedmont Virginia Coll. *(see Piedmont Virginia Comm. Coll.)*
Piedmont Virginia Comm. Coll. 405
Pierce Coll. 414 *(see also Franklin Pierce Coll., Los Angeles Pierce Coll.)*
Pierce Coll. at Puyallup *(see Pierce Coll. Puyallup)*
Pierce Coll. Dist. 11 *(see Pierce Coll. Fort Steilacoom, Pierce Coll. Puyallup)*
Pierce Coll. of Los Angeles *(see Los Angeles Pierce Coll.)*
Pierce Law Ctr. *(see Franklin Pierce Law Ctr.)*
Pierre's Sch. of Cosmetology 519
Pierre's Sch. of Cosmetology—Bangor 519
Pikes Peak Coll. *(see Pikes Peak Comm. Coll.)*
Pikes Peak Comm. Coll. 69
Pikeville Coll. 163
Pikeville Tech. Coll. *(see Big Sandy Comm. & Tech. Coll.)*
Pilgrim Bible Coll. *(see Oklahoma Wesleyan Univ.)*
Pillsbury Acad. *(see Pillsbury Baptist Bible Coll.)*
Pillsbury Baptist Bible Coll. 214
Pillsbury Coll. *(see Pillsbury Baptist Bible Coll.)*
Pima Comm. Coll. Dist. *(see Pima County Comm. Coll. Dist.)*
Pima County Comm. Coll. Dist. 19
Pima Med. Inst. 19
Pima Med. Inst—Albuquerque 556
Pima Med. Inst—Mesa 446
Pine City Area Vocational-Tech. Sch. *(see Pine Tech. Coll.)*
Pine Coll. *(see Pine Tech. Coll.)*
Pine Manor Coll. 191
Pine Rest Christian Mental Health Services 678
Pine Tech. Coll. 214
Pinecrest Developmental Ctr. 674
Pinellas Tech. Edu. Ctr—Clearwater Campus 488
Pinellas Tech. Edu. Ctr—Saint Petersburg Campus 488
Pines Vocational-Tech. Sch. *(see Southeast Arkansas Coll.)*
Pineville Beauty Sch. 518
Pinnacle Career Inst. 230, 732

Pinnacle Career Inst—Lawrence 510, 728
Pinnacle Inst. of Cosmetology, Inc 573
Pioneer Adult Full-Service Ctr. *(see Pioneer Career & Tech. Ctr.)*
Pioneer Bus. Coll. in America, The *(see Duff's Bus. Inst.)*
Pioneer Career & Tech. Ctr. 583
Pioneer Comm. Coll. *(see Penn Valley Comm. Coll.)*
Pioneer Pacific Coll. 323
Pioneer Sch. *(see Hope Coll.)*
Pipo Acad. of Hair Design 622
Pitt *(see Pitt Comm. Coll., Univ. of Pittsburgh)*
Pitt Bradford *(see Univ. of Pittsburgh Bradford Campus)*
Pitt Coll. *(see Pitt Comm. Coll.)*
Pitt Comm. Coll. 291
Pitt Industrial Edu. Ctr. *(see Pitt Comm. Coll.)*
Pitt Tech. Inst. *(see Pitt Comm. Coll.)*
Pittsburg State Univ. 156
Pittsburg Univ. *(see Pittsburg State Univ.)*
Pittsburgh Acad. *(see Univ. of Pittsburgh)*
Pittsburgh Art Inst. *(see Art Inst. of Pittsburgh)*
Pittsburgh Beauty Acad. 599
Pittsburgh Beauty Acad. of Charleroi 599
Pittsburgh Beauty Acad. of Greensburg 599
Pittsburgh Beauty Acad. of New Kensington 599
Pittsburgh Catholic Coll. of the Holy Ghost *(see Duquesne Univ.)*
Pittsburgh Children's Hosp. *(see Children's Hosp. of Pittsburgh)*
Pittsburgh Fillmmakers' Sch. of Film, Video & Photography 599
Pittsburgh Inst. of Aeronautics 339
Pittsburgh Inst. of Art *(see Art Inst. of Pittsburgh)*
Pittsburgh Inst. of Mortuary Science 339
Pittsburgh Seminary *(see Pittsburgh Theological Seminary)*
Pittsburgh Tech. Inst. 339
Pittsburgh Theological Seminary 339
Pittsburgh Univ. *(see Univ. of Pittsburgh)*
Pittsburgh Veterans Affairs Healthcare System *(see Veterans Affairs Pittsburgh Healthcare System)*
Pitzer Coll. 51
Pivot Point Int'l. Acad. 503
Pivot Point Int'l. Cosmetology Research Ctr. *(see Pivot Point Int'l. Acad.)*

Pivot Point the Masters 503

PJA Sch., The 339

PJ's Coll. of Cosmetology 513

PJ's Coll. of Cosmetology—Clarksville 506

PJ's Coll. of Cosmetology—Richmond 506

Placer Coll. *(see Sierra Coll.)*

Placer Jr. Coll. *(see Sierra Coll.)*

Plainfield Coll. *(see North Central Coll.)*

Planned Parenthood Federation of America 699

Planned Parenthood of Minnesota/South Dakota 679

Planned Parenthood of the Rocky Mountains 658

Platt Coll. 51, 70, 317, 723 *(see also Platt Coll. San Diego, Western Coll. of Southern California)*

Platt Coll. San Diego 51

Platteville Normal Sch. *(see Univ. of Wisconsin—Platteville)*

Platteville State Teachers Coll. *(see Univ. of Wisconsin—Platteville)*

Plattsburgh Coll. *(see State Univ. of New York Coll. at Plattsburgh)*

Plattsburgh State Univ. *(see State Univ. of New York Coll. at Plattsburgh)*

Play Therapy Inst. *(see Family Therapy/Play Therapy Inst.)*

Plaza Beauty Sch. 612

Plaza Bus. Inst. 734 *(see also Plaza Coll.)*

Plaza Coll. 271, 734

Plaza Sch. of Beauty Culture 608

Plaza Sch. of Techno. 733

Plymouth State Coll. 732 *(see also Plymouth State Univ.)*

Plymouth State Univ. 243, 732

PMC Coll. *(see Widener Univ.)*

Point Loma Coll. *(see Point Loma Nazarene Univ.)*

Point Loma Nazarene Coll. *(see Point Loma Nazarene Univ.)*

Point Loma Nazarene Univ. 51

Point Park Coll. 736 *(see also Point Park Univ.)*

Point Park Univ. 339, 736

Polaris Adult Edu. Ctr. *(see Polaris Career Ctr.)*

Polaris Career Ctr. 583

Polaris Vocational Ctr—Adult Edu. *(see Polaris Career Ctr.)*

Police Deptartment of New Orleans *(see New Orleans Police Dept.)*

Politec Inst. 605

Polk Coll. *(see Polk Comm. Coll.)*

Polk Comm. Coll. 92

POLY Languages Inst. 467

Polygraph Inst. *(see Dept. of Defense Polygraph Inst.)*

Polytechnic Inst. 622 *(see also Polytechnic Univ.)*

Polytechnic Inst. of Brooklyn *(see Polytechnic Univ.)*

Polytechnic Inst. of New York *(see Polytechnic Univ.)*

Polytechnic of Dubrovnik *(see American Coll. of Management & Techno.)*

Polytechnic Univ. 271 *(see also Universidad Politecnica de Puerto Rico)*

Polytechnic Univ. of Puerto Rico *(see Universidad Politecnica de Puerto Rico)*

Polytechnic Univ. of the Americas 351 *(see also Universidad Politecnica de Puerto Rico)*

Pomona Coll. 51

Ponca City Beauty Coll. 589

Ponce el Colegio Paramédico *(see Ponce Paramedical Coll.)*

Ponce Paramedical Coll. 350

Ponce Sch. of Medicine 350

Ponce Tech. Sch., Inc. 605

Pontifica Universidad Catolica de Puerto Rico—Arecibo *(see Pontifical Catholic Univ. of Puerto Rico Arecibo Campus)*

Pontifica Universidad Catolica de Puerto Rico—Guayama *(see Pontifical Catholic Univ. of Puerto Rico—Guayama Campus)*

Pontifica Universidad Catolica de Puerto Rico—Mayaguez *(see Pontifical Catholic Univ. of Puerto Rico—Mayaguez Campus)*

Pontifica Universidad Catolica de Puerto Rico—Ponce *(see Pontifical Catholic Univ. of Puerto Rico—Ponce Campus)*

Pontifical Catholic Univ. of Puerto Rico—Arecibo Campus 350

Pontifical Catholic Univ. of Puerto Rico—Guayama Campus 350

Pontifical Catholic Univ. of Puerto Rico—Mayaguez Campus 350

Pontifical Catholic Univ. of Puerto Rico—Ponce Campus 350

Pontifical Coll. Josephinum 309

Pontificia Universidad Catolica de Chile—Sch. of Journalism 714

Pontotoc County Techno. Ctr. *(see Pontotoc Techno. Ctr.)*

Pontotoc Techno. Ctr. 589

Pope John XXIII National Seminary 730 *(see also Blessed John XXIII National Seminary)*

Port Arthur Coll. *(see Lamar State Coll—Port Arthur)*

Port Huron Hosp. 678

Port Saint Lucie Beauty Acad. 483

Port St. Lucie Beauty Acad. *(see Fort Pierce Beauty Acad.)*

Portage Lakes Career Ctr. 583

Porter Adventist Hosp. 657

Porter & Chester Inst. 476 *(see also Connecticut Sch. of Electronics)*

Porter Mem. Health System *(see Porter Valparaiso Hosp.)*

Porter Sch. of Engineering Design *(see Porter & Chester Inst.)*

Porter Valparaiso Hosp. 670

Porter's Valparaiso Hosp. *(see Porter Valparaiso Hosp.)*

Porterville Coll. 52

Portfolio Ctr. 494

Portland Art Inst. *(see Art Inst. of Portland)*

Portland Coll. *(see Pacific Northwest Coll. of Art, Portland Comm. Coll.)*

Portland Coll. of Art *(see Pacific Northwest Coll. of Art)*

Portland Comm. Coll. 323

Portland Comm. Coll. Dist. *(see Portland Comm. Coll.)*

Portland Culinary Inst. *(see Western Culinary Inst.)*

Portland Inst. of Art *(see Art Inst. of Portland)*

Portland Med. Ctr. *(see Providence Portland Med. Ctr.)*

Portland Sch. of Art *(see Maine Coll. of Art)*

Portland Society of Art *(see Maine Coll. of Art)*

Portland State Univ. 323

Portland Univ. *(see Portland State Univ., Univ. of Portland)*

Portland VA Med. Ctr. *(see Veterans Affairs Med. Ctr—Portland)*

Portland Veterans Affairs Med. Ctr. *(see Veterans Affairs Med. Ctr—Portland)*

Portsmouth Beauty Sch. of Hair Design 544

Portsmouth Naval Med. Ctr. *(see Naval Med. Ctr. Portsmouth)*

Post Coll. *(see Post Univ.)*

Post Univ. 74, 724

Poteau Beauty Coll. 589

Poteau Comm. Coll. *(see Carl Albert State Coll.)*

Poteau Jr. Coll. *(see Carl Albert State Coll.)*

Potomac Acad. of Hair Design 738 *(see also Heritage Inst.)*

Potomac Acad. of Hair Design—Falls Church 738

Potomac Coll. 79, 744

Potomac Inst. of Massage Training *(see Potomac Massage Training Inst.)*

Potomac Massage Training Inst. 478

Potomac State Coll. of West Virginia Univ. 420

Potsdam Coll. *(see State Univ. of New York Coll. at Potsdam)*

Potsdam Normal Sch. *(see State Univ. of New York Coll. at Potsdam)*

Potsdam State Teachers Coll. *(see State Univ. of New York Coll. at Potsdam)*

Poway Acad. of Hair Design 467

Powder Springs Beauty Coll. 494

Powell & Associates, Inc. *(see Wade Powell & Associates, Inc.; Wray K. Powell & Associates, Inc.)*

Poynter Inst. for Media Studies, The 488

Practical Bible Coll. 734 *(see also Davis Coll.)*

Practical Bible Training Sch. *(see Davis Coll.)*

Practical Coll. *(see Davis Coll.)*

Practical Nursing Ctr. of Detroit *(see Detroit Practical Nursing Ctr.)*

Practical Nursing Sch. of Akron *(see Akron Sch. of Practical Nursing)*

Practical Schools 723 *(see also Westwood Coll—Long Beach)*

Prairie Bible Coll. 433, 752

Prairie Bible Inst. *(see Prairie Bible Coll.)*

Prairie Coll. *(see Prairie Bible Coll.)*

Prairie Grad. Sch. *(see Prairie Bible Coll.)*

Prairie State Coll. 129

Prairie View A&M Univ. 383

Prairie View State Normal & Industrial Coll. *(see Prairie View A&M Univ.)*

Prater Way Coll. of Beauty, Inc. 756

Pratt Coll. *(see Pratt Comm. Coll.)*

Pratt Comm. Coll. 156

Pratt Inst. 271

Praxis Inst. 488, 725

Premier Edu. Group, LP *(see Seacoast Career Schools)*

Premier Hair Acad. 628

Premier Training, Inc. Dale Carnegie Training 446, 721

Premiere Career Coll. 467

Presbyterian Coll. 358 *(see also Joint Board of Theological Colleges)*

Presbyterian Female Coll. *(see Queens Univ. of Charlotte)*

Presbyterian Healthcare Services 685

Presbyterian Healthcare System *(see Presbyterian Hosp.)*

Presbyterian Hosp. 692 *(see also Oklahoma Health Ctr. at OU Med. Ctr.)*

Presbyterian Jr. Coll. *(see Saint Andrews Presbyterian Coll.)*

Presbyterian Sch. for Indian Girls *(see Univ. of Tulsa)*

Presbyterian Sch. of Christian Edu. *(see Union Theological Seminary & Presbyterian Sch. of Christian Edu.)*

Presbyterian-St. Lukes Ctr. for Health Sciences Edu. *(see HealthONE Ctr. for Health Science Edu.)*

Prescott Ctr. Coll. *(see Prescott Coll.)*

Prescott Coll. 19

Presentation Coll. 362

Pressley Prof. Sch. of Cosmetology *(see David Pressley Sch. of Cosmetology)*

Pressley Sch. of Cosmetology *(see David Pressley Sch. of Cosmetology)*

Preston & Olin Inst. *(see Virginia Polytechnic Inst. & State Univ.)*

Prestonsburg Comm. Coll. 729 *(see also Big Sandy Comm. & Tech. Coll.)*

Primary Children's Med. Ctr. 705

Prime Cut Acad. of Hair & Nail Artistry 628

Prince Edward Island Univ. *(see Univ. of Prince Edward Island)*

Prince George's Coll. *(see Prince George's Comm. Coll.)*

Prince George's Comm. Coll. 181

Prince George's Hosp. Ctr. 675

Prince Inst. of Prof. Studies 7

Prince Reg. Vocational-Tech. Sch. *(see Albert I. Prince Reg. Vocational-Tech. Sch.)*

Prince William Sound Coll. *(see Prince William Sound Comm. Coll.)*

Prince William Sound Comm. Coll. 11

Princeton Agribusiness Training Ctr. 489 *(see also Robert Morgan Vocational-Tech. Instute)*

Princeton Baptist Med. Ctr. 651

Princeton Ctr. for Teacher Edu. 554

Princeton Information Techno. Ctr. 600

Princeton Theological Seminary 248

Princeton Univ. 248

Principia Coll. 129

Prism Career Inst. 554

Prism Career Inst—Hammonton 732

Private Industry Council *(see Edu. & Techno. Inst.)*

Pro Way Hair Sch. 494

Prof. Beauty Sch. 638

Prof. Bus. Coll. 272, 734

Prof. Bus. Inst. 734 *(see also Prof. Bus. Coll.)*

Prof. Career Development Inst. 494

Prof. Career Inst. 723 *(see also PCI Coll.)*

Prof. Career Inst. of North Texas *(see North Texas Prof. Career Inst.)*

Prof. Careers Acad. *(see Acad. of Prof. Careers)*

Prof. Careers Inst. 142 *(see also Inst. of Prof. Careers)*

Prof. Careers Inst., Inc. 623

Prof. Chefs Inst. of the South 518

Prof. Cosmetology Edu. Ctr. 448

Prof. Cosmetology Inst., Ltd. 728 *(see also Salon Prof. Acad.)*

Prof. Development Inst. *(see United States Army Inst. for Prof. Development)*

Prof. Electrical Sch. 605

Prof. Golfers Career Coll. 52

Prof. Hair Design Acad. 644

Prof. Health Training Acad. 755

Prof. Inst. of Beauty 467

Prof. Massage Training Ctr. 539

Prof. Practice Management Assoc. Inst. *(see Pace Inst.)*

Prof. Psychology Sch. of Chicago *(see Chicago Sch. of Prof. Psychology)*

Prof. Psychology Sch. of Colorado *(see Colorado Sch. of Prof. Psychology)*

Prof. Psychology Sch. of Wisconsin *(see Wisconsin Sch. of Prof. Psychology)*

Prof. Sch. of Translation *(see Babel Univ. Prof. Sch. of Translation)*

Prof. Skills Inst. 309

Prof. Tech. Institution 605

Prof. Training Ctr. 92

Prof.'s Choice Hair Design Acad. 503

Prospect Hall Sch. of Bus. 725

Protestant Episcopal Theological Seminary in Virginia 405

Providence Coll. 353

Providence Coll. & Theological Seminary 433

Providence Hosp. & Med. Centers 678

Providence Portland Med. Ctr. 696

Providence Saint Joseph Hosp. 655

Providence Saint Peter Hosp. 707

Providence Services *(see Benefis Healthcare—West Campus)*

ProvidenceTheological Seminary *(see Providence Coll. & Theological Seminary)*

Provo Coll. 395

Pro-Way Hari Sch. 726

Pruonto's Hair Design Inst. 600

Pryor Beauty Coll. 590

Psychoanalysis Grad. Sch. of Boston *(see Boston Grad. Sch. of Psychoanalysis)*

Psychological Studies Inst. 108

Pueblo Coll. *(see Pueblo Comm. Coll.)*

Pueblo Comm. Coll. 70

Pueblo Jr. Coll. *(see Colorado State Univ—Pueblo)*

Puerto Rican Adventist Coll. *(see Universidad Adventista de las Antillas)*

Puerto Rico Barber Coll. 605

Puerto Rico Conservatory of Music *(see Conservatory of Music of Puerto Rico)*

Puerto Rico Evangelical Seminary *(see Evangelical Seminary of Puerto Rico)*

Puerto Rico Jr. Coll. *(see Universidad del Este, Universidad del Turabo, Universidad Metropolitana)*

Puerto Rico Sch. of Plastic Arts *(see Escuela de Artes Plasticas de Puerto Rico)*

Puerto Rico Tech *(see Puerto Rico Tech. Jr. Coll.)*

Puerto Rico Tech. Jr. Coll. 350

Puerto Rico Techno. & Commercial Coll. *(see Colegio Tecnologico y Comercial de Puerto Rico)*

Puerto Rico Univ. at Utuado *(see Univ. of Puerto Rico at Utuado)*

Puerto Rico Univ—Aguadilla *(see Univ. of Puerto Rico at Aguadilla)*

Puerto Rico Univ—Arecibo *(see Univ. of Puerto Rico at Arecibo)*

Puerto Rico Univ—Bayamon *(see Univ. of Puerto Rico at Bayamon)*

Puerto Rico Univ—Carolina *(see Univ. of Puerto Rico at Carolina)*

Puerto Rico Univ—Cayey *(see Univ. of Puerto Rico at Cayey)*

Puerto Rico Univ—Humacao *(see Univ. of Puerto Rico at Humacao)*

Puerto Rico Univ—Mayaguez *(see Univ. of Puerto Rico at Mayaguez)*

Puerto Rico Univ—Med. Sciences Campus *(see Univ. of Puerto Rico—Med. Sciences Campus)*

Puerto Rico Univ—Ponce *(see Univ. of Puerto Rico at Ponce)*

Puerto Rico Univ—Rio Piedras *(see Univ. of Puerto Rico at Rio Piedras)*

Puget Sound Christian Coll. 414

Puget Sound Coll. *(see Puget Sound Christian Coll.)*

Puget Sound Coll. of the Bible *(see Puget Sound Christian Coll.)*

Puget Sound Inst. of Techno. *(see Bryman Coll.)*

Puget Sound Univ. *(see Univ. of Puget Sound)*

Pulaski Tech *(see Pulaski Tech. Coll.)*

Pulaski Tech. Coll. 26

Punxy Beauty Sch. of Cosmetology Arts & Science 600

Purchase Coll. *(see State Univ. of New York Coll. at Purchase)*

Purdue North Central *(see Purdue Univ. North Central)*

Purdue Univ. 142

Purdue Univ. at Kokomo *(see Purdue Univ. Sch. of Techno. at Kokomo)*

Purdue Univ. at New Albany *(see Purdue Univ. Sch. of Techno. at New Albany)*

Purdue Univ. at South Bend/Elkhart *(see Purdue Univ. Sch. of Techno. at South Bend/Elkhart)*

Purdue Univ. at Versailles *(see Purdue Univ. Sch. of Techno. at Versailles)*

Purdue Univ. Calumet 142

Purdue Univ. Columbus *(see Indiana Univ-Purdue Univ. Columbus)*

Purdue Univ. Fort Wayne *(see Indiana Univ-Purdue Univ. Fort Wayne)*

Purdue Univ. Indianapolis *(see Indiana Univ-Purdue Univ. Indianapolis)*

Purdue Univ. North Central 143

Putnam Career & Tech. Ctr. 641

Pyramid Career Inst. 503

Q

Quaker City Inst. of Aviation *(see Aviation Inst. of Maintenance)*

Quality Systems Management Grad. Sch. *(see National Grad. Sch.)*

Quantum Helicopters 446

Quapaw Tech. Inst. 721 *(see also National Park Comm. Coll. at Hot Springs)*

Quapaw Vocational Tech. Sch. *(see National Park Comm. Coll. at Hot Springs)*

Queen City Coll. 612

Queen of the Holy Rosary Coll. 52

Queens Coll. *(see City Univ. of New York Queens Coll.; Queens Univ. of Charlotte; Rutgers, The State Univ. of New Jersey New Brunswick Campus)*

Queens Coll. of Charlotte *(see Queens Univ. of Charlotte)*

Queens Hosp. Ctr. 689

Queen's Med. Ctr. 665

Queen's Theological Coll. 433

Queen's Univ. at Kingston 712

Queens Univ. of Charlotte 291

Queensborough Comm. Coll. *(see City Univ. of New York Queensborough Comm. Coll.)*

Quest Career Coll. 583, 734

Quest Coll. *(see Kaplan Univ.)*

Quicny Coll. & Seminary *(see Quincy Univ.)*

Quillen VA Med. Ctr. *(see James H. Quillen Veterans Affairs Med. Ctr.)*

Quimby Coll. *(see Southwestern Coll.)*

Quinco Behavioral Health Systems 670

Quincy Coll. 191

Quincy Jr. Coll. *(see Quincy Coll.)*

Quincy Tech. Coll. *(see Vatterott Coll—Quincy)*

Quincy Univ. 129

Quinebaug Valley Coll. *(see Quinebaug Valley Comm. Coll.)*

Quinebaug Valley Comm. Coll. 74

Quinebaug Valley Comm-Tech. Coll. *(see Quinebaug Valley Comm. Coll.)*

Quinn Coll. *(see Paul Quinn Coll.)*

Quinnipiac Coll. *(see Quinnipiac Univ.)*

Quinnipiac Univ. 74

Quinsigamond Coll. *(see Quinsigamond Comm. Coll.)*

Quinsigamond Comm. Coll. 191

Quorum Health Resources, Inc *(see Ohio Valley General Hosp.)*

R

R. C. Leffke & Associates, Inc. 737 *(see also John M. Jennings & Associates, Inc.)*

R.D. Hairstyling Coll., Inc. 575

R.L. Heron & Associates, Inc. 569

Rabbi Isaac Elchanan Seminary *(see Rabbi Isaac Elchanan Theological Seminary)*

Rabbi Isaac Elchanan Theological Seminary 272 *(see also Yeshiva Univ.)*

Rabbi Jacob Joseph Sch. 248

Rabbi Joseph Sch. *(see Rabbi Jacob Joseph Sch.)*

Rabbinical Acad. Mesivta Rabbi Chaim Berlin 272

Rabbinical Coll. Beth Shraga 272

Rabbinical Coll. Bobover Yeshiva B'nei Zion 272

Rabbinical Coll. Ch'san Sofer 272

Rabbinical Coll. of America 248

Rabbinical Coll. of Long Island 272

Rabbinical Coll. of Ohr Shimon Yisroel 272

Rabbinical Coll. of Telshe 309

Rabbinical Seminary Adas Yereim 272

Rabbinical Seminary M'kor Chaim 272
Rabbinical Seminary of America 272
Radcliffe Coll. *(see Radcliffe Inst. for Advanced Study)*
Radcliffe Inst. for Advanced Study 188
Radford Coll. *(see Radford Univ.)*
Radford M. Locklin Tech. Ctr. 488
Radford M. Locklin Vocational-Tech. Ctr. *(see Radford M. Locklin Tech. Ctr.)*
Radford State Teachers Coll. *(see Radford Univ.)*
Radford Univ. 405
Radiation Therapy Sch. for Radiation Therapy 663
Radiation Therapy Services, Inc. *(see Radiation Therapy Sch. for Radiation Therapy)*
Radio & Television Acad. *(see Acad. of Radio & Television Broadcasting)*
Radio & Television Broadcasting Acad. *(see Acad. of Radio & Television Broadcasting)*
Radiography Sch. of Fort Wayne *(see Fort Wayne Sch. of Radiography)*
Radville Christian Coll. *(see Western Christian Coll.)*
Rain Star Univ. *(see RainStar Univ.)*
RainStar Coll. *(see RainStar Univ.)*
RainStar Sch. of Therapeutic Massage *(see RainStar Univ.)*
RainStar Univ. 19
Rainy River Comm. Coll. 214
Raleigh Inst. *(see Shaw Univ.)*
Ralph Nichols Group, Inc. 531, 730
Ralph R. Willis Career Ctr. *(see Ralph R. Willis Vocational Tech. Ctr.)*
Ralph R. Willis Vocational Tech. Ctr. 641
Ralph R. Willis Vo-Tech Ctr. *(see Ralph R. Willis Vocational Tech. Ctr.)*
Ralph's Virginia Sch. of Cosmetology, Inc. 738 *(see also Legends Inst.)*
Ramapo Coll. of New Jersey 248
Ramirez Coll. of Bus. & Techno. 350
Rancho Santiago Comm. Coll—Santa Ana *(see Santa Ana Coll.)*
Rand Grad. Sch. 723 *(see also Pardee Rand Grad. Sch.)*
Rand Grad. Sch. of Policy Studies *(see Pardee Rand Grad. Sch.)*
Randall VA Med. Ctr. *(see Malcom Randall Veterans Affairs Med. Ctr.)*
Randall Veterans Affairs Med. Ctr. *(see Malcom Randall Veterans Affairs Med. Ctr.)*
Randazzo Vocational Training Inst. *(see Gretna Career Coll. Training Inst.)*

Randolph Coll. *(see Randolph Comm. Coll.)*
Randolph Comm. Coll. 291
Randolph State Normal Sch. *(see Vermont Tech. Coll.)*
Randolph-Macon Coll. 405
Randolph-Macon Woman's Coll. 405
Range Tech. Coll. *(see Fond du Lac Tribal & Comm. Coll.)*
Range Tech. Coll—Hibbing *(see Hibbing Comm. Coll.)*
Rangely Coll. *(see Colorado Northwestern Comm. Coll.)*
Ranger Coll. 383
Ranger Jr. Coll. *(see Ranger Coll.)*
Ranken Coll. *(see Ranken Tech. Coll.)*
Ranken Tech. Coll. 230
Raphael's Salem Beauty Acad. 583
Raphael's Sch. of Beauty Culture 583
Raphael's Sch. of Beauty Culture, Inc. 583
Rapid City Hosp. *(see Rapid City Reg. Hosp.)*
Rapid City Reg. Hosp. 702
Rapides Hosp. *(see Rapides Reg. Med. Ctr.)*
Rapides Reg. Med. Ctr. 674
Rappahannock Comm. Coll. 406
Raritan Valley Coll. *(see Raritan Valley Comm. Coll.)*
Raritan Valley Comm. Coll. 248
Ras Al Khaimah Men's Coll. *(see Higher Colleges of Techno. Ras Al Khaimah Men's Coll.)*
Ras Al Khaimah Women's Coll. *(see Higher Colleges of Techno. Ras Al Khaimah Women's Coll.)*
Rasmussen Coll—Eagan Campus 214
Rasmussen Coll—Mankato Campus 214
Rasmussen Coll—Minnetonka Campus 214
Rasmussen Coll—St. Cloud Campus 214
Ratledge Coll. *(see Cleveland Chiropractic Coll.)*
RAV Sch. of Prof. Studies *(see Virginia Sch. of Techno.)*
Ravenscroft Beauty Coll. 506
Ravenswood Hosp. *(see Advocate Illinois Masonic Med. Ctr.)*
Ray Coll. of Design *(see Illinois Inst. of Art)*
Raymond Walters Coll. *(see Univ. of Cincinnati—Raymond Walters Coll.)*
Ray's Faith Acad. of Beauty Edu. 518
Razzle Dazzle Coll. of Hair Design 497
RCA Inst. *(see Tech. Career Inst., Inc.)*
RCC Inst. of Techno. 740
RCH Tech. Inst. 738

Reading Area Coll. *(see Reading Area Comm. Coll.)*
Reading Area Comm. Coll. 340
Reading Dispensary *(see Reading Hosp. & Med. Ctr.)*
Reading Hosp. & Med. Ctr., The 699
Reconstructionist Rabbinical Coll. 340
Recording Arts & Sciences Conservatory *(see Conservatory of Recording Arts & Sciences)*
Recording Arts Coll. *(see Coll. for Recording Arts)*
Recording Workshop of Los Angeles *(see Los Angeles Recording Workshop)*
Red River Area Vocational Tech. Sch. 695
Red River Area Vo-Tech Sch. *(see Red River Area Vocational Tech. Sch.)*
Red River Coll. 712
Red River Tech. Coll. *(see Univ. of Arkansas Comm. Coll. at Hope)*
Red River Vocational Tech. Sch. *(see Univ. of Arkansas Comm. Coll. at Hope)*
Red Rocks Coll. *(see Red Rocks Comm. Coll.)*
Red Rocks Comm. Coll. 70
Red Wing Seminary *(see Luther Seminary)*
Red Wing Tech. Coll. *(see Minnesota State Coll-Southeast Tech.)*
Red Wing/Winona Techincal Coll— Red Wing *(see Minnesota State Coll-Southeast Tech.)*
Redlands Coll. *(see Redlands Comm. Coll.)*
Redlands Comm. Coll. 317
Redlands Univ. *(see Univ. of Redlands)*
Redwoods Coll. *(see Coll. of the Redwoods)*
Redwoods Comm. Coll. Dist. *(see Coll. of the Redwoods)*
Reed Coll. 323
Reedley Coll. 52
Reformed Bible Coll. 203
Reformed Bible Inst. *(see Reformed Bible Coll.)*
Reformed Presbyterian Seminary *(see Reformed Presbyterian Theological Seminary)*
Reformed Presbyterian Theological Seminary 340
Reformed Theological Seminary 221
Refrigeration Sch., The 19
Regecny Beauty Inst. 731
Regency Beauty Acad. 731 *(see also Regency Beauty Inst.)*
Regency Beauty Inst. 534, 731
Regency Sch. of Hair Design 513
Regent Coll. 433

Regent Language Training U.S.A 488

Regent Univ. 406

Regent USA *(see Regent Language Training U.S.A)*

Regents Coll. *(see Excelsior Coll.)*

Regents Coll. of the Univ. of the State of New York *(see Excelsior Coll.)*

Reg. Hosp. of Columbus *(see Columbus Reg. Hosp.)*

Reg. Hosp. of Northwest Georgia *(see Northwest Georgia Reg. Hosp.)*

Reg. West Med. Ctr. 682

Regis Coll. 192, 433

Regis Coll. in the Univ. of Toronto *(see Regis Coll.)*

Regis Univ. 70

Reid Hosp. & Health Care Services 670

Reid Mem. Hosp. *(see Reid Hosp. & Health Care Services)*

Reid State Coll. *(see Reid State Tech. Coll.)*

Reid State Tech. Coll. 7

Reid Tech. Coll. *(see Reid State Tech. Coll.)*

Reignbow Beauty Acad. *(see Reignbow Hair Fashion Inst.)*

Reignbow Beauty Acad., Inc. 554

Reignbow Hair Fashion Inst. 554 *(see also Reignbow Beauty Acad., Inc.)*

Reinhardt Acad. *(see Reinhardt Coll.)*

Reinhardt Coll. 108

Reinhardt Jr. Coll. *(see Reinhardt Coll.)*

Reinhardt Normal Coll. *(see Reinhardt Coll.)*

Religious Consultation & Research Society *(see Psychological Studies Inst.)*

Remington Coll. 728

Remington Coll—Baton Rouge 729

Remington Coll—Cleveland 309, 734

Remington Coll—Colorado Springs 724

Remington Coll—Dallas 383, 737

Remington Coll—Denver 724

Remington Coll—Fayatteville 721

Remington Coll—Ft. Worth 737

Remington Coll—Honolulu 727

Remington Coll—Houston 383, 737

Remington Coll—Jacksonville 725

Remington Coll—Lafayette 173, 729

Remington Coll—Largo 725

Remington Coll—Little Rock 721

Remington Coll—Memphis 736

Remington Coll—Mobile 7, 721

Remington Coll—New Orleans 173, 729

Remington Coll—San Diego 52, 722

Remington Coll—Tampa 92, 725

Remington Coll—Tempe 721

Renaissance Sch. of Therapeutic Massage 628

Renaissance Therapeutic Massage Sch. *(see Renaissance Sch. of Therapeutic Massage)*

Renasci Acad. of Hair, Inc. 476

Rend Lake Coll. 130

Reno Bus. Coll. *(see Morrison Univ.)*

Reno Univ. *(see Univ. of Nevada, Reno)*

Rensselaer at Hartford *(see Rensselaer Polytechnic Inst. at Hartford)*

Rensselaer Polytechnic Inst. 272

Rensselaer Polytechnic Inst. at Hartford 74

Renton Coll. *(see Renton Tech. Coll.)*

Renton Tech. Coll. 414

Reporting Acad. of Virginia *(see Virginia Sch. of Techno.)*

Research Coll. of Nursing 230

Research Med. Ctr. 680, 681

Restaurant Sch. at Walnut Hill Coll., The 340

Resurrection Health Care *(see Saint Francis Hosp-Resurrection Health Care)*

RETS Edu. Ctr. *(see CHI Inst—RETS Campus)*

RETS Electronic Inst. *(see Brown Mackie Coll—Louisville)*

RETS Electronic Schools 527

RETS Inst. of Techno. 729 *(see also Brown Mackie Coll—Louisville)*

RETS Inst—Nutley 733 *(see also HoHoKus RETS—Nutley)*

RETS Med. & Bus. Inst. *(see Brown Mackie Coll—Louisville)*

RETS Tech. Ctr. 309

RETS Tech. Training Ctr. *(see TESST Coll. of Techno.)*

RETS Training Ctr. *(see Remington Coll—New Orleans)*

Reuben Allen Coll. 612

Reuben Allen Cosmetology Coll. *(see Reuben Allen Coll.)*

Revans Univ-The Univ. of Action Learning 724

Rex Healthcare 692

Reynolds Coll. *(see J. Sargeant Reynolds Comm. Coll.)*

Reynolds Comm. Coll. *(see J. Sargeant Reynolds Comm. Coll.)*

Reynolds Mem. Hosp., Inc. *(see B.M. Spurr Sch. of Practical Nursing)*

Rhode Island Beauty Acad. 736

Rhode Island Coll. 353 *(see also Comm. Coll. of Rhode Island)*

Rhode Island Comm. Coll. *(see Comm. Coll. of Rhode Island)*

Rhode Island Hosp. 700

Rhode Island Jr. Coll—Knight Campus *(see Comm. Coll. of Rhode Island)*

Rhode Island Sch. of Design 353

Rhode Island Univ. *(see Univ. of Rhode Island)*

Rhodec Int'l. 437

Rhodes Coll. 369 *(see also Everest Coll., James A. Rhodes State Coll., Springfield Coll.)*

Rhodes State Coll. *(see James A. Rhodes State Coll.)*

Rice Aviation, A Division of A&J Enterprises *(see Westwood Aviation Inst—Los Angeles)*

Rice Aviation, A Division of Northrop Rice USA *(see Northrop Rice Aviation Inst. of Techno., Westwood Aviation Inst—Los Angeles)*

Rice Belt Tech. Inst. *(see Phillips Comm. Coll. of the Univ. of Arkansas)*

Rice Bible Coll. & Seminary *(see Luther Rice Bible Coll. & Seminary)*

Rice Hosp. *(see Rice Mem. Hosp.)*

Rice Inst., The *(see William Marsh Rice Univ.)*

Rice Mem. Hosp. 679

Rice Seminary *(see Luther Rice Bible Coll. & Seminary)*

Rice Univ. *(see William Marsh Rice Univ.)*

Rich Mountain Coll. *(see Rich Mountain Comm. Coll.)*

Rich Mountain Comm. Coll. 26

Rich Mountain Vocational-Tech. Sch. *(see Rich Mountain Comm. Coll.)*

Richard Bland Coll. 406

Richard J. Daley Coll. *(see City Colleges of Chicago—Richard J. Daley Coll.)*

Richard J. Solove Research Inst. *(see Ohio State Univ.)*

Richard L. Roudebush Veterans Affairs Med. Ctr. 670

Richard Stockton Coll. of New Jersey 249

Richard's Beauty Coll. 467, 723 *(see also Marinello Sch. of Beauty— Huntington Beach)*

Richfield Sch., The *(see Automotive Training Ctr.)*

Richland Coll. 383 *(see also Richland Comm. Coll.)*

Richland Comm. Coll. 130

Richland Tech. Edu. Ctr. *(see Midlands Tech. Coll.)*

Richmond Area Multi-Services, Inc. 655

Richmond Area Vocational Sch. *(see Augusta Tech. Coll.)*
Richmond Baptist Theological Seminary *(see Baptist Theological Seminary at Richmond)*
Richmond Coll. *(see Richmond, The American Int'l. Univ. in London; Richmond Comm. Coll.; Univ. of Richmond)*
Richmond Comm. Coll. 291
Richmond Inst. *(see Virginia Union Univ.)*
Richmond Maxi-Ctr. *(see Richmond Area Multi-Services, Inc.)*
Richmond Prof. Inst. *(see Virginia Commonwealth Univ.)*
Richmond Sch. of Health & Techno. 738 *(see also RSHT Training Ctr.)*
Richmond Tech. Coll. *(see Richmond Comm. Coll.)*
Richmond Tech. Inst. *(see Richmond Comm. Coll.)*
Richmond Theological Seminary *(see Virginia Union Univ.)*
Richmond Univ. *(see Univ. of Richmond)*
Richmond VA Med. Ctr. *(see Veterans Affairs Med. Ctr—Hunter Holmes McGuire)*
Richmond Veterans Affairs Med. Ctr. *(see Veterans Affairs Med. Ctr— Hunter Holmes McGuire)*
Richmond, The American Int'l. Univ. in London 437
Rick J. Gallegos & Associates, Inc. 488
Rick's Coll. *(see Brigham Young Univ—Idaho)*
Rider Bus. Coll., The *(see Rider Univ.)*
Rider Coll. *(see Rider Univ.)*
Rider Univ. 249
Rider-Moore & Stewart Sch. of Bus. *(see Rider Univ.)*
Ridge Vocational-Tech. Ctr. 488
Ridge Vo-Tech Ctr. *(see Ridge Vocational-Tech. Ctr.)*
Ridgewater Coll. 214
Ridley Secretarial Sch. *(see Ridley-Lowell Bus. & Tech. Inst.)*
Ridley-Lowell Bus. & Tech. Inst. 569
Riggs Le Mar Beauty Coll. 583
Right Way Computer Training Centers 723
Ringling Sch. of Art & Design 92
Rio Grande Bible Inst. 383
Rio Grande Coll. *(see Univ. of Rio Grande & Rio Grande Comm. Coll.)*
Rio Grande Coll—Del Rio Campus 385 *(see also Sul Ross State Univ.)*

Rio Grande Coll—Eagle Pass Campus 385 *(see also Sul Ross State Univ.)*
Rio Grande Coll—Uvalde Campus 385 *(see also Sul Ross State Univ.)*
Rio Grande Comm. Coll. *(see Univ. of Rio Grande & Rio Grande Comm. Coll.)*
Rio Grande Inst. *(see Rio Grande Bible Inst.)*
Rio Grande Univ. *(see Univ. of Rio Grande & Rio Grande Comm. Coll.)*
Rio Hondo Coll. 52
Rio Salado Coll. *(see Rio Salado Comm. Coll.)*
Rio Salado Comm. Coll. 20
Ripon Coll. 426
Rising Spirit Inst. of Natural Health 494
Rita's Moorhead Beauty Coll. 731 *(see also Ing'enue Beauty Sch.)*
River Falls Normal Sch. *(see Univ. of Wisconsin—River Falls)*
River Falls State Teacher's Coll. *(see Univ. of Wisconsin—River Falls)*
River Falls Teacher's Coll. *(see Univ. of Wisconsin—River Falls)*
River Oak Ctr. for Children 655
River Parishes Coll. *(see River Parishes Comm. Coll.)*
River Parishes Comm. Coll. 173
River Valley Services *(see Connecticut Valley Psychology Internship)*
Riverland Coll—Austin *(see Riverland Comm. Coll—Austin)*
Riverland Comm. Coll—Austin 214
Riverside City Coll. 52, 724
Riverside Coll. *(see Riverside City Coll.)*
Riverside Comm. Coll. 724 *(see also Riverside City Coll.)*
Riverside Hairstyling Acad. 488
Riverside Health System *(see Riverside Reg. Med. Ctr.)*
Riverside Hosp. *(see Riverside Reg. Med. Ctr.)*
Riverside Methodist Hosp/Grant Med. Ctr. 694
Riverside Reg. Med. Ctr. 706
Riverside Sch. of Health Careers *(see Riverside Reg. Med. Ctr.)*
Riverside Univ. *(see Univ. of California, Riverside)*
Rivertown Beauty Sch. *(see Rivertown Sch. of Beauty)*
Rivertown Sch. of Beauty 494
Rivier Coll. 243
Rizzieri Aveda Sch. for Beauty & Wellness 554, 733

Rizzieri Inst. 733 *(see also Rizzieri Aveda Sch. for Beauty & Wellness)*
Rizzieri Salon *(see Rizzieri Aveda Sch. for Beauty & Wellness)*
RMD Computer, Inc. 731
Roane Coll. *(see Roane State Comm. Coll.)*
Roane Comm. Coll. *(see Roane State Comm. Coll.)*
Roane County Tech. Ctr. *(see Roane Jackson Tech. Ctr.)*
Roane Jackson Tech. Ctr. 642
Roane State Comm. Coll. 369
Roanoke Bible Coll. 292
Roanoke Classical Seminary *(see Manchester Coll.)*
Roanoke Coll. 406 *(see also Roanoke Bible Coll.)*
Roanoke Valley Coll. of Health Sciences *(see Jefferson Coll. of Health Sciences)*
Roanoke Valley Comm. Hosp. Coll. of Health Sciences *(see Jefferson Coll. of Health Sciences)*
Roanoke-Chowan Coll. *(see Roanoke-Chowan Comm. Coll.)*
Roanoke-Chowan Comm. Coll. 292
Roanoke-Chowan Tech. Coll. *(see Roanoke-Chowan Comm. Coll.)*
Roanoke-Chowan Tech. Inst. *(see Roanoke-Chowan Comm. Coll.)*
Rob Roy Acad., Inc—New Bedford 527
Rob Roy Acad., Inc—Taunton Campus 527
Rob Roy Acad., Inc—Worcester 527
Rob Roy Acad-Fall River Campus 527
Robert Gordon Inst. of Techno. *(see Robert Gordon Univ.)*
Robert Gordon Univ., The 718
Robert Gordon's Coll. *(see Robert Gordon Univ.)*
Robert Gordon's Inst. of Techno. *(see Robert Gordon Univ.)*
Robert J. Hochstim Sch. of Radiography *(see South Nassau Communities Hosp.)*
Robert M. Scherer & Associates, Inc. 467
Robert Morgan Vocational-Tech. Inst. 489
Robert Morgan Vo-Tech Inst. *(see Robert Morgan Vocational-Tech. Inst.)*
Robert Morris Coll. 130 *(see also Robert Morris Univ.)*
Robert Morris Univ. 340
Robert Paul Acad. of Cosmetology Arts & Sciences 523

Robert Wood Johnson Med. Sch. 251 *(see also Univ. of Medicine & Dentistry of New Jersey)*
Roberto-Venn Sch. of Luthiery 446
Roberts Acad. of Hair Design *(see Dallas Roberts Acad. of Hair Design)*
Roberts Bus. Inst. 757
Roberts Coll. *(see Roberts Wesleyan Coll.)*
Roberts Corporation *(see Ken Roberts Corporation)*
Roberts Univ. *(see Oral Roberts Univ.)*
Roberts Wesleyan Coll. 272
Robertson Coll. 713
Robeson Coll. *(see Robeson Comm. Coll.)*
Robeson Comm. Coll. 292
Robeson Tech. Coll. *(see Robeson Comm. Coll.)*
Robeson Tech. Inst. *(see Robeson Comm. Coll.)*
Rochester Athenaeum *(see Rochester Inst. of Techno.)*
Rochester Bus. Inst. 272
Rochester Coll. 203 *(see also Rochester Comm. & Tech. Coll.)*
Rochester Comm. & Tech. Coll. 214
Rochester Comm. Coll. *(see Rochester Comm. & Tech. Coll.)*
Rochester General Hosp. 689 *(see also Isabella G. Hart Sch. of Practical Nursing)*
Rochester Inst. of Techno. 273
Rochester Methodist Hosp. 680
Rochester Nazareth Coll. *(see Nazareth Coll. of Rochester)*
Rochester Tech. Coll. *(see Rochester Comm. & Tech. Coll.)*
Rochester Theological Seminary *(see Colgate Rochester Crozer Divinity Sch.)*
Rochester Univ. *(see Univ. of Rochester)*
Rock Valley Coll. 130
Rockcastle Area Techno. Ctr. 673
Rockcastle County Area Techno. Ctr. *(see Rockcastle Area Techno. Ctr.)*
Rockefeller Career Ctr. *(see John D Rockefeller IV Career Ctr.)*
Rockefeller Univ. 273
Rockford Bus. Coll. 130
Rockford Coll. 130
Rockford Female Seminary *(see Rockford Coll.)*
Rockford Health System *(see Rockford Mem. Hosp.)*
Rockford Hosp. *(see Rockford Mem. Hosp.)*
Rockford Mem. Hosp. 668

Rockford Midstate Coll. of Commerce *(see Rockford Bus. Coll.)*
Rockford Sch. of Bus. *(see Rockford Bus. Coll.)*
Rockhurst Coll. *(see Rockhurst Univ.)*
Rockhurst Univ. 230
Rockingham Coll. *(see Rockingham Comm. Coll.)*
Rockingham Comm. Coll. 292
Rockingham Mem. Hosp. 706
Rockland Coll. *(see Rockland Comm. Coll.)*
Rockmont Coll. *(see Colorado Christian Univ.)*
Rocky Mountain Coll. 235, 433
Rocky Mountain Coll. of Art & Design 70
Rocky Mountain Pastoral Care & Training Associates 657
Rocky Mountain Univ. of Health Professions 750
Rodgers & Associates *(see J. R. Rodgers & Associates, Inc.)*
Roffler-Moler Hairstyling Coll. 495
Roger Williams Univ. 354
Roger's Acad. of Hair Design, Inc. 506
Rogers Mem. Veterans Hosp. *(see Edith Nourse Rogers Mem. Veterans Hosp.)*
Rogers State Coll. *(see Rogers State Univ.)*
Rogers State Univ. 317
Rogers Univ. *(see Rogers State Univ.)*
Rogers Univ—Tulsa Campus *(see Oklahoma State Univ.)*
Rogers VA Med. Ctr. *(see Edith Nourse Rogers Mem. Veterans Hosp.)*
Rogie's Sch. of Beauty Culture 606
Rogue Comm. Coll. 323
Rolla Area Vocational-Tech. Sch. *(see Rolla Tech. Inst.)*
Rolla Tech. Ctr. *(see Rolla Tech. Inst.)*
Rolla Tech. Inst. 681
Rollins Coll. 92
Roman Acad. of Beauty Culture 554
Ron L. Straughan & Associates, Inc. 556
Ron Moore & Associates 590
Ronnie & Dorman's Sch. of Hair Design 518
Ronny J's Barber & Styling Coll. 623
Roosevelt Hosp. Ctr. *(see Saint Luke's-Roosevelt Hosp. Ctr.)*
Roosevelt Univ. 130
Rosalind Franklin Univ. of Medicine & Science, The 130, 727 *(see also Dr. William M. Scholl Coll. of Podiatric Medicine)*
Rosary Coll. *(see Dominican Univ.)*
Rosary Hill Coll. *(see Daemen Coll.)*
Rose Coll. *(see Rose State Coll.)*

Rose Polytechnic Inst. *(see Rose-Hulman Inst. of Techno.)*
Rose State Coll. 318
Roseburg Beauty Coll., Inc. 593
Rosedale Bible Coll. 309
Rosedale Bible Inst. *(see Rosedale Bible Coll.)*
Rosedale Coll. *(see Rosedale Bible Coll.)*
Rosedale Tech *(see Rosedale Tech. Inst.)*
Rosedale Tech. Inst. 340
Rose-Hulman Inst. of Techno. 143
Rosel Sch. of Cosmetology 503
Rosemead Beauty Sch., Inc. 467
Rosemont Coll. 340
Ross Bus. Inst. 467
Ross Bus. Inst—Clinton Township 731
Ross Med. Edu. Ctr. 489, 495, 531
Ross Med. Edu. Ctr—Detroit 731
Ross Med. Edu. Ctr—Taylor 731
Ross Med. Edu. Ctr—Waterford Campus 731
Ross Med. Inst. *(see Ross Med. Edu. Ctr.)*
Ross Tech. Inst. *(see Ross Med. Edu. Ctr.)*
Rosslyn Cosmetology Training Acad. *(see Rosslyn Training Acad. of Cosmetology, Inc.)*
Rosslyn Training Acad. of Cosmetology, Inc. 606
Rosston Sch. *(see National Inst. of Tech—Long Beach)*
Roswell Comm. Coll. *(see Eastern New Mexico Univ—Roswell)*
Rotterdam Sch. of Management *(see Erasmus Univ. Rotterdam)*
Roudebush VA Med. Ctr. *(see Richard L. Roudebush Veterans Affairs Med. Ctr.)*
Roudebush Veterans Affairs Med. Ctr. *(see Richard L. Roudebush Veterans Affairs Med. Ctr.)*
Rowan Coll. of New Jersey *(see Rowan Univ.)*
Rowan Tech. Coll. 729 *(see Maysville Comm. & Tech. Coll., Rowan-Cabarrus Comm. Coll.)*
Rowan Tech. Coll—Eastern Kentucky Campus *(see Maysville Comm. & Tech. Coll.)*
Rowan Tech. Coll—Eastern Kentucky Campus 729
Rowan Tech. Inst. *(see Rowan-Cabarrus Comm. Coll.)*
Rowan Univ. 249
Rowan-Cabarrus Coll. *(see Rowan-Cabarrus Comm. Coll.)*
Rowan-Cabarrus Comm. Coll. 292

Roxbury Coll. *(see Roxbury Comm. Coll.)*
Roxbury Comm. Coll. 192
Royal Beauty Careers 623
Royal Commission for Jubail & Yanbu *(see Yanbu Industrial Coll.)*
Royal Melbourne Inst. of Techno. 711
Royal Melbourne Inst. of Tech—Chiropractic Unit *(see Royal Melbourne Inst. of Techno.)*
Royal Univ. of America *(see Dongguk Royal Univ.)*
Royal Veterinary Coll. *(see Univ. of London—Royal Veterinary Coll.)*
Royale Beauty Coll. *(see Royale Coll. of Beauty)*
Royale Coll. of Beauty 467
Roy's of Louisville Beauty Acad. *(see Hair Design Sch.)*
RSHT Training Ctr. 633, 738
RTP Hispanic American Coll. 758
Rudae's Sch. of Beauty Culture 506
Rudy & Kelly Acad. of Hair & Nails 633
Rumsey Tech. Inst. *(see James Rumsey Tech. Inst.)*
Rural Psychology Predoctoral Internship Program of East Kentucky *(see Hazard ARH Reg. Med. Ctr.)*
Rush Univ. 130
Rush-Presbyterian-Saint Luke's Med. Ctr. 668
Russell Sage Coll. 273 *(see also Sage Colleges)*
Russelville Area Techno. Ctr. *(see Bowling Green Tech. Coll—Glasgow Techno. Campus)*
Russian & East European Partnerships, Inc. 544
Rust Coll. 221
Rust Univ. *(see Rust Coll.)*
Rutersville Coll. *(see Southwestern Univ.)*
Rutgers Coll. *(see Rutgers, The State Univ. of New Jersey New Brunswick Campus)*
Rutgers, The State Univ. of New Jersey Camden Campus 249
Rutgers, The State Univ. of New Jersey New Brunswick Campus 249
Rutgers, The State Univ. of New Jersey Newark Campus 249
Rutgers—Camden *(see Rutgers, The State Univ. of New Jersey Camden Campus)*
Rutgers—New Brunswick *(see Rutgers, The State Univ. of New Jersey New Brunswick Campus)*

Rutgers—Newark *(see Rutgers, The State Univ. of New Jersey Newark Campus)*
Rutland Reg. Med. Ctr. *(see New England Sch. of Radiologic Techno.)*
Ryerson Inst. of Techno. *(see Ryerson Univ.)*
Ryerson Polytechnic Univ. 740 *(see also Ryerson Univ.)*
Ryerson Polytech. Inst. *(see Ryerson Univ.)*
Ryerson Univ. 713, 740

S

S.D. Bishop State Jr. Coll. *(see Bishop State Comm. Coll.)*
S.J. Grant & Associates, Inc. 503
S.S. Cyril & Methodius Seminary *(see SS. Cyril & Methodius Seminary)*
S.W. Sch. of Bus. & Tech. Careers 623
SAA Coll. *(see Sch. of Advertising Art)*
SABER 755
Sac State *(see California State Univ—Sacramento)*
Sacramento City Coll. 52
Sacramento State Coll. *(see California State Univ—Sacramento)*
Sacred Heart Coll. *(see Newman Univ., Regis Univ.)*
Sacred Heart Hosp. 699 *(see also Avera Sacred Heart Hosp.)*
Sacred Heart Major Seminary 203
Sacred Heart Med. Ctr. 707
Sacred Heart Monastery *(see Sacred Heart Sch. of Theology)*
Sacred Heart Sch. of Theology 426
Sacred Heart Seminary *(see Sacred Heart Major Seminary)*
Sacred Heart Univ. 74 *(see Univ. of the Sacred Heart)*
Saddleback Coll. 53
Saddleback Coll—North Campus *(see Irvine Valley Coll.)*
SAE Inst. of Techno. 569
Safeguards & Security Central Training Acad. *(see National Training Ctr.)*
Safford Coll. of Beauty 721 *(see also Hair Acad. of Safford)*
Safford Hair Acad. *(see Hair Acad. of Safford)*
Sage Coll. 53, 722 *(see also Russell Sage Coll.)*
Sage Coll. of Albany 273 *(see also Sage Colleges)*
Sage Colleges, The 273
Sage Jr. Coll. of Albany *(see Sage Colleges)*
Sage Tech. Services 497, 541

Saginaw Chippewa Tribal Coll. 746
Saginaw Valley Coll. *(see Saginaw Valley State Univ.)*
Saginaw Valley State Coll. *(see Saginaw Valley State Univ.)*
Saginaw Valley State Univ. 203
Saginaw Valley Univ. *(see Saginaw Valley State Univ.)*
Saint Agnes Sch. of Nursing *(see Marian Coll. of Fond du Lac)*
Saint Albert's Coll. *(see Dominican Sch. of Philosophy & Theology)*
Saint Aloysius Acad. *(see Mount Aloysius Coll.)*
Saint Ambrose Univ. 149
Saint Andrew's Coll. 433
Saint Andrews Presbyterian Coll. 292
Saint Anne's Hosp. 677
Saint Anselm Coll. 244
Saint Anthony Central Hosp. 658
Saint Anthony Coll. of Nursing 130
Saint Anthony Hosp. 695
Saint Anthony's Allied Health & Nursing Inst. *(see Saint Vincent Catholic Med. Centers of New York)*
Saint Augustine Coll. 130
Saint Augustine Health Sciences Univ. *(see Univ. of St. Augustine for Health Sciences)*
Saint Augustine Tech. Ctr. *(see First Coast Tech. Inst.)*
Saint Augustine's Coll. 292
Saint Augustine's Seminary of Toronto 433
Saint Barnabas Health Care System *(see Monmouth Med. Ctr., Newark Beth Israel Med. Ctr., Saint Barnabas Med. Ctr.)*
Saint Barnabas Hosp. 689
Saint Barnabas Med. Ctr. 684
Saint Benedict Coll. *(see Coll. of Saint Benedict)*
Saint Benedict's Monastery *(see Coll. of Saint Benedict)*
Saint Bernard's Sch. of Theology & Ministry 273
Saint Bonaventure Univ. 273
Saint Camillus Campus 709
Saint Catharine Coll. 163
Saint Catherine Coll. *(see Coll. of Saint Catherine)*
Saint Cecilia Normal Sch. *(see Aquinas Coll.)*
Saint Charles Borromeo Seminary 340
Saint Charles Coll. *(see Saint Charles Comm. Coll.)*
Saint Charles Comm. Coll. 230
Saint Charles County Comm. Coll. *(see Saint Charles Comm. Coll.)*
Saint Charles Hosp. 689

Saint Charles Sch. of Massage Therapy 539
Saint Charles Seminary *(see Saint Charles Borromeo Seminary)*
Saint Christopher's Childrens Hosp. *(see Saint Christopher's Hosp. for Children)*
Saint Christopher's Hosp. for Children 699
Saint Clair Coll. of Applied Arts & Techno. 713
Saint Clair County Coll. *(see Saint Clair County Comm. Coll.)*
Saint Clair County Comm. Coll. 203
Saint Clara Coll. *(see Cardinal Stritch Univ., Dominican Univ.)*
Saint Clare's Hosp. 689
Saint Cloud Coll. *(see Saint Cloud Tech. Coll.)*
Saint Cloud Hosp. 680
Saint Cloud Regency Beauty Acad. 534
Saint Cloud State Coll. *(see Saint Cloud State Univ.)*
Saint Cloud State Teachers Coll. *(see Saint Cloud State Univ.)*
Saint Cloud State Univ. 215
Saint Cloud Tech. Coll. 215
Saint Cloud VA Med. Ctr. *(see Veterans Affairs Med. Ctr-Saint Cloud)*
Saint Edward's Acad. *(see Saint Edward's Univ.)*
Saint Edward's Coll. *(see Saint Edward's Univ.)*
Saint Edward's Univ. 383
Saint Elizabeth Coll. *(see Coll. of Saint Elizabeth)*
Saint Elizabeth Coll. of Nursing 273
Saint Elizabeth Health Ctr. 694
Saint Elizabeth Hosp. *(see Saint Elizabeth Med. Ctr.)*
Saint Elizabeth Med. Ctr. 673, 689 *(see also Saint Elizabeth Coll. of Nursing)*
Saint Elizabeths Hosp. 661
Saint Elizabeth's Hosp. 669
Saint Elizabeth's Hosp. Med. Ctr. 694
Saint Elizabeth's Med. Ctr. 677
Saint Francis Acad. *(see Saint Francis Coll., Univ. of Saint Francis)*
Saint Francis Career Coll. 467
Saint Francis Coll. 273, 736 *(see also Coll. of St. Francis—Saint Joseph Coll. of Nursing, Saint Francis Univ., Univ. of New England, Univ. of Saint Francis)*
Saint Francis Hosp. 665, 695 *(see also Bon Secours Saint Francis Hosp., Saint Francis Med. Ctr.)*
Saint Francis Hosp. & Health Centers 670

Saint Francis Hosp—Resurrection Health Care 666
Saint Francis Med. Ctr. 674, 684, 699 *(see also OSF Saint Francis Med. Ctr.)*
Saint Francis Med. Ctr. Coll. of Nursing *(see OSF Saint Francis Med. Ctr.)*
Saint Francis Normal Sch. *(see Marian Coll.)*
Saint Francis Sch. of Pastoral Ministry *(see Saint Francis Seminary)*
Saint Francis Sch. of Practical Nursing 689
Saint Francis Seminary 427
Saint Francis Solanus Coll. *(see Quincy Univ.)*
Saint Francis Univ. 340, 736 *(see also Univ. of Saint Francis)*
Saint Francis/Mount Sinai Hosp. 659
Saint Giles Coll. 468
Saint Gregory's Coll. *(see Saint Gregory's Univ.)*
Saint Gregory's Seminary *(see Athenaeum of Ohio)*
Saint Gregory's Univ. 318
Saint Hyacinth Coll. & Seminary 730
Saint Ignatius Acad. *(see Univ. of San Francisco)*
Saint Ignatius Coll. *(see John Carroll Univ., Univ. of San Francisco)*
Saint James Hosp. *(see Saint James Mercy Health System)*
Saint James Mercy Health System 689
Saint James Mercy Hosp. *(see Saint James Mercy Health System)*
Saint John Fisher Coll. 273
Saint John Health *(see Saint John Hosp. & Med. Ctr.)*
Saint John Health System *(see Providence Hosp. & Med. Centers, Saint John Health System Sch. of Med. Techno.)*
Saint John Health System Sch. of Med. Techno. 678
Saint John Hosp. & Med. Ctr. 678
Saint John Med. Ctr. *(see Saint John Hosp. & Med. Ctr.)*
Saint John Providence Park Hosp. *(see Providence Hosp. & Med. Centers)*
Saint John Vianney Coll. Seminary 92
Saint John's Child & Family Development Ctr. 655
Saint John's Coll. 131, 181, 253
Saint John's Episcopal Hosp. South Shore 690

Saint John's Hosp. *(see Saint John's Mercy Med. Ctr., Saint John's Reg. Health System, Saint John's Reg. Med. Ctr.)*
Saint John's McNamara Hosp. *(see Rapid City Reg. Hosp.)*
Saint John's Mercy Med. Ctr. 681
Saint John's Reg. Health System 681
Saint John's Reg. Med. Ctr. 655, 682
Saint Johns River Comm. Coll. 92
Saint John's Seminary 53, 192
Saint John's Seminary Coll. 723
Saint John's Univ. 215, 274
Saint Joseph Coll. 74 *(see also Coll. of Saint Joseph, Loras Coll., Southern Vermont Coll.)*
Saint Joseph Coll. of Nursing 133 *(see Coll. of St. Francis—Saint Joseph Coll. of Nursing, Univ. of Saint Francis)*
Saint Joseph Healthcare 673
Saint Joseph Hosp. 655 *(see also Saint Joseph Healthcare, Saint Joseph Med. Ctr., Windham Comm. Mem. Hosp.)*
Saint Joseph Jr. Coll. *(see Missouri Western State Univ.)*
Saint Joseph Med. Ctr. 699, 707
Saint Joseph Mercy Hosp. *(see also Mercy Med. Ctr. North Iowa, Mercy Med. Ctr. Sioux City)*
Saint Joseph Mercy Hosp—Oakland 678
Saint Joseph Reg. Health Ctr. 704
Saint Joseph Seminary Coll. 173
Saint Joseph Stake Acad. *(see Eastern Arizona Coll.)*
Saint Joseph's Calumet Coll. *(see Calumet Coll. of St. Joseph)*
Saint Joseph's Coll. 143, 274 *(see also Saint Joseph's Coll. of Maine)*
Saint Joseph's Coll. of Maine 176
Saint Joseph's Healthcare System, Inc. *(see Saint Joseph's Reg. Med. Ctr.)*
Saint Joseph's Hosp. 484 *(see also Inst. of Allied Med. Professions, Saint Joseph's Hosp. Health Ctr., Saint Joseph's Hosp. of Marshfield, Saint Joseph's Reg. Med. Ctr.)*
Saint Joseph's Hosp. Health Ctr. 690
Saint Joseph's Hosp. Health Ctr. Sch. of Nursing *(see Saint Joseph's Hosp. Health Ctr.)*
Saint Joseph's Hosp. of Marshfield 709
Saint Joseph's Med. Ctr. 675, 690
Saint Joseph's Normal Sch. *(see Alverno Coll.)*

Saint Joseph's Reg. Med. Ctr. 670, 684
Saint Joseph's Seminary 274
Saint Joseph's Univ. 340
Saint Lawrence Acad. *(see State Univ. of New York Coll. at Potsdam)*
Saint Lawrence Univ. 274
Saint Leo Coll. *(see Saint Leo Univ.)*
Saint Leo Coll. Preparatory Sch. *(see Saint Leo Univ.)*
Saint Leo Univ. 93
Saint Louis Christian Coll. 230, 747
Saint Louis Coll. *(see Saint Louis Christian Coll., Saint Louis Univ.)*
Saint Louis Coll. at Forest Park *(see Saint Louis Comm. Coll. at Forest Park)*
Saint Louis Coll. at Meramec *(see Saint Louis Comm. Coll. at Meramec)*
Saint Louis Coll. of Health Careers 230
Saint Louis Coll. of Pharmacy 230
Saint Louis Comm. Coll. at Florissant Valley 230
Saint Louis Comm. Coll. at Forest Park 231
Saint Louis Comm. Coll. at Meramec 231
Saint Louis Hair Acad., Inc. 539
Saint Louis Jr. Coll. *(see Chaminade Univ. of Honolulu)*
Saint Louis Pharmacy Coll. *(see Saint Louis Coll. of Pharmacy)*
Saint Louis Univ. 231
Saint Luke's Clinical Pastoral Edu. Ctr. 665
Saint Luke's Coll. 150, 231
Saint Luke's Coll. of Nursing & Health Sciences *(see Saint Luke's Coll.)*
Saint Luke's Episcopal Hosp. 704
Saint Luke's Health System *(see Saint Luke's Hosp.)*
Saint Luke's Hosp. 665, 682, 599 *(see also Mercy/St. Luke's Sch. of Radiologic Techno.,Marquette General Health System)*
Saint Luke's Hosp. Sch. of Clinical Science 671
Saint Luke's Hosp. Sch. of Nursing *(see Saint Luke's Coll.)*
Saint Luke's Med. Ctr. 694, 709 *(see also Rush-Presbyterian-Saint Luke's Med. Ctr.)*
Saint Luke's Mem. Hosp. Ctr. *(see Faxton-St. Luke's Healthcare)*
Saint Luke's-Roosevelt Hosp. Ctr. 690
Saint Margaret Mercy Healthcare Ctr. 670
Saint Mark's Hosp. 705

Saint Mark's Pastoral Care Ctr. *(see Saint Mark's Hosp.)*
Saint Martin's Coll. 738 *(see also Saint Martin's Univ.)*
Saint Martin's Univ. 414, 738
Saint Mary Acad. *(see Marygrove Coll.)*
Saint Mary Coll. 728 *(see also Coll. of Saint Mary, Marygrove Coll., Univ. of Saint Mary)*
Saint Mary Hosp. *(see Reg. West Med. Ctr.)*
Saint Mary Med. Ctr. 699
Saint Mary of the Lake Univ. *(see Univ. of Saint Mary of the Lake Mundelein Seminary)*
Saint Mary Seminary & Grad. Sch. of Theology 309
Saint Mary-of-the-Woods Coll. 143
Saint Mary's Acad. *(see Clarke Coll.)*
Saint Mary's Coll. 143 *(see also Saint Mary's Coll. of Madonna Univ., Univ. of Saint Mary of the Lake Mundelein Seminary)*
Saint Mary's Coll. of Ave Maria Univ. 731 *(see also Saint Mary's Coll. of Madonna Univ.)*
Saint Mary's Coll. of California 53
Saint Mary's Coll. of Maryland 181
Saint Mary's Female Seminary *(see Saint Mary's Coll. of Maryland)*
Saint Mary's Hosp. 659, 706 *(see also Inst. of Allied Med. Professions, Marquette General Health System, United Hosp. Ctr.)*
Saint Mary's Hosp. of Franciscan Sisters *(see All Saints Healthcare—St. Mary's Campus)*
Saint Mary's Jr. Coll. *(see Coll. of Saint Catherine)*
Saint Mary's Med. Ctr. 655, 708 *(see also All Saints Healthcare—St. Mary's Campus)*
Saint Mary's Seminary & Univ. 181
Saint Mary's Univ. 383 *(see also Saint Mary's Seminary & Univ., Saint Mary's Univ. of Minnesota)*
Saint Mary's Univ. & Seminary *(see Saint Mary's Seminary & Univ.)*
Saint Mary's Univ. of Minnesota 215
Saint Meinrad Sch. of Theology 143
Saint Michael Hosp. 709
Saint Michael's Coll. 398 *(see Coll. of Santa Fe, Univ. of St. Michael's Coll.)*
Saint Norbert Coll. 427
Saint Olaf Coll. 215
Saint Patrick's Seminary *(see Saint Patrick's Seminary & Univ.)*
Saint Patrick's Seminary & Univ. 53

Saint Patrick's Univ. *(see Saint Patrick's Seminary & Univ.)*
Saint Paul Bible Coll. *(see Crown Coll.)*
Saint Paul Bible Inst. *(see Crown Coll.)*
Saint Paul Coll. of Law *(see William Mitchell Coll. of Law)*
Saint Paul Coll-A Comm. & Tech. Coll. 215, 731
Saint Paul Sch. of Theology 231
Saint Paul Seminary Sch. of Divinity *(see Univ. of Saint Thomas)*
Saint Paul Tech. Coll. 731 *(see also Saint Paul Coll—A Comm. & Tech. Coll.)*
Saint Paul Theology Sch. *(see Saint Paul Sch. of Theology)*
Saint Paul's Coll. 406
Saint Peter's Coll. 249
Saint Peter's Hosp. 690
Saint Peter's Seminary 433
Saint Petersburg Coll. 93
Saint Petersburg Jr. Coll. *(see Saint Petersburg Coll.)*
Saint Petersburg Seminary *(see Saint Petersburg Theological Seminary)*
Saint Petersburg Theological Seminary 93
Saint Philip's Coll. 383
Saint Procopius Coll. *(see Benedictine Univ.)*
Saint Raphael Hosp. *(see Hosp. of Saint Raphael)*
Saint Raphael Seminary *(see Loras Coll.)*
Saint Rose Coll. *(see Coll. of Saint Rose)*
Saint Scholastica Coll. *(see Coll. of Saint Scholastica)*
Saint Stephen's Coll. *(see Bard Coll.)*
Saint Teresa Coll. *(see Avila Univ.)*
Saint Thomas Aquinas Coll. 274
Saint Thomas More Coll. *(see Coll. of Saint Thomas Moore, Thomas More Coll.)*
Saint Thomas More Inst. *(see Coll. of Saint Thomas Moore)*
Saint Thomas Univ. 93 *(see also Univ. of Saint Thomas)*
Saint Tikhon's Orthodox Theological Seminary 340
Saint Vincent Archabbey & Coll. *(see Saint Vincent Coll. & Seminary)*
Saint Vincent Catholic Med. Centers of New York 690
Saint Vincent Coll. & Seminary 340
Saint Vincent de Paul Reg. Seminary 93
Saint Vincent Health *(see Saint Vincent Indianapolis Hosp.)*

Saint Vincent Hosp. *(see Saint Vincent Infirmary Med. Ctr., Mercy Med. Ctr. Sioux City)*

Saint Vincent Hosp. at Worcester Med. Ctr. 677

Saint Vincent Hospitals & Health Services *(see Saint Vincent Indianapolis Hosp.)*

Saint Vincent Indianapolis Hosp. 670

Saint Vincent Infirmary Med. Ctr. 652

Saint Vincent Mercy Med. Ctr. 694

Saint Vincent Seminary *(see Saint Vincent Coll. & Seminary)*

Saint Vincent's Charity Hosp. 694

Saint Vincent's Coll. 75

Saint Vincent's Coll. of Nursing *(see Saint Vincent's Coll.)*

Saint Vincent's Hosp. *(see Providence Hosp. & Med. Centers, Saint Vincent's Med. Ctr.)*

Saint Vincent's Hosp. & Med. Ctr. 690

Saint Vincent's Med. Ctr. 663 *(see also Saint Vincent's Coll.)*

Saint Vincent's Med. Ctr. Sch. of Med. Techno. *(see Saint Vincent's Med. Ctr.)*

Saint Vladimir's Orthodox Theological Seminary 274

Saint Vladimir's Seminary *(see Saint Vladimir's Orthodox Theological Seminary)*

Saint Xavier Coll. for Women *(see Saint Xavier Univ.)*

Saint Xavier Univ. 131

Sakie Int'l. Coll. of Cosmetology 638

Salem Acad. *(see Salem Coll.)*

Salem Coll. 292 *(see also Salem Coll. of Hairstyling, Salem Comm. Coll., Salem Int'l. Univ.)*

Salem Coll. of Hairstyling 539

Salem Comm. Coll. 249

Salem Int'l. Univ. 420

Salem Normal Sch. *(see Salem State Coll.)*

Salem State Coll. 192

Salem Teachers Coll. *(see Salem State Coll.)*

Salem Univ. *(see Salem Int'l. Univ.)*

Salem VA Med. Ctr. *(see Veterans Affairs Med. Ctr—Salem)*

Salem-Teikyo Univ. *(see Salem Int'l. Univ.)*

Salina Area Tech. Sch. 510

Salina Tech *(see Salina Area Tech. Sch.)*

Salisbury Coll. *(see Salisbury Univ.)*

Salisbury Univ. 182

Salish Kootenai Coll. 235

Sally Esser Beauty Sch. 531

Salon Prof. Acad., The 508, 728

Salon Professionals Acad. Fargo, Inc., The 575

Salon Success Acad. 468

Salt Lake Acad. *(see Latter-Day Saints Bus. Coll.)*

Salt Lake City Coll. *(see Salt Lake Comm. Coll.)*

Salt Lake City Comm. Coll. *(see Salt Lake Comm. Coll.)*

Salt Lake City VA Med. Ctr. *(see Veterans Affairs Med. Ctr—Salt Lake City)*

Salt Lake City Veterans Affairs Med. Ctr. *(see Veterans Affairs Med. Ctr—Salt Lake City)*

Salt Lake Coll. *(see Salt Lake Comm. Coll.)*

Salt Lake Comm. Coll. 395

Salt Lake-Tooele Applied Techno. Coll. 750

Salter Sch., The 527

Salter Tech. Inst. *(see Louisiana Tech. Coll—Lamar Salter Campus)*

Salvation Army Coll. *(see Salvation Army Coll. for Officer Training at Crestmont)*

Salvation Army Coll. for Officer Training at Crestmont 53, 723

Salvation Army Coll. for Officers Training 723 *(see also Salvation Army Coll. for Officer Training at Crestmont)*

Salvation Army Crestmont Coll. 723 *(see also Salvation Army Coll. for Officer Training at Crestmont)*

Salvation Army Sch. for Officer Training 274

Salve Regina Univ. 354

Sam Houston State Univ. 383

Sam Houston Univ. *(see Sam Houston State Univ.)*

Samaritan Counseling & Edu. Ctr. 657

Samford Univ. 7

Sampson Coll. *(see Sampson Comm. Coll.)*

Sampson Comm. Coll. 292

Sampson Tech. Coll. *(see Sampson Comm. Coll.)*

Sampson Tech. Inst. *(see Sampson Comm. Coll.)*

Samra Univ. of Oriental Medicine 53

Samuel Huston Coll. *(see Huston-Tillotson Univ.)*

Samuel Merritt Coll. 53 *(see also California Coll. of Podiatric Medicine)*

Samuel Merritt Coll. of Podiatric Medicine *(see California Coll. of Podiatric Medicine)*

San Angelo Coll. *(see Angelo State Univ.)*

San Antonio Beauty Coll. #3 623

San Antonio Beauty Coll. #4 623

San Antonio Coll. 384

San Antonio Coll. of Med. & Dental Assistants 623 *(see also Career Centers of Texas—Corpus Christi)*

San Antonio Methodist Hosp. *(see Methodist Hosp.)*

San Antonio Philosophical & Theological Seminary *(see Oblate Sch. of Theology)*

San Antonio Training Division *(see Career Advancement & Applied Tech. Training Division)*

San Antonio Uniform Consortium *(see Wilford Hall Med. Ctr.)*

San Antonio VA Med. Ctr. *(see Veterans Affairs Med. Ctr—San Antonio)*

San Antonio Veterans Affairs Med. Ctr. *(see Veterans Affairs Med. Ctr—San Antonio)*

San Bernardino Coll. *(see San Bernardino Valley Coll.)*

San Bernardino County Dept. of Behavioral Health 655

San Bernardino County Mental HealthDept. *(see San Bernardino County Dept. of Behavioral Health)*

San Bernardino Valley Coll. 53

San Diego Art Inst. *(see Art Inst. of California—San Diego)*

San Diego Beauty Acad. *(see Bay Vista Coll. of Beauty, Je Boutique Coll. of Beauty, Poway Acad. of Hair Design)*

San Diego Bible Coll. & Seminary *(see Southern California Seminary)*

San Diego Christian Coll. 53, 722

San Diego City Coll. 53

San Diego Coll. *(see San Diego City Coll., San Diego Mesa Coll., Univ. of San Diego)*

San Diego Coll. for Women *(see Univ. of San Diego)*

San Diego Design Inst. *(see Design Inst. of San Diego)*

San Diego Foundation Coll. *(see Foundation Coll. San Diego)*

San Diego Golf Acad. *(see Golf Acad. of the Carolinas, Golf Acad. of San Diego)*

San Diego Inst. of Design *(see Design Inst. of San Diego)*

San Diego Jr. Coll. *(see San Diego City Coll.)*

San Diego Jr. Coll. & Vocational Sch. *(see San Diego City Coll.)*

San Diego Mesa Coll. 53

San Diego Miramar Coll. 54

San Diego Montessori Teachers Coll. *(see Montessori Teachers Coll. of San Diego)*
San Diego Naval Med. Ctr. *(see Naval Med. Ctr—San Diego)*
San Diego Normal Sch. *(see San Diego State Univ.)*
San Diego State Univ. 54
San Diego Univ. *(see San Diego State Univ., Univ. of San Diego)*
San Diego VA Med. Ctr. *(see Veterans Affairs San Diego Healthcare System)*
San Diego Veterans Affairs Med. Ctr. *(see Veterans Affairs San Diego Healthcare System)*
San Fernando Beauty Acad., Inc. 468
San Fernando Coll. of Law 723, 724
San Fernando Valley Coll. of Law *(see Univ. of West Los Angeles)*
San Fernando Valley State Coll. *(see California State Univ—Northridge)*
San Francisco Art Inst. 54 *(see Art Inst. of California—San Francisco)*
San Francisco City Coll. *(see City Coll. of San Francisco)*
San Francisco Coll. *(see American River Coll., San Francisco State Univ.)*
San Francisco Coll. of Mortuary Science *(see American River Coll.)*
San Francisco Conservatory of Music 54
San Francisco Management Coll. *(see Management Coll. of San Francisco)*
San Francisco Music Conservatory *(see San Francisco Conservatory of Music)*
San Francisco Seminary *(see San Francisco Theological Seminary)*
San Francisco State Coll. *(see San Francisco State Univ.)*
San Francisco State Normal Sch. *(see San Francisco State Univ.)*
San Francisco State Teacher's Coll. *(see San Francisco State Univ.)*
San Francisco State Univ. 54
San Francisco Theological Seminary 54
San Francisco Univ. *(see San Francisco State Univ., Univ. of San Francisco)*
San Francisco Veterans Affairs Med. Ctr. *(see Veterans Affairs Med. Ctr—San Francisco)*
San Jacinto Coll. Central 384
San Jacinto Coll. North 384

San Jacinto Coll. South 384
San Joaquin Coll. of Law 54
San Joaquin Delta Coll. 54
San Joaquin General Hosp. 655
San Joaquin Hosp. *(see San Joaquin General Hosp.)*
San Joaquin Valley Coll-Visalia 55
San Jose Bible Coll. *(see William Jessup Univ.)*
San Jose Christian Coll. *(see William Jessup Univ.)*
San Jose Christian Coll. 723
San Jose City Coll. 55
San Jose Coll. *(see San Jose City Coll.)*
San Jose Jr. Coll. *(see San Jose City Coll.)*
San Jose State Coll. *(see San Jose State Univ.)*
San Jose State Teachers Coll. *(see San Jose State Univ.)*
San Jose State Univ. 55
San Jose Univ. *(see San Jose State Univ.)*
San Juan Basin Coll. *(see San Juan Basin Tech. Coll.)*
San Juan Basin Tech. Coll. 472
San Juan Bautista Med. Sch. *(see San Juan Bautista Sch. of Medicine)*
San Juan Bautista Sch. of Medicine 350
San Juan Coll. 254 *(see also San Juan Basin Tech. Coll.)*
San Juan Sch. of Medicine *(see San Juan Bautista Sch. of Medicine)*
San Juan Technological Coll. *(see Univ. Coll. of San Juan)*
San Juan VA Med. Ctr. *(see Veterans Affairs Med. Ctr—San Juan)*
San Juan Veterans Affairs Med. Ctr. *(see Veterans Affairs Med. Ctr—San Juan)*
San Mateo Coll. *(see Coll. of San Mateo)*
San Rafael Baptist Inst. *(see Golden Gate Baptist Theological Seminary)*
Sand Springs Beauty Coll. 590
Sand Springs Coll. of Beauty *(see Sand Springs Beauty Coll.)*
Sandburg Coll. *(see Carl Sandburg Coll.)*
Sandersville Coll. *(see Sandersville Tech. Coll.)*
Sandersville Reg. Tech. Inst. 726 *(see also Sandersville Tech. Coll.)*
Sandersville Tech. Coll. 108, 726
Sandhills Coll. *(see Sandhills Comm. Coll.)*
Sandhills Comm. Coll. 292
Sandusky High Sch. Adult Edu. 584

Sanford-Brown Coll. *(see Colorado Tech. Univ.)*
Sanford-Brown Coll—Collinsville 503
Sanford-Brown Coll—Fenton 231
Sanford-Brown Coll—Granite City *(see Sanford-Brown Coll—Collinsville)*
Sanford-Brown Coll—Milwaukee 427
Sanford-Brown Coll—North Kansas City 732
Sanford-Brown Inst—Atlanta 108, 727
Sanford-Brown Inst—Dallas 623, 737
Sanford-Brown Inst—Elmsford 734
Sanford-Brown Inst—Garden City 734
Sanford-Brown Inst—Iselin 733
Sanford-Brown Inst—Jacksonville 93, 726
Sanford-Brown Inst—Landover 730
Sanford-Brown Inst—Lauderdale Lakes 726
Sanford-Brown Inst—New York 734
Sanford-Brown Inst—Philadelphia 726
Sanford-Brown Inst—Springfield 730
Sanford-Brown Inst—Tampa 726
Sanford-Brown Inst—White Plains 569
Sangamon State Univ. *(see Univ. of Illinois at Springfield)*
Sangamond State Univ. *(see Univ. of Illinois at Springfield)*
Sanpete Stake Acad. *(see Snow Coll.)*
Santa Ana Coll. 55
Santa Barbara Bus. Coll. 55
Santa Barbara Bus. Sch. *(see Westwood Coll—Los Angeles)*
Santa Barbara City Coll. 55
Santa Barbara Coll. *(see Santa Barbara City Coll., Santa Barbara Coll. of Oriental Medicine)*
Santa Barbara Coll. of Oriental Medicine 55
Santa Barbara Cottage Hosp. 655
Santa Barbara Oriental Medicine Coll. *(see Santa Barbara Coll. of Oriental Medicine)*
Santa Clara Coll. *(see Santa Clara Univ.)*
Santa Clara Univ. 56
Santa Fe Coll. *(see Coll. of Santa Fe, Santa Fe Comm. Coll.)*
Santa Fe Comm. Coll. 93, 254
Santa Maria Jr. Coll. *(see Allan Hancock Coll.)*
Santa Monica Coll. 56
Santa Monica Montessori Inst. 468
Santa Rosa Coll. *(see Santa Rosa Jr. Coll.)*
Santa Rosa Jr. Coll. 56
Santiago Canyon Coll. 56

Sanz Sch., Inc. 478
Sarah Lawrence Coll. 274
Sarasota County Tech. Inst. 489
Sarasota Sch. of Massage Therapy 489
Sarasota Tech. Inst. *(see Sarasota County Tech. Inst.)*
Sargeant Reynolds Coll. *(see J. Sargeant Reynolds Comm. Coll.)*
Sargeant Reynolds Comm. Coll. *(see J. Sargeant Reynolds Comm. Coll.)*
Saskatchewan Univ. *(see Univ. of Saskatchewan)*
Saskatoon Theological Union *(see Saint Andrew's Coll.)*
SAU Tech *(see Southern Arkansas Univ—Tech)*
Saudi Arabian Oil Company Training & Career Development 647
Saudi Aramco Training & Career Development Ctr. 647
Saudi Electricity Company—Eastern Region Branch 647
Sauk Valley Coll. *(see Sauk Valley Comm. Coll.)*
Sauk Valley Comm. Coll. 131
Savannah Art Coll. *(see Savannah Coll. of Art & Design)*
Savannah Coll. of Art & Design, The 108
Savannah River Coll. 108, 726
Savannah State Coll. *(see Savannah State Univ.)*
Savannah State Univ. 108
Savannah Tech. Coll. 108
Savannah Tech. Inst. *(see Savannah Tech. Coll.)*
Savannah Univ. *(see Savannah State Univ.)*
Savant Training & Techno. 737
Sawyer Coll. of Bus. *(see Sawyer Coll., Inc.)*
Sawyer Coll., Inc. 143
Sawyer Sch. 607, 736
Saybrook Grad. Sch. & Research Ctr. 56
Saybrook Inst. *(see Saybrook Grad. Sch. & Research Ctr.)*
Sayre Jr. Coll. *(see Southwestern Oklahoma State Univ. Sayre Campus)*
SC State *(see South Carolina State Univ.)*
Scandinavian Aviation Acad. 468
Scandinavian Flight Acad. *(see Scandinavian Aviation Acad.)*
Scarlet Oaks Career Development Campus *(see Great Oaks Inst. of Techno. & Career Development—Scarlet Oaks Campus)*

Scenic Mountain Med. Ctr. 704
Schenck Civilian Conservation Ctr. 573 *(see also Schenck Civilian Conservation Ctr.)*
Schenectady Coll. *(see Schenectady County Comm. Coll.)*
Schenectady County Coll. *(see Schenectady County Comm. Coll.)*
Schenectady County Comm. Coll. 274
Scherer & Associates, Inc. *(see Robert M. Scherer & Associates, Inc.)*
Schiller Int'l. Univ. 93
Schiller Univ. *(see Schiller Int'l. Univ.)*
Schilling-Douglas Sch. of Hair Design 477
Schillinger House of Music *(see Berklee Coll. of Music)*
Schoharie State Sch. of Agriculture *(see State Univ. of New York Coll. of Agriculture & Techno. at Cobleskill)*
Scholl Coll. of Podiatric Medicine *(see Dr. William M. Scholl Coll. of Podiatric Medicine)*
Sch. Dist. of the City of Erie 699
Sch. for Film & Televisiom, The *(see Sch. for Film & Television at Three of Us Studio)*
Sch. for Film & Television at Three of Us Studio 569
Sch. for Int'l. Training 398
Sch. of Acupuncture & Massage Therapy *(see Swedish Inst.: Sch. of Acupuncture & Massage Therapy)*
Sch. of Acupunture & Oriental Medicine of Arizona *(see Arizona Sch. of Acupunture & Oriental Medicine)*
Sch. of Advanced Air & Space Studies 3, 721
Sch. of Advanced Airpower Studies 721 *(see also Sch. of Advanced Air & Space Studies)*
Sch. of Advertising Art 309
Sch. of Art & Design at Montgomery Coll., The 181, 730 *(see also Montgomery Coll—Takoma Park Campus)*
Sch. of Art & Design of New England *(see New England Sch. of Art & Design at Suffolk Univ.)*
Sch. of Art Inst. of Chicago, The 131
Sch. of Automotive Machinists 623
Sch. of Aviation Medicine 626
Sch. of Bus. & Techno. 730
Sch. of Clinical Laboratory Science 657
Sch. of Communication Arts 292

Sch. of Computer Techno., Inc. *(see Int'l. Acad. of Design & Tech—Fairmont)*
Sch. of Continuing Studies *(see Granite State Coll.)*
Sch. of Creative Hair Designs, Inc., The 531
Sch. of Dance Connecticut 476
Sch. of Deep Muscle Therapy *(see Deep Muscle Therapy Sch.)*
Sch. of Design of Rhode Island *(see Rhode Island Sch. of Design)*
Sch. of Diagnostic Med. Sonography *(see Florida Inst. of Ultrasound, Inc.)*
Sch. of Electrical Techno. *(see Escuela Tecnica de Electricidad, Inc.)*
Sch. of European Healing Massage Therapy *(see European Healing Massage Therapy Sch.)*
Sch. of Evangelical Theology *(see Evangelical Sch. of Theology)*
Sch. of Forestry *(see Minot State Univ—Bottineau)*
Sch. of Hair Design 590
Sch. of Hairstyling, The 497
Sch. of Healing Arts of Colorado *(see Colorado Sch. of Healing Arts)*
Sch. of Health Care Sciences *(see United States Air Force Sch. of Health Care Sciences)*
Sch. of Health Careers, The 489
Sch. of Health Sciences Campus 3
Sch. of Holistic Esthetics *(see Hobble Creek Sch. of Holistic Esthetics)*
Sch. of Hotel & Hospitality Arts *(see Monteclaro: Escuela de Hoteleria y Artes Servicios de Hospitalidad)*
Sch. of Law at Queens Coll. *(see City Univ. of New York Queens Coll.)*
Sch. of Medicine at Morehouse Coll., The *(see Morehouse Sch. of Medicine)*
Sch. of Medicine—Wichita, The 156
Sch. of Modern Techno. *(see Modern Techno. Sch.)*
Sch. of Osteopathic Medicine of West Virginia *(see West Virginia Sch. of Osteopathic Medicine)*
Sch. of Physical Theater *(see Dell'Arte Internatial Sch. of Physical Theater)*
Sch. of Plastic Arts of Puerto Rico *(see Escuela de Artes Plasticas de Puerto Rico)*
Sch. of Prof. & Grad. Studies—Overland 152
Sch. of Prof. & Grad. Studies—Wichita 152

Sch. of Rural Public Health *(see Texas A&M Univ. System Health Science Ctr.)*
Sch. of Tech. Training *(see Platt Coll.)*
Sch. of Techno. at Kokomo 142
Sch. of Techno. at New Albany 142
Sch. of Techno. at South Bend/Elkhart 142
Sch. of Techno. at Versailles 142
Sch. of the Immaculate Conception *(see Seattle Univ.)*
Sch. of the Museum of Fine Arts, Boston 192
Sch. of Tomorrow 478
Sch. of Traditional Chinese Medicine of Colorado *(see Colorado Sch. of Traditional Chinese Medicine)*
Sch. of Urban Missions—New Orleans 746
Sch. of Visual Arts 274
Schoolcraft Coll. 203
Schreiner Coll. *(see Schreiner Univ.)*
Schreiner Univ. 384
Schuylkill Bus. Inst. *(see Schuylkill Inst. of Bus. & Techno.)*
Schuylkill Inst. of Bus. & Techno. 340
Schuylkill Training & Tech. Ctr. *(see Schuylkill Training & Techno. Ctr.)*
Schuylkill Training & Techno. Ctr. 600
Science & Arts Univ. of Oklahoma *(see Univ. of Science & Arts of Oklahoma)*
Science & Techno. Inst. of Central Pennsylvania *(see Central Pennsylvania Inst. of Science & Techno.)*
Scientific Coll. of Beauty & Barbering 644
Scientific Therapeutics Sch. of Alexandria *(see Alexandria Sch. of Scientific Therapeutics, Inc.)*
Scio Coll. *(see Mount Union Coll.)*
Scioto County Joint Vocational Sch. 584
Scioto County JVS *(see Scioto County Joint Vocational Sch.)*
Scot Lewis Beauty Sch—Crystal *(see Scot Lewis Sch-Paul Mitchell Partner Sch—Plymouth)*
Scot Lewis Sch. 727 *(see also Scot Lewis Sch-Paul Mitchell Partner Sch—Bloomington)*
Scot Lewis Sch. of Cosmetology *(see Scot Lewis Sch-Paul Mitchell Partner Sch—Bloomington)*
Scot Lewis Sch-Paul Mitchell Partner Sch—Bloomington 534
Scot Lewis Sch-Paul Mitchell Partner Sch—Plymouth 534
Scot Lewis Schools-Paul Mitchell Partner Sch—Boise 497

Scott & White Clinic in Temple 704
Scott & White Mem. Hosp. *(see Scott & White Clinic in Temple)*
Scott Coll. *(see Agnes Scott Coll., Scott Coll. of Cosmetology, Scott Comm. Coll.)*
Scott Coll. of Cosmetology 642
Scott Comm. Coll. 150
Scottsbluff Jr. Coll. *(see Western Nebraska Comm. Coll.)*
Scottsdale Coll. *(see Scottsdale Comm. Coll.)*
Scottsdale Comm. Coll. 20
Scottsdale Culinary Inst. 20
Scottsdale Educational Ctr. *(see Long Tech. Coll.)*
Scranton Ctr., The *(see Pennsylvania State Univ.)*
Scranton Univ. *(see Univ. of Scranton)*
Scripps Coll. 56
Scripps Institution of Oceanography *(see Univ. of California, San Diego)*
Scripps Research Inst., The 56
Seabury Divinity Sch. *(see Seabury-Western Theological Seminary)*
Seabury-Western Theological Seminary 131
Seacoast Career Schools 520
Seacoast Ctr. for Edu. 544
Sealey & Associates, LLC *(see C.J. Sealey & Associates, LLC)*
Searcy Beauty Coll. 449
Seark *(see Southeast Arkansas Coll.)*
Seattle Art Inst. *(see Art Inst. of Seattle)*
Seattle Central Coll. *(see Seattle Central Comm. Coll.)*
Seattle Central Comm. Coll. 414
Seattle Coll. *(see Seattle Univ.)*
Seattle Inst. of Art *(see Art Inst. of Seattle)*
Seattle Inst. of Oriental Medicine 414
Seattle Maritime Acad. *(see Seattle Central Comm. Coll.)*
Seattle Massage Sch. *(see Ashmead Coll.)*
Seattle Midwifery Sch. 638
Seattle Pacific Coll. *(see Seattle Pacific Univ.)*
Seattle Pacific Univ. 414
Seattle Seminary *(see Seattle Pacific Univ.)*
Seattle Seminary & Coll. *(see Seattle Pacific Univ.)*
Seattle Univ. 414
Seattle Vocational Inst. 414 *(see also Seattle Central Comm. Coll.)*
Sebring Career Schools 623
Second Dist. Agricultural Sch. *(see Arkansas Tech Univ.)*

Second Start *(see New Hampshire Career Inst.)*
Segal Inst. *(see EduTech Centers)*
Seguin Beauty Sch. 624
Self Mem. Hosp. *(see Self Reg. Healthcare)*
Self Reg. Healthcare 701
Selma Coll. *(see Selma Univ.)*
Selma M. Levine Sch. of Music *(see Levine Sch. of Music)*
Selma Univ. 743
Séminaire de Québec *(see Université Laval)*
Seminar L'Moros Bais Yaakov 569
Seminario Evangelico de Puerto Rico *(see Evangelical Seminary of Puerto Rico)*
Seminario Major San Juan Bautista *(see Pontifical Catholic Univ. of Puerto Rico—Ponce Campus)*
Seminario Major San Juan Bautista 350
Seminary Extension Independent Study Inst. 612
Seminary for Girls *(see Queens Univ. of Charlotte)*
Seminary of Denver *(see Denver Seminary)*
Seminary of Saint Patrick's *(see Saint Patrick's Seminary & Univ.)*
Seminary of Saint Petersburg *(see Saint Petersburg Theological Seminary)*
Seminary of St. Petersburg *(see Saint Petersburg Theological Seminary)*
Seminary of the Genesee Conference *(see Cazenovia Coll.)*
Seminary of the Immaculate Conception 274
Seminary of the Northwest *(see McCormick Theological Seminary)*
Seminary West of the Suwannee *(see Florida State Univ.)*
Seminole Coll. *(see Seminole Comm. Coll., Seminole State Coll.)*
Seminole Comm. Coll. 94
Seminole Jr. Coll. *(see Seminole Comm. Coll., Seminole State Coll.)*
Seminole State Coll. 318
SEMO Hairstyling Acad. 539
Sentara Norfolk General Hosp. Sch. of Health Professions *(see Sentara Sch. of Health Professions)*
Sentara Sch. of Health Professions 633
Seoul National Univ. 716 *(see also Seoul National Univ.)*

Sepulveda Ambulatory Care Ctr. 656
(see also Veterans Affairs Greater
Los Angeles Healthcare
System—Sepulveda)
Sepulveda VA Med. Ctr. (see Veterans
Affairs Greater Los Angeles
Healthcare System—Sepulveda)
Sepulveda Veterans Affairs Med. Ctr.
(see Veterans Affairs Greater Los
Angeles Healthcare System—
Sepulveda)
Sequoia Inst. 723 (see also
WyoTech—Fremont, WyoTech—
Sierra)
Sequoias Coll. (see Coll. of the
Sequoias)
SER Bus. & Tech. Inst. 731
SER-IBM Bus. Inst. (see SER-IBM Bus.
Inst.)
Sessions.edu 570
Seton Hall Coll. (see Seton Hall Univ.)
Seton Hall Univ. 250
Seton Hall Univ. Sch. of Theology (see
Immaculate Conception
Seminary)
Seton Hill Coll. (see Seton Hill Univ.)
Seton Hill Univ. 341
Seton Montessori of Clarendon Hills
(see Montessori Edu. Centers
Associated-Seton)
Settlement Music Sch. 600
Settlement Music Sch. of
Philadelphia, The (see Settlement
Music Sch.)
Settlement Sch. of Music (see
Settlement Music Sch.)
Seven Counties Services, Inc. (see
Jefferson County Internship
Consortium)
Seventh Ward General Hosp. (see
North Oaks Med. Ctr.)
Seventh-day Adventist Theological
Seminary (see Andrews Univ.)
Sewanee: The Univ. of the South (see
Univ. of the South)
Seward County Coll. (see Seward
County Comm. Coll.)
Seward County Comm. Coll. 156
Sewickley Valley Hosp. 699
SGV Honolulu (see Intercultural
Communications Coll.)
Shaarei Torah of Rockland (see
Yeshiva Shaarei Torah of
Rockland)
Shady Grove Adventist Hosp. 675
Shady Grove Hosp. (see Shady Grove
Adventist Hosp.)
Shands Jacksonville Med. Ctr. 95
Shane Global Village Honolulu (see
Intercultural Communications
Coll.)

Sharjah Men's Coll. (see Higher
Colleges of Techno. Sharjah
Men's Coll.)
Sharjah Univ. (see American Univ. of
Sharjah)
Sharjah Women's Coll. 717
Sharon General Hosp. (see Sharon
Reg. Health System)
Sharon Reg. Health System 699
Sharp HealthCare (see Sharp Mem.
Hosp., Sharp Mesa Vista Hosp.)
Sharp Mem. Hosp. 655
Sharp Mesa Vista Hosp. 655
Sharp's Acad. of Hairstyling 532
Shasta Bible Coll. (see Shasta Bible
Coll. & Grad. Sch.)
Shasta Bible Coll. & Grad. Sch. 56
Shasta Coll. 56
Shasta Comm. Mental Health Ctr. 656
Shasta Grad. Sch. (see Shasta Bible
Coll. & Grad. Sch.)
Shasta Mental Health Ctr. (see Shasta
Comm. Mental Health Ctr.)
Shaw Collegiate Inst. (see Shaw Univ.)
Shaw Sch. of Bus. (see Husson Coll.)
Shaw Univ. 292 (see also Rust Coll.)
Shawnee Beauty Coll. 590
Shawnee Coll. (see Shawnee Comm.
Coll.)
Shawnee Comm. Coll. 131
Shawnee Guidance Ctr. (see Family
Service & Guidance Ctr. of
Topeka, Inc.)
Shawnee Language Inst., The 588
Shawnee State Comm. Coll. (see
Shawnee State Univ.)
Shawnee State Univ. 310
Shawnee Univ. (see Shawnee State
Univ.)
Shear Acad. 759
Shear Ego Int'l. Sch. of Hair Design
570
Sheer Success, Inc. (see Acad. of
Cosmetology)
Shelby Bus. Coll. (see Sparks Coll.)
Shelby State Comm. Coll. (see
Southwest Tennessee Comm.
Coll.)
Sheldon Jackson Coll. 11
Shelton Coll. (see Shelton State
Comm. Coll.)
Shelton Comm. Coll. (see Shelton
State Comm. Coll.)
Shelton State Coll. (see Shelton State
Comm. Coll.)
Shelton State Comm. Coll. 7
Shenandoah Coll. (see Shenandoah
Univ.)
Shenandoah Coll. & Conservatory of
Music (see Shenandoah Univ.)

Shenandoah Conservatory of Music
(see Shenandoah Univ.)
Shenandoah Inst. (see Shenandoah
Univ.)
Shenandoah Seminary (see
Shenandoah Univ.)
Shenandoah Univ. 406
Shenango Valley Sch. of Bus. (see
Bus. Inst. of Pennsylvania)
Shepherd Coll. 739 (see also
Shepherd Univ.)
Shepherd Comm. Coll. (see Comm. &
Tech. Coll. of Shepherd)
Shepherd Univ. 420, 739
Shepherd Univ. Comm. & Tech. Coll.
(see Comm. & Tech. Coll. of
Shepherd)
Sherbrooke Univ. (see Université de
Sherbrooke)
Sheridan Coll. 713 (see also Northern
Wyoming Comm. Coll. Dist—
Sheridan)
Sheridan Tech. Ctr. 489
Sheridan Vocational-Tech. Ctr. (see
Sheridan Tech. Ctr.)
Sheridan Voc-Tech Ctr. (see Sheridan
Tech. Ctr.)
Sherman Chiropractic Coll. (see
Sherman Coll. of Straight
Chiropractic)
Sherman Coll. of Straight Chiropractic
358
Sherman Kendall's Acad. of Beauty
Arts & Science—Midvale 629
Sherman Kendall's Acad. of Beauty
Arts & Science—Salt Lake City
629
Shimer Coll. 131
Shippensburg State Coll. (see
Shippensburg Univ. of
Pennsylvania)
Shippensburg Univ. of Pennsylvania
341
Shirley Baker Career Inst. 737
Shoals Comm. Coll. (see Northwest-
Shoals Comm. Coll.)
Sh'or Yoshuv Rabbinical Coll. 274
Shore Beauty Sch. 554
Shore Mem. Health System (see
Shore Mem. Hosp.)
Shore Mem. Hosp. 684
Shoreline Coll. (see Shoreline Comm.
Coll.)
Shoreline Comm. Coll. 415
Shorter Coll. 109
Shreveport Job Corps Ctr. 518
Si Tanka Coll. (see Si Tanka Univ.)
Si Tanka Huron Univ. 736 (see also Si
Tanka Univ.)
Si Tanka Univ. 362, 736
Si Tanka Univ—Huron 736

Sibley Mem. Hosp. 661
Sidney's Hairdressing Coll., Inc. 510
Siebert Associates, Inc. 644
Siegal Coll. of Judaic Studies *(see Laura & Alvin Siegal Coll. of Judaic Studies)*
Siemann Edu. Systems, Inc. *(see DPT Bus. Sch.)*
Siena Coll. 275
Siena Heights Coll. 731 *(see also Siena Heights Univ.)*
Siena Heights Univ. 204, 731
Sierra Acad. of Aeronautics Tech. Inst. 468
Sierra Coll. 56
Sierra Coll. of Beauty 468
Sierra Nevada Coll. 241
Sierra Valley Bus. Coll. 468
Silicon Valley Coll. 56
Silicon Valley Univ. 57
Siloam Sch. of the Bible *(see John Brown Univ.)*
Silver Lake Coll. 427
Silver lake Coll. of the Holy Family *(see Silver Lake Coll.)*
Simi Valley Adult Sch. 656
Simmons Coll. 192 *(see also Hardin-Simmons Univ.)*
Simmons Inst. of Funeral Service 275
Simmons Sch. of Embalming & Mortuary Science *(see Simmons Inst. of Funeral Service)*
Simon Fraser Coll. *(see Simon Fraser Univ.)*
Simon Fraser Univ. 713
Simon's Rock Coll. of Bard 192 *(see also Bard Coll.)*
Simpson Bible Coll. *(see Simpson Univ.)*
Simpson Bible Inst. *(see Simpson Univ.)*
Simpson Coll. 150, 723 *(see also Simpson Univ.)*
Simpson Univ. 57, 723
Sinai Hosp. of Detroit *(see Sinai-Grace Hosp.)*
Sinai Samaritan Med. Ctr. *(see Aurora Sinai Med. Ctr.)*
Sinai-Grace Hosp. 678
Sin-American Med. Rehabilitation Assoc. *(see Samra Univ. of Oriental Medicine)*
Sincalir Coll. *(see Sinclair Comm. Coll.)*
Sinclair Comm. Coll. 310
Sinte Gleska Coll. *(see Sinte Gleska Univ.)*
Sinte Gleska Univ. 362
Sioux Falls Coll. *(see Univ. of Sioux Falls)*

Sioux Falls Univ. *(see Univ. of Sioux Falls)*
Sioux Valley Hosp. 702
Sioux Valley Hosp. USD Med. Ctr. *(see Sioux Valley Hosp.)*
Sioux Valley Hospitals & Health System *(see Sioux Valley Hosp.)*
Sir George Williams Univ. *(see Concordia Univ.)*
Siskiyous Coll. *(see Coll. of the Siskiyous)*
Sisseton-Wahpeton Coll. *(see Sisseton-Wahpeton Comm. Coll.)*
Sisseton-Wahpeton Comm. Coll. 363
Sistema Univeritario Ana G. Mendez—Universidad Metropolitana *(see Universidad Metropolitana)*
Sistema Universitario Ana G. Mendez Universidad del Turabo *(see Universidad del Turabo)*
Sistema Universitario Ana G. Mendez—Universidad del Este *(see Universidad del Este)*
Sisters Assumption Coll. *(see Assumption Coll. for Sisters)*
Sisters of Charity Hosp. 690
Sisters of Mercy Health System *(see Saint John's Mercy Med. Ctr., Saint John's Reg. Health System)*
Sitting Bull Coll. 297
Skadron Coll. 723 *(see also Bryman Coll.)*
Skadron Coll. of Bus. *(see Bryman Coll.)*
Skagit Valley Coll. 415
Skidmore Coll. 275
Skidmore Sch. of Arts *(see Skidmore Coll.)*
Skills Ctr. of Norfolk *(see Norfolk Skills Ctr.)*
SkillTech *(see Ctr. for Techno., Essex)*
Skin Inst., The 629
Skin Works Sch. of Advanced Skin Care 629
Skyline Coll. 57
Slater Industrial Acad. *(see Winston-Salem State Univ.)*
Slater Industrial & State Normal Sch. *(see Winston-Salem State Univ.)*
Slippery Rock Coll. *(see Slippery Rock Univ. of Pennsylvania)*
Slippery Rock State Normal Sch. *(see Slippery Rock Univ. of Pennsylvania)*
Slippery Rock Univ. of Pennsylvania 341
Sloan-Kettering Cancer Ctr. *(see Mem. Sloan-Kettering Cancer Ctr.)*
Smith Coll. 192

Smith Univ. *(see Johnson C. Smith Univ.)*
Smith-Hughes Vocational Sch. *(see Atlanta Tech. Coll.)*
Smith's Coll. *(see Paul Smith's Coll. of Arts & Sciences)*
Snead State Comm. Coll. 7
Snow Coll. 395
Snow Jr. Coll. *(see Snow Coll.)*
Software Advanced Technologies Inst. 723
Software Sense Computer Learning Ctr., Inc. 554
Sojourner-Douglass Coll. 182
Soka Univ. of America 57
Solano Coll. *(see Solano Comm. Coll.)*
Solano Comm. Coll. 57
Solaris Health System *(see John F. Kennedy Med. Ctr.)*
Solove Research Inst. *(see Ohio State Univ.)*
Somerset Christian Coll. 250, 733
Somerset Coll. *(see Somerset Christian Coll., Somerset Comm. Coll.)*
Somerset Comm. Coll. 163
Somerset County Area Vocational Tech. Sch. 699
Somerset County Techno. Inst. 250
Somerset County Vo-Tech Sch. *(see Somerset County Area Vocational Tech. Sch.)*
Somerset Med. Ctr. 685
Somerset Sch. of Massage Therapy 554
Somerset Tech. Coll. *(see Somerset Comm. Coll.)*
Sonoma Coll. 724
Sonoma Coll—Petaluma 57
Sonoma State Coll. *(see Sonoma State Univ.)*
Sonoma State Univ. 57
Sonoran Desert Inst. 446
Sotheby's Educational Studies *(see Sotheby's Inst. of Art)*
Sotheby's Inst. of Art 570
Soule Univ. *(see Southwestern Univ.)*
Sound Master Recording Engineer Sch/Audio-Video Inst. 468
South Africa Univ. *(see Univ. of South Africa (UNISA))*
South Alabama Univ. *(see Univ. of South Alabama)*
South Arkansas Coll. *(see South Arkansas Comm. Coll.)*
South Arkansas Comm. Coll. 26
South Bay State Coll. *(see California State Univ—Dominguez Hills)*
South Baylo Univ. 656
South Bend Commercial Coll. *(see Brown Mackie Coll—South Bend)*

South Bend English Inst. 588
South Carolina Area Trade Sch. *(see Denmark Tech. Coll.)*
South Carolina Area Trade Sch—Columbia Campus *(see Midlands Tech. Coll.)*
South Carolina Coll. *(see Univ. of South Carolina—Columbia)*
South Carolina Dale Carnegie Training *(see Dale Carnegie Training of South Carolina, LLC)*
South Carolina Dept. of Corrections *(see Watkins Pre-Release Ctr.)*
South Carolina Med. Coll. *(see Med. Univ. of South Carolina)*
South Carolina Med. Univ. *(see Med. Univ. of South Carolina)*
South Carolina Military Acad. *(see Citadel)*
South Carolina Sch. of Healing Arts *(see Charleston Sch. of Massage)*
South Carolina State Univ. 358
South Central Coll—Mankato 215, 731
South Central Comm. Coll. *(see Gateway Comm. Coll.)*
South Central Tech *(see South Central Coll—Mankato)*
South Central Tech. Coll—Albert Lea *(see Riverland Comm. Coll—Austin)*
South Central Tech. Coll—Faribault *(see South Central Coll—Mankato)*
South Central Tech. Coll—Mankato *(see South Central Coll—Mankato)*
South Central Tech. Coll—Mankato 731
South Coast Coll. 57
South Coast Coll. of Court Reporting *(see South Coast Coll.)*
South Coast Nuclear Medicine 656
South Coll. 293, 369, 726 *(see also Amherst Coll., South Univ.)*
South Dakota Dale Carnegie Training *(see Leadership Training Inst.)*
South Dakota Mines Sch. *(see South Dakota Sch. of Mines & Techno.)*
South Dakota Sch. of Mines & Techno. 363
South Dakota State Univ. 363
South Dakota Univ. *(see Univ. of South Dakota)*
South Florida Coll. *(see South Florida Comm. Coll.)*
South Florida Comm. Coll. 94
South Florida Inst. *(see Florida Southern Coll.)*
South Florida Inst. of Techno. 489

South Florida Med. Career Inst. *(see Med. Career Inst. of South Florida)*
South Florida Montessori Edu. Ctr. 489
South Florida State Hosp. 663
South Florida Univ. *(see Univ. of South Florida)*
South Georgia Coll. 109 *(see also South Georgia Tech. Coll.)*
South Georgia State Normal Coll. *(see Valdosta State Univ.)*
South Georgia Tech. Coll. 109, 726
South Georgia Tech. Inst. 726 *(see also South Georgia Tech. Coll.)*
South Hills Beauty Acad. 600
South Hills Bus. Sch. *(see South Hills Sch. of Bus. & Techno.)*
South Hills Sch. of Bus. & Techno. 341
South Lancaster Acad. *(see Atlantic Union Coll.)*
South Louisiana Beauty Coll. 518
South Louisiana Coll. *(see South Louisiana Comm. Coll.)*
South Louisiana Comm. Coll. 746
South Mountain Coll. *(see South Mountain Comm. Coll.)*
South Mountain Comm. Coll. 20
South Nassau Communities Hosp. 690
South Nassau Hosp. *(see South Nassau Communities Hosp.)*
South Park Coll. *(see Lamar Univ.)*
South Park Jr. Coll. *(see Lamar Univ.)*
South Philadelphia Beauty Acad. 736
South Piedmont Comm. Coll. 293
South Plains Coll. 384
South Plains Jr. Coll. *(see South Plains Coll.)*
South Puget Sound Coll. *(see South Puget Sound Comm. Coll.)*
South Puget Sound Comm. Coll. 415
South Seattle Coll. *(see South Seattle Comm. Coll.)*
South Seattle Comm. Coll. 415
South Suburban Coll. of Cook County 131
South Suburban Hosp. *(see Advocate South Suburban Hosp.)*
South Texas Barber Coll. 624
South Texas Bible Inst. at Houston *(see Mid-America Christian Univ.)*
South Texas Coll. 384, 737
South Texas Coll. of Law 384
South Texas Comm. Coll. 737 *(see also South Texas Coll.)*
South Texas Jr. Coll. *(see Univ. of Houston—Downtown)*
South Texas State Teachers Coll. *(see Texas A&M Univ—Kingsville)*
South Texas Veterans HealthCare System 704

South Texas Vo-Tech Inst—Brownsville 737
South Texas Vo-Tech Inst—McAllen 624
South Texas Vo-Tech Inst—Weslaco 624
South Univ. 109, 726
Southampton Coll. *(see Long Island Univ.)*
Southcentral Foundation—Alaska Native Med. Ctr. 651
Southcentral Tech. Inst. *(see Ivy Tech Comm. Coll. of Indiana—Sellersburg)*
Southcentral—Alaska Native Med. *(see Southcentral Foundation-Alaska Native Med. Ctr.)*
Southeast Applied Techno. Coll. 761
Southeast Area Vocational Tech. Sch. *(see Southeast Tech. Inst.)*
Southeast Arkansas Coll. 26
Southeast Arkansas Tech. Coll. *(see Southeast Arkansas Coll.)*
Southeast Coll. *(see City Colleges of Chicago—Olive-Harvey Coll., Remington Coll—Mobile)*
Southeast Coll. of Techno. *(see Remington Coll—Mobile)*
Southeast Comm. & Tech. Coll. *(see Southeast Kentucky Comm. & Tech. Coll.)*
Southeast Comm. Coll. 238, 729 *(see also Southeast Kentucky Comm. & Tech. Coll.)*
Southeast Florida Dale Carnegie Training *(see Southeast Florida Inst., Inc.)*
Southeast Florida Inst., Inc. 489
Southeast Inst. of Culinary Arts *(see First Coast Tech. Inst.)*
Southeast Inst. of Oriental Medicine *(see Acupuncture & Massage Coll.)*
Southeast Kansas Tech. Sch. 728 *(see also Coffeyville Comm. Coll.)*
Southeast Kentucky Coll. *(see Southeast Kentucky Comm. & Tech. Coll.)*
Southeast Kentucky Comm. & Tech. Coll. 164, 729
Southeast Missouri Hairstyling Acad. *(see SEMO Hairstyling Acad.)*
Southeast Missouri Hosp. Coll. of Nursing & Health Sciences 231
Southeast Missouri State Univ. 231
Southeast Missouri Univ. *(see Southeast Missouri State Univ.)*
Southeast Reg. Med. Command *(see Dwight David Eisenhower Army Med. Ctr.)*

Southeast Reg. Tech. Ctr. *(see Southeast Kentucky Comm. & Tech. Coll.)*
Southeast Sch. of Cosmetology 514
Southeast Tech *(see Minnesota State Coll-Southeast Tech.)*
Southeast Tech. Inst. 363 *(see also Ivy Tech Comm. Coll. of Indiana— Madison)*
Southeast Vocational Tech. Inst. *(see Southeast Tech. Inst.)*
Southeast Wisconsin Dale Carnegie Training *(see J. R. Rodgers & Associates, Inc.)*
Southeastern Baptist Coll. 221
Southeastern Baptist Theological Seminary, The 293 *(see also Temple Baptist Seminary)*
Southeastern Beauty Sch—Midtown 495
Southeastern Beauty Sch—North Lumpkin 495
Southeastern Bible Coll. 8
Southeastern Bible Inst. *(see Southeastern Univ.)*
Southeastern Bus. Coll. *(see Gallipolis Career Coll.)*
Southeastern Bus. Coll. 310
Southeastern Bus. Coll—Sandusky *(see Ohio Bus. Coll.)*
Southeastern Bus. Inst. *(see Southeastern Bus. Coll.)*
Southeastern Career Coll. 369
Southeastern Career Inst. 624 *(see also Southeastern Career Inst.)*
Southeastern Coll. *(see Southeastern Baptist Coll., Southeastern Baptist Theological Seminary, Southeastern Bible Coll., Southeastern Career Coll., Southeastern Tech. Coll.)*
Southeastern Coll. at Wake Forest *(see Southeastern Baptist Theological Seminary)*
Southeastern Coll. of the Assemblies of God 725 *(see also Southeastern Univ.)*
Southeastern Comm. Coll. 150, 293
Southeastern Illinois Coll. 131
Southeastern Illinois Jr. Coll. *(see Southeastern Illinois Coll.)*
Southeastern Louisiana Univ. 173
Southeastern Oklahoma State Univ. 318
Southeastern Paralegal Inst. *(see Southeastern Career Coll., Southeastern Career Inst.)*
Southeastern Pennsylvania Dale Carnegie Training *(see Leadership Inst., Inc.)*

Southeastern Sch. of Cosmetology 441
Southeastern Sch. of Neuromuscular & Massage Therapy, Inc. 489, 573, 609
Southeastern State Coll. *(see Southeastern Oklahoma State Univ.)*
Southeastern State Normal Sch. *(see Southeastern Oklahoma State Univ.)*
Southeastern State Teachers Coll. *(see Southeastern Oklahoma State Univ.)*
Southeastern Tech. Coll. 109, 727, 745
Southeastern Tech. Inst. 677, 727 *(see also Southeastern Tech. Coll.)*
Southeastern Univ. 79, 94, 725
Southern Adventist Univ. 369
Southern Alabama Coll. *(see Alabama Southern Comm. Coll.)*
Southern Alabama Comm. Coll. *(see Alabama Southern Comm. Coll.)*
Southern Alberta Inst. of Techno. 713
Southern Arizona Mental Health Corporation *(see Southern Arizona Psychology Internship Consortium)*
Southern Arizona Psychology Internship Consortium 652
Southern Arizona Veterans Affairs Health Care System 652
Southern Arizona Veterans Affairs Med. Ctr. *(see Southern Arizona Veterans Affairs Health Care System)*
Southern Arkansas Univ. 27
Southern Arkansas Univ—Tech 27
Southern Baptist Coll. *(see Williams Baptist Coll.)*
Southern Baptist Seminary *(see Southern Baptist Theological Seminary)*
Southern Baptist Theological Seminary, The 164
Southern Bible Coll. *(see Messenger Coll.)*
Southern Bible Inst. *(see Southwestern Christian Coll.)*
Southern Bus. Coll. *(see Ohio Bus. Coll.)*
Southern California Bible Coll. *(see Southern California Seminary)*
Southern California Bible Coll. & Seminary *(see Southern California Seminary)*

Southern California Coll. *(see Southern California Univ. of Health Sciences, Maric Coll— Anaheim, Vanguard Univ. of Southern California)*
Southern California Coll. of Chiropractic *(see Southern California Univ. of Health Sciences)*
Southern California Coll. of Court Reporting *(see Maric Coll— Anaheim)*
Southern California Coll. of Optometry 57
Southern California Counseling Ctr. 656
Southern California Inst. of Architecture 57
Southern California Inst. of Techno. 57
Southern California Reg. Occupational Ctr. 656 *(see also Southern California Reg. Occupational Ctr.)*
Southern California Seminary 57
Southern California Univ. *(see Univ. of Southern California)*
Southern California Univ. of Health Sciences 58, 723
Southern Careers Inst. 624
Southern Christian Coll. *(see Southern Christian Univ.)*
Southern Christian Univ. 8
Southern Coll. *(see Florida Southern Coll., Keiser Coll., Southern Adventist Univ., Southern Comm. Coll., Southern Coll. of Optometry, Southern Polytechnic State Univ.)*
Southern Coll. of Optometry 370
Southern Coll. of Seventh-day Adventist *(see Southern Adventist Univ.)*
Southern Coll. of Techno. *(see Southern Polytechnic State Univ.)*
Southern Colorado Jr. Coll. *(see Colorado State Univ—Pueblo)*
Southern Colorado State Coll. *(see Colorado State Univ—Pueblo)*
Southern Colorado Univ. *(see Colorado State Univ—Pueblo)*
Southern Comm. Coll. 441
Southern Connecticut State Coll. *(see Southern Connecticut State Univ.)*
Southern Connecticut State Univ. 75
Southern Educational Alliance 624
Southern Evangelical Seminary 293
Southern Idaho Coll. *(see Coll. of Southern Idaho)*
Southern Illinois Univ. Carbondale 131
Southern Illinois Univ. Edwardsville 132
Southern Indiana Univ. *(see Univ. of Southern Indiana)*

Southern Industrial Sch. *(see Southern Adventist Univ.)*
Southern Inst. of Cosmetology 449
Southern Jr. Coll. *(see Southern Adventist Univ.)*
Southern Louisiana Internship Consortium *(see Louisiana State Univ. Health Sciences Ctr. in New Orleans)*
Southern Maine Coll. *(see Southern Maine Comm. Coll.)*
Southern Maine Comm. Coll. 176, 730
Southern Maine Tech. Coll. 730 *(see also Southern Maine Comm. Coll.)*
Southern Maine Univ. *(see Univ. of Southern Maine)*
Southern Maryland Coll. *(see Coll. of Southern Maryland)*
Southern Methodist Coll. 358 *(see also Southern Methodist Univ.)*
Southern Methodist Univ. 384
Southern Mississippi Univ. *(see Univ. of Southern Mississippi)*
Southern Nazarene Univ. 318
Southern Nevada Coll. *(see Comm. Coll. of Southern Nevada)*
Southern Nevada Comm. Coll. *(see Comm. Coll. of Southern Nevada)*
Southern Nevada Univ. of Cosmetology 543
Southern New England Sch. of Law 192
Southern New Hampshire Univ. 244, 732
Southern New Jersey Dale Carnegie Training *(see Success Unlimited, Inc.)*
Southern New Jersey Tech. Sch. 554
Southern Normal Sch. of Bowling Green *(see Western Kentucky Univ.)*
Southern Ohio Coll. *(see Brown Mackie Coll—Cincinnati)*
Southern Ohio Coll—Findlay *(see Brown Mackie Coll—Findlay)*
Southern Ohio Coll—Northeast *(see Brown Mackie Coll—Cincinnati)*
Southern Oregon State Coll. *(see Southern Oregon Univ.)*
Southern Oregon Univ. 323
Southern Polytech *(see Southern Polytechnic State Univ.)*
Southern Polytechnic State Univ. 109
Southern Reg. Med. Ctr. 665
Southern Sch. of Beauty 590
Southern Seminary Coll. *(see Southern Virginia Univ.)*
Southern Seminary Jr. Coll. *(see Southern Virginia Univ.)*

Southern State Coll. *(see Southern State Comm. Coll.)*
Southern State Comm. Coll. 310
Southern State General & Tech. Coll. *(see Southern State Comm. Coll.)*
Southern Tech. Ctr. 725
Southern Tech. Coll. *(see Remington Coll—Lafayette)*
Southern Tech. Inst. 489 *(see also Southern Polytechnic State Univ.)*
Southern Texas Univ. *(see Texas Southern Univ.)*
Southern Training Sch. *(see Southern Adventist Univ.)*
Southern Union Coll. *(see Southern Union State Comm. Coll.)*
Southern Union Comm. Coll. *(see Southern Union State Comm. Coll.)*
Southern Union State Comm. Coll. 8
Southern Univ. *(see Birmingham-Southern Coll., Southern Univ. & Agricultural & Mechanical Coll. at Baton Rouge)*
Southern Univ. & A&M Coll. *(see Southern Univ. & Agricultural & Mechanical Coll. at Baton Rouge)*
Southern Univ. & Agricultural & Mechanical Coll. at Baton Rouge 173
Southern Univ. at New Orleans 174
Southern Univ. at Shreveport 174
Southern Univ. Law Ctr. *(see Southern Univ. & Agricultural & Mechanical Coll. at Baton Rouge)*
Southern Utah Univ. 395
Southern Vermont Coll. 398
Southern Virginia Coll. for Women *(see Southern Virginia Univ.)*
Southern Virginia Univ. 406
Southern Wesleyan Univ. 358
Southern West Virginia Coll. *(see Southern West Virginia Comm. & Tech. Coll.)*
Southern West Virginia Comm. & Tech. Coll. 420
Southern West Virginia Comm. Coll. *(see Southern West Virginia Comm. & Tech. Coll.)*
Southlake Ctr. for Mental Health 671
Southside Reg. Med. Ctr. 706
Southside Virginia Coll. *(see Southside Virginia Comm. Coll.)*
Southside Virginia Comm. Coll. 406
Southwest Acupuncture Coll. 254
Southwest Applied Techno. Coll. 761
Southwest Baptist Coll. *(see Southwest Baptist Univ.)*
Southwest Baptist Univ. 232
Southwest Ctr. for Advanced Studies *(see Univ. of Texas at Dallas)*

Southwest Coll. *(see City Colleges of Chicago—Richard J. Daley Coll., Coll. of the Southwest, Los Angeles Southwest Coll., Southwest Coll. of Naturopathic Medicine & Health Sciences)*
Southwest Coll. of Los Angeles *(see Los Angeles Southwest Coll.)*
Southwest Coll. of Naturopathic Medicine & Health Sciences 20
Southwest Colorado Area Vocational-Tech. Sch. *(see San Juan Basin Tech. Coll.)*
Southwest Episcopal Theological Seminary *(see Episcopal Theological Seminary of the Southwest)*
Southwest Florida Bus. Coll. *(see Southwest Florida Coll.)*
Southwest Florida Coll. 94
Southwest Georgia Coll. *(see Southwest Georgia Tech. Coll.)*
Southwest Georgia Tech. Coll. 109
Southwest Georgia Tech. Inst. *(see Southwest Georgia Tech. Coll.)*
Southwest Health Career Inst., Inc. 557
Southwest Hosp. of Houston *(see Mem. Hermann Southwest Hosp.)*
Southwest Inst. of Techno. *(see Border Inst. of Techno.)*
Southwest Inst. of Healing Arts 446
Southwest Inst. of Health Careers *(see Southwest Health Career Inst., Inc.)*
Southwest Inst. of Merchandising & Design *(see Border Inst. of Techno.)*
Southwest Inst. of Myotherapy *(see Southwest Inst. of Healing Arts)*
Southwest Inst. of Techno. 384, 737
Southwest Kansas Conference Coll. *(see Southwestern Coll.)*
Southwest Kansas Tech. Sch. 510
Southwest Los Angeles Coll. *(see Los Angeles Southwest Coll.)*
Southwest Minnesota State Univ. 215, 731
Southwest Mississippi Coll. *(see Southwest Mississippi Comm. Coll.)*
Southwest Mississippi Comm. Coll. 221
Southwest Missouri State Coll. *(see Missouri State Univ.)*
Southwest Missouri State Teachers Coll. *(see Missouri State Univ.)*
Southwest Missouri State Univ. 732 *(see also Missouri State Univ.)*

Southwest Naturpathic Coll. *(see Southwest Coll. of Naturopathic Medicine & Health Sciences)*

Southwest Sch. of Electronics 737 *(see also Southwest Inst. of Techno.)*

Southwest State Tech. Coll. *(see Bishop State Comm. Coll— Southwest Campus)*

Southwest State Univ. 731 *(see also Southwest Minnesota State Univ.)*

Southwest Tech. Inst. *(see Ivy Tech Comm. Coll. of Indiana— Southwest, Southern Arkansas Univ—Tech)*

Southwest Tennessee Coll. *(see Southwest Tennessee Comm. Coll.)*

Southwest Tennessee Comm. Coll. 370 *(see also Southwest Tennessee Comm. Coll.)*

Southwest Texas Coll. *(see Southwest Texas Jr. Coll.)*

Southwest Texas Jr. Coll. 384

Southwest Texas State Univ. 737 *(see also Texas State Univ—San Marcos)*

Southwest Univ. 174 *(see also Southwest Baptist Univ.)*

Southwest Virginia Coll. *(see Southwest Virginia Comm. Coll.)*

Southwest Virginia Comm. Coll. 406

Southwest Virginia Dale Carnegie Training *(see Lawrence-White Associates, Inc.)*

Southwest Virginia Inst. *(see Virginia Intermont Coll.)*

Southwest Wisconsin Coll. *(see Southwest Wisconsin Tech. Coll.)*

Southwest Wisconsin Tech. Coll. 427

Southwestern Adventist Coll. 737 *(see also Southwestern Adventist Univ.)*

Southwestern Adventist Univ. 385, 737

Southwestern Assemblies of God Coll. *(see Southwestern Assemblies of God Univ.)*

Southwestern Assemblies of God Univ. 385

Southwestern Baptist Seminary *(see Southwestern Baptist Theological Seminary)*

Southwestern Baptist Theological Seminary 385

Southwestern Baptist Univ. *(see Union Univ.)*

Southwestern Bible Coll. *(see Southwestern Christian Univ.)*

Southwestern Bible Inst. *(see Southwestern Assemblies of God Univ.)*

Southwestern Christian Coll. 385

Southwestern Christian Univ. 318

Southwestern Coll. 20, 58, 156, 254, 310 *(see also Southwestern Assemblies of God Univ., Southwestern Christian Coll., Southwestern Christian Univ., Southwestern Comm. Coll.)*

Southwestern Coll. of Bus. *(see Southwestern Coll.)*

Southwestern Coll. of Christian Ministries *(see Southwestern Christian Univ.)*

Southwestern Coll. of the Assemblies of God *(see Southwestern Assemblies of God Univ.)*

Southwestern Coll. of the Bible *(see Southwestern Assemblies of God Univ.)*

Southwestern Collegiate Inst. *(see John Brown Univ.)*

Southwestern Comm. Coll. 150, 293

Southwestern Connecticut Dale Carnegie Training *(see B. Dickson & Associates, LLC)*

Southwestern Conservative Baptist Bible Coll. *(see Southwestern Coll.)*

Southwestern Illinois Coll. 132

Southwestern Indian Polytechnic Inst. 254

Southwestern Inst. of Techno. *(see Southwestern Oklahoma State Univ.)*

Southwestern Jr. Coll. *(see Southwestern Adventist Univ.)*

Southwestern Michigan Coll. 204

Southwestern Montessori Training Ctr. 624

Southwestern Normal Sch. *(see Southwestern Oklahoma State Univ.)*

Southwestern Oklahoma State Coll. *(see Southwestern Oklahoma State Univ.)*

Southwestern Oklahoma State Univ. 318

Southwestern Oregon Coll. *(see Southwestern Oregon Comm. Coll.)*

Southwestern Oregon Comm. Coll. 323

Southwestern Paralegal Inst. *(see Southwestern Prof. Inst.)*

Southwestern Prof. Inst. 624

Southwestern State Coll. *(see Southwestern Oklahoma State Univ.)*

Southwestern State Coll. of Diversified Occupations *(see Southwestern Oklahoma State Univ.)*

Southwestern State Teachers Coll. *(see Southwestern Oklahoma State Univ.)*

Southwestern Tech. Coll. *(see Minnesota West Comm. & Tech. Coll—Granite Falls, Minnesota West Comm. & Tech. Coll— Jackson, Minnesota West Comm. & Tech. Coll—Pipestone, Southwestern Comm. Coll.)*

Southwestern Tech. Coll—Granite Falls *(see Minnesota West Comm. & Tech. Coll—Granite Falls)*

Southwestern Tech. Inst. *(see Minnesota West Comm. & Tech. Coll—Granite Falls, Minnesota West Comm. & Tech. Coll— Jackson, Minnesota West Comm. & Tech. Coll—Pipestone, Southwestern Comm. Coll.)*

Southwestern Union Coll. *(see Southwestern Adventist Univ.)*

Southwestern Univ. 385 *(see also Blinn Coll., Southwestern Christian Univ., Southwestern Univ. Sch. of Law)*

Southwestern Univ. Sch. of Law 656

Southwestern Wisconsin Dale Carnegie Training *(see Siebert Associates, Inc.)*

Sowela Tech. Comm. Coll. 174, 729

Spa Sch., The 584

Spa Tech Inst. 520, 730

Spalding Univ. 164

Spanish Coalition for Jobs, Inc. 503

Spanish-American Inst. 570

Sparks Coll. 503

Sparks State Tech. Coll. *(see George C. Wallace State Comm. Coll— Dothan)*

Spartan Coll. of Aeronautics & Techno. 318, 735

Spartan Sch. of Aeronautics 735 *(see also Spartan Coll. of Aeronautics & Techno.)*

Spartanburg Coll. *(see Spartanburg Tech. Coll.)*

Spartanburg Methodist Coll. 358

Spartanburg Reg. Med. Ctr. 701

Spartanburg Tech. Coll. 358

Spearfish Normal Sch. *(see Black Hills State Univ.)*

Specs Howard Sch. of Broadcast Arts Inc. 532

Spectrum Health—Butterworth Campus 678

Spelman Coll. 109

Spencer Coll. *(see Iowa Lakes Comm. Coll—Spencer Campus)*
Spencerian Coll. 164
Spertus Inst. of Jewish Studies 132
Spiritual Care & Edu. Ctr. 694
Spohn Hosp. *(see CHRISTUS Spohn Hosp. Corpus Christi—Mem.)*
Spokane Coll. *(see Pacific Lutheran Univ., Spokane Comm. Coll.)*
Spokane Comm. Coll. 415
Spokane Falls Coll. *(see Spokane Falls Comm. Coll.)*
Spokane Falls Comm. Coll. 415
Spokane Univ. *(see Northwest Christian Coll.)*
Spoon River Coll. 132
Sports Acad. *(see United States Sports Acad.)*
Spring Arbor Coll. *(see Spring Arbor Univ.)*
Spring Arbor Univ. 204
Spring Coll. *(see Springfield Coll.)*
Spring Creek Normal & Collegiate Inst. *(see Bridgewater Coll.)*
Spring Garden Coll. *(see Automotive Training Ctr.)*
Spring Grove Hosp. Ctr. 675
Spring Hill Coll. 8
Spring Inst. for Intercultural Learning 472
Spring Int'l. Language Ctr., Inc. 472
Spring Valley Montessori Teacher Edu. Program 707
Springfield & Clark County Tech. Edu. Program *(see Clark State Comm. Coll.)*
Springfield Beauty Acad., Inc. 633
Springfield Bus. Sch. *(see Springfield Coll.)*
Springfield Coll. 192, 232 *(see also Springfield Coll. in Illinois, Springfield Coll. of Beauty, Springfield Tech. Comm. Coll.)*
Springfield Coll. in Illinois 132
Springfield Coll. of Beauty 593
Springfield Coll. of Benedictine Univ. *(see Springfield Coll. in Illinois)*
Springfield Comm. Coll. *(see Springfield Tech. Comm. Coll.)*
Springfield Hosp. Ctr. 675
Springfield Jr. Coll. *(see Springfield Coll. in Illinois)*
Springfield Tech. Coll. *(see Springfield Tech. Comm. Coll.)*
Springfield Tech. Comm. Coll. 192
Springfield-Clark County Joint Vocational Sch. 584
Springfield-Clark County JVS *(see Springfield-Clark County Joint Vocational Sch.)*
Springhouse Computer Sch. 600

Springhouse Edu. & Consulting Services *(see Springhouse Computer Sch.)*
Sprunt Comm. Coll. *(see James Sprunt Comm. Coll.)*
Spurgeon Baptist Bible Coll. 725, 734 *(see also Piedmont Baptist Coll.)*
Spurr Sch. of Practical Nursing *(see B.M. Spurr Sch. of Practical Nursing)*
SS. Cyril & Methodius Seminary 204
St. Agnes Sch. of Nursing *(see Marian Coll. of Fond du Lac)*
St. Albert's Coll. *(see Dominican Sch. of Philosophy & Theology)*
St. Aloysius Acad. *(see Mount Aloysius Coll.)*
St. Ambrose Univ. *(see Saint Ambrose Univ.)*
St. Andrew's Coll. *(see Saint Andrew's Coll.)*
St. Andrews Presbyterian Coll. *(see Saint Andrews Presbyterian Coll.)*
St. Anne's Hosp. *(see Saint Anne's Hosp.)*
St. Anselm Coll. *(see Saint Anselm Coll.)*
St. Anthony Central Hosp. *(see Saint Anthony Central Hosp.)*
St. Anthony Hosp. *(see Saint Anthony Hosp.)*
St. Anthony Nursing Coll. *(see Saint Anthony Coll. of Nursing)*
St. Anthony's Allied Health & Nursing Inst. *(see Saint Vincent Catholic Med. Centers of New York)*
St. Anthony's Hosp. of Denver *(see Saint Anthony Central Hosp.)*
St. Augustine Coll. *(see Saint Augustine Coll.)*
St. Augustine Health Sciences Univ. *(see Univ. of St. Augustine for Health Sciences)*
St. Augustine Tech. Ctr. *(see First Coast Tech. Inst.)*
St. Barnabas Health Care System *(see Monmouth Med. Ctr., Newark Beth Israel Med. Ctr., Saint Barnabas Med. Ctr.)*
St. Barnabas Hosp. *(see Saint Barnabas Hosp.)*
St. Barnabas Med. Ctr. *(see Saint Barnabas Med. Ctr.)*
St. Benedict Coll. *(see Coll. of Saint Benedict)*
St. Bernard's Inst. *(see Saint Bernard's Sch. of Theology & Ministry)*
St. Bernard's Sch. of Theology & Ministry *(see Saint Bernard's Sch. of Theology & Ministry)*

St. Bonaventure Univ. *(see Saint Bonaventure Univ.)*
St. Catharine Coll. *(see Saint Catharine Coll.)*
St. Catherine Coll. *(see Coll. of Saint Catherine)*
St. Cecilia Normal Sch. *(see Aquinas Coll.)*
St. Charles Borromeo Seminary *(see Saint Charles Borromeo Seminary)*
St. Charles Coll. *(see Saint Charles Comm. Coll.)*
St. Charles Comm. Coll. *(see Saint Charles Comm. Coll.)*
St. Charles Hosp. *(see Saint Charles Hosp.)*
St. Charles Sch. of Massage Therapy *(see Saint Charles Sch. of Massage Therapy)*
St. Charles Seminary *(see Saint Charles Borromeo Seminary)*
St. Christopher's Childrens Hosp. *(see Saint Christopher's Hosp. for Children)*
St. Christopher's Hosp. for Children *(see Saint Christopher's Hosp. for Children)*
St. Clair Coll. of Applied Arts & Techno. *(see Saint Clair Coll. of Applied Arts & Techno.)*
St. Clair County Coll. *(see Saint Clair County Comm. Coll.)*
St. Clair County Comm. Coll. *(see Saint Clair County Comm. Coll.)*
St. Clara Coll. *(see Dominican Univ.)*
St. Clare Coll. *(see Cardinal Stritch Univ.)*
St. Clare's Hosp. *(see Saint Clare's Hosp.)*
St. Cloud Bus. Coll. *(see Rasmussen Coll—St. Cloud Campus)*
St. Cloud Coll. *(see Saint Cloud Tech. Coll.)*
St. Cloud Hosp. *(see Saint Cloud Hosp.)*
St. Cloud State Coll. *(see Saint Cloud State Univ.)*
St. Cloud State Teachers Coll. *(see Saint Cloud State Univ.)*
St. Cloud State Univ. *(see Saint Cloud State Univ.)*
St. Cloud Tech. Coll. *(see Saint Cloud Tech. Coll.)*
St. Edward's Acad. *(see Saint Edward's Univ.)*
St. Edward's Coll. *(see Saint Edward's Univ.)*
St. Edward's Univ. *(see Saint Edward's Univ.)*

St. Elizabeth Coll. *(see Coll. of Saint Elizabeth)*

St. Elizabeth Coll. of Nursing *(see Saint Elizabeth Coll. of Nursing)*

St. Elizabeth Hosp. *(see Saint Elizabeth Med. Ctr.)*

St. Elizabeth Med. Ctr. *(see Saint Elizabeth Coll. of Nursing, Saint Elizabeth Med. Ctr.)*

St. Elizabeths Hosp. *(see Saint Elizabeths Hosp.)*

St. Elizabeth's Hosp. *(see Saint Elizabeth's Hosp.)*

St. Elizabeth's Med. Ctr. *(see Saint Elizabeth's Med. Ctr.)*

St. Francis Acad. *(see Saint Francis Coll., Univ. of Saint Francis)*

St. Francis Career Coll. *(see Saint Francis Career Coll.)*

St. Francis Coll. *(see Saint Francis Coll., Univ. of New England)*

St. Francis De Sales Coll. *(see DeSales Univ.)*

St. Francis Hosp. *(see Bon Secours Saint Francis Hosp., Saint Francis Hosp., Saint Francis Med. Ctr.)*

St. Francis Hosp. & Health Centers *(see Saint Francis Hosp. & Health Centers)*

St. Francis Hosp-Resurrection Health Care *(see Saint Francis Hosp-Resurrection Health Care)*

St. Francis Med. Ctr. *(see OSF Saint Francis Med. Ctr., Saint Francis Med. Ctr.)*

St. Francis Normal Sch. *(see Marian Coll.)*

St. Francis Sch. of Practical Nursing *(see Saint Francis Sch. of Practical Nursing)*

St. Francis Seminary *(see Saint Francis Seminary)*

St. Francis Solanus Coll. *(see Quincy Univ.)*

St. Francis Univ. *(see Saint Francis Univ., Univ. of Saint Francis)*

St. Francis/Mount Sinai Hosp. *(see Saint Francis/Mount Sinai Hosp.)*

St. Gregory's Seminary *(see Athenaeum of Ohio)*

St. Gregory's Univ. *(see Saint Gregory's Univ.)*

St. Ignatius Coll. *(see John Carroll Univ.)*

St. James Hosp. *(see Saint James Mercy Health System)*

St. James Mercy Health System *(see Saint James Mercy Health System)*

St. James Mercy Hosp. *(see Saint James Mercy Health System)*

St. John Fisher Coll. *(see Saint John Fisher Coll.)*

St. John Health *(see Saint John Hosp. & Med. Ctr.)*

St. John Health System *(see Providence Hosp. & Med. Centers)*

St. John Health System Sch. of Med. Techno. *(see Saint John Health System Sch. of Med. Techno.)*

St. John Hosp. & Med. Ctr. *(see Saint John Hosp. & Med. Ctr.)*

St. John Med. Ctr. *(see Saint John Hosp. & Med. Ctr.)*

St. John Providence Park Hosp. *(see Providence Hosp. & Med. Centers)*

St. John's Child & Family Development Ctr. *(see Saint John's Child & Family Development Ctr.)*

St. John's Child Study Ctr. *(see Saint John's Child & Family Development Ctr.)*

St. John's Coll. *(see Saint John's Coll.)*

St. John's Hosp. *(see Saint John's Mercy Med. Ctr., Saint John's Reg. Health System, Saint John's Reg. Med. Ctr.)*

St. John's McNamara Hosp. *(see Rapid City Reg. Hosp.)*

St. John's Mercy Med. Ctr. *(see Saint John's Mercy Med. Ctr.)*

St. John's Reg. Health System *(see Saint John's Reg. Health System)*

St. John's Reg. Med. Ctr. *(see Saint John's Reg. Med. Ctr.)*

St. John's Seminary *(see Saint John's Seminary)*

St. John's Univ. *(see Saint John's Univ.)*

St. Joseph Coll. *(see Coll. of Saint Joseph, Loras Coll., Saint Joseph Coll., Southern Vermont Coll.)*

St. Joseph Coll. & Seminary *(see Saint Joseph Seminary Coll.)*

St. Joseph Healthcare *(see Saint Joseph Healthcare)*

St. Joseph Hosp. *(see Saint Joseph Healthcare, Saint Joseph Hosp., Saint Joseph Med. Ctr., Windham Comm. Mem. Hosp.)*

St. Joseph Jr. Coll. *(see Missouri Western State Univ.)*

St. Joseph Med. Ctr. *(see Saint Joseph Med. Ctr.)*

St. Joseph Mercy Hosp. *(see Mercy Med. Ctr. Sioux City, Mercy Med. Ctr. North Iowa)*

St. Joseph Mercy Hosp-Oakland *(see Saint Joseph Mercy Hosp-Oakland)*

St. Joseph Reg. Health Ctr. *(see Saint Joseph Reg. Health Ctr.)*

St. Joseph Stake Acad. *(see Eastern Arizona Coll.)*

St. Joseph's Calumet Coll. *(see Calumet Coll. of St. Joseph)*

St. Joseph's Coll. *(see Saint Joseph's Coll., Saint Joseph's Coll. of Maine)*

St. Joseph's Healthcare System, Inc. *(see Saint Joseph's Reg. Med. Ctr.)*

St. Joseph's Hosp. *(see Inst. of Allied Med. Professions, Saint Joseph's Reg. Med. Ctr.)*

St. Joseph's Hosp. Health Ctr. *(see Saint Joseph's Hosp. Health Ctr.)*

St. Joseph's Med. Ctr. *(see Saint Joseph's Med. Ctr.)*

St. Joseph's Normal Sch. *(see Alverno Coll.)*

St. Joseph's Reg. Med. Ctr. *(see Saint Joseph's Reg. Med. Ctr.)*

St. Joseph's Seminary *(see Saint Joseph's Seminary)*

St. Joseph's Univ. *(see Saint Joseph's Univ.)*

St. Lawrence Acad. *(see State Univ. of New York Coll. at Potsdam)*

St. Lawrence Univ. *(see Saint Lawrence Univ.)*

St. Leo Coll. *(see Saint Leo Univ.)*

St. Leo Coll. Preparatory Sch. *(see Saint Leo Univ.)*

St. Leo Univ. *(see Saint Leo Univ.)*

St. Louis Broadcast Ctr. *(see Broadcast Ctr.)*

St. Louis Christian Coll. *(see Saint Louis Christian Coll.)*

St. Louis Coll. *(see Saint Louis Christian Coll., Saint Louis Comm. Coll. at Forest Park, Saint Louis Comm. Coll. at Meramec, Saint Louis Coll. of Health Careers, Saint Louis Coll. of Pharmacy, Saint Louis Univ.)*

St. Louis Coll. at Forest Park *(see Saint Louis Comm. Coll. at Forest Park)*

St. Louis Coll. at Meramec *(see Saint Louis Comm. Coll. at Meramec)*

St. Louis Coll. of Health Careers *(see Saint Louis Coll. of Health Careers)*

St. Louis Coll. of Pharmacy *(see Saint Louis Coll. of Pharmacy)*

St. Louis Comm. Coll. at Forest Park *(see Saint Louis Comm. Coll. at Forest Park)*

St. Louis Comm. Coll. at Meramec *(see Saint Louis Comm. Coll. at Meramec)*

St. Louis Dale Carnegie Training *(see C.J. Sealey & Associates, LLC)*

St. Louis Hair Acad., Inc. *(see Saint Louis Hair Acad., Inc.)*

St. Louis Jr. Coll. *(see Chaminade Univ. of Honolulu)*

St. Louis Pharmacy Coll. *(see Saint Louis Coll. of Pharmacy)*

St. Louis Symphony Comm. Music Sch. *(see Saint Louis Symphony Comm. Music Sch.)*

St. Louis Tech 539 *(see also Saint Louis Tech)*

St. Louis Univ. *(see Saint Louis Univ.)*

St. Luke's Clinical Pastoral Edu. Ctr. *(see Saint Luke's Clinical Pastoral Edu. Ctr.)*

St. Luke's Coll. *(see Saint Luke's Coll.)*

St. Luke's Episcopal Hosp. *(see Saint Luke's Episcopal Hosp.)*

St. Luke's Health System *(see Saint Luke's Hosp.)*

St. Luke's Hosp. *(see Marquette General Health System, Mercy/St. Luke's Sch. of Radiologic Techno., Saint Luke's Coll., Saint Luke's Hosp., Saint Luke's Hosp. Sch. of Clinical Science)*

St. Luke's Hosp. Sch. of Clinical Science *(see Saint Luke's Hosp. Sch. of Clinical Science)*

St. Luke's Hosp. Sch. of Nursing *(see Saint Luke's Coll.)*

St. Luke's Med. Ctr. *(see Rush-Presbyterian-Saint Luke's Med. Ctr., Saint Luke's Med. Ctr.)*

St. Luke's Mem. Hosp. Ctr. *(see Faxton-St. Luke's Healthcare)*

St. Luke's-Roosevelt Hosp. Ctr. *(see Saint Luke's-Roosevelt Hosp. Ctr.)*

St. Margaret Mercy Healthcare Ctr. *(see Saint Margaret Mercy Healthcare Ctr.)*

St. Martin's Univ. *(see Saint Martin's Univ.)*

St. Mary Acad. *(see Marygrove Coll.)*

St. Mary Coll. *(see Coll. of Saint Mary, Marygrove Coll., Univ. of Saint Mary)*

St. Mary Grad. Sch. of Theology *(see Saint Mary Seminary & Grad. Sch. of Theology)*

St. Mary Hosp. *(see Reg. West Med. Ctr.)*

St. Mary of the Lake Univ. *(see Univ. of Saint Mary of the Lake Mundelein Seminary)*

St. Mary Seminary *(see Saint Mary Seminary & Grad. Sch. of Theology)*

St. Mary Seminary & Grad. Sch. of Theology *(see Saint Mary Seminary & Grad. Sch. of Theology)*

St. Mary-of-the-Woods Coll. *(see Saint Mary-of-the-Woods Coll.)*

St. Mary's Acad. *(see Clarke Coll.)*

St. Mary's Coll. *(see Saint Mary's Coll., Saint Mary's Coll. of California, Saint Mary's Coll. of Madonna Univ., Saint Mary's Coll. of Maryland, Univ. of Saint Mary of the Lake Mundelein Seminary)*

St. Mary's Coll. of California *(see Saint Mary's Coll. of California)*

St. Mary's Coll. of Madonna Univ. *(see Saint Mary's Coll. of Madonna Univ.)*

St. Mary's Coll. of Maryland *(see Saint Mary's Coll. of Maryland)*

St. Mary's Female Seminary *(see Saint Mary's Coll. of Maryland)*

St. Mary's Hosp. *(see All Saints Healthcare—St. Mary's Campus, Inst. of Allied Med. Professions, Marquette General Health System, Saint Mary's Hosp., United Hosp. Ctr.)*

St. Mary's Hosp. of Franciscan Sisters *(see All Saints Healthcare—St. Mary's Campus)*

St. Mary's Jr. Coll. *(see Coll. of Saint Catherine)*

St. Mary's Med. Ctr. *(see)*

St. Mary's Seminary & Univ. *(see Saint Mary's Seminary & Univ.)*

St. Mary's Univ. *(see Saint Mary's Univ.)*

St. Mary's Univ. & Seminary *(see Saint Mary's Seminary & Univ.)*

St. Mary's Univ. of Minnesota *(see Saint Mary's Univ. of Minnesota)*

St. Meinrad Sch. of Theology *(see Saint Meinrad Sch. of Theology)*

St. Michael Hosp. *(see Saint Michael Hosp.)*

St. Michael's Coll. *(see Coll. of Santa Fe, Saint Michael's Coll., Univ. of St. Michael's Coll.)*

St. Norbert Coll. *(see Saint Norbert Coll.)*

St. Olaf Coll. *(see Saint Olaf Coll.)*

St. Patrick's Seminary & Univ. *(see Saint Patrick's Seminary & Univ.)*

St. Patrick's Univ. *(see Saint Patrick's Seminary & Univ.)*

St. Paul Bible Coll. *(see Crown Coll.)*

St. Paul Bible Inst. *(see Crown Coll.)*

St. Paul Coll. of Law *(see William Mitchell Coll. of Law)*

St. Paul Coll—A Comm. & Tech. Coll. *(see Saint Paul Coll—A Comm. & Tech. Coll.)*

St. Paul Sch. of Theology *(see Saint Paul Sch. of Theology)*

St. Paul Seminary Sch. of Divinity *(see Univ. of Saint Thomas)*

St. Paul Tech. Coll. *(see Saint Paul Coll—A Comm. & Tech. Coll.)*

St. Paul Theology Sch. *(see Saint Paul Sch. of Theology)*

St. Paul's Coll. *(see Saint Paul's Coll.)*

St. Peter's Coll. *(see Saint Peter's Coll.)*

St. Petersburg Coll. *(see Saint Petersburg Coll.)*

St. Petersburg Jr. Coll. *(see Saint Petersburg Coll.)*

St. Petersburg Seminary *(see Saint Petersburg Theological Seminary)*

St. Petersburg Theological Seminary *(see Saint Petersburg Theological Seminary)*

St. Philip's Coll. *(see Saint Philip's Coll.)*

St. Procopius Coll. *(see Benedictine Univ.)*

St. Raphael Hosp. *(see Hosp. of Saint Raphael)*

St. Raphael Seminary *(see Loras Coll.)*

St. Rose Coll. *(see Coll. of Saint Rose)*

St. Scholastica Coll. *(see Coll. of Saint Scholastica)*

St. Stephen's Coll. *(see Bard Coll.)*

St. Teresa Coll. *(see Avila Univ.)*

St. Thomas Aquinas Coll. *(see Saint Thomas Aquinas Coll.)*

St. Thomas More Coll. *(see Coll. of Saint Thomas Moore, Thomas More Coll.)*

St. Thomas More Inst. *(see Coll. of Saint Thomas Moore)*

St. Thomas Univ. *(see Saint Thomas Univ., Univ. of Saint Thomas)*

St. Vincent Archabbey & Coll. *(see Saint Vincent Coll. & Seminary)*

St. Vincent Catholic Med. Centers of New York *(see Saint Vincent Catholic Med. Centers of New York)*

St. Vincent Coll. & Seminary *(see Saint Vincent Coll. & Seminary)*

St. Vincent de Paul Reg. Seminary *(see Saint Vincent de Paul Reg. Seminary)*

St. Vincent Health *(see Saint Vincent Indianapolis Hosp.)*

St. Vincent Hosp. *(see Mercy Med. Ctr. Sioux City, Saint Vincent Hosp. at Worcester Med. Ctr., Saint Vincent Indianapolis Hosp., Saint Vincent Infirmary Med. Ctr.)*

St. Vincent Hosp. at Worcester Med. Ctr. *(see Saint Vincent Hosp. at Worcester Med. Ctr.)*

St. Vincent Hospitals & Health Services *(see Saint Vincent Indianapolis Hosp.)*

St. Vincent Indianapolis Hosp. *(see Saint Vincent Indianapolis Hosp.)*

St. Vincent Infirmary Med. Ctr. *(see Saint Vincent Infirmary Med. Ctr.)*

St. Vincent Seminary *(see Saint Vincent Coll. & Seminary)*

St. Vincent's Coll. *(see Saint Vincent's Coll.)*

St. Vincent's Hosp. *(see Providence Hosp. & Med. Centers, Saint Vincent's Med. Ctr.)*

St. Vincent's Med. Ctr. *(see Saint Vincent's Coll., Saint Vincent's Med. Ctr.)*

St. Vladimir's Orthodox Theological Seminary *(see Saint Vladimir's Orthodox Theological Seminary)*

St. Vladimir's Seminary *(see Saint Vladimir's Orthodox Theological Seminary)*

St. Xavier Univ. *(see Saint Xavier Univ.)*

Stacey's Beauty Coll. *(see Stacey's Hands of Champions Beauty Coll., Inc.)*

Stacey's Hands of Champions Beauty Coll., Inc. 629

Stage One, The Hair Sch. 540

Stage One-Hair Sch., Inc. 518

Stamford Health System 659

Stamford Hosp. *(see Stamford Health System)*

Stanbridge Coll. 468

Standard Beauty Coll. of Oklahoma *(see Sand Springs Beauty Coll.)*

Standing Rock Coll. *(see Sitting Bull Coll.)*

Stanford Health Services *(see Lucile Packard Children's Hosp.)*

Stanford Univ. 58

Stanley Coll. *(see Stanly Comm. Coll.)*

Stanley Comm. Coll. *(see Stanly Comm. Coll.)*

Stanley Tech. Inst. 642

Stanly Coll. *(see Stanly Comm. Coll.)*

Stanly Comm. Coll. 293

Stanton Beauty Coll. 590 *(see also Southern Sch. of Beauty)*

Staples Tech. Inst. *(see Central Lakes Coll.)*

Star Career Coll. 606

Star Coll. of Cosmetology—Nacogdoches 624

Star Coll. of Cosmetology—Tyler 624

Star Tech. Inst—Philadelphia 600

Star Tech. Inst—Stratford 554

Star Tech. Inst—Upper Darby 600

Star Tech. Inst—Wilmington *(see Harrison Career Inst—Wilmington)*

Star Tecnical Inst—Delran *(see Harrison Career Inst—Delran)*

Stark Coll. of Techno. *(see Stark State Coll. of Techno.)*

Stark State Coll. of Techno. 310

Stark Tech *(see Stark State Coll. of Techno.)*

Stark Tech. Coll. *(see Stark State Coll. of Techno.)*

Stark Techno. Coll. *(see Stark State Coll. of Techno.)*

Starr King Sch. for the Ministry *(see Starr King Sch. for the Ministry)*

Starr King Sch. for the Ministry 58

State Agricultural Coll. & Model Farm *(see Iowa State Univ.)*

State Agricultural Coll. of Oregon *(see Oregon State Univ.)*

State Area Vocational-Tech. Sch. *(see Chattanooga State Tech. Comm. Coll.)*

State Area Vocational-Tech. Sch—Knoxville *(see Tennessee Techno. Ctr. at Knoxville)*

State Area Vocational-Tech. Sch—Memphis *(see Tennessee Techno. Ctr. at Memphis)*

State Barber & Hair Design Coll. Inc. 590

State Beauty Acad., Inc. 624

State Coll. at Boston *(see Univ. of Massachusetts Boston)*

State Coll. at Salem *(see Salem State Coll.)*

State Coll. of Arkansas *(see Univ. of Central Arkansas)*

State Coll. of Beauty Culture 644

State Coll. of Iowa *(see Univ. of Northern Iowa)*

State Coll. of Johnson *(see Johnson State Coll.)*

State Fair Coll. *(see State Fair Comm. Coll.)*

State Fair Comm. Coll. 232

State Hosp. of Oregon *(see Oregon State Hosp.)*

State Normal & Industrial Coll. *(see Florida Agricultural & Mechanical Univ., Univ. of North Carolina at Greensboro)*

State Normal & Industrial Sch. *(see Univ. of North Carolina at Greensboro)*

State Normal & Industrial Sch. for Women *(see James Madison Univ., Radford Univ., Univ. of Mary Washington)*

State Normal Coll. *(see Florida Agricultural & Mechanical Univ.)*

State Normal Sch. & Univ. at Marion, The *(see Alabama State Univ.)*

State Normal Sch. at Cheney *(see Eastern Washington Univ.)*

State Normal Sch. at Florence *(see Univ. of North Alabama)*

State Normal Sch. for Chico *(see California State Univ—Chico)*

State Normal Sch. for Women *(see James Madison Univ.)*

State Normal Sch., Los Angeles *(see Univ. of California, Los Angeles)*

State Normal Sch., Troy *(see Troy Univ.)*

State Sch. of Mines & Metallurgy in El Paso *(see Univ. of Texas at El Paso)*

State Teachers & Agricultural Coll. *(see Fort Valley State Univ.)*

State Teachers Coll. *(see Alabama State Univ., James Madison Univ., Univ. of Southern Mississippi, Univ. of West Alabama)*

State Teachers' Coll. at Frostburg *(see Frostburg State Univ.)*

State Teachers Coll. at New Paltz *(see State Univ. of New York at New Paltz)*

State Teachers Coll. at Shippensburg *(see Shippensburg Univ. of Pennsylvania)*

State Teachers Coll., Johnson City *(see East Tennessee State Univ.)*

State Tech *(see Pellissippi State Tech. Comm. Coll.)*

State Tech. Inst. & Rehabilitation Ctr. *(see Michigan Career & Tech. Inst.)*

State Tech. Inst. at Knoxville *(see Pellissippi State Tech. Comm. Coll.)*

State Tech. Inst. at Memphis *(see Southwest Tennessee Comm. Coll.)*

State Trade Sch. *(see Windham Reg. Vocational-Tech. Sch.)*

State Univ. at Albany *(see Albany State Univ.)*

State Univ. of Arizona *(see Arizona State Univ.)*

State Univ. of Cleveland *(see Cleveland State Univ.)*

State Univ. of Illinois *(see Illinois State Univ.)*

State Univ. of Iowa *(see Iowa State Univ., Univ. of Iowa)*

State Univ. of New York at Albany 275

State Univ. of New York at Binghamton 275

State Univ. of New York at Buffalo 275

State Univ. of New York at New Paltz 275

State Univ. of New York at Stony Brook 275

State Univ. of New York Broome Comm. Coll. 276

State Univ. of New York Clinton Comm. Coll. *(see Clinton Comm. Coll.)*

State Univ. of New York Coll. at Brockport 276

State Univ. of New York Coll. at Buffalo 276

State Univ. of New York Coll. at Cortland 276

State Univ. of New York Coll. at Fredonia 276

State Univ. of New York Coll. at Geneseo 276

State Univ. of New York Coll. at Old Westbury 276

State Univ. of New York Coll. at Oneonta 276

State Univ. of New York Coll. at Oswego 276

State Univ. of New York Coll. at Plattsburgh 277

State Univ. of New York Coll. at Potsdam 277

State Univ. of New York Coll. at Purchase 277

State Univ. of New York Coll. of Agriculture & Techno. at Cobleskill 277

State Univ. of New York Coll. of Agriculture & Techno. at Morrisville 277

State Univ. of New York Coll. of Arts & Science New Paltz *(see State Univ. of New York at New Paltz)*

State Univ. of New York Coll. of Environmental Science & Forestry 277

State Univ. of New York Coll. of Optometry 277

State Univ. of New York Coll. of Techno. at Alfred 277

State Univ. of New York Coll. of Techno. at Canton 277

State Univ. of New York Coll. of Techno. at Delhi 278

State Univ. of New York Coll. of Techno. at Farmingdale 278

State Univ. of New York Columbia-Greene Comm. Coll. *(see Columbia-Greene Comm. Coll.)*

State Univ. of New York Corning Comm. Coll. *(see Corning Comm. Coll.)*

State Univ. of New York Downstate Med. Ctr. *(see State Univ. of New York Health Science Ctr. at Brooklyn)*

State Univ. of New York Dutchess Comm. Coll. *(see Dutchess Comm. Coll.)*

State Univ. of New York Educational Opportunity Ctr. 690

State Univ. of New York Empire State Coll. 278

State Univ. of New York Genesee Comm. Coll. *(see Genesee Comm. Coll.)*

State Univ. of New York Health Science Ctr. at Brooklyn 278

State Univ. of New York Herkimer County Comm. Coll. *(see Herkimer County Comm. Coll.)*

State Univ. of New York Hudson Valley Comm. Coll. *(see Hudson Valley Comm. Coll.)*

State Univ. of New York Inst. of Techno. at Utica/Rome 278

State Univ. of New York Jamestown Comm. Coll. *(see Jamestown Comm. Coll.)*

State Univ. of New York Jefferson Comm. Coll. *(see Jefferson Comm. Coll.)*

State Univ. of New York Maritime Coll. 278

State Univ. of New York Nassau Comm. Coll. *(see Nassau Comm. Coll.)*

State Univ. of New York New York State Coll. of Ceramics at Alfred Univ. *(see New York State Coll. of Ceramics at Alfred Univ.)*

State Univ. of New York Niagara County Comm. Coll. *(see Niagara County Comm. Coll.)*

State Univ. of New York North Country Comm. Coll. *(see North Country Comm. Coll.)*

State Univ. of New York Onondaga Comm. Coll. *(see Onondaga Comm. Coll.)*

State Univ. of New York Orange County Comm. Coll. *(see Orange County Comm. Coll.)*

State Univ. of New York Rockland Comm. Coll. 279

State Univ. of New York Suffolk County Comm. Coll. *(see Suffolk County Comm. Coll—Ammerman Campus)*

State Univ. of New York Tompkins Cortland Comm. Coll. *(see Tompkins Cortland Comm. Coll.)*

State Univ. of New York Ulster County Comm. Coll. *(see Ulster County Comm. Coll.)*

State Univ. of New York Upstate Med. Univ. 279

State Univ. of New York Westchester Comm. Coll. *(see Westchester Comm. Coll.)*

State Univ. of North Carolina *(see North Carolina State Univ.)*

State Univ. of North Dakota *(see North Dakota State Univ.)*

State Univ. of Savannah *(see Savannah State Univ.)*

State Univ. of South Dakota *(see South Dakota State Univ.)*

State Univ. of Southern Connecticut *(see Southern Connecticut State Univ.)*

State Univ. of Tennessee *(see Tennessee State Univ.)*

State Univ. of West Georgia 727 *(see also Univ. of West Georgia)*

State Univ. of Western Connecticut *(see Western Connecticut State Univ.)*

State Vocational Sch. *(see Jefferson Comm. & Tech. Coll.)*

State Vocational-Tech. Sch. *(see T.A. Lawson State Comm. Coll.)*

Staten Island Coll. *(see City Univ. of New York Coll. of Staten Island)*

Staten Island Univ. Hosp. 690

Staunton Sch. of Cosmetology, Inc. 633

Stautzenberger Coll. 310

Stearns & Associates, Inc. 730 *(see also Dale Carnegie Training of Maine)*

Steinbach Bible Acad. *(see Steinbach Bible Coll.)*

Steinbach Bible Coll. 433

Steinbach Bible Inst. *(see Steinbach Bible Coll.)*

Steinbach Bible Sch. *(see Steinbach Bible Coll.)*

Steinbach Coll. *(see Steinbach Bible Coll.)*

Stella Adler Conservatory of Acting *(see Stella Adler Studio of Acting)*

Stella Adler Studio of Acting 570

Stenographic Inst. of Hawaii *(see Hawaii Bus. Coll.)*
StenoTech Career Inst. 554
Stenotype Acad. *(see New York Career Inst.)*
Stenotype Inst. of Jacksonville 489
Stenotype Sch. of Long Beach *(see South Coast Coll.)*
Stephen F. Austin State Normal Coll. *(see Stephen F. Austin State Univ.)*
Stephen F. Austin State Univ. 385
Stephens Coll. 232
Stephenville Beauty Coll. 624
Stephenville Coll. *(see Tarleton State Univ.)*
Stepping Stones Montessori Sch. 648
Sterling Coll. 156, 398
Sterling Sch. *(see Long Tech. Coll— East Valley)*
Sterling Secretaries of Law *(see Long Tech. Coll—East Valley)*
Stern Sch. of Bus. 270 *(see also New York Univ., NYU at Manhattanville Coll.)*
Stetson Univ. 94
Steubenville Coll. *(see Franciscan Univ. of Steubenville)*
Steubenville Univ. *(see Franciscan Univ. of Steubenville)*
Steven Beauty Coll. *(see Elaine Steven Beauty Coll., Inc.)*
Stevens Coll. *(see Patricia Stevens Coll., Thaddeus Stevens Coll. of Techno.)*
Stevens Inst. of Techno. 250
Stevens Point Normal Sch. *(see Univ. of Wisconsin—Stevens Point)*
Stevens Sch. of Techno. *(see Thaddeus Stevens Coll. of Techno.)*
Stevens Tech *(see Thaddeus Stevens Coll. of Techno.)*
Stevens Techno. Inst. *(see Stevens Inst. of Techno.)*
Stevens-Henager Bus. Coll. *(see Stevens-Henager Coll.)*
Stevens-Henager Coll. 395
Stevenson's Acad. of Hair Design 518
Stewart Bus. Coll. *(see Rider Univ.)*
Still Coll. *(see Des Moines Univ— Osteopathic Med. Ctr.)*
Still Univ. of Health Sciences *(see A.T. Still Univ. of Health Sciences)*
Stillman Coll. 8
Stillman Inst. *(see Stillman Coll.)*
Stillpoint Massage Therapy Program *(see Greenfield Comm. Coll.)*
Stillwater Beauty Acad. 590

Stockton Bus. Coll. *(see Humphreys Coll., MTI Bus. Coll. of Stockton Inc.)*
Stockton Coll. *(see Richard Stockton Coll. of New Jersey, San Joaquin Delta Coll.)*
Stockton Coll. of New Jersey *(see Richard Stockton Coll. of New Jersey)*
Stockton Jr. Coll. *(see San Joaquin Delta Coll.)*
Stone Acad. 73, 476
Stone Acad—Waterbury 724
Stone Child Coll. 235
Stone Child Comm. Coll. *(see Stone Child Coll.)*
Stone Coll. *(see National Sch. of Techno.)*
Stone Vocational-Tech. Ctr. *(see George Stone Vocational-Tech. Ctr.)*
Stone Vo-Tech Ctr. *(see George Stone Vocational-Tech. Ctr.)*
Stonehill Coll. 192
Stony Brook State Univ. *(see State Univ. of New York at Stony Brook)*
Stony Brook Univ. *(see State Univ. of New York at Stony Brook)*
Storrs Agricultural Coll. *(see Univ. of Connecticut)*
Storrs Agricultural Sch. *(see Univ. of Connecticut)*
Stout Inst., The *(see Univ. of Wisconsin—Stout)*
Stout Manual Training Schools *(see Univ. of Wisconsin—Stout)*
Stout State Coll. *(see Univ. of Wisconsin—Stout)*
Stout State Univ. *(see Univ. of Wisconsin—Stout)*
Stoutzenberger Coll—Findlay *(see Brown Mackie Coll—Findlay)*
Straight Coll. *(see Dillard Univ.)*
Strand Coll. of Hair Design 609
Stratford Coll. *(see Stratford Univ.)*
Stratford Univ. 406
Stratton VA Med. Ctr. *(see Veterans Affairs Med. Ctr—Stratton)*
Stratton Veterans Affairs Med. Ctr. *(see Veterans Affairs Med. Ctr— Stratton)*
Straughan & Associates, Inc. *(see Ron L. Straughan & Associates, Inc.)*
Strayer Bus. Coll. *(see Strayer Univ.)*
Strayer Univ. 79
Strayer Univ. Online Campus 80
Strich Coll. *(see Cardinal Stritch Univ.)*
Strich Univ. *(see Cardinal Stritch Univ.)*
Strong Mem. Hosp. 690
Stroudsburg Sch. of Cosmetology 600

Stroudsburg Univ. *(see East Stroudsburg Univ. of Pennsylvania)*
Stuart Sch. of Bus. Administration 733 *(see also Stuart Sch.)*
Stuart Sch. of Locksmithing *(see Charles Stuart Sch. of Locksmithing)*
Stuart Sch., The 555, 733 *(see also MedTech Coll.)*
Studio Art Centers Int'l. 570
Studio Jewelers, Ltd. 570
Stylemasters Beauty Acad. 612
Stylemasters Coll. of Hair Design 639
Styles & Profiles Beauty Coll. 612
Submarine Learning Ctr. 476
Suburban Tech *(see Suburban Tech. Sch.)*
Suburban Tech. Sch. 570 *(see also Branford Hall Career Inst— Bohemia)*
Success Development Group, Inc. 721 *(see also Premier Training, Inc. Dale Carnegie Training)*
Success Unlimited, Inc. 555
Suffolk Beauty Acad. 633
Suffolk County Comm. Coll— Ammerman Campus 279
Suffolk Univ. 193
Sul Ross State Teachers Coll. *(see Sul Ross State Univ.)*
Sul Ross State Univ. 385
Sul Ross Univ. *(see Sul Ross State Univ.)*
Sullivan & Cogliano Training Centers 756
Sullivan Coll. *(see Sullivan Univ.)*
Sullivan County Coll. *(see Sullivan County Comm. Coll.)*
Sullivan County Comm. Coll. 279
Sullivan Univ. 164
Summit Acad. OIC 534
Summit Acad. Opportunities Industrial Ctr. *(see Summit Acad. OIC)*
Summit Career Coll., Inc. 468
Summit Christian Coll. *(see Taylor Univ.)*
Summit Inst. 725, 726
Summit Pacific Coll. 433, 740
Sumter Area Tech. Coll. *(see Central Carolina Tech. Coll.)*
Sumter Area Tech. Edu. Ctr. *(see Central Carolina Tech. Coll.)*
Sumter Beauty Coll. 609 *(see also Sumter Beauty Coll.)*
Sunbridge Coll. 279
Suncoast Ctr. for Natural Health/Suncoast Sch. 726 *(see also SunCoast II—The Tampa Bay Sch. of Health/Suncoast Sch.)*

SunCoast II-The Tampa Bay Sch. of Health/Suncoast Sch. 490, 726

SunCoast Inst. of Techno. 726

Suncoast Sch. *(see SunCoast II—The Tampa Bay Sch. of Health/Suncoast Sch.)*

Sunstate Acad. of Hair Design 490, 725

SUNY at Albany *(see State Univ. of New York at Albany)*

SUNY at Binghamton *(see State Univ. of New York at Binghamton)*

SUNY at Buffalo *(see State Univ. of New York at Buffalo)*

SUNY at Morrisville *(see State Univ. of New York Coll. of Agriculture & Techno. at Morrisville)*

SUNY at Old Westbury *(see State Univ. of New York Coll. at Old Westbury)*

SUNY at Stony Brook *(see State Univ. of New York at Stony Brook)*

SUNY Brockport *(see State Univ. of New York Coll. at Brockport)*

SUNY Broome Comm. Coll. *(see State Univ. of New York Broome Comm. Coll.)*

SUNY Buffalo Educational Opportunity Ctr. *(see State Univ. of New York Educational Opportunity Ctr.)*

SUNY Canton *(see State Univ. of New York Coll. of Techno. at Canton)*

SUNY Clinton Comm. Coll. *(see Clinton Comm. Coll.)*

SUNY Cobleskill *(see State Univ. of New York Coll. of Agriculture & Techno. at Cobleskill)*

SUNY Coll. at Brockport *(see State Univ. of New York Coll. at Brockport)*

SUNY Coll. at Buffalo *(see State Univ. of New York Coll. at Buffalo)*

SUNY Coll. at Cobleskill *(see State Univ. of New York Coll. of Agriculture & Techno. at Cobleskill)*

SUNY Coll. at Cortland *(see State Univ. of New York Coll. at Cortland)*

SUNY Coll. at Fredonia *(see State Univ. of New York Coll. at Fredonia)*

SUNY Coll. at Morrisville *(see State Univ. of New York Coll. of Agriculture & Techno. at Morrisville)*

SUNY Coll. at New Paltz *(see State Univ. of New York at New Paltz)*

SUNY Coll. at Oneonta *(see State Univ. of New York Coll. at Oneonta)*

SUNY Coll. at Oswego *(see State Univ. of New York Coll. at Oswego)*

SUNY Coll. at Plattsburgh *(see State Univ. of New York Coll. at Plattsburgh)*

SUNY Coll. at Potsdam *(see State Univ. of New York Coll. at Potsdam)*

SUNY Coll. at Purchase *(see State Univ. of New York Coll. at Purchase)*

SUNY Coll. at Utica/Rome *(see State Univ. of New York Inst. of Techno. at Utica/Rome)*

SUNY Coll. of Agriculture & Techno. at Cobleskill *(see State Univ. of New York Coll. of Agriculture & Techno. at Cobleskill)*

SUNY Coll. of Agriculture & Techno. at Morrisville *(see State Univ. of New York Coll. of Agriculture & Techno. at Morrisville)*

SUNY Coll. of Environmental Science & Forestry at Syracuse *(see State Univ. of New York Coll. of Environmental Science & Forestry)*

SUNY Coll. of Medicine at Syracuse *(see State Univ. of New York Upstate Med. Univ.)*

SUNY Coll. of Techno. at Alfred *(see State Univ. of New York Coll. of Techno. at Alfred)*

SUNY Coll. of Techno. at Canton *(see State Univ. of New York Coll. of Techno. at Canton)*

SUNY Coll. of Techno. at Delhi *(see State Univ. of New York Coll. of Techno. at Delhi)*

SUNY Coll. of Techno. at Farmingdale *(see State Univ. of New York Coll. of Techno. at Farmingdale)*

SUNY Coll. of Techno. at Utica/Rome *(see State Univ. of New York Inst. of Techno. at Utica/Rome)*

SUNY Columbia-Greene Comm. Coll. *(see Columbia-Greene Comm. Coll.)*

SUNY Corning Comm. Coll. *(see Corning Comm. Coll.)*

SUNY Cortland *(see State Univ. of New York Coll. at Cortland)*

SUNY Dehli Coll. *(see State Univ. of New York Coll. of Techno. at Delhi)*

SUNY Downstate Med. Ctr. *(see State Univ. of New York Health Science Ctr. at Brooklyn)*

SUNY Dutchess Comm. Coll. *(see Dutchess Comm. Coll.)*

SUNY Empire State Coll. *(see State Univ. of New York Empire State Coll.)*

SUNY Farmingdale *(see State Univ. of New York Coll. of Techno. at Farmingdale)*

SUNY Genesee *(see Genesee Comm. Coll.)*

SUNY Genesee Comm. Coll. *(see Genesee Comm. Coll.)*

SUNY Genesseo *(see State Univ. of New York Coll. at Geneseo)*

SUNY Health Science Ctr. at Brooklyn *(see State Univ. of New York Health Science Ctr. at Brooklyn)*

SUNY Herkimer County Comm. Coll. *(see Herkimer County Comm. Coll.)*

SUNY Hudson Valley Comm. Coll. *(see Hudson Valley Comm. Coll.)*

SUNY Instittue of Techno. at Utica/Rome *(see State Univ. of New York Inst. of Techno. at Utica/Rome)*

SUNY IT *(see State Univ. of New York Inst. of Techno. at Utica/Rome)*

SUNY Jamestown Comm. Coll. *(see Jamestown Comm. Coll.)*

SUNY Jefferson Comm. Coll. *(see Jefferson Comm. Coll.)*

SUNY Maritime Coll. *(see State Univ. of New York Maritime Coll.)*

SUNY Nassau Comm. Coll. *(see Nassau Comm. Coll.)*

SUNY New Paltz *(see State Univ. of New York at New Paltz)*

SUNY New York State Coll. of Ceramics at Alfred Univ. *(see New York State Coll. of Ceramics at Alfred Univ.)*

SUNY Niagara County Comm. Coll. *(see Niagara County Comm. Coll.)*

SUNY North Country Comm. Coll. *(see North Country Comm. Coll.)*

SUNY Oneonta *(see State Univ. of New York Coll. at Oneonta)*

SUNY Onondaga Comm. Coll. *(see Onondaga Comm. Coll.)*

SUNY Optometry Coll. *(see State Univ. of New York Coll. of Optometry)*

SUNY Orange County Comm. Coll. *(see Orange County Comm. Coll.)*

SUNY Oswego *(see State Univ. of New York Coll. at Oswego)*

SUNY Plattsburgh *(see State Univ. of New York Coll. at Plattsburgh)*

SUNY Potsdam *(see State Univ. of New York Coll. at Potsdam)*

SUNY Purchase *(see State Univ. of New York Coll. at Purchase)*

SUNY Rockland Comm. Coll. *(see State Univ. of New York Rockland Comm. Coll.)*

SUNY Suffolk *(see Suffolk County Comm. Coll—Ammerman Campus)*

SUNY Tompkins Cortland Comm. Coll. *(see Tompkins Cortland Comm. Coll.)*

SUNY Ulster *(see Ulster County Comm. Coll.)*

SUNY Upstate Med. Univ. *(see State Univ. of New York Upstate Med. Univ.)*

SUNY Westchester Comm. Coll. *(see Westchester Comm. Coll.)*

SUNY-ESF *(see State Univ. of New York Coll. of Environmental Science & Forestry)*

Suomi Coll. *(see Finlandia Univ.)*

Suomi Theological Seminary *(see Lutheran Sch. of Theology at Chicago)*

Superior Normal Sch. *(see Univ. of Wisconsin—Superior)*

Superior Sch. of Hairstyling 510

Superior State Teachers Coll. *(see Univ. of Wisconsin—Superior)*

Surry Coll. *(see Surry Comm. Coll.)*

Surry Comm. Coll. 293

Susquehanna Career & Techno. Ctr. 600

Susquehanna Health System 699

Susquehanna Univ. 341

Sussex County Coll. *(see Sussex County Comm. Coll.)*

Sussex County Comm. Coll. 250

Sutter Med. Ctr. 656

Suwanee-Hamilton Tech. Ctr. 490

Sverdrup CRSS *(see Jacobs Facilities, Inc.)*

Swainsboro Coll. *(see Swainsboro Tech. Coll.)*

Swainsboro Tech. Coll. 109

Swainsboro Tech. Inst. *(see Swainsboro Tech. Coll.)*

Swanson's Driving Schools, Inc. *(see All-State Career Sch.)*

Swarthmore Coll. 341

Swayne Sch. *(see Talladega Coll.)*

Swedish American Hosp. 669

Swedish Bible Inst. of Chicago *(see Trinity Int'l. Univ.)*

Swedish Inst.: Sch. of Acupuncture & Massage Therapy, The 279

Swedish Med. Ctr. 658, 707

Swedish Sch. of Acupuncture & Massage Therapy *(see Swedish Inst.: Sch. of Acupuncture & Massage Therapy)*

SwedishAmerican Health System *(see Swedish American Hosp.)*

Sweet Briar Coll. 406

Swiss Hospitality Inst. Cesar Ritz *(see Int'l. Coll. of Hospitality Management Cesar Ritz)*

Swiss Hotel Assoc. Hotel Management Sch. "Les Roches" *(see "Les Roches" Sch. of Hotel Management)*

SWOSU at Sayre *(see Southwestern Oklahoma State Univ. Sayre Campus)*

Sylacauga Sch. of Nursing *(see Central Alabama Comm. Coll.)*

Sylvia's Int'l. Sch. of Beauty 624

Synergy Healing Arts Ctr. & Massage Sch. 601

Synergy Therapeutic Massage Ctr. & Training Sch. *(see Synergy Healing Arts Ctr. & Massage Sch.)*

Synergystic Arts & Sciences *(see Hobble Creek Sch. of Holistic Esthetics)*

Syracuse Sch. of Embalming & Sanitary Science *(see Simmons Inst. of Funeral Service)*

Syracuse Univ. 279

Syrian Protestant Coll. *(see American Univ. of Beirut)*

T

T. A. Lawson Coll. *(see T.A. Lawson State Comm. Coll.)*

T. A. Lawson Comm. Coll. *(see T.A. Lawson State Comm. Coll.)*

T. A. Lawson State Coll. *(see T.A. Lawson State Comm. Coll.)*

T.A. Lawson State Comm. Coll. 8

T.H. Pickens Tech. Ctr. 472

Tabor Coll. 156

Tacoma Coll. *(see Tacoma Comm. Coll.)*

Tacoma Comm. Coll. 415

Taft Coll. 58

Taft Jr. Coll. *(see Taft Coll.)*

Tai Hsuan Coll. of Acupuncture & Herbal Medicine *(see World Medicine Inst.)*

Tai Hsuan Foundation Coll. of Acupuncture & Herbal Medicine 727 *(see also World Medicine Inst.)*

Tai Sophia Inst. 182, 746

Talbot Sch. of Theology *(see Biola Univ.)*

Talent Acad. 736

Taliesin West *(see Frank Lloyd Wright Sch. of Architecture)*

TALK Int'l. 490

Talladega Coll. 8

Tallahassee Coll. *(see Tallahassee Comm. Coll.)*

Tallahassee Comm. Coll. 94

Tallahassee Federal Correctional Institution *(see Federal Correctional Institution—Tallahassee)*

Talmudic Coll. of Florida 94

Talmudical Acad. of New Jersey 250

Talmudical Inst. of Upstate New York 279

Talmudical Seminary Oholei Torah 279

Talmudical Yeshiva of Philadelphia 341

Tampa Bay Beauty Inst. 484 *(see also Jacksonville Beauty Inst., Inc.)*

Tampa Bay Dale Carnegie Training *(see Rick J. Gallegos & Associates, Inc.)*

Tampa Bay Sch. of Health *(see SunCoast II—The Tampa Bay Sch. of Health/Suncoast Sch.)*

Tampa Coll. *(see Florida Metropolitan Univ—Pinellas, Florida Metropolitan Univ—Tampa)*

Tampa General Hosp. 664

Tampa Univ. *(see Univ. of Tampa)*

Tampa VA Med. Ctr. *(see James A. Haley Veterans Affairs Med. Ctr.)*

Tampa Veterans Affairs Med. Ctr. *(see James A. Haley Veterans Affairs Med. Ctr.)*

TAMU Corpus Christi *(see Texas A&M Univ—Corpus Christi)*

TAMU Galveston *(see Texas A&M Univ. at Galveston)*

TAMU Kingsville *(see Texas A&M Univ—Kingsville)*

TAMU Texarkana *(see Texas A&M Univ—Texarkana)*

TAMU—Commerce *(see Texas A&M Univ—Commerce)*

TAP-This Valley Works Ctr. for Employment Training 750

Target Training Ctr. 555

Tarleton Coll. *(see Tarleton State Univ.)*

Tarleton State Univ. 385

Tarrant County Coll. Dist. 386

Tarrant County Jr. Coll. Northeast Campus *(see Tarrant County Coll. Northeast)*

Tarrant County Jr. Coll. Northwest Campus *(see Tarrant County Coll. Northwest)*

Tarrant County Jr. Coll. South Campus *(see Tarrant County Coll. South)*

Tarrant County Jr. Coll—Southeast Campus *(see Tarrant County Coll. Southeast)*

Tax Training Sch. *(see National Tax Training Sch.)*

Taxidermy Inst. of Pennsylvania *(see Pennsylvania Inst. of Taxidermy)*

Taxidermy Training Inst. of Colorado *(see Colorado Inst. of Taxidermy Training, Inc.)*

Taylor Andrews Acad. of Hair Design 629

Taylor Andrews, Inc. *(see Taylor Andrews Acad. of Hair Design)*

Taylor Bus. Inst. 132, 280

Taylor Corporation *(see E. J. Taylor Corporation)*

Taylor Seminary *(see Taylor Univ. Coll. & Seminary)*

Taylor Tech. Inst. 490

Taylor Univ. 143

Taylor Univ. Coll. & Seminary 434 *(see also Edmonton Baptist Seminary)*

Taylortown Sch. of Beauty 532

TCI Coll. of Techno. *(see Tech. Career Inst., Inc.)*

TDDS Tech *(see TDDS Tech. Inst.)*

TDDS Tech. Inst. 584, 734

TDDS-Prof. Training Ctr. 734 *(see also TDDS Tech. Inst.)*

Teachers Coll. of Columbia Univ. 280

Teachers Coll. of Connecticut *(see Central Connecticut State Univ.)*

Teachers Coll. of the City of Boston *(see Univ. of Massachusetts Boston)*

Teachers Training Sch. *(see Baltimore Hebrew Univ.)*

Tech Inst. of Georgia *(see CTEC Acad., Tech Inst. of Georgia)*

Tech. Career Inst. 490

Tech. Career Inst., Inc. 280

Tech. Ctr. of Jackson County *(see Roane Jackson Tech. Ctr.)*

Tech. Ctr. of Mercer County *(see Mercer County Tech. Edu. Ctr.)*

Tech. Ctr. of Mineral County *(see Mineral County Tech. Ctr.)*

Tech. Ctr. of Norfolk *(see Norfolk Tech. Vocational Ctr.)*

Tech. Ctr. of Roane County *(see Roane Jackson Tech. Ctr.)*

Tech. Coll. of Alamance *(see Alamance Comm. Coll.)*

Tech. Coll. of Albany *(see Albany Tech. Coll.)*

Tech. Coll. of Alexandria *(see Alexandria Tech. Coll.)*

Tech. Coll. of Athens *(see Athens Tech. Coll.)*

Tech. Coll. of Atlanta *(see Atlanta Tech. Coll.)*

Tech. Coll. of Bellingham *(see Bellingham Tech. Coll.)*

Tech. Coll. of Central Kentucky *(see Bluegrass Comm. & Tech. Coll—Central)*

Tech. Coll. of Central Ohio *(see Central Ohio Tech. Coll.)*

Tech. Coll. of Dakota County *(see Dakota County Tech. Coll.)*

Tech. Coll. of Denmark *(see Denmark Tech. Coll.)*

Tech. Coll. of Eastern Idaho *(see Eastern Idaho Tech. Coll.)*

Tech. Coll. of Fayetteville *(see Fayetteville Tech. Comm. Coll.)*

Tech. Coll. of Marion *(see Marion Tech. Coll.)*

Tech. Coll. of Middle Georgia *(see Middle Georgia Tech. Coll.)*

Tech. Coll. of Milwaukee *(see Milwaukee Area Tech. Coll.)*

Tech. Coll. of Moultrie *(see Moultrie Tech. Coll.)*

Tech. Coll. of North Central Kansas *(see North Central Kansas Tech. Coll.)*

Tech. Coll. of Northeast Kansas *(see Northeast Kansas Tech. Coll.)*

Tech. Coll. of Northeast Wisconsin *(see Northeast Wisconsin Tech. Coll.)*

Tech. Coll. of Northwest Kansas *(see Northwest Kansas Tech. Coll.)*

Tech. Coll. of Savannah *(see Savannah Tech. Coll.)*

Tech. Coll. of South Georgia *(see South Georgia Tech. Coll.)*

Tech. Coll. of Southwest Georgia *(see Southwest Georgia Tech. Coll.)*

Tech. Coll. of Southwest Wisconsin *(see Southwest Wisconsin Tech. Coll.)*

Tech. Coll. of Spartanburg *(see Spartanburg Tech. Coll.)*

Tech. Coll. of the Greater Madison Area *(see Madison Area Tech. Coll.)*

Tech. Coll. of the Lowcountry 359

Tech. Coll. of the San Juan Basin *(see San Juan Basin Tech. Coll.)*

Tech. Coll. of Vermont *(see Vermont Tech. Coll.)*

Tech. Coll. of West Georgia *(see West Georgia Tech. Coll.)*

Tech. Coll. of Western Wisconsin *(see Western Wisconsin Tech. Coll.)*

Tech. Coll. of York *(see York Tech. Coll.)*

Tech. Edu. Ctr. of Mercer County *(see Mercer County Tech. Edu. Ctr.)*

Tech. Edu. Ctr—Osceola 490

Tech. Edu. Coll. 473

Tech. Inst. in Chamblee *(see Southern Polytechnic State Univ.)*

Tech. Inst. of Alamance *(see Alamance Comm. Coll.)*

Tech. Inst. of Camden County 685

Tech. Inst. of Cape May County *(see Cape May County Tech. Inst.)*

Tech. Inst. of Cosmetology Arts & Sciences 590

Tech. Inst. of Mitchell *(see Mitchell Tech. Inst.)*

Tech. Inst. of New England *(see New England Tech. Inst. of Connecticut)*

Tech. Inst. of New Hampshire *(see New Hampshire Tech. Inst.)*

Tech. Inst. of Pittsburgh *(see Pittsburgh Tech. Inst.)*

Tech. Inst. of Texas County *(see Texas County Tech. Inst.)*

Tech. Inst. of Wichita *(see Wichita Tech. Inst.)*

Tech. Inst. of York *(see York Tech. Inst.)*

Tech. Learning Centers, Inc. 478

Tech. Metropolitan Sch. *(see Colegio Tecnico Metropolitano)*

Tech. Sch. of Ponce *(see Ponce Tech. Sch., Inc.)*

Tech. Sch. of Southern New Jersey *(see Southern New Jersey Tech. Sch.)*

Tech. Sch. of Southwest Kansas *(see Southwest Kansas Tech. Sch.)*

Tech. Trades Inst—Colorado Springs *(see Intellitec Coll—Colorado Springs)*

Tech. Trades Inst—Grand Junction *(see Intellitec Coll—Grand Junction)*

Tech. Univ. of Colorado *(see Colorado Tech. Univ.)*

Tech. Vocational Inst. of Albuquerque *(see Albuquerque Tech. Vocational Inst.)*

Technological Coll. of San Juan *(see Univ. Coll. of San Juan)*

Technological Coll. of the Municipality of San Juan 736 *(see also Univ. Coll. of San Juan)*

Techno. & Commercial Coll. of Puerto Rico *(see Colegio Tecnologico y Comercial de Puerto Rico)*

Techno. Ctr. of Casey County *(see Casey County Area Techno. Ctr.)*

Techno. Ctr. of Essex *(see Ctr. for Techno., Essex)*

Techno. Ctr. of Indiana County *(see Indiana Cosmetology Acad.)*

Techno. Ctr. of Pontotoc County *(see Pontotoc Techno. Ctr.)*

Techno. Ctr. of Rockcastle County *(see Rockcastle Area Techno. Ctr.)*

Techno. Coll. of Pennsylvania *(see Pennsylvania Coll. of Techno.)*

Techno. Coll. of the Delaware Valley *(see Pennsylvania Inst. of Techno.)*

Techno. Edu. Ctr. *(see Techno. Edu. Coll.)*

Techno. Edu. Coll. 310

Techno. Inst. of California *(see California Inst. of Techno.)*

Techno. Inst. of Erie *(see Erie Inst. of Techno.)*

Techno. Inst. of Hawaii *(see Hawaii Techno. Inst.)*

Techno. Inst. of New England *(see New England Inst. of Techno.)*

Techno. Inst. of New Jersey *(see New Jersey Inst. of Techno.)*

Techno. Inst. of New York *(see New York Inst. of Tech—Old Westbury)*

Techno. Inst. of Northern Alberta *(see Northern Alberta Inst. of Techno.)*

Techno. Inst. of Oregon *(see Oregon Inst. of Techno.)*

Techno. Inst. of Pennsylvania *(see Pennsylvania Inst. of Techno.)*

Techno. Inst. of South Florida *(see South Florida Inst. of Techno.)*

Techno. Inst. of Southern California *(see Southern California Inst. of Techno.)*

Techno. Sch. of Virginia *(see Virginia Sch. of Techno.)*

Teddy Ulmo Inst. 606

Teikyo Loretto Heights Univ. 70

Teikyo Post Univ. 724 *(see also Post Univ.)*

Teikyo Univ. *(see Teikyo Loretto Heights Univ.)*

Television Broadcasting Acad. *(see Acad. of Radio & Television Broadcasting)*

Telluride Inst. *(see Deep Springs Coll.)*

Telshe Rabbinical Coll. *(see Rabbinical Coll. of Telshe)*

Telshe Yeshiva—Chicago 132

Tempe Normal Sch. of Arizona *(see Arizona State Univ.)*

Tempe State Teachers Coll. *(see Arizona State Univ.)*

Temple Baptist Coll. 748

Temple Baptist Seminary 370

Temple Baptist Theological Seminary *(see Temple Baptist Seminary)*

Temple Coll. 386 *(see also Temple Univ.)*

Temple Jr. Coll. *(see Temple Coll.)*

Temple Seminary *(see Temple Baptist Seminary)*

Temple Univ. 342

Temple Univ. of Tennessee *(see Tennessee Temple Univ.)*

Temple VA Med. Ctr. *(see Veterans Affairs Med. Ctr—Temple)*

Temple Veterans Affairs Med. Ctr. *(see Veterans Affairs Med. Ctr—Temple)*

Tenet Healthcare Corporation *(see Forest Park Hosp.)*

Tennessee Acad. of Cosmetology— East Shelby Drive 612

Tennessee Acad. of Cosmetology— Highway 64 612

Tennessee Career Coll. 612

Tennessee Dept. of Health 702

Tennessee Health Dept. *(see Tennessee Dept. of Health)*

Tennessee Inst. of Electronics 737 *(see also Fountainhead Coll. of Techno.)*

Tennessee Polytechnic Inst. *(see Tennessee Technological Univ.)*

Tennessee Radio Service Sch. *(see Fountainhead Coll. of Techno.)*

Tennessee Sch. of Beauty, Inc. 612

Tennessee Sch. of Massage 613

Tennessee State Univ. 370

Tennessee Tech *(see Tennessee Technological Univ.)*

Tennessee Technological Univ. 370

Tennessee Techno. Ctr. at Athens 613

Tennessee Techno. Ctr. at Covington 613

Tennessee Techno. Ctr. at Crossville 613

Tennessee Techno. Ctr. at Crump 613

Tennessee Techno. Ctr. at Dickson 613

Tennessee Techno. Ctr. at Elizabethton 613

Tennessee Techno. Ctr. at Harriman 613

Tennessee Techno. Ctr. at Hartsville 613

Tennessee Techno. Ctr. at Hohenwald 613

Tennessee Techno. Ctr. at Jacksboro 613

Tennessee Techno. Ctr. at Jackson 613

Tennessee Techno. Ctr. at Knoxville 613

Tennessee Techno. Ctr. at Livingston 613

Tennessee Techno. Ctr. at McKenzie 614

Tennessee Techno. Ctr. at McMinnville 614

Tennessee Techno. Ctr. at Memphis 614

Tennessee Techno. Ctr. at Morristown 614

Tennessee Techno. Ctr. at Murfreesboro 614

Tennessee Techno. Ctr. at Nashville 614

Tennessee Techno. Ctr. at Newbern 614

Tennessee Techno. Ctr. at Oneida/Huntsville 614

Tennessee Techno. Ctr. at Paris 614

Tennessee Techno. Ctr. at Pulaski 614

Tennessee Techno. Ctr. at Ripley 614

Tennessee Techno. Ctr. at Shelbyville 614

Tennessee Techno. Ctr. at Whiteville 614

Tennessee Temple Coll. *(see Tennessee Temple Univ.)*

Tennessee Temple Univ. 370

Tennessee Univ. at Martin *(see Univ. of Tennessee at Martin)*

Tennessee Univ., Knoxville *(see Univ. of Tennessee)*

Tennessee Wesleyan Coll. 370

Terra Comm. Coll. *(see Terra State Comm. Coll.)*

Terra State Coll. *(see Terra State Comm. Coll.)*

Terra State Comm. Coll. 311

Terra Tech. Coll. *(see Terra State Comm. Coll.)*

Terranova & Associates, Inc. *(see Andrew Terranova & Associates, Inc.)*

Terrell State Hosp. 704

Territorial Normal Sch. in Edmond *(see Univ. of Central Oklahoma)*

Territorial Trade Sch. *(see Honolulu Comm. Coll.)*

Territorial Univ. of Washington *(see Univ. of Washington)*

Terry Children's Psychiatric Ctr. 660

TESST Coll. of Techno. 182, 633

TESST Electronic & Computer Inst. *(see TESST Coll. of Techno.)*

TESST Techno. Inst. *(see TESST Coll. of Techno.)*

Teterboro Sch. of Aeronautics 555

Texarkana Coll. 386

Texas A&I Univ. *(see Texas A&M Univ—Kingsville)*

Texas A&I Univ. at Corpus Christi *(see Texas A&M Univ—Corpus Christi)*

Texas A&I Univ. at Laredo *(see Texas A&M Int'l. Univ.)*

Texas A&M Int'l. Univ. 386

Texas A&M Univ. 386

Texas A&M Univ. at Galveston *(see Texas A&M Univ.)*

Texas A&M Univ. at Qatar 386 *(see also Texas A&M Univ.)*
Texas A&M Univ. System Health Science Ctr., The 386
Texas A&M Univ—Commerce 387
Texas A&M Univ—Corpus Christi 387
Texas A&M Univ—Kingsville 387
Texas A&M Univ—Texarkana 387
Texas Acupuncture Inst. *(see Acad. of Oriental Medicine at Austin)*
Texas Barber Coll. *(see Texas Barber Coll. & Hairstyling Schools)*
Texas Barber Coll. & Hairstyling Schools 625
Texas Beauty Coll. 737 *(see also Milan Inst. of Cosmetology)*
Texas Bus. Sch. *(see Texas Sch. of Bus.)*
Texas Career Coll. *(see Virginia Coll.)*
Texas Career Inst. 737
Texas Careers 625
Texas Chiropractic Coll. 387
Texas Christian Univ. 387
Texas Coll. 387 *(see also Texas A&M Univ—Kingsville, Texas Chiropractic Coll., Texas Coll. of Cosmetology, Texas Coll. of Traditional Chinese Medicine)*
Texas Coll. of Arts & Industries *(see Texas A&M Univ—Kingsville)*
Texas Coll. of Chiropractic *(see Texas Chiropractic Coll.)*
Texas Coll. of Cosmetology 625
Texas Coll. of Traditional Chinese Medicine 387
Texas Cosmetology Coll. *(see Texas Coll. of Cosmetology)*
Texas County Tech. Inst. 540
Texas Culinary Acad. 387
Texas Dept. of Mental Health & Mental Retardation *(see Terrell State Hosp.)*
Texas Eastern Univ. *(see Univ. of Texas at Tyler)*
Texas Inst. of Oceanography *(see Texas A&M Univ. at Galveston)*
Texas Inst. of Traditional Chinese Medicine *(see Texas Coll. of Traditional Chinese Medicine)*
Texas Int'l. Edu. Consortium 704
Texas Lutheran Coll. *(see Texas Lutheran Univ.)*
Texas Lutheran Univ. 387
Texas Maritime Acad. *(see Texas A&M Univ. at Galveston)*
Texas Med. Ctr. *(see Saint Luke's Episcopal Hosp., Univ. of Texas Health Science Ctr. at Houston)*
Texas Normal Coll. & Teacher Training Inst. *(see Univ. of North Texas)*

Texas Presbyterian Coll. *(see Austin Coll.)*
Texas Sch. of Bus. 625
Texas Southern Univ. 388
Texas Southmost Coll. *(see Univ. of Texas at Brownsville/Texas Southmost Coll.)*
Texas State Coll. for Women *(see Texas Woman's Univ.)*
Texas State Tech. Coll—Amarillo *(see Amarillo Coll—Amarillo Tech. Ctr.)*
Texas State Tech. Coll—Harlingen 388
Texas State Tech. Coll—Marshall 388
Texas State Tech. Coll—Waco 388
Texas State Tech. Coll—West Texas *(see Texas State Tech. Coll—West Texas at Sweetwater)*
Texas State Tech. Coll—West Texas at Abilene *(see Texas State Tech. Coll—West Texas at Sweetwater)*
Texas State Tech. Coll—West Texas at Breckenridge *(see Texas State Tech. Coll—West Texas at Sweetwater)*
Texas State Tech. Coll—West Texas at Brownwood *(see Texas State Tech. Coll—West Texas at Sweetwater)*
Texas State Tech. Coll—West Texas at Sweetwater 388
Texas State Tech. Inst. *(see Texas State Tech. Coll—Waco)*
Texas State Tech. Inst—Harlingen *(see Texas State Tech. Coll—Harlingen)*
Texas State Univ. for Negroes *(see Texas Southern Univ.)*
Texas State Univ—San Marcos 388, 737
Texas State—San Marcos *(see Texas State Univ—San Marcos)*
Texas Tech Univ. 388
Texas Tech Univ. Health Sciences Ctr. 388
Texas Tech Univ. Sch. of Medicine *(see Texas Tech Univ. Health Sciences Ctr.)*
Texas Tech. Coll. *(see Texas Tech Univ.)*
Texas Traditional Chinese Medicine Coll. *(see Texas Coll. of Traditional Chinese Medicine)*
Texas Traditional Chinese Medicine Inst. *(see Texas Coll. of Traditional Chinese Medicine)*
Texas Univ—Pan American *(see Univ. of Texas—Pan American)*
Texas Vocational Schools 625
Texas Wesleyan Univ. 389

Texas Western Coll. of the Univ. of Texas *(see Univ. of Texas at El Paso)*
Texas Woman's Univ. 389
Thaddeus Stevens Coll. of Techno. 342
Thames Valley State Tech. Coll. *(see Three Rivers Comm. Coll.)*
Thanh Le Coll., Sch. of Cosmetology 468
The Art Inst. of Los Angeles *(see Art Inst. of California—Los Angeles)*
The Art Inst. of Los Angeles—Orange County *(see Art Inst. of California—Orange County)*
The Bryman Sch. *(see Utah Career Coll.)*
The CAD Inst. *(see Univ. of Advancing Techno.)*
The Mount *(see Mount Saint Mary's Univ.)*
Theatre Sch. of the Neighborhood Playhouse *(see Neighborhood Playhouse Sch. of Theatre)*
Theda Clark Med. Ctr. 709
ThedaCare *(see Theda Clark Med. Ctr.)*
Thelma's Beauty Acad. 449
Theological Inst. of Connecticut *(see Hartford Seminary)*
Theological Seminary of Bangor *(see Bangor Theological Seminary)*
Theological Seminary of Chicago *(see Chicago Theological Seminary)*
Theological Seminary of Dallas *(see Dallas Theological Seminary)*
Theological Seminary of New Brunswick *(see New Brunswick Theological Seminary)*
Theological Seminary of New York *(see New York Theological Seminary)*
Theological Seminary of Princeton *(see Princeton Theological Seminary)*
Theological Seminary of Saint Petersburg *(see Saint Petersburg Theological Seminary)*
Theological Seminary of San Francisco *(see San Francisco Theological Seminary)*
Theological Seminary of St. Petersburg *(see Saint Petersburg Theological Seminary)*
Theology Sch. of Austin *(see Austin Grad. Sch. of Theology)*
Theology Sch. of Toronto *(see Toronto Sch. of Theology)*
Theology Sch. of Vancouver *(see Vancouver Sch. of Theology)*

Therapeutic Massage & Movement Inst. *(see Inst. for Therapeutic Massage & Movement)*

Therapeutic Massage Coll. of Phoenix *(see Phoenix Therapeutic Massage Coll.)*

Thibodaux Area Tech. Inst. *(see Louisiana Tech. Coll—LaFourche Campus)*

Thief River Falls Area Vocation Sch. *(see Northland Comm. & Tech. Coll.)*

Thiel Coll. 342

Thiel Hall *(see Thiel Coll.)*

Third State Normal Sch. *(see Saint Cloud State Univ.)*

Thomas Aquinas Coll. 58 *(see also Saint Thomas Aquinas Coll.)*

Thomas Area Tech. Sch. *(see Southwest Georgia Tech. Coll.)*

Thomas Coll. 176 *(see also Thomas Univ.)*

Thomas County Comm. Coll. *(see Thomas Univ.)*

Thomas County Vocational Sch. *(see Southwest Georgia Tech. Coll.)*

Thomas Edison State Coll. 250

Thomas J. Kiblen & Associates 468

Thomas Jefferson Coll. *(see Roosevelt Univ.)*

Thomas Jefferson Sch. of Law 58

Thomas Jefferson Univ. 342

Thomas Jefferson Univ. Hosp. *(see Thomas Jefferson Univ.)*

Thomas Jr. Coll. *(see Thomas Coll.)*

Thomas Law Enforcement Acad. *(see Pat Thomas Law Enforcement Acad.)*

Thomas M. Cooley Law Sch. 204

Thomas More Coll. 164 *(see also Thomas More Coll. of Liberal Arts)*

Thomas More Coll. of Liberal Arts, The 244

Thomas Nelson Coll. *(see Thomas Nelson Comm. Coll.)*

Thomas Nelson Comm. Coll. 406

Thomas Tech. Inst. *(see Southwest Georgia Tech. Coll.)*

Thomas Univ. 110

Thompson Academies *(see Great Lakes Inst. of Techno.)*

Thompson Edu. Direct 736

Thompson Hospice Inst. *(see John D. Thompson Hospice Inst.)*

Thompson Inst. 342

Thompson Sch. of Practical Nursing 398 *(see also Vermont Tech. Coll.)*

Thomson Edu. Direct *(see Penn Foster Career Sch.)*

Thomson Edu. Direct Ctr. for Degree Studies *(see Penn Foster Career Sch.)*

Thoreau Language Inst. 527

Thornton Comm. Coll. *(see South Suburban Coll. of Cook County)*

Thornton Jr. Coll. *(see South Suburban Coll. of Cook County)*

Three of Us Studio Sch. for Film & Television *(see Sch. for Film & Television at Three of Us Studio)*

Three Rivers Coll. *(see Three Rivers Comm. Coll.)*

Three Rivers Comm. Coll. 75, 232, 724

Three Rivers Comm-Tech. Coll. Mohegan Campus 724 *(see also Three Rivers Comm. Coll.)*

Three Rivers Jr. Coll. *(see Three Rivers Comm. Coll.)*

Thunderbird, The American Grad. Sch. of Int'l. Management 721 *(see also Thunderbird, The Garvin Grad. Sch. of Int'l. Management)*

Thunderbird, The Garvin Grad. Sch. of Int'l. Management 20, 721

Thuy Princess Beauty Coll. 468

Tidewater Coll. *(see Tidewater Comm. Coll.)*

Tidewater Comm. Coll. 407

Tidewater Tech 407 *(see also Tidewater Tech)*

Tidewater Tech Aviation *(see Aviation Inst. of Maintenance)*

Tiffin Acad. of Hair Design 584

Tiffin Univ. 311

Tilburg Univ. 716 *(see also Tilburg Univ.)*

Tillotson Coll. *(see Huston-Tillotson Univ.)*

Timken High Sch. Adult Career Tech. Programs *(see Adult Comm. Edu. Full Service Ctr.)*

Timken Mercy Hosp. *(see Mercy Med. Ctr.)*

Timken Mercy Med. Ctr. *(see Mercy Med. Ctr.)*

TLC NuWave Sch. of Cosmetology 759

Toccoa Falls Coll. 110

Toccoa Falls Inst. *(see Toccoa Falls Coll.)*

Togus VA Med. Ctr. *(see Togus Veterans Affairs Med. Ctr.)*

Togus Veterans Affairs Med. Ctr. 674

Tohono O'odham Comm. Coll. 743

Tokai Int'l. Coll. of Hawaii *(see Hawaii Tokai Int'l. Coll.)*

Tokai Univ. *(see Hawaii Tokai Int'l. Coll.)*

Toledo Acad. of Beauty Culture—North 584

Toledo Acad. of Beauty Culture—South 584

Toledo Bus. Coll. *(see Davis Coll.)*

Toledo Public Schools Adult Edu. Ctr. 584

Toledo Public Schools Ellis Ctr. *(see Toledo Public Schools Adult Edu. Ctr.)*

Toledo State Coll. of Medicine *(see Med. Univ. of Ohio)*

Toledo Univ. *(see Univ. of Toledo)*

Toledo Univ. of Arts & Trades *(see Univ. of Toledo)*

Tom P. Haney Tech. Ctr. 490

Tomball Coll. 382 *(see also North Harris Montgomery Comm. Coll. Dist.)*

Tompkins Cortland Coll. *(see Tompkins Cortland Comm. Coll.)*

Tompkins Cortland Comm. Coll. 280

Toni & Guy Hairdressing Acad. 446, 473

Tony & Guy Hairdressing Acad. *(see Toni & Guy Hairdressing Acad.)*

Topeka Provident Assoc. *(see Family Service & Guidance Ctr. of Topeka, Inc.)*

Topeka VA Med. Ctr. *(see Colmery-O'Neil Veterans Affairs Med. Ctr.)*

Topeka Veterans Affairs Med. Ctr. *(see Colmery-O'Neil Veterans Affairs Med. Ctr.)*

Torah Temimah Talmudical Seminary 280

Toronto Inst. of Med. Techno. *(see Michener Inst. for Applied Health Sciences)*

Toronto Montessori Inst. 646

Toronto Sch. of Theology 434

Toronto Univ. *(see Univ. of Toronto)*

Total Cosmetology Training Ctr. 639

Total Health Inst. *(see DeLeon Acad. of Esthetics)*

Total Look Cosmetology Sch. *(see Total Look Sch. of Cosmetology & Massage Therapy)*

Total Look Sch. of Cosmetology & Massage Therapy 508

Total Look Sch. of Massage Therapy *(see Total Look Sch. of Cosmetology & Massage Therapy)*

Total Tech. Inst. 584

Touch of Class Sch. of Cosmetology 625

Tougaloo Coll. 221

Tougaloo Southern Christian Coll. *(see Tougaloo Coll.)*

Touro Coll. 280

Touro Coll. of Liberal Arts & Sciences *(see Michigan Jewish Inst.)*
Touro Coll. of Osteopathic Medicine *(see Touro Univ—California)*
Touro Coll. Sch. of Health Sciences *(see Touro Coll.)*
Touro Law Ctr. *(see Touro Coll.)*
Touro Law Ctr. 280
Touro Univ. at Mare Island *(see Touro Univ—California)*
Touro Univ. Coll. of Osteopathic Medicine 280, 723 *(see Touro Coll., Touro Univ—California)*
Touro Univ. Int'l. 58 *(see also Touro Coll.)*
Touro Univ—California 58, 723
Touro Univ—Nevada *(see Touro Univ. Coll. of Osteopathic Medicine)*
Towson State Coll. *(see Towson Univ.)*
Towson Univ. 182
Toyota Manufacturing USA 729
Toyota Technological Inst. at Chicago 745
Tracy Clinic *(see John Tracy Clinic)*
Trades Sch. of Colorado *(see Colorado Sch. of Trades)*
Trade-Tech. Coll. of Los Angeles *(see Los Angeles Trade-Tech. Coll.)*
Traditional Acupuncture Inst. *(see Tai Sophia Inst.)*
Traditional Chinese Medicine Coll. of America *(see American Coll. of Traditional Chinese Medicine)*
Traditional Chinese Medicine Coll. of Hawaii 114
Traditional Chinese Medicine Sch. of Colorado *(see Colorado Sch. of Traditional Chinese Medicine)*
Trainign Solutions of Vermont *(see Vermont Training Solutions, Inc.)*
Training Ctr. of Connecticut *(see Connecticut Training Ctr.)*
Training Centers of Southern California *(see NTMA Training Centers of Southern California)*
Training Sch. for Christian Workers *(see Azusa Pacific Univ.)*
Training Sch. for Nurses *(see Research Coll. of Nursing)*
Training Solutions, Inc. 570
Trans Pacific Hawaii Coll. *(see TransPacific Hawaii Coll.)*
TransPacific Hawaii Coll. 114
Transpersonal Psychology Inst. *(see Inst. of Transpersonal Psychology)*
Transworld Schools 469
Transy Univ. *(see Transylvania Univ.)*
Transylvania Univ. 164
Travel Acad., The *(see Career Acad.)*
Travel & Trade Career Inst. 724
Travel Edu. Inst. 731

Travel Inst. of the Pacific 496
Travel Univ. Int'l. 724
Traverse City Beauty Coll. 532 *(see also Twin City Beauty Coll.)*
Traviss Tech. Ctr. 490
Traxler Sch. of Hair 731
Treasure Valley Coll. *(see Treasure Valley Comm. Coll.)*
Treasure Valley Comm. Coll. 323
Trend Barber Coll. 625
Trend Beauty Coll. 500 *(see also DuQuoin Beauty Coll.)*
Trend Setter's Acad. of Beauty Culture 514
Trend Setters Coll. of Cosmetology 503
Trend Setters Sch. of Cosmetology, Inc. 756
Trendsetters Florida Sch. of Beauty & Barbering 490
Trenholm State Tech. Coll. *(see H. Councill Trenholm State Tech. Coll.)*
Trenholm Tech *(see H. Councill Trenholm State Tech. Coll.)*
Trenton Bus. Coll., The *(see Rider Univ.)*
Trenton State Coll. *(see Coll. of New Jersey)*
Trevecca Coll. *(see Trevecca Nazarene Univ.)*
Trevecca Nazarene Univ. 370
Trevecca Univ. *(see Trevecca Nazarene Univ.)*
Tri County Beauty Coll. 584
Tri County Techno. Ctr. 590
Triangle Tech 342, 343
Triangle Tech—Sunbury 343
Tri-C *(see Cuyahoga Comm. Coll.)*
Tri-C Corporate *(see Cuyahoga Comm. Coll—Corporate Campus)*
Tri-C Eastern Campus *(see Cuyahoga Comm. Coll. Eastern Campus)*
Tri-C Metro Campus *(see Cuyahoga Comm. Coll. Metropolitan Campus)*
Tri-C Western Campus *(see Cuyahoga Comm. Coll. Western Campus)*
Tri-Cities Chaplaincy 707
Tri-Cities State Area Vocational-Tech. Sch. *(see Northeast State Tech. Comm. Coll.)*
Tri-Cities State Tech. Inst. *(see Northeast State Tech. Comm. Coll.)*
Tri-City Comm. Mental Health Ctr. 671
Tri-City Comprehensive Comm. Mental Health Ctr. *(see Tri-City Comm. Mental Health Ctr.)*
Tri-City Mental Health Ctr. 656

Tri-County Area Vocational-Tech. Sch. *(see Tri County Techno. Ctr.)*
Tri-County Beauty Acad. 503
Tri-County Career Ctr. 584
Tri-County Coll. *(see Tri-County Comm. Coll., Tri-County Tech. Coll.)*
Tri-County Comm. Coll. 293
Tri-County Industrial Edu. Ctr. *(see Tri-County Comm. Coll.)*
Tri-County Joint Vocational Sch. *(see Tri-County Career Ctr.)*
Tri-County JVS *(see Tri-County Career Ctr.)*
Tri-County Tech *(see Tri-County Tech. Coll.)*
Tri-County Tech. Coll. 359
Trident Tech *(see Trident Tech. Coll.)*
Trident Tech. Coll. 359
Trident Training Facility Bangor 738
Tri-Health Bethesda & Good Samaritan Hosp. *(see TriHealth Good Samaritan Hosp.)*
TriHealth Good Samaritan Hosp. 694
Tri-Hosp. CPE Ctr. of Northern Atlanta *(see Northern Atlanta Tri-Hosp. CPE Ctr.)*
Trillium Montessori Teacher Edu. Inst. of Taiwan 648
Trinidad & Tobago Coll. of Therapeutic Massage 648
Trinidad Coll. *(see Trinidad State Jr. Coll.)*
Trinidad State Jr. Coll. 70
Trininty Coll. *(see Trinity Baptist Coll.)*
Trinity Baptist Coll. 94
Trinity Bible Coll. 297
Trinity Bible Inst. *(see Trinity Bible Coll.)*
Trinity Christian Coll. 132
Trinity Coll. 75, 724 *(see also Trinity Bible Coll., Trinity Christian Coll., Trinity Int'l. Univ., Trinity Lutheran Coll., Trinity Univ., Univ. of Trinity Coll. in the Univ. of Toronto)*
Trinity Coll. at Miami *(see Trinity Coll. of Florida, Trinity Int'l. Univ.)*
Trinity Coll. Faculty of Divinity *(see Trinity Int'l. Univ.)*
Trinity Coll. of Florida 94
Trinity Coll. of Nursing *(see Trinity Coll. of Nursing & Health Sciences Sch.)*
Trinity Coll. of Nursing & Health Sciences Sch. 132
Trinity Coll. of Puerto Rico 606
Trinity Coll. of the Bible & Theological Seminary 745
Trinity Episcopal Sch. for Ministry 343
Trinity Evangelical Divinity Sch. *(see Trinity Int'l. Univ.)*

Trinity Health *(see Saint Joseph's Reg. Med. Ctr., Trinity Hosp.)*
Trinity Health System *(see Holy Cross Hosp., Trinity Hosp.)*
Trinity Hosp. 692 *(see also Advocate Trinity Hosp.)*
Trinity Int'l. Coll. *(see Trinity Int'l. Univ.)*
Trinity Int'l. Univ. 132
Trinity Law Sch. 132 *(see also Trinity Int'l. Univ.)*
Trinity Life Bible Coll. 58
Trinity Life Coll. *(see Trinity Life Bible Coll.)*
Trinity Lutheran Coll. 415
Trinity Lutheran Hosp. 680
Trinity Lutheran Seminary 311
Trinity Med. Ctr. *(see Trinity Coll. of Nursing & Health Sciences Sch.)*
Trinity Ministry Sch. *(see Trinity Episcopal Sch. for Ministry)*
Trinity Nursing Coll. *(see Trinity Coll. of Nursing & Health Sciences Sch.)*
Trinity Reg. Health System *(see Trinity Coll. of Nursing & Health Sciences Sch.)*
Trinity Seminary *(see Trinity Lutheran Seminary)*
Trinity Seminary & Bible Coll. *(see Trinity Int'l. Univ.)*
Trinity Seminary & Bible Inst. *(see Trinity Int'l. Univ.)*
Trinity Univ. *(see Trinity Int'l. Univ.)*
Trinity Univ. 80, 389, 724
Trinity Valley Coll. *(see Trinity Valley Comm. Coll.)*
Trinity Valley Comm. Coll. 389
Trinity West Campus *(see Trinity Coll. of Nursing & Health Sciences Sch.)*
Trinity Western Univ. 434
Triple Cities Coll. *(see State Univ. of New York at Binghamton)*
Triple Cities Sch. of Beauty Culture 570
Tripler Army Med. Ctr. 665
Tripler Med. Ctr. *(see Tripler Army Med. Ctr.)*
Tri-Rivers Career Ctr. 584
Tri-Rivers Ctr. for Adult Edu. *(see Tri-Rivers Career Ctr.)*
Tri-Rivers Vocational Tech. Ctr. *(see Tri-Rivers Career Ctr.)*
Tri-Rivers Vo-Tech Ctr. *(see Tri-Rivers Career Ctr.)*
Tri-Service Optician Sch. 660
Tri-State Acupuncture Coll. *(see Tri-State Coll. of Acupuncture)*
Tri-State Bible Coll. 311
Tri-State Bus. Inst. 342

Tri-State Coll. *(see Tri-State Bible Coll., Tri-State Univ.)*
Tri-State Coll. of Acupuncture 280
Tri-State Coll. of Massotherapy 584
Tri-State Cosmetology Inst—Doniphan Drive 625
Tri-State Cosmetology Inst—Gateway East 625
Tri-State Educational Systems, Inc. *(see Tri-State Semi Driver Training, Inc.)*
Tri-State Normal Coll. *(see Tri-State Univ.)*
Tri-State Semi Driver Training, Inc. 584
Tri-State Univ. 143
Triton Coll. 132
Trocaire Coll. 280
Trojan Beauty & Barber Coll. 761
Troup County Area Vocational Tech. Sch. *(see West Georgia Tech. Coll.)*
Troup Tech *(see West Georgia Tech. Coll.)*
Troy Askins Vo-Tech, Inc. *(see Askins Vo-Tech, Inc.)*
Troy Sch. of Beauty Culture 570
Troy State Coll. *(see Troy Univ.)*
Troy State Normal Coll. *(see Troy Univ.)*
Troy State Teacher's Coll. *(see Troy Univ.)*
Troy State Univ. 721 *(see also Troy Univ.)*
Troy State Univ. Dothan 721 *(see also Troy Univ. Dothan)*
Troy State Univ. in Montgomery *(see Troy Univ. Montgomery)*
Troy Univ. 8, 721
Troy Univ. Dothan 9, 721
Troy Univ. Montgomery 9
Truck Driving & Heavy Equipment Operating Training Site 486 *(see also National Training, Inc.)*
Truck Marketing Inst. 469
Truckee Meadows Coll. *(see Truckee Meadows Comm. Coll.)*
Truckee Meadows Comm. Coll. 241
Truett Coll. *(see Truett McConnell Coll.)*
Truett McConnell Coll. 110
Truman Coll. *(see City Colleges of Chicago—Harry S Truman Coll.)*
Truman State Univ. 232
Truman Univ. *(see Truman State Univ.)*
Trumbull Adult Training Ctr. *(see Trumbull Career & Tech. Ctr.)*
Trumbull Bus. Coll. 311
Trumbull Career & Tech. Ctr. 585
Trumbull Coll. *(see Trumbull Bus. Coll.)*

Trumbull Mem. Hosp. 694
TSTC Harlingen *(see Texas State Tech. Coll—Harlingen)*
TSTC Sweetwater *(see Texas State Tech. Coll—West Texas at Sweetwater)*
TSTC Waco *(see Texas State Tech. Coll—Waco)*
TSTC West Texas Abilene *(see Texas State Tech. Coll—West Texas at Sweetwater)*
TSTC West Texas at Sweetwater *(see Texas State Tech. Coll—West Texas at Sweetwater)*
TSTC West Texas Breckenridge *(see Texas State Tech. Coll—West Texas at Sweetwater)*
TSTC West Texas Brownwood *(see Texas State Tech. Coll—West Texas at Sweetwater)*
Tualatin Acad. & Pacific Univ. *(see Pacific Univ.)*
TUCOM Nevada *(see Touro Univ. Coll. of Osteopathic Medicine)*
Tucson Coll. 446
Tucson Coll. of Beauty 446
Tucson Design Coll. 20
Tucson Veterans Affairs Med. Ctr. *(see Southern Arizona Veterans Affairs Health Care System)*
Tucumcari Area Vocational Sch. *(see Mesalands Comm. Coll.)*
Tufts Univ. 193
Tulane Coll. *(see Tulane Univ.)*
Tulane Univ. 174
Tulane Univ. of Louisiana *(see Tulane Univ.)*
Tulare Beauty Coll. 469
Tulsa Coll. *(see Tulsa Comm. Coll.)*
Tulsa Comm. Coll. 318
Tulsa English Instsitute, The 589
Tulsa Job Corps Ctr. 758
Tulsa Jr. Coll. *(see Tulsa Comm. Coll.)*
Tulsa Tech *(see Tulsa Techno. Ctr—Broken Arrow, Tulsa Techno. Ctr—Lemley, Tulsa Techno. Ctr—Peoria, Tulsa Techno. Ctr—Riverside)*
Tulsa Techno. Ctr—Broken Arrow 590
Tulsa Techno. Ctr—Lemley 590
Tulsa Techno. Ctr—Peoria 590
Tulsa Techno. Ctr—Riverside 591
Tulsa Univ. *(see Univ. of Tulsa)*
Tulsa Vocational Tech. Ctr. *(see Tulsa Techno. Ctr—Broken Arrow, Tulsa Techno. Ctr—Lemley, Tulsa Techno. Ctr—Peoria, Tulsa Techno. Ctr—Riverside)*

Tulsa Vo-Tech Ctr. *(see Tulsa Techno. Ctr—Broken Arrow, Tulsa Techno. Ctr—Lemley, Tulsa Techno. Ctr—Peoria, Tulsa Techno. Ctr—Riverside)*

Tulsa Welding Sch. 591

Tunxis Coll. *(see Tunxis Comm. Coll.)*

Tunxis Comm. Coll. 75

Tunxis Comm-Tech. Coll. *(see Tunxis Comm. Coll.)*

Turabo Univ. *(see Universidad del Turabo)*

Turner Job Corps Ctr. 495

Turner Theological Seminary *(see Interdenominational Theological Ctr.)*

Turning Point Beauty Coll., Inc. 446

Turtle Mountain Coll. *(see Turtle Mountain Comm. Coll.)*

Turtle Mountain Comm. Coll. 297

Tusculum Coll. 370

Tuskegee Female Coll. *(see Huntingdon Coll.)*

Tuskegee Univ. 9

Tuttle Vocational-Tech. Ctr. *(see Francis Tuttle Vocational-Tech. Ctr.)*

Twin Cities Seminary *(see United Theological Seminary of the Twin Cities)*

Twin City Beauty Coll. 532

Tyler Barber Coll. *(see New Tyler Barber Coll.)*

Tyler Coll. *(see John Tyler Comm. Coll., Tyler Jr. Coll.)*

Tyler Comm. Coll. *(see John Tyler Comm. Coll.)*

Tyler Jr. Coll. 389

Tyler Sch. of Art *(see Temple Univ.)*

Tyler State Coll. *(see Univ. of Texas at Tyler)*

Tyndale Coll. & Seminary 740 *(see also Tyndale Univ. Coll. & Seminary)*

Tyndale Seminary *(see Tyndale Univ. Coll. & Seminary)*

Tyndale Univ. & Seminary *(see Tyndale Univ. Coll. & Seminary)*

Tyndale Univ. Coll. & Seminary 434, 740

Tyson & Associates *(see Lance Tyson & Associates Dale Carnegie Training of Northeast Ohio)*

U

U.P. Acad. of Hair Design, Inc. 532

U.S. Air Force Acad. *(see United States Air Force Acad.)*

U.S. Air Force Advanced Distributed Learning Inst. *(see United States Air Force Inst. for Advanced Distributed Learning)*

U.S. Air Force Inst. of Techno. *(see Air Force Inst. of Techno.)*

U.S. Air Force Sch. of Health Care Sciences *(see United States Air Force Sch. of Health Care Sciences)*

U.S. AMEDD Ctr. & Sch. *(see Brooke Army Med. Ctr.)*

U.S. Army Acad. of Health Sciences *(see United States Army Med. Dept. Ctr. & Sch.)*

U.S. Army Command & General Staff Coll. *(see United States Army Command & General Staff Coll.)*

U.S. Army DENTAC at Fort Bragg *(see United States Army DENTAC—Ft. Bragg)*

U.S. Army Dental Activity—Ft Bragg *(see United States Army Dental Activity—Ft Bragg)*

U.S. Army Dental Activity—Ft Jackson *(see United States Army Dental Activity—Ft Jackson)*

U.S. Army Dental Activity—Ft. Benning *(see United States Army Dental Activity—Ft Benning)*

U.S. Army Dental Activity—Ft. Carson *(see United States Army Dental Activity—Ft. Carson)*

U.S. Army Dental Activity—Tripler *(see Tripler Army Med. Ctr.)*

U.S. Army Dental Clinic Command *(see United States Army Dental Clinic Command)*

U.S. Army Dept. Headquarters *(see Dept. of Army Headquarters)*

U.S. Army Infantry Sch. *(see United States Army Infantry Sch.)*

U.S. Army Inst. for Prof. Development *(see United States Army Inst. for Prof. Development)*

U.S. Army Med. Dept. Ctr. & Sch. *(see Brooke Army Med. Ctr., United States Army Med. Dept. Ctr. & Sch.)*

U.S. Army Med. Dept. Schools *(see United States Army Med. Dept. Ctr. & Sch.)*

U.S. Army Med. Service Sch. *(see United States Army Med. Dept. Ctr. & Sch.)*

U.S. Army Ordnance Ctr. & Sch. *(see United States Army Ordnance Ctr. & Sch.)*

U.S. Army Ordnance Missile & Munitions Ctr. & Sch. *(see United States Army Ordnance Munitions & Electronic Maintenance Sch.)*

U.S. Army Polygraph Sch. *(see Dept. of Defense Polygraph Inst.)*

U.S. Army Quartermaster Ctr. & Sch. *(see United States Army Quartermaster Ctr. & Sch.)*

U.S. Army Transportation & Aviation Logistics Sch. *(see United States Army Transportation & Aviation Logistics Sch.)*

U.S. Army War Coll. *(see United States Army War Coll.)*

U.S. Army—Dental Activities *(see United States Army—Dental Activities)*

U.S. Bus. Sch. in Prague 273 *(see also Rochester Inst. of Techno.)*

U.S. Career Inst. 473

U.S. Coast Guard Acad. *(see United States Coast Guard Acad.)*

U.S. Defense Information Sch. *(see Defense Information Sch.)*

U.S. Grant Career Ctr. *(see U.S. Grant Joint Vocational Sch.)*

U.S. Grant Joint Vocational Sch. 585

U.S. Grant JVS *(see U.S. Grant Joint Vocational Sch.)*

U.S. Grant Mem. Univ. *(see Tennessee Wesleyan Coll.)*

U.S. Int'l. Univ. *(see Alliant Int'l. Univ—San Diego Scripps Ranch)*

U.S. Marine Corps Inst. *(see United States Marine Corps Inst.)*

U.S. Marine Corps Univ. *(see United States Marine Corps Univ.)*

U.S. Merchant Marine Acad. *(see United States Merchant Marine Acad.)*

U.S. Military Acad. *(see United States Military Acad.)*

U.S. Naval Acad. *(see United States Naval Acad.)*

U.S. Naval Air Tech. Training Ctr. *(see Naval Air Tech. Training Ctr.)*

U.S. Naval Air Tech. Training Ctr. *(see Ctr. for Naval Aviation Tech. Training)*

U.S. Naval Construction Training Ctr. *(see Ctr. for Seabees & Facilities Engineering)*

U.S. Naval Diving & Salvage Training Ctr. *(see Ctr. for Explosive Ordnance Disposal & Diving)*

U.S. Naval Postgraduate Sch. *(see United States Naval Postgraduate Sch.)*

U.S. Naval Sch. *(see United States Naval Acad.)*

U.S. Naval Surface Warfare Training Ctr. *(see Ctr. for Surface Combat Systems)*
U.S. Naval Tech. Training Ctr. *(see Ctr. for Information Dominance Corry Station)*
U.S. Naval War Coll. *(see Naval War Coll.)*
U.S. Navy & Marine Corps Intelligence Training Ctr. *(see Ctr. for Naval Intelligence)*
U.S. Navy Supply Corps Sch. *(see United States Navy Supply Corps Sch.)*
U.S. Penitentiary Atlanta *(see United States Penitentiary Atlanta)*
U.S. Sports Acad. *(see United States Sports Acad.)*
U.S.A. Beauty Sch. Int'l., Inc. 570
U.T.A. Mesivta of Kiryas Joel 280
UAE Univ. *(see United Arab Emirates Univ.)*
UAlbany *(see State Univ. of New York at Albany)*
UBTech *(see Upper Bucks County Area Vocational Tech. Sch.)*
UC Berkeley *(see Univ. of California, Berkeley)*
UC Berkeley Extension 59
UC Davis *(see Univ. of California, Davis)*
UC Davis Counseling Ctr. *(see Univ. of California, Davis)*
UC Irvine *(see Univ. of California, Irvine)*
UC Riverside *(see Univ. of California, Riverside)*
UC San Diego *(see Univ. of California, San Diego)*
UC Santa Barbara *(see Univ. of California, Santa Barbara)*
UC Santa Cruz *(see Univ. of California, Santa Cruz)*
UCLA *(see Univ. of California, Los Angeles)*
UCLA Extension 59
UConn Health Ctr. *(see Univ. of Connecticut Health Ctr.)*
UCPA Employment & Training 503 *(see also UCPA Employment & Training)*
UCSD/VA Psychlogy Internship Program *(see Univ. of California, San Diego)*
Uebehler Accosiates *(see Meyer Uebelher Associates, LLC)*
UH—Clear Lake *(see Univ. of Houston—Clear Lake)*
UH—Downtown *(see Univ. of Houston—Downtown)*

UH—Victoria *(see Univ. of Houston—Victoria)*
Uintah Basin Applied Techno. Coll. 750
Ulster Comm. Coll. *(see Ulster County Comm. Coll.)*
Ulster County Comm. Coll. 280
Ulster Univ. *(see Univ. of Ulster at Jordanstown)*
Ultima Coll. of Cosmetology *(see Artistic Beauty Colleges)*
Ultimate Med. Acad. 490
Ultrasound Diagnostic Sch. *(see Sanford-Brown Inst.)*
Ultrasound Diagnostic Sch—Atlanta 727
Ultrasound Diagnostic Sch—Dallas 737
Ultrasound Diagnostic Sch—Elmsford 734
Ultrasound Diagnostic Sch—Garden City 734
Ultrasound Diagnostic Sch—Iselin 733
Ultrasound Diagnostic Sch—Jacksonville 726
Ultrasound Diagnostic Sch—Landover 730
Ultrasound Diagnostic Sch—Lauderdale Lakes 726
Ultrasound Diagnostic Sch—New York 734
Ultrasound Diagnostic Sch—Springfield 730
Ultrasound Diagnostic Sch—Tampa 726
Ultrasound Diagnostic Sch—Trevose 726
Ultrasound Inst. of Florida *(see Florida Inst. of Ultrasound, Inc.)*
UM Dearborn *(see Univ. of Michigan—Dearborn)*
UMaine *(see Univ. of Maine)*
UMass Amherst *(see Univ. of Massachusetts Amherst)*
UMass Boston *(see Univ. of Massachusetts Boston)*
UMass Lowell *(see Univ. of Massachusetts Lowell)*
UMass Mem. Med. Ctr. *(see Univ. of Massachusetts Med. Sch.)*
UMass Worcester *(see Univ. of Massachusetts Med. Sch.)*
Umpqua Coll. *(see Umpqua Comm. Coll.)*
Umpqua Comm. Coll. 323
UM—St. Louis *(see Univ. of Missouri—St. Louis)*
Umstead Hosp. *(see John Umstead Hosp.)*
UM—Western *(see Univ. of Montana—Western)*

Undergraduate Sch. of Cosmetology *(see Univ. of Spa & Cosmetology Art)*
Unification Theological Seminary 280
Unified Industries Incorporated 633
Uniformed Services Univ. of the Health Sciences 182
Union Biblical Seminary *(see United Theological Seminary)*
Union Bus. Coll. *(see Peirce Coll.)*
Union Coll. 164, 238, 281
Union County Coll. 250
Union County Vocational-Tech. Schools 555
Union Inst. & Univ., The 311
Union Inst., The *(see Union Inst. & Univ.)*
Union Prof. Training Sch. *(see Hondros Coll.)*
Union Protestant Hosp. *(see United Hosp. Ctr.)*
Union PSCE *(see Union Theological Seminary & Presbyterian Sch. of Christian Edu.)*
Union Seminary *(see Union Theological Seminary & Presbyterian Sch. of Christian Edu.)*
Union Teological Seminary in Virginia *(see Union Theological Seminary & Presbyterian Sch. of Christian Edu.)*
Union Theological Seminary 281 *(see also Union Theological Seminary)*
Union Theological Seminary & Presbyterian Sch. of Christian Edu. 407
Union Univ. *(see Union Inst. & Univ.)*
Union Univ. 370
Union Univ—Albany Law Sch. *(see Albany Law Sch.)*
Unitech Acad. *(see Unitech Training Acad.)*
Unitech Training Acad. 518
United Arab Emirates Univ. 717
United Beauty Coll., Inc. 469
United Car & Truck Driving Sch. 469
United Church Seminary *(see Luther Seminary)*
United Edu. Inst. 469
United Electronics Inst. *(see National Inst. of Techno.)*
United Hosp. Ctr. 708
United Hosp/Children's Hosp. & Clinic 679
United States Air Force Acad. 70
United States Air Force Acad. Hosp. *(see 10th Med. Group/SGFL)*
United States Air Force Inst. for Advanced Distributed Learning 442

United States Air Force Inst. of Techno. *(see Air Force Inst. of Techno.)*

United States Air Force Sch. of Health Care Sciences 705

United States AMEDD Ctr. & Sch. *(see Brooke Army Med. Ctr.)*

United States Army Acad. of Health Sciences *(see United States Army Med. Dept. Ctr. & Sch.)*

United States Army Command & General Staff Coll. 156

United States Army DENTAC—Ft. Bragg 692

United States Army DENTAC—Ft. Campbell 673

United States Army DENTAC—WBAMC 705

United States Army Dental Activity—Fort Jackson 701

United States Army Dental Activity—Ft Benning 665

United States Army Dental Activity—Ft Bragg 665

United States Army Dental Activity—Ft. Carson 658

United States Army Dental Activity—Tripler *(see Tripler Army Med. Ctr.)*

United States Army Dental Clinic Command 675

United States Army Dept. Headquarters *(see Dept. of Army Headquarters)*

United States Army Infantry Sch. 495

United States Army Inst. for Prof. Development, The 634

United States Army Logistics Management Coll. 634

United States Army Management Staff Coll. 634

United States Army Med. Dept. Ctr. & Sch. 626 *(see also Brooke Army Med. Ctr.)*

United States Army Med. Dept. Schools *(see United States Army Med. Dept. Ctr. & Sch.)*

United States Army Med. Equipment & Optician Sch. *(see U.S. Army Med. Equipment & Optical Sch.)*

United States Army Med. Service Sch. *(see United States Army Med. Dept. Ctr. & Sch.)*

United States Army Ordnance Ctr. & Sch. 523 *(see also United States Army Ordnance Ctr. & Sch.)*

United States Army Ordnance Munitions & Electronic Maintenance Sch. 442

United States Army Polygraph Sch. *(see Dept. of Defense Polygraph Inst.)*

United States Army Quartermaster Ctr. & Sch. 634

United States Army Sch. of Aviation Medicine *(see Sch. of Aviation Medicine)*

United States Army Transportation & Aviation Logistics Sch. 634

United States Army War Coll. 343

United States Army-Dental Activities 705

United States Bus. Sch. in Prague *(see Rochester Inst. of Techno., U.S. Bus. Sch. in Prague)*

United States Coast Guard Acad. 75

United States Defense Information Sch. *(see Defense Information Sch.)*

United States Defense Language Inst. *(see Defense Language Inst. Foreign Language Ctr.)*

United States Indian Industrial Training Sch. *(see Haskell Indian Nations Univ.)*

United States Int'l. Univ. *(see Alliant Int'l. Univ—San Diego Scripps Ranch)*

United States Int'l. Univ—Africa 435

United States Marine Corps Inst. 478

United States Marine Corps Univ. 407

United States Merchant Marine Acad. 281

United States Military Acad. 281

United States Naval Acad. 182

United States Naval Aerospace Med. Inst. *(see Bureau of Medicine & Surgery Naval Operational Medicine Inst.)*

United States Naval Air Tech. Training Ctr. *(see Ctr. for Naval Aviation Tech. Training, Naval Air Tech. Training Ctr.)*

United States Naval Construction Training Ctr. *(see Ctr. for Seabees & Facilities Engineering)*

United States Naval Dental Ctr. Far East 715

United States Naval Dental Sch—Maxillofacial *(see Bureau of Medicine & Surgery Naval Dental Sch-Maxillofacial)*

United States Naval Diving & Salvage Training Ctr. *(see Ctr. for Explosive Ordnance Disposal & Diving)*

United States Naval Health Sciences Edu. & Training Command *(see Bureau of Medicine & Surgery (U.S. Navy))*

United States Naval Hosp. Corps Sch. *(see Bureau of Medicine & Surgery—Naval Hosp. Corps Sch.)*

United States Naval Postgraduate Sch., The 58

United States Naval Sch. *(see United States Naval Acad.)*

United States Naval Sch. of Dental Assisting *(see Bureau of Medicine & Surgery Naval Sch. of Dental Assisting)*

United States Naval Sch. of Health Science *(see Bureau of Medicine & Surgery Naval Sch. of Health Science)*

United States Naval Surface Warfare Training Ctr. *(see Ctr. for Surface Combat Systems)*

United States Naval Tech. Training Ctr. *(see Ctr. for Information Dominance Corry Station)*

United States Naval Undersea Med. Inst. *(see Bureau of Medicine & Surgery—Naval Undersea Med. Inst.)*

United States Naval War Coll. *(see Naval War Coll.)*

United States Navy AEGIS Training Ctr. *(see Ctr. for Surface Combat Systems)*

United States Navy & Marine Corps Intelligence Training Ctr. 738 *(see also Ctr. for Naval Intelligence)*

United States Navy Field Med. Service Sch. *(see Bureau of Medicine & Surgery—Field Med. Service Sch.)*

United States Navy Supply Corps Sch. 495

United States Navy Trident Training Facility *(see Trident Training Facility)*

United States Penitentiary Atlanta 665

United States Sports Acad. 9

United Talmudical Acad. *(see United Talmudical Seminary)*

United Talmudical Seminary 281

United Tech. Ctr. 642

United Theological Coll., The *(see Joint Board of Theological Colleges)*

United Theological Seminary 311

United Theological Seminary of the Twin Cities 215

United Tribes Tech. Coll. 297

Unity Coll. 176

Unity Institution of Liberal Arts & Sciences *(see Unity Coll.)*

Universal Beauty Sch. 490

Universal Career Counseling Ctr. 606

Universal Coll. of Beauty, Inc—South Vermont Avenue 469
Universal Coll. of Beauty, Inc—West 43rd Place 469
Universal Coll. of Healing Arts 542
Universal Healing Arts Coll. *(see Universal Coll. of Healing Arts)*
Universal Sch. of Beauty *(see Universal Beauty Sch.)*
Universal Tech. Inst. 20, 626, 721
Universal Techno. Coll. of Puerto Rico 350
Universal Therapeutic Massage Inst. 557
Universidad Adventista de las Antillas 350
Universidad Central del Caribe 350
Universidad de América de Puerto Rico *(see American Univ. of Puerto Rico)*
Universidad de las Americas, A.C. 436
Universidad de las Americas—Puebla 436
Universidad de Monterrey 436
Universidad del Este 351
Universidad del Puerto Rico en Ultado *(see Univ. of Puerto Rico at Utuado)*
Universidad del Puerto Rico—Aguadilla *(see Univ. of Puerto Rico at Aguadilla)*
Universidad del Puerto Rico—Arecibo *(see Univ. of Puerto Rico at Arecibo)*
Universidad del Puerto Rico—Bayamon *(see Univ. of Puerto Rico at Bayamon)*
Universidad del Puerto Rico—Carolina *(see Univ. of Puerto Rico at Carolina)*
Universidad del Puerto Rico—Cayey *(see Univ. of Puerto Rico at Cayey)*
Universidad del Puerto Rico—Humacao *(see Univ. of Puerto Rico at Humacao)*
Universidad del Puerto Rico—Mayaguez *(see Univ. of Puerto Rico at Mayaguez)*
Universidad del Puerto Rico—Ponce *(see Univ. of Puerto Rico at Ponce)*
Universidad del Puerto Rico—Recinto de Ciencias Médicas *(see Univ. of Puerto Rico—Med. Sciences Campus)*
Universidad del Puerto Rico—Rio Piedras *(see Univ. of Puerto Rico at Rio Piedras)*
Universidad del Sagrado Corazón *(see Univ. of the Sacred Heart)*

Universidad del Turabo 351
Universidad FLET 94
Universidad Interamericana de Puerto Rico de San German *(see Inter American Univ. of Puerto Rico San German Campus)*
Universidad Interamericana de Puerto Rico Escuela Optometria *(see Inter American Univ. of Puerto Rico Sch. of Optometry)*
Universidad Interamericana de Puerto Rico Facultad de Derecho *(see Inter American Univ. of Puerto Rico Sch. of Law)*
Universidad Interamericana de Puerto Rico Recinto de Aguadilla *(see Inter American Univ. of Puerto Rico Aguadilla Campus)*
Universidad Interamericana de Puerto Rico Recinto de Arecibo *(see Inter American Univ. of Puerto Rico Arecibo Campus)*
Universidad Interamericana de Puerto Rico Recinto de Barranquitas *(see Inter American Univ. of Puerto Rico Barranquitas Campus)*
Universidad Interamericana de Puerto Rico Recinto de Bayamon *(see Inter American Univ. of Puerto Rico Bayamon Campus)*
Universidad Interamericana de Puerto Rico Recinto de Fajardo *(see Inter American Univ. of Puerto Rico Fajardo Campus)*
Universidad Interamericana de Puerto Rico Recinto de Guayama *(see Inter American Univ. of Puerto Rico Guayama Campus)*
Universidad Interamericana de Puerto Rico Recinto de Ponce *(see Inter American Univ. of Puerto Rico Ponce Campus)*
Universidad Interamericana de Puerto Rico Recinto Metropolitano *(see Inter American Univ. of Puerto Rico Metropolitan Campus)*
Universidad Internacional de Mexico, A.C. *(see Alliant Int'l. Univ—Mexico City)*
Universidad Metropolitana 351
Universidad Politecnica de Puerto Rico 351
Universitat Mannheim *(see Univ. of Mannheim)*
Université de Montréal 713
Université de Sherbrooke 713
Université du Maine *(see Univ. of Maine at Fort Kent)*
Université Laval 713
Universiteit Maastricht *(see Maastricht Univ.)*

Universiteit Tilburg *(see Tilburg Univ.)*
Universiteit Utrecht *(see Univ. of Utrecht)*
Univ. at Albany *(see State Univ. of New York at Albany)*
Univ. at Buffalo *(see State Univ. of New York at Buffalo)*
Univ. at Lewisburg *(see Bucknell Univ.)*
Univ. Coll. Dublin 715
Univ. Coll. of Bangor 176 *(see also Univ. of Maine at Augusta)*
Univ. Coll. of Maryland *(see Univ. of Maryland Univ. Coll.)*
Univ. Coll. of San Juan 351, 736
Univ. Good Samaritan Ctr. 679
Univ. Health Ctr. *(see Detroit Receiving Hosp.)*
Univ. Health Sciences Ctr. (Consortium) *(see Univ. of North Texas)*
Univ. Hosp. 665
Univ. Hosp. in Birmingham, The 9
Univ. Laboratories of the Detroit Med. Ctr. *(see Detroit Med. Ctr. Univ. Laboratories)*
Univ. Med. Ctr. 652
Univ. of Action Learning at Boulder 724
Univ. of Advancing Computer Techno. 721 *(see also Univ. of Advancing Techno.)*
Univ. of Advancing Techno. 20, 721
Univ. of Akron, The 311
Univ. of Akron—Comm. & Tech. Coll., The *(see Univ. of Akron)*
Univ. of Akron—Wayne Coll. 311
Univ. of Alabama at Birmingham, The 9
Univ. of Alabama at Tuscaloosa *(see Univ. of Alabama)*
Univ. of Alabama Birmingham—Walker Coll. *(see Bevill State Comm. Coll—Walker Coll. Campus)*
Univ. of Alabama Health System *(see Univ. Hosp. in Birmingham)*
Univ. of Alabama in Huntsville, The 9
Univ. of Alabama, The 9
Univ. of Alaska Anchorage 11
Univ. of Alaska Fairbanks 11
Univ. of Alaska Southeast 12
Univ. of Alberta 752
Univ. of Alfred *(see Alfred Univ.)*
Univ. of Anderson *(see Anderson Univ.)*
Univ. of Arizona 21
Univ. of Arizona—Arizona Int'l. Coll. *(see Arizona Int'l. Coll.)*
Univ. of Arkansas at Fayetteville 27
Univ. of Arkansas at Fort Smith 27
Univ. of Arkansas at Little Rock 27

Univ. of Arkansas at Monticello 27
Univ. of Arkansas at Pine Bluff 27
Univ. of Arkansas Comm. Coll. at Batesville 27
Univ. of Arkansas Comm. Coll. at Hope 27
Univ. of Arkansas Comm. Coll. at Morrilton 28, 721
Univ. of Arkansas Cossatot Comm. Coll. *(see Cossatot Comm. Coll. of the Univ. of Arkansas)*
Univ. of Arkansas for Med. Sciences 28
Univ. of Aurora *(see Aurora Univ.)*
Univ. of Baltimore 182
Univ. of Bayamon *(see Bayamon Central Univ.)*
Univ. of Bellevue *(see Bellevue Univ.)*
Univ. of Boston *(see Boston Univ.)*
Univ. of Boulder *(see Univ. of Colorado at Boulder)*
Univ. of Bowie *(see Bowie State Univ.)*
Univ. of Bridgeport 75
Univ. of British Columbia 713
Univ. of Buffalo *(see State Univ. of New York at Buffalo)*
Univ. of Calgary 713
Univ. of California at Los Angeles *(see Univ. of California, Los Angeles)*
Univ. of California Southern Branch *(see Univ. of California, Los Angeles)*
Univ. of California, Berkeley 59
Univ. of California, Davis 59
Univ. of California, Hastings Coll. of the Law 59
Univ. of California, Irvine 59
Univ. of California, Los Angeles 59
Univ. of California, Riverside 59
Univ. of California, San Diego 59
Univ. of California, San Francisco 60
Univ. of California, Santa Barbara 60
Univ. of California, Santa Cruz 60
Univ. of Campbellsville *(see Campbellsville Univ.)*
Univ. of Central Arkansas 28
Univ. of Central Connecticut *(see Central Connecticut State Univ.)*
Univ. of Central Europe *(see Central European Univ.)*
Univ. of Central Florida 95
Univ. of Central Michigan *(see Central Michigan Univ.)*
Univ. of Central Missouri *(see Central Missouri State Univ.)*
Univ. of Central Oklahoma 319
Univ. of Central Washington *(see Central Washington Univ.)*
Univ. of Charleston, The 420
Univ. of Chattanooga *(see Univ. of Tennessee at Chattanooga)*

Univ. of Chicago 133
Univ. of Chicago Divinity Sch. *(see Univ. of Chicago)*
Univ. of Cincinnati 311
Univ. of Cincinnati, OMI Coll. of Applied Science *(see Univ. of Cincinnati)*
Univ. of Cincinnati—Clermont Coll. 312
Univ. of Cincinnati—Raymond Walters Coll. 312
Univ. of Colorado at Boulder 70
Univ. of Colorado at Colorado Springs 70
Univ. of Colorado at Denver 724 *(see also Univ. of Colorado at Denver & Health Sciences Ctr.)*
Univ. of Colorado at Denver & Health Sciences Ctr. 71, 724
Univ. of Colorado Health Sciences Ctr. 724 *(see also Univ. of Colorado at Denver & Health Sciences Ctr.)*
Univ. of Connecticut Health Ctr., The 76
Univ. of Connecticut, The 76
Univ. of Corpus Christi *(see Texas A&M Univ—Corpus Christi)*
Univ. of Cosmetology Arts & Sciences 626
Univ. of Dallas, The 389
Univ. of Dayton 312
Univ. of Delaware 77
Univ. of Denver 71
Univ. of Detroit Mercy 204
Univ. of Detroit, The *(see Univ. of Detroit Mercy)*
Univ. of Dixie *(see Tennessee Technological Univ.)*
Univ. of Dubuque 150
Univ. of Dubuque Theological Seminary *(see Univ. of Dubuque)*
Univ. of East Carolina *(see East Carolina Univ.)*
Univ. of East Central Oklahoma *(see East Central Univ.)*
Univ. of East Stroudsburg *(see East Stroudsburg Univ. of Pennsylvania)*
Univ. of East Tennessee *(see East Tennessee State Univ.)*
Univ. of Eastern Connecticut *(see Eastern Connecticut State Univ.)*
Univ. of Eastern Illinois *(see Eastern Illinois Univ.)*
Univ. of Eastern Kentucky *(see Eastern Kentucky Univ.)*
Univ. of Eastern Michigan *(see Eastern Michigan Univ.)*
Univ. of Eastern New Mexico *(see Eastern New Mexico Univ.)*

Univ. of Eastern New Mexico— Roswell *(see Eastern New Mexico Univ—Roswell)*
Univ. of Eastern Oregon *(see Eastern Oregon Univ.)*
Univ. of Eastern Washington *(see Eastern Washington Univ.)*
Univ. of East-West Medicine 656
Univ. of Edinboro *(see Edinboro Univ. of Pennsylvania)*
Univ. of Edingurgh, The 718
Univ. of Elizabeth City *(see Elizabeth City State Univ.)*
Univ. of Elon *(see Elon Univ.)*
Univ. of Emporia *(see Emporia State Univ.)*
Univ. of Evansville 143
Univ. of Findlay 312
Univ. of Florida 95
Univ. of Florida Forest Ranger Sch. *(see Lake City Comm. Coll.)*
Univ. of Florida Health Science Ctr. Jacksonville *(see Shands Jacksonville Med. Ctr.)*
Univ. of Georgia, The 110
Univ. of Glasgow 718
Univ. of Great Falls 235
Univ. of Guam 112
Univ. of Guelph 713
Univ. of Hampston *(see Hampton Univ.)*
Univ. of Hartford 76
Univ. of Hawaii at Hilo 114
Univ. of Hawaii at Manoa 114
Univ. of Hawaii at West Oahu 114
Univ. of Hawaii Ctr. on Kaua'I *(see Kaua'i Comm. Coll.)*
Univ. of Hawaii Honolulu Comm. Coll. *(see Honolulu Comm. Coll.)*
Univ. of Hawaii Kapi'olani Comm. Coll. *(see Kapi'olani Comm. Coll.)*
Univ. of Hawaii Kua'i Comm. Coll. *(see Kaua'i Comm. Coll.)*
Univ. of Hawaii Leeward Comm. Coll. *(see Leeward Comm. Coll.)*
Univ. of Hawaii Maui Comm. Coll. *(see Maui Comm. Coll.)*
Univ. of Hawaii Windward Comm. Coll. *(see Windward Comm. Coll.)*
Univ. of Health Sciences *(see Kansas City Univ. of Medicine & Biosciences)*
Univ. of Health Sciences 732
Univ. of Houston 389
Univ. of Houston—Clear Lake 390
Univ. of Houston—Downtown 390
Univ. of Houston—Victoria 390
Univ. of Idaho 116
Univ. of Idaho—Southern Branch *(see Idaho State Univ.)*
Univ. of Illinois at Chicago 133

Univ. of Illinois at Chicago Circle *(see Univ. of Illinois at Chicago)*
Univ. of Illinois at Springfield 133
Univ. of Illinois at Urbana-Champaign 133
Univ. of Indianapolis, The 144
Univ. of Iowa 150
Univ. of Iowa Hospitals & Clinics *(see Univ. of Iowa)*
Univ. of Jacksonville *(see Jacksonville State Univ.)*
Univ. of Judaism 60
Univ. of Kansas 156
Univ. of Kansas City *(see Univ. of Missouri—Kansas City)*
Univ. of Kansas Med. Ctr. 156
Univ. of Kansas Sch. of Nursing *(see Univ. of Kansas Med. Ctr.)*
Univ. of Kentucky 165
Univ. of Kentucky Extended Campus Programs in Paducah *(see Univ. of Kentucky)*
Univ. of La Verne 60
Univ. of La Verne—Athens Campus 740
Univ. of Lake Superior *(see Lake Superior State Univ.)*
Univ. of Langston *(see Langston Univ.)*
Univ. of LaVerne *(see Univ. of La Verne)*
Univ. of Leicester's Centre for Labour Market Studies 437
Univ. of Lincoln *(see Univ. of Nebraska—Lincoln)*
Univ. of London—External Programme 718
Univ. of London—London Bus. Sch. 718
Univ. of London—Royal Veterinary Coll. 718
Univ. of Long Island *(see Long Island Univ.)*
Univ. of Louisiana at Lafayette, The 174
Univ. of Louisiana at Monroe, The 174
Univ. of Louisville 165
Univ. of Louisville Hosp. *(see Univ. of Louisville)*
Univ. of Lowell *(see Univ. of Massachusetts Lowell)*
Univ. of Maine 176
Univ. of Maine at Augusta 176
Univ. of Maine at Farmington 177
Univ. of Maine at Fort Kent 177
Univ. of Maine at Machias 177
Univ. of Maine at Orono *(see Univ. of Maine)*
Univ. of Maine at Presque Isle 177
Univ. of Maine Law Sch. *(see Univ. of Southern Maine)*
Univ. of Management & Techno. 407

Univ. of Manchester 718
Univ. of Manitoba 713
Univ. of Mannheim 715
Univ. of Mary 297
Univ. of Mary Hardin-Baylor 390
Univ. of Mary Washington 407, 738
Univ. of Maryland Baltimore 183
Univ. of Maryland Baltimore County, The 183
Univ. of Maryland Coll. Park 183
Univ. of Maryland Eastern Shore 183
Univ. of Maryland Univ. Coll. 183
Univ. of Maryland Univ. Coll—European Division 740
Univ. of Massachusetts Amherst 193
Univ. of Massachusetts at Worcester *(see Univ. of Massachusetts Med. Sch.)*
Univ. of Massachusetts Boston 193
Univ. of Massachusetts Dartmouth 193
Univ. of Massachusetts Lowell 193
Univ. of Massachusetts Med. Ctr. at Worcester *(see Univ. of Massachusetts Med. Sch.)*
Univ. of Massachusetts Med. Sch. 193
Univ. of Massachusetts Worcester *(see Univ. of Massachusetts Med. Sch.)*
Univ. of Medicine & Dentistry of New Jersey 251
Univ. of Memphis, The 371
Univ. of Metropolitan London *(see London Metropolitan Univ.)*
Univ. of Miami 95
Univ. of Miami Leonard M. Miller Sch. of Medicine *(see Jackson Mem. Hosp.)*
Univ. of Michigan 204
Univ. of Michigan—Dearborn 204
Univ. of Michigan—Flint 204
Univ. of Minnesota Hosp. & Clinics *(see Fairview-Univ. Med. Ctr.)*
Univ. of Minnesota—Crookston 216
Univ. of Minnesota—Duluth 216
Univ. of Minnesota—Morris 216
Univ. of Minnesota—Twin Cities 216
Univ. of Mississippi 221
Univ. of Mississippi Med. Ctr. 221
Univ. of Missouri—Columbia 232
Univ. of Missouri—Kansas City 232
Univ. of Missouri—Rolla 233
Univ. of Missouri—St. Louis 233, 731, 732
Univ. of Mobile 10
Univ. of Monaco *(see Int'l. Univ. of Monaco)*
Univ. of Montana Western Montana Coll. *(see Univ. of Montana—Western)*
Univ. of Montana, The 235

Univ. of Montana—Coll. of Techno., The 235
Univ. of Montana—Helena Coll. of Techno., The 235, 732
Univ. of Montana—Missoula *(see Univ. of Montana)*
Univ. of Montana—Western 235
Univ. of Monterey *(see Universidad de Monterrey)*
Univ. of Montevallo 10
Univ. of Montréal *(see Université de Montréal)*
Univ. of Murray *(see Murray State Univ.)*
Univ. of Nebraska at Kearney 238
Univ. of Nebraska at Lincoln *(see Nebraska Coll. of Tech. Agriculture)*
Univ. of Nebraska at Omaha 238
Univ. of Nebraska Med. Ctr. 239
Univ. of Nebraska Sch. of Tech. Agriculture *(see Nebraska Coll. of Tech. Agriculture)*
Univ. of Nebraska—Lincoln 239
Univ. of Nebraska—Lincoln at Omaha *(see Univ. of Nebraska—Lincoln)*
Univ. of Nevada, Las Vegas 241
Univ. of Nevada, Reno 241
Univ. of New Brunswick 714
Univ. of New England 177
Univ. of New Hampshire 244
Univ. of New Haven 76
Univ. of New Mexico, The 254
Univ. of New Orleans 174
Univ. of New Orleans Lakefront *(see Univ. of New Orleans)*
Univ. of New South Wales, The 711
Univ. of New York *(see New York Univ.)*
Univ. of Niagara *(see Niagara Univ.)*
Univ. of Norfolk *(see Norfolk State Univ.)*
Univ. of North Alabama, The 10
Univ. of North Carolina at Asheville, The 293
Univ. of North Carolina at Chapel Hill, The 294
Univ. of North Carolina at Charlotte, The 294
Univ. of North Carolina at Greensboro, The 294
Univ. of North Carolina at Pembroke, The 294
Univ. of North Carolina at Wilmington, The 294
Univ. of North Dakota 297
Univ. of North Dakota—Lake Region *(see Lake Region State Coll.)*
Univ. of North Dakota—Williston *(see Williston State Coll.)*
Univ. of North Florida 95

Univ. of North Georgia *(see North Georgia Coll. & State Univ.)*
Univ. of North London *(see London Metropolitan Univ.)*
Univ. of North Texas 390
Univ. of North Texas Health Science Ctr. at Fort Worth 390
Univ. of Northeastern Illinois *(see Northeastern Illinois Univ.)*
Univ. of Northern Arizona *(see Northern Arizona Univ.)*
Univ. of Northern Colorado 71
Univ. of Northern Illinois *(see Northern Illinois Univ.)*
Univ. of Northern Iowa 150
Univ. of Northern Kentucky *(see Northern Kentucky Univ.)*
Univ. of Northern Michigan *(see Northern Michigan Univ.)*
Univ. of Northern Virginia 407
Univ. of Northwest Missouri *(see Northwest Missouri State Univ.)*
Univ. of Northwestern Ohio 312
Univ. of Northwestern Oklahoma *(see Northwestern Oklahoma State Univ.)*
Univ. of Notre Dame 144
Univ. of Oakland City *(see Oakland City Univ.)*
Univ. of Oklahoma 319
Univ. of Oklahoma City *(see Oklahoma City Univ.)*
Univ. of Oklahoma Med. Ctr. *(see Univ. of Oklahoma Health Sciences Ctr.)*
Univ. of Omaha *(see Univ. of Nebraska at Omaha)*
Univ. of Oregon 324
Univ. of Osteopathic Medicine & Health Sciences *(see Des Moines Univ—Osteopathic Med. Ctr.)*
Univ. of Ottawa 714
Univ. of Pennsylvania 343
Univ. of Philadelphia *(see Philadelphia Univ.)*
Univ. of Phoenix 21
Univ. of Phoenix Online Campus 22
Univ. of Pittsburg *(see Pittsburg State Univ.)*
Univ. of Pittsburgh 344
Univ. of Pittsburgh Med. Ctr. Northwest 344
Univ. of Pittsburgh Med. Ctr. Presbyterian 344
Univ. of Pittsburgh Titusville Campus *(see Univ. of Pittsburgh Titusville Campus)*
Univ. of Portland 324
Univ. of Prince Edward Island 714
Univ. of Puerto Rico at Aguadilla 351
Univ. of Puerto Rico at Arecibo 351

Univ. of Puerto Rico at Bayamon 351
Univ. of Puerto Rico at Carolina 351
Univ. of Puerto Rico at Cayey 351
Univ. of Puerto Rico at Humacao 351
Univ. of Puerto Rico at Mayaguez 352
Univ. of Puerto Rico at Ponce 352
Univ. of Puerto Rico at Rio Piedras 352
Univ. of Puerto Rico at Utuado 352
Univ. of Puerto Rico—Med. Sciences Campus 352
Univ. of Puget Sound 415
Univ. of Redlands 60
Univ. of Rhode Island 354
Univ. of Richmond 407
Univ. of Rio Grande *(see Univ. of Rio Grande & Rio Grande Comm. Coll.)*
Univ. of Rio Grande & Rio Grande Comm. Coll. 312
Univ. of Rochester 281
Univ. of Saginaw Valley *(see Saginaw Valley State Univ.)*
Univ. of Saint Ambrose *(see Saint Ambrose Univ.)*
Univ. of Saint Cloud *(see Saint Cloud State Univ.)*
Univ. of Saint Francis 133, 144 *(see also Saint Francis Univ.)*
Univ. of Saint Gregory *(see Saint Gregory's Univ.)*
Univ. of Saint Lawrence *(see Saint Lawrence Univ.)*
Univ. of Saint Louis *(see Saint Louis Univ.)*
Univ. of Saint Mary 157, 728
Univ. of Saint Mary of the Lake Mundelein Seminary 133
Univ. of Saint Mary's *(see Saint Mary's Univ.)*
Univ. of Saint Michael's Coll. 434
Univ. of Saint Thomas 216, 390
Univ. of Saint Xavier *(see Saint Xavier Univ.)*
Univ. of Salisbury *(see Salisbury Univ.)*
Univ. of San Diego 60 *(see also San Diego State Univ.)*
Univ. of San Francisco 60
Univ. of San Jose *(see San Jose State Univ.)*
Univ. of Sarasota 726 *(see also Argosy Univ. Sarasota)*
Univ. of Saskatchewan 714
Univ. of Science & Arts of Oklahoma 319
Univ. of Scranton 344
Univ. of Seattle *(see Seattle Univ.)*
Univ. of Sioux Falls 363
Univ. of Slippery Rock *(see Slippery Rock Univ. of Pennsylvania)*
Univ. of South Africa (UNISA) 436

Univ. of South Alabama 10
Univ. of South Carolina—Aiken 359
Univ. of South Carolina—Beaufort 359
Univ. of South Carolina—Columbia 359
Univ. of South Carolina—Lancaster *(see Univ. of South Carolina—Columbia)*
Univ. of South Carolina—Salkehatchie 359 *(see also Univ. of South Carolina—Columbia)*
Univ. of South Carolina—Spartanburg 736 *(see also Univ. of South Carolina—Upstate)*
Univ. of South Carolina—Sumter 359 *(see also Univ. of South Carolina—Columbia)*
Univ. of South Carolina—Union 359 *(see also Univ. of South Carolina—Columbia)*
Univ. of South Carolina—Upstate 359, 736
Univ. of South Dakota, The 363
Univ. of South Florida 96
Univ. of South, The 371
Univ. of Southeast Missouri *(see Southeast Missouri State Univ.)*
Univ. of Southeastern Louisiana *(see Southeastern Louisiana Univ.)*
Univ. of Southeastern Oklahoma *(see Southeastern Oklahoma State Univ.)*
Univ. of Southern California 61
Univ. of Southern Colorado 724 *(see also Colorado State Univ—Pueblo)*
Univ. of Southern Europe 740 *(see also Int'l. Univ. of Monaco)*
Univ. of Southern Georgia *(see Georgia Southern Univ.)*
Univ. of Southern Indiana 144
Univ. of Southern Maine 177
Univ. of Southern Mississippi, The 222
Univ. of Southern Nevada 682, 732
Univ. of Southern New Hampshire *(see Southern New Hampshire Univ.)*
Univ. of Southern Oregon *(see Southern Oregon Univ.)*
Univ. of Southern Utah *(see Southern Utah Univ.)*
Univ. of Southern Virginia *(see Southern Virginia Univ.)*
Univ. of Southwest Minnesota *(see Southwest Minnesota State Univ.)*
Univ. of Southwest Missouri *(see Missouri State Univ.)*
Univ. of Southwestern Georgia *(see Georgia Southwestern State Univ.)*

Univ. of Southwestern Louisiana *(see Univ. of Louisiana at Lafayette)*

Univ. of Southwestern Oklahoma *(see Southwestern Oklahoma State Univ.)*

Univ. of Spa & Cosmetology Art 503

Univ. of St. Augustine for Health Sciences 96

Univ. of St. Francis *(see Saint Francis Univ.)*

Univ. of St. Lawrence *(see Saint Lawrence Univ.)*

Univ. of St. Mary of the Lake *(see Univ. of Saint Mary of the Lake Mundelein Seminary)*

Univ. of Steubenville *(see Franciscan Univ. of Steubenville)*

Univ. of Stony Brook *(see State Univ. of New York at Stony Brook)*

Univ. of Syracuse *(see Syracuse Univ.)*

Univ. of Tampa 96

Univ. of Tennessee at Chattanooga, The 371

Univ. of Tennessee at Martin, The 371

Univ. of Tennessee Med. Ctr. *(see Univ. of Tennessee)*

Univ. of Tennessee, The 371

Univ. of Tennessee—Knoxville *(see Univ. of Tennessee, The)*

Univ. of Tennessee—Memphis Campus *(see Univ. of Tennessee Health Science Ctr.)*

Univ. of Texas at Arlington, The 390

Univ. of Texas at Austin, The 390

Univ. of Texas at Brownsville/Texas Southmost Coll., The 391

Univ. of Texas at Dallas, The 391

Univ. of Texas at El Paso, The 391

Univ. of Texas at San Antonio, The 391

Univ. of Texas at Tyler, The 391

Univ. of Texas Health Science Ctr. at Houston, The 391

Univ. of Texas Health Science Ctr. at Laredo, The *(see Univ. of Texas Health Science Ctr. at San Antonio)*

Univ. of Texas Health Science Ctr. at San Antonio, The 391

Univ. of Texas Med. Branch at Galveston, The 392

Univ. of Texas of Permian Basin, The 392

Univ. of Texas Southwestern Med. Ctr. at Dallas, The 392

Univ. of Texas—Pan American, The 392

Univ. of the Arts 344

Univ. of the Caribbean *(see Caribbean Univ.)*

Univ. of the Cumberlands 165, 728

Univ. of the Dist. of Columbia 80

Univ. of the East *(see Universidad del Este)*

Univ. of the Everglades *(see Everglades Univ.)*

Univ. of the Green Mountains *(see Univ. of Vermont)*

Univ. of the Incarnate Word 392

Univ. of the Ozarks 28

Univ. of the Pacific 61

Univ. of the Pacific States *(see Pacific States Univ.)*

Univ. of the Sacred Heart 352 *(see also Sacred Heart Univ.)*

Univ. of the Sciences in Philadelphia 344

Univ. of the Silicon Valley *(see Silicon Valley Univ.)*

Univ. of the State of Pennsylvania *(see Univ. of Pennsylvania)*

Univ. of the United Arab Emirates *(see United Arab Emirates Univ.)*

Univ. of the Virgin Islands 399

Univ. of the West 723, 743

Univ. of Tiffin *(see Tiffin Univ.)*

Univ. of Toledo 312

Univ. of Toronto 714 *(see also Knox Coll., Univ. of St. Michael's Coll., Wycliffe Coll.)*

Univ. of Towson *(see Towson Univ.)*

Univ. of Trinity Coll. in Univ. of Toronto, The 434

Univ. of Tulsa 319

Univ. of Ulster at Jordanstown 718

Univ. of Upper Iowa *(see Upper Iowa Univ.)*

Univ. of Urbana *(see Urbana Univ.)*

Univ. of Utah 395

Univ. of Utrecht 716

Univ. of Valley City *(see Valley City State Univ.)*

Univ. of Valparaiso *(see Valparaiso Univ.)*

Univ. of Vermont 398

Univ. of Victoria 714

Univ. of Villanova *(see Villanova Univ.)*

Univ. of Virginia 408

Univ. of Virginia Health System *(see Univ. of Virginia)*

Univ. of Virginia Med. Ctr. *(see Univ. of Virginia)*

Univ. of Virginia's Coll. at Wise, The 408

Univ. of Warwick 718

Univ. of Washington 416

Univ. of Washington State *(see Washington State Univ.)*

Univ. of Waterloo 714

Univ. of West Alabama, The 10

Univ. of West Florida 96

Univ. of West Georgia 110, 727

Univ. of West Los Angeles, The 61, 723, 724

Univ. of West Los Angeles—San Fernando Valley Campus 723

Univ. of Western Carolina *(see Western Carolina Univ.)*

Univ. of Western Connecticut *(see Western Connecticut State Univ.)*

Univ. of Western Illinois *(see Western Illinois Univ.)*

Univ. of Western Kentucky *(see Western Kentucky Univ.)*

Univ. of Western Michigan *(see Western Michigan Univ.)*

Univ. of Western New Mexico *(see Western New Mexico Univ.)*

Univ. of Western Ontario, The 714 *(see also Huron Univ. Coll. Faculty of Theology)*

Univ. of Western Oregon *(see Western Oregon Univ.)*

Univ. of Western Washington *(see Western Washington Univ.)*

Univ. of Wichita *(see Wichita State Univ.)*

Univ. of Windsor 714

Univ. of Wingate *(see Wingate Univ.)*

Univ. of Winnipeg 714

Univ. of Winona *(see Winona State Univ.)*

Univ. of Wisconsin at River Falls *(see Univ. of Wisconsin—River Falls)*

Univ. of Wisconsin Colleges 427

Univ. of Wisconsin Hosp. & Clinics 709

Univ. of Wisconsin—Eau Claire 427

Univ. of Wisconsin—Green Bay 428

Univ. of Wisconsin—La Crosse 428

Univ. of Wisconsin—Madison 428

Univ. of Wisconsin—Milwaukee 428

Univ. of Wisconsin—Oshkosh 428

Univ. of Wisconsin—Parkside 428

Univ. of Wisconsin—Platteville 428

Univ. of Wisconsin—River Falls 428

Univ. of Wisconsin—Stevens Point 429

Univ. of Wisconsin—Stout 429

Univ. of Wisconsin—Superior 429

Univ. of Wisconsin—Whitewater 429

Univ. of Wyoming 430

Univ. of Wyoming Northwest Ctr. *(see Northwest Coll.)*

Univ. Sch. of Turabo *(see Universidad del Turabo)*

Univ. System of New Hampshire Coll. for Lifelong Learning *(see Granite State Coll.)*

Univ. System of New Hampshire Sch. of Continuing Studies *(see Granite State Coll.)*

UPMC Presbyterian Shadyside *(see Univ. of Pittsburgh Med. Ctr. Presbyterian)*
Upper Bucks Inst. of Aeronautics 601
Upper Iowa Univ. 150
Upper Valley Joint Vocational Sch. 585
Upper Valley JVS *(see Upper Valley Joint Vocational Sch.)*
Upper Valley Teacher Inst. 544
UPR—Aguadilla *(see Univ. of Puerto Rico at Aguadilla)*
UPR—Aguidilla Reg. Coll. *(see Univ. of Puerto Rico at Aguadilla)*
UPR—Aguidilla Univ. Coll. *(see Univ. of Puerto Rico at Aguadilla)*
UPR—Arecibo *(see Univ. of Puerto Rico at Arecibo)*
UPR—Bayamon *(see Univ. of Puerto Rico at Bayamon)*
UPR—Carolina *(see Univ. of Puerto Rico at Carolina)*
UPR—Cayey *(see Univ. of Puerto Rico at Cayey)*
UPR—Humacao *(see Univ. of Puerto Rico at Humacao)*
UPR—Mayaguez *(see Univ. of Puerto Rico at Mayaguez)*
UPR—Med. Sciences Campus *(see Univ. of Puerto Rico—Med. Sciences Campus)*
UPR—Ponce *(see Univ. of Puerto Rico at Ponce)*
UPR—Rio Piedras *(see Univ. of Puerto Rico at Rio Piedras)*
UPR—Ultado *(see Univ. of Puerto Rico at Utuado)*
Upstate Med. Univ. *(see State Univ. of New York Upstate Med. Univ.)*
Upstate New York Talmudical Inst. *(see Talmudical Inst. of Upstate New York)*
Urban Coll. of Boston 193
Urban League of Chicago Computer Training Ctr. *(see Chicago Urban League Computer Training Ctr.)*
Urban Parish Program *(see Emmanuel Coll.)*
Urbana Univ. 312
Ursinus Coll. 344
Ursuline Acad. *(see Ursuline Coll.)*
Ursuline Coll. 312
USC Aiken *(see Univ. of South Carolina—Aiken)*
USC Lancaster *(see Univ. of South Carolina—Lancaster)*
USC Upstate *(see Univ. of South Carolina—Upstate)*
UT Austin *(see Univ. of Texas at Austin)*
UT Dallas *(see Univ. of Texas at Dallas)*

UT El Paso *(see Univ. of Texas at El Paso)*
UT Health Science Ctr. at Laredo *(see Univ. of Texas Health Science Ctr. at San Antonio)*
UT Health Science Ctr. at San Antonio *(see Univ. of Texas Health Science Ctr. at San Antonio)*
UT Pan Am *(see Univ. of Texas—Pan American)*
UT Permian Basin *(see Univ. of Texas of the Permian Basin)*
UT San Antonio *(see Univ. of Texas at San Antonio)*
UT Tyler *(see Univ. of Texas at Tyler)*
Utah Career Coll., The 395
Utah Coll. *(see Utah Career Coll.)*
Utah Coll. of Applied Techno. *(see Bridgerland Applied Techno. Coll., Davis Applied Techno. Coll., Ogden-Weber Applied Techno. Coll.)*
Utah Coll. of Massage Therapy 629 *(see also Arizona Sch. of Massage Therapy—Phoenix, Arizona Sch. of Massage Therapy—Tempe, Denver Sch. of Massage Therapy, Nevada Sch. of Massage Therapy—Las Vegas)*
Utah Coll. of Massage Therapy—Tempe *(see Arizona Sch. of Massage Therapy—Tempe)*
Utah Coll. of Midwifery 737 *(see also Midwives Coll. of Utah)*
Utah Dale Carnegie Training *(see Chatterton, Inc)*
Utah Electronic Coll. *(see Bridgerland Applied Techno. Coll.)*
Utah Massage Therapy Coll. *(see Utah Coll. of Massage Therapy)*
Utah Midwifery Coll. *(see Midwives Coll. of Utah)*
Utah Myotherapy Coll. *(see Myotherapy Coll. of Utah)*
Utah Sch. of Midwifery *(see Midwives Coll. of Utah)*
Utah State Univ. 396
Utah Tech. Coll. at Provo *(see Utah Valley State Coll.)*
Utah Trade Tech. Inst. *(see Utah Valley State Coll.)*
Utah Univ. *(see Univ. of Utah)*
Utah Valley Comm. Coll. *(see Utah Valley State Coll.)*
Utah Valley State Coll. 396
UTI—Arizona *(see Universal Tech. Inst.)*
Utica Coll. 281
Utica Coll. of Syracuse Univ. *(see Utica Coll.)*

Utica Homeopathic Hosp. *(see Faxton-St. Luke's Healthcare)*
Utica Mem. Hosp. *(see Faxton-St. Luke's Healthcare)*
Utica Sch. of Commerce 281
UTI—Houston *(see Universal Tech. Inst.)*
UTI—Illinois *(see Universal Tech. Inst.)*
UTI—Phoenix *(see Motorcycle & Marine Mechanics Inst., Universal Tech. Inst.)*
UTI—Southern California *(see Universal Tech. Inst.)*
Utrecht Univ. *(see Univ. of Utrecht)*
UVA Coll. at Wise *(see Univ. of Virginia's Coll. at Wise)*
UW Health *(see Univ. of Wisconsin Hosp. & Clinics)*
UW—Baraboo-Sauk County *(see Univ. of Wisconsin—Baraboo-Sauk County)*
UW—Barron County *(see Univ. of Wisconsin—Barron County)*
UW—Eau Claire *(see Univ. of Wisconsin—Eau Claire)*
UW—Fond du Lac *(see Univ. of Wisconsin—Fond du Lac)*
UW—Fox Valley *(see Univ. of Wisconsin—Fox Valley)*
UW—Green Bay *(see Univ. of Wisconsin—Green Bay)*
UW—La Crosse *(see Univ. of Wisconsin—La Crosse)*
UW—Madison *(see Univ. of Wisconsin—Madison)*
UW—Manitowoc County *(see Univ. of Wisconsin—Manitowoc County)*
UW—Marathon County *(see Univ. of Wisconsin—Marathon County)*
UW—Marinette County *(see Univ. of Wisconsin—Marinette County)*
UW—Marshfield-Wood County *(see Univ. of Wisconsin—Marshfield-Wood County)*
UW—Milwaukee *(see Univ. of Wisconsin—Milwaukee)*
UW—Oshkosh *(see Univ. of Wisconsin—Oshkosh)*
UW—Parkside *(see Univ. of Wisconsin—Parkside)*
UW—Platteville *(see Univ. of Wisconsin—Platteville)*
UW—Richland *(see Univ. of Wisconsin—Richland)*
UW—River Falls *(see Univ. of Wisconsin—River Falls)*
UW—Rock County *(see Univ. of Wisconsin—Rock County)*
UW—Sheboygan County *(see Univ. of Wisconsin—Sheboygan County)*

UW—Stevens Point *(see Univ. of Wisconsin—Stevens Point)*

UW—Stout *(see Univ. of Wisconsin—Stout)*

UW—Superior *(see Univ. of Wisconsin—Superior)*

UW—Washington County *(see Univ. of Wisconsin—Washington County)*

UW—Waukesha County *(see Univ. of Wisconsin—Waukesha)*

UW—Whitewater *(see Univ. of Wisconsin—Whitewater)*

V

VA Central Iowa Healthcare System *(see Veterans Affairs Central Iowa Healthcare System—Knoxville Division)*

VA Connecticut Healthcare System Newington *(see Greater Hartford Clinical Psychology Internship Consortium)*

VA Connecticut Healthcare System West Haven *(see Veterans Affairs Connecticut Healthcare System West Haven)*

VA Eastern Kansas Healthcare System *(see Colmery-O'Neil Veterans Affairs Med. Ctr., Dwight D. Eisenhower Veterans Affairs Med. Ctr.)*

VA Greater Los Angeles Healthcare System *(see Veterans Affairs Greater Los Angeles Healthcare System, Veterans Affairs Greater Los Angeles Healthcare System—Los Angeles, Veterans Affairs Greater Los Angeles Healthcare System—Sepulveda)*

VA Healthcare System of Ohio *(see Veterans Affairs Med. Ctr—Dayton)*

VA Illiana Health Care System *(see Veterans Affairs Illiana Health Care System)*

VA Med. Ctr. at Asheville *(see Veterans Affairs Med. Ctr—Asheville)*

VA Med. Ctr. at Decatur *(see Atlanta Veterans Affairs Med. Ctr.)*

VA Med. Ctr. at Durham *(see Veterans Affairs Med. Ctr—Durham)*

VA Med. Ctr. at East Orange *(see Veterans Affairs Med. Ctr—East Orange)*

VA Med. Ctr. at Manchester *(see Veterans Affairs Med. Ctr—Manchester)*

VA Med. Ctr. at Oklahoma City *(see Veterans Affairs Med. Ctr—Oklahoma City)*

VA Med. Ctr. at Philadelphia *(see Veterans Affairs Med. Ctr—Philadelphia)*

VA Med. Ctr. at San Juan *(see Veterans Affairs Med. Ctr—San Juan)*

VA Med. Ctr. at Wilkes-Barre *(see Veterans Affairs Med. Ctr—Wilkes-Barre)*

VA Med. Ctr. Atlanta *(see Atlanta Veterans Affairs Med. Ctr.)*

VA Med. Ctr. Honolulu *(see Veterans Affairs Pacific Islands Healthcare System)*

VA Med. Ctr. in Memphis *(see Veterans Affairs Med. Ctr—Memphis)*

VA Med. Ctr. of Alexandria *(see Alexandria Veterans Affairs Med. Ctr.)*

VA Med. Ctr. of Allen Park *(see Veterans Affairs Med. Ctr—Allen Park)*

VA Med. Ctr. of Ann Arbor *(see Veterans Affairs Med. Ctr—Ann Arbor)*

VA Med. Ctr. of Asheville *(see Veterans Affairs Med. Ctr—Asheville)*

VA Med. Ctr. of Baltimore *(see Veterans Affairs Med. Ctr—Baltimore)*

VA Med. Ctr. of Bath *(see Veterans Affairs Med. Ctr—Bath)*

VA Med. Ctr. of Bay Pines *(see Bay Pines Veterans Affairs Med. Ctr.)*

VA Med. Ctr. of Bedford *(see Edith Nourse Rogers Mem. Veterans Hosp.)*

VA Med. Ctr. of Birmingham *(see Veterans Affairs Med. Ctr—Birmingham)*

VA Med. Ctr. of Brooklyn *(see Veterans Affairs Med. Ctr—Brooklyn)*

VA Med. Ctr. of Buffalo *(see Veterans Affairs Med. Ctr—Buffalo)*

VA Med. Ctr. of Castle Point *(see Veterans Affairs Med. Ctr—Castle Point)*

VA Med. Ctr. of Chicago *(see Jesse Brown Veterans Affairs Med. Ctr.)*

VA Med. Ctr. of Cleveland *(see Veterans Affairs Med. Ctr—Cleveland)*

VA Med. Ctr. of Dallas *(see Veterans Affairs Med. Ctr—Dallas, Veterans Affairs Med. Ctr—Houston)*

VA Med. Ctr. of Dayton *(see Veterans Affairs Med. Ctr—Dayton)*

VA Med. Ctr. of DC *(see Washington DC Veterans Affairs Med. Ctr.)*

VA Med. Ctr. of Des Moines *(see Veterans Affairs Central Iowa Healthcare System—Knoxville Division)*

VA Med. Ctr. of Gainesville *(see Malcom Randall Veterans Affairs Med. Ctr.)*

VA Med. Ctr. of Hampton *(see Veterans Affairs Med. Ctr—Hampton)*

VA Med. Ctr. of Indianapolis *(see Richard L. Roudebush Veterans Affairs Med. Ctr.)*

VA Med. Ctr. of Knoxville *(see Veterans Affairs Central Iowa Healthcare System—Knoxville Division)*

VA Med. Ctr. of Leavenworth *(see Dwight D. Eisenhower Veterans Affairs Med. Ctr.)*

VA Med. Ctr. of Lexington *(see Lexington Veterans Affairs Med. Ctr.)*

VA Med. Ctr. of Loma Linda *(see Loma Linda Veterans Affairs Healthcare System)*

VA Med. Ctr. of Long Beach *(see Veterans Affairs Med. Ctr—Long Beach)*

VA Med. Ctr. of Mare Island *(see Veterans Affairs Northern California Health Care System—Mare Island)*

VA Med. Ctr. of Martinsburg *(see Veterans Affairs Med. Ctr—Martinsburg)*

VA Med. Ctr. of Miami *(see Miami Veterans Affairs Med. Ctr.)*

VA Med. Ctr. of Milwaukee *(see Veterans Affairs Med. Ctr—Milwaukee)*

VA Med. Ctr. of Minneapolis *(see Veterans Affairs Med. Ctr—Minneapolis)*

VA Med. Ctr. of Mountain Home *(see James H. Quillen Veterans Affairs Med. Ctr.)*

VA Med. Ctr. of Nashville *(see Veterans Affairs Middle Tennessee Healthcare System)*

VA Med. Ctr. of New Orleans *(see New Orleans Veterans Affairs Med. Ctr.)*

VA Med. Ctr. of New York City *(see Veterans Affairs Med. Ctr—New York City)*

VA Med. Ctr. of North Chicago *(see North Chicago Veterans Affairs Med. Ctr.)*

VA Med. Ctr. of Northport *(see Veterans Affairs Med. Ctr—Northport)*

VA Med. Ctr. of Palo Alto *(see Veterans Affairs Palo Alto Health Care System)*
VA Med. Ctr. of Perry Point *(see Veterans Affairs Med. Ctr—Perry Point)*
VA Med. Ctr. of Pittsburgh *(see Veterans Affairs Pittsburgh Healthcare System)*
VA Med. Ctr. of Portland, OR *(see Veterans Affairs Med. Ctr—Portland)*
VA Med. Ctr. of Richmond *(see Veterans Affairs Med. Ctr—Hunter Holmes McGuire)*
VA Med. Ctr. of Saint Cloud *(see Veterans Affairs Med. Ctr—Saint Cloud)*
VA Med. Ctr. of Salem *(see Veterans Affairs Med. Ctr—Salem)*
VA Med. Ctr. of Salt Lake City *(see Veterans Affairs Med. Ctr—Salt Lake City)*
VA Med. Ctr. of San Antonio *(see South Texas Veterans HealthCare System, Veterans Affairs Med. Ctr—San Antonio)*
VA Med. Ctr. of San Diego *(see Veterans Affairs San Diego Healthcare System)*
VA Med. Ctr. of San Francisco *(see Veterans Affairs Med. Ctr—San Francisco)*
VA Med. Ctr. of Seattle *(see Veterans Affairs Puget Sound Health Care System)*
VA Med. Ctr. of Sepulveda *(see Veterans Affairs Greater Los Angeles Healthcare System—Sepulveda)*
VA Med. Ctr. of Stratton *(see Veterans Affairs Med. Ctr—Stratton)*
VA Med. Ctr. of Tampa *(see James A. Haley Veterans Affairs Med. Ctr.)*
VA Med. Ctr. of Temple *(see Veterans Affairs Med. Ctr—Temple)*
VA Med. Ctr. of the Puget Sound *(see Veterans Affairs Puget Sound Health Care System)*
VA Med. Ctr. of Togus *(see Togus Veterans Affairs Med. Ctr.)*
VA Med. Ctr. of Topeka *(see Colmery-O'Neil Veterans Affairs Med. Ctr.)*
VA Med. Ctr. of Tucson *(see Southern Arizona Veterans Affairs Health Care System)*
VA Med. Ctr. of West Haven *(see Veterans Affairs Connecticut Healthcare System West Haven)*

VA Med. Ctr. of West Los Angeles *(see Veterans Affairs Greater Los Angeles Healthcare System)*
VA Med. Ctr. of West Palm Beach *(see Veterans Affairs Med. Ctr—West Palm Beach)*
VA Med. Ctr., Washington, DC *(see Washington DC Veterans Affairs Med. Ctr.)*
VA Med. Ctr—Little Rock *(see Central Arkansas Veterans Healthcare System)*
VA Med. Ctr—Phoenix *(see Carl T. Hayden Veterans Affairs Med. Ctr.)*
VA Northern California Health Care System *(see Veterans Affairs Northern California Health Care System—Mare Island, Veterans Affairs Northern California Health Care System—Martinez)*
VA Pacific Islands Healthcare System *(see Veterans Affairs Pacific Islands Healthcare System)*
VA Palo Alto Health Care System *(see Veterans Affairs Palo Alto Health Care System)*
Vacaville Psychiatric Program *(see California Dept. of Mental Health Vacaville Psychiatric Program)*
Valdosta Coll. *(see Valdosta Tech. Coll.)*
Valdosta State Coll. *(see Valdosta State Univ.)*
Valdosta State Univ. 110
Valdosta Tech. Coll. 110, 727
Valdosta Tech. Inst. 727 *(see also Valdosta Tech. Coll.)*
Valdosta Univ. *(see Valdosta State Univ.)*
Valencia Coll. *(see Valencia Comm. Coll.)*
Valencia Comm. Coll. 96
Valencia Jr. Coll. *(see Valencia Comm. Coll.)*
Valley Baptist Med. Ctr. 705
Valley Beauty Sch. 585
Valley Beauty Sch—Zanesville 585
Valley Career Coll. 469
Valley Career Coll., Inc. 735 *(see also Valley Med. Coll., Inc.)*
Valley City State Univ. 297
Valley City Univ. *(see Valley City State Univ.)*
Valley Coll. *(see Los Angeles Valley Coll., San Bernardino Valley Coll., Valley Career Coll.)*
Valley Coll. of Los Angeles *(see Los Angeles Valley Coll.)*
Valley Coll. of Tech—Beckley 420
Valley Coll. of Tech—Martinsburg 642
Valley Coll. of Tech—Princeton 420

Valley Forge Christian Coll. 344
Valley Forge Coll. *(see Valley Forge Christian Coll.)*
Valley Forge Military Acad. & Coll. *(see Valley Forge Military Coll.)*
Valley Forge Military Coll. 344
Valley Grande Acad. *(see Valley Grande Inst. for Academic Studies)*
Valley Grande Coll. of Health & Techno. 737 *(see also Valley Grande Inst. for Academic Studies)*
Valley Grande Inst. for Academic Studies 626, 737
Valley Health System *(see Valley Hosp., Winchester Med. Ctr., Inc.)*
Valley Hosp., The 685
Valley Med. Coll., Inc. 593, 735
Valley Union Seminary *(see Hollins Univ.)*
Valparaiso Hosp. *(see Porter Valparaiso Hosp.)*
Valparaiso Univ. 144
Van Sant Sch. of Bus. *(see Hamilton Coll—Omaha)*
Vance County Tech. Inst. *(see Vance-Granville Comm. Coll.)*
Vance-Granville Coll. *(see Vance-Granville Comm. Coll.)*
Vance-Granville Comm. Coll. 294
Vancouver Comm. Coll. 714
Vancouver ECE & Montessori Coll. 646
Vancouver Sch. of Theology 434
Vancouver Training Inst. Montessori Program 646
Vanderbilt Univ. 371
Vanderbilt Univ. Divinity Sch. *(see Vanderbilt Univ.)*
VanderCook Coll. of Music 133
Vanderschmidt Sch. *(see Westwood Coll—O'Hare Airport)*
Vanguard Coll. 434, 740
Vanguard Coll. of Cosmetology 518, 729
Vanguard Health Systems *(see Baptist Med. Ctr.)*
Vanguard Inst. of Techno. 626
Vanguard Tech. Inst. *(see Terra State Comm. Coll.)*
Vanguard Univ. of Southern California 61
Vanguard-Sentinel Adult Career Centers *(see Vanguard-Sentinel Joint Vocational Sch. Dist.)*
Vanguard-Sentinel Career Centers *(see Vanguard-Sentinel Joint Vocational Sch. Dist.)*
Vanguard-Sentinel Joint Vocational Sch. Dist. 585
Vantage Career Ctr. 585

Varner & Associates, Inc. *(see James E. Varner & Associates, Inc.)*
Vassar Coll. 281
Vatterott Coll. 233 *(see also L'Ecole Culinaire)*
Vatterott Coll. of Austin *(see Austin Bus. Coll.)*
Vatterott Coll. of Dallas *(see Court Reporting Inst. of Dallas)*
Vatterott Coll. of Houston *(see Court Reporting Inst. of Houston)*
Vatterott Coll—Deerfield 732
Vatterott Coll—Des Moines 151
Vatterott Coll—Quincy 503
Vatterott Coll—Spring Valley 239, 732
Vaughn Coll. of Aeronautics & Techno. 281, 733
VCU Sch. of the Arts in Qatar *(see Virginia Commonwealth Univ.)*
Vee's Sch. of Beauty Culture 504
Velma B's Beauty Acad. 626
Velvatex Coll. of Beauty Culture 449
Venango County Area Vocational Tech. Sch. 700
Venango County Vo-Tech Sch. *(see Venango County Area Vocational Tech. Sch.)*
Venango Techno. Ctr. *(see Venango County Area Vocational Tech. Sch.)*
Vennard Coll. 151
Ventura Coll. 61
Venus Beauty Sch. 601
Vermilion Comm. Coll. 217
Vermillion Coll. *(see Vermilion Comm. Coll.)*
Vermillion State Jr. Coll. *(see Vermilion Comm. Coll.)*
Vermont Agricultural & Tech. Inst. *(see Vermont Tech. Coll.)*
Vermont Coll. 311 *(see also Union Inst. & Univ., Vermont Coll. of Union Inst. & Univ.)*
Vermont Coll. of Cosmetology 630
Vermont Comm. Coll. *(see Comm. Coll. of Vermont)*
Vermont Inst. of Comm. Involvement *(see Burlington Coll.)*
Vermont Law Sch. 398
Vermont Sch. of Agriculture *(see Vermont Tech. Coll.)*
Vermont Tech *(see Vermont Tech. Coll.)*
Vermont Tech. Coll. 398
Vermont Training Solutions, Inc. 630
Vermont Univ. *(see Univ. of Vermont)*
Vernon Coll. 392
Vernon Jr. Coll. *(see Vernon Coll.)*
Vernon Reg. Jr. Coll. *(see Vernon Coll.)*
Vernon's Kansas Sch. of Cosmetology 510

Veterans Affair Med. Ctr—Roudebush *(see Richard L. Roudebush Veterans Affairs Med. Ctr.)*
Veterans Affairs Central Iowa Healthcare System—Knoxville Division 671
Veterans Affairs Connecticut Healthcare System Newington *(see Greater Hartford Clinical Psychology Internship Consortium)*
Veterans Affairs Connecticut Healthcare System West Haven 659
Veterans Affairs Eastern Colorado Healthcare System 658
Veterans Affairs Eastern Kansas Healthcare System *(see Colmery-O'Neil Veterans Affairs Med. Ctr., Dwight D. Eisenhower Veterans Affairs Med. Ctr.)*
Veterans Affairs Greater Los Angeles Healthcare System 656
Veterans Affairs Healthcare System of Ohio *(see Veterans Affairs Med. Ctr—Dayton)*
Veterans Affairs Illiana Health Care System 669
Veterans Affairs Med. & Reg. Office Ctr. *(see Veterans Affairs Pacific Islands Healthcare System)*
Veterans Affairs Med. Ctr. Atlanta *(see Atlanta Veterans Affairs Med. Ctr.)*
Veterans Affairs Med. Ctr. Honolulu *(see Veterans Affairs Pacific Islands Healthcare System)*
Veterans Affairs Med. Ctr. of Bay Pines *(see Bay Pines Veterans Affairs Med. Ctr.)*
Veterans Affairs Med. Ctr. of Bedford *(see Edith Nourse Rogers Mem. Veterans Hosp.)*
Veterans Affairs Med. Ctr. of Chicago *(see Jesse Brown Veterans Affairs Med. Ctr.)*
Veterans Affairs Med. Ctr. of Des Moines *(see Veterans Affairs Central Iowa Healthcare System—Knoxville Division)*
Veterans Affairs Med. Ctr. of Indianapolis *(see Richard L. Roudebush Veterans Affairs Med. Ctr.)*
Veterans Affairs Med. Ctr. of Knoxville *(see Veterans Affairs Central Iowa Healthcare System—Knoxville Division)*
Veterans Affairs Med. Ctr. of Leavenworth *(see Dwight D. Eisenhower Veterans Affairs Med. Ctr.)*

Veterans Affairs Med. Ctr. of Lexington *(see Lexington Veterans Affairs Med. Ctr.)*
Veterans Affairs Med. Ctr. of North Chicago *(see North Chicago Veterans Affairs Med. Ctr.)*
Veterans Affairs Med. Ctr. of Tampa *(see James A. Haley Veterans Affairs Med. Ctr.)*
Veterans Affairs Med. Ctr. of Togus *(see Togus Veterans Affairs Med. Ctr.)*
Veterans Affairs Med. Ctr. of Topeka *(see Colmery-O'Neil Veterans Affairs Med. Ctr.)*
Veterans Affairs Med. Ctr. of West Haven *(see Veterans Affairs Connecticut Healthcare System West Haven)*
Veterans Affairs Med. Ctr., Washington, DC *(see Washington DC Veterans Affairs Med. Ctr.)*
Veterans Affairs Med. Ctr—Alexandria *(see Alexandria Veterans Affairs Med. Ctr.)*
Veterans Affairs Med. Ctr—Allen Park 678
Veterans Affairs Med. Ctr—Ann Arbor 678
Veterans Affairs Med. Ctr—Asheville 682, 692
Veterans Affairs Med. Ctr—Baltimore 676
Veterans Affairs Med. Ctr—Bath 690
Veterans Affairs Med. Ctr—Birmingham 651
Veterans Affairs Med. Ctr—Brooklyn 690
Veterans Affairs Med. Ctr—Buffalo 691
Veterans Affairs Med. Ctr—Castle Point 691
Veterans Affairs Med. Ctr—Cleveland 695
Veterans Affairs Med. Ctr—Colmery-O'Neil *(see Colmery-O'Neil Veterans Affairs Med. Ctr.)*
Veterans Affairs Med. Ctr—Dallas 705
Veterans Affairs Med. Ctr—Dayton 695
Veterans Affairs Med. Ctr—DC *(see Washington DC Veterans Affairs Med. Ctr.)*
Veterans Affairs Med. Ctr—Decatur *(see Atlanta Veterans Affairs Med. Ctr.)*
Veterans Affairs Med. Ctr—Durham 692
Veterans Affairs Med. Ctr—East Orange 685

Veterans Affairs Med. Ctr—Gainesville *(see Malcom Randall Veterans Affairs Med. Ctr.)*
Veterans Affairs Med. Ctr—Hampton 706
Veterans Affairs Med. Ctr—Houston 705
Veterans Affairs Med. Ctr—Hunter Holmes McGuire 706
Veterans Affairs Med. Ctr—Little Rock *(see Central Arkansas Veterans Healthcare System)*
Veterans Affairs Med. Ctr—Loma Linda *(see Loma Linda Veterans Affairs Healthcare System)*
Veterans Affairs Med. Ctr—Long Beach 656
Veterans Affairs Med. Ctr—Manchester 683
Veterans Affairs Med. Ctr—Mare Island *(see Veterans Affairs Northern California Health Care System—Mare Island)*
Veterans Affairs Med. Ctr—Martinsburg 708
Veterans Affairs Med. Ctr—Memphis 702
Veterans Affairs Med. Ctr—Miami *(see Miami Veterans Affairs Med. Ctr.)*
Veterans Affairs Med. Ctr—Milwaukee 710
Veterans Affairs Med. Ctr—Minneapolis 680
Veterans Affairs Med. Ctr—New Orleans *(see New Orleans Veterans Affairs Med. Ctr.)*
Veterans Affairs Med. Ctr—New York City 691
Veterans Affairs Med. Ctr—North Chicago *(see North Chicago Veterans Affairs Med. Ctr.)*
Veterans Affairs Med. Ctr—Northport 691
Veterans Affairs Med. Ctr—Oklahoma City 695
Veterans Affairs Med. Ctr—Palo Alto *(see Veterans Affairs Palo Alto Health Care System)*
Veterans Affairs Med. Ctr—Perry Point 676
Veterans Affairs Med. Ctr—Philadelphia 700
Veterans Affairs Med. Ctr—Phoenix *(see Carl T. Hayden Veterans Affairs Med. Ctr.)*
Veterans Affairs Med. Ctr—Pittsburgh *(see Veterans Affairs Pittsburgh Healthcare System)*
Veterans Affairs Med. Ctr—Portland 696

Veterans Affairs Med. Ctr—Saint Cloud 680
Veterans Affairs Med. Ctr—Salem 696
Veterans Affairs Med. Ctr—Salt Lake City 705
Veterans Affairs Med. Ctr—San Antonio 705
Veterans Affairs Med. Ctr—San Diego *(see Veterans Affairs San Diego Healthcare System)*
Veterans Affairs Med. Ctr—San Francisco 656
Veterans Affairs Med. Ctr—San Juan 700
Veterans Affairs Med. Ctr—Sepulveda *(see Veterans Affairs Greater Los Angeles Healthcare System—Sepulveda)*
Veterans Affairs Med. Ctr—Stratton 691
Veterans Affairs Med. Ctr—Temple 705
Veterans Affairs Med. Ctr—Tucson *(see Southern Arizona Veterans Affairs Health Care System)*
Veterans Affairs Med. Ctr—West Los Angeles *(see Veterans Affairs Greater Los Angeles Healthcare System)*
Veterans Affairs Med. Ctr—West Palm Beach 664
Veterans Affairs Med. Ctr—Wilkes-Barre 700
Veterans Affairs Middle Tennessee Healthcare System 702
Veterans Affairs Northern California Health Care System—Mare Island 657
Veterans Affairs Northern California Health Care System—Martinez 657
Veterans Affairs Pacific Islands Healthcare System 665
Veterans Affairs Palo Alto Health Care System 657
Veterans Affairs Pittsburgh Healthcare System 700
Veterans Affairs Puget Sound Health Care System 707
Veterans Affairs San Diego Healthcare System 657
Veterans HealthCare System of South Texas *(see South Texas Veterans HealthCare System)*
Vici Beauty Sch. 644
Victor Valley Beauty Coll. 469
Victor Valley Coll. 61
Victor Valley Comm. Coll. *(see Victor Valley Coll.)*
Victoria Beauty Coll. 626
Victoria Coll., The 392

Victoria Jr. Coll., The *(see Victoria Coll.)*
Victoria Univ. in the Univ. of Toronto *(see Emmanuel Coll. of Victoria Univ.)*
Victory Health Services Inc. 669
Victory Hosp. *(see North Mem. Med. Ctr.)*
Victory Montessori Training Inst. 61
Vidalia Beauty Sch. 517
Video Symphony EnterTraining, Inc. 469
Villa Julie Coll. 183
Villa Madonna Coll. *(see Thomas More Coll.)*
Villa Maria Acad. for Girls *(see Immaculata Univ.)*
Villa Maria Coll. *(see Immaculata Univ.)*
Villa Maria Coll. of Buffalo 282
Villa Montessori Sch. 559
Village at Manor Park 710
Village for Families & Children, Inc., The 659
Village Sch. for Children, The 559
Villanova Coll. *(see Villanova Univ.)*
Villanova Univ. 345
Vincennes Beauty Coll. 506
Vincennes Univ. 144
Virgil's Beauty Coll. 591
Virgin Islands Univ. *(see Univ. of the Virgin Islands)*
Virginia Agricultural & Mechanical Coll. *(see Virginia Polytechnic Inst. & State Univ.)*
Virginia Beach Higher Edu. Ctr. *(see Norfolk State Univ.)*
Virginia Careers Acad. 738
Virginia Ctr. for Montessori Training 634
Virginia Christian Coll. *(see Lynchburg Coll.)*
Virginia Coll. 10
Virginia Coll. at Birmingham *(see Virginia Coll.)*
Virginia Coll. at Pensacola 96, 725
Virginia Coll. Online 10 *(see also Virginia Coll.)*
Virginia Coll—Salem 738 *(see also Virginia Coll. at Austin)*
Virginia Collegiate Inst. *(see Roanoke Coll.)*
Virginia Commonwealth Univ. 408
Virginia Commonwealth Univ. Sch. of the Arts in Qatar 408
Virginia Consortium Program in Clinical Psychology *(see Coll. of William & Mary, Eastern Virginia Med. Sch., Norfolk State Univ., Old Dominion Univ.)*

Virginia Episcopal Theological Seminary *(see Protestant Episcopal Theological Seminary in Virginia)*

Virginia Farrell Beauty Sch—Ferndale 532

Virginia Farrell Beauty Sch—Livonia 532

Virginia Farrell Beauty Sch—St. Clair Shores 532

Virginia Farrell Beauty Sch—Westland 532

Virginia Highlands Coll. *(see Virginia Highlands Comm. Coll.)*

Virginia Highlands Comm. Coll. 408

Virginia Inst. *(see Roanoke Coll., Virginia Intermont Coll.)*

Virginia Intermont Coll. 408

Virginia Jr. Coll. *(see Mesabi Range Comm. & Tech. Coll.)*

Virginia Learning Inst. Massage Therapy Sch. 738 *(see also National Massage Therapy Inst.)*

Virginia Marti Coll. of Art & Design 312, 734

Virginia Marti Coll. of Fashion & Art 734 *(see also Virginia Marti Coll. of Art & Design)*

Virginia Massage Sch. *(see Virginia Sch. of Massage)*

Virginia Military Inst. 408

Virginia Normal & Collegiate Inst. *(see Virginia State Univ.)*

Virginia Normal & Industrial Inst. *(see Virginia State Univ.)*

Virginia Polytechnic Inst. & State Univ. 408

Virginia Sch. of Hair Design 634

Virginia Sch. of Massage 634

Virginia Sch. of Techno. 634

Virginia Sewing Machines & Sch. Ctr. 470

Virginia State Coll. *(see Virginia State Univ.)*

Virginia State Coll. for Negroes *(see Virginia State Univ.)*

Virginia State Univ. 409

Virginia Tech *(see Virginia Polytechnic Inst. & State Univ.)*

Virginia Techno. Sch. *(see Virginia Sch. of Techno.)*

Virginia Theological Seminary *(see Protestant Episcopal Theological Seminary in Virginia)*

Virginia Union Univ. 409

Virginia Univ. of Lynchburg 751

Virginia Wesleyan Coll. 409

Virginia Western Coll. *(see Virginia Western Comm. Coll.)*

Virginia Western Comm. Coll. 409

Visbile Sch., Music & Worship Arts Coll. 749

Visions in Hair Design Inst. of Cosmetology 761

Vista Coll. *(see Northwest Vista Coll., Vista Comm. Coll.)*

Vista Comm. Coll. 61

Visual Arts Coll. *(see Coll. of Visual Arts)*

Visual Arts Sch. *(see Sch. of Visual Arts)*

Viterbo Coll. *(see Viterbo Univ.)*

Viterbo Univ. 429

Vocal Arts Acad. *(see Acad. of Vocal Arts)*

Vocational Ctr. of Norfolk *(see Norfolk Tech. Vocational Ctr.)*

Vocational Edu. Inst. *(see Instituto de Educacion Vocacional)*

Vocational Guidance Services 585

Vocational Inst. of Florida 755

Vocational Inst. of Seattle *(see Seattle Vocational Inst.)*

Vocational Sch. of Atlantic County *(see Atlantic County Vocational Tech. Sch.)*

Vocational Tech. Ctr. of Alaska *(see Alaska Vocational Tech. Ctr.)*

Vocational Tech. Sch. of Clarion County *(see Clarion County Area Vocational Tech. Sch.)*

Vocational Techno. Ctr. of Fayette County *(see Fayette Plateau Vocational Techno. Ctr.)*

Vocational-Tech. Sch. of Greater Johnstown *(see Greater Johnstown Career & Techno. Ctr.)*

Vogue Beauty Acad—Cleveland 585

Vogue Beauty Acad—Cleveland Heights 585

Vogue Beauty Sch. 495

Volunteer Beauty Acad. of Lawrenceburg 614

Volunteer Beauty Acad—Dyersburg 615

Volunteer Beauty Acad—Madison 615

Volunteer State Coll. *(see Volunteer State Comm. Coll.)*

Volunteer State Comm. Coll. 372

Volusia Comm. Coll. *(see Daytona Beach Comm. Coll.)*

Von Curtis Acad. of Hair Design *(see Paul Mitchell The Sch.)*

Von Curtis Acad. of Hair Design 737

Voorhees Coll. 359

W

W & J Coll. *(see Washington & Jefferson Coll.)*

W. W. Hastings Indian Hosp. 695

W. W. Holding Industrial Edu. Ctr. *(see Wake Tech. Comm. Coll.)*

W. W. Holding Tech. Inst. *(see Wake Tech. Comm. Coll.)*

W.L. Bonner Bible Coll. 749

Wabash Coll. 144

Wabash Valley Coll. 134

Wabash Valley Tech. Inst. *(see Ivy Tech Comm. Coll. of Indiana—Kokomo)*

Wackenhut Services, Inc—Savannah River Site 609

Wade Coll. 392

Wade Powell & Associates, Inc. 634

Wagner Coll. 282

Wake County Industrial Edu. Ctr. *(see Wake Tech. Comm. Coll.)*

Wake Forest Coll. *(see Wake Forest Univ.)*

Wake Forest Manual Labor Inst. *(see Wake Forest Univ.)*

Wake Forest Univ. 294

Wake Forest Univ. Baptist Med. Ctr. *(see Wake Forest Univ.)*

Wake Forest Univ. Divinity Sch. *(see Wake Forest Univ.)*

Wake Tech *(see Wake Tech. Comm. Coll.)*

Wake Tech. Coll. *(see Wake Tech. Comm. Coll.)*

Wake Tech. Comm. Coll. 294

Wake Tech. Inst. *(see Wake Tech. Comm. Coll.)*

WakeMed 692

Walden Univ. 217, 724, 731

Waldorf Coll. 151

Walker & Associates, Inc. 724 *(see also B. Dickson & Associates, LLC)*

Walker Coll. 4 *(see also Bevill State Comm. Coll.)*

Walker County Area Vocational-Tech. Sch. *(see Northwestern Tech. Coll.)*

Walker Inst. of Techno. *(see Lorenzo Walker Inst. of Techno.)*

Walker State Tech. Coll. *(see Bevill State Comm. Coll.)*

Walker Tech. Inst. *(see Northwestern Tech. Coll.)*

Walla Walla Coll. 416

Walla Walla Comm. Coll. 416

Wallace Coll. *(see Lurleen B. Wallace Comm. Coll., Wallace State Comm. Coll.)*

Wallace Comm. Coll. *(see George C. Wallace State Comm. Coll—Dothan, Lurleen B. Wallace Comm. Coll., Wallace State Comm. Coll.)*

Wallace Comm. Coll. Aviation Campus *(see George C. Wallace State Comm. Coll—Dothan)*

Wallace Comm. Coll. Selma *(see George Corley Wallace State Comm. Coll—Selma)*

Wallace State Coll. *(see Wallace State Comm. Coll.)*

Wallace State Comm. Coll. 10 *(see also George C. Wallace State Comm. Coll—Dothan, George Corley Wallace State Comm. Coll—Selma)*

Wallace State Jr. Coll. *(see Lurleen B. Wallace Comm. Coll.)*

Wallace State Jr. Coll. & Tech. Inst. *(see George Corley Wallace State Comm. Coll—Selma)*

Wallamet Univ. *(see Willamette Univ.)*

Walnut Hill Coll. Restaurant Sch. *(see Restaurant Sch. at Walnut Hill Coll.)*

Walnut Hill Coll. Restaurant Sch. *(see Restaurant Sch. at Walnut Hill Coll.)*

Walsh Coll. *(see Walsh Univ.)*

Walsh Coll. of Accountancy & Bus. Administration 205

Walsh Inst. *(see Walsh Coll. of Accountancy & Bus. Administration)*

Walsh Sch. of Bus. *(see Florida Metropolitan Univ—Pompano Beach)*

Walsh Univ. 313

Walter Reed Army Med. Ctr. 661

Walter Reed Health Care System *(see Walter Reed Army Med. Ctr.)*

Walters Coll. *(see Univ. of Cincinnati—Raymond Walters Coll.)*

Walters Comm. Coll. *(see Walters State Comm. Coll.)*

Walters State Coll. *(see Walters State Comm. Coll.)*

Walters State Comm. Coll. 372

Wards Corner Beauty Acad. 634

Warner Coll. *(see Warner Pacific Coll.)*

Warner Pacific Coll. 324

Warner Southern Coll. 96

Warren County Career Ctr. 585

Warren County Career Ctr. Adult & Comm. Edu. Workforce Training *(see Warren County Career Ctr.)*

Warren County Coll. *(see Warren County Comm. Coll.)*

Warren County Comm. Coll. 251

Warren County Vo-Tech Sch. *(see Warren County Area Vocational Tech. Sch.)*

Warren H. Wilson Vocational Jr. Coll. & Associated Schools *(see Warren Wilson Coll.)*

Warren Wilson Coll. 295

Warren Woods Vocational Adult Edu. 532

Warren Woods Vocational Ctr. *(see Warren Woods Vocational Adult Edu.)*

Wartburg Coll. 151

Wartburg Seminary *(see Wartburg Theological Seminary)*

Wartburg Theological Seminary 151

Warwick Acad. of Beauty Culture 607

Warwick Beauty Acad. *(see Warwick Acad. of Beauty Culture)*

Warwick Univ. *(see Univ. of Warwick)*

Washburn Coll. *(see Washburn Univ.)*

Washburn Municipal Univ. *(see Washburn Univ.)*

Washburn Univ. 157

Washburn Univ. of Topeka *(see Washburn Univ.)*

Washburne Culinary Inst. *(see City Colleges of Chicago—Kennedy-King Coll.)*

Washington Adventist Hosp. 676

Washington & Jefferson Coll. 345

Washington & Lee Univ. 409

Washington Art Inst. *(see Art Inst. of Atlanta)*

Washington Bible Coll. 183, 746 *(see also Capital Bible Seminary)*

Washington Bible Inst. *(see Washington Bible Coll.)*

Washington Bus. Sch. of Northern Virginia *(see Gibbs Coll—Vienna)*

Washington Coll. 183 *(see also City Colleges of Chicago—Harold Washington Coll., Trinity Coll., Univ. of Mary Washington, Washington & Jefferson Coll., Washington State Comm. Coll.)*

Washington Comm. Coll. *(see Washington County Comm. Coll., Washington State Comm. Coll.)*

Washington Conservatory of Music, Inc. 523

Washington County Adult Skill Ctr. 634

Washington County Career Ctr. *(see Career Ctr. Adult Tech. Training)*

Washington County Coll. *(see)*

Washington County Comm. Coll. 177, 730 *(see also Washington State Comm. Coll.)*

Washington County Hosp. *(see Washington Hosp.)*

Washington County Tech. Coll. 730 *(see also Washington County Comm. Coll.)*

Washington DC VA Med. Ctr. *(see Washington DC Veterans Affairs Med. Ctr.)*

Washington DC Veterans Affairs Med. Ctr. 661

Washington Foreign Mission Seminary *(see Columbia Union Coll.)*

Washington Hosp. Ctr. 661

Washington Hosp., The 700 *(see also Washington Adventist Hosp.)*

Washington Jr. Coll. *(see Pensacola Jr. Coll.)*

Washington Missionary Coll. *(see Columbia Union Coll.)*

Washington Sch. of Prof. Psychology *(see Argosy Univ. Seattle)*

Washington Sch. of the Bible *(see Washington Bible Coll.)*

Washington State Comm. Coll. 313

Washington State Dale Carnegie Training *(see Crace & Associates)*

Washington State Normal Sch. *(see Central Washington Univ.)*

Washington State Univ. 416

Washington Tech. Coll. *(see Washington State Comm. Coll.)*

Washington Tech. Inst. *(see Univ. of the Dist. of Columbia, Washington State Comm. Coll.)*

Washington Theological Union 80

Washington Township Metropolitan Sch. Dist. *(see J. Everett Light Career Ctr.)*

Washington Training Inst. *(see Columbia Union Coll.)*

Washington Univ. *(see George Washington Univ., Washington Univ. in St. Louis)*

Washington Univ. in St. Louis 233

Washington Vocational Sch. *(see Margaret Murray Washington Vocational Sch.)*

Washington-Holmes Area Tech. Ctr. *(see Washington-Holmes Area Vocational-Tech. Ctr.)*

Washington-Holmes Area Vocational-Tech. Ctr. 490

Washington-Holmes Vo-Tech Ctr. *(see Washington-Holmes Area Vocational-Tech. Ctr.)*

Washtenaw Coll. *(see Washtenaw Comm. Coll.)*

Washtenaw Comm. Coll. 205

Wash'-uh-taw Baptist Univ. *(see Ouachita Baptist Univ.)*

Watauga Acad. *(see Appalachian State Univ.)*

Waterbury Hosp. Health Ctr. 660

Waterbury State Tech. Coll. *(see Naugatuck Valley Comm. Coll.)*

Waterloo Area Vocational Sch. *(see Hawkeye Comm. Coll.)*
Waterloo Lutheran Seminary 434
Waterloo Univ. *(see Univ. of Waterloo)*
Waters Coll. *(see Edward Waters Coll.)*
Watkins Coll. of Art & Design 372
Watkins Film Sch., The *(see Watkins Coll. of Art & Design)*
Watkins Inst. *(see Watkins Coll. of Art & Design)*
Watkins Pre-Release Ctr. 701
Watkins Techno. Ctr. *(see Wes Watkins Techno. Ctr.)*
Waubonsee Comm. Coll. 134
Waukesha County Coll. *(see Waukesha County Tech. Coll.)*
Waukesha County Tech. Coll. 429
Waukesha Tech. Coll. *(see Waukesha County Tech. Coll.)*
Wausau Hosp. *(see Comm. Health Care Wausau Hosp.)*
Wausau Industrial Sch. *(see Northcentral Tech. Coll.)*
Waycross Coll. 110
Waycross Jr. Coll. *(see Waycross Coll.)*
Wayland Baptist Coll. *(see Wayland Baptist Univ.)*
Wayland Baptist Univ. 392
Wayland Literary & Tech. Institution *(see Wayland Baptist Univ.)*
Wayland Seminary *(see Virginia Union Univ.)*
Wayland Univ. *(see Wayland Baptist Univ.)*
Wayne Coll. *(see Univ. of Akron, Wayne Comm. Coll., Wayne State Coll.)*
Wayne Comm. Coll. 295 *(see also Wayne County Comm. Coll. Dist.)*
Wayne County Career Ctr. 585
Wayne County Coll. *(see Wayne County Comm. Coll. Dist.)*
Wayne County Comm. Coll. *(see Wayne County Comm. Coll. Dist.)*
Wayne County Comm. Coll. Dist. 205
Wayne County Joint Vocational Sch. *(see Wayne County Career Ctr.)*
Wayne County JVS *(see Wayne County Career Ctr.)*
Wayne State Coll. 239
Wayne State Univ. 205
Wayne Tech. Inst. *(see Wayne Comm. Coll.)*
Wayne Univ. *(see Wayne State Univ.)*
Wayne's Sch. of Unisex Hair Design *(see Mister Wayne's Sch. of Unisex Hair Design)*
Waynesburg Coll. 345
Weatherford Coll. 392
Weatherford Coll. of Southwestern Univ. *(see Weatherford Coll.)*

Webb Inst. 282
Webb Inst. of Architecture *(see Webb Inst.)*
Webber Coll. *(see Webber Int'l. Univ.)*
Webber Int'l. Univ. 97
Webber Univ. *(see Webber Int'l. Univ.)*
Weber State Univ. 396
Webster Coll. 726 *(see also Daniel Webster Coll., Gulf Coast Coll.)*
Webster Coll—Ocala 97
Webster Inst. of Techno. *(see Gulf Coast Coll.)*
Webster Tech 726 *(see also Gulf Coast Coll.)*
Webster Univ. 233
Wedgwood Christian Youth & Family Services 678
Welder Training & Testing Inst. 601 *(see also ICT: Sch. of Welding)*
Welding Sch. of Illinois *(see Illinois Welding Sch.)*
Welding Sch. of Tulsa *(see Tulsa Welding Sch.)*
Wellesley Coll. 193
Wells Coll. 282
WellSpan Health *(see WellSpan Health—York Hosp.)*
WellSpan Health-York Hosp. 700
Well-Spring Resources, Inc. *(see Massage Therapy Training Inst.)*
WELS Coll. of Ministry, The *(see Martin Luther Coll.)*
Welsh Neck Acad. *(see Coker Coll.)*
Wenatchee Valley Coll. 416
Wentworth Acad. *(see Wentworth Military Acad. & Jr. Coll.)*
Wentworth Coll. *(see Wentworth Inst. of Techno.)*
Wentworth Inst. of Techno. 194
Wentworth Jr. Coll. *(see Wentworth Military Acad. & Jr. Coll.)*
Wentworth Male Acad. *(see Wentworth Military Acad. & Jr. Coll.)*
Wentworth Military Acad. & Jr. Coll. 233
Wes Watkins Techno. Ctr. 591
Wesley Biblical Seminary 222
Wesley Coll. 77, 222 *(see also John Wesley Coll.)*
Wesley Int'l. Barber & Beauty Coll. *(see John Wesley Int'l. Barber & Beauty Coll.)*
Wesley Med. Ctr. 672
Wesley Seminary *(see Wesley Biblical Seminary)*
Wesley Theological Seminary 80
Wesleyan Coll. 110 *(see also Southwestern Univ., Wesleyan Univ.)*
Wesleyan Univ. 76

Wesleyan Univ. of Nebraska *(see Nebraska Wesleyan Univ.)*
Wesleyan Univ. of West Virginia *(see West Virginia Wesleyan Coll.)*
West Alabama Univ. *(see Univ. of West Alabama)*
West Boca Med. Ctr. 664
West Central Coll. *(see West Central Tech. Coll.)*
West Central Tech. Coll. 111
West Central Tech. Inst. *(see West Central Tech. Coll.)*
West Chester Acad. *(see West Chester Univ. of Pennsylvania)*
West Chester Normal Sch. *(see West Chester Univ. of Pennsylvania)*
West Chester State Coll. *(see West Chester Univ. of Pennsylvania)*
West Chester State Teacher's Coll. *(see West Chester Univ. of Pennsylvania)*
West Chester Univ. of Pennsylvania 345
West Coast Talmudic Seminary *(see Yeshiva Ohr Elchonon-Chabad/West Coast Talmudic Seminary)*
West Coast Ultrasound Inst. 470
West Coast Univ. 61
West Coll. *(see West Los Angeles Coll.)*
West Contra Costa Jr. Coll. *(see Contra Costa Coll.)*
West Florida Seminary, The *(see Florida State Univ.)*
West Florida Univ. *(see Univ. of West Florida)*
West Georgia Coll. *(see Univ. of West Georgia)*
West Georgia Coll. *(see West Georgia Tech. Coll., Univ. of West Georgia)*
West Georgia Tech. Coll. 111, 745
West Georgia Tech. Inst. *(see West Georgia Tech. Coll.)*
West Hills Coll. *(see West Hills Comm. Coll.)*
West Hills Coll—Lemoore *(see West Hills Comm. Coll—Lemoore)*
West Hills Comm. Coll. 61
West Hills Comm. Coll—Lemoore 744
West Holmes Career Ctr. *(see Ashland County-West Holmes Career Ctr.)*
West Jersey Health System 685
West Kentucky Comm. & Tech. Coll. 165, 729
West Kentucky Industrial Coll. *(see West Kentucky Comm. & Tech. Coll.)*
West Kentucky State Vocational-Tech. Sch. *(see West Kentucky Comm. & Tech. Coll.)*

West Kentucky TECH *(see West Kentucky Comm. & Tech. Coll.)*
West Kentucky Tech. Coll. 729
West Kentucky Vocational Sch. *(see West Kentucky Comm. & Tech. Coll.)*
West LA Coll. *(see West Los Angeles Coll.)*
West Liberty Coll. *(see West Liberty State Coll.)*
West Liberty State Coll. 420
West Liberty State Coll—Wheeling Campus *(see West Virginia Northern Comm. Coll.)*
West Los Angeles Coll. 61
West Los Angeles Univ. *(see Univ. of West Los Angeles)*
West Los Angeles VA Healthcare Ctr. *(see Veterans Affairs Greater Los Angeles Healthcare System)*
West Los Angeles Veterans Affairs Healthcare Ctr. *(see Veterans Affairs Greater Los Angeles Healthcare System)*
West Michigan Barbering Coll. *(see West Michigan Coll. of Barbering & Beauty)*
West Michigan Beauty Coll. *(see West Michigan Coll. of Barbering & Beauty)*
West Michigan Coll. of Barbering & Beauty 532
West Oahu Coll. *(see Univ. of Hawaii at West Oahu)*
West Palm Beach VA Med. Ctr. *(see Veterans Affairs Med. Ctr—West Palm Beach)*
West Palm Beach Veterans Affairs Med. Ctr. *(see Veterans Affairs Med. Ctr—West Palm Beach)*
West Penn Allegheny Health System *(see Allegheny General Hosp.)*
West Plains Campus of Southwest Missouri State Univ. *(see Missouri State Univ—West Plains)*
West Plains Residence Ctr. *(see Missouri State Univ—West Plains)*
West Point *(see United States Military Acad.)*
West Shore Coll. *(see West Shore Comm. Coll.)*
West Shore Comm. Coll. 206
West Side Inst. of Techno. 734
West Side Montessori Sch. Teacher Edu. Program 570
West Suburban Coll. *(see West Suburban Coll. of Nursing)*
West Suburban Coll. of Nursing 134
West Suburban Nursing Coll. *(see West Suburban Coll. of Nursing)*

West Suburban Sch. of Nursing *(see West Suburban Coll. of Nursing)*
West Tennessee Bus. Coll. 372
West Tennessee Coll. *(see Union Univ.)*
West Tennessee Normal Sch. *(see Univ. of Memphis)*
West Tennessee State Teachers Coll. *(see Univ. of Memphis)*
West Texas A&M Univ. 393
West Texas State Coll. *(see West Texas A&M Univ.)*
West Texas State Normal Coll. *(see West Texas A&M Univ.)*
West Texas State Teachers Coll. *(see West Texas A&M Univ.)*
West Texas State Univ. *(see West Texas A&M Univ.)*
West Valley Coll. 62
West Virginia Bus. Coll. 420
West Virginia Career & Tech. Ctr. 642
West Virginia Career Coll. *(see West Virginia Career Inst., West Virginia Jr. Coll., West Virginia Jr. Coll. at Morgantown, West Virginia Jr. Coll—Bridgeport)*
West Virginia Career Inst. *(see West Virginia Jr. Coll. at Morgantown)*
West Virginia Career Inst. 421
West Virginia Coll. *(see Mountain State Univ., West Virginia State Univ.)*
West Virginia Conference Seminary *(see West Virginia Wesleyan Coll.)*
West Virginia Grad. Coll. *(see Marshall Univ. Grad. Coll.)*
West Virginia Inst. of Techno. *(see West Virginia Univ. Inst. of Techno.)*
West Virginia Jr. Coll. 421 *(see also West Virginia Career Inst.)*
West Virginia Jr. Coll. at Morgantown 421 *(see also West Virginia Career Inst.)*
West Virginia Normal Sch. at Fairmont *(see Fairmont State Univ.)*
West Virginia Northern Comm. Coll. 421
West Virginia Preparatory Sch. *(see Potomac State Coll. of West Virginia Univ.)*
West Virginia Sch. of Osteopathic Medicine 708
West Virginia State Coll. 739 *(see also West Virginia State Univ.)*
West Virginia State Comm. & Tech. Coll. 421
West Virginia State Comm. Coll. *(see West Virginia State Comm. & Tech. Coll.)*

West Virginia State Tech. Coll. *(see West Virginia State Comm. & Tech. Coll.)*
West Virginia State Univ. 421, 739
West Virginia Trade Sch. *(see West Virginia Univ. Inst. of Techno.)*
West Virginia Univ. 421
West Virginia Univ. at Parkersburg 421
West Virginia Univ. Hospitals, Inc. *(see West Virginia Univ.)*
West Virginia Univ. Inst. of Techno. 421 *(see also Comm. & Tech. Coll. at West Virginia Univ. Inst. of Techno.)*
West Virginia Wesleyan Coll. 422
Westark Comm. Coll. *(see Univ. of Arkansas at Fort Smith)*
Westark Jr. Coll. *(see Univ. of Arkansas at Fort Smith)*
Westborough State Hosp. 677
Westbrook Coll. *(see Univ. of New England)*
Westchester Bus. Inst. 734 *(see also Coll. of Westchester)*
Westchester Coll. *(see Coll. of Westchester, Westchester Comm. Coll.)*
Westchester Comm. Coll. 282
Westchester Conservatory of Music *(see Music Conservatory of Westchester)*
Westchester County Med. Ctr. 691
Westchester Sch. of Beauty Culture 570
WestConn *(see Western Connecticut State Univ.)*
Westech Coll. 470
Western Area Vocational Tech. Sch. 700
Western Area Vo-Tech Sch. *(see Western Area Vocational Tech. Sch.)*
Western Baptist Coll. 735 *(see also Corban Coll.)*
Western Baptist Theological Seminary *(see Western Seminary)*
Western Bible Inst. *(see Colorado Christian Univ.)*
Western Branch of the Kansas Normal Sch. *(see Fort Hays State Univ.)*
Western Bus. Coll. 324
Western Career Coll. 62
Western Carolina Univ. 295
Western Christian Coll. 740
Western Coll. *(see Western Career Coll., Western Christian Coll.)*
Western Coll. of Southern California 62, 723
Western Colorado Coll. *(see Western State Coll. of Colorado)*
Western Connecticut State Univ. 76

Western Connecticut Univ. *(see Western Connecticut State Univ.)*
Western Culinary Inst. 324 *(see also Brown Coll.)*
Western Dakota Tech. Inst. 363
Western Evangelical Seminary *(see George Fox Univ.)*
Western Governors Univ. 396
Western Health Sciences Univ. *(see Western Univ. of Health Sciences)*
Western Hills Sch. of Beauty & Hair Design 585
Western Illinois Edu. Consortium *(see Sauk Valley Comm. Coll.)*
Western Illinois Univ. 134
Western Inst. of Science & Health 724 *(see also Sonoma Coll— Petaluma)*
Western Inst. of Science & Health— San Francisco *(see Sonoma Coll—San Francisco)*
Western Int'l. Univ. 23
Western Iowa Tech *(see Western Iowa Tech Comm. Coll.)*
Western Iowa Tech Comm. Coll. 151
Western Kentucky State Coll. *(see Western Kentucky Univ.)*
Western Kentucky Univ. 165
Western Maryland Coll. *(see McDaniel Coll.)*
Western Massachusetts Precision Inst. 527
Western Michigan Coll. *(see Western Michigan Univ.)*
Western Michigan Coll. of Edu. *(see Western Michigan Univ.)*
Western Michigan Univ. 206
Western Montana Coll. of the Univ. of Montana *(see Univ. of Montana— Western)*
Western Nebraska Coll. *(see Western Nebraska Comm. Coll.)*
Western Nebraska Comm. Coll. 239
Western Nebraska Tech. Coll. *(see Western Nebraska Comm. Coll.)*
Western Nebraska Vocational Tech. Sch. *(see Western Nebraska Comm. Coll.)*
Western Nevada Coll. *(see Western Nevada Comm. Coll.)*
Western Nevada Comm. Coll. 241
Western New England Coll. 194
Western New Mexico Univ. 254
Western Oklahoma Area Vocational Tech. Sch. 695
Western Oklahoma Coll. *(see Western Oklahoma State Coll.)*
Western Oklahoma State Coll. 319
Western Oklahoma Vo-Tech Sch. *(see Western Oklahoma Area Vocational Tech. Sch.)*

Western Ontario Inst. of Techno. *(see Saint Clair Coll. of Applied Arts & Techno.)*
Western Ontario Univ. *(see Univ. of Western Ontario)*
Western Oregon Univ. 324
Western Pennsylvania Dale Carnegie Training *(see Leadership Training Services, Inc.)*
Western Pennsylvania Hosp., The 700
Western Pentecostal Bible Coll. 740 *(see also Summit Pacific Coll.)*
Western Pentecostal Coll. *(see Summit Pacific Coll.)*
Western Piedmont Comm. Coll. 295
Western Pilgrim Coll. *(see Oklahoma Wesleyan Univ.)*
Western Reg. Med. Command *(see Madigan Army Med. Ctr.)*
Western Reserve Care System 695
Western Reserve Coll. *(see Case Western Reserve Univ.)*
Western Reserve Eclectic Inst. *(see Hiram Coll.)*
Western Reserve Univ. *(see Case Western Reserve Univ.)*
Western Sch. of Commerce *(see Humphreys Coll.)*
Western Sch. of Health & Bus. Careers 345
Western Science & Health Inst. *(see Sonoma Coll—Petaluma)*
Western Seminary 324
Western State Coll. of Colorado 71
Western State Normal Sch. *(see Western Michigan Univ., Univ. of Maine at Farmington)*
Western State Teachers Coll. *(see Western Michigan Univ.)*
Western State Univ. Coll. of Law 62
Western State Univ. Coll. of Law of San Diego *(see Thomas Jefferson Sch. of Law)*
Western States Chiropractic Coll. 324
Western States Coll. *(see Western States Chiropractic Coll.)*
Western Suffolk Board of Cooperative Educational Services *(see Western Suffolk BOCES)*
Western Suffolk BOCES 570
Western Tech *(see Western Tech. Inst.)*
Western Tech. Inst. 393
Western Texas Coll. 393
Western Theological Seminary 206 *(see Seabury-Western Theological Seminary)*
Western Truck Sch. *(see Western Pacific Truck Sch.)*
Western Univ. of Health Sciences 62
Western Washington Coll. *(see Western Washington Univ.)*

Western Washington Coll. of Edu. *(see Western Washington Univ.)*
Western Washington Univ. 416
Western Wisconsin Coll. *(see Western Wisconsin Tech. Coll.)*
Western Wisconsin Tech. Coll. 429
Western Wisconsin Tech. Inst. *(see Western Wisconsin Tech. Coll.)*
Western Wyoming Coll. *(see Western Wyoming Comm. Coll.)*
Western Wyoming Comm. Coll. 430
Westfield Coll. *(see Westfield State Coll.)*
Westfield Normal Sch. *(see Westfield State Coll.)*
Westfield State Coll. 194
Westfield State Teachers Coll. *(see Westfield State Coll.)*
WestGate Training & Consultation Network 701
Westhampton Coll. *(see Univ. of Richmond)*
Westhill Inst. *(see Westhill Univ.)*
Westhill Univ. 436
Westinghouse Electric Corporation 736
Westlawn Inst. of Marine Techno. 476
Westlawn Marine Techno. Inst. *(see Westlawn Inst. of Marine Techno.)*
Westlawn Sch. of Yacht Design *(see Westlawn Inst. of Marine Techno.)*
Westminster Choir Coll. 249 *(see also Rider Univ.)*
Westminster Choir Coll. of Rider Univ. *(see Rider Univ.)*
Westminster Coll. 233, 345, 396
Westminster Coll. & Bible Inst. *(see Wesley Coll.)*
Westminster Coll. of Salt Lake City *(see Westminster Coll.)*
Westminster Seminary *(see Westminster Theological Seminary)*
Westminster Seminary California *(see Westminster Theological Seminary in California)*
Westminster Theological Seminary 345 *(see also Wesley Theological Seminary)*
Westminster Theological Seminary in California 62
Westmont Coll. 62
Westmoreland Coll. *(see Westmoreland County Comm. Coll.)*
Westmoreland Comm. Coll. *(see Westmoreland County Comm. Coll.)*
Westmoreland County Coll. *(see Westmoreland County Comm. Coll.)*

Westmoreland County Comm. Coll. 345
Weston Jesuit Sch. of Theology 194
Weston Sch. of Theology *(see Weston Jesuit Sch. of Theology)*
Westside Tech *(see Orange Tech. Edu. Ctr—Westside Tech)*
Westwood Aviation Inst—Denver *(see Westwood Coll. of Aviation Tech—Denver)*
Westwood Aviation Inst—Houston 62, 737
Westwood Coll. of Aviation Tech—Broomfield *(see Westwood Coll. of Aviation Tech—Denver)*
Westwood Coll. of Aviation Tech—Denver 71
Westwood Coll. of Aviation Tech—Houston 737
Westwood Coll. of Aviation Tech—Los Angeles *(see Westwood Aviation Inst—Los Angeles)*
Westwood Coll. of Aviation Tech—Los Angeles 62
Westwood Coll. of Tech—Anaheim 724
Westwood Coll. of Tech—Chicago Loop 727
Westwood Coll. of Tech—Dallas 737
Westwood Coll. of Tech—Denver North 724 *(see also Westwood Coll—Denver North)*
Westwood Coll. of Tech—Denver South 724 *(see also Westwood Coll—Denver South)*
Westwood Coll. of Tech—DuPage 727 *(see also Westwood Coll—DuPage)*
Westwood Coll. of Tech—Fort Worth 737
Westwood Coll. of Tech—Inland Empire 724
Westwood Coll. of Tech—Long Beach 723, 724 *(see also Westwood Coll—Long Beach)*
Westwood Coll. of Tech—Los Angeles 724 *(see also Westwood Coll—Los Angeles)*
Westwood Coll. of Tech—O'Hare 727
Westwood Coll. of Tech—O'Hare Airport *(see Westwood Coll—O'Hare)*
Westwood Coll. of Tech—River Oaks 727
Westwood Coll. of Tech—Schiller Park *(see Westwood Coll—O'Hare)*
Westwood Coll. of Tech—Upland *(see Westwood Coll—Denver North)*
Westwood Coll—Anaheim 724
Westwood Coll—Chicago Loop 727
Westwood Coll—Dallas 737

Westwood Coll—Denver North 71, 724
Westwood Coll—Denver South 71, 724
Westwood Coll—DuPage 134, 727
Westwood Coll—Fort Worth 737
Westwood Coll—Houston South 737
Westwood Coll—Inland Empire 724
Westwood Coll—Long Beach 62, 724
Westwood Coll—Los Angeles 62, 724
Westwood Coll—O'Hare Airport 134
Westwood Coll—O'Hare Airport 727
Westwood Coll—River Oaks 727
Westwood Inst. of Tech—Houston South 737
Wharton Coll. *(see Wharton County Jr. Coll.)*
Wharton County Coll. *(see Wharton County Jr. Coll.)*
Wharton County Jr. Coll. 393
Whatcom Coll. *(see Whatcom Comm. Coll.)*
Whatcom Comm. Coll. 417
Wheaton Coll. 134, 194
Wheaton Female Seminary *(see Wheaton Coll.)*
Wheeling Hosp. 708
Wheeling Jesuit Coll. *(see Wheeling Jesuit Univ.)*
Wheeling Jesuit Univ. 422
Wheelock Coll. 194
Whelan Sch. of Practical Nursing *(see Marion S. Whelan Sch. of Practical Nursing)*
White Earth Coll. *(see White Earth Tribal & Comm. Coll.)*
White Earth Comm. Coll. *(see White Earth Tribal & Comm. Coll.)*
White Earth Tribal & Comm. Coll. 747
White Earth Tribal Coll. *(see White Earth Tribal & Comm. Coll.)*
White Pines Coll. *(see Chester Coll. of New England)*
White Pines Coll. 732
White River Vocational Tech. Sch. *(see Arkansas State Univ—Newport)*
Whitewater Normal Sch. *(see Univ. of Wisconsin—Whitewater)*
Whitewater State Teachers Coll. *(see Univ. of Wisconsin—Whitewater)*
Whitewater Tech. Inst. *(see Ivy Tech Comm. Coll. of Indiana—Richmond)*
Whitley Coll. *(see South Coast Coll.)*
Whitman Coll. 417
Whitman Seminary *(see Whitman Coll.)*
Whitney Tech *(see Eli Whitney Reg. Vocational-Tech. Sch.)*

Whitney Vocational-Tech. Sch. *(see Eli Whitney Reg. Vocational-Tech. Sch.)*
Whittier Acad. *(see Whittier Coll.)*
Whittier Coll. 62
Whitworth Coll. 417
Wichita Area Tech. Coll. 510
Wichita Area Vocational-Tech. Sch. *(see Wichita Area Tech. Coll.)*
Wichita Collaborative Psychology Internship Program *(see Wichita State Univ.)*
Wichita Falls Jr. Coll. *(see Midwestern State Univ.)*
Wichita State Univ. 157
Wichita Tech *(see Wichita Area Tech. Coll.)*
Wichita Tech. Coll. *(see Wichita Area Tech. Coll.)*
Wichita Tech. Inst. 510
Wichita Univ. *(see Wichita State Univ.)*
Widener Coll. *(see Widener Univ.)*
Widener Univ. 345
Wiggins Trade Sch. *(see Los Angeles Trade-Tech. Coll.)*
Wilbarger County Jr. Coll. Dist. *(see Vernon Coll.)*
Wilberforce Univ. 313
Wilbur Wright Coll. *(see City Colleges of Chicago—Wilbur Wright Coll.)*
Wiley Coll. 393
Wilford Hall Med. Ctr. 705
Wilkes Coll. *(see Wilkes Univ.)*
Wilkes Comm. Coll. 295
Wilkes Reg. Med. Ctr. 692
Wilkes Univ. 345
Wilkes-Barre Area Vocational Tech. Sch. 700
Wilkes-Barre General Hosp. 700
Wilkes-Barre VA Med. Ctr. *(see Veterans Affairs Med. Ctr—Wilkes-Barre)*
Wilkes-Barre Veterans Affairs Med. Ctr. *(see Veterans Affairs Med. Ctr—Wilkes-Barre)*
Wilkes-Barre Vo-Tech Sch. *(see Wilkes-Barre Area Vocational Tech. Sch.)*
Willamette Univ. 324
William & Catherine Booth Bible Coll. *(see William & Catherine Booth Coll.)*
William & Catherine Booth Coll. 434
William & Mary Coll. *(see Coll. of William & Mary)*
William Beaumont Hosp. Schools of Allied Health 679
William Carey Coll. 222
William F. Lea & Associates, Inc. 514
William Harper Coll. *(see William Rainey Harper Coll.)*

William Howard Taft Univ. 63
William J. Bogan Jr. Coll. *(see City Colleges of Chicago—Richard J. Daley Coll.)*
William Jennings Bryan Coll. *(see Bryan Coll.)*
William Jennings Bryan Univ. *(see Bryan Coll.)*
William Jessup Univ. 63, 723
William Jewell Coll. 233
William Lee Bonner Bible Coll. *(see W.L. Bonner Bible Coll.)*
William Marsh Rice Inst. *(see William Marsh Rice Univ.)*
William Marsh Rice Univ. 393
William Mitchell Coll. of Law 217
William Paterson Coll. of New Jersey *(see William Paterson Univ. of New Jersey)*
William Paterson Univ. of New Jersey 251
William Penn Coll. *(see William Penn Univ.)*
William Penn Univ. 151
William R. Moore Coll. of Techno. 615
William R. Moore Sch. of Techno. *(see William R. Moore Coll. of Techno.)*
William Rainey Harper Coll. 134
William Rice Univ. *(see William Marsh Rice Univ.)*
William Scholl Coll. of Podiatric Medicine *(see Dr. William M. Scholl Coll. of Podiatric Medicine)*
William Smith Coll. *(see Hobart & William Smith Colleges)*
William T. McFatter Tech. Ctr. 491
William T. McFatter Vocational-Tech. Ctr. *(see William T. McFatter Tech. Ctr.)*
William Tyndale Coll. 731
William Woods Coll. *(see William Woods Univ.)*
William Woods Univ. 233
Williams Baptist Coll. 28
Williams Coll. 194 *(see also Aurora Univ., Williams Baptist Coll.)*
Williams Univ. *(see Concordia Univ., Roger Williams Univ.)*
Williamsburg Reg. Manpower Training Ctr. *(see Williamsburg Tech. Coll.)*
Williamsburg Tech. Coll. 360
Williamsburg Tech., Vocational, & Adult Edu. Ctr. *(see Williamsburg Tech. Coll.)*
Williamson Christian Coll. 372, 749
Williamson Coll. *(see Williamson Christian Coll.)*
Williamson Free Sch. of Mechanical Trades, The 346

Williamson Mechanical Trades Sch. *(see Williamson Free Sch. of Mechanical Trades)*
Williamson Sch. of Trades *(see Williamson Free Sch. of Mechanical Trades)*
Williamson Trades Sch. *(see Williamson Free Sch. of Mechanical Trades)*
Williamsport Acad. *(see Lycoming Coll.)*
Williamsport Area Comm. Coll. *(see Pennsylvania Coll. of Techno.)*
Williamsport Dickinson Jr. Coll. *(see Lycoming Coll.)*
Williamsport Dickinson Seminary *(see Lycoming Coll.)*
Williamsport Hosp. & Med. Ctr. *(see Susquehanna Health System)*
Williamsport Sch. of Commerce *(see Newport Bus. Inst.)*
Williamsport Tech. Inst. *(see Pennsylvania Coll. of Techno.)*
Willis Career Ctr. *(see Ralph R. Willis Vocational Tech. Ctr.)*
Willis Vocational Tech. Ctr. *(see Ralph R. Willis Vocational Tech. Ctr.)*
Willis Vo-Tech Ctr. *(see Ralph R. Willis Vocational Tech. Ctr.)*
Williston Coll. *(see Williston State Coll.)*
Williston State Coll. 297
Willmar Comm. Coll. *(see Ridgewater Coll.)*
Willsey Inst. 571
Willsey Limited Rockland, Inc. *(see Willsey Inst.)*
Wilmington Coll. *(see Univ. of North Carolina at Wilmington)*
Wilmington Coll. 77, 313
Wilmington Commercial Coll. *(see Goldey-Beacom Coll.)*
Wilson & Associates, Inc. *(see Jerry Wilson & Associates, Inc.)*
Wilson Beauty Coll., Inc. *(see Pat Wilson Beauty Coll., Inc.)*
Wilson Coll. *(see)*
Wilson Coll. 346 *(see also Lindsey Wilson Coll., Warren Wilson Coll.)*
Wilson County Tech. Inst. *(see Wilson Tech. Comm. Coll.)*
Wilson Industrial Edu. Ctr. *(see Wilson Tech. Comm. Coll.)*
Wilson Rehabilitation Ctr. *(see Woodrow Wilson Rehabilitation Ctr.)*
Wilson Tech *(see Wilson Tech. Comm. Coll.)*
Wilson Tech. Coll. *(see Wilson Tech. Comm. Coll.)*
Wilson Tech. Comm. Coll. 295

Winchester Med. Ctr., Inc. 707
Windham Comm. Hosp. *(see Windham Comm. Mem. Hosp.)*
Windham Comm. Mem. Hosp. 660
Windham Mem. Hosp. *(see Windham Comm. Mem. Hosp.)*
Windham Reg. Vocational-Tech. Sch. 660
Windham Tech. High Sch. *(see Windham Reg. Vocational-Tech. Sch.)*
Windsor Univ. *(see Univ. of Windsor)*
Windward Coll. *(see Windward Comm. Coll.)*
Windward Comm. Coll. 114
Winebrenner Seminary *(see Winebrenner Theological Seminary)*
Winebrenner Theological Seminary 313
Wingate Coll. *(see Wingate Univ.)*
Wingate Univ. 295
Winner Inst. of Arts & Sciences 346
Winner Inst., Inc. 518
Winnipeg Bible Coll. *(see Providence Coll. & Theological Seminary)*
Winnipeg Univ. *(see Univ. of Winnipeg)*
Winona State Coll. *(see Winona State Univ.)*
Winona State Normal Sch. *(see Winona State Univ.)*
Winona State Teachers Coll. *(see Winona State Univ.)*
Winona State Univ. 217
Winona Tech. Coll. *(see Minnesota State Coll-Southeast Tech.)*
Winston-Salem Barber Sch. 574
Winston-Salem Bible Coll. 748
Winston-Salem Coll. *(see Winston-Salem Bible Coll.)*
Winston-Salem State Coll. *(see Winston-Salem State Univ.)*
Winston-Salem State Univ. 295
Winston-Salem Teachers Coll. *(see Winston-Salem State Univ.)*
Winston-Salem/Forsyth County Industrial Edu. Ctr. *(see Forsyth Tech. Comm. Coll.)*
Winter Park Tech *(see Orange Tech. Edu. Ctr—Winter Park Tech)*
Winthrop Coll. *(see Winthrop Univ.)*
Winthrop Training Sch. *(see Winthrop Univ.)*
Winthrop Univ. 360
Winthrop Univ. Hosp. 691
Wisconsin Coll. of Cosmetology, Inc. 644
Wisconsin Conservatory of Music, Inc. 644
Wisconsin Deaconess Training Sch. *(see Bellin Coll. of Nursing)*

Wisconsin English Second Language Inst. 644
Wisconsin Indianhead Tech. Coll. 429
Wisconsin Inst. of Techno. *(see Univ. of Wisconsin—Platteville)*
Wisconsin Lutheran Coll. 429
Wisconsin Med. Coll. *(see Med. Coll. of Wisconsin)*
Wisconsin Mining Sch. *(see Univ. of Wisconsin—Platteville)*
Wisconsin Mining Trade Sch. *(see Univ. of Wisconsin—Platteville)*
Wisconsin Music Conservatory *(see Wisconsin Conservatory of Music, Inc.)*
Wisconsin Sch. of Electronics *(see Herzing Coll—Madison)*
Wisconsin Sch. of Prof. Psychology 429
Wisconsin State Coll. & Inst. of Techno. *(see Univ. of Wisconsin—Platteville)*
Wisconsin State Coll. Oshkosh *(see Univ. of Wisconsin—Oshkosh)*
Wisconsin State Coll., La Crosse *(see Univ. of Wisconsin—La Crosse)*
Wisconsin State Coll—Stevens Point *(see Univ. of Wisconsin—Stevens Point)*
Wisconsin State Coll—Superior *(see Univ. of Wisconsin—Superior)*
Wisconsin State Coll—Whitewater *(see Univ. of Wisconsin—Whitewater)*
Wisconsin State Univ. at River Falls *(see Univ. of Wisconsin—River Falls)*
Wisconsin State Univ—La Crosse *(see Univ. of Wisconsin—La Crosse)*
Wisconsin State Univ—Platteville *(see Univ. of Wisconsin—Platteville)*
Wisconsin State Univ—Stevens Point *(see Univ. of Wisconsin—Stevens Point)*
Wisconsin State Univ—Superior *(see Univ. of Wisconsin—Superior)*
Wisconsin State Univ—Whitewater *(see Univ. of Wisconsin—Whitewater)*
Withlacoochee Tech. Inst. 491
Wittenberg Coll. *(see Wittenberg Univ.)*
Wittenberg Univ. 313
Wofford Coll. 360
Woman's Coll. of Alabama *(see Huntingdon Coll.)*
Woman's Coll. of Frederick *(see Hood Coll.)*
Woman's Coll. of the Univ. of North Carolina *(see Univ. of North Carolina at Greensboro)*

Woman's Univ. of Texas *(see Texas Woman's Univ.)*
Women's Christian Assoc. Hosp. 691
Women's Coll. of Georgia *(see Georgia Coll. & State Univ.)*
Won Inst. of Grad. Studies 749
Wood Coll. *(see John Wood Comm. Coll.)*
Wood Comm. Coll. *(see John Wood Comm. Coll.)*
Wood Construction Ctr. *(see Seattle Central Comm. Coll.)*
Wood County Board of Edu. Sch. of Practical Nursing *(see Wood County Vocational Sch.)*
Wood County Vocational Sch. 708
Wood Inst. 731
Wood Tobe-Coburn Sch. 282
Woodbury Bus. Coll. *(see Woodbury Univ.)*
Woodbury Coll. 398
Woodbury Univ. 63
Woodhouse Day Spa *(see Woodhouse Sch. of Wellness)*
Woodhouse Sch. of Wellness, The 760
Woodhull Med. & Mental Health Ctr. 691
Woodrow Wilson Jr. Coll. *(see City Colleges of Chicago—Kennedy-King Coll.)*
Woodrow Wilson Rehabilitation Ctr. 634
Woods Hole Oceanographic Institution 194
Woods Univ. *(see William Woods Univ.)*
Woodward Beauty Coll. 591
Wooster Coll. *(see Coll. of Wooster)*
Worcester County Free Inst. of Industrial Science *(see Worcester Polytechnic Inst.)*
Worcester Med. Ctr. *(see Saint Vincent Hosp. at Worcester Med. Ctr.)*
Worcester Polytechnic Inst. 194
Worcester State Coll. 194
Word of Life Bible Inst. 571
Word of Life Fellowship *(see Word of Life Bible Inst.)*
World Class Univ. 615
World Coll. 409
World Medicine Inst. 114, 727
World Mission Univ. 744
World Outreach Med. Inst. 755
World Training Acad., Inc. 758
World Vision Coll. of Cosmetology, Inc. 754
Worldwide Bus. Schools *(see KeySkills Learning, Inc.)*
Worldwide Educational Services 733
Worldwide Educational Services—Clifton 733

Worldwide Educational Services—Newark 733
Worldwide Language Resources, Inc. 520
Worsham Coll. of Mortuary Science 134
Worsley Inst. of Classical Acupuncture *(see Acad. for Five Element Acupuncture)*
Worthington Comm. Coll. *(see Minnesota West Comm. & Tech. Coll—Granite Falls)*
Worthington Jr. Coll. *(see Minnesota West Comm. & Tech. Coll—Granite Falls, Minnesota West Comm. & Tech. Coll—Worthington)*
Worthington State Jr. Coll. *(see Minnesota West Comm. & Tech. Coll—Granite Falls, Minnesota West Comm. & Tech. Coll—Worthington)*
Wor-Wic Coll. *(see Wor-Wic Comm. Coll.)*
Wor-Wic Comm. Coll. 183
Wray K. Powell & Associates, Inc. 635
Wright Beauty Acad—Battle Creek 532
Wright Beauty Acad—Portage 532
Wright Beauty Coll. *(see ICS The Wright Beauty Coll.)*
Wright Bus. Sch. 510
Wright Coll. *(see City Colleges of Chicago—Wilbur Wright Coll.)*
Wright Inst., The 63
Wright Sch. of Architecture *(see Frank Lloyd Wright Sch. of Architecture)*
Wright State Univ. 313
Wright-Patterson Med. Ctr. *(see 74th Dental Squadron/SGD)*
WTI—Wichita *(see Wichita Tech. Inst.)*
WVJC Bridgeport *(see West Virginia Jr. Coll—Bridgeport)*
WVJC Morgantown *(see West Virginia Jr. Coll. at Morgantown)*
WVU Tech *(see West Virginia Univ. Inst. of Techno.)*
Wyckoff Heights Med. Ctr. 691
Wycliffe Coll. 434
Wyoming Tech. Inst. 739 *(see also WyoTech, WyoTech—Blairsville, WyoTech—Boston, WyoTech—Fremont, WyoTech—Sacramento)*
Wyoming Tech. Inst—Blairsville 736
Wyoming Tech. Inst—Boston *(see WyoTech—Boston)*
Wyoming Univ. *(see Univ. of Wyoming)*
Wyoming Valley Day Tech. Inst. *(see Pennsylvania State Univ.)*
Wyomissing Polytechnic Inst. *(see Pennsylvania State Univ.)*

WyoTech 430, 739
WyoTech—Blairsville 346, 736
WyoTech—Boston 527, 730
WyoTech—Fremont 63, 723
WyoTech—Sacramento 63
Wytheville Comm. Coll. 409

X

Xavier Univ. 313
Xavier Univ. of Louisiana 174
Xenon Int'l. Sch. of Hair Design 511
Xenon Int'l. Sch. of Hair Design II 542
Xenon Int'l. Sch. of Hair Design III 473

Y

Yacht Restoration Sch. (see Int'l. Yacht
    Restoration Sch.)
Yakima Beauty Sch. Beauty Works
    639
Yakima Valley Coll. (see Yakima Valley
    Comm. Coll.)
Yakima Valley Comm. Coll. 417
Yale Child Study Ctr. (see Yale Univ.)
Yale Coll. (see Yale Univ.)
Yale Divinity Sch. (see Yale Univ.
    Divinity Sch.)
Yale Univ. 76
Yale Univ. Divinity Sch. 76
Yale-New Haven Hosp. 660
Yanbu Industrial Coll. 716
Yankton Sch. of Theology (see United
    Theological Seminary of the Twin
    Cities)
Yavapai Coll. 23
Yeshiva & Kolel Bais Medrosh Elyon
    282
Yeshiva & Kollel Harbotzas Torah 282
Yeshiva Beth Moshe 346
Yeshiva Beth Yehuda-Yeshiva Gedolah
    of Greater Detroit 206
Yeshiva Coll. (see also Yeshiva Coll. of
    the Nation's Capital, Yeshiva
    Univ.)
Yeshiva Coll. of the Nation's Capital
    746
Yeshiva Derech Chaim 282
Yeshiva D'Monsey Rabbinical Coll.
    282
Yeshiva Eitz Chaim (see Yeshiva Univ.)
Yeshiva Gedolah Imrei Yosef D'Spinka
    282
Yeshiva Gedolah Rabbinical Coll. 97
Yeshiva Karlin Stolin Beth Aaron
    V'Israel Rabbinical Inst. 282
Yeshiva Mikdash Melech 282
Yeshiva of Nitra-Rabbinical Coll.
    Yeshiva Farm Settlement 282
Yeshiva of the Telshe Alumni 282

Yeshiva Ohr Elchonon-Chabad/West
    Coast Talmudic Seminary 63
Yeshiva Shaar HaTorah Talmudic
    Research Inst. 283
Yeshiva Shaarei Torah of Rockland
    283
Yeshiva Toras Chaim Talmudical
    Seminary 71
Yeshiva Univ. 283
Yeshiva Zichron Aryeh 283
Yeshivas Novominsk 283
Yeshivath Viznitz 283
Yeshivath Zichron Moshe 283
YMCA Coll. (see Sinclair Comm. Coll.)
YMCA Sch. of Commerce (see
    Franklin Univ.)
Yo San Traditional Chinese Medicine
    Univ. (see Yo San Univ. of
    Traditional Chinese Medicine)
Yo San Univ. of Traditional Chinese
    Medicine 63
York Coll. 239, 734 (see also City
    Univ. of New York York Coll., York
    Coll. of Pennsylvania, York County
    Comm. Coll.)
York Coll. of Pennsylvania 346
York Collegiate Inst. (see York Coll. of
    Pennsylvania)
York County Acad. (see York Coll. of
    Pennsylvania)
York County Area Vocational Tech.
    Sch. 700
York County Coll. (see York County
    Comm. Coll.)
York County Comm. Coll. 177, 730
York County Tech. Coll. 730 (see also
    York County Comm. Coll.)
York County Tech. Edu. Ctr. (see York
    Tech. Coll.)
York County Vo-TechSchool (see York
    County Area Vocational Tech.
    Sch.)
York Hosp. (see WellSpan Health—
    York Hosp.)
York Jr. Coll. (see York Coll. of
    Pennsylvania)
York Tech. Coll. 360
York Tech. Inst. 346
York Univ. 714
Yorktowne Bus. Inst. 346
Young Harris Coll. 111
Youngstown Centre of Massotherapy
    585
Youngstown City Schools (see Choffin
    Career & Tech. Ctr.)
Youngstown Coll. of Bus. & Prof.
    Drafting (see ITT Tech. Inst.)
Youngstown State Univ. 313
Youngstown Univ. (see Youngstown
    State Univ.)
Your Sch. of Beauty Culture 504

Youth Co-op Training Inst. (see Youth
    Co-op Training Inst.)
Yuba Coll. 63
Yuba Comm. Coll. (see Yuba Coll.)
Yukon Beauty Coll. 591
Yuma Reg. Med. Ctr. 652

Z

Zane State Coll. 314, 734
Zaraphath Bible Inst. 733 (see also
    Somerset Christian Coll.)
Zayed Univ. 752
Zion Bible Coll. 354, 736
Zion Bible Inst. 736 (see also Zion
    Bible Coll.)
Zion Wesley Inst. (see Hood
    Theological Seminary)